Oxford Dictionary of
National Biography

Volume 7

Oxford Dictionary of National Biography

IN ASSOCIATION WITH
The British Academy

From the earliest times to the year 2000

Edited by
H. C. G. Matthew
and
Brian Harrison

Volume 7
Box–Browell

OXFORD
UNIVERSITY PRESS

OXFORD
UNIVERSITY PRESS

Great Clarendon Street, Oxford OX2 6DP

Oxford University Press is a department of the University of Oxford.
It furthers the University's objective of excellence in research, scholarship,
and education by publishing worldwide in

Oxford New York

Auckland Bangkok Buenos Aires Cape Town
Chennai Dar es Salaam Delhi Hong Kong Istanbul Karachi
Kolkata Kuala Lumpur Madrid Melbourne Mexico City Mumbai Nairobi
São Paulo Shanghai Taipei Tokyo Toronto

Oxford is a registered trade mark of Oxford University Press
in the UK and in certain other countries

Published in the United States
by Oxford University Press Inc., New York

British Library Cataloguing in Publication Data
Data available

Library of Congress Cataloging in Publication Data
Data available: for details see volume 1, p. iv

ISBN 0-19-861357-1 (this volume)
ISBN 0-19-861411-X (set of sixty volumes)

Text captured by Alliance Phototypesetters, Pondicherry
Illustrations reproduced and archived by
Alliance Graphics Ltd, UK
Typeset in OUP Swift by Interactive Sciences Limited, Gloucester
Printed in Great Britain on acid-free paper by
Butler and Tanner Ltd,
Frome, Somerset

LIST OF ABBREVIATIONS

1 General abbreviations

AB	bachelor of arts
ABC	Australian Broadcasting Corporation
ABC TV	ABC Television
act.	active
A$	Australian dollar
AD	*anno domini*
AFC	Air Force Cross
AIDS	acquired immune deficiency syndrome
AK	Alaska
AL	Alabama
A level	advanced level [examination]
ALS	associate of the Linnean Society
AM	master of arts
AMICE	associate member of the Institution of Civil Engineers
ANZAC	Australian and New Zealand Army Corps
appx *pl.* appxs	appendix(es)
AR	Arkansas
ARA	associate of the Royal Academy
ARCA	associate of the Royal College of Art
ARCM	associate of the Royal College of Music
ARCO	associate of the Royal College of Organists
ARIBA	associate of the Royal Institute of British Architects
ARP	air-raid precautions
ARRC	associate of the Royal Red Cross
ARSA	associate of the Royal Scottish Academy
art.	article / item
ASC	Army Service Corps
Asch	Austrian Schilling
ASDIC	Antisubmarine Detection Investigation Committee
ATS	Auxiliary Territorial Service
ATV	Associated Television
Aug	August
AZ	Arizona
b.	born
BA	bachelor of arts
BA (Admin.)	bachelor of arts (administration)
BAFTA	British Academy of Film and Television Arts
BAO	bachelor of arts in obstetrics
bap.	baptized
BBC	British Broadcasting Corporation / Company
BC	before Christ
BCE	before the common (*or* Christian) era
BCE	bachelor of civil engineering
BCG	bacillus of Calmette and Guérin [inoculation against tuberculosis]
BCh	bachelor of surgery
BChir	bachelor of surgery
BCL	bachelor of civil law
BCnL	bachelor of canon law
BCom	bachelor of commerce
BD	bachelor of divinity
BEd	bachelor of education
BEng	bachelor of engineering
bk *pl.* bks	book(s)
BL	bachelor of law / letters / literature
BLitt	bachelor of letters
BM	bachelor of medicine
BMus	bachelor of music
BP	before present
BP	British Petroleum
Bros.	Brothers
BS	(1) bachelor of science; (2) bachelor of surgery; (3) British standard
BSc	bachelor of science
BSc (Econ.)	bachelor of science (economics)
BSc (Eng.)	bachelor of science (engineering)
bt	baronet
BTh	bachelor of theology
bur.	buried
C.	command [identifier for published parliamentary papers]
c.	*circa*
c.	*capitulum pl. capitula*: chapter(s)
CA	California
Cantab.	Cantabrigiensis
cap.	*capitulum pl. capitula*: chapter(s)
CB	companion of the Bath
CBE	commander of the Order of the British Empire
CBS	Columbia Broadcasting System
cc	cubic centimetres
C$	Canadian dollar
CD	compact disc
Cd	command [identifier for published parliamentary papers]
CE	Common (*or* Christian) Era
cent.	century
cf.	compare
CH	Companion of Honour
chap.	chapter
ChB	bachelor of surgery
CI	Imperial Order of the Crown of India
CIA	Central Intelligence Agency
CID	Criminal Investigation Department
CIE	companion of the Order of the Indian Empire
Cie	Compagnie
CLit	companion of literature
CM	master of surgery
cm	centimetre(s)

Cmd	command [identifier for published parliamentary papers]
CMG	companion of the Order of St Michael and St George
Cmnd	command [identifier for published parliamentary papers]
CO	Colorado
Co.	company
co.	county
col. *pl.* cols.	column(s)
Corp.	corporation
CSE	certificate of secondary education
CSI	companion of the Order of the Star of India
CT	Connecticut
CVO	commander of the Royal Victorian Order
cwt	hundredweight
$	(American) dollar
d.	(1) penny (pence); (2) died
DBE	dame commander of the Order of the British Empire
DCH	diploma in child health
DCh	doctor of surgery
DCL	doctor of civil law
DCnL	doctor of canon law
DCVO	dame commander of the Royal Victorian Order
DD	doctor of divinity
DE	Delaware
Dec	December
dem.	demolished
DEng	doctor of engineering
des.	destroyed
DFC	Distinguished Flying Cross
DipEd	diploma in education
DipPsych	diploma in psychiatry
diss.	dissertation
DL	deputy lieutenant
DLitt	doctor of letters
DLittCelt	doctor of Celtic letters
DM	(1) Deutschmark; (2) doctor of medicine; (3) doctor of musical arts
DMus	doctor of music
DNA	dioxyribonucleic acid
doc.	document
DOL	doctor of oriental learning
DPH	diploma in public health
DPhil	doctor of philosophy
DPM	diploma in psychological medicine
DSC	Distinguished Service Cross
DSc	doctor of science
DSc (Econ.)	doctor of science (economics)
DSc (Eng.)	doctor of science (engineering)
DSM	Distinguished Service Medal
DSO	companion of the Distinguished Service Order
DSocSc	doctor of social science
DTech	doctor of technology
DTh	doctor of theology
DTM	diploma in tropical medicine
DTMH	diploma in tropical medicine and hygiene
DU	doctor of the university
DUniv	doctor of the university
dwt	pennyweight
EC	European Community
ed. *pl.* eds.	edited / edited by / editor(s)
Edin.	Edinburgh
edn	edition
EEC	European Economic Community
EFTA	European Free Trade Association
EICS	East India Company Service
EMI	Electrical and Musical Industries (Ltd)
Eng.	English
enl.	enlarged
ENSA	Entertainments National Service Association
ep. *pl.* epp.	*epistola(e)*
ESP	extra-sensory perception
esp.	especially
esq.	esquire
est.	estimate / estimated
EU	European Union
ex	sold by (*lit.* out of)
excl.	excludes / excluding
exh.	exhibited
exh. cat.	exhibition catalogue
f. *pl.* ff.	following [pages]
FA	Football Association
FACP	fellow of the American College of Physicians
facs.	facsimile
FANY	First Aid Nursing Yeomanry
FBA	fellow of the British Academy
FBI	Federation of British Industries
FCS	fellow of the Chemical Society
Feb	February
FEng	fellow of the Fellowship of Engineering
FFCM	fellow of the Faculty of Community Medicine
FGS	fellow of the Geological Society
fig.	figure
FIMechE	fellow of the Institution of Mechanical Engineers
FL	Florida
fl.	*floruit*
FLS	fellow of the Linnean Society
FM	frequency modulation
fol. *pl.* fols.	folio(s)
Fr	French francs
Fr.	French
FRAeS	fellow of the Royal Aeronautical Society
FRAI	fellow of the Royal Anthropological Institute
FRAM	fellow of the Royal Academy of Music
FRAS	(1) fellow of the Royal Asiatic Society; (2) fellow of the Royal Astronomical Society
FRCM	fellow of the Royal College of Music
FRCO	fellow of the Royal College of Organists
FRCOG	fellow of the Royal College of Obstetricians and Gynaecologists
FRCP(C)	fellow of the Royal College of Physicians of Canada
FRCP (Edin.)	fellow of the Royal College of Physicians of Edinburgh
FRCP (Lond.)	fellow of the Royal College of Physicians of London
FRCPath	fellow of the Royal College of Pathologists
FRCPsych	fellow of the Royal College of Psychiatrists
FRCS	fellow of the Royal College of Surgeons
FRGS	fellow of the Royal Geographical Society
FRIBA	fellow of the Royal Institute of British Architects
FRICS	fellow of the Royal Institute of Chartered Surveyors
FRS	fellow of the Royal Society
FRSA	fellow of the Royal Society of Arts

FRSCM	fellow of the Royal School of Church Music		ISO	companion of the Imperial Service Order
FRSE	fellow of the Royal Society of Edinburgh		It.	Italian
FRSL	fellow of the Royal Society of Literature		ITA	Independent Television Authority
FSA	fellow of the Society of Antiquaries		ITV	Independent Television
ft	foot *pl.* feet		Jan	January
FTCL	fellow of Trinity College of Music, London		JP	justice of the peace
ft-lb per min.	foot-pounds per minute [unit of horsepower]		jun.	junior
FZS	fellow of the Zoological Society		KB	knight of the Order of the Bath
GA	Georgia		KBE	knight commander of the Order of the British Empire
GBE	knight or dame grand cross of the Order of the British Empire		KC	king's counsel
GCB	knight grand cross of the Order of the Bath		kcal	kilocalorie
GCE	general certificate of education		KCB	knight commander of the Order of the Bath
GCH	knight grand cross of the Royal Guelphic Order		KCH	knight commander of the Royal Guelphic Order
GCHQ	government communications headquarters		KCIE	knight commander of the Order of the Indian Empire
GCIE	knight grand commander of the Order of the Indian Empire		KCMG	knight commander of the Order of St Michael and St George
GCMG	knight or dame grand cross of the Order of St Michael and St George		KCSI	knight commander of the Order of the Star of India
GCSE	general certificate of secondary education		KCVO	knight commander of the Royal Victorian Order
GCSI	knight grand commander of the Order of the Star of India		keV	kilo-electron-volt
GCStJ	bailiff or dame grand cross of the order of St John of Jerusalem		KG	knight of the Order of the Garter
GCVO	knight or dame grand cross of the Royal Victorian Order		KGB	[Soviet committee of state security]
GEC	General Electric Company		KH	knight of the Royal Guelphic Order
Ger.	German		KLM	Koninklijke Luchtvaart Maatschappij (Royal Dutch Air Lines)
GI	government (*or* general) issue		km	kilometre(s)
GMT	Greenwich mean time		KP	knight of the Order of St Patrick
GP	general practitioner		KS	Kansas
GPU	[Soviet special police unit]		KT	knight of the Order of the Thistle
GSO	general staff officer		kt	knight
Heb.	Hebrew		KY	Kentucky
HEICS	Honourable East India Company Service		£	pound(s) sterling
HI	Hawaii		£E	Egyptian pound
HIV	human immunodeficiency virus		L	lira *pl.* lire
HK$	Hong Kong dollar		l. *pl.* ll.	line(s)
HM	his / her majesty('s)		LA	Lousiana
HMAS	his / her majesty's Australian ship		LAA	light anti-aircraft
HMNZS	his / her majesty's New Zealand ship		LAH	licentiate of the Apothecaries' Hall, Dublin
HMS	his / her majesty's ship		Lat.	Latin
HMSO	His / Her Majesty's Stationery Office		lb	pound(s), unit of weight
HMV	His Master's Voice		LDS	licence in dental surgery
Hon.	Honourable		*lit.*	literally
hp	horsepower		LittB	bachelor of letters
hr	hour(s)		LittD	doctor of letters
HRH	his / her royal highness		LKQCPI	licentiate of the King and Queen's College of Physicians, Ireland
HTV	Harlech Television		LLA	lady literate in arts
IA	Iowa		LLB	bachelor of laws
ibid.	*ibidem*: in the same place		LLD	doctor of laws
ICI	Imperial Chemical Industries (Ltd)		LLM	master of laws
ID	Idaho		LM	licentiate in midwifery
IL	Illinois		LP	long-playing record
illus.	illustration		LRAM	licentiate of the Royal Academy of Music
illustr.	illustrated		LRCP	licentiate of the Royal College of Physicians
IN	Indiana		LRCPS (Glasgow)	licentiate of the Royal College of Physicians and Surgeons of Glasgow
in.	inch(es)		LRCS	licentiate of the Royal College of Surgeons
Inc.	Incorporated		LSA	licentiate of the Society of Apothecaries
incl.	includes / including		LSD	lysergic acid diethylamide
IOU	I owe you		LVO	lieutenant of the Royal Victorian Order
IQ	intelligence quotient		M. *pl.* MM.	Monsieur *pl.* Messieurs
Ir£	Irish pound		m	metre(s)
IRA	Irish Republican Army			

m. *pl.* mm.	membrane(s)
MA	(1) Massachusetts; (2) master of arts
MAI	master of engineering
MB	bachelor of medicine
MBA	master of business administration
MBE	member of the Order of the British Empire
MC	Military Cross
MCC	Marylebone Cricket Club
MCh	master of surgery
MChir	master of surgery
MCom	master of commerce
MD	(1) doctor of medicine; (2) Maryland
MDMA	methylenedioxymethamphetamine
ME	Maine
MEd	master of education
MEng	master of engineering
MEP	member of the European parliament
MG	Morris Garages
MGM	Metro-Goldwyn-Mayer
Mgr	Monsignor
MI	(1) Michigan; (2) military intelligence
MI1c	[secret intelligence department]
MI5	[military intelligence department]
MI6	[secret intelligence department]
MI9	[secret escape service]
MICE	member of the Institution of Civil Engineers
MIEE	member of the Institution of Electrical Engineers
min.	minute(s)
Mk	mark
ML	(1) licentiate of medicine; (2) master of laws
MLitt	master of letters
Mlle	Mademoiselle
mm	millimetre(s)
Mme	Madame
MN	Minnesota
MO	Missouri
MOH	medical officer of health
MP	member of parliament
m.p.h.	miles per hour
MPhil	master of philosophy
MRCP	member of the Royal College of Physicians
MRCS	member of the Royal College of Surgeons
MRCVS	member of the Royal College of Veterinary Surgeons
MRIA	member of the Royal Irish Academy
MS	(1) master of science; (2) Mississippi
MS *pl.* MSS	manuscript(s)
MSc	master of science
MSc (Econ.)	master of science (economics)
MT	Montana
MusB	bachelor of music
MusBac	bachelor of music
MusD	doctor of music
MV	motor vessel
MVO	member of the Royal Victorian Order
n. *pl.* nn.	note(s)
NAAFI	Navy, Army, and Air Force Institutes
NASA	National Aeronautics and Space Administration
NATO	North Atlantic Treaty Organization
NBC	National Broadcasting Corporation
NC	North Carolina
NCO	non-commissioned officer
ND	North Dakota
n.d.	no date
NE	Nebraska
nem. con.	*nemine contradicente*: unanimously
new ser.	new series
NH	New Hampshire
NHS	National Health Service
NJ	New Jersey
NKVD	[Soviet people's commissariat for internal affairs]
NM	New Mexico
nm	nanometre(s)
no. *pl.* nos.	number(s)
Nov	November
n.p.	no place [of publication]
NS	new style
NV	Nevada
NY	New York
NZBS	New Zealand Broadcasting Service
OBE	officer of the Order of the British Empire
obit.	obituary
Oct	October
OCTU	officer cadets training unit
OECD	Organization for Economic Co-operation and Development
OEEC	Organization for European Economic Co-operation
OFM	order of Friars Minor [Franciscans]
OFMCap	Ordine Frati Minori Cappucini: member of the Capuchin order
OH	Ohio
OK	Oklahoma
O level	ordinary level [examination]
OM	Order of Merit
OP	order of Preachers [Dominicans]
op. *pl.* opp.	opus *pl.* opera
OPEC	Organization of Petroleum Exporting Countries
OR	Oregon
orig.	original
OS	old style
OSB	Order of St Benedict
OTC	Officers' Training Corps
OWS	Old Watercolour Society
Oxon.	Oxoniensis
p. *pl.* pp.	page(s)
PA	Pennsylvania
p.a.	per annum
para.	paragraph
PAYE	pay as you earn
pbk *pl.* pbks	paperback(s)
per.	[during the] period
PhD	doctor of philosophy
pl.	(1) plate(s); (2) plural
priv. coll.	private collection
pt *pl.* pts	part(s)
pubd	published
PVC	polyvinyl chloride
q. *pl.* qq.	(1) question(s); (2) quire(s)
QC	queen's counsel
R	rand
R.	Rex / Regina
r	recto
r.	reigned / ruled
RA	Royal Academy / Royal Academician

RAC	Royal Automobile Club		Skr	Swedish krona
RAF	Royal Air Force		Span.	Spanish
RAFVR	Royal Air Force Volunteer Reserve		SPCK	Society for Promoting Christian Knowledge
RAM	[member of the] Royal Academy of Music		SS	(1) Santissimi; (2) Schutzstaffel; (3) steam ship
RAMC	Royal Army Medical Corps		STB	bachelor of theology
RCA	Royal College of Art		STD	doctor of theology
RCNC	Royal Corps of Naval Constructors		STM	master of theology
RCOG	Royal College of Obstetricians and Gynaecologists		STP	doctor of theology
RDI	royal designer for industry		*supp.*	supposedly
RE	Royal Engineers		suppl. *pl.* suppls.	supplement(s)
repr. *pl.* reprs.	reprint(s) / reprinted		s.v.	*sub verbo / sub voce*: under the word / heading
repro.	reproduced		SY	steam yacht
rev.	revised / revised by / reviser / revision		TA	Territorial Army
Revd	Reverend		TASS	[Soviet news agency]
RHA	Royal Hibernian Academy		TB	tuberculosis (*lit.* tubercle bacillus)
RI	(1) Rhode Island; (2) Royal Institute of Painters in Water-Colours		TD	(1) *teachtaí dála* (member of the Dáil); (2) territorial decoration
RIBA	Royal Institute of British Architects		TN	Tennessee
RIN	Royal Indian Navy		TNT	trinitrotoluene
RM	Reichsmark		trans.	translated / translated by / translation / translator
RMS	Royal Mail steamer		TT	tourist trophy
RN	Royal Navy		TUC	Trades Union Congress
RNA	ribonucleic acid		TX	Texas
RNAS	Royal Naval Air Service		U-boat	*Unterseeboot*: submarine
RNR	Royal Naval Reserve		Ufa	Universum-Film AG
RNVR	Royal Naval Volunteer Reserve		UMIST	University of Manchester Institute of Science and Technology
RO	Record Office		UN	United Nations
r.p.m.	revolutions per minute		UNESCO	United Nations Educational, Scientific, and Cultural Organization
RRS	royal research ship			
Rs	rupees		UNICEF	United Nations International Children's Emergency Fund
RSA	(1) Royal Scottish Academician; (2) Royal Society of Arts		unpubd	unpublished
RSPCA	Royal Society for the Prevention of Cruelty to Animals		USS	United States ship
			UT	Utah
Rt Hon.	Right Honourable		*v*	verso
Rt Revd	Right Reverend		v.	versus
RUC	Royal Ulster Constabulary		VA	Virginia
Russ.	Russian		VAD	Voluntary Aid Detachment
RWS	Royal Watercolour Society		VC	Victoria Cross
S4C	Sianel Pedwar Cymru		VE-day	victory in Europe day
s.	shilling(s)		Ven.	Venerable
s.a.	*sub anno*: under the year		VJ-day	victory over Japan day
SABC	South African Broadcasting Corporation		vol. *pl.* vols.	volume(s)
SAS	Special Air Service		VT	Vermont
SC	South Carolina		WA	Washington [state]
ScD	doctor of science		WAAC	Women's Auxiliary Army Corps
S$	Singapore dollar		WAAF	Women's Auxiliary Air Force
SD	South Dakota		WEA	Workers' Educational Association
sec.	second(s)		WHO	World Health Organization
sel.	selected		WI	Wisconsin
sen.	senior		WRAF	Women's Royal Air Force
Sept	September		WRNS	Women's Royal Naval Service
ser.	series		WV	West Virginia
SHAPE	supreme headquarters allied powers, Europe		WVS	Women's Voluntary Service
SIDRO	Société Internationale d'Énergie Hydro-Électrique		WY	Wyoming
			¥	yen
sig. *pl.* sigs.	signature(s)		YMCA	Young Men's Christian Association
sing.	singular		YWCA	Young Women's Christian Association
SIS	Secret Intelligence Service			
SJ	Society of Jesus			

2 Institution abbreviations

All Souls Oxf.	All Souls College, Oxford
AM Oxf.	Ashmolean Museum, Oxford
Balliol Oxf.	Balliol College, Oxford
BBC WAC	BBC Written Archives Centre, Reading
Beds. & Luton ARS	Bedfordshire and Luton Archives and Record Service, Bedford
Berks. RO	Berkshire Record Office, Reading
BFI	British Film Institute, London
BFI NFTVA	British Film Institute, London, National Film and Television Archive
BGS	British Geological Survey, Keyworth, Nottingham
Birm. CA	Birmingham Central Library, Birmingham City Archives
Birm. CL	Birmingham Central Library
BL	British Library, London
BL NSA	British Library, London, National Sound Archive
BL OIOC	British Library, London, Oriental and India Office Collections
BLPES	London School of Economics and Political Science, British Library of Political and Economic Science
BM	British Museum, London
Bodl. Oxf.	Bodleian Library, Oxford
Bodl. RH	Bodleian Library of Commonwealth and African Studies at Rhodes House, Oxford
Borth. Inst.	Borthwick Institute of Historical Research, University of York
Boston PL	Boston Public Library, Massachusetts
Bristol RO	Bristol Record Office
Bucks. RLSS	Buckinghamshire Records and Local Studies Service, Aylesbury
CAC Cam.	Churchill College, Cambridge, Churchill Archives Centre
Cambs. AS	Cambridgeshire Archive Service
CCC Cam.	Corpus Christi College, Cambridge
CCC Oxf.	Corpus Christi College, Oxford
Ches. & Chester ALSS	Cheshire and Chester Archives and Local Studies Service
Christ Church Oxf.	Christ Church, Oxford
Christies	Christies, London
City Westm. AC	City of Westminster Archives Centre, London
CKS	Centre for Kentish Studies, Maidstone
CLRO	Corporation of London Records Office
Coll. Arms	College of Arms, London
Col. U.	Columbia University, New York
Cornwall RO	Cornwall Record Office, Truro
Courtauld Inst.	Courtauld Institute of Art, London
CUL	Cambridge University Library
Cumbria AS	Cumbria Archive Service
Derbys. RO	Derbyshire Record Office, Matlock
Devon RO	Devon Record Office, Exeter
Dorset RO	Dorset Record Office, Dorchester
Duke U.	Duke University, Durham, North Carolina
Duke U., Perkins L.	Duke University, Durham, North Carolina, William R. Perkins Library
Durham Cath. CL	Durham Cathedral, chapter library
Durham RO	Durham Record Office
DWL	Dr Williams's Library, London
Essex RO	Essex Record Office
E. Sussex RO	East Sussex Record Office, Lewes
Eton	Eton College, Berkshire
FM Cam.	Fitzwilliam Museum, Cambridge
Folger	Folger Shakespeare Library, Washington, DC
Garr. Club	Garrick Club, London
Girton Cam.	Girton College, Cambridge
GL	Guildhall Library, London
Glos. RO	Gloucestershire Record Office, Gloucester
Gon. & Caius Cam.	Gonville and Caius College, Cambridge
Gov. Art Coll.	Government Art Collection
GS Lond.	Geological Society of London
Hants. RO	Hampshire Record Office, Winchester
Harris Man. Oxf.	Harris Manchester College, Oxford
Harvard TC	Harvard Theatre Collection, Harvard University, Cambridge, Massachusetts, Nathan Marsh Pusey Library
Harvard U.	Harvard University, Cambridge, Massachusetts
Harvard U., Houghton L.	Harvard University, Cambridge, Massachusetts, Houghton Library
Herefs. RO	Herefordshire Record Office, Hereford
Herts. ALS	Hertfordshire Archives and Local Studies, Hertford
Hist. Soc. Penn.	Historical Society of Pennsylvania, Philadelphia
HLRO	House of Lords Record Office, London
Hult. Arch.	Hulton Archive, London and New York
Hunt. L.	Huntington Library, San Marino, California
ICL	Imperial College, London
Inst. CE	Institution of Civil Engineers, London
Inst. EE	Institution of Electrical Engineers, London
IWM	Imperial War Museum, London
IWM FVA	Imperial War Museum, London, Film and Video Archive
IWM SA	Imperial War Museum, London, Sound Archive
JRL	John Rylands University Library of Manchester
King's AC Cam.	King's College Archives Centre, Cambridge
King's Cam.	King's College, Cambridge
King's Lond.	King's College, London
King's Lond., Liddell Hart C.	King's College, London, Liddell Hart Centre for Military Archives
Lancs. RO	Lancashire Record Office, Preston
L. Cong.	Library of Congress, Washington, DC
Leics. RO	Leicestershire, Leicester, and Rutland Record Office, Leicester
Lincs. Arch.	Lincolnshire Archives, Lincoln
Linn. Soc.	Linnean Society of London
LMA	London Metropolitan Archives
LPL	Lambeth Palace, London
Lpool RO	Liverpool Record Office and Local Studies Service
LUL	London University Library
Magd. Cam.	Magdalene College, Cambridge
Magd. Oxf.	Magdalen College, Oxford
Man. City Gall.	Manchester City Galleries
Man. CL	Manchester Central Library
Mass. Hist. Soc.	Massachusetts Historical Society, Boston
Merton Oxf.	Merton College, Oxford
MHS Oxf.	Museum of the History of Science, Oxford
Mitchell L., Glas.	Mitchell Library, Glasgow
Mitchell L., NSW	State Library of New South Wales, Sydney, Mitchell Library
Morgan L.	Pierpont Morgan Library, New York
NA Canada	National Archives of Canada, Ottawa
NA Ire.	National Archives of Ireland, Dublin
NAM	National Army Museum, London
NA Scot.	National Archives of Scotland, Edinburgh
News Int. RO	News International Record Office, London
NG Ire.	National Gallery of Ireland, Dublin

NG Scot.	National Gallery of Scotland, Edinburgh
NHM	Natural History Museum, London
NL Aus.	National Library of Australia, Canberra
NL Ire.	National Library of Ireland, Dublin
NL NZ	National Library of New Zealand, Wellington
NL NZ, Turnbull L.	National Library of New Zealand, Wellington, Alexander Turnbull Library
NL Scot.	National Library of Scotland, Edinburgh
NL Wales	National Library of Wales, Aberystwyth
NMG Wales	National Museum and Gallery of Wales, Cardiff
NMM	National Maritime Museum, London
Norfolk RO	Norfolk Record Office, Norwich
Northants. RO	Northamptonshire Record Office, Northampton
Northumbd RO	Northumberland Record Office
Notts. Arch.	Nottinghamshire Archives, Nottingham
NPG	National Portrait Gallery, London
NRA	National Archives, London, Historical Manuscripts Commission, National Register of Archives
Nuffield Oxf.	Nuffield College, Oxford
N. Yorks. CRO	North Yorkshire County Record Office, Northallerton
NYPL	New York Public Library
Oxf. UA	Oxford University Archives
Oxf. U. Mus. NH	Oxford University Museum of Natural History
Oxon. RO	Oxfordshire Record Office, Oxford
Pembroke Cam.	Pembroke College, Cambridge
PRO	National Archives, London, Public Record Office
PRO NIre.	Public Record Office for Northern Ireland, Belfast
Pusey Oxf.	Pusey House, Oxford
RA	Royal Academy of Arts, London
Ransom HRC	Harry Ransom Humanities Research Center, University of Texas, Austin
RAS	Royal Astronomical Society, London
RBG Kew	Royal Botanic Gardens, Kew, London
RCP Lond.	Royal College of Physicians of London
RCS Eng.	Royal College of Surgeons of England, London
RGS	Royal Geographical Society, London
RIBA	Royal Institute of British Architects, London
RIBA BAL	Royal Institute of British Architects, London, British Architectural Library
Royal Arch.	Royal Archives, Windsor Castle, Berkshire [by gracious permission of her majesty the queen]
Royal Irish Acad.	Royal Irish Academy, Dublin
Royal Scot. Acad.	Royal Scottish Academy, Edinburgh
RS	Royal Society, London
RSA	Royal Society of Arts, London
RS Friends, Lond.	Religious Society of Friends, London
St Ant. Oxf.	St Antony's College, Oxford
St John Cam.	St John's College, Cambridge
S. Antiquaries, Lond.	Society of Antiquaries of London
Sci. Mus.	Science Museum, London
Scot. NPG	Scottish National Portrait Gallery, Edinburgh
Scott Polar RI	University of Cambridge, Scott Polar Research Institute
Sheff. Arch.	Sheffield Archives
Shrops. RRC	Shropshire Records and Research Centre, Shrewsbury
SOAS	School of Oriental and African Studies, London
Som. ARS	Somerset Archive and Record Service, Taunton
Staffs. RO	Staffordshire Record Office, Stafford
Suffolk RO	Suffolk Record Office
Surrey HC	Surrey History Centre, Woking
TCD	Trinity College, Dublin
Trinity Cam.	Trinity College, Cambridge
U. Aberdeen	University of Aberdeen
U. Birm.	University of Birmingham
U. Birm. L.	University of Birmingham Library
U. Cal.	University of California
U. Cam.	University of Cambridge
UCL	University College, London
U. Durham	University of Durham
U. Durham L.	University of Durham Library
U. Edin.	University of Edinburgh
U. Edin., New Coll.	University of Edinburgh, New College
U. Edin., New Coll. L.	University of Edinburgh, New College Library
U. Edin. L.	University of Edinburgh Library
U. Glas.	University of Glasgow
U. Glas. L.	University of Glasgow Library
U. Hull	University of Hull
U. Hull, Brynmor Jones L.	University of Hull, Brynmor Jones Library
U. Leeds	University of Leeds
U. Leeds, Brotherton L.	University of Leeds, Brotherton Library
U. Lond.	University of London
U. Lpool	University of Liverpool
U. Lpool L.	University of Liverpool Library
U. Mich.	University of Michigan, Ann Arbor
U. Mich., Clements L.	University of Michigan, Ann Arbor, William L. Clements Library
U. Newcastle	University of Newcastle upon Tyne
U. Newcastle, Robinson L.	University of Newcastle upon Tyne, Robinson Library
U. Nott.	University of Nottingham
U. Nott. L.	University of Nottingham Library
U. Oxf.	University of Oxford
U. Reading	University of Reading
U. Reading L.	University of Reading Library
U. St Andr.	University of St Andrews
U. St Andr. L.	University of St Andrews Library
U. Southampton	University of Southampton
U. Southampton L.	University of Southampton Library
U. Sussex	University of Sussex, Brighton
U. Texas	University of Texas, Austin
U. Wales	University of Wales
U. Warwick Mod. RC	University of Warwick, Coventry, Modern Records Centre
V&A	Victoria and Albert Museum, London
V&A NAL	Victoria and Albert Museum, London, National Art Library
Warks. CRO	Warwickshire County Record Office, Warwick
Wellcome L.	Wellcome Library for the History and Understanding of Medicine, London
Westm. DA	Westminster Diocesan Archives, London
Wilts. & Swindon RO	Wiltshire and Swindon Record Office, Trowbridge
Worcs. RO	Worcestershire Record Office, Worcester
W. Sussex RO	West Sussex Record Office, Chichester
W. Yorks. AS	West Yorkshire Archive Service
Yale U.	Yale University, New Haven, Connecticut
Yale U., Beinecke L.	Yale University, New Haven, Connecticut, Beinecke Rare Book and Manuscript Library
Yale U. CBA	Yale University, New Haven, Connecticut, Yale Center for British Art

3 Bibliographic abbreviations

Adams, *Drama*
W. D. Adams, *A dictionary of the drama*, 1: *A–G* (1904); 2: *H–Z* (1956) [vol. 2 microfilm only]

AFM
J O'Donovan, ed. and trans., *Annala rioghachta Eireann / Annals of the kingdom of Ireland by the four masters*, 7 vols. (1848–51); 2nd edn (1856); 3rd edn (1990)

Allibone, *Dict.*
S. A. Allibone, *A critical dictionary of English literature and British and American authors*, 3 vols. (1859–71); suppl. by J. F. Kirk, 2 vols. (1891)

ANB
J. A. Garraty and M. C. Carnes, eds., *American national biography*, 24 vols. (1999)

Anderson, *Scot. nat.*
W. Anderson, *The Scottish nation, or, The surnames, families, literature, honours, and biographical history of the people of Scotland*, 3 vols. (1859–63)

Ann. mon.
H. R. Luard, ed., *Annales monastici*, 5 vols., Rolls Series, 36 (1864–9)

Ann. Ulster
S. Mac Airt and G. Mac Niocaill, eds., *Annals of Ulster (to AD 1131)* (1983)

APC
Acts of the privy council of England, new ser., 46 vols. (1890–1964)

APS
The acts of the parliaments of Scotland, 12 vols. in 13 (1814–75)

Arber, *Regs. Stationers*
F. Arber, ed., *A transcript of the registers of the Company of Stationers of London, 1554–1640 AD*, 5 vols. (1875–94)

ArchR
Architectural Review

ASC
D. Whitelock, D. C. Douglas, and S. I. Tucker, ed. and trans., *The Anglo-Saxon Chronicle: a revised translation* (1961)

AS chart.
P. H. Sawyer, *Anglo-Saxon charters: an annotated list and bibliography*, Royal Historical Society Guides and Handbooks (1968)

AusDB
D. Pike and others, eds., *Australian dictionary of biography*, 16 vols. (1966–2002)

Baker, *Serjeants*
J. H. Baker, *The order of serjeants at law*, SeldS, suppl. ser., 5 (1984)

Bale, *Cat.*
J. Bale, *Scriptorum illustrium Maioris Brytannie, quam nunc Angliam et Scotiam vocant: catalogus*, 2 vols. in 1 (Basel, 1557–9); facs. edn (1971)

Bale, *Index*
J. Bale, *Index Britanniae scriptorum*, ed. R. L. Poole and M. Bateson (1902); facs. edn (1990)

BBCS
Bulletin of the Board of Celtic Studies

BDMBR
J. O. Baylen and N. J. Gossman, eds., *Biographical dictionary of modern British radicals*, 3 vols. in 4 (1979–88)

Bede, *Hist. eccl.*
Bede's Ecclesiastical history of the English people, ed. and trans. B. Colgrave and R. A. B. Mynors, OMT (1969); repr. (1991)

Bénézit, *Dict.*
E. Bénézit, *Dictionnaire critique et documentaire des peintres, sculpteurs, dessinateurs et graveurs*, 3 vols. (Paris, 1911–23); new edn, 8 vols. (1948–66), repr. (1966); 3rd edn, rev. and enl., 10 vols. (1976); 4th edn, 14 vols. (1999)

BIHR
Bulletin of the Institute of Historical Research

Birch, *Seals*
W. de Birch, *Catalogue of seals in the department of manuscripts in the British Museum*, 6 vols. (1887–1900)

Bishop Burnet's History
Bishop Burnet's History of his own time, ed. M. J. Routh, 2nd edn, 6 vols. (1833)

Blackwood
Blackwood's [Edinburgh] Magazine, 328 vols. (1817–1980)

Blain, Clements & Grundy, *Feminist comp.*
V. Blain, P. Clements, and I. Grundy, eds., *The feminist companion to literature in English* (1990)

BL cat.
The British Library general catalogue of printed books [in 360 vols. with suppls., also CD-ROM and online]

BMJ
British Medical Journal

Boase & Courtney, *Bibl. Corn.*
G. C. Boase and W. P. Courtney, *Bibliotheca Cornubiensis: a catalogue of the writings … of Cornishmen*, 3 vols. (1874–82)

Boase, *Mod. Eng. biog.*
F. Boase, *Modern English biography: containing many thousand concise memoirs of persons who have died since the year 1850*, 6 vols. (privately printed, Truro, 1892–1921); repr. (1965)

Boswell, *Life*
Boswell's Life of Johnson: together with Journal of a tour to the Hebrides and Johnson's Diary of a journey into north Wales, ed. G. B. Hill, enl. edn, rev. L. F. Powell, 6 vols. (1934–50); 2nd edn (1964); repr. (1971)

Brown & Stratton, *Brit. mus.*
J. D. Brown and S. S. Stratton, *British musical biography* (1897)

Bryan, *Painters*
M. Bryan, *A biographical and critical dictionary of painters and engravers*, 2 vols. (1816); new edn, ed. G. Stanley (1849); new edn, ed. R. E. Graves and W. Armstrong, 2 vols. (1886–9); [4th edn], ed. G. C. Williamson, 5 vols. (1903–5) [various reprs.]

Burke, *Gen. GB*
J. Burke, *A genealogical and heraldic history of the commoners of Great Britain and Ireland*, 4 vols. (1833–8); new edn as *A genealogical and heraldic dictionary of the landed gentry of Great Britain and Ireland*, 3 vols. [1843–9] [many later edns]

Burke, *Gen. Ire.*
J. B. Burke, *A genealogical and heraldic history of the landed gentry of Ireland* (1899); 2nd edn (1904); 3rd edn (1912); 4th edn (1958); 5th edn as *Burke's Irish family records* (1976)

Burke, *Peerage*
J. Burke, *A general [later edns A genealogical] and heraldic dictionary of the peerage and baronetage of the United Kingdom* [later edns *the British empire*] (1829–)

Burney, *Hist. mus.*
C. Burney, *A general history of music, from the earliest ages to the present period*, 4 vols. (1776–89)

Burtchaell & Sadleir, *Alum. Dubl.*
G. D. Burtchaell and T. U. Sadleir, *Alumni Dublinenses: a register of the students, graduates, and provosts of Trinity College* (1924); [2nd edn], with suppl., in 2 pts (1935)

Calamy rev.
A. G. Matthews, *Calamy revised* (1934); repr. (1988)

CCI
Calendar of confirmations and inventories granted and given up in the several commissariots of Scotland (1876–)

CClR
Calendar of the close rolls preserved in the Public Record Office, 47 vols. (1892–1963)

CDS
J. Bain, ed., *Calendar of documents relating to Scotland*, 4 vols., PRO (1881–8); suppl. vol. 5, ed. G. G. Simpson and J. D. Galbraith [1986]

CEPR letters
W. H. Bliss, C. Johnson, and J. Twemlow, eds., *Calendar of entries in the papal registers relating to Great Britain and Ireland: papal letters* (1893–)

CGPLA
Calendars of the grants of probate and letters of administration [in 4 ser.: England & Wales, Northern Ireland, Ireland, and Éire]

Chambers, *Scots.*
R. Chambers, ed., *A biographical dictionary of eminent Scotsmen*, 4 vols. (1832–5)

Chancery records
chancery records pubd by the PRO

Chancery records (RC)
chancery records pubd by the Record Commissions

CIPM	*Calendar of inquisitions post mortem*, [20 vols.], PRO (1904–); also *Henry VII*, 3 vols. (1898–1955)
Clarendon, *Hist. rebellion*	E. Hyde, earl of Clarendon, *The history of the rebellion and civil wars in England*, 6 vols. (1888); repr. (1958) and (1992)
Cobbett, *Parl. hist.*	W. Cobbett and J. Wright, eds., *Cobbett's Parliamentary history of England*, 36 vols. (1806–1820)
Colvin, *Archs.*	H. Colvin, *A biographical dictionary of British architects, 1600–1840*, 3rd edn (1995)
Cooper, *Ath. Cantab.*	C. H. Cooper and T. Cooper, *Athenae Cantabrigienses*, 3 vols. (1858–1913); repr. (1967)
CPR	*Calendar of the patent rolls preserved in the Public Record Office* (1891–)
Crockford	*Crockford's Clerical Directory*
CS	Camden Society
CSP	*Calendar of state papers* [in 11 ser.: *domestic, Scotland, Scottish series, Ireland, colonial, Commonwealth, foreign, Spain* [at Simancas], *Rome, Milan,* and *Venice*]
CYS	Canterbury and York Society
DAB	*Dictionary of American biography*, 21 vols. (1928–36), repr. in 11 vols. (1964); 10 suppls. (1944–96)
DBB	D. J. Jeremy, ed., *Dictionary of business biography*, 5 vols. (1984–6)
DCB	G. W. Brown and others, *Dictionary of Canadian biography*, [14 vols.] (1966–)
Debrett's Peerage	*Debrett's Peerage* (1803–) [sometimes *Debrett's Illustrated peerage*]
Desmond, *Botanists*	R. Desmond, *Dictionary of British and Irish botanists and horticulturists* (1977); rev. edn (1994)
Dir. Brit. archs.	A. Felstead, J. Franklin, and L. Pinfield, eds., *Directory of British architects, 1834–1900* (1993); 2nd edn, ed. A. Brodie and others, 2 vols. (2001)
DLB	J. M. Bellamy and J. Saville, eds., *Dictionary of labour biography*, [10 vols.] (1972–)
DLitB	Dictionary of Literary Biography
DNB	*Dictionary of national biography*, 63 vols. (1885–1900), suppl., 3 vols. (1901); repr. in 22 vols. (1908–9); 10 further suppls. (1912–96); *Missing persons* (1993)
DNZB	W. H. Oliver and C. Orange, eds., *The dictionary of New Zealand biography*, 5 vols. (1990–2000)
DSAB	W. J. de Kock and others, eds., *Dictionary of South African biography*, 5 vols. (1968–87)
DSB	C. C. Gillispie and F. L. Holmes, eds., *Dictionary of scientific biography*, 16 vols. (1970–80); repr. in 8 vols. (1981); 2 vol. suppl. (1990)
DSBB	A. Slaven and S. Checkland, eds., *Dictionary of Scottish business biography, 1860–1960*, 2 vols. (1986–90)
DSCHT	N. M. de S. Cameron and others, eds., *Dictionary of Scottish church history and theology* (1993)
Dugdale, *Monasticon*	W. Dugdale, *Monasticon Anglicanum*, 3 vols. (1655–72); 2nd edn, 3 vols. (1661–82); new edn, ed. J. Caley, J. Ellis, and B. Bandinel, 6 vols. in 8 pts (1817–30); repr. (1846) and (1970)
DWB	J. E. Lloyd and others, eds., *Dictionary of Welsh biography down to 1940* (1959) [Eng. trans. of *Y bywgraffiadur Cymreig hyd 1940*, 2nd edn (1954)]
EdinR	*Edinburgh Review, or, Critical Journal*
EETS	Early English Text Society
Emden, *Cam.*	A. B. Emden, *A biographical register of the University of Cambridge to 1500* (1963)
Emden, *Oxf.*	A. B. Emden, *A biographical register of the University of Oxford to AD 1500*, 3 vols. (1957–9); also *A biographical register of the University of Oxford, AD 1501 to 1540* (1974)
EngHR	*English Historical Review*
Engraved Brit. ports.	F. M. O'Donoghue and H. M. Hake, *Catalogue of engraved British portraits preserved in the department of prints and drawings in the British Museum*, 6 vols. (1908–25)
ER	The English Reports, 178 vols. (1900–32)
ESTC	*English short title catalogue, 1475–1800* [CD-ROM and online]
Evelyn, *Diary*	*The diary of John Evelyn*, ed. E. S. De Beer, 6 vols. (1955); repr. (2000)
Farington, *Diary*	*The diary of Joseph Farington*, ed. K. Garlick and others, 17 vols. (1978–98)
Fasti Angl. (Hardy)	J. Le Neve, *Fasti ecclesiae Anglicanae*, ed. T. D. Hardy, 3 vols. (1854)
Fasti Angl., 1066–1300	[J. Le Neve], *Fasti ecclesiae Anglicanae, 1066–1300*, ed. D. E. Greenway and J. S. Barrow, [8 vols.] (1968–)
Fasti Angl., 1300–1541	[J. Le Neve], *Fasti ecclesiae Anglicanae, 1300–1541*, 12 vols. (1962–7)
Fasti Angl., 1541–1857	[J. Le Neve], *Fasti ecclesiae Anglicanae, 1541–1857*, ed. J. M. Horn, D. M. Smith, and D. S. Bailey, [9 vols.] (1969–)
Fasti Scot.	H. Scott, *Fasti ecclesiae Scoticanae*, 3 vols. in 6 (1871); new edn, [11 vols.] (1915–)
FO List	*Foreign Office List*
Fortescue, *Brit. army*	J. W. Fortescue, *A history of the British army*, 13 vols. (1899–1930)
Foss, *Judges*	E. Foss, *The judges of England*, 9 vols. (1848–64); repr. (1966)
Foster, *Alum. Oxon.*	J. Foster, ed., *Alumni Oxonienses: the members of the University of Oxford, 1715–1886*, 4 vols. (1887–8); later edn (1891); also *Alumni Oxonienses … 1500–1714*, 4 vols. (1891–2); 8 vol. repr. (1968) and (2000)
Fuller, *Worthies*	T. Fuller, *The history of the worthies of England*, 4 pts (1662); new edn, 2 vols., ed. J. Nichols (1811); new edn, 3 vols., ed. P. A. Nuttall (1840); repr. (1965)
GEC, *Baronetage*	G. E. Cokayne, *Complete baronetage*, 6 vols. (1900–09); repr. (1983) [microprint]
GEC, *Peerage*	G. E. C. [G. E. Cokayne], *The complete peerage of England, Scotland, Ireland, Great Britain, and the United Kingdom*, 8 vols. (1887–98); new edn, ed. V. Gibbs and others, 14 vols. in 15 (1910–98); microprint repr. (1982) and (1987)
Genest, *Eng. stage*	J. Genest, *Some account of the English stage from the Restoration in 1660 to 1830*, 10 vols. (1832); repr. [New York, 1965]
Gillow, *Lit. biog. hist.*	J. Gillow, *A literary and biographical history or bibliographical dictionary of the English Catholics, from the breach with Rome, in 1534, to the present time*, 5 vols. [1885–1902]; repr. (1961); repr. with preface by C. Gillow (1999)
Gir. Camb. opera	*Giraldi Cambrensis opera*, ed. J. S. Brewer, J. F. Dimock, and G. F. Warner, 8 vols., Rolls Series, 21 (1861–91)
GJ	*Geographical Journal*

Gladstone, *Diaries* — *The Gladstone diaries: with cabinet minutes and prime-ministerial correspondence*, ed. M. R. D. Foot and H. C. G. Matthew, 14 vols. (1968–94)

GM — *Gentleman's Magazine*

Graves, *Artists* — A. Graves, ed., *A dictionary of artists who have exhibited works in the principal London exhibitions of oil paintings from 1760 to 1880* (1884); new edn (1895); 3rd edn (1901); facs. edn (1969); repr. [1970], (1973), and (1984)

Graves, *Brit. Inst.* — A. Graves, *The British Institution, 1806–1867: a complete dictionary of contributors and their work from the foundation of the institution* (1875); facs. edn (1908); repr. (1969)

Graves, *RA exhibitors* — A. Graves, *The Royal Academy of Arts: a complete dictionary of contributors and their work from its foundation in 1769 to 1904*, 8 vols. (1905–6); repr. in 4 vols. (1970) and (1972)

Graves, *Soc. Artists* — A. Graves, *The Society of Artists of Great Britain, 1760–1791, the Free Society of Artists, 1761–1783: a complete dictionary* (1907); facs. edn (1969)

Greaves & Zaller, *BDBR* — R. L. Greaves and R. Zaller, eds., *Biographical dictionary of British radicals in the seventeenth century*, 3 vols. (1982–4)

Grove, *Dict. mus.* — G. Grove, ed., *A dictionary of music and musicians*, 5 vols. (1878–90); 2nd edn, ed. J. A. Fuller Maitland (1904–10); 3rd edn, ed. H. C. Colles (1927); 4th edn with suppl. (1940); 5th edn, ed. E. Blom, 9 vols. (1954); suppl. (1961) [see also *New Grove*]

Hall, *Dramatic ports.* — L. A. Hall, *Catalogue of dramatic portraits in the theatre collection of the Harvard College library*, 4 vols. (1930–34)

Hansard — *Hansard's parliamentary debates*, ser. 1–5 (1803–)

Highfill, Burnim & Langhans, *BDA* — P. H. Highfill, K. A. Burnim, and E. A. Langhans, *A biographical dictionary of actors, actresses, musicians, dancers, managers, and other stage personnel in London, 1660–1800*, 16 vols. (1973–93)

Hist. U. Oxf. — T. H. Aston, ed., *The history of the University of Oxford*, 8 vols. (1984–2000) [1: *The early Oxford schools*, ed. J. I. Catto (1984); 2: *Late medieval Oxford*, ed. J. I. Catto and R. Evans (1992); 3: *The collegiate university*, ed. J. McConica (1986); 4: *Seventeenth-century Oxford*, ed. N. Tyacke (1997); 5: *The eighteenth century*, ed. L. S. Sutherland and L. G. Mitchell (1986); 6–7: *Nineteenth-century Oxford*, ed. M. G. Brock and M. C. Curthoys (1997–2000); 8: *The twentieth century*, ed. B. Harrison (2000)]

HJ — *Historical Journal*

HMC — Historical Manuscripts Commission

Holdsworth, *Eng. law* — W. S. Holdsworth, *A history of English law*, ed. A. L. Goodhart and H. L. Hanbury, 17 vols. (1903–72)

HoP, *Commons* — *The history of parliament: the House of Commons* [1386–1421, ed. J. S. Roskell, L. Clark, and C. Rawcliffe, 4 vols. (1992); 1509–1558, ed. S. T. Bindoff, 3 vols. (1982); 1558–1603, ed. P. W. Hasler, 3 vols. (1981); 1660–1690, ed. B. D. Henning, 3 vols. (1983); 1690–1715, ed. D. W. Hayton, E. Cruickshanks, and S. Handley, 5 vols. (2002); 1715–1754, ed. R. Sedgwick, 2 vols. (1970); 1754–1790, ed. L. Namier and J. Brooke, 3 vols. (1964), repr. (1985); 1790–1820, ed. R. G. Thorne, 5 vols. (1986); in draft (used with permission): 1422–1504, 1604–1629, 1640–1660, and 1820–1832]

IGI — *International Genealogical Index*, Church of Jesus Christ of the Latterday Saints

ILN — *Illustrated London News*

IMC — Irish Manuscripts Commission

Irving, *Scots.* — J. Irving, ed., *The book of Scotsmen eminent for achievements in arms and arts, church and state, law, legislation and literature, commerce, science, travel and philanthropy* (1881)

JCS — *Journal of the Chemical Society*

JHC — *Journals of the House of Commons*

JHL — *Journals of the House of Lords*

John of Worcester, *Chron.* — *The chronicle of John of Worcester*, ed. R. R. Darlington and P. McGurk, trans. J. Bray and P. McGurk, 3 vols., OMT (1995–) [vol. 1 forthcoming]

Keeler, *Long Parliament* — M. F. Keeler, *The Long Parliament, 1640–1641: a biographical study of its members* (1954)

Kelly, *Handbk* — *The upper ten thousand: an alphabetical list of all members of noble families*, 3 vols. (1875–7); continued as *Kelly's handbook of the upper ten thousand for 1878* [1879], 2 vols. (1878–9); continued as *Kelly's handbook to the titled, landed and official classes*, 94 vols. (1880–1973)

LondG — *London Gazette*

LP Henry VIII — J. S. Brewer, J. Gairdner, and R. H. Brodie, eds., *Letters and papers, foreign and domestic, of the reign of Henry VIII*, 23 vols. in 38 (1862–1932); repr. (1965)

Mallalieu, *Watercolour artists* — H. L. Mallalieu, *The dictionary of British watercolour artists up to 1820*, 3 vols. (1976–90); vol. 1, 2nd edn (1986)

Memoirs FRS — *Biographical Memoirs of Fellows of the Royal Society*

MGH — Monumenta Germaniae Historica

MT — *Musical Times*

Munk, *Roll* — W. Munk, *The roll of the Royal College of Physicians of London*, 2 vols. (1861); 2nd edn, 3 vols. (1878)

N&Q — *Notes and Queries*

New Grove — S. Sadie, ed., *The new Grove dictionary of music and musicians*, 20 vols. (1980); 2nd edn, 29 vols. (2001) [also online edn; see also Grove, *Dict. mus.*]

Nichols, *Illustrations* — J. Nichols and J. B. Nichols, *Illustrations of the literary history of the eighteenth century*, 8 vols. (1817–58)

Nichols, *Lit. anecdotes* — J. Nichols, *Literary anecdotes of the eighteenth century*, 9 vols. (1812–16); facs. edn (1966)

Obits. FRS — *Obituary Notices of Fellows of the Royal Society*

O'Byrne, *Naval biog. dict.* — W. R. O'Byrne, *A naval biographical dictionary* (1849); repr. (1990); [2nd edn], 2 vols. (1861)

OHS — Oxford Historical Society

Old Westminsters — *The record of Old Westminsters*, 1–2, ed. G. F. R. Barker and A. H. Stenning (1928); suppl. 1, ed. J. B. Whitmore and G. R. Y. Radcliffe [1938]; 3, ed. J. B. Whitmore, G. R. Y. Radcliffe, and D. C. Simpson (1963); suppl. 2, ed. F. E. Pagan (1978); 4, ed. F. E. Pagan and H. E. Pagan (1992)

OMT — Oxford Medieval Texts

Ordericus Vitalis, *Eccl. hist.* — *The ecclesiastical history of Orderic Vitalis*, ed. and trans. M. Chibnall, 6 vols., OMT (1969–80); repr. (1990)

Paris, *Chron.* — *Matthaei Parisiensis, monachi sancti Albani, chronica majora*, ed. H. R. Luard, Rolls Series, 7 vols. (1872–83)

Parl. papers — *Parliamentary papers* (1801–)

PBA — *Proceedings of the British Academy*

Pepys, *Diary*	*The diary of Samuel Pepys*, ed. R. Latham and W. Matthews, 11 vols. (1970–83); repr. (1995) and (2000)
Pevsner	N. Pevsner and others, Buildings of England series
PICE	*Proceedings of the Institution of Civil Engineers*
Pipe rolls	*The great roll of the pipe for . . .*, PRSoc. (1884–)
PRO	Public Record Office
PRS	*Proceedings of the Royal Society of London*
PRSoc.	Pipe Roll Society
PTRS	*Philosophical Transactions of the Royal Society*
QR	*Quarterly Review*
RC	Record Commissions
Redgrave, *Artists*	S. Redgrave, *A dictionary of artists of the English school* (1874); rev. edn (1878); repr. (1970)
Reg. Oxf.	C. W. Boase and A. Clark, eds., *Register of the University of Oxford*, 5 vols., OHS, 1, 10–12, 14 (1885–9)
Reg. PCS	J. H. Burton and others, eds., *The register of the privy council of Scotland*, 1st ser., 14 vols. (1877–98); 2nd ser., 8 vols. (1899–1908); 3rd ser., [16 vols.] (1908–70)
Reg. RAN	H. W. C. Davis and others, eds., *Regesta regum Anglo-Normannorum, 1066–1154*, 4 vols. (1913–69)
RIBA Journal	*Journal of the Royal Institute of British Architects* [later *RIBA Journal*]
RotP	J. Strachey, ed., *Rotuli parliamentorum ut et petitiones, et placita in parliamento*, 6 vols. (1767–77)
RotS	D. Macpherson, J. Caley, and W. Illingworth, eds., *Rotuli Scotiae in Turri Londinensi et in domo capitulari Westmonasteriensi asservati*, 2 vols., RC, 14 (1814–19)
RS	Record(s) Society
Rymer, *Foedera*	T. Rymer and R. Sanderson, eds., *Foedera, conventiones, literae et cuiuscunque generis acta publica inter reges Angliae et alios quosvis imperatores, reges, pontifices, principes, vel communitates*, 20 vols. (1704–35); 2nd edn, 20 vols. (1726–35); 3rd edn, 10 vols. (1739–45); facs. edn (1967); new edn, ed. A. Clarke, J. Caley, and F. Holbrooke, 4 vols., RC, 50 (1816–30)
Sainty, *Judges*	J. Sainty, ed., *The judges of England, 1272–1990*, SeldS, suppl. ser., 10 (1993)
Sainty, *King's counsel*	J. Sainty, ed., *A list of English law officers and king's counsel*, SeldS, suppl. ser., 7 (1987)
SCH	Studies in Church History
Scots peerage	J. B. Paul, ed. *The Scots peerage, founded on Wood's edition of Sir Robert Douglas's Peerage of Scotland, containing an historical and genealogical account of the nobility of that kingdom*, 9 vols. (1904–14)
SeldS	Selden Society
SHR	*Scottish Historical Review*
State trials	T. B. Howell and T. J. Howell, eds., *Cobbett's Complete collection of state trials*, 34 vols. (1809–28)
STC, 1475–1640	A. W. Pollard, G. R. Redgrave, and others, eds., *A short-title catalogue of . . . English books . . . 1475–1640* (1926); 2nd edn, ed. W. A. Jackson, F. S. Ferguson, and K. F. Pantzer, 3 vols. (1976–91) [see also Wing, *STC*]
STS	Scottish Text Society
SurtS	Surtees Society
Symeon of Durham, *Opera*	*Symeonis monachi opera omnia*, ed. T. Arnold, 2 vols., Rolls Series, 75 (1882–5); repr. (1965)
Tanner, *Bibl. Brit.-Hib.*	T. Tanner, *Bibliotheca Britannico-Hibernica*, ed. D. Wilkins (1748); repr. (1963)
Thieme & Becker, *Allgemeines Lexikon*	U. Thieme, F. Becker, and H. Vollmer, eds., *Allgemeines Lexikon der bildenden Künstler von der Antike bis zur Gegenwart*, 37 vols. (Leipzig, 1907–50); repr. (1961–5), (1983), and (1992)
Thurloe, *State papers*	*A collection of the state papers of John Thurloe*, ed. T. Birch, 7 vols. (1742)
TLS	*Times Literary Supplement*
Tout, *Admin. hist.*	T. F. Tout, *Chapters in the administrative history of mediaeval England: the wardrobe, the chamber, and the small seals*, 6 vols. (1920–33); repr. (1967)
TRHS	*Transactions of the Royal Historical Society*
VCH	H. A. Doubleday and others, eds., *The Victoria history of the counties of England*, [88 vols.] (1900–)
Venn, *Alum. Cant.*	J. Venn and J. A. Venn, *Alumni Cantabrigienses: a biographical list of all known students, graduates, and holders of office at the University of Cambridge, from the earliest times to 1900*, 10 vols. (1922–54); repr. in 2 vols. (1974–8)
Vertue, *Note books*	[G. Vertue], *Note books*, ed. K. Esdaile, earl of Ilchester, and H. M. Hake, 6 vols., Walpole Society, 18, 20, 22, 24, 26, 30 (1930–55)
VF	*Vanity Fair*
Walford, *County families*	E. Walford, *The county families of the United Kingdom, or, Royal manual of the titled and untitled aristocracy of Great Britain and Ireland* (1860)
Walker rev.	A. G. Matthews, *Walker revised: being a revision of John Walker's Sufferings of the clergy during the grand rebellion, 1642–60* (1948); repr. (1988)
Walpole, *Corr.*	*The Yale edition of Horace Walpole's correspondence*, ed. W. S. Lewis, 48 vols. (1937–83)
Ward, *Men of the reign*	T. H. Ward, ed., *Men of the reign: a biographical dictionary of eminent persons of British and colonial birth who have died during the reign of Queen Victoria* (1885); repr. (Graz, 1968)
Waterhouse, *18c painters*	E. Waterhouse, *The dictionary of 18th century painters in oils and crayons* (1981); repr. as *British 18th century painters in oils and crayons* (1991), vol. 2 of *Dictionary of British art*
Watt, *Bibl. Brit.*	R. Watt, *Bibliotheca Britannica, or, A general index to British and foreign literature*, 4 vols. (1824) [many reprs.]
Wellesley index	W. E. Houghton, ed., *The Wellesley index to Victorian periodicals, 1824–1900*, 5 vols. (1966–89); new edn (1999) [CD-ROM]
Wing, *STC*	D. Wing, ed., *Short-title catalogue of . . . English books . . . 1641–1700*, 3 vols. (1945–51); 2nd edn (1972–88); rev. and enl. edn, ed. J. J. Morrison, C. W. Nelson, and M. Seccombe, 4 vols. (1994–8) [see also *STC, 1475–1640*]
Wisden	*John Wisden's Cricketer's Almanack*
Wood, *Ath. Oxon.*	A. Wood, *Athenae Oxonienses . . . to which are added the Fasti*, 2 vols. (1691–2); 2nd edn (1721); new edn, 4 vols., ed. P. Bliss (1813–20); repr. (1967) and (1969)
Wood, *Vic. painters*	C. Wood, *Dictionary of Victorian painters* (1971); 2nd edn (1978); 3rd edn as *Victorian painters*, 2 vols. (1995), vol. 4 of *Dictionary of British art*
WW	*Who's who* (1849–)
WWBMP	M. Stenton and S. Lees, eds., *Who's who of British members of parliament*, 4 vols. (1976–81)
WWW	*Who was who* (1929–)

Box, Betty Evelyn (1915–1999), film producer, was born on 25 September 1915 at 283 Beckenham Road, Beckenham, Kent, the youngest of the five children of Frank Edward Box (*d.* 1939×48), nurseryman, then serving as a private in the 11th battalion, Royal West Kent regiment, and his wife, Eva Annie Dowling, dressmaker. Her eldest brother was Sydney *Box (1907–1983), film producer. She was educated at Balgowan primary school, Sydenham, Bromley Road elementary school, Beckenham, and the girls' elementary school, Beckenham. She then trained as a commercial artist, and took courses in shorthand and accountancy. In the early 1930s she joined the Young Communists and the Gollancz Left Book Club, although her left-wing affiliations were short-lived. On 6 September 1939 she married Victor Albert Langfeld Taylor (*b.* 1913/14), motor mechanic, and son of Frederick Robert Taylor, guest house proprietor, of Bournemouth. The marriage ended in divorce in 1943.

In early 1942 Sydney Box asked Betty to help him run Verity Films, which was making wartime propaganda. At Verity she used her organizational skills, contributing to over 200 documentaries. Apart from the technical work of the cameramen and recordists, she turned her hand to anything, and when Rank appointed Sydney Box to Gainsborough in 1946, Sydney made her head of the Islington branch of the studio. She exerted considerable creative control over the dozen films she made at Gainsborough, and in films such as *Miranda* (1948) and *Here Come the Huggetts* (1948) she combined a lightness of touch with a lack of pretension and dogma.

The late 1940s were a turning point for Box, both personally and professionally. On 24 December 1948 (having formally changed her name by deed poll back to Box) she married Peter Edward Rogers (*b.* 1916), film producer, and son of Claude Edward Thomas Rogers, land surveyor. He became producer of the *Carry on* films, and with him Box shared a healthy pragmatism about popular taste and film profits. In the following year she met the director Ralph Thomas (1915–2001), with whom she collaborated for the rest of her career. As a producer–director team, Box and Rogers were a formidable combination. They worked for the Rank Organisation at Pinewood from 1949 to 1979, and their films are an index of the varying fortunes of the British film industry.

During the 1950s Box's organizational talents earned her the nickname Betty Box Office. *Doctor in the House* (1954) was one of the greatest hits of the 1950s, and was entirely Box's idea. Reading the Richard Gordon novel on a train, she realized its potential and set about restructuring it for the audience tastes of the period. Rank's executive producers, John Davis and Earl St John, were chary of the project. However, the film's box-office performance forced them to revise their policy. The popularity of the *Doctor* films became a handicap for Box. Every time she wanted to begin a more innovatory topic, another *Doctor* film was the price she had to pay. As the 1960s progressed these films, such as *Doctor in Clover*, (1966) were increasingly formulaic.

Some of Box's films of the 1950s and early 1960s did take risks with subject matter. *Conspiracy of Hearts* (1960), about Italian nuns who rescue Jewish children, was (for the period) unusually explicit about antisemitism, and *No Love for Johnnie* (1960) dealt with a Labour MP who succumbs to the blandishments of power. As the 1950s progressed, Box initiated films which combined a raised emotional temperature with foreign locations. *Campbell's Kingdom* (1957) and *The Wind cannot Read* (1958) were melodramas in the Hollywood manner. She attributed their success to their exotic settings, because 'I reckoned you got so much more screen value for the same amount of money' (McFarlane, 86). Only twice in that decade did her commercial instinct falter. She chose to make *A Tale of Two Cities* (1958) in black and white rather than Technicolor, mistakenly thinking that this would confer an art-house cachet onto the film. She was also offered the script of the first James Bond film, but felt that she was not suited to a spies-and-sex blockbuster.

In 1958 Box was appointed OBE for her services to the film industry. The same year marked a turning point in her career; after that, her films were no longer so profitable. This was not because she had lost her touch, but because the Rank Organisation, like the other big distribution combines, was too inflexible to respond to new themes and audiences. Box was ultimately inhibited by the company to which she had given her professional life. Many of her films in the 1960s, such as the spy spoofs *Hot Enough for June* (1963) and *Some Girls Do* (1969), were uneven, and her career ended with limp films such as *Percy* (1971) and *Percy's Progress* (1974).

Box had a broad definition of the producer's role: budget management, selection of the topic, nuancing of the script, selection of personnel. She was well served by actors, whose careers she often established, but was less well served by her scriptwriters, who often turned in ill-crafted scripts. She never felt disadvantaged as a woman in a man's industry, and thought it better to operate by charm than by confrontation. Although the only major woman film producer in Britain in the 1940s, 1950s, and 1960s, she was modest about her work. In 1992 she received the first UK Women in Film lifetime achievement award. She died of cancer at her home, The Oaks, Manor Lane, Gerrards Cross, Buckinghamshire, on 15 January 1999. She was survived by her husband, Peter Rogers. She had no children. Her autobiography, *Lifting the Lid*, was published posthumously in 2000.   SUE HARPER

Sources B. Box, *Lifting the lid* (2000) · S. Harper, *Women in British cinema: mad, bad and dangerous to know* (2000) · B. McFarlane, ed., *An autobiography of British cinema* (1997) · J. Ashby, 'Betty Box, the lady in charge', in J. Ashby and A. Higson, *British cinema past and present* (2000) · *Classic Images* (March 1996) · *The Guardian* (16 Jan 1999) · *The Times* (18 Jan 1999) · *The Independent* (18 Jan 1999) · *Daily Telegraph* (18 Jan 1999) · WWW · b. cert. · m. certs. · d. cert.

Archives FILM BFI NFTVA, interviews

Likenesses group portrait, photograph, 1940–49, repro. in *The Guardian* · photograph, 1949, repro. in *The Independent* · photograph, 1971, repro. in *Daily Telegraph* · photograph, repro. in *The Times*

Wealth at death £2,811,251—gross; £2,775,011—net: probate, 18 March 1999, CGPLA Eng. & Wales

Box [*née* Baker], **(Violette) Muriel** [*other married name* (Violette) Muriel Gardiner, Lady Gardiner] **(1905–1991)**, screenwriter and film director, was born on 22 September 1905 at Simla, Poplar Grove, New Malden, Surrey, the third child of Charles Stephen Baker (*d.* 1945), a clerk for the South Western Railway at Waterloo, and his wife, Caroline Beatrice, *née* Doney (1872–1961), variously a pupil teacher, a maid, and an assistant in a magic-lantern shop. Nicknamed Tiggy, she received her primary education at St Matthew's School, Tolworth, Surrey, and in 1915 she began attending Holy Cross Convent in Wimbledon, only to be expelled, primarily because she had not been baptized. She then transferred to Surbiton high school, where she began to take ballet lessons and also studied drama under actor–manager Sir Ben Greet. Contemporaneously, a chance meeting with Joseph Grossman of Stoll Pictures led to her securing work as an extra in *The Wandering Jew* and in the thriller series *The Old Man in the Corner* (both 1920).

Muriel Baker became more fully involved in films in 1929, when she quit her typing job at Barclays Corsets in Welwyn Garden City, Hertfordshire, to join the scenario department of British Instructional Pictures. With the advent of talkies she was promoted to read unsolicited manuscripts and she rapidly developed both a sure story sense and a keen ear for dialogue, which she exploited in a series of short pieces, written for the Welwyn Folk Players. However, her real education in film came on Anthony Asquith's *Tell England* (1930), on which she served as continuity clerk. She soon transferred to British International Pictures at Elstree, where one of her assignments was Alfred Hitchcock's *Number Seventeen* (1931). In 1932, while based at Michael Powell's 99 Company, she unsuccessfully auditioned for the Royal Academy of Dramatic Art, but found solace in aspiring playwright Sydney *Box (1907–1983). Following his divorce from Katherine Knight in 1934, he and Muriel Baker married at Holborn register office on 23 May 1935.

By this time Muriel Baker and Sydney Box had already published two collections of playlets, *Ladies Only* (1934) and *Petticoat Plays* (1935), which were written specifically for all-female amateur casts. Shortly after their début professional production, *Mr Penny's Tuppence*, opened at the Opera House, Blackpool, they completed the first of their twenty-two film scripts, *Alibi Inn* (1935), an undistinguished melodrama, which was directed by Pen Tennyson. As she later explained, 'I used to do the overall plot, then Sydney would start work on it and "diddy it up" wherever he could … it would usually go through five or six stages' (McFarlane, 89). Following the birth of their daughter, Leonora, on 5 November 1936, Muriel Box resumed her writing career with the little-seen play *Home from Home* (1939) and she received her first solo screenwriting credit on the Ministry of Information's *A Ride with Uncle Joe* (1939). She then rejoined Sydney at Verity Films, which by 1942 was the largest documentary operation in Britain. Muriel Box's directorial début, *The English Inn* (1941), was among the more than 100 information and training films that the company produced, yet, within a year, she had

(Violette) **Muriel Box (1905–1991)**, by unknown photographer

been removed from *Road Safety for Children*, as propaganda chief Arthur Elton believed that women were unsuited to directing.

Sydney Box, however, continued to exhibit unswerving faith in his wife and they coproduced *29 Acacia Avenue* in 1945 (although it was not released for another two years, as the strict Methodist J. Arthur Rank considered it to be unwholesome). By this time the Boxes had won an Academy award for their screenplay for *The Seventh Veil* (1945), one of the first features to take psychiatry seriously. Yet Muriel was still frustrated in her ambition to direct, with Michael Balcon refusing to give the go-ahead to her 1950 reworking of *Romeo and Juliet*, as he reckoned she could never command the respect of a feature crew. It took Sydney's formation of London Independent Producers for Muriel to make the breakthrough. Shot in just twenty-three days, *The Happy Family* (1952) made little critical or commercial impact, but *Street Corner* (1953), a female riposte to *The Blue Lamp*, *The Beachcomber* (1954), a sturdy remake of *The Vessel of Wrath*, and the stinging television satire *Simon and Laura* (1955) were more warmly received. In spite of the social awareness and technical assurance of her work, Box always found funding difficult and had to make the Children's Film Foundation's Napoleonic drama *The Piper's Tune* (1962) for a mere £22,000.

Shortly after directing her thirteenth and final feature, *Rattle of a Simple Man* (1964), Muriel Box separated from Sydney and turned her back on film to co-found the UK's first feminist publishing company, Femina, which boasted Vera Brittain among its board members. Muriel Box personally edited the imprint's first volume, *The Trial* *of Marie Stopes*, although all attempts to bring it to the screen foundered. She was divorced from Sydney Box in May 1969 and on 28 August 1970 she married Gerald Austin *Gardiner, Baron Gardiner of Kittisford (1900–1990), lord chancellor from 1964 to 1970. He was the son of Sir Robert Septimus Gardiner, company director, and the widower of Lesly Doris, only daughter of Alderman Edwin Trounson of Southport. Following her marriage Muriel Gardiner became an increasingly active campaigner for women's rights, notably assisting Lady Edith Summerskill in her bid to reform the divorce laws. She completed her own memoirs, *Odd Woman Out*, in 1974, and published a biography of her husband, *Rebel Advocate*, in 1983. Although never an innovative or bankable talent, Muriel Box was justly, if belatedly, hailed in the 1980s as an inspiration to women film-makers everywhere for managing to overcome the prejudices of a male-dominated industry. She died on 18 May 1991 at Mote End, Nan Clark's Lane, Mill Hill, London, which had been her home since before her marriage to Gerald Gardiner. She was survived by her daughter, Leonora; Gerald Gardiner had died sixteen months previously.   DAVID PARKINSON

Sources M. Box, *Odd woman out: an autobiography* (1974) · B. McFarlane, ed., *An autobiography of British cinema* (1997) · C. Merz, 'Muriel Box', *The St James women filmmakers encyclopedia*, ed. A. L. Unterburger (1999) · D. Quinlan, *Quinlan's film directors*, 2nd edn (1999) · *The Times* (22 May 1991) · *The Independent* (23 May 1991) · *The Independent* (30 May 1991) · *The Independent* (12 June 1991) · WWW · Burke, *Peerage* · b. cert. · m. cert. [Gerald Austin Gardiner] · d. cert.
Archives BFI, screenplays, diaries, and papers
Likenesses photograph, repro. in *The Times* · photograph, repro. in *The Independent* (23 May 1991) · photograph, BFI [*see illus.*] · photographs, London, Kobal collection · photographs, Ronald Grant archive · photographs, Huntley archive
Wealth at death £868,853: probate, 1 July 1991, *CGPLA Eng. & Wales*

Box, (Frank) Sydney (1907–1983), film-maker and writer, was born on 26 April 1907 in Beckenham, Kent, the son of Frank Box, a career soldier who was wounded in the First World War, and his wife, a seamstress whose maiden name was Dowling. As the eldest, Sydney helped his mother bring up his four siblings, while his father served as a quartermaster at a distant camp. She persuaded the eleven-year-old to enter a prize-winning one-act play in a local arts festival and, two years later, encouraged him to become a cub reporter on the *Kentish Times*.

Having taken a job in the City of London, Box began writing and producing plays for the Beckenham Dramatic and Operatic Society, where he met his first wife, Katherine Knight; they were married in 1929. However, 'her match did not strike on Sydney Box' (M. Box, 132) and the marriage was subsequently dissolved in 1934. Box began an affair with Muriel Baker (1905–1991) [*see* Box, (Violette) Muriel], a continuity clerk employed by film director Michael Powell, whom he met after his play, *Murder Trial*, won the Welwyn cup in 1932.

Sydney and Muriel began collaborating on a series of playlets, six of which were published as *Ladies Only* in 1934. In the following year *Not this Man* won the National Drama

Festival Award at the Old Vic, only for the press to denounce it as blasphemous. Box sued for libel, and the couple's lawyer advised them that living together would not impress the jury, so they married in Holborn register office on 23 May 1935. Their daughter, Leonora, was born on 5 November 1936.

By 1939 Box had over fifty plays, several librettos, and the book, *Film Publicity* (1937), to his credit. Yet, despite being invited to script commentaries for documentarist Ralph Smart, he remained a journalist. In addition to writing 'slightly imaginative news stories' (M. Box, 123) for *Renter* and *Today's*, he also worked as a weekend sub-editor on the *Christian Herald*, the *Evening News* and the *Evening Standard*, as well as contributing to several Beckenham journals.

However, in 1940 he formed Verity Films, with Jay Lewis, to produce commercials and documentaries. Rejected for national service on account of a leg disability, he threw himself into making government-sponsored shorts such as *The Soldier's Food* (1940). However, the War Office and similar agencies were notoriously slow payers, and the partnership dissolved acrimoniously in the spring of 1941. Undeterred, Box refloated the company with a loan from the Film Producers Guild and within a year it was the country's biggest producer of propaganda and training films.

Having bought out Green Park Productions, Box moved into features, with *The Flemish Farm* (1943) and *On Approval* (1944). Following a spell at Two Cities, he took a lease on the Riverside Studios and resumed independent production with *29 Acacia Avenue* (1945). However, his greatest triumph was *The Seventh Veil* (1945), a melodrama starring Ann Todd that not only became a huge commercial hit, but also landed Sydney and Muriel the Oscar for best original screenplay.

Flushed with success, Box accepted the offer of fellow Methodist J. Arthur Rank to become managing director of Gainsborough Studios. Muriel was placed in charge of script development and they produced a number of successful and diverse pictures, including Carol Reed's *Holiday Camp* (1947), the Margaret Lockwood costume drama *Jassy* (1947), and the Somerset Maugham adaptations *Quartet* (1948) and *Trio* (1950).

In her autobiography *Odd Woman Out*, Muriel summed up their working relationship: 'Sydney has a sanguine, buoyant temperament which helped him take everything in his stride with the minimum of fuss. He was an incurable optimist, I am an incurable pessimist, which created a neat balance' (M. Box, 138). A contemporary profile painted a less idyllic picture, however, alluding to the creative tension engendered by his short temper. Yet it also admired his energy and commitment: 'He bites off large lumps of life. But there's a baby face, a soft voice, refinement, sensitivity and the odd paradox of urbane naivety' (*John Bull*, 5 Oct 1946).

Dismayed by a frustrating stay at Pinewood Studios (1949–50), Box took a year-long sabbatical to tour France and the United States. On his return he founded London Independent Producers to make Muriel's *The Happy Family*

(1952). *Street Corner* (1953) and *The Beachcomber* (1954) followed and, with his younger sister, Betty *Box, also now making films, the Boxes seemed set to dominate the British film industry. Indeed, Noël Coward even dubbed them 'the Brontës of Shepherd's Bush'.

In 1959, while negotiating a Hollywood deal to make *William the Conqueror*, Box suffered a cerebral haemorrhage and handed over his affairs to his brother-in-law, Peter Rogers. However, he made a surprise return to cinema in 1963, when he launched an unsuccessful bid to acquire British Lion Films after it was put up for auction by the government. He finally bowed out of pictures with Muriel's *Rattle of a Simple Man* (1964) and devoted his energies to acting as a director of Tyne-Tees Television and managing his 300 acre dairy farm at Mill Hill. However, he still harboured hopes of turning London Independent Producers into an agency for small-screen talent and possibly even launching his own television station. But a series of heart attacks in 1967 persuaded him to emigrate to Perth, Australia.

Divorced from Muriel in May 1969, Box married Sylvia Knowles in July. In the same year he published his first novel, *Diary of a Drop-out*; three more books, all whodunnits, followed over the ensuing decade, during which time he also sat on the Western Australian Arts Council. Sydney Box died in Perth on 25 May 1983.   DAVID PARKINSON

Sources M. Box, *Odd woman out: an autobiography* (1974) · B. Box, *Lifting the lid* (2000) · *The Times* (26 Dec 1963) · *The Times* (26 May 1983) · *John Bull* (5 Oct 1946) · *Daily Express* (26 Sept 1959) · *The Observer* (5 Jan 1964) · *CGPLA Eng. & Wales* (1985) · www.uk.imdb.com, 8 April 2002
Archives BFI, corresp. and papers | Bodl. Oxf., corresp. with R. B. Montgomery
Wealth at death £11,418—in England and Wales: Australian probate sealed in England, 1 July 1985, *CGPLA Eng. & Wales*

Boxall, Sir Charles Gervaise (1851–1914), army officer and promoter of rail-mounted artillery, was born on 30 August 1851 at Delves House, Ringmer, Sussex, the second son of William Percival Boxall JP, of Cowfold, Sussex, and his wife, Caroline Money. Educated privately, then at Brighton College, Boxall married Eugenie Wiles in 1879. In 1873, he was commissioned into the 1st Sussex volunteer artillery (based in Brighton), part of the eastern division of the Royal Garrison Artillery. He developed an interest in rail-mounted artillery, possibly inspired by the armoured railway car containing an artillery battery that was used by the Union army in the closing stages of the American Civil War. In 1884 he published *The Armoured Train for Coast Defence in Great Britain*, outlining a new concept in the use of heavy artillery. Engaging the support of his commanding officer, Sir Julian Goldsmid, and officials of the London, Brighton, and South Coast Railway Company, he mounted a heavy gun on an armoured wagon and demonstrated its ability to fire in all directions. Although the concept of using rail-mounted artillery for coastal defence was never taken up during his lifetime, the invasion scare and shortage of tanks in 1940 resulted in 9.2 inch guns and 12 inch howitzers being set up on railway wagons pulled by their own trains and deployed at key sites along the south coast.

Boxall continued to serve with the same unit and was made lieutenant-colonel commanding in 1893, and honorary colonel in June 1896 following the death of Sir Julian Goldsmid. His long service in the volunteer movement was recognized by the award of the volunteer decoration in 1894 and his creation as a CB in 1897. Boxall listed his leisure pursuits as shooting and tree planting, but he had an interest in historical research and produced *Early Records of the Duke of Manchester's English Manorial Estates* in 1892.

On the outbreak of the Second South African War in 1899, Boxall is said to have originated the idea of sending the City of London Imperial Volunteers (CIV) to serve in southern Africa in support of the regular forces deployed there. On account of its entirely middle-class composition this unit received tremendous publicity, but in fact they were responding to a general call from the War Office to all volunteer infantry to send service companies to southern Africa. *The Times History of the War in South Africa* relates that the origin of the force was in a conversation between Field Marshal Lord Wolseley and A. Newton, the lord mayor of London. What is beyond doubt is that Boxall acted as secretary and depot commandant to the CIV and that he did go to southern Africa at some point. During the campaign armoured trains were constructed and used initially in defence of both Mafeking and Kimberley, as well as for more general patrol work. These carried light armament but, in keeping with Boxall's proposal, a captured Boer 'Long Tom' was mounted on a railway truck for use against its former owners. The second, or guerrilla, phase of the war meant that such heavy artillery was virtually useless. For his services in connection with the war Boxall was created a KCB in 1902.

Boxall served as a member of the committee considering the creation of the Territorial Army from 1906 to 1907, as a member of the Sussex Territorial Association, and as honorary colonel of the 1st home counties field artillery until his death. He died of a heart attack in the Royal Crescent Hotel, Brighton, on 6 March 1914.   PETER LEAD

Sources L. S. Amery, ed., *The Times history of the war in South Africa*, 3 (1905) · C. G. Boxall, *The armoured train for coast defence in Great Britain* (1884) · *Army List* (1899) · *Army List* (1913) · P. Dennis, *The Territorial Army, 1906–1940*, Royal Historical Society Studies in History, 51 (1987) · *The Times* (7 March 1914), 11 · O. S. Nock, *Encyclopaedia of railways* (1977) · H. W. Wilson, *After Pretoria: the guerrilla war*, 2 vols. (1902) · *WW* (1912) · b. cert. · d. cert. · private information (2004)
Likenesses group portrait, 1899? (with officers), repro. in Wilson, *After Pretoria*, vol. 1, p. 7
Wealth at death £68,097 17s. 1d.: probate, 8 May 1914, *CGPLA Eng. & Wales*

Boxall, John (1524/5–1571), administrator, was born at Bramshott, Hampshire, but the identity of his parents is unknown. He was admitted scholar of Winchester College in 1538 at the age of thirteen and proceeded to New College, Oxford, where he was admitted scholar on 9 October 1540 and fellow exactly two years later (vacating in October 1554). It is presumed he graduated in arts at a foreign university, as he supplicated for incorporation as MA at Oxford on 11 July 1554; at the same time he supplicated for the degree of BTh, which was conferred on 15 July. By February 1558 he had proceeded to the doctorate. He appears to have received no benefice before Mary's accession, but was thereafter amply supplied. In 1554 he was admitted rector of Bishop's Hatfield, Hertfordshire. On 15 October he was elected warden of Winchester College (vacated 9 November 1556). He composed a eulogistic account of the first two years of Mary's reign, to the time (spring 1555) when an heir to the throne was expected (BL, Royal MS 12.A.XLIX); this may have brought him recognition at court. In the same year he published a sermon preached before convocation in St Paul's Cathedral on 22 October. On 26 October he was presented by the crown to a canonry in Winchester Cathedral (vacated by February 1558). His formal move into the crown's service came on 23 September 1556 when he was appointed to the council 'at large' and also as master of requests and a councillor of that court. He probably owed his promotion to Stephen Gardiner, though explicit evidence is lacking. He was at once sent to take part in negotiations with the French over disputed territory in the marches of Calais; he was also (31 October) named a tax collector for Calais. On his return he was named as 'umpire' in a case before the court of requests (*Ancient State*, ed. Hill, 175).

Boxall evidently gave satisfaction in these tasks, as on 21 December he was further promoted to membership of the privy council. Between 28 and 30 March 1557 he succeeded Sir William Petre as one of the two principal secretaries. He subsequently (7 April 1558) received a patent for this office, with an annuity of £100 back-dated to 25 March 1557. It was the first time that the secretaryship had been thus formally conferred, an important stage in the development of the office even though Boxall's tenure of it was unremarkable. His inexperience was such that for several months Petre continued to draft state correspondence. Subsequently Boxall's main concern was foreign affairs, his colleague Sir John Bourne handling home matters. Boxall's secretaryship was dominated by the French war, and his chief business was with Thomas Gresham, arranging finance in the Low Countries, and Sir William Pickering, hiring troops there. In March 1558 Bourne resigned, leaving Boxall sole secretary for the rest of the reign. In September King Philip asked Boxall to be among those sent to treat for peace with the French, but the queen replied that he and the others whom the king named were too ill to leave their chambers; Arundel and Thirlby went instead.

Boxall's ecclesiastical career meanwhile advanced in breadth, if not in eminence. By 21 December 1556 he had become archdeacon of Ely (suggesting that Bishop Thirlby was his patron in a more general way). The queen gave him the deanery of Peterborough on 24 June 1557, and on 1 October the rectory of Overton, Hampshire. On 2 December he was instituted to the deanery of Norwich (vacated by 16 May 1558). On 20 December he was presented to the prebend of Newington in St Paul's Cathedral, in the crown's gift on this occasion. On 19 March 1558 he was appointed dean of Windsor with the associated deanery of

Wolverhampton, and on 21 July he became register of the Order of the Garter. By 25 June 1557 he had acquired the prebend of Ilton in Wells Cathedral. On 3 November he was presented by the crown to the prebend of Grantham Borealis in Salisbury Cathedral. On 5 December he was collated to the prebend of Stillington in York Minster. He also held the rectory of Bolton Percy, Yorkshire. With others he was granted wardship of the heirs of Sir Thomas Cornwallis and the earl of Pembroke (31 January and 5 July 1557) and on 21 May 1557 he received a reversionary grant of lands. On 18 July 1558 he was licensed to retain ten gentlemen or yeomen beyond any to whom he was already entitled, and on 17 October, a month before Mary's death, he was authorized to apply her signature by stamp. The queen and Cardinal Pole named him an overseer of their respective wills.

Boxall's secretaryship was immediately terminated at Elizabeth's accession. In the days on either side of Mary's death he co-operated amicably with his successor, Sir William Cecil, in handing over the papers of the office, though having to make the astonishing revelation that some documents left in the late queen's death chamber had been used to seal her corpse. It was afterwards suggested by Nicholas Sander that Elizabeth was particularly anxious to retain Boxall's services. But while Mary was still alive, Philip II's envoy noted that Elizabeth thought 'muy mal' of him (Rodríguez-Salgado and Adams, 322). Boxall tried to dissuade the queen from giving her assent to the Act of Uniformity. On 2 November 1559 Archbishop Parker was required to administer to him the subsequent oath; on his refusal he was deprived of all his remaining benefices. On 18 June 1560 he was committed to the Tower, where he was allowed some liberty in associating with the other prominent Catholic prisoners. In September 1563 the Tower was evacuated because of plague, and Boxall and Thirlby were committed to Parker's personal custody. Boxall spent the rest of his life in the archbishop's various residences. In June 1564 the council refused him permission to live elsewhere because one of the other Catholic prisoners had broken parole. In July 1569, while at Lambeth, Boxall asked to be allowed to visit his eighty-year-old mother, who was 'dangerously diseasid' (BL, Lansdowne MS 12, fol. 12). Boxall died at Lambeth Palace on 3 or 4 March 1571; his brothers Edmund and Richard were his executors. Boxall was a staunch Catholic, but his disapproval of the Marian persecution gained him esteem from his opponents; Richard Hilles, reporting his death to Bullinger, described him as 'a man of much moderation … and of gentle disposition' (Robinson, 2.183).

C. S. KNIGHTON

Sources T. F. Kirby, *Winchester scholars: a list of the wardens, fellows, and scholars of … Winchester College* (1888) • administration, PRO, PROB 6/1, fol. 171v • Emden, *Oxf.*, 4.65 • *Fasti Angl., 1541–1857*, [St Paul's, London], 47 • *Fasti Angl., 1541–1857*, [Canterbury], 91 • *Fasti Angl., 1541–1857*, [York], 54–5 • *Fasti Angl., 1541–1857*, [Bath and Wells], 71 • *Fasti Angl., 1541–1857*, [Salisbury], 46 • *Fasti Angl., 1541–1857*, [Ely], 13, 15, 42, 91 • *Fasti Angl., 1541–1857*, [Bristol], 119 • CPR, 1555–7, 104, 358, 368, 387, 404, 492; 1557–8, 99, 129, 142, 144, 249, 306, 312, 422–3, 434, 453–4 • PRO, State papers domestic, Elizabeth I, SP 12/1, nos. 5, 39; 23, no. 40 • *CSP dom., 1547–80*, 115, 117, 201; 1553–

8, 336, 359, 362, 375 · *CSP for.*, 1553–8, 302, 305, 339, 368–401 · *CSP for.*, 1558–9, 4–6, 86 · *CSP Spain*, 1554–8, 349, 359, 361 · *CSP Rome*, 1558–71, 64 · *APC*, 1554–6, 359; 1556–8, 26, 33, 70 · *Correspondence of Matthew Parker*, ed. J. Bruce and T. T. Perowne, Parker Society, 42 (1853), 65–6, 104, 122, 192–5, 217–18 · H. Robinson, ed. and trans., *The Zurich letters, comprising the correspondence of several English bishops and other with some of the Helvetian reformers, during the early part of the reign of Queen Elizabeth*, 1, Parker Society, 7 (1842), 255; 2, Parker Society, 8 (1845), 183 · *The ancient state, authoritie, and proceedings of the court of requests by Sir Julius Caesar*, ed. L. M. Hill (1975), 175 · 'The count of Feria's dispatch to Philip II of 14th November 1558', ed. M. J. Rodríguez-Salgado and S. Adams, *Camden miscellany, XXVIII*, CS, 4th ser., 29 (1984) · F. G. Emmison, *Tudor secretary: Sir William Petre at court and home* (1961), 201, 207–8, 209 · D. Loades, *Mary Tudor: a life* (1989), 379 · *The diary of Henry Machyn, citizen and merchant-taylor of London, from AD 1550 to AD 1563*, ed. J. G. Nichols, CS, 42 (1848), 238 · BL, Royal MS 12.A.XLIX · J. Strype, *The life and acts of Matthew Parker*, new edn, 3 vols. (1821), vol. 1, pp. 95, 280–81; vol. 3, pp. 298–9 · J. H. Pollen, ed., 'Dr Nicholas Sander's report to Cardinal Moroni', *Miscellanea, I*, Catholic RS, 1 (1905), 1–47 [from a transcript of Archivio segreto vaticano, Armaria 64:28, fols. 252r–274r], esp. 17, 40–41, 56 · BL, Lansdowne MS 12 · J. Pits, *Relationum historicarum de rebus Anglicis*, ed. [W. Bishop] (Paris, 1619), 869–70

Archives PRO, state papers, foreign, Mary, SP 69
Wealth at death see grant of administration of will, 8 March 1571, PRO, PROB 6/1, fol. 171v

Sir William Boxall (1800–1879), by Michel Angelo Pittatore, 1870

Boxall, Sir William (1800–1879), portrait painter and museum director, was born on 29 June 1800 in or near Oxford, the son of Thomas Boxall, clerk to the collector of excise, and the brother of Anne (d. 1846), later wife of the Revd Charles Boxall Longland. He was educated at Abingdon grammar school and entered the Royal Academy Schools on 26 March 1819, having already exhibited *Portrait of a Lady* at the academy in 1818. In order to study the old masters he made several study trips to Italy, for instance in 1827–8, 1833–6, and 1845. Hoping to establish himself as a history painter he early on painted scenes from mythology, religious texts, and English literature, for example, *Jupiter and Latona* (exh. RA, 1823), *The Contention of Michael and Satan for the Body of Moses* (exh. RA, 1824), and *Lear and Cordelia* (exh. RA, 1831). Of his allegorical works *Hope* (exh. RA, 1840) was considered the best. He also painted a few landscapes, including *View of the Turl with Exeter, Lincoln and Jesus Colleges and All Saints' Church, Oxford* (exh. RA, 1827).

In search of regular employment Boxall turned increasingly to portraiture and enjoyed some reputation in this field between the mid-1830s and the 1860s. He painted society celebrities and hostesses; leading literary, artistic, and intellectual figures of the day, such as his friend William Wordsworth (1831; NPG); and several high-ranking clergymen. His most important commission was a full-length portrait, *The Prince Consort as Master of the Trinity House* (exh. RA, 1859; Trinity House, London). His portraits were rarely acclaimed as good likenesses and sometimes criticized for their lack of finish; several were reproduced as mezzotints by Samuel Cousins. On 3 November 1851 he was elected an associate of the Royal Academy, and in 1863 a full academician (retiring from the academy in 1877); he exhibited eighty-six works at the academy between 1818 and 1880, eleven at the British Institution, and seven at the Society of British Artists in Suffolk Street. He was also elected an honorary academician of the Academy of San Fernando, Madrid, in 1868.

In February 1866 Boxall was appointed director of the National Gallery, succeeding Sir Charles Eastlake; thereafter he virtually ceased to paint. He may have been Eastlake's nominee and certainly was proposed by Gladstone. However, he was not the only, nor the preferred, candidate: the prime minister suggested Austen Henry Layard (under-secretary at the Foreign Office) and Queen Victoria proposed John Charles Robinson (superintendent of art at the South Kensington Museum); Edwin Landseer's name also was put forward. As director Boxall journeyed frequently through Europe to study and make notes on galleries and collections and also to survey pictures for potential acquisition (his papers remain in the National Gallery). He acquired several important paintings during his eight-year tenure, notably Carlo Crivelli's *Demidoff Altarpiece*, in 1868; Michelangelo's *Virgin and Child with Saint John and Angels* (the 'Manchester Madonna'), in 1870; and Mantegna's *Introduction of the Cult of Cybele at Rome*, in 1873. He also increased the gallery's collection of Dutch seventeenth-century paintings, buying Pieter de Hooch's *Woman and her Maid in a Courtyard* in 1869 and successfully negotiating the acquisition of Sir Robert Peel's collection in 1871. Two of his purchases caused controversy: the authenticity of both *Christ Blessing the Children* (the 'Suermondt Rembrandt', now attributed to Nicolaes Maes) and Michelangelo's *Entombment* was questioned in the House of Lords in 1869. During his directorship the gallery was reconstructed and extended by Edward Middleton Barry RA.

In 1871 Boxall expressed his wish to retire on account of ill health (he often complained of lameness and seems to have suffered from depression), but he was persuaded to stay on by the trustees and the prime minister until 20 February 1874. He aided the successful candidature of Fredric Burton as his successor. A close friend from the early 1850s of Eastlake and his wife, Lady Elizabeth (whose portrait he painted in 1854), Boxall acted as one of Eastlake's executors after his death. Subsequently, in 1867, he acquired, through Lady Eastlake, nine paintings from her late husband's collection, including Piero della Francesca's *St Michael* and Pisanello's *Virgin and Child with Saint George and Saint Anthony Abbot*, and also his library. Together with Lady Eastlake, Boxall also ensured that his predecessor's travel journals were collated and transcribed, and a copy deposited in the National Gallery.

Boxall received the degree of DCL from Oxford University in 1870, and a knighthood was conferred on him on 24 March 1871; he was also a fellow of the Royal Society. In character he was solitary and sensitive; his principal companion in his last years was his dog, Garibaldi. Among his closest friends were the sculptor John Gibson (for whom he acted as executor in 1864) and the painters Landseer and Thomas Webster. Boxall died, unmarried, at his home in London—14 Welbeck Street, Cavendish Square—on 6 December 1879, partly from congestion of the lungs, and was buried six days later at Kensal Green cemetery. The contents of his studio were auctioned at Christies on 8 June 1880.   SUSANNA AVERY-QUASH

Sources *DNB* · *The Times* (8 Dec 1879), 8 · *The Athenaeum* (13 Dec 1879), 769–70 · *Art Journal* (1880), 83 · J. D. Coleridge, 'Sir William Boxall, R.A.', *Fortnightly Review*, 33 (1880), 177–89 · J. Egerton, 'Sir William Boxall, R.A.', *National Gallery catalogues: the British school* (1998), 419–25 · M. Levey, 'A little-known director: Sir William Boxall', *Apollo*, 101 (May 1975), 354–9 · Graves, *RA exhibitors* · M. J. H. Liversidge, 'John Ruskin and William Boxall: unpublished correspondence', *Apollo*, 85 (Jan 1967), 39–44 · M. J. H. Liversidge, 'Boxall, Sir William', *The dictionary of art*, ed. J. Turner (1996)
Archives National Gallery, London, corresp., papers, and sketchbooks | National Gallery, London, corresp. with Ralph Nicholson Wornum
Likenesses W. Boxall, self-portrait, oils, c.1819 (aged nineteen?), National Gallery, London · M. A. Pittatore, oils, 1870, NPG [*see illus.*] · A. L. Merritt, oils, c.1875, RA · Elliott & Fry, carte-de-visite, NPG · F. Joubert, carte-de-visite, NPG · W. S. Landors, oils, V&A · J. & C. Watkins, carte-de-visite, NPG · engraving (after photograph by Messrs J. and C. Watkins), repro. in *ILN* (25 July 1863), 80
Wealth at death under £12,000: probate, 17 Dec 1879, *CGPLA Eng. & Wales*

Boxer, Charles Ralph (1904–2000), historian, was born in Sandown, Isle of Wight, on 8 March 1904, the second son of Hugh Edward Richard Boxer (1871–1915), army officer, and his wife, Jane, *née* Patterson (1876–1929). Educated at Wellington College (1918–21) and the Royal Military College, Sandhurst (1922–3), he was commissioned in the Lincolnshire regiment in 1924. After the opening of Japan to the wider world there had been a family connection with that then little-known country, which fascinated Boxer from boyhood. Consequently he was happy to be seconded to a Japanese regiment from 1930 to 1933. This began his lifelong quest to understand the East. He later served in Hong Kong, where he was chief of army intelligence from 1939 to 1941. On 8 June 1939 he married Ursula Norah Anstice Tulloch (1909–1996).

On 20 December 1941, during the Japanese invasion of Hong Kong, Boxer was wounded in action and left with a permanently crippled arm. He was a prisoner of war from 1941 until the end of the war. For much of the time he was kept in solitary confinement. Of those grim years he would say only 'At times, I even prayed' (personal knowledge). Yet he harboured no resentment against his captors, whose victim he was, but whose admirer he remained. Though he was a man of granite integrity, some misinterpreted his magnanimity, and after he was safely dead he was accused, in an article in *The Guardian* (24 February 2001), of having been a Japanese collaborator. Surviving fellow prisoners and colleagues were outraged, and thanks to their protests an article in the same paper (10 March 2001) quickly set the record straight.

In 1945 Boxer was divorced as a result of his widely publicized love affair with the American feminist writer Emily (Mickey) Hahn (1905–1997), with whom he had had a daughter before the invasion of Hong Kong. In November the same year he married Hahn in New York. They had a second daughter, and the marriage lasted fifty-two years. In 1947, on the grounds of disability, he retired from the army with the rank of major. In that same year he was surprised by the offer of the Camoens chair of Portuguese in King's College, London, a post he held until retirement in 1967, except for two years (1951–3) as professor of the history of the Far East in the School of Oriental and African Studies, London. From 1967 until 1979 he was research professor in Indiana University, and simultaneously (1969–72) professor of the history of the expansion of Europe at Yale University. In 1972 he retired from there as emeritus professor. After leaving the army he lived on the family estate in Broadmayne, Dorset, until 1955, when, in order to be nearer London, he moved to Little Gaddesden, Hertfordshire, which was his last home.

Even in his lifetime Boxer was something of a legend. He was forty-three when, without a degree to his name, he was catapulted into academia by the offer of the first of five university chairs in different subjects ranging from Portuguese and history to Dutch. These offers were not eccentric since even before the war 'Captain Boxer' was widely known in academic circles through more than eighty scholarly publications. His early interest in Japan led him to the study of the first Europeans to contact that strange culture: the Portuguese, the Dutch, and the Jesuits. In turn, this led him to international history in the broadest sense, both geographically and topically. The author of some 350 books and articles, his contributions to scholarship were recognized by election to the British Academy (1957) and a cascade of honorary degrees and fellowships. He twice refused official honours on principle, believing, with Wellington, that 'a soldier's duty is to deserve medals, not to get them'. In 1969, though an agnostic, he accepted a papal knighthood conferred for services to Catholic mission history. A lifelong bibliophile, he possessed an internationally known rare-book collection which was seized by the Japanese in 1941 for the Imperial Library in Tokyo. The jewel of that collection, the sixteenth-century Boxer codex, later came to be in the Lilly Library, Indiana, together with all his papers.

To the academic community Boxer brought a breath of fresh air, though his salty style sometimes disconcerted common rooms and startled committee meetings, for despite his background and patrician bearing he was something of a subversive who ignored convention and liked to deflate pomposity. He had little sympathy for the pretensions of the old imperial order, and he rejected any sense of European superiority. He was too little of a sentimentalist to be invariably mild, but to his numerous students he was unfailingly encouraging, imparting to them his own enthusiasm, and his belief in humanity and fairness. His pathbreaking approach to problems old and new inspired two generations of scholars in Europe and the United States.

In his last years failing eyesight ended Boxer's writing, but believing that 'old age is not for softies' he bore the trial in accordance with the stoical principles learned from the *Meditations* of Marcus Aurelius, to which he was introduced in prison camp. Shortly before his death he learned that the Charles Boxer chair of history had been established in King's College, London. He died at a nursing home in St Albans, Hertfordshire, on 27 April 2000 and was cremated at St Albans in May. He was survived by his two daughters, his second wife having predeceased him.

J. S. CUMMINS

Sources D. Alden, *Charles R. Boxer: an uncommon life* (Lisbon, 2001) · E. Hahn, *China to me* (1987) · 'Bibliography of C. R. Boxer', *Portuguese Studies*, 17 (Nov 2001), 247–76 · K. Cuthbertson, *Nobody said not to go* (Boston, 1998) · *The Independent* (29 April 2000) · *The Guardian* (16 May 2000) · *Daily Telegraph* (13 June 2000) · *WWW* · personal knowledge (2004)
Archives Indiana University, Bloomington, Lilly Library, MSS · King's Lond., papers | Bodl. Oxf., corresp. relating to the Society for the Protection of Science and Learning
Likenesses photograph, repro. in *Daily Telegraph* (13 June 2000) · photograph, repro. in *The Independent* (29 April 2000) · photographs, priv. coll.
Wealth at death £978,859: probate, 20 Oct 2000, *CGPLA Eng. & Wales*

Boxer, Edward (1784–1855), naval officer, was born at Dover. He entered the navy in July 1798, and after eight years' junior service, mostly with Captain Charles Brisbane, and for some short time in the *Ocean*, bearing Lord Collingwood's flag, was confirmed, on 8 June 1807, as lieutenant of the *Tigre* with Captain Benjamin Hallowell (afterwards Carew). On his promotion to flag rank in October 1811, he followed Hallowell to Malta, and continued, with short intermissions, under his immediate command, until he was confirmed as commander on 1 March 1815. In 1822 he commanded the *Sparrowhawk* (18 guns) on the Halifax station, and was posted out of her on 23 June 1823. From 1827 to 1830 he commanded the *Hussar* as flag captain to Sir Charles Ogle at Halifax. In August 1837 he was appointed to the *Pique*, which he commanded on the North American and West Indian stations; and early in 1840 was sent to the Mediterranean, where he conducted the survey of the position afterwards occupied by the fleet off Acre and took part in the bombardment and capture of

Acre in November. For his services he received the Turkish gold medal, and was made CB on 18 December 1840.

In August 1843 Boxer was appointed harbour-master at Quebec, and held that office until his promotion to flag rank, on 5 March 1853. In April 1854 he became port-admiral at Constantinople. Here he was responsible for collecting the boats used for the invasion of the Crimea, and was thereafter responsible for logistics and principal agent for transports. In December he undertook the special duties of superintendent at Balaklava, which the crowded shipping, the narrow limits of the harbour, and the complete lack of wharves and roads had reduced to a state of disastrous confusion. This, and more especially the 6 mile sea of mud between the harbour and the camp, gave rise to terrible suffering and loss. While many blamed the admiral-superintendent at Balaklava, he was in fact responsible for bringing order to the chaos, but despite this he was used as a scapegoat by the Admiralty, and even his commander-in-chief. In truth he ought to be remembered rather as the man who, at the cost of his life, remedied the evils which had given rise to such loss. He died of cholera on board the *Jason*, just outside the harbour, on 4 June 1855, and Lord Raglan in reporting his death wrote that he had worked very hard, in all weathers, and had rendered an essential service to the army by improving the landing-places and establishing wharves on the west side of the port, accelerating the disembarkation of stores and troops and improving communications with the shore. His wife had died on 25 January 1826, nearly thirty years before; he was survived by a numerous family.

Boxer 'was an able officer, placed in charge of something beyond the talent of any man to organise quickly' (Lambert, 212). After the war he was posthumously decorated.

J. K. LAUGHTON, rev. ANDREW LAMBERT

Sources A. D. Lambert, *The Crimean War: British grand strategy, 1853–56* (1990) · A. C. Dewar, ed., *Russian war, 1855, Black Sea: official correspondence*, Navy RS, 85 (1945) · Boase, *Mod. Eng. biog.* · *GM*, 2nd ser., 44 (1855) · O'Byrne, *Naval biog. dict.* · K. Bourne, *Britain and the balance of power in North America, 1815–1908* (1967)
Archives NMM, letter-books · Public Archives of Nova Scotia, Halifax, logbook | NAM, corresp. with Lord Raglan · PRO, corresp. with Stratford Canning, FO 352

Boxer, (Charles) Mark Edward [*pseud.* Marc] (1931–1988), cartoonist and magazine editor, was born on 19 May 1931 in Chorleywood, Hertfordshire, the only son and younger child of Lieutenant-Colonel (Harold) Stephen Boxer, garage owner and car salesman, and his wife, Isobel Victoria Hughlings Jackson. He was educated at Boarsted, at Berkhamsted School, and at King's College, Cambridge.

Boxer cut an immediate dash. To contemporaries his slender elegance, charm, and wit seemed immensely sophisticated, even intimidating. As a youth he appeared mature, as an adult boyish. In his first term he acted as Tybalt, all in white, for the Marlowe Society, and also drew for a comic magazine, *Granta*. He became editor the next year (1952), and took more interest in style than content; the content undid him. A poem contained the lines:

(Charles) **Mark Edward Boxer** [Marc] (1931–1988), self-portrait, 1976

> You drunken gluttonous seedy God
> You son of a bitch, you snotty old sod.

This was deemed blasphemous, and he was sent down for a week. Though he could have taken finals, he chose not to do so and left Cambridge in a hearse, followed by a crowd of perhaps a thousand protesters.

In London, Boxer worked briefly on the *Sunday Express*, a fashion magazine called *Ambassador*, and *Lilliput*, and drew for *The Tatler*. In 1957 Jocelyn Stevens, a Cambridge friend, bought *Queen* and made him art director. Boxer hired the best photographers, displayed their work to maximum advantage, and was a large contributor to the magazine's conspicuous success. In 1962 he was the editor who launched the *Sunday Times Magazine*. Of the first issue its proprietor, Roy Thomson, who was paying for it, commented 'This is awful, absolutely awful'; even so Thomson carried the losses and the magazine. It became one of the major developments in British journalism of its time— much copied but rarely equalled. Boxer remained as editor until 1965 and stayed on as assistant editor until 1979. He was a director of the *Sunday Times* in 1964–6. In 1965 a listings magazine, *London Life*, of which he was editorial director, came and went; his only spectacular failure.

Over the same years Boxer had become famous as the outstanding pocket cartoonist of his time, under the name Marc. His reputation was made at *The Times* (1969–83), where his work showed to best advantage, but he later worked for *The Guardian*. He had a detailed knowledge of the manners and customs of the establishment, the upper classes, and newly fashionable 'swinging London'. His own background and his left-wing views, conventional at the time, gave him the necessary distance. He did not deal directly with political issues, but reported what certain types would (revealingly) say about them. He also had an extraordinary eye for details of dress. He was cartoonist of the year in 1972. His caricatures, for profiles in the *New Statesman*, *The Observer*, the *London Review of Books*, and, after 1987, the *Sunday Telegraph*, were witty. Immediately pleasing because of his skill at catching a slightly distorted likeness, they were often sharp, even wounding. He said himself that the best compliment was when the subject asked if he could buy the original and then after a day or two reconsidered. He also developed, from one of Alan Bennett's ideas, the Stringalongs, who first appeared in a strip cartoon in *The Listener*. Based on friends, they were viewed without affection and with merciless accuracy. Among his most effective illustrations for books were those which appeared in Clive James's *The Fate of Felicity Fark* (1975) and *Britannia Bright's Bewilderment* (1976), and in Alan Watkins's *Brief Lives* (1982), and on the jackets of the novels of Anthony Powell. In 1980 he became a director of the publisher Weidenfeld and Nicolson, but he returned to magazines to edit *The Tatler* in 1983–6. This time a dowdy magazine had already been livened up by Tina Brown, and Boxer's job, successfully carried out, was to maintain its vitality and widen its appeal. In 1986 he was made editorial director of Condé Nast in Europe, and in 1987 editor-in-chief of *Vogue*. Thus he ended as he had begun; if he ever wished for a more serious role, there was no sign of it in his career. A stylish cricketer, he did everything that he did exceptionally well, and left a precise and amusing portrait of the world he lived in.

In 1956 Boxer married Lady Arabella Stuart, youngest daughter of Francis Douglas Stuart, eighteenth earl of Moray; they had a daughter and a son. In 1982 they were divorced and in the same year Boxer married the television newscaster Anna Ford, daughter of John Ford, Church of England clergyman. They had two daughters. Boxer died of a brain tumour on 20 July 1988 at his home, 1 Upper Butts, Brentford, London. He was cremated at Mortlake cemetery, London, and his ashes were scattered at King's College, Cambridge.　　　　MARK AMORY, *rev.*

Sources *The times we live in: the cartoons of Marc* (1978) [introduction by James Fenton] · M. Boxer, *The trendy ape* (1968) · M. Boxer, *Marc time* (1984) · M. Amory, ed., *The collected and recollected Marc* (1993) · *The Times* (21 July 1988) · private information (1996) · personal knowledge (1996) · CGPLA Eng. & Wales (1989)
Likenesses M. Boxer, ink, 1976, NPG; repro. in Amory, ed., *Collected and recollected Marc* [see illus.] · P. Blake, portrait, priv. coll.
Wealth at death £405,677: probate, 7 Feb 1989, CGPLA Eng. & Wales

Boxshall, Edwin George (1897–1984), Balkan specialist and intelligence officer, was born on 4 February 1897 in Bucharest, the only son and younger child of William George Boxshall (d. 1918), a butcher's son who ran a small ironworks in Romania, and his wife, Marie Meyer, formerly of Cologne. At the time of his son's birth, William

Boxshall was acting vice-consul and pro-consul at Bucharest. Boxshall was educated at the German Lutheran College in Bucharest, and never shed a vestigial foreign accent in his spoken English. Until the end of his life he counted in German. He had intended to study medicine at Cambridge, but his plans were disrupted by war and his father's stroke (1914). Following Romania's occupation by the central powers in 1916, he assisted the British military attaché in Bucharest, served on the British military mission at the temporary northern capital of Jassy with the rank of second lieutenant, and was British representative on the Inter-Allied Passport Control Commission. Captured by marauding Bolsheviks while on a border reconnaissance, he was condemned to death as a spy and spent his twenty-first birthday in a cell at Khotin Fort on the River Dniester writing farewell letters: when his ink ran out, he cut his finger and filled his pen with blood. An allied advance saved him on the eve of execution.

Later in 1918 Boxshall was evacuated from Jassy with the military mission and endured a month-long train journey through revolutionary Russia to Murmansk. He undertook other special duties for the War Office before returning to Romania with courage and ingenuity on an official mission in 1918. He married in April 1920 Elise (1896–1986), the beautiful, intelligent, and versatile third daughter of Prince Barbu Stirbey (1872–1946). They had one son and one daughter. Stirbey represented one of the ruling families of Wallachia under the Ottoman empire; his unique position in Romania as courtier, agrarian reformer, and man of business was to prove invaluable to Boxshall's work. Stirbey was administrator of the royal domains, lover of Queen Marie, signatory of the armistice arrangements (1918), and prime minister (1927, 1945), and he also engineered the renunciation in 1925 by the crown prince Carol of his right to the Romanian throne. He was related to leaders of both the liberal and conservative parties. Following the reversal of the prince's fortunes and his seizure of power as King Carol II, there was an attempt in 1931 to poison Stirbey (who later went into temporary exile in 1934) and Boxshall apparently went underground for a few weeks at the same time.

In the inter-war period 'Eddie' Boxshall represented British enterprises such as Nobel Industries (afterwards ICI) in Romania. His most important commercial work was for the armaments company Vickers, which in 1925 entered an ill-starred agreement with the Romanian government and the Reşiţa company (of which Stirbey was a director) to establish two national munitions factories at Copşa-Mică and at Cugir. Boxshall was the most shrewd, energetic, alert, and reliable of Vickers's overseas representatives. On their behalf he monitored the chicanery of the arms trade in the Balkans, with all its commercial, military, political, and diplomatic ramifications. He studied the court camarilla surrounding King Carol, and was perhaps the best-informed Englishman in south-eastern Europe. He was discreet and incorruptible in an environment that was sordid. For most of the inter-war period Boxshall was station chief of the Secret Intelligence Service in Bucharest, though his activities were always more wide-ranging. His business trips to the kingdom of the Serbs, Croats, and Slovenes sometimes covered intelligence activities: thus he recruited David Footman, of Glyn Mills Bank, during a night-time rendezvous in Kalemegdan Park, Belgrade.

In 1940 Boxshall returned to London and assumed Balkan line responsibilities for the Special Operations Executive (SOE); he later became lieutenant-colonel and MBE. It was doubtless at his instigation that his friend Max Auşnit, the Anglophile Jewish industrialist who had led the Reşiţa company, escaped from a Romanian prison and was flown to Egypt in a stolen German bomber in 1944. Boxshall felt an outsider in England (which he had only visited for a few months before 1940), and was socially and emotionally insecure; this manifested itself in subservience to his official superiors. He broadcast to Romania through the BBC and maintained crucial clandestine wireless contacts with Stirbey who in 1944 led secret armistice discussions at Cairo and later successful peace negotiations in Moscow.

Boxshall and his first wife had separated in 1939. They divorced in 1946, and he married, secondly, on 22 September 1949, Joyce Henriette (1902–1974), daughter of William Wallach, barrister, and formerly the wife of an Indian army officer, Jack Brittain Jones, and mistress of King George II of the Hellenes, who had died in 1947. 'Joyce was pretty, gentle, dark-haired, blue-eyed and intelligent' (Coats, 92). After the SOE was disbanded, Boxshall joined MI6 with the title of consultant to the Foreign Office (later the Foreign and Commonwealth Office (FCO)). In 1959 he was appointed custodian of the SOE archives following parliamentary criticism that authors and film makers were disseminating inaccurate information about the SOE because of the enforcement of official secrecy; Boxshall was employed to check the accuracy of statements made in material submitted to the FCO, and to provide factual information on wartime espionage. As much of the SOE's archives had been destroyed, Boxshall's phenomenally accurate memory was indispensable (though his instincts and habits were increasingly against disclosure). Boxshall, who retired in 1982, died of bladder and prostate cancer, on 26 January 1984, at the Middlesex Hospital, Westminster.

Boxshall was a tall, handsome, imposing man with steady judgement and sound instincts. He had no enthusiasms, sentimentality, or bugbears in his working life. Fluent in four languages, he was a gifted pianist and a competent horseman. He had exquisite manners, dashing physical elegance, whimsical humour, and a seductive charm with women of which he often took advantage. His one passion was skiing, which he pioneered in Romania; he was later an honorary citizen of Zürs in Austria, and skied until the age of seventy-six.

RICHARD DAVENPORT-HINES

Sources private information · H. Pakula, *The last romantic: a biography of Queen Marie of Romania* (1985) · R. P. T. Davenport-Hines, 'Vickers' Balkan conscience: aspects of Anglo-Romanian armaments, 1918–39', *Business in the age of depression and war*, ed. R. P. T. Davenport-Hines (1990), 253–85 · R. P. T. Davenport-Hines, ed.,

Markets and bagmen: studies in the history of marketing and British indus-trial performance, 1830–1939 (1986), 160–79 • I. Porter, *Operation autonomous* (1989) • P. Coats, *Of generals and gardens* (1976), 92–3 • *Daily Telegraph* (30 Jan 1984) • *Daily Telegraph* (1 Feb 1984) • *The Times* (7 Feb 1984) • *Daily Mail* (25 July 1979) • *The Times* (7 Feb 1959)
Archives CUL, Vickers' Archives, corresp. • priv. coll., family papers | PRO, foreign office archives, FO 391
Likenesses photographs, priv. coll.
Wealth at death £367,863: probate, 29 May 1984, *CGPLA Eng. & Wales*

Boyars [*née* Asmus]**, Marion Ursula** (1927–1999), pub-lisher, was born on 26 October 1927 in Berlin, Germany, the elder daughter of Johannes Asmus, an avant-garde art book publisher, and his wife, Hertha Feiner (1896–1943), a teacher. After her Jewish mother and non-Jewish father were divorced in 1933 Marion lived with her mother. She and her younger sister Inge were sent to boarding-school in Gland, Switzerland, after the Nazi violence against Jews became apparent, but were inadvisably brought back to Berlin early in 1938, and only later that year sent to Amer-ica. Marion's father was able to arrange for his daughters' support in New York during the war, and their mother sent them many letters. Hertha Feiner was a popular schoolteacher and affectionate mother, and was active culturally. Not being obviously Jewish, she was not arrested and sent to Auschwitz until 1943. It is believed that she committed suicide on the train. Her letters to her daughters were translated and published in 1999.

In America, Marion attended New York University. Before graduation she married George Lobbenberg (*d.* 1969), another German Jewish refugee, and she moved with him to England, where he started a woman's under-wear factory in Shrewsbury. Bored with the limitations of a small county town, she went to the new experimental University of Keele, where she obtained a degree in polit-ics, philosophy, and economics in 1954. After the birth of her daughters in 1955 and 1957 she moved to London, hav-ing separated from her husband.

Marion Lobbenberg began her publishing career by answering an advertisement from John Calder, who was seeking new capital. She liked the company's pro-gramme, but was dissuaded from investing by her accountant. Instead she worked unpaid for two years to learn the business and make up her mind whether she wanted to risk her alimony in a company which, although prestigious after its first decade for its political and liter-ary list, had never made a profit. When after the two years she took the plunge she had met many of the authors, who at that point included Samuel Beckett, Eugène Ion-esco, Alain Robbe-Grillet, Marguerite Duras, and other internationally known foreign figures, as well as lesser known British and American writers. Her investment, a modest one, bought her half the company in 1960, and she became one of the few women prominent in British pub-lishing during this period. Having divorced her first hus-band in 1962, she married Arthur Boyars (*b.* 1925/6), a liter-ary journalist and poet, on 8 May 1964. In the same year she insisted that the company's name be changed to Cal-der and Boyars.

By this time the company had a string of best-sellers, including Henry Miller's previously banned *Tropic of Can-cer*, and works by William Burroughs and Alexander Troc-chi, and other writers considered unconventional and daring, who had been acquired as the result of literary conferences organized by Calder for the Edinburgh and Harrogate festivals. Beckett and other European writers published by the firm became more fashionable and over-all sales were good. Boyars played a major role in finding new writers, largely from the United States, where she spent much of her time, while in Britain she mainly com-missioned books on social issues from well-known pun-dits and politicians. Her biggest discovery was Ivan Illich, the radical social and political thinker, who enjoyed guru status in the 1960s. In 1966 the firm was involved in a high-profile court case for having published Hubert Selby Jun.'s novel *Last Exit to Brooklyn*. The case was privately brought by Sir Cyril Black, Conservative MP, which led to a trial at the Old Bailey. In both trials the book was found obscene, but an appeal from John Mortimer on behalf of Calder and Boyars in 1968 reversed the decision. A public appeal brought in enough to pay the costs and keep the company solvent, but the case caused Marion, who had accepted the book, much distress. The trial led to the formation of the Defence of Literature and the Arts Society, of which she was a joint secretary.

A confrontation between Boyars and Calder over the running of the company led to Boyars, who thought she might do better on her own, deciding to split the firm and continue to publish under her own name as Marion Boyars Ltd. The division was announced in 1975 at a time when the two partners were dealing with a strike arising from the demand of some of the editorial staff for more say in editorial policy. Peter du Sautoy, retired chairman of Faber and Faber, agreed to adjudicate the company break-up, which was difficult and much disputed, but eventually it led to two parallel lists being issued from the same office. Until 1984 the two businesses continued at 18 Brewer Street, Soho, until Boyars moved her company, without notice, to Putney. She also opened a small New York office.

Thereafter Boyars's list had a more feminist emphasis, with a large concentration of fashionable personalities as authors. She also continued with the literary ones she had inherited from the division and acquired some new talent. Her knowledge of German enabled her to acquire several prestigious German writers, mainly of avant-garde char-acter. Her list also included Elias Canetti, Merce Cunning-ham, Georges Bataille, Ken Kesey, Michael Ondaatje, and Pauline Kael, the composers Erik Satie, Leoš Janáček, and Karlheinz Stockhausen, some Russian poets, especially Yevgeny Yevtushenko, and Eudora Welty and other Americans, whose reputation she successfully revived. Boyars was a small woman, with bright, sharp eyes. She was tough in negotiation, a characteristic that gave her a reputation less favourable than she would have wished, but fiercely loyal to her writers. She died of pancreatic cancer on 1 February 1999 at her home at 4 Hollywood

Mews, Chelsea. During her long illness her younger daughter took over the management of her company, and continued it after her death.   JOHN CALDER

Sources *The Independent* (9 Feb 1999) · personal knowledge (2004) · archives of Calder and Boyars · H. Feiner, *Before deportation: letters from a mother to her daughters, January 1939–December 1942*, trans. M. B. Dembo (1999)
Archives Institut Mémoires de l'Édition Contemporaine, Paris, fonds John Calder Publishers
Likenesses photograph, repro. in *The Times* (2 Feb 1999) · photograph, repro. in *The Guardian* (2 Feb 1999)
Wealth at death £755,538—gross; £694,096—net: probate, 10 May 1999, *CGPLA Eng. & Wales*

Boyce, George Price (1826–1897), watercolour painter, the son of George John Boyce (d. 1853) and his wife, Anne Price, was born on 24 September 1826 at Gray's Inn Terrace, Bloomsbury. His father was a prosperous London wine merchant, silversmith, and pawnbroker who lived near at least one of his pawnshops, in Theobald's Road. In 1840 the family moved into a spacious white stucco house in Park Place Villas, close to the Regent's Canal in Maida Hill. Among Boyce's four siblings were Matthias (b. 1829), who became a solicitor, and Joanna Mary *Boyce (1831–1861), the wife of the portrait painter and miniaturist Henry Tanworth Wells, and herself a distinguished painter of landscapes and figure subjects.

Boyce attended a boarding-school in Chipping Ongar, Essex, and later studied in Paris. In 1843 he was articled to an architect named Little, and four years later he was taken on by Wyatt and Brandon, an architectural firm. In the summers of 1846 and 1847 he travelled in Europe, making careful drawings of buildings and architectural detail. He seems, however, to have become increasingly despondent about his prospects as a professional architect, and it was perhaps in the course of a visit to north Wales in 1848 in company with John Seddon, a fellow architectural student, and his brother the landscape painter Thomas Seddon, that Boyce himself began to contemplate a career devoted to art. The following season, when painting at Betws-y-coed, Boyce first met David Cox, who over a period of several years was to give him encouragement and advice. Boyce's early drawing style, with its careful attention to the forms of nature and strong colour, may be judged from the 1851 watercolour *A Road Near Betws-y-coed* (Yale Center for British Art, New Haven). A diary entry from August of that year recorded Cox's response to a drawing done in Wales: 'Completed drawing from Church, which Mr Cox said looked like a Pre-Raffaelite drawing' (Surtees, 3).

Back in London, Boyce attended the drawing classes that the Seddons organized in their house in Gray's Inn Road; he also joined the Clipstone Street Artists' Association, where he had the opportunity both to draw from the nude model and engage in discussions about art. In the early 1850s his drawings were on occasions refused by the Royal Academy selection committees, although in 1853 he was represented by two works, one a view of the east end of Edward the Confessor's chapel at Westminster Abbey (V&A). Early in 1854 he stood for election to the Society of Painters in Water Colours, but without success. In the same year his *Babbacombe Bay* (Astley Cheetham Art Gallery, Stalybridge) was shown at the National Institution at the Portland Gallery.

Boyce was by this time a familiar figure on the Pre-Raphaelite fringe. From about 1851 he had known D. G. Rossetti and Ford Madox Brown, and in March 1852 (on the occasion of C. R. Leslie's Royal Academy lecture on landscape painting) he first met J. E. Millais. In 1854 Boyce entered upon a friendship with John Ruskin, who visited him at his chambers at 60 Great Russell Street to see the collection of drawings by Rossetti that he had formed. When, later in the same year, Boyce set out on a journey to Italy, he painted a series of subjects in Venice and Verona recommended by Ruskin, treating them with meticulous attention to detail and as records of architectural form. On one occasion Ruskin wrote to Boyce:

> I congratulate myself, in the hope of at last seeing a piece of St Mark's done as it ought to be done ... it answers precisely to your wishes, as expressed in your note, '*near* subject—good architecture—colour & light & shade'. (Surtees, 119)

On other occasions, however, both in Venice and in London, Boyce adopted a looser and more atmospheric style, drawing city views at night which anticipate the nocturnes of James Whistler.

In 1856 Boyce transferred to chambers at 15 Buckingham Street, overlooking the Thames, which he shared with the architect William Burges. In 1862 he took over Rossetti's rooms in Chatham Place, and in 1869 he commissioned Philip Webb to build him West House, in Glebe Place, Chelsea. Although Boyce was given to black moods, and was frustrated by the limited appreciation that his work received, his landscapes were admired by fellow artists and competed for by a progressive circle of collectors. In 1857 two of his drawings were borrowed for the Russell Square Pre-Raphaelite exhibition, as he recorded in a diary entry for 26 May 1857:

> Letter from H. T. Wells saying he and Rossetti had been to my studio and walked off with that sunset sketch, and the crypt of St Niccolo [*sic*] at Giornico, to exhibit with a collection of Pre-Raphaelite Painters' work at 4 Russell Place, Fitzroy Square. They will look ridiculously small and mindless by the side of Rossetti's and Millais' and Hunt's works. (MS diary entry)

In the event two works entitled *Sketch in North Wales* and *At Venice* were shown. In 1858 Boyce contributed to the American Exhibition of British Art, being represented by four watercolours in the Philadelphia showing of the exhibition, and by three at Boston (each was described in the American exhibition catalogues as having been 'Painted on the spot'). Boyce was a founder member of the Hogarth Club, which operated as an exhibition space and convivial meeting place between 1858 and 1862. He was also a member of the Medieval Society, and later one of the leading figures in the Society for the Protection of Ancient Buildings, known as Anti-scrape.

Although Boyce lived principally in London, he made frequent long sojourns in the countryside and abroad. In 1853 he travelled with Thomas Seddon to Dinan in Brittany, and then on to the Pyrenees, returning when news of his father's imminent death reached him. In 1856 he spent the summer and autumn of the year in the Italian Alps, followed by a visit to Paris, where he sought medical treatment for an injury to his hip. In 1861, following the death of his sister Joanna from puerperal fever in July, he departed for Egypt, where he lived with the painters Frank Dillon and Egron Lundgren in an old house at Giza, and where he remained until February 1862. When he remained in Britain during the summer and autumn seasons he made for remote parts of the countryside, where he looked for time-worn and unspoilt buildings and hidden corners of the landscape to paint. Boyce was particularly attracted to the Thames valley, favouring the villages of Pangbourne, Mapledurham, Whitchurch, and Streatley, upriver from Reading. The pattern of his life is indicated in a diary entry for 8 May 1860:

> To Academy again. Brought away my two drawings [refused for the summer exhibition] … Left London by the 4.50 for Reading … back to Caversham, where I had left my boat, and pulled up thence to Mapledurham, where arrived about nine. Just as I was landing, I fell into the water up to my chest.   (MS diary entry)

Among his best works are the views of Thames-side mills and farm buildings, such as *Mill on the Thames at Mapledurham* (Fitzwilliam Museum, Cambridge) and *Old Barn at Whitchurch* (Ashmolean Museum, Oxford). Other parts of the country which Boyce frequently visited were the Welsh marches, Surrey and Sussex, and Northumberland and the borders.

In 1864 Boyce was finally elected an associate member of the Society of Painters in Water Colours (he waited a further fourteen years to become a full member). In 1864 he exhibited his characteristic work *At Binsey, Near Oxford* (Cecil Higgins Museum, Bedford), and in the following year showed *From the Windmill Hills, Gateshead-on-Tyne* (Laing Art Gallery, Newcastle upon Tyne). Both drawings include buildings seen through screens of trees, and take viewpoints which cause the elements of the composition to overlap. This avoidance of the conventionally picturesque was remarked on by perceptive critics. In 1866 the critic of the *Art Journal* praised the works of one who, 'only a few seasons ago entered this gallery [of the Society of Painters in Water Colours] as an anomaly', on the grounds that

> Mr Boyce is singular in the choice of his subjects, inasmuch as he loves to plant his sketching stool just where there is no subject. Yet does he manage to make out of the most unpromising of materials a picture which for the most part is clever and satisfactory   (*Art Journal*, 28, 1866, 174–5)

Boyce was represented at the Society of Painters in Water Colours summer exhibitions from 1864 until 1890, and also sent works to the winter exhibitions from 1864–5 to 1877–8.

From 1867 Boyce suffered repeated attacks of typhoid fever, reputedly contracted when painting at Bridewell in the East End of London. He died at West House on 9 February 1897, following a stroke, and he was buried in the Boyce family tomb at Kensal Green cemetery. Boyce is remembered both as an artist and as a collector of paintings by artist contemporaries. His collection, which included among many notable works Rossetti's 1859 portrait of Fanny Cornforth, *Bocca baciata* (Museum of Fine Arts, Boston), was sold at Christies on 1–3 July 1897. He is also familiar to students of Victorian art as the author of a colourful and informative diary, which covers the years of his adult life up to 1875, in which year on 31 August he married a French woman called Augustine Aimée Caroline Soubeiran.   CHRISTOPHER NEWALL

Sources C. Newall and T. Egerton, *George Price Boyce* (1987) [exhibition catalogue, Tate Gallery, London] • V. Surtees, ed., *The diaries of George Price Boyce* (1980) • [F. G. Stephens], 'Mr. George Price Boyce', *The Athenaeum* (13 Feb 1897), 221 • A. E. Street, 'George Price Boyce', *Old Water-Colour Society's Club*, 19 (1941), 1–8 • A. Staley, *The Pre-Raphaelite landscape* (1973), 107–10 • MS diaries, priv. coll. • d. cert. • m. cert.
Archives priv. coll., MS diaries | BL, Philip Webb MSS • Bodl. Oxf., F. G. Stephens MSS • UCL, D. G. Rossetti MSS
Likenesses D. G. Rossetti, double portrait, pen-and-ink drawing, 1858 (with Fanny Cornforth), Carlisle Museum and Art Gallery • H. T. Wells, drawing, 1861, priv. coll.; repro. in Newall and Egerton, *George Price Boyce* • glass plate negative, 1861, NPG • H. T. Wells, group portrait • H. T. Wells, photographs
Wealth at death £20,520 2s. 1d.: administration, 6 March 1897, CGPLA Eng. & Wales

Boyce [married name Wells], **Joanna Mary** (1831–1861), genre painter, daughter of George John Boyce (d. 1853) and his wife, Anne Price, and younger sister of the watercolourist George Price *Boyce (1826–1897), was born in Gray's Inn Terrace, Bloomsbury, London, on 7 December 1831. Joanna's father was a wine merchant and pawnbroker in London. The Boyce family lived in Gray's Inn Terrace until 1840, when they moved to Park Place Villas in Maida Hill. As a child Joanna Boyce showed an interest in art, in which she was encouraged by her father, who took her to exhibitions and lectures (and in 1851 to the funeral of J. M. W. Turner). At the age of seventeen she was allowed to enrol at Cary's school of art. In April 1852 she visited Paris with her father so that she might study contemporary French painting. Later in the same year father and daughter, with George Price Boyce, stayed at Betws-y-coed in Wales. George Boyce's death in September 1853 was a great loss to Joanna; by contrast, Anne Boyce was not supportive of her daughter's ambitions as an artist, and there were occasions when Joanna was close to giving up painting.

Joanna Boyce received advice on her painting from Henry Tanworth *Wells (1828–1903), who had been a friend of George's since 1849. However, Wells, who was already established as a portraitist and miniaturist, seems to have little understood the progressive and challenging character of Joanna's painting, and his point of view contrasts significantly with that of her brother, with whom Joanna seems to have had a truer sympathy in artistic matters. In 1853 Joanna Boyce transferred to Leigh's school of art and in 1854 she attended classes at the Government School of Design. In the spring of 1854 Joanna Boyce was contemplating a period of training in either Düsseldorf or Munich. This did not materialize, but in the autumn of the year she did travel in Belgium and the Netherlands. During the early 1850s she was introduced to members of the London-based Pre-Raphaelite circle by her brother.

In September 1855 Joanna Boyce returned to Paris, on

this occasion in company with her mother and brother Bob. She hoped to be able to attend painting classes under Rosa Bonheur, but for some reason—perhaps to do with her mother's or Wells's influence—she went instead to the studio of Thomas Couture, where she attended life classes in the atelier reserved for female students. In her two-part article 'Remarks on some of the French pictures at the Paris Exhibition, 1855', which appeared in the *Saturday Review* (1 and 29 December 1855), Joanna Boyce deplored the influence of Ingres on contemporary French painting and praised works by Constant Troyon and Couture. She was commissioned by the same periodical to write a three-part review of the 1856 Royal Academy exhibition (*Saturday Review*, 10, 17, and 24 May 1856). Here she praised Millais's *Autumn Leaves* and Holman Hunt's *Scapegoat*, and also took her opportunity to lambaste the works of the academicians: 'In truth, there are but three or four out of the whole number to whose works we annually look forward with anything like longing or curiosity' (ibid., 24 May 1856, 79).

Joanna Boyce first exhibited in public at the National Institution in 1854 and in 1855 her painting *Elgiva* (priv. coll.) was shown at the Royal Academy. In a late edition of *Academy Notes* Ruskin described the work as 'so subtle, and so tenderly wrought' (*The Works of John Ruskin*, ed. E. T. Cook and A. Wedderburn, 1903–12, 14.30–31), and Ford Madox Brown called it simply 'the best Head in the rooms' (*The Diary of Ford Madox Brown*, ed. V. Surtees, 1981, 138). She exhibited a further eight works at the academy, including *The Departure: an Episode of the Child's Crusade* (priv. coll.) in 1860 and *The Veneziana* (priv. coll.) and *Peep-Bo!* (des.) in 1861. On at least two occasions works of hers were rejected by the academy selection committees: in 1856 *Rowena Offering the Wassail Cup to Vortigern* and in 1859 'No Joy the Blowing Season Brings' were refused. The latter was subsequently much admired in Ernest Gambart's 1859 winter exhibition at the French Gallery.

For a while Joanna Boyce resisted Henry Wells's proposals of marriage. In a postscript to a letter to him of June 1855 she announced that the 'intense love of independence, which has often been a bane to me' (Boyce family MSS) was being overcome, but on 10 February 1857 she still feared the loss of liberty that might go with marriage, for 'I have talents or a talent and with it the constant impulse to enjoy it,—not for notoriety or fame, but for the love of it and the longing to work' (ibid.). Later in 1857 they travelled together in Italy and, according to a plan which had been previously divulged to Joanna's siblings, were married on 7 December in Rome, their wedding being solemnized at the British consulate. After their return to England in March 1858 they set up house in 1859 in Upper Phillimore Gardens, and later had built a country house at Holmbury Hill in Surrey. They had three children—Sidney and Alice were the inspiration for various of their mother's last paintings. It was following the birth of her third child, Joanna Margaret, and as a result of ensuing gastroenteric fever that Joanna died, on 15 July 1861, at her home, 9 Upper Phillimore Gardens. She was buried in the Boyce family tomb at Kensal Green cemetery, her body subsequently being removed to rest with that of her husband after his death in 1903.

Friends and fellow painters were invited to see the works that remained in Joanna Wells's studio. D. G. Rossetti, Burne-Jones, F. M. Brown, and Watts were among those who expressed their admiration for her art. *The Spectator*'s obituarist concluded that 'no English-woman has ever set forth such mastery of style and such subtle qualities of painting as are impressed upon her works' (*The Spectator*, 20 July 1861, 783), and drew a parallel between her early death and that of Elizabeth Barrett Browning, which had occurred a month or so before. Joanna Wells was represented in the Royal Academy summer exhibition in the year after her death, with a painting entitled *A Bird of God* (priv. coll.). Five of her paintings were also included in the International Exhibition of 1862. She was represented in the 1901 Royal Academy exhibition 'Works by deceased British artists', and in 1935 an exhibition of thirty-one of her paintings was held at the Tate Gallery.

CHRISTOPHER NEWALL

Sources priv. coll., Boyce family MSS · *An exhibition of paintings by Joanna Mary Boyce* (1935) [exhibition catalogue, Tate Gallery, London] · P. G. Nunn, 'A centre on the margins', in E. Harding, *Re-framing the Pre-Raphaelites: historical and theoretical essays* (1995), 43–60 · *The Spectator* (20 July 1861), 783 · d. cert.
Archives priv. coll., family MSS
Likenesses T. H. Foley, bust, priv. coll.
Wealth at death under £20: probate, 7 Nov 1862, *CGPLA Eng. & Wales*

Boyce, Sir (Harold) Leslie, first baronet (1895–1955), businessman and politician, was born at Taree, New South Wales, Australia, on 9 July 1895, the third son of Charles Macleay Boyce (1868–1936) and his wife Ethel May Thorne (d. 1943). Boyce attended Sydney grammar school from 1911 to 1913 and maintained links with the institution thereafter. In 1924 he established the London branch of the Old Sydneian's Union and in 1952 he was host at a banquet of London members.

In 1915 Boyce joined the Australian Imperial Force and served as a second lieutenant in the 27th battalion in Egypt and Gallipoli. Promoted to lieutenant in the 27th battalion, he was seriously wounded in July 1916 while fighting on the western front and almost buried alive after being taken for dead. After a lengthy period of convalescence in Britain, he returned to Australia and made a deal with the minister of defence that if he personally raised an infantry unit within six weeks he would be allowed to return with it to active service in France. This he did.

Early in 1919 Boyce entered Balliol College, Oxford, as a colonial military student, supported by a Huth scholarship and scholarships from the Rhodes Trust, and graduated in 1921 having completed the shortened course in modern history. In 1922 he was called to the bar by the Inner Temple and between 1923 and 1926 he worked in commercial law, dealing mainly with cases of damage to British goods and property in the Middle East during the First World War. In 1922 he acted as technical adviser to the Australian representative before the permanent mandates commission of the League of Nations in Geneva. He was later appointed a substitute delegate and legal adviser to the Australian delegation at the third assembly of the league. On 16 July 1926 he married Maybery Browse Bevan (*d.* 1978), daughter of Edward Philip Bevan of Melbourne. They had three sons.

In 1931 Boyce became managing director and chairman of the struggling Gloucester Railway Carriage and Wagon Company. He implemented a plan of reorganization with 'energy and vision' (Amery, 132), economizing in key areas and recruiting his friend Leopold Amery onto the board of directors. The firm gained large orders for railway rolling stock from Canada and Queensland. Profitability was restored and expansion soon followed. Boyce remained managing director of the company until 1945 and chairman until his death. He also held positions with several other companies, sat on the executive committees of various national trade associations, and was chairman of the all-party parliamentary railway group.

In May 1929 Boyce was elected a Unionist MP for Gloucester, his adopted home. He was also high sheriff of Gloucester (1941–2). During the turmoil created by Lord Beaverbrook's empire free trade campaign, he played a minor part in attempts to conciliate the different factions within his party. Sharing a platform with Beaverbrook in Gloucester in February 1930, he stressed the possibilities for a *rapprochement* between Baldwin and the rogue press baron. In private he suggested a referendum to resolve the issue (Barnes and Nicholson, 16, 64, 65). In 1930 he accompanied the empire parliamentary delegation to Northern Rhodesia.

During the Second World War Boyce joined the Palace of Westminster company (35th London battalion) of the Home Guard. He also sat on the advisory committee of the Ministry of War Transport and in 1946 led a UK trade mission to China. He lost his Gloucester seat to a Labour opponent at the general election of 1945 and did not sit in parliament again.

As a successful barrister, politician, businessman, and financier, Boyce naturally also developed strong links with the City of London. He was elected alderman for the ward of Walbrook (1942–54), having stressed in his campaign the task of reconstruction that faced the war-ravaged City and the need to 'meet modern requirements, and yet preserve inviolate all the ancient rights and privileges, and our immemorial customs' (Guildhall Library, MS 14809). He was a liveryman of the Loriners' and Carpenters' companies and became master of the Loriners in 1951. He acted as sheriff of the City of London from 1947 to 1948 and lord mayor of London from 1951 to 1952.

Boyce's elevation to the ceremonial pinnacle of the City establishment elicited a variety of responses. The *Gloucester Journal* (17 November 1951) was keen to claim him as a son of the town, drawing parallels with his illustrious Gloucestershire predecessor, Dick Whittington. The London *Evening Standard* (9 November 1951) meanwhile dubbed the event the 'austerity Lord Mayor's Show', owing to a shortened procession that reflected Britain's post-war economic difficulties. For others imperial sentiment distracted attention from budget cuts. Boyce was widely acclaimed as the first dominions-born lord mayor of London, an association further cultivated when the lord mayor's day procession stopped at Australia House to receive an address of congratulation sent by Robert Menzies, the Australian prime minister. At his inaugural banquet Boyce claimed that the City of London remained 'the very heart and centre of the British Empire—still the greatest Empire the world has ever known' (lord mayor's day book, 1951). His Australian origins were later deemed especially significant when he presided over the presentation of the freedom of the City of London to Menzies on 4 June 1952. His career demonstrated the continuing strength of the imperial bond between Britain and the dominions during the decades that followed the Second World War.

Boyce was created KBE in 1944 and a baronetcy was conferred on him in November 1952 at the end of his year of office as lord mayor. His interests included freemasonry (he was senior grand deacon from 1948 to 1949 in the grand lodge of English freemasons) and the St John Ambulance Brigade. He was also one of his Majesty's lieutenants and a JP for the City of London, and sat as a commissioner of the central criminal court, a governor of the Royal Hospitals and chairman of the executive committees of the King George VI Memorial Fund and the King George VI Foundation. He died of heart failure on 30 May 1955 at the Royal Hospital, Southgate Street, Gloucester.

SIMON J. POTTER

Sources *The Times* (1 June 1955) · Burke, *Peerage* (1999) · *AusDB* · I. Elliott, ed., *The Balliol College register, 1833–1933*, 2nd edn (privately printed, Oxford, 1934) · d. cert. · lord mayor's day book, 1951, CLRO · minutes of the proceedings of the court of common council, 1952, City of London RO · GL, MS 14809 · *A history of the Gloucester Railway Carriage and Wagon Company* (1960) · *The empire at bay: the Leo Amery diaries, 1929–1945*, ed. J. Barnes and D. Nicholson (1988) · L. S. Amery, *My political life*, 3: *The unforgiving years* (1955) · *WWW*, 1951–60

Likenesses photograph, 1951, GL, Noble collection, C78/1951 · photograph, 1952, GL, Noble collection, C78/1952

Wealth at death £55,362 18s. 3d.: probate, 16 Aug 1955, *CGPLA Eng. & Wales*

Boyce, Sir Rubert William (1863–1911), pathologist, was born on 22 April 1863 at Osborne Terrace, Clapham Road, London, the second son of Robert Henry Boyce, originally of Carlow, Ireland, an engineer who was at one time principal surveyor of British diplomatic and consular buildings in China, and his wife, Louisa, daughter of Dr Neligan, a medical practitioner in Athlone, Ireland. Educated in Rugby and in Paris, Boyce then entered University College, London, to study medicine. In 1888 he obtained the diplomas of the Royal College of Physicians and the Royal College of Surgeons; he graduated MB in 1889. After periods of study at Heidelberg and Paris and under Victor Horsley at University College, London, Boyce was appointed assistant professor of pathology at the latter institution in 1892. In that same year he published *A Text-Book of Morbid Histology* which was renowned for its illustrations.

In 1894 Boyce was appointed to the newly endowed George Holt chair of pathology in University College, Liverpool, then part of the Victoria University, Manchester.

At Liverpool he quickly organized a laboratory of scientific pathology on modern lines and established a school of hygiene. In 1898 his department of pathology was installed in a fine building erected for it, and in the same year he was appointed bacteriologist to the city of Liverpool. In 1901 he married Kate Ethel (d. 1902), daughter of William Johnston, a Liverpool shipowner, of Woodslee, Bromborough, Cheshire; she died shortly after the birth of their daughter.

Boyce was on the senate of University College, and he favoured its development and expansion into an independent and autonomous university. As an officer both of the college and of the municipality he was able to promote the early success of Liverpool University, which was established in 1902. Four endowed chairs in the new university owed their creation mainly to him, namely, those of biochemistry, of tropical medicine, of comparative pathology, and of medical entomology, as did the university lectureship on tropical medicine.

Boyce was particularly interested in the relationship between Britain and its colonies, and this was reflected in his work at Liverpool. Through his influence a university fellowship was endowed for young medical graduates from the colonies. Boyce was also instrumental in the founding of the Liverpool School of Tropical Medicine, in April 1899, inspired by Joseph Chamberlain, then secretary of state for the colonies. Boyce secured funding for the school from Sir Alfred Jones, and became the first dean of the school. Ronald Ross was appointed director, filling a post which was soon associated with an endowed chair at the university. In 1901 Boyce took the lead in organizing a series of expeditions to the tropics to investigate diseases in their natural habitat. In the first six years of its existence, the school sent seventeen expeditions, which, though costly in money and indeed lives, produced rich knowledge. In 1905 Boyce himself went to New Orleans and British Honduras to study epidemics of yellow fever.

Boyce's scientific and administrative achievements received recognition. He was made a fellow of University College, London; in 1902 he was elected FRS for his work on nervous diseases; and in 1906 he was knighted. He was also a member of the Colonial Office's West African advisory board, and he served on the royal commissions on sewage disposal and on tuberculosis.

In September 1906, after a spell of exceptionally heavy work, Boyce suffered a stroke, but made a partial return to his university work after a year. In 1909 he visited the West Indies at the request of the government to report on yellow fever, and in 1910 he went to west Africa for the same purpose. In his enforced withdrawal from laboratory work Boyce sought to arouse concern for the problems of tropical sanitation by writing accounts for the general reader about the bearing of recent biological discoveries on the health and prosperity of tropical communities. His *Mosquito or Man* (1909), and his *Health Progress and Administration in the West Indies* (1910) influenced public opinion, and both went through a number of editions. The latest of his projects was the formation of a bureau of yellow fever

at Liverpool. The first issue of its bulletin was sent to press just before Boyce's death.

Boyce died at the age of forty-eight on 16 June 1911, from an apoplectic seizure, at his home, Park Lodge, Sefton Park Road, Liverpool, and he was buried at Bebington cemetery. The success of the Liverpool School of Tropical Medicine was the aim and reward of Boyce's later life. He was small, but active, and a born organizer. He often joked that the word 'cash' would be found written across his heart, a testament to his fund-raising skills.

C. S. SHERRINGTON, rev. CLAIRE E. J. HERRICK

Sources *Journal of Pathology and Bacteriology*, 16 (1911–12), 274–82 · C. S. S., *PRS*, 84B (1911–12), iii–ix · *The Lancet* (1 July 1911), 59–60 · *BMJ* (1 July 1911), 53–4 · *The Times* (19 June 1911) · private information (1912) · *CGPLA Eng. & Wales* (1911)
Likenesses W. T. Maud, gouache, 1899 · photograph, 1906, RS · R. E. Morrison, oils, U. Lpool · photograph, repro. in *The Lancet* · photograph, repro. in *Journal of Pathology and Bacteriology*
Wealth at death £6609 8s. 4d.: probate, 11 July 1911, *CGPLA Eng. & Wales*

Boyce, Samuel (d. 1775), playwright and poet, was originally an engraver, and held subsequently a place in the South Sea House. In 1751 he published *The Friend of Liberty: an Ode, to George Heathcote, Esq.; Late Alderman of the City of London*. This was followed by *The Rover, or, Happiness at Last: a Pastoral Drama* (in two interludes and in verse), which was published in 1752 but never acted (Baker, 3.226). In 1755 *An ode to the right honourable the marquis of Hartington, lord lieutenant of the Kingdom of Ireland* and *Paris, or, The Force of Beauty: a Poem in Two Cantos* were published; both were reprinted in Boyce's *Poems on Several Occasions* (1757).

This edition of Boyce's poems was published by subscription; the original subscribers included Miss Fanny Murray, Miss Middleton, Samuel Johnson, and David Garrick. *Poems on Several Occasions* has been described as an 'extremely uncommon' book (Williams, 74) and from a bibliophilic point of view the work is of particular interest because of the method of printing and resultant errors in the various print formats. The 'Subscriber's list' shows Garrick (whose copy contains an inscription to him from Boyce and to whom two poems are written) as having subscribed for a copy on 'Royal Paper'. The printing of the special paper copies before the ordinary ones reverses the common eighteenth-century printing practice. I. A. Williams states that *Poems on Several Occasions* is the first definite instance of this occurring in an eighteenth-century text (ibid., 75). Garrick's large-paper copy was sold after his death and later passed to the Britwell Library (ibid., 74).

Boyce's title for his collection is an apt one, as the forty-eight poems contained therein reflect a variety of styles and subject matter. Often Boyce frames his poems with classical allusions but his subject is predominantly eighteenth-century culture: in this he is typically Augustan. In 'Song' ('The sun in virgin lustre shone') the classical story of Damon and Sylvia is retold but the sentiments throughout reflect eighteenth-century morality. *Poems on Several Occasions* is of interest because of the manner in which the collection articulates eighteenth-century concerns of the day; it reflects contemporary cultural debate and politics, and is peppered with references to the famous.

Dominant themes in the collection include love, which is often represented in a classical pastoral setting and in some poems is yoked to a eulogization of Britishness. The theme of female chastity is wittily expressed in the satiric 'Song' ('The wicked wits, as fancy hits') which reverses the stereotypical anti-woman vein of much early eighteenth-century satire to reveal the double standards in masculine behaviour and contemporary sexual morality:

The muse shall here th' indicated clear,
And prove the crimes on you
(ll. 11–12)

There emerges a strong anti-French sentiment in the collection, clearly represented in a number of poems which reproduce chauvinist clichés about the insidious influence of 'Gallic' tastes. The eclectic nature of *Poems on Several Occasions* is evident in the range of the subject matter which includes humorous commentaries on drunkenness—'Song' ('Push around the brisk glass, I proclaim him an ass') and 'Epigram' ('Quoth Guz to his spouse, with his skin full of beer'). In 1771 Boyce wrote 'A New Occasional Prologue' for *Othello* produced at Covent Garden (Stone, 8.1595). He died on 21 March 1775.   GAIL BAYLIS

Sources I. A. Williams, 'Samuel Boyce's *Poems on several occasions*', *Book Collectors' Quarterly* (April 1934) · *The new Cambridge bibliography of English literature*, [2nd edn], 2, ed. G. Watson (1971), 644 · F. W. Bateson, *The Cambridge bibliography of English literature*, 2 (1940), 354 · D. E. Baker, *Biographia dramatica, or, A companion to the playhouse*, rev. I. Reed, new edn, rev. S. Jones, 3 (1812), 226 · G. W. Stone, ed., *The London stage, 1660–1800*, pt 4: *1747–1776* (1962), 1595 · *DNB*
Archives BL, C.145.b.19

Boyce, Thomas (*bap.* **1732**, *d.* **1793**), Church of England clergyman and writer, was baptized on 11 September 1732 at St Andrew's, Norwich, the son of John Boyce, brewer, and Abigal. He went to school in Norwich and Scarning, before matriculating at Gonville and Caius College, Cambridge, in 1750. He graduated BA in 1754 and MA in 1767. He was ordained deacon on 2 November 1755, served as curate at Cringleford, near Norwich, and was ordained priest on 29 May 1768. From 1780 until his death he was rector of Great Worlingham, Suffolk, and chaplain to the earl of Suffolk.

Boyce is the author of *Harold*, an eighty-six page verse tragedy which was published in 1786 in London by the author at his own expense (BL, 1344n.29). The play, dedicated to Lady Beauchamp, proctor of Longley Park in Norfolk, was never acted and it would appear from the lack of evidence of any reprints that the tragedy was not a success. A handwritten note on the front-sheet of the British Library copy states that Boyce stopped work on it when he became aware that Richard Cumberland's tragedy on the same subject was in rehearsal at Drury Lane and that the author was 'conscious of the inferiority of his own abilities'. *Harold* has been described as 'dull' (Genest, 6.8) and the noticeable lack of action in the play (there are no battle scenes) supports the opinion that the tragedy is a vehicle for sentimental moralizing rather than dramatic tension.

The note on the front-sheet of *Harold* refers to the author as being a writer of elegies as well as a dramatist. A sample of Boyce's elegies appears in *Thomas Boyce, a Specimen of Elegiac Poetry* (1773). In the 'Advertisement', the poet states: 'These two Poems are selected, merely as being the most correct, from a small number written in the same manner', and he claims that further publication would be dependent on the 'opinion of the Public upon this Specimen' as to 'whether the others merit further trouble or attention'. It would appear that the opinion of the 'Public' was not favourable as no more elegies were published. The two elegies in the collection are written in heroic couplets and, although technically correct, are conventional and sentimental. 'Elegiac I: On the Death of a Young Lady' praises 'Chloe', described as a 'milk-white Fawn' who gaily 'frisks and frolics round'. 'Elegiac II' concerns a lament for 'the natural Daughter of a Field Officer who fell in the course of the late War'. Its theme is the seduction of a young innocent country maid by the 'arts of a Villain' who quickly abandons her. Boyce died on 4 February 1793.   GAIL BAYLIS

Sources T. Boyce, *Harold: a tragedy* (1786) [BL, 1344 n.29; note on front-sheet] · *DNB* · Genest, *Eng. stage*, vol. 6 · D. E. Baker, *Biographia dramatica, or, A companion to the playhouse*, rev. I. Reed, new edn, 2 vols. (1782) · Venn, *Alum. Cant.* · IGI

Boyce, William (*bap.* **1711**, *d.* **1779**), composer, organist, and music editor, was born in Maiden Lane, London, and was baptized on 11 September 1711 at St James Garlickhythe, the youngest of four children of John Boyce (1673–1752), joiner and cabinet-maker, and his wife, Elizabeth, *née* Cordwell (*d.* 1740). His father, 'discovering in his son while an infant, a delight in musical sounds' (Hawkins), had him admitted to the choir of St Paul's Cathedral about 1719 under Charles King, master of the choristers. On the breaking of his voice he stayed on to study the organ as an articled pupil of the cathedral's organist, Maurice Greene, from 1727 to 1734.

Boyce's first professional appointment was as organist at the earl of Oxford's chapel, St Peter's, Vere Street, in 1734, and he taught the harpsichord, notably at Mr Cavaller's seminary for young ladies in Queen Square. He moved to St Michael Cornhill in 1736 in succession to the organist Joseph Kelway and remained there until 7 April 1768. By 1736 he had composed some fifteen anthems which were in use at the Chapel Royal, and on the death of John Weldon on 7 May 1736 he succeeded him as a composer to the Chapel Royal on 21 June, sharing some of the duties of the second organist, Jonathan Martin. Once again he was closely associated with Maurice Greene, who was the senior composer and organist to the Chapel Royal.

Boyce was a member of Greene's Apollo Academy, which had met in the Devil tavern, Temple Bar, since 1731. Several of Boyce's larger works for soloists, chorus, and orchestra were first heard there: the sacred cantata *David's Lamentation over Saul and Jonathan* (words by John Lockman,

William Boyce (*bap.* 1711, *d.* 1779), by Thomas Hudson, *c*.1745–50

April 1736), *The Charms of Harmony Display* (an ode to St Cecilia written by the Revd Peter Vidal, *c*.1738), and *See Famed Apollo and the Nine* (Lockman's ode to St Cecilia, 1739). Lord Lansdowne's masque *Peleus and Thetis* and Walter Hart's Pindaric ode *Gentle Lyre Begin the Strain* had both been set by Boyce and performed there by 1740. It was probably for the Apollo Academy that Boyce composed his most popular and enduring choral work, the serenata *Solomon* to a libretto by Edward Moore first heard in the autumn of 1742 and published the following May.

In the autumn of 1737 Boyce conducted the Worcester festival and was connected with the annual Three Choirs festival until at least 1756, though evidence for his visits is sparse. March 1747 saw the publication of Boyce's first instrumental music, *Twelve Sonatas for Two Violins and a Bass*, whose popularity is confirmed by the extraordinarily large subscribers' list attached. Burney wrote that Boyce's trio sonatas were 'not only in constant use, as chamber Music, in private concerts … but in our theatres, as act-tunes, and public gardens, as favourite pieces, during many years' (Burney, *Hist. mus.*, 3.620). He had a similar success with a set of *Eight Symphonys*, published by Walsh in January 1760, which comprised seven overtures originally composed for other works between 1739 and 1756 and a work which is sometimes known as the Worcester overture. He published a further set of *Twelve Overtures* at his

own expense in 1770, but these were less successful. Hawkins comments:

> The taste of the people at the time of the publication of these, was very unpropitious to their success: they had the misfortune to meet with compositions of [J. C.] Bach and Abel which had already gotten possession of the public ear. (Hawkins, ix)

Boyce was a successful songwriter in the pastoral idiom and some seventy-six solo songs are known. Many of them, along with his duets and cantatas, were popular at Vauxhall and Ranelagh pleasure gardens and found their way into published anthologies, the earliest being Bickham's *Musical Entertainer* of 1737. Between March 1747 and July 1759 Boyce published a series of six books containing selections from his garden and theatre pieces entitled *Lyra Britannica*.

When Garrick became manager of Drury Lane, Boyce, from 1749 to 1759, supplied him with songs and incidental music for thirteen productions, including Garrick's adaptations of Shakespeare. Boyce's afterpiece *The Chaplet*, to a libretto by Moses Mendez, first performed on 2 December 1749, was highly successful for a number of years. *The Shepherd's Lottery*, written by the same librettist, which opened on 19 November 1751, had fewer performances. His final work at Drury Lane was for Garrick's pantomime *Harlequin's Invasion*, which opened on the last day of 1759 and was written to celebrate the end of the 'year of victories'. It featured Boyce's most famous song, 'Heart of Oak', which has been associated with the Royal Navy ever since.

On 1 July 1749 Boyce was in Cambridge with a large assembly of singers and instrumentalists from London to conduct his ode *Here All thy Active Fires Diffuse*, with words by William Mason, commissioned for the installation of the duke of Newcastle as chancellor of the university. The following day he performed his doctoral exercise, the orchestral anthem 'O be joyful in God', in St Mary's Church, and on 3 July he received the degrees of bachelor and doctor of music. He remained in Cambridge for a further two days performing his earlier compositions *Peleus and Thetis*, Dryden's *Secular Masque*, and *Gentle Lyre Begin the Strain*. On his return to London he accepted an invitation to become organist of All Hallows-the-Great, where a new organ had been installed. He was appointed on 28 July 1749 but, according to the vestry minute book, was asked to resign on 21 March 1764, evidently owing to frequent non-attendance.

On the death of Maurice Greene in December 1755 Boyce succeeded him as master of the king's musick, although he was not officially sworn in until June 1757. This prestigious appointment required him to compose annual odes to texts by the poet laureate for the king's birthday and for new year's day which were performed at St James's Palace. He also received Greene's conductorship of the charity festival for the sons of the clergy held annually at St Paul's Cathedral, for which he composed the fine orchestral anthem 'Lord, thou hast been our refuge'. Boyce obtained his third royal appointment, organist to the Chapel Royal, on the death of John Travers in

June 1758, thereby becoming the first musician to hold all three royal positions simultaneously.

Following the death of Handel in April 1759, it fell to Boyce to compose the music for state occasions. He composed the orchestral anthem 'The Souls of the Righteous' for the funeral of George II in Westminster Abbey on 11 November 1760, the wedding anthem 'The king shall rejoice' for George III and Queen Charlotte at St James's Palace on 8 September 1761, and a set of eight anthems for the coronation in Westminster Abbey on 22 September. Boyce declined to set the text 'Zadok the Priest', claiming that Handel had provided an unsurpassable setting for the coronation of George II in 1727. Thereby Boyce inaugurated the tradition of performing Handel's anthem at every coronation thereafter.

By September 1756 Boyce had left his parental home in Joiner's Hall, where he had lived since 1723, and was living in Quality Court, Chancery Lane. On 9 June 1759 he married Hannah Nixon, which remains a chronological puzzle since their daughter Elizabeth was born on 29 April 1749. A son, William, was born on 25 March 1764, and by this time the family had moved to Kensington Gore. Hawkins implies that this was precipitated by Boyce's worsening deafness. He wrote in the 'Memoirs'

> that before the expiration of his apprenticeship, Boyce's organs of hearing were so sensibly affected, that in a short time he became little less than deaf … it deprived him in some degree of a source of both delight and improvement, but he considered music as a mental and not a sensual pleasure, and secretly and with advantage contemplated that harmony which he could but just hear.   (Hawkins, i)

This handicap may explain Boyce's scholarly interest in the history and science of music. In the 1730s he studied with the composer and musical theorist Johann Christoph Pepusch, with whom he shared an interest in earlier musical styles. Boyce in turn shared his knowledge with 'organists and young musicians desirous of improvement in the theory of sounds, the laws of harmony, and the art of practical composition' (Hawkins, vii). His notable pupils included Thomas Linley, John Stafford Smith, Charles Wesley, and Jonathan Battishill. During his life Boyce assembled a considerable music library of manuscripts and printed music which eventually contained Greene's collection bequeathed to him at his death. The sale catalogue of Christie and Ansell (14–16 April 1779) reveals its riches in the descriptions of its 267 lots. As late as November 1778 Boyce evidently visited Christ Church, Oxford, and made an inventory of Dean Aldrich's music books. Philip Hayes returned the list to the college after his death, and it was almost certainly Hayes who acquired for the music school of the University of Oxford a large portion of Boyce's own compositions in manuscript from Hannah Boyce. Also acquired, from where is not known, was the full-length portrait of Boyce painted by Thomas Hudson about 1745. These are now in the Bodleian Library. Other collections of Boyce's music manuscripts are in the British Library, the Royal College of Music, the Fitzwilliam Museum, Cambridge, and University College, Aberystwyth.

Boyce was an assiduous editor and brought to fruition John Alcock's and Maurice Greene's cherished but unfulfilled proposal to publish an uncorrupt corpus of church music, printed in score, to be placed in the hands of all cathedral and collegiate choirs. Boyce's wife stated that he achieved this with considerable financial loss to himself, but its influence on the repertory of English church music was to last for more than a century. *Cathedral Music* was published in three large volumes in 1760, 1768, and 1773. In his last years at Kensington, Boyce was writing a treatise on harmonic theory and corresponding with Marmaduke Overend on the science of music. This material is also in the Bodleian.

Boyce died of gout in Kensington on 7 February 1779 and was honoured with burial in the crypt of St Paul's Cathedral on the 16th. The funeral was attended by a large gathering of musicians and he was buried to the sound of his own music played on the organ and sung by the choirs of the Chapel Royal, St Paul's, and Westminster Abbey. Both Burney and Hawkins knew Boyce personally and describe him in their writings. Burney in Rees's *Cyclopaedia* writes:

> There is an original and sterling merit in his productions, founded as much on the study of our own old masters, as on the best models of other countries, that gives to all his works a peculiar stamp and character of his own, for strength, clearness, and facility, without any mixture of styles, or extraneous and heterogeneous ornaments.

Hawkins, in his 'Memoirs of Dr. William Boyce' of 1788, describes something of Boyce's character:

> He was endowed with the qualities of truth, justice, and integrity, was mild and gentle in his deportment, above all resentment against such as envied his reputation, communicative of his knowledge, sedulous and punctual in the discharge of the duties of his several employments, particularly those that regarded the performance of divine service, and in every relation of life a worthy man.
> (Hawkins, xi)

This is borne out by Boyce's support for charitable foundations. For Mercer's Hospital in Dublin he composed the orchestral anthem 'Blessed is he that Considereth the Sick' (1741), which he later introduced at the festival of the sons of the clergy at St Paul's. He composed and conducted the funeral music for the burial of the philanthropist Captain Thomas Coram at the Foundling Hospital on 3 April 1751. For the benefit of the Leicester Infirmary he composed the ode *Lo! On the Thorny Bed of Care*, with words by Joseph Cradock, performed in St Martin's Church, Leicester, in September 1774.

Together with Handel and other eminent musicians, Boyce was a founder member of the Fund for the Support of Decayed Musicians and their Families, inaugurated on 19 April 1738: it is known today as the Royal Society of Musicians of Great Britain. There is evidence to suggest from appeals made by his widow that Boyce himself died impoverished. To assist the family Philip Hayes selected and published two volumes of Boyce's services and anthems—the first in November 1780, the second in

1790—and in the year of Boyce's death Longman and Broderip published *Ten Voluntaries for the Organ or Harpsichord*, which is Boyce's only known set of keyboard works.

ROBERT J. BRUCE

Sources J. Hawkins, 'Memoirs of Dr William Boyce', in W. Boyce, *Cathedral music*, 2nd edn, 1 (1788), i–xi · Burney, *Hist. mus.*, 3.619–21 · C. Burney, 'Boyce, William', in A. Rees and others, *The cyclopaedia, or, Universal dictionary of arts, sciences, and literature*, 45 vols. (1819–20) · F. G. Edwards, 'Dr. Boyce', *MT*, 42 (1901), 441–9 · D. Dawe, 'New light on William Boyce', *MT*, 109 (1968), 802–7 · J. S. Bumpus, *A history of English cathedral music, 1549–1889*, 2 vols. [1908] · H. D. Johnstone, 'The genesis of Boyce's "Cathedral music"', *Music and Letters*, 56 (1975), 26–40 · R. McGuinness, *English court odes, 1660–1820* (1971) · E. Taylor, 'William Boyce and the theatre', *Music Review*, 14 (1953), 275–87 · H. Boyce, letter to the dean and chapter of Gloucester Cathedral, 24 Aug 1779, Gloucester Cathedral Archives, D 936 X126 stamp on letter · parish register, London, St James Garlickhythe, 11 Sept 1711 [baptism]

Archives Bodl. Oxf., MSS | Glos. RO, letters to Samuel Viner

Likenesses T. Hudson, oils, *c*.1745–1750, Examination Schools, Oxford [*see illus.*] · J. K. Sherwin, line engraving, 1775, BM · J. Russell, pastel drawing, 1776, NPG · J. K. Sherwin, line engraving, 1788, NPG · J. K. Sherwin, drawing (William Boyce aged sixty), repro. in *Musica Britannica*, 13, xxviii; formerly in possession of T. W. Taphouse in 1901 · oils (aged about sixty), Royal College of Music, London

Wealth at death possibly poor; library sold two months after his death; Philip Hayes published Boyce's services and anthems to benefit his family

Boycott, Arthur Edwin (1877–1938), pathologist and naturalist, was born at Hereford on 6 April 1877, the third son of William Boycott, solicitor, and his wife, Eliza Mellard. He was educated at Hereford Cathedral school, and gained the senior classical scholarship at Oriel College, Oxford, where he transferred to natural science, and obtained a first class in physiology in 1898. He received a senior demyship at Magdalen College in 1900 and completed his clinical training at St Thomas's Hospital, London, qualifying MB in 1902. He was elected to a prize fellowship at Brasenose College, Oxford. At Oxford Boycott was greatly influenced by Sir J. S. Burdon-Sanderson, J. S. Haldane, and James Ritchie.

In 1903 Boycott, who was by this time working at Guy's Hospital, London, assisted Haldane in investigating anaemia in Cornish miners, which turned out to be due to hookworm infestation (see his Milroy lectures to the Royal College of Physicians in 1911). He later joined Haldane in studying compressed-air disease, which affects deep-sea divers; their findings led to the introduction of decompression in stages. They also studied mountain sickness.

Boycott married, in 1904, Constance Louisa, daughter of Colonel Will Agg, of the 51st King's Own Yorkshire light infantry, who lived at Prestbury, near Cheltenham. They had two sons, of whom John Agg Boycott (1906–1979) became pathologist to St George's Hospital, London. Boycott graduated MD in the same year as his marriage, and became assistant bacteriologist at the Lister Institute, where he wrote on diphtheria and paratyphoid fever. In 1907 he returned to Guy's Hospital as Gordon lecturer in pathology, and also developed an interest in the blood. With his assistant, Claude Gordon Douglas, he studied the factors affecting blood volume. In later life, Boycott said that the experiment which had pleased him most was the demonstration that the rate of blood regeneration after haemorrhage was in inverse proportion to the size of the animal. He ultimately showed that oxygen tension was the factor controlling red cell production (haematopoiesis) and postulated that the circulating blood and haematopoietic tissue formed a single unit—the 'erythron'. In 1912 Boycott became professor of pathology in the University of Manchester and continued work on the function of the kidney in controlling the volume and composition of the blood.

In 1915 Boycott was appointed to the department of pathology at University College Hospital. He served on the Health of Munition Workers Committee and was commissioned to the Royal Army Medical Corps in 1917 to work at the chemical warfare experimental station at Porton Camp in Wiltshire. Here, he co-operated with Sir Joseph Barcoft in studying the experimental pathology of toxic gases. The First World War was a most unhappy time for a religious man with pacifist views. Boycott returned to University College Hospital medical school after the war, and in 1919 became its first Graham professor of pathology. He worked there until his retirement, due to tuberculosis, in 1935. Even during his time at Manchester, Boycott saw the role of the professor of pathology as advancing pathology as a science and not just as the day-to-day application of laboratory methods to clinical medicine. This was resented by his clinical colleagues.

If pathology was half of Boycott's life, natural history—conchology in particular—was the other. At the age of fifteen he published a catalogue of Herefordshire snails, which foreshadowed his distribution census of British land and freshwater snails. He was recorder of the Conchology Society from 1919 to his death. He studied the complex genetics of the handedness of the helical shell of *Lymnaea peregra* and, in a study involving breeding over 1 million snails, made the important observation that right-handedness was a Mendelian dominant and depended on the genetic make-up of the mother.

Boycott was elected FRS in 1914 and served on the Royal Society's council from 1929 to 1931. He became an FRCP in 1926, a great honour for a non-clinician, and received an honorary LLD from McGill University in 1924. He was on the executive committee of the Imperial Cancer Research Fund until 1935 and on the governing body of the Lister Institute from 1925 to 1938. He was also president of the section of pathology of the Royal Society of Medicine in 1928–30, and he was on the Medical Research Council in 1932–5. Boycott was joint secretary of the Pathological Society of Great Britain and Ireland, a body distinct from the Pathology Society of London, at its formation in 1906. He was involved in the purchase of the *Journal of Pathology and Bacteriology* and its transfer to the Society. Boycott emphasized clear and accurate expression and the use of statistics and abhorred double publication of the same data. He also helped to found the Pathological and Bacteriological Laboratory Assistants Association, the precursor of the Institute of Medical Laboratory Sciences.

Boycott was fluent and lucid as a writer and as a speaker, but was not practical enough for the liking of undergraduates, and had little influence on medical practice. He pursued knowledge for its own sake and regarded immediate utility as irrelevant. He was intensely hard working, and, although he enjoyed good-natured controversy, his influence was limited by his inability to compromise his firm convictions. Like his father, Boycott was politically conservative. He developed odd prejudices against the motor car and wireless. He died of tuberculosis at his son's farm, Ewen Farm House, near Cirencester, Gloucestershire, on 12 May 1938. He was survived by his wife.

J. A. BOYCOTT, *rev.* GEOFFREY L. ASHERSON

Charles Cunningham Boycott (1832–1897), by unknown engraver, pubd 1897 (after Lafayette)

Sources *The Lancet* (21 May 1938), 1190–92 · *Journal of Pathology and Bacteriology*, 47 (1938), 161–94 · *The Times* (18 May 1938) · A. E. Boycott, 'The Pathological Society of Great Britain and Ireland', *British medical societies*, ed. D'Arcy Power (1939) · J. Hatcher, *Gazette of the Institute of Medical Laboratory Sciences*, 24 (1980), 263–4 · *BMJ* (21 May 1938), 1133–4 · C. J. Martin, *Obits. FRS*, 2 (1936–8), 561–71 · *CGPLA Eng. & Wales* (1938)
Archives Medical Research Council, London, corresp. · NHM, corresp., notebooks, and files on mollusca
Likenesses Elliott & Fry, photograph, repro. in *Lancet* · Elliott & Fry, photograph, repro. in Martin, *Obits. FRS* · photograph, repro. in Hatcher, 'Arthur Edwin Boycott', 263 · photograph, repro. in *Journal of Pathology and Bacteriology*
Wealth at death £21,809 4s. 1d.: probate, 8 June 1938, *CGPLA Eng. & Wales*

Boycott [*formerly* Boycatt], **Charles Cunningham** (1832–1897), land agent, from whose surname the word 'boycott' is derived, was born on 12 March 1832, the eldest surviving son of Revd William Boycatt (who changed his name to Boycott in 1862), rector of Wheatacre, Burgh St Peter, Norfolk, and Elizabeth Georgiana, daughter of Arthur Beevor. He was educated in Blackheath and Woolwich, and in 1850 was appointed ensign in the 39th regiment. After leaving the army in 1852 with the rank of captain, he farmed 500 acres near Loughmask, co. Mayo, in Ireland. In 1873 he became agent for Lord Erne, who owned 12,000 acres in co. Mayo.

In 1879 the Land League was formed to fight against tenant evictions and to discourage people from taking a farm from which a tenant had been evicted. In 1880 the Land League demanded a 25 per cent reduction in the rents paid by Lord Erne's tenants, and in September Boycott had to be placed under police protection following mob attacks.

Meanwhile Charles Stewart Parnell, in a speech at Ennis on 19 September 1880, advised tenants who could not obtain the reductions they demanded to take action against their landlord or his agent by 'isolating him from his kind as if he were a leper of old' (Hammond, 192–3). Parnell was not the first to recommend this course of action: it had been used since the mid-century and by the Land League since 1879, when John Dillon urged that if any man took up land from which another had been evicted 'let no man speak to him or have any business transaction with him'. But Parnell's speech encouraged Lord Erne's tenants to apply this treatment to Boycott. (Kee, 211). Labourers refused to work for him, his walls were pulled down and his cattle scattered, he was unable to obtain provisions from the neighbourhood, and food had to be brought to him by steamer. He was hooted and spat on in the road, and only with great difficulty did he receive letters and telegrams.

Appeals to the government for assistance were at first made in vain, and on 18 October he sent a letter to *The Times* complaining of his treatment. A month later a party of fifty Ulstermen, chiefly from co. Cavan (afterwards known as 'emergency men'), volunteered to harvest Boycott's crops, and they were given an escort of 900 soldiers. This was seen as a victory by the Land League, which was able to boast that thanks to its actions it had taken nearly 1000 men to gather in the produce of one farm. The number of evictions declined as a result. Once the harvest was completed, Boycott went to the United States. On his return to Ireland in the autumn of 1881 he was mobbed at an auction at Westport, and his effigy was hanged and burnt. He also received letters signed 'Rory of the Hills', threatening him with the fate of Lord Leitrim, who had recently been murdered. But things gradually improved and by 1883 were back to normal.

In 1886 Boycott left Ireland and became agent for Sir Hugh Adair's estates, in Suffolk. Boycott soon lived down his unpopularity and he even took his holidays in Ireland, but he was unable to obtain any compensation from the government. On 12 December 1888 he gave evidence before the special commission appointed to investigate the charges made by *The Times* against the Irish leaders, though he was not cross-examined.

The word 'boycott' first came into use at the end of 1880. In the *Daily News* of 13 December it was printed in capitals. Joseph Gillis Biggar, MP for co. Cavan, was among those who used it to signify all intimidatory measures that stopped short of physical violence. It came into general use to describe measures used to isolate an institution or a country.

Boycott was a shortish man with a bald head, a heavy white moustache, and flowing white beard. In 1853 he married Annie, daughter of John Dunne. He died on 19 June 1897 at Priest's House, Flixton, Suffolk. He was survived by his wife.

G. LE G. NORGATE, *rev.* ANNE PIMLOTT BAKER

Sources L. C. Sanders, *Celebrities of the century: being a dictionary of men and women of the nineteenth century* (1887) · Boase, *Mod. Eng. biog.* · J. L. Hammond, *Gladstone and the Irish nation* (1938) · Walford, *County families* · *Daily News* (22 June 1897) · *Norfolk Chronicle* (26 June 1897) · R. Kee, *The laurel and the ivy: the story of Charles Stewart Parnell and Irish nationalism* (1993); repr. (1994) · 'Special commission to inquire into … allegations against certain MPs', *Parl. papers* (1890), 27.477, C. 5891 · W. E. Vaughan, *Landlords and tenants in mid-Victorian Ireland* (1994) · d. cert.

Likenesses pencil drawing, 1888, NG Ire. · engraving, pubd 1897 (after photograph by Lafayette), NPG [*see illus.*] · Spy [L. Ward], chromolithograph caricature, NPG; repro. in *VF* (29 Jan 1881)

Wealth at death £2229 6s. 7d.: probate, 18 Aug 1897, *CGPLA Eng. & Wales*

Boyd family (*per. c.*1300–*c.*1480), landowners and administrators, rose to prominence from a landed base in Ayrshire. The first member of the family to achieve national eminence was **Sir Robert Boyd** (*d.* 1333) under Robert I, even though he played an uncertain role in the early stages of the wars of independence. Certainly following the general submission of 1304 he entered English service as coroner of Ayr and Lanark, and he was still associated with English agents in early 1305. But he was part of Robert Bruce's entourage later in that year and rebelled with Bruce in early 1306, taking Rothesay, besieging Inverkip, and attacking the earl of Strathearn. After the battle of Methven he escorted the Scottish queen to Kildrummy, although the account of his capture there is unlikely to be true, as he was not executed. According to chronicle sources, he was with Bruce, now Robert I, on Rathlin in the winter of 1306–7, and accompanied Edward Bruce in an attack on Galloway in 1308. Thereafter he was prominent in all Robert I's campaigns, and attended that king's first parliament in 1309. It is very likely he fought at Bannockburn, following which he received the barony of Kilmarnock, forfeited by the former King John (John de Balliol), and the lands of Noddsdale in May 1315. Between 1309 and 1329 he witnessed a significant number of royal charters, although he was not constantly with the king. He is last recorded in the Scottish army at Halidon Hill on 19 July 1333—it is said that he was captured there and died soon afterwards.

Subsequent Boyds were less important for several generations. Sir Robert's great-grandson, Thomas Boyd (*d.* 1432), was briefly a hostage for James I's release from imprisonment in England in 1424. Thomas's son, Sir Thomas Boyd, was briefly imprisoned on 13 May 1424 as part of James I's attacks on the Albany Stewarts. In 1438 he killed Alan Stewart of Darnley, and was himself killed in revenge on 7 August 1439 by Alexander Stewart, in a feud over ambitions in the Lennox. He was succeeded by his son **Robert Boyd**, first Lord Boyd (*d.* 1481/2), who was involved in the murder of Sir James Stewart of Ardgowan on 31 May 1445. He was made a lord of parliament by James II in June 1452, along with a number of south-westerners, as a way of securing support in the wake of the king's murder of the eighth earl of Douglas. He witnessed the parliamentary forfeiture of the ninth earl of Douglas in June 1455, but was not particularly prominent in royal business at any time before 1466. Instead it is his

brother, Sir Alexander Boyd of Drumcoll, who is most visible in the governmental records. A bond of 10 February 1466 makes it clear that at this time Alexander, the keeper of Edinburgh Castle and chamberlain, was virtually a partner with Gilbert, Lord Kennedy, in the governorship of the young *James III. Lord Boyd used his brother's links with Kennedy to enable the coup of 9 July 1466, when he led the seizure of James III following the exchequer audit at Linlithgow and took him to his brother's stronghold at Edinburgh. A parliament of October 1466 appointed him guardian, and witnessed the king's declaration, undoubtedly made under duress, that Lord Boyd had acted on his orders. Alexander Boyd was then discarded. He was excluded from the parliamentary apologia, and by early 1467 Lord Boyd had assumed his brother's offices.

Self-aggrandizement was used to reinforce a very narrowly based regime. Boyd's son Thomas [*see below*] was made earl of Arran, and early in 1467 was married to the king's sister Mary, while his daughter Elizabeth married the earl of Angus. In contrast, very little patronage was given to those who had taken part in the coup, or were sympathetic to it. To the antagonism of the nobility was added the irritation of the now nearly adult king, angered by Arran's marriage to his sister. On 25 April 1468, in order to prop up his authority, and to avoid calling a hostile parliament, Boyd had to make an agreement with prominent members of the council, by which they promised to defend Boyd's guardianship.

Boyd's period of office saw one notable success, with the ratification on 8 September 1468 of the treaty of Copenhagen by which Margaret of Denmark was betrothed to James III, the 'annual'—the payment due to Norway since 1266—for the Western Isles was cancelled, and Orkney and Shetland were pawned to Scotland, in the first step to their subsequent annexation. But in the summer of 1469, while Lord Boyd was in England on embassy, and Arran still in Denmark, the king assumed control of government, presumably with the help of his councillors, and probably his half-uncles, the earl of Atholl and James Stewart of Auchterhouse. Lord Boyd, Arran, and Alexander Boyd were forfeited in parliament on 22 November 1469 for their treasonous seizure of the king three years before, although only the unfortunate Alexander was present to be executed. Lord Boyd had joined his son in exile in Bruges by early 1470. By 1471 he was in England, where Edward IV gave him a yearly pension of 200 marks, and was residing in Alnwick in 1475, to the annoyance of James III. He died in England in 1481 or 1482. He married Mariota, daughter of Sir John Maxwell of Calderwood, and had three sons.

The eldest of these, **Thomas Boyd**, first earl of Arran (*d.* before 1474), had been contracted on 20 January 1466 to marry Lord Kennedy's daughter, as part of Lord Boyd's wooing of the Kennedy regime. Instead, following the July 1466 coup, he was married to Princess Mary (*b.* 1451), elder sister of James III, and created earl of Arran by his father's influence, shortly before 26 April 1467. The marriage was undoubtedly unpopular, particularly with the king who later claimed to have wept at the wedding, as it was seen as a waste of a valuable dynastic commodity, not to mention an insult to the royal family. Arran's most important public role was as one of the ambassadors who concluded the treaty of Copenhagen in September 1468. When the Boyds fell in the summer of 1469 Arran was still abroad, and he was forfeited on 22 November. In October 1471 Arran, Lord Boyd, and Princess Mary attempted to return to Scotland. After stopping first in England, Mary went ahead, but was detained by the king. She was subsequently married to James, Lord Hamilton (d. 1479), a rising star in James III's council, probably following Arran's death, which took place in England, before 1474. Nevertheless, Margaret maintained a residual loyalty for her first husband's family, and in the crisis of 1482 made an (eventually) abortive attempt to secure the succession of her son with Arran, James, to the Boyd lordship. Arran remained in England until his death.

The rise of the Boyds was short-lived, generally unpopular, and unsustainable in the face of parliamentary hostility and the coming of age of the king. However, they were part of a larger process in the 1460s, by which successive factions, largely based on south-western support, played out the rivalries of their region on a national stage.

ROLAND J. TANNER

Sources N. Macdougall, *James III: a political study* (1982), 70–87, 88–9, 171 · G. W. S. Barrow, *Robert Bruce and the community of the realm of Scotland*, 3rd edn (1988), 146, 193 · *Scots peerage*, 5.136–50 · *APS*, 1124–1423, 459, 289; 1424–1567, 185–7, 77, 85–98 · C. McGladdery, 'Auckinleck Chronicle', *James II* (1990), 160–73 · W. Bower, *Scotichronicon*, ed. D. E. R. Watt and others, new edn, 9 vols. (1987–98), vol. 8, p. 241 · *CDS*, vols. 2, 4 · J. M. Thomson and others, eds., *Registrum magni sigilli regum Scotorum / The register of the great seal of Scotland*, 11 vols. (1882–1914), vols. 1–2 · G. Burnett and others, eds., *The exchequer rolls of Scotland*, 23 vols. (1878–1908), vol. 1; vol. 7, p. 500; vol. 8, p. 53 · P. F. Tytler, *History of Scotland*, 3rd edn, 3 (1845), 507 · J. Maidment, ed., *Miscellany of the Abbotsford Club*, 1 (1837) · R. Nicholson, *Scotland: the later middle ages* (1974), vol. 2 of *The Edinburgh history of Scotland*, ed. G. Donaldson (1965–75), 327 · [J. Barbour], *The Brus: from a collation of the Cambridge and Edinburgh manuscripts*, ed. C. Innes, Spalding Club, 28 (1856) · J. Stevenson, ed., *Chronicon de Lanercost, 1201–1346*, Bannatyne Club, 65 (1839), 212 · G. W. S. Barrow and others, eds., *Regesta regum Scottorum*, 5, ed. A. A. M. Duncan (1988), 6, 67, 165, 203, 258, 308, 373, 375

Archives NA Scot., papers | NA Scot., Ailsa charters

Wealth at death pension from Edward IV in England of 200 marks p.a.—Robert, Lord Boyd: *CDS*, vol. 4, nos. 1415, 1440

Boyd, Alan Tindal Lennox-, first Viscount Boyd of Merton (1904–1983), politician, was born on 18 November 1904 at Loddington, Bournemouth, the second of four children of Alan Walter Lennox Boyd (1855–1934), a barrister, and his second wife, Florence Anne (1870–1949), daughter of James Warburton *Begbie MD, of Edinburgh. His father's first wife, Clementina Louisa, had died in 1896, leaving him with a daughter, Phyllis; in 1925 his father altered the family name to Lennox-Boyd by deed poll.

Family, education, and Conservative politics Lennox-Boyd remembered his father as an unaffectionate figure who spent long periods away from his young family. Florence, by contrast, developed an almost obsessively close relationship with her four sons. Together, mother and sons

Alan Tindal Lennox-Boyd, first Viscount Boyd of Merton (1904–1983), by Elliott & Fry, c.1960

constituted what one acquaintance described as the 'Lennox-Boyd Mutual Admiration Society', an emotionally self-sufficient unit into which outsiders found it virtually impossible to break. George, Alan's elder brother, was briefly engaged to the daughter of Lord Baden-Powell. Yet neither George nor either of Alan's other brothers ultimately married, despite the fact that Donald was thirty-two when he died, Francis thirty-five, and George forty-one. His own marriage in December 1938 to Patricia Florence Susan Guinness (b. 1918), daughter of Rupert Edward Cecil Lee *Guinness, second earl of Iveagh, caused surprise in some quarters. Nevertheless it proved a success. It provided him with a witty and tolerant companion who bore him three sons, and it absolved him from financial worries for the remainder of his life. It also helped him to endure the tragic deaths of all three of his brothers between April 1939 and June 1944 and the loss of his mother in 1949.

Lennox-Boyd was educated at Sherborne School and Christ Church, Oxford (1923–7), where he read history. He was active in university politics and became president of the union (1926). His characteristic brand of high toryism—incorporating an unswerving faith in Britain's established institutions and a highly romanticized notion of Britain's 'Imperial mission'—was already fully in evidence. He was awarded the Beit essay prize for colonial history (1926), but like his hero Lord Curzon he failed to win a first, to his immense disappointment. At the 1929 general election he stood, unsuccessfully, for the Conservatives in the Gower division of Glamorgan. Shortly afterwards, he was selected to fight the far more promising seat of Mid-Bedfordshire. His chances of securing election received a severe blow in August 1931, when the sitting Liberal member, Milner Gray, joined the newly formed National Government as a junior minister. Lennox-Boyd came under sustained pressure from the Conservative leadership not to stand against Gray, but refused to withdraw from the contest, and thus earned himself the nickname the Wrecker of Mid-Beds. At the October 1931 general election he won the seat for the Conservatives without the support of central office and, thereafter, felt free to take an independent line on the back benches. He held Mid-Bedfordshire continuously until 1960, although it remained a marginal seat. During the 1930s he became one of Winston Churchill's most energetic supporters in the campaign against constitutional reform in India. His determined advocacy of the nationalist cause during the Spanish Civil War and his suggestion that the king of Italy should be recognized as the emperor of Abyssinia led to accusations that he was a fascist sympathizer.

Despite his reputation as a right-wing rebel, Lennox-Boyd's assured performances in the Commons won him a place in government in February 1938 as parliamentary secretary at the Ministry of Labour. Shortly after his appointment, he attracted fierce criticism when he publicly dismissed the notion that Britain should guarantee the borders of Czechoslovakia against German aggression. This caused a rift with Churchill which took years to repair. At the outbreak of war, despite his desire to enlist, he was persuaded by Chamberlain to become parliamentary secretary at the newly created Ministry of Home Security. He was moved again, to the Ministry of Food, before leaving the government at his own request in May 1940 to join the Royal Naval Volunteer Reserve. He served on a series of motor torpedo boats. His duties included escorting channel convoys on their perilous progress through the Strait of Dover. In November 1943, shortly after the vessel under his command had been damaged in an attack on a German convoy off the Hook of Holland, Churchill brought him back into the government as parliamentary secretary at the Ministry of Aircraft Production. Churchill appears to have regarded his military service as adequate atonement for his Chamberlainite past, and their friendship gradually recovered.

Colonial affairs In the caretaker government of May to July 1945 Lennox-Boyd remained at the Ministry of Aircraft Production. After the Conservatives' defeat in the 1945 general election, he became a leading figure in the active back-benchers group of Tory MPs whose self-imposed mission was to harry the Labour government by every means at their disposal. He had little sympathy for the domestic social agenda of the Attlee administration and he was fiercely critical of their handling of imperial affairs, particularly their record in India and Palestine. On the death of Oliver Stanley in 1950, he became the Conservatives' principal spokesman on colonial affairs. Following the Conservative victory of October 1951, Churchill appointed him minister of state at the Colonial Office, despite being advised by the cabinet secretary that the post was unnecessary and should be abolished. He remained at the Colonial Office for less than seven months before being transferred, against his wishes, to the Ministry of Transport and Civil Aviation. He accepted this appointment on the understanding that he would return to the Colonial Office as secretary of state on Oliver Lyttelton's departure. As minister of transport, he consolidated his reputation by successfully piloting through the house the government's contentious 1953 Transport Bill.

At the end of July 1954 Lennox-Boyd finally succeeded to the post of colonial secretary. Given his previous political record, he might have been expected to make every effort to impede constitutional development in the colonies. He certainly believed that British rule had conferred immense benefits on colonial peoples and that their interests would not be served by unnecessarily rapid transfers of power. Yet he also believed in supporting the judgement of his governors, and their preference, when faced with pressure from strong nationalist movements, was overwhelmingly for concession rather than confrontation. He proved willing to expedite Malaya's progress towards independence, and he presided, with far greater reservations, over the transfer of sovereignty in Ghana. His period as secretary of state coincided with a fashion, of which he fully approved, for federating groups of colonial territories. As minister of state he took part in the negotiations leading to the establishment of the Central African Federation, and as colonial secretary he oversaw the creation of federations in the West Indies and southern Arabia. None of these survived. While their existence could be justified on economic and strategic grounds, they proved highly vulnerable to regional tensions, the fear of domination by a particular ethnic group, and the rise of anti-colonial nationalism.

Some of the most intractable problems with which Lennox-Boyd had to deal could not be resolved by the simple concession of independence. One such case was Cyprus. In their efforts to restore peace and stability to the island following the outbreak of the EOKA campaign of violence in 1955, the freedom of manoeuvre enjoyed by Lennox-Boyd and the island's governor was severely restricted by the involvement of Downing Street, the Foreign Office, and the chiefs of staff. In Malta he was faced with the anomalous situation of a dependent territory seeking *closer* association with Great Britain. Negotiations on integration with the island's prime minister, Dom Mintoff, proved far less amicable than many independence struggles and ultimately achieved nothing.

In November 1958 Lennox-Boyd bowed to pressure from his family and undertook to leave the Commons at the next general election in order to assume the post of managing director of Guinness, which was due to fall vacant in

1960. He had already served as colonial secretary for over four years, and he had little interest in taking on any other senior post in government. At the time this decision was made, he and Macmillan were in broad agreement over the general direction of British colonial policy. In so far as disagreements had emerged before the beginning of 1959, it was Lennox-Boyd who had proved the more sympathetic towards the aspirations of colonial nationalists. His plans for a graceful retirement from politics were confounded, however, by events in Africa. On 3 March 1959 eleven 'hard-core' Mau Mau inmates died at the Hola detention camp in Kenya. A communiqué issued by the Kenya government linked the deaths to water poisoning. On the morning of 14 March 1959, just hours before he was due to tell a special meeting of his constituency party that he did not intend to contest the next general election, Lennox-Boyd was informed by the governor of Kenya, Sir Evelyn Baring, that the detainees had been beaten to death. Under the circumstances Lennox-Boyd could not announce his intention of leaving politics without appearing to assume responsibility, personally and on behalf of the government, for the Hola deaths and subsequent cover-up. He was persuaded by Macmillan to fight the next general election on the understanding that, shortly afterwards, he would be allowed to quit the Commons.

Lennox-Boyd retained his seat in October 1959 and in the summer of 1960 he was elevated to the House of Lords as the first Viscount Boyd of Merton. He sold his house in central London to the newly independent government of Nigeria and bought Ince Castle in Cornwall, a seventeenth-century house overlooking the Lynher estuary. Yet he remained extremely busy. Arthur Guinness & Co. Ltd claimed much of his time. He served initially as joint managing director, and then, following Sir Hugh Beaver's retirement at the beginning of January 1961, as sole managing director. He remained in the post until 1967 and then served as joint vice-chairman until 1979. He gave generously of his time to a wide variety of other organizations including the British Museum, VSO, the Overseas Service Pensioners' Association, and the British Leprosy Relief Association, many of which enabled him to remain in touch with Commonwealth affairs.

Lennox-Boyd became increasingly alarmed at what he regarded as the dangerously rapid pace of decolonization in Africa. A sign of his disenchantment with the colonial policy of the Macmillan government was his decision in 1962 to become joint patron of the recently established Monday Club. However, he resigned from this office in 1968 after the club publicly endorsed Enoch Powell's stance on immigration. He had opposed the imposition of controls on Commonwealth immigration while colonial secretary, and on a personal level he was repelled by racial prejudice, as the many guests from Africa and elsewhere in the Commonwealth who stayed at his home in Chapel Street would testify. In this as in so many other matters, as Sir Hugh Foot once remarked, 'his good nature and his good humour and his generous fairness repeatedly rescue him from the consequences of his reactionary policies'

(H. Foot, *A Start in Freedom*, 1964, 152). A large man (6 feet 5 inches in height), his physical stature was more than matched by a commanding personality of immense warmth and charm, which won him a far wider range of friends than might have appeared likely from the bare outlines of his career. In April 1979 he was sent as head of a team of observers from the Conservative Party to monitor the elections in Zimbabwe. He accepted the task with relish and performed it with great thoroughness, although his team's main conclusion—that the elections had been fairly conducted—ultimately proved unhelpful to Margaret Thatcher. On the evening of 8 March 1983 he was knocked down and killed by a car while crossing the Fulham Road in London. He was cremated in a private ceremony and his ashes buried in the grounds of St Stephen's Church in Saltash, Cornwall.   PHILIP MURPHY

Sources Bodl. Oxf., MSS Boyd · interview for the Oxford Colonial Records Project, Bodl. RH · PRO, Colonial Office MSS · D. Goldsworthy, ed., *The conservative government and the end of empire, 1951–1957*, 3 vols. (1994) · P. Murphy, *Alan Lennox-Boyd: a biography* (1999) **Archives** Bodl. Oxf., papers · Ince Castle, Cornwall, scrapbooks · PRO, Colonial Office MSS and other departmental MSS · PRO, corresp. relating to Cyprus and Malta · PRO, private office papers, AVIA 9 | Bodl. RH, corresp. with Arthur Creech-Jones · Bodl. RH, corresp. with Margery Perham · Bodl. RH, corresp. with R. R. Welensky · CAC Cam., corresp. with Buchan-Hepburn · CAC Cam., Churchill MSS · CAC Cam., corresp. with E. L. Spears · CUL, corresp. with Sir Peter Markham Scott · HLRO, corresp. with Lord Beaverbrook · Nuffield Oxf., corresp. with Lord Cherwell · U. Birm. L., MSS, corresp. with Lord Avon · U. Leeds, Brotherton L., corresp. with Henry Drummond-Wolff | SOUND Bodl. RH, recordings of Oxford Colonial Records Project interviews **Likenesses** photograph, 1956, Hult. Arch. · Elliott & Fry, photograph, c.1960, NPG [*see illus.*] **Wealth at death** £197,998: probate, 22 June 1983, *CGPLA Eng. & Wales*

Boyd, Andrew Kennedy Hutchison (1825–1899), Church of Scotland minister and author, was born on 3 November 1825 at Auchinleck manse, Ayrshire, the eldest son of James Boyd (1787–1865), minister of the Tron parish, Glasgow, and his wife, Jane Hutchison. He received his earliest education at Ochiltree parish school and then at Ayr Academy (1838–40). In 1840 Boyd moved to London, studying at King's College and then at the Middle Temple; he seemed likely to follow a career at the English bar, but in 1844 his life changed direction on his decision to enter the ministry of the Church of Scotland. He moved to study at the University of Glasgow, first in arts and then in divinity: he was a fine student, winning nine first prizes while studying divinity and receiving his BA in 1846. On completing his studies he was licensed by the presbytery of Ayr and preached his first public sermon in Greenock, Renfrewshire, in October 1850.

Boyd's ministry began in Edinburgh, as an assistant at St George's, with his first individual charge being at Newton upon Ayr (1851–4). This was followed by Kirkpatrick-Irongray (1854–9), St Bernard's, Edinburgh (1859–65), and finally by the first charge of St Andrews from 1865 until his sudden death in 1899. His considerable fame was based on a combination of his reputation as a preacher and on his popularity as a writer, as well as his contributions to debates within the Church of Scotland. His various achievements were recognized by the University of Edinburgh, which granted him the degree of DD in 1864 (when Boyd was only thirty-four); by the University of St Andrews, which awarded him an LLD in 1889; by the Church of Scotland, which elected him to its highest position, moderator of the general assembly, in 1890; and by King's College, London, which made him a fellow in 1895. Boyd married on 12 April 1854 Margaret Buchanan (d. 1895), with whom he had seven children. On 5 April 1897 he married his second wife, Janet Balfour (d. 1917).

It was during Boyd's time at Kirkpatrick-Irongray that relatively light ministerial duties allowed him the time to develop his skill as a writer, and it was by the initials under which he wrote—A. K. H. B.—that he was perhaps best known. He wrote articles for *Fraser's Magazine*, which were eventually published in three series as *The Recreations of a Country Parson* (1859, 1861, and 1878), and ran into many editions. His writings were also immensely popular in the United States, where the 1861 series of *The Recreations* went through twenty editions. Despite finding writing difficult and even painful, he wrote prodigiously, a mixture of essays, sermons, and reminiscences, including *The Graver Thoughts of a Country Parson* (3 ser., 1862, 1865, 1875), *Counsel and Comfort Spoken from a City Pulpit* (1863), and *Our Little Life: Essays Consolatory and Domestic* (2 ser., 1882, 1884). The semi-autobiographical works *Twenty-Five Years of St Andrews* (2 vols., 1892), *St Andrews and Elsewhere* (1894), and *The Last Years of St Andrews* (1896) provide a fascinating and readable glimpse into his life and times; a detailed diary combined with a tenacious memory meant that very little was forgotten. 'Many a time', said Boyd, 'have I wished that my memory was not nearly so good' (Boyd, *Last Years*, 2–3).

As a churchman Boyd's importance was fourfold. First, he was an extremely popular preacher—Robert Story said, 'I never knew a man more fond of preaching; and few preached better … with his earnest and almost emotional manner' (Story, 91). Second, Boyd was a prominent figure in the contentious late nineteenth-century debate about church and state, with his weight firmly behind the principle of the Church of Scotland remaining an established national church. Third, Boyd's numerous contacts with prominent Anglicans, including J. A. Froude, Richard Whately, A. W. Thorold, A. P. Stanley, H. P. Liddon and R. W. Church, gave the Church of Scotland a reputation and exposure in influential English circles which it would not otherwise have had; 'he made its name familiar, its ministry respected, and its history and character, to some extent at least, understood, among people who became interested in it for his sake' (ibid., 93). 'There is no gulf at all', Boyd claimed, 'between the best in the Church of Scotland and the best in the Church of England' (A. Boyd, *Sermons and Stray Papers*, 1907, 41). This view perhaps contributed to his fourth role in Scottish church life as a leading supporter of the move towards the increased use of liturgy in services. An enthusiastic proponent of the use of the Christian year, he was strongly in favour of a more liturgical service and was also instrumental in the Church

of Scotland's adoption of *The Scottish Hymnal*, approved in 1870. Although his views earned him unpopularity in places, his role was an important one in the general adoption of these principles within the Scottish church.

In the 1890s Boyd suffered recurring bouts of ill health from which he never recovered his customary energy, and in 1898–9 a period of illness persuaded him to go to Bournemouth to recuperate. He died there on 1 March 1899 from accidental poisoning, having taken carbolic lotion which he mistook for a sleeping draught. He was interred in the churchyard of St Andrews Cathedral, Robert Story, principal of the University of Glasgow, preaching his funeral sermon. JAMES LACHLAN MACLEOD

Sources W. Tulloch, 'Biographical sketch', in A. Boyd, *Sermons and stray papers* (1907) · D. Henderson, *Anecdotes and recollections of AKHB* (1900) · R. Story, *AKHB, life and work* (1899) · *Fasti Scot.* · *DNB* · A. L. Drummond and J. Bulloch, *The church in Victorian Scotland, 1843–1874* (1975) · [A. K. H. Boyd], *Twenty-five years of St Andrews*, 2 vols. (1892) · A. Boyd, *St Andrews and elsewhere* (1894) · A. Boyd, *Last years of St Andrews* (1896) · *A.K.H.B.: a volume of selections*, ed. C. Boyd (1914)
Archives Hunt. L., letters · NL Scot., letters | NL Scot., corresp. with *Blackwood's*
Likenesses T. Roger, photograph, repro. in Boyd, *Sermons and stray papers* · carte-de-visite, NPG
Wealth at death £13,253 16s. 10d.: confirmation, 26 June 1899, CCI

Boyd, Archibald (1803–1883), dean of Exeter, was born at Londonderry, the son of Archibald Boyd, treasurer of that city. After being educated at the local diocesan college he proceeded to Trinity College, Dublin, where he graduated BA in 1823, proceeding MA in 1834, and BD and DD in 1868. He officiated as curate and preacher in the cathedral of Londonderry 1827–42, and here first distinguished himself as an able and powerful preacher, as a controversialist, and as an author. At that time the controversy between the presbyterians and the episcopalians of the north of Ireland was at its height. Boyd came to the defence of the established church and preached a series of discourses in reply to attacks. These discourses attracted great attention, and were afterwards printed as *Sermons on the Church* (1838), *Episcopacy, Ordination, Lay-Eldership, and Liturgies* (1839), and *Episcopacy and Presbytery* (1841).

In 1842 Boyd was appointed perpetual curate of Christ Church, Cheltenham. With Francis Close, his fellow worker, he took part in a scheme for establishing additional Sunday schools, infant schools, and Bible classes, and campaigned for a public library. He became an honorary canon of Gloucester in 1857. He was also a rural dean of the diocese. From 1859 to 1867 he was vicar of Paddington.

On 11 November 1867 Boyd accepted the deanery of Exeter, which he held until his death. Like Dean Close, he was a preaching and a working dean. He was a firm but moderate evangelical, and a voluminous writer on the ecclesiastical questions of the day. Notable among his publications are *England, Rome, and Oxford* (1846), a history of the prayer book (1850), *Turkey and the Turks* (1853), and works on baptism (1865) and confession (1867). His name is connected with the Exeter reredos case. In 1872–3 the dean and chapter erected in the cathedral a stone reredos, on which were sculptured representations in bas-relief of the ascension, the transfiguration, and the descent of the Holy Ghost, with some figures of angels. In accordance with a petition presented by William John Phillpotts, chancellor of the diocese, the bishop (Frederick Temple) on 7 January 1874 declared the reredos to be contrary to law and ordered its removal. But Boyd's action was found by the privy council (on 25 February 1875) to have been legitimate (or at least not illegitimate). At Exeter, Boyd attempted to suppress vicars choral.

In the autumn of 1882 Boyd had an accident at Vienna from which he never fully recovered. He died at the deanery, Exeter, on 11 July 1883, bequeathing nearly £40,000 to various societies and institutions in the diocese of Exeter. His wife, Frances, daughter of Thomas Waller of Ospringe, and widow of the Revd Robert Day Denny, had died on 6 January 1877, and Boyd's considerable estate may have come from her.

G. C. BOASE, *rev.* H. C. G. MATTHEW

Sources *The Times* (12 July 1883) · *Devon Weekly Times* (13 July 1883) · *Devon Weekly Times* (20 July 1883) · Contem Ignotus, *The golden decade of a famous town* (1884) · P. Barrett, *Barchester: English cathedral life in the nineteenth century* (1993)

Archives Devon RO, estate and family corresp. and papers · LPL, corresp. with A. C. Tait

Likenesses S. Cousins?, mezzotint (after H. W. Phillips), BM

Wealth at death £134,298 4s. 8d.: probate, 17 Aug 1883, *CGPLA Eng. & Wales*

Boyd, Arthur Merric Bloomfield (1920–1999), artist, was born on 24 July 1920 at Open Country, 8 Wahroonga Crescent, Murrumbeena, Victoria, Australia, the second child and eldest son in the family of three sons and two daughters of (William) Merric Boyd, potter, and his wife, Doris Lucy Eleanor, *née* Gough, painter. His ancestors included Sir William à Beckett, the first chief justice of Victoria, and the state's first brewer, John Mills. His paternal grandparents were the New Zealand-born academic painter Arthur Merric Boyd and his wife, Emma Minnie à Beckett, also a painter. His maternal grandparents were a Royal Navy officer, Commander Bunbury Gough, and his wife, Evelyn Rigg, a newspaper publisher and penal reformer. The distinguished painter Penleigh Boyd and the novelist Martin Boyd were among his uncles. His four siblings were the potter and painter Lucy Boyd, the sculptor Guy Boyd, the painter and potter David Boyd, and the painter Mary Boyd, who married successively two distinguished Australian painters, John Perceval and Sidney Nolan.

Early life The only important career question in Boyd's life was *when* he would become an artist, and in which media. After attending the state school at Murrumbeena (then a country village, later a suburb of Melbourne) he left, aged fourteen, during the depression years and worked at the north Melbourne paint factory of his uncle Ralph Madder, while gaining a modest amount of formal artistic instruction at the National Gallery Art School in Melbourne. In

Arthur Merric Bloomfield Boyd (1920–1999), by Axel Poignant, 1962

1936 he went to live with his watercolourist grandfather, Arthur Merric Boyd, at Rosebud on the Mornington Peninsula and became, almost overnight, a full-time painter. As early as 1937 he was producing highly proficient landscapes in the manner of Arthur Streeton and in the tradition of Rupert Bunny and Charles Conder. In 1938 he went back to Murrumbeena and built his own separate studio in the grounds, using plans drawn up by his cousin, the distinguished architect Robin Boyd. He was a founder member of the Contemporary Art Society in Melbourne, but later drifted away. In 1939 he shared an exhibition with Polish-born Yosl Bergner at the Rowden White Library at the University of Melbourne. The following year he had his first full-scale exhibition (with Keith Nichol) at the Athenaeum Gallery in Melbourne. The paintings of this period were mostly conventional landscapes in the Bunny, Conder, Streeton mode, but, for a young man barely twenty years old, they were astonishingly fluent, accomplished, and above all professional. His formal teaching had been so exiguous that this precocious skill can be attributed only to inherited genes and innate virtuosity.

On 12 May 1941 Boyd joined the army in a light horse machine gun unit, for which he was eminently ill-suited; as soon as possible he applied to, and was accepted by, the more appropriate cartographic company, conveniently situated opposite the public library and National Gallery of Victoria. There he met his fellow artists Yvonne Lennie and Sidney Nolan. The latter became a lifelong friend, rival, and eventually brother-in-law. Boyd shared not only painting with Nolan but also a firm dislike of the military life. While in the army he was charged with appropriating military property: in this case, blankets for himself and Yvonne to sleep on in the studio which he managed to maintain during his military service. He escaped any significant punishment and was later discharged from the army on 25 March 1944, together with his friend John Perceval, who then married Boyd's sister Mary. Boyd himself married Yvonne Hartland Lennie, daughter of John Aim Lennie and Edna Latham Hartland, on 6 March 1945 at the house of Stanley Neighbour, the Baptist minister in Oakleigh, a suburb next to Murrumbeena. In 1946 their first child, Polly, was born. In the same year Boyd shared a significant exhibition with Nolan and Albert Tucker, again at the Rowden White Library.

Images of Australia The period 1945–8 was of great importance in Boyd's work. It produced an extraordinary series of religious paintings including *The Prodigal Son*, *The Expulsion*, and *Angel Spying on Adam and Eve* which, while dealing with episodes from the Old Testament, were also imbued with a rather sinister voyeuristic element. Another masterpiece from 1946–7 was his visionary *Melbourne Burning*, in which the influence of both Bosch and Brueghel could be clearly discerned. As it was many years before he travelled to Europe, this was the influence only of imagery in reproduction form, rather than technique; but it was clear that he was already a major painter.

In 1949 Boyd moved with Yvonne, Polly, and his new son Jamie, to the former à Beckett family home, The Grange at Harkaway, Victoria, where he painted dining-room murals commissioned by his uncle Martin Boyd and also painted his Berwick landscapes which, while relatively conventional compared with his religious subjects, significantly advanced Australian landscape painting beyond its previous rather academic boundaries. In 1949 he made painting expeditions to north-west Victoria, the Grampians, and the Wimmera, and in 1950 had his first retrospective exhibition at the David Jones Gallery in Sydney. In 1951 he travelled to central Australia, Alice Springs, and Aretunga, and won the Dunlop prize.

In 1952 Boyd had his first exhibition of ceramic paintings, a medium which he more or less invented. Although, for years, he produced painted ceramic sculptures of great ingenuity and originality, it was the ceramic paintings which he produced between 1952 and about 1965 which constituted his best work in this medium. He painted in translucent colours onto damp unbaked clay tiles, usually of about 50 cm x 56 cm, and then fired them in a biscuit kiln which completely transposed the paints, after which they were glazed and fired a second time to produce gleaming surfaces whose ravishing colours were almost iridescent. He received a major public commission to produce a large sequence of these tiles on the theme of Romeo and Juliet for the English Shakespeare quatercentenary celebrations and exhibition in 1964. In 1954 he was commissioned to create a ceramic pylon for the Melbourne Olympic swimming pool, which was installed in 1956, accompanied by a show of his ceramic sculptures.

In 1955 Boyd moved with his family to the beach suburb of Beaumaris on Port Phillip Bay. In 1956–7 he travelled in Gippsland and elsewhere in Victoria, painting landscapes, and becoming immersed in the Aborigine themes which produced *Love, Marriage, and Death of a Half-Caste*, later universally known as the Bride series. He showed these at the influential Australian Galleries in Melbourne in 1958 (the same year as the birth of his third child, Lucy). The paintings dealt with the grim, tormented, hunted, and persecuted lives of Australian Aborigines in a series of often large paintings in oil on board which constituted—together with the Ned Kelly paintings of Sidney Nolan—the most politically significant and the most vividly painted works of Australian art in the mid-twentieth century. As a study of Aborigine life they were at the opposite pole of the careful, neutral observation of the paintings of Russell Drysdale. There was in the Boyd pictures an element of romanticism, a distinct hint of the noble savage, but also a sense of almost violent compassion for the Aborigines' plight. Paintings such as *Shearers Playing for a Bride*, *Persecuted Lovers*, and *Bridegroom Drinking from a Creek* were overwhelming images of the threatened humanity of the Aborigine world, and Boyd's sheer bravura image-making rendered the best of these paintings unforgettable.

St Francis and Nebuchadnezzar In 1959 Boyd was a co-signatory of the Antipodean manifesto, together with his brother David, the art historian Bernard Smith, and fellow artists John Perceval (his brother-in-law), Charles Blackman, John Brack, and Robert Dickerson. In November the same year he sailed with his family to London. (He flew only once in his lifetime, to Paris in the company of Sidney Nolan, and did all the rest of his prodigious travelling by boat and car and train.) He rented a house at 13 Hampstead Lane, Highgate, and went on developing the Bride theme. His first London exhibition was at the Zwemmer Gallery in 1960 and in 1961 he took part in the 'Recent Australian Painting' show at the Whitechapel Art Gallery, where Bryan Robertson was the director. Robertson gave him a Whitechapel retrospective the following year which cemented his reputation with the English critics.

Boyd's exposure to the treasures of Britain and Europe's art galleries had a profound effect on his painting and he became an avid gallery goer, particularly in Italy (where he bought a house called Paretaio at Colleoli, in the commune of Palaio in Tuscany) as his growing sales and prices enabled him to prosper. In 1963 he showed his ceramic paintings at the Zwemmer Gallery in London and in 1964 had a major retrospective exhibition at the Art Gallery of South Australia. In 1964–5 he worked in several media on the subject of St Francis of Assisi. He did copious drawings, about twenty lithographs, and many pastels, yet another medium which he conquered and in which he demonstrated further virtuosity. Many of them were used as illustrations for the book *St Francis* (1968) by T. S. R. Boase, who had by that time become a much valued friend.

In 1966 Boyd began to paint his series devoted to Nebuchadnezzar, perhaps the most important post-Bride sequence and, of course, a harking back to earlier biblical and religious themes. Technically they were, if not an actual advance, certainly an interesting digression. He had, from his exposure to the experimentation of contemporary art, particularly Riopelle, been struck by the opportunities presented by very thick impasto painting. For the Nebuchadnezzar pictures he used not only coarse brushes and palette knife but also his fingers to get the effects he wanted. In Nebuchadnezzar he found an ideal subject, the king who was told by Daniel, 'Thou shalt be driven from men.' These paintings were full of Freudian ideas, and were also vehicles for Boyd's exploration of fantasy. His compassion for the mad, driven king was both absolute and very moving. The paintings made a tremendous impact when they were first shown at the Edinburgh Festival of 1969.

In 1967 Boyd had travelled to Portugal and visited the weavers at Portalegre, and established yet another medium within his *œuvre*, creating immensely successful woven versions of St Francis and Nebuchadnezzar. Having bought the large house at 13 Hampstead Lane in 1965, he also rented, from 1970, a modest cottage, Keeper's Cottage, Ramsholt, near Woodbridge, Suffolk, as a weekend retreat. Inevitably, within a matter of weeks, it became a second studio where, undisturbed by metropolitan life, he painted, if anything, more prolifically than ever. He did many Suffolk landscapes, etchings, drawings, and pastels and, while at Ramsholt, experimented with oil paintings on copper sheets which enhanced his brilliant sense of colour almost as dramatically as his ceramic tiles had done.

Bundanon and later works In 1971 Boyd was awarded a Creative Arts fellowship at the Australian National University at Canberra, received the Britannica Australian award for the arts, and paid his first visit to the Shoalhaven River, New South Wales. In 1973 he bought Riversdale, a deserted farm and derelict cottage on the Shoalhaven, and began to establish the substantial house and studio space which became a central part of his existence for the rest of his life. In 1979 he bought a house called Bundanon, also on the Shoalhaven. Over the next fifteen years he acquired further property along the river, sometimes jointly with Sidney Nolan, until there was a single, substantial riverfront estate which he handed over to the Bundanon Trust so that it could be deeded to the nation. The Bundanon estate and the shores of the Shoalhaven became a consuming passion.

In 1980 Boyd showed paintings of skate and other fish during the Adelaide Festival and painted many large works devoted to the landscape, the flora, and the fauna of his Suffolk retreat. In 1984 he was commissioned to do sixteen very large Shoalhaven paintings for the principal foyer of the Victoria State Theatre in Melbourne. He was also commissioned in that year to create a tapestry for the Great Hall of the federal parliament building in Canberra. This 180 square metres tapestry was woven at the Victoria Tapestry Workshop in Melbourne over a period of two years from 1984 to 1986, and was installed in 1987; in its scale, density, and colour it was quite overwhelming. Boyd's cause in later years was championed by the influential English art critic and founder editor of *Modern Painters*, Peter Fuller, whose essay *The Australian Scapegoat* (1986), setting out some of his arguments in favour of a return to figuration in art, appealed greatly to Boyd. Boyd returned the compliment by giving the same title to his series of large, powerful, and very violently coloured canvases of 1987.

In 1988 Boyd represented Australia for a second time at the Venice Biennale and in 1991 his paintings based on Mozart's opera *The Magic Flute*, done in 1990, were shown at the Sydney Opera House as part of the celebrations of the bicentenary of Mozart's death. They were also shown in New York at Boyd's first exhibition there. These engaging large-scale works were all that survived of a plan to create an Australian version of the opera. Boyd was a gifted theatre designer, his work ranging from Peter O'Shaughnessy's productions of *Love's Labours Lost* and *King Lear* in Melbourne in the 1950s to a remarkable ballet, *Electra*, first performed in London, at the Royal Opera House, Covent Garden, in 1963. The choreography was by Robert Helpmann and the music by Malcolm Arnold, and Boyd's sets and costume designs were not only striking and original but also an integral part of the success of the work.

Boyd was, in addition to his many other gifts, a remarkable portrait painter. As a twentieth-century portraitist he ranked with Kokoschka and Graham Sutherland and was far more successful in the genre than his much lauded fellow Australian William Dobell. He had the ability, whether with family and friends or with distinguished artists and scholars, to convey as good and accurate a likeness as any Royal Academician, but to go below the surface of that obvious likeness and reveal joy, fear, indeed the whole range of emotion, as well as an at times quite frightening perception of the sitter's character.

Throughout his career from 1966 onwards Boyd was a considerable book illustrator. Sometimes he simply produced illustrations in the conventional way for a pre-existing text, as with the novel by Taner Baybars *A Trap for the Burglar* (1965), or provided illustrations from among the work he was already doing as with T. S. R. Boase's *St Francis* in 1968, and his *Nebuchadnezzar* in 1972. Most important in his output of books, however, were his collaborations with the Australian poet Peter Porter. They were brought together by the publisher Tom Rosenthal, who suggested that they should collaborate on a mutually agreed theme. Both the relationship and the professional collaboration worked effectively and Boyd and Porter produced four notable books together, *Jonah* in 1973, *The Lady and the Unicorn* in 1975, *Narcissus* in 1984, and *Mars*, a particularly savage satire on war and the military mind, in 1988.

Some of the book illustrations were in fact etchings. Boyd was one of the major graphic artists of the twentieth century. Series after series poured from his presses, as lithographs, etchings, dry-points, etchings with aquatint, or collographs. These included series on Lysistrata (also a notable book), St Francis, Tuscany, and many individual works in which, despite his exuberance in colour, he concentrated on dark velvety blacks contrasting with an almost baroque extravagance of line.

Boyd was created OBE in 1970, AO in 1979, and AC in 1992. In 1993, at Sidney Nolan's memorial service at the National Gallery of Australia, the prime minister, Paul Keating, made public Boyd's spectacular generosity and the country's acceptance of the Bundanon gift. Boyd and his wife felt that Bundanon would be the perfect place in which to preserve the otherwise endangered works of art of several previous Boyd generations, and these were combined with literally thousands of works of art by Boyd himself in a combination of museum and study centre lovingly created by the Boyds. The house originally built in the 1840s was carefully extended and the grounds newly landscaped so that the entire estate could be opened and used by young Australian artists and students, as well as those studying Australian art history and members of the general public seeking a glimpse of the unique Boyd vision. In 1994 Boyd gave the Bundanon Trust the copyright in all his artistic work. In 1995 he was named Australian of the Year and in 1998 he opened stage one of the Bundanon Artists Centre.

Boyd was a stocky, strongly built man, slightly below average height, with a full head of fine dark hair which gradually turned grey and then white and which regularly fell over his forehead and would, if not regularly trimmed, have fallen over his always bright, blue, all-seeing, perpetually darting eyes. As he was always working, he gave off an aura of sumptuous untidiness in whichever apparently disordered, but always perfectly organized, studio he happened to be in or near, his clothes, hands, face, and even hair usually spattered with paint or ink. He had the ability, even when at a party and wearing a new and expensive bespoke three-piece suit, to look simultaneously stylish, elegant, and rumpled. He was a man who practised, partly genuinely and partly as a careful way of coping with the world's less appealing characters and situations, an extreme diffidence verging on the inarticulate. But this was largely the protective, self-created carapace of a man who always knew what he wanted and, supported by a lifelong marriage to a wife who looked after him admirably, usually got it. When in trusted company he could, after listening quietly for as long as half an hour at a time, destroy everyone else's argument, whether literary or artistic or even political, in a few exquisitely constructed sentences, reducing everyone to silence and puncturing quite a few over-large egos in the process.

Boyd made his last visit to England in 1998, returning to Australia in January 1999. He died, after a period of illness, at the Mercy Hospital in Melbourne on 24 April 1999. He was survived by his wife, Yvonne, and their three children. A memorial service was held at the National Gallery of Australia on 27 May 1999 at which the prime minister of Australia, John Howard, was among the speakers.

T. G. ROSENTHAL

Sources F. Philipp, *Arthur Boyd* (1967) · S. McGrath, *The artist and the river: Arthur Boyd and the Shoalhaven* (1982) · U. Hoff, *The art of Arthur Boyd* (1986) [incl. introduction by T. G. Rosenthal] · T. G. Rosenthal, 'Arthur Boyd: a memoir', *Art Review* (Nov 1999) · J. McKenzie, *Arthur Boyd: art and life* (2000) · *WWW* · personal knowledge (2004) · private information (2004)
Archives FILM BFI NFTVA, *The South Bank Show*, London Weekend Television, 23 March 1989
Likenesses A. Poignant, photograph, 1962, priv. coll. [*see illus.*] · photograph, repro. in Philipp, *Arthur Boyd* · photograph, repro. in McGrath, *The artist and the river* · photograph, repro. in Hoff, *Art of Arthur Boyd* · photograph, repro. in Rosenthal, 'Arthur Boyd: a memoir' · photograph, repro. in McKenzie, *Arthur Boyd* · photograph, repro. in *The Times* (26 April 1999) · photograph, repro. in *The Guardian* (28 April 1999) · photograph, repro. in *The Independent* (29 April 1999) · photograph, repro. in *Daily Telegraph* (29 April 1999)
Wealth at death Bundanon estate and many works of art given to Australian nation

Boyd, Benjamin (1801–1851), stockbroker and entrepreneur, was born on 21 August 1801, in the parish of St Peter Le Pauvre, London, second son of Edward Boyd (1770?–1844), merchant, and his wife, Janet, daughter of Benjamin Yule, of Wheatfield, Midlothian. By 1808 the family had moved from Surrey to an ancestral seat—Merton Hall, near Newton Stewart, in Wigtownshire, Scotland—where seven surviving sons and three surviving daughters were raised and educated.

Edward Boyd had substantial overseas commercial interests, and his eldest son achieved seniority in the East India Company. In 1825 Benjamin joined the London stock exchange, and by the late 1830s he was a director of the North British Insurance Company, the St George Steam Packet Company, the London Reversionary Interest Society and—with James Matheson and others—the Union Bank of London. Tall, charming, capable, and commanding, Boyd moved in the highest society, his lively intellect enhancing a natural charisma. Even one of the Rothschilds confessed to being captivated, regardless that in their negotiations 'I always lose money by him; he is such a screw' (Boyd, 94).

In October 1840 Boyd outlined to the Colonial Office his maturing plans for 'further developing the resources of Australia and its adjacent islands' (*Historical Records of Australia*, 21.54–6). He was assured of ready assistance for his proposals to introduce a steamship service (requiring ancillary harbours and coaling stations) between Antipodean settlements; but the response to his enquiries about the possible status of personal territory he might acquire in the south seas was equivocal. In preparation for these activities the Royal Bank of Australia had been floated in

March 1840 with a nominal capital of £1 million. Boyd, its chairman, held 6000 of its £50 shares, which carried a guaranteed dividend of 5 per cent for five years. He was also a director (and his brother Mark *Boyd the manager) of the Australian Wool Company, and of a private company, Boyd Brothers, both formed in November 1840. Dexterous financial shuffling created further ambiguous commitments. In substance the bank exchanged debentures with the wool company, transferring the considerable difference to Boyd, in cash. The North British Insurance Company advanced him £27,000 against other debentures, and the Union Bank lent the Royal Bank £30,000. The St George Steam Packet Company bought steamships with funds provided by the Union Bank.

Boyd set out for Australia in his superb, heavily armed, Royal Yacht Squadron brig *Wanderer* in October 1841. Among its company were his brother James, the artist Oswald Brierly, and Henry Sewell. Having reached Port Phillip on 10 June 1842, Boyd arrived at Sydney on 18 July and set up headquarters at Neutral Bay. Three steamships had preceded him, carrying passengers (including his brother Curwen), cargoes, supplies, bank personnel, and cash. A rudimentary steamship service was already under way, depending for re-coaling on Twofold Bay, south of Sydney. There, Boyd speedily developed a settlement at Boydtown, established a whaling station, and acquired extensive grazing rights in the hinterland. From Twofold Bay livestock, wool, and whaling produce were eventually shipped to Sydney, London, and other markets.

Boyd had arrived in New South Wales on the eve of a cataclysmic depression. Economic conditions and rampant hostility towards London banks required the diversion of Royal Bank funds into dependable assets, and by mid-1844 Boyd had acquired rights to over 400,000 acres of prime land. As a major landholder he successfully rallied opposition to the moderate land reforms of Governor George Gipps, and for a year from September 1844 he represented the independent-minded Port Phillip district in the New South Wales legislative council. He was also foundation president, in 1844, of the influential Pastoralists' Association that sent his squatter cousin, Archibald Boyd, to lobby in London, where colonial land and emigration issues were also canvassed by Mark Boyd and fellow investors. Employing hundreds of workers in various capacities, and with thousands of stock requiring supervision to make landholding viable, Boyd campaigned for cheaper labour, proposing the transfer of convicts from Van Diemen's Land, and finally importing Pacific islanders, with disastrous results. By 1847 Boyd's resources were desperately over-extended and restive Royal Bank shareholders replaced him with his cousin William Sprott Boyd, who arrived in Sydney in March 1848. The precipitate selling of his assets reportedly made Benjamin Boyd half-deranged; and, having safeguarded his own investment, his cousin William departed in early 1849, to be replaced by a liquidator.

On 26 October 1849 Boyd left Sydney in the *Wanderer* for the California goldfields. On 3 June 1851 he sailed from San Francisco to cruise in the Pacific, intent on finding a 'Papuan' base or 'republic'. At San Cristobal in the Solomon Islands he decided to negotiate for 'a tract of land, including Makira [Bay] for future commercial purposes' (Webster, 101), possibly mining for gold. However, on 15 October 1851 Boyd and a crew member failed to return from an early morning shore visit at the neighbouring island of Guadalcanal. After repulsing a native attack, the *Wanderer* set course for Australia, having failed to find positive evidence of Boyd's fate. When the crippled vessel was wrecked off Port Macquarie, Boyd's highland dress costume, his Bible, and a woman's portrait were salvaged. His estate, valued at less than £3000, passed to his creditor, the defunct Royal Bank of Australia.

MARGARET STEVEN

Sources M. Diamond, *Ben Boyd of Boydtown* (1995) · [F. Watson], ed., *Historical records of Australia*, 1st ser., 21, 23–4, 26 (1924–5) · J. Webster, *The last cruise of the Wanderer* (1863) · M. Boyd, *Reminiscences of fifty years* (1871) · H. P. Wellings, *Benjamin Boyd in Australia*, 11th edn · J. H. Watson, 'Benjamin Boyd, merchant', *Royal Australian Historical Society Journal and Proceedings*, 2 (1906–9), 141–9 · H. P. Wellings, 'Ben Boyd's labour supplies', *Royal Australian Historical Society Journal and Proceedings*, 19 (1933), 374–84 · H. P. Wellings, 'Benjamin Boyd in Riverina', *Royal Australian Historical Society Journal and Proceedings*, 20 (1934), 114–21 · H. P. Wellings, 'Benjamin Boyd's three steamers', *Royal Australian Historical Society Journal and Proceedings*, 21 (1935), 320–35 · G. P. Walsh, 'Boyd, Benjamin', *AusDB*, vol. 1 · T. Sykes, *Two centuries of panic* (1988) · old parochial register of births and baptisms, Penninghame, Wigtownshire, Scotland, 21 Aug 1801
Archives NA Scot., inventory of documents produced by Sir Mark Boyd, 213355 encl. in C 29/17/12h022 · priv. coll., Alan Lennox-Boyd MSS | Mitchell L., NSW, O. H. Brierly journals and diary · PRO, Royal Bank of Australia, court of chancery collection, PRO/90 · PRO, Colonial Office, governor's dispatches NSW, etc., Ser. CO 201
Likenesses oils (as a young man), priv. coll. · sketch, Mitchell L., NSW
Wealth at death under £3000: Walsh, 'Boyd', *AusDB*

Boyd, Edward [Eddie] **(1916–1989)**, playwright and scriptwriter, was born on 11 May 1916 at 5 Townhead Street, Stevenston, Ayrshire, probably the eldest of four children known to have been born to Samuel Joseph Boyd, dynamite worker (whose father, Edward, was from co. Antrim, Ireland), and his wife, Mary Chapman Gardiner (*d. c.*1925). When Eddie was seven his younger twin brothers died at three months; two years on, first another brother and then his mother died of diphtheria within twelve hours of each other.

After attending Ardrossan Academy, at fifteen Boyd went to London with 1s. 2d. in his pocket, and spent four nights sleeping on a bench on the Embankment and several months in a home for the destitute. While in London he wrote a short story entitled 'Home is the sailor', later accepted by the *Manchester Guardian*. He received a cheque for 3 guineas, which he did not know how to cash. He served in the Royal Air Force from September 1939 to November 1945, as what he called their 'worst navigator' (Davidson). During the war years he married, but no details of the union are known; he called it 'a fleeting piece of war-time frivolity' (Davidson). After the war he worked as a part-time editor for Collins, and became involved with the left-wing Unity Theatre in Glasgow as stage manager, actor, and producer, beginning an enduring association with the actor Roddy McMillan. On 9 September 1948 he married Kathleen Maxwell or Donaldson (b. 1924/5), actress, daughter of Joseph Harrison Maxwell, school teacher, with whom he had a daughter, Susan. After fourteen years the marriage ended acrimoniously. He lived with his third wife, Catherine Cassidy Thomson (b. 1946), college lecturer, daughter of William Thomson, iron moulder, for twenty years, and had a second daughter, Rachel (the union was formalized on 24 September 1987).

For most of his career Boyd was a freelance writer, who became associated with BBC radio in Scotland and worked for four years as a contract writer with Granada Television. His radio career began with the acclaimed play *The Candle of Darkness* (1954). In the 1960s he wrote a crime drama, *The Odd Man* (1962), which was much admired, and a surreal thriller, *The Corridor People* (1966), which was likened to *The Avengers* and *The Prisoner*. Both were for Granada. His script of *Robbery* (1967), a film starring Stanley Baker, was a co-winner of the Screen Writers' Guild award. In 1971 he was praised for his radio play *The Wolf Far Hence*. A one-off television drama entitled *Good Morning Yesterday* led to his most celebrated work, the BBC series *The View from Daniel Pyke* (1971–3), in which Roddy McMillan excelled as a superficially tough Glaswegian private detective. In 1978 Boyd had further success with a television adaptation of John Buchan's *Huntingtower*.

Boyd was inspired by the blues and *film noir*. Recalling Raymond Chandler, he said that he wanted to create art 'where it is least expected' (Davidson). A tall, stooped figure with the face of a Roman Stoic but with the learning of an erudite anarchist, he had a sense of humour at once dry and surreal, and a reputation for being both outspoken and enigmatic. The care and psychological depth he brought to the atmospheric thriller exercised a considerable influence on Scottish writing. He continued to write and to express independent views (including the view that Scottish theatre was dead) until the end of his life. Following several years of poor health he suffered a stroke in his home at 23 Hillhead Street, Glasgow, and died in Gartnavel General Hospital on 17 December 1989.

DOUGLAS BROWN

Sources J. Davidson, 'A personal view from the man who created Daniel Pyke', *The Scotsman* (11 May 1981) • R. J. Ross, 'The view from Eddie Boyd', *Cencrastus* (autumn 1987), 4–6 • 'Across the airwaves', *Cencrastus* (autumn 1987), 6–9 • *Who's who in Scotland*, 2nd edn (1988), 45–6 • R. Goring, ed., *Chambers Scottish biographical dictionary* (1992) • *Glasgow Herald* (19 Dec 1989) • *The Scotsman* (19 Dec 1989) • W. G. Smith, 'Remembering Eddie', *The Scotsman* (19 Dec 1989) • E. Boyd, 'Beating a retreat to the other dear green place', *The Scotsman* (26 March 1988) • d. cert. • b. cert. • m. certs. [Kathleen Boyd Maxwell; Catherine Cassidy Thomson]
Archives U. Glas. L., Scottish Theatre archive, script collection | FILM probably BBC Scotland • probably STV | SOUND probably BBC Radio Scotland • probably Radio Clyde

Likenesses photograph, 1987, repro. in 'Across the airwaves', *Cencrastus* • photograph, 1989, repro. in *The Scotsman* • A. MacDonald, photograph, repro. in *Cencrastus* (March 1988)

Boyd, Elizabeth [*pseud*. Louisa] (*fl.* **1727–1745**), poet and novelist, apparently lived in London throughout her productive years. All that is known about her life or family comes from a few statements in her published works. In *The Snail* (1745), the only issue of her proposed periodical, she speaks of her 'deceased Father having long and zealously serv'd the *Stuart* family in a creditable Employ' (p. 15); and in an 'Advertisement' added to *The Happy Unfortunate, or, The Female Page* (1732), she states she is publishing the novel:

> with a view of settling myself in a way of Trade; that may enable me to master those Exigencies of Fortune, which my long Illness hath for some Time past reduc'd me to suffer; That I may be capable of providing for my now ancient, indulgent Mother; whom Age, and the Charge of many Children hath render'd incapable of providing for herself. … I shall directly sell Paper, Pens, Ink … Almanacks, Plays, Pamphlets, and all Manner of Stationary Goods.

The 353 subscriptions, among them a large number from the nobility, presumably enabled her to open the shop, possibly at her address in George Court, Princes Street.

The novel is set in Cyprus, in the tradition of Arcadian romance, with a convoluted plot that demonstrates the evil effects of arranged or loveless marriages. Amanda, Boyd's learned heroine, articulates the matrimonial ideal when she says:

> A Man must be settled enough to form a certain Judgement, of his own Affections and Inclinations, before in my Opinion he's qualified for either a Husband, a Lover, or a Friend, which three Persons ought to be always blended in one, if Happiness is propos'd in the Connubials. (2.215–16)

The novel was reissued as *The Female Page* in 1737.

In 1733 Boyd published *The Humorous Miscellany, or, Riddles for the Beaux*, a small collection of songs, riddles, and occasional verse. Her other poems include *Variety* (1727); *Verses most Humbly Inscrib'd to his Majesty King George IId on his Birthday* (1730); *The Happy North-Briton* (1737); and *Glory to the Highest, a Thanksgiving Poem on the Late Victory at Dettingen* (1743). *Admiral Haddock, or, The Progress of Spain* (1739 or 1740), is a long patriotic poem in which she reviews the defeat of the armada in 1588 and praises the naval actions of 1739. Her ballad-opera, *Don Sancho, or, The Students' Whim … with Minerva's Triumph, a Masque* (1739), is a strange mix of comedy, necromancy, and masque, set in the garden of an Oxford college, where Don Sancho conjures up assorted spirits, including the ghosts of Shakespeare and Dryden. The piece was never performed but was given a reading in the green room of Drury Lane Theatre. Although Boyd frequently mentions her ill health, neither the cause nor date of her death is known.

JOYCE FULLARD

Sources E. Boyd, *The happy unfortunate, or, The female page* (1732); repr. with introduction by W. Graves (1972) • E. Boyd, *The Snail: or, The Lady's Lucubrations … by Louisa* (1745) • BL cat. • M. A. Schofield, 'Elizabeth Boyd', *Masking and unmasking the female mind: disguising romances in feminine fiction, 1713–1799* (1990), 30–33 • R. Lonsdale, ed., *Eighteenth-century women poets: an Oxford anthology* (1989), 194 • J. Todd, ed., *A dictionary of British and American women writers, 1660–*

1800 (1984) • J. Fullard, ed., *British women poets, 1660–1800: an anthology* (1990) • Blain, Clements & Grundy, *Feminist comp.*

Boyd, Henry (1748/9–1832), translator and Church of Ireland clergyman, was born in Dromore, co. Antrim, the son of Charles Boyd, a farmer. He was educated at Trinity College, Dublin (BA 1776), before becoming a priest. In 1785 he published a two-volume translation of Dante's *Inferno* in English verse, only the second of its kind, with a specimen of the *Orlando Furioso* of Ariosto. It was printed by subscription, and dedicated to the earl of Bristol, bishop of Derry. The dedication is dated from Killeigh, near Tullamore, which was presumably Boyd's parish at the time. In 1793 he published a volume of his own verse, *Poems Chiefly Dramatic and Lyric*.

In 1802 Boyd issued three volumes of an English verse translation of the whole *Divina commedia* of Dante, with preliminary essays, notes, and illustrations. The translation is important as the first English version of the complete *Divine Comedy* to be published. It was, however, limited by Boyd's view of the translator's role as that of contemporizer, and his adherence to neo-classical poetic strictures. He intended to make the work accessible to a contemporary audience, and so the model was condensed, altered, and bowdlerized, Boyd's six-line stanzas bearing no real correspondence to Dante's original tercets. The edition's value was in assisting to re-establish an audience for Dante, whose reputation had suffered a decline in the previous century. It was dedicated to Viscount Charleville, whose chaplain Boyd was until the Irish rising induced him to resign his post.

In 1805 Boyd published the *Penance of Hugo: a Vision*, translated from the Italian of Vincenzo Monti, with two additional cantos; and the *Woodman's Tale*, a poem written in the manner and metre of Spenser's *Faerie Queene*; but he was unable to find a publisher for his translation of Ercilla's long poem *Araucana*. By this time he had also become the vicar of Drumgath, but was possibly best-known until the day of his death as the vicar of Rathfriland, or as chaplain to the earl of Charleville. In 1807 he issued Petrarch's *Trionfi*, translated into English verse as the *Triumphs of Petrarch*; and in 1809, some notes of his on the fallen angels in *Paradise Lost* were published, with other notes and essays on Milton, under the editorship of the Revd Henry Todd, as *Some Account of the Life and Writings of John Milton*. Boyd died at Ballintemple, near Newry, co. Down, at an advanced age, on 18 September 1832.

B. C. SKOTTOWE, rev. NILANJANA BANERJI

Sources Nichols, *Illustrations*, 7.120, 149, 157, 171, 717 • H. Boyd, in *The divina commedia of Dante Alighieri*, trans. H. Boyd (1802) [dedication] • *GM*, 1st ser., 55 (1785) • *GM*, 1st ser., 102/2 (1832), 651 • R. Welch, ed., *The Oxford companion to Irish literature* (1996) • W. J. De Sua, *Dante into English: a study of the translation of the 'Divine comedy' in Britain and America* (1964) • Burtchaell & Sadleir, *Alum. Dubl.*
Archives Lpool RO, corresp. with William Roscoe
Likenesses attrib. T. Robinson, group portrait, oils, *c*.1801–1808 (*A political group at the bishop's palace at Dromore*), Castleward, co. Down, Northern Ireland

Boyd, Henry (1831–1922), Church of England clergyman and college head, the third son of William Clark Boyd, of Hackney, Middlesex, and his wife, Mary, daughter of William Steinmetz, was born in Holborn, London, on 26 February 1831. Educated at Hackney School, he went as a commoner to Exeter College, Oxford, matriculating in January 1849. He gained a second class in *literae humaniores* in 1852, the Ellerton theological essay prize in 1853, and the Denyer theological essay prize in 1856 and 1857, and graduated BA (1852), MA (1857), and BD and DD (1879). He was ordained in 1854 to the curacy of Belleau in Lincolnshire and in 1856 moved to that of Probus, near Truro, Cornwall.

From 1863 to 1874 Boyd was perpetual curate of St Mark's, Victoria Docks, Plaistow, in east London (gross income £300; population 12,954), where he worked devotedly. He rebuilt his church and was proud of his schools. His interest in local conditions made him a keen supporter of housing and sanitary reform. Eventually the strain of these exertions led to a serious breakdown and paralysis, and for several months he could not move. He recovered, but had to give up his work in the East End.

In 1874 the Hertford College Act was passed whereby Magdalen Hall, Oxford, was dissolved, and its principal and scholars incorporated as a college of the university under the old name of Hertford College; the earlier Hertford College had lasted from 1740 to 1818, and its site and buildings had been occupied by the members of Magdalen Hall since their move in 1822 from their premises next to Magdalen College. The passage of this measure, initiated by Richard Michell (1805–1877), principal of Magdalen Hall, was facilitated by the munificence of Thomas Charles Baring MP, who offered an endowment for fellowships and scholarships, restricted to Anglicans. This offer had been made first to Brasenose, his old college, but had been declined, as it was thought inconsistent with the University Tests Act of 1871. It was accepted by Hertford College, but the first fellowship examination was challenged by nonconformists, who lost their case in the Court of Appeal. Baring retained under the act of 1874 power to nominate the first fellows at Hertford, and in 1874 he nominated Boyd, who became also dean and divinity lecturer.

In March 1877, following Michell's death, Boyd was appointed principal of the college, and from then until his death, forty-five years later, the welfare of Hertford was his constant care. Baring's scholarships enabled Hertford to attract able undergraduates and even 'poach' some from other colleges and among the unattached students. Boyd encouraged sporting success as a means of raising Hertford's standing, and he, a notable figure in top hat and frock coat without an overcoat, attended sporting events. Through him in 1878 the boat club acquired a barge, and in 1881 Hertford was head of the river. Under Boyd's leadership Hertford prospered, and the number of undergraduates grew steadily. Boyd transformed Hertford. By an exchange of properties with the city council in 1898 the college acquired land at the other side of New College Lane. Using the architect Thomas Graham Jackson (1835–1924), he oversaw an ambitious building and rebuilding programme—'the building operations which will always be the great outward memorial of his Principalship' (*Hertford College Magazine*, 1922, 2)—including the construction of the new hall (1889) and the chapel (1908). The college buildings were divided by New College Lane. In 1899 Boyd proposed that they be joined by a bridge for fellows and undergraduates and a tunnel for servants and provisions. However, New College opposed the bridge, and the city council refused permission in 1899 and 1905. The proposed tunnel was approved in 1900, but Boyd decided against its construction. Persistent, in 1913 he again applied to build a bridge. New College no longer opposed, and the council approved. The bridge, designed by Jackson in 'a highly distinctive style combining English Jacobean with motifs from Venetian architecture' (Goudie, 56) and with 'Henricus Boyd' inscribed on the front, was opened in January 1914. This 'Bridge of Sighs' became one of the most famous, and most photographed, of Oxford sights.

Although Boyd had not previously taken an important role in university affairs, he was a competent, conservative vice-chancellor from 1890 to 1894. Reportedly his vice-chancellorship was 'a model of commonsense and good temper', and he maintained 'the old traditions of entertaining' (*Hertford College Magazine*, 1922, 3). His tact and courtesy enabled him to deal with men of all kinds, and to overcome many difficulties. As master (1896–7) of the wealthy Drapers' Company he much influenced its educational policy and directed its benefactions in turn to Cambridge and Oxford universities. The chief monument of his activity is the electrical laboratory (for the use of the Wykeham professor of physics), in Parks Road, designed by Jackson and erected in 1910.

In August 1914, when he was eighty-three, the outbreak of war interrupted Boyd's fishing holiday in Norway and obliged his return via Newcastle upon Tyne. The First World War moved him deeply, and he was greatly concerned about its disruption of university life. He felt doubts whether Oxford would ever recover from its effects—doubts which he lived long enough to see, in part at least, dispelled. During the war, with Hertford used for officer training, he acted as college chaplain and maintained chapel services. After the war he delegated his ordinary college work to the vice-principal, but continued to take chapel services and to entertain undergraduates.

Boyd held a simple Christian faith, and actively supported low-church causes such as Wycliffe Hall, the evangelical theological college. Optimistic, cheery, tactful, diplomatic, and determined, he was a generous benefactor of Hertford, and entertained much. In his latter years he was 'one of the most respected figures in the university, and his venerable persona lent an air of time-honoured eminence to a college that had only recently been called into being' (Goudie, 55). He enjoyed port, cigars, and whist. He was an open-minded Conservative, with a strong feeling for tradition and custom. In manner somewhat shy and reserved, he was a capable college and university administrator, and in private life an attractive companion. Reportedly his modesty, honesty of purpose, and humanity gained him the regard of men of varied type and conditions. He was a man of taste, much interested in art and architecture. An accomplished watercolourist, he filled portfolios with sketches of cathedrals and churches in Spain, France, and Algeria (a collection is in the Taylor Institution, Oxford).

Boyd's interest in undergraduate recreations resulted partly from his own enjoyment of sports and games. Tall and active, in his youth he was a climber and swimmer, and in middle age he spent much time golfing. He was one of the first to introduce golf at Oxford, and when he was vice-chancellor he reserved one afternoon a week for it. He was also devoted to fishing, and for many years during the long vacation salmon-fished in Norway.

Following influenza, Boyd died, unmarried, on 4 March 1922 in his lodgings at Hertford College, and was buried on 8 March in Holywell cemetery, Oxford. A memorial tablet was placed in Hertford chapel, and the Boyd memorial fund was established to assist necessitous junior members of the college.

ALFRED COCHRANE, *rev.* ROGER T. STEARN

Sources personal knowledge (1937) · private information (1937) · *Hertford College Magazine*, 9 (May 1914) · *Hertford College Magazine*, 10 (April 1921) · *Hertford College Magazine*, 11 (April 1922) · *Hertford College Magazine*, 12 (April 1923) · A. Goudie, ed., *Seven hundred years of an Oxford college: Hertford College, 1284–1984* [1984] · Crockford (1876) · Crockford (1892) · Crockford (1902) · *Hist. U. Oxf.* 7: *19th-cent. Oxf. pt 2* · Foster, *Alum. Oxon.* · C. Hibbert, ed., *The encyclopaedia of Oxford* (1988); pbk edn (1992) · S. G. Hamilton, *Hertford College* (1903) · *WWW*, 1916–28 · *CGPLA Eng. & Wales* (1922)

Archives Hertford College, Oxford, corresp. and papers, Ref. 44/2

Likenesses H. von Herkomer, oils, 1901, Hertford College, Oxford · J. P. Champion, photograph, *c.*1920, repro. in *Hertford College Magazine*, 11 (April 1922), facing p. 4 · S. Lund, photograph, NPG

Wealth at death £53,140 9s. 9d.: probate, 5 April 1922, *CGPLA Eng. & Wales*

Boyd, Hugh (1690–1765), entrepreneur, was born near Ballycastle, Antrim, one of three sons of William Boyd (*d.* 1727), rector of Ramoan, and Rose, daughter and heir of Daniel MacNeill of Dunaneeny. He married Anne McAlister (1685?–1776), daughter of Rundal McAlister of Kenbaan Castle, near Ballycastle; they had two sons, one mentally unbalanced, and two or three daughters. Boyd was manager of Ballycastle's long-established collieries in 1723, when he visited mines in Scotland, and in 1732 he bought a share in the enterprise. In 1736 he bought out the remaining partners and, on favourable conditions, acquired leases in perpetuity of the mines, the village of Ballycastle (then only a cluster of houses), and all the lands around it. He opened new galleries in the mines and brought water from a mile away to fall over the cliffs and power a large box-wheel to pump undersea workings.

The colliery, remote from its main market, Dublin, could only flourish if the harbour was improved and Boyd quickly sought government help. On 15 November 1737, parliament granted him £10,000 to build a harbour for thirty small ships. He received advice from a Liverpool architect, Thomas Steers, but supervised the work personally, encountering many difficulties; he had to divert two rivers to prevent sand being deposited, and built bridges over the new channels. He searched for Scottish and Welsh oak massive enough for piles, and had a ship built at Swansea to carry the unusually long timber. This, with three other vessels, was lost during the work. He built forges and dredging ships on site, and his 'wagonway' of wooden rails was one of the first tramways in Ireland.

Ambitious and spurred on by knowledge of the coast's dangerous winds and currents, Boyd decided to build a bigger harbour than specified, for ships up to 120 tons, and in 1743, unable through ill health to attend parliament, he wrote a detailed account of the works to justify increased expenditure. After spending £30,000 of his own and parliament's money he completed the harbour in 1748. Soon twenty Ballycastle ships traded in coal and other goods; in the 1740s, over 6000 tons of coal were produced annually. As part of an apparently coherent strategy of using the coal along with other local resources such as sand, sea salt, and bark from his timber imports, Boyd developed the town's existing salt industry, founded pioneering but short-lived glass, tanning, candle-making, and iron industries, and had a linen bleachgreen, salmon fishery, and brewery.

After only a few years, a hitherto unknown ship-worm rendered the harbour's wooden piers useless; they had to be replaced with stone, at extra cost, and gradually the harbour silted up. Parliament voted £3000 in 1763, but, displeased by Boyd's failure to send enough coal to Dublin, refused further help.

At one time, almost three hundred people worked for Boyd. He built houses for them, and sold subsidized bread and corn; in 1745, a year of scarcity, he claimed that his system of food distribution kept a hundred families alive. He was founding chairman in 1755 of one of the first farming societies in Ireland, he gave 20 acres for a charter school to educate thirty charity pupils, and built an inn and a fine stone church, costing £2769 4s. 7½d., at Ballycastle. In his will he left £50 annually to maintain Church of Ireland worship there. Boyd was described as a genuinely pious and modest man. He also provided for twenty almshouses beside the church for former employees or their widows, and £100 for clothing fifty-five old people.

On 15 June 1765, 'Colonel Boyd', so called because he was lieutenant-colonel in the County Antrim militia, died, probably at the Manor House, Ballycastle. He was buried in his new church. Despite his lengthy and complicated will, his descendants through mismanagement and bad luck allowed Boyd's achievements, and Ballycastle's prosperity, to dwindle away. Hugh Macaulay *Boyd was his grandson.   LINDE LUNNEY

Sources G. A. Wilson, 'The rise and decline of the Ballycastle coalfield and associated industries, 1720–1840', MA diss., Queen's University of Belfast, 1951 • J. E. Mullin, The Causeway coast (1974), 161–75 • H. Boyd, 'Ballycastle harbour: an account of the progress of Ballycastle harbour, together with a representation of the present state of the works (1743)', The Glynns, 9 (1981), 5–15 • H. A. Boyd, 'Trade and commerce in the area in the eighteenth century', The Glynns, 8 (1980), 13–19 • C. Dallat, 'Ballycastle's 18th century industries', The Glynns, 3 (1975), 7–13 • J. B. Leslie, ed., Clergy of Connor: from Patrician times to the present day (1993), 229 • A. Day, P. McWilliams, and N. Dobson, eds., Parishes of county Antrim, 9: North Antrim coast and Rathlin (1994), 101–2

Boyd, Hugh Macaulay (1746–1794), writer on politics, was born Hugh Macaulay on 16 April 1746 in Ballycastle, co. Antrim, the younger son of Alexander Macaulay (d. 1766), barrister and member of the Irish parliament, and his wife, formerly Miss Boyd (d. 1782). After attending the Revd Thomas Ball's school in Dublin, in 1760, at the age of fourteen, he began his studies at Trinity College, Dublin, and completed them in 1765. At some point in the later 1760s, following the death of his maternal grandfather Boyd in 1765, Hugh Macaulay changed his surname to that of this grandfather and received a small bequest. In 1766 his father died intestate and his estate passed to his eldest son, leaving Boyd without an income. This lack of money reputedly led him to abandon his hopes of an army career and to opt instead for a legal training. He moved to London, but instead of pursuing a place at the bar, he appears to have concentrated on his social life, quickly becoming immersed in the fashionable society of the capital, where his chess and conversation skills made him popular. He was soon able to count Edmund Burke, Catharine Macaulay, David Garrick, John Wilkes, and Joshua Reynolds among his wide circle of acquaintances. Boyd also frequently attended parliamentary debates, and was noted for his ability to memorize speeches. In December 1767, already experiencing the financial difficulties that were to dog him throughout his life, he was fortunate enough to marry a young woman with money, Frances Morphy. His career as a political writer took off in 1776, when he returned to Ireland and published an address to the electors of Antrim from 'a Freeholder'. Back in London, Boyd produced an edition of the earl of Chatham's speeches, and continued to write anonymous political material. In 1777 and 1778 he wrote pieces for the London newspapers in support of the nabob of Arcot, presumably hoping to secure his patronage. Writing on more general political matters, he sent letters to the Public Advertiser signed 'Democrates' and wrote for the London Courant as 'The Whig' in 1779 and 1780.

At this point in his life, whether due to foolish generosity or an extravagant lifestyle, Boyd had spent his wife's fortune, and was forced to seek employment abroad. In 1781 he travelled to Madras in order to work for the East India Company under Lord Macartney. The following year he travelled to Ceylon on a diplomatic mission to the king of Candy. He met with little success in his negotiations, and was subsequently captured by the French on his journey back to Madras. Once freed, he returned to India and embarked again on a journalistic career, running the Madras Courier during 1792, and launching the Indian Observer and the Hircarrah in 1793. However, his activities were cut short in the following year, and he died in Madras, apparently penniless, on 19 October 1794, survived by his wife, a son, Hugh Stuart *Boyd, and a daughter.

Hugh Boyd did not become famous until after his death, when a number of publications claimed that he was Junius, the pseudonymous writer of a series of letters to the Public Advertiser between 1769 and 1772 that was highly critical of the government. The secrecy surrounding Junius's identity, and the vitriolic nature of the attacks, made unmasking the author a source of great interest among the British public, even as late as the early nineteenth century. In 1800 Lawrence Dundas Campbell, an associate of Boyd, published an edition of his works which identified Hugh Boyd as Junius. John Almon, who had edited the *London Courant* when it published Boyd's letters under the pseudonym of The Whig, agreed with Campbell, and claimed to have recognized Boyd's handwriting when reading original manuscripts of Junius's letters. However, despite the certainty of men like Campbell, Almon, and others, modern scholarship does not attribute much weight to their claims.   HANNAH BARKER

Sources *The miscellaneous works of Hugh Boyd, the author of the 'Letters of Junius'*, ed. L. D. Campbell, 2 vols. (1800) · [G. Chalmers], *The author of Junius ascertained* (1819) · *The letters of Junius complete*, ed. J. Almon, 2 vols. (1806) · BL, Boyd to H. S. Woodfall, 4/7/1777 and 24/10/1777, Add. MS 27780 [fols. 37–9] · BL, letter of appointment, Add. MS 38408 [fol. 320] · L. Werkmeister, *The London daily press, 1772–1792* (1963) · *The letters of Junius*, ed. J. Cannon (1978) · *GM*, 1st ser., 84/1 (1814), 224 · *European Magazine and London Review*, 37 (1800), 339–41, 433–6
Archives BL, letters, Add. MSS 27780, 29150, 35126 · Bodl. RH, narrative of his embassy to Ceylon
Likenesses J. Brown, stipple, pubd 1795 (after R. Home), NPG · W. Evans, stipple, pubd 1799 (after a print by R. Home), NPG · C. Watson, stipple, BM, NPG; repro. in J. Almon, ed., *Letters of Junius* · portrait, repro. in L. D. Campbell, ed., *Miscellaneous works of Hugh Boyd*, frontispiece · portrait, repro. in J. Almon, ed., *Letters of Junius*, lx–lxi

Boyd, Hugh Stuart (1781–1848), Greek scholar, was born at Edgware, Middlesex, the son of Hugh Macaulay *Boyd (1746–1794) and his wife, Frances, *née* Morphy. His father had been born Hugh Macaulay, but prior to his son's birth had assumed the surname of his maternal grandfather, Hugh *Boyd (1690–1765), of Ballycastle, Ireland.

As a boy in Hampstead, Boyd studied Greek with a tutor named Spowers. He was admitted a pensioner of Pembroke College, Cambridge, on 24 July 1799 and matriculated on 17 December 1800, but left the university without taking a degree. He once claimed that he could repeat 3280 'lines' of Greek prose and 4770 lines of Greek verse.

On 16 September 1805 Boyd married a Jewish woman, Ann Lowry (d. 1834), daughter of William Lowry, a well-known engraver and FRS. They had one child, Ann Henriette, and lived in various furnished houses in England, financed by his Irish estates. In 1811 he contracted ophthalmia, which led to complete blindness. A move in 1825 to Great Malvern and a reading of Elizabeth Barrett's *Essay on Mind* (1826) led in 1827 to their correspondence and friendship. She read Greek aloud to him, and he tutored her in the language. The friendship flourished in 1831–2 when both were living in Sidmouth.

Boyd's original publications included *Luceria, a Tragedy* (1806) rejected by Drury Lane, and *A Malvern Tale and other Poems* (1814). His translations included *Select Passages from the Works of St Chrysostom, St Gregory Nazianzen etc* (1810) and the *Agamemnon of Aeschylus* (1803). *Thoughts on an Illustrious Exile* (1825) extolled the Waldensian Christians and praised Napoleon's religious toleration, while Boyd's staunchly Anglican, anti-papist stance is expressed in *The Fathers not Papist with Select Passages and Tributes to the Dead* (1834). Despite his pedantry and vanity Elizabeth Barrett supported the lonely widower after 1834, when he lived in London, first at St John's Wood, then at 21 Downshire Hill, Hampstead, and then again at St John's Wood. Her 1844 volume, which made her fame, recalled in 'Wine of Cypress' Boyd's hospitality at Malvern. In September 1846 she confided to him, uniquely, her impending elopement. Latterly, Boyd suffered from acute lumbago, and died at 1 Hawley Place, Kentish Town, London, from a paralytic stroke, on 10 May 1848. Elizabeth Barrett Browning published three sonnets in his memory.

WILLIAM HUNT, *rev.* JOHN D. HAIGH

Sources B. P. McCarthy, 'Introduction', *Elizabeth Barrett to Mr Boyd: unpublished letters of E. B. Browning to Hugh Stuart Boyd*, ed. B. P. McCarthy (1955), xi–xxxix · J. W. Etheridge, *The life of the Rev. Adam Clarke*, 2nd edn (1858), 382–4 · *N&Q*, 2nd ser., 5 (1858), 88, 175, 226 · *N&Q*, 2nd ser., 7 (1859), 284, 523 · *N&Q*, 3rd ser., 4 (1863), 458 · *GM*, 1st ser., 96/2 (1826), 623 · *GM*, 2nd ser., 30 (1848), 130 · C. E. Buckland, *Dictionary of Indian biography* (1906) · *BL cat.* · *Weldon's register of facts and occurrences*, 1st ser. (Aug 1860–July 1861), 56–8 · Allibone, *Dict.* · D. J. O'Donoghue, *The poets of Ireland: a biographical dictionary with bibliographical particulars*, 1 vol. in 3 pts (1892–3) · d. cert.

Boyd, James (1795–1856), schoolmaster and author, the son of a glover, was born at Paisley on 24 December 1795. After receiving his early education partly in Paisley and partly in Glasgow, he entered Glasgow University, where he gained some of the highest honours in the humanity, Greek, and philosophy classes. After taking his degrees of BA and MA (1817), he devoted himself for two years to the study of medicine, but, having abandoned this pursuit, entered the Divinity Hall of the University of Glasgow, and was licensed to preach the gospel by the presbytery of Dumbarton in May 1822. Towards the close of that year he removed to Edinburgh, where for three years he maintained himself by private tuition. In 1825 he was unanimously chosen house governor in George Heriot's Hospital, Edinburgh. The University of Glasgow conferred on him the honorary degree of doctor of laws in 1827. He married, on 24 December 1829, Jane Reid, eldest daughter of John Easton, an Edinburgh merchant. They had nine children.

Boyd became classical master at Edinburgh high school on 19 August 1829; from this time he edited published editions of a number of classical texts. For many years he was also secretary to the Edinburgh Society of Teachers. He died at his house in George Square, Edinburgh, on 18 August 1856, having taught for nearly twenty-seven years in the high school. He was buried at New Calton, Edinburgh, on 21 August. The affectionate respect in which he was held by his pupils was shown after his death. Two 'Boyd clubs' were formed in the Crimea during the Russian war by British officers who had been taught by him, and other societies were founded in his honour by his classes. At a meeting held in Edinburgh his friends and pupils subscribed for a medal, to be named the 'Boyd medal', and to be annually presented to the 'dux' of the class in the high school taught by Boyd's successor.

G. C. BOASE, *rev.* M. C. CURTHOYS

Sources Boase, *Mod. Eng. biog.* · J. Colston, *History of Dr Boyd's fourth high school class* (1873) · W. S. Dalgleish, *Memorials of the high school of Edinburgh* (1857) · W. C. A. Ross, *The Royal High School* (1934) **Likenesses** J. Henderson, lithograph, repro. in Dalgleish, *Memorials*, facing pp. 45–6

Boyd, Sir John, first baronet (1718–1800), merchant, was born on 29 December 1718 on St Kitts in the Leeward Islands, the only child of Augustus Boyd (1679–1765) and Lucy, daughter of Judge John Peters and Elizabeth Henderson. Augustus Boyd was a native of northern Ireland who, about 1700, left co. Donegal for St Kitts, the home of a maternal uncle. There he purchased and managed several sugar estates, and established a business supplying European goods to planters. Failing to win a seat on the St Kitts council, he moved to London and established a trade with eastern Caribbean planters. In 1735 Augustus Boyd took lodgings with his brother-in-law, James Pechell of Broad Street. There, as Pechell's partner, he immersed himself in commission merchandising.

John Boyd, however, expressed little interest in overseas trade. Soon after the family's arrival in London, he enrolled at Christ Church, Oxford, in 1737, to read classics. Only after completing his studies and touring the continent did he reluctantly return to the counting-house. In 1749 he married Mary Bumstead, the daughter of a prominent Warwickshire landowner. He subsequently acquired the lease to a 304 acre estate named Danson Hill in north-west Kent to accommodate their growing brood. After purchasing the freehold in 1759, he employed William Chambers to design a new Palladian villa.

In national politics Boyd cut a low profile, opting to petition and inform parliament rather than enter its ranks as a member. He commented on the taking of British ships by the Spanish and the protection of mercantile interests in the Tortola trade. At most times he was an ardent supporter of the king, the administration, and their efforts to expand and defend the empire. Characteristically, he endorsed George II's war against France in the late 1750s, and embraced George III's peace in 1763. Boyd was a stronger presence in company politics. In April 1753 he was elected a director of the East India Company, and he served on its court until 1764. In Leadenhall Street he took an active part in Indian affairs. He was a member of nine different committees, attended them regularly, and served as the company's deputy chairman in 1759–60. During the 1760s he allied himself with Laurence Sulivan. In 1763, for instance, he created ten new votes for Sulivan's consortium by splitting larger shareholdings into £500 lots, each of which entitled its holder to a vote, and, in the following year, successfully ran as one of Sulivan's supporters. He supported Sulivan's stand on the appointment of John Spencer as the company's president in Bengal, complained about the extraordinary powers given to Clive's select committee in Bengal, and resigned when Sulivan failed to secure the chairmanship. In April

1765, and again the following year, Sulivan placed Boyd on his list of approved candidates, but the support proved costly, and Boyd lost. Frustrated with the directors and aggrieved by the unwillingness of those he had helped to repay him, Boyd retired from the company.

More personal matters now came to the fore. Boyd's first wife having died in March 1763, he had assumed the charge of the upbringing of his children. Although he married Catherine Chapone (d. 1813) on 1 August 1766 and raised three children with her, they never replaced his first wife and children in his affections. After the death of his father, Boyd passed to his son-in-law John Trevanion and William Wood the management of the family's trading business, and himself turned to more congenial pursuits. As befitted a man who had risen above the world of the counting-house, he broadened his sights. In late 1772 he visited Spain, France, Belgium, and the Netherlands, he learned new languages, and he purchased works of art for his villa. George III created him a baronet in 1775 and more significant travel and collecting followed in 1775 and 1776. Despite such honours and pleasures, however, his life was not untroubled. Chief among his concerns were the Caribbean plantations he inherited from his father and grandmother. Always a drain on time, energy, and money, these estates ran him aground in the 1770s. Early in the decade, political intrigues swept the island; a hurricane destroyed many of his buildings, and fire destroyed much of what remained. The capture of the island by the French in 1779 eventually stopped the flow of all proceeds. On account of such tribulations, his finances fell into disarray. In 1771, desperately needing money to manage his affairs, he turned for immediate relief to Richard Oswald, a partner in a Sierra Leone slave transshipment factory, but the loan did little to solve his long-term financial problems, which were complicated by the bankruptcies of several merchants who owed him substantial amounts of money. Gloom shadowed him, professionally and personally, and he began to see everything in the blackest colours. The deaths of loved ones crushed his spirit: his son Augustus died in 1772, and his favourite, Mary Jane, in 1779. Relations with those who survived became increasingly strained. He withdrew entirely from London society, and spent most of his time at Danson, hidden away in one wing of the mansion. He spoke in monosyllables. He constantly wept. Only the arrival of Paul Benfield, a clerk in his office who had gone out to India and made a fortune, and Benfield's loan of £90,000 in 1779 steadied Boyd's affairs.

By the end of the American War of Independence Boyd had repaid his debts, but by that time he had lost all taste for business or society. He retired to the country and lived in virtual isolation with his wife, daughters, and servants. He turned inward, focusing on religious subjects and good deeds and administering local charities. But the philanthropies did not ease his mind, and he died, plagued by fear and loneliness, on 24 January 1800 at Danson Hill, where he was buried. To his second wife he left an annuity of £1200, £3000 cash, and his personal effects. His daughters received generous annuities and legacies. The residue of the estate went to his son John (1715–1815), who subsequently auctioned off the extensive collection of paintings and drawings.

DAVID HANCOCK

Sources D. Hancock, *Citizens of the world: London merchants and the integration of the British Atlantic community, 1735–1785* (1995) · J. G. Parker, 'The directors of the East India Company, 1754–1790', PhD diss., U. Edin., 1977 · R. Hutcherson, *The history of Danson* (1979) · W. Playfair, *British family antiquity*, 7 (1811), 200–01 · GEC, *Baronetage* · V. L. Oliver, ed., *Caribbeana*, 1–6 (1909–19) · Foster, *Alum. Oxon.* · *An account of the late dreadful hurricane, which happened on the 31st of August, 1772* (1772) · *Journal of the commissioners for trade and plantations*, [vol. 9]: *From January 1749/50 to December 1753* (1932) · *Journal of the commissioners for trade and plantations*, [vol. 11]: *From January 1759 to December 1763* (1935) · PRO, PROB 11/1336, sig. 82, fols. 255–8
Archives priv. coll. | BL, Keith MSS, Add. MSS 35516–35538 · BL OIOC, court of directors' minutes · Bodl. Oxf., Sulivan MSS · Hall Place, Bexley, Kent, Danson deeds and parish records · PRO, St Kitts original corresp., CO 152/19–30
Wealth at death see will, PRO, PROB 11/1336, sig. 82

Boyd, Sir John McFarlane (1917–1989), trade unionist and Salvationist, was born on 8 October 1917 in Motherwell, Lanarkshire, the only child of James Boyd, butcher, who died in the influenza epidemic of the following year, and his wife, Mary Marshall, who in 1920 married John Burns, collier, with whom she had two further sons. John was welcomed by his stepfather as his own son, but John Burns's earnings were irregular, and after the 1926 general strike he had no work until the outbreak of the Second World War. Boyd was therefore brought up in considerable poverty, and later recalled that until he was fourteen the only boots he possessed were supplied by the parish. He attended Hamilton Street elementary school and Motherwell and Glencairn secondary school, earning money for the family by delivering newspapers and milk. In 1932 he left school early to take up one of the few engineering apprenticeships at the Lanarkshire Steel Company and at the same time joined the apprentices' section of the Amalgamated Engineering Union (AEU). He thus added a second element to his future career, for he had at the age of ten joined the Salvation Army. In 1932 he signed the Salvationist articles of war, was sworn in as a senior soldier, and graduated to a BBb bass in the Motherwell corps; his tuba, he noted, was 'easy to play but heavy'.

It was with a reputation as an open-air boy preacher that in 1937 Boyd took up the cause of junior workers at the Lanarkshire mill, on the claim of the AEU for the right to negotiate on their behalf. He found himself as one of the youthful leaders of a strike, which spread countrywide and achieved the union's objective on the apprenticeship question. After nine years as a craftsman and shop steward he was elected assistant divisional organizer in 1946, divisional organizer in 1949, and executive councillor for division one (Scotland) in 1953, the youngest member of the union ever to attain that office. He retained this post until 1975 when, following the untimely death of Jim Conway in an aeroplane crash, he was elected general secretary of the AEU until his retirement in 1982. During almost three decades of working from AEU headquarters in London, Boyd held almost every post in the labour movement available to him: president of the Confederation of Shipbuilding and Engineering Unions in 1964; member of the general council of the Trades Union Congress in 1967–75 and 1978–82; and chairman of the Labour Party in 1967. He was also his union's chief negotiator in a number of industries including shipbuilding, atomic energy, electricity supply, paper making, iron and steel, and aluminium. He was a member of the council of the Advisory, Conciliation and Arbitration Service (1978–82); a director of the British Steel Corporation (1981–6), of the UK Atomic Energy Authority (1980–85), of Industrial Training Services Ltd from 1980, and of International Computers Ltd (UK) from 1984; and a governor of the BBC (1982–7). He was appointed CBE in 1974, knighted in 1979, elected a fellow of the Royal Society of Arts in 1982, and in 1981, perhaps to his greatest satisfaction, received the Salvation Army's order of the Founder.

Boyd was a tall, well-built, kindly man, craggy of face and rich in the intonations of the Clydesider. His devotion to the Salvation Army never faltered, nor his sincerity in combining this with his role as a trade unionist. To him they both were aspects of his mission of service. 'Yours, in the Joys of Service', the words with which he ended his address to members urging them to elect him as general secretary of the AEU in 1974, was to him no cant phrase. It was the expression of a form of Christian socialism pursued at a time when this had ceased to be fashionable, but recognizable as a creed which had inspired many of his forebears in the trade union movement.

Much of Boyd's time within the AEU was spent weaning it away from communist and extreme left-wing influence. When he retired in 1982 the committed left had only two seats on the seven-man AEU executive. His hand was behind the introduction of the secret postal ballot for the election of AEU full-time officials, which was regarded with disfavour by many unions at the time, but later universally accepted. He was a doughty negotiator, persistent, fair, but sometimes tetchy, who sought to update his own organization. In this he did not wholly succeed before his retirement, and he left much still to be done. His efforts to absorb the draughtsmen into the Amalgamated Union of Engineering Workers (AUEW) (as it was then called) proved, for both organizational and political reasons, to be an exercise in sentiment rather than reality. But he did much to leave his union in better condition than he found it. Above all, Boyd laid great emphasis on decency and trust; 'ye canna', he commented in disgust with an employers' representative who had abused his confidence, 'negotiate with liars'.

In 1940 Boyd married a fellow Salvationist, Elizabeth, daughter of James McIntyre, steelworker. They had two daughters. Boyd died on 30 April 1989 at his home at 24 Pearl Court, Cornfield Terrace, Eastbourne, Sussex.

ARTHUR MARSH, *rev.*

Sources G. Sharp, *Sir John Boyd* (1983) · *Militant moderate*, video, c.1980 · G. Laird, 'Sir John Boyd: a tribute', *AEU Journal* (June 1989) · J. B. Jefferys, *The story of the engineers, 1800–1945* [1946] · personal knowledge (1996) · *CGPLA Eng. & Wales* (1989)

Wealth at death £13,980: probate, 19 July 1989, *CGPLA Eng. & Wales*

Boyd, Sir John Smith Knox (1891–1981), bacteriologist, was born on 18 September 1891 at Largs, Ayrshire, the second of three sons (there were no daughters) of John Knox Boyd, an agent in the Royal Bank of Scotland, and his wife, Margaret Wilson Smith. He was educated at the local school in Largs and then entered Glasgow University in 1908 to study medicine; he graduated MB, ChB in 1913. After house appointments at Glasgow Royal Infirmary he sailed to Rangoon as a ship's surgeon. On his return in 1914 Boyd applied for a commission in the Royal Army Medical Corps. By December he was at Ypres. From France he moved to Salonika, and became medical officer to the divisional engineers in 1916. In this post he travelled widely through Mesopotamia, making his first acquaintance with tropical diseases. After some training in bacteriology, by 1917 he was in charge of a mobile laboratory where he worked on the treatment of malaria and studied the prevalent dysentery. He became a pathologist at Salonika in September 1918 but was invalided home in December with 'Spanish influenza'. In the same year he married Elizabeth (*d.* 1956), daughter of John Edgar, a Dumfriesshire station-master.

Having obtained a regular commission in the Royal Army Medical Corps, in 1920 Boyd was appointed to head the brigade laboratory at Nasirabad in Rajputana and later the district laboratory in Mhow, Central Provinces. He returned to London in 1923 and joined the staff of the Royal Army Medical College, where he became demonstrator and then assistant professor of pathology. He obtained the DPH at Cambridge in 1924. Back in India in 1929 with the rank of major he was given charge of laboratories in Bangalore and then Poona. In 1932 he was appointed assistant director of hygiene and pathology at the army headquarters, Simla. In 1936 he returned to Millbank to run the vaccine laboratory. He was awarded the Leishman medal in 1937 and promoted to lieutenant-colonel in 1938.

Boyd put the vaccine department of the army medical college on a war footing in 1939 and after its transfer to Tidworth it produced sufficient material for all the needs of the services during the Second World War. He organized a blood transfusion service for the Middle East forces and pioneered the preferential use of whole blood for transfusion in casualties with severe blood loss. During this time he built up some forty laboratories in that zone. He was mentioned in dispatches (1941). In August 1940 he was also given responsibility for pathology in the Middle East and in November 1943 he became deputy director of pathology to Twenty-First Army group. Promoted colonel in 1944 Boyd became a brigadier in the following year. In 1945 he became director of pathology for the War Office.

Boyd left the army medical staff in 1946 and became director of the Wellcome Laboratories of Tropical Medicine where he remained until 1955. In that year he became a Wellcome trustee and served until 1966; he also became deputy chairman in 1965 and a consultant to the trust until 1968. Boyd's first wife died in 1956 and in 1957 he married his secretary, (Ellen) Mary Harvey Bennett (1910–1968), daughter of Denis Harvey Murphy, company director, of Northwood, Middlesex, and Mary Ellen Dempsey. There were no children of either marriage.

Boyd was especially interested in the dysenteric diseases. He studied the difference between 'smooth' and 'rough' colonies of dysenteric bacterial strains, showing that the rough strain contained the group antigen common to all flexner types while the smooth strain lacked this group antigen but possessed its own specific surface antigen. This property made it possible to separate dysenteric bacilli into two groups subsequently called flexneri and boydii. Later, in the Middle East, Boyd was responsible for the first trials of sulphaguanidine in the treatment of dysentery. His work on malaria included the first studies on synthetic anti-malarial preparations, and his studies of typhus in India in 1916 showed that most cases of this disease were transmitted by the mite and the flea, and not by the tick as had been suspected. Boyd also had a special interest in bacteriophage. His experience with these 'bacterial viruses' led him to formulate a theory for the long-lasting immunity that occurs after recovery from yellow fever, based on the bacteriophage model.

Boyd was a member or chairman of many committees and was president of the Royal Society of Tropical Medicine and Hygiene (1957–9). He was awarded the Manson medal in 1968 and was elected MRCP in 1950, and FRCP and FRS in 1951. He graduated MD from Glasgow in 1948. He was an honorary FRCPE (1960) and FRSM (1965). He was made FRCPath (1968), honorary LLD, Glasgow (1957), and honorary DSc, Salford (1969). He was appointed OBE in 1942 and knighted in 1958.

Boyd was a deeply honest man of military bearing with a determination to see that his objectives were achieved. During his latter years he was a very formidable figure, but once he made a friend his loyalty was unshakeable. He was a keen golfer and bird-watcher. Boyd died on 10 June 1981 at Northwood, Middlesex.   P. O. WILLIAMS, *rev.*

Sources L. G. Goodwin, *Memoirs FRS*, 28 (1982), 27–57 · J. Boyd, unpublished diaries and papers, Royal Army Medical College, Millbank, London · Munk, *Roll*
Archives Royal Army Medical College, Millbank, London, diaries and papers · Wellcome L., journals and papers
Likenesses photograph, 1957, repro. in Goodwin, *Memoirs FRS* · W. Bird, photograph, RS · W. Stoneman, photograph, RS
Wealth at death £116,451: probate, 20 July 1981, *CGPLA Eng. & Wales*

Boyd, Margaret [Maggie] (1913–1993), schoolteacher and lacrosse player, was born on 17 January 1913 in Strasbourg, Alsace, Germany, the daughter and fourth of five children of Dr Harold de Haven Boyd, manager of a Manchester oil company, and his wife, Charlotte Elisabeth, *née* Austin. She was educated at Berkhamsted Girls' School in Hertfordshire and Wycombe Abbey in Buckinghamshire, the latter a school to which lacrosse had been introduced in 1896 by Francis Jane Dove. At school Boyd excelled in games and was an able pianist.

After training as a physical education teacher at Bedford College, Boyd taught first at Roedean School and then at

Berkhamsted until the beginning of the Second World War. During the war she motorcycled daily to Ashridge House, near Berkhamsted, where she worked as a physiotherapist. Finally she returned to Wycombe Abbey, first as a teacher in charge of physical education and subsequently also as a housemistress—positions she held until her retirement in 1975, though even then she often helped out when there was a staff shortage. As with most of her activities she participated to the fullest and at Wycombe, in addition to her specified duties, she co-ordinated the school appeal, was in charge of careers advice, organized the sixth-form social work in High Wycombe, played a major role in the seniors (old girls') association, and generally became renowned as 'a superb crisis handler' (*Wycombe Abbey Gazette*).

Boyd played lacrosse for Bedford College and then for Boxmoor Ladies. A strong defence wing, she gained her first England selection in 1934 and captained the national side from 1937 until 1951, playing on the first official English tour to the United States in 1949.

During the war the annual home nations' tournament was interrupted for the first time since its inception in 1913. Women's club lacrosse came virtually to a standstill, but the schoolgirl game continued, thanks very much to the work of Boyd; she scavenged for balls and other essential gear, placing advertisements in the national press which produced large quantities of equipment. In 1946 she established the national schools' tournament, held annually at the close of each season. This became a five-day competition, one of the trophies competed for being the Boyd cup.

When she finished playing international lacrosse Boyd worked on the staff of Winsor School in Boston, Maine, for three years. She also began to coach lacrosse in Maine and returned there annually for over twenty years to coach in summer camps. As a coach she had the ability to spot the potential in players and nurse it to fruition. On her return to Britain she moved into administration of the game, becoming vice-president of the English Women's Lacrosse Association in 1955 and holding the presidency from 1967 to 1972. In 1969 she organized and managed a combined British and United States team—the Pioneers—which made the first overseas tour to Australia and played exhibition games there and also in New Zealand, Hong Kong, Japan, and Holland. Two years later she was awarded the OBE for services to lacrosse.

In April 1972 Boyd was elected foundation president of the International Federation of Women's Lacrosse Associations when it was established at Williamsburg, Virginia. Essentially a modest person who was easily embarrassed, she took little personal credit for the worldwide development of the sport and the establishment of a world cup. She simply said that she was 'thrilled that the small beginning had blossomed into such a thriving organisation due to the outstanding leadership of the presidents that followed me' (*The Independent*). Others thought differently, and only a few days before her death she was elected to the lacrosse hall of fame in Baltimore, the first woman to gain that honour.

Boyd had a great sense of fun, often interrupting other teachers' lessons with notes requesting the solution to a particular clue in the *Times* crossword, of which she was a devotee. She was also a good golfer and bridge player. Never married, she died of heart failure on 21 November 1993 at her home, 16 Crossways, Berkhamsted, which she had shared with her sister Etheldreda, leaving an estate of £1,696,159. She gave £1000 of this to Wycombe Abbey with the wish that it be used for any seniors who needed financial help. WRAY VAMPLEW

Sources *The Times* (11 Dec 1993) · *The Independent* (13 Dec 1993) · *Wycombe Abbey Seniors' Supplement* (1994) · *Wycombe Abbey Gazette* (Nov 1975) · J. Arlott, ed., *The Oxford companion to sports and games* (1975) · b. cert. · d. cert.
Likenesses group photograph, 1936, repro. in *The Times*
Wealth at death £1,696,159—net: *The Independent* (19 March 1994)

Boyd, Mark (1804/5–1879), author, born in Surrey, near the Thames, was the son of Edward Boyd, merchant, of Merton Hall, Newton Stewart, Wigtownshire, and his wife, Janet, daughter of Benjamin Yule of Wheatfield, Midlothian. He was a brother of Benjamin *Boyd. He spent his childhood mainly on the Scottish estate, which was near the River Cree. Later he pursued an active business career in London, where he became the director of a Scottish insurance society, and an active promoter of the colonization of Australia and New Zealand. He travelled much in Europe and published an account in the *London and Shetland Journal* of a journey in the Orkney Isles in 1839. On 23 December 1848 he married Emma Anne, the widow of 'Romeo' Coates, who had been run over and killed in the previous February; she predeceased him.

Boyd was a minor author; in 1864 he published a pamphlet about Australia, where his brother had settled. This was followed by *Reminiscences of Fifty Years* (1871) and *Social Gleanings* (1875) the latter being written from Oatlands, Walton-on-Thames. He died at the Alexandra Hotel, Hyde Park, London (his home at the time), on 13 September 1879, aged seventy-four.

JENNETT HUMPHREYS, *rev.* DEAN WILSON

Sources *Annual Register* (1848) · *Annual Register* (1879) · *GM*, 2nd ser., 30 (1848), 648 · 'Boyd, Benjamin', *AusDB*, vol. 1 · *CGPLA Eng. & Wales* (1880)
Wealth at death under £450: revoked probate, 12 Feb 1880, *CGPLA Eng. & Wales* · under £450: administration with will, 12 Feb 1880, *CGPLA Eng. & Wales*

Boyd, Mark Alexander (1563–1601), humanist scholar and writer, was born on 13 January 1563, possibly in Galloway, the son of Robert Boyd of Penkill Castle, Ayrshire. James Boyd, archbishop of Glasgow, was his uncle. His family was descended from the first Lord Boyd, who was forfeited by James III; his father was the son of the first Boyd of Penkill. The chronology and detail of Mark Alexander Boyd's life are still uncertain, and much that has been said about him is difficult to verify. It is said, for example, that he assumed the name Alexander, but was baptized only as Mark. However, his printed works all refer to him as Marcus Alexander Bodius, indicating that the full name was how he was known by his contemporaries. He is also said to have begun his advanced education at the University of Glasgow, but to have left following some unscholarly behaviour, including burning his books and insulting his masters. However, his name does not appear in the published records of the university, and in later years he exchanged polite correspondence with the principal of the university, Patrick Sharp, and also dedicated a poem to him. From this, it looks rather that his departure to the continent was occasioned by something other than his own insubordinate behaviour towards the university.

In 1581 Boyd went to France, and he remained on the continent until 1595. He seems to have spent his time there alternately studying and soldiering. He began studying in Paris, and from there went to Orléans to study civil law. He then followed his uncle's example of thirty years previous, and went to Bourges to study under Jacques Cujas. He left for Lyons about 1584, probably because of an outbreak of plague. From Lyons he travelled to Italy, where he met Cornelius Varus, who became his friend and a great admirer of his poetry. He returned to France by 1587, when he took up soldiering on behalf of Henri III. After being wounded, he returned to his study of law, this time at Toulouse, but when forces opposing Henri III captured the city, he moved to Bordeaux.

In Bordeaux in 1590, one of Boyd's collections of poetry and prose, *Epistolae quindecim*, was printed by Simon Millange; the other collection printed in his lifetime, the *Epistolae heroides et hymni*, was printed at La Rochelle by Jérôme Haultin in 1592 (this collection carries the false imprint of Antwerp, but the typeface marks it out as an Haultin printing). These volumes contain a wide range of material, mostly in Latin, though there are some pieces in Greek and a treatise in French; there are also some other works by Boyd contained in manuscript, and these too are mostly in Latin.

Boyd's poetry includes two sets of 'Epistolae heroides', inspired by Ovid's poems, some of which are responses from the men addressed in Ovid's poems, and others of which extend the idea to other heroines, both mythical, such as Penelope, and historical, such as Julia Augusta. The manuscript version of these is dated 1588, two years prior to their printing. There are also seventeen 'Elegiae', seven only in manuscript, nine only in the 1590 printing, and one in both. The 'Hymni', mostly accounts of flowers and stories attached to them, are additionally interesting for their dedications to various figures, including James VI, the dauphin, and Patrick Sharp, principal of Glasgow University; these appear in the 1592 printing, together with a poem (not about a flower) in Greek. Among numerous epigrams on a range of topics there is an epitaph for James Boyd, Mark Alexander's uncle. There are also a few miscellaneous poems, including a Greek epigram also addressed to James VI.

Boyd's prose is equally varied, but apart from the letters it survives only in manuscript. Some of the work reflects his studies in law: there is, for example, a commentary on

Justinian's *Institutes*, dated 1591, and also a treatise called 'Jurisconsultus', dedicated to François Balduin, possibly the Belgian jurist, though Boyd cannot have met him. Political matters are also the concern of two other works: the first is in Latin, 'Politicus', a treatise about the qualities of a statesman, dedicated to John Maitland, Lord Thirlestane, in 1590, and the second is in French, 'Discours civiles sur le royaume d'Ecosse'. The latter is incomplete, however, since only one book survives out of the twelve promised in the introductory material.

Boyd's other treatise, 'Poeta', is also unfinished. It is dedicated to his friend Cornelius Varus and sets out to explore the nature and training of a poet. It is a theme to which Boyd returns in a letter to Varus, printed in the 1592 collection; in it he seems to imply that he is giving up his poetic endeavours, but not enough is known about Boyd's life to interpret that statement with any certainty. Another eighteen of Boyd's letters, often addressed to the dedicatees of the verse, were also included in the 1592 collection, although none is dated. Other letters survive in manuscript, six to a relative, Robert Boyd, dated 1595, and one from Patrick Sharp to Boyd, dated 1592.

More recently Boyd has become better known for the vernacular sonnet 'Fra banc to banc' than for his works in Latin or in French. For a number of reasons the ascription of the sonnet to Boyd has been questioned: his discussions of poetry are largely concerned with writing in Latin, though he is not hostile to vernacular writing; no other vernacular work of his survives; the poem survives only in a single contemporary print and two eighteenth-century manuscript copies, and its attribution in all of these is ambiguous. However, recent work on this matter concludes that the attribution should stand. It would seem likely that this piece too was written while Boyd was in France, since the style of the print is very similar to those of the printers responsible for printing Boyd's collections in the early 1590s.

Boyd returned to Scotland in 1595. At least some of his last years were spent as a tutor to the earl of Cassillis, involving another journey abroad, but he died in Scotland, at Penkill, on 10 April 1601, and was buried at the church at Dailly. While his current reputation may rest on his excellent though isolated sonnet in Scots, it is clear that he is better placed in the world of other Scottish Latin poets—such as George Buchanan, of whom he speaks so respectfully, and Arthur Johnston, who reprinted his works—for, like them, he participated in a European rather than a narrowly Scottish culture.

NICOLA ROYAN

Sources I. C. Cunningham, 'Marcus Alexander Bodius, Scotus', *The palace in the wild: essays on vernacular culture and humanism in late-medieval and Renaissance Scotland*, ed. L. A. J. R. Houwen, A. A. Mac-Donald, and S. L. Mapstone (Leuven, 2000), 161–74 • R. Donaldson, '"M. Alex: Boyde": the authorship of "Fra banc to banc"', *The Renaissance in Scotland: studies in literature, religion, history and culture*, ed. A. A. MacDonald and others (1994), 344–66 • R. Sibbald, *Scotia illustrata, sive, Prodromus historae naturalis* (1684), pt 2, bk 3, chap. 2 • D. Dalrymple, Lord Hailes, *Sketch of the life of Mark Alexander Boyd* [1786/1787] • *Scots peerage*, 5.136–82

Archives NL Scot., corresp. and family papers, NLS Adv. MS 15.1.7 · NL Scot., NLS MS 20759 · NL Scot., NLS MS 25417, fol. 144*r* · NL Scot., NLS MS Wodrow 4to, CIV, fol. 1*r*
Likenesses engraving, repro. in Sibbald, *Scotia illustrata* · portrait, repro. in Dalrymple, *Sketch of the life*

Boyd, Martin À Beckett [*pseud.* Martin Mills] (1893–1972), novelist, was born on 10 June 1893 in Lucerne, Switzerland, the fourth of the five children of Arthur Merric Boyd (1862–1940) and his wife, Emma Minnie (1858–1936), daughter of William Arthur Callendar À Beckett and his wife, Emma Mills. Both of Boyd's parents were talented landscape painters. At the time of Martin's birth they were touring Europe with Minnie's parents, on whose considerable wealth they depended. In 1890 the À Becketts had bought Penleigh House, a former À Beckett estate in Wiltshire, but just before the birth of Martin serious financial losses halved their income. Unable to maintain the Wiltshire property, they returned to Australia with the Boyds at the end of 1893. Penleigh House was later sold, but in Martin Boyd's novels it appears in idealized form as embodying a way of life from which Anglo-Australians like himself were forever exiled.

Martin Boyd was educated at Trinity grammar school in Melbourne, where a sense of religious vocation was nourished by the liberal Christian teachings of headmaster Canon George Merrick Long. In 1912 he entered St John's Theological College, Melbourne, but found its low-church teaching arid; he left in less than a year. His older brothers found their vocations in art: Merric became a potter and Penleigh a landscape painter. Martin was uncertain. Told that he must earn a living, he assented affably to the idea of becoming an architect and passed two pleasant, undemanding years with the Melbourne firm of Purchas and Teague. The First World War changed his life.

For the Boyds, England's war was their war. Arthur Merric Boyd came from a military family, and with three sons of military age (the eldest having died in childhood) it was unthinkable that none should be in uniform. Martin's instincts were pacifist, but when the casualty lists from Gallipoli appeared, he felt he had no choice. His brothers joined the Australian forces. Martin decided to apply for a commission in a British regiment: if he were to be killed, he said, at least he would have seen England. He sailed in August 1915, and after completing an officer's training course he joined the Royal East Kent regiment, known as the Buffs. Posted to France early in 1917, he spent a gruelling year in the trenches. He was the only officer of his battalion who was neither killed nor wounded in this period, and the psychological damage went deep. Outwardly he conformed; tall, handsome, and assured in his well-tailored uniform, he kept his dissenting pacifist self in check. In 1918 he transferred to the Royal Flying Corps, where the risk of death was even greater than in the trenches, but the horrors of hand-to-hand fighting were avoided. Boyd survived, physically unscathed, but returning to Melbourne in 1919 he felt displaced and restless. With a vague idea that he might write, he went back to England. His early poems, *Verses* (1919) and *Retrospect* (1920), reflect his disillusioned post-war mood.

With an allowance of £100 a year from his parents, Boyd worked for eighteen months for the London weekly *The British-Australasian*, edited by his uncle, Charles Chomley. On his thirtieth birthday in June 1923 he felt that he had achieved nothing; and although his wit and charm made him welcome at Mayfair dances and dinner parties, he was tired of the social round. The news from home that his favourite brother Penleigh had been killed in a car accident provided the catalyst: Martin was ready to renounce the world. He joined a community of Anglican Franciscan friars at Batcombe in Dorset whose mission to tramps and men just out of prison appealed to him, but instead of disinterested love and care for the needy he found muddle and petty quarrels. The main legacy of the Batcombe experience was his semi-autobiographical novel *Love Gods*, published in 1925 under the pseudonym Martin Mills.

In the 1920s and 1930s Boyd published eight novels. For *Love Gods*, *Brangane* (1926), and *The Montforts* (1928) he used the pseudonym Martin Mills, and for *Dearest Idol* (1929) he chose Walter Beckett. *Brangane* was based on the eccentric career of the Australian writer Barbara Baynton, whose brief marriage to her third husband, Viscount Headley, ended in 1924 with a much publicized divorce. Boyd's fictionalized version was not unsympathetic to Baynton but she saw it as a betrayal of friendship. *The Montforts*, a thinly disguised version of the history of his mother's family in Australia, also caused trouble. Yet there was one family story that Boyd did not tell. He never disclosed the fact that his maternal grandmother, Emma À Beckett, was a convict's daughter and that a convict's fortune, based on the brewing trade, sustained the Boyds' leisured life as artists. Social shame as well as reverence for his grandmother's memory outweighed the novelist's sense of a magnificent story, replete with ironies.

Writing under his own name in the 1930s, Boyd produced four deft social comedies of English life: *Scandal of Spring* (1934), *The Lemon Farm* (1936), *The Picnic* (1937), and *Night of the Party* (1938). These were well received but made him only a modest income. He spent his winters in Sussex, living cheaply in rented cottages, and in summer travelled in Europe. He did not marry and appeared to have no close emotional ties. Some friends were sure he was homosexual; others were doubtful; all agreed that the private self of the charming and sociable Boyd was intensely guarded.

His first autobiography, *A Single Flame* (1939), was written during the Munich crisis. In a candid assessment of his First World War experience Boyd tested his pacifist beliefs against his sense of the evil of Nazism. In his finest novel, *Lucinda Brayford* (1946), in which the renewal of his Christian faith also appears, the morality of war is a central concern.

With the death of Boyd's father in 1940, his share of his mother's estate was released. Buying a house in Little Eversden, near Cambridge, was an attempt at permanence, but he lived there only intermittently. In 1948, enriched and made confident by the success of *Lucinda Brayford*, he decided to go home. He bought his À Beckett grandparents' house at Harkaway, Victoria, in the hope of making it a family centre. After expensive renovations in neo-Georgian style, Boyd lost heart. His nephews gave affectionate welcome to this unknown uncle but thought the house project was a folly. The brilliant careers of painter Arthur Boyd and architect Robin Boyd were then just beginning. Martin gave Arthur his first big commission and bought several paintings; later he was generous to other family members, but he had left it too late to be part of their lives.

The great benefit from the Australian venture was the discovery of Boyd's grandmother's diaries, almost complete from 1855 to 1906. Here Martin had the basis of a family story, more subtly shaded than *The Montforts*, told from the perspective of a narrator who, like Boyd, has come home after a long absence. Martin Boyd took the diaries back to Europe, and completed his first 'Langton' novel, *The Cardboard Crown* (1952), in Italy. *A Difficult Young Man* (1955) and *Outbreak of Love* (1957) took the Langton family story to 1914. All three novels were well reviewed and as the royalties came in Boyd did not notice how his capital was shrinking. He left England permanently in 1957 and spent his last years in a series of *pensiones* in Rome. In the fourth Langton novel, *When Blackbirds Sing* (1962), he confronted his own war experience. Renouncing social comedy, he produced a spare, awkward novel that was a critical and commercial failure. Discouraged and by the mid-1960s comparatively poor, he led an increasingly lonely life, finding company at the English centre of the Roman Catholic church of San Silvestro. His closest tie was with an Italian boy, Luciano Trombini. That Boyd loved this clever, engaging youth is evident from his diaries; a physical relationship seems unlikely. Trombini recalled Boyd as a wonderful teacher, a civilizing influence, and a generous friend. After Trombini married and moved to Milan, Boyd's isolation deepened; a second autobiography, *Day of my Delight* (1965), shows his sense of displacement. When Rome became too expensive he moved to Ostia Lido, where he liked to swim and walk on the beach. In letters to friends he raged against nuclear weapons, capitalism, and pornography. He found solace in the beauty of the natural world and comedy in the small events of daily life.

In August 1971 Boyd underwent surgery for stomach cancer in the hospital of the Piccola Compagna di Maria in Rome, where after a brief respite he returned to die. Financial help from his nephews eased his last months, and he was elated to know that his novels, reprinted in Australia, were restoring his reputation. A few days before his death on 3 June 1972, he was received into the Roman Catholic church. His burial in Rome's protestant English cemetery, at which an Anglican vicar joined a Catholic priest in prayer, suggests the harmonies as well as the divisions of a complex personality.   BRENDA NIALL

Sources Martin Boyd papers, NL Aus. · M. Boyd, *Day of my delight: an Anglo-Australian memoir* (Melbourne, 1965) · M. Boyd, *A single flame* (1939) · B. Niall, *Martin Boyd: a life* (Melbourne, 1988) · B. Niall, *Martin Boyd: Australian bibliographies* (Melbourne, 1977) · diaries of Emma À Beckett, Bundanon Trust, Bundanon, Nowra, New South Wales · diaries of W. A. C. À Beckett, Bundanon Trust, Bundanon, Nowra, New South Wales

Archives NL Aus. | NL Aus., MSS relating to biography, B. Niall papers | SOUND NL Aus., oral history interview
Likenesses group photograph, c.1901 · photographs, c.1916–1969, repro. in Niall, *Martin Boyd: a life*; copies, NL Aus., Brenda Niall papers · photograph, c.1918, NL Aus.; repro. in Niall, *Martin Boyd: a life*, facing p. 83 · photograph, NL Aus., Brenda Niall papers
Wealth at death approx. A$2500; some furniture given to family members

Boyd, Sir Robert (d. 1333). *See under* Boyd family (*per. c.*1300–*c.*1480).

Boyd, Robert, first Lord Boyd (d. 1481/2). *See under* Boyd family (*per. c.*1300–*c.*1480).

Boyd, Robert, fifth Lord Boyd (c.1517–1590), nobleman, was the eldest son of Robert, fourth Lord Boyd (d. 1558), and Helen, daughter of Sir John Somerville of Cambusnethan. In 1535 he married Margaret (d. 1601), daughter of Sir John Colquhoun of Glins, with whom he had two sons, Thomas and Robert, and six daughters, Margaret, Helen, Egidia, Agnes, Christine, and Elizabeth. He succeeded to his father's title in 1558.

The power base of the Boyd family was in Ayrshire, which had a reputation for religious dissidence stretching back to the time of the Lollards of Kyle in James IV's reign. Consequently it is not surprising that Robert Boyd, like some of the other leading Ayrshire landowners, notably the earl of Glencairn and Lord Ochiltree, should have played a prominent role in the events surrounding the Reformation in 1559–60, at both a local and a national level. At Easter 1559 Boyd was nominated one of the lords of the congregation who would protect the protestant reformer John Willock while he engaged in theological debate with Quintin Kennedy, abbot of Crossraguel. The contest was scheduled to take place at St John's Kirk, Ayr, but Kennedy ultimately decided not to participate. Then in the summer of 1559, as the protestant revolution gathered force, Boyd joined Knox and his followers at Perth, and when it became apparent in July that victory was impossible without outside assistance he was among the signatories of a letter appealing to Queen Elizabeth for English support. On 4 November Henry Balnaves, a leading reformer, reported paying 500 crowns to Glencairn and Boyd, thereby helping to keep them loyal to the protestant cause. In February 1560 Boyd was one of the commissioners appointed to negotiate the treaty of Berwick, which guaranteed English military and naval aid against the French forces of the regent, Mary of Guise. Having witnessed the defeat of the latter in the summer of 1560, Boyd attended the convention at Edinburgh in January 1561 at which the Book of Discipline, the first blueprint for the kirk, was given parliamentary approval.

Mary's personal reign from 1561 to 1567 created something of a dilemma for Boyd. He obviously had a strong attachment to the queen, yet some of her actions dismayed him. Thus the announcement in the summer of 1565 of her marriage to Lord Darnley, who had been brought up a Roman Catholic, aroused his fears over her religious intentions and caused him to join Moray's faction against the queen. The upshot of this questionable move was Boyd's participation in the so-called chaseabout raid, a futile attempt at rebellion led by Moray in August–September 1565. After assembling initially in Boyd's home territory of Ayrshire, the insurgents briefly occupied Edinburgh at the end of August, but the absence of any substantial support either in Scotland or from England soon caused the revolt to fizzle out.

Summoned to stand trial for his actions, Boyd decided to seek reconciliation with Darnley, and in March 1566 he joined those who, in return for a pardon for their involvement in the chaseabout raid, signed a bond recommending that the queen's consort be given the crown matrimonial. In the event Boyd received his remission from Mary herself, when after Riccio's murder she astutely split her opponents by granting pardons to the previous year's rebels, but not to those who had assassinated her secretary. Then after the murder of Darnley in February 1567 Boyd showed himself in favour of the queen's marrying Bothwell. He was a member of the jury which acquitted the earl of involvement in Darnley's death, and also a signatory of the Ainslie bond supporting his proposed marriage to Mary. On 17 May he was made a privy councillor, and in the following month he was a leader in an (unsuccessful) attempt to hold Edinburgh for the queen.

However, it was after Mary was forced to abdicate (24 July 1567) that Boyd's loyalty to her became particularly conspicuous. It was far from unusual in sixteenth-century Scotland for political allegiance to be at odds with religious affiliation, in whole regions as well as in individuals. Boyd was a native of the protestant south-west, which was nevertheless a powerful bastion of support for the queen. This may have been due in part to the highly successful tour of Ayrshire which Mary made in 1563. Moreover, it is likely that Boyd, like many others, disapproved of Mary's enforced abdication, believing it could only lead to civil war and instability. On 13 May 1568 he fought for Mary at Langside, and in September, following a meeting of her supporters at Dumbarton, he was nominated a commissioner to represent the queen at the forthcoming inquiry into Mary's behaviour which Queen Elizabeth had instigated. Boyd's selection was endorsed by Mary and he joined Bishop John Lesley, Lord Herries, and the others for the proceedings first at York and later at Westminster. Mary seems to have trusted him without reservation, and in a letter to Cecil of 11 February 1569 asked that she could keep him and Lesley permanently with her. In February 1569, with the investigation completed, Boyd was given a safe conduct to return to Scotland, but instead lingered near Tutbury in Staffordshire, where Mary had recently been transferred; he remained in England for much of 1569, acting as a Marian agent and becoming involved in the complex marriage negotiations between Mary and the duke of Norfolk. One of his duties was to deliver, as a token of the duke's affections, a diamond which Mary promised to wear secretly until their wedding took place. Shortly afterwards, in June 1569, he travelled to Scotland and discussed with Regent Moray the possibilities of arranging Mary's divorce from the exiled Bothwell, but he then returned to England once more. Early in 1570 Boyd went back to Scotland and for more than a year was active

as one of the 'queen's men' in the civil war waged intermittently between 1570 and 1573. None the less, by August 1571 he had recognized the futility of continuing the struggle, and with other Marians submitted to the earl of Lennox's government.

The earl of Morton's appointment as regent in November 1572 marked the beginning of the most important phase in Boyd's career. For almost a decade he held a variety of positions in an administration whose political and religious affinities appealed to his own anglophile and protestant leanings. Having been restored to the privy council by Lennox's government on 7 September 1571, Boyd also became an extraordinary lord of session under Morton, and then, as the state assumed control of the kirk's finances, collector of the thirds of benefices. On 17 November 1572 he visited the deathbed of John Knox. Moreover, he was closely involved in the pacification of Perth, of 23 February 1573, when the Gordon and Hamilton families were reconciled to Morton—Boyd being one of the officials responsible for the execution of the settlement in the southern half of the country. As a reward for his services Boyd received various forfeitures, escheats, and wardships, and in 1575 he was appointed bailie and justiciar of Glasgow, where his nephew James Boyd of Trochrig had become archbishop two years previously. By 1577 Lord Boyd was receiving a yearly pension of 1000 marks from the thirds of the archbishopric and of Paisley Abbey.

Having remained loyal to the regent during the 1578 crisis, when according to one account he even criticized him for yielding too easily to his enemies, Boyd once more became prominent in government after Morton effected his recovery. Thus he served on the commission, holding discussions with the leaders of the kirk regarding the second Book of Discipline; he was nominated to be one of the roll of councillors who would be in permanent residence with the king at Stirling; he attended the conference of September 1578 which put the final touches to the reconciliation between Morton and the Argyll–Atholl faction; and in 1579 he was named as one of the royal officials responsible for implementing the government's attack on the Hamiltons.

Morton's overthrow at the end of 1580 signalled the start of a period of fluctuating fortunes for Boyd. In August 1582, undoubtedly unhappy with the policies of the Lennox–Arran government, he joined in the so-called Ruthven raid, the seizure of James VI by ultra-protestants. Less than a year later, however, the raiders were ousted and many of them, including Boyd, were forced to leave the country and seek refuge in England. Only at the end of 1585, when the king assumed personal control of the realm, did Boyd experience better times. Thus in 1586 he was restored to his position as an extraordinary lord of session; and in June of that year he was appointed a border commissioner for negotiations over a proposed Anglo–Scottish alliance. One of his final duties was the supervision of the tax levied to meet the costs of James VI's marriage to Anna of Denmark. Boyd died at Kilmarnock on 3 January 1590, five months before the king and his bride returned to Scotland, and was buried in the Laigh Kirk (Low Church) at Kilmarnock.

For over thirty years Boyd had been a conspicuous figure in Scottish affairs. Initially he was both a staunch Marian and an ultra-protestant with anglophile sympathies. Latterly, once Mary's cause was indisputably lost, his religious and political outlook dictated most of his actions. The policies pursued by Morton during his regency were highly sympathetic to a man of Boyd's views, making the 1570s the most successful period of his long career.

G. R. HEWITT

Sources CSP Scot., 1569–81 · Scots peerage, 5.155–63 · Reg. PCS, 1st ser., vols. 2–3 · D. Calderwood, The history of the Kirk of Scotland, ed. T. Thomson and D. Laing, 8 vols., Wodrow Society, 7 (1842–9), vol. 3 · M. Livingstone, D. Hay Fleming, and others, eds., Registrum secreti sigilli regum Scotorum / The register of the privy seal of Scotland, 6 (1963) · J. M. Thomson and others, eds., Registrum magni sigilli regum Scotorum / The register of the great seal of Scotland, 11 vols. (1882–1914), vol. 4 · J. Spottiswoode, History of the Church of Scotland, ed. M. Napier and M. Russell, 2, Spottiswoode Society, 6 (1851) · APS, 1567–92 · T. Thomson, ed., A diurnal of remarkable occurrents that have passed within the country of Scotland, Bannatyne Club, 43 (1833) · D. Moysie, Memoirs of the affairs of Scotland, 1577–1603, ed. J. Dennistoun, Bannatyne Club, 39 (1830) · A. I. Cameron, ed., The Warrender papers, 1, Scottish History Society, 3rd ser., 18 (1931) · G. R. Hewitt, Scotland under Morton (1982) · M. H. B. Sanderson, Ayrshire and the Reformation (1997)

Boyd, Robert, of Trochrig (1578–1627), theological writer and poet, was born in Glasgow, the son of James Boyd of Trochrig, archbishop of Glasgow (d. 1581) and his wife, Margaret Chalmers, daughter of James Chalmers, baron of Gaithgirth. Robert was about three years old when his father died and his mother took him and his younger brother, Thomas, to live at Trochrig in Ayrshire. Educated at Ayr grammar school, he studied divinity at Edinburgh University with Robert Rollock, the principal, and philosophy with Charles Ferme, graduating MA about 1594; fellow students included John Murray, Robert Scot, and James Watson. He decided to continue his education abroad, and sailed to Dieppe on 1 May 1597. From there he made his way to Orléans, staying in the house of a Monsieur Gris, settled in Tours for a year, and then spent eight months in Bordeaux before moving to Poitiers. On a visit to Montauban he met Monsieur de Dismes, professor at the protestant university there. His new friend persuaded him to stay, and he taught philosophy at Montauban for the next five years. He lectured for four hours each day, continued his studies in Latin, Greek, and Hebrew, and at night read divinity, permitting himself very little sleep.

It had always been Boyd's desire to enter the church, and in September 1604 he moved to Verteuil, where he was ordained as pastor of the Reformed church on 9 November. His friends in the academic world were anxious not to lose him, however, and in April 1605 his congregation agreed to release him so that he could go to Saumur to be both pastor and professor of philosophy at the protestant university. In 1608 he was given the chair of divinity. He twice visited Scotland during this period, but he felt that his future lay in France and in May 1611 he married Anna (d. in or before 1654), daughter of Sir Peter de Maliverne of 'Vineola'.

Three years later Boyd's happy family life was disturbed when he received a message from James VI and I instructing him to return to Scotland to be principal of Glasgow University. Although reluctant he could not refuse the royal command and he and his family left Saumur on 2 October 1614. He had agreed to a year's trial at Glasgow, where, as well as being principal, he taught theology, Hebrew, and Syriac and was minister at Govan. Admired in Saumur for his fluent French sermons he impressed his Scottish students, like John Livingston, and subordinates like Robert Blair, with his extempore lectures in flowing Latin, as well as his encyclopaedic knowledge of theology, and his personal kindness. His commentary on the epistle to the Ephesians, in progress while he was in France but published only after his death, as Robert Bidii … in epistolam Pauli Apostoli ad Ephesios (1652), was a vast work of astonishing learning, and he also wrote excellent Latin poetry, some of which was published in Hetacombe Christiana (1627) and translated by Sir William Mure in A Spirituall hymne (1628).

His first year satisfactorily accomplished, Boyd agreed to stay on at Glasgow, but as time passed he became embroiled in the controversy over whether the Church of Scotland should have bishops. He believed that it should not. James VI and I was angry when he opposed the five articles of Perth, and in 1621 Boyd resigned, retiring to Trochrig. In October 1622, however, he was invited to become principal of Edinburgh University and minister of Greyfriars church. He accepted, but as soon as James VI heard he wrote to the provost, bailies, and town council of Edinburgh telling them, 'we think his byding ther will do much evil and therefor … we command you to put him not only from his office but out of your town … unless he conform totally' (Wodrow, 189). Boyd refused to comply, and was deprived.

Back in Ayrshire, Boyd was in 1624 given hopes that he might be restored to his position as principal at Glasgow, but although he signed a qualified declaration of conformity he was not allowed to return. Instead, on 18 December 1625, he accepted an invitation to become minister of Paisley. Even there, however, he was not to have a peaceful life. He had always maintained a wide-ranging correspondence, which he continued, but while one relative, Lady Boyd, wrote to thank him for his care for her spiritual welfare, another was less appreciative. Marion Boyd, the widowed countess of Abercorn, had recently converted to Roman Catholicism. At her urging her second son, Claud, Lord Strabane, broke into Boyd's house, scattering his beloved books and hurling his furnishings into the street. Horrified, Boyd retreated once more to Trochrig and at the end of 1626 fell seriously ill with a painful swelling in his throat, caused by cancer. He travelled to Edinburgh to consult doctors, but died three weeks later, on 5 January 1627 at the age of forty-eight, leaving books worth £1551 and a reputation as 'a very learned and holy man, eminent both in the school and the pulpit' (John Row, in Wodrow, 241). André Rivet, brother-in-law of Pierre du Moulin and professor of theology at

Leiden, who had known him since his time in France, wrote a sympathetic life, which was in turn a source of Robert Wodrow's biography.

ROSALIND K. MARSHALL

Sources R. Wodrow, *Collections upon the lives of the reformers and most eminent ministers of the Church of Scotland*, 2 (1845), 3–361, app. iii–xxxiv · Glasgow register of testaments, 8 June 1627, NA Scot. · A. Grant, *The story of the University of Edinburgh during its first three hundred years*, 1 (1884), 244 · *Fasti Scot.*, new edn, 1.45; 3.162, 410 · DNB · *Scots peerage*, 5.151, 167 · C. Innes, ed., *Munimenta alme Universitatis Glasguensis / Records of the University of Glasgow from its foundation till 1727*, 4 vols., Maitland Club, 72 (1854), vol. 1, pp. 211–12, 215–16; vol. 3, p. 367 · H. M. B. Reid, *The divinity professors in the University of Glasgow, 1640–1903* (1923), 3, 7, 22, 89 · D. G. Mullen, *Scottish puritanism, 1590–1638* (2000)
Archives NA Scot., Glasgow register of testaments, 8 June 1627
Likenesses Rivers, engraving, 1795 (after unknown artist, U. Glas.), Scot. NPG; repro. in J. Pinkerton, *Iconographia Scotica* (1797) · J. Rogers, engraving (after unknown artist, U. Glas.), Scot. NPG; repro. in Chambers, *Scots* · portrait, U. Glas.
Wealth at death £2536 in Scotland; £211 sterling; books worth £1551: NA Scot., Glasgow register of testaments, 8 June 1627

Boyd, Sir Robert (*bap.* 1710, *d.* 1794), army officer, was baptized on 20 April 1710 at Richmond, Surrey, the son of Ninian Boyd (*b.* 1664) and his wife, Susanna Johnston. In later life he referred to 'an old college friend at Glasgow' (BL, Add. MS 24163, fols. 37–8), and he was probably the Robert Boyd who was entered as an 'Anglo-Scottus' at Glasgow University in 1726. From there Boyd evidently entered the army as a civilian storekeeper, the same profession as his father. According to a memorial written by Boyd in 1750, for the previous twelve years he had 'done the duties of deputy judge advocate and deputy commissary of the musters' (BL, Add. MS 32721, fol. 31) in Minorca for Sir Arthur Wescombe. Wescombe wanted to resign these offices to him. During the siege of Minorca on 19 May 1756 Boyd made a heroic attempt to reach Admiral John Byng's fleet in an open boat with a message from the garrison commander, General William Blakeney. Consequently he was called as a witness at Byng's court martial.

On 25 March 1758 Boyd was made a lieutenant-colonel; he then served five campaigns on the staff of the marquess of Granby as commissary general to the Hessian troops serving as part of the allied forces in Germany under the command of Prince Ferdinand of Brunswick. From the German campaign he wrote detailed letters to his political masters in England. It was apparently Boyd's back upon which Prince Ferdinand scribbled the news of his victory at Minden in August 1759 which Boyd took to England. On 13 January 1760 he bought a company in the 1st foot guards. At this time he narrowly avoided being promoted to command a regiment in India, Lord Clive recommending him as 'one of the best, if not the best officer in the King's service' (Russell, 34). Boyd claimed thirty-two years' service abroad in 1762, and with peace in the offing he attempted to secure future employment; firstly he hoped to be employed with the Hessian troops until their contract ended in the summer of 1763: 'this doceur' (BL, Add. MS 38200, fol. 91) would help him furnish his new house in Queen Anne Street in London. His ultimate aim was a governorship which would allow him

to retire to England on an income not dissimilar to that he had enjoyed in Minorca. In 1764 Boyd was enlisting Prince Ferdinand in his quest for employment. On 18 September 1765 Boyd exchanged his company of guards for one in the 39th foot regiment, of which he became colonel on 6 August 1766. On 25 May 1768 he was named lieutenant-governor of Gibraltar, where his regiment had been posted. He became a major-general in 1772.

In May 1773 Boyd landed back on Gibraltar, and as acting governor began work on the 'king's bastion', a fortress able to accommodate 800 men and twenty-six cannon and mortars. Boyd was still there in 1776 with a new governor, General George Augustus Eliott, not yet arrived. In August 1776 he referred to his family being with him; but little is known about his wife, Arabella (*d.* 1791), except that she was similar in age to her husband. Boyd finally left in spring 1777, the year he was promoted lieutenant-general. He returned to play a key role in the defence of besieged Gibraltar from 1779 to 1782 and suggested the use of red hot shot to disable the enemies' floating batteries. Political faction was rife in the garrison, with Boyd a noted client of the opposition in parliament (John Pitt, second earl of Chatham, had served as his aide-de-camp); one of his enemies, Colonel Charles Ross, called his troops the 'storekeepers regiment' (Russell, 83), and Boyd was often at loggerheads with Governor Eliott.

With the siege over, Ross even objected, unsuccessfully, to the inclusion of Boyd's name in an address of thanks from the House of Commons in December 1782. However, Boyd had to act as royal commissioner when Eliott was installed with the Order of the Bath in April 1783. On 28 January 1785 Boyd was himself made a knight of the Bath, but he had to wait until 19 May 1788 for his investiture. In January 1791 Boyd was back in Gibraltar as governor, leaving his wife at home for she died at Albyns, Essex, on 12 November 1791. He attained the rank of general on 12 October 1793. Boyd died in Gibraltar on 13 May 1794, aged eighty-four, and was buried in the king's bastion. His will mainly dealt with his stock in three per cent consolidated Bank of England annuities, the beneficiaries being nieces and nephews.

STUART HANDLEY

Sources J. Russell, *Gibraltar besieged, 1779–1783* (1965) · will, PRO, PROB 11/1247, sig. 354 · C. Innes, ed., *Munimenta alme Universitatis Glasguensis / Records of the University of Glasgow from its foundation till 1727*, 3, Maitland Club, 72 (1854), 231 · IGI · Walpole, *Corr.*, 11.117; 20.583–4; 21.3 · BL, Add. MS 32721, fol. 31 · BL, Add. MS 24163, fols. 37–8, 161 · BL, Add. MS 38200, fols. 91, 288–9 · BL, Add. MS 6860, fols. 86–7 · GM, 1st ser., 61 (1791), 1069 · N. B. Leslie, *The succession of colonels of the British army from 1660 to the present day* (1974), 78 · DNB
Archives BL, journal, Add. MSS 38605–38606 · NAM, letter-book | BL, letters to Lord Grantham, Add. MSS 24159–24163 · PRO, letters to Lord Chatham, PRO 30/8 · PRO, corresp. with F. J. Jackson, FO 353
Likenesses line engraving, pubd 1783, BM, NPG · J. Hall, line engraving, pubd 1785 (after A. Poggi), BM, NPG · C. Watson, stipple, pubd 1785 (after J. Smart), BM, NPG · plaster medallion (after W. Tassie), Scot. NPG
Wealth at death see will, PRO, PROB 11/1247, sig. 354

Boyd, Robert (1808–1883), physician and asylum superintendent, was born in Ireland. He was educated at Edinburgh University, graduating MD in 1831. He became a member of the Royal College of Surgeons in 1830. In 1836 he was elected a licentiate of the Royal College of Physicians, London, and in 1852 became a fellow. Boyd's early medical career is unclear, but it is likely that he was involved in hospital medicine as he published a number of articles in the 1830s in *The Lancet*, *Medical Gazette*, *Edinburgh Medical Journal*, and the *Provincial Medical and Surgical Journal*. By 1836 he appears in the records of the Marylebone guardians as an assistant apothecary at the workhouse infirmary, and would seem to have worked his way up becoming successively house surgeon and, in 1840, resident physician. He took a special interest in the pauper lunatics who were housed in a specialist ward within the workhouse.

Boyd was an important pioneer of the care of the insane in workhouses at a time when official policy was to move parish paupers into county asylums. In the absence of sufficient space in the county asylum at Hanwell he demonstrated that it was possible to run an effective lunatic ward within a workhouse infirmary setting, thus obviating the need to move patients far away from their local area. This post also provided plentiful opportunities for general clinical experience. In 1840 for example he applied to the board of guardians for permission to use a small room adjoining the boys' bathroom for the purpose of trying scientific experiments. In a later paper on tumours of the brain Boyd commented that he had been present at 1039 post-mortems at Marylebone. During the 1840s he was also listed as a lecturer in medicine, and by this period had married Isabella (*b.* 1814), herself from Ireland, and together they had two sons and four daughters.

In 1849, as a result of his experience at Marylebone workhouse, which contained almost 2000 inmates, Boyd became superintendent and physician to the new county asylum at Wells, in Somerset, a post he held until 1868. This post provided an ideal opportunity for Boyd to further his keen interest in pathological medicine. Like many superintendents, though, he found the bureaucratic aspects of the job, and opposition to local initiative from the central lunacy commission, frustrating. In 1859 for example he and the county asylum visiting magistrates petitioned the commissioners unsuccessfully for permission to create a special asylum for epileptic patients, who constituted over 13 per cent of all inmates at Somerset. He wanted further specialist facilities created for other categories of mentally ill people so that their illnesses could be studied more carefully. From 1869 until 1875 Boyd was living in Bolton Row, Mayfair, in private practice, but he then became proprietor and physician of Southall Park private asylum.

Boyd was interested in medical politics and was a member of the Medico-Psychological Association. In 1870 he was elected president and took the opportunity to remind members of the importance of workhouse infirmaries as a source of learning in morbid anatomy and insanity for students. Unlike many hospitals which had selective admission criteria, workhouses took patients with most diseases. This might well have applied to patients with general paralysis of the insane about whom he wrote a

landmark article the following year, identifying that it was as much a disease of the general nervous system as of the brain. Using evidence from 924 deaths at Somerset Asylum, of whom 162 (18 per cent) had the disease, Boyd did 155 post-mortems, establishing a 4:1 ratio of men to women, and finding evidence of similar changes in the spinal cord and brain. In 1873 Boyd's commitment to pathological medicine led him to support a move to remove Henry Maudsley from the editorship of the *Journal of Mental Science*. Maudsley's degenerationist ideas and pessimism had led him to denigrate colleagues' research and the resulting treatments. When Harrington Tuke was made president that year Boyd proposed that editorship of the association's journal should become a function of the presidency which would have ousted Maudsley from a position in which he had been able to promote his ideas.

Like most asylum superintendents Boyd published annual reports with statistics of the establishments he managed, but he also contributed a number of other important papers to the literature of pathology and psychological medicine. He produced sixteen articles for the *Journal of Mental Science* including 'Statistics of pauper insanity', 'Diseases of the nervous system', and 'Treatment of the insane poor', several of which were related to mental health policy. His earlier medical papers included pioneer work on comparative measurement of the weight of different body organs at different ages, and more especially of the brain.

Boyd, like most Victorians, had a range of private interests. He was a fellow of the Zoological Society and pursued antiquarian studies. In the 1860s he corresponded with the Revd George Gordon, an old university friend, on the subject of Roman coins and pottery. Boyd had a robust and powerful physique, was reserved and taciturn in nature, and in speech was steady, weighing his words carefully. He was a popular man, noted for his kindness, and his general regard for patients. On 14 August 1883, together with one of his sons, Captain William Boyd, two patients, and the cook, he tragically lost his life in a fire at his private asylum, while going back into the building to save the inmates.   NICK HERVEY

Sources *BMJ* (18 Aug 1883), 353 · directors and guardians' minutes, Marylebone, LMA, P89/MRY 1/523–529 · *The Lancet* (25 Aug 1883), 352–3 · *Medical Registers* (1848–83) · d. cert. · census returns, 1881 [Robert Boyd and Isabella Boyd]
Archives Elgin Museum, Elgin, Moray, letters to George Gordon
Wealth at death £7456 1s.: probate, 13 Sept 1883, CGPLA Eng. & Wales

Boyd, Thomas, first earl of Arran (*d.* before **1474**). *See under* Boyd family (*per. c.*1300–*c.*1480).

Boyd, Sir Thomas Jamieson (1818–1902), publisher and philanthropist, was born on 22 February 1818 at 16 Charlotte Street, Leith, the eldest of three sons of John Boyd, corn merchant, and his wife, Anne, daughter of Thomas Jamieson. John Boyd's brother George Boyd was a partner with Thomas Oliver in the Edinburgh publishing house of Oliver and Boyd, and when, in 1843, Oliver retired and George Boyd died, John Boyd became a partner and his sons Thomas, John, and Thomson joined the staff of Oliver and Boyd. On 6 June 1844 Thomas Boyd married Mary Ann, daughter of John Ferguson, surgeon, of Edinburgh.

Nothing is known about Boyd's education; but under his regime, and with the help of his younger brothers, Oliver and Boyd attained a prominent place in the trade for its educational and reference books. Its profitability freed Boyd to a great extent for a second career in public service. He was an active and prominent member of the Merchant Company of Edinburgh; he was elected master in 1869, at the age of fifty-one, and later held the office for two further periods. In this capacity he was chiefly responsible for reforming the four educational charitable institutions governed by the Merchant Company, namely, George Watson's, James Gillespie's, and Daniel Stewart's hospitals, which educated boys, and the Maiden Hospital, which educated girls. These 'hospitals' had been founded by members of the Merchant Company to care for and educate children of poor merchants. The scheme was approved by government and by a provisional order issued in July 1870 under the Endowed Institutions (Scotland) Act. Under the order the institutions expanded into fee paying day schools with open admission. Bursaries and scholarships were established to support those who proceeded to further education, while industrial and evening schools were made available for children of the industrious poor. A chair of commerce was endowed at Edinburgh University, the first of its kind in Scotland. The operation was successful and the scheme was taken as a model by the English endowed school commissioners.

Boyd also promoted another great Edinburgh institution, the new Royal Infirmary at Lauriston, erected on the site formerly occupied by George Watson's Hospital. Boyd was chairman of the committee which raised £320,000, the largest sum ever to have been subscribed in the city for a charitable purpose. The prince of Wales (later King Edward VII) laid the foundation stone in 1870. The infirmary was formally opened on 29 October 1879; in the absence of any royal personage able to undertake this duty, Boyd himself performed the opening ceremony, presiding over a vast gathering eager to see this impressive new building for 500 patients, which was considered to be the largest and best-equipped in Europe.

Boyd entered the town council in 1875 as a representative for St Leonard's ward. In 1877 he was elected lord provost of Edinburgh; he was re-elected in 1880 and held office until the end of 1882. During his provostship the new Edinburgh Dock at Leith was opened by the duke of Edinburgh on 26 July 1881. In the following month, when Queen Victoria held a review of Scottish volunteers, Boyd, who was an honorary colonel of the Queen's Edinburgh regiment, was knighted by her at Holyrood Palace, on 25 August.

Boyd also served as curator of Edinburgh University from 1879 to 1885, as a commissioner for northern lighthouses from 1877 to 1882, and as a commissioner for Scottish Educational Endowments from 1882 to 1889; and he did useful work as chairman for ten years of the Scottish Fishery Board. In 1896 the publishing house of

Oliver and Boyd was taken over by George and James Thin and John Grant, and Boyd retired from the firm in the following year.

After relinquishing all other public duties Boyd continued to act as director of the Union Bank of Scotland and of the Scottish Provident Institution until within two months of his death. Boyd was made FRS and DL, and he was a JP and an elder of the United Free Church. He died at his home, 41 Moray Place, Edinburgh, on 22 August 1902, and received a public funeral at the Dean cemetery. His wife had died on 21 February 1900, leaving their two sons and six daughters.

G. Le G. Norgate, *rev.* Anita McConnell

Sources W. M. Parker, 'The house of Oliver and Boyd: a record from 1778–1948', typescript, Edinburgh Public Libraries · *The Scotsman* (30 Aug 1879), 5 · *The Scotsman* (12 Oct 1880), 3 · *The Scotsman* (23 Aug 1902), 6 · *The Scotsman* (27 Aug 1902), 6 · *Petition and schemes under the Endowed Institutions (Scotland) Act regarding: i. George Watson's Hospital, ii. the Merchant Maiden Hospital, iii. Daniel Stewart's Hospital, iv. James Gillespie's Hospital and Free School*, Edinburgh Merchant Company (1870) · A. Logan Turner, *Story of a great hospital: the Royal Infirmary of Edinburgh, 1729–1929* (1937), 228, 258–9 · J. Grant, *Cassell's old and new Edinburgh*, 3 vols. [1880–83], vol. 3, pp. 288–9 · *The Times* (23 Aug 1902) · *DNB*

Likenesses O. Leyde, oils, Edinburgh Merchant Company · portrait, repro. in *The Graphic* (10 Sept 1881) · wood-engraving (after bust by W. Brodie), NPG; repro. in *ILN* (27 July 1872)

Boyd, Walter (1753–1837), financier, was born on 18 November 1753 in Scotland. He had at least one brother. He was possibly educated in Amsterdam, and he seems to have served an apprenticeship with a merchant house there or in France. From 1774 to 1781 he managed farms in Lincolnshire, leaving without any definite prospects.

Boyd's subsequent career developed from a connection with Sir Robert Herries and his brothers, Charles and William. The Herries were merchants in London and Barcelona, and also had a major stake in the London Exchange Banking Company which supplied facilities to travellers in Europe to cash cheques. It is not clear how Boyd was introduced to the Herries, but he was soon in touch with William when the latter was established by his brother Robert as a merchant and banker in Ostend in 1780. As a result of his connections with William Herries, Boyd became associated with Veuve Nettine et Fils of Brussels, bankers to the Austrian administration. In 1782, Herries and Édouard Walckiers, a partner of Veuve Nettine et Fils who married Dieudonnée Nettine, established the Banque Particulière dans les Pays-Bas Autrichiennes, and appointed Boyd and his fellow Scot, John William Ker, as *secrétaires de direction* (personal secretaries to the directors).

In 1785 the two ambitious Scots entered a six-year partnership as Boyd, Ker et Cie and opened a bank in Paris. Boyd built up an extensive network of correspondents in France, the Netherlands, and London, drawing in particular on Veuve Nettine et Fils in Brussels, Herries in London, and Hope & Co. in Amsterdam. His main business was foreign exchanges and dealing in securities, but his interests were wide: he probably acted as the agent of Robert Herries in supplying American tobacco to the farmers general; he was banker to Thomas Jefferson; he acted for English visitors to Paris; he made loans to the aristocracy; and he was involved in factional fights for control of the Compagnie des Indes. It was around this time that he married Harriet Anne Hooke Goddard, daughter of Thomas Goddard of London; they had three sons and four daughters. She died on 10 January 1833; one son, Robert, and all the daughters, survived their father. According to Lady Elizabeth Spencer-Stanhope, Boyd stood

> in a pre-eminent position, admitted, as an Englishman, to those highest circles which were closed to the monied men of France, and aspiring to that commanding influence in the commercial world which although often maintained in England is seldom countenanced in France. (HoP, *Commons*)

In 1791 the partnership was renewed for a further six years with the addition of three 'commandite' partners, who provided additional capital without sharing in risks. One was Boyd's young cousin Walter; more important were Édouard Walckiers and François Laborde-Méréville. Although Walckiers was an adviser to the emperor Joseph II and a director of the royal treasury, he had taken a leading part in the insurrection of 1789 and fled to Paris: he supplied 1.5 million livres of capital. François Laborde-Méréville was the son of a wealthy Bayonne banker who married Rosalie de Nettine, the sister of Dieudonnée. In 1789 Laborde-Méréville opposed Jacques Necker's scheme for financial reform before the national assembly, and instead proposed—probably with Boyd's support—to set up a private bank which would pay off state debts and reform the collection of taxes, in return for the right of note issue. Although the scheme came to nothing, Boyd was confident that his new partners would bring both capital and connections.

At first political turmoil gave opportunities for speculation on the exchanges. He formed a group, with Hope & Co., and Harman, Hoare & Co. in London, to play the market; he joined with Charles Herries in selling gold and silver bullion to anxious French investors. But by 1792 Boyd was sufficiently concerned by the political situation to establish a base in London. He left Paris in September 1792 and was followed by Ker and Laborde-Méréville in 1793. The Paris bank remained in the charge of the younger Walter Boyd, who was arrested on suspicion of being an enemy agent. Although he was released, the situation was precarious: the National Convention was demanding that large bills be drawn on London, Amsterdam, and Hamburg to pay for corn imports. In August 1793 the younger Boyd and Walckiers made an agreement to protect the firm by handing it to Antoine Geneste, the firm's cashier, who would run it without risk; Boyd and Walckiers were limited partners with the right to reclaim the business. Boyd and Walckiers soon fled the country, but Geneste was executed in 1794 and the assets of the bank were seized.

Boyd had meanwhile re-established his business in London, in association with the nabob Paul Benfield (d. 1810). Benfield had gone to India as an architect in the East India Company army in 1764, subsequently resigning his commission to become contractor for the ramparts at Madras, as well as lending large sums to the nawab of the Carnatic to finance his war with the raja of Tanjore. When the governor of Madras reinstated the raja, the nawab refused to repay Benfield; Benfield plotted to kidnap the governor, and was ordered home by the East India Company. He purchased an estate, and was elected to parliament in 1780; but in 1781 he returned to India before being ordered home in 1788 by Cornwallis. Benfield was one of the most notorious nabobs, and even a friend called him 'exacting, dissatisfied and ambitious' (Cope, 39). The important point for Boyd was that Benfield was rich. The new firm of Boyd, Benfield & Co. was formed in 1793, and Benfield subscribed £25,000; he also supplied the funds for Boyd's own share of £60,000 by purchasing French annuities from Boyd, Ker et Cie, which were then placed in the new firm. The firm was, therefore, a combination of Benfield's Indian wealth with Boyd's financial skill.

Boyd soon started to play the exchanges, and in May 1794, on the advice of Veuve Nettine et Fils, he contracted for a loan of £3 million to Austria to finance the war in the Austrian Netherlands. He faced opposition both from the Austrian envoy in London, who preferred to deal with a leading bank, and from the contractors of the British loan who had secured an agreement from Pitt that there should be no competition for funds. Boyd urged Pitt to condone the loan. Why, he asked, should London 'forego the advantages of being as it were the Banker of Europe?' Remittances would, he argued, be paid 'in such a manner as that *produce* and *manufactures* may make the principal part of it' (Cope, 48–9). Pitt permitted the loan to proceed, but Boyd faced severe difficulties when the advance of the French removed the collateral for the loan provided by the revenues of the Austrian Netherlands. The Austrians pressed Boyd to meet his commitments, and one possible solution was for the British government to guarantee the loan to its ally. Boyd's own preference was to make the Austrian loan convertible into consols. The issue became a major element in diplomatic negotiations between the two countries, and was further complicated by the Austrians' need for another loan of £3 million at a time when a large British loan was planned. The outcome was a consortium headed by Boyd, Benfield & Co., which included the Goldsmids, Thellussons, and other leading houses, to contract for a loan of £18 million to Britain and £6 million to Austria. Boyd had, through his contacts with the Austrian Netherlands, become the leader of the syndicate contracting for British government loans. It was, remarked *The Times* 'the greatest money negotiation that ever took place in this or in any other country at one time' (13 Dec 1794).

The generous terms secured by Boyd were attacked in both Austria and London, where concern was expressed by the Bank of England, the City, and the Commons. He obtained a further loan contract in 1796, without competition and on favourable terms which led to a committee of enquiry; and he entered into an agreement to make advances to the Treasury through a somewhat devious procedure involving bills of exchange drawn on Hamburg, which led to questions in the Commons. Nevertheless, the syndicate obtained the contract for a further loan for £7.5 million in 1796, again without competition. 'There is', said the *Morning Chronicle*, 'but one booth in the fair' (HoP, *Commons*).

Doubtless as a means of self-defence, in 1796 Boyd joined Benfield as the second member of parliament for Shaftesbury. But more serious problems were appearing. Boyd, Benfield was holding large amounts of loan, and could not sell it without a fall in prices and a loss of their premium. In April 1796 Boyd invited leading bankers to a meeting to establish a rival credit institution to the Bank of England in order to force the bank to advance money to the government and introduce a more generous discount policy. This was a sign of mounting desperation. In the late 1790s the situation was bleak, as members of the Boyd network experienced difficulties. Walckiers failed in 1796, owing the firm £66,000, and Charles Herries in London in 1798, owing the firm £188,000; the advances to Veuve Nettine could not be realized. Boyd revealed the position to Pitt and Dundas, but an advance of £40,000 was not enough to maintain the position. Boyd turned to Benfield for assistance to draw on funds in India, but this was not easily achieved: most of Benfield's assets were bonds of the nawab of the Carnatic which could be sold only at a heavy discount. Tension built up with Benfield, who was aggrieved at the heavy losses on his remittances from India. Pitt, issuing a new loan of £18 million in 1797, bowed to pressure and opted for an open subscription. But in April 1798, a syndicate headed by Boyd, and including Thellusson and Goldsmid, obtained a new loan without competition. The terms were not favourable, and there were soon problems as the price of the stock fell. In October 1798 Boyd was not invited to join his former colleagues in the syndicate and early in 1799 his partnership with Benfield was dissolved. By March 1800 he was bankrupt.

The situation was transformed in 1801 by peace with France: the chance of regaining his lost assets took Boyd to France. When war resumed in 1803, he was interned. He was able to play some small role in international finance, in relation to Spanish payments to France, but these were years of general inactivity and frustration. He survived as a result of the charity of friends: a fund was raised for him, to which Huskisson and Walter Scott subscribed. A legacy of £1000 to his wife contributed to their support. 'Her love for her children and her attachment to me', he wrote to a partner of Hope & Co., 'has given her always so to say supernatural strength, which has sustained us all!' (Cope, 167). She was allowed to return to England in 1811, but Boyd regained his freedom only in 1814.

Boyd at once started a campaign to regain his assets from the French government. The first payment was received by 1816, and by 1821 he was able to repay the debts against Boyd, Benfield & Co. in full. The creditors granted him an allowance of about £50,000, and in 1823 he invested £33,000 in consols and purchased Plaistow Lodge, near Bromley in Kent, the former home of the banker Peter Thellusson, for £17,000. He was returned to

parliament, representing Lymington between 1823 and 1830. When he died at Plaistow on 16 September 1837 he left net personalty of £180,000 which was, presumably, the remnants of his French fortune. He was clearly a financier with flair, who was able to exploit a well-developed network of contacts in France, the Netherlands, and London. The loss of his French assets had gravely weakened his position, but through his ability to tap the funds of Benfield and also to utilize his ties with the Austrian Netherlands, Boyd was able to secure a position in the market for British government loans which was remarkable and unsustainable. Perhaps there are two people who deserve more sympathy: the unfortunate Geneste, who was guillotined, and Benfield, whose considerable landed estate was sold in 1801 to meet the demands of his creditors, and who died in poverty in Paris in 1810.

MARTIN DAUNTON

Sources S. R. Cope, *Walter Boyd: a merchant banker in the age of Napoleon* (1983) · HoP, *Commons* · *The Times* (13 Dec 1794)
Archives BL, letters to Huskisson, Add. MS 38738 · Trinity Cam., corresp., incl. William Pitt
Wealth at death £180,000——net personalty: PRO, death duty registers, IR 26/1442

Boyd, William (1685–1772), minister of the Presbyterian General Synod of Ulster, was probably a son of Thomas Boyd (*d.* 1699), Presbyterian minister of Aghadowey, co. Londonderry. He graduated MA at Edinburgh University in 1702, was licensed by the Route presbytery in 1707, and ordained at Macosquin, co. Londonderry, on 31 January 1710.

In March 1718 nine Presbyterian ministers, mostly from co. Londonderry, and more than three hundred of their members petitioned Colonel Samuel Shute, governor of New England, declaring their 'sincere and hearty inclination to transport ourselves to that very excellent and renowned Plantation, upon our obtaining from His Excellency suitable encouragement' (Bolton, 324). Boyd, deputed bearer of the petition, was favourably received in Boston. Although neither he nor any of the nine clergy themselves emigrated, James McGregor, minister of neighbouring Aghadowey (1701–18), arrived with some of his flock at Boston in August 1718. They settled at Haverhill, New Hampshire, and renamed it Londonderry.

Throughout his career Boyd took a prominent part in the non-subscription controversy in the General Synod of Ulster. He was among the majority of ministers who voluntarily subscribed the Westminster confession of faith at synod in 1721; and in 1724 he was a member of a committee appointed to draw up articles against Thomas Nevin, minister of Downpatrick (1711–44), accusing him of impugning the deity of Christ. On 25 April 1725 Boyd was installed by the Londonderry presbytery at Taughboyne, with a promised stipend of £50. The congregation had been without a minister since William Gray left for Usher's Quay, Dublin, in 1721. Gray returned to the neighbourhood of Taughboyne in 1727 and, without obtaining presbytery approval, began organizing a congregation in a disused corn kiln at nearby St Johnston. Following arbitration before church courts, Gray was deposed from the ministerial office and Boyd vindicated. In 1731 synod declared 'that Mr. Boid's character stands clear and unexceptionable & that his Doctrine and conversation has been suitable to his station & office as a minister of the Gospel' (*Records of the General Synod of Ulster*, 2.166). The St Johnston congregation was admitted to synod the same year.

Boyd was elected moderator of synod in 1730. At Antrim, in 1731, his sermon to synod was entitled 'A good conscience a necessary qualification of a gospel minister', and it was directed against a famous discourse by the non-subscribing minister of Antrim, John Abernethy, entitled *Religious Obedience Founded on Personal Persuasion*, which had been published in 1720. As an orthodox subscriber to the Westminster confession Boyd maintained that 'conscience is not the supreme lawgiver, the unerring witness, the infallible judge; it always bears respect unto God' (Witherow, *Memorials, 1731–1800*, 4). In 1734 he was an unsuccessful candidate for the clerkship of the general synod. In 1739 he took the lead against a licentiate, Richard Aprichard, who had scruples about some doctrines in the confession and who eventually withdrew from the synod. A number of presbyteries voiced concern at the synod in 1747, complaining of 'sundrie Errors and corruptions creeping in upon the Church' (*Records of the General Synod of Ulster*, 2.329). Boyd and eight other divines were appointed to draw up a 'Serious Warning' to be read from the pulpits against 'several dangerous errors that sap the very foundations of Christianity' (*Records of the General Synod of Ulster*, 2.330). These errors were in regard to such doctrines as original sin, the satisfaction of Christ, the Trinity, and the authority of scripture. The warning concluded by exhorting all to continue 'steadfast in the faith, that has been handed down to us … contained in the sacred scriptures of the Old and New testaments & summarily abridged in our Westminster Confession of faith, larger and shorter Catechisms' (ibid.).

Boyd was a constant attender at presbytery, general synod, and the sub-synod of Londonderry, where he was clerk from 1747 until 1766. He was appointed a trustee of the synod's Widows of Ministers Fund in 1761, and at that year's meeting of synod was a member of the group responsible for drawing up an address to George III. His last recorded appearance at the general synod was in 1770. Boyd married, but no details about his wife are known. He died on 2 May 1772 and was buried at Taughboyne.

ALEXANDER GORDON, *rev.* W. D. BAILIE

Sources *Records of the General Synod of Ulster, from 1691 to 1820*, 3 vols. (1890–98) · MS, minutes of the sub-synod of Derry, 1706–36, Presbyterian Historical Society, Belfast · MS, minutes of the sub-synod of Derry, 1744–1802, Presbyterian Historical Society, Belfast · J. McConnell and others, eds., *Fasti of the Irish Presbyterian church, 1613–1840*, rev. S. G. McConnell, 2 vols. in 12 pts (1935–51) · C. K. Bolton, *Scotch Irish pioneers in Ulster and America* (1910) · T. Witherow, *Historical and literary memorials of presbyterianism in Ireland, 1731–1800* (1880) · A. G. Lecky, *The Laggan and its presbyterianism* (1905)

Boyd, William, **fourth earl of Kilmarnock** (1705–1746), Jacobite army officer, the son and heir of William Boyd, third earl of Kilmarnock (1683/4–1717), and his wife,

Euphemia (*b.* 1684, *d.* in or before 1729), daughter of William, eleventh Lord Ross, was born on 12 May 1705 and baptized twelve days later at Kilmarnock. Styled Lord Boyd until succeeding his father in September 1717, he was educated at Glasgow University. During the 1715 Jacobite rising the third earl, a country whig by political background, raised a regiment in support of the government and the young Lord Boyd accompanied him on campaign.

Kilmarnock inherited an encumbered estate, and his straitened circumstances were made worse by what he later confessed was a 'careless and dissolute life' marked by 'vanity, and addictedness to impurity and sensual pleasure' (Foster, 10–11). In politics he long followed the lead of Sir Robert Walpole and the Campbells. He was a regular voter in peers' elections, invariably supporting the ministry's candidates. In the hotly contested election of 1734, opposition peers noted that he had been brought from France at government expense, and that he and his wife each received pensions of £200.

It is as a Jacobite, however, that Kilmarnock is best known. After Walpole's fall his pension was stopped, and he was drawn to the Stuart cause mainly because he saw it as an opportunity to retrieve his broken fortune. He later told the duke of Argyll:

> for the two Kings and their rights, I cared not a farthing which prevailed; but I was starving, and, by God, if Mahommed had set up his standard in the Highlands I had been a good Mussulman for bread, and stuck close to the party, for I must eat.   (Lenman, 256–7)

A likely contributing factor was the Jacobite leanings of his in-laws. On 15 June 1724 Kilmarnock, a lifelong member of the Church of Scotland, had married Lady Anne Livingston (*bap.* 1709, *d.* 1747), an episcopalian, whose father, James, fifth earl of Linlithgow and fourth earl of Callendar, had been attainted for his participation in the 'Fifteen. Through her maternal aunt, Lady Kilmarnock was also the presumptive heir of the countess of Erroll. A rumour circulated that the latter had threatened to disinherit the Kilmarnocks if the earl did not come out for the Young Pretender, Charles Edward Stuart.

Kilmarnock had no part in planning the rising of 1745 and joined the Jacobites only in October, after Charles Edward had visited Callendar House, near Falkirk, part of his wife's inheritance. One of the few lowland peers to join the rising, Kilmarnock wrote to his wife that 'I am now in my Boots to join the Prince' and that 'every Scotsman in his senses will go the same way' (Bailey, 25–6). He quickly became prominent in the Jacobite leadership and was named to the privy council. In the internal politics of the movement, he generally followed the prince's lead. He commanded a troop of Horse Guards on the march into England and later distinguished himself at the battle of Falkirk (17 January 1746), where his knowledge of local topography proved useful. (On the same occasion, Lady Kilmarnock was said to have contributed to the Jacobite victory by entertaining Henry Hawley, commander of the government army, with a leisurely breakfast at Callendar House, delaying his reaction to the Jacobite attack.) At the battle of Culloden (16 April 1746) Kilmarnock's troop formed part of the Jacobite reserve and fought dismounted. He was captured when, in the closing stages of the battle, he mistook royal dragoons for a Jacobite regiment.

Originally imprisoned at Inverness, Kilmarnock was later brought to London, where in late July he was tried for high treason in the House of Lords along with the earl of Cromarty and Lord Balmerino. Kilmarnock pleaded guilty and repented of his part in the rising. At the trial Horace Walpole noted that he looked younger than his forty-one years, 'tall and slender, with an extreme fine person', and that he behaved with 'a most just mixture between dignity and submission' (Walpole to Sir Horace Mann, 1 Aug 1746, Walpole, *Corr.*, 19.281). Though he won much sympathy, Kilmarnock and the other Jacobite lords were convicted and condemned to death. He still hoped for mercy, and the duke of Hamilton, Lady Townshend, and others pleaded for his life. Only Cromarty was pardoned, however, and Kilmarnock and Balmerino were beheaded on 18 August 1746 on Tower Hill. Kilmarnock, dressed in black, met his end bravely and acknowledged in a final statement that his was a just punishment. Though he and Balmerino parted as friends, the latter remained defiantly Jacobite and went to the block protesting his loyalty to the Stuarts.

The topic of their last conversation—whether, on the eve of Culloden, Jacobite orders had specified that no quarter be given government troops—became and has remained a subject of controversy. Though both men denied knowledge of such an order, Kilmarnock acknowledged that while a prisoner at Inverness he had heard that the duke of Cumberland had in his possession a no-quarter order signed by Lord George Murray, the Jacobite general. Some felt that Cumberland suspected Kilmarnock's complicity in the alleged no-quarter decision and that this had doomed his plea for mercy. (None of the surviving copies of the order in Murray's hand includes the no-quarter phrase, and doubts exist about the authenticity of the order that came into Cumberland's hands.)

Attainted, Kilmarnock's titles and estates were forfeited at his death. His eldest son, James, Lord Boyd, who had fought on the government side at Culloden, successfully regained them through litigation in 1751; in 1758 he inherited the earldom of Erroll from his great-aunt. Kilmarnock, whose head was reunited with his body in the coffin and not displayed, was buried on the day of his execution in the chapel of St Peter ad Vincula in the Tower.

The highest-ranking peer to be executed for participation in the 'Forty-Five, Kilmarnock's dramatic death was easily the most memorable feature of his career. In repudiating his actions in the rising he played the part expected of the condemned in the eighteenth century, though Balmerino's defiance made the latter the preferred hero in Jacobite tradition.   WILLIAM C. LOWE

Sources DNB · J. Foster, *An account of the behaviour of the late earl of Kilmarnock, after his sentence, and on the day of his execution* (1746) · Walpole, *Corr.*, vols. 9, 19 · F. McLynn, *The Jacobites* (1985) · G. B. Bailey, *Falkirk or paradise! The battle of Falkirk Muir, 17 January 1746* (1996) · W. Robertson, *Proceedings relating to the peerage of Scotland, from January 16, 1707 to April 29, 1788* (1790) · *Scots peerage*, vol. 5 · *Report on the manuscripts of Lord Polwarth*, 5 vols., HMC, 67 (1911–61) · D. Szechi, 'The Jacobite theatre of death', *The Jacobite challenge*, ed. E. Cruickshanks and J. Black (1988), 57–73 · F. J. McLynn, *Charles Edward Stuart: a tragedy in many acts* (1988) · B. Lenman, *The Jacobite risings in Britain, 1689–1746* (1980) · GEC, *Peerage*, new edn · W. A. Speck, *The Butcher: the duke of Cumberland and the suppression of the 45* (1981) · A. M. Smith, *Jacobite estates of the Forty-Five* (1982) · K. Tomasson and F. Buist, *Battles of the '45* (1962) · T. Salmon, *A short view of the families of the Scottish nobility* (1759)

Archives NL Scot., MS 16604 [contains letters from Kilmarnock to his wife]

Likenesses N. Parr, etching, engraving, 1746, NL Scot.; repro. in *Memoirs of the lives and families of the lords Kilmarnock, Cromertie and Balmerino* · J. Basire, engraving, Scot. NPG · N. Parr, line engraving, NPG · attrib. A. Ramsay, oils, Dick Institute, Kilmarnock · engraving, Scot. NPG · line engraving, BM · mezzotint · print (execution of Kilmarnock and Balmerino), repro. in J. Black, *Culloden and the '45* (1990), 191 · stipple, NPG

Wealth at death financial straits widely known; bankrupt: McLynn, *Jacobites*, 82

Boyd, Zachary (1585–1653), preacher and university administrator, was born in Kilmarnock, Ayrshire, of unknown parentage. He matriculated at Glasgow University in 1601, and graduated MA from St Andrews in 1607. Perhaps encouraged by his cousin Robert Boyd of Trochrig he completed his education at the protestant University of Saumur, where he was eventually appointed regent professor in 1611. Boyd declined the principalship in 1615 and he returned to Scotland in 1623. After living for a short time in the households of Sir William Scott in Elie (probably Sir William Scott of Clerkington, d. 1656) and the marquess of Hamilton, Boyd was called to the Barony parish in the suburbs of Glasgow, where he remained for the rest of his life.

Boyd enjoyed a long-time relationship with Glasgow University. He was elected dean in 1631, and was re-elected in 1633 and 1635. In 1634, and again in 1635 and 1645, he was elected rector, and in 1644 he was appointed vice-chancellor. Boyd married Elizabeth Fleming of Glasgow, who died in 1636, and Margaret Mure, who outlived him. Both marriages were childless. Remembered for his generosity towards Glasgow University, Boyd bequeathed it assets of approximately 20,000 marks. The source of his income remains a mystery.

Boyd was a supporter of the national covenant of 1638, and, like other Scots presbyters, he viewed Cromwell and his Independents as a threat to Scottish presbyterian government. An apocryphal story is told of how Boyd remained at his post, even while the magistrates and ministers of Glasgow fled in the face of Cromwell's army. Pagan indicates that when Cromwell and his officers appeared at the cathedral church, Boyd 'railed on them all to their very face in the High Church' (Pagan, 43–4). Cromwell's response was to invite Boyd for dinner, and the two were said to have spent the night together talking and praying.

Much of Boyd's published work is religious poetry of dubious merit. Samuel Colvil's observation is fairly typical when he wrote, 'bad lines many times causeth more mirth than good ones. Where one laughs the poems of Virgil, Homer, Ariosto, Du Bartas … twenty will laugh at those of … Mr. Zacharie Boyd' (Colvil, sig. A7r). Others were kinder, as when John Sleazer argued that Boyd's reputation as a bad poet was 'grossly exaggerated'. Boyd's published poetry appears in three separate collections: *The Garden of Zion* (1644), *The Psalms of David in Meeter* (1644), and *Scriptural Songs or Holy Poems* (1645), all of which are retellings of biblical stories. Two other collections of verse, the *Four Evangels* and *Zion's Flowers, or, Christian Poems for Spiritual Edification*, were never published, except for four of the poems of *Zion's Flowers*, brought out in 1855 by the Edinburgh bibliophile Gabriel Neil. Boyd's reputation as a bad poet was not helped when his metrical paraphrase of the Psalms was passed over by the commissioners of the general assembly, although he eventually did play a role in the development of the psalter, and merited a special thanks of the general assembly minuted on 1 January 1650.

Boyd's reputation as a poet has unquestionably influenced opinion about his prose, which is certainly worthy of attention as a revealing barometer of seventeenth-century Scottish religiosity. While his most important published prose work, *The Last Battell of the Soule in Death*, is long and prolix, it possesses a dramatic realism making it an important contribution to the tradition of the *ars moriendi*. Boyd's strength, though, was as a preacher, and his sermons exhibit a robustness that leaves Boyd well placed in relation to others who wrote in the plain style. A staunch Calvinist, Boyd took very seriously the special role of the preacher in the calling of God's elect to his true church. Only a handful of Boyd's sermons were published during his lifetime, *A Sermon of Preparation to the Communion* and *A Sermon for the Day of the Sacrament* (1629) and *Two Orientall Pearles, Grace and Glory* (1629). Boyd did leave behind, however, 254 unpublished sermons and devotional works currently housed in Glasgow University Library, which Boyd himself organized into a number of collections in anticipation of publication. His unpublished works cover a range of issues, including the need for church reform, the nature of the purified church, the role of preaching in the reform church, and the importance of rigorous spiritual self-examination.

Boyd died in Glasgow in 1653 and was buried there.

DAVID W. ATKINSON

Sources D. W. Atkinson, *Selected sermons of Zachary Boyd*, STS, 4th ser., 17 (1989) · G. Neil, introduction and appendix, in Z. Boyd, *Four poems from 'Zion's flowers', or, Christian poems for spiritual edification*, ed. G. Neil (1855) · J. M. Long, *Glasgow and the barony thereof: a review of three hundred years* (1895) · Chambers, *Scots.*, rev. T. Thomson (1875) · J. Sleazer, *Theatrum Scotiae* (1693); repr. (1855) · J. Pagan, *Sketch of the history of Glasgow* (1847) · [W. Thomson], ed., *Deeds instituting bursaries, scholarships, and other foundations, in the College and University of Glasgow*, Maitland Club, 69 (1850) · S. Colvil, *Mock poem, or, Whigs supplication* (1681)
Archives U. Glas. L., MSS 380–394, 400–401
Likenesses Trotter, line engraving, 1795, NPG · oils, U. Glas.

Boyd-Carpenter. For this title name *see* Carpenter, John Archibald Boyd-, Baron Boyd-Carpenter (1908–1998).

Boydell, John (1720–1804), engraver and printseller, the eldest of the seven children of Josiah Boydell (1691–1757?), surveyor and land steward, and his wife, Mary (1693/4–1777), was born at Dorrington in Shropshire on 19 January 1720. Like other men of his day he was disinclined to lose a year of his life to the change in calendar, and so always gave the year of his birth in old style, as 1719.

Youth and training, 1720–1750 As a child Boydell spent much time with his grandfather John (*d.* 1731), who was vicar of Ashbourne and rector of Mapleton, Derbyshire, and who instilled in him by the age of eight an enduring respect for moral rectitude. When he was twelve he moved with his family to Hawarden, Flintshire, where his father was land steward to Sir John Glynne. In 1739 he went to London to work for a Mr Cradock, before a place was found for him as house steward to John Lawton, MP for Newcastle under Lyme. Lawton refused Boydell's demand for a wage of 12 guineas per annum, and Boydell considered emigrating to the East Indies, but instead he walked back to Wales and his sweetheart Elizabeth, the daughter of Edward Lloyd, of the Fords, near Oswestry. Suddenly, he discovered his vocation:

> A large Print of Hawarden Castle and the Country adjacent drawn by Mr. Badeslade and engraved by Wm. Harry Toms in London was just finished. I admired it to a great degree, finding it was an employment that many have got a livelihood by—I thought I should like to Follow the art of Engraving. My Friends enquired of Mr. Badeslade relating to my wishes, wrote to Mr. Toms who offered to take me on trial. ('Autobiography', 82–3)

In 1741, at the advanced age of twenty, Boydell was bound apprentice to Toms for a £50 premium. Elizabeth promised to wait for him.

For the next six years Boydell lived with Toms in Union Court, Holborn. At first he copied prints after Claude and Poussin. He was advised to draw at the St Martin's Lane Academy and attended there five nights a week. His master was 'subject to be in Liquor, and very Outrageous and at such times striking his Servants and beating the wainscott with his fist' ('Autobiography', 85). But, to Boydell, Toms was 'very civil' and 'us'd to call me Mr Boydell—althou' an Apprentice' (ibid.). Boydell had little time for his colleagues in Toms's studio. Louis-Philippe Boitard, he recalled, 'lost much time in taking snuff', while Jean Baptiste Chatelain, who was paid by the hour, 'would often come for half an hour receive sixpence go and spend it amongst bad women in Chick Lane and Black-boy Alley' (ibid., 83). Boydell himself would have made the perfect model for Hogarth's industrious apprentice. In 1746 he engraved a large plate of Penzance and paid Toms a further £30 to release him from his final year's service. After two years as a journeyman, lodging with a stationer called Wroughton, he considered himself able to support a wife, and in 1748 he went back to Wales to marry Elizabeth Lloyd. He took with him four drawings by Gainsborough and four copperplates and, having engraved these, spent his honeymoon summer drawing views of Snowdonia, the Welsh castles, and the High Peak for later publication. Four views near Ipswich after Gainsborough and a view of

John Boydell (1720–1804), by Sir William Beechey, 1801

Wrexham church were published in December 1748. His initial method of selling his prints was to:

> carry them in the Morning my self in a Portfolio to all the Print Shops in the City. In the afternoon to all in the West End of Town, brought what I received and always gave it to my Wife to take care of. (ibid., 86)

He worked hard. During 1750 he published twenty-eight landscapes.

Foundations of the business, 1750–1770 By 1751, having amassed a total capital of £150, Boydell took the bold decision to purchase the freedom of the City in the Stationers' Company and take a shop, with the sign of the Unicorn, at the corner of Queen Street in Cheapside. In old age he told Joseph Farington that 'his wife was alarmed at the boldness of this determination & wept at the danger of incurring such expence' (Farington, *Diary*, 1415). Within a year he took two apprentices: his brother Thomas paid no fee, but Richard Ford, son of an art auctioneer, brought both £40 and, in his father, a valuable ally. Boydell realized quickly that the main demand both from collectors and for decoration was for foreign prints, so he determined to equip himself to deal internationally. He taught himself French, with a grammar, a dictionary, and *Les aventures de Télémaque*, and by attending a foreign chapel at St James. By degrees he accustomed himself 'to speak and write the Language which enabled me to Correspond with Foreigners—which was of great service to me' ('Autobiography', 84). In particular he got to know the leading Parisian printseller Pierre-François Basan.

During the next few years Boydell's business strategy took shape. He was an active committee man, taking livery in the Stationers' Company on 2 April 1754 and becoming common councillor for the ward of Cheap in 1758. In January 1756 he was selected to retail prints published by the Society of Antiquaries for a 20 per cent commission. Meanwhile he expanded his stock of plates by buying others secondhand. Joseph Goupy's plates comprised one of his first major acquisitions, in 1755, and he bought Picart's *Impostures Innocentes* in 1756. It was only now that he began speculative publishing. Boydell joined the Society for the Encouragement of Arts, Manufactures, and Commerce in 1760 and immediately undertook publication of the paintings that won its major prizes. He had commissioned a young landscape specialist, William Woollett, to engrave a Claude in 1760. Now he commissioned Woollett to engrave two paintings by Richard Wilson and two by the brothers Smith of Chichester; he also commissioned François Ravenet to engrave the prizewinning history painting. This venture proved highly profitable. Woollett's *Niobe*, in particular, drew great critical accolades and sold very well abroad, helping Boydell to pay for his imports in kind rather than in cash. Boydell then launched a major initiative billed as *A Collection of Prints, Engraved from the most Capital Paintings in England*. The original proposal was for seven numbers at a guinea per number. A subscription for 251 copies was headed by the king, the princess dowager, and the earl of Bute. Boydell himself engraved several prints for the collection, but he was wise enough to realize that he himself would never be more than a pedestrian engraver. His claim for this enterprise was that it would give talented young English engravers an opportunity to try their hand at engraving history pictures, and, although he gave some of the most important engravings to experienced expatriates such as François Ravenet, this major enterprise did help to establish several promising artists [see Boydell, John, engravers]. The prints also sold very well abroad: even among subscribers almost a third were foreigners. Boydell presented the first complete volume to the king in 1769.

The great merchant printseller, 1770–1790 As Boydell's *Collection* took shape he moved to a larger house at 90 Cheapside. A second volume was completed in 1772. Into this some English paintings by William Hogarth, Benjamin West, and Nathaniel Dance were introduced. A third volume, compiled in 1773, consisted entirely of republished prints from celebrated plates that Boydell had acquired secondhand. He added two more volumes before 1786. The *Collection* was the backbone of Boydell's empire, but he substantiated his position as the publisher of the finest works of art in Britain with two further projects. In 1775 he announced plans to engrave the Walpole collection at Houghton Hall, Norfolk, before it was sold to Catherine the Great of Russia and to publish the duke of Devonshire's book of designs by Claude. In addition he published a number of fine mezzotints of paintings by Rembrandt.

When it came to publishing contemporary paintings Boydell was only one of several notable figures, but he was nevertheless responsible for the publication of some of the most impressive paintings of the period. He was the publisher of Joseph Wright of Derby's *Orrery* (1768), *Air Pump* (1769), *Blacksmith's Shop* (1771), and *Iron Forge* (1773), which are among the finest mezzotints ever engraved. He published Reynolds's celebrated history painting *Ugolino* (1774) and several paintings by the court favourites Dance, Johann Zoffany, and West. He cemented his place in royal favour with huge mezzotints of the king's paintings *Regulus's Return to Carthage* (1771) and *Hannibal Swearing Enmity to the Romans* (1773), by West. Boydell owned only a third share with Woollett and Ryland in West's *Death of Wolfe* (1775), but this proved to be an enormously successful plate, and after the untimely deaths of Ryland and Woollett he acquired the whole copyright. Now Boydell began to work on a munificent scale. In 1779 he bought from West *Alfred the Great Dividing his Loaf with the Pilgrim* and presented it to the Stationers' Company, turning his generosity to account through an engraving of it by Sharp. In 1784 Boydell paid Copley £800 for *The Death of Major Peirson*. He acquired Hogarth's plates in 1786.

Boydell's shop, with its grand second-floor showroom (10 ft x 70 ft) lit from above, with pictures displayed on hinged screens, became a tourist attraction. In the inner gallery he displayed paintings that he had bought and published together with the portraits of artists who had painted and engraved them for him. Over the chimney was *The Death of Major Peirson*.

Meanwhile Boydell's career in public office continued. Apart from a brief interruption in 1771, he was common councillor for Cheap until 1782, in which year he became an alderman. He was commonly thereafter referred to as Alderman Boydell. He served as sheriff in 1785, as master of the Stationers' Company in 1783–4, and as steward of the Marine Society in 1785. He was closely associated with the Royal Academy and a regular guest at their dinners, and he made not infrequent visits to court. Elizabeth Boydell died on 27 January 1781 and was buried at St Martin Pomeroy on 4 February 1781. Thereafter, Boydell's household was run by his niece Mary. He took her brother Josiah *Boydell into partnership in 1786.

At a dinner at Josiah Boydell's house in West End, Hampstead, in November 1786 Boydell eagerly embraced a proposal that he might publish a series of prints illustrating the works of Shakespeare. The project rapidly took shape, and proposals dated 1 December 1786 were published in the press. The Boydells and the bookseller George Nicol proposed the works of Shakespeare edited by George Steevens, with typography by Bulmer and paper by Whatman. These would be embellished with one series of large and another series of small prints, all taken from specially commissioned paintings by artists led by Joshua Reynolds and Angelica Kaufmann and engravers led by Caroline Watson and Francesco Bartolozzi. The alliance between the Boydells and Nicol was cemented when Mary married the bookseller on 8 September 1787. A rejected suitor, an apothecary named Elliot, was so desperate that he attempted to shoot her from close range but, 'Providentially, though they were so close as to set fire to the lady's cloack, yet by the balls glancing on her stays, she received only a slight contusion under the shoulder' (*British Mercury*, 1787, 152). In September the newly-weds went with John Boydell to Paris, where they dined with Boydell's principal correspondent, Basan.

To house the Shakespeare paintings a new gallery was built in Pall Mall. Reynolds was given an advance of £500 to secure his first contribution, but the Boydells immediately fell out with Gainsborough, who wanted equal pay, and soon after with Wright of Derby, whose *Romeo and Juliet* they then rejected. The fact was that they could not, or would not, afford to pay the best artists enough to secure their services. The problem was even more acute with engravers. To engrave large prints in line took a very long time, and the best engravers already had their hands full with work of their own. Josiah Boydell, who had the management of the project, chose to have most of the prints engraved in stipple—chiefly, perhaps, for the sake of speed—and many were given to inexperienced young artists, who nevertheless had to be paid 300 guineas a plate. The gallery opened in May 1789 with thirty-four paintings by eighteen artists on show: 20,000 people visited, 6600 catalogues were sold, and 100 names were added to the subscription. The last figure might have been disappointing but, with Boydell's more ambitious projects, success or failure rested on sales abroad. At home his triumph was complete. He was chosen as lord mayor for 1790–91 and his niece Mary acted as his mayoress.

Decline and death, 1790–1804 When the first 'Shakspeare' prints (Boydell used the contracted form of the name) came out in 1792 they were not well received. The grandiloquent claims that had been made for the project as a forum for British history painting now rebounded on the publishers. The painters blamed the engravers. West told Farington that 'He had looked over the Shakespere Prints and was sorry to see them of such inferior quality'. He complained of a 'general defficiency in respect of drawing' and 'did not wonder many subscribers had declined to continue their subscriptions' (Farington, *Diary*, 2331). Others were more critical of the paintings, few of which showed much flair. The engraver William Byrne blamed the publishers, telling Farington that:

> J. Boydell had ruined publications by his manner of managing the Shakespeare work, which had been sacrificed to a narrow economy; That the subscriptions to it had fallen off near two thirds. Alderman Boydell is excused, the blame is imputed to J. Boydell. (ibid., 631)

Well into his seventies, the alderman seemed undaunted by this set-back, though he admitted to Farington that these days:

> if He rises at 5 in the morning He is obliged to lay on a couch for an Hour in the course of the day.—He said He had always been an early riser and a moderate eater. He said he drank milk in the morning, which agreed with him & he thought did him more service than anything. (Farington, *Diary*, 209)

About 1794 he presented the corporation of London with twenty-four paintings, most of which had been commissioned for publication and had been hanging in 90 Cheapside. But perhaps even he was feeling the strain of his business difficulties. The problems with Shakespeare were dwarfed by the disastrous effect on the European trade in luxury goods of the French invasions of the Netherlands and the Rhineland. By 1797 it was clear that the Boydells were in trouble. By November 1803 they were in debt to the tune of £41,000 and had to stop payments. Their bank had loaned £12,000 with the houses in Pall Mall and Cheapside as security, but there were worries about bankruptcy. They had applied to parliament for leave to conduct a lottery to raise money by disposing of the Shakspeare Gallery and its contents. Josiah Boydell hoped the lottery would raise £80,000 (and it did raise £78,000), but before it could be drawn the great alderman was dead.

Josiah Boydell told Farington that his uncle had caught a cold by going to the Old Bailey to do his duty as an alderman on a damp, foggy day; he died, presumably at his house in Cheapside, on 12 December 1804. Farington noted that he was opened after his death and all the material parts were in so good a state that it was thought he might have lived ten years longer had this accidental complaint not attacked him. He was buried at St Olave Jewry on 19 December 1804. Some time later, his niece Mary Nicol bequeathed money to pay for a bust and memorial tablet to be placed in the church.

In his public pronouncements Boydell tended to suggest that he had created an export business in British prints single-handedly and that his Shakspeare Gallery provided the first opportunity for British history painters. This was a great exaggeration. John Landseer was not afraid to assert that fine engravers such as Strange, Ryland, and Woollett had done more for the reputation of British engraving than Boydell, and other publishers had helped to ensure that contemporary British art was widely respected long before the Shakspeare Gallery was projected. Nevertheless, Boydell was the most important single print publisher during the period in which British art rose to European prominence. Moreover, his shrewd selection of paintings for publication and of fine young engravers to interpret them produced, especially in the 1760s and 1770s, some of the most distinguished (and profitable) copperplates to be crafted in Britain. No print publisher before or since has ever exerted as much influence on the course of British art. TIMOTHY CLAYTON

Sources 'An autobiography of John Boydell, engraver', ed. W. B. Jones, *Flintshire Historical Society Publications*, 11 (1925), 81–7 • Farington, *Diary* • S. Bruntjen, *John Boydell, 1719–1804: a study of art patronage and publishing in Georgian London* (1985) • W. H. Friedman, *Boydell's Shakespeare Gallery* (1976) • D. F. McKenzie, ed., *Stationers' Company apprentices*, [3]: *1701–1800* (1978) • A. B. Beaven, ed., *The aldermen of the City of London, temp. Henry III–[1912]*, 2 vols. (1908–13) • 'Sketch of the life and character of Alderman Boydell', *European Magazine*, 21 (1792), 243 • *Morning Post* (14 Nov 1786) • S. von la Roche, *Sophie in London, 1786* (1947), 237–9 • A. Graves, 'Boydell and his engravers', *The Queen* (30 July 1904), 178–9 • J. Parry, *Extraordinary characters of the nineteenth century* (1805) • G. M. Rubinstein, 'Richard Earlom (1743–1822) and Boydell's *Houghton gallery*', *Print Quarterly*, 8 (1991), 2–27 • *Annual Register* (1804) • *GM*, 1st ser., 74 (1804), 1177–8 • C. A. White, *Sweet Hampstead and its associations* (1903) • correspondence, Free Library of Philadelphia, Philadelphia, John Frederick Lewis collection of autographs of engravers • will, PRO, PROB 11/1421, sig. 152 • J. Evans, *A history of the Society of Antiquaries* (1956), 117–18 • T. Clayton, *The English print, 1688–1802* (1997)

Archives Flintshire RO, Hawarden, autobiography | Birm. CA, letters to Matthew Boulton
Likenesses V. Green, mezzotint, pubd 1772 (after J. Boydell), BM, NPG • attrib. studio of Reynolds, double portrait, oils, *c*.1775 (with his wife), Sir Thomas Adams Grammar School, Newport, Shropshire • J. Gillray, caricature, etching with aquatint, 1789 (*Shakespeare sacrificed*) • J. Graham, oils, 1792, Stationers' Hall, London • J. Gillray, caricature, etching with aquatint, 1797 • W. Beechey, oils, 1801, Guildhall Art Gallery, London [*see illus.*] • A. Van Assen, etching, 1804 (after J. Parry) • T. Barks, bust, V&A • W. Beechey, oils, second version, NPG • J. Condé, stipple (after A. Pope), BM, NPG; repro. in *European Magazine* (1792) • J. Gillray, caricature, etching (*A peep into the Shakespeare Gallery*) • H. Meyer, stipple (after G. Stuart), BM, NPG; repro. in *Contemporary portraits* (1814) • F. Wheatley, group portrait, drawing (*Interior of the Shakespeare Gallery*), V&A

Boydell, John, engravers (*act.* 1760–1804), printmakers, came to prominence in the rapid expansion of the Boydell publishing business in the later 1760s. With his career as a printmaker coming to a close around 1760, John *Boydell (1720–1804) emerged as the most important employer of engravers in late eighteenth-century London. Still listing himself as an importer of prints in the early 1760s, by 1770 he was exporting to the European market, marking the maturation of the British school. The network of engravers whose talents he employed reflects both the patriotic concerns of the publisher, in being dominated by indigenous artists, and the commercial nature of his ventures. Boydell did not raise a school as such, but rather cultivated a variety of talents, calling on these according to the nature of the project in hand. All of Boydell's engravers worked in a variety of genres and for different publishers.

Aside from the high-profile engravers Francesco Bartolozzi (1728–1813) and Lewis Schiavonetti (1765–1810), Boydell employed a number of foreigners, notably the brothers Haid and the brothers Facius, and the French printmaker Jean Baptiste Michel [*see below*]. The brothers **Johann Gottfried Haid** (1710–1776) and **Johann Elias Haid** (1739–1809) were members of a distinguished artistic family from Augsburg, the place of their birth. Johann Gottfried was trained by his father, Johann Lorenz Haid, and Johann Elias by his elder brother. They worked almost exclusively for Boydell during a period in London from 1764 to 1767, producing prints after Zoffany, Reynolds, and the old masters. After that date Johann Elias returned to Augsburg, where he died in 1809, while Johann Gottfried went to Vienna to teach at the new Kupferstecher-Academie; he died in that city in 1776. The brothers **Johann Gottlieb Facius** (*b. c*.1750, *d.* in or before 1813) and **Georg Siegmund Facius** (*b. c*.1750, *d.* in or before 1813) were both born in Regensburg about 1750. Specialists in stipple-engraving, they studied in Brussels, where their father was Russian consul. They were working exclusively for Boydell in London from 1776, and collaboratively they engraved and stippled for him several plates after William Hamilton and Angelica Kauffmann, James Barry's *Birth of Venus* (1778), and reproductions of Sir Joshua Reynolds's stained-glass windows for New College, Oxford (1785). Georg Facius also showed miniatures at the Royal Academy between 1785 and 1788, giving addresses in Leicester Fields and Soho. The brothers contributed four large-format plates to the *Shakspeare Gallery*, being paid the higher rate of £367. In 1798 Farington reported that one or other Facius was among the many foreigners imprisoned, but he was bailed out by Boydell. One of their last jobs for Boydell was a plate after West's *Ascension*, published on 2 January 1797, though they were still active in 1813. **Jean Baptiste Michel** (1738/1748–1804), born in Paris in 1738 or 1748, studied in that city under Pierre Chenu (1718–1780), who had also worked for Boydell. Michel moved to London about 1780 and specialized in engravings combining line and stipple techniques. His first print for Boydell was *William de Albanac presents his three daughters to Alfred III, king of Mercia*, after West (published 9 November 1782), and plates for the *Houghton Gallery*. He also worked on two of the large-format plates for the *Shakspeare Gallery*, and was paid the higher rate of £367. He is said to have produced more than thirty plates for Boydell over the years. Michel died in 1804.

Boydell's claim to have reinvigorated a native school of printmaking is borne out by the careers of a number of British-born engravers whose talents he actively cultivated. Prominent among these is the printmaker and draughtsman **Richard Earlom** (1743–1822), the son of William Earlom and his wife, Margaret, baptized on 14 May 1743 at St Sepulchre, Holborn, where his father was the vestry clerk. He is said to have been introduced to the painter G. B. Cipriani through a neighbour in Cow Lane, Smithfield, a coach-maker who mended the lord mayor's coach (decorated by the Italian artist). He studied with Cipriani, and at the St Martin's Lane Academy and the duke of Richmond's gallery of casts. From 1757 to 1766 he frequently won premiums and prizes for drawing and for engraving at the Society of Arts, including in 1765 a premium for an original drawing of *Numa Pompilius Refusing the Roman Sovereignty*. He exhibited his prize-winning drawing of *The Dancing Faun* with the Free Society of Artists in 1762, and in 1767 exhibited the drawing after West of his *Story of Pyrrhus* (engraved by John Hall and published by Boydell in 1769). In 1773 he went to Houghton Hall, Norfolk, with George and Joseph Farington and Josiah Boydell to copy works in the collection, published by Boydell as *The Houghton Gallery* (1774–88). His outstanding achievements for Boydell were the fifty-one plates after Cipriani intended for use by art students and the 300 plates after Claude, published as the *Liber veritatis* (1777–1819). He was paid the unusually high rate of £420 for the single large engraving he created for the *Shakspeare Gallery*, Fuseli's *Lear*. Although he worked predominantly for Boydell throughout his career, he also produced prints for the publishers Robert Sayer (notably the mezzotint after Zoffany's *Royal Academicians*, 1773), Laurie and Whittle, and B. B. Evans. He continued to work for Boydell & Co. after John Boydell's death. A son, Thomas, is said to have died in 1789 aged only seventeen. Earlom is estimated to have produced more than 500 engravings, seventy portraits, sixty mezzotints, and many illustrations, including mezzotints to Thornton's *The Temple of Flora* (1799/1807) and Woodburn's *Portraits of Characters Illustrated in British History* (1810). He is noted as a considerable technical

innovator, combining mezzotint with other techniques with particular delicacy. By 1817 his eyesight was failing, and he had retired from art. He died on 9 October 1822, at Exmouth Street, Clerkenwell, leaving an estate valued at nearly £14,000, largely benefiting his widow and the children of his deceased daughter.

The printmakers employed by Boydell generally worked over a range of genres. **Thomas Cook** (1744/5?–1818), a pupil of Simon Francis Ravenet, was a relatively minor figure who none the less undertook a range of projects for the publisher. In 1770 he won a silver pallet for drawing outlines of the human figure at the Society of Arts. Cook worked as a printmaker in a number of contexts, producing portraits for the *Gentleman's Magazine* and frontispieces for book publishers, as well as a number of single plates in different genres for Boydell. He was most famous for his reproductions of the works of Hogarth, published as *Hogarth Restored* in 1806. These were much scorned for their inferior technique. He also engraved the reduced reproductions of Hogarth for Nichols and Stevens's *Genuine Works of William Hogarth* (1808–17). Cook died in 1818, probably in April, according to the *Gentleman's Magazine*, at the age of seventy-four, which may identify him as the Thomas Cook, son of William Cook and his wife, Judith, baptized at St Luke's, Old Street, on 18 January 1745.

Working primarily on reproductions of works by modern artists was **Joseph Collyer the younger** (1748–1827), born on 14 September 1748, the son of Joseph *Collyer the elder (1714/15–1776), a translator and writer, and his wife, Mary *Collyer, *née* Mitchell (1716/17–1762), also a writer. He was a pupil of Anthony Walker (*c*.1726–1765), an engraver who worked for Boydell in the early 1760s (notably on Woollett's *Niobe* plate). On Walker's death, Collyer continued to study with the engraver's brother, William Walker. In 1761 he won a prize for drawing at the Society of Arts. Collyer enrolled as an engraver at the Royal Academy Schools on 14 March 1771, giving his age as '22 last Sept'. Having come to the notice of Boydell, he engraved for him a plate after Teniers, and subsequently reproduced works by contemporary artists, including Wheatley and Reynolds. He produced one large plate and two smaller prints for the *Shakspeare Gallery* and also worked as a book illustrator. He exhibited engravings at the Society of Artists exhibitions of 1770, 1778, and 1780, and at the Free Society of Artists in 1779. Collyer was made an associate of the Royal Academy in 1786, and, with Earlom and James Fittler [see below], was proposed as a director of the charitable Society of Engravers vaunted, unsuccessfully, in 1788. He exhibited engravings at the Royal Academy in 1789 and 1791–2, and intermittently from 1797 to 1822, giving his address as 8 Constitution Row, Gray's Inn Road. He was appointed portrait engraver to Queen Charlotte, and was a member of the Stationers' Company, becoming master in 1815. He died at his home on Constitution Row on 24 December 1827.

A number of Boydell's engravers specialized in landscape imagery. Said to have been of French extraction, **Daniel Lerpinière** (1745–1785) was born in London. With

Fittler, he was Boydell's prime engraver of marines. He was a pupil of Francis Vivares, whose manner he followed in his own line-engravings. He exhibited with the Free Society of Artists between 1773 and 1779 and in 1783, giving addresses in Vauxhall Road and Lambeth. Lerpinière seems to have worked exclusively for Boydell from the mid-1770s. He collaborated with Fittler on the large plates of the naval engagements of George Farmer and Captain Pearson, after Paton, issued by Boydell in 1780. In a list of plates issued in 1784 Boydell says he paid the engraver as much as 150 guineas for his print of *The Relief of Gibraltar*, after Paton, and 40 guineas each for *Morning* and *Evening*, after Cuyp and Pynaker respectively. Lerpinière died at Walcot Place, Lambeth, in 1785. **James Fittler** (1758–1835) was born in London in October 1758. In 1776 he exhibited two sketches, including a portrait of General James Wolfe, with the Free Society of Artists, giving his address as 'At Mr Fittler's, Wells Street, near Germain Street, St James's'. He enrolled at the Royal Academy Schools as a student of engraving in April 1778, giving his age as '22 next Oct.', and in 1781 married Elizabeth Johnson. He exhibited at the academy from 1788 to 1824 and was elected an associate in 1800. Fittler was appointed marine engraver to George III. He also contributed one large plate and four small illustrations to the *Shakspeare Gallery*. In 1790–91 he co-published with John Love *Views of Weymouth*, and he was copublisher with Robert Bowyer in 1795 of an illustrated Bible, losing, according to Farington, £1500 in the venture. None the less, he later appears as publisher of engravings after John Claude Nattes's views of Scotland (1804) and a folio set of reproductions of Raphael's *Cartoons* (1810). According to Farington, his daughter married a hatter who went bankrupt, further aggravating Fittler's financial difficulties. His last published works were illustrations to Dibdin's *Aedes Althorpinae* (1822), after which he appears to have retired from art; his drawings and prints were sold off at Sothebys on 14–16 July 1825. He died at Turnham Green on 2 December 1835 and was buried in the churchyard of St Nicholas, Chiswick.

Among the many engravers in the employ of Boydell specializing in landscape was **James Peak** [Peake] (c.1730–c.1782), who may have been the son of James and Elizabeth Peak baptized at St Sepulchre, Holborn, on 2 May 1731. Intermittently between 1761 and 1771 he showed engravings with the Society of Artists, giving an address in Fleet Street and then 'At Mr Perrin's, Watchmaker, facing St Clement's Church'. He produced etched views and prints in a great variety of genres, although predominantly landscape. For Boydell he worked on plates after Claude, George Smith of Chichester, Richard Wilson, and Pillement. His name appears as both Peak and Peake in the original exhibition catalogues and even on published prints. He is believed to have died around 1782. **Francis Chesham** (1749–1806) exhibited engravings at the Society of Artists in 1777–8 and 1780. He worked for a number of publishers, specializing particularly in landscape views, although he also engraved, for instance, the designs of Charles Catton for the third volume of *The English Peerage*

(1790). For Boydell, he engraved the plate of *Admiral Parker's Victory* (1782), after Robert Dodd, and two of George Robertson's views of Coalbrookdale, the others being by Lowry and Fittler. **John Pye** (b. 1746, d. after 1789) was a pupil of Thomas Major and won first prize in the competition for drawing the human figure at the Society of Arts in 1760. Between 1769 and 1773 he exhibited engravings with the Society of Artists, giving addresses at Lincoln's Inn Fields, Fenchurch Street, and finally 19 Cornhill. He enrolled as a student at the Royal Academy Schools in March 1777, giving his age as thirty-one. Pye specialized in landscape etchings, and for Boydell in the mid-1770s he produced plates after Cuyp, Claude, and Rembrandt and prints after Vernet and Kauffmann. Pye is said to have used the talents of **Samuel Middiman** (1750–1831) on plates published under his name only. Middiman was apprenticed in 1767 to William Byrne (1743–1805), an engraver who had studied with Aliamet and Wille in Paris, and who worked for Boydell in the later 1760s. Middiman is also said to have worked with Woollett and Bartolozzi. He exhibited at the Free Society of Artists in 1771 and showed drawings and prints with the Society of Artists from 1772 to 1777, giving addresses in St James's Square and then Wells Street, Oxford Road. In 1780–82 and 1795–7 he exhibited drawings and stained drawings at the academy, giving addresses in Margaret Street, Winchester Row, and Warren Place. On 5 April 1788 he married Martha Woodyer at St Pancras. Middiman produced three large plates and one smaller illustration for the *Shakspeare Gallery*. As a specialist landscape etcher his skills were much in demand, and he is said to have worked on many plates issued under the sole name of other engravers, for instance John Pye. He produced the fifty-three plates for *Select Views in Great Britain* (1814) and sixteen plates for *Picturesque Castles and Abbeys in England and Wales* (1807–11). About 1812 he gave up engraving and appears to have turned to landscape painting, exhibiting pictures at the British Institution in 1810–11 and again in 1824. He died on 20 December 1831 at Cirencester Place, Westbourne Park.

Although Boydell's print production was dominated by landscapes and reproductions of old masters, his most significant contribution to British art can be considered the patriotic *Shakspeare Gallery* project conceived in 1786. Boydell employed more than forty different engravers for the large-format and quarto versions of the gallery's prints. A number of high-profile engravers, including William Sharp, Bartolozzi, Schiavonetti, and Earlom, were employed on a handful of the plates, being paid exceptionally high rates. **Francis Legat** (1755–1809) can be considered in this company. Born in Edinburgh, he studied at the Trustees' Academy in that city under Alexander Runciman and was a pupil of the engraver Andrew Bell (1726–1810). In 1780 he moved to London, lodging at 22 Charles Street. His first prints for Boydell were *The Continence of Scipio*, after Poussin (published 1784), and *Mary, Queen of Scots*, after Gavin Hamilton (published 1786). Although he produced only four large prints for the *Shakspeare Gallery*, he was among the best paid of the engravers to work on the project. He was rewarded £500 by Boydell for engraving Barry's *Lear and Cordelia* and £450 for West's *Hamlet*; only Bartolozzi and Sharp were paid more. By 1790 he had moved to Sloane Square, and in 1797 was living in Pleasant Row, where his mother died in 1799. In 1796 he exhibited at the academy *A Girl and Pigeons* and in 1800 *Maternal Solicitude*, indicating forays into original sentimental imagery. He later lodged with a Mr Proctor at Charles Street, Middlesex Hospital, the address given in the 1800 academy exhibition catalogue; this supports reports of financial difficulties later in life, despite his being appointed historical engraver to the prince of Wales. He died on 7 April 1809, apparently in a state of depression, and was buried at St Pancras Church.

More prolific in their contributions to the *Shakspeare Gallery* were Anker Smith, John Peter Simon [*see below*], and Robert Thew [*see below*]. **Anker Smith** (1759–1819), printmaker and miniature painter, was born in London, the son of William Smith, a silk merchant in Cheapside, and his wife, Mary, and was baptized at All Hallows, Honey Lane, on 5 March 1759. After a period at the Merchant Taylors' School, in 1777 he was articled to his maternal uncle, the attorney John Hoole, but encouraged by James Heath he turned instead to art. From 1779 to 1782 he studied with the engraver Taylor, and then worked as an assistant to Heath. In 1787 he was commissioned to engrave for Bell's *British Poets*, and from the same date he was employed as a line-engraver for Boydell and contributed ten small plates to the *Shakspeare Gallery*. In 1794 and from 1796 to 1800 he exhibited engravings and miniatures at the Royal Academy, and in 1797 he was made an associate of the academy. The catalogues record addresses in Chelsea, Old Bond Street, and finally Upper Ranelagh Street. Smith married Charlotte Susannah Snape, at St Andrew by the Wardrobe, on 1 November 1791. They had a daughter, Charlotte (*b.* 5 Nov 1792), and three sons who went on to be artists: **Frederick William Smith** (*bap.* 1797, *d.* 1835), a sculptor and pupil of Chantrey, who died young on 18 January 1835; Edwin Dalton Smith (*bap.* November 1800), a miniature painter; and **Herbert Luther Smith** (*bap.* 1809, *d.* 1870), a painter. He also adopted and trained his nephew the miniature painter William Charles Ross. Anker Smith was one of the original governors of the Society of Engravers, formed in London in 1803, and he produced illustrations after Singleton for editions of *The Arabian Nights* (1802), *Gil Blas* (1809), and *Don Quixote* (1818). He died of apoplexy in London on 23 June 1819, his death being announced at the academy on 5 July that year.

John Peter Simon (1764?–*c*.1810) enrolled at the Royal Academy Schools on 31 December 1778, giving his age as '14 1st August last', though most authorities give his date of birth as about 1750. Specializing in stipple, Simon contributed to Worlidge's *Collection of Drawings from Curious Antique Gems* (1768) and produced many prints after contemporary British artists, notably William Hamilton and Reynolds. He contributed to Boydell's *Houghton Gallery*, engraved individual plates, notably after Thomas Gainsborough's *The Woodman* (published 1791), and produced fifteen large plates and four small plates for the *Shakspeare*

Gallery. This output included the small version of Opie's *Capulet Finds Juliet Dead* (1792), which was rejected by Boydell, who later commissioned William Blake to produce an alternative version. Simon's plates for the gallery are marred by the poor reproduction of the etched underdrawing. He is said to have died around 1810. **Robert Thew** (1758–1802) was born at Patrington, Yorkshire, the son of an innkeeper. He was reportedly brought up as a cooper, although it is also said that he served in his youth as a professional soldier. In 1783 he settled in Hull and either taught himself engraving or, more probably, received some training from a local practitioner. Despite these lowly beginnings, Thew came to the notice of Boydell, and from 1790 he worked very extensively on the *Shakspeare Gallery*. He produced twenty-one of the large-format reproductive prints. Thew, who was appointed engraver to the prince of Wales, died at Roxley, Stevenage, in July 1802.

MARTIN MYRONE

Sources T. Dodd, 'Memoirs of English engravers, 1550–1800', BL, Add. MSS 33394–33407 · S. Bruntjen, *John Boydell, 1719–1804: a study of publishing and patronage in Georgian London* (1985) · W. H. Friedman, *Boydell's Shakespeare Gallery* (1976) · A. Graves, 'Boydell and his engravers', *The Queen* (July 1904–July 1905) · J. Strutt, *A biographical dictionary, containing an historical account of all the engravers, from the earliest period of the art of engraving to the present time*, 2 vols. (1785–6) · W. Pope and F. Benwick, eds., *The Boydell Shakespeare Gallery* (1996) · J. T. Smith, *Nollekens and his times*, 2 vols. (1828) · D. Alexander and R. Godfrey, *Painters and engraving: the reproductive print from Hogarth to Wilkie* (1980) [exhibition catalogue, Yale U. CBA, 1980] · T. Clayton, *The English print, 1688–1802* (1997) · J. Pye, *Patronage of British art* (1845) · Society for the Encouragement of Arts, Manufactures, and Commerce, *A register of the premiums and bounties given by the Society … 1754 to 1776* (1778) · Farington, *Diary* · G. M. Rubinstein, 'Richard Earlom and Boydell's Houghton gallery', *Print Quarterly*, 8 (1991), 2–27 · DNB

Archives Birm. CA, letters to Matthew Bourton [John Boydell]

Boydell, Josiah (1752–1817), artist and publisher, was born on 18 January 1752 at the Manor House, Hawarden, Flintshire, the fourth of nine children of Samuel Boydell (1727–1783), farmer, and his wife Ann, *née* Turner (1725–1764). Apprenticed in 1766 to his uncle, John *Boydell, for seven years, he studied painting under Benjamin West and mezzotint engraving under Richard Earlom. His later, principal, plates included *Charles I*, *Jane Wenman* (after Van Dyck and published in 1778 and 1779, respectively) and the frontispiece to *Liber veritatis* (a self-portrait of Claude Lorrain).

When John Boydell undertook to publish engravings after the paintings in Houghton Hall, Norfolk, prior to their imminent export to the empress of Russia, Josiah Boydell, with Joseph and George Farington, made the necessary drawings in preparation for the engravers. While in Norfolk he married, on 6 December 1774, Jane North (*fl.* 1760–1820), granddaughter of Sir Roger North. They were to have several children, one of whom, John North Boydell, became involved in the family publishing business. An accomplished artist as well as engraver, Josiah Boydell exhibited at the Royal Academy between 1772 and 1779, giving his addresses in London as 90 Cheapside (1772–3), Great Castle Street, Leicester Fields (1776), and Southwood, Highgate (1779). He was adept at portraiture and historical painting, and his output included a portrait of Alderman John Boydell (exh. Royal Academy, 1772); one of his wife (when Miss North) in the character of Juno (exh. Royal Academy, 1776), and one of himself and his wife (exh. Royal Academy, 1776). Though not identified conclusively, the latter may be the portrait in Newport Adams School, Shropshire. He painted pictures for John Boydell's Shakspeare Gallery (receiving £157 10s. each for scenes from 1 *Henry VI* and 3 *Henry VI*, and £105 each for two scenes from 2 *Henry IV*). His *Field of Battle Near Towton* was presented to the City of London by John Boydell (this decayed and was subsequently disposed of just prior to the Second World War), together with *The Battle of Agincourt* (of which the City has no record).

While living at West End, Hampstead, Josiah Boydell helped form the Hampstead infantry in 1798 and became their captain. After its standing down he became lieutenant-colonel commandant of the subsequently formed Loyal Hampstead Volunteers from 1803. After his uncle's death in 1804 he succeeded John Boydell as alderman of Cheap ward and was in control of the print publishing business at Cheapside of which he had formerly been a partner. Although his business acumen was not equal to that of his uncle, he was as enthusiastic towards promoting the arts in England. His *Suggestions towards forming a plan for the encouragement … of the arts … in this country in two letters addressed to Robert Udney, dated 22 & 23 December 1801* (1805) reveals a sincere believer in the importance of the arts to the country's economy. His own artistic talent was generally underestimated. It was of some 'surprise, that an artist of such promise, is not to be found among the Royal Academicians' (*The Times*, 3 April 1790). A member of the Royal Society of Arts from 1790 and master of the Stationers' Company (1811–12), he was forced to resign his aldermanic status in 1809 owing to ill health. Having suffered respiratory problems for some years, he died at his home at Halliford, Middlesex, on 27 March 1817 and was buried in Hampstead church. Examples of his work are in the Guildhall Library, London.   L. A. FAGAN, *rev.* VIVIENNE W. PAINTING

Sources E. E. Newton, 'A forgotten Hampstead worthy', *Transactions of the Hampstead Antiquarian and Historical Society* (1899), 119–36 · E. T. Evans, 'The Hampstead Volunteers', *Hampstead Annual* (1905–6), 28–42 · private information (2004) [NAM; Guildhall Art Gallery, London] · Graves, *RA exhibitors* · A. B. Beaven, ed., *The aldermen of the City of London, temp. Henry III–[1912]*, 2 vols. (1908–13) · apprentice indenture, CLRO, CF1/1039 · m. cert. copy, Mercers' Hall, London, E3/38 · *Cheshire Sheaf*, 3rd ser., 9 (1912), 105 · Folger, MS Y.d. 369 · J. Boydell, *Suggestions towards forming a plan for the encouragement … of the arts … in this country, in two letters addressed to Robert Udney, dated 22 & 23 December 1801* (1805)
Likenesses G. Stuart, oils, 1783–7, Holburne of Menstrie Museum, Bath · W. Miller, group portrait, oils, before 1793 (*The ceremony of swearing in the lord mayor, 1782*), Guildhall Art Gallery, London · B. Smith, engraving (after W. Miller, before 1793), Guildhall Print Room, London · F. Wheatley, group portrait, drawing (*Interior of the Shakespeare Gallery*), V&A

Boyd Orr. For this title name *see* Orr, John Boyd, Baron Boyd Orr (1880–1971).

Boye, Rice (*fl. c.*1629–1636), Church of England clergyman and separatist minister, preached in the west country at some point in the late 1620s, most probably in Gloucestershire, although the precise location of his cure is unknown. About 1629 he found himself in conflict with Edward Norice (or Norris), the godly preacher of Tetbury, over the question of how believers were supposed to pray for temporal blessings, such as wealth, prosperity, and health. Their dispute was initially conducted in the pulpit, through the private exchange of manuscripts and letters, and at least on one occasion at a well-attended meeting at the Berkeley home of Edward Chetwind, dean of Bristol. Boye maintained that Christians were to pray for such blessings in an absolute and unconditional manner, just as they were to pray for the unconditional spiritual blessings God offered through his absolute promises to the faithful; he further argued that those who were not granted such temporal blessings had been denied God's grace because they lacked true faith in his absolute promises. This peculiar position may perhaps have been an outgrowth of the antinomian opinions spreading at the fringes of the godly community in the 1620s and 1630s, for Norice insinuated that Boye was associated with the notorious antinomian John Traske, whose career as an itinerant, unbeneficed preacher brought him through Gloucestershire in these years. Antinomians such as Traske argued vigorously that divine grace was absolutely and wholly unconditional, flowing solely from belief in the promise (which was itself taken to be the free gift of God); meanwhile, they criticized mainstream puritans who, in their view, contaminated the doctrine of free grace by imposing rigorous, legalistic conditions and exacting religious duties on aspiring saints. The polemic against Norice—whom Boye habitually denounced as a 'justiciary', or legalist—mirrored this antinomian critique, and was probably part of a broader conflict unfolding within the godly community during the early decades of the century.

On Norice's account, it was at least partly as a result of their dispute and its aftermath that Boye turned away from the Church of England. By 1635, when Boye finally attacked Norice in print (in *The Importunate Begger for Things Necessary*), he had moved to London and affiliated himself with the underground Southwark 'semi-separatist' congregation that had been founded by Henry Jacob (he would soon be joined by Traske). At some point in the early 1630s the Jacob church splintered, with Boye allegedly attaching himself to the more radical group surrounding John Duppa, who promoted a rigid and total separation from the established church. During these years Boye also became deeply involved in the importation and distribution of illegal books against the Laudian regime. In 1637 he was among those named in the Star Chamber bill against Burton, Bastwick, and Prynne. According to the future Fifth Monarchist Edmund Chillendon, in 1636 Boye, then living in Coleman Street, had approached Chillendon with fifty copies each of Prynne's *Newes from Ipswich* and the *Divine Tragedy*, all of which Chillendon then forwarded to Norwich for sale. Apart from a further counterblast to Norice in 1636, nothing more is known of Boye's career, which despite its obscurity serves to shine a spotlight on the outermost margins of the puritan community, where separatism, religious heterodoxy, and the illicit book trade flourished to the frustration of the Laudian authorities.   DAVID R. COMO

Sources D. Como, *Blown by the spirit: puritanism and the emergence of an antinomian underground in pre-civil war England* [forthcoming] · C. Burrage, *The early English dissenters in the light of recent research, 1550–1641* (1912) · E. Norice, *A treatise, maintaining that temporall blessings are to bee sought and asked with submission to the will of God* (1636) · E. Norice, *The new gospel, not the true gospel* (1638) · PRO, SP 16/346/58, fol. 132r · PRO, SP 16/349/52, fol. 101r–v · M. Tolmie, *The triumph of the saints: the separate churches of London, 1616–1649* (1977)

Boyer, Abel (1667?–1729), lexicographer and journalist, was most probably born on 24 June 1667, at Castres in the upper Languedoc, the son of Pierre Boyer, one of the two chief magistrates or consuls of Castres, and Catherine Campdomerc (*b*. 1651), the eighth child of the marriage of Eleazar Campdomerc and Sara De Terson. As magistrate, his father had suffered suspension from office and was fined for his commitment to protestantism. It was from Pierre Campdomerc, his maternal uncle, that Abel Boyer apparently got his first rudiments of learning.

Education In 1683 or 1684 Boyer embarked upon the first formal educational training for which there is evidence. He entered the nearby protestant academy of Puylaurens (formerly Montauban), as his uncle had done before him. He enrolled as a student of theology, apparently aiming to follow a family tradition and become a minister in the Huguenot church. Among the alumni of Montauban was Pierre Bayle, a close friend of one André Terson, a member of Boyer's mother's family. However, Boyer's studies at Puylaurens were curtailed in March 1685 when the academy was suppressed by royal decision. Some time after the revocation of the edict of Nantes in October, Boyer fled France for the Netherlands.

In 1687 poverty may have obliged Boyer to serve briefly in the army of the Dutch republic, as did many other Huguenots at the time. The experience, if it took place, may have contributed to his later close technical interest in things military which, he claimed in 1696, was based partly on what he had seen of some of the battlefields of Flanders. However, he soon resumed his interrupted studies at the University of Franeker in Friesland. According to Pierre Bayle, who had declined in 1684 the offer of the chair of philosophy at Franeker, Boyer attended courses in philosophy and theology, and also in mathematics and fortification—then regarded not only as connected studies, but as regular parts of the education of a gentleman.

When Boyer left the Netherlands some time after 11 July 1689, he took with him to England a letter of introduction from Bayle to Bishop Burnet, recently consecrated as the bishop of Salisbury and well known to Bayle as a scholar with a passionate concern for the plight of the Huguenots. In October 1690 Boyer is recorded as having received a payment of 15*s*. out of the Royal Bounty Fund as a student in divinity, and it seems reasonable to give credence to the claim of Boyer's first contemporary obituarists—his

Abel Boyer (1667?–1729), by François Chéreau the elder (after Hans Hysing)

widow, Mary, and a cousin—that his first employment in England was writing and preparing for publication in 1691 Dr Thomas Smith's edition of William Camden's letters. In July 1691 Boyer was established in the family of Sir Benjamin Bathurst, comptroller of the household of the prince and princess of Denmark, and was then, or soon after, appointed French and Latin tutor to Bathurst's eldest son, Allen.

From tutor to author Boyer's own first published work, *The compleat French master for ladies and gentlemen: being a new method, to learn with ease and delight the French tongue* (1694), was, as its subtitle suggests, French without tears, a genre of literary production then much in vogue, and it enjoyed immediate and lasting popular favour throughout the eighteenth century in Britain, Europe, and North America. In the hope of courtly preferment as French teacher in the household of the duke of Gloucester (the son of Prince George of Denmark and Princess Anne), it was dedicated to the duke and, according to Boyer's preface to the eighth edition of 1721, had been encouraged by Anne herself. At the time of Boyer's death the work had gone through ten editions.

In 1695 Boyer published his *Character of the Virtues and Views of the Age*, with a fulsome preface to 'the much honoured Allen Bathurst'. The following year he published *A Geographical and Historical Description of those Parts of Europe which are the Seat of War*, which was dedicated to the duke of Ormond, one of the Denmarks' circle of friends. In the second half of 1698 Boyer appeared as a translator in the publication of *Ductor historicus*, a historical work by the French priest and theologian Pierre Le Lorrain de Vallemont. In dedicating this work to John, Lord Churchill, Boyer acknowledged the Churchill family's repeated encouragements in his endeavours to serve the public.

In 1699 Boyer published his *Royal Dictionary*, which he had begun in 1694 or thereabouts, and which was dedicated to the duke of Gloucester, with, as Boyer claimed, the knowledge, favour, and encouragement of Princess Anne. The work was something of an innovation in England in announcing a particular and unusual view of language as a changing, living thing. It did this by citing recent and living writers as sources or authorities, and by attempting to convey the variety of meanings of a word according to word usage as found in their works.

Apart from giving Boyer entrance into English intellectual and social circles, the *Royal Dictionary* also made him a European man of letters. Immediately upon its publication, and well into the second half of the eighteenth century, the work was published—and pirated—across Europe. However, the record of European publication, though impressive, is dwarfed by the reception in England. Nineteen editions each of the *Royal Dictionary* and the *Royal Dictionary Abridged* were published in London between 1699 and 1797. The *Royal Dictionary* found a place in the libraries of scholars, public figures (including Dr Johnson), politicians, and clerics; increasingly, however, it found its main use in the classroom. But for Boyer himself the most important consequence of the *Royal Dictionary* seems to have been the encouragement it gave him, perhaps above all financially, to abandon tutoring and to make a living as a writer: not a year went by between 1699 and his death in 1729 without publication.

Annalist, historian, propagandist, man of letters In 1700 two publications came from Boyer's pen: a translation of Racine's *Iphigénie*, entitled *Achilles*, which saw a few performances at Drury Lane, and an aid to the learning of French by English speakers, and of English by foreigners, entitled *The Wise and Ingenious Companion, French and English*. In 1701 there was a return to military history in *The Draughts of the most Remarkable Fortified Towns of Europe*, and in 1702–3 he published in three volumes *The History of King William the Third*, the first complete published account of William's life and reign. In *A Geographical and Historical Description* Boyer had described William as 'our Glorious Monarch' (p. 1). The possessive pronoun is significant: Boyer wrote of England as if he were an Englishman, though he remained proud of his French roots.

Boyer had intended originally to carry his *William III* as far as the coronation of Queen Anne. He made good that promise with *The History of the Reign of Queen Anne Digested into Annals* (1703–13), concerned more with British than with continental affairs, and Boyer took particular pride in his coverage of parliamentary affairs, including parliamentary debates. In the same year as he began the *Annals*

he started, or was already engaged in, a manuscript newsletter service, and by 1714 he was well known as a newsletter writer, willing to write a letter every post for a guinea a month. In 1704 he also became something of an intelligence agent, employed, and possibly paid, by Robert Harley, then secretary of state for the northern department.

In July 1705, in response to a plea from Abel Roper, the publisher of Boyer's *William III* and of his *Annals*, Boyer agreed to write for the thrice-weekly newspaper the *Post Boy*, as the author of its foreign coverage. Boyer later claimed that he had turned around the fortunes of the paper within a year. Good fortune also came his way in 1706 when he achieved naturalization at his second attempt. However, in August 1709 he fell out with Roper, and in a pre-emptive coup Boyer took over the newspaper himself; he continued to write for it under that title and under the title the *True Post Boy* until April 1710.

In 1710 Boyer hoped to renew the patronage that Robert Harley had conferred upon him in 1704, and dedicated to him his *Annals* for that year. The 'small place' for which he petitioned was that of gazetteer, editor of the only officially authorized government newspaper, the *London Gazette*, the office having become vacant probably in August upon the resignation of its holder, Richard Steele (R. P. Bond, 71, n. 57). Unfortunately, in his concern to prove his loyalty to Harley, Boyer crossed swords with Jonathan Swift: although the appointment of gazetteer fell to Henry St John, the secretary of state for northern affairs, it was to Swift that St John deferred in all matters of the press.

Boyer first attacked Swift in the March issue of a new periodical, the *Political State of Great Britain*, which Boyer had begun in January 1711. The journal—which provided a register of monthly occurrences across Britain, America, and Europe, abstracted pamphlets and books, offered observations on trade and public finance, and reported regularly on current parliamentary debates—was Boyer's enduring historical monument, and he compiled it until his death. It was also the main vehicle for Boyer's lifelong feud with Swift. In September 1711 the feud approached its climax, with the publication by Boyer of *An Account of the State and Progress of the Present Negotiation of Peace*, a reply to Swift's *New Journey to Paris*. The next month, at Swift's prompting, St John charged Boyer with seditious libel, and required him to provide a recognizance of £200 as surety for his appearance at the court of queen's bench to answer the charge against him. However, as a result of intercession by Harley, now earl of Oxford and first lord of the Treasury, Boyer was discharged at the end of the Michaelmas term; in respect of the gazetteership, however, he was disappointed, passed over twice, in both cases in favour of creatures of Swift.

Stung, Boyer now sought to position himself as an ardent supporter of the Hanoverian succession. Initially he continued to attack the proposed peace between Britain and France in the *Political State*. He claimed to be acting as an impartial reporter of the arguments on both sides, but gave the whigs the best of the argument, congratulating them on having won not only the argument but also the overwhelming support of the political nation. Boyer was freer to express a personal opinion as a pamphleteer than as the compiler of a periodical that laid claim to be a paper of record. In summer 1713 he translated a learned, wide-ranging, and widely circulated attack on the folly of the peace, written originally in French by another Huguenot refugee, Jean Dumont, entitled *Les soupirs de l'Europe etc., or, The groans of Europe at the prospect of the present posture of affairs*; this was followed by a translation of a work by André-François Deslandes, entitled *A Philological Essay, or, Reflections on the Death of Free-Thinkers*.

Having in these publications acted as a conduit of French culture, Boyer engaged in cultural traffic in the opposite direction, providing the first French translation of Addison's *Cato* in 1713. Whether or not Addison's *Cato* and Boyer's translation of it can be considered political acts is unclear, but what is certain is that most of Boyer's publications of the following year were deliberately political, designed to restore connections with those (like the Marlboroughs) who had assisted him in the past, to distance himself still further from Oxford and Bolingbroke, and to demonstrate his own zeal for the Hanoverian succession. In the *Memoirs of the Life and Negotiations of Sir William Temple* (1714) Boyer made of Temple's life as diplomat and servant of the crown a tract for his own times. The work branded Oxford and Bolingbroke as Jacobites, just as they had abandoned negotiations with the Pretender (James Stuart) and were facing the difficult task of establishing their loyalty to the Hanoverian succession. This was made more difficult with Boyer's publication on 1 July 1714 of letters from Anne to Sophia, the dowager electress of Hanover, to the elector of Hanover (later George I), and to the duke of Cambridge (later George II). These gave an unwelcome public airing to the divisions between the Hanoverian court and Anne and her government, and cast doubt upon the professions of private and public zeal for the Hanoverian succession by Bolingbroke and Oxford. Two days later Bolingbroke issued a warrant for Boyer's arrest: he was bound over in a recognizance of £100 and ordered to present himself at the court of queen's bench on the first day of the next term. However, the action was overtaken by events: on 27 July Oxford was dismissed, on 1 August Anne died and was succeeded peacefully by George I, on 31 August Bolingbroke was dismissed, and on 29 November Boyer was discharged.

Boyer expected some return for his services and sufferings for the Hanoverian cause, and his impatience at the delay in this was evident in an advertisement of April 1716 heralding the publication of his *Compleat and Impartial History of the Impeachments of the Last Ministry*. However, neither the advertisement nor the work itself won Boyer the gazetteership he still seems to have coveted most: once again, he was passed over. None the less, one favour soon came his way from James Stanhope, shortly to become secretary of state for northern affairs. In November or December 1716 Boyer published a defence of the ministry's northern policies, *The Interest of Great Britain*, which was written, according to Boyer, at the particular request of Stanhope, with materials provided by the minister. In his dedication to Stanhope, Boyer saluted him as a patron nonpareil, but there is no evidence that Stanhope did anything more for Boyer.

Boyer continued to serve Stanhope and also to hound Oxford; Oxford, awaiting his trial for treason in the Tower and nurturing his antipathy towards whig journalists, awarded the palm of his opprobrium to Boyer as 'the greatest scoundrel in the world that understands neither French nor English' (BL, Portland loan, 29/38/6). A week before Oxford was due to come to trial, in June 1717, Boyer, accused of being the author of *Minutes of the Negociations of Mons*, denied the charge and instead proclaimed the tract a forgery of a kind that pointed unmistakably to Daniel Defoe as its author. Defoe responded at once with a *tu quoque* decrying Boyer as 'the scum of Hackney Scribblers', a mercenary plagiarist who clumsily cobbled together the works of others, cheated his booksellers, and practised openly almost all abominable vices; Defoe even attempted to publish a newspaper advertisement describing Boyer, now fifty and still apparently unmarried, as a sodomite (*Portland MSS*, 5.537). Boyer ostentatiously disdained from replying, though he continued to snipe at Defoe in the *Political State* long afterwards.

In August 1718 Boyer published anonymously *Animadversions and Observations*, a lengthy and closely argued defence of the government's financial policies in reply to an attack on them from the disaffected whig Archibald Hutcheson. Though concerned primarily with the detail of financial policy and with praising the excellent financial judgement of ministers, without 'any Design to make my Court to any Body', Boyer ranged beyond finance to applaud the government's foreign policy, revisiting ground he had covered in *The Interest of Great Britain* in 1716, and to clear the crown of blame for the party quarrels which had accompanied the accession of George I (p. 88). He also took up the defence of his fellow Huguenot refugees in England, praising their large contribution to public funds in perilous times, to the growth of manufacture and of trade, and to raising Britain to an unprecedented peak of prosperity and contentment. In contrast, the only other separate publication by Boyer in that year was far removed from high politics, though it showed him once again in cantankerous dispute with a fellow writer: he accused John Ozell, with the latter's new translation of Fenelon's *Télémaque*, of plagiarizing a 1699 version of which Boyer had been a translator.

However, the spat with Ozell contributed to a much more serious confrontation with the government in April and May 1722. Having been alerted in a letter from Edmund Curll, the publisher of Ozell's translation of *Télémaque*, to the publication in the March issue of the *Political State* of a libel against Walpole, the government apprehended Boyer and obliged him to enter a recognizance for the huge sum of £500. Salt was further added to the wound as the author of the libel was Archibald Hutcheson, though Boyer claimed that he had provided abstracts in order to expose its author to the detestation he deserved. The threat of punishment and the large pecuniary penalty were evidently seen as sufficient to ensure better behaviour in future, as no further legal action was taken. Boyer occasionally took a more critical line, even crossing swords with a former hero, Bishop Benjamin Hoadly (with whom he had sided during the Bangorian controversy of 1717), in Hoadly's capacity as government propagandist, and by 1729 he was taking up a somewhat isolationist position in respect of Europe.

Final years Towards the end of 1722 Boyer produced what he regarded as his greatest work, *The History of the Life and Reign of Queen Anne*, essentially a reformed version of the *Annals* and the early volumes of the *Political State*. In the following year Boyer was able to complete the work in his new home he had built for himself in Five Field Row near Chelsea College, in a fashionable and then distinctly whiggish suburb of London; he had lived previously—since 1708 at least—at a property which had doubled as a shop in Queen's Court, King Street, near Covent Garden. Chelsea was also noted for its good air, which could have been a consideration for a sickly man. By January 1729 Boyer complained of having been housebound for more than a year and 'under the disadvantage of a crazy Constitution, broken with Age, constant Labour, and a Compilation of a stubborn Gout and Rheumatism, and the remains of a long fit of Ague and Fever' (*Political State*, 37, 1729, preface).

Poor health and general decrepitude were not Boyer's only difficulties. In February 1729 he was threatened with arrest by the House of Commons for having breached parliamentary privilege by publishing abstracts of the *Votes* in the *Political State*. Boyer huffed and puffed, but heeded the warning, immediately ceasing to report current proceedings in parliament, summarizing them only after the end of the parliamentary session. This was Boyer's last brush with authority, but he continued pen in hand, living only long enough to see into print a revised and enlarged edition of his *Royal Dictionary*, a further edition of his *Theory and Practice of Architecture*, which he had first published in 1703, and the tenth edition of his *Compleat French-Master*. He also completed *The Grand Theatre of Honour, Nobility, and Chivalry*, in French and English, taking the history no further than the tenth century on the grounds that he wished not to offend the niceties of certain reigning princes, and planned a second volume to cover parts of Europe omitted in the first. However, he died on 16 November 1729, presumably at his home in Chelsea, a month before *The Grand Theatre* was published.

Boyer retained to his end a sense of double identity; in the month before he died he described himself as 'Gallo-Britannus' (*Political State*, 37, 1729, 298). This was reflected in his will, made in December 1727. It reveals the existence of a daughter (said to be about three years old in 1729) named Pierre Catherine, presumably in memory of his parents. The bulk of his estate was left to her, with instructions that his executors—his wife and his cousin, the latter certainly a French Huguenot by origin—should turn everything into money and invest it in the Bank of England. As an institution that owed much to Huguenot expertise and investment, and that was distinctly whiggish from its start and thereafter, it was a fitting resting place for the fiscal remains of someone of Boyer's origins and loyalties. He was buried in Chelsea Old Church yard on 19 November 1729.   G. C. GIBBS

Sources BL, Add. MSS 4226; 28167; Portland loans, 29/38/6; 29/127/4; 29/163 · HLRO, British Record Association, deposit no. 833 · *The manuscripts of the House of Lords*, new ser., 12 vols. (1900–77), vol. 11 · *JHL*, 18 (1705–9), 164 · UCL, Huguenot Library, Bounty papers, MS 4/1 · Bodl. Oxf., MSS Smith 46, 48, 59 · PRO, SP 35/31; SP 44/77, fols. 126–9, 152; SP 44/81, fols. 49–50, 55 · GL, MS 11936/15, fol. 444 · parish register, Chelsea Old Church, 1704–47, LMA · R. P. Bond, ed., *Studies in the early English periodical* (1957) · *The manuscripts of his grace the duke of Portland*, 10 vols., HMC, 29 (1891–1931) · J. Sutherland, *Defoe* (1937) · A. Boyer, *The political state of Great Britain*, 38 (1729), 604–6 · P. Desmaizeaux, *Bibliothèque raisonnée des ouvrages des savans de l'Europe*, 3, pt 1 (1729), 471 · J. Flagg, 'Abel Boyer: a Huguenot intermediary', *Studies in Voltaire*, 242 (1986) · G. C. Gibbs, 'Abel Boyer Gallo-Anglus glossographus et historicus, 1667–1729: his early life, 1667–1689', *Proceedings of the Huguenot Society of London*, 23/2 (1978), 87–98 · G. C. Gibbs, 'Abel Boyer: from tutor to author', *Proceedings of the Huguenot Society*, 24 (1983–8), 46–59 · G. C. Gibbs, 'Abel Boyer: the making of a British subject', *Proceedings of the Huguenot Society of Great Britain and Ireland*, 26/1 (1994) · G. C. Gibbs, 'Abel Boyer and Jonathan Swift: a "French dog" bites back', *Proceedings of the Huguenot Society of Great Britain and Ireland*, 27/2 (1999), 211–31 · E. Haag and E. Haag, *La France protestante*, 2nd edn, 6 vols. (Paris, 1877–88), vol. 4, p. 492 · G. Tournier, 'La famille de Campdomerc', *Bulletin de la Société d'Histoire Protestante Française* [Paris], 70 (1921), 226–39 · P.-D. Bourchenin, *Études sur les academies protestantes en France au XVIe et au XVIIe siècles* (Paris, 1882) · poor rates collecting books, parish of St Paul, Covent Garden, City Westm. AC · will, PRO, PROB 11/633, sig. 294

Archives BL, 'The political state of Great Britain for the month of April, 1711', Add. MS 70274 | BL, letters to Robert Harley, loan MS 29

Likenesses J. Basire, engraving, HLRO · F. Chéreau the elder, engraving (after H. Hysing), BL, NPG [*see illus.*]

Boyes, John Frederick (1811–1879), classical scholar, was born in London on 10 February 1811, the son of a Yorkshireman, Benjamin Boyes. His father being then resident in Charterhouse Square, in October 1819 Boyes entered Merchant Taylors' School. After a very creditable school career extending over nearly ten years, he went in 1829 as Andrew's civil law exhibitioner to St John's College, Oxford, having relinquished a scholarship which he had gained in the previous year at Lincoln College. He graduated BA in 1833 (MA 1835), taking a second class in classics. Soon afterwards he was appointed second master of the Forest School, Walthamstow, and eventually succeeded to the headmastership, which he held from 1844 to 1848. Among a large circle of discriminating friends, he enjoyed a high reputation for culture and scholarship. The fruits of his extensive reading and literary taste were to be seen in his published works: *Illustrations of the tragedies of Aeschylus and Sophocles, from the Greek, Latin, and English poets* (1844); *English Repetitions, in Prose and Verse* (1849); *Life and Books, a Record of Thought and Reading* (1859); and *Lacon in Council* (1865). The closing years of his life were largely devoted to practical benevolence, in the exercise of which he was as humble as he was liberal. He died at 10 St James's Terrace, Harrow Road, London, on 26 May 1879, leaving a widow, Charlotte Augusta Cobourg Boyes.

C. J. ROBINSON, rev. M. C. CURTHOYS

Sources C. J. Robinson, ed., *A register of the scholars admitted into Merchant Taylors' School, from AD 1562 to 1874*, 2 (1883), 211 · private information (1885) · J. G. Tanner, *Sermon* (1879), preface, appx · Boase, *Mod. Eng. biog.* · V. Sillery, *St John's College biographical register, 1775–1875* (1987) · *CGPLA Eng. & Wales* (1879)

Wealth at death under £18,000: probate, 10 July 1879, *CGPLA Eng. & Wales*

Boyesku, Euphrosyne Parepa de. *See* Rosa, Euphrosyne Parepa- (1836–1874).

Boyle, Charles, fourth earl of Orrery (1674–1731), politician and Jacobite conspirator, was born in Little Chelsea near Kensington, Middlesex, on 28 July 1674, not 1676 as stated in the *Dictionary of National Biography*, and was baptized on 1 August at St Mary's, Kensington, the youngest son of Roger Boyle, second earl of Orrery (1646–1682), and his wife, Lady Mary Sackville (1648–1710), daughter of Richard Sackville, fifth earl of Dorset. His grandfather was Roger *Boyle, first earl of Orrery, a Cromwellian minister and playwright, and his great-uncle was the natural philosopher Robert *Boyle.

Upbringing, education, and literary career Following the separation of his parents in the 1670s, Boyle was brought up by his mother at Knole in Kent, the seat of his uncle, Charles *Sackville, sixth earl of Dorset. Educated first at a school in Sevenoaks and then at St Paul's School, London, he matriculated at Christ Church, Oxford, in 1690, aged fifteen, where he studied with Francis Atterbury, later bishop of Rochester and a co-conspirator for the Jacobite cause. A 'studious man not given to the lifestyle of many peers' sons' (Bennett, 380), Boyle was the only nobleman to take a degree from the college during a thirty-year period.

Boyle's abilities undoubtedly generated respect and led to his involvement in a famous episode, recalled in Swift's *Battle of the Books*, during the long-running controversy between the 'ancients' of Christ Church and 'moderns' led by the Cambridge classicist Richard Bentley. To showcase the talents of their young scholar, the dean of Christ Church, Henry Aldrich, had assigned Boyle to translate the *Epistles of Phalaris*, a collection of letters supposedly the work of a Sicilian dating from the fifth century BC. However, Boyle believed that his research on the *Epistles* (which, via a third party, required him to consult the collection at the king's library at St James's, Westminster) had been hindered by Bentley, the collection's custodian. His incomplete edition appeared in 1695, a year after his graduation, and contained a prefatory remark concerning Bentley's disobliging manner which proved the catalyst for the controversy. Embarrassed and insulted, within four years Bentley had produced two dissertations on the epistles which disproved Phalaris's authenticity; subsequent rejoinders to Bentley (principally *Dr Bentley's Dissertation on the Epistles of Phalaris … examin'd*, 1698), though attributed to Boyle, were almost certainly written by Atterbury and fellow Oxford ancients. Boyle's Oxford

years also saw the development of a wide-ranging intellectual curiosity evident in his growing personal library (ultimately consisting of 10,000 volumes, and now preserved at Christ Church), which constitutes a comprehensive corpus of medical and scientific treatises between 1690 and 1730. Elected a fellow of the Royal Society in 1706, Boyle later supported the Quaker horologist and scientific instrument-maker George Graham, whose tellurion—an instrument to display the motion of the moon, sun, and earth—was renamed the orrery after the earl.

After Oxford, Boyle also continued to produce works of literary scholarship, as well as satirical poems and a play, *As you Find it* (1703), on the then popular theme of marital discord and reconciliation. In addition to George Graham, Orrery supported several prominent writers of the day, including the poet Elijah Fenton, whose *Oxford and Cambridge Miscellany Poems* (1708) contained two of the earl's lyrical verses, and the dramatists Thomas Southerne and George Farquhar, whose most celebrated work, *The Recruiting Officer*, was based on his experiences in Boyle's (then Orrery's) Irish regiment.

Political career, 1695–1714 Boyle's public career began with his election to the family borough seat at Charleville, co. Cork, which he represented from 1695 to 1699. In 1701 he ran, successfully, for election to one of the borough seats for Huntingdon. His defeated opponent, John Pedley, disputed the election, and in a petition accused Boyle of improprieties including the intervention of an unnamed peer who with 'Swords & Clubs' had threatened to 'menace, assault, and strike the Recorders of the said Borough and others of the Petitioner's Voters' (*JHC*, 13.333). Boyle denounced these charges in the Commons, and Pedley's petition was later withdrawn. However, Francis Wortley, borough recorder and a fellow Huntingdon MP, whom Boyle mildly ridiculed in his speech, confronted him in a duel in Hyde Park on 27 March 1701. In a bitter struggle Boyle was seriously wounded and spent several months recuperating. Following his brother's death in 1703, he was raised to the Irish peerage as fourth earl of Orrery. Voting fairly consistently along tory lines, he was re-elected for Huntingdon in subsequent elections. In the year after his ennoblement he purchased a colonel's commission and thereafter held the colonelcies of three major regiments of foot. His military career was aided by a long-standing friendship with John, second duke of Argyll, who arranged for his award of the order of knight of the Thistle.

On 30 March 1706 Orrery married Lady Elizabeth Cecil (c.1687–1708), sister of the sixth earl of Exeter, at a ceremony at Burghley House. On 2 January 1707 their only child, John *Boyle (styled Lord Boyle and later fifth earl) was born, the countess dying in June of the following year. Orrery never remarried, although from at least 1718 he maintained an intimate relationship with Margaret Swordfeger (d. 1741), the wife of his secretary, who became his consort and mistress. With her Orrery had two sons, Charles and Boyle, and two daughters, Clementina and

Martha Sophia, names which belie the earl's by then well-formed Jacobite sympathies.

During 1709 and 1710 Orrery participated in three military campaigns in Flanders, and was involved in fierce fighting at Malplaquet and the siege of Béthune. Now a major-general in the prestigious Royal Scots Fusiliers (1710), he advised the first minister, Robert Harley, on military reforms designed to offset the influence of their mutual political opponent, the duke of Marlborough. From 1711 to June 1713 he served as the queen's envoy-extraordinary at Brussels and The Hague. His attachment to Harley also brought him a place on the privy council (1711) and a seat in the Lords as Baron Boyle of Marston, Somerset. Yet growing dissatisfaction with the apparent duplicity of Harley (now earl of Oxford) prompted him to follow Argyll into opposition in 1713.

Jacobite politics Following the Hanoverian succession Orrery was designated lord lieutenant of Somerset and lord of the bedchamber to George I. Within two years, however, he was a victim of Argyll's fall from court grace following the duke's unacceptably close intrigues with the prince of Wales. Forced to dispose of his regiment and commission, Orrery joined the dissident whigs under Argyll's leadership, a relationship which was instrumental in his conversion to the Jacobite cause. As a disgruntled former courtier with diplomatic, military, and political experience, Orrery was a valuable individual for the exiled Stuarts and was now sought out by the Jacobite secretary of state, the earl of Mar. By late 1717 Orrery had embraced Jacobitism, although his ongoing circumspection and caution in correspondence drew criticism from fellow conspirators. A firm believer in the need for a sizeable foreign army as an essential requirement of a successful Jacobite invasion, he also insisted that the Stuarts guarantee the security of the Anglican church to their potential supporters.

After 1716 Orrery became a permanent member of the parliamentary opposition, joining forces with staunch tories and suspected Jacobites, and engaging in numerous foolhardy protests designed to annoy the whig ministries of Stanhope, Sunderland, and Walpole. By the early 1720s he was instrumental in many of these protests and has often been included in the handful of tory leaders associated with the Atterbury conspiracy of summer 1722, which resulted in the execution of Christopher Layer for treason in the following year. In fact, while undoubtedly close to Bishop Atterbury, and receiving a military commission from James Edward Stuart, the Jacobite Pretender, Orrery almost certainly did not advocate or assist in the planning of the conspiracy, and was then otherwise engaged in raising money to return tories to parliament.

None the less, Orrery's association with Layer and Atterbury prompted his arrest and imprisonment in the Tower from late September 1722 to March of the following year. His release on bail of £50,000 was granted only after desperate appeals from his family and medical testimonials claiming that his life was in danger. After a protracted convalescence Orrery resumed his parliamentary opposition, as well as his Jacobite activities, assisted after 1725 by a close friend and fellow officer, Colonel William Cecil. In 1725 he undertook the second of his missions (the first being in 1720) to the French court to solicit support for the Jacobite cause. The former was hindered by its coinciding with the financial crisis caused by the collapse of the Mississippi Company; the second failed largely as a result of its emissary's timidity. Plans for a third journey were underway when Orrery died at his house in Downing Street, Westminster, on 31 August 1731. He was buried on 11 September at Westminster Abbey.

Orrery's will reveals the extent to which relations had broken down between the fourth earl and his son, John, who now inherited the Irish and English titles. The worsening relations had been prompted by John's dislike of Margaret Swordfeger, a sentiment he shared by the late 1720s with his new in-laws, the earl and countess of Orkney. This opposition prompted Orrery to draft a will which, to the disgust of his legitimate heir, entitled Margaret and her children to a generous provision of nearly £10,000 to be supplemented by the fifth earl if required. Following Margaret's death in 1741, her two eldest children sought to collect their mother's bequest in full, but were cut off by the fifth earl following Clementina's marriage to a Roman Catholic. The fourth earl's claim that John lacked the 'Inclination either for Entertainment or Knowledge which study and Learning afford' (will, PRO, PROB 11/646, fols. 241–2) led him to bequeath his library and instrument collection to Christ Church, Oxford. Although father and son were reconciled before the fourth earl's death, his will was never revised.

LAWRENCE B. SMITH

Sources Royal Arch., Stuart papers · diplomatic correspondence of Charles, fourth earl of Orrery, 1711–13, BL, Add. MS 37209 · L. B. Smith, 'Charles Boyle, 4th earl of Orrery, 1674–1731', PhD diss., U. Edin., 1994 · E. Budgell, *Memoirs of the life and character of the late earl of Orrery, and of the family of the Boyles, particularly … Charles earl of Orrery* (1732) · Harvard U., Houghton L., Orrery papers, MS Eng. 218.1–25 · will, PRO, PROB 11/646 · diplomatic correspondence of Charles, fourth earl of Orrery, Jan 1710/11 Dec 1713, PRO, State Papers, foreign, Flanders, 77/60–62 · BL, Boyle papers, Add. MS 10388 [includes manuscript copy of Orrery's maiden speech in the House of Commons, 15 Feb 1700/1] · S. Lambert, ed., *House of Commons sessional papers of the eighteenth century*, vol. 3 (1975) · military and diplomatic corresp. of Charles, fourth earl of Orrery, to the duke of Marlborough, BL, Add. MS 61154 · 'Mary Caesar's journal, 1729–1740', BL, Add. MS 62558 · corresp. of Charles, fourth earl of Orrery and Henry Paget, first earl of Uxbridge, 1723–5, BL, Add. MS 61830 · countess of Cork and Orrery [E. C. Boyle], ed., *The Orrery papers*, 2 vols. (1903) · letters of Charles, fourth earl of Orrery, to Brettridge Badham, NL Ire., MS 4177 · 'Leases, letts, and accounts passed by Charles earl of Orrery … of his estate of Marston in Somersetshire on Lady day 1714 to his death 28 August 1731', MSS, priv. coll. · 'The letters of Henry St John to the earl of Orrery, 1709–1711', ed. H. T. Dickinson, *Camden miscellany, XXVI*, CS, 4th ser., 14 (1975), 137–200 · H. T. Dickinson, ed., 'Letters of Bolingbroke to the earl of Orrery, 1712–1713', *Camden miscellany, XXXI*, CS, 4th ser., vol. 44 (1992), 349–71 · *Calendar of the Stuart papers belonging to his majesty the king, preserved at Windsor Castle*, 7 vols., HMC, 56 (1902–23) · Orrery papers, W. Sussex RO, Petworth House archives · [F. Atterbury], *A short review of the controversy between Mr. Boyle, and Dr. Bentley … (1701) · The reasons which induc'd her majesty to create the right honourable Charles, earl of Orrery, and James, duke of Hamilton, peers of Great Britain* (1711) · E. Cruickshanks, 'Lord Cowper, Lord Orrery, the duke of Wharton, and Jacobitism', *Albion*, 26 (spring

1994), 27–40 · G. V. Bennett, *The tory crisis in church and state, 1688–1730: the career of Francis Atterbury, bishop of Rochester* (1975) · GEC, *Peerage*

Archives BL, diplomatic corresp., Add. MS 37209 · Harvard U., Houghton L., letter-books, business letters, and papers · MHS Oxf., collection, scientific instruments · priv. coll., 'Leases, letts, and accounts passed by Charles earl of Orrery … of his estate of Marston in Somersetshire on Lady day 1714 to his death 28 August 1731', MSS · PRO, State Papers, foreign, Flanders, diplomatic corresp., Jan 1710/11–Dec 1713, 77/60–62 | BL, Add. MS 61830 · BL, military and diplomatic corresp. to duke of Marlborough, Add. MS 61154 · BL, Portland Papers · BL, letters of Sir Robert Walpole, Lord Townshend, etc., Add. MS 9148 · NL Ire., MS 4177 · Royal Arch., Stuart papers · Royal Bank of Scotland, London, group archives, Glyn Mills/Childs Bank account, CH/14, CH/15

Likenesses engraving, *c*.1690, repro. in H. C. Beeching, *Francis Atterbury* (1909) · C. Jervas, oils, 1706, NPG · oils, 1707, repro. in Orrery papers · oils?, *c*.1708, priv. coll. · B. Baron, engraving, NPG; repro. in E. Budgell, *Lives of the Boyles* (1732); copy, priv. coll., Dr. Richard Sharp, U. Oxf. · G. Vertue, engraving

Wealth at death very wealthy; was able to leave £10,000 to mistress, also left £10,000 worth of books

Boyle, Constance Antonina [Nina] (1865–1943), women's rights campaigner, was born in Bexley, Kent, on 21 December 1865, the second daughter and fifth of the six children of Robert Boyle (1830–1869), great-grandson of the second earl of Glasgow and a captain in the Royal Artillery, and his wife, Frances Sydney Fremoult Sankey (*d.* 1909), daughter of Francis Fremoult Sankey MD. Little is known about her early life or education.

About the turn of the century Nina Boyle spent years in South Africa, including performing hospital duty during the Second South African War, in which two of her brothers also served. She also worked as a journalist, and during this time commenced her activism for women's rights, founding the Women's Enfranchisement League of Johannesburg. After returning to Britain in 1911, she became active in the Women's Freedom League (WFL), which had been formed in 1907 after a split within the Women's Social and Political Union (WSPU) over autocratic control by the Pankhursts, and which adopted civil disobedience and propaganda tactics in preference to the occasionally more violent methods used by the WSPU.

Boyle became head of the WFL's political and militant department in 1912. She wrote extensively for *The Vote* (the journal of the WFL) and took a leading role in the league's campaigns and numerous demonstrations. She was arrested on several occasions and imprisoned three times. Partly as a means of improving the treatment of women by the police—particularly given her own experiences—and also as part of the WFL's aim to make all employment areas open to women, Boyle attempted to gain approval for women to be employed as special constables. When this was officially refused, in the autumn of 1914 Boyle, with Margaret Damer Dawson of the National Vigilance Association, established the first voluntary women's police force, the Women's Volunteer Police Corps (WVP). The WVP represented also an attempt within the women's movement to begin to challenge male control of the law—particularly in regard to sexual matters. In correspondence with Asquith in 1914, Boyle complained in regard to the possible revival of the Contagious Diseases

Act that it was unjust that male officers should police laws that were 'almost exclusively concerned with matters in which women are involved to a greater extent than men' (Levine, 57). But it was the policing of such matters that led to divisions within the WVP. From the first the corps had acted at least to some extent as 'moral police', concentrating on young women and prostitutes loitering near railway stations used by servicemen. This type of work became officially sanctioned, but Boyle split away from the organization over the use of the WVP to enforce a curfew on women of 'loose character' near a service base in Grantham. Boyle saw this as a 'slur upon *all* women' (Carrier, 17). Dawson, the organizational strength in the WVP, carried on and developed the corps into the women police service, ultimately leading to official acceptance of women as police officers. In late 1916 Boyle went to Macedonia and Serbia to do war relief work, for which she was awarded the Samaritan order of Serbia and the allied medal.

Although women over thirty gained the vote in 1918, there was some doubt as to whether women were eligible to stand for parliament. In March 1918 Boyle attempted to stand as a WFL candidate in the Keighley by-election. Although her nomination was rejected because of a technical flaw, the returning officer's willingness to accept her candidature established the desired principle.

During the 1920s and 1930s Boyle remained active in a broad range of women's organizations. She campaigned on behalf of the National Union of Women Teachers, the Women's Election Committee, the Open Door Council (which aimed to remove protective barriers that restricted women's employment opportunities), and also organizations concerned with the welfare of women and children in developing countries. She was particularly active in the Save the Children Fund (SCF). In 1921 she went to the USSR to work in an SCF famine relief programme, she wrote articles for SCF publications, and she made frequent speeches as an SCF representative. On 20 May 1936 the SCF honoured her with a tribute at the Lyceum Club.

In 1920 Boyle had a novel, *Out of the Frying-Pan*, published. Although it was not received particularly well by reviewers, she went on to write a string of adventure romance novels ending with *Good Old Potts* in 1934. In many of her books 'remarkably capable' women were apparent (*TLS*, 12 March 1925, 173), and the reviewer of her 1927 work, *The Rights of Mallaroche*, thought readers should enjoy the book 'then go back to p.289 to smile at the feminism which Miss Boyle has kept hot from her suffragette days' (*TLS*, 27 Oct 1927, 769).

Boyle was a committed and principled activist whose actions led in part to increased opportunities for women to be involved in both the making and the enforcement of the law. Her courage and determination for her causes were remembered as being complemented by a developed sense of humour and modesty. She never married. She died in a nursing home at 99 Cromwell Road, London, on 4 March 1943, and was cremated at Golders Green on 9 March.   MARC BRODIE

Sources Burke, *Peerage* [Glasgow] · R. M. Douglas, *Feminist Freikorps: the British voluntary women police, 1914–1940* (1999) · J. Carrier, 'The control of women by women: the women police', *Bulletin of the Society for the Study of Labour History*, 26 (1973), 16–18 · P. Levine, '"Walking the streets in a way no decent woman should": women police in World War I', *Journal of Modern History*, 66 (1994), 34–78 · *TLS* (12 Aug 1920) · *TLS* (8 Nov 1923) · *TLS* (12 March 1925) · *TLS* (27 Oct 1927) · *TLS* (6 June 1929) · *TLS* (6 March 1930) · *TLS* (9 July 1931) · *TLS* (17 May 1934) · *The Vote* (1911–18), *passim* · *World's Children* (1927–38), *passim* · *The Times* (6 March 1943), 1 · P. Brookes, *Women at Westminster: an account of women in the British parliament, 1918–1966* (1967) · M. Mulvihill, *Charlotte Despard: a biography* (1989) · *DNB*
Wealth at death £1302 10s.: probate, 1 Oct 1943, *CGPLA Eng. & Wales*

Boyle, Sir Courtenay Edmund (1845–1901), civil servant, was the elder son of the two sons and a daughter of Captain Cavendish Spencer Boyle (1814–1868), 72nd regiment, and Rose Susan (d. 1902), daughter of Colonel C. C. Alexander RE. He was born on 21 October 1845 in Kingston, Jamaica, where his father was then stationed. Vice-admiral Sir Courtenay Boyle (1770–1844) was his grandfather, and Edward Boyle, seventh earl of Cork, his great-grandfather. Sir Cavendish Boyle (1849–1916), at one time governor of Newfoundland and Mauritius, was his younger brother. He was educated at Charterhouse, where he was a good classical scholar and captain of the cricket eleven. A Latin speech which he made at school before leaving for Oxford attracted the notice of Thackeray, who was present on the occasion as an old Carthusian. He gained an open junior studentship at Christ Church, Oxford, which was supplemented by an exhibition from his school. Although well read in classics, with an extraordinary memory for quotation, he only took a second class in moderations in 1865 and a third class in *literae humaniores* in 1868 (BA; MA, 1887). He was a distinguished university sportsman: he played in the Oxford cricket eleven against Cambridge in 1865–7, when he kept wicket, and he represented Oxford against Cambridge in real tennis in 1866–7.

Soon after Boyle left Oxford, Lord Spencer, to whom he was related and who was viceroy of Ireland in Gladstone's first administration (1868–74), took him on his staff in Dublin, first as assistant private secretary and then as private secretary. After acting as assistant inspector of the English Local Government Board from 1873, Boyle was appointed in 1876 inspector for the eastern counties. On 20 April 1876 he married Lady Muriel Campbell (d. 1934), daughter of the second earl of Cawdor.

In 1882, when Spencer went back to Ireland as viceroy, Boyle, still holding his inspectorship, again became his private secretary, and was on the scene of the Phoenix Park murders almost immediately after they had taken place. In 1885 he accompanied the prince and princess of Wales on their tour of Ireland, received the CB, and was made assistant secretary to the Local Government Board. An anonymous article by him strongly opposing Irish home rule appeared in the *Quarterly Review* (April 1885), one of several contributions by him to periodical literature on questions of public policy.

In May 1886 Boyle was appointed by A. J. Mundella, the president of the Board of Trade, assistant secretary in charge of the board's railway department. His appointment came at a sensitive time, when the railway companies' freight charges were under attack in parliament for placing British manufacturers and farmers at a disadvantage with their foreign competitors. He was involved with Lord Balfour of Burleigh in the lengthy and highly complex inquiry which led to a revision of railway rates and the passage of the Railway and Canal Traffic Act (1888) and the Regulation of Railways Act (1889). State regulation of electric lighting and traction also dated from this period and, advised by the physicist Lord Kelvin, he chaired the committee during 1890–91 which formulated the legal definitions of the ohm, the ampere, and the volt. He successfully adjudicated between the experts and prepared the legislation which settled the standards of measurement in electricity. He was also a member of Lord Rayleigh's committee on the National Physical Laboratory, in which he took a close interest; he backed the funding of 'pure' scientific research.

Boyle was knighted (KCB) in 1892, and in 1893 he was promoted to be permanent secretary of the Board of Trade in succession to Sir Henry Calcraft (1836–1896). His period of office marked the beginning of a departure from the strict policy of *laissez-faire* established in the department by T. H. Farrer. He valued the work of specialists such as Llewellyn Smith, who headed the newly created labour department. The Conciliation Act of 1896 gave the board an arbitration role in industrial disputes, Boyle himself having settled a dispute in the boot and shoe trade in 1895. Like the majority report of the royal commission on labour, he believed the key to industrial peace lay in organized employers dealing with well-run trade unions on the basis of legally binding collective agreements (see his article on 'Conciliation and arbitration in trade disputes', *Edinburgh Review*, 391, January 1900, 1–21). He was critical of employers who refused to negotiate with unions and in 1896 tried to persuade Lord Penrhyn to meet workers' representatives during the notorious north Wales quarry dispute.

Boyle also chaired an inter-departmental committee set up in 1897 by C. T. Ritchie, president of the Board of Trade, to consider means of monitoring the foreign competition faced by British exporters in overseas markets. This led to the setting up in 1899 of the commercial intelligence branch, another significant extension to the Board of Trade's work. He remained as permanent secretary until his sudden death at his London home, 11 Granville Place, Portman Square, on 18 May 1901. He was buried at Hampton, Middlesex. His widow survived him; there were no children.

As an official, Boyle was a very hard worker, who arrived at his office at abnormally early hours. He was clear and practical and a great believer in method, as was shown by his little books *Hints on the Conduct of Business, Public and Private* (1900) and *Method and Organisation in Business* (1901). He made a very good chairman of a committee. He was not only a strong and capable civil servant but also a scholar with an aptitude for writing in prose and verse, a man of society with a great gift for after-dinner speaking, and a sportsman. He kept up his interest in cricket and advocated cricket reform in *The Times* under the pseudonym of An Old Blue. Fishing was his favourite sport in later life, and, while at the Board of Trade, he worked hard for the improvement of the salmon-fishing laws and was largely responsible for a royal commission on the subject. He edited in 1901 *Mary Boyle: her Book*, autobiographical sketches by an aunt [*see* Boyle, Mary Louisa].

C. P. LUCAS, *rev.* M. C. CURTHOYS

Sources *The Times* (21 May 1901) · *Wisden* (1902) · *Annual Register* (1901) · private information (1912) · *Nature*, 64 (1901), 82–3 · *Leading men of London: a collection of biographical sketches* (1895) · *Wellesley index* · W. H. G. Armytage, 'The railway rates question and the fall of the third Gladstone ministry', *EngHR*, 65 (1950), 18–51 · R. Davidson, 'Llewellyn Smith, the labour department and government growth, 1886–1909', *Studies in the growth of nineteenth-century government*, ed. G. Sutherland (1972), 227–62 · H. A. Clegg, A. Fox, and A. F. Thompson, *A history of British trade unions since 1889*, 1 (1964)
Wealth at death £28,251 0s. 7d.: probate, 1 March 1902, *CGPLA Eng. & Wales*

Boyle, David, Lord Shewalton (1772–1853), advocate, was born on 26 July 1772 at Irvine, Ayrshire, the fourth son of Patrick Boyle (1717–1798), of Shewalton, army chaplain and landowner, and of his second wife, Elizabeth (*d.* 1832), daughter of Alexander *Dunlop (1684–1747), professor of Greek at the University of Glasgow; Patrick Boyle was the third son of John, second earl of Glasgow. Boyle was educated at the University of St Andrews from 1787 to 1789 and then at the University of Glasgow, where he studied law with John Millar, the whig pupil of Adam Smith and in his day the most famous teacher of law in Britain. Boyle was called to the Scottish bar on 14 December 1793. His abilities and connections impressed Lord Melville, political manager of Scotland, on whose recommendation he became solicitor-general for Scotland in May 1807, in the duke of Portland's administration. In the general election of the following month he became MP for Ayrshire, which he continued to represent until his appointment on 23 February 1811 to the court of session as Lord Boyle. He was appointed lord justice clerk on 15 October 1811. He was sworn on 11 April 1820 a member of the privy council. In 1837, on succeeding to the estate of his elder brother, he changed his judicial title to Lord Shewalton.

Boyle practised as an advocate and gained a good reputation. He increased his political value by dynastic marriage, on 24 December 1804, to an heiress from the landed gentry of his native county, Elizabeth, eldest daughter of Alexander Montgomerie of Annick, brother of the twelfth earl of Eglintoun; she died on 14 April 1822. They had six sons and five daughters. Boyle married secondly, on 17 July 1827, Camilla Catherine, eldest daughter of David *Smythe of Methven, Lord Methven, a Scottish judge. She died on 25 December 1880, leaving three sons and one daughter. One of Boyle's daughters by his first marriage, Helen, married the advocate and philanthropist Sir Charles Dalrymple Fergusson, fifth baronet, and was mother to the colonial governor Sir James Fergusson.

David Boyle, Lord Shewalton (1772–1853), by Sir John Watson-Gordon, exh. RA 1848

Boyle's sons by his second marriage included George David *Boyle, who became dean of Salisbury in 1880.

After acting as lord justice clerk for nearly thirty years, Boyle was appointed lord justice-general and president of the court of session, on the resignation of Charles Hope, Lord Granton. Boyle resigned office on 5 May 1852, declining the baronetcy which was offered to him. He died at Shewalton on 4 February 1853 and was buried at Dundonald, Ayrshire, on 11 February.

ARTHUR H. GRANT, *rev.* MICHAEL FRY

Sources HoP, *Commons, 1790–1820*, vol 3. · *Scots peerage*, vol. 4 · *GM* [passim] · G. Brunton and D. Haig, *An historical account of the senators of the college of justice, from its institution in MDXXXII* (1832) · *Caledonian Mercury* (7 Feb 1853) · *Glasgow Herald* (7 Feb 1853) · *The Times* (9 Feb 1853)
Archives NL Scot., justiciary notebooks · NRA Scotland, priv. coll., corresp. and papers | BL, corresp. with Sir Robert Peel, Add. MSS 40350–40490, *passim*
Likenesses J. Watson-Gordon, oils, exh. RA 1848, Parliament House, Edinburgh [*see illus.*] · R. M. Hodgetts, mezzotint (after miniature by W. J. Newton), NPG · P. Park, bust, Society of Solicitors in the Supreme Courts of Scotland, 2 Abercromby Place, Edinburgh · J. Steell, marble statue, Faculty of Advocates, Parliament Hall, Edinburgh · J. Steell, plaster statue, Scot. NPG · J. Watson-Gordon, study for oil painting, oil on millboard, Scot. NPG

Boyle, Sir Dermot Alexander (1904–1993), air force officer, was born on 2 October 1904 at Belmont House, Rathdowney, Queen's county, Ireland, one of five children and the second of the three sons of Alexander Francis Boyle, estate agent, and his wife, Anna Maria, *née* Harpur. He was educated at St Columba's College, Dublin, from where he entered the newly established RAF College, Cranwell, in 1922.

After graduating in 1924 Boyle flew with 17 squadron at Hawkinge and then on air policing duties in Iraq, quickly gaining invaluable experience of air operations. Next, having qualified as a flying instructor, he was able to demonstrate his exceptional piloting skills in display flying at Hendon and elsewhere. In the 1930s he served with the Auxiliary Air Force, spent three years on the headquarters staff in India dealing with airmen's personal affairs, and later became chief flying instructor at Cranwell. He married on 5 September 1931 Una (*b.* 1907/8), daughter of the late Edward Valentine Carey, rubber planter. They had two sons and a daughter.

When the war started Boyle went to France with the advanced air striking force and ended up arranging its evacuation. Duties followed at Bomber Command headquarters, in command of a Hampden bomber squadron, and in 1941 in the Cabinet Office secretariat, where he gained an invaluable insight into the higher realms of policy making. He then commanded Stradishall, a large Bomber Command station, before becoming senior air staff officer in 83 group, one of the major tactical formations specially set up for the invasion of north-west Europe.

The war over, Boyle attended the Imperial Defence College, served as assistant commandant at the RAF Staff College, and directed personnel matters in the Air Ministry before returning to the bomber world in command of 1 group. Here his primary task was to see the RAF's first jet bomber, the Canberra, into squadron service. A wonderful aircraft, he called it, and he often flew it himself, most notably in 1952 when he led a flight on a 24,000 mile tour of South America. In 1953 he moved on to become commander-in-chief, Fighter Command, where after taking charge of the queen's coronation review at Odiham he oversaw the introduction of another of the RAF's great post-war aircraft, the Hunter. He was made KCVO and KBE in 1953, and GCB in 1957.

Boyle took over as chief of air staff from Sir William Dickson on 1 January 1956—despite never having served on the Air Council, the usual prerequisite. He was the first incumbent not to have served in the First World War, and also the first Old Cranwellian. Lord Trenchard, the founder of the RAF College, had always looked forward to the day when a former cadet would reach the top of the RAF and none was more delighted when Boyle was appointed. Sadly, the new chief of air staff's first engagement was to attend the great man's funeral.

Soon afterwards Boyle became embroiled in the mounting crisis that followed Egypt's nationalization of the Suez Canal. While the military planning and preparations occupied much of his time, Boyle himself refused to become involved in the politics. He knew nothing of the Israeli connections, though he certainly shared his colleagues' misgivings about a situation in which the prime minister, Anthony Eden, was being steadily overwhelmed. His task was essentially to ensure that the RAF could play its part in operation Musketeer, and he shared the credit for the success of the air offensive carried out by the RAF in co-operation with the Fleet Air Arm and the French air force.

Boyle now faced problems of a different order in the course of a new major defence review. Inspired by the government's conviction that large savings in expenditure on conventional forces were essential to the improvement of Britain's economic performance, Duncan Sandys, the minister of defence, wrote a white paper which caused consternation around the RAF. Admittedly Boyle applauded one key aspect, its confirmation of the role of the V-bomber force in providing the United Kingdom's nuclear deterrent, in which he was a passionate believer. Sandys's other ideas were anathema, in particular his prediction that the advent of missiles could mean the end of manned fighter aircraft, and Boyle—deciding that resignation would serve no purpose—resolved to defend his corner. While he had no choice but to accept heavy cuts, especially in Fighter Command and Germany, he sought the backing of many influential friends, notably when he staged a special 'Prospect' conference in London in April 1958. Here, in the presence of 300 important personalities in public life, he affirmed that the air staff still saw the manned aircraft as the ultimate means of defence. Amid the subsequent political uproar the prime minister, Harold Macmillan, had to come to the rescue in the House of Commons. Boyle trod somewhat more carefully from now on, but in tours to bases throughout the world he sought to keep the RAF itself informed about developments and to restore its personnel's belief in themselves and confidence in their future. His was a timely demonstration of inspired leadership whose result, as he himself later put it, was to preserve the fabric of the RAF.

Many other matters, too, engaged Boyle's attention, including an attempt by the navy, strongly encouraged by Lord Mountbatten when he became chief of defence staff, to take over the aircraft of Coastal Command, and a full-scale study of the future roles of air transport. In the nuclear field there were the successful tests of Britain's hydrogen bomb at Christmas Island; the agreement to deploy the American Thor nuclear missile in the United Kingdom—a decision which Boyle supported since it brought the RAF into a new field of technology and would help prepare for the advent of Britain's intercontinental ballistic missile, Blue Streak; and the growing questions about Blue Streak itself, coupled with the possible acquisition of the air-launched Skybolt in its place. Moreover—a major achievement—he persuaded Sandys to agree to the development of the RAF's new strike and reconnaissance aircraft, the TSR 2.

At the end of 1959 Boyle handed over the post of chief of air staff to Sir Thomas Pike and accepted new challenges both in industry and in continuing connections with the RAF. As vice-chairman of the British Aircraft Corporation from 1962 to 1971 his service experience was invaluable for many aircraft projects, including the multi-role combat aircraft (MRCA), which eventually became the Tornado. The cancellations, on the other hand, horrified him, especially that of the TSR 2 in 1962; he simply could not believe that Sir Charles Elworthy, then chief of air staff, had gone along with it. Boyle also found time to guide the establishment of the RAF's own museum, at Hendon; as the first chairman of its board of trustees from 1965 to 1974 he provided much of the inspiration for this widely admired RAF institution. The RAF Benevolent Fund, of which he was deputy chairman, and the RAF Club, of which he was president, also owed him much, and to the end of his life he maintained his interest in the modern RAF, in its history, and in Cranwell, his alma mater.

Boyle died at Sway, Hampshire, on 5 May 1993, survived by his wife. He was one of the great father figures of the RAF. Superb flying ability, great staff skills, inspiring leadership, dominating presence, power to command an audience, charm, kindliness: such qualities made him one of the most respected and best-loved of all the RAF's high commanders.   HENRY A. PROBERT

Sources D. Boyle, *My life: an autobiography* (1989) [privately published] · H. Probert, *High commanders of the RAF* (1991) · official RAF records · *The Times* (7 May 1993) · *The Independent* (8 May 1993) · *WWW* · private information (2004) · personal knowledge (2004) · b. cert. · m. cert.
Archives Royal Air Force Museum, Hendon, department of research and information services, papers
Likenesses photograph, repro. in *The Times* · photograph, repro. in *The Independent*
Wealth at death £18,852: probate, 15 July 1993, *CGPLA Eng. & Wales*

Boyle [*née* Savile], **Dorothy, countess of Burlington** (1699–1758), portrait painter and caricaturist, was born in London on 13 September 1699 and baptized on 24 September at St James's, Piccadilly, the elder daughter of William Savile, second marquess of Halifax (1665–1700), and his second wife, Lady Mary Finch (*bap.* 1677, *d.* 1718), daughter of Daniel Finch, second earl of Nottingham and seventh earl of Winchilsea. At the age of eighteen Dorothy, with her younger sister Mary, inherited the Halifax estates and thus became a highly marriageable proposition. On 21 March 1721 she married the 'architect earl', Richard *Boyle, third earl of Burlington (1694–1753).

Henceforward the couple's lives chiefly revolved around three houses: Burlington House, Piccadilly; Chiswick House, Middlesex; and Londesborough in the West Riding of Yorkshire. William *Kent, painter, designer, and landscape gardener, shared their lives for nearly thirty years. Kent had responded to the announcement of Lord Burlington's engagement by hoping that Lady Dorothy's fortune would help to finance the redecoration of Lord Burlington's houses: 'I hope the vertu will grow stronger in our house & architecture will floresh more' (Harris, *Palladian Revival*, 70). He was not disappointed.

Dorothy Boyle, countess of Burlington (1699–1758), by William Kent, *c.*1735 [painting in the garden room at Chiswick House]

Lady Burlington took a keen interest in design, particularly in the creation of the Burlingtons' new villa at Chiswick; she also shared her husband's love of music and the theatre. Husband and wife extended friendship and patronage to David Garrick over some six years. Lady Burlington, self-appointed chaperone of the Viennese opera singer Eva Maria Veigel (Violette), painted her portrait and arranged her marriage to Garrick, but he came to resent Lady Burlington's domination and their correspondence ended. Her friendship with Alexander Pope was more equable; Pope assisted her from 1732 in preparing the papers of her grandfather George Savile, marquess of Halifax ('the Trimmer'), for publication in 1750. She served for ten years (1727–37) as one of Queen Caroline's eight ladies of the bedchamber and received permission to copy portraits in the Royal Collection. Off duty she rode to hounds.

Chiefly Lady Burlington took pleasure in portraiture. She was largely self-taught, having learnt by copying. Visiting Burlington House in 1743 George Vertue observed that the 'great room' was 'adorned with many crayon painted heads—the works of her Ladyship mostly all of them Coppyd from excellent pictures'. Vertue assumed that Kent had 'instructed [her] in the Art of drawing & painting in crayons' (Vertue, *Note books*, 3.140) but Kent's contribution was chiefly in liberating Lady Burlington in the direction of informal pen and ink sketches. She quickly developed a liking for him, referring to him as Kentino or the 'little Signor'. They evidently drew frequently in each other's company, each using an energetic pen and ink line, which sometimes makes it difficult to distinguish the work of one from the other among drawings from the so-called Kent–Burlington albums at Chatsworth. Kent drew Lady Burlington painting in oils at her easel, seated in the garden room at Chiswick which he designed for her, and painting the double portrait of her daughters which is now at Hardwick Hall. Her chalk drawing of Kent seated at a table, sketching, is one of several impromptu sketches of interiors with figures; she seems not to have tackled landscape.

Most of Lady Burlington's portraits, whether pencil studies or developed into oils, are of her daughters, the most accomplished being *Lady Charlotte Boyle* (c.1740–1745; Chatsworth, on long loan to Chiswick House). Otherwise, apart from a portrait in oil of Princess Amelia (uniquely signed 'D. Burlington/pinx^t'), she asked only family and friends to sit for her. But, as Horace Walpole noted, she also had a 'talent for caricatura'—for catching swift likenesses, often sardonically inscribed, on whatever fragment of paper or card came to hand. About thirty of these survive, including a sketch of Alexander Pope playing cards and a study of Queen Caroline on her deathbed, later inscribed by Pope with irreverent verse. Lady Burlington also concocted an operatic caricature by combining figures taken from Marco Ricci and Joseph Goupy into a new composition, showing the castrato Farinelli singing a duet with the dumpy Francesca Cuzzoni, with the impresario Heidegger in the background in a rage; the result, etched by Joseph Goupy, was published in 1734. Two chalk drawings by Lady Burlington are in the British Museum (Dept. of Prints and Drawings).

Correspondence between Lord and Lady Burlington over the years suggests that their relationship was amicable; each was in the habit of addressing the other as 'My dear Child', while a letter from Lord Burlington to his wife (23 September 1735) declares that 'Hearing from you, is the most agreeable thing in the world to me'. In Jean-Baptiste Van Loo's portrait group *The Third Earl of Burlington with his Wife and Two Daughters* (1739; collection Trustees of the Lismore estate) Lady Burlington is depicted holding a palette of oil colours. Behind her is a black servant, almost certainly James Cambridge, of whose head she made a sensitive pencil study. The two daughters are Dorothy and Charlotte, only survivors into adulthood of a son and three daughters born to the Burlingtons between 1724 and 1731. Dorothy married Lord Euston in 1741, dying unhappily within a year; Lady Burlington's portrait of her from memory was engraved by John Faber jun., privately published for friends. The younger daughter, Charlotte, married (1749) William Cavendish, marquess of Hartington, later fourth duke of Devonshire, and died in 1754, leaving four children; it is through that marriage that material relating to Lady Burlington (including all drawings and correspondence mentioned here and not otherwise located) is at Chatsworth.

Lord Burlington died in 1753, leaving everything to his countess for her lifetime. Overtaken by illness and solitude Lady Burlington fell to raging: Walpole reported to Seymour Conway on 19 September 1758 that 'she breaks out all over—in curses and blasphemies' (Walpole, *Corr.*, 37.571–2). She died in her bedchamber in Chiswick House on 21 September 1758.　　　　　　　　　　JUDY EGERTON

Sources S. Jenkins, 'Lady Burlington at court', *Lord Burlington: the man and his politics*, ed. E. Corp (1998), 149–79 · M. de Novellis, *Pallas unveil'd: the life and art of Lady Dorothy Savile, countess of Burlington (1699–1758)* (1999) [exhibition catalogue, Orleans House Gallery, Twickenham] · J. Harris, *The Palladian revival: Lord Burlington, his villa and garden at Chiswick* (1994) [exhibition catalogue, Montreal, Pittsburgh, and London] · J. Harris, *William Kent, 1685–1748: a poet on paper* (1998) [exhibition catalogue, Sir John Soane's Museum, London, 30 Oct – 19 Dec 1998] · J. D. Hunt, *William Kent: landscape garden designer* (1987) [illustr. catalogue of Kent's landscape and related drawings, 109–71] · T. C. Barnard and J. Clark, eds., *Lord Burlington: architecture, art and life* (1995) [Van Loo portrait group no. 268] · *The letters of David Garrick*, ed. D. M. Little and G. M. Kahrl, 1 (1963) · W. Feaver, *Masters of caricature: from Hogarth and Gillray to Scarfe and Levine*, ed. A. Green (1981) · parish register, St James's, Piccadilly, 24 Sept 1699 [baptism] · GEC, *Peerage*, new edn, 2.432–3 · Vertue, *Note books*

Archives Chatsworth House, Derbyshire, Devonshire MSS
Likenesses W. Aikman, oils, c.1700–1725, Chiswick House, London · C. Jervas?, oils, c.1722–1725, Chatsworth settlement, Derbyshire · W. Kent, pen, ink, and water on paper, c.1735, Chatsworth settlement, Derbyshire [*see illus.*] · J. B. van Loo, oils, 1739, Lismore estate

Boyle [*formerly* O'Boyle], **Sir Edward**, **first baronet** (1848–1909), barrister, was born in London on 6 September 1848, the elder son of Edward O'Boyle (d. 1865), civil engineer, of London, and his wife, Eliza (d. 1888), daughter of James Gurney of Culloden, Norfolk. He was educated privately for the army, but instead became a surveyor, and was elected a fellow of the Surveyors' Institution in 1878.

On 18 March 1874 Boyle married Constance Jane, younger daughter of William Knight of Kensington Park Gardens, businessman and magistrate; they had two children: a son, Edward, who succeeded Boyle in the baronetcy, and a daughter, Constance Beryl Bertha (b. 31 March 1882).

After some twenty years' practice as a surveyor, Boyle left that profession for the bar, to which he was called at the Inner Temple on 17 November 1887. He rapidly acquired a lucrative practice as an expert in rating and compensation cases, using the experience gained in his former profession, and took silk in 1898. He stood as a Conservative candidate in Hastings in 1900, and in Rye in 1903, both unsuccessfully. He was created a baronet on 14 December 1904. In the arbitration concerning the purchase by the Straits Settlements government of the Tanjong Pager Dock Company in 1905, Boyle acted as the arbitrator nominated by the company under the authority of a special ordinance. At the general election in January 1906 he was returned MP for Taunton, but ill health compelled his retirement from parliament in 1909.

Boyle was joint author of three important legal treatises, two of which dealt with the subjects in which he had specialized, rating and compensation. He travelled widely and was a fellow of the Royal Geographical Society. He died at his London residence, 63 Queen's Gate, on 19

March 1909. His son owned a portrait of him by the Hon. John Collier and another in the robes of a KC by Herbert Olivier, a replica of which he presented to the Surveyors' Institution.

C. E. A. BEDWELL, *rev.* CATHERINE PEASE-WATKIN

Sources *The Times* (20 March 1909) · Burke, *Peerage* · *Law List* (1908) · *Dod's Parliamentary Companion* (1907) · *CGPLA Eng. & Wales* (1909) · d. cert.
Archives NRA, papers
Likenesses J. Collier, portrait, priv. coll. · H. Olivier, portrait; replica, Royal Institution of Chartered Surveyors, London
Wealth at death £110,331 4s. 10d.: probate, 3 June 1909, *CGPLA Eng. & Wales*

Boyle, Edward Charles Gurney, Baron Boyle of Handsworth (1923–1981), politician, was born at 63 Queen's Gate, Kensington, London, on 31 August 1923, elder son in the family of two sons and one daughter of Sir Edward Boyle (1878–1945), second baronet, barrister, writer, and company director, and his wife, Beatrice (*d.* 1961), daughter of Henry Greig, of Belvedere House, Kent. His grandfather Sir Edward Boyle (1848–1909), created the first baronet in 1904, also a barrister, had been Conservative MP for Taunton from 1906 to 1909. The name Gurney derived from the surname of the first baronet's mother.

Boyle was educated at Eton College and Christ Church, Oxford, and showed early talent in the directions of his future life, writing and politics. At Eton he was president of the Political Society and editor of the *Eton Chronicle*. At Oxford he was president of the union, active in Conservative politics, and in 1947 half of a university debating team (with Tony Benn) which toured the United States. He succeeded his father as baronet in 1945, having already had three years as a temporary civil servant at the Foreign Office, and so went up to Oxford with the first post-war generation, aged twenty-two. Though he left Oxford in 1949 with only a third-class degree in history, which seemed to belie his recognized intellectual abilities, he was already seen as a coming man who would achieve much—more indeed than he ever did achieve. Sir Edward Heath, a close friend as well as a political associate, felt that Boyle's 'intellectual characteristics … comprised a wide breadth of interest, a remarkable store of information, and a phenomenal memory for everything that he encountered, but his was not a mind full of innovative ideas or of penetrating analysis' (*DNB*). Though they shared what Heath called 'deep-seated and moderate convictions which guided him all through his life' (ibid.) there was an intellectual difference between the leader Heath, who cogitated mainly to promote action, and the follower Boyle, who enjoyed philosophical reflection for its own sake, and was not always quick to make up his mind. This divergence of approach was a barrier both to Boyle's eventual advancement at the top and to Heath getting the best out of the Conservative colleague who most nearly shared his own outlook.

After Oxford, Boyle was assistant editor of the *National Review*, but while still an undergraduate had been selected as Unionist candidate for Birmingham, Perry Barr. He

Edward Charles Gurney Boyle, Baron Boyle of Handsworth (1923–1981), by Godfrey Argent, 1969

fought and lost the seat in the general election of 1950, aged only twenty-six, but established connections with Birmingham which lasted for the rest of his political career. He comfortably won the Handsworth constituency, then safely Conservative, at a by-election in November 1950, and retained the seat until he went to the Lords in 1970. Birmingham was, though, an uncomfortable base for a moderate like Boyle, for its Conservatism tended to the right, especially when coloured immigration affected the city's politics soon after Boyle became one of its MPs. He was not a comfortable member of the Birmingham Conservative members' group in the Commons, refused to campaign for immigration restrictions, and in the 1960s had difficulties with his local party, notably in the aftermath of Enoch Powell's race speech in 1968, delivered in the city, when the rising Monday Club began to stir up his local activists against him.

When Churchill's Conservatives regained office in 1951, Boyle was appointed parliamentary private secretary to the under-secretary for air, moving on to be parliamentary secretary at the Ministry of Supply in July 1954 (younger even than Churchill himself when first given office in 1906), and became economic secretary to the Treasury in 1955. Apart from a single interruption, he spent the rest of his Commons life on the front bench, and even that interval was short: friends who organized a celebration of his resignation in November 1956 in protest at the Suez invasion found that he was back in office as a junior education minister under Macmillan in January 1957 before they could actually hold the party. Difficulties with his constituency following his stand over Suez led him to consider leaving politics to take up the permanent post of head Treasury representative in Delhi, as he confided to his friend Tony Benn, but he decided to stick with his departmental position.

In 1959 Boyle returned to the Treasury as financial secretary, and then went back to the cabinet post of minister of education in 1962. He stayed at education until his party lost office in 1964, and then returned after an unhappy period as shadow home secretary (1964–5) to be education spokesman in opposition. Economics and education, the two fields in which he took the greatest personal interest, were also therefore the only departments where he ever acted as minister or shadowed for any lengthy period in opposition. Consequently Boyle never had opportunities to develop as a political all-rounder. A modest and easygoing man, he even allowed himself in 1964 to be demoted from minister of education to minister of state at the larger Department of Education and Science (though retaining his cabinet seat), when Alec Douglas-Home needed the secretaryship of state for Quintin Hogg.

During his two periods at the Treasury, Boyle proved a capable minister, with an unusually good grasp for a minister in that generation of the economics involved. The chancellor, R. A. Butler, had wanted him as a junior treasury minister after seeing his impressive performance at supply, and Boyle thereafter remained close to Butler, strongly backing him for the premiership in 1963. During 1955 he had to carry a heavy responsibility, since Butler had to cope simultaneously with an economic crisis, personal ill health, and a dying wife. He worked well enough with Macmillan when he replaced Butler at the end of the year, though he was unable to persuade him even of the economic risks of the Suez adventure, and it was this that ensured his rapid return to office when Macmillan became prime minister. He had delayed his Suez resignation until after the cease-fire, not wanting to divide the country while British troops were under fire, but stuck to his own guns to the extent of abstaining in the no-confidence debate that followed, one of only eight Conservative MPs to do so. During the Profumo crisis of 1963 he seriously considered resignation once again, and the many letters from friends which urged him to do so indicated the reputation for personal integrity that he enjoyed.

Boyle was unlucky that he twice arrived at the Treasury after a pre-election boom had over-heated the economy, so that the naturally expansionist Boyle was forced to help implement the credit squeezes of 1955–6 and 1961–2. He did, though, willingly help Heathcoat Amory as chancellor in resisting Macmillan's demand for tax cuts even during a boom in 1960. He was thought to have done well at the Treasury on both occasions, and the whips and party managers were happy to see him progress upwards, offering as he did a youthful, unstuffy, and modern face to a party increasingly jaded during thirteen years in office. When Macmillan reshuffled his team and gave Boyle his first cabinet posting at education in 1962, he identified the Etonian and Harrovian baronets Boyle and Sir Keith Joseph as his modernizing 'beavers', who would help to project a forward-looking image, while he himself contributed continuity and experience. Given his lifestyle, private means, and the intense knowledge of classical music which made him a knowledgeable conversationalist, a regular visitor to Glyndebourne, and the would-be author of a book on the composer Gabriel Fauré, Boyle was never exactly convincing in this role of classless, modern man.

At education Boyle assisted Geoffrey Lloyd in a modest expansion programme in 1957–9, and then pursued a far more active one of his own from 1962. His introduction to the published Newsom report on secondary schooling has been hailed as 'a momentous breakthrough in official thinking', since he took the opportunity to reject the idea of fixed intelligence levels which had underpinned the tripartite system set up in 1944, and demanded instead that all children should have 'an equal opportunity of *acquiring* intelligence and of developing their talents and abilities to the full'. He naturally therefore welcomed comprehensive schools, but at the same time, as a staunch believer in academic standards, could not also accept the demise of the grammar school (Cook and McKie, 172). It fell to Boyle to announce the government's acceptance of the Robbins report into higher education when published in 1963, and so dramatically to accelerate the rate of expansion in the university sector during the decade, during which student numbers doubled and expenditure on universities approximately tripled. His seven honorary degrees (four of them before he himself abandoned the Commons for the common room) and his pro-chancellorship of the new University of Sussex (1965–70) testified to the belief that he had as a minister made a material impact on tertiary education.

In opposition after 1964 the Home and Education portfolios were both responsibilities where Boyle's innate moderation conflicted with the party's right wing, and he was sometimes indeed attacked at party conferences as a surrogate for his friend and leader Heath. These were not therefore happy times for him politically, since he was reluctant to adopt even the rhetoric of a party moving to the right. Heath has recalled that Boyle 'repeatedly refused' the offer of other front-bench positions at this time (DNB), but Boyle was not offered such positions as shadow chancellor which would have both engaged his interest and reflected his seniority. He was, for example, one of the few Conservative frontbenchers interested enough to find out in the later 1960s about the emerging monetarist school of economics, which swept his party in the next generation, but he was also a supporter of incomes policies. Frustrated by lack of progress, he decided in 1969 to retire from the Commons and become directly involved in education as vice-chancellor of the University of Leeds. He could thus from 1970, in Heath's words, 'express his views and implement his policies without constant interference from those taking part in the political battle' (ibid.). Boyle became a life peer in July

1970 and, in deference to his new non-political role, sat on the cross-benches in the House of Lords. In June 1981, shortly before his death, he was made a Companion of Honour.

After he moved to Leeds, Boyle's admired fair-mindedness secured his appointment as chairman of the top salaries review board, and in a time of rapid inflation he was instrumental in ensuring that politicians were steeled to the always difficult task of ensuring fair remuneration for the highest-paid public servants. At Leeds he was a diplomatic vice-chancellor during the later period of the student unrest which had begun in 1968, a difficult manager for student radicals to hate. He was fully committed to the university and its members, actively involved in its affairs, and recognized to have done his job so well that he was in 1977–9 chairman of the Committee of Vice-Chancellors and Principals. It was characteristic of Boyle that he preferred meeting and dealing with students in Leeds to the national leadership of the university sector.

Boyle was, thought Anthony Sampson in 1962, one of the few 'radically minded men' within modern Conservatism, though he had:

> a nineteenth century look to him: he is a huge rubicund baronet who wears formal clothes, and talks with unconcealed learning … He walks like a bear, with a formidable shuffle, and he has the broad interests and the leisureliness of a cultivated squire.   (Sampson, 89)

He was a persuasive rather than an oratorical speaker, and a man who rarely enjoyed scoring party political points in debate. Indeed, for a politician he had like Keith Joseph the near-fatal weakness of always being able to see the case against whatever position he was advancing, and in many cases sharing some sympathy with it too. This made him a sometimes dithering frontbencher, for example, over secondary education, where he would not adopt an all-out defence of grammar schools, yet could not commit himself wholeheartedly to comprehensives and then seek to persuade Conservatives to join him there. He was, though, a courageous man, unshakeably committed to the defence of reason and of moderate causes, for example, on race relations; when contesting the Powellite drift within the Conservative Party in 1965–70 he constantly proclaimed the need for understanding on both sides as a multiracial society developed. He symbolized a civilized, centrist, conciliatory style of Conservatism; in 1980 there were reports that he was involved in discussions about the formation of a centre party. His withdrawal to the House of Lords in 1970 provoked expressions of regret about the lack of intellectuals in the House of Commons, and the reflection in a *Times* leader that British politics failed to attract sufficient 'men of powerful mind' of the type which he represented (*The Times*, 3 June 1970, 11).

In his earlier years Boyle had been a high Anglican, and though he moved steadily towards agnosticism as he aged, he never lost that passion for service to the community which his early beliefs and family background had engendered. In later life he suffered from ill health, and died at his home, the vice-chancellor's lodge, 10 Grosvenor Road, Leeds, on 28 September 1981. He had never married, and the baronetcy passed to his brother, Richard Gurney Boyle (1930–1983).   JOHN RAMSDEN

Sources U. Leeds, Brotherton L., Boyle MSS · Trinity Cam., Butler MSS · Bodl. Oxf., conservative party archive · personal knowledge (2004) · *DNB* · *The Times* (29 Sept 1981) · *Daily Telegraph* (29 Sept 1981) · T. Benn, *Years of hope: diaries, letters, and papers, 1940–1962* (1994) · S. Brittan, *Steering the economy: the role of the treasury* (1969) · C. Cook and D. McKie, eds., *Decade of disillusion: Britain in the sixties* (1972) · C. Knight, *The making of conservative education policy in postwar Britain* (1990) · R. Lamb, *The Macmillan government: the emerging truth* (1995) · J. Ramsden, *The age of Churchill and Eden, 1940–1957* (1995) · J. Ramsden, *The winds of change: Macmillan to Heath, 1957–1975* (1996) · A. Sampson, *The anatomy of Britain* (1962) · A. Seldon, *Churchill's Indian summer: the conservative government, 1951–1955* (1981) · J. Vaizey, *In breach of promise: Gaitskell, Macleod, Titmuss, Crosland, Boyle: five men who shaped a generation* (1984)

Archives U. Leeds, Brotherton L., corresp. and papers |SOUND BL NSA, current affairs recordings

Likenesses G. Argent, photograph, 1969 [*see illus.*]

Wealth at death £180,018: probate, 17 Dec 1981, *CGPLA Eng. & Wales*

Boyle [*née* Gordon], **Eleanor Vere** (1825–1916), illustrator and author, was born on 1 May 1825 at Auchlunies, Aberdeenshire, the youngest of the nine children of Alexander Gordon (1783–1873) of Auchlunies, son of George, third earl of Aberdeen, and his wife, Albinia Elizabeth, daughter of Richard Cumberland and Lady Albinia Cumberland, daughter of George, third earl of Buckinghamshire. Her mother was an amateur painter. Her early childhood was spent at Auchlunies and she was educated at home. She often visited Maryculter, the seat of her uncle General Gordon, in the nearby valley, and even after the family moved to Hampton Wick in 1833 they frequently travelled north, particularly to Ellon Castle, Aberdeenshire, which her father inherited in 1840. She also went regularly to Hampton Court, where her grandmother, Lady Albinia Cumberland (formerly maid of honour to Queen Charlotte, wife of George III), occupied grace-and-favour apartments.

On 23 September 1845, at a ceremony in St George's Hanover Square, Eleanor Gordon married the Hon. and Revd Richard Cavendish Townshend Boyle (1812–1886), the youngest son of Edmund, eighth earl of Cork and Orrery. Her husband was vicar of Marston Bigot, Somerset, and in 1847 became chaplain-in-ordinary to Queen Victoria. They lived at Marston rectory, Marston Bigot, at that time a remote and old-fashioned area, spending their holidays in Switzerland, the south of France, and Italy. The first of their five children was born in 1846, the fifth and last in 1854.

Although Boyle undoubtedly received art instruction as a child, it was not until the birth of her own children that she developed her talent—under the influence of the works of Albrecht Dürer, the Pre-Raphaelites, and John Ruskin's *Modern Painters*, and with the benefit of informal advice from William Boxall, Charles Eastlake, and Thomas Landseer; the latter taught her to etch. Between 1852 and 1877 Boyle (who was known professionally as E. V. B. or the Hon. Mrs Richard Boyle) illustrated fourteen books, the majority fairy tales or nursery rhymes. *Child's Play* (1852) with seventeen drawings (the first time nursery rhymes had been illustrated) and *A Children's Summer* (1853) with eleven etchings on steel by the artist (illustrating prose by her cousin, Mary Boyle, and verse by W. M. Call) won praise from John Ruskin, Thomas Landseer, Tom Taylor, and Francis Turner Palgrave, and led to the suggestion that she should be included, with Lady Waterford, in John Millais's sketching club project of 1854. There followed *Waifs and Strays from a Scrap-Book* (1862), *Woodland Gossip* (1864), *A Leaflet from a German Christmas Tree* (1865), *In the Fir Wood* (1866), *The Story without an End* (1868), *A Dream Book* (1870), a new translation of Hans Christian Andersen's *Fairy Tales* (1872), *Beauty and the Beast* (1875), *The Magic Valley, or, Patient Antoine* by Eliza Keary (1877), and *A New Child's Play* (1877). She also illustrated Thomas Gray's *Elegy Written in a Country Churchyard* (for *Favourite English Poems* published by Sampson Low in 1859) and Lord Tennyson's *May Queen* (1861). Idealized children, often in mysterious natural surroundings with meticulously rendered plants and animals, predominate in her illustrations, most of which, from the 1860s, were reproduced photographically and some subsequently printed in colour. Boyle also exhibited fourteen designs for illustrations and independent works at the Society of Female Artists (Society of Lady Artists from 1869) (1859–79), five at watercolour exhibitions of the Dudley Gallery (1872–80), thirteen at the latter's black and white exhibitions (1877–80), and three at the Grosvenor Gallery (1880, 1881). Constantly involved with charitable work in her husband's parish, Eleanor Boyle often used the proceeds from her sales and publications for good causes: she financed the provision of fresh drinking water in Lower Marston and refurbished her husband's church.

About 1871, on Richard Boyle's retirement, the family moved to Huntercombe Manor, near Burnham in Buckinghamshire, where Boyle re-created the extensive garden, planting roses on a large scale and 20,000 snowdrops. From 1878, when her husband suffered a stroke, Boyle's artistic output lessened considerably and she devoted herself to writing. Nature, gardens, and what she called 'the day of small things, of Nature's delicate masterpieces' (E. V. Boyle, *The Peacock's Pleasaunce*, 1908, 92) were her main subjects in ten books published between 1884 and 1908, many illustrated with small black and white vignettes. *Days and Hours in a Garden*, dedicated to her husband, who died in 1886, was her most popular work, ten editions appearing between 1884 and 1898. Also successful were *Ros rosarum ex horta poetarum* (1885), an anthology of poetry about roses to which Tennyson and Bulwer-Lytton contributed verses, and *Seven Gardens and a Palace* (3rd edn, 1900)—a collection of essays by Eleanor Boyle reprinted from the *Anglo-Saxon Review*, *Blackwood's Magazine*, *Country Life*, the *National Review*, and the *Pall Mall Magazine*—describing gardens she had known since her childhood. She presented a copy of this last work to her friend Queen Alexandra.

Boyle's views on art were also published. A patroness of the Frome School of Art since its foundation in 1868, she

twice addressed its students (in 1870 and 1899), encouraging a 'patient following of Nature for love of Nature's truth' and education of 'the perception of beauty' while decrying impressionism and the 'profoundly joyless' art inspired by Burne-Jones (E. V. Boyle, *The Peacock's Pleasaunce*, 1908, 249, 258, 253). She herself continued to sketch; in 1902 an exhibition was held of her work entitled 'Sketches, dreams and drawings' at Leighton House, Kensington, London. Her last work, drawn for Tennyson in 1911, was *Love hath us in the Net*.

Much of Eleanor Boyle's considerable wealth having been lost as a result of unwise investments by her son-in-law, a banker (to whom her fortune was entrusted after the death of her husband), her old age was spent in comparative poverty. She died in Brighton on 29 July 1916 and was buried in Marston Bigot churchyard.

CHARLOTTE YELDHAM

Sources M. McGarvie, 'Eleanor Vere Boyle (1825–1916) (E. V. B.), writer and illustrator: her life, work and circle', *Transactions of the Ancient Monuments Society*, new ser., 26 (1982), 94–145 • E. C. Clayton, *English female artists*, 2 vols. (1876) • F. Reid, *Illustrators of the sixties* (1928) • J. Soden and C. Baile de Laperrière, eds., *The Society of Women Artists exhibitors, 1855–1996*, 4 vols. (1996) • F. Hays, *Women of the day: a biographical dictionary of notable contemporaries* (1885) • V. Surtees, *Sublime and instructive* (1972) • S. Houfe, *The dictionary of British book illustrators and caricaturists, 1800–1914* (1978) • exhibition catalogues (1872–80) [Dudley Gallery; watercolour: 1872, 1878, 1880; black and white: 1877–80] • exhibition catalogues (1880–81) [Grosvenor Gallery, London] • *The Times* (18 Aug 1916)
Archives Ebberston Hall, North Yorkshire, Fenton archives
Likenesses W. Boxall, portrait, 1846, priv. coll.
Wealth at death £2325 4s. 4d.: probate, 9 Oct 1916, CGPLA Eng. & Wales

Boyle, George David (1828–1901), dean of Salisbury, born at Edinburgh on 17 May 1828, was the eldest child of David *Boyle, Lord Shewalton (1772–1853), a Scottish judge, and his second wife, Camilla Catherine (d. 1880), eldest daughter of David Smythe of Methven. As 'a small, shy child' he saw Sir Walter Scott in his father's study (Boyle, 2). Educated first at Edinburgh Academy and by a private tutor, he went in 1843 to Charterhouse School. In June 1846 he matriculated at Exeter College, Oxford, went into residence in April 1847, and graduated BA in 1851 and MA in 1853. In London, as at Edinburgh, family connections brought him, while a schoolboy, the acquaintance of persons of literary distinction, and he developed a precocious interest in the Oxford Movement. However, the influence of John Campbell Shairp, whom he met first in 1838, and who became a lifelong friend, preserved him from partisanship (his recollections of Shairp are included in W. Knight's *Principal Shairp and his Friends*, 1888). Ordained deacon in 1853 and priest in 1854, Boyle was from 1853 until 1857 curate of Kidderminster under Thomas Legh Claughton, and from 1857 to 1860 curate of Hagley. In 1861 he married Mary Christiana, daughter of William Robins of Hagley. They had no children.

In 1860 Boyle 'had three offers of new work at once' and he chose the incumbency of St Michael's, Handsworth, Birmingham (Boyle, 203). He entered into the public life of Birmingham, especially on its educational side, was a governor of King Edward VI's School, and numbered among his friends men differing as widely as John Henry Newman, George Dawson, and Robert William Dale. In 1867 Boyle became vicar of Kidderminster, where he won general confidence. He was chairman of the first school board for Kidderminster, acted as arbitrator in an industrial dispute, promoted the building of an infirmary, and greatly developed the church schools.

In 1880 Boyle was appointed dean of Salisbury. A sum of £14,000 was spent on the cathedral under his direction. His love of literature and his acquaintance with men of affairs continued to widen his interests. On ecclesiastical controversy, in which he took no active part, he exercised a moderating influence. His *Recollections* suggests a tendency to broad-churchmanship growing out of high-churchmanship. He considered contributing to *Essays and Reviews* (1860) but did not do so. He died suddenly of heart failure at Salisbury on 21 March 1901, his wife surviving him. A mural tablet and a window to his memory are in Salisbury Cathedral.

Boyle edited with notes a selection from Clarendon's history (1889); he also published his *Recollections* (1895) and a small volume entitled *Salisbury Cathedral* (1897).

A. R. BUCKLAND, *rev.* H. C. G. MATTHEW

Sources G. D. Boyle, *Recollections* (1895) · *The Times* (22 March 1901) · *Guardian* (27 March 1901) · *Guardian* (12 Nov 1901) · Foster, *Alum. Oxon.* · W. Knight, *Principal Shairp and his friends* (1888)
Archives NL Scot., letters to Sir Charles Dalrymple
Likenesses oils, Church House, Salisbury · portrait, repro. in Boyle, *Recollections*
Wealth at death £2540 7s. 1d.: probate, 14 Aug 1901, *CGPLA Eng. & Wales*

Boyle, George Frederick, sixth earl of Glasgow (1825–1890), Tractarian layman, was born on 9 October 1825, the first of two children of George Boyle, fourth earl of Glasgow (1765–1843), and his second wife, Julia (1796–1868), daughter of Sir John *Sinclair, bt, of Ulbster. The fourth earl had three children from his first marriage, the eldest surviving son, James, succeeding him as fifth earl. In 1844 Boyle went to Christ Church, Oxford, and graduated BA in 1847. At the university Boyle became an adherent of the Oxford Movement, and for the rest of his life he devoted his time and fortune to promoting Tractarianism, mainly in Scotland but also in England.

In 1847, together with Walter, eighteenth Lord Forbes, Boyle endowed the foundation of St Ninian's Cathedral, Perth, as a Tractarian establishment and the first cathedral to be built in Scotland since the sixteenth-century Reformation. The foundation had received the support of Patrick Torry, bishop of the diocese, but its ritualism and English Anglo-Catholic clergy alienated his successor, Charles Wordsworth. Although Boyle and Forbes sympathized with Wordsworth they were not prepared to forsake entirely the cathedral's Tractarian inspiration. Boyle continued his support of St Ninian's until 1885, when some £9000 which he had bestowed was needed to pay his debts. In 1849 Boyle endowed another Tractarian establishment, the College of the Holy Spirit, at Millport on the island of Great Cumbrae, one of his estates in the Firth of

Clyde and his customary residence. It was to be a Tractarian theological college, but remoteness prevented its success. However, the college became the cathedral of the Isles in the diocese of Argyll and the Isles in 1874.

On 29 April 1856 Boyle married Montagu (1835/6–1931), daughter of George Ralph, third Lord Abercromby, and his wife, Louisa Penuel Forbes, and they had two daughters. Montagu was the beloved niece of Bishop Alexander Penrose Forbes, which further cemented the friendship between these two leading Scottish Tractarians. Boyle was an active confidant and supporter of the bishop during the eucharistic controversy in the Scottish Episcopal church between 1857 and 1860, acting as a moderating influence on the more militant of the bishop's supporters among the Episcopalian clergy. Boyle also campaigned for Bishop Forbes in the struggle to save the use of the Scottish communion office in the Episcopal church in the early 1860s. His hopes for Anglican–Roman Catholic reunion led to him becoming for a time one of the more moderate proprietors of the *Union Review*, founded in 1863 as the organ of the Association for the Promotion of the Unity of Christendom and the mouthpiece of the most ultra-Romanist Anglo-Catholics. Boyle was the most sustained and prominent of a number of aristocratic lay supporters and financiers of Tractarianism who facilitated the spread of the Oxford Movement in the Scottish Episcopal church, in recognition of which he was one of the chief mourners at the funeral of E. B. Pusey in 1882.

Boyle was elected MP for Bute in 1865 and retained his seat until 1869, when he succeeded his half-brother as sixth earl of Glasgow. He inherited the family seat of Crawford Priory, Fife, and was deputy lieutenant of Renfrewshire and Fife and lord clerk register of Scotland. But his overly generous Tractarian endowments and a sudden fall in land prices caused his bankruptcy in 1885, and he died in comparative poverty on 23 April 1890 at 32 Palmerston Place, Edinburgh. He was buried at the cathedral of the Isles, the institution that he had founded.

ROWAN STRONG

Sources Dundee University Archives, George Boyle MSS · NA Scot., George Boyle MSS · R. Strong, *Alexander Forbes of Brechin* (1995) · W. Perry, *The Oxford Movement in Scotland* (1933) · J. Wordsworth, *The episcopate of Charles Wordsworth, bishop of St Andrews* (1899) · *Debrett's Peerage* (1970) · M. Lochhead, *Episcopal Scotland in the nineteenth century* (1966) · GEC, *Peerage* · m. cert. [Scotland] · d. cert. [Scotland]
Archives NA Scot., corresp. and papers · University of Dundee, corresp. · University of Dundee, corresp. and papers relating to the college and collegiate church of the Holy Spirit | Cumbrae College, Cumbrae, Brechin MSS · University of Dundee, letters to Alexander Forbes

Boyle, Helen (1869–1957), physician and specialist in the treatment of mental illness, was born in Dublin on 19 November 1869, the eldest of the five children of Richard Warneford Boyle (d. 1900), a banker, and Alice Mary (d. 1921), *née* Chambers. She was educated at home and at the Höhere Tochterschule in Bonn, Germany, where her mother and siblings had moved in 1882 as a result of her father's bankruptcy and her parents' informal separation.

In 1890 Helen Boyle entered the London School of Medicine for Women. In 1893 she took the Scottish triple qualification in medicine, becoming licentiate of the Royal College of Physicians of Edinburgh, the Royal College of Surgeons of Edinburgh, and the Royal Faculty of Physicians and Surgeons of Glasgow. She also received her certificate in midwifery. She took her MD (Brussels) in 1894 and became a member of the British Medical Association. During the same year Boyle began working part time at the Canning Town Medical Mission, and between 1895 and 1897 worked as fourth medical assistant at the London County Council Claybury Asylum, probably because mental health was, due to its low status, one of the few areas of work open to women doctors. While there she collaborated in some of Sir Frederick Mott's early experiments in psychopathology, and became the first person to identify and isolate bacillary dysentery as an infective condition among mental patients.

In 1897 Boyle began work full time at the Canning Town Medical Mission as superintendent, working particularly with women struggling with poverty and stress. It was her experience at Canning Town that laid the foundation stone for her life's work. She commented on that time:

> I saw mental patients being manufactured in the rough, as it were. I met them every day at the dispensary and in people's houses. I saw them, to my mind, neglected and maltreated until after days, months or years, according to their resisting power, they were turned into the finished product—lunatics—and were certified. (Boyle, 1)

It was there that she decided to devote her life to preventative work with women in the early stages of mental illness.

In mid-1897 Boyle and her colleague Mabel Jones moved to Brighton to work as the town's first female general practitioners. In 1899 they founded the Lewes Road Dispensary for Women and Children in a poor area of Brighton. Its popularity, and Helen Boyle's concern about the preponderance of women suffering from untreated mental illness, resulted in the foundation in 1905 of the Lady Chichester Hospital for Women with Nervous Diseases. It was the first hospital of its kind in England. Both the hospital and dispensary were extremely successful, resulting in the expansion of both. The dispensary, concentrating on physical ailments, began to take in-patients, and in 1912 expanded into a medical hospital for women and children, which in 1917 became the New Sussex Hospital for Women and Children. In 1915 Helen Boyle went to Serbia for five months to the Reserve Hospital in Vrnjatchka Banja as part of the Royal Free Hospital team, and for her services was awarded the order of St Sava. This action was typical of Boyle's desire to become involved in pioneer work in areas where she could be most useful.

Throughout her professional life Helen Boyle was at the forefront of the developing speciality of psychiatry, and in 1924 she gave evidence to the royal commission on lunacy and mental disorder, and again in 1930 prior to the passing of the Mental Treatment Act. In 1928 she became a member of the council of psychiatry section of the Royal Society of Medicine. Boyle was involved in the founding of several societies: the Brighton Guardianship Society (1913), the Medical Women's Federation (1917), and the International Medical Women's Federation (1922). In 1923 she co-founded and was made vice-chairman of the National Council for Mental Hygiene (which later became MIND), and in 1924 became part of Archbishop Temple's Church's Council of Healing. In 1953 she was made a member of the *comité d'honneur* of the World Federation for Mental Health.

While continuing her work at the Lady Chichester Hospital, in 1930 Boyle became honorary consultant for nervous diseases at the Royal Sussex Hospital, and in 1937 was appointed honorary consultant for early nervous disorders at the Royal County Hospital. In 1939 she became the first woman president of the Royal Medico-Psychological Association.

Among Boyle's works were 'Case of juvenile general paralysis' (1899), 'Some points in the early treatment of mental and nervous cases (with special reference to the poor)' (1905), 'The ideal clinic for the treatment of nervous and borderland cases' (1924), and 'Watchman, what of the night?' (1939), all published in the *Journal of Mental Science*; 'Diagnosis and treatment of the milder forms of the manic depressive psychosis', which appeared in *Proceedings of the Royal Society of Medicine* (1930); and 'The mental hygiene movement' in *Mental Health* (1944). Her main leisure interests were poetry, walking, beagling, and her friends—who were numerous. She possessed a general enthusiasm for life, enormous energy, and great interest in people.

In 1948 the National Health Service took over the Lady Chichester Hospital for Women with Nervous Diseases, and Helen Boyle retired, although she remained in private practice until she died on 20 November 1957 at her home, Rockrose, Pycombe, Hove, Sussex. She was buried at All Saints' Church, Hove on 4 December. She was unmarried.

EMMA MILLIKEN

Sources C. L. Hingston and C. Vince, *Medical Women's Federation Journal* (Jan 1958) · *The Times* (4 Dec 1957) · *Medical Directory* (1895–1957) · *Medical Register* (1895–1957) · *The women's who's who, 1934–5: an annual record of the careers and activities of the leading women of the day* (1934) · private information (2004) · H. Boyle, *Twenty-one years of pioneer work: a record and an appeal* (1926) · E. Pryor, *Claybury: a century of caring* (1993) · *The Times* (5 Dec 1957)
Archives E. Sussex RO · priv. coll. · Royal Free Hospital, London | Wellcome L., Medical Women's Federation MSS
Likenesses photograph, 1939, Aldrington House, Hove · photograph, repro. in *Journal of Mental Science* (Sept 1939) · photographs, priv. coll.
Wealth at death £25,292: priv. coll.

Boyle, Henry, Baron Carleton (1669–1725), politician, was born on 12 July 1669, the third and youngest son of Charles Boyle, Baron Clifford of Lanesborough (1639–1694), and his first wife, Lady Jane Seymour (d. 1679), the youngest daughter of William, second duke of Somerset. He was a scion of a prominent Anglo-Irish aristocratic family; his grandfather was Richard *Boyle, second earl of Cork. After Westminster School he was commissioned into the army, almost certainly through the offices of his uncle Laurence *Hyde, earl of Rochester. He did not share the legitimist views of his Hyde relations, however, adopting instead the moderate whiggery of his father. In November 1688 he had joined the desertion of James II for the prince of Orange. He entered parliament for Tamworth, his father's old constituency, in May 1689, but after losing the seat at the general election in 1690 went to Ireland to run his grandfather's huge estates in counties Cork and Waterford. He served briefly in the Irish parliament, where he was noted for his great skill and 'quickness'. In 1692, having resigned his army commission, he was elected MP for Cambridge University, of which his cousin the third duke of Somerset was chancellor. Identifying himself with the 'country' opposition, he shone as a speaker and scrutineer of government activity, and obtained election to the commission of accounts during the years 1695–7. Tiring of opposition, however, he crossed to the court party during the winter of 1697–8, and his effective advocacy of the court's financial measures brought him appointment as a lord of the treasury in May 1699 and advancement to chancellor of the exchequer in 1701, which latter office he retained until 1708. From 1704 until 1715 he was also both lord treasurer of Ireland and lord lieutenant of the West Riding of Yorkshire. Urbane and superior, he avoided political infighting wherever possible, preferring the steady routines of treasury business, from which he profited handsomely.

Following the 1705 election, when he became MP for Westminster, Boyle emerged as one of Godolphin's chief lieutenants in the lower house, and in February 1708 he replaced Robert Harley as secretary of state in the southern department. His leadership over the court whigs, the high point of his career, ceased, however, towards the end of 1709 as the ministry succumbed increasingly to the dominance of the junto whigs. Early in 1710 he was a manager in the Sacheverell trial, but, unable to face the battles engendered by ascendant toryism, he declined re-election later in the year and withdrew from politics altogether. Following Queen Anne's death in 1714 he was, inevitably, tipped for the highest offices under the incoming whig ministry, but received only a barony. He supported Lord Sunderland's government during the 'whig schism' and in 1721 was appointed to the cabinet rank of lord president; he was retained as such by Walpole. Boyle died, unmarried, at his London residence, Carleton House, on 14 March 1725, leaving estates in Oxfordshire, Wiltshire, and Petersham in Surrey, plus a personalty in excess of £27,000. According to Lady Mary Wortley Montagu, Carleton was the real father of Kitty Hyde [see Douglas, Catherine, duchess of Queensberry and Dover], daughter of Jane *Hyde, countess of Clarendon and Rochester, and her husband, Henry, Lord Hyde. The veracity of the story remains unclear, but certainly both Kitty and Jane benefited in money and jewellery from Carleton's will. He was buried in the family vault at Londesborough, Yorkshire, on 31 March 1725. A. A. Hanham

Sources 'Boyle, Hon Henry', HoP, Commons · C. B. Realey, The early opposition to Sir Robert Walpole, 1720–27 (1931) · DNB
Archives BL, corresp. with Lord Townshend and the duke of Marlborough, Add. MSS 33273, 36795, 38498–38499; Egerton MSS 892–894 · BL, corresp. with Charles Whitworth, Add MSS 37356–37358 passim · Bodl. Oxf., corresp. with Lord Townshend · NL Ire., corresp. with William Congreve · PRO NIre., letters to Lord Coningby
Likenesses J. Houbraken, line engraving, 1741 (after G. Kneller), BM, NPG; repro. in T. Birch, The head of illustrious persons of Great Britain … with their lives and characters, 2 vols. (1743–51) · G. Kneller, portrait, Hardwick Hall, Derbyshire
Wealth at death more than £27,000, excl. estates in Oxfordshire, Wiltshire, and Surrey: 'Boyle, Hon Henry'

Boyle, Henry, first earl of Shannon (1681×7–1764), speaker of the Irish House of Commons, was born in Castlemartyr, co. Cork, Ireland, the second son of Lieutenant-Colonel Henry Boyle (c.1650–1693) of Castlemartyr and Mary O'Brien, daughter of Murrough *O'Brien, first earl of Inchiquin (c.1614–1674), the commander of protestant forces in Munster in the 1640s. His father was killed in Flanders in 1693 while fighting with the duke of Marlborough's army. He was a member of the Church of Ireland, and was educated at Westminster School, where he became queen's scholar in 1702, and then at Christ Church, Oxford, where he matriculated in March 1705; both institutions were high tory and had strong connections with the Boyle family. In 1705 he succeeded to the family estate, a minor one within the Cork Boyle family, after the death of his older brother, Roger. He served as MP for Midleton, co. Cork, from 7 July 1707 to 2 November 1713, then for Kilmallock, co. Limerick, from November 1713 to October 1714, and finally for co. Cork from October 1715 until 17 May 1756. He was sworn of the privy council on 28 April 1733 and in November 1733 was appointed chancellor of the exchequer, a post which he held for three separate periods. He was elected speaker of the Irish House of Commons on 4 October 1733 and sat in the chair until 17 April 1756, when he went to the Lords. He was appointed to the Irish revenue board on 12 September 1735 and was first commissioner until 5 April 1739. He was also a long-serving lord justice, holding that position fifteen times between 1734 and 1764. On 16 April 1756 he was made baron of Castlemartyr, Viscount Boyle of Brandon, and earl of Shannon and was granted a £2000 per annum pension for thirty-one years.

Boyle continued the rebuilding work at Castlemartyr, which had been destroyed in 1689, and he improved the demesne and the borough town, preferring this to his Dublin residence in Henrietta Street. He was awarded an honorary degree of LLD from Trinity College, Dublin, in July 1735 and, on his being raised to the peerage, was given the position of governor of co. Cork on 3 May 1756. Boyle married twice, first in 1715 to Catherine (d. 1725), daughter of Childly Coote and his wife, Catharine Sandys, of Killester, co. Limerick; she died childless on 5 May 1725. Then he married a distant cousin, Henrietta Boyle (1701–1746), sister of the third earl of Burlington and youngest daughter of Charles Boyle, second earl of Burlington, and his wife, Juliana Noel, on 22 September 1726. They had five sons (three of whom died young) and one daughter; Henrietta Boyle died on 13 December 1746. The children included Boyle's heir, Richard (1728–1807), who became second earl of Shannon in December 1764.

Henry Boyle, first earl of Shannon (1681x7–1764), by John Brooks, pubd 1742

For a thirty-year period from 1734 to 1764 Boyle was perhaps the leading Irish politician in both the House of Commons and Dublin Castle. He was described as a deep politician; in appearance he was most open, and in reality most reserved. Contemporaries often underestimated him, mistaking country gentleman manners and a preference for residence in Castlemartyr over fashionable Henrietta Street as a sign of bucolic indifference. Boyle was, however, the most effective undertaker or Irish parliamentary manager before 1800, with his wielding of patronage, his electoral interest, and, above all, his sense of his own and other MPs' honour. He owed his political power primarily to his Commons following, estimated in 1753 at a total of forty members. His interest was not based on his own land, although he controlled the boroughs of Castlemartyr and Clonakilty in co. Cork, but on his family connections and political guile. One of his connections was with the Brodrick family, later viscounts Midleton and absentees, who first returned him as an MP. By the late 1720s he had become the manager of both their interest in co. Cork and also, through marriage, of the interest of the third earl of Burlington. By 1729, when the Commons speaker William Conolly died, Boyle considered standing as his successor but did not. Four years later he was strong enough to be the unrivalled candidate with his 'Munster squadron' of MPs, so named at the time because of their regional base in counties Cork and Waterford. He married to this parliamentary strength his control of the Irish revenue board in the 1730s, which gave him patronage over a thousand minor posts. He soon gave up his revenue post,

however, and relied instead on his influence in the Commons, thus making him a different type of undertaker from William Conolly or John Ponsonby. His appointment as lord justice for the first of many times in 1734 and then as chancellor of the exchequer, a sinecure worth £800 per annum, marked his recognized place in the Dublin Castle administration after that date.

Boyle's period as speaker and chief undertaker was largely a quiet one because there was no serious threat of a money bill between 1733 and 1753. Despite this, successive viceroys all distrusted him, partly because he openly opposed unpopular government measures, like the unsuccessful effort to introduce regulations to stop the smuggling of wool to France in 1741, and partly due to his indispensability. This distrust began with the duke of Dorset in 1733, who hesitated about appointing the new speaker of the Commons one of his lords justices, especially after Boyle refused to support legislation to repeal the Test Act. His relationship with subsequent viceroys during the 1730s and 1740s was one of cautiousness on both sides and was marked by his refusal to break fully with his country's past; for example, he demanded and gained government support both for popular anti-Catholic measures and for the use of crown revenues to aid the Irish economy and the local interests of the gentry through the building of canals, the spreading of tillage, and the development of linen manufacturing. The good relations broke down after 1750 with the premature attempt of the duke of Dorset to replace Boyle as speaker and lord justice in order to satisfy the ambitions of Archbishop George Stone and the Ponsonby family. Boyle was now in his sixties and the prospect of retirement must have appealed. However, he chose to resist and a battle soon ensued over the rights of the Irish parliament to dispose of the revenues it raised and also over the use, by Boyle and his allies, of a growing Anglophobia among Irish protestants inside and outside parliament. After the money bill was rejected in the 1753–4 session the Dublin parliament was prorogued by Dorset, and Boyle was dismissed from all his government offices. Yet, with the prospect of war with France and the worries about another disrupted parliamentary session, Dorset was replaced in March 1755 and the new viceroy, the marquess of Hartington, was authorized to negotiate a settlement with Boyle. The outcome of this was his retirement as speaker and his creation as first earl of Shannon in April 1756. Boyle's patriotism had been called into question several times by pamphleteers during the 1750s crisis and his 1756 settlement was compared with William Pulteney's apostasy in the wake of Walpole's fall in 1742. Despite this vocal criticism he kept his electoral interest intact and was persuaded to return as a lord justice in April 1758 in order to prop up the administration of the duke of Bedford. Although he served as a lord justice for another three terms this was in order to give the government extra parliamentary credibility rather than to enable him to remain an active politician.

Shannon died from an attack of gout in the head on 27 December 1764 at his home in Henrietta Street, Dublin, and was buried in St Patrick's Cathedral, Dublin, on 31 December. By the time of his death he had created a remarkable rise in fortunes for his branch of the Cork family, coming from minor beginnings to create an electoral interest and landed estate which survived him.

EOIN MAGENNIS

Sources J. L. McCracken, 'The undertakers of Ireland and their relations with the viceroy, 1724–1771', MA diss., Queen's University, Belfast, 1941, 76–88 • E. Hewitt, ed., *Lord Shannon's letters: a calendar of the letters written by the 2nd earl of Shannon to his son Viscount Boyle, 1790–1802* (1982), xxiii–xl • D. O'Donovan, 'The Money Bill crisis of 1753', PhD diss., University College Dublin, 47–52 • PRO NIre., Shannon MSS • J. Lodge, *The peerage of Ireland*, rev. M. Archdall, rev. edn, 7 vols. (1789) • GEC, *Peerage* • Foster, *Alum. Oxon.* • *Old Westminsters*, vol. 1 • *GM*, 1st ser., 34 (1764), 46
Archives Chatsworth House, Derbyshire, letters • NL Ire. • PRO NIre., corresp. and papers
Likenesses J. Brooks, mezzotint, pubd 1742, NG Ire., NPG [*see illus.*] • S. Slaughter, oils, 1744, Palace of Westminster, London; version, NG Ire. • brass medal, 1753, BM • J. van Nost, marble bust, 1754, Rotunda Hospital, Dublin • Irish school, oils (*Henry Boyle, earl of Shannon, speaker, Irish House of Commons, 1682–1764*), NG. Ire

Boyle, Henry Edmund Gaskin

Boyle, Henry Edmund Gaskin (1875–1941), anaesthetist, was born on 2 April 1875 in Christ Church, Barbados, the only child of Henry Eudolphus Boyle, manager of the Hope and Bannatyne estates in Christ Church, and his wife, Elizabeth, daughter of Benjamin Law Gaskin, a member of the Barbados house of assembly. Boyle attended the local schools of Codrington and Harrison before leaving Barbados for England in 1894 and enrolling at St Bartholomew's Hospital medical school, London. He qualified MRCS LRCP in 1901. An intensely loyal 'Barts man', Boyle was a keen sportsman and played both rugby and cricket for the hospital.

Boyle's first post, in August 1901, was as casualty officer at Bristol Royal Infirmary. He returned to Barts as junior resident anaesthetist in April 1902 and was appointed senior resident administrator of anaesthetics in 1905 at a salary of £350 per annum. Later that year he became non-resident assistant administrator of the department of anaesthetics. During this time he wrote a popular textbook entitled *Practical Anaesthetics* (1907), which went through two further editions. On 1 October 1925 he became anaesthetist to St Bartholomew's Hospital; he resigned on health grounds in February 1939, and the following July he was elected to the honorary position of consulting anaesthetist to the hospital, a position he filled until his death.

In his initial researches, with Somnoform, Boyle developed an apparatus for its administration; however, the drug never became popular. He then worked with intratracheal insufflation techniques before developing what was to become his most famous contribution to anaesthesia: a continuous-flow oxygen, nitrous oxide, and ether apparatus. In 1912 Boyle met the New York anaesthetist James T. Gwathmey, who had designed a continuous-flow anaesthetic apparatus that included a water-sight flow-meter for oxygen and nitrous oxide. He persuaded Boyle to obtain one of these devices, and having used it Boyle then asked Coxeters to manufacture a similar apparatus that would have a gas tight fitting for English

cylinders (a problem with the Gwathmey machine). Known as Boyle's nitrous oxide-oxygen-ether outfit, it was first used at Barts in September 1917 and a short report describing its use in more than 3600 cases appeared in 1919. Over the next two decades Boyle constantly modified this apparatus. Further refinements took place after his death, and although the name of 'Boyle's machine' was dropped it remained essentially as he had designed it throughout the rest of the century. Boyle had been made a captain in the Royal Army Medical Corps in September 1914, and he was appointed OBE in 1920 because of his work in caring for wounded soldiers in London during the war. He made other important contributions to anaesthesia, developing a special laryngotomy tube and then the Boyle–Davis gag that was used for decades in tonsil surgery. He also introduced one of the first Sorensen electrical suction apparatuses ever used in Britain.

Boyle married a widow, Mildred Ethel Green, daughter of John William Wildy, of Coutts Bank, on 3 September 1910. He had one step-daughter. Affectionately known as Cocky, he was a man of great personal charm, a social person renowned for his rotund frame, hearty laugh, and fund of amusing stories. He entertained lavishly and this might have accounted for his considerable financial difficulties later in life. He received no financial gain from any of his inventions. Boyle was a founder member of the editorial board of the *British Journal of Anaesthesia*, an original member of the Association of Anaesthetists of Great Britain and Ireland, and one of the first two examiners for the diploma in anaesthesia. He was a member of the Society of Anaesthetists that evolved into the anaesthetic section of the Royal Society of Medicine. He was a staunch supporter of this latter group and was elected president for 1923. He was created FRCS in 1935.

Boyle died in London on 15 October 1941 at the Royal Cancer Hospital, Chelsea. He was cremated two days later at Golders Green, and was survived by his wife. In January 2000, the department of anaesthesia at St Bartholomew's Hospital was renamed the Boyle department of anaesthesia.

DAVID J. WILKINSON

Sources F. T. Evans, *British Journal of Anaesthesia*, 18 (1942), 43–4 • C. F. Hadfield, 'Eminent anaesthetists: H. E. G. Boyle', *British Journal of Anaesthesia*, 22 (1950), 107–17 • private information (2004) [D. Golding] • H. E. G. Boyle, 'New inventions: nitrous oxide-oxygen-ether outfit', *The Lancet* (8 Feb 1919), 226 • H. E. G. Boyle, 'A few impressions', *St Bartholomew's Hospital Journal*, 29 (1921–2), 46–8 • d. cert. • m. cert. • *Medical Directory*
Archives Bristol RO, faculty meeting minutes, BR1, 25693 • St Bartholomew's Hospital, London, archives, minute books of various committees, HA3/25, HA3/26, HA1/30, HA1/31, HA3/56, HA3/58, HA3/38, HA3/42, HA3/46
Likenesses two portraits, St Bartholomew's Hospital, London

Boyle, John

Boyle, John (1563–1620), Church of Ireland bishop of Cork, Cloyne, and Ross, was born in Kent, the eldest son of Roger Boyle and Joan Naylor, daughter of John Naylor of Canterbury, and brother of Richard *Boyle, first earl of Cork (1566–1643). The brothers' education suggests that their parents were of at least yeoman status. John Boyle was educated at King's School, Canterbury, and matriculated, with his brother Richard, from Corpus Christi College, Cambridge, in 1583. He gained the degrees of BA (1587), MA (1591), and BD (1598), then obtained the rectory of Elstree, Hertfordshire, and in 1610 that of Great Stanmore, Middlesex. On 5 February 1611 he was collated to the prebend of Bishopshill in the diocese of Lichfield. He is sometimes described as dean of Lichfield. With financial assistance from his brother Richard he secured the degree of DD at Cambridge in 1614, thus opening the prospect of episcopal office, but he still needed to undergo considerable expense to secure the duke of Buckingham's support for his appointment as bishop of the diocese of Cork, Cloyne, and Ross. He surrendered his other livings and was consecrated in 1618, one of a number of Cork's kinsmen to secure strategic church livings in Munster. Following an accident, resulting in a broken leg, he died at Cork on 10 July 1620, and was buried at Youghal.

J. T. GILBERT, rev. JUDITH HUDSON BARRY

Sources N. Canny, *The upstart earl: a study of the social and mental world of Richard Boyle, first earl of Cork, 1566–1643* (1982) · H. Cotton, *Fasti ecclesiae Hibernicae*, 6 vols. (1845–78) · W. M. Brady, *Clerical and parochial records of Cork, Cloyne, and Ross*, 3 vols. (1863–4) · *Fasti Angl.* (Hardy) · A. Ford, *The protestant Reformation in Ireland, 1590–1641*, 2nd edn (1997)

Boyle, John, fifth earl of Cork and fifth earl of Orrery (1707–1762), biographer, was born in Glasshouse Street, London, on 2 January 1707. He was the only son of Charles *Boyle, fourth earl of Orrery (1674–1731), and his wife, Lady Elizabeth Cecil (c.1687–1708), daughter of the fifth earl of Exeter. He never knew his mother and saw little of his father, a soldier and diplomat. He was educated at home, being tutored from 1713 by the poet Elijah Fenton, his father's secretary, and from November 1717 at Westminster School. He matriculated from Christ Church, Oxford, on 16 August 1723, and two years later, now styled Lord Boyle, left Oxford without a degree and departed for a continental tour, ostensibly to complete his education but also disguising his father's Jacobite mission.

On 9 May 1728, soon after coming of age, Boyle married, in London, Lady Henrietta (d. 1732), daughter of George *Hamilton, first earl of Orkney. As Henrietta's parents strictly forbade her association with her father-in-law and his mistress Margaret Swordfeger (d. 1741) the already uneasy relationship between Lord Boyle and his father grew worse. The fourth earl not only made generous provision in his will for Mrs Swordfeger and their children but, unjustly declaring that his legitimate son had never demonstrated 'Inclination either for the Entertainment or Knowledge which Study and Learning afford' (will, PRO, PROB 11/646/341–342), he bequeathed most of his immense personal library to Christ Church. Struggling between filial deference and devotion to his wife Lord Boyle lamented: 'I lost my Mother before I knew I had one; I have a Father but he seems not to know he has a Son' (*Orrery Papers*, 1.83). There was a reconciliation in 1730, but the fourth earl died on 28 August 1731, with his will unamended.

Profound personal tragedy struck the new earl of Orrery

again, on 22 August 1732, with the death of Henrietta on the couple's arrival in Ireland. Orrery was left with three small children: Charles (b. 27 Jan 1729), Hamilton (b. 3 Feb 1730), and Elizabeth (b. 7 May 1731). Compounding his grief was his financial predicament; he had assumed his father's debts of over £20,000 but, owing to negligence and the dishonesty of his father's agent, his Irish estates were far less profitable than had been expected. For eighteen years he pursued lawsuits, attempting to regain sums due.

On 30 June 1738, in Dublin, Orrery married Margaret Hamilton (1710–1758), of Caledon, co. Tyrone, with a fortune of about £3000 p.a.; shortly after the marriage she pledged her diamonds as security for her husband's debts. The pair enjoyed domesticity, and, unlike his own father, Orrery deeply cherished time spent with his growing family. He and Margaret had three children: Lucy, Catherine, and Edmund (b. 21 Nov 1742). At Oxford in 1743 he was created MA (University College) and DCL. He took his seat in the House of Lords on 7 November 1735 but he shunned public affairs wherever possible, preferring instead the rural tranquillity of his estate at Marston, Somerset, or his wife's house at Caledon.

Orrery began his political career as a tory and Jacobite. In parliament he associated with Bolingbroke, and attacked the ministry in 1739; he also communicated with the exiled Stuart court and involved himself in Jacobite schemes before the rising of 1745. He joined signatories who asked Louis XV to dispatch 10,000 troops and was designated a member of the council of regents for Prince Charles Edward in 1743. A Jacobite prisoner disclosed his name to a Lords committee in 1746 but it decided against his prosecution. He was reportedly still toasting James Stuart publicly as late as 1747 but he was also turning towards the opposition court of Frederick, prince of Wales. By 1749 he was listed as a potential office-holder on Frederick's accession, but Frederick died in 1751 and soon afterwards Orrery withdrew from politics. His finances were so hopelessly confused that he was obliged to place his estates in the hands of trustees for the benefit of his many creditors and, in September 1754, to retire with his wife and daughter Lucy to live more economically in Italy. He became acquainted with Horace Mann, the British consul in Florence, whom he convinced of his loyalty to George II; on his return to England in late 1755 he began to receive a secret service pension of £800 p.a. that continued until his death.

Orrery was on intimate terms with Alexander Pope from the early 1730s until the latter's death; his acquaintance with Swift began in 1732, during the dean's waning years. His correspondence with both figures suggests deep friendship and an undying mutual respect; he was instrumental in the publication of their letters and other works. His own best-known work is his popular and controversial *Remarks on the Life and Writings of Dr. Jonathan Swift* (1751), in the form of a series of letters to his son Hamilton. Though *Remarks* elicited hostile contemporary criticism modern studies applaud Orrery's reasoned objectivity, his creative innovation in utilizing the epistolary method in biography, and his judicious consultation of reliable, first-hand sources, which compensated for his limited acquaintance with Swift.

Orrery's other works include translations of two of Horace's odes (1741); a translation of Pliny's letters (1751), dedicated to his son Charles (which was overshadowed by a more academic edition in the same year); and *Letters from Italy in the Years 1754 and 1755*, published posthumously in 1773, which is filled with perceptive social and cultural observations. He also contributed anonymous essays to periodicals, but arguably his greatest literary contribution is as a letter-writer. A two-volume selection from letters now at Harvard, edited by Emily Boyle, countess of Cork and Orrery, (*The Orrery Papers*, 1903), poignantly unveils a complicated, hypersensitive individual; an affectionate, attentive father and passionate, devoted husband; and a conscientious landlord of Irish estates whose pungent commentaries about the backward, unsophisticated country around him are both hilarious and informative. Orrery's letters display a man striving for literary recognition not solely because of his family's historical legacy; his unpleasant youthful memories; and the fact that his leisure and innate abilities lent facility to such endeavours. Orrery encouraged other authors, including Fenton, Thomas Southerne, Elizabeth Rowe, Mary Barber, Samuel Bowden, Lewis Theobald, and Charlotte Lennox; Johnson said that had he 'been rich, he would have been a very liberal patron' (Boswell, *Life*, 5.238).

Lady Orrery died in London on 24 November 1758, followed by her elder stepson, Charles, on 16 September 1759. Orrery lived on until 16 November 1762, when, at Marston, complications from his long-time affliction with gout ended his life; he was buried at St John's, Frome. Contrary to common misconceptions his lands had not been augmented by the Cork estates of his cousin Richard, earl of Cork and Burlington, upon the latter's death in 1753; all Orrery received was the Cork title.

Johnson called Orrery 'feeble-minded' and said that his conversation 'was like his writings, neat and elegant, but without strength. He grasped at more than his abilities could reach; tried to pass for a better talker, a better writer, and a better thinker, than he was' (Boswell, *Life*, 5.238). Yet Lady Mary Wortley Montagu remarked in 1754 that despite the inherent flaws in Orrery's *Remarks*, it clearly established its author as 'a Poet, a Patriot, a Philosopher, a Physician, a Critic, a compleat Scholar, and a most excellent Moralist, shining in private Life as a submissive Son, a tender Father, and zealous Friend' (*Complete Letters*, 3.56). If her usually acerbic criticism is not the sole motivation for her comments, a re-examination of the man and his writings lends it credence.

LAWRENCE B. SMITH

Sources Harvard U., Houghton L., Orrery papers, MS Eng. 218.1–26 · countess of Cork and Orrery [E. C. Boyle], ed., *The Orrery papers*, 2 vols. (1903) · will, Nov 1728, PRO, PROB 11/646, sig. 236 [Charles Boyle, fourth earl of Orrery] · J. Boyle, fifth earl of Cork and Orrery, *Letters from Italy in the years 1754 and 1755* (1773) · W. King, letters to John, 5th earl of Orrery, 1738–45, Bodl. Oxf., MS Eng. hist. d. 103 · M. Prince, 'The literary life and position in the eighteenth century of John, earl of Orrery', PhD diss., Smith College, 1948 · Royal Arch., Stuart papers · J. Boyle, fifth earl of Cork and Orrery, *Remarks on the life and writings of Dr. Jonathan Swift* (1751) · *The correspondence of Alexander Pope*, ed. G. Sherburn, 5 vols. (1956) · Boswell, *Life* · 'Letters of John, 5th earl of Orrery, 1743–62', Bodl. Oxf., MS Eng. misc. d. 103 · 'Letters of Charles, 4th earl of Orrery and John, 5th earl of Cork and Orrery, to Brettridge Badham', NL Ire., MS 4177 · 'The life of Lysander, translated from Plutarch by the Hon. Charles Boyle, afterwards earl of Orrery ... with the addition of some ... memoranda respecting him, in the handwriting of his son, the Hon. John Boyle, 1730', BL, Add. MS 10388 · J. Lodge, *The peerage of Ireland*, rev. M. Archdall, rev. edn, 7 vols. (1789) · M. McGarvie, *The book of Marston Bigot: the story of Marston House and the earls of Cork and Orrery* (1987) · GEC, *Peerage*, new edn, vol. 3 · L. B. Namier, *The structure of politics at the accession of George III*, 2nd edn (1957) · G. F. R. Barker and A. H. Stenning, eds., *The Westminster School register from 1764 to 1883* (1892) · L. B. Smith, 'Charles Boyle, 4th earl of Orrery, 1674–1731', PhD diss., U. Edin., 1994 · E. Cruickshanks, *Political untouchables: the tories and the '45* (1979) · *The complete letters of Lady Mary Wortley Montagu*, ed. R. Halsband, 3 vols. (1965–7) · D. Dickson, 'An economic history of the Cork region in the 18th century', PhD diss., University College Dublin, 1977 · J. Boyle, fifth earl of Cork and Orrery, *Remarks on the life and writings of Dr. Jonathan Swift*, ed. J. Fróes (2000) · *The correspondence of Jonathan Swift*, ed. H. Williams, 5 vols. (1963–5) · Walpole, *Corr.*, vol. 17 · T. Prior, *A list of the absentees of Ireland, and the yearly value of their estates and incomes spent abroad* (1729) · court of chancery records, 1737, PRO, 11/620; 1748, 11/1315

Archives BL, writings, Add. MS 4466 · Harvard U., Houghton L., papers · NL Ire., estate corresp., MSS 4177, 13252, 13255 · priv. coll., 'Leases, letts and accounts passed by Charles earl of Orrery ... of his estate of Marston in Somersetshire' · Royal Bank of Scotland, London, archives, Glyn Mills/Childs bank account of fifth earl of Orrery, CH/15 · U. Nott. L., description of journey to Dungannon, MS PwV166 [copy] · Yale U., Beinecke L., accounts, Add. MS 10388 | BL, corresp. with Thomas Birch, Add. MS 4303 · BL, corresp. with Thomas, duke of Newcastle, Add. MSS 32868–32941 · Bodl. Oxf., letters to Herbert Bowen, MS Eng. misc. d. 97 · PRO NIre., D/2433; D/2707 · Royal Arch., Stuart papers · Wilts. & Swindon RO, Stourhead archive, 'An account written by Margaret, countess of Cork and Orrery, of an estrangement between the earl and Henry Hoare, annotated by the latter', 383.909

Likenesses attrib. I. Seeman, oils, c.1740–1749, NPG; repro. in J. F. Kerslake, *Early Georgian portraits*, 2 (1977) · J. Faber junior, mezzotint, 1741, AM Oxf.; repro. in Cruickshanks, *Political untouchables* · attrib. Du Pan, group portrait, repro. in Boyle, ed., *Orrery papers*, 2; formerly priv. coll., sold in 1905 · C. Jervas, portrait, priv. coll. · oils, repro. in J. F. Kerslake, *Early Georgian portraits*, 2 (1977)

Boyle, Katherine. See Jones, Katherine, Viscountess Ranelagh (1615–1691).

Boyle, Mary. See Rich, Mary, countess of Warwick (1624–1678).

Boyle [née Monckton], **Mary** [Maria], **countess of Cork and Orrery** (1746–1840), literary hostess, was born on 21 May 1746, the youngest child and only surviving daughter of John Monckton, first Viscount Galway (1695–1751) and his second wife, Jane (d. 1788), fourth daughter of Henry Warner Westenra, of Rathleagh, Queen's county, Ireland. Her father was a British MP and office-holder in Great Britain and Ireland, and was made an Irish peer in 1727.

From her youth, Mary (or Maria) Monckton was interested in literature and the world of ideas. She was, from her earliest years, marked out to become a member of the select and aristocratic club of women whose means and temperament allowed them to pursue the interests of the

Mary Boyle, countess of Cork and Orrery (1746–1840), by Sir Joshua Reynolds, *c.*1777–8

'blue stocking'. In her twenties she established herself as a patroness of the London political and literary beau monde. While still in her mother's house in Charles Street, Berkeley Square, she entertained many considered to be persons of genius and talent, including James Boswell, Samuel Johnson, and Edmund Burke. Johnson was said to be fond of her company and Boswell recounted an incident in 1781 at the house in Berkeley Square, where she delighted and indeed 'enchanted the Sage' (Boswell, 4.109). Discussing her own literary opinions with Johnson, Miss Monckton argued for the 'pathetick' (ibid.) quality of Laurence Sterne's writings. While Johnson, who held a deep antipathy for Sterne, denied these qualities in Sterne's works, Miss Monckton held to her conviction that Sterne's was an affecting literary talent. Maintaining that she had been deeply moved by her reading of Sterne, she was not discouraged by Johnson's dismissive pronouncement; 'that is because, dearest, you're a dunce' (ibid.). When not in London, Miss Monckton lived with her brother Colonel John Monckton (1739–1830) at Fineshade, Northamptonshire.

Describing her appearance in 1782 with a characteristically acid, feminine attention to detail, Fanny Burney

remarked that Miss Monckton was 'one of those who stand foremost in collecting all extraordinary or curious people to her London conversaziones, which like those of Mrs. Vesey, mix the rank and the literature, and exclude all besides' (*Diary and Letters*, 2.123). She continued by observing that Miss Monckton was 'between thirty and forty, very short, very fat' (ibid., 124). Nevertheless, she conceded Miss Monckton to be 'handsome, splendidly and fantastically dressed' (ibid.) and 'rouged not unbecomingly' (ibid.). Beyond her appraisal of Miss Monckton's physical attributes, Burney speculated as to her subject's social ambitions, suggesting that Miss Monckton was 'evidently and palpably desirous of gaining notice and admiration' (ibid.). Still, she concluded of Monckton, 'she has an easy levity in her air, manner, voice and discourse' (ibid.). If Fanny Burney's praise was mixed, Miss Monckton nevertheless succeeded in gaining the notice of James Boswell and of inspiring a more ardent admiration in that notorious roué. Having enjoyed considerable hospitality at one of Miss Monckton's evenings, Boswell felt the need the following morning to account for his behaviour and to 'give what had happened the most ingenuous turn … by the following verses' (Boswell, 4.110). He wrote a poem to Miss Monckton, assuring her that it was neither from the company of 'the excellent Montrose', the conversation of 'Graham's wit', nor 'from generous wine' but from 'your bright eyes … intoxication flashed'. Conceding that his actions were 'not enlightened though enflamed', Boswell made his demurral 'victim at once to wine and love' and his entreaty, 'I hope Maria you'll forgive' (ibid.).

While in her mother's house, Miss Monckton advanced her role as social and artistic patron by sponsoring the émigré French ballet and inviting dancers such as Mademoiselle Theodore to her home. A one-time member of Noverre's ballet troupe, formerly of the Opéra in Paris, Theodore travelled to London in 1781 along with the rest of Noverre's company. In 1782 Horace Walpole wrote to Anne Fitzpatrick, countess of Upper Ossory, of seeing the French ballerina dancing a minuet with Richard Edgcumbe, later second earl of Mount Edgcumbe, at one of Miss Monckton's evenings. In addition to her interests in dance and literature, Miss Monckton was very keen to fashion and promote theatrical careers. She attempted to share her critical appreciation of the theatre with Dr Johnson as early as 1775. Insisting that Johnson accompany her to the Drury Lane to hear a performance by Sarah Siddons, she once again encountered the critical and social irritability of Johnson. 'Well madam,' he complained, 'if you desire it I will go. See her I shall not, Hear her I shall not' (*Diary and Letters*, 2.143). Johnson's irritation was such that he gave repeated accounts of this artistic, if not social, ordeal to mutual friends and acquaintances over the years.

On 17 June 1786, in her mother's house in Charles Street, Berkeley Square, Miss Monckton married Edmund Boyle, seventh earl of Cork and seventh earl of Orrery (1742–1798), who had divorced his first wife in 1782. They had no children. Her marriage may have subdued her intrepidity with the London literati. Certainly during the dozen years of her marriage very little was reported of her. After her husband's death, the dowager Lady Cork revived her 'passion for entertaining persons of note' (*DNB*) and turned her attentions towards a more political guest list. Although her evenings were attended by the prominent and the promising from both political parties, including Viscount Castlereagh, George Canning, Sir Robert Peel, and Lord John Russell, her sympathies were decidedly whig. Her dinners and receptions provided the social space for the constructive and informal negotiation of business. In her later years her guests included such luminaries as the prince regent (afterwards George IV), Richard Brinsley Sheridan, Lord Byron, Sir Walter Scott, and Sydney Smith. In her journal for 1811 Mary Berry described one of Lady Cork's parties as 'curious' and another as 'a great assembly'. Of the evening, she remarked, 'the Prince was there and all the world' (*DNB*).

Lady Cork remained a lively wit and curious intellect until the end of her life. Even in her later years her memory was considered remarkable. As an example, she could still, when well past eighty, recite most of Pope's *Iliad*. As Catherine Bury, countess of Charleville, writing to Amelia Opie in 1809, observed, 'Lady Cork's activity in pursuit of amusement is a pleasant proof of vivacity and spirit surviving youth' (C. L. Brightwell, *Memorials of the Life of Amelia Opie*, 1854, 139). C. R. Leslie, writing in 1834, could still confirm that judgement. Remarking that while 'Lady Cork is very old, infirm and diminutive … her features are delicate and her skin fair, and notwithstanding her great age she is very animated' (*Autobiographical Recollections*, 1.136–7), he concluded that 'the old lady, who was a lion hunter in her youth, is as much one now as ever' (ibid., 1.137) and 'wholly taken up' with John Gardner Wilkinson, the explorer, another guest. She was certainly able to exert a powerful impression on the social and political sensibility of literary London even in her final years and after. Leslie's assessment is echoed in the view that Dickens used Lady Cork as the template for Mrs Leo Hunter in *The Pickwick Papers*. Benjamin Disraeli, who knew Lady Cork well, is said to have described her accurately as Lady Bellair in his 1837 novel *Henrietta Temple*.

Although the most accomplished portrait of Lady Cork was probably that by Sir Joshua Reynolds, perhaps the most characteristic rendering of her was a sketch made by her niece, Miss Anna Maria Monckton of Somerford. Beneath the sketch is written, perhaps by Lady Cork herself,

Look at me,
I'm 93,
And all my faculties I keep;
Eat, drink, and laugh, and soundly sleep.
(*DNB*)

Lady Cork died at her home in New Burlington Street, London, on 30 May 1840, and was buried either in the Monckton vault at Brewood, Staffordshire, or at Fineshade, Northamptonshire. PAMELA EDWARDS

Sources D. H. Monckton, *A genealogical history of the family of Monckton* (1887) • *Annual Register* (1840) • *Bentley's Miscellany*, 19 (1846), 293 • Boswell, *Johnson*, ed. G. B. Hill, [another edn], 4 (1887) • *Diary and letters of Madame D'Arblay* (1778–1840), ed. C. Barrett and A. Dobson, 6 vols. (1904–5), vol. 4 • Farington, *Diary*, 9.3499 • Walpole, *Corr.*, vol. 33 • C. J. Hamilton (1904) • C. R. Leslie and T. Taylor, *Life and times of Sir Joshua Reynolds*, 2 vols. (1865) • *Autobiographical recollections of the late Charles Robert Leslie, R.A.*, ed. T. Taylor (1860); repr. with introduction by R. Hamlyn (1978) • *DNB* • GEC, *Peerage* • Burke, *Peerage* (1999)

Likenesses J. Reynolds, oils, *c*.1777–1778, Tate collection [*see illus.*] • J. Reynolds, oils, 1779, Fineshade Abbey, Northamptonshire • A. M. Monckton, sketch, 1839; known to be in Sommerford in 1894 • H. P. Briggs, oils • J. Jacobe, mezzotint (after J. Reynolds)

Boyle, Mary Louisa (1810–1890), writer, was born on 12 November 1810 at Cavendish Square in London, the fifth of the six children of Captain (later Admiral) Sir Courtenay Boyle (1770–1844) and his wife, Carolina Amelia, *née* Poyntz (1773–1851). In Boyle's chronologically vague memoirs, posthumously edited by her nephew as *Her Book* (1901), she describes an early memory of watching chained convicts at work on the wharf at Sheerness, where her father was commissioner of the dockyard. After he had taken up an appointment with the Navy Board, the family moved into apartments attached to the offices at Somerset House. Some time later her father 'took up abode in Upper Berkeley Street', and 'my mother and the rest of the family settled at Hampton Court' where they remained until 1840 (Boyle, 39). After this they moved to Millard's Hill, a home on the Somerset estate of her mother's brother-in-law, where Mary was still resident ten years later.

Boyle was educated in Brighton, at Miss Poggi's, a school first located in Regency Square, then at Brunswick Terrace. In her twenties Boyle attempted to establish herself as a novelist with *The State Prisoner* (1837) and *The Forester: a Tale of 1688* (1839). *The Bridal of Melchia* (1844), published in the year of her father's death, is a dramatic sketch in accomplished but slavishly Shakespearian unrhymed iambic pentameters. She was able to put her passion for the theatre to more practical effect after meeting Dickens at Rockingham Castle in 1849. Dickens, impressed by her acting ability, engaged both her and one of her brothers to play in several amateur performances. He also published Boyle in *Household Words*. 'My Mahogany Friend'—a title concocted by Dickens himself, after he had heavily cut the piece and then written delicately to discourage her from having ambitions as an author—appeared on 8 March 1851. In *Tangled Weft* (1865), a short volume containing two stories, Boyle took note of Dickens's arguments in favour of 'compactness'. The second story especially, 'Mildred Fawkener', deserves to be preserved as an example of high-minded Victorian romantic fiction.

In addition to her friendship with Dickens—she was among those present in the garden at Gad's Hill in 1870 on the day of his death—Mary Boyle is also remembered in association with Alfred Tennyson, whom she did not meet until 1882. Tennyson, whose son Hallam married Mary's niece Audrey, addressed one of the most poignant poems of his old age 'To Mary Boyle'. Although she had established a London home, at South Audley Street, much of her life had been spent moving from one country house to another, including Althorp, the home of her cousin Lord Spencer. In addition to her fiction, her publications included poetry and a biographical catalogue of the portraits at Longleat. Mary Boyle died of a cerebral haemorrhage on 7 April 1890, at 71 Oakley Street, London, her home at the end of her life. MICHAEL THORN

Sources M. Boyle, *Her book*, ed. C. Boyle (1901) · *The letters of Charles Dickens*, ed. M. House, G. Storey, and others, 6 (1988) · N. MacKenzie and J. MacKenzie, *Dickens: a life* (1979) · Boase, *Mod. Eng. biog.*
Wealth at death £3034 4s. 8d.: probate, 19 April 1890, CGPLA Eng. & Wales

Boyle, Michael (1580?–1635), Church of Ireland bishop of Waterford and Lismore, was born in London, the third son of Michael Boyle (d. 1596), a merchant, and his wife, Jane Peacock, and younger brother of Richard *Boyle, archbishop of Tuam. He entered Merchant Taylors' School, London, in 1587, and proceeded to St John's College, Oxford, in 1593. He graduated BA (5 December 1597), MA (25 June 1601), BD (9 July 1607), and DD (2 July 1611), and became a fellow of his college. He was appointed vicar of Finedon in Northamptonshire. Though esteemed for his learning and prudence, Boyle's subsequent rise in Irish ecclesiastical circles owed much to his relative Richard Boyle, first earl of Cork. In 1613 he was appointed to the archdeaconries of Cork and Cloyne and the prebend of Glanworth. In 1614 he became dean of Lismore and by 1619 was bishop of Waterford and Lismore. He married twice; his first wife was Dorothy Fish, daughter of George Fish of South Hill, Bedfordshire, and his second Christian, daughter of Thomas Bellott of Chester, but he had no children by either marriage. He held until death the chancellorship of Lismore and Cashel and the treasurership of Waterford. Boyle died at Waterford on 27 December 1635, where he was buried in the cathedral of the Blessed Trinity. J. T. GILBERT, rev. ELIZABETHANNE BORAN

Sources The whole works of Sir James Ware concerning Ireland, ed. and trans. W. Harris, 1 (1739), 539 · J. Lodge, The peerage of Ireland, rev. M. Archdall, rev. edn, 1 (1789), 144–5 · W. H. Rennison, ed., Succession list of the bishops, cathedral and parochial clergy of the dioceses of Waterford and Lismore (1920), 28, 42, 52, 56, 165 · Wood, Ath. Oxon., 1st edn, 2.88 · J. B. Leslie, 'Biographical index', MS copy, Representative Church Body Library, Dublin, vol. 1, p. 125 · W. M. Brady, Clerical and parochial records of Cork, Cloyne, and Ross, 1 (1863), 311 · H. Cotton, Fasti ecclesiae Hibernicae, 2nd edn, 1 (1851), 280 · Wood, Ath. Oxon.: Fasti (1815), 275, 292, 321, 344 · Foster, Alum. Oxon. · C. J. Robinson, ed., A register of the scholars admitted into Merchant Taylors' School, from AD 1562 to 1874, 1 (1882), 30 · W. A. Phillips, ed., History of the Church of Ireland, 3 (1933), 27, 42 · The Lismore papers, first series: autobiographical notes, remembrances and diaries of Sir Richard Boyle, first and 'great' earl of Cork, ed. A. B. Grosart, 5 vols. (privately printed, London, 1886), vol. 2, p. 411; vol. 4, p. 257

Boyle, Michael (1609/10–1702), lord chancellor of Ireland and Church of Ireland archbishop of Armagh, was the eldest son of Richard *Boyle (c.1574–1645), archbishop of Tuam between 1638 and 1645, and his wife, Martha, daughter of Richard or John Wright of Catherine Hill. A member of a cadet branch of the prolific tribe of Boyles which colonized public offices and the established Church of Ireland, Michael Boyle graduated BA from Trinity College, Dublin, in 1637. In the same year he was incorporated as MA at Trinity College, Oxford. Local links immediately secured his preferment to the parish of Clonpriest, one of the richest in the diocese of Cloyne. In 1640

he was advanced to the deanery of Cloyne. Enjoyment of these emoluments was soon interrupted by the outbreak of the confederate war and personal tragedy. Boyle, who had married, probably in the late 1630s, Margaret, daughter of George *Synge, bishop of Cloyne, lost his wife and their only daughter in 1641 when they drowned at sea. At about the same time Boyle offered his services as chaplain to the protestant forces in the province of Munster and later in the 1640s Boyle married the Hon. Mary, daughter of Dermod O'Brien, fifth Baron Inchiquin, and sister of Murrough *O'Brien, first earl of Inchiquin. They had three sons and six daughters. Boyle's new connections (the sixth baron was commander of the protestant army) may have assisted him into the post of chaplain-general. His skills as an emissary were soon revealed. He seems to have followed his brother-in-law in aligning with Charles I rather than the Westminster parliament in 1648. He was looked upon as the head of the protestant clergy of Munster who remained loyal to the Stuarts throughout the revolutions of the late 1640s. As such, Inchiquin addressed to him queries about the stance of the clergy, some of whom were acknowledging the regime which had succeeded the executed Charles I.

Unlike many of his colleagues and some within his own family, Boyle stayed aloof from the new government. Continuing in Munster, he provided one of several channels through which the exiled royalists could be informed of opinion and opportunities in the area. In December 1652 he was with his kinsman Richard *Boyle, second earl of Cork, the head of the Boyles in Ireland. He also attended the wedding at Youghal in 1656 of one of Cork's daughters. Again, in the uncertain time late in 1659, Boyle dined with Cork. It is likely that Boyle travelled covertly between England and Ireland during the interregnum. Boyle's loyalty was acknowledged and his losses recompensed when he received lands formerly owned by Sir Hardress Waller in 1660. The grant was confirmed in the Act of Settlement of 1662.

Boyle's unimpeachable loyalty and his considerable sufferings brought his advancement to the bishopric of Cork in August 1660. He also held six sinecures in the diocese until attacked for doing so by his kinsman the earl of Orrery, lord president of Munster. Boyle's capacity for business, especially to safeguard the material interests of the church, attracted favourable notice. In addition, his record, coupled with diplomacy, enabled him to escape the suspicions to which those in his family such as Orrery and Cork, who had collaborated with the previous regime, were prone. In the autumn of 1660 he was sent to London to advance the claims of the established Church of Ireland for compensation. In 1661 the Irish convocation chose him as one of its agents to solicit in England: a tribute to his skills and perhaps to the links with English bishops and courtiers forged during the 1650s. In November 1661 he appeared before the English council, but meetings with the lord chancellor, the earl of Clarendon, and Gilbert Sheldon, bishop of London, convinced him that the Irish church had pitched its claims too high. The lord lieutenant, the duke of Ormond, backed his translation to the archdiocese of Dublin in November 1663. Already Boyle had been sworn of the Irish privy council, but his more regular presence in Dublin meant that he frequently attended. As an astute observer of politics, both secular and ecclesiastical, he was valued by Ormond as an informant. In 1665 his skills, together with the political interest which he commanded (particularly in Munster), led to his appointment as lord chancellor. Boyle accurately protested that he lacked any great proficiency in the law. On occasion he had expressed dislike of the common lawyers, and hoped that the clergy might no longer be harassed in the courts. Initially Boyle deputed much of the work of chancery to a keeper of the seal. However, this stratagem did not deflect the criticism of those opposed on principle to the choice of a cleric and those simply contemptuous of Boyle. He sought to improve chancery procedures to the extent of issuing orders for its regulation in 1668. These were repeated in 1673 and 1685, perhaps indicating that they had had only a limited effect.

The office of lord chancellor brought Boyle additional patronage, fees, and further chances of surreptitious enrichment. In 1672 his rents alone yielded £1941. In 1686 he was listed among a score in Ireland worth more than £2000 p.a. A sign of his increasing wealth was the acquisition of a country property at Blessington, in co. Wicklow. During the 1670s he erected a large mansion there, which was lavishly embellished and furnished. He also undertook the improvement of the archiepiscopal residence of St Sepulchre's in Dublin. Detractors pointed not just to this unabashed enjoyment of his wealth, but to delays and partiality in chancery and to torpor in his diocese. On 8 March 1673 it was alleged that under the 'proud and insolent' Boyle, the whole kingdom groaned (Conway, letter, de Vesci MSS, H/15). These criticisms did not lessen the confidence of the administration in his abilities. Boyle skilfully picked his way through the contending factions within the Irish council. In 1677 it was rumoured that he might be translated to Canterbury in succession to Sheldon. Early in 1679 Ormond, again lord lieutenant, had him translated to the primatial see of Armagh. He was named three times to the triumvirate of lords justices who governed in the absence of a lord lieutenant or lord deputy.

Complaints were voiced that Boyle as lord chancellor had allowed overt or covert Catholics to be included in the county commissions of the peace. To some Irish protestants this seemed the more culpable as the panic over the Popish Plot spread to Ireland. Boyle's marriage into the O'Brien family, the earls of Inchiquin, some of whom had remained Catholic, was also used to embarrass him politically. However, with the storms of the Popish Plot and exclusion weathered, and a tory reaction setting in, he was vulnerable to attack on other grounds. Some noted that he had not purged the magistracy of all who had served the Cromwellians. The truth was that Boyle, whatever his failings as a judge, was too closely identified with the English protestant interest in Ireland to join enthusiastically in the restitution of Catholics to offices and lands. As the political atmosphere altered under James II,

he was replaced as chancellor in 1686. The lord lieutenant at the time praised Boyle as an able and loyal servant of the crown, but admitted that he had a large following beyond his dependants in chancery. As archbishop of Armagh he retained considerable power, but did nothing openly to challenge the Catholic *revanche*.

Increasing incapacity, first physical and then mental, diminished Boyle's influence. Already in 1689 he was thought 'decrepit' (J. Bonnell to J. Strype, 19 April 1689, BL, Stowe MS 746, fol. 191). He did not join wealthy protestants fleeing from Ireland. However, in 1690 he quickly rallied to the new monarchs, hoping thereby to prevent any religious settlement which might comprehend or tolerate the dissenters. When archbishop of Dublin, although his see contained a sizeable population of protestant nonconformists, he had protected individuals against the full rigour of the laws, but he did not favour a general toleration. By 1697, reportedly both blind and deaf, he left other, younger bishops such as Narcissus Marsh, Samuel Foley, William King, and Nathaniel Foy to devise and apply measures to invigorate the established church, although Boyle's inactivity, it was felt, frustrated reform. Before old age slowed him, however, during more than three decades as a bishop he had deployed legal rather than spiritual weapons in the battle against the many adversaries of the Church of Ireland. Concurrently, in the traditions of his family, he enriched himself. Boyle died on 10 December 1702 at his house in Oxmantown, near Dublin, in the ninety-third year of his age, and was buried in St Patrick's Cathedral, Dublin.

Murrough Boyle, first Viscount Blessington (1648–1718), government official, was the son and heir of Michael Boyle and his second wife, Mary. Murrough matriculated from Trinity College, Dublin, on 18 August 1662, and was MP for Kilmallock during 1665–6. He married Mary (*d.* 1668), daughter of John *Parker, archbishop of Dublin. They had one daughter. Mary died on 13 September 1668, and in November 1672 Boyle married Lady Anne (*d.* 1725), daughter of Charles Coote, second earl of Mountrath. They had two sons and two daughters. On 23 August 1673 Boyle was created Viscount Blessington in the peerage of Ireland. He was governor of Limerick and constable of Limerick Castle from 1679 until 1692. Blessington was inclined to drama rather than politics, writing a play, *The Lost Princess*, which has been described as 'truly contemptible' (Baker, 1.58). Blessington died on 26 April 1718 at Island Bridge, Dublin, and was buried on 29 April with his father in St Patrick's Cathedral, Dublin. His widow died on 5 April 1725 and was buried on 11 April in the same vault. The title was inherited by his son Charles (*d.* 1732), who died without issue, whereupon his peerage became extinct.   TOBY BARNARD

Sources Report on the manuscripts of the late Reginald Rawdon Hastings, 4 vols., HMC, 78 (1928–47), vol. 4 · Calendar of the manuscripts of the marquess of Ormonde, new ser., 8 vols., HMC, 36 (1902–20) · Journals of the House of Lords in the kingdom of Ireland, vol. 1 · Petworth House, Orrery MSS, general ser., 28; 29 · V&A NAL, Forster Library, Ormonde papers · NL Ire., de Vesci MSS, H/4; H/15 · Bodl. Oxf., MSS Carte 45, 37, 53, 215; MS Rawl. C. 984, fols. 85–86b; MS Add. C. 306 · M. Boyle, two letters to Orrery, 10 Feb 1671/1672–17 Feb 1671/1672,

Harvard U., Houghton L., Orrery MSS, MS 218 22F · diary of the second earl of Cork, Chatsworth House, Derbyshire, Lismore MS 32/31 · J. Jones, letter to W. Legge, 28 June 1665, Staffs. RO, Dartmouth papers, D1778/iii/O/19, 3 · *The manuscripts of the earl of Dartmouth*, 3 vols., HMC, 20 (1887–96) · BL, Althorp MS B 6 · charges of Bennet against Lord Chancellor Boyle, 1673, NL Ire., MS 17845 · J. Ware, *The whole works*, 2 vols. (1744), vol. 1, pp. 130, 357, 569 · *The correspondence of Henry Hyde, earl of Clarendon, and of his brother, Laurence Hyde, earl of Rochester*, ed. S. W. Singer, 1 (1828), 289–90 · *A collection of such of the orders heretofore used in chancery, with such alterations and additions thereunto as Michael lord arch-bishop of Dublin … hath thought fit at present to ordain* [n.d., 1668?] · *Rules and orders appointed to be observed in the high court of chancery in Ireland* (1685) · B. de Breffny, 'The building of the mansion at Blessington, 1672', *GPA Irish Arts Review Yearbook*, 5 (1988), 73–7 · Burtchaell & Sadleir, *Alum. Dubl.*, 88 · GEC, *Peerage*, new edn · D. E. Baker, *Biographia dramatica, or, A companion to the playhouse*, rev. I. Reed, new edn, rev. S. Jones, 3 vols. in 4 (1812)

Archives Bodl. Oxf., corresp., Carte MSS · Hunt. L., corresp. · NL Ire., letters · PRO, corresp., SP 63 | BL, letters to Lord Essex, Stowe MSS 200, 208, 209 · NL Ire., corresp. with duke of Ormond · NL Ire., de Vesci MSS, accounts and MSS · TCD, corresp. with W. King

Likenesses D. Loggan, line engraving, BM, NPG · R. Purcell, mezzotint (after G. Soest), BM

Boyle, Murrough, first Viscount Blessington (1648–1718). *See under* Boyle, Michael (1609/10–1702).

Boyle, Richard, first earl of Cork (1566–1643), landowner and administrator, was born at Preston, near Faversham in Kent, on 13 October 1566, the second son of Roger Boyle (*d.* 1576), landowner, and his wife, Joan, daughter of Robert Naylor. Roger Boyle, a cadet of a Herefordshire family, was able to send his eldest sons to Cambridge. Richard went from King's School in Canterbury to Corpus Christi College in 1583. His studies were continued at the Middle Temple, where he attached himself as a clerk to Sir Richard Manwood, chief baron of the exchequer. Soon he was noticed by a Kentish neighbour, Sir Edward Waterhouse, who was chancellor of the Irish exchequer.

Early career, 1588–1603 In 1588 Boyle travelled with Waterhouse to Ireland. He later contended that he had arrived with a gold bracelet, a diamond ring, and £27 3s. in his purse: not negligible assets. In Ireland, following the earl of Desmond's uprising in the southern province of Munster, opportunities abounded. English authority had to be restored, partly through confiscating the estates of the defeated. An unscrupulous opportunist, Boyle abandoned the ailing Manwood and turned to Sir Geoffrey *Fenton as his principal patron. Fenton, as secretary to the council and escheator, presided over the confiscations and parallel search for 'concealed' lands which the crown claimed as its own. He was also a confidant of Lord Burghley. Through Fenton, Boyle secured the powerful post of deputy escheator. In this capacity he oversaw much of the detail of identifying, valuing, and leasing the confiscated lands. The work gave Boyle great chances for both legitimate and illicit gains and, applying himself energetically to the tasks, he quickly mastered the intricate procedures and profited. He granted large tracts at low rents to cronies and clients and kept some—especially in the western province of Connaught—for himself.

Boyle's personal holdings were further enlarged when

Richard Boyle, first earl of Cork (1566–1643), by Isaac Oliver, *c.*1610–15

on 6 November 1595 he married Joan, daughter of William Apsley and coheir to lands around Limerick. Joan died giving birth to a stillborn child on 14 December 1599. They had no other children. Boyle's blatant exploitation of the system in which he was officially involved and the meagre profits for the crown aroused growing criticism. These attacks also reflected the factionalism within the English administration in Dublin, where Boyle's principal patron, Fenton, was at loggerheads with Sir William Fitzwilliam, the lord deputy. Boyle, through whom Fitzwilliam planned to ruin Fenton, was threatened with arrest. He survived this threat, only to face another from the newly arrived treasurer-at-war, Sir Henry Wallop, in January 1596. Evidence of Boyle's malpractices accumulated, and he was arrested later in the year. When a new English lord deputy, Thomas, Lord Burgh, arrived in 1597, it was rumoured that Boyle might be executed for felony. Instead Burgh died, and the threat was temporarily lifted. However, Boyle's evident chicanery meant that he remained a target for 'reformers' in the Irish administration. In 1598 he withdrew discreetly to Munster, only for rebellion to break out there, forcing him to return to London and to work at the Middle Temple. Still he was haunted by his activities in Ireland, as the warring groups carried their complaints to England. Again, luck favoured Boyle. Adversaries died. Also, the appointment of Sir George Carew as lord president of Munster enabled Boyle to attach himself to a new patron. He promptly purchased the clerkship of the presidential council of Munster, and with it a chance to re-establish himself in the province.

Carew smoothed Boyle's return to favour with the London government. He also prepared the ground for perhaps

Boyle's greatest coup. Sir Walter Ralegh, who had been granted enormous acreages of the forfeitures in Munster during the earlier plantation, had decided to unload them. Boyle bought the Ralegh holdings, for a bargain price of £1500. Much of the money for this purchase was supplied by the £1000 portion of his second wife, Catherine (c.1588–1630), a daughter of Sir Geoffrey Fenton. They married on 25 July 1603 and had seven sons—including Richard *Boyle (1612–1698), Roger *Boyle (1621–1679), and Robert *Boyle (1627–1691)—and eight daughters, including the future Katherine *Jones (1615–1691) and Mary *Rich (1624–1678). Again, Carew was the vital intermediary to the match. Boyle was knighted on the day of his marriage. With over 42,000 acres, Boyle was pre-eminent among the newcomers in Munster and potentially one of the richest men in Ireland. His perspective changed. The defence, consolidation, and exploitation of his estates henceforth preoccupied him. Residence and direct oversight were identified as crucial to success. Boyle rapidly developed an unrivalled familiarity with the physical and human geography of his properties, concentrated around the fertile lower reaches of the River Blackwater on the borders of counties Cork and Waterford, but with outlying portions further to the west. He also assembled a trusted and talented team of subordinates. Relations, including an elder brother, John *Boyle, were encouraged to set up in the area. At the same time he needed to protect his wealth against the envious. Technically he was already contravening the government ban on any single undertaker holding more than 10,000 acres in the plantation. These insecurities obliged him to participate in politics, in both Ireland and England. Another strategy was to hold office in Ireland, in order to increase his influence over policy.

Irish magnate, 1604–1629 The vagaries of the early Stuarts constantly threatened to disturb those lately established on Irish estates. Monarch and ministers, short of money, suspected what adventurers in Ireland such as Boyle had surreptitiously accumulated. Successive administrations considered devices by which the incumbents might be forced to disgorge some of what they held. In the event the danger of antagonizing the likes of Boyle made the government cautious. Instead, in 1606, through a commission for defective titles, the new proprietors were encouraged to buy secure titles for what they held by paying the government sums by way of composition. Boyle was particularly insecure after Ralegh was arrested and his possessions seized by the crown. Boyle protected himself by activity at court during 1604–5 and, as a result, he received a fresh grant of Ralegh's Irish lands from the king. But his rights to some of his other acquisitions remained open to challenge. Accordingly Boyle exerted himself with the officials in Dublin to protect what he had earlier gained through the system of escheats. He beat off a challenge in the 1613 parliament, in which he sat as member for Lismore. Boyle had acquired this ancient settlement, and secured its recent incorporation as a borough. By 1614 he had procured a patent which promised to put his possession of lands beyond challenge. At the same time his

wealth and importance were acknowledged by his appointment to the Irish privy council on 15 February 1613. Moving with increasing confidence within the Dublin administration, he formed alliances with the officials, some of whom—like Boyle—were on the way to regional eminence and whose methods of personal enrichment differed little from his.

Meanwhile Boyle took his estate in hand. Through tenancies, ecclesiastical patronage, and appointments in his boroughs he fashioned a settlement responsive to his own interests and highly profitable to himself. It was also designed as a model of what the resident and vigilant proprietor could achieve in Ireland. Simultaneously a peaceful and protestant island would be achieved and the English protestant interest advanced. Subsequently, and in part thanks to his own talents for self-advertisement, Boyle was held up as an exemplary landlord. There was no gainsaying his success in enriching himself. By 1640 his Irish rents probably yielded an annual £18,000. Only the Butlers, a much older-established family, rivalled this wealth in Ireland. Even in English terms his income put Boyle on a par with the richest noblemen. And it was with such noblemen that he wanted to rank.

In the venal world of early Stuart Ireland it was easy enough to gain a title. Created Lord Boyle, baron of Youghal, on 6 May 1616, Boyle was advanced to the earldom of Cork on 6 October 1620. A subsidiary title, Viscount Dungarvan, was used by his heir. For these distinctions he apparently paid £4500. In 1628 his younger sons Lewis and Roger were created Viscount Boyle of Kinalmeaky and Lord Broghill respectively on account of their father's services. In all, eleven of his children survived into adulthood. These children were used to advance their father both politically and socially. Their marriages were intended to strengthen ties with the dominant personality at the English court, Sir George Villiers, the future duke of Buckingham, and with the Clifford and Howard dynasties. In Ireland the same strategy linked the Boyles to the ancient and locally important Barrys, earls of Barrymore, and Fitzgeralds, earls of Kildare.

Despite this thickening web of connections, Cork felt insecure. He was still affected by the inherent instability caused by factional manoeuvrings in Dublin and London. He also attracted the jealousy of other settlers, the resentment of those whom he had displaced, and the suspicions of the administration that it had been tricked by him. In Ireland he faced the hostility of the lord deputy from 1615, Sir Oliver St John, whose own patronage and profiteering had been considerably depleted by Cork's activities. On his side, Cork needed to treat St John warily, since behind him stood the much more potent figure of George Villiers, the king's favourite. Villiers, thanks to St John, realized that Ireland could add substantially to his own wealth and influence. Others, hopeful of prospering from Ireland, cultivated Villiers and St John, and might come to threaten Cork's enormous acquisitions. Settlers in Munster, headed by Cork, were further perturbed by the interest of Villiers and St John in annexing the profitable export trade from Ireland to their system of patents and monopolies. This threatened to divert potential profits away from the newcomers in Ireland and in 1621 they counter-attacked. Sir John Jephson, a landowner in Munster, levelled charges against St John in the English House of Commons. St John was duly recalled, but the mood in England, encouraged alike by Buckingham and the lord treasurer, Cranfield, was to view Ireland as an asset to the king (and themselves), the potential of which had yet to be fully realized.

New inquiries into what had happened during the recent plantations and what might next be achieved shone a searchlight into the shadowy practices of Cork, but he was saved from immediate action by the crown to recover some of what it had lost when Cranfield was toppled in 1624. At the same time Cork hoped to ingratiate himself with Buckingham. Notwithstanding Cork's courtesies and caresses, however, Buckingham remained an uncertain ally, the more so as he was willing to entertain the complaints of Cork's adversaries from Ireland, notably the lord chancellor, Adam Loftus.

Buckingham's death in 1628 reduced the pressure to investigate Cork's Irish ventures but Cork, well aware that to be secure in Ireland he needed friends in England, set about cultivating new patrons, the then powerful lords Coventry and Goring and Humphrey May. As a result he received a fresh grant of much of his disputed property in 1629. This favour was eased by a loan from Cork of £15,000 to the crown. An even clearer sign of his high standing was his appointment on 8 August 1629, in tandem with his rival, Adam, Viscount Loftus, as lord justice of Ireland, a post he retained until a new lord deputy sailed to Dublin in 1633.

Lord justice and lord treasurer, 1629–1639 As a lord justice Cork headed the English government of Ireland and had arrived at the plenitude of his power. His authority and status matched his wealth. Critics contended that he misused his office for personal gain. A wish to avenge himself on his old opponents made his rule divisive and—in some quarters—hated. Some whom he offended subsequently harassed him throughout the 1630s. The most serious quarrel developed over the finances and Cork was soon ranged against the vice-treasurer, Francis Annesley, Lord Mountnorris. The latter was briefly superseded, leaving Cork in effective control of the exchequer. This temporary situation was made more permanent when, in October 1631, Cork secured the lord treasurership, paying a mere £300 for it. More positive, although hardly disinterested, were Cork's schemes while lord justice to strengthen the protestant settlers, of whom he was now clearly the most successful. He believed the government should lighten taxes and subsidize ventures to create industries of the type—textiles, iron making, timber trades, and glass manufacture—which he had encouraged in south Munster. Further measures, such as a tougher enforcement of the penalties for religious recusancy, were advocated to weaken the already enfeebled Catholics. Ireland, Cork contended, would thrive only if peace prevailed. Otherwise the export trade would be interrupted. The exploitation of natural resources, practised vigorously on

Cork's estates, threatened to exhaust many of them simply for short-term gain. Cork, however, was prepared to justify the felling of woodlands and reclamation of bogs and waste as 'commonwealth work' (Ranger, 'Career', 131), since it destroyed the habitats of the indigenous Irish Catholics. More constructively, he sponsored urban development. Some towns in his bailiwick—Youghal, Dungarvan, and Lismore—were long established. Others, notably Tallow and Bandon, owed much to Cork's investment.

In 1633 the installation of a new lord deputy, Thomas, Lord Wentworth, once again caused Cork anxiety as to how he and his possessions would be treated. At first Wentworth proceeded circumspectly, and was thought broadly to agree with the anti-Catholic measures favoured by Cork. The earl also hoped that a projected marriage of his heir with a niece of Wentworth would ease the situation. However, Mountnorris, since his recall from Ireland, had endeared himself to Wentworth and so prejudiced the latter against Cork. Seeing favour drifting away from Cork, old opponents, fair-weather friends, and erstwhile associates deserted him. Wentworth, bent on restoring and enhancing royal authority over Ireland, saw Cork as the personification of all that had undermined it in recent decades and decided to make an example of him by stripping him of many of the church lands and other of his properties, on the grounds that they had been acquired illegally or were enjoyed on forged evidence. Simultaneously a more trivial dispute arose over the desire of Cork to raise a monument in the Dublin cathedral of St Patrick to his second wife. The monument was placed at the east end of the cathedral where the altar had formerly stood, a theologically sensitive position which attracted objections from Wentworth and the Laudian Bishop Bramhall of Derry. In addition, the monument came to symbolize the way in which Cork had commandeered so many assets of the church, sometimes by installing kinsmen and clients as bishops and deans, and through that and other devices securing beneficial leases on church lands. Wentworth, in alliance with Archbishop Laud and Bishop Bramhall, backed a campaign to recover the wealth of the church in Ireland detained by powerful laypeople and Cork offered a conspicuous target.

Wentworth was at first uncompromising in his determination to humble Cork but intermediaries in England and Ireland eventually worked out a settlement whereby Cork was fined £15,000 and surrendered his impropriations, but retained his lease on Youghal. No sooner was this protracted negotiation concluded than other parts of Cork's empire came under attack. The lord president in Munster, Sir William St Leger, unleashed by Wentworth, hounded Cork in his locality. The earl mobilized his contacts in the English privy council and court, and from 1636 spent more time in England, where in Dorset and Somerset he had bought land. His eldest son, thanks to marriage to the Clifford heiress, was inserting himself into the English aristocracy. Younger sons, after protracted education on the continent, followed the same path. All could work to their father's advantage, and shield him against what increasingly looked like a vendetta on Wentworth's part. Indeed, the lord deputy's aggression in Ireland created a coalition against him but Cork, for all his dislike of Wentworth, did not actively abet this group. He preferred to consolidate his position by building up alliances in London with Goring and Sir Thomas Stafford, the illegitimate son of his old boss Carew. On the fringes of the circle of the queen, Cork still refrained from any open criticism of Wentworth. In 1639 he demonstrated his loyalty by sending three of his sons to wait on the king as he prepared to fight the Scottish covenanters. Cork's good standing was indicated publicly in June 1640, when he was added to the English privy council.

Final years, 1640–1643 In Ireland the summoning of parliament in 1640 allowed a concerted attack on Wentworth, by this time earl of Strafford, chiefly through his subordinates who remained in Ireland and in office. By 1640 Cork controlled six parliamentary boroughs in south Munster, and had influence in another four. Although he used this patronage to advance his own interest, he did not direct these members to attack Strafford. In England, too, he abstained from the scheming to bring down the lord deputy. However, once the impeachment began, he backed it. Sweeter still was the removal of many of Strafford's supporters from the Irish administration. At last Cork was freed from the meddlesome inquiries into what he had or had not done to amass his possessions. But full enjoyment of these riches was frustrated when the Irish Catholics rose. The uprising, originating in Ulster in October 1641, gradually spread into Munster. The property and persons of recent settlers, like the Boyles, were particular targets. From his seat at Lismore, the former bishop's palace, Cork organized resistance. Several of his sons were sent to fight the insurgents; one, Lewis, Lord Kinalmeaky, was killed in action at Liscarrol in September 1642. Arms and equipment were shipped in through his port of Youghal. The expense, coupled with the loss of rents, burdened Cork but, in acting to save his and co-religionists' holdings, he also looked to a future in which protestant power would be increased. He joined the campaign of Irish protestants to use the rebellion to justify further expropriation of Catholic-owned property. By 1643 the fiercely anti-Catholic in Ireland, such as Cork, found themselves at odds with Charles I and his deputy Ormond. Unable to defeat the insurgents in either Ireland or England, the king authorized a truce with the Irish adversaries in September 1643. This cessation strained Cork's attachment to the royalist cause. Since acquiring his great stake in Ireland, his attitude towards official policy had altered. Distant regimes were judged ultimately on the freedom that they allowed to buccaneers like himself. Concessions to the local Catholics were strenuously but—in 1643—unsuccessfully opposed. Cork, having retreated to his enclave of Youghal, died on 15 September 1643, and was buried in St Mary's Abbey, Youghal. It fell to his sons to sustain and finance the war effort in the region. Through flexible strategies reminiscent of Cork's, they saved and

subsequently enlarged the extensive settlement which would be regarded by Oliver Cromwell as the model for a placid and prosperous protestant Ireland. Others, less sympathetic to these freebooters, felt that they personified both a system which sacrificed Irish to English interests, and the licence granted to rapacious adventurers from England, Wales, and Scotland.

Cork composed an autobiography through which he hoped to impress contemporaries and later generations with what he had accomplished. He allowed that divine favour had assisted his rise. Indeed, he adopted 'God's providence is mine inheritance' (GEC, *Peerage*) as his motto. Inevitably his account exaggerated the gradient of his rise, and glossed over much of his ruthlessness. The plantation over which he presided was built on the wreckage of earlier civilizations, not all of which were totally effaced. Cork was prepared to marry children into families which belonged to those earlier settlements. Similarly he used the compliant among them as his auxiliaries. He was happy to take over ancient buildings in Lismore and Youghal as his principal residences. Although they were enlarged and furnished sumptuously, their essential characters were not altered. Rivals, whether among the older Catholic or newer English communities, were relentlessly harried. Cork had a vision of a protestant Ireland which he set out to realize on his own estates. Much of it was lifted from an idealized lowland England, and did not always fit the conditions of southern Ireland. Silently he dropped some of his ambitions and adjusted to indigenous ways. Just as there was no denying that Cork had scrambled to the top of Irish protestant society, he also attracted new settlers to the region, so altering it permanently. Impressive as the achievements looked, his protestant towns were too fragile to withstand the Catholic onslaught after 1641. The protestant population in the Munster countryside, increased perhaps to 22,000, remained puny. Much that he had built so painstakingly was destroyed and had to be refashioned after 1649. Nevertheless, Cork had laid durable foundations for a dynasty which for more than a century would dominate the economy, society, and politics of Munster, Ireland, and even England. His reputation as the nonpareil of the industrious English settler, carefully fabricated by his own writings, survived long after he had died. Similarly, vestiges of what he had achieved were visible under his successors, from the 1750s the dukes of Devonshire, into the twenty-first century.

TOBY BARNARD

Sources Chatsworth House, Derbyshire, Lismore MSS · Lismore MSS, NL Ire. · A. B. Grosart, ed., *Lismore papers*, 10 vols., 1st and 2nd ser. (1886–8) · T. O. Ranger, 'The career of Richard Boyle, first earl of Cork, in Ireland, 1588–1643', DPhil diss., U. Oxf., 1959 · T. O. Ranger, 'Richard Boyle and the making of an Irish fortune, 1588–1614', *Irish Historical Studies*, 10 (1956–7), 257–97 · P. J. S. Little, 'Family and faction: the Irish nobility and the English court, 1632–42', MLitt diss., TCD, 1992 · N. Canny, *The upstart earl: a study of the social and mental world of Richard Boyle, first earl of Cork, 1566–1643* (1982) · V. Treadwell, *Buckingham and Ireland, 1616–1628*, Dublin (1998) · D. Townshend, *The life and letters of the great earl of Cork* (1904) · M. MacCarthy-Morrogh, *The Munster plantation: English migration to*

southern Ireland, 1583–1641 (1986) · H. F. Kearney, Strafford and Ireland, 1633–40 (1958) · GEC, Peerage, new edn · Venn, Alum. Cant.
Archives Balliol Oxf., autobiography · BL, corresp. with marginal notes; autobiography, Add. MS 19832 [copies] · NL Ire., estate corresp. · Trustees of the Chatsworth Settlement, Derbyshire, corresp., diary | PRO NIre., corresp. with earl of Kildare, D3078 · Sheff. Arch., Wentworth Woodhouse MSS
Likenesses I. Oliver, miniature, c.1610–1615, NPG [see illus.] · stipple and line engraving, pubd 1803, NG Ire. · tomb effigy on monument, Youghal, Cork, Éire
Wealth at death approx. £18,000 p.a. in rents: Ranger, 'The career of Richard Boyle'

Boyle, Richard (c.1574–1645), Church of Ireland archbishop of Tuam, was the second son of Michael Boyle (d. 1596), merchant, of London, and Jane, daughter of William Peacock, and was an elder brother of Michael *Boyle (1580?–1635), bishop of Waterford and Lismore. He was admitted to Corpus Christi College, Cambridge, in 1590, graduated BA in 1595, proceeded MA in 1598, and was incorporated MA at Oxford on 16 July 1601. Foster refers to his holding the vicarage of Finedon, Northamptonshire, in 1606 (Foster, Alum. Oxon., 1.163), but his ecclesiastical career was based in Ireland, where the influence of his cousin Richard Boyle, first earl of Cork, ensured his steady rise in ecclesiastical circles. He became warden of Youghal on 24 February 1603, dean of Waterford on 10 May 1603, dean of Tuam in May 1604, archdeacon of Limerick on 8 May 1605, and bishop of Cork, Cloyne, and Ross on 22 August 1620. By 30 May 1638 he was advanced to the see of Tuam. On the outbreak of the Irish rising in 1641 he retreated with Dr John Maxwell, bishop of Killala, and others to Galway for protection, where, when the town rose in arms against the garrison, his life was saved through the influence of the earl of Clanricarde. After a time in Bristol he returned to Cork, where he died on 19 March 1645 and was buried in the cathedral of St Fin Barre. Ware commends him for having repaired more churches and consecrated more new ones than any other bishop of his time (Whole Works of Sir James Ware, 1.566). By his marriage to Martha, daughter of Richard or John Wright of Catherine Hill, Surrey, he left two sons and nine daughters. His eldest son, Michael *Boyle (1609/10–1702), became archbishop of Armagh, while his second son, Colonel Richard Boyle, died at Drogheda in 1649.

T. F. HENDERSON, rev. ELIZABETHANNE BORAN

Sources The whole works of Sir James Ware concerning Ireland, ed. and trans. W. Harris, 1 (1739), 566, 616 · J. Lodge, The peerage of Ireland, rev. M. Archdall, rev. edn, 1 (1789), 144–6 · W. M. Brady, Clerical and parochial records of Cork, Cloyne, and Ross, 3 (1864), 52–4 · H. Cotton, Fasti ecclesiae Hibernicae, 2nd edn, 1 (1851), 139, 225, 278, 406 · Wood, Ath. Oxon., new edn, 1.293 · Venn, Alum. Cant., 1/1.196 · Foster, Alum. Oxon. · J. B. Leslie, ed., 'Tuam biographical succession lists', Representative Church Body Library, Dublin, 8 · R. Mant, History of the Church of Ireland, 1 (1840), 563 · W. A. Phillips, ed., History of the Church of Ireland, 3 (1933), 12, 42, 46, 89, 91 · W. H. Rennison, ed., Succession list of the bishops, cathedral and parochial clergy of the dioceses of Waterford and Lismore (1920), 37, 62, 83, 114 · The Lismore papers, first series: autobiographical notes, remembrances and diaries of Sir Richard Boyle, first and 'great' earl of Cork, ed. A. B. Grosart, 5 vols. (privately printed, London, 1886), vol. 2, pp. 355–6; vol. 3, p. 238; vol. 4, pp. 261–2; vol. 5, p. 250 · C. McNeill, ed., The Tanner letters, IMC (1943), 73
Archives Chatsworth House, Derbyshire, letters

Boyle, Richard, first earl of Burlington and second earl of Cork (1612–1698), royalist army officer and politician, was born on 20 October 1612 at Youghal, co. Cork, the second child but eldest surviving son of Richard *Boyle, first earl of Cork (1566–1643), and his wife, Catherine Fenton (c.1588–1630), daughter of Sir Geoffrey *Fenton. His siblings included the natural philosopher Robert *Boyle, Roger *Boyle, first earl of Orrery, Katherine *Jones, Viscountess Ranelagh, and Mary *Rich, countess of Warwick. From 16 October 1620, when his father was ennobled, the child was known by his father's subsidiary title of Viscount Dungarvan. Knighted by the Irish lord deputy in 1623, he studied briefly at Oxford in 1629–30 and was then sent on a more extended continental tour. He visited both Saumur and Paris in 1633. The care which had been devoted to his education was also evident in the way his ambitious father negotiated his marriage. On 3 July 1634 he married Elizabeth Clifford (1613–1691), daughter of Henry *Clifford, fifth earl of Cumberland. The alliance connected Boyle, the son of an arriviste in protestant Ireland, with an ancient aristocratic house. It brought the prospect of substantial English estates concentrated in Yorkshire, Westmorland, and Cumberland which in time would transform this branch of the Boyles from Irish to English grandees. Dungarvan was further connected with nobles powerful at court, such as the earls of Pembroke and Salisbury. He flourished in this environment, though his extravagance alarmed his father. A measure of his standing was the fact that he was selected to greet the Venetian ambassador in 1638, and the presence of the king and queen at the christening of his heir, Charles, on 17 November 1639. In the latter year he had hastened to the king's side as preparations began for a war against the Scots.

Dungarvan was elected to the Short and Long parliaments in 1640 for the Westmorland borough of Appleby, an area where the Cliffords' influence was strong. However, he sailed back to Ireland at the time of the uprising in autumn 1641. In November 1641 the English parliament commissioned him to command a cavalry troop, and he took part in Irish engagements in the region where the family's property lay, notably the battle of Liscarroll in September 1642. In November he sailed to England, to seek aid for the protestants of the region; he returned to Ireland in July 1643, but in the event defence of the Boyles' Irish interests was deputed to his younger brothers, and Dungarvan returned once again to England. There his adherence to the king's cause led to his being disabled from sitting in parliament on 10 November 1643 and, on 4 November 1644, to his being granted an English peerage as Baron Clifford. Already in 1643 he had succeeded to the Irish earldom of Cork. Although he was not conspicuous as a royalist commander, the importance of the family into which he had married ensured that the parliamentarian authorities monitored his activities. The victorious parliament penalized him. He had paid a fine of £1631 to recover the English estates by the end of May 1650. Not until 1653 did he regain full control of his much more valuable Irish holdings under the terms of the Dublin treaty of 1647. He removed himself discreetly to the continent in the later 1640s, and for a time was with the exiled royalist lord lieutenant, Ormond, at Caen.

Cork returned to Ireland on 28 May 1651, and there attended to the repair of his estate, which his wife had already begun. Once more discretion was his watchword, since members of the occupying army and administration eyed him suspiciously. Nevertheless in private he remained loyal to the liturgy of the proscribed Church of England, and manifested the personal piety which continued for the rest of his life. The enforced attention to his patrimony gave him an intimate knowledge of its human and physical geography, and in no small measure explained its subsequent prosperity. By the 1670s it was probably yielding an annual £30,000, making its owner the richest man in Ireland. From 1655, under the more congenial regime of Henry Cromwell, Cork undertook modest local duties. In 1658 he was appointed a justice of the peace for counties Cork and Waterford. He also welcomed the itinerating lord deputy to his estates in the summer of 1658, and had political discussions with him when in Dublin. In December 1659, as confusion threatened to envelop Ireland and England, Cork positioned himself in London. Along with others from protestant Ireland he schemed to prevent the dispossessed Irish Catholics being treated generously.

Cork was appointed a privy councillor in Dublin in December 1660, and installed in his father's office of lord treasurer on 6 July 1661. The second office, essentially a sinecure, conferred precedence and a daily allowance of £1. It was symptomatic of Cork's limited political influence that he was not consulted about proposed reforms of the Irish revenue despite being nominal head of its administration. The lord treasurership had, nevertheless, given him the disposal of posts in the revenue with which to gratify the politically powerful and his own dependants. His high standing at the English court, together with his wealth, his wife's lineage, and his past services to the Stuarts (especially the queen mother, Henrietta Maria) secured advancement to an English earldom—of Burlington (or Bridlington)—in 1665. Other posts, such as governor (the equivalent of lord lieutenant) of counties Cork and Waterford and military governor of Hawlbowline Fort in Cork harbour (1662), attested to his pre-eminence as a proprietor in the region. For similar reasons he was appointed lord lieutenant of the West Riding of Yorkshire, a position he held briefly in 1667 and from 1679 to 1687, and recorder of York (1685–8). But the manner in which the king asked him to vacate the lord lieutenancy in 1667 in favour of Buckingham, newly reconciled to the court, was a reminder of Burlington's light political weight. Nor could royalist ultras forget how he had compromised with the Cromwellians. As one of the latter remarked, Burlington 'was a cautious man that had no mind to venture too far for fear of his great estate, and so seemed to carry fair with all parties' (*Memoirs of Sir John Reresby*, ed. A. Browning, 1936, 306). In 1667 he had absented himself from the proceedings against the disgraced Clarendon, into whose family his own had recently

married. His attitudes towards exclusion and the accession of William III and Mary II were deliberately opaque. In the end, the safety of his valuable Irish holdings overrode other considerations. Oversight of the distinct Irish and English estates necessitated a peripatetic life. In 1667 he acquired the carcass of Sir John Denham's London mansion in Piccadilly, which was completed with a grandeur consonant with the Burlingtons' new dignity; they moved into Burlington House the following year. In 1682 an estate at Chiswick, in Middlesex, was bought, to which in 1684 the family moved permanently. After 1686 advancing years and disturbed conditions prevented further voyages to Ireland. Predeceased by his wife (in 1691) and his eldest son, Charles, Viscount Dungarvan and Lord Clifford (in 1694), he died at Chiswick House on 15 January 1698 and was buried at Londesborough, his Yorkshire seat, on 8 February. He was succeeded by his grandson Charles.   TOBY BARNARD

Sources diary of Richard Boyle, second earl of Cork, 1651–73, Chatsworth House, Derbyshire · journal of Elizabeth Clifford, countess of Cork and Burlington, Chatsworth House, Derbyshire · Chatsworth House, Derbyshire, Lismore MSS · NL Ire., Lismore MSS · BL, Althorp MS B 3–7 · *The Lismore papers*, ed. A. B. Grosart, 10 vols. in 2 series (privately printed, London, 1886–8) · Keeler, *Long Parliament* · T. C. Barnard, 'Land and the limits of loyalty: the second earl of Cork and first earl of Burlington', *Lord Burlington: architecture, art and life*, ed. T. C. Barnard and J. Clark (1995), 167–99 · P. J. S. Little, 'Family and faction: the Irish nobility and the English court, 1632–42', MLitt diss., TCD, 1992 · T. C. Barnard, 'The protestant interest', *Ireland from independence to occupation, 1641–1660*, ed. J. Ohlmeyer (1995), 218–40 · PRO, PROB 11/448, quire 259 · A. Swatland, *The House of Lords in the reign of Charles II* (1996) · letters to Ormond, Bodl. Oxf., MS Carte 215 · PRO NIre., D 638/6/1 · Borth. Inst., PR LON 2, fol. 18*v* · GEC, *Peerage*

Archives BL, corresp., B3–7 · Chatsworth House, Derbyshire, corresp.; diary · NL Ire., corresp. and papers · NL Ire., Lismore MSS | BL, letters to Lord Essex, Stowe MSS 200–212, *passim* · Bodl. Oxf., corresp. with Ormond, Carte MSS · Bodl. Oxf., Clarendon MSS, corresp. with Clarendon · Chatsworth House, Derbyshire, Lismore and Londesborough MSS, Bolton Abbey MSS · W. Yorks. AS, Leeds, letters to Sir John Reresby

Likenesses P. Lely, oils, *c.*1670, Buccleuch estates, Selkirk · A. Van Dyck, oils, Chatsworth House; photograph, NPG · oils (after A. Van Dyck), Chatsworth; version, NPG · oils (after A. Van Dyck), Knole, Kent

Boyle, Richard, third earl of Burlington and fourth earl of Cork (1694–1753), architect, collector, and patron of the arts, was born on 25 April 1694 at Burlington House, Piccadilly, London, the only son of Charles Boyle, second earl of Burlington and third earl of Cork (*d.* 1704), and Juliana (1672–1750), daughter and heir to Henry Noel, second son of the fourth Viscount Campden. He was educated at home, and at his father's death on 9 February 1704 he succeeded to his titles and estates. In 1715 Burlington was made lord treasurer of Ireland and governor of co. Cork and was sworn of the Irish privy council. In the same year he became vice-admiral of the county of York and lord lieutenant of the East and West Ridings of Yorkshire. Burlington was sworn of the privy council of England on 15 May 1729. His nomination as knight of the Garter came on 18 May 1730, and he was installed at Windsor on 18 June 1730. On 21 June 1731 he was made captain of the band of

Richard Boyle, third earl of Burlington and fourth earl of Cork (1694–1753), by Jonathan Richardson the elder, c.1717–19

pensioners. His legal claim to the barony of Clifford was granted on 25 May 1737. In May 1733 Burlington resigned all his offices, apparently because George II failed to honour a promise to appoint him to a high household office, probably that of lord treasurer. Until that date he was a supporter of Walpole's government but in the pre-sessional forecast of January 1734 was listed as against the ministry. He attended the House of Lords only intermittently after coming of age in 1715, and showed particular interest in debates and committees concerned with Ireland, Yorkshire, and other personal interests.

Burlington was elected a fellow of the Royal Society on 1 November 1722 and a fellow of the Society of Antiquaries on 5 February 1724. On 21 March 1721 he married Dorothy Savile (1699–1758), lady of the bedchamber to Queen Caroline [see Boyle, Dorothy], eldest daughter and coheir of William Savile, marquess of Halifax, and Mary, daughter of Daniel Finch, earl of Winchilsea. They had three daughters: Dorothy (1724–1742), who married George, earl of Euston; Juliana (1727–1731); and Charlotte (1731–1754).

Burlington owned four principal seats, three of which were acquired by his great-grandfather Richard, the first earl of Burlington and second earl of Cork, by marriage and purchase. He resided annually in three of these seats: his London town house, Burlington House in Piccadilly; his suburban seat on the Thames at Chiswick in Middlesex; and his country seat at Londesborough in the East Riding of Yorkshire. His Irish seat of Lismore Castle in co. Waterford, located on a vast estate numbering some 42,000 acres in the counties of Cork and Waterford, was the original family seat purchased by Richard, the first

earl of Cork, from Sir Walter Ralegh in 1602. Although his Irish estates provided the major source of revenue for his architectural projects on his English estates, Burlington never visited Ireland.

Burlington and architecture Architecture was Burlington's outstanding area of contribution to the arts. Like his fellow aristocrat and contemporary Henry Herbert, ninth earl of Pembroke, Burlington was an 'Architect earl', who practised architecture not from economic necessity but as a passionate avocation. Surprisingly, he showed no interest in architecture during his grand tour of 1714–15. While on it, he purchased a number of paintings and several drawings, made the acquaintance of William Kent, and indulged his passion for music: he returned to England with three Italian musicians. Like Lord Shaftesbury, who in his 1712 *Letter Concerning Art, or Science of Design* argued for a national architecture based upon classical precedents, Burlington aimed to place England within the mainstream of the classical tradition. His architecture—with its didactic, lucid character—was intended to demonstrate that England could create an architecture worthy of Rome. It was the centrepiece of an elaborately orchestrated campaign, with Burlington as the spokesman for the revival of an English classical style whose content he would dictate.

The traditional view of Burlington as a whig nobleman has been challenged. It has been argued that Burlington led a double life in service to the Jacobite cause, that his public life and architectural endeavours were a subterfuge for clandestine political activity in support of the exiled Stuarts, and that his grand tour and 1719 Italian sojourn served as opportunities for both cultural enrichment and political contacts with the exiled Stuart court. Burlington's reliance on the Stuart architect Inigo Jones as a cornerstone of his architecture is interpreted as a return not merely to Jonesian classicism but also to the early Stuart court, and as a reaffirmation of the divine right of kings (Barnard and Clark). Jacobite sympathies could explain one important early architectural commission: the Westminster School dormitory, a building erected under the aegis of the Jacobite dean of Westminster Abbey, Francis Atterbury. However, Burlington's record in the House of Lords, and his conduct during the Jacobite risings of 1715 and 1745, give no hint of Jacobite sympathies, and it is extremely doubtful that his architecture is encoded with Jacobite symbolism or that his architectural patronage reflected Jacobite leanings. Until more than circumstantial evidence is produced, Burlington's putative crypto-Jacobite proclivities must remain in the realm of speculation.

Burlington's interest in architecture began during the four and a half years between his two Italian sojourns. About 1717 he was probably responsible for replacing James Gibbs with Colen Campbell as the architect responsible for remodelling Burlington House. This change reflects his evolving tastes from Gibbs's baroque classicism to Campbell's more rigorous classicism based on the architecture of Andrea Palladio. Under Campbell's tutelage at Burlington House and in the garden at Chiswick,

Burlington learned the practical aspects of architecture. When he returned to Italy in 1719 he had made architecture his muse. In Venice and the Veneto he studied Palladio's architecture, recorded annotations of his impressions in a prepared copy of Palladio's *I quattro libri dell'architettura*, and purchased a large collection of Palladio's drawings of his reconstructions of the Roman baths. On returning to London in November 1719, Burlington began what became his lifelong architectural project: the transformation of his suburban estate at Chiswick, Middlesex.

Burlington was one of the most rigorous practitioners of the English classical architectural movement known as Palladianism. His architecture is didactic in character and is based upon the architecture of Inigo Jones, Palladio, and classical Rome, as represented in Palladio's drawings and in his treatise *I quattro libri dell'architettura*. Like Alberti, Burlington believed that the visual arts should provide moral instruction: for him classical architecture was a mute but eloquent language capable of conveying ideas and stimulating the imagination visually and intellectually.

With two notable exceptions Burlington's executed designs were for town or country houses and were executed for his fellow aristocrats and members of his family. At Chiswick he designed a suburban villa with its gardens and garden buildings. In the garden at Oatlands, Surrey, he designed a small villa (*c*.1725) for the seventh earl of Lincoln. He also designed: the huge Belvedere Tower (1725–7) for Sir Robert Furnese at Waldershare Park, Kent; an octagonal temple (1743) at Woburn Farm, Surrey, for Sir Philip Southcote; a summer house (*in situ* by 1744) for Sir Robert Clifton at Clifton Hall, Nottinghamshire; and wings (*c*.1733) to Petersham Lodge, Surrey, for the first earl of Harrington. For his brother-in-law Charles, Lord Bruce, he designed a country house at Tottenham Park, Wiltshire, begun in 1721, with wings added about 1730–38 and an octagonal building and banqueting house (1743) in the garden. Also for Lord Bruce he designed a *pied-à-terre* (1726–7) at Round Coppice, Iver Heath, Buckinghamshire, located halfway between his Wiltshire country house and London, and interior alterations to Warwick House (1726–7), his London residence.

Burlington also designed five town residences, of which, however, only three were built. Two were erected on land behind Burlington House that he had provided for a town house development in 1717: one for Lord Mountrath (*c*.1721) and the other for General Wade (1723). His third London town house was designed for the second duke of Richmond at Whitehall (1733–4). The two unexecuted designs were a sumptuous London residence for the earl of Bath and an elegant house for Colonel James Gee (*c*.1722) at Bishop Burton in the East Riding of Yorkshire. He also designed five institutional buildings: York assembly rooms (1731–2), Westminster School dormitory (1722–30), Chichester Council House (1730), a hospital, and Sevenoaks School and almshouses (*c*.1724). Of these, only the assembly rooms and dormitory were erected.

Tottenham Park, Wiltshire—Burlington's only country house—was designed for his brother-in-law Charles, Lord Bruce, to replace the family seat destroyed by fire. Burlington's work at Tottenham Park spanned his entire architectural career, from 1721 to 1743. Henry Flitcroft, Burlington's personal draughtsman and architectural assistant, executed the drawings and was the site architect for at least the first building phase. Although Tottenham Park was Burlington's first and largest commission, he was in full command of his architectural ideas, and designed a house containing architectural elements that would become his architectural leitmotifs, and bearing allusions to the architecture of Jones and Palladio.

Begun in 1721, the front elevation of Tottenham Park was a slightly recessed three-bay central section crowned by a cupola, reminiscent of the north elevation of Amesbury Abbey, a nearby country house then believed to be by Inigo Jones (later attributed to John Webb) and owned by Burlington's uncle Lord Carleton. Its tall, two-storey corner towers punctuated by Serliana windows (often referred to as Palladian or Venetian windows) recall towers found in many of Palladio's villa designs in Burlington's drawing collection and similar towers on the villas Pisani and Thiene in Palladio's treatise. Large expanses of wall punctuated by single and double hung windows dominate the front elevation, giving it an emphatic rhythm. In addition to the house, Burlington designed two service buildings facing each other across the courtyard. Their façades are pared-down versions of Palladio's design for a small villa in Burlington's drawing collection, but without the recessed Serliana entrance portal and the robust aedicular windows flanking it.

In the early 1730s Burlington added elaborate wings to the front and garden elevations of Tottenham Park. On the garden elevation, corner towers matching those on the front elevation were added, but without Serliana windows. Defining the central section was an impressive freestanding, hexastyle, Ionic portico with an Italianate rusticated podium, derived from the podium of Burlington's villa at Chiswick. The wings consisted of a series of individual units, or small buildings, each with its own roof and fenestration. This, which Rudolf Wittkower terms the 'staccato principle' (Wittkower, 155), is a defining characteristic of the villa and Link Building at Chiswick. The elevations at the end of each wing have Serliana windows with Ionic capitals and a full entablature flanked by niches and Italianate rusticated quoins at the corners. In 1743 Burlington designed two garden buildings for Tottenham Park: a 70 foot Tuscan banqueting house and an octagonal garden building.

From 1720 Burlington transformed his suburban estate at Chiswick into a paradigm of classical architecture, with buildings exemplifying his architectural theory and practice. His first act was to complete the formal garden begun before his 1719 Italian trip. Every aspect of the garden was made subservient to its architecture, with each of the four garden buildings representing aspects of the architecture of Inigo Jones, Palladio, and classical Rome. At the end of the east *allée* of the *patte d'oie* Burlington designed a diminutive rustic building whose front elevation was modelled on Jones's vineyard gate at Oatlands Palace, Surrey; buildings attributed to Campbell and Gibbs probably occupied the termini of the west and central *allées*. Along the western boundary of the garden Burlington designed two buildings. Overlooking an apsidal pool within its own garden enclosure stood a (now demolished) banqueting house featuring a portico with a pair of Tuscan columns patterned after the Tuscan portico of Jones's St Paul's Church, Covent Garden. To the south, in its own garden enclosure, a tetrastyle Ionic temple was erected, a miniature version of two famous classical Roman buildings, the Pantheon and the Temple of Fortuna Virilis, both depicted in great detail in Palladio's treatise. The Ionic temple faces an orange-tree garden in the form of an amphitheatre. It consists of three concentric grass terraces where tubs of orange trees were placed during the summer months. From the circular pool at the centre of the orange-tree garden rises a stone obelisk on a pedestal. Burlington's fourth garden building (also now demolished), was an orangery located on the eastern boundary of the estate. There are two extant orangery designs: a domed and arcaded one, inspired by Palladio's thermal drawings, such as the Baths of Agrippa; and a seven-bay design with a gigantic, superimposed Corinthian portico in the manner of Palladio's Venetian church façades. As the domed and arcaded orangery design could function successfully as a greenhouse, it was probably this design that was erected.

Burlington now embarked on a more ambitious project by designing an extraordinarily idiosyncratic villa (1726–9) facing the Thames. Erected in close proximity to an existing Jacobean house, the villa at Chiswick was designed without the amenities of a residence, which the earlier house provided. To confirm this symbiotic relationship, the villa and house were connected by the so-called Link Building and loggia in the early 1730s. Diminutive in size and jewel-like in the intensity of its architectural detailing, the villa is a paean to Jones, Palladio, and classical Rome. Its design was based upon Palladio's two famous suburban villas, La Rotonda at Vicenza and the Villa Foscari, near Venice. Palladio's standard Corinthian order in his treatise defines the exterior and interior. The free-standing hexastyle portico derives from Palladio's Villa Foscari, but was dramatically altered by the addition of a boldly rusticated podium. This rustication was inspired by that defining Palladio's Palazzo Thiene (Vicenza), which Burlington described as 'certainly the most beautifull modern building in the world'. For the portico's capitals, Burlington deviated from Palladio's Corinthian order and selected the luxuriant Corinthian capitals from the Temple of Castor and Pollux in the Roman Forum, as illustrated in Palladio's treatise. The Serliana windows on the side and garden elevations and the thermal windows in the drum of the dome also derive from Palladio's Roman bath drawings.

The villa's innovative floor plan consists of simple geometric forms. Circles, semicircles, octagons, squares, and rectangles create a circular flow of space unlike the traditional linear spatial disposition of English domestic architecture. Burlington's novel treatment of such space derives from Palladio's Roman bath drawings and his Palazzo Thiene, in which similar spatial configurations were employed. The rooms on the piano nobile of the villa bristle with sumptuous architectural detailing, deriving in large part from Inigo Jones and to a much lesser degree from Palladio and classical Rome. There is nothing perfunctory or merely decorative about the interiors of the villa. The architectural detailing is a lexicon of classical architecture and is intended to be a standard for others to follow.

Burlington designed his villa as a temple to the arts. It functioned as a place for contemplation, entertainment, and the exhibition of art. Lord Hervey's scathing epigram based on the Roman poet Martial suggests that the villa did not function as a residence:

> Possess'd of one great hall for state,
> Without a place to sleep or eat;
> How well you build let flattery tell,
> And all mankind how ill you dwell!
> (Hervey, 1.574)

The walls of the piano nobile were lined with Burlington's painting collection, interspersed with pieces from his sculpture collection and gilt furniture designed by William Kent. In such an ambience, Burlington could escape the formalities of the nearby Jacobean house to study, work on his architectural projects, and meet friends. The circular flow of space and the openness of the floor plan also made the piano nobile an ideal place for musical gatherings and entertainments, with the Serliana windows providing views of the formal garden and glimpses of Burlington's garden architecture.

In contrast to his suburban villa at Chiswick, the York assembly rooms (1731–2) are the finest public statement of Burlington's architectural principles. With an unprecedented archaeological fidelity and reliance upon Palladio as his guide to classical Rome, Burlington created a building that was a precursor to neo-classicism. Austere on the exterior, clearly and sumptuously articulated on the interiors, the assembly rooms functioned as a place for the nobility and gentry of town and county to meet and entertain. From Palladio's drawings of the Roman baths came the severe five-bay arcaded front elevation of the assembly rooms (now demolished), as well as the apsidal and domed circular rooms surrounding the Great Assembly Room. With this room, Burlington attempted to rival the ancients, creating a modern version of Vitruvius's Egyptian Hall for dancing and other entertainments. Relying upon Palladio's reconstructions of the Egyptian Hall and the Roman basilica, he combined these to create a peripteral hall of forty-four Corinthian columns supporting a clerestory, and in accordance with Vitruvius and Palladio, an open loggia around the building at the clerestory level to view the activities in the Great Assembly Room.

Burlington's opinion and imprimatur on classical architecture were sought by his fellow peers. With Lord Pembroke, he oversaw Roger Morris's remodelling of Castle Hill, Devon (1729–*c*.1740), for Lord Clinton; his advice was solicited about details such as the proportions of the hall entablature. For Sir Mark Pleydell at Coleshill, Berkshire (1744), the chimney-stacks at the angles of the house were rebuilt at the direction of Burlington and the earl of Leicester. With the assistance of William Kent, Burlington was instrumental in formulating the design of Holkham Hall (c.1734), the Norfolk country house of his friend the earl of Leicester. For the earl of Carlisle at Castle Howard, Yorkshire, Daniel Garrett designed and obtained Burlington's approval for the addition to Nicholas Hawksmoor's mausoleum of an elaborate staircase based on the one at the villa at Chiswick (1737–42). In 1727, as part of his campaign to create an English classical architecture, Burlington paid for repairs to the Tuscan portico of Jones's St Paul's Church, Covent Garden, and in 1733 similarly for Jones's Barber–Surgeons' Hall, London. To save Jones's Beaufort House gate from demolition, Burlington had it removed from Hans Sloane's Chelsea garden in 1733, and re-erected in his garden at Chiswick.

Through influence wielded behind the scenes, Burlington placed a contingent of his Palladian architectural protégés in positions throughout the office of works. At the core of the English architectural establishment, the office of works was responsible for the care and the design of royal buildings. William Kent, whom Burlington promoted as a history painter and then architect and landscape architect, was appointed first master carpenter (1726), then master mason and deputy surveyor (1735). Henry Flitcroft held a number of positions, among them the clerkship of works at St James's, Whitehall, and Westminster (1726). Isaac Ware, architect, author, and translator, held several offices, among them clerk of the works at Windsor (1729) and Greenwich (1732–3). Even such minor protégés as Daniel Garrett and Stephen Wright were also given positions in the office of works.

Burlington's art collections Burlington's art collections, although not large by the standards of the day, reflected not only his fondness for Italy but also his architectural interests. His painting collection, hung at Burlington House and in the villa at Chiswick, consisted mainly of works from the Italian baroque by such artists as Annibale Carracci, Domenichino, Pietro da Cortona, and Carlo Maratta. In addition, Burlington owned a representative sample of paintings by Dutch masters, including Rembrandt, as well as English family portraits. His small sculpture collection, located primarily at Chiswick, expressed his devotion to the classical tradition. Three full-length Roman statues, which according to Daniel Defoe were excavated from Hadrian's villa, stood in the garden along with sphinxes, a boar, and other statues modelled on classical prototypes by John Cheere, Giovanni Battista Guelfi, and Peter Scheemakers. John Michael Rysbrack's full-length statues of Palladio and Jones flanked the stairs to the piano nobile of the villa.

Burlington's most important collection was that of his architectural drawings. The collection consisted of the single largest corpus of Palladio's architectural drawings, including his reconstructions of the Roman baths and other Roman monuments. Jones's architectural drawings

as well as his masque drawings, the drawings of John Webb, Jones's pupil, and a miscellaneous collection of sixteenth- and seventeenth-century drawings, mainly Italian, also formed part of the collection. Complementing this was a superb architectural library consisting of virtually all published editions of architectural treatises and texts, beginning with a mid-fifteenth-century incunabulum on vellum of Vitruvius's *Ten Books of Architecture*.

Burlington's drawing collection was not only indispensable to his own architecture: he also employed it as a means to disseminate his architectural principles. He made the collection available to his protégés for study and inclusion in their architectural treatises and design books. In 1727 William Kent published a lavishly illustrated two-volume folio, *The Designs of Inigo Jones*, for which Burlington probably provided a subvention. The majority of the book's designs came from Burlington's drawing collection, including the ground-plans, elevations, and a section of the tribune of the villa at Chiswick. In 1731 Isaac Ware published the *Designs of Inigo Jones and Others*. Ware too was deeply indebted to Burlington, and informed his readers that the unexecuted designs in his text were at Burlington House. The majority of the plates in Ware's publication were devoted to designs by Inigo Jones, including those for the chimney-pieces erected in Burlington's villa; gate piers designed by Burlington for Chiswick were also included. Another publication supported by Burlington was Thomas Malie's publication *A New and Accurate Method of Delineating All the Parts of the Different Orders in Architecture* of 1737, a translation of Revesi Bruti. Burlington advocated the translation of Bruti's 1627 text, read Malie's manuscript, and encouraged him to publish it; consequently the text was dedicated to him. With the publication of a selection of Palladio's drawings of the Roman baths, Burlington wrapped himself in Palladio's mantle. In his treatise *I quattro libri dell'architettura* Palladio promised but failed to publish his drawings of the Roman baths; Burlington completed the master's work by publishing *Fabbriche antiche disegnate' da Andrea Palladio Vicentino*. Although 1730 is the stated publication date of the *Fabbriche*, it probably was not published until later in the decade. Of the fewer than 100 copies published, Burlington gave most to his friends and fellow *cognoscenti*. Burlington was also intimately involved with Isaac Ware's 1738 English translation of Palladio's influential treatise, published as *The Four Books of Architecture*. Ware dedicated his publication to Burlington, stating that he was given 'free access to your study, wherein many of the original drawings of Palladio, besides those which compose this work, are preserved'. Burlington also revised and corrected Ware's translation and probably provided a subvention for its publication.

Burlington and music Music was Burlington's other great passion. Unlike his interest in architecture, which occupied him for approximately twenty-five years, his devotion to music was constant and continual. Throughout his life Burlington patronized composers, librettists, musicians, and the Italian opera, and held musical performances in his various residences. He undoubtedly acquired his love of music, and in particular the Italian opera, from his mother, Juliana, dowager countess of Burlington, who was its ardent champion. The libretto of *Antioco*, an Italian opera by Francesco Gasperini, was dedicated to her, and George Frideric Handel may have stayed at Burlington House during his first brief London sojourn of 1710–11. On his return to London in 1712, Handel was given an apartment at Burlington House, where he wrote the opera *Amadigi di Gaula* (1715), the libretto of which is dedicated to Lord Burlington.

On his grand tour Burlington was never without music. He rented harpsichords and other instruments in Rome, Florence, Venice, and Paris for musical performances in his lodgings, and his grand tour account book records that he attended the opera in Rome and Florence. In Rome Burlington acquired the musical services of the string players Filippo Amadei and the brothers Pietro and Prospero Castrucci, who joined his entourage on its homeward journey through Italy and France. Supported and sponsored by Burlington, the Castrucci brothers settled in England, where they played at private musical gatherings in his residences and performed with opera orchestras in London and Dublin. Amadei, a cellist and composer, was also supported by Burlington and he too played for Burlington's musical gatherings and gave concerts, as well as composing for and playing in Handel's opera orchestra. Unlike the Castrucci brothers, Amadei eventually returned to Italy.

As his account books indicate Burlington was an ardent supporter of public musical events throughout his life, attending operas, masques and Handel's oratorios. His support of the Italian opera, whose performances dominated London's musical life during the first third of the eighteenth century, was unswerving. He was a member of the board of directors of the Royal Academy of Music from its inception in 1719 until its demise in 1728. The academy was formed to provide financial support for the Italian opera with the ultimate goal of making it self-supporting, and each director was required to subscribe £200. Burlington pledged a sum far in excess, £1000. In 1728, however, the academy collapsed, its finances in disarray and torn asunder by internal feuding between Handel and an Italian faction led by the composer Giovanni Bononcini, the librettist Paolo Rolli, and the castrato Senesino. From the dissolution of the academy came two rival opera companies: the Second Academy of Music (1729–33), led by Handel, and the Opera of the Nobility (1733–7), led by Rolli. Although Burlington was a founder member of the Opera of the Nobility, he did not let his support for the rival opera company prevent him from attending Handel's oratorios. Throughout the 1740s until his death in 1753, he purchased boxes for family and friends.

Both the opera and London's Italian community provided Burlington with an opportunity to immerse himself in the Italian language and culture he so admired. Furthermore, his association with them may well have played an important role in the development of his architectural ideas. During the early years of the century Burlington knew a number of Italian literary figures who were members or partook of the tenets of the Accademia dell'Arcadia, a literary society founded in 1690 in Rome. The Arcadians' aim was to purge Italian literature of its mannered excesses by returning to the literary exemplars of classical Rome and the Renaissance. Like the Arcadians, Burlington's architectural principles were founded upon a classical revival. He may well have discussed and refined his concepts of a classical revival with fellow Arcadians Pietro Grimani, the Venetian ambassador with whom he established a lifelong friendship, and Paolo Rolli, leader of London's Italian opera community, who dedicated his opera libretto *L'Astarto* to Burlington and taught his daughters Italian.

Burlington and literature Although primarily remembered for his architectural patronage, Burlington was one of the great literary patrons of his day. The wide spectrum of his literary interests is reflected in the variety of the thirty-nine publications dedicated to him. These range from art and architecture, literature, and music to sermons and scientific works. The most famous dedication is Alexander Pope's *Epistle to Burlington* (1731), which contains the classic statement of Burlington's architectural principles:

> You too proceed! making falling Arts your care,
> Erect new wonders, and the old repair;
> Jones and Palladio to themselves restore,
> And be whate'er Vitruvius was before.

Burlington's major support for writers came through his munificent patronage of publication subscriptions. Not only did he subscribe to ninety-seven separate publications, but in many instances he subscribed for more than one copy. The majority of his subscriptions were devoted to literature (twenty-eight) and history (twenty-six), with only nine to architecture, and the remainder to travel, music, science, and religion. He was an ardent supporter of contemporary poets, subscribing for six copies of Alexander Pope's translation of Homer's *Iliad* (1715–20) and five copies of *The Odyssey* (1725), five copies of Matthew Prior's *Poems* (1718), five copies of James Thomson's *The Seasons* (1730), and fifty copies of John Gay's *Poems on Several Occasions* (1720). Another form of patronage that Burlington extended to writers and artists was residence at Burlington House. William Kent, described by Horace Walpole as 'a proper priest' to Burlington's 'Apollo of Arts' (Walpole, 56) and Burlington's artistic confidant, was a permanent resident and the poet John Gay, whose *Epistle to Burlington* was part of his *Poems on Several Occasions*, was a guest for long periods during the 1720s.

Alexander Pope, however, was *primus inter pares* among the artists and writers Burlington supported. With Kent, Pope was a member of Burlington's inner circle and a friend and confidant of Lady Burlington. The earl's deep and abiding friendship with him went beyond mere patronage and was based on mutual artistic and aesthetic ideals. Burlington's library contained more of Pope's works than any other poet, including numerous editions as well as an early manuscript and a presentation copy of his *Epistle to Burlington*. Burlington shielded Pope and his family from anti-Catholic sentiment and provided legal assistance during the publication of Pope's at times scurrilous *Dunciad* (1728). In 1718 he offered Pope free tenancy of a plot of land behind Burlington House. Pleading that he could not afford to build a house on the plot, Pope declined the offer. At Pope's Thames-side villa, Burlington paid for the remodelling of the interiors and for the stone for the remodelling of the portico. Regarding his villa, the poet wrote to Burlington:

> that there should be nothing Durable in my building which I was not to owe to Chiswick. I am sure there will be nothing in it Beautiful besides, nor (I believe) in this nation, but what is owed to the Lord of Chiswick.   (*Correspondence of Alexander Pope*, 3.341–2)

Death and reputation Judging from his many portraits, Burlington was of average height and of slight build, small-boned, with delicate features, brown eyes, a high forehead, and a receding chin. So closely are his public and private personae intertwined that it is extremely difficult to separate the man from his deeds. His high-minded idealism made him the object of ridicule by his contemporaries. His architectural ideals were lampooned by William Hogarth in the satirical engraving *Masquerades and Operas* (also referred to as 'The bad taste of the town', 1723–4, British Museum, London) and he was the butt of sarcastic remarks by lords Chesterfield and Hervey, and Sarah, duchess of Marlborough, among others. Walpole's comment is probably a fair assessment of Burlington's personality: 'Never was protection and great wealth more generously and more judiciously diffused than by this great person, who had every quality of a genius and artist, except envy' (Walpole, 53).

Burlington died on 3 December 1753 at Chiswick and was buried in the family vault at Londesborough on 15 December 1753. Charlotte, his youngest daughter and sole heir, married William Cavendish, fourth duke of Devonshire. She inherited the barony of Clifford, and the Boyle family's landholdings in Ireland, Yorkshire, and elsewhere passed to the Devonshire family. Burlington's personal belongings, papers, and art collection are at Chatsworth, the Devonshire family's country seat in Derbyshire. His drawing collection is divided between Chatsworth and the Royal Institute of British Architects, London, given in trust by the eighth duke of Devonshire in 1894.

During the nineteenth century Burlington's accomplishments were denigrated. The villa at Chiswick was variously attributed to Campbell and Kent, and at the turn of the century it was let as a mental institution. Burlington was excluded from James Fergusson's *History of the Modern Styles of Architecture* (1846) and Inigo Jones credited with designing Chiswick Villa. Reginald Blomfield in his *A History of Renaissance Architecture in England, 1500–1800* (1897) claimed that Burlington paid Campbell, Kent, and others to design buildings to which he affixed his name. In the early twentieth century J. Alfred Gotch in his *The English Home from Charles I to George IV* simply dismissed Burlington, characterizing him as merely dabbling in design.

With the rise of architectural history after the First World War Burlington's reputation was slowly revived. The American historian Fiske Kimball led the way with a careful analysis of Burlington's autograph designs, followed by Rudolf Wittkower, who acknowledged Burlington's architectural accomplishments but diminished him in comparison with Kent. Not until Burlington's inclusion in Howard Colvin's *A Biographical Dictionary of English Architects, 1660–1840* (1954) was his significant contribution to British architecture properly acknowledged.

PAMELA DENMAN KINGSBURY

Sources A. Collins, *The peerage of England*, ed. B. Longmate, 5th edn, 8 vols. (1779) · GEC, *Peerage*, vol. 2 · J. Lodge, *The peerage of Ireland*, 1 (1754) · trustees of Chatsworth, Chatsworth House, Derbyshire, Burlington MSS · A. Shaftesbury, 'A letter concerning the art, or science of design', *Characteristicks of men, manners, opinions, times*, 3 (1733) · T. C. Barnard and J. Clark, eds., *Lord Burlington: architecture, art and life* (1995) · E. Corp, ed., *Lord Burlington: the man and his politics* (1998) · R. Wittkower, 'Lord Burlington and William Kent', *Archaeological Journal*, 102 (1945), 151–64 · Chatsworth House, Derbyshire, Devonshire collection · RIBA BAL, Burlington–Devonshire collection · *The parish of St James, Westminster*, 1/2, 2/2, Survey of London, 30, 32 (1960–63) · Colvin, *Archs.* · D. Defoe, *A tour thro' the whole island of Great Britain*, 2 (1742) [with additions by S. Richardson] · A. Palladio, *I quattro libri dell'architettura di Andrea Palladio* (Venice, 1601) [Burlington's annotated copy, Chatsworth House, Derbyshire] · A. Palladio, *The four books of Andrea Palladio's architecture*, trans. I. Ware (1738) · John, Lord Hervey, *Some materials towards memoirs of the reign of George II*, ed. R. Sedgwick, 2 (1931); repr. (1970) · York assembly rooms minute book and account books, 1729–58, York City RO · H. M. Colvin and others, eds., *The history of the king's works*, 5 (1976) · H. Walpole, *Anecdotes of painting in England*, ed. R. Wornum, new edn, 3 vols. (1849); repr. (1876), vol. 3 · E. Harris and N. Savage, *British architectural books and writers, 1556–1785* (1990) · G. E. Dorris, *Paolo Rolli and the Italian circle in London, 1715–1744* (1967) · W. Dean and J. M. Knapp, *Handel's operas, 1704–1726* (1987) · *Alexander Pope: selected poetry and prose*, ed. W. K. Wimsatt (1965) · *The correspondence of Alexander Pope*, ed. G. Sherburn, 3 (1956) · F. Kimball, 'Burlington Architectus', *RIBA Journal*, 34–5 (1926–8) · J. Carré, *Lord Burlington (1694–1753): le connaisseur, le mécène, l'architecte* (Clermont-Ferrand, 1993)

Archives BL, corresp., B3–7 · Chatsworth House, Derbyshire, MSS, incl. corresp., account books, land deeds, leases, etc. · NL Ire., corresp. | PRO NIre., letters to first earl of Shannon · York City RO, York assembly rooms minute book and account books

Likenesses G. Kneller, group portrait, *c.*1700, Chatsworth House, Derbyshire; copy, NPG · J. Smith, mezzotint, 1701 (after G. Kneller), BM, NPG · G. Kneller, oils, 1716, Chatsworth House, Derbyshire · J. Richardson the elder, oils, *c.*1717–1719, NPG [*see illus.*] · mezzotint, 1731–3, BM, NPG · J. Faber junior, mezzotint, 1734 (after G. Kneller), BM, NPG · G. Knapton, oils, 1743, Chatsworth House, Derbyshire · J. B. van Loo, group portrait, Ireland; trustees of the Lismore Estate

Boyle, Richard Vicars (1822–1908), civil engineer, born in Dublin on 14 March 1822, was the third son of Vicars Armstrong Boyle of that city, a descendant of a branch of the Boyles of Kelburn, Ayrshire, who had migrated to the north of Ireland in the seventeenth century. His mother was Sophia, eldest daughter of David Courtney, of Dublin. After education at a private school and two years' service on the trigonometrical survey of Ireland he became a pupil to Charles Blacker Vignoles. After his training he was engaged on railway construction in Ireland, at first as assistant to William Dargan, who employed him on the Belfast and Armagh and Dublin and Drogheda Railways. In 1845, under Sir John Benjamin Macneill, he surveyed and laid out part of the Great Southern and Western Railway, and in 1846–7 was chief engineer for the Longford and Sligo Railway. In the autumn of 1852 he laid out railways and waterworks in Spain as chief assistant to George Willoughby Hemans.

Boyle married, in 1853, Eléonore Anne, daughter of W. Hack of Dieppe; their only son died in infancy. In the same year he was appointed a district engineer on the East Indian Railway, stationed first at Patna, later at Arrah (Shahabad), where he was caught up in the Indian mutiny. After having survived a week-long siege by mutineers in Arrah, he, in quick succession, sustained an injury from a horse kick and suffered shipwreck. After a sea trip to Penang and Singapore to recover his health, he returned to Arrah early in 1858. For his services Boyle received the mutiny medal and a grant of land near Arrah. In 1868, after leaving the East Indian Railway Company, he became a first-class executive engineer in the Indian public works department, but was soon recalled to England by private affairs. He was made CSI in 1869. From 1872 to 1877 he was in Japan as engineer in chief for the imperial Japanese railways. With English assistants he laid out an extensive system of railways in Japan and left about 70 miles of completed line in full working order. In 1882 he presented a paper on the Rokugo river bridge, Japan, to the Institution of Civil Engineers, of which he became an associate on 10 January 1854 and member on 14 February 1860. He joined the Institution of Electrical Engineers in 1874. On retiring in 1877 from professional work Boyle and his wife travelled extensively. He died at his home, 3 Stanhope Terrace, Hyde Park, London, on 3 January 1908, and was buried at Kensal Green on 9 January. He was survived by his wife.　　　　　W. F. SPEAR, rev. ANITA MCCONNELL

Sources *Journal of the Institution of Electrical Engineers*, 41 (1908), 868 · *The Times* (6 Jan 1908), 4c · *The Times* (11 Jan 1908), 10b [funeral] · *PICE*, 174 (1907–8), 372–4 · *Engineering* (10 Jan 1908), 45 · C. Ball, *The history of the Indian mutiny*, 2 vols. (1858–9), vol. 2 · G. B. Malleson, *Recreations of an Indian official* (1872) · *CGPLA Eng. & Wales* (1908)

Wealth at death £14,039 17s. 6d.: resworn probate, 7 Feb 1908, *CGPLA Eng. & Wales*

Boyle, Robert (1627–1691), natural philosopher, was born on 25 January 1627 at Lismore Castle in the province of Munster, Ireland, the fourteenth child and seventh and youngest son of Richard *Boyle, first earl of Cork (1566–1643), lord high treasurer of Ireland, and his second wife, Catherine (c.1588–1630), daughter of Sir Geoffrey *Fenton, a literary scholar and principal secretary of state for Ireland. His father, known as the Great Earl, was one of the self-made men of the seventeenth century; having arrived in Ireland in 1588 with virtually no money, he lived to be one of the wealthiest subjects in the kingdom. Of Boyle's thirteen surviving brothers and sisters, many went on to subsequent eminence. They included Richard *Boyle, first earl of Burlington and second earl of Cork, Katherine *Jones, Viscountess Ranelagh, Roger *Boyle, first earl of Orrery, and Mary *Rich, countess of Warwick. Their prominence evidently owed at least something to

Robert Boyle (1627–1691), by Johann Kerseboom, c.1689–90

the formative influence of their father's strong personality; he was alone responsible for his children's upbringing after the death of his wife in 1630. Some of Boyle's siblings (such as Mary, later countess of Warwick) seem to have had a somewhat tempestuous relationship with the Great Earl, but Boyle's recollection was that he was his father's special favourite; this did not, however, preclude the earl's insisting that Robin, as his parents called him, should, like his elder brothers, be sent away from home at an early age, by which time Boyle had evidently acquired the stutter which he was never fully to overcome.

Early life and education In 1635, when he was eight, Boyle was sent to Eton College with his brother Francis, later Viscount Shannon. The boys were placed under the tutelage of the headmaster, John Harrison. From the outset Boyle distinguished himself by his studiousness: 'he prefers Learning afore all other vertues or pleasures' (Maddison, *Life*, 11n.), his father was informed, though Boyle subsequently recalled his lack of 'Inclination to Latin' (Hunter, *Boyle by Himself*, 26) which had to be rectified at a later date. He also commented in retrospect on the taste for history and for the gallant deeds of heroes of antiquity that he developed at this time; his enthusiasm, he claimed, was especially for the writings of Quintus Curtius and Sir Walter Ralegh. At Eton he was first introduced to romances, and specifically the story of Amadis de Gaule, while he discovered the virtues of algebra as a means to control his thoughts. In 1638 their father took Boyle and his brother away from Eton, and for a while they were tutored by William Douch, a clergyman to whom

Cork had given the vicarage of Stalbridge in Dorset, where his chief English estate was situated.

In 1639, again in the company of his brother, Boyle embarked on a continental tour. Their guardian in their travels was Isaac Marcombes, a French protestant who had earlier conducted Boyle's elder brothers on a similar tour. After travelling through France, they settled at Geneva, Marcombes's home town, where they stayed for twenty-one months. Boyle's studies during this stay and during his subsequent stay at Geneva in 1642–4 covered a range of topics including ethics, history, natural philosophy of a fairly conservative variety, and fortification. In his autobiography Boyle recounted a conversion experience which he had at this time, occasioned by an awe-inspiring thunderstorm, which he claimed had a formative influence on his entire subsequent life.

In 1641 the two Boyle boys and Marcombes set out for Italy. Boyle's recollections of this visit are again recounted in his autobiography, including their visit to Florence, where he heard of the death of Galileo, whose works he was just then perusing, and to Rome, where he visited the sights and observed the pope with the disdain appropriate to a well-born young protestant. Subsequently the party returned to France, where problems arose due to the outbreak of the Irish rising and the sudden termination of the funds that they had been receiving from their father. As a result, while Francis returned to Ireland to fight, Boyle spent two more years studying in Geneva.

Boyle returned to England in 1644 and initially spent some months in London: virtually the only surviving record of this episode is his vivid later recollection of his homecoming and reunion with his sister Lady Ranelagh, with whom he had already developed an especially close relationship and in whose house he stayed for four and a half months. In 1645 Boyle moved to Stalbridge, Dorset, where his father had bequeathed him the manor house and estate. There Boyle spent much of the next decade, though it is possible that he travelled to France in 1645, while from February to April 1648 he visited the Netherlands. He also travelled regularly to London, and it was probably during these visits that he took part in the activities of a body called the 'Invisible College', which has been the subject of intense speculation on the basis of brief references in three of Boyle's letters of 1646–7, though none of these gives more than vague clues as to its personnel and aims. In addition, from 1647 onwards, correspondence survives between Boyle and the intelligencer Samuel Hartlib, who frequently reported on Boyle's views and activities in his *Ephemerides* from 1648 until the end of the 1650s.

At Stalbridge in the mid-1640s Boyle embarked quite self-consciously on a career as a writer. Contrary to what might be expected from his later publications, his efforts were not initially devoted to science. His first project (in 1645–6) was his *Aretology*, a somewhat stilted treatise on 'Ethicall Elements' intended to lay down the rudiments of morality as a basis for the pursuit of virtue. Subsequently Boyle experimented with other literary genres, and the

best of his compositions of this period display a real vigour and solicitude for stylistic elegance. Among them were pious essays, and reflections on scriptural passages and events which formed the basis of his later *Occasional Reflections* (1665). Others were influenced by his reading of French romances, including imaginary lives, speeches, and a romance, *The Martyrdom of Theodora and of Didymus*, said by Dr Johnson to be the first work 'to employ the ornaments of romance in the decoration of religion' (J. Boswell, *Life*, 1.312): the romance was partially published in much altered form in 1687, though the original version also survives. Other compositions included letters presenting moralistic prescriptions to fictional addressees, a number of which survive, some of them forming part of an ambitious work of which one part was ultimately to appear in modified form as *Some Motives and Incentives to the Love of God* (1659), usually referred to by its running title, *Seraphic Love*.

Two other significant writings of this phase in Boyle's career are his autobiographical 'Account of Philaretus during his minority' of 1648 or 1649, which recalls memories of his childhood and continental travels, and his 'Invitation to a free and generous communication of secrets and receits in physick', addressed to Hartlib and almost certainly written in 1649, which was to become Boyle's first published work in 1655. This was a formative period in Boyle's life, even though his writing subsequently shifted to quite different topics. The concern for morality seen in his writings of this period was the source of the concern for probity and self-control that he internalized and sought to exemplify in later life. In addition, remnants of his literary aspirations survived.

The turn to science In 1649–50 a major change in Boyle's preoccupations occurred. Most importantly, in 1649 he successfully set up a laboratory at his house in Stalbridge; the experiments that this enabled him to carry out seem immediately to have fascinated him to an extent that transformed his career, and from that summer onwards his work shows an enthusiasm for experimental knowledge that had earlier been missing, though a legacy of his earlier aspirations may be discerned in his ambition to put such experimental knowledge to apologetic use. Writings that survive from this period display an acute concern about the threat of irreligion posed by the predominant Aristotelian natural philosophy of the day, combined with a conviction that the best means to offset this was a recourse to experimental data. His empirical investigations at this point concerned a range of chemical and alchemical trials involving mercury and other substances, while he also refers to his use of a microscope to observe the minute structure of living things, and reveals a preoccupation with collecting data about 'effluvia' and other natural phenomena that foreshadows later interests. Intellectually his mentors at this stage in his career were such sixteenth-century and early seventeenth-century authors as Paracelsus, Bernardino Telesio, Francis Bacon, Tommaso Campanella, and J. B. van Helmont. Boyle also expressed his sense of solidarity with 'the Chymists', and it was evidently in a chemical context that he first encountered atomist ideas to which he gave expression in his treatise 'Of the atomicall philosophy' (c.1652–4). Moreover, he forged links with other figures who shared his interests, notably Hartlib's son-in-law, Frederic Clodius, and the American alchemist George Starkey, with whose instructions Boyle prepared alchemical products, including a philosophical mercury and the Helmontian drug *ens veneris*.

A further key development of the years around 1650 was that Boyle became interested in the biblical languages— Greek, Hebrew, Chaldaic, Syriac, and Arabic—and in the scholarship that had been devoted to the elucidation of biblical and classical history since the Renaissance. The stimulus to the former, Boyle attributed to the scholar and divine James Ussher, archbishop of Armagh. Its fruit is to be seen particularly in the 'Essay of the holy scriptures' (c.1652–4), part of which has survived in manuscript, while part of it he adapted to form his *Some Considerations Touching the Style of the Holy Scriptures*, published in 1661. Such interests were shared by Boyle's friend and west country neighbour John Mallet, and were discussed in letters between the two men. To this episode can be traced the expertise in biblical languages which Boyle retained for the rest of his life and by which contemporaries were impressed.

Between June 1652 and July 1654 Boyle spent all but about three months in Ireland. The reasons for this visit are not entirely clear, but they probably related to the Boyle family's landed interests there. In Ireland Boyle had contact with William Petty, then in Dublin, who apparently introduced him to anatomical dissection, a topic on which he reported with enthusiasm in letters to Hartlib. At this time he also wrote 'a short essay concerning chemistry, by way of a *judicium de chemia & chemicis*', which apparently contained the germ of his critique of 'vulgar chymists' in his *Sceptical Chymist* (1661). Towards the end of his Irish stay Boyle fell seriously ill with an anasarca or dropsy: complications developed, which he vividly recounted in his later years, and these affected not least his eyesight, which he claimed never fully recovered. The result of this was that for the rest of his life Boyle was dependent on amanuenses to write his ideas down for him, and this gave his style a digressiveness reflecting his actual manner of speaking, which contrasts with the pursuit of elegance according to literary models which characterized his writings of the mid- to late 1640s.

Interregnum Oxford Late in 1655 or early in 1656 Boyle moved to Oxford, joining the lively group of natural philosophers centred on Wadham College under the auspices of John Wilkins, who had been intruded as warden there by the parliamentary commissioners; the group also included such figures as the Anglican physician Thomas Willis. After Wilkins moved to Trinity College, Cambridge, in 1659, its meetings took place at Boyle's lodgings in the High Street. The significance of this group for the later development of English science has often been emphasized, and it clearly had a major impact on Boyle. It was now that he seriously confronted the writings of the

major continental natural philosophers, notably Gassendi and Descartes, refining and modernizing the ideas that he had acquired from the essentially Renaissance authors whom he had encountered earlier in the decade. In the case of Descartes, though Boyle had been aware of his writings earlier, he claimed that the figure who 'made him understand Des Cartes' Philosophy' was Robert Hooke, who entered Boyle's employ at this time and helped him in some of his crucial experiments (J. Aubrey, *Brief Lives*, ed. A. Clark, 1898, 1.411).

In addition, it seems that at this time Boyle discovered more of the intrinsic interest of knowledge about the natural world, as against the apologetic motives that had dominated his initial espousal of experimental learning earlier in the 1650s. He now also became aware of a further threat which a reformed natural philosophy might have to withstand, namely that posed by the ideas of Thomas Hobbes, whose version of the mechanical philosophy had been attacked as pernicious and implicitly atheistic by one of the leading figures in the Oxford group, Seth Ward, earlier in the 1650s. The threat of materialistic atheism which Hobbes seemed to exemplify added a new dimension to Boyle's apologetic concerns, which was to remain with him for the rest of his life.

The late 1650s, following Boyle's move to Oxford, saw an extraordinarily intense programme of research and writing on his part. The numerous books on different aspects of natural philosophy which he now began or completed set the pattern for his entire subsequent intellectual career, and it was on them that his later impact was substantially based. At this time he wrote the bulk of *Some Considerations Touching the Usefulness of Experimental Natural Philosophy* (1663, 1671): the first part, which celebrates the religious value of study of the natural world, had been begun earlier but was revised and extended at this time, while the first section of the second part, dealing with the value of science to medicine, was apparently now newly written. This immense compilation—which, in the course of expounding its theme, divulged a vast number of cures which Boyle had come across and tried—was to prove his most extensive medical work and it was widely cited in the debates on medical practice of the time. Boyle also wrote extensively on the application of science more generally, and some sections of these writings were to be published as the second section of part 2 of *Usefulness* in 1671, though others were abandoned. A key aim of this section was to show that practical inventions and advancements in technique are grounded in theoretical natural philosophy, and to defend the new experimental sciences against critics who doubted their social utility.

More important still was Boyle's *Certain Physiological Essays* (1661). This collection comprised a series of essays presenting a very subtle view of experiments and their rationale, and illustrating the way in which they could be deployed to provide an empirical foundation for Boyle's version of the mechanical philosophy, in which natural changes and sensory effects could be attributed to interactions between minute bodies that he called corpuscles.

He adopted the name corpuscularianism to avoid the irreligious overtones that atomism had inherited from classical antiquity. In addition to the essays on experimentation generally, which included two key discourses on the significance of unsuccessful experiments, Boyle also laid out some of his specific experimental findings in this collection, perhaps most crucially in 'A physico-chymicall essay, containing an experiment with some considerations touching the differing parts and redintegration of salt-peter'—often referred to by Boyle as his 'Essay on nitre'. There he experimentally demonstrated how the changes that could be brought about in saltpetre by chemical means could be explained entirely in terms of the size and motion of corpuscles, without the need for any of the explanations in terms of 'forms' and 'qualities' associated with traditional scholastic science.

Boyle was later to pursue these ideas in various other works, the most notable of which was his *The Origin of Forms and Qualities* (1666), in which he attacked the predominant scholasticism of the period, trying to wean his contemporaries away from the essentially qualitative modes of thinking associated with Aristotelian ideas, and to indicate the superior intelligibility of mechanical explanations of phenomena. This was accompanied by more extensive collections of experimental and observational data intended to vindicate corpuscularian explanations of the natural world, begun while he was at Oxford, the most notable of which were *Experiments and Considerations Touching Colours* (1664) and *New Experiments and Observations Touching Cold* (1665). These writings were an important source for Locke's well-known distinction between 'primary' and 'secondary' qualities.

In the late 1650s Boyle wrote his most famous work, *The Sceptical Chymist* (1661), a somewhat discursive dialogue which attacked both the peripatetic doctrine of four elements and the Paracelsian view of the *tria prima*, while at the same time attempting to persuade the 'chymists', from whom he had initially learned so much as an experimenter, that they needed to adopt a more philosophical approach in their study of nature. Like *Certain Physiological Essays*, the work also sought to vindicate corpuscular explanations of chemical reactions, in the course of doing so retailing much information about experimental investigations which Boyle had carried out.

Alongside this, Boyle's *New Experiments Physico-Mechanical, Touching the Spring of the Air and its Effects* (1660), written in a relatively short period in 1659 and published almost as soon as it was finished, recounted experiments using a vacuum chamber or 'air pump' which he constructed with the assistance of Hooke. Rejecting the scholastic notion that nature could not tolerate a vacuum, he showed how it was perfectly possible to produce one, and this enabled him to illustrate the characteristics and functions of the air by studying the effects of its withdrawal on flame, light, and living creatures. He also argued that certain characteristics of the air could only be explained in terms of the ingenious hypothesis that it had a certain weight and 'spring'. Subsequent to the publication of the *New Experiments*, and partly as a result of the well-publicized controversies which followed it, the 'air pump' became part of the standard equipment of laboratories, and was widely diffused throughout scientific Europe.

Apart from his scientific work, Boyle's Oxford period was also notable for the religious contacts that he made. The most important of these was with the Calvinist theologian Thomas Barlow, then Bodley's librarian, who was to become bishop of Lincoln in 1675. Barlow was well known for his skill in cases of conscience, or casuistry, and—both at this time and later—he provided Boyle with much advice on such matters; in 1659 he also acted as an intermediary between Boyle and the former regius professor of divinity, Robert Sanderson, whom Boyle had offered to remunerate if he prepared for publication his celebrated casuistical lectures, given at Oxford in the 1640s before he was ejected by the parliamentary visitors. At this point in Boyle's life his active engagement with missionary projects first became apparent: in 1660 he paid the cost of printing a translation into Arabic by the scholar Edward Pococke of Grotius' *De veritate religionis Christianae*, and over the next few years he contributed to the cost of the publication of a Turkish catechism and New Testament and helped the Lithuanian exile Samuel Chylinski, who had translated the Bible into his native language and was seeking to get it published. From this time also dates Boyle's concern with evangelizing the North American Indians.

The Restoration and its aftermath The aftermath of the Restoration in 1660 saw a peak of public activity on Boyle's part, something which he had shunned hitherto. In 1660 he encouraged his friends Sir Peter Pett and Thomas Barlow to write tracts on the pressing political question of what degree of toleration was desirable and practicable. He was also a member of the council for foreign plantations from 1661 to 1664, and in 1662 became governor of the Company for the Propagation of the Gospel in New England. A note made by Bishop Gilbert Burnet on an interview with Boyle later in his life records that both the earl of Clarendon and the earl of Southampton tried to encourage Boyle to become a bishop, an invitation that he declined on the grounds that 'he never felt the Inward Vocation so he should be in an Imployment against the grain with him' (Hunter, *Boyle by Himself*, 33).

Of the activities that Boyle embarked on in the aftermath of the Restoration, only one proved sustained, his governorship of the New England Company; otherwise, the chief long-term legacy of this burst of involvement with the public sphere on Boyle's part was a grant to him from Charles II of impropriations of former monastic lands in Ireland. This may initially have been intended to support the profuse experimental activity which Boyle had already been carrying on in the 1650s and which was to continue for the rest of his life but—evidently at least partly due to recriminations that followed the grant on the part of disappointed applicants, notably representatives of the Irish church—Boyle resolved to spend the proceeds on 'pious uses', in supporting both the Irish clergy and the evangelical activity in New England to which he was by this time committed.

The most significant change in Boyle's career about 1660 was that he began to publish. Prior to 1659, Boyle's only publication was a tract addressed to Hartlib (composed in 1649) that appeared in *Chymical, Medicinal, and Chirurgical Addresses Made to Samuel Hartlib Esquire* (1655). In 1659 Boyle orchestrated the publication of an English translation of a brief work by the Dutch anatomist Lodewijk de Bils, *The Coppy of a Certain Large Act ... Touching the Skill of a Better Way of Anatomy of Mans Body*, and his care over its promotion foreshadows his later concern about his own writings. The same year also saw the publication of *Seraphic Love*, while from 1660 onwards a veritable torrent of works followed, beginning with *New Experiments ... Touching the Spring of the Air* and including many of the works composed in the 1650s. Boyle's writings were published not only in English; he also made careful arrangements to have them translated into Latin by Oxford dons and others, and their subsequent publication by booksellers in Oxford and London ensured that they were widely read in the international scholarly community. Indeed, it is not surprising that one of his publishers later claimed that he had become known throughout Europe as 'the English philosopher'.

It was a tribute to the new-found celebrity that Boyle enjoyed in the early 1660s that he was the subject at this time of published attacks, particularly on his first scientific book, *New Experiments ... Touching the Spring of the Air*. Works criticizing this were brought out by Thomas Hobbes, by the English Jesuit Francis Linus, and by the Dutch scholar Anthony Deusing, and Boyle replied at length to Hobbes and Linus, disposing of Deusing in briefer comments in the preface to the Latin edition of his defence against Linus. In the course of elaborating his views, in *A Defence of the Doctrine, Touching the Spring and Weight of the Air*, Boyle divulged what later became known as Boyle's law, namely that the quantitative relationship between the volume and pressure of a gas was an inverse one; in Boyle's language that 'pressures and expansions [are] in reciprocal proportion' (*Works*, 3.59).

The controversy with Hobbes has proved of much interest to historians, partly because it involved an attack on the newly established Royal Society combined with an attack on Boyle's methods of investigation. Boyle explicitly recognized this feature of Hobbes's approach: 'though some things in the Title Page [and] in the Book it self seem to make the chief Design of it to be the Disparagement of the Society', he wrote, 'yet the Arguments are for the most part levelled at some Writings of mine', and he expressed his surprise that an experienced writer would publicly attack an institution supported by his own patron, the duke of Devonshire. For his part, in *An Examen of Mr T. Hobbes's 'Dialogus'* (1662), Boyle used the opportunity to strengthen the grounds for experimental knowledge by contrasting it with Hobbes's method of arguing from plausible hypotheses, declaring that 'on the occasion of Mr *Hobbs*'s Building a great part of his philosophy upon no surer a ground ... we may hence learn how little Reason there is to blame me, as he is pleas'd to do, for making Elaborate Experiments' (*Works*, 3.115, 120).

Such controversy did not affect the rise of Boyle's star, which had been enhanced by the foundation in 1660 of the Royal Society, devoted to experimental philosophy of the kind pursued by the group at Oxford to which Boyle had belonged in the 1650s. He was present at the society's inaugural meeting on 28 November 1660, and was active at its meetings throughout its early years. He also benefited from the promotional activities on behalf of the society and the new science undertaken at this time by its first secretary, Henry Oldenburg, who had been a close contact of Boyle since he had tutored Boyle's nephew Richard Jones, later first earl of Ranelagh, in the 1650s. The most significant of Oldenburg's initiatives was his inauguration in 1665 under the society's auspices of the *Philosophical Transactions*: in addition to carrying frequent contributions by Boyle—some of them almost of book length—the new journal included fulsome reviews of each of his books as they came out. Boyle was also praised as emblematic of the Royal Society's scientific work in Joseph Glanvill's apologia, *Plus ultra* (1668). The significance of the society for Boyle's intellectual activities in the 1660s is underlined by the fact that it was in response to its request for a report on the work of the French natural philosopher Blaise Pascal, in 1664, that he wrote his *Hydrostatical Paradoxes* (1666).

During the 1660s Boyle continued to live in Oxford, and on 8 September 1665 he was created doctor of physic there, the only academic degree he ever acquired. However, the journal books of the Royal Society reveal that he was frequently in London from 1661 onwards, and in 1665–6 he was clearly in the capital throughout the episode involving the perplexing Irish 'stroker' (so called because he seemed to heal people by stroking their bodies), Valentine Greatrakes, in the debate over whom Boyle became involved when an iconoclastic tract on the subject was dedicated to him by the controversialist and physician Henry Stubbe. Boyle objected to Stubbe's explanation of the phenomenon both on scientific and on theological grounds, and subsequently he took a close interest in Greatrakes's cures, attending more than sixty healing sessions, and in one instance participating in the stroking himself.

In 1668 Boyle left Oxford and moved to London, where for the rest of his life he shared a house in Pall Mall with his sister Lady Ranelagh, the closeness of his relations with whom was commented on by contemporaries; even this sojourn, however, was punctuated by occasional stays in lodgings elsewhere in London and in the country. Boyle seems to have settled in well at the Pall Mall house, with his own quarters and even his own laboratory, which was evidently located in a 'back-house'. The laboratory became a well-known place of encounter with him, and was much frequented by foreign and other visitors. Indeed, such an attraction for visitors from overseas did the great philosopher become that John Evelyn claimed that 'one who had not seene Mr Boyle, was look'd-on as missing one of the most valuable Objects of our Nation' (Hunter, *Boyle by Himself*, xlii).

Later years and death In 1670 Boyle suffered a severe stroke which, in the words of his sister Mary, brought him to 'deathes doore'. Thereafter, his activity at the Royal Society dwindled and he kept more to himself, but he was as active as ever in his publishing activity. His profuse experimental work of the 1650s and 1660s continued throughout the following decade, being represented perhaps most notably by his *Experiments, Notes, &c., about the Mechanical Origin or Production of Divers Particular Qualities* (1675), aimed (like his earlier books) to vindicate corpuscular explanations against scholastic ones. He also brought out sequels to his *New Experiments … Touching the Spring of the Air* in which experiments using a vacuum pump were expounded, the last, first published in Latin in 1680, largely written by his then assistant, Denis Papin. In addition Boyle investigated the intriguing properties of phosphorescence in *Aerial Noctiluca* and *Icy Noctiluca* (1680–2).

In the 1670s Boyle also published a variety of shorter, more controversial treatises. Despite his professed reluctance to become involved in controversy, he attacked Henry More in *An Hydrostatical Discourse* (1672) for More's misuse of Boyle's experimental findings and he returned to the attack on Hobbes; he also published an attack on the chemists who he felt were exaggerating the explanatory power of the interaction between acid and alkali. In addition, he published more speculative treatises such as *Of the Systematical or Cosmical Qualities of Things* (1670), while the late 1670s apparently saw a peak in Boyle's interest in alchemy. In 1676 he published an article in the *Philosophical Transactions* on the incalescence of mercury with gold, which stimulated a revealing response from Newton (who did not think that such matters ought to be revealed in public). In 1678 Boyle brought out a short tract, *Of a Degradation of Gold Made by an Anti-Elixir*. These publications reflected an exceptional intensity at this time in Boyle's contact with people who claimed to have witnessed alchemical processes, together with a burst of epistolary communication with a shadowy circle of French alchemists in which Boyle's chief contact was one Georges Pierre.

The decade was also notable for the publication of theological writings by Boyle, some of them works which he had compiled in the 1660s but had put to one side at that time, such as *Excellency of Theology, Compar'd with Natural Philosophy* (1674), to which was appended an important shorter work by Boyle, 'Considerations about the excellency and grounds of the mechanical hypothesis', often regarded as the classic exposition of his philosophy.

In the last decade of Boyle's life his experimental programme was expressed in such works as *Experiments and Considerations about the Porosity of Bodies* (1684) and his treatise on mineral waters. He also brought out his *Experimenta et observationes physicae* (1691), the last work published in his lifetime, which invokes an explicitly Baconian inspiration for its combination of experimental and reported data. However, perhaps the most important works that Boyle published in this decade represented his mature reflections on major theological and philosophical issues, notably *A Discourse of Things above Reason* (1681),

A Free Enquiry into the Vulgarly Receiv'd Notion of Nature (1686), *A Disquisition about the Final Causes of Natural Things* (1688), and *The Christian Virtuoso* (1690). In these he made a profound contribution to contemporary debates regarding the true relationship between God and the natural world, and man's potential for comprehending this.

Various works by Boyle on medical topics also appeared. These were the first such publications since the medical section of his *Usefulness* published in 1663. In the aftermath of that work, Boyle had considered developing the rather guarded criticisms of orthodox medical practice that it contained into an outright assault on the contemporary 'methodus medendi'. Though he wrote at least part of this work, however, he decided against publishing it. Instead, his later publications in this field dealt mainly with what might be described as 'medical science', comprising his *Memoirs for the Natural History of Human Blood* (1684), *Of the Reconcileableness of Specifick Medicines to the Corpuscular Philosophy* (1685), and *Medicina hydrostatica* (1690). He also brought out a collection of medical recipes in 1688; initially this was privately printed but a properly published edition appeared posthumously in 1692, with sequels appearing thereafter. The 1680s also saw Boyle take a leading part in a project for making salt-water sweet, for which his nephew Captain Robert Fitzgerald obtained a patent in 1683 but which met with only partial success.

Boyle's active religiosity is much in evidence in the later years of his life. His philanthropy was well known and he backed various projects such as that for the publication and distribution of the Bible in Gaelic, both in Ireland and in the Scottish highlands; he also supported the churchman Burnet while he was producing his seminal *History of the Reformation of the Church of England* in 1680. In that year Boyle refused to become president of the Royal Society, attributing his decision to his reluctance to take the oaths required under the Test Acts—reflecting a 'scrupulosity' much in evidence in his later years. Various epistolary discourses on casuistical questions addressed to him by Barlow survive from the early 1680s, while a more extraordinary survival comprises Boyle's own notes on his confessional interviews with Bishop Gilbert Burnet and Bishop Edward Stillingfleet in 1691, which reveal his extreme scruples on matters of conscience affecting his financial affairs, and the blasphemous thoughts that assailed him. Such scruples also influenced his approach to the natural world, since a further interview with Burnet—who evidently replaced Barlow as Boyle's chief confidant in the last years of his life—makes clear Boyle's ambivalence about alchemy on the grounds that the insights which it offered might be illicitly achieved by malevolent spirits.

By the later 1680s Boyle's health was declining. In 1688 he issued a strange broadsheet advertisement apologizing for the imperfection of his publications and blaming it on his anxiety to put as much as possible into print before it was too late. He also curtailed his preparedness to receive visitors. In 1689 he resigned his governorship of the Company for the Propagation of the Gospel in New England on health grounds. It was apparently due to further worries about his health in the summer of 1691 that he drew up an elaborate will on 18 July, though he continued to add codicils dealing with various aspects of his affairs thereafter; his solicitousness about such matters was enhanced by concern over his finances due to the unsettled state of Ireland at the time. A climax of activity in cataloguing his papers in that year evidently reflected a similar sense that his death was not far off.

Boyle's beloved sister Lady Ranelagh died on 23 December 1691 and he himself died a week later, in the early hours of 31 December 1691; he was buried in the chancel of St Martin-in-the-Fields on 7 January 1692, when the funeral sermon was preached to 'a vast crow'd' by Gilbert Burnet (Maddison, *Life*, 185). That year and the next saw the publication of posthumous works under the aegis of John Locke. One of the numerous codicils to Boyle's will provided for the setting up of a series of lectures for the defence of the Christian religion against atheists and others, the so-called Boyle lectures. The first series of these was delivered by the scholar and divine Richard Bentley in 1692. Other charitable bequests under Boyle's will followed later in the 1690s and into the early eighteenth century.

Boyle's thought and influence The central fact of Boyle's life from his adolescence onwards was his deep piety, and it is impossible to understand him without doing justice to this. His friends remarked after his death how 'the very Name of God was never mentioned by him without a Pause and a visible stop in his Discourse' (Hunter, *Boyle by Himself*, 48), and this slightly disconcerting habit was symptomatic of the overriding significance for him of his deep theism. Burnet's funeral sermon rightly stressed how Boyle's life was devoted to the service of God and to the defence and propagation of the Christian religion, which he carried out by various means. One was by deploying for charitable purposes the wealth that he acquired both by his high birth and by the grant of impropriations to him by Charles II at the Restoration. His support for missionary enterprises was supplemented by philanthropy on a smaller scale: throughout his life he devoted funds to the support of the needy, be they rural ministers in Ireland, impecunious scholars, or religious refugees from overseas, notably Huguenots. He was similarly solicitous in placing the medical expertise that he acquired in the course of his career at the disposal of the necessitous, aspiring in this to a truly Christ-like role.

Boyle's chief lifework, however, was the pursuit of his religious goals by means of intellectual activity. In the 1640s his preoccupation was the encouragement of piety and of high standards of morality among his peers. Thereafter, his concern was above all with promoting his theistic ends by utilizing the findings from the profuse study of nature in which he engaged from about 1650 onwards. Boyle was fiercely hostile to views of nature that he saw as detracting from a proper appreciation of God's power in his creation. Among these, his principal target was the Aristotelian world view which was prevalent in his day, though he was equally hostile to other intellectual traditions which he saw as pernicious, notably the materialism

associated with Hobbes, which contemporaries frequently saw as indistinguishable from atheism.

The activities in which Boyle engaged in order to confront these threats were twofold, and both were pursued with an energy amounting to obsessiveness which characterized him in all areas of his life. That which emerged earliest was writing. Apart from his published books, which number more than forty and comprise some 3 million words, further evidence of his activity as a writer survives in the Boyle archive, including drafts, notes, and sections of works that were not published in his time, some of which have been printed since, notably in volumes 13 and 14 of the new edition of his *Works*. Though he sometimes expressed diffidence about the manner in which he expressed himself, Boyle was generally content with the message that he put across in his numerous publications. Indeed, he was highly self-conscious about his *œuvre*, with strong views about authorship and the threat to it posed by plagiarism. In the 1660s he was behind various proposals put to the Royal Society to register authorship, and his defensiveness about his own writings grew as his life went on, particularly due to the extent to which he believed that he was the victim of intellectual piracy by writers and publishers in the 1670s.

Equally important was the second leading activity of Boyle's intellectual career, the experimentation which developed from about 1650. From the summer of 1649 Boyle spent much of his time in his laboratory, ceaselessly investigating chemical and other phenomena. The results of this appear not only in Boyle's published works but also among his papers, which include profuse accounts of repeated trials made over many years. Indeed, Boyle was an experimenter *par excellence*, both in theory and practice, eclectically building on precedents provided in the writings of Francis Bacon and in the procedures of the practical 'chymists' and other craftsmen which he consciously sought to graft into natural philosophy. In part he did so through the consideration that he gave to the method and rationale of experiments in *Certain Physiological Essays* and other works. Equally important was his experimental practice, which displayed an extraordinary ingenuity in devising trials which would reveal significant information about the phenomena he studied, combined with an unprecedented precision in observing their outcome. Indeed, Boyle's experimentation, like his writing—and, for that matter, his soul-searching in his spiritual life—was inspired by the obsessiveness that characterized everything he did, ensuring that he was never satisfied until sure that he had penetrated the innermost core of a subject.

Having executed his experiments, Boyle's persona as writer came to the fore, and he went to great pains to provide a detailed account of them so that others could follow as closely as possible the procedures that he had used in reaching the results that he reported. His hope was that his readers would accept the 'matters of fact' that he had established, whatever rival interpretations might be based on them. Indeed, his experimental accounts from the late 1650s onwards used increasingly sophisticated strategies to deal with the fact that it was impossible to reproduce all the exact circumstances of an experiment accurately in writing, providing a model for others which was widely followed. However, he did not limit himself to observations that he had made himself. He also included accounts of phenomena that he had been told of by others or had read about in books, a practice for which he explicitly cited the example of Bacon. Such books as his histories of cold and colours, or his later *Experimenta et observationes physicae*, are made up of a patchwork of such material, which Boyle saw as offering the basis on which a science of nature would ultimately be constructed.

When it came to the conclusions that might be derived from such data, Boyle was a little more ambivalent. He was hostile to the premature systematization that he saw as having blighted much science prior to his time, and the result was that he showed a reluctance to draw conclusions for which he was criticized by some more rationalistic thinkers of his day, such as Christian Huygens and Gottfried Wilhelm Leibniz. Nevertheless his empirical activity was underwritten by clear explanatory goals. In particular, from the 1650s to the end of his life he never swerved from his conviction that the universe was best understood according to mechanical principles, and he ceaselessly urged the superiority of these to the Aristotelian and other alternatives that flourished in his day. Such principles appealed to him not least because he saw them as supremely compatible with God's active role in the world.

Though Boyle took it for granted that explanations should be formulated in primarily mechanical terms he acknowledged that there might be intellectual differences within this basic framework, and his own views were quite flexible. Thus his interpretation of chemical phenomena took it for granted that corpuscles were endowed with chemical, as against strictly mechanical, principles, while various of the explanations that he adduced invoked 'intermediate causes', such as the concepts of weight and elasticity in the air. His corpuscularianism was itself eclectic, drawing on a range of sources and including concepts such as 'dregs' or 'denseness' which might be seen as at odds with a strict interpretation of the mechanical philosophy. Boyle had no illusions about the complexity of the world—it was partly for this reason that he was so insatiable in collecting information about it—and this was reflected by the interpretations of it that he formulated.

Indeed, Boyle ranged perhaps surprisingly far in the phenomena that he took seriously, with a truly Baconian sense that primacy should be given to establishing whether phenomena actually existed rather than dismissing them according to a priori criteria. Thus he toyed with the notion that there were 'cosmical qualities' transcending purely mechanistic laws in the universe, and he was also fascinated by authenticated reports of supernatural phenomena, on the grounds that these vindicated the reality of God's power in the world. His interest in alchemy fits into this context, since he was perfectly prepared to believe that unexpected phenomena of the kind that it revealed were real. Matters were complicated by his ethical qualms as to whether such knowledge might be illicit and hence to be avoided on moral grounds, but against this was the consideration that alchemy appeared to offer an empirical bridge between the natural and the supernatural realms which might provide irrefutable evidence of God's existence.

Boyle's major preoccupation was the relationship between God's power, the created realm, and man's perception of it, a topic on which he wrote extensively, in books mainly published in the 1680s though the views that they expressed may be traced in embryonic form in his earlier writings. In them Boyle laid stress on the extent to which God's omniscience transcended the limited bounds of human reason, taking up a position that contrasted with the rather complacent rationalism of contemporary divines such as Joseph Glanvill. He also reflected at length on the proper understanding of final causes, and in conjunction with this provided one of the most sophisticated expositions of the design argument in his period. Indeed, Boyle's significance for the history of science depends almost as much on the profound views on difficult issues put forward in these philosophical writings as it does on his experimental treatises.

In terms of his affiliations in the religious scene of his day, Boyle was somewhat independent. He conformed to the Church of England in 1660, and specifically stated his allegiance to the idea of a visible church, but he was unusually tolerant towards Catholics by the standards of most English protestants of his day, and he was singularly uninterested in many of the doctrinal debates by which the contemporary English church was riven. He also showed a marked sympathy for the views of those who, unlike him, felt unable to conform to the Anglican church at the Restoration, and his contacts extended even to those described at the time as 'enthusiasts'. The ecclesiastical group with whom he seems to have had the least sympathy were the high-churchmen who were in the ascendant during the Restoration decades, and there is some truth in a loose characterization of Boyle as a 'latitudinarian', so long as this is understood in a fairly flexible manner, as reflecting a general inclination to religious tolerance and a stress on the fundamentals of Christianity, rather than an insistence on comprehension along lines laid down by a triumphalist Anglican church. Equally important was his view that differences among Christians should be minimized in favour of an attack on atheists whose ideas all could agree in deprecating, which was to be institutionalized in the Boyle lectures.

As for Boyle's political views, in his mature years he was closely associated with the establishment and had personal contact with each of the Restoration monarchs. Prior to 1660 his primary commitment seems to been to political stability; although his views at that time (as later) remain substantially inscrutable, contemporaries noted that he always referred to the government of the day 'with an exactness of respect' (Hunter, *Boyle by Himself*, 25). He was also committed to national prosperity, taking an active interest in economic improvement and in maximizing the effectiveness of the navy. On the other hand, it is revealing that the brief period of active involvement in such affairs on his part which occurred in the early 1660s ended in disillusionment, and there is some evidence of his dissatisfaction with the *laissez faire* attitudes of the Restoration government. Boyle's sympathies seem to have been more with the egalitarian and interventionist ideals represented by Samuel Hartlib and his associates in the interregnum, with whom he had had close contacts. There is evidence that, in the later decades of the century, Boyle's strong feelings about the plight of the poor placed him somewhat at odds with the prevailing orthodoxy, especially on medical matters, where his views continued to echo the aspirations of the interregnum reform movement.

These were views, however, which Boyle publicly expressed only in muted form. Although scrutiny of his unpublished papers reveals strong feelings on such topical issues, these views only marginally affected his public persona. Neither were most contemporaries aware of the more stressful aspects of his religiosity, including the doubts that he suffered and the tortured conscience with which he had to live. During his career Boyle learned how to capitalize on those of his characteristics which went down well with his contemporaries, and to keep the more ambivalent aspects of his ideas to himself. Publicly, the image of Boyle in the eyes of most of his contemporaries, which is also the image which has come down to posterity, was one of serenity, of a lofty transcendence of the mundanities of the world in the pursuit of higher goals of truth and piety. This view was formulated with brilliant clarity in Burnet's funeral sermon, which heavily influenced the first full life of Boyle by Thomas Birch, published in 1744. Birch's *Life* has been the basis of almost all subsequent accounts of Boyle, while Birch and his collaborator, Henry Miles, also influenced his retrospective image by the extent to which they tidied up his archive, more or less consciously clearing away material which they saw as irrelevant to the image of the great and good man which they purveyed. The view of him that resulted was not untrue but merely incomplete. When their omissions are corrected, and Boyle is placed back into his proper historical context, he remains a remarkable figure. Today the achievement of this icon of the new science seems no smaller than it did to his early admirers.

Michael Hunter

Sources *The works of Robert Boyle*, ed. M. Hunter and E. B. Davis, 7 vols. (1999–2000) · T. Birch, 'The life of the Hon. Robert Boyle', in *The works of the Hon. Robert Boyle*, ed. T. Birch, 2nd edn (1772), 1.vi–cl · M. Hunter, ed., *Robert Boyle by himself and his friends* (1994) [incl. Boyle's 'Account of Philaretus during his minority'] · R. E. W. Maddison, *The life of the Honourable Robert Boyle, F. R. S.* (1969) · R. E. W. Maddison, 'The portraiture of the honourable Robert Boyle', *Annals of Science*, 15 (1959), 141–214 · *The correspondence of Robert Boyle*, ed. M. Hunter, A. Clericuzio, and L. M. Principe (2001) · M. Hunter, *Letters and papers of Robert Boyle: a guide to the manuscripts and microfilm* (1992) · J. F. Fulton, *A bibliography of the Hon. Robert Boyle*, 2nd edn (1961) · M. Hunter, *Robert Boyle reconsidered* (1994) [incl. bibliography of writings on Boyle, 1941–93] · M. Hunter, 'How Boyle became a scientist', *History of Science*, 33 (1995), 59–103 · M. Hunter, 'Casuistry in action: Robert Boyle's confessional interviews with Gilbert Burnet and Edward Stillingfleet', *Journal of Ecclesiastical History*, 44 (1993), 80–98 · L. M. Principe, 'Virtuous romance and romantic virtuoso: the shaping of Robert Boyle's literary style', *Journal of the History of Ideas* (1995), 377–97 · L. M. Principe, 'Newly discovered Boyle documents in the Royal Society's archive: alchemical tracts and his student notebook', *Notes and Records of the Royal Society*, 49 (1995), 57–70 · L. M. Principe, 'Style and thought of the early Boyle: discovery of the 1648 manuscript of *Seraphic love*', *Isis*, 85 (1994), 247–60 · J. T. Harwood, ed., *The early essays and ethics of Robert Boyle* (1991) · N. Canny, *The upstart earl: a study of the social and mental world of Richard Boyle, first earl of Cork, 1566–1643* (1982) · A. Clericuzio, 'A redefinition of Boyle's chemistry and corpuscular philosophy', *Annals of Science*, 47 (1990), 561–89 · C. Webster, *The great instauration: science, medicine and reform, 1626–1660* (1975) · R. G. Frank, *Harvey and the Oxford physiologists: a study of scientific ideas and social interaction* (1980) · M. Boas, 'An early version of Boyle's *Sceptical Chymist*', *Isis*, 45 (1954), 153–68 · R. M. Sargent, *The diffident naturalist: Robert Boyle and the philosophy of experiment* (1995) · S. Shapin and S. Schaffer, *Leviathan and the air-pump: Hobbes, Boyle and the experimental life* (1985) · T. Birch, *The history of the Royal Society of London*, 4 vols. (1756–7) · *A brief account of Mr Valentine Greatrakes and divers of the strange cures by him lately performed* (1666) · M. B. Hall, 'Acid and alcali in seventeenth-century chemistry', *Archives Internationales d'Histoire des Sciences*, 34 (1956), 13–28 · R. E. W. Maddison, 'Robert Boyle and the Irish Bible', *Bulletin of the John Rylands Library*, 41 (1958), 81–101 · A. Chalmers, 'The lack of excellency of Boyle's mechanical philosophy', *Studies in the History and Philosophy of Science*, 24 (1993), 541–64 · M. Hunter, 'The reluctant philanthropist: Robert Boyle and the "Communication of secrets and receits in physick"', *Religio medici: medicine and religion in seventeenth-century England*, ed. O. P. Grell and A. Cunningham (1996), 247–272 · M. Hunter, 'Boyle versus the Galenists: a suppressed critique of seventeenth-century medical practice and its significance', *Medical History*, 47 (1997), 322–61 · L. M. Principe, *The aspiring adept: Robert Boyle and his alchemical quest* (1998) · J. W. Wojcik, *Robert Boyle and the limits of reason* (1997) · M. Hunter, *Robert Boyle (1627–91): scrupulosity and science* (2000)
Archives BL, Birch papers · BL, Sloane papers · Chatsworth House, Derbyshire, corresp., accounts and papers · GL, corresp. with commissioners of New England · NL Ire., Orrery papers, letters and papers · NL Ire., Ormonde papers · Queen's College, Oxford, Barlow papers · RS, letters to Henry Oldenbury · University of Sheffield, Hartlib papers
Likenesses W. Faithorne, line engraving, c.1659, BM, NPG · attrib. J. Riley, oils, 1682, RS · J. Smith, mezzotint, 1689 (after J. Kerseboom), BM, NPG · J. Smith, mezzotint, 1689, BM, NPG · J. Kerseboom, oils, c.1689–1690, RS [*see illus.*] · C. R. Berch, medal, 1729 (after ivory medallion by J. Cavalier, 1690) · J. M. Rysbrack, marble bust, 1733, Royal Collection · W. Faithorne, portrait, AM Oxf. · J. Kerseboom, oils, other versions, NPG; Hardwick Hall, Derbyshire · sculpture (as a child), St Patrick's Cathedral, Dublin, tomb of the first earl of Cork
Wealth at death £10,000: Maddison, *Life*, 198

Boyle, Roger (1617/18?–1687), Church of Ireland bishop of Clogher, was a younger brother of Robert Boyle, bishop of Ferns, and may have been the son of Robert Boyle (d. 1665), vicar of Carrickmacross, co. Monaghan. He was educated at Trinity College, Dublin, where he became a scholar in 1638 and was elected a fellow in 1646. Following the outbreak of the rebellion in 1641 he went to England and became tutor to Lord Paulet, in whose family he remained until the Restoration. In 1661 he became rector of Carrigaline and of Ringrone in the diocese of Cork, and in October 1662 became dean of Cork. On 12 September 1667 he was promoted to the see of Down and Connor, a diocese with large numbers of protestant nonconformists. He bowed to pressure from Bishop Leslie of Raphoe and moved to excommunicate local presbyterian clergy, but was apparently restrained by the primate, Archbishop Margetson. On 21 September 1672 he was translated to the see of Clogher.

Boyle had a reputation for piety and learning, and was the author of *Inquisitio in fidem Christianorum hujus saeculi* (1665) and *Summa theologiae Christianae* (1681), the latter prompted by the lack of 'a corpus of Theology which would be agreeable to the Anglican church in every part' (Bolton, 40–41). His commonplace book on various subjects, together with an abstract of Sir Kenelm Digby's treatise on the nature of bodies, is preserved in manuscript in Trinity College Library, Dublin. He died at Clones, co. Monaghan, on 26 November 1687, said to be in his seventieth year, and was buried in the church there. James II did not appoint a successor, granting the revenues of the see to the Roman Catholic bishop, Patrick Tyrrel.

T. F. HENDERSON, *rev.* JASON Mᶜ ELLIGOTT

Sources *The whole works of Sir James Ware concerning Ireland*, ed. and trans. W. Harris, 2 vols. in 3 (1739–45, [1746]) · H. Cotton, *Fasti ecclesiae Hibernicae*, 6 vols. (1845–78) · J. B. Leslie, *Clogher clergy and parishes* (1929) · Burtchaell & Sadleir, *Alum. Dubl.*, 2nd edn · F. R. Bolton, *The Caroline tradition of the Church of Ireland* (1958)
Archives TCD, commonplace book

Boyle, Roger, first earl of Orrery (1621–1679), politician and writer, was the twelfth child and third son to survive of Richard *Boyle, first earl of Cork (1566–1643), and his second wife, Catherine Fenton (c.1588–1630). He was born at the family's principal seat of Lismore Castle, co. Waterford, on 25 April 1621. Thanks to his father's standing as the largest proprietor in the southern part of the province of Munster, the boy was ennobled as Baron Broghill on 28 February 1628. The title derived from the estate in the north of co. Cork with which his father endowed the youth. In 1630 Broghill entered Trinity College, Dublin, but by 1632 had removed to England. There, on 17 March 1636, he was admitted into Gray's Inn, at the same time as an elder brother, Lewis, Viscount Kinalmeaky. Soon afterwards he departed on a continental tour under a French protestant, Isaac Marcombes. As well as travelling through France and Italy, he lodged for a time in Geneva with the Calvinist theologian Diodati. These experiences deepened Broghill's attachment to the protestantism already strong in his family. They also introduced him to contemporary continental culture, which later influenced his writings, his architectural projects, and his interests in military theory and practice. On his return to England he gravitated towards a smart court set. His entry into it was eased by his elder brother Richard *Boyle, later first earl of Burlington, already familiar with this world, and by Broghill's own suavity. His father sent him to attend the king at Berwick as he prepared to fight the Scots in 1639. The standing within England of Broghill and his family was further acknowledged—and enhanced—when, on 27 January 1641, he married Lady Margaret Howard (1623–1689), a daughter of Theophilus *Howard, second earl of Suffolk. She came with a portion of £5000. This helped towards the purchase of an estate at Marston Bigod

Roger Boyle, first earl of Orrery (1621–1679), by unknown artist

in Somerset, which would prove convenient as he shuttled regularly between England and Ireland.

War in Ireland Either shortly before or after the outbreak of the rising in October 1641 Broghill returned to Ireland. Much of the defence of his own and his relations' property fell to him. He soon showed his mettle as soldier and politician. In part through a ruse he repulsed the force which was besieging his father's castle at Lismore in February 1642. In November 1642 he sailed to England with his elder brother Dungarvan to solicit supplies and reinforcements. In July 1643 he returned to organize defences. Nominally subordinate to the provincial commander, Inchiquin, he continued to be employed on missions to the English parliament. In July 1644 he and Inchiquin explained publicly that they could no longer be bound by the truce which the lord lieutenant, Ormond, on behalf of Charles I, had signed the previous September with the insurgents. The Munster leaders turned to the English parliament to relieve them in their extremity. Broghill was now appointed governor of the port of Youghal, much of which was owned by the Boyles. In 1645 he was commissioned as a general of horse in the province, and in December that year deputized for Inchiquin. Increasingly, the latent rivalry between the two generals expressed itself in open disagreements over tactics. Broghill regarded Westminster, where he had long-standing and close links, as the best hope of relief for protestant Ireland. He backed the appointment by parliament of Philip Sidney, Viscount Lisle, as viceroy and commander in Ireland in 1646. Lisle belonged to the political grouping at Westminster in which Broghill had friends and relations. Under Lisle he could reasonably expect his own standing to rise and the plight of Munster to be alleviated. Lisle's commission affronted the king's own lieutenant, Ormond, and alarmed Inchiquin. In 1647 the latter defected to the beaten Charles I. As a consequence, divisions among Munster protestants widened ominously. Personally Broghill gained from his parliamentarian affiliation. In February 1648 he was granted £2000 towards his arrears of pay, and the following month was appointed master of the ordnance. But Lisle's expedition failed in its larger aims, leaving the protestants of south Munster still vulnerable to the Catholic forces.

By 1649, with the king executed and Cromwell with an army campaigning in Ireland, Broghill was expected to dissociate himself from the new order and follow his brothers Richard (now second earl of Cork) and Francis (later Viscount Shannon) into foreign exile. Instead, in circumstances which have always been surrounded with mystery and even fantasy, he was persuaded, seemingly by Cromwell himself, to serve the revolutionary regime. Irish protestants like Broghill, whose holdings had been overrun by the insurgent Catholics throughout the 1640s (and earlier), reckoned that only England could secure their return and guarantee their secure enjoyment for the future. Any incumbent English regime, even when it had originated in regicide, if able to aid protestant Ireland, could be accepted and supported. Now that a Commonwealth had been established, Broghill did not scruple to enlist its backing for a campaign to restore himself and his protestant neighbours to what they had lately lost. The personal intervention of Cromwell with Broghill, a story which originated with the latter's chaplain, was hardly needed to persuade him where his interests now lay. On behalf of the new English republic, he threw himself into soldiering across a terrain that he knew intimately. He helped the English commanders to victory in their southern Irish campaigns. In April 1650 he had the satisfaction of assisting in the defeat of his former ally and commander Inchiquin. At Macroom in co. Cork he captured the Catholic bishop of Ross, Boetius MacEgan, a notable warrior. He also joined in the protracted siege of Limerick, alongside Ireton. He was again rewarded: in February 1651 he was made lieutenant-general of the ordnance and was granted sizeable tracts of confiscated lands with a yearly yield of £1000. These grants promised to ease, but did not end, the chronic indebtedness which beset him. Like so many of his protestant neighbours in Munster, deprived of the bulk of his rents throughout the war, he had resorted to desperate expedients, including the mortgaging of his Somerset property. The cumulative effects of these financial devices dogged him for much of the 1650s, and encouraged compromises with a regime which might assist.

A wider stage: the 1650s Radicals within the English army and Irish administration doubted the firmness of Broghill's attachment to their cause, and lost no chance to asperse him. They worried lest he—and through him his extensive kindred and clientele among the settlers established before 1641—secure disproportionate influence. They feared, too, that he might blunt the edge of the reforming government in Dublin. Others, notably the new ruler of Ireland from 1655, Henry Cromwell, were more favourably impressed. So, seemingly, was Oliver Cromwell. In March 1655 Broghill was appointed for a year to head the civil government of Scotland as lord president of the council in Edinburgh. Without any discernible Scottish links, he tackled this brief energetically. Foremost among his tasks was the need to win over the Presbyterian clergy, the more intransigent of whom still prayed publicly for Charles Stuart. Using diplomacy, blandishments, and bullying, he quietened the implacable. But, at best, the calm was temporary. Broghill, nevertheless, acquired clerical contacts which he valued. In 1660, when measures in Ireland, England, and Scotland had to be synchronized, he exploited his Scottish informants. Moreover, his knowledge of their principles made him sympathize with their predicament after 1660. In Edinburgh as lord president he attempted to build a coalition among locals friendly towards the Cromwellian protectorate. This quest paralleled what Henry Cromwell, who regularly sought his advice, was attempting in Dublin, and may have prefigured the calculations of the group that offered Oliver Cromwell the crown in 1657.

In 1654 and 1656 Broghill was elected to the Westminster parliament for co. Cork. In 1656 he had also been returned for Edinburgh, for which he preferred to sit. In preparation for his own and his allies' returns he had demonstrated his forte for electioneering. Within the parliaments his skills as manager and as deviser of constitutions were displayed. Irish protestants, a minority, needed pliancy both to protect their vulnerable privileges and to exert an influence greater than their small numbers would merit. This flexibility marked his political approach to settling the three nations in the aftermath of war, reconquest, and regicide. Unusually among his contemporaries he knew each of the three at first hand. The wars had given him the chance to operate in this larger arena. But he did so sequentially rather than simultaneously. Even at a time when Britain and Ireland were united, throughout much of the 1650s, the practical impossibility of maintaining a presence in each country defeated even the most energetic like Broghill. His stay in Scotland was brief and his impact there limited, but he retained a better sense of problems in civil society and the church common to all the Cromwellian and Stuart territories.

Stability and prosperity were his lodestones. In the parliament of 1654–5, which included representatives of Scotland and Ireland, he was one of those who sought—unavailingly—to avert a collision between the republicans and the supporters of the Cromwellian protectorate. Outspoken as a critic of rule by the military, adopted during the experiment of the major-generals between 1655 and 1656, he advocated kingship. This device was intended to win over to Cromwell more of the political élites on which government had relied before 1642. He had already moved the regime in Scotland in this direction, through conciliation of local civilians. Henry Cromwell, in Dublin since the summer of 1655, under Broghill's prompting also explored this approach. The hope was that, once Oliver Cromwell had become king, he too would be backed by the propertied in England and Wales, and could reduce his political dependence on the soldiery. Cast down when, in May 1657, Cromwell refused the kingly title, but not the rest of the settlement in 'The humble petition and advice', he retired to his Irish estates. These had recently been augmented by the belated passage of an ordinance which conferred on him confiscated properties in co. Cork, including Blarney Castle and Ballymaloe. This bounty, worth well in excess of £1000 annually, had first been proposed in 1651 but was authorized only on 26 June 1657.

Broghill was soon cajoled back into public life by, among others, Henry Cromwell. In January 1658 he took his place in the Cromwellian second chamber, the other house. It was rumoured that he might be added to the council of state, but was not. After Richard Cromwell succeeded his father as protector in September 1658, Broghill's power grew. English radicals within the army disliked—and perhaps exaggerated—his role. By July 1659 these adversaries again controlled the government, in Ireland as well as in England. Now back in south Munster, he lost his military commands. He bided his time, too wily to reveal his thoughts and contacts. He imposed a similar discipline on his followers in Ireland, lest they jeopardize all by any premature display of preferences.

Restoration politician and protestant leader, 1660–1679
Others acted in Dublin to oust the English republicans and to summon a representative assembly in February 1660. Broghill's importance within his native country was recognized, not just by his return for both co. Waterford and Dublin University to this assembly. In January 1660 he had been named by the restored Rump in London as one of its three commissioners to rule Ireland. In the Dublin Convention he diverged from other protestant leaders, notably his fellow commissioner Sir Charles Coote, in his Fabian tactics. Not until Charles II's return had become a certainty did he unequivocally endorse it. He was reluctant to have the king restored unconditionally. Nor was he enthusiastic about allowing the episcopalian Church of Ireland its pre-war pre-eminence. In danger of falling behind the unsullied royalists, in May 1660 he hurried to London. There his voice, stridently hostile to Catholics and the Irish, added to the clamour to retain the essentials of the Cromwellian land settlement. Broghill, and those whom he represented in southern Ireland, had gained much from the recent redistributions, and were reluctant to surrender their booty. He ingratiated himself with the king, who, on 5 September 1660, advanced him to the Irish earldom of Orrery. Thanks to his wife's family, the Howards, he was elected for Arundel to the Westminster Convention of 1660 and the 1661 parliament. On 10 October 1660 he was entrusted, as lord president, with the government of his home province of Munster. On 26 October he was once more a member of the trio to which, as lords

justices, the care of Ireland was deputed. In this capacity he implemented much but determined little, since the vital decisions were taken in London. He concealed his own misgivings as he enforced legal conformity to the re-established state church and harassed dissenters, particularly the Scottish Presbyterians of Ulster. He was obliged to order the return of their old properties to a few favoured Catholics. He was mortified when, with the arrival in July 1662 of the lord lieutenant, Ormond, he was relegated to his regional presidency. Ormond, the king's man in Ireland throughout the 1640s, personified an unswerving loyalism; Orrery apparently the opposite. To these differences was added a personal antipathy, masked behind civilities. He scarcely concealed his contempt for his apparently indolent and insouciant superior, whose talents, he believed, were surpassed by his own.

In addition to the lord presidency, on 22 June 1662 Orrery was commissioned as sergeant-major-general. He was further entrusted with the government of the strategically sensitive city of Limerick and co. Clare. Interpreting his remit broadly, he felt empowered to interfere in any matter which might touch the safety of protestant Ireland. He repeatedly contrasted his own vigilance with Ormond's culpable neglects. He made play with the dense web of kinship which tied Ormond to many Catholic notables. Eager to demonstrate his importance, he refashioned his seat on his north co. Cork estate and renamed it Charleville. Later he was reckoned to have spent £20,000 on these works. Not only did he hold his presidential court there, he aspired to transform the newly incorporated borough into a model of what other settlers might achieve. He founded a school to which the sons of the provincial squirearchy were enticed. Foreign artisans, mostly protestant refugees from the Low Countries and France, were installed in the hope of reviving the depressed textile industries. These prestigious operations resembled those undertaken by his rival Ormond. But for Orrery, as a younger son, such lavish expenditure overtaxed his resources. His income, from lands and offices, seldom exceeded £4000 p.a. Clandestine opportunities for enrichment certainly abounded in the 1650s and 1660s, and it was widely assumed that he availed himself of them. In 1668 it was alleged that he had received over £44,000 from two separate sources. Yet, by the lax standards which prevailed in seventeenth-century Ireland, such profiteering was regarded as a matter of pride not shame. In the main he spent what he received on sustaining the magnificent equipage as a regional potentate rather than enlarging permanently the fortune of his family.

Orrery used his office in Munster to demonstrate how the affairs of protestant Ireland should be conducted. The province, with its long and remote coasts, might be surprised by the Dutch, French, or privateers. Accordingly, he enjoined watchfulness on underlings. He attended closely to the internal affairs of the boroughs under his charge, many of which contained settlers who had arrived only in the 1650s and who might incline to republicanism or religious dissent. He was equally wary of the Catholics, still by far the largest component in the local population. He strenuously opposed moves to readmit them to a share of their former properties and power. His care, justified by the vulnerable situation of Munster, was also intended to point up the casualness with which Ormond treated international and domestic threats. By 1666, with a risk of invasion by the French, he was urging military preparedness. He put faith in locally recruited militias, to be composed exclusively of protestants. These would perpetuate the military arrangements that had underpinned the original plantations in Munster in the time of his father, and revived an idea that he had put to Henry Cromwell.

A shrewd self-publicist, Orrery intended that his own assiduity should be contrasted with Ormond's supposed neglects. These comparisons were intended to strengthen his claims on the Irish viceroyalty. Driven by envy of Ormond, he abetted those, in England and Ireland, scheming to topple the lord lieutenant. In particular, he struck up a tactical alliance with the restlessly ambitious second duke of Buckingham. In 1669 they triumphed. Yet the dismissal of Ormond did not bring Orrery to power, as he had hoped. Rumours had circulated that he might even be appointed to a great office of state (such as the lord chancellorship) in England. Instead, he too was attacked. In November 1669 moves to impeach him were begun at Westminster. Alleged misconduct in the government of Munster was the main charge. He trounced his accusers. But the episode revealed how isolated and insecure he had become. Another sign of declining repute came with the suppression on 30 July 1672 of the Munster presidency. He was consoled with a generous pension and other marks of status, and retained a military command. Reassured that no personal slight had been meant, nevertheless it was clear that he was out of step with a movement more friendly towards the Catholics. Henceforward he lacked a formal position, other than as peer, privy counsellor, and army officer, from which to shape policy. However, this did not silence him. He monotonously accused those responsible for Ireland of misunderstanding its needs. Moreover, he carried his message into England, where between 1674 and 1676 he attended the Commons.

Ideas, writings, and character Soon after Charles's restoration Orrery had countered the lobbying of the Irish Catholics hopeful of regaining their lost property and influence. In 1662 he published two tracts, *The Irish Colours Displayed* and *An Answer of a Person of Quality to a Scandalous Letter*, in which he rebutted the contention of a Catholic apologist, Peter Walsh, that many of his co-religionists had loyally supported the Stuarts. This issue of loyalty to the dynasty was one well calculated to embarrass the pliant Orrery. He reverted to it in his plays, several of which were performed in the 1660s. His ability to express—and sometimes to create—the anxieties of the beleaguered Irish protestant minority gave him a larger role. The protestant interest, both as idea and actuality, owed much to his unscrupulous industry. In his formulation the earlier construct of 'the English of Ireland' to denote those loyal to English authority evolved into one in which confession—protestantism—not ethnicity was the defining quality. In time, and assisted by Orrery's descendants,

such as Henry *Boyle, first earl of Shannon, the idea of the protestant interest underwent a further transmutation: into the Irish protestant ascendancy of the eighteenth century.

The vigour and fluency with which Orrery advanced the opinion that the Irish protestants were the only secure foundation for English rule in the island established him as the foremost spokesman for that interest. Furthermore, he had acted on his beliefs. He steered his neighbours through the hazards of the confederate wars and the Cromwellian occupation. He busied himself in the 1650s and 1660s to secure material advantages not just for his immediate family, but for the larger protestant community. He first realized the electoral potential of the Boyles' huge possessions in co. Cork and co. Waterford. In the successive elections of 1654, 1656, 1659, 1660, and 1661 his activities can be detected. His circumspect elder brother Cork willingly deputed this task to his more adept junior. His political aptitudes, glimpsed occasionally in his dealings with the Long Parliament, were perfected in the interregnum. Diplomacy was needed to achieve even a limited understanding with the warring Presbyterian ministers in the Scotland of the mid-1650s. Managerial and rhetorical dexterity was evident as he organized the enthusiasts for kingship at Westminster in 1657. The same can be sensed in his handling of the Dublin Convention in the spring of 1660. In the Irish parliament of 1661–6 he boasted how he led a cohort of 'Orreronians': at least twenty-five members for Munster constituencies. They formed the nucleus of a larger following through which he could guide hesitant MPs into enacting the controversial Restoration settlement. The lord lieutenant, Ormond, was happy to let him act as his undertaker in the parliament. These tastes of power left him embittered when, after 1672, he was denied his formal primacy as lord president of Munster or any adequate outlet for what he regarded as his transcendent abilities.

From the 1640s Orrery, like other protestant lobbyists from Ireland, encouraged the English and Irish authorities to act on the axiom that confession was now the surest index of political reliability. He identified religious differences as the dynamic in the troubled recent history of Ireland. This opinion was encouraged by his reading, experiences, and reflection. He subscribed to the widespread view that Catholicism, both as political doctrine and as theological system, undermined society. He was suspected of exaggerating Irish Catholics' untrustworthiness and inflating the fears of Irish protestants to further his own career, yet, in his analyses of past and present troubles in Ireland, he treated of more than confessional differences. Conquest, and the resultant expropriation of the older vintages of landowners (almost invariably Catholics), embittered the defeated. These grievances, he predicted, would never vanish. The Catholic majority would watch for a chance to reverse the decision of recent wars, so that the utmost vigilance would henceforward be required. Orrery, in his military, administrative, and private capacities, exercised it. When necessary, he used spies, double agents, and deceit. It was alleged, indeed, that he kept a spy in the king's bedchamber, Ned Progers, who purloined and passed to his paymaster confidential letters from the likes of Ormond. He also insisted that the settlers in Munster stay on alert and that he, even after he had been deposed as lord president, should keep armaments at his houses.

For the same reasons, Orrery tried to prevent the readmission of Catholic traders into the walled towns in 1672–3. But such exclusions no longer suited either the English government or the Irish economy. His strident denunciations of the official indulgence of the dangerous reached a crescendo during the Popish Plot, when his old rival, Ormond, again ruled the kingdom. Even those who shared his apprehensions were wearied by the monotony and shrillness with which he voiced them. One by one he estranged leading politicians of his time, not only Clarendon and Ormond, but those closer to him in outlook, such as Essex and Shaftesbury. His unremitting anti-Catholicism grated on the king. Appointed to the English privy council in 1665, he was removed in April 1679.

Orrery owed much of his contemporary and later celebrity to his voluminous writings. He published poems, a lengthy romance, *Parthenissa*, in the French mode, as well as his plays. *Parthenissa*, never completed, occupied its author intermittently from the 1640s onwards. The dramas attracted the notice of contemporaries, being performed to acclaim in London and Dublin. From the 1630s he had mingled easily with writers: first Suckling and Davenant, later—in the 1650s—Cowley, and then (during the 1660s) Katherine Phillips. Dryden admired his rhymed dramatic couplets. His easy command of literary genres fitted well with his self-projection as courtier and wit. For a time he stood high at the courts of Charles I, his son, and Henry Cromwell. But his vanities and jealousies tarnished his reputation. In the plays themes of honour, loyalty, and betrayal suggested that, despite their sometimes exotic settings—Sicily for *The General*, Hungary for *Mustapha*, and in *Tryphon* the history of the Maccabees—they expressed the dilemmas that had beset him during his tortuous career. Although imitative of the modes of the age, and ironically derivative from French models at a time when he scorned France, their fluency excited admiration. The same virtuosity, schooled in the adolescent travels and later campaigning, led him to write a pioneering *Treatise on the Art of War*, published in 1677. Typically he bragged that it was the first comprehensive manual in English. A second volume was intended, but, if finished, was never printed. He may also have contemplated a fuller history of his times. Stimulated in the mid-1670s by the renewed interest in the controversial passages of the 1640s, he had the leisure to compose such an account. Arthur Annesley, earl of Anglesey, an erstwhile collaborator, engaged on a similar design, enquired after his death about his manuscripts. Nothing is known to have survived.

Towards the close of his life, incapacitated and in pain after a botched operation to ease his gout, Orrery composed devotional poems on the chief festivals of the churches of England and Ireland, which would be published posthumously. As he prepared for death, he subscribed to a conventional protestant orthodoxy. Nevertheless, he was still worried enough about the mounting Catholic menace to advocate protestant union. He entrusted his school at Charleville to a nonconformist minister ejected from his English parish. In addition he kept in touch with the veteran dissenter Richard Baxter and his schemes to comprehend orthodox presbyterians. In Ireland especially, the protestant presence was too puny readily to tolerate internal divisions, which could only hearten the Catholics. Ever the polymath, he also designed buildings. The grandiose seat at Charleville may have resulted from his fertile brain. The Charles Fort, commanding the entrance to Kinsale harbour, also owed much to his architectural skills. It further embodied his obsession with the physical defence of Ireland; here against possible Dutch or French invaders. Yet, Ormond received more praise than Orrery for erecting the bastion. He died at his second home in co. Cork, Castlemartyr, on 16 October 1679 and was interred two days later in the family vault at Youghal.

Constantly overshadowed or thwarted by others whom he regarded as less capable, Orrery's tactlessness alienated the important and probably cost him the highest offices. A contemporary recorded why he was regarded so ambivalently. His vanity 'would not let him be content with what he had of the king's favour unless he held it with ostentation'. Thus, when ill in London, he had persuaded the king publicly to visit him in his lodgings, and so attracted admiring attention which flattered his self-esteem. His 'devising head' and 'towering wit' were turned to destructive ends and left him with a sorry reputation for duplicity. 'He certainly had many qualities of a great man, affable, eloquent, liberal and stout, but he wanted sincerity and as he was still aspiring to be uppermost gave himself no rest but was intriguing to the world's end' ('Account of Restoration politics', Dublin Public Libraries, Gilbert MSS 207, pp. 12–17; 227, p. 246).

TOBY BARNARD

Sources W. Sussex RO, Orrery papers [30 vols.] · NL Ire., MSS 32–36 · Morrice's life of Orrery, NA Ire., MS 473 · NA Ire., Orrery MSS, MS 2449 · letters to Orrery, Harvard U., Houghton L., Orrery papers, MS 218.22F · Orrery papers, 2 vols., V&A NAL, Forster Library · corresp. with Essex, BL, Stowe MSS 200–217 · diary of the second earl of Cork, Chatsworth House, Derbyshire, Lismore MSS · Chatsworth House, Derbyshire, Lismore MSS · E. Milward, ed., *A collection of the state letters of … Orrery* (1742) · *Calendar of the manuscripts of the marquess of Ormonde*, new ser., 8 vols., HMC, 36 (1902–20) · K. M. Lynch, *Roger Boyle, first earl of Orrery* (1965) · T. C. Barnard, 'The political, material and mental culture of the Cork settlers', *Cork: history and society—interdisciplinary essays on the history of an Irish county*, ed. P. O'Flanagan and C. G. Buttimer (1993), 309–52 · E. MacLysaght, ed., *Calendar of the Orrery papers*, IMC (1941) · *The dramatic works of Roger Boyle, earl of Orrery*, ed. W. S. Clark, 2 vols. (1937) · P. J. S. Little, *The political career of Roger Boyle, Lord Broghill, 1636–1600*, PhD diss., U. Lond., 2000 · *The Lismore papers*, ed. A. B. Grosart, 10 vols. in 2 series (privately printed, London, 1886–8) · Burtchaell & Sadleir, *Alum. Dubl.*, p. 89 · T. Morris, funeral sermon

Archives BL, corresp. and papers, Add. MS 25287 · BL, Add. MSS 37206–37208 · BL, Add. MSS 46929–46954 · BL, Eg MS 3327 · BL, Eg MS 3340 · Chatsworth House, Derbyshire, corresp. · Harvard U., MS 218.22F · Hunt. L., corresp. · Hunt. L., letters and literary MSS · NL Ire., corresp. and papers · NL Ire., MSS 32–36 · NRA, priv. coll., corresp. and papers · Petworth House, West Sussex, MSS · V&A,

corresp. and papers relating to Ireland | BL, letters to Lord Essex, Stowe MSS 200–212 · BL, letters to Sir J. Mallet, Add. MS 32095 · Bodl. Oxf., Carte and Clarendon MSS · Bodl. Oxf., Rawlinson MSS A., Thurloe state papers · NL Ire., corresp. with the duke of Ormond

Likenesses J. Mynde, line engraving, BM, NPG · portrait, repro. in Lynch, *Roger Boyle*; formerly in possession of Patrick Boyle · portrait, NPG [*see illus.*]

Boyle, William (1853–1923), playwright, was born on 4 April 1853, at Dromiskin, co. Louth; his father may have been Christian Boyle, a farmer. He was educated at St Mary's College, Dundalk, subsequently joining the civil service in London, and acting as an excise officer until 1914. *A Kish of Brogues* (1899) was a collection of tales and poems based on the country life of his childhood. On 25 April 1905 the Abbey Theatre in Dublin staged his first play, *The Building Fund*, which dealt with rural life in a realistic and unromanticized manner. Many critics of the Abbey policy at the time, which was faulted for being either too poetic or for making a travesty of Irish character (as was said of J. M. Synge's *The Playboy of the Western World*), welcomed Boyle's familiar style and accuracy. Boyle was, in fact, drawing upon an older set of conventions than that which the Abbey (founded 1904) was seeking to form for itself; his models were those of Victorian melodrama and farce in their Dublin manifestations: stereotypical characters, stock situations, humorous brogue, broad comedy, and sentiment. Yeats thought his work vulgar and yet recognized its commercial appeal, a consideration of some importance for a theatre heavily dependent on the goodwill of its patron, the English heiress, Annie Horniman. Nevertheless Yeats 'nearly had a fit' when Boyle told him he wrote poetry, but relaxed when he was reassured that it was merely comic verse (Hogan and O'Neill, 59).

Boyle returned to the Abbey with *The Eloquent Dempsey* (20 January 1906) and repeated his popular success with this study of small-town politics and patriotism. It was followed by *The Mineral Workers* (20 October 1906), dealing with the conflict between modernization and tradition in the countryside, as a young industrialist seeks to set up a smelting plant in an area exclusively given over to farming, and after much opposition, some of it politically motivated, who triumphs. Once again, Boyle found more favour with the popular reviewers than he did with Yeats and the Abbey directorate. When the controversy blew up over Synge's *Playboy* (January 1907) Boyle withdrew his three plays from the Abbey repertory in protest against the staging of a play which, in his view, calumniated Irish character. Lady Gregory, who distrusted Boyle as much as Yeats did, commented on his departure: 'that's a rotten branch gone' (Hogan and others, 183).

Boyle returned, however, with another play of rural realism, *Family Failing* (28 March 1912), which was less well received. After retiring from his post in London he returned to his native place to build a house on the spot where the family one had been. He became a magistrate, which effectively estranged him from the very people he

had hoped to become closer to on his return. Out of sympathy with the Easter rising of 1916, he went back to England where he died at his home, 16 Ardbeg Road, Dulwich, London, on 6 March 1923, survived by his wife, Maud. A nationalist who distrusted Yeats and the Irish literary movement, and a realist who yet could not tolerate the Irish country people being (as he put it) 'misrepresented', his emotional tensions were the source of his dramatic energy and his irascibility.   ROBERT WELCH

Sources R. Hogan and others, eds., *The Abbey Theatre: the rise of the realists, 1910–1915* (1979) · R. Hogan and M. J. O'Neill, eds., *Joseph Holloway's Abbey Theatre* (1967) · R. Hogan, ed., *Dictionary of Irish literature*, rev. edn, 1 (1996), 183 · d. cert.

Archives NL Ire., letters to Joseph Holloway · NL Ire., letters to D. J. O'Donoghue

Wealth at death £798 10s. 2d.: administration, 18 April 1923, CGPLA Eng. & Wales

Boyle, William Henry Dudley, twelfth earl of Cork and twelfth earl of Orrery (1873–1967), naval officer, was born, together with a twin sister, at Hale, Farnham, on 30 November 1873, the second of the four sons in a family of nine of Colonel Gerald Edmund Boyle (*d.* 1927) and his wife, Lady (Elizabeth) Theresa Pepys (*d.* 1897), daughter of the first earl of Cottenham. He entered the *Britannia* as a naval cadet in 1887 and two years later went to sea as a midshipman in the *Monarch* of the channel squadron, later transferring to the *Colossus* in the Mediterranean. In later life he used to claim that it was his service in this ship which was responsible for his future career in the navy, since it brought him into contact in very early life with officers of outstanding ability and dedication, and in fact no fewer than six of the seven lieutenants serving in the *Colossus* later reached flag rank. He married on 24 July 1902 Lady Florence Cecilia Keppel (*d.* 1963), daughter of William *Keppel, seventh earl of Albemarle; there were no children of the marriage.

As a commander Boyle served in the naval intelligence department in the Admiralty in 1909–11, and on promotion to captain in 1913 was appointed naval attaché in Rome, a post in which he was still serving when Italy joined the allies during the First World War. In 1915 he returned to sea in command of the *Fox*, serving in the Red Sea and Indian Ocean. At the same time he was senior officer of the Red Sea patrol, and as such was called upon to support some of the irregular operations of T. E. Lawrence, with whom he worked in close and cordial co-operation. He returned home in 1917 to command the *Repulse* in the Grand Fleet, serving as flag captain to Rear-Admiral Richard Phillimore and subsequently to Rear-Admiral Sir Henry Oliver. In 1918 he transferred to the *Lion*, where he was flag captain and chief of staff to Vice-Admiral Sir William Pakenham, serving in the rank of commodore, second class. At the end of the war he was appointed CB.

Boyle was promoted rear-admiral in 1923 and served as second in command of the 1st battle squadron in the Atlantic Fleet, and later as rear-admiral commanding the 1st cruiser squadron in the Mediterranean. On promotion to vice-admiral in 1928 he commanded the Reserve Fleet, and followed that appointment as president of the Royal Naval College, Greenwich, and vice-admiral commanding the Royal Naval War College in charge of the senior officers' war course. Having been appointed KCB in 1931, in 1932 he reached the rank of admiral and in the following year became commander-in-chief, Home Fleet, flying his flag in the *Nelson*. During this appointment he succeeded his kinsman as twelfth earl of Cork and Orrery (1934).

In normal circumstances Cork's command of the Home Fleet would have been his last appointment and he would have been placed on the retired list on its completion, but the unexpected death of Admiral Sir William Fisher in 1937 left a vacancy in the Portsmouth command and Cork was appointed to the post. He remained as commander-in-chief Portsmouth for the normal period of two years during which a vacancy occurred in the list of admirals of the fleet and he was selected to fill it (January 1938).

Cork had left Portsmouth by the start of the Second World War and was unemployed, but being exceedingly fit physically and full of energy and drive, he offered his services to the Admiralty for an active employment. An early opportunity arose with the command of the force provisionally arranged by the war cabinet to assist Finland, then under unprovoked attack by Russia, but it foundered on the rock of Norwegian and Swedish neutrality which effectively barred all means of access. But before that expedition was finally cancelled, the German attack on Norway was launched on 8 April 1940 and he was given the appointment of flag officer, Narvik, with the force originally destined for Finland being switched to the capture of Narvik and the destruction of the iron ore trade from that port to Germany. His joint military commander was Major-General P. J. Mackesy, who had preceded him to Norway, and the two men met for the first time at Harstad, a small port north of Narvik, which had been selected as the main base for the operation, to discover, as Cork described in his official dispatch, that they had left London with diametrically opposed views. This was hardly surprising in view of Cork's naval reputation as a fiery leader, and the expedition began on a sour note. It was not eased by the failure in England to load the transports tactically, so that the weapons most urgently needed on arrival were stowed at the bottoms of the holds and were therefore the last to be unloaded. The impasse between naval and military theories of attack on Narvik were partially solved five days later when the war cabinet gave Cork supreme command of the expedition, but by then the overall effect of the campaign of Norway was becoming academic in relation to the European war as a whole. In the event, Narvik was eventually captured by Cork's expedition and the iron ore loading installations in the port destroyed, but the force had to be withdrawn and Narvik abandoned to the Germans the following week. During this operation Cork had the unusual distinction of flying his union flag at sea as an admiral of the fleet, which officially made him senior to the commander-in-chief, Home Fleet, Admiral Sir Charles Forbes, who was in overall command of the naval side of the whole campaign, but this anomaly passed without incident.

The Narvik operation was the final episode of Cork's active career, although in 1941 he was sent to Gibraltar to inquire into the circumstances of the indecisive naval action off Spartivento, in which the pursuit of a fleeing Italian fleet had been called off by Admiral Sir James Somerville, commanding force H, in the belief that they were too fast to be caught and that no good purpose could be served by chasing the enemy to within range of shore-based aircraft. The result of Cork's inquiry completely vindicated Somerville's decision.

Cork had no further naval employment. He was now sixty-nine years old, and in his now exalted rank there was no avenue of active service left open to him. He became president of the Shaftesbury Homes and *Arethusa* training ship in 1942 and served in that position until 1953.

Cork was small in stature with fiery red hair, and was familiarly known as Ginger throughout the navy. He always wore a monocle which perhaps enhanced his aristocratic appearance, and right up to the end of his very long life he had a commanding presence, walking very upright with his shoulders back. Although a strict disciplinarian, he was regarded with affection by officers and men who served with him. He died at his home, 7 Knaresborough Place, London, at the age of ninety-three on 19 April 1967, and was succeeded, as thirteenth earl of Cork and Orrery, by his nephew, Patrick Reginald Boyle.

PETER KEMP, *rev.*

Sources Earl of Cork and Orrery [W. H. D. Boyle], *My naval life, 1886–1941* [1942] · personal knowledge (1981) · S. W. Roskill, *The war at sea, 1939–1945*, 3 vols. in 4 (1954–61) · *The Times* (20 April 1967) · *WWW* · Burke, *Peerage* (1980) · *CGPLA Eng. & Wales* (1967)
Archives JRL, corresp. with Auchinleck, reports, etc. | FILM BFI NFTVA, news footage · BFI NFTVA, advertising film footage (Shaftesbury Homes)
Likenesses W. Stoneman, two photographs, 1930–42, NPG
Wealth at death £7381: probate, 23 Aug 1967, *CGPLA Eng. & Wales*

Boyne. For this title name *see* Ogilvy, Sir Patrick, of Boyne, Lord Boyne (*d.* in or after 1705); Hamilton, Gustavus, first Viscount Boyne (1642–1723).

Boyne, John (1750s–1810), watercolour painter and engraver, was born in co. Down, Ireland. His father was originally a joiner by trade, but afterwards held an appointment in the victualling office at Deptford for many years. Boyne was brought to England when about nine years old, and subsequently articled (*c.*1770) in London to the landscape engraver William Byrne (1743–1805), who is principally known for his antiquarian engravings after Thomas Hearne. After his apprenticeship had ended, he attempted to work independently but, apparently, lack of application and a dissipated lifestyle worked against him. Unsuccessful as an engraver, he embarked on a more congenial career, joining a company of strolling actors near Chelmsford. He appeared in several plays, and assisted in a farce entitled *Christmas*. However, soon wearying of life as an actor he returned to London in 1781, and took up a trade of pearl-setting, being employed by a Mr Flower, of Chichester Rents, Chancery Lane. Later he appears as a master in a drawing school, first in Holborn, and then in Gloucester Street, Queen Square, where Thomas Heaphy and James Holmes were his pupils.

Boyne exhibited eighteen pieces, mainly classical, Shakespearian, and biblical subjects, at the Royal Academy between 1788 and 1809, giving his London addresses as 11 Great Turnstile, Lincoln's Inn Fields (1788), 34 Gloucester Street, Queen Square (1791–1801), and from 1802, 43 Penton Place, Pentonville. Boyne died at the last address on 22 June 1810. His most important artistic works were watercolour heads of Shakespearian characters, resembling those of John Hamilton Mortimer, some of which were engraved; other significant works include *Assignation*, *A Sketch to the Memory of the Duke of Bedford*, *The Muck Worm*, and *The Glow Worm*. Boyne's best work is probably the large Rowlandson-like watercolour *Meeting of Connoisseurs* (V&A), a scene in an artist's studio which includes a self-portrait; it was engraved in stipple by T. Williamson. The British Museum holds *The Quack Doctor* and a head of King Lear in black chalk and wash; other examples of Boyne's work are in the Royal Collection at Windsor and the Fitzwilliam Museum, Cambridge.

L. A. FAGAN, *rev.* MARTYN ANGLESEA

Sources Redgrave, *Artists* · Graves, *RA exhibitors* · W. G. Strickland, *A dictionary of Irish artists*, 2 vols. (1913) · I. O. Williams, *Early English watercolours and some cognate drawings by artists born not later than 1785* (1952) · Mallalieu, *Watercolour artists*
Likenesses J. Boyne, self-portrait, watercolour (*A meeting of connoisseurs*), V&A · T. Williamson, stipple (after J. Boyne)
Wealth at death 'idle and dissipated'; 'reckless in his habits and always poor': Redgrave, *Artists*

Boys, Sir Charles Vernon (1855–1944), physicist and inventor, was born at the rectory, Wing, Uppingham, Rutland, on 15 March 1855, the eighth child of five sons and four daughters of the rector, Charles Boys, and his wife, Caroline Goodrich Dobbie.

Education and early career Boys was devoted to his father whose skills he learned to emulate in model making, carpentry, and home-made fireworks at a precociously early age. Probably educated at home and locally up to the age of fourteen, he went to Marlborough College in 1869. There he soon exercised his ingenuity in covertly refurbishing the school clock without permission, and quietly subverting many other rules of conduct without ever being caught. In his second year, however, Boys's attention was focused on science by the tutelage of G. F. Rodwell, who proved to be the great inspiration of his scientific career; indeed Boys praised Rodwell throughout his life and, nineteen years later, dedicated his first book to him.

From December 1872 to 1876 Boys studied for an associateship in metallurgy and mining at the Royal School of Mines in Jermyn Street, London. There he studied metallurgy under John Percy, and in the Science Schools at South Kensington he learned chemistry from Frankland and was trained in physics by Frederick Guthrie. Boys clearly made an impact on the last, for soon after he started work in a colliery in 1876 he was invited back to South Kensington as Guthrie's laboratory assistant. During the late 1870s Boys was also employed as a teaching

Sir Charles Vernon Boys (1855–1944), by John Collier, 1915

assistant by Percy in addition to undertaking occasional school instruction, but Boys's inventive capacities soon came to the fore. In 1880 he constructed an integrating machine that embodied the principles of calculus learned from the works of Isaac Todhunter, and, after showing this new device to the Physical Society of London in 1881, Boys soon became a recognized expert in the field of mechanical calculation; he was no less an expert on the physics of bicycles and the Otto dicycle. In the same year Guthrie made him a life member of the Physical Society and regularized Boys's position at the renamed Normal School of Science by appointing him as a salaried demonstrator.

Reluctant teacher In Guthrie's laboratory in the early 1880s Boys developed a new expertise in electrical science, supplementing the revised 1884 edition of Guthrie's *Magnetism and Electricity* with a chapter on telephones, dynamos, and measurement techniques. By 1885–6 time for his own inventive work was curtailed since Guthrie's ill health obliged Boys to teach theoretical subjects for which he had little taste, and the number of students studying in the laboratory had swelled greatly. One of these, the young H. G. Wells, later complained for example that the 'extremely blond' and 'largely inaudible' Boys had left Wells largely unenlightened on thermodynamics; having 'galloped' through an hour of opaque exposition, Boys had simply 'bolted' back to the apparatus in his private room to continue with his invention (H. G. Wells, *Experiment in Autobiography*, 1.211). A later student of Boys, Sir Richard Gregory, recalled him supervising only advanced students, and apart from infrequent cross-examinations generally leaving them to their own devices. Boys would not be seen for days on end while working on a practical problem, but upon solving it he would sometimes rush into the students' laboratory whooping like a tribal warrior and jumping over tables in his manic excitement.

Bubbles and fibres After Guthrie died in 1886 Boys not only took on the demonstratorship of the Physical Society, but also took over temporarily as acting professor. He was disappointed to have to stand down in favour of the Oxford trained Arthur Rücker, who was appointed professor at the Normal School in 1887. Rücker and Boys soon published together on optical techniques for showing electrical stress, and it was doubtless Rücker's research on liquid films that first got Boys interested in the physics of soap bubbles. Boys's expertise in this area was publicly displayed in a series of Royal Institution Christmas lectures later published in *Soap Bubbles, Their Colours and the Forces which Mould Them* (1890, many editions and translations), and this remains the definitive account of the topic. The prodigious talent that Boys had in experimental matters was recognized by the award of a fellowship of the Royal Society in 1888 and his promotion to assistant professor in the same year. In the ensuing twelve years Boys undertook important research on the properties of quartz, especially as fibres in torsional suspensions, and high-speed photographic techniques.

In 1887 Boys deployed a fine quartz fibre in a radiomicrometer that was so remarkably delicate that it could detect the heating effect of a candle over a mile away. Working at night in his father's rural garden in the following year Boys was able to detect the differential heat reflections from different areas of the moon; conversely, his fastidious efforts to detect terrestrial heating by individual stars effectively demolished claims by previous experimenters to have found evidence of this effect. During 1890 and 1891 Boys further enhanced the sensitivity of his fibres by shooting an arrow attached to fused quartz across a room, the fluid solidifying as a long fine thread of unprecedented strength. He employed these fibres in attempts to improve upon Henry Cavendish's determination of the gravitational constant 'G': finding the environment of Exhibition Road too disturbed, even at night, Boys removed his experiments to the basement of the Clarendon Laboratory in Oxford where he worked alone after nocturnal shunting duties at the railway station had been completed. Between 1894 and 1895 Boys was thus able to achieve a precision of five significant figures—a result that was unsurpassed for decades, and led to his award of the Royal Society medal in 1896. In the midst of all this he cultivated a new technique with a rotatory lens in 1893 which enabled the flight of bullets to be photographed for the first time. Such accomplishments made Boys the doyen of British experimental physicists for decades thereafter.

Boys married Marian Amelia Pollock, daughter of Henry Pollock, master of the supreme court of justice, in 1892. This partnership produced a son, Geoffrey Vernon Boys (1893–1945), later secretary of the Institution of Naval

Architects, and a daughter, Margaret Angela (1896–1937), who married Malcolm Carruthers. While Boys continued to invent and experiment with enormous zeal even in the earliest years of his marriage, he was now obliged to supplement his modest salary to support not only his wife and young family, but also his impecunious elderly father. To this end Boys endured the duties of a University of London examiner, and from 1893 also undertook lucrative work as expert witness in patent cases, being employed by the Dunlop tyre company as one of a very small number of specialist witnesses. In later decades his expertise was called upon in a wide range of legal disputes, most prominently in cases concerning Marconi's patents for wireless telegraphy and attempts by J. A. Fleming to prolong the patent on his thermionic valve.

Liberated by gas Boys gave up his assistant professorship in 1897, also resigning his honorary positions as demonstrator and librarian for the Physical Society, to become a metropolitan gas referee. This slightly more remunerative new position enabled him to continue his inventive activity without the onerous duties of teaching. Not only did he have access to the workshops at the gas referees' official premises at 66 Victoria Street in Westminster for quantitative work on the thermal and illuminating powers of gas, but he also hired rooms in the same building for use as private workshop and laboratory. Here he researched alone, extending his high-speed photographic techniques to the study of lightning flashes, although this method was not taken up in practical application until 1928–33 in the USA and South Africa. Here Boys also developed the many practical jokes for which he was cherished by his scientific contemporaries, firing smoke rings at or dropping water bombs on unsuspecting pedestrians in the street below—studiously avoiding such reprehensible conduct in front of his own son, however. Although a solitary labourer, Boys was not unsociable in his leisure time, being a founder member of the Automobile Club, later the RAC, in 1898. He also frequented such clubs as the Athenaeum and Savile, and was long a central figure in the Royal Society Club, endearing himself to many with his generosity, sympathy, and puckish humour.

During the first decade of the twentieth century Boys's reputation in the world of science was still in the ascendant. He was appointed president of section A of the British Association for the Advancement of Science in 1903, and acted as president of the Roentgen Society in 1906–7. At the same time Boys's private life became difficult as Marian found his idiosyncratic behaviour increasingly intolerable. Boys could not understand why the sociable and well-connected Mrs Boys objected to his drinking cooled tea from a saucer and not bothering to dress for dinner when tired after work. Moreover, his dogmatic and unorthodox views on the correct modes of handling coal fires and of cooking vegetables cannot have improved domestic harmony. Boys was sufficiently understanding of Marian's romantic affair with A. R. Forsyth to agree to a divorce in 1910 so that she could remarry. Boys thereafter lived as a bachelor, having rooms at Palace Street in Westminster, spending evenings at his clubs, and weekends at his house in Hampshire. Having few hobbies other than crosswords and geometrical puzzles, he spent most of his time in his workshop and friends were often invited down to admire his heroic deeds of invention such as novel sundials and the dipleidoscope for astronomical time determinations.

Following his divorce Boys threw himself into his work in Victoria Street with even greater vigour. He worked collaboratively with J. S. G. Thomas in new techniques of gas calorimetry from 1913, and on liquid films and bubbles in 1911–12 patents. During the First World War Boys gave military advice on ballistics, edited and amplified Jervis-Smith's posthumous *Dynamometers* (1915), and served as president of the Physical Society of London in 1916–17. It was from 1920 that the ever sprightly Boys's public service became most prominent. As one of the three gas referees employed throughout the entire country as stipulated by the Gas Act of 1920, Boys worked on means of gauging the calorific value of gas consumed in a household, so that its price might be related to its thermal value and not merely to its volume. He developed a recording calorimeter that incorporated a 'thinking machine' which automatically corrected for pressure fluctuations, and worked on it constantly until 1934 when he was finally satisfied with a model that was then widely adopted. It was at this time that Boys, with typically scant respect for orthodox conduct, arranged to melt down both the Rumford medal he was awarded for his calorimetric researches in 1924 and his Royal Society medal, so that he could donate the gold to Marlborough College to finance the award of science prizes at his alma mater.

1935 was a most eventful year for Boys, despite the loss of vision in one eye after a cataract operation two years previously, and a severe impairment in his hearing. Not only did he publish *The Natural Logarithm*, a pamphlet inspired by decades of pondering Todhunter's book *Algebra* with a very practical eye, but he was also honoured with a knighthood. At his eightieth birthday celebrations at the Royal Society Club his friend and later obituarist R. A. S. Paget composed a memorable song with the immortal refrain 'Boys will be Boys'. The octogenarian polymath revealed his great horticultural expertise in *Weeds, Weeds, Weeds* (1937), and did not retire as a gas referee until 1939—even then continuing to act as a consultant adviser until 1943. That year also saw his last paper presented at the Physical Society on a device for drawing ellipses.

Boys died at his country home, Bourneside, St Mary Bourne, Andover, Hampshire, on 30 March 1944, and was buried at St Mary Bourne. He was cherished by physicists for his contributions to apparatus and applied science long after his humorous, boyish antics had been forgotten. GRAEME J. N. GOODAY

Sources R. A. S. Paget, 'Sir Charles Boys, FRS', *Proceedings of the Physical Society*, 56 (1944), 397–403 · Lord Rayleigh [R. J. Strutt], *Obits. FRS*, 4 (1942–4), 771–88 · C. T. R. Wilson, 'Sir Charles Vernon Boys', *Nature*, 155 (1945), 41–2 · A. G. Lowndes, 'Sir Charles Boys', *Nature*, 155 (1945), 147 · *Nature*, 133 (1934), 677 · J. S. G. T., 'Dr Boys on gas calorimetry', *Nature*, 133 (1934), 710–11 · R. V. Jones, 'Boys, Charles Vernon', *DSB* · Physical Society of London, *Proceedings of Jubilee Meetings* (1924), 21–3 · b. cert. · d. cert.
Archives ICL · Sci. Mus., notes relating to gravitational experiments; further notes relating to gravitational experiments | CUL, letters to Sir George Stokes
Likenesses photograph, 1900–40, repro. in Rayleigh, *Obits. FRS*, facing p. 771 · J. Collier, portrait, 1915 [*see illus.*] · R. Paget, pen sketch, 1929, Athenaeum, London
Wealth at death £36,500 15s. 6d.: probate, 14 June 1944, CGPLA Eng. & Wales

Boys [Boschus], **David** (*d.* after 1465), prior of Gloucester, joined the Carmelite order in Gloucester and graduated BTh at Oxford. He lectured at both Oxford and Cambridge and travelled abroad, furthering his studies at other universities. He went to Rome, where he is said to have preached many sermons. While lecturing at Oxford he collected the works of his fellow Carmelite, John Barningham (*d.* 1449), and donated them to the Carmelite library at Cambridge. He was chaplain to Eleanor, duchess of Gloucester, and probably also to Duke Humphrey (*d.* 1447). In later years he returned to Gloucester, where he was prior until his death after 1465. He was noted for his love of the contemplative life, meditating long hours on the scriptures and rarely leaving his cell. He wrote six books, all lost, including 'On human immortality', 'Against the Moslems', 'On the doctrine of the spirit', and 'On true innocence'. RICHARD COPSEY

Sources J. Bale, Bodl. Oxf., MS Selden supra 41, fol. 181 · BL, J. Bale, Harley MS 3838, fols. 101v–102, 208v–209 · J. Bale, *Illustrium Maioris Britannie scriptorum … summarium* (1548), fol. 203 · Bale, *Cat.*, 1.589–90 · Emden, *Oxf.* · Emden, *Cam.* · *Commentarii de scriptoribus Britannicis, auctore Joanne Lelando*, ed. A. Hall, 2 (1709), 454–5 · A. T. Bannister, ed., *Registrum Johannis Stanbury, episcopi Herefordensis* (1918), 156 · C. de S. E. de Villiers, ed., *Bibliotheca Carmelitana*, 2 vols. (Orléans, 1752), vol. 1, p. 379; vol. 2, p. 902

Boys, Edward (1599–1667), Church of England clergyman, born in Hoad Court, Blean, Kent, and baptized on 21 December 1599 in Canterbury Cathedral, was the fifth of ten children of Thomas Boys (*d.* 1625), of Hoad Court, gentleman, and his first wife, Sarah (*d.* 1602), daughter of Richard *Rogers, dean of Canterbury and suffragan bishop of Dover. Educated at Eton College, Boys matriculated as a pensioner from Corpus Christi College, Cambridge, in Easter term 1620. Subsequently elected a scholar, he graduated BA in 1624 and proceeded MA in 1627. With his election to a fellowship at Corpus in 1631 Boys embarked on an academic career: in 1634 he received the degree of BD and the same year held the appointment of university preacher.

In 1640, however, Boys was presented to the living of Mautby, a tiny village in Norfolk, by the antiquary and landowner William Paston, his contemporary at Corpus. Freed from the obligations of his college fellowship in 1641, on 22 March that year Boys married, by licence at Canterbury Cathedral, Mary Herne, a widow related through marriage to a Norfolk gentry family; there were no children. Thereafter he appears to have lived out the years of conflict and Commonwealth quietly in Mautby, in

Edward Boys (1599–1667), by William Faithorne the elder, pubd 1672

his time 'a Country Village consisting onely of four Farmers' (Boys, sig. a 2). His editor, Roger Flynt, another Corpus contemporary, maintained that Boys's retirement was the result of reticence and modesty. More likely Boys was outspoken in his support of Charles I and deemed it expedient to seek the seclusion of a country parish. The leanings of his friends suggested as much: Paston was knighted by Charles I in 1641, Flint was sequestered for delinquency before May 1645, and Joseph Hall, Boys's bishop at Norwich and an admirer of his preaching, was expelled from the diocese about 1647. On 22 May 1651 Boys's library of 2000 books, the parish register, and the parsonage house were all destroyed by fire.

Like many of his contemporaries Boys made obedience to the king a strong element in sermons preached after the restoration of 1660. Of the sixteen published posthumously by Flynt in 1672 four bore directly on this theme; the occasion of one of these ('Carolus redux') can be precisely dated (7 July 1666). Boys died at Mautby on 10 March 1667 and was buried in the chancel of his church. In his will he left £10 to his old college to add to gifts made during his lifetime: an edition of Binius's *Concilia generalia* presented in September 1641 and two volumes of holograph sermons by his uncle John Boys (1571–1625), dean of Canterbury.　　　　　　　　WILLIAM RICHARDSON

Sources Venn, *Alum. Cant.* · R. Hovenden, ed., *The register booke of christeninges, marriages, and burialls within the precinct of the cathedrall and metropoliticall church of Christe of Canterburie*, Harleian Society, register section, 2 (1878) · E. Boys, *Sixteen sermons preached on several occasions* (1672) · R. Masters, *The history of the College of Corpus Christi and the B. Virgin Mary … in the University of Cambridge* (1753) · F. Blomefield and C. Parkin, *An essay towards a topographical history of the county of Norfolk*, [2nd edn], 11 vols. (1805–10) · J. Spurr, *The Restoration Church of England, 1646–1689* (1991) · M. R. James, *A descriptive catalogue of the manuscripts in the library of Corpus Christi College, Cambridge*, 2 vols. (1909–12) · Kent parish registers

Likenesses W. Faithorne the elder, engraving (aged sixty-six), BM, NPG; repro. in Boys, *Sixteen sermons* [*see illus.*]

Boys, Edward (1785–1866), naval officer, son of John *Boys (1749–1824) and his wife, Mary, daughter of the Revd Richard Harvey. He entered the navy in 1796, and after serving in the North Sea, on the coast of Ireland, and in the channel, was in June 1802 appointed to the frigate *Phoebe*. On 4 August 1803, Boys, when in charge of a prize, was captured by the French, and remained a prisoner of war for six years, until, after many daring and ingenious attempts, he succeeded in escaping. On his return to England he was made lieutenant (effective from 25 May 1809) and served mostly in the West Indies until the peace. On 8 July 1814 he became commander, but, with the post-war naval reduction, he had no further employment afloat, though from 1837 to 1841 he was superintendent of Deal dockyard. On 1 July 1851 he retired with the rank of captain.

Immediately after his escape, and while in the West Indies, Boys wrote for his family an account of his adventures in France; the risk of jeopardizing his French friends made him keep this private, and although abstracts from it had found their way into the papers it was not until 1827 that he was persuaded to publish it, as *Narrative of a Captivity and Adventures in France and Flanders between the Years 1803–9*; this was the source from which Captain Marryatt, the author of *Peter Simple*, drew much of his account of his hero's escape—more perhaps than from the previously published narrative of the naval officer Henry Ashworth's adventures. Boys also published in 1831 *Remarks on the Practicability and Advantages of a Sandwich or Downs Harbour*.

Boys had married Elizabeth, *née* Sayer; they had three sons and three daughters. He died at 14 Blomfield Terrace, Harrow Road, Paddington, London, on 6 June 1866. His second son was Admiral Henry *Boys (1820–1904), captain of the *Excellent* and superintendent of the Royal Naval College at Portsmouth, 1869–74, director of naval ordnance from 1874 to 1878, and second in command of the Channel Fleet in 1878–9; after his retirement he served on the board of the Maxim Nordenfelt Gun Company, and as governor of the Marine Society.

J. K. LAUGHTON, rev. ANDREW LAMBERT

Sources W. H. Boys, *Memoir of the naval services of Admiral Henry Boys* (privately printed, Liverpool, 1913) · D. Syrett and R. L. DiNardo, *The commissioned sea officers of the Royal Navy, 1660–1815*, rev. edn, Occasional Publications of the Navy RS, 1 (1994) · E. Boys, *Narrative of a captivity and adventures in France and Flanders … 1803–9* (1827) · O'Byrne, *Naval biog. dict.* · Boase, *Mod. Eng. biog.* · CGPLA Eng. & Wales (1866)

Wealth at death under £1500: resworn probate, June 1867, *CGPLA Eng. & Wales* (1866)

Boys, Henry (1820–1904), naval officer, was born on 30 September 1820 at Upper Deal, Kent, the second son of Captain Edward *Boys RN (1785–1866), superintendent of Deal dockyard from 1837 to 1841, and his wife, Elizabeth, *née* Sayer. His younger brother Richard also joined the navy but was killed in action against pirates on the Moroccan coast in May 1846. Boys was educated at Ramsgate School before joining HMS *Edinburgh* in 1837. Her captain, William Wilmot Henderson, was a local political and naval friend of his father. *Edinburgh* was active on the coast of Syria in 1840; Boys was noted for his conduct at Beirut under heavy fire on 2 October. He was slightly wounded at the bombardment of Acre on 3 November. Between 1841 and 1845 he served in HMS *Illustrious*, flagship of the West Indies station. He impressed everyone he served under with his professionalism and personality, and with his father's active solicitation and the support of Captain Henderson he secured promotion: on 15 February 1846 he was commissioned as a lieutenant of the *Snake*, 16 guns, on the west African station. Edward Boys persuaded the liberal Admiralty board to recall his son. The *Snake* disappeared at sea after Boys left. He qualified in gunnery before returning to west Africa, in 1849, where he distinguished himself in the campaign to end the illegal Atlantic slave trade.

Back in Britain in 1851 Boys then followed his patron Henderson to the Brazil station, Henderson's position as commander-in-chief guaranteeing Boys's promotion to commander, which occurred on 14 May 1853. Henderson died, but Boys remained on the Brazil station, almost dying of yellow fever. Again in Britain in 1856 he married, and on 17 October 1857 was promoted captain. In 1863 his old shipmate Captain Robert Hall, then private secretary to the first lord of the Admiralty, secured his appointment to HMS *Pelorus* destined for China; there he transferred into HMS *Barrosa* and he remained on station until 1866. During his absence his parents died. In July 1867 Boys took command of HMS *Warrior* for her second commission in the channel. In this fine ship he consolidated his reputation as an outstanding officer. He was involved in securing the queen from an alleged Fenian plot to kidnap her from the grounds of Osborne, and she visited the ship, a rare honour. In August 1868 *Warrior* and *Royal Oak* collided, but Boys was acquitted of responsibility. The following year he commanded three ships towing a huge floating dock from Madeira to Bermuda, and manoeuvred the dock into Bermuda harbour. He was then appointed captain of the gunnery training ship *Excellent*, the most important captain's command in the service. He remained five years, with many of the future leaders of the navy serving on his staff, including John Fisher, with whom he co-operated on the early development of torpedoes. In February 1872 Boys commanded the naval brigade sent to the thanksgiving service at St Paul's Cathedral, for the recovery from typhoid of the prince of Wales, the first occasion when the navy took the place of honour on a royal ceremonial occasion.

In May 1874 Boys followed his lifelong friend and immediate predecessor at *Excellent*, Arthur Hood, as director of naval ordnance. He was responsible for weapons during a period of rapid technical progress and applied his profound understanding of the sea and gunnery to the development of new systems. His regime, like that of Hood, was one of steady if unspectacular progress. In April 1875 he went to Malta on HMS *Devastation*, the first capital ship without sails, to report on her sea-keeping and massive 35 ton guns. Promoted rear-admiral on 30 July 1875 he worked closely with his friends, the controller Admiral Houston Stewart, the secretary Admiral Robert Hall, and the second sea lord Admiral Hood. In 1878 Boys took a sea command. Initially he commanded the Reserve Fleet, mobilized when the channel squadron went to the Mediterranean. Next he was second in command of a fleet under Admiral Cooper Key, preparing for service in the Baltic. Later he investigated the tragic explosion of a 12 inch Armstrong RML gun on the battleship *Thunderer*, establishing that the gun had been double-loaded, and ensuring the end of muzzle-loading guns in the Royal Navy.

Boys came ashore in mid-1879, served on committees concerned with port defences and small arms, and reported on gun trials. On 1 April 1881 he became vice-admiral. After promotion to full admiral on 1 June 1885 he retired. He became a director of the Nordenfelt Gun Company and the Barrow Shipbuilding Company until they were bought by Vickers. He was twice chairman of the Royal United Services Institution, and remained a vice-president until his death. He was also a governor of the Marine Society. He remained active until his final year, and died at Blackheath on 16 March 1904. Boys was a fine seaman, a careful innovator, and an effective leader. His early career was made by his father and local political friends, but his merits ensured his continued success as a captain and admiral. He was one of the modernizers of the navy.

ANDREW LAMBERT

Sources W. H. Boys, *Memoir of the naval services of Admiral Henry Boys* (privately printed, Liverpool, 1913) • O'Byrne, *Naval biog. dict.* • R. F. MacKay, *Fisher of Kilverstone* (1973) • W. L. Clowes, *The Royal Navy: a history from the earliest times to the present*, 7 vols. (1897–1903), vols. 6–7 • J. G. Wells, *Whaley: the story of HMS Excellent, 1830 to 1980* (1980) • A. D. Lambert, *Warrior* (1987) • Kelly, *Handbk* (1891) • Boase, *Mod. Eng. biog.* • E. Longford, *Victoria RI* (1964) • P. Magnus, *King Edward the Seventh* (1964)
Wealth at death £5979 13s. 10d.: probate, 1904, CGPLA Eng. & Wales

Boys, John (*bap.* 1571, *d.* 1625), dean of Canterbury, was born at Elmton, in Eythorne, Kent, and baptized on 12 November 1571 at Eythorne, the sixth of ten children of Thomas Boys (1528–1600) of Eythorne, gentleman, from a family established in east Kent since at least 1380, and his wife, Christian Searles (*d.* 1587), daughter and coheir of John Searles of Wye. Boys entered the King's School, Canterbury, about 1581 and was admitted pensioner at Corpus Christi College, Cambridge, in April 1586. He graduated BA in 1590 and proceeded MA in 1593. That year he moved to Clare College, a migration apparently caused by his annoyance that a vacant Kentish fellowship at Corpus had been given instead to a native of Norfolk; he proceeded BD

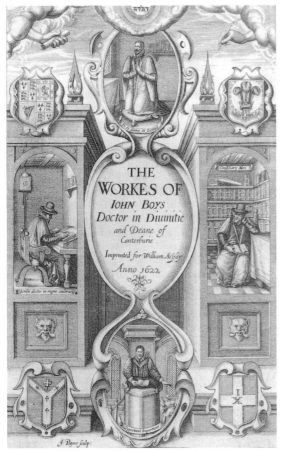

John Boys (*bap.* 1571, *d.* 1625), by John Payne, pubd 1622

from Clare in 1600. In 1597 Boys was presented to the rectory of Betshanger in Kent through the influence of his uncle Sir John Boys (*d.* 1612), recorder of Canterbury, and in the same year Archbishop John Whitgift gave him the mastership of Eastbridge Hospital in Canterbury. Boys appears to have lived at Betshanger and to have begun to cultivate the art of preaching for, in addition to being presented by Whitgift with the further living of Tilmanstone in Kent in 1599, he preached at Paul's Cross for the first time that year and again on 8 February 1601, when his sermon coincided with a commotion in the cathedral caused by the attempted rebellion of Robert Devereux, second earl of Essex. In 1603 Boys was given a third Kent living, the rectory of Hollingbourne, and on 4 October the following year married Angela Bargrave (*d.* 1645), daughter of Robert Bargrave of Bridge, near Canterbury. There were no children.

Boys never lost sight of his debt to Cambridge. The foundation of his work was, he said, laid there: John Overall, then a fellow at Trinity College, had taken a special interest in him and the university nurtured his interest in the pulpit. Boys's anonymous eulogist heard him say that 'he never missed publique Sermon at St Maries, during all the time of his abode there, save twice' (*Remaines*, sig. b). He preached in Latin at the university church in 1599 and

again in 1605 when he received the degree of DD. Soon afterwards Boys began the project that was to bring him renown and, eventually, preferment—a systematic exposition, through printed sermons, of the church's prescribed lectionary. It was a project well suited to the protestant milieu being developed at Canterbury by Thomas Neville, dean from 1597 to 1615, and it occupied Boys for the next decade. During this time he took 'paines in preaching every weeke, if not at his owne charge, yet there where was more need' (ibid., sig. a3) and the result was eleven books of 'postils' published between 1609 and 1617. Such was the popularity of his volumes that sales were large and rapid. Further impressions were soon required and twelve separate reissues have survived for the period from 1610 to 1616.

By 1610 Boys's influence was being felt at Canterbury, where Neville reviewed the preaching obligations of the cathedral clergy and instituted a rota of liturgically based expository sermons. Nevertheless, the progress of Boys's career was slow. According to contemporaries his lack of advancement was because 'a great prelate in the church' bore him ill will 'for mutual animosities betwixt them, whilst gremials in the university' (Fuller, 2.155). Boys preached at Ashford during the primary visitation of Archbishop Richard Bancroft in September 1607, but his only preferment during Bancroft's tenure at Canterbury was his appointment by James I in 1610 as one of seventeen founding fellows of the ill-fated King's College, Chelsea, where, under the provostship of Matthew Sutcliffe, the fellows' task was to counter the controversial literature of Catholic writers. One fruit of this work was Boys's sermon at Paul's Cross on the anniversary in 1613 of the Gunpowder Plot (5 November), in which he also commended the lottery set up in 1612 to help refinance the Virginia Company.

With the succession of George Abbott to Canterbury, Boys's work to promote a preaching ministry found an enthusiastic patron and finally secured him preferment. In 1618, upon resigning the vicarage at Tilmanstone, he was awarded the rectory of Great Monaghan and in May 1619 the deanery at Canterbury. In 1620 he was made a member of the court of high commission, in 1622 he collected together his books and five miscellaneous sermons, publishing them as his *Workes*, and in 1624 he sat in the convocation at London on behalf of the clergy in his diocese. Boys presided over a significant expansion of the cathedral's musical life which, he maintained, much aided the due observance of the prayer book. In his time at Canterbury the cathedral also retained the strongly protestant tenor that Neville had inaugurated, centred on the pulpit: to this Boys brought the predestinarian Calvinism typical of the late Elizabethan and Jacobean church. The subsequent choice as dean in succession to Boys of his brother-in-law, the conservative Isaac Bargrave, signalled a move in the direction of Laudianism.

Boys probably had independent means. He appears to have inherited his father's house and he was able to maintain a spacious household in his official residence at Chartham, where he refurbished the fabric. Three months after preaching before Charles I at Canterbury Boys died in his study at Elmton in Eythorne on 26 September 1625; he was buried in the cathedral four days later. Six years after his death fifteen further sermons were published as the *Remaines of … John Boys*, 'that reverend and famous postiller'. Boys's widow, Dean Bargrave's sister, erected a monument to her husband, possibly by Nicholas Stone and now considered 'an outstanding example of the discovery of the surface quality of marble' (Collinson and others, 522); it depicts Boys standing in his library. In 1631 Boys's eulogist maintained that 'there were in his time, and yet are few soules … that taste not of his books' (*Remaines*, sig. a) and he was, it seems, one of the great book collectors of his time, quoting liberally in his published work from an exceptionally wide range of contemporary literature, including Shakespeare.

Boys's writings were translated into German and published in Strasbourg in 1683 and 1685; an edition appeared in Philadelphia in 1849. The continuing appeal and convenience to clergy of Boys's exposition of the Anglican lectionary is attested to by C. H. Spurgeon in his *Commentating and Commentaries* (1876), while in 1906 Charles Higham, a prominent theological bookseller in London, reported a continuing 'steady demand' for Boys's *Workes*, 'which is still much used by clergy' (priv. coll.).

WILLIAM RICHARDSON

Sources Venn, *Alum. Cant.* · *The workes of John Boys* (1622) · *Remaines of that reverend and famous postiller, John Boys* (1631) · P. Collinson, P. N. Ramsay, and M. Sparks, eds., *A history of Canterbury Cathedral* (1995) · R. Masters, *The history of the College of Corpus Christi and the B. Virgin Mary … in the University of Cambridge* (1753) · M. J. Sparks and E. W. Parkin, '"The deanery", Chartham', *Archaeologia Cantiana*, 89 (1974), 169–82 · *DNB* · M. Maclure, *The Paul's Cross sermons, 1534–1642* (1958) · Fuller, *Worthies* (1840) · A. Chalmers, ed., *The general biographical dictionary*, new edn, 32 vols. (1812–17) · C. E. Woodruff and H. T. Cape, *Schola Cantuariensis* (1908) · [M. D. Forbes], ed., *Clare College, 1326–1926*, 2 vols. (1928–30) · Wood, *Ath. Oxon.: Fasti*, new edn · BL, Bishop White Kennett's biographical collections, Lansdowne MS 984, no. 45 · M. R. James, *A descriptive catalogue of the manuscripts in the library of Corpus Christi College, Cambridge*, 2 vols. (1909–12) · P. Clark, *English provincial society from the Reformation to the revolution: religion, politics and society in Kent, 1500–1640* (1977) · parish register, Eythorne, 12 Nov 1571, CKS [baptism] · parish register, Patricksbourne, 4 Oct 1604, CKS [marriage]

Archives CCC Cam., holograph sermons or 'postils', MSS 215, 216

Likenesses J. Payne, four line engravings, pubd 1622, BM, NPG [*see illus.*] · J. Cole, line engraving (after N. Stone?), NPG · N. Stone?, marble effigy on monument, Canterbury Cathedral; repro. in Collinson, Ramsay, and Sparks, eds., *History of Canterbury Cathedral* · oils, Canterbury Cathedral, deanery; repro. in L. Behrens, *Under thirty-seven kings* (1926), 60

Boys, Sir John (*bap.* 1607, *d.* 1664), royalist army officer, was baptized at Chillenden parish church, Kent, on 5 April 1607, second of the six children of Edward Boys (*d.* 1661) of Goodnestone-next-Wingham, Kent, and his wife, Jane (*d.* 1620), daughter of Edward Saunders of Northbourn in Kent. It does not appear that John Boys attended university. As eldest son he was heir to the estate at Bonnington in Goodnestone, the main seat of his family since at least the mid-fourteenth century. At the age of twenty-one Boys was indicted for the manslaughter in Canterbury of a

vagrant, Thomas Alcock, by 'a blow on the head with a fire pan' (*CSP dom.*, 1629–31, 336) but he was pardoned in November 1630. Three years later, on 8 March 1634, he married Lucy (*d.* in or before 1650), daughter of John Denne of St Stephen's near Canterbury; they had five daughters.

Before the civil war Boys spent 'divers years as a soldier abroad' (BL, Add. MS 18891, fol. 15), probably in Ireland. He was a captain in the army raised by Charles I against the Scots in 1640; in February 1642 he was at Chester recruiting for the Irish army to oppose the Catholic Confederate rebels and by November, with civil war in England, he was appointed lieutenant-colonel in the royalist foot regiment of John Savage, second Earl Rivers. In September 1643, in the aftermath of the first battle of Newbury, Boys was appointed governor of nearby Donnington Castle. It had a strong barbican tower but otherwise only a modest curtain wall described by William Camden as 'windows on all sides, very lightsome' (Money, 135). The castle had strategic significance in controlling the London to Bath road and was positioned between the royalist headquarters at Oxford and the parliamentarians in London; Boys constructed earthworks around it before defending it from two assaults during the summer of 1644. Knighted by Charles I in the days before the second battle of Newbury in October 1644, Boys was made colonel and repulsed a further attack on the castle. During the subsequent winter parliament raised money for a final siege and Boys surrendered Donnington on 1 April 1646 only after John Dalbier's troops blasted it with a 15 inch 'mortar-piece' (Money, 207).

In September 1646 Boys was in the Netherlands but he was back at Bonnington in November. Now basing himself in Kent, he played the leading role in the county uprising of 1648 which followed the attempt of parliament to ban the traditional celebration of Christmas. He was among those framing a country petition in May with its threat of armed resistance, and following the subjugation of Maidstone and Canterbury by parliamentarian forces in June Boys escaped to the Netherlands. Late in July he sailed with Prince Charles for Yarmouth, but plans to raise Norfolk for the king and relieve Colchester came to nothing. A fortnight later Boys attempted to raise Kent at Deal but in the skirmish that ensued he was shot. 'The buckle of his hanger gave some stop to the bullet' and he was captured (*Packets of Letters*, 7). Boys escaped with sequestration and made composition of his fines in April 1649. Following the death of his first wife he married Ann Brockman on 12 December 1650 at Newington-next-Hythe, Kent; after her death about 1653 he married Elizabeth, Lady Finch (*d.* 1672?), daughter of Sir John Fotherby of Barham, Kent, and widow of Sir Nathaniel Finch.

Boys was arrested and imprisoned in the spring of 1651 and again in February 1655 with a few close colleagues on suspicion of planning military insurrection. In 1658 Boys was listed in succession to Rivers as colonel in the Kent royalist army and was supplying money to Charles Stuart in Brussels. By June 1659 it was the opinion of Sir Edward Hyde that Boys was 'as fit a person to be Major General …

as any man; and, if I am not deceived, is well beloved generally in the country' (Newman, 39) and that summer he received a royal commission 'to treat with subjects formerly in rebellion' in Kent (Everitt, 303). In January 1660 with his aged father and others Boys 'designed and propounded' a county petition that called for free elections and he was briefly reimprisoned in Dover Castle (*Mercurius Politicus*, 26 Jan–2 Feb 1660, 1068); thereafter he was one of those who plied the English Channel carrying correspondence between Edward Montagu, first earl of Sandwich, and Charles.

With the dissolution of the Rump Parliament in February there was a final republican effort to divide opinion in Kent but Boys and others issued a counter-declaration on 20 April on behalf of the gentry 'who adhered to the King' which rejected any 'revengeful thoughts and actions' (Everitt, 312–13). The following day Boys dined with Montagu's follower Samuel Pepys along with 'some other gentlemen, formerly great Cavaliers'. To Pepys he 'seemed a fine man' and they met again at sea in mid-May, Boys on his way back from the Brill and still closely involved in the preparations that culminated two weeks later in the restoration of Charles II (Pepys, 1.112, 106).

In July 1660 Boys was rewarded with the customership of Dover and in April 1662 he was appointed deputy governor of Duncannon Fort, co. Wexford. He died at Ross, co. Wexford, on 8 October 1664, having been on active service in Ireland during 1663–4, and was buried in Goodnestone church. Boys was survived by his third wife, Elizabeth, and three of his daughters who, in 1666, sold the Bonnington estate to Thomas Brome. WILLIAM RICHARDSON

Sources A. Everitt, *The community of Kent and the great rebellion, 1640–60* (1966) · W. Money, *The first and second battles of Newbury* (1884) · P. R. Newman, *Royalist officers in England and Wales, 1642–1660: a biographical dictionary* (1981) · Pepys, *Diary*, vol. 1 · BL, Rupert correspondence, Add. MS 18891 · *Packets of letters from Scotland, Berwick, Newcastle, and York to members of the House of Commons* [1648] [Thomason tract E 446(3)] · *Mercurius Politicus* (26 Jan–2 Feb 1660) · E. Peacock, *The army lists of the roundheads and cavaliers* (1874) · M. Wood, *Donnington Castle: official guide book* (1964) · Thurloe, *State papers* · W. A. Shaw, ed., *Calendar of treasury books*, 1, PRO (1904), 1660–1667 · *CSP dom.*, 1629–20; 1660–61 · M. A. E. Green, ed., *Calendar of the proceedings of the committee for compounding … 1643–1660*, 5 vols., PRO (1889–92) · H. F. Hore and P. H. Hore, eds., *History of the town and county of Wexford*, 6 vols. (1900–11) · C. Dalton, *Irish army lists, 1661–1685* (1907) · W. Kennet, *A register and chronicle … containing matters of fact … towards … a true history of England* (1728) · parish register, Chillenden · parish register, Goodnestone-next-Wingham · parish register transcript, Hackington · parish register, Newington-next-Hythe · grave monument, Kent, Goodnestone-next-Wingham church

Archives BL, corresp., Add. MSS 18891, 28001–28004

Likenesses portrait, exh. National Portrait Exhibition 1866; formerly in possession of Revd Thomas Boys in 1871 · Stow, engraving (after portrait), repro. in Money, *First and second battles* · oils, repro. in Money, *First and second battles*; formerly in possession of the Hammond family, St Albans Court, Nonington, Kent, in 1920s · portrait (version); formerly in possession of Judge Boys of Barne, Ontario, 1909

Wealth at death bequests of £3000 in total to daughters: will, 1664

Boys, John (*bap.* 1621, *d.* 1661), translator and antiquary, was baptized on 14 November 1621 at St Mary Northgate,

Canterbury, the only son of John Boys (1590–1640) of Hoad Court, Blean, Kent, and Mary (or Margaret), daughter of Martin *Fotherby, bishop of Salisbury. His grandfather Thomas Boys of Canterbury (*d.* 1625), otherwise Thomas of St Gregory's or Dr Thomas of Fredville, had inherited the estate from his uncle, Sir John Boys of St Gregory's Priory, 'a man of much note in his profession of the law' who died childless in 1612 (Hasted, 3.565). Boys's immediate family on both sides was closely connected with Canterbury Cathedral for several generations.

Little is known about Boys's education, profession, or settled residence. He was admitted to the Inner Temple in November 1640 and took the protestation oath in Blean in January 1642. With his wife, Ann (*d.* 1712), daughter of Dr William Kingsley, archdeacon of Canterbury Cathedral, Boys had some six children, all of whom, including the youngest, Damaris (*b.* 2 May 1658), were born in the city of Canterbury.

Like several cousins and prominent Kentish men Boys was a committed loyalist, embroiled in the political upheavals of the time. On 24 January 1660 he presented a 'Declaration of the nobility, gentry, ministry and communalty of the county of Kent' to the mayor at the town hall of Canterbury. The magistrates found the petition for a free parliament offensive, as Boys narrates in his 'Vindication of the Kentish declaration' of the same day; unlike some friends, he narrowly escaped imprisonment. On 28 February 1660, with Sir John Boys of Bonnington, a kinsman acclaimed for his defence of the royalist stronghold Donnington Castle, Boys presented 'A letter of thanks to his excellency the L. General Monk' at Whitehall, 'according to the order and advice of east Kent' on the news that excluded members would be returned to parliament. 'A speech' to be delivered on Charles II's landing at Dover on 25 May 1660 'was prevented therein by reason his majesty made no stay at all in that town'; so Boys sent a copy (all these documents were printed at the end of his *Aeneas his Descent into Hell* of 1661, under the title 'Certain pieces relating to the publick').

Boys's principal contributions to the field of letters are his translations in 1661 of books 3 and 6 of Virgil's *Aeneid*: first, *Aeneas his Descent into Hell: as it is Inimitably Described by the Prince of Poets in the Sixth of his Aeneis*, and, second, *Aeneas his Errours, or, His Voyage from Troy into Italy: an Essay upon the Third Book of Virgils Aeneis*. No single separate translation of either of these books had yet appeared, while translations of other single books or parts of the *Aeneid* were common, especially of books 2 and 4. Both translations are accompanied by Boys's commentaries 'wherein all passages Critical, Mythological, Philosophical and Historical, are fully and clearly explained' (title-page, book 6). Boys cites numerous classical commentaries on the body politic and the public weal. His works, full of overt references to contemporary politics and undisguedly royalist, follow Virgil's 'double design': 'the one was (in general) to represent heroical virtue in the person of his most accomplish'd Aeneas'; 'The other was (in particular) to celebrate the Name and Family of Emperor Augustus' ('Preface to the

Reader, book 6'). Before and immediately after the Restoration, most published translations of the *Aeneid* were similarly royalist, or loyalist. Book 6 congratulates Sir Edward Hyde on his succession as lord chancellor, praising his loyalty to the king; book 3 commends Lord Cornbury, Clarendon's son, to follow his father's illustrious example.

Boys's verse compares badly with earlier verse translations of books 3 and 6, by Thomas Phaer, John Vicars, John Ogilby, and James Harrington, while his pentameters are better than Stanyhurst's hexameters. His heroic couplets mostly follow the sense of Virgil's lines; sometimes the rhymes were deemed felicitous enough for imitation by his successors, Richard Maitland and John Dryden. But Boys's ambitions were not poetic. They were purely against 'the fanaticks' in name of the 'sober' royalist cause. In their appreciation of the classical spirit of Virgil and his hero, Aeneas, most translators of the *Aeneid* until the end of the century were similarly dedicated to the public weal. Yet no published version is as bald a statement of commitment or *pietas*, of which the inclusion of those dated and signed documents involving public events at the end of book 6 is a testimony. They 'are monuments of loyalty rather than wit: I was always Master of a better heart than head, and ever gloried more in sincere and honest thoughts, then in trim and adorn'd expressions' (*Aeneas his Descent*, 217). Book 6 ends with a Virgilian-styled epigram in Latin and English, honouring Charles II, and 'A Satyr', both dated 'Canter. Sept. 30. 1656'. The latter appeared as a dedicatory poem in William Somner's *Dictionarium* (1659). Book 6 also has commendatory verses by Boys's cousin Charles Fotherby and Thomas Philipot. Both Somner and Philipot's father, John, acknowledge Boys's learning and antiquarian interests in respectively *Dictionarium* and *Villare Cantianum*. For the latter, published by Thomas as his own in 1659, Boys also wrote a dedicatory poem.

Boys died on 18 March 1661. Like his father and five of his children, including his heir, John, a colonel who was knighted for his services, he was buried in Blean parish church. His wife later married Sir Richard Head, and was buried in Canterbury Cathedral in 1712.

E. M. KNOTTENBELT

Sources parish register, Canterbury Cathedral Archives, U3/100/1/1 · parish registers, Canterbury Cathedral Archives [parishes of Blean (U3/62/1/1), St Mary Northgate (U3/103/1/1), Eythorn (U3/151/1/1)] · W. H. Cooke, ed., *Students admitted to the Inner Temple, 1547–1660* [1878], 308 · H. A. C. Sturgess, ed., *Register of admissions to the Honourable Society of the Middle Temple, from the fifteenth century to the year 1944*, 1 (1949), 96 · J. Foster, *The register of admissions to Gray's Inn, 1521–1889, together with the register of marriages in Gray's Inn chapel, 1695–1754* (privately printed, London, 1889), 156 · J. Venn and J. A. Venn, *Matriculations and degrees, 1544–1659* (1913), 88 · Venn, *Alum. Cant.*, 1/1.195–6 · Foster, *Alum. Oxon.*, 1500–1714, 1.164 · *DNB* · 'Boys, Sir John (1607–1664)', *DNB* [cousin] · 'Boys, Edward (1599–1667)', *DNB* [uncle] · 'Boys, John (1571–1625)', *DNB* [great-uncle, dean of Canterbury] · 'Fotherby, Martin (1549?–1619)', *DNB* [father-in-law, bishop of Salisbury] · 'Rogers, Richard (1532?–1597)', *DNB* [grandmother's father] · 'Somner, William (1598–1669)', *DNB* · 'Philipot, John (1509?–1645)', *DNB* · 'Philipot, Thomas (d. 1682)', *DNB* · E. Hasted, *The history and topographical survey of the county of*

Kent, 1 (1778), iv, 63, 103; 3 (1790), vol. 1, pp. iv, 63, 103; vol. 3, p. 565 · Berry, *County genealogies, Kent* (1830), 438–45 · T. Corser, *Collectanea Anglo-poetica, or, A … catalogue of a … collection of early English poetry*, 2, Chetham Society, 55 (1861), 323–5 · R. C. F. Baker, 'Protestation returns: House of Lords records', transcription in preparation for publication, Institute of Heraldic and Genealogical Studies, Northgate, Canterbury · Cowper, *Memorial inscriptions in Canterbury Cathedral* (1897), 16, 49, 219, 274, 286 · will of Thomas Boys, Canterbury Cathedral Archives, 46, fol. 232 · W. Somner, *The most accurate history of the ancient city and famous cathedral of Canterbury* (1661), 297, 322–3 · W. Somner, *Dictionarium Saxonica-Latino-Anglicanum* (1659) · T. Philipott, *Villare Cantianum* (1659), 61, 124–5, 169–70, 178, 252–3 · Kennet, *Life of Mr Somner* (1693), 37–8, 116–17 · *Fasti Angl., 1541–1857*, [Canterbury], 12, 15, 36 · L. B. Behrens, *Under thirty-seven kings* (1926), esp. 55–63 · IGI

Wealth at death see Berry, *County genealogies*, 440, 445; Hasted, *The history*, vol. 3, p. 565

Boys, John (1749–1824), agriculturist, only son of William Boys of Barham, Kent, and Ann, daughter of William Cooper of Ripple, was born in November 1749. He had a farm at Betshanger, near Deal, Kent, and later at Each, Kent, and was a successful farmer, well known for his breed of Southdown sheep.

Boys was one of the commissioners of sewers for east Kent, and did much to promote the drainage of the Finglesham and Eastry Brooks. At the request of the board of agriculture he wrote *A General View of the Agriculture of the County of Kent* (1796), followed by *An Essay on Paring and Burning* (1805). He was much quoted in encyclopaedias, and his books were translated into French and widely circulated in France. He also contributed to Arthur Young's *Annals of Agriculture* (1784).

In 1774 Boys married Mary, daughter of the Revd Richard Harvey, former vicar of Eastry-cum-Word. They had eight sons, including Edward *Boys, naval officer, and five daughters. Boys died on 16 December 1824 at Wingham, Kent.

T. F. HENDERSON, *rev.* ANNE PIMLOTT BAKER

Sources GM, 1st ser., 95/1 (1825), 86–7 · W. Berry, *County genealogies: pedigrees of the families in the county of Kent* (1830)

Boys, Thomas (1792–1880), biblical scholar and writer, was born on 17 June 1792 at Sandwich, Kent, the only son of Rear-Admiral Thomas Boys of Kent. He was educated at Tonbridge grammar school and entered Trinity College, Cambridge, on 13 October 1808. He was made a scholar and a Smythe exhibitioner in 1810, and graduated BA (1813) and MA (1817). After university he entered the army with a view to becoming a military chaplain. He was active under Wellington in 1813 in the Peninsular War, was wounded at the battle of Toulouse, and gained the Peninsular medal. After his return Boys was ordained deacon, in 1816, and priest, in 1822. On 8 January 1822 he married a Miss Somers, of High Wycombe, Buckinghamshire. While in the Peninsula he had translated the Bible into Portuguese so accurately that his version was adopted there by Catholics and protestants alike, and Don Pedro I of Portugal publicly thanked him for his gift to the nation.

Boys soon established a reputation as a prolific writer and a Hebrew scholar. In 1821 he issued a volume of sermons, which was followed in 1824 by *Tactica sacra*, a book expounding a theory that there were similarities between the arrangement of New Testament writings and the parallelism used in writings of the Jewish prophets. In 1825 he published *A Key to the Book of Psalms* (reissued as *A Key to the Psalms*, edited by E. W. Bullinger, in 1890), and in 1827 he wrote *A Plain Exposition of the New Testament*. Drawing inspiration from B. W. Noel's *Remarks on the Revival of Miraculous Powers in the Church*, he published *The Suppressed Evidence* in 1832, and in 1844 he brought out his first work of history, *Protestantism in Papal Europe*. Boys also taught ancient Hebrew to Jewish students at Hackney College, Middlesex, from 1830 to 1832, and he became professor of Hebrew at the Missionary College, Islington, in 1836; while holding this last post, he revised several versions of the Vulgate, including Deodati's Italian Bible and the Arabic Bible.

Boys was a frequent contributor to *Blackwood's Edinburgh Magazine*, where he published sketches and papers, including 'My Peninsular medal', which was serialized from November 1849 to July 1850. In 1848 he was appointed vicar of Holy Trinity, Hoxton, London. In addition to the many learned papers which he published under his own name, he also used the pseudonym 'Vedette'. As well as writing about history, Hebrew scholarship, and his military experiences, he also wrote twelve papers on Chaucer and contributed to *Notes and Queries*. Boys died at his home, 23 Leighton Road, Kentish Town, London, on 2 September 1880. His daughter, Frances Georgiana, survived him. RONALD BAYNE, *rev.* SINÉAD AGNEW

Sources Venn, *Alum. Cant.* • Boase, *Mod. Eng. biog.* • Ward, *Men of the reign*, 104 • *The Times* (13 Sept 1880), 8 • *The Times* (14 Sept 1880), 8 • Allibone, *Dict.* • J. Hutchinson, *Men of Kent and Kentishism* (1892) • *Men of the time* (1875) • CGPLA Eng. & Wales (1880) • GM, 1st ser., 92/1 (1822), 176

Wealth at death under £600: administration, 17 Sept 1880, CGPLA Eng. & Wales

Boys, Thomas Shotter (1803–1874), topographical watercolour painter and printmaker, was born on 2 January 1803 at Pentonville, near London, the son of a salesman. He was apprenticed on 4 February 1817 to the London engraver George Cooke. His earliest recorded prints are an etching of 1823 after an antique vase in Baron Denon's collection, which he exhibited at the Society of British Artists the following year, and an engraving after Claude Lorrain's *Cephalus and Procris Reunited by Diana* (National Gallery, London). When his apprenticeship to Cooke ended in 1823 Boys moved to Paris where he soon became the protégé and companion of the British artist Richard Parkes Bonington. Bonington introduced Boys to a circle of influential patrons, artists, and literati which included Eugène Delacroix, Baron Charles Rivet, and Prosper Merimée. Boys continued to work for Cooke, and he exhibited four reproductive engravings at the Paris Salon of 1827–8, but as his friendship with Bonington intensified, his professional interests shifted from engraving to watercolour painting. It was undoubtedly from Bonington that he learned the subtleties of this technique, which he later imparted to his own pupils William Callow, Ambrose Poynter, and Edward John Poynter. Boys, in turn, may

have instructed both Bonington and the French landscape painter Paul Huet in the art of etching.

While many of Boys's earliest watercolours tend to be copies of other artists' works, especially Bonington's popular Parisian and Italian subjects, he eventually developed an independent and original style within a few years of Bonington's death in 1828. His most enduring achievements are the hundreds of *plein-air* and finished watercolours that date to his years of residence in Paris from 1831 to 1837. By submitting many of these to public exhibitions, he contributed to the revival of watercolour painting in France. At the 1833 Salon Boys exhibited seven watercolour views of Paris, Venice, Rouen, Chester, and Salisbury Cathedral—the last now at the Yale Center for British Art. His address at the time, 19 rue de Bouloy, was the same as that of Callow and the French artists Pierre-Jules Jollivet, Pierre-Toussaint-Frédéric Mialhe, and Henri-Joseph, baron de Triqueti. The last's manuscript catalogue of Bonington's prints, preserved in the library of the École des Beaux-Arts, Paris, claims that Boys finished Bonington's only etching, *Bologna, the Leaning Towers*.

In 1834 Boys again exhibited at the Paris Salon three watercolour views of Béthune and Paris. During the 1830s he also mastered the art of lithography. Between 1833 and 1845 Boys was a mainstay of the *Picardie* and *Languedoc* volumes of Baron Isidore Taylor's magisterial *Voyages pittoresques et romantiques dans l'ancienne France*. He also collaborated with A. Rouargue in the publication of *Architecture pittoresque dessinée d'après nature* (1835). As early as 1830 Boys had envisioned a series of etched views of Paris to rival Thomas Girtin's *Picturesque Views of Paris and its Environs* (1803), but the project was abandoned in favour of a publication in 1839 of twenty-six chromolithographs titled *Picturesque Architecture in Paris, Ghent, Antwerp, Rouen, etc.* published by Charles Hullmandel. This series of landscape and architectural views, derived from Boys's own watercolours and produced with the technical assistance of Hullmandel, ranks as one of the most innovative ventures in the history of printmaking. It brought Boys both a modicum of international celebrity and a commendation from King Louis-Philippe. He published his lithographic *Series of Views in York* (1841) the same year he was elected a full member of the New Watercolour Society, where he exhibited annually until the year of his death. Equally successful was his publication *Original Views of London as It Is* (1842), which introduced a vivacity previously unknown in the architectural delineation of this metropolis. He was now at the apex of his powers and popularity. In 1842–3 he made several excursions to Germany and to Prague in an effort to expand his repertoire of landscape subjects. He also painted a few oils at this time such as *Greenwich from Observatory Hill* (exh. Society of British Artists, 1858). Like so many of the landscape draughtsmen of his generation, Boys had modelled his style on Bonington's virtuoso handling and brilliant colouring. As his career progressed, however, he seemed incapable of changing this style to accommodate the public's increasing demand for larger, more highly detailed paintings. By 1850 Boys had spent his creative capital, and his financial fortunes began a steady and steep decline. For the last twenty years of his life he worked intermittently as a drawing master and a reproductive lithographer in London, but he died in oblivion and near poverty on 10 October 1874 at 30 Acacia Road, St John's Wood, leaving a widow, Celestine Marie Barbe Boys. It is one of the tragedies in the history of British art and printmaking that Thomas Shotter Boys was unable to sustain the great promise of his work of the 1830s.

Boys was prolific, and his watercolours grace most of the public collections in England. In North America, the Yale Center for British Art owns a large and representative group, while the Houghton Library, Harvard University, has many of the working drawings and tracings for *London as It Is* and *Picturesque Architecture in Paris, Ghent, Antwerp, Rouen, etc.* PATRICK NOON

Sources Bryan, *Painters* (1866) · W. Callow, *William Callow, RWS, FRGS: an autobiography*, ed. H. M. Cundall (1908) · H. Stokes, 'Thomas Shotter Boys', *Walker's Quarterly* [whole issue], 18 [1926] · E. B. Chancellor, '*Original views of London as it is*' by *Thomas Shotter Boys* (1926) · E. B. Chancellor, '*Picturesque architecture*' by *Thomas Shotter Boys* (1928) · *R. P. Bonington and his circle*, Burlington Fine Arts Club (1937) · J. R. Abbey, *Travel in aquatint and lithography, 1770–1860*, 2 vols. (1956–7) · G. von Groschwitz, 'The prints of Thomas Shotter Boys', *Prints*, ed. C. Zigrosser (1962), 191–215 · M. L. Twyman, *Lithography, 1800–1850* (1970) · J. Roundell, *Thomas Shotter Boys* (1974) · *Thomas Shotter Boys* (1974) [exhibition catalogue, Nottingham University Art Gallery] · P. Noon, 'Bonington and Boys: some unpublished documents at Yale', *Burlington Magazine*, 123 (1981), 294–300 · M. Pointon, *The Bonington circle: English watercolour and Anglo-French landscape, 1790–1855* (1985) · P. Noon, *Richard Parkes Bonington: on the pleasure of painting* (1991) [exhibition catalogue, Yale U. CBA and the Petit Palais, Paris] · *CGPLA Eng. & Wales* (1874)
Likenesses E. A. Lessore, ceramic plaque, 1856, NPG
Wealth at death under £100: administration, 26 Oct 1874, *CGPLA Eng. & Wales*

Boys, William (1700–1774), naval officer, was born at Deal on 25 June 1700, the eldest son of William Boys (d. 1756?), a woollen draper, and his wife, Jane Laurence (d. before 1756). His parents were devout nonconformists, and Boys was initially educated for the ministry; however, the passing of the 1714 Schism Act caused a change of plan, and that same year he went to sea in a merchant ship. Three years later he joined the Royal Navy for a voyage to the East Indies as a midshipman in the *Prince Frederick*. In 1725 he shipped as second mate of the South Sea Company's slaver the *Luxborough Galley*. On 25 June 1727, homeward-bound from the West Indies, the ship was lost by fire in mid-Atlantic. Boys and twenty-two others escaped in a sixteen-foot open boat without food or water. After thirteen days six of them had survived to reach Newfoundland by living on the bodies of their dead shipmates.

This horrific experience confirmed Boys in his austere piety, and for the rest of his life he fasted and prayed in memory of his deliverance between 25 June and 7 July every year. Boys returned to England and then went to work for a while as a factor on a West India plantation; he next re-entered the navy as a master's mate on the flagship in the Downs. On 5 May 1735 he was promoted lieutenant. By 1739 he was second lieutenant of the *Dunkirk*,

which in 1741 was sent to reinforce Admiral Vernon's forces in the West Indies. On 8 June 1741 Vernon made him commander of the fireship *Aetna* at William Pulteney's request, and sent him home with dispatches. He then commanded the sloop *Baltimore*, and on 25 June 1743 became captain of the frigate *Greyhound*. He took command of the *Princess Louisa* (60 guns) in 1744 and next year went to the East Indies again, this time in the *Pearl* (40 guns).

At the outbreak of the next war in 1755 Boys became flag-captain of Vice-Admiral Thomas Smith's flagship the *Royal Sovereign* in the Downs. In 1759 he was made a commodore under Smith's command in the *Preston* (50 guns), watching Dunkirk. After the French privateer François Thurot escaped with a small squadron on 15 October, Boys pursued him northwards, for a while cruised off Scotland, and on his return was made commander-in-chief at the Nore. On 4 July 1761 he retired from sea service to be lieutenant-governor of Greenwich Hospital, and he was still in this post when he died on 4 March 1774 while visiting his children in Deal. He and his wife, Elizabeth Pearson of Deal, are buried beside his parents at the Congregational chapel there, where he had been baptized. His eldest son, William *Boys, was a surgeon and topographer; his eldest daughter, Jane, married another; his son Pearson followed him into the navy but never rose above lieutenant; and his daughter Elizabeth married the future Admiral Sir Henry Harvey.

A fine seaman, an efficient and hard-working administrator, and a shrewd judge of men, Boys was particularly in his element as Smith's flag-captain in the Downs, within a mile of his birthplace; his extensive knowledge of the local waters and the local people (especially the Deal pilots and smugglers, overlapping categories, several of whom were his kinsmen) was of great usefulness. As a pious nonconformist who entered the navy from the merchant service while in his thirties and rose on merit alone to be a commander-in-chief, he made a career which would have been typical of the state's navy under Cromwell, and showed it was still feasible under George II.

N. A. M. RODGER

Sources W. Boys, *An account of the loss of the Luxborough Galley* (1787) · copy of Boys's own narrative of the loss of the *Luxborough Galley* with an attached biographical notice compiled by his daughter, Elizabeth Harvey, NMM, MS 81/041 [uncatalogued] · J. Charnock, ed., *Biographia navalis*, 5 (1797), 233–9 · S. Pritchard, *The history of Deal* (1864), 190–91 · *The Vernon papers*, ed. B. McL. Ranft, Navy RS, 99 (1958), 249 · lieutenant's passing certificate, PRO, ADM 107/3, p. 248 · will, PRO, PROB 11/995, fol. 282 · PRO, ADM 1/655, 715–17, 927 and 1487 [includes Boys's official corresp. with the admiralty, 1756–60] · will, CKS, PRC 32/64/69 [William Boys senior] · PRO, RG4/1003, fol. 15v · L. Boys Behrens, *Love smugglers and naval heroes: being historical notes of the eighteenth century* (1929)
Archives PRO, official corresp. with admiralty, ADM 1/655, 715–717, 927, 1487
Likenesses stipple, NMM
Wealth at death left £4700 in consols and South Sea stock: will, PRO, PROB 11/995, fol. 282

Boys, William (1735–1803), surgeon and topographer, was born in Deal, Kent, on 7 September 1735, the eldest son of Commodore William *Boys (1700–1774), afterwards lieutenant-governor of Greenwich Hospital, and Elizabeth Pearson of Deal. He practised as a surgeon in Sandwich and devoted much of his spare time to literature and scientific research. Descended from an ancient Kent family, he added to the distinguished reputation of the Sandwich branch of the Boys family by working as a historian. As his home, the White Friars, was within a mile of Richborough Castle, the Roman Rutupium, he naturally investigated its history. He also became renowned for deciphering ancient manuscripts and inscriptions, for zealously collecting antiquities connected with Sandwich, and for his studies in astronomy, natural history, and mathematics.

In 1759 Boys married Elizabeth (1738–1761), daughter of Henry Wise, a Sandwich jurat; they had two children. In 1761 he was elected jurat and acted with his wife's father; in the same year Elizabeth died. The following year he married Jane Fuller (d. 1783), coheir of her uncle, John Paramor of Statenborough; they had eight children. In 1767 Boys was elected mayor of Sandwich. In his first publication, published anonymously at Canterbury in 1775, he presented the case for Sandwich against a parliamentary bill to enable the commissioners of sewers to make the Stonar Cut, which it was thought would destroy Sandwich harbour. In 1776 he was elected FSA and in 1782 he again served as mayor. He was also a magistrate and was prominent in the public business of his town and neighbourhood.

In the same year as the death of Boys's second wife, 1783, John Duncombe published his *Antiquities of Reculver*, which included much information that had been supplied by Boys. In 1784 *Testacea minuta rariora* was published, which contained plates and descriptions of the tiny shells found by Boys on the seashore near Sandwich. The book was put together by George Walker as Boys was too preoccupied with his profession. None the less, in 1786 Boys issued proposals for publishing his *Collections for a History of Sandwich* at a price to cover only its expenses, and placed his materials in the hands of the printers in Canterbury. The first part appeared in 1788 but there was considerable delay and anxiety over the second and final part, which was eventually published in 1792 but at great pecuniary loss to Boys. This is the work for which he is best known and it occupied the principal part of his life. A quarto volume of 877 pages, it is an outstanding book which was compiled and edited with great knowledge and ability, illustrated beautifully by the author himself. It is notable for a chapter on natural history and for recording the results of his exhaustive explorations of Richborough Castle.

In 1787 Boys published his *Account of the Loss of the Luxborough*, reporting a case of cannibalism, in which his father had been one of the men compelled to resort to the extreme of cannibalism in order to preserve life. Thomas Pennant recorded that in his parlour Boys hung a series of pictures portraying the terrible circumstances. The account appears in full in the *History of Greenwich Hospital* (1789) by John Cooke and John Maule. In 1792 Boys sent Dr Simmons his 'Observations on Kit's Coity House', which,

being read at the Society of Antiquaries, appeared in volume 11 of *Archaeologia*. Despite increasing ill health and having led a busy life, Boys was prominent among an army of helpers to the great Kent historian Edward Hasted. He undertook detailed fieldwork in east Kent, which was conveyed and used by Hasted. They subsequently corresponded, became estranged, and then were reconciled. Described as calm, stolid, and full of facts, Boys partnered William Boteler as Hasted's main support in completing the first edition of his *History of Kent* under immense difficulties. Boys was a member of the Linnean Society and contributed frequently to the *Gentleman's Magazine*. A new tern found by him at Sandwich was named Sterna Boysii after him by Latham in his *Index ornithologicus*. In 1789 Boys had been appointed surgeon to the sick and wounded seamen at Deal and in 1796 he gave up his Sandwich practice to live in Walmer, but returned to Sandwich in 1799. His health having declined, he suffered apoplectic attacks in 1799 and died of apoplexy on 15 March 1803, aged sixty-seven. He was buried in St Clement's Church, Sandwich, where there is a Latin epitaph to his memory.

JENNETT HUMPHREYS, rev. JOHN WHYMAN

Sources A. Winnifrith, *Men of Kent and Kentish Men: biographical notices of 680 worthies of Kent* (1913), 88–9 · J. Simson, *Eminent men of Kent* (1893), 131 · J. Boyle, *In quest of Hasted* (1984), 16, 18, 19, 20, 26, 27, 30, 32, 33, 41, 43, 45, 46, 67, 127 · F. W. Cook, 'Kentish bibliographical notes', *Archaeologia Cantiana*, 41 (1929), 175–9, esp. 177–8 · F. W. Hardman, 'Stonar and the Wantsum Channel, pt 1: physiographical', *Archaeologia Cantiana*, 53 (1941), 62–80, esp. 69 · C. Matson, 'William Rolfe: a noted Sandwich antiquarian', *Archaeologia Cantiana*, 76 (1961), 180–85, esp. 181–2 · C. Matson, 'Men of Kent, pt 1: boys of Bonnington', *Archaeologia Cantiana*, 79 (1964), 70–76, esp. 74 · C. Matson, 'Men of Kent, pt 2: Harvey of Eastry', *Archaeologia Cantiana*, 80 (1965), 98–106, esp. 101 · F. Hull, 'The coming of the barons, 1403', *Archaeologia Cantiana*, 87 (1972), 1–8, esp. 1 · J. Boyle, 'Sand discoveries about Edward Hasted and his *History of Kent*', *Archaeologia Cantiana*, 97 (1981), 235–59, esp. 241–5, 249, 256 · E. W. Parkin, 'The ancient Cinque Port of Sandwich', *Archaeologia Cantiana*, 100 (1984), 189–216, esp. 189 · J. Boyle, 'Hasted in perspective', *Archaeologia Cantiana*, 100 (1984), 295–304, esp. 298, 303 · *GM*, 1st ser., 73 (1803), 293, 421–3 · Nichols, *Illustrations*, 4.676; 6.613, 653, 685, 687 · E. Hasted, *The history and topographical survey of the county of Kent*, 2nd edn, 10 (1800), 111, 113, 441 · Nichols, *Lit. anecdotes*, 9.24–7nn.

Archives BL, family papers, Add. MSS 33896, 34106, 44918, 45389, 45499–45505 · CKS, notes and extracts relating to the history of Kent · East Kent Archives Centre, Dover, notes and extracts relating to history of Sandwich · Linn. Soc., drawings of molluscs | Warks. CRO, letters to Thomas Pennant

Likenesses portrait, Sandwich Guildhall, Mayor's parlour

Boyse, Joseph (1660–1728), Presbyterian minister and religious writer, was born at Leeds on 14 January 1660, one of sixteen children of Matthew Boyse, clothesworker, and Elizabeth Jackson. His father was a puritan and former elder of the church at Rowley, New England, and was afterwards resident for about eighteen years at Boston, Massachusetts, before returning to Leeds. On 16 April 1675 Joseph Boyse entered Richard Frankland's academy at Kendal and in 1678 studied at Edward Veal's academy in Stepney. In 1679 he began to preach at Glassenbury, near Cranbrook, in Kent, and ministered there for almost a year. In 1681 he became domestic chaplain to the dowager countess of Donegal in Lincoln's Inn Fields, and in 1682 ministered for six months in the Brownist church in Amsterdam, though retaining his Presbyterian principles. But for the penal laws he would have settled in England. In 1683, on the death of his friend Timothy Haliday, he was persuaded to succeed him in Dublin as colleague to Dr Daniel Williams, then minister of Wood Street. When Williams resigned in 1687 Boyse remained, and here he continued to exercise his ministry for the remaining forty-one years of his life. In 1699 he married Rachel Ibbetson of Leeds; they had three children: Samuel *Boyse, who became a gifted poet; Joseph, who probably died in infancy; and a daughter, who married a Mr Waddington.

Boyse's ordination sermon in Dublin was preached by John Pinney, ejected from Broadwindsor, Dorset. During the greater part of his ministry Boyse was a noted advocate of the Presbyterian cause, defending Presbyterian rights and liberties, and setting forth the teachings of the Christian faith in sermons and pamphlet literature. Early on he came into conflict with William King, chancellor of St Patrick's Cathedral, Dublin, and subsequently bishop of Derry and archbishop of Dublin. King had attacked the Presbyterians in his 'Answer' to Peter Manby, a former dean of Derry who had converted to Catholicism. This led Boyse to publish his first work, *Vindiciae Calvinisticae*, in 1688, in which he rejected King's definition of the church as those who profess the religion of Christ and live under lawful spiritual governors, insisting that the true church can only be defined in relation to the truth for which it stands. Though forcefully argued, Boyse's pamphlet breathed an eirenical spirit, and concluded with a plea for co-operation and mutual respect between episcopal and reformed churches in spite of deep differences of judgement and practice.

Boyse was to cross swords with King again. In 1690 he published an important political pamphlet vindicating the Revd Alexander Osborne of Newmarket from a charge against him by Walker, governor of Derry, that he was Tyrconnell's spy. An interesting printed letter is extant in the British Library entitled *Great News from the Camp before Limrick in a Letter from J. Boyse of Dublin to Tho. Parkhurst*. It is dated 28 August 1690 and claims to be the 'last letter from Limrick that can be given credit to' (*Great News from the Camp before Limrick*, 1690). It contains many vivid details of the siege. In 1693 he published a volume entitled *Sacramental Hymns* intended to supplement the psalter at communion services. In 1694 and 1695 Boyse resumed his controversy with King, who had tried to prove to the dissenters in the diocese of Derry that their ways of worship, and not those of the established church, fell short of what scripture taught. In his *Remarks* (1694) Boyse produced a major work of controversy, ably answering King's arguments and demonstrating factual inaccuracies. King replied by publishing a second edition of his work, together with a further *Admonition*. Boyse responded with *A Vindication of the 'Remarks'* (1695). Both works contain a wealth of fascinating information about congregational life and worship among the dissenters in Ireland, both north and south. Boyse was now firmly established as a

formidable and scholarly controversialist, and a liberal-minded dissenter in the tradition of Richard Baxter, whose works he so often quoted.

The year 1695 was one of considerable literary activity on Boyse's part, including a sermon on the death of Queen Mary and two pamphlets arguing the case for a bill of indulgences for the dissenters. This marked the beginning of his involvement in the campaign to repeal the Test Acts. His pamphlet of 1695, *The Case of the Protestant Dissenters in Ireland*, argued strongly against the illogicality of the current toleration *de facto* but not *de jure*, and pleaded the excellent service rendered by dissenters during the revolution. It takes strong theological exception to Anglican communion being made a test for civil and military office. In answer to two replies from Tobias Pullen, bishop of Dromore, and Anthony Dopping, bishop of Meath, Boyse published *The Case of the Protestant Dissenters—Vindicated*. The position of the dissenters worsened after the Test Act of 1704. Threat of rebellion in 1715 led to a number of dissenters defying the law and endeavouring to serve the crown. A bitter attack on them by Dr William Tisdal, vicar of Belfast, elicited a reply from Boyse in 1716 entitled *Remarks on a Pamphlet Issued by William Tisdal DD*. The issue was to remain a pressing one for the dissenters until the passing of the Toleration Act of 1719 which, although it fell short of their ultimate hopes, was clearly the most they could get at that time.

Boyse's sermon before the Societies for the Reformation of Manners was published in 1698. In 1701 he published *Family Hymns for Morning and Evening Worship*, all of them based on psalms, and including a melody line and bass part.

Boyse entered into the controversy precipitated by the case of Thomas Emlyn, who had been appointed as Boyse's colleague at Wood Street in 1691, and who, unknown to Boyse, or to the congregation, had parted company with the orthodox doctrines of the Trinity and the person of Christ, and had become an Arian. For eleven years he exercised a popular ministry in Wood Street, but one member of his congregation, a physician, who for a time had studied theology, became concerned at consistent omissions in Emlyn's preaching and, after having discussed the matter with Boyse, he and Boyse confronted him with their suspicions. Emlyn readily admitted his convictions, but Boyse felt the matter must be brought before the Dublin ministers, who decided to depose him. Emlyn insisted on writing an account of what had happened, and later published his *Humble Inquiry into the Scripture Account of the Lord Jesus Christ* (1702). As a result Emlyn was tried and convicted of blasphemy and imprisoned from 16 June 1703 until 21 July 1705. Boyse set out to defend the orthodox doctrine in *A Vindication of the True Deity of our Blessed Saviour* (1703). In his very first work Boyse had spoken out against Socinianism, and in a letter written to Robert Wodrow in 1720 there is clear evidence that his abhorrence of those who denied the Trinity remained unaltered.

Boyse also published funeral sermons on the death of Elias Travers (1705) and of William Cairns (1707). In 1708 he brought out a two-volume edition of some of his sermons. The most controversial was 'The office of a scriptural bishop', which drew forth a reply from two Dublin curates, Edward Drury and Matthew French. The sermon was printed separately in 1709 and Boyse added a lengthy postscript in which he replied to the two clergy. This work had the distinction of being burned by the common hangman by order of the Irish House of Lords in November 1711. He continued the controversy on ministerial orders in 1712 by a lengthy work entitled *A Clear Account of the Ancient Episcopacy*, in which he sought to defend the reformed doctrine of ministry. The death of Queen Anne and the accession of George I in 1714 led to the publication of two sermons, while in 1716 he published a funeral sermon for Sir Arthur Langford and an ordination sermon for Dr John Leland, disappointing in that it says nothing about Leland, who was to become a man of such eminence.

Boyse was consistently opposed to Roman Catholicism. In the years 1687 and 1688 he had preached about the principal points of difference and composed a catechism (now lost) for his young people to highlight these concerns. In 1718 he launched an attack upon Catholicism in a sermon entitled *Popery Proved to be a Different Gospel*, together with a lengthy preface.

Boyse also became deeply involved in the struggle over subscription, which was to monopolize the debates of the synod of Ulster for nearly a decade. He was present at the synod in Belfast in 1721 as a commissioner from Dublin. In 1721, together with Nathanael Weld and Richard Choppin, Boyse wrote a letter to Dr Victor Ferguson, secretary of the Belfast Society. In 1722 Boyse's was the major hand in a preface to John Abernethy's *Seasonable Advice* and in the later *Postscript* (1724). Both works plead for charity and offer a *via media* solution. Boyse and his friends were concerned for the preservation of doctrinal orthodoxy while at the same time wanting charity and comprehensiveness to be the marks of ecclesiastical fellowship.

Boyse preached at the 1722 synod in Londonderry, and the sermon was published in 1723 in a personal letter to the northern ministers pleading with them not to sever connections with their non-subscribing brethren. In 1724 he published funeral sermons for Mrs Mary Choppin and Dr Duncan Cumyng, and a volume of sermons entitled *Discourses on the Four Last Things*. He then published a *Vindication of a Private Letter* (1726) in answer to John McBride's charges that the Dublin ministers were partisan and working for the non-subscribers. It reflects not only Boyse's own views on subscription but his deep personal sorrow at the course of events that inevitably was to end in rupture. The last work he himself was to publish was a sermon preached in 1727, *The Sole Headship of Christ*, in opposition to the claims of Roman Catholicism.

The zenith of Boyse's career as a writer came only a few months before his death with the publication of his collected works by a London press. They occupy two huge folios usually bound as one, and are the earliest, if not the only, folios published by a Presbyterian minister in Ireland. The volumes went out with a recommendation signed by Edmund Calamy and a number of other London

ministers. They contain a number of important sermons and treatises not hitherto published, as well as omitting one or two works. At the end of the first volume there are two works of great significance on the doctrine of justification revealing a close affinity between Boyse's theology and that of Richard Baxter. Early in his own career some of the Dublin ministers had charged Boyse with Pelagianism. The charge had evidently been answered satisfactorily. On the issues of justification and election, however, it is clear that Boyse, like Baxter, stood for a modification of Calvinism, and this difference in emphasis and direction brought him into conflict with the authoritarian views of some of his contemporaries. In the second volume, as well as two pieces on the Roman controversy, there is a fascinating attack on the Quakers, which called forth a reply shortly before Boyse's death from a Dublin schoolmaster, Samuel Fuller.

To survey Boyse's writing is to be impressed not only by the range of its subject matter but by the breadth of his learning and skill as a debater. While often polemical, he produced excellent pastoral and devotional material. His warm humanity and sincere personal grief over the bitter divisions of his latter years are reflected not only in his formal writings but in what personal correspondence has survived, notably his letters to Ralph Thoresby of Leeds. It would also appear that some sort of personal memoir had been written by Boyse himself, and valuable quotations from it are made in Choppin's funeral sermon.

Boyse's final years were marked by increasing ill health and by sadness at the irresponsible behaviour of Samuel, his son. For several months before the end he was unable to carry out his duties. He died in Dublin on 22 November 1728.

Boyse was a most conscientious pastor and preacher. He did not possess the natural gifts of a clear, strong voice, nor skills of elocution, yet his preaching had a deep effect upon his hearers. His sermons were well argued and firmly based upon the exposition of scripture which was a hallmark of the puritan tradition. Like Baxter he was comprehensive in his churchmanship. Indeed southern Presbyterianism, with its more English ethos, had a less rigid view of church government than was the case in Scotland and the north of Ireland.

Boyse had a passion for theological education. He himself was a product of the dissenting academies and was a 'patron' of the academy of Dr Thomas Dixon in Whitehaven. In co-operation with the other Dublin ministers he helped to provide training in divinity for students, and was instrumental in setting up an academy in Dublin and attracting as its teacher the brilliant Francis Hutcheson.

Boyse played a significant part in the life of Dublin, giving with a generosity that exhausted his slender means, encouraging reformation of manners, and speaking out on behalf of French protestant refugees. He composed the Latin inscription on the original pedestal (1701) of the equestrian statue of William III that once occupied a place of prominence in College Green, Dublin.

One of the ironies of history is that a man of such eminence, who was referred to by contemporaries as 'the great Mr Boyse', should be so largely forgotten by historians of Irish Presbyterianism until recent times. Perhaps it was his unpopular stand in the subscription controversy or the fact that he stood largely outside the dominant Ulster Scots ethos of later Irish Presbyterianism. Perhaps it lay in the fact that the age that followed was weary of doctrinal controversy, and in such an age the liberal puritanism of Boyse may well have seemed largely irrelevant.

A. W. GODFREY BROWN

Sources DNB · R. Choppin, *A funeral sermon occasion'd by the death of Mr Joseph Boyse* (1728) · A. W. G. Brown, *The great Mr Boyse* (1988) · T. Witherow, *Historical and literary memorials of presbyterianism in Ireland, 1623–1731* (1879) · J. S. Reid and W. D. Killen, *History of the Presbyterian church in Ireland*, new edn, 2–3 (1867) · [J. Hunter], ed., *Letters of eminent men, addressed to Ralph Thoresby*, 2 vols. (1832) · *Diary of Ralph Thoresby FRS*, ed. J. Hunter, 2 vols. (1830) · T. Emlyn, *Works*, 14th edn, 3 vols. (1746), 1 · G. Mathews, *An account of the trial … of … Thomas Emlyn* (1839) · *Records of the General Synod of Ulster, from 1691 to 1820*, 3 vols. (1890–98) · J. Armstrong, 'An appendix, containing some account of the Presbyterian churches in Dublin', in J. Armstrong and others, *Ordination service … of the Rev. James Martineau* (1829)

Archives BL, corresp. with T. Steward · W. Yorks. AS, Leeds, Yorkshire Archaeological Society, letters to Ralph Thoresby

Wealth at death reputed to have died in 'straitened circumstances': DNB

Boyse, Samuel (1702/3?–1749), poet, son of Joseph *Boyse (1660–1728), a dissenting minister, and his wife, Rachel (*née* Ibbetson), was born in Dublin and educated at a private school there. He was said to have been eighteen when he entered Glasgow University, where he was an undergraduate by February 1721, the year in which his elegy on the theologian John Anderson (1668–1721) was published. His father probably intended him for the Presbyterian ministry, but, under-age, he married a tradesman's daughter, Emilia Atchenson, and abandoned his studies. He returned to Dublin with his wife and her sister, where they sponged on Joseph until his death in November 1728. Samuel's young daughter died in 1726 and was mourned in his verse. He wrote a letter on liberty in James Arbuckle's *Dublin Weekly Journal* (11 February 1727).

Boyse went to Edinburgh, where his collection *Translations and Poems* (1731), dedicated to the countess of Eglinton, attracted over 250 subscribers. Some poems were 'sacred to conjugal love' and addressed to his wife in Ireland, though it was said that Boyse knew she was having affairs. Boyse found patrons among members of the Scottish nobility to whom he dedicated several separately published poems, but he was unresponsive to their offers of help. Shiels said that the duchess of Gordon gave Boyse an introduction for a post in the customs, but the day on which he should have presented himself was stormy, so he chose to lose the post rather than face the rain. This may be an embellishment of the fact that Boyse refused an offered post in the excise because its duties required 'a Strength and Application beyond my Capacity' and because he believed his education fitted him for more respectable callings, such as nobleman's secretary or librarian, or grand-tour tutor (Boyse to Sir John Clerk, 24 May 1733).

Debts drove Boyse from Edinburgh after 1734. He went to London, but failed to take advantage of introductions to influential men such as Alexander Pope and the future Lord Mansfield. Boyse's wife, with at least one child, had rejoined him, though the pair followed irregular courses to the extent that both were poxed by different partners. Begging letters, including many to eminent dissenters who were friends and admirers of Boyse's father, together with verse writing, much of it for magazines, provided the family's uncertain income. For instance: in 1737 *The Olive, an Heroic Ode* earned Boyse 10 guineas from its dedicatee, Sir Robert Walpole; in 1738 Robert Dodsley gave him only 2 guineas for translations from Voltaire; and in 1739 Boyse's follow-up begging letter to Sir Hans Sloane asked him to replace the bad shilling he had given to Mrs Boyse the night before. Shiels saw Boyse when he had pawned his clothes and

> sat up in bed with the blanket wrapt about him, through which he had cut a hole large enough to admit his arm, and placing the paper upon his knee, scribbled in the best manner he could the verses he was obliged to make. (Shiels, 5.169)

At this time, though, Boyse wrote his best work. His *Deity* (1739), a long poem in heroic couplets on the attributes of God, shows a firm religious conviction and an intellectual strength quite out of keeping with the disorder of its author's life.

Boyse published a second collection, *Translations and Poems* (1738) and continued as a hack. Throughout the summer of 1740 he was employed by Edward Cave in French translation, which his friend Samuel Johnson said he did well; in the following winter he could find only the slavish labour of index making. Then he modernized two of Chaucer's *Canterbury Tales* for 3d. a line in George Ogle's edition (1741). Most of Boyse's poems appeared fugitively in journals, but *The Praise of Peace*, translated from the Dutch (1742), and *Albion's Triumph*, on the victory at Dettingen (1743), achieved separate publication. In July 1742, arrested for debt, he wrote a desperate letter to Cave and obtained half a guinea on account for *The Praise of Peace* and 'The Triumphs of Nature' (on Stowe gardens). Cave paid Boyse by the hundred lines, later requiring him to produce what he called the 'long hundred'; Boyse signed his work in the *Gentleman's Magazine* 'Y' or Alcaeus. Three begging letters of 1744 are printed in *Notes and Queries* (March 1986, 78–80). This was the pattern of his entire literary life. He squandered what little he had, so was still obliged to pawn his clothes from time to time, but was ingenious enough to invent a paper collar and cuffs to conceal his lack of a shirt in public. Johnson once collected money to redeem Boyse's clothes, which two days later were pawned again. 'The sum (said Johnson) was collected by sixpences, at a time when to me sixpence was a serious consideration' (Boswell, *Life*, 4.407n.).

Boyse had some connection with Reading, Berkshire. His *Miscellaneous Works … for the Amusement of the Fair Sex* was published there in 1740, and one of its light amatory poems was addressed to 'The Reading Muses'. Emilia Boyse died in Reading some time between 1745 and June

1747, and was buried at the expense of the parish. Her widower, unable to afford mourning clothes, tied half a yard of black ribbon round the neck of the lap-dog that he carried about whenever he affected to be a man of fashion. He took to drink, but managed to compile an *Historical Review* of the period 1739 to 1745 and an *Impartial History* of the Jacobite rising of 1745 (published in Reading, 1747–8, by David Henry, Cave's brother-in-law). For writing and proof-correcting these substantial, rushed works he was paid half a guinea a week. On the title pages he is called 'MA', but there is no evidence that he ever took a degree.

Boyse returned to London and, some two years after the death of Emilia, married again. His second wife, a cutler's widow, originally from Dublin, was uneducated, but 'well enough adapted to his taste' (Shiels, 5.172), and it seems that she induced him to live more regularly and to dress decently. He now expressed remorse for his former life in a poem called 'The Recantation'. After a lingering phthisis, resulting from injuries sustained either from being run over by a coach when drunk or from being assaulted in the street by two or three soldiers, he died in lodgings near Shoe Lane, off Fleet Street, in May 1749. His friend Francis Stewart, Johnson's amanuensis, tried to collect money for a decent funeral, but failed because potential donors had all been sponged upon so often by Boyse during life; so he was buried as a pauper, only with the distinction that the burial service was separately performed over his corpse.

Boyse's last works were *A Demonstration of the Existence of God* (1749), translated from Fénelon, and a classical handbook, *The New Pantheon, or, Fabulous History of the Heathen Gods*, published posthumously in 1753 and often reprinted in a version revised and corrected by William Cooke (*d.* 1780). Boyse's *Deity* received wide publicity when Henry Fielding (who had commended it in *The Champion*, 12 February 1740) praised it again in the introduction to book 7 of *Tom Jones* (February 1749), prompting a new edition of the poem a month later. Boyse's friend, Dr William Cuming of Dorchester, said that he 'was of a middle size, of a thin habit, slovenly in his dress, which was increased by his necessities, very near-sighted, and his hearing imperfect' (Nichols, *Select Collection*, 6.348). Shiels testifies that, besides his literary attainments, Boyse had a taste for painting and for music, and an extensive knowledge of heraldry (Shiels, 5.174).   JAMES SAMBROOK

Sources R. Shiels, *The lives of the poets of Great Britain and Ireland*, ed. T. Cibber, 5 (1753), 160–76 · J. Nichols, ed., *A select collection of poems*, 8 vols. (1780–82), vol. 2, pp. 161–3n; vol. 6, pp. 328–31, 344–8nn; vol. 8, pp. 288–90nn · Boswell, *Life*, 4.407n. · A. Kippis and others, eds., *Biographia Britannica, or, The lives of the most eminent persons who have flourished in Great Britain and Ireland*, 2nd edn, 2 (1780), 533–7 · Nichols, *Lit. anecdotes*, 9.777 · S. Boyse, ten letters to Sir John Clerk of Penicuik, 1730–35, NA Scot., GD 18/4515, 4517–4522 · A. Sherbo, 'Three letters of Samuel Boyse and a poem by Cowper (?)', *N&Q*, 231 (1986), 78–80 · C. Innes, ed., *Munimenta alme Universitatis Glasguensis / Records of the University of Glasgow from its foundation till 1727*, 4 vols., Maitland Club, 72 (1854) · H. L. Piozzi, 'Anecdotes', in *Johnsonian miscellanies*, ed. G. B. Hill, 1 (1897), 147–351, esp. 228 · D. F. Foxon, ed., *English verse, 1701–1750: a catalogue of separately printed poems with notes on contemporary collected editions*, 2 vols. (1975) · A. Chalmers,

'The life of Boyse', *The works of the English poets from Chaucer to Cowper*, 14 (1810), 515–23
Archives BL, letters to Thomas Birch, Add. MS 4301, fols. 242–249 · BL, letters to Edward Cave, Stowe MS 748, fols. 180–181 · BL, letters to Sir Hans Sloane, Sloane MS 4056, fols. 51, 141 · NA Scot., corresp. with Sir John Clerk of Penicuik

Bozon, Nicholas (*fl. c.*1320), Franciscan preacher and Anglo-Norman writer, produced a substantial literary output, but very little information about his life survives. He himself says that he was 'del ordre de freres menours', and that he was 'ordenours', which probably means that he had the right to administer absolution (a right much sought after by the mendicants). It has been suggested that he belonged to the Bozon family of Norfolk, and that he may have studied at Oxford. It is likely that he belonged to the friary in Nottingham (he refers to the rivers Trent and Derwent as if they are familiar to him). He writes in Anglo-Norman, but sometimes quotes a proverb or a pithy saying in English, and sometimes uses an English word (like 'wapentak'). Works attributed to him (either by himself or by scribes) include allegories in verse (such as the *Char d'orgueil*, or the *Passion*, in which Christ is a lover-knight who, wearing the arms of his squire Adam, fights Belial in order to rescue his beloved, Mankind), several poems on the Virgin Mary, a number of saints' lives in verse, some lively sermons in verse, and the *Plainte d'amour*, a powerful satire on corruption, which may well have been inspired by the bull *Exivi de paradiso* (1312). The poem *De bonne femme la bounté* in BL, Add. MS 46919, is also now commonly attributed to him. The best-known, however, is the *Contes moralisés* (probably written after 1320), a collection of prose stories and *exempla* illustrating some moral point, which were perhaps intended to be used in sermons. It includes animal fables, contemporary anecdotes, and material drawn from bestiaries or natural history. The stories are told in a vivid and direct manner, and show a curiosity about the world and human behaviour and a practical and down-to-earth attitude.   DOUGLAS GRAY

Sources A. Thomas, *Histoire littéraire de la France* (1924), vol. 36 of *Histoire littéraire de la France*, 400–24 [incl. work list] · M. D. Legge, *Anglo-Norman in the cloisters* (1950), 85–9 · M. D. Legge, *Anglo-Norman literature and its background* (1963), 229–32 · M. A. Klenke, *Dictionnaire des lettres françaises: le moyen âge* (1964), 549 · N. Bozon, *Contes moralisés*, ed. P. Meyer and L. T. Smith, Société des Anciens Textes Français, 29 (1889)
Archives BL, Add. MS 46919

Brabazon [*formerly* Sharpe], **Hercules Brabazon** (1821–1906), watercolour painter, was born Hercules Brabazon Sharpe on 27 November 1821 in Paris, the second of the four children of Hercules Sharpe (*d.* 1858) and his wife, Anne (*d.* 1837x40), daughter of Sir Anthony Brabazon, first baronet, of co. Mayo. Sharpe spent the first years of his life in Paris, where he and his mother and father, elder brother William, and younger sister Anne, lived in a hotel on the rue de Rivoli. The family's main residence in England was Blackhall Manor, co. Durham; however, in 1832 the family settled at their new estate at Oaklands, near Sedlescombe, Sussex.

Sharpe was educated at Dr Hooker's Preparatory School

Hercules Brabazon Brabazon (1821–1906), by John Singer Sargent

in Northiam, Sussex, and from there proceeded to Harrow School in 1835. He was of a quiet and reserved temperament, finding pleasure in art and music. Sharpe was unhappy at Harrow, and in 1837 he transferred to the École Privat in Geneva. In 1840 he went up to Trinity College, Cambridge, and graduated with an honours degree in mathematics in 1844. Sharpe's father wanted his son to study law after leaving Cambridge, and in May 1843, some months before his graduation, Sharpe was admitted to Lincoln's Inn. Sharpe was a strong character, and his interests in art and music were deeply felt. He resolved to study both these subjects in Rome, and after graduating from Cambridge in 1844 he left England to do so. His father hoped to encourage him to return by reducing his allowance, but even though the consequences of this meant that he had to live in conditions of hardship, Sharpe remained in Rome and enrolled at the Accademia di Santa Cecilia (music) and the Accademia di San Luca (art).

In 1847 Sharpe's elder brother William died. As his brother's heir he succeeded to the family estates in Connaught which had belonged to his mother's brother, Sir William John Brabazon, second baronet, who had died unmarried in 1840. Under the terms of the will of his late uncle, he changed his name from Hercules Brabazon Sharpe to Hercules Brabazon Brabazon. He now enjoyed financial independence and was free to pursue his artistic aims. In 1848, when Brabazon sailed from Naples to visit Spain, he began what was to be a life devoted to painting, travel, and the study of works both by old masters and by contemporary artists. The paintings of Velázquez, which Brabazon first encountered in the Prado, Madrid, inspired and influenced him throughout his life, as did the works of J. M. W. Turner. His earlier and careful sketches from nature show the influence of David Cox, Peter DeWint, and William Müller, but as he gained in confidence and colour sense, he worked more and more in the manner of

Turner's later sketches, making a free use of bodycolour. Brabazon made many studies after the works of artists whom he admired (after Velázquez, Turner, Rembrandt, Constable, Goya, and Watteau, among others, and after contemporary artists, such as Manet). He termed such studies his 'souvenirs', and they are transcripts into his own language rather than copies, revealing his deep understanding of earlier and of contemporary art, and his excellence as a draughtsman as well as a painter, who through careful observation could render the human face and figure with insight and sensitivity.

When his father died in 1858, Brabazon inherited Oaklands which he invited his brother-in-law, Major Combe, to manage. Brabazon divided his time between Oaklands, London, and in travelling abroad. He made frequent journeys to Italy, France, Spain, and Switzerland; he made three tours of the Nile to the borders of Egypt and the Sudan between 1868 and 1877, and undertook three journeys to India in 1870, 1875, and 1876. He would return with hundreds of watercolours in which he aimed always at freshness of impression, handling his colour with directness and simplicity. He was skilled at representing depth and perspective, as *Side Canal Venice* (Tate Collection) and *Monaco* (Tate Collection) show. These paintings demonstrate the harmony of colour that is a characteristic of his work, often achieved using only three or four pigments. *Side Canal Venice*, an unforced study, painted freely and quickly in the open air, is representative of his painting style.

Brabazon described himself as living 'for Art and Sunshine' (Beetles, 7), and he was committed to developing his abilities as a painter, but it was not until he reached the age of seventy that he was induced to exhibit or sell his watercolours. He was a quiet and gentle man who looked upon his drawings as being those of a gentleman amateur; however, many of his friends were professional artists who recognized the beauty and originality of his works. Brabazon was elected a member of the Burlington Fine Arts Club in 1867; there he met John Ruskin and the two became friends. Brabazon accompanied Ruskin on a sketching tour of Amiens in 1880, and Sir Herbert Jekyll remembered Ruskin stating in 1882 that 'Brabazon is the only man since Turner at whose feet I can sit and worship and learn about colour' (*Hercules Brabazon Brabazon*, 1989, no pagination). In 1885 Brabazon met the American artist John Singer Sargent, who encouraged him to exhibit. In 1891 Brabazon was elected a member of the New English Art Club and felt honour bound to exhibit two paintings (*Venice* and *Lago Maggiore*) in its winter exhibition of 1891, and two (*The Rigi* and *Malaga*) in its summer exhibition of the following year. The paintings were immediately well received and in 1892 Brabazon yielded to Sargent's persuasion and held his first one-man exhibition at the Goupil Gallery in Bond Street. Sargent helped to hang the exhibition and wrote the preface to the catalogue. Sixty-six watercolours were sold immediately, although Brabazon gave the money he received for them to charity. He had further one-man exhibitions at the Goupil Gallery in 1894,

1898, 1899, and 1905. He became a founder member of the Pastel Society in 1899, and while he came to this medium late in life he used it with skill and sensitivity. In February 1906 he exhibited with the International Society of Sculptors, Painters, and Gravers.

During his last two years Brabazon was confined to his rooms at Oaklands, where he died peacefully in his sleep on 14 May 1906. He never married. Sargent was a pallbearer at the funeral, and Brabazon was buried in the churchyard at Sedlescombe. Brabazon's folios, containing over 2000 drawings, were bequeathed to his niece, Mrs Harvey Brabazon Combe, who converted an old tithe barn at Sedlescombe into a gallery; the Brabazon Art Museum opened on 30 June 1910. The family estate of Oaklands, however, encountered serious financial difficulties in the 1920s, and in 1926 Brabazon's relatives sold the works that they had inherited. The consequences of 3199 of Brabazon's works entering the London art market over twenty-seven months damaged his reputation because of the great decline in their value, which some took to be representative of their quality. Since the 1980s, however, his reputation has been revived through a series of exhibitions at Chris Beetles Ltd, London. The British Museum, the Victoria and Albert Museum, the Tate collection, and the Metropolitan Museum of Art, New York, hold examples of Brabazon's work.

MARTIN HARDIE, rev. JESSICA KILBURN

Sources C. Beetles, Art and sunshine: the work of Hercules Brabazon Brabazon, NEAC, 1821–1906 (1997) • C. L. Hind, Hercules Brabazon Brabazon, 1821–1906: his art and life (1912) • H. T. Brabazon Combe, Notes on the life of H. B. Brabazon (1910) • Hercules Brabazon Brabazon, 1821–1906 (1989) [exhibition catalogue, Chris Beetles Ltd, London, 1989] • Hercules Brabazon Brabazon, 1821–1906 (1983) [exhibition catalogue, Leicester Polytechnic Exhibition Hall and Sothebys, London, 1983; presented by Chris Beetles Ltd] • A. Weil, 'The strange eclipse of Hercules Brabazon Brabazon: a missing chapter in British art history', Hercules Brabazon Brabazon, 1821–1906, and the New English Art Club (1986) [exhibition catalogue, Chris Beetles Ltd, London, Oct 1986] • Chris Beetles summer show (1998) [exhibition catalogue, Chris Beetles Gallery, London, 1998] • Chris Beetles summer show (1999) [exhibition catalogue, Chris Beetles Gallery, London, 1999] • H. Sharpe, Genealogical history of the family of Brabazon (1825) • G. Reynolds, English watercolours (1989) • d. cert.
Archives U. Glas., MacColl MSS C279, C286, P26 • U. Glas., Whistler MS B181
Likenesses pencil drawing, 1855, priv. coll.; repro. in Beetles, Art and Sunshine • W. Rothenstein, chalk drawing, 1894, BM • J. S. Sargent, oils, 1900, NMG Wales • W. Rothenstein, chalk drawing, NPG • J. S. Sargent, oils, NPG [see illus.] • J. S. Sargent, pencil drawing, repro. in Hercules Brabazon Brabazon, 1821–1906 (1983) [exhibition catalogue, Chris Beetles Ltd, London, 1983]
Wealth at death £39,271 8s. 6d.: probate, 3 July 1906, CGPLA Eng. & Wales

Brabazon, John Theodore Cuthbert Moore-, first Baron Brabazon of Tara

(1884–1964), aviator and politician, was born in London on 8 February 1884, the younger son in the family of two sons and two daughters of Lieutenant-Colonel John Arthur Henry Moore-Brabazon (1828–1908), landowner, of Tara Hall, co. Meath, Ireland, and his wife, Emma Sophia (d. 1937), the daughter of Alfred Richards, of

John Theodore Cuthbert Moore-Brabazon, first Baron Brabazon of Tara (1884–1964), by Sir Cecil Beaton, 1940

Forest Hill. He was educated at Harrow School (1898–1901) and at Trinity College, Cambridge, where he read engineering but did not take a degree. Attracted to the mysteries of the early internal combustion engine even while at school, he spent his university vacations as an unpaid mechanic to Charles S. Rolls, the pioneer of motor cars. On leaving Cambridge, Moore-Brabazon became an apprentice in the Darracq works in Paris, from which he graduated as an international racing driver. In 1907 he won the Circuit des Ardennes in a Minerva. He had married on 27 November the previous year Hilda Mary (d. 1977), the only daughter of Charles Henry Krabbé, who farmed an estate in Buenos Aires; they had two sons.

As an aviator, Moore-Brabazon soon exchanged the tranquil pleasures of the balloon for a Voisin aircraft resembling a huge box kite. In it he became the first Englishman to pilot a heavier-than-air machine under power in England. The flight took place over the Isle of Sheppey in May 1909, lasted rather more than a minute, and ended in a crash which nearly cost him his life. This courageous enterprise brought him, in March 1910, the first pilot's certificate to be issued by the Royal Aero Club. Some years later he set a whimsical fashion among motorists by acquiring the number plate FLY 1. In October 1909, piloting a machine made by the Short brothers, he won a prize of £1000 offered by the Daily Mail for the first English aircraft to fly 1 mile. But, after witnessing the death of his friend Rolls in an air crash nine months later, he was persuaded by his wife to abandon flying until the outbreak of war in 1914. Moore-Brabazon served with the Royal Flying Corps on the western front and specialized in the development of aerial reconnaissance and photography. His qualities of leadership and mechanical flair brought him the regard and friendship of that exacting commander Hugh Trenchard. He rose to the rank of lieutenant-colonel, was awarded the MC, received three mentions in dispatches, and became a commander of the Légion d'honneur.

In 1918 Moore-Brabazon's brother officer Lord Hugh Cecil encouraged him to stand for parliament as a Conservative. He was elected for the Chatham division of Rochester, a seat which he held until his defeat in 1929. From 1931 to 1942, when he was created a peer, he sat for Wallasey. Fearlessly ebullient, he delivered his maiden speech within two days of entering the house and in 1919 was rewarded by an invitation to become parliamentary private secretary to Winston Churchill, the newly appointed secretary of state for war and air. From 1923 to 1924 and from 1924 to 1927 he was parliamentary secretary to the Ministry of Transport. Under his direction the London docks remained open to receive shipments of food during the general strike of 1926. In the same year he steered through the Commons a bill to rationalize the electricity industry. He supported Churchill's pleas for a more spirited policy of rearmament throughout the era of appeasement, and his loyalty was recognized when in October 1940 he replaced Lord Reith as minister of transport in the wartime coalition and was sworn of the privy council. After seven months spent largely in making good the dislocation caused by enemy air raids he became minister of aircraft production. He had many friends in the industry and both in and out of office kept abreast of its technical developments, particularly the jet engine invented by Frank Whittle. He also restored a more orderly regime in the ministry after the inspired piracy by which his predecessor, Lord Beaverbrook, had ensured a desperately needed flow of fighter planes. In February 1942, however, when a speech at a private luncheon leaked into the newspapers, he was alleged to have expressed the hope that the German and Russian armies would annihilate each other. Although he had done as much as any minister to keep Britain's Russian allies supplied with aircraft, whatever the cost to Britain's own war effort, Churchill asked for his resignation. He accepted his dismissal with characteristic good humour and was consoled with a peerage.

That was the end of Moore-Brabazon's political career but not of his influence on aviation. He became chairman of the committee that planned the construction of civil aircraft in the post-war years, not least the huge and beautiful machine that bore his name but never flew commercially. He was also elected president of the Royal Aero Club, president of the Royal Institution, and chairman of the Air Registration Board. As a father figure of aeronautical enterprise he never ceased to insist that speed should if necessary be sacrificed to safety, comfort, economy, and prestige. In 1953 he was appointed GBE.

It is unlikely that Moore-Brabazon would have achieved cabinet rank except in a wartime administration led by Churchill. Although he brought an inventive and industrious mind to his ministerial duties, he had no great regard for the niceties of procedure or administration, and his genial presence, heralded by a cigarette in its holder and sustained by the humour of an after-dinner speaker, failed to inspire confidence in his more staid colleagues. With characteristic panache he was one of the last to wear a top hat in the House of Commons. He could be endearingly irreverent. In youth he had flown with a pig as his passenger in order to confound a familiar adage; and the speech that caused his downfall in 1942 echoed in tone his retort to the major who in the early days of the First World War had ordered him to obey his superior officer: '*Superior officer? Senior, if you please, sir.*'

Tall, muscular, and deceptively ponderous, he excelled at several sports well into his eighth decade. Except during the two world wars he braved the Cresta run at St Moritz every year from 1907 until his death. Three times he won the Curzon cup, the blue riband of tobogganing. He was a member of the Royal Yacht Squadron and in 1952 captain of the Royal and Ancient Golf Club of St Andrews. He died at Grangewood, Longcross, near Chertsey, Surrey, on 17 May 1964 and was succeeded by his elder son, Derek Charles (*b.* 1910); the younger son died in 1950. The second baron died in 1974 and was succeeded by his only son, Ivon Anthony (*b.* 1946). KENNETH ROSE, *rev.*

Sources Lord Brabazon of Tara [J. T. C. Moore-Brabazon], *The Brabazon story* (1956) • *The Times* (18 May 1964) • private information, 1981 • Burke, *Peerage* (1999) • *CGPLA Eng. & Wales* (1964)

Archives Royal Air Force Museum, Hendon, papers | CAC Cam., corresp. with A. V. Hill • CUL, corresp. with Sir Samuel Hoare • ICL, corresp. with Herbert Dingle • Nuffield Oxf., corresp. with Lord Cherwell | FILM BFI NFTVA, *Celebrity*, 19 Aug 1959 • BFI NFTVA, news footage • IWM FVA, actuality footage • IWM FVA, news footage | SOUND IWM SA, 'British civilian aviator recalls the early days of powered flight', BBC, 1959, 17783 • IWM SA, oral history interview • IWM SA, recorded talk

Likenesses C. Beaton, photograph, 1940, NPG [*see illus.*] • W. Stoneman, photograph, 1944, NPG • F. Eastman, oils, 1951, Royal Air Force Museum, Hendon; [on loan from Royal Aero Club] • A. E. Cooper, oils, 1958, Royal Air Force Museum, Hendon • A. E. Cooper, pastel drawing, 1958, NPG • W. Bird, photograph, 1962, NPG • D. McFall, bronze bust, 1964, Royal Institution of Great Britain, London • O. Birley, oils, priv. coll.

Wealth at death £46,650: probate, 9 July 1964, *CGPLA Eng. & Wales*

Brabazon, Mary Jane, countess of Meath (1847–1918). *See under* Brabazon, Reginald, twelfth earl of Meath (1841–1929).

Brabazon, Reginald, twelfth earl of Meath (1841–1929), politician and philanthropist, was born on 31 July 1841 in a house near Belgrave Square, London, the second son of William Brabazon (1803–1887), styled Lord Brabazon and from 1851 eleventh earl of Meath, and his wife, Harriot (1811–1898), the second daughter of Sir Richard Brooke, sixth baronet, and his wife, Harriot Cunliffe. His elder brother, Jacques le Normand, died of diphtheria in 1844, near Naples, but Reginald survived and, as Lord Brabazon, was educated from 1851 to 1854 at a private school at Whitnash, near Leamington Spa, before attending Eton College (1854–9). The Spartan regime at Eton is recalled in his autobiography, *Memories of the Nineteenth Century* (1923), which tells of a master who accused boys of 'spinelessness' for brushing snow off their knees, pointing out that, if their forefathers had 'minded a little snow', then Canada would not have been added to the empire. On leaving

Reginald Brabazon, twelfth earl of Meath (1841–1929), by Sir William Orpen, exh. RA 1929

school he went to learn German from 1860 to 1861 in Bückeburg, near Hanover, and in 1863 passed into the Foreign Office as a clerk by competitive examination.

On 7 January 1868 Brabazon married Lady Mary Jane Maitland [**Mary Jane Brabazon**, countess of Meath (1847–1918)]. The daughter of Thomas *Maitland, eleventh earl of Lauderdale (1803–1878), and his wife, Amelia (d. 1890), the daughter of William Young, she was born on 15 March 1847. The marriage produced four sons and two daughters. Brabazon moved into the diplomatic service, and his first appointment to the embassy in Berlin (1868–70), during the period of the Franco-Prussian War, led to his alienation from Germany. He also served at The Hague (1870) and in Paris (1871–3), before abandoning diplomacy, at the insistence of his in-laws, on being posted as second secretary to the 'remote' outpost of Athens. Brabazon remained unemployed without pay, at the disposal of the diplomatic service, until he finally resigned in 1877. He and his wife went to live at Rivermead, Sunbury, Middlesex, in 1873 and decided to devote their prodigious energies and enthusiasms to 'the consideration of social problems and the relief of human suffering' (Brabazon, *Memories of the Nineteenth Century*, 201). Brabazon embarked on a career of public philanthropy that was to span several decades, from the time of the handsome, black-bearded aristocrat of the 1870s to the bald, white-bearded, benevolent Santa Claus of the 1920s.

In 1874 Brabazon became honorary secretary of the Hospital Saturday Fund Committee and started the Dublin Hospital Sunday movement, and in 1879 became the first chairman of the Young Men's Friendly Society, later the Church of England's Men's Society. In 1882 he founded the Metropolitan Gardens Association, of which he was chairman until his death, but it was as an alderman of the London county council (1889–92, 1898–1901) and first chairman of its parks committee that London is indebted to him for the preservation of so many of its open spaces, and for parks, gardens, and playgrounds covering thousands of acres, the lungs of the metropolis. Lady Brabazon not only supported her husband's schemes but also devoted her own time and money to philanthropic endeavours, such as the Workhouse Concert Society. In 1885 she set up the Ministering Children's League, whose members pledged to help those in suffering by doing at least one kind deed every day.

On 7 January 1887 Brabazon was invited to speak on the National Association for Promoting State-Directed Colonization, begun in 1884, of which he was both chairman and president, to a meeting held in Clerkenwell, London, under the hostile auspices of the Social Democratic Federation. The working-class audience was ready for 'a warm time with a real live Lord' and his speech was frequently interrupted, one man shouting, 'I should like to cut off your head', to which he replied, 'If they could prove to him that cutting off his head would save the starving poor, he was quite willing that it should be cut off' (Brabazon, *Memories of the Nineteenth Century*, 232–4). In May 1887, on his father's death, he succeeded to the title as the twelfth earl and inherited 14,717 acres, along with Killruddery, near Bray, co. Wicklow, Ireland, and Eaton Court in Herefordshire with 695 acres.

Lord Meath, an ardent Conservative, Unionist, and imperialist, began to promote the movement for the recognition of an empire commemoration day, with which his name is chiefly associated, after reading in 1896 of a ceremony in Hamilton, Ontario, at which the British flag was hoisted and children sang the national anthem. The first public meeting to promote the idea of celebrating Queen Victoria's birthday, 24 May, as 'Empire day' did not take place until 24 May 1904, but four years later official British recognition of such a day was turned down in the Commons by a 68-vote majority, the figures being received with loud Irish nationalist and Labour cheers. Meath succeeded in obtaining British government support for Empire day only in 1916, a decade after it had become a statutory holiday in most of the dominions; the war against Germany, as much as his incessant propaganda efforts, brought final recognition. In 1922, a year after his retirement from active involvement, Empire day became affiliated to the Royal Colonial Institute, and 80,000 schools throughout the empire were said to participate.

While campaigning for Empire day, Meath was also a zealous supporter of Lord Roberts's campaign for national military service, had founded the Lads' Drill Association (1899–1906), afterwards incorporated in the National Service League, and become chairman and president of the Duty and Discipline movement (1912–19), as well as scout commissioner for Ireland (1911–28). Many of these causes are now seen as an establishment-led reaction to the weakening of parental discipline and the questioning of authority in an age of gradual emancipation from Victorian values and domestic tyranny. Meath wrote and edited several books, mostly collections of his articles or essays, promoting the campaigns to which he devoted his time. He died on 11 October 1929 at 40 Eaton Square, the residence in London of his sister Lady Kathleen Brabazon, and was buried at Delgany, co. Wicklow, on 16 October 1929. Lady Meath, who had predeceased him on 4 November 1918, was buried on 7 November at Bray, also in co. Wicklow.

JOHN SPRINGHALL

Sources Earl of Meath [R. Brabazon], *Memories of the nineteenth century* (1923) · Earl of Meath [R. Brabazon], *Memories of the twentieth century* (1924) · J. O. Springhall, 'Lord Meath, youth and empire', *Journal of Contemporary History*, 5 (1970), 97–111 · J. A. Mangan, 'The grit of our forefathers', *Imperialism and popular culture*, ed. J. M. MacKenzie (1986), 113–39 · *The diaries of Mary, countess of Meath*, ed. R. Brabazon, 2 vols. (1928) · Earl of Meath [R. Brabazon], *Brabazon potpourri* (1928) · GEC, *Peerage*
Archives Killruddery, near Bray, co. Wicklow, Ireland | FILM BFI NFTVA, actuality footage
Likenesses Bassano, photograph, 1895, NPG · W. Stoneman, photograph, 1924, NPG · W. Orpen, oils, exh. RA 1929, NPG [*see illus.*] · J. Russell & Sons, photograph, NPG · bronze bust, Royal Commonwealth Society, London · memorial plaque, Ottershaw church, Surrey · relief medallion on memorial, Lancaster Gate, London
Wealth at death £45,720 4s. 3d.: probate, 26 Nov 1929, *CGPLA Eng. & Wales*

Brabazon, Sir Roger (*b.* in or before 1247?, *d.* 1317), justice, was the son of William le Brabazon and his wife, Amice, and may have been born at Mowsley in Leicestershire. Between 1275 and 1289 he was in the service of Edward I's brother, Edmund of Lancaster, regularly acting as his attorney in the making of final concords and doing other kinds of legal business for him. It was at Edmund's request that he received his first judicial commissions in 1285, 1287, and 1288. These were to inquire into wrongdoing by Edmund's other bailiffs and stewards in various counties, and into poaching in Edmund's parks, and to hold eyres in Edmund's forests in Lancashire and Yorkshire. When Ralph Hengham and William Saham were removed from the court of king's bench, probably at the end of Hilary term 1290, after being convicted of official misconduct, Brabazon joined the court as a junior justice.

During 1291–2 Brabazon played a prominent role in the hearing of the 'great cause', on Edward's behalf requiring the Scots to acknowledge Edward's overlordship over Scotland at the initial meeting at Norham in May 1291; acting as one of Edward's auditors; pronouncing Edward's final judgment, which awarded the Scottish throne to Balliol in December 1292; and defending Edward's right to hear appeals from Scotland, against the actions of his erstwhile deputies there, in England a few days later. He also played a role in the preparation of the tendentious 'official' notarial record of part of these proceedings made by Master John of Caen. When Gilbert of Thornton died in late August 1295 Brabazon replaced him as chief justice of king's bench. He retained the chief justiceship for over twenty years, until his retirement on grounds of age and ill health on 23 February 1316.

Roger Brabazon married Beatrice, the widow of William

of Kilby, between 1281 and 1284. Beatrice was one of two daughters of Warin of Bassingbourn and his wife, Albreda. Through her mother Beatrice was coheir to Henry Biset with her sister Constance, the wife of Walter Bek, and from him Beatrice inherited the manor of West Allington in Lincolnshire. Brabazon and his wife subsequently exchanged this manor for the lands allotted to Constance on the division of the Biset inheritance, including East Bridgford in Nottinghamshire. The two sisters were also coheirs to the lands held by their uncle John of Sproxton at Coleby in Lincolnshire and at Sproxton and elsewhere in Leicestershire. Brabazon probably himself inherited lands at Mowsley in Leicestershire and Great Rollright in Oxfordshire. His main property acquisitions were at Garthorpe in Leicestershire (close to Sproxton) and Sibbertoft in Northamptonshire, just across the county border from Mowsley. He also acquired a house and other properties in London near Aldersgate.

Brabazon died on either 13 or 14 June 1317, without surviving issue, and his lands passed to his brother Matthew. He also had a brother Thomas who was in clerical orders and on whom he settled property. The John Brabazon who died *c.*1302 was probably also a brother. This John was probably the father of the Roger Brabazon junior, or Roger Brabazon clerk, who is once described as Roger the judge's nephew, and who like his uncle was in the service of Edmund of Lancaster (and his wife, Blanche), as also of the Master John Brabazon who was one of Roger's executors. Roger the elder's wife, Beatrice, had died by 1304, and after her death he granted lands to the Lincolnshire Premonstratensian house at Newbo to establish a chantry for her as well as for himself. Shortly before his own death, Brabazon also endowed a chantry in Westminster Abbey to pray for his own soul and for the souls of his erstwhile patron Edmund of Lancaster and Edmund's wife, Blanche. He was buried in St Paul's Cathedral, not far from his London home, which was sold by his executors to another notable royal judge, Hervey Staunton.

PAUL BRAND

Sources *Chancery records* · Common bench plea rolls, PRO, CP 40 · King's bench plea rolls, PRO, KB 27 · court of common pleas, feet of fines, PRO, CP 25/1 · Cartulary of John of Woodford, BL, Cotton Claudius MS A.xiii · E. L. G. Stones and G. G. Simpson, eds., *Edward I and the throne of Scotland, 1290–1296*, 2 vols. (1978) · [M. T. Martin], ed., *The Percy chartulary*, SurtS, 117 (1911) · W. Stubbs, ed., *Chronicles of the reigns of Edward I and Edward II*, 2 vols., Rolls Series, 76 (1882–3) · *CIPM*, 6, no. 82 · R. R. Sharpe, ed., *Calendar of wills proved and enrolled in the court of husting, London, AD 1258 – AD 1688*, 1 (1889), 272

Brabazon, Sir William (*d.* 1552), lord justice of Ireland, was the son of John Brabazon, a gentleman of Eastwell, Leicestershire; his mother's maiden name was Chaworth. At an unknown date he married Elizabeth, daughter and coheir of Nicholas Clifford of Holme, Kent; they had two sons and two daughters. William was a protégé of Thomas Cromwell. In April 1534 he was dispatched by the chief secretary to the northern marches of England to prepare for Lord Dacre's arrest. He was appointed under-treasurer, receiver-general, and treasurer-at-war in Ireland on 26 August 1534, holding this position until his death. From 1534 he was a member of the privy council of Ireland.

A virulent opponent of the Kildares, Brabazon was involved in killing 100 of Fitzgerald's galloglass near Naas in March 1535 and campaigned against Fitzgerald in Allen in early August. At that time he withstood the advance of Geraldine forces in co. Kildare, earning the praise of senior members of the Irish council. Later that month he and Lord Deputy Grey negotiated agreements with O'More and O'Connor. In April of the following year he overran MacMurrough's country. Grey departed Dublin in late July 1536 to negotiate with the earl of Desmond and the O'Briens, and left Brabazon in charge of defending Dublin, re-edifying Powerscourt, erecting defences at Fassaroe, and reconstructing the bridge and fortresses at Athy and Woodstock. Brabazon seconded Archbishop Browne's speech in parliament supporting the bill against papal authority and jurisdiction, a stance which is said to have spurred the members of the house to vote in favour of the bill.

The manner of his administration earned Brabazon a stiff reprimand from Henry VIII in February 1537. Before April, Archbishop Browne made allegations of fraud and peculation against Brabazon. In May Brabazon accompanied Grey on a campaign into the lordships of MacGeoghegan and O'Connor. He campaigned against the earl of Desmond and O'Carroll in August. In October 1538 he unsuccessfully tried to negotiate an agreement with MacMurrough. Later that month he accompanied Grey on a raid on Kavanagh's lordship, and they both travelled to Ulster in an effort to expel the Scots. In 1539 he was appointed a commissioner to take surrenders of monastic properties. The following year he went to England to testify at the impeachment of Lord Leonard Grey. In the summer of that year he was accused of misappropriation of the new crown possessions and an audit carried out in 1540–41 unveiled his vast acquisitions and financial malpractice.

On 12 October 1543 Brabazon was appointed lord justice of Ireland, and held office from 10 February to 11 August 1544. In summer 1544 he sent 700 men to serve at the siege of Boulogne. On 16 February 1546 he was again appointed lord justice for a term lasting from 1 April to 16 December 1546. In July he drove O'More and O'Connor from co. Kildare, marched into Offaly, and garrisoned Dangan in Offaly and Ballyadams in Leix (Laois). In mid-December St Leger returned and criticized Brabazon for having goaded both Gaelic lords into rebellion. In 1547 Brabazon became constable of Athlone Castle. In spring 1548 he attended St Leger in suppressing the seditious practices of Viscount Baltinglass's sons in Kildare. In February 1550 he was elected lord justice by the council following the death of Francis Bryan and held office until 10 September 1550. He negotiated an agreement between the earls of Desmond and Thomond at Limerick in March, and campaigned against Charles MacArt Kavanagh in August. On 20 January 1551 he was appointed joint under-treasurer with his son-in-law Andrew Wise. He was nominated a commissioner of the court of wards on four occasions, in 1545, 1547, 1548, and 1550. He died while campaigning in Ulster in July 1552. His heart is said to have been interred with his ancestors in Eastwell and his remains were buried in the chancel of St Catherine's Church, Dublin, where a monument was erected in his memory.   MARY ANN LYONS

Sources PRO, state papers, Ireland, Edward VI, SP 61 · *LP Henry VIII*, vols. 7–21 · *State papers published under … Henry VIII*, 11 vols. (1830–52), vol. 2, pt 3; vol. 3, pt 3 · H. Sharpe, *Genealogical history of the family of Brabazon* (1825) · J. Lodge, *The peerage of Ireland*, rev. M. Archdall, rev. edn, 1 (1789) · *CSP Ire.*, 1509–73 · *Holinshed's chronicles of England, Scotland and Ireland*, ed. H. Ellis, 6 (1808) · R. Cox, *Hibernia Anglicana, or, The history of Ireland from the conquest thereof by the English to the present time*, 1 (1689) · C. Brady, *The chief governors: the rise and fall of reform government in Tudor Ireland, 1536–1588* (1994) · S. G. Ellis, *Ireland in the age of the Tudors* (1998) · S. G. Ellis, *Tudor frontiers and noble power: the making of the British state* (1995) · B. Bradshaw, *The dissolution of the religious orders in Ireland under Henry VIII* (1974) · J. S. Brewer and W. Bullen, eds., *Calendar of the Carew manuscripts*, 1: 1515–1574, PRO (1867) · M. C. Griffith, ed., *Calendar of inquisitions formerly in the office of the chief remembrancer of the exchequer*, IMC (1991) · J. Morrin, ed., *Calendar of the patent and close rolls of chancery in Ireland, of the reigns of Henry VIII, Edward VI, Mary, and Elizabeth*, 1 (1861) · *The Irish fiants of the Tudor sovereigns*, 4 vols. (1994) · N. B. White, ed., *Extents of Irish monastic possessions, 1540–41*, IMC (1943) · G. Mac Niocaill, ed., *Crown surveys of lands, 1540–41, with the Kildare rental begun in 1518*, IMC (1992) · J. L. J. Hughes, ed., *Patentee officers in Ireland, 1173–1826, including high sheriffs, 1661–1684 and 1761–1816*, IMC (1960) · T. W. Moody and others, eds., *A new history of Ireland, 9: Maps, genealogies, lists* (1984)
Archives NL Ire., corresp. [microfilm] | PRO, corresp., SP 61, Ireland, Edward VI
Wealth at death allegedly had Ir£12,000 owing on account in 1551: Ellis, *Ireland in the age of the Tudors*

Brabourne. For this title name see Hugessen, Edward Hugessen Knatchbull-, first Baron Brabourne (1829–1893).

Brabourne, Theophilus (1590–1662), Church of England clergyman and religious controversialist, was born at Norwich, the elder of two sons of Henry Brabourne, a hosier with puritan sympathies, who wanted Theophilus to 'prove a godly minister' (Brabourne, *A Reply*, 94). He was educated at the Norwich Free School until he was fifteen, and at seventeen, instead of proceeding to Cambridge, he was sent to London as a wholesale agent in the family business. Clergy with puritan leanings were already being silenced for non-compliance, and Henry Brabourne reasoned that it was not an auspicious time for his son to take holy orders. Theophilus remained in London until his marriage, about 1619, to Abigail, daughter of Roger and Joane Galliard of Ashwell Thorpe, a union which was to produce five children. He then returned to Norwich, and with a renewed interest in ministry applied himself to study under the tutelage of 'three able divines' (ibid.)—compensation, perhaps, for a lost undergraduate training. In 1621 he took the MA degree, and in September of that year he was ordained by Thomas Dove, bishop of Peterborough and formerly dean of Norwich, thus becoming one of a very few to have been ordained in the Anglican tradition without having received a formal university education. He was licensed for the Norwich diocese in April 1622, and in 1630 was noted as curate at Catton in Norfolk. Details of his clerical appointments are meagre, and by 1654 he had relinquished active ministry to devote his time to study, writing, and the management of his not inconsiderable properties. He had by then achieved notoriety as a heretic, and had established a reputation as an able writer and controversialist.

Brabourne's claim to recognition rests in his vigorous and sustained sabbatarianism, particularly his *Discourse upon the Sabbath Day* (1628), the first work in the English language to advocate observance of Saturday as the sabbath, and its sequel, *A Defence of … the Sabbath Day* (1632). These works were catalysts in the development of seventh day doctrine and practice in early seventeenth-century England, and their influence was to extend well beyond their own day and beyond English shores. Although Cox is incorrect in regarding Brabourne as the founder of the Seventh Day Baptists (Cox, 1.157–8), it is none the less true that the *Discourse* and the *Defence*, together with Brabourne's other works on the sabbath, contributed significantly to the adoption of seventh day principles by Baptists and others in the seventeenth century and later. Brabourne, however, remained an Anglican, eschewed believers' baptism, and wishing to avoid schism did not openly observe the seventh day himself, fearing that it would bring confusion 'to see a few keep Saturday for Sabbath, and a multitude to keep Sunday' (T. Brabourne, *A Defence*, 1632, 229). Despite this reticence few argued the necessity of seventh day observance more cogently or consistently, or with more adverse effects, than Brabourne. Between 1628 and 1660 he published in all ten works which wholly or in part advocated the Saturday sabbath. Brabourne's theology of the sabbath derived from a threefold conviction: that the moral law as expressed in the ten commandments was perpetually binding; that the practice of Christ and the early church necessitated observance of the seventh day; and that the identity of the seventh day, despite changes in the calendar and arguments to the contrary, remained indisputably Saturday. Later sabbatarian apologists would return to the arguments found in his writings, but it was Brabourne who laid the foundation for a revival in the English-speaking world of an ancient practice that was to continue into the twenty-first century.

The appearance of the *Defence* in 1632 had unforeseen consequences. Alexander Gordon believed that its publication was one of the reasons that induced Charles I to reissue the so-called Book of Sports in 1633 (Gordon, 567). For Brabourne himself it marked the beginning of a journey to the court of high commission and Newgate gaol. The *Defence* was boldly dedicated to Charles, who referred it to Francis White, bishop of Ely, for a response. White's reply, *A treatise of the sabbath-day … a defence of the orthodoxal doctrine of the Church of England against sabbatarian novelty*, appeared in 1635, too late to prevent the spread of Brabourne's 'heresy', which White himself admitted might already 'have poisoned and infected many people with this Sabbatarian error, or some other of like quality' (White, 'Epistle Dedicatory'). It was also too late for Brabourne. By October 1633 he was in prison, and in April and June of 1634 he found himself before the court of high commission charged with holding and disseminating 'erroneous, heretical, and judaical opinions' (*CSP dom.*, 1634–5, 126). He admitted authorship of the *Defence* and to

holding sabbatarian views, 'as much bound to keep the Saturday Sabbath as the Jews were before the coming of Christ' (ibid.), and was pronounced a Jew, a heretic, and a schismatic. It was ordered that he be deprived of all ecclesiastical privileges, deposed from holy orders, excommunicated, fined £1000, and required to make a public retraction of his errors at such time and place and in such form as the court should approve.

Brabourne was remanded in custody pending further consideration of his case and the possibility of handing him over to the secular authority should he persist in his views. One of his prosecutors, Sir Henry Marten, moved during the trial that the old anti-Lollard legislation *De haeretico comburendo* be brought against him, and only the personal intervention of William Laud prevented it. Brabourne remained in gaol for the next eighteen months while proceedings continued. Eventually in February 1636 he was released, having finally agreed to a submission acceptable to the court. Although it was received as a recantation, Brabourne later claimed that he had only retracted the word 'necessarily' in the statement 'Saturday ought necessarily to be our Sabbath'. This had been 'rashly maintained', he agreed, but withdrawal of the word 'necessarily' had been but the retraction 'of a rash word, not the matter' (Brabourne, *A Reply*, 100–01). It was, it seems, the only element of the original sentence that was finally imposed.

Brabourne returned to Norwich and, after keeping a low profile for some years, resumed publication in the 1650s on a range of topics. His *Change of Church Discipline* (1653) and *The Second Part of the Change of Church Discipline* (1654), which advocated a form of Erastianism against the papal system, and against presbyterians and Independents, attracted the wrath of a local presbyterian, John Collings (or Collins), a bitter opponent of all non-presbyterians. A vitriolic exchange ensued between Collings and Brabourne which quickly degenerated into a mutual attack *ad hominem*, bringing no credit to either party, and in which Collings taunted Brabourne over his lack of education and aborted ministry, calling him a 'Boltpoak, Weaver, Hostler, Maltster, and now a non-sensical scribbler' (J. Collings, *A New Lesson for the Indoctus Doctor*, 1654, title-page). Brabourne, undeterred, continued to advocate observance of Saturday, in opposition to Daniel Cawdrey, joint author with Herbert Palmer of the important *Sabbatum redivivum*, and against Jeremiah Ives and Edward Warren, both of whom had also opposed him over the seventh day. He also published on other issues. There are eight known pamphlets from his pen in the 1650s and 1660s, in addition to his works on the sabbath and the exchanges with Collings, in which he defended the authority of the king and parliament, supported the oath of allegiance, advocated liberty of conscience, and attacked the Church of England. In *The Humble Petition of Theophilus Brabourne unto the Honourable Parliament* (1661) he returned to the temporal power of the church, arguing that archbishops and bishops should 'own the king's supremacy' in fact as well as in theory, claiming that the structure of the Church of

England had been taken from the papal system and maintaining that Charles I had 'unadvisedly' delegated ecclesiastical power to his bishops (T. Brabourne, *Humble Petition*, 1661, 2, 8–9). In *Sundry Particulars Concerning Bishops* (1661) he called for a radical restructuring of the Church of England, including abolition of the office of bishop, on the grounds that Anglican orders were derived from Rome, and that the money could be put to better use.

Brabourne died at Norwich between 28 April 1662, when a codicil was made to his will, and 4 November, when it was proved. He was predeceased by his wife and four of their five children. His estate, consisting largely of property and land, was left mainly to his surviving daughter and her children and to his thirteen other grandchildren, with the exception of a few small bequests and with provisions for outstanding debts to be settled from rental income. He left £10 for 'the poor Sabbath-keepers in Norwich, to be distributed by Mr Pooly [Christopher Pooley] and his elders'. Brabourne's wider legacy to posterity, however, remains his writing on the sabbath, the influence of which is still evident today.   BRYAN W. BALL

Sources *CSP dom.*, 1633–6 • B. W. Ball, *The seventh-day men: sabbatarians and sabbatarianism in England and Wales, 1600–1800* (1994) • R. Cox, *The literature of the sabbath question*, 2 vols. (1865) • T. Brabourne, *Answer to Cawdrey* (1654), 75 • T. Brabourne, *A reply to the indoctus Doctor Edoctus* (1654) • A. Gordon, 'Theophilus Brabourne, M. A.', *Sabbath Memorial*, 49–50 (Jan–April 1887), 565–70 • W. H. Hart, *Index expurgatorius Anglicanus, or, A descriptive catalogue of the principal books printed or published in England, which have been suppressed*, 1 vol. in 5 pts (1872–8), pt 3 • K. L. Parker, *The English sabbath: a study of doctrine and discipline from the Reformation to the civil war* (1988) • D. S. Katz, *Philo-Semitism and the re-admission of the Jews to England, 1603–1655* (1982) • F. White, 'Epistle dedicatory', *A treatise of the sabbath-day* (1635) • J. Hunt, *Religious thought in England from the Reformation to the end of the last century*, 1 (1870) • B. Brook, *The lives of the puritans*, 2 (1813) • *DNB* • will, Norfolk RO, NCC wills 1662, OW80

Wealth at death seemingly financially impoverished; sundry debts and small legacies to be paid from income of six houses and attached land in Norwich; also land at Ludham, Norfolk: will, Norfolk RO, Norwich, NCC wills 1662, OW80

Brabrook, Sir Edward William (1839–1930), civil servant, was born on 10 April 1839 at 10 Cornhill in the City of London, the first son and second of three children of Edward Brabrook (1798–1858) and his second wife, Grace Darby, *née* Sommers (1800–1856). His father was a warehouse manager, and the family occupied the upper three floors of the business premises at 10 Cornhill. After early education by a governess, at the age of seven Edward William was sent to the private City Commercial School of William Pinches, where he eventually became head boy. In 1851, following the forced resignation of his father due to illness, the family moved to a small house in Westminster, and Edward William took work as an accountant and bookkeeper for various merchants. He then became assistant, and subsequently private secretary, to the actuary Arthur Scratchley. He carried out research for Scratchley's various publications on life insurance, friendly societies, and savings banks, and this led to an informal training in actuarial matters. At this time he was a member of a number of small dining clubs, was an

active contributor to *Notes and Queries*, and was elected to a fellowship of the Society of Antiquaries in 1860. His parents were both active Wesleyan Methodists, as was Edward William until he retired from the society in 1861.

On 10 May 1862 Brabrook married Emily Caroline Withers (1841–1900), daughter of Robert Withers, a law clerk, and their first son was born in November the same year. In 1863 he became a student of Lincoln's Inn, and was called to the bar in 1866. During his early married life he began what was to become a lifelong commitment to a wide variety of learned societies, gaining fellowships of the Anthropological Society of London (1864), the Institute of Actuaries (1864), the Royal Society of Literature (1865), and membership of the London and Middlesex Archaeological Society (1865). In 1869 the defining moment of his professional career occurred when the then chief registrar of friendly societies, J. Tidd Pratt, offered Brabrook the post of assistant registrar at an annual salary of £500. Pratt died the following year, and after an interval during which the royal commission on friendly societies considered the future of the registry, J. M. Ludlow was appointed chief registrar, and Brabrook became assistant registrar for England, at a salary of £900 per annum. In 1892 he succeeded Ludlow as chief registrar, a post he held until 1904 when, at the age of sixty-five, he reached the formal retirement age for civil servants and received his pension of £875 per annum.

In his official capacity Brabrook took responsibility for compiling and publishing data on friendly societies, and appeared as a witness before the royal commissions on labour and on the aged poor, and various select committees on building, friendly, and co-operative societies. He wrote extensively on the law relating to working-class self-help institutions, producing legal guides for industrial and provident (co-operative) societies (1869), trade unions (1871), and savings banks (1905), updating Tidd Pratt's *Law of Friendly Societies* from the eighth (1873) to the thirteenth (1897) editions, and writing, with Arthur Scratchley, a guide to the law of building societies (1882). He contributed articles on building societies, friendly societies, and savings banks to the *Encyclopaedia Britannica*. His *Provident Societies and Industrial Welfare* (1898) was the most comprehensive contemporary survey of working-class self-help institutions, and his published lectures, *Institutions for Thrift* (1905) were a strong statement of his beliefs about the economic and moral advantages of self-help. In retirement he strongly opposed the introduction of non-contributory old-age pensions and of national insurance, believing that paternalistic state involvement in welfare provision would undermine working-class independence and self-help. He was made a companion of the Bath in 1897, and was knighted in 1905 in recognition of his services to the friendly society movement.

Brabrook's family, resident in Lewisham until 1892, and then in Balham, grew rapidly, with his wife bearing three sons and eight daughters between 1862 and 1885. The years 1895 to 1902 were clouded by domestic bereavement: two of his daughters died in a bathing accident at St Leonards in 1895, his eldest son Edward (secretary of the

Building Societies Association) died in 1898, his wife died in 1900, and a third daughter died in 1902. On 25 March 1914 he married his spinster sister-in-law, Flora Maud Withers (1856–1925).

These events did not significantly interrupt Brabrook's associational activities: he was elected to membership of the Athenaeum in 1889, and served as president of the Anthropological Institute (1895–7), vice-president and treasurer of the Royal Society of Literature (1896–1915), vice-president of the Statistical Society (1900), president of both the anthropology (1898) and economic (1903) sections of the British Society for the Advancement of Science, president of the London and Middlesex Archaeological Society (1910), vice-president of the Society of Antiquaries, president of the Folk Lore Society (1901), and chair of the thrift sub-committee and member of council of the Charity Organization Society, and he contributed many short notes to the proceedings of these societies. His presidential addresses to the Anthropological Institute are remarkable for the absence of any engagement with the conceptual or empirical questions debated by late Victorian anthropologists.

In his later years Brabrook, a profusely bearded figure, lived at Langham House, 8 Stafford Road, Wallington, Surrey, where he died of a brain haemorrhage on 20 March 1930. He was buried at Norwood cemetery on 23 March, after a service at Christ Church Presbyterian Church, Wallington.   PAUL JOHNSON

Sources E. Brabrook, *Sir Edward Brabrook, C. B.: some notes on his life* (1930) [privately printed, London] · *The Times* (21 March 1930) · *WWW* · *Debrett's Peerage* · J. Foster, *Men-at-the-bar: a biographical hand-list of the members of the various inns of court*, 2nd edn (1885) · b. cert. · m. certs. · d. cert. · P. H. J. H. Gosden, *Self-help: voluntary associations in the 19th century* (1973) · P. Johnson, *Saving and spending: the working-class economy in Britain, 1870–1939* (1985)
Archives Bishopsgate Institute, London, letters to G. Howell · UCL, letters to F. Galton · University of Bristol Library, letters to J. Beddoe
Likenesses photograph, repro. in *Some notes*, frontispiece · photograph (on ninetieth birthday), repro. in *Some notes*, 48
Wealth at death £14,819 3s. 5d.: resworn probate, 2 May 1930, CGPLA Eng. & Wales

Brace, William (1865–1947), trade unionist, was born at Risca, Wales, on 23 September 1865, one of six children of Thomas and Ann Brace. At the age of twelve he went straight from the local board school to work underground at the coal pit. He later worked at Celynnen and Aber-carn collieries before being elected as miners' agent in 1890. In the same year he married Nellie, daughter of William and Harriet Humphreys. They had two sons and a daughter; their eldest son was killed in the First World War, but Ivor Llewellyn became chief justice of North Borneo.

Brace's career fell into two unequal parts. From 1890 to 1920 he was a trade unionist and politician; from 1920 until he retired in 1927 he was in the civil service where, his obituary in the *Western Mail* argued, he did his best work. His real significance, however, was as a miners' leader who perceptibly shaped union activity in the south Wales coalfield. The guiding principle of his union career was his striving for unity. His first battle in this cause came

early. The Miners' Federation of Great Britain (MFGB) had been launched at a meeting held in Newport in 1889, which Brace, then a working collier, took two days off to attend. However, the south Wales miners held aloof, except for the tiny enclave grandiosely named the Monmouth and South Wales District Miners' Union, which had chosen Brace as its agent. There were two stumbling-blocks to unity: the minority of unionized miners in south Wales were loosely organized into a number of separate districts; and wages were tied to the price of coal by a sliding scale, which, with its illusion of automaticity, sapped the motivation towards unionism. The system was stoutly defended by Mabon (William Abraham), the dominant figure on the miners' side for over a generation.

It was this third obstacle that Brace confronted, carrying his campaign throughout the coalfield. Accused by Mabon of bringing 'an English influence' as a lackey of the MFGB, Brace described Mabon as 'a tool … in the hands of the employers'. In an extraordinary slander suit in 1893 Mabon was awarded £500 damages. Brace turned defeat into triumph, however: he astutely displayed the legal demands (which he ignored) at his meetings, mockingly declaiming 'if me and my union and all our household furniture were sold up it would not come to five hundred shillings' (Arnot, *South Wales Miners*, 1.32). His tireless and—it was widely agreed—peerless oratory, combined with the obduracy of the coal-owners, slowly eroded support for the sliding scale. The culmination was the five-month stoppage of 1898 when the victorious coal-owners, led by the unbending W. T. *Lewis, later first Baron Merthyr, insisted on a humiliating settlement which alienated even Mabon.

Despite this setback, Brace profited from defeat in a number of ways that contributed to unity among Welsh miners. A small and significant step was a reconciliation between Brace and Mabon: a greater achievement was the immediate formation of the South Wales Miners' Federation (SWMF) commonly known as the 'Fed'. Another major development occurred in January 1899, when Brace and Mabon attended the annual conference of the MFGB as 'penitent Welshmen', and successfully applied for membership. Brace was miners' agent for Monmouthshire from 1890 to 1920, the first vice-president of the SWMF from 1898 to 1911, and then president until 1920. He was also on the executive committee of the MFGB from 1900 to 1920 (with a wartime break from 1915 to 1918).

Almost inevitably Brace's industrial activity was paralleled by a political career. He was elected MP for South Glamorgan in 1906, holding the seat as a Liberal in the two elections of 1910 despite the fact that the MFGB had affiliated to the Labour Party in 1909. In 1918 he was returned unopposed for Abertillery. From 1915 to 1919 he was a junior minister as under-secretary for home affairs. Although considered likely to be offered high office under a future Labour government, Brace suddenly resigned his seat and union offices in 1920 to become chief labour adviser to the ministry of mines. He took this step because of the bitterness with which the union's new young Turks (and notably A. J. Cook, Noah Ablett, and S. O. Davies) successfully attacked his advice on the settlement of the datum line strike of 1920. Even a quarter of a century later Brace asserted that his opponents 'had gone wild' (Arnot, *South Wales Miners*, 2.196–7).

If unity was one guiding light for him, another was religion. Brace's strong faith was expressed in his will ('any civilisation worth having must be established on the fundamentals of the Christian religion') which included bequests to two Baptist chapels (and their neighbouring hospitals) in Abertillery and Newport. A lifelong abstainer, he was the 'best-dressed trade unionist of his generation' (*Western Mail*) with his immaculate morning coat and silk hat, while his striking presence was emphasized by his flowing, black, handlebar moustache. He was an inspiring speaker, and like Bevan after him he honed his talent by declaiming to the wind on Welsh mountain tops; fittingly, his last speech, strong as ever, was at a celebratory dinner to welcome the creation of the National Union of Miners. Brace died aged eighty-two at his home, 60 Allt yr yn Avenue, Newport, on 12 October 1947, after a long illness.   JOHN WILLIAMS

Sources R. P. Arnot, *South Wales miners / Glowyr de Cymru: a history of the South Wales Miners' Federation*, [1] (1967) · R. P. Arnot, *South Wales miners / Glowyr de Cymru: a history of the South Wales Miners' Federation*, [2] (1975) · *Western Mail* [Cardiff] (14 Oct 1947) · N. Edwards, *History of South Wales Miners' Federation*, 1 (1938) · R. Gregory, *The miners and British politics, 1906–1914* (1968) · L. J. Williams, 'The Monmouthshire and South Wales Coalowners' Association', MA diss., U. Wales, Aberystwyth, 1955 · R. P. Arnot, *The miners: a history of the Miners' Federation of Great Britain*, 1: ... 1889–1910 (1949) · F. Bealey and H. Pelling, *Labour and politics, 1900–1906: a history of the Labour Representation Committee* (1958) · H. A. Clegg, A. Fox, and A. F. Thompson, *A history of British trade unions since 1889*, 1 (1964) · *WWW* · *South Wales Argus* (13 Oct 1947) · *South Wales Argus* (15 Oct 1947) · *South Wales Argus* (17 Oct 1947)

Likenesses photograph, repro. in Arnot, *South Wales miners*, vol. 1

Bracebridge [Brasbrigg], **John** (*fl. c.*1420), priest and book collector, was a priest at the Bridgettine abbey of Syon, at Isleworth in Middlesex. He may be identifiable with the John Bracebrigge who was headmaster of Boston School from 1390, and of Lincoln School from 1406 to 1420. If the identification is accepted, it would appear that in the latter year Bracebridge left Lincoln for Syon. The early sixteenth-century catalogue of books belonging to the brethren at Syon (now Cambridge, Corpus Christi College, MS 141) lists 110 volumes (most of them containing several works) as having been given by Bracebridge, making him substantially the library's chief benefactor. Although theology predominates, his gifts cover a very wide range of subjects, including secular history, canon law, philosophy, medicine, and grammar; under this last occurs a *catholicon*, a grammatical dictionary in two volumes which may well have been written by Bracebridge himself. Like most of the abbey's books, these seem to have been lost at the dissolution, but two of Bracebridge's gifts, both composite volumes, survive in Cambridge libraries, as Trinity College, MS 15.2, and St John's College, MS 1.11.

MARIOS COSTAMBEYS

Sources R. Sharpe, *A handlist of the Latin writers of Great Britain and Ireland before 1540* (1997) · M. Bateson, ed., *Catalogue of the library of*

Syon Monastery, Isleworth (1898) · Emden, *Oxf.*, 1.239–40 · N. Orme, *English schools in the middle ages* (1973), 126

Bracegirdle, Anne (*bap.* **1671**, *d.* **1748**), actress and singer, was born in Northamptonshire, the third surviving daughter of Martha, *née* Furniss, and Justinian Bracegirdle, 'Coachman, Coachmaker or Letter-out of Coaches', according to her admirer Anthony Aston (Aston, 8). Family wills reveal that surviving siblings were named Frances, Martha, Hamlet, and John. Anne was baptized, probably as an infant, at St Giles, Northampton, on 15 November 1671 and was about seventy-seven when she died in 1748, rather than eighty-five, as recorded on her tombstone in Westminster Abbey. She 'had the good Fortune to be well placed, when an Infant, under the care of Mr. Betterton and his Wife, whose Tenderness she always acknowledges to have been Paternal; Nature formed her for the Stage' (Betterton, 26). Anne first appears in performance records on 12 January 1688, when she is listed as member of the United Company, although anecdotal evidence from Betterton suggests that she may have been a child performer with the company, playing the page in Thomas Otway's *The Orphan* as early as 1680. Downes records that during the 1688 season she was mainly cast in supporting roles, such as Atelina in William Mountfort's *The Injured Lovers*, Lucia in Thomas Shadwell's *The Squire of Alsatia*, and Emmeline in Dryden's *King Arthur*.

The following season, on 20 November, Anne Bracegirdle played her first breeches part, Semernia in Aphra Behn's *The Widow Ranter*. She was to become very popular in breeches parts, and often delivered prologues in male garb. Aston recalls: 'she was finely shap'd, and had very handsome Legs and Feet; and her Gait, or Walk was free, manlike, and modest; when in Breeches', although he noted: 'she had a Defect, scarce perceptible, viz. Her Right Shoulder a little protended, which, when in Men's Cloaths, was covered by a Long or Campaign Peruke' (Aston, 10). She also played Marcelia in George Powell's *The Treacherous Brothers* and Biancha in Mountfort's *The Successful Strangers*. On 16 March 1690 she probably replaced Mrs Boutell to create one of her most famous roles, Statira in Nathaniel Lee's *The Rival Queens*, playing opposite Mountfort's Alexander. Colley Cibber recalls the impact of her performance: 'If any thing could excuse that desperate Extravagance of Love, that almost frantick Passion of Lee's Alexander the Great, it must have been when Mrs Bracegirdle was his Statira' (Cibber, 142). By the 1690s Anne was performing in more significant roles, such as Lady Anne in *Richard III* and Desdemona in *Othello*, and was regularly sent out to charm audiences with prologues and epilogues. Cibber, who joined the United Company in 1690, remembers her:

blooming to her Maturity; her Reputation as an actress gradually rising with that of her Person ... she had no greater claim to Beauty than what the most desirable Brunette might pretend to. But her Youth and lively Aspect threw out such a Glow of Health and Chearfulness, that on the Stage few Spectators that were not past it could behold her without Desire. It was even a Fashion among the Gay and Young to have a Taste or Tendre for Mrs. Bracegirdle. (Cibber, 72)

Anne Bracegirdle (*bap.* 1671, *d.* 1748), by William Vincent [as Semernia, the Indian queen, in *The Widow Ranter* by Aphra Behn]

This fashionable devotion was to have tragic consequences on 9 December 1692, when the infatuated Captain Hill and violent Lord Mohun attempted to abduct Mrs Bracegirdle. The attempt failed and she retreated to her home in Howard Street, but Hill loitered outside, vowing revenge on Mountfort, whom he perceived to be his rival in love. When Mountfort appeared at the scene, apparently by chance, Hill ran him through and killed him. Whether Bracegirdle and Mountfort were lovers is not clear, but this was certainly implied in the novelized version of the story, *The Players' Tragedy*, rushed into print in early 1693. The tragedy kept Anne off the stage until after Lord Mohun's trial and acquittal in February 1693, when she returned as Lady Trickitt in Thomas Southerne's *The Maid's Last Prayer*. Neither this role, nor her Araminta in William Congreve's first play, *The Old Bachelor*, was a great success, but by April her performance in Thomas D'Urfey's *The Richmond Heiress* had re-established her popularity. This role, like her part in D'Urfey's *Don Quixote, Part II* the following year, made use of her strong singing voice. John Eccles helped to train her and provided many popular songs. When Dryden saw *The Richmond Heiress*, he thought 'the Singing was wonderfully good, And the two [Dogget and Bracegirdle] sung better than Redding and Mrs Ayloff, whose trade it was' (*BDA*).

By 1694 Anne Bracegirdle was one of the leading players of the United Company, recognized for her triumphs in pathetic tragedy, her lively comic sensibility, and her singing prowess. But all was not well within the company under Christopher Rich's management. Cibber remembers that Rich, 'under Pretence of bringing younger Actors forward, order'd several of Betterton's and Mrs Barry's chief Parts to be given to young Powel and Mrs Bracegirdle'. Powell accepted, but 'Mrs Bracegirdle had a different way of thinking, and desir'd to be excus'd from those of Mrs Barry' (Cibber, 154). Rich's attempts to divide and rule failed, as the 'petition of the players' of 1694 preserved in the lord chamberlain's records (PRO LC 7/3) indicates. Mrs Barry petitioned against the splitting of her annual benefit where 'a third part of the profitt of Mrs Barry's play [was taken] from her to give to Mrs Bracegirdle'. In article 12 of the petition, Mrs Bracegirdle made a bid for her own annual benefit of an old play, very reasonably offering to defray the house charges and, 'what ever she can gett above by the Assistance of her freinds [*sic*] is all she desires for her self'. Cibber recounts that, after a private hearing with King William, Betterton, Barry, and Bracegirdle received their licence for a new company at Lincoln's Inn Fields on 25 March 1695.

Anne Bracegirdle became a shareholder and a key figure in the newly licensed company. She was considered enough of an attraction, playing Angelica in the theatre's opening production of Congreve's *Love for Love*, to be given both the prologue and epilogue to perform. Her contribution to the financial success of the new enterprise is tacitly acknowledged in the prologue to *Love for Love*, where she explains how the theatre was set up:

> By Bribery, errant Brib'ry let me die:
> I was their Agent, but by Jove I swear
> No honourable Member had a Share,
> … I preferr'd my poor Petition
> And brib'd ye to commiserate our Condition.
> (W. Congreve, *Love for Love*, lines 35–7, 46–7)

The early years for the new company were difficult, yet Anne consistently proved to be a draw for audiences. She played a range of leading roles during the next few years, among them Isabella in Gildon's *Measure for Measure* and Bellinda in Vanbrugh's *The Provoked Wife*. She had several parts written for her by Congreve, with whom she apparently developed an intimate relationship. She played Almeria in his *The Mourning Bride* and, most famously, on 5 March 1700 opened as Millamant in *The Way of the World*. The following year Congreve thought her Venus, in his *The Judgment of Paris*, 'performed to a miracle' (*BDA*). Tom Brown waxed very satirical on the relationship between Congreve and the reputedly chaste Bracegirdle in his *Amusements Serious and Comical*. He quipped that:

> tis *the way of the World*, to have an Esteem for the fair sex, and she-looks to a Miracle when she is acting a Part in one of his own Plays … he Dines with her almost ev'ry day, yet She's a Maid, he rides out with her, and visits her in Publick and Private, yet She's a Maid; if I had not a particular respect for her, I should go near to say he lies with her, yet She's a Maid.
> (Brown, 51)

Several poems of the time implied that Congreve and Bracegirdle had married, although there is no evidence of this. Another writer who created roles for her, but in a different vein, was Nicholas Rowe, who wrote pathetic, tragic heroines such as Selima in *Tamerlane*, Lavinia in *The Fair*

Penitent, and Semanthe in *Ulysses*. The Barry–Bracegirdle combination in these plays, which coupled villainess and pathetic heroine, proved to be a popular box-office draw. Anne also captured the headlines during 1701 as Victoria in Southerne's *The Fatal Marriage* and the following year as Evandra in Shadwell's *Timon of Athens* and Cordelia in Tate's *King Lear*.

Together with Betterton and Barry, Anne Bracegirdle appears to have had a controlling influence in the financial running of the Lincoln's Inn Fields company. When Queen Anne came to the throne, it is these three that are named on the players' petition asking for protection against those reformers who wanted the theatres closed. By 1703 John Verbruggen, a leading player and also a signatory on the shareholding agreement, was complaining that the accounts were kept secret and that 'Mr. Betterton Mrs Barry & Mrs Bracegirdle have made Gains to themselves of benefit plays & other wise' (Downes, 253). The 'Three Ruling B—'s' are satirized in the dedication to the anonymous play *The Lunatick* (1705), which prophesies the end of their 'abuses' when the Haymarket Theatre opens. By 1705 Mrs Bracegirdle's weekly earnings were assured at £3, rising to as much as £5 when profits were good. By 1707 her earnings equalled those of the other leading players, Barry, Betterton, Powell, and Wilks—probably in excess of £120 annually. The 1706–7 season saw what Congreve dubbed 'another revolution' as the companies reorganized, and Mrs Bracegirdle moved to the Queen's Theatre, Haymarket, under the management of Owen Swiny. She played a few new roles, including Aspasia in Beaumont and Fletcher's *The Maid's Tragedy* and Harriet in George Etherege's *The Man of Mode*, but this season was her last on the stage. Several reasons have been mooted for her departure. Betterton recounts a contest set up between Bracegirdle and the company's rising young actress, Ann Oldfield. They were to play the title role in Betterton's *The Amorous Widow* on consecutive nights; in the event, Oldfield 'charm'd the whole Audience to that Degree, they almost forgot they had ever seen Mrs. Bracegirdle … which so much disgusted her celebrated Antagonist, that in a short time after she quitted the Stage'. The anonymous life of Ann Oldfield published in 1730 suggests a further twist, that 'Mrs. Oldfield's benefit, being allowed by Swiney [Swiny] to be in the season before Mrs. Bracegirdle's, added so much to the affront that she quitted the stage immediately' (Genest, 2.375). It is possible that Anne's financial position was adversely affected by the younger talent and the reorganization of the companies. After a final performance on 18 February 1707 as Lavinia in Betterton's *Caius Marius*, Anne Bracegirdle quit the stage, 'nor could she be persuaded to return to it, under new Masters, upon the most advantageous Terms, that were offered her' (Cibber, 143). She returned to the stage only once more, for the benefit of her old ally Betterton, in her famed role as Angelica in *Love for Love*. One or two mezzotints captured her in action, but her grandest portrait is as an emblematic figure, standing at the feet of William III's horse in Kneller's huge painting of 1697.

It is not clear how Anne Bracegirdle supported herself after her departure from the stage, but she was helped by bequests and contributions from her admirers. The earl of Scarsdale left her £1000 in his will, proved on 2 January 1708. Whatever Anne's actual relationship with such figures, she maintained a reputation for modesty. Aston called her 'that *Diana* of the Stage', and even suggested that her chaste behaviour had financial rewards:

> The Dukes of Dorset and Devonshire, Lord Hallifax, and other Nobles, over a Bottle, were all extolling Mrs. Bracegirdle's virtuous Behaviour, *Come*, says Lord *Hallifax*,— *You all commend her Virtue, &c. but why do we not present this incomparable woman with something worthy her Acceptance?* His Lordship deposited 200 Guineas, which the rest made up 800, and sent her with Encomiums on her Virtue. (Aston, 10)

As Gildon has his Critick quip, she 'has got more money be dissembling her Lewdness, than others by professing it' (Gildon, 70). When Mrs Barry died she left Anne £220 in her will, to preserve her from 'any debt of the Playhouse', which implies that Mrs Bracegirdle may still have had a financial interest in the theatre, although she appeared to spend the remaining thirty-nine years of her life out of the public eye. In the early 1740s she moved from Howard Street to the home of Mr Chute, where she died on Monday 12 September 1748. She was buried at Westminster Abbey on 18 September. In her will she left £10 to the poor, £400 to her nephew Justinian, and £100 to Mrs Ann Hodge, spinster. The remainder she left to her niece Martha.

J. MILLING

Sources Highfill, Burnim & Langhans, *BDA* · C. Cibber, *An apology for the life of Mr. Colley Cibber* (1740) · T. Betterton, [W. Oldys and others], *The history of the English stage* (1741) · J. Milhous, *Thomas Betterton and the management of Lincoln's Inn Fields, 1695–1708* (1979) · A. Aston, *A brief supplement to Colley Cibber, esq.: his 'Lives of the late famous actors and actresses'* [n.d., c.1747] · C. Gildon, *A comparison between two stages* (1702) · Genest, *Eng. stage* · J. Downes, *Roscius Anglicanus*, ed. J. Milhous and R. D. Hume, new edn (1987) · J. Haynes, 'Anne Bracegirdle', *TLS* (2 May 1986) · L. Hook, 'Anne Bracegirdle's first appearance', *Theatre Notebook*, 13 (1958–9), 133–6 · T. Brown, *Amusements serious and comical* (1700)
Likenesses G. Kneller, group portrait, 1697 (with William III), Hampton Court · Kneller, sketch, c.1697, Houghton Hall, Norfolk · J. Smith, portrait, 1737, Garr. Club · T. Bradwell, portrait, 1755, Garr. Club · J. Stow, line engraving, pubd 1811 (after Harding), BM, NPG · F. H. van den Hoven, engraving, repro. in *Deliciae musicae* (1696), title-page · J. Smith, mezzotint (as Semernia in *The widow Ranter*), V&A · attrib. W. Vincent, mezzotint (as Placentia in *Beauty in distress*), V&A · W. Vincent, mezzotint, BM, NPG [*see illus.*]
Wealth at death over £510: Highfill, Burnim & Langhans, *BDA*, 2.581

Bracegirdle, John (*d.* 1614), Church of England clergyman and poet, whose place and date of birth are unknown, matriculated as a sizar at Queens' College, Cambridge, in 1588, and was granted BD in 1602. Previous accounts of his life state that he was the son of John Bracegirdle (*d.* 1585), vicar of Stratford upon Avon, and that he was born in Cheshire, but this seems unlikely as this Bracegirdle's will mentions neither marriage nor children. Following university Bracegirdle was ordained priest in Lincoln by

Bishop William Chaderton on 14 May 1598, after which followed a series of clerical appointments in Sussex: as rector of St John's-sub-Castro, Lewes, on 21 November 1598, which he held until 1602; rector of St Thomas-in-the-Cliffe in 1599; vicar of Rye on 12 July 1602; vicar of West Firle on 29 January 1602; and finally vicar of Peasmarsh on 31 July 1606.

Bracegirdle's only known work is in manuscript: 'Psychopharmacon, the mindes medicine, or, The phisicke of philosophie', in five books and dated 1602; it survives as BL, Add. MS 11401. This is a translation into English of Boethius with the prose translated into blank verse, and the verse into different forms of rhyme; it is dedicated to Thomas Sackville, later earl of Dorset, who as Lord Buckhurst presented him with the vicarage of Rye. This may indicate that Bracegirdle had puritan leanings which Sackville wished to promote; east Sussex was notorious for puritanism from the 1570s onwards and Rye reportedly had a puritan mayor in 1610. The gentry were known to encourage educated ministers who could preach well and Bracegirdle was licenced to preach throughout the diocese on 29 January 1604.

Bracegirdle was married to Sarah Blaxton (1580–1639), one of nine children of Henry Blaxton (d. 1606), chancellor of Chichester Cathedral, and his wife, Joan Nunn (d. 1607). Bracegirdle and his wife had at least one son, also called John, who was baptized in 1607 in Rye, and possibly one daughter, Rebecca.

Bracegirdle's 'Psychopharmacon' included a promise to produce further work but any other literary intentions he may have had were terminated with his death in early 1614, and he was buried on 8 February at St Mary's Church, Rye. As his will is missing it is not known how his finances stood; the plurality of his livings might suggest he was seeking to supplement a low income but the more learned clergy frequently held several offices. In 1614 his wife married another clergyman, William Stonard (c.1571–1637), parson of Ashurst, Sussex.　　　　　C. BATEY

Sources Cooper, *Ath. Cantab.* · W. C. Renshaw, 'Some clergy of the archdeaconry of Lewes and South Malling deanery', *Sussex Archaeological Collections*, 100 (1962), 220–77, esp. 226 · G. S. Butler, 'The vicars of Rye and their patrons', *Sussex Notes and Queries*, vol. 13, 274–5 · W. D. Peckham, *Chichester institutions, 1601–1614* · P. R. Jenkins, 'The condition of the clergy of the diocese of Chichester, 1601–1640', BA diss., 1981, Wilts. & Swindon RO, MP1982 · G. R. Axon, 'He baptised Shakespeare', *Cheshire Life*, 18/11 (1955) · W. H. Challen, 'Henry Blaxton, DD', *Sussex Notes and Queries*, 14 (1954–7), 221–5 · E. H. W. Dunkin, ed., *Calendar of Sussex marriage licences*, Sussex RS, 12 (1911), 48 · J. G. Bishop, 'Lancelot Andrewes, bishop of Chichester', *The Chichester Papers*, 33 (1963), 11 · P. Clark, *English provincial society* (1977) · J. Saunders, *A biographical dictionary of Renaissance poets and dramatists, 1520–1650* (1983) · *VCH Sussex*, 2.33 · A. Fletcher, *A county community in peace and war: Sussex, 1600–1660* (1974)

Bracey [*née* Phillips], **Joan** (1656?–1685?), highwaywoman, was the daughter of John Phillips, a wealthy farmer in Northamptonshire. The principal source of evidence relating to Joan is Alexander Smith's *A Complete History of the Lives and Robberies of the most Notorious Highwaymen*, first published in 1719. Although it has been demonstrated that

Smith's work was historically inaccurate no other authenticating evidence about Joan has yet come to light. Captain Johnson's account of Joan, published in 1755, appears to copy wholesale, with some embellishments, from Smith's earlier work. Smith claims that when she was about twenty-four she was courted and seduced by the highwayman Edward Bracey (1654–1685), who hoped to secure a marriage portion from the match. He further suggests that Joan soon joined Edward on the road and that they committed innumerable highway robberies together, always passing for husband and wife, though they were never officially married.

The Braceys made enough money, Smith continues, to enable them to give up the road and open an inn in the suburbs of Bristol. Joan's great beauty meant that 'all the gay young fellows of the place came to drink with Madam Bracey' (Rayner and Crook, 1.300) and, though she encouraged her many admirers to spend their money, she appears to have remained faithful to Edward and to have enjoyed duping her would-be lovers. According to Smith one suitor, an eminent merchant named Day, was robbed of his money and clothes as a result of one of Joan's tricks. He was told that, with her husband away, Joan awaited him in her bedchamber. Day was shown into an adjoining room by a maidservant and asked to undress before she would take him to Joan's bedroom. Naked to his shirt, and in darkened rooms for the sake of modesty, Day was shown to a room that he believed to be Joan's but which in fact led to the back lane behind the inn. To the lifelong amusement of his friends, concludes Smith, Day was able to explain his nakedness on his way home only by pretending to be mad.

Another cheat related by Smith was performed on a young man called Rumbald, the heir to an estate of £100 on the death of an uncle. In debt to the Braceys, he was threatened by Joan until he agreed to rob on the highway with Edward and another companion. A robbery was staged, whereupon Joan said that she would turn evidence and have Rumbald hanged unless he agreed to make over the reversion of his estate to her.

Smith states that the inn gained such a scandalous reputation that the Braceys were forced to leave and to resume their former course of life. For the remainder of Joan's career she and Edward 'committed a great many robberies together on the highway', with Joan usually in male disguise. Joan was eventually caught, although Edward and another companion escaped, during a robbery on the Loughborough Road, near Nottingham. According to one modern account she was executed at the end of Wilford Lane, in Nottingham, on 15 April 1685 and her body taken to a village in Sherwood Forest for burial.

BARBARA WHITE

Sources A. Smith, *A complete history of the lives and robberies of the most notorious highwaymen*, ed. A. L. Hayward, 5th edn (1719); repr. (1926) · J. L. Rayner and G. T. Crook, eds., *The complete Newgate calendar*, 1 (privately printed, London, 1926) · P. Pringle, *Stand and deliver: the story of the highwayman* (1951) · P. Haining, *The English highwayman: a legend unmasked* (1991) · [Captain Johnson], *The lives and adventures of the German princess* (Mary Carleton), *Mary Read, Anne*

Bonny, Joan Philips, Madam Churchill, Betty Ireland, and Ann Hereford (1755)

Bracken, Brendan Rendall, Viscount Bracken (1901–1958), politician and publisher, was born on 15 February 1901 at Church Street, Templemore, co. Tipperary, the second son and third of the four children of Joseph Kevin Bracken (1852–1904), builder and monumental mason, and his second wife, Hannah Agnes Ryan (1872–1928). His father belonged to the Irish Republican Brotherhood. His temperamental mother aspired to gentility. Widowed in 1904, she had by 1908 moved her family (including two stepdaughters) to Dublin. There Brendan, a bright and unruly child, attended St Patrick's national school, Drumcondra, until 1910, when he transferred to the O'Connell School, run by the Christian Brothers. Distressed by his misbehaviour, Mrs Bracken sent him in 1915 to Mungret, a Jesuit boarding-school near Limerick, but he bolted and ran up hotel bills. A family friend, Patrick Laffan, had a brother in New South Wales; the tearaway was shipped off to join him in 1916 (a draconian response rendered more explicable perhaps by the boy's jealousy of his mother's attachment to Laffan). Bracken led a precarious life in Australia. Sacked from a sheep farm, he worked intermittently at schools in Echuca, Sydney, and Orange, and avoided vagrancy by visiting convents as a student of church history. Loss of faith did not ever diminish his love of the ecclesiastical. He read voraciously, talked incessantly, and latched onto new acquaintances with alacrity.

After returning to Ireland in 1919, Bracken found his mother, now Mrs Patrick Laffan, embroiled in a bitter dispute with his siblings over money. He left them to it and headed for England, where he purported to be an Australian, this being the time of the Anglo-Irish War. Henceforth he would not willingly admit to Irish or Roman Catholic roots. Later, when famous, he deliberately made a mystery of his background (while giving financial assistance to relatives whom he hardly ever saw). Claiming to be a graduate, he earned enough from teaching jobs in Lancashire to afford to spend autumn 1920 as a pupil at Sedbergh public school, posing as a fifteen-year-old orphan—though tall, burly, and contemptuous of authority. The old school tie won him transient employment at preparatory schools at Rottingdean and Bishop's Stortford, where he told tall stories about friends in high places. Late 1922 found him in London working part-time for the *Empire Review*, a monthly journal run by Oliver Locker-Lampson. One of its contributors, J. L. Garvin, took a shine to the eager young 'Australian' and introduced him to various figures in politics and journalism. One was Winston Churchill, for whom Bracken at once manifested an extraordinary enthusiasm. Churchill put him to good use as an election helper in 1923–4. Bracken did not discourage a rumour that he was Winston's illegitimate son.

In December 1923 another new associate, Major J. S. Crosthwaite-Eyre of the publishers Eyre and Spottiswoode, invited him to edit a number of the *Illustrated Review*. Bracken repackaged it as *English Life* and gained entrée to London salons in return for publicity puffs. His social success was that of an unconventional 'character': a

Brendan Rendall Bracken, Viscount Bracken (1901–1958), by unknown photographer, 1941

loud-mouthed know-all, impervious to rebuffs, who gatecrashed parties and insulted everyone with reckless abandon. His witty cracks were as renowned as his preposterous lies. When caught out, he would simply laugh. Charlatanism comprised a part of his entertainment value, and his looks did him no harm: a big pale face, a slightly flattened nose, wire spectacles, blackened teeth, and a shock of crinkly carrot-coloured hair which sat on his head like a bad wig. His accent was hybrid Irish-Australian-Cockney, and a cigarette usually dangled from his lip. Casual observers saw in Bracken the unconscious rudeness of a natural barbarian. In truth there was no such simplicity about him. To clergymen and headmasters, for example, he could appear serious, sensitive, idealistic, and even spiritual. Perceptive associates understood that here was a personality so contradictory that attempts to distinguish bogus traits from genuine would be futile.

Crosthwaite-Eyre, for one, thought highly of Bracken. His drive and intelligence merited a seat on the board of Eyre and Spottiswoode in January 1926. *The Banker*, their new periodical, was Bracken's idea. Now he induced this old-fashioned firm to plunge headlong into financial journalism, acquiring in 1928 the *Financial News* (a City daily), the *Investors' Chronicle*, the *Liverpool Journal of Commerce*, and a half-stake in *The Economist*. While projecting the image of a press baron, Bracken was actually only a modest shareholder in Financial Newspaper Proprietors Ltd, the subsidiary which ran these titles, yet he did earn £3000 a year as editor of *The Banker*, chairman of the *Financial News*, and managing director of *The Economist*. His chauffeur-driven

Hispano-Suiza may have helped impress the Conservatives of marginal North Paddington, who adopted him as candidate for the general election of 1929. He scraped home after a boisterous campaign, but quickly had to refocus on business, as the profits of the financial press plummeted after the Wall Street crash. Though always a moody and unpredictable employer, Bracken appreciated that specialist papers rely on high standards and to deliver these he picked the right men: Paul Einzig and Maurice Green, for example. His own editorial interventions did not amount to much. Still, by 1934, when he became chairman, Financial Newspaper Proprietors Ltd was prospering once more with a livelier style of economic news.

In parliament Bracken rekindled his relationship with Churchill, who, now politically isolated again, found time for the extrovert who so warmly agreed with him on all the great issues of the day. Baldwin, often the target of their criticism, famously described Bracken as the faithful *chela* (Hindi for a slave-like votary of a guru). Indeed, this was no normal political alliance: Bracken readily met Churchill's demand for hero-worship, applauding his wisdom, excoriating his foes, running his errands, and touting his journalism. The older man enjoyed the vehemence, flippancy, sarcasm, and zest of an acolyte who shared something of his own way with words. Even Clementine Churchill ultimately recognized that this insufferable interloper had a talent for laughing her husband out of melancholy. Many, however, viewed their intimacy as proof of Churchill's bad judgement.

To the Commons, Bracken preached the gospel of Winston on India, armaments, and foreign policy. Economics elicited his own voice, though, advocating *laissez-faire*. North Paddington saw him only infrequently, as he loved the social whirl of Westminster. There in 1930 he had bought 8 North Street (renamed Lord North Street in 1937). It was a Georgian house, and he furnished it in period, becoming a connoisseur of architecture, antiques, and rare books. He courted a couple of society beauties, Lady Pamela Smith and Penelope Dudley Ward, and liked people to think that he remained unmarried because the latter had rejected him. His self-assurance faltered in the presence of nubile women. He was probably celibate. An object of fascination to amateur psychologists, he never truthfully confided much in anybody.

When Churchill was made first lord of the Admiralty in September 1939, Bracken became his parliamentary private secretary. No one intrigued harder to get Winston into Downing Street, for Bracken revelled in the role of brash, tough, cynical, political 'fixer'. Sworn of the privy council in June 1940 (despite royal doubts), he moved into no. 10 so as to be always on hand for 'the Boss'. Their midnight bouts of wild talk and hard drinking (often with Lord Beaverbrook) were grist to the mill of Churchill's critics, yet even they could never decide whether Bracken was evil genius or court jester. Day in, day out, he had the prime minister's ear. He brought him the gossip, spread his message, and helped him develop his ideas through discussion. The detail of such influence is elusive, but Bracken tended to show more interest in people than in

policies. Junior appointments and honours were his province, with his power varying inversely with the premier's preoccupations. Churchill, for example, let him handle church patronage. Bracken meanwhile hinted at knowing all the secrets. Never a simple 'yes man', he could get away with saying things to his chief that nobody else would dare to utter. Their violent quarrels were soon forgotten, and Winston made a joke of having to humour 'poor dear Brendan'.

Bracken's promotion to minister of information on 21 July 1941 raised eyebrows—and turned out to be a masterstroke. The department, located at Senate House, Bloomsbury, was notoriously discordant and despised. Trapped between news-hungry journalists and tight-lipped defence staff, it had alienated both. Suddenly Bracken's aggressive energy shocked the ministry out of its malaise, while his decisive leadership clarified its purpose—which was not to try and stimulate patriotism or good cheer, but simply to supply as much news about the war as possible within the constraints of military security. Exploiting his link to Churchill he badgered the War Office, Admiralty, and Air Ministry into speeding up the flow of information and ending excessive censorship. The public, he argued, could be trusted to interpret war news more maturely.

The minister might shirk his paperwork, yet he knew how to handle the media—ever available and ready to comment, never defensive or condescending. American correspondents particularly liked the informality of his weekly press conferences, when he embroidered the official communiqués with anecdotes and *faux* indiscretions. Old habits died hard: he loved to tell of a mythical brother in the navy. Interdepartmental rows were common, especially with the Foreign Office. In the political warfare executive, Bracken feuded ferociously with Hugh Dalton over propaganda to enemy-occupied countries. On the other hand he soothed relations between the government and the BBC, whose independence he safeguarded by differentiating sharply between overseas broadcasting (needing close supervision) and domestic broadcasting (as free as the press). By 1943 the Ministry of Information was running so effectively that its political head seemed bored with it. He left routine to the director-general, Cyril Radcliffe, and concentrated on aiding the prime minister.

Bracken had become one of the most influential figures outside the war cabinet. Not many Conservative MPs had advanced so far during the coalition years. He was first lord of the Admiralty in the caretaker government formed on 25 May 1945. But perhaps Bracken and the Ministry of Information had been merely a happy coincidence: an unusual minister for an unusual ministry. As Beaverbrook hoped otherwise, the *Daily Express* gave him unwonted publicity during the general election, headlining his opposition to planning, Keynesianism, and extravagant welfare schemes.

Bracken was disproportionately blamed for the Conservative defeat in July 1945, when he lost his seat. A by-election in Bournemouth returned him in November, yet his whipping-boy role was affirmed: for disaffected backbenchers, decrying Bracken was a coded way of sniping at Churchill, a party leader beyond open reproach. It did not matter that he shadowed fuel and power with provocative flair; root-and-branch anti-socialism embarrassed tory reformers. In business he flourished. Thanks to his late friend, Sir Henry Strakosch, he chaired the Union Corporation from 1945. He may not have known much about its South African mines, but his phenomenal range of contacts justified his fee. In September 1945 he merged the *Financial News* with the *Financial Times* (another chairmanship for him) and in 1951 he launched *History Today*.

Bournemouth East and Christchurch retained Bracken in parliament in February 1950 and October 1951. Then in November he retired from politics after declining the Colonial Office in Churchill's government. Viscount Bracken of Christchurch, created in January 1952, never took his seat in the Lords. His vitality, previously so great, had grown fitful. Some were pleased to say that he had mellowed; others found him morose. Acute sinusitis was a factor. He could still be quite his old self when browbeating *Financial Times* staff. His 'Men and matters' column appeared weekly until 1955. Public schools were his passion, carried almost to excess. He made major benefactions to Sedbergh and chaired its board of governors. His death at Flat 121, Grosvenor House, Park Lane, London, on 8 August 1958 was caused by cancer of the throat. The body was cremated without ceremony at Golders Green.

Brendan Bracken had made his way by a quick brain, audacity, and turbulent forcefulness. Those who knew him best vowed that under his thick defensive shell there beat a heart of gold. Maybe they sentimentalized him in reaction to others who portrayed him only as a bully, boor, or grotesque. His generosity, though real, was capricious. He was a uniquely successful minister of information, and it is ironic how an incurable romancer improved the openness of wartime news management. Not until the 1970s were the facts of his early life clarified. Bracken is remembered as Churchill's loyal supporter through thick and thin and also as an oddity.   JASON TOMES

Sources C. E. Lysaght, *Brendan Bracken* (1979) • A. Boyle, *Poor dear Brendan* (1974) • *My dear Max: the letters of Brendan Bracken to Lord Beaverbrook*, ed. R. Cockett (1990) • *The diaries of Sir Robert Bruce Lockhart*, ed. K. Young, 2 (1980) • I. McLaine, *Ministry of morale* (1979) • D. Kynaston, *The Financial Times: a centenary history* (1988) • Lord Moran, *Churchill: the struggle for survival, 1940–1965* (1966) • P. Einzig, *In the centre of things* (1960) • J. Colville, *The fringes of power* (1985) • Hansard 5C • R. S. Churchill, *Twenty-one years* (1965) • J. Ramsden, *The age of Churchill and Eden, 1940–1957* (1995) • *DNB* • b. cert.
Archives Bodl. Oxf., corresp. with Lord Monckton; corresp. with third earl of Selborne • Borth. Inst., corresp. with Lord Halifax • CAC Cam., corresp. with P. G. Buchan-Hepburn • CAC Cam., corresp. with P. Einzig • CAC Cam., corresp. with Lord Halifax [copies] • CAC Cam., corresp. with Sir E. L. Spears • CUL, corresp. with Sir S. Hoare • HLRO, corresp. with Lord Beaverbrook • HLRO, corresp. with Viscount Davidson • JRL, letters to the *Manchester Guardian* • Nuffield Oxf., corresp. with Lord Cherwell • PRO, corresp. with Sir E. Bridges, CAB 127/330 • PRO, corresp. with Sir S. Cripps, CAB 127/76 • TCD, corresp. with T. Bodkin • U. Birm. L., corresp. with Sir A. Eden | FILM IWM FVA, actuality footage • IWM FVA, news footage | SOUND IWM SA, oral history interview • IWM SA, recorded lecture
Likenesses photograph, 1941, Sci. Mus., Science and Society Picture Library [*see illus.*] • R. Lutyens, charcoal, 1956–9, CAC Cam., Bracken Library • U. Nimptsch, bust, 1956–9, Bracken House, Cannon Street, London • photographs, repro. in Lysaght, *Brendan Bracken*
Wealth at death £145,735 5s. 6d.: probate, 1958

Bracken, Henry (*bap.* 1697, *d.* 1764), writer on farriery and surgeon, was baptized on 31 October 1697 at St Mary, Lancaster, the son of Henry Bracken, a local innkeeper who held a number of minor offices with the Lancaster corporation. After a grammar-school education at Lancaster he was apprenticed to Dr Thomas Worthington, a Wigan physician. At the end of his apprenticeship about 1717, Bracken went to London and spent a few months as a pupil of St Thomas's Hospital but was disappointed with the lack of cadavers. He next went to Paris to the Hôtel Dieu where he found plenty of opportunity for dissection and was able to attend midwifery cases through the intercession of the English ambassador, the earl of Stair. On 29 August 1730 he matriculated at the University of Leiden, where he attended Boerhaave's lectures for eighteen months, though this was in a non-graduate capacity. After an unsuccessful attempt to establish himself in London, Bracken set himself up as a physician, surgeon, and man-midwife in Lancaster. Bracken married Ann Hopkins in January 1720 and may have been the Henry Bracken who married Susannah X. Bracken about 1725.

Having already written on both human and equine medicine, Bracken published his most famous and best-selling work, *Farriery Improved, or, A Compleat Treatise upon the Art of Farriery*, in two volumes in 1738. Its popularity sprang from Bracken's robust language and common-sense solutions, which were grounded as much in his first-hand knowledge of the general care and feeding of horses, as in his application of Newtonian medicine to their treatment. The work ran to twelve editions. Bracken also published several other popular works on farriery, a number of medical articles, and substantial monographs on midwifery and the stone.

Bracken experienced mixed fortunes in his public and private life. Between 1726 and 1731 he held a variety of offices for the Lancaster corporation, such as auditor, chamberlain, and bailiff, but was politically marginalized for most of the next two decades. During the 1730s he was also engaged in a protracted dispute with Peter Kennedy MD, the author of a treatise on the eye. A staunch Roman Catholic tory, Bracken was imprisoned for allegedly abetting the Jacobite rising of 1745. His imprisonment, which was possibly instigated by local enemies, was short-lived. He was discharged without trial, and it appears there were no grounds for his arrest. Personal tragedy followed. Bracken, who had already lost three infant daughters, now lost his only son to fever—contracted when he had visited his father in prison. Bracken recovered from his setbacks and was elected mayor of Lancaster in 1748 and again in 1758. He died at Lancaster on 13 November 1764.   MAX SATCHELL

Sources D. Harley, 'Ethics and dispute behaviour in the career of Henry Bracken of Lancaster: surgeon, physician and manmidwife', *The codification of medical morality*, ed. R. Baker and others (1993), 47–71 · *DNB* · F. Smith, *The early history of veterinary literature and its British development*, 4 vols. (1919–33); repr. (1976), vol. 2, pp. 29–39 · R. W. Innes Smith, *English-speaking students of medicine at the University of Leyden* (1932), 29 · J. F. Smithcors, 'William Gibson, surgeon, farrier, on fevers', *Medical History*, 2 (1958), 210–20 · *IGI*

Brackenbury, Charles Booth (1831–1890), army officer, born in Bayswater, London, on 7 November 1831, was the third son of William Brackenbury (*d.* 1844), lieutenant, 61st foot (1809–16), of Aswardby, Lincolnshire, and his wife, Maria (*b. c.*1798), daughter of James Atkinson of Newry, co. Down, and widow of James L. Wallace. He belonged to an old Lincolnshire family, well represented in nearly all the nineteenth-century British wars. William Brackenbury served in the same regiment as his elder brother, Sir Edward *Brackenbury (1785–1864), and was wounded at Talavera and Salamanca. Sir Henry *Brackenbury (1837–1914) was Charles Brackenbury's brother.

Charles Brackenbury obtained a cadetship at the Royal Military Academy, Woolwich, on 8 July 1847, was commissioned second lieutenant, Royal Artillery, on 19 December 1850, and became lieutenant on 27 September 1852. He served in the Crimea from June 1855, with the chestnut troop of the horse artillery. Having been promoted second captain on 17 November 1857, he was sent to Malta. In March 1860 he was appointed assistant instructor in artillery at the Royal Military Academy, and in February 1864 assistant director of artillery studies at Woolwich. He became first captain on 9 February 1865, and was a boundary commissioner under the 1867 Reform Act.

During the Austro-Prussian War of 1866 Brackenbury was the *Times* correspondent with the Austrian army, and was at the battle of Königgrätz (Sadowa)—riding with Benedek under fire at Chlum—and reported the naval battle of Lissa. He was the *Times* correspondent in the Franco-Prussian War, accompanying Prince Frederick Charles in the Le Mans campaign; and in the Russo-Turkish War of 1877, when he crossed the Balkans with Count Gourko.

Brackenbury became regimental major on 5 July 1872, and lieutenant-colonel on 15 January 1876. In September 1873 he was attached to the recently established intelligence branch of the War Office, as acting deputy assistant adjutant-general then deputy assistant adjutant-general (April 1874 to March 1876). In 1875 he lectured at the Royal United Service Institution on 'The intelligence duties of the staff abroad and at home', showing the disparity in size between the intelligence branch and continental staffs, and calling for upgrading and enlargement of the former. From April 1876 to June 1880 he was superintending officer of garrison instruction at Aldershot, and from July 1880 to June 1885 superintendent of the gunpowder factory at Waltham Abbey, Essex. He was promoted colonel in the army on 15 January 1881, and in the regiment on 1 October 1882. He commanded the artillery in the south-eastern district, as colonel on the staff, from 8 May 1886 until 2 June 1887, when he was appointed director of

Charles Booth Brackenbury (1831–1890), by C. W. Walton

artillery studies at Woolwich. His title was changed on 1 October 1889 to 'director of the artillery college', and he was given the temporary rank of major-general.

On 6 April 1854 Brackenbury married Hilda Eliza, daughter of Archibald Campbell of Quebec, her majesty's notary, and they had six sons and three daughters. Two sons joined the Indian staff corps, and died in India—Charles Herbert, of typhoid fever contracted in the Bolan Pass in 1885; Lionel Wilhelm, killed at Manipur in 1891.

Unlike many officers Brackenbury had no Indian service or colonial war experience, but he had witnessed continental great-power war. Impressed and influenced by the Prussian army, he became one of the 'Prussophile', 'continentalist' school in Britain, ignoring the American Civil War and urging copying from the Prussians, including replacement of line formation by 'swarm'. He advocated continental offensive doctrine and criticized preoccupation with minimizing losses, claiming 'the side which has the greatest moral force wins' (Bailes, 103). Like other continentalists he became quite rigid in his views. He urged army reform and innovation including tactical change, large-scale manoeuvres, Royal Artillery higher education, and a general staff with a chief of staff. In the early 1870s he advocated machine guns, and in 1878 he advocated iron shields (separate from the gun, not attached as was later the case) to protect field artillery gunners from infantry fire and shrapnel. In the *Contemporary Review* he warned against military unpreparedness and the danger of invasion.

Wanting to increase pressure for army reform, Brackenbury after 1884 became friendly with Spenser Wilkinson and they discussed military issues. Brackenbury criticized Wolseley and the duke of Cambridge, and urged Wilkinson to demand a chief of staff and army organization ready for war. Wilkinson later described Brackenbury as 'one of the most accomplished officers of the progressive school, a master of his profession and a clear exponent of its principles' (Gwynn and Tuckwell, 2.389). Sir Charles Dilke, following the collapse of his career with the 1885 Crawford divorce scandal, took up the cause of army reform and cultivated senior officers, seeking expertise. He contacted Brackenbury, who from 1887 advised and assisted him with his articles and books on defence including *The Present Position of European Politics* (1887), *The British Army* (1888)—Dilke wrote in his unpublished memoirs of the articles from which he compiled the books, 'the first two … were entirely from my hand, whereas the others of that series were largely Charles Brackenbury's' (BL, Add. MS 43941)—and *Problems of Greater Britain* (1890); these works publicized British defence inadequacies and demanded reform. As Brackenbury was on the active list his role was not disclosed: he wrote to Dilke, 'I am obliged to maintain a strict incognito' (BL, Add. MS 43913, fols. 204–5). Brackenbury was also a friend of George Meredith and discussed military issues with him.

Brackenbury's main publications were *European Armaments in 1867* (based on articles in *The Times*, in 1867)—mostly on ordnance, and including his assessment of the Gatling gun, *The Constitutional Forces of Great Britain* (1869), *Foreign Armies and Home Reserves* (from *The Times*, 1871), *Frederick the Great* (1884), and *Field-Works: their Technical Construction and Tactical Application* (1888), in a series of military handbooks he edited. His contributions to the *United Service Institution Journal* (vols. 15–28) included papers on 'The military systems of France and Prussia in 1870' (15), 'The winter campaign of Prince Frederick Charles, 1870–71' (15), 'The intelligence duties of the staff' (19), and 'The latest development of the tactics of the three arms' (27.439). He frequently contributed to *The Times*, and once to the *Nineteenth Century*.

Brackenbury's cousin Edward Brackenbury (1848–1907), Royal Artillery, in 1870 married Emilie ('Mimi') Shaw, sister of Flora Shaw (1852–1929). Brackenbury's wife disliked housekeeping and found her children rather burdensome, and in the late 1870s and early 1880s Flora Shaw lived with Brackenbury's family at Aldershot and Waltham Abbey in the role of housekeeper–governess. She became a quasi-filial close friend of Brackenbury, consulting him on her problems, and in the later 1880s he used his contacts, including Spenser Wilkinson—to whom he described her in 1889 as 'not only clever, but graceful and womanly' (Spenser Wilkinson MSS, 9011-42-133-17)—to try to advance her career in journalism.

In February 1890, following overwork, Brackenbury fainted in the street in Woolwich and 'went down to a zero of strength' (Spenser Wilkinson MSS, 9011-42-133-20). Following convalescence, he resumed his duties. Returning from his work at Woolwich to his home in Chelsea, he died suddenly on 20 June 1890 in a first-class railway carriage, between Maze Hill and London Bridge, following a heart attack, and was buried with military honours at Plumstead cemetery, Woolwich.

E. M. LLOYD, *rev.* ROGER T. STEARN

Sources *The Times* (21 June 1890) · NAM, Spenser Wilkinson MSS · BL, Dilke MSS · H. Brackenbury, 'A letter from Salamanca', *Blackwood*, 165 (1899), 376–84 · private information (1901) · H. H. R. Bailes, 'The influence of continental examples and colonial warfare upon the reforms of the late Victorian army', PhD diss., U. Lond., 1980 · E. M. Spiers, *The late Victorian army, 1868–1902* (1992) · T. G. Fergusson, *British military intelligence, 1870–1914* (1984) · S. Gwynn and G. M. Tuckwell, *The life of the Rt. Hon. Sir Charles W. Dilke*, 2 vols. (1917) · W. S. Hamer, *The British army: civil–military relations, 1885–1905* (1970) · Boase, *Mod. Eng. biog.* · E. M. Bell, *Flora Shaw (Lady Lugard DBE)* (1947) · H. Brackenbury, *Some memories of my spare time* (1909) · *Hart's Army List* (1889) · *Army List* (1889) · *Annual Register* (1890) · Burke, *Gen. GB* (1937) · *CGPLA Eng. & Wales* (1890)
Archives NAM, letters to Spenser Wilkinson · Tyne and Wear Archives Service, Newcastle upon Tyne, letters to Lord Rendel
Likenesses C. W. Walton, lithograph, NPG [*see illus.*] · wood-engraving, repro. in *ILN* (28 June 1890)
Wealth at death £3550 1s. 9d.: probate, 23 July 1890, *CGPLA Eng. & Wales*

Brackenbury, Sir Edward (1785–1864), army officer, a direct descendant of Sir Robert *Brackenbury, lieutenant of the Tower of London in the time of Richard III, was second son of Richard Brackenbury of Aswardby, Lincolnshire, and his wife, Janetta, daughter of George Gunn of Edinburgh. Having entered the army as an ensign in the 61st regiment in 1803, and become a lieutenant on 8 December 1803, he served in Sicily, in Calabria, at Scylla Castle, and at Gibraltar (1807–8), and in the Peninsula from 1809 to the end of the war in 1814. At the battle of Salamanca he alone captured a gun guarded by four soldiers, and repeatedly showed distinguished bravery.

On 22 July 1812 Brackenbury was promoted captain, and after the war was attached to the Portuguese and Spanish army from 25 October 1814 to 25 December 1816, when he was placed on half pay. He served as a major in the 28th foot from 1 November 1827 to 31 January 1828, when he was again placed on half pay. His foreign services were further recognized by his being made a knight of the Portuguese order of the Tower and Sword in 1824, a knight of the Spanish order of St Ferdinand, and a knight commander of the Portuguese order of St Bento d'Avis.

Brackenbury, who was knighted by the king at Windsor Castle on 26 August 1836, was a magistrate and deputy lieutenant for the county of Lincoln. He attained to the rank of lieutenant-colonel on 10 January 1837, and ten years afterwards sold out of the army. Brackenbury's first marriage was on 9 June 1827, to Maria, daughter of the Revd Edward Bromhead of Reepham near Lincoln; they had a son, who died in 1845. Secondly, in March 1847, he married Eleanor (d. 1862), daughter of Addison Fenwick of Bishopwearmouth, co. Durham, and widow of W. Brown Clark of Belford Hall, Northumberland; they had a son born in 1848. Brackenbury died at his home, Skendleby Hall, near Spilsby, Lincolnshire, on 1 June 1864.

G. C. BOASE, *rev.* JAMES LUNT

Sources GM, 3rd ser., 17 (1864), 123 · R. Cannon, *The sixty-first regiment* (1837), 24, 31, 67 · Boase, *Mod. Eng. biog.*
Wealth at death under £4000: probate, 2 Sept 1864, *CGPLA Eng. & Wales*

Brackenbury, Hannah (1795–1873), philanthropist, was born at Leyland, Lancashire, on 17 November 1795, second of the three surviving children of Francis Brackenbury and his wife, Sarah Blackledge. Nothing else is known of her life until 1844, when she moved from Manchester to Hove, accompanied by her ailing brother, James Blackledge Brackenbury (1793–1844), with whom she had been living. He had made a fortune as a solicitor working for railway pioneers. He died at Hove on 31 October 1844, apparently a widower. When his only child, Harriette Mary Brackenbury (1833–1861), and his bachelor brother Ralph Brackenbury (1797–1864) died, the family money converged on Hannah Brackenbury. Publicly, she was the 'last in lineal descent of the ancient family of Brakenbury of Denton and Sellaby in the County of Durham'. Privately, she was more diffident. Robert Surtees (1779–1834) had worked out a pedigree for this family from 1222 to 1677, but he could not trace later descendants. Her father was probably the Francis Brackenbury born in 1769 who is mentioned by Surtees as a member of a yeomanly cadet branch which flourished near Richmond, Yorkshire, in the eighteenth century.

In 1865 Hannah Brackenbury had an income of about £7000 per annum. She distributed about £100,000 in philanthropy between 1865 and 1872. William Henry Rooper (formerly incumbent of St Andrew's Church, Hove, which she attended) was an influential adviser, and so was Edward Lewis, J. B. Brackenbury's partner. Rooper was her agent in correspondence with Robert Scott, master of Balliol College, Oxford, which led (1865–72) to her endowment of eight Brackenbury scholarships at the college. She wanted to help students with ambitions in law or medicine, the professions of her brothers, and was persuaded that history and natural science were the appropriate foundations. Balliol was chosen because she believed that her medieval ancestors had been closely involved with the Balliol family. In fact, the only clear Balliol–Brackenbury connection is the Brackenbury tower of Barnard Castle, the main Balliol seat in England. This led Scott to joke that she might like to build a Brackenbury tower at Balliol. She took this bait, and eventually paid for most of the reconstruction of the Balliol Broad Street front (1867–8). She also established six Brackenbury scholarships at Manchester grammar school.

Although in precarious health, Hannah Brackenbury was still a firmset, strong-looking woman, and in vigorous possession of her faculties; Rooper did not find her an easy person to direct or to keep to her intentions. From late 1868 she usually dropped the c in her surname, apparently thinking the spelling Brakenbury more authentic. In 1869 the Brakenbury mortuary chapel was attached to the church of St Nicolas, Portslade, at her expense, and she paid for new school buildings which were opened nearby in 1872. In her lifetime she was also a major benefactor to Owens College, Manchester (mostly for medicine), to Richmond School, Yorkshire (for Brackenbury scholarships), and to the Ardwick and Ancoats Dispensary in Manchester (for the first Ancoats Hospital building with beds).

Hannah Brackenbury died at home (31 Queen Adelaide Crescent, Hove), of heart failure after a short illness, on 28 February 1873, and was interred on 7 March in the vault beneath the Brakenbury Chapel. Probate was granted based on a valuation under £160,000. Her lengthy will made provision for her housekeeper-companion Alice King; there were bequests for many friends and their children; the University of Durham received £9000 for professorships; but the greater part of her estate was distributed among numerous hospitals, asylums, and charities (mostly medical).

JOHN JONES

Sources *Manchester Guardian* (5 March 1873) · *Brighton Gazette* (6 March 1873) · inscriptions, St Nicolas, Portslade, Brakenbury Chapel · Hove Reference Library, Autograph Collection · R. Surtees, *The history and antiquities of the county palatine of Durham*, 4 (1840), 16–21 · W. H. Chaloner, *The movement for the extension of Owens College Manchester, 1863–73* (1973), 20 · J. Thompson, *The Owens College: its foundation and growth* (1886), 427, 454, 458 · L. P. Wenham, *The history of Richmond School, Yorkshire* (1958), 98, 101–2, 115, 125 · J. Middleton, *Saint Nicolas's School, Portslade, Sussex: a history* (1990) · d. cert. · *CGPLA Eng. & Wales* (1873)
Archives Balliol Oxf. · Hove Central Library, Sussex
Wealth at death under £160,000: probate, 13 March 1873, *CGPLA Eng. & Wales*

Brackenbury, Sir Henry (1837–1914), army officer, who belonged to an old Lincolnshire family, was born at Bolingbroke, Lincolnshire, on 1 September 1837, the youngest son of William Brackenbury (*d.* 1844) of Aswardby, a veteran of the Peninsular War, and his wife, Maria (*b.* *c.*1798), the daughter of James Atkinson of Newry, co. Down, and the widow of James L. Wallace. Major-General Charles Booth *Brackenbury (1831–1890) was his brother. He was educated at Tonbridge School (1846–9) and Eton College (1850–52) before studying law in a notary's office in Quebec. In 1853 he received an ensign's commission in the Canadian militia, but after the outbreak of the Crimean War he returned to England and studied at the Royal Military Academy, Woolwich (1855–6). He was commissioned lieutenant in the Royal Artillery on 7 April 1856.

After service at Devonport, Brackenbury volunteered for active duty during the Indian mutiny. Having reached India in August 1857 he served in central India but was invalided home in 1858. He was posted back to Woolwich and became depot adjutant in 1860 and later a cadet company commander. At Woolwich he began to study his profession seriously and to contribute articles to professional journals and to *Fraser's Magazine* and other national periodicals. His publications included *The Last Campaign of Hanover* (1870) and *The Tactics of the Three Arms* (1873). From 1877 he contributed to *Blackwood's Magazine*. He supported the Cardwell reforms and advocated further reform.

In 1861 Brackenbury married Emilia (*d.* 1905), the daughter of Edmund Storr Halswell FRS and the widow of Reginald Morley. She was eight years older than he was, and he married her in order to pay off his debts. He regretted the

Sir Henry Brackenbury (1837–1914), by F. B. Ciolina, 1904

marriage almost immediately, and the couple soon ceased to live together. Moreover, Brackenbury was a notorious philanderer. In Natal in 1875, for example, he had an affair with the wife of Theophilus 'Offy' Shepstone. After Emilia's death, on 9 September 1905, Brackenbury married later that year Edith Maud Desanges, the daughter of the military painter Louis Desanges. There were no children from either marriage.

After being promoted captain in August 1866, Brackenbury succeeded Edward Hamley as professor of military history at the Royal Military Academy in 1868. He regularly visited Europe to study recent battlefields and went to observe the Franco-Prussian War, writing his impressions for *The Standard*. In September 1870 he was invited to superintend the work of the British National Society for Aid to the Sick and Wounded (later the British Red Cross), and returned to England in January 1871 with both French and German decorations.

Brackenbury made the acquaintance of Garnet Wolseley in December 1872 and, when Wolseley was given command of the Asante expedition the following year, wrote offering to serve under him. Brackenbury became Wolseley's assistant military secretary and a member of his 'ring' [see Wolseley ring]. He served in most of the major actions of the campaign, and back in England wrote a semi-official history, *The Ashanti War: a Narrative* (1874). He was promoted major in April 1874 and in 1875 accompanied Wolseley, as assistant military secretary, to Natal. Rewarded with a brevet lieutenant-colonelcy in October

1875, he returned to regimental duty. In July 1878 Wolseley took him as assistant adjutant and quartermaster-general to Cyprus, where he remained to reorganize the police. When Wolseley assumed direction of the Anglo-Zulu War Brackenbury joined him in July 1879 as military secretary, and later succeeded George Colley as Wolseley's chief of staff for the campaign against the Pedi chief Sekukuni.

Wolseley had quickly recognized Brackenbury's administrative talents. He described him as 'not one of the cleverest, but *the* cleverest man in the British Army' (Maurice and Arthur, 224) and wrote, 'he is method itself' (Harvie, 13). Wolseley advanced Brackenbury's career, despite opposition from the duke of Cambridge, the commander-in-chief, who regarded him as a dangerous radical, 'a very dangerous man' (Harvie, 17). At the same time Wolseley accepted that Brackenbury's selfishness made him very unpopular in the army. As Wolseley put it, Brackenbury was a 'worshipper of his own vile body more than most men I have known in the world' (Wolseley's journal, 27 July 1878). Moreover, Lady Wolseley took a violent dislike to the sallow-featured 'black Brack' and his 'putty nose and bilious complexion' (Wolseley to wife, 4 June 1879, Wolseley MSS, W/P 8/4), to the extent that Wolseley promised her in 1880 not to take Brackenbury as his chief of staff should he secure the Indian command. Most officers found his affected manner and speech—he pronounced his name Whackenbaywe—repulsive. He belittled his subordinates and on campaign repeatedly grumbled.

With Colley having been chosen to succeed Wolseley in Natal, Brackenbury went directly to India in February 1880 to succeed Colley as private secretary to the viceroy, Lord Lytton. Lytton was recalled in July 1880 and Brackenbury, who was made CB, became military attaché in Paris in January 1881. While on leave in May 1882 he was offered, on Wolseley's recommendation, the appointment of under-secretary for police and crime in Ireland, following the murder of Lord Frederick Cavendish. Within three months, however, Brackenbury resigned, hoping for active service with Wolseley in Egypt. The queen and Gladstone were incensed that he had 'abandoned his post at a most critical moment' (Ponsonby to Queen Victoria, 21 July 1882, Royal Archives, D34/60), and he was refused permission to go to Egypt and placed on half pay. He filled his time writing, and turned down the chance to be the Conservative Party's chief agent.

In 1883 Brackenbury returned to regimental service at Gibraltar. In August 1884 he was rescued by Wolseley and joined the Gordon relief expedition as deputy assistant quartermaster-general. In December 1884, although he had no operational command experience, he was made chief of staff to Wolseley's river column and succeeded to its command when William Earle was killed at Kirbekan in February 1885: controversially he decided to retire rather than advance. Buller wrote that Brackenbury was 'detested by everyone in his camp' (*Relief of Gordon*, 201). He successfully extracted the column from the Sudan and was promoted major-general in June 1885. He described his experiences in *The River Column* (1885).

Perpetually short of money, Brackenbury desperately needed further employment and came close to leaving the army before, through Wolseley's influence, he was appointed deputy quartermaster-general at the War Office, with the title of director of military intelligence, in January 1886. Under his direction the intelligence branch achieved the status of a full (and virtually autonomous) directorate in 1887 with direct access to the commander-in-chief. Among his subordinates was Charles à Court (later Repington), who considered him 'brilliant'. Not only did Brackenbury provide a comprehensive military intelligence service, he also undertook a much needed revision of the army's mobilization scheme in 1886. Effectively, Brackenbury's work underpinned the acceptance of the two-corps standard implicit in the Stanhope memorandum of 1888. Brackenbury was the only military member of the 1888 royal commission, chaired by Lord Hartington, on military and naval organization. He was widely believed to be the source of the Hartington report's recommendation to abolish the post of army commander-in-chief and replace it with a continental-style chief of staff. Wolseley and others were convinced that Brackenbury wanted the post for himself, though he had first advocated such an appointment in 1866. Such a change was unacceptable to the queen, and the government rapidly distanced itself from the report. In 1890, following the publication of Spenser Wilkinson's *The Brain of an Army*, Brackenbury wrote secretly to Wilkinson urging him to continue to press for a chief of staff: 'but pray don't quote me on the subject' (Luvaas, 260).

Brackenbury was promoted lieutenant-general in April 1888 and in August 1889 was the joint author with Major-General Newmarch of a memorandum establishing the government's preferred strategy, in the event of a war against Russia, of amphibious operations on Russia's peripheries. This was opposed by the Indian army's 'forward school', which sought to fight beyond the north-west frontier and demanded massive reinforcements to do so. In April 1891 Brackenbury was sent to India as a military member of the viceroy's council by the desire of Lord Salisbury to introduce a degree of realism into Indian military planning. To some extent he became converted to the strategic views of Lord Roberts, the commander-in-chief in India, but his earlier memorandum remained the orthodoxy. Roberts considered him able but some of his views unsound, and found him less congenial than Sir George Chesney (whom he succeeded) and Chesney's predecessors. In 1892, with Roberts's retirement approaching, some saw Brackenbury as a possible successor, but in a memorandum to the viceroy he effectively excluded himself, and Sir George White was appointed. Brackenbury oversaw changes in the Indian army's organization, mobilization, and intelligence services, as well as financial reforms.

Brackenbury was appointed KCB, previously denied him by Cambridge's hostility, in 1894, and the KCSI on leaving India in April 1896. His service in India had cleared yet more debts, but, now supporting both his sister and his brother's widow, he needed further employment. He turned down Bermuda as too expensive a command, while Wolseley, now intensely suspicious of him, blocked his candidature for quartermaster-general at the War Office. Instead he became president of the ordnance committee in May 1896 and, with the temporary rank of general, director-general of ordnance in February 1899. The ordnance department was responsible for supplying not only ordnance proper, but also a vast range of 'warlike stores, clothing and necessaries'. Brackenbury struggled with the manifold deficiencies of munitions production during the Second South African War, achieving some success in equipping the army with its wartime needs. In 1900 he arranged the secret, unprecedented purchase from Germany of eighteen batteries of Ehrhardt 15-pounder quick-firing field guns. Also in 1900 he pressed the cabinet for artillery rearmament, and he secured the appointment of an equipment committee under Sir George Marshall. In 1903 Lord Esher suggested Brackenbury for his proposed War Office reorganization committee, but Sir George Clarke was appointed. Brackenbury suffered from ill health, but he completed his term of office and retired in February 1904. Promoted GCB in 1900, he was sworn of the privy council on his retirement. He had become colonel commandant of the Royal Artillery in November 1897. His memoirs, *Some Memories of my Spare Time*, appeared in 1909. He died at the Excelsior Hotel Regina, Nice, France, on 20 April 1914. IAN F. W. BECKETT

Sources H. Brackenbury, *Some memories of my spare time* (1909) · H. Brackenbury, *The Ashanti war*, 2 vols. (1874) · H. Brackenbury, *The river column* (1885) · E. M. Spiers, *The late Victorian army, 1868–1902* (1992) · *The South African diaries of Sir Garnet Wolseley, 1875*, ed. A. Preston (1971) · *The South African journal of Sir Garnet Wolseley, 1879–1880*, ed. A. Preston (1973) · *In relief of Gordon: Lord Wolseley's campaign journal of the Khartoum relief expedition, 1884–1885*, ed. A. Preston (1967) · I. F. W. Beckett, 'The Stanhope memorandum of 1888: a reinterpretation', *BIHR*, 57 (1984), 240–47 · C. Trebilcock, 'War and the failure of industrial mobilisation, 1899–1914', *War and economic development: essays in memory of David Joslin*, ed. J. M. Winter (1975), 139–64 · T. G. Fergusson, *British military intelligence, 1870–1914* (1984) · W. S. Hamer, *The British army: civil–military relations, 1885–1905* (1970) · W. C. Beaver, 'The development of the intelligence division and its role in aspects of imperial policy making, 1854–1901: the military mind of imperialism', DPhil diss., U. Oxf., 1976 · J. Luvaas, *The education of an army: British military thought, 1815–1940* (Chicago, IL, 1964) · F. Maurice and G. Arthur, *The life of Lord Wolseley* (1924) · J. H. Lehmann, *All Sir Garnet: a biography of Field-Marshal Lord Wolseley* (1964) · Boase, *Mod. Eng. biog.* · *WWW* · Burke, *Peerage* (1907) · I. Harvie, '"A very dangerous man": a profile of Henry Brackenbury', *Soldiers of the Queen*, 96 (1999), 12–17 · *Roberts in India: the military papers of Field Marshal Lord Roberts, 1876–1893*, ed. B. Robson (1993) · *CGPLA Eng. & Wales* (1914) · G. Wolseley, journal, PRO, WO 147/6 · Hove Central Library, Wolseley MSS · Royal Arch.

Archives BL OIOC, papers, MS Eur. D 735 · Hove Central Library, autobiographical collection, corresp. · Royal Artillery Institution, Woolwich, London, papers, MD/1085 | BL, corresp. with H. O. Arnold-Forster, Add. MSS 50306, 50325, *passim* · BL, Lansdowne MSS, L (5) 15 · CKS, letters to Edward Stanhope · Devon RO, Buller MSS, 2065M/SS4/27 · Hove Central Library, letters to Lord and Lady Wolseley · NAM, letters to Earl Roberts, 7101-23-11 · NL Scot., corresp. with Blackwoods · PRO, corresp. with Sir J. C. Ardagh, PRO 30/40

Likenesses F. B. Ciolina, photograph, 1904, repro. in H. Brackenbury, *Some memories of my spare time* (1909) [see illus.] · photograph,

repro. in *Celebrities of the Army* (1900) · portrait, probably Royal Artillery · print (after photograph by Denque & Co), NPG
Wealth at death £5704 1s. 6d.: probate, 1914

Brackenbury, Joseph (1787–1864), poet and Church of England clergyman, was born on 27 September 1787 at Langton by Partney, Lincolnshire, the third son of the Revd William Brackenbury (1753/4–1824) and his wife, Juliet (d. 1790), the daughter of Benet Langton, of Langton Hall, Lincolnshire. He matriculated at Bene't College (later Corpus Christi), Cambridge, in Michaelmas term 1806, and became a scholar there. In 1810 he published by subscription his *Natale solum, and other Poetical Pieces*, and on 11 December 1810 he married Mary (1788–1862), daughter of Colonel Richard Brackenbury of Aswardby, Lincolnshire, and his wife, Janetta, *née* Gunn. They were to have four sons and three daughters. Brackenbury took his BA in 1811 and was ordained priest in the same year. He served as chaplain to the Madras establishment between 1818 and 1820. From 1828 to 1860 he was chaplain and secretary to the Magdalen Hospital, Blackfriars Road, Southwark, London. In 1862 he became rector of Quendon, Essex, and he died there, in the rectory, of apoplexy, on 31 March 1864, aged seventy-six.

JENNETT HUMPHREYS, *rev.* MEGAN A. STEPHAN

Sources Venn, *Alum. Cant.* · Burke, *Gen. GB* (1937) · [J. Watkins and F. Shoberl], *A biographical dictionary of the living authors of Great Britain and Ireland* (1816) · Boase, *Mod. Eng. biog.* · T. Cooper, *A new biographical dictionary: containing concise notices of eminent persons of all ages and countries* (1873) · *GM*, 3rd ser., 17 (1864), 668 · J. Brackenbury, *Natale solum, and other poetical pieces* (1810) · d. cert. · IGI · CGPLA Eng. & Wales (1864)
Wealth at death under £800: resworn probate, Nov 1864, CGPLA Eng. & Wales

Brackenbury, Sir Robert (d. 1485), knight, was the second son of Ralph Brackenbury of Denton in the parish of Gainford, co. Durham. The nearby lordship of Barnard Castle was held by Richard, duke of Gloucester, in the right of his wife, Anne Neville, from 1474, and Robert Brackenbury had probably entered the duke's service by 1477, when ducal retainers witnessed his father's grant to him of land in School Aycliffe, co. Durham. By 1479 Brackenbury was treasurer of Gloucester's household and one of the duke's feoffees. Two years later, in 1481, he acquired the manor of Selaby, co. Durham. Brackenbury's prospects were transformed by Gloucester's accession in 1483. He was not at Richard's coronation, but less than a fortnight later, on 17 July, he was made constable of the Tower of London for life and master of the mint and keeper of the king's exchange in the Tower—one of relatively few northerners to receive major office in the south so early in the reign.

Brackenbury was thus constable of the Tower when Richard is believed to have ordered the death of his nephews, Edward V and Richard, duke of York, although no chronicler associates him directly with their deaths. Early writers give no details, and the version current after the execution of Sir James Tyrell in 1502 was that Brackenbury had hesitated to carry out their murder, and Richard accordingly commanded Tyrell to kill them. The most that can be said is that the scale of Brackenbury's subsequent reward makes it unlikely that his role in the affair had offended the king.

After Buckingham's rebellion of October 1483, which involved many of Edward IV's local servants, Richard used land and office forfeited by the rebels to move trusted northern associates into the areas most badly affected by the rising. In March 1484, Brackenbury, by now an esquire of the king's body, was given extensive land in Kent for his good service against the rebels. One of the manors, Ightham Mote, apparently became his home in the county. He was added to the Kent commissions of the peace in July 1484 and was made sheriff in November. He was also made receiver-general of the forfeited lands and goods of rebels in Kent, Surrey, and Sussex. His local influence was recognized by Archbishop Thomas Bourchier, who made Brackenbury his steward in March 1484. Brackenbury and his wife, Agnes, were enrolled within the confraternity of Christ Church, Canterbury.

Brackenbury was evidently regarded as one of the king's most reliable supporters in the south-east, and his range of activities kept him busy. In July 1484 he was forced to delegate responsibilities because of 'other arduous business touching the king's right' (PRO, KB 9/951/28). In addition to his local offices he was one of Richard's commissioners in the office of admiral and a royal councillor. He was knighted around Christmas 1484 and became a knight of the king's body. He continued to receive royal patronage, and by the end of the reign his gains from royal service were probably of the order of £500 p.a., which made him one of the best-rewarded of Richard's household servants. Not all his gains came directly from the king. A fellow knight of the body, the Essex landowner Sir Thomas Montgomery, made over one of his own offices to him, while the rebel John Forster escaped attainder in 1483 by conveying land to Brackenbury, and early in the next reign Margaret Beaufort was seeking to recover silver and gilt cups which Brackenbury had taken. His influence was recognized by the scholar Pietro Carmeliano of Brescia, who dedicated his poem on St Catherine to him.

Brackenbury fought in Richard's army at Bosworth and was killed there on 22 August 1485. He was attainted, and his land forfeited, in the first parliament of Henry VII. The attainder was reversed in 1489 in favour of his two daughters, Anne and Elizabeth. Brackenbury's bastard children were explicitly denied any immediate share in the restoration, although his illegitimate son was to inherit if Anne and Elizabeth died childless. That son was still alive in 1499 when he was bequeathed £40 in the will of Thomas Barowe, who had been Gloucester's chancellor, but there is no record of his death. Elizabeth, still unmarried, made her will in 1504. She then held Selaby, which she ordered to be sold by her feoffees, and the money to be used to pay her debts, including those to the dowager duchess of Norfolk, Elizabeth Talbot, 'to whom I am especially bound' (PRO, PROB 11/14, fol. 163v). There is no mention in the will of her sister, Anne.

ROSEMARY HORROX

Sources PRO · BL · *Chancery records* · *RotP* · R. Horrox, *Richard III, a study of service*, Cambridge Studies in Medieval Life and Thought, 4th ser., 11 (1989) · A. J. Pollard, '"St Cuthbert and the Hog": Richard III and the county palatine of Durham, 1471–85', *Kings and nobles in the later middle ages*, ed. R. A. Griffiths and J. Sherborne (1986), 109–29 · *Registrum Thomae Bourgchier … 1454–1486*, ed. F. R. H. Du Boulay, CYS, 54 (1957) · *Ninth report*, 3 vols., HMC, 8 (1883–4) · W. Campbell, ed., *Materials for a history of the reign of Henry VII*, 2 vols., Rolls Series, 60 (1873–7)

Brackenbury, Robert Carr (1752–1818), Methodist preacher, was born at Panton House in Lincolnshire and baptized on 28 April 1752, the first child of Carr Brackenbury and Isabella, daughter of William Booth of Ashby Puerorum. He was educated at Felsted School and, from 20 May 1769, at St Catharine's College, Cambridge, which he entered with the intention of taking holy orders, but it was here that a spiritual crisis turned him from his original purpose. No more is known of his Cambridge days, and in 1776 he came under the influence of John Wesley.

From this time until the end of Wesley's life (1791) Brackenbury and Wesley met on several occasions at Brackenbury's home at Raithby in Lincolnshire, in addition to those occasions when Wesley invited Brackenbury to accompany him on his travels. In 1779 they went on a tour to Scotland, and twice (in 1783 and 1786) they journeyed to the Netherlands. In July 1779 Wesley paid his first visit to Raithby, while Brackenbury was building the hall that was to be his future home. On the estate Brackenbury built a small chapel over the stables, which Wesley opened. When Wesley visited Horncastle later the same year 'the wild men were more quiet than usual; I suppose, because they saw Mr Brackenbury standing by me, whom they knew to be in Commission for the Peace' (*Journal of John Wesley*, 6.242–3). Wesley and Brackenbury also corresponded frequently. Brackenbury was one of a small number present at City Road, London, when Wesley died on 3 March 1791.

Brackenbury married twice. His first wife, Jane, died on 3 March 1782, at the age of twenty-four, 'after a short Life of great troubles and adversities', as her monument in Raithby church records. In 1795 Brackenbury married second Sarah (d. 1847) of Loughborough, daughter of Henry Holland, a captain in the Loughborough Volunteers.

Brackenbury's most important work as a Methodist preacher was in the Channel Islands, where he was sent by Wesley in 1783 at the request of soldiers who were stationed there. He worked there in the face of much opposition and spent money building chapels. In 1790 he returned to the mainland and met a Methodist from Frome who instructed him to visit and preach on the Isle of Portland. Brackenbury spent some time in Portland but moved to other places according to his own inclinations, building chapels at his own expense, helping others financially, and supporting many charities. He wrote poetry and several hymns. He was never ordained yet Wesley made him a member of the legal hundred and his name appeared in the minutes of conference along with all of Wesley's preachers.

Brackenbury's life was dogged by ill health, which affected his spiritual state and led to periods of depression. He was of a nervous disposition yet had great courage when faced with a violent crowd. Thomas Jackson, one of Wesley's preachers, described him thus:

> rather below the middle size, portly and well proportioned, with an open and placid countenance, rather reserved, but gentlemanly in his manners. In the pulpit his address was calm, but impressive; his sermons were received … by the Methodist congregations with gratitude and respect. (Jackson, 74–5)

There is no known portrait of him, except in silhouette.

Brackenbury expressed a wish that nothing should be written about him after his death, with the result that his widow destroyed any material that would have been useful for a substantial biography. He died at Raithby on 11 August 1818 and was buried in the chancel of Raithby church, near his first wife. The *Gentleman's Magazine* reported his death as being:

> In his 66th year … a celebrated character of the turf, though possessed of an ample future, he was for many years a zealous preacher among the Methodists, and is stated to have bequeathed £1,600 for the spreading of the Gospel. (*GM*)

His will, made in 1816, shows that he owned property in the Isle of Portland, Loughborough, Charnwood Forest, and a number of Lincolnshire villages, in addition to his home in Raithby.   WILLIAM LEARY

Sources R. Smith, *Raithby Hall: memorial sketches of R. C. Brackenbury esq.* (1859) · R. D. Moore, *Methodism in the Channel Islands* (1952) · *The journal of the Rev. John Wesley*, ed. N. Curnock and others, 8 vols. (1909–16); repr. (1938) · *The letters of the Rev. John Wesley*, ed. J. Telford, 8 vols. (1931) · T. R. Leach, 'The preaching squire: Robert Carr Brackenbury, 1752–1818', *The Lincolnshire historian* (1964) · 'The will of R. C. Brackenbury', *Proceedings of the Wesley Historical Society*, 33 (1961–2) · *GM*, 1st ser., 88/2 (1818), 376 · T. Jackson, *My own life and times* (1873) · Venn, *Alum. Cant.*
Likenesses silhouette, repro. in *Wesleyan Conference Handbook* (1925)

Brackenridge, Hugh Henry [*formerly* Hugh Montgomery Breckenridge] (1748–1816), writer and judge, was born Hugh Montgomery Breckenridge, probably at Ballivulune, near Campbeltown, Argyllshire, the only son of William Breckenridge, a farmer. Impoverished following the Jacobite rising, the family emigrated to the Barrens, York county, Pennsylvania, in 1753. Hugh was an able scholar and quickly learned to render Horace into Scots. At the age of fifteen he became a pupil schoolmaster in rural Maryland, and, younger than most of his students, he asserted his authority by 'felling one unruly brute with a fire log' (*Princetonians*, 139).

From 1768 to 1774, Breckenridge attended the College of New Jersey at Princeton, supporting himself as a schoolmaster. His college friends were James Madison, later president of the United States, and Philip Freneau, the poet. He and Freneau collaborated on *Father Bombo's Pilgrimage* (1770), often considered the first novel written in America, and on a declamatory poem, *The Rising Glory of America*, which Breckenridge, a big man with a booming voice, first read in public. He graduated in divinity, continued as a backwoods teacher, writing plays for his pupils, and then, during the American War of Independence, became a fiery army chaplain, and wrote two plays: *The Battle of Bunkers-Hill* (1776) and *The Death of General Montgomery* (1777).

Having religious doubts, Breckenridge resigned a year after he was licensed to preach by the Philadelphia presbytery. He then studied law, was admitted to the Philadelphia bar, and in 1781 settled in Pittsburgh. It was about this time that he changed his middle name to Henry, and altered the spelling of his last name, reasoning that 'the bulk of the same stock spelt it so' (Newlin, *DAB*, 3.340). In what was then still a frontier village, he helped to found the *Pittsburgh Gazette*, opened a bookshop, and helped to establish what became the University of Pittsburgh. Although he disliked the native people of the frontier, he none the less defied public opinion in 1785 with his defence of an Indian accused of the murder of two white settlers, and described the case in detail in *The Trial of Mamachtaga* (1785). That year he married a Miss Montgomery with whom he had a son, Henry Marie, in 1786. She died in 1788 and in 1790 he married Sabina (or Sofia) Wolfe, with whom he had two sons, born in 1797 and 1801, and a daughter, born in 1804.

A whig, and later a disciple of Jefferson, Brackenridge entered politics, but was, perhaps, too principled to last; his race for a seat in congress in 1794 was unsuccessful. He mediated in the 'Whiskey Insurrection' of 1793–4, a fiscal and constitutional dispute, but satisfied neither side, and in 1795 he published a vivid account of the controversy. Brackenridge contributed significantly to early American jurisprudence, becoming a judge in the Pennsylvania supreme court (1799–1811), codifying and adapting laws, and compiling the influential *Law Miscellanies* (1805–14) which represented 'an important contribution to an ongoing debate about the place of English common law in American jurisprudence' (Newlin, *DAB*, 3.342). Brackenridge's legal career was characterized by a logical approach and a caustic wit. He was also known for certain eccentricities of dress and behaviour, for example his tendency to lounge with his feet up in court.

A 'mission to explain' made Brackenridge a prolific writer. He is now chiefly remembered for his novel, the brilliant social and political satire *Modern Chivalry: the Adventures of Captain John Farrago, and Teague O'Regan, his Servant* (1792–1804). The humour of this work emanates from the contrast between a patrician intellectual master, perhaps based on Brackenridge himself, and his assertive servant. Frequently revised, and written in the picaresque style of Cervantes and Smollett, with the latter of whom Brackenridge has been compared, *Modern Chivalry* was a best-seller for fifty years. Present-day critical evaluation confirms its worth as the first considerable American novel. Brackenridge's Scottishness is most often encountered in his poetry, although there is a well developed Scottish character, the servant Duncan Ferguson, in *Modern Chivalry*, and as late as 1811, Brackenridge wrote the sentimental *Epistle to Sir Walter Scott*, inspired by *The Lady of the Lake*. A modern edition of his works has a glossary of Scottish words.

Brackenridge moved to Carlisle, Pennsylvania, in 1801, and by 1803 he had become trustee of Dickinson College there, and worked to reduce its religious affiliation. He died in Carlisle on 25 June 1816, and was buried a member of the masonic order and of the honor roll of the Society of St Andrew.   LOUIS STOTT

Sources D. Marder, *Hugh Henry Brackenridge* (1967) · C. M. Newlin, 'Brackenridge, Hugh Henry', *DAB* · C. M. Newlin, *Life and writings of Hugh Henry Brackenridge* (1932) · S. M. Lloyd, 'Brackenridge, Hugh Henry', *ANB* · H. M. Brackenridge, 'Biographical notice', *Southern Literary Messenger*, 8 (Jan 1842), 1–19 [repr. in early editions of *Modern chivalry*] · R. A. Harrison, *Princetonians, 1769–1775: a biographical dictionary* (1980)

Brackley. For this title name *see* Egerton, Thomas, first Viscount Brackley (1540–1617).

Brackley, Herbert George (1894–1948), air force officer and airline executive, was born in Islington, London, on 4 October 1894, the second of the seven children of George Herbert Brackley, a master tailor, and his wife, Lilian Sarah Partridge. The family later moved to Kent and Brackley was educated at Sevenoaks grammar school. In 1912 he joined Reuters and in April 1915 was commissioned in the Royal Naval Air Service and learned to fly at Eastchurch. By the end of that summer he was a bomber pilot in France. In 1918 he transferred to the newly formed Royal Air Force and took command of a bomber squadron equipped with new Handley Page o/400 bombers. At the time of his demobilization in March 1919 Brackley had attained the rank of major, flown seventy bombing raids and was the holder of the DSO, the DSC, the French Croix de Guerre and the Belgian order of the Crown.

Returning to civilian life, Brackley joined the Handley Page Company and took one of its four-engined bombers to Newfoundland in a bid to make the first direct crossing of the Atlantic. Beaten in the attempt by John Alcock and Arthur Whitten Brown, he turned the large aircraft westwards and made the first flight from Newfoundland to New York, following this with a number of pioneer flights in the United States. In early 1920 he set off on another maiden flight, this time from London to Cape Town, but crashed near Khartoum. For the rest of the year, as chief pilot for the Handley Page Transport Company, he flew commercial services with the civil version of the HP o/400 from London to Paris, Cologne, and Brussels. In 1921 Brackley accepted an invitation to join the British air mission to Japan which undertook the organization and training of the Japanese naval air service. In 1922 he married Frida Helena, elder daughter of Robert Mond; they had two sons and one daughter.

Early in 1924, when the principal British air transport companies were amalgamated to form Imperial Airways, Brackley, having returned from his Japanese assignment, was appointed air superintendent. This position, which he was to hold for the next fifteen years, gave him responsibility for the airline's operations, training, and route development. It was during his service with Imperial Airways that Brackley, already an experienced bomber pilot, advanced the technique of commercial aircraft operation. He improved the working conditions of commercial pilots as well as developing standards of passenger comfort in aircraft. He was also responsible for the selection and testing of Imperial Airways' new aircraft including the airline's many flying boats, a type on which he became a particular expert.

Brackley's honest and straightforward manner was appreciated by the company's flying staff, whose relations with the Imperial Airways management were otherwise poor. Indeed, Brackley's role as an intermediary between the general manager, George Woods-Humphery, and the pilots was vital to the airline's expansion. A man of exceptional energy and dedication, Brackley personally carried out route surveys, making expeditions to every corner of the airline's network, and supervising the preparation of bases and airfields.

When Imperial Airways was merged with British Airways in 1939 to form the state-owned British Overseas Airways Corporation (BOAC), Brackley was disappointed not to be made operations manager of the new undertaking. However, with the outbreak of the Second World War, he returned to the Royal Air Force, where his wide experience of transport operations was applied first in staff posts in Coastal Command and afterwards in the position of senior air staff officer in RAF transport command. His knowledge of flying boats was of particular value in the development of anti-submarine tactics with the Short Sunderland, a military version of the C Class flying boats which Imperial Airways had introduced onto its Empire routes in 1936. In 1941 Brackley was appointed CBE and in 1943 promoted to the rank of air commodore. The following year he was a member of the British delegation to the Chicago conference on international civil aviation and at the end of hostilities he returned to commercial air transport as special assistant to Lord Knollys, the chairman of BOAC. Among his achievements was the successful evacuation of a large number of people to Pakistan at the time of the division of India in 1947.

In early 1948 Brackley became chief executive of the recently formed British South American Airways Corporation (BSAA), taking over the job after the sudden departure of Air Vice-Marshall Don Bennett. It was in this capacity that he undertook a major inspection tour of the airline's operations in South America and was drowned while swimming at Rio de Janeiro on 15 November 1948. He was buried at Blakeney, Norfolk, where he had lived in the Old Rectory. Soon after his death BSAA was merged with BOAC.

Brackley's untimely death deprived British civil aviation of one of its most able and experienced figures. A modest man, who should have received greater recognition for his work at Imperial Airways, he belonged to that first influential generation of air transport pioneers which emerged from the testing ground of British air operations in the First World War, and included George Woods-Humphery and William Sholto Douglas, later Lord Douglas, chairman of British European Airways in the 1950s.   PETER J. LYTH

Sources DNB · F. H. Brackley, 'Brackles' (1952) · P. Masefield, 'Brackley, Herbert George', DBB

Archives Royal Air Force Museum, Hendon, papers
Wealth at death £15,097 17s. 8d.: probate, 19 Feb 1949, CGPLA Eng. & Wales

Bracton, Henry of. See Bratton, Henry of (d. 1268).

Bradberry, David (1735–1803), Independent minister, was born at Reeth, in the North Riding of Yorkshire, on 12 November 1735; nothing is known of his parents. He was a convert of George Whitfield, and in 1759 he began a course of ministerial training at Mile End Academy, Middlesex, but he terminated his course prematurely in February 1762 in order to take up an appointment as assistant to the Revd John Sayers at Alnwick, Northumberland. He remained there until 1764, when he moved to Wellingborough as minister at Cheese Lane Independent Chapel. He appears to have resigned from this post in the summer of 1767, when he moved to Kent as a supply preacher. After preaching to the congregation at the Ebenezer Chapel in Ramsgate on 10 October 1767 he was invited to become its pastor but, while agreeing to preach there on a regular basis, he did not accept pastoral responsibility until April 1769 and was not ordained until 24 October 1770. He continued at Ramsgate with considerable success for eighteen years.

On 14 August 1785 Bradberry accepted the invitation to become minister at Cannon Street Chapel, Manchester. There he soon incensed some of the members of the congregation, and especially the Scottish members, by his attempts to remove the ruling elders from office and to break up the semi-Presbyterian form of church government. This dispute led in 1788 to a considerable secession of members from the church and to the establishment by the seceders of Mosley Street Chapel. Bradberry resigned from Cannon Street, probably in 1795, and for a time was minister at Grovers' Hall, London. His final ministerial appointment was in 1797 at Kennington, Surrey.

Bradberry was not a prolific writer and is credited with just three published works, of which the only one of any note is a poem entitled Tetelestai: the Final Close (1794). He died in London on 13 January 1803 and was buried in Bunhill Fields. His funeral oration was given by the Revd John Humphries of Dead Man's Place, Southwark, and his funeral sermon was preached by Robert Simpson of Hoxton.   W. E. A. AXON, rev. M. J. MERCER

Sources C. Surman, index, DWL · B. Nightingale, Lancashire nonconformity, 6 vols. [1890–93], vol. 5 · T. Timpson, Church history of Kent (1859) · A. G. Hurd, These 300 years: the story of Ramsgate Congregational Church, 1662–1962 (1962) · W. E. A. Axon, ed., The annals of Manchester: a chronological record from the earliest times to the end of 1885 (1886) · J. A. Jones, ed., Bunhill memorials (1849) · Mile End Academy, student lists, 25 Sept 1754–, DWL, NCA 105/3ii, 105/4

Bradbridge, William (1507–1578), bishop of Exeter, was born in Chichester, the son of a wealthy mercer. His father, who was on good terms with the dean and chapter of Chichester, had at least two other sons; one was brought up to succeed him, while William and Augustine were destined for the church. In the mid-1520s William was sent to Magdalen College, Oxford, and became a fellow there in 1529, the year in which he determined for his BA. The only college office he appears to have held was that of supervisor of ale in 1532. He had vacated his fellowship by 1534 and in 1535 was collated to the vicarage of Willingdon, Sussex, by the dean and chapter of Chichester. In 1539 he was admitted to the degree of BTh. In 1542 Willingdon was replaced by the Sussex vicarage of East Dean, followed in 1547 first by that of West Thorney and then by the rectory of West Tarring, also in Sussex. He held the latter until he became a bishop.

Bradbridge appears to have weathered all the changes in religion of the mid-sixteenth century, remaining in England and in post throughout both Edward's and Mary's reigns, although his brother Augustine was among the Marian exiles. In 1554 William became warden of St Mary's Hospital, Chichester, while on 17 March that year he was instituted prebendary of Lyme and Halstock in Salisbury Cathedral. He renewed his links with Chichester Cathedral when on 7 January 1559 he was installed as prebendary of Sutton there, and in 1562 succeeded Augustine as chancellor of that diocese. Later that year he is recorded as selling old vestments and other furnishings in London to raise money for the chapter. William Bradbridge may well have owed much of his preferment after 1558 to the influence of his brother, and also to the favour of William Barlow, bishop of Chichester from 1559 to 1568. Not only did Augustine marry Barlow's eldest daughter, but he and William seem to have been the only members of his chapter whom the bishop felt able to trust with tasks of discipline and reform.

It is possible that Barlow's support put William Bradbridge into the circle of patronage around Sir William Cecil—explaining, perhaps, why on 29 March 1563 he was presented by the crown to the deanery of Salisbury. In the same year he aligned himself with the reformers in convocation by voting for the six articles proposing the abrogation of ceremonies, and signing the petition for the reformation of discipline. In 1565 he became rector of Ditchling, Sussex, regularizing his position in 1570 when he was dispensed to hold three benefices. In spite of his continuing connection with Sussex he was diligent at Salisbury in performing his duties as dean, regularly attending chapter meetings, and for several years held the position of keeper of the muniments, which required residence in the cathedral close.

It might well have looked as if his deanery was the most that Bradbridge would achieve, but early in 1571 he became bishop of Exeter. Royal assent was granted on 26 February and he was consecrated on 18 March. Well over sixty, he was one of the oldest men to be made a bishop under Elizabeth. His diocese was a poor one, and in 1572 he was dispensed to hold the livings of Lazant, Cornwall, and Newton Ferrers, Devon, *in commendam*. There were equivocal aspects to his religious position. He is unlikely to have pleased the godly in his diocese when within forty-eight hours of his consecration he made his 26-year-old nephew William Marston his chancellor. Yet he was also a firm supporter of the meetings of reformist clergymen known as 'prophesyings', and himself sometimes acted as their moderator, reporting to Archbishop Grindal in 1576 how 'Great profit groweth thereby, I do persuade myself,

for that I see the people delight to hear and gladly do resort, the clergy become studious in the tongues and grow ripe in the Scriptures' (Collinson, 238). Nevertheless he had difficulties with both Catholics and puritans. In 1576 he failed to make any impression on a group of Cornish Catholics who obdurately refused to come to church, and a year later had to deal with the schoolmaster of Liskeard who caused scandal by denouncing as valueless oaths taken on the Bible, 'because it is nothing but ink and paper' (Rowse, 334).

Bradbridge seems to have been an isolated figure as bishop. He usually lived not in his palace at Exeter but at Newton Ferrers, where he convened the episcopal audience court in the parsonage. He is not recorded as a preacher; indeed, after his death the second earl of Bedford likened him to a dumb dog. He attended parliament in 1571, 1572, and 1575, and at Christmas 1577 broke with his usual practice by attending the quarter sessions in Exeter. He also acted as visitor of Exeter College, Oxford. But much of his time was devoted to farming; by the time of his death he owned a flock of 100 sheep and lambs and some 3 dozen horses, pigs, and cattle. Some of his lay deputies, most notoriously Henry Borough, his sub-collector of taxes, took advantage of his absences from Exeter to line their own pockets. By 1577 the bishop had begun to suspect that he was being deceived. He was reassured by Borough and his associates, to the extent that Bradbridge 'rejoicing drank to the gentlemen, and said that he would not be indebted to the queen for anything' (Heal, 'Clerical tax collection', 116), but doubts soon recurred, and he initiated inquiries once more. Such precautions came too late, however, and when he died the bishop owed £1235 to the exchequer, most of it for taxes embezzled by Borough.

Unmarried, and consequently without the support a wife could have given him, Bradbridge appears eventually to have found the burdens of his office too much, and on 11 March 1576 he wrote to Cecil, now Lord Burghley, asking to be allowed to return to his deanery at Salisbury, which he mistakenly believed was vacant: 'If it please your lordship to send me hence, and to restore me to the place from whence I came, you could never do me such a pleasure' (Strype, 2/2.35–6). In the event Bradbridge stayed in office, and died suddenly and alone at Newton Ferrers on 27 June 1578. His poverty was such that his executors could not afford a fitting burial; he was interred on the north side of Exeter Cathedral choir.

Bradbridge published nothing, and his episcopate aroused little enthusiasm, either at the time or later. His younger contemporary John Hooker offered the lukewarm verdict that:

> he was a professor of divinitie, but not taken to be so well grounded as he persuaded himselfe, he was zelous in religion, but not so forwarde as he was wished to be. In his latter daies he delighted to dwell in the countrie, which was not so much to his liking, as troublesome to his clergie, & to such as had anie sutes unto him. (*Holinshed's Chronicles*, 3.1309)

A century later a local historian described him, with some

generosity, as 'a man only memorable for this, that nothing memorable is recorded of him saving that he well governed this church about eight years' (Izacke, 135–6).

KENNETH CARLETON

Sources Emden, *Oxf.*, 4.66 • J. R. Bloxam, *A register of the presidents, fellows … of Saint Mary Magdalen College*, 8 vols. (1853–85), vol. 2 • J. A. Vage, 'The diocese of Exeter, 1519–1641: a study of church government in the age of the Reformation', PhD diss., U. Cam., 1991 • R. Holinshed and others, eds., *The third volume of chronicles, beginning at Duke William the Norman*, ed. J. Hooker (1587), incl. Hooker's catalogue of bishops of Exeter • J. Strype, *Annals of the Reformation and establishment of religion … during Queen Elizabeth's happy reign*, new edn, 2/2 (1824), 35–6 • *Calendar of the manuscripts of the most hon. the marquis of Salisbury*, 2, HMC, 9 (1888) • R. Izacke, *Antiquities of the city of Exeter* (1677) • M. Hobbs, ed., *Chichester Cathedral: an historical survey* (1994) • A. L. Rowse, *Tudor Cornwall*, 2nd edn (1969) • F. O. White, *Lives of the Elizabethan bishops of the Anglican church* (1898) • *Fasti Angl., 1541–1857*, [Chichester] • *Fasti Angl., 1541–1857*, [Salisbury] • F. Heal, *Of prelates and princes: a study of the economic and social position of the Tudor episcopate* (1980) • P. Collinson, *Archbishop Grindal, 1519–1583: the struggle for a reformed church* (1979) • R. B. Manning, *Religion and society in Elizabethan Sussex* (1969) • F. Heal, 'Clerical tax collection under the Tudors: the influence of the Reformation', *Continuity and change: personnel and administration of the church in England, 1500–1642*, ed. R. O'Day and F. Heal (1976), 97–122

Wealth at death owed £1235 to the exchequer

Bradbrook, Muriel Clara (1909–1993), literary scholar, was born on 27 April 1909 in Glasgow, the eldest child of Samuel Bradbrook (*d.* 1928) and his wife, Annie Wilson, née Harvey (*b.* 1872). Samuel Bradbrook was superintendent of HM water guard, first at Glasgow and then at Liverpool. Muriel Bradbrook was educated at Hutcheson's School, Glasgow, and at Oldershaw School, Wallasey, from where she proceeded to Girton College, Cambridge. She graduated with a double first in English in 1930 and was Ottilie Hancock research fellow at the college from 1932 to 1935. In 1935 she was made an official fellow.

During the Second World War Bradbrook worked in London for the Board of Trade, and returned to Cambridge as university lecturer in 1945. Even before that she had already published five books of literary criticism: *Elizabethan Stage Conditions* (1932), *Themes and Conventions of Elizabethan Tragedy* (1935), *The School of Night: Study of the Literary Relationships of Sir Walter Ralegh* (1936), *Andrew Marvell* (1940), written in collaboration with Gwyneth Lloyd Thomas, and *Joseph Conrad: Poland's English Genius* (1941). While busy in London with her war work she managed to write one more book, *Ibsen the Norwegian: a Revaluation*, published in 1946. Having learned Dano-Norwegian so as to be able to read Ibsen's early work in the original, Bradbrook placed great emphasis on the poetic power of his language. She devotes a chapter to some of his more significant lyrical poems and links the themes of several of them with particular aspects of some of the plays written later. In the preface she wrote, 'The book was written during the intervals of war work in London, where many of Ibsen's countrymen shared the night watches with me, and on one occasion rescued me and my manuscript from the debris of a flying bomb.' This book, and two or three others of hers, are telling testimonies to the breadth of

her range. There is, for example, an excellent commentary on Beckett's *En attendant Godot* in chapter 1 of *Literature in Action* (1972). Although a specialist in Elizabethan and Jacobean literature (especially dramatic literature), Bradbrook saw poetry, from Aeschylus to Beckett, as being all of a piece, the finest and truest expression of the human spirit.

Bradbrook was one of the earliest of twentieth-century critics to begin the rehabilitation of Elizabethan drama *as drama*, that is to say to undertake the task of restoring it, whole and undiluted, to the theatre. She was herself an avid theatregoer, trenchantly critical of productions that did less than justice to the text but quick and eager to praise moments of truth perceived and visual poetry realized. Often, both in her writing and in her lectures, she expressed her disapproval of the nineteenth-century tendency to regard Shakespeare as 'mere literature': even the great A. C. Bradley comes under her lash in this regard. The essay for which she won the Harness prize was the basis of her first book: *Elizabethan Stage Conditions* (1932). For the second edition in 1962 she wrote a brief prefatory note:

> Some sentences in this essay may sound less than just to that great Shakespearean, Harley Granville Barker. When as a youthful student I wrote them, I knew that Granville Barker was one of the adjudicators for the Harness Prize, and was determined not to curry favour. So I slapped the examiner. I have not forgotten his genial kindness then and would like to say now how much I have always admired his work.

Throughout the 1950s and 1960s Bradbrook's work on Shakespeare and the Elizabethans continued to be greeted with superlatives by the best critics of the day: 'The sanest and most stimulating book about Shakespeare to have appeared since the war', said Kenneth Muir about *Shakespeare and Elizabethan Poetry* (1951); Frank Kermode, in 1962, described *The Rise of the Common Player*, published in that year, as 'A highly original book, which constantly illuminates the drama of the period … A rich, rewarding book'. And James Reeves said the same book 'has the merit of integrating literary history with sociology, instead of separating it off in the manner of earlier writers on the theatre'.

The University of Cambridge appointed Bradbrook reader in 1962 and professor of English in 1965 (the English faculty's first woman professor). In 1968 she was appointed mistress of Girton. At various times during her career she held visiting professorships at Santa Cruz (California), Kuwait, Seoul, Tokyo, Kenyon College (Ohio), and Rhodes University, South Africa. Reputed to have been tentative, and even somewhat disorganized and vague in everyday matters in her early days at Girton, when she became chairman of the English faculty she very quickly established a reputation for vigorous action and firm decision (with, perhaps, just a touch of the authoritarian). Her clashes with Dr George Steiner, for instance, are still part of Cambridge folklore. But her capacity for clarity of vision, imaginative planning, and sheer hard work was never anywhere in question.

At the personal level Bradbrook was kind, patient, generous to a fault, and quite without any arrogance or pretentiousness. Her judgement was shrewd without being shrewish, her conversation witty without being facetious. To dozens of her professional colleagues and scores of her former students she was affectionately known as Brad; to her many friends outside her immediate Cambridge circle she was Mollie, though she always wrote as M. C. Bradbrook. In 1969 she had written a history of Girton under the ironic title, *The Infidel Place*. Girton was, in a very special sense, her second home, the centre of her life and of her remarkable career. She never married. She retired in 1976 and was recognized by Girton as a life fellow.

In all Bradbrook wrote some seventeen books, several quite brilliant and none negligible. She died at her home, 91 Chesterton Road, Cambridge, on 11 June 1993, and was cremated in Cambridge on 22 June. She left an estate of £705,250, much of it bequeathed in trust for her brother Samuel J. Bradbrook for life, but reverting absolutely to Girton College on his death.   ERIC SALMON

Sources Girton Cam., Bradbrook MSS · *The Times* (16 June 1993) · *The Independent* (16 June 1993) · 'Preface', M. C. Bradbrook, *Elizabethan stage conditions*, 2nd edn (1962) · personal knowledge (2004)
Archives Girton Cam., MSS
Likenesses photograph, repro. in *The Times* · photograph, repro. in *The Independent* · photographs, Girton Cam.
Wealth at death £705,250: *The Times* (23 Sept 1993)

Bradburn, Samuel (1751–1816), Methodist minister, was born in Gibraltar on 5 October 1751, the youngest son of the thirteen children of Isaac Bradburn (1719–1794), a gardener turned army private, and his wife, a Mrs Bold (1722–1775), the daughter of Samuel Jones, a Wrexham gardener. Samuel was apprenticed to a Chester shoemaker in 1764, and despite minimal schooling later acquired some knowledge of Latin, Greek, and Hebrew. After a strict Anglican upbringing he indulged in drinking and gambling, with occasional attacks of conscience, until his conversion in 1769. After joining the Methodists in 1770 he became a travelling preacher in 1774. In 1779 he was accused of Arianism by Dr Thomas Coke but exonerated.

In the divisions after John Wesley's death over relations with the Church of England, Bradburn supported those wishing for Methodist ordinations and sacraments. His *The Question 'Are Methodists Dissenters?' Fairly Examined* (1792) portrayed Methodism as not fully identifiable with Anglicanism or dissent, and free to shape its own ethos. Ordained by fellow Methodists in 1792, Bradburn alienated 'Church Methodists' in Bristol that year and supported the Lichfield plan (1794) for a quasi-episcopal Methodist government. He was suspected of 'democratical' sentiments, though his 'Rights of Man' language was mainly applied to religious toleration and Methodist lay rights. From 1795, however, alarmed by government threats against Methodism, he attacked the radical Methodists led by Alexander Kilham. He was president of the Methodist conference for 1799–1800, but was suspended from the ministry during 1802–3, apparently for drunkenness, possibly aggravated by chronic inability to keep out of debt.

Bradburn published only a few pamphlets and sermons, and an account of John Wesley's character (1791). Despite his popularity as a leading preacher ('the Methodist Demosthenes'; Stevens, 1.125) Bradburn attracted criticism for being unduly witty, satirical, and eccentric in and out of the pulpit, though he was careful of his appearance and powdered his wig. Despite these shortcomings he was a favourite of Wesley's, who engineered his first marriage on 28 June 1778 to Elizabeth Nangle of Dublin (1755/1757–1786), persuading her guardians to consent and marrying the couple forthwith in their parlour. (Praying for guidance about marriage Bradburn added 'But, O Lord, let it be Betsy'.) On 10 August 1786 he married Sophia Cooke (1758/9–1834), daughter of a Gloucester surgeon. Of his six sons, and either one or two daughters, only a daughter survived him. Bradburn's last years were clouded by physical and mental illness. He died in Long Lane, Southwark, on 26 July 1816 and was buried near Wesley's tomb in the New Chapel burial-ground, City Road, London on 2 August 1816. He was survived by his second wife, who died on 16 March 1834.   HENRY D. RACK

Sources E. W. Bradburn, *Memoirs of the late Rev. Samuel Bradburn* (1816) · T. W. Blanshard, *The life of Samuel Bradburn, the Methodist Demosthenes* (1870) · W. R. Ward, *Religion and society in England, 1790–1850* (1972) · A. Stevens, *The history of the religious movement of the eighteenth century, called Methodism*, rev. J. Willey, 3 vols. (1863–5) · L. Tyerman, biography of S. Bradburn, JRUML, Methodist archives, MAB B1234 · *The letters of John Pawson*, ed. J. C. Bowmer and J. A. Vickers, 3 vols. (1994–5) · *Methodist Magazine*, 39 (1816), 709
Archives JRL, Methodist Archives and Research Centre, corresp., diaries, and papers; family corresp. · JRL, letters and sermons
Likenesses S. Freeman, engraving (after portrait by D. Orme, W. Orme), repro. in Bradburn, *Memoirs*, frontispiece · attrib. D. Orme, W. Orme, portrait, repro. in Bradburn, *Memoirs*, frontispiece · line engraving, BM; repro. in *Arminian Magazine* (1785) · portrait, repro. in Blanshard, *Life of Samuel Bradburn*, frontispiece

Bradbury, George (*bap.* 1643, *d.* 1696), judge, was baptized at St Martin-in-the-Fields on 28 August 1643, the eldest son of Henry Bradbury of St Martin's Fields, Middlesex, and Barbara Carew. He was admitted to Queen's College, Oxford, in 1659, and entered the Middle Temple on 28 June 1660. He received an MA on 28 September 1663 and was called to the bar on 17 May 1667. For some time his practice in court was inconsiderable. He is first listed as junior counsel on 3 June 1684 against Lady Ivy in a suit in which she asserted her title to lands in Shadwell. The deeds on which she relied were of doubtful authenticity, and Bradbury won commendation from Lord Chief Justice Jeffreys for pointing out that the deeds described Philip and Mary by a title which they did not assume until some years after the date which the deeds bore. When Bradbury repeated his comment, Jeffreys responded: 'Lord, sir! you must be cackling too; we told you your objection was very ingenious, but that must not make you troublesome. You cannot lay an egg but you must be cackling over it' (Foss, *Judges*, 7.311). Bradbury's name next occurs in 1681, when he was a trustee, along with the earl of Shrewsbury and Hon. Charles Bertie, of the marriage settlement of one of the Carys of Tor Abbey.

Bradbury may have been an intermediary used by the

conspirators involved in the revolution of 1688. He was certainly involved in the events in London in December 1688. According to Roger Morrice, Bradbury was one of the lawyers summoned to attend the peers on 21 December on the nomination of the earl of Dorset, 'for he does the business of that family' (Beddard, 184). When he attended—along with Maynard, Holt, Pollexfen, and Atkins—on the following day, he helped to draft the order for removing papists from London. He also attended on 24 December when the peers debated how to call a free parliament. He was called to the bench of his inn on 7 February 1689, and was in heavy demand in the months following the revolution as a counsel in cases before the House of Lords. These included being assigned as counsel for Sir Adam Blair and others, who were impeached for dispersing proclamations of King James. On the recommendation of Shrewsbury and the duke of Norfolk, on 12 February 1689 he was appointed cursitor baron of the exchequer. He retained his place until his death on 12 February 1696. His will contains no mention of a marriage; his house 'being the sign of the White Lyon in the Strand' (PRO, PROB 11/430/28) was left to his nephews and heirs in turn, the sons of his brother, Henry.

STUART HANDLEY

Sources Foss, *Judges*, 7.311–12 · Sainty, *Judges*, 140 · R. Beddard, ed., *A kingdom without a king: the journal of the provisional government in the revolution of 1688* (1988), 151–9 · IGI · will, PRO, PROB 11/430, sig. 28 · *The manuscripts of the House of Lords*, 4 vols., HMC, 17 (1887–94), vol. 2 · *Calendar of the Stuart papers belonging to his majesty the king, preserved at Windsor Castle*, 7 vols., HMC, 56 (1902–23), vol. 6, p. 50 · *CSP dom.*, 1689–90, 378 · Foster, *Alum. Oxon.* · H. A. C. Sturgess, ed., *Register of admissions to the Honourable Society of the Middle Temple, from the fifteenth century to the year 1944*, 1 (1949), 163 · *Herald and Genealogist*, 8 (1874), 107 · *State trials*, 10.616, 626

Bradbury, Henry Riley (1831–1860), writer on printing, the eldest son of William *Bradbury (1800–1869), co-owner of the printing and publishing firm Bradbury and Evans, and his wife, Sarah, was born in London. In 1850 he went to Vienna to study at the imperial printing office. There he became acquainted with the art of nature printing, a process whereby natural objects are impressed into metal plates, from which electrotypes are taken that can be used in relief printing. Bradbury afterwards claimed that he invented this process, but the imperial printer, Alois Auer, in *Discovery of the Natural Printing Process* (Vienna, 1854, in English, German, Italian, and French), published six facsimile letters from Bradbury purporting to indicate that he first saw the process in Vienna. Certainly Bradbury brought the process back to Britain and there perfected it. In 1855 he produced in folio the fine 'nature-printed' plates to *Ferns of Great Britain and Ireland*, written by Thomas Moore, curator of the Chelsea Botanic Gardens, and edited by the eminent botanist John Lindley (1859). These were followed by the plates to William Grosart Johnstone's and Alexander Croall's *Nature-Printed British Sea-Weeds* (4 vols., 1859–60), a copy of which G. H. Lewes asked John Blackwood to obtain for him. Bradbury consolidated his knowledge of nature printing first in a lecture on 11 May 1855 at the Royal Institution (London, 1856), translated badly into German by an employee of

Bradbury and Evans to counteract Auer's *Das Benehmen eines jungen Engländers namens Henry Bradbury* (Vienna, 1854) and his *Discovery*. Bradbury's amplified disquisition, *Autotypography, or, Art of Nature-Printing*, was printed for private circulation in 1860.

Bradbury lectured to the Royal Institution on 9 May 1856 about a different topic, the ease with which banknotes were being forged; this was published under the title *On the Security and Manufacture of Bank Notes* by his father's firm in 1856, and illustrated with plates by John Leighton FSA. About this time Bradbury established his own firm, Bradbury and Wilkinson, in Fetter Lane, London. In 1860 he produced *Specimens of Bank-Note Engraving* incorporating samples of banknote paper manufactured by T. H. Saunders.

On 14 May 1858 Bradbury again addressed the Royal Institution, this time attempting 'to illustrate … the power and the spread of printing as an intellectual agent in the destinies of man' (Bigmore and Wyman, 1.77). This address, issued in 1858 as *Printing: its Dawn, Day, and Destiny*, reviewed letterpress, intaglio, chemical, photographic, siderographic, and electro processes. Over the next two years Bradbury worked up a prospectus for a folio treatise on the graphic arts of the nineteenth century. Before this could be put into production, however, on 2 September 1860 Bradbury committed suicide in Cremorne Gardens by drinking soda water laced with prussic acid. Dickens speculated to W. H. Wills that the family's 'strong influence' kept the story out of the papers; George Holsworth, employee of *All the Year Round*, believed Bradbury was depressed because one of Frederick Mullet Evans's daughters was marrying another, but Dickens doubted 'whether any blurred vision of that most undesirable female … ever crossed his drunken mind' (letter of 4 Sept 1860, *Letters of Charles Dickens*, 302–3). The firm Bradbury founded had moved about 1859 to Farringdon Street, London, and continued under the name Bradbury, Wilkinson & Co.

ROBERT L. PATTEN

Sources *DNB* · E. C. Bigmore and C. W. H. Wyman, eds., *A bibliography of printing*, 2nd edn, 2 vols. (1945) · *American dictionary of printing and bookmaking* (1894) · *The letters of Charles Dickens*, ed. M. House, G. Storey, and others, 9 (1997) · Boase, *Mod. Eng. biog.*, vol. 1 · *The George Eliot letters*, ed. G. S. Haight, 9 vols. (1954–78) · *The letters and private papers of William Makepeace Thackeray*, ed. G. N. Ray, 4 vols. (1945–6) · R. G. G. Price, *A history of Punch* (1957) · catalogue [BM]
Archives Bodl. Oxf., corresp. with Evans
Wealth at death under £7000: administration, 19 Oct 1860, CGPLA Eng. & Wales

Bradbury, Joan (c.1450–1530). *See under* Women traders and artisans in London (*act.* c.1200–c.1500).

Bradbury, John Swanwick, first Baron Bradbury (1872–1950), civil servant, was born at Winsford, Cheshire, on 23 September 1872, the only surviving son of John Bradbury (d. 1889), oil merchant, and his wife, Sarah (d. 1901), daughter of William Cross, of Winsford. He was educated at Manchester grammar school and at Brasenose College, Oxford, where he held a scholarship and gained first classes in classical moderations (1893), *literae humaniores* (1895), and modern history (1896). He was then successful

John Swanwick Bradbury, first Baron Bradbury (1872–1950),
by Elliott & Fry, 1920s

in the open competitive examination for first division clerkships in the civil service.

After a short time in the Colonial Office Bradbury was transferred to the Treasury. His selection at the end of 1905 to be private secretary to Asquith, chancellor of the exchequer in the newly appointed Liberal government, marked him out for advancement. When Lloyd George succeeded Asquith in April 1908, Bradbury became head of the Treasury's first (finance) division. In that capacity he helped to prepare the 1909 budget—Lloyd George's 'people's budget', which was blocked by the Lords and did not become law until April 1910, after a general election. He had not long emerged from the strenuous work which this demanded when he became deeply involved in Lloyd George's health insurance project. Lloyd George assigned the task of planning this vast scheme to Bradbury and William Braithwaite of the Inland Revenue, assisted by Lloyd George's private secretary, R. G. Hawtrey. When the National Insurance Bill became law the Treasury had also to take the initiative in building up a new administrative machine. Bradbury became an insurance commissioner and a member of the national health insurance joint committee (1911–13) without relinquishing his post at the Treasury. He married in 1911 Hilda Maude (d. 1949), daughter of William Arthur Kirby, chartered accountant, of Hampstead. They had one daughter and two sons.

In 1913, when Sir Robert Chalmers resigned the permanent secretaryship of the Treasury, it was decided to appoint two joint permanent secretaries. The choice fell

on the forty-year-old Bradbury, who had charge of the purely financial functions, and Sir Thomas Heath, who attended to the administrative side. They were later rejoined by Chalmers. Bradbury's knowledge of British financial institutions was unparalleled outside the City of London at that time.

In the financial crisis on the outbreak of war in August 1914 Bradbury saw immediately that what was needed was an issue of paper money of small denomination. (Before the war gold sovereigns were in circulation, and the smallest-denomination bank note was for £5.) This would both economize on gold and reduce the risk of a run on the banks. By a combination of swift action and ingenious improvisation he was able to provide a new issue of currency notes within a week. The £1 and 10s. notes, issued by the Treasury to the banks, bore a facsimile of his signature and were long known as 'Bradburys'.

Throughout the war Bradbury remained the government's chief financial adviser. Among his numerous contributions to war finance was the innovation, in 1916, of war savings certificates for small investors. These were to remain an important instrument of UK government borrowing in peacetime as well as in both world wars. In January 1918 he was appointed to the committee, chaired by Lord Cunliffe, on currency and foreign exchanges after the war. The UK had been effectively but not legally off the gold standard during the war: the Cunliffe committee took for granted an eventual return to gold at the pre-war par (though without a return to internal gold circulation) and concerned itself with the arrangements for a period of transition which was expected to last ten years. Bradbury's influence shows in its main recommendations for a cessation of government borrowing after the war, for the gradual reduction and eventual elimination of the currency note issue, and for the renewed use of the bank rate mechanism. In making these recommendations he was concerned more to prevent further inflation after the war than to bring about an early return to the gold standard. In the summer of 1919 he arranged within the Treasury that any increases in currency notes had to be matched by setting aside Bank of England notes. As an inflationary post-war boom gathered pace this trick reduced bank's reserves and forced the chancellor to allow interest rates to rise dramatically in the winter of 1919–20.

The treaty of Versailles brought Bradbury a new sphere of work. He left the Treasury in 1919 to become principal British delegate to the reparation commission. The five years which followed gave ample scope for his gifts of tact, judgement, and humour. The Dawes report of 1924 owed much to Bradbury, who was 'indefatigable behind the scenes with ideas and formulae' according to one close observer (Grigg, 169). He was also deeply involved in the contentious decision of the UK government to return to gold in April 1925. He was appointed in 1924 to the committee on the currency and Bank of England note issues chaired at first by Sir Austen Chamberlain and then by Bradbury himself, and he was consulted again by the chancellor of the exchequer, Winston Churchill, and the prime minister when the decision was taken. As in 1918

Bradbury was cautious and pragmatic rather than doctrinaire in his advice. In January 1925 he was raised to the peerage as Baron Bradbury of Winsford, shortly before his retirement from the civil service, having played a significant part in its twentieth-century evolution. He had been appointed CB in 1909, promoted KCB in 1913 and GCB in 1920. He was an honorary fellow of Brasenose (1926) and an honorary LLD of Cambridge and Manchester (1925).

From 1925 to 1929 Bradbury was chairman of the National Food Council and also for a time a government-appointed director of the Anglo-Persian Oil Company. He was chairman of the Bankers' Clearing House Committee and president of the British Bankers' Association (1929–30 and 1935–6). A member of the Macmillan committee on finance and industry in 1929–31, he dissented from its report, finding himself 'in disagreement with most of the conclusions'. His own conclusions were that the gold standard should be maintained at the existing parity; that the domestic currency and banking systems needed only minor improvements not radical reform; and that 'the best contribution which the State can make to assist industry and promote employment is strict economy in public expenditure and lightening the burden of debt by prudent financial administration' ('Memorandum of dissent by Lord Bradbury', committee on finance and industry, *Report*, Command 3897, 1931, 263–81).

Bradbury was described as 'tall, but with a slight stoop, his face pale and rather deeply lined, with a jowl, not actually prominent, but indicative of a bull-dog tenacity' (*DNB*). Contemporaries attributed his successful public career, in part, to this quality of tenacity, combined with a sense of humour, a tolerant outlook, and a capacity for witty comment. He died in London, where he had lived, on 3 May 1950.

SUSAN HOWSON

Sources DNB · S. Howson, *Domestic monetary management in Britain, 1919–38* (1975) · D. E. Moggridge, *British monetary policy, 1924–1931: the Norman conquest of $4.86* (1972) · P. J. Grigg, *Prejudice and judgment* (1948) · B. B. Gilbert, *The evolution of national insurance in Great Britain: the origins of the welfare state* (1966) · J. M. Keynes, 'War and the financial system, August 1914', *Economic Journal*, 24 (1914), 460–86 · H. N. Bunbury, ed., *Lloyd George's ambulance wagon: being the memoirs of William J. Braithwaite, 1911–1912* (1957) · CGPLA Eng. & Wales (1950)
Archives PRO, papers, T170 · PRO, British delegation to reparation commission, corresp., and MSS of Sir John Bradbury, T 194/4–13 · PRO, Treasury finance files, T160 | BLPES, Braithwaite MSS · Bodl. Oxf., corresp. with H. H. Asquith · HLRO, corresp. with Stanley Baldwin and Andrew Bonar Law · Lpool RO, corresp. with seventeenth earl of Derby
Likenesses Elliott & Fry, photograph, 1920–29, NPG [*see illus.*] · A. E. Orr, portrait, priv. coll. · Quiz [P. Evans], caricature, NPG; repro. in *Saturday Review* (3 Oct 1925)
Wealth at death £39,890 10s. 4d.: probate, 26 July 1950, CGPLA Eng. & Wales

Bradbury, Sir Malcolm Stanley (1932–2000), writer and literary scholar, was born on 7 September 1932 at Nether Edge Hospital, Sheffield, the elder of the two sons of Arthur Bradbury (1899–1985) and his wife, Doris, née Marshall (1898–1993). His father's family came from Macclesfield, Cheshire, and his mother's from Sheffield, Yorkshire. Arthur Bradbury was a railwayman who ended his

Sir Malcolm Stanley Bradbury (1932–2000), by Richard Whitehead, 1993

career as an advertising manager in British Rail. Because of his father's occupation, and the disturbances of the Second World War, Bradbury lived in several different places in early childhood, but the family settled in Nottingham, where he attended West Bridgford grammar school from 1943 to 1950. He took justifiable pride in the fact that while still a schoolboy he had short stories published in the *Nottinghamshire Guardian*, the newspaper that had published D. H. Lawrence's first story. In 1950 he went to University College, Leicester, then a very small institution that prepared students for the external degrees of London University, and obtained a first in English in 1953. He had already started the novel that became *Eating People is Wrong*. He was offered a postgraduate scholarship by the University of London which he took up at Queen Mary College, though he worked mainly in the round reading-room of the British Museum. He obtained his MA (then a two-year research degree) with a thesis on the influential 'little magazines' of the modern literary era, and he was soon publishing parts of it in similar magazines, as well as contributing more light-hearted pieces to periodicals like *Punch*. From an early age, therefore, creative, scholarly, and popular journalistic strands were intertwined in his writing career.

Bradbury had developed a strong interest in American literature (in those days a rather esoteric option for students of English literature) and in 1955–6 he went to America as an English-Speaking Union fellow and postgraduate instructor at the University of Indiana, Bloomington, 'teaching the comma and underlining' (as he liked to say) in freshman English while laying the foundations of his future research on American literature. That year was a formative experience. The American way of life was both a provocation to satire and a foil against which to appreciate the very different flaws and follies of the British society to which he returned in 1956, to enrol for a PhD on American literary expatriates at the University of Manchester (obtained in 1962). In 1958–9 he returned to America, as a British Association for American Studies fellow, attached to Yale University. Bradbury was keenly interested in the then fashionable discipline of sociology, and his humorous journalistic pieces at this time, subsequently collected in *Phogey* (1960) and *All Dressed Up and Nowhere to Go* (1962), were a kind of popular sociology of style and behaviour. The witty observation of contemporary manners in different cultures was to be a consistent feature of his novels.

Bradbury had always suffered from a heart condition, which curtailed his participation in sports, and no doubt encouraged his literary and intellectual pursuits, in childhood and youth. In 1958 he underwent what is reputed to be the first hole in the heart operation carried out in Britain. It was a traumatic experience which left its trace on the closing chapters of *Eating People is Wrong*—indeed the author finished that book in hospital with a pessimistic sense of urgency. Happily the operation was successful, and the following year was something of an *annus mirabilis* for him. On 17 October 1959 he married Florence Betty (Elizabeth) Salt, a librarian in Nottingham whom he had known for some years; he obtained his first academic post, as tutor in literature and drama in the extramural department of the University of Hull; and he had his first novel published.

Eating People is Wrong was deservedly acclaimed by reviewers and immediately established Bradbury as a significant new voice in English fiction. Perhaps inevitably, because of its satirical take on academic life and episodes of high farce, it was linked with Kingsley Amis's *Lucky Jim*, though it has a more intellectual underlying theme, one which was to recur in Bradbury's work: the plight of the liberal humanist who lacks the strength, and perhaps the will, to resist those forces in contemporary society whose influence he most deplores.

In 1961 Bradbury was appointed to a lectureship in the English department of the University of Birmingham. Another young lecturer and novelist in the department was David Lodge. The two men became fast friends, and in due course collaborators (with a talented undergraduate, Jim Duckett) on a satirical stage revue, *Between these Four Walls*, produced by the Birmingham Repertory Theatre in 1963. In 1965 Bradbury published his second novel, *Stepping Westward*, in which a provincial English novelist comes to a university in the middle of America to be writer in residence and fails abysmally to understand the political intrigues in which he is involved. In the same year Bradbury accepted a pressing invitation from the newly founded University of East Anglia (UEA) at Norwich to accept a lectureship with a mandate to develop

American studies there. He was to remain at UEA for the rest of his academic life, retiring in 1995 as professor of American studies. To the general public, however, he was better known as co-founder (with Sir Angus Wilson) and later sole director of an MA course in creative writing. From small beginnings (in its first year, 1970, the course had only one student, Ian McEwan) this grew into the most successful and prestigious course of its kind in the country, whose graduates have made a significant contribution to contemporary British fiction over the years. Many of them have paid tribute to Bradbury's generosity and tact as a teacher.

Bradbury's own fictional masterpiece was perhaps *The History Man* (1975). Its anti-hero, sociology lecturer Howard Kirk, who believes that Marx has provided him with the plot of history, which happens to coincide conveniently with his own desires for domination of other people, became one of the mythical figures of contemporary culture, especially after the success of the BBC's television serialization of the novel, adapted by Christopher Hampton, in 1980. *The History Man* received the Royal Society of Literature's Heinemann award, and Bradbury's next novel, *Rates of Exchange*, was shortlisted for the Booker prize in 1983. This is set in the imaginary eastern European country of Slaka, for which Bradbury invented a colourful history and geography and a language full of Slavic syllables and English puns. (He even wrote and separately published a spoof guidebook called *Why Come to Slaka?*) The educated Slakans speak an expressive broken English and run rings round the naïve English linguistics lecturer whose visit drives the plot. This novel, and the next one, *Dr Criminale* (1992), revealed Bradbury's sympathetic fascination with the plight of intellectuals under repressive communist regimes prior to the collapse of the Soviet empire, and the various strategies they used to survive. The amusing surface comedy of cross-cultural manners in these novels covers some dark, disturbing ideas about history and politics, and the final joke is usually on the feeble representatives of liberal democracy.

If Bradbury's novels were more widely spaced in time than his admirers would have liked, this was partly because he laboured to perfect them and revised them endlessly, but partly too because he spread his energies so widely. He was, for instance, one of the first English literary novelists to become actively involved in television drama, having his first teleplay, *The After Dinner Game* (written with Christopher Bigsby) produced by the BBC in 1975. At the other end of his career he wrote two ambitious original television mini-series, *The Gravy Train* (1990) and *The Gravy Train Goes East* (1991), satirizing bureaucracy and corruption in a Europe dominated by the EU and shaken up by the collapse of communism. Some of his finest work for television included adaptations of other writers' work, notably John Fowles's *The Enigma*, Tom Sharpe's *Porterhouse Blue*, and Stella Gibbons's *Cold Comfort Farm* (later released as a feature film). He contributed episodes to some of the most popular British television crime series, such as *A Touch of Frost*, *Dalziel and Pascoe*, and *Kavanagh QC*.

Like most writers who venture into this field of endeavour, he wrote many screenplays that were never produced. The frustrations of the screenwriter's life found comedic relief in his novella *Cuts* (1987).

Throughout his academic career, and after his retirement, Malcolm Bradbury continued to publish works of criticism and scholarship too numerous to list here—though mention must be made of his astonishingly comprehensive *The Modern British Novel* (1993; rev. 2001), and *Dangerous Pilgrimages: Transatlantic Mythologies and the Novel* (1995), the finest fruit of his long study of American–European literary relations. He edited classic novels and reference books and anthologies. He wrote hundreds of, probably more than a thousand, book reviews in newspapers and magazines (and never a spiteful or destructive one). He took the function of criticism very seriously, but he was also capable of carnivalizing it, as in his parodic biography of a fictitious continental post-structuralist theorist, *Mensonge* (1987).

Bradbury was chairman of the Booker prize judges in 1981, and was involved in the award of several other literary prizes. He travelled frequently abroad, to conferences or on lecture tours for the British Council, and presided for many years over an influential seminar organized by the council at Cambridge every summer, at which a select gathering of foreign academics, writers, translators, and literary journalists encountered a procession of some of Britain's most distinguished authors. He was in his element on these occasions, which involved a good deal of socializing. Malcolm Bradbury enjoyed the kind of party of which the chief constituents are good talk and good wine, and his stamina on these occasions was legendary.

Physically Bradbury was tall, but never used his height to intimidate. His manners were gentle, his voice was light. His speech had no perceptible class or regional accent, though in later life it acquired an attractive, slightly patrician drawl. When he read from his own work his delivery had a distinctive rising and falling intonation. He possessed a whole spectrum of laughs, from an infectious giggle to a full-throated guffaw. His long, handsome face, surmounted by dark wavy hair that became thinner and grizzled in later years, was the face of an intellectual, the broad brow furrowed with the traces of thought; but there were laugh lines around the eyes and the mouth was always apt to break into a smile. When he wrote on the typewriter or computer, the tip of his tongue flickered and curled between his lips as if in sympathy with the difficulty and delicacy of the task.

Bradbury was a man of letters of a kind unusual in modern times, and of perhaps unique versatility. For his services to literature he was appointed CBE in 1990 and was knighted in 2000. He was a fellow of the Royal Society of Literature, and the recipient of numerous honorary degrees, fellowships, and visiting professorships.

Bradbury could not have achieved so much without the devoted support and assistance of his wife, Elizabeth. Nevertheless the work rate he set himself took its toll on his health. He contracted a rare respiratory disease called cryptogenic organizing pneumonia which progressed alarmingly in 2000 and failed to respond to the customary treatment. This prevented him from properly enjoying the publication of his long-awaited novel *To the Hermitage* in the spring of that year. In form and content this was quite a new departure, deftly splicing together a wry, Shandean self-portrait with a vivid historical evocation of the philosopher Denis Diderot, whose encyclopaedic intellectual energy he admired, and whose disappointments stirred his sympathies. The moving elegiac conclusion to that novel soon acquired an extra poignancy.

Malcolm Bradbury died at Priscilla Bacon Lodge, Coleman Hospital, Norwich, on 27 November 2000, attended by his wife and their two sons, Matthew and Dominic. He was buried on 4 December in the churchyard of St Mary's parish church, Tasburgh, a village near Norwich where the Bradburys owned a second home. Though he was not an orthodox religious believer, he respected the traditions and socio-cultural role of the Church of England, and enjoyed visiting churches in the spirit of Philip Larkin's famous poem 'Churchgoing'.

A memorial service held at Norwich Cathedral in February 2001 was attended by over 500 people, an indication of how sadly Bradbury was missed in many different walks of life. In the English literary world he left a gap which could hardly be filled, because of the variety of his talents and the breadth of his interests. His friends cherished the memory of his wit, his sociability, his gentleness, and his generosity of spirit towards fellow writers.

DAVID LODGE

Sources L. Henderson, ed., *Contemporary novelists*, 5th edn (1991) · 'Malcolm Bradbury', contemporary writers leaflet, 1992, Book Trust and the British Council · *The Guardian* (28 Nov 2000) · A. Motion and K. Ishiguru, 'Tributes', *The Guardian* (28 Nov 2000) · I. McEwan and D. Lodge, 'Farewell to a friend', *The Guardian* (29 Nov 2000) · *The Times* (28 Nov 2000) · *Daily Telegraph* (28 Nov 2000) · *Debrett's People of today* (1999) · private information (2004) [Elizabeth Bradbury, widow]

Archives University of Indiana, Bloomington | FILM U. Birm. L., video interview with David Lodge, discussion of *The history man*

Likenesses photographs, 1975, Hult. Arch. · R. Whitehead, photograph, 1993, NPG [*see illus.*]

Bradbury, Thomas (1676/7–1759), Independent minister and religious controversialist, was born at Alverthorpe, near Wakefield, where his father, Peter Bradbury (1639/40–1699), a tailor, was a leading member of a dissenting meeting; his mother was Mary (d. 1723). Peter Nayler, the minister at Alverthorpe, had been ejected from West Houghton in Lancashire in 1662, and it was he who began the young Bradbury's education, noting his unusually retentive memory. After attending the free school at Leeds, Bradbury entered Timothy Jollie's dissenting academy at Attercliffe. Oliver Heywood records in his diary meeting the student Bradbury and giving him books. The two later corresponded. A particular influence on Bradbury was Thomas Whitaker, minister of Call Lane, Leeds, a man of orthodox views who befriended him and took him into his home. Bradbury visited Whitaker regularly until his death in 1710 and then edited a collection of his sermons.

Bradbury's ministry began in 1697 when he supplied the

Thomas Bradbury (1676/7–1759), by John Faber junior, 1749 (after Mary Grace)

vacant pulpit at Beverley. While there, he corresponded with George Keith, the self-styled Christian Quaker, and received copies of Keith's narratives of the proceedings at Turners' Hall. In 1699 he became assistant minister at Newcastle upon Tyne, first to the elderly Dr Richard Gilpin, then to his successor, Benjamin Bennet. His popularity with the congregation led to a disagreement with Bennet, and in September 1701 he received, but did not pursue, an invitation to the church in Mark Lane in London, which then called Isaac Watts.

Bradbury's first publication, *Christus in coelo*, was a selection of his Newcastle sermons. It appeared in 1703, and the following year Bradbury became assistant to John Galpin, minister at Stepney. Almost immediately he was invited to Yarmouth as co-minister with Samuel Wright but rejected the call. A letter to Bradbury in April 1704 from Jeremiah White, Oliver Cromwell's former chaplain, suggests that a faction of the congregation at Newcastle may have invited him to return. He remained at Stepney, however, until his public ordination as minister of the former Moravian meeting-house in Fetter Lane, London, on 10 July 1707, where he succeeded Benoni Rowe. Bradbury's *Confession of Faith* shows him to have been a firm Calvinist. Its publication ran to five editions by 1729.

Lively minded, with an easy way of public speaking, a good presence, and an arresting turn of phrase, Bradbury quickly attracted a large congregation and was appointed to a number of lectureships, notably at Salters' Hall and the Weigh House. He was a Merchants' lecturer at Pinners' Hall for over fifty years.

Bradbury emerged to public notice in London at a time when the toleration of dissenters was being threatened by the preaching of Dr Henry Sacheverell and other high-churchmen, and by the incitement of the mob against them. The incoming tory ministry of 1710 intensified the pressures on dissenters through the Occasional Conformity Act of 1711 and the Schism Act of 1714. Bradbury became an outspoken defender of religious liberty and supporter of the Hanoverian succession. His highly political sermons every 5 November, the anniversary of King William's landing in England as well as of the Gunpowder Plot, were notorious, but popular. Typical was 'The lawfulness of resisting tyrants', preached in 1713 and published in 1714, which ran to four editions. Most of his political sermons were included in his *Works*, published posthumously in 1762.

Some on his own side thought Bradbury too outspoken. *A Friendly epistle by way of reproof from one of the people called Quakers, to T B, a dealer in many words* appeared in 1715 from the pen of Daniel Defoe. Bradbury's practice of resorting to a tavern after preaching each 5 November to eat, drink, and sing raucously 'The Roast Beef of Old England' attracted the criticism of both Isaac Watts and George Whitefield, who thought his behaviour unbecoming in a minister. But Bradbury, whose motto was *Pro Christo et patria* (for Christ and country), had made his mark. Queen Anne was said to have called him Bold Bradbury and to have tried to quieten him with a bishopric. The mob burnt his meeting-house in March 1710 and threatened him, but he escaped. According to his grandson, an assassin sent to kill him was converted by one of his sermons. Bradbury, alerted by a pre-arranged signal that Queen Anne had at last died—a handkerchief falling from the gallery as he preached—prayed for King George and boasted afterwards that he had been the first to proclaim the new reign. When attending the new court with other dissenting ministers in their black gowns to present a loyal address, he was asked by a courtier, 'Pray sir, is this a funeral?', to which Bradbury replied, 'Yes Sir, it is the funeral of the Schism Act, and the resurrection of liberty'. These stories are well vouched for, if perhaps embroidered in the telling. However, the report that after Queen Anne's death he preached on the text 'Go, see now this cursed woman and bury her, for she is a king's daughter' is probably apocryphal, though he would have been capable of it.

In 1719 Bradbury became caught up in the Salters' Hall dispute. The trustees of four dissenting meetings in Exeter had barred three of the four ministers for refusing to subscribe to the declaration concerning the divinity of Christ and then appealed to the London ministers for guidance. A gathering of ministers of the three denominations at Salters' Hall duly considered a letter of advice designed to restore peace in Exeter. The draft, however, did not address the doctrinal issue. Bradbury moved a new clause affirming belief in the Trinity. This was lost by four votes, arguably because some thought the procedure out of order. At the resumed meeting Bradbury therefore proposed that before considering the advice further those present should subscribe to a declaration of belief in the Trinity. When the moderator, Joshua Oldfield, refused to put the proposal to the meeting, upwards of sixty ministers, led by Bradbury, moved to the gallery and subscribed their signatures to the declaration, while the smaller number who remained below did not. Each side then sent separate letters to Exeter, similar in the advice offered on resolving disputes between ministers and their congregations, but with marked differences in the forthrightness of commitment to trinitarian belief.

Bradbury's leading part in the dispute made him a target in the ensuing pamphlet war—designed, he said, to destroy his reputation. The political charge against him was that the disunity he had caused among dissenters was of comfort only to their political enemies, and he lost a prominent whig politician, Shute Barrington, from his congregation. Barrington was thought to have written one of the highly personal attacks on Bradbury, *A Letter of Advice to the Protestant Dissenters* (1720). The religious charge was that he was a creed-maker who did not use the language of scripture and was trying to threaten liberty of religious belief. Bradbury's defence, in *An answer to the reproaches cast on those ministers who subscribed to their belief in the eternal Trinity* (1719), was that the original letter of advice to Exeter had been intended to be a screen for Arian ministers, and that the expression of trinitarian belief he had proposed was one to which dissenting ministers were required by law to assent, or had been drawn from the Westminster assembly's catechism. A move to exclude him from the Pinners' Hall lectures failed. The anti-Arian lectures held at Fetter Lane were an outcome of this simmering dispute. They were published as *The Power of Christ* (1724).

Bradbury's stand received support from outside dissent as well as within. William Wake, archbishop of Canterbury, himself beset by some prominent questioners of trinitarian doctrine, wrote to Bradbury on 5 September 1721: 'I am glad to see that amidst our other much lesser differences we all stand fast and agree in contending for the faith as it was delivered to the saints' (Wilson, 3.521). Bradbury's most considered response to the issue behind the dispute was *The Mystery of Godliness* (1726), in which he put forward a scriptural basis for belief in the divinity of Christ.

While many regarded Bradbury as heroic and forthright, his delight in argument and controversy, and his inability to tolerate compromise or control his wit, led to a series of disputes. Though old friends, there was a serious falling out when Bradbury criticized Isaac Watts's *Psalms* (1719) and forbade the use of Watts's 'whims' in his services. He was scornful of Watts's essay *The Christian Doctrine of the Trinity* (1722) and of Watts's other efforts for accommodation with the anti-trinitarians. Relations between them were not helped by Bradbury's open dislike of two of Watts's closest friends, his co-pastor, Samuel Price, and the author of *The History of the Puritans*, Daniel Neal. The correspondence between the two men on these subjects does neither credit. In 1728 Bradbury had a disagreement with his deacons over a minor money matter, and led his supporters to New Court, Carey Street, where

the two congregations successfully united under his ministry. That he could still call on friends of weight is shown by the speed with which he was able to clear a substantial debt on New Court. In the same year he quarrelled with the philanthropist William Coward, who resented Bradbury's advice on his will. Coward dismissed Bradbury from the Little St Helen's lectures, to which he had been appointed in 1726, though his continuing value as a protagonist led to an invitation to take part in the famous Lime Street lectures in defence of Calvinism in 1730. Like some other Independents he criticized Philip Doddridge for his accommodating attitude to the Methodists, but—this short-lived disagreement apart—the two men maintained good relations throughout. Bradbury supported Doddridge's students as a member of the Congregational Fund Board and Doddridge sought him out as preacher and dining companion whenever he was in London.

Bradbury married Mary Richmond (d. 1765), reportedly a widow of means, on 1 August 1717. They had two daughters. In 1744 one daughter married John Winter, an agent for the army and brother of Bradbury's successor at New Court, Richard Winter. Their son Dr Robert Winter, also later minister at New Court, helped preserve his grandfather's memory. The other daughter was married in 1768 to George Welch, a banker, who with Thomas Wilson founded the Societas Evangelica and Hoxton Academy in 1778. Bradbury's brother, Peter, who had been his assistant minister at Fetter Lane, continued at New Court until he married money. He resigned in 1731 and retired to an estate in Yorkshire.

Doddridge feared that an illness in 1738 had brought Bradbury 'near Eternity' (*Calendar*, ed. Nuttall, 518). Another in 1743 also concerned his friends. These, however, appear to have been the only interruptions of his sixty-two years' active ministry. He remained to the end a popular, patriotic preacher and an uncompromising leading figure in orthodox dissent among the Independents. Of all his collected sermons *The Christian's Joy in Finishing his Course* (1713), from before the years of theological controversy, was said to have given him most personal satisfaction. He preached his last sermon on 12 August 1759, the anniversary of the accession of George I, and fell ill shortly afterwards. He died, aged eighty-two, on 9 September 1759 and was buried in Bunhill Fields on 15 September. The next day, a Sunday, Richard Winter, his successor, and Thomas Hall, Independent minister at Moorfields, preached funeral sermons at New Court. His widow survived him and was buried on 28 September 1765.

JOHN HANDBY THOMPSON

Sources W. Wilson, *The history and antiquities of the dissenting churches and meeting houses in London, Westminster and Southwark*, 4 vols. (1808–14), vol. 3, pp. 504–35 · J. G. Miall, *Congregationalism in Yorkshire* (1868), 229, 304, 374 · D. Bogue and J. Bennett, *History of dissenters, from the revolution in 1688, to … 1808*, 3 (1810), 489–95 · *Calendar of the correspondence of Philip Doddridge*, ed. G. F. Nuttall, HMC, JP 26 (1979), letters 385, 411, 422, 484, 489, 518, 605, 623, 946, 948, 1549–50 · *The posthumous works of Isaac Watts DD*, 2 vols. (1779), vol. 2, pp. 168–233 · J. Browne, *A history of Congregationalism and memorials of the churches in Norfolk and Suffolk* (1877), 242 · J. H. Turner, T. Dickenson, and O. Heywood, eds., *The nonconformist register of baptisms,* *marriages, and deaths* (1881), 96, 148, 212, 290 • J. Hunter, *The rise of the old dissent, exemplified by the life of Oliver Heywood* (1842), 385 • *The Rev. Oliver Heywood … his autobiography, diaries, anecdote and event books*, ed. J. H. Turner, 4 (1885), 248 • Salter's Hall tracts, DWL • A. P. Davis, *Isaac Watts* (1943), 25, 58–61, 112, 114, 216–17 • 'Thomas Gibbons diary: extract', *Transactions of the Congregational Historical Society*, 1 (1901–4), 391 • R. Winter, *A sermon occasioned by the death of the Rev. T. Bradbury* (1759) • T. Hall, *A sermon occasioned by the death of T. Bradbury* (1759) • BL, Sloane MS 4276, fols. 6 and 220 • Thomas Bradbury's account of his youthful religious experience, BL, Add. MS 4275, fol. 87r • T. Bradbury, *The duty and doctrine of baptism* (1749), preface • Stepney church book, Tower Hamlets RO, TH/8337/1, fols. 10r–211r

Likenesses G. Vertue, line engraving, 1725 (after T. Gibson, 1725), BM • J. Faber junior, mezzotint, 1749 (after M. Grace), BM, NPG [*see illus.*] • J. Spilsbury, mezzotint (after M. Grace) • G. White, mezzotint (after T. Gibson), BM, NPG • engravings, repro. in Wilson, *History and antiquities of dissenting churches*, vol. 3, facing pp. 504, 533

Wealth at death wealthy, but money allegedly his wife's: Bogue and Bennett, *History of dissenters*

Bradbury, William (1800–1869), printer, was born in Bakewell, Derbyshire. As a young man he lived for a time in Lincoln, where he may have worked as an apprentice compositor under Captain Felix Joyce, whom he later employed in his own establishment. Bradbury moved to London in 1824 and began a printing business at 76 Fleet Street in partnership with his brother-in-law William Dent. In 1826 Bradbury married a woman named Sarah; two of his sons, Henry Riley *Bradbury (1831–1860) and William Hardwick *Bradbury (1832–1892), followed him into the printing business. Between 1828 and 1830 William Bradbury and Dent moved the firm to Bolt Court, then to Oxford Arms Passage, and finally to Warwick Lane, in the process taking on another partner and changing the name to Bradbury, Dent, and Manning. In 1830 that firm dissolved, and Bradbury formed a partnership with the printer Frederick Mullett *Evans (1803–1870) in Bouverie Street, Whitefriars. In July 1833 Bradbury and Evans moved the printing works to nearby Lombard Street, eventually occupying the length of this small street with offices and warehouses. Here they installed a large, steam-driven cylinder press of the latest design, made by Middleton & Co., well suited for the demanding printing requirements of newspapers and periodicals. This and some twenty smaller machines were kept running round the clock six days a week, with men working in relays, thus achieving a level of productivity that soon gained Bradbury and Evans a reputation as one of the most efficient printing firms in Britain.

An early and long-continued speciality of the firm was legal printing, beginning with work for Bradbury's friend William Maxwell, who had set up as a law publisher in nearby Bell Yard in 1830. This connection persisted into the next generation: Bradbury's son William Hardwick later became a prominent shareholder and director of the Maxwell firm and a friend of Maxwell's son. Parliamentary reports were another source of revenue. The firm printed several weekly newspapers, acquired as steady clients such London publishing houses as those recently established by Edward Moxon, Alexander Smith, and Edward Chapman and William Hall, and formed a lucrative relationship with the Chambers brothers in Edinburgh, for whom it printed *Chambers's Edinburgh Journal* and the popular *Cyclopedia*. Rapid expansion—the business soon employed some 200 compositors alone—and a growing specialization in illustrated periodicals and fine-art printing kept Bradbury constantly on the lookout for suitably skilled workmen. In the late 1830s he sought help from William Chambers in finding experienced young compositors, and in 1843 he explained, in a court case involving a dismissed workman's claim, that only a limited number of pressmen were capable of bringing off good impressions from woodcuts, and that as a printer of illustrated periodicals he was compelled to keep such men, at the liberal wage of 36s. a week, permanently employed. With their extensive works Bradbury and Evans were able to step in when other printers needed help on large jobs with tight deadlines, sometimes printing the *London Journal* and even once the *Illustrated London News*. As head of the firm Bradbury, with his long experience and exacting temperament, was personally involved in all aspects of the daily work on the printing shop floor, closely supervising the more difficult jobs and holding his men to a high standard. Years later his partner Evans remarked on Bradbury's excellent taste as a printer and his influence in raising the quality of printing in England. A firm upholder of such ancient printing traditions as the annual Waygoose celebration of masters and men, Bradbury was known for his liberality, paying unusually high wages to his workmen and being quick to recognize and reward exceptional skill.

The connection with Chapman and Hall brought Bradbury into close relations with Charles Dickens, whose serial novels *The Pickwick Papers* (1836–7) and *Nicholas Nickleby* (1838–9) Bradbury and Evans printed. In the spring of 1839, when Bradbury's young daughter who 'used to play about between the two rooms in Bouverie Street' died (John Forster to Bradbury, 13 March 1839; Sawyer, 61), Dickens wrote to assure Bradbury of his 'earnest and sincere sympathy and warm regard' and of his fellow feeling, having himself lost 'a young and lovely creature'—his sister-in-law Mary Hogarth—nearly two years previously (*Letters of Charles Dickens*, 1.515–16 and n.). Dickens, his wife Catherine, and her sister Georgina Hogarth grew fond of the Bradburys over the years. Dickens nicknamed Bradbury 'Beau B' and lampooned his provincial accent; Georgina did a killing imitation of Mrs Bradbury. At one memorable party on 20 December 1855 the Bradburys entertained Dickens, John Forster, and the *Punch* staff to 'the very best cooked dinner' Dickens had 'ever sat down to' in his life. Afterwards, he wrote to Catherine, Mrs Bradbury told him about the time when her husband, in her absence, had burnt down the marital bed and secretly replaced it. When, on the first occasion after her return home, she composed her 'luxuriant and gorgeous figure' between the sheets, she started up and said, 'William, where his me bed?—This is not me bed—wot has append William—wot ave you dun with me bed' (*Letters of Charles Dickens*, 7.769–70).

In the autumn of 1841, when the new comic weekly *Punch* was foundering financially despite critical praise and the best efforts of such writers as Mark Lemon, Douglas Jerrold, and Henry Mayhew, Bradbury and Evans were approached for assistance. The firm lent the enterprise £150 and became their printers, but were reluctant to become proprietors. At last, however, Lemon persuaded them to buy the editors' shares of the periodical outright for £200, and after acquiring the engraver Ebenezer Landell's share and the magazine's debts they became sole proprietors at the end of 1842. With the help of their client Chambers's London agent, W. S. Orr & Co., a wider distribution to the trade was accomplished, and under Lemon's skilful editorship *Punch* quickly began to make headway, achieving a circulation of some 40,000 copies a week by the 1840s and becoming a mainstay of British middle-class life (Altick, 38). The magazine quickly became a mainstay of the Bradbury and Evans firm as well, bringing in over £10,000 a year by the 1860s. Bradbury and Evans hosted a weekly dinner for the men of *Punch* at which Bradbury was a frequent presence in the early years, and the magazine's staff formed the centre of the proprietors' social circle. At an early stage in *Punch*'s life Bradbury had attempted to press Lemon to use its pages to promote a railway in which he had invested, but Lemon so firmly rebuffed him that the editorial management of the magazine maintained an independence from the proprietors for ever afterwards. Bradbury concurred with Evans in constantly agreeing to loans and advances for members of the staff, essentially acting as bankers to the often improvident *Punch* men and thereby earning their steadfast loyalty and affection. In creating a stable and productive atmosphere this combination of kindliness and shrewdness contributed substantially to the magazine's success. *Punch* remained the one unalloyed and continuing success of the firm for the rest of Bradbury's life and beyond, a success that he and Evans constantly strove, and failed, to duplicate in other ventures.

William Makepeace Thackeray had served on the *Punch* staff for several years when he brought to Bradbury and Evans his first full-length novel, after trying to place it elsewhere; published in numbers as *Vanity Fair* in 1847-8, it took the literary world by storm. Although Thackeray soon left *Punch* out of dissatisfaction with both its politics and its rate of pay, the firm maintained warmly cordial relations with him and published *Pendennis* (1848-50), *The Newcomes* (1853-5), and *The Virginians* (1857-9), as well as several minor works. Thackeray also published with George Smith, who in 1864, after the author's death, finally bought out Bradbury and Evans's copyrights. But Thackeray always considered Bradbury's firm his principal publishers, and the connection proved a rewarding one for both parties. Other authors with whom the firm enjoyed a good working relationship as book publishers were Robert Surtees, whose sporting novels were memorably illustrated by John Leech, the famed war correspondent William Howard Russell, and Charles Knight, whose *English Cyclopedia* was a valuable property, as well as such members of the *Punch* circle as Gilbert à Beckett, Percival

Leigh, Douglas Jerrold, Mark Lemon, Shirley Brooks, and Francis Burnand. Relations with Anthony Trollope and Wilkie Collins, for each of whom Bradbury and Evans published one novel, were not so happy.

Remembered as the 'keenest man of business that ever trod the flags of Fleet Street' (Spielmann, 36), Bradbury possessed an entrepreneurial boldness reflected in a letter of 1849 in which he assured his partner, 'I'm all for going ahead! Unless the ground is quite cut beneath us' (Bradbury to Evans, n.d., Bodl. Oxf.). Bradbury and Evans's main concern was to keep their extensive presses running consistently, a goal that led them to publish a number of periodicals besides *Punch*, including the *Army and Navy Gazette*, the *Horticultural Register*, edited by Bradbury's friend Joseph Paxton, and Charles Wentworth Dilke's *Gardener's Chronicle and Agricultural Gazette*, and to print many others such as *Chambers's* and the *Family Herald*. However, when in 1844 Dickens asked the firm to take over publishing his serial fiction and other works, Bradbury and Evans hesitated. They did not know how to market serials and thought Chapman and Hall ought to continue the job. Further negotiation resulted in Dickens transferring most of his business to Bouverie Street, though Chapman and Hall, shareholders in the copyright of most of Dickens's previous publications, were publishers of record for reprints and some other titles. From 1844 to 1859 Bradbury and Evans printed and published Dickens's new work; all the parties involved enjoyed large profits as Dickens's reputation and readership skyrocketed.

The Dickens connection led to other entanglements, one of them a costly venture in which Bradbury played an active role. At the urging of Paxton the firm agreed in 1845 to back and publish a new morning newspaper, the *Daily News*, as a Liberal rival to the powerful paper *The Times*, setting up extensive offices in Whitefriars and engaging a large staff. Dickens contracted on 3 December that year to edit the paper at a salary of £2000 a year and plunged into the work with his usual energy. But he quickly became disaffected with the project. Bradbury's clumsy interference with the editorial management of the paper and his brusque treatment of the editor's father particularly infuriated Dickens, who soon abandoned the editorship and forbore even to meet Bradbury face to face for some time afterwards. Dilke, editor of *The Athenaeum*, took control of the finances from April 1846, and within a year the newspaper had been transferred to William King Hales of 8 Lombard Street. As major investors Bradbury and Evans incurred losses well in excess of their initial investment of £22,500. Some portion of that loss, however, must have been made up by the profits from Dickens's weekly magazine *Household Words* (March 1850–May 1859), in which Bradbury and Evans owned a quarter-share. A great success in its own right, that magazine also introduced important mid-Victorian writers to the firm, including Wilkie Collins, Elizabeth Cleghorn Gaskell, and Harriet Martineau.

In November 1858 the relationship with Dickens, who up to then had been generally pleased with Bradbury and Evans both as printers and as publishers, turned suddenly and irreversibly sour. Because *Punch* did not insert Dickens's public statement about his separation from his wife, Dickens moved to dissolve the *Household Words* partnership and to discontinue its publication. He succeeded in buying the title and stock from the firm at auction, and he folded it into a new journal, *All the Year Round*. Bradbury and Evans attempted to counteract this competition with *Once a Week*, which they had at first hoped would feature Thackeray's fiction as its main attraction. These hopes were dashed when Thackeray took up the editorship of George Smith's *Cornhill Magazine* at a princely sum and committed any new writings to that magazine and publisher. In the event the partners chose not to create a permanent staff for the new periodical, as they had with *Punch*, but to throw its pages open to a shifting variety of authors, under the editorship of Samuel Lucas, and to distinguish its contents by means of copious illustrations by such leading artists as John Everett Millais, Holman Hunt, Frederick Sandys, and the young George Du Maurier. Just as Bradbury had tried to interfere in the daily management of *Punch* and in that of the *Daily News*, so, too, did the first editors of *Once a Week* complain of the proprietors' second-guessing of their decisions. Though the magazine started bravely, featured such talented writers as George Meredith and Harriet Martineau, and kept up a higher standard of woodcut illustration than any other periodical of its time, it lost ground steadily over the succeeding decade and was at last sold to James Rice in 1869. Long-term success eluded the firm in most of its other periodical ventures as well, including the *Ladies Companion* (1849–50), Albert Smith's *The Month* (1851) with illustrations by John Leech, and for a brief period in 1852–3 the sporting magazine *The Field*, then edited by Mark Lemon and also illustrated by Leech. Full or partial ownerships in the *London Journal*, the *Literary Gazette*, and the *Gentleman's Magazine* were likewise disappointing.

In his middle years Bradbury experienced personal as well as professional misfortune. His son Henry committed suicide on 2 September 1860, allegedly distraught because one of Evans's daughters had refused him. Bradbury was plagued by periods of ill health that frequently interfered with his active involvement in the business. Less sociable, and perhaps less socially adept, than his junior partner, he came to find the rambunctiousness of the famous weekly *Punch* dinners too much for his nerves. Both Bradbury's son William Hardwick and his daughter Edith married into the family of Thomas and William Agnew, the prominent Manchester-based art dealers, who soon brought much needed capital to the firm. On 1 November 1865 Bradbury made a rare appearance at a special *Punch* dinner held at the Albion Hotel to announce his and Evans's formal retirement in favour of their sons, the bringing in of the Agnews as partners, and the change of the firm's name to Bradbury Evans & Co. After a protracted bout of bronchitis Bradbury died, survived by his wife, at his family's long-time residence, 13 Upper Woburn Place, Tavistock Square, London, on 11 April 1869.

ROBERT L. PATTEN and PATRICK LEARY

Sources *The letters of Charles Dickens*, ed. M. House, G. Storey, and others, 12 vols. (1965–2002) · J. Forster, *The life of Charles Dickens*, ed. J. W. T. Ley (1928) · *The letters and private papers of William Makepeace Thackeray*, ed. G. N. Ray, 4 vols. (1945–6) [with 2 vol. suppl., ed. E. F. Harden (1994)] · M. H. Spielmann, *The history of 'Punch'* (1895) · R. L. Patten, *Charles Dickens and his publishers* (1978) · R. D. Altick, *'Punch': the lively youth of a British institution, 1841–1851* (1997) · C. Fox, *Graphic journalism in England during the 1830s and 1840s* (1988) · D. Dixon, 'Bradbury and Evans', *British literary publishing houses, 1820–1880*, ed. P. J. Anderson and J. Rose, DLitB, 106 (1991) · 'Incidents of my life', *London, Provincial, and Colonial Press News* (Sept 1886), 17–20; (Dec 1886), 17–21 · P. L. Shillingsburg, *Pegasus in harness: Victorian publishing and W. M. Thackeray* (1992) · 'Some London printing offices: no. 5: Bradbury, Agnew & Co.', *London, Provincial, and Colonial Press News* (Nov 1884), 27–9 · 'Mr Punch at dinner: centenary of a famous printery', *British and Colonial Printer and Stationer* (28 Jan 1926), 63–4 · P. A. H. Brown, *London publishers and printers, c.1800–1870* (1982) · H. R. Fox Bourne, *English newspapers: chapters in the history of journalism*, 1 (1887) · W. E. Buckler, '*Once a Week* under Samuel Lucas, 1859–65', *Publications of the Modern Language Association of America*, 67 (1952), 924–41 · G. G. Grubb, 'Dickens and the *Daily News*: preliminaries to publication', *Nineteenth Century Fiction*, 7 (Dec 1951), 174–94; 'Dickens and the *Daily News*: resignation', *Nineteenth Century Fiction*, 7 (June 1952), 19–38 · W. B. Todd, *A directory of printers and others in allied trades, London and vicinity, 1800–1840* (1972) · M. W. Maxwell, 'The development of law publishing, 1799–1974', *Then and now, 1799–1974: commemorating 175 years of law bookselling and publishing* (1974), 121–36 · *The Times* · *Punch* (24 April 1869) · C. J. Sawyer, *Dickens v. Barabbas* (1930)

Archives *Punch* library, London, account books and letters · Yale U., Beinecke L. | Bodl. Oxf., Bradbury and Evans papers

Likenesses A. Bassano Ltd, photograph, repro. in Spielmann, *History of 'Punch'*, 37

Wealth at death under £8000: probate, 5 June 1869, *CGPLA Eng. & Wales*

Bradbury, William Hardwick (1832–1892), publisher, second son of William *Bradbury (1800–1869), co-owner of the printing and publishing firm Bradbury and Evans, and his wife, Sarah, was born in London in December 1832. After attending a private school in Brighton, he attended University College School in Gower Street, London, from 1843 to 1848. Originally intended for the bar, Bradbury soon gravitated to the family business, spending two years working in publishing and bookselling in Dublin before entering the Bradbury and Evans publishing house in Bouverie Street, London. It is said that Bradbury and his brother Henry Riley *Bradbury joined Frederick Evans, son of their father's partner Frederick Mullet Evans, in printing the sheets of Charles Dickens's *David Copperfield* (20 parts as 19, May 1849–November 1850), being careful to let no other employees know what the next instalment would contain.

Until summer 1858 the firm's relations with Dickens, one of their most profitable authors, remained cordial; they continued to publish his novels and his weekly serial, *Household Words*. But during spring that year Dickens separated from his wife, Catherine, and in June he published in *The Times* (7 June) and in *Household Words* (12 June) a statement declaring that his 'domestic trouble' had been 'amicably composed', and that rumours involving other people 'are abominably false'. Though he never asked his publishers to insert the announcement in *Punch*, Dickens felt so aggrieved because it did not appear there that he initiated what proved to be a long and complicated severing of his contractual relations with the firm. In March 1859 Dickens announced a rival journal, *All the Year Round*, into which he folded *Household Words* when Bradbury and Evans auctioned it off two months later on 16 May. Dickens purchased the copyright and stock for £3500. He estimated that the stock was worth about £1600; he sold it, with some other stock and plates, to Chapman and Hall on 19 May for £2500. Bradbury and Evans countered with a new periodical of their own, *Once a Week*, edited by Samuel Lucas and illustrated by many of the leading *Punch* artists. But after encouraging initial sales and contributions from Harriet Martineau, Alfred Tennyson, and George Henry Lewes, among others, the circulation sank to about 35,000 by the mid-1860s. (It was eventually sold in 1869.) During this period Bradbury and Evans were entangled in complicated legal suits with Dickens, and Dickens's eldest son, Charley, was engaged to Evans's daughter Bessie (Elizabeth Matilda Moule Evans, *d.* 1907), whom he married on 19 November 1861.

In the midst of these troubles, on 2 September 1860, Bradbury's older brother Henry committed suicide. The family house at 13 Upper Woburn Place, Dickens reported to W. H. Wills, 'looked grim and dry, with all the blinds down, brooding in a hot, dusty, tearless, frozen kind of way, at the unsympathetic street' (*Letters of Charles Dickens*, 302, 4 Sept 1860). Henry had gone into business for himself as a 'nature printer', but he had often worked as well in his father's firm. After his brother's death W. H. Bradbury crossed over from the publishing side of the firm to assume the supervision of its extensive and demanding printing business. It was a bad time for the firm. Dickens cut his former publishers. He did not attend Charley's wedding and he never again spoke to Frederick Mullet Evans. When Dickens learned that Charley was going into partnership with Bessie's brother Frederick Moule Evans in the Postford Paper-Making Company, he was unhappy (ibid., 508 and n. 3). During the 1860s several of the firm's periodicals, including the *Gardener's Chronicle and Agricultural Gazette* and *Once a Week*, were sold off. And the founding partners grew weary. In 1865 both retired. W. H. Bradbury and Frederick Moule Evans took over from their fathers. Shortly after Henry's death Bradbury had married Laura, sister of the art dealer William *Agnew (1825–1910) [*see under* Agnew family]. The couple had three daughters and one son. When Evans decided to withdraw from the firm in 1872, refinancing with Agnew money produced new family partners and a new company name: Bradbury, Agnew & Co.

Bradbury, who assumed the position of chairman, kept *Punch*, but otherwise ceased to publish books and periodicals, although until 1885 he maintained the tradition of an annual dinner at the Bedford in September celebrating the publication of *Punch's Almanack*. He died at his home, Oak Lodge, Nightingale Lane, Clapham, Surrey, on 13 October 1892. His estate was proved on 9 December at £33,034 0s. 6d. His son W. Lawrence Bradbury succeeded as joint managing director alongside William Agnew.

ROBERT L. PATTEN

Sources Boase, *Mod. Eng. biog.*, vol. 4 · M. H. Spielmann, *The history of 'Punch'* (1895) · R. L. Patten, *Charles Dickens and his publishers* (1978) · *The letters of Charles Dickens*, ed. M. House, G. Storey, and others, 9 (1997) · D. Dixon, 'Bradbury and Evans', *British literary publishing houses, 1820–1880*, ed. P. J. Anderson and J. Rose, DLitB, 106 (1991) · *DNB* · *The Times* (14 Oct 1892) · *CGPLA Eng. & Wales* (1892)
Archives Bodl. Oxf., Bradbury and Evans corresp.
Likenesses A. Bassano Ltd, photograph, repro. in Spielmann, *History of 'Punch'*, 37
Wealth at death £33,034 0s. 6d.: probate, 9 Dec 1892, *CGPLA Eng. & Wales*

Braddell [*née* Busse], **Dorothy Adelaide** (1889–1981), designer and decorative artist, was born at 129 Inverness Terrace, Paddington, London, on 30 June 1889, the daughter of Jacob Levine Busse, stockbroker, and his wife, Annie Leonie Stiebel. After attending Miss Manville's school and King's College, London, she studied art at Regent School Polytechnic and at the Byam Shaw School of Art, and won a national gold medal for decorative design. On 12 September 1914, in Paddington, she married the architect Darcy Braddell (1884–1970), with whom she had a son and a daughter. For much of her early career she worked in advertising and display with a client list that included leading national companies such as Shell-Mex Ltd, Viyella, and Allied Ironfounders. However, her lasting reputation lay in her work in domestic interior and kitchen design, much of which was seen in prestigious exhibitions ranging from 'British Art in Industry', at the Royal Academy (1935), to 'Britain Can Make It', at the Victoria and Albert Museum, London (1946). Her work also featured frequently at the *Daily Mail* Ideal Home exhibitions, for which she often contributed articles on domestic planning to the accompanying publications.

An important client for many years after the end of the First World War was Shell-Mex Ltd, for whom Braddell produced advertisements as well as many vivid watercolours of English towns and villages that were used for a variety of publicity materials. In line with the newly founded Campaign for the Preservation of Rural England, Shell-Mex Ltd had become increasingly committed to promoting environmentally sensitive advertising and signage. These included what Braddell described as 'inn signboard' advertising—painted pictorial boards hanging from posts. Although often connected to individual petrol stations they also featured the roads on which they were positioned through the use of illustrative vignettes. For example the Pioneer filling station at Kingston Hill, on the London to Portsmouth road, featured St Paul's Cathedral, the Hog's Back, and a sailing galleon. Braddell also produced an innovative set of large-scale pictorial designs to detract from the ugliness of many railway bridges spanning roads. Although advertising Shell they also featured distances from towns co-ordinated with colourful images of sightseeing attractions in the region. Her work for Shell also encompassed a variety of exhibition stands, including that at the 1932 Motor Show, where she adopted a markedly art deco style with recessed lighting, modernist chromium-plated steel furniture, and zebra-skin-like furnishing fabrics. Many art deco features were also incorporated into her Viyella stand for William Hollins & Co. at the Ideal Home Exhibition of the same year, especially in the decorative metal-and-glass lighting strip at cornice level. Her dexterity enabled her to move through a variety of styles, depending on the context and the aspirations of her clients. For example when designing the Crosse and Blackwell stand at the Nation's Food Exhibition at Olympia in 1925 she looked back to the period when the company was founded by drawing on the architecture of London baroque churches for the pavilion, with attendants dressed in period costume.

Between the 1930s and 1950s Braddell devoted a considerable amount of energy to rational interior design and domestic planning, very much in tune with the aims of the campaigning Electrical Association for Women and contemporary thinking on scientific management in the home. Alongside other socially committed British women pioneers of domestic design and planning in the 1930s—such as Caroline Haslett, Anne Shaw, Edna Moseley, and Elizabeth Denby—Braddell has been undervalued in accounts of British inter-war design. Though socially and professionally well connected the fact that their work was largely centred on the home, itself seen as an essentially feminine domain, has resulted in a comparative lack of recognition. Their contemporary male counterparts, whose masculine values dominated significant committees such as that of the Council for Art and Industry, established by the Board of Trade late in 1933, suffered no such adverse compartmentalization.

While undertaking many commissions for private clients Braddell also worked for a number of commercial companies, often acting—unusually for a woman at that time—in a consultancy capacity. Much of her domestic planning design was seen in exhibitions at home and abroad, and mainly featured domestic room settings, especially kitchens. These included the 'British Art in Industry' exhibition (1935), the Empire Exhibition (Glasgow, 1938), the 'Britain Can Make It' exhibition (1946), and the annual Ideal Home exhibitions, which were always held in central London. She was also involved in design for a much younger audience—for instance in that for the self-contained and innovatory Children's Exhibition at the 1937 Ideal Home Exhibition, which occupied a prominent area and was geared to attracting the interest of children. Clothes, furniture, games and toys, books, and food were 'presented in such a way as to delight children … yet with a view of guiding their tastes in the right direction' (publicity pamphlet 1937, V&A, archive of art and design cuttings files). The brightly coloured display featured Alice in Wonderland, Peter Pan, and other children's favourites radiating around the central feature of 'Piccaninny Circus', topped by the *Daily Mail* cupid.

For many years Braddell showed many kitchens in a variety of styles at the ever popular Ideal Home exhibitions. For example at the 1933 exhibition she showed a 'commonsense kitchen', a 'gas kitchen', a 'basement kitchen' (which also served as a sitting room for two maids), a 'kitchen–living-room' for a small country house, and a 'luxury kitchen' (with a central chromium steel and armour-plated glass working table and modern tubular

steel furniture). Highlighting her approach she wrote: 'I think it can be truly said that good planning is the first essential of labour-saving' (Braddell, typescript, V&A, AAD/1980/2). Much of her work featured Aga cookers (manufactured in England by Allied Ironfounders) incorporated into modern, labour-saving settings with integrated work surfaces and built-in cupboards. She also worked closely with manufacturers on appliance design itself, most notably with the Parkinson Stove Company. Her room settings also featured in a number of significant international exhibitions, most importantly in the British pavilion at the Paris Exhibition of 1937, where all the designs shown were selected by the Council for Art and Industry. Her combined kitchen, scullery, pantry, and maid's sitting room for a small country house was designed to be run either by the owner or the maid. Built-in units and integrated worktops, together with Bakelite telephone and radio, conveyed a modern vision of the kitchen where functional, social, and leisure spaces were seen as one. After the Second World War she continued to look forward to better standards of design and planning in the domestic environment, as displayed at the 'Britain Can Make It' exhibition of 1946, mounted by the recently formed Council of Industrial Design.

Dorothy Braddell continued to be busy into the 1960s, as her daybooks testify. She died at Quinton House, Lower Quinton, Warwickshire, on 27 April 1981. Examples of her drawings and prints are held in the Victoria and Albert Museum, London.   JONATHAN WOODHAM

Sources V&A NAL, AAD/1980/2 [129 items, c.1920–61] • D. Braddell, drawings and prints, V&A, department of prints and drawings • E. Lomas, *Guide to the archive of art & design, Victoria & Albert Museum* (2001) • D. Braddell, 'The bathroom', *Design for Today*, 2 (Feb 1934), 57–53 • *ArchR*, 74 (July 1933) [British industrial art issue] • *ArchR*, 82 (Sept 1937) [Paris exhibition issue] • J. Attfield and P. Kirkham, eds., *A view from the interior*, rev. edn (1995) • *Illustrated souvenir: the Royal Academy exhibition of British art in industry* (1935) [exhibition catalogue, RA, 1935] • J. M. Woodham, 'British art in industry, 1935', *Design and industry* (1980), 39–44 • J. M. Woodham, 'Women, design and the state in the interwar years', *Women designing: redefining design in Britain between the wars*, ed. J. Seddon and S. Worden (1994), 40–45 [exhibition catalogue, University of Brighton Gallery, 7–31 March 1994] • b. cert. • m. cert. • d. cert. • *CGPLA Eng. & Wales* (1981)
Archives V&A NAL, papers
Wealth at death £31,148: probate, 18 June 1981, *CGPLA Eng. & Wales*

Braddock, Edward (*bap.* 1695, *d.* 1755), army officer, was baptized at St Margaret's, Westminster, on 2 February 1695, the son and namesake of an officer (eventually a major-general) in the Coldstream Guards and his wife, Mary. The elder Edward Braddock (1664–1725) obtained an ensigncy for his son in the Coldstreams in October 1710, and he then progressed by purchase: lieutenant, 1716; captain-lieutenant, 1734; captain (line rank of lieutenant-colonel), 10 February 1736; second major, with army rank of colonel, 1743; first major, 1745; and lieutenant-colonel, 1745. Before the War of the Austrian Succession, which created opportunities for advancement, his pace of promotion was rather slow. Braddock probably did not participate in, and certainly did not command, any action during the war, but instead handled administrative assignments. Seeking advancement, in February 1753 he left the Coldstreams to become colonel of the 14th foot: he spent 1753–4 with the regiment at Gibraltar, where he also served as acting governor. Of his governorship Walpole later reported: 'he made himself adored, and where scarce any governor was endured before' (Walpole, 20.496). In April 1754 he was promoted major-general.

During the autumn of 1754 Braddock was given command of an expedition to North America. The duke of Cumberland, captain-general and formerly colonel of the Coldstreams, seems to have been instrumental in placing him in charge. Braddock's task was twofold: he was to put the British colonies on a war footing; and, beginning with the seizure of Fort Duquesne, on the forks of the Ohio River, he was to sweep the French back into Canada and ultimately seize Quebec and Montreal. Despite the immensity of the assignment, Braddock was given only two regiments to work with, the 44th and 48th foot, both of which were undermanned. It does not appear that he had sought this position, and he is reported to have said: 'we are sent like sacrifices to the altar' (Bellamy, 1.194).

Braddock sailed from Cork in December 1754 and disembarked at Hampton, Virginia, on 20 February 1755. His first initiative was to co-ordinate the war preparations of the various colonies, but, despite government directives that exalted his authority, he was soon complaining over a lack of co-operation. On 15 April, at a conference in Alexandria, he did win the approval of five governors for a co-ordinated offensive, but he was unsuccessful in his attempt to persuade them to establish a common fund to finance the war. While in Virginia, Braddock became convinced that he needed to have a large contingent of Native Americans to accompany his expedition, yet, when his agents succeeded in recruiting several hundred of them, Governor James Glen of South Carolina helped persuade these warriors to stay at home.

Nor did Braddock find more co-operation after he joined his army at Fort Cumberland (Wills Creek, Maryland) on 10 May. The troops were poorly supplied and much of the food was spoiled. When he pressed contractors to fulfil their obligations they demanded extra time and raised their prices. Only in early June was this problem alleviated, as Benjamin Franklin was able to provide some wagons and provisions. Yet another problem that Braddock faced at Wills Creek was the quality of his troops. The two British regiments had been augmented by drafts and by recruitment in America, but as late as 8 June Braddock was writing to Cumberland's secretary: 'the whole of the Forces are now assembled, making about two thousand Effectives, the greatest part Virginians, very indifferent Men, this Country affording no better; it has cost infinite pains and labor to bring them to any sort of Regularity and Discipline' (Pargellis, *Military Affairs*, 54). Nevertheless, when the army finally marched, on 10 June, Braddock expressed optimism. The march proceeded slowly, and he became concerned that if the pace did not quicken Fort Duquesne would be reinforced before his army arrived (as

did in fact happen). On 16 June Braddock ordered a division of his army, leaving about one-third of the men (and most of the wagons) to proceed at their own pace, under the command of Thomas Dunbar, colonel of the 48th.

By the early afternoon of 9 July Braddock's army was within 10 miles of Fort Duquesne when it was suddenly confronted by a force of about 800 men, more than three-quarters of them Native Americans, the rest French or Canadian. The enemy force had actually intended to ambush the British as they were fording the Monongahela, but it improvised quickly, as the Native Americans raced down the flanks of Braddock's army and caught it in a crossfire, while the French held the front. Within minutes many of the officers in Braddock's vanguard were killed or incapacitated, and the men fell back. Braddock himself was with the main body of his army, and it appears that on hearing the firing in the front he sent forward a detachment, which, however, soon encountered the retreating vanguard and became enmeshed with it. The three hours that followed found Braddock's army in the same confused state, helpless in the face of enemy fire. Braddock attempted to rally his men, but to no avail, and finally he was shot in the chest—possibly by one of his own men—and the army retreated, two-thirds of the men having been killed or wounded. On 13 July, in Dunbar's camp at Great Meadows near Fort Necessity, some 60 miles back in the direction of Wills Creek, Braddock surrendered his command and died. He was buried there the following day on the road. His grave was discovered in 1812, and in 1913 a monument was raised over it.

A lifelong bachelor, Braddock left his estate to a protégé, the actress George Anne Bellamy, and to John Calcraft, an army agent he mistakenly believed to be her husband. Like many officers, he had for years indulged himself at the gaming tables of London and Bath, and contemporary rumour linked him with several women. Regardless of his lifestyle, however, the fortune he bequeathed was significant—£7000, according to Bellamy—if not large.

Contemporaries portrayed Braddock as hot tempered. It may be that as he aged he attempted to rein in his temper, and an officer who served with him 1746–8 wrote that Braddock, 'by having been now and then taken down, is greatly reformed' (*Frankland-Russell-Astley MSS*, 354). The issue of his temper is related to a second: that he was a martinet. Even among his peers he seems to have had a reputation for harshness. Bellamy recalled an incident when he, at her request, interceded for 'a poor fellow [about] to be chastised'. The officer that he spoke to asked him, 'How long since he had divested himself of brutality', to which Braddock responded, 'You never knew me insolent to my inferiors' (Bellamy, 3.55). But the characterization of Braddock as a fierce disciplinarian persisted, and it had particular consequence in America, where reports of his harshness fed a negative stereotype of British officers.

Braddock's historical significance is tied entirely to his expedition in North America and particularly to the battle that concluded it. For the most part, the assessment by contemporaries and historians alike has been harsh. As the officer in command of an army that suffered an overwhelming and bloody defeat he must accept some responsibility, but it would be simplistic to place all the blame on him. The assignment given him by the government was wholly unreasonable, especially considering the troops and the resources he was allowed. The lack of co-operation from the governors—which, in the case of Glen, amounted to virtual sabotage—hampered his progress, as did the dilatoriness of the contractors. At the battle itself Braddock was undermined by the troops, who ignored his orders to re-form and move against the enemy, and by the ineptitude of some subordinate officers, particularly Lieutenant-Colonel (later Major-General) Thomas Gage, who commanded the vanguard. The image that lingers, of Braddock stubbornly attempting to fight a conventional 'European' battle in an American forest against an irregular force, may misrepresent his tactics during the engagement and certainly underestimates the obstacles that he faced.

PAUL E. KOPPERMAN

Sources P. E. Kopperman, *Braddock at the Monongahela* (1978) · L. McCardell, *Ill-starred general: Braddock of the Coldstream guards* (1958) · W. Sargent, *The history of an expedition against Fort Duquesne in 1755: under Major-General Edward Braddock* (1855) · J. K. Lacock, 'Braddock Road', *Pennsylvania Magazine of History and Biography*, 38 (1914), 1–37 · *DNB* · S. Pargellis, 'Braddock's defeat', *American Historical Review*, 41 (1935–6), 253–69 · G. A. Bellamy, *An apology for the life of George Anne Bellamy*, ed. [A. Bicknell], 4th edn, 5 vols. (1786) · *Report on the manuscripts of Mrs Frankland-Russell-Astley of Chequers Court, Bucks.*, HMC, 52 (1900) · S. Pargellis, ed., *Military affairs in North America, 1748–1765: selected documents from the Cumberland papers in Windsor Castle* (1936) · Walpole, *Corr.*, vol. 20 · parish register, St Margaret's, City Westm. AC

Archives BL, Add. MS 4478B · CUL, biographical papers · Historical Society of Western Pennsylvania, Pittsburgh, corresp. and MSS [copies] · NA Canada, notebooks and journal · PRO | BL, Newcastle MSS, Add. MSS 32853–32855 · Royal Arch., Cumberland MSS

Likenesses H. B. Hall, etching, 1781, repro. in McCardell, *Ill-starred general*

Wealth at death £7000

Braddock [*née* Bamber], **Elizabeth Margaret** [Bessie] (1899–1970), trade union activist and politician, was born at Zante Street, Liverpool, on 24 September 1899, the elder daughter of Hugh Bamber, bookbinder, and his wife, Mary, daughter of Andrew Little, an Edinburgh lawyer. Mary Bamber became national organizer of the Union of Distributive and Allied Workers and was a passionate socialist, once described by E. Sylvia Pankhurst as the finest fighting platform speaker in the country.

Bessie Bamber left elementary school at fourteen to take a job filling seed packets for 5*s.* a week; later she worked for a draper and subsequently for the Co-op, where she joined the union movement of which she was to be a lifelong member. Her main interest, however, was in politics. From socialist Sunday school she moved to the Independent Labour Party, leaving this in 1920 because she found it insufficiently radical, and going on to join the recently formed Communist Party of Great Britain instead. In 1924 she repudiated communism and returned to the labour movement.

Elizabeth Margaret [Bessie] **Braddock** (1899–1970), by unknown photographer, 1958 [centre, with Myles White (left) and Jack Braddock (right)]

On 9 February 1922 Bessie married John *Braddock (known as Jack; 1892–1963) who shared her political and social interests. They had no children. Their marriage, which was very close, lasted until Jack's death in 1963: by then the Braddocks had become legendary in the politics of Merseyside. He became leader of the Liverpool city council; she was a member of the city council from 1930 to 1961, for the last six years as an alderman.

In 1936 Bessie Braddock was adopted as the prospective parliamentary candidate for the Exchange division of Liverpool. Because of the extension of the life of the 1935 parliament as a consequence of the war, she had to wait until 1945 to fight an election, which she won with a majority of 665. She was the first Labour candidate to be returned for that constituency and the first woman MP for a Liverpool seat. She was elected to the Labour Party national executive committee in 1947 and remained an MP until 1970, despite an attempt by her local party to oust her in 1955 because of her right-wing position.

Bessie Braddock became one of the notable personalities of the House of Commons, and in 1952 she was the first woman MP to be suspended from a sitting. Always outspoken—and there were some who found her language over-rich for the Palace of Westminster—she was defiant in her support of working people. She argued passionately for better housing, education, and welfare services for the poor, and was a particularly strong advocate of the National Health Service, making herself an expert on mental health. She was also a defender of the sport of boxing. A large woman, who confessed to weighing 15 stone, she championed the manufacture of outsize clothes at modest prices. She was not gracious to those whose arguments she rejected, whether they came from the opposition or her own party, as Aneurin Bevan and Michael Foot were both, at different times, to discover.

Deeply antagonistic towards the left, she opposed Bevanism. When offered a post in the Labour government of 1964 she refused, saying that she could do more fighting for the government in Liverpool. Thus she stayed on the back benches, retained her roots in Merseyside, and fought for the people and ideals which she had always supported. She died in Liverpool on 13 November 1970.

ELIZABETH VALLANCE, *rev.*

Sources *The Times* (14 Nov 1970) · *Sunday Times* (15 Nov 1970) · J. Braddock and E. Braddock, *The Braddocks* (1963) · private information (2004) · M. Toole, *Bessie Braddock MP* (1957) · *WWBMP*, vol. 4 · *The Times guide to the House of Commons* (1945–70)
Archives Lpool RO, papers
Likenesses photograph, 1916, repro. in Braddock and Braddock, *The Braddocks*, 6–7 · photograph, 1922, repro. in Toole, *Bessie Braddock*, 48–9 · photograph, 1945, repro. in Toole, *Bessie Braddock*, frontispiece · photograph, 1958, repro. in Braddock and Braddock, *The Braddocks*, frontispiece [*see illus.*]
Wealth at death £20,141: probate, 22 Jan 1971, *CGPLA Eng. & Wales*

Braddock, John [Jack] (1892–1963), politician, was born on 26 July 1892 at 10 Derby Street, Hanley, Staffordshire, the son of John Braddock (1858–1907), pottery worker and later school-board officer, and his wife, Mary (*née* Cummings). He was brought up in a family closely involved in the growing labour and socialist movement around the beginning of the twentieth century. His father was a socialist who was elected to the Hanley school board as a Labour member. Little is known of Braddock's mother, except that her brother, John Cummings, was chairman of the bricklayers' union in north Staffordshire. Braddock's upbringing was by no means poor, with his father earning £160 a year about the time of his birth.

Braddock received an elementary school education, which finished at the time of his father's death, in 1907, when he became a clerk in a draper's shop. Later he took up an apprenticeship in a wagon-building firm, and had soon organized a strike there, for which he was suspended. Having completed his apprenticeship, Braddock left in 1913 at the age of twenty-one to seek employment and adventure elsewhere. He worked in various towns, and joined the Independent Labour Party. In 1915 he arrived in Liverpool, intending to emigrate to Canada, but instead stayed on in the city.

A lifelong teetotaller, Braddock became involved in local trade union and Independent Labour Party and socialist circles. Through these activities he met his future wife, Bessie Bamber (1899–1970) [*see* Braddock, Elizabeth Margaret], the daughter of a well-known socialist organizer in the city, Mary Bamber. He also came to the notice of the police for the first time by forming a branch of the Industrial Workers of the World, a US-based anarcho-syndicalist organization. After the war, with Bessie and Mary Bamber, he became a founder member of the Communist Party of Great Britain. He became embroiled in the activities of the communist-influenced National Unemployed Workers' Movement (NUWM), and came to wider public attention for the first time. On 12 September 1921 members of an NUWM demonstration occupied the Walker Art Gallery in Liverpool, and were attacked by police. Braddock was one of the organizers, although he did not join in the occupation and escaped injury, but he was prosecuted along with 156 others. The main defendants, including Braddock, received nominal sentences, and the conduct of the police was severely criticized by the court.

By now Braddock was living with Bessie Bamber, and on 9 February 1922 he married her at the Liverpool register office. The marriage lasted for forty-one years until Braddock's death. The couple had no children, their political commitments being their first responsibility. Braddock continued to attract police attention: in 1923 he was tried and acquitted on a charge of possessing arms intended for the IRA. His communist connections meant that he was unemployed from about 1920 to 1925, but he and his wife became increasingly at odds with the centralized leadership of the Communist Party, and they both resigned in August 1924. The Braddocks' political future now lay with the Labour Party.

Braddock served on the Merseyside Council of Action during the 1926 general strike, and later that year became an agent for the Co-operative Insurance Society, which was to be the main source of his income for the rest of his life. He became prominent in the Fairfield Labour Party, and in April 1929 was elected as a delegate to the Liverpool Trades Council and Labour Party. In December 1929 he was elected unopposed at a by-election as councillor for the Everton ward. This was one of Labour's safest seats, which Braddock was to hold until he became an alderman in 1955. He was proposed for the parliamentary seat of Everton in 1935, but rejected it in favour of maintaining his local work. His wife, Bessie, was also elected to the council in 1930, and together they became the main protagonists of a left-wing faction within the party. They worked with the NUWM and on campaigns such as anti-fascism and support for the republican cause in Spain. In 1937 he spent six weeks in Spain visiting the International Brigades. Such activities brought the Braddocks into conflict with the predominantly right-wing and Catholic leadership of the party.

The most sensational event in this phase of Braddock's career took place in 1932. In September of that year the NUWM organized a demonstration in Liverpool, following the major riots that had taken place in Birkenhead. Clashes between police and the unemployed broke out during the Liverpool protest. Braddock claimed to have been in the Kardomah Café at the time, but his NUWM past came back to haunt him when he was later arrested at his home and charged with inciting a riot. Sixteen witnesses supported his alibi, but thirteen policemen attested that they had seen him at the riot, and he was sentenced to six months' imprisonment. He spent five weeks in Walton gaol, successfully fighting his campaign for re-election to the council from there, and eventually was acquitted on appeal in London, returning to a hero's reception in Liverpool.

Braddock's career took a different turn in the 1940s, as he abandoned his radical past and moved into the mainstream of the party. His elevation in the party hierarchy was fortuitous. In 1943 he was elected deputy leader of the Labour group as a compromise candidate who was the least unacceptable to the Catholic caucus. Two years later the Labour leader, Luke Hogan, was elected as lord mayor, and Braddock took his place as leader for a twelve-month term of office. Hogan fell out with the party while mayor and never resumed the leadership, so Braddock stayed on by default. Along with Bessie in parliament, he became increasingly identified with the right wing of the party, and was a vocal critic of communism in the cold-war atmosphere of the late 1940s.

In 1955 Braddock became the first Labour leader of the Liverpool council, although his first term of office, until 1961, was not marked by unqualified success. Labour prioritized the construction of high-rise flats, and oversaw the development of overspill estates, in contradiction to election promises and with long-term social consequences that were not all positive. Pledges to foster comprehensive education were unfulfilled. His achievement in attracting large transnational firms to the area was a positive gain as far as employment was concerned, although many of these firms were to leave the city later. Braddock's successful wooing of Ford to its Halewood site was probably his greatest and longest-lasting achievement. Within the Labour Party left-wing opposition to Braddock grew, culminating in a revolt over council rent rises in 1960–61. Labour lost control of the city in 1961, and Braddock clung on to the leadership by only three votes in May 1962. His party was returned to power in May 1963, but Braddock failed to make any further significant mark before his sudden death.

On 12 November 1963 Braddock collapsed at an official function in the Walker Art Gallery, the scene of his first public notoriety. He had suffered a heart attack, and died before he reached hospital. He was cremated at the Liverpool crematorium, Anfield, on 15 November, in a non-religious ceremony.

Being quite short and stocky in stature, Braddock was an unprepossessing figure, although in later years he was famous for his extravagant wide-brimmed hats. He has been rather fancifully compared to an American 'boss politician', ruling autocratically over an undemocratic political 'machine'. This comparison misses the mark, for British municipal politics did not allow the patronage necessary for real machine politics, and within his broad-church party Braddock was never able to eliminate opposition. Not least, as many of those who knew him will aver, he was not the overpowering personality that his reputation might suggest, paling in contrast with his fiery wife, Bessie.   SAM DAVIES

Sources M. Toole, *Mrs Bessie Braddock MP* (1957) · J. Braddock and B. Braddock, *The Braddocks* (1963) · *Liverpool Daily Post* (13 Nov 1963) · *Liverpool Daily Post* (14 Nov 1963) · *Liverpool Daily Post* (16 Nov 1963) · *Liverpool Daily Post* (24 May 1955) · Liverpool Central Library, Liverpool trades council and labour party MSS · S. Davies, 'Times of change: Liverpool trades council, 1948–1998', *The Liverpool labour movement, 1848–1998*, ed. J. Dye (1998) · M. Nightingale, ed., *Merseyside in crisis* (1980) · S. Davies, *Liverpool labour: social and political influences on the development of the labour party in Liverpool, 1900–1939* (1996) · R. Baxter, 'The Liverpool labour party, 1918–1963', DPhil diss., U. Oxf., 1969 · P. J. Waller, *Democracy and sectarianism: a political and social history of Liverpool, 1868–1939* (1981) · *The Times* (13 Nov 1963) · *The Times* (16 Dec 1963) · b. cert. · m. cert. · d. cert.

Archives Liverpool Central Library, Liverpool trades council and labour party MSS

Likenesses photograph, 1958, repro. in Braddock and Braddock, *The Braddocks*, frontispiece; *see illus. in* Braddock, Elizabeth Margaret (1899–1970) · photographs, *Liverpool Daily Post*, photographic archive · photographs, *Liverpool Echo*, photographic archive

Wealth at death £2203 13s. 0d.: probate, 6 Dec 1963, *CGPLA Eng. & Wales*

Braddocke, John. *See* Bradock, John (1655/6–1719).

Braddon, Sir Edward Nicholas Coventry (1829–1904), politician in Australia, born at Skisdone Lodge, St Kew, Cornwall, on 11 June 1829, was the third and only surviving son of Henry Braddon, solicitor, of an old Cornish family, and his wife, Fanny, daughter of Patrick White of Limerick. Mary Elizabeth *Braddon, the novelist, was his younger sister. Educated at a private school in Greenwich and at University College, London, in 1847 he joined the mercantile firm of Bagshaw & Co., his cousins, in Calcutta; but left them in 1850 or 1851 to manage a number of indigo factories near Krishnagar. He transferred to the government railways shortly before the Santal rising of July 1855, in the course of which he saw military action. During the Indian mutiny he served in a volunteer force in Purnea under Sir George Adney Yule. On 19 October 1857 he was appointed an assistant commissioner for Deoghar in the Santal district. On 1 May 1862 he became superintendent of excise and stamps in Oudh, and on 1 July 1871 inspector-general of registration. Upon the amalgamation of Oudh and the North-Western Provinces his position was abolished and being offered no other, much to his annoyance, he retired on a pension in 1878 and went to live on the north-west coast of Tasmania.

Here Braddon was elected to the house of assembly in 1879 as member for West Devon. By 1886 he was acknowledged as leader of the (liberal) opposition. On 30 March 1887 he joined an administration in which Philip Oakley Fysh became premier while he led the assembly as minister for lands and works and also for education. On 29 October 1888 he was appointed Tasmanian agent-general in London, where he was successful in negotiating loans for private and public works in the colony. In 1891 he was made KCMG. He returned to Tasmania in 1893 and on 19 December, having been re-elected to his old seat, helped turn out the government which had recalled him. On 14 April 1894 he became premier, in which capacity he represented Tasmania at the 1897 jubilee celebrations and colonial conference in London, where he was sworn of the privy council. In that year he also received the honorary degree of LLD at Cambridge. His term of office, during the latter part of which he was treasurer as well as premier, came to an end on 12 October 1899, after he had been censured by the assembly for exerting political pressure on two civil servants.

Braddon was the first Tasmanian minister to have extensive prior experience in public administration and his abilities were readily acknowledged, though his incisive methods, learnt in India, at times shocked many. His government was progressive, though he was one of its more conservative members. It stabilized the finances of the colony, encouraged economic development, enacted social reforms, and introduced proportional representation.

Braddon was a strong supporter of the federation of the Australian colonies. In 1898, at the federal conference at Sydney, he carried a clause in the Constitution Bill ensuring that for the first ten years three-quarters of federal customs revenues would be returned to the states. Tagged the 'Braddon blot' by the larger colonies, its adoption ensured the support of the smaller colonies for federation. In 1901 Braddon was elected by a large majority senior member for Tasmania in the first parliament of the commonwealth of Australia, and in 1903 he was re-elected in the interests of Free Trade; at the 1951 jubilee he was the founding father honoured by Tasmania.

Although known for his sarcastic turn of phrase and cynical wit, Braddon was well respected, both in his local community and throughout the colony. He was an enthusiastic sportsman and was the author of *Life in India* (1872) and *Thirty Years of Shikar* (1895). He married twice: first, on 24 October 1857, Amy Georgina, daughter of William Palmer of Purnea (died in 1864, leaving two sons and three daughters); second, on 16 October 1876, Alice Harriet (died in or after 1904), daughter of John H. Smith, with whom he had one daughter. Braddon died on 2 February 1904 at his residence, Treglith, Leith, Tasmania, and was buried privately in the Pioneers' cemetery at Forth, though a state funeral was offered. M. N. SPROD

Sources S. Bennett, 'Braddon, Sir Edward', *AusDB*, vol. 7 · S. Bennett, 'Braddon in India', *Tasmanian Historical Research Association, Papers and Proceedings*, 26 (1979), 70–107 · D. Denholm, 'Edward Nicholas Coventry Braddon, 1829–1904: his contribution to Tasmanian politics, 1879–1899', BA diss., University of Tasmania, 1963 · J. Reynolds, 'Premiers and political leaders', *A century of responsible government in Tasmania*, ed. F. C. Green (1956), 192–203 · *Mercury* [Hobart] (3 Feb 1904) · *Tasmanian Mail* (6 Feb 1904) · *The Times* (3 Feb 1904) · P. Mennell, *The dictionary of Australasian biography* (1892), 52–3 · B. Burke, *A genealogical and heraldic history of the colonial gentry*, 1 (1891); repr. (1970), 331 · S. Bennett and B. Bennett, *Biographical register of the Tasmanian parliament, 1851–1960* (1980) · *Cyclopedia of Tasmania* (1900), 52–3 · *Australian commonwealth parliamentary debates*, 18 (1904), 14
Archives Archives Office of Tasmania, letters to James Smith [copies in the University of Tasmania, Hobart] · NL Scot., corresp. with *Blackwood's*
Likenesses photograph, repro. in *Cyclopedia of Tasmania*, 2 vols. (Hobart, 1900), vol. 1, p. 2 · photograph, repro. in S. Bennett, 'A home in the colonies: Edward Braddon's letter to India from North West Tasmania, 1878', *Papers and Proceedings* [Tasmanian Historical Research Association], 27/4 (1980) · photographs, Archives Office of Tasmania, Tasmania
Wealth at death £8720—value for probate in Tasmania: *AusDB* · £679—value for probate in New South Wales: *AusDB*

Braddon, Laurence (d. 1724), lawyer, was the second son of William Braddon of Treworgy, in St Genny's, Cornwall. He was admitted to the Middle Temple on 20 November 1677.

When Arthur Capel, earl of Essex, sent to the Tower of London for his part in the Rye House plot of 1682, was found dead in the Tower on 13 July 1683, Braddon decided that he had been murdered, and began to collect evidence to prove this. He was soon arrested, and on 7 February 1684 he and Hugh Speke were tried before the court of king's bench, accused of a conspiracy to spread the belief that the earl of Essex was murdered by his keepers, on the order of the court, and of attempting to suborn witnesses to testify to this. Braddon was found guilty on all the counts, was fined £2000, and kept in prison until William III landed in 1688. He was called to the bar on 24 November 1693, and in February 1695 he was appointed solicitor to the wine licence office at a salary of £100 a year.

Most of Braddon's works concern the death of the earl of Essex. *Enquiry into and Detection of the Barbarous Murther of the Late Earl of Essex* (1689) was probably written by him, and he was the author of *Essex's Innocency and Honour Vindicated* (1690), *Murther will out* (1692), *True and Impartial Narrative of the Murder of Arthur, Earl of Essex* (1729), and *Bishop Burnet's Late History Charg'd with Great Partiality and Misrepresentation* (1724), which claimed that Burnet's history was full of misrepresentations to make people believe that Essex committed suicide. Braddon also published *The Constitutions of the Company of Watermen and Lightermen* (1708), and an *Abstract of the Rules, Orders, and Constitutions* of the same company (1708). In *The Miseries of the Poor are a National Sin, Shame, and Danger* (1717) he argued for the establishment of guardians of the poor and inspectors for the encouragement of arts and manufactures. In 1721 he brought out *Particular Answers to the most Material Objections Made to the Proposal for Relieving the Poor*. Braddon died on 29 November 1724.

W. P. COURTNEY, rev. ANNE PIMLOTT BAKER

Sources *State trials*, vol. 9 · *N&Q*, 3rd ser., 4 (1863), 500 · *Biographia Britannica, or, The lives of the most eminent persons who have flourished in Great Britain and Ireland*, 7 vols. (1747–66) · Boase & Courtney, *Bibl. Corn.* · H. A. C. Sturgess, ed., *Register of admissions to the Honourable Society of the Middle Temple, from the fifteenth century to the year 1944*, 1 (1949)

Braddon [married name Maxwell], **Mary Elizabeth** (1835–1915), novelist, was born on 4 October 1835, at 2 Frith Street, Soho Square, London, the youngest of the three children of Henry Braddon, a Cornish solicitor, and his wife, Fanny White (d. 1868), an Irish journalist from co. Cavan. Sir Edward *Braddon was her elder brother. When she was four, her parents' marriage broke down owing to her father's financial irresponsibility and infidelity, and Fanny moved to Sussex with her children. In 1843 the family settled in Kensington, London, where Mary received a good education at Scarsdale House, a private girls' school.

At the age of twenty-two Braddon began an acting career with a touring company, determined to raise herself and her mother from barely genteel poverty. She took the stage name Mary Seyton, and usually played the parts of middle-aged women rather than those of young girls. She was accompanied by her mother as chaperone on her travels, mainly to Beverley and Hull in Yorkshire. Towards 1859 she began working on short stories and a collection of poems, *Garibaldi and other Poems* (published in 1861),

Mary Elizabeth Braddon (1835–1915), by William Powell Frith, exh. RA 1865

encouraged by an older Yorkshire admirer, identified as 'Mr Gilby' from letters. Later that year Gilby supplied her with enough money to enable her to leave off acting for six months and concentrate on writing. It would not be Braddon's first brush with Victorian proprieties.

Braddon wrote a number of 'penny dreadful' short stories which from September 1860 were published in the *Welcome Guest*, the *Halfpenny Marvel*, and other cheap fiction magazines owned by the publisher John Maxwell (1820–1895). During 1860 her first novel, *Three Times Dead*, had appeared, but its reception did not hint at the popularity she would later enjoy. Towards the end of 1860 her friendship with Gilby had ended acrimoniously, probably because by January 1861 she was working as editorial assistant for Maxwell. Maxwell was married with five children, and his wife, Mary Ann Crowley, was confined in a Dublin mental institution. By June Braddon and her mother had moved into Maxwell's house at 26 Mecklenburgh Square, Soho, London, Braddon passing as Maxwell's wife and acting as stepmother to his children.

Braddon was becoming weary of the penny dreadful stories that provided her with a regular income, writing to her long-term friend and patron Edward Bulwer-Lytton, 'The amount of crime, treachery, murder, slow poisoning and general infamy required by the halfpenny reader is something terrible' (Wolff, *Sensational Victorian*, 126). However, in July 1861 Maxwell's magazine *Robin Goodfellow* began to serialize the first chapters of *Lady Audley's Secret*, the first of the two 'bigamy novels' which made her name. When *Robin Goodfellow* failed, *Lady Audley* was transferred

to the *Sixpenny Magazine*, where it caught the attention of the publishers Edward and William Tinsley. The novel was a runaway success, prompting nine editions within the year. The two circulating library giants, Mudies and the Library Company, competed with each other to buy the largest number of copies, and by February 1863 at least three different adaptations were performed on the London stage.

Within a year Braddon had supplied her readers with a companion volume in *Aurora Floyd* (1862), where a passionate, raven-haired horsewoman elopes with her groom before marrying respectably into the squirearchy. Both Braddon's transgressive heroines are plagued by the inconvenient return of their first husbands, and both resort to desperate measures when threatened with exposure. *Aurora Floyd* was serialized in *Temple Bar*, causing an unprecedented run on the magazine, and, like *Lady Audley's Secret*, appeared in several different adaptations in London theatres. Although Wilkie Collins's *The Woman in White* (1860) and Mrs Henry Wood's *East Lynne* (1861) had prompted the invention of the term 'sensation fiction', Braddon's two novels soon came to exemplify the new genre. Together they made her a fortune which enabled her to buy Lichfield House, a Georgian mansion in Richmond, Surrey, yet they also brought an unwelcome personal notoriety.

Lady Audley was a new kind of heroine, whose blonde, blue-eyed, wax-doll beauty suggested the bland passivity of a Laura Fairlie or Rosamund Lydgate, yet masked ambition, bigamy, and homicide. While Aurora Floyd did not resort to murder, an infamous scene where she horsewhips her blackmailer, causing her hair to fall down and her clothes to become disarrayed, underlined an unladylike excess of sexuality. Although Henry James pointed out that, as Braddon's heroines sated their passions within marriage, her novels might be 'indecent, if you like, but not immoral', it was a distinction few reviewers granted (James, 263). Margaret Oliphant spoke for many when she complained, 'This eagerness for physical sensation is represented as the natural sentiment of English girls' (Oliphant, 'Novels', 263).

Braddon's success forced her private life into the public sphere. By 1864 her relationship with Maxwell could not be concealed—they had two children, and expected a third—and so, early that year, an advertisement was placed in two London papers announcing a 'recent marriage' between the couple (Wolff, *Sensational Victorian*, 98). However, Mary Ann Crowley's brother-in-law, Richard Brinsley Knowles, denied the marriage in every paper that printed it, and subsequent reviews accused Braddon of immorality, both in fiction and, through less and less veiled innuendo, in life. The *Quarterly Review* accused her of supplying 'the cravings of a diseased appetite' (QR, April 1863), while in the *North British Review* Fraser Rae pointedly alluded to her disreputable acting past, earlier career in the penny dreadfuls, and equivocal marital status, noting, 'She has temporarily succeeded in making the literature of the kitchen the favourite reading of the drawing room' (*North British Review*, Sept 1865). Margaret Oliphant went further still, bitingly suggesting that Braddon's love of bigamy was 'an invention which could only have been possible to an Englishwoman knowing the attractions of impropriety and yet loving the shelter of the law' (Oliphant, 'Novels', 263).

During the four years following *Lady Audley's Secret* Braddon defied her critics by publishing eight novels, often writing several novels for serialization at once; as she remarked to Bulwer-Lytton, 'I have never written a line that has not been written against time' (Wolff, *Sensational Victorian*, 134). Although accused of beginning 'the reign of bigamy as an interesting and fashionable crime' and inventing 'the fair haired demon of modern fiction' (Oliphant, 'Novels', 263), after *Aurora Floyd* she turned to more decorous drawing-room fiction. *Eleanor's Victory* (1863), *The Doctor's Wife* (1864), and *The Lady's Mile* (1866) were gentler 'society' novels. In 1866 Maxwell founded the *Belgravia Magazine*, a fiction journal which would be edited by Braddon for ten years and carried serials of many of her novels. Later that year her third child died, but she continued to write through a period of depression, publishing her twentieth novel by 1868. However, the death of her sister in October, followed by that of her mother a month later while Braddon was heavily pregnant, prompted a severe nervous collapse, complicated by puerperal fever and postnatal depression. She did not begin to convalesce until June 1869.

Drawing upon her stage experience, Braddon began to write plays in 1871, but none was produced. *The Lovels of Ardel* (1872) was her next major novel, a domestic saga in the vein of *The Lady's Mile*, and *To the Bitter End*, a 'sensational' tale of seduction and betrayal, followed a year later. Meanwhile, in September 1874, the scandal that had been bubbling under for the past decade broke when Mary Ann Crowley died in Dublin, and her brother-in-law Richard Knowles placed prominent death notices in the national papers phrased to underline the irregularity of Braddon's domestic life. Her marriage on 2 October 1874, as soon as the law allowed, emphasized the illegitimacy of her five surviving children. Scandalized, the servants at Lichfield House all gave notice, and the Maxwells were forced to leave Richmond for Chelsea for a year to allow local gossip to die down.

Towards the end of the 1870s Braddon became a keen reader of Zola, and her novels accordingly began to display a movement towards social radicalism. *Joshua Haggard's Daughter* (1876), set in a Devon fishing village, was influenced by Braddon's reading of Zola and Hardy. A year later she began editing *The Mistletoe Bough*, a Christmas fiction annual, another profitable venture with Maxwell. In 1878 *Vixen*, which like *Aurora Floyd* starred a 'pretty horsebreaker' heroine of wilful passions, was serialized in *All the Year Round*. *Vixen*, one of Braddon's favourites, was praised for being 'in Miss Braddon's later but better manner', and the *Saturday Review*, a long-standing critic of 'sensation fiction', looked forward to 'the pleasure of seeing her books given away as prizes in a school for young ladies' (*Saturday Review*, 47, 1879, 280–82). However, an undercurrent of quasi-incestuous sexual obsession permeated the blameless domestic plot, alluding to the 'sensation' genre Braddon had helped to create. The heroine's mother delivered one of the great lines of Victorian respectability, 'It is worse than a crime, Violet, it is an impropriety'.

During the 1880s Braddon continued to write 'for the Circulating library and the young lady readers who are its chief supporters' with undiminished vigour (Wolff, 'Devoted disciple', 150). By 1892 her sixtieth novel had appeared, and she and Maxwell were sufficiently well known to appear in George Gissing's *New Grub Street* (1892) as Mr and Mrs Jedwood, the corrupt publisher and the best-selling novelist who supports him. However, Maxwell was by then an invalid, and *Like and Unlike* (1892), contrasting a prostitute with a compromised society hostess, was the last novel that Braddon would be able to write for some time. Maxwell died from influenza on 5 March 1895, after a long illness. Later that year one of Braddon's novels, *Sons of Fire*, became a test case in a campaign by the circulating libraries to replace the expensive three-volume novel in favour of a cheaper one-volume format. Her resistance marked a crisis in the fate of the three-decker.

In 1907 Braddon became seriously ill after a stroke, and only partly recovered, having to walk with a cane for the rest of her life. Her son, the novelist William Babington Maxwell (1866–1938), and his family moved into Lichfield House to care for her. She died there on 4 February 1915, and was buried in Richmond cemetery. During her lifetime she had published over eighty novels, and *Lady Audley's Secret* had never been out of print. More recently, literary critics, following Elaine Showalter, have reappraised Braddon's 'sensation' fictions as 'carefully controlled female fantasies' of protest, rebellion, and escape subversive of the constraints imposed by the Victorian ideology of 'separate spheres' (Showalter, 163). During the 1990s *Eleanor's Victory* and *Vixen* were republished by Pocket Classics, and scholarly editions of *Aurora Floyd* and *Lady Audley's Secret* were issued in the Oxford World's Classics series.

KATHERINE MULLIN

Sources R. Wolff, *Sensational Victorian: the life and fiction of Mary Elizabeth Braddon* (1979) • H. James, 'Miss Braddon', *The Nation* (9 Nov 1865) • E. M. Casey, 'Other people's prudery: Mary Elizabeth Braddon', *Tennessee Studies in Literature*, 27 (1984), 72–82 • E. Showalter, *A literature of their own: from Charlotte Brontë to Doris Lessing* (1991) • R. L. Wolff, ed., 'Devoted disciple: the letters of Mary Elizabeth Braddon to Sir Edward Bulwer-Lytton, 1862–1873', *Harvard Library Bulletin*, 22 (April 1974), 5–35, 129–61 • M. Oliphant, 'Novels', *Blackwood*, 102 (1867), 263 • [H. L. Mansel], 'Sensation novels', *QR*, 113 (1863), 481–514 • W. F. Rae, 'Miss Braddon's novels', *North British Review*, 43 (1865), 180–205 • 'Miss Braddon', *Saturday Review*, 47 (1879), 280–82 • M. Oliphant, 'Sensation novels', *Blackwood*, 91 (1862), 564–84

Archives Harvard U., Houghton L., notebooks and literary MSS | BL, letters to T. H. Escott, Add. MS 58786 • Herts. ALS, letters to Lord Lytton • Women's Library, London, letters to Bram Stoker

Likenesses W. P. Frith, oils, exh. RA 1865, NPG [*see illus.*] • J. E. Hyett, bronze relief memorial, exh. Ra 1917, Richmond parish church • H. Harcal, caricature, NPG • lithograph, NPG

Wealth at death £68,112 1s. 3d.: probate, 29 June 1915, CGPLA Eng. & Wales

Brade, William (*c*.1560–1630), violinist and composer, spent much of his working life in Germany, where he made a considerable impact as a player, teacher, and composer. He held numerous court positions, principally in Denmark and with various members of the Brandenburg and Brunswick dynasties. Brade spent about four years at the Brandenburg court before travelling to Copenhagen to take up a position at the court chapel of Christian IV in November 1594. He remained there until September 1596, when once again he returned to Brandenburg. He was back at the Danish court from September 1599 until February 1606 (though he seems to have visited Berlin in 1603). He then moved to the court of Count Ernst III of Holstein-Schaumburg in Bückeburg. At Easter 1608 he left to join the town music (*Ratsmusik*) of Hamburg. He returned to Bückeburg in 1611 for a further two years, but his threat to return to Hamburg unless he was paid a salary of 1000 thalers (more than twice what he had received during his earlier period of employment at this court) brought him into conflict with his patron. Count Ernst took steps to warn the Hamburg authorities about this 'mischievous, wanton fellow' and his disruptive wife. Brade did, however, return to Hamburg at Easter 1613 (having organized an exchange with the leader of the *Ratsmusik*).

Residence in Hamburg, which was a centre of music publishing, must have acted as a stimulus to Brade. He had had fifteen dances included in the first volume of the anthology *Ausserlesener Paduanen und Galliarden* (1607) and a couple more in the second volume (1609). But during his first two periods of residence in the city he produced two books of his own instrumental music, *Newe ausserlesene Paduanen, Galliarden, Canzonen, Allmand und Coranten* (1609) and *Newe ausserlesene Paduanen und Galliarden* (1614), the latter a collection of six-part (and mostly paired) pavans and galliards. These are more contrapuntally sophisticated than his later dance collections. The 1609 collection was also published in Antwerp.

Brade is next heard of in 1614 at the court of Duke Friedrich III of Schleswig-Holstein at Holstein-Gottorp, but by mid-1615 he was back in Copenhagen. Another collection of five-part dance music, *Newe ausserlesene liebliche Branden, Intraden, Mascharaden, Balletten, All'manden, Couranten, Volten, Aufzüge und frembde Tänze*, appeared in Lübeck and Hamburg in 1617. In 1618 he was in Halle as a member of the household of Christian Wilhelm von Brandenburg, where he styled himself 'kapellmeister by appointment to the prince of Magdeburg'. (He seems to have held a similar rank at Güstrow with the duke of Mecklenburg.) He moved to Berlin as court kapellmeister to the elector Johann Sigismund of Brandenburg in 1619, but in August 1620 returned to the Danish court. Brade's last collection of instrumental music, *Newe lustige Volten, Couranten, Balletten, Padoanen, Galliarden, Masqueraden, auch allerley Arth newer frantzösischer Täntze*, another set of social dances, was published in Berlin in 1621 (having perhaps been set in train during his residence there). In 1622 he took up his last court position, as director of the court kapelle of Schleswig-Holstein. As the Thirty Years' War spread to this region, Brade sought safety in Hamburg, which was neutral. He became kapellmeister of the theatre in 1625, and it seems that he may have been involved with the *Gymnasium*. Brade died in Hamburg on 26 February 1630. Four years later the poet and theologian Johann Rist referred to him as 'the famous English string player'.

Brade seems to have had some distinguished pupils. He taught Nicholas Bleyer at Holstein-Gottorp, and it seems likely that he taught Johann Schop and David Cramer in Hamburg. He can thus be seen as a formative influence in the development of north German violin playing. He seems to have taken some pride in his origins, styling himself *Wilhelm Brade Englisch* on the title-pages of several publications. He clearly maintained his contacts with English musicians—and not just with those who spent all or part of their working lives in north Germany and Denmark. The 1617 publication contains arrangements of twenty of the most popular dances from Jacobean court masques (and a number of other dances which are in a similar style and might possibly originate from the same source).

PETER WALLS

Sources B. Thomas, introduction, in W. Brade, *Pavans, galliards and canzonas* (1982) · W. Braun, *Britannia abundans: deutsch-englische Musikbeziehungen zur Shakespearezeit* (1977) · P. Holman, *Four and twenty fiddlers: the violin at the English court, 1540–1690*, new edn (1993) · C. R. Huber, 'The life and music of William Brade', University of North Carolina, 1965 · A. Moser, *Geschichte des Violinspiels*, ed. H. J. Nösselt (1966) · P. E. Mueller, 'The influence and activities of English musicians on the continent during the late sixteenth and early seventeenth centuries', Indiana University, 1954 · C. A. Price, ed., *The early baroque era* (1993) · I. Spink, ed., *The seventeenth century* (1992) · *New Grove*

Bradeston, Thomas, Lord Bradeston (*d.* 1360), soldier and royal councillor, was probably the son of Robert de Bradeston, a minor landowner of Breadstone, Gloucestershire. The Bradestons were close allies of the Berkeleys of Berkeley Castle, their near neighbours, and Thomas probably began his career in the Berkeleys' service. In 1321 he was involved alongside Maurice, Lord Berkeley (*d.* 1326), in the marchers' rebellion against Edward II and the Despensers. As a result of his action, he suffered forfeiture and temporary imprisonment, but by 1325 he appears to have made his peace with the regime, and he played no active part in the events of Edward II's downfall.

In 1328, after the accession of Edward III, Bradeston became an esquire in the royal household, probably owing his introduction to royal service to his then patron, Thomas, Lord Berkeley (*d.* 1361), whose wife, Margaret, was daughter of Roger (V) Mortimer, Queen Isabella's lover. Bradeston quickly developed a close association with the new king, who was a few years his junior, and from the time of the latter's arrest of his mother at Nottingham in 1330 Bradeston's career advanced rapidly. In 1339 he was raised to the rank of knight-banneret and from 1346 until his death he was summoned to parliament as a lord. He appears to have been a man of considerable energy and administrative capacity, and he was on occasion employed in diplomacy, but it was primarily as a soldier that he distinguished himself. In the decade and a half from 1330 he scarcely absented himself from a single important campaign. In 1333 he led a retinue on the expedition to Scotland, and was present at the victory over the Scots at Halidon Hill near Berwick. Between 1338 and 1340 he accompanied Edward on his early campaigns against the French in the Low Countries. In 1341 he again accompanied the king to the Low Countries and in 1342 he took part in one of the three expeditions to Brittany. Very likely his greatest services were rendered in the thirteen months of campaigning that followed Edward's invasion of France in July 1346. He contributed to the mighty victory over the French at Crécy on 26 August, and was present at the year-long siege of Calais. In the wake of the surrender of Calais on 4 August 1347 he was rewarded with a grant in fee of property in the town.

In many of the expeditions in which he participated Bradeston fought alongside Sir Maurice Berkeley of Uley, Gloucestershire, the younger brother of Thomas, Lord Berkeley. John Smyth of Nibley, the seventeenth-century historian of the Berkeley family, described Bradeston as Sir Maurice's 'inseparable companion-in-arms' (Saul, 77), and it is possible that a formal relationship of brotherhood-in-arms existed between the two. In the local politics of Gloucestershire Bradeston showed himself a consistent upholder of the Berkeley interest, and his peacetime retinue, which probably numbered two or three knights and half a dozen esquires, operated largely as a sub-retinue of theirs. The powerful sponsorship that he enjoyed, both locally and at court, allowed him ruthlessly to further his personal and dynastic interests in the county. At some time in the 1340s the people of King's Barton near Gloucester, which Bradeston held at farm, petitioned the king for redress of grievance against him and his officers, saying that when at court he behaved like a 'little saint' ('un sainturel'), while in his own county he was like a 'raging lion' ('lyon rampant'; Saul, 267). Despite, or perhaps because of, his oppressive lordship, Bradeston showed a strong streak of conventional piety. He founded chantries in his local chapelry at Breadstone and in the parish church at Winterbourne, where he resided, and it has been suggested that he paid for the great east window of St Peter's Abbey, Gloucester (now Gloucester Cathedral), and for wall paintings, partly extant, in Winterbourne church. He died on 25 August 1360, leaving a widow, Agnes, who died in 1369; a first wife, Isabel, sister of Sir Walter Paveley, had been alive in the 1340s. Bradeston's heir was his grandson Thomas, aged eight; his eldest son, Sir Robert, had predeceased him in the 1350s.

NIGEL SAUL

Sources Chancery records · GEC, Peerage · PRO, Chancery, Warrants for the Great Seal (series 1), C 81 · PRO, Chancery Treaty Rolls, C 76 · R. Austin, 'Notes on the family of Bradeston', Transactions of the Bristol and Gloucestershire Archaeological Society, 47 (1925), 279–86 · CIPM, 10, no. 614 · N. Saul, Knights and esquires: the Gloucestershire gentry in the fourteenth century (1981)

Bradfield, Henry Joseph Steele (1805–1852), colonial official and author, was born on 18 May 1805 in Derby Street, Westminster, London, where his father, Thomas Bradfield, was a coal merchant. In 1825 he published *Waterloo, or, The British Minstrel: a Poem*. He had trained as a surgeon,

and on 26 April 1826 left England aboard the schooner *Unicorn* with Lord Cochrane's expedition to Greece, where he took part in several engagements on land and sea. After his return he published *The Athenaid, or, Modern Grecians, a Poem* (1830) and *Tales of the Cyclades, Poems* (1830), and in 1839 he edited a work entitled *A Russian's Reply to the Marquis de Custine's 'Russia'*.

On 1 September 1832 Bradfield received a commission as *sous-lieutenant* in the Belgian *Bataillon étranger* and was appointed to the 1st regiment of lancers. At one time he held a commission in the Royal West Middlesex militia. He was appointed stipendiary magistrate in Tobago on 31 December 1835, and was transferred to Trinidad on 13 May 1836. He was reappointed to the southern or Cedros district on 13 April 1839, but soon returned to England following a quarrel with another colonial officer. In 1841 he returned to the West Indies as private secretary to Colonel Macdonald, lieutenant-governor of Dominica, and in 1842 he acted as colonial secretary in Barbados. Charges connected with the earlier quarrel were, however, renewed, and the government cancelled his appointment.

From then on Bradfield lived very precariously, drawing on his moderate literary talents: among some contributions he made to the *Gentleman's Magazine* were articles on 'The last of the Paleologi' in January 1843, and a 'Memoir of Major-General Thomas Dundas and the expedition to Gaudaloupe' later the same year. Latterly, he was almost a professional beggar; he committed suicide by swallowing prussic acid, and was found dead in the St Albans Hotel, Charles Street, Westminster, on 11 October 1852.

G. C. BOASE, rev. LYNN MILNE

Sources G. Cochrane, Wanderings in Greece (1837) · GM, 2nd ser., 39 (1853), 102 · Morning Post (13 Oct 1852), 4 · Morning Post (15 Oct 1852), 6 · d. cert.

Bradford. For this title name *see* Newport, Francis, first earl of Bradford (1619–1708); Bridgeman, Selina Louisa, countess of Bradford (1819–1894).

Bradford, Sir Edward Ridley Colborne, first baronet (1836–1911), administrator in India and police officer, was born on 27 July 1836 at Hambleden Cottage, Buckinghamshire, the second son of William Mussage Kirkwall Bradford (1806–1872), who was rector successively of Rotherfield Greys, Oxfordshire; Weeke, Hampshire; and West Meon, Hampshire. His mother, Mary (1810–1894), was the elder daughter of Henry Colborne Ridley, rector of Hambleden and younger brother of Sir Matthew White Ridley, third baronet.

Bradford was educated at a private school at Henley-on-Thames and from the age of ten at Marlborough College. A teenage illness cut short his schooling and in 1853 he accepted a cadetship in the East India Company's Madras army and joined the 2nd Madras light infantry at Jalna. In 1855 he was promoted to lieutenant and transferred to the 6th Madras cavalry at Mhow in central India.

On the outbreak of war with Persia in 1856 General John Jacob selected Bradford to organize a corps of irregular cavalry in Persia, but this project was abandoned and he was instead attached to a troop of 14th light dragoons,

Sir Edward Ridley Colborne Bradford, first baronet (1836–1911), by Henry Tanworth Wells, 1900

with whom he served at the capture of Muhammara. He returned to India in mid-1857 eager to help suppress the rebellion then raging in the north and centre of the country. As adjutant of the left wing 6th Madras cavalry he was initially engaged in skirmishes with insurgent chiefs near Jubbulpore and in the Sagar and Nerbudda districts, but he later transferred to Mayne's irregular cavalry (subsequently the 1st regiment of Central India horse), of which on 25 October 1858 he became second in command. His leadership in decisive battles against the forces of Tantia Topi, insurgent commander of Cawnpore, on 19 and 25 October 1858 won him praise in dispatches 'for his great influence over the native soldiery, his excellent tact and judgment'. He remained with Mayne's horse throughout 1859 and into 1860, mopping up the last of the insurgents. In September 1860, his health sapped by his long stretch of active soldiering, he was ordered home to recuperate. He returned to India in 1862, whereupon he was appointed political assistant in west Malwa in addition to his military duties.

On 10 May 1863 Bradford's hopes of further military glory were dashed by a hunting accident. Returning from a hunting party near Guna which had dispatched eighteen tigers, he went after one remaining tiger, failed to kill it outright, and was attacked and severely mauled, in consequence of which his left arm had to be amputated. Although he resumed as soon as possible his former pursuits of hunting and shooting, his military career was over and he turned instead to the Indian political service.

In 1874, after serving as political agent in Jaipur, Baghelkhand, Bharatpur, and Mewar, Bradford was appointed general superintendent of the thuggee and dacoit department, which had outgrown its original remit of policing criminal communities to become a form of secret police, tracking down cases of sedition and politically motivated crime. Four years later, in March 1878, Bradford was appointed chief commissioner of Ajmer and given supreme control of relations with the Rajput princes. In this role he persuaded several princes of the desirability of introducing railways and basic social reforms into their territories. He was the model of a paternalistic adviser, lauded by his colleagues for his 'magnetic influence' over the Rajput chiefs and nobles. In reality he was a stern figure with an impeccable military bearing and a handy reputation for having survived a round with a tiger, which, when coupled with his very real power as political chief in Rajputana, made it difficult for any petty prince to withstand his 'advice'. In private he was dismissive of the princes in his charge, accusing them almost without exception of laziness, vanity, stupidity, and guile.

Because of his connections with India's extant royalty, Bradford was attached to the staff of both the duke of Edinburgh on his visit to India in 1870 and the prince of Wales on his visit in 1875. In 1889 he accompanied Prince Albert Victor on his Indian tour. In June 1885 he was made KCSI, and two years later was on the point of becoming resident at Hyderabad when Lord Cross offered him the post of secretary to the political and secret department of the India Office in London, an offer he accepted not least because it enabled him to keep his family together. He had married on 17 June 1866 Elizabeth (Lizzie) Adela (d. 1896), third daughter of Edward Knight of Chawton House, Hampshire, a nephew of Jane Austen. Only four of their six children had survived childhood in India and at the time of Lord Cross's offer Bradford had been preparing to send the younger ones home to England with their mother.

Bradford adapted quickly to the ethos of the political and secret department; in order to avoid discussion of the government of India's political work in either the press or parliament he undertook to settle contentious issues by corresponding privately with Sir Mortimer Durand, who was both foreign member of the government of India and a long-standing friend.

In February 1889 Bradford turned down the governorship of the Cape, but in June 1890, after some hesitation, he accepted the post of chief commissioner of the Metropolitan Police Force of London, an appointment which continued a trend within the London force of hiring senior officers from the relatively illiberal policing traditions of Ireland and the colonies. Bradford inherited a discontented constabulary, teetering on the brink of a general strike over pay and conditions. Within days of taking office, however, he had dismissed thirty-nine strikers for insubordination and embarked on a course of remedial measures, which included an increase in stations and signal boxes to reduce the areas covered by individual constables and an enhanced recreational programme. As chief of police he oversaw the public demonstrations connected with the diamond jubilee and the funeral of Queen Victoria, the coronation of Edward VII, the relief of Ladysmith and Mafeking, and several rallies against unemployment. He retired on 4 March 1903. He was made aide-de-camp to the queen in 1889, KCB in 1890, GCB in 1897, GCVO in 1902, a baronet on 24 July 1902, and extra equerry to Edward VII in 1903 and to George V in 1910.

After his retirement from public service Bradford acted as chairman of a committee to inquire into the wages of postal servants, but his chief interest was hunting. He hunted several days a week with the Bicester, Warwickshire, Heythrop, and Whaddon chase hounds. He died suddenly at his house in London, 50 South Audley Street, Westminster, on 13 May 1911 and was buried four days later in the churchyard at Chawton, Hampshire, beside his first wife, who had died in 1896. In 1898 he had married, secondly, Edith Mary, daughter of William Nicholson of Basing Park, Hampshire, formerly high sheriff of the county and MP for Petersfield. She survived him with a daughter and two sons of his first marriage. His eldest son, Montagu Edward, born in 1867, joined the Indian Civil Service and died in India in 1890. His second son, Evelyn Ridley (1869–1914), lieutenant-colonel in the Seaforth Highlanders, succeeded to the baronetcy. He was killed in action in France on 14 September 1914.

KATHERINE PRIOR

Sources DNB · Burke, *Peerage* (1959) · B. Porter, *The origins of the vigilant state* (1987) · BL OIOC, Cadet MSS · BL OIOC, Durand MSS · *The Times* (15 May 1911)

Archives BL OIOC, Durand MSS

Likenesses W. W. Ouless, portrait, c.1887, Mayo College, Ajmer, India · photograph, before 1887, BL · wood-engraving, 1890, NPG; repro. in *ILN* (28 June 1890) · H. T. Wells, drawing, 1900, NPG [*see illus.*] · M. B. Constant, portrait, 1901, priv. coll. · Spy [L. Ward], chromolithograph caricature, NPG; repro. in *VF* (15 Nov 1890) · portrait, repro. in *Strand Magazine* (Feb 1896)

Wealth at death £17,039 15s. 4d.: resworn probate, 3 July 1911, CGPLA Eng. & Wales

Bradford, John (c.1510–1555), evangelical preacher and martyr, was a native of the parish of Manchester. His parents are said to have been of gentle birth, but little is known for certain of his family, except that he had at least three sisters. He attended Manchester grammar school, and was grateful for the rest of his life for the education he received there.

Conversion Between 1544 and 1547 Bradford was employed by Sir John Harington of Exton, Rutlandshire, the vice-treasurer of the English army in France, whom he may have met when Harington was serving in the north for the 1542 Scottish campaign. Harington's French responsibilities included the king's interests and properties at Boulogne, and it is probable that Bradford served as his assistant there. His employment proved far from uncontroversial, however, and he found himself suspected of peculation, at the expense of both the crown and his employer, whom he was alleged to have defrauded of £140. The details remain obscure. When the affair was brought up by Bishop Gardiner in 1553, Bradford denied any offence against Harington, whose own shady dealings

complicate in their turn the issue of his employee's possible, but improbable, offence against the crown.

Bradford does not appear to have had any particular penchant for military affairs, and it is not surprising that in 1547 he should have left Boulogne, and on 8 April enrolled at the Inner Temple. Coinciding with this change in career, and even more momentous, was his religious conversion. Crucial roles in this event were played by Thomas Sampson, who stimulated his interest in theology, and by Hugh Latimer, whose fiery preaching evidently so impressed Bradford that he voluntarily began a process of restitution with regard to his offences in France. Further underlining his personal renewal, he also sold a number of valuables and distributed the proceeds among the needy, and thereafter, as Foxe put it, 'he gave himself wholly to the study of the holy scriptures' (*Acts and Monuments*, 7.143). He never married, but as far as possible remained on affectionate terms with members of his family. His sister Margaret married Roger Beswick, who became a devoted protestant, but, although his other sisters and his mother seem to have remained conservative in religion, Bradford never ceased to show himself concerned for their spiritual welfare; this is particularly apparent in letters he wrote to his mother, for instance on 24 February 1554 and 24 June 1555.

Bradford also changed course with regard to his chosen career, as he took full advantage of the growing opportunities to study the new learning. As with others of that generation who were inclined towards humanism, his initial foray into the classics seems modest enough, being a translation of Petrus Artopoeus and John Chrysostom published in 1548 as *The Divisyon of the Places of the Lawe and of the Gospell* (ESTC 822). In the early summer of the same year he gained admission to St Catharine's College, Cambridge, where he clearly met with approval, since on 19 October 1549 he was awarded the degree of MA, following examination by James Pilkington, future bishop of Durham. Three days later he wrote to his friend John Traves, anticipating his election to a fellowship at Pembroke College through the good offices of its master, Nicholas Ridley, who turned out to have been in disputation with Edwin Sandys, master of St Catharine's, as to which college should secure Bradford's services. By the following month he was a fellow of Pembroke, a position he claimed he had never sought, and found himself in the company of Edmund Grindal, and acted as tutor to John Whitgift when the latter arrived in Michaelmas term 1550. It is a sign of his developing eminence that he should also have formed an intimate friendship with the Strasbourg theologian Martin Bucer, who came to Cambridge in 1549. According to Sampson, Bradford kept a sort of journal during his time in Cambridge, recording the important events and thoughts of each day, as an aid to his development as a servant of Christ.

Evangelical preacher Bucer intended that Bradford should become a preacher, while Bradford protested that he needed further study before he could take on such a role. But on 10 August 1550 Ridley, now bishop of London, ordained him deacon, gave him a preaching licence, and appointed him one of his own chaplains. On 24 August 1551 he was collated to the prebend of Kentish Town in St Paul's Cathedral, and in December following he was made one of six chaplains in ordinary to the king; it is a sign that Bradford had come to be regarded as a member of a protestant preaching élite that his colleagues should have been Grindal, John Knox, John Harley, Andrew Perne, and William Bill. It was intended that at any one time two should be serving at court, while the others travelled through the country preaching reformation. It is unclear how much time Bradford spent away from London, but he certainly preached in Lancashire and Cheshire during 1552, his own writings attesting to a ministry which centred upon Manchester but extended to such places as Liverpool, Bolton, Stockport, and Westchester. His effectiveness was greatest in southern Lancashire, where he spoke to large crowds and attracted a number of converts, though without making much impression upon the gentry of the region. Back at Westminster, he and his fellow chaplains used the Lenten season of 1553 as the occasion for a controversial pulpiteering campaign against sin in high places; Bradford himself went so far as to hold up the duke of Somerset, executed less than a year earlier, as an exemplar of unrighteousness. Sampson records this sermon as having been delivered in the presence of the king himself, and as proclaiming the imminence of divine judgment.

This episode shows that he was not a man to be daunted by authority, and Bradford also proved himself both courageous and responsible in the immediate aftermath of Edward VI's death. On 13 August 1553, accompanied by John Rogers, he acted swiftly to calm disturbances provoked by the Catholic Gilbert Bourne in a sermon at Paul's Cross, risking his safety to the extent that a dagger thrown at Bourne grazed his own clothing. Then during the afternoon he preached in Bow church, Cheapside, and according to Foxe 'reproved the people sharply for their seditious demeanour' (*Acts and Monuments*, 7.145). By temperament meek and self-effacing, neither now nor later did Bradford shrink from danger, though he and his comrades became increasingly vulnerable to the dictates of Queen Mary's government. A few days after he had assisted the authorities in the task of crowd control he was summoned before the council in the Tower, where the queen was then resident, and charged with preaching seditious sermons. Imprisoned in the Tower, he was at first incarcerated alone, but was then moved to the place known as the 'Nun's bower' with Edwin Sandys. They stayed there for five months. It was clearly government policy to keep the leading protestant prisoners on the move, however, perhaps in the hope of disorientating them, and on 6 February 1554 the two men were separated, Bradford being taken to another room in the Tower, which he shared with Cranmer, Ridley, and Latimer. On 11 or 12 March the latter were removed to Oxford, and on the 24th Bradford left for Southwark and the king's bench prison there.

Prisoner and disputant The king's bench prison became something like a 'mother-house' for people charged with heresy; apart from Bradford, its inmates included Robert Ferrar, Rowland Taylor, and John Philpot. Bradford spent some ten months imprisoned here, though his sympathetic character, along with the favour of the knight marshal, Sir William Fitzwilliam, secured for him an unusual amount of freedom. Foxe records that he was given leave to preach twice daily, and even to administer the sacraments. But Bradford's acknowledged holiness of life could not prevent serious theological disputes from arising among the protestant prisoners. He was a leading representative of what was becoming the theological mainstream among Edwardian evangelicals, with a bent decidedly, if not radically, Calvinistic, and increasingly influenced by ideas from Geneva and Strasbourg adapted to English circumstances. Not everyone, however, was eager to jump on the predestinarian bandwagon, and in south-east England, in particular, there was a good deal of interest in countervailing ideas, often also of continental origins. There emerged a group of so-called 'free-willers', led by Henry Harte, who 'repudiated with violence the predestinatory doctrines of Calvin' (Dickens, 328). The result was a spirited debate on the issues of election and free will, conducted through discussions, correspondence, and writings, in and around the various gaols in which protestants had been imprisoned by Queen Mary's government. For the latter the divisions among their opponents provided a cause for satisfaction and matter for propaganda, but for the evangelical cause they were the source of much grief, as its leaders struggled to present a united front to their adversaries by reclaiming as many as possible of the people whom they regarded as their confused or ill-taught brethren.

In these disputes Bradford played a leading part, not only by endeavouring to keep order in the prisons, where feelings sometimes ran very high, but also through his writings. He was in constant correspondence with his opponents, composing such treatises as *To a Free-Willer* in 1554, and *To Certain Free-Willers* on 1 January 1555, and when matters looked particularly critical he also appealed to Cranmer, Ridley, and Latimer in Oxford. With Taylor, Ferrar, and Philpot he forwarded to the imprisoned bishops a text by Harte with the comment:

> The effects of salvation they so mingle and confound with the cause, that if it be not seen to more hurt will come by them, than ever came by the papists, inasmuch as their life commendeth them to the world more than the papists. (*Writings*, 2.170–71)

Ridley, at least, took the matter seriously, composing a treatise (probably now preserved among the Fairhurst papers in Lambeth Palace Library) in which he took up a position identical to Bradford's own, rejecting misconceived notions of both free will and predestination in favour of the doctrine of God's election and justification by faith in Christ. It would appear that the party of moderate predestinarianism prevailed, and that a number of free-willers defected to it. Thus Bradford rejoiced over a certain Skelthrop, declaring that God 'hath given him to see his truth at the length, and to give place to it' (ibid., 2.243), but Harte remained obdurate, prompting

Bradford's ally John Careless to exclaim 'God convert him or confound him shortly' (*Acts and Monuments*, 8.164).

As well as having to confront theological opposition while in prison, Bradford also had once more to face charges of financial mismanagement. Outside assistance was essential if the protestant prisoners were not to risk starvation, and since Bradford was effectively their leader it fell to him to organize the equitable distribution of the donations, whose contributors included Nicholas Ridley and a number of godly women, including Lady Vane from Holborn, Mrs Anne Warcup, and Anne Boleyn's former silkwoman, Joan Wilkinson. He was now accused not of peculation but of favouring his own supporters at the expense of the free-willers when he handed out alms. One of the latter named John Trewe brought such a charge, which Bradford denied with feeling, asserting that he had always been concerned for the well-being of his opponents, and had even devoted to it money intended for his private use. Such unfairness would certainly have been out of character for Bradford, but the allegation underlines the difficulties of his position, that he should have been responsible for the well-being of a number of fellow prisoners whose theological position he was at the same time attacking. The challenges of leadership required unlimited patience and godly wisdom.

Temptations of election Another, and to him doubtless more important, aspect of Bradford's prison ministry was the pastoral one of giving comfort to people who were agonizing over their assurance of salvation. It was a ministry which extended outside the confines of prison, to members of London's godly congregations who looked to him for guidance. Their doubts stemmed largely from the same deterministic doctrines which had prompted debate between Bradford and the free-willers. Thus Margery Coke, greatly disturbed by 'temptations of election', appealed to Bradford for comfort and received a sympathetic response (23 July 1554), even though he was himself in the grip of fever at the time. Some two weeks later Joyce Hales required similar assistance as she wrestled with the same dilemma. Indeed, she became a regular correspondent of Bradford, who faithfully consoled her 'with texts and images from Matthew's gospel and Romans. He intended to lift her from a deep spiritual crisis, and yet find words which would be applicable to his own, or any Protestant's, plight' (Wabuda, 249).

It was to Mistress Hales that Bradford dedicated his *Defence of Election*, a substantial treatise in which he declares confidently that 'Faith of God's election ... is of all things which God requireth of us, not only most principal, but also the whole sum: so that "without this faith" there is nothing that we do that can "please God"' (*Writings*, 1.307). In another passage he assures readers 'that election is so certain that the elect and predestinate to eternal life shall never finally perish or err to damnation finally' (ibid., 1.314), and he concludes with a firm yet moderate (or 'infralapsarian') statement of the Calvinist position: 'But they, because they cannot by their curious reason see how election should be before God, and yet follow Adam's fall to us, therefore they come with their witless,

unreasonable, arrogant and very detestable "hows"' (ibid., 1.330). He also composed two briefer works, *A Treatise of Election and Free-will* and *A Brief Sum of the Doctrine of Election and Predestination*, again covering controversial ground:

> God's foresight is not the cause of sin or excusable necessity to him that sinneth: the damned therefore have not nor shall have any excuse, because God, forseeing their condemnation through their own sin, did not draw them, as he doth his elect, unto Christ. (ibid., 1.219)

Bradford could also assume a less partisan and more pastoral voice, however, as in his *Sermon on Repentance*, speaking as if God were appealing through himself:

> If, when we hated him and fled away from him, he sent his Son to seek us; who can think otherwise than now we loving him, and lamenting because we love him no more, but that he will for ever love us? (*Writings*, 1.75)

It is not surprising that men and women anticipating a violent death for their faith should have thought much of their place in the next life. Bradford composed *A Very Godly Prayer of one Standing at the Stake Ready to be Burnt for Christ's Gospel's Sake*, and expressed the ultimate hope of his flock in his *Meditation of the Blessed State and Felicity of the Life to Come*:

> Thy angels will gather them together, and they shall meet thee in the clouds, and be always with thee. They shall hear this joyful voice, 'Come, ye blessed of my Father, possess the kingdom prepared for you from the beginning'. (ibid., 1.275)

Condemnation and death The demands of prison life on Bradford's physical and emotional resources were very great, making it hard to understand how he was able to manage with only four hours' sleep a night, as Foxe records that he did. He enjoyed the companionship of his associates after his meals, but soon turned to reading and prayer. As the Marian persecution gathered momentum at the beginning of 1555, he needed all his strength. Bradford was examined three times at Winchester on 22, 29, and 30 January, and at the last of these sessions he was condemned as a heretic. But although the burning of John Rogers on 4 February might have led him to expect a quick end, he did not suffer until nearly five months later, being held first in the Clink and then in solitude in the Compter in the Poultry, in what was known as the Grocers' Hall court. The reason for the delay was undoubtedly the anxiety of the Catholic authorities to undermine his influence in his native Lancashire, either by executing him there, as was at first expected, or by securing his recantation. On 19 February the writ for his execution was withdrawn and Bradford was subjected to repeated conferences and examinations during that month, March, and April. Among the eminent churchmen and theologians who came to debate with him were Nicholas Heath, archbishop of York, George Day, bishop of Chichester, and the Spanish divines Alfonso de Castro and Bartolomé Carranza. At one point he was told he could take refuge abroad if only he would recant. His importance was as apparent to his enemies as it was later to be to his protestant successors. In the words of John Strype, Bradford was a man 'of whose worth the papists themselves were so sensible, that they took more pains to bring him off from the profession of religion, than any other' (Strype, 3/1.363–4).

Bradford held firm, and late on 30 June 1555 he was taken back to Newgate. He finally went to the stake at Smithfield on the following day, accompanied by John Leaf, a much younger man, and wearing a new shirt made for him for the occasion by one of his supporters, a Mrs Marler. Foxe describes him as 'somewhat tall and slender, spare of body, of a faint sanguine colour, with an auburn beard' (*Acts and Monuments*, 7.145), a representation confirmed by his portrait (in Hampstead Public Library), which shows a sombre scholar-preacher, characteristic of the mid-sixteenth century. Before all else a godly man, he was concerned 'to make to himself a catalogue of all the grossest and most enorme sins, which in his life of ignorance he had committed' (*Writings*, 1.33). But there was also a very pleasant and compassionate side to his personality, which even the Jesuit Robert Parsons acknowledged, remarking that Bradford was 'of a more soft and mild nature than many of his fellows' (Loane, 159). It was this combination of qualities which enabled Bradford to give a leadership in prison which was of fundamental importance for the evangelical cause, both at the time and later. In the words of William Haller:

> But besides being the hero and author of one of the most striking tales in the whole *Book of Martyrs*, Bradford also left materials which enabled Foxe to present him as a prototype of all the physicians of the soul who would presently be undertaking the spiritual direction of more and more of Elizabeth's subjects.   (Haller, 207)

D. ANDREW PENNY

Sources The acts and monuments of John Foxe, ed. J. Pratt, [new edn], 7 (1877) • D. A. Penny, *Freewill or predestination: the battle over saving grace in mid-Tudor England* (1990) • M. L. Loane, *Pioneers of the Reformation in England* (1964) • *The writings of John Bradford*, ed. A. Townsend, 1 vol. in 2 pts, Parker Society, 31 (1848–53) • W. Haller, *Foxe's 'Book of martyrs' and the elect nation* (1963) • J. Strype, *Ecclesiastical memorials*, 3/1 (1822) • A. G. Dickens, *The English Reformation* (1964) • C. Haigh, *Reformation and resistance in Tudor Lancashire* (1975) • HoP, *Commons, 1509–58*, 2.298–300 • *DNB* • J. Ridley, *Nicholas Ridley: a biography* (1957) • D. MacCulloch, *Thomas Cranmer: a life* (1996) • D. D. Wallace, *Puritans and predestination: grace in English protestant theology, 1525–1695* (1982) • S. Wabuda, 'Henry Bull, Miles Coverdale, and the making of Foxe's Book of martyrs', *Martyrs and martyrologies*, ed. D. Wood, SCH, 30 (1993), 245–58

Archives Emmanuel College, Cambridge, letters of the martyrs, MSS 260–262

Likenesses Passe, line engraving, BM, NPG; repro. in H. Holland, *Herōōlogia* (1620) • engraving, repro. in E. Baines, *History of Lancashire*, vol. 2, p. 243 • portrait, Hampstead Public Library • portrait, Pembroke Cam.

Bradford, John [Siôn] (1706–1785), poet and antiquary, was the son of a Richard Bradford (*fl. c.*1700–1750) who lived at Y Pandy, Betws Tir Iarll, in upper Glamorgan. Little definite is known of his father, but he was probably a weaver, fuller, and dyer, as his son became. A tradition existed in the family that the Bradfords, who had their own coat of arms, had moved to Betws from Bradford-on-Avon in the early seventeenth century.

Bradford became a prominent figure among the small,

cultured fraternity of bards that emerged in upper Glamorgan during the first half of the eighteenth century and played an important role in the literary renaissance that occurred in the county at that time. He appears to have applied himself diligently in his youth to studying the ancient Welsh bardic traditions and collecting Welsh manuscripts. There is some evidence that he acquired several of the manuscript volumes of the cultured Powel family of Tir Iarll. He was undoubtedly acquainted with the works of many English authors and literary critics, and it is said that some of the English volumes he had acquired were still in the possession of his descendants in the nineteenth century. However, very little of his verse is now extant, and the few surviving examples do not suggest that he was endowed with much poetic ability. A staunch nonconformist, he acquired some repute as a rationalist, and the works of some of the more prominent eighteenth-century deists made a deep impression on him. He was known to the influential Morris circle in north Wales, and he corresponded with both William Wynn (1709–1760) of Llangynhafal and Lewis Morris (1701–1765), the celebrated Welsh poet and scholar, who described Bradford, in a characteristically sarcastic manner, as 'the Prime of South Wales Poets'. He was elected a member of the Honourable Society of Cymmrodorion, London.

The most talented of his pupils was the renowned Welsh literary forger Iolo Morganwg (Edward Williams; 1747–1826), who, after Bradford's death, invented many stories about his erudition and his connection with the druidic and Unitarian bardic system which, he claimed, had uniquely persisted in Glamorgan throughout the centuries, and especially in Tir Iarll. Iolo frequently maintained that it was in Bradford's manuscripts that he had found many of the details that were later shown to be the product of his own fertile imagination. Much that was written about Bradford in the nineteenth century must, therefore, be treated with the greatest caution.

Bradford was buried on 6 June 1785 in Betws and his will was proved at Cowbridge on 11 October that year. After specifying certain sums he bequeathed to his daughters and to his wife, Alice, he left the remainder of his possessions entirely to his son, Richard, who was blind. However, his will contained no reference to his collection of books and manuscripts. He expressed the wish to be buried 'with my ancestors in the parish church of Betws in a decent manner without any funeral pomp and with as little expense as decency will admit of'. In July 1785, approximately a month after his death, William Thomas (1727–1795), the schoolmaster of St Bride's-super-Ely, wrote in his diary, which is a valuable chronicle of events in Glamorgan in his day: 'Was lately buried at Betws near Bridgend John Bradford a fuller and a dyer of 80 yrs of age. a great disbater and a Nominated Deist or a freethinker.' Nevertheless, the Betws parish registers show that he was a churchwarden in 1767–8 and that his son, Richard, served in a similar capacity in 1787–8.

After John Bradford's death his son, Richard, continued to work as a weaver and fuller in Betws. An employee of his, named David James, who played a prominent role in the Unitarian movement in Tir Iarll and its neighbourhood, married a niece to Richard Bradford. Their great-granddaughter became the wife of John Kyrle Fletcher, a well-known bookseller in his day in Newport, Monmouthshire. C. W. LEWIS

Sources G. J. Williams, *Traddodiad llenyddol Morgannwg* (1948), 237–40, 267–72 · C. W. Lewis, 'The literary history of Glamorgan from 1550 to 1770', *Glamorgan county history*, ed. G. Williams, 4: *Early modern Glamorgan* (1974), 535–639, esp. 614–16 · G. J. Williams, *Iolo Morganwg a chywyddau'r ychwanegiad* (1926), 163–6 · parish register, 1767–8, Betws Tir Iarll, Glamorgan · NL Wales, Llanover collection · Cardiff MS 4.877, fol. 235 · BL, MS 14929, fol. 54 · *Cylchgrawn Cymdeithas Hanes Eglwys Methodistiaid Calfinaidd Cymru*, 34 (1949), 47 · I. Morganwg [E. Williams], *Poems, lyric and pastoral*, 2 vols. (1794), 2.218–19 · W. O. Pughe, ed., *The Cambrian register*, 1 (1796), 343

Bradford, John (1750–1805), Church of England clergyman and Independent minister, was born at Hereford, the son of John Bradford, a clothier. He was brought up as an Anglican and educated at Hereford grammar school before proceeding to Wadham College, Oxford, whence he matriculated on 25 June 1767 and graduated BA in 1771. After leaving Oxford, Bradford became curate at Frelsham in Berkshire. He later confessed that he began his curacy as an avowed Arian but experienced a conversion to Trinitarianism and became decidedly Calvinistic in his religious convictions. While still an Anglican clergyman he agreed to preach in several chapels belonging to the Countess of Huntingdon's Connexion, but this was frowned on by the church authorities and in 1780 he was dismissed from his living at Frelsham.

Bradford then joined the countess's connexion and for several years supplied various chapels in south Wales and the west midlands including Bridge Street, Walsall, and Virgin's End (later Mayers Green), West Bromwich. His most unusual supply was preaching at the old playhouse in Birmingham, which had been purchased by the countess for use as a chapel. There Bradford preached from a pulpit positioned at the front of the stage. His preaching proved very popular and the entire theatre was sometimes crammed with an appreciative audience. However, the desire for a settled ministry led him to leave the connexion and accept in 1786 charge of the independent congregation at the newly opened Paradise Chapel in Bartholomew Street, Birmingham. While there he published (1792) *A Collection of Hymns*, some of which were written by himself. This collection of 280 hymns, avowedly antinomian, proved popular at the time but very few of these hymns are in common usage today. His other notable literary work, also published in 1792, was his *Notes to Bunyan's 'Pilgrim's Progress'*, extracts from which later appeared as footnotes in volume 3 of George Offor's edition of Bunyan's works.

Bradford, who had married about 1779 and had a family of twelve children, remained at Bartholomew Street until 1797, when financial circumstances forced him to accept the more lucrative position of minister at the City Chapel

in Grub Street, London. There he 'ministered with great acceptation till his death' on 16 July 1805 (Jones, 15). He was buried in Bunhill Fields, London.

J. H. THORPE, *rev.* M. J. MERCER

Sources Surman, index of nonconformist ministers, DWL · J. A. Jones, ed., *Bunhill memorials* (1849) · J. Gadsby, *Memoirs of hymn writers and compilers of 17th and 18th centuries* (1855) · [A. C. H. Seymour], *The life and times of Selina, countess of Huntingdon*, 2 vols. (1839) · *The whole works of John Bunyan*, ed. G. Offor, 3 vols. (1862) · J. Julian, ed., *A dictionary of hymnology*, rev. edn (1907) · Foster, *Alum. Oxon.*

Bradford, Sir John Rose, baronet (1863–1935), physician and physiologist, was born in London on 7 May 1863, the only son of Abraham Rose Bradford, naval surgeon, and his wife, Ellen, daughter of Nicholas Littleton. Both parents came from Saltash, near Plymouth, where Littletons had for many years been general practitioners in the neighbourhood. Bradford was educated at University College School, London, and after a year spent learning French at Bruges he entered University College, London, in 1881, as a medical student. Inspired by the teaching of E. R. Lankester, Bradford gained a first class in zoology in 1883 when he graduated BSc. He remained fascinated by the subject, but turned to medicine as a career. He was awarded gold medals in anatomy and physiology in 1884, and in medicine in 1889, when he became MD (Lond.). He also conducted laboratory research, and in 1885 William Bayliss and Bradford published in the *Proceedings* of the Royal Society the first of a series of papers on the electrical changes accompanying nervous stimulation of the salivary glands.

Allowing for a brief period of residence in 1886 as house physician, Bradford's teaching in anatomy and his research in physiology continued to be his main occupation until 1889. He was then appointed to the staff of University College Hospital as assistant physician, with Henry Head as his first clinical clerk. As clinical duties became Bradford's main priority, he joined the staff of the National Hospital for Diseases of the Nervous System, Queen Square, as assistant physician, and was there from 1893 to 1896. He continued his physiological research, aided by much-sought-after research studentships. In this work he attempted to analyse the physiology of the nerve supply to the viscera; he began with the innervation of the blood vessels of the lungs, and moved on to that of the kidneys. But in this research he was outpaced by J. N. Langley. Bradford then turned his attention to kidney diseases, and became recognized as an authority in this branch of medicine.

As professor-superintendent of the Brown Animal Institution from 1895 to 1903 Bradford carried on the tradition of Sir Victor Horsley and Charles Sherrington. The high value of Bradford's physiological studies led to his election in 1894 as FRS at the age of only thirty-one. He was elected FRCP in 1897, and delivered the Goulstonian lecture in 1898, the Croonian lectures in 1904, and the Harveian oration in 1926. In 1899 he married Mary (*d.* 1937), daughter of Thomas Ffoulkes Roberts, of Llanidloes, Montgomeryshire, sometime mayor of Manchester, and niece of the physician Sir William *Roberts; they had no children.

In 1900 Bradford became full physician at University College Hospital, and soon afterwards he ceased all sustained research. He then devoted himself to his teaching duties and to the advancement of scientific thought. He was a pioneer of the idea that all scientific research which is allied or ancillary to medicine should be brought into association with clinical practice. It was this ideal, present in all of his work, which marked him out as a leader in the medical profession. Bradford served on the hospital staff until 1923, and was one of the best clinical teachers to have graced that school. His lectures were clear and informative, despite being delivered without notes, and he was also a source of great encouragement to students on the wards.

Bradford's friendship with David Bruce aroused an interest in tropical medicine, and he sought clinical experience in this field by serving as physician at the Royal Naval Hospital at Greenwich from 1905 to 1919. In 1907 he became a member of the tropical diseases committee of the Royal Society, and in 1908 he was foremost in planning the Sleeping Sickness Bureau which developed into the Tropical Diseases Bureau of the London School of Tropical Medicine. He was senior medical adviser to the Colonial Office from 1912 to 1924. In the Royal Society itself Bradford served from 1908 to 1915 as secretary in the biological section, a post that had not been given to a practising physician for more than eighty years. This enabled him to advance further the relationship of the society with government departments, especially with regard to the study of tropical diseases. He was on the governing body of the Lister Institute from 1899 to 1918 and chairman from 1912 to 1914, and the creation of the Beit Trust for fellowships in medical research in 1909 was largely due to the guidance of Bradford and James Kingston Fowler.

At the outbreak of the First World War Bradford relinquished his interests in London and served in France from 1914 to 1919 as consulting physician to the British expeditionary force, with the rank of major-general, Army Medical Service; he was appointed CB in 1915 and CBE in 1919. Towards the end of that time Bradford conducted a bacteriological study of some of the non-suppurative diseases prevalent in the army. From this he claimed that he and his colleagues had discovered the viruses of trench fever, nephritis, and influenza. However, these claims did not hold because, in this instance, his techniques of study were inaccurate.

Bradford was president of the Royal College of Physicians from 1926 to 1931, and in 1928 he conducted the college celebrations of the tercentenary of the publication of Harvey's *De motu cordis*. He was vice-chairman of the governing body of University College, London, from 1922 to 1932, and chairman in 1932. He was appointed KCMG in 1911 and in 1931 was created a baronet. The universities of Cambridge, Edinburgh, Durham, Dublin, and Christiania conferred honorary degrees upon him. In 1924 he was the

(unsuccessful) Conservative candidate for the parliamentary seat of the University of London.

Tall, and possessing an air of authority, Bradford had a gift for organization. Although stubborn in opinion, he was a warm and helpful man, who was well liked. Bradford died at his home, 8 Manchester Square, London, on 7 April 1935. The baronetcy became extinct on his death.

T. R. ELLIOTT, *rev.* TIM O'NEILL

Sources *BMJ* (13 April 1935), 805–7 · *The Lancet* (13 April 1935), 906–9 · *The Times* (8 April 1935) · T. R. Elliot, *Obits. FRS*, 1 (1932–5), 527–35 · F. W. S. Craig, *British parliamentary election results* (1972) · election certificate, RS
Archives Wellcome L., letters to the Barlow family · Wellcome L., corresp. with Lister Institute
Likenesses R. Schwabe, oils, University College Hospital, London · photograph, RS; repro. in Elliot, *Obits. FRS*
Wealth at death £22,886 9s. 9d.: probate, 22 May 1935, *CGPLA Eng. & Wales*

Bradford, Robert John (1941–1981), Methodist minister and politician, was born in Roe Valley District Hospital, Limavady, co. Londonderry, on 8 June 1941, the seventh child of George Bradford, a labourer and later a milkman, and his wife, Lily, *née* Wright. His parents, who were wartime evacuees from Belfast, soon separated and, after his mother contracted tuberculosis in 1943, he was raised by foster parents (a shipyard worker and his wife, Jimmy and Sadie Nicholson) in Belfast's Sandy Row area. He was educated at Blythe Street primary school and Linfield secondary intermediate school, which he left aged fifteen. After working as an errand-boy, he had an under-eighteen trial for Sheffield Wednesday Football Club; he later drew on his skills in the House of Commons team. But he soon returned to Belfast and to night school where, supported by clerical work at a linen mill, he began to prepare for the Methodist ministry. He studied at Edgehill College, an affiliate of Queen's University, in the years 1965–8, and reacted against the predominant liberal religious values, instead espousing fundamentalist, evangelical theology. Ordained in June 1970, he became minister at Suffolk in south-west Belfast. He married a nurse, Norah Evangeline Thompson of Donaghadee, whose late father had also been a Methodist minister, on 5 December 1970. They adopted a baby daughter, Claire, in 1976.

Suffolk was one of the newer and less stable Roman Catholic–protestant interfaces in Belfast, and by 1972 Bradford was surrounded by a violent struggle between protestants and Catholics for control of housing and territory—republicans burnt down his church hall. Bradford joined the Orange order, and contested the Northern Ireland assembly election in 1973, unsuccessfully, on behalf of William Craig's short-lived Vanguard Unionist Progressive Party. By the time of the British general election of February 1974, Ulster Unionist politics were in turmoil. Many of the upper-middle-class Unionists who supported Brian Faulkner's efforts to implement a compromise political settlement were swept aside. Bradford was elected for Belfast South as a Vanguard member of the United Ulster Unionist Coalition (UUUC), defeating the sitting Faulknerite. In November 1975 he transferred allegiance within the coalition to the Ulster Unionist Party (UUP), believing that his election pledge precluded any further involvement in Craig's efforts to implement 'emergency power-sharing'.

Although continuing to oppose any 'imposed power-sharing' by the British government, and seeing no prospect of reconciling republicanism with unionism, Bradford remained a strong advocate of devolution, believing that neither of the main British parties could be trusted with the security of Northern Ireland. During these years Enoch Powell, supported by James Molyneaux, was influential in counselling the opposing, integrationist view within the party. When the party leadership fell vacant in September 1979, Bradford ran against Molyneaux. He was not successful, though the party returned to an agreed devolutionist position during the 1980s.

During his few years in public life Bradford was not a leading influence on party policy. But his outspoken and strongly evangelical style brought him a considerable popular following. He once declared that 'the problems of Northern Ireland are the result of three things ... the Roman Catholic Church, International Marxism and ecumenical confusion' (Bradford, 106). The most important dimension to his political life was the personal link he was able to maintain between the Ulster Unionists and Ian Paisley's Democratic Unionist Party (DUP) after the early demise of the UUUC. Paisley later claimed, in the House of Commons on 16 November 1981, that the original decision of Bradford to stand for parliament had been taken at his home, though this is not confirmed by Norah Bradford's memoir. In 1979–80 Bradford attempted unsuccessfully to forge a common UUP/DUP policy on the Thatcher government's early devolution plans. In August 1981 he again appealed for Unionist unity, as parliament increased the number of Northern Ireland parliamentary seats from 12 to 17, but the UUP and DUP were unable to agree on a division of seats. At the time of his death he and Paisley were planning a joint tour to counter Irish Republican Army propaganda in the USA. Paisley and his DUP colleagues were ejected from the House of Commons on 16 November 1981 for their behaviour during the debate following Bradford's death, in which Paisley claimed that 'his death comes nearer to me and my colleagues than to anyone else in the House of Commons' (The Times, 17 Nov 1981). Paisley read the lesson at Bradford's funeral.

In his career Bradford, as a robust spokesman for populist political and religious views, helped to retain for the Unionist Party the support of many hardline protestants who might otherwise have defected to the DUP. He opposed the extension of homosexuality law reform to Northern Ireland, and he considered the Fair Employment Agency unnecessary. Shortly after entering parliament he resigned from the Irish Methodist church in protest at its ecumenical direction, though retaining his ordained status through annual summer missions to Methodist communities in Mississippi and neighbouring states. In 1978 he joined with Paisley to interrupt a service celebrating the 500th anniversary of the birth of Sir Thomas More, the first Roman Catholic mass to be held in the Palace of Westminster since the Reformation, believing it to be 'a blasphemous heresy against the Articles of the Established Church' (The Times, 7 Aug 1978). A prominent advocate of restoring the death penalty for the murder of members of the security forces, he called in February 1981 for the home secretary to use powers under the Treason Act of 1351 for this purpose.

On 14 November 1981 Robert Bradford was shot dead by the Provisional IRA at his constituency surgery held at the Finaghy Advice Centre, Finaghy, Belfast. In the event his murder was one of fewer than a dozen assassinations of elected representatives during the Ulster troubles. It may have been the first carried out by the Provisional IRA. Why he was singled out is not entirely clear. His prominent advocacy of capital punishment probably played a part, as did the heightened climate of bitterness that followed the deaths of the IRA hunger strikers in summer 1981. The location of his south Belfast constituency surgery close to strongly republican areas certainly made him a relatively easy target. His murder provoked immense anger in the protestant community, and secretary of state James Prior was roughly handled as he attended the funeral. Though a Methodist minister to the end, Bradford was buried from a Presbyterian church at Dundonald, in east Belfast, on 17 November. His widow, Norah, later supported the conciliatory policy of Northern Ireland first minister David Trimble at a key moment in the aftermath of the Belfast agreement of 1998.   A. C. HEPBURN

Sources The Times (16–19 Nov 1981); (20 May 1978); (24 May 1978); (29 May 1978); (7 April 1978); (19 Nov 1979); (23 Nov 1979); (3 Feb 1981); (3 July 1981); (28 Aug 1981) · N. Bradford, A sword bathed in heaven: the life, faith and cruel death of Robert Bradford MP (1984) · Daily Telegraph (20 Aug 1979) · J. Prior, A balance of power (1986) · CGPLA NIre. (1981) · b. cert. · m. cert.
Likenesses photograph, repro. in The Times (16 Nov 1981)
Wealth at death £500: administration, 4 Dec 1981, CGPLA NIre.

Bradford, Roland Boys (1892–1917), army officer, was born on 23 February 1892 at Carwood House, Witton Park, Bishop Auckland, co. Durham, the fourth son and the fourth of five children of George Bradford (1845–1911), colliery manager, and his wife, Amy Marion Andrews, of Willesborough, Kent. He was educated at Polam Grange and at Epsom College. A keen sportsman but not academically gifted, he was interested at Epsom chiefly in the cadet corps, in which he became a section commander. Initially undecided on a future career, he joined the Church Lads' Brigade on leaving school and in April 1910 was appointed second lieutenant to the local Territorial Force. These experiences led him to determine upon a career in the regular army, and on 22 May 1912 he was gazetted as second lieutenant to the 2nd battalion of the Durham light infantry (DLI).

The First World War presented Bradford, a highly ambitious young officer, with an opportunity to demonstrate his exceptional talents. He was promoted lieutenant on 25 September 1914 and quickly began to emerge as an officer of remarkable ability; within six months of his arrival on the western front his qualities were officially recognized, and on 18 February 1915 he received the Military Cross. His flair for soldiering was acknowledged by rapid promotion; by May 1915 he had attained the rank of adjutant to the 7th battalion, DLI. In April 1916 he was transferred to the 9th battalion, as second-in-command; he was then appointed its commanding officer, and on 4 August promoted lieutenant-colonel.

Within a few months of his transfer to the 9th battalion, DLI (50th division) Bradford had established himself as a spirited and courageous leader. Wounded in fierce fighting around Mametz Wood in September 1916, he refused to be denied the privilege of leading his men into attack and, once engaged in the fight, carried a wounded man back under heavy fire to the assembly trench. His tenacious fighting spirit was again in evidence on 1 October 1916, when the 9th battalion moved to Eaucourt l'Abbaye in support of the main attack. Heavy fighting had resulted in the 47th and 50th divisions losing touch. A battalion in the leading line had suffered very severe casualties, its commander was wounded, and the right flank of the division had become dangerously exposed to the enemy's fire. Recognizing the critical state of battle Bradford asked for permission to command the exposed battalion in addition to his own. With skilful leadership of the two battalions he succeeded in rallying the attack, captured and defended the objective, and secured the flank. For his gallant conduct in this action he was awarded the Victoria Cross.

Bradford's heroic battlefield exploits do not, however, fully account for the deep affection in which he was regarded by those under his command. He had a determined and uncompromising leadership style, expecting the highest level of professionalism from his men, yet this was tempered by a compassionate regard for those under his command. His religious beliefs were central to his life, and he genuinely felt that the Christian faith could be as beneficial to his men as it was to him. He therefore introduced the custom that one verse of the hymn 'Abide with me' should be sung every evening, insisting that 'it should be no mere catch-phrase with us. It means we realise that there is Someone who really abides with us, and who will help us to help ourselves' (*Brigadier-General R. B. Bradford*, 102). He inculcated a strong sense of spiritual unity and purpose within the battalion and felt the loss keenly when any man under his command was killed. He almost always attended their burials, and on one occasion dug the grave of a young officer with his own hands.

On 5 November 1917 Roland was promoted brigadier-general, to command the 186th brigade of the 62nd division, thus becoming at the age of twenty-five the youngest general in the British army. His new battalions were part of the West Riding division of territorials that formed the centre of the attack in the battle of Cambrai. On the eve of battle he requested a list of places where padres could be found during the attack, and expressed the opinion that their presence in such circumstances was as important as that of any general. Despite initial allied success the Cambrai offensive provoked a fierce German counter-attack. Bradford was killed in action on 30 November 1917, when his headquarters, near lock 7 on the

Canal du Nord, was hit by a stray shell. He was buried in Hermies British cemetery, near Havrincourt, France. He was unmarried. There are memorials to him in St Cuthbert's Church, Darlington; Queen Elizabeth Sixth Form College, Darlington; St Paul's Church, Witton Park, co. Durham; Holy Trinity Church, Darlington; and at the Territorial Drill Hall, Darlington, known as the 'Bradford armoury'. John Buchan and Douglas Haig were among those who paid tribute to his outstanding talent and personality.

Two of Bradford's brothers also were killed in the war: James Barker Bradford, a lieutenant in the DLI who had won the Military Cross, died in France on 14 May 1917; George Nicholson Bradford, a lieutenant-commander in the Royal Navy, was killed during the Zeebrugge raid on 23 April 1918, and the Victoria Cross was posthumously awarded him for his actions. The General Bradford Memorial Fund was opened to honour the three brothers, and the contributions used to build the Bradford entrance at Darlington Memorial Hospital.   LESLEY COLLINS

Sources *Brigadier-General R. B. Bradford, V.C., M.C. and his brothers* (privately printed, 1918) · www.geocities.com/bradcrem/bradford_index.htm, Jan 2002 · b. cert.
Archives Durham RO, Durham County Hall archives
Likenesses photographs, repro. in www.geocities.com/bradcrem/bradfordrbb_biog.htm · photographs, Durham County Hall
Wealth at death £10,042 3s. 0d.: probate, 1918, *CGPLA Eng. & Wales*

Bradford, Roy Hamilton (1921–1998), politician, was born in Ligoniel, north Belfast, on 7 July 1921, the son of Joseph Hamilton Bradford, of Rockcorry, co. Monaghan, and his wife, Isabel Mary, *née* McNamee, of Donemana, Tyrone. His father's background in the south of Ireland helps explain Bradford's lifelong easy acquaintance with the Republic of Ireland and many of its leading figures. After studying at the Royal Belfast Academical Institution, he went in 1940 as a foundation scholar to Trinity College, Dublin, still a redoubt of southern unionism. There he took the gold medal in modern languages. After graduating in 1942 with a first-class degree in German and French, he worked in army intelligence in France, Belgium, and Germany from 1943 to 1947. In 1950 he went to live in London where, aside from insurance and restaurant interests (he co-owned a Covent Garden restaurant with the film director John Schlesinger), he worked as a writer and broadcaster for BBC and ITV. He published a number of short stories in the London *Evening Standard*, and in 1960 published his first novel, *Excelsior*. He married Hazel Elizabeth Lindsay (d. 1994), a former chairwoman of the Ulster Unionist Party, and daughter of Captain W. Lindsay, of Belfast, in 1946. They had two sons, Conor and Tobias (Toby).

Bradford entered Stormont as Ulster Unionist MP for the Victoria ward, east Belfast, defeating David Bleakley of the Northern Ireland Labour Party, in 1965. He was seen as a liberal modernizer, close to the prime minister Terence O'Neill, and by 1966 he was assistant chief whip with responsibility for reorganizing the Ulster Unionist Party. In 1968 he was promoted chief whip, with a seat in the cabinet. From 1967 to 1969 he served simultaneously as parliamentary secretary to the Ministry of Education, and from 1969 to 1971 he was minister of commerce. Thereafter, he was from 1971 to 1972 minister of development. He maintained a rapport both with his working-class protestant constituency and with the political and journalistic worlds of Britain and the Republic of Ireland.

Bradford later published a novel, *Last Ditch* (1981), which barely fictionalized the struggle by the Northern Ireland cabinet against direct rule from Westminster, imposed in March 1972. In the Northern Ireland assembly elected in June 1973, he was the Ulster Unionist Party member for East Belfast. He supported his party leader, Brian Faulkner, in negotiating a power-sharing administration and was head of the department of the environment in the subsequent executive. His conservative economic views jarred with those of his colleagues in the Social Democratic and Labour Party, particularly the veteran socialist Paddy Devlin. Bradford was the only member of the executive to stand in the Westminster general election of February 1974. Canvassing under the banner 'Ulster Unionist pro-assembly', he lost the seat of North Down to the united Ulster Unionist coalition candidate, James Kilfedder, by a margin of over 16,000 votes.

Bradford was unhappy with the Sunningdale deal, agreed in December 1973, which proposed a council of Ireland to supplement power-sharing, and his relations with his fellow executive ministers deteriorated. In May 1974, when the loyalist Ulster Workers' Council called a strike in an effort to scupper Sunningdale, he was most vocal in counselling negotiations with the strikers. Ministers in the Social Democratic and Labour Party in particular suspected him of leaking information to the Ulster Workers' Council on the deployment of troops, which he opposed. Twice he offered his resignation to Faulkner. In June 1974, a month after the fall of the executive, he left Faulkner's Northern Ireland Unionist Party and reverted to the anti-Sunningdale official Unionist Party, by then led by Harry West. He criticized the secretary of state for Northern Ireland, Merlyn Rees, for trying to appease the IRA and Ulster Volunteer Force. In the Westminster general election of October 1974 he urged his constituents to vote for the hardliner William Craig for the Belfast East seat.

Bradford's political stage now narrowed. In 1974 he failed to win election to the Northern Ireland convention, but in 1989 he was elected to North Down borough council, where he later served as mayor. He remained a member of the council until his death. He retained a prominent voice through journalism, writing for the *Belfast News-Letter*. He attacked the Anglo-Irish agreement of 1985 but supported Sinn Féin's involvement in the peace process in the 1990s. He was chairman of the Northern Ireland European Movement from 1977, then president from 1987. His last work, *Rogue Warrior of the SAS: the Life of Lt.-Col. R. B. 'Paddy' Mayne, DSO*, co-written with Martin Dillon, was published in 1987. He died in Belfast on 2 September 1998 and was survived by his two sons, his wife, Hazel, having predeceased him.

Bradford observed the limits of Unionist toleration of change in Northern Ireland, but his urbanity and familiarity with non-Ulster milieux permitted him to remain relatively detached from the passions of the troubles. This stymied a prolonged career at the forefront of populist politics, but made him an authoritative and respected commentator.   MARC MULHOLLAND

Sources S. Elliot and W. D. Flackes, *Northern Ireland: a political directory, 1968–99* (1999) · J. F. Harbinson, *The Ulster Unionist party, 1882–1973: its development and organisation* (1973) · D. Hume, *The Ulster Unionist party, 1972–1992* (1996) · R. Fisk, *The point of no return: the strike which broke the British in Ulster* (1975) · *Daily Telegraph* (4 Sept 1998) · *The Times* (7 Sept 1998) · *The Independent* (9 Sept 1998) · *The Guardian* (11 Sept 1998) · WWW

Archives PRO NIre., political, professional, and business papers

Likenesses photograph, 1970, repro. in *Daily Telegraph* · photograph, 1974, repro. in *The Guardian* · photograph, repro. in *The Times* · photograph, repro. in *The Independent*

Bradford, Samuel (1652–1731), bishop of Rochester, was born on 20 December 1652 in St Ann Blackfriars. He was the son of William Bradford, a citizen of London and parish officer during the plague. He was educated at St Paul's School, and then, when that school closed owing to the plague and the fire of London, he went to Charterhouse. He was admitted to Corpus Christi College, Cambridge, in 1669. He matriculated on 27 March 1672; however, owing to some scruples concerning subscriptions, declarations, and oaths, he did not take the BA. On leaving university he returned home and began to study medicine and then religion. After 'a free conversation with some of the best and ablest divines in London' and with the encouragement of Dr Benjamin Whichcote (Lamb, 215), Bradford reconciled his initial scruples and decided to take orders but, as he was too old to return to university, Archbishop Sancroft admitted him to the degree of MA in 1680 by royal mandate. He subsequently became a private tutor in the families of a number of gentlemen. Following the revolution of 1688, Bradford went to London and was ordained deacon on 15 June 1690, and then priest on 5 October the same year by Bishop Compton. At the beginning of 1691, on the recommendation of William Lloyd, John Tillotson, Edward Stillingfleet, Richard Kidder, John Williams, and Thomas Tenison, Bradford was elected as minister of St Thomas's, Southwark, by the governors of St Thomas's Hospital.

Soon after, Bradford was made lecturer of St Mary-le-Bow, Southwark, and was employed at Carlisle House, Lambeth, by Archbishop Tillotson as the tutor to his two grandsons. Following the death of the incumbent of St Mary's, the parishioners, without Bradford's knowledge, attempted to persuade the archbishop to give the rectory to Bradford. Tillotson did so, although he was not happy at the parishioners' attempt to influence his decision. Bradford was installed as rector of St Mary-le-Bow in November 1693, at which time he resigned his cure of St Thomas's and his lectureship, against the wishes of his parishioners. Bradford was friendly with William Whiston. Whiston reported that as rector of St Mary-le-Bow, Bradford, with the assistance of Whiston, refused communion to Lady Caverly, as she was cohabiting with Sir John Hubern. However, as Hubern refused to marry the lady even after Bradford and Whiston had entreated him to do so, Bradford relented and allowed Lady Caverly to receive communion in the future, despite Whiston's advice to the contrary. Similarly, Bradford refused communion to Sir Charles Duncomb, as Duncomb was reported to be keeping a prostitute in his home. Bradford maintained this ban when Duncomb failed to rectify the situation.

Soon after his appointment to St Mary-le-Bow, Bradford took up the lectureship of All Hallows, Bread Street. On 13 July 1697 Bradford was incorporated at Oxford. At some point Bradford married Jane Ellis, the daughter of Captain Ellis of Medbourne in Leicestershire. Together they had one surviving son, William (c.1696–1728), who became archdeacon of Rochester and vicar of Newcastle upon Tyne. They also had two daughters, Jane, who married Reuben Clarke, archdeacon of Essex, and Susanna, who married John Denne, vicar of St Leonard, Shoreditch.

Bradford appears to have been a low-churchman. He was close friends with a number of prominent low-church divines, to whom he owed much of his career advancement. It was probably for his low-church views that he gained the favour of William III, who had a preference for moderate churchmanship. William was so impressed by a sermon which Bradford preached in front of him on 30 January 1698 that he ordered that it should be published and in March made Bradford royal chaplain-in-ordinary, a position he continued to hold under Queen Anne. Bradford continued to preach on many public occasions, often choosing to speak on the importance of Christian unity and charity.

Whiston, a radical low-churchman and Arian, went so far as to imply in his memoirs that Bradford was sympathetic to Arianism. However, his sermons, a number of which were published, do not indicate such views and the eighteenth-century historian John Lamb records that Bradford wrote to Whiston to deny this claim, asserting 'I can as freely and honestly declare myself no Arian as you do that you are one' (Lamb, 228). Bradford's low-church connection can also be seen in his appointment as Boyle lecturer in 1699. The Boyle lectures had been set up in 1691 by the latitudinarian Robert Boyle and were financially supported by the low-church archbishop, John Tenison. Their aim was to defend Christianity from attack through the reconciliation of divine revelation and reason and, as both the historians Margaret Jacob and John Gascoigne have shown, the appointment of lecturers was subject to a strong low-church influence. As lecturer Bradford preached eight sermons on 'The credibility of the Christian revelation, from its intrinsick evidence', which were later published in 1739 in a collection of Boyle lectures. Bradford was also a whig, as well as a low-churchman, committed to both the revolution and the protestant succession. It is probably for this reason that Thomas Hearne described him as 'a most sad, dull, vile wretch' (*Remarks*, 8.126).

Bradford was created DD by Queen Anne when she visited Cambridge University on 16 April 1705, and he later received the prebend of Westminster, into which position he was installed on 23 February 1707. However, Anne's reign witnessed a revival of high-church influence in both the political and ecclesiastical establishment and Bradford's religious and political views hindered his career advancement. This was particularly true of 1710, when partisan animosity was at its height. At the beginning of 1710 Queen Anne offered Bradford the bishopric of St David's. As this was a poor bishopric, Bradford accepted on the proviso that he should be able to hold his prebend of Westminster in commendam. Following the Sacheverell trial and the subsequent growth of tory influence in the government, however, Bradford's request was refused and so he was forced to decline the offer of the bishopric. A little later he was again hindered by the tory party when he lost the position of vice-chancellor of Cambridge University to the tory Dr Gooch, by ninety-five votes to fifty-one.

Bradford's career prospects improved with the whig ascendancy following the accession of George I. On 20 May 1716 he was elected master of Corpus Christi College, Cambridge, a position he continued to hold until 1724. In April 1718 he was offered the bishopric of Carlisle in the place of the deprived high-churchman and tory, Francis Atterbury, and was consecrated by William Wake on 1 June 1718. At first many of the northern gentry, who supported Atterbury, were opposed to their new bishop, but Bradford soon won their approval. On 19 July 1723 he was translated to the bishopric of Rochester, and in the same year he was made dean of Westminster. Bradford also held the position of dean of the honourable Order of the Bath and was a member of the Society for the Propagation of the Gospel in Foreign Parts. Bradford died on 17 May 1731 and was buried, as he had requested in his will, in the north cross aisle of Westminster Abbey. His wife survived him.

REBECCA LOUISE WARNER

Sources *Masters' History of the college of Corpus Christi and the Blessed Virgin Mary in the University of Cambridge*, ed. J. Lamb (1831) · Venn, *Alum. Cant.* · W. Whiston, *Memoirs of the life and writings of Mr William Whiston: containing memoirs of several of his friends also* (1749) · T. Birch, *The life of the Most Reverend Dr John Tillotson, lord archbishop of Canterbury* (1752) · *GM*, 1st ser., 1 (1731) · C. M. L. Bouch, *Prelates and people of the lake counties: a history of the diocese of Carlisle, 1133–1933* (1948) · *The London diaries of William Nicolson, bishop of Carlisle, 1702–1718*, ed. C. Jones and G. Holmes (1985) · PRO, PROB 11/645, sig. 163, fols. 154r–155r · BL, Lansdowne MS 1013, fol. 238 · Christ Church Oxf., Wake MS 21, fol. 135 · M. C. Jacob, *The Newtonians and the English revolution, 1689–1720* (1976) · J. Gascoigne, *Cambridge in the age of the Enlightenment* (1989) · *Remarks and collections of Thomas Hearne*, ed. C. E. Doble and others, 8, OHS, 50 (1907)
Likenesses oils, Westminster Abbey, deanery

Bradford, Samuel Clement (1878–1948), librarian and information scientist, was born on 10 January 1878 at 14 Olmar Street, Ossory Road, Camberwell, London, the son of Samuel Joseph Bradford, a commercial clerk, and his wife, Katherine Lucy Lipscombe. Bradford was trained as a chemist, obtaining a London degree via study at night school. Then in 1899 he joined the staff of the Science Museum Library at South Kensington, initially to work both on the collections and in the library. In 1901 he moved full-time into the library, though his career there was not without its interruptions. On 22 September 1906 he married Cora Mabel (*b.* 1880/81), daughter of Walter Monnery, a manufacturer's agent; there were no children. In the years just before the First World War he was put in charge of the chemistry collections in the museum, and during the war was seconded to the National Physical Laboratory and the chemical warfare department. The Science Museum expected qualified staff to carry out research in their own speciality; Bradford's research was mainly concerned with the theory of solutions and the properties of colloids, for which work he obtained a London DSc. However, library activities dominated his interests, and it is for these that he is primarily remembered.

From the start of his career Bradford realized that the rapid expansion of scientific literature was creating increasing problems for the rapid retrieval of relevant information. He decided that such retrieval would best be aided by employing the most detailed subject classification possible. He saw particular potential in a system of classification that was then being developed on the continent by H. La Fontaine and P. Otlet. This system subsequently became the universal decimal classification (UDC), and Bradford became one of its strongest champions. His opportunity to introduce it into the Science Museum came after the First World War. He was appointed assistant keeper in 1922 and three years later took over as chief librarian when the incumbent retired. He was subsequently promoted to keeper in 1930.

During this period Bradford came into close contact with Professor A. F. C. Pollard at Imperial College. Their discussions of classification led to the formation of the British Society for International Bibliography in 1927. The society became a major focus, especially via the Science Museum Library, for disseminating knowledge of the UDC in the UK. Bradford's leading role in the society led to an increasing international involvement. In particular, he became a lifelong supporter of the International Federation for Documentation based at The Hague. In the event, his own attempt to establish a subject index of scientific literature at South Kensington, based on the UDC, ultimately proved unsuccessful.

His concern with the problems of information retrieval caused Bradford to examine closely the coverage of scientific literature by abstracting and indexing services. This led in the 1930s to a study of how articles devoted to a particular topic were scattered across a range of different journals. On the basis of his results, Bradford formulated his 'law of scattering', which became one of the basic concepts of information science. It describes quantitatively the distribution of articles on a particular topic, ranging from a small core of journals containing many relevant articles to a large number of peripheral journals containing only occasional relevant articles. Bradford argued that such scattering meant that no individual abstracting or indexing service could cover exhaustively all the literature on a given topic. Instead, he pressed for the establishment of an international network of collaborating institutions for such work.

Throughout the inter-war period Bradford concentrated

on developing the outreach of the Science Museum Library. He believed that aiding easy information retrieval in the UK entailed the creation of a national science library. He further believed that the Science Museum Library could be expanded to fulfil this role. During the 1920s and 1930s Bradford tried to obtain support for such an expansion. Though backed by the Science Museum authorities, he encountered considerable and continuing opposition from the Board of Education, which financed the library's activities. By persistence, and by cutting several corners, he managed to build up staff numbers, library stock, and the range of library activities. By the time he retired at the end of 1937 his library was in many ways functioning as the national library that he claimed it to be, not least as regarded loans of scientific publications. As a result of Bradford's efforts, the Science Museum Library after his death came, indeed, to form the basis for the National Lending Library at Boston Spa—subsequently an essential component of the British Library.

Bradford's main hobby was cultivating roses, and he published a book on the subject after he retired. A small man, immaculately dressed, he was remembered by colleagues as always wearing a rose in his button-hole during the growing season. Bradford's most influential publication—a book entitled simply *Documentation* (1948)—was also published in retirement, shortly before his death. It has since become recognized as one of the founding publications of what is now called information science. Bradford died at his home, Mulberry Cottage, 8 Marryat Road, Wimbledon, on 13 November 1948. A. J. MEADOWS

Sources [E. M. R. Ditmas], 'Obituary', *Journal of Documentation*, 4 (1948), 169–74 · D. Follett, *The rise of the Science Museum under Henry Lyons* (1978) · [M. Gosset], 'S. C. Bradford', *Journal of Documentation*, 33 (1977), 173–6 · D. J. Urquhart, 'S. C. Bradford', *Journal of Documentation*, 33 (1977), 177–9 · *CGPLA Eng. & Wales* (1949) · b. cert. · m. cert. · d. cert.
Likenesses photograph, Sci. Mus.
Wealth at death £1333 16s. 1d.: probate, 13 Jan 1949, *CGPLA Eng. & Wales*

Bradford, Sir Thomas (1777–1853), army officer, the eldest son of Thomas Bradford of Woodlands, near Doncaster, and Ashdown Park, Sussex, and his wife, daughter of William Otter, of Welham, Nottinghamshire, was born on 1 December 1777. He entered the army as ensign in the 4th regiment on 20 October 1793. In 1795 he was promoted major into the Nottinghamshire fencibles, at that time stationed in Ireland. He served with the forces opposing the 1798 Irish uprising, and in 1801 was promoted brevet lieutenant-colonel and appointed assistant adjutant-general in Scotland. He was summoned to the colours as a major in 1805, and served with Auchmuty as deputy adjutant-general in 1806 in the expedition to South America.

In June 1808 Bradford accompanied the force under Sir Arthur Wellesley to Portugal, and was present at the battles of Vimeiro and Corunna. On his return to England he became assistant adjutant-general at Canterbury, and lieutenant-colonel in succession of the 34th and 82nd regiments in 1809. In 1810 he was promoted colonel, and took command of a brigade in the Portuguese army. In this capacity he proved most successful and, during the attack on the Arapiles in the battle of Salamanca especially, directed his brigade with distinction. In 1813 he was promoted major-general and made a *mariscal de campo* in the Portuguese service; he was then put in charge of a Portuguese division, which he commanded at Vitoria, the siege of San Sebastian, and in the battle of the Nive. In the fighting before Bayonne he was so severely wounded that he had to return to England.

In 1814 Bradford was placed on the staff of the northern district, and in January 1815 made KCB; he was also awarded the Portuguese order of the Tower and Sword. He missed the battle of Waterloo, at which his younger brother, Lieutenant-Colonel Sir Henry Holles Bradford KCB, who had also been a staff officer in the Peninsula, was killed. He commanded the 7th division of the army of occupation in France from 1815 to 1817, and the forces in Scotland from 1819 until he was promoted lieutenant-general in May 1825. He then became commander-in-chief of the troops in the Bombay presidency, a post he retained for four years. He was colonel, 94th regiment, in 1823–9, and, on returning to England in 1829, became colonel, 30th regiment. In 1831 he was made GCH and in 1838 GCB. In November 1841 he was promoted general, and in 1846 exchanged the colonelcy of the 30th for that of the 4th regiment. Bradford was twice married. He and his first wife had two sons and three daughters who survived infancy. His second wife was the widow of Lieutenant-Colonel Philip Ainslie; they also had children. Bradford died at 13 Eaton Square, London, on 28 November 1853.

H. M. STEPHENS, rev. DAVID GATES

Sources Boase, *Mod. Eng. biog.* · *GM*, 2nd ser., 41 (1854), 315–16 · J. Philippart, ed., *The royal military calendar*, 3 vols. (1815–16) · D. Gates, *The Spanish ulcer: a history of the Peninsular War* (1986) · T. Pakenham, *The year of liberty: the story of the great Irish rebellion of 1798* (1969)
Archives Suffolk RO, Bury St Edmonds, extracts from his letters relating to the defence of Ypres and Tournay
Likenesses W. J. Edwards, stipple and line print (after G. Sanders), NPG

Bradford, William (1590–1657), a founder of Plymouth Colony, was born in Austerfield, Yorkshire, and baptized there on 19 March 1590, the third child and only son of William Bradford (*c*.1560–1591) and Alice Hanson (1562–1597), both from Austerfield yeoman families.

Childhood and study In early childhood he suffered the loss by death first of his father (July 1591), then of his paternal grandfather (1596), with whom he was living following his mother's remarriage, and finally his mother (1597). At the age of seven he was taken in by two uncles, Robert and Thomas Bradford, who brought him up as a farmer.

Where and for how long Bradford went to school is not known, though his aptitude for learning must have been evident in his childhood. Cotton Mather, his earliest biographer, wrote that 'he was a person for *study* as well as *action*' who ultimately commanded not only the classical languages taught in the schools of the day, Latin and

Greek, but also both Dutch and French. Finally, he took up and mastered Hebrew (Mather, 1.104–5). He apparently had no formal university training.

About the age of twelve he became interested in religion and came under the influence of Richard Clyfton, a puritan minister in Babworth, Nottinghamshire, about 10 miles from Austerfield. It was a life-shaping connection, leading soon to Bradford's involvement with a separatist puritan congregation at Scrooby, where Clyfton was associated with John Robinson, a younger minister who would become the pastoral leader of the Scrooby congregation after their move from England to the Netherlands. At Scrooby the congregation met in the home of William Brewster, who became Bradford's mentor and lifelong friend. Writing much later, Bradford recalled the essential puritan principles that compelled the congregation to leave England: they wished to worship God 'according to the simplisitie of the Gospell; without the mixture of mens inventions' (*History of Plymouth Plantation*, 1.8). They believed the established church's insistence on worship practices that had 'no warrante in the word of God' furthered the work of Satan. Together with the 'tiranous power of the prelates' (ibid., 1.18) who tried to enforce universal conformity by imprisoning or silencing nonconforming ministers, these conditions were intolerable to those seeking a purer form of worship. So they 'joyned them selves (by a covenant of the Lord) into a church estate' (ibid., 1.21–2). This covenanted church became the primary source of their identity as a community thenceforth.

Emigration to America Bradford's narration of the Scrooby separatists' emigration from England gives dramatic details of the unexpected separation of men and women, the detention of some in gaols by English authorities— Bradford was confined for a brief time in Boston, Lincolnshire—and their eventual crossing to the continent despite a fierce storm in the North Sea that nearly wrecked them on the Norwegian coast. The congregation was reunited in Amsterdam by the summer of 1608. After about a year there, with John Robinson as sole pastor, the congregation moved to Leiden, where they resided from 1609 until some left for North America in 1620.

Initially faced with 'the grimme and grisly face of povertie' (*History of Plymouth Plantation*, 1.37), the people integrated themselves into Dutch society by taking up useful trades. Bradford became a weaver of fustian, a material made of cotton and silk. In 1611, at the age of twenty-one, he inherited the family property in England, which he sold, reinvesting in a house and business in Leiden. On 10 December 1613, he married the sixteen-year-old Dorothy May (*d.* 1620), recently of Amsterdam but originally from Wisbech in Cambridgeshire.

The congregation's residence in Leiden coincided with a twelve-year truce between the Netherlands and Spain in the Thirty Years' War. Anticipating the expiry of that truce in 1621, and recognizing increased clashing of their own convictions with the more worldly life of their Dutch neighbours, several members of the church, including

Bradford, began as early as 1617 to negotiate for authorization to establish a colony in North America. Anticipating emigration, he sold his house in Leiden in 1619. Financial backing was raised from English investors—'merchant adventurers'—who expected a profitable return from the enterprise.

A small ship, the *Speedwell*, took the 'pilgrims', as Bradford called them, from the Dutch port at Delftshaven to Southampton, where they joined the larger *Mayflower* for the transatlantic voyage, though neither ship is named in Bradford's narrative. His prose in *Of Plimmoth Plantation* captured the emigrants' emotional state:

> They went aborde, and their freinds being with them, where truly dolfull was the sight of that sadd and mournfull parting; to see what sighs and sobbs and praires did sound amongst them, what tears did gush from every eye, and pithy speeches peirst each harte. ... But the tide (which stays for no man) caling them away that were thus loath to departe, their Reve[ren]d pastor [Robinson] falling downe on his knees, (and they all with him,) with watrie cheeks commended them with most fervente praiers to the Lord and his blessing. (*History of Plymouth Plantation*, 1.124-5)

The Bradfords left behind their only child, John, who rejoined his father seven years later. On 5 August 1620 some 102 colonists finally embarked from Southampton, a minority of whom were from the core puritan group in Leiden, the rest being servants or 'strangers', people committed to the colonial project but not to the spiritual community. The smaller ship proved unseaworthy and had to be left behind, necessitating a second departure, this time from Dartmouth, on 6 September.

The Plymouth Colony After a two-month sea crossing the ship was blown off course in approaching North America and took refuge in Cape Cod Bay rather than going farther south as originally planned. The *Mayflower* anchored at the eastern end of Cape Cod, near what is now Provincetown, on 11 November 1620. On that day forty-one men, including Bradford, signed an agreement that became known as the Mayflower compact in which they agreed to 'covenant, and combine our selves togeather into a civill body politick, for our better ordering and preservation' and to submit to 'the generall good of the Colonie' (*History of Plymouth Plantation*, 1.191). Their arrival was followed shortly by Dorothy's drowning in the bay, an unexplained occurrence that remains one of the mysteries of the Plymouth settlement. Miles Standish then led a group of men, including Bradford, in initial explorations on land which included their first encounters with American Indians. The exploration party guided the entire group's landing at Plymouth on 15 December 1620. The timing of their arrival could hardly have been worse, as Bradford says in the most dramatically eloquent passage in his famous history:

> And for the season it was winter, and they that know the winters of that cuntrie know them to be sharp and violent, and subject to cruell and feirce stormes, deangerous to travill to known places, much more to serch an unknown coast. Besides, what could they see but a hidious and desolate wildernes, full of wild beasts and willd men? and what multitudes ther might be of them they knew not. Nether could they, as it were, goe up to the tope of Pisgah, to vew

from this willdernes a more goodly cuntrie to feed their hopes; for which way soever they turnd their eyes (save upward to the heavens) they could have little solace or content in respecte of any outward objects. For summer being done, all things stand upon them with a wetherbeaten face; and the whole countrie, full of woods and thickets, represented a wild and savage heiw.   (ibid., 1.155-6)

Bradford's earliest writing about the Plymouth experience was probably as an anonymous contributor to a work now known as *Mourt's Relation*, whose chief author was Edward Winslow. It gives a partial account of the first year's experience at Plymouth but, because it is in large measure a promotional tract, omits mention of the deaths of half of the colonists in the first winter and spring. Among the other early casualties was John Carver, the colony's first governor, in April 1621. Bradford was chosen to replace him and, discovering an aptitude for leadership, was re-elected in thirty-one of his remaining thirty-six years. In the years when he was not elected governor, he served as an 'assistant', or magistrate. Ten years after the founding, in 1630, Bradford began to write his more comprehensive account of the colony's history, *Of Plimmoth Plantation*, the single most important source of information about Plymouth Colony and Bradford himself, though he avoids details of purely personal autobiography and refers to himself throughout simply as 'the Governor'. He there gives explicit details of the devastation of the population by scurvy and other causes in the initial months.

Success in raising a crop in the first year, thanks to help from the American Indians with seed corn and farming methods, led to the thanksgiving briefly described in both *Mourt's Relation* and *Of Plimmoth Plantation*. About two years after Dorothy's death Bradford wrote to a widow and mother of two sons, Alice Carpenter Southworth (c.1590-1670), whom he had known in Leiden, asking her to join him in Plymouth. They were married on 14 August 1623, and ultimately had two sons and a daughter, William, Joseph, and Mercy.

Despite the thanksgiving celebration, scarcity of provisions and the threat of starvation or undernourishment continued for the first five years. One cause of this was the arrival of uninvited individuals, sent by authority of the merchant adventurers, who were solely concerned with 'their particular'—their own financial gain. The earliest such arrivals brought few provisions or other essentials, so became a drain on the scarce resources of the community. Such problems were aggravated by the failure of the key person among the investors, Thomas Weston, to keep his promises of support to the colonists. The colony would continue to be harassed by unfaithful or treacherous individuals who posed repeated challenges to the wisdom and resolve of Governor Bradford and his fellow magistrates. His patience, wisdom, diplomatic skill, and self-sacrificing commitment made him the effective leader the colony needed.

Of particular importance to the early success of the colony were a few key American Indians who allied themselves with the English settlers and advised them in their relations with the larger Indian presence in the area. These included Tisquantum (Squanto), sole survivor of the Patuxet people, Samoset, an Algonquian, and Hobomok, a Wampanoag, all of whom had learned English from previous contact with English explorers and fishermen. With Squanto as intermediary, Bradford's government came to an important peace agreement with Massasoit, chief of the Wampanoag, a treaty that survived until the time of Massasoit's son Metacom, known to the English as King Philip. Bradford's public approach to the natives of the area was similar to that described in Captain John Smith's writings about his experience in Virginia, where dialogue and a desire for co-operation were backed up by the threat of firm physical force. Bradford followed a policy of seeking peaceful relations with the neighbouring American Indians. Throughout his career he enforced a strict policy requiring that all land must be purchased before it could be settled. Another manifestation of his government's respect for their humanity was the prosecution, conviction, and execution of three Englishmen in 1638 for the murder of a Narragansett man.

The major enemies of the colony, Bradford discovered, were not the native people but Englishmen. In particular, Thomas Morton, who established a separate colony at Mount Wollaston, offended the Plymouth colonists' sense of how best to relate to their neighbours when his colonists gave guns to the American Indians and their men behaved with wanton abandon with the Indian women. Bradford's government reacted sternly in capturing Morton, whom Bradford called the 'lord of misrule', and shipping him back to England. Other culprits were the first minister, John Lyford, sent by the adventurers in London, and his companion John Oldham, a self-interested trader. Bradford intercepted letters that exposed Lyford as a hypocrite who was undermining the colony by making false reports to the London backers. His past, Bradford learned, included expulsion from Ireland for sexual offences while a minister there, and later womanizing and adulteries. Both Lyford and Oldham were expelled.

Bradford's governorship was also troubled until the mid-1630s by the colony's major financial difficulties. Isaac Allerton, one of the Leiden émigrés and a son-in-law of the revered Brewster, proved unworthy of the governor's trust. In 1627 Bradford and eleven others had bought out the joint stock company for £1800 and thus accepted responsibility for the colony's troubled finances. They entrusted Allerton to conduct their business abroad but, in seeking personal profit, he ran the colony into much greater debt, to the personal loss of Bradford. After Allerton's dismissal a sadder but wiser Bradford concluded that 'Even amongst freinds, men had need be carfull whom they trust' (History of Plymouth Plantation, 2.121). In 1630 the Warwick patent from the Council for New England named Bradford as the sole proprietor of the colony. He immediately included as joint owners all of the original settlers—the 'Old Comers'. Finally, responding in 1639 to a rare challenge to his authority, Bradford signed over his privileges as proprietor to all the freemen of the

colony. A consistent mark of his leadership was his valuing community cohesiveness above personal gain.

Character and achievement No portrait of Bradford exists, but his belongings at his death included a violet-coloured cloak, a red waistcoat, and a suit with silver buttons (Smith, 270), belying the common misconception that puritans were averse to colourful adornment. His lifelong love of learning was manifest in his possession of Plymouth's second-largest library. Late in life he demonstrated his intellectual vitality in various literary efforts. He wrote the first of three 'dialogues' in 1648. It recalls for the younger generation the exemplary lives and values of the original Scrooby members. The second dialogue has not survived, but the third, written in 1652, defends the validity of the congregational form of church government. Like many other first-generation New England puritans, Bradford also wrote poetry; seven of his poems are still extant. In his early sixties he returned to his study of Hebrew in the hope that by reading the original language of the scriptures, he would be able 'to see how the words, and phrases lye in the holy texte, and to discerne somewhat of the same, for my owne contente' (Meyer, 14).

His personal and political skills brought him success as a leader and ensured the survival of Plymouth Colony. But Bradford's most important and lasting claim to distinction is his chronicle of Plymouth Colony's creation and early years, *Of Plimmoth Plantation*. The fullest history of early American colonial experience and a work exemplifying the strength of the 'plain style', this book describes the expatriate pilgrims' experience until 1646, the last year for which he included any details, writing only the dates '1647' and '1648' on the final page. While scholars have differed on whether the book is most characterized by a tone of sadness or a theme of hope, it is, throughout, the clearest example in the literature of American colonization of 'providential history'—an interpretation of human experience as governed by God's providence. While showing the shortcomings of people and the decline of community cohesiveness, a wrenching source of 'greefe and sorrow of hart' in his old age, he still saw life's experience as the work of a beneficent God. Bradford died on 9 May 1657 in Plymouth, where he was buried.

SARGENT BUSH, JUN.

Sources W. Bradford, *History of Plymouth plantation, 1620–1647*, ed. W. C. Ford, 2 vols. (1912) [orig. title *Of Plimmoth plantation*] • W. Bradford, 'A dialogue or 3d conference betweene some yonge-men borne in New-England, and some ancient-men, which came out of Holand and old England, concerning the church, and the governmente thereof', *Proceedings of the Massachusetts Historical Society*, 11 (1870), 407–464 [introduction by C. Doune, pp. 396–406] • W. Bradford, 'A dialogue, or, The sume of a conference between som younge men borne in New-England and sundery ancient men that came out of Holland and old England *anno domini* 1648', *Publications of the Colonial Society of Massachusetts*, 22 (1920), 115–41 • *William Bradford: the collected verse*, ed. M. G. Runyan (1974) • *A journal of the pilgrims at Plymouth: Mourt's relation, a relation or journal of the English plantation* (1622); repr. with an introduction by D. B. Heath (1963) • I. S. Meyer, ed., *The Hebrew exercises of Governor William Bradford* (1973) • B. Smith, *Bradford of Plymouth* (1951) • G. D. Langdon, *Pilgrim colony: a history of New Plymouth, 1620–1691* (1966) • C. Mather, *Magnalia Christi Americana*, 7 bks in 2 vols. (1820) • P. D. Westbrook,

William Bradford (1978) • P. Gay, *A loss of mastery: puritan historians in colonial America* (1966) • D. Levin, 'William Bradford: the value of puritan historiography', *Major writers of early American literature*, ed. E. Emerson (1972), 11–31 • A. B. Howard, 'Art and history in Bradford's *Of Plymouth plantation*', *William and Mary Quarterly*, 28 (1971), 237–66 • R. Daly, 'William Bradford's vision of history', *American Literature*, 44 (1973), 557–69 • J. Rosenmeier, '"With my owne eyes": William Bradford's *Of Plymouth plantation*', *Typology and early American literature*, ed. S. Bercovitch (1972), 69–105 • W. P. Wenska, 'Bradford's two histories: pattern and paradigm in *Of Plymouth plantation*', *Early American Literature*, 13 (1978), 151–64 • D. Laurence, 'William Bradford's American sublime', *Publications of the Modern Language Association of America*, 102 (1987), 55–65
Archives Mass. Hist. Soc. • Massachusetts State Archives, Boston, *Of Plimmoth plantation*
Wealth at death £900: Smith, *Bradford*, 314; will and inventory, *The Mayflower Descendant*, 2 (1900), 228–34

Bradford, William (1663–1752), printer, was born in Barwell, Leicestershire, on 20 May 1663, the son of William Bradford (*d.* 1667) and his wife, Ann, and was baptized in the parish church there on 30 May. Though the baptism took place in the Anglican church, according to law, it seems probable that his parents were members of the Society of Friends because he learned the printing trade in London with Andrew Sowle, at the sign of the Crooked Billet in Holloway Lane, Shoreditch; by the time Bradford was freed on 3 December 1684, Sowle was the exclusive, though not official, printer to the Quakers, although he had to operate clandestinely much of the time. When a client and fellow Friend, William Penn, proposed his new colony in North America in 1682, Sowle no doubt arranged for his former apprentice to join Penn there in 1685 as the colony's first printer, based in the Oxford township, near Philadelphia. Bradford married Sowle's eldest daughter, Elizabeth (*d.* 1731), on 28 April 1685, prior to his departure, and their first child, Andrew, was born in Philadelphia about 1686. In 1690 Bradford helped construct William Rittenhouse's new paper mill near Philadelphia, the first in the English colonies, which supplied his paper needs for many years.

As holder of a contract with the Quakers, Bradford was expected to be in the service of the dominant political establishment, led by Thomas Lloyd and his supporters in the yearly meeting of Friends. Bradford, however, came to align himself with a heterodox Quaker, George Keith, in his criticism of the establishment, publishing some of Keith's broadsides and pamphlets. In August 1692 Bradford and his distributor John McComb were tried and eventually gaoled by the quarter sessions court for printing works without an imprint, a violation of the same Licensing Act of 1662 as had bedevilled Bradford's old master, Sowle. Bradford's press and type were seized during his arrest but they were returned to him after he had completed his sentence on his petition to the provincial council in April 1693. Meanwhile, Bradford, reading the political climate of Pennsylvania correctly, had applied to be, and received appointment as, public printer in New York that same month. As in Pennsylvania, he would become the first printer in the colony and settlement, then only a small Anglo-Dutch village. He lived first in

Pearl Street in Manhattan; from 1698 he was resident in Stone Street.

Although Bradford found it difficult to collect his stipend from the royal governors—he did not receive full payment until 1717—his life in Manhattan was mainly harmonious. He was appointed public printer of New Jersey in 1702, concurrently with his New York post, and in 1710 became clerk of the New Jersey assembly. Meanwhile his New York printing office turned out a steady stream of job work, session laws, almanacs, and religious tracts, some of considerable interest—such as the Book of Common Prayer in the Mohawk language, for the use of missionaries. By 1700 Bradford had returned to the Anglican fold and he became a vestryman of Trinity parish in 1703. His Quaker friend George Keith had also converted to the Church of England and, as a representative of Dr Thomas Bray's Society for the Propagation of the Gospel in Foreign Parts, he engaged in an energetic campaign to proselytize Friends in the middle colonies, with publications printed by Bradford. Bradford maintained cordial relations with English Quakers, however, importing books and other publications for resale from his sister-in-law Tace *Sowle, who had inherited her father Andrew's business in London. In 1713 Bradford's son Andrew, having learned the trade in his father's office, returned to Philadelphia to open a printing establishment there. When Benjamin Franklin, aged seventeen, left Boston in 1723 to seek his fortune with William Bradford, Bradford introduced him to the two printers then operating in Philadelphia, his son Andrew and Samuel Keimer.

From 1714 Bradford was living in the north-west corner of Hanover Square. In 1725 he started New York's first newspaper, the *New-York Gazette*. To support his enterprises he was operating a paper mill in Elizabethtown, New Jersey, by 1728, and acquiring real estate in the vicinity. At some point following the death of his wife in 1731, Bradford married a woman named Smith. John Peter Zenger, his former apprentice, was brought to trial in 1734 for libelling the royal government, but Bradford, now seventy-one years old, remained studiously neutral during the celebrated case. In the same year he moved elsewhere in Hanover Square, but by 1737 he was back in Pearl Street where he lived until his death. He retired from his businesses in 1744 and died at home on Saturday evening, 23 May 1752, having that morning, aged eighty-nine, according to Isaiah Thomas, 'walked over a great part of the city' (Thomas, 461). He was buried before the end of the month in Trinity churchyard on Wall Street, New York.

Bradford was not a distinguished printer, or newspaper editor, or bookseller, but he was a pioneering figure in all three of these professions in colonial America. His principal talents appear to have been in the realm of human relationships: he acquired and kept friends and acquaintances in many spheres, on both sides of the Atlantic.

CALHOUN WINTON

Sources H. Amory and D. D. Hall, eds., *The colonial book in the Atlantic world* (2000) • A. J. Wall, 'William Bradford, colonial printer', *Proceedings of the American Antiquarian Society*, 73 (1963), 361–84 • A. J.

DeArmond, *Andrew Bradford: colonial journalist* (1949) • I. Thomas, *The history of printing in America*, rev. 2nd edn (1970) • E. B. Bronner and D. Fraser, *William Penn's published writings, 1660–1726: an interpretive bibliography* (1986) • ESTC • C. W. Miller, *Benjamin Franklin's Philadelphia printing, 1728–1766: a descriptive bibliography* (1974) • R. S. Mortimer, 'The first century of Quaker printers', *Journal of the Friends' Historical Society*, 40 (1948), 37–49; 41 (1949), 78–84 • D. F. McKenzie, ed., *Stationers' Company apprentices*, [2]: *1641–1700* (1974) **Archives** New York Historical Society, MSS

Bradick, Walter (1705/6–1794), merchant, of unknown parents, was a trader at Lisbon when he was ruined by the earthquake which destroyed that city in 1755. On returning to England he had the further misfortune to lose his eyesight, and in 1774, on the nomination of the queen, he was admitted to Sutton's Hospital (the Charterhouse), London, where he died on 19 December 1794, aged eighty-eight.

An obituary in the *Gentleman's Magazine* claims that Bradick was the author of *Choheleth, or, The Royal Preacher* (1765), an anonymous paraphrase of Ecclesiastes in Miltonic blank verse, dedicated to George III. However, according to a manuscript note by the Methodist preacher Joseph Sutcliffe in a copy of the 1824 reprint of *Choheleth*, the poem was written by Dennis Furley, said to be the merchant whose miraculous escape from death in the Lisbon earthquake is recounted in John Wesley's *Journals* (8 February 1768). His son was John Wesley's disciple and correspondent, the Revd Samuel Furley (1732?–1795). Peter Hall (1803–1849) suggested that the Hebrew scholar Robert Lowth (1710–1787) wrote *Choheleth* (*GM*, 1830).

JAMES SAMBROOK

Sources *GM*, 1st ser., 65 (1795), 83 • N. Higgins, ed., *A paraphrase on the book of Ecclesiastes* [1824] [annotation by J. Sutcliffe, U. Edin. copy] • *GM*, 1st ser., 100/2 (1830), 386 • *The letters of the Rev. John Wesley*, ed. J. Telford (1931); repr. (1960) • *DNB*

Bradlaugh, Alice (1856–1888). *See under* Bonner, Hypatia Bradlaugh (1858–1935).

Bradlaugh, Charles (1833–1891), politician and freethinker, was born on 26 September 1833 at home at 31 Bacchus Walk, Hoxton, London, the eldest of seven children born to Charles Bradlaugh, a solicitor's clerk, and his wife, Elizabeth Trimby, a former nursemaid. He was baptized at St Leonard, Shoreditch, on 8 December 1833, and educated at local elementary day schools and St Peter's Sunday school, Hackney Road, where he became a teacher.

While preparing for confirmation in 1849, Bradlaugh questioned the doctrines of the church. Pressure to conform caused him to leave home and he took lodgings with Elizabeth Sharples Carlile, the widow of Richard Carlile, and her family at the Warner Street temperance hall. He gave his first public lecture—'The past, present and future of theology'—10 October 1850. Having failed to earn his living as a coal merchant, in December 1850 he enlisted in the 7th dragoon guards and was posted to Ireland. This had a deep effect on his political views. In 1852 his father died, and the following year a legacy from his great-aunt

Charles Bradlaugh (1833–1891), by Walter Sickert, exh. New English Art Club 1890

was used to purchase his discharge; he took a job as errand boy (and was soon promoted to clerk) with Thomas Rogers, a solicitor of 70 Fenchurch Street. On 5 June 1855 he married Susannah (Susan) Lamb Hooper at St Philip's, Stepney. Their first child, Alice *Bradlaugh [*see under* Bonner, Hypatia Bradlaugh], was born on 30 April 1856 at their home at 4 West Street, Bethnal Green; Hypatia *Bonner followed on 31 March 1858, and Charles on 14 September 1859.

Bradlaugh lived a double life: professionally, he was a skilled lawyer, though nominally only a solicitor's clerk; privately, he was also a free thought and radical lecturer with a growing national reputation. To protect his employer's name, in 1855 he adopted the pseudonym Iconoclast, with which he kept his identities apart until 1868. From November 1858 he edited a free thought periodical, *The Investigator*, which failed in August 1859, and he was then invited to co-edit the *National Reformer*, with which his name was associated as editor (1860–64; 1866–1890) and owner (from 1862) until his death. Bradlaugh also became noted in radical politics: at the Hyde Park Sunday trading riots (July 1855); in support of Felice Orsini, the would-be assassin of Napoleon III (1858); and in campaigns for an extension of the franchise in Britain (from 1859).

The Bradlaughs moved from Bethnal Green to 3 Hedger's Terrace, Cassland Road, Hackney, in 1857 and to Elysium Villa, Northumberland Park Road, Tottenham, in 1859. After a brief return to the City at 12 St Helen's Place, Bishopsgate, in 1862, they settled in 1864 at Sunderland Villa, next door to their former Tottenham address, and advertised for a second servant. Having failed to secure articles from Rogers, in 1858 Bradlaugh was apprenticed clerk to Thomas Harvey, who also refused to article him and eventually went bankrupt. He then moved to Montague Leverson, a radical with equally dubious business dealings, who articled him in June 1862, but the two men parted in 1864. After this, Bradlaugh supplemented his earnings from lecturing and journalism with freelance legal and financial work, notably for the Naples Colour Company (1866–9). He was soon several hundreds of pounds in debt and his wife was becoming an alcoholic in the company of a former army friend, the poet James Thomson. In 1870 Sunderland Villa was given up, and Susan Bradlaugh and the two girls went to live with her parents in Midhurst, Sussex; young Charles died of kidney failure in July; and Bradlaugh himself rented two rooms at 29 Turner Street, Commercial Road, Stepney, where he dedicated himself full-time to propagandism.

During this period of crisis Bradlaugh took a leading part on the executive of the Reform League (1865–7) and formed the National Secular Society with himself as president (1866), a post he was to retain (except during 1871–4) until 1890. In 1867 he helped the Fenians draft their manifesto, and in 1868 he was prosecuted for failing to deposit a surety of £400 in respect of the *National Reformer*, which led in 1869 to the repeal of this last 'tax on knowledge'. In 1870 he took up the cause of the French republicans, influenced by the republican Vicomtesse Mina de Brimont Brassac, through whom he became acquainted with Prince Jérôme Napoleon, who lent him money. His reputation as a leading radical was further enhanced in the 1870s, when he led the short-lived republican movement in Britain and published his two most successful lectures, *The Land, the People and the Coming Struggle* (1871) and *The Impeachment of the House of Brunswick* (1872); he also founded the National Republican League in 1873.

In 1868 and twice in 1874 Bradlaugh unsuccessfully contested a parliamentary seat at Northampton, and he made financially unsuccessful lecture tours of the United States in 1874 and 1875. A legacy of £2500 enabled him to move in February 1877 from Turner Street to 20 Circus Road, St John's Wood, quite near Annie Besant, who had joined the National Secular Society in 1874 and become his closest friend. Susan Bradlaugh died in May 1877 and Alice and Hypatia moved in with their father. Further notoriety came in 1877, when Bradlaugh and Besant began the Freethought Publishing Company to re-issue Charles Knowlton's birth-control pamphlet *The Fruits of Philosophy* (1832), which had been prosecuted for obscenity. After a trial which gave extensive publicity to the idea of birth control, Bradlaugh and Besant were sentenced to six months' imprisonment but the verdict was quashed on a technicality.

In 1880 Bradlaugh was elected junior Liberal MP for Northampton. He applied to substitute an affirmation for the oath on grounds of unbelief. A select committee ruled against this, so Bradlaugh asked to take the oath, which was also refused. He became a symbol of people against parliament. Opposition to him was based partly on political expediency by a small group of Conservative backbenchers and partly on outrage against his atheism, republicanism, and advocacy of birth control. For five years he outwitted the best legal brains in several court cases to defend himself from heavy fines for having voted without being first sworn. He successfully recontested Northampton in 1881, 1882, 1884, and 1885, and on four occasions pleaded his case at the bar of the house. A government bill to change the law was defeated by three votes in 1883 and not until after the general election of 1886 did the speaker overrule opposition and allow Bradlaugh to take the oath. In 1888 he secured an act to permit parliamentary affirmations.

By this time Bradlaugh's opposition to socialism, publicized on 17 April 1884 in a debate with H. M. Hyndman on *Will Socialism Benefit the English People?*, had made his radical individualism appear less threatening. He was a hardworking MP, who gathered evidence for the royal commission on market rights and tolls, secured a select committee on perpetual pensions, sat on the royal commission on vaccination (1889), and championed native rights in India, which brought him recognition as back-bench 'member for India'. In December 1889 he attended the Indian National Congress in Bombay.

Bradlaugh was one of the best orators and champions of the popular cause in Victorian Britain, but by the late 1880s he was increasingly out of touch and ill with cardiac asthma and hereditary kidney weakness (Bright's disease). He died at home in Circus Road on 30 January 1891 and was buried next to his daughter Alice (who died of meningitis in 1888) at Brookwood necropolis on 3 February. He was survived by Hypatia, who married Arthur Bonner, a printer, in 1885.   EDWARD ROYLE

Sources H. B. Bonner and J. M. Robertson, *Charles Bradlaugh: a record of his life and work … with an account of his parliamentary struggle, politics and teachings, by John M. Robertson*, 4th edn, 2 vols. (1898) · D. Tribe, *President Charles Bradlaugh, MP* (1971) [incl. full bibliography of Bradlaugh's writing] · W. L. Arnstein, *The Bradlaugh case: a study in late Victorian opinion and politics* (1965); repr. as *The Bradlaugh case: atheism, sex, and politics among the late Victorians* (1983) · F. D'Arcy, 'Charles Bradlaugh and the world of popular radicalism, 1833–91', PhD diss., U. Hull, 1979 · E. Royle, *Radicals, secularists and republicans: popular freethought in Britain, 1866–1915* (1980) · E. Royle, ed., *The Bradlaugh papers* (1975) · J. P. Gilmour, ed., *Champion of liberty: Charles Bradlaugh* (1933) [with a bibliography compiled by H. B. Bonner] · J. Saville, ed., *A selection of the political pamphlets of Charles Bradlaugh, with a preface and biographical notes* (1970) · *Humanity's gain from unbelief, and other selections from the works of Charles Bradlaugh*, ed. H. B. Bonner (1929) · R. Manvell, ed., *The trial of Annie Besant and Charles Bradlaugh* (1976) · E. Royle, 'Charles Bradlaugh, free thought and Northampton', *Northamptonshire Past and Present*, 6 (1978–83), 141–50 · R. E. Quinault, 'The fourth party and the Conservative opposition to Bradlaugh, 1880–1888', *EngHR*, 91 (1976), 315–40 · J. Rich, 'The Bradlaugh case: religion, respectability and politics', *Australian Journal of Politics and History*, 21 (1975), 38–51 · N. H. Sinnott, 'Charles Bradlaugh and Ireland', *Journal of the Cork Historical and Archaeological Society*, 2nd ser., 77 (1972), 1–24 · *National Reformer* (8 Feb 1891) · baptism cert.

Archives Bishopsgate Institute, London, corresp., papers, and family papers · Bodl. Oxf., corresp. · Hackney Archives, London, papers · Shoreditch Public Library, Pitfield Street, London, artefacts | BL, corresp. with W. E. Gladstone, Add. MS 44111 · BL OIOC,

letters to William Digby, MS Eur. D 767 · Co-operative Union Arch-
ive, Manchester, letters to George Holyoake · Glos. RO, corresp.
with Sir Michael Hicks Beach · HLRO, corresp. with Sir H. B. W.
Brand · Northampton Library, Thomas Adams MSS, relating to
Bradlaugh's election contests · PRO, papers relating to Regina *v*
Bradlaugh and Besant

Likenesses A. Millière, photograph, 1866–9, repro. in Gilmour,
ed., *Champion of liberty*, facing p. 32 · W. Sickert, oils, exh. New English Art Club 1890, National Liberal Club, London [*see illus.*] ·
W. Sickert, pencil drawing, 1890, NPG · W. Sickert, oils, 1891, Man.
City Gall. · F. Verheyden, bronze bust, 1893, repro. in Gilmour, ed.,
Champion of liberty, facing p. 102; stolen from Brookwood necropolis, Woking · C. Holding, plaster bust, 1894, National Secular Society, Bradlaugh House, 47 Theobald's Road, London · G. Tinworth,
terracotta statue, 1894, Abington Square, Northampton ·
F. Verheyden, bust, marble, 1897, Shoreditch Public Library, Pit-
field Street, London · J. Collier, portrait, 1918; photograph, South
Place Ethical Society, Conway Hall, Red Lion Square, London ·
H. Furniss, pen-and-ink caricature, NPG · F. C. Gould, double portrait, chalk caricature (with F. O'Driscoll), NPG · S. P. Hall, pencil
drawings, NPG · Spy [L. Ward], chromolithograph caricature, NPG;
repro. in *VF* (12 June 1880) · W. Strang, etching, BM, NPG · cartoons,
repro. in Gilmour, ed., *Champion of liberty* · photographs (between
the ages of twenty and fifty-seven), repro. in Gilmour, ed., *Champion of liberty*

Wealth at death £4586 4s. 0d.: probate, 21 March 1891, CGPLA
Eng. & Wales

Bradlaw, Sir Robert Vivian (1905–1992), dentist, was born
on 14 April 1905 at 7 Rathmines Road, Blackrock, Dublin,
the son of Philip Archibald Bradlaw, dentist, and his wife,
Henrietta Louise, *née* Samuel. He was a member of a large
family with medical and dental connections. His father
died when Bradlaw was in his early teens, and he completed his general education at Cranleigh after he and his
mother had moved to England. He subsequently studied
both dentistry and medicine in London at Guy's Hospital,
gaining his LDS in 1926 and MRCS LRCP in 1928. After
qualifying he did a spell as a ship's surgeon, visiting the
Far East, and also undertook some private dental practice.
He also held part-time academic appointments, as a demonstrator at the Royal Dental Hospital in Leicester Square,
where he undertook research into the nerve supply of
dentine, and at the National Hospital in Queen Square.

By the mid-1930s Bradlaw had decided on the longer-
term direction of his career, resolving to devote himself in
part to advancing the discipline of dental surgery, which
was still emerging as a learned profession, and at the same
time establishing himself in the burgeoning dental academic world. In 1936 he was appointed to the newly established chair of dental surgery at the then small dental
school at Newcastle upon Tyne, within the University of
Durham. He became dean, and with considerable vision
began the transference of function and power from visiting consultants, who hitherto had been the only people
available to run dental schools, to a system involving a
core of full-time staff who not only could teach but who
also, like their medical counterparts, possessed the
expertise and responsibility to advance knowledge. He
acted also as a consultant to the ministries of Pensions and
Supply and the Royal Navy, and served on two influential
national bodies, the Central Health Services Council and
the government's standing dental advisory committee, of

which he became chairman. His influence on dental education during this period was far-reaching and profound,
and in the post-war years the developments he had instituted in Newcastle became the model for fundamental
changes in the pattern of undergraduate dental education
throughout the country.

However, by the late 1930s Bradlaw's interests were
extending on a broader front to encompass postgraduate,
as well as undergraduate, dental education, and also the
professional political processes governing the provision
of the country's dental services. He made a substantial
impact nationally in these areas during the war years and
afterwards, when his forward-ranging vision was ahead of
that of most of his contemporaries. As dean of the Newcastle dental school he served as a member of the Dental
Board of the United Kingdom, the governing body of the
profession operating under the auspices of the General
Medical Council. In 1943 he became a member of the
Teviot committee, set up by the minister of health to consider the measures needed to improve dental education,
research, and legislation. One recommendation in the
final report of the committee in 1946 was that the Dental
Board should be replaced by an independent General Dental Council. Bradlaw was also involved with other luminaries, including Sir Alfred Webb Johnson, Sir Wilfred
Fish, and Sir William Kelsey Fry, in setting up a faculty of
dental surgery within the Royal College of Surgeons of
England. This was established by supplemental charter in
1947 and, in recognition of his major contribution, Bradlaw was appointed as the first dean of the faculty. He was
Hunterian professor at the Royal College of Surgeons in
1955, receiving the Colyer gold medal in the same year and
the honorary gold medal of the college in 1968. During his
period as dean he initiated the examination for the fellowship in dental surgery, analogous to the FRCS in general
surgery. In 1974 he delivered the first Bradlaw oration at
the Royal College of Surgeons.

In 1960, after twenty-four years of notable contribution
to the university and its dental school, Bradlaw left Newcastle and returned to London to become dean and director of studies at the Institute of Dental Surgery, director
of the Eastman Dental Hospital, and professor of oral
medicine in the University of London, posts which he held
until he retired in 1970. He was an accomplished lecturer,
his field of special interest being the manifestations in the
mouth of general disease. His presentations were
enriched with knowledge and experience gained from his
own research. In 1954 he received the British Dental Association's Howard Mummery prize for his work on oral
syphilis, and was also a recipient of the Tomes prize.

Under the Dentists Act 1956, the General Dental Council
was created to replace the Dental Board of the United
Kingdom. Bradlaw, a member of the new council from the
outset, became president in 1964, succeeding Sir Wilfred
Fish, previously chairman of the Dental Board. He retired
as president in 1974. In his presidential address in 1973 he
advocated the inclusion of items of preventive dental
treatment in the National Health Service's general dental
service scale of fees—an innovative concept for its time.

He was also very active in the British Dental Association, serving as a member of its representative board, and as president of the association in 1974.

As well as holding various postgraduate qualifications and diplomas, Bradlaw was the recipient of many honours, including doctorates from ten universities. Of particular satisfaction to him was the degree of doctor of civil law awarded by the University of Newcastle upon Tyne in 1965. In 1975 he was made an honorary fellow of the Royal Society of Medicine. He was also chevalier de la santé publique (France); knight, order of St Olaf (Norway); and commander, order of Homayoun (Iran). He was appointed CBE in 1950 and knighted in 1965.

Bradlaw was a widely read, cultivated man with diverse interests, including cooking, eighteenth-century paintings, Chinese and Korean celadon ware china, fashioning pottery, and cultivating orchids. All these subjects were studied with the same dedication that he devoted to his professional activities. In his Newcastle days he liked in addition to shoot and fish, while golf was a challenge which he pursued with vigour. Some time during mid-life he became a Roman Catholic, deriving great spiritual comfort from his religion for the rest of his life. Although essentially a private man, he was also a sociable and convivial host. His unobtrusive kindnesses were appreciated by many, yet he had a dignified, serious demeanour which appeared formidable to subordinate colleagues. He was a shrewd judge of junior colleagues' abilities and potential, and gave valuable career guidance to many. His wit and self-deprecating sense of humour were well known; when he arrived for a meeting at the University Senate House on the morning his knighthood was announced, he recounted with much glee how, in the railway carriage on his way into London, one avid reader of *The Times* turned to his neighbour and said 'look at the people they give knighthoods to these days' (private information). He never married. He died on 12 February 1992 at Stoke Goldington, near Newport Pagnell, Buckinghamshire, the place to which he had retired. In his will he requested that there should be no announcement of his death and no memorial service.   Martin C. Downer

Sources British Dental Association archives, London · *Guy's Hospital Gazette* (6 Feb 1965) · *British Dental Journal*, 118 (1965), 541 · *British Dental Journal*, 122 (1967), 371 · *The Probe* (1973), 274-6 · *The Probe* (1974), 240-43 · G. H. Leatherman, 'The toast is Sir Robert Bradlaw', *British Dental Journal*, 158 (1985), 280-81 · *British Dental Journal*, 172 (1992), 293 · *British Dental Journal*, 173 (1992), 158 · *The Times* (2 March 1992) · *The Independent* (17 March 1992) · *WWW*, 1991-5 · Burke, *Peerage* · b. cert. · personal knowledge (2004) · private information (2004)
Archives British Dental Association, London · General Dental Council, London · RCS Eng.
Likenesses Rickard, bust, 1972, RCS Eng. · A. Zinkeisen, oils, General Dental Council, London · photograph, repro. in *The Times* · photograph, repro. in *British Dental Journal*, 172/7 (1992), 293
Wealth at death £470,816: probate, 12 May 1992, *CGPLA Eng. & Wales*

Bradley, Andrew Cecil (1851–1935), literary scholar, was born on 26 March 1851 at Park Hill, Clapham, Surrey, the youngest son of the twenty-one children of Charles *Bradley (1789–1871), notable evangelical preacher and leader of the so-called Clapham Sect, and Emma Linton, his second wife. Francis Herbert *Bradley (1846–1924) was his elder brother, George Granville *Bradley (1821–1903) his half-brother, and Sir George Grove (1820–1900) his brother-in-law.

Oxford and philosophy Bradley entered Cheltenham College in 1864. He was elected to an exhibition at Balliol College in 1868 and went up to Oxford in the following year. There he found himself in an extraordinary circle of talent: A. C. Swinburne, J. A. Symonds, R. L. Nettleship, Bernard Bosanquet, J. Cook Wilson, Scott Holland, Evelyn Abbott, John McCunn, Edward Caird, and Herbert Asquith were his contemporaries or at least lingering presences, and most of these remained his friends and confidants for the rest of their lives. In 1871 he took a second in classical moderations (Mackail implies that his languages were not impeccable) but redeemed himself in 1873 with a first in *literae humaniores* which Benjamin Jowett called 'brilliant'. In 1874 he was elected to a Balliol fellowship and in 1875 won the chancellor's prize for an English essay, 'Utopias, ancient and modern', and was in line for a permanent appointment. He was advised that his best chance was in history and so he went to Berlin, where Heinrich von Treitschke had just assumed the chair of history, to acquire the latest in Germanic scholarship.

Symonds's letters picture Bradley in his Oxford years as something of a poet and an aesthete ('poets like Bradley and Swinburne rave about *Italia unita*'; *Letters of John Addington Symonds*, 2.285). A devotion to Giuseppe Mazzini remained with him throughout his life; Bradley apparently lectured on him early in his career but, characteristically, did not publish anything on Mazzini until he revised a chapter in C. E. Vaughan's *Studies in the History of Political Philosophy before and after Rousseau* (1925).

Fifty years after entering Balliol, Bradley told a friend that his soul had been saved by Mazzini and Thomas Hill Green. Green was already the resident tutor when Bradley began his undergraduate studies, and he offered a counterweight to Jowett's rationalist scepticism and an ethical route by which troubled Victorian souls could find self-realization outside conventional religious observance. Mackail locates a spiritual crisis in Bradley's life in the year before he went to Balliol—'a strong, even violent reaction from the atmosphere of rigid evangelicism in which he had grown up' (Mackail, 386), emphasizing the literal truth of scripture and need for a personal sense of sin. Against this Green offered the panacea of idealist philosophy and, even more effectively, an imperative of social justice, a new sense of guilt, a new call to self-sacrifice. Edward Caird spoke in 1883 not only for Bradley but for his generation when he wrote, 'There are not a few among the Oxford men of the last fifteen years to whom … [Green's] existence was one of the things that gave reality to the distinction between good and evil' (A. Seth and R. B. Haldane, eds., 'Preface' to *Essays in Philosophical Criticism*, 1883, 7). Bradley belonged to the inner circle of Green's disciples, and when Green died in 1882 it was

Bradley who was entrusted with the publication of Green's *Prolegomena to Ethics* (1883).

Devotion to Green meant sharing in some of the tension between Green and Jowett. Jowett was suspicious of idealism as yet another *system* of beliefs, and Bradley seems to have come under suspicion of proselytizing. He says in a letter of 1875, 'I must try to convince him [Jowett] that I can attend to grammar and I do not want to proselytise' (Bradley to Green, spring 1875, Oxford, Balliol College). His essay, 'Aristotle's conception of the state', published in Evelyn Abbot's *Hellenica* (1880), shows, however, how closely Greek studies and the struggle for social justice were connected in Bradley's mind. As far as his career was concerned, it became clear that the only way forward lay outside Balliol. Green seems to have persuaded Bradley not to accept a lectureship at New College, and in a letter of 1881 confesses that this was probably a mistake: 'I did not then forecast … the persistency of [Jowett's] opposition—not, as it is needless to say, to you personally—but to that kind of teaching being given in the college in which you could be most useful' (Green to Bradley, 23 June 1881, Balliol College). This remark comes accompanying a suggestion that Bradley might consider taking up a professorship in the new University College in Liverpool. Two chairs seemed open to him, one in modern literature and history, the other in philosophy and political economy, and in his application he left it to the electors to decide in which capacity he could best serve the university. They chose Bradley for the first option and gave the other post to his Balliol contemporary John McCunn. The Oxford onlookers were puzzled that Bradley had not been chosen for the philosophy post. He thought of himself as a student of philosophy and in his application he had stated that 'during the last nine years I have worked most at philosophy, especially in its application to morals, politics and literature' (application to University College, Liverpool). And indeed his published work continued to display his primary interest in this field. About 1882 he was involved in a project, begun by Green and completed by Bosanquet, Nettleship, and others of his disciples, to translate the logic and metaphysics of Hermann Lotze (published 1884), Metaphysics III falling to Bradley's lot. In 1897 he edited Nettleship's *Philosophical Lectures and Remains*, prefixed with a selection of Nettleship's letters, mostly to Bradley himself. These make clear the kinds of questions which obsessed this group—questions of appearance and reality, of inner and outer life, of the one and the many. In these terms it is not surprising, though it puzzled Oxford onlookers, that in 1888 Bradley was considered a possible candidate for the Waynflete chair in metaphysics and morals. But he himself indicated that he did not wish to stand.

Liverpool and literature The move from philosophy to literature (Liverpool eventually cancelled the requirement to teach history) had already been prepared for by Bradley's work in extramural lecturing. As early as 1879 he had been invited by the Association for Promoting the Education of Women to lecture on literature under its auspices, and it was this experience, he said, which made him see

that the work he was best fitted for was to bring his analytical powers to bear on the experience of poetry.

Enthusiasm for democracy did not stretch so far as to allow Bradley to accept Liverpool as a natural home (although he continued in later life to return to Hoylake and West Kirby for sea-breezes and golf). In 1885 he asked to be considered for the new Merton chair of English literature. But Oxford appointed A. S. Napier, trained in Germanic philology. In 1889 he transferred from Liverpool, though the move only took him to another large industrial city, Glasgow. But this time he was in an ancient university and one which was already home to Oxford academics, such as Edward Caird, soon to be master of Balliol, and his brother, John Caird, principal of the university. Bradley's appointment was ridiculed by Henry Du Pré Labouchère, as was the simultaneous appointment of Gilbert Murray to the chair of Greek, as a choice of persons without national reputation. The relationship between Bradley and Murray was cemented by better bonds than this, however, as they shared liberal ideals and mutual admiration. Murray, writing at the end of his life, notes that 'the close friendship of Andrew Bradley was one of the most precious influences in my life' (*Gilbert Murray*, 96). Their letters are filled with abhorrence for war and imperialism, and royal pomp and establishment snobbery, and with enthusiasm for female suffrage, the education of women, and a national theatre. Glasgow, however, offered a powerful challenge to egalitarianism. Large and responsive but unbearably rowdy classes ('a set of savages whom it is a loathsome drudgery to teach'; Bradley to G. Murray, 10 Nov 1892, Bodl. Oxf.) and perpetual lecturing duties imposed strains that ground down both of them. In 1899 ill health forced Murray to resign and Bradley was not far behind him, retiring in 1900 in the hope (so often expressed) to lead a 'literary life'. But he did not pursue his ambition without regrets. As early as 1902 he is found complaining of the loss of any sense of 'usefulness': in Glasgow 'the contact with the men kept me sweeter … but I remember the *grind* with horror' (ibid., 20 Jan 1902). And much later, writing to Lady Mary Murray, he goes even further, saying 'I wouldn't myself have missed my years in a great business city, and I don't suppose you would' (Bradley to M. Murray, 12 June 1920, Bodl. Oxf.). It is in these Glasgow years that one hears the strongest expression of his desire to attach his ideals to some political movement: 'What I want to do is to read and think again about "questions" and find out what to think' (ibid., 26 Dec 1900). He felt himself 'like thousands of people … separated from the liberalism of their youth' but 'at a loss what to make for'. Socialism obviously interested him. In 1898 he speaks of Albert Schäffle's *Quintessence of Socialism* (which Bosanquet had translated) as 'very interesting' and he has 'some ideas simmering for my Fabian paper' (ibid., 30 Dec 1898). But to give persuasive force to his ideals and relate them to his literary life he had to approach them from a different angle.

Shakespearean Tragedy In 1901 came the opportunity that in some sense Bradley's career was waiting for—election to the Oxford professorship of poetry. This involved not only a return to the centre of his emotional life—a centre from which the rest of his career had been an exile—but also a demand that he use his return to justify his choice of 'a literary life'. The appointment (for five years) offered little guidance how this could be done, but the necessity to formulate the argument produced his masterpiece, *Shakespearean Tragedy* (1904), together with its companion volume, *Oxford Lectures on Poetry* (1909). In these lectures he was finally able to answer the Oxford objection that literary criticism was likely to be 'mere chatter about Shelley' and his own fear that it was 'mere idle voluptuousness' (Bradley to G. Murray, 3 Feb 1901, Bodl. Oxf.). He did this by bringing the moral seriousness which attached to the Oxford Greats syllabus of Greek texts and Greek philosophy to bear on a combination of modern (English) literature and modern (German) philosophy. In the four 'great' tragedies of Shakespeare (neither comedies nor histories have a role in the argument) he finds a poetic vision capable of sustaining a search for ethical understanding, so that 'what imagination loved as poetry, reason might love as truth' (A. C. Bradley, *Oxford Lectures on Poetry*, 394).

The underpinning of the argument in *Shakespearean Tragedy* comes from Aristotle as modified by Hegel's theory of the ethical substance of the universe. The fates of tragic heroes 'embodied in a poetic experience of which they are but aspects' become in fact representations of that call to self-sacrifice in the interest of a higher truth which Green had offered to his followers. Likewise the 'reality' posited of the characters can be seen to reflect Green's demand that these followers test their ideals against real life.

It is this high seriousness which drives Bradley's incessant effort to test ultimate meanings against the concrete facts of the lives depicted in the plays (in such notes as 'Where was Hamlet at the time of his father's death'). In theatrical terms this is absurd, and later critics such as L. C. Knights in *How many Children had Lady Macbeth?* (1933) ridiculed such analyses as the irrelevant pipe dreams of a bookish don. Bradley's letters do in fact show him continuously concerned with the theatrical productions of his own day; but this is not the concern which drives *Shakespearean Tragedy*, nor is it the concern which sustained its reputation. It was as a defence of the scrupulosity and seriousness of literary criticism that this was a necessary book for the early generations of English literary scholarship.

Final years In the years after the professorship of poetry, Bradley found himself once again caught in the contradiction between his literary and his social ideals. He was oppressed by a sense of failure. Not that he lacked honours; he was made an honorary fellow of Balliol, was awarded honorary doctorates from Liverpool, Glasgow, Edinburgh, and Durham, and was offered (but declined) the King Edward VII chair at Cambridge. In 1907 and 1908 he gave two series of Gifford lectures (for a 'colossal' stipend). He was pleased by the warmth of the reception he received in Glasgow but dissatisfied with his own performance. The first set of lectures was published posthumously as *Ideals of Religion* (1940) but the second could not be revised into any shape which seemed acceptable.

The First World War was, of course, a great sorrow to him, particularly in terms of the Germanophobia it produced. He refused to believe that the philosophers who had inspired his youth had any connection with German militarism. In 1915 he participated, with Murray and Bosanquet, in a series of lectures on the 'International Crisis'. His talk, 'International morality: the United States of Europe', reflected his undimmed Mazzinian vision of a truly democratic future and argued for the separation of the German philosophic tradition from the present conflict.

Good works remained, however, within Bradley's grasp. He was an enthusiastic supporter of the Workers' Educational Association. He laboured tirelessly to establish the study of English literature in schools and universities as a democratically accessible basic element in education. He was, as his obituary pointed out, 'father and moving spirit' (*English Association Bulletin*) to the English Association (set up in 1906 on the model of the Classical Association) and he sought to interest nationally important people in its welfare ('some of the big schoolmasters are beginning to take their English teaching seriously'; Bradley to R. Bridges, 27 Feb 1910, Bodl. Oxf.). Time was running out for him, however. The melancholy and ill health which had plagued him all his life became a predominant theme of his correspondence. Never having married, he lived in London with his sister, Marian (Mrs de Glehn), and in 1927 saw through the press the second edition of his brother F. H. Bradley's *Ethical Studies*. But in the main he saw himself as a spent force. His *Miscellany* volume, published in 1929, is generally agreed to show a loss of power. Bradley died in his sister's care at his home, 6 Holland Park Road, Kensington, London, on 2 September 1935.

G. K. HUNTER

Sources letters to Gilbert and Lady Mary Murray, Bodl. Oxf. · letters to and from T. H. Green, Balliol Oxf. · *The letters of John Addington Symonds*, ed. H. M. Schueller and R. L. Peters, 3 vols. (1967–9) · testimonials in favour of A. C. Bradley's application to University College, Liverpool, Bodl. Oxf., MS G. A. Lancs. 8°179 · testimonials in favour of A. C. Bradley's application for the Merton chair in Oxford University, Bodl. Oxf., MS G. A. Oxon. 4°84 · J. W. Mackail, 'Andrew Cecil Bradley, 1851–1935', *PBA*, 21 (1935), 385–92, esp. 386 · *DNB* · J. H. Muirhead, ed., *Bernard Bosanquet and his friends* (1935) · K. Cooke, *A. C. Bradley and his influence* (1972) · G. K. Hunter, 'A. C. Bradley's *Shakespearean tragedy*', *Essays and Studies by Members of the English Association*, new ser., 21 (1968) · *The Times* (4 Sept 1935) · *English Association Bulletin*, 81 (Nov 1935), 17 · M. Richter, *The politics of conscience: T. H. Green and his age* (1964) · *Gilbert Murray: an unfinished autobiography, with contributions by his friends*, ed. J. Smith and A. Toynbee [1960] · b. cert. · d. cert.

Archives Balliol Oxf., papers · Bodl. Oxf., lecture notes | BL, corresp. with Macmillans, Add. MS 55017 · Bodl. Oxf., corresp. with Robert Bridges, etc. · Bodl. Oxf., letters to Gilbert Murray · Bodl. Oxf., letters to Lady Mary Murray · JRL, letters to Samuel Alexander · NRA, priv. coll., corresp. with Sir Oliver Lodge

Likenesses W. Stoneman, photograph, 1917, NPG · G. Henry, oils, U. Glas.

Wealth at death £30,014 12s. 2d.: probate, 13 Nov 1935, *CGPLA Eng. & Wales*

Bradley, Charles (1789–1871), Church of England clergyman and author, was born at Halstead, Essex, in February 1789. His parents, Thomas and Ann Bradley, were both of Yorkshire origin, but settled in Wallingford, where their son Charles, the elder of two sons, passed the greater part of the first twenty-five years of his life. He married in 1810 Catherine Shepherd of Yattenden, took pupils, and edited several school books. He was, for a time after his marriage, a member of St Edmund Hall, Oxford, but was ordained on reaching the age of twenty-three, without proceeding to a degree. Like several others who attended St Edmund Hall at that time, he was a pronounced evangelical.

In 1812 Bradley became curate of High Wycombe. There for many years he combined the work of a private tutor with the sole charge of a large parish. Among his pupils were William Smith O'Brien, the Irish nationalist, and Bonamy Price, later professor of political economy in the University of Oxford. Bradley's powers as a preacher soon attracted attention. He made the acquaintance of William Wilberforce, the commentator Thomas Scott, Daniel Wilson, and other evangelicals. His sermons, published in 1818 and dedicated to Lord Liverpool, sold well, with an eleventh edition in 1854.

In 1825 Bradley became vicar of Glasbury in Brecknockshire. That year he published more sermons which also sold well. He retained the living of Glasbury until his death, but in 1829 became the first incumbent of St James's Chapel, Clapham—the heart of evangelicalism—where he lived, with some periods of absence, until 1855.

By this time Bradley's reputation as a preacher was fully established. His striking face and figure and dignified and impressive delivery added to the effect produced by the substance and style of his sermons, which were prepared and written with unusual care and thought. Further volumes of his sermons were published in 1831, 1836, 1842, and 1853. They had a very large circulation, and were widely preached in other pulpits than his own, not only in England and Wales, but in Scotland and America. Sales declined in the 1860s, but a volume of selections was published in 1884. Bradley's sermons presented the evangelical gospel straightforwardly in attractive and simple English. He also published hymns.

Bradley was the father of a numerous family. With his first wife, who died in 1831, he had thirteen children, of whom twelve survived him. The eldest of six sons was the Revd C. Bradley of Southgate, a prominent educationist. His fourth son was George Granville *Bradley, master of University College, Oxford, and dean of Westminster. By his second marriage in 1840 with Emma, daughter of John Linton, he also left a large family, among whom were Francis Herbert *Bradley, philosopher, and Andrew Cecil *Bradley, literary scholar. Bradley spent the last period of his life at Cheltenham, where he died at 19 Royal Parade on 16 August 1871.

G. G. BRADLEY, rev. H. C. G. MATTHEW

Sources Crockford (1871) · Foster, *Alum. Oxon.* · Boase, *Mod. Eng. biog.*
Wealth at death under £4000: probate, 19 Sept 1871, *CGPLA Eng. & Wales*

Bradley, Edward [*pseud.* Cuthbert Bede] (1827–1889), author and Church of England clergyman, the second son of Thomas Bradley, a surgeon, was born in Swan Street, Kidderminster, Worcestershire, on 25 March 1827. His family had literary pretensions: his brother, Thomas Waldron Bradley, published two novels, *Grantley Grange: Benedicts and Bachelors* (1874) and *Nelly Hamilton* (1875); and an uncle, William Bradley of Leamington Spa, Warwickshire, was the author of *Sketches of the Poor by a Retired Guardian*. Edward Bradley was educated at Kidderminster grammar school and in 1845 went to the newly established University College, Durham. His undergraduate career was assisted by a Thorp and a foundation scholarship. He graduated with a fifth-class degree (there were then seven classes in all) in 1848 and took his licentiate in theology in 1849. He was ordained by the bishop of Ely (Turton) in November 1850 to the curacy of Glatton-with-Holme, Huntingdonshire, and during his four years at Glatton he published in the *Illustrated London News* an account of the draining of Whittlesea Mere, then being carried out by William Wells of Holmewood. In 1854 he was appointed curate of Leigh in Worcestershire and in 1857 vicar of Bobbington, Staffordshire. On 7 December 1858 he married Harriet Amelia, daughter of Samuel Hancocks, an ironmaster, of Wolverley, Worcestershire. They had two sons, Cuthbert Edward and Henry Waldron, the latter of whom also became a clergyman. Bradley served as rector of Denton-with-Caldecote, Huntingdonshire, from 1859 to 1871 and in the latter year was appointed to his first permanent living, Stretton, Rutland, with a stipend of £300. At Stretton he carried out an extensive restoration of the church (1881–2) at a cost of nearly £2000, the money being partly raised by a series of lectures and public readings he gave in Manchester, Leeds, Birmingham, and towns and cities in the midlands. In 1883 he was presented with the living of Lenton-with-Hanby, near Grantham, Lincolnshire, by Lord Aveland.

Bradley first adopted the pseudonym Cuthbert Bede when publishing some undergraduate verses in *Bentley's Miscellany* in 1846. The name honours the two tutelary saints of Durham. Despite the later vast popularity of his Verdant Green books he appears to have had little direct knowledge of Oxford undergraduate life. It was once assumed that what knowledge he had had been acquired during the eighteen-month gap between his Durham licentiate and his first curacy, but there is little or no evidence of an extensive sojourn in the university. His brother, Thomas Waldron Bradley, insisted in an article in *Berrows Worcester Journal* (23 November 1895) that he had stayed in Oxford for only a matter of days (Hutton, 2), and it would seem that many of the supposedly Oxonian adventures of Verdant Green derive from Bradley's own experience and observation of undergraduate life in Durham. The series of pen-and-ink drawings (in the manner of the caricaturist Richard Doyle) entitled *Ye Freshmonne his Adventures at Univ. Coll. Durham* (pts 1 and 2 at University College, Durham), having been shown to Mark Lemon at *Punch*, were altered on Lemon's advice to form the illustrations of 'The Adventures of Mr Verdant Green, an Oxford Freshman' which were eventually published in the *Illustrated London News* on 13 and 17 December 1851. Surviving drawings of Durham student life are also reproduced in Bradley's series of etchings entitled *College Life* (published in Oxford, Cambridge, and Durham in 1849–50). The etchings were much admired by George Cruikshank and John Leech, the former at one time allowing Bradley to watch him at work. Bradley was also acquainted with men in the *Punch* circle, notably Albert Smith and Douglas Jerrold, and he contributed papers to *Punch* from 1847 to 1855, including in 1853 the series *Mr Peterloo Brown's Examination of the Oxford Statutes* (25.68–9, 77–8, 103–4). The curtailment of the publication of his Verdant Green drawings in the *Illustrated London News* persuaded him to add an extended narrative to his pictures. Nevertheless, despite his existing reputation, he had some initial difficulty in placing with a publisher *The Adventures of Mr Verdant Green, an Oxford Freshman by Cuthbert Bede BA, with 90 Illustrations by the Author*. It was eventually issued by Nathaniel Cooke of the Strand, London, as one of his shilling paperback Books for the Rail in October 1853. *The Further Adventures of Mr Verdant Green, an Oxford Undergraduate* appeared in 1854 and *Mr Verdant Green, Married and Done For* in 1857. The first edition of *The Adventures of Mr Verdant Green* sold out in Oxford on the first day and the continuing success of the three narratives was affirmed when the outright copyright was acquired by James Blackwood in 1858 and a collected cloth-bound edition was issued. (By 1870 it had sold 100,000 copies.) Hippolyte Taine records in *Notes sur l'Angleterre* in 1872 that Oxford friends recommended three novels to him from which to get the flavour of Oxford life: Thackeray's *Pendennis*, Thomas Hughes's *Tom Brown at Oxford*, and 'un petit roman assez gai, illustré par l'auteur'—*The Adventures of Mr Verdant Green*.

None of Bradley's other literary work achieved either the success or the fame of the Verdant Green novels of the 1850s. *Little Mr Bouncer and his Friend Verdant Green* (1873) lacks their vigour and lightness of touch. Apart from the *Illustrated London News* and *Punch* the young Bradley had contributed to Albert Smith's periodicals *The Months*, *The Man in the Moon*, and *Town and Country Miscellany*. He later published essays, verses, and sketches in journals as various as *Sharpe's London Magazine* (1853–5), *All the Year Round*, *The Field*, *St James's*, the *Gentleman's Magazine*, *Once a Week*, *Leisure Hour*, the *Churchman's Family Magazine*, *The Quiver*, *Fores's Sporting Notes and Sketches*, and the *Boy's Own Paper*. He devised a regular double acrostic column for the *Illustrated London News* from 30 August 1856 (claiming to have reintroduced the double acrostic to England) and contributed steadily to *Notes and Queries* (1852–86). He is also credited with having designed one of the first Christmas cards (published by Lambert of Newcastle upon Tyne in 1847) and was, as the satirical illustrations to his *Photographic Pleasures Popularly Portrayed with Pen and Pencil* (1855) suggests, wittily informed about the contemporary fashion for photography (both amateur and professional).

Bradley also wrote works for children, including *Nearer and Dearer: a Tale out of School* (1857), in which a boy tries various schemes to outwit the security measures of a local girls' school; *Fairy Fables* (1858); *Funny Figures by a Funnyman* (1858), a book of nonsense in the tradition of Edward Lear; and *Happy Hours at Wynford Grange: a Story for Children* (1858). Some of his later books include *Glencreggan, or, A*

Highland Home in Cantire (1861), *The Curate of Cranston, with other Prose and Verse* (1862), *Tour in Tartan Land* (1863), *The White Wife, with other Stories, Supernatural, Romantic and Legendary* (1865), *Mattins and Mutton's, or, The Beauty of Brighton* (1866), *A Holiday Ramble in the Land of Scott* (1869), *Figaro at Hastings, St Leonards* (1877), and *Fotheringay and Mary Queen of Scots* (1886).

Bradley died at the vicarage at Lenton, Lincolnshire, on 12 December 1889, and was interred in the churchyard at Stretton, Rutland; his wife survived him. As a young man, then closely shaven and very pale, Bradley had been introduced to Douglas Jerrold as 'Mr Verdant Green'. 'Mr Verdant Green?' said Jerrold, 'I should have thought it was Mr Blanco White.' A carte-de-visite photograph of Bradley (Durham University Library) is reproduced in Katherine M. Hutton's *Durham University Journal Special Supplement* (1994). Other portraits appear in the *Boy's Own Paper* (February 1890) and in M. H. Spielmann's *The History of 'Punch'* (1895).   ANDREW SANDERS

Sources K. M. Hutton, 'The adventures of Mr Verdant Green, or, An idea in need of a publisher', *Durham University Journal*, suppl. (1994) · DNB · BL cat. · Durham University Library cat. · *Durham University Journal*, 9 (1890), 10, 35 · *The Times* (13 Dec 1889), 5 · Crockford (1888) · M. H. Spielmann, *The history of 'Punch'* (1895), 491–5 · H. Gernsheim, 'Cuthbert Bede (the Rev. Edward Bradley, 1827–1889), Robert Hunt FRS (1807–1887), and Thomas Sutton (1819–1875)', *One hundred years of photographic history: essays in honor of Beaumont Newhall*, ed. Van Deren Coke (1975), 59–67 · J. T. Fowler, *Durham University: earlier foundations and present colleges* (1904), 100–02, 286 · *Grantham Journal* (14–21 Dec 1889) · N&Q, 7th ser., 8 (1889), 500 · '"Cuthbert Bede" and the University of Durham', *Durham University Journal*, 9 (1891), 150 · 'Who invented Christmas cards?', *Durham University Journal*, 21 (1918), 484 · 'Cuthbert Bede', *Durham University Journal*, 9 (1890), 70, 89 · m. cert. · CGPLA Eng. & Wales (1890)
Archives Noris Library and Museum, St Ives, corresp. and papers · U. Durham L., corresp. and papers | BL, corresp. and business transactions with Richard Bentley and his successors, Add. MSS 46617–46664, *passim* · Bodl. Oxf., letters to Bertram Dobell · NL Scot., letters to William Blackwood & Sons
Likenesses carte-de-visite, repro. in Hutton, 'The adventures of Mr Verdant Green' · photograph, repro. in Hutton, 'The adventures of Mr Verdant Green', *Durham University Journal special supplement* (1994)
Wealth at death £1103 3s. 10d.: probate, 13 Feb 1890, CGPLA Eng. & Wales

Bradley, Francis Herbert (1846–1924), philosopher, was born at Clapham, Surrey, on 30 January 1846, son of Charles *Bradley (1789–1871), an Anglican clergyman of evangelical persuasion, and his second wife, Emma, daughter of John Linton. Bradley's father was a leading figure in the influential Clapham Sect. He had twenty-one children with his two wives and was generally feared by them, although apparently least by Francis Herbert. One of his brothers, A. C. *Bradley, the Shakespearian critic, was professor of poetry at Oxford and of English literature at Glasgow, and Gifford lecturer at Glasgow in 1907. A much older half-brother, George Granville *Bradley, was headmaster at Marlborough when Bradley was a pupil there (1861–3), after transferring from Cheltenham College (1856–61). Bradley was a diligent child and good at sport, though not to the extent of one of his sisters who in

Francis Herbert Bradley (1846–1924), by Reginald Grenville Eves [posthumous]

the 1880s played tennis in the Wimbledon championships.

An attack of typhoid fever brought Bradley's schooldays to an end but in 1865 he went up to University College, Oxford. He graduated in Greats in 1869 but with only a second-class degree. As a result Bernard Bosanquet, whom Bradley always admired greatly, was awarded the fellowship at University College for which they had both competed. Bradley, after a period as a schoolteacher, eventually gained a fellowship at Merton College in 1870. This was tenable for life so long as he remained unmarried, which he did. The fellowship was one of the last without any tutorial or lecturing commitments. Apart from occasional meetings with visiting postgraduates, which reportedly were willingly and courteously given, he kept to the terms of his engagement. As befitted the author of *Ethical Studies* (1876), he was most punctilious in fulfilling the college duties consequent upon his station as a fellow.

Despite remaining unmarried and despite the cloistered and severely academic character of his life, Bradley was without doubt a man who enjoyed amorous experience of some depth. The 'E... R...' to whom he dedicated *Appearance and Reality* (1893) and the second edition of *Principles of Logic* (1922) is believed to be a Madame or Mademoiselle Radcliff. This side of his personality, together with his wry and immensely attractive sense of humour, as well as his masterly control of language, come out most forcibly in his *Aphorisms*. In regard to Bradley's use of language, T. S. Eliot (whose unpresented doctoral thesis at Harvard was published in 1964 under the title *Knowledge*

and Experience in the Philosophy of F. H. Bradley), when reflecting on why Bradley's writings and personality are prone to fascinate readers, saw one of the reasons as lying in what he took to be, for its purposes, his 'perfect style'. In June 1871 Bradley contracted a severe kidney illness, the effects of which stayed with him for the rest of his life. Anxiety, tiredness, and cold were all likely to bring on severe illness and it was partly for reasons of health that he spent long periods abroad. The retired existence which this illness compelled meant that from 1871 the account of his life is almost entirely given in the account of his philosophical writing.

Moral philosophy Bradley's first book, *Ethical Studies* (1876), remains in some ways perhaps his most attractive work. In it he is most explicit with respect to the influence that Hegel had on him, although even at this early stage he makes it quite clear that this admission does not constitute agreement. At places in *Ethical Studies* there is, no doubt, stylistic excess but in general it is written with the passion and intellectual vigour of a young man setting out to confront the presuppositions of a local philosophical establishment: presuppositions which in the 1960s were to re-emerge in Anglo-Saxon philosophy in a way that has ensured the continuing relevance of the book.

Bradley confronts the establishment in regard to the very purpose of moral philosophy. Any generalized moral scepticism is rejected as incoherent. Morality in human societies, and the moral consciousness of normal human individuals, are undeniable facts. The purpose of moral philosophy is theoretical, not practical. It is concerned fundamentally with the nature of the moral as the sphere within which, in particular historical contexts, the distinction between moral and immoral is in diverse ways drawn, not with any attempt to establish universal practical principles for delineating the moral from the immoral. Thus the proper task of the philosopher is to achieve a systematic understanding of the interrelated phenomena, psychological and sociological, which are conditions of the existence of morality and thus of both morality and immorality in the individual life. It is not fundamentally the philosopher's task to evaluate the relative worth of the diverse moralities that have existed and it is never his task to bring about 'improvements' in such moralities. Equally, it is never his task to attempt the construction of either a universal moral almanac or an algorithm of pure reason to guide human beings in those moral decisions the proper making of which will be essential to their achievement of satisfaction, or real happiness, in life as a whole: which will, in other words, be essential to achievement in their lives of a sustainable and harmonious self-realization.

The ideals of duty for duty's sake and pleasure for pleasure's sake, essential to Kant's ethical theory and hedonistic utilitarianism respectively, are inadequate to the task of moral philosophy thus conceived. In particular, neither can provide an intelligible account of the good, or final end of morality, if this is to be construed as the systematic self-realization of a human life as a whole. Pleasures as momentary and successive states of a feeling-self will constitute a series of particulars extended in time *ad infinitum* in which past and future particulars will exist, at any waking moment, at best, only as ideas. The greatest happiness, conceived quantitatively as achievement of the greatest number in an unlimited series of pleasures, is a goal the realization of which is unintelligible: there is no such sum. At any moment a feeling-self can enjoy simply what is present to it and, no matter what pleasures it may have had in the past, the individual could never at any moment be any nearer its goal of the greatest number than when it was born. If, on the other hand, by 'greatest quantity of happiness' is meant 'as much as, in the circumstances of its life, is open to the individual' then, according to the hedonistic psychology, *that* amount will always be had by any sentient individual.

Bradley does not purport to make a scholarly criticism of Kant. However, in effect he argues that if the theoretical schema implicit in Kant's transcendental psychology is taken seriously with its dichotomous dualism of faculties (thought and reason on the one hand, sensibility, and therefore inclination, on the other) the supreme principle of practical reason, in having its origin in an active faculty which is *ex hypothesi* strictly universal for finite sentient subjects, must remain purely formal and empty. No universal rationally binding content could have its ground in the contingent character of our inclinations even if this character was—like, according to Kant, the forms of our cognitive sensibility—common to all members of the human species. The only duty for duty's sake that pure reason could deliver to the will of a sentient individual would be 'realize non-contradiction'. So Bradley rejects the idea that a human being, as the possessor of a moral will, can be properly conceived (as it is in terms of the psychological schema essential to Kant's transcendental idealism) as a rational but intrinsically isolated transcendental subject.

For Bradley any human being, capable of coming to possess a contentful moral will that is constrained by a particular array of duties, must be regarded irreducibly as a historically located individual, the subject of a specific upbringing in particular socio-historic circumstances. For any normal human being the content of its moral will must derive fundamentally from the duties associated with its station—a station the functions of which, and the consequent duties and rights of which, will be related to those of other stations within the social institutions jointly constitutive of the social organism in which it lives its life. Moreover, on Bradley's view the contents of an individual's good will—the will of the good self as opposed to that of the bad self—and its motivation to realize that will ought so to derive. However, Bradley was well aware that the force of such an imperative must depend in obvious ways on the moral character of the state (family, society, and so on) in which the individual lives and on the individual having anything that could properly be called a station within that context. For instance, Bradley notes how the contingency of being in work can be essential to moral self-realization. Hence only under *ceteris paribus*

conditions can an individual be expected morally to identify its inner will with the objective will of the state (family, society, and so on) and thus be expected to achieve its self-realization in realizing, to the very best of its abilities, purposes intrinsic to the wider social wholes within which it lives. It will be the normal way for a human being to do so but, for the above and other contingent reasons, Bradley makes it clear that more or less frequently individuals—without thereby being immoral—will not be able to see, or acknowledge in their hearts, their lives as realizable in that sort of way. Thus Bradley concludes that 'My Station and its Duties' cannot by themselves provide a sufficient answer to the question 'What is morality?'.

In order to see how it needs supplementation Bradley proceeds to sketch in some detail the inner structure of the moral consciousness. For a consciousness located within the moral sphere there can be no conflict between the moral and the non-moral: hence the peculiarity of the question 'Why should I be moral?' To be an individual self-consciously located within the moral sphere is to apprehend certain demands on one's actions—namely those of morality—as unconditional. Correspondingly, the moral consciousness will demand that the individual in the various spheres of activity constitutive of its life strives to realize, at each juncture, its best self to the very best of its ability. For the individual, this best self will be an ideal self. It will be ideal both as a thinkable object with part of its content at any waking moment still simply intended to be realized in fact—and thus far, in one sense of the term, still unreal; and also as a self that at every point succeeds in meeting the demands of morality that bear on it, in the activities constitutive of its life, completely. Morality, given the unconditional nature of its demands, cannot expect any less of the good will than that it aims at complete fulfilment of those demands, in other words, that the individual identifies in its will totally with its good self and aims at moral perfection in the realization of itself. Such an ideal self should operate as a regulative ideal in an individual's experience and will often—especially at an early stage in the development of moral consciousness—present itself in individual form, that is, the idea of an actual person will often constitute the template for an individual's ideal self.

Given this structure to moral consciousness, two distinct kinds of conflict will inevitably be prone to qualify the moral experience of a self-conscious human being: conflicts of will arising from the individual's liability to identify itself with its bad-self as opposed to its good-self; and conflicts arising, at particular junctures, as a result of incompatible demands on its will which present themselves to the individual equally as duties, that is, as *prima facie* unconditional claims. The latter kind of conflict, Bradley maintains, cannot be resolved by deduction from general principles. Any judgement as to which duty is, in the given circumstance, to override must be of an intuitive character.

Normally the duties bearing on a human being's will, and determining the actions of the individual, so far as it identifies with its good self, will be those arising from its station, or stations, within a particular social organism (state, society, family, and so on). However, Bradley insists that genuinely moral claims that extend beyond the call of the duties of social morality can present themselves in the consciousness of an individual and these can conflict with the claims of social morality. Those that he mentions are the demands for self-realization that can fall on the will of the artist, or scientist. Such a process of self-realization need only be incidentally and indirectly social and yet its achievement can often cause conflict with the proper fulfilment of duties that derive from the individuals' stations within the social organism. Moreover, Bradley allows that claims of what he calls 'cosmopolitan' morality can bear on an individual's will through a conception of goodness that is not tied to the morality of any particular time or country.

Finally, Bradley maintains that reflection on the structure of moral consciousness will show morality to be unsatisfactory in a way which implies a higher form of consciousness: namely that of religion. For convenience Bradley proceeds to illustrate the structure of the religious consciousness in the form it has, in particular, within the protestant Christian life. (There is, of course, no suggestion that the religious consciousness will have internal to it a metaphysically adequate conception of reality.)

For morality, neither in the world of things in space and time nor in the consciousness of individuals is what exists in fact what ought to be. The ideal self, for morality, is at best a merely regulative ideal which if *per impossibile* it were realized in a finite individual would entail the elimination of the opposing poles of good and bad self that are necessary for the existence of moral experience. By contrast, the object of the religious consciousness is a realized ideal self and for the religious consciousness the finite individual's will, so far as it is good, will be made to coincide with the will of that realized ideal self, with the will of God. In fulfilment of his faith the individual must strive to die to his private, unreal, self—die, that is, to those aspects of will that have separated him, and humankind in general, from a primordial identity with God. In his thoughts and actions in the world (a world which, for faith, is itself the realization and ultimate triumph of the divine will) he must place his whole self in the 'hands of God'. However, Bradley insists that religion cannot properly be seen as adding any specific practical content of its own to the good will which, normally and with the qualifications noted, must remain that determined by an individual's station and its duties. By faith the spirit and ultimate motivation with which the good will is exercised will be transformed, but thus transformed morality must survive, without additional content, in its fulfilment within the religious life.

Epistemology and metaphysics The classification of Bradley's philosophy as Hegelian and idealist is not enlightening, and he was himself reluctant to accept these descriptions. A fundamental element in Bradley's philosophy is his rejection of the conception of an inner mind, or part-active, part- passive, thinking-cum-percipient subject,

conceived as existing in some relation to a human being. Such a thing might be thought of as an independently existent reality (for example Cartesian dualism) or as an entity metaphysically supervenient on a human being's brain (for example, Locke on a physicalist construal and contemporary scientific realism), or as a phenomenalist construction out of independently existent sensory data (for example the Humean and logical positivist tradition), or as a transcendental ego (for example, the Kantian tradition and the early Wittgenstein). Bradley makes it clear both in his *Principles of Logic* (1883) and *Appearance and Reality* that the thinking subjects he is concerned with are *irreducibly* sentient creatures, human and otherwise, living their lives in what he calls 'our real world': in other words, in the world of geographical space and historical time which a normal adult human being will be able to think of, at any waking moment, as containing its body and its activities present, past, and future, bodily and otherwise. Bradley describes mind, or soul, as a characteristic of a normal adult human being, as a 'late development' both evolutionarily and within the span of the individual human life. He insists there is no reason to accept a Cartesian break between humans and lower animal species with respect to mental faculties. The break, in so far as it exists, is one of degree and is a function of our species-wide linguistic ability. Within the history of the normal individual human life the development of mind proper will be piecemeal and coincide with the individual's gradually increasing mastery of the use of language 'for social purposes'. Hence, like that of his successors at Oxford, Collingwood and Ryle, Bradley's concept of mind is Aristotelian in tenor and radically anti-Cartesian.

Correspondingly, Bradley's centrally important conception of immediate sentient experience is not to be construed in terms of a causal-input model. Immediate experience is not to be construed either, as with Descartes, as a momentary deliverance of sensations into an independently existent self-conscious mind; or, as with Locke, as a momentary deliverance into a brain—a collocation of independently existent physical stuff—momentarily experiencing itself; or, as with Kant, as a deliverance of sensations from the *ex hypothesi* unknowable independently existent reality to a transcendental subject which, in virtue of the form of its inner sense, will appear in its consciousness, in so far as it also has a faculty of apperception, as orderable in a unique linear time-series. The paradigm for Bradley's conception of a finite centre of immediate experience is that enjoyed, at a waking moment, by a human infant at an early pre-linguistic stage or by an animal (like one of his much loved dogs), which—in lacking mastery of the requisite dating-and-placing vocabulary from a natural language—could not have the capacity to think systematically about particular times, past and future, and particular locations in space, in pointable directions, outside its present perceptual environment.

According to Bradley's epistemology, the metaphysician's independently existent reality will be immediately given in the present activities, bodily and otherwise, of such a finite centre. However, it could only be present fragmentarily in ideal form within such an experience and not in the complex systematic ways in which it will be present at successive moments in the thought-embedded sense perceptions and activities constitutive of a normal adult human being's waking life. On the other hand, Bradley insists that in the case of the adult human experience, no matter how systematic its discursive knowledge in the various spheres of its interests might become, there must always be a background sentience, a knowing-and-being-in-one, in which reality will be immediately given, and out of which ideal contents, and thus specific objects of its consciousness, will present themselves in one way and another, more or less inchoately, as inputs to its various standing systems of thought.

Thus Bradley's epistemology succeeds in being both realist and empiricist in a way that the above mentioned theories do not, in that he takes a sentient individual's experience at each waking moment to provide a fundamental point of cognitive and practical access, immediate and discursive, to an independently existent reality. Moreover, Bradley takes it to be a *sine qua non* of a human being possessing, to any significant degree, systematic knowledge of any specific sphere of reality (in history, geography, the special sciences, morality, religion, literature, metaphysics, and so on) that it should acquire an ability to exercise at waking moments the ideal construction of our real world. Having this complex of logically interrelated conceptual capacities amounts to having what G. E. Moore called the 'common sense view of the world'.

However, in his metaphysics Bradley argues that the key concepts exercised in the ideal construction of our real world (the concepts of time, space, movement, rest, cause and effect, activity and passivity, self and not-self, and so on) can be shown to involve contradictions which have their source in the very nature of our intrinsically abstract and partial predicative thinking. Thus he maintains that the source of the contradictions is not merely latent in the egocentric historical and geographical thinking essential in practice in our daily lives. It will be latent in any of the specific systems of discursive knowledge we might in our lives acquire. For practical purposes this is not important and we can, when such contradictions actually arise in the development of specific systems of knowledge, at least in principle, resolve them by bringing the conflicting ideal contents together, with suitably modified meanings, within the context of more comprehensive systems of thought (as with the modification that took place in the physicist's concept of space-time when Einsteinian relativity theory supplanted Newtonian mechanics).

Within the special sciences, on Bradley's view, the practical success of a more comprehensive theory will be evidence of the greater degree of its truth relative to that of the narrow pre-existing theory. However, against the pragmatist Bradley was adamant that the nature of truth was not to be elucidated in terms of the notion of practical success. On the contrary, the more comprehensive theory will work better because of its greater degree of truth. Or, in Bradley's alternative terminology, the system of objects that can be thought of via the concepts internal to the more comprehensive theory will have a greater degree of reality than the system of objects cognitively accessible through the supplanted theory.

In metaphysics, on Bradley's view, given the intrinsically partial nature of the theories of the natural scientist and the contradictions inevitably latent in them, physicalism of the sort currently popular among metaphysicians is not a coherent option. Nevertheless, Bradley sees philosophical logic as giving a glimmer of light at the end of the metaphysical tunnel. Given the premiss that for any true negative judgement there must be some feature of reality in virtue of which it is true, Bradley concluded that an independently existent reality must have a character in virtue of which no internally inconsistent system of ideal contents can conceivably be true of it. He designates this character harmoniousness. Further, Bradley reasons that since any system of ideal contents by which a finite individual could have discursive knowledge of reality will have contradictions latent in it, none of the systems of objects of our discursive knowledge could conceivably be, in the metaphysician's sense, independently existent or absolutely real. Only an immediate experience—a knowing-and-being-in one within which no distinction could be drawn between ideal content and reality known through the exercise of that content, and thus an experience in that respect analogous to the merely sentient phases of a finite life—could conceivably be independently existent. He concludes therefore that the Absolute must be an all-encompassing harmonious immediate experience in which all finite sentient life in this or any world must have its source and within which all the conflicting aims and activities of finite creatures must achieve, somehow transformed and perfectly fulfilled, ultimate realization.

However, it is necessary to be careful in understanding the term 'experience' in this context. Bradley insists that almost the whole point of his metaphysics is to avoid the trap of taking one (or more) of the ontological categories of thing existing within our real world and attributing absolute, or unconditional, reality to the favoured sort while relegating to a merely phenomenal existence, and metaphysically to absolute unreality, all other objects of our knowledge. It follows that the use of the word 'experience', in Bradley's characterization of the Absolute, must be understood neutrally with respect to the mind–body distinction that we ordinarily draw within our real world. Nevertheless, it is clear that Bradley holds that metaphysics must take the idea of a human sentient life with all its multiform conflicting aims, values, activities, and sufferings as the irreducible source from which it, by an extension of meaning, can get an inkling of the ultimate nature of the independently existent reality which it strives in very general terms to characterize coherently.

Bradley received several honours during his career. In 1889 the University of Glasgow conferred on him the degree of LLD. He was elected to the Kongelige Danske Videnshabernes Selskab (the Royal Danish Academy of

Science and Letters) in 1921, to the Reale Accademia Nazionale dei Lincei in 1922, and to the Reale Istituto Lombardo of Milan in 1923. He declined on the grounds of his health to join the British Academy at its foundation but was unanimously elected an honorary fellow in 1923. In June 1924 he was made a member of the Order of Merit. He lived at Merton College from his election until late in the summer of 1924, at which time he was still fully engaged in his philosophical work. Symptoms of blood poisoning then led to his removal to the Acland Nursing Home, Banbury Road, Oxford, where he died after a few days' illness on 18 September 1924. He was buried in Holywell cemetery, Oxford, in the same grave as a younger brother who had been drowned in the Thames in 1866. Bradley was the dominant figure within British philosophy in the last quarter of the nineteenth century and in the early years of the twentieth. During the twentieth century his influence declined rapidly under the influence of the formal logic-based analytical philosophy associated with Russell, Moore, Frege, and Wittgenstein. Under the influence of Wittgenstein's later work, the philosophical relevance of formal logic was once again placed in question in a way not totally dissimilar from Bradley's. His writings have, in consequence, received something of a revaluation, and a respectable secondary literature on them has begun to develop.   Guy Stock

Sources G. R. G. Mure, 'Francis Herbert Bradley: towards a portrait', *Encounter*, 16/1 (1961), 28–35 · T. S. Eliot, 'F. H. Bradley', *Selected essays*, 2nd edn (1934), 406–17 · T. S. Eliot, *Knowledge and experience in the philosophy of F. H. Bradley* (1964) · *DNB* · *WWW*
Archives Merton Oxf., corresp. and papers | JRL, letters to Samuel Alexander · McMaster University, Hamilton, Ontario, corresp. with Bertrand Russell · NL Scot., letters to Lord Haldane · U. Newcastle, Robinson L., corresp. with Bernard Bosanquet
Likenesses R. G. Eves, oils (posthumous), Merton Oxf. [*see illus.*] · photograph, Merton Oxf.
Wealth at death £10,492 1s. 5d.: resworn probate, 14 Nov 1924, *CGPLA Eng. & Wales*

Bradley, George (1816–1863), journalist, was born at Whitby in Yorkshire, and apprenticed to a firm of printers in his home town. After being a reporter for several years on the *York Herald* he was appointed editor of the *Sunderland and Durham County Herald*, and about 1848 became editor and one of the proprietors of the *Newcastle Guardian*. In 1843 Bradley published *A concise and practical system of shorthand writing, with a brief history of the progress of the art, illustrated by sixteen engraved lessons and exercises.*

Bradley seems to have lived mainly in Newcastle where he was, for some time, an influential member of the town council. He was married, but it is not known if he and his wife, Sarah, had any children. Bradley died at Newcastle on 14 October 1863.

                            Thompson Cooper, *rev.* Joanne Potier

Sources *Whitby Times* (23 Oct 1863) · J. E. Rockwell, *The teaching, practice and literature of shorthand* (1884), 82
Wealth at death under £1500: administration with will, 6 Jan 1864, *CGPLA Eng. & Wales*

Bradley, George Granville (1821–1903), dean of Westminster and schoolmaster, born at High Wycombe on 11 December 1821, was the fourth son of Charles *Bradley

George Granville Bradley (1821–1903), by John Jabez Edwin Mayall, pubd 1883

(1789–1871) and his first wife, Catherine Shepherd (d. 1831). The literary scholar A. C. *Bradley and the philosopher Francis Herbert *Bradley were his half-brothers. In 1829 the family moved to Clapham, Surrey, where in 1834 Bradley became a pupil at the grammar school under Charles Pritchard. In August 1837 he was admitted to Rugby School under Thomas Arnold and placed in the upper fifth form. On 20 March 1840 he was admitted a scholar of University College, Oxford, where his tutors were Travers Twiss and Piers Calverley Claughton, but he was more influenced by a younger fellow, Arthur Penrhyn Stanley, of whom he published *Recollections* (1883) and to whose biography by R. E. Prothero (1883) he contributed. In 1844 he was one of four in the first class in classics and in October was elected fellow of his college. In 1845 he won the Latin essay prize.

Bradley did not reside on his fellowship but joined Archibald Campbell Tait's staff at Rugby School. There he soon won renown both as a teacher and as a housemaster. When in 1849 Edward Meyrick Goulburn succeeded Tait there was trouble at Rugby, and Bradley, working with his colleague, T. S. Evans, saved the school from disaster. On 18 December 1849 he married Marian (d. 27 Nov 1910), fourth daughter of Benjamin Philpot, vicar-general and archdeacon of Sodor and Man. She was 'a woman of rigid views' (Green, 8). They had two sons and five daughters, of whom Arthur Granville, Margaret Louisa *Woods, and Emily were published writers.

In 1858 the headmastership of Marlborough College was vacated by George Edward Lynch Cotton, who until

1852 had been one of Bradley's colleagues at Rugby, and by Cotton's desire Bradley succeeded him. He took orders on his appointment. He had no easy post. Though Cotton had begun to relieve the school of its money troubles, there was still a heavy debt, and memories of disorder were not extinct. By good management, by raising the fees, and by increasing the numbers, Bradley not only removed the debt but was able to add greatly to the school buildings.

It was said of Bradley that he quelled disorder by 'inspired invective' (Butcher), and that 'the first contact with Bradley was a little paralysing; it produced the effect of an intellectual torpedo shock' (Bradley, 199). His friend Stanley learned from him 'the sense of constant, stimulating, provoking, advancing pressure' (ibid., p. 200). Bradley kept most of the teaching of the sixth form in his own hands, and was especially successful in teaching Latin prose, while he widened the old curriculum by reading with his boys Joseph Butler's *Analogy* and modern historical works. His *Practical Introduction to Latin Prose Composition* (1881) was used in schools for a generation. He supervised the general teaching by a monthly 'review' of each form; in the presence of the master he took the boys through some of the work which they had been doing, and spared neither boy nor master. At the same time by the gentler side of his nature he made the boys his friends.

To both sides Tennyson bore witness by sending his son Hallam 'not to Marlborough but to Bradley' (Bradley, 200). Bradley had first met Tennyson in 1841, when they were both on a visit to Edmund L. Lushington at Park House near Maidstone; when in 1860 Bradley took a house near Farringford, Tennyson's house in the Isle of Wight, the acquaintance was renewed and soon ripened into the closest friendship. At this time Marlborough won more scholarships at Oxford than any other school, Rugby alone coming at all near it. The fame of Marlborough crossed the channel, and when in 1866 the French government sent Demogeot to study the English public-school system, he had instructions to visit Marlborough, and was warmly welcomed by Bradley.

In 1870 Bradley left Marlborough for Oxford, succeeding as master of University College F. C. Plumptre, a head of the old-fashioned kind with a modified interest in learning. The college had never lacked men of ability among its scholars, but most of the commoners read only for a 'pass' degree and had the reputation of being a 'rackety mirthloving' set. Bradley was determined to raise the standard of industry and insisted that every commoner should read for an honours degree. Some consequent unpopularity was increased by an edict banishing dogs from the college, but he had his way, and he strengthened his position by bringing back James Franck Bright from Marlborough as tutor in history, and importing from Cambridge his former Marlborough pupil Samuel Henry Butcher as a tutor in classics. Moreover, contrary to the practice of heads of houses, he took an active part in the teaching. His lectures on Sophocles, Cicero, and Latin prose attracted many undergraduates from other colleges. Entrance to his own

college became competitive and its graduates prominent in public life. In 1880 Bradley was nominated in succession to Lord Selborne a member of the university commission, and his services were rewarded by a canonry of Worcester. In 1881 the death of his old friend Stanley vacated the deanery of Westminster, and Bradley was chosen by Gladstone to take his place, the appointment being made despite stiff resistance from the queen. The broad-church tradition within the abbey was thus maintained.

Once more Bradley found himself in a difficult situation, for Stanley left the abbey's finances and fabric in disrepair. After long negotiations and much opposition Bradley induced the government to act. The ecclesiastical commissioners were empowered to provide a sum for immediate repairs and an income for the future, but one so small that it had to be supplemented by the proceeds of a suppressed canonry. Thus the building was saved. Bradley's daughter Emily Tennyson Bradley (later Smith) wrote several works on the abbey. In 1889, at Bradley's instigation, a parliamentary commission was appointed to consider the question of space for future monuments and interments. As a substitute for interments Bradley extended the system of memorial services. The chief burials in his time were those of Darwin, Browning, Tennyson, and Gladstone, while the chief ceremonials were the jubilee service of Queen Victoria on 21 June 1887 and the coronation of Edward VII on 9 August 1902. After Stanley's example Bradley used to take parties of working men round the abbey weekly in spring and summer. In the proceedings of convocation he took some part and, though he left the Liberal Party on the home-rule question, his ecclesiastical liberalism was never shaken. After the coronation he resigned the deanery on 29 September 1902, and retired to Queen Anne's Gate, where he died on 13 March 1903. He was buried in the south aisle of the nave of the abbey by the grave of Atterbury.

JOHN SARGEAUNT, *rev.* H. C. G. MATTHEW

Sources *The Times* (13 March 1903) · *The Times* (16 March 1903) · A. G. Bradley, A. C. Champneys, and J. W. Baines, *A history of Marlborough College* (1893) · F. D. How, *Six great schoolmasters* (1904) · Gladstone, *Diaries* · S. H. Butcher, 'The late Dean Bradley', *Fortnightly Review*, 79 (1903), 103–14 · V. Green, *Love in a cool climate: the letters of Mark Pattison and Meta Bradley, 1879–1884* (1985)
Archives Westminster Abbey, London, official corresp. | BL, letters to G. L. Craik, Add. MS 61895 · BL, W. E. Gladstone MSS, Add. MSS 44466–44519, *passim* · Bodl. Oxf., letters to Friedrich Max Muller and Georgina Max Muller, MSS Eng. c 2808, c 2809, e 2711, d 2369 · CUL, letters to B. F. Westcott · Durham Cath. CL, letters to S. B. Lightfoot · King's AC Cam., letters to Oscar Browning · LPL, corresp. with Edward Benson · LPL, corresp. with and recollections of A. C. Tait
Likenesses B. Stone, photograph, 1902, Birmingham Reference Library · L. Dickinson, oils, Rugby School · J. J. E. Mayall, woodburytype photograph, NPG; repro. in T. Cooper, *Men of mark: a gallery of contemporary portraits* (1883) [see illus.] · W. W. Ouless, oils, Marlborough College · Spy [L. Ward], caricature, chromolithograph, NPG; repro. in *VF* (29 Sept 1888) · cabinet photograph, NPG · oils, Westminster Abbey, London, deanery · photograph, Westminster Abbey, London, deanery
Wealth at death £21,713 1s. 5d.: probate, 16 June 1903, *CGPLA Eng. & Wales*

Bradley [*née* Layfield], **Helen** (1900–1979), painter and writer, was born on 20 November 1900 at Lees, near Oldham, Lancashire, the first of the four children of Frederick Layfield and his wife, Jane Anne, *née* Shaw. Her father was a supplier of small items of hardware to shops in the Oldham area. In 1911 the family moved from Lees to Frederick Street in Oldham, where Helen Layfield attended Clarksfield School, which she left at the age of thirteen. At the prompting of the headmaster she entered for, and won, the John Platt scholarship at Oldham Art School. Despite the fact that her uncle, Charles Edward Shaw (*fl.* 1879–1895), was a professional artist, her father thought it an unsuitable career for a young woman. He allowed her to study jewellery and embroidery instead but she was forced to postpone her education in 1914 with the outbreak of the war.

In 1926 Helen Layfield married the flower painter and textile designer Thomas Bradley (1900–1993), who had also studied at Oldham Art School; they had two children, Peter and Elizabeth. It was not until Helen Bradley was sixty-five years old that she first exhibited the nostalgic narrative paintings for which she became well known. Her intention, at first, was to show her grandchildren what life had been like when she was a child. Over the next fourteen years, until her death only a week before she was due to be appointed MBE, she developed and popularized a unique style combining image and text, lucid description, and high fantasy.

L. S. Lowry's industrial scenes provide the most obvious parallel to Helen Bradley's work and, indeed, Lowry knew of and commented favourably on her paintings. Her style is far more anecdotal, however, and unashamedly sentimental, reflecting the homely, down-to-earth personality which would make her as popular a television chat-show guest as she was an artist. Her paintings and accompanying texts illustrate the period from 1904 to 1908. The main characters are her three maiden aunts, her mother, Helen herself, her younger brother George Bradley (d. 1989), Miss Carter (who wore pink), and the object of her affections, Mr Taylor, the bank manager. They are usually pictured on holiday in Blackpool or Southport, taking walks in Salford's Peel Park, or on excursions to the shops or the market. A strain of whimsical, even bizarre, humour runs through the later series of paintings, *In the Beginning*, based on stories recounted by Helen's great-aunt Jane in which God makes some very unexpected personal appearances in the streets of Oldham and Manchester.

Sometimes dismissed as a 'naïve' painter, the distinctive appearance of Helen Bradley's work represents a fusion of specific sources adapted to a very particular purpose. The absence of shading and her use of rich colours, decorative patterning, and simplified forms can be traced back to an interest in Persian and Mughal miniatures. As she said:

> All these people painted a story … The Turks also painted stories, about a kind of super-giant, and they simplified their art. They painted horses which had generals on them very big, and all the men very little, which absolutely tickled me pink. (Stafford, 5)

When she lived in London in the 1940s, she saw an exhibition of paintings by the Dutch artist Hendrick Avercamp (1585–1634), whose skies, similar to those in the paintings of J. M. W. Turner, inspired the atmospheric backdrops to her scenes of the industrial north. She also encountered works by the Chinese artist Gao Qipei (1672–1734), whose lyrical and calligraphic approach to landscape is most evident in her watercolours.

Helen Bradley wrote and illustrated four books, the first of which, *And Miss Carter Wore Pink: the Diary of an Edwardian Childhood*, was published in 1971. Practically a household name in the 1970s, she appeared twice on Russell Harty's television chat shows and was a frequent guest on the television programmes *Pebble Mill at One* and *Jackanory*. Helen Bradley died at her home, 2 Green Villa Park, Wilmslow, Cheshire, on 19 July 1979. She was cremated at Prestbury crematorium on 23 July and a service of thanksgiving was held at the United Reformed church in Wilmslow on the same day. Her estate was valued for probate under the name Nellie Bradley. Her paintings have continued to command high prices at auction and have regularly featured in retrospective exhibitions in the 1980s and 1990s, including Warrington Museum and Art Gallery in 1991 and in Osaka, Japan, in 1993. The Museum and Art Gallery, Salford, owns *It was a Beautiful Place* …, a view in Peel Park, and there are further works in the Atkinson Art Gallery, Southport, and Oldham Art Gallery. Miss Carter Publications, which Helen Bradley and her husband, Tom, were instrumental in setting up, continued in the late twentieth century to promote her work through limited-edition prints and reproductions.

STEPHEN WHITTLE

Sources J. Stafford, *Helen Bradley* (1974) [exhibition catalogue, Oldham Art Gallery, Oldham, 1974] · V. A. J. Slowe, *Helen Bradley* (1989) [exhibition catalogue, Abbot Hall Gallery, Kendal, 1989] · H. Bradley, *And Miss Carter wore pink: scenes from an Edwardian childhood* (1971) · H. Bradley, *Miss Carter came with us* (1973) · H. Bradley, *"In the beginning" said Great Aunt Jane* (1975) · H. Bradley, *The queen who came to tea* (1978) · *CGPLA Eng. & Wales* (1979) · Miss Carter Publications, Bolton · private information (2004)

Likenesses C. Harrison, oils, *c.*1975, priv. coll. · photograph, 1977, Miss Carter Publications, Bolton · photograph, 1979, Miss Carter Publications, Bolton

Wealth at death £222,211: probate, 2 Oct 1979, *CGPLA Eng. & Wales*

Bradley, Henry (1845–1923), philologist and lexicographer, born at Manchester on 3 December 1845, was the only child of the marriage of John Bradley (1791/2–1871) of Kirkby in Ashfield, Nottinghamshire, and his second wife, Mary Spencer (1804/5–1870), of Middleton by Wirksworth, Derbyshire. From 1846 his father, a fire-clay agent who had been a farmer and partner in a mill, lived at Brimington, near Chesterfield, and Bradley attended Chesterfield grammar school from 1855 to 1859. In that year his family moved to Sheffield, where in 1863 he became corresponding clerk to a cutlery firm. During the interval, appointments as a tutor and companion allowed him to read widely and study languages, for which he had a great natural aptitude. His office work gave him opportunities of developing this interest, and during the twenty years in which he remained in his post he not only mastered several modern European languages, but acquired a knowledge of the classical tongues, as well as a considerable acquaintance with Hebrew.

In 1872 Bradley married Eleanor Kate, daughter of William Hides, of Sheffield; they had one son and four daughters. In January 1884, partly for economic reasons and partly on account of his wife's health, he moved to London, where for some years he supported his family by miscellaneous literary work, of which reviewing formed an important part. A review by him in the *Academy* for February and March 1884 of the first part of the *New English Dictionary* drew attention to his unusual knowledge of English philology, and brought about an association with the dictionary which led to his being appointed one of its editors in 1889, a position which he retained for the rest of his life, becoming senior editor on the death of Sir James Murray in 1915. In 1891 he received the honorary degree of MA from Oxford University, and in 1914 that of DLitt. After working for some time in a room at the British Museum, he moved permanently to Oxford in 1896, and lived for many years in North House in the University Press quadrangle. In 1896 he was elected a member of Exeter College and in 1916 a fellow of Magdalen College. From 1892 he received a civil-list pension in recognition of his services to learning. He was president of the Philological Society for three periods between 1890 and 1910, and was elected FBA in 1907. From the time of his settling in Oxford the dictionary became his main occupation, though he continued to write numerous articles and reviews, and produced two or three separate publications. With the exception of one or two periods of ill health, he was able to carry on his work, despite his age, until his death.

During his first years in London, in addition to his extensive reviewing of philological and other books, Bradley wrote a number of articles for those volumes of the dictionary which cover the letters B, C, and D. He also compiled the volume on *The Goths* (1888) for the Story of the Nations series, a work written in a popular style but based on a careful study of original sources. For the Oxford University Press he prepared a revised edition of F. H. Stratmann's *Middle English Dictionary*, which appeared in 1891 and was at that time the most complete special dictionary for that period of the language. An edition of Caxton's *Dialogues* for the Early English Text Society (1900), the popular and highly successful *Making of English* (1904), and the British Academy paper 'Spoken and written language' (1913; issued in book form in 1919) complete the list of Bradley's separate works. He was involved with his friend Robert Bridges in founding the Society for Pure English (1919). In addition his numerous articles and notes on both linguistic and literary points in Old and Middle English are important contributions in these fields, and show his wide knowledge, sound judgement, and originality of thought. Not a few of them contain brilliant discoveries or suggestions that have been readily accepted by other scholars.

Bradley's earliest independent work arose from his interest in the history and origin of British place names,

and his later contributions to this subject were of great value in setting the study on a sounder philological and historical basis than previously. Although he undertook no large work of his own, his searching reviews of the publications of others not only exhibited their defects but made clear the principles on which the scientific investigation of place names must be conducted. Of his special articles in this field the most important were those on *Ptolemy's Geography of the British Isles* (1885) and *English Place-Names* (1910).

The share which Bradley took in the *Oxford English Dictionary*, from the date when he devoted most of his time to that work, was the editing of the letters E, F, G, L, M, S–Sh, St, and part of W, amounting in all to 4590 pages out of a total of 15,487, and including several difficult portions of the vocabulary. The treatment of these, and the work as a whole, naturally gave opportunity for his unusual qualifications as a scholar: his extensive knowledge of ancient and modern languages, his thorough grasp of philological principles, his retentive and accurate memory, and his rare powers of analysis and definition. In some respects the dictionary necessarily limited his range, and by its claims on his time restricted his contributions to other fields of learning or literature in which he was equally fitted to excel. This was most evident to those who knew him most intimately, and by personal contact could realize that under a quiet and unassuming manner he possessed outstanding intellectual powers.

After a short illness, Bradley died at his home, 173 Woodstock Road, Oxford, on 23 May 1923. He was survived by his wife.   W. A. CRAIGIE, *rev.* JENNY MCMORRIS

Sources 'Bradley, Henry', *The Oxford companion to the English language*, ed. T. McArthur (1992), 147 · *The collected papers of Henry Bradley* (1928) · historical introduction, *Supplement to the Oxford English dictionary* (1933) · personal knowledge (1937) · d. cert. [John Bradley] · d. cert. [Mary Bradley] · *CGPLA Eng. & Wales* (1923)
Archives BL, corresp. with Macmillans, Add. MS 55034 · Bodl. Oxf., corresp. with R. S. Bridges · U. Glas. L., letters to George Neilson
Likenesses Hills & Saunders, photograph, *c.*1913, NPG · W. Stoneman, photograph, 1917, NPG · E. Hall, photograph, 1922, NPG · Elliott & Fry, photograph, NPG · photograph, NPG
Wealth at death £3601 10*s*. 4*d*.: probate, 24 Aug 1923, *CGPLA Eng. & Wales*

Bradley, Humphrey (*fl.* 1584–1625), designer of land drainage systems, was possibly the son of John Bradley (*fl.* 1561–1568), concierge of the English trading house at Bergen op Zoom, Brabant, who was married to Anna van der Delft. He first appears in England in 1584, when he submitted to secretary Walsingham a lengthy and able 'advys' on the cost of improvements to Dover harbour, though he was not employed on the scheme.

In 1589 Bradley was involved in various local drainage schemes: on the River Ouse in Cambridgeshire, the Nene near Wisbech, and the Witham in Lincolnshire. He was the first to see the need of and to plan for a single comprehensive drainage scheme for the whole of the fens, and on 3 December 1589 he presented a treatise on the topic to Lord Burghley. Access to Burghley was probably assisted by Bradley's marriage on 27 June 1589, in London, to Anna

Sermantens from Delft, whose uncle, Joachim Ortell, was one of the Dutch diplomatic representatives in London. Bradley proposed that, since all the fenlands were above sea level, a simple gravitational drainage system would be sufficient, obviating the need for mills and machinery; this anticipated the system of straight new cuts later employed by Vermuyden. Bradley suggested that 'the greatest impediments to all good drainage projects live in the minds and the imaginations of men' (Darby, 264) and that privy council inaction over his scheme owed much to the selfish interests of individual landowners and counties.

In a letter of 3 March 1592 Bradley claimed to have leased from Lord Lumley all the coal on his manor at Hartlepool, but it is unclear if he ever developed the enterprise. Two further submissions to Burghley in March and April 1593 contained a comprehensive survey of the fenland economy and topography, and sensibly suggested that the variety of tenures demanded an act of parliament and crown finance to compel agreement. Although in the Netherlands he was reputed to be a skilled dyker, it is unlikely that Bradley had any experience of very large-scale drainage (as opposed to land reclamation by embankment). His suggested drainage methods seem woefully inadequate, and his assessment that the work could be completed by 700–800 men in six months for £5000 was hopelessly optimistic, given Vermuyden's later experiences. Yet the reason for Burghley's rejection of the scheme was probably not its technical defects but Bradley's failure to win financial patronage when well-placed groups of prospective English undertakers had a rival interest in fen drainage.

Bradley finally left England in 1594. Two years later he was sent to France by the states general of the United Provinces to aid Henri IV in land reclamation and drainage for strategic military purposes. On the establishment of peace, he was appointed on 1 January 1599 'maître des digues du royaume', which conferred a practical monopoly of land drainage throughout France. Initial difficulties were remedied by a royal edict (1607), which established a new body, the Association pour le Desséchement des Marais et Lacs de France, whose members secured the necessary capital and shared in land allocation on completion of the work. Backed by Sully, the king's chief minister, and with strong connections at court, Bradley presided over extensive drainage works in the Auvergne, Languedoc, and Saintonge. He was unable to persuade Sully to have Rouen joined to Marseilles by connecting Joigny on the River Seine to Dijon on the Saône, but overall his work in France seems to have been successful.

Bradley was alive in France in 1625 and probably dead by 1639. His private life is glimpsed only in his letters to and from his wife, and in the baptism of two children, Joachim (1592) and Sara (1594), at the Dutch church at Austin Friars, London.　　　　　　　　　　　　　　　　　　BASIL MORGAN

Sources L. E. Harris, *The two Netherlanders: Humphrey Bradley and Cornelis Drebbel* (1961) · H. C. Darby, *The draining of the fens*, 2nd edn (1956); repr. (1968) · *CSP dom.*, *1581–94* · le comte de Dienne, *Histoire du desséchement des lacs et marais en France avant 1789* (1891) · APC, *1598–90*

Bradley, James (*bap.* **1692**, *d.* **1762**), astronomer, was born in Sherborne, Gloucestershire, and baptized there on 3 October 1692, the third son of William Bradley, a descendant of a family from Bradley Castle, co. Durham, and Jane Pound, of Bishop's Canning, Wiltshire, whom William Bradley married in 1678.

Early years and education Bradley was educated at Northleach grammar school and at Balliol College, Oxford, where he was admitted as a commoner in March 1711. He took his BA in October 1714 and his MA in June 1717, after which he initially pursued a career in the church. He was ordained deacon on 24 May 1719 by the bishop of London, and in July became vicar of Bridstow in Monmouthshire, immediately after being ordained a priest by Hoadly, the bishop of Hereford. The parish of Bridstow was in the gift of the bishop of Hereford, to whom Bradley later also became chaplain. In addition, he was presented with the sinecure from a small parish in Pembrokeshire, which was said to have been procured for Bradley from the prince of Wales with the help of the prince's secretary, the amateur astronomer Samuel Molyneux. However, from the point of view of his later career Bradley's early years were most significant for the contact he had with a maternal uncle, the Revd James Pound, one of the leading astronomical observers in England, who had worked both with Edmond Halley, the second astronomer royal, and with Sir Isaac Newton. From 1707 Pound was rector of Wansted in Essex, where he devoted much of his time to observing. From at the latest 1715 he was joined in this activity by his nephew; from that date Bradley's handwriting appeared regularly in the Wansted observing books. Pound provided the young Bradley with occasional financial assistance, and also nursed him through smallpox in 1717, but his most profound influence on his nephew was through the fostering of his interests in astronomy. In March 1716 Bradley wrote to the Royal Society about the aurora, and in 1718 Halley published two observations by Bradley in the *Philosophical Transactions of the Royal Society*, describing the young man's observing abilities in glowing terms. In November of that year Bradley was elected a fellow of the Royal Society. His duties as a clergyman were clearly light and, after his appointment as vicar of Bridstow, he continued to visit Wansted and to make astronomical observations from there.

Savilian professor of astronomy Bradley changed career in the autumn of 1721 when, following the death of John Keill, he was appointed Savilian professor of astronomy in the University of Oxford, with the support of the lord chancellor, George Parker (later earl of Macclesfield), and of Martin Foulkes (later president of the Royal Society). On his appointment, on 31 October 1721, he resigned his livings in the church. By this time Bradley had already made significant contributions to observational astronomy. He was particularly interested in the motions of Jupiter's satellites, and used his own observations to correct available astronomical tables, potentially a very

James Bradley (*bap.* 1692, *d.* 1762), by Thomas Hudson, *c.*1742–7

valuable activity for other astronomers, who all relied on such tables. In addition, he had made and published observations of two nebulae—at Halley's request—and observations of the double stars Castor and gamma Virginis, as well as observations of the planet Mars.

Having taken up the appointment at Oxford, it is not clear how much time during the first few years Bradley actually spent at the university apart from delivering his lectures; his inaugural lecture was read on 26 April 1722. However, following the appointment he was able to devote himself full-time to astronomy, for which he continued to use his uncle's observatory at Wansted. Nor did James Pound's death in November 1724 mark the end of Bradley's association with the place. Pound left no will, and Bradley continued to use the same instruments and to reside in Wansted with his uncle's widow.

Discovery of aberration It was about a year after his uncle's death that Bradley began the work which led to his first major discovery in astronomy. His friend Samuel Molyneux was interested in trying to measure the annual parallax of the stars, a tiny apparent motion of the stars caused by the actual annual motion of the earth around the sun, from which it would be possible to calculate distances to the nearest stars. Detecting such a movement would, moreover, finally provide observational confirmation of Copernicus's heliocentric theory. In particular, Molyneux wished to repeat an attempt to measure the annual parallax of the star gamma Draconis, first made by the natural philosopher Robert Hooke in 1669. To do so, he installed a zenith sector specifically designed for the purpose on his estate at Kew, and in December 1725 he invited Bradley to assist him in observing. Gamma Draconis was selected

because it crosses the meridian (culminates) almost overhead, thereby allowing observers to ignore the problem of the refraction of light through the earth's atmosphere, which affects the positions of all celestial objects nearer the horizon. Theory predicted that gamma Draconis would culminate at its most southerly point in December; its position at culmination should then gradually shift northwards every day over the following months, to its most northerly point in June, and back again over the following six months. To the astronomers' surprise, however, gamma Draconis did not do this. Instead, after December it continued to culminate at more southerly points, reaching its most southerly point in March and its most northerly point in September. The overall change in position over the six months was about 40 seconds of arc (that is, about one hundredth of a degree). In an attempt to identify the cause of this movement, Bradley decided to observe other stars and obtained his own zenith sector from the instrument maker George Graham, which he set up at Wansted. From August 1727 he observed a number of stars over a year and discovered that each displayed a comparable annual motion. A possible explanation apparently came to him while sailing on the Thames, when he noticed that the vane at the top of the mast changed direction as the boat turned although the wind continued to blow from the same direction. The analogous explanation for the apparent shift in position observed in the stars, he suggested, was that it resulted from a combination of the transmission of light at a finite speed from the star and the annual movement of the earth around the sun. This phenomenon—known as the aberration of light—was first described by Bradley in a letter to Halley, read to the Royal Society in January 1729. From his observations and theory, Bradley was able to calculate the speed of light: he stated that light took 8 minutes and 12 seconds to travel from the sun to the earth. He was also able to say with some authority that annual stellar parallax, the phenomenon he and Molyneux had set out to measure, must, in the stars observed, be exceedingly small (less than 1 second of arc, and therefore beyond the accuracy of the instruments available to Bradley and his contemporaries); otherwise, with the high precision instruments they had used, they would certainly have detected it. The consequence of this was that the distance to the nearest stars must be even more immense than had previously been believed.

In 1729 Bradley assumed the added role of lecturer in experimental philosophy at Oxford, giving his lectures in the Ashmolean Museum. He continued presenting these lectures for more than thirty years, to groups of on average more than fifty students. Two years after this appointment he failed in an attempt to be appointed keeper of the museum, but in 1732 he finally moved to Oxford to occupy a house in New College Lane, to which his professorship entitled him. His aunt, Mrs Pound, accompanied him and stayed in Oxford until her death in 1737. Most of the astronomical instruments from the house in Wansted were also moved, with the exception of the Graham zenith sector, which remained in Essex. Bradley had good reason to leave the instrument where it was and he made regular visits back to Wansted to use it for the continued observation of the stars he had started to track in the work leading to his discovery of aberration.

Appointment as astronomer royal By the early 1740s, therefore, Bradley was well established as a leading member of the astronomical community in Britain. During his years at Oxford he had also started to correspond with leading astronomers on the continent of Europe, including Pierre Louis de Maupertuis, through whom he became familiar with the work of Alexis Claude Clairaut and Pierre le Monnier, among others. Thus when Edmond Halley died in 1742, Bradley was an obvious candidate to succeed him. It has been reported that Halley himself was keen that Bradley should replace him, that he had been willing to resign in the younger man's favour, but that he died before he was able to do so. Bradley also continued to have the support of the earl of Macclesfield, who wrote in support of his candidature. On 3 February 1742 Bradley was appointed astronomer royal, and within three weeks the University of Oxford had awarded him a DD.

Bradley took up his new appointment in June 1742, but on his arrival at Greenwich he found the observatory and its instruments in a state of neglect. One of the main instruments, an 8 foot radius iron quadrant made by Jonathan Sisson under George Graham's supervision, was wedged against the roof of the quadrant house, and the sextant house had been taken over by pigeons. Before he could start a programme of observing from Greenwich, therefore, Bradley had to ensure that the instruments could be used. As well as inviting Graham and Sisson to reset the quadrant and the observatory's transit instrument, he and other fellows of the Royal Society petitioned the king for new instruments and a new building to house them. As a result a new quadrant and transit instrument were commissioned from John Bird, and a new building was started.

Meanwhile, during his early years at the Royal Greenwich Observatory Bradley both continued his previous programmes of work and turned his attention to the requirements of the new post. The observatory had been established in 1675 for a specific reason: to assist navigation, through the production of accurate tables of the positions of celestial bodies. Once the existing instruments were restored and placed in position, therefore, Bradley started to observe stellar culminations, using the transit instrument, and to help him in this he trained his nephew John Bradley. In the second half of 1742 more than 1500 transit observations were recorded. Much of the Bradleys' time was spent re-examining the positions of the brightest stars in the sky, as the astronomer royal grappled with the complexities of allowing for the different phenomena which cause the observed positions of celestial objects to appear to have shifted from their actual positions. In addition to taking into account the recently discovered effect of aberration, Bradley was aware of the need to consider precession (arising from the periodic movement of the earth's axis, similar to that of a spinning top) and the refraction of light through the earth's atmosphere. Refraction was a particularly difficult effect to allow for, as it varies according to the angular height, or altitude, of the object being observed and the local conditions (temperature and pressure) of the atmosphere. By concentrating on establishing, as far as possible, the positions of the brightest stars, Bradley would then be able to use the framework of those stars to increase the accuracy of the observatory's data on other celestial objects, especially those in the solar system. As well as concentrating on determining accurate positions for the brightest, so-called fixed, stars, during his early years at Greenwich, Bradley was responsible for a series of lunar observations and for observations of three comets (in 1743, 1744, and 1748). The observations of the moon were significant, as he corresponded about them with a number of astronomers in continental Europe. Through this correspondence he pursued his and the observatory's interest in the problem of determining longitude at sea and, it has been argued, sowed the seeds for the eventual launch of the *Nautical Almanac*, published by the Greenwich observatory annually since 1767.

Discovery of nutation In the course of this work Bradley also continued to pursue a personal programme of observing. Having made the discovery of aberration, he was still concerned about the observations of the stars he had made with the zenith sector at Wansted. In his initial analysis of the data he had considered a different explanation of the apparent motion exhibited: that it resulted from a periodic 'nodding', or nutation, of the earth's polar axis, brought about by the moon's gravitational pull on the earth, as predicted by Newton's theory. Bradley quickly eliminated this as the explanation of the particular observations he had made, but continued to wonder about the possibility of detecting evidence of such a nutation. Detecting and measuring the effect would provide a means of calculating the earth's spheroidicity and thus of settling the dispute between the Newtonians and those who followed the line of the French astronomer Jacques Cassini over whether the earth was elongated or flattened at the poles. From the observational point of view, one of the main problems was that, in theory, the earth's axis would take over eighteen years to complete a nutational cycle. Nevertheless, Bradley decided in the late 1720s to observe for what would be a full cycle; he continued the work for the necessary period, travelling to Wansted to make the observations, as all observations had to be made using the same instrument from the same spot. By early 1747 the observing programme was finished and the data analysed. Bradley then wrote to the earl of Macclesfield, a letter which was read to the Royal Society in February 1748. In it, Bradley announced his detection of nutation and confirmed the Newtonian model of the earth, flattened at the poles. By the time these results were published there was already separate observational confirmation of the shape of the earth from French expeditions to northern Sweden and to Peru to measure, by trigonometrical means, the length of a degree of arc of the earth's surface in each location. But Bradley's work in establishing the existence of a nutation of the earth's axis, together with his earlier detection of aberration, provided observational confirmation both of Copernicus's heliocentric solar system and of Newton's principle of universal gravitation. In 1748, following his announcement of nutation, Bradley was awarded the Royal Society's Copley medal.

Around the time of the announcement of nutation, Bradley started to receive formal international recognition for his achievements in astronomy. In 1746 he became a member of the Royal Academy of Berlin and in July 1748 a foreign associate of the Académie Royale des Sciences in Paris. Two years later he became a corresponding member of the Imperial Academy of Sciences in St Petersburg, and he subsequently assisted the academy by overseeing the construction by Bird of a quadrant made especially for them; in 1754 he became a full member of the academy. Three years later he was chosen to be a member of the institute in Bologna. Further recognition also came at home from the crown. When Bradley succeeded Halley in 1742 his income was £100 per annum, a rate which had not changed since John Flamsteed's appointment as the first astronomer royal in 1675. From this the incumbent had to pay for the running of the observatory. However, in the late 1740s Bradley received a single payment from the state of £1000 to meet the costs of re-equipping the observatory, and in 1752, in an acknowledgement of his skills and understanding as an astronomer and his contributions to navigation and trade, he was personally granted a pension from the crown of £250 per annum.

The Greenwich observations, 1750–1762 At about this point in his career Bradley was offered, but refused, the opportunity to return to work in the church by taking over the living from the parish of Greenwich. He preferred instead to continue at the Greenwich observatory, devoting himself full-time to the pursuit of astronomy. From 1750, almost until his death in 1762, he organized a very thorough programme of observations. Following the completion of the observations at Wansted, and of the building work at Greenwich, the zenith sector was moved to the Greenwich observatory. From then, Bradley concentrated all his effort on Greenwich and on gathering many volumes of observations. Over the twenty years for which he was astronomer royal, more than 900 folio pages in thirteen volumes were filled, the majority being recorded in the second half of his tenure. However, the observations were not published during his lifetime, and on his death they were removed from the Greenwich observatory by the executors of his estate. Their claim was that, since the pension awarded to Bradley in 1752 was in recognition of his personal abilities as an astronomer, and not a result of his office, the observations were not the property of the crown.

On 25 June 1744 Bradley had married Susannah Peach (*d.* 1757) of Chalford, Gloucestershire, and in 1746 a daughter, also named Susannah, was born. On her father's death, therefore, she inherited the Greenwich observations, held in trust for her until she came of age. When she reached the age of twenty-one, however, Susannah handed the papers to an uncle, the Revd Samuel Peach,

who refused a request from the board of longitude to surrender them. He left them to his elder son, John, who was equally unwilling to relinquish such valuable documents without what he regarded as due recompense. A legal case claiming ownership of the observations was prepared by the crown, but in 1776 John's younger brother, Samuel junior, who had become the legal heir of the papers on his marriage to Susannah Bradley, presented them to Lord North, chancellor of the University of Oxford. North gave them to the university on the condition that they be published by the Clarendon Press. The press, however, took more than twenty years to produce any publication. It was thus 1798 before the first volume of Bradley's observations appeared. When the volume was finally published, it included tables of aberration (in the equatorial plane) of sixteen stars, a catalogue of over 380 of the brightest fixed stars, and lunar latitudes and longitudes from the 1750s. A second volume, covering observations from the last six years of Bradley's time at Greenwich, appeared in 1805. By this time, one of the main problems associated with publishing was that the raw data, up to forty years after the observations were made, were not especially useful. The task of 'reducing' the data—that is, allowing for all the phenomena, including aberration, nutation, precession, refraction, and all the characteristics of the instruments used for observing, which affect the apparent position of the object on the celestial sphere—was not started until after the second volume was published. Then the young German astronomer Friedrich Wilhelm Bessel was encouraged by his fellow countryman and mentor Wilhelm Olbers to tackle the huge complexities. The work took Bessel more than ten years and resulted in his *Fundamenta astronomia* (1818), recognized by his contemporaries as one of the most significant contributions to positional astronomy; it confirmed Bessel as a leading authority. Starting with Bradley's observations, Bessel established a degree of accuracy previously unknown in positional astronomy. Bradley's observations were also revisited in the second half of the nineteenth century by the astronomer Arthur Auwers, who carried out a new reduction involving more data than had been known to Bessel. The outcome was three volumes of Bradley's observations, published between 1882 and 1903, and, it has been argued, marking the foundation of all modern star positions.

Interests in astronomical precision Bradley's significance in the history of stellar positional astronomy is therefore clear. But his responsibilities as astronomer royal went beyond keeping track of the fixed stars, and his personal interests in astronomy were not limited to observing stellar positions. One of his keenest concerns, closely allied to his primary work in gathering celestial positions, was in the accurate measurement of time. In the early 1730s the instrument maker George Graham built a clock which beat sidereal seconds, and used it in London to gather data on the clock's time-keeping at that latitude and temperature. He sent the results to Bradley. The clock was then shipped to Jamaica to one Colin Campbell, who carried out similar tests and also sent the results to Bradley. From the data, Bradley, then at Oxford, was able to demonstrate that, having allowed for differences in temperature, in Jamaica the clock slowed by about two minutes per day in comparison with its performance in London, in keeping with Newton's theory of gravity for the earth as an oblate spheroid. Bradley was also able to calculate how much the length of the pendulum would have to be altered at different latitudes to compensate for the associated differences in gravitational pull. A decade later, shortly after his appointment as astronomer royal, Bradley returned to the question of the length of a clock's pendulum, and set up a series of experiments to determine the length of a seconds pendulum at Greenwich as part of his programme to establish the observing ground rules for his tenure at the observatory. Later still in his career he must have been involved once again in the question of time-keeping, but in a wider context. Although there is no clear documentary evidence of Bradley's participation, as astronomer royal he is very likely to have had a role in England's adoption of the Gregorian calendar in 1752.

Bradley's fascination with accuracy of time and position led him to investigate the physical phenomena affecting both. In addition to the new phenomena he himself identified, he turned his attention to refraction, and derived a set of tables for use at the observatory. His main work in this area came in the early 1750s, after the new instruments were in place, when he made use of the new Bird quadrant and analysed the effect of temperature and pressure on the observations. Over the same period, and with the same instrument, he also set about determining as precisely as possible the latitude of the Greenwich observatory, a fundamental measurement for all observing programmes.

Throughout his career in astronomy, Bradley addressed himself to issues of instrumentation. Having early on proved his skill in the use of telescopes with very long focal lengths, in 1723 he helped James Pound carry out trials with a reflecting telescope designed by James Hadley. After this Bradley himself experimented with grinding his own specula. He was not particularly successful in this, but he achieved a level of skill and understanding which allowed him personally to undertake many of the necessary repairs to the instruments at Greenwich. Although he was not especially successful at making mirror surfaces, unlike many of his contemporaries he was interested in using reflecting telescopes. In 1732 he was involved in trials at sea of a sextant made by Hadley and was very impressed with the instrument. By the time he succeeded Halley at Greenwich he was adept at assessing the performance of individual instruments. As in his approach to all aspects of his work, accuracy was the key, and he worked assiduously during the early years at the Greenwich observatory to reform and improve the performance of its range of instruments. For instance, in 1745 he added an improved micrometer screw to the 8 foot Graham quadrant to enable readings accurate to half a second of arc to be made.

Interests in the solar system Much of the remainder of Bradley's working life was spent in observing the solar system. Following his early work on the motion of Jupiter's satellites, he returned in the mid-1720s to observing the satellites, using his own observations from London of the eclipses of the four main satellites (the 'Medicean' stars discovered by Galileo) and comparing them with similar observations made from New York and Lisbon. From these observations, and the differences in the times of the disappearance and reappearance of each as it passed behind the body of Jupiter, he was able to deduce the differences in longitude between the three observing places. He reported his results to the Royal Society in 1726. During the programme of observations, he also noted the very different paths followed by each of the satellites. In keeping with his approach to all observing programmes—driven by a wish to improve the accuracy of all observational data—he set out to improve existing tables of the satellites' motions and to understand why the moons moved as they did. His investigations continued into the 1730s, when he deduced a formula interrelating the motions of all four satellites based on their mutual gravitational attraction.

Bradley's interests extended to the rest of the solar system. In 1719, with his uncle James Pound, he observed the planet Mars when at opposition (that is, directly opposite the sun) with the aim of obtaining an improved value for the solar parallax, and hence of the distance between the earth and the sun. The value they obtained suggested the sun was further away than had previously been supposed. In addition, throughout his career as astronomer, in common with almost all astronomers of the period, Bradley followed the paths of comets as they passed within observing distance of the earth. For three, those passing in 1723, 1737, and 1757, he wrote short papers, presenting his raw observations and his reductions of them, calculating the comets' elements, and giving details of their physical appearance, including the tail and nucleus and the comets' magnitudes. Bradley also made detailed notes of his observations of the comet of 1744, which was extremely bright, equalling the brightness of Jupiter at times, and that of 1748. He exchanged information on comets with several overseas astronomers, including Benito Suarez, a Jesuit observer in Paraguay, and the French astronomer Abbé de Lacaille.

Other solar system phenomena and characteristics also attracted Bradley's attention. Early on in his work in astronomy he measured the diameters of the visible discs of the planets; as early as 1715 he measured Jupiter using a telescope with a focal length of over 200 feet, indicating a significant level of skill as an observer. Four years later he attempted to make measurements of Saturn, including the diameters of the inner and outer rings, observations which required a great deal of care. His interest in Saturn was rekindled more than a decade later when he observed the planet around the time when the rings were edge on to the earth, and therefore invisible for a while. His observations of the reappearance of the rings in 1730 are the only ones to have survived from that date. These observations are also of interest historically, as, unusually for the period, Bradley used a reflecting rather than a refracting telescope to make them. Bradley was also interested in Mercury and Venus, and made measurements of the diameters of both in 1722. Towards the end of his time as astronomer royal he returned to a consideration of Venus as, in 1761, a rare transit of the planet was due (a transit, an apparent crossing of the sun's surface by a planet, is an event which takes place in pairs, eight years apart, about every century). Bradley's particular interest in this phenomenon, apart from its rarity, came from his wish to use the observations to improve the accuracy of the value of the solar parallax. He was aware of the need to observe the transit from two widely separated locations, and decided that Java and the island of St Helena should be chosen. By the late 1750s Bradley himself was too frail to contemplate such a journey. Instead he sent his then assistant at Greenwich, Charles Mason, to Java, and persuaded the Royal Society to send the young astronomer Nevil Maskelyne to observe the transit from St Helena. In the event, neither expedition was destined to produce results: Mason failed to reach Java in time, as he travelled through areas involved in the Seven Years' War and was delayed by enemy action, and for Maskelyne the weather in St Helena was unfavourable. Maskelyne's career in astronomy, however, had much brighter prospects: by the mid-1760s he was himself astronomer royal.

Final years During his period as astronomer royal Bradley employed four assistants, the first of whom was his nephew John Bradley, who worked with him for nine years. He was succeeded in 1751 by Gael Morris, who was Bradley's assistant for five years, and then Charles Mason, who worked at Greenwich from 1757 until he set off for Java in 1760. By the time Bradley was joined by the last of his assistants, Charles Green, he had been suffering for some time from a variety of ailments; he also became increasingly concerned that he was losing his powers of reasoning. After his wife's death in 1757 he maintained close contact with her family, and as physical illness set in he went to stay with them at Chalford in Gloucestershire. He was cared for there by a local doctor, Dr Lewis, and by Dr Daniel Lysons from Oxford. On 13 July 1762 he died from the illness, a chronic abdominal inflammation. He was buried near his wife and his mother at Minchinhampton, Gloucestershire. A brass plate, with an inscription by Dr Blayney (later regius professor of Hebrew in the University of Oxford) was fixed to an altar tomb in the churchyard and later moved into the church to protect it from thieves. Almost seventy years after Bradley's death a dial was erected at Kew to mark the spot where he began the observations which led to the discovery of aberration and of nutation.

During his lifetime Bradley was held in high esteem by his peers. Halley recognized his talent very quickly, and Newton once described him as the best astronomer in Europe. From the eulogies to Bradley following his death, it is equally clear that he was held in considerable esteem by his contemporaries. He was reported to have been humane, benevolent, and kind, a dutiful son, an indulgent husband, a tender father, and a steady friend. Although he was not particularly wealthy, he supported members of his family when he could. In his will he left annuities to his widowed sisters, Mary Mills and Elizabeth Jenner, and ensured his daughter, Susannah, was properly educated and cared for until she came of age. His books were left to Samuel Peach junior, and his nephews William Dallaway and John Peach were appointed as executors of his will and as joint guardians to Susannah.

For most of his life Bradley was healthy and must have had considerable stamina to sustain such a heavy programme of observing for so many years. When not observing, much of his work involved the meticulous, methodical, but unglamorous reduction of the data gathered. To identify the phenomena of aberration and nutation he needed a great deal of determination and patience, as well as enormous skill as an observer. These particular strengths he called upon in all his astronomical endeavours, which meant that his legacy to later astronomers was highly significant. Although he published comparatively little during his lifetime, his papers on aberration and nutation were key publications for the discoveries themselves and for the development of the notion of precision in astronomy; he also produced a number of papers, mainly concerning comets and other solar system objects. Moreover, the observations he made laid the basis for positional astronomy for over a century and a half. Knowing how and the precise extent to which the positions of celestial objects were affected by what could be termed 'local' phenomena—that is, those resulting from the instrument, the conditions around the observatory, and the motions both of the earth's axis and of the earth's orbit—allowed Bradley and later astronomers to concentrate upon characteristics intrinsic to the objects themselves. While, as has been pointed out by late twentieth-century historians, Bradley was not alone in Europe in taking positional astronomy so seriously, he was known to be a leading authority throughout his years as astronomer royal. Moreover, through his diligence in recording data at Greenwich, his legacy was tangible, reappearing in the form of basic astronomical tables in the early nineteenth and early twentieth centuries—tables which were heralded, literally, as epoch-making by astronomers of those eras.

MARI E. W. WILLIAMS

Sources *Miscellaneous works and correspondence of the Rev. James Bradley*, ed. [S. P. Rigaud] (1832); repr. (1972) · J. Bradley, 'An account of a new discovered motion of the fix'd stars', *PTRS*, 35 (1727–8), 637–61 · J. Bradley, 'Concerning an apparent motion observed in some of the fixed stars', *PTRS*, 45 (1748), 1–48 · *DNB* · A. F. O'D. Alexander, 'Bradley, James', *DSB* · E. G. Forbes, *Greenwich observatory*, 1: *Origins and early history (1675–1835)* (1975) · F. W. Bessel, *Fundamenta astronomiae pro anno MDCCLV deducta ex observationibus viri incomparabilis, James Bradley, in specula astronomica Grenovicensi per annos 1750–1762 institutes* (1818) · G. F. A. Auwers, *Neue Reduktion der Bradley'schen Beobachtungen aus den Jahren 1750 bis 1762*, 3 vols. (1882–1903) · J. Bradley, *Astronomical observations made at the Royal Observatory … MDCCL to … MDCCLXII*, ed. [T. Hornsby and A. Robertson] (1798–1805) · W. McCrea, 'James Bradley, 1693–1762', *Quarterly Journal of the Royal Astronomical Society*, 4 (1963), 38–40 · W. McCrea, 'The significance of the discovery of aberration', *Quarterly Journal of the*

Royal Astronomical Society, 4 (1963), 41–3 · R. Woolley, 'James Bradley, third astronomer royal', *Quarterly Journal of the Royal Astronomical Society*, 4 (1963), 47–52
Archives BL, observations on Halley's comet, Add. MS 4439 · Bodl. Oxf., corresp. and papers · CUL, Royal Greenwich Observatory archives, observations, star catalogues, and papers · MHS Oxf., lectures · UCL, lectures, notebooks and treatises
Likenesses T. Hudson, oils, *c.*1742–1747, RS [*see illus.*] · oils, after 1747, NMM, Greenwich, Royal Observatory · oils, *c.*1833–1840 (after T. Hudson), NPG · oils, *c.*1833–1840 (after J. Faber), NPG · J. Faber junior, engraving (after T. Hudson), repro. in *National Portrait Gallery catalogue*, pl. 80
Wealth at death £360; plus sufficient to fund three annuities totalling at least £135 p.a.: will, *Miscellaneous works*, ed. Rigaud

Bradley, Katharine Harris (1846–1914), poet, collaborated with her niece **Edith Emma Cooper** (1862–1913) to publish verse under the pseudonym Michael Field. The aunt was born in Birmingham on 27 October 1846, the daughter of Charles Bradley (1810–1848), tobacco manufacturer of a Derbyshire family (who died of cancer when she was only two), and his wife, Emma Harris (1812–1868). Katharine became her own spelling of what at her birth had been Catherine (and on her death certificate was Katherine), although her preference for a series of male nicknames and pseudonyms meant that her own name was rarely used.

Katharine Bradley's much older sister Emma Harris Bradley (1835–1889) had married James Robert Cooper (1818–1897), merchant, about 1860, and in 1861 or 1862 their household was joined by Katharine and her widowed mother (who, like the father, died of cancer). Edith Emma Cooper was born to Emma and James Cooper in High Street, Kenilworth, on 12 January 1862. After the birth of a second daughter, Amy, Emma Cooper became an invalid, and Katharine took over from her sister the upbringing and education of her young niece Edith, tending her as a mother. Katharine had similarly been educated at home, by private tutors, but in 1868 attended the Collège de France in Paris and later (1874) attended Newnham College, Cambridge, for a vacation course studying the classics. The whole family moved to Stoke Bishop, near Bristol, in 1879, and Katharine and her niece Edith attended courses there at University College. They joined the debating society, arguing eloquently for causes like women's suffrage and anti-vivisection (Sturgeon, 20). Katharine was briefly a disciple of Ruskin, being swayed in the 1870s by his moral and aesthetic teachings. She joined his Guild of St George in January 1875, but was ejected in 1877 for her confessed atheism (T. S. Moore and D. C. S. Moore, chapter 7).

In 1875 Katharine had published her first volume of lyrics, *The New Minnesinger*, under the name Arran Leigh; in 1881 the collaboration with Edith took shape in their joint publication of *Bellerophôn* under the names Arran and Isla Leigh. Their aim was to write great verse tragedies based on historical subjects, calling up the male Elizabethan tradition and eschewing modern realism (they admired Rossetti and Pater): they likened themselves to Beaumont and Fletcher. Dorothy Wordsworth was the only other English woman they ranked as a poet at this time.

In 1884, with the publication of the verse dramas *Callirrhöe* and *Fair Rosamund*, their joint pseudonym Michael Field was born. 'He' was hailed by critics (including Robert Browning) as a major new voice: 'a poet of distinguished powers', 'something almost of Shakespearean penetration', 'a fresh gift of song' (Sturgeon, 27–8). The disguise was not penetrated until after the publication of *Long Ago* (1889), based on fragments of Sappho. Just as Katharine had predicted, 'the report of lady authorship will dwarf and enfeeble our work at every turn' (T. S. Moore and D. C. S. Moore, 6). Calling them his 'two dear Greek women', Browning remained an admirer of their work, as did Swinburne, Wilde, Meredith, and Yeats. But after it was known that Michael Field was two spinsters his works were shunned, until at length they resorted to anonymity and found success in 1905 with *Borgia*. Lionel Johnson was the only critic ever to praise as they felt they deserved. Nevertheless, they published twenty-seven tragedies, eight volumes of lyrics, and a masque, and had one (prose) play, *A Question of Memory*, briefly staged in London; it was produced by J. T. Grein for the Independent Theatre Society in 1893.

Their collaboration was close-knit and closely guarded: 'we are closer married [than the Brownings]', they maintained in *Works and Days* (T. S. Moore and D. C. S. Moore, 16). Katharine (nicknamed Michael) was the short, energetic, vivacious, outgoing partner who loved to study Greek, and who managed their business correspondence; Edith (Henry) was tall, shy, pallid, reflective, of a keener and steadier intellect, more given to Latin than Greek; she kept the accounts. Their economic independence allowed them to remain lifelong worshippers of beauty—'life was one of their arts', as one contemporary remarked (Sturgeon, 36). Both women enjoyed continental travel with frequent trips to the art galleries of Europe; *Sight and Song* (1892), a series of lyrics centred on various paintings by old masters, was one of the fruits. They issued much of their work through private presses in small, beautifully decorated editions, many designed and published by the artists Charles Shannon and Charles Ricketts, editors of *The Dial*, who became their close friends. From about 1885 their partnership had blossomed into a romantic love and they formed a sexual union, at first joyous but later clouded by various guilts. Edith's much-loved father died while walking in the Alps in 1897; his body was not recovered for many months. Edith took the news as a punishment, but he left money that enabled the pair to set up house together for the first time, at Richmond in 1899. Her mother (Katharine's sister) had died in 1889.

In 1907 Edith turned to the Catholic church, remaining a devotee until her death. Katharine at first feared losing her, but then joined her, choosing for her own confessor their friend Father John Gray, poet and probable homosexual. The two women remained devoted companions until their deaths within nine months of each other, both of cancer. Katharine concealed her own illness while nursing Edith, who died on 13 December 1913 at 1 The Paragon, Petersham Road, Richmond. Katharine published *Poems of Adoration*, Edith's last work, in 1912, and her own, *Mystic*

Trees, in 1913. Each was signed Michael Field. After Edith's death, Katharine published early poems by Edith in *Dedicated* (1914), also slipping in one of her own, 'reverting to the pagan' (Sturgeon, 57):

> In the old accents I will sing, my Glory, my Delight,
> In the old accents, tipped with flame, before we knew the
> right.

Katharine died at The Cottage, Haidkesyard, Armitage, Staffordshire, on 26 September 1914; she had been dressing to go to mass. Katharine and Edith were buried together in the St Mary Magdalen cemetery, Mortlake, and a marble tomb was made for them by Charles Ricketts in 1926; it has since disappeared, however, possibly because of deterioration or damage. Twenty-nine volumes of the diaries of Katharine Bradley and Edith Cooper ranging over the period from 1888 to 1914 are housed in the British Library: selected excerpts were published in 1933 as *Works and Days*. Their verse writing is uneven, their plays are marred by an indulgence in archaisms, but many of their lyrics are fine, especially the more passionate love poems. VIRGINIA H. BLAIN

Sources M. Sturgeon, *Michael Field* (1922); repr. (New York, 1975) · T. S. Moore and D. C. S. Moore, eds., *Works and days: from the journal of Michael Field* (1933) · L. Johnson, 'Michael Field', *The poets and the poetry of the nineteenth century*, ed. A. H. Miles, 9 (1907) · I. C. Treby, *The Michael Field catalogue: a book of lists* (1998) · Michael Field letters, Bodl. Oxf. · M. Field, letters, Morgan L. · unpublished Michael Field journals, BL · b. cert. · d. cert. **Archives** BL, corresp. and diaries, Add. MSS 45851–45856, 46776–46804, 46866–46867, 61713–61724 · Bodl. Oxf., corresp. and literary MSS | BL, corresp. with Sir Sydney Cockerell, Add. MS 52707 · BL, letters of Michael Field to Alice Trusted · Bodl. Oxf., letters of E. E. Cooper to her parents and to K. Bradley · Bodl. Oxf., letters to Elkin Mathews · Harvard University, near Florence, Italy, Center for Italian Renaissance Studies, letters from K. Bradley and E. E. Cooper to Bernard Berenson (1892–1914), 50135 · NL Scot., letters to John Gray **Likenesses** C. Ricketts, miniature (with Edith Emma Cooper), FM, Cam.; repro. in Sturgeon, *Michael Field* · C. Shannon, drawing (with Edith Emma Cooper), Birmingham Art Gallery; repro. in Moore and Moore, eds., *Works and days*, 4 · portrait (with Edith Emma Cooper), repro. in Sturgeon, *Michael Field* · portrait (with Edith Emma Cooper), repro. in Moore and Moore, eds., *Works and days* **Wealth at death** £9447 8s. od.—Edith Emma Cooper: probate, 5 Feb 1914, *CGPLA Eng. & Wales*

Bradley, Martha (*fl.* 1740s–1755), writer on cookery, is known today only through her one monumental book, *The British Housewife*, which was published as a part-work from January to October 1756 and eventually came out in book form in 1758. The book is a complete manual for the housewife, the cook, the housekeeper, the gardener, and the farrier, with monthly sections of advice and recipes which cover every aspect of domestic management in the middle of the eighteenth century. The author herself was a professional cook who worked in Bath in the 1740s. She perfected her craft by her practical experience and her knowledge of earlier cookery books: she used and adapted recipes by such predecessors as Mary Eales (*Mrs Mary Eales's Receipts*, 1718), Patrick Lamb (*Royal Cookery*, 1710; 3rd edn, 1726), Vincent La Chapelle (*The Modern Cook*, 1733), and Hannah Glasse (*The Art of Cookery*, 1747). A reference to William Hogarth's *Analysis of Beauty* (1.70), published in 1753, establishes that Martha Bradley's book was written after that date. The publisher's note that Mrs Bradley's papers, including a valued family manuscript recipe collection, were all lodged with him (*The British Housewife*, 1.369) suggests that she was dead by the time her work began to be published.

Martha Bradley is one of the most important cookery writers of the eighteenth century, not only because her book is one of the most comprehensive of its kind but also because she discusses the merits and difficulties of the dishes, gives information on European as well as English cookery, and tells the reader what is old-fashioned and what is up to date. In an age when most cookery books were simply compilations Mrs Bradley's book stands out for the author's personal involvement in her recipes. GILLY LEHMANN

Sources M. Bradley, *The British housewife* (1756)

Bradley, Ralph (1716–1788), lawyer, probably born at Greatham, co. Durham, the son of Nicholas Bradley (*d.* 1784) and his wife, Margaret Bunting (*d.* 1720), was a contemporary of James Booth, who has been called the patriarch of modern conveyancing.

Bradley was admitted to the Middle Temple on 22 November 1751 and called to the bar on 10 June 1757. He practised at Stockton-on-Tees with great success for upwards of half a century. He is said to have managed the concerns of almost the whole county of Durham, and, though a provincial counsel, his opinions were everywhere received with the greatest respect. His drafts, like Booth's, were reputedly prolix to excess, but some of them remained long in use as precedents in the northern counties.

Bradley published in London in 1779 *An Enquiry into the Nature of Property and Estates as Defined by English Law*. A posthumous compilation, *Practical Points, or, Maxims in Conveyancing*, appeared in London in 1804, edited by J. Ritson. This was a collection of Bradley's notes on points of practice, and the technical minutiae of conveyancing as they were suggested in the course of his professional life. Ritson was a contemporary and fellow townsman of Bradley. The latter by his will left a considerable sum, estimated at £40,000, on trust for the purchase of books calculated to promote the interests of religion and virtue in Great Britain, and the happiness of mankind. However Lord Thurlow, by a decree in chancery, set aside this charitable disposition in favour of his next of kin. Bradley died at Stockton-on-Tees on 28 December 1788, and was buried in the parish church of Greatham, where a monument was erected to his memory on the north side of the chancel. ROBERT HARRISON, rev. DAVID IBBETSON

Sources R. Surtees, *The history and antiquities of the county palatine of Durham*, 3 (1823), 340 · will, PRO, PROB 11/1175 fol. 206 · litigation on will, PRO, C 33/475 pt. 2 fol. 579 · *GM*, 1st ser., 58 (1788), 1184 · H. A. C. Sturgess, ed., *Register of admissions to the Honourable Society of the Middle Temple, from the fifteenth century to the year 1944*, 1 (1949), 344 · J. Hutchinson, ed., *A catalogue of notable Middle Templars: with brief biographical notices* (1902) · J. F. Waller, ed., *The imperial dictionary of universal biography*, 3 vols. (1857–63) · *Sweet and Maxwell's Legal*

bibliography of the British commonwealth of nations, 2 vols. (1957) · C. Davidson and T. C. Wright, *Davidson's precedents and forms in conveyancing*, 4th edn., 5 vols. (1864–77)
Likenesses memorial, Greatham parish church, co. Durham
Wealth at death £40,000: Surtees, *History*, vol. 3, p. 340n.

Bradley, Richard (1688?–1732), botanist and writer, was interested in gardening from his childhood. He lived mostly in the vicinity of London. He was elected a fellow of the Royal Society of London on 1 December 1712, having been nominated by one of his patrons, Robert Balle. Another friend, James Petiver, an affluent apothecary and insatiable collector in all fields of natural history, helped arrange for Bradley to travel to the Low Countries in May 1714, following Petiver's route of 1711 and apparently carrying letters of introduction. In a letter to Petiver in 1714 Bradley sent blessings to his own children, which indicates that he was probably married at that time, though no details of a first wife are known. While there, though without medical training, he began practising medicine, and wrote to Petiver for recipes of medicines, which were duly sent.

In 1716 Bradley published two brief articles in the *Philosophical Transactions of the Royal Society* that attest more to his enthusiasm for botany than to scientific ability. Some of his many publications in horticultural periodicals contain original observations, but most were popular writings which could earn him a living. His writings, expertise, and personality attracted a few wealthy patrons, most notably James Brydges, first duke of Chandos, who hired him to advise and supervise his plantings at Canons in Middlesex. By November 1717 Brydges was sending him funds to pay his debts. However, in December 1719 Brydges complained of his having mismanaged £460, and their relationship ended.

Bradley had only a slight acquaintance with Sir Hans Sloane when he embarked for the Low Countries, but Petiver obtained for him a letter of introduction from Sloane, and when Bradley returned in October, he added to Sloane's collections. Bradley dedicated two publications to Sloane and also cited his works. By June 1723 he knew Sloane well enough to ask his advice about whether to leave the country because of an 'unfortunate affair at Kensington, whereby I lost all my substance, my expectations, and my friends' (BL, Sloane MS 3322, fol. 50).

Four months later Bradley optimistically asked Sloane to support his application for the botany chair at Oxford being endowed by William Sherard, but Sherard's condition for the endowment was that it go to Johann Jacob Dillenius. In 1724 Bradley was appointed the first professor of botany at Cambridge. Bradley's immediate successors in that chair were first John Martyn and later John's son, Thomas. Long after Bradley's death Thomas Martyn claimed that 'Bradley was never of any university' and that he obtained the appointment 'by means of a verbal recommendation from Dr Sherard to Dr Bentley; and pompous assurances that [Bradley] would procure the University a public Botanic Garden by his own private purse and personal interest' (Egerton, 'Relationship', 60, 73n.).

Bradley was unable to arrange for a botanical garden, but he did write and publish two sets of course lectures, on general and practical botany (*Ten Practical Discourses*, 1727) and on pharmaceutical botany (*A Course of Lectures upon the Materia medica*, 1730). Although Thomas Martyn also claimed that Bradley did not teach, the subtitle of the latter work says these lectures were read 'in the Physick Schools at Cambridge'. Bradley's early ecological ideas—on the balance of nature and biological productivity—added to his reputation.

Hence, about 1730, Bradley married Mary, a woman of some means who believed he was also a doctor. He died in Charterhouse Lane, London, on 5 November 1732. His final illness consumed all his wife's wealth, and after his death she wrote to Sir Hans Sloane saying that she and her child were destitute. FRANK N. EGERTON

Sources B. Henrey, *British botanical and horticultural literature before 1800*, 2 (1975), 424–54; 3 (1975), 14–18 · F. N. Egerton, 'Richard Bradley's relationship with Sir Hans Sloane', *Notes and Records of the Royal Society*, 25 (1970), 59–77 · F. N. Egerton III, 'Richard Bradley's illicit excursion into medical practice in 1714', *Medical History*, 14 (1970), 53–62 · F. N. Egerton, 'Richard Bradley's understanding of biological productivity: a study of eighteenth-century ecological ideas', *Journal of the History of Biology*, 2 (1969), 391–410 · F. N. Egerton, 'Changing concepts of the balance of nature', *Quarterly Review of Biology*, 48 (1973), 322–50 · G. D. Rowley, introduction, in *Collected writings on succulent plants* (1964), vii–xxiv · R. Williamson, 'John Martyn and the Grub-street Journal, with particular references to his attacks on Richard Bentley, Richard Bradley', *Medical History*, 5 (1961), 361–74 · R. Williamson, 'The germ theory of disease: neglected precursors of Louis Pasteur (Richard Bradley, Benjamin Martin, Jean-Baptiste Goiffon)', *Annals of Science*, 11 (1955), 44–57 · S. M. Walters, *The shaping of Cambridge botany* (1981), 15–29 · F. A. Stafleu and R. S. Cowan, *Taxonomic literature: a selective guide*, 2nd edn, 1, Regnum Vegetabile, 94 (1976), 300–01 · Desmond, *Botanists*, 84 · D. E. Allen, *The naturalist in Britain: a social history* (1976) · A. Stevenson, *Catalogue of botanical books in the collection of Rachel McMasters Miller Hunt*, 2 (1961)
Archives U. Cam., department of plant sciences | BL, letters to Sir Hans Sloane and J. Petiver, Sloane MSS 1968, 3322, 4045–4049, 4065
Wealth at death none; spent wife's wealth, leaving her destitute: Egerton 'Richard Bradley's relationship with Sir Hans Sloane', 72; Henrey, *British botanical and horticultural literature*

Bradley, Robert [Buddy] (1908–1972), choreographer, was born in Harrisburg, Pennsylvania, on 24 July 1908, the son of Robert Louis Bradley and his wife, Georgia Marguerite, *née* Walker. He was educated at Harrisburg high school, and on leaving school was apprenticed as a sign writer. He made his stage début as a dancer in 1926 at the Lincoln Square Theatre, New York, in a revue with Florence Mills. He then became the dance teacher and arranger for a number of Broadway musicals. In addition to Fred Astaire and his sister Adele, he coached many stars, including Mae West, Ruby Keeler, Lucille Ball, and Eleanor Powell. However (like other black choreographers) he was never credited for choreographing a show with a white cast in America. In 1928 he rechoreographed *Greenwich Village Follies*, even though Busby Berkeley's name appeared as choreographer in the programme. In 1968 he said: 'They called me in to patch them up when they realized how bad the dancing was. I never saw half the shows my stuff appeared in. I wasn't invited, and besides I was too busy teaching' (Stearns and Stearns, 162).

Fred Astaire suggested that Jessie Matthews persuade the impresario Charles B. Cochran to invite Bradley to London to stage the dances for her show *Ever Green* (the title originally had two words) at the Adelphi Theatre in 1930. With a score by Rodgers and Hart, this became Matthews's greatest hit, and Bradley received his first choreographic credit. After *Ever Green*, he collaborated with Matthews again in *Hold my Hand* at the Gaiety Theatre in 1931. By the end of the decade he had choreographed over thirty musicals in London, including Cole Porter's *Anything Goes* (1935), and *Blackbirds of 1936* (1936), which featured the Nicholas Brothers. He made his first appearance on the London stage in *Cochran's 1931 Revue*, and in 1943, in addition to choreographing *It's Time to Dance* with Jack Buchanan and Elsie Randolph, he also featured in the production as Buddy. In 1932 he collaborated with Frederick Ashton in creating Britain's first jazz ballet, *High Yellow*, in which Alicia Markova starred. He also created a cabaret act for the ballet dancers Vera Zorina and Anton Dolin.

In 1934, at Jessie Matthews's request, Bradley was signed by Gaumont-British to choreograph her dances for the film version of *Evergreen*, in which he made his one and only screen appearance, dancing with some children on the pavement of a London street in the spectacular production number 'Springtime in your Heart'. He and Matthews also collaborated on *It's Love Again* (1936), *Head over Heels* (1937), *Gangway* (1938), and *Sailing Along* (1938). Ralph Reader was credited as the dance arranger for *First a Girl* (1935), although Bradley helped out. The Bradley–Matthews partnership was one of the most important in the history of dance, and yet books about the history of British musical theatre and cinema largely ignored Bradley's contribution. One of the few exceptions was John Kobal's *Gotta Sing, Gotta Dance* (1971). Kobal wrote:

> Her usual choreographic collaborator, an American resident in England, Buddy Bradley, must have understood Jessie Matthews and her abilities as a dancer almost as well as she

did herself. There is hardly ever a moment in her dances that is not lyrical and harmonious or which looks awkward for her to do. She feels the music. At times she almost seems to *be* the music, always anticipating the next movement—not just clever choreography, but her body's intuitive expression of the pleasure she gets from dancing.   (Kobal, 95)

Matthews herself recalled:

> We worked on most of my films together marvellously well! We created together. Had he tied me down to his one type of dancing, I would have rebelled. I was a classical dancer, and I added to the classical arabesques, the high kicks of musical comedy. Buddy then added the coloured rhythm.   (Kobal, 100)

Bradley choreographed a number of other British film musicals of the 1930s, including *Radio Parade of 1935* (1934), *Brewster's Millions* (1935), *Oh, Daddy* (1935), and *This'll Make you Whistle* (1936). He also choreographed a number of pre-war and early post-war television variety shows for the BBC. Broadcast live from Alexandra Palace, these included *Night Lights* (1939), *Variety in Sepia* (1947), *Black Magic* (1949), and a television version of the West End revue *Sauce Tartare* (1949). As choreographer, Bradley was responsible for Jessie Matthews taking over from Zoe Gail in *Sauce Latter Tartare* at the Cambridge Theatre in 1949. It was the last time they worked together, though he did make a guest appearance in BBC television's *This is your Life* tribute to Matthews in 1961.

Bradley's teaching career continued to flourish after the Second World War. In 1950 the Buddy Bradley Dance School in London had over 500 students. It remained in operation until 1968 when he decided to return to New York. He died there on 17 July 1972, at the Beth Israel Hospital. He was survived by his wife, Dorothy. They had no children.   STEPHEN BOURNE

Sources S. Bourne, 'Harlem comes to London', *Black in the British frame: black people in British film and television, 1896–1996* (1998) · M. Stearns and J. Stearns, *Jazz dance: the story of American vernacular dance* (New York, 1968) · 'Our Busby Berkeley', *Film Weekly* (25 Jan 1935) · 'He gives the stars their legs', *Picturegoer Weekly* (7 March 1936) · J. Kobal, *Gotta sing, gotta dance: a pictorial history of film musicals* (1971) · C. Valis Hill, 'Buddy Bradley: the "invisible" man of

Robert Bradley (1908–1972), by unknown photographer, 1934 [centre, in the musical *Evergreen*]

Broadway brings jazz tap to London', *Proceedings of the Society of Dance History Scholars* (14–15 Feb 1992) • J. Parker, ed., *Who's who in the theatre*, 12th edn (1957) • C. V. Hill, 'Bradley, Buddy', *ANB* • *Variety* (26 July 1972)

Likenesses photograph, 1934, repro. in Bourne, *Black in the British frame*, following p. 116 • photograph, 1934, Hult. Arch. [*see illus.*]

Bradley, Thomas (1599/1600–1673), Church of England clergyman, was born in Berkshire. He matriculated from Exeter College, Oxford, on 9 May 1617, aged seventeen. He graduated BA on 21 June 1620, became chaplain to George Villiers, duke of Buckingham, and accompanied him on the expedition to France in 1627. In 1629 a ship's captain named Richard Plumleigh applied to the privy council to take Bradley with him on the expedition to France. He became rector of the Yorkshire parishes of Castleford and Ackworth in 1630 and 1631 respectively; both livings were in the gift of Charles I. At some point he became chaplain to Frances Savile (*d.* in or after 1651), daughter of John *Savile, first Baron Savile (1556–1630), whom he married in May 1631. Their eldest son was born on Christmas day 1632.

At the outbreak of civil war Bradley travelled to the royalist headquarters at Oxford and was created DD on 20 December 1642. He acted as chaplain to Charles I during this period, and ministered to the royalist troops at the siege of Pontefract in 1644. He was sequestered from his livings in 1644, and his library was treacherously appropriated by a friend to whom he had entrusted it in an attempt to avoid its seizure by parliament. In 1645 he was assessed at £300 by the committee for advance of money, and on 13 April 1647 his wife was granted fifths from both his Yorkshire livings. He described some of his sufferings in the published version of a sermon in defence of 'the Feast of the Nativitie' delivered at Winchester on Christmas day 1650, *Comfort from the Cradle* (1651). In 1655 he urged the lord protector and the council of state to adopt his scheme for raising large sums of money through the extortion of first fruits and tithes. He subsequently published *A Present for Caesar*, in which he called himself 'a friend and servant to the Commonwealth' (3r–3v), urging Cromwell to implement his scheme, provoking a response from Rice Vaughan in *First Fruits and Tenths of Ecclesiastical Livings* (1657). After the Restoration, in an attempt at vindication, *Appello Caesarem* (1661), Bradley maintained that his scheme had been designed to secure the Church of England and provide a steady revenue for the Stuarts after their return from exile. Whatever the truth of this claim, he conveniently neglected to mention that he had expected to receive significant financial benefits from the adoption of his scheme.

In 1661 Bradley styled himself 'an Episcopal-Presbiterian', perhaps an endorsement of Archbishop Ussher's scheme for primitive episcopacy. He was made a prebendary of York in 1660 and was canon of the cathedral between 1666 and 1670. In 1665 he petitioned the queen for presentation to the rectory of Castleford as a reward 'for his services at home and abroad to the King' (*CSP dom.*, 1665–6, 139). By 1669 he had regained possession of Ackworth. Bradley was 'an excellent preacher' and 'a

ready and acute wit'. However, *A Sermon Preached at Yorke* (1663), which attacked the excise and argued that magistrates should punish those, like rack-renting landlords, enclosers, and speculators, who oppressed the poor, was censured, and he was forced to recant some of his words in his next assize sermon that August, published as *Cesars due, and the Subjects Duty* (1663). His sermons of the later 1660s are largely concerned with the theme of man's mortality; *Nosce te ipsum* and *The Second Adam*, both assize sermons from 1668, were followed by *Elijahs Nunc dimittis* (1669), described as 'the authors own funeral sermon'. In July 1670 Charles II wrote to the archbishop of York recommending Toby Convers to the prebend in York which 'Dr Bradley is intending to resign' (*CSP dom.*, 1660–70, 311). He died in 1673.

SIDNEY LEE, *rev.* JASON MᶜELLIGOTT

Sources Walker rev., 389–90 • Foster, *Alum. Oxon.* • *CSP dom.*, 1625–73 • Wood, *Ath. Oxon.*, new edn, 3.719 • Wood, *Ath. Oxon.: Fasti* (1815), 392 • Wood, *Ath. Oxon.: Fasti* (1820), 52 • M. A. E. Green, ed., *Calendar of the proceedings of the committee for compounding … 1643–1660*, 5 vols., PRO (1889–92) • M. A. E. Green, ed., *Calendar of the proceedings of the committee for advance of money, 1642–1656*, 3 vols., PRO (1888) • T. Bradley, *Comfort from the cradle* (1650)

Bradley, Thomas (1751?–1813), physician, was a native of Worcestershire, where for some time he ran a school. He was recognized as being a skilled mathematician and was a member of the Society of Friends. About 1786 he gave up teaching and, deciding on a career in medicine, went to Edinburgh, where he graduated MD in 1791. His dissertation was published as *De epispasticorum usu in variis morbis tractandis* (1791). Bradley settled in London, and on 22 December 1791 was admitted licentiate of the Royal College of Physicians. From 1794 to 1813 he was physician to the Westminster Hospital, during which time he acted as private tutor to John Ayrton Paris, who later became an eminent physician. For many years Bradley was editor of the *Medical and Physical Journal*. He published a revised and enlarged edition of J. Fox's *New Medical Dictionary* (1803), and also *A Treatise on Worms, and other Animals which Infest the Human Body* (1813). According to the *Gentleman's Magazine*:

> His retired habits in early life did not fit him for the great stage of the Metropolis, to which he proved unequal, rather from diffidence than from want of professional knowledge. He was in truth, more read in books than in men, and therefore disdained to pursue the arts which ensure success; and as he always hesitated like a genuine mathematician, to draw conclusions from uncertain premises, he appeared to less advantage in the side chamber, than bolder and less conscientious practitioners who possessed but a small portion of his knowledge. (*GM*, 97–8)

Bradley died in St George's Fields, London, at the close of 1813. [ANON.], *rev.* MICHAEL BEVAN

Sources *GM*, 1st ser., 84/1 (1814) • Munk, *Roll* • P. J. Wallis and R. V. Wallis, *Eighteenth century medics*, 2nd edn (1988) • S. C. Lawrence, *Charitable knowledge: hospital pupils and practitioners in eighteenth-century London* (1996)

Likenesses N. Branwhite, group portrait, stipple, pubd 1801 (after *Institutors of Medical Society of London* by S. Medley), BM

Bradley, William (1801–1857), portrait painter, was born on 16 January 1801 in Manchester. Little is known of his family or parents, except that his father was remembered

William Bradley (1801–1857), self-portrait

as an inventive and ingenious man; his death left Bradley an orphan by the age of three. Bradley became a shop assistant in the local firm of Weight, Armitage & Co. for 3s. a week. He had a natural facility for drawing and, after leaving this job when he was sixteen, Bradley set himself up as an artist outlining profiles for 1s. apiece and giving sketching lessons. According to his obituary in the Art Journal of 1857, he advertised himself as a 'portrait, miniature, and animal painter, and teacher of drawing' (p. 272). About 1822 the American-born painter Mather Brown, who was highly favoured by the Mancunians, gave him some lessons and possibly introduced him to Sir Thomas Lawrence.

Shortly thereafter, at the age of twenty-one, Bradley moved to London and quickly established himself as a portrait painter. Lawrence showed great interest in Bradley's ability, frequently appraising his work, and serving as an inspiration. While in London, between 1823 and 1846, Bradley exhibited twenty-one individual portraits and one group portrait at the Royal Academy, and thirteen paintings, largely fancy pictures, at the British Institution, as well as several pictures at the Free Society of Artists. Bradley was a perceptive artist with great talent in the use of colour, light, and shade, and in giving striking resemblances to his portraits. He painted many notable subjects including William Ewart Gladstone; this portrait was later engraved as a mezzotint by William Walker for the art collector Robert Vernon (exh. RA, 1827). Bradley had close ties to Manchester and often returned there for short visits; in

1833 he and his fellow portrait painter Benjamin Rawlinson Faulkner went to Manchester for a longer stay. They both worked in the studio of the landscape painter Charles *Calvert in Princes Street and in the same year Bradley married Calvert's eldest daughter; a few months later he and his wife returned to London. His pupils included the portraitists William Percy and Thomas Henry Illidge, both of whom exhibited at the Royal Academy.

Bradley suffered increasingly from failing health, and in 1847 he, his wife, and their children returned to Manchester. He continued to devote himself to his painting, but his physical and mental health deteriorated to the extent that he could do little and he became misanthropic, spending months at a time in his studio. Bradley's family was devoted to him and his wife and daughter attended to him until his very last hours, when he died of typhoid fever on 4 July 1857 in his rooms at Newall's Buildings, Market Street, Manchester. In his obituary the Art Journal made an appeal to the public, and particularly to Bradley's sitters, to assist his widow in the maintenance and education of their four children, who had been left in poverty by Bradley's death. DELLA CLASON SPERLING

Sources Art Journal (1857), 272 · J. -A. Dréolle, 'Nécrologie: William Brandley [sic], C. Turner, John Birch et Thomas Crawford', L'Artiste (1857), 153 · Redgrave, Artists, 50 · Graves, RA exhibitors, 1 (1905), 265 · Graves, Brit. Inst., 61 · Graves, Artists, 3rd edn, 33 · A. Graves, A century of loan exhibitions, 1813–1912 (1913), vol. 1, p. 99 · DNB · Thieme & Becker, Allgemeines Lexikon, 4.506 · R. Parkinson, ed., Catalogue of British oil paintings, 1820–1860 (1990), 9–10 [catalogue of V&A] · d. cert. · B. Stewart and M. Cutten, The dictionary of portrait painters in Britain up to 1920 (1997), 106
Likenesses W. Bradley, self-portrait, drawing, Manchester City Galleries [see illus.]
Wealth at death very little money if any: Art Journal, 272; Dréolle, 'Nécrologie'

Bradmore, John (d. 1412), surgeon, was resident in London from at least 1377 until his death. He married twice; his first wife, Margaret, with whom he had a daughter, Agnes, died some time after May 1410, and he married again without delay. His son, Nicholas, was born after his death to his second wife, Katherine.

In 1386 John Bradmore and his brother Nicholas, also a surgeon, were accused of false coining, but were pardoned. John later supported Nicholas in another brush with the law, but appears himself to have led a peaceful and blameless life.

Some time between 1403 and his death Bradmore compiled a lengthy surgical treatise in Latin, which he entitled Philomena; this survives as BL, Sloane MS 2272. A Middle English translation of part of this work, made after his death, appears in BL, Harley MS 1736, and extracts from the Latin text in Oxford, All Souls College, MS 73. In his treatise Bradmore gives details of several cases of interest, chief among which is his treatment of Henry, prince of Wales, later Henry V, for a facial wound received at the battle of Shrewsbury in 1403. An arrowhead entered the prince's face beside his nose and became lodged in the bone. After various others had failed to remove the arrowhead Bradmore devised and made an instrument to remove it without further damage to the surrounding flesh. His subsequent treatment of the wound is given in detail. Bradmore had been connected with the royal household since at least 1399, in which year he treated the master of the king's pavilions, William Wyncelowe, for an extensive abdominal wound resulting from a failed suicide attempt. Full details of this case are also given in *Philomena*. Bradmore received payments from the royal household for fees and robes in 1403 and 1406, and appears also to have received an annuity of 10 marks from the prince of Wales. His appointment in 1408 to the office of searcher of the port of London brought a further annual payment of £10.

An oath taken before the mayor and aldermen in the Guildhall in April 1390 appears to have appointed Bradmore, with three others, to be in some way overseer of surgery within the city of London. In 1390–91 and again in 1402 he treated monks in Westminster Abbey Infirmary. He was clearly prosperous, and from 1391 he began to acquire property within the parish of St Botolph, Aldersgate, city of London, in which he was resident. From 1391 until his death he lived in a tenement situated on the east side of Aldersgate Street, opposite the parish church. In 1399 he purchased the adjoining garden. At the time of his death he owned four tenements, one of which he bequeathed to his daughter, Agnes, and the remaining three to his second wife, Katherine, and her child. Shortly after his death his widow's property was assessed in the lay subsidy roll of 1412 as having an annual rental value of £4 3s. 6d.

Bradmore and his first wife, Margaret, were among the founder members in 1377 of the fraternity of the Holy Trinity in the parish of St Botolph, Aldersgate. In 1400 he was churchwarden of the parish church, and in 1409–10 he was master of the fraternity of the Trinity. In his will he bequeathed a cloth of silk to this fraternity and money to the lesser fraternity of Sts Fabian and Sebastian in the same church. In addition, the reversion of the property left to his daughter, his wife, and her expected child was bequeathed to the fraternity of the Holy Trinity if the child should die without legitimate heirs (and indeed the property was in the hands of the fraternity by 1447). Bradmore died on 27 January 1412 in his home parish, and was buried in the church of St Botolph, where a monument commemorating him and both his wives existed before the great fire of 1666.   S. J. LANG

Sources P. Basing, ed., *Parish fraternity register*, London RS (1982) [edn of BL Add. MS 37664] • *Chancery records* • exchequer various accounts, PRO, E101/404/21 • BL, Harley MS 319 [royal accounts] • CLRO, Husting rolls • R. R. Sharpe, ed., *Calendar of letter-books preserved in the archives of the corporation of the City of London*, [12 vols.] (1899–1912), vol. H • B. Harvey, *Living and dying in England, 1100–1540: the monastic experience* (1993) • J. C. L. Stahlschmidt, ed., 'Lay subsidy temp. Henry IV: original documents', *Archaeological Journal*, 44 (1887), 56–82 • J. Stow, *A survey of London*, rev. edn (1603); repr. with introduction by C. L. Kingsford as *A survey of London*, 2 vols. (1908); repr. with addns (1971) • R. T. Beck, *The cutting edge: early history of the surgeons of London* (1974) • S. J. Lang, 'John Bradmore and his book *Philomena*', *Social History of Medicine*, 5 (1992), 121–30
Archives All Souls Oxf., MS 73 • BL, Sloane MS 2272; Harley MS 1736

Wealth at death approx. £4 3s. 6d.—annual rental value: Stahlschmidt, ed., 'Lay subsidy temp. Henry IV'

Bradock [Braddocke], **John** (1655/6–1719), Church of England clergyman and theological author, was born in Shropshire; his parents' names are not known. On 6 May 1671 he was admitted as a pensioner to St Catharine's College, Cambridge. Having matriculated in 1673 he graduated BA in 1675, proceeded MA in 1678, and held a fellowship from 1680 until 1688. In 1687 the university vice-chancellor sent him, together with George Stanhope, with letters to James II's ministers petitioning the king to revoke a mandate to confer a degree of MA on a Benedictine monk without the statutory oaths being taken.

About 1689 Bradock moved to Kent, where he became chaplain to Sir James Oxenden, bt, of Dene, and curate to John Batteley, rector of Adisham. In 1694 he was nominated by the archbishop of Canterbury, Thomas Tenison, to the perpetual curacy of Folkestone, which he resigned for the vicarage of St Stephen alias Hackington, to which he was presented by Batteley, archdeacon of Canterbury, on 30 March 1699. In 1703 he was appointed one of the Six Preachers of Canterbury Cathedral. Ofspring Blackall, his friend and contemporary at St Catharine's, made him his chaplain when he became bishop of Exeter in 1708, although 'he got nothing by it, but the Title' (BL, Add. MS 5863, fol. 114v). He was collated to the mastership of Eastbridge Hospital, Canterbury, on 12 January 1710.

Bradock wrote *The doctrine of the fathers and the schools consider'd: concerning the articles of a Trinity of divine persons and the unity of God*, part the first (1695). In it he defended William Sherlock's *Vindication of the Doctrine of the Holy and Ever Blessed Trinity* (1690), against Robert South's *Animadversions upon Dr Sherlock's Book* (1693). Examining patristic, scholastic, and later writers on the Trinity he aimed to demonstrate that '*Three Divine Persons* may be orthodoxly stiled *Three Infinite Minds or Spirits*' (p. iv). He was answered by Thomas Holdsworth in *Impar conatui* (1695). The proposed second part concerning the unity of God, *Deus unus et trinus*, was almost ready for publication when it was suppressed at the direction of Archbishop Tenison, who did not wish the controversy prolonged. James Bonnell wrote to John Strype in 1699 that he feared Bradock was 'warping towards Socinianism, by an Account he gave me of Something he was about to publish'.

Bradock died at his vicarage on 14 August 1719, aged sixty-three, and was buried in the chancel of Hackington church.   ANDREW STARKIE

Sources BL, Add. MS 5863 [Cole's 'Alphabetical collections for an Athenae Cantab. B'], fol. 114v • Venn, *Alum. Cant.* • E. H. W. Dunkin, C. Jenkins, and E. A. Fry, eds., *Index to the act books of the archbishops of Canterbury, 1663–1859*, British RS, 55 (1929), 63 (1938), 95

Bradock, Thomas (1555/6–1607), Church of England clergyman and translator, was born at Southwark, the son of Thomas Bradocke. He was admitted to Westminster School by 1570, and then attended Greyfriars School. In June 1573 he matriculated at Corpus Christi College, Cambridge, migrating to Gonville and Caius by 12 May 1574 when aged eighteen, and then to Christ's. Here he graduated BA in 1577, proceeding MA (1580) and BTh (1593). He was a fellow from 1579 until 1587. In 1584 he was incorporated MA, and made proctor, in the University of Oxford. Bradock seems to have been sympathetic to the puritan tendency in the church. In 1579 he and the other fellows of Christ's signed a protest on behalf of Hugh Broughton, who had been stripped of his fellowship by the master; his signature also appears on a letter from the fellows to Lord Burghley, thanking him for mediating in a dispute involving the vice-chancellor, Dr John Copcot, and Sampson Sheffield. He was ordained priest in April 1580.

On 1 March 1588 Bradock was elected master of the free school at Reading and though he had resigned by 4 April the following year this short tenure coincided with the last months as a pupil at the school of William Laud, the future archbishop. On 8 April 1591 he was instituted to the rectory of Stanstead Abbots, Hertfordshire, but resigned the living before 20 September 1593. On 20 August 1593 he and Elizabeth Graves were granted a licence to marry. Soon after he was instituted to the rectory of Navenby, Lincolnshire, which he held until 1599. From Navenby he seems to have gone to the parish of Wittersham, Kent, where he died; Elizabeth Bradock was granted the administration of his estate on 19 November 1607.

Bradock is chiefly remembered for his translation into Latin of the defence issued by Bishop John Jewel of his *Apologia pro Ecclesia Anglicana* against the criticisms of the Catholic controversialist Thomas Harding. The translation was published in Geneva in 1600, in order that foreign scholars might understand the nature of the controversy to which Jewel's *Apologia* had given rise since its publication in 1562. It was dedicated to John Whitgift, archbishop of Canterbury, 'who has filled the diocese with learned men'. Bradock is also remembered for having given books to the library of his former college of Christ's.　　　STEPHEN WRIGHT

Sources *Reg. Oxf.*, 2/1.352 • Venn, *Alum. Cant.*, 1/1.199 • J. Peile, *Biographical register of Christ's College, 1505–1905, and of the earlier foundation, God's House, 1448–1505*, ed. [J. A. Venn], 1 (1910) • J. Strype, *Annals of the Reformation and establishment of religion … during Queen Elizabeth's happy reign*, new edn, 2–3 (1824) • J. M. Guilding, ed., *Reading records: diary of the corporation*, 1 (1892) • *Old Westminsters* • *VCH Berkshire*, vols. 2–3 • R. Newcourt, *Repertorium ecclesiasticum parochiale Londinense*, 1 (1708) • Wood, *Ath. Oxon.: Fasti* (1815), 228–9 • L. Duncan, ed., 'Kentish administrations, 1604–49', *Archaeologia Cantiana*, 20 (1893), 1–48 • C. W. Foster, ed., *The state of the church in the reigns of Elizabeth and James I*, Lincoln RS, 23 (1926) • J. Lewis, ed., 'Stanstead Abbotts', *Transactions of the East Hertfordshire Archaeological Society*, 2/1 (1902–4), 27–31

Bradshaigh [*née* Bellingham], **Dorothy**, Lady Bradshaigh (*bap.* **1705**, *d.* **1785**), letter writer, was baptized on 21 March 1705 at Rufford, Lancashire, the younger of the two daughters of William Bellingham (*c.*1660–1718), son of James and Elizabeth Bellingham of Levens, Westmorland, and his wife, Elizabeth, daughter of William Spencer of Ashton, Lancashire, and widow of Robert Hesketh of Rufford (*d.* 1697). The Bellinghams were a prominent landed family, but the estate inherited by Dorothy's father in 1693 had been squandered by his elder brother Alan (1656–1693), and Levens Hall, the Bellingham home for more than a century, had been sold. Called to the bar in 1686,

William Bellingham seems to have practised the law for a while, but his marriage of 1703 restored his fortunes and provided the Rufford home in which Dorothy and Elizabeth *Echlin, his coheirs, were raised with their half-sister, Elizabeth Hesketh (1694–1776). He also seems to have retained some Bellingham lands in Poulton, near Lancaster, so that his death in 1718 (little regretted by a daughter to whom 'he had made himself indifferent … by his cool and awful behaviour') left her 'the mistress of a considerable fortune' (*Correspondence of Samuel Richardson*, 4.272–3).

It is likely that Dorothy Bellingham then lived in the Preston household of Edward Stanley (1689–1776), afterwards earl of Derby, who had married Elizabeth Hesketh in 1714, and of whom she later spoke as being 'not only a Brother, but a Father' (V&A, Forster MSS, XI, fol. 19). She was resident in Preston at the time of her marriage on 6 April 1731 to Roger Bradshaigh (1699–1770) of Haigh, near Wigan, who became fourth baronet on the death of his father in 1747. The courtship was complex (she later described herself as 'one who obstinately refused her lover for nine years, and was prevailed upon to alter her condition in the tenth'; *Correspondence of Samuel Richardson*, 4.260), but on marriage they became a devoted couple. They reportedly honoured the debts incurred by the 'parliamentary *mania*' of the third baronet, and from 1742, when they took over Haigh Hall, they lived quietly on 'a straitened income' (*GM*, 74, 1804, 900). Sir Roger restored the estate by exploiting its deposits of cannel (a high-grade, jet-like coal, from which, as though to blazon the source of their returning wealth, Lady Bradshaigh built a summer house). The house was briefly commandeered by the Jacobite army in 1745, but otherwise there was little to disturb an existence which Lady Bradshaigh divided between social pursuits in Lancashire and London, and practical or charitable tasks which included cow-doctoring, training fallen women for service, and endowing an almshouse for retired miners. There were no children, and the baronetcy became extinct at Sir Roger's death.

Lady Bradshaigh owes her place in literary history to her voluminous correspondence with the novelist Samuel Richardson, which Richardson circulated in manuscript and considered publishing as 'the best Commentary that cd. be written on the History of Clarissa' (*Selected Letters of Samuel Richardson*, 336). Elaborate ruses surrounded the early exchanges, which began when Lady Bradshaigh addressed him in two anonymous letters of July 1748, pleading for a happy ending to *Clarissa*, the serial publication of which was then in progress. Richardson replied by advertising in the *Whitehall Evening Post*, and for the next eighteen months she besieged him with letters written under the pseudonym Belfour, which elicited in reply (along with much sparring and banter) some of his most revealing literary statements. Lady Bradshaigh disclosed her identity only in February 1750, and the two at last met in March. Thereafter she consolidated her position as the most intimate and influential member of Richardson's literary circle, voicing her instinctively sentimental responses to the novels with an eloquence that remained unaffected by her distaste for learning in women. Richardson did not exaggerate when telling her that *Sir Charles Grandison* (1753–4) was 'owing to you … more than to any one Person besides' (ibid., 319), and the influence persisted in revisions later made to the work in response to her marginal annotations. In his final months he borrowed her annotated copies of *Pamela* and *Clarissa*, apparently with a view to undertaking comparable revisions. Many of her letters appeared in Barbauld's *Correspondence of Samuel Richardson* (1804); the *Clarissa* annotations, with Richardson's marginal responses and her sketch of an alternative ending, were published in 1998.

Robust in personality and appearance, Lady Bradshaigh described herself in 1749 as 'middle-aged, middle-sized, a degree above plump, brown as an oak wainscot, a good deal of country red in her cheeks' (*Correspondence of Samuel Richardson*, 4.300–01). She was probably right to see herself in the vivacious Charlotte of *Sir Charles Grandison*, and the same identification was made by her sister, Lady Echlin, who recalled her rebellious nature in youth and still found her, in middle age, 'this ungovernable Lady B—' (*Correspondence of Samuel Richardson*, 5.31). Her great-niece reported that she 'carried a dash of Miss Do [her childhood nickname] to the latest period of her valuable existence' (*GM*, 74, 1804, 900). She died at Haigh, and was buried in the Bradshaigh family vault at All Saints, Wigan, on 21 August 1785.   THOMAS KEYMER

Sources T. C. D. Eaves and B. D. Kimpel, *Samuel Richardson: a biography* (1971) • *The correspondence of Samuel Richardson*, ed. A. L. Barbauld, 6 vols. (1804) • V&A NAL, Forster Library, Richardson papers • parish register, Croston, Lancashire • parish register, All Saints, Wigan, Lancashire • *Selected letters of Samuel Richardson*, ed. J. Carroll (1964) • Betha [E. (Palmer) Budworth], *GM*, 1st ser., 74 (1804), 899–900 • Betha [E. (Palmer) Budworth], *GM*, 1st ser., 83/2 (1813), 307 • *VCH Lancashire* • HoP, *Commons, 1660–90* • HoP, *Commons, 1715–54* • T. Keymer, 'Richardson, Incognita, and the *Whitehall Evening Post*', *N&Q*, 237 (1992), 477–80 • J. Barchas and G. D. Fulton, eds., *The annotations in Lady Bradshaigh's copy of 'Clarissa'* (1998) • A. J. Hawkes, Bradshaigh pedigree, *Chetham miscellanies*, Chetham Society, new ser., 8 (1945), i • A. D. Bagot, *Levens Hall* [1963] • GEC, *Baronetage* • Burke, *Peerage* (1840) • J. Burke and J. B. Burke, *A genealogical and heraldic history of the extinct and dormant baronetcies of England, Ireland, and Scotland* (1838) • J. Foster, ed., *Pedigrees recorded at the herald's visitations of the counties of Cumberland and Westmorland* (1891) • J. Nicolson and R. Burn, *The history and antiquities of the counties of Westmorland and Cumberland*, 2 vols. (1777) • W. P. Baildon, ed., *The records of the Honorable Society of Lincoln's Inn: admissions*, 1 (1896) • J. A. Wood, 'The chronology of the Richardson–Bradshaigh correspondence of 1751', *Studies in Bibliography*, 33 (1980), 182–91 • A. L. Reade, 'Samuel Richardson and his family circle [pt 4]', *N&Q*, 12th ser., 11 (1922), 383–6

Archives Hunt. L., annotated copy of *Sir Charles Grandison* (vol. 7 only) • NL Scot., papers in Crawford Muniments • Princeton University, New Jersey, Robert H. Taylor collection, annotated copy of *Clarissa* | V&A, Forster MSS, letters to Richardson

Likenesses E. Haytley, double portrait, oils, 1746 (with her husband), History Shop, Wigan • attrib J. Highmore, double portrait, oils, c.1750 (with her husband), repro. in Kerslake, *Early Georgian portraits* (1977), vol. 2, pl. 689a; priv. coll. • engraving (after C. Watson), repro. in Barbauld, ed., *Correspondence of Samuel Richardson*, vol. 5

Wealth at death substantial: will, 1786, PRO, PROB 11/1139, fols. 276v–289v

Bradshaigh [*alias* Barton], **Richard** (1601/2–1669), Jesuit, was born in Lancashire, the third son of Roger Bradshaigh (*d.* 1641) of Haigh Hall, Lancashire, and his wife, Anne Anderton, daughter of Christopher Anderton of Lostock. He was one of a large family which produced five Catholic priests and three nuns. Educated at the English College, St Omer, 1622–3, as were several of his brothers, he was admitted to the English College, Rome, on 4 October 1623 and entered the Society of Jesus on 28 August 1625. He spent his noviciate in Rome, was sent to Flanders in 1628, and studied at Liège where he was ordained priest on 19 August 1632. He held a series of posts at St Omer, returned to England in 1638–9, and became a professed father on 22 July 1640 at Ghent, under the name Richard Barton. By 1641 he was acting as rector of the province's college for higher studies at Liège. In the later 1640s he was resident in Paris, acting as procurator of the English Jesuit province in 1655, and as provincial from 15 April 1656. At some point he crossed to England witnessing, in London, the fall of the republic and the Restoration. While in Paris he appears to have been instrumental in effecting the conversion to Catholicism of the only son of John Cosin, bishop of Durham. He promoted the establishment of the Poor Clare convent at Rouen, where his sister Mary Ignatius (born Ellen Bradshaigh; *d.* 1673) was to serve as abbess, and the Benedictine convent at Boulogne, for which he secured a notable benefaction. Possibly he was the author of a work directed against bishop John Bramhall's 1658 work on the succession of protestant bishops, though this was more probably the work of Peter Talbot. From 1660 until his death there, on 12 February 1669, he undertook an 'efficient and popular rectorship' (Chadwick, 173) of the English College, St Omer.   R. M. ARMSTRONG

Sources T. M. McCoog, *English and Welsh Jesuits, 1555–1650*, 1, Catholic RS, 74 (1994), 113 • H. Foley, ed., *Records of the English province of the Society of Jesus*, 1 (1877), 227–32; 7 (1882–3), 78 • A. Kenny, ed., *The responsa scholarum of the English College, Rome*, 2, Catholic RS, 55 (1963) • Gillow, *Lit. biog. hist.* • A. M. C. Forster, 'The chronicles of the English Poor Clares of Rouen [pts 1–2]', *Recusant History*, 18 (1986–7), 59–102, 149–91 • C. Hibbard, 'The contribution of 1639: court and country Catholicism', *Recusant History*, 16 (1982–3), 42–60 • A. Neville, 'English Benedictine nuns in Flanders, 1598–1687', ed. M. J. Rumsey, *Miscellanea, V*, Catholic RS, 6 (1909), 1–72, esp. 47 • T. H. Clancy, *English Catholic books, 1641–1700: a bibliography* [1974] • H. Chadwick, *St Omers to Stonyhurst* (1962)

Bradshaigh, Sir Roger, first baronet (1628–1684), politician and colliery owner, was born at Haigh Hall, Haigh near Wigan in Lancashire, on 13 January 1628, the eldest surviving son of James Bradshaigh (1598–1631) of Haigh and his wife, Ann, fourth daughter of Sir William Norris of Speke. James Bradshaigh died before his father, whose estate was taken into crown wardship on his death in 1641, passing to Roger in 1649. The Bradshaighs were adamant Roman Catholics: four of Roger Bradshaigh's uncles were Jesuits in the English mission, and a fifth was a Carmelite; two aunts and a sister were nuns at Gravelines and Rouen. However the court of wards and liveries put Roger under the guardianship of protestants John Fleetwood of Penwortham and William Radcliffe of Manchester, and in 1641 he became an Anglican 'by his choice, not by his chance' (HoP, *Commons*). He was entrusted to the earl of Derby, with whose son he was educated in the Isle of Man during the first civil war, when the parliamentarian sympathy of Radcliffe combined with the Bradshaighs' royalism to secure Haigh from any intrusion. In 1647 Bradshaigh married Elizabeth (*d.* 1695), daughter of William Pennington of Muncaster. They were to have seven children, two of whom survived, including his heir, Sir Roger Bradshaigh, second baronet (1649–1686). Bradshaigh's wife was devoutly Anglican, and 'his own religion is such that he is no friend at all to us [Roman Catholics]' (Nicholas Blundell, quoted in Hawkes, 39), but he was imprisoned at Chester on suspicion of royalist sympathies in 1651. Assurances given to secure his release prevented his joining the earl of Derby's support of the Pretender's invasion, crushed by Lilburne at the battle of Wigan Lane (on the Haigh estate) on 25 August 1651.

Bradshaigh was heavily engaged with the Lancashire commission of forfeited estates on behalf of kinsmen and other local families in the 1650s. Seven of his relatives or wards were threatened with or suffered dispossession, and Bradshaigh organized purchases for some of the latter. In 1660 he was elected to the pre-Restoration parliament, knighted on the accession of Charles II, and appointed a deputy to the earl of Derby as lord lieutenant of Lancashire. A fine soldier, he was an energetic captain of a troop of horse and responsible for reorganizing the county militia. His assiduity in pursuit of 'phanaticks' and conventicles balanced Derby's firm action against papists, whom Derby accused Bradshaigh of protecting. Certainly he remained a close friend of a number of prominent Roman Catholics, including Viscount Molyneux of Croxteth, the 'popish recusant convict' created lord lieutenant of Lancashire by James II in 1687, appointing twelve 'convicted papists' as deputies (Kenyon MS 611). The duplicity of the Lancashire lieutenancy in the 1660s and 1670s ensured reasonable order in a disaffected county renowned for extreme Catholic and puritan sympathies, continually unsettled by rumoured rebellions and plots. Bradshaigh's role in post-Restoration government was acknowledged in his appointment as high sheriff of Lancashire and to a baronetcy, pursued to indulge his courtier son, in 1679. He was MP for Lancashire from 1660 to 1678, and also served as mayor of Wigan in 1661 and 1681.

Bradshaigh's forebears included notable scholars, poets, and divines. However, although he had a good library and was an enthusiastic correspondent of Lancastrian friends in London, who sent him the latest fashions in books and clothes, Sir Roger was businesslike and practical. He leased a glassworks to John Blackburne of Westby; he had a pottery where John Dwight, who patented porcelain-making processes at the Fulham pottery in 1671 and 1684, worked for a time; and he built the forge and slitting mill which were the embryo of the Haigh ironworks (which, with the colliery, formed the nucleus of the gigantic Wigan Coal and Iron Company in the nineteenth century).

The colliery was the basis of Haigh's other industries and of the estate's fortunes. It was renowned for fuel from the cannel seam, which carried a high premium in the market. The seam was deep, given the current mining technology, and plagued by water and gas. Sir Roger was responsible for bringing it into secure and continuous heavy production, and for establishing Haigh colliery as one of the largest and the longest-worked in Lancashire. He formulated the Haigh colliery orders, which ensured that operations could be systematically supervised and developed and, according to subsequent testimony by the third baronet, he spent 'every shilling he could lay his hands on' on the great Haigh sough, which he surveyed and engineered personally (quoted in Cox, 124). Two-thirds of a mile long and 147 feet below ground at its deepest, this tunnel of 6 feet x 4 feet with ten ventilation pits took from 1652 to 1670 to construct and cost a great deal of money. It drained vast coal reserves and provided knowledge (meticulously recorded 'for my posterity' in the orders) about many coal seams, including the cannel, 'the root, basis and stamina' of Haigh (earl of Crawford and Balcarres, 19).

Bradshaigh died at Chester on 31 March 1684, and was buried at Wigan. His wife survived him. His heir, the second baronet, died three years later. Despite Sir Roger's heavy capital investment, income from the colliery carried the estate through the deaths without financial jeopardy. Widows' jointures amounting to £660 per annum were paid for many years by his grandson, who by 1729 was drawing an income of £1900 a year from the Haigh estate, over half of which came from the cannel. The sough which made this possible was 'the greatest engineering achievement in England down to the building of the Eddystone lighthouse', according to the twenty-eighth earl of Crawford (Hawkes, 19). It served collieries in Haigh and Aspull for 300 years until mining ceased, and still runs freely. The three generations of Bradshaighs who followed Sir Roger spent most of their time at court. The male line failed in 1770, when the Haigh estates and businesses passed through an heiress to Alexander Lindsay, sixth earl of Balcarres, in 1780.   JOHN LANGTON

Sources HoP, *Commons* · A. J. Hawkes, 'Sir Roger Bradshaigh of Haigh, knight and baronet, 1628–1684: with notes of his immediate forbears', *Chetham miscellanies*, Chetham Society, new ser., 8 (1945), i–vi, 1–73 · 'Sir Roger Bradshaigh's letter book', *Transactions of the Historic Society of Lancashire and Cheshire*, 63 (1911), 120–73 · Earl of Crawford and Balcares, 'Haigh Cannel', *Transactions of the Manchester Statistical Society* (1933–4), 1–23 · J. Langton, *Geographical change and industrial revolution: coalmining in south west Lancashire, 1590–1799* (1979) · 'Observations upon the government in Lancashire and the changes therein', 27 Aug 1687, Kenyon MS 611 · J. Hatcher, *Before 1700: towards the age of coal* (1993), vol. 1 of *The history of the British coal industry* (1984–93) · M. Cox, 'Sir Roger Bradshaigh, 3rd baronet, and the electoral management of Wigan, 1695–1747', *Bulletin of the John Rylands University Library*, 37 (1954–5), 120–64, esp. 124

Archives Man. CL, letter-book · NL Scot., corresp. and papers | Gredlington Hall, Shropshire, Kenyon MSS · Lancs. RO, letters to Roger Kenyon · NL Scot., Crawford MSS · priv. coll., letters to Roger Kenyon · Wigan Archives Service, Leigh, Haigh colliery orders

Likenesses oils, 1946, repro. in A. J. Hawkes, 'Sir Roger Bradshaigh of Haigh', facing p. 10; Wigan Public Library, 1946
Wealth at death letters of administration and inventory, 17 June 1687, granted at Chester

Bradshaigh, Sir Roger, third baronet (*bap.* 1675, *d.* 1747), politician and coal owner, was baptized on 29 April 1675, the first son of Sir Roger Bradshaigh, second baronet (*c.*1649–1687), of Haigh Hall, Lancashire, and his wife, Mary (*d.* 1733), the daughter and coheir of Henry Murray of Berkhamsted, Hertfordshire, groom of the bedchamber to Charles I, and his wife, Anne, Viscountess Bayning. His paternal grandfather, Sir Roger *Bradshaigh, first baronet, had been responsible for establishing the Haigh colliery as one of the largest in Lancashire. The rich seam of cannel coal was systematically mined by successive generations of the family. If, however, the Bradshaighs were in the forefront of the burgeoning coal industry of southwest Lancashire, they also demonstrated that region's dogged resistance to the Reformation, retaining their Roman Catholic loyalties into the seventeenth century. Bradshaigh's father, who succeeded to the title and family estates in March 1684, was bedevilled by accusations of Catholic sympathies, but while sitting for Lancashire in the parliament of 1685 was listed among the opposition to James II. Upon his death, on 17 June 1687, he was succeeded by the twelve-year-old Roger, whose care was entrusted to Peter Shakerley, Bradshaigh's great-uncle and the tory governor of Chester Castle.

Shakerley's influence on the young Bradshaigh was initially considerable. In 1690 Bradshaigh supported Shakerley's return to parliament for Wigan, and when he himself became active in politics in the mid-1690s his beliefs were of the same stridently tory stamp as those of his guardian. In 1695, while still a minor, he was elected to parliament for Wigan, a seat he was to hold uninterrupted for the following fifty-two years. The year after his election he initially refused to sign the Association declaring William III the 'rightful and lawful king', and for the rest of the decade he remained opposed to the predominantly whig ministries. In 1699, however, a disagreement between Bradshaigh and Shakerley concerning money led to a cooling of their relationship and marked a distinct shift in Bradshaigh's political sympathies. Having distanced himself from Shakerley, he fell into the political orbit of two leading north-west whigs, James Stanley, tenth earl of Derby, and Richard Savage, fourth Earl Rivers, for whom Bradshaigh's brother Henry was then aide-de-camp. Throughout the first decade of the eighteenth century Bradshaigh allied himself with the whigs, going so far in 1710 as to vote for the impeachment of the high-church cleric Henry Sacheverell. At the end of this year, however, he followed Rivers in transferring his political support to the tory ministry of Robert Harley. After the Hanoverian succession he returned to the whig fold, and voted with successive whig ministries until his death.

Bradshaigh's partisan vacillations make his political career difficult to explain in party terms, and from 1700 onwards he should instead be viewed as a consistent court supporter who gave his vote to successive ministries, be they whig or tory. His decision to abandon his fervent toryism of the 1690s seems, however, to have been the result of persistent financial pressures forcing him to trim his sails to the prevailing political wind in the hope of receiving official patronage, rather than a more altruistic belief in the need to support the monarch's ministers.

The development of the colliery at Haigh had been expensive, particularly under the first baronet. When Bradshaigh succeeded to the family estates he found them heavily indebted. His finances were also drained by the cost of maintaining the family interest at the borough of Wigan, a quarrelsome constituency where political disputes frequently led to prolonged and expensive court cases. The financial problems consequent upon these debts were of such an order that even the £600 per annum Bradshaigh received upon his marriage on 22 June 1697 to Rachel (*d.* 1743), the daughter of Sir John Guise, second baronet, of Elmore, Gloucestershire, failed to alleviate his difficulties, which were at their worst in the 1700s and 1710s. His alliance in the 1700s with the earl of Derby and the Earl Rivers may well have been made in the hope that they would be able to use their influence to gain him a profitable government place, and it seems likely that when in 1706 Bradshaigh obtained the colonelcy of regiment of foot it was in the hope that the salary of £800 per annum would alleviate some of his financial worries. He surrendered this commission in 1709, and in the same year was forced to obtain an act of parliament enabling him to sell part of his family's estates in order to pay family debts and the portions of his siblings. His continuing need for a patron willing to give him financial assistance led, between 1710 and 1714, to a series of letters from Bradshaigh to Robert Harley requesting loans, gifts, and government office. Some funds were forthcoming, and it was no doubt in the hope that such aid would continue that Bradshaigh supported whig ministries after the Hanoverian succession. By the 1720s his financial difficulties had diminished somewhat, the income from his mining interests having increased. His position remained, however, less than comfortable. Bradshaigh and his wife had four sons and three daughters, and in order to lessen the burden his family placed upon his estates he obtained, in the 1720s and 1730s, places in the army and at court for his younger sons.

Bradshaigh was exceptionally proud of his lengthy parliamentary service, and when responding in 1727 to Thomas Wooton's enquiry for material for his *Baronetage* was at pains to point out that he 'has sat in Parliament as a Member for that place [Wigan] ever since [1695] which is now above 32 years, this is more then [*sic*] be said of any gentleman of his age in England' (BL, Add. MS 24120, fol. 140). The pride Bradshaigh took in the longevity of parliamentary service perhaps lay in the fact that his career as an MP was remarkable for few other reasons; no account has yet been discovered of his delivering a single speech in the Commons. His concern to remain in parliament was evident when in 1742 he settled his estates upon his eldest son's marriage, as he took great care to ensure that he would be left an estate sufficient to qualify him for a seat in the Commons. Though Bradshaigh had completed half a century's continuous service for Wigan he nevertheless took the trouble in 1745 and 1746 to establish an interest against the next general election, but such efforts were cut short by his death on 25 February 1747. That he had experienced financial problems until the end of his life was clear from the debts of £8000 which he left at his death, and from the fact that his small personal estate was seized by Hoare's Bank. He was succeeded in his title and estates by his eldest son and namesake, but the male line of the Bradshaighs failed in 1770, and in the nineteenth century their Lancashire estates, and profitable coalmines, descended by marriage to Alexander Lindsay, sixth earl of Balcarres.   RICHARD D. HARRISON

Sources A. J. Hawkes, 'Sir Roger Bradshaigh of Haigh, knight and baronet, 1628–1684: with notes of his immediate forbears', *Chetham miscellanies*, Chetham Society, new ser., 8 (1945), i–vi, 1–73 · M. Cox, 'Sir Roger Bradshaigh, 3rd baronet, and the electoral management of Wigan, 1695–1747', *Bulletin of the John Rylands University Library*, 37 (1954–5), 120–64 · HoP, *Commons* [draft] · NL Scot., Bradshaigh MSS, Crawford MSS · BL, Add. MS 24120, fol. 140 · G. S. Holmes, *British politics in the age of Anne*, rev. edn (1987)
Archives Lancs. RO, letters · NL Scot., corresp. and papers | NL Scot., Crawford MSS · priv. coll., letters mainly to George Kenyon
Wealth at death debts totalling £8000: will, PRO, PROB 11/756, sig. 199, cited Cox, 'Sir Roger Bradshaigh' · settled bulk of estate on eldest son, 1742

Bradshaw, Ann Maria. *See* Tree, (Anna) Maria (1801/2–1862).

Bradshaw, George (1801–1853), compiler of railway guides, only son of Thomas Bradshaw and his wife, Mary Rogers, was born at Windsor Bridge, Pendleton, Salford, Lancashire, on 29 July 1801. His parents, although of limited means, gave him a good education, placing him under the care of a Mr Coward, a Swedenborgian minister. He then studied at a school kept by a Mr Scott at Overton, Lancashire. On leaving school he was apprenticed to J. Beale, a Manchester engraver, who had acquired some reputation by the execution of the plates of *The Art of Penmanship Improved*, by Duncan Smith (1817). In 1820 he accompanied his parents to Belfast and there established himself as an engraver and printer, but, not finding sufficient work, he returned to Manchester the following year. For some time he had been interested in the engraving of maps, and in 1827 he decided to concentrate on that branch of art. The first map projected, engraved, and published by him was one of Lancashire, his native county. This was followed in 1830 by his map of the canals of Lancashire, Yorkshire, and the surrounding region. This map eventually became one of a set of three known as *Bradshaw's Maps of Inland Navigation*.

On 16 May 1839 Bradshaw married Martha, daughter of William Darbyshire of Stretton, near Warrington. They had two sons, Christopher and William. Also in 1839, soon after the commencement of the railway system, he produced *Bradshaw's Railway Time Tables*, a small book, bound in cloth, price 6*d*. In 1840 a fuller edition appeared under the new title of *Bradshaw's Railway Companion*, which also contained sectional maps, and was sold at 1*s*. It was an

George Bradshaw (1801–1853), by Richard Evans, 1841

occasional rather than a regular publication and was supplemented by a monthly time sheet. In December 1841 no. 1 of *Bradshaw's Monthly Railway Guide* appeared, in a yellow wrapper, which became famous worldwide. Another publication was *Bradshaw's Continental Railway Guide*, known colloquially as 'the foreign *Bradshaw*'. It was printed in Manchester, but the first number was published in Paris in June 1847. He also published *Bradshaw's General Railway Directory and Shareholders' Guide*, which first appeared in 1849.

When Bradshaw produced his first *Monthly Railway Guide* a small format and small print were used. For the numerous footnotes and addenda the type was minuscule. This presented a challenge to Victorian opticians to produce spectacles which were serviceable for reading *Bradshaw*—an essential companion for railway travellers. You did not simply 'look up' train times: you 'studied' *Bradshaw*. But the word 'Bradshaw' became synonymous with incomprehensibility: the guide was pilloried in *Punch* and *Vanity Fair* and was the subject of music-hall jokes. When the actress Fanny Kemble was asked what she read to send her to sleep she replied: 'Why, the foreign *Bradshaw*, of course.' The monthly *Bradshaw* continued publication until 1961, 108 years after its founder's death. From a relatively early date it was consulted for other information besides the times of departure and arrival of trains. From 1858 for example it recorded the departure times of steamboats and the rise and fall of tides. It played a large part in making the British time-conscious.

When he was a young man Bradshaw joined the Society of Friends, and was active with Richard Cobden and other Quakers and radicals in holding peace conferences, in the attempts to establish an ocean penny postage, and in other philanthropic labours. He was largely responsible for organizing 'Friends of Peace' congresses in Brussels (1848), Paris (1849), and Frankfurt (1850). Part of his time he devoted to the establishment of schools for the poor. Bradshaw joined the Institution of Civil Engineers as an associate in February 1842. In August 1853 he went to Norway on a tour combining business and recreation, and on 6 September, while on a visit to a friend in the neighbourhood of Christiania, he contracted cholera and died in a few hours. He was buried in Norway, in the cemetery belonging to the cathedral of Christiania, at Opoto, on the 11th.   G. C. BOASE, *rev.* PHILIP S. BAGWELL

Sources G. R. Smith, *The history of Bradshaw* (1939) · C. E. Lee, *The centenary of Bradshaw* (1940) · P. Fitzgerald, *The story of Bradshaw's Guide* (1896) · E. Lomax, 'Bradshaw the timetable man', *Antiquarian Book Monthly Review*, 2 (1975) · P. H. Emden, *Quakers in commerce: a record of business achievement* (1939) · H. R. de Salis, *Bradshaw's canals and navigable rivers of England and Wales* (1906) · *Bradshaw's Continental Railway Guide* (1847) · *Bradshaw's General Railway Directory and Shareholders' Guide* (1847–1923) [title varies] · *Manchester Guardian* (17 Sept 1853), 7 · *PICE*, 13 (1853–4), 145–9 · *The Athenaeum* (27 Dec 1873), 872 · *The Athenaeum* (17 Jan 1874), 95 · *The Athenaeum* (24 Jan 1874), 126 · *N&Q*, 6th ser., 8 (1883), 45, 92, 338; 11 (1885), 15
Archives Birm. CA, letters to railway companies · Man. CL · University of Leicester
Likenesses R. Evans, oils, 1841, NPG [*see illus.*] · stipple, pubd 1853, NPG

Bradshaw, Henry (*d.* 1513), scholar and hagiographer, was a Benedictine monk of the abbey of St Werburgh, Chester. He was probably professed in the mid-1490s since he was ordained subdeacon in 1499 and deacon and priest the following year. Although there is no evidence to corroborate Anthony Wood's statement that he was sent to Oxford, his scholarly interests and achievements are demonstrated in his life of the seventh-century St Werburh, written in English in verse form, and completed in the year of his death. There are four known surviving copies of this work, which was printed in 1521 in London by Richard Pynson; two of these are in the Bodleian Library, Oxford, one in the British Library, and one in the York Minster Library. The text was edited by C. Horstmann for the Early English Text Society in 1887.

Bradshaw's aim was to 'wryte a legende good and true And translate a lyfe into Englysshe' of the 'noble princes … abbess gracyous … Protectryce of the Cytee [of Chester]' (Horstmann, *Life of Saint Werburge*, 12). However, that he was no mere translator is clear from the many details that he provided from historical sources including Bede, Gerald of Wales, and Ranulf Higden, who had been a Chester monk–historian 150 years earlier. He also mentions a 'Passyonary', that is, a book of saints' lives, which was then in the abbey library. This probably refers to a four-volume set of which only the first volume survives, as MS 3 in the library of Gray's Inn, London; its index is complete and shows the entry for St Werburh to have been in volume 3.

Bradshaw's literary technique illustrates the continuing influence of John Lydgate (*d.* 1450) in, for example, the latter's tendency to extensive inflation of the narrative,

though without the ostentatious display from which some of Lydgate's work suffers. Despite his awkward and unpolished versification, the vigour of Bradshaw's style, the dramatic presentation of characters and events, and the sensitivity and humour expressed in speeches and descriptive passages, all hold the reader's interest. Moreover, the frequent exhortations to the reader underline the author's commitment to honour the saint and furnish a model of Christian piety and devotion for the 'marchaunt men havyng litell lernyng' and 'rude people' who will be edified by the 'noble historye' (Horstmann, *Life of Saint Werburge*, 199, 100).

The length of this work (over 5600 lines) is explained by the fact that interwoven with the saint's life and miracles is a chronicle recording not only her royal ancestry but also an account of the foundation of the city of Chester, its minster, and later its abbey. For the chronicle, while Bradshaw may have used the *Annales Cestrienses*, he must have had access to other sources which would also have furnished him with material for a now lost Latin work, *De antiquitate et magnificentia urbis Cestrie*, attributed to him by Anthony Wood. A poem by another hand, entitled 'A Balade to the Auctour', printed by Pynson with the life of St Werburh, states that Bradshaw died in 1513.

JOAN GREATREX

Sources H. Bradshaw, *The life of Saint Werburge of Chester*, ed. C. Horstmann, EETS, 88 (1887) · Register of John Arundel, Lichfield Joint RO · Wood, *Ath. Oxon.*, new edn, vol. 1 · C. Cannon, 'Monastic productions', *The Cambridge history of medieval English literature*, ed. D. Wallace (1999) · D. Pearsall, *Old English and Middle English poetry* (1977) · A. J. Horwood, ed., *A catalogue of the ancient manuscripts belonging to the Honourable Society of Gray's Inn* (1860) · R. C. Christie, ed. and trans., *Annales Cestrienses, or, Chronicle of the abbey of S. Werburg at Chester*, Lancashire and Cheshire RS, 14 (1887) · J. Tait, ed., *The chartulary or register of the abbey of St Werburgh, Chester*, 2 vols., Chetham Society, new ser., 79, 82 (1920–23) · R. V. H. Burne, *The monks of Chester, the history of St. Werburgh's Abbey* (1962) · H. Phillips, 'Aesthetic and commercial aspects of framing devices: Bradshaw, Roos and Copland', *Poetica, an international journal of linguistic-literary studies*, 43 (1995), 37–42 · H. Bradshaw, *The holy lyfe and history of Saynt Werberge* (1521)
Archives BL · Bodl. Oxf. · York Minster Library

Bradshaw, Henry (*c.*1500–1553), judge, was the only surviving son of William Bradshaw of Wendover, Buckinghamshire, who died in 1537. He was admitted to the Inner Temple from Barnard's Inn in 1521. Although he was temporarily put out of commons for quarrelling in 1529, he was called to the bar about that time and became a bencher in 1536 when he gave his first reading. He served as double reader in 1542, notwithstanding that he had the king's letters to be excused (as a law officer), and was treasurer for three years from 1544. It was probably during the 1540s that he erected chambers in the inn, known for a while as Bradshaw's Rents; these were on the east side of what became Tanfield Court, near the present library staircase.

Bradshaw married Jane (*d.* 1598/9), daughter of John Hurst of Kingston and widow of William Mainwaring (*d.* 1529) of East Ham, Essex; they had four sons and four daughters. In 1540 he was appointed solicitor-general, and he was promoted to attorney-general in 1545. The latter appointment enabled him to act as a justice of assize, and he went on the midland circuit from 1545 until his death. Edward VI renewed his office of attorney-general, which he held until 21 May 1552 when he became chief baron of the exchequer in succession to Sir Roger Cholmeley. He did not take the coif, but his arms were displayed in the windows of Serjeants' Inn, Fleet Street, where barons of the exchequer seem sometimes to have been given privileges. After little more than a year in office, he died on 27 July 1553, and was buried at Halton in Buckinghamshire.

Besides his paternal estate at Wendover, Bradshaw also left estates and houses at Halton (where he kept a study) and at Noke in Oxfordshire, where his widow lived on until her death. By his will, made in 1546, he established a charity under which his executors were to hire eight craftsmen 'well instructyd in their misteris' to live in Wendover, Halton, and Noke and 'take and instructe in their mysteres and handycraftes such poor folke and childreyn bothe men and women kynde as shalbe put to them' by his widow or his heirs, or the vicar of Wendover; they were to be fed, clothed, and lodged out of the profits of their own labours (PRO, PROB 11/36, fols. 122v–124). This arrangement was to last for twenty years. There are three kneeling figures of Bradshaw on memorial brasses: in a long gown on his father's brass at Wendover and in judicial robes both on his own monument at Halton and on his wife's at Noke.
J. H. BAKER

Henry Bradshaw (1831–1886), by unknown engraver (after Sir Hubert von Herkomer, 1881)

Sources F. A. Inderwick and R. A. Roberts, eds., *A calendar of the Inner Temple records*, 1 (1896) · Sainty, *King's counsel* · Sainty, *Judges* · W. Dugdale, *Origines juridiciales, or, Historical memorials of the English laws*, 3rd edn (1680), 328 · will, PRO, PROB 11/36, sig. 17 · will, PRO, PROB 11/93, sig. 30 [wife's will] · W. Lack, H. M. Stuchfield, and P. Whittemore, *The monumental brasses of Buckinghamshire* (1994), 99, 100, 230–31 · inquisition post mortem, PRO, C 142/90/42 · PRO, REQ 1/5, fols. 124, 147v
Likenesses brass effigy on monument, Wendover, Buckinghamshire · brass effigy on monument, Halton, Buckinghamshire · brass effigy on monument, Noke, Oxfordshire

Bradshaw, Henry (*bap.* **1601**, *d.* **1662**). *See under* Bradshaw, John, Lord Bradshaw (*bap.* 1602, *d.* 1659).

Bradshaw, Henry (**1831–1886**), librarian and scholar, the third son and fifth child of Joseph Hoare Bradshaw and Catherine, daughter of Richard Stewart of Ballintoy, co. Antrim, was born at 2 Artillery Place, Finsbury Square, London, on 2 February 1831. His father, a partner in Hoare's Bank, belonged to an Irish branch of the Bradshaw family of Lancashire, Cheshire, and Derbyshire. Bradshaw was educated at Temple Grove, East Sheen, and then in 1843 entered Eton College, first as an oppidan and then, following the collapse of his family's fortunes and his father's death, aged sixty-one, in 1845, as a colleger; he became captain of the school. In 1850 he proceeded as a scholar to King's College, Cambridge. Rather than take his BA without examination, as members of the college were then entitled, Bradshaw chose to sit the classical tripos: he gained a second class in 1854. In February 1853 he had obtained a fellowship of his college; but lacking the resources to remain in Cambridge, he took employment

under a friend from King's, George Williams, as a schoolmaster at St Columba's College, near Dublin, an institution that combined Irish patriotism with high-church Anglicanism. In Dublin he found kindred interests with J. H. Todd, but after Williams returned to Cambridge Bradshaw followed in 1856. In 1857–8 and 1863–5 he served as dean of his college, where he took an active part in its reform.

Bradshaw, who inherited from his father an important library of Irish printed books formed during the early nineteenth century, had taken a close interest in the older collections in the university library as an undergraduate, and he now turned to it to earn a living. His first appointment, from November 1856 to October 1858, was as principal assistant. In imagining that he would be able to concentrate on his own researches into its manuscripts and early printed books, he hoped for more than was either realistic or acceptable. A post more suited to his inclinations and knowledge was instead created for him in 1859; and he thus found himself charged with the parts of the library that stood in most need of his abilities. During the next few years he helped in preparing the printed catalogue of manuscripts (1856–67) and rediscovered much that had been neglected or forgotten. These included the tenth-century Book of Deer, the early Welsh glosses on a ninth-century manuscript of Juvencus, and the forgotten manuscripts of the protestant Waldensians, which Bradshaw redated authoritatively. He also began his study of Chaucer manuscripts, beginning with those in the university library and gradually extending his work until he could set them out in groups. Although attempts were made to persuade him to edit Chaucer himself, and he issued a pamphlet on the ordering of the *Canterbury Tales* in 1868, most of his work here was absorbed into the editions prepared for the Chaucer Society by F. J. Furnivall and then into the Clarendon edition by W. W. Skeat. In general, Bradshaw preferred to avoid public controversy, but in 1863 he spoke out strongly against the claim by Constantine Simonides to have written the Codex Sinaiticus. Although he learned sufficient of oriental languages to identify the manuscripts in his care, his interests lay in the West.

Above all, Bradshaw concentrated on fifteenth-century printing, beginning with the library's substantial collection of books printed by Caxton: much of his knowledge was used (not always with full comprehension) by William Blades in his life of Caxton (1861–3). Mainly studying books printed in England, the Low Countries, and the Rhine valley, Bradshaw established the foundations of modern bibliographical method. By identifying printed types with individual presses he mapped out much of the previously obscure history of early printing: two 'memoranda' on the subject appeared in 1870–71. Equally fundamentally, he realized the importance of linking codicological evidence to textual and other bibliographical questions. Although he never propounded the principles of his work, he was much influenced by the systematic analysis of coleoptera by G. R. Crotch, a colleague in the university library. He once summed up his method in a letter to F. J. Furnivall: 'Arrange your facts vigorously and get them plainly before you, and let them speak for themselves, which they will always do' (Prothero, 349). Bradshaw's methods may be seen in more detail in his published correspondence with J. W. Holtrop and M. F. A. G. Campbell of The Hague, as well as in his analyses of several major auctions where the books were catalogued with insufficient knowledge: he published that for the De Meyer sale (at Ghent) in 1870, but others survive in his notebooks. He extended his ordering of fifteenth-century presses, by country, town, and printer, even to the shelves of the university library, sometimes dismembering volumes in order to accommodate their contents to his bibliographical view.

With his election as university librarian in 1867 Bradshaw at last found himself in control of the library, of whose needs he was keenly aware. His predecessor, J. E. B. Mayor, had begun the task of reform. But although the library acquired books and manuscripts, by purchase (often at prices extraordinarily low even for the time) and by donation, on a scale never before seen in Cambridge, Bradshaw was less successful as an administrator than as a bibliographer and scholar. His presidential address to the Library Association in 1882 appeared as a further 'Memorandum', and Bradshaw appended to it a wealth of everyday detail. Under his eye, the library's collections took on much of their modern shape, and benefactors—including, most notably, Samuel Sandars (1837–1894)—were actively encouraged; but he possessed an endless ability to procrastinate and it was left to his successors to confront the increasingly urgent need for more space. His own

gifts, partly by bequest, included his collection of Irish books and many incunabula.

Even as his international reputation increased, Bradshaw continued his researches throughout his librarianship: into the medieval organization of Lincoln Cathedral; into early English liturgy; into the Gutenberg Bible; into medieval libraries; into the earliest printing in Cambridge. He was an energetic traveller among European libraries; but little of this appeared in print, and his notebooks, now in Cambridge University Library, remain an unpublished mine of observation and analysis. He published no book, but instead issued a series of brief 'Memoranda'; much of his antiquarian work was published in the papers of the Cambridge Antiquarian Society. Generous in sharing his knowledge, to the despair of his contemporaries he was often a poor correspondent; and he was reluctant to extend his ideas from particular examples to generalization. Inevitably, much of his work is to be found in the publications of others, such as Robert Willis and J. W. Clark's *Architectural History* of Cambridge (1886), Francis Procter and Christopher Wordsworth's *Breviarium ad usum Sarum* (1879–96), and Christopher Wordsworth's *Statutes of Lincoln Cathedral* (1892–7). His liturgical studies are commemorated in the Henry Bradshaw Society, founded in 1890 for the 'editing of rare liturgical texts'.

Short, stoutly built, clean-shaven, and with closely cropped hair, Bradshaw usually managed to control a naturally quick temper. He died, unmarried, from heart failure on 10 February 1886 in his rooms in King's College: he was buried on 15 February in the college chapel. His collected papers, edited by Francis Jenkinson, were published in 1889.

DAVID MCKITTERICK

Sources G. W. Prothero, *A memoir of Henry Bradshaw* (1888) • A. C. Benson, *The leaves of the tree: studies in biography* (1911) • [C. E. Sayle], *A catalogue of the Bradshaw collection of Irish books in the University Library, Cambridge*, 3 vols. (1916) • J. C. T. Oates, *A catalogue of the fifteenth-century printed books in the University Library, Cambridge* (1954) • D. McKitterick, *Cambridge University Library, a history: the eighteenth and nineteenth centuries* (1986) • P. Needham, *The Bradshaw method* (1988) • R. Stokes, *Henry Bradshaw* (1984) • Venn, *Alum. Cant.* • J. W. Clark, *Old friends at Cambridge and elsewhere* (1900), 292–301 • A. E. B. Owen, 'Henry Bradshaw and his correspondents', *Transactions of the Cambridge Bibliographical Society*, 11 (1996–9), 480–97

Archives BL, notes on visitation to Ely, Egerton MS 2655 • CUL, corresp. and papers • King's AC Cam., corresp. and papers, many relating to literary research and librarianship | Bath Royal Literary and Scientific Institution, letters to Leonard Blomefield • BL, corresp. with Sir Arthur Hamilton-Gordon, Add. MS 49272, *passim* • CUL, corresp. with W. M. Conway • JRL, letters to Nichols family • King's AC Cam., letters to Oscar Browning • NRA, priv. coll., letters to Sir Norman Moore • U. Birm., corresp. with Edward Arber • UCL, London, corresp. with Karl Pearson

Likenesses H. von Herkomer, oils, 1881, King's Cam. • W. H. Thornycroft, marble bust, exh. RA 1888, CUL • engraving (after H. von Herkomer, 1881), NPG [*see illus.*]

Wealth at death £1838 15s.: resworn administration, April 1887, CGPLA Eng. & Wales (1886)

Bradshaw, James (*bap.* 1613, *d.* 1685), clergyman and ejected minister, was baptized at Bolton, Lancashire, on 7 November 1613, the son of John Bradshaw (*d.* 1662) of Darcy Lever Hall in that parish and his first wife, Alice, daughter of Robert Lever. He was admitted plebeian to Brasenose College, Oxford, in January 1630, matriculated in December 1631, graduated BA in April 1634, and proceeded MA in January 1637. Some time before 17 September 1648, when their first child was baptized, James married Elizabeth, the daughter of Benjamin Childe, rector of Cotesbach in Leicestershire: in a fine entanglement of family relationships, James's father's third wife was Benjamin Childe's widow, if not also Elizabeth's mother. James and Elizabeth are known to have had four sons and six daughters, of whom one son and one daughter died in infancy.

By 1642 Bradshaw was curate of Turton, Lancashire, where he signed the protestation. Shortly after he was admitted rector of the wealthy living of Wigan following the deprivation of the previous incumbent, Bishop John Bridgeman of Chester. As the parliamentarian forces advanced on Lathom House, defended by the countess of Derby, in February 1644, Bradshaw urged them on from his pulpit, taking as his text Jeremiah 15: 14: 'And I will make thee to passe with thine enemies, into a land which thou knowest not: for a fire is kindled in mine anger, which shall burne upon you'. As a royalist account sourly observed, he set about:

> by as many markes and signes as ever hee had given of Antichrist, proving the Lady Derby to bee the scarlett whore and the whore of Babylon, whose walls he made as flatt and as thin as his discourse. Indeed, before he dispatch't his prophecy hee thump't 'em downe, reserveing the next verse to bee a triumph for the victor.   (Ormerod, 163)

The seven towers of Lathom House he compared to the seven horns of the Beast.

Bradshaw became a prominent figure in the presbyterian establishment in Lancashire. In December 1644 he was named by parliamentary ordinance one of the ministers empowered to ordain pending the final settlement of the ecclesiastical order and he was appointed a representative of the fourth Lancashire classis in 1646. In 1648 he was a signatory to the Lancashire clergy's assertion of presbyterian orthodoxy, *The harmonious consent of the ministers of the province within the county palatine of Lancaster, with their reverend brethren the ministers of the province of London*. In May 1649 he was signatory to a letter to London congregations appealing for relief for his war-torn parish and its neighbourhood, afflicted 'with a three-corded scourge of sword, pestilence, and famine, all at once afflicting it' (Ormerod, 277). The commissioners who surveyed the churches of Lancashire in June 1650 reported that Bradshaw was 'a painefull able preaching minister, and hath observed the cure upon the Lordes dayes' (Bridgeman, 3.465). However, they also noted a sign of his disaffection from the republican regime. He had failed to observe the fast day on 13 June, ordained to atone for the nation's ingratitude for its recent deliverances and to unite the people against the foreign and domestic enemies of God's cause by a parliament preparing for 'a New and Bloody War' with Scotland (*An act appointing Thursday the thirteenth of June 1650 to be kept as a day of solemn fasting and humiliation*). The following year, when the earl of Derby attempted to raise Lancashire for

Charles II and was crushed near Wigan in late August, Bradshaw was arrested (one of a number of presbyterian clergy in the county brought in under suspicion) and was only released in November upon his own bond of £400. At the beginning of 1653 Bradshaw lost the rectory of Wigan. This was not because of his political disaffection but because the benefice had become legally vacant with the death of the sequestered Bishop Bridgeman in November 1652. The trustees of the late Sir John Hotham, who had acquired the advowson about 1641, appointed his son Charles as the new rector.

From 1653 to 1657 Bradshaw served as curate of the chapel of Ellenbrook in Worsley parish, Lancashire, as such attending, and occasionally acting as moderator of, meetings of the Manchester classis. In January 1657 he was admitted curate of Macclesfield, Cheshire. Bradshaw's book of sermon notes, densely written in a crabbed hand, would seem to belong to his years at Ellenbrook and Macclesfield; it is now held in the British Library (BL, Add. MS 63608).

Bradshaw seems to have regarded the rituals of the restored monarchy with the same distaste that he had for the republic's. On 30 May 1662 (by when there had been plenty of time for disillusion with the new regime to set in) the Cheshire magistrate Sir Thomas Legh complained that Bradshaw persisted in 'his nonconformity to the present Government in all poynts as high as ever, for yesterday he would not celebrate as a day of thanksgiving for his sacred ma[jes]tie's Restauration &c. although he be commanded thereunto by an Act of Parliament' (*Calamy rev.*, 68–9). Bradshaw's ejection from Macclesfield followed shortly after, and he retired to Darcy Lever Hall, which he had inherited upon his father's death on 1 May 1662. In 1664 he entered his coat of arms and pedigree at the herald's visitation of the county, and two years later was paying tax on seven hearths. He did not entirely give up his vocation for the life of a minor country gentleman. For a while he had liberty to preach at nearby Westhoughton chapel in Deane parish, and later a kinsman connived at his reading some of the prayers at Bradshaw chapel in Turton parish without having had to subscribe to the Thirty-Nine Articles. Nevertheless, the ageing Bradshaw did not take out a licence under the declaration of indulgence in 1672. Bradshaw died in 1685 and was buried at Bolton on 26 February. He was survived by his wife and succeeded by his eldest son, John Bradshaw (*bap.* 1653, *d.* 1706).   TIM WALES

Sources *Calamy rev.*, 68–9 · G. T. O. Bridgeman, *The history of the church and manor of Wigan, in the county of Lancaster*, 3, Chetham Society, new ser., 17 (1889), 461–73 · [C. B. Heberden], ed., *Brasenose College register, 1509–1909*, 2 vols., OHS, 55 (1909), 159 · G. Ormerod, ed., *Tracts relating to military proceedings in Lancashire during the great civil war*, Chetham Society, 2 (1844) · W. Dugdale, *The visitation of the county palatine of Lancaster, made in the year 1664–5*, ed. F. R. Raines, 3 vols., Chetham Society, 84–5, 88 (1872–3), vol. 1, p. 51 · *The nonconformist's memorial … originally written by … Edmund Calamy*, ed. S. Palmer, [3rd edn], 1 (1802), 337–8 · W. A. Shaw, ed., *Minutes of the Manchester presbyterian classis*, 3 vols., Chetham Society, new ser., 20, 22, 24 (1890–91) · J. Bradshaw's sermon notes, BL, Add. MS 63608 · *The* *harmonious consent of the ministers of the province within the county palatine of Lancaster, with their reverend brethren the ministers of the province of London* (1648) · *CSP dom.*, *1651–2*, 1

Archives BL, sermon notes, Add. MS 63608

Bradshaw, James (*bap.* 1635, *d.* 1702), clergyman and ejected minister, was born at Hacken, Bolton parish, Lancashire, and baptized on 16 March 1635 in Bolton parish church. He was the son of Laurence Bradshaw of Darcy Lever, Bolton parish, and Margaret Holmes. He attended Bolton grammar school and matriculated from Corpus Christi College, Oxford, in 1653. He did not graduate but was further educated by his uncle, William Holmes, vicar of Guilsborough, Northamptonshire. He was ordained by the fourth Lancashire classis (Warrington) and was settled at Hindley chapel in the parish of Wigan by 1658. He was in the royalist rising under Sir George Booth in 1659. Bradshaw was ejected from Hindley in 1662.

Unfortunately for the nonconformists in the chapelries of Wigan parish, the rectory of Wigan was held *in commendam* by the bishop of Chester. Even tolerant Restoration bishops such as John Wilkins and John Pearson, who were happy to ignore the preaching ministry of nonconformists in the chapels of ease in the remoter parts of their diocese, could not ignore them in their own parish. Hindley chapel stood vacant until 1668 when a conformist minister could be found but Bradshaw seems to have remained in the parish. 'Mr Bradshaw of Hindley' appears in a list of seven 'nonconformist secluded prtended Ministers and such as frequently hould Conventicles', produced by the JP Sir Roger Bradshaigh in August 1665 (Nightingale, *Quaker Movement*, 205). Bradshaigh, one of the Lancashire deputy lieutenants, was a fierce opponent of nonconformists in the county. He had Bradshaw arrested and sent to Lancaster gaol for preaching at Blackrod, Bolton parish, in May 1669. At the assizes Bradshaw had to promise not to preach unless he read prayers or had licence from the bishop. He was to find an ingenious way around this restriction.

Upon the indulgence Bradshaw was licensed on 1 May 1672 as a presbyterian teacher at Hindley, with his house licensed as a meeting-place. He gained access to Rainford chapel, Prescot parish, in 1673 and retained it until his death in 1702. He did this with the collaboration of neighbouring clergy who occasionally read the prayer book service and preached for him. On 19 October 1680 one poor unfortunate appeared before the Chester church court for having his child baptized by Bradshaw. He complained that the vicar of Upholland was indisposed and, besides, he was under the impression that Bradshaw was a 'lawfull minister'. Bishop Pearson was unwilling to proceed against peaceable ministers preaching in the remote chapelries and so Bradshaw remained undisturbed. He was one of the Monday lecturers in Bolton and was briefly imprisoned during Monmouth's rebellion. He had Rainford Chapel certified as a dissenting place of worship at the quarter sessions held at Ormskirk on 22 July 1689. When he took the association oath in 1696 he described himself as minister of Rainford. He received a grant from the Common Fund from 1690 until 1701 and took an active part in the Lancashire provincial assembly between 1694 and 1700. He preached at the provincial assembly meeting in Warrington on 10 August 1697 and was the provincial's moderator at Warrington on 8 August 1699. Bradshaw died in 1702 after sustaining a leg injury while riding on a preaching tour. Rainford Chapel was recovered by the Church of England.

Bradshaw produced only two known printed works: *The Sleepy Spouse of Christ Alarm'd* (1677) and *Faiths Trial and Triumph* (1702). He had a large family and a poor congregation and living. His wife's name is unknown, and as she is not mentioned in his will it is likely that she died before him. Two of his children, a son (*d.* 1678) and a daughter (*d.* 1684), are buried at Upholland, where he lived, and more burials appear in the 1690s. His son Ebenezer was ordained on 22 June 1694, alongside Edmund Calamy, at Samuel Annesley's meeting-house in London, the first public ordination in London by presbyterians after the Restoration. He was minister of the protestant dissenting congregation in Ramsgate, Kent, and died on 11 March 1741, aged eighty.

JONATHAN H. WESTAWAY

Sources E. Axon, 'Ellenbrook Chapel and its 17th century ministers', *Transactions of the Lancashire and Cheshire Antiquarian Society*, 38 (1920), 3–34, esp. 15–18 · A. Gordon, ed., *Cheshire classis: minutes, 1691–1745* (1919), 159–60 · *Calamy rev.*, 68–9, 502 · W. A. Shaw, ed., 'Minutes of the United Brethren, 1693–1700', *Minutes of the Manchester presbyterian classis*, 3, Chetham Society, new ser., 24 (1891), 349–65 · A. Sparke, ed., *The registers of the parish church of Bolton* (1913), 142 · J. Lowe, 'The case of Hindley Chapel, 1641–1698', *Transactions of the Lancashire and Cheshire Antiquarian Society*, 67 (1957), 45–74 · G. T. O. Bridgeman, *The history of the church and manor of Wigan, in the county of Lancaster*, 1, Chetham Society, new ser., 15 (1888), 461–72, 695, 700, 722, 745, 758, 760, 778 · A. Brierley and A. E. Hodder, eds., *The registers of the church of St Thomas the Martyr, Upholland, in the county of Lancaster*, Lancashire Parish Register Society (1905), 159, 172, 174 · D. J. Browning and F. R. Pope, eds., *The register of the chapel of Rainford*, Lancashire Parish Register Society, 119 (1980), 123 · E. Calamy, ed., *An abridgement of Mr. Baxter's history of his life and times, with an account of the ministers, &c., who were ejected after the Restauration of King Charles II*, 2nd edn, 2 vols. (1713), vol. 2, pp. 16, 123 · E. Calamy, *A continuation of the account of the ministers … who were ejected and silenced after the Restoration in 1660*, 2 vols. (1727), vol. 1, pp. 17, 140 · E. Calamy, *An historical account of my own life, with some reflections on the times I have lived in, 1671–1731*, ed. J. T. Rutt, 2nd edn (1830), 349 · *Catalogue of the library … founded pursuant to the will of … Daniel Williams*, 2 (1841), 432 · F. Gastrell, *Notitia Cestriensis, or, Historical notices of the diocese of Chester*, ed. F. R. Raines, 2/2, Chetham Society, 21 (1850), 213–14 · *DNB* · G. Hadfield, *The Manchester Socinian controversy* (1825), 140 · R. Halley, *Lancashire: its puritanism and nonconformity*, 2 vols. (1869), vol. 1, pp. 391, 473; vol. 2, pp. 97, 105, 108 · A. J. Hawkes, 'Sir Roger Bradshaigh of Haigh, knight and baronet, 1628–1684: with notes of his immediate forbears', *Chetham miscellanies*, Chetham Society, new ser., 8 (1945), i–vi, 1–73 · B. Nightingale, *Early stages of the Quaker movement in Lancashire* (1921), 95, 98, 131, 202, 205, 206 · B. Nightingale, *Lancashire nonconformity*, 6 vols. [1890–93], vol. 4, pp. 4–5, 173 · *The nonconformist's memorial … originally written by … Edmund Calamy*, ed. S. Palmer, [3rd edn], 1 (1802), 337; 2 (1802), 364 · W. A. Shaw, ed., *Minutes of the Bury presbyterian classis, 1647–1657*, 2 vols., Chetham Society, new ser., 36, 41 (1896–8), 26, 31, 35, 43, 50, 109, 216 · W. A. Shaw, ed., *Minutes of the Manchester presbyterian classis*, 3 vols., Chetham Society, new ser., 20, 22, 24 (1890–91), 418–19 · J. Westaway, 'Scottish influences upon the reformed churches in north west England, c.1689–1829: a study of the ministry within the congregational and presbyterian churches in Lancashire, Cumberland and Westmorland', PhD diss.,

University of Lancaster, 1997 · will, 22 Aug 1701, Lancs. RO, MS WCW

Archives DWL, John Evans, 'List of dissenting congregations and ministers in England and Wales, 1715–29', MS 38.4

Wealth at death £50 bequeathed; bulk of estate in Hindley to brother-in-law, wife, and nephew: will, Lancs. RO, MS WCW

Bradshaw, James (1717–1746), Jacobite army officer, was born in Manchester, the only son of a wealthy Roman Catholic family in trade. He attended the Manchester Free School, where he studied classics, before being apprenticed in 1734 to Charles Worral, a Manchester factor who traded at the Golden Ball, Lawrence Lane, London. The death of his father in 1740 brought Bradshaw back to Manchester, where in 1741 he married a Miss Wagstaff and formed a partnership with James Dawson. After the death of both his wife and their only child in 1743, Bradshaw fell into a deep depression. In November 1745 he joined Charles Edward Stuart at Carlisle, recruited in Manchester at The Bell inn, and served as a member of the council of war. He was commissioned as a captain in the Manchester regiment under Colonel Francis Townley. On the march to Derby, he paid his men from his own purse, headed the company at Clifton Moor, and attended the Young Pretender at Carlisle. After quarrels with Townley, he transferred to Lord Elcho's life guards in early 1746, with whom he fought at Falkirk.

Captured at Culloden on 16 April 1746, Bradshaw was held prisoner in a nearby church with the wounded, then transported to London on the ship *Jean of Leith*. In London he was imprisoned in the new gaol, Southwark, and tried for treason at St Margaret's Hill on 27 October 1746. On the advice of his friends, his counsel told the court that the death of his wife and child had made Bradshaw insane, a defence consistent with his demeanour and dress during the trial, at which he behaved in a manner the court thought nonchalant. Found guilty and sentenced to death for high treason, he used his gallows speech to decry the treatment of Jacobite prisoners at the hands of the government, claiming that the wounded had been stripped, starved, and denied medical assistance from surgeons, whose instruments had been confiscated. He denied that he was insane, and declared his loyalty to both the Jacobite cause and the Church of England. He was hanged on Kennington Common on 28 November 1746.

JENNETT HUMPHREYS, *rev.* MARGARET D. SANKEY

Sources State trials, 18.415–24 · B. G. Seton and J. G. Arnot, eds., *The prisoners of the '45*, Scottish History Society, 3rd ser., 13–15 (1928–9) · R. Forbes, *The lyon in mourning, or, A collection of speeches, letters, journals … relative to … Prince Charles Edward Stuart*, ed. H. Paton, 3 vols., Scottish History Society, 20–22 (1895–6)

Bradshaw [*alias* White], **John** [*name in religion* Augustine of St John] (**1575/6–1618**), Benedictine monk, was born near Worcester, the third son of John Bradshaw, a citizen of Worcester who 'bore office in that towne … executing … the office of one of the chiefest Magistrates of the towne', and his wife, Anne Warmestrey, through whom he was related to a number of prominent families, including the Crofts of Croft Castle (McCann and Connolly, 244). Both his parents were Roman Catholics. He was educated at the

free school in Worcester. The Jesuit Edward Oldcorne was chaplain at Hindlip, near Worcester, and it was most likely through him that young Bradshaw was introduced to Henry Garnett, the Jesuit superior, who sent him to St Omer. On 21 February 1596 he arrived at the English College at Valladolid. The Jesuit superiors recognized his leadership qualities and he was made prefect over his companions. During a dangerous illness in the winter of 1598–9 he vowed to become a religious if his life were spared. Already several English youths in Rome had joined the Italian monks of Monte Cassino and other Benedictine monasteries with the hope of one day returning to England. He was the first of a stream of students to leave the seminary for the monastery of San Benito in Valladolid in April 1599. After a month's postulancy he was sent to the abbey of San Martino, Compostela, where he was received as a novice on 26 May and took the programmatic name of Augustine. In 1600 he was professed with four others (one of them being John (Leander) Jones), who had followed him from the seminary. He then went to the University of Salamanca. On 5 December 1602, in spite of the opposition of the Jesuits, Clement VIII granted formal permission to the English Benedictines, both in Spain and in Italy, to return to their country as missionaries. As soon as the news arrived he set out for England with three others on 26 December and arrived just as Elizabeth was dying.

Bradshaw had been appointed superior over his companions. He seems to have worked at first in his native county. He is also very likely the White mentioned as a priest haunting Worcestershire and the neighbouring counties. So many young Englishmen desired to join the Benedictines that it was soon evident that steps must be taken to find a spot more accessible than Spain for a monastery in which English subjects could be trained. So in the spring of 1604 he set out again to attend the general chapter of the Spanish Benedictines and lay before his superiors the plan. On his way he called upon the nuncio in Paris, and there it was that most likely his attention was first directed to Douai as a suitable position for the proposed foundation, it being a university town with rich abbeys close at hand. The Spanish abbots agreed to the proposal, and he returned to England with the title of vicar-general over the monks working there.

During the early part of 1605 Bradshaw was naïvely engaged in a scheme for purchasing a toleration for English Catholics from the government, high hopes being raised by the accession of James I. Garnett, the Jesuit superior, had lately failed in a similar attempt, and was less sanguine in his views of the government's intentions. When Bradshaw's negotiations proved unsuccessful, he blamed the Jesuits for their failure.

In the autumn of 1605 Thomas Arundell, first Baron Arundell of Wardour, had taken command of an English regiment in the service of the Archduke Albert against the Dutch, who no longer had the support of England, which had made peace with Spain in 1604. He brought Augustine Bradshaw out of England with him to be chaplain-general of that regiment. Coniers, a Jesuit, also joined the camp at Ostend as one of the chaplains, but he by no means liked being under the command of the Benedictine chaplain-general. All other plans failing, it was determined to get rid of him by procuring the dismissal of Lord Arundell. The regiment was mutinous and riven with factions suspecting each other of being agents of the English government and secretly in league with the Dutch. James Blount, one of the officers, was sent, with recommendations 'to blast his late colonel' at the Spanish court, and succeeded so well that at the end of May 1606 Lord Arundell and almost half of the officers were cashiered, and with them, of course, the chaplain-general.

Meanwhile Bradshaw was also battling with opposition to the monastic foundation in Douai which he began in 1606 and for which he had enlisted the patronage of the wealthy and influential Philippe de Caverel, abbot of St Vaast in Arras. The many defections to local Benedictines of students at the English colleges at Rome and Valladolid made his project unwelcome to Thomas Worthington, president of the English College, Douai, which was then in a rather parlous condition. Worthington's efforts to get the Benedictine foundation prohibited by appealing to Caraffa, the nuncio in Brussels, and then to Rome, were supported by Robert Persons, who thought the conversion of England would be best secured by a unitary mission under firm Jesuit leadership and that the Benedictine monasteries there, if recovered, should not be restored to the Benedictines, but be at the disposal of the church in general. The local Jesuits also feared that the school the Benedictines intended to open would compete with their own establishment in St Omer. But with his characteristic address and adroitness Bradshaw outmanoeuvred these objectors and by 1609 not only did St Gregory's Priory at Douai, the ancestor of the present Downside community, receive full ecclesiastical and civil authorization, but amicable relations between the principal contenders became normal thereafter. In the thick of these troubles Bradshaw acquired, in December 1605, a former collegiate church at Dieulouard, Lorraine (therefore in French territory), to be a possible refuge in case the Douai scheme came to nothing. Here came to be established the monastery of St Laurence which, at the French Revolution would transfer to England and settle at Ampleforth.

While engaged in this struggle Bradshaw was able to help the secular clergy. He obtained, from the munificent Caverel, Arras College in Paris as a house of study for the English clergy who were to devote themselves to writing. The house was to be a counter-blast to Chelsea College, lately established for anti-Catholic controversialists by James I. In 1611 Bradshaw founded St Benedict's Monastery at St Malo with the help of Gabriel Gifford, later to be archbishop of Rheims, in order to relieve the pressure of numbers at Dieulouard.

As vicar-general, Bradshaw was constantly in England superintending the numerous subjects who were working on the mission. In 1614 there were over eighty. Before Persons's death (1610) Bradshaw began his negotiations for a reunion of all English Benedictines into one congregation. Three groups had emerged. The monks from Italy (never more than a dozen) had secured for two of their own men, Edward Maihew and Vincent Sadler, an aggregation to the monastery of Westminster, then represented by its last survivor, old Father Robert (or Sigebert) Buckley. These two, who were joined later on by a third (19 December 1609), therefore represented the historic English Benedictine congregation. Bradshaw's Anglo-Spanish subjects were numerous: they possessed houses and men. The Italians had neither; the old English had only the succession. These two latter parties were desirous of a union, and Bradshaw entered enthusiastically into the project. What would suit the smaller bodies would be for the Anglo-Spanish monks to furnish men, money, and houses, while the others acted as superiors. The incongruity of such an arrangement did not seem to strike Bradshaw, who, on 13 February 1610, signed an agreement of ten articles. His precipitate action was greatly resented by the rest of his brethren, and the monks at Douai appealed to their ultimate superior, the general of the Spanish Benedictines, and Bradshaw was summoned to Spain in 1612. The result was that he was removed from his vicarship as well as from the priorship of St Gregory's, where there was much discontent with his over-strict regime, and John (Leander) Jones was set up in his place. The union with the old English congregation was eventually brought about under more equitable terms. But Bradshaw was as resilient as ever. On his way back from Spain he came to the notice of the famous Capuchin Joseph du Tremblay, Richelieu's *éminence grise*. The friar was then engaged in his work of reforming certain abbeys, and had lately taken a special interest in the order of Fontevrault. Under his influence the abbess, Louise de Bourbon, with her coadjutor, Antoinette d'Orléans, was desirous of restoring monastic observance in the houses of monks and nuns subject to her rule. Bradshaw was recommended by Tremblay 'as one full of zeal, sanctity, ability, and energy'. He began his work in October 1613, and was so successful that he was called to a like work in the abbeys of Chelles, Remiremont, and Poitiers. He also became engaged in a projected union of the monks of Fontevrault with the English monks at Douai. But, although this would have been of material advantage to the latter, further reflection showed the vicar-general that it would drain the mission of men and be a tax beyond the strength of his English monks. So the matter was dropped, and he was withdrawn. In 1615 he was sent to found a house for English monks in Paris, and for one year presided over its destinies. This evolved into St Edmund's Priory, Paris, whose community later settled at Douai Abbey, near Reading. In 1616, having a well earned reputation for observance, he was sent to reform the Cluniac priory of Longueville, near Rouen, where he died, aged forty-two, on 4 May 1618 and where he was buried.

Bradshaw was a frank, open-minded man, with a singular winning way, which always made a striking first impression. His generous nature led him into impetuous actions which caused difficulties a more prudent man would have escaped. It is perhaps open to question whether he would have succeeded so well as he did had he not had the help of such men as John Roberts and John (Leander) Jones to supply the deficiencies of his character.   E. L. TAUNTON, rev. DAVID DANIEL REES

Sources J. McCann and H. Connolly, eds., *Memorials of Father Augustine Baker and other documents relating to the English Benedictines,* Catholic RS, 33 (1933) · D. Lunn, *The English Benedictines, 1540–1688* (1980) · B. Weldon, *Chronological notes … of the English congregation of the order of St Benedict* (1881) · H. Connolly, *Some dates and documents for the early history of our house, 1: our establishment as a community at Douay* (1930) · P. Guilday, *The English Catholic refugees on the continent, 1558–1795* (1914) · L. Owen, *The running register* (1626) · R. H. Connolly, 'The first six', *Downside Review,* 46 (1928), 31–49 · T. B. Snow, *Obit book of the English Benedictines from 1600 to 1912,* rev. H. N. Birt (privately printed, Edinburgh, 1913) · E. Bishop, 'The beginning of Douay convent', *Downside Review,* 16 (1897), 21–35
Archives Monastic Archives, Silos, Spain, MSS · Monte Cassino Abbey, Italy, MSS · Westm. DA, MSS
Likenesses portrait, Spetchley Park, Worcestershire

Bradshaw, John, Lord Bradshaw (*bap.* 1602, *d.* 1659), lawyer, politician, and regicide, was born at Wibersley, in the parish of Stockport, Cheshire, and baptized on 10 December 1602 at St Mary's, Stockport, the second surviving son of Henry Bradshaw (*d.* 1654) of Marple Hall and Wibersley, and Catherine Winnington (*d.* 1604) of Offerton in the same county. His grandfather, also Henry, descended from a respectable Derbyshire family, was described as a yeoman, but having purchased Marple in the break-up of the estate of Sir Edward Stanley early in the reign of James VI and I, the Cheshire Bradshaws were of comfortable gentry standing.

Early life As a youth Bradshaw is said to have attended Stockport Free School, Bunbury School, elsewhere in Cheshire, and Middleton School, Lancashire. He entered Gray's Inn on 26 May 1620 and was called to the bar on 23 April 1627. Typically described as an obscure Cheshire attorney, Bradshaw appears nevertheless to have been at least reasonably well connected. His mother's family apparently had dealings with Sir Benjamin Rudyard, surveyor of the court of wards. In 1630 a John Bradshaw was appointed as steward of the manor of Glossop, which belonged to Thomas Howard, earl of Arundel. The manor lay close to the Cheshire home of the future lord president, but it has proved difficult to establish incontrovertibly whether it was he who served the earl. Bradshaw was also related to Sir Humphrey Davenport, lord chief baron of the exchequer from 1632.

Bradshaw was certainly already well connected in his native Cheshire, and it was here that his legal career began. He corresponded with the Leghs of Lyme, and once took a letter from Sir Peter to the earl of Bridgewater. Subsequently he enjoyed the patronage of Sir William Brereton, his neighbour and kinsman. Sir George Booth also appears to have been well enough disposed towards him. His clients at law included the brewers and bakers of Chester; the borough of Congleton; and families such as the Fittons of Chester and the Booths of Twemlow. He also represented John Milton (to whom he may have been related) in a chancery case in 1647, an engagement perhaps typical of those which prompted Clarendon's

John Bradshaw.

John Bradshaw, Lord Bradshaw (*bap.* 1602, *d.* 1659), by unknown engraver

remark that he was 'much employed by the factious' (Clarendon, *Hist. rebellion,* 4.475). This would appear to have marked the beginning of one of Bradshaw's most signal friendships.

Bradshaw's activities as a lawyer raised him to prominence in the affairs of his provincial homeland. In 1637 he became mayor of Congleton, and later became high steward there, serving in that capacity until May 1656. He was also chosen steward of Newcastle under Lyme by the mayor, bailiffs, and burgesses on 31 August 1641; he held this office, which entailed certain judicial responsibilities in the town, until his death. On 3 January 1638 he married a local woman, Mary (*bap.* 1596, *d.* in or before 1658), daughter of Thomas Marbury of Marbury. Bradshaw's legal practice made him wealthy. By 1640 he retained no fewer than five servants.

The civil war Lucrative as his legal career had been in peacetime, the 1640s were the making of John Bradshaw. He first rose to prominence in the City of London in 1643. Against the backdrop of revelations about Waller's plot to betray the capital into royalist hands, under-sheriff Richard Gibbs died, leaving a vacancy for a judge in the Wood Street sheriffs' court. Common council and the court of aldermen vied for the right to nominate a successor. On 18 July Alderman John Langham nominated Bradshaw for the vacant post, and sought the backing of the council. But Bradshaw's appointment was challenged by Richard Proctor, the preferred candidate of the lord mayor and court of aldermen. On 21 September 1643 Bradshaw was accepted as its nominee by the common council in preference to the other two candidates, Proctor and William Steele, Bradshaw's fellow Cheshireman. On 25 September, the day MPs took the solemn league and covenant, Bradshaw was sworn as judge accordingly. The resulting legal case in the king's bench (after 1649 the upper bench) was not resolved in Bradshaw's favour until 1656, although he had himself sat on the bench in the sheriffs' court since his appointment, and had been authorized to appoint a deputy in 1649. The early phase of this dispute also took place against the backdrop of an argument among parliamentarian militants over the command of militia forces in the City, an argument in which Bradshaw appears to have taken a prominent part himself, as well as the debate in the City over the principle of the 'general rising', the all-out military strategy favoured by 'war party' sympathizers in London.

Bradshaw entered the national stage as a parliamentarian lawyer in the rapidly expanding world of state and administrative advocacy. His first important engagement was as counsel to the committee for compounding with delinquents. Such was the importance of his role at the heart of this sensitive business that by January 1647 he was referred to as being 'as it were Attorney General' (BL, M636/8, Verney Correspondence, unfoliated). That year, he also acted as counsel to the committee for the visitation of Oxford.

It was in the service of the state that Bradshaw now came to make a real impact on national affairs. On 23 October 1644, the third anniversary of the outbreak of the Irish rising, Bradshaw joined the legal team appointed by the Commons on the king's behalf for prosecution of the Irish rebel Lord Maguire. In June 1647 he was junior counsel in the trial of Judge David Jenkins. He acted as principal counsel when Lieutenant-Colonel John Lilburne successfully appealed the Star Chamber judgment against him before the House of Lords on 13 February 1646.

It has been suggested that Bradshaw's retention on Lilburne's behalf reflected partisan calculation by an Independent faction at Westminster working at this time to protect the future Leveller as part of their political warfare with the presbyterians. When the lower house began to recruit its membership upon the gradual resumption of peace from 1645, Bradshaw had certainly figured in the plans of the emergent Independent interest. In November that year he failed to obtain election to a seat for Newcastle under Lyme, much to the disappointment of his patron Brereton, the parliamentary commander in Cheshire and north Wales. On the other hand, despite initial enthusiasm Brereton appears to have dropped Bradshaw from his designs on a seat for the city of Chester the following year. On 8 October 1646, having been nominated by the Commons as a commissioner of the great seal along with Sir Rowland Wandesford and Sir Thomas Bedingfield, Bradshaw was rejected by the Lords. It has been remarked that 'we must suppose that this employment was [sought for] him through the influence of his great clients in the House of Commons' (M. Noble, *Lives of the English Regicides*, 2 vols., 1798, 1.48).

After some initial resistance to his nomination in the Commons, the House of Lords sent down an ordinance making Bradshaw chief justice of Chester, Flint, Montgomery, and Denbigh on 12 March 1647, which passed the Commons on the 16th. It has been claimed that on 18 March following he was also chosen by the Lords as one of the eight judges responsible for the Welsh great sessions. But the ordinance for appointing judges to go on circuit in Wales discussed in the Commons and the Lords on 19 and 20 March left the matter of appointment to the commissioners of the great seal. In any case, as justice of Chester, Bradshaw would have been responsible for the circuit in the three north Wales counties specified by his patent. On 12 October 1648 Bradshaw was one of those created serjeants-at-law by parliament, on which occasion his sponsors were his Cheshire patrons Booth and Brereton.

The trial of Charles I On 10 January 1649 Bradshaw was appointed lord president of the high court of justice set up to try Charles I, of which he had been appointed a member by the first unicameral act of parliament in English history [see also Regicides]. Conventionally it is claimed that Bradshaw was appointed to and then chaired this unprecedented tribunal only because he was the only judicial figure of any rank who could be persuaded to participate in proceedings. However, Bradshaw, along with Serjeant Nicholas, Roger Hill, and Francis Thorpe, had all been nominated to sit in the court first projected under the terms of an ordinance which was rejected by the House of Lords on 2 January 1649. All four judges were then also named to the high court of justice as it was established on 6 January, and all four were absent from the court's first two meetings. That Bradshaw was singled out from among these judicial figures on 10 January to preside over the trial may owe a great deal to the factional machinations which influenced the way in which the trial was conducted. Bradshaw was closely linked, through the sheriffs' court and the Salters' Hall subcommittee for the command of the city militia, with those elements within the common council of the City of London which had staged a successful coup to seize control over the corporation from the lord mayor and aldermen in December and January. Since the trial was itself predicated on the notion of the constitutional supremacy of the House of Commons, it is likely that Bradshaw commended himself as a potential chairman of the high court of justice due to his association with one of the constituencies in English politics with the clearest interest in maintaining the new constitutional dispensation—represented in the court itself by commissioners Robert Tichborne and Owen Rowe.

Bradshaw became the focus of every effort to conduct the trial with dignity and a veneer of legal formality. His title was to be observed outside the court in Westminster Hall, as well as within. He was given smart apartments in New Palace Yard, and later in the dean's house at Westminster Abbey. Each day's proceedings began with the lord president's ceremonial entry into the great hall, a mace and sword of state going before. On the final day of the trial he was noted to have worn a scarlet gown. There is no contemporary evidence to support the legend that he wore a beaver hat lined with plates of steel for the duration of the trial, for fear of assassination attempts.

As lord president, the deputed spokesman of the king's judges, Bradshaw also played a crucial role himself in the conduct and handling of the trial, having been directed by his fellow commissioners to deal directly with the king. The immense drama of the trial derives in large part from Bradshaw's oratorical duelling with Charles, whom the lord president undoubtedly skewered in the course of some of the most important exchanges of the four days of public trial. Bradshaw's influence was apparent on the first day when it was he who decreed that the king ought to sit facing his judges, rather than off to the side, as some judges had wished. On the third day, 23 January, Bradshaw appears to have attempted effectively to rule the king contumacious after his sixth refusal to plead to the charge, and thereby to precipitate a move to condemnation the following day. In this he was overruled by his colleagues. On the final day of the trial, 27 January, Bradshaw had been instructed by his fellow judges to allow the king to offer 'anything' he might wish to say to the court before it proceeded to judgment. Charles duly proposed a trilateral conference with his Lords and Commons in camera. Bradshaw's attempt to brush aside this suggestion was overruled, prompting the high court's short withdrawal to the court of wards to consider the proposal. When it reconvened, Bradshaw had to tell the king that his judges had declined his offer. Nevertheless, clearly under strict instruction from the other judges, he offered Charles two further opportunities to propose something more acceptable. The king's failure to do any such thing was the cue for Bradshaw to enter the history books as the only Englishman ever to hand down sentence of death upon his sovereign.

The Commonwealth Bradshaw was commissioned to chair the high court of justice subsequently set up to try and condemn several royalist delinquents, the duke of Hamilton (tried as the earl of Cambridge), the earl of Holland, Arthur Lord Capel, Lord Goring (alias the earl of Norwich), and Sir John Owen. On 14 February 1649 Bradshaw was among the forty-one peers, politicians, judges, and soldiers chosen by MPs to sit on the new council of state set up by the Rump as the principal executive organ of the Commonwealth of England and Ireland. Tied up with the trials in Westminster Hall, Bradshaw was unable to attend the council's early meetings. Nevertheless, on 10 March, the day after the executions in palace yard, he was appointed lord president of the council by his colleagues at the board, making him in effect England's first elected executive head of state, albeit somewhat indirectly. Two days later he made his first appearance in the temporary council chamber at Derby House, attending with unrivalled diligence thereafter. It may have been his influence which secured for John Milton appointment to the office of secretary for foreign tongues to the council. The journalist Marchamont Nedham, who, like Milton, was remembered years later in a codicil to the lord president's will, also appears to have benefited from Bradshaw's patronage.

Bradshaw held the chair of the council until 26 November 1651, when his office went into rotation, apparently to Bradshaw's great discontent. He held on to his seat at the board comfortably at the next election in the Commons house, however, and himself served as the first rotating

president. He also polled very respectably in the council election of November 1652, continued as a councillor until the dissolution of the Rump, serving once more as lord president in January 1653, and was a member of standing committees on foreign affairs and trade, among others. He retained the title of Lord Bradshaw for the remainder of his political career.

Bulstrode Whitelocke remarked that at the council board Bradshaw 'spent much of their time in his long speeches, a great hindrance to … business' (*The Diary of Bulstrode Whitelocke, 1605–1675*, ed. R. Spalding, Records of Social and Economic History, new ser. 13, 1990, 234). But Whitelocke also supported the first attempt to appoint Bradshaw to the chancellorship of the duchy of Lancaster, defeated by twenty-five votes to twenty-one on 16 July 1649. Bradshaw was awarded a short-term commission a fortnight later, but does not appear to have been entrusted with the revised duchy seals, nor the chamber in Westminster where duchy business was conducted. Nevertheless, despite obvious controversy among MPs about the status of the duchy jurisdiction, his commission was periodically revived and renewed, until 17 September 1653, when it was split with Thomas Fell.

One of Bradshaw's most politically sensitive roles during the Commonwealth was as chairman of the court for relief on articles of war. In this capacity he was responsible, from June 1649, for protecting the claims of individuals who had negotiated their capitulation with army officers during the wars in England, only to find that the terms they had been granted were not subsequently respected by parliament and its local committees. The court sat in adjudication of numerous such claims in the early 1650s, frequently ruling that the articles of war ought to be upheld in the face of decisions taken at Westminster or in the provinces. On one or two notable occasions, as in the case of Sir John Stowell, the court's rulings caused uproar among those who had purchased confiscated estates in good faith, only to find their title questioned on the grounds of prior claims to the benefit of articles. The whole issue contributed greatly to the growth of political tensions during the Commonwealth era.

The former lord president was eclipsed somewhat in the wake of the dissolution of the Rump, and was at times clearly rather out of sorts with the protectorate. It is popularly held that Bradshaw defied Cromwell on 20 April 1653, warning the lord general when he came to dissolve the council of state, having just ejected parliament, that 'no power under heaven can dissolve them but themselves' (S. R. Gardiner, *History of the Commonwealth and Protectorate, 1649–1660*, 2, 1897, 265). But there is no direct evidence of this. Certainly Bradshaw was not in the chair that day, as Ludlow's account would appear to imply. Having no formal record of the day's business in the council chamber, it is impossible to say whether he was present at all, or even whether the council actually sat.

The protectorate Bradshaw managed to cling onto his official suite of rooms at Whitehall after the meeting of Barebones Parliament, occasion for the ousting of many of his colleagues from the palace, and he continued to serve in the court for relief on articles of war. But after the inauguration of the protectorate Bradshaw's political position became precarious. In February 1654, the protector's council had recommended that Bradshaw be sent a new patent as chief justice of Chester, but evidently this was insufficient to salve the wounds inflicted less than a year earlier. When the first protectorate parliament met in September 1654 one newsbook reported that 'Lord Bradshaw', one of the MPs for Staffordshire, had been a candidate for speaker. About this time Milton praised Bradshaw for his role in condemning Charles I, an action which 'liberty herself … has entrusted to eternal memory' ('The second defence of the English people', *Complete Prose Works of John Milton*, vol. 4 pt 1, 1966, 637).

Bradshaw was in the van of the attack made by the 'Commonwealthsmen' on the new constitution which commenced almost as soon as the new MPs had settled into their seats. He rapidly fell under the suspicion of the new regime. His official appointments became a particular bone of contention, and he was forced to confront the lord protector in defence of his patent appointing him chief justice of Chester in 1654. He was dismissed in August, but successfully faced down his opponents, going on circuit, official sanction for which was granted in September.

Although Bradshaw appears to have been included in the Cheshire commission for securing the peace of the Commonwealth, set up to assist the new major-general in 1655, it is hard to see how he could have been omitted from a body whose support among the leaders of Cheshire society was thin at best. In August 1656 the major-general whose jurisdiction included Cheshire, Tobias Bridge or Bridges, managed to prevent Bradshaw's return as MP for the county, principally by persuading the leading gentry to exclude him from the slate. According to Bradshaw's brother, Henry, the popular candidacy of the chief justice was not forced, as his proposed running-mate, Sir William Brereton, would almost certainly have come off very much the worse if it had come to a vote. Subsequent attempts to secure Bradshaw a seat in the City of London came to nothing. He had become an open opponent of the regime by now, Monck having received intelligence the year before that he had conspired with other opponents of the Cromwellian regime to kidnap the colonel as a prelude to overthrowing the army leadership. Fresh attempts were made to deprive Bradshaw of his judicial office at Chester in August 1656. According to Noble, he was deprived, though if this were indeed so, by July 1659 he had certainly been reinstated.

Bradshaw was elected to sit in Lord Protector Richard Cromwell's parliament as MP for Cheshire in 1659, at least in part thanks to the intervention of the sheriff, John Legh of Booths, who moved the poll at a crucial moment to Bradshaw's home town, Congleton. Bradshaw took his seat only after considerable opposition to his return in the parliamentary privileges committee had been borne down, the vote in the house giving Bradshaw a bare majority of seven. The election itself contributed not a little to the rising of Booth in the county a few months later, it having been suggested that Bradshaw's appeal to the 'birthright' of freeholders, even Quakers, to exercise their political will free from gentry control forced upon Booth and his confederates the realization that they were left with no option other than 'fighting to preserve their way of life' (Morrill, *Cheshire, 1630–1660*, 298).

Nevertheless, Bradshaw had been heaped with rewards for his services in the course of the 1650s. In August 1649 parliament voted him land worth £2000 per annum from the estates of the earl of St Albans (marquess of Clanricarde) and Lord Cottington. The former included Summer Hill, which in 1645 had been sequestered and granted to Clanricarde's half-brother, the earl of Essex, and Tonbridge Park, Kent (in the same parish as Summer Hill). The Cottington estate included the manors of Feltham and Hanworth in Middlesex, plus other properties in that county, as well as Berkshire, Hampshire (including Fremantle Park), Kent, Somerset, and Wiltshire. In the latter county, the properties included Hatch, the manor of Fonthill Gifford, and land in the parish of Tisbury. Subsequently Bradshaw also acquired Farrockline House, forfeit for the treason of a Lancashire gentleman, by which time he was apparently living at Greenway Hall, Bagnall, Staffordshire. He had supposedly also acquired the estate of his brother-in-law, John Fallowes, the heavily indebted lord of Fallowes Hall, Alderley, Cheshire, who was married to Anne Bradshaw.

Last days The restoration of the Commonwealth saw Bradshaw once again in the saddle, though by now ill. He was a member of the council of state appointed in May 1659, and in the following month became one of three new commissioners for the great seal. Within days he had written to parliament asking to be relieved temporarily of his duties as seal commissioner. He attended the house on 22 July to take the requisite oath. He rose from his deathbed to denounce the military usurpers who once more disrupted the Rump in October, and reputedly declared with almost his dying breath that had he to try the king again he would do it willingly. His old associate Marchamont Nedham reported that John Bradshaw, whom he described as 'my Noblest Friend', died at Dean's House, Westminster on 31 October 1659. The cause of death was described as 'quartan ague', usually taken to be malaria or malaria-like symptoms. He was buried in Westminster Abbey on 22 November; his wife, who predeceased him, was also buried there. They left no surviving children. Bradshaw had bequeathed his estate to his wife, with reversion to his nephew, Henry, towards whom the lord president had apparently shown some affection during his lifetime. Henry senior [*see below*] chided his son's choice of studies at Christ's in 1652, as ill requital of 'your uncles indulgencie in sufferinge you to make your owne choise what to studie' (Bodl. Oxf., MS top. Cheshire e.3, fol. 15v).

On 15 May 1660 it was resolved that Bradshaw, although dead, should be attainted by act of parliament, together with Cromwell, Ireton, and Pride, all of whom had died before the Restoration. As early as 3 May 1654 Bradshaw had been specially excepted from any future pardon in a proclamation issued by Charles II. On 12 July 1660 the sergeant-at-arms was ordered to deliver to the house Bradshaw's goods. On 4 December 1660 parliament directed that:

> the bodies of Bradshaw, Cromwell, and Ireton 'should be taken up from Westminster' and hanged in their coffins at Tyburn. This indignity was duly perpetrated on 30 Jan 1661. The regicides' heads were subsequently exposed in Westminster Hall and their bodies reburied beneath the gallows. (*DNB*)

The remains of Bradshaw's wife were translated to Westminster Abbey churchyard on 9 September 1661. At least one legend has Bradshaw surviving the Restoration, then making good his escape, incognito, to Jamaica, where he died and was buried, a memorial inscription advising passers-by that they 'never, never forget that rebellion against tyrants is obedience to God' (Chester City Archive, Earwaker Collection, 'Bradshaw of Congleton', CR63/1/72/1; extract from *Leek Times*, 3 Dec 1892).

Assessment Throughout his public career Bradshaw fairly consistently aligned himself with more radical elements in English politics, first in the City, then at Westminster, favouring the drive for outright military victory over the king, followed by the redistribution of the power of the crown away from existing élites. At the king's trial he was in a position to put forward for the benefit of posterity some very strong views about the nature of authority in the English state, and the subjection of the crown to laws made by the representatives of the English people. Inevitably, calculations of political advantage were bound up with the articulation of his principled convictions. In January 1649 the best hope of securing those convictions had seemed to lie, paradoxically, in securing the compliance of the king. The growing desperation of the trial commissioners was voiced in Bradshaw's admonitions, repeated over and over even in the face of the king's utter contempt, that Charles plead to the charges against him, thereby accepting the jurisdiction of the high court of justice, and hence the authority of the Commons to legislate independently of the crown and House of Lords. When this strategy failed and the monarchy soon after fell, Bradshaw found himself at the helm of the council of state, the new executive authority whose first and most pressing task was the final destruction of the Levellers, the only supporters of something more genuinely approaching the reality of 'popular sovereignty' in the aftermath of regicide. Simultaneously, Bradshaw had a hand in drafting legislation to alleviate hardships faced by victims of delinquent landlords. Yet as a leading light of the judicial establishment, he was allied with powerful military interests in the frontline of a struggle to uphold property and its interests during the 1650s, even when these clashed with those who had carried the burden of the struggle against the king in the provinces of England. His public stance at the election of 1656 was more of a response to the hostility of Cheshire society towards his candidacy, than a belief in social and political egalitarianism. However, it probably did in part reflect some of the 'antiformal' potential inherent in his religious outlook and associations.

Bradshaw's elder brother, **Henry Bradshaw** (*bap.* 1601, *d.* 1662), parliamentarian army officer, was baptized on 23 January 1601 in St Mary's, Stockport. In 1630 he married Mary Wells (*bap.* 1606, *d.* 1643), and in 1644 he married his second wife, Anne Bowdon (*fl.* 1644–1660). On 6 July 1646 he signed a Cheshire petition for the establishment of the presbyterian church. He performed military service for parliament during the civil wars and Commonwealth, commanding in September 1651 the Macclesfield militia at Worcester, where he was wounded. He:

> sat on the court martial which tried and condemned the earl of Derby and other loyalists at Chester in 1652; was charged with this offence at the Restoration; was imprisoned by order of parliament from 17 July to 14 August 1660; was pardoned on 23 February 1661; and, dying at Marple, was buried at Stockport on 15 March [1662]. (*DNB*)

SEAN KELSEY

Sources *DNB* · pedigree of Bradshaw and Isherwood of Marple, Ches. & Chester ALSS, CR63/1/73 · J. Foster, *Register of admissions to Gray's Inn, 1521–1881* (privately printed, London, 1887) · journals, CLRO, court of common council, vol. 40, fols. 68v, 69v, 71, 74v, 75; vol. 41, fols. 131v–34v · repertories of the court of aldermen, CLRO, vol. 56, fols. 194, 199v, 206, 209v, 243v–4, 246v · *JHL*, 9 (1646–7), 30, 55, 75 · *JHC*, 3 (1642–4), 648, 651, 674 · *JHC*, 5 (1646–8), 113 · *JHC*, 6 (1648–51), 132, 141, 261, 271, 272, 443, 599 · *JHC*, 7 (1651–9), 43, 112, 241, 277, 320, 367 · *JHC*, 8 (1660–67), 88 · *IGI* · *CSP dom.*, 1639, 301–2; 1648–54, 411; 1656–7, 50, 117 · *The letter books of Sir William Brereton*, ed. R. N. Dore, 2 vols., Lancashire and Cheshire RS, 123, 128 (1984–90) · A. C. Gibson, 'Original correspondence of the Lord President Bradshaw', *Transactions of the Historic Society of Lancashire and Cheshire*, new ser., 2 (1861–2), 41–74 · A. C. Gibson, 'Every-day life of a country gentleman of Cheshire in the 17th century', *Transactions of the Historic Society of Lancashire and Cheshire*, new ser., 3 (1862–3), 67–92 · J. P. Earwaker, *East Cheshire: past and present, or, A history of the hundred of Macclesfield*, 2 (1880), 65–77 · G. Ormerod, *The history of the county palatine and city of Chester*, 2nd edn, ed. T. Helsby, 3 (1882), 843–7 · J. G. Muddiman, *The trial of Charles I* (1926?) · P. J. Pinckney, 'Bradshaw and Cromwell in 1656', *Huntington Library Quarterly*, 30 (1966–7), 233–40 · J. S. Morrill, *Cheshire, 1630–1660: county government and society during the English revolution* (1974) · J. S. Morrill, 'Parliamentary representation', *VCH Cheshire* · K. Lindley, *Popular politics and religion in civil war London* (1997), 311–19 · J. T. Peacey, 'John Lilburne and the Long Parliament', *HJ*, 43 (2000), 625–45 · J. L. Chester, ed., *The marriage, baptismal, and burial registers of the collegiate church or abbey of St Peter, Westminster*, Harleian Society, 10 (1876) · JRL, Legh of Lyme MSS
Archives PRO, letters and state MSS, State Papers 25
Likenesses W. Dobson, double portrait, oils (with Hugh Peters), Helmingham Hall, Suffolk; negative, Courtauld Inst. · M. Vandergucht, line engraving, BM, NPG; repro. in E. Ward, *The history of the grand rebellion*, 3 vols. (1713) · engraving, NPG [*see illus.*]
Wealth at death disposed of extensive real estate in Berkshire, Hampshire, Kent, Middlesex, Somerset, and Wiltshire; bequests of several thousand pounds, though many were cancelled in final codicil: Earwaker, *East Cheshire*, vol. 2, pp. 73–7

Bradshaw, John (*b.* 1658/9), convicted criminal, was born in Maidstone, Kent, the son of Alban Bradshaw, an attorney. He matriculated on 23 February 1674, aged fifteen, from Corpus Christi College, Oxford, and was admitted as a scholar on 20 April.

It was later charged that early in the morning of 13 July 1677 Bradshaw and another scholar, Robert Newlin, had broken into the chamber of John Wickes, a senior fellow of Corpus, in order to rob him. They attacked the sleeping Wickes with a hammer, but its head flew off the handle and the victim survived. His assailants were placed in custody at the college but Newlin, through the connivance of his uncle, the college president, Dr Robert Newlin, escaped. Bradshaw was imprisoned in Oxford Castle. Condemned to death at the assizes on 27 July, he petitioned the king, and on the 31st a warrant for his reprieve was issued, apparently through the influence of Arthur Annesley, earl of Anglesey. However, it seems that there was pressure to have this decision reversed. On 13 September Annesley wrote to Secretary Sir Joseph Williamson conceding that Bradshaw 'will not be fit to continue of a college after such an offence' but urging that the reprieve be not rescinded: 'I beseech you therefore, the man being young and of great parts and learning, to move his Majesty that he may be transported' (*CSP dom.*, 1677–8, 357); on 8 October the vice-chancellor of the university, Dr Henry Clarke, certified that such a course would not adversely affect discipline.

It seems very unlikely that the death sentence was imposed, but was Bradshaw banished, or pardoned? Anthony Wood suggested the latter, for after remaining in prison for a whole year Bradshaw 'retired soon after to his own country' of Kent, where he 'taught a petty school'. At university 'a perfect atheist', he later 'turned quaker, was a preacher among them', and finally, in 1685, converted to Catholicism (Wood, 4.619). There is no evidence to confirm Wood's attribution to him of the pamphlet *The Jesuite Countermin'd, or, An Account of a New Plot* (1679). Whoever was the author of this ultra-loyalist work seems very unlikely to have shortly become a Quaker, or a Roman Catholic, and these denominations have no record of John Bradshaw. His later career remains a matter for speculation, and the place and date of his death are unknown.

STEPHEN WRIGHT

Sources Foster, *Alum. Oxon.* · Wood, *Ath. Oxon.*, new edn · T. Fowler, *The history of Corpus Christi College*, OHS, 25 (1893) · *CSP dom.*, 1677–8

Bradshaw, Lucretia (*d. c.*1755). *See under* Folkes, Martin (1690–1754).

Bradshaw, Nicholas (1574/5–1655), Church of England clergyman, was born in Buckinghamshire. Like others of his kin he went to Balliol College, Oxford, from where he matriculated on 6 November 1590, aged fifteen, and graduated BA on 21 April 1594. Having become a fellow in 1595, he proceeded MA on 31 March 1599 and BD on 29 November 1605. Presented by William Woodford to the rectory of St Mildred, Bread Street, London, on 27 June 1604, within the next few years he resigned his fellowship and married Margaret, daughter of George Cromer (*c.*1552–1631) of London and his wife, Anne (*c.*1555–1610). Their eldest child, Anne, was born before 1609, and was perhaps the Anne, daughter of Nicholas Bradshaw, baptized at St Margaret Pattens on 15 March 1606 or 1607.

On 5 December 1606 Bradshaw was also instituted as rector of Ockham, Surrey. Here he had a ministry of over forty-eight years and baptized seventeen more children from George (18 June 1609) to Polycarpus (28 March 1634); fifteen lived to adulthood. His sole publication was a thirty-folio verse, *Canticum evangelicum summam sacri evangelii continens* (1635), dedicated to Sir Arthur Mainwaring. A rare copy found its way into the Huth collection; in 1864 William Carew Hazlitt had a copy given by the author to his friend Robert Kerr.

By 1645 Bradshaw had been sequestrated from Bread Street, but he kept Ockham through the civil war and Commonwealth. Margaret Bradshaw died on 21 April 1648 and Bradshaw himself on 15 January 1655. A memorial was erected in the chancel of his church, where he was buried, near to an inscription to their Cromer grandparents, by four of his sons, James, Richard, Robert, and Nathanael.

VIVIENNE LARMINIE

Sources O. Manning and W. Bray, *The history and antiquities of the county of Surrey*, 3 (1814), 125, 128 · Foster, *Alum. Oxon.* · *N&Q*, 3rd ser., 6 (1864), 143 · G. Hennessy, *Novum repertorium ecclesiasticum parochiale Londinense, or, London diocesan clergy succession from the earliest time to the year 1898* (1898), 339, s.79 · IGI [Ockham parish register; St Margaret Patten parish register] · *Walker rev.*, 42 · J. Jones, *Balliol College: a history*, 2nd edn (1997), 326 · STC, 1475–1640

Bradshaw, Penelope (*d.* 1753/4), compiler of cookery books, is known only through her writings. According to the title-page of one of her books, *Bradshaw's Valuable Family Companion* (12th edn, 1752), she had worked for several noble families for many years; another title-page, in *The Family Jewel* (7th edn, 1754), states that she had had a forty-year career as a professional housekeeper to an aristocratic family. This information is, however, open to serious doubt, since the 1754 edition was almost certainly published after her death and the publishing history of her books shows that the title-pages were embellished in an unscrupulous fashion to increase sales.

Bradshaw's books combine cookery and confectionery with household hints and remedies; the various editions, with slightly different titles and considerable variations in the number of pages, appeared between 1748 and 1754. The title is sometimes *Bradshaw's Valuable Family Jewel*, sometimes *Bradshaw's Family Companion*, sometimes *The Family Jewel*; all are variations on the same book. Since the date of the tenth edition of the first title (1748) is earlier than that of the fifth edition (1749) it seems certain that the edition numbers are spurious, designed to suggest rapid sales. To produce her book, Bradshaw took recipes from Edward Lambert's *The Art of Confectionary* (*c.*1744) and others from Eliza Johnston's *The Accomplish'd Servant Maid* (1747). She did this quite openly: an unnumbered 1748 edition of *Bradshaw's Valuable Family Jewel* states that the book was 'Begun by Mrs Eliza Johnson [*sic*], and now finished by Mrs Penelope Bradshaw and Mr Lambart [*sic*], Confectioner' and the preface describes 'Mrs Johnston' as her 'dear Relation'. (Edward Lambert was a confectioner with a shop in St Albans Street, Pall Mall.) In this version of the book Bradshaw's own contribution is minimal—three recipes and brief general directions on cooking methods; the remaining material is taken from Lambert (she took all but three of his recipes) and Johnston (she took all but thirty-nine of hers). Other shorter versions of the book reproduce some of the material from Lambert and Johnston, with virtually all of the remainder lifted from Hannah Glasse's *The Art of Cookery, Made Plain and Easy* (1747), the borrowings disguised by abridging and rephrasing the general advice and by halving or doubling the quantities in the recipes. In 1754 the book, now entitled *The Family Jewel*, was revised by 'E. H.' and much new material was added. The revision, coupled with the fact that the book was no longer printed for the author, as it had been up to 1753, but for R. Whitworth, suggests that Bradshaw had died by 1754.   GILLY LEHMANN

Sources F. Lucraft, 'A study of *The compleat confectioner* by Hannah Glasse (*c*.1760), part one', *Petits Propos Culinaires*, 56 (1997), 23–35 · V. Maclean, *A short-title catalogue of household and cookery books published in the English tongue, 1701–1800* (1981) · P. Bradshaw and E. Lambert, *Bradshaw's valuable family jewel*, 10th edn (1748) · P. Bradshaw, *The family jewel*, 7th edn (1754)

Bradshaw, Percy Venner [P. V. B.] **(1877–1965)**, illustrator and art teacher, was born at 10 Mountford Road, Hackney, London, on 27 November 1877, the son of William Bradshaw, a warehouseman who later worked as a commercial traveller for a hosiery company, and his wife, Frances Ann, *née* Venner. His grandfather was a Baptist minister and he had an elder brother, Bart, and a younger sister. He was educated at Haberdashers' Aske's School, Hatcham, London, where his tutor was Robert Blair, later chief education officer of the London county council. Having failed to gain a junior clerkship in the civil service he left school at the age of fourteen and became a clerk in an advertising agency while studying art at evening classes at Goldsmiths' College and Birkbeck College, London. After selling, at fifteen, his first drawing (a heading for the correspondence page) to *Boy's Own Paper* for half a guinea (then more than his week's wages) and another to *Chums*, he transferred to the agency's art department. At the age of eighteen he resigned and turned full-time freelance cartoonist and illustrator, contributing to *Boy's Own Paper*, *Home Chat*, *Sunday Companion*, and other journals published by Harmsworth, Newnes, and Pearson. He then won first prize in a competition run by *The Artist* magazine (he drew a jester's head) and briefly worked on the art staff of the *Daily Mail* (with Oliver Onions, Bernard Lintott, and Charles Folkard) before freelancing again for *Tatler*, *The Sketch*, *The Bystander*, and *Windsor Magazine*. He also began writing articles for the *Daily Graphic* and, having produced many illustrations for stories in *Boy's Own Paper*, wrote and illustrated the first of many serials, 'The Fourth Form Ferret', for the paper in 1905. In addition he designed picture postcards (producing as many as 150 in a year) and, a great theatregoer, also wrote scripts for the music-hall comedians Arthur Roberts and Walter Passmore. A great admirer of the work of Phil May—'one of my artistic heroes' (Bradshaw, *Brother Savages*, 55)—and the illustrators Hablot K. Browne (Phiz), Gordon Browne, Alfred Pearse, and Fred Barnard, Bradshaw's own work in black

and white and watercolour was accomplished but otherwise conventional in its approach, and he usually signed his drawings either P. V. Bradshaw or P. V. B.

A series Bradshaw was commissioned to write for *Boy's Own Paper* ('Black and white drawing as a profession') received so many letters that he decided to found the Press Art School correspondence course in 1905 with capital of £100 bequeathed to him by a man he met at a party. His first pupil was Leo Cheney—later to create the most famous version of the Johnnie Walker whisky trademark figure. Other celebrated pupils included W. L. Ridgewell, Alan D'Egville, Kenneth Bird (Fougasse; later art editor of *Punch*), Honor Appleton, Joe Lee, David Ghilchik, Peter Fraser, Chas Grave, Norman Pett, Stan Terry, Bertram Prance, and, in more recent times, Ralph Steadman. During the First World War his students also included twelve generals, the Hon. John Jacob Astor (later first Baron Astor, proprietor of *The Times*), and Lieutenant Leefe Robinson VC, who shot down the first Zeppelin airship in Britain. The school (of which he was principal for more than fifty years) was at first run from his home but later moved to the twenty-two-room Tudor Hall, in Forest Hill, London— once the home of Baroness Burdett-Coutts—where he had his own presses. In 1914 Bradshaw published the first of twenty portfolio brochures entitled *The Art of the Illustrator*, which featured interviews with distinguished artists and illustrators of the day, and he later produced a number of instructional and historical books such as *Art in Advertising* (1925), *I Wish I Could Draw* (1941), and *I Wish I Could Paint* (1945). By 1916 the school was enrolling 3000 new students a year and employed more than 20 staff, and by 1943 more than 4000 drawings by its pupils had appeared in *Punch* alone. Bradshaw also enlisted help from magazine art editors and art directors of book publishing houses to give advice to pupils, and his consultant staff included Bert Thomas, Heath Robinson, Fred Pegram, Leo Cheney, and Harry Rountree. Following his success, rival companies such as the ABC School of Drawing (1912) and Charles E. Dawson's Art Course were set up.

Pronounced unfit for military service, Bradshaw was a special constable during the First World War. After the war he produced hundreds of postcards for companies such as Raphael Tuck and Moss and Misch, worked part-time for Royds advertising agency (1930), and from 1933 was London sales organizer for the printer Sun Engravings of Watford. The school, however, continued and a special supplementary course, 'Caricature and humorous drawing', was introduced in 1936. During the Second World War he served as a fire-watcher and wrote humorous verse for allied newspapers, published as *Marching On* (1943). In addition he wrote a popular series of articles about cartoonists—'They Make Us Smile'—in *London Opinion* in the 1940s (later published as books) and a number of volumes of reminiscences.

A keen actor, Bradshaw met his wife, Mabel Bennett, when they both played in an amateur dramatic company production. Two of their children, Peter and Wendy, were named in honour of their godfather, J. M. Barrie, author of *Peter Pan*. A member of the London Sketch Club (1912),

Bradshaw was elected to the Savage Club in 1922 and later served on its committee, writing its official history in 1958. He died in Hither Green Hospital, Lewisham, London, on 13 October 1965, aged eighty-seven.

MARK BRYANT

Sources P. V. Bradshaw, *Drawn from memory* (1943) · P. V. Bradshaw, *Brother savages and guests* (1958) · M. Bryant, *Dictionary of twentieth-century British cartoonists and caricaturists* (2000) · M. Bryant and S. Heneage, eds., *Dictionary of British cartoonists and caricaturists, 1730–1980* (1994) · M. Felmingham, *The illustrated gift book, 1880–1930* (1988) · W. O. G. Lofts and D. J. Adley, *The men behind boys' fiction* (1970) · *Who's who in art* · M. Horn, ed., *The world encyclopedia of cartoons* (1980) · b. cert. · d. cert. · *CGPLA Eng. & Wales* (1966)
Likenesses T. Purvis, caricature, repro. in M. Norgate and A. Wykes, *Not so savage* (1976), 96 · S. Strube, caricature, repro. in Bradshaw, *Drawn from memory*, 118 · B. Thomas, caricature, repro. in Bradshaw, *Drawn from memory*, 106 · photograph, repro. in Bradshaw, *Drawn from memory*
Wealth at death £25,000: probate, 4 Jan 1966, *CGPLA Eng. & Wales*

Bradshaw, Richard (*bap.* 1610, *d.* 1685), merchant and diplomat, was baptized at Pennington, Aspull, Lancashire, on 25 August 1610; his parents are unknown. A merchant of Chester, he was elected to the common council of the city on 14 July 1637, replacing Randle Finchett, deceased. In that year he married Katherine, daughter of former mayor of Chester John Fitton, niece of Sir George Booth, and cousin of Sir William Brereton's first wife, Susanna.

During the civil war Bradshaw was quartermaster-general in Sir William Brereton's troop and was one of the twelve parliamentary commissioners chosen to accept the surrender of Chester in February 1646. It had been prearranged by the committee for the revenue that (on the surrender of Chester) Bradshaw be its customer, splitting the post previously conjoined with Liverpool. It was recommended that the best servants were those 'who have not only lost their estates but done good service to the Parl[iament]' (*Letter Books*, 1.309).

In 1649 Bradshaw was elected mayor of Chester, but by June 1650 he had been chosen deputy of the Company of Merchant Adventurers in the Hanseatic city of Hamburg, a position in which he revealed himself keen to defend the company's interests in the Baltic. He also acted as the sole resident for the Commonwealth; letters addressed to him as 'Lord Resident for the state of England in Hamburg' may account for Richard Bradshaw's confusion with his distant kinsman John Bradshaw, president of the council of state. In his dual role Bradshaw encountered hostility towards the English state, despite the senate of Hamburg's 'loose expression' of neutrality (DDL 411, 28 June 1650), and was the target of intrigues by the Dutch, local residents, and English and Scottish exiles in the city. Throughout his residency in Hamburg he was periodically chosen deputy and then ousted again. Meanwhile Bradshaw provided in his reports a running commentary on events in Britain, particularly counselling against trusting any moves made by the Scots, and praising 'Honest Cromwell' for his victories. Any good news he urged be written up in Latin and circulated abroad to counter malignant counter-propaganda (DDL 411, 9 July 1650). He also sent reports of Baltic affairs and the actions of continental powers to Gualter Frost, secretary to the council of state, and Marchamont Nedham—assessments of foreign affairs were determined by confessional alliances. A member of the English congregation in Hamburg, his vigilance against Catholics was particularly pronounced.

Bradshaw acted in Hamburg with David Hochstetter and his partner, Slingsby Bethel. He was unswervingly loyal to the Commonwealth and careful in his descriptions of it. Despite speaking slightingly of Machiavelli's religion, he seems to have been influenced by his thought. Bradshaw was one of very few who referred to the Commonwealth as a 'republic'—possibly because continental diplomacy involved dealing in Latin. He counselled the English state to implement stringent actions to establish 'respect and owninge of Englands Republique', rather than affection, because continental powers sought to 'swallowe upp little Englands Com[mon]wealth' (DDL 411, 26 Nov 1650).

Under the protectorate Bradshaw continued in office and in his unswerving service of authority. Throughout his residency in Hamburg he consistently identified as 'malignants' and supporters of Charles Stuart opponents of the English state and those who made his work difficult. However, opposition to Bradshaw's position in Hamburg under the protectorate may have come from republican anti-Cromwellians. While he continued to work with Hochstetter, their previous co-operation with Slingsby Bethel turned to hostility when Bethel supported Bradshaw's rival, Francis Townley. The dispute was framed in terms of a generational split between hotheaded young men, disrespectful of seniority and the 'graver sort' (MS Rawl. A, 4.222, 5.85). Bradshaw complained of harsh words and physical attacks and wrote several self-vindications. He suggested combining the company structures of London and Hamburg, restricting the council to twenty-four of the older merchants (with the younger generation observing and learning how to run a trading venture), which would elect a court of thirteen, continuing for not more than five or six years. Authority within the company should be restricted to men 'of known good lyfe and conversation, wel affected to the government of the state, and not under the age of 30' (ibid., 4.476). Underlying the battle with the 'implacable generation' was probably a more political conflict. Bradshaw complained of Townley's 'Machiavellian' religion. The associated action of republicans such as Bethel, with royalist plotters against the protectorate, and their mutual joy at news of Cromwell's rumoured death, imply that royalist–republican collaboration may have extended to the Baltic.

Bradshaw had been joined by his wife in Hamburg in November 1650 and their youngest child died there in 1655, news of which he claimed his opponents had celebrated with fiddling and dancing. Katherine sent missives to England to support her husband, complaining of his poor treatment at the hands of English and foreigners alike. She was anxious for his health when in April 1657 detailed instructions came for Bradshaw to undertake a mission to the tsar of Russia in support of the Swedes, which involved travelling through plague areas. Bradshaw himself, appreciating the political hazards of an embassy to the 'Royalist-infested' court in Moscow, told Thurloe that the appointment had 'put me into a straight between the danger of such an employment and my duty to obey' (Venning, 227). However, on 12/22 May he finally accepted the commission, asking that John Drury, formerly resident in Prussia and currently ambassador to Switzerland, might accompany him. They arrived at Riga on 29 May/8 June, where they waited in vain for a safe conduct to proceed further. Meetings in the succeeding months with envoys of the tsar and local officials achieved nothing. In February 1658 Bradshaw assured Thurloe that 'nothing shall be wanting on my part ... that the mediation may yet take effect for ... the advantage of the Protestant cause' (Venning, 229), but he had been overtaken by events. Charles X's victories transformed the balance of power in the Baltic in Sweden's favour, and Bradshaw's mission became in consequence of much less importance. By 28 February/8 March he had returned to Königsberg in Prussia, *en route* for Hamburg, and wrote informing Thurloe that he had concluded that, since he could not succeed in Russia, he should resume his neglected duties as consul.

In 1659 Bradshaw returned to England and on 22 November he attended the funeral in Westminster Abbey of his kinsman John Bradshaw. In January 1660 he was one of the commissioners of the navy. By the time he drew up the first draft of his will in March 1680 he was living on his estates in Pennington, Lancashire. By 12 December 1683, when he made an amendment, his wife Katherine had died. He himself died in 1685 (after his last addition to the document on 19 May), probably in Pennington, leaving his lands in Lancashire and at Idston in Cheshire to his sons, Byron and George, and several grandchildren. His daughter Susanna Wentworth resigned her executorship to her brother Byron on 26 October that year.

SARAH BARBER

Sources Lancs. RO, Farington papers, DDL 411 · Thurloe state papers, Bodl. Oxf., MS Rawl. A, vols. 2–7 · *The letter books of Sir William Brereton*, ed. R. N. Dore, 1, Lancashire and Cheshire RS, 123 (1984) · *The letter books of Sir William Brereton*, ed. R. N. Dore, 1, Lancashire and Cheshire RS, 123 (1984) · M. J. Groombridge, ed., *Calendar of Chester city council minutes, 1603–1642*, Lancashire and Cheshire RS, 106 (1956) · W. F. Irvine, ed., *Marriage licences granted within the archdeaconry of Chester in the diocese of Chester*, 4, Lancashire and Cheshire RS, 61 (1911) · T. Venning, *Cromwellian foreign policy* (1995) · will, 1703, Lancs. RO, WCW Richard Bradshaw · *DNB* · parish register, Leigh St Mary, Wigan History Shop, MF1A 15/1
Archives Lancs. RO, letters, DDL 411 | Bodl. Oxf., Thurloe state papers, MS Rawl. A

Bradshaw, Thomas (*fl.* 1591), poet, was the author of *The Shepherds Starre* (1591). Beyond this fact, however, very little is known of him. The title-page of *The Shepherds Starre* describes Bradshaw as 'a Gentleman late of the Right worthie and honorable the Lord Burgh, his companie & retinue in the Briell in North-holland'. The work itself is dedicated jointly to Burgh and to the earl of Essex. A prefatory letter written by Alexander Bradshaw, brother of

Thomas, appears immediately after the dedication; if it is to be believed, Alexander Bradshaw took advantage of his brother's absence in Holland to publish *The Shepherds Starre* without Thomas's knowledge: 'Brother, I have made bolde to publish the booke which you left me to my private use. I was moved thereunto by your friends, and my favourers heere in England.' Preliminary poems by I. M. and T. G. (Thomas Groos) deal with Bradshaw's departure from England. The volume itself consists of 'A Paraphrase upon the third of the Canticles of Theocritus', in both verse and prose. Bradshaw may have been one of the three men named Thomas Bradshawe who matriculated at Oxford University in the 1580s.

SIDNEY LEE, *rev.* ELIZABETH GOLDRING

Sources T. Bradshaw, *The shepherds starre* (1591) · Foster, *Alum. Oxon.*

Bradshaw, William (*bap.* 1570, *d.* 1618), Church of England clergyman and religious controversialist, was baptized in the parish church of St Peter, Market Bosworth, Leicestershire, on 27 October 1570. He was the son of Nicholas Bradshawe, a descendant of a once important Lancashire family, and was one of six children, having three brothers and two sisters.

Education The family lived in poverty, and it was a benevolent uncle who paid for Bradshaw's early education at the grammar school in Worcester. When his uncle died Bradshaw was forced to suspend his studies and return to Bosworth, his father hoping he would train in a more practical occupation. About 1586–7, after several years at home, his education resumed, when George Ainsworth, the master of the grammar school at Ashby-de-la-Zouch, took him into the school there. At Ashby, Bradshaw was introduced to a puritan community which greatly influenced the formation of his religious opinions.

Bradshaw gained the reputation of being a diligent and gifted student, and went to Emmanuel College, Cambridge, in 1588, matriculating at Easter of the following year. Emmanuel too was reputed for its puritan character. His tutor there was Nathaniel Gilby, then fellow of the college, who was a son of Anthony Gilby, the Marian exile and radical leader of the Elizabethan puritan movement. Bradshaw received financial assistance from Sir Edward and Sir Francis Hastings, on whom his father also depended, on the recommendation of the puritan minister Arthur Hildersham, a distant relation of the Hastings family, and lecturer at Ashby-de-la-Zouch. At this early stage Bradshaw already knew many important puritan figures, both lay and clerical, and boasted influential patrons. Having graduated BA early in 1593 and proceeded MA in 1596 he hoped to gain a fellowship. However, the college statutes prohibited the appointment of more than one fellow from each county, and in 1595 the post for Leicestershire had been awarded to Joseph Hall, a future bishop of Norwich, who had been Bradshaw's fellow pupil at Ashby grammar school. Sir Edward Hastings offered Bradshaw a clerical living, but he declined, considering himself not yet ready to enter the ministry. His next move was again shaped by the influential patrons he continued to accrue.

Developing nonconformity Sir Edward Hastings continued to support Bradshaw financially, but it was not long before Laurence Chaderton, master of Emmanuel College, secured him a fellowship at Sidney Sussex College, Cambridge. Chaderton was a moderate puritan who had formed a close personal and professional relationship with Bradshaw at Emmanuel. Even in later years, when it became clear that Bradshaw's brand of nonconformity was more radical than his own, he continued to be both a patron and friend. The building of Sidney Sussex College was, however, still incomplete, so in the interim Chaderton suggested that Bradshaw take up a post as tutor to the children of Sir Thomas Leighton, governor of Guernsey. Bradshaw arrived in Guernsey at the end of 1597, and it was during his time there that he forged 'a lasting affection' with Thomas Cartwright, the presbyterian reformer, who in 1576 had implemented a full-blooded presbyterian religious settlement in Guernsey, and was now a preacher at Castle Cornet (Gataker, 27). A correspondence between them endured until Cartwright's death, and their friendship was commemorated by Bradshaw in his preface to the second edition of Cartwright's *A Treatise of Christian Religion* (1616). As Cartwright acknowledged in a letter to Chaderton, Bradshaw's ministry on the island was popular, but despite offers from the Leighton family to stay he returned to England in early December 1598. After nearly drowning at Harston Mills on his way up to Cambridge from London, Bradshaw took up his fellowship at Sidney Sussex, sharing a room with Thomas Gataker, who subsequently became his biographer. Soon afterwards Bradshaw was ordained in the Church of England, and at the request of several prominent local gentlemen became an itinerant preacher and lecturer at Abington and Steeple Morden in Cambridgeshire, also participating in a weekly lecture with other godly ministers at Bassingbourn.

In 1599 Bradshaw published anonymously his first work, *A Triall of Subscription*, in which he urged ministers not to subscribe to the three articles, even for the sake of expediency. This idea struck at the very heart of the moderate puritanism of men such as Chaderton. Bradshaw also showed himself to be uncompromising over the issue of the supposedly 'indifferent' ceremonies, which to him were simply popish and unlawful. He urged his fellow ministers to conform only to the dictates of their own conscience, and not to succumb to the call from prelates and moderates alike for a 'politique subscription' (Bradshaw, *A Triall of Subscription*, Middelburg, 1599, fol. A5v). Unsurprisingly, it was not long before Bradshaw was in trouble with the university authorities. Later that year the bishop of London, Richard Bancroft, complained to the vice-chancellor and the master of Sidney Sussex, James Montague, that Bradshaw had organized the distribution of a book by John Darrell, the preacher and exorcist, through a local tailor, in which Darrell attacked Samuel Harsnet, Bancroft's chaplain. During the 1590s Darrell had preached at Ashby, where he met Bradshaw, but had got into trouble with the authorities over his exorcisms. On 26 May 1599 he appeared before the high commission accused by Harsnet of being an impostor. He was convicted of the charges, deprived of his ministry, and imprisoned in the Gatehouse. Bradshaw left Cambridge voluntarily until the controversy died down, and spent several months in Abington and Steeple Morden exercising his ministry. He was offered several preaching positions in the area, but accepted none and eventually returned to Cambridge about 1600.

Beginnings in the ministry In July 1601, on the advice of godly friends in London, Bradshaw left Cambridge for good, to answer a call to a lectureship at Chatham, Kent, again on Chaderton's recommendation. Bradshaw was popular at Chatham, and according to Gataker was elected 'by joynt consent' of the congregation after an examination of his spiritual suitability (Gataker, 36). On 25 April 1602 Sir Francis Hastings wrote to the archbishop of Canterbury, John Whitgift, asking him to confirm Bradshaw's appointment. As Bradshaw was already a reputed nonconformist, Hastings was obliged to assure the archbishop in a letter of 25 April that Bradshaw would 'not offer any disturbance to the peace of the Church either in word or action' (*The Letters of Sir Francis Hastings, 1574–1609*, ed. C. Cross, Somerset RS, 69, 1969, 82). His petition was unsuccessful, however, for some ministers from the neighbouring villages had already reported Bradshaw to the bishop of Rochester, John Young, for being 'a man not conformable to the Rites of the Church, nor well-affected to the present Government' (Gataker, 36). Having sent a spy to hear Bradshaw preach the bishop charged him with teaching the heretical doctrine, 'that a man was not bound to love God, unless he were sure that God loved him' (ibid., 41). On 26 May 1602 Bradshaw was summoned to appear the next morning before the bishop of London and the archbishop of Canterbury at Shorne, to answer the charge of expounding false and ungodly doctrine. Although Bradshaw offered to clear himself of the charges he was merely asked to subscribe, which he refused, and was consequently prohibited from preaching. Gataker suggests that Bancroft had shown a particular dislike of Bradshaw since the Darrell case, and sent spies to his home in an attempt to catch him breaching the conditions of his suspension. A petition 'to restore unto us our Vertuous and faithful Teacher' was sent to the bishop of Rochester from the Chatham congregation and its minister John Philips, but was rejected, and Bradshaw had little choice but to move to London (ibid., 42).

Reformer and polemicist The next chapter of Bradshaw's life began with a visit to Leicestershire, during which his friend Arthur Hildersham secured for him a post in the household of Alexander Redich, a puritan gentleman of Newhall in Derbyshire. Bradshaw accepted the position and spent the rest of his life in the service of the Redich family. Redich procured a preaching licence for Bradshaw from William Overton, bishop of Coventry and Lichfield, and awarded him the somewhat meagre maintenance of £10 a year. Bradshaw once again found himself nestled within the confines of the established church, protected by powerful patrons and, this time, a sympathetic bishop. About 1604 Alexander Redich temporarily moved to London, taking Bradshaw with him. Redich had become intimately involved in the puritan petitioning campaign at the beginning of James I's reign, and on 7 December 1604 presented a petition for religious reform to James I in the name of several prominent Lancashire JPs. Hildersham had presented a similar petition six days previously on behalf of the Lincolnshire ministry, and with such close associates involved in such activities Bradshaw was no doubt informed of, if not involved in, the mobilization of support for reform at this time. While in London Bradshaw was asked to preach at the nearby Christchurch in Newgate Street, and was subsequently chosen by the vestry to be the permanent lecturer, but was obstructed from doing so by the bishop of London. His thoughts then turned to marriage, to a widow of his former congregation named Katherine Wiginton. He had considered this while at Chatham, and more than two years after their original betrothal they were married on 9 September 1604 in St Mary's Church, Chatham. Bradshaw returned to London with his new bride, but penury forced them to live apart for some time, his wife earning a living as a tutor of children.

It was between 1604 and 1606 that Bradshaw was most active as a polemicist for the nonconformist cause, producing a string of controversial writings which sought to take the puritan movement in a new direction. He was a key figure in the propaganda campaign headed by the puritan printer William Jones, who published many of Bradshaw's works from his secret press. The most important of these works was *English Puritanisme: containeing the maine opinions of the rigidest sort of those that are called puritanes* (1605). Written after the failure of the puritan agenda at the Hampton Court conference it addresses the vexed issue of church government head on, attacking episcopacy as unscriptural and advocating the autonomy of the individual congregation. According to Bradshaw 'every Companie, Congregation or Assemblie of men, ordinarilie joyneing together in the true worship of God, is a true *visible church* of Christ ... equall and of the same power and authoritie', an idea which challenged the notion of a hierarchical national church (Bradshaw, *English Puritanisme*, 1605, 5). Although he retained the presbyterian offices of pastors, elders, and deacons, he dispensed with the idea of a superstructure of synods, which had appeared so threatening to the concept of the royal supremacy. His solution was to deprive the episcopate of its rights and powers, a system which he considered as much of a menace to the king's authority as presbyterianism, and return them all to the king. Civil obedience was central to Bradshaw's theology, and was a theme which he explored in many of his works.

These ideas became known to contemporary critics as 'the new-found parish-discipline', and were pivotal in the development of a non-separatist congregationalism within the puritan movement (George Downame, *A Sermon Defending the Honourable Function of Bishops*, 1605, fol.

A4r). Bradshaw's ideas had an ostensible affinity with those of congregational separatists such as Francis Johnson and Henry Ainsworth, and Bradshaw expended much polemical energy refuting the charge of separatism and schism. Indeed, the essence of his vision was its syncretic fusion of a fierce criticism of the unreformed elements of the English church, with a continued allegiance to it as a 'true' visible church which could not be lawfully abandoned. As the title of the book suggests it represented the beliefs of 'the rigidest sort' of nonconformists, and was no doubt partly an attempt to lead the puritan movement to fresh ideological terrain. Its promotion of congregational ideas and strict ceremonial nonconformity was an inspiration to later generations of congregationalists, yet also in its own milieu was a brave attempt to solicit the happy marriage between ecclesiastical congregationalism and civil hierarchy through the promotion of grass-roots change. In 1610 William Ames translated it into Latin, in order to make the text available to the European academic community, an indication of its growing importance and influence. Ames and Bradshaw were close associates, and in 1614 Ames wrote the preface for Bradshaw's *The Unreasonablenesse of the Separation*. Gataker testifies to their further collaboration on the publication of Bradshaw's *A Treatise of Justification* (1615).

The church authorities became aware of Bradshaw's activities and his complicity in the printing of illicit puritan books, and sent two pursuivants to his house to search for manuscripts. His pregnant wife ingeniously hid the manuscripts in a hole between two chimneys, and nothing was found. Nevertheless, she was ordered to appear before the high commission to answer questions about her husband's activities, but after one appearance the case was dismissed for lack of evidence. Bradshaw continued to publish unlicensed tracts, and was almost certainly one of the anonymous authors of *An Answere to a Sermon Preached*, published in 1609, possibly in collaboration with the puritan activist Richard Sherwood, which attacked George Downame's *jure divino* defence of episcopacy of 1608. This is corroborated by Gataker, who claimed that 'the greatest part of that which was done in that grand *Controversie* with Doctor *Downham* concerning *Episcopacie*' was indeed written by Bradshaw (Gataker, 55).

Quieter times Bradshaw continued to be a frequent visitor to London throughout his life, but after the birth, about 1605, of his first child, John, who was baptized in Threadneedle Street, he returned to Derbyshire with his family. He finally settled in Stanton Ward, near Newhall, and preached in the parish church in the village of Stapenhill. During his many years there Bradshaw produced several works of edification, mainly for use by members of the Redich household, some of which were published posthumously by Gataker, who testified to Bradshaw's abilities in 'dissolving of difficult cases of conscience' (Gataker, 51). Bradshaw spent much of his life performing his pastoral duties in and around Newhall, and as these works show, considered his role as godly preacher and instructor in the Word, as important as his role as polemical writer. In his pastoral writings Bradshaw dealt with common godly dilemmas such as the meaning of marriage, coming to terms with death, and how believers should prepare themselves for receiving the sacrament. His *Meditation of Mans Mortalitie*, published by Gataker in 1621, was inspired by the death in 1613 of his great friend Alexander Redich, and was intended for the private use of Redich's daughter, Grace, Lady Darcy. In all his edificatory works Bradshaw demonstrated a typically Calvinist world-view, stressing the importance of cohesion within the persecuted community of the godly elect, and identifying popery as the ultimate enemy.

In his guise as humble preacher Bradshaw took his ministry beyond his own parish, and was one of several divines who met regularly for preaching and discussion at Ashby-de-la-Zouch, Repton, and Burton upon Trent. His colleagues, who included Arthur Hildersham, referred to him as 'the weighing divine', because of his skills in debate and mediation (Gataker, 52). Although such exercises had been an integral part of the godly experience for many years the 1604 canons insisted that such exercises must be authorized by the bishop. So when the Arminian and anti-puritan Richard Neile became bishop of Coventry and Lichfield in 1611 the Ashby group, along with many other such groups in the area, was suppressed. It is likely that the Ashby exercise caused Neile particular concern, as Edward Wightman, the last man in England to be burnt for heresy (a case over which Neile presided), had regularly attended it.

Last years, death, and significance In Bradshaw's later years he devoted much of his energies to denouncing separatism, which allowed him to emphasize, despite his nonconformity, his allegiance to the Church of England. Bradshaw took part in several private conferences between separatists and non-separatists, helping to reinforce his image as a loyal member of the established church. *The Unreasonablenesse of Separation*, published in 1614, was an attempt to disclaim the charges of separatism levied at him and his associates. He urged the godly to continue communicating with the English church, as long as they 'doe not actually communicate in those corruptions, but onely in the true parts of Gods worship' (fol. L1r). His desire to unite the godly community is illustrated further in his *Treatise of Justification* (1615). Within the context of the disagreements over the issue of justification abounding within, and threatening to divide, godly London society, Bradshaw struck a conciliatory middle ground, a fact which emphasizes the respect and seniority he enjoyed among his contemporaries.

In spite of Bradshaw's lifelong nonconformity he managed to elude church censure for much of his later life. However, on returning to Derbyshire in 1617 after one of his regular trips to London he was suspended from preaching by the bishop's chancellor. The prohibition was swiftly lifted after both Bradshaw and a friend successfully petitioned the bishop for its repeal. In 1618, after travelling to London to attend Alexander Redich's widow, Katharine, at her home in Chelsea, Bradshaw was taken ill, and he died soon afterwards of a 'malignant fever' (Gataker, 50). His will was witnessed on 2 May by Arthur

Hildersham. According to Gataker, Bradshaw had three sons, one of whom died, and a daughter, but his will suggests that he made provision only for his sons, for his worldly possessions were to be divided into three equal parts, one to his wife and two to each of his children. He was buried at St Luke's, Chelsea, on 16 May 1618. His body was carried 'on the shoulders of six of his Reverend Brethren of the Ministry', after which Gataker preached the funeral sermon to a large contingent of the London godly community (Gataker, 51). His son John, later pastor at Etchingham, Sussex, and author of several published works, issued Bradshaw's *A Discourse of Sinne Against the Holy Ghost* in 1649.

Gataker's biography depicts Bradshaw as a modest and even-tempered man who commanded respect from both moderates and radicals. This being said, Bradshaw's innovation and radicalism, in print if not in lifestyle, should not be underestimated. As Gataker commented, he was not 'one that kept his Talent wrapt up in a Napkin; though he were cooped up mostly in an obscure corner, through the harsh courses of those, that would not suffer his Light to shine forth in any eminent place' (Gataker, 51). Along with Henry Jacob, Bradshaw was responsible for the first articulation in print of congregational ideas in a non-separatist context, and was hailed by later generations, in old and New England as one of the fathers of congregationalism. In his own day he was not only a celebrated controversialist, but also the epitome of the scrupulous godly pastor.

VICTORIA GREGORY

Sources Venn, *Alum. Cant.* · T. Gataker, 'The life and death of Master William Bradshaw', *The lives of thirty-two English divines*, in *A general martyrologie*, 3rd edn (1677), 25–60 · M. Curtis, 'William Jones: puritan printer and propagandist', *Library*, 5th ser., 19 (1964), 38–66 · P. Lake, *The boxmaker's revenge* (2001) · P. Lake, 'William Bradshaw, Antichrist and the community of the godly', *Journal of Ecclesiastical History*, 46 (1985), 570–89 · P. Lake, *Moderate puritanism and the Elizabethan church* (1982) · A. F. Scott Pearson, *Thomas Cartwright and Elizabethan puritanism* (1925) · 'Darrel, John', *DNB* · 'Wightman, Edward', *DNB* · 'Hall, Joseph', *DNB* · 'Gataker, Thomas', *DNB* · S. Bendall, C. Brooke, and P. Collinson, *A history of Emmanuel College, Cambridge* (1999) · P. Collinson, 'Lectures by combination: structures and characteristics of church life in 17th-century England', *Godly people: essays on English protestantism and puritanism* (1983), 399–428 · B. W. Quintrell, 'The royal trust and the puritans, 1604–5', *Journal of Ecclesiastical History*, 31/1 (1980), 41–58 · IGI · parish register, Chatham, St Mary, 9 Sept 1604, CKS [marriage] · parish register, Chelsea, St Luke, LMA, LMA P74/LUK/161, fol. 37r, 16 May 1618 [burial]

Wealth at death see will, 1618, PRO, PROB 11/131, fol. 365v

Bradshaw, William (*fl.* 1700), literary hack, is known only for the remote possibility that he had a hand in the history of the work known in English as *The Turkish Spy* (1687–94). The source for this statement lies in the bookseller John Dunton's *Life and Errors of John Dunton* (1705). Dunton, the accuracy of whose statements is often doubtful, bases his opinion on his ability to recognize Bradshaw's style. He writes 'Mr. *Bradshaw* was the best-accomplished hackney-author I have met with; his genius was quite above the common size, and his style was incomparably fine.' Dunton then tells of Bradshaw's making off with money and books and never seeing him again. He continues 'In a little time after [the robbery] was published the first volume of the Turkish Spy; and so soon as I saw it, the very style, and manner of writing, convinced me that Bradshaw was the author.' Dunton later encountered Bradshaw's wife who told him that:

> Dr. *Midgely* had engaged him in a work which would take up some years to finish … Dr. *Midgely* owned to me he was well acquainted with Mr. Bradshaw, and said he was very ingenious, but unhappy, and something indebted to him. After this, I had no more intelligence of Mr. Bradshaw; but the Turkish Spy was for some years published, volume after volume; so that it is very probable (for I cannot swear I saw him write it) that Mr. William Bradshaw was the author of the Turkish Spy. Were it not for this discovery, which was never made known before, Dr. Midgely had gone off with the honour of that performance. (Nichols, *Lit. anecdotes*, 1.413–14)

Dr Robert Midgley is considered the best candidate for the authorship of *The Turkish Spy*, although the basis for the claim is founded solely on external evidence.

Dunton is also the sole authority for the statements that Bradshaw 'designed for the Ministry, till he had finished his studies' and that 'he writ for me the Parable of the Magpies, and many thousands of them sold' (Nichols, *Lit. anecdotes*, 1.413). *The Parable of the Black-Birds and the Mag-Pies Vindicated* (1691), an allegory on the history of England from the reign of Charles I to the accession of William III, is usually attributed to E. Thompkins. Nothing else is known of Bradshaw.   ARTHUR SHERBO

Sources Nichols, *Lit. anecdotes* · BL cat.

Bradshaw, William (1671–1732), bishop of Bristol, was born on 10 April 1671 at Abergavenny, Monmouthshire, the son of William Bradshaw, described as gentleman. He entered New College, Oxford, in 1692 and later became a fellow. He graduated BA in 1697, proceeded MA in 1699, and was ordained deacon on 4 June 1699, and priest on 26 May 1700. After a spell within the university—he was proctor and senior preacher there in 1711—he was, reportedly, chaplain to Charles Trimnell, the bishop of Norwich, who was influential in whig circles. In 1717 Bradshaw was appointed to a prebend at Canterbury Cathedral and to the living of East Peckham, Kent; he held the latter until 1722, and later that year became rector of Fawley, Hampshire. On 24 May 1723 he was appointed canon of Christ Church, Oxford, at the same time receiving the degree of DD by diploma. Courting whig interests he went on the grand tour of Europe as tutor to the duke of Devonshire's second son.

In 1724 Bradshaw was appointed to the bishopric of Bristol; he held the deanery of Christ Church concurrently *in commendam*, which was normal at that time because of the poverty of the Bristol diocese (the poorest English see, with a value of £400 a year). His tenure of the deanery was turbulent. Described by Hearne as a convinced whig with 'much of the same principles with Bradshaw the regicide' (*Remarks*, 10.53), Bradshaw was a whig dean in a predominantly tory chapter; perhaps even more significant, unlike his predecessors who had been mostly Christ Church men he had no previous connection with the college. The choleric, though convivial, Bradshaw became well known in

William Bradshaw (1671–1732), by Enoch Seeman, 1718

Christ Church for his disputes with colleagues, and in particular with the subdean, Thomas Terry. In 1728 this reached such a stage of mutual vituperation that when Bradshaw refused to allow the college to grant Terry a new coach house, the latter, a contemporary noted, 'gave the dean very foul language. The dean was wise enough to make his return in the same dialect. The quarrel lasted long, to the great diversion of all present' (*Portland MSS*, 7.414). His subordinates pretended to forget his name, called him John Bradshaw (after the regicide), or failed to remove their caps as they passed. One modern commentator has written that 'the accumulation of slights and insults was enough to drive the dean to drink, and seems to have done so, for Hearne believed that it was "excessive drinking that shortened his life"' (Bill, 49; *Remarks*, 11.138).

Bradshaw died at Bath, after a long illness, on 16 December 1732, and was buried in Bristol Cathedral. The stone slab formerly over his tomb near the bishop's throne is now no longer visible. Two of his sermons have been published, one preached in St Paul's on 5 November 1714, the other before the House of Lords on 30 January 1730, the anniversary of the execution of Charles I.

WILLIAM MARSHALL

Sources *Fasti Angl.* (Hardy), 1.218; 2.524; 3.497, 570 · Foster, *Alum. Oxon.* · *A catalogue of all graduates … in the University of Oxford, between … 1659 and … 1850* (1851) · J. Welch, *The list of the queen's scholars of St Peter's College, Westminster*, ed. [C. B. Phillimore], new edn (1852), 31 · subscription book, 1721–3, Hants. RO, Winchester diocesan records, 21M65/F1/10 · visitation book, diocese of Winchester, 1722–3, Hants. RO · R. O'Day and F. Heal, eds., *Princes and paupers in the English church, 1500–1800* (1981) · E. G. W. Bill, *Education at Christ Church, Oxford, 1660–1800* (1988) · *Remarks and collections of Thomas Hearne*, ed. C. E. Doble and others, 11 vols., OHS, 2, 7, 13, 34, 42–3,

48, 50, 65, 67, 72 (1885–1921) · *The manuscripts of his grace the duke of Portland*, 10 vols., HMC, 29 (1891–1931), vol. 7 · will, PRO, PROB 11/657, fols. 209–11
Likenesses E. Seeman, oils, 1718, Christ Church Oxf. [*see illus.*]

Bradshawe, Nicholas. *See* Bradshaw, Nicholas (1574/5–1655).

Bradstreet [*née* Dudley], **Anne** (1612/13–1672), poet, probably born in Northampton, was the eldest daughter and second of the five children of Thomas Dudley (1576–1653) and his first wife, Dorothy, *née* Yorke (1581/2–1643), who had married in Northampton on 25 April 1603. According to Cotton Mather, her mother was 'a *gentlewoman* both of good *estate* and good *extraction*' (Adlard, 26); Bradstreet described her in an epitaph as a woman of 'unspotted life', 'Religious in all her words and ways' (*Works*, ed. Hensley, 204). Her father, a man of great 'Natural and Acquired Abilities' and 'excellent *Moral* Qualities' (Mather, 1.20) who encouraged his daughter in both her studies and her writing, she greatly admired for his unwavering commitment to public service and for his 'love to true religion' (*Works*, ed. Hensley, 202). On the recommendation of William Fiennes, first Viscount Saye and Sele, in 1619 he became steward to Fiennes's future son-in-law Theophilus Clinton, fourth earl of Lincoln (*c*.1600–1667), at Sempringham, Lincolnshire. Like both Fiennes and Clinton, afterwards parliamentarians, Dudley was a man of puritan conviction, much influenced by the Northamptonshire minister John Dod. About 1625 the Dudley family moved to Boston, to enable Dudley to join the congregation ministered to by the eminent puritan John Cotton. By then his daughter would have had the opportunity to become acquainted with her future husband, Simon *Bradstreet (*bap.* 1604, *d.* 1697), the son of Simon Bradstreet (*d.* 1621), nonconformist puritan vicar of Horbling, Lincolnshire, since, after his father's death, he served as a member of Lincoln's household under Dudley. They married in 1628, when Simon Bradstreet was steward to Francis Rich, dowager countess of Warwick, at Leighs Priory, Essex. In March 1630 they sailed, with Thomas and Dorothy Dudley, from Southampton at the very start of the puritan 'great migration' to New England on board John Winthrop's flagship, the *Arbella*. It was, says Mather, Anne Bradstreet who persuaded her husband to emigrate (Mather, 2.19).

Bradstreet later addressed to her children for their 'spiritual advantage', 'not to set forth myself, but the glory of God' (*Works*. ed. Hensley, 240), a short reflective account of her experience which confirms what might be inferred of her upbringing, temperament, and convictions from these puritan connections. From the age of six or seven her conscience was sensitive to wrongdoing. Prone to blame herself for her moral failings, she 'found much comfort in reading the Scriptures'. At the age of fourteen or fifteen she grew 'more carnal, sitting loose from God', but about the age of sixteen she was restored to faith through recovery from an attack of smallpox (ibid., 241). The only recorded reference Bradstreet makes to the challenge of emigration exemplifies puritan acquiescence to the divine will:

> After a short time I changed my condition and was married, and came into this country, where I found a new world and new manners, at which my heart rose. But after I was convinced it was the way of God, I submitted to it and joined to the church at Boston.   (ibid., 241)

This was the church of which Cotton was afterwards chosen minister on his arrival in New England in 1633. Her poetry returns repeatedly to this tension between the duty of Christian patience and the pain of human experience and disappointment.

The *Arbella* reached Salem on 12 June 1630, to find the previous year's settlers, in Dudley's words, 'in a sad and unexpected condition' (*Works in Prose and Verse*, xxx), many dead, the survivors weak and sickly, with barely two weeks' provisions. Since Salem could not provide for them, the new arrivals had to move elsewhere. The Bradstreets settled briefly at Charlestown, then at Boston, and then (in December 1630) at Cambridge (then called Newtown). About 1635 they moved to Ipswich (Agawam), and between 1640 and 1644 they made their final home in Andover (Merrimack). Though she herself made no direct intervention in the political or religious life of Massachusetts, Bradstreet's was one of the most politically significant families in seventeenth-century New England. Both her father, 'a principal founder and pillar of the colony' (Morton, 167), and her husband held a succession of public offices, both serving several terms as governor of Massachusetts. God having kept her 'a long time without a child, which was great grief to me, and cost me many prayers and tears' (*Works*. ed. Hensley, 241), in 1633 or 1634 Bradstreet gave birth to Samuel, the first of eight children (Dorothy, Sarah, Simon, Hannah, Mercy, Dudley, and John).

Bradstreet's *The tenth muse lately sprung up in America, or, Severall poems, compiled with great variety of wit and learning … by a gentlewoman in those parts* was published in London in 1650 (Thomason's copy is dated 5 July). The prefatory material identified the 'gentlewoman' as Anne Bradstreet, 'at present residing in the Occidental parts of the World, in America, alias Nov-Anglia' (*Works*. ed. Hensley, 8) but the unsigned address to the reader, apparently written by her brother-in-law John Woodbridge (1613–1695), husband of her sister Mercy and minister at Andover, states that the book is published 'without [Bradstreet's] knowledge, and contrary to her expectation' (ibid., 3) in order to prevent the publication by others of imperfect copies from manuscripts in circulation. The project was clearly well planned (*The Tenth Muse* carried eight commendatory poems) and, whether or not she had any inkling of it, Bradstreet certainly took her poems sufficiently seriously to have dedicated a manuscript collection of them to her father (himself a writer of verse) as early as 20 March 1642, and already to have written a full apologia for her writing, as though anticipating its appearance in print (included as 'The Prologue' in *The Tenth Muse*). In the later poem 'The Author to her Book' she professed dismay at this unauthorized publication, but her response was to revise her texts and to add new poems for an authorized second edition, which appeared in Boston posthumously in 1678.

The fact of this publication is itself sufficiently remarkable to secure Bradstreet's fame. She was the first English woman and the first New Englander to publish a collection of original poems, and so may claim to be both the first female poet and the first colonial poet in English, and a radical figure. In 'The Prologue' she is very well aware of the contemporary prejudice against women's engagement in intellectual and artistic activity:

I am obnoxious to each carping tongue
Who says my hand a needle better fits,
A poet's pen all scorn I should thus wrong,
For such despite they cast on female wits.
(*Works*. ed. Hensley, 16)

In 'The Prologue' and in other poems such as her elegy on Queen Elizabeth, who

hath wip'd off th'aspersion of her sex,
That women wisdom lack to play the rex
(ibid., 196)

Bradstreet issued a direct challenge to prevailing notions of woman's place and duty.

The Tenth Muse is shaped by the protestant Renaissance tradition. Four long four-part poems, or quaternions (modelled on a lost poem by Bradstreet's father entitled the 'Four Parts of the World'), on the four elements, the four humours, the four ages of man, and the four seasons of the year, and an incomplete poem entitled 'The Four Monarchies', later abandoned after 3500 lines when 'My papers fell a prey to th'raging fire' (*Works*, ed. Hensley, 178) in 1666, make up the major part of the collection. These are ambitious pieces which show considerable reading in natural philosophy, biblical commentary, history, and classical literature. They draw on approved protestant models and exemplars (Spenser, Sidney, Du Bartas, the Ralegh of the *History of the World*), but the essentially plain manner of Bradstreet's end-stopped lines, closed heroic couplets, and unmodulated iambic metre, attempts none of their rhetorical and metaphorical elaboration. The author's puritan commitment is most evident in the unequivocally parliamentarian sympathies of 'A Dialogue between Old England and New', dated 1642, which attributes the civil war to the countenancing of 'Idolatry' and 'foolish superstitious adoration' by 'mighty men' who further popery (*Works*, ed. Hensley, 182).

Bradstreet's distinctive achievement, however, rests on her thirty-five short lyrical and meditative poems, dating largely from the 1650s and 1660s. Some of these were first printed in the 1678 edition, others not until 1867 when John Harvard Ellis first printed in his edition texts preserved in the Andover manuscript, a small leather-bound notebook kept by Bradstreet (with entries also in the hand of her son Simon). They are remarkable for the specificity of their domestic occasions, the intimacy of their address, and their unaffected articulation of personal feeling. Many are addressed to Bradstreet's husband, children, and grandchildren and they take up with the everyday: her son's departure for England; the arrival of letters from her absent husband; apprehensions before childbirth; the

burning of their house; illness and bereavement. Protestantism had encouraged marital love as a fit poetic subject, and as an ideal it was hymned by Spenser and Milton; but Bradstreet was the first poet in English to publish explicitly marital love lyrics.

There is very little in any of these poems which can be attributed to Bradstreet's American habitation. The scenes depicted derive from Renaissance pastoral and from biblical story, rather than from observation: America is figured as the wilderness of Israel's desert wanderings. 'Contemplations' describes an autumn evening walk by the River Merrimack, but its principal affinities are with the Renaissance emblem and puritan sermon, reading the 'Book of the creatures' as a revelation of the divine will.

Throughout her life Bradstreet suffered recurrent bouts of what she came to call 'my old distemper of weakness and fainting' (*Works*, ed. Hensley, 257), the occasion of several of her poems. She endured a particularly severe and prolonged period of illness in the first half of 1661. That

No fainting fits shall me assail,
Nor grinding pains my body frail

is one of the promises of heaven to which she looks in her last poem, dated 31 August 1669 (ibid., 294). Besides ill health, she mentions among the chastening experiences by which she grew in grace 'losses in estate' (ibid., 242) of which the most severe was the destruction of the Bradstreets' home by fire in 1666, when their collection of over 800 books, a remarkable collection for that date in New England, was burnt. Bradstreet died of consumption at Andover, Massachusetts, on 16 September 1672. Her place of burial is not known.

Bradstreet enjoyed considerable reputation among younger contemporaries such as Edward Phillips, who included her in his chapter in *Theatrum poetarum* (1675) entitled 'Women among the moderns eminent for poetry' (p. 254), Bathsua Makin, who spoke of her as 'an excellent poet' (p. 20) in her *Essay to Revive the Ancient Education of Gentlewomen* (1673), and Cotton Mather, who in *Magnalia Christi Americana* (1702) saluted her poems as 'a Monument for her Memory beyond the Statliest Marbles' (2.17), but then her reputation fell sharply away, with (it seems) no published reference to her thereafter until the early nineteenth century. John Berryman's long poem *Homage to Mistress Bradstreet* (1956) is evidence of the revival of her reputation in the twentieth century.   N. H. KEEBLE

Sources *The works of Anne Bradstreet in prose and verse*, ed. J. H. Ellis (1867); repr. (1932) · *The works of Anne Bradstreet*, ed. J. Hensley (1967) · *The complete works of Anne Bradstreet*, ed. J. R. McElrath and A. P. Robb (1981) · C. Mather, *Magnalia Christi Americana*, 7 bks in 1 vol. (1702) · *John Winthrop's journal: 'History of New England', 1630–1649*, ed. J. K. Hosmer, 2 vols. (1908); repr. (1959), 190–98 · B. Makin, *An essay to revive the antient (sic) education of gentlewomen* (1673) · E. Phillips, *Theatrum poetarum, or, A compleat collection of the poets, especially the most eminent of all ages* (1675) · G. Adlard, *The Sutton-Dudleys of England and the Dudleys of Massachusetts* (1862) · A. Jones, *The life and work of Thomas Dudley, the second governor of Massachusetts* (Boston and New York, 1899) · J. K. Piercy, *Anne Bradstreet* (1965) · E. W. White, *Anne Bradstreet, the tenth muse* (1971) · R. F. Dolle, *Anne Bradstreet: a reference guide* (Boston, MA, 1990) · R. Rosenmeier, *Anne*

Bradstreet revisited (1991) • H. Morton, *Chronicles of the pilgrim fathers* (1910) [with an introduction by J. Masefield]
Archives Stevens Memorial Library, North Andover, Massachusetts, Andover MSS [on deposit at Harvard U.]

Bradstreet, Dudley (1711–1763), adventurer and spy, was born in Tipperary, where his father had obtained considerable land under the Cromwellian grants. His father's wealth was much reduced by debts, and Dudley, who was the youngest son, was looked after by a foster father in Tipperary. He became a trooper, but soon left the army and traded briefly and unsuccessfully as a linen merchant and then as a brewer. He spent the next few years involved in various financial ventures, in Ireland and England. His elder brother, Simon (1693–1762), was trained as a barrister and was created a baronet in 1759.

During the Jacobite rising of 1745 Bradstreet was employed by government officials to spy on the rebels and obtain information on the movements of Prince Charles Edward Stuart and his army. Under the name Captain Oliver Williams, he assumed the character of a devoted adherent to the Stuart cause and gained access to the Jacobite council at Derby. He may have helped to bluff the Jacobites into the retreat from Derby and described the episode in considerable detail in his memoirs, *The Life and Uncommon Adventures of Captain Dudley Bradstreet* (1755). Though he never received payment or an army commission from the government, which he claimed were promised to him, he was rewarded with a gift of £120 from George II.

Bradstreet seems to have lived for a while as a confidence trickster or conjuror. His last show was as a 'bottle conjuror', which he performed in January 1748. He dramatized these exploits into a five-act play entitled *The Magician, or, The Bottle Conjuror*, which was performed four times in London; on the fifth night the play seems to have been suppressed by the magistrates of Westminster. Bradstreet returned to Ireland, where he owned a small property, and tried to trade as brewer in co. Westmeath. This proved unsuccessful, not least because of his disputes with the local excisemen. In an attempt to supplement his income, he published his memoirs in 1755 and, two years later, *Bradstreet's lives: being a genuine history of several gentlemen and ladies, all living within these ten years past, remarkable for their virtues, or their vices*.

Bradstreet died at Multifarnham, co. Westmeath, in 1763.   J. T. GILBERT, *rev.* S. J. SKEDD

Sources *The life and uncommon adventures of Captain Dudley Bradstreet*, ed. G. S. Taylor (1929) • *Dublin Journal* (1763) • GEC, *Baronetage* • F. McLynn, *The Jacobite army in England, 1745: the final campaign* (1983)

Bradstreet, John (1714–1774), army officer, was born on 21 December 1714 in Annapolis Royal, Nova Scotia, and was baptized Jean-Baptiste Bradstreat. His mother, Agathe de Saint-Étienne de la Tour (*b.* 1690, *d.* after 1739), was of a prominent Acadian family; his father, Edward Bradstreet (*d.* 1718), was a lieutenant in the 40th foot. In 1735 Bradstreet's mother obtained an ensigncy in the 40th for him. During service at Canso, Nova Scotia, and while prisoner after Canso was captured by the French (May 1744), he acquired first-hand knowledge of Louisbourg, and upon his release he provided Sir William Shirley, governor of Massachusetts, with a plan for its capture. Shirley lauded him for the initiative, as well as for the role that Bradstreet, serving as lieutenant-colonel in the 1st Massachusetts regiment, played in the expedition that took Louisbourg (16 June 1745). Bradstreet was named town major to the new garrison, but was soon accused of profiteering, and in August 1747 he departed to take up an appointment as lieutenant-governor of St John's, Newfoundland. In late 1751 he journeyed to England, where he won the friendship of several influential men.

In early 1755 Bradstreet returned to America, now a captain in the newly reconstituted 51st foot (he had originally been commissioned on 5 September 1745). Shirley assigned him to shore up the defences at Oswego and prepare it to serve as a base for an expedition against Niagara. This assignment involved him in diplomacy with the Native Americans, which Sir William Johnson saw as meddling. The Niagara enterprise foundered, but Shirley gave Bradstreet command of the central effort projected for 1756, the taking of Fort Frontenac (Cataraqui). This plan, too, was aborted, and Bradstreet devoted much of 1756 to an able, though ultimately unsuccessful, effort to prevent the French from taking Oswego. On 3 July, while leaving Oswego, Bradstreet's force was attacked by a larger body of French and Native Americans but fought off the enemy.

Although the 51st was broken in late 1756, Bradstreet was commissioned captain in the Royal Americans on 8 March 1757. He gained the trust of Shirley's successor, Lord Loudoun, and, when in late 1757 Loudoun was abruptly replaced by James Abercromby, Bradstreet was able to ingratiate himself with the new commander-in-chief, while in Britain a mentor secured him promotion to lieutenant-colonel. Bradstreet played a key role in moving men and supplies for the attack on Ticonderoga, and although the expedition ended disastrously he distinguished himself in his management of the evacuation. He had in fact gained a wide reputation for his logistical ability, and Wolfe identified him as one of the 'three or four excellent' military men who were Americans: 'Bradstreet for the battles and for expeditions is an extraordinary man' (*Stopford-Sackville MSS*, 2.261).

Despite Ticonderoga, Bradstreet persuaded Abercromby that it was feasible to move against Fort Frontenac, and the general provided him with an army of 3600 men. Desertion and disease quickly reduced the force, and Abercromby began to question whether the expedition would proceed, but on 6 August Bradstreet wrote to him: 'shou'd the Numbers be reduced [to] 1000 Men … with them I will do my best' (*Correspondence of William Pitt*, 1.324). After embarking at Oswego on 20 August, Bradstreet crossed Lake Ontario and took the weakly defended fort eight days later. Before levelling the fort he seized furs and goods valued at 800,000 livres and distributed this plunder among the troops, reserving none for himself. He also destroyed the small French fleet on the lake. This victory weakened the French position in the Great Lakes and precipitated their withdrawal from the Ohio valley. Pitt praised Bradstreet for his 'Success in the difficult Enterprize against Cadaraqui, which he had planned with so much Judgement, and executed with equal Activity and Resolution' and communicated the king's 'most particular Satisfaction in his Zeal and Bravery' (*Correspondence of William Pitt*, 1.422). Bradstreet was now promoted colonel, retroactive to 20 August 1762.

Bradstreet fulfilled mainly administrative functions for the remainder of the war. While serving at Albany as deputy quartermaster-general he accumulated enough wealth to prompt rumours of profiteering. But he desired another military command, and the Pontiac War furnished the occasion. In 1764 he was given command of an expedition to lift the siege of Detroit and punish hostile Native Americans that it encountered. Bradstreet relieved Detroit without opposition on 27 August, less than a month after leaving Niagara. Nevertheless, his policy of making treaties with hostile tribes, rather than intimidating them through force, angered Major-General Thomas Gage, the commander-in-chief, and Johnson also criticized his performance. Furthermore, when Bradstreet attempted to return across Lake Erie in late October, storms cost the lives of many of his men.

Gage was now openly hostile, and although Bradstreet resumed his duties as deputy quartermaster-general at Albany his operations were hamstrung by the commander-in-chief. In late 1772 he was promoted major-general, but even this was merely part of a general promotion of men who had been colonels since 1762. Bradstreet continued to work through contacts in London, hopeful of enhancing his wealth and influence. He also attempted to purchase from the Native Americans a tract of 300,000 acres, but in July 1773 the Board of Trade advised that the sale be voided.

Bradstreet died in New York, of cirrhosis and dropsy, on 25 September 1774 and was buried the following day, with full military honours, at Trinity Church. His estate included £15,000 plus 15,000 acres. He left behind a wife, the former Mary Aldridge, who before marrying him had been married to his cousin. She and Bradstreet were estranged, and at the time of his death she was living in Britain with their two daughters.

PAUL E. KOPPERMAN

Sources W. G. Godfrey, *Pursuit of profit and preferment in colonial North America: John Bradstreet's quest* (1982) · 'The claims of Col. John Bradstreet to lands in America', *Proceedings of the American Antiquarian Society*, new ser., 19 (1908), 151–81 · *Report on the manuscripts of Mrs Stopford-Sackville*, 2 vols., HMC, 49 (1904–10) · *Correspondence of William Pitt, when secretary of state, with colonial governors and military and naval commissioners in America*, ed. G. S. Kimball, 2 vols. (1906) · *Correspondence of William Shirley*, ed. C. H. Lincoln, 2 vols. (1912) · S. Pargellis, ed., *Military affairs in North America, 1748–1765: selected documents from the Cumberland papers in Windsor Castle* (1936) · *The papers of Sir William Johnson*, ed. J. Sullivan and others, 14 vols. (1921–65)
Archives American Antiquarian Society, Worcester, Massachusetts, corresp. and MSS | Harvard U., corresp. with Thomas Gage · Hunt. L., letters to James Abercromby · Hunt. L., Loudoun MSS · PRO, corresp. with Sir Jeffrey Amherst, WO34 · U. Mich., corresp. with Thomas Gage

Wealth at death £15,000—also 15,000 acres

Bradstreet, Robert (1766–1836), poet, son of Robert Bradstreet, was born at Higham, Suffolk. He was educated by the Revd T. Foster, rector of Halesworth, before being admitted on 4 June 1782 to St John's College, Cambridge, where he took his BA degree in 1786 and his MA in 1789. Bradstreet owned an estate at Bentley in Suffolk, with a mansion called Bentley Grove. He lived abroad for several years and witnessed many of the scenes of the French Revolution, which he supported in his youth. He married in France, but, as was the fashion, this marriage was dissolved soon afterwards and, on his return to England, in 1800 he married Miss Adham of Mason's Bridge, near Hadleigh, Suffolk. Bradstreet was the author of *The Sabine farm: a poem, into which is interwoven a series of translations, chiefly descriptive of the villa and life of Horace, occasioned by an excursion from Rome to Licenza* (1810). For some time he settled at Higham Hall, Raydon, with his large family, but in later years he lived in various places, until he died at Southampton on 13 May 1836.

THOMPSON COOPER, *rev.* S. C. BUSHELL

Sources *London Packet* (20–23 May 1836), 1 c1 · *GM*, 1st ser., 103/2 (1833), 420 · Venn, *Alum. Cant.* · Watt, *Bibl. Brit.*

Bradstreet, Sir Samuel, third baronet (c.1735–1791), judge, was the younger son of Sir Simon Bradstreet (1693–1762), an Irish barrister who was created an Irish baronet on 14 July 1759, and his wife, Ellen (d. 1779), the third daughter of his paternal uncle. He attended the Revd Thomas Ball's school in Dublin and matriculated as a fellow-commoner at Trinity College, Dublin, on 13 December 1752. He did not, however, take a degree; he was admitted to the Middle Temple on 29 January 1753 and called to the Irish bar in Hilary term 1758.

After only eight years of practice at the bar Bradstreet was appointed to the recordership of Dublin on 14 July 1766, and king's counsel *ex officio* in 1767. On 19 January 1771 he married Elizabeth (d. 1799), the only daughter and heir of James Tully MD of Dublin, with whom he had four sons. He succeeded to the baronetcy, as third baronet, on the death of his brother Simon in 1773, and was elected MP for the city of Dublin in the Irish House of Commons in 1776. He was re-elected in October 1783 but stood down the following year on his elevation to the king's bench. He spoke frequently in the Commons and was noted for his independence, which earned him the sobriquet Slippery Sam. In October 1781 he introduced the Habeas Corpus Bill and also a bill designed to prevent the removal of judges on grounds other than judicial misbehaviour. Both were eventually enacted and stand as milestones in the history of individual rights and judicial independence within Ireland.

Bradstreet was appointed to king's bench in January 1784; at the same time his fellow MPs Alexander Crookshank and Peter Metge were appointed, respectively, to the court of common pleas and the exchequer. The appointments were made to increase the number of judges in each of the Irish common-law courts from three to four, a proposal which had been mooted for many years and which both Bradstreet and Crookshank had initially opposed in the Commons. Barrington cites Bradstreet as one of a number of independent spirits in the Commons who was effectively bought off by governmental preferment, but this is probably unfair. On his appointment to high judicial office it was much more to his credit that he should terminate or at least reduce his involvement in the highly-charged politics of the time.

In 1788 Bradstreet presided at the Maryborough assizes, where Captain (afterwards Major-General Sir) Robert Rollo Gillespie was tried for the murder of William Barrington, younger brother of Sir Jonah Barrington. Gillespie had shot Barrington following the young man's bloodless duel with Lieutenant M'Kenzie, and Bradstreet in his summing up advised that it was a clear case of murder. However, a jury dominated by military men returned a verdict of justifiable homicide, and Gillespie was eventually able to resume his military career. Also in 1788, and again in 1789 (on the death of Lord Chancellor Lifford), Bradstreet was appointed a commissioner of the great seal, along with Robert Fowler, archbishop of Dublin, and Sir Hugh Carleton, chief justice of the court of common pleas.

Bradstreet died at his seat at Booterstown, near Dublin, on 2 May 1791, and was succeeded in the baronetcy by his eldest son, Simon. NATHAN WELLS

Sources GEC, Baronetage · F. E. Ball, The judges in Ireland, 1221–1921, 2 (New York, 1927) · Burtchaell & Sadleir, Alum. Dubl., 2nd edn · W. E. Hume-Williams, A short history of the Irish parliament, 1782–1800 (1912) · C. J. Smyth, Chronicle of the law officers of Ireland (1839) · J. Barrington, Personal sketches of his own times, 1 (1827), 169, 176 · E. Keane, P. Beryl Phair, and T. U. Sadleir, eds., King's Inns admission papers, 1607–1867, IMC (1982) · H. A. C. Sturgess, ed., Register of admissions to the Honourable Society of the Middle Temple, from the fifteenth century to the year 1944, 1 (1949)

Bradstreet, Simon (*bap.* **1604**, *d.* **1697**), colonial governor, was baptized on 18 March 1604 at Horbling, Lincolnshire, the son of Simon Bradstreet (*d.* 1621), puritan clergyman, and his wife, Margaret. The Revd Bradstreet had been one of the overseers of Emmanuel College, Cambridge. Simon remained at grammar school until the age of fourteen, at which time he was taken into the family of Theophilus Clinton, fourth earl of Lincoln. Eight or nine years later Dr John Preston persuaded Lord Lincoln to allow Simon to go to Emmanuel and serve as a tutor to Lord Rich. When Rich failed to arrive, according to Cotton Mather, Bradstreet returned briefly to the household of the earl of Lincoln, and then became steward to the dowager countess of Warwick.

Bradstreet joined the group planning a puritan colony in New England, and in March 1630 was named secretary of the Massachusetts Bay Company. He was chosen an assistant in the following month, shortly before he accompanied Governor John Winthrop to the New World on the *Arbella*. He served as an assistant (councillor and justice of the peace) in the Massachusetts Bay colony for the next forty-nine years. Though an assistant himself, he generally stood against exercises of discretionary magisterial authority. He served on important committees and helped to organize the United Colonies of New England, a confederation of the Massachusetts, Connecticut, New Haven, and Plymouth colonies. Bradstreet was one of the commissioners of the United Colonies, serving for thirty-three years. In 1662 he represented Massachusetts as an agent to Charles II. He received confirmation of the colony's charter, but the king demanded greater religious toleration and Bradstreet temporarily lost some of his popularity in Massachusetts when he returned as the bearer of these tidings. But in 1678 he was chosen deputy governor, and in the following year he was elected governor of the colony.

Bradstreet was a moderate who became increasingly unpopular with those who wished to resist royal attacks on the colony's charter. Despite this he was re-elected governor annually until the charter was revoked in 1684. When the colony was subsumed into the dominion of New England in 1686, he refused a seat on the dominion council on the grounds that the new government lacked a representative assembly. Following the revolt that overthrew the dominion in April 1689, he was made a member of the council of safety that ran the colony's affairs until a popular convention voted to resume the old charter government. Bradstreet again served as governor until the arrival in May 1692 of William Phipps, the first governor appointed under a new royal charter.

Bradstreet's first wife was Anne Dudley [see Bradstreet, Anne (1612/13–1672)], daughter of Thomas Dudley, head steward of the earl of Lincoln's estates, whom he married in 1628. She achieved note as a distinguished poet. Much of her poetry described aspects of their family life, most famously the poem 'To my Dear and Loving Husband', which begins with the lines 'If ever two were one, then surely we'. The couple had four sons and four daughters. After Anne's death on 16 September 1672 Bradstreet moved to Boston, and on 6 June 1676 he married Anne Gardner (*bap.* 1633, *d.* 1713), the daughter of Emanuel Downing and niece of John *Winthrop. Following the establishment of the new charter government they moved to Salem, where Bradstreet died on 27 March 1697 and was buried.

A moderate in matters of both religion and politics, Bradstreet became a symbol of continuity with the founders in his last decades. The longest-surviving member of the colony's original leadership, he was referred to by Cotton Mather as 'the Nestor of New England'.

FRANCIS J. BREMER

Sources R. Johnson, 'Bradstreet, Simon', ANB · N. B. Shurtleff, ed., Records of the governor and company of the Massachusetts Bay in New England, 5 vols. in 6 (1853–4) · E. W. White, Anne Bradstreet (1971) · M. Hall, Edward Randolph and the American colonies (1960) · R. Johnson, Adjustment to empire (1981) · C. Mather, Magnalia Christi Americana, 7 bks in 1 vol. (1702) · R. C. Anderson, ed., The great migration begins: emigrants to New England, 1620–1633 (1995) · S. E. Morison, The founding of Harvard College (1935)
Likenesses portrait, Boston Athenaeum
Wealth at death extensive landed estate in New England (over 1500 acres in Massachusetts alone): will, Anderson, ed., The great migration begins, 210–12

Bradwardine, Thomas (c.1300–1349), theologian and archbishop of Canterbury, was of obscure origins. The sequence of his academic career would suggest that he was born about 1300, rather than 1290, as surmised by Henry Savile, editor of the only printed edition of Bradwardine's main work, his *De causa Dei contra Pelagium*, published in London in 1618. Although Chichester is now generally taken to have been Bradwardine's birthplace, that view, in part at least, rests on a misreading of the reference to Chichester in *De causa Dei*; it is named there merely as the place where his father was living, and there is no suggestion that Bradwardine was born there, or of how long his father had lived there. Bradwardine's family may have originated from the village of Bredwardine, a few miles to the west of Hereford, which in 1331 was forfeited to the king; but there is no known connection.

Early career, 1321–1339 Bradwardine's name first appears in 1321 as a fellow of Balliol College, Oxford. By 1323 he was a fellow of Merton College. Membership of Balliol was reserved for those not yet masters of arts. Merton, however, was for those studying for one of the higher faculties, especially theology. Bradwardine must, therefore, have graduated master of arts by 1323. He would then have had to perform three years' necessary regency (teaching) in the arts faculty, compulsory for new masters of arts. It therefore seems probable that he would have enrolled for the theological faculty in 1325, after the completion of his three years. He was twice elected university proctor, in November 1325 and January 1327, and was one of the university's representatives in its dispute with the archdeacon of Oxford in May 1328. There is no evidence for an earlier belief that it was in his capacity as proctor that Bradwardine visited the papal court at Avignon, and that while there he heard a dispute on future contingents in which a celebrated Toulouse master took part. It has been suggested that the latter was the Franciscan Pierre Aureole. But Aureole died in 1322, probably before Bradwardine had graduated master of arts and three years before he became proctor. It seems much more likely that the occasion was between 1335 and 1336, after Bradwardine had been made a papal mandatory in February 1335. He may have participated in the disputation; and his own question on future contingents (ed. Genest, in *Recherches Augustiniennes*) probably dates from two or three years previously. His concern with the problem was therefore of long standing, and culminated in the third and last book of *De causa Dei*, which was devoted to it.

Bradwardine spent until 1335 at Merton, perhaps then joining the household of Richard Bury (d. 1345), bishop of Durham and chancellor, and his circle of scholars. He had already been made a canon of Lincoln, with the prebend of St Botolph's, Lincoln, by papal provision in 1333, having become a bachelor of theology; he was still called a bachelor of theology in 1336 when he received a benefice in the gift of the bishop of Chichester. In the following year he was appointed chancellor of St Paul's, London, a position he held until 1349. The chancellor carried responsibility for the teaching of theology, and it seems plausible that Bradwardine was himself already a master of theology. In

that case, his period of regency in the theological faculty—which need not have lasted for longer than a year—would have been completed by 1337, and he could have become a master of theology in 1336. Such a chronology would have enabled Bradwardine to take up his appointment at St Paul's, and then to become a royal chaplain in 1339, without having to return to Oxford to lecture there. Instead these two appointments mark a change from an academic to a public career. Henceforth Bradwardine's fortunes followed the king's, until he was translated to Canterbury in 1349.

Royal service, 1339–1349 Bradwardine's *De causa Dei* certainly suggests that he did not return to Oxford, though it clearly originated there, in lectures given in response to the request of his fellow Mertonians, to whom it is addressed. The lectures were designed to combat the nefarious doctrines of those whom he called the 'modern Pelagians'. But, where in the first two books he remarks, in passing, that he was writing in Oxford, in the third book he refers only to London in a similar context of using it as an example. He may well have written, or finished, the third book after he had left Oxford, perhaps from lectures at St Paul's. His post-epistle to his Mertonians clearly implies that he was no longer among them to do what he was enjoining on them, namely, to restore discipline; he also apologized for the delay in completing the work because of the demands of other time-consuming business, suggesting involvements that had taken him away from academic life. Despite proposals for an earlier date, that of 1344, found in all the extant manuscripts of *De causa Dei*, would seem to be the correct one.

The culmination of Bradwardine's royal service was on Edward III's expedition to France in 1346, which issued in the English victory at Crécy, on 21 August, to which Bradwardine was an eyewitness. There is, however, no evidence that—as was once believed—he had also gone on an earlier journey with Edward to Flanders and the Rhine in 1338. After the subsequent English victory over the Scots at Nevilles Cross, on 17 October 1346, Bradwardine was appointed one of the negotiators to make peace with France. He himself celebrated the king's double triumph in his victory sermon, *Sermo epinicius*, preached before the king and assembled nobles shortly after Nevilles Cross; it was delivered in English, but preserved in a Latin version. The sermon, on a text from 2 Corinthians 2: 14, expressed in popular form, with a strong infusion of jingoism, Bradwardine's central theological concern, that God is the sole author of all good, and grants victory freely to whom he wills, who are always the virtuous.

The nature of the occasion is testimony to Bradwardine's high standing. That was confirmed when, on 30 August 1348, following the death of John Stratford, archbishop of Canterbury, Bradwardine was elected by the monks of Canterbury as Stratford's successor. But they offended the king for having failed first to obtain his licence to elect, and they were compelled to choose the dying John Ufford instead. Ufford, however, died before his consecration; and this time, on 4 June 1349, Bradwardine was duly elected, and consecrated by Pope Clement VI six weeks later, on 19 July, at Avignon. Bradwardine's election as archbishop of Canterbury broke the prevailing tendency to exclude eminent theologians from the higher offices in the church. Whether he was the exception because of his reputation, or because of the growing dearth of alternative candidates resulting from the black death, which had by then had a devastating effect, must be a matter of speculation. In the event it was of no consequence, for on 26 August 1349 Bradwardine himself died from plague at Canterbury, having been archbishop for thirty-eight days. He was buried at Canterbury.

Mathematical writings Bradwardine continued the combination of mathematician, scientist, and theologian characteristic of Oxford since the time of Robert Grosseteste (*d.* 1253). In his own lifetime and the following centuries he was scarcely, if at all, less eminent as a mathematician than as a theologian, as may be gauged from the early printing of his works on geometry, arithmetic, and motion: *Geometria speculativa* (Paris, 1495; Valencia, 1503), *Arithmetica speculativa* (Paris, 1495; Valencia, 1503), *Tractatus de proportionibus* or *De velocitate motuum* (Paris, *c.*1481; ed. and trans. H. L. Crosby, 1955; repr. 1961). These, in addition to his logical exercises on insolubles (*Insolubilia*, ed. Roure, 205–326) and his unpublished tractate on the continuum, as well as a treatise on fallacies (attributed to him) and a collection of physical questions, date from his period of regency in the arts faculty and his early years in the theological faculty. So may an aid to memory, and a rhyming composition on numbers, also unpublished. So far no extant manuscripts have been identified of other works ascribed to him, including astronomical tables.

Of the above works, Bradwardine's *Tractatus de proportionibus* was of far-reaching significance. It gave a new mathematical direction to the study of the mechanics of motion in all its forms, which was taken up and developed by his younger Mertonian colleagues and successors. It was widely read at Paris and other continental universities in the second half of the fourteenth century and the fifteenth century; and it continued to be influential until the time of Galileo. In this treatise Bradwardine was concerned to reaffirm mathematically, against apparent anomalies, Aristotle's doctrine that movement only occurs when force is greater than resistance, and that no motion results when there is an equilibrium of forces or where a resistant force is greater than a motive force. Bradwardine sought to show that force and resistance are related exponentially in a geometrical ratio, rather than by a simple arithmetical difference. Hence, to produce twice the velocity, the proportion of force to resistance must be squared, not doubled, and cubed for triple the velocity and so on. This formula applied not only to the cause of motion, 'in relation to the forces of the movers to the things moved' (dynamics), the subject of chapter 3, but also to 'the magnitudes of the things moved and of the space traversed' in time (kinematics), the subject of chapter 4. Although the distinction between dynamics and kinematics was only incidental to Bradwardine's enterprise of finding a universal rule that would govern each of these

facets, it became established largely as a consequence of his differentiation of them.

Bradwardine, however, remained bounded by the language of Euclid's *Elements*, which prevented him from being able to express his concepts in the most appropriate mathematical form; and his so-called 'word-algebra', of using letters for variables, was more a shorthand, used extensively in philosophical discussion. Yet notwithstanding these limitations, and the almost complete absence of empirical corroboration, Bradwardine's *Tractatus* marked a new phase both in formulating physical theory in mathematical terms, virtually for the first time in the middle ages, and in setting subsequent themes for investigation, above all the measurement of instantaneous change (that is, change at any given instant) in every kind of motion, rather than the definition of completed change, as in Aristotle's rules. By the seventeenth century both approaches had been superseded by the improved methods and understanding that Bradwardine had helped to initiate.

Bradwardine the theologian Bradwardine's *Tractatus de proportionibus* was published in 1328; by then he had turned to the study of theology. Henceforth he became a theologian and a churchman. He seems already to have undergone a literal, Pauline conversion, brought about by a changed comprehension of the words from Romans 9: 16: 'So it depends not upon man's will or exertion, but upon God's mercy.' He recounted in *De causa Dei* how, when he was in the arts faculty, he fell, in his foolishness and vanity, into the error of Pelagius:

> I rarely used to hear anything about grace, except perhaps in an equivocal manner; but every day I learned that we are masters of our own free acts, and that it is in our power to do either good or evil, to be virtuous or vicious, and many similar things.   (Bradwardine, *De causa Dei*, 308)

At first, whenever he heard a passage from St Paul read in church, extolling grace and depreciating free will, such as from his letter to the Romans 9: 16, he was displeased, because towards grace he was graceless. But afterwards, even before he had become a theological student, the words appeared to him like a beam of grace, and he seemed to see that the grace of God preceded all merits in time and nature; and that, in both respects, God antecedently willed that he who merited should be saved, and antecedently worked the merits in an individual before the individual himself. For God was the first mover in all movements. 'I therefore give my thanks to him who gave me this grace as a gift' (Bradwardine, *De causa Dei*, 308).

De causa Dei *De causa Dei* was the outcome of that revelation, some fifteen years later, and the passage from Romans 9: 16 was the most cited text in it. For the years between, apart from the question on future contingents, mentioned earlier, and a recently discovered manuscript collection of other questions, in which it is included, and which appear to have formed part of Bradwardine's lost commentary on the *Sentences*, there are no other known surviving theological works from Bradwardine's time in the theological faculty. His commentary on the *Sentences*, which, at Oxford, came in the seventh year of the theology course, would probably have been delivered in the academic year 1332–3; and the question on future contingents could have come from the third of the four books of the *Sentences*. Whatever its provenance, that question represented an early theological exercise, which, as already indicated, was the forerunner of the third book of *De causa Dei*. *De causa Dei*, therefore, remains Bradwardine's surviving theological monument.

Although primarily a polemic, its nearly 900 printed folio pages approximate also, in scale and range, to a theological *summa*, touching all those facets of God's nature and his governance of creation that concern human free will, grace, merit, predestination, divine foreknowledge, revelation, necessity, and contingency. Together they cover many of the same topics as a commentary on the *Sentences*, albeit not in the same compendious manner. *De causa Dei* follows the characteristic scholastic combination of reason and authority. The contrast between the two components is, if anything, accentuated by its geometrical form, as a body of interrelated axioms, theorems, proofs, conclusions, and corollaries, beginning with proofs for God's existence. The arguments themselves are in the accepted disputatory logical mode, drawing, like any such work, upon the recognized canon of doctrines from Bradwardine's predecessors, extending from Aristotle and Augustine to Thomas Aquinas and Duns Scotus (d. 1308). They are complemented by the appeal to the authority of the Bible, which stood supreme as the word of God and the rule of faith, supported by the testimony of the saints and fathers, and other inspired individuals, pre-eminent among them Augustine, arch-opponent of the Pelagians of his own day and doctor of grace, who set the tone for Bradwardine's own re-enactment of many of the same attitudes.

Like Augustine, Bradwardine saw himself as the defender of Christian truth; and a feature of *De causa Dei* is the sustained citation of supporting names and texts, often for pages at a time, in that conviction. In addition to Augustine, from whom Bradwardine derived both his doctrine of grace and his general outlook, he took from Aristotle the concept of a first unmoved mover as one of his two proofs for God's existence. The other was from Anselm's idea of God as the highest good, than whom a more perfect cannot be conceived. To Thomas Aquinas he owed the order of causes between God, as first cause, and his creatures, as second causes, in which the first cause was not only the immediate mover and conserver of every second cause but the prior and more immediate mover and cause in any created action. Here, as throughout, Bradwardine brought his own interpretation to established notions. God was thus what he termed necessary coeffector or pre-effector of everything created, including the free acts of the human will.

Divine coefficiency and issues of necessity This doctrine of divine coefficiency has long been widely interpreted as determinism; and only in more recent years has that view been seriously and justifiably challenged. For Bradwardine, divine coefficiency did not mean the negation of human free will; it was its condition, and merely expressed philosophically the theological truth stated in St John's gospel 15: 5, the most repeated text after Romans 9: 16, that 'Without me, you can do nothing'. That dependence upon God as first and most immediate cause and conserver derived from the difference between a necessary being, who was eternal and uncaused, and a possible being, which owed its existence to another cause, and so of itself was merely contingent—a contrast earlier adopted by Duns Scotus. Bradwardine also followed Scotus in locating the source of all necessity and contingency in God's will as the cause of all creation. The contingency and freedom in both God's will and the human will lay in the power of each to choose between contraries, a power that they retained even after having chosen between them.

Bradwardine, however, in keeping with his principle of divine coefficiency was, in contrast to Duns Scotus, equally concerned to stress the necessity inseparable from God's willing. Here he adopted a distinction between what he called antecedent and consequent necessity, which went back to Anselm. They represented the two indivisible facets of God's power as first cause and creator: antecedent necessity was his efficacious and sovereign will in contingently giving existence to everything that he willed; consequent necessity was the order that resulted from his willing as the effect of antecedent necessity. Had he willed differently, antecedently, as he was infinitely free to have done, he would have decreed a different order consequently. Thus, far from divine necessity's negating contingency—the common charge of Bradwardine's opponents—the two were concomitant; without the necessity entailed in the fulfilment of God's antecedent willing, there would be nothing to exist contingently as the consequence of his willing, including human free will. In that sense, God necessitated free will, as he necessitated everything else, as its first cause and necessary coeffector.

Grace and free will These were the bases of Bradwardine's rejection of the claims by the 'modern Pelagians', who remained anonymous, for the independent powers of human free will at the expense of the need for grace and the certainty of God's revelation of future events. These claims were widespread in Bradwardine's day, especially at Paris and Oxford, but they spread to the universities throughout the continent. Those whom he called the 'modern Pelagians' did not belong to any one school; nor were the two issues of grace and future contingents always found together in the same thinker or treated in the same manner. They were each part of a contemporary debate about the contingency of creation and God's power to have ordered it differently: in particular to have done directly what he ordinarily did through intermediaries, where no contradiction was entailed. That applied to created grace as the requisite for justification and merit.

The doctrine of the dispensability of created grace, which in its contemporary form derived from Duns

Scotus, was upheld by a wide spectrum of both Scotists and those influenced by Ockham; but it was by no means confined to them, and continued to find support during the fifteenth century. Bradwardine's 'modern Pelagians' were drawn from among its contemporary supporters, including probably Ockham, as a leading exponent of the dispensability of intermediaries, but hardly Scotus, whom he treated as an authority. What, to Bradwardine, was Pelagianism, through elevating the natural powers of the human will above the need for a supernatural gift, was for his opponents the opposite, by making God's will the arbiter in deciding to reward someone directly instead of through the gift of grace. It had nothing to do with the human will's power to transcend its natural limitations or to compel God's reward, but involved only God's freedom to choose how his will would be done. Bradwardine's hostility to the apparent autonomy conferred on human free will was further exacerbated by the paradoxes suggested by his opponents in the name of God's omnipotence, appearing to denude grace of any intrinsic goodness or inherent necessity. The disputes on future contingents had a comparable effect, calling into question the certainty of revelation about the future through the prophets and Christ. The freedom of the future was being made to derogate from the determinateness of God's decrees. *De causa Dei* was designed to restore their immutability.

There were three main areas of dispute. Two concerned grace; the third future contingents. The first of the two on grace held that its presence was not necessary in order to be justified and saved, but that an act of free will could be directly rewarded by God; the second—and, for Bradwardine, the most widespread and insidious—maintained that grace could be merited congruously (*de congruo*), as a moral claim upon God to award it. Both therefore subverted the eternally decreed order of grace and salvation, founded upon God's prevenient grace, as had earlier been revealed to Bradwardine; the second also destroyed the gratuitousness of grace, turning it from a gift into an object to be sold. The only merit that Bradwardine recognized was that which came from first possessing grace (*de condigno*).

The same prerequisite applied not only to justification and salvation and all the theological virtues, but also to the moral and philosophical virtues. God's necessary coefficiency was needed in all actions, good and bad. The difference was that good actions had to be preceded by God's freely bestowed grace, without which man was incapable of doing good or loving God; but, when a man sinned, God only co-acted in the action as an action: its sinfulness was from the intention of the human will. From that standpoint both grace and sin were the expression of man's impotence as a second cause, as much as the outcome of the central events of Christian history. In his dismissal of the intrinsic worth of created actions, and his conception of God, as always effecting, but never permitting, Bradwardine went beyond tradition. Over future contingents, the central issue was contained in what Bradwardine called the common opinion, originating with Aristotle, that only propositions about past and present events were determinately true or false; but propositions about future events were of what was yet to come, and so were contingent, neither true nor false. That appeared to make God's knowledge of the future equally contingent, entailing its mutability and the uncertainty of his revelation about the future, which could be falsified. Otherwise, everything would be eternally determined, which would negate free will. Bradwardine's reply was contained in the interplay of God's antecedent and consequent necessity, making all created time, as their outcome, the future as well as the past and present, both necessary and contingent, in having been immutably willed from eternity. While God, by his antecedent will, could have caused a different past, present, and future, the sequence that he has willed was necessary by his consequent necessity, guaranteeing the certainty of his revelation.

Although the defence of God's cause against the usurpations of human powers was *De causa Dei*'s primary objective, its subsidiary concern was to nullify the threat both to God's will and man's will from any kind of countervailing naturalistic or astral determinism. *De causa Dei* is punctuated by refutations of articles containing such doctrines, condemned at Paris in 1277, which it meets in the same way by reaffirming God's omnipotence to the exclusion of all rivals to it.

Influence and significance Bradwardine was one of the central thinkers of the fourteenth century. His influence can be seen upon the discussions of his contemporaries and successors, as well as in Chaucer's coupling of his name, in the 'Nun's Priest's Tale' (line 422), with the names of Augustine and Boethius on God's foreknowledge and man's free will. If his influence on John Wyclif (d. 1384) or the sixteenth-century reformers is no longer accepted, it was prominent in the renewed controversies over future contingents in the sixteenth and seventeenth centuries, attested by the printing of *De causa Dei* in 1618, and again in 1656. Theologically he remains a controversial figure, with no agreement over the exact character of his thought beyond its undoubted Augustinian inspiration. Despite enthusiastic defenders in the sixteenth and seventeenth centuries, he came in the eighteenth century to be increasingly regarded as a theological determinist, who upheld the prevenience of God's will to the point of denying human liberty or autonomy. He was accordingly branded unorthodox, sometimes heretical, and accused of going beyond tradition. That view prevailed until recently. His own terminology did not help him, especially expressions like 'antecedent necessity' to denote God's actions towards his creatures. Since the late 1950s, however, there has been a change of view and a growing tendency to reject these assertions. Bradwardine's doctrines are now taken to be in keeping with tradition, albeit sometimes framed in a novel way. He did not deny free will, and he upheld the contingency of creation against claims for the influence of natural necessity. Even his notion of divine coefficiency said nothing that Aquinas had not said before him. This more recent emphasis restores a needed balance to the assessment of Bradwardine. If he still does not appear to conform completely to tradition, his system was more than an essay in divine omnipotence at the expense of human freedom.

GORDON LEFF

Sources T. Bradwardine, *De causa Dei contra Pelagium* (1618) · *Thomas of Bradwardine, his Tractatus de proportionibus: its significance for the development of mathematical physics*, ed. and trans. H. L. Crosby (1955) · J.-F. Genest, *Prédétermination et liberté créée à Oxford au XIVe siècle* (Paris, 1992) · J.-F. Genest, ed., 'Le *De futuris contingentibus* de Thomas Bradwardine', *Recherches Augustiniennes*, 14 (1979), 249–336 · H. A. Oberman, *Archbishop Thomas Bradwardine: a fourteenth-century Augustinian* (1957) · H. A. Oberman and J. A. Weisheipl, 'The *Sermo epinicius* ascribed to Thomas Bradwardine', *Archives d'Histoire Doctrinale et Littéraire du Moyen Âge*, 25 (1958), 295–329 · *Thomas of Bradwardine, his Tractatus de proportionibus: its significance for the development of mathematical physics*, ed. and trans. H. L. Crosby (1955); repr. (1961) · A. C. Crombie, *Augustine to Galileo : the history of science, AD 400-1650*, 2 vols. (1952); rev. edn as *Medieval and early modern science* (Garden City, NY, 1959) · P. Vignaux, *Justification et prédestination au XIVe siècle* (1934) · E. J. Dijksterhuis, *The mechanization of the world picture* (1961) · J. A. Weisheipl, 'The interpretation of Aristotle's *Physics* and the science of motion', *The Cambridge history of later medieval philosophy: from the rediscovery of Aristotle to the disintegration of scholasticism, 1100-1600*, ed. N. Kretzmann, A. Kenny, and J. Pinborg (1982), 521–36 · G. Leff, *Bradwardine and the Pelagians* (1957) · J.-F. Genest and K. Tachau, 'La lecture de Thomas Bradwardine sur les *Sentences*', *Archives d'Histoire Doctrinale et Littéraire du Moyen Âge*, 57 (1990), 301–6 · M. L. Roure, 'La problématique des propositions insolubles au XIIIe siècle et au début du XIVe siècle', *Archives d'Histoire Doctrinale et Littéraire du Moyen Âge*, 37 (1970), 205–326 · Emden, *Oxf.*

Bradwell. For this title name *see* Driberg, Thomas Edward Neil, Baron Bradwell (1905–1976).

Brady, Sir Antonio (1811–1881), Admiralty official, naturalist, and social reformer, was born at Deptford, London, on 10 November 1811, the eldest son of Anthony Brady of the Deptford victualling yard, then storekeeper at the Royal William victualling yard, Plymouth, and his wife (whom he married on 20 December 1810), Marianne, daughter of Francis Perigal and Mary, *née* Ogier, both of Huguenot descent. He was related to Hugh Brady, bishop of Neath, Nicholas Brady, author of a metrical version of the Psalms, and Maziere Brady, judge. He was educated at Colfe's School, Lewisham, Kent, and then entered the civil service as a junior clerk in the Victoria victualling yard, Deptford, on 29 November 1828.

On 18 May 1837 Brady married Maria, eldest daughter of George Kilner of Ipswich. They had a son and two daughters. From the date of his marriage he lived at Maryland Point, Forest Lane, Stratford, Essex. Having served there and at Plymouth and Portsmouth, he was, through the recommendation of Sir James Graham, promoted to headquarters at Somerset House as a second-class clerk in the accountant-general's office on 26 June 1844. He was gradually promoted until in 1864 he became registrar of contracts, and having played an important part in reorganizing the office, he was made the first superintendent of the

Admiralty's new purchase and contract department on 13 April 1869, on an increased salary of £1000 a year. He held this appointment until 31 March 1870, when he retired on a special pension. He was knighted by the queen at Windsor on 23 June 1870 for his services to the Admiralty.

After his retirement Brady devoted himself to charitable work and science, perhaps particularly where these overlapped—as with his advocacy of sanitary reform, technical education for the poor, and the preservation of open space for the recreation of the poor. He was widely remembered for his part in the campaign to preserve Epping Forest. He chaired and addressed a mass meeting in 1871 to protest against its enclosure and was a founder and trustee of the Forest Fund which was established to help save the forest. About 1871 he was appointed a judge in the verderer's court for the forest of Epping, and continued in that office after the administration of the forest passed to the corporation of London under the act of 1878. He was associated with church work of all kinds, particularly among the poor. He published in 1869 *The Church's Works and its Hindrances, with Suggestions for Church Reform*. The establishment of the Plaistow and Victoria Dock Mission, the East London Museum at Bethnal Green for the promotion of technical art and science, and the West Ham and Stratford Dispensary owed much to Brady. He was particularly interested in sanitary reform and in relieving the distress caused by cholera epidemics.

Brady was a member or fellow of the Ray, Paleaeontological, Microscopical, Palaeontographical, Meteorological, and Geological societies. He was an original life member of the British Association for the Advancement of Science and was especially active on its geological section. In 1844 his attention had been attracted to the deposits of brickearth in the valley of the Roding at Ilford, within a mile of his home. He began collecting the rich series of mammalian remains in the brickearths of the Thames valley, comprising among others the skeletons of the tiger, wolf, bear, elephant, rhinoceros, horse, elk, stag, bison, ox, and hippopotamus. Brady wanted his extensive and valuable collection—part of which was described in his *Catalogue of Pleistocene Mammalia from Ilford, Essex* (1874, London, privately printed)—to go to the East London Museum, but it went instead to the British Museum (Natural History) at South Kensington. Brady acknowledged his indebtedness to William Davies FGS of the British Museum, who helped him to preserve the otherwise very crumbly fossil remains. He died suddenly, having suffered from angina pectoris, at his residence, Maryland Point, 7 Forest Lane, Stratford, Essex, on 12 December 1881. He was buried in the family vault at St John's churchyard, Stratford, on 16 December. Brady was survived by his wife, his son, Nicholas, rector of Wennington, Essex, and his daughters, Fanny Maria, who married William *Emery, archdeacon of Ely, and Elizabeth Kilner.

G. C. BOASE, *rev.* ELIZABETH BAIGENT

Sources *Transactions of the Essex Field Club*, 3 (1884), 94–101 · R. V. Hamilton, *Naval administration* (1890) · Boase, *Mod. Eng. biog.* · *Stratford and Essex Advertiser* (16 Dec 1881) · *Stratford and Essex Advertiser*

(23 Dec 1881) • H. Woodward, *Nature*, 25 (1881–2), 174–5 • *The Guardian* (14 Dec 1881), 1782 • *CGPLA Eng. & Wales* (1882) • *Ecological Magazine* (1882), 93
Archives Essex RO, Chelmsford, family corresp. and papers • NHM, corresp. relating to Pleistocene collection | LPL, letters and papers to A. C. Tait relating to Plaistow and Victoria Dock Mission **Likenesses** Pearson, engraving (after T. Scott, after photograph by Maull & Co.), repro. in *Transactions of the Essex Field Club*, 95 **Wealth at death** £21,240 12s. 1d.: probate, 4 Feb 1882, *CGPLA Eng. & Wales*

Brady [*née* Hutchinson], **Elizabeth** (1803–1874), headmistress, was born on 28 March 1803 in Upper Street, Islington, London, the second of the three children of Jacob Hutchinson (1772–1837), grocer, and his wife, Elizabeth, daughter of Thomas Barringer and his wife, Martha. Both her parents were Quakers, but her father was disowned by the Society of Friends in 1806 for not paying his debts and the family subsequently moved to Norwich where Elizabeth, her sister, brother, and mother were all placed under the care of the local Quaker meeting. However, she returned to London at the age of eight when she was sent to the Friends' school at Islington and remained there after completing her education to train and work as a teacher.

In 1825 the Friends' school moved to new premises in Croydon, Surrey, and it was here that Elizabeth met Edward Foster Brady, the son of Edward and Elizabeth Brady of Hertford. Another former pupil of the Islington school, Brady arrived to take up a position as schoolmaster in 1826 after having spent time on the continent recovering from consumption and the two were married in Croydon on 5 November 1828.

After the marriage, Elizabeth Brady continued to teach and in 1833 she and her husband were appointed as joint superintendents of the school. The couple were devoted to each other and in the first six years of their marriage produced three children: Bedford Foster in 1829, Elizabeth in 1831, and Anna Jane in 1834. However, Edward's health deteriorated in the mid-1830s and he became an invalid. After his death in 1838, Elizabeth stayed on as superintendent of the school but eventually left in 1842 to become headmistress of the Quaker girls' school at Castlegate and the Mount in York. Her health was also rather delicate and in 1846 she was forced to resign her position to take a complete rest from teaching. But her great natural energy and strength of perseverance enabled her to recover and in 1848 she established her own school for the daughters of Friends at Edgbaston in Birmingham.

Elizabeth Brady remained deeply attached to the principles of the Society of Friends throughout her life. A tender and gentle woman, she inspired great affection from her pupils and was a loving and devoted mother, as well as a keen supporter of many philanthropic causes including the anti-slavery movement, the Peace Society, and Dorcas Meetings.

After twenty-one years of running her own school, Elizabeth Brady decided to retire and planned to devote more time to the work of the Society of Friends. But her health deteriorated and she spent the last five years of her life an invalid. She died (as a result of chronic bronchitis and a stroke) at her home, 79 Gough Road, Edgbaston, on 22 May 1874, and was buried on the 27th at Wiltonberry Aston, Birmingham. MARGARET A. E. HAMMER

Sources *Annual Monitor* (1876) • 'Dictionary of Quaker biography', RS Friends, Lond. [card index] • Boase, *Mod. Eng. biog.* • *CGPLA Eng. & Wales* (1874) • d. cert.
Wealth at death under £4000: probate, 30 June 1874, *CGPLA Eng. & Wales*

Brady, Henry Bowman (1835–1891), naturalist and pharmacist, was born on 23 February 1835 at Gateshead, the son of Henry Brady (1805–1883), a medical practitioner and amateur naturalist, and his wife, Hannah Bowman (1802–1872) of One Ash Grange, Derbyshire. His older brother, George Stewardson Brady, went on to achieve international recognition for his work on Ostracoda. He had seven other brothers and sisters. He was educated at two Quaker schools (Ackworth and Tulketh Hall near Preston), and the moral values of the Religious Society of Friends, inculcated in him at an early age, were to remain with him throughout his life.

Brady left school in 1850, went on to study pharmacy in what was later to become the Newcastle College of Medicine, and, on graduating in 1855, set himself up as a pharmacist in Newcastle upon Tyne. His energy and organizational ability were soon evident. He was largely responsible for the foundation of the British Pharmaceutical Congress and served as its treasurer (1864–70) and president (1872–3). He also served on the council of the Pharmaceutical Society and was a member of its board of examiners. Moreover, he did much to promote the scientific education of pharmaceutical chemists, and was instrumental in transforming the *Pharmaceutical Journal* (to which he was a regular contributor) from a monthly to a weekly publication. He received many accolades from his professional colleagues, and was elected honorary member of the American Pharmaceutical Association, the Philadelphia College of Pharmacy, and the pharmaceutical societies of St Petersburg and Vienna.

Notwithstanding the many and varied demands on his time, Brady was able to publish papers on Foraminifera (Protozoa) from the 1860s. Significant milestones in his early foraminiferological career were the publications of monographs on the genera *Loftusia* and *Parkeria*, with William Benjamin Carpenter in 1869, and on Permo-Carboniferous non-fusulines, in 1876. He numbered among his other co-authors William Kitchen Parker and Thomas Rupert Jones. His philosophical trademark was a broad concept of the species and of intraspecific variability, and an associated conservatism in the establishment of new specific names. In 1876 he retired from business to devote the remainder of his life to the full-time study of Foraminifera. In 1884 he published the seminal *Report on the Foraminifera Dredged by HMS Challenger*. The text, written in a delightfully idiosyncratic style, set new standards of comprehensive presentation of information, while the colour plates, whose production was personally supervised by Brady, are of a standard of accuracy and artistry rarely matched before or since.

Brady received many awards and honours in recognition of his signal services to natural science, particularly in later life. He was elected in 1859 a fellow of the Linnean Society, in 1864 a fellow of the Geological Society, and in 1874 a fellow of the Royal Society, on whose council he served in 1888. In that year he also joined the Zoological Society, and received an honorary doctorate from the University of Aberdeen. He was appointed as corresponding member of the Imperial Geological Institute of Vienna and an honorary member of the Royal Bohemian Museum, Prague, and in 1887 received a gold medal from the Austrian emperor Franz Joseph I for services to the Imperial (Hof) Museum in Vienna, to which, through his colleague Felix Karrer, he sent a set of slides of Foraminifera from the Austro-Hungarian north pole expedition (dealt with in the *Challenger* report).

Brady was something of a gentleman traveller and journeyed twice around the world. His interest in the flora and fauna he encountered frequently prompted him to write short pieces. On his last overseas trip, in 1889–90, he fell seriously ill with dropsy. On his return, he took up residence in Bournemouth. He died, unmarried, at the town's Mansion Hotel, from bronchitis and emphysema, on 10 January 1891. He was buried that month in Jesmond old cemetery in Newcastle. His personal and professional integrity and stoic fortitude in the face of chronic ill health were combined with a sense of humour that on occasion led him to desert his usual staid demeanour and endeared him to his friends.   ROBERT WYNN JONES

Sources DNB · C. G. Adams, 'Henry Bowman Brady, 1835–1891', *Foraminifera*, ed. R. H. Hedley and C. G. Adams, 3 (1978), 275–80 · R. W. Jones, 'The *Challenger* expedition (1872–1876), Henry Bowman Brady (1835–1891) and the *Challenger* Foraminifera', *Bulletin of the British Museum (Natural History)* [Historical Series], 18 (1990), 115–43 · R. W. Jones, *The Challenger Foraminifera* (1994) · M. Foster, 'Henry Bowman Brady', *Nature*, 43 (1890–91), 299 · J. W. Steel and others, *A historical sketch of the Society of Friends … in Newcastle and Gateshead, 1653–1898* (1899) · d. cert. · *Newcastle Daily Chronicle* (15 Jan 1891)
Archives Newcastle Central Library, local studies department · NHM · RS, corresp. · U. Edin. L. | GS Lond., letters to Charles Moore
Likenesses photograph, c.1868–1870, Newcastle Central Library, local studies department; repro. in Jones, *Challenger Foraminifera* · photograph, 1880–1889?, NHM; repro. in Adams, 'Henry Bowman Brady' · D. Smith, two photographs, 1886, NPG
Wealth at death £7840 13s. 4d.: resworn probate, July 1891, CGPLA Eng. & Wales

Brady, Hugh (*c.*1527–1584), Church of Ireland bishop of Meath, was born at Dunboyne in that county. Tradition describes him as a son of Sir Denis O'Grady of co. Clare but this may be incorrect. There is no evidence that O'Grady lived at Dunboyne nor any allusion to O'Grady kin in Hugh Brady's correspondence. Brady's will, however, suggests that he had several Brady kin in the area of north Meath and it is likely that the bishop's father was a resident of Dunboyne. A Donald Brady is described, about 1540, as a 'true and lawful' man of the neighbourhood (White, 60); he occupied land near Ratoath, where Bishop Brady had a house, and at Personstown where the bishop held property at his death. The link is speculative but weight is added in that Bishop Brady already possessed property at Dunboyne at his appointment to the diocese; this suggests that he held it by inheritance.

Elizabeth I described Hugh Brady as a graduate of Oxford (though his name is not in any college register). Brady obtained the patronage of the future secretary, William Cecil, marrying a widow who may have been related to the Cecil family. By 1562 Brady was rector of St Mary Aldermary in London, a prestigious parish and a centre of reform. In 1563 the queen, impressed by his 'learning and sufficiency', appointed him to Meath (Morrin, 1.484). Brady may have been over-sanguine about the prospects of religious reform in Ireland; by March 1564 he wrote to Cecil that he lived in a 'sea of troubles' and had 'rather be a stipendary priest in England than bishop of Methe in Ireland' (PRO, SP 63/10/30).

Though the lord deputy, Sir Henry Sidney, described Brady as a 'godly minister and a good servant to your Highnesse' (PRO, SP 63/55/38), the bishop made little headway with reform. His clergy were 'ragged', his funds were 'scant', and the people 'scarcely to be won' (PRO, SP 63/10/30). He was an active member of the Irish privy council and in 1572 was credited with hazarding his person in the field against the followers of James Fitzmaurice. Convinced that reform depended on well-educated native clergy, he frequently urged that buildings at St Patrick's Cathedral be converted to a university. In this he was vigorously opposed by the archbishop of Dublin, Adam Loftus, who appears to have had a personal antipathy towards him.

After the death of his first wife Brady married, in 1568, Alice, daughter of the lord chancellor of Ireland, Robert *Weston. Their first son, Luke, was born in 1570, followed by two more sons, Nicholas and Gerard, and a daughter, Elizabeth. In 1576 Brady initiated an episcopal visitation which discovered 'the very walls of the churches down', with many clergy living on 'the gain of masses' (PRO, SP 63/55/38). By 1581 he wrote despairingly that 'everything therein groweth from evil to worse' (PRO, SP 63/97/19). From the late 1570s a majority of the Irish privy council believed that physical force was the most effective way of ensuring the pacification and conversion of the people. Brady was unenthusiastic about this approach and appears to have become a rather isolated figure towards the end of his life.

Hugh Brady died in February 1584 and was buried near the parish church at Dunboyne, where his grave can still be seen. He was survived by his second wife. Although he was the most conscientious of the Irish Elizabethan bishops, the circumstances in which he found himself meant he could achieve little. Archbishop Loftus, who had so thwarted Brady's attempts to establish a university at Dublin, eventually became provost of the new Trinity College, and is regarded by many as its founder. In this he gained an accolade which Brady had, perhaps, done more to deserve.   HELEN COBURN WALSHE

Sources PRO, state papers, Elizabeth, SP 63, Ireland · W. M. Brady, *Clerical and parochial records of Cork, Cloyne, and Ross*, 3 vols. (1863–4) · N. B. White, ed., *Extents of Irish monastic possessions, 1540–41*, IMC (1943) · J. S. Brewer and W. Bullen, eds., *Calendar of the Carew*

manuscripts, 6 vols., PRO (1867–73) • 'Calendar of fiants, Henry VIII to Elizabeth', *Report of the Deputy Keeper of the Public Records in Ireland*, 7–22 (1875–90), appxs • J. Morrin, ed., *Calendar of the patent and close rolls of chancery in Ireland, of the reigns of Henry VIII, Edward VI, Mary, and Elizabeth*, 1 (1861), 484

Wealth at death uncertain; lands, some possessions, debt of £160: will, PRO, state papers, Elizabeth, SP 63/110/18

Brady, John (*d.* 1814), government official and author, was employed as a clerk in the victualling office. He was the author of *Clavis calendaria, or, A Compendious Analysis of the Calendar*, published in two volumes in 1812; this popular survey reached a third edition three years later. Brady died on 5 December 1814 at Kennington, Surrey. An abridgement of his work appeared in the year of his death and extracts were reprinted in *The Credulity of our Forefathers* (1826). In the same year there appeared *Varieties of literature: being principally selections from the portfolio of the late John Brady*, compiled by his son John Henry Brady.

THOMPSON COOPER, *rev.* PHILIP CARTER

Sources [J. Watkins and F. Shoberl], *A biographical dictionary of the living authors of Great Britain and Ireland* (1816)

Brady, Sir Maziere, first baronet (1796–1871), judge, was born in Dublin on 20 July 1796, the second son of Francis Tempest Brady (1763–1821), manufacturer of gold and silver thread, and his wife, Charlotte, *née* Hodgson. In 1812 Brady entered Trinity College, Dublin; in 1814 he obtained a scholarship and twice won the vice-chancellor's prize for English verse. He obtained his BA in 1816, his MA in 1819, and was called to the Irish bar in the Trinity term of 1819. Brady was first married in 1823, to Eliza Anne, *née* Buchanan (*d.* 1858), of Dublin; they had five children. After her death he married Mary, *née* Hatchell, of Dublin.

In 1833, under the ministry of Earl Grey, Brady, as an avowed Liberal, was appointed one of the commissioners to inquire into the state of the Irish municipal corporations. In 1837 he became solicitor-general for Ireland in succession to Stephen Woulfe (1787–1840), and he became attorney-general in 1839. In the following year he was promoted to the bench as chief baron of the court of exchequer. He was raised to the bench of the Irish court of chancery, somewhat reluctantly, in 1846. Reputed to be one of the best chief barons and one of the poorer lord chancellors, he had been promoted to the higher post in line with Lord Russell's policy of 'Ireland for the Irish'. In 1850 he became the first vice-chancellor of the Queen's University, whose founding principles he warmly advocated.

From 1853 to 1858 Brady again served as lord chancellor of Ireland and he took up the post for a third time in 1859, after which he held it through the second administrations of Lord Palmerston and Earl Russell until the overthrow of the latter in 1866. He retired amid general regret on 28 June 1866. Although a protestant, he was a committed emancipist and had fought the infiltration of the co. Down magistracy by Orange justices. In 1869 he was created a baronet by W. E. Gladstone.

Brady died at his home, 26 Upper Pembroke Street, Dublin, on 13 April 1871. His interests had included not only legal, political, and educational matters, but also geology, which he pursued as a hobby. At the time of his death he was a member of the national Board of Education, and president of the Irish Art Union and of the Academy of Music; he is remembered for his attempts to have a national gallery of Ireland established. He was succeeded in his estates and title by his eldest son, Francis William Brady QC. A portrait by Jones hangs in the National Gallery of Ireland.

ARTHUR H. GRANT, *rev.* SINÉAD AGNEW

Sources F. E. Ball, *The judges in Ireland, 1221–1921*, 2 vols. (1926) • O. J. Burke, *The history of the lord chancellors of Ireland from AD 1186 to AD 1874* (1879) • Ward, *Men of the reign* • Boase, *Mod. Eng. biog.* • J. Hutchinson, ed., *A catalogue of notable Middle Templars: with brief biographical notices* (1902) • D. J. O'Donoghue, *The poets of Ireland: a biographical dictionary with bibliographical particulars*, 1 vol. in 3 pts (1892–3) • J. Wills and F. Wills, *The Irish nation: its history and biography*, 4 vols. (1871–5) • *Debrett's Peerage* • J. S. Crone, *A concise dictionary of Irish biography* (1928) • [J. H. Todd], ed., *A catalogue of graduates who have proceeded to degrees in the University of Dublin, from the earliest recorded commencements to … December 16, 1868* (1869) • *Freeman's Journal* [Dublin] (14 April 1871) • *Freeman's Journal* [Dublin] (18 April 1871) • *Daily News* (15 April 1871) • *Irish Times* (18 April 1871) • *The Times* (15 April 1871) • *The Times* (19 April 1871)

Archives TCD, corresp. | Bodl. Oxf., corresp. with Lord Kimberley

Likenesses T. A. Jones, oils, NG Ire.

Wealth at death under £20,000: probate, 12 May 1871, *CGPLA Ire.*

Brady, Nicholas (1659–1726), poet and Church of England clergyman, was born at Bandon, co. Cork, on 28 October 1659. He was the great-grandson of Hugh Brady, first protestant bishop of Meath, and son of Major Nicholas Brady (*fl.* 1641–1687), a protestant Irish army officer, and his wife, Martha, daughter of Luke Gernon, a Munster provincial judge.

Brady was educated under Dr Tindall at St Finbarre's School, Cork, until he was twelve years old, and then under Dr Busby at Westminster School, where he was king's scholar in 1673 and captain. He was elected to a Westminster studentship at Christ Church, Oxford, in December 1678 and matriculated on 4 February 1679, but was sent down for some unknown offence in 1682. He migrated to Trinity College, Dublin, from where he graduated BA (1685) and MA (1686). He was ordained priest at Cork in September 1687, became domestic chaplain to Edward Wetenhall, bishop of Cork and Ross, and, under Wetenhall's patronage, obtained a prebend in Cork Cathedral on 9 July 1688, and subsequently the livings of Ballymoney, Drinagh, and Kilmeen—all of them poor by English standards.

When many protestant clergy fled the Roman Catholic ascendancy effected by James II's viceroy, Brady remained in Ireland and earned favour among Jacobites by preaching the divine right of kings and non-resistance. In February 1689 the protestants of Bandon overpowered the viceroy's garrison and declared for William III, whereupon James II ordered his general, Justin MacCarthy, to burn the town, but Brady had sufficient interest with MacCarthy to persuade him to waive the burning and settle for an indemnity of £1500 ready money.

On 29 June 1690 Brady married Laetitia (*d.* 1748), daughter of Richard Synge (*d.* 1688), archdeacon of Cork, and

more durable because the musical setting was by Henry Purcell.

Brady was commissioned on 23 April 1694 as chaplain to Colonel Sir Richard Atkins's foot regiment and soon afterwards he became chaplain to William III and Queen Mary. He was now employed on the work that made his name: a metrical translation of the psalms in collaboration with another protestant Irish clergyman, Nahum Tate, poet laureate, and, like Brady, a protégé of the earl of Dorset. Tate's and Brady's *New Version of the Psalms of David* (1696), and the supplement to it, with other 'hymns' (1700), was smoother than the well-established old metrical version by Sternhold and Hopkins and so more satisfying to modern taste. It especially pleased whigs with occasional political allusions: for instance 'The prince, who slights what God commands, / Expos'd to scorn must quit his throne' (Psalm 107: 40). William III, to whom the *New Version* was dedicated, made an order in council on 3 December 1696 allowing it to be used in 'all such Churches … as shall think fit to receive the same'. Bishop William Beveridge complained in posthumously published 'critical observations' (1710) that its wit and fancy were unscriptural, but 'Tate and Brady' gradually displaced 'Sternhold and Hopkins' and was widely used in Anglican churches until the mid-nineteenth century. It ran to over three hundred editions.

Brady resigned St Katharine Cree in June 1696, when he was appointed perpetual curate of Richmond chapelry, Surrey, by the vicar of Kingston, Gideon Harding, having been invited to Richmond 'by the gentlemen of that place, in consequence of a high esteem they had conceived for him during a retreat which he had made thither, while he was translating the Psalms' (Kippis, 2.565). Brady was also esteemed by Trinity College, Dublin, for on 15 November 1699 he was awarded the degrees of BD and DD: Dr Pratt, a senior fellow and future provost of the college, travelled to England to make the award. Brady was vicar of Stratford upon Avon from 10 November 1702 to 16 October 1705, a living he owed to the earl of Dorset, and on 21 February 1706 he was presented to the rectory of Holy Trinity, Clapham, Surrey, by Dame Rebekah Atkins, mother of Colonel Sir Richard Atkins. In each case Brady continued to hold and reside in his Richmond living: his curacy was 'deemed independent of' the vicar of Kingston (Manning and Bray, 1.433), so Brady retained it when Harding died in 1713. Brady was also chaplain to Queen Anne and subsequently to Caroline, princess of Wales.

According to Brady's grandson, the whole of his various preferments amounted to £600 p.a. (Kippis, 2.565), but his expensive habits and love of hospitality obliged him to keep a school at Richmond. The school was given a useful puff by Richard Steele in *The Spectator* (no. 168, 12 September 1711), and so was probably more profitable than a scheme launched by Brady in 1713 to publish a blank-verse English translation of Virgil's *Aeneid* by subscription for 4 guineas: two in hand, two on delivery of the last volume. The first six books (Latin and English texts, with notes) appeared, as planned, between 1714 and 1716, but the remainder was not published until 1726 and is extremely

Nicholas Brady (1659–1726), attrib. Hugh Howard

granddaughter of Edmond Synge, bishop of Cork. There were four sons and four daughters of this marriage, but two daughters and one son died in infancy. Also in 1690, Brady, now an outspoken and zealous Williamite, was deputed by the citizens of Bandon to go to London to petition parliament for redress of their grievances when King James was in Ireland. He was appointed curate of St Katharine Cree on 16 July 1691, and lecturer of St Michael's, Wood Street; he also became chaplain to James Butler, second duke of Ormond. Brady now relinquished his Irish preferments and settled with his growing family in England. The first of his many published sermons was preached on 26 November 1691, 'the Thanksgiving-day for the preservation of the King and the reduction of Ireland' (title-page).

Brady's dull tragedy, *The Rape, or, The Innocent Imposters*, concerning fifth-century Goths and Vandals, was staged at Drury Lane in May 1692, thanks to the dramatist Thomas Shadwell's interest with Charles Sackville, earl of Dorset, and was published in the same year. Shadwell wrote the epilogue; Brady wrote a dedication to Dorset in which he mentioned his own (unspecified) sufferings for William III's government and the protestant religion. His play sank with scarcely a trace, though it was recast after Brady's death and acted four times at Lincoln's Inn Fields (25–8 November 1729). Brady's anonymous 'Ode on St Cecilia's Day', first publicly sung on 22 November 1692, proved rare. The work was evidently not widely available in its day: Samuel Johnson writes:

> Dr Brady attempted in blank verse a translation of the *Eneid*, which, when dragged into the world, did not live long enough to cry. I have never seen it, but that such a version there is, or has been, perhaps some old catalogue informed me. (Johnson, 1.453)

Brady was a fashionable preacher not only in his own churches but at court and before city livery companies. A hundred of his sermons appeared in print, the last of which were published in 1730 by his eldest son, Nicholas (1692–1768), vicar of Tooting. Brady died at Richmond on 20 May 1726 and was buried in Richmond church on 26 May. His widow was buried beside him on 5 August 1748.

JAMES SAMBROOK

Sources T. Cibber [R. Shiels], *The lives of the poets of Great Britain and Ireland* (1753), vol. 4, pp. 62–4 · A. Kippis and others, eds., *Biographia Britannica, or, The lives of the most eminent persons who have flourished in Great Britain and Ireland*, 2nd edn, 5 vols. (1778–93), vol. 2, pp. 564–5 · G. Bennett, *History of Bandon* (1869), 221–4, 272–9 · private information (2004) [Mrs J. Curthoys] · *Old Westminsters*, 1.115 · Burtchaell & Sadleir, *Alum. Dubl.*, 2nd edn · H. Cotton, *Fasti ecclesiae Hibernicae*, 6 vols. (1845–78), vol. 1, p. 221; vol. 5, p. 41 · R. Newcourt, *Repertorium ecclesiasticum parochiale Londinense*, 1 (1708), 381 · J. C. C. Smith, *Parish registers of Richmond, Surrey* (1905) · W. Van Lennep and others, eds., *The London stage, 1660–1800*, pt 1: *1660–1700* (1965) · *The complete works of Thomas Shadwell*, ed. M. Summers (1927), vol. 5, pp. 403–4 · O. Manning and W. Bray, *The history and antiquities of the county of Surrey*, 3 vols. (1804–14), vol. 1, p. 433; vol. 3, pp. 371, 379 · C. Dalton, ed., *English army lists and commission registers, 1661–1714*, 6 vols. (1892–1904), vol. 2, p. 257; vol. 3, p. 390 · J. H. Bloom, *Shakespeare's church* (1902), 145 · E. G. W. Bill, *Education at Christ Church, Oxford, 1660–1800* (1988), 160 · R. Bagwell, *Ireland under the Stuarts*, 3 (1916), 202–3 · S. Johnson, *Lives of the English poets*, ed. G. B. Hill, [new edn], 3 vols. (1905), vol. 1, p. 413; vol. 2, p. 249 · *CSP dom.*, 1686–7, 358 · J. Julian, ed., *A dictionary of hymnology*, rev. edn (1907), 919–20 · C. Spencer, *Nahum Tate* (1972)

Likenesses attrib. H. Howard, oils, NG Ire. [see illus.]

Brady, Richard [Risteard Mac Brádaigh] (*d.* **1607**), Roman Catholic bishop of Kilmore, was a member of the ancient Mac Brádaigh family, probably from Cúil Brighde (Castletara) in Breifne-O'Reilly (in his day renamed Cavan). Donagh Mooney, who knew him well and who is the main source of our information about him, said he was a Connaught man; he could have been born across the Cavan border in co. Leitrim but still in old Breifne. His father's name was Cathal Maol Mac Brádaigh, and Richard (Risteard) was the eldest of six sons, the others being Tadhg, Uilliam, Seán, Eoghan, and Séamus. He studied civil and canon law, probably at Salamanca, and may have been ordained priest there before returning to Ireland and entering the Franciscan order in the Cavan friary. Noted for holiness and learning, he was minister provincial for about three years in 1573–1576. He was appointed bishop of Ardagh by Gregory XIII in January 1576, and then bishop of Kilmore (embracing co. Cavan) in March 1580. Walter Harris, who thought Brady was bishop of Kilmore before 1576, was annoyed by the crown's neglect of that diocese and wrote scathingly about him, 'a delegate of the Pope's, that usurped it, dispersing abroad seditious bulls

and such like trash'. The crown appointed John Garvey to Kilmore in January 1585, and Brady was a marked man.

In December 1590 Miler Magrath, the archbishop of Cashel, apprehended a Walter Farannan who testified against Bishop Brady, saying that the powerful Nugent family were in contact with the duke of Parma and that Brady was their go-between; but there is no evidence that he left Ireland. Nevertheless, by May 1591 secret plans were afoot to apprehend him. A letter addressed to Philip II of Spain dated Enniskillen, 8 May 1593, asking for military aid for O'Neill and O'Donnell, was signed by five Irish leaders and six bishops, including Edmund Magauran, archbishop of Armagh, his senior suffragan Redmond O'Gallagher, bishop of Derry, and Bishop Brady. After the deaths of the other two, Brady would have become vice-primate of all Ireland (*c.*1601), and the leading representative of the Catholic church in the country; but he may have resigned from his see by then. His nephew Risteard, Tadhg's son, got involved in the on-going war, and was captured and executed in Mullingar in 1601, and that must have been a heavy blow.

Brady lived an austere life, much given to prayer and the administration of his diocese in as far as circumstances allowed. He lived for the most part in friaries, Multyfarnham (Westmeath) in particular, wore the Franciscan habit, and followed the friars' horarium. As a senior bishop in Armagh archdiocese he was a target for government forces; we are told that he was arrested three times in all, imprisoned and ransomed twice. On 1 October 1601 Multyfarnham was attacked by Sir Francis Shane, who seized Bishop Brady and others. They were taken to Shane's castle at Ballymore (about midway between Mullingar and Athlone), where Brady advised the young Donagh Mooney to consider carefully before taking the vows of a Franciscan in those dangerous times. The bishop, who was too old and infirm to be taken as a prisoner to Dublin in winter, was placed in custody near Ballymore and was conveyed to the capital later. He was set free when a large ransom was paid by his friends in the summer of 1602. He rejoined the friars at Multyfarnham where small huts had been erected and reconstruction had begun. But all was again destroyed by soldiers under Sir Francis Rushe on 25 July 1604; the friars were carried off to Dublin, and the weak Bishop Brady, unable to stand or ride easily, was stripped of his garments and thrown into a hole full of stones, thorns, and nettles, while he prayed for his captors. He was rescued and brought back to Multyfarnham. Mooney wrote, 'Having laid aside the episcopal burden, he lived for a long time helpless as an infant, but withal a gracious and lovable old man.' About July 1606 he received Tadhg O'Corcoran, Miler Magrath's servant, who asked to be reconciled to the Catholic church but who a short time later betrayed some of the plans for the flight of the earls, O'Neill and O'Donnell, in 1607. Brady died at Multyfarnham in September of the same year, and was buried near the entrance to the church. His name was placed on a list of prelates who suffered for their faith that appeared in David Rothe's *De processu martyriali* printed in 1619. There was a long vacancy between Brady's death and the papal appointment of Hugh O'Reilly as bishop of Kilmore in 1625.

IGNATIUS FENNESSY

Sources D. Mooney [D. Moneyus], 'Brussels MS 3947. De provincia Hiberniae s. Francisci', ed. B. Jennings, *Analecta Hibernica*, 6 (1934), 12–138, esp. 49, 93–8, 108, 112 • R. L. Browne, ed. and trans., 'A history of the Franciscan order in Ireland', *The Franciscan Tertiary*, 6/11 (March 1896) • P. O'Connell, *The diocese of Kilmore* (1937), 330–31, 386–92, 553 • T. O'Donnell, *Franciscan Abbey of Multyfarnham* (1951), 27–31, 39–41 • C. Eubel and others, eds., *Hierarchia Catholica medii et recentioris aevi*, 2nd edn, 3, ed. W. van Gulik, C. Eubel, and L. Schmitz-Kallenberg (Münster, 1923), 116, 217 • M. K. Walsh, 'Archbishop Magauran and his return to Ireland', *Seanchas Ardmhacha*, 14 (1990–91), 75–6 • C. P. Meehan, *The rise and fall of the Irish Franciscan monasteries and memoirs of the Irish hierarchy in the seventeenth century*, 5th edn (1877), 40–45, 171 • C. P. Meehan, *The fate and fortunes of Hugh O'Neill, earl of Tyrone, and Rory O'Donel, earl of Tyrconnel*, 3rd edn (1886), 72–4 • C. Mooney, 'Some Cavan Franciscans of the past', *Breifne*, 1 (1958), 19–20 • W. M. Brady, *The episcopal succession in England, Scotland, and Ireland, AD 1400 to 1875*, 1 (1876), 280–81, 291–2 • P. F. Moran, ed., *Spicilegium Ossoriense*, 1 (1874), 71–2 • *CSP Ire.*, 1588–92, 360–61, 365, 375, 393; 1603–08, 566 • *The analecta of David Rothe, bishop of Ossory*, ed. P. F. Moran (1884), 383 • *The whole works of Sir James Ware concerning Ireland*, ed. and trans. W. Harris, 1 (1739), 230 • 'Papers relating to the Nine Years' War', *Archivium Hibernicum*, 2 (1913), 301 • S. O' R. MacBradaigh, 'Teallach Cearbhuill: the genealogy of MacBradaigh of Cúil Brighde in Cavan', *Breifne*, 5/7 (1976), 149–57 • I. Fennessy, 'Richard Brady OFM, bishop of Kilmore, 1580–1607', *Breifne*, 9/36 (2000), 225–42

Brady, Robert (*c.*1627–1700), historian and physician, was born at Denver, near Downham Market, Norfolk, the son of Thomas Brady, attorney, and Mary, daughter of Thomas Whick of West Walton, Norfolk. He was educated at Downham School, under Mr Gilbert, and in 1644 was admitted as a sizar to Gonville and Caius College, Cambridge, where he was a scholar, 1644–50, and from where he graduated BA in 1648. He was about to proceed MB in 1650 when his education was interrupted as he was forced to flee the country.

Brady had been declared a traitor and had his goods sequestered following the hanging of Edmund Brady, presumed to be his brother, at Norwich in December 1650, to prevent a threatened royalist insurrection in Norfolk. To ensure his safety Brady travelled via the Netherlands to the king's garrison in the Isles of Scilly. After its surrender in May 1651 and having failed to settle in France, Brady obtained articles to return to England. On returning to Cambridge in 1652 he graduated MB in 1653, but his political connections prevented him from taking his MD in 1658, and also led to his being imprisoned at Great Yarmouth for six months during this period. For the last years of the Commonwealth he maintained himself by practising medicine, assisting unofficially in his college's affairs, and acting as an agent for the Norfolk royalists, providing, as he later put it, 'many services tending to his Majesty's Restauration' (Pocock, 'Robert Brady', 187).

Following the Restoration Brady was created MD by the king's letters in September 1660. He remained at Gonville and Caius; when the master, Dr Bachroft, decided to retire in December of that year Brady was chosen, on Bachroft's recommendation, to succeed him, although he had never held a fellowship and was not a choice the fellows would have freely made themselves. His mastership was uneventful. In 1677, after some years of campaigning for the post, he succeeded Francis Glisson as regius professor of physic. He was admitted a fellow of the Royal College of Physicians on 12 November 1680.

However, it is as a historian, rather than a physician, that Brady is best known. The date he began historical research is unknown, but the first mention of his work appears in a letter he wrote in 1675 to Sir Joseph Williamson, secretary of state, in which he set out his intention to write a full history of England and asked for assistance to do so. The work would, he hoped,

> begett in farre the greater and most considerable part of the people a Cheerfull submission and Obedience, as also a firm adherence to the present Government both in support and defence of it, Notwithstandinge the suggestions and insinuations of any sort of man whatsoever to the contrary. (Pocock, 'Robert Brady', 188)

The first of Brady's works, *A Full and Clear Answer to a Book Lately Written by Mr Petyt*, was published in February 1681, at the height of the exclusion crisis and on the eve of the Oxford parliament, to which he was returned. It pointed out the illogicality of the whig attack on Sir Robert Filmer's assertion of the crown's sovereignty over parliament. His work was criticized in the Commons by Sir William Jones and would probably have been 'called into question and burnt' if the parliament had lasted for another two days (*Life and Times of Anthony Wood*, 533). The timing of this work underlines the nature of his project. Brady's prime concern at all times was with bolstering the royalist cause; he viewed his critics not as academic rivals, but as writers 'with design to promote Sedition, and in expectation of Rebellion, and the destruction of the Established Government' (Brady, 326). His other principal works were *An Introduction to the Old English History* (1684), an assemblage of tracts rebutting rival historical theories, and *A Complete History of England*, a controversialist work dedicated to James II in which the historical narrative is formed from linked chronicles and prefaced with interpretative notes; the first volume appeared in 1685. His books made much use of records held in the Tower of London, and both were probably written under government auspices.

Brady's works are notable for their development of a new critical historical awareness and method. Royalist historians had generally been unsuccessful in challenging the dominant interpretation of English history established by Sir Edward Coke. This centred on the ahistorical idea of an ancient constitution and immemorial law unchanged by history, and which therefore predated and existed independently of the monarchy. It was a tradition which even denied the existence of the Norman conquest in its preoccupation with marginalizing the crown. If the law had depended on a conqueror's will it would forever depend on his and his successor's permission. In the hands of Restoration whig historians, such as William Petyt, William Atwood, and James Tyrell, this had become a powerful weapon against any extension of the royal prerogative. Brady's desire to overturn this politically limiting consensus led him to reject Coke and, following Sir Henry Spelman's lead, to recognize the importance of feudalism, imposed by the Normans, as the source of English law and the central reality of Norman and Angevin society. In its treatment of past society as understandable only in its own terms, this was an achievement which should, according to Pocock, be 'reckoned as one of the most important occurrences in the history of our historiography' (Pocock, *Ancient Constitution*, 198).

Brady was also active in parliamentary politics. He was involved in Norfolk politics during the election of 1679, when he nearly stood for his university but withdrew in favour of Sir William Temple, and was elected to the 1681 parliament and again in 1685. During the latter parliament he was reasonably active, particularly as a member of seven committees, among them one to bring in a clause forbidding resolutions to alter the succession. This work must have been particularly satisfying in light of the views on hereditary monarchy he had set out in *A True and Exact History of Succession* in 1681. Brady was also a JP for Middlesex and Westminster in 1687–9, and, as such, examined one of the minor figures of the Rye House plot.

In 1682 Brady was appointed physician-in-ordinary to Charles II, a post he retained under James II, and spent much time in attendance upon the court over the ensuing years. He was granted a salary of £300 to take custody of the records at the Tower of London in 1686, although he was not, as has sometimes been suggested, keeper, this being an office held by Sir Algernon May, an obscure gentleman living in Ireland at that time. The next year he joined James II in his visit to Oxford when the king attempted to impose a Roman Catholic president on Magdalen College. Brady assisted by identifying precedents for Nathaniel Johnston's royalist tract, *The King's Visitorial Power Asserted*. As physician he was one of those who deposed to the birth of the prince of Wales in 1688. His involvement with the Stuarts continued to the very end: at the urging of Bishop Turner of Ely he made a last minute attempt to dissuade James from flight at Rochester in December 1688. Following the revolution Brady remained master of Gonville and Caius, certifying in 1691 that he and the fellows had taken the oath of allegiance. Although he accepted the new regime, his well-known allegiance to the Stuarts left him vulnerable. In 1693 Brady was accused by a group of Royal College of Physicians fellows who supported the new regime of having killed a Mrs Campneis by treating her red face with a special ointment, leading him to complain to the college censors that he was 'calumniated' against.

Brady was to write no further historical works of any note and, with other royalists, was ordered to turn over the Tower records to his old adversary Petyt in March 1689. The second volume of his *Complete History* was published in 1690, but it contained only chronicle material without interpretation. The same year saw the appearance of his *Treatise of Cities and Boroughs*, a rather confused work presumably written some years earlier in support of Charles

II's revision of the charters. It is sometimes suggested that he wrote the nonjuring tract *An Inquiry into the Remarkable Instances of History and Parliamentary Records*, published in 1691, but this remains uncertain. His historical work was heavily criticized and rejected by the historians of the new regime and remained generally ignored and forgotten for much of the eighteenth and nineteenth centuries.

Brady was married to Jane (1623–1679), daughter and coheir of Luke Constable of Swaffham. Brady died on 19 August 1700 and was buried in St Mary's Church, Denver, Nolfolk, leaving the bulk of his land and money to Gonville and Caius College.   PATRICK WALLIS

Sources Venn, *Alum. Cant.* · Munk, *Roll* · A. Kippis and others, eds., *Biographia Britannica, or, The lives of the most eminent persons who have flourished in Great Britain and Ireland*, 2nd edn, 5 vols. (1778–93) · J. G. A. Pocock, 'Robert Brady, 1627–1700: a Cambridge historian of the Restoration', *Cambridge Historical Journal*, 10 (1950–52), 186–204 · R. Brady, *An introduction to the old English history* (1684) · J. G. A. Pocock, *The ancient constitution and the feudal law* (1957); repr. (1967) · *The life and times of Anthony Wood*, ed. A. Clark, 5 vols., OHS, 19, 21, 26, 30, 40 (1891–1900) · F. Blomefield and C. Parkin, *An essay towards a topographical history of the county of Norfolk*, [2nd edn], 11 vols. (1805–10) · HoP, *Commons* · A. W. Hughes Clarke and A. Campling, eds., *The visitation of Norfolk … 1664, made by Sir Edward Bysshe*, 1, Harleian Society, 85 (1933) · *DNB*

Archives BL, SL MSS 2251, 3310, 28600–28601, 30330; notes from the journals of Parliament, ST MS 360 · Bodl. Oxf., transcript copies of his treatise on parliament

Likenesses E. Harding, stipple, 1799, BM, NPG, Wellcome L. · oils, Gon. & Caius Cam.

Wealth at death £500 and estate in Denver to college; £40 life interest on estate to niece: Venn, *Alum. Cant.*

Brady, Thomas, styled Baron Brady (1752/3–1827), army officer in the Austrian service, was born in Ireland, either at Cootehill or Cavan, between October 1752 and May 1753. He entered the Austrian service as a cadet in infantry regiment 15 (Pallavicini, later Fabris) on 21 November 1769, was promoted ensign on 3 April 1774 and lieutenant on 30 November 1775, and was advanced to the rank of first lieutenant on 20 March 1784. During the War of the Bavarian Succession (1778–9) he distinguished himself at the skirmish of Habelschwerdt (18 January 1779). On 15 May 1788 he was transferred to the general staff and promoted captain. In Austria's last Turkish war he served with the Austrian army corps in Croatia and received, on 15 November 1788, the knight's cross of the military order of Maria Theresa for personal bravery at the storming of Novi (3 October 1788), where he was wounded. He was appointed major on the general staff on 28 March 1790.

In the war against revolutionary France Brady served in the Netherlands and distinguished himself at the battle of Neerwinden (18 March 1793). He was promoted lieutenant-colonel and commander of the Tyrolese sharpshooters on 1 April 1793, then colonel-commander of infantry regiment 55 (Murray) on 11 February 1794. He served in Germany in 1795–6 and was promoted major-general on 6 September 1796. He then transferred to the Austrian army in Italy before it was forced back onto Austrian soil. At the head of a grenadier brigade he fought the last encounter of the First War of Coalition at Judenburg, Styria, on 4 April 1797. In October 1797 he was nominated military and civil governor of the Venetian province of Albania, which, following the peace treaty of Campoformido, passed into Austrian hands.

Brady was made Feldmarschall-Leutnant on 18 January 1801, commanded a division in Bohemia, and officiated as military and civil governor of Dalmatia and Albania from October 1803 until February 1806. During the 1809 campaign he was in command of a division of the 2nd army corps and particularly distinguished himself at the battle of Aspern (21–2 May 1809). For reasons of health he was retired with the rank of Feldzeugmeister on 3 September 1809. He had received the title of imperial chamberlain in 1801, the honorary colonelcy of the 1st regiment of infantry (Kaiser) in 1803, and the title of privy councillor in July 1804. At some time after 1787 he had married a Countess Degen, who predeceased him. Brady died in Vienna on 16 October 1827. His heir was a James O'Brady.

MICHAEL HOCHEDLINGER

Sources Österreichisches Staatsarchiv, Vienna, Haus-, Hof-, und Staatsarchiv, Staatskanzlei Geheime Räte · Österreichisches Staatsarchiv, Vienna, Kriegsarchiv, Direktionsakten 194/1914 · Österreichisches Staatsarchiv, Vienna, Allgemeines Verwaltungsarchiv, Adelsakten Brady 1758, 1763, 1815 · H. Meynert and J. Hirtenfeld, *Oesterreichisches Militärkonversationslexikon* (1851), vol. 1, p. 484 · J. Hirtenfeld, *Der Militär-Maria-Theresien-Orden und seine Mitglieder* (1857), vol. 1, p. 241ff. · C. von Wurzbach, *Biographisches Lexikon des Kaiserthums Österreich*, 60 vols. (Vienna, 1856–91), vol. 2, p. 107 · *DNB* · A. von Wrede, *Geschichte der k. und k. Wehrmacht*, 5 vols. (Vienna, 1898–1905) · *Österreichisches biographisches Lexikon, 1815–1950*, 1 (1957), 105 · E. Schmidhofer, 'Das irische, schottische und englische Element im kaiserlichen Heer', PhD diss., University of Vienna, 1971

Likenesses F. Deiwel, silhouette, Indian ink drawing, Österreichische Nationalbibliothek, Vienna, Bildarchiv-Porträtsammlung

Brady, William (1881–1960), bookmaker, was born in Yorkshire Street, Salford, son of John Brady, commission agent, and his wife, Mary, *née* Hanoran. Known as Billy, he attended St John's Cathedral Boys' School in Salford and went to work with his two brothers at a local cable manufacturing business. He played rugby league for the factory team and later for Salford as a half-back. Brady and his brothers took bets at work, giving them to their father when they went home.

Since the passing of the Betting Houses Act in 1853 cash betting on horse-races away from the racecourse had been unlawful, but the activity remained popular among working-class people. In 1902 the Bradys were caught by the management and were sacked. Billy Brady then became a full-time illegal bookmaker. It is likely he took bets on the street, but in 1906 the Street Betting Act forced bookies into spots more protected from the police. The housing in Salford was mostly two-up, two-down and at the rear of each terrace there ran a common entry or passage. Brady set up a pitch in the backyard of the family's home: his punters (or customers) came up the entry and handed him their bets and cash over the yard's wall.

During the First World War Brady served with the Royal Army Service Corps, becoming a sergeant and taking part in the battle of the Somme. On leave in 1915 he married his fiancée, a shop assistant called Ellen Devine (*b.* 1883/4), on Christmas day; they had three daughters and two sons.

His wife helped greatly in his bookmaking business, which he expanded after his discharge. He took over several pitches and was acknowledged as the biggest bookmaker in Salford. Most bookies protected themselves against large pay-outs by imposing a limit on the amount that could be won on a certain kind of bet. Brady was regarded as the founder of no-limit betting. He had a large notice painted on the end of his pitch proclaiming 'world record payout' to an old lady who had won several hundred pounds for an outlay of 6*d*.

Street bookies were decried by some people as immoral and unchristian. Others felt they drew the working class away from political action and encouraged wasteful spending. These negative images were reinforced by Walter Greenwood in his powerful novel *Love on the Dole*, written in 1933. Set in Hanky Park, Salford, it features the notorious bookie, Sam Grundy. Small and fat with beady eyes, sporting diamonds of a preposterous size and a collection of gold pendants, spade guineas, and masonic emblems, suggestively Grundy boasts that he has no limits.

Many working-class people, however, looked on street bookies more positively. A former detective recalled Brady 'as a benefactor of the Catholic church rather than a criminal, despite the illicit status of his business' (Davies, 155). This opinion was widespread locally, and he was regarded as a good churchman and family man with a strong social concern, who sponsored parties and outings for the young and underprivileged. A governor of many schools, he was said to have an affable disposition and be unassuming and modest. He died at home at Southwood, Old Hall Lane, Worsley, Salford, on 12 September 1960, the year in which off-course cash betting was legalized. Following a requiem mass at St John's Cathedral, Salford, he was buried at St Mary's cemetery, Wardley. He was survived by his wife.

CARL CHINN

Sources private information (2004) · Celia Brady, letter; James Cush, letter 1; John L. W., letter 2; Tom Carroll, letter 2, U. Birm. L., special collections department, Carl Chinn bookmaking letters · A. Davies, *Leisure, gender and poverty: working-class cultures in Salford and Manchester, 1900–1939* (1992) · C. Chinn, *Better betting with a decent feller: bookmakers, betting and the British working class, 1750–1990* (1991) · interviews with Billy Brady, priv. coll., Andrew Davies Interviews · W. Greenwood, *Love on the dole* (1933) · m. cert. · *CGPLA Eng. & Wales* (1960)

Wealth at death £15,320 17*s*. 4*d*.: probate, 29 Nov 1960, *CGPLA Eng. & Wales*

Brae, June [*real name* June Telfer Bear] (1917–2000), ballet dancer, was born at St Ives, Ringwood, Hampshire, on 17 May 1917, the daughter of John McMillan Bear, a civil engineer, and his wife, May Alfreda Byerley. She travelled as a child to China with her parents, and at an early age, in addition to a conventional local education, began ballet training in classes taught in Shanghai by the eminent Russian émigré Georgy Goncharov. A fellow student at the same time was the future Margot Fonteyn. The two girls became close friends, and in her autobiography Fonteyn described the young June Bear as an unusually expressive dancer, whose serious involvement in the classes prompted Fonteyn to give closer attention to Goncharov's teaching.

Fired in turn by the reports Fonteyn and her mother brought back from their visits to London of the dancers they saw and, in particular, of the teaching there by the famous Nicholas (Nicolay Gustavovich) Legat, Mrs Bear determined that her daughter should pursue further ballet studies in England. June went to Legat for advanced training and, later, to Paris for further study with other Russian teachers, notably Mathilde Kshesinskaya. Finally, in 1933, she joined the Sadler's Wells Ballet School founded by Ninette de Valois, and two years later she graduated into the emerging Vic–Wells Ballet.

Her first professional appearances were as June Bear, but according to de Valois's brother, the photographer Gordon Anthony, de Valois 'didn't care for the idea of performing bears in her company' (Anthony), so changed June's surname anagrammatically to Brae, and she used that form throughout her career. By then she had the physical allure of a Hollywood star of that era and could well have succeeded in that métier, with her dramatic gifts in addition to balletic skills. These quickly became evident in her first major roles, from the Other Woman in de Valois's *Prometheus* and the romantic Caroline in Antony Tudor's *Jardin aux lilas* (both 1936) to her most memorable creation of the formidably aggressive Black Queen in de Valois's chess-game ballet *Checkmate* (1937).

During this time June Brae was also regularly teamed with another leading dancer, Pamela May, in ballets requiring a pairing of female soloists (*Giselle*, *Les patineurs*, *Swan Lake*), and they, with Fonteyn, became the company's most popular stars in the 1930s. Brae had the distinction of dancing the first British Lilac Fairy when *The Sleeping Beauty* (then called *The Sleeping Princess*) was first produced at Sadler's Wells in 1939. She was remembered in this role as 'the essence of graceful charm and authoritative dignity' by Gordon Anthony (Anthony, 354), whose professional photographs of her are in the Theatre Museum, London. By nature she was gentle, vivacious, and radiant of personality, much loved by friends and colleagues, and adored by audiences, to whom she responded with good humour and sociable spirit.

On 15 February 1941 June Brae married David Lucas Breeden (b. 1917/18), then a pilot officer in the Royal Air Force, whom she had earlier met while on tour in Cambridge and with whom she had a daughter and a son. She was obliged to undergo surgery in 1942, and spent the rest of the war years in retirement from the stage in order to be with her husband and family. In 1946 she was persuaded back by Ninette de Valois to lead the new, separate company that 'Madam' was forming at Sadler's Wells to replace the nominal Sadler's Wells Ballet when the latter became resident at Covent Garden. She was nevertheless cast in the leading role of the Ballerina in the first new ballet created in the post-war Covent Garden, Robert Helpmann's *Adam Zero*, and also took the leading role in Andrée Howard's *Assembly Ball* for the new Sadler's Wells

Opera Ballet (later the Theatre Ballet), where the necessarily young and untried troupe benefited particularly from Brae's authority and experience; meanwhile she herself achieved the hitherto unique distinction of performing leading roles in two new ballets premièred within forty-eight hours (8–10 April 1946).

During her two years with the second company Brae took on several existing roles new to her, of which the most eloquent (for many admirers) was perhaps the estranged Bride in Howard's hauntingly restrained *La fête étrange* (based on Alain Fournier's *Le grand Meaulnes*). She took her definitive retirement from dancing in 1950, and made only one later appearance, in January 1981 at a gala to celebrate fifty years of Sadler's Wells Theatre since its reopening by Lilian Baylis. Brae joined some other former dancers to appear in the Hogarthian orgy scene in de Valois's *The Rake's Progress*, after which de Valois was heard to comment that henceforth she wanted none but married women to perform that scene. Otherwise Brae settled with her husband and family in their new home at Bath, where David Breeden predeceased his wife. She survived through a protracted illness to die from bronchopneumonia and dementia in a Bath nursing home, Heather House in Bannerdown Road, Batheaston, on 3 January 2000.

NoËL GOODWIN

Sources *The Guardian* (13 Jan 2000) · *The Times* (14 Jan 2000) · *Daily Telegraph* (4 Feb 2000) · *The Independent* (4 Feb 2000) · personal knowledge (2004) · private information (2004) · G. Anthony, 'Pioneers of the Royal Ballet: June Brae', *Dancing Times* (April 1970), 354 · M. Clarke, *Dancing Times* (Feb 2000), 409 · P. May, *Dancing Times* (Feb 2000), 411 · M. Clarke, *The Sadler's Wells Ballet* (1955) · M. Fonteyn, *An autobiography* (1975) · b. cert. · m. cert. · d. cert.
Likenesses G. Anthony, photograph, 1937, repro. in *The Guardian* · photograph, c.1937, repro. in *The Times* · photograph, 1937, repro. in *Daily Telegraph* · G. Anthony, photographs, Theatre Museum, London · photograph, repro. in *The Independent*

Bragg, Sir (William) Lawrence (1890–1971), physicist and crystallographer, was born on 31 March 1890 at 58/60 Lefevre Terrace, Adelaide, Australia, the elder son (the younger, Robert, was killed at Gallipoli in 1915) and eldest of the three children of Sir William Henry *Bragg (1862–1942), physicist, and his wife, Gwendoline (1869–1929), daughter of Sir Charles *Todd, government astronomer of South Australia.

Education Bragg was educated in Adelaide at Convent School (1895–7), at Queen's preparatory school (1898–1901), and at St Peter's College, Adelaide, the leading Church of England school in South Australia (1901–5). Always ahead of his age group he left school at fifteen to enter the University of South Australia, at Adelaide, in 1905, where he read mathematics, with subsidiary courses in physics and chemistry, in his father's department. He graduated with first-class honours in mathematics in 1908. Most of his tuition was from his father: he had a desk in his office and was drawn into detailed discussion of his father's developing research work on the nature of X-rays.

In 1909 Bragg's family moved to England, where his

and potassium chloride in a study described as 'the great breakthrough to actual crystal-structure determination and to the absolute measurement of X-ray wavelengths' (Ewald, 69).

The X-ray spectrometer provided a more powerful method of analysing crystal structures than Laue photographs and Bragg worked in Leeds during the summer of 1913, using the instrument to analyse a number of mineral structures while his father concentrated mainly on spectroscopic studies of the X-rays. Together they determined the structure of diamond. For this body of work, described in *X-Rays and Crystal Structure* (1915), written by Bragg in collaboration with his father, they were jointly awarded the Nobel prize for physics in 1915. Aged twenty-five at the time, Bragg was still known as the youngest ever Nobel prizewinner two decades after his death.

Bragg served throughout the First World War, first in the Leicestershire Royal Horse Artillery and then, from August 1915, as officer in charge of sound ranging, a method of locating enemy guns from the sound of their firing. He was awarded the MC (1918), appointed OBE (1918), mentioned in dispatches three times, and rose to the rank of major.

In 1919 Bragg returned briefly to the lectureship and fellowship at Trinity College, Cambridge, to which he had been appointed in 1914, but left for Manchester in the autumn, where he had been appointed Langworthy professor of physics in succession to Sir E. Rutherford. There he created the leading school of crystallography, to some degree in competition with his father who established another school at the Royal Institution. They seem to have agreed that Bragg should study metals and minerals, and crystal physics more generally, while his father concentrated on organic structures.

In 1921 Bragg was elected FRS and in December that year he married Alice Grace Jenny, the daughter of Albert Hopkinson, a Manchester physician who became, in retirement, a demonstrator in anatomy in Cambridge, and his wife, Olga Cunliffe-Owen. Bragg had met his future wife in 1919 in Cambridge, where she was reading history at Newnham College. Over the period 1924–35 they had two boys and two girls. The elder son, Stephen, an aeronautical engineer with Rolls-Royce, subsequently became vice-chancellor of Brunel University, while the younger, David, inherited the artistic talents of his father and grandmother. The elder daughter, Margaret, married Mark Heath, ambassador to the Holy See 1982–5, and Patience, the younger, an authority on dyslexia, married David Thomson, younger son of Bragg's old friend Sir G. P. Thomson. In later years Bragg's wife was a JP, mayor of Cambridge, chairman of the Marriage Guidance Council, and wrote amusing articles in the *Manchester Guardian*.

Bragg's achievements in Manchester included the introduction of the idea of atomic radii; experimental verification of the theory of X-ray diffraction from perfect and imperfect crystals; the derivation of experimental atomic scattering factors for sodium and potassium that stimulated theoretical work by D. R. Hartree; the development

Sir (William) Lawrence Bragg (1890–1971), by Elliott & Fry

father had been appointed professor of physics at Leeds University, and Bragg entered Trinity College, Cambridge. He read part one of the mathematical tripos (first class, 1910) and part two of the natural sciences tripos (physics), graduating in 1912 with first-class honours.

Research, marriage, and chair at Manchester, 1912–1937 In the summer of 1912 Friedrich, Knipping, and Laue in Munich discovered the diffraction of X-rays by crystals and in the autumn of that year Bragg showed, first, that the phenomenon can be simply understood in terms of the reflection of X-ray waves by planes of atoms in the crystals (according to Bragg's law) and, second, that the observed effects are capable of revealing the detailed arrangements of the atoms in the crystals. In this single piece of work, which was described to a meeting of the Cambridge Philosophical Society on 11 November 1912, he opened the way to the detailed study of the wave nature of X-rays and, at the same time, began the X-ray analysis of crystal structures that has since revealed the arrangement of the atoms in all kinds of substances from the chemical elements to viruses. Both of these new opportunities for research were quickly exploited. His demonstration of X-ray reflection from mica in December 1912 led immediately to his father's development of the X-ray spectrometer, and the discovery that each element emits a characteristic X-ray spectrum of definite wavelengths; this led in turn to the discovery of the atomic numbers of the elements by H. G. J. Moseley. At the same time Bragg himself quickly determined the atomic arrangements in sodium of methods for analysing increasingly complex structures, including especially the Fourier method of calculating the electron density distribution in a crystal—following a suggestion by his father; the demonstration that X-ray analysis is properly regarded as a branch of optics; and the development, with E. J. Williams, of the theory of order–disorder changes. In structural studies his main achievement was the analysis of a wide range of silicate mineral structures that led to a detailed understanding of silicate chemistry, but he also promoted the study of metals and alloys by A. J. Bradley and others that underlies modern solid-state physics.

This work is described in about a hundred original papers and reviews published in leading scientific journals, especially *Proceedings of the Royal Society*, *Philosophical Magazine*, *Nature*, and *Zeitschrift für Kristallographie*. In addition Bragg wrote: *The Crystalline State: a General Survey*, which appeared in 1933 as the first volume of a projected series to be edited jointly by father and son; *Electricity* (1936), an account of his Christmas lectures at the Royal Institution in 1934; and *Atomic Structure of Minerals* (1937), based on his Baker lectures at Cornell University in 1934. The volume *Electricity* was translated into many languages, including Czech, Finnish, and Japanese.

Despite his great productivity at Manchester, and the availability to him of a steady stream of postgraduate researchers—for which he felt great gratitude—Bragg was not always happy there. A possible post at Cambridge in 1929 did not materialize, and he refused the offer of a chair at Imperial College, London, in the same year. His mother's death in that year, coupled with his professional disappointments, a difficult relationship with his father, and the effects of the economic crash on his Manchester environment led him to an emotional crisis in 1930, during which his health broke down. However, he recovered quickly in the following year, and his move from industrial Didsbury to rural Alderley Edge, in 1933, helped him face the world with renewed vigour.

Cavendish professor, 1938–1954 Bragg became director of the National Physical Laboratory in November 1937 but he occupied the post for less than a year, being appointed Cavendish professor of physics at Cambridge in March 1938 in succession to Rutherford, who had died the previous October. Thus he followed Rutherford in a major chair for the second time, much to the disappointment of nuclear physicists, who had hoped to see one of their number continue Rutherford's work in Cambridge. Their opposition was the occasion for C. G. Darwin's memorable remark: 'nuclear physics is a passing phase' (Phillips, 110). In the event nuclear physics remained the largest single activity in the Cavendish Laboratory but Bragg concentrated mainly on promoting the development of other new lines of research. Even in his first year, which was taken up increasingly with preparations for war, he made further advances in X-ray optics, strengthened the study of metals in the crystallographic laboratory, and enthusiastically supported the crystallographic studies of proteins by M. F. Perutz, which had been started under the

influence of J. D. Bernal and were to be Bragg's chief research interest for the rest of his career.

Bragg played no part in the war research that was conducted in the Cavendish but he acted as consultant to the sound ranging section in the army (the method was still useful and was employed, furthermore, in plotting the trajectories of the V 2 rockets) and to the Admiralty on underwater detection by the use of sound waves (asdic or sonar). He also served on committees set up by the Ministry of Supply to keep its scientific activities under review and as a member of the advisory council of the Department of Scientific and Industrial Research. In 1941 he spent six months in Ottawa, Canada, as scientific liaison officer, and in 1943 he visited Sweden to re-establish contacts with Swedish scientists.

Bragg was knighted in 1941 and his father, still at the Royal Institution, wrote to Lorna Todd, his sister-in-law in Adelaide: 'Isn't that fine? … He will have to be Sir Lawrence: we can't have confusion worse than ever … In spite of all care, people mix us up and are apt to give me a first credit on occasions when he should have it' (Caroe, 177). This was an issue that had bothered Bragg—William or Willy to family and close friends—since the earliest days, when his father, as an established senior scientist, was invited to describe Bragg's original work at the Solvay Conference on Physics in 1913, and it was still a sore point with him long after his father's death in 1942.

From 1939 to 1943 Bragg was president of the Institute of Physics. While working hard to maintain the activities of the institute and foster discussion about the needs of the post-war world, he was mainly responsible for the creation of the X-ray analysis group to promote X-ray research in both universities and industry. At the end of the war he also contributed to the formation of the International Union of Crystallography, of which he was the first president, and the publication of its journal *Acta crystallographica*.

After the war Bragg reorganized the Cavendish Laboratory, giving each research section as much autonomy as possible. The principal activities included nuclear physics; low temperature physics; radio physics, which embraced radio astronomy under Martin Ryle (of particular interest to Bragg as a further example of physical optics); and the crystallography and metal physics which were his chief concern. In 1946 he was awarded a royal medal of the Royal Society. Work on protein crystallography had been maintained during the war and in 1947 he persuaded the Medical Research Council to set up a research unit on the molecular structure of biological systems at the Cavendish Laboratory. This was the origin of the MRC Laboratory of Molecular Biology—and the site of the preliminary work which later led to the determination of the structure of DNA and, with Bragg's active participation, to the subsequent breakthrough to protein structure analysis.

During this Cambridge period Bragg published a further ninety papers and reviews in scientific journals despite his firm adherence to the principle that he would be listed only as an author if he had made a significant contribution to the work; he was general editor of two further volumes of *The Crystalline State* (1948 and 1953).

At the Royal Institution, 1954–1966 In 1954 Bragg left Cambridge to become resident Fullerian professor and director of the Davy–Faraday Laboratory at the Royal Institution in London. There he maintained the traditional activities but sought to involve industry more closely through corporate membership. His association with industry and his interest in the industrial development of research had begun during his Manchester days, when he was in contact with local firms and with the Shirley Institute. Among other initiatives at the Royal Institution, he began an intensive programme of lectures for schoolchildren, gave popular science lectures on television, and built up a research team that collaborated with Kendrew and Perutz in the first successful studies of protein structures (myoglobin and haemoglobin) and was the first, in 1965, to determine the structure of an enzyme (lysozyme).

In this period Bragg collaborated with G. F. Claringbull in writing *The Crystalline State*, volume 4, entitled *Crystal Structures of Minerals* (1965), and he wrote another sixty papers, mainly reviews and published versions of lectures though they included, in his last original scientific paper, 'The determination of the co-ordinates of heavy atoms in protein crystals' (*Acta crystallographica*, 11, 1958, 70–75), a contribution that was important in the structure analysis of tobacco mosaic virus. Characteristically this method depended on the careful analysis of a few measurements, carried out by hand, and owed nothing to the growing dominance of digital computers in the development of the subject. On the international scene he was chairman of the Solvay Conferences on Physics (1948–61), and president of the International Science Hall at the Brussels Exhibition in 1958.

By the time of his retirement in 1966 Bragg had made the Royal Institution again a leading centre of scientific research and, thanks in large part to the impact of television, a focus for the popular exposition of science to a wider audience than ever before. In recognition of his overall achievements he was rather belatedly awarded the Copley medal of the Royal Society in 1966 and appointed CH in 1967. During his career he had been awarded honorary degrees by eleven universities.

Character and scientific legacy Bragg had a stocky build, a somewhat military appearance resembling his father, and a diffident manner. He was not self-confident in public affairs and he found committees and personal relations generally difficult to handle. He was essentially a private man who delighted in reading, painting, gardening, birdwatching, sailing, and domestic activities with his wife and family. But he wrote quickly and vividly, his public lectures were models of popular exposition, he had a profound grasp of classical physics, and he brought about an important scientific revolution. Through his development and promotion of X-ray crystallography in three major scientific appointments, Bragg transformed our understanding of the natural world: modern mineralogy, metallurgy, chemistry, and molecular biology were completely restructured as a result of his discoveries. Only two weeks before his death he completed the text of his last book, *The Development of X-Ray Analysis* (1975), which summarized these advances in his characteristically lively style. Ironically this work, which challenged the dominance of nuclear and quantum physics as *the* modern scientific disciplines, was carried out almost entirely in physics departments; the struggles for recognition of himself and his associates are a study in the emergence of new disciplinary boundaries.

Bragg died of cancer in Ipswich General Hospital, Suffolk, on 1 July 1971 and was cremated at Ipswich crematorium on 6 July after a funeral service in Waldringfield church near his country home.

DAVID PHILLIPS (LORD PHILLIPS OF ELLESMERE)

Sources D. Phillips, *Memoirs FRS*, 25 (1979), 75–143 · P. P. Ewald, ed., *Fifty years of X-ray diffraction* (1962) · J. M. Bijvoet, W. G. Burgers, and G. Hägg, eds., *Early papers on diffraction by crystals*, 2 vols. (1969–72) · J. G. Crowther, *The Cavendish Laboratory, 1874–1974* (1974) · G. M. Caroe, *William Henry Bragg, 1862–1942: man and scientist* (1978) · J. D. Watson and F. H. C. Crick, 'A structure for deoxyribose nucleic acid', *Nature*, 171 (1953), 737 · D. W. Green, V. I. Ingram, and M. F. Perutz, 'The structure of haemoglobin-IV: sign determination by the isomorphous replacement method', *PRS*, 225A (1954), 287–307 · C. C. F. Blake and others, 'Structure of hen egg white lysozyme', *Nature*, 206 (1965), 757–63 · private information (2004) · W. L. Bragg, draft autobiography, Royal Institution of Great Britain, London

Archives Bodl. Oxf., papers relating to Society for Protection of Science and Learning · CUL, corresp. relating to Cavendish Laboratory · Medical Research Council, London, corresp. · Royal Artillery Institution, Woolwich, London, papers · Royal Institution of Great Britain, London, corresp. and papers | Bodl. Oxf., corresp. with Dorothy Hodgkin; corresp. with Sir David Phillips · CAC Cam., corresp. with Sir Edmund Bullard; corresp. with Sir James Chadwick; corresp. with Archibald Vivian Hill · CUL, corresp. with Ulick Richardson Evans · CUL, corresp. with Francis John Worsley Roughton · IWM, corresp. with Sir Henry Tizard · Nuffield Oxf., corresp. with Lord Cherwell · Rice University, Houston, Texas, Woodson Research Center, corresp. with Sir Julian Huxley · U. Leeds, Brotherton L., corresp. with Edmund Stoner

Likenesses photograph, 1913, University of Manchester, department of physics and astronomy · photograph, 1926, Trinity Cam. · photograph, c.1930, University of Manchester, department of physics and astronomy · photographs, 1942–50, Hult. Arch. · W. Stoneman, photograph, 1943, NPG · R. J. Burn, chalk drawing, 1950, Trinity Cam. · T. Cuneo, group portrait, oils, 1962, Royal Institution of Great Britain, London · L. Meitner-Graf, photograph, 1962, Royal Institution of Great Britain, London · Dring, pastel, 1965, priv. coll. · J. Mills, bronze bust, 1966, Royal Institution of Great Britain, London; copies, Cavendish Laboratory, U. Cam., Manchester, department of physics and astronomy · J. Mills, bronze bas relief, 1967, Royal Institution of Great Britain, London · G. Argent, photograph, 1970, NPG · H. Bhabha, sketch, U. Cam., Cavendish Laboratory · Elliott & Fry, three photographs, NPG [*see illus.*] · group photographs (at Solvay conferences), RS · photographs, Royal Institution of Great Britain, London · photographs, U. Cam., Cavendish Laboratory · photographs, University of Manchester · three photographs, RS

Wealth at death £34,969: probate, 18 Oct 1971, *CGPLA Eng. & Wales*

Bragg, Philip (*d.* **1759**), army officer and politician, was commissioned an ensign in the 1st foot guards on 10 March 1702. He fought at Blenheim and on 25 August 1704

was made a captain in the regiment of Brigadier Tatton (afterwards Gilbert Primrose's). For the remainder of the war he campaigned in Flanders; he is listed as having been present at Malplaquet. In 1710 and 1711, following his appointment as lieutenant-colonel of the earl of Ilay's regiment (6 May 1709), he served as aide-de-camp to the duke of Marlborough. Bragg's advancement was urged by John, Earl Poulett, and Anthony Henley MP.

By 1 June 1715 Bragg had returned to Primrose's regiment (later the 24th foot). He entered the 3rd foot guards as captain and lieutenant-colonel on 17 March 1727 and between 1733 and 1735 was master of the Royal Hospital, Kilmainham. On 10 October 1734, after two years as lieutenant-colonel of William Hargrave's regiment, he succeeded to the colonelcy of the 28th foot, an appointment that lasted twenty-five years and which gave rise to the regimental nickname 'the Old Braggs'. In 1742, as a newly promoted brigadier-general, Bragg accompanied Lord Stair to Flanders. Further promotions to major-general on 5 July 1743 and lieutenant-general on 10 August 1747 followed. In September 1748, with the end of the War of the Austrian Succession, the duke of Cumberland took the unprecedented step of trying to disband the 28th foot in favour of a younger regiment. Cumberland's justification was the 28th foot's 'most infamous condition' (Royal Archives, Cumberland MS 39/143). Yet, as even Cumberland recognized, Bragg could not be held responsible for this. He was a general officer on the Irish staff and had been unable to oversee his regiment while it served in Flanders. It was left to the duke of Dorset, who as lord lieutenant of Ireland had been Bragg's patron, to secure the intervention of the Pelham ministry and save his client's command.

Bragg then entered the Irish parliament and represented the borough of Armagh from 1749 until his death, in Dublin, on 6 June 1759. His estate was valued at £7000, from which his will left £1000 (and his Dublin home) to Ann, the widow of Captain Robert Saunders, and the bulk of what remained to Lord George Sackville, the third son of the duke of Dorset and a former lieutenant-colonel of Bragg's regiment.   ALASTAIR W. MASSIE

Sources C. Dalton, ed., *English army lists and commission registers, 1661–1714*, 5–6 (1902–4); repr. (1960) · C. Dalton, *George the First's army, 1714–1727*, 2 vols. (1910–12) · Royal Arch., Cumberland MSS, 39/143, 40/283, 41/113, 41/118 · 'Memorial of Major-General Philip Bragg', March 1746, PRO, SP 63/409, fol. 107 · PRO, PROB 11/851 (384) · BL, Add. MS 35354, fol. 397 · BL, Blenheim MSS, Add. MS 61284, fols. 71, 73; 61589, fol. 98 · *Fourth report*, HMC, 3 (1874), 229 [Earl De La Warr MSS] · *GM*, 1st ser., 12 (1742), 108 · *GM*, 1st ser., 29 (1759), 293 · *Journals of the House of Commons of the kingdom of Ireland*, 8–11 (1753–61) · E. Childers and R. Stewart, *The story of the Royal Hospital, Kilmainham* (1921)

Archives PRO, SP 63/409, fol. 107 | BL, Blenheim MSS · BL, Hardwicke MSS · Royal Arch., Cumberland MSS

Wealth at death £7000: *Fourth report*, HMC, 3 (1874), 229 [Earl De La Warr MSS]

Bragg, **Sir William Henry** (1862–1942), physicist, was born at Westward, near Wigton in Cumberland, on 2 July 1862, the eldest of the three sons of Robert John Bragg

Sir William Henry Bragg (1862–1942), by Randolph Schwabe, 1932

(1830–1885), a merchant navy officer who became a farmer at Stoneraise Place, Westward. His mother, Mary (1833–1869), the daughter of Robert Wood, perpetual curate of Westward, died when he was seven years old. After her death he lived with his uncle William Bragg for six years in Market Harborough, Leicestershire, where he attended the grammar school. He went on to King William's College, Isle of Man, in 1875, and in 1881 entered Trinity College, Cambridge, as a scholar studying mathematics. Third wrangler in part I of the tripos in 1884, Bragg graduated with first-class honours in 1885.

Teaching in Australia, 1886–1909 Bragg accepted the Elder professorship at the University of Adelaide in 1886. While his responsibilities included lecturing on applied mathematics, he was primarily teaching physics, much of which he had not covered in his mathematical training at Cambridge. Bragg was forced to teach himself a great deal of this material. Soon after his arrival he met Gwendoline (1869–1929) whose father Charles *Todd FRS, postmaster-general and government astronomer of South Australia, had been instrumental in bringing Bragg to Adelaide; they married in 1889. They had three children, (William) Lawrence *Bragg (1890–1971), Robert (*b.* 1892), and Gwendoline Mary (*b.* 1907). The expenditure of Bragg's energies on teaching, lectures, and demonstrations, combined with the priority he gave to family life, meant that he published only three research papers in the eighteen years from his arrival until 1904, two in Australian journals. It was in this year that his research career might be said to have begun.

As president of section A (covering astronomy, mathematics, and physics) of the Australian Association for the Advancement of Science, Bragg presented 'On some recent advances into the theory of the ionization of gases' at their January 1904 meeting in Dunedin, New Zealand. Bragg discussed recent international developments in physics, which he decided to follow up with a series of experiments on the absorption of alpha particles. Through the years of instruction and demonstration Bragg had acquired considerable experimental skill, and was probably the first in Australia to set up an X-ray tube following their discovery in 1895. These skills became crucial as he embarked on his research career, and his work was received with interest abroad. Bragg's early results on alpha particles were seen as a confirmation of some predictions of Ernest Rutherford, the rising expert on radiation, who in the same year published a textbook, *Radio-Activity*, the first in its field. Bragg's research and publications catapulted him into the forefront of physicists attempting to explain the various newly discovered forms of radiation. He was elected FRS in 1907, and in 1908 was invited to take up the Cavendish professorship in physics at the University of Leeds.

Research on radiation Bragg arrived in 1909, and during his first three years at Leeds continued his research on radiation including alpha particles, beta rays, gamma rays, and X-rays. He continued to develop and make use of ionization chamber techniques and favoured a corpuscular model of some of these phenomena. In particular, he became an early champion of the particle-like nature of X-rays through one such corpuscular theory, the neutral pair hypothesis. This was the proposal that X-rays were corpuscles each made up of a pair of positive and negative particles, accounting for a combination of high penetration and weak ionization characteristics. By 1912 he became aware of the need for a theory which had both particle and wave aspects. While he was partially vindicated by the wave–particle duality of electromagnetic radiation supported by quantum mechanics, Bragg's specific mechanisms were only briefly supportable by his experimental evidence. In 1912 Bragg brought much of his work during this period together in his *Studies in Radioactivity*. The relationships formed and techniques developed during this time were very significant in the next phase of his research, which was to come in response to new experimental results coming out of Germany.

Discovery of X-ray crystallography, 1912–1915 In the summer of 1912 the results of some experiments done at Arnold Sommerfeld's institute at the University of Munich began to be received with great interest both within Germany and abroad. Bragg had briefly corresponded with Sommerfeld the year before and, as one of the top British physicists in the field, he was one of the first in the country to get news of these results. Max von Laue, with the assistance of W. Friedrich and P. Knipping, had produced a number of photographic plates displaying symmetrical patterns of spots. The spots had been created by the multiple deflection of a single beam of X-rays after passing through a crystal of zinc-blende, and these results led to the conclusion that X-rays could interfere in crystals and that consequently they should be considered as electromagnetic waves. This result was of crucial importance to a wide group of scientists working at the time, most notably those interested in the physics of radiation and those interested in the structure of matter, the crystallographers.

Bragg, working with his son William Lawrence, was among the first in Britain to begin to tackle the problem of explaining Laue's photographic plates. Laue's own explanation, that the crystal's symmetrical arrangement of atoms acted as a sort of diffraction grating, was soon questioned by Bragg and others, including Röntgen himself. Laue's formulae correctly predicted some of the spots' positions on the photographic plates, but the result seemed to be independent of the wavelength of the radiation. This was a major problem as wavelength was one of the crucial parameters for a wave explanation of the phenomenon. In addition, Bragg was faced with pressure from the crystallographers to take into account the parameters imposed by their discipline; among these were the Miller indices, which described the internal geometry of crystalline substances. Bragg was even publicly challenged to take crystallographic details into account by A. E. H. Tutton in the pages of *Nature*.

Acting in part on his son's suggestion, Bragg attempted to defend his corpuscular view of X-rays by proposing that Laue's spots were caused by X-ray corpuscles passing through gaps in the crystal structure. This explanation was soon superseded by his son's masterful synthesis of crystal structure concepts and wave mechanics. In this solution the spots were considered to be due to reflections from classes of reflecting planes within the crystal structure, each denoted by a set of Miller indices. This approach accounted for all of the spots and was dependent on wavelength and internal crystal symmetry. Bragg and his son immediately followed up with a very fruitful collaboration in which they began to explore crystal properties and structures. The techniques and tools they developed, the ionization spectrometer for example, drew heavily on Bragg's past work and expertise. These techniques became the basis of an entire field of scientific research, that of X-ray crystallography, which was to develop along many different lines in subsequent years, notably resulting in the discovery of the DNA double helix four decades later.

The year 1915 saw many changes in Bragg's life including the closure of the early period of collaboration with his son on X-ray diffraction. This was marked by the joint publication of *X-Rays and Crystal Structure*, which came to be the first basic text for the field of X-ray crystallography. This same year both Braggs, father and son, shared the Nobel prize in physics for their work over the previous three years. In addition there were changes in Bragg's academic life as he left Leeds for London to become the Quain professor of physics at University College. In terms of X-ray crystallographic work Bragg temporarily lost momentum owing to war research; he became a member of the Admiralty board of invention and research resulting in a period of time at the Naval Experiment Station at Hawkcraig and at Harwich working on submarine detection. War research, the completion of the work with his son Lawrence, and perhaps the loss of his younger son Robert in the Dardanelles that same year, all meant that X-ray crystallographic research did not become a full-time endeavour again until after the war.

Royal Institution, 1923–1942 Bragg was recognized for his war research by being made CBE (1917) and KBE (1920). His research environment changed again when he succeeded Sir James Dewar in the joint post of Fullerian professor of chemistry at the Davy–Faraday Research Laboratory and director of the Royal Institution in 1923. Bragg brought his students across from University College and established a very important centre of early X-ray crystal structure physics in the Davy–Faraday Laboratory. Among distinguished scientists who trained and worked there were Kathleen Lonsdale and J. D. Bernal. The area of research was limited to the structure of organic substances by unwritten agreement with his son, who worked on inorganic structures. His role at the Royal Institution provided a platform for Bragg's interest in communicating with a non-scientific audience. He was renowned for his skills of presentation and demonstration, notably through the regular Christmas lectures for young people. These were characterized by elegant means of explaining technical concepts, and several of them were published as books, including *The World of Sound* (1920) and *The Nature of Things* (1925). His wife died in 1929, only a few years after they had moved into the director's residence at the Royal Institution.

Although he had been awarded the Royal Society's Rumford medal in 1916, and been made an honorary fellow of Trinity College, Cambridge, in 1920, it was only after becoming director of the Royal Institution that Bragg began to be seen as one of the great statesmen of science in his day. In 1928 he presided over the Glasgow meeting of the British Association. He received the Royal Society's Copley medal in 1930 and served as president of the Physical Society from that year until 1932. In 1931 he was honoured with the Order of Merit, and served as president of the Royal Society from 1935 to 1940. He was often called upon to present scientific issues to a non-scientific audience; his 1941 Riddell memorial lecture at Durham University, 'Science and faith', provides a retrospective insight into his scientific career. He saw science as a collection of observations of nature, and the role of the researcher to arrange and extend the scope of these observations. Significantly, he observed that experimental physics often involved steps of faith in the pursuit of these objectives. It was this role to which he was committed until his death, at the director's residence in the Royal Institution, 21 Albemarle Street, London, on 12 March 1942. He was cremated on 19 March after a funeral in London, and a plaque was placed in Chiddingfold church, Surrey.   Talal Debs

Sources E. N. da C. Andrade, *Obits. FRS*, 4 (1942–4), 277–300 · P. Forman, 'Bragg, William Henry', *DSB* · Lord Rayleigh [J. W. Strutt], *Proceedings of the Physical Society*, 54 (1942) · L. Hoddeson, E. Braun, J. Teichman, and S. Weart, eds., *Out of the crystal maze: chapters from the history of solid-state physics* (1992) · R. H. Stuewer, 'William H. Bragg's corpuscular theory of X-rays and γ rays', *British Journal for the History of Science*, 5 (1970–71), 258–81 · W. L. Bragg, 'The diffraction of short electromagnetic waves by a crystal', *Proceedings of the Cambridge Philosophical Society*, 17 (1912–14), 43–57 · W. H. Bragg, 'On the properties and natures of various electric radiations', *London, Edinburgh, and Dublin Philosophical Magazine*, 6th ser., 14 (1907), 429–49 · A. E. H. Tutton, 'The crystal space-lattice revealed by Rontgen rays', *Nature*, 90 (1912–13), 306–9, esp. 307 · W. H. Bragg, 'Science and faith', Riddel memorial lecture, U. Durham, 7 March 1941 · L. Badash, 'Rutherford, Ernest', *DSB* · G. M. Carol, *William Henry Bragg: man and scientist* (1978) · private information (2004) · d. cert.

Archives Bodl. Oxf., corresp. relating to Society for Protection of Science and Learning · Royal Institution of Great Britain, London, corresp. and papers · RS, letters to Royal Society · U. Leeds, Brotherton L., notebook | CAC Cam., corresp. with A. V. Hill · CUL, corresp. with Lord Rutherford · Ransom HRC, letters to Sir Owen Richardson · Trinity Cam., corresp. with Sir Joseph John Thomson | FILM BFI NFTVA, current affairs footage

Likenesses W. Stoneman, photographs, 1920–38, NPG · E. Kennington, pencil drawing, 1927, Trinity Cam. · W. Nicholson, oils, 1932, Royal Institution of Great Britain, London · R. Schwabe, pencil drawing, 1932, NPG [*see illus.*] · C. E. S. Phillips, oils, 1939, Royal Institution of Great Britain, London · H. Knight, oils, RS · T. Purvis, pen-and-ink drawing, Royal Institution of Great Britain, London · W. Rothenstein, drawing, Carlisle; [in possession of city of Carlisle

Wealth at death £27,039 5s. 0d.: probate, 5 May 1942, *CGPLA Eng. & Wales*

Bragge, William (1823–1884), civil engineer and steel manufacturer, was born at Birmingham on 31 May 1823, the third son of Thomas Perry Bragge, a manufacturing jeweller. After some years of general tuition, Bragge studied practical engineering with two Birmingham firms, and in his leisure applied himself closely to the study of mechanics and mathematics. In 1845 he entered the office of a civil engineer, and soon after engaged in railway surveying. He acted first as assistant engineer and then as engineer-in-chief of part of the line from Chester to Holyhead.

Through the recommendation of Sir Charles Fox, Bragge was sent out to Brazil as the representative of Messrs Belhouse & Co., of Manchester, becoming superintending engineer for the construction of gas works in the city of Rio de Janeiro. This was followed by the survey of the first railway constructed in Brazil—the line from Rio de Janeiro to Petropolis—for which he received several distinctions from the emperor, Don Pedro. The emperor in later years visited Bragge at Sheffield. From Brazil, Bragge went to Buenos Aires, where he initiated gas, railway, and water works.

In 1858 Bragge left South America. He joined John Brown and John D. Ellis in a partnership which ran John Brown & Co.'s Atlas works in Sheffield. Bragge served as managing director alongside Ellis, with responsibilities for foreign trade. He was an accomplished linguist, and travelled across Europe, Russia, Egypt, and America. The rolling of armour plates, the manufacture of steel plates, the adoption of the helical railway buffer-spring, and other developments of the emerging heavy steel industry were matters in which he rendered other effective aid to his firm. In 1870 Bragge was chosen to be master cutler of Sheffield, and he was instrumental in the founding of Weston Park Museum, which included exhibitions of cutlery. The same year he was elected as a councillor in Sheffield, becoming chairman of the libraries committee and later an alderman. He was also active in the working men's club movement and the National Education League, and he was president of the School of Art.

In 1872 Bragge resigned his position of managing director to his firm, which had been converted into a limited company in 1864, and went over to Paris as engineer to the Société des Anglais, which had for its object the utilization of the sewage of a large part of Paris. The scheme proved unsuccessful, and resulted in a heavy monetary loss to the promoters. In 1876 Bragge returned to his native town of Birmingham, settling there, and developing a successful firm for the manufacture of watches by machinery on the American system. He played an active role in the life of Birmingham and its district. He was elected as a non-council representative on the city's libraries committee, and in the adjoining area of Handsworth he was a member of the local board.

In spite of his business commitments, Bragge found time to add to his numerous collections. Among these was a unique Cervantes collection, which included nearly every work written by or relating to the great Spanish writer. This collection, which consisted of 1500 volumes, Bragge presented to his native town, but it was destroyed in the fire at the Birmingham Free Library in 1879. A cabinet of gems and precious stones which Bragge collected from all parts of Europe was purchased for the Birmingham Art Gallery. The most remarkable collection formed by Bragge consisted of 13,000 pipes and smoking apparatus from all over the world, and many samples of snuff and tobacco; in 1880 Bragge published his *Bibliotheca nicotiana*, a catalogue of books about tobacco and objects connected with its use. This and a notable collection of manuscripts were later dispersed.

Bragge was a fellow of the Society of Antiquaries, of the Anthropological Society, of the Royal Geographical Society, and of many foreign societies.

On 14 July 1846 Bragge married Martha Beddow, the daughter of James Beddow, a druggist, and a sister of the Revd George Beddow; they had at least one son. Bragge died at his home, 59 Hall Road, Handsworth, on 6 June 1884. For some time before his death he was almost totally blind. He was buried at the old cemetery, Key Hill, Birmingham, on 10 June. G. B. SMITH, *rev.* CARL CHINN

Sources Birmingham Daily Post (9 June 1884) · Sheffield Daily Telegraph (9 June 1884) · Sheffield and Rotherham Independent (9 June 1884) · J. T. Bunce, History of the corporation of Birmingham, 2 (1885) · The Times (10 June 1884) · Brief hand list of the Cervantes collection, presented to the Birmingham Free Library, reference department, by William Bragge, 1874 · A. J. Grant, Steel and ships: the history of John Brown's (1950) · C. J. Erickson, British industrialists: steel and hosiery, 1850–1950 (1959) · m. cert.
Archives John Brown plc, London, John Brown & Co. business records
Likenesses E. W. Wyon, marble medallion, c.1866, Mappin Art Gallery, Sheffield
Wealth at death £8536 0s. 6d.: probate, 3 Sept 1884, CGPLA Eng. & Wales

Braham, John (1777?–1856), singer, was probably born on 20 March 1777 in London. The year of his birth has often been given as 1774, but two accounts published during his lifetime—in *The Harmonicon* (10, 1832, 1), and in the *Illustrated London News* (20 March 1852, 245)—clearly state 1777, a date also inferable from Sainsbury's *Dictionary of Musicians* (1827). Details of his early life are obscure. He was probably the youngest of the (at least) nine children of John Abraham, a German Jew (*d.* after 1779), and his wife, Esther Abrams (*d.* after 1798), and it is likely that he was educated at the Great Synagogue in Duke's Place, Aldgate, London. Following his father's death, his uncle, the tenor Michael Leoni (Myer Lyon), took responsibility for his care and taught him singing. He made his first stage appearance on 21 April 1787, when, using the form of his name by which he became famous, he sang at Covent Garden, where his solos included Arne's 'The soldier tir'd of war's alarms'. Between June 1787 and August 1788 he sang in at least five more performances at the Royalty, Covent Garden, and Haymarket theatres. On Leoni's emigration to Jamaica, Braham became a protégé of the financiers the Goldsmid brothers.

Early career Braham's voice settled as a tenor, and in 1794 he sang at Bath. Here he studied under Venanzio Rauzzini and met the internationally famous soprano Nancy *Storace (1765–1817) and her brother, the composer Stephen Storace, who engaged him to sing in his forthcoming opera *Mahmoud*, given its première (after the composer's death) on 30 April 1796 at Drury Lane. This work established the nineteen-year-old singer at the forefront of his profession. On 26 November 1796 he appeared at the King's Theatre in Grétry's *Zémire et Azor* and later performed in operas by Sacchini and Martín y Soler. To sing at the Italian Opera House was an extraordinary attainment for a Briton. Performances of sacred music added to his reputation.

By now Braham and Nancy Storace had established a relationship which outwardly lasted nearly twenty years. On 10 August 1797 she drew up a will bequeathing Braham £2000, and later that month they embarked on a highly successful continental tour which lasted until 1801. After eight months in Paris, where they sang to an audience that included Napoleon and Josephine and met Napoleon's brother Jerome, they went to Florence and performed in operas by Moneta and Basili. Braham deeply impressed Giacomo Davide, then the leading Italian tenor. For the season of December 1798 to March 1799 he sang at La Scala, Milan, in Nasolini's *Il trionfo di Clelia*, alongside another internationally famed British singer, the soprano Elizabeth Billington, whom he mortified by

John Braham (1777?–1856), by unknown artist, c.1834

imitating her favourite embellishments. (Later they were reconciled.) At Genoa he took composition lessons from Isola. In August 1799 Braham and Storace moved to Livorno, where they met Horatio Nelson and Emma Hamilton and the queen of Naples. On 26 December 1800, at Venice, they sang in an incomplete version of Cimarosa's *Artemisia*; the composer had recently died, and on 28 January 1801 Braham sang in his requiem mass. At Trieste they sang in Martín y Soler's *Una cosa rara*, then returned to London via Vienna and Hamburg.

Growing celebrity On 9 December 1801 Braham and Storace appeared at Covent Garden in *Chains of the Heart*, an indifferent piece by Mazzinghi and Reeve. Greater acclaim attended *The Cabinet* in February 1802. Braham wrote the music for his own part in this collaborative work, a practice that he maintained until 1828; he also composed all the music for *The English Fleet in 1342* (1803) and *The Paragraph* (1804). On 3 May 1802 Storace gave birth to their son, William Spencer Harris Braham. Braham was engaged at the King's Theatre for its seasons of 1804 to 1806. In 1805 his benefit performance of *Una cosa rara* 'drew one of the most crowded audiences ever known in that house, the overflowing of the pit actually filling the stage, until it was with great difficulty the performers could get on and off' (*The Harmonicon*, 10, 1832, 3). On 27 March 1806 he sang the role of Sesto in *La clemenza di Tito*—the first British performance of an opera by Mozart. His fees grew apace. At Drury Lane, where he was also engaged during 1805, his salary rose from £30 per week to £48 per week in 1807–8, and a benefit performance

brought more than £365. In 1809 he sang at the Theatre Royal, Dublin, for the unparalleled sum of 2000 guineas for fifteen nights. So popular was he that this engagement was extended to thirty-six nights at the same rate. Compositions and teaching (Nelson's wife was once a pupil) brought additional income.

The height of his powers It was said that 'Non c'è in Italia tenore come Braham' ('there is no tenor like Braham in Italy'; *The Harmonicon*, 10, 1832, 1). The *Quarterly Musical Magazine and Review* asserted that Braham possessed 'the most extraordinary genius and aptitude for the exercise of his profession that was ever implanted in a human being' (1, 1818, 86). His virtuoso technique, clear enunciation, and vividly dramatic interpretations were outstanding. In his prime his range was from low A to high F, including high C in full voice. As was conventional, he transferred to falsetto for high notes, but surpassed other performers in disguising this change. His admirers and social circle included the very highest members of society. George IV once postponed a royal concert which coincided with Braham's benefit. Charles Lamb declared, 'The little Jew has bewitched me … Braham's singing, when it is impassioned, is finer than Mrs. Siddons's or Mr. Kemble's acting! and when it is not impassioned it is as good as hearing a person of fine sense talking' (C. Lamb and M. Lamb, 2.351). (Lamb later wrote slightingly of Braham's conversion to Christianity.) His poor acting was accepted for the sake of his singing; Sir Walter Scott remarked that 'Braham was a beast of an actor, but an angel of a singer' (Warrack, 352). But he was frequently attacked for singing 'too much to the gallery' (*ILN*, 20 March 1852, 246). The *Quarterly Musical Magazine and Review* accused him of doing 'all that man could do to corrupt the taste, insult the understanding of his audience, and to lower his own estimation' (3, 1821, 386). His compositions give little guide to his vocal qualities, for they were tailored to the amateur market. His best-known work, 'The Death of Nelson' (incorporated in *The Americans* of 1811), was modelled on Méhul's French Revolutionary *Chant du départ*.

Domestic alterations Storace's husband, from whom she had long been separated, died in 1806, and thus she and Braham could have married, but they did not do so. Their relationship was at an end by 1815, when Braham had an affair with a Mrs Wright. The case came to public attention, and on 2 March 1816 there were disapproving reactions when he appeared at the King's Theatre; on 16 March he was hissed at Drury Lane. On 23 July Mr Wright brought an action against Braham for criminal conversation, and was awarded £1000 in damages. The architect John Soane acted as intermediary between Braham and Storace. Braham hotly disputed Storace's claim to ownership of various items, raging, 'She will have to my latest Breath my Abhorrence and Contempt. … Mean—Malicious and Despicable Wretch!!!' (26 March 1816). Storace replied, 'I have ever acted towards him with the greatest Honor and disinterestedness' (6 April 1816). Inevitably the increasingly bitter exchanges disturbed Spencer, then a schoolboy at Winchester College.

Braham soon left Mrs Wright. On 11 November 1816 he married the seventeen-year-old Frances (Fanny) Elizabeth Bolton (1799–1846) in Manchester. They made an odd, if devoted, couple: Braham, the senior by more than twenty years, was short (5 feet 3 inches), swarthy, and accounted very ugly; Fanny, the daughter of a Manchester dancing-master, was very tall, blonde, and considered a beauty. She was also completely stage-struck and socially ambitious. Between 1819 and 1829 they had six surviving children: the duke of Sussex was godfather to the second son, Augustus. Meanwhile, Nancy Storace died on 24 August 1817—her death, some suggested, hastened by the impact of Braham's marriage. Her will of 1797 was still in force, but Braham passed his inheritance to Spencer. Nancy's mother, Elizabeth Storace (whose funeral, in May 1821, Braham attended), took responsibility for the boy.

Braham's career continued unabated. In October 1819 he received 25 guineas per appearance at Drury Lane, with a minimum of twenty appearances, plus a benefit performance, and on 23 July 1824 he sang in the first major English production of Weber's opera *Der Freischütz*, at the Lyceum, for a weekly fee of £150. At the York festival of September 1825 he received 250 guineas. Here his repertoire included works by Handel (Braham was renowned for 'Deeper and deeper still … waft her angels' from *Jeph-tha*), Haydn, Salieri, Bishop, and Rossini. On 12 April 1826, at Covent Garden, he created the role of Huon in Weber's *Oberon*. Conscious that 'Braham knows his public, and is their idol' (Warrack, 352), at the singer's request Weber reluctantly altered his part (one item, 'Ruler of this awful hour', was added on the eve of the première). When Weber died soon afterwards, Braham was one of the committee responsible for the funeral arrangements, and he sang in Mozart's Requiem at the funeral service on 21 June 1826.

By 1830 Braham possessed a fortune estimated at £90,000, and he signed a twenty-one-year lease, at £250 per annum, for The Grange, a large property in Brompton, London. He favoured operatic works in the English mould, which had spoken sections and opportunities for interpolations of music of his own choice, and were thus less wearing vocally. He continued to divide opinion. In 1829 the visiting Belgian scholar Fétis reported that his voice was 'ruined, and he roars' (*The Harmonicon*, 7, 1829, 277); yet in November 1831 he was described as 'this ever-blooming favourite', his music in Auber's *Fra Diavolo* being 'rendered more effective here [Drury Lane] than even in Paris' (*The Harmonicon*, 9, 1831, 310), and in the Handel commemoration festival held at Westminster Abbey in 1834 he 'surpassed himself' (Mount Edgcumbe, *Musical Reminiscences*, 4th edn, 1834, 247–9). His contact with royalty continued: during the York festival of September 1835 he lunched with the future Queen Victoria and her mother, the duchess of Kent.

Theatrical ventures and financial difficulties In 1832 Braham had exclaimed, 'Thank God! I am not', when asked by a parliamentary committee if he were a theatre proprietor

('Select committee on dramatic literature', 1530). But, at the urging of his wife, on 18 May 1835 he became co-manager, with Frederick Yates, of the Colosseum, Regent's Park, investing £30,000, and on 20 May he purchased the site for a new theatre, which he opened as the St James's on 14 December 1835 at the cost of £26,000. Among the works given at the St James's in 1836–7 were three by Charles Dickens, including the unsuccessful *The Village Coquettes*, with music by J. P. Hullah, in which Braham took part.

Braham's theatrical ventures proved disastrous and cost him the financial fruits of his career. He was forced to revise plans for retiring, accepting engagements with minor performers such as Fanny Dickens (the author's sister). Braham was now in his sixties, and his voice dropped to the baritone range. In 1838 and 1839 he sang the title roles in Mozart's *Don Giovanni* and Rossini's *Guillaume Tell* at Drury Lane. His last stage appearance was in the latter work, on 7 February 1839. His financial worries remained. On 23 September 1840 he sang in Mendelssohn's *Lobgesang* under the composer's direction in the Birmingham festival, and on 1 October 1840 he left with his wife and eighteen-year-old son Charles, a tenor, for an American tour in an attempt to recoup losses. They returned to England on 25 January 1843. Braham gave concerts in London and the provinces with Charles and Hamilton, another son with aspirations as a singer, often accompanying himself at the piano. There were vain calls in the press for a government pension. His wife's theatrical enthusiasms and extravagance exacerbated the situation. She died on 16 February 1846, having suffered from a heart complaint. Braham's eldest daughter, Frances [see Fortescue, Frances Elizabeth Anne Parkinson- (1821–1879)], had married as her second husband the seventh Earl Waldegrave, a match that provided more rank than hard cash. She none the less provided financially for many members of her extended family, and on 30 November 1846 offered her father £2000 to discharge his debts and proposed to arrange an income of £600 per annum for life, which Braham accepted. Despite this injection of cash, during July 1849 he was compelled to go to Brussels while his creditors were pacified. In July 1851, to Braham's great annoyance, Spencer, now an Anglican clergyman who had become a minor canon at Canterbury Cathedral, officially changed his surname to Meadows, apparently because of scandals among his irascible half-family. Braham sang seldom. He gave his final concerts at Exeter Hall in March 1852, aged seventy-five. He had first appeared at Covent Garden sixty-five years previously. By now Sims Reeves was the leading British tenor. In 1853 Braham again went to the continent to avoid bankruptcy and imprisonment for debt, though he soon returned. After an illness he died peacefully at his home in Conduit Street, Hanover Square, London, on 17 February 1856, and was buried in Kensal Green cemetery.

For over thirty years Braham was a dominating character in British musical life. During much of this time he was the only native male singer of international quality, though he compromised artistic standards by pandering to audiences. The final twenty years of his life were darkened by financial worry. Nevertheless, in the words of *The Athenaeum's* obituary, 'Braham had enjoyment of life and of his art to the last' (*The Athenaeum*, 23 Feb 1856, 241).

GEORGE BIDDLECOMBE

Sources 'Memoir of John Braham', *The Harmonicon*, 10 (1832), 1–4 · *The Harmonicon*, 7 (1829), 277 · O. W. Hewett, *Strawberry fair: a biography of Frances, Countess Waldegrave, 1821–1879* (1956) · Highfill, Burnim & Langhans, *BDA* · *ILN* (20 March 1852), 245–6 · Sir John Soane's Museum, London, Nancy Storace MSS · 'Sketch of the state of music in London', *Quarterly Musical Magazine and Review*, 3 (1821), 379–99, esp. 386–7 · G. Brace, *Anna Susanna: Anna Storace, Mozart's first Susanna* (1991) · J. Girdham, 'The last of the Storaces', *MT*, 129 (1988), 17–18 · C. B. Hogan, ed., *The London stage, 1660–1800*, pt 5: *1776–1800* (1968) · J. Warrack, *Carl Maria von Weber*, 2nd edn (1976) · *The works of Charles and Mary Lamb*, ed. E. V. Lucas, 7 vols. (1903–5), vols. 1–2 · D. Reynolds, ed., *Weber in London, 1826* (1976) · *The Times* (24 July 1816), 3 · J. M. Levien, *The singing of John Braham* (1945) · playbills, 1839, Drury Lane Theatre · 'Select committee on dramatic literature', *Parl. papers* (1831–2), vol. 7, no. 679 · *Oxberry's Dramatic Biography*, 3/41 (1825), 145–59

Archives Som. ARS, corresp. and papers | Sir John Soane's Museum, London, Nancy Storace MSS · Som. ARS, Strachey MSS

Likenesses oils, *c*.1800, Garr. Club · etching, 1802 (after R. Dighton), NPG · A. Cardon, stipple, pubd 1806 (after J. G. Wood), BM, NPG · S. De Wilde, drawing, 1819, NPG · miniature, *c*.1834, NPG [*see illus.*] · R. Dighton, drawing, NPG · W. M. Thackeray, pencil sketch, V&A · forty-two prints, Harvard TC

Braham, John Robert Daniel (1920–1974), air force officer, was born at the manse, Holcombe, Somerset, on 6 April 1920, the only son (there was also a daughter) of Ernest Goodall Braham, a Church of England clergyman and himself a Royal Flying Corps pilot in the First World War, and his wife, Ethel Randall. He was educated at Taunton School, Somerset, but left before he was seventeen to work in the Lancashire county police as a boy clerk in Wigan. In December 1937 he applied for a short-service commission in the RAF, and to his evident amazement was accepted and sent for elementary flying training in 90 m.p.h. Tiger Moths. He received his wings at Shawbury near Shrewsbury in 1938. Though chafing to fly single-engined fighters, by the outbreak of war he was still flying twin-engined Blenheim F1 night fighters in 29 squadron from Debden, Essex. With several pilots called John already in his squadron, Braham's radio call sign became Bob, and this remained his service nickname for the rest of his career.

On 24 August 1940, flying from Digby, Lincolnshire, Braham downed his first victim—a Norwegian-based Heinkel III night intruder— over the North Sea off Spurn Head. In 1941 he teamed up with his remarkable navigator and operator of the then new airborne AI radar set, William James Gregory, known as Sticks because of his proficiency as a drummer. This pair became the most formidable night-fighting combination in the RAF. By 12 November the thrice-decorated Braham had destroyed twelve enemy aircraft and in 1942 he was posted to command 141 squadron at Ford, near Chichester, Sussex, as the youngest wing commander in the RAF. After a period supporting Coastal Command based at Predannock, Cornwall, in 1943 Braham was switched to the experimental task of escorting bomber streams over Europe. For this purpose sensitive Serrate detectors were fitted into Beaufighters—aircraft which had been developed by the Bristol Aircraft Company from the 'Britain First', with substantial private sponsorship.

In February 1944, after his twentieth victory, nineteen of them at night, Braham was taken off intruder and escort work and put in charge of night operations at 2 light bomber group headquarters. Typically he extracted an understanding from his air officer commanding, Basil Embry, that he would still be allowed a 'ration' of operational flights. After he had raised his score to twenty-nine, and now uniquely entitled to wear the ribbons of both the DSO and the DFC, each with two silver rosettes denoting two bars, Braham's luck ran out over Denmark on 25 June 1944. He was jumped by a Focke Wulf FW 190 flown by the German ace Robert Spreckels, and forced down on to a Danish beach. Braham flew 316 operational sorties and was hit eleven times in forty-one attacks on his aircraft. He also survived five crash landings.

Braham was developing combat fatigue. Despite his consummate low-flying ability he had already had a brush with some trees and had also once even grazed the ground in a Mosquito. Some felt he owed his life to spending the last ten months of the war in Stalag Luft 3 at Sagan, near Breslau. But for the intervention of a lone SS soldier in black battledress, he and his navigator, the Australian Donald Walsh, might well have been lynched by a hostile crowd aboard the train carrying them to interrogation. Braham was liberated by the British 11th armoured division near Lübeck on 2 May 1945. He was wearing the tunic in which he had been shot down. Depressed by what he perceived as a work-shy post-war Britain, Braham in May 1952 sailed with his wife and his three young sons to take up a commission in the Royal Canadian Air Force. He was posted as a group captain to SHAPE headquarters in Paris in 1960.

Since 1914 only ten British officers had ever been six times decorated for gallantry. Braham, who was one of these, uniquely achieved a seventh decoration: in 1951 he was awarded the AFC for hazardous developmental work on all-weather fighter aircraft. He was also awarded by the Belgians their Croix de Guerre and the order of the Crown. His book '*Scramble!*' was published in London in 1961 and described frankly and modestly the unrelenting exploits of one of the sharpest thorns in the side of the Luftwaffe. In April 1941 he married Joan Helen, the daughter of Edward Hyde, a grocer, of Leicester. Braham died in Halifax, Nova Scotia, on 7 February 1974.

NORRIS MCWHIRTER, *rev.*

Sources J. R. D. Braham, '*Scramble!*' (1961); repr. (1985) · D. F. Aris, unpublished biography of Braham, Ministry of Defence, Air Historical branch

Likenesses photographs, repro. in Braham, '*Scramble!*'

Braham, Robert (*fl.* 1555), literary editor, is known to posterity solely by his 'pistle to the reader' that prefaces the edition of John Lydgate's *Troy Book*, published by Thomas

Marshe in 1555. Braham offers a critique of earlier versions of the Troy legend, particularly William Caxton's *Recuyell of the Histories of Troy* (1476) which he feels trivialized its subject, making it more 'worthye to be numbered amongest the trifelinge tales of Robyn Hode, & Beuys of Hampton, than remain as a monument to so worthy a history'. He also criticizes Richard Pynson's 1513 edition of Lydgate's work: 'suche was the ignorance of both the prynter and correctour … that the sentence and consequentlye the historye is so confused and obscured, that in most places, there can be almost nothinge gathered therof'. There is some irony in this judgement since, in the view of the modern editor of the *Troy Book*, Marshe's edition is 'the poorest of all the texts' (Lydgate, 61). Braham does praise Lydgate himself ('the verye perfect disciple and imitator of the great Chaucer') as well as Chaucer's first editor, William Thynne.

A. S. G. EDWARDS

Sources J. Lydgate, *Lydgate's Troy book: AD 1412–20*, ed. H. Bergen, 4, EETS, extra ser., 126 (1935), 62–5

Brahms, Caryl. *See* Abrahams, Doris Caroline (1901–1982).

Braid, James (1795–1860), surgeon and hypnotist, son of James Braid and his wife, Anne Suttie, was born on 19 June 1795 at Ryelaw in a detached part of the parish of Portmoak, Kinross, Scotland. His father owned land in Ryelaw and in neighbouring Walkerton, near Leslie, Fife. Braid was apprenticed to the surgeons Charles Anderson (father and son) in Leith, and he also attended classes at Edinburgh University in 1812–14; he obtained the diploma of LRCS (Edinburgh) in 1815. On 17 November 1813 he married Margaret Mason or Meason at St Cuthbert's Church, Edinburgh; they had a son, James (*b.* 1822), and a daughter. In 1816 Braid was appointed surgeon to Lord Hopetoun's mines at Leadhills, Lanarkshire, and in 1825 set up in private practice at Dumfries, where he was briefly in partnership with William Maxwell, a friend of Robert Burns. On the recommendation of a Mr Petty, a Mancunian patient, Braid moved to Manchester, and by 1828 he was established there at 67 Piccadilly. He remained in Manchester for the rest of his life, his final address being 212 Oxford Street. His competence as a surgeon won him a solid practice and his geniality many friends. He was also noted for his compassion towards patients too poor to pay a fee.

Braid published papers on the surgical treatment of club-foot and of strabismus, in which he seems to have specialized, but it is entirely for his work with hypnosis that he is remembered. His interest in this subject began in November 1841, when he attended a demonstration by the French mesmerist Charles Lafontaine. After reflecting on Lafontaine's performances, and experimenting for himself, Braid came to believe that he had discovered the key to mesmeric phenomena and cures. Beginning on 27 November 1841 he set forth his views and demonstrated his methods in a series of five public lectures (reported in detail in the *Manchester Guardian* and the *Manchester Courier*); and the ideas and practices there first adumbrated took firmer shape in his only full-length book, *Neurypnology, or, The Rationale of Nervous Sleep* (1843). Braid

James Braid (1795–1860), by unknown engraver, 1851

held that the 'mesmeric sleep' (to which he gave the name 'hypnotism') was not due to the transfer of 'mesmeric fluid' or 'animal magnetism' from operator to patient, but was a peculiar nervous state, not to be equated with sleep and probably involving changes in cerebral circulation. It was most readily induced by protracted visual fixation of a small bright object held above the eyes and about 8 to 15 inches away.

This 'nervous sleep' had two phases. In the first there was a great exaltation of all the special senses except vision, and of some mental faculties, together with a disposition to retain limbs in positions in which they had been placed. After a while these limbs assumed a cataleptic rigidity, and the patient began to pass into a second phase in which there was a general tonic rigidity of the musculature and a 'profound torpor' of the organs of special sense. The pulse, however, was greatly accelerated. Particular limbs or sense organs could be restored to functioning by directing a brief current of air at them or (in the case of limbs) by administering pressure or a blow over the rigid muscles. The muscular rigidity inhibited circulation in the affected limbs, and redirected blood to the brain, nervous system, and other parts. When a limb was released from rigidity blood flowed into it with especial vigour. It was to these changes in circulation that Braid attributed the curative effects of hypnotism, of which he cited numerous examples from his own practice. Subjects might be returned to normal wakefulness by blowing on or lightly pressing their eyeballs.

At this period Braid believed in, and thought he had achieved, the phenomena of 'phrenomesmerism' (the effects of mesmerically stimulating the various phrenological 'organs'), and he advanced a somewhat specious physiological (non-mesmeric) explanation of them. He did not subsequently refer to these supposed phenomena, no doubt because he quickly developed a sound appreciation (not then common) of the various possible sources of error in hypnotic and related experimentation.

Braid never wrote a full-scale revision of his ideas,

though he intended to do so. His later, considerably changed, views were developed in a series of articles and pamphlets, several of them responses to contemporary publications. The most significant, perhaps, are *The Power of the Mind over the Body* (1846), *Magic, Witchcraft, Animal Magnetism, Hypnotism, and Electro-Biology* (1852), and *Hypnotic Therapeutics, Illustrated by Cases* (1853). Braid continued to induce the 'hypnotic sleep' principally, though not entirely, by his eye fixation technique, and he continued to regard that sleep as divided into two stages, which he now termed the 'sub-hypnotic or partial state of the nervous sleep' and the 'full or double consciousness stage of the sleep'. The former was a state of 'monoideism' in which, through concentrating upon some indifferent object, the critical faculties were stilled, and imagination, swayed by suggestion and self-suggestion, took control. The stage of 'double consciousness' was a further development of the preceding state, attained by only a limited number of subjects. The subject entered a sleep-like or somnambulic state, usually with retained responsiveness to suggestion, and afterwards could not remember what took place unless once again put into the hypnotic sleep.

As for the hypnotic treatment of ailments, in addition to the beneficial effects of physically induced changes in the circulation Braid now postulated a direct influence of the mind, stimulated by appropriate suggestions—on particular mental and physiological functions and organs. His own practice utilized both approaches.

Braid died at 212 Oxford Street, Chorlton upon Medlock, Manchester, after a few hours of illness, on 25 March 1860, and was buried at the parish church of Neston, Cheshire. He was survived by his wife, son, also a surgeon, and daughter. He was described by a correspondent in the *Manchester City News* (16 February 1895) as having 'massive imperturbable features, reminding one of a colossal Egyptian head', with 'a full, penetrating eye … brilliantly dark'. The various pictures of Braid which appear in books on hypnotism derive, often at several removes, from a lithograph by Edward Cocking.

Braid's writings are characterized by robust common sense and sound medical knowledge rather than by any special scientific or literary gifts. His work on hypnosis gained some recognition from the British medical profession during his lifetime, but after his death was largely forgotten. Towards the end of the nineteenth century he began to be hailed, because of his later emphasis on 'suggestion' as the clue to many hypnotic and related phenomena, as a forerunner of the celebrated Nancy school of hypnotism. However his direct influence on that school was probably slight. He may have had a more direct influence on the rival school of the Salpêtrière in Paris. During the 1860s a number of French medical men, following E. Azam, P. Broca, and J. P. Durand de Gros, had begun to try out Braid's earlier methods and ideas as laid down in *Neurypnology*. The work of these writers (nicknamed 'Braidists') was known at the Salpêtrière, where in the late 1870s, under the direction of the great neurologist J. M. Charcot, hypnotism first became a scientifically acceptable subject of study. The Salpêtrière school thought of hypnotism as having physiologically definable stages (catalepsy, lethargy, and somnambulism), initiated and terminated by particular physical stimuli. This has a marked similarity to Braid's early ideas.

ALAN GAULD

Sources J. M. Bramwell, 'James Braid: his work and writings', *Proceedings of the Society for Psychical Research*, 12 (1896–7), 127–66 · G. Fletcher, 'James Braid of Manchester', *BMJ* (26 Oct 1929), 776–7 · N. M. Kravis, 'James Braid's psychophysiology: a turning point in the history of psychiatry', *The American Journal of Psychiatry*, 145 (1988), 1191–206 · A. Gauld, *A history of hypnotism* (1992), 230, 279–88 · J. M. Bramwell, *Hynotism: its history, practice and theory* (1930), 21–9, 40–41, 278–94, 460–67 · *The Lancet* (31 March 1860) · *Medical Times and Gazette* (7 April 1860), 355 · letter, *Medical Times and Gazette* (14 April 1860), 386 · *Manchester Guardian* (26 March 1860) · *Manchester Courier* (31 March 1860) · parish register (birth), Portmoak, Perth and Kinross Council Archives, 19 June 1795 · CGPLA Eng. & Wales (1860) · IGI

Likenesses E. Cocking, lithograph, 1850–54, JRL · lithograph, 1851, Wellcome L., London [*see illus.*]

Wealth at death under £3000: administration, 9 May 1860, CGPLA Eng. & Wales

Braid, James (1870–1950), golfer, was born at Liberty Place, Elie, Fife, on 6 February 1870, the son of James Braid, ploughman and later forester, and his second wife, Mary Harris. He began very early to play golf, was a caddie, and won boys' competitions. Elie and its immediate neighbour Earlsferry were then a nursery of famous golfers—notably the brothers Jack and Archie Simpson, and Douglas Rolland, a cousin of Braid's—and the boy James on leaving school at thirteen was anxious to take up golf professionally. His parents did not approve and he was apprenticed to a joiner in a neighbouring village. His golf was thus confined to Saturday afternoons and summer evenings, but at sixteen he had won the scratch medal of the Earlsferry Thistle club with a record score. At nineteen he went to work as a joiner in St Andrews, where he played with Hugh and Andrew Kirkaldy and other leading golfers, and at twenty-one he moved to Edinburgh. There he joined the Edinburgh Thistle club and won the important amateur competition open to all Edinburgh golfers on the Braid hills.

In the autumn of 1893 Braid's boyhood friend Charles Ralph Smith, then head clubmaker at the Army and Navy Stores in London, suggested that Braid should work under him, and although he had never then made a club, he accepted the offer and headed south. He remained at the stores for nearly three years, playing weekend golf on London courses. In 1894 he played in his first open professional competition at Stanmore, where he finished fifth, and soon after was tenth in the open championship at Sandwich. He first became widely known at the end of 1895, through halving an exhibition match with John Henry Taylor, then open champion, at West Drayton.

In 1896 Braid was appointed professional at Romford, where he stayed until 1904, when he became the first professional at Walton Heath: he remained there for the rest of his life. After his match with Taylor, Braid became recognized as one of the best golfers of the day, a very long driver and a magnificent iron player, although his putting remained a weak point for several years until he adopted the aluminium club with which he became one of the best putters of his time. He was second in the championship of 1897, beaten by one stroke by Harold Hilton. He won it for the first time at Muirfield in 1901 with a score of 309. About this time Harry Vardon, Braid, and Taylor emerged as the three leading golfers under the name of the Triumvirate, although Braid did not win the open again until 1905 at St Andrews with 318. He won at Muirfield in 1906 with 300, at Prestwick in 1908 with a wonderful score of 291, and at St Andrews in 1910 with 299. He was thus open champion four times in six years, then a unique achievement.

Braid also won the *News of the World* tournament—officially recognized as the professional match-play championship—in 1903, 1905, 1907, and 1911, and the French championship in 1910. His eyes, into which lime had accidentally been thrown when he was a boy, had always troubled him to some extent and did so more as he grew older. This may explain his winning no more great events after 1911, although he remained a very fine golfer, and in 1927, at the age of fifty-seven, was runner-up to Archie Compston in the *News of the World* tournament over his beloved Walton Heath.

Braid played no outstanding single challenge match during his career, but several foursomes; in particular that in 1905 in which he and Alexander Herd for Scotland met Vardon and Taylor for England. It was played over four links—St Andrews, Troon, Lytham and St Anne's, and Deal—and the Englishmen won by thirteen up and twelve to play. Braid never ceased to play with a youthful enthusiasm: he could usually be relied upon to go round Walton Heath in a score under the number of his own years, and on his eightieth birthday, a wet stormy day, he holed the course in 81. In his later years he did much work as a golf architect, travelling extensively throughout the British Isles; he helped to lay out, among many other courses, Gleneagles and Blairgowrie, and also remodelled some of the historic championship links such as the medal (now the championship) course at Carnoustie. Braid married on 18 November 1898 Minnie Alice (1874–1939), daughter of Henry Wright, labourer of Upminster, with whom he had two sons: James (*b.* 1899) and Harry Muirfield (*b.* 1901), both of whom subsequently worked in the whisky trade. He died in a nursing home at 31 Queen's Gate, London, on 27 November 1950, after an operation, and was buried at St Peter's Church, Walton on the Hill.

In his best years Braid weighed 12 stone 6 pounds and he was 6 feet 1½ inches in height. He was a man of quiet and reserved nature, who would never rashly commit himself, and he possessed great discretion and common sense. The latter qualities were vital in somebody whose regular playing companions at Walton Heath included at various times Lloyd George, Churchill, Edward, prince of Wales (the future Edward VIII), Lord Riddell, and Dr W. G. Grace. As a player he combined a cool, steady nerve with dash and boldness. He had a natural dignity, a pleasant sense of humour, and a remarkable power of inspiring affection among all who knew him. A shrewd businessman and negotiator, Braid was instrumental in the foundation of the Professional Golfers' Association, and was made an honorary member of the Walton Heath and Royal and Ancient golf clubs. A room was named in his honour in the clubhouse at Walton Heath, and was adorned with memorabilia from a golfing life of unique richness, variety, and success.

BERNARD DARWIN, *rev.* RICHARD FISHER

Sources J. Braid, *Advanced golf* (1908) · B. Darwin, *James Braid* (1952) · J. F. Moreton, *The golf courses of James Braid* (1996) · J. Braid and others, *A book of golf*, ed. E. F. Benson and E. H. Miles (1903) · H. Leach, *Great golfers in the making* (1907) · *Golf*, Badminton Library (1902) · private information (1959) · personal knowledge (1959)
Archives clubhouse of the Walton Heath golf club, Surrey, memorabilia, clubs, balls, photographs, etc. relating to him | FILM BFI NFTVA, news footage
Likenesses C. Flower, group portrait, 1913, Royal and Ancient Golf Club, St Andrews; *see illus. in* Vardon, Henry William (1870–1937) · J. Gunn, portrait, Walton Heath golf club, Surrey, NPG · B. Partridge, caricature, pen, pencil, and water colour, V&A · Spy [L. Ward], caricature, lithograph, repro. in *VF* (26 June 1907) · photograph, Walton Heath golf club, Surrey · photographs, repro. in J. F. Moreton, *James Braid* (1996)
Wealth at death £29,297 6*s.* 7*d.*: administration, 17 March 1951, CGPLA Eng. & Wales

Braidley, Benjamin (1792–1845), religious author, the son of Benjamin Braidley, a farmer, was born at Sedgefield, co. Durham, on 19 August 1792. He was apprenticed to a firm of linen importers in Manchester, and in 1813 became an active worker in the Bennett Street Sunday schools. In 1815 1635 pupils received prizes for regular attendance, and in 1816 2020 scholars were on the rolls of the schools. By the 1830s his was the largest Anglican Sunday school in Manchester. In 1830 Braidley was constable, and in 1831 and 1832 boroughreeve of Manchester. He was also high constable of the hundred of Salford. In 1835 he was twice unsuccessful Conservative candidate for Manchester. Braidley visited America in 1837, and his diary during his visit shows his great interest in education, the slavery question, and religion, seen from an evangelical standpoint. He was a commission agent, and became wealthy, but through the failure of the Northern and Central Bank he lost the greater part of his fortune.

Braidley was the author of *Sunday School Memorials* (1831), which has short biographies of persons connected with the Bennett Street Sunday schools. This work, some portions of which first appeared in the *Christian Guardian*, passed through four editions, the last of which, greatly enlarged, was published in 1880 as *Bennett Street Memorials*. Braidley also contributed to the *Shepherd's Voice*, a religious magazine, and wrote several tracts in a local controversy about the doctrines of the Church of Rome. He died, unmarried, of 'apoplexy' on 3 April 1845.

E. C. A. AXON, *rev.* H. C. G. MATTHEW

Sources W. Harper, *Memoir of Benjamin Braidley* (1845) · H. Taylor, 'Memoir', *Bennett Street memorials: a record of Sunday school work*, ed. G. Milner (1880)
Likenesses portrait, repro. in Taylor, 'Memoir'

Braidwood, James (1800–1861), fire officer, was born at Edinburgh, the son of a builder and cabinet-maker. His grandfather, a strict sabbatarian, was one of the 'Bowhead saints'. After attending Edinburgh high school he trained blanket, he entered the cellar and removed two kegs of gunpowder stored there.

Such was Braidwood's reputation that in the summer of 1832, when the insurance companies agreed to co-operate in running the London Fire Engine Establishment, he was appointed superintendent in overall command of the new joint force. He welded the previously competing units into a single brigade, which came into being on 1 January 1833. His men were unable to save the Houses of Parliament (16 October 1834) which, being uninsured public buildings, were not strictly the force's responsibility, but by some accounts they were instrumental in saving Westminster Hall. The 120 full-time firemen still represented a comparatively small force, but they succeeding in dealing with major fires which broke out in London during the 1850s, and were called upon to deal with the Windsor Castle fire in March 1853. His paper on fires delivered to the Royal Society of Arts in 1856 showed some modifications in his practice since his earlier treatise; he came to prefer recruiting former seamen to the fire service, citing their discipline, experience of 24-hour watches, and willingness to live in the confined quarters of a fire station. He was noted as kind to his men, who held him in great affection. He was on call all night through a speaking tube beside his bed at his Watling Street headquarters, where the gaslight in his bedroom was always illuminated so that he could respond quickly to an emergency.

Braidwood, who became an associate of the Institution of Civil Engineers in 1833, applied his knowledge of building structures to encourage fire prevention. In his evidence (17 June 1843) to the royal commission on the state of large towns and populous districts, he advocated airtight floors in all buildings and brick dividing-walls in domestic buildings. Acting as an unofficial adviser on fire prevention to the government and other bodies, he pressed for building regulations to take fire risks into account. He made many practical improvements to fire engines and fire escapes. He was married to Mary Ann Jane Braidwood, with whom he had six children. He also had one stepson and supported two of his own unmarried sisters.

Braidwood died in the course of his duties on 22 June 1861 at Tooley Street, London, the scene of an enormous fire which broke out in six-storey riverside warehouses packed with inflammable materials. Investigating the blaze on its first night (it raged for two weeks, setting the Thames ablaze with molten tallow), he was crushed and buried under a wall when a warehouse containing saltpetre exploded; the iron fire-resisting doors, which Braidwood had recommended to be installed in all such warehouses, had been left open. His body was recovered two days later and was buried at Abney Park cemetery on 29 June. Queen Victoria sent her condolences to his widow, and his funeral procession, the longest since that for the duke of Wellington, stretched for a mile and a half.

One of the last of the insurance company fire chiefs, Braidwood was the most celebrated firefighter of his time, and his death was marked by many memorials. Yet he was a quiet, unassuming man, who avoided the pomp and

James Braidwood (1800–1861), by unknown photographer

as a surveyor, working for a while in his father's business. In October 1824, when the Edinburgh Fire Engine Establishment was founded, he was appointed the first master of fire engines. In the following month (15 November 1824) the great fire of Edinburgh broke out in the High Street, burning down the steeple of the Tron Church. Braidwood could do little to prevent the fire's advance, but in its aftermath imposed his authority on the new brigade. Dividing the city into districts, he drilled his men weekly at 4 o'clock in the morning and soon developed an efficient force. A measure of his success was a marked reduction in the proportion of fires which resulted in total losses to property. He described his pioneering firefighting methods in *On the construction of fire engines and apparatus, the training of firemen, and the method of proceeding in cases of fire* (1830). He preferred to recruit firemen from the building trade, on the grounds of their familiarity with structures and, in the case of slaters, fearlessness on rooftops. He believed it to be essential that water should be directed at the root of the flames, regarding the practice of directing hoses from the safety of the street as generally ineffective, and was credited with establishing the distinctive principle of British fire-fighting that, under the command of their officers, firemen should enter burning buildings to reach the source of the fire. During the commotion of a fire he gave orders to his men through coded signals using a high-pitched bosun's pipe. His own coolness and daring were conspicuous during a fire in an ironmonger's shop in Hunter's Square; covered in a wet paraphernalia of continental fire brigades. Although acknowledged as the leading authority in his field, he always gave serious consideration to advice from any quarter. He was a man of deep piety, belonging to Dr Cummings's Church of Scotland congregation in London, and taking part in the charitable work of organizing ragged schools. His greatest achievement was to apply order and science to the practice of tackling fires. His collected papers, published posthumously as *Fire Prevention and Fire Extinction* (1866), embodied principles which were still regarded as tenets of good fire brigade organization a century later (Blackstone, 105). A plaque was erected to his memory in Tooley Street, near the spot where he met his death. M. C. CURTHOYS

Sources 'Memoir', J. Braidwood, *Fire prevention and fire extinction* (1866) · *GM*, 3rd ser., 11 (1861), 212 · G. V. Blackstone, *A history of the British fire service* (1957) · P. G. M. Dickson, *The Sun Insurance office, 1710–1860* (1960) · C. Knight, ed., *The English cyclopaedia: biography*, 6 vols. (1856–8) · S. Maunder, *The biographical treasury*, new edn, rev. W. L. R. Cates (1870) · d. cert.

Likenesses figure, Staffordshire china, c.1850, repro. in Blackstone, *History of the British fire service*, 193 · Jeens, engraving, repro. in Braidwood, *Fire prevention and fire extinction*, frontispiece · engraving, repro. in Blackstone, *History of the British fire service*, 193 · photograph, London Fire Brigade [*see illus.*]

Wealth at death £5000: probate, 27 July 1861, CGPLA Eng. & Wales

Braidwood, Thomas (1715–1806), teacher of deaf people, was born in Scotland and educated at Edinburgh University. He was for some time assistant in the grammar school at Hamilton, and afterwards opened a mathematical school in Edinburgh. In 1764 a boy of thirteen named Charles Sherriff, who had lost his hearing at the age of three, was placed with him to learn writing; in a few years Braidwood had taught him to speak. At about the end of 1768 some lines purporting to be by Sherriff, on seeing Garrick act, appeared in the London newspapers and called attention to the case. In 1807 these were reprinted in the *Gentleman's Magazine*, in which a writer who signed himself A said the verses were really written by Caleb Whitefoord as a means of getting an introduction to Garrick. Sherriff became a successful miniature painter in London, Bath, Brighton, and the West Indies. Lord Monboddo, in his *Of the Origin and Progress of Language* (1773), wrote that Sherriff 'both speaks and writes good English'. On the other hand A said he never could understand Sherriff, whom he knew well.

Encouraged by his success with Sherriff, Braidwood devoted himself to the teaching of the mute from his address at Craigside House (later 93 and 95 Dumbiedyke Road), Edinburgh. His only mechanical aid was a small silver rod 'about the size of a tobacco-pipe', flattened at one end and having a bulb at the other; this he used to place the tongue in the correct positions. Hugh Arnot, in his *History of Edinburgh* (1779), said of Braidwood's method that 'He shows them the use of words in expressing visible objects, and their qualities. After this he proceeds to instruct them in the proper arrangement of words, or grammatical construction of language' (Law, 188). From about 1770 Braidwood was assisted by his relative John

Braidwood. Samuel Johnson visited the institution in 1773 and called it a 'subject of philosophical curiosity … which no other city has to show; a college of the deaf and dumb, who are taught to speak, to read, to write, and to practise arithmetic'. He set a sum for the pupils and 'wrote one of his *sesquipedalia verba*', which was pronounced to his satisfaction. He said of the pupils that they 'hear with the eye'; they numbered 'about twelve'. Arnot said that the pupils were 'mostly from England, but some also from America'. Francis Green mentions that there were 'about twenty pupils' in 1783. Braidwood also taught sign language.

In 1783 Braidwood moved his academy to London, the king, according to Green, having promised £100 a year from his private purse to help to make it a public institution. Braidwood established himself at Grove House, Mare Street, Hackney, where he died on 24 October 1806, in his ninety-first year. John Braidwood, his partner, was born in 1756, married Thomas Braidwood's daughter in 1782, and died on 24 September 1798, at Hackney, of a pulmonary complaint. He was survived by his wife, two sons, Thomas and John, and two daughters. The academy was continued by his widow and his sons.

ALEXANDER GORDON, *rev.* MICHAEL BEVAN

Sources *GM*, 1st ser., 77 (1807), 37–8, 130, 305–6 · A. Law, *Education in Edinburgh in the eighteenth century* (1965), 187–90 · O. Checkland, *Philanthropy in Victorian Scotland* (1980) · F. Green, *"Vox oculis subjecta": a dissertation on the … art of imparting speech … to the naturally deaf and … dumb … by a parent* (1783)

Brailes, William de (*fl. c.*1230–1260), manuscript artist, whose signature, W. de Brail', appears in two illustrated manuscripts of the mid-thirteenth century, is almost certainly identifiable as the William de Brailes named in five Oxford property deeds of c.1230–1260. Although the documents do not specify William's trade, one deed names him as witness along with three illuminators, three bookbinders, and a parchment maker. He lived in Catte Street, approximately on the present site of All Souls College chapel, within the area around St Mary's Church where the Oxford book trade was concentrated. Differences of style within the manuscripts containing the signature show that he worked with several other artists. Art historians have concluded that William de Brailes was the head of a workshop of manuscript artists based at his tenement in Catte Street.

Brailes's name implies that he came originally from Upper or Lower Brailes (Warwickshire), near Shipston-on-Stour. His signature in the manuscripts accompanies a depiction of a tonsured figure who does not wear the habit of any religious order. William was probably a clerk in minor orders. One of the Oxford documents mentions that he had a wife, Celena.

Brailes and his assistants decorated about a dozen surviving manuscripts. These include several Bibles; a psalter; sets of illustrated leaves which probably originally belonged to two psalters; and the earliest surviving fully illustrated English book of hours. The decoration of this group of manuscripts comprises full-page pictures, mostly of Old and New Testament scenes; historiated and

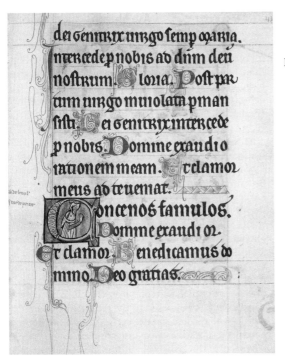

William de Brailes (*fl. c.*1230–1260), manuscript illumination

ornamental initials; and colourful line-fillers which occasionally include representations of animals, birds, and fish. Characteristic of the workshop are long ornamental extensions to the initials. The extensions occupy the borders and frame the accompanying text. The figure style of the workshop is vigorous if somewhat coarse. Colours are subdued, with dark and light blue, brown, and pink predominating.

Brailes also decorated one page of a psalter possibly made in London, and may therefore have spent part of his career away from Oxford. Paintings of four apostles and an angel on the vault of the chapter house of Christ Church Cathedral, Oxford, are in his style. These may show that he occasionally worked as a wall painter, or at least supplied designs for wall paintings.

William de Brailes and his workshop exemplify a significant development in later medieval book production. In the thirteenth century the decoration of manuscripts was passing out of the hands of the religious houses to artists who were grouped together within the towns and who worked for patrons both lay and ecclesiastical. The William de Brailes workshop in Oxford is the first workshop to which a name and a definite location can be assigned and whose products can be identified.

TIMOTHY GRAHAM, *rev.*

Sources S. G. Cockerell, *The work of W. de Brailes* (1930) · G. Pollard, 'William de Brailles', *Bodleian Library Record*, 5 (1954–6), 202–9 · M. Rickert, *Painting in Britain: the middle ages*, 2nd edn (1965), 104–6 · N. Morgan, *Early Gothic manuscripts*, 1 (1982), nos. 68–74 · C. Donovan, *The de Brailes hours* (1991) · J. Alexander and P. Binski, eds., *Age of chivalry: art in Plantagenet England, 1200–1400* (1987), nos. 314, 436 [exhibition catalogue, RA]

Likenesses manuscript illumination, BL, Add. MS 49999, fol. 43 [*see illus.*] · portrait, repro. in Alexander and Binski, eds., *Age of chivalry*, pl. 436, p. 388

Brailsford, Henry Noel (1873–1958), journalist and author, was born on 25 December 1873 in Mirfield, Yorkshire, the elder child and only son of Edward John Brailsford (1841–1921), a prominent Wesleyan Methodist preacher, and his wife, Clara Pooley (1843–1944), daughter of Henry Pooley. Most of Brailsford's childhood was spent in Scotland, where his father served as a circuit minister, successively in Edinburgh, Greenock, Blairgowrie, and Glasgow. He attended George Watson's College in Edinburgh (1883–4) and the high school of Dundee (1885–90) before receiving a bursary at Glasgow University. Rebelling against the puritanical regimen of his upbringing, Brailsford became estranged from his father, whose attempt to shield him from immorality by imposing teetotalism and a distinctive outfit had only made him self-conscious. At Glasgow, he studied classics and philosophy under Gilbert Murray, E. C. Caird, and A. C. Bradley, graduating MA in 1894 with first-class honours in logic and moral philosophy and second-class honours in Latin and Greek, and winning Thomas Logan prize as the most distinguished arts graduate of his year. The outstanding undergraduate in a generation that included John Buchan and Robert Horne, Brailsford was also a founder of the university Fabian Society and a frequent contributor to the *Glasgow University Magazine*. After brief stints at Balliol College, Oxford, and the University of Berlin, he returned to Glasgow as Clark fellow in mental philosophy and as assistant to Robert Adamson, lecturing to women undergraduates at Queen Margaret's College; on 29 September 1898 he married one of his pupils, Jane Esdon Malloch [*see* Brailsford, Jane Esdon (1874–1937)].

When Adamson terminated his appointment after a year, Brailsford applied unsuccessfully for a post at the University College of North Wales in 1896. Abandoning hope of an academic career, he turned to journalism, becoming sub-editor of the *Scots Pictorial* in 1897. It offered so little scope for his literary ambitions that he soon resigned to enlist in the Philhellenic Legion, a volunteer force fighting alongside the Greeks against the Ottoman Turks. Inspired by a romantic attachment to Hellenism, Brailsford, who suffered a minor wound in Thessaly, was soon disabused of his Byronic impulses. He returned to Scotland to resume his career, recounting his war experiences in his first book and only novel, *The Broom of the War-God* (1898). This attracted the attention of C. P. Scott, who dispatched Brailsford to Crete and Thessaly as a special correspondent for the *Manchester Guardian*, his initial foreign assignment for the newspaper. In addition he distributed barley to Christian inhabitants of Crete as relief agent for the Grosvenor House committee.

Although Brailsford continued to write intermittently for the *Guardian*, including a stint in Manchester as a leader writer in 1905, the lack of a regular berth prompted his move to London in 1899, where he established himself as a leader writer for a series of Liberal, anti-imperialist

Henry Noel Brailsford (1873–1958), by unknown photographer, 1942

newspapers: the *Morning Leader* (1899–1900), *The Echo* (1902–5), *The Tribune* (1906–7), and the *Daily News* (1907–9), resigning from the last, along with his friend H. W. Nevinson, over its refusal to disavow forcible feeding of suffragettes. In addition he was a frequent contributor to the weekly *Speaker* (1899–1906) and a staff member of its successor, *The Nation*, throughout H. W. Massingham's term as editor (1907–22). His leaders and articles earned him a reputation as an authority on Russia, Egypt, and the Balkans and an incisive critic of British foreign and imperial policies.

Beginning with the South Africa Conciliation Committee, Brailsford participated actively in agitation on behalf of liberation movements abroad and befriended foreign revolutionaries residing in London. Membership of the Balkan committee and familiarity with the region made him the obvious choice to lead a British relief mission to Macedonia for five months in 1903–4, distributing food and organizing medical assistance in Ochrida and Monastir. His first-hand experience informed his second book, *Macedonia* (1906), a cultural survey that became for many years the standard work. A member of the Friends of Russian Freedom and an associate of Peter Kropotkin, Feliks Volkhovsky, David Soskice, and Theodore Rothstein, Brailsford was approached by Russian acquaintances in 1904 seeking a British passport to facilitate an exile's return to Russia incognito. Despite assurances that the passport would not implicate him in violence, it was found on a terrorist killed by his own bomb in a St Petersburg hotel. In response to an official Russian protest, Brailsford was tried, convicted of conspiracy in July 1905 for obtaining a passport under false pretences, and fined £100. In May 1907 he interceded with the philanthropist Joseph Fels on behalf of Russian Social Democratic Party delegates, including Lenin and Trotsky, then meeting in London, and managed to secure a loan of £1700 for their return passage.

Raised in Liberal nonconformist culture, Brailsford became disenchanted with the Liberal Party and the Fabian Society, finding both insufficiently critical of British imperialism. In 1907 he joined the Independent Labour Party in protest against the government's handling of the Denshawai incident in Egypt. His oppositional stance angered his newspaper owners, but editors like Massingham and A. G. Gardiner tolerated his outspoken attacks on British policies. When the *Daily News* sent him to Egypt in 1908, despite his avowed nationalist sympathies, he used the opportunity to condemn British neglect of native education and complicity in child labour. He was also unalterably opposed to the Anglo-Russian entente, which he felt would impede constitutional development and encourage Russian expansion in Persia.

In 1909, at the instigation of his wife, a militant suffragette, Brailsford became active in the suffrage campaign. As a leader of the Men's League for Women's Suffrage, he sought to mediate between militants and constitutionalists. Such initiatives proved as fruitless as those of the conciliation committee, which Brailsford, its honorary secretary, devised to secure an inter-party legislative compromise. In 1910 he was adopted as a women's suffrage candidate in South Salford to oppose Hilaire Belloc, but withdrew when a pro-suffrage Liberal was nominated.

Brailsford's principled resignation from the *Daily News* meant a serious loss of income, not remedied until he became a regular contributor to the *New Republic* (1914–46) and the *Daily Herald* (1917–22). He turned increasingly to books and political pamphlets, most notably with *Shelley, Godwin and their Circle* (1913), a minor classic published in the Home University Library. In 1913 he served on the Carnegie commission of inquiry into the origins of the Balkan wars and was one of the principal authors of its report. Under the influence of J. A. Hobson, he identified economic imperialism as a cause of emerging international tension. In *The War of Steel and Gold* (1914), a seminal text for those on the left formulating a socialist foreign policy, Brailsford urged the satisfaction of German economic and territorial demands in order to relieve international conflict. His subsequent dissent during the First World War derived less from pacifist scruples than from his belief in mutual culpability. Within the Union of Democratic Control and the Labour Party Advisory Committee on International Questions he advocated a negotiated peace and a generous settlement. In *A League of Nations* (1917), he proposed an inclusive world organization responsible for overseas investment, an equitable distribution of raw materials, and the means to enforce its decisions militarily. His ideas gained notoriety not merely in Britain, but among President Woodrow Wilson's advisers as well.

After his defeat as Labour candidate for the Montrose burghs in 1918, Brailsford toured central Europe, graphically reporting on the devastation in Germany, Poland, and Hungary in a series of articles subsequently incorporated into *Across the Blockade* (1919) and *After the Peace* (1920). He warned repeatedly that unless the vindictive settlement were rectified, economic collapse and resurgent militarism would ensue in Germany. As one of the first Western journalists admitted to the Soviet Union in 1920, he was favourably impressed by the economic and educational strides made since the revolution but critical of the suppression of dissent. His initial enthusiasm, recorded in *The Russian Workers' Republic* (1921), was tempered after exposure to Stalinism during a second visit in 1927.

In 1922 Brailsford was appointed as editor of the *New Leader*, the restructured Independent Labour Party (ILP) weekly. Balancing ideological exhortation with cultural enrichment, it acquired an international reputation during the four years of his editorship. Without neglecting practical politics or industrial affairs, it attracted leading artists and intellectuals to its roster. As editor, Brailsford wrote a substantial portion of each week's issue, using it as a pulpit from which to preach reconciliation with Germany and the Soviet Union and to expound the living wage programme, derived from Hobson's underconsumptionist theory. The plan, coupled with state-financed family allowances and reinforced by banking and import controls, was explicated in Brailsford's *Socialism for Today* (1925) and became the cornerstone of ILP unemployment policy. Despite the *New Leader*'s recognized impact on the socialist movement in the 1920s, Brailsford's conflicts with the ILP's Scottish leaders, as well as dwindling circulation figures, led to his dismissal in 1926.

After his editorship ended, Brailsford travelled widely, attending socialist conferences abroad, lecturing in the United States, and visiting the Soviet Union in 1927 and India in 1930. *Olives of Endless Age* (1928) and *Property or Peace?* (1934) elaborated his views on internationalism and the connections between capitalism and war, while *Rebel India* (1931) espoused the cause of Indian self-government. Despite dissatisfaction with inter-war Labour governments, he repudiated the ILP's decision to disaffiliate, associating himself instead with the ostensibly loyal Socialist League. He later favoured collaboration with the Communist Party to achieve working-class unity, signed the 1937 unity manifesto, and was briefly involved with *Tribune*. During the 1930s he began to write weekly columns for *Reynolds's News* and joined the staff of the *New Statesman*, the two periodicals with which he was most closely identified for the remainder of his career. In London and in India Brailsford became acquainted with Gandhi and Nehru and for the next fifteen years was among the staunchest British friends of Indian freedom.

Although he had been one of the foremost critics of the Versailles treaty and a supporter of disarmament, the outbreak of the Spanish Civil War convinced him that an anti-

fascist alliance, including the Soviet Union, was imperative. More than any other event during his lifetime, the Spanish conflict aroused his passionate idealism. Only with difficulty could friends dissuade him from enlisting in the International Brigades, his age notwithstanding. He chaired the Labour Spain Committee, a pressure group advocating an active pro-loyalist policy. It was Spain that converted him from a belief in concessions to avoid war to military resistance to fascism. His denunciation of the Munich agreement was among the strongest indictments to appear in the British press. He also spoke out forcefully against the Soviet purge trials, earning the enmity of the Communist Party.

During the Second World War Brailsford broadcast frequently in the BBC Overseas Service and wrote *From England to America* (1940), a plea for American entry into the war. He befriended refugees, assisting many to find homes or secure passage to North America. His unabated affinity for German culture and conviction that Nazism was an aberration led him to argue for magnanimity in *Our Settlement with Germany* (1944), a stance that incurred considerable opprobrium. In 1944, fifty years after completing his degree, he received from the University of Glasgow an honorary degree of LLD.

Brailsford's first marriage failed, ending in separation in 1921. In 1930–38 he lived with the artist Clara *Leighton (1898–1989), who subsequently migrated to the United States. On 10 July 1944 he married Evamaria Perlmann Jarvis (1914–1988), a divorced German refugee. After the war deteriorating health curtailed his ability to undertake foreign assignments, but he went to India to report on provincial elections for *Reynolds's* in 1945, to Germany in 1947, and to Yugoslavia in 1950. Retiring from journalism in the 1950s, he devoted himself to his final book, *The Levellers and the English Revolution* (1961), still incomplete when he died of a stroke at the West London Hospital, London, on 23 March 1958. He had no children.

Brailsford belonged to a long tradition of radical writers and pamphleteers, linked intellectually as much to Paine and Shelley as to Marx and Hobson. Moving from liberalism to quasi-revolutionary socialism, he clung to the ideal of political democracy. More than a journalist, he remained throughout his career a tireless dissenting voice, never wavering in his quest for international conciliation, social justice, and the liberation of subject peoples.

F. M. LEVENTHAL

Sources F. M. Leventhal, *The last dissenter: H. N. Brailsford and his world* (1985) • F. M. Leventhal, 'Brailsford, Henry Noel', *DLB*, vol. 2 • K. Martin, ed., *Editor: a second volume of autobiography, 1931–1945* (1968) • A. M. Scott, diary, U. Glas. L. • H. W. Nevinson, diaries, Bodl. Oxf. • A. F. Havighurst, *Radical journalist: H. W. Massingham* (1974) • private information (2004) • b. cert. • m. cert.
Archives BL, corresp. with Society of Authors, Add. MS 63215 • Labour History Archive and Study Centre, Manchester, corresp.; corresp. and papers; press cuttings, pamphlets | BLPES, corresp. with the independent labour party • Bodl. Oxf., letters to Gilbert Murray • Bodl. Oxf., H. W. Nevinson diaries • JRL, Guardian archives, letters to the *Manchester Guardian* • King's Lond., Liddell Hart C., corresp. with Sir B. H. Liddell Hart • Labour History Archive and Study Centre, Manchester, Communist Party MSS, letters to R. Palme Dutt • Man. CL, Manchester Archives and Local Studies,

Manchester Suffrage MSS, letters to Millicent Fawcett · priv. coll., Clare Leighton MSS · U. Sussex, Kingsley Martin MSS | FILM BFI NFTVA, documentary footage | SOUND BBC WAC · BL NSA, documentary recording · BL NSA, performance recording **Likenesses** C. Leighton, oils, 1930?–1939? · F. M. Leventhal, photographs, 1938–47 · photograph, 1942, priv. coll. [*see illus.*] **Wealth at death** £693 6s.: administration, 27 May 1958, CGPLA Eng. & Wales

Brailsford [*née* Malloch], **Jane Esdon** (1874–1937), suffragette, was born on 3 April 1874 in Elderslie, Renfrewshire, one of the six children of John Malloch (*d*. 1898), a Scottish cotton manufacturer, and his wife, Margaret Marion McLeod. On leaving Paisley grammar school, she matriculated in 1893 at Glasgow University, where she studied philosophy and Greek, the latter under Gilbert Murray, for whom she developed a passionate, if unrequited, attachment. She was also a founder of the Glasgow University Fabian Society, launched in the spring of 1896. A headstrong young woman, widely acknowledged as a promising Hegelian, she possessed remarkable beauty, which not only made her the cynosure of a host of undergraduate contemporaries, but was later to arouse the ardour of Henry W. Nevinson and Wilfrid Scawen Blunt. After completing her studies in 1896, she went to Oxford where she attended Somerville College for one year before returning to Glasgow and eventually consenting to marry her persistent suitor and former philosophy instructor, Henry Noel *Brailsford (1873–1958).

Immediately after a civil marriage ceremony on 29 September 1898, Jane Brailsford accompanied her husband to Crete, where he was serving as a foreign correspondent for the *Manchester Guardian*. In 1903 the Brailsfords travelled to Macedonia to report on the Bulgarian insurgency, later returning for five months in 1903–4 as relief agents following an uprising against Turkish rule. In addition to assisting her husband to distribute food and relief funds collected by the Macedonian Relief Committee, Jane Brailsford administered a hospital in Ochrida until a bout of typhus forced her to return to England. During the years in which H. N. Brailsford gained prominence as a leader writer and foreign correspondent for a succession of Liberal daily and weekly newspapers, Jane Brailsford attempted to discover her own creative outlets, first as a novelist and later as an actress, but to no avail. Whether she was impeded because she was a woman or simply because, despite earlier promise, she lacked talent is unclear, but her efforts to build a reputation for herself other than as an adjunct to her husband and as an occasional participant in radical campaigns proved abortive.

An advocate of votes for women, Jane Brailsford joined the National Union of Women's Suffrage Societies but, impatient with constitutionalist moderation, she began to participate in militant demonstrations, shifting her affiliation to the Women's Social and Political Union (WSPU) in 1909. Inspired by the selfless dedication of militant leaders, she was among a dozen suffragettes, including Lady Constance Lytton, who resolved to undertake acts of violence in Newcastle on 9 November 1909 to protest against the forcible feeding of women prisoners. After attacking a barricade with a concealed axe as a symbolic

revolutionary act, Jane Brailsford was taken into custody and sentenced to the second division for a month. As the wife of a notable journalist she received preferential treatment—she was not forcibly fed—and was released after three days of imprisonment. Arrested again during a WSPU demonstration on 21 November 1911, she was sentenced to seven days in the second division at Holloway prison. It was a propensity for impetuosity coupled with deep-seated frustration that led her to invest such energy in WSPU activity between 1909 and the end of 1912. Her yearning for a cause to which she could wholeheartedly commit herself and her ambition for notoriety were temporarily satisfied in franchise agitation.

When Frederick and Emmeline Pethick-Lawrence were expelled from the WSPU in October 1912, Jane Brailsford resigned from the organization in disgust and quarrelled with her husband over militant tactics, to which he was opposed. She later suffered severe depression and a physical breakdown, possibly precipitating the uncontrolled drinking that blighted her later years. Regarding marriage as a form of subjugation, she never concealed her repugnance for her husband, whom she treated with contempt. At her insistence they had no children. In 1913 the Brailsfords parted, only to be reconciled temporarily a year later when they moved to Welwyn. In 1921 they separated permanently, although she refused to agree to a divorce. By the late 1920s Jane Brailsford, incapacitated by alcoholism, was living alone in Kew, London. She died on 9 April 1937 at 385 High Road, Chiswick, Middlesex, of pneumonia and cirrhosis of the liver.

F. M. LEVENTHAL

Sources F. M. Leventhal, *The last dissenter: H. N. Brailsford and his world* (1985) · H. W. Nevinson, *More changes, more chances* (1925) · H. W. Nevinson, diaries, Bodl. Oxf. · A. M. Scott, diary, U. Glas. L. · private information (2004) · b. cert. · m. cert. · d. cert. **Likenesses** photograph, priv. coll.

Brailsford, John (*b.* 1692), poet, was born on 10 May 1692 in London, the son of John Brailsford, tinman or pewterer. He was educated at the Merchant Taylors' School (which he entered on 12 March 1701) and St John's College, Cambridge, where he was admitted as a sizar on 29 June 1709; he graduated BA in 1712 and MA in 1717. In both places he was the friend of Ambrose Bonwicke (1691–1714), the nonjuror. After acting as curate at Blaston in Leicestershire he became rector of Kirkby in Ashfield, Nottinghamshire. His *Derby Silk-Mill*, a descriptive poem in imitation Miltonic verse, was published in Nottingham in 1739; there is a copy of this rare work in Derby Public Library. Brailsford may have been the John Brailsford who married Elizabeth Headley on 3 November 1719 at Blore Ray, Staffordshire. His son John *Brailsford, born at Blore Ray in 1721 or 1722, is separately noticed.

THOMPSON COOPER, rev. W. B. HUTCHINGS

Sources D. F. Foxon, ed., *English verse, 1701–1750: a catalogue of separately printed poems with notes on contemporary collected editions*, 2 vols. (1975) · S. F. Creswell, *Collections towards the history of printing in Nottinghamshire* (1863) · J. R. Tanner, ed., *Historical register of the University of Cambridge … to the year 1910* (1917) · Venn, *Alum. Cant.* · C. J. Robinson, ed., *A register of the scholars admitted into Merchant Taylors' School, from AD 1562 to 1874*, 1 (1882) · IGI

Brailsford, John (1721/2–1775), Church of England clergyman, was born at Blore Ray, Staffordshire, son of the Revd John *Brailsford (b. 1692), also an Anglican clergyman. His mother may have been Elizabeth Headley, who married a John Brailsford at Blore Ray, Staffordshire, on 3 November 1719. He was educated first at a school in Mansfield, Nottinghamshire, and then went up in 1741 to Emmanuel College, Cambridge; he received his BA in 1744, and an MA in 1766. Ordained priest in 1746, he served as vicar of North Wheatley, Nottinghamshire, and as chaplain to Francis, Lord Middleton. In 1761 he published *The Nature and Efficacy of the Fear of God in Private and Public Life*, an assize sermon preached at Warwick; this was followed by *Thirteen Sermons on Various Subjects*, published in Birmingham the year after his death.

In 1766 Brailsford was appointed to the headmastership of the free school in Birmingham, a position he held until he died on 25 November 1775.

THOMPSON COOPER, rev. ROBERT BROWN

Sources Venn, *Alum. Cant.* · N. Carlisle, *A concise description of the endowed grammar schools in England and Wales*, 2 vols. (1818) · J. Cooke, *The preacher's assistant* (1783)

Brailsford, Mary Ann (bap. 1791, d. 1852), originator of the Bramley's Seedling apple, was baptized at Southwell, Nottinghamshire, on 20 May 1791, the eldest daughter of Charles Brailsford (d. 1812) and his wife, Elizabeth Dickinson (d. 1837). In 1809 the family moved to 73 Church Street, Southwell, a dwelling which in the twentieth century became famous as Bramley Tree Cottage. It was in 1809 that Mary decided to plant some pips of an apple that her mother was preparing for a fruit pie; one pip germinated and, when the seedling grew too big for the pot, Mary planted it out in the garden of their cottage. In 1812, following her father's death, the property passed to her mother. On 20 May 1813 Mary married John Bucklow (d. 1819); she left the family home and took no further interest in the apple tree, which would probably not have borne fruit until it was ten to fifteen years old.

On 25 July 1820 the widowed Mary married Richard Hindley (d. 1836), a farmer of Charle's Yard, Newark, near Newark, where their son Richard Brailsford Hindley (1821–1900) and a daughter, Catherine, who died in infancy, were born. When her mother died, in 1837, Mary and her married sister Diana Aram inherited the cottage, which they sold in the following year. On 28 November 1846 it was purchased by a butcher, Matthew Bramley (1796–1871), owner of the White Lion, Easthorpe, who lived in the cottage until his death. Mary Hindley died at Clark's Yard, Newark on 17 February 1852, oblivious of her part in the development of Britain's most popular cooking apple of the twentieth century. She was buried in the churchyard of St Giles at Holme.

The apple's potential was first recognized by **Henry Merryweather** (1839–1932), nurseryman, born at Southwell, Nottinghamshire, on 24 January 1839, the son of Henry Merryweather (b. 1803), a gardener, and his wife, Ellen Trusswell. After a brief education, in 1854 Henry joined his father, who had been a gardener at Norwood Hall, at the nursery he had shortly afterwards established

specializing in the production of strawberries. In 1857 Merryweather, then seventeen, encountered the Revd Arthur Tatham's gardener, George Musson, carrying a basket of impressive apples that had come from the tree in Bramley's garden. Having secured permission to take cuttings for grafting Merryweather began to build up his stock, selling Bramley's Seedling apples locally from the early 1860s. The strain did not receive more than local fame until 1876, when it was first exhibited in London and was highly commended by the Royal Horticultural Society. In 1883 it was given a first class certificate, a nationally important accolade for the apple variety, which led to its being grown throughout the country.

Although on occasions Merryweather gave Bramley the credit for raising the apple he explained in his 1892 catalogue that the variety was a chance seedling from a pip sown by Brailsford. Henry deserves the credit for not only recognizing the apple's potential, but also for his efforts in popularizing it to become Britain's leading cooking apple.

Merryweather continued to expand Southwell Nurseries. He popularized the growing of peaches, nectarines, and apricots trained to grow fan shaped against south facing walls in order to catch the sun and warmth. He developed many new varieties of fruit and roses, of which the Merryweather damson was a prolific cropper. His marriage to Elizabeth produced four sons, Ernest John, John Edward, Alfred George, and William Henry, and established a dynasty of leading nurserymen. Merryweather was an influential figure in civic administration and was appointed JP for Nottingham in 1912. In later life he still continued to play an active part in the internationally famous horticultural business which he had assisted his father to establish. He died on 8 October 1932 at Southwell.

The precise origin of the apple pips Brailsford planted is unclear but it would almost inevitably have been the result of cross-pollination of two of the many apple trees grown in the Southwell area. Most of the best varieties of apples were chance findings promoted by nurserymen from plants grown from pips or seeds, hence the use of the term 'seedling' to denote their origins. The resulting plants differ considerably, producing fruit of widely varying quality; their value cannot be appreciated until they begin to bear fruit. Once an improved strain is identified it is reproduced by grafting the stems onto other rootstocks. The Bramley apple is a triploid, very vigorous, and partial tip-bearing tree. It is a heavy cropper of large well-flavoured apples with their own distinct taste and appeal, producing a crisp, dry juice with a delightful piquancy.

The development of this prolific variety was a historical accident. While Mary Brailsford deserves the credit for having raised the Bramley's Seedling apple this possibly ought to be shared with her mother, who refrained from uprooting it during its early years, when its ultimate value was questionable. Mary's son Richard Brailsford Hindley, who was for many years deputy clerk to the county magistrates at Newark, appreciated his mother's contribution in this sphere and, by passing this information on to his own children, helped to establish an oral tradition that was uncovered by L. Lefroy's pioneering research in the Second World War. Though Bramley gave his name to what became the most popular culinary apple in Britain it is evident that he played little part in the actual rearing of the tree, being no more than a cipher in its production. By the late twentieth century the variety was grown in an area greater than that of all other cooking apples combined.   JOHN MARTIN

Sources A. Simmonds, *The origins of Bramleys seedlings* (1945) · P. Pomeroy, *The Bramley apple seedling* (1982) · H. H. Grace, letter, *Gardener's Chronicle* (2 Jan 1943) · L. Lefroy, *Gardener's Chronicle* (Aug 1944) · R. Merryweather, *The Bramley: a world famous cooking apple* (1992) · A. Simmonds, *A horticultural who was who* (1948) · M. Hadfield, *A history of British gardening* (1960) · R. Sanders, *The English apple* (1988) · R. Hogg, *The fruit manual*, 5th edn (1884) · gravestone, St Giles's Church, Holme, Nottinghamshire [R. Hindley] · d. cert.
Likenesses drawing, Merryweather Garden Centre, Southwell, Nottinghamshire, Bramley Apple Exhibition

Brain, Dennis (1921–1957), horn player, was born on 17 May 1921 in London, the son of Aubrey Brain (1893–1955) and his wife, Marion Beeley. He was born into a horn-playing dynasty of which, despite his premature death, he became the most distinguished member. His grandfather was Alfred Edwin Brain (1860–1929), a former military man who became a member of the London Symphony Orchestra's horn section known as 'God's own quartet'. Dennis Brain's uncle, Alfred Brain (1885–1966), was also an exponent of the instrument and made a successful career both before and after his emigration to the USA in 1923. His father, Aubrey Brain, played in the London Symphony Orchestra before taking up in 1930 the position of principal horn in the BBC Symphony Orchestra: he was the leading exponent of the instrument in Britain at that time. Every member of the household was musical; Brain's mother was at one time a singer at Covent Garden. Having shown a precocious interest in the horn while at St Paul's School, Norwich, Brain studied with his father at the Royal College of Music, London, with the organ as his second study. His public début came in 1938 when he played Bach's 'Brandenburg' concerto no. 1 (which features two concertante horn parts) with his father in the Queen's Hall, London, under the baton of Adolf Busch. Soon he was playing chamber music with ensembles including the Griller and Busch quartets and making broadcasts for the BBC.

During the Second World War Brain was principal horn in the RAF central band and symphony orchestra. The second horn player, Norman del Mar, also a composer, conductor, and musicologist, became a close friend. Brain made twenty-six solo appearances in the wartime National Gallery concerts organized by Dame Myra Hess, in a range of works including the Mozart horn quintet (K407) and the Brahms trio for horn, violin, and piano (op. 40), which became his signature works in later years. His career as a professional orchestral player began in October 1942 in the Sidney Beer Orchestra, soon renamed the National Symphony Orchestra. As early as 1943 he recorded Mozart's fourth horn concerto with the Hallé Orchestra, followed in 1944 by the Beethoven sonata for

Dennis Brain (1921–1957), by Howard Coster, 1956

piano and horn, op. 17, with Dennis Matthews. Brain's recordings, most of all the 1953 performances of the four Mozart horn concertos with the Philharmonia Orchestra conducted by Herbert von Karajan, were an outstanding success in both artistic and commercial terms.

Brain's involvement with contemporary composers began in 1942 when, as a member of the RAF Orchestra, he played scores by Benjamin Britten for American radio broadcasts. His virtuosity inspired Britten to write elaborate horn solos. The composer was persuaded to write for him the *Serenade for Tenor, Horn, and Strings* (op. 31, 1943), a major landmark in British music, which Brain, the tenor Peter Pears, and the Boyd Neel Orchestra recorded with Britten conducting in 1944. Also written for Brain were horn concertos by Elisabeth Lutyens (1946), Gordon Jacob (1951), Malcolm Arnold (1946), and Paul Hindemith (1949), which greatly enlarged the solo repertory of the instrument. He also gave in 1948 the second performance of Richard Strauss's virtuoso second horn concerto (1942).

Dennis Brain's innocent, boyish sense of fun endeared him to his orchestral colleagues; short and stocky with an infectious grin, he would indulge in the innocent japery which gained him, del Mar, and the flautist Gareth Morris the nickname the Three Musketeers. His legendary appetite for rich foods eventually took a toll on his figure. Brain and del Mar would frequently appear with dance and jazz bands in addition to fulfilling RAF and other professional engagements. His sense of fun found its ultimate outlet in 1956 when he performed a Mozart horn concerto on a hosepipe at a Hoffnung festival concert. He knew nothing of anxiety and, as del Mar recalled, 'it seemed as if the pitfalls of this notoriously unreliable instrument simply never occurred to him' (*DNB*). In 1944 Brain met Yvonne (*b. c.*1926), daughter of Edward Ralph Coles, a bank accountant from Petersfield. A piano student at the Royal College of Music, she was five years his junior. They were married on 8 September 1945 and had two children.

From 1946 until his death, as orchestral player and soloist, Dennis Brain was one of the dominant musical personalities of the London scene. He was appointed principal horn of the Philharmonia Orchestra, whose début on 27 October 1945 marked a new era in British orchestral playing. From its foundation by Sir Thomas Beecham in 1946, the rival Royal Philharmonic Orchestra also competed for Brain's presence. A highlight of his career came in 1952 when Toscanini conducted the Brahms symphonies with the Philharmonia at the new Festival Hall, where Brain's unmatched warmth and nobility in the great solo passages for horn were universally admired.

Initially, like his father, Brain used a narrow-bore French instrument with piston valves, but in 1951 he adopted a German double horn which produced a fuller tone. His playing was remarkable for its virtuosity—he was capable of a flawless rendering of 'The Flight of the Bumble Bee' on this most treacherous instrument—but perhaps more so for a sensitivity of phrasing and ebullient sense of sheer enjoyment which have rarely been matched. A critic in 1951 described him as 'an alchemist, turning copper into gold' (Pettitt, 114). He was active in the studios, and many surviving recordings, notably those of the Mozart, Strauss, and Hindemith horn concertos, capture his art at its finest. In his last years Brain sought to expand his range beyond the limited repertory of the horn: he founded wind ensembles and a small chamber orchestra, which he had begun to conduct.

Brain was a keen motorist, buying a series of increasingly fast cars, a passion that he shared with the conductor Herbert von Karajan. A copy of the magazine *Autocar* was spotted on his music stand as he recorded the Mozart horn concertos, playing from memory. This enthusiasm led to tragedy when, on 1 September 1957, he was killed aged thirty-six at Hatfield while driving back from the Edinburgh Festival. Lavish tributes were offered by musicians around the world.   TIM BARRINGER

Sources S. J. Pettitt, *Dennis Brain: a biography*, 2nd edn (1989) [with bibliography] · R. Lewis Marshall, *Dennis Brain on record: a comprehensive discography* (Newton, Mass., 1996) · Grove, *Dict. mus.* · CGPLA *Eng. & Wales* (1957) · *DNB* · M. Meckna, 'The legacy of Dennis Brain', *Horn Call*, 21/2 (April 1991), 1–5
Archives FILM BFI NFTVA, documentary footage | SOUND BL NSA, 'Music critic Felix Aprahamian describes Dennis Brain's organ playing and assesses his influence as a horn player', 1LP0058897 S2 BD4 C1 BBC · BL NSA, *Talking about music*, 151, 1LP0200074 S1 BD1 BBC TRANSC · BL NSA, oral history interview · BL NSA, performance recordings
Likenesses H. Coster, photograph, 1956, NPG [see illus.] · photographs, repro. in Pettitt, *Dennis Brain*
Wealth at death £30,109 1s. 5d.: probate, 7 Nov 1957, CGPLA *Eng. & Wales*

Brain, Walter Russell, first Baron Brain (1895–1966), physician and medical administrator, was born at Clovelly, Denmark Road, Reading, on 23 October 1895, the only son and elder child of Walter John Brain, solicitor, and his wife, Edith Alice, daughter of Charles Smith, architect. At Mill Hill School he studied classics, since he was intended for the law. His hobbies were English literature, writing, and natural history. He wanted to do science, but this was not allowed by his parents. In 1914 he entered New College, Oxford, as a commoner to read history, which he disliked. Disapproving strongly of war, he joined the Friends' Ambulance Unit in 1915 and was sent to work in York. Moving later to the King George Hospital, London, he became attached to the X-ray department, where he met Stella (*b.* 1896), daughter of the physician Reginald Langdon Langdon-Down. They married on 8 September 1920. Brain attended evening classes at Birkbeck College and in 1919 went back to New College to read medicine. He was taught by J. B. S. Haldane, Charles Scott Sherrington, Julian Huxley, and H. C. Bazett. He took a shortened course for the BA (1919) and obtained the Theodore Williams scholarship in physiology (1920). He entered the London Hospital in October 1920, graduated BM BCh (Oxon.) in 1922, proceeded DM in 1925, and was elected FRCP in 1931.

Brain joined the newly formed medical unit at the London Hospital. Through the influence of Henry Head and George Riddoch he took up neurology. He was appointed physician to Maida Vale Hospital in 1925, assistant physician to the London Hospital in 1927, and he was physician to Moorfields Hospital in 1930–37. Brain made four important contributions to neurology. With A. Dickson Wright and Marcia Wilkinson he showed that the median nerve could be paralysed by compression at the wrist in the carpal tunnel; surgical relief of this would restore function. With D. W. C. Northfield and M. Wilkinson he demonstrated the importance of backward protrusion of the intervertebral disc in the cervical spine as a cause of paralysis of the legs; this has since been recognized as a very common neurological disturbance. He described damage to the brain and peripheral nerves in cancer, particularly cancer of the lung. As a consequence the British Empire Cancer Campaign established at the London Hospital a unit for the investigation of carcinomatous neuropathies, of which Brain was the director until his death. And he showed that the great protrusion of the eyes which is usually associated with an overactive thyroid gland could occur in its absence; he called this endocrine exophthalmos. He was an excellent and scholarly physician, not an experimentalist.

Brain had originally considered making a career in psychiatry. He never lost his interest in affairs of the mind, and particularly the problem of perception. *Mind, Perception and Science* (1951), the Riddell lectures on *The Nature of Experience* (1959), and a book, *Speech Disorders* (1961), were the outcome. From the time he was elected to the London Hospital, Brain earned his livelihood as a physician in consulting practice, in which he was very successful. He had a remarkable memory and a flair for exposition, resulting in a book, *Diseases of the Nervous System*, first published in 1933 and reaching its sixth edition in 1962. His book with E. B. Strauss, *Recent Advances in Neurology*, was first published in 1929 and had gone into seven editions by 1962. He also wrote *Some Reflections on Genius, and other Essays* (1960), *Doctors Past and Present* (1964), *Science and Man* (1966), *Tea with Walter de la Mare* (1957), and *Poems and Verses* (1961). He edited *Brain* from 1954. Eighteen books and more than 150 papers were a remarkable output for a busy Harley Street physician, especially when his public service is considered. He achieved it by interest, industry, and a remarkable capacity for using every minute, particularly those spent in the back of his motor car. It was thus that he wrote *Dialogues of Today*, published anonymously in *The Lancet* during 1959 and reprinted as *Socrates on the Health Service* (1960), which had a profound effect on the ethos of the new service.

In public Brain was a shy, silent man. He once wrote: 'There are two international languages of religion: the Latin of the Roman Catholic Church, and the silence of the Quakers.' His elegant after dinner speeches, full of wit and learning, came as a surprise to the uninitiated.

Russell and Stella Brain were a partnership from their meeting in the X-ray department until Brain's death. They had two sons and a daughter, to whom they were devoted. The Brains joined the Society of Friends in 1931 and were subsequently regular attenders at the meeting-houses on Sundays. He gave the Swarthmoor lecture in 1944, 'Man, society and religion', in which he stressed the importance of a social conscience. This conscience of his led him to take on a variety of public services. He became chairman of the medical council of the London Hospital during the war, defending the interests of those who were away on active service. He became a member of King Edward's Hospital Fund for London and chairman of its hospital service plan. In 1950 he succeeded Lord Moran as president of the Royal College of Physicians, London, retaining this office until 1957. His wide interests, experience, and sympathy, and his lucid mind earned him the respect and admiration of the profession, the administrators, and the law makers. He proved a medical statesman of wisdom, insight, and stature. He was a member of the royal commission on marriage and divorce in 1952, of the royal commission on mental certification and detention in 1954; chairman of the distinction awards committee from 1962, of the interdepartmental committee on drug addiction in 1958, and of the standing committee on drug addiction in 1966. He was president of the British Association for the Advancement of Science in 1963–4.

Brain was knighted in 1952, created a baronet in 1954, and made Baron Brain of Eynsham in 1962. He was elected FRS in 1964 and an honorary fellow of New College, Oxford, in 1952. He received honorary degrees from Oxford, Manchester, Southampton, Wales, Belfast, and Durham. He was an honorary fellow of the royal colleges of physicians of Edinburgh and of Ireland, the royal colleges of surgeons of England, of obstetricians and gynaecologists, and of physicians and surgeons of Glasgow, the Royal Australasian College of Physicians, the American

and South African colleges of physicians, and the Faculty of Radiologists. He was president of the Association of Physicians (1956), of the Association of British Neurologists (1960), of the International Society of Internal Medicine (1958), of the Family Planning Association from 1956, and of the Migraine Trust which, as one who had been a sufferer, he was active in founding in 1966. Brain was an honorary member of American, French, German, and Spanish neurological societies, and of the Swiss Academy of Medicine. He gave the Rede, Eddington, and Linacre lectures at Cambridge, the Riddell lectures at Durham, the Bryce lecture at Oxford, and the Osler oration in Canada. He was awarded the Osler medal for 1960 at Oxford.

Brain died at his home, Hillmorton, Coombe Hill Road, Kingston, Surrey, on 29 December 1966, working to the end; his last working day was devoted to arranging a new issue of *Brain*. A meeting in his memory was held at Friends' House, London, on 10 February 1967. He was succeeded by his elder son, Christopher Langdon (*b.* 1926). His younger son, Michael, became assistant professor of medicine at McMaster University, Ontario, in 1969.

GEORGE PICKERING, *rev.*

Sources G. W. Pickering, *Memoirs FRS*, 14 (1968), 61–82 • private information (1981) • personal knowledge (1981) • *The Times* (3 Jan 1967), 12g • *The Times* (11 Feb 1967), 10c • *BMJ* (7 Jan 1967), 56–7; (21 Jan 1967), 180; (4 Feb 1967), 308 • b. cert. • m. cert. • d. cert. • J. D. Gordan, 'Doctors as men of letters', *Bulletin of the New York Public Library*, 68 (1964), 600 • *ILN* (7 Jan 1967), 12 • *Nature*, 213 (1967), 132
Archives RCP Lond., corresp. and papers • Wellcome L., MSS and material relating to the Family Planning Association | Rice University, Houston, Texas, Woodson Research Center, corresp. with Sir Julian Huxley
Likenesses W. Stoneman, photograph, 1952, NPG • J. Epstein, bronze bust, 1959, RCP Lond. • W. Bird, photograph, 1962, NPG
Wealth at death £30,340: probate, 28 Feb 1967, CGPLA Eng. & Wales

Braine, Bernard Richard, Baron Braine of Wheatley (1914–2000), politician, was born on 24 June 1914 at 212 Pitshanger Lane, Ealing, London, the son of Arthur Ernest Braine, civil servant, and his wife, Elsa Marie, *née* Hoffacher. His father, who worked as a staff clerk in the Admiralty, was an enthusiastic member of the Fabian Society. Braine was educated at Hendon county grammar school. He then became a clerical officer in the Inland Revenue. On 21 December 1935 he married Kathleen Mary (1913/14–1982), daughter of Herbert William Faun, of East Sheen, Surrey, a pensioner of the royal Irish constabulary. They had three sons: Richard (*b.* 1939), Michael (*b.* 1942), and Brendon (*b.* 1945).

Unlike his father Braine became an enthusiastic Young Conservative, and was elected as a national vice-chairman in 1938. A vigorous campaigner against appeasement—and against Oswald Mosley's fascists—he enlisted in the North Staffordshire regiment, as a private, in 1940 and served in west Africa, south-east Asia, and Europe. From relatively humble origins he rose quickly within the army, attending the Staff College, Camberley, and securing attachment to the staff of Lord Mountbatten. He ended the war as a lieutenant-colonel.

Once the war was over Braine decided to pursue a career

in politics. He fought the safe Labour seat of Leyton East in 1945 before winning selection for Billericay, after enhancing his reputation as a lecturer on policy issues. The Conservatives had fared particularly badly in Essex at the general election of 1945, winning only three of the twenty-six seats. In 1950 there were only twenty-four seats, but the Conservatives won eleven of them. Braine's own majority was relatively slender, at just over 4000, but he remained in the Commons until he retired, in 1992. As a result of boundary changes he represented Billericay only until 1955, but after this he was returned for South-East Essex (1955–83) and Castle Point (1983–92).

Braine's wartime experience reinforced his interest in the Commonwealth. Before the war his high conception of Britain's imperial role placed him on the progressive wing of his party, and in social background he could be compared with other rising Conservative stars like Edward Heath. But his career stalled in the mid-1950s as the 'wind of change' began to blow in an uncongenial direction. He was not alone in combining a distaste for apartheid with an assumption of white racial superiority, and he was an outspoken supporter of the Suez invasion of 1956. On both of these issues his fiery rhetoric brought attention to the fact that he was out of step with policy developments that party leaders regarded as a regrettable necessity.

In October 1960 Braine was given his first official post within the government, as parliamentary under-secretary to the minister of pensions. But this proved a brief staging post. After only four months he joined the Commonwealth Relations Office, again as a parliamentary under-secretary, under Duncan Sandys. Although Harold Macmillan's policy towards the Commonwealth was not to his taste this appointment seemed to offer the chance of a constructive contribution in his favourite area. But after Macmillan's reshuffle of July 1962 Braine was transplanted again, this time to the Ministry of Health, where he served as parliamentary secretary to Enoch Powell. The two very different characters were already firm friends, and Powell regarded Braine as an efficient minister. Yet it was a strange twist that united them at Health, and although Braine continued to defend Powell through future controversies he mingled his admiration with a sense of perspective, voting for Reginald Maudling rather than for his old friend in the leadership election of 1965.

When the Conservatives fell from office in October 1964 Braine's ministerial career was over. He served as deputy shadow spokesman on Commonwealth affairs (under Maudling) but again raised questions about his judgement by speaking out against the sanctions that the Labour government imposed on the illegal Smith regime in Rhodesia. In theory, at least, Braine did not oppose eventual majority rule, but he feared the consequences of excessive haste. It was a delicate balance to strike, and those who defended Smith on these grounds were easily denounced by their opponents as racists who wanted to perpetuate white political dominance. With Heath as leader of the party Braine's views seemed more outdated than ever, but he continued to hope for promotion.

Unusually for an imperialist he at least shared some of Heath's enthusiasm for Europe, and he helped to found the British–German parliamentary group. But when the Conservatives won the general election of 1970 his only reward was the post of deputy chairman of the Commonwealth Parliamentary Association. In that capacity he became a staunch upholder of Britain's link with the Falkland Islands, but at the time this seemed like yet another of his quixotic causes. He was knighted in 1972—a reward perhaps for having avoided open rebellion at a time when the Heath government was regularly hounded by disappointed right-wing backbenchers. He even proved amenable to persuasion on subjects like immigration, where he wholeheartedly agreed with the implacable Powell.

In 1974 the Conservatives suffered two general election defeats, but Braine clung on at South-East Essex. By this time he was a highly popular constituency MP, devoting much of his remarkable energy to local causes. In particular he was ferocious in resisting the construction of a third London airport at Foulness, in Essex; later he extended this opposition to the alternative Essex site: Stansted. Once he had developed a principled objection to a development in his own back yard he usually applied this across the board. Thus his bitter objection to chemical plants in his constituency—which inspired a record-breaking filibustering speech in the Commons, lasting for more than three hours—was extended to environmental hazards generally, including the nuclear plant at Windscale. Among his other causes were teetotalism and the prosecution of war criminals.

When Margaret Thatcher became prime minister in 1979 it was far too late for Braine to hope for preferment. He was, however, sworn of the privy council in 1985, in recognition of his diligent and lengthy service. In 1987 he became father of the house, but this made no difference to his campaigning outlook. Retirement did not come until the 1992 election, when he was almost seventy-eight. A peerage allowed him to retain his parliamentary platform but his final years were marred by loneliness (his wife died in 1982) and ill health. He moved to a nursing home in Benfleet, Essex, and died in Southend Hospital on 5 January 2000, of heart disease. He was survived by his three sons.

Braine never achieved the high office that he sought, but he became one of the best-known of backbenchers. A large, debonair man with an elegant moustache, by the end of his career in the Commons he could easily have been mistaken for a traditional tory knight of the shires. His views on subjects such as immigration reinforced this (inaccurate) impression. In truth while others from similar backgrounds managed to straddle the divide between the old and the new Conservative parties he was stranded in no man's land. In outlook he was too open-minded to be classed as a stereotypical right-winger, but he backed up his votes against 'progressive' legislation with violent speeches, and this characteristic ensured that he was generally labelled as a desperate reactionary. Perhaps the best image of Braine was formed by his fellow back-bencher Alan Clark during a debate on the Argentinian invasion of the Falklands in April 1982. Clark, whose background and attitude to politics provide a fascinating contrast to those of his subject, pictured Braine delivering 'One of his great ham displays of indignation. So splutteringly bombastic that in a curious kind of way he makes the House, that most cynical of audiences, pay attention' (Clark, 313). Clark seems to have overlooked the possibility that the house listened because on this, like so many of his favourite subjects, the anachronistic Braine was almost alone in speaking out with true, if tactless, sincerity.

MARK GARNETT

Sources *The Times* (6 Jan 2000) · *The Guardian* (7 Jan 2000) · *The Independent* (7 Jan 2000) · *Daily Telegraph* (8 Jan 2000) · *WWW* · Burke, *Peerage* · A. Clark, *Diaries: into politics* (2000) · S. Heffer, *Like the Roman: the life of Enoch Powell* (1998) · b. cert. · m. cert. · d. cert.
Archives Essex RO, Southend, papers
Likenesses photograph, 1955, repro. in *The Independent* · photograph, 1964, repro. in *The Guardian* · photograph, 1990, repro. in *The Times* · photograph, repro. in *Daily Telegraph*
Wealth at death £438,687: probate, 9 May 2000, *CGPLA Eng. & Wales*

Braine, John Gerard (1922–1986), writer, was born on 13 April 1922 in Bradford, the elder child and only son of Fred Braine, a sewage-works inspector, and his wife, Katherine Josephine Henry. By religion his father was a Methodist, his mother a Roman Catholic; he was brought up in the latter faith. He was educated at St Bede's Roman Catholic Grammar School, Bradford, and attended the Leeds School of Librarianship—his mother had worked as a librarian. In 1938–40 he was in rapid succession a furniture shop assistant, bookshop assistant, laboratory assistant, and progress chaser. Between 1940 and 1951 he was an assistant librarian at Bingley Public Library, becoming chief assistant in 1949. This part of his career was interrupted in 1942–3 by service in the Royal Navy, from which he was invalided out. In 1951 tuberculosis necessitated a long spell in hospital, from which he did not emerge until 1954. Over the next three years he worked as branch librarian successively at Northumberland and West Riding of Yorkshire county libraries. He had been writing various items, including a verse play, without much success for some time, and now, in 1957, published his first novel, *Room at the Top*. Although earlier rejected by four publishers, this book immediately took its place as one of the significant novels of the post-war period. Its author's lack of a conventionally prolonged education may well have contributed to its freshness and vigour, and its story, of the material ascent and emotional coarsening of Joe Lampton, a northern working-class lad, owed something to a tradition of provincial writing that had become weakened. Before long its sales reached 100,000 in hardback and the film rights had been sold before publication. Within four months Braine was able to give up his career as a librarian and devote himself to writing. The film appeared in 1958.

Braine's second novel, *The Vodi* (1959), an excursion into the supernatural influenced by his hospital experiences, has never done anything like so well either commercially or in esteem, but in his third, *Life at the Top* (1962, filmed

John Gerard Braine (1922–1986), by Mark Gerson, 1962

1965), he returned to Joe Lampton, now a capable but disaffected executive, and to commercial success. None of Braine's later novels, of which the last, *These Golden Days*, appeared in 1985, attracted the attention the Lampton books received. Joe enjoyed a kind of resurrection as the protagonist of two television series, *Man at the Top* (1970 and 1972), and several of Braine's other novels were effectively adapted for television.

It is difficult not to see in Braine's career after 1962 a decline in literary standards of performance as well as of popularity and standing with the public. Inexorably he came to be seen as a man if not of one book then of one character, the uncertainly attractive and far from inexhaustible Lampton. What at one stage had passed as a harsh northern critique of the affluent south seemed more and more to slide into tolerance at best. More than this, in the absence of the narrative thrust of the earlier novels, the general treatment and style was revealed as flatly pedestrian. Autobiography or wish-fulfilment took the place of invention, to the point of occasional embarrassment in late works such as *One and Last Love* (1981). Besides fiction, he published a critical study, *J. B. Priestley* (1978), and a handbook called *Writing a Novel* (1974), which, together with much sound practical advice to the tyro, includes a heartfelt warning, poignant in retrospect, of the dangers of success. He pursued a more ephemeral calling as a political polemicist in writing and in public appearances. At first a supporter of unilateral nuclear disarmament and other left-wing causes, he moved suddenly and spectacularly to the right, calling for the return of hanging and the ending of all foreign aid.

Though possessing strong views and vociferous dislikes, Braine showed no animosity towards anyone. He was indeed a man of great natural sweetness. Pale, chubby, bespectacled, a serious cigarette smoker and drinker with a perpetual look of being out of condition, he had an expression of settled gloom that easily lightened into a genial smile. He showed an endearing pleasure in his prosperity and no resentment when his star began to fade.

In 1955 Braine married Helen Patricia, daughter of William Selby Wood, engineering fitter. They had a son and three daughters. The family moved from Bingley to Woking in 1966. Braine died of a gastric haemorrhage on 28 October 1986, in a Hampstead hospital.

KINGSLEY AMIS, rev.

Sources D. Salwak, *John Braine and John Waine, a reference guide* (1980) · *The Times* (30 Oct 1986) · *New Statesman* (21 March 1975) · *CGPLA Eng. & Wales* (1987)
Archives U. Leeds, Brotherton L., diaries, notebooks, and literary papers · W. Yorks. AS, Bradford, diaries, notebooks, and literary papers
Likenesses M. Gerson, photograph, 1962, NPG [*see illus.*] · photographs, 1971–4, Hult. Arch.
Wealth at death under £40,000: probate, 11 Feb 1987, *CGPLA Eng. & Wales*

Braithwaite, Anna (1788–1859). *See under* Braithwaite, Joseph Bevan (1818–1905).

Braithwaite, John (*bap.* 1633, *d. c.*1680), Quaker apologist and missionary, was born at Cartmel, Lancashire, and baptized there on 24 March 1633; he was the son of James Braithwaite of Newton, in that parish.

Braithwaite became a Quaker in 1652 after meeting George Fox; the latter recorded in his journal how he noticed the young man taking notes during a minister's sermon at the chapel of Newton in Cartmel, and relates that he soon 'came to be convinced and became a fine minister of the gospel' (*Journal of George Fox*, 1.46). Some time after this, in 1656, he travelled to Somerset, where he is included in a quarterly meeting record concerning 'the first publishers of trueth in the County of Somerset' (Morland, 57) which states that 'Thomas Briggs and John Braithwaite of Lancashiere also did publish trueth about the same time, in severall market townes, and had severall meetings in the same County' (ibid., 58). In 1658 he visited a friend confined in Ilchester gaol, but was 'unmercifully beaten by a wicked gaoler and not suffered to come in' (Besse, 1.584). On another occasion, he and Thomas Briggs were also imprisoned for preaching at Salisbury.

Braithwaite wrote only three tracts, which were published around the time of the Restoration. Lamenting the state of England in 1660, in *A Serious Meditation upon the Dealings of God with England* (n.d.), he writes, 'Oh how is thy silver become dross! And thy liberty become bondage! Oh how art thou gone backward and not forward!' (p. 2). In another tract, entitled *The Ministers of England* (1660), he discusses the nature of ministry, objecting to tithe-taking and other practices.

John Braithwaite would appear to have died about 1680, or perhaps before this time, and in Somerset, for Quaker records state that he, 'being a young man, there finished his testimony by death' (Morland, 58). If the same man, this seems somewhat curious as he would actually have been around forty-seven years old and therefore not particularly young. Two other men with the same name are recorded in the Quaker digest registers for Lancashire: John Braithwaite of High Wray who was buried at Colthouse, Lancashire, in April 1671 and John Breathwet who was buried in the October of the same year.

CAROLINE L. LEACHMAN

Sources *The journal of George Fox*, ed. N. Penney, 1 (1911) · S. C. Morland, ed., *The Somersetshire quarterly meeting of the Society of Friends, 1668–1699*, Somerset RS, 75 (1978) · J. Besse, *A collection of the sufferings of the people called Quakers*, 1 (1753) · J. Whiting, *Persecution expos'd: in some memoirs relating to the sufferings of John Whiting and many others of the people called Quakers* (1715) · J. Smith, ed., *A descriptive catalogue of Friends' books*, 1 (1867) · *DNB* · Quaker digest registers for Lancashire
Archives RS Friends, Lond., Swarthmore MSS, vol. 3 (MS vol. 354)

Braithwaite, John (1696–1740), soldier and diplomatist, was the second of three sons born to John Braithwaite (1666–1739), a member of a prominent Westmorland family, and his wife, Silvestra Cooke (*d.* 1739). In his preface to his *History of the Revolutions in the Empire of Morocco* (1729), John Braithwaite relates how he began his adventurous career at a young age in Queen Anne's fleet, although there is no record of this in any official naval list. He states that his service began 'with a letter from Queen Anne' (J. Braithwaite, preface), which perhaps suggests irregular service in a privateer by 'letters of marque' and therefore not in the Royal Navy. His later military career is better documented. On 15 September 1716 he was commissioned second lieutenant in the 23rd foot, later the Royal Welsh Fusiliers. On 19 August 1718 he became ensign to Lieutenant-Colonel James Gee in the 3rd foot guards.

In his twenties Braithwaite accompanied as secretary his kinsman Christian Cole, British resident at Venice, with whom he travelled extensively in Europe. On his return to London he took up service in the army once more and commanded for the duke of Montagu in the expeditions to St Lucia and St Vincent. While on half-leave his seemingly inexhaustible appetite for travel took him to Spain, Italy, the Balearic Islands, and finally Portugal. When in Lisbon in 1727 he heard about the siege of Gibraltar and volunteered at once. Carried in a British man-of-war, he was the first to enter the besieged fortress, and was very well regarded by both the garrison and the fleet. He then crossed the straits to Morocco to resume his second career as a diplomat by joining the British consul-general, John Russel, in his expedition to the emperor Mawlay Isma'il. During his time in Morocco Braithwaite took daily notes of the events from July 1727 to February 1728 and published them in *The History of the Revolutions in the Empire of Morocco*. The work is a very detailed account of an empire that was strategically important to Great Britain; it achieved a list of over 400 subscribers, many of whom were army officers. On his return to London, Braithwaite determined to leave the regular army and to join the Royal African Company, to whom his book is dedicated. He was appointed chief merchant and governor of Cape Coast Castle in the Gold Coast Colony, then administered by the Royal African Company. His friends saw his book through the press and arranged for its translation into Dutch, German, and French editions that were published in 1729, 1730, and 1731.

In 1730 Braithwaite married Sylvia (1714–1799), who had been born in Amsterdam. They had two daughters, Silvia and Caroline, and a son, Sir John Braithwaite (1739–1803), soldier, who was created first baronet on 18 December

1802. In 1740 Braithwaite again took ship aboard a Baltic merchantman. In an engagement with a Spanish privateer off the coast of Sicily he died as he had lived for much of his life, right in the thick of the action. His will was certified on 29 April 1740 and proved on 27 August 1740 in favour of his widow. She died in 1799 and was buried in Westminster Abbey. John Braithwaite's career has been much confused with the exploits of his younger cousin Admiral Richard Braithwaite (1728–1805) and with those of his son.

STANLEY LANE-POOLE, *rev.*
WILLIAM RONALD BRAITHWAITE

Sources NAM · pedigree, General Sir G. C. Boughton-Braithwaite, 1805, Coll. Arms · J. Braithwaite, *The history of the revolutions in the empire of Morocco* (1729) · G. E. Braithwaite, *The Braithwaite clan* (privately printed, London, 1974)

Braithwaite, John, the elder (*bap.* 1760, *d.* 1818), engineer and diver, was baptized at St Albans Abbey, Hertfordshire, on 20 July 1760, the second son of five children of William Braithwaite (*bap.* 1732, *d.* 1800), whitesmith and engine maker, and Mary Crowther (*c.*1730–1803). His family had run an engine-making shop in St Albans since 1695. John, though the younger son, became the leader of the business which manufactured pumps and engines for the brewing industry and other trades.

The family had left St Albans in 1768 and by 1782 the firm was established in Portland Street, near Soho Square, then a major centre of engineering in London. The Braithwaites now used their knowledge of pumps and hydraulics to exploit a lucrative area of business in salving goods from shipwrecks. They built a diving machine probably along the lines of the wooden or metal diving bells that had been used since the sixteenth century. According to their claims, the design was a significant improvement, but its details were kept secret. Its first recorded use was in 1783, when John Braithwaite descended to the wreck of the *Royal George*—Admiral Richard Kempenfelt's flagship, which had gone down off Spithead the previous year while preparing to lead the fleet bound for the relief of the siege of Gibraltar. He recovered her sheet anchor, many guns, and the ship's bell now displayed at the National Maritime Museum in Greenwich.

After this success Braithwaite and his brother William bought a 40 ton sloop and in 1785 sailed to Gibraltar to salvage the guns from French and Spanish floating batteries sunk by the British artillery during the siege. The brass cannon found a ready market at auction but the iron cannon proved unsaleable so the brothers presented them to the emperor of Morocco at his seaport of Salé.

Between August 1787 and February 1791 Braithwaite brought up goods from the East Indiaman *Hartwell*, wrecked after a mutiny on her maiden voyage in 1787 on the Rifona Reef off Boavista, one of the Cape Verde Islands. As well as facing technical challenges the Braithwaites here encountered armed opposition from American privateers seeking to raid the salvaged cargo. Their spirited defence was reported in *The Times*. The tiny *Endeavour*, lightly armed and with a crew of only nine, engaged the five pirate vessels for over an hour, finally driving them off at the cost of only minor injuries. Braithwaite returned with £38,000 in Spanish dollars, 7000 pigs of lead, and 360 boxes of tin. He also brought back Eliza or Elizabeth Doile (*c.*1775–1814), a Verdian planter's daughter, and they married at St Pancras parish church on 3 June 1794, the anniversary of the Boavista skirmish.

Home waters provided the next major project. The Indiaman *Earl of Abergavenny* sank in Weymouth Bay in 1805 while on charter as a troopship; in the following year, Braithwaite raised goods worth £105,000, mostly coin. Again, technical innovation played a part: he devised and used machinery for sawing apart ships' timbers underwater and blew up the wreck with one of the first known underwater gunpowder charges.

This success enabled Braithwaite to retire. He bought a small estate, the Old Manor House at Westbourne Green, near Paddington, then on the north-western edge of London and convenient for his town house and works in the New Road (now Euston Road). The business was continued by two of his seven sons, John *Braithwaite (1797–1870) and Francis (1796–1823), though all of them worked in related engineering occupations. He died at home on 5 February 1818 of a pistol-shot wound to his spine, sustained three days before when attacked by a highwayman near the entrance lodge to his estate. He was buried two days later in St Pancras Church, and left a fortune of £30,000.

WILLIAM RONALD BRAITHWAITE

Sources *The Times* (22 Sept 1786) · *The Times* (6 Feb 1818) · *GM*, 1st ser., 54 (1784), 550, 632 · *GM*, 1st ser., 88/1 (1818), 644 · *The Mechanics Magazine*, 13 (1830) · 'John Braithwaite', *Journal of the Society of Arts*, 18 (1869–70), 885 · priv. coll., Braithwaite MSS · parish register, St Albans Abbey, 17 Dec 1732, 20 July 1760 [baptism] · parish register, 30 Dec 1800, 14 Sept 1803 [burial] · parish register, St George's, Mayfair, 8 March 1750 [marriage] · parish register, St Pancras Church, London, 3 June 1794 [marriage] · parish register, St Pancras Church, London, 7 Feb 1818 [burial]
Archives priv. coll., family papers | FILM Historical Diving Society, London, diving video
Likenesses oils, *c.*1808, priv. coll.
Wealth at death £30,000: will, 1813, LMA

Braithwaite, John, the younger (1797–1870), engineer, was born on 19 March 1797 at 1 Bath Place, New Road, Euston, London, the third of the seven sons of John *Braithwaite, the elder (*bap.* 1760, *d.* 1818), engineer and diver, and his wife, Eliza or Elizabeth Doile (*c.*1775–1814), who came from the Cape Verde Islands. After being educated at Walter Lord's School, Mitcham Road, Tooting, in Surrey, he joined his father's workshop, where he gained experience of practical engineering and became a skilled draughtsman.

In 1808 Braithwaite's father purchased the Old Manor House at Westbourne Green, near Paddington, and lived here with his family until 1818, when he died, leaving the estate to all his sons and the business to Francis and John. When Francis died in 1823, John Braithwaite carried on the business alone and added to it by starting to make high-pressure steam engines. In 1817 he reported before the House of Commons upon the Norwich steamboat explosion, and in 1820 he ventilated the House of Lords using air-pumps. In 1822 he constructed a donkey engine, and in 1823 cast the statue of the duke of Kent by Sebastian Gahagan, which was erected in Portland Place, London.

Braithwaite was introduced to George and Robert Stephenson in 1827, and about the same time became acquainted with Captain John Ericsson, who then had many new ideas. In 1829 Braithwaite and Ericsson constructed for the Rainhill trials the locomotive engine *The Novelty*. This engine was the first one ever to run a mile within a minute (56 seconds); but the trials were entered rather late, and *The Novelty*, probably constructed somewhat hastily, failed to complete the course. Nevertheless, some contemporary accounts of the event were enthusiastic about the engine, and although Braithwaite did not win the contest with his machine, he still received orders for two locomotives—though of a different design—for the opening of the Liverpool and Manchester Railway.

At this time Braithwaite (with Ericsson) manufactured the first practical steam fire-engine, which was ultimately destroyed by a London mob. It had, however, previously been effective at the fires at the English Opera House and the Argyle Rooms in 1830, and at the conflagration of the houses of parliament in 1834. It threw 150 gallons of water per minute to a height of 90 feet, burnt coke, and got up steam in about 20 minutes; but it was looked upon with so much jealousy by the fire brigade of the day that Braithwaite had to withdraw it. He, however, soon constructed four others of larger dimensions, two of which, in Berlin and Liverpool respectively, gave good service.

In 1830 Braithwaite and Ericsson took out a patent (no. 5903) for an improved method of manufacturing salt from brine, and in the same year had to fight an important lawsuit, which they lost. This was brought by Lord Cochrane and Alexander Galloway, who claimed that one of their patents had been infringed by Braithwaite and Ericsson's patent on 'Furnaces of steam boilers and pneumatic apparatus for creating atmospheric draught therein' (1829, no. 5763). In 1833 Braithwaite built a caloric engine in conjunction with Ericsson. The following year he ceased to take an active part in the management of the works in the New Road, but instead began to practise as a civil engineer for public works, and was largely consulted at home and abroad, particularly on the capabilities and improvement of locomotive engines.

In 1834 the Eastern Counties Railway was projected and laid out by Braithwaite in conjunction with Charles Blacker Vignoles. The act of incorporation was passed in 1836, and Braithwaite was soon after appointed engineer-in-chief for its construction. He adopted a 5 foot gauge, and upon that gauge the line was constructed as far as Colchester, the works, however, being made wide enough for a 7 foot gauge. On the recommendation of Robert Stephenson it was subsequently altered to the national gauge of 4 ft 8½ in. Later Braithwaite advocated a still narrower gauge. He ceased to be officially connected with the Eastern Counties Railway on 28 May 1843, but while engineer of the company he brought in American excavating and pile-driving machinery for the construction work.

In 1835 Braithwaite published a *Supplement to Captain Sir John Ross's narrative of a second voyage in search of a north-west passage, containing the suppressed facts necessary to an understanding of the cause of the failure of the steam machinery of the Victory*, in an effort to explain the breakdown of a steam boiler which he and Ericsson had installed, in the belief that the ship was being equipped for experimental purposes and not for a challenging sea voyage. Sir John Ross published a reply in the same year.

Braithwaite was joint founder of the *Railway Times*, which he started in conjunction with J. C. Robertson as editor in 1837, and he continued as sole proprietor until 1845. He undertook the preparation of plans for the Direct London and Exeter Railway, but the panic of the period, and his connection with some speculative ventures, necessitated the winding up of his affairs in 1845. Braithwaite had, in 1844, a share in a patent for extracting oil from bituminous shale, and works were erected near Weymouth, which, but for his financial difficulties, might have been successful.

Some years before, in 1836–8, Ericsson and Braithwaite had fitted a screw propeller to an ordinary canal boat, which started from London along the canals to Manchester on 28 June 1838, returning by way of Oxford and the Thames to London. Although the operation of the boat was successful, the experiment was abandoned because of the restricted draught of the canals and the competition of the railways, which took away the traffic.

In 1844, and again in 1846, Braithwaite was often on the continent surveying railway lines in France, and on his return he was employed to survey Langstone harbour in 1850, and to build the Brentford brewery in 1851. By this time, Braithwaite and his wife, Caroline Amelia (1803/4–1878) were living at 39 Bedford Square, London, with their daughter and two sons, and from now on he practised mainly as a consulting engineer, advising on patents for various engineering projects. His patents on heating, lighting, and ventilating had appeared in 1846 (no. 11046) and 1847 (no. 11546), and in 1857 a report he had written was published in *Guideway Steam Agriculture* by P. A. Halkett.

Braithwaite became a member of the Institution of Civil Engineers on 13 February 1838, and at the time of his death he was one of the oldest members of the Society of Arts, having been elected in 1819; he was also a life governor of seventeen charitable institutions.

In appearance, as a photograph of him in later years shows, Braithwaite was a handsome, well-built man with thick wavy hair and a short bushy beard. He was always kind and hospitable, and treated his employees and apprentices well. His conversation was lively and often humorous and instructive, and his willingness to help inventors was well known. A practical engineer of talent, John Braithwaite should be remembered for the part he played in the early development of railways, and especially for *The Novelty*, which competed so valiantly against Stephenson's *Rocket* at the Rainhill trials.

Braithwaite died very suddenly from a stroke at just

before midnight on 24 September 1870 at 6 Clifton Gardens, Paddington, London; his remains were interred in Kensal Green cemetery. He was survived by his wife.

G. C. BOASE, rev. CHRISTOPHER F. LINDSEY

Sources PICE, 31 (1870–71), 207–11 · *Journal of the Society of Arts*, 18 (1869–70), 885 · W. Braithwaite, 'A short history of the Braithwaites', *Family Tree Magazine* (Sept 1992), 8–9 · P. A. Hayward, *Hayward's patent cases, 1600–1883*, 2 (1987), 102–34 · W. C. Church, *Life of John Ericsson*, 1 (1890) · F. E. Hansford, 'John Braithwaite', *St. Pancras Journal* (May 1955), 4–5 · W. L. Rutton, 'Westbourne Green: a retrospect', *Home Counties Magazine*, 2 (1900), 17, 275–7, 279 · *The Mechanics Magazine*, 13 (1830), 235–7, 308–12, 377–88, 417–19 · T. F. T. Baker, ed., *A history of the county of Middlesex: Hampstead and Paddington parishes*, 9 (1989), 180, 230 · K. R. Gilbert, *Fire fighting appliances* (1969) · C. Tomlinson, ed., *Cyclopedia of useful arts and manufactures*, 2 vols. (1852–4) · K. H. Vignoles, *Charles Blacker Vignoles: romantic engineer* (1982) · d. cert.

Archives BL, letters patent and railway plans · Inst. CE, sketches and other items · National Museums and Galleries on Merseyside, original cylinder of *The Novelty* · Sci. Mus., replica of *The Novelty*, incorporating parts of the original | Sci. Mus., Rastrick's Rainhill notebook and other items connected with Braithwaite and Ericsson

Likenesses F. C. Lewis, lithograph, c.1830 (after J. Boaden), NPG; repro. in *Mechanics' Magazine* (1830) · W. Black & Co., lithograph, 1869, Sci. Mus. · copperplate on wood, Sci. Mus. · photograph, Sci. Mus.

Braithwaite, **Sir John Bevan** (1884–1973), stockbroker, was born on 22 November 1884 at Islington, London, the younger son of Joseph Bevan *Braithwaite (1855–1934), a stockbroker, and his wife, Anna Sophia Gillett. Both parents belonged to long-established and well-connected Quaker families. John was educated at Leighton Park School, Reading, and at Owens College, Manchester (later Manchester University). He then followed his elder brother into the stockbroking firm of Foster and Braithwaite, of which their father was, from 1888 until 1922, the senior partner. He became a member of the stock exchange in 1907, and in the following year he was made a partner in the firm.

Braithwaite married in 1908 Martha Janette Baker (d. 1972), the daughter of Joseph Allen Baker (1852–1918), an engineer, a member of the London county council from 1895 to 1906, and Liberal MP for Eastern Finsbury from 1905 until his death. The couple had two sons and a daughter, and lived for most of their married life in Hampstead Garden Suburb.

Soon after Braithwaite became a partner in Foster and Braithwaite, it became apparent that the firm was facing severe financial problems. Losses had been made as a result of the firm's activities in company promotion and in trading on the stock exchange on its own account. Deeply shocked by these discoveries, Braithwaite told his father that he considered such activities to be 'nothing less than dangerous gambling' and inappropriate for a 'strong ancient & honoured & impregnable City House' (Reader, *A House in the City*, 126–7). They had brought the firm, he said, close to 'the possibility of failure. … it has been before my mind like a nightmare day & night more or less continually' (ibid., 127). The remedy he advocated was 'hard work & self-denial' (ibid., 131), which in the

event contributed to the salvation of Foster and Braithwaite and provided Braithwaite with his own guideline through life.

During the First World War, Braithwaite served with the Friends' Ambulance Unit. Afterwards he returned to the firm, where, in the 1920s, the new direction in which its policy took it, eschewing speculation, met with the approval of his 'somewhat austere cast of mind' (Reader, *A House in the City*, 133). In the inter-war years he began to take a greater interest and participate in the affairs of the stock exchange. In 1937 he was elected to its governing body, the committee for general purposes.

Braithwaite's view of the role and function of the stock exchange, shaped by his formative experiences with Foster and Braithwaite, gained wider support, particularly after the Second World War. He considered that the stock exchange could not continue to act as a private club but that it had a public duty, and therefore should be publicly accountable. When the new council of the stock exchange was formed in 1949, Braithwaite was elected as its chairman, a post he held for ten years. During that time it was largely due to him that the visitors' gallery was opened, that the stock exchange employed an advertising agency, and that, in 1950, a compensation fund for members' clients was established. In all of these he faced considerable opposition, but his powerful personality won the day. He was knighted in 1953.

Sir John continued to press for wider shareholding among the public. Not untypical of his views was a speech he made in 1956: 'If only some of the hundreds of millions that are poured down the drain each year on betting on horses, dogs and football could be attracted into investment in British industry, what a fine start could be made' (Reader, *A House in the City*, 173).

Braithwaite was a director of the London Electric Lighting Company (the firm with which his father had had a long connection) from 1934 to 1948, and its chairman from 1943 to 1948. He was a governor of the London School of Economics from 1953 to 1964. Although his influence had long been paramount at Foster and Braithwaite, he did not become its senior partner in name until 1963. He held the office until he retired in 1971. Braithwaite's retirement, and the time to indulge more fully his lifetime interests in literature, music, and photography, was short. He died at his home, 85 Hampstead Way, Hampstead Garden Suburb, London, on 5 April 1973.

JUDY SLINN

Sources W. J. Reader, 'Braithwaite, Sir John Bevan', *DBB* · W. J. Reader, *A house in the City* (1979) · *WWW* · *CGPLA Eng. & Wales* (1973) · *The Times* (6 April 1973) · d. cert.

Archives GL, Foster and Braithwaite MSS

Likenesses photographs, stock exchange, London, Foster and Braithwaite

Wealth at death £133,737: probate, 18 June 1973, *CGPLA Eng. & Wales*

Braithwaite, **Joseph Bevan** (1818–1905), barrister and Quaker minister, was born on 21 June 1818 in Highgate, Kendal; with his twin sister he was the youngest of the nine children of Isaac Braithwaite (1781–1861), dyestuff manufacturer and drysalter, and Anna Braithwaite, both parents being of long-standing Quaker families. His mother, **Anna Braithwaite** (1788–1859), Quaker minister, was born on 27 December 1788 at Birmingham, eleventh of the fourteen children of Charles *Lloyd (1748–1828), banker, and Mary Lloyd, née Farmer (1751?–1821). It was a cultivated family circle. Anna married Isaac Braithwaite of Kendal in 1808, her sister Mary (1784–1822) having married his brother George (1777–1853) in 1806. Her brother Charles *Lloyd (1775–1839) and his wife settled at Brathay Lodge, near Ambleside in Westmorland, and her sister Priscilla married Christopher Wordsworth, master of Trinity College, Cambridge. In 1815 her meeting recorded its unity with her vocal ministry and, besides many journeys in Britain and Ireland throughout her life, she thrice visited America (1823–4, 1825, 1827–9), on the latter two occasions with her husband. Her theology was uncompromisingly evangelical and, like other English ministering Friends then visiting America, she vigorously opposed the 'unsound' part-mystical, part-rationalist teaching of Elias Hicks and his anti-authoritarian followers, who considered the visitors a major cause of the separations of 1827–8 which rent American Quakerism for over a century. In 1835 Isaac Crewdson, a near connection of her husband, published *A Beacon to the Society of Friends*, provoking widespread controversy and resulting, particularly in Manchester and Kendal meetings, in substantial secession from the society, including five of her seven surviving children. For some years Anna Braithwaite suffered from a spinal affliction and after 1851 she ventured little from home or the family's summer residence at Scotby, near Carlisle. She died at Kendal on 18 December 1859, and her body was interred in the Quaker burial-ground there.

Joseph Bevan Braithwaite, educated at the Friends' school, Stramongate, Kendal, thus grew up in an atmosphere charged with religious excitement and controversy. Indeed, he was about to resign his Quaker membership and was writing a pamphlet against the Friends when, with his cousin George Stacey Gibson, he attended the Britain yearly meeting of 1840. This experience determined him to cast in his lot with the society. For a career Braithwaite turned to the law and, after being articled (1834–40) to a Kendal solicitor, went to the London chambers of John Hodgkin. He was called to the bar in 1843 but, because of an impediment in his speech, did not practise in court. His pupils remembered gratefully the time and attention he gave them, though Edward Fry recalled him as 'a very dry lawyer, who loved ... even the ghost of dead questions, with a warm affection' (A. Fry, *Memoir of Sir Edward Fry*, 1921, 46).

From 1840 until his death Braithwaite belonged to Westminster Friends' meeting, in which he soon started to speak: his gift in the ministry was acknowledged in 1844. He had in his teens studied not only Latin and New Testament Greek but also Hebrew, and in 1834 Joseph John Gurney made him a generous gift of books, the foundation of Braithwaite's substantial library and considerable reputation as a patristic scholar. After Gurney's death in 1847 the mantle of evangelical leadership among British Quakers

fell increasingly on Braithwaite, whose first substantial work was the editing of Gurney's *Memoirs* (2 vols., 1854). A conservative biblical scholar, he was never a literalist; an evangelical, he was also a mystic; a stammerer, he was a frequent and eloquent minister. He married on 27 August 1851 Martha Gillett (1823–1895), also an acknowledged minister, the daughter of a Quaker banker of Banbury, Oxfordshire; they had nine children, including the stockbroker Joseph Bevan *Braithwaite. After ten years at 65 Mornington Road, Regent's Park, London, the family moved in 1861 to 312 Camden Road, Martha's banker brother George Gillett and his family moving to 314. Braithwaite's legal practice enabled him to travel extensively among Friends in Britain, Ireland, and France (sometimes accompanied by his wife) and he five times visited America (1865, 1876, 1878, 1884, 1887). In return there was a constant stream of American and other visitors to the Braithwaite home. He thus became both well-known and influential on both sides of the Atlantic. His work for the Bible Society brought him into contact with central and southern Europe and the Middle East. He inherited his mother's aversion to the Hicksites and he was responsible for the declaration of faith adopted by the 1887 conference of American orthodox yearly meetings at Richmond, Indiana, and was grieved that British Friends declined to endorse it. In the 1850s he would 'meet religious doubts and difficulties in a comprehending, sympathetic spirit' (T. Hodgkin, *The Friend*, new ser., 45, 1905, 766), but from the later 1860s he was more defensive of religious orthodoxy and his family was discouraged, on raising some new point, to be told that '*my* views on all these subjects were settled more than sixty years ago' (Thomas and others, 88).

In 1869 Braithwaite joined the committee of the British and Foreign Bible Society and made two journeys on its behalf to eastern Europe (1872, 1883–4). He had a wide range of friendships: poets and prelates, Anglicans and free churchmen—and, unusual for the time, Roman Catholics. John Bright, who once called him 'the Quaker Bishop of Westminster', noted his ministry appreciatively, mentioning 'concluding passages eloquent and beautiful' and a 'sermon remarkable for brevity and force' (J. T. Mills, *John Bright and the Quakers*, 2, 1935, 48–9). Braithwaite was clean-shaven and dignified in mien: his face emanated benign calm. He was an early riser and for much of his life would be in his study by five o'clock, inviting his children to join him. He enjoyed them and his grandchildren and it was far from a solemn household. He died at 312 Camden Road, London, on 15 November 1905, and his body was interred in the Quaker burial-ground at Winchmore Hill, London.   EDWARD H. MILLIGAN

Sources A. L. Thomas and others, *J. Bevan Braithwaite: a friend of the nineteenth century, by his children* (1909) · J. B. Braithwaite, *Memoirs of Anna Braithwaite* (1905) · H. Lloyd, *The Quaker Lloyds in the industrial revolution* (1975), 220–33 · *Annual Monitor* (1906), 3–41 · *The Friend*, new ser., 45 (1905), 780, 814–17, 863–4 · *The Friend*, 18 (1860), 21 · digest registers of births, marriages, and burials, RS Friends, Lond.

Archives NL Scot., corresp. and papers · RS Friends, Lond., corresp., papers, memoranda, and commonplace books | RS

Friends, Lond., Lloyd MSS · RS Friends, Lond., Anna Braithwaite MSS · Wellcome L., corresp. with John Hodgkin
Likenesses C. A. Gandy, photograph, 1875, RS Friends, Lond. · J. Deane Hilton, photograph, 1883, RS Friends, Lond. · A. B. Durand, engraving (Anna Braithwaite; after W. Dunlop), RS Friends, Lond. · J. H. Hogg, photograph (Anna Braithwaite; after daguerreotype?), RS Friends, Lond.
Wealth at death £14,742 7s. 2d.: probate, 20 March 1906, CGPLA Eng. & Wales

Braithwaite, Joseph Bevan (1855–1934), stockbroker, was born on 5 October 1855 at 65 Mornington Road, Regent's Park, London, one of the three sons and six daughters of Joseph Bevan *Braithwaite (1818–1905), barrister, and his wife, Martha Gillett (1823–1895), daughter of a Banbury banker. Both the Braithwaite and the Gillett families belonged to the Society of Friends which, over the century or so before Joseph's birth, had many members whose dedication to business enterprise, combined with marriages made almost exclusively within the group, gave them an influence far outweighing their numerical strength. Quaker families, to many of whom young Joseph was related, held dominant positions in financial institutions in the City of London, as well as in the banking, brewing, railway, iron and steel, and confectionery industries.

Joseph Braithwaite was educated at Quaker schools in Kendal (the Braithwaites had long been established there) and at Grove House, Tottenham, in north London, and he then began to read for the bar. However, in 1876 he changed direction and joined the City stockbroking firm of Foster and Braithwaite. Founded by Quakers in 1825, it was by the 1870s largely owned by its senior partner, Joseph's uncle, Isaac Braithwaite (1810–1890). Isaac had provided for his succession within the firm, with the introduction of two of his sons, so that Joseph cannot have had great hopes of advancement when he joined; but the death of Alfred Braithwaite, one of Isaac's sons, created an opening in 1880 and Joseph became a partner at the age of twenty-five. In 1881 he married Anna Sophia Gillett, daughter of the banker Jonathon Gillett, a connection through his mother's family; they had two sons, Jonathon Frederick (1883–1962) and John Bevan *Braithwaite (1884–1973).

In the 1880s Isaac Braithwaite's plans for the future direction of Foster and Braithwaite were blighted by what the firm's historian has described as a 'concatenation of death and dereliction of duty' (Reader, *A House in the City*, 92)—that is, the premature death of Isaac's second son in the business in 1885 and the sudden departure of another partner, apparently guilty of embezzlement. As a result, when Isaac Braithwaite retired in 1888, Joseph Braithwaite succeeded him as senior partner.

Braithwaite's principal interests did not lie in stockbroking; indeed his obituarist in the *Financial Times* noted that he 'seldom entered the Stock Exchange' (1 Dec 1934). His skills lay rather with finance and its provision, and these were applied particularly in the last two decades of the nineteenth century, to the advantage of the new and rapidly developing electricity industry. Braithwaite's interest in electricity reflected a strong technical bent and an enthusiasm for engineering and scientific matters which lasted all his life; he had an astronomical observatory built on his house at Muswell Hill in north London.

It was on Braithwaite's recommendation that Foster and Braithwaite played a major part in the launch on the stock exchange in the early 1880s of the first electric-lighting companies, in the shape of the Anglo-American Brush Electric Light Corporation and its various satellite companies. Investing in electricity was at that time highly speculative, as the collapse after the stock market boom of 1882—and the drop in Foster and Braithwaite's profits—clearly evidenced. Joseph Braithwaite himself became chairman in 1882 of the Great Western Electric Power and Light Company, and he devoted considerable time to the development of generating stations at Bristol and Cardiff.

In the 1890s as head of the firm Braithwaite, assisted by his two partner cousins, Cecil Braithwaite and Ronald Savory, led the firm into company promotion on a much larger scale than ever before. Prominent among the companies that the firm promoted on the stock exchange, either by placing their shares or by underwriting them, were electrical undertakings. Braithwaite became a director of several companies which were financially and contractually linked, and he formed a connection which lasted for the rest of his life with the Electric and General Investment Corporation (established in 1890) and the City of London Electric Lighting Company (established in 1891); he became chairman of both of these in 1906 and remained so until 1934.

Braithwaite was elected a member of the Institution of Electrical Engineers in 1893 and he became a close associate of Emile Garcke (1856–1930), an electrical engineer who played a significant part in the creation of the electricity supply industry. Equally significant was the role played by Braithwaite in providing finance for the new industry, and his ability to do so was underpinned by his position in Foster and Braithwaite.

The firm's activities in company promotion in other areas were less successful, and in the years leading up to 1914 unwise investments in such doubtful enterprises as the Piccadilly Hotel and the Kansas City, Mexico, and Orient Railway Company took Foster and Braithwaite close to disaster. Its survival was due to changes introduced by Braithwaite's younger son, John, who had become a partner in 1908, rather than to any initiative taken by the senior partner himself. Joseph Braithwaite remained the titular head of Foster and Braithwaite until he retired in 1922. He died on 30 November 1934 at his Somerset home, Blencathara, Sea View Road, Burnham-on-Sea.

JUDY SLINN

Sources W. J. Reader, 'Braithwaite, Joseph Bevan', DBB · W. J. Reader, *A house in the City* (1979) · A. M. Taylor, *Gilletts: bankers at Banbury and Oxford* (1964) · *Financial Times* (1 Dec 1934) · CGPLA Eng. & Wales (1935) · d. cert.
Archives GL
Likenesses photographs, repro. in Reader, 'Braithwaite, Joseph Bevan'
Wealth at death £35,469: Reader, 'Braithwaite, Joseph Bevan' · £30,875 18s. 6d.: probate, 1835

Braithwaite [*married name* Lawrence], **Dame** (**Florence**) **Lilian** (1873–1948), actress, was born in Ramsgate on 9 March 1873, the daughter of the Revd John Masterman Braithwaite (1846–1889), then a curate and later vicar of Croydon, and his wife, Elizabeth Jane, daughter of Colonel Thomas Sidney Powell CB of the 53rd regiment. She was the eldest of seven children, five of them boys, of whom two achieved distinction in the services (Colonel Francis Powell Braithwaite and Vice-Admiral Lawrence Walter Braithwaite). A third became European manager of the *Christian Science Monitor*. Lilian was educated at Croydon and Hampstead high schools and in Dresden, Germany. Starting as an amateur actress, her ambition to become a professional aroused a storm of family protest which, however, she managed to overcome and, joining the Shakespearian company of William Haviland and Gerald Leslie Lawrence (1873–1957), she sailed for South Africa and made her first professional appearance at Durban in 1897. She married Lawrence in the same year, and their daughter, Joyce Carey (1898–1993), was born after their return to London. The marriage ended in divorce. Her first appearance in London was in 1900 with Julia Neilson in *As You Like It* at the Opera House, Crouch End; she then played in Paul Kester's *Sweet Nell of Old Drury* at the Haymarket Theatre. In 1901 she joined Frank Benson and appeared in a Shakespeare season at the Comedy Theatre. A tour with George Alexander then followed and she appeared under his management at the St James's Theatre, 1901–4.

Braithwaite's ethereal beauty and undoubted talent brought many offers of engagements, and she now embarked upon a West End career that was to end only with her death. Among her early parts were Lady Hermione Wynne in *The Flag Lieutenant* by W. P. Drury and Leo Trevor, and Mrs Panmure in A. W. Pinero's *Preserving Mr Panmure*; in 1912 she appeared as the Madonna in C. B. Cochran's production of the mystery spectacle *The Miracle* at Olympia; in 1913 she was Mrs Gregory in *Mr Wu*, by Harry Vernon and Harold Owen, with Matheson Lang, and in 1921 she was Margaret Fairfield in *A Bill of Divorcement* by Clemence Dane. Tall, dark, serene, and lovely, she appeared regularly and successfully in play after play, becoming identified in the minds of theatregoers with beautiful suffering heroines and drawing-room dramas at the Haymarket Theatre. In 1924, however, there came a great change in her career when she accepted at short notice the part of Florence Lancaster in Noël Coward's *The Vortex* at the Everyman Theatre, later transferring to the West End and then appearing in the same part in New York. With the shingled, promiscuous Florence, Lilian Braithwaite gained recognition as a dramatic actress and said goodbye for ever to suffering heroines. Her parts at this time included the possessive matriarch of Sidney Howard's *The Silver Cord* and other dramatic roles.

In 1928 Braithwaite's *métier* changed again. She appeared as a 'ten per cent lady' in Ivor Novello's *The Truth Game* at the Globe Theatre and made an enormous success as a light comedienne. The public now could not have enough of this actress who made such malicious remarks in such honeyed accents, and a succession of successful

Dame (Florence) Lilian Braithwaite (1873–1948), by Charles Sims, exh. RA 1902

comedies followed one another, among them *Flat to Let*, *Fresh Fields*, *Family Affairs*, *Full House*, *The Lady of La Paz*, *Bats in the Belfry*, *Comedienne*, and *Tony Draws a Horse*. Nevertheless, she twice reverted to more dramatic roles with Elizabeth in *Elizabeth, la femme sans homme* at the Haymarket Theatre (1938) and Lady Mountstephan in *A House in the Square* (1940) at the St Martin's Theatre.

In 1940 Braithwaite went to the Theatre Royal, Drury Lane, to work for the Entertainments National Service Association and in 1943 she was appointed DBE. In December 1942, in her seventieth year, she entered upon her greatest success of all with the part of Abby Brewster in Joseph Kesselring's *Arsenic and Old Lace* at the Strand Theatre, which ran until the beginning of March 1946. She died in London on 17 September 1948, confident that her illness was but a passing thing and that soon she would be rehearsing a new play. She rehearsed, said Noël Coward, 'with a dry, down to earth efficiency which was fascinating to watch'. Her popularity as an actress was inclined to make serious students of the drama underrate her great ability—her grace, her perfect technique, her exquisite timing. She was a wise and witty woman whose *bons mots* have passed into theatrical history, and her work for theatrical charities was never ending. She also acted for the cinema and appeared in many British productions. Her last and most noteworthy appearance was in *A Man about the House* (1947).　　　DIANA MORGAN, *rev.* K. D. REYNOLDS

Sources J. Parker, ed., *Who's who in the theatre*, 6th edn (1930) · N. Coward, *Present indicative* (1937) · *WWW* · personal knowledge (1959) · *CGPLA Eng. & Wales* (1948)

Likenesses C. Sims, portrait, exh. RA 1902, Garr. Club [*see illus.*] · R. S. Sherriffs, ink and grey wash caricature, 1937, NPG · Mrs

A. Broom, photographs, NPG · H. van Dusen and Hassall, lithograph, NPG · H. Speed, portrait, priv. coll. · postcard, NPG
Wealth at death £78,764 0s. 4d.: probate, 9 Dec 1948, *CGPLA Eng. & Wales*

Braithwaite, Richard Bevan (1900–1990), philosopher, was born on 15 January 1900 in Banbury, Oxfordshire, the eldest in the family of three sons and one daughter of William Charles Braithwaite, of Banbury, barrister, banker, and historian of Quakerism, and his wife, Janet, daughter of Charles C. Morland, of Croydon. He was educated at Sidcot School, Somerset (1911–14), Bootham School, York (1914–18), and as a scholar at King's College, Cambridge (1919–23), where he became a wrangler in part two of the mathematical tripos (1922), and gained a first class in part two of the moral sciences tripos (1923).

In 1924 Braithwaite was elected to a fellowship at King's College, which he retained until his death. He was successively a university lecturer in moral sciences (1928–34), Sidgwick lecturer (1934–53), and Knightbridge professor of moral philosophy (1953–67). He did much to foster the philosophy of science in Cambridge, lecturing on it regularly for the philosophy tripos (his lectures on probability being particularly memorable). He also brought it into the natural sciences tripos, working with the historian Herbert Butterfield to found the department of history and philosophy of science.

Braithwaite's own work was in the Cambridge tradition of scientifically informed philosophy exemplified by Bertrand Russell, J. M. Keynes, Frank Ramsey, and C. D. Broad. His mathematical training showed most clearly in his philosophy of science, notably in his explication of the concept of probability invoked in modern science. This culminated in *Scientific Explanation* (1953), the published version of his Trinity College Tarner lectures of 1945–6, a classic work whose influence ranks him as a methodologist of science with Sir Karl Popper and Carl Hempel.

Braithwaite's philosophy ranged far wider than the philosophy of science. His 1955 inaugural lecture, *Theory of Games as a Tool for the Moral Philosopher*, showed the significance for moral and political philosophy of modern theories of games and decisions. His 1955 Eddington lecture, *An Empiricist's View of the Nature of Religious Belief*, showed his long-standing concern with religion. In this he was greatly influenced by his Quaker upbringing, as in the pacifism, later rejected, that made him serve in the Friends' Ambulance Unit in the First World War. He eventually joined the Church of England, being baptized and confirmed in King's College chapel in 1948.

Braithwaite took a keen interest in public affairs, and was active in college and university politics. He took especial satisfaction in helping to promote the grace admitting women to membership of Cambridge University, and thus to its degrees. His principal recreation was reading novels.

It was the way Braithwaite philosophized that most inspired his students, colleagues, and friends. In height and weight he may have resembled the average Englishman, but not in his intellectual exuberance. In discussion, even in old age, deaf, with spectacles and thinning hair, sometimes apparently asleep, his attention rarely flagged; and the intensity of his contributions—often prefaced with roars of 'Now look here, I'm sorry …'—was a continual refutation of the popular dichotomy of reason and passion. His curiosity was boundless, his grasp of issues quick and complete, his comments clear, forceful, and original. No one could be more passionate in the rational pursuit of truth, nor less concerned to impress, dominate, preach, or be taken for a guru. He was a great scourge of the obscure, the portentous, the complacent, and the slapdash—diseases to which philosophy is always prone and to which his incisive irreverence was the perfect antidote.

Braithwaite received an honorary DLitt from Bristol University in 1963, and was visiting professor of philosophy at Johns Hopkins University in 1968, the University of Western Ontario in 1969, and the City University of New York in 1970. He was president of the Mind Association in 1946, and of the Aristotelian Society in 1946–7. In 1957 he became a fellow of the British Academy and in 1986 a foreign honorary member of the American Academy of Arts and Sciences. In 1948 he helped to found what later became the British Society for the Philosophy of Science, of which he was president from 1961 to 1963.

In 1925 Braithwaite married Dorothea Cotter, daughter of Sir Theodore *Morison, principal of Armstrong College, Newcastle upon Tyne, which later became Newcastle University. She died in 1928, and in 1932 he married Margaret Mary (d. 1986), daughter of Charles Frederick Gurney *Masterman, a noted Liberal MP and member of the 1914 cabinet. They had a son and a daughter. Braithwaite died of pneumonia on 21 April 1990 at The Grange, a nursing home in Bottisham, near Cambridge. His ashes were interred in King's College chapel, Cambridge.

D. H. MELLOR, *rev.*

Sources M. Hesse, 'Richard Bevan Braithwaite, 1900–1990', *PBA*, 82 (1993), 367–80 · *Annual Report of the Council* [King's College, Cambridge] (1990) · private information (1996) · private information (2004) [T. Adkins] · personal knowledge (1996) · *CGPLA Eng. & Wales* (1990)
Archives King's AC Cam., notes, lectures, and press cuttings
Likenesses photograph, 1952, Hult. Arch.
Wealth at death £148,072: probate, 16 Oct 1990, *CGPLA Eng. & Wales*

Braithwaite, Sir Walter Pipon (1865–1945), army officer, was born on 11 November 1865 at Alne, near Easingwold, Yorkshire, the youngest son and twelfth child of the vicar, the Revd William Braithwaite (d. 1870), and his wife, Laura Elizabeth Pipon, daughter of the seigneur of Noirmont, Jersey. Braithwaite was educated at Bedford School and the Royal Military College, Sandhurst. He was commissioned into the Somerset light infantry in 1886 and saw service with the 2nd battalion in the later stages of the Third Anglo-Burmese War, being mentioned in dispatches. On 25 April 1895 he married Jessie Adine (1868/9–1950), the daughter of a London banker, Caldwell Ashworth. They had one son, who was killed on the first day of the battle of the Somme in 1916. Although unsuccessful in the entrance examination, in 1898 Braithwaite secured a nomination to the Staff College. On passing out he was sent to South Africa as a special service officer on the outbreak of war in 1899. He served on the staff throughout the war, first as a brigade-major and then as deputy assistant adjutant-general, taking part in most of the major actions from the relief of Ladysmith onwards. He was mentioned in dispatches three times, and in 1900 he was breveted major.

A popular and capable officer, Braithwaite had proved his bravery under fire and his considerable aptitude for staff work in wartime, and in peacetime his competence and charm facilitated his continued rise in the army. After the war he joined the staff of the southern command, first under Sir Evelyn Wood and then Sir Ian Hamilton. In 1906 he was appointed an instructor at the Staff College and promoted lieutenant-colonel. In 1909 Braithwaite was promoted colonel and transferred to the directorate of staff duties at the War Office, then under Sir Douglas Haig. In 1911 he was appointed commandant of the Indian Army Staff College, Quetta, into which he introduced the new continental approach to staff work which had been inculcated into the home army since the Second South African War.

On the outbreak of war in 1914 Braithwaite returned to the War Office as director of staff duties, and in 1915 was selected to be Sir Ian Hamilton's chief of staff for the Gallipoli campaign. In a campaign noted for its inefficient organization and the ineptitude of its senior commanders Braithwaite proved an exception. He carried out his duties with distinction; in his first dispatch Hamilton praised Braithwaite as the best chief of staff he had ever met. However, Braithwaite's policy of screening his chief from the growing criticism of the campaign by the fighting troops would suggest that at times he took loyalty to his superior too far. Braithwaite was promoted major-general in 1915, and on his recall to England in October 1915 was given command of the 62nd (2nd West Riding) division, a second-line territorial division then in training. Braithwaite took the division to France in 1917 where it joined Sir Hubert Gough's Fifth Army. The untested division endured a bloody baptism of fire in the fighting round Bullecourt in April and May. By the end of the year Braithwaite, an excellent leader and trainer of men, had moulded the division into an effective fighting formation, which was to acquit itself well in the battle of Cambrai in November 1917, and again during the 1918 German spring offensive. In August, to the regret of his division, Braithwaite was promoted to command the 22nd corps but in September he was transferred to the 9th corps in the Fourth Army, which he led in the advance to victory.

After the war Braithwaite served with the army of the Rhine, and then held in succession the western command in India, the Scottish command, and the eastern command. In 1927, having been promoted general in the previous year, he was appointed adjutant-general to the forces and a member of the army council, acting at the same time as an aide-de-camp general to the king. At the end of a long military career, while serving on the army council,

Braithwaite was reluctant to accept the need for the mechanization of the British army. He was appointed CB in 1911 and promoted KCB in 1918 and GCB in 1929. He was appointed to the French Légion d'honneur, was a grand officer of the order of the crown of Belgium, and received the French and Belgian Croix de Guerre. Following his retirement in 1931 he became governor of the Royal Military Hospital, Chelsea, a position he held until 1938. He was colonel of the Somerset light infantry from 1929 until 1938, and in 1933 was appointed Bath king of arms. On leaving Chelsea, Braithwaite destroyed all his military papers.

Braithwaite died suddenly on 7 September 1945 at his home, The Ricks, Rotherwick, near Basingstoke.

J. E. EDMONDS, rev. WILLIAM PHILPOTT

Sources King's Lond., Liddell Hart C., B. Liddell Hart MSS · I. Hamilton, *Despatches from the Dardanelles* (1916) · H. R. Winton, *To change an army: General Sir John Burnett-Stuart and British armoured doctrine, 1927–1938* (1988) · J. E. Edmonds, ed., *Military operations, France and Belgium, 1918*, 1, History of the Great War (1935) · J. E. Edmonds, ed., *Military operations, France and Belgium, 1918*, 5 vols., History of the Great War (1935–47) · m. cert. · C. F. Aspinall-Oglander, ed., *Military operations: Gallipoli*, 2 vols., History of the Great War (1929–32) · private information (1959) · personal knowledge (1959) · *CGPLA Eng. & Wales* (1946) · Venn, *Alum. Cant.*
Archives CUL, corresp. with Lord Hardinge |FILM BFI NFTVA, news footage
Likenesses W. Stoneman, photographs, 1919–43, NPG
Wealth at death £1771 2s. 10d.: probate, 7 Jan 1946, *CGPLA Eng. & Wales*

Braithwaite, William John (1875–1938), civil servant, was born at the rectory, Great Waldingfield, Suffolk, on 1 June 1875, the second son of the Revd Francis Joseph Braithwaite (d. 1889), rector of Great Waldingfield, and his wife, Mary Hopkinson. He was educated at Winchester College and at New College, Oxford, where he held a scholarship and won first classes in classical moderations (1896) and *literae humaniores* (1898). He took a very high place (sixth) in the civil-service examinations in 1898 and entered the Inland Revenue. Here he established himself as a first-rate official, preparing the work for the innovative land taxes introduced in the budget of 1909, and conducting an inquiry into local income taxes in Switzerland and Germany in 1910. He was made assistant secretary of the Board of Inland Revenue in 1910, and was called to the bar by the Inner Temple in 1911. He married on 2 June 1908 Lilian Grace, daughter of Andrew Duncan of Chislehurst, with whom he had one son and one daughter.

The high point of Braithwaite's career was his work on the national health insurance scheme which formed part 1 of the National Insurance Act of 1911. The scheme instigated the first state-organized programme to provide for the health needs of a workforce vastly changed by nineteenth-century industrialization and urbanization. A large part of the workforce was compelled to pay regular contributions into an insurance fund. These contributions were matched by employers and the Treasury to underpin a fund which could pay out a range of health benefits on sickness, disablement, medical treatment, maternity care, and sanatorium attendance. As a former resident (1898–1903) at Toynbee Hall, the university settlement in the East End of London, Braithwaite had, like his friend and near contemporary, William Beveridge, a familiarity with social problems. He was picked by Lloyd George, then chancellor of the exchequer, to go to Germany to carry out the initial investigation of how social insurance schemes operated there. In November 1910 he became Lloyd George's principal assistant in devising the detail of a scheme for Britain. His skills assisted Lloyd George in developing practicable working arrangements in which approved insurance societies were retained as the main local administrative agents. He also bolstered the chancellor in pressing on with the reform despite a lack of clear support from elsewhere within either the government or the civil service.

In conducting this work Braithwaite was deeply committed to state-organized social improvement but simultaneously constrained by respect for the principles of self-help, operating through voluntary associations, and limited government. As the editor of his memoirs later put it, he was a 'philosophic radical' who 'had an idealist's belief that the keenness and zeal in the cause of self-government found in the small country Friendly Society in which he was interested could be developed in the whole working-population' (*Ambulance Wagon*, 14). Unfortunately for Braithwaite, he was deemed too young and inexperienced to be appointed chairman of the National Health Insurance Commission, that oversaw the implementation of the scheme. This role fell to Sir Robert Morant who, following the Fabian views of the Webbs, would have preferred a non-contributory state-funded scheme and one which was directly managed by government agencies rather than by the non-governmental insurance societies. Braithwaite was made secretary to the joint committee responsible for initial implementation in 1912, but his relations with Morant were deeply strained. Overworked and on the verge of a breakdown, he was persuaded to take a holiday, and on his return he was induced to take the post of special commissioner of income tax in 1913. He held this post until his retirement in 1937.

Throughout his career Braithwaite was a respected public official. He was rather slow in his speech and paternal in manner but overall amiable and well liked. He 'had an immense capacity for work, marked organizing ability, and possessed in a high degree the quality of carrying through to a finish any task he had begun' (*Ambulance Wagon*, 14). In 1937 he was appointed a CB. In practice, however, Braithwaite was sidelined from an involvement in central policy for a considerable portion of his career. He was also denied recognition for his major role in what proved one of the key landmarks in the origins of the twentieth-century British welfare state. Not until the publication in 1957 of his memoirs, based on his diaries, which provide an invaluable insight into the creation of national insurance, did he receive thorough recognition of his achievements. This has been confirmed by the work of later historians researching into the public records.

In his spare time Braithwaite's major commitment was

to the Northeyites' Boys' and Men's Club in Limehouse. This dated back to his residence in Toynbee Hall, when he helped the club's founder, Cyril Jackson. Braithwaite later took over the club's management, a role he kept for the rest of his life. His major contribution was a 12 acre sports ground at Hainault, comprising football and cricket pitches, a swimming pool, and pavilions. He organized both the fund-raising and the construction of the facilities. These were later passed to the London Playing Fields Society. His retirement came to a tragically abrupt end when he died at the British Hospital, Port Said, Egypt, on 14 March 1938 on his way home from the Far East.

JONATHAN BRADBURY

Sources *Lloyd George's ambulance wagon: being the memoirs of W. J. Braithwaite, 1911–1912*, ed. H. Bunbury (1957) · *WWW* · b. cert. · B. B. Gilbert, *The evolution of national insurance in Great Britain* (1966) · J. Harris, *William Beveridge: a biography*, 2nd edn (1887) · J. Grigg, *Lloyd George: the people's champion, 1902–1911* (1978) · A. Briggs and A. Macartney, *Toynbee Hall: the first hundred years* (1984) · H. J. Hardy, ed., *Winchester College, 1867–1920: a register*, 2nd edn (1923)
Archives BLPES, papers relating to the 1911 National Insurance Act | HLRO, Lloyd George papers · PRO, Bradbury papers
Likenesses photograph, repro. in Bunbury, ed., *Lloyd George's ambulance wagon*, facing p. 9
Wealth at death £7656 3s. 11d.: resworn probate, 1938, *CGPLA Eng. & Wales*

Brakelond, Jocelin of (*fl.* 1173–*c*.1215), Benedictine monk and biographer, probably came from Brakelond Street in Bury St Edmunds, Suffolk. He professed at Bury in 1173 and Samson, the future abbot, was his novice master. He became the prior's chaplain, but within four months of Samson's election to the abbacy (1182) was appointed his chaplain, an office that he held until 1188. Apparently he held no other office until *c*.1197 when he became guest-master, remaining so until at least 1200. His later career is obscure. This is partly because his biography of Samson, which is also a source of autobiographical information, ends in 1202, and partly because at least two Bury monks were called Jocelin in his day. Davis and Thomson identify him with Jocellus (Jocelin), sub-cellarer and then, with a brief intermission, cellarer from 1197 to *c*.1206–9. However, this identification faces the problem that he never states in his biography of Samson that he was sub-cellarer and cellarer, although he does mention that he was guest-master. His identification by Rokewode, Arnold, and Butler, as the almoner who occurs between 1206 and 1209 and in 1215, seems preferable, although this identification entails accepting that the story of Henry of Essex, recounted to the writer by Jocelin the almoner—'a man of great piety, powerful in word and deed' (*Chronicle*, ed. Butler, 68 [author's trans.]) was an interpolation. This is quite possible. It reads like one, and its inclusion *in textu* in the two earliest manuscripts (BL, Harley MS 1005, fols. 121–63, and the badly burnt Cotton MS Vitellius D.xv, fols. 1–28) does not prove the contrary, because both are fair copies of the last half of the thirteenth century. The date of Jocelin's death is unknown, but he probably died and was buried at the abbey.

Jocelin's earliest recorded literary work was a now lost

hagiography of St Robert, the boy 'saint' supposedly 'martyred' by the Jews in Bury in 1181, but his fame rests on his biographical chronicle of Abbot Samson written c.1203, a work rightly regarded as a classic. It is a biography set in the framework of conventual history. It ends in 1202, ten years before Samson's death. Jocelin wrote mainly from memory, based on intimate knowledge. When Samson's chaplain, 'I lived with him night and day', and 'noted many things and stored them in my memory' (*Chronicle*, ed. Butler, 36, 26). The biography reflects a change of attitude on Jocelin's part after 1188, when he ceased being Samson's chaplain. Until then he tends to eulogize Samson. He was, indeed, accused of flattery—of 'hunting after favour and popularity … of passing over certain things in silence, where silence was wrong' (*Chronicle*, ed. Butler, 105)—a charge which he denied, though he clearly admired and was fond of Samson. But after 1188 he becomes more critical and presents the convent's point of view. He particularly supports the cellarer in his disputes with the abbot. (He, as guest-master, had close links with the cellary which financed the provisioning of guests.) But he remains judicious to the end and never quite loses sympathy for Samson.

Jocelin was a learned man. He writes simple, lucid Latin, and quotes freely from the Bible and from such classical authors as Horace, Ovid, and Virgil (probably using a florilegium). But the distinctive feature of his narrative is its immediacy and humanity. As a writer he has affinities with, for example, the contemporary humanist Gerald of Wales (*d.* 1220x23) and with Adam of Eynsham (*d.* in or after 1233), but no one else in medieval England left such an intimate picture of an abbot, nor of life in the cloister. Jocelin himself emerges as a kindly man of simple piety. He, along with the other monks, wept for joy when St Edmund's body and even the martyr's cup were found intact after the terrible fire in St Edmund's shrine in 1198. He preferred the quiet life, having no ambition for administrative power. When Samson complained to him about the worries of office, Jocelin raised his hands to heaven and exclaimed 'Almighty God, grant that such anxiety may never be mine!' (*Chronicle*, ed. Butler, 36). He was an affectionate man: he grieved at the loss of the friendship of a fellow monk, his benefactor, owing to an injudicious remark made at the time of the abbatial election of 1182.

Jocelin describes Samson's appearance and character in a set piece and his narrative has many details revealing Samson's aspirations, feelings, and behaviour. Thus, he has an anecdote illustrating Samson's austerity. When Jocelin was a novice he heard it said that whatever dish was placed before Samson he never liked to have it changed. Once when Jocelin was serving at table he put this to the test, giving Samson a 'very black and broken dish' (*Chronicle*, ed. Butler, 40). Samson was unmoved, but Jocelin repented and changed it for a better dish, at which Samson was angry. An example of Jocelin's many graphic descriptions of life in the cloister is the account, much of it in naturalistic direct speech, of the monks' confabulations before the abbatial election of 1182. The monks were agreed that the elect should be a good man, but some

stressed the need that he should be learned, so that he could preach in chapter and to the people, while the main concern of others was that he should be an able administrator. But the younger men proposed a certain man who, though still a novice, was 'industrious, literate and of noble birth' (*Chronicle*, ed. Butler, 14), saying that the senior monks were decrepit old men.

Jocelin was very interested in, and had an excellent understanding of, the abbey's business affairs. He gives much information, for example, about the market in the town, where abbot and convent bought much of their supplies, specifying its regulations and describing Samson's dealings with the burgesses who traded there. He did not rely on memory alone for the biography. Possibly he had kept contemporary notes and used them as a source. He certainly made much use of documents. He incorporated two *in extenso*—the list of the abbey's churches which he himself had compiled and given to Samson as a new year's gift, and Samson's survey of the abbey's knights' fees. Documents also underlie a number of passages. Some of the relevant documents survive and comparison with the passages in question demonstrates the accuracy of the narrative. Altogether, Jocelin's biography of Samson is not only outstanding as a piece of literature, but is also an invaluable historical source.   ANTONIA GRANSDEN

Sources *The chronicle of Jocelin of Brakelond: concerning the acts of Samson, abbot of the monastery of St Edmund*, ed. H. E. Butler (1949) · *Chronica Jocelini de Brakelonda*, ed. J. G. Rokewode, CS, 13 (1840) · T. Arnold, ed., *Memorials of St Edmund's Abbey*, 1, Rolls Series, 96 (1890), 209–336 · *The kalendar of Abbot Samson of Bury St. Edmunds*, ed. R. H. C. Davis, CS, 3rd ser., 84 (1954) · R. M. Thomson, ed., *The chronicle of the election of Hugh, abbot of Bury St Edmunds and later bishop of Ely* (1974) · B. P. McGuire, 'The collapse of a monastic friendship: the case of Jocelin and Samson of Bury', *Journal of Medieval History*, 4 (1978), 369–97 · A. Gransden, *Historical writing in England*, 1 (1974), 381–5 · A. Gransden, 'Jocelin of Brakelond's biography of Abbot Samson', *17th International Congress of Historical Sciences*, 2 (1992), 1138–46 · *Jocelin of Brakelond, chronicle of the abbey of Bury St Edmunds*, trans. D. Greenway and J. Sayers (1989)
Archives BL, Cotton MS Vitellius D.xv, fols. 1–28 · BL, Harley MS 1005, fols. 121–163

Bramah, Ernest. *See* Smith, Ernest Brammah (1868–1942).

Bramah [Bramma], **Joseph** (1749–1814), engineer and inventor of locks, was born on 2 April 1749 at Stainborough Lane Farm, near Barnsley, Yorkshire; he was the second son in the family of three sons and two daughters of Joseph Bramma (1713–1800), a farmer, and his wife, Mary Denton (1711?–1774). After a simple education at Silkstone town school, he was apprenticed to a local carpenter, Thomas Allott of Stainborough Fold. He then moved to London, where he obtained employment as a cabinetmaker. His marriage to Mary Lawton (1749/50–1815), daughter of Francis Lawton of Mapplewell, near Barnsley, took place about 1783. At their home in London at 124 Piccadilly, and later in Pimlico next to Bramah's works in Eaton Street, they brought up their five children—a daughter and four sons, three of whom subsequently entered the family business.

While carrying out work connected with the fitting of water closets, Bramah found the Cumming model, then being installed, to have certain defects. To make it more reliable he replaced the usual slide valve with a hinged flap valve, thereby reducing the risk of the system freezing in cold weather. A patent (1778) was obtained for the new closet, which he started to manufacture in a Denmark Street workshop. By 1797 nearly six thousand of them had been made, and production continued well into the nineteenth century.

In 1783 Bramah joined the Society of Arts, where he attended some technical discussions on locks before going on to perfect and patent his own design in 1784. For this he devised a series of notched sliders which made the lock difficult to pick and gave it a better reputation for security than earlier designs. He put forward his ideas in *A Dissertation on the Construction of Locks* (1788?), and as his lock became known, Bramah realized that some mechanization of production was required if he was to keep up with demand, especially as the mechanisms were complicated and slow to make by hand.

To tackle the problem Bramah enlisted the help of a bright young engineer, Henry *Maudslay, who joined his company in 1789. Bramah's ideas and Maudslay's practical skills were subsequently combined to design and build the various tools, which included a sawing machine, a spring-winding machine, and milling cutters. These were all successfully completed about 1790—an achievement of some note in the history of machine tool development.

By the time Bramah's second patent on locks appeared in 1798 he had probably already made his now famous offer of 200 guineas to anyone who could open his lock without a key. This prize remained unclaimed during his lifetime; but in 1851 Alfred Charles Hobbs, an American locksmith in London for the Great Exhibition, managed to pick the lock after fifty-one hours of work. He received the prize, but the lock's good reputation survived and was even enhanced by the long time Hobbs had taken to open it.

Bramah's most important invention, however, was the hydraulic press (1795), developed out of a long-standing interest in water power, which he had already put to good use in his hydrostatical machine and boiler (1785) and fire engine (1793). The press, with its ingenious self-tightening collar to prevent fluid loss, could convert a small force into a much larger one by using the pressure created by the compression of a liquid in a cylinder of the machine. It was ideal for tasks such as extracting oil and moisture, pressing cloth, or testing the strength of materials, and it still retains many other applications in industry.

Throughout his career Bramah also produced a number of minor inventions. Among these were a beer engine (1797); a planing machine (1802); a paper-making machine (1805); a banknote numbering and dating machine (1806), of which at least thirty were purchased by the Bank of England; an early but not very practical form of fountain pen (1809); and also an unusual machine (1809) for producing multiple pen nibs from a single quill. Not all of his ideas were fully exploited at the time, however. Although he foresaw screw propulsion for ships, suggested methods for extruding and forming materials, and pointed out the advantages of ring mains for domestic water supplies, he did not live to see these become part of everyday life.

In appearance Bramah was probably well-built and of medium height, with dark hair and well-defined features. A religious man, he had a good sense of humour and was cheerful and kind to his workmen. His intelligence, strong personality, and capacity for hard work must have contributed greatly to his success in business.

Bramah died at Pimlico on 9 December 1814 after catching a cold which turned to pneumonia. He was buried in the churchyard of St Mary's, Paddington, on 16 December, and a commemorative tablet, erected by public subscription, was subsequently placed in Silkstone church near his Yorkshire birthplace.

Bramah was typical of many inventors of the time; not only did he create original designs, but he had a great talent for improving on the ideas of others. As well as the range of his inventions and their usefulness, he was notable for his ingenious machine tools, his understanding of the value of publicity (as with his lock prize), and for his ability to supply a reliable quality product in order to achieve commercial success.

CHRISTOPHER F. LINDSEY

Sources I. McNeil, *Joseph Bramah: a century of invention, 1749–1851* (1968) · J. Wilkinson, *Worthies, families and celebrities of Barnsley and the district* (1883), 225–51 · H. W. Dickinson, 'Joseph Bramah and his inventions', *Transactions* [Newcomen Society], 22 (1941–2), 169–86 · C. Tomlinson, ed., *Cyclopedia of useful arts and manufactures*, 2 vols. (1852–4) · K. R. Gilbert, *The machine tool collection: catalogue of exhibits, with historical introduction*, new edn (1966) · *GM*, 1st ser., 84/2 (1814), 613 · W. C. Brown, 'Biographical memoir of Mr Joseph Bramah', *New Monthly Magazine*, 3 (1815), 208–13 · S. Smiles, *Industrial biography: iron-workers and tool-makers* (1863) · parish register (burial), St Mary's, Paddington

Archives BL, letters patent · Sci. Mus., engineering drawings, Bramah Lock papers, and historic items | Bramah Security Equipment Ltd, London, information and historic items

Likenesses portrait, *c*.1799, Institution of Mechanical Engineers, London · J. F. Skill, J. Gilbert, E. Walker, and W. Walker, group portrait, pencil and wash drawing, 1855–8 (*Men of Science living in 1807–1808*), NPG

Wealth at death under £45,000: PRO, death duty registers, IR26-631 [PCC 1-204/5]

Bramall, Sir (Ernest) Ashley (1916–1999), politician and educationist, was born at 31 Brunswick Road, Hove, on 6 January 1916, the elder of two sons (the younger later became Field Marshal Lord Bramall) of Major Edmund Haselden Bramall (1889–1964) and his wife, Katharine Bridget Westby (1887–1984). He was educated at Westminster School and, after a period of ill health and on doctor's advice, at Canford School, Dorset. At Magdalen College, Oxford, he read politics, philosophy, and economics. Perhaps influenced by his mother's strongly held socialist views, he became chairman of the Oxford University Labour Club and treasurer of the Oxford Union. On coming down from Oxford with a second-class honours degree in 1938, he read for the bar at the Inner Temple. On 2 September 1939 he married Margaret Elaine Taylor (*b*. 1916), a social worker, with whom he had two sons. The marriage

Sir (Ernest) Ashley Bramall (1916–1999), by unknown photographer, 1967

was dissolved in 1950. Soon after war broke out in September 1939 he joined the Northamptonshire yeomanry and later the Reconnaissance Corps but was soon selected to attend the army Staff College, Camberley. At the end of his course he was posted to the operational staff of the headquarters of home forces with the rank of major. Home forces had some responsibility for mounting operation Overlord—the invasion of Normandy—and also for the deception plan—operation Fortitude—in which he played a leading part. Bramall's knowledge of German proved a useful asset in an operation that successfully persuaded the German commanders not to deploy their Fifteenth Army to repel the D-day landings.

Immediately after the war Bramall was involved in the work of reconstruction in the British zone of Germany. His part in re-establishing a democratically based trade union movement was one that he later recalled with pride. He then left the army to enter national politics. At a by-election in 1946, held just as bread rationing took effect, he won the seat in Bexley for Labour with a sharply reduced majority. He then combined his work as MP with his interrupted legal studies. He was called to the bar by the Inner Temple in 1949. His particular legal interest then and later was in housing law. On 23 September 1950 he married Germaine (Gery) Margaret Kraft, née Bloch (b. 1920), a translator, with whom he had one son. At the general election in that same year he lost the Bexley seat to Edward Heath by 133 votes and, in two subsequent attempts, did not regain it.

Bramall's interests turned from national politics to the local government of London. He became a member of

Westminster city council, as an alderman, and shortly afterwards became leader of the Labour opposition on the council. At a London-wide level he was elected in 1961 to the London county council (LCC) as the member for Bethnal Green. He remained a member of the LCC and of the Greater London council that succeeded it for the next twenty-seven years.

In 1964, aged forty-eight and at the height of his powers, Bramall embarked on his educational work in London. He became the Labour Party's chief whip on the inner London education authority (ILEA) as it carried forward the educational functions of the LCC on the creation of the Greater London council. After a period when he led Labour in opposition, he became the leader of the authority on 29 April 1970, and remained in that role until 9 May 1981. It was a unique achievement. Over the 120 years of its existence, from the days of the London school board to those of the LCC and then the ILEA, Bramall was the only person to lead the largest education authority in western Europe uninterruptedly for more than ten years. His dedication to this onerous and, at the time, unpaid task is illustrated by the fact that, during these years, he took the chair at 164 out of 165 policy committee meetings, at which all the main issues affecting the ILEA's responsibilities were debated and closely scrutinized.

As leader of the authority Bramall presided over difficult times. Falling birth rates, after decades of expansion, meant that contraction had to be managed. Within a decade the number of secondary schools had to be reduced from 223 to 182, and twenty-seven colleges became fifteen. At the same time the composition of the population of inner London was changing. Over 500,000 people had moved from the inner city to be replaced by a new population of some 250,000, mostly from overseas, many with home languages other than English. Teachers moved away from London with a moving population. There were serious staff shortages and new challenges to be met at every level, from the provision of nursery places to the financing of five polytechnics, all subsequently to gain university status. At times, there were also uneasy relationships with national government.

Bramall confronted these challenges with high principles, a commanding grasp of detail, and formidable skill in debate. As a lawyer he brought to any issue affecting people a strong sense of natural justice. To that he added a determination to uphold constitutional proprieties. It was not for a local authority, in his view, to defy—though it might strongly and publicly oppose—government decisions on local government expenditure. In 1979 that approach, which required substantial reductions to the authority's planned expenditure, brought him into direct conflict with many of his colleagues and only narrowly did he win the day. On two points of principle, with the support of his closest colleagues, he exerted the full weight of his convictions. Corporal punishment in primary schools was ended in January 1973 and, leading the way that others subsequently followed, in 1981 at all London's secondary schools. And, after years of debate and indecision, selection to secondary schools by means of examinations at 11+ was ended in 1977. This development proved far less contentious, both at the time and subsequently, than many had expected. Between 1975 and 1977, thirty-nine public notices were issued, affecting the future of forty-eight schools. To fewer than half these notices were objections made in the form laid down by statute, namely by ten or more local government electors or by borough councils.

While leading the ILEA and being ultimately responsible for a revenue budget of some £900 million, Bramall undertook time-consuming work of national importance. For these and other services he was knighted in 1975. His national work included chairing the newly formed council of local education authorities. For five years he also served as leader of the employer's side of the Burnham committee, whose function was to settle the level of teachers' pay. To this complex and for the most part unrewarding task he brought a degree of patience that, for a person who did not always suffer even sensible people gladly, was wholly admirable.

In 1981 Bramall was displaced as leader of the authority by his own party in one of those political convulsions that even at the time seemed unwise, and subsequently proved damaging to the future security of London's education service. Neither then nor later did he allow that reverse to deflect him from his commitment to education and the good governance of London's institutions. His concern for music and the expressive arts, both in his public and in his private life, was lifelong and, in part, reflected in the achievements of his son, Anthony, as a chief conductor in Germany. In semi-retirement he continued to take a direct and influential interest in individual schools and colleges. Among these was Pimlico School, of whose governors he remained chairman until 1994 and a member until shortly before he died. He was for many years chairman of both Westminster College and the City and Islington College. He also served as a governor of the Museum of London, and was a member of the council of City University and chairman of the National Council on Drama Training. His long and profoundly influential contribution to local government and its institutions, and to the London education service in particular, continued until the end of his life.

Sir Ashley died of prostate cancer on 10 February 1999, after a short illness, at Trinity Hospice, Clapham, London. He was cremated on 15 February 1999 at the West London crematorium, Kensal Green. He was survived by his wife.

PETER NEWSAM

Sources *The Times* (11 Feb 1999) · *The Guardian* (12 Feb 1999) · *The Independent* (12 Feb 1999) · *Daily Telegraph* (15 Feb 1999) · WWW · private information (2004) [Lady Bramall; Field Marshal Lord Bramall; Mair Garside] · personal knowledge (2004) · b. cert. · m. certs. · d. cert. · CGPLA Eng. & Wales (2000)

Archives NRA, priv. coll., papers

Likenesses photograph, 1946, repro. in *The Independent* · photograph, 1967, Hult. Arch. [see illus.] · photograph, repro. in *The Times* · photograph, repro. in *The Guardian* · photograph, repro. in *Daily Telegraph*

Wealth at death £228,467: probate, 2000

Brambell, Francis William Rogers (1901–1970), zoologist, was born on 25 February 1901 at Combridge House,

Francis William Rogers Brambell (1901–1970), by Lafayette, 1927

Sandycove, near Dublin, the eldest of three sons (one of whom died in infancy) of Louis Alfred Brambell (1867–1955), an accountant at the Guinness Brewery in Dublin, and his wife, Amelia Jane Mary Rogers (1869–1951). He was educated at Aravon School (1911–14), and was then coached privately for entry to Trinity College, Dublin. He graduated BA in 1922, gained a BSc (subsequently transformed into an MSc) in 1923, and in 1924 took the first PhD to be awarded by Trinity College. In October 1924 he went, with an 1851 Exhibition scholarship, to University College, London, where he worked on the development of the reproductive systems, especially those of the domestic hen and the mouse. By 1927, having published a substantial body of work and obtained a DSc (London) for his cytological studies, he was appointed to a lectureship in zoology at King's College, London. In the same year, on 27 December, he married Margaret Lilian (b. 1901), daughter of William Adgie of Leeds, whom he had met while she was a student at the London School of Economics. They had a daughter (Anne Elizabeth; b. 1928) and a son (Michael; b. 1932). In 1930 Brambell published his first book, *The Development of Sex in Vertebrates*. In the same year, at the age of just twenty-nine, he was appointed to the Lloyd Roberts chair of zoology at the University College of North Wales, Bangor.

At Bangor, Brambell extended his work on mammalian reproduction from laboratory animals to comparative studies of wild species. Having begun with voles and shrews, at the beginning of the Second World War he and his colleagues transferred their attention to the wild rabbit. While seeking an explanation for the loss of whole litters of rabbits in early pregnancy, Brambell and I. H. Mills noticed the presence of fibrinogen and fibrin in the yolk sac cavity of the blastocyst. This suggested that proteins were passing from mother to young, and further experiments, in which the passive immunization of does resulted in the passage of antibodies into the yolk sac a few hours later, confirmed that proteins could pass across the placenta from mother to embryo. This was at variance with then current theories of placental permeability, and had enormous implications for the whole theory of immunization. Brambell spent the rest of his scientific career working on the issues that arose from this discovery, and his last book, published only a week before his death, was *The Transmission of Passive Immunity from Mother to Young* (1970).

In the post-war years Brambell rose from prominence at Bangor to be a leading national figure in the scientific establishment. Soon after his arrival at Bangor he had started an annual course on marine biology, from which initiative grew the Marine Sciences Laboratory at Menai Bridge. In 1953 he persuaded the Agricultural Research Council to set up a unit of embryology and mammalian reproduction under his direction at Bangor. He held numerous administrative positions in the university and various national learned societies, was elected to a fellowship of the Royal Society in 1949, and from 1960 to 1968 was a member of the University Grants Committee, latterly as chairman of its biology subcommittee.

In 1964 Brambell took up the position for which he is best remembered. Earlier that year Ruth Harrison had published *Animal Machines*, a critique of what she called 'factory farming'. It articulated the current concerns of many, and of the animal welfare movement in particular. In an attempt to cool down an increasingly heated debate by exposing it to some scientific rigour, the government created a technical committee to enquire into the welfare of animals kept under intensive livestock husbandry systems. The permanent secretary at the Ministry of Agriculture, Fisheries and Food (MAFF), Sir John Winnifrith, was instrumental in Brambell's appointment to chair the committee. Other members included senior MAFF civil servants and veterinary surgeons. After several meetings it became clear that a coherent account of the principles of animal welfare was required, against which differing views, attitudes, and propositions could be assessed. This was largely written by Brambell. After long discussion by the committee it emerged virtually unchanged as the fourth chapter of the committee's report.

The Brambell report, published in 1965, made many recommendations, among which were a new act of parliament to safeguard the welfare of farm animals, and the establishment of an advisory committee; it also suggested minimum space provisions for intensively housed cattle, pigs, and poultry, and advocated the prohibition of de-beaking of poultry, tail-docking and indoor tethering

of pigs, and provision of restricted livestock diets. Subsequent writers, from both sides of the animal welfare debate, considered the report a seminal document and it was translated into several languages. Its proposal that all animals should, at least, have the freedom to stand, lie down, turn around, groom themselves, and stretch their limbs became known as the 'five freedoms'. These five freedoms dominated discussion of animal welfare in Europe for many years, even though some felt that they concentrated excessively on one aspect of behaviour—comfort seeking—to the exclusion of others, such as health and security. In fact such criticisms reflected a narrow reading of the report, which in other parts of Brambell's crucial fourth chapter gave full weight to these other desiderata.

Brambell recognized that some of the report's detailed recommendations lacked scientific justification and so might be open to criticism from the livestock industry. Nevertheless he felt that his committee should take a lead, and that unless it made specific recommendations about husbandry standards it would be avoiding the issue. The government did indeed establish the Farm Animal Welfare Advisory Committee (FAWAC), later the Farm Animal Welfare Council, which in 1968 produced the first codes of practice for the welfare of livestock. Many animal welfare activists felt that the codes reflected the dominance of the FAWAC by those representing the interests of producers. In a letter to *The Times* Brambell and other members of his committee voiced their dissatisfaction with them, and especially with their provisions for the stocking densities of poultry. Their report, they felt, had involved compromise to arrive at political acceptability; now the codes represented 'a compromise on a compromise for which no case other than commercial expediency exists' (*The Times*, 23 June 1969, 9). In the short term, perhaps, the Brambell report might not have achieved its objectives; in the long run it clearly had much influence.

Brambell retired in 1968. About 6 feet tall, of medium build, with (in his sixties) greying hair and a moustache, he was firmly but softly spoken, with a trace of an Irish accent. He was regarded as an excellent lecturer, and had a large stock of anecdotes, many of them concerning his exploits as a Home Guard officer during the war. The secretary of the Brambell committee later recalled that Brambell's impatience with shoddy arguments was coupled with a 'mild and engaging sense of humour' (private information). He derived pleasure from working with animals without over-sentimentalizing them. While regarding it as natural for humans to kill animals for food, he felt that they also had a duty to care for them, and he had a deep dislike of cruelty to animals. He was created CBE in 1966. He died at his home, Y Gwylain, Menai Bridge Road, Bangor, on 6 June 1970, and was buried three days later at St James's Church, Bangor. He was survived by his wife. Following his death the new zoology laboratories at Bangor were named after him.   PAUL BRASSLEY

Sources C. L. Oakley, *Memoirs FRS*, 19 (1973), 129–71 · private information (2004) · *DNB* · F. W. Rogers Brambell and others, letter, *The Times* (23 June 1969), 9 · R. Garner, *Animals, politics and morality*

(1993) • R. Moss, ed., *Livestock, health and welfare* (1992) • J. Webster, *Animal welfare* (1994) • d. cert. • *The Times* (8 June 1970)

Archives U. Wales, Bangor, Brambell Laboratories

Likenesses Lafayette, photograph, 1927, NPG [*see illus.*] • F. C. Blair, oils, *c.*1965, priv. coll.; copy, Brambell Laboratories, U. Wales, Bangor • photograph, repro. in Oakley, *Memoirs FRS*

Wealth at death £33,370: probate, 30 Nov 1970, *CGPLA Eng. & Wales*

Brambell, (Henry) Wilfrid (1912–1985), actor, was born on 22 March 1912 at 6 Edenvale Road, Rathgar, co. Dublin, one of at least two sons of Henry Lytton Brambell, a cashier at the Guinness brewery, and his wife, Edith Marks (*b. c.*1879), a former opera singer. He gave his first public performance at the age of two, when he sang 'Three Mice went into a Hole to Spin', 'Mister Bear', and 'There are Fairies at the Bottom of my Garden' to some of the first hospitalized casualties of the First World War. Following his parents' divorce, he was brought up by his Aunt Louisa, who encouraged him to sing in local choirs and act in school productions. After leaving Kingstown grammar school, he enrolled at the Abbey School in Dublin, where he not only appeared in end-of-term shows such as George Bernard Shaw's *Fanny's First Play* but also took minor roles at the Abbey Theatre itself, most notably in Shaw's *The Showing up of Blanco Posset*.

Brambell supplemented his income in the early 1930s by working as an office junior at the sporting supplement of the *Irish Times* and at the *Irish Field and Gentleman's Gazette*. He also continued singing and, in 1938, won a gold medal for his performance in Mendelssohn's oratorio *St Paul*. However, as he later recalled,

> one night I had a row with an aunt and my voice broke. From then on, I was a bass-baritone. It seemed so stupid. Me standing there filling a hall with a great booming voice—and only a shrimpish, skinny five-foot-six behind it. I gave it up immediately. (*Weekend*)

Having toured with the Entertainments National Service Association during the Second World War, Brambell gained repertory experience in places as far-flung as Swansea, Bristol, Bromley, and Chesterfield. He also worked in revue, opposite comedians George and Arthur Black, and made the first of his thirty-three feature films. Some sources credit him with an appearance in Alfred Hitchcock's *The 39 Steps* (1935), but in his autobiography, *All Above Board* (1976), Brambell clearly states that his début came in Carol Reed's *Odd Man Out* (1946).

However, it was on stage that Brambell made a greater impression in the early 1950s. Having co-starred with Liam Redmond in *Happy as Larry* at the Criterion Theatre, he began a career-long liaison with Shakespeare's mechanicals. Yet he also moved into television, most notably by playing a drunk in *The Quatermass Experiment* (1953). Indeed, Brambell was so much in demand in this period that he earned the nickname Old Neverstop. However, his private life was less auspicious. In August 1948 he married a 34-year-old divorcée, Mary Josephine (Molly) Hall, daughter of Patrick McGurk, a trade union official. However, seven years after their marriage Molly became pregnant by a lodger, and the couple divorced in 1955. Tragically, she died in New Zealand a year later, and Brambell

(Henry) Wilfrid Brambell (1912–1985), by Vivienne, 1960s

claimed to have remained celibate for a decade. However, in 1962, accused of importuning for immoral purposes in a London lavatory, he was conditionally discharged.

About this time Brambell's career took an unexpected upturn. Fresh from his success in Disney's *In Search of the Castaways* (1961), and having impressed in the Granada drama *No Fixed Abode*, he was cast as Albert Edward Ladysmith Steptoe in an episode of the BBC's *Comedy Playhouse* series, entitled *The Offer* (5 January 1962). Directed by Duncan Wood and scripted by Tony Hancock's writers, Ray Galton and Alan Simpson, this depicted the fractious relationship between a seedy rag-and-bone man and his ageing bachelor son, Harold. The co-star was Harry H. Corbett as the son (despite the fact that Brambell was only thirteen years Corbett's senior). Such was the success of the play that a six-part series was suggested. Fearing overexposure and typecasting, Brambell initially refused to sign up. But eventually he relented and the first episode of *Steptoe and Son* was broadcast on 7 June 1962.

The show became an instant classic and ran for twenty-seven episodes in four series to November 1965, when Galton and Simpson decided to quit while they were ahead. However, they soon began adapting the format for the radio, and six series were broadcast between 1966 and 1976. Brambell and Corbett also appeared in a fifteen-minute sketch at the 1963 royal variety performance, although they apparently earned the queen's displeasure with a spin-off single, 'Steptoe and Son at Buckingham Palace', which failed to make the charts. Toothless, dishevelled, and routinely dismissed as a 'dirty old man', Albert employed cunning and pathos both to humiliate the socially ambitious Harold and to prevent him from leaving home. Almost every story-line turned on this interdependence and generational antagonism, prompting the television correspondent of *The Times* to opine in 1962, '*Steptoe and Son* virtually obliterates the division between comedy and drama'. Public demand ensured that the sitcom returned to the BBC in March 1970, and it ran for a further twenty-eight episodes over four series to October 1974. There were also two Christmas specials and two feature films, *Steptoe and Son* (1972) and *Steptoe and Son Ride Again* (1973). The success of *Steptoe and Son*—which has continued to be rebroadcast—made Brambell a wealthy man.

Away from Steptoe, Brambell reached possibly his biggest audience as Paul McCartney's grandfather in The Beatles' first feature, *A Hard Day's Night* (1964). However, he was less fortunate with his Broadway début, *Kelly* (1965), which closed after just one performance. Yet he did taste stage success in Neville Coghill's musical version of *The Canterbury Tales* (1967), as Scrooge in *A Christmas Carol* (1970), and in the Old Vic's 1976 revival of *The Ghost Train*, by Arnold Ridley. His film career contained fewer highs, although it was not without its curios, such as playing Alice B. Toklas in *The Adventures of Picasso* (1978). Following treatment for cancer, Brambell died in the Westminster Hospital, Westminster, London, on 18 January 1985. He left the bulk of his estate, and his flat in Pimlico, to a close friend and flatmate, Yussof Bin Mat Saman.

DAVID PARKINSON

Sources W. Brambell, *All above board: an autobiography* (1976) • *The Times* (19 Jan 1985) • '20 fings wot you never knew about Harold and his dirty old man', *News of the World* (19 June 1988) • *Steptoe and son*, website • *Daily Mail* (19 Jan 1985) • *Weekend* (30 Dec 1970) • m. cert. • d. cert.
Archives FILM BFI NFTVA • National Museum of Photography, Film and Television, Bradford | SOUND BBC WAC • BL NSA, performance recordings
Likenesses Vivienne, photograph, 1960–69, NPG [*see illus.*] • group portrait, photograph, 1963, Hult. Arch. • photograph, 1970, Hult. Arch.
Wealth at death £170,720: probate, 16 May 1985, *CGPLA Eng. & Wales*

Brame [*née* Law], **Charlotte Mary** (1836–1884), novelist and benefactor, was born on 1 November 1836, at Rosary House, 35 Castle Street, Hinckley, Leicestershire, the eldest of the nine children of Benjamin Law (1814–1859), superintendent registrar and clerk to the Poor Law Union, and his wife, Charlotte (1814–1877), sister of Robert Heathcoat. Charlotte Brame's parents were devout Roman Catholics, and at Charlotte's birth they were master and matron of the workhouse. Although well-to-do by most standards, the family never forgot the poor; Charlotte's father was a generous benefactor and she followed his example throughout her life. Her father was also the local correspondent for the *Leicester Journal*, and encouraged his daughter to write; she published her poems in the local press from an early age. Initial fears for Charlotte's health prompted a baptism by a lay person which was regularized a year later, and poor health was to dominate the rest

of her life. Early education in Hinckley was followed by convent schools in Bristol and Preston and by a finishing school in Paris. On her return to England, Charlotte secured positions as a governess in Dover, Brighton, and then Leicestershire. It was at this time that she wrote and submitted stories to the Roman Catholic periodical *The Lamp*.

Charlotte's character was described at her death as

one of the brightest, best and most estimable of women, purely noble and charming to a fault. She possessed a cheerful mind, a vivid poetic imagination, was gifted with a wonderful memory and had keen perception and insight into character. She had a glowing passionate love of flowers and had in society a marvellous conversational power and charm. (*Leicester Chronicle*, 29 Nov 1884)

On 7 January 1863 Charlotte married Phillip Edward Brame (1839–1886), a London-based jeweller and the son of John Brame, a Baptist minister. He was never an astute businessman, however, and his business fortunes declined along with his health and sanity. He was given to drinking and his behaviour became increasingly erratic, so that Charlotte was impelled to write, in order to support the family. Her stories appeared in popular weekly publications such as *Bow Bells*, the *London Reader*, and the *Family Herald*. She was incredibly prolific, writing somewhere in the region of 130 novels during her lifetime. Charlotte Brame's fiction was invariably set in English country houses, and her characters were beautiful and wealthy heiresses, eligible bachelors, and aged and wise matriarchs. Against this milieu, she reworked the theme of love in all of its multifarious aspects—old love, young love, jealousy, suspicion, misalliance, and improvident marriage. High morals such as honour, a sense of duty, and self-sacrifice are lauded as the greatest of virtues. The books also contain strong descriptive passages, some of which are drawn from her associations with Leicestershire.

The Brame family settled at 1 Albert Street and 42 Delancey Street, Camden Town, London. Charlotte had nine pregnancies, but only four of her children lived to maturity, all of which took a toll on her own already less than robust health. She secured a permanent position on the staff of the *Family Herald*, but business failure forced the family to move to Cheetham, Manchester, where they lived first at 68 York Street and then 47 Elizabeth Street. For health reasons the family then moved to Brighton. The only existing handwriting by Charlotte Brame are three letters in which she describes fears over failing health, worries about family finances, and expressions of loneliness. The family returned to Rosary House, Hinckley, in 1879. Charlotte continued to write, sending manuscripts to the London editors, and, in spite of her domestic concerns, she performed many acts of charity.

Charlotte Brame's death at Rosary House, on 25 November 1884, was unexpected and painful. Large numbers attended her funeral before interment in Ashby Road cemetery, Hinckley. She died owing money and all her children were taken into guardianship at her death. As a tragic sequel, Phillip Brame committed suicide in May

1886. A commemorative blue plaque was set on her house and a brass memorial plaque was placed in St Peter's Church, Hinckley.

During her lifetime, Charlotte Brame did not receive the income to which she was entitled because her stories were shamelessly pirated in America, especially in the *New York Weekly*, many appearing under imposed pseudonyms such as Bertha M. Clay, Caroline M. Barton, and Mrs Florence Norton. Her books were extremely popular, and continued to attract a worldwide audience into the twentieth century. Translations were made into Spanish, Polish, and Arabic. Several of the works were dramatized, and two of the Bertha Clay titles were used as the basis for films; *Wife in Name Only* (1923) starred Tyrone Power. A contemporary contributor to the *Family Reader*, Charles Garvice, reproduced some of Charlotte Brame's works, and during the 1940s and 1950s Wright and Brown reprinted a large number of the titles. The Lythway Press, in the 1960s, also reprinted several of the stories, and other editions have appeared. Her enduring if unobtrusive presence is indicated by a passing reference in Frank McCourt's *Angela's Ashes* (1996):

> Mam says she wants to join the Library too, but it's a long walk from Laman's house, two miles, and would I mind getting her a book every week, a romance by Charlotte M Brame or any other nice writer.

In her short lifetime, Charlotte Brame was one of the unsung women authors of the nineteenth century. Her literary endeavours, in a male-dominated field, her works of charity, and her personal stamina and resilience, in the face of family tragedy and ill health, represent a triumph in adversity.   GREGORY DROZDZ

Sources G. Drozdz, *Charlotte Mary Brame: Hinckley's forgotten daughter* (1984) · Allibone, *Dict.* · *Leicester Chronicle* (29 Nov 1884) · m. cert. · d. cert. · *CGPLA Eng. & Wales* (1885)
Archives Leics. RO, Hinckley grammar school papers, letters, DE 1243/430/1–3 · priv. coll., letter
Likenesses photograph, repro. in H. J. Francis, *History of Hinckley* · photographs, priv. coll.
Wealth at death £1030: administration, 1 Jan 1885, *CGPLA Eng. & Wales*

Bramfield [Bromfield], **Edmund** (*d.* 1393), Benedictine monk and bishop of Llandaff, presumably came from Bramfield in east Suffolk. His natal surname was probably Halesworth. He professed at Bury St Edmunds in or before 1350, and studied at Gloucester College, Oxford, graduating doctor of theology in 1373. Soon after his return to Bury St Edmunds the general chapter of black monks of the southern province appointed him its proctor in the papal curia. This appointment was probably at the instance of his abbot, John Brinkley, who was then one of the chapter's two presidents. It would appear that Bramfield was already a troublemaker at Bury St Edmunds, since he was made to promise before departure for Rome to procure nothing in the curia detrimental to the abbey's interests. Nevertheless, following Abbot Brinkley's death on 31 December 1378 Bramfield obtained provision to the abbacy from Urban VI on 12 March 1379, in violation of the

Statutes of Provisors of 1351 and 1365. In addition the convent had already elected an abbot, John Timworth, in the normal way, with royal licence and assent.

The consequent conflict between Bramfield and Timworth, between papal power and royal prerogative, became a *cause célèbre* which received much attention in contemporary monastic chronicles, especially in those of Thomas Walsingham. Bramfield returned to England and, with the support of a minority of the monks and a powerful group of the townsmen of Bury St Edmunds, entered the abbey on 11 October 1379. He acted as abbot for four days, but was summoned to appear before the king or his council, and on 15 October was arrested together with his main adherents and imprisoned in the Tower of London. As they made no satisfactory reply before the king's council to the accusation that they had breached the Statutes of Provisors, they were committed for trial in the court of king's bench. Bramfield was tried at Westminster on 23 February 1380 and condemned to imprisonment in the grim dungeon of Corfe Castle. However, at the petition of the monks of Bury St Edmunds, he was sent instead to the less severe confinement of Nottingham Castle. During the peasants' revolt of 1381 the insurgents at Bury were led by a Thomas Halesworth, apparently Bramfield's brother. They demanded Edmund's release and installation as abbot, but he remained imprisoned for another four years.

At length, after protracted negotiations, King Richard induced Urban to confirm Timworth's election: on 22 June 1385 the process of Timworth's election was repeated, and he received papal confirmation and blessing in London by Urban's commissary. Meanwhile, Urban had translated Bramfield to the abbacy of La Grande Sauve in the diocese of Bordeaux. Richard released him from Windsor Castle, where he was then being held, and gave him permission to travel to La Grande Sauve. Bramfield, however, went instead to the Roman curia and there held the office of master of theology in the schools of the Apostolic Palace. Abbot Timworth died on 16 January 1389 and on 14 June his successor, William Cratfield, received papal confirmation and blessing in Rome. Perhaps it was to prevent Bramfield from renewing his claim to the abbacy of Bury St Edmunds that Urban provided him to the bishopric of Llandaff: he consecrated him on 20 January 1390. Bramfield died on 10 June 1393 and was buried in Llandaff Cathedral.

The assertion of John Leland and Thomas Tanner that Bramfield was a writer cannot be substantiated.

ANTONIA GRANSDEN

Sources 'Electio Johannis Tymworth', *Memorials of St Edmund's Abbey*, ed. T. Arnold, 3, Rolls Series, 96 (1896), 113–37 · *Thomae Walsingham, quondam monachi S. Albani, historia Anglicana*, ed. H. T. Riley, 2 vols., pt 1 of *Chronica monasterii S. Albani*, Rolls Series, 28 (1863–4), vol. 1, p. 415; vol. 2, pp. 1–4, 68, 125, 180 · L. C. Hector and B. F. Harvey, eds. and trans., *The Westminster chronicle, 1381–1394*, OMT (1982), 394 · G. B. Stow, ed., *Historia vitae et regni Ricardi Secundi* (1977), 53, 55–7, 80, 121, and nn. · *Gesta abbatum monasterii Sancti Albani, a Thoma Walsingham*, ed. H. T. Riley, 3 vols., pt 4 of *Chronica monasterii S. Albani*, Rolls Series, 28 (1867–9), vol. 2, p. 407 · R. L. Storey, 'Papal provisions to English monasteries', *Nottingham Medieval Studies*, 35

(1991), 77–91, esp. 82–8 · *Chancery records* · M. D. Lobel, *The borough of Bury St Edmunds* (1935), 150–54 · R. Sharpe, *A handlist of the Latin writers of Great Britain and Ireland before 1540* (1997), 107 · Emden, *Oxf.*, 1.275–6

Bramhall, John (*bap.* 1594, *d.* 1663), Church of Ireland archbishop of Armagh, was born in Pontefract, Yorkshire, and baptized in St Giles's Church there on 18 November 1594, the eldest of six children of Peter Bramhall (*d.* 1635) of Carleton, Pontefract; his mother's name is unknown. He attended grammar school in Pontefract and then went to Cambridge, where he was admitted to Sidney Sussex College on 21 February 1609. He graduated BA in 1612. Archbishop Toby Matthew ordained him deacon in York Minster on 24 December 1615 and priest on 22 December 1616, the year he proceeded MA.

Early career in Yorkshire Bramhall began his ministry as assistant curate at St Martin's Micklegate, York, where he became rector on 2 August 1617. Less than a year later, on 24 June 1618, Christopher Wandesford presented him to the rectory of South Kilvington, near Thirsk. On 10 November he married a clergyman's widow, Ellen Collingwood (*née* Halley), who brought with her a substantial library.

Bramhall's career continued at a steady pace in the next decade. He proceeded BD in 1623, and became a prebendary of Ripon Cathedral on 20 March that year, subdean in 1624, and master of the Hospital of St John the Baptist in 1625. Bramhall's reputation as an able disputant and preacher was acquired mainly because of an unlicensed public disputation with two Catholic priests at Northallerton in 1623. The debate centred on transubstantiation, utraquism, and the visibility of the church. John Vesey, Bramhall's late seventeenth-century biographer, claimed that he had driven his opponent to affirm 'that eating was drinking and drinking was eating in the bodily sense'. Vesey was gilding the lily somewhat because the phrase, in fact, was Bramhall's own. It does capture well, though, the sense of 'zeal' rather than 'discretion' which he later said was animating him at the time of the Spanish match, when 'religion in England seemed to our country people (though without any ground) to be placed *in aequilibrio*' (*Works*, 3.540). Defence of the Church of England came to be a pillar of his future reputation. In the short term, after a light rebuke from Matthew, he was employed by the archbishop, and was thus led into ecclesiastical administration, the other dominant concern of his life. In 1627 he took up residence in Ripon, although he retained South Kilvington until 1633.

In 1621 Bramhall had preached to the York convocation on the pope's 'unlawful usurpation of jurisdiction over the Britannic churches'. This was a theme to which he returned in 1630 for his doctoral disputation, 'that Papacy was either the procreant or conservant cause, or both the procreant and conservant cause, of all the greater controversies in the Christian world' (*Works*, 3.540). With his patron, Wandesford, he was placed that year on the York high commission. Two years later he was granted by the crown the prebend of Huisthwaite in York Minster; both Bishop

William Laud and Wandesford's friend Sir Thomas Wentworth, lord president of the council of the north, took an interest in securing the appointment for him.

First Irish career When impeached in March 1641 Bramhall declared: 'I was moved (it was not my seeking) to come here into Ireland for the good and settlement of this church' (Hunt. L, Hastings MS 16064). He arrived in Ireland with Wentworth and Wandesford on 23 July 1633. On 4 August, in his new capacity as chaplain to the lord deputy, he preached on the text 'tu es Petrus' ('thou art Peter'; Matthew 16: 18), holding 'the church of Rome to be only schismaticall and the Pope to be a patriarch' (Dublin City Library, Gilbert MS 169, fol. 211). On 3 September he became treasurer of Christ Church Cathedral, Dublin, where he rapidly settled down to business. This shift from direct confrontation with Catholics to a new concentration on restoring and guarding the temporalities of the established church epitomized Dublin Castle's approach to ecclesiastical affairs for the rest of the decade. Bramhall became prime agent of that policy by acting as chief negotiator, arbitrator, and enforcer. Virtually no transaction concerning church lands or revenues across Ireland's twenty-six dioceses was made without, at very least, his knowledge and, more usually, his active participation. In letters to Laud he listed the many ills of the Irish church—pluralism, long leases, defective taxation records, systematic undervaluations, illegal impropriations—and determined to tackle all of them.

Of the many clergy with Yorkshire connections who were rapidly promoted at this time Bramhall's rise was swiftest of all. On 1 October 1633 he succeeded by royal patent to the archdeaconry of Meath. This lucrative benefice was the equivalent of a deanery, since this diocese had no chapter. He was nominated to Derry on 9 May 1634 and consecrated in the chapel of Dublin Castle on 26 May by James Ussher, archbishop of Armagh, and bishops Anthony Martin of Meath, Robert Echlin of Down and Connor, and Richard Boyle of Cork. Despite his excellent connections and great service he never became, as was widely expected, a privy councillor. The idea was mooted by Laud and Wentworth in 1634, and they even toyed with making him lord chancellor in 1638, but it is likely that it was more convenient to refer petitions from the council board to Bramhall rather than having him sit on it. Indeed some clergy asked for referral to the bishop of Derry in their petitions.

Bramhall's success in recovery of church revenue lay not just in his powerful backers but also in his command of detail. Most of 1634 was spent gathering information, most notably during a regal visitation of Munster. His southern circuit offered an opportunity to persuade the two Boyle bishops, Richard of Cork and Michael of Waterford and Lismore, to join in a complaint against their cousin Richard Boyle, earl of Cork, for usurpation of church lands. Bramhall was also involved in deliberately publicized actions concerning lands in Killaloe and Clonfert, where there had been collusion between bishops and landowners. The immediate effect was to bring large-scale impropriators and lessees of church lands such as the earls of Ormond and Clanricarde into negotiations with him. Such rapidly acquired practical experience made him instrumental in the drafting and passing of four acts concerning temporalities in the parliament of 1634–5. These new statutes created a uniform system of leasing which stemmed the flow of revenue away from the church and rendered collusive and destructive leasing virtually impossible. He also carried a petition through convocation for the restoration of royal appropriations to the church, which Charles granted in April 1635. Along with the royal grant went his own quite effective scheme for buying in appropriations. Then in 1638 he engineered the revival of a distinct diocese of Cloyne after a space of 209 years by overturning a suspect fee-farm. By the end of the 1630s Bramhall's assiduous and often gleeful pursuit of the historical entitlements of the Church of Ireland had created serious strains. Clerical revenues grew greatly, but grew on the back of more effective tithe collection and radically renegotiated leases, and always under a shadow of prerogative action. Accordingly landowners, both protestant and Catholic, identified Bramhall as the leader of a clerical estate which had been re-endowed at their expense.

From the outset Bramhall had advocated adoption by the Irish church of the Thirty-Nine Articles and the English canons of 1604. He quickly discovered in convocation (which started on 21 July 1634) that many bishops and clergy were resistant to any change which did not uphold, in some manner, the 101 Irish articles of 1615. By December, after a blistering confrontation between Wentworth and leading clerics, the Thirty-Nine Articles were received without either confirmation or denial of the Irish articles. Attention then shifted in the spring of 1635 to composition of a book of canons. Here Bramhall was forced to adapt, though not very graciously, to the realities of persistent opposition to an unaltered book of English canons. Initially he viewed framing a few canons to cater for the exigencies of the Irish scene as an unfortunate necessity, but then spotted an opportunity. He began to work very hard on what became a more distinctive code, an 'improvement' on 1604. While Bramhall kept Laud informed of events in Dublin and referred some drafts to him, it is likely that some of the most distinctive features of the 1634 book, such as provision for auricular confession, the requirement that communion tables be placed at the east end, mandatory use of a silver cup, and very much tightened ministerial subscription, were his work. It has been said that he opposed inclusion of canons allowing for the use of the Irish language on the grounds that it contravened a 1536 statute for the English 'order, habit and language'. Yet while he had no great enthusiasm for Irish, it is far more likely that his anxiety was fuelled by problems attendant on provision for clerks to read parts of the service in parishes where the incumbent was anglophone. Such an arrangement could be seen to diminish the centrality of the priest, the ordained minister, which was the particular stamp he sought to leave on the canons.

After the strains of convocation Bramhall diligently avoided any show of triumph and worked closely with Ussher, who had been very nettled by proceedings, on recovery of rights and property. The primate tried to move into semi-retirement, and begged Bramhall to see to it that he would not be named as a member of the new Irish court of high commission. This court first sat on 27 February 1636, and during its existence Bramhall was the most active episcopal member. Surviving evidence indicates that this was a busy tribunal occupied above all with clerical income and property. Yet it became synonymous with attacks on those who favoured, or even appeared to favour, the Scottish national covenant. Bramhall clearly disliked and distrusted the Scots, and viewed nonconformity as a particular national disease. As early as 1634 he denounced the clergy of Down and Connor as 'absolute irregulars, the very ebullition of Scotland' (Shirley, 41). For their part Scottish sources, especially accounts of a conference in August 1636 between Henry Leslie, bishop of Down and Connor, and a group of godly ministers, depict Bramhall as a hectoring bully, more in love with force than reason. He did play a part in rendering Ulster too uncomfortable for a number of ministers, who then fled the country only to warn their conventicling counterparts of the oppressions in Ireland. His deep antipathy to Archibald Adair, bishop of Killala, who was accused of speaking favourably of the covenant in August 1639, led to his being dubbed Bishop Bramble and the Irish Canterbury. These labels stuck fast. As a commissioner for the Londonderry plantation from November 1638 he was motivated primarily by a desire to ensure that the lands did not fall into Scottish hands.

The next Irish parliament in 1640 appeared at first to Bramhall as an opportunity to complete a programme of reconstruction of revenues. The House of Commons presented forty-four grievances about clerical exactions on 17 June, and Dublin Castle promptly lost control of parliament. Equally promptly Bramhall became a focus of the ire of Irish landowners. On 7 November the Irish remonstrance marked out high commission as a leading grievance. On 3 December Wandesford, who had succeeded Strafford as lord deputy, died in office, and two days later Bramhall's close business associate John Atherton, bishop of Waterford and Lismore, was hanged for sodomy. Bramhall's own impeachment in Dublin naturally followed on that of Strafford at Westminster. Very general articles were drawn up against him by Lord Chancellor Richard Bolton, Sir George Radcliffe, and Chief Justice Gerard Lowther and read into the record of the Commons on 4 March 1641. It quickly became apparent, however, that there was considerable doubt about the right of the Irish parliament to impeach. Proceedings fizzled out by July, though Bramhall was not formally discharged until April 1644. None the less the action did ensure he was unable to appear in Strafford's defence. From February 1641 onwards the Irish Commons entertained a flood of petitions against his decisions arrived at on reference from the privy council. Over the months that followed queries about the legality of the mechanisms used to recover church lands gave way to annulments or leave to appeal, and the patent of the 1636 high commission was overthrown. So even before the rebellion of October 1641 the best part of Bramhall's labours had been swept away.

Exile According to Archbishop Ussher, Strafford had pressed him the night before his execution to remember the bishop of Derry to King Charles. Once out of confinement in early 1642 Bramhall travelled north to his diocese, where his family were still resident. John Vesey offers an uncorroborated story of an attempt by Sir Phelim O'Neill to entrap Bramhall and of artillery being turned on his episcopal residence by hostile Derry citizens. Certainly rising presbyterian feeling combined with his now dangerous notoriety made a return to England prudent. After a brief visit to Oxford, by 30 September he was back in Ripon, where he attached himself to William Cavendish, marquess of Newcastle. In 1643 he produced his first printed work, *Serpent Salve*, by far the longest reply to *Observations upon His Majesty's Late Papers and Expresses* (1642). An itch to reply, to rebuff, was the main force behind virtually all of Bramhall's subsequent works, and when not a controversialist he tended to write on request. After Marston Moor, Bramhall sailed with Newcastle from Scarborough, landing at Hamburg on 8 July 1644. Apart from roughly a year's spell in Ireland he spent the entire period up to the Restoration on the continent.

Bramhall passed most of the period 1644–8 at Brussels, probably with Sir Henry de Vic, the king's resident, providing Church of England services for English merchants there and at Antwerp. Although he already knew James Butler, marquess of Ormond, they formed an excellent working relationship in the late 1640s. Just before his departure for Ireland in September 1648 Ormond assured the bishop that he would invite him over as soon as conditions permitted. This happened either just prior to, or just after, the 1649 peace, because by late spring Bramhall was again in Ireland, this time acting as the lord lieutenant's general agent. Letters show him to have been active in Kilkenny, south Galway, Limerick, and Clare. His apparent success led to his appointment on 9 March 1650 as procurator-general and special commissioner to take the royal share of prizes and booty captured after the peace of 17 January 1649. Despite Clanricarde's protection, which allowed him to use the prayer book service in Portumna and encourage James Dillon, earl of Roscommon, to profess his faith in the Church of England as he was dying, his presence clearly irritated Catholics and may have been partly responsible for his departure in March 1650 well in advance of Ormond. He was fortunate in being able to slip out into open sea despite coming close to two parliamentary ships patrolling the Shannon. Oliver Cromwell's alleged remark that 'he would have given a good sum of money for the Irish Canterbury' (Vesey, 28) shows he was still considered a good catch. Parliament's 1646 articles of peace stipulated that he should not be pardoned, as did the 1648 proposals, and he was also excluded from the 1652 Indemnity Act.

On his return to the continent in time for, from his perspective, the alarming political developments of 1650, Bramhall had the minor consolation of administering communion to a kneeling Charles II at Breda on 26 May before his voyage to Scotland. His other significant liturgical involvement with the Stuarts was his confirmation of James duke of York, Henry duke of Gloucester, and Princess Mary. Over the next decade much of his energy was devoted to managing part of Ormond's domestic finances and mainly in acting as a prize commissioner. This was an itinerant time, his correspondence indicating that he constantly moved between The Hague, Antwerp, Brussels, Ghent, Utrecht, and Flushing, with occasional trips further afield. At some point, probably in the latter half of 1652, he made 'a tedious and chargeable voyage into Spain' (Berwick, 105–8). The story, which is to be found in biographies from Vesey on, that the Inquisition had circulated his picture as a wanted man, seems highly improbable. As prize commissioner he had occasion to act as auctioneer of vessels and their cargo. Such activities drew scathing comments from Edward Nicholas and led to at least one serious clash between Bramhall and Edward Hyde. Nicholas viewed Bramhall's 1652 conversations with John Lilburne at Bruges as a bizarre proceeding. Relations were not enhanced in 1653 when Bramhall assisted in spreading a rumour started by Sir Richard Grenville that Hyde was in receipt of a secret pension. Yet by 1658 Hyde was sending Bramhall gifts and complimenting him on the quality of his latest publication, *Schism Guarded and Beaten Back* (The Hague, 1658).

Between 1649 and 1658 Bramhall wrote seven books. Much of his posthumous fame rests on exchanges with Thomas Hobbes on liberty and necessity. Their controversy had its roots in a philosophical discussion which took place at Newcastle's Paris residence in 1645. Neither disputant intended publishing, but as Hobbes's part was printed, without his permission, in 1654 as *Of Liberty and Necessity*, Bramhall felt obliged to go to press with *A Vindication of True Liberty from Antecedent and Extrinsical Necessity* (1655). Bramhall, a libertarian in his understanding of human freedom, produced two more pamphlets, while Hobbes, a determinist, one more. The bishop's defence was lively and robust and highly intelligent, but not especially original. The same bright forcefulness is manifest in his other books, which consist mainly of discourses against Catholics on the one hand and 'sectaries' on the other. Bramhall jumped in where he perceived the need to be greatest, adopted a defensive posture, and championed the traditions and origins of the Church of England in print as he had upheld the rights and endowments of the Church of Ireland in revenue raising.

Starting with his *Answer to M. de la Millitière* (The Hague, 1653), Bramhall embarked on a series of works denying that the English church had gone into schism and defending its claim to apostolic succession. These were all topical pieces—Théophile Brachet de la Millitière had written an open letter to Charles II inviting him to become a Catholic, and Richard Smith, bishop of Chalcedon and leader of England's Catholics, had levelled the charge of schism. Later, in the posthumously published *Vindication of Himself and the Episcopal Clergy from the Charge of Popery* (1672), Bramhall was again replying, this time to Richard Baxter's *Treatise of Gratian Religion* (1672). These tracts all depended heavily on the appeal to the past and tart rejoinders to those who alleged novelty or upheaval:

> I make not the least doubt in the world but that the Church of England before the Reformation and the Church of England after the Reformation are as much the same church as a garden before it is weeded and after it is weeded is the same garden. (*Works*, 1.113)

As the 1650s went on those loyal to the old establishment became anxious about episcopal succession. Apart from the paucity of consecrators, and the age and unwillingness of many of those left, there were legal difficulties, since there were no deans and chapters to elect on foot of a royal *congé d'élire*. From 1652 Bramhall repeatedly suggested direct nominations to Irish sees, since no election was necessary, and then translation as appropriate to England. Events were to dispel these anxieties. Bramhall went to Brussels in 1659 when the court moved there. He crossed back into England with the king in May 1660 or very soon afterwards, and was certainly at Westminster on 15 June, when rumours already had begun to circulate that he would be given the archdiocese of York.

Restoration prelate Bramhall was nominated as archbishop of Armagh and primate of all Ireland on 1 August 1660, though his impending promotion had been common knowledge for over a month. He was showered with congratulatory letters, and this last phase of his life began in a celebratory, almost triumphal, manner. On 27 January 1661 he devised and carefully managed an elaborate liturgy for a collective consecration of two archbishops and ten bishops in St Patrick's Cathedral, Dublin. This vigorous display of protestant religious and civil hegemony was presided over by the new primate, assisted by three other survivor bishops, John Leslie of Raphoe, Griffith Williams of Ossory, and Robert Maxwell of Kilmore, to the strains of an anthem specially composed by Dean William Fuller:

> Angels look down and joy to see
> like that above, a monarchy
> Angels look down and joy to see
> Like the above, an hierarchy.
> (D. Loftus, *Proceedings … in Christchurch*, 1662)

Jeremy Taylor, bishop-consecrate of Down and Connor, delivered a sermon rhapsodizing on episcopacy. The event was a double triumph for Bramhall because his crafted solemnities were matched by the hard fact that, with Ormond, he had picked the entire bench.

Most of Bramhall's other business in these years did not provide him with anything of the same level of satisfaction or success. He duly took his place as a leading public figure. At their first meeting on 8 May 1661 the Irish Lords elected him speaker. On 13 July convocation made a solemn declaration thanking him for his services to the Church of Ireland, highlighting in particular his role in the 1634 convocation. All records of his impeachment were erased from the parliamentary rolls. In January 1662 the Lords appointed a committee to press the crown for some special recognition of his long service and many sufferings. However, in the greater political sphere all the ritual words and gestures had no matching substance. His

strategy centred on reverting to the position obtaining prior to October 1641 and resurrecting some of his earlier schemes for church endowments. In 1662 he did succeed in carrying a bill for union and division of parishes which had fallen in 1640, but his endless lobbying for a uniform tithing system and long leases for bishops had no issue. Over the winter of 1661 bishops John Parker of Elphin and Michael Boyle of Cork, agents of the Irish convocation in London, had a very tough time in the negotiations surrounding an Act of Settlement for Ireland. It was very hard for them to secure the primate's desired remission of the clerical taxes of first fruits and twentieth parts, and they intimated there was little real enthusiasm for lavish re-endowment. Although Bramhall kept proposing to return to repeat his earliest Irish activity by carrying out a regal visitation to draw up a full and accurate taxation book for the whole country, the mandate was not issued until May 1663, a scant month before his death. Correspondence between Michael Boyle and Bramhall during this time offers a sharp contrast between the rising, energetic new man and an older man whose health and once formidable powers of concentration were now failing.

Bramhall did make what he called his 'northern visitation' during August 1661. His own diocese did not have the substantial presbyterian population to be found in Derry and Down and Connor. Although the Church of Ireland had been restored faster than its English counterpart, the kingdom continued to operate under the (intermittently suspended) 1560 Uniformity Act until 1665. Bramhall and his bishops had formally read and approved the 1662 prayer book in September of that year, but Edward VI's second book was not superseded until 1666. Bramhall's own dealings with ministers ordained by presbyteries indicate not, perhaps, a new moderation on his part, but a desire to ensure the established church was as comprehensive as possible within certain bounds. He did this by underlining the status of the Church of Ireland as the national church and the consequent legal necessity of canonical procedures in order to retain a benefice. Those who accepted his offer were, in effect, conditionally re-ordained. Some acquiesced, but sixty-one Ulster presbyterians were deprived. Bramhall and Ormond had worked to make sure Jeremy Taylor was given Down and Connor and George Wilde Derry. Both bishops were harshly critical of presbyterians and favoured coercion. Bramhall even resisted Taylor's translation out of the north in April 1661, writing to Sir George Lane that his work in 'the reformation of that schismatical part of the country was not yet complete' (Bodl. Oxf., Carte MS 221, fol. 172). His policy at this time appears to have been to offer a legalistic solution to those interested in compliance, leaving the rigorous attentions of his suffragans to the more determined nonconformists.

On 3 January 1663 Bramhall made a will leaving £5200 in cash and estates in Meath, Tyrone, and Dublin. The will also referred to his 'paralytical infirmities' (Berwick, 4), the effects of two earlier strokes. His final stroke came on 23 June 1663 while attending the court of claims in a case between himself and Sir Audley Mervyn. He did not regain consciousness, and died about 3 a.m. on Saturday 25 June. His funeral was held on 16 July, and he was buried in Christ Church, Dublin. Jeremy Taylor preached a fulsome sermon, in the course of which he became the first to present Bramhall as an Anglican 'father': 'in him were visible the great lines of Hooker's judiciousness, of Jewel's learning, of the acuteness of bishop Andrewes' (*Works*, 1.lxxxv). Ellen Bramhall made her will in 1665, and apparently died soon afterwards. The Bramhalls had three sons and three daughters, of whom the eldest, Isabel, married Sir James Graham, son of the earl of Menteith. The descent from their daughter of Francis Rawdon (later Rowdon-Hastings), second earl of Moira and first marquess of Hastings, explains the presence among the Hastings manuscripts of the bulk of John Bramhall's surviving papers.

Reputation Bramhall's busy career during the 1630s is important for the light it sheds on Wentworth's viceroyalty and on Laud's plans for the churches in all three kingdoms. Only a little of this work survived 1641, and was salvaged in the Restoration period. Accordingly most attention has been given to the writings of his exile years, which first appeared in John Vesey's edition of his collected works in 1676. The writings were prefaced by the first full biography, *Athanasius Hibernicus*, which depicts him as a quintessential Anglican dedicated to the *via media*. This portrait has endured, and accounts for his selection as one of the Caroline divines in the nineteenth-century *Library of Anglo-Catholic Theology*. The editor of his works, A. W. Haddan, was critical of Bramhall's prose style, but T. S. Eliot was kinder: 'his phrases are lucid and direct and occasionally have real beauty and rhythm' (T. S. Eliot, *Selected Essays*, 1951, 361). Eliot also viewed him as a link between the Lancelot Andrewes generation and that of Jeremy Taylor, and praised him for taking up the cudgels against Hobbes. This has been the tenor of most assessments of his life, and he has been remembered chiefly by association with more famous figures such as Ussher, Laud, Hobbes, and Wentworth. Since 1922 he has been commemorated more directly in the Church of Ireland. A chair, dated 1661, most probably made for his enthronement as archbishop, has been used in St Patrick's Cathedral, Armagh, for consecrations of bishops, ordination of priests and deacons, and at confirmations.

JOHN McCAFFERTY

Sources Hunt. L., Hastings MSS 14080, 15153–15173, 15948–15960 · Strafford papers, vols. 6 and 7, Sheffield City Libraries · state papers, Ireland, PRO, SP 63/254–60, 270–77, 304–7 · J. Vesey, *Athanasius Hibernicus, or, The life of the most reverend father in God, John Lord primate of Armagh* (1676) · E. Berwick, *The Rawdon papers* (1819) · *The works of the most reverend father in God, John Bramhall*, ed. A. W. Haddan (1842–5) · W. E. Collins, 'John Bramhall', *Typical English churchmen from Parker to Maurice*, ed. W. E. Collins (1902), 81–119 · W. Ball-Wright, *A great Yorkshire divine of the 17th century* (1899) · E. P. Shirley, ed., *Papers relating to the Church of Ireland, 1631–9* (1874) · J. D. McCafferty, 'John Bramhall and the reconstruction of the Church of Ireland, 1633–1641', PhD diss., U. Cam., 1996 · W. J. Sparrow Simpson, *Archbishop Bramhall* (1927) · Venn, *Alum. Cant.* · E. B. Fryde and others, eds., *Handbook of British chronology*, 3rd edn, Royal Historical Society Guides and Handbooks, 2 (1986)
Archives Hunt. L., corresp. | Bodl. Oxf., Ormonde MSS, Carte papers · PRO, state papers, Ireland, SP 63

Likenesses stained-glass memorial window, 1860–1940, St Patrick's Cathedral, Armagh · E. Harding, stipple, 1996 (after oil painting), NPG · H. B. Hall, engraving (after portrait in possession of the archbishops of Armagh), repro. in Bramhall, *Works* · oils, Sidney Sussex College, Cambridge · portrait, priv. coll.
Wealth at death £5200 in cash; plus estates in Meath, Tyrone, and Dublin: will, repr. in Berwick, *Rawdon papers*

Bramis [Bramus], **John** (*fl.* 14th cent.), Augustinian friar and writer, belonged to his order's priory at Thetford in Norfolk. He is known only as the translator of the fourteenth-century Anglo-Norman verse 'family romance' of *Waldef* into Latin prose: the text of his *Historia regis Waldei*, which is extant in a single manuscript (Cambridge, Corpus Christi, MS 329), shows him to be a competent though not inspired translator. Bramis's origin is unknown; Waldef, a semi-legendary East Anglian king, would have been a figure of local interest in Thetford.

The bibliographers Thomas Tanner (1674–1735) and John Bale (1495–1563) also conflate Bramis with Bromus, supposed author of a compilation used as the source for a pedestrian Latin history, the *Historia compendiosa de regibus Britonum*. This text, formerly attributed to the twelfth-century historian Ralph de Diceto, is in fact mainly an abridgement of Geoffrey of Monmouth's *Historia regum Britanniae*. All the passages for which Bromus is cited occur in Geoffrey's work, and the *Historia compendiosa* ends with a general *haec Brome*, which suggests that it may originally have been a reference to Geoffrey's work, perhaps under an abbreviated form of its more usual contemporary title of *Gesta* (or *Historia*) *Brittonum*. Although not by Diceto, the *Historia compendiosa* is still probably too early to be based on a text by Bramis, as one of its extant manuscripts is actually older than the Anglo-Norman *Waldef* that Bramis translated.

PETER DAMIAN-GRINT

Sources J. Bramis, *Historia regis Waldei*, ed. R. Immelmann (1912) · Tanner, *Bibl. Brit.-Hib.*, 121–2 · Ralph de Diceto, 'Historia compendiosa de regibus Britonum', *Historiae Britannicae, Saxonicae, Anglo-Danicae scriptores XV*, ed. T. Gale (1691), 551–9 · F. Thin [F. Botevile], 'Catalogo scriptorum hist.', *The chronicles of England, Scotlande and Irelande*, ed. R. Holinshed and others (1589) · Londiniensis [John Caius], *De antiquitate Cantabrigiensis academiae* (1568), 149 · J. Bale, *Illustrium Maioris Britannie scriptorum ... summarium* (1548) · *DNB* · *The Historia regum Britannie of Geoffrey of Monmouth*, ed. N. Wright, 1: *Bern, Bürgerbibliothek, MS 568* (1985) · J. C. Crick, *The Historia regum Britannie of Geoffrey of Monmouth*, 4: *Dissemination and reception in the later middle ages* (1991) · T. D. Hardy, *Descriptive catalogue of materials relating to the history of Great Britain and Ireland*, 3 vols. in 4, Rolls Series, 26 (1862–71), 337 · BL, Arundel MS 220, fols. 95–99b · BL, Cotton MS Julius D.vi
Archives CCC Cam., MS 329

Bramley, Frank (1857–1915). *See under* Newlyn school (*act.* 1882–c.1900).

Bramley, Fred (1874–1925), trade unionist, was born on 27 September 1874 in the small community of Pool, near Otley, in the West Riding of Yorkshire, the son of Alfred Bramley, a journeyman engineer and travelling local preacher, and his wife, Anne Elizabeth *née* Oates. Nothing is known of his mother's background, or of other children from the marriage.

After an elementary education in Bradford, Bramley began an apprenticeship as a cabinet-maker. He continued to study in his spare time, however, and remained active in adult education in later life; at his death he was president of the Workers' Educational Association. Bramley spent his youth in Bradford, then a stronghold of the Independent Labour Party (ILP). He became a member of the ILP, as well as the trades council, and a lecturer on social and economic questions and travelling salesman and lecturer for the socialist newspaper *The Clarion*. In 1898 he married Mary Jane; they had two children, John and Elsie. After 1903 he campaigned vigorously against tariff reform and in 1906 conducted his first *Clarion* van tour of London with Fred Hagger. *The Clarion*, edited by Robert Blatchford, sold widely not only at newsagents but through touring campaigns conducted in vans, by bicycle, and even on foot by *Clarion* ramblers. The van tours were a notable means of spreading socialist ideas in the capital.

After moving to London, where he resumed work as a cabinet-maker, Bramley became an active member of the National Amalgamated Furnishing Trades Association, which had been established in 1902 as a result of fusion between the Alliance Cabinet-makers' Association and the Scottish Cabinet-makers. Alexander Gossip became national secretary in 1905, and Fred Bramley, by then prominent in union affairs, succeeded James O'Grady as national organizer in 1912. Until the outbreak of war in 1914 he was continuously involved in trade disputes which characterized those years of labour unrest, especially the lock-outs in Liverpool, Manchester, and Nottingham and the bitter furniture dispute of 1912–13 at High Wycombe. In this conflict, employers who had recently formed a federation from thirty-one leading firms were establishing factory furniture making, which had grown out of, and developed alongside, a large domestic industry. This new factory furniture manufacturing industry was very competitive, employed increasing numbers of women, and was marked by weak union organization, except among the highly skilled.

During the twelve-week dispute, foot and mounted police reinforcements were brought in from outside, notably from the London metropolitan force. Bitter, sometimes violent, conflict ensued, and Bramley organized anti-violence brigades in order to protect pickets from police, as well as soup kitchens to feed the families of those locked out. After the government's chief industrial commissioner Sir George Askwith began arbitration, an agreement was signed in February 1914. This greatly improved previous practice, defined grades and wages clearly, and protected women.

Like many leading members of the ILP, Bramley opposed British entry into war in August 1914, but combined increasingly important trade union activities with political ones. He helped form the London branch of the Labour Party, becoming its chairman between 1916 and 1919, and was an active campaigner for women's suffrage. He stood unsuccessfully as Labour candidate in an Aberdeen South by-election in 1907, and was defeated at Devonport in 1918 and Chatham in 1922. In 1915 he was elected to the TUC's parliamentary committee, but the following year resigned on appointment as assistant secretary to the TUC, a post he held until 1923. In those years he built a national reputation and played an important part in decisive change at the TUC. With Harry Gosling and others he persuaded the 1920 and 1921 congresses to create a thirty-two man general council to replace the parliamentary committee, and this became general staff of the whole trade union movement, co-ordinating its economic and political response to the trade depression which struck in March 1921.

When C. W. Bowerman retired in 1923, Bramley succeeded him to become the first full-time secretary general to the TUC, resigning as prospective parliamentary candidate for Reading. He was then in a perfect position to complete the reforms he had put in train at the TUC and shape policy on the new general council. The problems facing him were formidable, and he suffered increasingly from heart disease, but he achieved much during his brief tenure of office. He was an effective administrator, creating new specialist services for research, publicity, and legal questions. During the first Labour government in 1924 he helped resolve the locomotive engineers' strike in January and the complex London transport strike in March.

Bramley travelled widely in Europe and continued the strongly anti-communist line he had taken since 1917. Yet his political position was in some ways ambivalent. At the 1921 Labour Party conference he vigorously opposed affiliation with the communists, but was equally strongly opposed to military intervention in Soviet Russia. Later, he warmly supported A. A. Purcell's efforts in 1924–5 to establish an Anglo-Russian advisory trade union committee. He was a member, with Purcell and George Hicks, of the TUC delegation to Russia, where the communists found him an effective and sympathetic negotiator.

Bramley believed that while communism had to be resisted in Britain, the TUC must try to form links with the Russian working class. The relationship which he successfully fostered between British and Soviet unions collapsed only after he died suddenly of a heart attack at the age of fifty-one on 10 October 1925 while in the Netherlands for a meeting of the International Federation of Trade Unions in Amsterdam. The procession which followed his coffin to Amsterdam railway station stretched a quarter of a mile and represented all sections of the Dutch working-class movement, including communists, socialists, and syndicalists.

Bramley's death occurred during the nine-month interim between Red Friday of July 1925 and the general strike of May 1926. After the strike's failure, his successor Walter Citrine and other anti-communist labour leaders like Ernest Bevin were able to use the general council Bramley had helped create to shape TUC policy. Citrine regarded his rugged, stockily built, clean-shaven fellow Yorkshireman with warm affection, and noted that they shared a talent for playing the cornet in brass bands, though Bramley was much the more gifted musician.

Famed also for his droll sense of humour and great capacity for friendship, Bramley was survived by his wife, son, and daughter. He was cremated at Golders Green crematorium, Middlesex.   PATRICK RENSHAW

Sources DLB · D. Martin and others, *Dictionnaire biographique de mouvement ouvrier international*, 1 (1979) · WWW · *The Labour who's who* (1924) · A. Bullock, *The life and times of Ernest Bevin*, 1 (1960) · D. F. Calhoun, *The united front: the TUC and the Russians, 1923–1928* (1976) · H. A. Clegg, A. Fox, and A. F. Thompson, *A history of British trade unions since 1889*, 1 (1964) · B. C. Roberts, *The Trades Union Congress, 1868–1921* (1958) · G. A. Phillips, *The general strike: the politics of industrial conflict* (1976) · R. Martin, *Communism and the British trade unions, 1924–1933* (1969) · Lord Citrine [W. M. Citrine], *Men and work: an autobiography* (1964) · *Beatrice Webb's diaries, 1912–1924*, ed. M. I. Cole (1952) · b. cert. · *The Times* (12 Oct 1925)
Archives London Metropolitan University, TUC collections, official report of the British trade union delegation to Russia · U. Warwick Mod. RC, MSS 929/21.12.1–6
Wealth at death £802 4s. 3d.: administration, 13 Nov 1925, CGPLA Eng. & Wales

Brampton. For this title name *see* Hawkins, Henry, Baron Brampton (1817–1907).

Brampton, Sir Edward [Duarte Brandão] (*c.*1440–1508), soldier and merchant, was born in Lisbon *c.*1440, reputedly the illegitimate son of Rui Barba and the wife of a Jewish blacksmith. About 1468 he travelled to England and converted to Christianity. As was usual in such cases, the king of England stood godfather. Brampton may have fought for Edward IV during the political upheavals of 1469–71. In 1472 he was given joint command of an armed force sent to sea to resist the king's enemies. In October that year he was made denizen and rewarded 'for his good service to the king in many battles' with property in London. In the following year he was commissioned to raise mariners for service against the king's enemies.

Brampton may have been the namesake 'of the king's household' who entered Lincoln's Inn in 1475, although he can rarely have been in England in the next few years. He came to the attention of Charles, duke of Burgundy, in 1475, presumably as a consequence of the English invasion of France that year, and remained in Burgundy until the duke's death. He was back in Edward IV's service by 1479, when he was a gentleman usher of the chamber. In the following year he received a major grant of land in Northamptonshire formerly held by Isabel Peche, who had died in 1479. In 1481 Brampton served under John Howard, later first duke of Norfolk (*d.* 1485), on the naval expedition against the Scots, commanding a Portuguese carvel. By 1482 he had become an esquire of the king's body and was made captain and governor of Guernsey. He remained in the royal household under Richard III, who knighted him and gave him further land in Northamptonshire and London in 1484. In March 1485 he was sent to Portugal to pursue negotiations for a bride for the recently widowed king, and was thus out of England when Richard III was killed at Bosworth.

From the mid-1470s Brampton maintained extensive business interests. He was master of the Drapers' Company of London in 1477–8, and in the latter year appears buying goods abroad for the royal wardrobe. He lent money to both Yorkist kings, repayment generally being made from the customs due on goods shipped by him. He also developed trading interests in Portugal. In return for financial help to Alfonso V he was renaturalized as a Portuguese subject in August 1479 and given trading privileges; in Portugal he was known as Duarte Brandão.

After Bosworth, Brampton did not return to the English court. His grants were cancelled by the new regime, and he pursued his career elsewhere, settling initially in Bruges and returning to Portugal in 1487. It was during this period that he came to know Perkin Warbeck (*d.* 1499), who later claimed to be Edward IV's son, Richard, duke of York. Warbeck's knowledge of the Yorkist court, which impressed contemporaries, may have come partly from Brampton, although there is nothing to associate him with the conspiracy itself. Brampton was finally pardoned by Henry VII in 1489. There is no evidence that he returned to England, though his son was knighted by Henry VII in 1500.

The grant of land made to Brampton in 1480 describes Isabel Peche as his late wife. She was the daughter of William Vaux of Northampton, and the widow of William Tresham (*d.* 1450). On Tresham's death she married William Peche of Lullingstone, Kent, who outlived her. At her death, Isabel is elsewhere described as Peche's wife, and the nature of her liaison with Brampton is thus uncertain. By 1487 Brampton had remarried; his wife is named variously as Catherine de Bahamonde and Margaret Boemond. His licence to settle in Portugal in 1487 refers to his children, but his only known child is Henrique Brandão (*d.* 1515). Edward Brampton died in Lisbon on 11 November 1508.   ROSEMARY HORROX, *rev.*

Sources I. Arthurson, *The Perkin Warbeck conspiracy, 1491–1499* (1994) · C. Roth, 'Perkin Warbeck and his Jewish master', *Transactions of the Jewish Historical Society of England*, 9 (1918–20), 143–62 · C. Roth, 'Sir Edward Brampton, alias Duarte Brandão: governor of Guernsey, 1482–5', *Report and Transactions* [Société Guernesiaise], 16 (1955–9)

Bramston, Francis (*bap.* 1619, *d.* 1683), judge, was baptized on 10 August 1619 at St Lawrence Jewry and St Mary Magdalen, Milk Street, the third son of Sir John *Bramston the elder (1577–1654), lawyer and judge, and his first wife, Bridget, daughter of Sir Thomas *Moundeford, physician of Milk Street, London. He was educated at the celebrated school of Thomas Farnabie or Farnaby in Goldsmith's Alley, Cripplegate, before being admitted in 1634 to Queens' College, Cambridge, where he graduated BA (1637) and MA (1640). According to the master, Dr Martin, he showed 'learning and industry and a great sobriety' (*Autobiography*, 28–9), but he had a weak constitution. Although made a fellow of his college, his plans for a career in the church seem to have been abandoned in favour of the law. He had been admitted to the Middle Temple on the same day as his elder brother Moundeford on 16 September 1634 and he was called to the bar on 24 June 1642.

Bramston spent the ensuing four years in travel in France and Italy, falling in with John Evelyn and his friend Henshaw at Rome in the spring of 1645, and again at Padua and Venice in the autumn of that year. On his return to England he devoted himself to the study and practice of the law. Nothing much is known about him until the Restoration, when he was made steward of some of the king's courts in Essex and of the liberty of Havering in the same county. He was made a bencher of his inn on 30 October 1663. In 1664 he represented Queens' College in the litigation over the election of Simon Patrick to the presidency, and in the following year was appointed one of the counsel to the university, with a fee of 40s. per annum. In 1668 he was appointed reader at the Middle Temple, his subject being the statute 3 Jac. c.4, concerning popish recusants. The banquet which, according to the custom, he gave on this occasion (3 August) is described by Evelyn, who was present, as 'so very extravagant and great as the like hath not been seen at any time' (Evelyn, 3.512). In attendance were the duke of Ormond, Lord Privy Seal Robartes, the earl of Bedford, Lord Bellasyse, and Viscount Halifax, besides 'a world more of earls and lords'. In November 1669 he was admitted to the degree of serjeant-at-law, presenting to the king a ring with the motto *Rex legis tutamen*, and was appointed steward of the court of common pleas at Whitechapel with a salary of £100 per annum.

In 1676 Bramston was seen by Sir Richard Wiseman as a potential rival to his own cousin and brother-in-law Sir William Wiseman in a pending by-election at Maldon. Wiseman hoped that 'the king would please to make the serjeant a judge. I know he will make a good judge' (Browning, 3.105). According to his brother, Bramston 'was of low stature, well set, and inclining to fat', but he also had the requisite qualities for the bench: 'he had a good measure of knowledge in the civil law, and in school divinity, an excellent historian, and thoroughly studied in the common law, which he made his profession' (*Autobiography*, 31). His qualifications were eventually recognized on 17 June 1678 when he was created a baron of the exchequer. However, he was dismissed on 29 April 1679, without reason assigned, along with judges Wild, Thurland, and Bertie. It was supposed that either Sir William Temple or Lord Chancellor Finch was at the bottom of the affair. On 4 June a pension of £500 a year was granted him, of which only the first three terminal instalments were paid him. At Bramston's death, which occurred at his chambers in Serjeants' Inn on 27 March 1683, it was three years and six months in arrears. He was buried on 30 March in Roxwell church, Essex. He died heavily in debt; his brother John *Bramston the younger, his executor and heir, made persistent efforts to get in the amount due in respect of his pension, and succeeded in 1686 in recovering £1456 5s.; the balance was, as he plaintively puts it, abated in costs. Bramston never married, nor (despite some accounts) was he knighted.

STUART HANDLEY

Sources *The autobiography of Sir John Bramston*, ed. [Lord Braybrooke], CS, 32 (1845), 28–32, 97, 163 · M. W. Helms and P. Watson, 'Bramston, John', HoP, *Commons, 1660–90*, 1.710–13 · Sainty, *Judges* · Baker, *Serjeants* · Evelyn, *Diary*, 2.470; 3.512 · A. Browning, *Thomas Osborne, earl of Danby and duke of Leeds, 1632–1712*, 3 (1951), 105 · Foss, *Judges*, 7.57–9 · *Report on the manuscripts of Allan George Finch*, 5 vols., HMC, 71 (1913–2003), vol. 2, p. 42 · H. A. C. Sturgess, ed., *Register of admissions to the Honourable Society of the Middle Temple, from the fifteenth century to the year 1944*, 1 (1949), 130 · Venn, *Alum. Cant.* · DNB · IGI

Wealth at death in debt: Bramston, *Autobiography*, 163

Bramston, James (1694?–1743), poet and Church of England clergyman, was the son of Francis Bramston, of Chelmsford, Essex, colonel of a guards regiment, and Sarah, daughter of Sir William Glascock. His great-grandfather was Sir John *Bramston (1577–1654), lord chief justice of the king's bench, and his grandfather was Sir Moundeford Bramston (d. 1679), master in chancery. Bramston entered Westminster School in 1704 as a bishop's boy or lord's scholar and was elected queen's scholar ('aged 14') in 1708; he was admitted to Christ Church, Oxford, on 5 June 1713 (he matriculated on 23 June, 'aged 18') and was elected to a Westminster studentship on 22 December. He contributed Latin poetry to university and Christ Church collections, graduated BA in 1717 and MA in 1720, and became a praelector at Christ Church until his studentship was terminated in 1722.

Though admitted to the Middle Temple on 20 May 1718, Bramston made his career in the church. He was ordained deacon at Oxford on 12 June 1720 and priest at Winchester on 5 March 1721. On 21 June he was appointed chaplain to the 2nd dragoon guards, and by 1724 he was married.

On 10 March 1724 Bramston was instituted as rector of Lurgashall, near Midhurst in Sussex. He gave communion plate to the church, and its chancel was rebuilt partly at his expense. The 'fame and proofs' of his 'colloquial wit' were still remembered at Lurgashall in the early nineteenth century (Dallaway, 2.1.365). His wit had wider circulation too, for he was known to Alexander Pope, who complimented him as a preacher in *The Dunciad* (1728, 3.200), and praised his *Art of Politicks* (1729) (*The Correspondence of Alexander Pope*, ed. G. Sherburn, 1956, 3.173). This satire in heroic couplets is a creative adaptation of Horace's *Ars poetica*. Bramston's next satire, *The Man of Taste* (March 1733), also in heroic couplets, was occasioned by Pope's *Epistle to Burlington* and satirizes the targets Pope would attack in his *New Dunciad* (1742). Bramston's *Ignorami lamentatio super legis communis translationem ex Latino in Anglicum* (1736), dedicated by 'Ambi-dexter Ignoramus' to 'Dulmannum', is a high-spirited satire on lawyers, written in dog Latin hexameters. His last poem, *The Crooked Sixpence* (1743), a Miltonic parody, is an ingeniously feminized imitation of John Philips's *Splendid Shilling*.

On 10 July 1739 Bramston was instituted again to Lurgashall, and on the same day was instituted to the vicarage of Westhampnett, near Chichester. On 5 November he was appointed domestic chaplain to the second earl of Ashburnham (1724–1812); on 9 November he became vicar of Harting and rector of nearby Chalton (both places between Petersfield and Portsmouth). His rapid acquisition of pluralities in two dioceses may have been owing to favour in high places: in November 1738 Henry Pelham (the future prime minister) recommended Bramston to his brother the duke of Newcastle 'with regard to a little affair in Sussex' (BL, Add. MS 32691, fol. 438). Bramston retained all his benefices until death. Towards the end of his life he resided in Blendworth, the neighbouring parish to Chalton. He died on 22 December 1743 and was buried at Chalton on 30 December. His wife, Elizabeth, survived him and was sole beneficiary of his will. *The Art of Politicks* and *The Man of Taste* were reprinted in Dodsley's *Collection of Poems*, 1 (1748). JAMES SAMBROOK

Sources *Old Westminsters*, vols. 1–2; suppl. 1 · J. Bramston, *The man of taste* (1733); repr. with introduction by F. P. Lock (1975) · C. Dalton, ed., *George the First's army, 1714–1727*, 2 (1912), 202 · *Remarks and collections of Thomas Hearne*, ed. C. E. Doble and others, 8, OHS, 50 (1907), 178 · Foster, *Alum. Oxon.* · W. D. Peckham, 'Chichester diocese institutions', E. Sussex RO [typed list] · J. Dallaway, *A history of the western division of the county of Sussex*, 2/1 (1819), 365 · BL, Add. MS 32691, fol. 438 · *The autobiography of Sir John Bramston*, ed. [Lord Braybrooke], CS, 32 (1845), xx · transcript of Harting church book, Society of Genealogists · F. G. Stephens and M. D. George, eds., *Catalogue of prints and drawings in the British Museum, division 1: political and personal satires*, 3 (1877), p. 403, no. 2510 ['Scotch tast in vista's'] · D. F. Foxon, ed., *English verse, 1701–1750: a catalogue of separately printed poems with notes on contemporary collected editions*, 2 vols. (1975) · Bramston's will
Archives BL, Add. MS 32691, fol. 438

Bramston, James Yorke (1763–1836), vicar apostolic of the London district, was born on 18 March 1763 at Oundle in Northamptonshire, the elder son of John Bramston, a solicitor, and his wife, Elizabeth Yorke, daughter of the Revd Edward Yorke, vicar of Oundle. He was educated at Oundle School, but the report in the *Dictionary of National Biography* of his having been at Cambridge is due to a confusion with his younger brother, John William, who was admitted to Trinity College in 1777. Originally intended for the Indian Civil Service or the navy, James finally decided on the law, and on 26 April 1785 was entered as a student at Lincoln's Inn. Although he was never called to the bar, he studied for nearly four years under the distinguished Catholic lawyer Charles Butler. In 1790 he was received into the Catholic church by the Revd Arthur O'Leary, the Franciscan missioner at Soho. Though eager to begin studying at once for the priesthood, in deference to his father's wishes he remained in England until 1792, when he entered the English College, Lisbon. Ordained in 1796, he stayed in Lisbon for a further five years, ministering chiefly to the British community, and earned a reputation for tireless charity during the epidemic which swept the city in 1800. He returned to England the following year, and in 1802 was appointed by the vicar apostolic of the London district, John Douglass, to the poorest of all the Catholic missions in the capital, St George-in-the-Fields, Southwark. There he remained as the priest-in-charge for nearly twenty-three years. In 1808 he was a founder member of the Board of British Catholics, formed to negotiate for political and religious concessions with the government. Its readiness to compromise, and its support for a policy of giving the laity a voice in the appointment of bishops, were vigorously opposed by Joseph Milner, the foremost defender of hierarchical authority, who denounced it as the tool of its aristocratic patrons.

In 1812 William Poynter, vicar apostolic of the London district, appointed Bramston his vicar-general. In 1814 Bramston went to Rome with Poynter, and on 5 April 1815,

at Genoa, Poynter asked Pope Pius VII to appoint Bramston as his coadjutor. The appointment was blocked by Milner, and eight years were to elapse before it was secured. On 29 June 1823 Bramston was consecrated by Poynter at St Edmund's College, near Ware, as bishop of Usulae *in partibus infidelium*. On the death of Poynter in November 1827, Bramston succeeded him as vicar apostolic of the London district. His personal geniality, legal experience, and long service on the London mission were strong qualifications for the office, though he was by now increasingly handicapped by ill health. When the Catholic Emancipation Bill was passed in 1829 he greeted it with reserve, warning the faithful in his new year pastoral letter of 1830 not to compromise their spiritual identity. He continued to treat Milner with disarming mildness, while privately describing him as 'the author of more mischief against the Catholic Church than Luther himself' (Ward, *Eve*, 182). From 1834 Bramston was debilitated by increasing corpulence, and in the spring of 1836 began to suffer from erysipelas in the right foot, which made it impossible for him to walk. He died at Southampton on 11 July 1836, and was buried at St Mary Moorfields, London. His remains were translated to St Edmund's College, near Ware, in 1899.

Johnsonian in temperament and physique, an entertaining conversationalist, and a discerning judge of character, Bramston was at ease with all classes of society, being especially noted for his charity towards the poor. His fluency in Italian was an advantage in his relations with Rome, while his wide social contacts, skill in the conduct of business, and familiarity with English law and custom peculiarly fitted him to manage the affairs of the Catholic community, at a critical moment in its history, with unobtrusive discretion. 'A Popish priest grafted on to a Protestant lawyer', he once remarked, 'should be a switch for the devil himself' (Ward, *Eve*, 8).

G. MARTIN MURPHY

Sources B. N. Ward, *The eve of Catholic emancipation*, 3 vols. (1911–12) · B. Ward, *The sequel to Catholic emancipation*, 2 vols. (1915) · G. Anstruther, *The seminary priests*, 4 (1977), 45–6 · Gillow, *Lit. biog. hist.*
Archives St George's Roman Catholic Cathedral, Southwark, London, Southwark Roman Catholic diocesan archive, corresp. relating to Gibraltar · Westm. DA, diary of journey to Rome · Westm. DA, corresp., papers, and diary | Ushaw College, Durham, corresp. with John Lingard · Ushaw College, Durham, letters to E. Winstanley
Likenesses H. Robinson, stipple, pubd 1828 (after W. Derby), NPG · W. Derby?, oils, *c*.1833, repro. in Ward, *Sequel to Catholic emancipation*, 1.12 · W. Holl, stipple, pubd 1836, NPG · A. Ramsay, oils, St Edmund's College, near Ware, Hertfordshire
Wealth at death £3000: probate, 1836 [8/229]

Bramston, Sir John, the elder (1577–1654), judge, was born on 18 May 1577 at Malton, Essex, the eldest son of Roger Bramston and his wife, Priscilla, widow of Thomas Rushee and daughter of Francis Clovile. Priscilla's ancestors had long resided in Chelmsford hundred, Essex, but Roger came from a London family. After their marriage he settled at Boreham, the residence of Priscilla's first husband. John attended Malton grammar school, before matriculating at Jesus College, Cambridge, in 1593. He left without a degree, entered the Middle Temple on 26 October 1597, and was called to the bar there on 7 June 1605. A year later he married Bridget, daughter of Thomas Moundeford MD. She was described as a 'beautiful' and pious person, who was also 'a very observant wife' and 'tender mother' (*Autobiography*). Together they had a large family, including their sons Sir John *Bramston the younger (1611–1700), whose own autobiography is an important source for his father's life, and the judge Francis *Bramston (*bap.* 1619, *d.* 1683).

In 1607 Bramston was selected counsel and made solicitor for the University of Cambridge with an annual fee of 40s. Lent reader at the Middle Temple in 1623, he lectured on the Henrican Statute of Limitations (32 Henry VIII c. 2), and he delivered a second reading in the following autumn, when his subject was fraudulent conveyances (13 Elizabeth I c. 5). On 22 September of the same year he was called to the degree of serjeant-at-law, initially choosing the duke of Buckingham as his patron, but when this was disallowed because Buckingham had already been selected by another lawyer, Bramston named the earl of Warwick and Lord Petre of Writtle instead.

During the second half of the 1620s Bramston's practice grew steadily, and, though never a member of parliament, he appeared in several cases of political significance. In 1626 he was named one of the counsel for the earl of Bristol, who was being impeached by the House of Lords. In 1627 he represented Sir Thomas Darnel and Sir John Hevingham, two of the 'five knights', who had been committed to the Fleet for refusing to contribute to the forced loan. Appointed by the court at short notice because Darnell was having trouble finding a lawyer who would take his case, Bramston did not deny that the king had the right to commit the subject to prison, but he applied for a writ of habeas corpus on the grounds that the charges against his clients were not specific enough to enable the judges to decide whether the defendants should continue to be detained. In 1628 Bramston was chosen one of the counsel for the City of London on the motion of Sir Heneage Finch, then recorder, who was a close friend and connection by marriage. In 1629 he was one of the counsel for several of the nine members of the House of Commons (including Sir John Eliot, Denzil Hollis, John Selden, and William Coryton) who had been indicted for making seditious speeches in parliament. Next year the bishop of Ely (John Buckeridge) appointed him chief justice of his diocese.

His first wife having died some years earlier, in 1631 Bramston made a journey to Ireland to marry Elizabeth Brereton, daughter of Lord Brabazon of Ardee and sister of the earl of Meath, who was the widow first of George Montgomery, bishop of Clogher, and secondly of Sir John Brereton, a king's serjeant in Ireland. Formalizing revival of an old attachment that had been frustrated in their younger years by the opposition of Elizabeth's father, the ceremony took place at Kilruddery, near Dublin. His interest in his new wife's estates led Bramston to maintain an interest in Irish affairs during the 1630s, while in the meantime his career in England continued to prosper. He was made a queen's serjeant on 26 March 1632, and his promotion to king's serjeant on 8 July 1634 was followed by a knighthood on 24 November. Along with Sir John Bankes, he was during the same period assigned by the privy council to find ways of enforcing more effectively the monopoly of the recently created Society of Soapmakers of Westminster by preventing the importation or manufacture of any soap outside of its control. According to a letter of Archbishop Laud the king also selected Bramston, along with Bankes and Solicitor-General Sir Edward Littleton, to find a way to augment the incomes of poor vicars. In January 1635 Bramston made a report on the legality of a commission to inquire into offenders against recent proclamations concerning forestallers and regrators and the power of such a commission to make financial compositions with the delinquents. Although refraining from giving a judgment on the 'conveniency and fitness' (*CSP dom.*, *1635*, 467) of the proposal, he concluded that the commission itself would be legal so long as it was clear that only the king's pardon, and not a composition, could exonerate offenders.

Royalist involvement Following the death of Sir Thomas Richardson, Bramston was appointed chief justice of the king's bench on 14 April 1635, and in the same year he purchased his estate at Skreens near Roxwell in Essex from the son of Lord Treasurer Weston for the sum of £8000. According to the diarist and judge Sir Richard Hutton, Bramston's appointment was generally applauded, but it soon involved him in the legal and political controversies associated with the king's plan for the levy of ship money. In November 1635 Bramston joined with the other judges in agreeing that the measure could be legally extended from port towns, where it had traditionally applied, to inland areas as well. At the request of the king, in February 1637 he signed an extrajudicial decision by all of the judges that affirmed the king's right to make the levy at such times as he thought fit. According to his son, however, Bramston's own view was that the charge could only be made in times of necessity, therefore he refused to agree to the collective opinion until he was told by the older judges that it was customary for all of them to subscribe to the opinion of the majority. When the case testing ship money (*R. v. Hampden*) came to trial in 1637 Bramston, speaking last, explicitly endorsed many of the arguments that chief justice of the common pleas, Sir John Finch, had made in favour of the king. He declared that the king could make the charge on the subject in 'case of necessity, *pro bono publico*' (*State trials*, 3.1248). It was no more than what every subject owed to the commonwealth in time of danger, and there was in any case a difference between 'a tallage on the people and a service in case of necessity' (ibid.). Nevertheless, aware that the outcome of the case had already been decided by a majority who ruled for the king, Bramston ultimately agreed with the opinion of chief baron Sir Henry Davenport that Hampden should have the verdict on the purely technical grounds that the writs failed to identify to whom the assessed money should be paid.

Although not as severe as those levelled at some of his colleagues, articles of impeachment, which cited his extrajudicial opinions in connection with ship money but not his judgment in *R. v. Hampden*, were laid against Bramston by the Long Parliament on 21 December 1640. With the exception of agreeing that he had participated in the extrajudicial opinion of November 1635, Bramston denied all of the charges against him, including his alleged failure to grant a prohibition in a tithe case that was being heard in the Norwich ecclesiastical courts. Although the impeachment never came to trial, the House of Lords required Bramston to find bail for £10,000, which was provided by his sons-in-law, Sir William Palmer and Sir Thomas Dyke, and he became liable to immediate committal and forfeiture of his bail if he left London.

This last condition became critical when the king ordered Bramston to join him in Yorkshire on 29 July 1642. According to his son, a consideration weighing on his mind at this time was the possibility that in the event of war his position as chief justice of king's bench would require him to act as chief coroner of England, a role that would have given him the unenviable responsibility of viewing the body of any man slain in battle against the king and declaring him attainted and liable to forfeit his property. Even so, his son also says that Bramston attempted to use his connections in the Lords in order to gain permission to leave London, but this was denied. Claiming that he was too old to travel by horseback, and that a journey north by coach would almost certainly lead to his apprehension by the supporters of parliament, he sent two of his sons, John and Francis, to inform the king of his predicament. Evidently unsympathetic, Charles told the young men that their father was 'not soe old but he may indure the journey well; his presence is necessary for my service, and he must come' (*Autobiography*, 84). Still either unwilling or unable to comply, Bramston was discharged from his office on 10 October 1642. According to Clarendon, Bramston, a man of great learning and integrity, had not intended any disfavour to the king, and his son suspected that Charles's actions were in no small part a reaction to the lobbying of Bramston's successor, Sir Robert Heath, even though Heath himself later wrote a solicitous letter to Bramston explicitly denying the aspersion and promising to remind the king not to forget him.

On 10 February 1643 Bramston received a patent appointing him a king's serjeant, and parliament at the same time began to solicit his co-operation, though with no more than limited success. The terms of peace offered the king at Oxford on 1 February proposed his reappointment as lord chief justice of the king's bench, though with the proviso that he should serve during good behaviour ('quamdiu se bene gesserit'), rather than at the king's pleasure. Described as an 'Assistant to the House of Peers' (*JHC*, 3.677), he was consulted in 1644 in connection with the trial of Macquire and MacMahon, two prisoners who had escaped from the Tower and had been retaken. According to his son, Sir John himself travelled from Essex to London on Christmas day 1646 in order to quiet speculation that he might be offered the great seal. In 1647

it was again proposed to make him one of the commissioners of the great seal, and in April the House of Commons resolved that he should be appointed a justice of the court of common pleas. Once again, according to his son, Bramston called on the help of his political friends in order to avoid, rather than refuse, these appointments. Even in the last year of his life Oliver Cromwell, then lord protector, sent for him privately, and urged him to accept reappointment as chief justice, but Bramston excused himself. He said that he was old, and having failed to give satisfaction in his previous spell in office, he thought that he should meddle no more in public affairs.

In his last months Bramston sometimes attended church services at Lincoln's Inn, where he enjoyed the sermons of James Ussher, the archbishop of Armagh. After a short illness he died on 22 September 1654 at his house at Skreens. Of middle height—in youth slight and active, in later years stout without being corpulent—he was buried in Roxwell parish church alongside his second wife, who died in 1647. Nicholas Fuller characterized Bramston as 'one of deep learning, solid judgment, integrity of life, and gravity of behaviour' (Fuller, *Worthies*, 1.511). According to his son, he was

> a very patient hearer of cases, free from passion and partiality, very modest in giving his opinion and judgment … which he usually did with such reasons as often convinced those that differed from him and the auditory. Even the learned lawyers learned of him, as I have heard Twisden, Wild, Windham, and the admired Hales, and others acknowledge often. (*Autobiography*, 95–6)

A Latin epitaph, attributed to Cowley, was placed on his tomb in 1732.   CHRISTOPHER W. BROOKS

Sources DNB · *The autobiography of Sir John Bramston*, ed. [Lord Braybrooke], CS, 32 (1845) · *State trials*, vol. 3 · JHC, 3 (1642–4) · B. Whitelocke, *Memorials of the English affairs*, new edn (1732) · Essex RO, Chelmsford, D/DEB [twenty-eight letters, and other papers of Bramston] · Baker, *Serjeants* · *The diary of Sir Richard Hutton, 1614–1639*, ed. W. R. Prest, SeldS, suppl. ser., 9 (1991) · C. T. Martin, ed., *Minutes of parliament of the Middle Temple*, 4 vols. (1904–5) · Clarendon, *Hist. rebellion* · CSP dom., 1626–45 · Fuller, *Worthies* (1840) · Bodl. Oxf., MS Bankes 64/8 · *Articles of accusation exhibited by the Commons House of Parliament now assembled against Sir John Bramston … Sir Robert Berkley … Sir Francis Crawley … Sir Humphrey Davenport … Sir Richard Weston … Sir Thomas Trevor* (1641) · Venn, *Alum. Cant.* · H. A. C. Sturgess, ed., *Register of admissions to the Honourable Society of the Middle Temple, from the fifteenth century to the year 1944*, 3 vols. (1949)
Archives LPL, corresp. and MSS | Essex RO, Chelmsford, letters and MSS, incl. draft relating to the articles of impeachment against him and MSS relating to Essex clothworkers, D/DEB
Likenesses oils, Colchester Museum; version, NPG

Bramston, Sir John, the younger (1611–1700), politician and autobiographer, was born in the family home in Whitechapel, London, and was baptized on 11 September 1611, eldest son and fourth of nine children of Sir John *Bramston (1577–1654), chief justice of king's bench, and his first wife, Bridget, daughter and coheir of Thomas Moundeford, physician, of Milk Street, London. Francis *Bramston was a younger brother. Bramston's complaint that his schoolmaster, Andrew Walmsley of Blackmore, Essex, brutally flogged his brother Moundeford prompted the boys' transfer to a more competent master, Thomas

Farnaby of Cripplegate, London, about 1624. Bramston went to Wadham College, Oxford, in 1627 for nearly three years and entered the Middle Temple, where he was called to the bar in 1635. He was chamber fellow and lifelong friend of Edward Hyde, later earl of Clarendon. On 19 November 1635 he married Alice (d. 1648), daughter of Anthony Abdy, a clothworker and alderman, of Lime Street, London, leasing a house in Charterhouse Yard. They had six sons and four daughters.

Bramston practised law until 'the drums and trumpets blew [his] gown over [his] ears' (Autobiography, ix, 103). At the outbreak of civil war he sold his chambers on his father's advice. He lived on his early success at the bar and a settled estate from his father. Following his wife's child-bed death on 11 February 1648, after a pregnancy troubled by accidents and an induced delivery, he and the surviving children spent winters with his sister Porter and her family and summers with his father at Skreens near Chelmsford, Essex. In 1635 the elder Bramston had bought this manor from Lord Treasurer Portland's second son for £8000. After his father's death in 1654 Bramston inherited Skreens, living there and in houses or lodgings in or near London.

The leading source for his life is The Autobiography, a lively, disorganized memoir, part autobiography, part journal, intended to preserve for his descendants 'something of my father and myself' (Autobiography, 4). To counter life's impermanence he proposed two themes: his father's and his constancy to the royalist, tory, and court cause; and their complete adherence to the doctrine and discipline of the Church of England. Bramston held both these principles imperative to Restoration. His first venture into politics had been an abortive attempt to enter parliament at the second 1640 general election as a burgess for Bodmin, Cornwall. A double return led to his petition to the committee of privilege, which accepted his contention that he received 'the popularity of the major part of the select number' (Autobiography, 160), but this finding was never reported to the house. Instead, John Pym's nephew, Anthony Nicholl, held the seat from 1641 to about 1648. This and his father's impeachment nurtured the Bramstons' 'malignancy' towards the parliamentary and army leadership.

Bramston, however, remained quiet during the civil wars and interregnum, sometimes gathering with about fifty family members and friends at Skreens. Since valuable holdings near London did not encourage intransigence, attendance at prayer book services was the extent of their noncompliance. Religious consistency helped him rebut accusations of Roman Catholicism brought by local political opponent Henry Mildmay in 1672 and heard before the privy council. Mildmay's witness, Ferdinando de Macedo, a Portuguese, gave false evidence, which elicited damaging testimony from people he had duped.

Bramston entered parliament as knight of the shire for Essex in 1660 at the top of the poll, and returned in 1661, apparently for the second seat. Charles II conferred the honour of knight of the Bath at his coronation on 23 April 1661, when Bramston refused hereditary distinction by declining a baronetcy. His new dignity cost £500 in fees and finery. After a quiet beginning in the convention he served actively in the Cavalier Parliament as committee member, reporter to the House of Lords, and teller, especially on legislation concerning the ecclesiastical settlement and economic regulation. He was a burgess for Maldon in the first 1679 parliament and the sole 1685 parliament, and contested a third election there. In addition, between 1660 and 1688 Bramston was justice of the peace, deputy lieutenant and vice-admiral of Essex, high steward of Maldon, and committee member for parliamentary tax assessment.

Bramston kept up his autobiography until a month before his death at eighty-eight. Of Christmas day 1699 he wrote

> I thank God I went [to church], received the Communion at the rails, this being the first time the Communion hath been celebrated since the table was railed in, and the pulpit removed, and I praise God I have been free of the cold ever since. (Autobiography, 413)

He died on 4 February 1700, at Skreens, leaving Anthony, his third son and heir, and was buried near his wife and father in the chancel of Roxwell parish church on 14 February.   THOMAS M. COAKLEY

Sources The autobiography of Sir John Bramston, ed. [Lord Braybrooke], CS, 32 (1845) · G. Hampson and G. Jagger, 'Essex', HoP, Commons, 1660–90, 1.228–30 · G. Hampson and G. Jagger, 'Maldon', HoP, Commons, 1660–90, 1.234–6 · M. W. Helms and G. Hampson, 'Bramston, John', HoP, Commons, 1660–90, 1.710–13 · CSP dom., 1660–88 · D. Hirst, The representative of the people? voters and voting in England under the early Stuarts (1975) · D. Brunton and D. H. Pennington, Members of the Long Parliament (1954) · Keeler, Long Parliament · F. G. Emmison, Guide to the Essex Record Office, 2nd edn (1969) · J. Stow, A survay of London, rev. edn (1603); repr. with introduction by C. L. Kingsford as A survey of London, 2 vols. (1908); repr. with addns (1971) · DNB

Archives Essex RO, family MSS · Essex RO, legal and official papers, incl. lieutenancy resolutions, list of names of deputy-lieutenants, papers as vice-admiral of Essex, orders from the privy council to the lord lieutenant, instructions and expenses incurred on knighthood, and papers on charges of Roman Catholicism · LPL, papers | Bodl. Oxf., letters to John Morris · Essex RO, memorandum from clerk of House of Commons on parliamentary attendance [priv. coll.] · Essex RO, Skreens (Roxwell) estate MSS · Essex RO, Weston family MSS

Bramwell, Sir Byrom (1847–1931), physician and neurologist, was born on 18 December 1847 at Dockray Square, North Shields, Northumberland, the eldest son of John Byrom Bramwell (1823–1882), a general medical practitioner in North Shields, and his wife, Mary, daughter of Thomas Young, a shipowner. Bramwell was academically successful at Cheltenham College, where he also played football and cricket for the school. His time there is marked by a memorial plaque in the college chapel. In 1865 he became a student at the medical school at Edinburgh (as his father had done) and the details of his days there can be found in the entertaining address he gave to the Edinburgh Royal Medical Society fifty years later. Bramwell was not only an academic: he captained the university cricket eleven, fished (he lodged for a time with William Stewart, author of The Practical Angler), and was popularly known as 'the baron'.

After graduation in 1869 Bramwell was made house surgeon to James Spence, the professor of surgery at Edinburgh. He was also invited to become Thomas Laycock's assistant in the chair of medicine there, but he felt duty bound to help his ailing father in the medical practice built up by his grandfather. Between 1869 and 1874 he continued in the family practice and obtained a number of local appointments. However, he did not abandon his ambition to become a teacher of medicine, and in 1872 he was appointed lecturer in medical jurisprudence and pathology at Durham University. In 1874 he moved to Newcastle upon Tyne to become the physician and pathologist at Newcastle Royal Infirmary. In 1875 he received a gold medal for his MD thesis, 'Reports on clinical cases'.

In 1879 Bramwell took what was then a risky step for an English 'outsider' and moved to Edinburgh. He became a fellow of the Royal College of Physicians of Edinburgh in 1880, but his first year in the city was difficult: his private practice earned him 5 guineas. However, he persevered and his reputation grew after he became a lecturer in the Edinburgh extramural school of medicine. Between 1892 and 1897 he lectured on clinical medicine to women students and invited male students to attend weekly outpatient clinics. These occasions were so popular that Bramwell published a fortnightly series entitled *Studies in Clinical Medicine*. In time his practice flourished and in 1895 he was appointed principal medical officer to the Scottish Union and National Insurance Company. Bramwell's hospital career was also successful: in 1882 he was appointed pathologist at the Edinburgh Royal Infirmary, in 1885 he became assistant physician, and in 1897 he was made physician—a post he held until his retirement in 1912. He was also physician to the Chalmers Hospital from 1887 to 1918. His failure to secure the chair of medicine at Edinburgh on the death of Thomas Grainger in 1900 was a severe disappointment to him.

Bramwell's real love was teaching, and while a physician on the wards he published accounts of his Wednesday clinics in the journal *Clinical Studies* between 1903 and 1910. As well as being an enthusiastic teacher, Bramwell was also a prolific author. He published reports of cases throughout his clinical career and also wrote about the practice, teaching, and general aspects of medicine. In addition to nine volumes of clinical reports, he produced ten books, an *Atlas of Clinical Medicine* (3 vols., 1892–6), and more than 160 papers. Of the textbooks, *Intracranial Tumours* (1888) is the most important. His *Diseases of the Spinal Cord* (1881) was also an international success, being translated into German, French, and Russian. In *Anaemia and some Diseases of the Blood-Forming Organs and Ductless Glands* (1899) Bramwell surveyed another large area of medicine by reviewing 14,777 cases. He also published *Lectures on Aphasia* (1897). The collected volumes of *Clinical Studies* and his *Atlas* consolidate and illustrate Bramwell's teaching sessions.

Although president of the Royal College of Physicians of Edinburgh from 1910 to 1912, Bramwell was no mere medical politician. In 1923 he was president of the Association of Physicians at its meeting in Edinburgh and in the same year he became the first clinician to be elected a fellow of the Royal College of Physicians in London under the special rule allowing the election of distinguished physicians who were not members of that college. He had been elected a fellow of the Royal Society of Edinburgh in 1886, and also received the honorary degree of LLD from Edinburgh, Birmingham, and St Andrews, and of DCL from Durham. He was a member of many foreign medical societies, and was knighted in 1924.

In 1872 Bramwell married his second cousin, Martha (d. 1918), daughter of Edward Crighton, of North Shields. They had three sons, two of whom qualified in medicine, and at least one daughter. In Edinburgh Bramwell lived and worked in Drumsheugh Gardens. He also used Baberton House (near Threipmuir Loch) as a summer residence. After the death of his wife in 1918 he moved to another Edinburgh address, 10 Heriot Row, where he stayed with his cousin. Bramwell was an expert angler, and he enjoyed watching cricket at Lord's or the Oval in London and the rugby internationals in Edinburgh. He became fascinated by astronomy and his son thought that his father would have taken it up as a profession if his life was to begin again.

Bramwell died at his address in Edinburgh on 27 April 1931. A memorial service was held in St Mary's Episcopal Cathedral three days later, after which a private burial took place. Members of his family found Bramwell affectionate, generous, unselfish, and devoted to the welfare of his children. S. A. Kinnier Wilson, one of his house physicians who became a distinguished neurologist, also described him as 'big, kindly, critical, and unruffled' (*BMJ*, 1825).   IAIN MILNE

Sources B. Ashworth, *The Bramwells of Edinburgh* (1986), 13 · E. Bramwell, *Proceedings of the Royal Society of Edinburgh*, 51 (1930–31), 224–31 · *BMJ* (9 May 1931), 823–6 · R. W. Philip, *Edinburgh Medical Journal*, 3rd ser., 38 (1931), 444–7 · B. Bramwell, 'The Edinburgh medical school, and its professors in my student days', *Edinburgh Medical Journal*, 3rd ser., 30 (1923), 133–56 · A. L. Turner, *History of the University of Edinburgh, 1883–1933* (1933) · *The Lancet* (9 May 1931) · *CGPLA Eng. & Wales* (1931)
Likenesses D. Alison, oils, *c.*1923, Royal College of Physicians of Edinburgh · A. S. Watson, photograph, Wellcome L.

Bramwell, Sir Frederick Joseph, baronet (1818–1903), mechanical engineer, was born on 7 March 1818 in Finch Lane, Cornhill, City of London. He was the third son of George Bramwell, a partner in the firm of Dorrien & Co., bankers, of Finch Lane. His mother was Elizabeth Martha Frith. His elder brother, George *Bramwell, Baron Bramwell, attained eminence at the bar and on the bench. After attending the Palace School, Enfield, Frederick was apprenticed in 1834 to John Hague, a mechanical engineer, whose works in Cable Street, Wellclose Square, were later bought by the Blackwall Rope Railway. Hague invented a system for driving trains by means of atmospheric pressure, which was adopted with some success on a short railway in Devon. Bramwell, impressed by the concept, joined another of Hague's pupils, Samuel Collett Homersham, about 1845, in proposing a scheme for an atmospheric railway in a low-level tunnel from Bank via Charing Cross to Hyde Park Corner. The details of the

Sir Frederick Joseph Bramwell, baronet (1818–1903), by Frank Holl

scheme (including hydraulic lifts to raise the passengers) were worked out, but nothing came of it (see Bramwell's paper to the Institution of Mechanical Engineers at Plymouth in 1899, reprinted in *Engineering*, 68, 246–80). Equally unsuccessful was a more modest proposal to construct an experimental atmospheric railway from Waterloo Station over Hungerford suspension bridge to Hungerford market. In Hague's engineering works Bramwell also studied methods of steam propulsion on roads, and while still an apprentice came to know Walter Hancock, who first constructed a successful road locomotive. The development of steam carriages was short-lived, having been killed off by the development of the railways. On completion of his apprenticeship Bramwell became chief draughtsman and later manager in Hague's office. Under his supervision in 1843 a locomotive of 10 tons in weight was constructed for the Stockton and Darlington Railway.

On leaving Hague's employ Bramwell became manager of an engineering factory in the Isle of Dogs, and was connected with the Fairfield railway works, Bow, then under the management of William Bridges Adams. In 1847 Bramwell married his first cousin, Harriet Leonora (1814/15–1907), daughter of Joseph Frith. They had three daughters. The second, Eldred, married Sir Victor Horsley FRCS. In 1853 Bramwell set up in business on his own account, and soon left the manufacturing side of his profession almost exclusively for the legal and consultative side. His gift for describing complicated mechanical details in clear and simple language, intelligence, power

of rapidly assimilating information, wit, and presence made him an invaluable witness in scientific and especially patent cases. Yet it was not until he was over forty that he made £400 in any one year. In 1860 he took with reservations an office at 35A Great George Street, Westminster. Thenceforth his practice as a consultant rapidly increased; within ten years his income grew very large.

Bramwell was among the first to practise regularly as a scientific witness or technical advocate. His information was always up to date although he acknowledged his bias. He devised ingenious models to illustrate his evidence. In parliamentary committee rooms, where he dealt almost entirely with questions of civil engineering, Bramwell soon gained as great a reputation as in the law courts. An authority on waterworks engineering, he was permanently retained by all eight London water companies. In later life he was chiefly in demand as an arbitrator, where his forensic capacity and judicial acumen found full scope. He was not responsible for any important engineering works, but as chairman of both the East Surrey Water Company from 1882 until his death and of the Kensington and Knightsbridge Electric Lighting Company he supervised the construction of much of the companies' works. He designed and built a sewage disposal scheme for Portsmouth, which had certain original features from the low levels of parts of the district.

Bramwell, whose only relaxation was in variety of work, was indefatigable in honorary service to the various societies and institutions of which he was a member. Here he showed to advantage his exceptional gifts of oratory and his powers of historical survey. He joined the Institution of Mechanical Engineers in 1854, was elected to the council in 1864, and became president in 1874. He was especially devoted to the Institution of Civil Engineers, founded in 1818, to which he was elected in 1856, becoming president in 1884. He was a vice-president of the Institution of Naval Architects, and served many years on its council. He became a member of the British Association for the Advancement of Science in 1865 and for many years he regularly attended the annual meetings. He was president of section G (mechanical science, afterwards engineering) in 1872 and 1884. In 1888 he was elected president of the association. He was always a leading spirit at the convivial Red Lion dinner, one of the more light-hearted functions of the association. In 1874 he joined the Society of Arts, and for twenty-eight years he served continuously on its council, of which he was chairman in 1881 and 1882. From 1885 to 1900 he was honorary secretary of the Royal Institution.

Bramwell was a liveryman of the Goldsmiths' Company, having been apprenticed to his father 'to learn his art of a banker'. He was prime warden of the company in 1877–8. As representative of the company on the council of the City and Guilds of London Institute for the promotion of technical education (established in 1878) he became the first chairman, and filled the post with energy and efficiency until his death. He was knighted on 18 July 1881. He was also chairman of the second inventions exhibition in 1885.

In later life Bramwell was constantly employed by the government on various departmental committees, including the ordnance committee from 1881 to his death. In 1886 he delivered a paper in Birmingham on the metallurgy of gun metals and the problems of construction to withstand large forces. Many honorary distinctions were accorded him. He was elected to the fellowship of the Royal Society in 1873, and in 1877–8 served on its council. In 1875 he was elected a member of the Société des Ingénieurs Civils de France. He was made DCL of Oxford in 1886 and of Durham in 1889; LLD of McGill University, Montreal, in 1884, and of Cambridge in 1892. He was created a baronet in 1889.

Bramwell remained essentially pragmatic and his interests were mainly in applied science, the developments of which he eagerly followed in his own time, and anticipated with something like prophetic insight. As early as 1874 he criticized inefficient uses of energy resources, referring to the use of coal as cruelly wasteful. On the issue of passenger safety his prescience may be noted in his call for improved communication between trains and 'those in the signal houses'. In a speech in 1881 he predicted that fifty years hence the internal combustion engine would have superseded the steam engine. Active to the last, Bramwell died on 30 November 1903 at his residence, 1A Hyde Park Gate, London, from cerebral haemorrhage, and was buried at Hever in Kent, where he possessed a small property. Lady Bramwell survived her husband and died in 1907. The baronetcy became extinct on Bramwell's death.   B. P. CRONIN

Sources Institution of Mechanical Engineers: Proceedings (1874) · Institution of Mechanical Engineers: Proceedings (1903), 767, 913–15 · A. R. Stock, ed., Institution of Mechanical Engineers: Proceedings (1940) [index] · F. J. Bramwell, 'Some reminiscences of steam locomotion on common roads', Engineering (17 Aug 1894), 222–3 · list of candidates, 1873, RS · The Engineer (4 Dec 1903) · H. T. Wood, Journal of the Society of Arts, 52 (1903–4), 67–9 · R. Richardson and R. Thorne, The Builder illustrations index, 1843–1883 (1994), 541 · The Times (1 Dec 1903) · WWW · personal knowledge (1912) [DNB]

Archives UCL, corresp. and papers | BL, letters to Professor Owen and John Hall Gladstone · Institution of Mechanical Engineers, London, archives, letter to Professor Stokes

Likenesses E. O. Ford, marble bust, Royal Institution of Great Britain, London · F. Holl, oils, Inst. CE [see illus.] · S. Lucas, oils, RSA · Spy [L. Ward], chromolithograph caricature, NPG; repro. in VF (27 Aug 1892)

Wealth at death £102,061 4s. 9d.: resworn probate, 1904, CGPLA Eng. & Wales · £90,957 17s. 8d.: double probate, 22 Nov 1904, CGPLA Eng. & Wales

Bramwell, George William Wilshere, Baron Bramwell (1808–1892), judge and political pamphleteer, was born at 22 Finch Lane, Cornhill, London, on 12 June 1808, the son of George Bramwell, banker, and his wife, Elizabeth Martha, née Frith. Frederick Joseph *Bramwell was his younger brother. He was educated at the Revd Martin Ready's school at Peckham, and then at the Palace School, Enfield, under Dr George May, and served an apprenticeship as a clerk in his father's bank. Admitted to Lincoln's Inn in 1830 and the Inner Temple in 1836, Bramwell at first practised as a 'special pleader', and was not called to the bar until 1838. In 1830 he had married Jane Silva (d. 1836)

George William Wilshere Bramwell, Baron Bramwell (1808–1892), by London Stereoscopic Co., after 1862

and they had two daughters; by Bramwell's later account the wedding took place in New York without banns or licence. Bramwell became a bencher of the Inner Temple and queen's counsel in 1851, and established himself as the acknowledged leader of the home circuit, earning £8000 during his final year at the bar. He was appointed a judge as baron of the exchequer in 1856, on which he was also knighted. After serving twenty years in the court of exchequer, Bramwell was appointed lord justice of appeal in 1876, a privy councillor the same year, and created Baron Bramwell of Hever on 3 February 1882. In 1882 he was also elected a fellow of the Royal Society. Although he was not appointed a lord of appeal, Bramwell sat for many years hearing appeals in the House of Lords until his death in 1892.

As a judge Bramwell has been described as 'domineering, entertaining, and consciously concerned to mould the law to ends which he favoured'. Indeed, in the words of P. S. Atiyah, Bramwell's primary interest to the historian of nineteenth-century law is because 'he made no secret of his political convictions, and because it is not difficult to trace the influence of these convictions on his legal judgments in a wide variety of cases' (Atiyah, 374). Bramwell's political principles were those of the classical school of nineteenth-century liberalism, and he sincerely believed that the principle of laissez-faire permeated the common law of England. Holding that the state should not interfere in bargains freely struck between adult individuals, Bramwell considered Herbert Spencer to be 'the profoundest thinker of the age' and on at least one occasion he cited Ricardo in a judgment. In his 1888 presidential address to the economics section of the British Association for the Advancement of Science, Bramwell remarked that there was only one really important principle of political economy and that was the principle of laissez-faire.

Bramwell's advocacy of freedom of contract was far

from sophisticated, but was deeply held and forcefully expressed, and entered directly into many of his judgments. For example, in *British and American Telegraph Co.* v. *Colson* he dissented from the view—now an accepted principle of English law—that an offeror was bound by a posted letter of acceptance which went astray. In Bramwell's view a man should only be bound by a contract to which he gave a clear assent. Similarly, he was unsympathetic towards the development of quasi-contract, on the grounds that someone should not be obliged to pay for a benefit which he had received but for which he had not agreed to pay. Thus in *Boulton* v. *Jones*, he was willing to contemplate that a person was free of all liability to pay for goods he had consumed simply because they had been supplied to him in error.

Bramwell also opposed the development of workmen's compensation on the grounds that the bargain struck between an employer and a workman was reached on the basis of the latter's understanding of all the risks to which he was exposed. Since the workman was, in effect, already being paid for exposing himself to the risk of injury, the workman's wages excluded any right to compensation. Bramwell expressed this point clearly in his dissenting judgment in *Smith* v. *Charles Baker & Sons*. In this case he remarked:

> it is a rule of good sense that if a man voluntarily undertakes a risk for a reward which is adequate to induce him, he shall not, if he suffers from the risk, have a compensation which he did not stipulate.   (*Smith* v. *Charles Baker & Sons*, 1891)

He expressed similar views when called as a witness to give evidence before the 1876 parliamentary select committee on employers' liability.

Bramwell's strict adherence to the principles of *laissez-faire* liberalism can also be found in his summing-up in perhaps the most famous case in which he was involved, *R.* v. *Druitt* in 1867. The case involved Druitt and several others who were officials of an Operative Tailors' Protection Association, and who had been indicted for carrying out picketing in an illegal manner and with intimidation during a tailors' strike in the spring of that year. In his summing-up Bramwell stated:

> The public has an interest in the way in which a man disposes of his industry and his capital; and if two or more persons conspire by threats, intimidation, or molestation to deter or influence him in the way in which he should employ his industry, his talents, or his capital they are guilty of a criminal offence.   (Fairfield, 30)

Although Druitt and the other defendants were found guilty, Bramwell dismissed them without passing any sentence but with a stern warning about what he saw as the tyranny and injustice of their behaviour.

Bramwell did not confine his advocacy of *laissez-faire* principles to the courtroom. He became a founder member of the Liberty and Property Defence League in 1882, established by Lord Wemyss to combat the rising tide of 'state socialism'. In so doing Bramwell associated himself with a group of political writers and pamphleteers, including Auberon Herbert and Wordsworth Donisthorpe, who were stout defenders of the principles

of *laissez-faire* liberalism in the closing decades of the nineteenth century. Bramwell himself authored a number of pamphlets on behalf of the league including *Laissez Faire* (1884) and *Drink* (1885), the latter of which sold 100,000 copies. In *Laissez Faire* Bramwell expressed his political creed in simple, direct, and unambiguous terms. *Drink* was, as might be expected, an anti-prohibitionist tract which defended an Englishman's right to choose for himself what he wanted to drink. Bramwell was also a regular contributor to the letters page of *The Times* newspaper, where, usually under the signature 'B', he protested against various legislative proposals to interfere with freedom of contract and mounted a strong defence of free trade. Although a Liberal for much of his life, he joined many others of his classical Liberal views in breaking with Gladstone in 1886 over Irish home rule.

During his career Bramwell also made two significant contributions to law reform. He was a member of the common law procedure commission appointed to inquire into the process, practice, and system of pleadings in the superior courts. Its report led to the Common Law Procedure Act of 1852. Bramwell also served as a member of the mercantile law commission which reported on (among other things) limited liability for companies. Although the mercantile law commissioners were unable to reach agreement on the principle of limited liability in their first report, Bramwell himself had no doubts about the correct answer. He insisted that the introduction of limited liability would merely involve removing a restriction in the law, leaving individuals free to conclude whatever bargains they saw fit. He gave short shrift to the idea that the law should:

> interfere to prevent, for their own sakes, any persons from entering into any agreement they may be willing to form ... [F]or the purpose of protecting the parties themselves, I say the State ought not to interfere, but to leave every man to the most zealous and best informed of all protectors, himself. (*Parl. papers*, 1834, 27.468)

Ultimately, the principle of limited liability was enacted by parliament in the Companies Act, 1862. Bramwell claimed responsibility for the invention of the term 'Limited' to describe a company so formed.

In 1861 Bramwell married his second wife, Martha Sinden, who died childless on 5 June 1889. Bramwell himself died at home at Four Elms, Edenbridge, Kent, on 9 May 1892. A member of the Cremation Society of England, he was cremated without ceremony four days later at the chapel of the society at St John's, Woking, Surrey.

M. W. TAYLOR

Sources C. Fairfield, *Some account of George William Wilshere, Baron Bramwell of Hever* (1898) · P. S. Atiyah, *The rise and fall of freedom of contract* (1979) · A. W. B. Simpson, ed., *Biographical dictionary of the common law* (1984) · *The Times* (10 May 1892) · *The Times* (14 May 1892) · GEC, *Peerage* · Burke, *Peerage* (1889) · CGPLA Eng. & Wales (1892)

Archives Bodl. Oxf., corresp. with Sir William Harcourt · Bodl. Oxf., corresp. with J. E. Thorold Rogers · UCL, corresp. with Edwin Chadwick

Likenesses London Stereoscopic Co., photograph, after 1862, NPG [*see illus.*] · Spy [L. Ward], chromolithograph caricature, repro. in *VF* (29 Jan 1876) · photograph, repro. in Fairfield, *Some account of*

George William Wilshere … Bramwell, frontispiece · portrait, repro. in *ILN* (1 March 1856) · portrait, repro. in *ILN* (21 May 1892) · portrait, repro. in *ILN* (2 July 1892)
Wealth at death £61,474 18s. 3d.: probate, 18 June 1892, *CGPLA Eng. & Wales*

Bramwell, William (1759–1818), Methodist preacher, was born in Elswick, Lancashire, in February 1759, the tenth of eleven children of George Bramwell, a farmer, and his wife, Elizabeth, devout Anglicans. After a village education William was apprenticed to a Liverpool merchant in 1775, then to a Preston currier. After being converted while receiving communion he joined the Methodists, met John Wesley, and began to preach, one of his early converts being Ann Cutler (1759–1794). In 1786–7 he became an itinerant preacher in Kent, but then served mainly in northern towns. In July 1787 Bramwell married Ellen Byrom (d. 1828); they had four children.

Bramwell was the most successful Wesleyan revivalist of his generation, particularly in the Yorkshire revival of 1792–6. He used groups to pray for those undergoing conversion. Having received the gift of 'entire sanctification' he forcefully preached the possibility of receiving this instantaneously by faith, which, with the emotional scenes in his meetings, recalled early Methodism, though he kept tight control of proceedings. His work was admired in America and in revivalist circles inside and outside Wesleyanism. He supported female preaching, opposing restrictions on it by the Wesleyan conference in 1803, though advising the leading preacher, Mary Barritt (later Taft), to submit.

Bramwell was criticized by Wesleyan leaders hostile to revivalism and emphasizing pastoral discipline. On several occasions he appeared to offer leadership to seceders but then retreated. This was so in his dealings with Alexander Kilham in Sheffield (1797) and James Sigston and the 'Kirkgate Screamers' at Leeds in 1803. That year he resigned from the Wesleyan Methodists and appeared to be about to lead a secession of the Manchester Band Room Methodists and Christian Revivalists in Macclesfield, but under great pressure returned to Wesleyanism. This behaviour hindered him from achieving high office, though he was nominated chairman of the Manchester district on the eve of his death.

Bramwell acquired some knowledge of the biblical languages. He was the author of *A Short Account of the Life and Death of Ann Cutler* (1796) and an abridgement of Samuel D'Oyley's translation *The Salvation Preacher* (1800), which seems to have disappointed its readers.

Bramwell stood about 5 feet 9 inches or 5 feet 10 inches tall, with legs which seemed too slender for a figure inclined to stoutness but curbed by diet. He had a dark complexion, black hair, and piercing eyes. Vigorous and ascetic in his habits, he was an inveterate early riser for prayer, in which he had great power. He had a clear, flexible voice, preaching graphically on the horrors of hell and mercilessly condemning sin. He was credited with 'discerning spirits' (perceiving strangers' sins).

Bramwell was an outstanding example of the persistence of the revivalist tradition within Wesleyanism, though also of the strains this was now creating, while his methods anticipated the more self-conscious organized revivalism of the American Charles Finney (1792–1875). He died at Leeds on 13 August 1818 of a stroke and was buried three days later at Westgate Hill near Birstall, Yorkshire.   HENRY D. RACK

Sources J. Sigston, *Memoirs of the life and ministry of Mr William Bramwell*, 3rd edn, 2 vols. (1821) · *Memoirs of the life and ministry of Rev. William Bramwell by members of his family* (1848) · T. Harris, *The Christian minister in earnest: memoirs of Rev. William Bramwell* (1846) · J. Everett, *Wesleyan takings*, 3rd edn (1841) · W. R. Ward, *Religion and society in England, 1790–1850* (1972) · J. Baxter, 'The great Yorkshire revival, 1792–96', *Sociological Yearbook of Religion*, ed. M. Hill, 7 (1974), 46–76 · J. Kent, *Holding the fort: studies in Victorian revivalism* (1978) · C. N. Wawn, 'Christian ministry characterised by William Bramwell', *Wesleyan Methodist Magazine*, 72 (1849), 254–62, 362–73 · JRL, MAM PLP 13.35 · *The letters of John Pawson*, ed. J. C. Bowmer and J. A. Vickers, 3 vols. (1994–5) · [J. Blackwell], *Life of Alexander Kilham* (1838) · R. Carwardine, *Transatlantic revivalism: popular evangelicalism in Britain and America, 1790–1865* (1978) · IGI
Archives JRL, Methodist Archives and Research Centre
Likenesses probably by W. Ridley, engraving (aged thirty-two), repro. in Sigston, *Memoirs of … William Bramwell*, frontispiece

Brancaster, John of [John de Brancastre] (d. 1218), administrator, was a Norfolk man, taking his name from Brancaster in that county. The Richard of Brancaster (also known as Richard Ruffus) who preceded John in the prebend of Liddington in Lincoln Cathedral, and who in 1207 granted him the vicarage of Brancaster, may have been an older brother. John of Brancaster is first recorded about 1194, witnessing a charter of Archbishop Hubert Walter. It is impossible to say whether he was then attending Hubert as justiciar or as primate, but he was certainly employed in the king's chancery by November 1198, when he begins to appear as one of the senior clerks named in royal instruments as acting in the place of the chancellor. On Richard I's death he passed immediately into the service of John, witnessing one of the latter's charters at Dieppe on 21 May 1199, over a week before his coronation. Brancaster returned to England with John, and later accompanied the king to Normandy in 1201 and 1203, while in November 1204 he was sent on an undefined errand to Flanders. Thereafter his appearances as a witness of royal acts become relatively infrequent, no doubt because he was more often employed away from court. In 1206 he and Hugh of Chalcombe were responsible for tallaging a number of midland counties, while in January 1207 he was given custody of the vacant abbey of Ramsey, Huntingdonshire, a responsibility he retained until December 1209.

Brancaster remained loyal to John during the interdict on the kingdom and the excommunication of the king. But unlike his principal colleagues among the chancery clerks, Hugh and Jocelin of Wells, he did not become a bishop, the highest office he attained being that of archdeacon of Worcester, to which he had been appointed by 4 June 1200. He also obtained the livings of Frodingham, Lincolnshire, Kimberley, Norfolk, Topcroft, Norfolk, and probably Badingham, Suffolk, in addition to the prebend of Liddington and vicarage of Brancaster, while on several occasions he received gifts of wine from the king. He was at least sometimes active as archdeacon; in 1212 he received royal letters presenting Richard Marsh to Kempsey church, Worcestershire, while two years later a charter was presented in the bench recording how Brancaster, while the see of Worcester was vacant, had instituted a parson in the disputed church of Eckington, Worcestershire. He was still alive on 4 May 1218, but had died before the end of that year. HENRY SUMMERSON

Sources Chancery records (RC) · Pipe rolls, 2–12 John · L. Landon, The itinerary of King Richard I, PRSoc., new ser., 13 (1935) · Fasti Angl., 1066–1300, [Lincoln], 83 · Fasti Angl., 1066–1300, [Monastic cathedrals], 106 · J. H. Round, ed., Calendar of documents preserved in France, illustrative of the history of Great Britain and Ireland (1899), 35–6 · Curia regis rolls preserved in the Public Record Office (1922–), vols. 1–7 · Ann. mon., 1.64; 4.410 · W. H. Hart and P. A. Lyons, eds., Cartularium monasterii de Rameseia, 1, Rolls Series, 79 (1884), 228–32 · C. R. Cheney and E. John, eds., Canterbury, 1193–1205, English Episcopal Acta, 3 (1986) · C. Harper-Bill, ed., Norwich, 1070–1214, English Episcopal Acta, 6 (1990) · H. G. Richardson, ed., Memoranda Roll I John, new ser., 21, PR Society (1943) · S. Painter, The reign of King John (1949) · V. Brown, ed., Eye Priory cartulary and charters, 1, Suffolk RS, Suffolk Charters, 12 (1992), 64–5

Branch [née Parry], **Elizabeth** (1672x87–1740), murderer, was born either in Bristol or at Norton St Philip, Somerset, the youngest daughter of a ship's surgeon. Her father, who later 'acquir'd a handsome Fortune' as a shipmaster, gave Elizabeth £2000 upon her marriage to Benjamin Branch (d. c.1730), a gentleman farmer from Hemington, Somerset, with an estimated income of £300 per annum. Elizabeth, whose particularly brutal treatment of her servants would earn her the epithet of 'the Cruel Mistress', seems to have been viewed with abhorrence by contemporaries in part because, as 'a Gentlewoman of great Substance', she made such an ill use of her authority (Cruel Mistress, 9). As Branch herself conceded in her dying speech, she served as a graphic reminder of what could befall 'Masters and Mistresses of Families' who, instead of checking their passions, allowed themselves to be led by them 'from one degree of Cruelty to another' (ibid., 35).

All accounts of Elizabeth Branch's life agree that she very early manifested clear signs of a violent and 'savage' temper. She was reported to have been born with 'a Tooth in her Head', which, it was claimed, 'denotes … a fierce, barbarous and cruel Disposition'. As a child, 'contrary to the natural Inclination of her Sex', Elizabeth 'used to catch Flies and kill them' and 'lov'd to torment Dogs and Cats'; later she graduated to ill-using her father's servants. However, after being warned by her friends that 'this Temper … would never recommend her to a Husband', Elizabeth 'thought fit to suspend or Stifle it' until, as 'Mistress of a Family', she could 'gratify' her most cruel impulses with impunity (Cruel Mistress, 32). Indeed, Elizabeth was no sooner married than she began to mistreat her servants, starving and beating them 'on the slightest Occasion'. Moreover, Branch was not only a cruel mistress but a bad mother who, 'not content with being cruel herself … train'd her Daughter up in the same Disposition' (ibid., 32–3). Her daughter **Elizabeth** [Betty] **Branch** (d. 1740), murderer, 'often cut open Mice and Birds, torturing them for three Hours together before they expir'd'. She was

thought to have received 'such barbarous Notions' from her mother, 'a great Reader', whose favourite story was 'that of Nero, who ript up his Mother's Belly to see how he was born' (Inhumanity and Barbarity, 31). After the death of Benjamin Branch—who was believed to have exercised a restraining influence—mother and daughter became so infamous that no one but 'Strangers, Strollers in the Country' or the children of 'Poor Person[s]' would consent to enter their service (Cruel Mistress, 33).

On 13 February 1740, according to the testimony of the dairymaid Anne James, the Branches' servant-maid Jane Buttersworth, a parish ward about thirteen years old (General Evening Post), was sent out on an errand to a neighbouring farm. Upon her return Elizabeth and Betty, convinced that she had loitered along the way, fell furiously upon the unfortunate girl—striking her with rods, broomsticks, shoes, or any other object that came to hand. According to one report, Jane was beaten for 'almost seven Hours' (Daily Post) and finally expired after sustaining injuries that, in the words of a surgeon who examined her body, 'were enough to have kill'd the stoutest Man' (Cruel Mistress, 23). Elizabeth and Betty, claiming that Buttersworth had died of natural causes, refused to allow anyone to see the body, which they hastily buried 'in the dead of Night' (Daily Gazetteer; Cruel Mistress, 22).

The suspicious circumstances surrounding Buttersworth's death soon gave rise to 'a general Muttering among the Neighbours', several of whom privately exhumed the corpse and brought it to a surgeon to be examined. The Branches, who had the 'worst of Characters for their ill Usage of their Servants', were promptly apprehended, and on 31 March 1740 tried at the Somerset assizes for murder (Cruel Mistress, 28). Despite having hired an eight-man defence counsel and (it was rumoured) offering bribes to both witnesses and jurymen, the Branches made but a feeble defence—claiming that Buttersworth had injured herself in a 'Fit', or that her wounds had been inflicted after her death by malicious neighbours. During a sensational six-hour trial, in which one former servant testified that the Branches had on one occasion viciously beaten him and forced him to eat his own excrement, 'old Mrs. Branch appear'd very little concerned' and was even reported to have 'several Times kick'd' one of the prosecution witnesses as she stood at the bar. The jury, without even retiring to deliberate, delivered a verdict of guilty (Daily Gazetteer; Trial of Mrs. Branch, 21).

Elizabeth and Betty Branch were executed at Ilchester on 3 May 1740. Fearful lest they be 'torn in pieces' by an angry mob, the two women were 'at their own Request' escorted to the gallows very early in the morning and hanged 'before Six o'Clock, to the great Disappointment of several Thousands of People, that came far and near on purpose to see a publick Example made of two Wretches that so much deserv'd it' (Malefactor's Register, 3.12; Daily Post; Cruel Mistress, 35). They were both buried in Ilchester churchyard. ANDREA MCKENZIE

Sources The trial of Mrs. Branch, and her daughter, for the murder of Jane Buttersworth, 2nd edn (1740) · The cruel mistress, being, the genuine *trial of Elizabeth Branch, and her own daughter, for the murder of Jane Buttersworth ... together with an account of their lives* (1740) · *Inhumanity and barbarity not to be equal'd, being an impartial relation of the barbarous murder committed by Mrs. Elizabeth Branch and her daughter, on the body of Jane Buttersworth, their servant* [1740] · *Remarkable trials and interesting memoirs of the most noted criminals*, 2 vols. (1765) · *The malefactor's register, or, The Newgate and Tyburn calendar*, 5 vols. (1779?) · *General Evening Post* (1–4 March 1740) · *Daily Gazetteer* (15 April 1740) · *Daily Post* [London] (13 May 1740) · *London Magazine*, 9 (1740), 191–3, 241 · *GM*, 1st ser., 10 (1740), 258

Likenesses portraits, repro. in *The cruel mistress* (1740)

Wealth at death considerable; income of £200–£300 p.a.; plus approx. £2000 inherited from father: *Cruel mistress*; *Trial of Mrs. Branch*; *Daily Gazetteer*

Branch, Elizabeth (d. 1740). *See under* Branch, Elizabeth (1672×87–1740).

Branch, Thomas (*fl.* 1738–1753), legal writer, is a figure about whom almost nothing is known apart from his published works. The first of them, *Thoughts on Dreaming* (1738), was subtitled, 'An enquiry into the nature of the human soul'. His other work, *Principia legis et aequitatis* (1753) presented, in alphabetical order, a collection of maxims, definitions, and remarkable sayings relating to law and equity. It became highly commended as a students' textbook, both in Britain and in America. A reference in the *Gentleman's Magazine* to the 'lady of Thomas Branch, Esq.' is ambiguous, but may imply that he was still alive in December 1769.

          J. M. Scott, *rev.* Robert Brown

Sources W. T. Lowndes, *The bibliographer's manual of English literature*, ed. H. G. Bohn, [new edn], 6 vols. (1864) · *GM*, 1st ser., 39 (1769), 608

Brancker, Thomas (1633–1676), mathematician, was born at Barnstaple, Devon, in late August 1633, the son of Thomas Brancker (d. 1633). His father had attended Oriel and Exeter colleges in Oxford, taken up a post teaching in Ilminster, Somerset, in the early 1620s, and become headmaster of the high school in Barnstaple about 1630. The family was related to the Brounckers of Lancashire and thence to Sir William Brouncker, the first president of the Royal Society. Brancker matriculated at Exeter College, Oxford, on 27 November 1652. He gained his BA on 15 June 1655 and was elected as a probationer fellow at the end of the same month, rising to full fellow on 10 July of the following year. Having taken his MA on 22 April 1658 he began a career as a preacher. He also studied mathematics and chemistry under the guidance of Peter Stahl of Strasbourg. The latter had come to Oxford at the suggestion of Robert Boyle and taught Ralph Bathurst and Christopher Wren, among others.

While still at Oxford, in 1662, Brancker published a short treatise on globes, *Doctrinae sphaericae adumbratio una cum usu globorum artificialium*. However, soon after this he was expelled from his fellowship for refusing to conform his preaching to the ceremonies of the Church of England. He moved to Cheshire where, having apparently resolved to conform, he took holy orders and was appointed as the minister of Whitegate near Northwich. At some point after his arrival in Cheshire he married Hannah Meyrick of Leicester.

Brancker had begun the translation of an algebra by Heinrich Rahn in 1662, which he completed in 1665 and prepared to send to the press. Hearing that John Pell (who had been Rahn's tutor) was in London, Brancker sent him a copy for his comments. Pell made various alterations and reworkings of Rahn's problems; he also suggested that Brancker should include a 'Table of incomposits' and showed him the method for calculating it. This table showed the odd numbers between 1 and 99,999 with the prime numbers indicated and the lowest prime factor given for all the others. This book was finally published in 1668 as *An Introduction to Algebra, Translated out of the High-Dutch into English*. The translation was highly acclaimed and even acknowledged in an early paper in the *Philosophical Transactions*.

From the dating of the preface to *An Introduction* it appears that Brancker was still at Whitegate in 1668. However, having come under the patronage of William, Lord Brereton (owing to his ability in mathematics and chemistry), he was granted the living of Tilston, near Malpas. He soon after gave up this post in order to become master of Macclesfield School. He remained in Macclesfield until his death there on 26 November 1676, and was buried in the parish church. His monument spoke of him as a mathematician, chemist, natural philosopher, and linguist, and stated that he had studied 'under the auspices of the Hon. Robert Boyle'.   H. K. Higton

Sources Foster, *Alum. Oxon.* · Wood, *Ath. Oxon.* · S. P. Rigaud and S. J. Rigaud, eds., *Correspondence of scientific men of the seventeenth century*, 2 vols. (1841) · *N&Q*, 5th ser., 11 (1879), 41, 174, 344 · *DNB* · *IGI*

Brancker, Sir William Sefton (1877–1930), army and air force officer, was born at Woolwich on 22 March 1877, the elder of the two sons of Colonel William Godefroy Brancker (1834–1885), Royal Artillery, of Erbistock, Ruabon, Denbighshire, and his wife, Hester Adelaide, the daughter of Major-General Henry Charles Russel, Royal Artillery. The Branckers were an old Anglo-German family long resident in England. After his father's death he was educated at Bedford School (1891–4) and the Royal Military Academy at Woolwich. He was commissioned in the Royal Artillery in September 1896 and served in the Second South African War from 1900 to 1902, when he was wounded and mentioned in dispatches. He was promoted captain in 1902 and in the following year, after a spell in England, was sent to India, where he held a variety of staff and instructional appointments; he passed out of the staff college at Quetta in December 1907. On 7 April 1907 he married May Wynne, the daughter of Colonel Spencer Field, of the Royal Warwickshire regiment; they had one son. While in India, Brancker made useful contacts among higher officers, including Major-General Sir Thompson Capper, with whom he went to visit the Manchurian battlefields. He also learned Hindustani, Pushtu, and Tibetan and enjoyed sports of all sorts, participating in a great deal of pig-sticking and big-game shooting.

Brancker first flew in India, on 15 January 1911, when he became the first air passenger in that country. The next day he carried out the army's first aerial reconnaissance, during manoeuvres at Aurangabad, when he was an observer in a Bristol biplane piloted by Henri Jullerot. He left India in April 1912 and was posted to the 43rd battery of the Royal Field Artillery at Deepcut under Major E. B. Ashmore. That summer he flew frequently with the newly formed Royal Flying Corps (RFC), and in February 1913, after a spell of language study in Germany, he was promoted major and posted to the aviation section of the military training directorate at the War Office. He took his Royal Aero Club pilot's certificate—no. 525—at Brooklands on 18 June 1913 and afterwards passed through the short course at the Central Flying School at Upavon. In October he joined the staff of the director-general of military aeronautics, Sir David Henderson. When Henderson took command of the RFC in France on the outbreak of war in August 1914, Brancker was appointed deputy director, effectively taking charge of military aviation at the War Office. He now worked directly under the new secretary of state, Lord Kitchener.

At almost their first meeting Kitchener gave Brancker orders to prepare for 'a vast expansion' of air power. When Brancker suggested that Kitchener's New Armies would require about fifty squadrons, other departments 'were cynically unbelieving as to the possibility of such a creation'. Kitchener, though, wrote against Brancker's estimate: 'Double this. K.' (Macmillan, 68). Brancker thus became largely responsible for the early expansion of the RFC. His duties took him frequently to France, as he tried to fit the new technology into the old management structure. He approached his work with 'the energy and freedom from convention which was part of his nature', employing buccaneering methods to cut through War Office red tape (*Aeroplane*, 8 Oct 1930, 798). In August 1915 Henderson returned to the War Office and Brancker, now a lieutenant-colonel, went to France to command 3 wing of the RFC. He returned to England in December 1915 as brigadier-general in command of the northern brigade, and in February 1916 he moved to St Omer as temporary commander of the RFC. Shortly afterwards, in March, he returned to the War Office, where he became director of air organization.

In his periods of command in the field Brancker proved that he was not just a desk man. Short, dapper, and monocled, he was high-spirited and charming, with a cheerful approach to life. He flew constantly and badly, of which he was 'characteristically unashamed' (*Aeroplane*, 8 Oct 1930, 798). In February 1917 he became deputy director-general of military aeronautics, a role that brought him into close contact with Major-General Sir Hugh Trenchard, and in June he was promoted major-general. Trenchard both liked and trusted Brancker and came increasingly to confide in him. Such regard was not, however, universal. His outspokenness earned him the enmity of General Sir William Robert Robertson and, in October 1917, demotion to an overseas posting as major-general in command of the RFC, Middle East, at Cairo. He was recalled early in January 1918 to a seat on the newly formed Air Council as controller-general of equipment. In May he headed a special air mission to the United States and in August he became master-general of personnel. He 'took for granted in women those qualities of steadfastness and good sense' (Macmillan, 435) which the armed services required, and supported their employment in the Royal Air Force.

Brancker left the service in January 1919 to develop civil aviation, which, like Sir Frederick Sykes, he believed to be the future. He was created KCB (1919) in recognition of his war service and gazetted air vice-marshal, retired, in August; in June 1918 he had been the first recipient of the Air Force Cross. He now joined George Holt Thomas in the Air Travel and Transport Company and helped to organize the first London to Paris airline. Sir Frederick Tymms said of him that he was 'sometimes, not without reason, called the father of civil aviation in Europe' (*Journal of the Royal Aeronautical Society*, 1966, 321). He became an apostle of civil aviation and a tireless speaker, counsellor, and technical expert, voluble in English, French, and German. Brancker spoke foreign languages 'as badly and as recklessly as he flew, and got away with it just as successfully' (*Aeroplane*, 8 Oct 1930, 800). In the United States he helped the passage of the Air Mail Act of 1926 and the creation of the Daniel Guggenheim Fund for the promotion of aeronautics. He used his many contacts with good effect and when president of the Royal Aeronautical Society (1925–6; he was on the council from 1924 to 1930) persuaded the Guggenheim Fund to restore the society to credit with a gift of $25,000. Brancker could give letters of introduction to the most important people in aviation and maintained his contacts at banquets and other social activities. While he loved to dance until dawn, he always arrived punctually at his office at nine o'clock next morning. He was a stickler for keeping to a schedule, a key to how he achieved so much.

On 22 May 1922 Brancker returned to the Air Ministry as director-general of civil aviation, an appointment he held until his death. He threw himself wholeheartedly into his work at the ministry. Whether in allocating subsidized routes before 1924 to the various companies or, after the formation of Imperial Airways, in seeking the best prices for the 'chosen instrument', he was always direct in his approach. He was perhaps too tolerant over the enforcement of air navigation laws, but he helped to start the flying club movement and attended virtually every air meeting while in office, getting to know all the officials of all the clubs. He persuaded George V to present the king's cup for air races in Britain and encouraged long-distance flyers such as Norman Macmillan, his biographer, and Amy Johnson. Brancker's proselytizing style alarmed and even shocked the Foreign Office, and Sir Samuel Hoare, as secretary of state for air, had frequently to intervene to limit the damage done. Hoare later recalled: 'No one, however, could bear any lasting resentment against Brancker's indiscretions. They were obviously the effects of his burning zeal. He would be the first to say "*mea culpa*" and the first to commit them again' (Templewood, 96).

Brancker was one of the founders, in 1919, and a permanent member, of the International Convention on Aerial Navigation (ICAN), and a founder, in 1928, of the Guild of

Air Pilots and Air Navigators. He was a director and president (1928–9) of the Institute of Transport. In January 1930 he consented to become the first president of the British Gliding Association, hoping thereby to encourage youth flying. In November 1924 he flew with Alan Cobham and A. B. Elliott in a DH50 to Rangoon, surveying the air route to India for commercial purposes. They returned in March 1925. In 1927 he flew on the inaugural Imperial Airways flight to India, and he later flew on the corresponding flight to Kenya.

Although he was a proponent of airship services when Charles Dennistoun Burney's scheme of 1922 offered long-distance opportunities that aeroplanes could not match, by 1930 Brancker was less enamoured of the idea. In 1928 he had given his opinion that 'the supremacy of the airship for transoceanic voyages would wane before the competition of great flying-boats' (Macmillan, 410). As the head of civil aviation he heard a great deal about the shortcomings of the R101 airship and personally witnessed the demoralized atmosphere at the construction plant at Cardington, Bedfordshire. He was assigned a place on the inaugural flight to India, in October 1930, and days before departure sought a meeting with the Labour secretary of state, Lord Thomson, to express his serious misgivings. Thomson, though, was under political pressure to justify the enormous government expenditure on R101 and was determined to press on, even though the airship had not completed a full-power air trial. He invited Brancker to vacate his seat on the flight, all but offering a white feather. Brancker, who never lacked courage, dutifully boarded the ill-fated rigid, which left for India at 6.30 p.m. on Saturday 4 October. He was among the forty-eight passengers and crew who were killed in the early hours of the following morning, when the airship burst into flames after hitting the ground at Allonne, near Beauvais, France. He was buried, with the other victims, in a common grave at the cemetery at Cardington, next to the Royal Airship Works where the R101 had been made.

Sefton Brancker's brilliant organizing capacity played an important part in the development of the RFC during the First World War and of civil aviation in the years afterwards. He could be tactless and at times conveyed the air of a journalist in search of a story rather than a departmental head. Some who judged him superficially suspected a lack of depth and poise. In fact he was gifted with unusually clear vision, tempered by shrewd common sense. 'He simply forced aircraft upon the notice of all and sundry, and his energy was only equalled by his ability' (*Flight*, 10 Oct 1930, 1105).   ROBIN HIGHAM

Sources N. Macmillan, *Sir Sefton Brancker* (1935) · *The Aeroplane* (8 Oct 1930) · *Flight* (10 Oct 1930) · R. Higham, *The British rigid airship* (1967) · R. Higham, *Britain's imperial air routes* (1960) · N. Shute, *Slide rule* (1954) · B. Collier, *Heavenly adventurer: Sefton Brancker and the dawn of British aviation* (1959) · *The Times* (1 Jan 1931), 15e · W. Raleigh and H. A. Jones, *The war in the air*, 6 vols. (1922–37), vols. 1–3 · A. Boyle, *Trenchard* (1962) · *Journal of the Royal Aeronautical Society* (1966) · Viscount Templewood, *Empire of the air: the advent of the air age, 1922–1929* (1957) · *WWW* · C. Chant, *Aviation: an illustrated history* (1978)

Archives NRA, papers | Durham RO, corresp. with Lord Londonderry · PRO, AIR files, RFC · PRO, AIR files, DCA | FILM BFI NFTVA, documentary footage · BFI NFTVA, news footage · IWM FVA, actuality footage | SOUND BBC WAC · IWM FVA, oral history interview

Likenesses F. Dodd, charcoal and watercolour drawing, 1918, IWM · L. F. Roslyn, bronze bust, 1919, IWM · H. Coster, photographs, c.1926, NPG · B. Partridge, pencil drawing, 1929, NPG · J. Lavery, portrait · H. Wrightson, portrait, repro. in *LondG* (1 Jan 1919) · photographs, IWM

Wealth at death £6990 2s. 10d.: probate, 24 Dec 1930, CGPLA Eng. & Wales

Brand [*née* Ogle], **Barbarina**, **Lady Dacre** (1768–1854), poet and playwright, was born on 9 May 1768, the third daughter of Admiral Sir Chaloner Ogle, baronet (*d.* 1816), and Hester, youngest daughter and coheir of John Thomas DD, bishop of Winchester. She was educated at home, and in 1789 she married Valentine Henry Wilmot (*d.* 1819) of Farnborough, Hampshire, an officer in the guards, with whom she had a daughter, Arabella (1796–1839). After his death, on 4 December 1819 she married Thomas Brand, twentieth Baron Dacre (1774–1851); they had no children.

Lady Dacre was one of the most accomplished women of her time, an excellent horsewoman, sculptor, and a French and an Italian scholar, as well as a writer of some note. In 1821 her poetical works were privately printed in two octavo volumes, under the title *Dramas, Translations, and Occasional Poems*. They include four dramas, the first of which, *Gonzalvo of Cordova*, was written in 1810 and was indebted to de Florian's *Gonzalve de Cordone* (1791). The next, *Pedarias, a Tragic Drama*, was written in 1811, its story being derived from *Les Incas* of Marmontel. Her third dramatic work was *Ina*, a tragedy in five acts, the plot of which was set in Saxon England. It was produced at Drury Lane on 22 April 1815, under the management of Sheridan, to whose second wife, the daughter of Dr Ogle, dean of Winchester, Lady Dacre was related. It was not sufficiently successful to induce its repetition. It was printed in 1815, as produced on the stage, but in Lady Dacre's collected works she restored 'the original catastrophe, and some other parts which had been cut out'. The fourth drama was entitled *Xarifa*. Lady Dacre's book also contains translations of several of the sonnets of Petrarch. Ugo Foscolo's *Essays on Petrarch* of 1823 are dedicated to Lady Dacre, and the last forty-five pages of the work are occupied by her translations from Petrarch. Her *Translations from the Italian*, principally from Petrarch, were privately printed at London in 1836. She also wrote several plays and comedies for amateur theatres which were successfully put on at Hatfield and The Hoo. Lady Dacre was a prolific letter-writer who shared a correspondence with other literary women such as Joanna Baillie, Mary Mitford, and Catherine Maria Fanshawe.

In addition to her other accomplishments, Lady Dacre was an excellent amateur artist, and excellent in modelling animals, particularly the horse. In 1831 she edited *Recollections of a Chaperon*, followed in 1835 by *Tales of the Peerage and Peasantry*, both collections of short stories published anonymously, but written by her daughter Arabella, who had married the Revd Frederick Sullivan, vicar of Kimpton, Hertfordshire. Lady Dacre was devastated by Arabella's death in 1839, and this and her own increasing deafness made it difficult for her to socialize. She died in Chesterfield Street, Mayfair, Westminster, on 17 May 1854.   THOMPSON COOPER, rev. REBECCA MILLS

Sources G. Lyster, ed., *A family chronicle derived from notes and letters selected by Barbarina, the Hon. Lady Grey* (1908), 13, 186 • J. Shattock, *The Oxford guide to British women writers* (1994), 125 • review, *QR*, 49 (1833), 228–47 • *GM*, 2nd ser., 42 (1854), 296–7 • J. Martin, *Bibliographical catalogue of books privately printed*, 2nd edn (1854), 276, 466 • GEC, *Peerage*, new edn
Archives U. Durham L., corresp. and papers | BL, letters to Sir Anthony Panizzi, Add. MSS 36714–36715, 36726 • Devon RO, letters to Lady Morley and Therese Villiers • NL Scot., corresp. with Lord Lynedoch • U. Leeds, Brotherton L., corresp. with Ichabod Charles Wright
Likenesses H. Seymour, drawing (aged seventy-five), repro. in Lyster, ed., *A family chronicle*, 186

Brand, Sir David (1837–1908), advocate and local politician, was born in Glasgow on 27 December 1837, the eldest son of Robert Brand, a linen merchant, and his wife, Elizabeth, daughter of Robert Thomson. He was educated at Glasgow Academy and the universities of Glasgow and Edinburgh before studying at Heidelberg where he graduated doctor of jurisprudence. He was admitted a member of the Faculty of Advocates in 1864. In 1877 he married Elizabeth Findlay, daughter of Robert Findlay Dalziel of Paisley. A Liberal in politics, Brand was active in the registration courts in the interest of that party. He was involved in Gladstone's successful Midlothian election campaign (1880) and was rewarded with a position of advocate-depute in the Liberal government from 1880 to 1885. In 1885 he was appointed sheriff of the county of Ayr.

Brand was appointed chairman of the Crofters' Commission established by the Crofters' Holdings (Scotland) Act of 1886. The commission—consisting of Brand and two colleagues—was established to review rents and arrears, evaluate compensation for improvements, and administer common grazings regulations in the seven crofting counties of the north of Scotland. The first two years of the commission's work were a period of intense land agitation in the highlands. The commission acted as a peripatetic land court and its presence in the areas of unrest, its uncomplicated procedure, willingness to hear evidence in Gaelic, and a quickly established reputation for fairness, played a major role in helping to quell the agitation. Brand's part in this achievement was crucial. The fact that he assumed the chairmanship of the commission without any previous involvement in highland affairs worked in his favour, as he was able to approach issues with an open mind and an unblemished reputation. The workload of the commission in its early years was massive: between 1886 and 1893 the commission made decisions on the rents of over 14,000 crofts. On average they reduced crofting rents by about one third and cancelled about two thirds of the arrears which had arisen during the years of agitation since 1882.

Brand's legal expertise was important in the work of the commission, which was, essentially, a court of law. The

difficulties were enormous; crofting was an entirely novel legal code and a radical departure from established land law in Scotland. The commission had to establish a body of precedence in this difficult area; the fact that very few of its decisions were the subjects of appeals is testimony to Brand's sure touch.

In the early 1890s the workload of the commission was decreasing and Brand chaired the royal commission (highlands and islands) in 1892. This body had the remit of identifying land being used for grazing or sport which could be transferred to crofters. Brand's political skills were taxed by the job of chairing a fractious and unpopular royal commission. The commission's report was greeted with derision and the government showed no signs of wishing to implement its recommendations before losing office in 1895.

Brand was also a member of the congested districts board, established in 1897 to implement the Conservative policy of land purchase in the highlands. This body was underfunded and found highland crofters to be lukewarm towards the notion of land purchase. Brand was one of the authors of the report of the Crofters' Commission 'on the social condition of the people of Lewis in 1901, as compared with twenty years ago', published as a parliamentary paper in 1902 and retaining a permanent value as a survey of crofting life in the Hebrides. In June 1907 he was knighted. By then his health was failing and for the last two years of his life he played little active role in the Crofters' Commission or on the congested districts board. Brand died at his home, 42 Coates Gardens, Edinburgh, on 22 January 1908 and was buried at Dean cemetery, Edinburgh on 25 January. He was survived by his wife, son, and three daughters.   EWEN A. CAMERON

Sources E. A. Cameron, *Land for the people: the British government and the Scottish highlands, 1880–1925* (1996) • 'Sir David Brand, advocate', *Scots Law Times* (6 July 1907), 41–2 • *Scots Law Times* (25 Jan 1908), 138–9 • *Ayrshire Post* (24 Jan 1908) • *The Scotsman* (26 Jan 1908) • *Ayr Advertiser* (30 Jan 1908) • *CCI* (1908)
Archives NA Scot., department of agriculture and fisheries files, AF67/1–31
Likenesses photograph, repro. in 'Sir David Brand'
Wealth at death £12,832 6s. 9d.: confirmation, 11 May 1908, *CCI*

Brand, Hannah (1754–1821), actress and playwright, was born on 19 November 1754 in Norwich, the daughter of John Brand, a tanner, and his wife, Hannah. She was the younger sister of the clergyman and pamphleteer John *Brand (1743–1808). There were two other sisters; Mary, the elder, kept a school at Norwich in conjunction with Hannah before the latter abandoned teaching for the stage. She made her début in January 1792 with the Drury Lane company at the King's Theatre (Opera House) in the Haymarket, in her own tragedy, *Huniades*. The *London Chronicle* (17 January 1792) recorded that 'the first four acts were received with great applause', but the work proved too long for the continued approbation of the audience. Brand, announced as making 'her first appearance upon any stage', deprived it of what chance it might have had with an actress of more experience as the heroine, although the editors of the *Biographia dramatica* remembered her performance as 'marked by force and discrimination'. The play was withdrawn, but a shorter version was reproduced on 2 February with the title *Agmunda*. This experiment proved no more successful than the first, and piece, heroine, and author vanished from London.

Two years later, on 20 March 1794, Brand appeared at the York theatre, playing Lady Townly in Vanbrugh's *The Provoked Husband*. Her manager there, Tate Wilkinson, complained of her old-fashioned dress, provincial accent, conceit, and contradictory passions. All of these provoked the audience, and her performance 'met with rude marks of disgustful behaviour' (Wilkinson, 4.158). She remained in York until the last night of the season (21 May 1794), when she appeared in her own play, *Agmunda*, in which she was derided. In the summer she performed in Liverpool with no greater success. Wilkinson suggests that neither she nor her plays had any chance of succeeding on the stage, though she attributed her defeat to the jealousy of Mrs Siddons and the rest of the Kembles. Apart from these and other eccentricities, she possessed 'many good and shining qualities', was estimable in her private character, and was endowed with a good understanding.

In 1798 Brand published in Norwich, by subscription, a volume of *Plays and Poems*, containing: the full-length version of her own play under its original title, two English adaptations of plays by Corneille and Destouches, and some miscellaneous poems. After her failure on the stage she again became a governess. She was hired by a former pupil, a married woman, but Brand's eccentric conduct was the cause of much unpleasantness between husband and wife.

Brand died in March 1821. Her will was proved in London on 19 October 1821, and left small bequests of books and money to her sisters and other relatives. The remainder, £200, was left to Mary Ware, a widow, of Norfolk.

JOSEPH KNIGHT, *rev.* K. A. CROUCH

Sources Highfill, Burnim & Langhans, *BDA* · C. B. Hogan, ed., *The London stage, 1660–1800*, pt 5: *1776–1800* (1968) · T. Wilkinson, *The wandering patentee, or, A history of the Yorkshire theatres from 1770 to the present time*, 4 vols. (1795) · *London Chronicle* (17 Jan 1792) · *London Chronicle* (19 Jan 1792) · *London Chronicle* (2 Feb 1792) · Genest, *Eng. stage* · W. Beloe, *The sexagenarian, or, The recollections of a literary life*, ed. [T. Rennell], 2 vols. (1817) · D. E. Baker, *Biographia dramatica, or, A companion to the playhouse*, rev. I. Reed, new edn, rev. S. Jones, 3 vols. in 4 (1812) · Nichols, *Illustrations* · H. Brand, *Proposals for publishing by subscription one volume in octavo plays and poems, by Miss Hannah Brand* (1797) · H. Brand, *Plays and poems* (1798) · *IGI*
Wealth at death approx. £300; small bequests of just over £100; remainder of £200 in 50 per cent annuities: Highfill, Burnim & Langhans, *BDA*

Brand, Henry Bouverie William, first Viscount Hampden (1814–1892), politician and speaker of the House of Commons, born on 24 December 1814, was the second son of Henry Otway Brand, twenty-first Baron Dacre, and his wife, Pyne, second daughter of the Hon. and Very Revd Maurice Crosbie, dean of Limerick. The barony of Dacre had passed through the female line to the Fiennes family, from them to the Lennards, and from them to Charles Trevor Roper, eighteenth Baron Dacre (1745–1794); the

Henry Bouverie William Brand, first Viscount Hampden (1814–1892), by Lombardi, 1860s

eighteenth baron's sister Gertrude married Thomas Brand of The Hoo, Hertfordshire, father of Thomas Brand, twentieth Baron Dacre (whose wife was Barbarina *Brand, Lady Dacre), and great-grandfather of Viscount Hampden.

Brand was educated at Eton College. He did not go to a university, and on 16 April 1838, when twenty-three years of age, married Elizabeth Georgina (1817/18–1899), daughter of General Robert Ellice (1784–1856). His political career began in 1846, when he became private secretary to Sir George Grey, home secretary. From 6 July 1852 he sat as Liberal member for Lewes until 1865, when he was returned for Cambridgeshire, which he continued to represent until his elevation to the peerage. He was a whip under Palmerston from 17 April 1855 to 1 March 1858. For a few weeks in the spring of 1858 Brand was keeper of the privy seal to the prince of Wales, and on 9 June 1859 he became parliamentary secretary to the Treasury. He held this post under Palmerston and Russell until July 1866 and he continued to act as senior Liberal whip for the two years during which the Liberals were in opposition, importantly developing the role of the whips' office in elections. When Gladstone took office in 1868 Brand was not included in the administration, his place as whip being taken by George Grenfell Glyn, afterwards Baron Wolverton, but when John Evelyn Denison (afterwards Viscount Ossington) resigned the speakership of the House of Commons in February 1872, Brand was elected without opposition to succeed him.

Brand's long tenure of the position of party whip caused doubts as to his fitness for the speakership, but these were soon solved by Brand's impartial performance of his duties; he endeared himself to the house by his uniform suavity, and in 1874, when Disraeli returned to office, Brand was, on 5 March, on the motion of Henry Chaplin, unanimously re-elected speaker. The development of systematic obstruction under Parnell's auspices placed Brand in a position of unprecedented difficulty, and on 11 July 1879 Parnell moved a vote of censure on him for having ordered two clerks to take minutes of the speeches, on the ground that he had no power to do so; the motion was lost by 421 to 29 votes. Brand had in the same parliament some difficulty in dealing with Samuel Plimsoll.

After the general election of 1880 Brand was once more, on the motion of Sir Thomas Dyke Acland on 30 April, unanimously elected speaker, but the return of the Parnellite home-rulers in increased numbers added to his difficulties, and their obstructive tactics culminated in the debate on W. E. Forster's motion for leave to introduce his Coercion Bill. The sitting, which began on 31 January 1881, was by these means protracted for forty-one hours until 9 a.m. on 2 February. Brand, who had left the chair at 11.30 on the previous night, then returned, and controversially ended the debate by refusing on his own responsibility to hear any more speeches. The strict legality of his action was doubtful, but it was justified by sheer necessity. It was the first check imposed upon members' power of unlimited obstruction; next day, in consultation with Brand, Gladstone introduced resolutions reforming the rules of procedure.

Brand's tenure of the speakership was henceforth relatively uneventful; he worked closely with Gladstone on developing rules of procedure, attending the cabinet on 30 January and 2 February 1882 (possibly a unique attendance by a speaker). He received the unusual honour of GCB at the close of the 1881 session, and in February 1884 resigned the chair on the ground of failing health. He was granted the usual pension of £4000 and on 4 March was created Viscount Hampden of Glynde, Sussex. His choice of title was probably determined by his descent in the female line from John Hampden. For the rest of his life he devoted himself to agricultural experiments at Glynde, particularly in dairy farming. He was made lord lieutenant of Sussex, and in 1890 succeeded his elder brother, Thomas Crosbie William, as twenty-third Baron Dacre. Brand and his wife, who died at Lewes on 9 March 1899, aged eighty-one, had five sons, including Henry Robert *Brand, second Viscount Hampden (1841–1906), colonial governor, and five daughters. He died at Pau on 14 March 1892, and was buried at Glynde on the 22nd, a memorial service being held on the same day in St Margaret's, Westminster.   A. F. POLLARD, rev. H. C. G. MATTHEW

Sources GEC, *Peerage* · Gladstone, *Diaries* · A. F. Thompson, 'Gladstone's whips and the general election of 1868', *EngHR*, 63 (1948), 189–200 · *The Times* (16–23 March 1892) · *The Times* (10 March 1899)
Archives Chatsworth House, Derbyshire, letters to duke of Devonshire · HLRO, diaries, corresp., and papers | BL, corresp. with W. E. Gladstone, Add. MSS 44193–44195 · BL, corresp. with Lord Halifax, Add. MS 49556, *passim* · BL, corresp. with Lord Iddesleigh, Add. MS 50021, *passim* · BL, corresp. with Sir Stafford Northcote, Add. MS 50021 · Bodl. Oxf., letters to Benjamin Disraeli · Bodl. Oxf., corresp. with Lord Kimberley · Borth. Inst., corresp. with Lord Halifax · Bucks. RLSS, letters to Baron Cottesloe · Co-operative Union, Holyoake House, Manchester, letters to George Holyoake · ICL, letters to Lord Playfair · NL Scot., corresp. with Sir George Grey · PRO, corresp. with Lord John Russell · U. Southampton L., corresp. with Viscount Palmerston
Likenesses Lombardi, carte-de-visite, 1860–69, NPG [*see illus.*] · F. Holl, oils, 1885, Palace of Westminster, London · F. Holl, portrait, The Hoo, Welwyn, Hertfordshire · Lock & Whitfield, woodbury-type photograph, NPG; repro. in T. Cooper, *Men of mark: a gallery of contemporary portraits* (1876) · London Stereoscopic Co., carte-de-visite, NPG · F. Sargent, etching (aged sixty-nine), BM · J. J. Tissot, chromolithograph caricature, NPG; repro. in *VF* (16 Nov 1872)
Wealth at death £54,752 9s. 10d.: probate, 30 July 1892, CGPLA Eng. & Wales

Brand, Henry Robert, second Viscount Hampden (1841–1906), colonial governor, was born on 2 May 1841 at Government House, Devonport, Devon, the eldest of the five sons in the family of ten children of Henry Bouverie William *Brand, first Viscount Hampden (1814–1892), an army officer and later speaker of the House of Commons, and his wife, Elizabeth Georgina (1817/18–1899), the daughter of General Robert Ellice (1784–1856). He was educated at Rugby School before being commissioned in 1858 in the Coldstream Guards, and served for a period as aide-de-camp to Viscount Monck, governor-general of Canada; he retired from the army in October 1865 with the rank of captain.

On 21 January 1864 Brand married Victoria Alexandrina Leopoldine (d. 1865), the daughter of Sylvain van de Weyer, Belgian minister of state. She died in childbirth less than two years later, and on 14 April 1868 he married Susan Henrietta (d. 1909), the daughter of Lord George Henry Cavendish. They had three daughters and six sons, the fourth being the merchant banker Robert Henry *Brand, Baron Brand (1878–1963).

In 1868 Brand was elected as a Liberal for the seat of Hertfordshire, but he was defeated in 1874. He then immediately stood for Stroud, where the election had been declared void on petition. Although he was successful, he was himself unseated shortly afterwards by legal challenge. In 1880 he was returned to parliament for the Stroud constituency and he served as surveyor-general of the ordnance from 1883 to 1885. He opposed Irish home rule and stood unsuccessfully for Cardiff as a Liberal Unionist in the general election of 1886. In 1892 he succeeded to his father's titles.

In 1895 Hampden was appointed governor of New South Wales. His term there has been described as being 'remarkable as one of political calm' (Cunneen). He resigned from his position eighteen months earlier than expected, to deal with the 'urgent private affairs' (*The*

Times, 23 Nov 1906) of his heir's marriage. Hampden had a very keen interest in sport and had pointedly noted that New South Wales could not be 'called a sporting country' (Cunneen), lacking as it did good hunting and shooting. Undoubtedly the highlight of his tenure as governor was the celebration of the queen's diamond jubilee, an event which encouraged his provision in the colony of 'hospitality on an unusual scale' (*The Times*, 23 Nov 1906).

Hampden died on 22 November 1906 at his home, 5 Grosvenor Gardens, London, of Bright's disease, and was buried on 27 November at Kimpton, Hertfordshire.

MARC BRODIE

Sources *The Times* (23 Nov 1906), 10 · Burke, *Peerage* (1894) · C. Cunneen, 'Brand, Henry Robert', *AusDB*, vol. 9 · *DNB* · *Sydney Morning Herald* (26 Feb 1899) · GEC, *Peerage* · *CGPLA Eng. & Wales* (1907)
Archives BL, corresp. with E. T. H. Hutton, Add. MSS 50082, *passim* · BL, letters to G. D. Ramsay, Add. MS 46450 · Mitchell L., NSW, Carruthers MSS · NL Aus., Barton MSS
Likenesses J. Collier, portrait, The Hoo, Welwyn · Newman, group portrait, photograph (with family), Mitchell L., NSW · T. Roberts, oils, Government House, Sydney · Spy [L. Ward], chromolithograph caricature, NPG; repro. in *VF* (15 March 1884) · wood-engraving (after photograph by Russell & Sons), NPG; repro. in *ILN* (22 June 1895)
Wealth at death £177,405 14s. 8d.: probate, resworn, 1907, *CGPLA Eng. & Wales* (1907)

Brand, Herbert Charles Alexander (1839–1901), naval officer, was born on 10 July 1839 at Bathwick, Somerset, the son of Charles Brand and his wife, Caroline Julia Sanders. He entered the navy in December 1851, and as a midshipman served on the flagship *Britannia* in the Black Sea in 1854, and in the *Colossus* in the Baltic in 1855. He was appointed in 1856 to the *Calcutta*, going out to China as the flagship of Sir Michael Seymour (1802–1887). While in her, he was present at the destruction of the junks in Fatshan (Foshan) Creek, at the capture of Canton (Guangzhou), and at the capture of the Taku (Dagu) forts in 1858. Afterwards, as a sub-lieutenant of the *Cruiser*, he took part in the unsuccessful attack on the Taku forts (25 June 1859), and the next day received from the commander-in-chief his promotion to lieutenant. In 1865, still a lieutenant, he commanded the gun-vessel *Onyx* on the West Indian station, and supported the military in suppressing the revolt in Morant Bay, Jamaica, and sat as president of the questionable court martial held, by order of the general in command, on the leaders. The court found them guilty, following which (by order of the governor, Edward Eyre) they were executed. For this service Brand was officially thanked by the governor, the general, and the assembly; but in Britain humanitarians brought charges of murder against Alexander Nelson and Brand. On 10 April 1867 they were brought up for trial at the Old Bailey, when Lord Justice Cockburn told the grand jury that the circumstances had justified the application of martial law; the grand jury consequently found 'no true bill', and the prisoners were discharged. If Brand had been a more discreet man, he would probably have received a reward from the government for his services; but he permitted his temper to rule his action and wrote several ill-judged letters to his principal accusers, notably Charles Buxton MP. Their publication showed him as a quarrelsome bully. These letters forced the Admiralty to the conclusion that he could not be promoted, and although employed in the command of a gun-vessel on the Irish coast during the Fenian troubles, he was virtually shelved some time before his retirement with the nominal rank of commander in July 1883. He lived at 8 Bathwick Hill, Bath, and died at Bath on 10 June 1901.   J. K. LAUGHTON, *rev.* ANDREW LAMBERT

Sources *The Times* (11 June 1901) · G. Heuman, *The killing time: the Morant Bay rebellion in Jamaica* (1994) · B. Semmel, *The Governor Eyre controversy* (1962) · *Annual Register* (1867) · H. Hume, *Life of Edward John Eyre* (1867) · personal knowledge (1901) · *CGPLA Eng. & Wales* (1901)
Wealth at death £318 18s. 3d.: probate, 9 July 1901, *CGPLA Eng. & Wales*

Brand, James (1831–1909), public works contractor, was born on 20 September 1831 in Montrose, Forfarshire, the son of Charles Brand (*d.* 1885), mason and contractor, from a Kincardine family, and his wife, Margaret Falconer. He had at least one brother. After leaving school in Montrose he was apprenticed for three years to his uncle William Brand, who was in charge of enlarging Ardross Castle, overlooking the Firth of Cromarty, for Alexander Matheson the opium trader. In 1851 he began to work for his father as clerk of works for the building of the Episcopal church at Arbroath. Charles Brand was part of a consortium which successfully tendered for the extension of the Aberdeen Railway to Inverness, and James Brand worked with him on the sections of the line for which he was responsible. He became manager of the firm in 1853. His father, as part of another consortium, contracted for sections of the Great North of Scotland Railway (GNSR), and was allocated the section between Elgin and Keith. Brand worked there as contract agent in 1856–8, and saw the completion of the route from Aberdeen to Inverness; he was taken into partnership with his father in 1859, forming the company Charles Brand & Son. In 1863 Brand married Jane, daughter of William Gordon, procurator fiscal in Banffshire, and shortly after this was received into the Roman Catholic church. The couple had five sons, two of whom became Jesuit priests, and three daughters, two of whom became nuns.

During the 1860s the firm was active in railway construction in north and north-east Scotland. It built the line from Keith to Dufftown for the GNSR, opened in 1862, and the section of the highland railway between Bonar Bridge and Golspie. In the late 1860s it expanded into lowland Scotland and then undertook a series of contracts on the Glasgow tramways from 1870, the first to be tendered by Glasgow corporation. Work began in 1878 on an important contract building Grangemouth docks, and the firm went on to build docks in Dumbarton, 1880–84, and Donegal quay in Belfast, 1882–5.

Charles Brand retired in 1882, and James Brand became sole partner. In that year the firm began work on the eastern section of the Glasgow City and District Railway, the first underground line to be built in Glasgow. It took four years to build because of the technical difficulties of tunnelling underneath buildings in the city centre, often through waterlogged sand, and also the problem of blasting through boulder clay: only 7 yards of tunnel a month were completed while tunnelling under Buchanan Street. This work led to contracts for the Glasgow District subway, to build sections under the River Clyde: this used cable traction, the same system as the San Francisco cable cars, powered by stationary steam engines above ground. Tunnelling began in 1891 and the subway opened in December 1896, only to close again on the first day after an accident. Brand also helped to build the Glasgow Central Railway for the Caledonian Railway: in order to excavate the busy streets in the centre of Glasgow nearby buildings had to be underpinned, and there were problems with water from the River Clyde seeping into the workings. This line opened in 1895. Using expertise gained in Glasgow, the firm was to carry out many contracts for the London underground after the First World War.

A new partnership was formed in 1903, including Brand's third son, Harry, and after this Brand began to retire from the business. He had been a member of Glasgow parish council since 1875 and chairman of the merged Glasgow parish in 1898–1901. As chairman of the hospitals committee he succeeded in getting the council to build a large new general hospital. In 1904 he sat on the Glasgow municipal commission on the housing of the poor. Brand was also active in the Catholic community of Glasgow, serving on the Scottish Catholic schools committee, and was chairman of the Caledonian Catholic Association. He died on 15 January 1909 in Bournemouth, survived by his wife.   ANNE PIMLOTT BAKER

Sources DSBB · Engineering (22 Jan 1909) · M. Barclay-Harvey, A history of the Great North of Scotland railway, 2nd edn (1949) · H. A. Vallance, The Great North of Scotland railway (1965) · W. A. C. Smith and P. Anderson, Illustrated history of Glasgow's railways (1993) · B. Kettle, The Glasgow underground (1989) · CGPLA Eng. & Wales (1909)
Likenesses drawing, repro. in DSBB, vol. 1, p. 135
Wealth at death £113,593 18s. 9d.: confirmation, 17 April 1909, CCI

Brand, Sir Johannes Henricus [Jan Hendrik] (1823–1888), president of the Orange Free State, son of Sir Christoffel Joseph Brand (1797–1875), speaker of the Cape house of assembly, and his wife, Catharina Fredrica, née Kuchler (bap. 1797, d. 1868), was born in Cape Town on 6 December 1823. He received Dutch and English schooling at Tot Nut van 't Algemeen and at the South African College, entered Leiden University in May 1843, and graduated LLD in 1845. After qualifying at the Inner Temple, London, in 1849, he returned to practise at the Cape bar, and from 1851 also taught law at the South African College, becoming a professor in 1858. In 1851 he married Johanna Sibella, née Zastron (d. 1898), daughter of the Cape registrar of deeds; they had eight sons and three daughters.

In 1854 Brand was elected to the house of assembly for Clanwilliam. He was an aggressive, fearless speaker, particularly on topics falling within his professional competence. But an offer to stand for the Orange Free State presidency ended his Cape career. He succeeded, took office on

2 February 1864, and remained president until his death, being chosen for the office again in 1869, 1874, 1879 and 1884.

Brand's Orange Free State (OFS) became known as a 'model republic', partly because it was mistakenly thought to have no ethnic problem, and more accurately because of its 1854 constitution, and as a result of Brand's efforts to promote its administrative and educational systems, its international recognition, and (from a poor start) its economic strength. He steered his country through several crises, especially over frontier lands which his own burghers took or coveted, and over British challenges to the political claims of his own state.

The Sotho had fought successfully under Moshoeshoe against the OFS in 1858–9 to retrieve lost lands in the Caledon valley. When border troubles broke out again in 1864, OFS commandos defeated the Sotho, who ceded most of their grazing lands to the Boers, but then resumed the conflict in 1867. Intervention by Sir Philip Wodehouse, the high commissioner, led Brand, reluctantly, to give back some Sotho territory in return for a British take-over of Basutoland and its frontier problems (1868–9). In 1871 the Cape government assumed responsibility, but provoked the Sotho in 1880 by demanding the surrender of guns lawfully acquired by Sotho workers on the diamond fields. Brand was not pleased when, in 1884, Britain resumed control over Basutoland as a protectorate. OFS farmers looked upon Basutoland as their labour reserve. Coincidentally, there was also friction among the seTswana-speaking Rolong of Thaba'Nchu, over whom Moshoeshoe had claimed paramountcy, and whose land lay near the Sotho–OFS frontier. When Chief Samuel murdered his rival Sepinare, Brand took over the territory but let his burghers colonize much of their land.

After the discovery of diamonds on his western border in 1867, Brand claimed sovereignty over the territory, where some farmers had OFS titles, on the ground of Britain's abandonment of responsibility north of the Orange River in 1854, and a surveyor's report which placed the border of Waterboer's Griqua territory west of the diamond fields. Britain argued that the OFS land claims were inconclusive, that the diamond area was within Griqua territory, and that the influx of diggers into the area required controls which only Britain could provide. Brand demanded international arbitration, but Britain appointed Lieutenant-Governor Keate of Natal to make an award instead. Keate supported the British view, confirming that the Griqua chief was a territorial sovereign in his own right. In 1871 Waterboer placed his state under British control, and Brand protested in vain.

The incorporation of Griqualand West was part of a plan to federate southern Africa, launched by Disraeli's colonial secretary Lord Carnarvon in 1875. Though his proposal to hold a conference in London won support in the eastern Cape and in Natal, it was opposed by the Cape government and the Transvaal. Brand agreed to a conference on 'native problems' and the control of firearms, but rejected the separate representation of Griqualand West.

He went to London in 1876 to reject the federal plan, and a dubious court judgment in the same year overturned Keate's ruling that the Griqua chief had territorial rights, sufficiently strengthening Brand's hand to enable him to negotiate a monetary payment in return for his recognition of the Keate award.

Trying to keep federalism alive, Britain annexed the Transvaal by a coup in 1877, an act which Brand angrily denounced, urging Britain to restore self-government to the territory. When the Transvaalers successfully rebelled in 1880–81, Brand's neutrality enabled him to act as broker in the negotiation of the Pretoria convention of 1881, whereby the Transvaal regained its autonomy while recognizing British suzerainty. For this performance, and with the approval of his executive council (for he was no longer a British subject), in 1882 Brand accepted appointment as GCMG.

The discovery of gold on the Witwatersrand in 1886 transformed the regional balance of economic power, underscoring the need for improved communications and closer fiscal relations between the various states. Being centrally placed, the OFS had a special interest here. Brand first achieved telegraphic links with the coastal colonies, then began to work for a customs union so as to gain a reasonable share of revenue on goods conveyed between the OFS and the outside world. Kruger's Transvaal insisted on independent access to world trade through Delagoa Bay; but groundwork which Brand prepared led to a customs convention with the Cape shortly after his death. Railway links were more problematic because the Cape and Natal competed for freight, Kruger insisting on a Delagoa Bay line against the wishes of transport riders in the OFS. Brand wanted lines from both the Cape and the Transvaal, or none at all. After his death the OFS government decided, with Transvaal assent, to admit the Cape line first.

Fearing the effects of Afrikaner nationalism on his bi-cultural European community, in 1881 Brand verbally attacked a branch of the Afrikaner Bond, a Cape political movement, for trying to establish itself in the OFS. He also discouraged efforts to promote an unlimited anti-imperial alliance with the Transvaal, while endorsing the right of the northern republic to maintain its independence unimpaired.

Brand died from a heart complaint on 14 July 1888. A friend of Britain and of the Transvaal, he had the understanding of a person of diverse roots—'thoroughly English', yet belonging to an exclusively Afrikaner family, and emotionally loyal to the Dutch Reformed church. G. D. Scholtz noted a symbolism linking Brand's father's launch of the newspaper *De Zuid Afrikaan* with the essentially South African outlook of his son—albeit one which took white lordship for granted, reflecting the perspective of the majority of the white population in his day.

T. R. H. DAVENPORT

Sources G. D. Scholtz, *President J. H. Brand* (1957) [Afrikaans] · M. C. E. van Schoor, 'Brand, Johannes Henricus', *DSAB* [guide to sources in Afrikaans] · T. B. Barlow, *President Brand and his times*

(1972) [incl. bibliography] · W. W. Collins, *Free Statia*, new edn (1965) · J. G. Fraser, *Episodes in my life* (1922) · C. F. Goodfellow, *Great Britain and South African confederation, 1870–1881* (1966) · J. J. Oberholster, *Die Anneksasie van Griekwaland-Wes* (Cape Town, 1946) · P. B. Sanders, *Moshoeshoe: chief of the Sotho* (1975) · D. M. Schreuder, *Gladstone and Kruger* (1969) · J. van der Poel, *Railway and customs policies in South Africa, 1885–1910* (1933) · *The Times* (17 July 1888) · *Friend of the Free State and Bloemfontein Gazette* (17 July 1888) · *Zuid-Afrikaan* (17 July 1888) · *Cape Argus* (16 July 1888)
Archives National Archives of South Africa, Bloemfontein, priv. coll. · priv. coll. | PRO, corresp. with Lord Carnarvon, PRO 30/6 · Netherlands, J. A. Loudon MSS
Likenesses C. W. H. Schroder, drawing, repro. in Collins, *Free Statia* · oils, National Museum of Cultural History, Pretoria, South Africa · photograph (in middle age), repro. in G. Lagden, *The Basutos* · photograph (in old age), repro. in Barlow, *President Brand* · statue, Bloemfontein, South Africa · wood-engraving, NPG; repro. in *ILN* (2 April 1881)

Brand, John (*d.* 1600), Church of Scotland minister, was a canon of the Augustinian abbey of Holyrood, Edinburgh, when he made his first recorded contact with the cause of religious reform. In 1560 he was sent by Archbishop John Hamilton of St Andrews to John Knox with a message which expressed sympathy for some aspects of religious reform, but urged restraint and the preservation of the existing church structure in the interests of social stability. This approach had no effect on Knox, and although it is not known how far Brand was himself directly involved in the negotiations, these contacts and the prevailing atmosphere in Edinburgh soon had the effect of causing him to join the reformed church as a minister. Having been examined by John Spottiswood, superintendent of Lothian, he was admitted as minister of the Canongate in 1564, in succession to John Craig. Subsequently he also became minister of Edinburgh Castle. On 5 January 1568 he was appointed chaplain of St Ninian beside Trinity College, Edinburgh. The extant kirk session records show that the parish of the Canongate was well administered from the time of Brand's admission.

Brand was one of the signatories of the letter sent from a meeting of ministers at St Andrews in September 1566 to Theodore Beza, with comments on the second Helvetic confession. At the assembly of June 1567 he was appointed to a commission to confer with crown nominees to consider ecclesiastical jurisdiction and authority as laid down by an act of that assembly. His strong support for the king's party during the troubles of 1571 led to his being banished from Edinburgh for a time. But after a bond had been drawn up on 2 July 1572 a truce was declared on the 31st; the exiles returned and several hundred hagbutters and pikemen marched up the Canongate, with Brand and John Durie, his colleague in Leith, at their head. As a result, within three weeks the queen's party had lost control of the town council to that of the king. The regent subsequently commanded that £58 be paid to Brand out of the thirds of benefices in consideration of his banishment. With his restoration complete, on 24 November he preached before the three estates when they met in the council house in Edinburgh to elect James Douglas, fourth earl of Morton, as regent.

Following the demotion of Ninian Hamilton, a pre-Reformation canon of St Giles who had been first exhorter and later minister of Duddingston, to the position of reader, Brand was given the oversight of that parish in 1574; he probably remained minister until the admission of Charles Lumsden in 1588. Thereafter he was frequently a member of deputations sent by the general assembly to the regent and privy council and later to the king. He was appointed to pronounce excommunication against Alexander Gordon, bishop of Galloway, and he was selected by several assemblies to enforce other decisions concerning the episcopate: in April 1577 he replaced John Spottiswood in summoning Patrick Adamson, archbishop of St Andrews; in July 1580 he warned Adam Bothwell, bishop of Orkney, to appear before the assembly; and in 1581 and 1582 he was one of the commissioners who met with the king to discuss the case of Robert Montgomerie, archbishop of Glasgow, whom James appointed but whom the kirk forbade to take office. Brand was one of the ministers who attended the earl of Morton before his execution on 2 June 1581. He preached at the opening of the general assembly of April 1582 in the absence of David Lindsay, the previous assembly's moderator. In 1583 he was one of the assessors to the moderator of the October assembly.

During the last decade of his life Brand was appointed the visitor of the churches in Tweeddale; later, with others, to the presbytery of Lothian; and finally within months before his death to the presbytery of Peebles. After the passing of the Black Acts of May 1584, he was among those summoned to subscribe them before the privy council in August. At first he demurred, but he finally signed them along with John Craig in December, an act which caused difficulties for several ministers who were still refusing to sign. Two years later, after these problems had been overcome, he was appointed to an assembly commission to deprive unsuitable ministers. He remained active within the general assemblies and his parish until his death in Edinburgh on 2 September 1600.

Brand was married twice. With his first wife, Elizabeth Johnston, he had a son, James, who on 27 June 1573 received a royal presentation to the chaplaincy of St Thomas-in-the-Canongate for seven years for his sustentation at school, and who had an illegitimate child with Beatrice Delarasche in 1588. With his second wife, Abigail Smith, he had two daughters and a son, John, who as a student at the University of Edinburgh was beheaded in 1615 for murdering William King, an illegitimate son of James King, advocate.   DUNCAN SHAW

Sources Fasti Scot., 1.17, 23 · C. H. Haws, Scottish parish clergy at the Reformation, 1540–1574, Scottish RS, new ser., 3 (1972), 36 · A. B. Calderwood, ed., The buik of the kirk of the Canangait, Scottish RS, old ser., 90 (1961) · D. Calderwood, The history of the Kirk of Scotland, ed. T. Thomson and D. Laing, 8 vols., Wodrow Society, 7 (1842–9), vol. 2, p. 396; vols. 3–4; vol. 5, p. 87 · T. Thomson, ed., Acts and proceedings of the general assemblies of the Kirk of Scotland, 3 pts, Bannatyne Club, 81 (1839–45)

Brand, John (1669–1738), Church of Scotland minister and author, was born in Canongate, Edinburgh, in August 1669, the son of John Brand, of Polish descent, baker in Canongate, and Janet Barclay of the Pearston family. He was educated at schools in Musselburgh and Canongate, but on his mother's death (c.1682, of bronchitis contracted at field preachings) and before his father's remarriage, he was 'kept at home to take care of the house' ('Memoirs', 4). However, he matriculated at Edinburgh at Candlemas (2 February) 1684, graduating on 9 July 1688. He then entered the divinity school and was licensed in May 1693.

Apart from summer jobs in Haddingtonshire, Galloway, and Ayrshire, Brand had travelled little when 'Duke William Hamilton and his religious Duchess' ('Memoirs', 2) heard him preach in Canongate Kirk and decided that he should be called to Bo'ness, Linlithgowshire, 'a place I was never in and for what I remember never heard of till called to preach there' (ibid., 22). On 3 January 1694 he was ordained and inducted to the parish where, in spite of a call to Elgin and the offer of the chair of Hebrew at Aberdeen, he remained for the rest of his life. Bo'ness was the second port in Scotland, with a population of over two thousand, a huge task for a young man of twenty-four, but Brand took it on with enthusiasm, and concerned himself with every aspect of life—social, economic, medical, criminal (he had strong but not wholly unsympathetic views on smuggling), and religious. His parishioners included Sir Robert Hamilton, the covenanting general, whose dying words he recorded.

As Brand was unmarried for his first years as a minister, the general assembly sent him through the country on visitations. In the winter of 1694–5 he was in Aberdeenshire and Moray (he met his future wife in Aberdeen), in the summer of 1699 he went to Dumfries and Galloway (returning by way of Greenock to preach on one of the Darien ships), and in April 1700 he went to Orkney and Shetland.

It is this journey, recounted in *A Brief Description of Orkney, Zetland, Pightland Firth and Caithness* (1701; republished in J. Pinkerton, *Voyages and Travels*, 1809, vol. 3, and then separately in 1883), by which Brand is remembered. It is dedicated to the duke of Hamilton who had asked him to publish it, 'and no doubt there was in me something of a fond inclination to appear an author' ('Memoirs', 98). The journey was extremely unpleasant, but, once in the islands, Brand recorded what he saw and heard in detail. His is a valuable record of life in the northern islands. He talks of 'personable and comely' people (*Brief Description*, 1809 edn, 741), of longevity, language, and agriculture, of fishing and sea fowl, of 'ancient monuments, strange accidents and some other things not only curious and delectable but also profitable to the judicious' (ibid., 754). Witches were still a scourge, though the brownies had been stamped out at the Reformation, and he recounts the capture of a mermaid, but these last things aside, his book remains of immense value as a picture of life in those islands at the turn of the eighteenth century. It was the first work to deal comprehensively with the northern islands, though it draws in some respects on James Wallace's *Description of Orkney* (1693), and it was not until the production of the Statistical Accounts of the 1790s that any further work of consequence on the islands appeared.

Having returned from his Orkney and Shetland journey, on 5 September 1700 Brand married Elizabeth Mitchell (d. 1729), daughter of the provost of Aberdeen, and from then on his life centred on his parish and his family of five sons and six daughters. He kept a diary from the time he went to Bo'ness, which, between 1727 and 1730, he wrote out in the form of memoirs for the benefit of his children, whom he adored. This remarkable account is an important record of the life of a minister in the immediate post-revolution period. Brand was involved peripherally with Darien, since so many of his parishioners went there, and in 1705 he visited the unfortunate crew of the *Worcester* in their death cell. In 1703 he published a broadsheet entitled *Plain Grounds of Presbyterian Government*, which was suppressed by the city council of Edinburgh, but otherwise he was only an informed if unoriginal commentator on the events of the day.

Brand died in Bo'ness in July 1738 and was succeeded as minister of Bo'ness by his son William. He was 'of full body' ('Memoirs', 38), and resembled the small sandy-haired and red-faced Alexander Shields, one of the Darien ministers, for whom he was occasionally mistaken.

PATRICK CADELL

Sources 'Memoirs of John Brand', NL Scot., MS 1668 · kirk session records of Bo'ness, NA Scot., CH2/540 · J. Brand, *A brief description of Orkney* (1701)
Archives NL Scot., memoirs

Brand, John [Fitzjohn] (1743–1808), Church of England clergyman and political writer, was born on 6 November 1743 in Norwich, the son of John Brand, a tanner, and his wife, Hannah. His sisters, Mary and Hannah *Brand, ran a well-regarded seminary for French education at Norwich. Hannah also became known as an actress, author, and defender of the rights of women. Brand is said to have spent several years travelling on the continent before university, during which time he pursued his interests in science and literature. The extent and itinerary of his travels as well as the details of how he supported himself are unknown, as the family was impoverished following the death of his father. Having matriculated in January 1762, he took a BA degree at Caius College, Cambridge, in 1766 and proceeded MA in 1772.

While at Cambridge, Brand gained a reputation as a skilled mathematician, graduating as fifth wrangler in his tripos. His poetic work *Conscience* (1772) was composed as an entry for Seaton's prize at Cambridge but was submitted too late for entry. Its subsequent publication gained him some attention and favourable reviews, but not enough encouragement to persist with this branch of literature. Despite only slender prospects of preferment he took holy orders and after a 'tedious apprenticeship' (Nichols, *Illustrations*, 6.531) as a curate took up the post of reader at St Peter Mancroft, Norwich, and was in 1775 presented to the vicarage of Wickham Skeith in Suffolk by

John Woodehouse. Here, while subsisting on a small living, he married his servant, a poor and unsophisticated woman (of whom further details are unknown), and together they had a large family. Having taken up the profession of letters in order to supplement his meagre income, Brand produced translations, reviews, and occasional pieces on the subject of 'political arithmetic' in the *British Critic* and other papers, which brought him to the favourable attention of some well-placed figures, including the lord chancellor, Alexander Wedderburn, Lord Loughborough, who secured for Brand the rectorship of St George, Southwark, London, in 1797. The value of this position was substantially increased by act of parliament in 1807, and Brand could, at last, look forward to the prospect of a secure and comfortable lifestyle for his final years.

Growing debate on the subject of the reform of the poor law was the occasion for his first sustained study and writing on economics. Poor rates roughly doubled in the third quarter of the eighteenth century, and this fact focused the attention of local office-holders and administrators and caused a number of schemes for revision or reform to be put forward, of which the best-known came from the lawyer and MP Thomas Gilbert. Gilbert proposed the incorporation of neighbouring groups of parishes in order to facilitate an efficient and cost-effective expansion of the workhouse system while at the same time reining in the expenses of outdoor relief. Brand's response, contained in his *Observations on some of the Probable Effects of Mr Gilbert's Bill* (1776), broadly supported Gilbert's proposals while making a number of careful predictions about the projected costs and advantages of the plan, as well as scrutinizing other works on the same subject. His own work was also based upon a careful scrutiny of data contained in the registers of local workhouses. Brand also called for improved provision for the education of the poor and discussed the probable moral influence of changes to the system of administering poor relief. He rejected the common complaint that the burden of taxes had risen alarmingly over the eighteenth century, arguing instead that although price inflation had produced this appearance, in fact taxes had remained constant at about the same level since 1713. This contention, based on a distinction between what he termed fiscal charge and fiscal burden—the higher fiscal charge being more than compensated for by a larger national product resulting in roughly the same fiscal burden—brought him into public dispute with the philosopher and calculator Richard Price, who had constantly warned of the deleterious consequences of a growing national debt. Brand's later *Alteration of the Constitution of the House of Commons and the Inequality of the Land Tax* (1793) was based on a substantial review of statistics and fiscal calculations, including those of Price.

The near famine conditions of the years 1799–1800 prompted Brand to respond to a burgeoning public discourse with *A determination of the average depression of the price of wheat in war below that of the preceding peace* (1800). This argued and attempted to demonstrate by statistical evidence that grain prices in fact tended to be lower under conditions of war than during peacetime. This improbable hypothesis was perhaps influenced by Brand's tory sympathies and a desire to counter the cause of the radical and whig anti-war movement, which had gained popular support for its argument that a return to peace would reduce the price of corn. His distinctive and original political views were further expounded in other pamphlets, notably his *Historical Essay on the Principles of Association in a State* (1796).

In consequence of some peculiarities of manners and speech picked up during a youthful sojourn in France, Brand was labelled with the teasing nickname Abbé Brand. A number of tales testified to his eccentricity. Once, following a literary dispute in which he felt his name had been besmirched, he challenged a nephew of Richard Price to an impromptu pugilistic contest. Sadly, Brand came off worst, retiring with a broken rib. It is not known when he married, but his obituaries recorded 'eight orphans wholly unprovided for' (*GM*). He died on 23 December 1808 in Lambeth, London. R. D. SHELDON

Sources DNB · Nichols, *Illustrations*, vol. 6 · J. Brand, *A defence of the pamphlet ascribed to John Reeves Esq.* (1796) · *GM*, 1st ser., 78 (1808), 1134 · Venn, *Alum. Cant.*
Likenesses line engraving, BM

John Brand (1744–1806), by unknown artist

Brand, John (1744–1806), antiquary and topographer, was born on 19 August 1744 at Washington in co. Durham, where his father, Alexander Brand, was the parish clerk. Little is known of his mother, Elizabeth Wheatley, who died shortly after he was born. When his father remarried Brand was sent to live in Gateshead with his maternal uncle and aunt, Anthony and Anne Wheatley, with whom he maintained close relations for the rest of his life. He was educated at Newcastle grammar school under the Revd Hugh Moises, a formidable pedagogue who was responsible for promoting a number of northern scholars. Here Brand developed a taste for classical learning which he kept up in the years after he left school. In 1758 he was bound apprentice to his uncle, a cordwainer, and he was admitted to the freedom of the company in 1768. His mentor, Hugh Moises, was instrumental in interesting other patrons in sending him to Oxford, where he matriculated at Lincoln College in 1768, holding a Lord Crewe scholarship, and graduated BA in 1775. By this point he had already been ordained some years: he served first the curacy of Bolam, Northumberland, before moving to the curacy of St Andrew's, Newcastle, in June 1773, and on 6 October 1774 he was presented by Matthew Ridley to the perpetual curacy of Cramlington, about 8 miles from Newcastle, a living which he retained until his death. In 1778 Brand was appointed under-usher to the grammar school where he had formerly been a pupil and he became usher in 1781. By 1784 he had moved to London: the duke of Northumberland, an early and supportive patron, presented him to the rectory of the united parishes of St Mary-at-Hill, Lovat Lane, and St Mary Hubbard, and in 1786 he appointed Brand as one of his domestic chaplains. Brand also acted in the capacity of secretary and librarian to the duke. In 1778 he had been elected to the Society of Antiquaries and the move to London coincided with his election as resident secretary to the society, with a salary of 20 guineas per annum, to which office he was annually re-elected until his death in 1806.

Brand's initial publications were of poetry, the first being a *Collection of Poetical Essays* in 1765, followed by *On Illicit Love* in 1775. These poetical effusions were followed by the antiquarian works for which he is better known today. His first major publication, *Observations on Popular Antiquities* (1777), was essentially an expansion and revision of *Antiquitates vulgares* by another Newcastle antiquary of the early eighteenth century, Henry Bourne. Bourne's work had become expensively scarce and Brand's *Popular Antiquities* found a ready market and sold rapidly, appealing to the eighteenth-century interest in customs and manners and the nostalgia of an urbanizing age for the rural customs of the past. Brand carried on collecting materials for a revised edition of *Popular Antiquities* for the rest of his life and he acquired a large amount of additional information from the statistical enquiries in Scotland instigated by Sir John Sinclair. A second edition was planned in 1795, but Brand was apparently overwhelmed by the task of arranging systematically so much material and he did not live to complete the project. Instead the collections were purchased after his death by a bookseller for £600 and were incorporated into a new edition by Sir Henry Ellis, published in 1813. Charles Knight & Co. published a new edition of *Popular Antiquities* with additional materials and a fresh index in 1841, and in 1870 William Carew Hazlitt published another version, condensing and reorganizing the material, which—having been gathered over the course of many years—was chaotic and often contradictory. Brand has been criticized for his lack of system, the confusion of his notes, and his reliance on often inaccurate secondhand authorities. Nevertheless, the volume gathered huge quantities of miscellaneous material, providing a starting point for other, more rigorous, enquiries, and made a significant contribution to the emerging discipline of folklore studies.

Brand's publisher for *Popular Antiquities* had been the Newcastle bookseller Thomas Saint, and it appears to have been Saint who first suggested to Brand that he should undertake a revision of Bourne's other work, *The History of Newcastle*. Saint had considerable input into the volume: it was at his insistence that it was dedicated to the mayor and common council of Newcastle and it was his suggestion that Brand should compile what was essentially volume two, on the trade and political economy of the town, to broaden the appeal to the non-specialist reader. Saint fell ill before the history was completed and he died on 31 July 1788. Publication was therefore relinquished to the London publishers Messrs White and Davis. The history, published by subscription in two volumes in 1789, with engravings by James Fittler, which alone cost £500, had a print run of 1000, unusually large for a work of its kind, and the whole impression was sold off at a low price. At the time the reputation of the volume was said to have been damaged by this glut in the market. The history was, moreover, widely criticized as being dull, too detailed and parochial—it certainly lacked the vivacity and anecdotal detail to be found in Bourne. The history was deeply conservative and supportive of the corporation at a time when the town's oligarchy was being subjected to persistent attack. However, today it is highly valued for the wealth of erudition and research that it contains. The lack of an index was also much deplored, but this problem was mitigated by William Dodd's compilation of an index for the Society of Antiquaries of Newcastle upon Tyne in 1881.

After 1789, Brand published no other works, although he did contribute several papers to *Archaeologia*. He continued to collect materials and left copious amounts of manuscript collections relating to both the history of Newcastle and popular antiquities. By the time of his death he had amassed an extensive and valuable library of books and manuscripts, particularly strong in early printed works of English literature, many of which he annotated and embellished with pen and ink sketches of the authors. The auction of his library in 1807 lasted over thirty-seven days, and the sale of the 8611 articles raised over £17,000. Brand died suddenly on 11 September 1806, in his own home—the rectory at St Mary-at-Hill—at his breakfast table, from an apoplectic fit. He was buried on 24 September in the chancel of St Mary-at-Hill. He never married and left his entire estate to his aunt Anne Wheatley of Hanover Square, Newcastle. Mrs Wheatley had continued to manage Brand's affairs in Newcastle during his

absences and in return Brand had always been affectionately considerate for her welfare.

Brand's lack of system in compiling his material was apparently mirrored in his career as secretary to the Society of Antiquaries. After his death the society's accounts were found to be in complete disorder, muddled with his own private papers. Members grumbled that he did not answer letters, and his duties to the duke, often demanding his presence at Alnwick, conflicted with the requirements of the society. He made little lasting impact on the affairs of the society beyond compiling a return for the select committee for public records on the historical manuscripts in the society's possession in March 1800. Although his obituary claimed that he filled his parochial duties with regularity and punctuality, he was twice prosecuted for non-residence as he lived in accommodation provided by the Society of Antiquaries in Somerset House for a number of years, while letting out his parsonage at St Mary-at-Hill. Contemporaries reported that he was generous with his time and knowledge and enjoyed the company of his close friends, although he was 'somewhat repulsive to strangers' (*GM*, 881). R. H. SWEET

Sources newspaper cutting (origin not specified), Northumbd RO, Newcastle upon Tyne, ZAN MI7/198 · *GM*, 1st ser., 76 (1806), 881 · R. Welford, *Men of mark 'twixt Tyne and Tweed*, 3 vols. (1895) · Nichols, *Lit. anecdotes*, 9.651–3 · J. Evans, *A history of the Society of Antiquaries* (1956) · *Letters of John Brand to Mr Ralph Beilby* (1825) · *Analytical Review*, 5 (1789) · *DNB* · IGI

Archives BL, list of mayors and sheriffs of Newcastle, Egerton MS 2425 · Bodl. Oxf., papers incl. interleaved copy of *Observations on popular antiquities* · Gateshead Local Studies Library, materials collected by him · Northumbd RO, Newcastle upon Tyne, corresp., memorandum book, and prayers · S. Antiquaries, Lond., materials collected by Brand and diary, M5448A · S. Antiquaries, Lond., diary, historical collections and papers, MSS 220, 317, 448, 752 · U. Newcastle, Robinson L., memoir | BL, corresp. with R. S. Vidal and others, Add. MS 41313

Likenesses T. Coram, etching, NPG · line drawing, repro. in Welford, *Men of mark* · miniature, watercolour, Laing Art Gallery, Newcastle upon Tyne [*see illus.*] · self-portrait, sketch, Northumbd RO, Newcastle upon Tyne · silhouette, line engraving, NPG; repro. in J. Brand, *The history and antiquities of the town and county of Newcastle upon Tyne*, 2 vols. (1789), frontispiece

Wealth at death estate originally valued at under £800, excl. sale of library for £17,000: Welford, *Men of mark*

Brand, Sir (Christopher Joseph) Quintin (1893–1968), air force officer, was born in Beaconsfield, near Kimberley in South Africa, on 25 May 1893, the son of Edward Christopher Joseph Brand, an inspector in the Johannesburg criminal investigation department. Educated at the Marist Brothers' College, Johannesburg, he served with the South African defence force in South-West Africa in 1914–15. After developing an interest in powered flight he transferred to the Royal Flying Corps (RFC) in England, serving on the western front and, in the later stages of the First World War, in home defence.

During a night-time German raid on Chatham on 3–4 September 1917, Flossie Brand and two other officers of 44 squadron led by Captain Gilbert Ware Murlis Green were granted permission to take off in single-seater Sopwith

Camel fighters. These had previously been allowed to fly only during daytime, with night flying restricted to the slower and more trusted machines with two or more crew. Although the three officers failed to intercept any enemy planes, they patrolled the Thames estuary in the dark for some forty minutes, demonstrating that there was no great risk in flying the 'unstable' fighters at night. Edward Bailey Ashmore described their sortie as 'perhaps the most important event in the history of air defence' (Cole and Cheeseman, 302).

In the last German air raid of the First World War, on 19–20 May 1918, Brand, who was commanding 112 squadron, was credited with bringing down near Faversham one of three Gotha bombers dispatched by British fighter pilots on that occasion. According to observers he 'narrowly escaped being burned himself, when the flaming machine shot past him to its doom in the sea' (Hammerton). For this he was awarded the DSO in addition to his other decorations, MC (1917) and DFC (1918).

After the First World War, Brand, a flight lieutenant in the newly formed RAF, took part in the last of three historic flights during 1919 and 1920 undertaken in Vickers Vimy bombers, following John William Alcock's and Arthur Whitten Brown's transatlantic flight, and the flight of Ross Macpherson Smith and Keith Smith from England to Australia. In December 1919 the Air Ministry announced that the air route from Cairo to Cape Town was established, after landing sites along the way had been surveyed and prepared. On 4 February 1920 Brand and Pierrie (later Pierre) van Ryneveld (1891–1972), a South African who had also served in the RFC during the war, started out from England (taking off from Brooklands) in their Vimy, named *Silver Queen*, reaching Cairo on 9 February. On the next stage of their journey, to Khartoum, they crashed near Wadi Halfa on 11 February, only the engines proving salvageable. These were fitted to a new airframe, renamed *Silver Queen II*, and their flight was resumed from Cairo on 22 February, reaching Bulawayo on 5 March. A further accident, when taking off for Pretoria, grounded them, but a DH9 (Voortrekker) supplied by the South African government enabled them to complete their flight; they arrived in Cape Town on 20 March 1920, to be greeted by a telegram from George V. Their journey of some 6200 miles had taken just over 109 flying hours. On their return to England they were honoured with a banquet attended by Winston Churchill, secretary of state for air, and both aviators were knighted (KBE). Their pioneering African flight was re-enacted in 1999.

On 9 June 1920, at St Peter and St Paul's Roman Catholic Church, Ilford, Brand married Marie Winifred Charlotte (d. 1941), the daughter of Patrick William Vaughan, a customs and excise officer. They had two sons and a daughter. In 1929, promoted wing commander, he was posted to Egypt as second in command at the Abu Qir aircraft depot, then from 1932 to 1936 served as director-general of aviation in Egypt, with the rank of group captain from 1935. After returning to Britain he was deputy director (1936)

and director (1937–9) of maintenance at the Air Ministry, with the rank of air commodore (1938).

Promoted air vice-marshal, Brand was one of the four group commanders under Hugh Dowding (the others being Keith Park, Trafford Leigh-Mallory, and Richard Saul) in charge of the air defence of Britain during the battle of Britain. He was placed in command of 10 group, which became operational in July 1940 with ten squadrons responsible for the defence of south Wales and southern England west of Portsmouth. He got on well with Park, whose command covered south-east England, and co-operated in providing him with reinforcements at crucial times, an indication of his support for the strategy and tactics of Park and Dowding in confronting raids by the Luftwaffe. His rapid deployment of squadrons in support of Park when there were threats to aircraft factories or aerodromes to the west and south-west of London stemmed from his agreement with Park that it was 'more essential to get a small number of squadrons quickly to the point requested than to delay whilst his squadrons are forming up into wings' (Orange, 124). The latter tactic, known as the big-wing, advocated by Leigh-Mallory and his pilot Douglas Bader, and the subject of much controversy, achieved a larger number of enemy hits, but often too late to prevent the enemy bombers reaching their targets; by the time a wing was formed, the damage had been done and the enemy was in retreat. Brand was present at the crucial meetings to discuss the future employment of Fighter Command held in September and October 1940 which led to the removal of Dowding and Park. Brand was transferred to command 20 training group in 1941 and retired from the RAF in November 1943.

On 18 October 1943, following the death of his first wife, Brand married her younger sister, Mary Mildred Vaughan, with whom he had a daughter. They lived in Surrey until 1952, when they moved to Rhodesia. Brand died at Umtali on 7 March 1968.   C. J. B. Joseph

Sources *The Times* (9 March 1968) · *WWW* · Kelly, *Handbk* (1948) · Burke, *Peerage* (1967) · m. cert. · J. A. Hammerton, ed., *War in the air* (1935) · C. Cole and E. F. Cheeseman, *The air defence of Great Britain, 1914–1918* (1984) · V. Orange, *Park: the biography of Air Chief Marshal Sir Keith Park* (2001) · R. Higham, *Britain's imperial air routes, 1918 to 1939: the story of Britain's overseas airlines* (1968) · S. Bungay, *The most dangerous enemy: a history of the battle of Britain* (2000) · J. P. Ray, *The Battle of Britain: new perspectives* (1994)

Brand, Robert Henry, Baron Brand (1878–1963), merchant banker and public servant, was born on 30 October 1878 in Kensington, London, the seventh child and fourth son of Henry Robert *Brand, second Viscount Hampden of Glynde (1841–1906), soldier, Liberal MP, and colonial governor, and his second wife, Susan Henrietta (d. 1909), younger daughter of Lord George Henry Cavendish. He had five brothers, one of whom died in childhood, and three sisters. He was educated at Marlborough School (c.1889–1898) and at New College, Oxford, from 1898, where he took a first in modern history in 1901; he was thereupon elected a fellow of All Souls, and he remained a fellow (with intervals) until his death.

Robert Henry Brand, Baron Brand (1878–1963), by Elliott & Fry

Brand's background and family traditions drew him towards service in the empire: his father had been governor of New South Wales and was an influential Liberal Imperialist and friend of Viscount Milner, governor of the Cape Colony and high commissioner for South Africa. Brand's university days had been overshadowed by the Second South African War; and with the end of that war in 1902 it was clear that there was exciting work to be done in South Africa. Through his father's influence he joined Milner's staff in Johannesburg in December 1902 and became thereby a member of 'Milner's kindergarten', a group of Oxford-educated young men devoted to the ideal of the empire.

Brand was never a man of action; his weak heart would have precluded this in any case, but his inclinations and his talents drew him towards administration. Milner recognized this talent and Brand successively became assistant secretary, acting secretary, and, in March 1904, permanent secretary to the inter-colonial council of the Transvaal and the Orange River Colony. The council was responsible for the administration of the reconstruction loan intended to finance the rebuilding and development of the region. Much of Brand's own work centred on the activities and development of the newly merged central South African Railway system, dealing with arguments over tariffs and freight rates among the four colonies. This was a frustrating exercise which helped to convince him that political unification was the only practical solution.

Brand's primary claim to importance in South African

history was the work he did in 1908–9 as secretary of the Transvaal delegates at the South African National Convention. He had gained the trust of the Transvaal leaders and, most importantly, of J. C. Smuts, to whom he acted as personal assistant. Together they prepared a draft constitution for the new union, and Brand 'was able to underpin Smut's vision and tactical skill with a firm basis of theoretical rigour and practical foresight' (DNB). Brand's period in South Africa strengthened his faith in the British empire as a force for peace and prosperity in the world. He retained an interest in South African affairs, acting as South Africa's financial representative at the Genoa conference in 1922.

Brand returned to London in 1909 to help with the passage of the South Africa Act through parliament, but he intended to return to South Africa to settle. However, he fell ill with influenza and missed his boat, and while awaiting the next an opportunity presented itself which changed the course of his life. R. M. Kindersley proposed that he join the merchant bank Lazard Brothers. Lazards was then emerging as one of London's most prestigious accepting and issuing houses, in the 1920s issuing the sterling bonds of governments, regional states, and municipalities, especially in Europe, and winning market share from more established houses by aggressive marketing and negotiation. From 1919 the business interests of W. D. Pearson, later first Viscount Cowdray, included a large shareholding in Lazards.

After some negotiation Brand agreed to join Lazards; he received an initial salary of £2000 plus 5 per cent of the firm's annual profits. Soon after he became a managing director, a position he held until 1944; he remained a director of Lazards until he retired in 1960. Brand developed a strong belief in international finance as an instrument for international co-operation and peace, and he used the skills acquired in and the financial security provided by merchant banking, in carrying out a number of political responsibilities.

Brand's heart condition kept him out of the fighting in 1914, but with Lloyd George's advent as minister of munitions in 1915 Brand was swept into government service. The stimulus for Lloyd George's new position was an armaments crisis; attempts to increase the supply of shells had included purchasing them abroad, but the result was chaotic, and Brand was sent to Canada to sort out procedures. With the establishment of the imperial munitions board in Ottawa, Brand acted as its liaison officer in London with the Ministry of Munitions until the end of the war. The crux involved the financing of Canadian munitions and, as British spending power declined, London looked to Washington. As a financier responsible for munitions, Brand was the ideal person to send to Washington, where he acted as deputy chairman of the British war mission in 1917–18. He then went to Paris, to act as financial adviser to Lord Robert Cecil, chairman of the supreme economic council, during the peace conference.

At this point both Brand and Lazards decided that he should concentrate on banking, and he turned down further requests from the British government. Nevertheless, he acted as adviser or delegate to various European financial conferences during the inter-war years. He had long been interested in Germany and indeed had written in 1915 an approving report on the German banking system, and it was therefore appropriate that he was appointed a member both of the expert committee which advised the German government on the stabilization of the Deutschmark in 1922 and of the 'standstill' committee appointed in July 1931 to advise on the short-term credits caught in the German banking crisis. Brand's approval of Germany did not extend to Hitler: by 1933 he thought the Nazi regime a threat to the international order.

Brand served as a member of the Macmillan committee on finance and industry from 1929 to 1931. He argued for cheap money and against wholesale protection, and was generally in sympathy with the liberal ideals of fellow member J. M. Keynes, with whom he had happily worked both at Versailles and on the expert committee on the German Deutschmark. Drawing on his knowledge of German banking he proposed a closer integration of finance and industry, arguing the need for new first-class institutions set up specifically to issue industrial securities, which, unlike most City establishments, would maintain a close and continuing relationship with their client companies.

Brand spent the years 1941–6 primarily in Washington, serving as head of the British food mission in 1941–4, chairman of the British supply council in North America in 1942 (when he had to rescue it from the strains of departmental and personal jealousies) and again in 1945–6, and British Treasury representative in 1944–6. As Treasury representative he joined Keynes in the acrimonious and difficult negotiations for the ending of 'lend-lease' and for the US and Canadian loans to Britain, and as a UK delegate at the Bretton Woods and Savannah conferences in 1946, which established the International Monetary Fund and the International Bank for Reconstruction and Development.

During Brand's earlier sojourn in America he had married (in 1917) Phyllis Langhorne, daughter of a Virginia landowner and auctioneer, Charles Dabney Langhorne, and sister of Nancy Astor (he was a close friend of the Cliveden circle). They had two daughters and a son who was killed in action in 1945. Brand was devastated by his wife's death in 1937; a very practical effect of his marriage to a prominent American, however, was to provide social and personal contacts which he could use, in conjunction with his own long experience of North America, in navigating the rocks and whirlpools of wartime Washington.

After the war Brand remained essentially a banker, but his wide interests ensured a sheaf of extra-curricular duties. He was a director of the Times Publishing Company Ltd from 1925 to 1959, a member of the General Advisory Council of the BBC from 1951 to 1956, president of the Royal Economic Society from 1952 to 1953, and a director of Lloyds Bank Ltd. He had been appointed CMG in 1910 and honorary DCL at Oxford in 1937, but only after the death of his son would he accept a peerage, in 1946 becoming Baron Brand of Eydon.

Lord Brand was one of those quietly powerful men— one of 'the great and the good'—who, while not holding elected public office, are repeatedly called upon by policy makers, domestic and foreign. He was a strong proponent of Anglo-American co-operation, especially in the economic sphere. It did him no harm that his writings, which included *The Union of South Africa* (1909), *War and National Finance* (1921), *Why I am not a Socialist* (1923), and numerous articles, especially in the journal *The Round Table*, though lucid, tended to be dull. He possessed intelligence, practical common sense, and the authority derived from his own success: he was undeniably sound, and in later years a man of the utmost *gravitas*. He was also 'a man of the utmost charm, with a soft voice and a mild, short-sighted appearance' (*DNB*).

Lord Brand died at the Old Vicarage, Firle, near Lewes, Sussex, on 23 August 1963. KATHLEEN BURK

Sources Bodl. Oxf., MSS Brand · *WWW* · Burke, *Peerage* · *The collected writings of John Maynard Keynes*, ed. D. Moggridge and E. Johnson, 23–4 (1979); 26 (1980) · J. E. Kendle, *The Round Table movement and imperial union* (1975) · K. Burk, *Britain, America and the sinews of war, 1914–1918* (1984) · *DNB* · *The Times* (24 Aug 1963) · *Minutes of evidence taken before the committee on finance and industry*, ed. H. P. Macmillan, 2 vols. (1931) · d. cert. · HLRO, Lloyd George papers
Archives Bodl. Oxf., corresp. and papers; round table corresp. | BLPES, letters to Edwin Cannon · BLPES, corresp. with the editors of the *Economic Journal* · Bodl. Oxf., corresp. with Lionel Curtis · Bodl. Oxf., corresp. with Lord Monckton · Bodl. Oxf., letters to countess of Selborne · CAC Cam., corresp. with Sir Ralph Hawtrey · King's AC Cam., corresp. with John Maynard Keynes · NA Scot., corresp. with Philip Kerr · NA Scot., letters to Lord Ralph Kerr and Lady Ann Kerr
Likenesses J. de Glehn, pencil and chalk drawing, 1935, Eydon Hall · A. Mason, pencil drawing, 1956, Eydon Hall · G. Bruce, oils, 1963, priv. coll. · Elliott & Fry, photograph, NPG [*see illus.*] · photographs, priv. coll.
Wealth at death £79,158 4s. 3d.: probate, 15 Oct 1963, *CGPLA Eng. & Wales*

Brand, Thomas (*bap.* 1635, *d.* 1691), nonconformist minister, was baptized on 8 May 1635 at Leaden Roding, Essex, the son of Thomas Brand (*c.*1597–1654), Church of England clergyman, of Great Hormead, Hertfordshire, who was archdeacon of Cardigan from July 1629 and rector of Leaden Roding from 1627 until his death in 1654. The young Thomas was educated at school in Bishop's Stortford, Hertfordshire, and at Merton College, Oxford, where he matriculated on 24 June 1653. On 15 May 1656 he was admitted as a student to the Middle Temple and on 26 June 1657 he was allocated to the chamber of George Baker of the utter bar, in Inner Temple Lane. He graduated BA from Oxford in 1660. In the interim, through the influence of Dr Samuel Annesley, he was persuaded to join the ministry.

About 1659 Brand became chaplain in the family of Dame Bridget Roberts, widow of Sir Howland Roberts, at her house at Glassenbury, in Cranbrook, Kent, a place later described as 'the sanctuary for divine worship, for the spreading of religion through the country' (Annesley, foreword). In this pious household, 'Reading the scripture, or catechising or singing of psalms, accompanied family Prayer twice every day'. The chaplain acted also as tutor to Lady Roberts's four young children. He:

> constantly rose, if in health, at five o'clock, and continued in his study till family prayer, and then to his study again, till a little before noon; and after dinner when he had walked, or discoursed a little, he returned to his study, saying 'I must to my business' … After supper he came down with great cheerfulness. (Annesley, 14–15)

Brand preached at Glassenbury twice every Sunday, and often preached locally. Indeed his efforts to found religious exercises took him beyond the borders of the county, for 'God sent him to a borough in Sussex' where he set up a meeting and persuaded other ministers to take turns in preaching there (ibid., 18). On 20 April 1672 he was licensed to preach at the chapel adjoining the Robertses' house. In 1674, following the death of Daniel Poyntel of nearby Staplehurst, Brand was invited to take charge of the congregation there. Having first made it his business to find for Lady Roberts 'a worthy successor, whose great piety and ministerial abilities were beyond the vulgar' (ibid.), Brand moved to Staplehurst. There he was ordained minister. Soon he was 'near marrying a young gentlewoman, but before the time appointed for the marriage, Christ took her to himself' (ibid., 24). About two years later he married a widow, whose name is unknown; all their several children appear to have died young.

It is unclear quite how long Brand remained in his ministry or why he left it. Annesley recorded obscurely that, 'After some years in Staplehurst he was morally forced to another situation. The arguments for his remove took hold of his conscience'. Perhaps about the time of the arrival of Samuel French as minister of Staplehurst in the winter of 1684–5 Brand moved from Kent and settled at Bishop's Hall, once the residence of Bishop Bonner, near Bethnal Green. There he founded an academy, in which he was assisted from about 1689 by John Ker MD, who had taught dissenters in Dublin. According to Samuel Palmer, who attended before 1698, the syllabus included logic, metaphysics, and natural philosophy and appears to have been extremely rigorous. In 1690 there were nine students, financed by scholarships of the Presbyterian Fund. Brand 'had a singular dexterity at insinuating himself into the affections of young people, and overcoming their unwillingness to be instructed' (Annesley, 40). It was probably also while at Bethnal Green that he 'hired a writing master, to come into some families in order to teach some servants who had no time to go to school, to learn to write and cast accounts' (ibid., 53).

There is much testimony as to Brand's generosity, made possible by the estate inherited from his father, which he averred that 'he would squeeze … as long as he lived' (Gordon, 221). His charitable expenditure was estimated at £300 per year. He is reported to have underwritten much of the cost of reprinting 20,000 copies of Joseph Alleine's *Treatise on Conversion*, altering the title to a *Guide to Heaven*

and arranging its free distribution. He and his friends also sold bibles below cost price to all who would promise not to resell them, and Brand maintained children of poor parents, setting them to trades. Dr Earle, many years a distinguished minister of the presbyterian congregation in Hanover Street, London, was one of his protégés. Brand died at Stepney on 1 December 1691, and was buried in Bunhill Fields.   STEPHEN WRIGHT

Sources S. Annesley, *Memoirs of the Rev. Thomas Brand (with a sermon preached on the occasion of his death), by the Rev. Samuel Annesley, LL.D.* (1692) • A. Gordon, ed., *Freedom after ejection: a review (1690–1692) of presbyterian and congregational nonconformity in England and Wales* (1917) • J. T. Cliffe, *The puritan gentry besieged, 1650–1700* (1993) • H. McLachlan, *English education under the Test Acts: being the history of the nonconformist academies, 1662–1820* (1931) • H. A. C. Sturgess, ed., *Register of admissions to the Honourable Society of the Middle Temple, from the fifteenth century to the year 1944*, 3 vols. (1949) • Foster, *Alum. Oxon.* • E. H. Brine, *Congregationalism at Staplehurst* (1947) • E. Bailey, *Struggles for conscience, or, The religious annals of Staplehurst* (1862) • W. Tarbuck, ed., 'Briefs in the parish of Cranbrook', *Archaeologia Cantiana*, 14 (1882), 206–22 • 'Early nonconformist academies', *Transactions of the Congregational Historical Society*, 6 (1913–15), 20–24 • C. T. Martin, ed., *Minutes of parliament of the Middle Temple*, 4 vols. (1904–5), vol. 3 • *Calamy rev.* • *IGI* • *Old Westminsters*

Brandard family (*per. c.*1825–1898), printmakers, came to prominence with **Robert Brandard** (1805–1862), printmaker and painter, who was born at Birmingham, and baptized on 31 January 1805 at St Philip's, Birmingham, the eldest son of Thomas Brandard (*d.* 1830), engraver and copperplate printer, of Barford Street, Deretend, Birmingham, and his wife, Ann. A member of the Birmingham school of engravers, Robert Brandard learned the rudiments of his profession from his father, and probably studied also at J. V. Barber's Great Charles Street Academy and under the engraver William Radclyffe. In 1824 he became a pupil in London of the landscape engraver Edward Goodall, and about a year later set up professionally in Islington. He joined the Artists' Annuity Fund in 1827 and signed the 1837 petition to the king on the admission of engravers to the Royal Academy. Robert is primarily known for his landscape and topographical prints after works by contemporary painters such as Clarkson Stanfield, Augustus Callcott, J. F. Herring, Richard Westall, and most notably J. M. W. Turner, whom he met through Goodall. Many of his metal-engraved prints after Turner's paintings were produced under the supervision of the artist, who considered Robert to be one of the six best contemporary engravers (Rawlinson, lxvi). One of his earliest engravings to attract attention was *Sans souci* after Thomas Stothard, which appeared in the first volume of William Pickering's *The Bijou* (1828). Other journals to which he contributed include the *Literary Souvenir*, *Friendship's Offering*, *The Keepsake*, the *Landscape Annual*, and *Heath's Picturesque Annual*. His first important book illustration commission was for eight plates after William Brockedon for his *Illustrations of the Passes of the Alps* (1828–9). Many others followed, among them twenty-one plates after William Henry Bartlett for N. P. Willis's *American Scenery* (1840) and *Canadian Scenery* (1842), seven after Stanfield and William Collins for Walter Scott's Waverley novels, and three vignettes after George Cattermole and others for Baroness Calabrella's *Evenings at Haddon Hall* (1846). Five engravings of pictures in the Royal Collection were included in S. C. Hall's *The Royal Gallery* (c.1855). Among his wood-engraved work are illustrations to Charles Knight's *London* (1841–2). Of his various steel- or copper-engraved reproductions of Turner's work, those for *Picturesque Views in England and Wales* (1838), *Rivers of France* (1837), *The Poetical Work of Sir Walter Scott* (1834), and *The Poetical Works of John Milton* (1835) are among the most successful, the Scott plates earning him 60 guineas each. Between 1851 and 1866 fifteen of his plates appeared in the *Art Journal*, of which the eight after Turner were subsequently published in *The Turner Gallery* (c.1878), most notably *Rain, Steam and Speed* (1860), *The Snowstorm* (1861), and *Whalers—the 'Erebus'* (1861). The latter, one of Robert's last engravings, was considered by a contemporary to be 'a gem on which his reputation may well rest', while others regarded his large plate of *Crossing the Brook* (1842), exhibited with *The Snowstorm* at the International Exhibition of 1862, as his finest (Hunnisett, 24). From his home address in Eynsford, Kent, he jointly published with J. Hogarth *Scraps of Nature*, two volumes of etchings made between 1842 and 1851 of the coast and Weald of Kent, examples of which were included in the *Art Journal* (1875). According to one obituary 'quiet, unobtrusive, and gentlemanly in manner' (*Art Journal*), Robert was esteemed by everyone who knew him. His pupils included his brother-in-law, Mr (possibly William) Floyd, and James Clayton Bentley. He died at his home, 2 Campden Hill Villas, Kensington, London, on 7 January 1862, survived by his wife, Elizabeth. Between 1831 and 1858 he exhibited frequently at the British Institution, Royal Academy, Society (later Royal Society) of British Artists, and New Watercolour Society. Examples of his work are held at the Victoria and Albert Museum and British Museum, London; the Fitzwilliam Museum, Cambridge; Leicester City Museums; and Blackburn Museum Art Collection.

Robert's brother **John Brandard** (1812–1863), lithographer, was born at Birmingham, and baptized on 13 March 1812 at St Martin's, Birmingham. He began his career as an engraver, mainly of commercial designs. He married on 17 January 1833 Maria Chater at Edgbaston, Birmingham. Their five children were all baptized at St Pancras Old Church, London, between 1835 and 1845. One of the earliest and most skilful English lithographic artists, he became well known in the 1840s for his music-cover illustrations, his reputation enhanced by his close association with the eminent London lithographic printers M. and N. Hanhart, with whom he was exclusively employed for many years. His chromolithographs are characterized by delicate colouring, and smooth, even tone achieved by the use of high-quality paper and a close attention to detail in the preparation of lithographic stones. For this and other tasks John constantly employed two assistants, thus greatly increasing his output. Stage subjects were his speciality, ballet and opera in particular. His prints of dancers, many sketched from life, were admired by Degas, their oval faces and mouths, and

pointed hands and feet characteristic of John's figure style. Celebrities depicted include Carlotta Grisi as La Péri in *Giselle* (1844), and Lucille Grahn in *Catarina* (1846). Idealized images of Queen Victoria, Prince Albert, and other members of the royal family feature regularly on music covers, notably for titles published by Jullien & Co., such as *The Court Ball March*. Military and comic scenes recur on song and music sheets, as do portraits of women, later issued as single prints. Many of his colour lithographs appeared also in black and white. Lithographic landscapes include views of Hastings and illustrations to *Kenilworth and its Castle Illustrated* (c.1865) to which Robert also contributed. John also designed fancy title-pages and ornamental borders for various musical albums, books of beauty, and pocket books. A direct reference to the illustrator is included in one of the verses to *The Polka-Mania*: 'And graphic Brandard takes the whim—But let his pencil speak for him'. The initials J. B. appear on some of the early titles, but more often his work was signed J. Brandard. He made—and spent—money freely, often charging as much as 20 guineas for a print. (The average price for a cover was 3*s*. to 4*s*.) An imposing, dandified figure, he liked to be seen arriving at Drury Lane or Covent Garden in his own coach. He died at his home, 8 Southampton Place, Chalk Farm, London, on 15 December 1863. Extensive collections of his work are held at Reading University; at the Theatre Museum, Covent Garden, Victoria and Albert Museum, and British Museum, London; and at the Bodleian Library, Oxford. His son Walter Brandard (*bap.* 1842) also drew some music titles.

Another brother, **Edward Paxman Brandard** (1819–1898), printmaker and painter, was born probably at Birmingham. He was baptized on 19 September 1820 at St Martin's, Birmingham. On his father's death in 1830 he was apprenticed to Robert, whose studio Turner frequently visited. Edward was said to be the last to work under the personal superintendence of Turner as well as the last of the steel engravers (Hunnisett, 18). Of his prints after Turner, *Apollo and Daphne in the Vale of Tempe* and *The Bridge of Sighs* were published in *The Turner Gallery*. Etchings include *The Hay Wain* and *Salisbury Cathedral* after Constable, and his own *Meadows at Marlow in the Thames* for *The Portfolio*, 14 (1883). Edward frequently contributed to books on topography, history, art, and architecture: engravings after T. Allom for G. N. Wright's *China* (1843) were followed by a succession of plates and vignettes, many after W. H. Bartlett, for books such as W. Beattie's *The Danube* (1844), Conybeare and Howson's *Life and Epistles of St Paul* (1854), and B. Woodward's *General History of Hampshire* (1863). Some of his prints of the 1860s and 1870s, such as *Laufenburg* for *Picturesque Europe* (1876–9), were engraved after Miles Birket Foster. Edward contributed numerous plates to the Art Union of London. Between 1853 and 1887 thirteen appeared in the *Art Journal*. He exhibited at a number of London galleries from 1849 to 1885, including the British Institution (where his prices ranged from 4 guineas to 25 guineas), Royal Academy, New Watercolour

Society, and Society of Painter-Etchers. He died on 3 February 1898 at Aysgarth, Kingston Road, New Malden, Surrey, leaving a widow, Susannah. He was then living at 1 Albion Grove, Thornhill Road, Barnsbury, London. Examples of his work are held at the Victoria and Albert Museum and British Museum, London. A sister, Annie Caroline Brandard, a landscape painter, exhibited at the Royal Academy (1838, 1883, and 1884).   JOANNA SELBORNE

Sources DNB · B. Hunnisett, *An illustrated dictionary of British steel engravers*, new edn (1989) · R. K. Engen, *Dictionary of Victorian engravers, print publishers and their works* (1979) · R. K. Engen, *Dictionary of Victorian wood engravers* (1985) · Redgrave, *Artists* · W. G. Rawlinson, *The engraved work of J. M. W. Turner*, 2 vols. (1908–13) · Bryan, *Painters* (1964) · *Art Journal*, 24 (1862), 46 · *ILN* (19 Feb 1898), 249 · M. H. Grant, *A dictionary of British etchers* (1952) · Mallalieu, *Watercolour artists* · W. E. Imeson, *Illustrated music-titles and their delineators: a handbook for collectors* (1912) · D. Spellman and S. Spellman, *Victorian music covers* (1969) · C. Haill, *Victorian illustrated music sheets* (1981) · Graves, *RA exhibitors* · Graves, *Brit. Inst.* · J. Johnson, ed., *Works exhibited at the Royal Society of British Artists, 1824–1893, and the New English Art Club, 1888–1917*, 2 vols. (1975) · J. Thackray Bunce, introduction and biographical notes, *Exhibition of engravings by 19 Birmingham men* (1877) [exhibition catalogue, Royal Birmingham Society of Artists, Birmingham, 1877] · A. M. Hind, *A history of engraving and etching*, 3rd edn (1923); repr. (1963) · M. H. Grant, *A dictionary of British landscape painters, from the 16th century to the early 20th century* (1952) · S. Houfe, *The dictionary of 19th century British book illustrators and caricaturists*, rev. edn (1996) · I. Mackenzie, *British prints: dictionary and price guide*, rev. edn (1998) · S. H. Pavière, *A dictionary of Victorian landscape painters* (1968) · Wood, *Vic. painters* · C. W. Beaumont, 'Some prints of the romantic ballet', *Print Collectors' Quarterly*, 18 (July 1931), 221–43 · C. W. Beaumont and S. Sitwell, *The romantic ballet in lithographs of the time* (1938) · S. Sitwell, *The romantic ballet from contemporary prints* (1948) · I. Guest, *A gallery of romantic ballet* (1965) · E. Beresford Chancellor, 'Early lithographs on sheet music', *The Connoisseur*, 93 (1934), 258–61 · Hall, *Dramatic ports.* · *Engraved Brit. ports.* · IGI · CGPLA *Eng. & Wales* (1862) [Robert Brandard] · CGPLA *Eng. & Wales* (1863) [John Brandard] · CGPLA *Eng. & Wales* (1898) [Edward Paxman Brandard]

Likenesses photograph (Edward Paxman Brandard), repro. in Hunnisett, *Illustrated dictionary of British steel engravers*, 18

Wealth at death under £2000—Robert Brandard: probate, 20 Jan 1862, CGPLA *Eng. & Wales* · under £100—John Brandard: probate, 4 Jan 1864, CGPLA *Eng. & Wales* · £95—Edward Paxman Brandard: probate, 9 March 1898, CGPLA *Eng. & Wales*

Brandard, Edward Paxman (1819–1898). *See under* Brandard family (*per. c.*1825–1898).

Brandard, John (1812–1863). *See under* Brandard family (*per. c.*1825–1898).

Brandard, Robert (1805–1862). *See under* Brandard family (*per. c.*1825–1898).

Brande, William Thomas (1788–1866), chemist, was born on 11 February 1788 at 10 Arlington Street, London, the youngest of the six children of Augustus Everard Brande (1746–1834), apothecary, and his wife, Ann, *née* Thomas (1753–1837). Brande was a scion of a wealthy family of apothecaries with appointments to the Hanoverian and London courts stretching back to near the beginning of the eighteenth century. Brande's father, born in Hanover

William Thomas Brande (1788–1866), by Maull & Polyblank, 1855

(naturalized 1784), was apothecary to Queen Charlotte between 1783 and 1801.

Education From about 1794 until 1797 Brande received a rudimentary classical education at a private school in Kensington. Between 1797 and 1801 he attended Westminster School, where he made fair progress in classical and general knowledge. In the latter year Brande's father retired from the court and moved to Chiswick. As a consequence Brande met the chemist Charles Hatchett, who had a small chemical manufacturing business there and who was to exercise an immense influence over Brande's choice of career and its course. Hatchett had a private laboratory in Roehampton where he allowed Brande both to assist him and to undertake his own chemical experiments. This inculcated in Brande a taste for chemistry which never left him. Although his father wished him to enter the church Brande decided to study medicine—then the only route to a career in chemistry. His decision may explain the rather strained relationship which Brande had with his family; his father's will made much less provision for him than for his siblings.

From 2 February 1802 until 6 February 1810, Brande was indentured to his elder brother, Everard Brande (1776–1868), who was then running the family business in Arlington Street. During his apprenticeship he visited Hanover where he pursued scientific and linguistic studies at Göttingen and Brunswick following the peace of Amiens in 1802. When the war recommenced on 18 April

1803 Brande had difficulty returning to London; he escaped via Hamburg on a Dutch ship. By 1804 he had resumed working with his brother and in the same year he also commenced studying at the Great Windmill Street school of medicine and at St George's Hospital, where he studied chemistry under George Pearson and Friedrich Accum. According to Brande, at this time his brother 'threw every obstacle in the way of my chemical progress that was decently in his power'. Nevertheless, he 'found time … to read, and often to experiment in my bedroom late in the evening' (Taylor, iii).

Chemical studies and teaching It seems that in 1801 Brande, still at Westminster School, was introduced to Humphry Davy who had then just been appointed professor of chemistry at the newly founded Royal Institution. On his return from Hanover, Brande renewed his acquaintance and 'as a result, his zeal in the pursuit of chemistry was greatly augmented' (Taylor, iii). From 1805 he started to attend Davy's lectures at the Royal Institution and occasionally absented himself from Arlington Street or Great Windmill Street in order to do so. In 1808 Brande and Davy were among the founders of the Animal Chemistry Club.

Despite his youth and family opposition Brande was able to conduct original chemical research, some of which was published in the *Philosophical Transactions of the Royal Society*. Such was his ability that in 1808, four years after he started studying there, Brande was lecturing at Great Windmill Street. This gave him membership of the London lecturing circle and in the next few years he delivered lectures on pharmaceutical chemistry at the medical school in Cork Street and on materia medica for Pearson. In 1809, at the age of twenty-one, he was elected a fellow of the Royal Society.

In 1812 Davy resigned his professorship of chemistry at the Royal Institution. Hatchett, who was a manager of the institution, seems to have been influential in ensuring that Brande was invited to give a series of lectures on chemistry in 1812 and then in securing his appointment as Davy's replacement in 1813 at an annual salary of £200. Brande moved into the Royal Institution and later in the year was also appointed superintendent of the house. Brande also replaced Davy in giving lectures on agricultural chemistry to the board of agriculture, but gave only one series before the board was dissolved the following year. In 1813 he was also appointed professor of chemistry to the Society of Apothecaries. Brande's appointment to the Royal Institution marked an important change in his career. Unlike most other lecturers in the period, who earned their living by giving itinerant lectures, Brande was now permanently in an institution made famous by Davy and possessing the best-equipped laboratory in Britain. This did not mean, however, that he ceased giving lectures elsewhere. For instance, in 1819 he delivered the first lecture and course at the newly built London Institution, which had been founded in imitation of the Royal Institution, and he gave other courses there in later years.

Brande's meteoric rise within the London scientific community was confirmed during 1813 by his election to membership of the Royal Society Club and by the award of the society's Copley medal for a paper on experiments dealing with the alcoholic content of wine and other drinks. In 1816 he succeeded W. H. Wollaston, at the latter's suggestion, as one of the two secretaries of the society, a position he held for the following ten years. By 1818 he was sufficiently financially secure to marry the younger daughter of his patron, Anna Frederica Hatchett (1797–1881). His marriage on 4 July entailed his moving out of the Royal Institution; the couple first lived in Clarges Street and from 1824 to 1828 they lived in Grafton Street. They had two sons and three daughters.

According to Brande's later recollection:

> from 1815 to 1848, I also delivered a series of lectures and demonstrations on theoretical and practical chemistry in the Laboratory below [the main lecture theatre of the Royal Institution]. They were intended for all denominations of students, and were given thrice weekly, from October to May. They were the first lectures in London in which so extended a view of chemistry, and of its applications, including technical, mineralogical, geological, and medical chemistry, was attempted. (Brande, 168)

These lectures were mainly attended by students from Great Windmill Street and, from 1828, from St George's Hospital. Initially he delivered these courses alone with the help of Michael Faraday, who as the assistant chemist at the Royal Institution was responsible, until 1825, for preparing and executing lecture demonstrations for Brande. In 1824 Faraday gave some of the lectures and from the following year the course was given jointly. In 1846 Brande tried to drop them but was persuaded to continue, though at a reduced level. Brande also gave many courses of Saturday lectures on specific topics at the Royal Institution, delivered twenty-eight Friday Evening discourses between 1826 and 1852, and gave seven series of Christmas lectures between 1834 and 1851.

Publications, consultancy, and later life Brande's lectures at the Royal Institution served, at least initially, as the basis for his major publications. In 1817 he published *Outlines of Geology* (2nd edn, 1829) while in 1819 his *Manual of Chemistry* appeared; both were based on his lectures. The *Manual of Chemistry* became a hugely successful and influential textbook and formed the model for many subsequent chemical textbooks by other authors. It went through six English editions by 1848 and was translated into several languages. He repeated the formula with his *Manual of Pharmacy*, which, published in 1825, had reached its third edition by 1833. Then followed his *Dictionary of Materia medica* (1839) and the highly successful *Dictionary of Science, Literature, and Art*, published in 1842. This latter went through many editions and was still being published posthumously in 1875. His last major publication, *Organic Chemistry* (1854), was based on his last course of lectures at the Royal Institution, in 1852. The link between Brande's publications and the institution also extended to his editing, between 1816 and 1830, the *Quarterly Journal of Science* which, although not an official publication of the Royal Institution, was nevertheless closely connected with it. It contained original papers, details of lectures given at the institution, summaries of papers published in overseas journals, and book reviews, and provided a quick route to publication for those associated with the Royal Institution. Faraday helped Brande with the work, preparing summaries of papers, and when Brande was away was completely in charge. The *Quarterly Journal* was a valuable general science journal at a time when there were very few such.

Brande was active in promoting the study of chemistry. In 1836 he was one of the original members of the senate of the University of London and in 1846 was appointed an examiner in chemistry, a post he retained until 1858. He was one of the founders of the Chemical Society in 1841 and was among its first vice-presidents, a post he held from 1841 to 1846. He was president from 1847 to 1849, during which period he oversaw the incorporation of the society and commencement of publication of its *Quarterly Journal*.

In 1823 the government consulted Brande on the manufacture of iron and steel to be used as dies for coins at the Royal Mint. This was the start of his long association with the mint in which, once again, Hatchett seems to have played some initiating role. Two years later Brande was appointed clerk of the irons and superintendent of machines. Though these posts involved much administrative work they provided an annual income of £700 and accommodation at the mint which the Brandes occupied after leaving Grafton Street. Following the royal commission of 1848 the organization of the mint was reformed and in early 1852 Brande was appointed at an annual salary of £900 to the newly created post of superintendent of the coining and die department, a post he held until death. One of the requirements of the reformed mint was that employees must have no other paid employment so Brande had to resign his professorships at the Society of Apothecaries (of which he was master for the year 1851–2) and the Royal Institution, though he was made an honorary professor there. He also had to cease consultancy work for the various London water companies. He had undertaken this kind of work for many years and in the preceding three had played a major role in the extremely controversial issue of how to provide a new water supply for London.

Brande's contribution to science and its practical application was recognized by the award of a DCL by the University of Oxford in 1853. Nevertheless, most of his contemporaries believed that he had not fulfilled his early promise. According to John Davy, Davy became 'very much disappointed' with Brande, whom he believed to be 'mercenary and had no lofty views' (Berman, 132–3). Brande was not a brilliant lecturer when compared with his predecessor at the Royal Institution, Davy, or with his successor, Faraday, but these are hardly fair comparisons and the fact that he was able to sustain his lectures to medical students and others for more than thirty years certainly helped keep the institution in a reasonable financial state. A contemporary noted that Brande was 'distinguished for the clearness of his [lecturing] style, for the

methodical arrangement of his matter, as well as for the admirable selection and performance of his experimental illustrations' (*JCS*). Nor, unlike Davy and Faraday, did Brande make any scientific discovery of major importance. Yet in the application of science to medicine, to water analysis, and to coining, Brande made a significant contribution to bringing science and technology together in the nineteenth century. He died on his seventy-eighth birthday at his country house in Tunbridge Wells on 11 February 1866 and was buried in Norwood cemetery. He was survived by his wife and children.

FRANK A. J. L. JAMES

Sources C. H. Spiers, 'William Thomas Brande, leather expert', *Annals of Science*, 25 (1969), 179–201 · W. T. Brande, 'Resignation of Professor Brande', *Notices of the Proceedings at the Meetings of the Members of the Royal Institution*, 1 (1852), 168–9 · A. S. Taylor, *PRS*, 16 (1867–8), ii–vi · E. Ironmonger, 'William Thomas Brande (1788–1866)', *Proceedings of the Royal Institution of Great Britain*, 38 (1960–61), 450–61 · E. Ironmonger, 'Further thoughts on W. T. Brande', *Proceedings of the Royal Institution of Great Britain*, 44 (1971), 262–73 · M. Berman, *Social change and scientific organization: the Royal Institution, 1799–1844* (1978) · *The correspondence of Michael Faraday*, ed. F. A. J. L. James, [4 vols.] (1991–) · C. Hamlin, *A science of impurity: water analysis in nineteenth century Britain* (1990) · A. A. Tulley, 'The chemical studies of William Thomas Brande, 1788–1866', MSc diss., U. Lond., 1970 · *JCS*, 19 (1866), 509–11

Archives Linn. Soc. · RCP Lond. · Royal Institution of Great Britain, London · RS · Wellcome L. | U. Texas, Herschel MSS

Likenesses Troye, plaster relief, c.1820, NPG; copy, Royal Institution, London · H. W. Pickersgill, oils, exh. RA 1830, Royal Institution of Great Britain, London · L. Wyon, lithograph, 1847, Royal Institution of Great Britain, London · Shappen, group portrait, lithograph, pubd 1850 (*Celebrated English chemists*; after daguerreotypes by Mayall), BM · Maull & Polyblank, photograph, 1855, NPG [*see illus.*] · H. Weigall, oils, exh. RA 1859, Apothecaries' Hall, London · T. Bridgford, lithograph, BM · M. Gauci, lithograph (after L. Wyon), BM · C. W. Sharpe, stipple and line print (after L. Wyon), BM, NPG

Wealth at death under £3000: probate, 23 March 1866, *CGPLA Eng. & Wales*

Brander, Gustavus (1719/20–1787), merchant and antiquary, was born in either London or Sweden, and was the son of Charles Brander (1681–1745) and his wife, Margaret (1687–1757). The family was of Swedish descent. Gustavus was trained in the Scandinavian trade, which he carried on with great success in the City. He was a director of the Bank of England from 1761 to 1779. Having inherited the fortune of his uncle John Spicker, he employed much of his wealth in forming collections of historical interest. Among his principal curiosities was the magnificent chair in which the first emperor of Germany was said to have been crowned. Engraved upon it in polished iron were scenes from Roman history, from the earliest times to the foundation of the empire. Brander was a fellow of the Society of Antiquaries (1749) and of the Royal Society (1754), a trustee of the British Museum (1761), and a founder member of the Society for the Encouragement of Arts (1754). He communicated papers on his Alexandrian Pillar and on the nuptial medal of Henry VII to the Society of Antiquaries in the 1750s. While he lived in London in partnership with Abraham Spalding, his library and pictures narrowly escaped the fire which destroyed their house in White Lion Court, Cornhill, on 7 November 1766. After this he moved to Westminster, and eventually to Hampshire, where he purchased the site of the old priory at Christchurch. Having built a villa and laid out gardens near the priory remains, he married, in January 1780, Elizabeth Lloyd (b. 1726), widow of John Lloyd, vice-admiral of the blue, and daughter of Mr Gulston (or Gulson) of Widdial, Hertfordshire.

As was common at the time, Brander was interested in science as well as antiquities. In 1755 he communicated an account of the effect of lightning on the Danish church in Wellclose Square to the *Philosophical Transactions* (54.298). His collection of fossils found in the cliffs about Christchurch and the coast of Hampshire aroused the interests of naturalists. Copperplate engravings of them, accompanied by a scientific Latin description by Daniel Solander, were published as *Fossilia Hantoniensia collecta, et in Museo Britannico deposita, à Gustavo Brander* in 1766. From a manuscript in Brander's possession, Samuel Pegge printed *The Forme of Cury: a Roll of Antient English Cookery, Compiled about the Year 1390* (1780). The most celebrated of his historical manuscripts, however, was the 'Winton Doomsday' and the accompanying Anglo-Saxon sacramentary. These were purchased by the Society of Antiquaries at the sale of his library in 1790.

In the winter of 1786 Brander had just completed the purchase of a house in St Albans Street in London, when he was seized by an illness which caused his death, in London or Christchurch, on 21 January 1787, aged sixty-seven. He was buried in Christchurch Priory.

THOMPSON COOPER, *rev.* D. G. C. ALLAN

Sources GM, 1st ser., 57 (1787), 94 · memorial inscription, Christchurch Priory, Hampshire · minutes, RSA · minutes, S. Antiquaries, Lond. · Nichols, *Lit. anecdotes*, 6.260 · typescript notes on bank directors, Bank of England Museum, London · T. Mortimer, *The merchant's directory* (1763) · IGI
Archives RS, letters and papers, 2.477; 3.58, 69 · S. Antiquaries, Lond., Antiquaries MSS, 156, 212 | BL, letters to Thomas Birch, Add. MS 4301, fols. 287–91 · BL, letters to Daniel Solander, Add. MS 29533, fol. 55 · BL, letters to Thomas Percy, Add. MS 32329, fol. 87 · Bodl. Oxf., corresp. with John Charles Brooke
Likenesses N. Dance, oils, BM
Wealth at death £1807 cash bequests; £620 in annuities; land and property: will, PRO, PROB 11/1149, fols. 23v to 26v

Brandis, Sir Dietrich (1824–1907), forester and botanist, born at Bonn on 31 March 1824, was the eldest son of Christian August Brandis (1790–1867) and his wife, Caroline Hausmann, a Hanoverian, who was a pioneer in social work. His father, son of the court physician at Copenhagen, after studying at Göttingen and Kiel universities, was *Privatdocent* at Copenhagen and Berlin universities, secretary to the Roman historian Niebuhr when ambassador at Rome (1816–21), and from 1822 to his death in 1867 was, save for three years' absence in Greece (1837–9), professor of philosophy at Bonn. Appointed *Kabinetsrat* (privy councillor) by Otho, king of Greece, in 1837, the elder

Brandis spent that and the two following years with his family at Athens, where the archaeologist Ernst Curtius acted as their tutor. Of Dietrich's younger brothers, Bernhard (1826–1911) obtained a reputation as a physician, while Johannes was private secretary to Augusta, the German empress.

Dietrich, after early education at Bonn, commenced botanical pursuits at Athens, studying under Fraas and accompanying Link on excursions. Having returned to Bonn in August 1839, he attended the Royal High School and university there. Subsequently he studied botany at Copenhagen under Schouw, at Göttingen under Grisebach and Lantzius-Beninga, and again at Bonn with Treviranus. He became PhD of Bonn on 28 August 1848, and *Privatdocent* in 1849.

In 1854 Brandis married Rachel, daughter of Joshua *Marshman, Indian scholar and missionary, and widow of Joachim Otto Voigt (1798–1843), Danish surgeon and botanist. This marriage determined his career. His wife's sister was the wife of General Sir Henry *Havelock. When Pegu in Burma was annexed in 1852, the valuable teak forests were being depleted by unscrupulous adventurers, and in 1855 General Havelock was consulted. On his suggestion the governor-general, Lord Dalhousie, put Brandis in charge of the threatened forests on 16 January 1856. Next year his commission was extended to include all Burmese forests, and by 1861 he had instituted controls that curbed private traders. His professional duties precluded much scientific study, but his interest in botany was maintained, and on 5 May 1860 he was elected a fellow of the Linnean Society. In 1862 he was asked to advise the government of India on general forest policy. The problem was difficult because rights of public user everywhere prevailed. Brandis, overcoming official and popular opposition, devised an efficient system of eliminating or adequately curtailing these rights; he also suggested the co-ordination and strengthening of the provincial departments which had control of the forests, and on 1 April 1864 he was appointed inspector-general of Indian forests.

During 1863–5 and 1868–70 he toured extensively, establishing state forest management in northern India. His provincial reports show a keen interest in evaluating community forest management. In the debate among officials prior to the second Forest Act of 1878 he steered a middle course between advocates of total state control of forests and votaries of village control. While on furlough in 1866 he arranged for the continental training of candidates for employment in forestry work.

Invalided on 4 February 1871, Brandis was on duty in England from 12 April 1872 until 22 May 1873 completing *The Forest Flora of North-West and Central India*, commenced by Dr John Lindsay Stewart. Prepared at Kew, this work, published in 1874, established Brandis's botanical reputation; he was elected FRS on 3 June 1875, and appointed CIE on 1 January 1878. After his return to India he founded in 1878 a school for Indian foresters at Dehra Dun. During

1881–3 he inaugurated a sound system of forest management in Madras. On 24 April 1883 he retired from Indian service, with a special honorarium and valedictory notice. As administrator and as professional forester he had proved himself equally eminent. His dual role as architect of the Indian forest department and as a sympathizer of community control added to his stature. Although his bid to reconcile the two strands did not succeed, he anticipated the dilemmas the Indian environmental movement faced subsequently.

After settling in Bonn, Brandis, who inherited his mother's social interests, instituted a working men's club. At the same time he resumed his botanical studies, examining specimens collected by himself or sent from Calcutta. While he had been absent from Simla on duty at Madras during 1881–3, it had been proposed to provide an English training instead of the existing continental training of forestry officers for India. Accordingly in 1885 a forestry school was established at Cooper's Hill, Surrey, and although Brandis thought the step to be premature, he joined the board of visitors. On 16 February 1887 he was promoted KCIE. On 10 October 1888 he agreed to supervise the practical continental training of British students. He performed this duty from 1888 to 1896, not only for British students but also for the young foresters of the United States forest department. His services and expert knowledge were recognized by the honorary degree of LLD from Edinburgh in 1889, and the grade of Prussian professor in 1890. In 1898 his university gave him a jubilee diploma; on 22 November 1905 he received a message of thanks from Theodore Roosevelt. Brandis's work was a powerful formative influence on Gifford Pinchot, the founder of American forestry.

After 1896 Brandis again confined his attention to botanical work, dividing his time from 1897 to 1900 between London and Bonn. In 1901 he settled in Kew in order to prepare a botanical forest manual. There he resided until November 1906, when he finally returned to Bonn. His great work *Indian Trees*, which he completed while suffering from a painful illness, was published in London in November 1906. It is a model of botanical exactitude and a monument to enthusiasm and perseverance.

Brandis's first wife had died at Simla in 1863, and in 1867 he married secondly, at Bonn, Katharine, daughter of Dr Rudolph Hasse. By his second marriage he had four sons and three daughters; three children died young. Brandis died at 27 Bonnertalway, Bonn, on 29 May 1907, and was buried in the family grave in the old cemetery.

DAVID PRAIN, rev. M. RANGARAJAN

Sources H. Hesmer, *Leben und Werk von Dietrich Brandis (1824–1907)* (1975) · E. Wilmot, 'Sir Dietrich Brandis', *Indian Forester*, 33 (1907), 305–8 · 'D. Brandis: the founder of forestry in India', *Indian Forester*, 10 (1884), 347–54 · R. Guha, 'Dietrich Brandis and Indian forestry: the road not taken', Nehru Memorial Museum and Library, New Delhi · D. Brandis, 'Indian forestry', 1897, Oriental University Institute, Woking, esp. 29–46 · E. P. Stebbing, *The forests of India*, 3 vols. (1922–7), esp. 1.163–4; 2.463 · B. Ribbentrop, *Forestry in British India* (1900), esp. 100–16 · BL OIOC · National Archives of India, New Delhi · J. L. Stewart and D. Brandis, *The forest flora of north-west and central India* (1874), xiv · W. S. [W. Schich], *PRS*, 80B (1908), iii

Archives Bodl. Oxf., corresp. with Lord Kimberley

Likenesses G. H. Siebert, pastel, 1867; last known at Elberfeld · photograph, 1906, RBG Kew

Wealth at death £338 0s. 1d.: probate, 22 Jan 1908, *CGPLA Eng. & Wales*

Brandon. For this title name *see* individual entries under Brandon; *see also* Hamilton, James, fourth duke of Hamilton and first duke of Brandon (1658–1712); Campbell, Elizabeth, duchess of Argyll and *suo jure* Baroness Hamilton of Hameldon [Elizabeth Hamilton, duchess of Hamilton and Brandon] (*bap.* 1733, *d.* 1790); Hamilton, Alexander Douglas-, tenth duke of Hamilton and seventh duke of Brandon (1767–1852); Hamilton, William Alexander Anthony Archibald Douglas-, eleventh duke of Hamilton and eighth duke of Brandon (1811–1863); Hamilton, Nina Mary Benita Douglas-, duchess of Hamilton and Brandon (1878–1951); Hamilton, Douglas Douglas-, fourteenth duke of Hamilton and eleventh duke of Brandon (1903–1973).

Brandon, Charles, first duke of Suffolk (*c*.1484–1545), magnate, courtier, and soldier, was the second but only surviving son of Sir William Brandon (*d.* 1485) and his wife, Elizabeth Bruyn (*d.* 1494) of South Ockendon. The manner of Sir William's death, killed at Bosworth bearing Henry VII's standard, prepared the way for his son's fame. Charles's grandfather, Sir William Brandon of Wangford and Southwark, survived to 1491, a trusted figure in the government of Suffolk; but more important for Charles's advancement was the career of his uncle, Sir Thomas *Brandon, one of Henry VII's leading courtiers. Charles probably grew up in his household, moving on naturally to serve the king.

Rise to power By about 1503 Charles Brandon waited on Henry VII at table and by 1507 he was an esquire for the body. More excitingly, by 1505–6 he was one of the company of king's spears, martial young gallants active in jousts and courtly display. By the end of the reign he was also master of the horse to Henry Bourchier, earl of Essex, one of the most prominent nobles at Henry's court. Though he first jousted publicly at the tournament to celebrate Prince Arthur's marriage to Katherine of Aragon in 1501 and waited on the prince the morning after his wedding, he does not seem to have held a post either in Arthur's household or in that of Prince Henry. This did not prevent him from forming close bonds with Henry, nor did the difference in their ages. Henry normally chose his friends from his coevals; Brandon was unusual in that although he was some seven years older than Henry VIII, and eventually predeceased him, he remained his lifelong intimate. Prince Henry watched Brandon and his friends joust at court in his father's last years and on his accession soon made them central to the tournaments and revels of his own court. The all-gilt armour Brandon wore as one of the six challengers at the coronation tournament of 1509 was a sign of things to come.

Charles Brandon, first duke of Suffolk (*c*.1484–1545), by unknown artist, *c*.1540–45

In the first three years of Henry's reign Brandon shared the limelight at court with a number of contemporaries who also joined him in financial and romantic ventures: Edward Howard, Thomas Knyvet, Henry and Edward Guildford. Howard's and Knyvet's deaths in the war of 1512–13 left Brandon increasingly alone at the head of their circle and he took an ever more distinctive part in the king's entertainments. In revels he began to be the only participant dressed identically with the king, in jousts to be the king's sole partner in challenging the rest of the court. By 1513–14 contemporaries recognized him as the king's principal favourite, a complementary figure to the rising minister Thomas Wolsey.

Favour brought rewards and responsibilities. At Brandon's uncle's death in January 1510 he succeeded him as marshal of the king's bench and in November 1511 he added the parallel post of marshal of the king's household. This gave him control over the prisons of both jurisdictions in Southwark and made him an influential figure in the borough, where he continued to live in the house that had been his grandfather's and uncle's. In October 1512 he became master of the horse in succession to Knyvet, giving formal shape to his close involvement with the king's horses, hunting, and jousts. Stewardships of royal estates, keeperships of royal houses, and offices in Wales were all steadily added to his portfolio. His status rose in leaps and bounds: knighted on 30 March 1512, elected a knight of the Garter on 23 April 1513, created Viscount Lisle on 15 May 1513. Promotion into the peerage was made possible by his betrothal to Knyvet's eight-year-

old stepdaughter, Elizabeth Grey, heir to the barons Lisle, whose wardship he had purchased from the crown. The title was also intended to facilitate his exercise of increasingly responsible military commands.

In the naval campaign of 1512 Brandon and Henry Guildford had captained one of Henry's largest ships, the *Sovereign*, but watched helplessly as another, the *Regent*, burnt with Knyvet aboard. The following spring Brandon was chosen to lead a landing force to Brittany, but the expedition was aborted. His chance for glory came that autumn, as Henry invaded France in person. Brandon raised a large retinue of 1831 men, mostly through his offices in Wales. He served as high marshal of the army, in charge of discipline, and led the vanguard of the king's ward, some 3000 men. He took no great part in the fighting of the early part of the campaign, but at the siege of Tournai he led a successful assault on one of the city gates which was instrumental in persuading the citizens to surrender to Henry. When handed the keys of the city, the king passed them to Brandon, who led his troops in to occupy it. Soon afterwards Henry granted him the outlying castle of Mortain. No wonder Margaret of Austria's agent with the English army reported that Brandon was a 'second king' (*LP Henry VIII*, 1/2, no. 2171).

Charles Brandon's rise was capped on 1 February 1514 with his creation as duke of Suffolk. On the same day Thomas Howard, earl of Surrey, became duke of Norfolk, the reward for his victory at Flodden. In this context Brandon's creation may have been as much a celebration of Henry's victories in France as of his favourite's merits. Some contemporaries found it shocking. Erasmus compared the over-promoted master of the horse to a drunken stable-hand in a satire of Persius, in a comment he prudently edited out of the 1519 edition of his letters. Others thought the promotion was intended to equip Brandon to marry Margaret of Austria, regent of the Netherlands, with whom he had flirted during Henry's visits to her court in 1513. When rumours spread around Europe and betting on the likelihood of such a match opened in London, Margaret was shocked. She demanded Henry scotch the rumours and cancel Brandon's projected visit to the Netherlands to raise troops for the next year's campaigning, and the king complied.

The strength of Margaret's reaction owed much to the frailty of her political position in the Netherlands and much to her own tragic experience of marriage, but it probably also reflected Brandon's murky and reprehensible marital history to date. Not only was he currently contracted to marry young Lady Lisle; between 1503 and 1510 he had married twice under controversial circumstances. His first wife was Anne Browne, daughter of Sir Anthony Browne and gentlewoman to the queen. He contracted to marry her and she became pregnant, but in summer 1506 he abandoned her to marry her widowed aunt, Dame Margaret Mortimer. On 7 February 1507 he had licence of entry on Dame Margaret's lands, which he rapidly began to sell. By the end of the year, probably

£1000 or more in profit, he was negotiating the annulment of this marriage on the multiple grounds of his consanguinity with Dame Margaret, the consanguinity of his two wives, and the consanguinity of his grandmother with Dame Margaret's first husband. Early in 1508 he secretly married Anne Browne in Stepney church, later repeating the ceremony publicly in St Michael Cornhill. At some point between 1506 and 1509 they had a daughter, Anne, whose legitimacy was later questioned, depending as it did upon the exact sequence of events. In the summer of 1510 their second, indisputably legitimate, daughter, Mary, was born. Her mother died shortly afterwards. At this time or later Brandon also fathered three bastards, Charles, later Sir Charles Brandon of Sigston (d. 1551), Mary, who married Robert Ball of Scottow, and Frances, who married successively the Lincolnshire gentlemen William Sandon and Andrew Bilsby. His reputation in such matters was thus scarcely unspotted when he embarked on a still more spectacular marital venture.

Marriage to the French queen In summer 1514 Wolsey brokered peace between Henry and Louis XII of France, a peace sealed by Louis's marriage to Henry's sister *Mary (1496–1533). In the autumn Suffolk led a jousting embassy to the wedding celebrations. Louis's death in January brought him to France again, charged with escorting Mary home. At Paris, in mid-February, without Henry's permission, they wed. Many at the English court were outraged. Henry was angry, though perhaps not surprised: Mary had apparently asked him for a free choice of husband should Louis die, Suffolk had discussed the possibility of a marriage before he left England, and once in France they asked the king's permission to marry on their return. Mary took the blame on herself, Suffolk excused himself with the consideration that he 'newar sawe woman soo wyepe' (BL, Cotton MS Caligula D. vi, fol. 186r), and early in May the king met them at Birling in Kent as they travelled home. On 13 May at Greenwich they married in public. Henry's displeasure was mollified by the surrender of Mary's jewels and plate, half her dowry, the wardship of the now redundant Lady Lisle, and a further £24,000 payable over twelve years from the profits of Mary's dower lands in France.

In the years that followed, Suffolk and his new duchess spent long periods away from court. On 1 February 1515 Henry had granted him what remained of the confiscated estates of his predecessors, the Pole dukes of Suffolk, situated in East Anglia with outliers in Oxfordshire, Berkshire, and other counties. Now he had to set about reconstituting the landed basis of the Poles' power by buying out the grantees to whom Henry VII and Henry VIII had alienated many of their manors, and making that power effective by his presence. Charles and Mary alike were welcome in Norfolk and Suffolk, fêted by towns, monasteries, and gentlemen. Their presence was also encouraged by Henry and Wolsey, concerned at the treasonable activities of Richard de la Pole, an exile patronized by the French as a Yorkist pretender. But Suffolk never managed to reconstruct the entire Pole estate, and his following among the local gentry was too heavily dependent on the loyalty of his extended but not very powerful cousinage, especially the Wingfield clan.

Mary's French connections also complicated Suffolk's political life. Her dower income from France, when it could be made to flow freely, amounted to some £4000, even after Henry's share had been deducted, and as such was probably larger than his income from all other sources, certainly more than his net landed income of about £1500 in 1523. French ambassadors thus tended to treat him as a hired spokesman at the English court, and his unguarded enthusiasm for Anglo-French amity led to his exclusion from the making of foreign policy at sensitive moments. Worse, Wolsey and Henry used his chronic indebtedness as a political leash to ensure that he did not help the French too much. But although he was no longer the 'second king' he had been, he had not lost the king's favour. At court he continued to star in the king's jousts, from 1517 as Henry's leading opponent rather than his team-mate, and he sued successfully for various grants, most notably the reversion to the office of earl marshal, national arbiter in matters of heraldry and chivalry, which he filled from the death of the second duke of Norfolk in 1524. By the early 1520s he seems to have learned to distance himself from French interests and in 1523 Henry had no qualms about appointing him to command an army of more than 11,000 men to invade northern France.

War and local power Brandon was to co-operate with an army from the Habsburg Netherlands under Floris, count of Buren, to strike deep into France with the aim of exploiting the rebellion of Charles, constable of Bourbon. He reached Calais on 24 August, but problems of supply, plague, and co-ordination with his allies delayed the junction of the armies and the effective start of the campaign until 1 October. Thereafter progress was stunning. On 18 and 20 October Ancre and Bray fell, opening the way across the Somme. On 28 October Montdidier surrendered. French sentries at Pont-Ste Maxence, halfway from Montdidier to Paris, saw Suffolk's outriders. Chains were strung across the streets of Paris, the rich evacuated their goods to Orléans, and the bells of the city fell silent, ready to signal the English attack. But Suffolk and Buren, under orders to meet with Bourbon, headed not south but east towards Champagne, where the constable's campaign had petered out long before. They took more towns and castles, but by 11 November they were at Prémont, almost back on the borders of Habsburg territory. Then the coldest night in living memory froze their tired army into mutinous retreat. Suffolk stopped at Valenciennes, hoping to resume the campaign in the spring, but it became evident that his allies' priorities lay elsewhere. By mid-December he was at Calais and early next year he was home.

Suffolk was named to command armies again in 1524 and 1528, once against France and once against the Netherlands, but both campaigns were cancelled. Instead he made his contribution to Henry's foreign adventures by working with Thomas Howard, third duke of Norfolk, to maintain good order in East Anglia. In spring 1525 they negotiated for a generous contribution to the amicable grant to fund a new campaign in France, then confronted protesters against the levy. Similarly, in 1528 they worked to regulate grain supplies in a year of famine and appease unrest caused by the suspension of the cloth trade to the Netherlands. Meanwhile, a rapprochement with the French, whose support Henry sought in his bid for the annulment of his marriage to Katherine of Aragon, gave Suffolk a role in Anglo-French diplomacy. This culminated in an embassy to France in May–June 1529, though he was unable to prevent the peace of Cambrai between France and the Habsburgs.

Friendship with France made Mary's dower revenues flow more freely than ever before. The money was welcome for several reasons. Suffolk's profits from royal office were declining. He had surrendered the mastership of the horse and the marshalcies in the wake of his marriage. Then, in 1525, in the reorganization of Welsh government associated with Princess Mary's sending to Ludlow, he lost the chief justiceship of north Wales, the constableship of Caernarfon Castle, and the receiverships and chief stewardships of the marcher lordships of Bromfield, Yale, and Chirk, offices he had collected between 1509 and 1513. He had exercised the offices largely through deputies, mostly local men like Sir William Gruffydd of Penrhyn, but had used the revenues under his control as a liberal source of credit, a source choked off in 1525.

Meanwhile Suffolk had a growing family. His children from his marriage to Mary were still young: Henry, born on 11 March 1516, had died by 1522, but there followed Frances, born on 16 or 17 July 1517, Eleanor, born between 1518 and 1521, and another Henry, born in 1522 and created earl of Lincoln in 1525. The daughters of his marriage to Anne Browne, in contrast, were old enough to need husbands. For Anne he had purchased the wardship of Edward Grey, fourth Baron Powis, in 1517, and they were married by March 1525. For Mary he managed to buy the marriage of Thomas Stanley, second Baron Monteagle, and they were married in late 1527 or early 1528. In November 1527 he concluded negotiations with Wolsey and other councillors for a still more important match. For £2666 13s. 4d., payable over nine years, he bought for his son and heir the marriage of the king's ward Katherine Willoughby (1519–1580) [see Bertie, Katherine], daughter and heir to the lately deceased William, eleventh Baron Willoughby de Eresby, whose estates in Lincolnshire and East Anglia would prove a splendid addition to the Brandon patrimony.

A final expense was Suffolk's ambition to build notable houses. Already in the years after his creation as duke he had rebuilt his uncle's house in Southwark as Suffolk Place, a large brick palace decorated with fashionable terracottas. In the late 1520s and early 1530s he built its counterpart in East Anglia, Westhorpe, a moated brick courtyard house of considerable size with terracotta plaques and battlements, ornate chimneys and painted glass, oak-

panelled rooms, a statute of Hercules, and well-stocked parks and gardens. He later claimed it cost him £12,000. Only fragments of either house survive.

Political and personal troubles By February 1529 ambassadors were naming Suffolk as one of Wolsey's enemies at court. He seems not to have opposed the cardinal as vigorously as Norfolk and the Boleyns, but on his embassy to France he was certainly happy to enquire of François I whether he thought Wolsey was obstructing the king's divorce. As Wolsey fell from power in October, Suffolk took up the role as a leading councillor for which his status and the king's confidence fitted him, being appointed president of the king's council. But as the new regime settled down from 1530, his attendance in council and parliament was erratic, his influence limited, and his position uncomfortable. He found the missions Henry sent him on to humiliate Katherine of Aragon distasteful, his relations with Anne Boleyn were poor, and his son's powerful claim to the throne as the only legitimate and English-born grandson of Henry VII drew unwelcome attention. In spring 1533 Norfolk demanded that Suffolk relinquish to him the office of earl marshal and Henry made Suffolk comply. Followers of Norfolk murdered Suffolk's client Sir William Pennington in the Westminster sanctuary in 1532, but were readily pardoned. This seems to have been part of a wider rivalry in East Anglia between the affinities of the two dukes which exposed the continuing weaknesses of Brandon's local following.

Personal setbacks mounted in this period too. Suffolk's wife, Mary, died on 25 June 1533 at Westhorpe and was buried in Bury St Edmunds Abbey. His son Henry, earl of Lincoln, died on 8 March 1534. One son-in-law, Baron Monteagle, turned out so feckless that Suffolk had several times to take over his lands and pay his debts, while the other, Baron Powis, found his wife so adulterous that he kidnapped her lover in a night-time raid and ended their marriage by a formal separation. On the other hand, more promising marriages were arranged for his younger daughters, Frances to Henry Grey, marquess of Dorset, and Eleanor to Henry, Lord Clifford, heir to the earldom of Cumberland. And, startlingly, Suffolk himself married again in September 1533: his fourth wife was the fourteen-year-old Katherine Willoughby, originally intended as his son's bride. More romantic commentators thought it was the shock that killed young Lincoln, but Suffolk had ensured that the Willoughby estates would not leave his line, an assurance confirmed by the birth of a son, again named Henry, on 18 September 1535, and of another, Charles, in 1537 or 1538. Katherine's lands were all the more significant because Mary's death necessitated a financial reckoning with the crown, one which cost the duke all his Oxfordshire and Berkshire estates and Suffolk Place in Southwark.

Lincolnshire magnate The fall of Anne Boleyn in spring 1536 drew Henry's senior councillors into renewed prominence, but what brought Suffolk back to the forefront of national affairs was the outbreak of the Lincolnshire revolt in October and the ensuing Pilgrimage of Grace. Appointed the king's lieutenant to suppress the Lincolnshire rebels, he advanced fast from Suffolk to Stamford, gathering troops as he went; but by the time he was ready to fight, the rebels had disbanded. On 16 October he entered Lincoln and began to pacify the rest of the county, investigate the origins of the rising, and prevent the southward spread of the pilgrimage, still growing in Yorkshire and beyond. Only two tense months later, as the pilgrims dispersed under the king's pardon, could he disband his 3600 troops and return to court. There the king commanded him to move his home to Lincolnshire, and from spring 1537 he set about doing so.

The Willoughby estates and the close-knit following of gentlemen who had administered them for the duchess's father and widowed mother formed the core of Suffolk's power in the county. Establishing himself as the dominant local magnate required much more. In April 1537 the king gave him Tattershall Castle as an imposing base. By late summer Suffolk was preparing for a wholesale exchange of his East Anglian estates, including the lands of Leiston Abbey and Eye Priory granted to him in April 1537 in reward for his service against the rebels, for monastic property and other crown land in Lincolnshire and elsewhere. Negotiations took until September 1538 but the result was to make Suffolk indisputably the greatest landowner in Lincolnshire, with a dense belt of estates spread across the centre of the county. The lands he had been granted in other counties he sold off, ready to invest in more Lincolnshire land as it became available in the years ahead. Effective lordship also required the duke's presence, and after spending May and June 1537 in East Anglia he spent much time in Lincolnshire. He oversaw Lord Hussey's execution in July 1537, moves against vagabonds in 1538, and musters in spring 1539.

Activity in Lincolnshire did not mean alienation from the court. Suffolk seems to have worked effectively with Thomas Cromwell. He served on the increasingly well-defined privy council. In the household reforms of 1539 he was appointed to the great mastership of the household, an upgraded version of the lord stewardship. He led both the party which met Anne of Cleves on her arrival at Dover on 27 December 1539 and the team which negotiated with her the terms of her divorce from the king in July 1540. He took no great part in the politics of Cromwell's fall but, as ever, increased in prominence as a symbol of stability at a time of political turmoil.

Last years Suffolk's health was poor at times in the 1540s but this did not prevent his taking a major part in Henry's last wars against France and Scotland, while between campaigns he sat more regularly in the privy council than ever before, as a senior statesman and military expert. Although he does not appear to have been a notably imaginative general, he won the praise of several of his contemporaries; the verdict of Ellis Gruffydd, that 'he was the flower of all the captains of the realm and had the necessary patience to control soldiers', at least hints at

qualities of leadership (Davies, 25). In October and November 1542 he guarded the northern border while Norfolk and others invaded Scotland. From January 1543 to March 1544 he was the king's lieutenant in the north. Based mostly at Darlington, from there he supervised regional government and border warfare, dealt with the Scottish nobles sympathetic to Henry's plans to marry Prince Edward to the infant Mary, queen of Scots, and planned for a major invasion which he never had the chance to command. Nevertheless, his work laid the basis for the capture of Edinburgh by Edward Seymour, earl of Hertford, in May 1544.

By then Suffolk had been called away to France, where although now aged about sixty he led the siege of Boulogne with conspicuous bravery and skill, from July to November 1544 commanding the king's ward in the huge army which eventually captured the town. Though Henry arrived for the final stages of the siege, it was Suffolk whom he invited to ride in to occupy Boulogne on 14 September. Keeping it in the face of French resurgence was another matter, and Henry was irate when Suffolk and Norfolk retreated to Calais on 3 October, leaving John Dudley, Viscount Lisle, to hold the new conquest. But the king soon relented, and in February 1545 Suffolk got his reward, the lands of Tattershall College for less than half the standard price.

In these years Suffolk worked happily with fellow councillors of various religious and political allegiances, from the conservatives Thomas, Baron Wriothesley, William Paulet, Baron St John, and Sir Anthony Browne, who would all serve as executors of his will, to the reformists Hertford and Lisle. His own religious position remained ambivalent. His personal preferences seem to have been conservative: his chapel was graced by six choristers and statues of saints and he requested dirges in his will. Many of the clergy he patronized were former monks (to whom he would not need to pay pensions from his former monastic lands if he provided them with benefices instead) or were estate or household administrators. Others were clearly conservatives in doctrine and prospered under Queen Mary. But some were committed protestants: the renegade Scottish Dominican Alexander Seton, the future bishop of Norwich John Parkhurst, Archbishop Cranmer's protégés Thomas Lawney and Richard Marsh. Some were favourites of the duchess, who from her husband's last years was moving in the reformist circles at court around Queen Katherine Parr, while yet others were linked to clients of the duke. Suffolk's ambiguous position, like the king's, may well have been adopted in an effort to reconcile the conflicting demands of those who called on his good lordship in a period of increasing religious polarization. The merchants who sold the lead he stripped from monasteries and the artists he patronized—including Hans Holbein, from whom he commissioned various works including delightful miniatures of his sons—gave him other links to the networks of reformist religion.

The consolidation of Suffolk's Lincolnshire estates continued and with it the construction of a following in county society more coherent and powerful than anything he had managed in East Anglia, though several leading knightly families resisted his hegemony. His local eminence was displayed when the king, on his way to York in 1541, stayed with Suffolk at Grimsthorpe, the Willoughby house he had extended with a new court. By 1545 his landed income was higher than it had ever been, at perhaps £2100 net, plus some £900 from the Willoughby estates. When he died of unknown causes at Guildford, on 22 August 1545, fresh from fortifying Portsmouth and still preparing to lead an army to the relief of Boulogne, the financial and political legacy he left to his sons was a strong one. All was owed to the favour of the king, who decreed Suffolk should be buried at St George's Chapel, Windsor, as he was on 9 September, a fitting reward for his dogged fulfilment of his motto, *Loyaulte me oblige*.

The young dukes Charles Brandon left two sons, **Henry Brandon** (1535–1551) and **Charles Brandon** (1537/8–1551), successively second and third dukes of Suffolk. Aged only ten when his father died, Henry faced a long minority. His wardship was granted to his mother in May 1546 for £1500 and he was set to study at court with Prince Edward, under Richard Coxe, John Cheke, and Roger Ascham. Henry and Charles were knighted at Edward's coronation, where Henry carried the orb. Henry was active at Edward's court, revelling with the king in March 1547, running at the ring in May 1550, and dressing up as a nun in a masque in June. In April 1550 he travelled briefly to France as a hostage for the fulfilment of the treaty of Boulogne. In May 1550 it was suggested he might marry the duke of Somerset's daughter Anne, but his mother dismissed the idea on the grounds that the children should wait until they knew their own minds in such matters. Meanwhile he and his brother pursued their formal education, enrolling at St John's College, Cambridge, in 1549.

When the sweating sickness struck Cambridge in summer 1551, Henry and Charles Brandon moved out to Buckden in Huntingdonshire, but too late. Both had contracted the disease. Henry died on 14 July. Charles survived him by only half an hour and they were buried together at Buckden. Thomas Wilson, Walter Haddon, Parkhurst, Cheke, and three dozen other Cambridge and Oxford scholars praised their learning, piety, and virtues unstintingly and lamented their passing in a volume of Latin and Greek verse and prose, published in 1551. Wilson, who had tutored them, also chose them as the subjects of his exemplary oration of praise in *The Arte of Rhetorique* (1553). Even allowing for the conventions of such works it seems that they were young men of considerable promise whose loss was keenly felt.

With them their father's direct line expired. The Suffolk title was granted to Brandon's son-in-law Dorset in October 1551, while his daughters and aunts and their respective descendants bickered over his lands. The duchess went on to a new marriage, Marian exile, and Elizabethan fame. The fateful consequences of Charles Brandon's marriage to Mary Tudor were to haunt their granddaughters Jane, Katherine, and Mary Grey in 1553 and beyond. Meanwhile the memory of the duke of Suffolk outlived the extinction

of his line, as 'a duke famous at home and abroad' (MacCulloch, 245). In the seventeenth century he was remembered as Henry's jousting partner, in the nineteenth and twentieth either as a reprobate—as in Richard Davey's book *The Sisters of Lady Jane Grey and their Wicked Grandfather* (1911)—or as the French queen's dashing suitor, as played by Richard Todd in the 1953 Disney film *The Sword and the Rose*. For historians he has long been in the shadow of his wives and his royal master, but has more recently attracted attention as one of the great survivors of Henry's lethal court.

S. J. GUNN

Sources S. J. Gunn, *Charles Brandon, duke of Suffolk, c.1484–1545* (1988) • GEC, *Peerage*, new edn, 12/1.454–62 • *LP Henry VIII* • S. J. Gunn, 'The duke of Suffolk's march on Paris in 1523', *EngHR*, 101 (1986), 596–634 • S. J. Gunn and P. G. Lindley, 'Charles Brandon's Westhorpe: an early Tudor courtyard house in Suffolk', *Archaeological Journal*, 145 (1988), 272–89 • M. B. Davies, 'Boulogne and Calais from 1545 to 1550', *Fouad I University Bulletin of the Faculty of Arts*, 12 (1950), 1–90 • D. MacCulloch, 'The *Vita Mariae Angliae Reginae* of Robert Wingfield of Brantham', *Camden miscellany, XXVIII*, CS, 4th ser., 29 (1984), 181–301 • E. Read, *Catherine, duchess of Suffolk* (1962) • T. Wilson and others, *Vita et obitus duorum fratrum Suffolciensium* (1551) • T. Wilson, *The arte of rhetorique* (1553) • M. Dowling, *Humanism in the age of Henry VIII* (1986) • J. Loach, *Edward VI* (1999) • *The chronicle and political papers of King Edward VI*, ed. W. K. Jordan (1966)

Archives BL, Cotton MSS, corresp. and papers • BL, corresp. relating to negotiations with Scotland, Add. MSS 32648–32656 • Lincs. Arch., estate and household records • PRO, estate and household records

Likenesses attrib. J. Gossaert al. Mabuse, double portrait, panel painting, c.1515–1520? (with Mary Tudor), priv. coll. • L. Hornebolte, miniature, c.1530 (Charles Brandon?), Louis de Wet collection • panel painting, c.1540–1545, NPG [*see illus.*] • H. Holbein, miniatures, 1541 (Henry Brandon and Charles Brandon), Royal Collection

Brandon, Charles, third duke of Suffolk (1537/8–1551). *See under* Brandon, Charles, first duke of Suffolk (*c*.1484–1545).

Brandon, Lady Frances. *See* Grey, Frances, duchess of Suffolk (1517–1559).

Brandon, Henry, second duke of Suffolk (1535–1551). *See under* Brandon, Charles, first duke of Suffolk (*c*.1484–1545).

Brandon [*formerly* Brandeis], **(Oscar) Henry** (1916–1993), journalist, was born on 9 March 1916 in Liberec, Bohemia—then part of the Austro-Hungarian empire, but shortly to become part of Czechoslovakia—the only child of a banker in Prague whose family name was Brandeis. After secondary education in his native country he studied in Lausanne, Switzerland, and at the Charles University of Prague. In 1939, as Hitler's armies swept into Czechoslovakia, he decided, given his Jewish origins, to emigrate to England. His father had died in 1935 and his mother planned to join him as soon as he was settled: that this proved impossible was one of the great sorrows of his life, and fifty-four years later he was buried, by his own wish, beside his parents in Bratislava.

Arriving in England without a word of the language, Brandon enrolled at the London School of Economics and found employment of a sort in a briar pipe factory. He was lucky enough to fall in with Iain Lang, the foreign editor of the *Sunday Times*, who encouraged him to aim at serious journalism. His first article for the *Sunday Times* appeared in December 1939, under the heading 'Economic havoc in Prague'. A year later, the paper sent him, by now speaking English proficiently, on a three-month assignment to report on American defence industries. In the event, he remained working in the USA for four years and in 1943 he joined the staff of the paper, after which he became a war correspondent in north Africa, Italy, and France. At the end of the war he reported on the peace conferences and diplomatic meetings in Paris, London, and Moscow, as well as on the early stages of the United Nations in New York.

By the time he was appointed to the key post of Washington correspondent for the *Sunday Times* in 1949—a move supported by Ian Fleming, then Kemsley Newspapers' foreign manager—Brandon had come a long way from his modest beginnings. To a good brain and retentive memory he had added wide knowledge of the issues and personalities of post-war politics and diplomacy, and had also won a deserved reputation for discretion—not a characteristic of most journalists. His own political inclinations, if any, were never made apparent, which is perhaps why so many politicians trusted him. As Washington correspondent for the *Sunday Times*—a post he held until 1983—he established and maintained a unique relationship with successive American political leaders and influential people. This enabled him to report with singular accuracy on the evolution over a period of thirty-four years of American foreign, defence, and economic policies, especially in the context of the Anglo-American alliance. Among the impressive list of his American contacts and friends were Dean Acheson, President John Kennedy and his wife, Jacqueline, and brother Robert, McGeorge Bundy (Kennedy's national security adviser), Robert McNamara, presidents Lyndon Johnson, Richard Nixon, and Ronald Reagan, Henry Kissinger (this was an especially close relationship), Katherine (Kay) Graham (the owner of the *Washington Post*), a long stream of British ambassadors, and many others. There was no other representative of a foreign media concern in Washington who enjoyed the access he did. Nor was this extensive network confined to the USA: because of his reputation and standing in Washington, he came to know, inform, and entertain leading British figures ranging from George Brown and Harold Lever to Edward Heath and Margaret Thatcher.

A journalist for a weekly paper is under less pressure than one filing two or three messages daily. Brandon was able to spend his week garnering information from friends and contacts, so that Sunday after Sunday he could reveal to his readers what was going on, or was due to go on, in Washington's seats of power. To those readers, that is, who read him. This was not popular journalism, in the modern and not always favourable sense. It was aimed at a relatively small group of politicians, policy-makers, diplomats, and foreign-affairs communities in London, Paris, and perhaps Moscow. And for all its quality of content,

this meant, especially as the readership of the *Sunday Times* widened, that his material often had to be rearranged, sometimes rewritten, by his London editors. The task was made doubly necessary by the fact that English was not his native tongue. He acquiesced in the practice, though he occasionally expressed regret at the loss of a treasured but abstruse allusion. He won numerous prizes for his journalism, and was appointed CBE in 1985.

The high esteem in which Brandon was held in Washington added greatly to the international lustre of the *Sunday Times*, but his individualism did not make him always an easy colleague on his own ground, which he defended with an unshakeable sense of possession. A good skier, a respectable tennis player, and an interesting if somewhat slow-paced talker, he was welcome at many Washington dinner tables. But it was noticeable that on such occasions he tended to direct most of his attention to the newsworthy rather than to the lesser lights who might be present—a habit common to many eager journalists. His marriage, in 1970, to Mabel Hobart Wentworth, former wife of Eric Wentworth, did much to smooth these rough edges and to induce a more relaxed manner. He was devoted to their daughter, Fiona. Mabel Brandon later became the social secretary to the White House during the first administration of President Reagan. The Brandons entertained extensively in a splendid house whose garden marched with that of the British embassy. No other foreign correspondent lived in such state, which may perhaps explain the rather grudging attitude towards him of some of Brandon's journalistic colleagues.

As well as his regular contributions to the *Sunday Times*, Brandon wrote several books, most of them expanding ground already covered in his journalism. Thus *In the Red: how Sterling Came in from the Cold* (1967) described the events leading up to the devaluation of the pound that year. *The Retreat of American Power* (1973) analysed the foreign policy of Nixon and Kissinger, and was published in Britain, Germany, and Japan as well as in the USA. His autobiography, *Special Relationships* (1988), containing some shrewd judgements of men and events, was well received in America but made little impact in the UK. His last book was *In Search of a New World Order: the Future of US–European Relations* (1992).

After his retirement Brandon continued to live in Washington, where he was made a senior scholar-in-residence at the Brookings Institute. He maintained his literary output with contributions to American publications, and also produced two small volumes of discussions of foreign policy, under the Brookings imprint. He was a cultivated man; his published interviews with artists and writers were proof, if such were needed, that his interests and range were by no means confined to politics. The kind of 'top people's' journalism to which Brandon was recruited and which he continued to practise had become by the time of his retirement largely a thing of the past. But nothing should detract from his achievements at the height of his Washington career, when his insider knowledge was deemed to be so important that the Nixon administration authorized the tapping of his telephone. It was, in its disagreeable way, a special kind of tribute.

Brandon died at the Queen Square Neurological Hospital, London, on 20 April 1993, of a cerebral haemorrhage. After his death his widow and daughter, helped by donations from more than 150 friends in Britain and the USA, established the Henry Brandon memorial fellowships, one of whose aims is to take Czech and Slovak journalists to the USA to study the workings of a free press. FRANK GILES

Sources O. Brandon, *Special relationships* (1988) · *WWW, 1991–5* · *The Times* (22 April 1993) · *The Independent* (23 April 1993) · personal knowledge (2004) · private information (2004)
Likenesses photograph, repro. in *The Times* · photograph, repro. in *The Independent*
Wealth at death £28,243 effects in England: probate, 10 Sept 1993, *CGPLA Eng. & Wales*

Brandon, Henry Vivian, Baron Brandon of Oakbrook (1920–1999), judge, was born on 3 June 1920 in St Botolph's Nursing Home, Richmond Road, Worthing, Sussex, the younger son of Captain Vivian Ronald Brandon RN and his wife, Joan Elizabeth Maud Simpson. His father was a naval officer taken prisoner of war by Germany during the First World War for allegedly spying off the North Sea coast. Henry Brandon was educated firstly at Durston House, Ealing, whence he gained a scholarship to Winchester College in 1933. At Winchester he was second on the roll of scholars and won several college prize medals. He also excelled at rugby fives, soccer, and Winchester football. In 1939 he went to King's College, Cambridge, to read classics with the Stewart of Ranloch scholarship, but his university career was interrupted by the outbreak of war. He was commissioned in the Royal Artillery. Serving in Madagascar, he was awarded the MC for directing his regiment's fire by radio from a motorcycle deep behind the Vichy French lines. He also served in India and Burma, and ended the war as a major.

Brandon returned to Cambridge in 1945 and graduated in 1946 with a first in law, a half-blue in rugby fives, and an abiding passion for cricket. In the same year he was called to the bar by the Inner Temple as an entrance scholar and Yarborough Anderson scholar. He spent his early years at the bar at 7 King's Bench Walk, a small set of chambers with a mixed practice within the Probate, Divorce, and Admiralty jurisdiction, that strange rag-bag of specialities that had grown out of the old ecclesiastical court jurisdiction. He built up a thriving practice in all three branches, the only man then at the bar to do so. The clarity of his intellect, the lucidity of his opinions, and the incisiveness of his advocacy ensured that he received instructions outside these fields and he encroached on the territory of the leading set of commercial chambers, 3 Essex Court. On 28 December 1955 he married Jeanette Rosemary Janvrin (*b.* 1930/31), a private secretary. Four children soon followed, three sons and a daughter. Taking silk in 1961 Brandon became the leader of choice for the leading Admiralty solicitors, but his career in the front row was short-lived.

In 1966, at the age of forty-six, Brandon was appointed a

Henry Vivian Brandon, Baron Brandon of Oakbrook (1920–1999), by Jimmy Sime, 1961

judge of the High Court in the Probate, Divorce, and Admiralty Division, and was knighted. He was the sole Admiralty judge. What had counted in the Admiralty court up to then was a knowledge of good seamanship—preferably from personal experience—and dexterity with the dividers and parallel rule. It was almost considered bad form to take a point of law. Now there came a judge who over the next twelve years scrutinized, spring-cleaned, and put in order every corner of the complex Admiralty jurisdiction. 'What is the authority for that?', he would ask with almost monotonous regularity—not, as counsel sometimes suspected, in order to tease them or be difficult for its own sake—but because he genuinely wanted to know and insisted on knowing before making up his mind. He delighted in debate and playing devil's advocate, but woe betide the ill-prepared counsel appearing before him: he would mercilessly expose sloppy preparation. He set himself the highest standards, and expected the same of those who appeared before him.

The Family Division (as it became under the Administration of Justice Act of 1970) was not exempt from his scrutiny: he applied the same exacting standards to this work, but combined it with a special understanding of human foible and frailty. 'A man may be a mouse in the witness box and a lion outside', he once commented (*Daily Telegraph*). And when a Roman Catholic woman tried to convince him that her religious scruples prevented her from committing adultery, he remarked that 'human beings tend to do things which are inconsistent with their scruples' (ibid.). Brandon's work in this division, particularly after the major statutory reforms introduced in 1971, drew on all his many powers and gifts. His reliable judgement combined with his deep understanding of human nature and love of family life fully equipped him for this work, which he relished as a contrast to the Admiralty cases.

When the Admiralty court was transferred to the Queen's Bench Division under the 1970 legislation, Brandon declined to go with it, feeling that life on circuit was incompatible with his family commitments, so he sat as an 'additional judge of the Queen's Bench Division' on secondment from the Family Division. This obstinacy no doubt contributed to the delay of his elevation to the Court of Appeal, until 1978. In the Court of Appeal he quickly established himself as authoritative across the much wider field of law found there. He rapidly became a highly respected member of the court and relished the more collegiate atmosphere produced by sitting in divisions of three rather than alone. In 1981 he was promoted a lord of appeal in ordinary; it was as Baron Brandon of Oakbrook in the House of Lords that he achieved his full potential.

As one of the law lords, Brandon regularly gave the leading opinion in cases across the whole field of English law. The published law reports bear the best witness to his outstanding powers of analysis; his clear tabulation of principle would often be regarded as almost a codification of that area of the law. But Brandon insisted that the courts' decisions be securely founded on statutory provisions or other established sources. In *Richards* v. *Richards* (1983), for example, he expressed astonishment that the courts had, without examining or having proper regard to the relevant statutory framework, developed the practice of making so-called 'ouster' orders, turning spouses out of the only accommodation they had. In the result, he agreed that the first-instance judge had been wrong to make such an order in a case in which the judge had said he considered it to be 'thoroughly unjust' to do so. Again in the *Gillick case* (1985) he took his stand on the fact that legislation treated sexual intercourse between a man and a girl under sixteen as unlawful; and he (unlike the three of his colleagues constituting the majority) believed that it necessarily followed that anyone—whether a parent, a doctor, or a social worker—who gave contraceptive advice was thereby necessarily guilty of encouraging or facilitating the commission of a criminal offence. Such decisions did not give Brandon a reputation for liberalism, but his view was that it was the courts' function to apply the law rather than to decide cases in accordance with the judge's social and political preferences. Thus in 1991 he was among the law lords who ruled that a husband could be convicted of raping his wife. In the *Spycatcher* case in 1987 he considered that the government ban on publication of extracts from Peter Wright's book should be continued, although he accused the attorney-general of trying to 'impose the kind of censorship the Soviet government imposes' (*The Times*).

If Lord Denning had been the innovative architect, Lord Brandon was the skilled surveyor who did his best to ensure that the foundations of English law remained sound and that developments were firmly based in precedent. He would identify clearly the governing principles which, once identified, pointed almost inevitably to the result of an appeal. This ability to isolate principle from previous case law was his greatest legacy to English law and the forensic process.

Those who knew Henry Brandon well off the bench experienced deep friendship, consistent kindness, and unswerving loyalty, mixed with a subtle and occasionally wicked sense of humour. The younger generation interested him, and they were enthralled by his readiness to engage them in lively debate. Outside his work, his abiding love and concern was for his wife and large, close family: he was, first and last, a devoted husband, father, and family man. Lord Brandon died on 24 March 1999 at Stratton Manor Nursing Home, Diddies Road, Stratton, Bude, Cornwall, having suffered for some years from Parkinson's disease. He was cremated.   PAUL COLERIDGE

Sources *The Times* (25 March 1999) · *Daily Telegraph* (25 March 1999) · *The Independent* (29 March 1999) · *WW* · Lord Phillips of Worth Matravers, memorial speech, 12 July 1999 · personal knowledge (2004) · private information (2004) · b. cert. · m. cert. · d. cert.
Likenesses J. Sime, photograph, 1961, Hult. Arch. [*see illus.*] · F. Blunt, photograph, 1973, Hult. Arch. · photograph, repro. in *The Times* · photograph, repro. in *Daily Telegraph* · photograph, repro. in *The Independent*

Brandon, John (*b.* **1644/5**), Church of England clergyman, the son of Charles Brandon, a physician of Maidenhead, was apparently born near Bray, Berkshire. He matriculated at Oriel College, Oxford, as a commoner on 15 February 1662, aged seventeen, and graduated BA on 11 November 1665.

Anthony Wood reports that Brandon 'entertained for some time certain heterodox opinions, but afterwards being orthodox' took holy orders. He lived at Wargrave and was rector of Finchinhampstead, both in Berkshire, and for some years preached a weekly lecture at Reading. All his works had as a central concern the dangers of that heterodoxy which it would appear had so attracted him in his youth. *To pyr to aiōnion, or, Everlasting Fire No Fancy* (1678) provided a belated attack on the Baptist Samuel Richardson's denial of the reality of hell-fire in his *Of the Torments of Hell* (1657), a work already challenged by Nicholas Chewney in 1660 in *Hell, with the Everlasting Torments Thereof Asserted*. The book was dedicated to Henry, earl of Starlin (Sterling), dated as from Wargrave, 20 July 1676. Brandon expressed deep concern that 'some men live, as if hell and its everlasting sorrows were but scarecrows, and melancholy fancies', which he described as 'a devilish doctrine' (Brandon, *To pyr*, sig. A2). Another work of Brandon's concerned the afterlife, *Happiness at hand, or, A plain and practical discourse of the joy of just men's souls in the state of separation from the body* (1687), a work dedicated to Dr Robert Woodward, chancellor of the diocese of Salisbury, in which Brandon asserted that 'the soul of man remains alive after his body is dead', in answer to the 'brutish' notion that 'men die (in all respects) as the beasts that perish' (Brandon, *Happiness at Hand*, 11, 2–3). His third publication, *A Forme of Sound Words, or, A Brief Family-Catechisme* (1682), in itself a contribution to a well-worn genre of pastoral writing, again reflected his anxieties about the threat of atheism and unbelief, and included a section 'Proofs that there is a God'. His date of death is as yet unknown.   SIDNEY LEE, *rev.* CAROLINE L. LEACHMAN

Sources Wood, *Ath. Oxon.*, new edn, 4.505–6 · Foster, *Alum. Oxon.* · I. Green, *The Christian's ABC: catechisms and catechising in England, c.1530–1740* (1996) · D. P. Walker, *The decline of hell: seventeenth-century discussions of eternal torment* (1964) · P. C. Almond, *Heaven and hell in Enlightenment England* (1994) · J. Brandon, *To pyr to aiōnion, or, Everlasting fire no fancy* (1678) · J. Brandon, *Happiness at hand, or, A plain and practical discourse of the joy of just men's souls in the state of separation from the body* (1687)

Brandon, John Raphael Rodrigues (1817–1877), architect and writer, was born in London on 5 April 1817, the second of six children of Joshua de Isaac Moses Rodrigues Brandon and his wife, Sarah. He was a pupil of J. Dédeau in Alençon, France, and in 1836 was articled to the architect Joseph T. Parkinson. Although fairly successful in private practice, which he carried on from 1841 to 1847 with his brother Joshua Arthur Rodrigues Brandon [*see below*] at Beaufort Buildings, Strand, he is best-known as an author. Both brothers were ardent students of Gothic architecture, and together they wrote a series of three works on Early English ecclesiastical architecture. The most important of these is *Parish Churches* (1848), which consists of a series of perspective views of sixty-three churches selected from most of the counties of England, accompanied by plans of each drawn to a uniform scale and a short textual description. Their *Analysis of Gothic Architecture* (1847) consists of a collection of more than 700 examples of doors, windows, and other details of existing ecclesiastical architecture compiled from actual measurements taken from little-known parish churches throughout the country, with remarks on the various classes of items. The last of the series, *Open Timber Roofs of the Middle Ages* (1849), is a collection of perspective and geometric and detail drawings of thirty-five of the best roofs found in different parish churches in eleven different English counties, with an introduction containing information on the timber roofing of the middle ages. The drawings given show at a glance the form and principle of construction of each roof. The work

> serves the one useful and necessary purpose of showing practically and constructively what the builders of the middle ages really did with the materials they had at hand, and how all those materials, whatever they were, were made to harmonise. (*The Builder*, 35, 1877, 1051)

For this reason, the Brandon brothers' works became pattern books, serving as a source of design for nineteenth-century architects.

Brandon exhibited designs at the Royal Academy between 1838 and 1874, including, in 1843, in the names of Brandon and Blore, a design for Colchester town hall, built in 1845; and in 1853, together with Robert Ritchie, a design for the interior of the Catholic Apostolic Church (since 1963 the church of Christ the King, the university church of London University). The Catholic Apostolic Church in Gordon Square, London, was built between 1850 and 1854 and, though reproducing features recorded by the Brandon brothers in their scholarly works, this extremely large church was criticized by a contemporary for its lack of originality of design (*RIBA Sessional Papers*, 10). Recent scholars, however, have drawn attention to the combination of thirteenth- and fifteenth-century Gothic precedents in its design, which offer a tangible record of the Brandon brothers' study of ecclesiastical architecture (see Stamp and Amery, 40–41). With his brother, Brandon had also previously designed several stations and engine-houses on the London to Croydon railway in the 1840s. These included chimneys disguised as the bell-towers of early Gothic churches, and the buildings were carried out in a medieval manor-house style. He also built, altered, and restored many churches. Among those he built were the small church of St Peter's in Great Windmill Street, London (1848; dem.), and Holy Trinity Church, Knightsbridge (1861; dem.). In 1860 Brandon became a fellow of the Institute of British Architects, but despite his scholarly knowledge of medieval and Gothic architecture, he failed to become a successful architect. This, together with the early death of his brother Joshua, and the death of his wife and child, unbalanced his already oversensitive temperament. On 8 October 1877 he committed suicide by shooting himself in the head at his chambers, 17 Clement's Inn, Strand.

Joshua Arthur Rodrigues Brandon (1822–1847), architect and author, was born on 9 February 1822 and had before his early death at the age of twenty-five attained what promised to become a considerable practice, particularly in church architecture, for which his studies along with his brother and the fame of their joint publications so well fitted him. With his brother he built the new corn exchange at Colchester, Essex (1845); Portswood Chapel (1847) and Christ Church (1846–7), Southampton, Hampshire (1847); and All Saints' Church, Sculthorpe, Norfolk (1847). He died on 11 December 1847 at 11 Beaufort Buildings, Strand.   ANNETTE PEACH

Sources *Dir. Brit. archs.* · L. D. Barnett and others, eds., *Bevis Marks records: being contributions to the history of the Spanish and Portuguese Congregation in London*, 5 vols. (1940–93) · *The Builder*, 35 (1877), 1041, 1051–2 · *The Builder*, 5 (1847), 603 · E. Jamilly, 'Anglo-Jewish architects, and architecture in the 18th and 19th centuries', *Transactions of the Jewish Historical Society of England*, 18 (1953–5), 127–41, esp. 135–6 · Graves, *RA exhibitors* · G. Stamp and C. Amery, *Victorian buildings of London, 1837–1887: an illustrated guide* (1980), 40–41 · *The architect's, engineer's, and building-trades' directory* (1868) · *Catalogue of the drawings collection of the Royal Institute of British Architects*, Royal Institute of British Architects, 20 vols. (1969–89) · C. Barry, *Sessional Papers of the Royal Institute of British Architects* (1877–8), 10 · d. cert. [Joshua Arthur Rodrigues Brandon]

Archives RIBA, biography file · RIBA, MSS collection | RIBA, nomination papers, Fv3 [missing]

Brandon, Joshua Arthur Rodrigues (1822–1847). *See under* Brandon, John Raphael Rodrigues (1817–1877).

Brandon, Katherine. *See* Bertie, Katherine (1519–1580).

Brandon, Richard (*d.* 1649), common hangman and probable executioner of Charles I, was the son of Gregory Brandon, whom he succeeded in the post of common hangman. His father was certainly hangman of London by 1611, when he was living in Rosemary Lane, Whitechapel, with Alice, his wife. The same year, on 8 January, he was convicted at Middlesex sessions of the manslaughter of Simon Morton, but escaped by pleading benefit of clergy. In 1617 a bizarre jape in the College of Heralds, played by the York herald on Garter (or possibly Clarenceux) king of arms, saw Gregory Brandon being granted a coat of arms. This led to the imprisonment of the two heralds and considerable mirth among Brandon's Whitechapel cronies. It has been suggested that the title 'esquire' popularly given to successive London hangmen was a direct result of this incident.

Richard Brandon, sometimes called 'young Gregory' by his contemporaries (indeed, for a time, the gallows at Tyburn was referred to as 'the Gregorian tree'), is believed to have assisted his father in his later years as hangman, and to have succeeded him (*c.*1639), allegedly claiming the post by inheritance. As notorious a character as his father, he is said to have prepared himself for his calling from an early age by decapitating cats and dogs. In 1641 Brandon was a prisoner in Newgate on a charge of bigamy, from which he seems to have cleared himself—possibly twice. He also lived in Rosemary Lane, with his wife, Mary, but it is unclear whether she was his original wife or an allegedly bigamous one. Brandon seems to have prided himself on his dextrous use of the axe, product of an unerring eye and a steady hand, and he apparently never needed to strike more than once. Those executed by him during the 1640s included the earl of Strafford (1641), Sir Alexander Carew (1644), Sir John Hotham and his son, and Archbishop Laud (1645). After the death sentence was passed on Charles I (28 January 1649), Brandon is said to have refused to carry out the execution; but on 30 January he was taken to the scaffold at Whitehall by a troop of horse and, masked, with false beard and periwig, decapitated the king with a single blow. Within an hour of the execution he allegedly received £30 for his pains, together with a handkerchief from the king's pocket, and an orange stuck full of cloves which he sold for 10s. In March 1649 he executed the earl of Holland, the duke of Hamilton, and Lord Capel, all with the same axe he had used on the king. Brandon died, reputedly full of remorse for taking the king's life, on 20 June 1649, and was buried the next day in Whitechapel churchyard. In the burial register, which calls him 'a ragman', a marginal note, in a different hand, added: 'This R. Brandon is supposed to have cut off the head of Charles the First' (Bland, 17).

After 1649 royalist rumour-mongers suggested that Brandon did indeed refuse to execute the king, and that the deed had been done by two troopers, Hulet and Walker, from the regiment of the regicide John Hewson. Other suggestions included the Scottish judge, Lord Stair, Hugh Peters, and Colonel George Joyce, who had been active in promoting the king's trial. An ill-informed French source confidently claimed that Fairfax and Cromwell personally executed the king. Even late into the seventeenth century various eccentric hermits and aged exhibitionists still claimed the sinister honour. After the Restoration, William Hulet was formally tried (October 1660) for his part in the king's execution, convicted by a jury, and sentenced to death, but he was later pardoned and released. The weight of probability suggests that Brandon was indeed the executioner. Three pamphlets in the Thomason collection, published in 1649, proclaim his confession to the deed. The pardon and release of Hulet, the skill with which the executioner delivered the single blow, Brandon's acknowledged presence at Whitehall on the fateful day, the statement on his burial certificate, the testimony of his widow—all these have convinced most historians, from S. R. Gardiner to C. V. Wedgwood, that Brandon wielded the fateful axe.   BASIL MORGAN

Sources J. Bland, *The common hangman* (1984) · *DNB* · C. V. Wedgwood, *The trial of Charles I* (1964) · P. Sidney, *The headsman of Whitehall* (1905) · B. Bailey, *Hangmen of England* (1989) · *N&Q*, 2 (1850) · *N&Q*, 2nd ser., 9–11 (1860–61) · J. G. Muddiman, *The trial of King Charles the First* (1928) · *The last will and testament of Richard Brandon, esquire* (1649) · *The confession of Richard Brandon the hangman—upon his death bed* (1649) · *A dialogue, or, A dispute between the late hangman and death* (1649)

Brandon, Samuel (*fl.* 1598), writer, is known only as the author of *The Tragicomoedi of the Vertuous Octavia* (1598). The play, probably written as a closet drama, draws heavily both on Sir Thomas North's translation of Plutarch and on Samuel Daniel's *Cleopatra* (Brandon, ed. McKerrow, v). That Brandon chooses to call his play a 'tragicomoedi' is presumably due to the fact that the eponymous heroine, who oscillates throughout between love for Antony and jealousy of Cleopatra, survives her difficulties (Collier, 3.78). Since its appearance in 1598, *Octavia* has been reprinted only twice: in 1909 by the Malone Society and in 1912 by Tudor Facsimile Texts. Although the work has been criticized for its disregard of the Aristotelian unities, its 'feebly drawn' characters, and its 'unimpassioned' speeches, it is not wholly without merit: along with George Chapman's *Seven Books of the Iliad*, which also appeared in 1598, Brandon's *Octavia* introduced the Greek compound epithet to English readers (Collier, 3.74–8). Two epistles between Octavia and Mark Antony are appended to the play and dedicated to Maria Thynne. The play itself is dedicated to her mother, Lucy Touchet, Lady Audley.

JOSEPH KNIGHT, *rev.* ELIZABETH GOLDRING

Sources J. P. Collier, *The history of English dramatic poetry*, 2nd edn, 3 vols. (1879) · S. Brandon, *The virtuous Octavia* (1598), ed. R. B. McKerrow (1909) · S. Brandon, *The virtuous Octavia*, ed. J. S. Farmer (1912) · D. E. Baker, *Biographia dramatica, or, A companion to the playhouse*, rev. I. Reed, new edn, 2 vols. (1782) · G. Langbaine, *An account of the English dramatick poets* (1691) · Arber, *Regs. Stationers*, vol. 3 · W. W. Greg, ed., *A companion to Arber* (1967) · E. K. Chambers, *The Elizabethan stage*, 4 vols. (1923), vol. 3, p. 236

Brandon, Sir Thomas (*d.* 1510), courtier and diplomat, was the third son of Sir William Brandon of Southwark (*d.* 1491) and his wife, Elizabeth Wingfield (*d.* 1497). With his eldest brother, William, who had been attainted for his part in the rebellion against Richard III of 1483, and John

Risley, he fled from East Mersea in November 1484 to join Henry Tudor in exile. Two months later he was offered a pardon by Richard III, as was the rebel garrison of Hammes, which he had daringly reinforced at the head of a party of thirty of Tudor's supporters. He presumably declined the offer, for he was in favour with Henry VII from the beginning of the reign, though there is no evidence that he fought at Bosworth (unlike his brother William, who carried Tudor's standard and was cut down by Richard III in person). In the spring of 1487 he commanded a naval force, in 1492 served on the French campaign, and was knighted after the battle of Blackheath in 1497. He sat in council on occasion and served the king as a diplomat, once in 1503 on a mission to Maximilian, king of the Romans, at Cologne and Antwerp, but more often in dealing with foreign ambassadors in England. In 1506 he led the party of courtiers dispatched to the south coast to meet Philip the Fair, duke of Burgundy, on his unexpected arrival in England.

An esquire for the king's body by September 1486, Brandon was an active courtier much involved with the king's horses and hawks. He took part in the baptism and knighting of Prince Arthur and the knighting of Prince Henry, jousted at court in 1494, and cut a splendid figure at the marriage of Prince Arthur and Katherine of Aragon in 1501, wearing a gold chain worth some £1400. From 1501, and probably from 1499, he served as master of the horse, a post to which he was reappointed by Henry VIII. He was also marshal of the king's bench prison in Southwark, as his father had been. He seems to have lived mostly in Southwark, where he leased part of the bishop of Winchester's manor. It is symptomatic of the concentration of his career at court that he was never named to any commission of the peace, though he was a commissioner for the aid of 1504 in Southwark and Suffolk.

In 1507 Brandon was elected to the Order of the Garter. His various grants from the king included the wardships of two successive lords Say in 1491 and 1509, the keepership of Freemantle Park, and the manor of Duddington. More significant still was the king's support for his marriage to two wealthy widows. Between August 1495 and May 1496 he married Anne Fiennes, daughter of Sir John Fiennes and Alice Fitzhugh, and granddaughter of Richard Fiennes, Lord Dacre of the South (d. 1483). She was the widow (as his third wife) of William, marquess of Berkeley (d. 1492). She died on 10 September 1497 and was buried in St George's Chapel, Windsor. Between August 1502 and February 1503, having paid £100 for the king's assistance in persuading the lady in question, Sir Thomas was married again, this time to Elizabeth Dynham (d. 1516), sister and coheir of John, Lord Dynham (d. 1501), and widow successively of Fulk Bourchier, Lord Fitzwarine (d. 1479), and Sir John Sapcotes (d. 1501).

Each of Brandon's marriages brought him control over substantial estates in the western counties, though the first led him into a dispute with Maurice Berkeley, and the second may have lain behind repeated trouble between him and Robert, second Lord Willoughby de Broke. His wives and his court service brought him considerable wealth despite the small extent of his own landed estate: bequests of cash and plate in his will totalled nearly £1000. Sir Thomas's career seemed set to continue prosperously under Henry VIII. He was an active councillor, retained his previous offices, and was appointed warden and chief justice of the royal forests south of Trent on 2 June 1509. But he died on 27 January 1510 and was buried on the 29th at the London Blackfriars. His heir was his nephew Charles *Brandon, first duke of Suffolk (c.1484–1545), but his will also made large provision for Lady Jane Guildford, widow of Sir Richard Guildford (d. 1506), whose servants had cared for him in his last illness; she in turn requested prayers for his soul in her will of 1538. His widow took a vow of celibacy before Bishop John Fisher (d. 1535) on 21 April 1510 and died on 19 October 1516, being buried in the priory of St Mary Overie, Southwark.   S. J. GUNN

Sources PRO · Chancery records · LP Henry VIII, vol. 1/1 · GEC, Peerage, new edn, vols. 2, 5 · J. Gairdner, ed., Letters and papers illustrative of the reigns of Richard III and Henry VII, 2 vols., Rolls Series, 24 (1861–3) · B. André, Historia regis Henrici septimi, ed. J. Gairdner, Rolls Series, 10 (1858) · W. Campbell, ed., Materials for a history of the reign of Henry VII, 2 vols., Rolls Series, 60 (1873–7) · A. H. Thomas and I. D. Thornley, eds., The great chronicle of London (1938) · Joannis Lelandi antiquarii de rebus Britannicis collectanea, ed. T. Hearne, [3rd edn], 6 vols. (1774) · R. Virgoe, 'Sir John Risley (1443–1512), courtier and councillor', Norfolk Archaeology, 38 (1981–3), 140–48, esp. 143 · The Anglica historia of Polydore Vergil, AD 1485–1537, ed. and trans. D. Hay, CS, 3rd ser., 74 (1950) · will, PRO, PROB 11/16, sig. 29 · J. Smyth, The Berkeley manuscripts: the lives of the Berkeleys ... 1066 to 1618, ed. J. Maclean, 3 vols. (1883–5) · C. G. Bayne and W. H. Dunham, eds., Select cases in the council of Henry VII, SeldS, 75 (1958) · register of John Fisher, CKS, DRb/Ar 1/13, fol. 37 · R. Fox, bishop's register, Hants. RO, Winchester diocesan records, 21M65/A1/20, fols. 59r–60r · Bodl. Oxf., MS Ashmole 1109, fol. 111r · inquisition post mortem, PRO, E 150/677/2

Wealth at death over £1000—bequests of cash and plate: will, PRO, PROB 11/16, sig. 29

Brandram, Samuel (1824–1892), reciter, born in London on 8 October 1824, was the only son of William Caldwell Brandram. He was educated at Merchant Taylors' and King's College schools in London and Trinity College, Oxford, from where he graduated with a BA in 1846 and received an MA three years later. At the university he was best known as an athlete. After leaving Oxford he became a student at Lincoln's Inn, and was called to the bar on 22 November 1850. He practised as a barrister until 1876, when, being short of money, he became a professional reciter.

From his university days, when he took part with Frank Talfourd in founding the first Oxford Dramatic Society, Brandram had shown great aptitude for the stage, and was also well known for his singing of ballads. During his vacations he used to act with the Canterbury Old Stagers and the Windsor Strollers. He first appeared as a reciter at Richmond, and very soon met with success. He had been a student of Shakespeare from his schooldays, and, although his miscellaneous programmes were admired, he was seen at his best when he gave a whole play of Shakespeare or Sheridan. He would recite in an almost complete form some dozen plays, among which *Macbeth* was his favourite, along with *Hamlet*, *A Midsummer Night's*

Dream, and *The Tempest*. He had an excellent memory and his voice was so flexible that he could give the three witches in *Macbeth* three distinct voices, and could make a convincing Portia, Ophelia, or Miranda. Brandram found northern audiences the most responsive, and Manchester became his favourite town. In course of time he married Julia Murray (*d.* 1907), an actress in Charles Kean's company, and eventually they had three sons and three daughters.

In 1881 Brandram published *Selected Plays of Shakespeare, Abridged for the Use of the Young*; it reached a fourth edition in 1892. The more important passages were printed in full, while short narratives supplied the place of the others. *Brandram's Speaker: a Set of Pieces in Prose and Verse Suitable for Recitation, with an Introductory Essay on Elocution* appeared in 1885. The same year Brandram also issued a further volume of *Selections from Shakespeare*. He became an honorary examiner of the Polytechnic School of Elocution and vice-president of the Richmond Athenaeum and devoted much time to promoting charitable goals. His last two recitals, at the Star and Garter, Richmond, and at Steinway Hall, were benefits. Brandram died at 6 Bentinck Street, Cavendish Square, London, on 7 November 1892, and was buried on the 10th in Richmond cemetery.

G. Le G. Norgate, rev. Nilanjana Banerji

Sources *The Era* (12 Nov 1892) · *ILN* (19 Nov 1892) · J. Foster, *Men-at-the-bar: a biographical hand-list of the members of the various inns of court*, 2nd edn (1885) · *Era Almanack and Annual* (1893) · W. K. R. Bedford, *Blackwood*, 153 (1893), 256–61 · *The Athenaeum* (12 Nov 1892), 674 · Foster, *Alum. Oxon.* · d. cert. · *CGPLA Eng. & Wales* (1892)
Likenesses J. E. Mayall, cabinet photograph, NPG · portrait, repro. in *ILN*
Wealth at death £1044 4s. 11d.: probate, 28 Nov 1892, *CGPLA Eng. & Wales*

Brandreth, Jeremiah [called the Nottingham Captain] (1786/1790–1817), revolutionary politician, is of unknown parentage. In the absence of information about his parentage or early life, rumour abounded following Brandreth's apprehension for his part in the Pentrich rising of 1817. To some, his sallow complexion suggested either a Gypsy or Irish provenance, while Thomas Denman, his defence counsel, likened him to a corsair; others believed he had been a sailor or a whitesmith and that he came from Exeter. His background, however, was less exotic. He was born in Wilford, Nottinghamshire, although the date is uncertain, into a long-established but hard-pressed family of framework-knitters from Sutton in Ashfield. It seems he spent some time in the army, but otherwise probably remained in the hosiery districts: he became a stockinger and married a local woman, Ann Bridget, in 1811. Indeed, it is possible that the mysterious Brandreth went silent to the gallows in order to protect colleagues in the secret networks of local protest, the east midlands underground which linked the Luddite industrial outbreaks of 1811–16 to the ill-fated political rising of 1817.

Plans for a general rising gathered momentum after the introduction of repressive legislation in 1817 to curb the radical meetings, societies, and newspapers which had flourished amid post-war distress and dislocation. Central planning meetings were held at Wakefield; these were attended by the veteran Jacobin Thomas Bacon of Pentrich as the Derbyshire delegate. Brandreth's involvement was at regional level, an extension perhaps of his alleged former role as a Luddite captain in the hosiery districts. He was a member of the north midland committee to which Bacon reported. At Wakefield, Bacon and the delegates agreed there should be simultaneous uprisings in the towns of the midlands and the north, a concentration of forces round Nottingham, and then a march on London. To ascertain likely support, Joseph Mitchell was deputed to tour the country: he soon acquired a travelling companion, W. J. Richards, the infamous Oliver the Spy.

Whether Oliver acted as *agent provocateur* or simply as an informer is not clear; furthermore, there is no concrete evidence of a meeting between Oliver and Brandreth. At the time Brandreth was living in Nottingham on parish relief at Wilford, out of work like many others in the 'Derbyshire Ribs' trade. He left Nottingham on 5 June, ahead of Oliver's last visit, to mobilize the villagers of Pentrich, Bacon's home base, in readiness for the rising finally fixed, after two postponements, for the night of 9 June. By this time several district delegate meetings had already been raided and there were considerable suspicions about Oliver. Brandreth, however, proceeded with his mission to lead the Derbyshire insurgents into Nottingham in sure expectation of the establishment of a provisional government. On the night of the 9th he led a contingent of men, over 100 strong, through pouring rain on the 14 mile march, stopping at houses *en route* to demand arms and support. On one occasion a farm labourer was accidentally shot, almost certainly by Brandreth. They arrived in Nottingham, wet and demoralized, to be confronted by a force of hussars ready in waiting. Brandreth managed to escape, but was eventually discovered and apprehended in a village in Nottinghamshire, whence he returned penniless to his wife (who was expecting their third child), having twice been turned off ships at Bristol bound for America. Tried by a special commission in Derby (where a veil was drawn over Oliver's role) the Nottingham Captain was executed at Nuns Green, Derby, on 7 November 1817 along with two of his lieutenants, William Turner and Isaac Ludlam, fellow members of the north midland committee.

Despite the persistent efforts of the prison chaplain to elicit a confession and establish the details of his past, Brandreth revealed nothing before his execution. His prison letters to his wife attest to a fair standard of literacy but they are devoid of explanation or recrimination. Other than his actions, Brandreth left no record of what Thomas Denman described as his stern and inflexible patriotism. In the absence of evidence, there has been much speculation and controversy about his motives and qualities as a Regency revolutionary. Some historians, critical and dismissive of the underground tradition, have branded him a 'desperate fellow', an impulsive and unrealistic hot-head who duped the credulous folk of Pentrich into foolish violence by his commanding personality and promises of roast beef, plum pudding, newly coined money, and pleasure trips on the River Trent (White, 176–7). Others depict Brandreth in heroic stature; a community-bred, working-class activist, leader of 'one of the first attempts in history to mount a wholly proletarian insurrection, without any middle-class support' (Thompson, 733). In this debate, there is no place for the traditional interpretation of Brandreth as the tool and dupe of Oliver the Spy. JOHN BELCHEM

Sources DNB · J. Stevens, *England's last revolution: Pentrich, 1817* (1977) · R. J. White, *Waterloo to Peterloo* (1968) · E. P. Thompson, *The making of the English working class*, new edn (1968) · M. I. Thomis, 'Brandreth, Jeremiah', *BDMBR*, vol. 1
Archives PRO, Home Office papers, corresp., HO 40/6; HO 42/165, 171
Likenesses Neele, stipple (after W. Pegg), BM · W. G. Spencer, drawing, ink on ivory, BM · coloured etching, BM, NPG · prints, Derbyshire County Library

Brandreth, Joseph (1746–1815), physician, the son of Thomas Brandreth, was born in Ormskirk, Lancashire, and graduated MD in Edinburgh in 1770. His thesis, *De febribus intermittentibus* ('On the intermittent fevers'), was published in the same year and dedicated to his father, *patri optimo* ('best of fathers'), and to William Cullen, *praeceptori spectatissimo et amico vero* ('most watchable teacher and true friend'). Nothing is known about Brandreth's family and early education other than it was not privileged.

Although his success was attributed to his own industry and talents, Brandreth also had the good fortune to succeed about 1776 to the successful Liverpool practice of Matthew Dobson. He went on to become a successful physician and active participant in the civic life of Liverpool. Awarded the freedom of the city in 1802, his house, a mansion built in 1680 (and since demolished), was described as 'tolerably large' (Picton, 2.147). Brandreth was physician to the busy Liverpool Dispensary from its beginning in 1778 (with 2062 patients in the first year) and was, according to the *Dictionary of National Biography*, primarily responsible for the charity's foundation, though there is no remaining evidence to confirm this. Two years later he joined the staff of the Liverpool Infirmary, where he remained active until 1810. He was also physician to the new Fever Hospital and to the lunatic asylum of Liverpool, and he was a generous subscriber to the building fund for the Liverpool Medical Institution. Twice president (1800 and 1804) of the Liverpool Medical Library, which from 1779 was run from the dispensary, Brandreth was also active in what was then the Liverpool Library at the Lyceum; established in 1758, this was probably the first circulating library in Britain.

Nothing is known of Brandreth's wife, but the couple had at least two sons and a daughter: Joseph was a surgeon and practised in Liverpool, whereas Thomas Shaw *Brandreth (1788–1873) was an inventor and classical scholar; Catharine married William Rowe Lyall, dean of Canterbury. In 1791 Brandreth wrote a letter on the therapeutic effects of bathing feverish patients in cold water and vinegar which was published in *Medical Commentaries*. He was

on the board that decided upon the suitability of surgeons applying for jobs on slave ships, and may also have been a lecturer, since he enjoyed a reputation for an excellent memory. Brandreth died in Liverpool on 10 April 1815 'after a long and painful illness' (*Monthly Repository*, 254).

Brandreth's historical significance lies in his participation in institutional transformations in the medical world of Liverpool and not, despite his attentiveness to medical science, from any outstanding contributions to medical knowledge. His thesis on fevers appears not to have had any impact on the profession. Brandreth's opinions on the use of cold water and vinegar in typhus (Cullen's word for fevers that included delirium and stupor) perhaps originated with him but we cannot be sure; according to his colleague James Currie, it was a therapy also practised by others at the infirmary. The treatment was unorthodox: following humour-based theories of fever which had been in place for more than 2000 years, most practitioners and patients believed fever to be caused, not cured, by the sudden exposure of hot bodies to a cold environment. Hence most therapies for fever involved warming, not cooling, the patient. It was Currie, however, who wrote extensively on the cold-water therapy, and who made the most of the discovery.

Despite his 'unexampled success' (*GM*, 472) and 'considerable celebrity' (Picton, 2.147), through lack of evidence of his life and its course of events Brandreth is condemned to be recalled (if at all) as an instance of a type of medical reformer rather than celebrated as the rich subject that he probably was; his activity in Liverpool life and society, and his role in the dispensary, recalls his better-known London contemporary J. C. Lettsom, another successful physician dedicated to the reform of metropolitan life. However, Brandreth was held with affection and esteem, according to the obituary in the *Monthly Repository*, and made long-lasting friendships; he brought to his patients a face lined with 'deep thought' and 'anxious care', married with 'the smile of kindness and benevolence' (p. 254). L. A. F. DAVIDSON

Sources *Liverpool Mercury* (14 April 1815); repr. in *GM*, 1st ser., 85 (1815), 472 · *Monthly Repository*, 10 (1815), 254 · T. H. Bickerton and R. M. B. MacKenna, *A medical history of Liverpool from the earliest days to the year 1920*, ed. H. R. Bickerton (1936) · J. A. Picton, *Memorials of Liverpool*, rev. edn, 2 (1875) · G. McLoughlin, *A short history of the first Liverpool Infirmary* (1978) · J. A. Shepherd, *A history of the Liverpool Medical Institution* (1979) · L. G. Wilson, 'Fevers', *Companion encyclopedia of the history of medicine*, ed. B. W. F. Bynum and R. Porter, 1 (1993), 382–411 · W. F. Bynam and V. Nutton, eds., *Theories of fever from antiquity to the Enlightenment* (1981) · *British medicine in an age of reform* [London 1987], ed. R. French and A. Wear (1991) · *DNB* · E. Evans, *Catalogue of engraved British portraits*, 2 [1853], 49
Likenesses E. Scriven, line and stipple engraving (after J. Allen), NPG · W. Ward, mezzotint, BM · portrait, repro. in Bickerton, *Medical history of Liverpool*

Brandreth, Thomas Shaw (1788–1873), inventor and classical scholar, was born on 24 July 1788 in Cheshire, the son of the physician Joseph *Brandreth (1746–1815). He attended Eton College and later entered Trinity College, Cambridge, where he took his BA degree in 1810, with the distinctions of second wrangler, second Smith's prizeman, and chancellor's medallist, and his degree of MA in 1813. He was elected to a fellowship at his college, was called to the bar, and practised at Liverpool, but his liking for scientific inventions interfered with his legal career. He was elected a fellow of the Royal Society in 1821. He had previously invented his logometer, or 10 foot gunter rule. He also invented a friction wheel and a double-check clock escapement, all of which he patented. His scientific pursuits led to a close friendship with George Stephenson, and he became one of the directors of the Liverpool and Manchester Railway, but resigned shortly before its completion. He was actively involved in the survey of the line, especially the section across Chat Moss. The government limitation of railway speed to 10 miles an hour, which threatened to destroy the hopes of the promoters of steam locomotion, led Brandreth to invent a machine in which the weight of a horse was utilized on a moving platform, and a speed of 15 miles an hour was expected. However, the success of the *Rocket* locomotive soon established the supremacy of steam, and Brandreth's invention was used only where steam power proved too expensive, as in Lombardy and in some parts of the United States.

Brandreth married, in 1822, a daughter of Ashton Byrom, of Fairview, near Liverpool; they had two daughters, and five sons. His scientific pursuits and a move to London, where he had few legal contacts, considerably reduced his practice. He was offered a position as a judge in Jamaica, but decided instead to retire to Worthing and devote himself to the education of his children. At Worthing he resumed his classical studies, and pursued a learned and difficult inquiry into the use of the digamma in the Homeric poems, publishing the results in a treatise entitled *A Dissertation on the Metre of Homer* (1844). He also published a text of the *Iliad* with the digamma inserted and Latin notes. This was followed by a line by line translation of the *Iliad* into blank verse (1846), which was well received as an accurate and scholarly version. He also took a lively interest in the affairs of Worthing, and was largely instrumental in perfecting the extensive water and drainage improvements of the town, where he was chairman of the first local board, and JP for West Sussex. He died at Worthing on 27 May 1873.

STANLEY LANE-POOLE, *rev.* R. C. COX

Sources private information (1885) · Venn, *Alum. Cant.* · election certificate, RS

Wealth at death under £40,000: resworn probate, Oct 1873, *CGPLA Eng. & Wales*

Brandt, Augustus Ferdinand (1835–1904), merchant banker, was born on 3 April 1835 at Archangel in Russia, the eldest son of Wilhelm Brandt (1802–1857), merchant, and his wife, Pauline Amburger. He came from a German merchant family that had been prominent in Russia's international trade since the end of the eighteenth century, with an agency in London from 1805. His early life was spent in Archangel and then St Petersburg, where his father headed the trading house Wilhelm Brandt & Co. He was educated at the private school of Dr Carl May in that city, and then travelled to England to serve a commercial apprenticeship with the Liverpool firm Blessig, Braun & Co.

With the premature death of his father in 1857 the 21-year-old Brandt returned briefly to St Petersburg to co-manage Wilhelm Brandt & Co. However, he was most anxious to make a career in London; in 1858, with that end in mind, he persuaded his uncle, Edmund Brandt, who ran the London branch, E. H. Brandt's Sons & Co., to change places with him and move to St Petersburg. In 1863 Brandt married Elisabeth Oesterreich (1835–1922); they had at least two sons.

Brandt's brother-in-law, Hermann Loehnis, a partner in Bunge, Loehnis & Co., New York, joined Brandt's London house in 1858. At the end of the same year his father's cousin, Adolphus Brandt, retired, and Brandt was able to strengthen his control over the London firm. This was subsequently reinforced by his younger brothers Alfred Ernst and Arthur Henry also joining the family business, when the company's name became Wilhelm Brandt's Sons & Co., under which it traded until well into the twentieth century. Another important stage came in 1865 when the London house and that in St Petersburg were separated—Augustus left the St Petersburg firm and his uncle Edmund left the London one.

Under Brandt's guidance the British firm scaled down its trading activities in Russia, where it had acted as commission agent for the sale of Russian staples such as timber and grain and for the import into Russia of colonial products for the account of the Archangel and St Petersburg houses. It shifted its focus to other parts of the world—to India, Japan, and Argentina, selling these countries' products on commission. The St Petersburg house, Wilhelm Brandt & Co., was liquidated in 1878, and in 1885 the connection with the rapidly growing Russian firm of E. H. Brandt was severed too. Thereafter, the chief trading connection that Wilhelm Brandt's Sons & Co. had with Russia was in grain dealings with Blessig & Co., St Petersburg, run by Brandt's schoolfriend Edward Blessig. Brandt did, however, purchase substantial shareholdings in two Russian textile concerns, the Voskresensky and the Yekaterinhof mills, jointly with another friend, the Bremen-born textile magnate, Baron Ludwig Knoop.

The Russian link still proved profitable for Brandt. His inheritance of £10,000 from his father's will in 1857 had been turned into a private fortune of £25,000 by the time of his marriage in 1863. When Hermann Loehnis withdrew from the firm in 1877, his 25 per cent share of the firm was worth £44,000, indicating that the total capital of the firm at that time was £176,000.

Profitable contacts were also established in Argentina and most notably with the Buenos Aires firm of Ernesto Tornquist & Co., which became one of Argentina's leading export houses and, later still, the country's largest private bank. Initially its dealings with Brandts involved the export of grain and other commodities, but later it came to include banking and stock-exchange dealings. Brandts were able to offer large-scale credit facilities to the Argentina firm.

As a consequence of the crisis at Barings in 1890, which Brandts helped to alleviate by contributing £25,000 (a substantial, if modest, sum) to the guarantee fund, the firm established links with Argentina's only large-scale meat-freezing plant, owned by the Sansinena family, who were forced to suspend payments. The company was reorganized as the Sansinena Company, with creditors such as Baring Brothers being paid off with shares in the new company. Over the years Brandt bought small blocks of these shares, which initially traded at a heavy discount, and when the company's profits improved during the Second South African War, Brandts acquired a substantial block of the Sansinena shares held by Barings.

In 1886 Brandt made an unsuccessful attempt to expand the firm's Indian business through the purchase of the Calcutta house, C. Scholvin & Co. Its name was changed to A. H. Brandt, under the charge of Augustus's youngest brother, Arthur Henry Brandt, whom he had taken into partnership in 1880. In order to promote the new venture Brandt invested in the newly established Hamburg–Calcutta line and managed to secure for it exclusive representation in Calcutta. Despite this the branch never really prospered and it closed in 1892.

Wilhelm Brandt's Sons & Co. also moved into the insurance business, initially as agents and brokers in order to secure cover with underwriters on the merchandise the company was shipping or had financed. Because of its reputation in this field the firm's partners were invited onto the boards of several major British insurance companies. Between 1871 and 1875 Augustus Brandt served as a director of the Marine Insurance Company Ltd.

Although Brandt and his wife moved to Hamburg in 1880 for health reasons, he continued to exercise control over the affairs of the company through the medium of postal and telegraph communications. His closest friend here was Max Schinkel, who in the 1880s was deputy chairman of the Norddeutsche Bank, Hamburg's leading banking house. Through this link Wilhelm Brandt's Sons & Co. enhanced its prestige in Hamburg banking circles by securing the Norddeutsche Bank's acceptance business. However, this declined after 1895, when the Norddeutsche Bank was taken over by the Disconto-gesellschaft, which set up its own London branch.

At the beginning of 1895 Brandt brought his two eldest sons, Augustus Philip and Henry Bernard, into the partnership. A few months later his younger brother Alfred Ernst died of tuberculosis. Shortly afterwards disagreements between Brandt and his brother Arthur Henry resulted in the latter's withdrawing his one-third share of the firm's capital and setting up on his own account as Arthur H. Brandt & Co.

Despite such vicissitudes, Wilhelm Brandt's Sons & Co. under Augustus Brandt's guidance achieved a position among the first rank of accepting houses in London. It continued to flourish and to extend its geographical spread. By 1904 the firm had a clerical staff of more than eighty and a capital of £750,000. The essence of Brandt's commercial strategy had been to make the business of acceptance credits the core of his firm's commercial operations. Additionally he had sought to restrict business to firms with a first-class reputation.

Brandt died at Hamburg on 24 January 1904, leaving an estate in Britain of almost £1 million. His policies were continued with great success by his sons and, by the outbreak of the First World War, Wilhelm Brandt's Sons & Co. was one of the leading merchant banks in the City of London.　　　STUART THOMPSTONE

Sources E. Amburger, 'Wilhelm Brandt and the story of his enterprises', 1937 · E. Amburger, *Deutsche in Staat, Wirtschaft und Gesellschaft Russlands: die Familie Amburger in St Petersburg, 1770–1920* (Wiesbaden, 1986) · U. Nott., Brandt MSS · C. F. Menke, 'Die wirtschaftlichen und politischen Beziehungen der Hansestädte zu Russland im 18. und frühen 19. Jahrhundert', diss., Göttingen, 1959 · S. R. Thompstone, 'The organisation and financing of Russian foreign trade before 1914', PhD diss., U. Lond., 1991 · CGPLA Eng. & Wales (1904)
Archives U. Nott. | BLPES, Wilhelm Brandt's Sons & Co. MSS
Likenesses P. de Laszlo, portrait, priv. coll.
Wealth at death £913,836 16s. 6d.: probate, 21 April 1904, CGPLA Eng. & Wales

Brandt, Francis Frederick (1819–1874), barrister and author, was born at Gawsworth rectory, Cheshire, the eldest son of the Revd Francis Brandt (d. 1854), rector of Aldford, Cheshire, from 1842 to 1850, and Ellinor, second daughter of Nicholas Grimshaw, twice mayor of Preston, Lancashire. He was educated at nearby Macclesfield grammar school, entered the Inner Temple in 1839, and practised for some years as a special pleader.

Called to the bar on 30 April 1847, Brandt took the north Wales and Chester circuit. He was a successful and popular leader of the Chester and Knutsford sessions, where he was particularly adept with local juries in criminal trials, had a fair business in London, especially as an arbitrator or referee, was one of the revising barristers on his circuit, and was employed for many years as a reporter for *The Times* in the common pleas. About 1864 he was offered and declined an Indian judgeship.

In his earlier days Brandt wrote in magazines and in *Bell's Life*, and he later produced several books. Apart from one novel, *Frank Morland's Manuscripts, or, Memoirs of a Modern Templar* (1859), all were on subjects connected with sports or gaming, though Brandt never indulged in either. His first book, *Habet! A Short History on the Law of the Land as it Affects Pugilism* (1857), attempted to defend the legality of prize-fighting. His most substantial was *Games, Gaming, and Gamesters' Law* (1871), a book of considerable legal and antiquarian research, which reached a second edition.

Convivial and humorous, Brandt was a familiar and popular figure in the courts and his inn, where he lived unmarried in chambers at 8 Fig Tree Court. Until his health deteriorated he was a zealous member of the Inns of Court rifle corps, but he suffered increasingly from a severe neuralgic complaint. His death, at his chambers on 6 December 1874, was the result of inflammation of the lungs. He was buried in Highgate cemetery.

G. C. BOASE, rev. PATRICK POLDEN

Sources *Law Times* (19 Dec 1874), 125 · *Solicitors' Journal*, 19 (1874–5), 106 · *The Times* (8 Dec 1874) · G. Ormerod, *The history of the county*

palatine and city of Chester, 2nd edn, ed. T. Helsby, 2 (1882), 760 · *VCH Lancashire*, 7.74 · Boase, *Mod. Eng. biog.* · Allibone, *Dict.*
Wealth at death   under £9000: resworn probate, Dec 1875, *CGPLA Eng. & Wales*

Brandt, Hermann Wilhelm [Bill] (1904–1983), photographer, was born on 2 May 1904 in Hamburg (though he later encouraged the belief that he was born in south London), the second of four sons (there were no daughters) of Ludwig Walter Brandt, merchant (who had been brought up in London), and his wife, Lili Merck. Perhaps because of the English connections of his family and the high feelings caused by the First World War, Brandt's schooldays were intensely unhappy. He contracted tuberculosis in his youth and at the age of twenty was sent to a sanatorium in Davos, Switzerland. Two and a half years later he travelled to Vienna, seeking a cure by means of psychoanalysis, but doctors there pronounced him free of the disease. Through his younger brother Rolf, he became part of the brilliant artistic circle of Dr Eugenie Schwarzwald. She placed Brandt in the studio of Trude Fleischmann, a leading portrait photographer, to learn photography. There he met Eva Boros, who was to become his first wife. Perhaps through the agency of Dr Schwarzwald, Ezra Pound sat for Brandt in 1928. The poet provided an introduction to Man Ray, in whose Paris studio the young photographer served as an assistant for three months in 1929–30. Brandt always spoke of this period with enchantment. He was thrilled by the films of Dalí and Buñuel and inspired by the enormous new possibilities offered by the surrealist movement in its heyday.

Brandt continued his apprenticeship in Paris, making observant street photographs which became part of his classic *œuvre*. In typically cosmopolitan style, he married his Hungarian wife, Eva (daughter of Joseph Boros), in Barcelona in 1932. They settled in London and Brandt began to publish his photographs in the *News Chronicle*. His first impressions of England were collected in his first book, *The English at Home* (1936). The book is notable for its pointed contrasts of upper- and working-class life, but also for Brandt's sheer relish for the mysteries and rituals of Englishness. He had privileged access to these through various Brandt uncles and their households. Friends and family acted out various roles in Brandt's photographs. His master in the art of documentary photography, or photojournalism, was the Paris-based Transylvanian Brassai, whose beneficial influence was even more in evidence in Brandt's *A Night in London* (1938). Influenced by J. B. Priestley's *English Journey* (1934) and the widespread concerns aroused by the Jarrow crusade (1936), Brandt and his wife travelled to Yorkshire and the north-east in 1937. He made the definitive images of coal-searchers, although these were not published until the next decade, and of the bleak beauty of the (then) coal-black cities such as Halifax. Soon he was photographing the eerie tranquillity of blacked-out London during the phony war. He had a stimulating editor and friend in Tom Hopkinson, for whom he worked with great creativity and productiveness at *Lilliput* (founded 1936) and *Picture Post* (founded 1938). In the 1940s he also began to take commissions

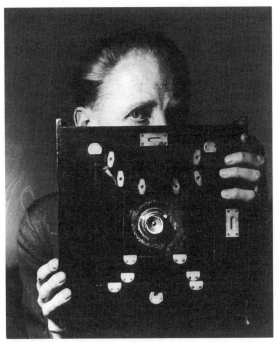

Hermann Wilhelm [Bill] **Brandt** (1904–1983), by Laelia Goehr, 1945

from Carmel Snow, the dashing editor of *Harper's Bazaar*, through which Brandt's work became well known to an American audience. Aside from the magazines, Brandt received other commissions. For the Ministry of Information he produced his famous photographs of London's makeshift bomb shelters in underground stations and their rows of sleeping occupants. For the National Buildings Record he photographed major monuments. During the 1940s Brandt produced two more great series: his portraits of young writers and his landscapes. The former included such stars as Elizabeth Bowen (to whose writings he was particularly drawn), Robert Graves, and Dylan Thomas. The landscapes—a reflection of national identity in a time of war—feature places associated with the Brontës, Thomas Hardy, Dr Johnson, and others. The series originally appeared in *Lilliput* and was republished, with further images, in Brandt's third classic book, *Literary Britain*, introduced by John Hayward, in 1951.

In 1944 Brandt embarked on yet another exploration. He acquired a mahogany and brass-view camera with a wide-angle lens. It was actually a Kodak camera made for police work, but Brandt used it to photograph the nude. The ground glass yielded only an indistinct image of the subject, and Brandt had to work almost 'blind'. He later said that he chose this camera because he wanted to see differently, 'like a mouse, a fish or a fly'. The wide-angle lens dramatically expanded and diminished the figure like an episode from *Alice in Wonderland*, a book in which Brandt—like other surrealists—delighted. Brandt's vision of the nude was more directly informed by his admiration for Arp, Matisse, Moore, and Picasso. The series began in domestic interiors but was later extended to beaches in southern England and northern France. Brandt found that a Hasselblad with a Superwide lens could give him the same results as the old Kodak, and he also used the newer camera for his later portraits. *Perspective of Nudes* appeared in 1961, followed by a career survey, *Shadow of Light*, in 1966. These books, and a retrospective exhibition at the Museum of Modern Art, New York (1969), and the Hayward Gallery, London (1970, followed by a UK tour), brought Brandt to the attention of a new generation. Lucky pilgrims were welcomed by Brandt to his second-floor flat in Airlie Gardens, Kensington, to find an enchanting interior that was at once Victorian, surrealist, and contemporary, with stuffed seabirds recalling his landscapes, Brandt's own collages formed of beach-combed seaweeds and shells, and lively modern painted reliefs by his brother Rolf. They found that Brandt himself was unexpectedly boyish, fond of laughter—and lovable. He was also genuinely modest. He must have charmed a large audience when he claimed, in a BBC television documentary about him, that 'anyone could have taken' his famous picture of maids ready to serve dinner (1936).

It was mainly because of Brandt that the climate of opinion about photography changed in Britain. Photography was habitually thought of as the preserve of celebrity portraitists, commercial dullards, and fashionable chancers, but Brandt showed that photography could be informed by the imagination and create works of subtle, profound, visual art. This was recognized by many accolades in his later years: an honorary degree from the Royal College of Art in 1977, an award as royal designer for industry in 1978, and an honorary fellowship from the Royal Photographic Society in 1980. He was represented by Marlborough Fine Art in London and New York and exhibited and published widely until his death.

Bill Brandt—Billy to his closest friends—was tall, fair-haired, slim, and handsome, with a beautiful smile and a surprisingly hearty laugh. He always kept a slight accent, but in later life he refused to admit to being German or even to speaking the language (although he was never naturalized). Tom Hopkinson said that Brandt had a voice 'as loud as a moth'. He was ultra-sensitive, private, and shy, and suffered from diabetes. Despite his apparent frailty, Brandt was—for many—the most vigorous, compelling, and poetic photographer working in Britain in modern times. His archive is kept at his former home in London; a major retrospective was held at the Edwynn Monte Gallery, New York, in 2001.

Brandt's second wife, whom he met in the early 1940s, was Marjorie (*d.* 1971), daughter of Henry James Becket. On 21 December 1972 he married Dorothy Anne (Noya) Kernot, widowed daughter of Ivan Leslover. Brandt died at St Stephen's Hospital, Chelsea, London, on 20 December 1983.   COLIN FORD, *rev.* MARK HAWORTH-BOOTH

Sources C. Connolly and M. Haworth-Booth, *Bill Brandt: Shadow of light*, 2nd edn (1977) • M. Hiley, *Bill Brandt: nudes, 1945–80* (1980) • A. Ross, *Bill Brandt: portraits* (1982) • M. Haworth-Booth, *Bill Brandt: literary Britain*, 2nd edn (1984) • M. Haworth-Booth and D. Mellor, *Bill Brandt, behind the camera* (1985) • N. Warburton, *Bill Brandt: selected texts and bibliography* (1993) • M. Gasser, 'Bill Brandt in Switzerland and Austria', *History of Photography*, 21/4 (1997), 303–13 • personal knowledge (2004) • m. cert. [Dorothy Anne Kernot] • d. cert.
Likenesses L. Goehr, photograph, 1945, V&A [*see illus.*] • R. Hill, photograph, repro. in Warburton, *Bill Brandt*, frontispiece

Brandwood, James (1739–1826), Quaker minister, was born on 11 November 1739 at New House, Entwistle, near Rochdale, where his parents were yeoman farmers. In adulthood Brandwood practised as a land surveyor and conveyancer, and is also said to have acted as the steward of the Turton estate, near Bolton. After a visit to the Friends' meeting at Crawshawbooth, Brandwood ceased to attend the Anglican services at Turton Chapel. He joined the Quakers in 1761, and a meeting was shortly afterwards settled at Edgworth, near Bolton, where he lived for many years. His religious views deprived him of his fair share of his inheritance and he received only an annuity of £25.

As a recognized minister of the Society of Friends, Brandwood visited various parts of England, and in 1787 went to Wales in the company of James Birch. During the first decade of the nineteenth century Brandwood appears to have taken a much less active role in meetings, and in 1813 he ceased to be an acknowledged minister. He was reinstated in 1824, when he settled at Westhoughton, also near Bolton, whereupon he visited many of the southern meetings. He died, unmarried, on 23 March 1826 and was buried in the Quaker burial-ground at Westhoughton. A selection of his letters and papers, dating from 1782 to 1823 and dealing with matters of religious experience, was edited by John Bradshaw of Manchester, who published the volume in 1828.

W. E. A. AXON, *rev.* PHILIP CARTER

Sources *Letters and extracts of letters of James Brandwood*, ed. J. Bradshaw (1828) • J. C. Scholes, *Biographical sketch of James Brandwood* (1882) • J. Smith, ed., *A descriptive catalogue of Friends' books*, 2 vols. (1867); suppl. (1893)

Brangwyn, Sir Frank William (1867–1956), artist, was born at 24 rue du Vieux Bourg, Bruges, on 13 May 1867; his forenames were registered in Bruges as François Guillaume. He was the first son of William Curtis Brangwyn (1839–1907), an ecclesiastical architect, church decorator, and craftsman of Welsh origin, born in Buckinghamshire, and of Eleanor Griffiths (*b.* 1842), who came from Brecon. They were Roman Catholics. Brangwyn had two elder sisters and was followed by three brothers. His father, a follower of Pugin, had worked for G. E. Street before moving to Bruges, where he carried out a number of mural paintings, frescos, and mosaics, as well as designing several important buildings and, notably, being responsible for the reconstruction of the church of St André (Sint Andries). He also designed textiles and ran a workshop in which local craftsmen were trained. The family returned to London in 1875, having made a substantial contribution to the cultural life of Bruges; William Curtis Brangwyn then worked on the design of Tower Bridge with Sir Horace Jones.

At the age of eight Frank Brangwyn was sent to Westminster City School, where he remained until he was

Sir Frank William Brangwyn (1867–1956), by Emil Otto Hoppé, 1909

twelve. He was a poor and erratic scholar, frequently playing truant and preferring to help in his father's workshop. His father sent him to draw in the South Kensington Museum, where he was befriended and encouraged by Harold Rathbone, a former pupil of Ford Madox Brown, and by Arthur Heygate Mackmurdo, a protégé of John Ruskin, who founded the Century Guild. Mackmurdo introduced the young Brangwyn to William Morris, who employed him (c.1882–1884) as a glazier and, later, on inlay work, embroidery, and wallpapers. Brangwyn also began to develop as a painter, and in 1885, when still in his teens, he exhibited *A Bit on the Esk* (oil, now lost) at the Royal Academy. It was bought by a shipowner. A passion for the sea led Brangwyn to join the Royal Naval Volunteer Reserve for a period and he rapidly gained a reputation for seascapes and landscapes. He persuaded the purchaser of *A Bit on the Esk* to let him travel on board a freighter which sailed in 1888 to Constantinople and the Black Sea. From this voyage he returned with a great many paintings and studies, and painted his largest and most ambitious composition, *Burial at Sea* (oil, 1890; Art Gallery and Museum, Glasgow), which was executed in a style influenced by the realist painters Jules Bastien-Lepage and H. H. La Thangue, grey and close-toned in general colour. It was awarded a medal at the Paris Salon of 1891. An approach which was to become more characteristic, however, was shown in *The Golden Horn, Constantinople* (oil, 1890; Toledo, Ohio), which is vigorously painted and in brighter colours. Another long sea journey was undertaken in 1890, when

Brangwyn visited Antwerp, the coast of Spain, Tunis, Tripoli, Jaffa, Constantinople, Izmir, Trebizond, and Galatz. On his return to England in 1891 he held his first one-man show, 'From Scheldt to Danube', at the Royal Arcade Gallery, Bond Street, London. Subsidized by Larkin's Gallery he revisited Spain in 1891 in the company of the Scottish colourist Arthur Melville, who influenced Brangwyn decisively to intensify his use of colour. Brangwyn travelled on to South Africa and possibly also to Zanzibar.

In 1892 Brangwyn began to do illustrations for *The Graphic*, and his international reputation had grown to the point that he became a corresponding member of the Munich Secession. A visit to Morocco in 1893 confirmed his admiration for Delacroix, and Brangwyn's fresh, bright colour and lively handling of paint, remarked on with admiration by Wassily Kandinsky in his *Über das Geistige in der Kunst* (1912), was further developed. *The Slave Market* (oil; Atkinson Art Gallery, Southport) and *The Buccaneers* (oil; Washington University Art Gallery, St Louis), both of 1892, are evidence of this influence. A work similar in style, *Market in Morocco*, was bought by the French government in 1895.

In 1895 Samuel Bing commissioned Brangwyn to decorate the façade of his new, and soon to be celebrated, art gallery, L'Art Nouveau, in Paris. A striking design of horizontal stripes, with two ornamental friezes of stylized floral motifs and others evoking Japanese woodcuts, made a sensational impact, as did his decoration, *Dancing*, for the entrance hall during the first 'Salon de l'art nouveau'. His carpet of this period, 'La vigne' (Stedelijke Musea, Bruges), resembles William Morris's 'Trellis' wallpaper in composition; at the same time his prolific creative output of paintings, architectural decorations, and applied art placed him at the heart of the European avant-garde. He became a corresponding member of the Vienna Secession, when it was formed in 1897, and was invited along with other foreign artists, such as Rodin and Whistler, to exhibit in their first exhibition in 1898.

Between 1902 and 1920 Brangwyn executed a prodigious number of mural commissions, including monumental series or panels for Skinner's Hall in London; for the Venice Biennale (where he was awarded a gold medal); for Leeds City Art Gallery; Lloyd's Register; the county court house, Cleveland, Ohio; the Manitoba legislative building, Winnipeg; Christ's Hospital, Horsham, and the state capitol of Missouri in Jefferson City, as well as mosaics for St Aidan's Church, Leeds, and interiors for R. H. Kitson's Casa Cuseni, Taormina, in Sicily. Brangwyn was a prolific artist in many media, designing metalwork, furniture, textiles, ceramics, and glass, as well as making many powerful etchings, lithographs, and woodcuts. A consistent feature of his painting, drawing, and graphic art was his homage to work—to physical effort—expressed in Michelangelesque terms; he always regarded himself as a man of the people and identified himself with their labour. Brangwyn was made an associate of the Royal Academy in 1904, and a Royal Academician in 1919. At that period his fame was worldwide. Honours were conferred on him by the ruling families, the governments, the academies, and the leading institutions of many countries, including France, Germany, the Netherlands, Belgium, and Italy. During the First World War, as an official war artist, he mainly concentrated on propaganda posters.

After the war Brangwyn was given what he regarded as his most important commission; this was for a series of large murals to cover the north and south walls of the royal gallery in the House of Lords. The Lords had decided, in 1924, that there should be a memorial to the peers and members of their families who had died in the recent conflict. Lord Iveagh offered to pay for the whole work and in 1926 he gave the commission to Brangwyn. Brangwyn first designed a series of compositions based on scenes of battle, to harmonize in subject matter and colour with the existing long murals by Daniel Maclise, which are on the east and west walls. After Brangwyn had worked for two years, however, Lord Iveagh could not accept the grim realities depicted (*A Tank in Action*, tempera on canvas, 1925–6, is now in the National Museum and Gallery of Wales, Cardiff) and asked Brangwyn to start afresh on a quite different scheme. The new series, in radiant colours, was to evoke instead the beauty of the dominions and colonies which had fought for the British. These, the *British Empire Panels*, are a celebration of the people, the flora, and the fauna of those lands in a profusion of mainly tropical vegetation. They are flamboyant, flat, and decorative in their effect. In 1930 five of the sixteen large panels were set up in the royal gallery for inspection by the Royal Fine Arts Commission. Their report was adverse. Despite vigorous public support from Royal Academicians, including Sickert, the Lords voted against the scheme. Brangwyn was devastated by this blow. Some compensation was afforded in 1934, when the corporation of Swansea acquired the panels, which were installed in the Guildhall, where they may still be seen.

Although Brangwyn continued to execute major commissions, such as that for the Rockefeller Center in New York (1932), he tended to become reclusive. Contributory factors in this were events in his private life. On 28 January 1896 he had married Lucy Ray, a nurse. They were not to have children and in time their marriage became unhappy; Brangwyn took a mistress, with whom he had a son, who did not take his father's name and who was brought up in the dominions. Lucy Brangwyn became an alcoholic and died in 1924. Her death contributed to Brangwyn's increasing pessimism and hypochondria (he suffered from sciatica, rheumatism, and an umbilical rupture, but began to talk of dying many years before he died, aged eighty-nine). He was also saddened and angered by developments in modern art; he was aware that his work was now ignored by many critics or regarded as old-fashioned. Although he did not attend any church he became intensely religious.

During the 1930s Brangwyn began to dispose of many of his possessions. His friend Comte Albert de Belleroche negotiated a gift of over 400 works to Bruges, in 1936, for the establishment of a permanent museum in Brangwyn's native city. At the same time Brangwyn also donated a substantial collection to the William Morris Museum, Walthamstow. In 1941 he was knighted, and in 1952 the Royal Academy held a retrospective of 470 of his works, Brangwyn being the first living academician to be so honoured. A museum of Brangwyn and of de Belleroche was established in 1947 at Orange in France. He was a stocky figure, a little below average height, with a round head, plump cheeks, and a short nose; he had emphatic eyebrows, wore his hair to one side, and for long periods in youth and age was bearded. He died on 11 June 1956 at his home, The Jointure, in Ditchling, Sussex.

ALAN WINDSOR

Sources R. Brangwyn, *Brangwyn* (1978) · Stedelijke Musea Brugge, *Collectie Frank Brangwyn* (1987) · R. Charles, *Frank Brangwyn centenary*, Arts Council of Wales (1967) [exhibition catalogue, NMG Wales, 1967] · *The Times* (13 June 1956) · W. Shaw-Sparrow, *Frank Brangwyn and his work* (1910) · W. de Belleroche, *Brangwyn talks* (1944) · B. Dolman, ed., *A dictionary of contemporary British artists*, 1929, 2nd edn (1981) · R. Cork, *A bitter truth: avant-garde art and the Great War* (1994) · *CGPLA Eng. & Wales* (1956) · DNB
Archives Brangwyn Museum, Bruges, Belgium, MSS · William Morris Museum, Walthamstow, London, letters and cartoons | BL, letters to A. H. Knighton-Hammond, Add. MS 52538 · JRL, letters to M. H. Spielmann · Ransom HRC, corresp. with John Lane · V&A, corresp. with Sir James Morton · William Morris Gallery, letters to Eleanor Pugh, stained glass cartoons
Likenesses W. Hodgson, pencil and watercolour drawing, 1892, NPG · A. L. Coburn, photogravure, 1904, NPG · P. May, chalk drawing, c.1904, NPG · E. O. Hoppé, platinum print, 1909, NPG [*see illus.*] · A. Drury, bronze bust, 1918, Herbert Art Gallery, Coventry · F. W. Brangwyn, self-portrait, oils, 1920, Uffizi Gallery, Florence · E. Lumsden, etching, 1921, William Morris Gallery, London · A. de Belleroche, chalk drawing, 1922, Brangwyn Museum, Bruges, Belgium · P. Evans, chromolithograph, ink, 1922, NMG Wales · A. B. Sava, sculpture, 1925–1930?, Ferens Art Gallery, Kingston upon Hull · L. Thomson, two photographs, 1926, NPG · J. Simpson, charcoal drawing, 1930–39, Carlisle City Art Gallery · J. Simpson, etching, 1930–39, NPG · L. Ginnett, chalk drawing, 1936, NPG · J. Kerr-Lawson, oils, c.1936, Ferens Art Gallery, Kingston upon Hull · A. H. Knighton-Hammond, sanguine drawing, 1937, NPG · A. Toft, bronze statuette, 1938, William Morris Gallery, London; bust, NMG Wales · A. Toft, bust, 1938, Brangwyn Hall, Swansea · A. H. Knighton-Hammond, etching, 1939, NPG · F. W. Brangwyn, self-portrait, conté, 1940, priv. coll. · A. John, chalk drawing, 1947, William Morris Gallery, London · F. W. Brangwyn, self-portrait, drawing, William Morris Gallery, London · F. W. Brangwyn, self-portrait, drawing, Dundee City Art Gallery · F. W. Brangwyn, self-portrait, drawing, Ferens Art Gallery, Kingston upon Hull · J. Simpson, pencil and watercolour drawing, William Morris Gallery, London · J. Simpson, woodcut with watercolour wash, William Morris Gallery, London · S. Spurnier, black and red chalk drawing, NPG · photograph, NPG
Wealth at death £39,162 0s. 10d.: probate, 7 Aug 1956, *CGPLA Eng. & Wales*

Bransby, James Hews (1783–1847), Unitarian minister and writer, was born in Ipswich, the son of John Bransby (1762?–1837), an instrument maker, fellow of the Royal Astronomical Society, author of a treatise entitled *The Use of the Globes* (1791), and editor of the *Ipswich Magazine* in the single year of its existence, 1799. The son abandoned his father's Calvinism for heterodoxy and studied for the Unitarian ministry in the academy maintained at Exeter from 1799 to 1804 by Timothy Kenrick and Joseph Bretland. In 1803 he was invited to become minister at Cross Street Chapel, the 'new meeting' opened on 30 October 1802 for the old Presbyterian congregation at Moretonhampstead, south-west of Exeter on the edge of Dartmoor. There he kept a school. Among the eight boarders was John Bowring, whose *Autobiographical Recollections* contain some amusing particulars. Not very wise nor very honest, Bowring said of Bransby, but he had 'some knowledge, more taste, and was full of pleasant anecdote' (*Recollections*, 46), and he was encouraging to the young Bowring. The boys, however, having discovered his 'little fibs and … little dishonesties' (ibid.), made him the butt of schoolboy pranks, some connected with his passionate pursuit of 'Miss Saucer-Eyes', otherwise Sarah (*d.* 1841), the daughter of Jacob Isaac (*d.* 1818), General Baptist minister in the town. In 1803 or 1804 the two married; there were no children.

In 1805 Bransby moved to Wolverhampton Street Chapel in Dudley, where he again kept a preparatory school for boys. He was well liked, but increasing concern was caused by his eccentricities, particularly as he developed a tendency perhaps best described as kleptomania. At length he committed a breach of trust involving forgery, but he was not prosecuted on condition of his leaving Dudley in 1828 for ever. He retired to Wales and supported himself by teaching, editing a paper, and odd literary jobs. His peculiarities continued, for he would borrow a manuscript and, after improvements, send it to a magazine as his own. An irresistible impulse led him on one occasion to revisit Dudley for a few hours; as he stood gazing at his old meeting-house he was recognized, but spared. Late in life he occasionally preached again. He died very suddenly at Bron'r Hendref, near Caernarfon, on 4 November 1847.

Bransby was a frequent contributor to the *Christian Reformer* and published, besides some school compilations, topographical guides and accounts of interesting occurrences in Wales and elsewhere. He also produced in 1842 an excellent edition of John Evans's *Sketch of the Various Denominations of the Christian World*, originally published in 1794. Bransby left behind him a mass of very compromising papers, which fell accidentally into the hands of Franklin Baker and were probably destroyed.

ALEXANDER GORDON, *rev.* R. K. WEBB

Sources J. Kenrick, 'The dissenting academy at Exeter', *Monthly Repository*, 13 (1818), 229 · *Monthly Repository*, 17 (1822), 434–5 [obit. sermon on Lindsey Priestley] · *Christian Reformer, or, Unitarian Magazine and Review*, 9 (1842), 64 · *Christian Reformer, or, Unitarian Magazine and Review*, new ser., 3 (1847), 760 · *Autobiographical recollections of Sir John Bowring*, ed. L. B. Bowring (1877), 44–9 · *GM*, 2nd ser. (1837), 452

Archives Dudley Archives and Local History Service, Coseley, Staffordshire, letters · JRL, corresp.

Branston family (*per. c.*1800–*c.*1880), engravers, came into prominence with **(Allen) Robert Branston** (1778–1827), who was born at Lynn, in Norfolk, the son of a copperplate-engraver and heraldic painter. He was taught to engrave on wood by his father. At the age of eighteen Robert moved to Bath, before settling in London in 1799. With his wife, Harriet, he had three sons, the first of whom, George Augustus, was baptized at St Mary, Lambeth, on 3 October 1800. In London he supported himself initially by embellishing musical scores and lottery bills with wood-engravings. Later he provided many wood-engravings for well-produced books, which helped significantly to revive this art form. He also aided the cause by training several apprentices, including John and Charles Thompson; A. J. Mason and G. Watts; his nephew, George Wilmot Bonner; and his sons, Frederick William and Robert Edward Branston [*see below*]. As a result of these endeavours, he has been called the leader of the London school of black-line engraving, a school which largely depended on others for its designs. He signed his work 'R. Branston sc', Branston, or RB. He died in Brompton, London, in 1827.

According to his contemporary Samuel Redgrave, Robert Branston 'engraved the figure well, and excelled with gradations of light in indoor scenes' (Redgrave, 52). Many vignettes of human subjects were commissioned from him to illustrate books, such as Robert Bloomfield's *Wild Flowers* (1806), George Marshall's *Epistles in Verse* (1812), and a reprint of James Puckle's *The Club* (1817), where he engraved figures after designs by John Thurston such as *Critic*, *Envioso*, and *Lawyer*. Thurston's *Cave of Despair* from Spenser's *Faerie Queene* was also engraved by Robert for William Savage's *Practical Hints on Decorative Printing* (1822). This is probably his most important plate, and it rivalled Charlton Nesbit's engraving of *Rinaldo and Armida* in the same volume. By contrast, Robert's representations of animals and nature were less successful, especially when compared with the work of Thomas Bewick. Chatto and Jackson, for instance, declared that 'in the representation of trees and natural scenery Branston almost uniformly failed' (Chatto and Jackson, 536).

Robert Edward Branston (*bap.* 1803, *d.* 1877) was baptized on 26 June 1803 at St Martin-in-the-Fields, Westminster, London. Like his father, he was prolific. It is sometimes impossible to disentangle their work for on occasion they both signed themselves Branston. Like his brother, Frederick, Robert produced several plates for French publications, notably *Paul et Virginie* (1838), and, like his father, he produced a plate for William Savage's *Practical Hints on Decorative Printing* (1822): *Passage Boats* after A. W. Callcott, about which Savage remarked positively. On 26 May 1830 he married at St Giles, Camberwell, Surrey, Caroline Martha Lunn (*d.* 6 Sept 1880), with whom he had a daughter, Ann Mary, baptized in the same church on 26 March 1832.

During his life Robert Edward Branston went into business with several engravers. Between 1829 and 1835 he formed a partnership with John Wright at 4 New London Street. The majority of their work (signed B&W or BW) was printed by Charles Whittingham the elder. They produced, for instance, engravings for publications by Edward Turner Bennett, including *The Tower Menagerie* (1829) and *The Gardens and Menageries of the Zoological Society Delineated* (2 vols., 1830–31), and for John Britton's *Picturesque Antiquities of the English Cities* (1830). They apprenticed John Greenaway. Branston's second business partner was

Charles Whiting, with whom he collaborated at Beaufort House, the Strand, until 1840. Whiting had acquired William Congreve's process for security printing in colours, so Whiting and Branston specialized in polychrome lottery tickets and banknotes. After the firm disbanded, Branston moved to 35 (later 76) Fleet Street, and immediately created an association with James Henry Vizetelly and a Mr Whitehead, while Ebenezer Landells acted as an engraving supervisor. By the time the firm folded in 1841 it had published *The Boy's Own Book* and had trained W. H. Wills (as well as, for a while, his cousin G. W. Bonner). Robert's last joint venture was with a pupil, William Dickes, who later became a prominent colour printer. Branston and Dickes worked from 36 St Andrew's Hills, and together they developed a method for printing in relief from a metal plate, a technique used to reproduce a drawing by A. W. Callcott in William Savage's *Dictionary of the Art of Printing* (1841). Robert Edward Branston died at his home in Denmark Hill, Camberwell, on 6 January 1877.

Frederick William Branston (*bap.* 1805) was baptized on 20 January 1805 at St Luke, Old Street, Finsbury, London. He spent his life in London, residing for some time at 4 Crescent Place, New Bridge Street (1848), and 48 Paternoster Row (1849). Many of his engravings of the 1830s were produced for French publications: for magazines, including the *Magasin Pittoresque*, and books, including Léon de Laborde's *Essais de gravure* in 1833 and *Les évangiles* in 1838, which had designs after Théophile Fragonard. He also produced wood-engravings by well-known native artists for best-selling English publications, for instance, after William Harvey's designs for James Northcote's *Fables* (1828); and after J. Franklin, E. M. Ward, H. J. Townsend, and J. Paton for Samuel Carter Hall's publications, such as his *Book of British Ballads* (1842) and *Nursery Tales* (1845). He signed his work: F. W. Branston, Fred Branston, or 'F. Branston sc'.

More obscure members of the family include the wood-engravers Charles Branston (*fl.* 1856–1878) and Elizabeth Branston (*fl.* 1832–1834). Some addresses from London trade directories are known for them. Charles is listed as working at 21 Tavistock Terrace, Upper Holloway (1856); 4 Beaufort Buildings, the Strand (1863); 6 Fetter Lane, Fleet Street (1866); 4 Salisbury Court (1876–7); and at 13 Edith Road, Peckham (1876), from where he established the firm of Branston & Co. (*fl.* 1878–1891). Elizabeth, meanwhile, worked for a time at 13 Golden Terrace, White Conduit Fields (1832–4). Proof impressions of engravings by members of the Branston family are in the British Museum and the Victoria and Albert Museum, London, and the Bodleian Library, Oxford. SUSANNA AVERY-QUASH

Sources W. J. Linton, *The masters of wood-engraving* (1889), 157, 162, 164, 170, 173–8, 180, 191, 192, 197, 201, 215 · W. Chatto, J. Jackson, and H. G. Bohn, *A treatise on wood-engraving*, 2nd edn (1861), 535–8, 544–5, 634 · C. J. Courtney Lewis, *The story of picture printing in England during the nineteenth century* [1928], 10, 13–14, 20, 23, 59–60, 62, 101, 178–9 · R. K. Engen, *Dictionary of Victorian engravers, print publishers and their works* (1979) · 'Branston, Allen Robert', *DNB* · S. Houfe, *The dictionary of 19th century British book illustrators and caricaturists*, rev. edn (1996) · G. Wakeman, *Victorian book illustration: the technical revolution* (1973), 45 · R. McLean, *Victorian book design and colour printing*, rev. edn (1972), 35, 51, 197 · P. Gusman, *La gravure sur bois en France au XIXe siècle* (Paris, 1929), 153 · Redgrave, *Artists* · Bryan, *Painters* (1903–5) · Thieme & Becker, *Allgemeines Lexikon* · IGI · CGPLA *Eng. & Wales* (1877) [Robert Edward Branston]

Wealth at death under £14,000—Robert Edward Branston: probate, 26 Feb 1877, CGPLA *Eng. & Wales*

Branston, Frederick William (*bap.* 1805). *See under* Branston family (*per.* c.1800–c.1880).

Branston, (Allen) Robert (1778–1827). *See under* Branston family (*per.* c.1800–c.1880).

Branston, Robert Edward (*bap.* 1803, *d.* 1877). *See under* Branston family (*per.* c.1800–c.1880).

Brant, Joseph [Thayendanegea] (1743–1807), leader of the Mohawk Indians, was born in 1743, probably in March, in or near Cuyahoga (near present-day Akron, Ohio). His parents, Peter Tehowaghwengaraghkwin and Margaret (*fl.* 1735–1780), were ordinary Mohawks with limited links to the tribe's leading families.

Early years Widowed, Margaret returned to her home at the Canajoharie Mohawk village in New York between 1746 and 1750. She had Joseph baptized there, his Mohawk name translating as 'two sticks of wood bound together'. She also remarried, but her new husband died fighting the Catawbas, and in 1753 she married a prominent Mohawk hereditary chief, Brant Canagaraduncka, from whom Joseph took his surname. Through his stepfather, Joseph and his elder sister, Molly *Brant, came to the attention of the powerful superintendent-general of Indian affairs, Sir William Johnson. Molly became Johnson's common-law wife and an important figure in Mohawk politics.

As a young warrior, Brant fought as one of the British-allied Mohawks in the Seven Years' War. Afterwards, Johnson sent him in 1761 to Moor's Indian Charity School in Lebanon, Connecticut, where he studied under the Revd Eleazar Wheelock. He learned to speak, read, and write English well, and studied such subjects as Hebrew, Greek, Latin, and agriculture, impressing Wheelock as a considerate and modest youth in the process. Both Brant and his patrons assumed that he would undertake further studies and become a missionary, but instead he returned to Canajoharie after only two years at school. As one of Johnson's extended network of Mohawk connections, Brant joined fellow tribesmen during the early stages of the Pontiac War (1763–7) to help the crown suppress the Native nations that had risen against the British.

In 1765 Brant married Neggen Aoghyatonghsera, or Margaret (*d.* 1771), a young Oneida woman from a prominent family. They had two children, Isaac and Christiana, and enjoyed a comfortable life at Canajoharie. As a product of the colonial middle ground, Joseph supported his family through hunting and fishing as well as by both traditional and European-style farming, and by trading, guiding, and translating for the British Indian department. After Margaret's death, in 1773 Brant, following Mohawk custom, married her half-sister, whose name may have been Susanna. The local Anglican priest thought such a marriage was inappropriate, so a German

Joseph Brant (1743–1807), by Gilbert Stuart, 1786 [detail]

minister officiated at the wedding. Despite this incident and exposure to dissenting protestantism at school Brant remained a conscientious Anglican; he translated parts of the Book of Common Prayer and other religious texts into Mohawk, although, like many aboriginal Christians, he did not abandon traditional beliefs entirely.

The American War of Independence Even though his origins were humble, Brant emerged as a leader among the Mohawks in the late 1760s and early 1770s (with some influence among the Oneidas as well). He advanced because of his own intelligence and energy, his prosperity which attracted a following, his marriages to prominent women, and his ability to serve both his people and the British as a cultural broker.

During this period he struggled to prevent the loss of tribal independence and the unwanted alienation of Mohawk land to settlers who regularly used deceit to acquire coveted aboriginal farms and hunting territories. At one point, unable to gain redress through official channels, a frustrated Brant led twenty warriors to assault one of the most aggressive speculators, George Klock, who, like many of the worst exploiters of Native land rights, supported the revolutionary cause as the thirteen colonies slid towards rebellion.

With the outbreak of hostilities, Brant joined a loyalist and Native force that marched north in May 1775 to guard the approaches to Montreal. During this time, the governor of Quebec, Guy Carleton, promised the Mohawks that they would keep their lands and offered them compensation for any losses they might sustain in fighting for the crown. Carleton's declarations promised to resolve

many of Brant's concerns and helped to affirm his loyalty. Nevertheless, his earlier experiences had made him so wary of white ways that he decided to travel to London in late 1775 to seek confirmation and redress for earlier encroachments. Imperial officials offered to fulfil the commitments made in Montreal, providing that the Mohawks remained faithful during the rebellion. While in London Brant became something of a celebrity before leaving for America in June 1776. *En route*, he fought as a marksman when his ship came under attack from a privateer. He landed on crown-held Staten Island, participated in military operations in that region, and then journeyed back to the Mohawk valley through enemy lines.

There Brant recruited Natives, as well as members of the white and black communities to fight for the crown. Headquartered primarily near Fort Niagara on Lake Ontario 'Captain' Brant spent the rest of the war leading his volunteers in operations against the rebels. His objectives were to rescue loyalists and Iroquois (Cayugas, Mohawks, Oneidas, Onondagas, Senecas, and Tuscaroras) from rebel-controlled regions, defend Six Nations territory, and deny the revolutionaries the abundant foodstuffs produced on the frontier. Brant's followers, particularly his Natives, also wanted to win the honours and rewards that Iroquois men could earn through combat in a society that valued the warrior spirit.

Despite extensive propaganda to the contrary, Brant was a comparatively humane combatant in the bitter conflict that pitted former neighbours against each other. That propaganda contributed many myths about Brant: claims that he exercised far more control over Iroquois affairs than was possible in Six Nations politics and that he was descended from Mohawk nobility, and claims that portrayed him in pejorative terms, such as 'the Monster Brant' of Thomas Campbell's popular 1809 poem *Gertrude of Wyoming*.

Some of Brant's many actions included the siege of Fort Stanwix and the battle of Oriskany, as well as raids against numerous settlements, such as Cobbleskill and Cherry Valley. Because the loyalist and Iroquois attacks were so effective, George Washington dispatched a large army in 1779 to destroy Iroquois villages and farms. Brant participated in the failed defence of Iroquoia (modern upstate New York), most notably at the battle of Newtown. The success of the rebel assault forced the majority of Six Nations people to flee west to Fort Niagara, to spend the rest of the war in squalid refugee camps. However, the expedition did not force the pro-crown Iroquois out of the conflict, and war parties, often headed by Brant, continued to inflict death and destruction upon their enemies until 1781.

Brant's second wife died in 1778 or 1779. His third marriage, in 1779, was to Catharine Adonwentishon (d. 1837). The couple were to have seven children: Joseph, Jacob, Margaret, Catharine, Mary, John, and Elizabeth. Catharine's father was the important fur trader and Indian agent George Croghan. Her mother came from a prominent Mohawk family, which allowed Catharine to rise to the status of matron of the Turtle clan, while her half-brother,

Henry, succeeded to the important civil and hereditary chieftainship of Tekarihoga at about the time of her marriage. (Joseph belonged to the Wolf clan.) Both Catharine and Henry used their influence to help advance Joseph's ambitions for leadership.

During these years Brant had a farm (at present-day Lewiston, New York), near the Iroquois refugee camps at Niagara, where he kept black slaves and built an Anglican chapel. However, the war took its toll on him, as was shown in 1781 by the first of a growing series of accounts of drunken, brawling behaviour.

Canada and the Ohio country The treaty of Paris that ended the American War of Independence left Brant feeling betrayed: Britain failed to address Native objectives, and the border with the new republic was located too far north to protect most aboriginal territory on the frontier—territory that the tribes and loyalists largely controlled at the end of hostilities. Brant declared angrily, 'England had Sold the Indians to Congress' (Allan Maclean, quoting Brant to Frederick Haldimand, 13 May 1783, Haldimand MSS, BL, Add. MS 21763, 2.108). In light of the disaster of 1783, Brant and some other Iroquois leaders decided to resettle in British territory along the Grand River on the north shore of Lake Erie. They chose the Grand because of its proximity to both the predominantly Algonkian nations of the Ohio country and the Senecas of western New York (the most numerous of the Iroquois tribes). Thus, the site held out the promise of fulfilling Brant's new dream, that of forming a confederation of all of the tribes of the lower Great Lakes to defend their lands and interests in the face of anticipated white expansion. In 1784 the British agreed to the move and granted a tract to the Six Nations. By 1785, 1850 people, roughly one-third of the Iroquois in New York, had moved to the Grand. They comprised members of all the Iroquois tribes, along with Delawares and others who had lived among them before the revolution. This was a significant event in Iroquois history, heralding the birth of what would become the largest Six Nations community in the Great Lakes region. It also marked the rise of Brant from being primarily a Mohawk leader to being one with much broader influence among all the Iroquois.

Brant used his personal resources and his influence with crown officials to construct a chapel on the Grand (still extant at the beginning of the twenty-first century), open a school, recruit a physician, and establish a masonic lodge. He also promoted European agricultural practices to improve his people's material well-being and to help them adapt to the erosion of older subsistence patterns. Like some other Six Nations leaders, Brant believed that agricultural prosperity would enable Native society to resist unwanted aspects of white culture and foreign administrative control. Change, however, came slowly because most Iroquois preferred their ancestral ways of living.

Shortly after moving to the Grand, Brant began to worry about the exact nature of the British government's land grant. He had assumed that the large tract had been given in fee simple, thus allowing the tribes to lease or sell superfluous parts of it to generate capital to provide investment income to benefit the Iroquois. However, crown officials argued that the Six Nations only had the right to occupy the land, and therefore were limited to selling their right of occupancy to surplus territory. Furthermore, sales could be made solely to the government, which paid much less for occupancy rights than private speculators might offer for the land itself. Frustrated with the government's attitude and wanting to obtain the compensation promised in Montreal and London in 1775 and 1776, as well as hoping for promises of British military support should the Great Lakes tribes again go to war with the United States, Brant journeyed to England in 1785–6. He obtained the compensation he sought, but failed to resolve the land issue or secure any meaningful military commitment.

Undaunted by his set-backs in London, Brant spent the rest of his life working to change government policies. Many within the Iroquois world mistrusted his motives or did not want to sell land because they hoped to maintain traditional ways of life. Others preferred to have chiefs other than Brant lead the alienation process. Internal Iroquois divisions were aggravated by the aggressive political and diplomatic actions of colonial officials who exploited government restrictions and their personal links to Iroquois leaders to advance the interests of the crown—and sometimes themselves—at the expense of the Six Nations. In desperation, Brant used whatever weapons he could find to achieve his goals. While participating in negotiations with the Americans to address Iroquois concerns within the United States, he made sure that the British knew about his efforts in order to raise doubts about his loyalty and thereby gain concessions. During the mid-1790s, when British officials in Canada were worrying about foreign invasion, he spread rumours that he might join the king's enemies or lead an uprising within British territory. At one point, he took a large war party with him to a meeting with colonial officials in order to intimidate them. While a violent breach was unlikely, Brant correctly thought that threats might prompt officials to make concessions in meeting his wishes to sell and lease land. Rumours and threats were consistent with traditional Iroquois diplomatic practices, and were intended to force other powers to respond to their demands. Nevertheless, they represented a departure for Brant, whose support for the crown had been comparatively forthright until the end of the American War of Independence. The change demonstrated his growing political maturity and his recognition of British willingness to sacrifice the interests of the Six Nations.

South-west of the Grand, the Ohio nations fought the Americans between 1787 and 1794 to preserve their territory against American settlement. Brant and other Six Nations chiefs feared losing their land in New York (and perhaps Canada) if they joined the western tribes in what they assumed would be a doomed struggle without British support. Although deeply distrustful of the United States and willing to fight if necessary, the Iroquois leaders tried to persuade the western tribes to negotiate a boundary acceptable to the Americans. Instead, the western tribes rejected the advice of the Six Nations, were defeated, and lost most of their lands in the disputed region. In the process, Brant's efforts to establish a pan-tribal confederacy collapsed, as did his efforts to reunite the Six Nations, now split by the international border, with the result that Iroquois resident in Canada and America gradually went their separate ways.

In 1795, during the frontier tensions and controversies over land rights, Brant and his son Isaac (who was something of a rogue) got into a fight. Joseph inflicted a knife wound that later became infected. Isaac died and Joseph was plunged into deep, self-recriminating grief. Although the circumstances surrounding the attack are unclear, Joseph's opponents within the Six Nations may have urged Isaac to murder his father. Political assassination by a family member was a traditional way of getting rid of someone, especially a person who had become 'too great' in Iroquois minds, and such threats had been made before in Brant's career. Another son, John (Ahyonwaeghs), rose to leadership after 1815, but he was only a little boy at the end of the eighteenth century. Casting about for an able assistant, Brant adopted a mixed Scottish–Cherokee individual, John Norton (Teyoninhokarawen), into the Mohawk tribe in 1798 or 1799 to become a chief and ultimately his successor.

Later years In 1802 or 1803 Brant left his Grand River home to take up residence at Burlington Bay, Upper Canada, on Lake Ontario, where he lived comfortably in the European style. (While he derived some of his wealth from farming and other enterprises, much of it came from government pensions and land grants as well as presents offered to help maintain the British–Iroquois alliance.) However, he continued to play an active role in Iroquois affairs. On his deathbed in his Burlington home on 24 November 1807, Brant's last words, directed at Norton, were supposedly, 'Have pity on the poor Indians: if you can get any influence with the great, endeavor to do them all the good you can' (Stone, 2.499).

The cause of Brant's death is uncertain, although his health had become frail, partly because of heavy drinking and recurring malaria. He was buried near his Burlington home. His family inherited his two houses, hundreds of acres of land, a government pension, and other assets totalling a substantial legacy by the frontier standards of the time. In 1850, with much ceremony, his remains were reinterred in the graveyard beside the little chapel he had built at Brantford on the Grand River in 1787.

The fundamental challenge faced by the Iroquois in Brant's time was how to resist the ever-constricting limitations on their independence and subsistence patterns as they dropped to a numerically insignificant status in a growing sea of European and American settlers. Earlier in his career Brant strove to address the challenge by earning favour through a vigorous loyalty to the crown in its struggles on the frontier. After the disaster of the American War of Independence, he tried to create new political and economic structures so that his people could exercise as much independence as possible and live comfortably within their changing environment. He also worked to force white officials to live up to the promises and obligations they had made to the Iroquois over the years. Ultimately, he enjoyed only modest successes in holding back unwanted control of Iroquois affairs. Internally, Native politics were too fragmented for one person to muster majority opinion behind any particular political and economic programme, and his modernizing tendencies put him in a minority position in relation to most Six Nations people. Externally, white officials had gained so much power over the Iroquois by the time Brant emerged as a leader that they were well placed to thwart most of the challenges he might pose to them.   CARL BENN

Sources I. T. Kelsay, *Joseph Brant, 1743–1807: man of two worlds* (1984) · W. L. Stone, *Life of Joseph Brant—Thayendanegea*, 2 vols. (1838) · C. M. Johnson, ed., *The valley of the Six Nations: a collection of documents on the Indian lands of the Grand River* (1964) · *The journal of Major John Norton, 1816*, ed. C. F. Klinck and J. J. Talman (1970), 270–85 · B. Graymont, 'Thayendenegea', *DCB* · B. Graymont, *The Iroquois in the American revolution* (1972) · C. M. Johnson, 'Joseph Brant, the Grand River lands and the northwest crisis', *Ontario History*, 55 (1963), 267–82 · A. F. Hunter, ed., 'The probated wills of men prominent in the public affairs of early Upper Canada', *Papers and Records [Ontario Historical Society]*, 23 (1926), 328–51 [will, 18 Oct 1805] · D. W. Boyce, ed., 'A glimpse of Iroquois culture history through the eyes of Joseph Brant and John Norton', *Proceedings of the American Philosophical Society*, 117 (1973), 286–94

Archives Joseph Brant Museum, Burlington, Ontario, artefacts · NA Canada, MSS · Royal Ontario Museum, Toronto, artefacts | Archives of Ontario, Toronto, Russell MSS; Simcoe MSS · BL, Haldimand MSS · NA Canada, Indian affairs papers · Wisconsin Historical Society, Madison, Draper MSS

Likenesses G. Romney, oils, 1776, National Gallery of Canada, Ottawa · miniature, *c.*1780–1799, Joseph Brant Museum, Burlington, Ontario · J. F. Rigaud, oils, 1786; copy, New York State Education Department, Albany; original now lost · attrib. G. Stuart, oils, 1786, New York State Historical Association, Cooperstown · G. Stuart, oils, 1786, Syon House, Middlesex [*see illus.*] · W. Berczy, watercolour, 1794–1807, Musée du Séminaire de Québec, Quebec City · C. W. Peale, oils, 1797, Independence National Historical Park, Philadelphia · W. Berczy, oils, *c.*1797–1807, Royal Ontario Museum, Toronto · E. Ames, oils, 1806, New York Historical Association, Cooperstown · W. Berczy, oils, *c.*1808, priv. coll. · statue, 1886, Brantford, Ontario · W. Berczy, oils, National Gallery of Canada, Ottawa · print, repro. in *London Magazine* (1776)

Wealth at death two homes, hundreds of acres of land, moveable property, and a pension: Hunter, ed., 'The probated wills'

Brant, Molly [Konwatsi tsiaienni, Degonwadonti] (*c.*1736–1796), leader of the Mohawk Indians, was born a Mohawk, one of the six native North American nations which comprised the Iroquois confederacy and whose homeland was in present-day New York state. Brant may have been born at Canajoharie in upstate New York. Because Mohawk Iroquois society was non-literate when she was born and kept no written records, little information about Brant's early life is known. Her father was Peter Tehowaghwengaraghkwin, and her mother Margaret. All Iroquois societies were matrilineal and matrilocal, and women were traditionally the primary breadwinners—farmers in an agricultural society—and consequently often played important political roles. Molly (Mary) Brant may have been a 'clan mother' or 'matron' which would have entitled her to appoint clan chiefs, to eject them from office if she found their leadership lacking, and to deliberate along with other matrons in political councils of the nation.

Molly Brant spent her childhood at Cuyahoga in the Ohio valley (considered Iroquois hunting grounds at the time) and at Canajoharie (a Mohawk village on the Mohawk River) where she may have attended an Anglican mission school; later in life she wrote letters in English which provide evidence of excellent penmanship, although it is possible that she dictated these letters. Brant seems to have been interested in diplomacy, as she accompanied an Iroquois diplomatic delegation to Philadelphia in 1754–5, probably listening and watching as a diplomatic apprentice. Having been widowed in the mid-1740s, Molly's mother remarried twice, secondly to an influential Mohawk chief, Brant Canagaraduncka. He was a friend of Sir William *Johnson (1715?–1774), the Irish baronet who developed a real estate empire in the British province of New York and a bureaucratic career as superintendent of Indian affairs for the northern department of the British colonial administration in North America from 1755 until his death in 1774.

In the late 1750s Johnson was grooming Molly's younger brother Joseph *Brant as a political protégé. As legend has it, he became smitten with Molly when she leapt onto the back of a horse at a militia muster and rode around the grounds attracting attention with her flamboyant style. They entered into a marital relationship which was probably recognized according to Mohawk rite, although not in the Anglican church, the closest thing to an established church in the frontier area of provincial New York in the mid-eighteenth century. Johnson already had three children with a German woman who served as his housekeeper at Fort Johnson and Johnson Hall, his residences in the Mohawk valley (the most sophisticated and luxurious dwellings in the area). He and Brant had eight children together, for whom he provided in his will along with his three other offspring. Perhaps more important than heirs to Johnson, however, was, as observers noted, that the Brant–Johnson union was 'a matter of state policy, as it increased his influence with all the Indians' (Brant MS F15:61). Molly Brant was known among British colonial officials; Daniel Claus, Johnson's successor in charge of Indian affairs, commented that 'one word from her [was] more taken Notice of by the Five Nations [Six Nations Iroquois confederacy] than a thousand from any white man without exception' (Haldimand MS B114:63).

Brant not only played hostess at Johnson Hall in the 1760s and 1770s but also seems to have presided unofficially over the daily running of the British Indian department (headquartered there) in Johnson's absences, and used the associated expense accounts to curry favour with Iroquois and European political acquaintances. The more generous she was with blankets, clothing, rum, and other backcountry necessities, the greater her influence until she became certainly the most influential Mohawk woman in the region, at least from the perspective of written documents. But although she socialized with and entertained important British colonial figures, she always dressed in Mohawk rather than European fashion, even if the materials used for her frocks, leggings, and moccasins were the finest available. Brant also refused to speak English, always using an interpreter instead. Johnson perhaps did not mind this, since he spoke Mohawk as well, but undoubtedly there was tension over her role beyond household management. He had been known for his disapproval of the political role that many Iroquois women were accustomed to filling, having at least once refused to allow female involvement at a political meeting of several Indian groups at Johnson Hall.

During the American War of Independence, shortly after Johnson's death in 1774, Brant spent much of her energy attempting to keep the Mohawks and all of the Iroquois loyal to the British cause. British officials consciously cultivated good relations with her for this reason, and rebel forces were afraid of her influence. She spied for the British during the war and helped determine the outcome of military events in August 1777 at Oriskany, New York. She was known for the haranguing speeches she gave to neutral or pro-American Iroquois leaders at Iroquois political meetings. She and her family suffered personal privation, the pillaging of her home, refugee flight, and permanent exile from the Mohawk valley homeland because of her loyalty to the British empire.

Even after the war and the disappointing failure of British negotiators at the Paris peace talks to defend the interests of the Iroquois who had fought on the British side, Molly Brant remained enamoured of the British connection. Rather than live among her own people at the new Six Nations reserve community north-west of their homeland, in the new colony of Upper Canada (of which her brother Joseph Brant was the unofficial leader), she chose to live in the new British town of Kingston, also in Upper Canada, and was a founder member of the town's first Anglican church. Her daughters married into the Upper Canadian élite: army officers, an Indian department surgeon, and a magistrate and legislative assembly member, while her one surviving son lived a traditional Iroquois life on the Six Nations reserve. Molly Brant died on 16 April 1796 in Kingston and was buried at St George's Anglican Church there.

Molly Brant could be seen as a paradoxical figure: both pro-Iroquois and pro-British. Speaking and dressing as a Mohawk, and encouraging her children to do likewise, sheltering, feeding, and clothing Iroquois people during their diaspora period—these cast her in a staunchly traditional Iroquois light. She argued on behalf of her nation to the British colonial government before, during, and after the American War of Independence, protecting their interests and rights. Brant always identified herself fiercely with her people. Yet she also involved her people in a war which resulted in dispossession. Although she did not plan or anticipate the result of the war, she did bind her people to a European government that betrayed them at the treaty table and that after 1783 increasingly regarded native North Americans as subject rather than sovereign peoples. Yet despite the government's attitude towards her people, Brant remained pro-British until her death. Perhaps most striking about Molly Brant was that she was able to find a niche in pre-revolutionary North America, between two cultures, and was able to function effectively in both while maintaining the appearance of an Iroquois woman. She was a politically powerful Mohawk woman, despite the waning of female political roles in that society and despite, or perhaps partly because of, her husband.   GRETCHEN L. GREEN

Sources State Historical Society of Wisconsin, Draper Collection, Brant MSS, ser. F · NA Canada, Haldimand papers, MG21-Add. MS B114 · *The papers of Sir William Johnson*, ed. J. Sullivan and others, 14 vols. (1921–65) · *Daniel Claus' narrative of his relations with Sir William Johnson and experiences in the Lake George fight*, ed. A. S. Walcott (1904) · E. B. O'Callaghan and B. Fernow, eds. and trans., *Documents relative to the colonial history of the state of New York*, 15 vols. (1853–87) · *The journal of Major John Norton*, ed. C. F. Klinck and J. J. Talman (1970) · Loyalist claims, bundle 11, Archives of Ontario · PRO, audit office 13, loyalist ser., vols. 89–90 · *The diary of Mrs. John Graves Simcoe*, ed. J. Robertson (1911) · B. Graymont, 'Koñwatsi tsiaiʔéñni', *DCB*, vol. 4 · I. T. Kelsay, *Joseph Brant, 1743–1807: man of two worlds* (1984) · H. P. Gundy, 'Molly Brant, loyalist', *Ontario History*, 45 (1953), 97–108 · G. Green, 'Molly Brant, Catharine Brant, and their daughters: a study in colonial acculturation', *Ontario History*, 81 (1989), 235–50 · R. S. Allen, 'Brant, Molly', *ANB*

Branthwaite, William (1563–1619). *See under* Authorized Version of the Bible, translators of the (*act.* 1604–1611).

Brantingham, Thomas (*d.* 1394), administrator and bishop of Exeter, took his name from Brantingham in the East Riding of Yorkshire, where he later held the sub-manor of Thorp; his father's name was John, and he was doubtless related to Ralph Brantingham, a veteran clerk and chamberlain of the exchequer who was disgraced in 1365. The pedigree in the printed edition of his episcopal register is very suspect. He does not seem to have attended university and had no degrees.

Brantingham himself said that he had served Edward III and Queen Philippa 'from our adolescence to our time as a bishop' (Hingeston-Randolph, vii). He was certainly a clerk of the exchequer by 18 December 1349, having been presented by the king to the rectory of Barnwell St Andrew, Northamptonshire, on 24 June previous. In all he received seventeen presentations from Edward III (mainly rectories at first, prebends later), four of which proved invalid; even his hold on the treasurership of Wells Cathedral (19 July 1367) was contested throughout by a cardinal with a papal provision. His exclusive reliance on the crown meant that his preferments lay all over the country, with no sign of independent support even in Yorkshire.

A financial account for the year between February 1353 and February 1354 names Brantingham as an attorney for the comptroller of the household. He was appointed cofferer on 5 October 1359, with executive responsibility for finance during the French campaign of 1359–60. From 1361 to 1368, during the truce with France, he was treasurer, and receiver of the mint, of Calais, and was employed in various negotiations with the duke of Burgundy and other business connected with the defence of the English pale there. On 27 June 1369, as soon as war broke out again, Brantingham was appointed treasurer of the realm, the first for thirteen years with any financial

experience. The issue roll for 1369/70, the first full year of his treasurership, was published by the Record Commission in 1835, in a translation by Frederick Devon. It has been argued that William Wykeham, now chancellor, deliberately caused the king to employ men of straw in order to monopolize real influence. Brantingham at least was not that, and neither was he a client of Wykeham, even though the paths of their careers intertwined. Financing the war proved disastrously difficult, and the war went badly. Critics of the regime in parliament caused Wykeham to lose office on 24 March 1371, Peter Lacy, keeper of the privy seal, two days later, Brantingham on the 27th. It has been suggested that the replacement of these officials by three laymen denoted anti-clericalism, or at least concern that as clerics they were too sheltered from accountability; alternatively, that they were seen as lukewarm for war; or, simply, that Wykeham had made too many enemies not to be a vulnerable scapegoat.

Brantingham found departure from government service painless. In July 1369 he had been elected to the see of Hereford, but the pope had then provided William Courtenay. However, on 4 March 1370 Brantingham was provided to the see of Exeter, which Courtenay would certainly have preferred for reasons of family, wealth, and status. It seems that Brantingham had outrun Courtenay, rather than vice versa. He was consecrated on 12 May 1370, and received the temporalities on the 16th. Once ousted from office Brantingham went to see his new diocese in July 1371 and launched himself into a thorough primary visitation of both Devon and Cornwall, and, a rarity, was back in Cornwall again in July 1372. Although he did attend parliaments in the following years, he made himself a very active resident diocesan; whether this extended from predictable financial zeal to newfound pastoral talent is not clear.

On the accession of Richard II, with the king a minor and consensus the government's objective, Brantingham was recalled as treasurer on 19 July 1377 after a year of severe political crisis, from which, unlike Wykeham, Brantingham had stood well apart, avoiding even the arrangement in the Good Parliament of 1376 that all recent treasurers should give a public account of their record. His diocese was to see very little of him until, having witnessed the Commons in parliament vote all three infamous poll taxes, he resigned once more on 1 February 1381; the chronicler Walsingham says he was dismissed. If that was so, and probably it was, the bishop soon had reason to be grateful, given the fate of his successor, Robert Hales, in the popular revolt that year.

Brantingham went home at once after leaving office, conducting another energetic triennial visitation of Cornwall in May and June, having been unable to act thus in 1378; he undertook further visitations in 1384, 1387, and 1390. He appears from his register to have been a keen diocesan, not a disgraced politician marking time. He attended parliaments with a reputation rising as current affairs grew worse. In November 1381, and in 1382 and 1384, he was one of the Lords appointed to confer with the Commons (a sign of trust in him on both sides), and in

November 1381 was on a commission to reform the king's household. In 1385 he was made a comptroller of the parliamentary subsidy, and in the same year, with serious crisis again in sight, was one of those nominated to inquire into the king's debts.

In October 1386 matters came to a head, and the king's chief officers were impeached, or at least forced to resign, in the Wonderful Parliament. Eleven lords, of the highest reputation and carefully not chosen as partisan, of whom Brantingham was one, were appointed to supervise reform of the king's household and rule. However, Brantingham was not among those who defied Richard's attempts to overthrow this arrangement in 1387 or took extreme action against his remaining advisers in 1388. His non-involvement was confirmed freely by the resurgent king in 1397, even after the bishop's death—Richard declared that Brantingham had been innocent and loyal.

Indeed, when Richard II declared himself of age on 3 May 1389, and looked to loosen the restraints put upon him in the previous year, he made a point of changing the chief officers. Brantingham was brought back from his diocese on 4 May to the treasurership; thereby, the king declared his own freedom of choice, but also that he would choose the most reputable. Perhaps this recall was always purely symbolic, or simply to make the king's assertiveness more difficult to oppose, but perhaps, also, Brantingham now found the office just too demanding. Before 12 August, with no replacement for some days, he resigned. On the 26th Richard, on account of Brantingham's age and services to Edward III and himself, excused him from future attendance at parliaments and councils.

There are signs that Brantingham had been slowing up recently, and, although he managed his tour of Cornwall in 1390, his health seems to have declined markedly in November, confining him to Chudleigh and Clyst St Mary, both in Devon, the latter entirely from October 1391. There he made a predictably meticulous will on 13 December 1393, in which he requested burial on the north side of Exeter Cathedral nave before the altar in his prepared tomb. The will showed an exclusive focus on his household, the cathedral, and diocese, with no mention of kin, but gifts of rings and ornaments to Wykeham, Courtenay, and Bishop Ralph Ergum, his elderly neighbour at Wells and a fellow Yorkshireman. Sturdy to the end he died at Clyst St Mary a full year later, on 23 December 1394. The contents of his tomb were despoiled in 1646, supposedly for religious reasons.

R. G. DAVIES

Sources F. C. Hingeston-Randolph, ed., *The register of Thomas de Brantyngham, bishop of Exeter*, 2 vols. (1901–6) · Tout, *Admin. hist.*, vol. 3 · J. R. L. Highfield, 'The relations between the church and the English crown during the pontificates of Clement V and John XXII, 1305–1334', DPhil diss., U. Oxf., 1951 · R. G. Davies, 'The episcopate in England and Wales, 1375–1443', PhD diss., University of Manchester, 1974, 3.xlviii–ix · *Fasti Angl., 1300–1541*, [Exeter] · exchequer, lord treasurer's remembrancer, enrolled accounts, wardrobe and household, PRO, E 361/4 m. 2 · F. Devon, ed. and trans., *Issue roll of Thomas de Brantingham*, RC (1835)
Archives Devon RO, Exeter diocesan records, register

Branwhite, Charles (1817–1880), landscape painter, was born at 58 Queen Square, in Bristol, on 7 June 1817, the second son of Bristol's outstanding miniature portrait painter Nathan Cooper *Branwhite (1774/5–1857) and his wife, Hannah (b. 1778). Nathan was himself the son of the poet Peregrine *Branwhite (bap. 1745, d. c.1795) of Lavenham, Suffolk. Charles Branwhite studied under his father, initially pursuing sculpture and winning silver medals for bas-reliefs at the Society of Arts, London, in 1837 and 1838 and exhibiting portrait busts at the Bristol Society of Artists in 1839 to considerable acclaim. He took up painting, however, perhaps inspired by the example of his friend William James Müller, whose broad and fluent style and choice of local landscape subjects he at first emulated. Branwhite exhibited at the British Institution from 1843, showing there annually until 1857, with snow and frost scenes predominating. He showed intermittently at the Royal Academy from 1845 to 1856. He was elected an associate of the Society of Painters in Water Colours on 12 February 1849, exhibiting there for thirty years but never becoming a full member. J. L. Roget in his history of the society wrote patronizingly of Branwhite's 'very rapid and popular style of execution' and of such lavish use of body colour 'that many of his drawings may be regarded as works in distemper' (Roget, 336). However Branwhite was a passionate angler and many fine watercolours of river scenes in Devon and Wales reflect a more personal enthusiasm for the landscape itself rather than merely for striking pictorial and technical effects. He was a substantial shareholder in the West of England Bank, whose collapse may have aggravated the heart disease from which he had suffered for several years before his death at his home, Bramford House, Westfield Park, Clifton, Bristol, on 15 February 1880. He was buried at Arnos Vale cemetery, Bristol, five days later. He left a widow, Mary Ann Mayes (who may have been his second wife); a son, Charles Brooke, and a daughter, Ellen Elizabeth.

Charles Branwhite's elder brother, Nathan Branwhite (1813–1894), did some fine watercolour portraits of his family (City Museum and Art Gallery, Bristol), exhibited in Bristol in 1839 some watercolours of landscapes, and executed the marble bust of W. J. Müller in Bristol Cathedral. The younger of Nathan's and Charles's two sisters, Rosa, was a professional landscape painter of delicate watercolours, mostly of river and meadow scenes in England and Wales. She married W. J. Müller's younger brother, Edmund Gustavus Müller (1816–1888), a landscape painter of modest talent. Charles Branwhite's son, Charles Brooke Branwhite (1851–1929), was a successful Bristol landscape painter in oils and watercolour, also specializing in winter scenes and landscapes in Wales and the south-west of England.

FRANCIS GREENACRE

Sources artist's scrapbook, 1924, City Museum and Art Gallery, Bristol, MSS Bristol [incl. obits] · *Bristol Times and Mirror* (21 Feb 1880) · *ILN* (20 March 1880) · *Art Journal*, new ser., 19 (1880), 208 · J. L. Roget, *A history of the 'Old Water-Colour' Society*, 2 vols. (1891) · MS bound vol. of proofs of reviews of exhibitions, City Museum and Art Gallery, Bristol · *DNB* · Graves, *RA exhibitors* · Graves, *Brit. Inst.* ·

F. Greenacre, *The British School of Art, Francis Danby and painting in Bristol, 1810–1840* (1973) • *Bristol in 1898–1899, Contemporary biographies*, vol. 2 • L. Lambourne and J. Hamilton, eds., *British watercolours in the Victoria and Albert Museum* (1980) • will
Archives City Museum and Art Gallery, Bristol • V&A
Likenesses G. W. Braikenridge, watercolour, *c.*1835, City Museum and Art Gallery, Bristol • N. C. Branwhite, two watercolours, City Museum and Art Gallery, Bristol • wood-engraving (after photograph by J. H. Morgan), NPG; repro. in *ILN*
Wealth at death under £6000: probate, 15 March 1880, *CGPLA Eng. & Wales*

Branwhite, Nathan Cooper (1774/5–1857), miniature painter and engraver, was born in St Albans, Hertfordshire, the eldest son of Peregrine *Branwhite (*bap.* 1745, *d. c.*1795), minor poet and shopkeeper of Lavenham, Suffolk. He trained as an engraver under Isaac Taylor, an engraver and draughtsman, but became established as a miniaturist working in watercolour on ivory, exhibiting thirteen miniatures at the Royal Academy between 1802 and 1828. By 1810 he had settled in Bristol, where he became the leading miniature painter in the years from 1810 to 1840. He retained a subsidiary practice as an engraver, reproducing some of his own portraits but more usually other artists' work in the form of stipple engravings, many of medical or clerical subjects. These included a series of plates for the *Methodist Magazine* in 1807. Branwhite's best work dates from the 1810–40 period, and he was considered by his contemporaries to produce well-drawn and accurate likenesses of his subjects. He was an influential figure in artistic circles in Bristol, which included such figures as Francis Danby and James Johnson, with whom he was well acquainted, and he helped to organize the first exhibition of the work of Bristol artists in 1824–5. His lost drawing of Danby is now known only through a surviving photograph (Greenacre, *Danby*, frontispiece).

Branwhite and his wife, Hannah (*b.* 1778), had at least four children, of whom two sons, Nathan (1813–1894) and Charles *Branwhite (1817–1880), became artists. Nathan Branwhite junior practised as a miniaturist and portrait painter, working in a style close to his father's, and Charles became a successful painter of landscape watercolours, mainly of Wales, Somerset, and Devon. Branwhite died at the age of eighty-two on 18 March 1857 at 7 West Clifton Terrace, Bristol. An important group of his oil paintings, miniatures, and drawings, including two self-portraits, is in the collection of the City Museum and Art Gallery, Bristol.   V. REMINGTON

Sources F. Greenacre, *The Bristol school of artists: Francis Danby and painting in Bristol, 1810–1840* [1973], 181–9 [exhibition catalogue, City Museum and Art Gallery, Bristol, 4 Sept – 10 Nov 1973] • F. Greenacre, *Francis Danby, 1793–1861* (1988) [exhibition catalogue, City of Bristol Museum and Art Gallery and Tate Gallery, London, 1988] • B. Stewart and M. Cutten, *The dictionary of portrait painters in Britain up to 1920* (1997) • D. Foskett, *Miniatures: dictionary and guide* (1987), 498 • B. S. Long, *British miniaturists* (1929), 46 • L. R. Schidlof, *The miniature in Europe in the 16th, 17th, 18th, and 19th centuries*, 1 (1964), 107 • Thieme & Becker, *Allgemeines Lexikon* • Graves, *RA exhibitors* • *DNB* • census returns for parish of St Augustine-the-Less, Bristol, 1851 • d. cert.

Likenesses N. C. Branwhite, two self-portraits, oils on panel, *c.*1820, City Museum and Art Gallery, Bristol

Branwhite, Peregrine (*bap.* **1745**, *d. c.***1795**), poet, was baptized at Lavenham in Suffolk on 22 July 1745, the son of Rowland Branwhite and his wife, Sarah, *née* Brooke. He was brought up to the bombazine trade, which he carried on for some time at Norwich. He was not very successful, however, as he seems to have paid more attention to books than to the shop. He afterwards established a branch of the St Anne's School (London) at Lavenham, and conducted it personally for some years. He wrote: *Thoughts on the Death of Mr. Woodmason's Children, Destroyed by Fire 18 Jan 1782* (published anonymously); *An elegy on the lamented death of Mrs. Hickman, wife of the Rev. Thomas Hickman of Bildeston, Suffolk, who died 7 Sept 1789, when but just turned of 19* (1790); *Astronomy, or, A Description of the Solar System* (1791); and *The Lottery, or, The Effects of Sudden Affluence* (manuscript). A year or two before his death he moved to Hackney. He died at 32 Primrose Street, Bishopsgate Street, London, about 1795. Among his children was Nathan Cooper *Branwhite, miniature painter and engraver.
                           THOMPSON COOPER, *rev.* REBECCA MILLS

Sources BL, Add. MS 19166, fol. 234
Archives BL, Add. MS 19166, fol. 234

Braose, Philip de. *See* Briouze, Philip de (*d.* before 1201).

Braose, William (III) de. *See* Briouze, William (III) de (*d.* 1211).

Brasbridge, Joseph (1744–1832), autobiographer, was born on 17 March 1744 in Buckinghamshire, the son of 'an inland farmer' (Brasbridge, 1st edn, 2), Rowland Brasbridge, and his wife, Mary; he was baptized at St Mary's, Aylesbury, on 28 March 1744. Having moved to London, he established himself in late 1770 as partner to Mr Slade, a shopkeeper trading in silverware at 98 Fleet Street. In the following year he married his partner's sister, but soon after the birth of a son (19 March 1776) his wife died: together with the later death of his son at only eight years old, this precipitated a crisis in his life, and led to the dissolution of the partnership and a period of unwise living. Friends, however, rallied to his aid, and he was able to resume business in a property adjacent to his earlier partnership. He was married a second time, to Elizabeth Greenhill, at St Albans Abbey, on 7 October 1788. Two children ensued from the union: a daughter, who died aged twenty-eight years after injuries sustained on falling from a small carriage that was being wheeled by Brasbridge himself, and a son, who died in 1819 from a fever obtained while helping others. At this time Brasbridge and his wife gave up business, and retired to a cottage at Herne Hill. There, after a tour to Monmouthshire to visit a long-standing and generous client, he returned via Tintern, Bristol, and the Isle of Wight, and settled to write his autobiography: this was published in 1824 as *The Fruits of Experience, or, Memoir of Joseph Brasbridge, Written in his 80th Year*.

Brasbridge declares that his aim in writing was the hope

that his life would 'be found equally productive of warning to the dissipated and of encouragement to the industrious' (Brasbridge, 1st edn, 1), and his volume gives as much attention to his peccadilloes as to his prudence. First his story immerses itself in an account of life at 'the tavern club, the card party, the hunt, the fight' (ibid., 3), and the inevitable consequence of bankruptcy, and then it describes how, with the support of friends (notably the bookseller John Pridden) he re-established himself, traded successfully, joined the ranks of the worthy, and held office as a governor of Bridewell Hospital.

At the time of publication Brasbridge's memoir was received by the anti-banausic literati with amusement and disdain; today, as well as standing as an early example of an autobiography, it offers literary access to the social life of commerce viewed from the inside. Although his work is based neither on a diary nor on a ledger of transactions, such absence of factual support delights rather than irritates, and enables the reader to learn of the parties to his fall and of those who contributed to his success. In scene after scene of the first part of his book we meet his fellow tradesmen, printers, drapers, wax chandlers, carpenters, and sugar bakers, for example; in the second part, however, what might be termed the city at play becomes instead a review of the upwardly mobile, and we are introduced not only to country gentlemen and planters from the Indies placing orders for silver plate, but also to John Moore (a future archbishop of Canterbury), Lady Hamilton, and Mrs Piozzi, who was intrigued by a new line in papier mâché tea-trays adorned with figures from Etruscan vases derived from the recent discoveries at Herculaneum. That many of his anecdotes refer to events a decade or more before Brasbridge was writing reminds us that his focus was on the highlights of his experience—and adds to the attractiveness of his writing. After preparing his life and also his will, which is dated to 1827 at St Albans, Brasbridge died at Highgate on 28 February 1832; his wife survived him.   PAUL FOSTER

Sources J. Brasbridge, *The fruits of experience* (1824); 2nd edn (1824) · *Blackwood*, 16 (1824), 428–38 · *GM*, 1st ser., 94/1 (1824), 234–8 · *GM*, 1st ser., 102/1 (1832), 567–8 · *IGI* · *DNB* · private information (2004) [Bucks. RLSS]

Likenesses engraving, repro. in Brasbridge, *Fruits of experience*

Brasbridge, Thomas (1536/7–1593), Church of England clergyman and author, was (according to Anthony Wood) of a Northamptonshire family, but (by his own account) spent his childhood at Banbury, including a period of plague, probably the mid-1540s. He may have been the son of a Banbury couple, William Brasbridge (*d.* 1576) and Alice (*d.* 1580). He was elected a demy of Magdalen College, Oxford, in 1553 aged sixteen, graduated BA on 18 November 1558, and became a fellow in 1561 after a probationary fellowship (apparently fruitless) at All Souls in 1558. Ordained by Grindal in 1560, he studied both divinity and medicine, and remained to tend the plague-stricken during the epidemic of 1563–4. Having proceeded MA on 20 October 1564 and become Magdalen bursar in 1565 and dean of arts and then vice-president in 1572 and 1574, his academic career none the less stalled in the latter year

with an unsuccessful supplication in April for the degree of BD.

A dedication to Henry Hastings, earl of Huntingdon, of an exposition of *Abdias the Prophet* (1574) bore no obvious fruit in the shape of ecclesiastical preferment. Brasbridge had apparently left Magdalen before the controversy over the 1575 decanal election—initially, if Wood is correct, to mix medical practice and preaching at Banbury, but certainly later to reside in London, teaching and tending plague victims. It was his further experience of the disease which (together with indebtedness to one William Turner) underlay *The Poore Man's Jewel, that is to say, a Treatise of the Pestilence* (1578). The work reveals that by this time Brasbridge was married, although it does not give his wife's name.

In 1581 Brasbridge was presented by the crown to the vicarage of Banbury. Here he laid the foundations for the 'precise' reputation of the town, later to be consolidated by William Whately. Inevitably he became involved in the factional struggle between two local gentlemen, John Danvers, a defender of maypoles, and Sir Anthony Cope, who was of conventicling tendencies (according to Danvers) and the dedicatee of the 1592 edition of Brasbridge's *Poore Man's Jewel*. In 1589 Danvers's daughters were charged with attacking Brasbridge, not only with fists but with knives, and the following year Brasbridge's opponents were able to exploit his aversion to vestments and the sign of the cross to bring about his deprivation. Ninety-five parishioners, claiming the countenance of Sir Francis Knollys, sought to support Brasbridge by voluntary subscription to continue as a preacher (a role in which he had a certain reputation) against papists who, it was implied, would otherwise flourish under Danvers's influence. Brasbridge died three years later aged fifty-six, leaving a widow, Anne, and an unpublished commentary (finally published in 1615) on Cicero dedicated to the scholar and dean of Winchester Laurence Humphrey (1527–1590). Brasbridge was buried at Banbury on 11 November 1593. Administration of his will was granted to his widow on 15 March 1594.   JULIAN LOCK

Sources B. J. Blankenfeld, 'Puritans in the provinces: Banbury, Oxfordshire, 1554–1660', PhD diss., Yale U., 1985, chaps. 3, 6 · W. D. Macray, *A register of the members of St Mary Magdalen College, Oxford*, 8 vols. (1894–1915), vol. 2 · Foster, *Alum. Oxon.* · J. R. Bloxam, *A register of the presidents, fellows ... of Saint Mary Magdalen College*, 8 vols. (1853–85), vol. 2, pp. lxxii, cvi; vol. 4, p. 146 · Wood, *Ath. Oxon.* · A. Beesley, *The history of Banbury* (1841) · W. Potts, *History of Banbury* (1958) · T. Brasbridge, *The poore man's jewell, that is to say, a treatise of the pestilence*, 2nd edn (1592) · J. S. W. Gibson, ed., *Baptism and burial register of Banbury, Oxfordshire*, 1: 1558–1653, Banbury Historical Society, 7 (1965–6) · *Banbury wills and inventories, 1: 1591–1620*, ed. J. S. W. Gibson, Banbury Historical Society, 13 (1985) · J. S. W. Gibson and E. R. C. Brinkworth, eds., *Banbury corporation records: Tudor and Stuart*, Banbury Historical Society, Records section, 15 (1977), 59–60 · E. R. C. Brinkworth, 'The inventory of Thomas Brasbridge', *Cake and Cockhorse*, 3 (1965–8), 71–4 · information for privy council, 1589, PRO, SP 12/223/47 · J. Strype, *The history of the life and acts of the most reverend father in God Edmund Grindal*, new edn (1821), 53–4

Archives BL, petition to Lord Burghley, Lansdowne MS 64, fols. 45–6

Wealth at death £47 17s. 3d.; vicarage valued at £22 p.a.: Brink-worth, 'The inventory'; Gibson, ed., *Banbury wills*, 127–8; *Valor ecclesiasticus*

Brasbrigg, John. *See* Bracebridge, John (*fl. c.*1420).

Brass, John. *See* Brasse, John (1790–1833).

Brass, Sir Leslie Stuart (1891–1958), lawyer and public servant, was born at 29 Trafalgar Square, Chelsea, London, on 12 November 1891, the son of Lot Brass, mechanical engineer, and his wife, Elizabeth Harnor. He was educated at St Paul's School, and from 1910 to 1914 at Christ Church, Oxford, where he took a surprising third class in both moderations and greats—surprising because in his long career he demonstrated intellect and application of the highest order.

Defective eyesight made him unfit for military service, and Brass joined the Home Office in October 1915 as a temporary clerk in the criminal division. He was called to the bar in 1920 by the Inner Temple but never practised in the courts. He stayed in the criminal division until 1936. His work covered all aspects of the criminal law and the criminal courts, and he extended his expertise by membership of a number of departmental committees and conferences, for example on territorial waters, the hours of duty of staff at Broadmoor Institution, the suppression of counterfeiting, and the codification of international law.

As a result Brass worked up a practice helping and advising many parts of the Home Office on legal matters, while he was still concerned with the policy and administrative issues of the criminal division. This was recognized by his appointment as assistant legal adviser in 1936. He became legal adviser to the Home Office in 1947, a position which he held until his retirement in 1957.

As legal adviser to the Home Office Brass contributed greatly to many difficult issues where a balance had to be struck between individual liberty, the rule of law, and democratic pressures. He was a superb practitioner of the art of integrating legal expertise with government administration. His knowledge and experience were vast. He was much respected by parliamentary draftsmen, and lawyers in other government departments often sought his advice. He was appointed CBE in 1942 and was knighted in 1950.

Brass inspired respect and affection. Meetings with him were discursive and punctuated by long pauses for reflection. He analysed the issues and the options and some red herrings too, but his interlocutor usually left with a sound and legally viable view on the way forward. He was not completely at ease with ministers. He did not always deal with official files quickly, and the time and care that he sometimes devoted to giving an elaborate explanation of the delay might, it was thought, have been enough to dispose of the substance of the file. For many years he argued that it was too difficult to make wife maintenance orders enforceable between England and Scotland, as the two legal systems were so different, even though there was enforceability between England and much of the Commonwealth. A decision to make the change was taken during his absence from the office.

Brass's formal dress (always a stiff wing collar, black jacket, waistcoat, striped trousers, and boots) was offset by a puckish manner and squeaky voice. Outside the office he was kindly and hospitable within a select circle. He lived for some time in a hotel and was a churchwarden. He was unfamiliar with many everyday matters. When he decided to take a holiday, he would go to a mainline station and see where the trains were going to that day. Each year on Remembrance Sunday, his office, which was opposite the Cenotaph, was occupied by the ladies of the royal family. To decorate the room he arrived on the Saturday morning with an armful of flowers—buying them by the pound, it was said.

Many who knew Brass were astounded to learn of his marriage, on 29 October 1955, shortly before his retirement, to Jessie Buchanan West, the widow of John T. West, a Glasgow surgeon, and daughter of Neil Buchanan, a financial adviser. Brass died suddenly of heart failure in Western Road, Hove, Sussex, on 17 November 1958.

BRIAN CUBBON

Sources *The Times* (17 Nov 1958) · *WWW* · b. cert. · m. cert. · d. cert. · private information (2004) · *CGPLA Eng. & Wales* (1959)
Archives PRO, corresp. and papers, HO 189
Wealth at death £258,270 3s. 10d.: administration, 3 April 1959, *CGPLA Eng. & Wales*

Brass, William [Bill] (1921–1999), demographer and statistician, was born in Edinburgh on 5 September 1921, the only son and second of the three children of John Brass (1892–1962), engineer, and his wife, Margaret Tait, *née* Haig (1893–1968), dressmaker. Family circumstances were not easy: his father was gassed in the First World War and never fully recovered. Compulsory attendance at Presbyterian services during childhood had no enduring effect, although the other family commitment, to the Labour Party, proved more robust, leading to active campaigning during the 1945 election. He was educated at the Royal High School, Edinburgh, and began his undergraduate studies at Edinburgh University in 1940, gaining a war honours degree in mathematics and physics. From 1943 to 1946 his talents were directed to the war effort, where as scientific officer in the Royal Naval Scientific Service he worked on anti-submarine devices, statistical studies of electrical interference, and torpedo ballistics. He resumed his studies at Edinburgh University in 1946 and in 1947 completed his classified degree, an MA in mathematics and natural philosophy. Before university Brass learned no physics: his transition from the Latin and Greek at school was a source of some pride.

In January 1948 Brass joined the colonial service as a statistician in the East African statistical department, of which he was deputy director from 1953 to 1955, working *inter alia* on the East African medical survey. East Africa awoke his lifelong interest in the demography of the developing world, in those days little-developed despite its growing importance. Brass's arrival coincided with a major step forward in methods of conducting early colonial censuses. Previously it had been thought impossible to conduct them with European methods, by house-to-house visits by trained enumerators with printed schedules. Constructing demographic pictures from simple material began the lines of enquiry which dominated his career. He married Betty Ellen Agnes Topp (b. 1926) on 6 September 1948 while serving in Nairobi. She was then a schoolteacher, teaching mathematics, applied mathematics, and statistics. They had two daughters.

In 1955 Brass was appointed lecturer in the department of statistics at Aberdeen University, and was promoted in 1963 to senior lecturer. A year's leave of absence at the office of population research, Princeton University, facilitated the collaboration with Ansley Coale and others which yielded *The Demography of Tropical Africa* (1968), a pioneering work in a subject where knowledge is more often moved forward by papers in journals than by books.

In 1965 Brass became reader in medical demography at the London School of Hygiene and Tropical Medicine, where he remained for the rest of his professional life. Promoted in 1972 to professor of medical demography, he served as head of the department of medical statistics and epidemiology from 1977 to 1982. There with colleagues he developed his own distinctive approach, expanding the subject through new teaching and institutional arrangements. In 1970 he set up an MSc in medical demography (later the MSc in population and health), which proved a high road to a demographic career for many students. In 1974, with support from the overseas development administration he set up the Centre for Overseas Population Studies, which he directed until 1978. In that year its remit expanded with funding from the Economic and Social Research Council, and it became the Centre for Population Studies which Brass directed until his retirement in 1988.

Brass's interests were varied, but the essence of his achievement is his invention of a new armoury for demography: the 'indirect' or 'Brass' methods of demographic estimation. These provided a way to answer hitherto unanswerable questions about the demography of the third world: a 'demographer's stone' to turn base data into gold. From the middle of the twentieth century, as Brass's career developed, the demographic action was in the developing countries. There, annual population growth of up to 4 per cent generated populations where up to 50 per cent were aged under fifteen, hampering development and the relief of poverty. Without registration of births and deaths, and with censuses prone to serious error, demographic science could neither analyse adequately these momentous developments, nor identify early, crucial indications of the spread of family limitation.

With creative mathematical imagination and profound understanding of how populations worked, Brass realized that accurate estimates of mortality, the numbers of births, the spacing of children, and their trends could be derived from information which had little direct relationship to the desired measure. Thus conventional measures of fertility, normally derived from expensive registration systems in conjunction with censuses, could instead be derived from answers to simple questions in censuses and surveys about the number and survival of children, spouses, and parents. This growing suite of Brass methods, employed throughout the world, forms the basis of many estimates today used by the United Nations and other bodies, and even in historical demography. They included such innovations as the estimation of infant and child mortality from the proportions of children lost to women of given ages. Brass, tending to assume that data were guilty until proved innocent, showed how survey questions on births (suspected of bias) could yield accurate estimates of past fertility. His elegant and parsimonious 'model life table' methods employ the regularities in human mortality patterns to convert fragmentary data on deaths into scientifically usable statistics on lifetime risks of dying.

Further innovations provided mortality estimates for adults from the proportions of their children who were orphans. However, when data had improved and actual patterns of family building became better known, it turned out that an apparent, implausible, rise in fertility in earlier years had been correctly reported by the women concerned. It had not arisen because older women had, as supposed, under-reported their children, an assumption which Brass publicly regretted with characteristic sensitivity.

Brass turned his hand to many other areas, illuminating difficult topics such as household structure, and population projection, where he championed the importance of 'period' rather than the 'cohort' measures then more fashionable. He showed how subtle techniques of measurement could lift the cloud of pessimism about the birth-rate in modern societies. International fame gave him many opportunities to indulge his taste for travel, art, and archaeology.

Simplicity and directness were Brass's hallmarks. His students wondered at his ability to convey complex ideas with straightforward robust language, in an easily mimicked—and to some impenetrable—gravelly Scots accent. He solved problems with simple innovative ideas and a stubby pencil, then generously handed over solution and credit to students and colleagues. Hence Brass was greatly liked as well as universally admired, a combination by no means universal in academic life. His kindness and generosity extended to the hospitality of his home and his assumption of the persona of Santa Claus at children's parties.

Brass felt that there were fewer real demographers in the UK than actually claimed that title, a consequence of his belief in the central importance of mathematical models and technique as the defining property of the subject. Some felt, however, that his exceptional prominence in so small a subject in the UK distorted the field towards measurement of third-world phenomena, distracting it from the fundamental task of their explanation, and giving priority to demography over population studies.

Brass was the towering figure in British demography in his day, with an international reputation. He was president of the British Society for Population Studies (1975–7), became a fellow of the British Academy in 1979 and served on its council for three years. He was also president of the International Union for the Scientific Study of Population. In 1978 he won the prestigious Mindel C. Sheps award from the Population Association of America, and in 1981 he was appointed CBE. In 1984 he was elected a foreign associate of the US National Academy of Sciences. He became an emeritus professor on his retirement from the London School of Hygiene, and was elected an honorary fellow in 1997. He remained professionally active, working at the Netherlands Institute for Advanced Study, the Australian National University, with the US National Academy of Sciences, the Latin American centre CELADE, and other professional and charitable bodies, until he suffered a major stroke in 1997.

During his time at the London School of Hygiene, Brass lived with his wife in Muswell Hill, London. Following his stroke in 1997, he moved to a nursing home in Chalfont St Peter, Buckinghamshire, where he lived until his death on 11 November 1999. He was buried at Chalfont St Peter. His wife survived him.   DAVID COLEMAN

Sources 'William Brass, 1921–1999', *PBA*, 111 (2001), 413–26 · *The Independent* (19 Nov 1999) · *The Guardian* (20 Nov 1999) · G. Feeney, introduction, *Brass tacks*, ed. B. Zaba and J. Blacker (2001), 1–6 · private information (2004) [Betty Brass, wife; John Blacker; Dr Gigi Santow; Dr Richard Smith; Evelyn Dodd] · personal knowledge (2004) · *WW*

Brasse [Brass], **John** (1790–1833), educational writer, was the son of George Brass, a stonemason and sexton, of Richmond, Yorkshire. Lame from birth, he was nominated to a foundationer's place at Richmond grammar school, where he was taught by James Tate. A fund was raised to maintain him at Trinity College, Cambridge, where he was admitted as a sizar in 1807. He was made a scholar in 1810, graduated BA as sixth wrangler in 1811, and proceeded MA (1814), BD (1824), and DD (1829). He was a fellow of his college from 1811 until his marriage in 1817 to Isabella Milner of Richmond. Ordained deacon in 1813 and priest in 1814, he was vicar of Aysgarth, Yorkshire, from 1817 until 1824, when he was presented by his college to the living of Stotfold, Bedfordshire, to the augmentation of which he donated £500. He remained vicar of Stotfold until his death at Theobalds, Cheshunt, in 1833. His death was reported in May 1833; his wife had died on 28 November 1832. His friend, the politician Matthew Talbot Baines, also educated at Richmond grammar school and Trinity College, Cambridge, was one of his executors. He was survived by a daughter, Frances Jane, and a son, John Readshaw Brasse, who was admitted to Jesus College, Cambridge in 1840.

Brasse edited Euclid's *Elements of Geometry* (1825?), and the *Oedipus Rex* (1829, 1834), *Oedipus Coloneus* (1829), *Trachiniae* (1830), and *Antigone* (1830) of Sophocles. He published a Greek Gradus in 1828, which was reissued, in two volumes, at Göttingen, edited by C. F. G. Siedhof, in 1839–40, and in England, edited by the Revd F. E. J. Valpy, in 1847. He spelt his name Brass in early life, and Brasse in later years.   SIDNEY LEE, *rev.* M. C. CURTHOYS

Sources *GM*, 1st ser., 102/1 (1832), 582 · *GM*, 1st ser., 103/1 (1833), 473–4 · H. J. Rose, *A new general biographical dictionary*, ed. H. J. Rose

and T. Wright, 12 vols. (1853) · Venn, *Alum. Cant.* · will, PROB 11/1818/424 · *Letters of James Tate*, ed. L. P. Wenham (1965)

Brassey [*née* Allnutt], **Anna** [Annie], **Lady Brassey** (1839–1887), traveller, was born in London on 7 October 1839, daughter of John Allnutt and his first wife, Elizabeth Harriet, only child of John Fassett Burnett of May Place, Crayford, Kent. Her mother died when she was in infancy and she lived with her grandfather at Clapham, and afterwards with her father in Chapel Street and Charles Street, Berkeley Square. On 9 October 1860 she married at St George's, Hanover Square, London, Thomas *Brassey (1836–1918), created Baron Brassey in 1886, liberal politician and writer on naval affairs, eldest son of Thomas *Brassey, the railway contractor. They had one son and four daughters. She and her husband lived at Beauport Park, near Hastings, and then at Normanhurst Court, Catsfield, Sussex, a house which they built in 1870. She busied herself with the management of the estate and with good works in the neighbourhood, as well as in being a leader of society. She was also drawn into politics by her husband's, eventually successful, attempts to enter parliament.

Annie Brassey made her name as a traveller on ocean voyages with her husband, and as a travel writer with accounts of their journeys. *The Flight of the Meteor* (1866) and *A Cruise in Eothen* (1872) described journeys in the Mediterranean and to North America. Their success encouraged the Brasseys to embark on a circumnavigation of the globe and on 1 July 1876 they set sail from Chatham in Thomas Brassey's new 531 ton, three-masted, topsail schooner *Sunbeam*, with its 350 horsepower steam engine, which had been launched in 1874. They were forty-four on board: the Brasseys and their children, a small party of friends, a professional crew, and a complete domestic staff.

Their way lay across the south Atlantic, through the Strait of Magellan into the Pacific Ocean, continuing by way of Tahiti, Hawaii, and Japan to Penang and thence to Ceylon, Aden, and the Red Sea. While the *Sunbeam* passed through the Suez Canal, Annie Brassey and the children went overland to Cairo to visit the pyramids, rejoining the party at Alexandria. Their arrival at Hastings on 27 May 1877 completed the eleven-month voyage. It had been a complete success, uneventful except for a dangerous flooding of the decks in a high sea off Ushant and their rescue of the crew of a ship on fire near Rio. The monotony of the days at sea was varied by excursions ashore, planned and led by Annie Brassey to the colourful street markets of Rio, Valparaiso, and Singapore, and to scenes of natural beauty in Tahiti, Ceylon, and Hawaii with its thrilling volcanoes.

The voyage was to make Annie Brassey a celebrity not because she had been round the world in a luxury yacht, but because she struck exactly the right note in her book about the adventure, using the entries in her journal to describe rambles ashore and daily life afloat: this was lively enough with five children under fourteen, a dog, three birds, and a kitten aboard. *A Voyage in the Sunbeam* (1878) was a solid work of 508 pages with maps and wood-

Anna Brassey, Lady Brassey (1839–1887), by Bassano, 1883

engravings. It was a best-seller overnight, reached its nineteenth edition in 1896, and was translated into French, German, Italian, Swedish, and Hungarian. A contemporary criticized her style as 'gossiping' and unintellectual, but it was conceded that she wrote 'with fluency and accuracy' (Adams, 577). There followed *Sunshine and Storm in the East* (1880) and *In the Trades, Tropics and the Roaring Forties* (1885), which described voyages to Cyprus and Constantinople and to the West Indies and Madeira and which, although less popular than *A Voyage in the Sunbeam*, had a wide circulation. In September 1885 the *Sunbeam* took W. E. Gladstone to Norway; he wrote his election manifesto during the voyage. Annie Brassey described the journey in an article in the *Contemporary Review* (48, October 1885, 480).

During her voyages Annie Brassey made large collections of natural and ethnological curiosities which she displayed at exhibitions at Hastings in 1881 and 1885, and at South Kensington in 1883. As busy ashore as afloat, she took an especial interest in the St John Ambulance Association, for which she was elected dame chevalière of the order of St John of Jerusalem in 1881. She left England on 16 November 1886 in the *Sunbeam* on her last voyage, undertaken for the sake of her health. She visited India, Borneo, and Australia, but contracted malaria and died at sea on 14 September 1887 and was buried at lat. 15°50″ S, long. 110°38″ E at sunset on the same day. An account, edited by Lady Broome, *The Last Voyage*, was published in 1889.

The cruises of the *Sunbeam* may have resembled family picnics rather than voyages of discovery, but Annie Brassey, who inspired and organized them, is not to be denied the status of a true traveller. A poor sailor, never really well at sea, she dared all it could do to her, in order that she might visit the farthest corners of the earth. As her husband wrote, 'the voyage would not have been undertaken and assuredly it would never have been completed without the impulse derived from her perseverance and determination' (Brassey, preface).

E. H. MARSHALL, *rev.* DOROTHY MIDDLETON

Sources W. H. D. Adams, *Celebrated women travellers of the nineteenth century* (1896) · P. Kemp, ed., *The Oxford companion to ships and the sea* (1988) · T. Brassey, preface, in A. Brassey, *A voyage in the Sunbeam* (1889) · *Annual Register* (1887) · private information (1901) · Burke, *Peerage*

Likenesses Bassano, photograph, 1883, NPG [*see illus.*] · F. Grant, oils; at Normanhurst Court in 1901 · lithograph, BM · lithograph, NPG

Wealth at death £21,424: resworn administration with will, Nov 1888, *CGPLA Eng. & Wales*

Brassey, Thomas (1805–1870), civil engineering contractor, was born on 7 November 1805 at Buerton, near Audlem, Cheshire, the son of John Brassey, landowner, and his wife, Elizabeth. He had two brothers and one sister. Brassey attended Mr Harting's school in Chester and then, at the age of sixteen, was apprenticed to a land surveyor and agent named Lawton. Five years later, having become Lawton's partner, Brassey went to live in Birkenhead where he augmented the experience which he had acquired in road surveying and improvement, including work under Thomas Telford on the London to Holyhead road, by engaging in property development in the new town.

Among his achievements in these years was the building of a new road from Tranmere to Bromborough with a bridge over Bromborough pool. A meeting with George Stephenson at Storeton quarries, Wirral, when the engineer was looking for stone for Sankey Viaduct during the construction of the Liverpool and Manchester Railway (1826–30), proved a significant turning point in Brassey's career. His competence in business apparently so impressed Stephenson and his assistant, Joseph Locke, that they later encouraged Brassey, who still had only the most slender experience of civil engineering work, to compete with some of the country's leading contractors for the Penkridge contract of the Grand Junction Railway (Birmingham to Warrington). This and subsequent major work under Locke on the London and Southampton and Glasgow, Paisley, and Greenock railways had by the summer of 1841 earned him at least £500,000 and laid the foundations of his career as a railway builder. On 27 December 1831 Brassey married Maria Faringdon (*d.* 1877), daughter of Joseph Harrison of Liverpool and Birkenhead; she strongly encouraged Brassey to extend his career as a railway contractor. The Brasseys had four children: John, who died very young, Henry Arthur, Victor, and Thomas *Brassey.

Thomas Brassey (1805–1870), by George Zobel (after Frederick Newenham, in or before 1850)

The 1840s saw Brassey embark on a series of assignments which made him the greatest international civil engineering contractor of his time. His initial achievements outside Britain came in France where, in partnership with William Mackenzie, Brassey successfully tendered first for the line from Paris to Rouen and then its extensions to Dieppe and Le Havre. Either with Mackenzie or alone, Brassey eventually contributed to the construction of approximately 870 miles of railway in France, including the lines connecting Orléans and Bordeaux, Amiens and Boulogne, and Mantes and Cherbourg. An extraordinary event associated with his work in France was the collapse in January 1846 of the huge Barentin Viaduct on the Rouen to Le Havre line which occurred partly through the use of mortar of an inferior quality.

The successful completion of the railways between Paris and the channel coast proved the springboard for contracts in Spain, Belgium, the Netherlands, Italy, Switzerland, Denmark, Norway, Austria, Poland, Ukraine, and Romania totalling approximately 3000 miles of line throughout continental Europe by the time of Brassey's death. They included the first substantial railway tunnel in Switzerland, the Hauenstein between Basel and Olten, and the construction of track at considerable height on both sides of the approaches to the Mont Cenis Tunnel.

Outside Europe, Brassey was responsible for about 1550

miles of railway. He worked in Australia, Argentina, Algeria, Brazil, and India, but his most demanding assignment, and one of the least profitable, was the building and equipping of the Grand Trunk Railway of Canada which he undertook in partnership with S. M. Peto, E. L. Betts, and W. Jackson. This entailed making the majority of the railway linking Toronto with Montreal and Quebec and the construction of a tubular bridge of massive proportions across the St Lawrence at Montreal. In order to provide the vast quantities of materials and equipment for the line and bridge, the contractors set up Canada Works, Birkenhead, which, under the management of George Harrison, Brassey's brother-in-law, and William Heap, made the locomotives, excavating machinery, bridge sections, and other components for Canada. After four years' work, the first train ran from Toronto in October 1856, and across the bridge in 1859.

The outbreak of the Crimean War brought a request to Brassey, Peto, and Betts from the government for the construction of a line about 7 miles long from the port of Balaklava for the carriage of supplies required by the allied forces besieging Sevastopol. The speedy completion of this line in 1855 played a significant part in securing victory and alleviating the suffering of the troops.

Despite the demand for his services abroad, Brassey did not neglect opportunities at home. In the 1840s the partnership of Brassey, Mackenzie, and John Stephenson obtained two contracts on the Chester and Holyhead Railway and responsibility for the entire lengths of the Lancaster and Carlisle, Trent Valley (Rugby to Stafford), and Caledonian (Carlisle to Glasgow and Edinburgh) lines; the combined tender price of this work was £2.84 million. Among his contributions to other major projects in this decade were part of the North Staffordshire Railway, the route of the Great Northern Railway from King's Cross to Peterborough, and lines to connect the Caledonian Railway with Forfar, via Stirling and Perth.

The promotion of many secondary lines in rural areas in the second half of the nineteenth century meant that contractors were often expected not only to build but also to finance railway companies, and sometimes even manage their traffic. Brassey showed no reluctance to participate in this process and made major purchases of shares or accepted debentures as the contractor of several lines, including the Salisbury and Yeovil, Ringwood, Christchurch, and Bournemouth, and Hereford, Ross, and Gloucester. More conventional business arrangements in the 1860s saw him engaged in work of national importance with contracts on the Midland Railway's Bedford to St Pancras route. His contribution to the British network finally came to approximately 1900 miles of line.

Although Brassey was predominantly a railway builder, his achievements included two projects of first-rate importance outside that field. The opening of Victoria Dock in 1855, as constructed by Brassey, Peto, and Betts, gave London its first dock designed for steamships and served by railways. In the 1860s, in association with Henry Harrison and Alexander Ogilvie, he completed the middle level sewer (Kensal Green to Bow) of the new drainage system of London designed by J. W. Bazalgette.

The financial crisis of 1866 began in banking and spread to many other forms of business, including civil engineering. Brassey avoided the bankruptcy which overtook Peto but lost, it is believed, about £1 million. The construction of the Grand Trunk Railway, his joint ownership of Victoria Dock, and the leases of Danish lines and the London, Tilbury, and Southend Railway were at one time or another a burden on his financial resources.

The reputation for integrity and generosity of spirit accorded to Brassey in his lifetime endured throughout the twentieth century. He was not afflicted by the insularity of outlook of some others in his profession. He admired American methods of manufacture and, in common with Locke, saw much merit in the system of railway promotion adopted in France. The extent of his commitments compelled him to delegate considerable authority to talented agents, such as James Falshaw and Stephen Ballard, who then operated largely without interference. In return, they, and, it is said, many of his navvies, regarded him with respect and even affection. Brassey accepted two foreign honours as a matter of courtesy but eschewed all suggestion of awards in Britain. Although a wealthy man he was without venal instinct or desire for an ostentatious lifestyle. His greatest achievement was to raise the status of the civil engineering contractor to the eminence already attained in the mid-nineteenth century by the engineer.

The first signs of a serious deterioration in Brassey's health appeared in 1867 and he died of a brain haemorrhage on 8 December 1870 in the Victoria Hotel, St Leonards, Sussex, where he had lived for some years. A member of the Church of England, he was buried at the parish church, Catsfield, Sussex. He died one of the wealthiest of the self-made Victorians, leaving an estate of almost £3.2 million in the United Kingdom, but, on the evidence of records at an early point in his career, considerable assets abroad. His sons entered Liberal politics and society. Some of his money benefited the Bodleian Library, Oxford, via his son Thomas.   DAVID BROOKE

Sources A. Helps, *Life and labours of Mr Brassey* (1872); repr. (1969) · *PICE*, 33 (1871–2), 246–51 · *The Engineer*, 30 (1847), 406 · T. Brassey, *Work and wages* (1872) · C. Walker, *Thomas Brassey: railway builder* (1969) · J. Millar, *Thomas Brassey, railway builder, re Canada Works, Birkenhead* (1993) · A. W. Currie, *The Grand Trunk Railway of Canada* (1957) · M. Chrimes, *Civil engineering, 1839–1889: a photographic history* (1991) · *CGPLA Eng. & Wales* (1871) · d. cert.
Archives Flintshire RO, Hawarden, contracts and papers relating to the construction of railways in Italy · Inst. CE, tender for the construction of the Taw Valley railway | Inst. CE, business records of Messrs Mackenzie and Brassey
Likenesses M. Wagmüller, marble bust, 1871, Inst. CE · G. B. Black, lithograph, BM · M. Wagmüller, bust, Chester Cathedral · G. Zobel, engraving (after F. Newenham, in or before 1850), Inst. CE [*see illus.*] · carte-de-visite, probably Inst. CE; repro. in Chrimes, *Civil engineering*, 26 · engraving, National Railway Museum, York · portrait, repro. in A. Helps, *Life and labours of Mr Brassey* (1872), frontispiece
Wealth at death under £3,200,000 in UK: double probate, March 1871, *CGPLA Eng. & Wales* (1871) · over £2,000,000—trust fund: *The Times* (6 Feb 1871)

Brassey, Thomas, first Earl Brassey (1836–1918), politician, was born at Stafford on 11 February 1836, the eldest son of Thomas *Brassey (1805–1870), civil engineering contractor, of Buerton, Cheshire, and his wife, Maria Faringdon (d. 1877), second daughter of Joseph Harrison of Liverpool. He was educated at Rugby School and University College, Oxford, where he took honours in the school of law and modern history (1859). His father's railway enterprises led to school holidays being spent partly at Portsmouth, where he acquired his love of the sea and interest in maritime affairs, and partly in France, where he obtained a sound knowledge of the French language. Other holidays and Oxford vacations were spent in yachting cruises, a pastime in which he took great interest throughout his life. He was elected to the Royal Yacht Squadron a year after leaving Oxford. Brassey decided not to follow his father's profession but to join the parliamentary bar, and he became a pupil of John Buller, the leading parliamentary draftsman of the day. He was called to the bar in 1866, but soon abandoned a legal career for politics. Having already stood unsuccessfully as a Liberal for Birkenhead in 1861, he was elected for Devonport in June 1865, but, before taking his seat, was defeated at the general election a few weeks later. He failed at a by-election at Sandwich in 1866, but was successful at Hastings in 1868 and retained that seat until 1886.

From his entry into parliament until 1880 Brassey worked hard and laboriously at the subjects in which he was interested: wages, the condition of the working classes, and employers' liability; naval matters of every department, administration of the dockyards, naval pay, shipbuilding and design, organization of the naval reserves, and the creation of the Royal Naval Volunteer Artillery (1873). He compiled useful volumes entitled *Work and Wages* (1872), *Foreign Work and English Wages* (1879), *British Seamen* (1877), *The British Navy* (1882–3), an encyclopaedic work in five volumes, and *Sixty Years of Progress* (1904). The character of his work and his conception of his duty in public life are aptly described in his own preface to *The British Navy*:

> Few men have entered the House of Commons with more slender share of what are usually described as parliamentary talents than the humble individual who writes the present introduction; and if, by devotion to special subjects, he has gained the confidence of the public, his experience may perhaps encourage others.

There is no doubt that Brassey's untiring industry contributed greatly to the reforms in naval administration and maritime policy that were being evolved as the conditions of the old sailing navy and marine rapidly passed away. Besides his parliamentary work he published articles in the leading reviews, wrote letters to *The Times*, issued pamphlets, and read papers and lectures at public institutions, nearly always on labour questions or naval and marine affairs. He spent part of every parliamentary recess at sea in his yacht, Gladstone accompanying him in 1885, and in 1876–7 he made a tour round the world, an account of which is given in his first wife's popular book,

Thomas Brassey, first Earl Brassey (1836–1918), by London Stereoscopic Co.

Voyage in the 'Sunbeam' (1878). The later voyages of the *Sunbeam* Brassey described in his book *'Sunbeam' R. Y. S.*, published a few months before his death. R. T. Pritchett was his artist on these voyages. Brassey was the first private yachtsman to be given the certificate of master mariner after examination. Although he was never happier than when afloat in his yacht, he never undertook a long voyage unless it was to fulfil some public purpose; and in 1916 he handed over the *Sunbeam* to the government of India for hospital work during the war.

In 1880 Brassey joined Gladstone's second administration as civil lord of the Admiralty, and held this office for four years. In 1881 he was created KCB in recognition of his services to the naval reserves, and in 1884 he was made parliamentary secretary to the Admiralty, a position which he held until the end of that parliament (1885). As civil lord his administrative responsibility was limited to the control of the works department and of Greenwich Hospital. He was more interested in other branches of naval affairs, and employed himself in writing detailed memoranda on all kinds of subjects for the benefit of his colleagues, who appreciated his keen interest in naval matters; but his productions, while full of facts, seldom led to any concrete conclusion, and the effect of them was rather to ventilate the subject than to produce any tangible results. His short term as parliamentary secretary and spokesman of the Admiralty did not add to his reputation, for he was no parliamentary debater nor was he quick at taking up points made against his department in the House of Commons. Brassey was not included in Gladstone's 1885 government. He supported home rule, and was defeated at Liverpool in the general election of 1886. In that year first appeared *Brassey's Naval Annual*, which was for many years the most authoritative survey of naval affairs throughout the world. He was raised to the peerage as Baron Brassey of Bulkeley, Cheshire, in Gladstone's resignation honours (1886).

Brassey served as lord-in-waiting to the queen from 1893 to 1895, when he was appointed governor of Victoria. His administration of Victoria coincided with the movement for the federation of the Australian colonies, and he played a considerable part in bringing this measure into effect. The queen's assent to the Commonwealth Act was given a few months after his departure (1900). He won a large measure of popularity among the people of Victoria and displayed his usual industry in lecturing and speaking on naval defence, imperial federation, and industrial subjects.

After his return to England, Brassey was an incessant advocate, both at the Institution of Naval Architects, of which he was president (1893–6), and in the House of Lords, of the employment of armed merchant ships as cruisers for the protection of British trade routes. His instinct was always to make the best use of material ready to hand rather than embark on the expense of new weapons. He preferred rearming old battleships and subsidizing merchant cruisers to new construction, and using fishermen as reservists to increasing the personnel of the navy. He did not appreciate the inadequacy of these measures in the days when scientific development had so far advanced and formidable rivals were creating powerful modern fleets.

In 1906 Brassey was promoted GCB and in 1908 he was appointed lord warden of the Cinque Ports. At the coronation of George V (1911) he was created Earl Brassey and Viscount Hythe. Brassey was married twice. His first wife, whom he married in 1860, was Anna (1839–1887) [*see* Brassey, Anna], the only child of John Allnutt, of Charles Street, Berkeley Square, London. She was a devoted helper in his parliamentary career and in his yachting voyages, and published accounts of many of their journeys; she died at sea in 1887 off Port Darwin. They had one son, Thomas Allnutt, second Earl Brassey, and four daughters. In 1890 Brassey married the Hon. Sybil de Vere Capell (*b.* 1858), the youngest daughter of Viscount Malden, and granddaughter of the sixth earl of Essex, with whom he had one daughter. He died in London on 23 February 1918. The second Earl Brassey, a generous benefactor to the Bodleian Library and to Balliol College, Oxford, died without issue in 1919 and the title became extinct.

V. W. BADDELEY, *rev.* H. C. G. MATTHEW

Sources GEC, *Peerage* · A. Brassey, *The last voyage* (1889) · A. Brassey, *A voyage in 'The Sunbeam'* (1878) · T. Brassey, *Recent letters and speeches* (1879) · Gladstone, *Diaries*

Archives Bishopsgate Institute, London, letters to George Howell · BL, corresp. with W. E. Gladstone, Add. MSS 44433–44789, *passim* · Bodl. Oxf., corresp. with Lord Kimberley · Bodl. Oxf., corresp. with Lord Selborne · CUL, corresp. with Lord Hardinge · NL Aus., corresp. with Alfred Deakin · NL Scot., corresp. mainly with Lord Rosebery · U. Newcastle, corresp. with Walter Runciman

Likenesses Ape [C. Pellegrini], chromolithograph caricature, NPG; repro. in *VF* (6 Oct 1877), pl. 260 · London Stereoscopic Co., two photographs, NPG [*see illus.*] · oils (after F. Holl), Indian Institute, Oxford

Wealth at death £134,805 17s. 5d.: probate, 21 Nov 1918, *CGPLA Eng. & Wales*

Bratby, John Randall (1928–1992), artist, was born on 19 July 1928 at a nursing home in Wimbledon, the first of two children of George Alfred Bratby (1887–1947), wine taster, and his wife, Lily Beryl Randall (1897–1945). The Bratbys traced their roots to Derbyshire, while the Randalls were a London family. Instability marked the Bratbys, with Bratby's grandfather dying in an insane asylum, and an uncle confined for life in a mental institution. George Bratby was to manifest symptoms of mental illness, and the shadow of this darkened Bratby's own life, and made him at times fearful for his sanity. It was not a happy childhood. From an early age, Bratby was aware of his father's frightening paranoid energy: a man quite capable of believing there were hidden microphones in his chimney, or that the radio could listen to you just as you could hear it. There were constant rows between his parents, and there was little warmth or affection in the home. Later, the increasingly deranged and now unemployed George Bratby embarrassed his son by wandering the suburban streets of Norbiton in sandals and casual clothes while everyone else was going to work.

At school, Bratby was shy, unpopular, and bullied. He did not distinguish himself at lessons. Coupled with his miserable home life, this led him to create an alternative world: he resold school buns at breaktime, wrote pornographic stories for the reading of which he charged, and trained himself as a boxer. Not until he was seventeen did he begin to show any real aptitude for art, and then it was due to the inspired teaching of Harold Watts, who recognized the potential in Bratby's sketches of boxers. Conscripted, Bratby was swiftly discharged on account of his extreme myopia, but managed to obtain an ex-service grant, with which, at Watts's encouragement, he went on to study at Kingston School of Art (1947–50). There he discovered the extraordinary determination to succeed which took him on to the Royal College of Art (RCA; 1951–4), and his early fame.

Bratby believed that he had inherited his father's energy, and that it was this which gave him the drive to paint. The artistic impulse he attributed to his mother's family. Painfully shy and often aggressive because of it, he was unsuited to art school camaraderie, and found academic training uncongenial. At Kingston he failed the intermediate exam in arts and crafts, and was forced to leave. But by this point, painting was his life-raft, and he continued to paint and draw obsessively. He managed to produce a body of work, awkward but not without talent, which convinced the professor of the Slade School of Fine Art to offer him a postgraduate place. Bratby, with what was to become typical cheek and canniness, managed to swap his Slade place for one at the Royal College, which he considered a superior institution. It was while a student at

John Randall Bratby (1928–1992), self-portrait, 1954 [*Peterborough Joans*]

the RCA that the Bratby myth began to coalesce. According to his own later slightly embarrassed account he frequented prostitutes and was tempted into physical violence. He lived wildly, splurging his grant and then having to stow away in the attics of the college (from which he and his paintings were once summarily ejected), or begging and sleeping rough in Hyde Park. His work matched his lifestyle. Influenced by the down-to-earth realism of Sickert, Bratby depicted the seedier aspects of his surroundings, and would be found in the college studios painting a dustbin, or setting up his easel in a lavatory. The style of his painting was correspondingly crude and vigorous—he favoured thick pigment in sombre colours. The professor of painting at the college, Carel Weight, thought him the most talented student he had ever had. On 2 April 1953 he married his fellow RCA student Jean Esme Oregon Cooke (b. 1927). A sculptor and potter, Cooke subsequently became a painter of real distinction.

In 1954 Bratby had the first of a series of one-man exhibitions at the acclaimed Beaux Arts Gallery, and his public career was launched. He began to win prizes: first in the John Moores junior section (1957), and Guggenheim awards (1956, 1958). In 1954 he first exhibited a painting at the Royal Academy, becoming an associate in 1959, and a Royal Academician in 1971. With his trademark thick paint and his flair for publicity (he had a talent for leaking stories to the press), Bratby soon became not only a folk hero in the art schools of Britain, but a household name. At first the critics' response was overwhelmingly supportive, with the *Sunday Times* comparing Bratby's rendition of a cornflake packet favourably with Velázquez's *Rokeby Venus*. In 1956 he was chosen to represent Britain at the Venice Biennale, along with the other so-called kitchen sink painters—Edward Middleditch, Jack Smith, and Derrick Greaves. A major early painting, *Still-Life with Chip Frier*, was that year bought by the Tate Gallery. Other examples of his work are in the Museum of Modern Art, New York, and the Victoria and Albert Museum, London.

In 1957 Bratby was commissioned to paint the pictures for the film of Joyce Carey's novel *The Horse's Mouth*, starring Alec Guinness as its bohemian artist-hero. He exhibited his work in America, and bought a house in Blackheath. Then, in 1960, he was suddenly dropped by the influential critics, as abstraction and pop art seized their collective attention. Although he remained a thoroughly popular artist, selling well until the end of his life, Bratby's critical reputation slumped, to show the first signs of reassessment only in 1990. From 1960 onwards, his behaviour must be seen in the context of early success painfully followed by what he saw as consignment to art historical limbo.

Disillusioned with painting, and perhaps having momentarily overworked his seam, Bratby took up writing, producing a stream of luridly autobiographical illustrated novels, beginning with *Breakdown* in 1960. This was followed by *Breakfast and Elevenses* (1961), *Brake-Pedal Down* (1962), *Break 50 Kill* (1963), and a host of unpublished sequels and short stories. Bratby was driven to be prolific: in his writing he was as compulsive and compelling as in his painting. A portrait series begun in 1967 eventually numbered more than 1500 pictures. Meanwhile, in 1970 Bratby suffered a crisis in his life and art, adopting a highly charged Fauvist palette and threatening his marriage with increasingly wayward behaviour. He drank heavily and pursued young ladies. There were several driving offences. Then in 1974 he met Patricia (Patti) Prime (*b.* 1931), an actress, through a lonely hearts column. In 1975 he was divorced from Jean Cooke. He married Patti on 4 May 1977, and a period of relative stability ensued.

As Bratby grew older, he tended to work frenetically, and then spend up to half the rest of the year travelling abroad on the proceeds. As he scrawled late in life on a Missoni carrier bag: 'I do not want to be right and broke, I'd rather be wrong and in funds.' If the paintings sometimes suffered as a result, there was usually still some trace of the Bratby genius to transform and reinvent what he saw with urgent physicality. The intensity of his early work created a hard act even for Bratby to follow, while his popularity in the media tended to militate against his genuine achievement. He died outside his home in Hastings, the Cupola and Tower of the Winds, Belmont Road, on 20 July 1992, and was cremated at Hastings crematorium on 29 July. He was survived by his wife, Patti.

ANDREW LAMBIRTH

Sources private information (2004) · A. Clutton-Brock, *Painters of today: John Bratby* (1961) · J. Bratby, *Stanley Spencer's early self-portrait* (1969) · R. Gibson, *John Bratby portraits* (1991) · A. Lambirth, *Venice: the Hemingway suite* (1991) · *The Times* (22 July 1992) · *The Times* (28 July 1992) · *The Times* (30 July 1992) · *The Independent* (23 July 1992) · *The Independent* (30 July 1992)

Archives Tate collection, papers | priv. coll., Patti Bratby MSS · priv. coll., Jean Cooke MSS · priv. coll., Julian Hartnoll MSS · priv. coll., Bob Simm MSS

Likenesses J. R. Bratby, self-portrait, pencil, 1954, Tullie House, Museum and Art Gallery, Carlisle [*see illus.*] · J. R. Bratby, self-portrait, oils, 1955, Man. City Gall. · J. R. Bratby, self-portrait, pencil, 1956–7, Arts Council, London · J. R. Bratby, self-portrait, oils, 1957, Walker Art Gallery, Liverpool · photographs, 1961–73, Hult. Arch. · J. R. Bratby, self-portrait, oils, 1963, NPG · J. R. Bratby, self-portrait, oils, 1967, NPG · J. R. Bratby, self-portrait, oils, 1990 (with Patti), NPG · photograph, repro. in *The Times* (22 July 1992) · photograph, repro. in *The Times* (28 July 1992)

Wealth at death £143,914: probate, 19 Aug 1993, *CGPLA Eng. & Wales*

Brathwaite, Richard (1587/8–1673), poet and writer, was born at Burneshead Hall, Kendal, the second surviving son of Thomas Brathwaite (*d. c.*1610), barrister, and Dorothy Bindloss of Westmorland. There were seven children of this union. Although there are no entries of his birth in the parish register, a portrait found at Dodding Green, Kendal, was painted in 1626 and describes him as 'aged 38'. Brathwaite makes reference to his childhood in later writings such as *A Spirituall Spicerie* (1638). A minor writer of the seventeenth century, he nevertheless published copious volumes stretching across a wide generic range. Authorship of some attributed texts is disputed.

Brathwaite went to Oriel College, Oxford (*c.*1604), and in 1621 dedicated *Times Curtaine Drawne, or, The Anatomie of Vanitie* to 'his deare foster-Mother, the Universitie of Oxford'. From there he proceeded to Cambridge, probably to Pembroke College since he was under the authority of Lancelot Andrewes, who was master of the college until 1605. From 1609 onwards, Brathwaite trained in law at Gray's Inn, London, but when his father died about 1610 he apparently concentrated on managing the family estates left him in his father's will.

Although his writing alludes to contemporary London and to the court (which, despite his royalist leanings, he was not averse to satirizing), it is not clear how far Brathwaite was part of the contemporary London literary scene. References to him in the writings of others are rare, although he certainly knew Thomas Heywood, and scholars now suggest possible co-authorship of texts with Thomas Randolph. Thomas Nabbes dedicated *The Unfortunate Mother* to him in 1640. Dedicatees of his own work tend to be predictable patrons, significant aristocrats at the court, such as Henry Wriothesley, earl of Southampton (dedicatee of *The Schollers Medley* in 1614), and Henry Somerset, earl of Worcester (recipient of *The Arcadian Princesse* in 1635).

On 4 May 1617 Brathwaite married Frances Lawson (*d.* 1633) at Hurworth, near Neasham in co. Durham. She was the daughter of James Lawson of Neasham. They had nine children (five sons and four daughters). During these years Brathwaite, as well as writing, concentrated on his estate

Richard Brathwaite (1587/8–1673), by William Marshall, pubd
1638

and on county-based duties. He was a local justice of the
peace and captain of the trained bands in Westmorland,
as well as a deputy lieutenant of the county. Brathwaite's
older brother, Sir Thomas, died in 1618 leaving one son,
George, but from this time onwards Richard appears to
have assumed the headship of the family.

On 7 March 1633 Brathwaite's own wife, Frances, died.
In 1634 he wrote a series of elegies in her memory: *Anniversaries upon his Panarete*. He married again on 27 June 1639
after a lengthy period of mourning. His second wife was
Mary, daughter of Roger Crofts of Kirtington, Yorkshire.
Anniversaries upon his Panarete teasingly describes her as a
'widow' but there is no evidence to confirm her status as
such. They had one son, who became renowned as a naval
captain: Sir Strafford Brathwaite, eventually killed in a
sea-fight with Algerian pirates.

Richard Brathwaite's two chief periods of authorial
productivity were between 1611 and 1622 and 1630 and
1641, but he continued to publish in the 1650s and 1660s.
In 1611 he published a collection of poems entitled *The
Golden Fleece*. Writing at this point still seems a family
affair—there are references to squabbles over his father's
will and the volume is dedicated to his uncle and older
brother. In 1614 he published a book of pastorals, *The Poet's
Willow*, a moral treatise entitled *The Prodigals Teares* which
is on the theme of vanity, and *The Schollers Medley* (reissued
in 1638 and 1651 as *A Survey of History, or, A Nursery for Gentry*). This last text is a prose text which interrogates the discipline of history (dividing the topic into areas such as divine, discursive, moral, and 'Mixt' history) and the office of
a historian. Ancient Roman and Greek historians are a
focus of particular praise. The variation between these
three volumes, all issued in the same year, indicates
Brathwaite's literary versatility.

Brathwaite's *Love's Labyrinth* (1615) includes a poetic
reworking of the story of Pyramus and Thisbe. 1617 saw *A

Solemne Joviall Disputation, a prose treatise on drinking. Its
second section bears the title 'The smoaking age, or, The
man in the mist: with the life and death of tobacco'. This
was published anonymously and a Latin version by 'Blasius Multibibus' appeared in 1626. Brathwaite regularly
published under pseudonyms. In 1619 the verse-text *A New
Spring Shadowed* by 'Musophilus' appeared. *Essaies upon the
Five Senses* appeared in 1620, and in 1621 Brathwaite wrote a
collection of pastorals entitled *The Shepheards Tales* and
Times Curtaine Drawne; the former contains satires,
eclogues, and odes of a largely conventional nature in
which shepherds share dialogues on unrequited love and
birds such as lapwings and nightingales are celebrated;
the latter is a long poem on the subject of grief. Another
collection of pastorals, which reprinted material from *The
Shepheards Tales*, was issued in that year: *Nature's Embassies,
or, The Wilde-Mans Measures, Danced Naked by Twelve Satyres*.
Figures from history and classical literature are used here
to embody certain faults or sins such as adultery (Clytemnestra), blasphemy (Caligula), and incest (Tereus). Also
published in that year was *Panedone, or, Health from Helicon*,
a collection of emblems, epigrams, and elegies. *Britain's
Bath* in 1625 includes an elegy on the earl of Southampton.

From the second period of activity dates what was
Brathwaite's most renowned work for many years: a satire
which had been originally published in Latin and pseudonymously, *Barnabae itinerarium, or, Barnabee's Journal*, by
Corymbaeus (1638). This didactic and satirical text
describes four journeys between Kendal (Brathwaite's
home) and London. The route taken is different in each
instance. It is a remarkable example of the trend for topographical writings in the 1630s, but in its rollicking style it
also prefigures some of the picaresque novels of the eighteenth century. Recently, however, Brathwaite has come to
be most commonly associated with the lengthy conduct
books he wrote in the 1630s: *The English Gentleman* (1630)
and *The English Gentlewoman* (1631), both of which went
through several editions and expansions in his lifetime.
These books offer rules for social conduct and etiquette.
*The English gentleman, containing sundry excellent rules, or
exquisite observations tending to the direction of every gentleman,
of selecter ranke and quality, how to demeane or accommodate
himselfe in the manage of publike or private affaires*, which was
dedicated to Philip, earl of Pembroke and Montgomery,
looks at such topics as the dangers that attend on youth,
and expounds on such themes as 'Disposition', 'Education', 'Vocation', 'Recreation', and 'Acquaintance'. *The English gentlewoman, drawne out to the full body: expressing what
habiliments doe best attire her, what ornaments doe best adorne
her, what complements doe best accomplish her*, as its title suggests, is rather more exercised about appearance and
social obedience than its male counterpart. Sections here
include 'Apparell', 'Behaviour', 'Complement', 'Decency',
and 'Honour'. This text is dedicated to the earl of Pembroke's wife, Lady Anne Clifford. Both texts have become
important documents for social historians and for those
interested in cultural practice.

Following the publication of these manuals in 1630 and

1631, Brathwaite published *Whimzies* in 1631, *Novissima Tuba, or, The Last Trumpet* in 1632 (a religious poem in Latin which was translated by John Vicars in 1635), and *Raglands Niobe* in 1635—a poem in memory of Elizabeth, wife of Edward Somerset, Lord Herbert. Brathwaite's elegy on his own wife *Anniversaries upon his Panarete* had been published the year before.

As well as being skilled in Latin, Brathwaite knew Italian since in 1635 he published a translation of Silesio's prose fiction, as *The Arcadian Princesse, or, The Triumph of Justice* ('I have heere sent you an Italian plant translated to an English platte' he told the earl of Worcester), which tells the story of Themista's descent to earth and attempt to reform the corrupt world. This could be read as having a political subtext in the period of Charles I's personal rule (1629–40). In 1636 R. B., presumed to be Brathwaite, wrote *The Lives of All the Roman Emperors* and in 1638 *The Psalmes of David*. It has been suggested that Brathwaite may have co-authored *Cornelianum dolium* with Thomas Randolph in 1638, and possibly the publication *The Penitent Pilgrim* (1641), and although the evidence for this seems slim, certainly there are internal parallels with his other publications. In 1639 an 'R. B. Esq.' also wrote *An Epitome of All the Lives of the Kings of France*. Most intriguingly, a publication of 1638–9 has been attributed to Brathwaite; this is *The Fatal Nuptiall*, an elegy on the victims of a ferry accident in Lake Windermere in 1638.

According to a self-reference in *A Spirituall Spicerie* (1638), Brathwaite dedicated himself to poetry and dramatic writing. No plays by him are extant, but one of his most interesting creations has received critical attention for both its dramatic and its political qualities. *Mercurius Britanicus, or, The English Intelligencer* (1641) is a dramatic pamphlet or playlet, originally published in Latin but later translated into English. The title-page claims that it was acted at Paris 'with great Applause', and it has been suggested that the second earl of Leicester may have sponsored this performance since its limited but firm criticism of Charles I's personal rule chimed with his political sympathies (Butler, 'A case study', 952–3). Twenty-seven characters are listed in the dramatis personae, including a chorus of parliament men and the ghost of Coriolanus (a thinly veiled portrait of the recently executed earl of Strafford). The subject is the infamous ship money trial of 1638. The main action is a trial in which the defendants are the twelve judges of the court of exchequer who had, in 1638, given Charles the fatal advice to levy on his subjects ship money, the ultimate resistance to which has been read by some historians as making a crucial contribution to the outbreak of civil war in 1642, and who had tried the test case in which John Hampden had challenged the levy's legality. One of those judges was Sir Richard Hutton, Brathwaite's now deceased godfather. *The Prodigals Teares* had been dedicated to Hutton; *Astraea's Tears* (1641) is Brathwaite's elegy for him, and he is treated with most leniency by the text. Hutton had, along with Sir George Croke and Sir John Denham, pronounced in favour of Hampden, so Brathwaite's defence of all three

had strong justification. The two judges who had supported Hampden only on technical grounds are indicted along with the remaining seven who found for the king and who are clearly blamed for their 'evil counsel'. The text provides a fascinating insight into the contemporary debate about ship money and vivid confirmation of a presumed tendency to blame the king's advisers rather than the king himself for bad decision making. *The Schollers Medley* was republished as *A Nursery for Gentry* (1638), and contained references to the 'Halcyon days' of the 1630s which imply that Brathwaite was not entirely hostile to Charles I's personal rule.

The years before the civil war saw a rush of texts: *Ar't Asleepe Husband?* (1640), a collection of lectures on moral themes; *The Two Lancashire Lovers, or, The Excellent History of Philocles and Doriclea* (1640, by 'Musaeus Palatinus'), a prose romance; and *Astraea's Tears*. The war—in which Brathwaite is believed to have fought, on the royalist side—then leads to a pause in proceedings, but by 1651 Brathwaite is back in print: *A Strappado for the Devil* is a volume of satires directly based on George Wither's *Abuses Whipt and Stript*. The satirical element dominates Brathwaite's creations of the 1650s: *A Mustur Roll of the Evill Angels* (1655), an account in prose of famous heretics; *Lignum vitae* (1658); and *The Honest Ghost* (1658). 1659 also saw the publication of *Panthalia, or, The Royal Romance* by one 'R. B.'.

Following the restoration of the monarchy in 1660 Brathwaite withdrew to his Yorkshire estate in East Appleton. He remained active in the manor of Catterick where he became a trustee of a free school. He continued to publish at this time, beginning with his panegyric poem, *To His Majesty* (1660). A political satire, *The Chimney's Scuffle*, was published in 1662. 1665 saw *The Captive Captain*, a prose-verse medley, and *A Comment upon Two Tales of … Geoffrey Chaucer, Knight*, an interesting example of literary criticism. Brathwaite's 1665 political satire, *Regicidium*, like *Mercurius Britannicus*, evidences dramatic qualities.

Although his prolific output has not gained much critical or popular attention since his lifetime, Brathwaite's *œuvre* is of growing importance as evidence of a gentleman's literary activity in the seventeenth century as well as of particular approaches to social and political issues. He died at his home in East Appleton, near Catterick, aged eighty-five on 4 May 1673 and was buried on 7 May in the parish church.   JULIE SANDERS

Sources M. W. Black, 'Richard Brathwaite: an account of his life and works', PhD diss., University of Pennsylvania, 1928 · DNB · M. Butler, 'A case study of Caroline political theatre: Brathwaite's *Mercurius Britannicus*', HJ, 27 (1984), 947–53 · J. Haslewood, preface, in R. Brathwaite, *Barnabae itinerarium, or, Barnabee's journal*, ed. J. Haslewood, 9th edn, 1 (1820) · J. Knowles, 'Marlowe and the aesthetics of the closet', *Renaissance configurations*, ed. G. McMullan (1998) · S. Roberts, 'Women reading', *Renaissance configurations*, ed. G. McMullan (1998) · B. Ravelhofer, '"Virgin wax" and "hairy menmonsters": unstable movement codes in the Stuart court masque', *The politics of the Stuart court masque*, ed. D. Bevington and P. Holbrook (1999), 252–3 · S. Wiseman, *Drama and politics in the English civil war* (1998) · M. Butler, *Theatre and crisis, 1632–1642* (1984) · R. Brathwaite, *A strappado for the devil* (1878) · R. Brathwaite,

Barnabae itinerarium, ed. J. Haslewood (1876) · R. Brathwaite, *Nature's embassies* (1876)
Likenesses portrait, 1626, repro. in Black, 'Richard Brathwait' · W. Marshall, line engraving, BM, NPG; repro. in R. Braithwaite, *A survey of history* (1638) [*see illus.*] · R. Vaughan, line engraving, BM; repro. in R. Braithwaite, *The English gentlemen* (1630)

Brattle, Thomas (1658–1713), astronomer and college administrator in America, was born in Boston, Massachusetts, on 20 June 1658, the second of the eight children of Thomas Brattle (*c*.1624–1683), a merchant, and his wife, Elizabeth Tyng (1638–1682). The elder Thomas was one of the wealthiest men in the colony, which he served in many capacities, including as a representative in the general court and as a militia captain. His son Thomas attended the Boston Latin school in preparation for Harvard College, from which he received the degree of AB in 1676 and AM in 1679. To qualify for his second degree he pursued higher mathematics, a subject in which he was already better informed than any of his New England contemporaries. This facility enabled him in 1680 and 1681 to calculate the orbit of Halley's comet from his own observations. Sir Isaac Newton learned of Brattle's work, reported anonymously to the Royal Society, and cited it in the *Principia*.

In 1682 Brattle travelled to England, where he established relationships with Sir Robert Boyle and members of the Anglican clergy. Touring Britain and France, he also cultivated an interest in architecture. When he returned to Boston in 1689, he carried with him both valuable contacts and the latest word on British culture. When his father died in 1683, he had inherited a substantial estate. Free from material worries, he served the public interest as he understood it upon his return from England. For two decades beginning in 1693 he served as the treasurer of Harvard College. In 1698 he was also probably behind the design of Stoughton Hall, Harvard's (and New England's) first Georgian college building. And in 1699 he took the lead in establishing Boston's Brattle Street Church. An expression of ecclesiastical reform impulses alive in eastern Massachusetts at the end of the seventeenth century, the church broke away from common local practice by omitting public testimonies of religious experience by candidates for admission to communion and by granting its minister an unusual measure of authority over its affairs. More orthodox contemporaries, led by Increase Mather and Cotton Mather, protested against these innovations, but the church quickly won favour among Boston's more refined residents. To promote the congregation, Brattle provided the land for its meeting-house, which he probably designed. He died in Boston on 18 May 1713, and was buried there in King's Chapel burial-ground. He never married.

William Brattle (1662–1717), minister in America, brother of Thomas, was born in Boston on 22 November 1662, the third son and fourth child of Thomas and Elizabeth Brattle. After preparation at the Boston Latin school he entered Harvard College in 1676. He graduated AB in 1680 and AM in 1683. Two years later he began a career that bound him to Cambridge, Massachusetts, for the

remainder of his life. In 1685 President Increase Mather appointed him a tutor in the college. Mather lived in Boston throughout his presidency, so Brattle and fellow tutor John Leverett shared immediate responsibility for the college. The young instructors encouraged toleration and intellectual curiosity in their students, many of whom read widely in Anglican and Enlightenment writings as a consequence. Brattle's Cartesian *Compendium of Logic* was used in classes at Harvard until about 1765.

Brattle resigned his tutorship in 1696 in favour of the pulpit of the First Church in Cambridge, which ordained him on 25 November. In his new post he remained an important figure at the college. Harvard students attended the Cambridge church, so they heard his sermons regularly. He also served on both of the college's governing bodies, the corporation and the board of overseers. Many of the reforms that Thomas Brattle introduced at the Brattle Street Church were anticipated in Cambridge, notably private rather than public relations of religious experiences.

William married Elizabeth Hayman (1676–1715) on 3 November 1697. They had two sons. William *Brattle (1706–1776), the only one of their children to survive to adulthood, became a general in the provincial militia and a member of the governor's council. After Elizabeth's death, *c*.1716 Brattle married Elizabeth Gerrish Green (1673–1747). He died in Cambridge on 15 February 1717.

CONRAD EDICK WRIGHT

Sources R. A. Kennedy, 'Thy patriarchs' desire: Thomas and William Brattle in puritan Massachusetts', PhD diss., U. Cal., Santa Barbara, 1967 · C. K. Shipton, *Sibley's Harvard graduates: biographical sketches of graduates of Harvard University*, 17 vols. (1873–1975), vol. 2, pp. 489–98; vol. 3, pp. 200–07 · E.-D. Harris, ed., *An account of some of the descendants of Capt. Thomas Brattle* (1867) · R. Kennedy, 'Thomas Brattle and the scientific provincialism of New England, 1680–1713', *New England Quarterly*, 63 (1990), 584–600 · R. Kennedy, 'Thomas Brattle: mathematician–architect in the transition of the New England mind, 1690–1700', *Winterthur Portfolio*, 24 (1989), 231–45 · W. B. Sprague, *Annals of the American pulpit*, 1 (1857), 236–8 · R. Kennedy, ed., *Aristotelian and Cartesian logic at Harvard* (1995) · A. B. Forbes, 'William Brattle and John Leverett, FRS', *Publications of the Colonial Society of Massachusetts*, new ser., 28 (1935), 222–4 · T. W. Baldwin, ed., *Vital records of Cambridge, Massachusetts*, 2 vols. (1914–15) · J. Savage, *A genealogical dictionary of the first settlers of New England*, 4 vols. (1860–62), vol. 1, pp. 238–9 · 'Percival and Ellen Green', *New England Historical and Genealogical Register*, 15 (1861), 106 · R. D. Joslyn, ed., *Vital records of Charlestown, Massachusetts, to the year 1850*, 1 (1984), 98 · 'Capt. Thomas Brattle and his men', *New England Historical and Genealogical Register*, 41 (1887), 274–7 · W. H. Whitmore, *The Massachusetts civil list for the colonial and provincial periods, 1630–1774* (1870), 124
Archives Harvard U., records as college treasurer · RS, scientific papers | NMM, letters to John Flamsteed

Brattle, William (1662–1717). *See under* Brattle, Thomas (1658–1713).

Brattle, William (1706–1776), colonial politician and army officer in America, was born on 18 April 1706 in Cambridge, Massachusetts, the only surviving son of Congregational minister William *Brattle (1662–1717) [*see under* Brattle, Thomas], of that town, and Elizabeth Hayman

(1676–1715). His parents were both natives of Massachusetts; his father, along with his childless uncle Thomas *Brattle, had founded the Brattle Street Church in Boston as a more tolerant alternative to the strict anti-Anglican puritan establishment. The sole heir of both his father and prosperous uncle, William entered Harvard College in 1718 and graduated AB in 1722. Unlike his forebears, however, he had little talent for preaching, and cut no figure in either medicine or law, in which he also dabbled. Brattle's true calling lay in organizing the Massachusetts militia (of which he rose to be commander as brigadier-general in 1760) and participating in provincial politics. Brattle was married twice: in 1727 to Katherine Saltonstall (1704–1752), daughter of a Massachusetts governor, and on 2 November 1755 to Martha Fitch Allen (1704–1763), widow of Boston representative James Allen.

A jovial, pleasure-loving man whose enemies dubbed him Brigadier Paunch (*Proceedings of the Massachusetts Historical Society*, 62.20), Brattle's family connections placed him among the Massachusetts élite. Having been elected to the assembly in 1729 by the voters of Cambridge, where he served until elevated to the council in 1756, Brattle plunged into the political fray from the start. Notable events of eighteenth-century Massachusetts can be followed through his participation. In the early 1740s he opposed the Great Awakening and quarrelled with the evangelist George Whitefield—who accused his beloved Harvard College of irreligiosity—before joining the rest of Massachusetts in turning his religious zeal against the French and their American Indian allies during King George's War and the Seven Years' War. A partisan of William Shirley, governor between 1741 and 1756, Brattle nevertheless emerged in the 1760s as a leader of the opposition to British policy to regulate the colonies, now promoted by Governor Francis Bernard and Lieutenant-Governor Thomas Hutchinson. Brattle's greatest moment came in the autumn of 1765. In lieu of the traditional pope-day (or Guy Fawkes day) celebration on 5 November, in which Boston's North and South End mobs battled for the possession of effigies of the pope and Stuart Pretender, General Brattle joined with the popular leader, Ebenezer Mackintosh, in heading a procession which symbolized that the respectable militia and the disreputable mob had linked forces. In turn Brattle's election to the provincial council was vetoed by the governor in 1769, whereupon Cambridge promptly returned him to the assembly.

Brattle's split with the resistance came in January 1773. He thought it reasonable that the salaries of judges should be fixed to secure their independence from both the governor and the assembly, and published letters in the major Boston newspapers presenting his case. From then on Brattle could be counted among the increasing numbers of the old political élite who, while initially having opposed British policy, feared that the growth of popular politics threatened the social order. Governor Hutchinson promoted Brattle to major-general for this change of heart. Brattle thereafter appeared prominently at the increasingly futile displays of royal authority as head of the militia, and joined others of his class to sign a testimonial defending Hutchinson. As head of the militia Brattle may have stalled the outbreak of the revolution by several months: in July 1774 he persuaded Governor Thomas Gage to seize munitions being gathered for possible resistance at the powder-house in Medford. Unfortunately Gage dropped a letter of Brattle's, which warned of plans 'to meet at one minute's warning equipt with arms and ammunition' (29 Aug 1774, Artemas Ward MSS, vol. 2), in the streets of Boston. The patriots recovered and publicized it. Brattle was forced to flee Cambridge to the British lines, whereupon a crowd helped itself to his fine wine cellar. Having left Boston with the British on evacuation day (17 March 1776), Brattle, who had been ailing for over a year, died in Halifax, Nova Scotia, on 25 October. His son Thomas, who convinced the patriots that he was a true revolutionary although he had earlier posed as a loyalist in England, inherited the mansion on Brattle Street, Cambridge, which was still standing well over two centuries later.

WILLIAM PENCAK

Sources C. K. Shipton, 'Brattle, William', *Sibley's Harvard graduates: biographical sketches of those who attended Harvard College*, 7 (1945), 10–23 · W. Pencak, *War, politics and revolution in provincial Massachusetts* (1981) · Mass. Hist. Soc., Artemas Ward MSS
Archives American Antiquarian Society, Worcester, Massachusetts · Mass. Hist. Soc.
Likenesses portrait, repro. in Shipton, 'Brattle, William', 11
Wealth at death insolvent: Shipton, 'Brattle, William', 23

Bratton [Bracton], **Henry of** (d. 1268), justice and supposed author of the legal treatise known as *Bracton*, was probably born at Bratton Fleming near Barnstaple in Devon. Neither his parentage nor the date of his birth is known.

Bratton as clerk and justice Bratton's first appearance in surviving records is in March 1238, when his agreement with Stephen Fleming was enrolled on the plea roll of the court of *coram rege*. This indicates that he had by then become a clerk of William of Raleigh (d. 1250), the court's only professional justice. William of Raleigh had been presented to the rectory of Bratton Fleming by King John in 1212. Bratton's recruitment into Raleigh's service must be connected with Raleigh's possession of the rectory of Bratton's home village. Bratton had probably been in Raleigh's service for some years before 1238, though for just how long is uncertain. Soon after Raleigh left the court on being elected bishop of Norwich in 1239, Bratton was taken into the king's service and put on an annual retainer of 40 marks a year (in February 1240). This has been taken to indicate that he was by then a senior clerk with a long period of service to Raleigh. All that is certain, however, is that he was by then sufficiently senior to have been entrusted with the custody of Raleigh's plea rolls and also those of the justice whom Raleigh had himself served as clerk, Martin of Pattishall (d. 1229). He was ordered to surrender them to the exchequer in 1258 and can be shown to have been in possession of them in 1247. He had probably been in continuous possession of them ever since 1239.

Bratton received only the first year's payment of his

retainer, perhaps because he sided with Raleigh in a dispute with the king over Raleigh's election in 1240 to the see of Winchester. He then disappears from view until 1245. By then he had become rector of the Lincolnshire church of Gosberton and received, thanks to Raleigh, a papal dispensation to hold two additional benefices with cure of souls. It was also in 1245 that Bratton received his first judicial appointment, sitting as a junior justice on the eyres of Lincolnshire and Nottinghamshire. Although he was also appointed to act as justice of the Yorkshire eyre and of eyres in four other northern counties the following year, the final concords indicate that he did not act. Bratton's next judicial appointment was as a junior justice of the court where he had previously served as a clerk, the court of *coram rege*. He probably became a justice of the court in October 1247 and served initially until June 1251. By February 1249 he had also become a canon of Wells Cathedral, holding the prebend of Whitchurch in Binegar: just the kind of preferment that came the way of successful clerics in royal service. He was reappointed to the court of *coram rege* in July 1253 and served there until late June 1257. Between 1251 and 1258 he authorized (generally with others) a number of mandates enrolled on the close rolls, and some of the authorizations identify him as a member of the king's council. They include a mandate to the justices of the common bench in 1256, on the computation of the year and a day allowed to men essoined of bed-sickness in leap years, and another mandate of the same year which suggests the existence of legislation requiring seignorial assent for alienations in mortmain. He was probably involved in drafting some, if not all, of these mandates.

Between 1257 and his death in 1268 Bratton's main judicial activity was as an assize justice in the south-west of England. Although appointed to hold sessions of the special eyre for the remedying of local grievances in Gloucestershire, Worcestershire, and Herefordshire late in 1259, it seems unlikely that he ever acted. The close roll also has a memorandum belonging to February 1267 noting that he and others had been appointed to hear the complaints of the disinherited, but again it seems unlikely that he acted. During the same period Bratton was presented to two Devon rectories (Combeinteignhead and Bideford), was briefly (in 1264) archdeacon of Barnstaple, and then held the chancellorship of Exeter Cathedral from 1264 until his death. By 1262 he also held a prebend in the bishop of Exeter's Sussex collegiate church of Bosham. Bratton died, unmarried, in 1268, probably in the autumn (possibly on 30 October). He was buried in the nave of Exeter Cathedral where his executors established a chantry in his memory. A chantry was also established for him at Wells.

The treatise known as Bracton Henry of Bratton was long thought to have been the author of the legal treatise known as *Bracton*. As may be deduced from its more formal alternative title *De legibus et consuetudinibus Angliae*, it is the most ambitious English legal work of the middle ages, apparently conceived on a grand scale as an overall survey and discussion of the whole of the common law as it was being applied in the king's courts in England, with supporting citations of actual decided cases, and the reproduction of writ and enrolment formulas currently in use. The extant treatise is evidently only part of the work as originally envisaged, but even so the work is around ten times the length of the only previous English legal treatise, *Glanvill*. The main topics covered are the acquisition and transmission of property rights, criminal law, and the working of the different kinds of real action for the recovery or assertion of rights over land and other forms of real property. Most manuscripts divide up the work into four or five books, but this division is an artificial one and the basic unit of composition appears to be the 'title'. Each 'title' is in turn composed of a number of independent paragraphs. *Bracton* is clearly the work of an author with a knowledge of Roman and canon law as well as English common law, though there has been a long debate among legal historians about how expert the author really was in the 'learned law'. It is clear that the author did make use of Roman law to fill gaps in his English materials. He also drew on Roman law for some of the more abstract organizing principles of the treatise. Despite the size of the book it survives in about fifty different manuscripts, most of them written during the last two decades of the thirteenth century or the first half of the fourteenth century.

The problem of authorship The ascription of the treatise to Henry of Bratton can be traced back to within a few years of his death. The first folio of one of the earliest surviving manuscripts of *Bracton* has an inscription recording that this is 'beginning of the book of lord H. de Bratton' and early in 1278 Robert of Scarborough acknowledged having received a loan of 'the book which lord Henry of Bratton composed', evidently a copy of the treatise. When the book found its way into print in 1569, the unknown editor (T. N.) not only ascribed authorship of the treatise to Bratton, but also adopted a reading of one passage near the beginning of the treatise (found only in a minority of surviving manuscripts) in which the authorial 'I' was extended to 'I Henry of Bratton'. The same anonymous editor also transformed Bratton's surname into 'Bracton', the name by which both justice and book have generally been known since. Bratton's authorship of the treatise went unchallenged both by his late nineteenth-century editor, Sir Travers Twiss, whose six-volume edition, published in the Rolls Series, appeared between 1878 and 1883, and by George Woodbine, whose four-volume edition appeared between 1915 and 1942. Woodbine did not believe that everything found in the various manuscripts of *Bracton* (especially in their margins) was necessarily from the pen of Bratton, and went to some pains to distinguish those *addiciones* he regarded as from the pen of Henry of Bratton from those which could not be 'Bractonian'. Other twentieth-century scholars (H. Kantorowicz, T. F. T. Plucknett, and H. G. Richardson) conducted a long debate about how far the muddled state of the text of *Bracton* as it now exists was the responsibility of Bratton and how far the responsibility of one or more redactors working before or after his death. The most recent editor of the text, S. E. Thorne, when his edition began to appear in 1968, showed no signs of doubt about Bratton's authorship. It was only when the final two volumes of his new edition appeared in 1977 that Thorne challenged the long consensus by arguing that Bratton was only the reviser of a work originally composed by someone else. Thorne's view is now generally, though not universally, accepted by scholars, though some of his arguments have needed to be revised in detail in the light of subsequent criticism.

The main argument against Bratton's authorship of major parts of the treatise relates to the date when those parts were written. Although it had long been known that the treatise cites mainly cases of the 1220s and early 1230s the general consensus before 1977 was that it had been written during the 1250s and that the author had deliberately chosen cases of an earlier period as an authoritative source for the doctrine of the treatise. It now seems clear that parts of the text must have been written earlier than the enactment of the provisions of Merton of 1236, as several passages relating to changes made by that legislation are clearly additions to a text originally complete without them. Other parts of the text giving writ forms can be shown to have been written before 1237, for the writs have limitation date formulas which were in use before that year, or are most readily explicable as crudely and inaccurately altered versions of such formulas. Material added to the section on replevin relating to the action of recaption, and to the section on the assize *utrum* relating to its use by laymen as well as clerics, likewise suggests original composition of both of those sections earlier than *c*.1240. Other evidence pointing to a date no later than the early 1230s for parts of the treatise is the inclusion of a form of judicial commission apparently last used in 1226 and of a special set of articles of the eyre used at the Shipway session of the Kent eyre of 1227; references to the use of the essoin of the general summons at the eyre (no longer in use after 1234); and to the action of warranty of charter as a way for tenants to stop distraint for services not specified in their charters (not found after the mid-1230s). Bratton is not a plausible candidate for a treatise of which much had already been written by the mid-1230s, for he can hardly by then have acquired the requisite degree of legal expertise. A much more plausible candidate is the William of Raleigh whom Bratton served as clerk, and who had been the clerk of Martin of Pattishall before Pattishall's retirement in 1229. His authorship best explains the author's knowledge of what Pattishall said and did in court, and his occasional use of the great justice's first name.

Bratton and *Bracton* The manuscript of the treatise evidently passed to Bratton. Raleigh may have hoped that Bratton would keep the treatise up to date and make the necessary revisions that would allow it to pass into wider circulation. Bratton certainly did make some revisions. He may well (as Thorne suggested) have been responsible for adding material connected with William of Raleigh's period as senior justice of the court of *coram rege*. He may also have been responsible for other revisions that produced two opposing and unreconciled viewpoints in the text of the treatise. Bratton is also the most likely reviser

of a passage that deals with errors in the names included in writs. His first name and surname are used to illustrate errors in syllables ('Henricus de Brothtona' for 'Henricus de Brattona' and letters ('Henricus de Brettona' for 'Henricus de Brattona'). His too is the name used to illustrate an error in the dignity held by the plaintiff ('Henry de Bratton precentor' for 'Henry de Bratton dean'). It was also presumably Bratton who was responsible for the second preface added to the treatise, which talks of greater men who are 'foolish and insufficiently instructed, who climb the seat of judgment before learning the laws', and of how they pervert laws and customs by deciding cases more by their own will than by the authority of the laws, and of the compiler writing for 'the instruction at least of lesser men' and going back to the 'ancient judgments of just men ['vetera judicia justorum'], searching through … their deeds, their *consilia* and *responsa*' (*De legibus et consuetudinibus Angliae*, 2.19). This was clearly Bratton's apologia for not updating the treatise: it had hardly been necessary when the treatise was originally written, for then the cases cited were much more nearly contemporary. It was certainly Bratton who was responsible for the incorporation of references to cases which he had himself determined or which involved him of various dates between the mid-1240s and the mid-1250s.

After the mid-1250s Bratton seems largely to have abandoned work on the treatise. It does not include any references to the changes made by the provisions of Westminster of 1259. Nor did he alter those passages in the treatise that dealt with seignorial attempts to control mortmain alienations, or the computation of the year and a day allowed to tenants who essoined themselves of bedsickness, in the light of the mandates of 1256 relating to both these subjects with whose issue he was closely involved. Given the amount of effort that had been invested in the treatise, its apparent abandonment by its author more than a decade before his death, and at a time when he certainly remained active, has always seemed puzzling. It becomes much less puzzling if it was not the author, but a reviser, who was giving up the unequal struggle to try and keep (or rather bring) the treatise up to date. The treatise does not seem to have gone into general circulation until after Bratton's death, and it may well be the fact that it was found among his possessions at his death that explains why the treatise came so soon to be ascribed to him.

'Bracton's Note Book' In 1884 Paul Vinogradoff discovered a manuscript in the British Museum containing about two thousand transcripts of enrolments taken from the plea rolls of the courts over which Martin of Pattishall and William of Raleigh presided as justices during the period from 1217 to 1239–40. Noting the coincidence between these enrolments and the cases cited in *Bracton*, Vinogradoff suggested that the manuscript was 'drawn up for Bracton and annotated by him or under his direction' (*Bracton's Note Book*, 1.xviii). F. W. Maitland gave the collection the name *Bracton's Note Book* when he published it in 1887. He saw it as an essential working tool for the author of *Bracton*, evidence of how he had set to work by first selecting material from rolls belonging to Pattishall and Raleigh and then having it copied into his notebook. Maitland saw that there was one major difficulty with this hypothesis. Of the five hundred or so cases cited in the treatise, only about two hundred are actually to be found in the notebook. His answer was to conjecture that it was the sole survivor of what had originally been two or more such notebooks. The connection between treatise and notebook was generally accepted until 1977. It was again Thorne who cast doubt on the supposed relationship. Bratton had certainly possessed the notebook and been responsible for at least part of its contents. But major parts of the notebook were first copied from the rolls and annotated by or under the direction of others, and it was doubtful whether the notebook was in fact used, or could have been used, in the composition of the treatise. Some connection with the treatise none the less remains a possibility. Even if not used in composing the treatise, it may still have been intended for use in revising it, or even as a companion to it for those without ready access to the rolls containing the cases cited in the treatise.

PAUL BRAND

Sources P. Brand, 'The age of Bracton', *PBA*, 89 (1996), 65–89 · H. de Bracton, *On the laws and customs of England*, ed. G. E. Woodbine, trans. S. E. Thorne, 4 vols. (1968–77) · *Bracton's note book*, ed. F. W. Maitland, 3 vols. (1887) · J. L. Barton, 'The mystery of Bracton', *Journal of Legal History*, 14 (1993), 1–42 · C. A. F. Meekings, *Studies in 13th century justice and administration* (1981) · PRO, court of king's bench, curia regis rolls, KB 26/168 m 24d

Archives BL, Add. MS 12269 · Middle Temple, London, papers

Brawne [*married name* Lindon], **Frances** [Fanny] (1800–1865), fiancée of John Keats, was born on 9 August 1800 in the West End of London, the first of five children of Samuel Vernon Brawne (1778–1810), a businessman 'of no commercial reputation' (Motion, 324), and Frances (1772–1829), daughter of John Ricketts. The main event in Fanny's life as far as posterity is concerned was her love affair with the poet John *Keats (1795–1821) from the time of the beginning of his *annus mirabilis* of autumn 1818 until his death in 1821.

Fanny Brawne came from a middle-class background and was reasonably well educated, at least in literature and languages, speaking French and undertaking translations from German. She first met Keats in the late autumn of 1818 in Hampstead and by June 1819 they had an 'understanding' which, probably by October, had become an official, albeit secret, engagement. In view of Keats's poor financial situation and Fanny's youth, her mother disapproved of the affair. In fact, Fanny's mother was by no means the only person to disapprove of the relationship: Charles Brown apparently considered Fanny to be 'superficial and vain' and 'flirtatious' with 'every man she met' (Richardson, 31), and a number of other friends of Keats, including J. H. Reynolds and his family, Joseph Severn, and Charles Dilke, similarly regretted the attachment. For Keats, though, while he described Fanny in December 1818 as 'elegant, graceful, silly, fashionable and strange', 'monstrous', 'flying out in all directions', a '*Minx*' with a 'penchant … for acting stylishly' (*Letters of John Keats, 1814–*

Frances [Fanny] **Brawne (1800–1865)**, by unknown artist, c.1833

1821, 2.8, 13), she was the 'one passion' of his short life (Houghton, 1), a passion which was to be characterized by an intensity of emotion which often slid into jealousy. When Keats's candid and passionate letters to Fanny were published in 1878, the insecurity and jealousy that they expressed, although evidence of a certain emotional instability on his part, none the less contributed to her reputation as a fickle and superficial lover of the increasingly famous poet. As her biographer notes, nineteenth-century commentators 'drew Fanny Brawne as they wanted her to be: a common, shallow, faithless, calculating flirt' (Richardson, 144), and her reputation was rescued only after the publication of her letters to Fanny Keats in 1936. Both Keats's sense of distrust and the ensuing disapproval were exacerbated by the poet's tuberculosis which, from the autumn of 1819 onwards, made him seem to be the helpless victim of Fanny's apparently wilful and unfaithful nature. Even when he was living next door to the Brawne family in Wentworth Place, Hampstead, the nature of Keats's illness often meant he found it distressing either to be with Fanny or to contemplate her being away from him. After he left for Italy in September 1820 he became so distressed by his feelings for Fanny that he was able neither to write directly to her nor read her letters to him. There seems to be little doubt that, fuelled by Keats's early death, the often painful emotions expressed in his letters to her, and the antagonism of his circle towards her, Fanny's influence on the poet was misrepresented as profoundly negative by a romanticizing later nineteenth century. In fact, it is significant that Keats wrote many of the poems for which he is most well known soon after meeting Fanny, and it is undoubtedly the case that his relationship with her was influential in the shaping of his greatest work.

After Keats's death, Fanny remained in Hampstead and mourned him through the 1820s, befriending his sister as she had promised him she would. After her mother's death in 1829 Fanny became financially independent and, on a visit to France in 1833, in Boulogne met Louis Lindo (later Lindon; 1812–1872), whom she married on 15 June 1833. Of Spanish or Portuguese extraction and from a wealthy Jewish merchant and banking family, Louis Lindon seems to have held a number of positions, including working as an officer for the British Legion in Spain and as a wine merchant in London later in life. Until the 1850s, when they settled in London, the Lindons lived on the continent, especially in Germany, where they can be traced in Düsseldorf, Heidelberg, and Freiburg, and where Fanny gave birth to two sons and a daughter. Fanny died at 34 Coleshill Street, Pimlico, London, on 4 December 1865. She was buried in Brompton cemetery on 9 December.

ANDREW BENNETT

Sources J. Richardson, *Fanny Brawne* (1952) · H. E. Rollins, ed., *The Keats circle: letters and papers and more letters and poems of the Keats circle*, 1 (1965) · W. J. Bate, *John Keats* (1963) · Lord Houghton, *Life and letters of John Keats* [n.d.] · A. Motion, *Keats* (1997) · *Letters of Fanny Brawne to Fanny Keats (1820–1824)*, ed. F. Edgcumbe (1936) · *Letters of John Keats to Fanny Brawne*, ed. H. B. Forman (1878) · *The letters of John Keats, 1814–1821*, ed. H. E. Rollins, 2 vols. (1958) · R. Gittings, *John Keats* (1968)
Archives BL, MS, 'Nickel List and his merry men', Add. MS 45566 · Keats House, Hampstead, London, letters to Fanny Keats
Likenesses A. Edouart, silhouette, *c.*1829, Keats House, Hampstead, London · miniature, *c.*1833, Keats House, Hampstead, London [*see illus.*] · ambrotype, *c.*1850, Keats House, Hampstead, London

Braxfield. For this title name *see* Macqueen, Robert, Lord Braxfield (1722–1799).

Bray [*née* Kempe; *other married name* Stothard], **Anna Eliza** (1790–1883), novelist and writer, was born on 25 December 1790 in Newington, Surrey, the daughter of John Kempe, a porteur d'or at the Royal Mint, and Ann, daughter of James Arrow and Elizabeth Jerdan Arrow of Berkshire. She had one brother, Alfred *Kempe (*c.*1785–1846), a noted antiquary. Her education was private, at the home of one of her mother's cousins, a Miss Wrather, and it was interrupted by illness. Her brief attempt at an acting career was also interrupted by illness. With the help of her father she took painting lessons with Thomas Stothard; he referred her to his son Charles Alfred *Stothard (1786–1821) as a pupil, and the two were married in February 1818. While on their honeymoon in France, Anna Stothard wrote letters to her mother and brother describing the beauties and antiquities of the countryside, collected in her first publication in 1820 as *Letters Written during a Tour through Normandy, Brittany, and other Parts of France in 1818*.

Anna Stothard's husband, an artist, had a particular interest in statuary and funerary art. During the first year of her marriage she accompanied him as he sketched works of art found mainly in parish churches and she researched local histories and customs. They would collaborate on each other's projects. In May 1821 Charles Alfred Stothard fell from a ladder in a church in Beer Freers, Devon, where he had been sketching a painted ceiling; he struck his head on a pew and died. Anna Stothard, who was pregnant, gave birth to the couple's only child, Blanche Anna Eliza Stothard, on 29 June 1821, but the child died on 2 February 1822. She published a memoir of her husband in the *Gentleman's Magazine* (June 1821) and, later, as *Memoirs, including Original Journals, Letters, Papers, and Antiquarian Tracts of the Late Charles Alfred Stothard* (1823). In 1832 her brother Alfred assisted her in publishing Stothard's *The Monumental Effigies of Great Britain*, to which he contributed an introductory essay.

Anna Eliza Stothard married the Revd Edward Atkyns *Bray (1778–1857), vicar of Tavistock, Devon, in 1822. Both her *Autobiography* and the 'Memoir' she wrote as a preface to his *Poetical Remains* are silent on details of how the two met and on other personal information. His poetry, however, indicates that they had an affectionate and companionate relationship and that they both shared in each other's writing work. He included some of his verse and antiquarian descriptions of Dartmoor in his wife's fiction.

By 1826 Bray had devoted herself full-time to writing fiction, publishing *DeFoix, or, Sketches of the Manners and Customs of the Fourteenth-Century* (1826). In 1828 she published *The White Hoods* and *The Protestant*, followed by *The Talba* and *Fitz of Fitz-Ford: a Legend of Devon* in 1830. In her *Autobiography* she maintained that she spent about three months writing each work of fiction, and the correction of proofs often overlapped with the writing of the next novel. Of these first works, *The Protestant* generated public controversy because of its anti-Catholicism. It was published during the Catholic emancipation debates, and about this time Bray and Robert Southey began a correspondence, though Bray recalled that it was Southey's interest in *The Talba*, not *The Protestant*, which first led him to write to her. Attracted to her talents in descriptive writing and to her sensitivity to local history, he suggested that she gather the stories of her Devon area, and this became *A Description of the Part of Devonshire Bordering on the Tamar and the Tavy* (1836), a three-volume collection of stories and information she compiled between February 1832 and October 1835. Her efforts led to her acquaintance with Maria Colling, a local servant–poet, whose works Bray edited as *The Fables and other Pieces of Verse by Maria Colling* (1831) and to which Southey contributed a brief life of the poet.

While writing the Devon history Bray was also writing a historical epistolary novel, *Trelawny of Trelawne*, begun in 1834 and published in 1837. As background for her romantic plot she read seventeenth-century love letters between two Trelawny first cousins lent to her by a member of that family, but in Bray's story it is the Catholic church, not members of the Trelawny family, which opposes the marriage of the hero and heroine. In 1839 she published *Trials* of the Heart, another regional historical romance, and she travelled with her husband to Switzerland. From her notes and their travel journals she composed The Mountains and Lakes of Switzerland, with a Descriptive Sketch of other Parts of the Continent (1841). Three more novels followed between 1842 and 1848.

In 1845 Bray's first collected works, The Novels and Romances of Anna Eliza Bray, in ten volumes, was published by Longmans. In 1851 she published a biography of Thomas Stothard for John Murray. Widowed in 1857, and childless, she moved to London to reside closer to her brother's family. In 1859 she published Handel: his Life, Personal and Professional with John Ward, London's leading music publisher, and edited Edward Bray's Poetical Remains. An eleven-year gap in her publishing career ended in 1870 with The Revolt of the Protestants of the Cévennes, the first history in English of this eighteenth-century revolt; The Good St Louis and his Times (1872); and Joan of Arc and the Times of Charles the Seventh, King of France (1874). In her final years she published three more novels, in 1871, 1874, and 1880, and at the time of her death was editing a new edition of her novels for Chapman and Hall. An odd episode in her later life was the accusation that in 1816 she had stolen a piece of the Bayeux tapestry, but her name was cleared, primarily through the efforts of The Times.

Bray died on 21 January 1883 at her home at 40 Brompton Crescent, London. Her nephew John Alfred Kempe was one of her executors and the editor of her Autobiography (1884), which ended in 1843 with Southey's death. Her plans to complete the work beginning with letters between herself and Southey's widow, Caroline Bowles, were not realized. The Autobiography, though reticent on personal details and imprecise about the events of her daily life, is an invaluable record of her writing processes and her literary career and as an example of female autobiographical writing in the nineteenth century. Bray's career was varied, her output consisting of twelve historical novels and twelve works of non-fiction, issuing from some of London's best publishing houses, including John Murray, Longmans, Bentley, and Chapman and Hall. As a novelist she aimed to create 'living history' in her narratives, and she was careful to construct each novel's period and setting with sufficient accuracy. She was attracted to themes of inheritance in jeopardy, and to obstructions to independence and personal choice.

BEVERLY E. SCHNELLER

Sources E. A. Baker, The age of Dickens and Thackeray (1936), vol. 5 of The history of the English novel · G. C. Boase, 'Anna Eliza Bray and her writings', Library Chronicle, 1 (1884), 126 · B. Schneller, 'Anna Eliza Bray', British women writers: a critical reference guide, ed. J. Todd (1989) · B. Schneller, 'Anna Eliza Bray', British Romantic novelists, 1789–1832, ed. B. K. Mudge, DLitB, 116 (1992), 49–54 · The life and correspondence of Robert Southey, ed. C. C. Southey, 6 vols. (1849–50) · Autobiography of A. E. Bray, ed. J. A. Kempe (1884) · CGPLA Eng. & Wales (1883)
Archives BL, corresp. and papers · W. Sussex RO, papers | Syracuse University, New York, corresp. with Caroline Bowles · Trinity Cam., letters to Dawson and Mary Turner · W. Sussex RO, letters to Alfred Bray Kempe and J. E. Kempe
Likenesses W. Brockedon, black and red chalk drawing, 1834, NPG · F. C. Lewis, stipple (after a miniature by W. Patten), BM, NPG · engraving, repro. in Kempe, ed., Autobiography of A. E. Bray, frontispiece
Wealth at death £15,906 7s. 11d.: probate, 23 Feb 1883, CGPLA Eng. & Wales

Bray [née Hennell], **Caroline** (1814–1905), children's writer, the eighth and youngest child of James Hennell (1782–1816), traveller and later partner in the mercantile house of Fazy & Co., Manchester, and his wife, Elizabeth (1778–1858), daughter of Joel Marshall of Loughborough, was born at 2 St Thomas's Square, Hackney, Middlesex, on 4 June 1814. Her father died, aged thirty-three, less than two years after her birth. Her brother Charles Christian *Hennell (1809–1850) and her sisters Mary *Hennell (1802–1843) and Sara *Hennell (1812–1899) were also writers. Cara, as she was known, was educated at home with her sisters, and was, like them, briefly a governess. According to her sister Sara, she was successful, despite her quiet, modest manner, in gaining and keeping children's attention, a gift she showed later in the educational books she wrote for children (Hennell).

On 26 April 1836 Cara married Charles *Bray (1811–1884), a wealthy Coventry ribbon manufacturer, philanthropist, and author. The Hennells were Unitarians, but Bray held more sceptical views, which his wife never wholly shared. Distressed by the anti-religious views Bray expressed on their honeymoon in Wales, Cara asked her brother Charles to investigate the evidence of the truth of the gospels. The result was Charles Hennell's Inquiry Concerning the Origin of Christianity (1838), which concluded against the miraculous elements in the life of Christ, but retained a reverence for his moral example. Cara herself henceforward held a reverent but uncommitted view of Christianity. The Brays had no children, but in 1846 they adopted Elinor, who was Bray's child with another woman.

In 1841 Cara and her sister Sara were introduced to Mary Ann Evans (to be known later as George Eliot the novelist), with whom both sisters became close friends. Cara's watercolour portrait of her, done in 1842, and one of her father, Robert Evans, were presented by the artist to the National Portrait Gallery in 1899. The correspondence with Mary Ann Evans, which began in 1842, was interrupted in 1854, when Cara was shocked by her friend's setting up home with the married George Henry Lewes, but resumed in 1856 or 1857, and continued until George Eliot's death in 1880. J. W. Cross (whom George Eliot had married in 1880) largely based his biography on this correspondence. In June 1859 Cara visited her friend in London—their first meeting for five years—and was told the secret of her authorship of Adam Bede.

In 1840 Charles Bray had bought a house near Coventry known as Rosehill, where Mary Ann Evans was a frequent guest, as were Harriet Martineau, Ralph Waldo Emerson on his visits from America, the publisher John Chapman, Herbert Spencer, the celebrated Edinburgh phrenologist George Combe, and many other leading writers and thinkers, mostly of a liberal and reforming tendency. Charles Bray retired from business in 1856, and the following year he and Cara sold Rosehill, moving to nearby Ivy

Cottage. Between 1859 and 1881 they spent part of each year at Laurie Park, a house they owned near the Crystal Palace at Sydenham in south-east London.

In 1860 Cara published the first of her books for children, *Physiology for Common Schools*, an unpretentious work describing the body's functions and explaining the importance of a healthy diet and personal hygiene. Other books followed, some in the form of improving children's stories, which, though moralizing, are refreshingly undogmatic and light in tone. Cara Bray was a lifelong supporter of the Society for the Prevention of Cruelty to Animals, acting as founder and honorary secretary of the Coventry branch from 1874 to 1895. Many of her children's books, including *Our Duty to Animals* (1871), address the importance of human kindness to animals. Her books are quietly impressive, expressing the sweet nature to which George Eliot, among others, paid tribute in her letters and journals.

After her husband's death in October 1884 Cara continued to live at Ivy Cottage, St Nicholas Street, Coventry, where she died of heart failure, aged ninety, on 21 February 1905. She was buried in Coventry cemetery on 24 February 1905. ROSEMARY ASHTON

Sources S. S. Hennell, *A memoir of Charles Christian Hennell* (1899) · *Coventry Herald* (24 Feb 1905) · G. S. Haight, *George Eliot: a biography* (1968) · *The George Eliot letters*, ed. G. S. Haight, 9 vols. (1954–78) · Cara Bray, engagement diary, MS, Coventry Central Library · C. Bray, *Phases of opinion and experience during a long life* (1884) · J. W. Cross, ed., *George Eliot's life as related in her letters and journals*, 3 vols. (1885)
Archives Coventry Central Library, diary and commonplace book | Yale U., Beinecke L., George Eliot–George Henry Lewes collection
Likenesses S. Hennell, miniature, 1833, Coventry Central Library
Wealth at death £387 14s. 4d.: probate, 16 May 1905, CGPLA Eng. & Wales

Bray, Charles (1811–1884), freethinker and social reformer, was born in Coventry on 31 January 1811, the son of a wealthy ribbon manufacturer. Ill as a child, Bray was sent out of the city at an early age and attended a boarding-school from the age of nine to fourteen, after which he went to a school at Isleworth, Middlesex. At the age of seventeen he was apprenticed in a London warehouse, where his health collapsed twice (in 1829 and 1830). While in London, Bray was converted from a half-hearted Methodism to a zealous evangelicalism and, following his return to his father's warehouse at Coventry in 1830, made his first public appearance on the platform of a meeting of the Bible Society. However, following a series of discussions with Unitarian friends of his parents, Bray underwent a period of intense religious doubt, and emerged as a sceptic of all denominational religion. He also came to embrace philosophical necessitarianism, believing that all things necessarily act in accordance with the laws of their own nature. In 1841 he published his account of this process in *The Philosophy of Necessity, or, The Law of Consequences as Applicable to Mental, Moral and Social Science*; a second edition, cast entirely in phrenological language, appeared in 1863, funded by subscription.

Bray was an early supporter of national undenominational education and, following his father's example of founding schools on the Wilderspin system, helped found a mechanics' institution in Coventry in 1835 with the money gained by his taking over the family business following his father's death that year. It was while preparing a course of lectures for the institution that summer that Bray began his lifelong interest in phrenology. A mix-up with a London bookseller meant that he received George Combe's *Phrenology*, rather than a work on physiology by Andrew Combe. Initially opposed to the system, Bray became wildly excited by the prospect of the existence of a science that purported to explicate the natural laws of the mind and thus provide the cerebral machinery by which the philosophy of necessity worked. Bray conducted a course of lectures on phrenology at the mechanics' institution in 1836 and, following his first didactic work (*The Education of the Body*, 1837), published his first phrenologically influenced work, *The Education of the Feelings: a Moral System for Secular Schools*, in 1838, having just joined the newly established Phrenological Society.

On 26 April 1836 Bray married Caroline, daughter of James Hennell and younger sister of Mary Hennell, Sara Sophia Hennell, and Charles Christian Hennell. Caroline *Bray (1814–1905), herself an author, introduced her husband to Mary Ann Evans (George Eliot; *see* Evans, Marian), whom she sought to persuade of the truth of phrenology.

As a committed non-sectarian, Bray encouraged secular models of social organization. He attended the so-called 'commencement of the millennium' at Harmony Hall, Queenwood, on 1 May 1842 and though not an Owenite, he took an interest in the progress of socialism and communism. Appended to the first edition of *The Philosophy of Necessity* was an essay detailing the history of socialist communities, written by his sister-in-law Mary Hennell. In 1844 Bray published a neo-Owenite *Essay upon the Union of Agriculture and Manufactures, and upon the Organization of Industry*. Although less optimistic of the inevitability of progress than Owen and the Owenites, Bray was a believer in the scientific basis of social reform. In 1843 he helped establish the Coventry Labourers' and Artisans' Co-operative Society and promoted co-operation through the *Coventry Herald* (which he bought in 1846 and owned until 1874). The society soon comprised a thousand shareholding members and expanded to buy looms, pigs, coal, and a flour mill.

Sceptical of the claims of democracy, Bray believed that it was co-operation and colonization (both on home wastes and abroad) that would deliver mankind from anarchy and social dissolution. He successfully campaigned to secure Co-operative Society members land on which to dig gardens, and, with the ex-Owenite John Collier Farn, established a midlands missionary project that promoted other forms of self-help. In 1845 Bray established a short-lived working men's club, which sought to provide wholesome recreation for the respectable working class. In his autobiography Bray attributed his failure to gain re-election to the city council in 1846 to the damage which the Co-operative Society and working men's club allegedly did to the trade of local publicans and shop-keepers (Bray, 68).

With the collapse of the Coventry Co-operative Society in 1860 (through the policy of giving credit, which Bray opposed), Bray retired from public life. He had earlier (in 1856) ceased his involvement in ribbon manufacture and had moved in 1857 from a country house, Rosehill (which he had bought in 1840), to the adjacent Ivy Cottage. He did, however, remain closely involved in the activities of the Coventry Provident Dispensary for the forty-five years from the start of his involvement in 1837. Established in 1830, the dispensary provided medical advice and treatment to working-class members who paid a weekly penny subscription.

Bray was also interested in mesmerism and spiritualism and joined James Silk Buckingham's British and Foreign Institute in Hanover Square. Although unconvinced by demonstrations of the latter, he speculated, in *On Force, its Mental and Moral Correlates* (1866), that the human body transmitted thought in a similar fashion to warmth, emanating from a reservoir capable of being tapped by clairvoyants. He also published a pamphlet on the same subject, in the Scott series, entitled *Illusion and Delusion* (1873), and delivered a paper before the Psychological Society of Great Britain, published as *Natural Law: as Automatic Mind or Unconscious Intelligence* (1874).

Bray continued to write phrenological works throughout his life. In 1871 he attempted to rationalize Combe's system with modern science in *A Manual of Anthropology, or, Science of Man Based on Modern Research*, though perversely the following year he dropped the phrenological nomenclature from *The Education of the Feelings* to improve sales of the new (4th) edition. At the close of his life Bray was still attempting to convince the scientific élite of the truth of phrenology. He read a paper on 'Cerebral psychology' before a meeting of the Psychological Society of Great Britain in 1878, and followed this by publishing his *Psychological and Ethical Definitions on a Physiological Basis* in 1879.

Bray died at his home in Coventry on 5 October 1884, survived by his wife. They had no children, though Bray had an illegitimate daughter. Although his published works were idiosyncratic, polemical, and unpopular, Bray's lifelong support of liberal and humanitarian causes ensured that a life spent 'zealously endeavouring to discern the truth' (Bray, 1) was not wasted in irrelevant system-building.   MATTHEW LEE

Sources C. Bray, *Phases of opinion and experience during a long life* (1884) · D. de Guistino, 'Bray, Charles', *BDMBR*, vol. 1 · R. Cooter, *Phrenology in the British Isles: an annotated historical biobibliography and index* (1989) · J. F. C. Harrison, *Robert Owen and the Owenites in Britain and America: the quest for the new moral world* (1969)

Archives Holyoake House, Manchester, Co-operative Union archive, corresp. with G. J. Holyoake · NL Scot., corresp. with George Combe

Likenesses H. Adlard, line print (aged seventy-two; after photograph), BM, NPG

Wealth at death £285 3s. 9d.: probate, 23 Dec 1884, *CGPLA Eng. & Wales*

Bray, Edward Atkyns (1778–1857), poet and writer, the only son of Edward Bray (d. 1816), solicitor, and manager of the Devon estates of the duke of Bedford, and his wife, Mary, daughter of Dr Brandreth of Houghton Regis, Bedfordshire, and widow of Arthur Turner, was born at the Abbey House, Tavistock, on 18 December 1778. As his mother would not allow him to be sent to a public school, he was educated privately at home and at Alphington in Exeter. At an early age he showed an aptitude for languages, drawing, and poetry. He was also interested in antiquities and history. Following his father, Bray became a student at the Middle Temple in 1801 and was called to the bar in 1806. He served on the western circuit until 1811, when he decided to become a clergyman. Bray was ordained by the bishop of Norwich, and in 1812, by the favour of the duke of Bedford, became the vicar of Tavistock and the perpetual curate of Brent Tor. Almost immediately after ordination he entered himself at Trinity College, Cambridge, and took the degree of BD as a ten-year man in 1822. He resided in Tavistock for the rest of his life. He married Anna Eliza, *née* Kempe (1790–1883) [*see* Bray, Anna Eliza], the widow of Charles Alfred Stothard, in 1822. The couple had no children.

Bray published *Sermons from the Works of the most Eminent Divines of the 16th, 17th, and 18th Centuries* (1818), a collection of forty examples which he hoped would aid young preachers in their composition and delivery of sermons; *Discourses from Tracts and Treatises of Eminent Divines* (1821); *Select Sermons by Thomas Wilson, Bishop of Sodor and Man*; and a volume of his own, *Discourses on Protestantism* (1829). In 1820 he published *Lyric Hymns*. He also contributed to the *Classical Journal* on ancient poetic metre and published essays on the Italian sonnet. After Bray's death, Anna Eliza Bray collected and published his *Poetical Remains* (2 vols., 1859) and also *A Selection from the Sermons, General and Occasional, of Rev. E. A. Bray* (2 vols., 1860). Volume one of the *Poetical Remains* contained his juvenilia, as well as thirty-three sonnets, ten patriotic odes, and occasional poems, translations from Italian and Greek, and a variety of amatory songs in the seventeenth-century style. The second volume included fifty-five pages of occasional verse, largely on domestic life and scenes; ballads; poetical tales and other juvenilia; the fifty-nine lyric hymns; and a variety of epigrams and inscriptions. The 'Druidical and other inscriptions', original triplets and couplets designed to be inscribed on stones to line a garden walk, were featured in Anna Eliza Bray's topographical study of the Devon area, *A Description of the Part of Devonshire Bordering on the Tamar and the Tavy* (1836). Several of her twenty-four historical novels included poetry by her husband in her characters' letters and in song.

In 1839, when the couple travelled to Switzerland, Bray kept a travel journal which his wife later incorporated into her *The Mountains and Lakes of Switzerland* (1841). In 1835 and again on Christmas day 1836 the Brays entertained the poet Robert Southey in the vicarage; he had come to know Anna Eliza Bray through her fiction and they had corresponded. In a letter of January 1837 Southey provided one of the only external descriptions of the Bray home: he wrote that the gardens were large and well designed, that the view of the Tavy was pleasant, and that he was impressed with his hosts' engraved pewter dinner service, something which he had not seen since his childhood.

Edward Atkyns Bray suffered throughout his life with symptoms that suggested a respiratory problem. In August 1856 he lost his footing on a path in his garden, fell, and struck his back against an ornamental granite boulder. The consequent spinal injury made him a bedridden invalid for the rest of the year. During his recovery he wrote the occasional poems which were later included as 'Leaves from the hortus siccus' in volume two of his collected poetry. Bray died of complications from the fall and from his respiratory ailment on 16 July 1857 at Tavistock. He was buried at a well-attended funeral on 23 July in the abbey church at Tavistock. According to the 'Memoir' prefixed to the *Poetical Remains* by Anna Eliza, Bray was respected by his clerical colleagues, a conscientious pastor, and a scholarly man. His proposed antiquarian history of Dartmoor was left unfinished at his death.

W. P. COURTNEY, *rev.* BEVERLY E. SCHNELLER

Sources Mrs Bray, 'Memoir', in *Poetical remains, social, sacred, and miscellaneous of the late Edward Atkyns Bray*, ed. Mrs Bray, 1 (1859), vii–lii · Venn, *Alum. Cant.* · A. E. Bray, *A true description of the … Tamar and the Tavy*, new edn (1879), vol. 2, pp. 304–73
Likenesses R. J. Lane, lithograph, NPG · W. Patten, engraving, repro. in Bray, *Poetical remains*, frontispiece

Bray, Henry (*b.* before 1248, *d.* 1311×13), administrator, first appears in surviving records, but already in a responsible position, in 1269. He is therefore likely to have been born some years before 1248. He was the son of William de Bray of Hinton, near Woodford Halse in Northamptonshire. His use of the title *magister* indicates that he had received a university education, presumably at Oxford. In the late 1260s and early 1270s he is to be found as the business agent of the west midland baron John de Verdon.

In 1273 Bray became a king's clerk. His first royal commission was levying arrears of a clerical tenth granted to the king. Later the same year he was appointed to the custody of various Welsh castles and honours that had come into the king's hands on the death of George de Cantilupe, lord of Abergavenny, at about the beginning of November. In 1275 he surrendered custody of Cilgerran but retained Abergavenny itself until 1281, and was embroiled during this period in a number of disputes with the tenants of the honour. In 1281 he was commissioned by the king to search the chirograph chests for all deeds relating to Jewish debts which had come into the king's hands through the forfeiture of the creditors concerned, and then to levy those debts for the king. Shortly afterwards he was also given the status of a justice of the Jews. He was paid as such until 1287, and in 1290 was still in possession of a key to the Jewish treasury, but it is doubtful whether he actually served as a justice for most of this period, since in February 1283 he was appointed to the full-time position of escheator of England south of Trent.

Bray held this position until May 1290, when he was arrested and sent to the Tower of London and his lands seized, probably as the result of an allegation made against him in the course of the 'state trials' of 1289–93.

The contemporary chronicler Bartholomew Cotton records that Bray attempted to drown himself *en route* for the Tower, and that he also tried to dash his brains out while in custody, but he came to no harm and by October had been released and begun paying a fine. By Easter term 1292, however, he was back in the Tower and his lands once more in the king's hands, apparently after a second conviction. Although the amount of his fine was fixed at 2000 marks as early as October 1292, he remained in prison in the Tower, and later in Winchester Castle, until 1294, when his release was obtained in return for a promise by Bray and his sureties to pay the fine off at the rate of 300 marks a year. In 1299 he reached an agreement with the king, granting the latter some of the Northamptonshire lands he had acquired in return for a remission of all the king's financial claims against him. He was never again employed directly by the king.

There is no evidence that Henry Bray was ever married, and by 1284 he had taken orders in the church that were incompatible with married status. He is, however, known to have had a son, also named Henry. He was still alive at the end of 1311 but was dead by September 1313.

PAUL BRAND, *rev.*

Sources court of common pleas, plea rolls, PRO, CP 40 · exchequer, memoranda rolls of the king's remembrancer, PRO, E 159 · *Chancery records* · *Bartholomaei de Cotton … Historia Anglicana*, ed. H. R. Luard, Rolls Series, 16 (1859) · T. F. Tout and H. Johnstone, eds., *State trials of the reign of Edward the First, 1289–1293*, CS, 3rd ser., 9 (1906)

Bray, John (*d.* 1381?), physician and botanist, is first recorded in September 1372, when John of Gaunt, duke of Lancaster (*d.* 1399), granted him £10 yearly from Kingston Manor, Dorset, for his services, with a living befitting a chamberlain, two horses and a servant, and 3*s.* a day when on actual service with the duke. Next year the keeper of Wimbourneholt (also in Dorset) was instructed to provide Master John with a tenth from the income of his property, and in 1375 Bray was still being paid a £10 annuity.

Late in 1376 Bray was named as royal physician in the household of Edward III. His professional standing is shown by the substantial financial rewards which he obtained for his services. In October 1376 he was granted 20 marks (£13 6*s.* 8*d.*) a year, and also £12 from the abbess and convent of Shaftesbury. Bray's wife, Joan, aged and infirm, was in April 1377 sent to the Shaftesbury convent by the king's command, with a grant for her maintenance for life. In the same year William Montagu, earl of Salisbury (*d.* 1397), granted Bray a pension of £5 a year. By 1378 Bray's annuity from Shaftesbury was confirmed, naming him as 'physician of the late King' (*CPR*, 1377–81, 136), and retaining him to stay with the young Richard II.

Bray's Shaftesbury annuity was transferred to a yeoman of the king's chamber 'in like manner as John Bray, physician, deceased', from 6 August 1381 (*CPR*, 1381–5, 37). Bray was the author of a glossary of herbs and medicines in Latin, French, and English, *Sinonoma de nominibus herbarum*, preserved in BL, Sloane MS 282, fols. 167*v*–173*v*.

This is probably the most accurate of the many lists of synonyms of the time. It is also possible that he was identical with the John Braize whose 'Practica medicine' is preserved in BL, Sloane MS 521, fols. 128r–159v.

JOHN HARVEY

Sources C. H. Talbot and E. A. Hammond, *The medical practitioners in medieval England: a biographical register* (1965), 125 · 'Sinonoma de nominibus herbarum secundum magistrum Iohanne Bray; liber cynonum editus a magistro J. B. de nominibus artem phisicalem et sirurgicum tangentibus in genere', BL, Sloane MS 282, fols. 167v–173v · J. Harvey, *The Black Prince and his age* (1976), 123–4, 176 · *CClR, 1374–7*, 538 · *CPR, 1377–85*

Archives BL, Sloane MS 282, fols. 167v–173v · BL, Sloane MS 521, fols. 128r–159v

Wealth at death very highly paid specialist during last nine years of life; left various annuities amounting to over £40, besides allowances for himself and wife: *CPR, 1377–85*

Bray, John Francis (1809–1897), socialist and writer, was born on 26 June 1809 in Washington, DC, USA, the eldest of seven children of John Bray, comedian and singer, and his wife, Sarah Hunt. His ancestors were primarily farmers and cloth manufacturers who had worked in or near Huddersfield, Yorkshire, for several generations. His father grew up in Yorkshire but emigrated to the United States in 1805 on being offered an engagement in Washington.

In May 1822 when Bray was nearly thirteen, his father returned to England because of ill health, taking his family with him, but died just a few days after their arrival in Leeds. His father's sister, with whom they were staying, subsequently apprenticed John to a printer in Pontefract. After continuing his apprenticeship at Selby, he spent a period as an itinerant journeyman printer before returning to Leeds to secure employment for a time (1833–4) on the *Voice of the West Riding*, one of the more notable of the many unstamped papers of the period.

It was during the early 1830s and as a result of his experiences as a journeyman printer that Bray first began to consider, write, and discourse upon social and industrial questions and, in particular, the impoverished condition and economic vulnerability of the labouring classes. Between December 1835 and February 1836 he published five 'Letters for the People' in the *Leeds Times*, and in November 1837 he delivered a series of lectures to the Leeds Working Men's Association, of which he was treasurer.

In his addresses to the association Bray was quite clear that only a programme of fundamental economic and social change would emancipate labour and as the association came to embrace the political objectives of the Charter, Bray ceased, therefore, to participate in its affairs. There is no evidence of any subsequent involvement in Chartism.

Both the letters and the lectures prefigured the work for which he has since been primarily remembered, *Labour's Wrongs and Labour's Remedy, or, The Age of Might and the Age of Right*, which was published in weekly numbers in 1838 and as a whole in 1839. In this work Bray explained labour's impoverishment as the consequence of a system of unequal exchanges between capitalist and labourer. It

was this which 'enable[d] one class to live in luxury and idleness, and doom[ed] another to incessant toil' (*Labour's Wrongs*, 49). Further, as a result of the working-class indigence which eventuated, deficient demand had become an endemic feature of existing economic arrangements and so the labouring classes suffered not just exploitation but absolute destitution when, in periods of general economic depression, their labour became surplus to requirements.

Taking his stand on the labour theory of value Bray looked to the creation of a system of 'universal labour and equal exchanges [of labour for labour]' (*Labour's Wrongs*, 109). To this end he advocated the ownership and control of the means of production 'by society at large' (ibid., 170) on the basis of worker-controlled joint-stock companies subject to the overall direction of local and national boards of trade. While, therefore, he was undoubtedly influenced by the communitarian socialism of Robert Owen, he rejected the limiting idea of self-sufficient co-operative communities and advocated instead central planning of the production, pricing, and distribution of goods, together with the allocation of resources.

In his critical use of the labour theory of value Bray may have influenced Marx, who certainly read him in that 1844–6 period when he embraced it. Marx also commented positively, if critically, upon Bray in *The Poverty of Philosophy* and his *Theories of Surplus Value*. That said, *Labour's Wrongs* was indifferently reviewed and in May 1842, shortly after its publication, Bray returned to the United States, though not before drafting *A Voyage from Utopia* (1841–2) as a riposte to those who had categorized the prescriptions of the former work as 'impracticable' and 'visionary'. However *A Voyage*, a ponderous satire on the manners and social customs of Britain, America, and France, lacked the analytical sharpness of the 1839 work and was not in fact published until 1957.

In 1844 Bray married the daughter of a cabinet-maker; they had six children, only one of whom survived into adulthood. Bray and his family settled in Lapeer county, Michigan, before moving to Pontiac in 1848, where in 1851 he took charge of a local paper, *The Jeffersonian*. When that folded, he was employed for a time with the *Detroit Enquirer* between 1853 and 1855, and it was during this period that he wrote *The Coming Age*, which was to provide a critical discussion of spiritualism in eight parts. However, only two were published (1855).

By the late 1850s Bray was cultivating a small 6 acre farm and between 1856 and 1865 owned and managed a daguerreotype gallery. However, he continued to write and in 1864 a 44-page tract entitled *American Destiny: What Shall it be Republican or Cossack?* was published in New York. The work defended the right of the southern states to secede from the Union as the cornerstone of republicanism and argued that the maintenance of that right was a crucial barrier to the emergence of despotism ('Cossackism'). Throughout the 1860s and 1870s Bray also contributed short articles and letters on socialism and labour questions to a wide variety of American papers. These included, among others, the *Irish World*, *Denver*

Labour Inquirer, *Hartford Examiner*, *John Swinton's Paper*, *Detroit Socialist*, *The Spectator*, *Chicago and Cinncinnati Socialist*, and *Milwaukee Emancipator*.

In the 1870s and 1880s Bray was active in the American labour movement. He accepted an invitation from the Socialist Labor Party of Detroit to speak at an eight-hour demonstration in 1879. He would have been nominated in 1880 for the US presidency on the Greenback Labor Party ticket if the socialist delegates had not walked out of the convention in Chicago. In May 1886 he was initiated into the syndicalist Knights of Labor. In addition he wrote several pamphlets for the Detroit Socialist Tract Association, under whose auspices his last major work, *God and Man a Unity*, was published in 1879, a book which unsuccessfully attempted to fuse theological critique with socialist political economy.

In Bray's last letter, in the *Paterson Labor Standard* of 12 September 1896, he continued to plead eloquently the cause of 'oppressed labor against the numerous tyrannies it groans under'. He died from catarrhal consumption at his son's farm near Pontiac, Michigan, USA, on 1 February 1897. His wife predeceased him in 1876.

NOEL THOMPSON

Sources H. J. Carr, 'A critical exposition of the social and economic ideas of John Francis Bray', PhD diss., U. Lond., 1943 · M. Jolliffe, 'John Francis Bray', *International Review for Social History*, 4 (1939), 1–36 · H. J. Carr, 'John Francis Bray', *Economica*, new ser., 7 (1940), 397–415 · M. F. Lloyd Pritchard, introduction, in J. F. Bray, *A voyage from Utopia*, ed. M. F. Lloyd Pritchard (1957) · D. Martin and J. Saville, 'Bray, John Francis', *DLB*, vol. 3 · E. Lowenthal, *The Ricardian socialists* (1911) · C. K. Yearly, *Britons in American labor: a history of the influence of the United Kingdom immigrants on American labor, 1820–1914* (1957) · J. P. Henderson, 'An English communist, Mr Bray [and] his remarkable work', *History of Political Economy*, 17 (1985), 73–95 · J. E. King, 'Utopian or scientific? A reconsideration of the Ricardian socialists', *History of Political Economy*, 15 (1983), 345–73 · G. D. H. Cole, *Socialist thought: the forerunners, 1789–1850* (1959) · N. Thompson, *The market and its critics: socialist political economy in nineteenth century Britain* (1988) · M. Beer, *A history of British socialism*, 2 vols. (1940)

Archives BLPES, MSS, incl. autobiographical sketch · U. Leeds, Brotherton L., family corresp. · U. Mich., Labadee College | Col. U., Seligman collection, drafts and cuttings

Likenesses photographs, repro. in Pritchard, 'Introduction'

Bray, Sir Reginald More (1842–1923), judge, was born at Shere, near Guildford, Surrey, on 26 September 1842, the elder son of Reginald Bray JP, of Shere, and his wife, Frances, daughter of Thomas Norton *Longman, the publisher [*see under* Longman, Thomas (1699–1755)]. He came from a distinguished family, which included not only the Tudor statesman and architect Sir Reginald Bray, but also Sir Thomas More; Bray's paternal grandmother was the sister of the economist T. R. Malthus. His younger brother, Sir Edward Bray, was later judge of Marylebone county court. Bray eventually succeeded to the large estate in Surrey which had been in the family since the end of the fifteenth century, and all his non-professional interests were local.

Bray was educated at Harrow School and then won a scholarship to Trinity College, Cambridge, where he graduated BA as twelfth wrangler in 1865. Having read in chambers with Charles James Watkin Williams, he was called to the bar by the Inner Temple in 1868. In the same year he married Emily Octavia, fourth daughter of a neighbouring landowner, Arthur Kett Barclay, of Bury Hill, Dorking; they had four sons and four daughters.

Bray joined the south-eastern circuit, 'devilled' for J. P. Murphy QC, and built up a respectable common-law practice. In 1891 he was made recorder of Guildford—a position which he held until 1904—and became a bencher of his inn. He did not become queen's counsel until 1897, after an unusually long career as a junior. He had a varied practice. In 1904, for example (his last year at the bar), the House of Lords reversed three decisions of the Court of Appeal which had decided against him on such diverse matters as local government law (*Caterham UDC* v. *Godstone RDC*), domicile in relation to liability for legacy duty (*Winans* v. *Attorney-General*), and the right to light (*Colls* v. *Home and Colonial Stores*).

Bray served on several occasions as commissioner of assize, and in June 1904, after the resignation of Mr Justice Bruce, he was appointed by Lord Halsbury to be a judge of the King's Bench Division and was knighted. Although this promotion came somewhat late Bray sat on the bench for eighteen years, until he reached the age of seventy-nine. He was considered by his peers to be one of the ablest puisne judges, sitting frequently in divisional courts and as a third member in the Court of Appeal. His knowledge of principles, his keen insight, and his robust common sense were exhibited in many reported judgments, such as those contained in *Sanday* v. *British and Foreign Marine Co.* (1915, restraint of princes), the Slingsby legitimacy case (1916), and *Reeve* v. *Jennings* (1910, a novel point under the Statute of Frauds).

A conservative in theological matters, Bray would not admonish an Anglican clergyman who had refused communion to a man who had married his deceased wife's sister (*R. v. Dibdin*, 1909) and was in favour of exempting Anglican Easter collections from income tax (*Cooper v. Blakiston*, 1907). Both of these judgments were overturned by higher courts, but he did have one success: his judgment that the West Riding local educational authority should pay for religious instruction in a non-provided school (*R. v. West Riding CC*, 1906) was accepted by the House of Lords.

In March 1923 Bray became ill while sitting in court. He died at 17 The Boltons, Kensington, London, on 23 March 1923 and was buried at Shere. He was survived by his wife and children.   P. A. LANDON, *rev.* HUGH MOONEY

Sources *CGPLA Eng. & Wales* (1923) · private information (1937)

Likenesses J. Collier, portrait, Manor House, Shere, near Guildford, Surrey · Spy [L. Ward], caricature, NPG; repro. in *VF* (17 Oct 1906)

Wealth at death £107,338 7s. 2d.: probate, 19 June 1923, *CGPLA Eng. & Wales*

Bray, Sir Reynold [Reginald] (*c*.1440–1503), administrator, was the eldest son of Richard Bray, gentleman and surgeon (*d.* 1469/70?), and his second wife, Joan Troughton (*d.* 1474).

Early career to 1485 Bray was born, probably in the early 1440s, in the parish of St John, Bedwardine, Worcestershire. Nothing is known of his early years until he is found by 1465 in the service of Lady Margaret Beaufort and her second husband, Henry, Lord Stafford, for whom he was receiver-general. Throughout the later 1460s Bray's private account books show him travelling widely on behalf of Margaret and Henry Stafford and managing both their estates and their legal affairs. He continued in Margaret Beaufort's service after Stafford's death in 1471, moving with her to Lancashire, and remained in that service even after 1485, although latterly he largely acted through deputies. There are at least two recorded early contacts with Henry Tudor, the future Henry VII, the first when Bray was sent to Weobley in September 1469 with money for the boy to buy a bow and arrows; and the second when Bray accompanied Henry to a meeting with the restored Henry VI in 1470. In the 1470s he was also employed on occasion in positions of trust by Lady Margaret's new husband, Thomas, Lord Stanley, acting for Stanley in delicate negotiations with Elizabeth Woodville, and purveying equipment for his lord's expedition to France in 1475 in the king's company, and in which he appears himself to have participated. Either Stanley patronage, or more probably that of William, Lord Hastings, exercised through the duchy of Lancaster, secured his return for the parliamentary seat of Newcastle under Lyme, Staffordshire, in 1478.

By about 1475 Bray had married Katherine Hussey (d. 1506), then aged about thirteen, the younger daughter and coheir of Nicholas Hussey, a former victualler of Calais. The marriage appears to have been brokered by Richard Guildford, who was married to the sister of the husband of Bray's own sister, Joan Isaac, and a future comptroller of Henry VII's household. Katherine herself advanced first in the household of Margaret Beaufort, and then in that of Henry VII's queen, Elizabeth of York. Katherine brought him estates in Berkshire, Sussex, and Hampshire, and it was to be with the alias 'of Harting, Sussex', that Bray would obtain a pardon from Richard III, on 5 January 1484, for all offences, including treason: that is, for his conspiratorial share in the rebellion against Richard of 1483. In this Bray is said to have acted as go-between between Margaret Beaufort and John Morton, then bishop of Ely, and to have recruited, or collaborated with, Sir Giles Daubeney, Sir John Cheney, and Guildford. One of his mainpernors for the pardon was William Cope, then his servant, and later to become cofferer of Henry VII. Bray's role as conspirator and fund-raiser for the successful invasion by Henry Tudor in 1485, which brought him to the throne as Henry VII, is known primarily from the *Anglica historia* of Polydore Vergil, but tends to be confirmed both by payments reimbursing him after 1485, and from the immediate preferment he received at the hands of the new king.

King's servant On 13 September 1485 Bray was appointed chancellor of the duchy of Lancaster. Following the reopening of the exchequer after Michaelmas he acted jointly with the London merchant Avery Cornburgh as under-treasurer of the exchequer. He was knighted at the coronation, on 28 October. On 28 February 1486 the king, by word of mouth, appointed Bray treasurer of England, an office he held until 10 July of the same year, when he was replaced by John, Lord Dynham, conventionally appointed by letters patent. Bray, however, in an unusual relationship continued to act jointly with Dynham in the exchequer in matters such as the taking of bonds from sheriffs and other officers, and for the leasing of lands; and was in effect jointly treasurer with Dynham during some of the king's more prolonged absences from proximity to London. He was feed by Dynham himself with the manor of Horley, Oxfordshire. Bray also continued to negotiate for loans on behalf of the king, and to make loans to the crown in his own name, and became intimately involved in the management of revenues raised or audited outside the exchequer, at times acting in direct conjunction with the king in his chamber.

Bray had some oversight of the customs revenues, and shipped wool in his own and the king's name, taking bottom in the king's ship the *Sovereign*. He was treasurer for war for the French expedition of 1492. Other offices granted by the king include that of chief justice of the forests south of Trent, an office to which he was appointed jointly in survivorship with John, Lord Fitzwalter, on 14 January 1486, and then with Giles, Lord Daubeney, from 24 November 1493. Bray's appointment to offices in the Welsh marches, in the north of England, and in the duchy of Chester, was the prelude to their reform under the direction of the council, and led to the extension of Henry VII's unique brand of personal kingship into the regions concerned. Other grants of stewardships, parkerships, and other estate offices, both in crown lands, in lands of the duchy of Lancaster, and in lands held temporarily by the crown, mirror Bray's own areas of regional interest or, where held in survivorship, his association with Richard Empson and patronage of John Hussey, later Lord Hussey. In 1491, 1495, and 1497 he was returned as MP for Hampshire, in which he held land in Freefolk in right of his wife, and Flood by purchase. More crucially, he held the custody of the castle of Carisbrooke and the farm of the Isle of Wight from the crown, occupying both from 1488 but with a formal grant only in 1495, and was also steward of the lands of the duke of Buckinghamshire, then a minor, for much of the decade. As a knight of the king's body he was a member of the king's household. He was habitually appointed to the bench in nine counties, although he sat regularly only in Middlesex and Surrey, as well as to commissions of oyer and terminer, gaol delivery, sewers, and the like.

The rewards of office In a series of grants made by Henry VII, beginning with the estate offices and then converted first to lease and then, in 1490 to a grant of the lands in tail male, and finally, in June 1492, in fee simple, Bray acquired Eaton (now known as Eaton Bray), Houghton Regis, and Totternhoe, with their appurtenances in Bedfordshire and Buckinghamshire, forfeited by John, Lord Zouche. In 1495 he further secured his title by intervening with Henry VII to obtain Zouche's restoration in blood, and by making an additional payment of £1000 to Zouche himself. By the late 1490s he was building at Eaton in brick and stone under the oversight of his receiver, John Cutte. His other main estates were centred on Clewer, Berkshire, and Shere, near Guildford, Surrey, close to his mother's burial place at Guildford, to Margaret Beaufort's palace at Woking, and to Claygate, where he held office from the crown. Shere he acquired in 1486 by a life grant from Thomas Butler, earl of Ormond, purchasing it outright in 1495. Chelsea, Middlesex, was purchased through the intervention of Margaret Beaufort. Since the inventory of his goods shows a substantial store of stuff at Blackfriars and Coldharbour, he may also have held property there, or perhaps continued to reside in Margaret Beaufort's mansion at Coldharbour, where he and his wife had rooms. Almost all Bray's estates, which at their greatest extent were in eighteen counties, were acquired by gift and purchase after 1485, some through manipulation of his political might.

From 1485 until his death Bray was one of the most powerful and omnicompetent of the king's councillors, but his importance for the history of the reign of Henry VII cannot be explained conventionally in terms of office or title. It lies in his long and loyal service to the king's mother, Margaret Beaufort, and to Henry VII himself. To Polydore Vergil he was *pater patriae, homo severus* ('father of his country, a man of gravity'; *Anglica historia*, 128), with ready access to the king, and freedom to rebuke as well as to influence him, a verdict repeated in less flattering terms both by the chroniclers and foreign envoys. As chancellor of the duchy he presided from *c.*1499 over the novel institution of the council learned, meeting in the duchy chamber to direct a penal system of bonds, and the enforcement of the prerogative to the king's benefit; and after his death a number of those offices and functions performed by Bray in intimate association with the king in his chamber and council became more institutionalized, including oversight of wardships, and the extra exchequer audit of accounts. His influence with the king was widely recognized, sometimes feared, and marked by a succession of fees, offices, benefits, and requests to act as executor or supervisor of wills, and requests for his direct intervention with the king for grants of grace and favour, for which both his own correspondence and the accounts of the king's chamber, among other sources, show him to be a focal point. With a few other leading councillors Bray received a French pension from 1492, epitomized by Raimondo da Soncino, the Milanese ambassador, in the comment that 'and as these leading satraps are very rich, the provision has to be very large' (*CSP Milan*, 1.325). In 1494 the University of Oxford appointed him its steward. He was named executor for the king in 1491 and 1496; other testamentary appointments as executor or supervisor include John, Cardinal Morton (who also left a legacy to Bray's nephew, Reynold, as his godson); Edward Story, bishop of Chichester; Thomas Langton, bishop of Winchester; John, Lord Dudley; and Edward, Viscount Lisle, and his wife.

The man and his works Bray had no real known cultural interests, and to the author of the great chronicle he was 'playn and rowth in spech' (*Great Chronicle*, 325), although Thomas Linacre, a noted humanist as well as a physician, attended his deathbed, and Bray and his wife funded works at Pembroke and Jesus colleges, Cambridge. An early association with the London merchant Henry Colet was continued, at least by Katherine, as a friendship with his humanist son John Colet, later dean of St Paul's, who was appointed by Katherine as her executor. His connections with the household of Margaret Beaufort, continuing active until his death, brought him the friendship of William Smith, from 1495 bishop of Lincoln, and of Hugh Oldham, who deputized for Bray in his receivership. Although there is no evidence to support his nineteenth-century reputation as an architect, he was directly engaged in at least three major building projects, and in lesser works at several other of his own houses. The works at Eaton were on a scale that suggests a substantial manor house in the most advanced idioms of the early Tudor style, and in which he was assisted by a gift of stone from the dean of Windsor, Christopher Urswick; and the substantial stores of materials left at his death at Edgcote, Northamptonshire, where Henry VII had visited him in September 1498, suggest that he also intended building there. At Bath he was associated with Bishop Oliver King in building the new cathedral. At Windsor he funded the south aisle and other work at St George's Chapel, continuing his interest even after the king had transferred his attention to Westminster, where Bray, with others, laid the foundation stone for the king's new chapel and intended burial place on 24 January 1503.

Bray was elected a knight of the Garter in 1501. The aisles of St George's are heavily decorated with his arms and his badge of the hemp-brake, and he is buried in a chantry chapel there. There is no monument, but a coffin thought to be his was discovered when the vault was opened in 1740. The representation of Bray in the 'Magnificat window' of the priory at Great Malvern is entirely conventional, showing him bovine and beardless, kneeling in a tabard of his pre-1497 arms. The latter were augmented at Blackheath, where he was dubbed a knight-banneret, quartering thenceforward the arms of the ancient Northamptonshire family of Bray. Sir Reynold Bray died, childless, on 5 August 1503. His immediate heirs were to be the sons of his brother, John, for the two younger of whom he had arranged marriages to the children of his sister-in-law, Constance, and her husband, Henry Lovell, in a concern for dynastic continuity which consistently ran beyond mere profit. These plans proved abortive. After litigation before the council, his estates were divided in 1510 between Edmund Bray, the eldest of John's sons, and Sir William Sandys, married to Margery, daughter of Sir Reynold's elder half-brother, who was also named John. The real extent of Bray's wealth is unknown. As early as 1491 he was able to contribute as much as £500 to a benevolence to the crown, and Dugdale, though he cites no evidence, estimated the value of Bray's purchases of land after 1497 as more than 100 marks (£666 13s. 4d.) per annum. Perhaps the truest measure of his resources is the rapidity with which his executors paid a substantial proportion of fines totalling 6200 marks which were imposed after his death—2500 marks by February 1505.

M. M. CONDON

Sources will, PRO, PROB 11/13, sig. 26 · chancery close rolls, PRO, C 54/378 · PRO, exchequer, king's remembrancer, inventories of goods and chattels, E 154/2/10 · PRO, CIPM, C 140/33, no. 47 · PRO, exchequer, exchequer of receipt rolls, E 401 · Westminster Abbey Muniment Room, London, WAM 5472, 16026, 16051, 32407 · M. M. Condon, 'From caitiff and villein to Pater Patriae: Reynold Bray and the profits of office', *Profit, piety and the professions in late medieval England*, ed. M. A. Hicks (1990), 137–68 · M. M. Condon, 'Ruling elites in the reign of Henry VII', *Patronage, pedigree and power in later medieval England*, ed. C. D. Ross (1979), 109–42 · *The Anglica historia of Polydore Vergil, AD 1485–1537*, ed. and trans. D. Hay, CS, 3rd ser., 74 (1950) · *Three books of Polydore Vergil's 'English history'*, ed. H. Ellis, CS, 29 (1844) · A. H. Thomas and I. D. Thornley, eds., *The great chronicle of London* (1938) · R. Somerville, *History of the duchy of Lancaster, 1265–1603* (1953) · 'The Brays of Shere', *The Ancestor*, 6 (1903), 1–10 · Stonyhurst College, Lancashire, MS 60 · *CSP Milan* · T. Habington, *A survey of Worcestershire*, ed. J. Amphlett, 2 vols., Worcestershire Historical Society (1895–9)

Archives Westminster Abbey Muniment Room, London, antiphons · Westminster Abbey Muniment Room, London, letters and papers | Guildford Muniment Room, Guildford, Onslow MSS · Stonyhurst College, Lancashire, MS 60 · Westminster Abbey Muniment Room, London, account rolls Eaton Bray · Westminster Abbey Muniment Room, London, Stafford household books

Likenesses J. Carter, etching (after watercolour drawing), BM; repro. in J. Carter, *Specimens of ancient culture and painting* (1790) · stained glass window, priory church, Great Malvern, Worcestershire; repro. in Somerville, *Duchy of Lancaster* · watercolour drawing (after stained glass window), Stanford Hall, Leicestershire

Wealth at death see will, PRO, PROB 11/13, sig. 26; PRO, C 54/378; inventory, PRO, E 154/2/10

Bray, Thomas (*bap.* 1658, *d.* 1730), Church of England clergyman, was born at Bray's Tenement, Marton, Shropshire, the son of Richard Bray, a poor farmer, and his wife, Mary. He was baptized at the parish church for Marton, Chirbury, on 2 May 1658. He attended Oswestry grammar school before matriculating at All Souls College, Oxford, on 12 March 1675 (probably as a servitor performing tasks for the fellows), graduating BA on 11 November 1678. As he could not afford the fee he proceeded MA from Hart Hall only (since he could not remain a member of All Souls without becoming a fellow) on 12 December 1693. He became a schoolmaster until he reached the canonical age of twenty-three in 1681, when he was ordained deacon, and priest the next year, by Thomas Wood, bishop of Coventry and Lichfield.

Parish duties and catechism Bray became curate of a parish near Bridgnorth in Shropshire, but soon attracted the notice of Sir Thomas Price of Park Hall, near Castle Bromwich, Warwickshire. In 1682 Price made him his chaplain and secured for him from Sir Andrew Hacket, the patron, the living of Lea Marston in the same county. He was chosen to preach an assize sermon at Warwick, which was heard by Simon, Lord Digby, who was so impressed that he recommended him to his brother William who, succeeding to the title in 1685, presented him to the rectory of Over Whitacre. Bray held the two adjacent Warwickshire livings in plurality. Each was worth less than £20 per annum, but later Lord Digby endowed Over Whitacre

Thomas Bray (*bap.* 1658, *d.* 1730), by unknown artist

with a gift of glebe lands and tithes and obtained a grant from Queen Anne's Bounty. Lord Digby was also patron of another Warwickshire parish, Sheldon, and after its rector, Digby Bull, resigned rather than take the oath of loyalty to William and Mary he appointed Bray, in 1690, to this parish of 500 people.

Bray married about 1685, but no record of the date or place of the wedding has been discovered, and only the forename of his wife, Elenor, is known. They had a son in 1687 and a daughter in 1688, but Elenor died later in the latter year. Bray married, on 3 November 1698, Agnes Sayers of Clerkenwell, Middlesex. They had four children, all of whom died young.

Following the revolution of 1688 the bishops of the church were anxious that its people should be well instructed in its beliefs in the face of the challenge it had faced from both nonconformists and Roman Catholics over the previous decade. In 1695 Thomas Tenison, archbishop of Canterbury, issued injunctions under the authority of the crown requiring the clergy to observe the fifty-ninth canon calling for regular catechizing of the young on Sundays. Bray believed in the need for this, and the next year contributed to a long-established genre, composing the first volume of his *Catechetical Lectures*, which, based upon his method of teaching in his parish, was designed to assist the clergy in explaining the catechism to their congregations. This volume was published by the 'authoritative injunctions' of William Lloyd, bishop of Coventry and Lichfield, to whom it was dedicated. Though the other intended three volumes were never published this volume sold out at 3000 copies and realized a profit of

£700. Bray gained great prestige through this. His name became well known in the capital, and he secured the approval of the bishop of London, Henry Compton.

Parish libraries in America and England This approval brought Bray a venture in America. In 1690 a local revolution had led to the overthrow of Roman Catholic control of the colony of Maryland, and Francis Nicolson, who became governor shortly afterwards, secured a privileged position for the Church of England there and actively encouraged measures to promote and benefit it, such as by building residences for the clergy. In 1691 the colonial assembly passed an act to divide the colony into parishes and to appoint a legal maintenance for the clergy in each parish. The bishop of London was responsible for the oversight of the church outside the British Isles, and in 1695 Nicolson requested Compton to send over a clergyman to act as the bishop's commissary or agent, who would provide pastors for the parishes and oversee their work. Compton selected Bray for the post, which he accepted. Nicolson approved of his appointment and, in order to add to the prestige of the church in the colony, requested him to take the degrees of BD and DD at Oxford. This he did at Magdalen College on 17 December 1696, though he found it difficult to afford the fees. He received no allowance for expenses and had to sell his own small effects and raise money on credit.

By autumn 1695 Bray had moved to London, paying £20 a year for his lodging and a servant and appointing a curate at £30 a year to take charge of Sheldon, but he was faced with legal difficulties. An order in council declared the Maryland assembly's act invalid because it wrongly stated that the laws of England were in force in the colony, and it was considered advisable that Bray should not go out there until an amended act was passed.

Meanwhile Bray set out to gain missionaries who would go to the vacant parishes in Maryland as soon as the new act was passed. He found that it was mainly unbeneficed clerics and those with poor livings who were willing to undertake such a distant and uncertain assignment, and they could not afford to buy the books which he considered they needed. He determined to provide libraries for them. He told Compton that only if he and other bishops would support such a scheme would he continue with his task. The two archbishops and five bishops declared, 'We look upon this design as what will tend very much to propagate Christian knowledge in the Indies. ... And therefore, we shall contribute cheerfully towards promoting these parochial libraries' (Thompson, 16).

In December 1695 Bray printed *Proposals for Encouraging Learning and Religion in the Foreign Plantations*, a plea for libraries for the overseas clergy. This assisted his public appeal for subscriptions towards the project. Among his supporters was Princess (afterwards Queen) Anne, who gave him a 'noble benefaction' of £44, and he founded his 'premier library' at Annapolis, the new capital of Maryland which was named after her. Before his death he had founded thirty-nine libraries, some having more than a thousand volumes, in North America, as well as many others overseas.

In 1697 Bray published *An essay towards promoting all necessary and useful knowledge, both divine and human, in all parts of his majesty's dominions, both at home and abroad*, containing lists of recommended books. This aimed at extending the libraries to the Church of England. He reckoned that at least 400 incumbents or curates with a stipend of £10 or £15 a year were too poor to obtain books. One of his strongest beliefs was in the need to uphold the dignity and authority of the English clergy. Their ignorance through such poverty prevented them from confuting the attacks that were being made upon them, not only by dissenting 'Enthusiasts and Antinominians', but increasingly by 'Atheists, Deists and Socinians' so that 'all veneration to the priestly craft is worn off' (Rose, 178). He proposed a revival of the ancient, largely obsolete rural deaneries so that libraries could be provided for these groups of parishes. During his lifetime more than eighty such libraries were founded in many parts of the country.

In order to place his work on a permanent basis Bray wished to obtain an endowment for the libraries. In 1697 parliament was considering a bill to assign certain lands 'given to superstitious uses', which had been taken over by the crown, to the maintenance of Greenwich Hospital, and Bray and his friends petitioned that a part of them should be appropriated to the 'propagation of true religion in our foreign plantations'; but all the lands went to Greenwich Hospital. In 1698 he asked the king for the grant of some arrears of taxes due to the crown and even followed the king to the Netherlands to secure this, but the arrears were found to be almost valueless (Thompson, 33–5).

The founding of the SPCK These efforts having failed Bray now gained the support of Compton and 'several worthy persons' to form an organization for doing this. He planned it to be 'a Protestant Congregation or Society' which was to work in a similar way to the Congregatio de Propaganda Fide of the Roman Catholic church. He termed it the Society for Promoting Christian Knowledge (SPCK) and declared its purpose to propagate Christian teaching at home and abroad through encouraging libraries and charity schools, circulating books and pamphlets, and supporting missionaries to both settlers and native peoples in the colonies. It was founded by Bray and four lay friends who met on 8 March 1699. Largely through Bray's vigorous leadership the society met frequently—sixty times in the first year—and increased its number by electing further members, both clerical and lay. Bray had originally intended to obtain a charter for it from the crown, but this was not done and it remained a voluntary society.

Though Bray in his ecclesiastical outlook sympathized with the high-church conception of the authority of the episcopate and the importance of the sacraments, he regarded the purpose of the SPCK as pragmatic rather than doctrinal. It included among its earliest members men of differing views who agreed about its purpose. Bray himself was no nonjuror and under Queen Anne became a supporter of the Hanoverian cause. 'Good Dr. Bray', William Whiston recalled, 'said how happy and religious the nation would become when the House of Hanover came and was very indignant when Mr Mason said that matters would not be mended when that family came thither' (W. Whiston, *Memoirs, Written by Himself*, 1753, 134).

The voyage to Maryland After his second marriage Bray moved to another house in London 'for myself and family' at a rent of £30, to which he probably took his children from Sheldon. He still had only his stipend from Sheldon to meet his many expenses and could not receive, until he went to Maryland, the salary of £400 allotted to him as commissary. He was offered two preferments in London to supplement this—the endowed but titular post of sub-almoner to the royal household and the parish of St Botolph, Aldgate, 'but he declined all offers that were inconsistent with his going to Maryland, as soon as it should become proper to take that voyage' (*Publick Spirit*, 21).

After waiting two years, Bray resolved, whatever the legal position, that he ought now to go to Maryland. His efforts in England had by now ensured that the colony, with a population of about 25,000, possessed thirty parishes, of which about half had clergy. He set out on 16 December 1699, borrowing money and selling his personal belongings to pay for his passage. Knowing that naval chaplains and other seagoing clergy were often detained in ports he founded libraries for them at Gravesend, Deal, and Plymouth. He arrived in Maryland on 18 March 1700 and, though a new governor had now been appointed who was less supportive of him, he at once set about 'repairing the breach made in the settlement of the parochial clergy' (Thompson, 48) and planning to send them a full supply of books.

On 22 May Bray held a general visitation of the clergy of the province at Annapolis and delivered his charge to them. He had meant to stay on in Maryland, but though he had been there for only two months the clergy urged him to go back to England and seek to have the law for the establishment of the church in Maryland, which had been twice rejected at Westminster, re-enacted with the royal assent. And they trusted he could find and bring back good men to place in the vacant parishes. He hoped to see the act passed and return in the spring.

Back in England Bray found that the Quakers were seeking to secure the defeat of the act. He refuted them in a printed memorial, but found that the act would not soon come into effect, and after making an unsuccessful attempt to obtain a bishop for Maryland he resigned his office of commissary. The act was finally approved later. He had himself met all the cost of his voyage and expenses. A friend, Thomas Thynne, first Viscount Weymouth, gave him £300 and two others £50 each, but he characteristically spent it all on his undertakings.

One of Bray's prominent activities was to continue to press for the extension of bishops to America. He was entitled to speak for the case of Maryland, but he supported the idea of the establishment of four bishoprics, in Jamaica, Barbados, Virginia, and Maryland. His motive was to uphold the constitution of the church:

It seems requisite to consecrate bishops for these parts as we of the Church would be thought to believe the truth and force of our own arguments brought to prove the *Jus Divinum* of episcopacy and the necessity of bishops (where possibly they may be had) to constitute the national and regular part of the Catholic Church. (Thompson, 71)

The work of the SPCK and founding of the SPG Bray's most prominent undertaking, however, was the work of the SPCK. It had grown rapidly during his absence and was now busily engaged in several activities, the most prominent remaining the establishment of libraries and the provision of charity schools. The education of children in these schools was conducted along definite church principles. In accordance with Bray's ideas it was based upon the catechism, and he insisted that confirmation was 'both greatly necessary and of regular benefit in the Church of Christ' (Rose, 181). In addition the SPCK helped the religious societies by distributing their literature and investigated prison conditions after Bray had visited Bridewell and Newgate. The society supported the establishment of parish workhouses, designed to provide profitable employment and moral reform for their inmates, and it inspired the provision of voluntary hospitals and infirmaries, maintained by subscription, for the indigent sick.

Indeed, Bray considered that its work was now so extensive that part should be assigned to a separate society. This, unlike the SPCK, was to be a corporate society, and on 16 June 1701 he received the charter for the Society for the Propagation of the Gospel in Foreign Parts (SPG). It held its initial meeting in Lambeth Palace, and the archbishop of Canterbury became its first president. Its purpose was to enable the Church of England to support its clergy in the English colonies 'for the instruction of the King's loving subjects in the Christian religion' and to evangelize the native peoples there (Pascoe, 3–8). Having been the virtual initiator of both these pioneering church societies Bray wished now to hand over their management to others, and some time in winter 1703–4 he returned to Sheldon.

St Botolph, Aldgate Bray continued to hold this Warwickshire parish in plurality and in 1706 was again offered (and this time accepted) the living of St Botolph, Aldgate. He moved in spring 1708 to his new parish, which a survey of London church life six years later stated was 'a large and populous parish, wherein are above one thousand dwelling houses'. His parishioners were given daily morning and evening prayers and many special sermons and lectures as well as generous care for the poor (J. Paterson, *Pietas Londiniensis*, 1714). He set the congregation to sing the new metrical psalms of Nahum Tate and Nicholas Brady in place of the older ones of Thomas Sternhold and John Hopkins. Ralph Thoresby in his diary noted in 1723 Bray's diligence and conscientiousness as a pastor. He recorded that he 'walked to the pious and charitable Dr. Bray's in Aldgate and was extremely pleased with his many pious, useful and charitable works'. The next Sunday, having heard Bray read prayers and preach twice excellently and catechize the charity school children, he stated:

I was extremely surprised at the prodigious pains so aged a person takes; he is very mortified as to the world and has taken abundance of trouble to have a new church erected in this large parish, though it would lessen the revenue £100 per annum to him. (*The Diary of Ralph Thoresby*, ed. J. Hunter, 2 vols., 1830, vol. 2, 15 and 26 May 1723)

And it was doubtless due to his influence that Sir John Cass founded in 1710 his charity school near the church.

As the incumbent had to do in many London city parishes Bray had to provide for many poor people. He left money to establish a fund for continuing his 'prayers with catechetical exercises and reading proper discourses to the poor in the workhouse belonging to St. Botolph, Aldgate' and arranged that if any future incumbent should decline this 'use of the desk' another church was to be sought where this could be done. He left also 'suits of mean but new apparel of mantuas and petticoats' for the use 'of the poor women of both parts of the parish … who are observed to come most frequently to church on the Lord's day and weekdays so that they may be decently clothed and not afraid to come' (Thompson, 88). It was during these years that his wife, Agnes, died.

Dr Bray's Associates Despite the demands of this busy parish Bray continued with his other activities. Prominent was his early concern for erecting libraries. He was pleased when Sir Peter King, afterwards lord chancellor, secured the passing of an act 'for the better preservation of parochial libraries in England' (Thompson, 90). And when he was in the Netherlands he had spoken about the spiritual condition of the black population in the West Indies and North America to King William's secretary at The Hague, the Sieur D'Allone, who made a bequest in his will for their instruction, amounting by the time D'Allone died in 1723 to £900 invested in South Sea annuities. In that year Bray had a dangerous illness and was uncertain about his future health, so he founded his third organization, Dr Bray's Associates, a group to continue his work of 'founding clerical libraries and supporting negro schools'. Shortly before his death he extended the associates into a charitable organization, which was confirmed by a decree of chancery in 1731; it still exists today.

Bray was an early and active supporter of Thomas Coram's Foundling Hospital, first planned in 1722 though not built until 1739, nine years after Bray's death. Coram for a time lived with Bray, and was encouraged by him in involving himself with the provision of missionary work and parish libraries in North America.

In 1727 'an acquaintance made a casual visit to Whitechapel prison, and his representation of the miserable state of the prisoners had such an effect on the doctor that he applied himself to solicit benefactions to relieve them' (Thompson, 99–100), and Bray sent his missionary candidates to visit them. Through this he came to know General James Edward Oglethorpe, who joined the associates and induced others to do so. And towards the end of 1729, within six weeks of his death, Bray suggested to Oglethorpe that there should be a colony in America for released debtors and the unemployed poor, which led to the foundation of Georgia in 1732. As a trustee of Bray's estate and in accordance with Bray's known interest Oglethorpe used some of Bray's property to aid the settlement of poverty-stricken families in the colony.

Later writings and death Bray had also continued with his writing. His publications during this period included an expression of his anti-popish outlook. The SPCK and the SPG had made early corresponding contacts with the reformed churches on the continent. During the War of the Spanish Succession both societies were active in their support of the protestant cause, and from 1709 they urged the case of protestant minorities to be considered in any forthcoming peace treaty. In 1712, as negotiations proceeded at Utrecht, they—and Bray in particular—solicited material from their continental correspondents for a collection of treatises to remind protestant rulers of the true nature of popery, which Bray published as *Papal usurpation and persecution as it has been exercised in ancient and modern times … designed as supplemental to the Book of martyrs*, consisting of 'Choice and learned treatises of celebrated authors … ranged and digested into as regular an history of the subject as the nature of the subject would admit' (Rawlinson, 39). Bray published the work anonymously for fear of assassination. Only one volume appeared, as he had to lay the second aside after spending much time compiling materials for it. He bequeathed his collection of anti-Catholic works to Sion College; it is now in Lambeth Palace Library. According to Richard Rawlinson, Bray

was indeed so great a master of the Papal history, that few authors could be presum'd able with equal accuracy and learning to trace the origin and growth of those exorbitant powers which are claimed by the See of Rome. (Rawlinson, 39)

Other writings were *Promordia bibliothecaria* (1726), containing 'several schemes of parochial libraries, laid down to proceed by a general progression from strength to strength'; and *Missionala* (1727), being 'a collection of missionary pieces relating to the conversion of the heathen, both the African Negroes and the American Indians' (title-page).

Bray's health was now failing, and he engaged a succession of curates. After becoming bedridden late in 1729 he died in London on 15 February 1730, and was buried at St Botolph, Aldgate. 'I am called a *Projector*', he wrote about himself in 1699 in his *Bibliotheca catechetica*, '(a very mean and contemptible character with such as are accounted men of wisdom) upon the account of these designs I am continually forming' (Thompson, 103). He was indeed a projector, and most of the designs of this remarkable cleric, who was not a great divine and secured no higher preferment than a London parish, prospered and succeeded to a greater extent than he could have expected and are still effectual today. As a result of his powerful supportive influence among the Anglicans in America they were able, assisted later in the eighteenth century, to withstand the shock and upheaval of the War of Independence and to continue their existence afterwards by the establishment of the protestant episcopal church in the United States. And another later consequence of his work was the ability of the Church of England to identify itself with the cause of religious learning and social welfare in the UK as well as embarking upon the cause of overseas missions and beginning the process which was to lead it to become the centre of the worldwide Anglican communion.   LEONARD W. COWIE

Sources H. P. Thompson, *Thomas Bray* (1954) · *Publick spirit illustrated in the life and designs of the Reverend Thomas Bray D.D.* (1746); reprinted with additions by H. J. Todd (1808) · W. K. Lowther Clarke, *A history of the SPCK* (1959) · W. K. Lowther Clarke, *Eighteenth-century piety* (1944) · E. McClure, ed., *A chapter in English church history: being the minutes of the Society for Promoting Christian Knowledge for … 1698–1704* (1888) · E. L. Pennington, *The Rev Thomas Bray* (Church Historical Society, Philadelphia, 1934) · L. W. Cowie, *Henry Newman: an American in London, 1708–43* (1956) · J. H. Overton, *Life in the English church, 1660–1714* (1885) · N. Sykes, *Church and state in England in the XVIII century* (1934) · R. Rawlinson, 'A short historical account of the life and designs of Thomas Bray, D.D.', in B. C. Steiner, *The Rev. Thomas Bray: his life and selected works relating to Maryland*, Maryland Historical Society, 37 (1901), 11–50 · W. S. Perry, ed., *Historical collections relating to the American colonial church*, 1: *Virginia* (1870); 4: *Maryland* (1878) · F. L. Hawks, *Contributions to the ecclesiastical history of the United States*, 2 vols. (1839) · C. F. Pascoe, *Two hundred years of the SPG: an historical account, 1701–1900* (1901) · A. A. Ettinger, *James Edward Oglethorpe: imperial idealist* (1936) · C. Rose, 'The origins and ideals of the SPCK, 1699–1716', *The Church of England, c.1689–c.1833: from toleration to tractarianism*, ed. J. Walsh, C. Haydon, and S. Taylor (1993), 172–90 · E. Duffy, '*Correspondence fraternelle*: the SPCK, the SPG, and the churches of Switzerland in the War of the Spanish Succession', *Reform and Reformation: England and the continent, c. 1500–1750*, ed. D. Baker, SCH, Subsidia, Subsidia, 2 (1979), 251–80 · P. Slack, *From reformation to improvement: public welfare in early modern England* (1999)
Archives LPL, papers · NRA, notebook | LPL, corresp. relating to the Society for the Propagation of the Gospel
Likenesses portrait, United Society for the Propagation of the Gospel, London [*see illus.*]
Wealth at death £655 in South Sea annuities: Thompson, *Thomas Bray*, 100

Bray, Thomas (1749–1820), Roman Catholic archbishop of Cashel and Emly, was born in Fethard, co. Tipperary, the son of John Bray, wine merchant, and his wife, Margaret Power. Educated at the Irish College, Paris, and at St Guard, Avignon, he received a doctorate in divinity from Congregatio de Propaganda Fide, Rome, in 1773. He was ordained to the priesthood at Paris in 1774 before returning to Ireland to serve in his native diocese. In 1782 he was appointed vicar-general of the diocese, and in October 1792 he was consecrated archbishop of Cashel and Emly, in succession to James Butler.

Bray administered the diocese at a critical period, and throughout the 1790s he joined his fellow bishops in their condemnation of the French Revolution and the associated radicalism of the United Irishmen. He supported the Act of Union, confident that the emancipation promised by Pitt would follow, but he was determined to resist the establishment of a royal veto or state pension for the Catholic clergy.

Bray's pastoral priority was education and the introduction of Tridentine discipline and order following the disruption of the penal era. To this end he published the comprehensive *Statua synodalia* (2 vols., Dublin, 1813). The first volume, based on the statutes of a diocesan synod of 1810, reiterated the decrees of the Council of Trent on the sacraments and on ecclesiastical discipline. Its counsels against the 'excesses' associated with the celebration of patterns (popular religious festivals on saints' days), weddings, wakes, and the 'savage customs of howling and bawling at funerals' (p. 87) reflected the church's determined opposition to important aspects of traditional culture. To this Bray added the council's decree against duelling, papal condemnations of freemasonry, and historical sketches of archbishops of Cashel. The second volume contains a series of pastoral instructions to be read in English or in Irish at the chapels of the diocese throughout the liturgical year.

Bray died on 9 December 1820 and was buried in his cathedral, popularly known as the 'Big Chapel', which he had erected in Thurles in 1809.

THOMPSON COOPER, rev. DÁIRE KEOGH

Sources C. Meagher, 'Calendar of the papers of Dr Bray, archbishop of Cashel and Emly (1792–1820)', *Journal of the Cork Historical and Archaeological Society*, 2nd ser., 73 (1968), 81–113; 74 (1969) · K. Whelan, 'The Catholic church in county Tipperary, 1700–1900', *Tipperary: history and society*, ed. W. Molan and T. McGrath (Dublin, 1985), 215–54
Archives Cashel Roman Catholic Diocesan Archive, Thurles, papers

Bray, William (d. 1643), Church of England clergyman, matriculated as a pensioner from Trinity College, Cambridge, in the Easter term of 1613, graduating BA from Christ's College in 1617 and proceeding MA in 1620. He was ordained deacon in the diocese of Lichfield in September 1620, and priest in September 1621. He began his clerical career as an unbeneficed lecturer in London, where, according to William Prynne, he established a reputation as 'a great zelot and Precisian' and 'an earnest preacher against Altars and prophane Sabbath-breakers' (Prynne, 312, 331). Later, however, he was appointed chaplain to William Laud; it is not clear precisely when he took up this position, but Laud later wrote that 'he had been my chaplain above ten years in my house' (*Works of … William Laud*, 4.294), suggesting that Bray may have taken up the post soon after Laud's appointment as bishop of London in 1628.

One of Bray's duties as Laud's chaplain was to license books for the press. In this capacity he played an important role in expediting the publication of Sir Henry Spelman's *Concilia* (1639): he wrote to Spelman in 1635 looking forward to the completion of 'your much desired British Councels' (BL, Add. MS 34600, fol. 25) and his signature and imprimatur appear on the autograph manuscript of the work (Bodl. Oxf., MS Tanner 288, fol. 36). As a rule he seems to have been averse to religious controversy: he expunged some anti-Catholic material from Daniel Featley's *Sermons* (1636), and it was alleged at Laud's trial that on being asked to license Sir Anthony Hungerford's *Advice to a Son* (1639) he had replied that 'there were some harsh phrases in it, which were better left out, because we were upon a way of winning the Papists' (*Works of … William Laud*, 4.278). However, Sir Edward Dering later declared that in comparison with his fellow licenser Samuel Baker, 'I ever held Dr Bray the more moderate man' (Dering, sig. d4r), an assessment supported by an incident in 1637 when the Derbyshire puritan minister John Hieron and several of his parishioners were summoned to Lambeth to answer charges of nonconformity. Baker refused to discharge them, but they then went to Bray, 'who courteously received them, and went with them to Sir John Lamb, and obtained their discharge' (Porter, sig. D3v).

Bray proceeded BD in 1631 and on 5 May 1632 was presented to the rectory of St Ethelburga, Bishopsgate, London. He resigned on 2 April 1633 on becoming vicar of St Martin-in-the-Fields. Both livings were in the gift of Laud (as bishop of London), who later declared of Bray: 'I found him a very able and an honest man, and had reason to prefer him to be able to live well; and I did so' (Works of … William Laud, 4.294). As vicar of St Martin, Bray was involved in a protracted dispute with the earl of Bedford, who had financed the building of the new church of St Paul, Covent Garden, and sought to have it separated from the parish of St Martin. The dispute was settled in 1638 on terms that were broadly favourable to Bray: it was ordered that St Paul's should remain a chapel of ease within the parish of St Martin, and that Bray should appoint a curate to serve the church at an annual stipend of £100. Bray also received several pieces of higher preferment: on 11 June 1632 he was appointed a prebendary of St Paul's Cathedral, and on 13 November 1637 a canon of Canterbury. He proceeded DD in 1639. Some authorities also identify Bray as vicar of Chaldon Herring, Dorset, but this may result from confusion with another man of the same name, who was ordained deacon in the diocese of Salisbury on 21 December 1616 (Yale University, Beinecke Library, Gen. MSS, vol. 295).

One of the books licensed by Bray was John Pocklington's Sunday No Sabbath (1636), which Prynne regarded as 'the most prophane and scurrilous [work] ever yet printed' because of its anti-sabbatarian views (Prynne, 312). On 12 March 1641 Bray was summoned before the House of Lords and asked whether he had licensed this and another work by Pocklington, Altare Christianum (1637), to which he replied:

> that he did licence them both, and read them over, but not so cautiously as he should have done; for which he is heartily sorry, and confessed he is now of another opinion than he was when he licensed and approved those two books. (JHL, 4.183)

He was ordered to preach a recantation sermon at St Margaret's, Westminster, which was later published as A Sermon of the Blessed Sacrament of the Lords Supper (1641). In this sermon, Bray declared himself 'a true Protestant of the Reformed Church of England' and repudiated 'that most dangerous and destructive doctrine of Transubstantiation'; he then listed the errors in Pocklington's two books, and confessed his regret at having licensed 'all these erroneous and offensive passages'. On 16 April 1641, it was reported to the Lords that Bray had preached the sermon 'with ingenuity and candour'; and it was duly ordered 'that he be discharged from any further trouble

concerning this business' (JHL, 4.219). On 12 January 1643 the House of Commons appointed Dr John Wincopp to serve the cure of St Martin-in-the-Fields, on hearing that Bray had deserted the parish three months previously and joined the royalist army. On 3 October the house made a further order granting Wincopp the use of Bray's library, and on 15 December it was noted that the living was vacant owing to Bray's death.　　　　　　ARNOLD HUNT

Sources [W. Prynne], A quench-coale, or, A briefe disquisition and inquirie (1637) · G. Radcliffe, The earl of Strafforde's letters and dispatches, with an essay towards his life, ed. W. Knowler, 2 vols. (1739) · The works of the most reverend father in God, William Laud, ed. J. Bliss and W. Scott, 7 vols. (1847–60) · W. Bray, A sermon of the blessed sacrament of the Lords supper (1641) · R. Porter, The life of Mr John Hieron (1691) · E. Dering, A discourse of proper sacrifice (1644) · collections relating to Westminster, BL, Harley MS 1831 · JHC · JHL · Walker rev. · G. Hennessy, Novum repertorium ecclesiasticum parochiale Londinense, or, London diocesan clergy succession from the earliest time to the year 1898 (1898) · Fasti Angl., 1541–1857, [St Paul's, London] · Fasti Angl., 1541–1857, [Canterbury] · Venn, Alum. Cant.
Archives BL, letters to Sir Henry Spelman, Add. MS 34600

Bray, William (1735/6–1832), antiquary, the fourth and youngest son of Edward Bray (1687–1739), of Shere in Surrey, and his wife, Anne (1695–1774), daughter of the Revd George Duncomb, was born in Shere and baptized there on 7 November 1736. In 1746 he joined his elder brothers, George and Edward, at Rugby School. A third brother, Charles, had died in infancy in 1735. On leaving school he was articled to Mr Martyr, an attorney, at Guildford, whom he left in November 1757 for further instruction from Mr Addersley of New Inn. On 28 November 1757 he was sworn in as an attorney of the king's bench. He married, at Guildford on 28 September 1758, Mary Stephens (b. 1734), daughter of Henry Stephens of Wipley, near Worplesdon, Surrey. They had eight children, of whom only a son, Edward, and two daughters lived to maturity. His wife died on 14 December 1796.

Bray's success as a solicitor owed as much to his personality as it did to his energy and professional ability. In 1761 he became a clerk of the board of green cloth through the patronage of John Evelyn of Wotton. Although the post, which gave him responsibility for the accounts of the royal household, required Bray to live in London, its light demands enabled him to develop a successful legal practice in Great Russell Street, which acted for many families and charities in Surrey, London, and Middlesex. Principal of these charities was that of Henry Smith, for which Bray was treasurer from 1769. He was also a director of the Equitable Assurance Society between 1774 and 1827.

Bray's interest in history was developed by his legal work and contact with other Surrey antiquaries. He was elected a fellow of the Society of Antiquaries in 1772, was treasurer of the society from 1803 to 1823, and contributed twenty-nine articles to Archaeologia. His first publication, A Sketch of a Tour into Derbyshire and Yorkshire, the result of one of his antiquarian tours, was published anonymously in 1777, but the second edition appeared under his name in 1783. In 1800 he privately printed Collections Relating to

Henry Smith, which remains a useful source for the history of Smith's charity and provided materials for Bray's next work, the completion of Owen Manning's *History and Antiquities of Surrey*. He had been in contact with Manning from an early stage in the project, and they became close friends. Manning's blindness from 1796 and his death in 1801 jeopardized the project and Bray, helped by Richard Gough, undertook its completion with characteristic speed and commitment. The first volume was issued in 1804, the second in 1809, and the third in 1814. As steward of many Surrey manors, Bray was uniquely placed for detailed topographical study based upon the county's records, and in the course of the work he visited every parish, gaining access to all but two of the county's churches. The history is a model of its kind. He was disappointed by its lack of illustrations, but this encouraged some owners, notably Richard Percival and Robert Barclay, to collect and commission illustrations to incorporate in their own copies. Bray's last major literary labour, in collaboration with William Upcott, was *Memoirs Illustrative of the Life and Writings of John Evelyn*, published in 1818 in two volumes and enlarged to five volumes in 1827. His transcription of Evelyn's diary was immediately popular but the edition was flawed by his errors in transcription as well as the alterations he made to the manuscript to improve the story and to omit subjects he considered indelicate. His achievement, however, had been to bring Evelyn's diary to public attention. This was also his intention for the More-Molyneux manuscripts at Loseley House, near Guildford, where his arrangement of the documents throughout the 1820s enabled later scholars, notably A. J. Kempe and J. C. Jeaffreson, to publish their own reports on these important records. Bray planned, but did not publish, a history of the royal household and prepared a study of Domesday Book. He contributed forty-seven articles to the *Gentleman's Magazine* and died at Shere on 21 December 1832, aged ninety-six. A memorial is erected to him in the church at Shere, where he was buried on 29 December.

JULIAN POOLEY

Sources Surrey HC, Bray papers, G52/-, G85/- · LMA, Bray Warren archive, 4031 · F. E. Bray, 'Extracts from the diary of William Bray, the Surrey historian', *Surrey Archaeological Collections*, 46 (1938), 26–59 · B. Board, 'Surrey', *English county histories: a guide*, ed. C. R. J. Currie and C. P. Lewis (1994), 375–84 · J. Simmons, introduction, in O. Manning and W. Bray, *The history and antiquities of the county of Surrey*, 1 (1974), v–vii · *GM*, 1st ser., 103/1 (1833), 87–8 · Evelyn, *Diary* · *VCH Surrey* · J. Evans, *A history of the Society of Antiquaries* (1956) · *Seventh report*, HMC, 6 (1879) [W. More-Molyneux (Loseley MSS)] · R. Percival, 'The history and topography of the county of Surrey, commenced by O. Manning, continued by W. Bray, illustrated by Percival', BL, Crach. 1. Tab. I. b. I · R. Barclay, 'Illustrations of Surrey', Surrey HC, 4348 · monumental inscriptions, Shere parish church, Surrey · parish register (marriage), Guildford, St Mary, 1758 · parish register (burial), Shere parish church, 1832 · parish register (baptism), Shere parish church, 1736, Surrey HC
Archives BL, Add. MS 6409, misc. corresp. · Bodl. Oxf. · Equitable Life Assurance Company, Aylesbury · Surrey HC, G52/-, G85/-, 1499 | BL, Upcott MSS, Add. MS 15951 · Bodl. Oxf., corresp., incl. letters to John Nichols and J. B. Nichols · LMA, letter-books from his solicitor's practice, 4031/- · S. Antiquaries, Lond., general corresp. files · Surrey HC, letters to Lord Midleton · Yale U., Beinecke L., Osborne collection, Nichols MSS
Likenesses J. Linnell, portrait, 1832, priv. coll.; repro. in Bray, *Extracts from the diary of William Bray* · J. Linnell, mezzotint, pubd 1833 (after his portrait), BM, NPG · J. Miers, silhouette, V&A
Wealth at death £16,000: will, 1833, PRO; death duty registers, PRO, IR 26/1311, fol. 19

Bray, William Trewartha [Billy] (1794–1868), Bible Christian preacher, was born at Twelveheads, in the parish of Kea, near Truro, on 1 June 1794, the only son and eldest of three children (one of the daughters was of unsound mind) of William Bray, Methodist tin miner, and his wife, Ann, daughter of Robert and Jane Trewartha of Chengenter, Gwennap. At the age of seventeen he left home to pursue his trade as a tin miner in Devon, and succumbed to drink and a profligate lifestyle.

After seven years Bray returned to Cornwall and on 16 July 1821, at Kea church, he married Joanna, also a lapsed Methodist. The manner of Bray's conversion, gradually accomplished in November 1823, assisted by the reading of John Bunyan's *Visions of Heaven and Hell* and driven by fear of the consequences of drunkenness for his family life, indicated that a remarkable revivalist was about to emerge. The crucial step began with a determination to rise and pray in the middle of the night; he continued in prayer the following morning, and took for spiritual nourishment the Bible and Wesley's hymnbook. It was only afterwards that he roared away his 'load' at the Bryanite (or Bible Christian) meeting.

Twelveheads was near Wesley's revival centre at Gwennap pit; Bray's grandfather had been one of his converts and had helped to build the Twelveheads chapel. Bray now became a locally celebrated revivalist on his own account, becoming a local preacher in 1824 and labouring outside as well as within the Bible Christian denomination, to which he gave lifelong allegiance. He built many chapels with his own hands, including his first at Bethel, Cross Lanes.

The distinctive thing about Billy Bray which made him a legend in his lifetime and made his biography one of the Methodist best-sellers of the century was an immediate apprehension of the divine glory which issued naturally in leaping, dancing, and cheerful controversy with the world. His claim that 'if they were to put me into a barrel, I would shout glory out through the bunghole!' was not a facetious pose, but the normal expression of an irrepressibly good-humoured Christian. His charismatic leadership included an emphasis on prayer, healing, and reverence for the sabbath, as well as a vehement dislike of drinking and smoking. He died on 25 May 1868 at Twelveheads and was buried in Baldhu.   W. R. WARD, *rev.*

Sources F. W. Bourne, *Billy Bray: the King's Son* (1871) · C. Davey, *The Glory Man: a new biography of Billy Bray*, pbk edn (1979) · T. Shaw, *A history of Cornish Methodism* (1967)

Braybroc, Henry de. *See* Braybrooke, Henry of (d. 1234).

Braybroke, Robert de. *See* Braybrooke, Robert (1336/7–1404).

Braybrooke. For this title name *see* Griffin, John Griffin, fourth Baron Howard de Walden and first Baron Braybrooke (1719–1797); Griffin, Richard, second Baron Braybrooke (1750–1825); Griffin, Richard, third Baron Braybrooke (1783–1858); Neville, Richard Cornwallis, fourth Baron Braybrooke (1820–1861).

Braybrooke [Braybroc], **Henry of** (*d.* 1234), sheriff and justice, was the only son of Robert of Braybrooke, who had risen from obscurity late in Richard I's reign to become, under King John, sheriff of Bedfordshire and Buckinghamshire, Northamptonshire, and Rutland, and who accumulated under-tenancies concentrated in Northamptonshire, Leicestershire, Bedfordshire, Buckinghamshire, and Essex, largely by redeeming the mortgages of landholders who had become hopelessly indebted to Jewish moneylenders. As part of the transaction involved in paying off the debts of Wischard Ledet, who held the honour of Chipping Warden, Northamptonshire, Wischard's daughter and heir, Christiana, was married to Henry of Braybrooke, so that in 1222 Braybrooke succeeded his father-in-law as lord of the honour.

Henry of Braybrooke proved to be cast in the same mould as his father. Succeeding Robert as sheriff on the latter's death in 1211, he raised ever greater revenues from his shires for the king. Father and son were listed by Roger of Wendover among John's evil counsellors. In June 1213, moreover, John commissioned Henry to take charge of repairs to Northampton Castle. Nevertheless, in 1215 Henry of Braybrooke went over to the barons, though it is not clear why he did so. According to Wendover he held out against swearing to the liberties espoused by the barons until well into 1215. But the appointment of Geoffrey de Martigny as constable of Northampton in April, shortly before it was besieged by baronial forces, probably indicates that by then the king was taking no chances with Braybrooke, who within a month was included among those rebels whose forfeiture John specifically ordered. Braybrooke joined the rebels in London. He had lost Bedfordshire and Buckinghamshire in 1214. Now, in the wake of Magna Carta, he was formally replaced as sheriff of his remaining shires; but when hostilities were renewed in September, the king began distributing Henry's former estates to others.

Following John's death Braybrooke continued to side with Prince Louis of France against those acting for the young Henry III. Shortly after Easter 1217 he defended Mountsorrel Castle against the royalists, and he narrowly escaped capture at the rebel rout at Lincoln in May. But when the treaty of Lambeth ended the civil war in September, he submitted to the king, and most of his lands were restored forthwith.

Henceforth Braybrooke served the new regime faithfully. He was never a sheriff again, but he acted frequently as a royal justice, chiefly in Bedfordshire and Buckinghamshire. In the summer of 1224, in a measure directed against Falkes de Bréauté (*d.* 1226), Braybrooke was commissioned to hear assizes of novel disseisin from Bedfordshire and Buckinghamshire in Dunstable from 10 June. He

had been handpicked for the job: as the chronicler Ralph of Coggeshall and Bréauté himself pointed out, he was an enemy of the Bréautés, perhaps in part because he was a vassal of William de Beauchamp (*d.* 1260), who had been deprived of Bedford Castle for rebellion against John, and was still trying to recover it from Falkes de Bréauté. Bréauté, who had been replaced as sheriff of the two counties in January, was convicted of sixteen disseisins; it is likely that his brother William, then in control of Bedford, also lost lands. As Braybrooke made his way to the assembly that the king had summoned in Northampton, he was captured and imprisoned by William de Bréauté. The seizure and allegedly brutal treatment of a royal justice provoked outrage. Falkes did not instruct William to back down, and royal forces besieged Bedford from 20 June until Braybrooke was released and the garrison surrendered on 14 August. The king then issued orders for the demolition of the castle, to be implemented by Walter of Pattishall (*d.* 1232), Falkes de Bréauté's replacement as sheriff, and by Henry of Braybrooke. Braybrooke's loyalties may have been torn, for William de Beauchamp did not want the castle destroyed, but loyalty to the king prevailed.

Thereafter Braybrooke frequently sat as a justice, in Lincolnshire and Yorkshire as well as Bedfordshire and Buckinghamshire. The last recorded occasion was in 1231. He was dead by 13 April 1234, for on that date the king took his widow Christiana's homage for the lands that had escheated on her husband's death. Henry and Christiana had three children: their heir, Wischard Ledet, who was to die on crusade in the Holy Land in 1241 with Christiana's second husband, Gerard de Furnival; John of Braybrooke; and Margery, who was married to Simon of Pattishall, son and heir of Walter. Braybrooke bequeathed his body to Bushmead Priory, Bedfordshire, of which he was a benefactor.   GEORGE GARNETT

Sources BL, Braybrooke cartulary, Sloane MS 986 · *Chancery records* [PRO and RC] · Pipe rolls · Paris, *Chron.* · *Memoriale fratris Walteri de Coventria / The historical collections of Walter of Coventry*, ed. W. Stubbs, 2 vols., Rolls Series, 58 (1872–3) · *Radulphi de Coggeshall chronicon Anglicanum*, ed. J. Stevenson, Rolls Series, 66 (1875) · W. W. Shirley, ed., *Royal and other historical letters illustrative of the reign of Henry III*, 2 vols., Rolls Series, 27 (1862–6), 236, no. ccvi · W. Farrer, *Honors and knights' fees … from the eleventh to the fourteenth century*, 3 vols. (1923–5) · G. H. Fowler, ed., *Cartulary of the abbey of Old Wardon*, Bedfordshire Historical RS, 13 (1930) · D. A. Carpenter, *The minority of Henry III* (1990) · H. G. Richardson, *The English Jewry under Angevin kings* (1960) · S. Painter, *The reign of King John* (1949) · *CIPM*, 1.259 · *Close rolls of the reign of Henry III*, 14 vols., PRO (1902–38)

Braybrooke [*née* Jolliffe], **June Guesdon** [*pseud.* Isobel English] (1920–1994), writer, was born at 15 Kensington Court Place, London, on 9 June 1920, the belated second daughter of John Mayne Jolliffe (1885–1957), a Welsh civil servant at the Ministry of Pensions, and his wife, May Guesdon (1885–1966), a Tasmanian of Huguenot descent whose ambitions to be a professional singer were thwarted by domestic obligations. June contracted tuberculosis of the spine at the age of two and spent much of her early childhood in Brittany undergoing a salt-water cure, a period recalled in her novel *Every Eye* (1956). From the age of eight she was educated at La Retraite, a convent school in Burnham-on-Sea in Somerset, after which she attended secretarial college in London. She subsequently worked with the poet and critic Kenneth Allott, who taught her literature. She was presented at court in 1937, and had unfulfilled ambitions to become a professional pianist.

During the Second World War, June had a brief job as a secretary with MI5, abruptly curtailed when it was discovered she had written a letter to her sister in occupied Belgium, innocently describing her work. On 1 July 1941 she married Ronald Dundas Orr-Ewing (1913–1988), a junior executive officer with the Metropolitan Police, then serving with the air force, and lived with him at 9 Airlie Gardens in Kensington. He subsequently joined the Home Office as an inspector of prisons, and it was he who first encouraged her to write. They had one daughter and were divorced amicably in 1953.

On 5 December 1953, having converted to Roman Catholicism, June married Neville Patrick Bellairs Braybrooke (1923–2001), writer and editor, and the couple moved into a small house bought for them by Neville Braybrooke's mother at 10 Gardnor Road on the southern edge of Hampstead Heath. On her marriage certificate June described herself as a writer, but it was not until the following year that she published her first book, *The Key that Rusts*, under the name Isobel English, the pseudonym she used for all her writing. This subtle and complex novel is narrated by a woman who observes, with a mixture of coolness and compassion, the disastrous affair between her older brother and a friend. Stevie Smith welcomed a 'very sagacious and very original voice—a voice of our times, ironical and involved, and yet a very peculiar voice' (quoted in preface to Persephone edition of *Every Eye*, viii).

In 1956 June Braybrooke published her second and what is perhaps her finest novel, *Every Eye*, an elliptical account of a young woman travelling by train to Ibiza, then untamed, on her delayed honeymoon; the narrative is intercut with memories of her childhood and the complicated network of adult relationships spun around her. Sharply observed and beautifully written, this is an exquisite miniature. 'I don't believe you ever see anything dead on, only at a peculiar angle through the corner of your eye', the heroine's husband says, and this describes Braybrooke's own method (*Every Eye*, Persephone edn, 18). Her third and last novel, *Four Voices* (1961), is equally idiosyncratic, a comedy of (mostly bad) manners set in London. The voices that narrate the story in skilful counterpoint are those of a man, two of his former wives (one a genteel and son-smothering Roman Catholic, the other a splendidly rackety drunk), and his prospective daughter-in-law. Parts of the book were dramatized on television.

Braybrooke published short stories in numerous periodicals and anthologies, collecting (at the suggestion of Elizabeth Bowen, a great admirer) thirteen of them in *Life after All* (1973), which was awarded the Katherine Mansfield prize. Mansfield is a character in Braybrooke's one play, *Meeting Point* (1976), along with Virginia Woolf and Emily Brontë. It was inspired by an item in a bookseller's catalogue which referred to a man claiming that Emily Brontë was seduced by her father, had a baby, and that he was the baby's son. The play was never produced, but was published in the *New Review* (vol. 3, no. 29). She also collaborated with the illustrator Barbara Jones on *The Gift Book* (1964), a decorative and humorous A–Z of different sorts of presents, most of them useless and unwelcome.

The Braybrookes were a highly literary couple, their lives devoted to books, and many of their friends were writers. Among these were Muriel Spark, who provided the titles of Braybrooke's last two novels (and whose own reception into the Catholic church the Braybrookes sponsored), and Olivia Manning, whose biography they wrote together, and which Neville Braybrooke completed after his wife's death. June Braybrooke also wrote introductions to reissues of several of Manning's books under the Virago imprint. From 1969 the Braybrookes divided their time between Gardnor Road and a house they bought at 29 Castle Road in Cowes on the Isle of Wight.

June Braybrooke suffered from debilitating migraines and frequent writer's block, the latter largely a result of her perfectionism. She said she always had to make 'many, many drafts before anything respectable appears' (jacket copy of *Four Voices*). Describing herself as 'a very private sort of person' (quoted in *Friends and Friendship*, 95), she shunned publicity, refusing almost every request for an interview, and concentrated instead on her writing, encouraged not only by her two husbands but also by admirers such as Bowen and Smith. Of striking appearance, she was immaculately turned out even when unwell, often sporting the jewellery she developed a passion for collecting ever since first hearing the 'Jewel Song' from Charles Gounod's *Faust*. Characteristic of her elegance was her habit of wrapping the typescripts of her novels in a silk scarf before delivering them to her publisher. She wrote at a hospital table while lying, fully clothed, on her bed. Her physical fragility is nowhere apparent in her books, however, which although informed by her religious beliefs are not in the least pious: they are tough, funny, and written in a sinewy prose with not a word wasted. Her output was small but absolutely distinct. June Braybrooke died of leukaemia at the Royal Free Hospital in Camden, London, on 30 May 1994. She was buried in Hampstead cemetery, Fortune Green, London, on 8 June.

PETER PARKER

Sources N. Braybrooke, preface, in I. English, *Every eye* (2000) · personal knowledge (2004) · private information (2004) · K. Dick, ed., *Friends and friendship* (1974) · b. cert. · m. certs. · d. cert.
Likenesses E. de Maré, photograph, 1956, priv. coll.
Wealth at death under £125,000: probate, 28 July 1994, *CGPLA Eng. & Wales*

Braybrooke [Braybroke], **Robert** (1336/7–1404), bishop of London, was born at Colmworth, Bedfordshire, a younger son of Sir Gerard Braybrooke of Colmworth and his wife, Isabella, probably a daughter of Sir Reginald Hampden of Great Hampden, Buckinghamshire. His father was MP for the county no fewer than sixteen times, and the family's landed pedigree can be traced from at least the mid-twelfth century. The bishop was recognized as kin by *Richard II, through the family of Wake of Liddell; most probably, Lora Wake, the bishop's grandmother, was great-aunt to *Joan of Kent, the king's mother. The bishop's brothers were Sir Gerard (*d.* 1403), Nicholas (*d.* 1399), a resident archdeacon of Cornwall, Henry (*d.* 1362), and Reginald, a clerk who served the bishop. Their sisters were Katherine (*d.* 1384), prioress of Clerkenwell, Middlesex, and Alice, who married Sir John Kentwood. Their son, Reginald Kentwood (*d.* 1441), was made archdeacon of London by his uncle in 1400. Robert Braybrooke himself was a BA of Oxford University by 1358, BCL by 1360, and a licentiate by 27 October 1381; the timetable of his university career suggests a date of birth in the mid-1330s. Having taken orders, he was papally provided to the rectory of Hinton, Cambridgeshire, in 1360. In January 1363 he enjoyed preferment on the petition of Joan of Kent, whose service he may have entered. On 20 April 1376 he was proctor for the archdeacon of Canterbury in the enthronement of Bishop Thomas Arundel at Ely.

The accession of Richard II brought Braybrooke into immediate prominence. He was appointed as the boy's secretary on 20 August 1377, while on 12 June 1380 he was appointed to the embassy to seek Richard's marriage with Anne of Bohemia. He was on this mission from 18 June to 1 December, and soon after his return was appointed to make a firm treaty with Charles IV of Bohemia, Anne's father, on 26 December, and was away once more from 2 January to 23 March 1381. Braybrooke meantime had switched between rectories twice and obtained three cathedral prebends. More handsomely, on 17 March 1377 he obtained the archdeaconry of Cornwall, and was also elected dean of Salisbury some time after 13 August 1379, being confirmed on 28 February 1380.

On 11 May 1381 Braybrooke was appointed to conclude the king's marriage and bring Anne of Bohemia back to England. He left London on 12 May and preceded the bride back to England on 20 September. Meantime, after the murder of Archbishop Sudbury in the peasants' revolt, William Courtenay had been translated to Canterbury, and Braybrooke papally provided to fill his place at London on 9 September 1381. Resigning as king's secretary in October, he received the temporalities on 27 December and was consecrated at Lambeth on 5 January 1382. Much to the annoyance of Courtenay, who had not yet received the pallium to complete his succession to Canterbury, it was decided that the royal marriage must perforce be conducted by Braybrooke at Westminster on 20 January as dean of the province. Robert's particular closeness to the couple perhaps helped underwrite this strict observance of form.

Braybrooke's career, calmly successful thus far, suddenly met a crisis. There was widespread anger at the government's dismissal of the highly respected Richard, Lord Scrope, from the chancellorship on 11 July 1382, and the two-month interval before Braybrooke was appointed in his place on 9 September suggested both that it had not been planned ahead and that Braybrooke was indeed no obvious choice. His background inevitably also suggested

that the government intended to replace an experienced and independent great officer of state with someone who would simply do whatever the household required, at a time when the latter was being severely criticized. In parliament in October, Braybrooke compounded the offence by trying to attribute to it decisions actually taken in a council of nobles. There was furious protest in the assembly, and Braybrooke's position was hopeless. He resigned on 10 March 1383.

The court seems to have kept Braybrooke at arm's length hereafter, which actually allowed him to achieve an increasingly respected position in broader public life, and to avoid altogether the far harsher attacks on the king's circle in the years that followed. Joan of Kent named him as an executor and her 'very dear' or 'dearest' friend on 7 August 1385 (Nichols, 78), and perhaps her death did help to dilute the bishop's intimacy with the royal family. On 23 October 1385 he was able to effect a reconciliation between the king and Archbishop Courtenay, though he failed to achieve the more difficult reconciliation between Richard and his uncle, Thomas of Woodstock. When the major political crisis of the mid-reign reached its peak in February 1388, Braybrooke was one of the five respected magnates who were chosen to wait upon and supervise the king, who was in effect under arrest by his political opponents but being accorded full formal honour. On 3 June 1388 he celebrated the mass to mark the end of the Merciless Parliament, but there is no evidence that he had done more than acquiesce in what had happened there.

Braybrooke was not to play any integral part in government hereafter, but was a regular choice for commissions requiring public weight and enjoyed the king's personal confidence. On 28 November 1390 he was on the commission to execute judgment in the notorious *Scrope* v. *Grosvenor* heraldic dispute. Before 27 April 1391 he had been engaged in the sensitive matter of providing a marble tomb for the king's older brother, Edward, who had died as a child. In late 1393 the king gave him a diamond. Shortly after 25 February 1395 Braybrooke and the chancellor, Archbishop Thomas Arundel of York, went to Ireland, reportedly to ask Richard II to come back to England as soon as possible to deal with domestic problems. Braybrooke himself returned to London by 2 May.

Braybrooke was appointed on 14 January 1397, and again on 14 July, as an attorney for Roger Mortimer, fourth earl of March, who was taking up the lieutenancy of Ireland. He himself was appointed as chancellor of Ireland on 15 October 1397, but apparently did not take up the post. He joined with Walden in 1398 to intervene with the king on behalf of the city of London for protection against the behaviour of the king's substantial Cheshire bodyguard. In 1399 he was awarded the marriage of William, Lord Latimer's heir, which he regranted to Elizabeth, Lady Clifford. On 16 April 1399 he was a witness to Richard II's will at Westminster, and then accompanied the king to Ireland, being absent from his diocese from 14 May to 29 August. He had returned with the king as far as Milford

Haven, Pembrokeshire, but apparently did not accompany him on the final dash towards Cheshire and the showdown with Henry Bolingbroke. He adjusted smoothly to the deposition of Richard II, receiving Bolingbroke in his episcopal palace and celebrating mass at the coronation. As in the previous reign, he attended council meetings quite often but seems to have had no specific part in government.

Throughout his episcopate Braybrooke lived mainly in his palace by the cathedral or at his other palace in Stepney, but at least twice a year he paid substantial visits to the country parts of his diocese. A full register (although the surviving volume stops abruptly at the end of 1401 as regards institutions, and soon after in the sections for other forms of business), together with extensive household accounts, have allowed his domestic administration to be studied in detail. In his early years he had annoyed the citizenry of London, first when publicly supporting the legislation of 1382 in restraint of preachers, and then, by contrast, being less than zealous in enforcing legislation against prostitution, which the city always banished firmly to the other side of the river. In 1385 he threatened excommunication against anyone buying or selling in the cathedral precinct, playing ball games there, or shooting at birds on the cathedral roof. In 1386 he established a festival day in the cathedral for St Earconwald. Much later, on 26 April 1398, he addressed the long-running abuse whereby the resident canons of the cathedral obliged any would-be newcomer to their number to promise to spend at least 700 marks upon them in open hospitality and entertainment in his first year, a custom that had reputedly reduced the canons in residence to just two (more probably four or five, including dignity-holders). The bishop gained a writ from the king threatening a fine of £4000 if the chapter did not conform forthwith to the election regulations of Salisbury, then enjoying an unrivalled reputation. The resident membership of the chapter actually sank to one in the 1440s.

The ending of the extant register in 1401–2, and Braybrooke's ceasing to attend any royal councils at about the same time, perhaps suggest that he was in physical decline in his last years. On 24 July 1403 he was named as an executor and legatee of Bishop William Wykeham, but the testator was himself an ancient and may not have known the condition of one of his last old friends. Braybrooke himself did make a will, but it has not survived. He died on 28 August 1404 and was buried in St Paul's Cathedral. His body was disinterred when work began on the rebuilding of the cathedral after the great fire. Its uncorrupted state made it an object of veneration to the élite few who were allowed to see it. The dean refused to sell bits of Braybrooke at any price. The countess of Oxford (presumably the actress Hester Davenport) therefore manipulated an opportunity to gnaw off his genitals.

R. G. DAVIES

Sources L. H. Butler, 'Robert Braybrooke, bishop of London (1381–1404) and his kinsmen', DPhil diss., U. Oxf., 1952 · Braybrooke's register, GL, MS 9531/3 · Emden, *Oxf.*, 1.254–5 · R. G. Davies, 'The episcopate in England and Wales, 1375–1443', PhD diss., University of Manchester, 1974, 3.l–liv · [J. Nichols], ed., *A collection of … wills … of … every branch of the blood royal* (1780) · N. Saul, *Richard II* (1997) · HoP, *Commons, 1386–1421*, 1.343–6

Archives GL, register, MS 9531/3 · GL, household accounts

Brayfield, John James (1752/3–1821), writer on sport, was the only son of Sarah Brayfield (1732/3–1820) of Camberwell, Surrey, and possibly of George Brayfield (d. 1785), a former governor of London's St Bartholomew's Hospital, who died suddenly in the Strand in September 1785. On 27 December 1773 he married Elizabeth Childs (d. in or after 1821) at St Leonard, Shoreditch, London. Little more is known of Brayfield's life apart from what appears in an obituary in the *Sporting Magazine* for March 1821. This describes him as a lifelong habitué of London fairs, boxing matches, races, and 'diversions of every kind' from the 'ring made by the first rate amateurs of the fancy' (that is prizefights) down to the weekly badger-baiting in Black Boy Alley. The latter pastime was said to have been stopped by the intervention of the Society for the Reformation of Manners in 1803, though a later revival is possible. To this catalogue of spectacles Brayfield also added public hangings, being a 'constant at Newgate executions'.

Brayfield was almost certainly the J. J. B. responsible for some of the more interesting and perceptive contributions to the sporting press during the early nineteenth century. The *Sporting Magazine's* essay 'On the art of swimming' (June 1811), for example, was aimed at young readers, particularly those whom 'pleasure or other motives' took to the coast. J. J. B. provided a discussion of buoyancy aids such as corks and bladders (of which he approved), and his thoughts on the best way to learn: walking into the sea breast-deep and then repeatedly throwing an egg towards the shore and then diving towards the object. In a more substantial article two years later, 'The importance of regulating the diversions of people', J. J. B. drew attention to the then widespread alarm at the degeneracy of modern popular recreations, such as gurning, sack-racing, and competitions to eat hot puddings, which he considered a far cry from the former pastimes of long bow or cudgel play. Equally deplorable was the equation of cards and dice as the 'chief sports' of the 'quality of both sexes'. His recommendation that country gentlemen encourage 'manly and innocent sports' was both a means of fostering wellbeing and an instrument of social control by making the tenantry 'brave and good subjects'.

Brayfield is thought to have lived in the parish of St Giles, Camberwell. He died aged sixty-eight and, according to the parish registers of St Botolph, Aldersgate, London, was buried, probably at St Botolph's, on 16 February 1821. He was survived by his wife, Elizabeth, who was later described as living in St Luke's parish, Middlesex, and who received an annuity in Brayfield's will (PRO, PROB 11/1642, sig. 248). Other bequests were made to a grandson, J. J. B. Willis, the son of Brayfield's natural daughter married to a John Willis.

DENNIS BRAILSFORD

Sources *Sporting Magazine* (March 1821), 283 · *GM*, 1st ser., 90/1 (1820), 283 · will, PRO, PROB 11/1642, sig. 248 · parish registers, St Botolph, Aldersgate, London · *IGI*

Wealth at death see will, PRO, PROB 11/1642, sig. 248

Brayley, (John) Desmond, Baron Brayley (1917–1977), glass manufacturer and politician, was born at 10 Mervyn Street, Rhydyfelin, near Pontypridd, Glamorgan, on 29 January 1917, the only son of Frederick Brayley, a café owner, and his wife, Jennie Bassett. He was educated at Pontypridd grammar school, which he left at the age of seventeen to join the regular army in the Royal Artillery, becoming a physical-training instructor. During the Second World War he served in the Army Air Corps with distinction in the African desert campaigns, and was awarded the MC for gallantry in 1942. He went on to Crete and Sicily, where he received a mention in dispatches. From an earlier marriage to Irene Wisden he was presumably divorced, for on 18 August 1945 he married Flight Officer Queenie Elizabeth Selma Bee (b. 1912/13), daughter of Horace Bee, estate agent; they had two daughters. The marriage was dissolved in 1960.

In 1946 Brayley joined the Phoenix Glass Company of Bristol, rising to managing director in the 1950s. In the process he became a wealthy man and was noted in Bristol for his free-spending habits and interest in horse-racing. In 1961 he became chairman of, and a major shareholder in, the Canning Town Glass Works, a bottle-manufacturing firm in London, which he was instrumental in developing. He had been a lifelong member of the Labour Party and did not allow success and wealth to affect his loyalty to it or to blur his early memories of poverty in Wales. He was a generous benefactor to the party and donated 60,000 shares in the Canning Town Glass Works to its funds. Harold Wilson first met Brayley through Lord Wigg, a close political ally and paymaster-general in his 1964 government. Wigg, a former regular soldier, shared Brayley's devotion to the army and his interest in horse-racing, while self-made, flamboyant, and wealthy entrepreneurs always seemed to appeal strongly to Wilson. When the Labour government was defeated in 1970, Wilson recommended Brayley for a knighthood in his resignation honours list, citing his services to the Bristol Labour Party.

Brayley was, however, little known in the party and there was much adverse comment when Wilson made him a life peer in 1973. This was intensified when he was appointed parliamentary under-secretary for defence in March 1974. A few months later rumours began to circulate about his business affairs before becoming a minister. On taking office he had sold his shares in the Canning Town Glass Works for £1 million but on 7 September he was named at a shareholders' meeting as owing the company £16,515 for expenses which had been queried by the auditors; at one stage the company was claiming £200,000 from Brayley and similar sums from other directors. Although Brayley claimed ignorance of this, concern over allegations affecting a minister's business interests led the president of the Board of Trade to order on 15 September an inquiry under the Companies Act, and Brayley, after consulting Wilson, resigned from the government. Coming in the midst of the general election campaign

these events were embarrassing enough for the Labour Party, but the more so when Brayley's close association with Wilson, and his gift of shares to the party, became known. After Brayley's resignation there were further allegations about misuse of the company's funds. Brayley sued the owners of the *Daily Mail* for its disclosure of internal company documents, but in July 1976 he was arrested on five charges of fraud, which he strongly denied. Litigation began but the main issues had not come to trial when Brayley died of abdominal cancer, on 16 March 1977, at Cardiff Royal Infirmary, and the case was closed without the truth ever being known. The administration of his estate showed assets of £87,091 but these were far exceeded by his liabilities. It was a tragic end to the career of a man of great talents and, his friends always insisted, of high honour, whose death, they believed, had been accelerated by the shame of a scandal not of his wilful doing. Nor had he been prepared for the glare of publicity surrounding his ministerial appointment, even before the storm broke over his business life.

Brayley was always noted for his work for charities, particularly those helping mentally handicapped people and those in his native Pontypridd, but not until after his death did the full extent of his personal generosity become known through tributes published in *The Times*. The controller of the Royal Artillery Benevolent Fund wrote of his 'boundless generosity' to the regiment, and the chairman of the Middlesex sessions, Ewen Montagu, paid tribute to his unfailing readiness to meet anonymously appeals for financial help for prisoners and their families in distress or to assist their rehabilitation on release. In 1961 Brayley became a freeman of the City of London. In 1970 he was appointed an honorary colonel-commandant of the Royal Artillery and in the same year became a deputy lieutenant for Greater London. He was, from 1968, a JP for Middlesex. He had been a noted sportsman and athlete, and an army championship boxer. He held his own private pilot's licence.

IAN WALLER, *rev.* ANITA MCCONNELL

Sources *The Times* (2 July 1976), 26d–f · *The Times* (29 July 1976), 1f · *The Times* (17 March 1977), 21f–h · *The Times* (19 March 1977), 16g · 'The man from Canning Glass', *Sunday Times* (15 Sept 1974), 12a · *The Times* (14 Sept 1974), 2a · b. cert. · m. cert. [Queenie Bee] · d. cert.
Likenesses photograph, repro. in *The Times* (14 Sept 1974), 2a
Wealth at death £87,091: administration, 30 May 1979, CGPLA Eng. & Wales

Brayley, Edward Wedlake (1773–1854), topographer and archaeologist, born in Lambeth, London, was apprenticed to one of the most eminent enamellers in London. While an apprentice he met John Britton. They both had literary and artistic aspirations, and longed to be free of their existing trades. They formed a close friendship, which lasted for sixty-five years, and collaborated to produce illustrated volumes on topographical subjects. They began their literary partnership with a song called 'The Powder Tax, or, A Puff at the Guinea Pigs', written by Brayley and sung by Britton at a discussion club at the Jacob's

Well, Barbican, London. The ballad was very popular, and 70,000 or 80,000 copies of it were sold.

In 1800 the two friends became joint editors of *The Beauties of England and Wales* and, having concluded arrangements with a publisher, made a walking tour from London through several western and midland counties to north Wales, in search of materials. They gradually acquired an adequate, if not profound, knowledge of topography and archaeology. The first six volumes were jointly executed by Brayley and Britton, the former being largely responsible for the text, the latter for the illustrations. Brayley produced volumes 7, 8, and 10 alone. The work ran to twenty-five volumes; but, after disagreement with the publishers, the two authors withdrew from the undertaking in 1814, and other writers, including the Revd Joseph Nightingale and James Norris Brewer, took their place, completing the work in 1816. The work is important because of its sheer scale and completeness, the mass of information it records, and its relatively early date: but the editors depended on existing scholarship and, where this was lacking, for example in Brayley's *Huntingdonshire*, they could add little.

After the end of his apprenticeship Brayley worked for the enameller Henry Bone, preparing and firing plates for small pieces of jewellery and large landscapes. He continued to write topographical works, which were a testament more to his energy than to his scholarship. He also turned his hand to fiction, poetry, geology, natural history, and other subjects, often writing with co-authors. His most important work was probably a *History of Surrey* (5 vols., 1841–8). His topographical works bear scrutiny because of his competence in a range of scientific, literary, and artistic subjects, a breadth of knowledge which few other contemporary topographers could match. Brayley was elected a fellow of the Society of Antiquaries in 1823, and in 1825 he was appointed librarian and secretary of the Russell Institution at 55 Great Coram Street, London, which offices he held until his death. He published catalogues of the library (1826, 1849).

Brayley probably married his wife, Ann (c.1771–1850), some time before the birth of their eldest son, Edward William *Brayley, in 1801 or 1802. He and his two younger brothers, who died of consumption, had a cheerless upbringing as their father tried to instil into them his own habits of relentless industry. Brayley died at 55 Great Coram Street on 23 September 1854 from cholera. He was survived by his eldest son and daughter.

THOMPSON COOPER, *rev.* ELIZABETH BAIGENT

Sources J. Britton, *A brief memoir of Edward Wedlake Brayley … from the Gentleman's Magazine* (privately printed, London, 1855) · J. Britton, *The autobiography of John Britton*, 3 vols. in 2 (privately printed, London, 1849–50) · *The Athenaeum* (30 Sept 1854), 1170 · *GM*, 2nd ser., 42 (1854), 538, 582 · C. Knight, ed., *The English cyclopaedia: biography*, 6 vols. (1856–8) [suppl. (1872)] · J. R. Abbey, *Scenery of Great Britain and Ireland in aquatint and lithography, 1770–1860* (1952) · C. R. J. Currie and C. P. Lewis, eds., *English county histories: a guide* (1994) · Boase, *Mod. Eng. biog.* · *GM*, 2nd ser., 34 (1850), 336
Archives Bodl. Oxf. | BL, letters to Philip Bliss, Add. MSS 34568, 34570 · BL, letters as sponsor to the Royal Literary Fund · Bodl. Oxf., letters to various people, incl. Mark Noble and Sir Thomas Phillipps · Dorset Studies Centre, Exeter, Westcountry Studies Library, copies of documents relating to Devon · NHM, letters to members of the Sowerby family

Brayley, Edward William (1801/2–1870), writer and lecturer on science, the eldest son of Edward Wedlake *Brayley (1773–1854), topographer, and his wife, Ann (c.1771–1850), was born in London. He was educated, together with his brothers Henry and Horatio, under an austere system. Secluded from all society except that of their tutors, the boys led a cheerless and monotonous life: denied pocket-money, they were not even allowed to take a walk without a tutor. Henry and Horatio both died of pulmonary tuberculosis. Brayley went on to study science in the London Institution and the Royal Institution, where he attended W. T. Brande's lectures on chemistry. He is known to have married, but his wife's name is not known.

Early in life, following in his father's footsteps, Brayley was interested in topographical literature, and wrote the historical descriptions in *Ancient Castles of England and Wales* (2 vols., 1825). However, he soon abandoned antiquarian studies and devoted his attention to scientific investigation. He had already published in the *Philosophical Magazine* (1824) a paper on luminous meteors, a subject which occupied his attention to nearly the end of his life. He subsequently published a variety of scientific papers in different journals, especially the *Philosophical Magazine*, to which he contributed editorial assistance between 1823 and 1844. In 1829 and 1830 he was engaged by Rowland Hill (and Hill's father and brother) to take charge, as lecturer and tutor, of a department of instruction in physical science in their schools of Hazelwood near Birmingham, and Bruce Castle, Tottenham, near London. The schools did not, however, succeed, although Brayley explained their educational principles in *The Utility of the Knowledge of Nature Considered; with Reference to the General Education of Youth* (1831).

Brayley became joint librarian of the London Institution in 1834 and held that position until 1865; at that point the institution named him principal librarian, as well as professor of physical geography, and he held those titles until his death. He offered popular scientific lectures in many London institutions, including the Royal Institution, the London Mechanics' Institution, the Belgrave, Russell, and Marylebone institutions, and especially the London Institution, where he first lectured in 1828 and last in 1869. Between 1840 and 1864 he lectured there almost annually, most often on the subjects of meteors and meteorology, mineralogy, physical geography, and such variants as 'peat' or 'metalliferous deposits'. He also held forth on recent eclipses, Lord Rosse's telescopes, Hall's condensing apparatus, the remains at Pompeii, and photogenic drawing. He delivered extended educational courses as well as popular evening soirées; as a salaried librarian he also substituted on short notice for other lecturers. He occasionally delivered discourses on special subjects at the celebrated Friday evening meetings of the Royal Institution; in one, on 11 May 1838, he attempted to show that the chemical theory of volcanoes once advanced by Humphry Davy could be subsumed within the more recent belief that volcanoes arose from variations in isothermal surfaces within the earth. Such synthesis and popular exposition of different research findings was a characteristic of his work.

Brayley's scientific interests were diverse, and his career resisted specialization. While many of his publications and lectures concerned meteorology, geology, and geochemistry, others embraced astronomy, physical anthropology, palaeontology, and taxonomy. He made few original contributions and did little field or laboratory research. Instead his writings (facilitated by his library position) reflected wide and voluminous reading, on which basis he reviewed literature, suggested possibilities for further research, and advanced synthetic hypotheses. Thus he argued that rock basins were the product of natural forces, not the artificial creations of the druids; that the Papuans were the aboriginal inhabitants of the Indian subcontinent; that brine springs might contain potassium salts; and that in the animal kingdom the powers of producing heat and light varied inversely with each other. Most of his work commented on the ideas of others: his law of animal heat and light reflected the taxonomy of William Sharp Macleay, he attempted to harmonize the volcanic theories of Davy and Herschel, and he moved from an apparent endorsement of William Buckland's creationism, in 1831, to an acceptance of the uniformitarian principle in 1865, when he concluded that the earth had been formed from the gradual coalescence of meteors.

Brayley prepared the thirteenth (and last) edition of Samuel Parkes's *Chemical Catechism* (1834), a work supplementing popular institutional lecturing which had circulated widely and been translated into several languages since its initial 1806 publication. To the biographical division of the *English Cyclopaedia* he contributed the lives of several men of science; and to the arts and sciences division of the same work the articles on meteors, correlation of physical forces, refrigeration of the globe, seismology, waves and tides, and winds. Especially in his capacity at the London Institution, he gave assistance to several men of science in conducting their works through the press. Most notable among these was William Robert Grove, whose important *Correlation of Physical Forces* (1846) was based on lectures delivered at the London Institution. Luke Howard's *Barometrographia* (1847) explicitly acknowledged Brayley's assistance. It is noteworthy that when Grove first achieved the decomposition of water by heat there were only three persons present besides himself—namely Faraday, Gassiot, and Brayley.

Brayley was elected a fellow of the Royal Society in 1854; he was an original member of the Zoological and Chemical societies, a corresponding member of the Societas Naturae Scrutatorum at Basel, and a member of the American Philosophical Society. He died, a widower, on 1 February 1870, at his home, 53 Oakley Road, Islington, London, of heart disease.   J. N. HAYS

Sources J. C. Cutler, 'The London Institution, 1805–1933', PhD diss., University of Leicester, 1976 · J. N. Hays, 'The London lecturing empire, 1800–1850', *Metropolis and province: science in British culture, 1780–1850*, ed. I. Inkster and J. Morrell (1983), 91–119 · private information (1885) · C. Knight, ed., *The English cyclopaedia: biography*, 6 (1858) · M. L. Cooper and V. M. D. Hall, 'William Robert Grove and the London Institution, 1841–1845', *Annals of Science*, 39 (1982), 229–54 · J. N. Hays, 'Science in the City: the London Institution, 1819–1840', *British Journal for the History of Science*, 7 (1974), 146–62 · I. R. Morus, 'Correlation and control: William Robert Grove and the construction of a new philosophy of scientific reform', *Studies in History and Philosophy of Science*, 22 (1991), 589–621 · *CGPLA Eng. & Wales* (1870) · *DNB* · *The Times* (4 Feb 1870) · *GM*, 2nd ser., 34 (1850), 336

Archives RS, corresp. with Sir John Herschel

Wealth at death under £1500: administration with will, Feb 1870, *CGPLA Eng. & Wales*

Brayne, John (*c*.1541–1586), grocer and financier, was the eldest child of Thomas Brayne (*d*. 1562), a tailor (nominally a girdler), and his wife, Alice Barlow (*d*. 1566), of the parish of St Stephen, Coleman Street, London, who married on 22 January 1541. John Brayne was apprenticed on 13 March 1554 to John Bull, a grocer in Bucklersbury, London. He completed his apprenticeship, married Margaret Stowers (*d*. 1593) [*see below*] at St Dionis Backchurch on 14 January 1565, and became a successful grocer with a house and business in Bucklersbury. By 1573 the Braynes had had four children, Robert (*b*. 1565), Roger (*b*. 1566), Rebecca (*b*. 1568), and John (*b*. 1573). All were baptized at St Stephen Walbrook, the church for the eastern half of Bucklersbury, and all soon died, at least three of them in infancy. Fatefully for Brayne, his sister Ellen had married the joiner turned player James Burbage, also of St Stephen, Coleman Street, on 23 April 1559.

Brayne undertook financial ventures that had nothing to do with groceries, and it is for two of these that he is remembered. The earlier of the two was the building in 1567 of a professional playhouse, apparently the first purpose-built one in the British Isles since Roman times. It was east of Aldgate, near Mile End, in a court or yard belonging to a farmhouse called the Red Lion. Brayne hired one carpenter to build scaffolds for spectators and another to build the stage, and he quarrelled with both. The playhouse was not elaborate, since he probably spent only about £15 on it. It was to be ready by 8 July 1567 so that a play called *The Story of Sampson* could take place there, but nothing more is known about the place, or whether James Burbage had anything to do with it. Brayne's first known financial involvement with Burbage is a loan they made jointly in 1568.

Burbage was instrumental in Brayne's later memorable venture. Burbage bought a lease, dated 13 April 1576, on part of the dissolved priory of Holywell in Shoreditch. There, in an open space, he meant to build the first large and costly public playhouse, to be called The Theatre. The lease ran until 25 March 1597, but Burbage probably thought of it as running until 1607, because a clause provided that he could have up to ten more years if he spent £200 on old buildings there during the first ten years. Also, he could dismantle and remove the playhouse while the lease was in force. However, because Burbage had nothing like enough money for the scheme, he took in Brayne, who joined him without a written contract. Brayne was to supply most of the funds needed to erect the building, and Burbage was to have the lease put into both their names. Once the playhouse was open, the takings would pay the running costs and yield profits, most of which would go to Brayne until his investment and Burbage's were the same; then the two would share costs and profits. Brayne, now childless, spoke, according to Burbage, of leaving his share of the enterprise to Burbage's children.

The scheme went awry from the beginning. Burbage and Brayne planned to spend about £200 but actually spent about £700. They had to borrow money, then mortgage the lease. Brayne, and even his wife, had to join in putting up the building. He had to sell his house and business in Bucklersbury and moved to Shoreditch; in 1577–8 he ceased to be active as a grocer. He and Burbage soon fell into bitter and occasionally violent quarrels about who had spent how much and taken how much in profits. Because the lease was mortgaged, Burbage could not add Brayne's name to it. Instead, he gave Brayne bonds worth £600 guaranteeing that he would do so. The name was never added, however, and the bonds proved uncollectable. Brayne drew up a will in 1578 and left the Burbages out of it. Neither he nor his wife ever recouped his losses on The Theatre, but the Burbages prospered.

Brayne tried another investment in January 1580 with at least some help from Burbage. He acquired a lease for twenty-four years on The George inn in Whitechapel, into which he moved. This venture, however, came to echo that at The Theatre, and proved as disastrous to Brayne. Since the place was not functioning as an inn, Brayne, without a written contract, took an old friend, Robert Miles, goldsmith, as a partner; Miles was to restore the inn trade and share expenses and profits with Brayne. Miles also moved into the place, which did become an inn again, but not for long. Brayne quarrelled as bitterly with Miles as he did with Burbage, and eventually Miles controlled the lease. Brayne died, partly at least, because of a violent quarrel with Miles, and was buried in the churchyard of St Mary Matfelon, Whitechapel, on 15 June 1586. He was bankrupt and had hidden his goods and himself from creditors.

Brayne's widow, **Margaret Brayne** (d. 1593), convinced herself that Miles was responsible for her husband's death, and Miles ejected her from The George. She pursued him at law for murder and sued him for a share in The George. Soon she evidently gave birth to a child, Katherine, and she and Miles became close friends. He readmitted her to The George, though not to a share in it, and in 1588, supported and financed by Miles, she sued Burbage for half The Theatre or the £600 that Burbage's bonds to Brayne were in theory worth. The Burbages counter-sued, claiming that Brayne was childless when he died. They called Miles an adulterer and a 'murdring knave' and Margaret Brayne a 'murdring ho[r]' (Wallace, 100, 105, 115, 121). They believed, apparently, that Miles was Katherine Brayne's father and that he and Margaret Brayne had conspired to kill her husband.

The Burbages squeezed Margaret Brayne out of the ownership of The Theatre in 1589. The mortgage had long been forfeit, and the mortgagee, John Hyde, legally owned the lease. He, however, was ready to return it to Burbage and Brayne's widow in return for his money, of which only about £30 was still owing. Burbage's son, Cuthbert, got his patron, Walter Cope, an official in the entourage of the lord treasurer, to ask Hyde to give the lease to Cuthbert if Cuthbert paid the money. Cuthbert did so, and Hyde gave him the lease on condition that the Burbages give Margaret Brayne a proper share in the place. The Burbages became owners outright but did not honour the condition.

Margaret Brayne died of plague and was buried in the churchyard of St Mary Matfelon on 13 April 1593. In her will (8 April) she made Miles her heir. She left him not only her goods and her lawsuits but also Katherine Brayne, insisting that the child was her husband's and hoping that Miles would be good to her. She owed Miles so much money, she said, that all her goods 'will nothinge countervaile' (Wallace, 153–4). Katherine Brayne also died of plague three months later; she was buried in the churchyard of St Mary Matfelon on 23 July. Miles carried on Margaret Brayne's lawsuits until 1595, when the court decided that it would not continue to hear the case until Miles had pursued the bonds of 1578 in the common law courts. This was apparently not worth his while, and, in effect, the Burbages had won. In 1597 Miles began another lawsuit against them on Margaret Brayne's behalf but soon dropped it. Because the landlord of The Theatre refused to renew the lease after the first ten years or on favourable terms in 1597–8, Burbage's sons had The Theatre pulled down in the Christmas season of 1598–9 and its timbers carried to Bankside for use in building the Globe.

HERBERT BERRY

Sources C. W. Wallace, *The first London theatre* (1913) · W. Ingram, *The business of playing: the beginnings of the adult professional theater in Elizabethan England* (1992) · H. Berry, 'Shylock, Robert Miles, and events at the theatre', *Shakespeare Quarterly*, 44 (summer 1993), 182–201 · H. Berry, 'A handlist of documents about the theatre in Shoreditch', *Shakespeare's playhouses* (1987), 19–44 · H. Berry, 'The first public playhouses, especially the Red Lion', *Shakespeare Quarterly*, 40 (summer 1989), 133–45 · parish register, St Michael Bassishaw, London [marriage of Thomas Brayne and Alice Barlow], 22 Jan 1541 · parish register, St Stephen, Coleman Street, London · records of the Grocers' Company, London · parish register, St Dionis Backchurch, London, 14 Jan 1565 [marriage] · parish register, St Mary Matfelon, Whitechapel, London, 15 June 1586, 13 April 1593 [burials] · records of the London commissary court [wills of John Brayne and Margaret Brayne] · H. Berry, 'John Brayne and his other brother-in-law', *Shakespeare Studies*, 30 (2002), 93–8

Brayne, John (d. 1654), clergyman and Seeker, was settled by parliament as minister of St John's, in the Soke, Winchester, from the late 1640s until his death. His fame rests on the flurry of tracts he published in his last years, and little is known of his background. He may have come from Somerset: one tract was dedicated to his kinsman Thomas Churchey of Wincanton, and he may be identical with the John Brayne of Crewkerne, a gentleman's son who entered New Inn Hall, Oxford, in 1636, aged twenty-two.

He was certainly fluent in the classical languages and Hebrew, and was once described as 'Dr Brayne' (*CSP dom.*, 1654, 289).

By the later 1640s Brayne had developed radical political and religious ideas. In September 1647 he had a vision of the impending downfall of monarchy in England, France, and Spain, heralding the reign of Christ on earth. He sent this prophecy to the MP John Lisle, and it circulated in the army. In 1649 he revealed that General Thomas Fairfax ('and none else'; Brayne, *The Gospel-Pattern*, sig. A2) was the avenging angel of Revelation 14: 16, and that God would use the army to restore the true church, paving the way for the calling of the Jews. In the same year he welcomed news from France of the overthrow of Cardinal Mazarin, 'the first of the foolish virgins' (Brayne, *Babels Fall*, 19), and predicted an English invasion of Scotland to root out presbyterianism. This prophecy too was sent to Lisle. Other works reveal connections with the members of the Rump Parliament John Pyne and William Sydenham, and with the millenarian polymath John Sadler, 'a dear and faithful friend' (Brayne, *An Exposition*, sig. A2).

Brayne's primary interest lay in the nature of the church. He regarded all existing churches as false, believing that the true church would emerge only at the end of the 1260 years in the wilderness (Revelation 12: 6), which would be in 1666. There were, however, some true ministers, typified by the two witnesses of Revelation 20, and it was in this sense that he described himself as 'an unworthy witness' of the Lord (Brayne, *The New Earth*, title page). Such ministers were to preach the gospel (as Brayne did four or five times a week), but should not administer the sacraments. He devoted much thought to the shape of the future church. In 1648 he wrote to the Westminster assembly, criticizing the presbyterian system it had devised, but the only result was the suspension of his augmentation at Winchester. His own studies led him towards a much modified congregationalism, with a threefold ministry of evangelists, pastors, and teachers. Church members would observe the seventh-day sabbath and practise adult baptism; all others would continue to keep the first-day sabbath, and would be barred from the sacraments. Brayne also held idiosyncratic views on the hereafter. His version of mortalism distinguished between the soul, remaining with the body until the last judgment, and the spirit, which God quickened only in the elect and which returned straight to heaven. Those with such an awakened spirit might be blessed in this life with divine dreams and revelations. His views on predestination and the Trinity were remarkably conventional.

Like the Fifth Monarchists, Brayne saw the judicial laws of the Old Testament as an essential part of Christ's reign. He supported parliament's measures against blasphemy and the Adultery Act of 1650, though he regarded them as inadequate and insufficiently close to scripture. He also advocated sweeping changes in education. He attacked Latin authors as profane, wanted schools to use only biblical and early Christian writings in teaching Greek, and urged greater study of Hebrew. Existing translations of the Bible were so faulty, he complained, that they should

be called in. Astrology was condemned as the doctrine of demons. Brayne had considerable influence on other millenarian and spiritual writers. His polemical tracts drew replies from, among others, John Gadbury, the astrologer, and the Baptist Peter Chamberlen (1601–1683). Brayne was buried in Winchester on 20 February 1654. He had died in poverty, and in August of that same year the council of state settled a pension of £30 on his widow, Dorcas, and their eight small children.   BERNARD CAPP, *rev.*

Sources J. Brayne, *Babels fall* (1649) · J. Brayne, *The churches going in* (1649) · J. Brayne, *The new earth* (1653) · J. Brayne, *A vision, which one Mr Brayne … had* (1649) · *CSP dom.*, 1652–5 · parish register, Winchester, St John's, Hants. RO [burial] · J. Brayne, *The gospel-pattern for the government of gospel-churches* (1649) · J. Brayne, *An exposition upon the canticles* (1651)

Wealth at death died in poverty; widow awarded pension of £30

Brayne, Margaret (d. 1593). *See under* Brayne, John (c.1541–1586).

Brayne, William (d. 1657), army officer, was the son of Thomas Brayne. In 1653 he was made lieutenant-colonel of a regiment in the English army in Scotland commanded by Colonel William Daniel. In June 1654 he was given command of troops withdrawn from Irish service and based in the most remote parts of Scotland, short of supplies, and unable to live off the land. By June 1655 he was governor of Inverlochy, one of the five garrison strongholds of the English in Scotland, with jurisdiction over Lochaber and surrounding districts and a wide remit to 'use all the other good and convenient ways and means to bring the inhabitants of the said bounds to a more civil life and conversation'. This involved the strict application of martial law, in the absence of any framework of English common law (Thurloe, *State papers*, 3.521). Broghill described Brayne as 'a person of parts, honnesty, affectionate to the government, and one I have found very serviceable here' (Thurloe, *State papers*, 4.500).

Brayne's demonstration of resourcefulness, organization, and ability to administer in circumstances in which normal legal frameworks could not be established was rewarded by Cromwell with dispatch to the newly captured territory of Jamaica. Appointed commander-in-chief there, he sailed from Kinsale and, short of water, landed first at Barbados before reaching Jamaica in December 1656. He had already deduced that the soldiers he was transporting from Scotland and Ireland would make poor planters. Despite meagre resources, he surveyed the state of Barbados, encouraged settlers to migrate thence to Jamaica, systematically established the troops from Scotland and Ireland at Port Morant, and planned a fort at the mouth of the harbour there and a garrison at Cagway (later Port Royal). He urged the encouragement of trade with the Dutch in order to develop the fledgeling colony and lessen the risk of a Hispano-Dutch alliance. He employed a German from Brazil who knew how to domesticate native cattle and set about trying to entice settlers from Nevis and St Kitts. Depressed by the unwillingness of the soldiers to settle ('laisie and unsetled, expecting to be always maintayned at the publique chardge'), the slowness and paucity of supplies, and repeated bouts of fever, he asked to be relieved of his post after one year. 'A retired country life will be much fitter for me', he declared to Thurloe (Thurloe, *State papers*, 6.111). He seems to have been a man of some integrity, opposing the appointment of Colonel Holdip (or Holdep) because he bore a reputation for cruelty, and repeatedly asking for ratification of his authority to act alone, everyone else having left or died. Brayne finally succumbed to fever on 2 September 1657. A testimony to his indefatigability was left by his successor, Colonel Edward D'Oyley, who complained that full command was too heavy a burden, and requested that he be joined by Colonel Barrington, whose 'genius much inclined to the way of plantation' (ibid., 6.453). SARAH BARBER

Sources *CSP col.*, vol. 1 · Thurloe, *State papers* · F. D. Dow, *Cromwellian Scotland, 1651–1660* (1979)
Archives Bodl. Oxf., Thurloe state papers

Brazil, Angela (1868–1947), children's writer, was born at 1 West Cliff, Preston, Lancashire, on 30 November 1868, the younger daughter and fourth child of Clarence Brazil (1831–1899) and his wife, Angelica McKinnell (1835/6–1915). The Brazils were of Irish descent and Angela was proud of her 'Celtic' ancestry, but with her dark hair and eyes she resembled in appearance her half-Spanish mother. Clarence Brazil worked in the Lancashire cotton trade and the family moved around the area accordingly. In 1873 they moved to Egremont on the Mersey, in 1877 to Manchester, in 1884 to Bolton, and ultimately to near Bury. In her autobiographical *My Own Schooldays* (1925) Angela presented a picture of a happy, cultivated, professional family, but she may not have been telling the whole truth and there are hints of financial and other difficulties.

Angela Brazil was educated at a small private school in Wallasey, then at the preparatory department of Manchester high school, and finally at Ellerslie, a more exclusive girls' school. After the family moved to Bolton she boarded in the school hostel; during her last year she became academic head of the school, but there was no prefect system and the title bestowed no authority. Nor did the school then do much in the way of games or drama, though it was strong musically. (She liked to present herself as musical, though her audiences disagreed.)

After leaving school Angela Brazil and her elder sister studied at Heatherley's Art School in London; sketching, like botany, was a lifelong hobby. Apart from a shadowy episode as a governess she apparently lived at home, eventually keeping house for a doctor brother. After her father died in 1899 she, her mother, and her sister moved to a cottage in the Conwy valley, where they had had a holiday home since 1883, and for some years travelled extensively in Europe and the Near East. (In the 1920s the Welsh cottage was given up and she bought one in Polperro, Cornwall.) In 1911 Angela Brazil moved with her brother to Coventry, where their sister joined them after their mother's death in 1915. They remained together for the rest of their lives, joining fully in the social and cultural activities of

Angela Brazil (1868–1947), by Lafayette, c.1934

the city and attending St Michael's Church. Although she was said to be shy, she was hospitable and encouraging to young people.

Angela Brazil was over thirty before she began to publish (her first publication being a book of children's plays) and not until 1906 did she put her mother's boarding-school experience into fictional dress, producing *The Fortunes of Philippa*. Forty-seven school stories followed it, the last published in the year before her death. So vast was Angela Brazil's contribution to the girls' school story that she is popularly supposed to have invented it, but in fact it had been emerging as a separate genre for over twenty years before her first essays in it. She gained her pre-eminence by a prolific output and a concentration on the genre, so that by the 1920s she was recognized as the leading writer of girls' school stories.

Though nearly all of Angela Brazil's books have a school setting, the plots of most depend on external circumstances, usually the unravelling of a mystery: they are about schoolgirls rather than schools. Romantic scenery, unusual names (for example Aldred, Gipsy, Ulyth, Winona, Avelyn, Lesbia, Ingred, Mavis, and Merle), and devoted friendships abound; her descriptive writing is flowery and her famous use of slang ('blossomy', 'twiggezvous', 'ripping', and the like) startling. Her characters are not especially memorable and tend to the artistic rather than the sporty. In her best works, such as *A Fourth Form Friendship* (1911), *A Pair of Schoolgirls* (1912), *The Youngest Girl in the Fifth* (1913), *For the Sake of the School* (1915), *The Head Girl of the Gables* (1919), and others, some personal dilemmas are convincingly presented and worked through, but this was an aspect which died out of her books, to their disadvantage. On the whole, too, few of her heroines appear to have much concept of adult life.

This was both Angela Brazil's strength and her weakness. She identified very closely with her heroines, and her books gained in originality by this level of presentation—she did not, as earlier writers had done, take a superior authorial stand. Perhaps she herself, as the petted youngest of her family, had never had to grow up mentally. The result was that her books were both enthralling to the young and easy to grow out of. The other major school-story writers attract adult enthusiasts: Brazil does not. She is enjoyed now for her unconscious humour, not as a stylish creator of plots and characters. But there is no doubt that her books—which, with posthumous reprints, spanned fifty years—were in their time enormously popular and financially successful. Angela Brazil died on 13 March 1947 at her home, 1 The Quadrant, Warwick Road, Coventry, a wealthy woman, having neither created nor significantly shaped her chosen genre but leaving a name still synonymous with it.   HILARY CLARE

Sources A. Brazil, *My own schooldays* (1925) · G. Freeman, *The schoolgirl ethic: the life & work of Angela Brazil* (1976) · S. Sims and H. Clare, *The encyclopaedia of girls' school stories* (2000), vol. 1 of *The encyclopaedia of school stories*, ed. R. Auchmuty and J. Wotton · b. cert. · d. cert. · census returns, 1881
Archives Coventry Central Library, papers, incl. 'fan mail'
Likenesses Lafayette, photograph, *c.*1934, NPG [*see illus.*] · photographs, repro. in Brazil, *My own schooldays* · photographs, repro. in Freeman, *The schoolgirl ethic* · photographs, repro. in A. Marshall, *Life's rich pageant* (1984)
Wealth at death £38,914 9s. 0d.: probate, 23 Aug 1947, CGPLA Eng. & Wales

Breadalbane. For this title name *see* Campbell, John, second marquess of Breadalbane (1796–1862).

Breadalbane and Holland. For this title name *see* Campbell, John, first earl of Breadalbane and Holland (1634–1717); Campbell, John, third earl of Breadalbane and Holland (*bap.* 1696, *d.* 1782).

Breakspear, Nicholas. *See* Adrian IV (*d.* 1159).

Breakwell, Thomas (1872–1902), the first English Baha'i convert, was born at Ellen Street, Woking, Surrey, on 31 May 1872, the youngest of the five children of Edward Breakwell, blacksmith, and his wife, Elizabeth, *née* Knight. He received his elementary education at the local school, and subsequently emigrated with his family to the United States. He found well-paid and responsible work at a southern cotton mill, which enabled him to spend his summer vacations in Europe.

In the summer of 1901 Breakwell made the acquaintance of May Ellis Bolles, a Canadian then living in Paris. She had been the first person in France to accept the Baha'i faith, and, at the personal request of 'Abdual-Bah', the eldest son and appointed successor of Baha' Allah, the founder of the faith, she had remained in France to spread the Baha'i message. Bolles left an account of her first meeting with Breakwell: 'It was like looking at a veiled light. I saw at once his pure heart, his thirsty soul, and over all was cast the veil which is over every soul until it is rent

asunder by the power of God in this day.' She went on to describe him as 'of medium height, slender, erect, and graceful with intense eyes and an indescribable charm. ... I discerned a very rare person of high standing and culture, simple, natural, intensely real in his attitude toward life and his fellow men'. Filled with enthusiasm, he gave up his plans for travel and set off for Egypt to meet 'Abd al-Baha'. This was the first visit by an English pilgrim; 'Abd al-Baha' instructed him to resign his position in the cotton mill (which employed child labour) and to devote himself to the faith. Breakwell returned to Paris, where he threw himself into teaching the Baha'i message: many enrolled in his classes.

Breakwell's parents (who had moved back to England) arrived in Paris to attempt to persuade their son to return with them to London: his health was rapidly declining and he was found to have advanced consumption. He refused to leave Paris, as 'Abd al-Baha' had asked him to stay, and persuaded his father of the truth of his faith. Breakwell died in the Maison Municipale de Santé, Paris, on 13 June 1902. Shortly before his death he had written a letter to 'Abd al-Baha''s secretary, Dr Yunis Khan, saying: 'Suffering is a heady wine; I am prepared to receive that bounty which is the greatest of all; torments of the flesh have enabled me to draw much nearer to my Lord.' In 1957 the guardian of the Baha'i faith referred to Thomas Breakwell as: 'one of the three luminaries shedding brilliant lustre on the annals of the Irish, English and Scottish Baha'i communities'.   PHILIP HAINSWORTH

Sources private information (2004) · M. Maxwell, *Bahá'í World*, 7 (1936–8), 707–11 · O. Z. Whitehead, *Some early Bahá'ís of the West* (1977)
Likenesses photograph, *c.*1902, possibly Baha'i World Centre, Israel

Brearley, Harry (1871–1948), metallurgist, was born on 18 February 1871 at 23 Spital Street, Sheffield, the youngest of five sons and the eighth of nine children of John Brearley, steelworker, and his wife, Jane Senior. Brearley's father was 'an expert steel melter and also an expert ale-supper' (Brearley, *Knotted String*, 20); his mother, a blacksmith's daughter, took in washing to help raise her large family. He grew into a delicate child, whose slum upbringing—and especially his mother's hard life—sowed the seeds of his later socialism. Educated at Woodside board school, at the age of twelve Brearley worked briefly in the crucible steel furnaces alongside his father at Thos Firth & Sons (an experience he immortalized in *Steel-Makers*, 1933). By 1883 he had gravitated to Firth's laboratories, where he washed bottles. The firm's chemist, James Taylor—a crucial influence on Brearley—encouraged him to study metallurgy. By the age of twenty Brearley had become a laboratory assistant and was apprenticed for a premium of £50. Shortly afterwards, now earning about £2 a week and describing himself as a metallurgical chemist, he married, on 23 October 1895, Helen Theresa Crank (1874–1955), the daughter of James Crank, a coal dealer.

Brearley progressed rapidly in his chosen profession and in 1901 he left Firths to start a new laboratory at another Sheffield steelworks, Kayser Ellison. While there, he wrote the first of his technical texts (with Fred Ibbotson), *The Analysis of Steelwork's Materials* (1903). Brearley returned to Firths in 1903, after its merger with John Brown & Co. After a spell as chief chemist at Firth's Salamander works at Riga, in 1907 Brearley became the first director of a newly created research division—the Brown-Firth Research Laboratories.

In May 1912, while researching steel for small arms, Brearley made trials with low carbon steels containing about 12 per cent chromium. These steels had the happy ability (due to the formation of a chromium oxide film on the steel's surface) to resist corrosion, a fact recognized by Brearley almost immediately. He also saw the commercial possibilities of the product and alerted Firths. According to Brearley, Firths showed little interest, and he was left to find a use for it. He suggested that it might be useful for cutlery, a view vindicated when one of Sheffield's cutlery firms succeeded in 1914 in making knife blades from the alloy. Stainless (or as it was then known, 'rustless') steel had arrived, and by the First World War commercial production in Sheffield was well under way.

Brearley's claims as stainless steel's discoverer did not go unchallenged. In America the metallurgist Elwood Haynes had pre-empted his chromium formula; while in Germany, Eduard Maurer and Benno Strauss at Krupps had patented, in 1912–13, a chromium nickel stainless alloy that was to have even more potential than Brearley's composition. Nevertheless, Brearley's claim as the pioneer of the commercial development of martensitic stainless steel (the type used in cutlery) can be accepted. An individualist of socialist leanings, he intended sharing in the credit and rewards of his discovery, an attitude which led to many disputes with his employers. In 1915 he left Firths and became a works manager of Brown Bayley's steelworks in Sheffield, a company he was to be associated with until his death. Remarkably, stainless steel was never patented in Britain (the discovery appears to have spread so quickly in Sheffield that patenting was not thought worth while). However, Firths and Brearley (after they had settled their differences) soon tied up the rights on stainless steel in the USA, Canada, Italy, France, and Japan, so that any Sheffield firm intending to export to these countries needed a licence from the Firth-Brearley Stainless Steel Syndicate—an organization founded in 1917, which made good profits for Firths and Brearley in the 1920s.

In 1920 Brearley was awarded the Bessemer gold medal by the Iron and Steel Institute. Five years later he became a director of Brown Bayleys, and shortly afterwards, at about the age of fifty-five, he began enjoying a period of semi-retirement on the rewards of stainless steel. He wrote several books, notably an evocative autobiography, *Knotted String* (1941). In 1942 he established the Freshgate Trust Foundation, a charity which he hoped would 'help lame dogs over stiles'. Brearley lived at Walton, near Chesterfield, and later in life moved to Livermead, Torquay, where he died at his home, Walton Cottage, 21 Mead Road, on 14 July 1948. He was cremated at Efford crematorium, Plymouth, on 16 July. He left £80,881 gross, of which he bequeathed £1000 a year to his widow for life (his only child, Leo, born in 1896, had died in Australia in 1946) and the remainder to the Freshgate Foundation.

GEOFFREY TWEEDALE

Sources H. Brearley, *Knotted string* (1941) · H. Brearley, *Harry Brearley, stainless pioneer: autobiographical notes* (1989) · J. Trueman, 'The initiation and growth of high alloy (stainless) steel production', *Historical Metallurgy*, 19 (1985) · G. Tweedale, *Sheffield steel and America: a century of commercial and technological interdependence, 1830–1930* (1987) · G. Tweedale, *Steel city: entrepreneurship, strategy, and technology in Sheffield, 1743–1993* (1995) · R. D. Gray, *Alloys and automobiles: the life of Elwood Haynes* (1979) · British Steel Stainless, *75 years of stainless steel, 1913–1988* (1988) · G. Tweedale, *Giants of Sheffield steel* (1986) · private information (2004) · b. cert. · m. cert. · *CGPLA Eng. & Wales* (1948)

Archives Firth-Brearley Stainless Steel Syndicate, records · Firth-Brown Ltd, company records · Sheff. Arch.

Likenesses photographs, repro. in Tweedale, *Giants of Sheffield steel* · photographs, repro. in Brearley, *Stainless pioneer*

Wealth at death £80,881 16s. 2d.: probate, 1 Oct 1948, *CGPLA Eng. & Wales*

Brearley, Molly Root (1905–1994), educationist, was born on 28 March 1905 at Rosebank, 2 Priory Avenue, Hastings, Sussex, the daughter of Dr Hermon Brearley (1876–1940), professor of music and organist, and his wife, Mabel Daisy, *née* Root (1880–1962), pianist and piano teacher. She was the eldest of three children and attended a small private school in Hastings for children from seven to eighteen. She later speculated that her teacher, who held an English degree, had Froebelian connections. Activities included nature study, reading and listening to the great works of literature, and painting and drawing. The house was full of pictures (the teacher's father was an RA) which the children discussed. Brearley recalled: 'She made school entirely delightful and so full of interest that I really believe no-one was ever bored' (Brearley, 12). When she was eleven her father was appointed to the post of cathedral organist at Blackburn and she was sent to Blackburn high school, leaving in 1924 to study English at Liverpool University. Illness interrupted her studies and she left Liverpool with a teacher's certificate in 1928 and was appointed to a post at Kettering Girls' High School, where her duties were to teach junior English, history, and games. She remained at Kettering for nearly ten years, leaving in April 1938, and she described the school as 'well-run and enlightened' (Brearley, 12). During this period she was active in the Girl Guides, serving as a county trainer, and gaining the blue cord diploma. She also worked with Brownies and cadet groups and claimed that she learned most from these activities (Brearley, 12), although the school had some features associated with progressive schools of the period, including unstreamed classes and restricted amounts of homework.

It was during this period that Brearley's interest in Froebel teaching developed, and she took the two-year National Froebel Union teacher's certificate by private study in 1932–3, gaining a first class, and completed the trainer's diploma in 1937. This qualification entitled the holder to teach in a training college and required a term's practical teaching which Brearley completed at Bedford Training College, which was then a Froebel college. The ethos at Bedford appealed to her and she returned there in 1938 to take up a post as kindergarten mistress at The Crescent, in charge of seventy children under seven years old. Other duties included lecturing to college students in principles of education. Bedford was a reception area during the Second World War and Brearley worked in the children's clubs opened by the local authority, and was also involved in fire watching. At Bedford prison and at St Albans Diocesan Orphanage and Training Home for Girls she taught reading, an activity reflecting her own passion for literature and her desire to give others the skills to appreciate books. In the post-war period she became involved in courses established to promote basic education to refugees and others as part of European reconstruction. She wrote numerous articles on reading and produced the Queensway Reading scheme with Lois Neilson, published by Evans in the 1960s.

Brearley moved to her next post, as lecturer in the faculty of education at Birmingham University, in 1944, and was initially involved in training for infant and junior teaching. In 1949 she was awarded an official degree by the university and began to work in the pioneering remedial centre at Selly Wick established by Professor Fred Schonell. Her colleagues there included W. D. Wall and Mia Kellmer Pringle, and their work involved training educational psychologists and remedial teachers, and providing a service to schools. It was unique at the time for its combination of service provision with an active research programme by university staff and students. The academic rigour which characterized her work was utilized to promote a child-centred approach to the education of children who appeared to be failing. It was at this time that Brearley became interested in the work of Jean Piaget and Susan and Nathan Isaacs, and she later wrote that this 'served to give me a stronger theoretical framework which contradicted nothing I had learnt from Froebel' (Brearley, 14). Her belief in the importance of Piaget's ideas led her to publish *A Teacher's Guide to Reading Piaget* with Elizabeth Hitchfield in 1966, a book designed to make his difficult ideology accessible to practising teachers.

Brearley was appointed to the post of principal of the Froebel Educational Institute in 1955, succeeding her friend Eglantyne Mary Jebb, and introduced a number of innovative diploma courses for teachers as well as encouraging cross-faculty collaboration in teaching the BEd. A colleague recalled: 'For years old students would say that one of the courses which made a great impression was the first year study combining child development with maths or science or movement and so on' (Athey, *A Personal Appreciation*, 3). This approach was reflected in the book she edited with Froebel staff, *Fundamentals in the First School* (1969). During her period as principal Brearley served on the committees of numerous organizations. She had been an active member of the National Froebel Foundation since the 1940s, serving on the members' committee, the joint examination board, the standing committee, and, most notably, the governing body, for which she was vice-chair in 1973. As a member of the Schools' Broadcasting

Council of the BBC during the 1960s she worked on television and radio programmes, as both adviser and broadcaster. She made a major contribution to two television series produced by Eileen Molony, *Growth and Play*, aimed at parents, and *The Springs of Learning*, as well as to the radio series *Parents and Children*. She also served on committees of the University of London, including the committee of principals, and maintained close links with the Nursery Schools Association (later the British Association of Early Childhood Education), the Pre-School Playgroup Association, and the World Organization for Early Childhood Education. She was an editorial consultant for the journal *Education 3–13* for many years.

In 1963 the Central Advisory Council for Education was asked to consider the subject of primary education and the transition to secondary school. The council, chaired by Bridget Plowden, produced its report *Children and their Primary Schools* in 1967. As a member of the council Brearley was able to influence this key—and controversial—report. Its general ethos was encapsulated in the first line of chapter two: 'At the heart of the educational process lies the child' (Department of Education and Science, Central Advisory Council for Education, *Children and their Primary Schools*, 1967, 7). A colleague commented: 'She was an indefatigable worker and an outstanding communicator. It is doubtful whether a single bit of authentic research was missed by members of that Committee' (Athey, 'Ten years on', 2).

Brearley cared for all children, and throughout her career she supported projects which sought to remedy the kinds of educational failure identified by the Plowden committee. At the Froebel Educational Institute, together with Joyce Bishop, chair of the Froebel governing body, she raised funds for the Project for the Study of Educational Failure in Underprivileged Children, which ran from 1971 to 1972. Following on from this, the Froebel Nursery Project was established in 1973, with funding from the Leverhulme Trust, and continued to 1978. The research carried out during this project, grounded in a Piagetian and constructivist pedagogy, was published by Chris Athey in 1990 under the title *Extending Thought in Young Children*.

After her retirement in 1970 Brearley initially remained close to the Froebel Institute before moving to Radford Semele, near Leamington Spa, in 1975. She continued to lead an active life, running courses for teachers into her eighties and travelling to New York to hold six-week summer schools for teachers and children in the Bronx at the Community Resources Institute, sponsored by the Ford Foundation. She was also invited to Canada to participate in the summer schools held at the University of British Columbia. Her love of literature led her to join the Poetry Society and to lecture on her favourite poets, particularly John Clare. She retained her affection for the Froebel Institute and continued to write for *The Link*, the magazine of the Michaelis Guild representing past Froebel students, until 1992.

A tall, elegant woman, Brearley could be a formidable

critic with a rapier-like command of language, demanding the same commitment from her staff as she herself displayed. A colleague recalled another aspect to her personality:

> It may seem like a fairy story when I say that I found Academic Board meetings exciting because we were discussing real issues that people felt passionate about. Issues that would influence the future … Lots of us found those years both fascinating and FUN. (Athey, *A Personal Appreciation*, 2)

Brearley was appointed CBE in 1965 for her services to education, and her portrait, by William Evans, hangs in the Adam Room of Froebel College. She died just one day before her eighty-ninth birthday, on 27 March 1994, from heart failure at South Warwickshire Hospital, Warwick; she was cremated at Oakley Wood crematorium, Leamington Spa, on 7 April 1994. She never married.

Jane Read

Sources private information (2004) [E. Bevan-Roberts, formerly Hitchfield; A. Brearley] · C. Athey, *A personal appreciation of Molly Brearley* (1999) · *The Link* (1994) · *Daily Telegraph* (9 April 1994) · *The Times* (2 April 1994) · 'A thanksgiving for the life of Molly Brearley CBE, 1905–1994', miscellaneous deposited material, University of Surrey, Roehampton, London, Froebel College, FACS/FE1/8–5 BRE · M. Brearley, 'What Froebel has meant to me', *The Link* (1982), 12–14 · C. Athey, 'Ten years on: a retrospective account of the Froebel Early Education Project', unpubl. report, 1999 · dossier on Molly Brearley, U. Lpool L., special collections and archives, A. 076 · annual reports, 1955–70, Incorporated Froebel Educational Institute · governing body minutes and various committee minutes, National Froebel Foundation archive · contributor files, School Broadcasting Council files, BBC WAC · PRO, Plowden report MSS, ED 146/64–93; ED 207/1–14 · d. cert. · b. cert.
Archives BBC WAC · PRO, Department of Education MSS · University of Surrey, Roehampton, London, Froebel College, MSS, FACS/FE/1/8–5 BRE
Likenesses W. Evans, oils, 1969, University of Surrey, Roehampton, London, Froebel College · photograph, repro. in *The Times*
Wealth at death £234,112: probate, 15 June 1994, *CGPLA Eng. & Wales*

Breathnach, Éadbhard. *See* Walsh, Edward (1805–1850).

Bréauté, Sir Falkes de (d. 1226), soldier and royal favourite, was of obscure Norman parentage. One reasonably reliable source, which described him as 'small in stature but very valiant', stated that he was the son of a Norman knight by a concubine (Michel, 173), and in the mid-twelfth century there was indeed a knightly family at Bréauté, a village in the Pays de Caux near modern Le Havre. Most chroniclers, however, allege that he was of servile origin, often referring to him contemptuously by his first name only, and even presenting that name as a mere nickname.

Early career, 1204–1215 The Bréauté family does not appear to have held lands in England before 1204, and it is probable that Falkes, with at least three brothers and one sister, abandoned his native Normandy for England following the French king's conquest of the duchy in 1204. There is no contemporary evidence to support the later assertion that he was first employed as a royal door-keeper, but some that he was a poor royal sergeant. He may have been

Sir Falkes de Bréauté (*d.* 1226), drawing

sent to Poitou on royal service in January 1206; he was certainly the royal sergeant to whom King John entrusted Glamorgan and Wenlock in February 1207. He was probably knighted about this time, and was soon made constable of Carmarthen, Cardigan, and the Gower. He gained a fearsome reputation in the chronic warfare of the Welsh marches; in 1212, for instance, the king ordered him to destroy the Welsh abbey of Strata Florida because it was supporting the king's enemies. However, Bréauté was often employed elsewhere in royal service, including in Flanders and Poitou, and seems to have won high favour with John. He was frequently with John in England from January 1215 onwards, and it was later alleged, quite wrongly, that he was one of the foreign mercenaries condemned in Magna Carta. More plausibly, he was numbered among the royalists who swore to abide by the charter's terms and the decisions of the twenty-five baronial leaders.

Rise to power, 1215–1217 The renewal of war between the king and barons in autumn 1215 offered Bréauté great opportunities for advancement, and he soon demonstrated his ruthless and dauntless character, as well as his unquestioning loyalty to the Angevin kings, earning the lasting hatred of barons and monastic chroniclers alike. His activities ranged far and wide across central England. On 28 November 1215 he took Hanslope, Buckinghamshire, a castle of William Mauduit; soon after, William de Beauchamp's castle at Bedford also fell to him, and he probably received it in perpetual grant from the king. Early in 1216 John divided his army around London between the earl of Salisbury and four 'alien' captains, including Bréauté, while the king himself headed northwards to ravage the lands of the rebels. Then, when Prince Louis of France came to England to claim the throne in June, Bréauté was sent to hold Oxford against the resurgent baronial forces. On 17 July, he and the earl of Chester sacked Worcester, whose citizens had come to terms with Louis.

In September or October 1216 King John rewarded Bréauté with the hand of Margaret, the newly widowed wife of Baldwin de Revières (d. 1216), son and heir of William, earl of Devon (d. 1217). Margaret was also the daughter and heir of Warin Fitzgerald, the royal chamberlain, and of Warin's wife, Alice de Courcy, the heir of the Courcys of Stoke Courcy (Stogursey), Somerset. As a result Bréauté was made 'the equal of an earl' by his marriage (*Memoriale fratris Walteri de Coventria*, 2.253). He immediately took control of the Isle of Wight, as Margaret's dower, and soon received Stogursey as her inheritance and became chamberlain to the exchequer. When John died suddenly on 19 October, Falkes de Bréauté was one of the executors of his will. He was also one of the royalist barons who issued a revised version of Magna Carta on 12 November 1216, under the leadership of the regent, William Marshal the elder, and Guala the papal legate.

Bréauté continued to fight for Henry III as loyally and as ruthlessly as he had served King John. Holding six midland counties, Bréauté represented a major obstacle to Prince Louis and the rebel barons, for although the royalists soon lost Hertford and Cambridge, Bréauté retained the castles of Oxford, Buckingham, Northampton, and Bedford. It was during this struggle for central and eastern England that Bréauté's men committed their worst atrocities. On 22 January 1217 they fell upon the town and abbey of St Albans, perhaps because it had come to terms with Prince Louis only ten days earlier, albeit under compulsion. After unspeakable barbarities against the townsmen, they turned upon the abbey, killed the abbot's cook, and extorted 200 marks by threatening to burn the abbey. Bréauté's followers also afflicted the monks of Wardon, Bedfordshire. He made restitution to both abbeys, but St Albans, at least, regarded his penance as a sham, designed only to please his wife.

At the end of February Bréauté headed south in a royalist army which failed to relieve the besieged port of Rye. Returning north, he raided and captured the Isle of Ely. He then played a critical part in the campaigns that culminated in the royalist victory at Lincoln (20 May) and the dashing of Prince Louis's hopes of the crown of England. Bréauté joined the earl of Chester in besieging the rebel fortress of Mountsorrel, Leicestershire. In consequence,

the rebels divided their forces perilously: while Louis himself remained at the siege of Dover with half his army, the remainder of the rebels and French marched north to relieve Mountsorrel. Having achieved this, they set off to assist a rebel force that was besieging the royalist garrison of Lincoln Castle; but the main royal army now arrived under the earl marshal and the bishop of Winchester, and forced a battle in the very streets of Lincoln. Before the engagement Bréauté led his men into Lincoln Castle, from whose walls his crossbowmen raked the Franco-baronial army in the streets below. He then sallied forth into the city with such audacity that he was captured, but was rescued by his followers, and fought on until the arrival of the other royalist forces settled the issue. Even his detractors acknowledged Bréauté's role in the royalist victory, against numerically superior forces. Characteristically, his fierce espousal of the cause of Henry III was matched by a reluctance to release a number of his prisoners, once peace had been established between Prince Louis and the royalists in September.

The conflicts within the minority government, 1218–1222 The royalist triumph in 1217 marked the climax of Bréauté's career, and the court even celebrated Christmas at his expense at Northampton. Thereafter, however, he was one of a number of the victors of 1217 who were alienated in the years of peace by the policies of the justiciar, Hubert de Burgh (d. 1243), particularly over the resumption of royal castles and manors which officials like Bréauté were holding for their own profit. For several years, however, Bréauté's position was almost unassailable. As a leading figure in the government of the young king, he was able to deflect the judgments made against him in general and local eyres in 1218 and 1219, while himself serving as a justice in Essex, Hertfordshire, and East Anglia. In March 1218, after the death of the old earl of Devon, he received the honour and castle of Plympton, Devon, as his wife's dower, together with the custody of his stepson, the young heir to the earldom. He continued to hold the shrievalties of six midland counties, and Rutland between 1218 and 1221 as well. Yet his greatness depended upon the favour of the regency, since all these grants were revocable; moreover, his wife's Courcy inheritance was hotly contested in the courts by her elder half-sister, Alice of Cornhill, wife of the former rebel Hugh de Neville (d. 1234).

More dangerous were the enmities Bréauté had made among the royalists themselves. William Marshal the younger (d. 1231) had had to pawn four manors to him during the war, and struggled bitterly to recover them. Bréauté made other enemies as a sheriff and defender of the king's interests: the earl of Salisbury grew to loathe him for supporting Nicola de la Haie as constable of Lincoln Castle against the earl's private ambitions, and with Robert de Courtenay even planned a raid against Bréauté's lands in Devon. These disputes all threatened serious disturbance between 1218 and 1222. Such quarrels underlined the fragility of Bréauté's position, for, unlike the earls of Pembroke and Salisbury or Robert de Courtenay, he had no independent landed base and so could ill afford to offend the magnates of England. His survival increasingly depended upon the support of such great men as Ranulf (III), earl of Chester (d. 1232), and Peter des Roches, bishop of Winchester (d. 1238), who were disenchanted with the rule of Hubert de Burgh and his allies.

Bréauté appears to have been only too well aware that he was despised as a low-born alien. About 1222, during a dispute as sheriff of Northamptonshire with John Marshal (d. 1235), Bréauté exclaimed that Marshal and 'all the native-born men of England' were traitors, who wished nothing more than to restart the war: but all England, he cried, would not be big enough for the war he would wage against them! Perhaps as alarming to the justiciar was Bréauté's boast that not even thirty pairs of royal letters would make him change his mind (Shirley, 1.220–22). His frustration with the selfishness of those nobles in the regency who impeded his duties as sheriff did not prevent Bréauté's obstructing all attempts by the regency to recover the royal demesnes that he himself held.

The winter crisis, 1223–1224 For a time these tensions were papered over. In July 1222 Bréauté and Hubert de Burgh co-operated in suppressing a citizens' revolt in London. At the justiciar's behest, Bréauté seized three of the ringleaders, including a former sheriff of London called Constantine Fitzalulf, and executed them without trial outside the city, ignoring Constantine's offer of 15,000 marks in return for his life. Bréauté and de Burgh then arrested and mutilated the other leaders of the revolt. Bréauté also took a strong force to the royal army of Montgomery which humiliated Llywelyn ab Iorwerth (d. 1240) in September 1223. But Hubert de Burgh's growing ascendancy drove Bréauté, Chester, and their allies ever closer in opposition to him, until the strains within the regency boiled over. On 9 November 1223 de Burgh fled with the king to Gloucester, while the earls of Chester and Gloucester, the count of Aumale, and Bréauté attempted to seize the Tower of London a few days later. A new civil war was averted by the mediation of Archbishop Langton, but at a stormy parley in London on 4 December, the bishop of Winchester, the earl of Chester, and Bréauté left together in high umbrage. Bréauté and the 'schismatics' headed north, celebrating Christmas at Leicester while the king and his court lay at Northampton. However, outnumbered and threatened with excommunication, the earl of Chester and his allies went to Northampton, where, on 29 or 30 December, they agreed to resign their castles and shrievalties to the king. Bréauté lost Hertford Castle and the shrievalties of Oxford and Northampton immediately, and the shrievalty of Bedfordshire by 18 January. Thereafter he ceased to be present at the major councils of the realm.

The siege of Bedford Castle, 1224 At this juncture Falkes de Bréauté was still by no means isolated, and the archbishop and his suffragans were probably at pains to avoid further damaging rifts: they held a ceremony of reconciliation between the regency and the 'schismatics' in late April,

which Bréauté attended. Yet by June 1224 he had become separated from his allies, and his isolation led to his downfall. The crisis of the previous winter had given both strength and initiative to Hubert de Burgh the justiciar, who was henceforth unlikely to suffer any resistance from Bréauté to the recovery of royal domains. In February the government decided to remove him from custody of the earl of Devon's lands and heir, rejecting Bréauté's plea that Plympton Castle was his wife's dower. Bréauté ignored this order and continued to hold Plympton. He also refused to surrender Bedford Castle, and paid no heed to claims that his enemies now laid against him in the courts. He was soon threatened with a trumped-up capital charge of breach of the peace in Bedfordshire; this was adjourned in June, but assize justices at Dunstable found him guilty of sixteen cases of wrongful disseisin (some chroniclers allege over thirty).

On 16 June William de Bréauté, Falkes's brother and constable of Bedford Castle, seized one of the justices, Henry of Braybrooke, a personal enemy of both Bréautés, who Falkes later claimed had been despoiling his lands without judgment. William's move was foolhardy in the extreme, for the king and his magnates were then gathering at Northampton, only 20 miles away, to discuss the defence of Poitou against the king of France. William de Bréauté refused to release the captured justice on 19 June, and so the king and magnates laid siege to Bedford Castle the following day. Archbishop Langton forthwith excommunicated the garrison and Falkes as well. Falkes de Bréauté later claimed, somewhat implausibly, that he had gone to Bedford on 17 June to release the captured justice, but the constable had hidden with his captive in a wood. But whether or not Bréauté had connived in his brother's action, he now decided to support William and resist the regency's attempts to cow him. Having lavished great care upon the defences of Bedford Castle and installed a sizeable garrison of English and Normans, he probably expected the castle to hold out long enough—for a year, he allegedly claimed—until the earl of Chester and others intervened on his behalf; indeed, it was to the earl of Chester's lands that he now retreated.

Bréauté had reckoned without the determination of the justiciar and archbishop, the weakness of Chester and the other 'schismatics', and the resources of the crown for a siege; above all, the young king was furious that the suppression of Bréauté in England might cost him his province of Poitou, as indeed it did. Men were mustered from several shires to work the great siege-engines, in the construction of which an entire wood was felled, and a general aid was granted by the nobles and clergy. The eight-week siege of Bedford impressed contemporaries by its ferocity: six knights and over two hundred common soldiers and labourers were killed by the missiles of the garrison, which spurned all offers to parley. By early August, Bréauté, evading the knights sent after him and fleeing to Llywelyn's lands, began to despair of aid: the earl of Chester, indeed, had joined the royal army for a time in July, and King Henry ignored all entreaties from the earl and Welsh prince on Bréauté's behalf. Eventually Bréauté met the bishop of Coventry near Chester and agreed to submit through him; on 12 August the king granted him a safe conduct to go from Coventry to Northampton. Yet notwithstanding Bréauté's imminent submission the royal army forced the surrender of Bedford on 14 August, after the fourth assault, and on the following day William de Bréauté and almost the entire garrison, numbering more than eighty knights and men-at-arms, were refused pardon and hanged.

The fate of his brother and followers, and the loss of Bedford, left Falkes de Bréauté a broken man; on 19 August he submitted to Henry III, pleading for forgiveness and resigning all his possessions, including Stogursey and Plympton. Faced with the prospective loss of her inheritance and dower, his wife, Margaret, immediately sought a divorce, on the grounds that she had been forced into the marriage eight years beforehand: she was unsuccessful in this plea, but remained in the king's custody and succeeded in recovering some of her lands. In London on 25 August, meanwhile, Bréauté made a formal surrender of all his lands and was absolved. Papal letters on his behalf arrived too late to help him. In October he chose exile rather than judgment by his peers, well aware of the hatred he had aroused among the barons. At the coast he tearfully begged his escort, William (IV) de Warenne, earl of Surrey, to tell the king that he had disturbed the peace in England solely at the behest of the great men of the realm.

Exile and death, 1224–1226 The miserable remainder of Bréauté's life is easily told. Arriving in Normandy, he was imprisoned by Louis VIII in Compiègne, in revenge for his defeat of the French in England in 1217, but either papal intervention or his crusader's badge (assumed in 1221) saved him from death, and he was released at Easter 1225. He then spent several months in Rome, where he laid a lengthy defence of his actions before the pope. This *querimonia*, a remarkable document taking up some fourteen pages in the printed edition of Walter of Coventry's *Memoriale*, was probably drawn up with the assistance of Robert Passelewe (d. 1252), who accompanied Bréauté to Rome. By way of a decidedly partial account of Bréauté's recent misfortunes—attributed to the malice of Archbishop Langton, Hubert de Burgh, and others unnamed—it begged the pope to ensure justice for a man excommunicated without cause, one who should be under papal protection as a crusader. Intended to secure papal support for Bréauté's reinstatement in England, it certainly appears to have aroused sympathy for him at the curia.

Departing for England, Bréauté was captured in Burgundy in August 1225 by a knight whom he had once imprisoned in England, but papal intervention secured his release. Meanwhile the papal nuncio, Master Otto, implored Henry III to restore his wife and lands to Bréauté, but without success. Bréauté afterwards resided at Troyes, but was expelled from the kingdom of France in 1226 because he refused to do homage to Louis VIII (r.

1223–6). He returned to Rome and was again promised papal help, but some time after 18 July he died at the church of San Ciriaco, allegedly from eating a poisoned fish, and was buried there. He had appointed Guala, the former legate to England, as the executor of his will and guardian of his son. This son, the only child of his marriage to Margaret de Revières, was possibly the Thomas de Bréauté who held a small portion of her inheritance in Oxfordshire in 1255. The dying Bréauté was said to have confessed that he had deposited 11,000 marks with the templars in London, from whom Henry III tried to recover them.

Assessment Falkes de Bréauté was variously described as the 'scourge of the earth', the 'rod of the Lord's fury', and 'a most evil robber' (*Memoriale fratris Walteri de Coventria*, *Memoriale*, 2.268–9; Paris, *Historia Anglorum*, 2.131; Paris, *Chron.*, 3.12). If Matthew Paris gives the most lurid details concerning him, it remains true that most other chroniclers also condemned him, while contemporary letters attest his unpopularity among the nobility, and the court rolls tell much of his rapacity as a sheriff and soldier.

Yet it is difficult to pinpoint exactly why Bréauté aroused such odium. Although the horrors of his pillages in eastern England appear to have been real enough, they were not unique. He sought to line his own pockets no more than many others among the regency, while he was often hated for reviving royal rights rather than for the pursuit of his own ambitions. Certainly incipient English insularity tarred Bréauté, a Norman, with the brush of the 'alien-born' Poitevins and Tourangeaux with whom King John had surrounded himself. But it was his pride and insolence, in one of low birth, that characterized the anecdotes told about him: his disdain for his peers and his aspiration to be the mightiest baron in England were widely noted. When the abbot of St Albans complained that Bréauté's millpond had damaged some of the abbey's crops at Luton, Bréauté expressed regret that he had not destroyed the entire yield. He was a benefactor of Newnham Priory, Bedfordshire, but the canons there remembered him chiefly for the destruction of their great church at Bedford to enlarge Bedford Castle, even though he probably did so on King John's orders, and they contributed stones for mangonels at the siege of Bedford.

With such forcefulness and insolence, Falkes de Bréauté won the affection of no one except his war-bands: Pope Honorius III, the bishop of Winchester, Llywelyn, and the earl of Chester all gave him support at different times, but were not so concerned for his welfare as to save him from ruin; and even his wife deserted him when the opportunity presented itself. Isolated and hated by 1224, Bréauté failed to see that he was no longer serving the king's interests and that he had become a menace to the peace of the realm; his proud refusal to recognize his true position in England eventually caused his ruin.   D. J. POWER

Sources Paris, *Chron.* · *Ann. mon.*, vols. 1, 3, 4 · *Memoriale fratris Walteri de Coventria | The historical collections of Walter of Coventry*, ed. W. Stubbs, 2 vols., Rolls Series, 58 (1872–3) · F. Michel, ed., *Histoire des ducs de Normandie et des rois d'Angleterre* (Paris, 1840) · *Radulphi de*

Coggeshall chronicon Anglicanum, ed. J. Stevenson, Rolls Series, 66 (1875) · *Gesta abbatum monasterii Sancti Albani, a Thoma Walsingham*, ed. H. T. Riley, 3 vols., pt 4 of *Chronica monasterii S. Albani*, Rolls Series, 28 (1867–9) · *Matthaei Parisiensis, monachi Sancti Albani, Historia Anglorum, sive … Historia minor*, ed. F. Madden, 3 vols., Rolls Series, 44 (1886–9) · *Rogeri de Wendover liber qui dicitur flores historiarum*, ed. H. G. Hewlett, 3 vols., Rolls Series, [84] (1886–9) · *The historical works of Gervase of Canterbury*, ed. W. Stubbs, 2 vols., Rolls Series, 73 (1879–80) · T. Stapleton, ed., *De antiquis legibus liber: cronica majorum et vicecomitum Londoniarum*, CS, 34 (1846) · Chancery records (RC) · PRO · P. Chaplais, ed., *Diplomatic documents preserved in the Public Record Office*, 1 (1964), 1101–272 · W. W. Shirley, ed., *Royal and other historical letters illustrative of the reign of Henry III*, 1, Rolls Series, 27 (1862) · *Curia regis rolls preserved in the Public Record Office* (1922–) · Pipe rolls · J. Godber, ed., *The cartulary of Newnham Priory*, 1 vol. in 2 pts, Bedfordshire Historical RS, 43 (1963–4) · L. Delisle and others, eds., *Recueil des actes de Henri II, roi d'Angleterre et duc de Normandie, concernant les provinces françaises et les affaires de France*, 4 vols. (Paris, 1909–27) · K. Norgate, *The minority of Henry III* (1912) · D. A. Carpenter, *The minority of Henry III* (1990) · J. Le Maho, *L'apparition des seigneuries châtelaines dans le Grand-Caux à l'époque ducale*, Archéologie Médiévale, 6 (1976), 3–148 · VCH Oxfordshire, vol. 6 · GEC, *Peerage*, new edn, vols. 4, 8
Likenesses M. Paris, portrait (at death), repro. in Carpenter, *Minority of Henry III*, pl. 14 · drawing, CCC Cam., MS 16, fol. 64v [*see illus.*]

Brechin, Sir David (*b.* before **1278**, *d.* **1320**), soldier and landowner, was the son of Sir William Brechin, son of Henry, illegitimate son of David, earl of Huntingdon (*d.* 1219); his mother was Elena, daughter of Alexander Comyn, earl of Buchan. His father died between 1286 and June 1291 (when no claim to the Scottish throne was submitted by him); on 10 December 1292 David was still a minor, though of marriageable age. He was presumably of age when doing homage to Edward I in August 1296, and must have fought against him at Dunbar, for he was bound to serve Edward in France in 1297. He returned to Scotland and took up the patriotic cause; as a knight he was in the retinue of Robert Bruce, earl of Carrick, at Peebles on 20 August 1299, and was wounded in an assault on the English garrison of Lochmaben in September 1301. He submitted to Edward with the rest of the Scottish community in February 1304, renewing his homage with his wife, Margaret, at Stirling on 7 July.

The killing of John Comyn of Badenoch in February 1306 threw Brechin, given his kinship with the Comyns of Buchan, firmly into the anti-Bruce camp, and he seems to have been taken prisoner at Brechin Castle by John Strathbogie, earl of Atholl, in April–May 1306. After the defeat of Bruce and Atholl at Methven on 19 June 1306 he was freed, and was active as a commander for Edward I and Edward II. He served with others of the Anglo-Scottish leadership at Ayr in July–August 1307, when they collectively borrowed 5000 merks from Sir Ralph de Monthermer. Thereafter he went north to be keeper of Aberdeen Castle and with Sir John (I) Mowbray, guardian north of Tay, and inadequate forces resisted Robert I's guerrilla campaign between Aberdeen and Inverness after September 1307. Having compelled the invalid king to withdraw from Slioch at Christmas, they encountered increasing difficulty in 1308; finally on 23 May 1308 their force broke and

fled at Inverurie. Robert ravaged Buchan, took Aberdeen, and cleared the north-east. At Christmas 1308 Forfar fell, but a truce protected the remaining English position. About this time (when there are many writs to and about pro-English Scots) the only reference to Brechin is a gift of wine by Edward II on 8 July 1308 or 1309. He must have been taken prisoner, presumably at Brechin again, in 1309, and then pretended to submit to King Robert, for on 15 June 1310 he was an adherent of the Scots seeking to submit to Edward.

This Brechin did, apparently with the help of his wife, and in March 1312 claimed that he had been in command at Dundee, with thirty men-at-arms, from 24 June 1311. Although his men were still there, he must have gone to Edward II at York by early February 1312, to obtain help for the beleaguered garrison, which surrendered in early April. On 20 April he was made keeper of Berwick, with orders to send men to relieve Dundee, but when its fall was known, he was relieved of Berwick (3 May). Perhaps he had sailed to Dundee, for he was seized once more, nothing being heard of him until his wife had leave on 4 October 1314 to go to Scotland to secure his freedom. The threat of forfeiture in November 1314 probably moved him to adhere to Robert I, but he was never in that king's favour. In 1317 he made overtures to Edward II through Andrew Harclay, recently released as a prisoner from Scotland, and was offered the English king's peace, yet he stayed in Scotland. In 1318–20 he witnessed two charters of Robert I, before becoming involved in the mysterious conspiracy which took him and others to trial in parliament in August 1320, just three months after his wife had sealed on his behalf the letter to the pope in defence of Scottish freedom, the Declaration of Arbroath.

Brechin's crime, for which, despite being a knight, he was hanged at Perth in August 1320, is said by Barbour to have been that he knew of, but did not reveal, the conspiracy. This is difficult to believe, since the same source ascribes to William Soulis both authorship of the plot and the desire to take the throne—and he was only imprisoned. Barbour's story comes from an Umfraville source very sympathetic to Brechin (Barbour calls him the 'good' Sir David), which sought an excuse for Gilbert Umfraville's desertion of King Robert in 1320 in the harsh treatment of Brechin. It is much more likely that the aim of the conspirators was to secure a Balliol restoration without English lordship and that Brechin was deeply involved. Some who were tried were acquitted, so the justice was not Edwardian in a ruthless rage; one might reasonably be surprised that Brechin survived so long in Robert I's Scotland.

About 1299 Brechin married Margaret, heir of Bunkle and widow of Sir John Stewart, who was killed at Falkirk in 1298. She died after October 1314 and he married again. His second wife was Margery Ramsay, called 'de Rame[sei]' on her seal of 1320. His only known child, born of his first marriage, was a daughter, Margaret, who married Sir David Barclay; he received Brechin's lands from Robert I.

A. A. M. DUNCAN

Sources J. Barbour, *The Bruce*, ed. A. A. M. Duncan (1997) · J. Stevenson, ed., *Illustrations of Scottish history, from the twelfth to the sixteenth century*, Maitland Club, 28 (1834) · *CDS*, vols. 2–3, 5 · *Scots peerage*, 2.216–22

Bredon, Simon (*d.* 1372), physician and astronomer, came from Winchcombe, Gloucestershire, and by 1330 was a fellow of Merton College, Oxford, where he remained probably until 1348. In 1333 he visited the papal court at Avignon in the course of university administration. Academically he was notable in undertaking higher studies in both theology and medicine, and drew on both subjects in his later career. From 1348 he held a variety of ecclesiastical preferments. By 1355 he was in the service of Richard (II) Fitzalan, earl of Arundel (*d.* 1376), probably as a medical adviser, and in 1358 was at Hertford, attending Joan (*d.* 1362), the wife of David II of Scotland, from whom she was becoming estranged. In 1365 he was involved in a legal dispute as a result of his refusing to attend the prior of St Pancras at Lewes, where he had been a medical adviser since 1361, a post which he held in conjunction with his wardenship of the hospital of New Work at Maidstone. However, in his will of 1368 Bredon described himself as canon of Chichester and rector of Biddenden (Kent), which he presumably regarded as his principal positions.

A variety of mathematical, astronomical, and medical works have been ascribed to Bredon, but with the dearth of scholarly work on him much doubt remains. The Boethian arithmetic ascribed to him in Cambridge University Library, MS Ee.3.61, and other manuscripts seems simply to be an expanded version of a work often attributed to his older Merton contemporary Thomas Bradwardine (*d.* 1349). As Olaf Pedersen has shown, the *Theorica planetarum* often listed under his name is more properly attributed to Walter Bryt. Nor can the long work on arithmetic and its applications ascribed to him in a manuscript in the Bodleian Library, Oxford (MS Bodley 465) be regarded as genuine, not least because of its references to work by Nicole Oresme (*d.* 1382); the hand, moreover, should probably be regarded as Elizabethan rather than fifteenth-century, as often stated.

Possibly Bredon's most important work was his commentary on part of Ptolemy's *Almagest*, but this seems to have been the subject of scant scholarly study. He was certainly highly regarded as an astronomer; both John Ashenden (*d.* in or before 1368?) and Thomas Werkworth refer to him as in 1340 equating the motion of the eighth sphere 'with the greatest diligence', and his reputation extended to the sixteenth century, where he figured as one of John Dee's heroes of English science. In Oxford, Bodleian MS Digby 179, he is credited with a Latin translation (more probably, if by him, a revision or paraphrase of an existing one) of Ptolemy's astrological *Tetrabiblos*. There is also a treatise on the astrolabe ascribed to him in the British Library, Harley MS 321, and he certainly owned astrolabes. On the medical side, there is extant a small part of what probably was (or would have been) a huge medical work, the *Trifolium*: it seems to have contained little that was original and what survives has been described as 'excruciatingly dull' (Talbot, 'Simon Bredon', 22).

Examples of Bredon's hand are scattered among a fair number of medieval manuscripts, in particular what is now Oxford, Bodleian, MS Digby 178. A. G. Watson has shown that a large part of this, together with two manuscripts from the British Library, formerly constituted a single manuscript, which was probably one of those bequeathed by Bredon to Merton College. Among the items ascribed to Bredon's own hand are some marginal notes on square numbers, followed by notes on citations to the *Conics* of Apollonius of Perga that had been made by the thirteenth-century Polish scholar Witelo in book 1 of his *Perspectiva*. (These have puzzled recent scholars in that some of the relevant parts of Apollonius's work are not otherwise known to have existed in Latin in the thirteenth century.) Bredon gives the enunciations of Witelo's Propositions I.129 and I.131, and then remarks, *mirabilis et falsa* ('wonderful and false'), with a short explication. Witelo's expression is obscure and, allowing that he did not fully understand Witelo's intent, Bredon's criticisms have some force.

In his will of 1368 Bredon left cash, plate, vestments, scientific instruments, and especially books to a variety of individuals and institutions. Among the latter Merton College figured prominently, and among the former were William Heytesbury (*d.* 1372/3), the famous Mertonian logician and natural philosopher, whom Bredon also appointed as one of his executors. Bredon left his body to be buried at Battle Abbey if he died within a day's journey of it, and this is what may well have happened after his death in 1372.   GEORGE MOLLAND

Sources C. H. Talbot, 'Simon Bredon (*c.*1300–1372): physician, mathematician, and astronomer', *British Journal for the History of Science*, 1 (1962–3), 19–30 · Emden, *Oxf.* · C. H. Talbot, 'Bredon, Simon', *DSB* · F. M. Powicke, *The medieval books of Merton College* (1931) · *Richard of Wallingford: an edition of his writings*, ed. and trans. J. D. North, 3 vols. (1976) [Lat. orig., with parallel Eng. trans.] · J. D. North, 'The western calendar—"intolerabilis, horribilis, et derisibilis": four centuries of discontent', *Gregorian reform of the calendar: proceedings of the Vatican conference to commemorate its 400th anniversary* [Vatican 1982], ed. G. V. Coyne, M. A. Hoskin, and O. Pedersen (1983), 75–113; repr. in J. D. North, *The universal frame: historical essays in astronomy, natural philosophy, and scientific method* (1989), 39–77 · O. Pedersen, 'The problem of Walter Brytte and Merton astronomy', *Archives Internationales d'Histoire des Sciences*, 36 (1986), 227–48 · A. G. Watson, 'A Merton College manuscript reconstructed: Harley 625; Digby 178, fols. 1–14, 88–115; Cotton Tiberius B.IX, fols. 1–4, 225–35', *Bodleian Library Record*, 9 (1973–8), 207–17 · J. A. Weisheipl, 'Repertorium Mertonense', *Mediaeval Studies*, 31 (1969), 174–224 · M. Clagett, ed., *Archimedes in the middle ages*, 5 vols. (1964–84) · *Witelonis Perspectivae liber primus: Book 1 of Witelo's 'Perspectiva'*, ed. S. Unguru (1977) · S. Bredon, 'Trifolium', Bodl. Oxf., MS Digby 160, fols. 102–219 · J. B. Post, 'Doctor versus patient: two fourteenth-century lawsuits', *Medical History*, 16 (1972), 296–300
Archives BL · Bodl. Oxf., MS Digby 160, fols. 102–219 · Bodl. Oxf., MSS Digby 178, 179
Wealth at death considerable fortune in money, plate, books, and other personal property: will, Powicke, *Medieval books*, 82–6

Bree, Robert (*bap.* 1758, *d.* 1839), physician, was baptized at Solihull, Warwickshire, on 13 September 1758, the eldest of the nine children of Robert Bree (*b.* 1724), surgeon apothecary, and his wife, Mary, *née* Milward (*b. c.*1730). The Brees were a medical family, though Joseph Foster described Bree's father as a gentleman in 1775, the year that Bree left King Henry VIII School in Coventry to enter University College, Oxford. He graduated BA in 1778 and MA in 1781, and he also studied medicine at Edinburgh in 1780–81 as a pupil of John Brown (1735–1788), who advocated the therapeutic values of alcohol. Bree was admitted an extra-licentiate of the College of Physicians on 31 July 1781, and became MB in 1782 and MD on 12 July 1791. In 1781 he replaced Anthony Fothergill as physician at Northampton General Hospital but, unable to make a living there in competition with William Kerr, Bree moved in June 1784 to Leicester, where he had a large and lucrative practice. While there he married a Miss Johnson, from an old-established Leicestershire family. Bree held an honorary appointment at Leicester Infirmary, and he was a subscriber and the chairman of the governors in 1784. He was also one of the three physicians attending the Leicester Lunatic Asylum. However, chronic asthma caused him to retire from practice in 1793 and he served as a Leicestershire militia captain in East Anglia for a year (1794–5), a period which seems to have reduced his asthma.

Bree moved to Birmingham in 1796 and took a house in Edmund Street; he later moved to the Old Square. In March 1801 he was appointed one of the four honorary physicians at Birmingham General Hospital, a post from which he resigned on 18 March 1806; he also served the General Dispensary and, in 1803, with Edward Johnstone was one of the physicians advising the newly founded loyal volunteers in the town. From Birmingham, Bree moved to Hanover Square, London, where he attended the duke of Sussex, an asthmatic. He was admitted a candidate, on 31 March 1806, and fellow, on 23 March 1807, of the Royal College of Physicians; he was censor in 1810, 1819, and 1830, and Harveian orator in 1827. On 11 February 1808 he was elected FRS. He was vice-president of the Medical and Chirurgical Society in 1812. Bree gave up practice, still suffering from asthma, in 1833, and died at his home, Park Square West, Regent's Park, London, on 6 October 1839.

Bree published *A practical enquiry into disordered respiration: distinguishing the species of convulsive asthma, their causes and indications of cure* (1797), as well as papers on consumption, splenitis, and cholera (1799, 1811, and 1832).

ARTHUR H. GRANT, rev. JOAN LANE

Sources *Public characters of 1805* (1805) · E. R. Frizelle and J. D. Martin, *The Leicester Royal Infirmary, 1771–1971* (1971) · E. R. Frizelle, *The life and times of the Royal Infirmary at Leicester* (1988) · F. F. Waddy, *A history of the Northampton General Hospital, 1743–1948* (1974) · J. A. Langford, ed., *A century of Birmingham life … 1741–1841*, 2 vols. (1870–71) · J. Hill and R. K. Dent, *Memorials of the Old Square* (1897) · *GM*, 2nd ser., 12 (1839), 545 · Munk, *Roll* · Solihull register, Warks. CRO, DRB 64/2 · personal record, RS · U. Edin. · General Hospital governors' minutes, Birmingham Archives, MS 1423/1 · Foster, *Alum. Oxon.*

Breeks, James Wilkinson (1830–1872), administrator in India and anthropologist, was born at Warcop, near Borough, Westmorland, on 5 March 1830, the son of Richard and Elizabeth Breeks. He was educated at Blackheath proprietary school, and in 1847, on the recommendation of his uncle, Major Wilkinson, obtained a writership in the East India Company's Madras civil service.

Breeks arrived in India in December 1849. In July 1852 he was posted as assistant to the collector and magistrate of Bellary. In March 1855 he joined the accountant-general's office as an assistant and two years later became Canarese translator to the Madras government. In November 1858, after ten weeks as civil auditor for the Punjab, Breeks returned to the accountant-general's office. In April 1861 he became private secretary to the governor of Madras, Sir William *Denison, whose eldest daughter, Susan Maria, he married on 19 February 1863.

In 1864 Breeks returned to Britain with the intention of resigning the service on the grounds of ill health. He became a partner in the large China merchant house of Dent & Co. in London, but in 1867 the firm collapsed and he was forced back to India. Possibly on the representations of his father-in-law, the India Office took the unusual step of allowing him to rejoin the civil service.

From 4 January 1868 Breeks officiated as civil and sessions judge at Chittoor. In the following August he was appointed commissioner of the Nilgiris, a district with its headquarters at Ootacamund, the European sanatorium of the south. He and his wife were popular among Ooty's expatriates, probably not least because Breeks's years in the commercial world had rubbed off some of the reserve and officiousness of the typical civilian. As a couple they were praised for rising above the cliques and parochiality of a fashionable hill resort. They patronized many local educational and charitable undertakings and Breeks was further admired as a keen and able cricketer.

In 1871 the trustees of the Indian Museum at Calcutta called upon the government of India to assemble collections of artefacts which would illustrate 'the state of the arts among the aboriginal and other jungle peoples in India and its Dependencies'. In Madras Breeks was authorized to investigate the aboriginal peoples of the Nilgiris, of whom the Todas were the most well known. Breeks took to this early anthropological work enthusiastically, although with little of the systematization that would characterize the efforts of the next generation of official anthropologists. In addition to his collection for the museum, he drafted a lengthy and detailed report on the four tribes that he investigated, the Todas, Kotas, Kurumbas, and Irulas, before dying of a liver infection, contracted during his research in the hills, on 6 June 1872. The report, edited by his widow and illustrated with a large number of albumen prints, was subsequently published by government authority as *An Account of the Primitive Tribes and Monuments of the Nilagiris* (1873).

Breeks was survived by his wife, three sons, and a daughter. In his memory, the European residents at Ootacamund founded the Breeks Memorial School for the children of poor Europeans and Eurasians.

KATHERINE PRIOR

Sources *Overland Athenaeum and Daily News* [Madras] (12 June 1872) · *Madras Mail* (7 June 1872) · BL OIOC, Haileybury MSS · ecclesiastical records, BL OIOC · *An account of the primitive tribes and monuments of the Nilagiris. By the late James Wilkinson Breeks*, ed. [S. M.

Breeks] (1873) · C. A. Bayly, ed., *The raj: India and the British, 1600–1947* (1990), no. 389 [exhibition catalogue, NPG, 19 Oct 1990 – 17 March 1991]
Likenesses C. Silvy, carte-de-visite, 1860, NPG
Wealth at death under £3000: probate, 26 Sept 1872, *CGPLA Eng. & Wales*

Breen, James (1826–1866), astronomer, was born at Armagh, Ireland, on 5 July 1826, the second son of Hugh Breen, who superintended the lunar reductions at the Royal Observatory, Greenwich. In 1842, at the age of sixteen, he was engaged as a calculator at Greenwich, but exchanged the post for that of assistant in the Cambridge observatory in August 1846. In 1854 he published *The planetary worlds: the topography and telescopic appearance of the sun, planets, moon, and comets*, a useful little work, suggested by discussions on the plurality of worlds, showing considerable acquaintance with the history of the subject as well as the practical familiarity conferred by the use of one of the finest refractors then in existence. After twelve years' enthusiastic co-operation with James Challis, Breen resigned his appointment towards the end of 1858 and pursued the study of literature in Paris. In 1860 he went to Spain, and observed the total eclipse of the sun (18 July) at Camuesa with Wray and Buckingham of the Himalaya expedition. In the following year, after some months in Switzerland, he settled in London and studied literature and languages. He read much at the British Museum, and contributed regularly, but for the most part anonymously, to the *Popular Science Review* and other periodicals. He was elected a fellow of the Royal Astronomical Society in 1862. He had made arrangements for the publication of a work on stars, nebulae, and clusters, of which two sheets were already printed, before the consumption from which he suffered put an end to his plans. He died at 119 Pentonville Road, London, at noon on 25 August 1866, and was buried with his father at Nunhead cemetery.

A. M. CLERKE, *rev.* JOSEPH GROSS

Sources *Monthly Notices of the Royal Astronomical Society*, 27 (1866–7), 104 · Boase, *Mod. Eng. biog.*
Wealth at death under £200: probate, 3 Oct 1866, *CGPLA Eng. & Wales*

Bregowine [Bregwin] (*d.* 764), archbishop of Canterbury, succeeded Archbishop Cuthbert in 761. Two post-conquest lives of Bregowine were written at Christ Church, Canterbury, but contain little reliable information. Osbern of Canterbury claimed that he was a continental Saxon of noble parentage, brought up (somewhat improbably) as a Christian, drawn to Canterbury by the reputation of Archbishop Theodore (*d.* 690). Eadmer says that he owed his election to Æthelberht II of Kent (*r.* 725–62), but this may be little more than guesswork. All that can be said is that he was probably not, unlike his predecessors Tatwine, Nothhelm, and (perhaps) Cuthbert, of Mercian origin, though Mercian influence was growing in Kent during his episcopate. In 764 Offa of Mercia gave Islingham, Kent, to Bishop Eardwulf of Rochester, a grant made at Canterbury 'with the agreement and permission of our archbishop Bregowine' (*AS chart.*, S 105): 'the first occasion when a Mercian king granted bookland in Kent

in his own name' (Brooks, 112). The political tension between Offa and Cynewulf of Wessex contributed to Christ Church's loss of the minster at Cookham in what is now Berkshire, an area long disputed between Mercian and West Saxon kings. The church and its estate had been granted to Christ Church by Æthelbald of Mercia in the time of Archbishop Cuthbert, but after Cuthbert's death in 760, Cynewulf regained the region; two former members of Cuthbert's household then stole the title-deeds of Cookham and delivered them to the West Saxon king, who, despite Bregowine's protests, appropriated the minster and its lands (*AS chart.*, S 1258). Bregowine may have been able to acquire other lands for his church, but the early archives of Christ Church are lost; a chance survival, dated 762, records a grant of land in Canterbury itself, near Queningate, by Dunwald, thegn of King Æthelberht II, whose deed of gift acknowledges Bregowine's consent (*AS chart.*, S 1182).

Dunwald's gift was made as he was about to depart on a pilgrimage to Rome. Bregowine himself had visited Rome at some point, where he made the acquaintance of the Englishman Lul, archbishop of Mainz, disciple and successor of Archbishop Boniface. In a letter to Lul, Bregowine recalls their former meeting and expresses the wish to maintain spiritual and earthly friendship with the communities on the continent; he also informs Lul of the death, on 28 December, of another former pilgrim to Rome, the Kentish abbess Bugga, who had asked to be remembered to him.

What little is known about Bregowine suggests a man who strove to maintain both the endowment of his church and its wider spiritual associations. He died in 764, the date of his death being variously remembered as 24, 25, and 26 August, and was buried in the baptistery of Christ Church, where a cult later developed. In 1121–2 a German monk, Lambert, attempted to obtain his body for a monastery abroad, but died before he could fulfil his plan. It was perhaps this attempt to remove his remains which led to their translation into the chapel of St Gregory in the recently completed choir of the Romanesque cathedral in 1123, and Eadmer's composition of his life of St Bregowine.

ANN WILLIAMS

Sources N. Brooks, *The early history of the church of Canterbury: Christ Church from 597 to 1066* (1984) · *English historical documents*, 1, ed. D. Whitelock (1955) · A. W. Haddan and W. Stubbs, eds., *Councils and ecclesiastical documents relating to Great Britain and Ireland*, 3 (1871) · Eadmer, 'Vita S. Bregwini', *Patrologia Latina*, 159 (1854) · R. W. Southern, *Saint Anselm and his biographer: a study of monastic life and thought, 1059–c.1130* (1963)

Brekell [Breikell], **John** (*bap.* 1698, *d.* 1769), Presbyterian minister, was baptized in the parish of North Meols, Lancashire, on 28 January 1698, the son of Barnaby Breikell (1669–1728) and Jennett Thomasson. He was educated for the ministry at Nottingham under John Hardy. His first known settlement was at Stamford, apparently as an assistant, but he did not stay long. According to the Evans list, by 1729 he was assistant to Christopher Bassnett at the Key Street Chapel in Liverpool, and a letter of Henry Winder's, now lost, dated 2 June 1730, mentions him as a

Liverpool minister. His first entry in the Key Street baptismal register is on 6 April 1732, and he may have been admitted to the status of a colleague, after ordination, in April 1732. On 11 November 1736 he married Elizabeth Molyneux; they subsequently had five children. On Bassnett's death on 22 July 1744 Brekell became sole pastor.

During his long ministry Brekell published twenty-one books. In 1745 he corresponded with Philip Doddridge, discussing Doddridge's *Practical Discourses on Regeneration*, and Doddridge may have been the patron of Brekell's first publication, *The Christian warfare, or, A critical and practical discourse of making our calling and election sure: with an appendix concerning the persons proper to be admitted to the Lord's supper* (1742). After the 1745 Jacobite rising Brekell published several works in defence of the Hanoverian state, including an attack on the Manchester nonjuror Thomas Deacon's *A Full, True and Comprehensive View of Christianity*. An accomplished Hebrew and Greek scholar, he published a sermon on the word 'Euroclydon' in 1744, and in 1758 published his views opposing the introduction of vowel-points into the Masoretic text of the Old Testament. He also defended infant baptism in reply to John Gill, and engaged in print with Joseph Mottershead over the expediency of baptizing sick and dying infants.

Brekell's ministry was carried out against the background of a serious decline in the dissenting interest in Liverpool. In the 1750s and 1760s many leading lay members conformed, and in 1763 John Henderson, minister of the Benn's Garden Chapel, followed suit. In 1750 a group of theologically advanced Lancashire ministers proposed a reform of dissenting worship and the introduction of a liturgy. A bitter dispute over an ordination in Warrington in May 1750 led to the formation of 'private associations' within the district without Brekell's initial knowledge. These associations discussed reforming the practice of ordination among protestant dissenters and then 'turned their attention to another object, viz. The introducing set Forms of prayer among the Dissenters' (John Brekell to George Benson, 10 Sept 1751, Unitarian College collection, MS Box B1 11). Brekell opposed the plans for the liturgy in 1758, but the proposals had a huge influence in Liverpool. Leading members of the Benn's Garden and Key Street chapels who objected strongly to extempore prayer, yet who were unwilling to conform, issued on 16 October 1760 a request for a rational liturgy. Under the leadership of Thomas Bentley, subsequently Josiah Wedgwood's business partner, these dissenters built the Octagon Chapel in 1763 and established a new liturgy, published as *A Form of Prayer and a New Collection of Psalms* (1763). Brekell, whom Bentley believed represented a rather conservative Presbyterian hierarchy, collaborated with the new minister of the Benn's Garden Chapel, William Enfield, to publish *A New Collection of Psalms Proper for Christian Worship* in 1764. He published a further work on public prayer in 1765 and a pamphlet on church music in 1766.

From 1767 Brekell was assisted in his ministry by Philip Taylor, who succeeded him as minister. He did not live to see the Octagon Chapel experiment founder in 1776, as he

died on 28 December 1769. He was buried in the Toxteth Park Chapel. His ministry covered the period between the rise of the evangelical liberalism of Doddridge and the avowal of Socinianism by Joseph Priestley, to whose *Theological Repository* Brekell contributed in his later years under the sobriquet Verus. His religious beliefs undoubtedly modified over time: in *The Divine Oracles* (1749) he asserts the sufficiency of scripture against human traditions, which was then almost an article of faith among the Arminian dissenters, yet he sided with Athanasius against the Arians. His later treatment of the atonement showed Socinian influence, though he stood firm on the question of Christ's person. Henry Taylor, recalling him in 1822, wrote that he judged from Brekell's

> private conversation that he was an Arian. My friend, Dr Enfield who, some years after his death, had access to his papers, however, told me that from them he could ascertain him to have been in fact a Socinian. He passed with his people as an orthodox man; and from an idea, then very prevalent among free thinking ministers, he considered it his duty not to endanger his usefulness among them by shocking their prejudices. (Nightingale, 6.123)

JONATHAN H. WESTAWAY

Sources A. Gordon, MS additions to 'Brekell, John', *DNB*, JRL · *DNB* · letter from John Brekell to Samuel Bourne, Liverpool, 2 April 1751, JRL, Unitarian College collection, MS Box B1 11 · B. Nightingale, *Lancashire nonconformity*, 6 vols. [1890–93], vol. 6, pp. 118–39 · eleven letters from John Brekell to George Benson, 1745–57, JRL, Unitarian College collection, MS Box B1 11 · will, 8 Sept 1770, Lancs. RO, MS WCW · A. D. Holt, 'Benn's Garden Chapel', *Unitarian Historical Society Transactions*, 10/2 (1951–4), 91–101 · A. Holt, *Walking together: a study in Liverpool nonconformity, 1688–1938* (1938) · H. Brierley, *The parish registers of North Meols, 1594–1731*, Lancashire Parish Register Society, 66 (1929), 24, 28, 41–2, 43, 45–6, 50, 52, 54, 73, 107, 120 · J. Brekell, letter to George Benson, 15 Dec 1738, Lancs. RO, Sir Cuthbert Grundy papers, MS DDX 207/1/12 [containing an exposition of the word 'Euroclydon'] · *Calendar of the correspondence of Philip Doddridge*, ed. G. F. Nuttall, HMC, JP 26 (1979), 215 · R. Halley, *Lancashire: its puritanism and nonconformity*, 2 vols. (1869), vol. 2, pp. 324, 410n. · H. McLachlan, *English education under the Test Acts: being the history of the nonconformist academies, 1662–1820* (1931), 12 · D. Thom, 'Liverpool churches and chapels, their destruction, removal, or alteration: with notices of clergymen, ministers, and others [pt 1]', *Proceedings and Papers of the Historic Society of Lancashire and Cheshire*, 4 (1851–2), 139–41, 144–5 · J. Toulmin, *Memoirs of the Rev. Samuel Bourn* (1808), 177, 182

Archives JRL, Unitarian College collection, letters to George Benson, MS box B1 11 · JRL, Unitarian College collection, letter to Samuel Bourne, MS box B1 11 · Lancs. RO, letters to George Benson, Sir Cuthbert Grundy papers, MS DDX 207/1/12

Wealth at death see will, 8 Sept 1770, Lancs. RO, MS WCW

Brema, Marie [*real name* Mary Helen Fehrman] (1856–1925), singer, was born Mary Helen Fehrman on 28 February 1856 at 6 Grove Park, Toxteth, Liverpool, the daughter of Diederich Fehrman, a German merchant, and his wife, Cora Wooster Davis from Virginia. In 1874 she married Arthur Frederick Nicholas Braun (*b.* 1854), a commission merchant. A mezzo-soprano, she took singing lessons in 1890 with Bessie Cox, professor at the Guildhall School of Music, and George Henschel, and made her concert début on 23 February 1891 at a Saturday Popular Concert at St James's Hall, Piccadilly, under the name Bremer (a reference to her father's birthplace, Bremen). She made her opera début later that year, at the Shaftesbury Theatre, London, taking the role of Lola in the first English production of *Cavalleria rusticana*. Her career took off rapidly: in 1892 she stepped in at short notice to sing Guinevere in Bemberg's *Elaine* at Covent Garden when Blanche Deschamps-Jehin fell ill, and was a great success, returning in 1893 to sing Siebel in Gounod's *Faust*.

Marie Brema was the first British singer to appear at Bayreuth: Cosima Wagner engaged her for the 1894 festival, at a time when many of Wagner's original singers had retired and she needed new artists. As Ortrud in the first Bayreuth *Lohengrin*, Brema was the success of the festival; she also sang Kundry in *Parsifal*, and returned in 1896 and 1897 to sing that role as well as Fricka in *Das Rheingold*. After her Bayreuth season in 1894, she became internationally known as a Wagnerian singer. She toured America later that year with the Damrosch opera company, and was engaged for the 1895–6 season by the Metropolitan Opera Company in New York, where she made her début on 27 November 1895 as Brangäne in *Tristan und Isolde*, the first opera to be sung in the original German in that city. She sang Brünnhilde in *Die Walküre*, Ortrud in *Lohengrin*, Amneris in *Aida*, and also Orfeo in Gluck's *Orfeo ed Euridice*, a role she was to repeat many times, to great acclaim. She returned to the Metropolitan for the 1898–9 season, taking the part of Fidès in Meyerbeer's *Le prophète* as well as singing Fricka and Brünnhilde, and she made two appearances there in 1899–1900. She was a great success at the Paris Opéra when she sang Brangäne under Charles Lamoureux in 1899, and thereafter sang there often; she was the first to sing Brünnhilde in *Götterdämmerung* in German in Paris, under Hans Richter in 1902. In Brussels she was a sensation as Dalila in Saint-Saëns's *Samson et Dalila*. At Covent Garden she sang in the 1897 and 1898 seasons, and in the 1901 season she created the part of Beatrice in C. V. Stanford's *Much Ado about Nothing*. She made her final appearance at Covent Garden at the beginning of 1907, when she sang Fricka and Ortrud during the winter season of German opera.

In England Marie Brema made frequent appearances on the concert platform, especially at the important provincial festivals, including the Three Choirs Festival, in which she first performed in 1897 at Hereford, and she gave the first performances of several new works by British composers, notably singing the role of the Evil Spirit in Parry's oratorio *King Saul* at the Birmingham festival in 1894. She was a soloist in Elgar's *The Light of Life* at the Worcester festival in 1899, and it may have been this that led to her engagement to sing the part of the Angel at the first performance of Elgar's *The Dream of Gerontius*, conducted by Hans Richter on 3 October 1900 at the Birmingham festival. While she was a success in *Gerontius*, she seems to have been the only redeeming feature in what was otherwise a disastrous performance, although not all critics found her suited to the role. Elgar's friend Rosa Burley, while agreeing that Brema was the only singer to have any grasp of the emotions the music was meant to express, described her as 'a goddess from Valhalla if ever there was one' and as unsuitable for the part (Burley and

Carruther, 141–2). Elgar is said to have written the part for Clara Butt and felt that the tessitura did not suit Brema very well, but he asked her to sing it again at the performance he was to conduct himself at the 1902 Three Choirs Festival in Worcester Cathedral; she fell ill and was replaced by Muriel Foster, who became first choice for the Angel for many years to come. Brema sang the part only three more times, in 1903–4.

Although her voice was fading, Brema continued to perform until the First World War. She organized 'Miss Marie Brema's Opera Season', a series of operas sung in English and conducted by Frank Bridge at the Savoy Theatre in 1910–11, and sang Orfeo in her own production of *Orfeo ed Euridice*. The season also included the first English performance of *La Pompadour* (1902), by the Hungarian composer Emanuel Moór, and a new version of Handel's *L'Allegro ed il Penseroso*, with singers performing off-stage and a series of tableaux on the stage. In 1912 she toured the provinces with the Denhof opera company, and sang in the *Ring* cycle at the Wagner festival in Brussels.

Marie Brema taught at the Royal Manchester College of Music from 1912 and was appointed professor of singing there in 1913 (although she continued to live in London), and as director of the opera class she produced a student opera every year. She died on 22 March 1925 at 117 Cecil Street, Manchester. Her daughter, Tita Brand, an actress, was married to the Belgian poet Emile Cammaerts: her translation of his version of *The Two Hunchbacks*, a Belgian fairy tale, with incidental music by Frank Bridge, was first performed on 15 November 1910 as part of Brema's opera season at the Savoy Theatre, and Elgar wrote and conducted the background orchestral music for the recitation by Tita Brand of Cammaerts's poem *Carillon* at the Queen's Hall on 7 December 1914.   ANNE PIMLOTT BAKER

Sources G. Hodgkins, ed., *The best of me: a Gerontius centenary companion* (1999) · *The Times* (24 March 1925) · R. Burley and F. C. Carruther, *Edward Elgar: the record of a friendship* (1972), 141–2, 197–8 · M. Kennedy, *The history of the Royal Manchester College of Music, 1893–1972* (1971) · 'Miss Marie Brema's opera season', *MT*, 51 (1910), 789 · H. Rosenthal, *Two centuries of opera at Covent Garden* (1958) · G. Fitzgerald, *Annals of the Metropolitan Opera* (1990), 91 · F. Spotts, *Bayreuth: a history of the Wagner Festival* (1994) · *New Grove*, 2nd edn · H. S. Wyndham and G. l'Epine, eds., *Who's who in music* (1913) · Brown & Stratton, *Brit. mus.* · *IGI* · *WW* · b. cert. · d. cert.

Likenesses photograph, 1896, repro. in Spotts, *Bayreuth* · photograph, repro. in *The Times*, 18 · photograph, repro. in Hodgkins, ed., *The best of me*, 179

Breman [Braman], **John** (*bap.* 1627, *d.* 1703), army officer, politician, and conspirator, was baptized on 27 March 1627 at Alton, Hampshire, the eldest surviving son of Thomas Braman (*d.* 1661), mercer of Alton. He first appears in 1647 as one of the regimental agitators of the New Model Army horse regiment of Colonel Nathaniel Rich. The regiment was prominent in opposing parliament's demand to disband and he and his fellow agitator Nicholas Lockyer may have drawn up the regiment's petition of grievances in the spring of that year.

Breman remained with Rich's regiment until December 1654 when, now a lieutenant, he was implicated in the so-called Overton Plot, when papers criticizing the protectorate were circulated among troops in Scotland. Together with four fellow officers he was court-martialled in February 1655, cashiered, required to post bond for his good behaviour, and sent to England. Breman evidently remained on good terms with Rich, who had broken with Cromwell the previous year and had been deprived of his regiment, for when Rich was restored to his regiment in July 1659 by the Rump Parliament, Breman returned to it as well, now as a captain. Swiftly promoted major, he induced his troops to join a mutinous garrison at Portsmouth that had declared for parliament in December in the wake of an army coup, and which Rich's regiment had been sent to suppress. Rich, who had temporized with the coup, acquiesced in Breman's action, and when the regiment returned to London at the end of the month Breman was included in parliament's thanks. General Monck responded by removing Rich from his command on 26 February 1660. He and Breman tried to contest the order, but, on 1 March, Rich surrendered his commission, and Breman was dismissed as well.

Breman remained under close surveillance. In April he was arrested on suspicion of complicity in Colonel John Lambert's projected rising. A plot to free him from custody along with the former major-general James Berry was subsequently reported. In September 1661 the erstwhile parliamentary radical Praisegod Barebone visited him in prison. Breman and Berry were among those sent to the Tower for closer confinement on 18 May 1662, and Breman was later sent to Windsor Castle. In 1664 he admitted knowledge of weapons that had been brought into England from the Netherlands and New England. Upon his release the following year he returned to private life in Chichester, Sussex, worshipping as an Independent and apparently maintaining his links to radical activists such as Colonel Henry Danvers. His first wife, Sarah, died in 1657 and about 1665 he married Elizabeth (d. in or before 1696), widow of William Marlow of Itchingfield, Sussex, and daughter of Edward Osborne of Hartlip, Kent. However, the ceremony may have been performed by a fellow nonconformist, casting doubt over the marriage's validity.

In 1678 Breman was offered a commission by an old comrade in arms, Colonel Richard Norton, to serve in Flanders under Colonel George Legge, but declined, citing ill health and his long absence from military service. Two months later, however, he was observed with the prominent republican John Wildman, and was soon actively involved in the politics of the exclusion crisis. Breman served for Chichester in the parliaments of 1679, 1680, and 1681, and at the dissolution of the latter he was reportedly in correspondence with the veteran radicals John Gladman and Richard Rumbold. A consistent supporter of exclusion, he was described in September 1681 as 'a great fanatic' (Zaller, 93) and dissenters were reported to be supporting him for a county seat in the next election.

Breman remained a visible figure. In October 1682 he was projected as one of the leaders of a cavalry regiment in a plot promoted by the earl of Essex to seize Whitehall on behalf of the duke of Monmouth, the exclusionist candidate for the throne. In February 1683 he and his brother-in-law Richard Farringdon helped mount a demonstration in Chester on behalf of Monmouth. That same month his name appeared on a list of radicals purportedly plotting to raise an insurrection in London, perhaps in connection with a plot to assassinate the duke of York, the heir to the throne. In late July he was arrested and imprisoned in the Tower in connection with the planned general insurrection known as the Rye House Plot on the urging of the bishop of Chichester, who described him as a 'desperate' enemy to the king and 'as bad as a plague' locally (Zaller, 94). In October he successfully petitioned for his release, promising 'that he would live a private retired life etc and not serve in Parliament' (DWL, Morrice entring book P, 383). However, in July 1685 he conspired in Monmouth's abortive rising and was again arrested.

Breman was among the nonconformists briefly courted by James II in 1687 and 1688. In December 1687 he was appointed to a commission of inquiry to investigate unreported fines against dissenters and recusants in the previous ten years. The following May he was included in the Sussex commission of the peace, and in September he received both court and dissenter backing as a candidate for parliament. None the less he joined William of Orange's invasion army in November. In July 1689 he appeared as the major of a volunteer regiment of horse composed of London citizens, whose colonel was William himself. More substantial reward came in 1692 when he was appointed deputy governor of the Isle of Wight. On about 22 September 1696 he married his third wife, Elizabeth, widow of Thomas Mathew of High Street, Lewes, Sussex, and daughter of Thomas Meeres of Glynleigh House, Westham, in the same county. After this marriage he moved to Lewes and died on 25 August 1703. He was buried at All Saints', Lewes, and was survived by his wife.

ROBERT ZALLER

Sources CSP dom., 1660–61, 567; 1661–2, 82, 376, 449; 1677–8, 679, 680; 1680–81, 473; Jan–June 1683, 70, 358, 375, 385; July–Sept 1683, 3, 8, 111, 137; 1683–4, 38, 63 · B. D. Henning, 'Braman, John', HoP, Commons, 1660–90, 1.709–10 · The Clarke papers, ed. C. H. Firth, 4 vols., CS, new ser., 49, 54, 61–2 (1891–1901) · C. H. Firth and G. Davies, The regimental history of Cromwell's army, 2 vols. (1940) · R. L. Greaves, Deliver us from evil: the radical underground in Britain, 1660–1663 (1986) · R. L. Greaves, Secrets of the kingdom: British radicals from the Popish Plot to the revolution of 1688–89 (1992) · D. R. Lacey, Dissent and parliamentary politics in England, 1661–1689 (1969) · R. Zaller, 'Breman, John', Greaves & Zaller, BDBR, 93–4 · N. Luttrell, A brief historical relation of state affairs from September 1678 to April 1714, 6 vols. (1857) · R. Morrice, 'Ent'ring book', DWL, Morrice MS P · IGI

Wealth at death ordered property to be sold to provide £450 for widow; residue to be divided among nephews and nieces: Henning, 'Braman, John'

Brembre, Sir Nicholas (d. 1388), merchant and mayor of London, is of unknown origins, though he may have been related to Sir Thomas Brembre, or Bramber, a wealthy and well-connected royal clerk who was receiver of the king's chamber from c.1347 to 1354, and keeper of the privy seal in 1354–5. One of Thomas's associates was John Stodey, a rich London vintner, and some time before 1369 Nicholas married Idonia, one of Stodey's four daughters.

Nicholas Brembre himself was a member of the Grocers' Company, but, like many leading London merchants, made his fortune from wool. Possibly supported by Sir Thomas, in 1365 he was the biggest exporter of wool in London, shipping an 'almost incredible 1432 sacks' (Lloyd, 251). His marriage helped to consolidate his standing among the capital's principal merchants, with whom, and more especially with the merchants of the staple and (to his detriment, since it linked him with men suspected of exploiting their control of the city's food supply) the victuallers, he was to be associated throughout his career. Though he continued to deal in wool, for instance exporting 286 sacks in the year 1380/81, and leaving 150 sacks at his death, he also invested in property. In London his holdings were worth nearly £60 per annum at his death, and he had manors in Kent and Middlesex as well.

The London in which Brembre's career developed was always apt to disorder, but by the early 1370s was becoming tense and violent to an exceptional degree. Perennially contentious issues like the competition between native and alien merchants, and the friction between victualling and non-victualling guilds, were exacerbated by the effects of plague (there was another visitation in 1369), of a growing scarcity of specie, and of the weakness of the central government in the declining years of Edward III and the early years of Richard II. There were no French victories to compensate for heavy taxation; indeed, the government was unable to keep the seas safe for English shipping, thereby putting at risk both London's trade and her food supply. But successive kings needed the city's wealth, and though (as always) distrustful of the Londoners both for their habitual turbulence and for their potential weight in national politics, they were consequently ready to interfere in the affairs of the capital whenever they saw advantage in doing so. Opponents of the court followed suit.

In 1372 Brembre was elected sheriff. This first foray into civic politics was perhaps prompted by concern for the security of the wool trade after the Franco-Castilian victory at La Rochelle on 22 June. In the following year, with William Walworth, he became mayor of the Westminster staple. He was also one of the London merchants who in the early and mid-1370s sought greater influence with the crown by co-operating to make loans. However, in 1376 London's four MPs, who included Brembre's associates Walworth and John Pyel, supported the attacks made on the court in the Good Parliament of that year, while in the aftermath of the parliament opponents of the ruling oligarchy, led by John Northampton, whose rivalry with Brembre was to do much to disturb the peace of London for over a decade, took advantage of dissension within the city to secure changes in its government. Moreover the Londoners had aroused the enmity of John of Gaunt, duke of Lancaster, who attacked the judicial privileges of the city, prompting riots against him in February 1377. As part of London's subsequent bid to achieve reconciliation with the government, in which Gaunt was now dominant, the mayor, Adam Stable, was dismissed on 21 March, and replaced by Brembre.

At the head of a regime in which the wool merchants were dominant Brembre secured a new charter for London, issued on 4 December 1377, which confirmed the city's privileges and restricted the trading rights of non-citizens. But in spite of his efforts to maintain order, the city remained volatile. On 8 March 1378 one of Brembre's sheriffs, the goldsmith Nicholas Twyford, hindered the mayor from making an arrest after a riot between the goldsmiths and pepperers, and was consequently deprived of his office. At about this time, too, a mob broke into the London house of Thomas of Woodstock, earl of Buckingham, who at the Gloucester parliament of October 1378 announced his intention of impeaching Brembre for the attack. Brembre, no longer mayor, persuaded the earl to drop his complaint in return for a gift of 100 marks, but could not save the previous year's charter, which was annulled.

Brembre displayed strength of character during the peasants' revolt of 1381. According to Froissart, he was responsible for summoning the London militia and surrounding the insurgents after Wat Tyler was killed at Smithfield on 15 June. Knighted by Richard II shortly afterwards, he was licensed to act against former rebels in and around London. In November 1381 Northampton was elected mayor, and remained in office for two years. His introduction of ordinances establishing a free trade in foodstuffs was probably of little concern to those wealthy merchants who made most of their money from other forms of trade, and who may have hoped that Northampton's influence with John of Gaunt would help defend the general interests of the city. Brembre, however, was unconvinced. He did not vote for Northampton's re-election in 1382, and sought to increase his own influence with the king by securing loans for him from London. His misgivings were confirmed when Northampton secured a parliamentary statute that barred the victuallers from holding judicial office in the city—an act potentially highly detrimental to the grocers—even though it also restored the privileges London had lost in 1378.

In 1383 Northampton sought a third term as mayor. This time Brembre opposed him. The election was held in a tense atmosphere, amid allegations that Northampton was using force to prevent his opponents from voting. Brembre was victorious because, according to the *Westminster Chronicle*, he had the king's approval. Having failed to persuade Gaunt to have the election annulled, Northampton organized resistance to the new mayor, on 7 February 1384 summoning a large gathering which he led through the city. Hearing about the assembly while he was at dinner, Brembre hurried to the scene and ordered Northampton to accompany him. Northampton refused, whereupon Brembre arrested him and his brother. Further disturbances followed, and on 11 February one John Constantine, a cordwainer who was probably a relation of Northampton by marriage, was tried and executed in Cheapside on Brembre's initiative for trying to raise an insurrection. Brembre subsequently promoted Northampton's prosecution for treason before the king, who sentenced him to life imprisonment.

On 26 November 1383 Brembre had obtained a further new charter for the city, rescinding the prohibition against victuallers holding office. Although his position in London's factional politics was essentially that of an upholder of the traditional oligarchy, represented by aldermen who were predominantly drawn from among the great merchants, he nevertheless sought to allay the fears of the lesser crafts who had supported Northampton, for instance by refusing to reinstate the fishmongers' monopoly of the retailing of fish. Nevertheless some of his actions as mayor caused resentment, such as his insistence that the London guilds should present their ordinances for approval by the city authorities. In 1384 he was re-elected mayor. Brembre was opposed by Nicholas Twyford. To prevent any disturbances he concealed armed men in the Guildhall, who rushed out as soon as a cry went up for Twyford, so that the latter's supporters fled. The *Westminster Chronicle* notes that although some people 'as far as they dared' called this election into question, 'Brembre none the less remained mayor throughout the ensuing year, with the especial approval of the king' (*Westminster Chronicle*, 103). That approval was undoubtedly linked to Brembre's ability both to lend money himself to the king—£1333 6s. 8d. in September 1382, for instance, and nearly £1000 in December 1384—and to organize corporate loans from the city.

In 1385 Brembre was elected mayor for a third term. By now he was becoming increasingly identified with the inner circle of the king's friends and advisers who dominated the government, and perhaps it was for that reason that in November 1386, apparently with Brembre's support, the fishmonger Nicholas Exton became mayor. In August 1387 Brembre attended the council at Nottingham at which King Richard questioned the judges as to the legality of the commission established by parliament in the previous year to investigate the government of the realm, and then, as opposition to the king grew, in November went back to London with Richard, subsequently trying to rally support for him there. He was later accused of having caused the citizens to swear an oath of allegiance to the king against his enemies. On 14 November, Brembre was one of the five royal favourites to be accused of treason by the *lords appellant. The latter were headed by Thomas of Woodstock, who may have continued to feel a personal hostility towards Brembre. On 26 December, following the battle of Radcot Bridge, Exton admitted the appellants to London, and on 1 January 1388 Brembre was arrested and imprisoned in Gloucester Castle.

Brembre's trial for treason, which took place before parliament at Westminster, began on 17 February. He faced numerous charges, including one of having had twenty-two Newgate prisoners summarily executed, as well as of accroaching the royal power and resisting the appellants. Refused a copy of the accusations, he pleaded 'guilty of nothing' as each charge was read out to him. He offered to rebut the charges by battle, but this was disallowed. When the king tried to defend him, 305 of those present threw down their gauntlets in support of the accusations.

Twelve peers were deputed to examine the charges, but reported that Brembre had done nothing worthy of death. Representatives of the London guilds were asked to say if he was guilty, but without result. Finally the mayor, aldermen, and recorder were summoned. Asked if they thought Brembre was aware of the treasons alleged by the appellants, they replied that 'they supposed he was aware rather than ignorant of them'. The recorder was then asked 'What, in that case, does that law of yours say?', to which he replied that 'anyone who, having knowledge of such matters, concealed instead of disclosing them, would be, and would deserve to be, punished by the loss of his life' (*Westminster Chronicle*, 315). This sufficed to secure his conviction, and on 20 February Brembre suffered the penalties of treason, being drawn on a hurdle to Tyburn and there hanged. He was buried in the church of the London Greyfriars.

Brembre died bravely. He recited prayers from the office for the dead on his way to the gallows, and on the scaffold 'his contrition and piety moved almost all the bystanders to tears' (*Westminster Chronicle*, 315). A wealthy man, his possessions at his death included £1073 in gold nobles. His widow married Sir Baldwin Raddington, the comptroller of the king's wardrobe. In London, Brembre remained a controversial figure, so much so that in 1391 the city authorities forbade any discussion of his or Northampton's opinions, as likely to provoke disorder. Clearly a man of great ability, he had the pre-eminent virtue of loyalty. His friend John Pyel (who was a mercer, a fact that shows that Brembre could make alliances that cut across trade rivalries), in his will of 1379, made an explicit profession of his faith in Brembre's trustworthiness, while his loyalty to Richard II cost him his life. At the same time, although he several times showed himself willing to conciliate political opponents, the fate of John Constantine, and, perhaps, some of the accusations made against him in 1388, both at his trial and in the pages of hostile chroniclers, show that he was as capable of using strong-arm methods as his adversaries. Perhaps it is true to say that Brembre was a man whose misfortune it was to be undone by his virtues as well as by his shortcomings.

ANDREW PRESCOTT

Sources L. C. Hector and B. F. Harvey, eds. and trans., *The Westminster chronicle, 1381–1394*, OMT (1982) · *Knighton's chronicle, 1337–1396*, ed. and trans. G. H. Martin, OMT (1995) [Lat. orig., *Chronica de eventibus Angliae a tempore regis Edgari usque mortem regis Ricardi Secundi*, with parallel Eng. text] · R. Bird, *The turbulent London of Richard II* (1949) · P. Nightingale, *A medieval mercantile community: the Grocers' Company and the politics and trade of London, 1000–1485* (1995) · C. Barron, *Revolt in London: 11th to 15th June 1381* (1981) · T. H. Lloyd, *The English wool trade in the middle ages* (1977) · A. B. Beaven, ed., *The aldermen of the City of London, temp. Henry III–[1912]*, 2 vols. (1908–13) · R. R. Sharpe, ed., *Calendar of letter-books preserved in the archives of the corporation of the City of London*, [12 vols.] (1899–1912), vol. H · A. H. Thomas and P. E. Jones, eds., *Calendar of plea and memoranda rolls preserved among the archives of the corporation of the City of London at the Guildhall*, 6 vols. (1926–61) · H. T. Riley, ed., *Memorials of London and London life in the XIIIth, XIVth, and XVth centuries* (1868) · Tout, *Admin. hist.*, vols. 3–4 · A. Tuck, *Richard II and the English nobility* (1973) · A. Goodman, *The loyal conspiracy: the lords appellant under Richard II*

(1971) • G. Holmes, *The Good Parliament* (1975) • S. L. Thrupp, *The merchant class of medieval London, 1300–1500* (1948)
Wealth at death £60 p.a. from property in London: Thrupp, *Merchant class*, 326 • manors in Kent and Middlesex

Bremer, Sir James John Gordon (1786–1850), naval officer, was born on 26 September 1786, the son of Lieutenant James Bremer RN (*d.* 1786) and his wife, Ann, daughter of Captain James Norman RN. He was entered as a first-class volunteer on board the guardship *Sandwich* at the Nore in 1794. This was only for a few months; in October 1797 he was appointed to the Royal Naval College at Portsmouth, and was not again embarked until 1802, when he was appointed to the *Endymion* as a midshipman under Captain Philip Durham. For the next fourteen years he was actively and continuously serving in different parts of the world. He was made lieutenant on 3 August 1805, commander on 13 October 1807, and captain on 7 June 1814, but had no opportunities for any special distinction. He married, on 27 March 1811, Harriet (*d.* 1846), daughter of Thomas Wheeler of Waterford, and widow of the Revd George Henry Glasse. They had two sons and four daughters, the eldest of whom married Captain (afterwards Admiral) Sir Leopold Kuper. On 4 June 1815 Bremer was made a CB, and on 24 October 1816, while in command of the frigate *Comus*, he was wrecked on the coast of Newfoundland. In February 1824 he was sent, in command of the *Tamar*, to choose a site for a British settlement on the north coast of New Holland, which would enable British merchants to break the Dutch trade monopoly in the East Indies. He sailed from Sydney and chose a site (Fort Dundas) on the western shore of Melville Island, Australia. In September he took formal possession, left a garrison and convicts, and in November sailed to India. He continued an enthusiast for the expansion of British trade in the Malay areas. On 25 January 1836 he was made a KCH, and in the following year was appointed to the frigate *Alligator*, and again went out to Australia, where, attempts to colonize Melville Island having failed, he formed a settlement at Port Essington, which he left in June 1839; it failed and was abandoned in 1849. From there he returned to India, where, by the death of Sir Frederick Maitland in December 1839, he was left senior officer for a few months, until superseded by Rear-Admiral Elliot in July; he was again senior officer in the following November, when Admiral Elliot invalided, until the arrival of Sir William Parker in August 1841. Sir Gordon Bremer had thus the naval command of the expedition to China during the greater part of the years 1840–41, with the local rank of commodore, for which services he received the thanks of parliament, and was made KCB on 29 July 1841. In April 1846 he was appointed second in command of the channel squadron, with his broad pennant in the *Queen*, and in the following November was appointed commodore-superintendent of Woolwich Dockyard, a post he held for the next two years. He attained his flag on 15 September 1849, but died a few months later, on 14 February 1850, at Compton, near Plymouth. Bremer was an able sea officer, but one incapable of rising to the opportunities opened up in China. 　　J. K. Laughton, *rev.* Andrew Lambert

Sources G. S. Graham, *Great Britain in the Indian Ocean: a study of maritime enterprise, 1810–1850* (1967) • G. S. Graham, *The China station: war and diplomacy, 1830–1860* (1978) • *AusDB* • *GM*, 2nd ser., 33 (1850), 534 • O'Byrne, *Naval biog. dict.*

Bremner, David (1818/19–1852). *See under* Bremner, James (1784–1856).

Bremner, James (*c.*1712–*c.*1780). *See under* Bremner, Robert (*c.*1713–1789).

Bremner, James (1784–1856), civil engineer and shipbuilder, was born at Keiss, in the parish of Wick, Caithness, on 25 September 1784, the youngest of nine children of James and Janet Bremner. He resembled his soldier father in his robust physique and in his fearless character, which emerged early in life. He received a limited education before, in 1798, being apprenticed to the Greenock shipbuilders Steele and Carswell, later Robert Steele & Co. While there he was able to study the improvements made to Greenock harbour in 1804. He went to sea as a ship's carpenter and made two voyages to North America. It was his intention to set up as a shipbuilder in Canada, but he was dissuaded by friends and he returned to Wick about 1809. There he married Christina Sinclair (1791–1856), with whom he had five daughters and three sons. His sons all followed their father's calling as engineers and **David Bremner** (1818/19–1852) showed particular promise as resident engineer for the Clyde Trust before his premature death at the age of thirty-three.

James Bremner established a shipyard at Pulteneytown, on the eastern side of Wick, where he is said to have built fifty-six vessels in all. Experience of the ferocity of the local seas and his intuitive command of engineering principles informed his work on harbour construction. In all he was engaged on nineteen such projects, mainly around Caithness, including major works at Lossiemouth and Pulteneytown itself. Through his friendship with Sir John Sinclair, he was introduced to Marc Isambard Brunel and also to Thomas Telford, who took him to the Institution of Civil Engineers. Bremner was elected a corresponding member of the institution in 1833 and received a Telford medal in 1844 for his papers on harbour construction.

His skill in the lucrative business of salvage was proven on numerous occasions and he is credited with raising or refloating 236 vessels during his career. His ingenuity was well illustrated when he used the timber cargo of a ship to make a raft with which to salvage it. When the steamship *Great Britain* was stranded in Dundrum Bay and extensive efforts to refloat her by Brunel and others proved unavailing, Bremner was at last approached. Assisted by his eldest son, Alexander, he successfully refloated the vessel in September 1847. By this time Bremner was ordinarily engaged as the Wick agent of the Aberdeen, Leith and Clyde Shipping Company, in which role Hugh Miller encountered him. Miller felt regret that a man of such singular talents could have reached this stage in life only to occupy a position far below his worth. He described him as the 'Brindley of Scotland' (Miller, 387) in tribute to his untutored genius, but there was little about Bremner himself which suggested any consciousness of underachievement.

In personality he was both humorous and forceful, with a quick temper more than offset by his open-handed generosity. Joseph Mitchell wrote of him as 'very amusing, making friends with every one he meets by his kindly and rattling manner and the liberality of his payments' (Mitchell, 1.229). In 1845 Bremner published a *Treatise on the Planning and Constructing of Harbours* which drew on his experiences. At the Great Exhibition of 1851 he exhibited plans and models relating to his various endeavours. He died suddenly at his home in Harbour Place, Pulteneytown, on 12 August 1856, three months after his wife.

G. C. BOASE, rev. LIONEL ALEXANDER RITCHIE

Sources PICE, 16 (1856–7), 113–20 · J. Bremner, *Treatise on the planning and constructing of harbours: in deep water, on submarine pile-driving; the preservation of ships stranded; and raising of those sunk at sea; on principles of lately patented inventions* (1845) · J. Mowat, *James Bremner, wreck raiser* [1973] · *Memoir of the late Mr James Bremner, CE* (1856) · A. S. Cowper and I. Ross, eds., *Caithness monumental inscriptions (pre 1855)*, 2 (1992), 43–4 · J. Mitchell, *Reminiscences of my life in the highlands*, 1 (1883), 227–41 · H. Miller, *The cruise of the Betsey* (1858), 382–7 · *John O'Groat Journal* (26 Nov 1993)
Likenesses portrait, c.1833

Bremner [Brymer], **Robert** (c.1713–1789), music publisher, may have been born in Edinburgh on 9 September 1713, the son of John Brymer and Margaret Urie, possibly episcopalians whose occupations are unknown, and, if this identification is correct, younger brother to **James Bremner** (c.1712–c.1780), composer and music teacher, who may have been the James Brymer baptized in Edinburgh on 15 August 1712. Although nothing is known of Robert's early life, he probably had a musical background and access to capital when he started his Edinburgh music business in 1754.

By 1755 Bremner was supplying music to the influential Edinburgh Musical Society, and seemed confident of his future, since he married Margaret Bruce on 30 May 1756 in Edinburgh; their children were Charles (b. 11 Feb 1759), James (b. 6 Aug 1760), and Ellen. In 1756 Bremner also published his own *Rudiments of Music*, which supported the remarkable reform of Scottish Presbyterian church music started by the former English soldier Thomas Channon in Aberdeenshire.

Of psalm-singing's past, Bremner wrote that:

there arose such a Mass of confusion and Discord as quite debased this the noblest part of Worship. This they called the old Way of singing, for which there were many Advocates, though in fact it was the new, or rather no Way at all. (Johnson, 'Bremner', 187)

Bremner's solution included canticles, anthems, new psalms, and, remarkably, a canon by William Byrd, all part of 'the first official expansion of the [church] repertory beyond the "twelve" [statutory psalms]' (Johnson, *Music and Society*, 179).

In 1757 Bremner published Nicolo Pasquali's best-seller *Thorough-Bass Made Easy* and began issuing his own skilfully arranged *Collection of Scots Reels or Country Dances* (1757–61), which included the first tunes published and

identified as strathspeys. A successful businessman, he purchased William McGibbon's books and music, on that composer's death, and in 1759 reprinted his Scots tune collections in four volumes.

Both Robert and his brother James worked for the Edinburgh Musical Society, which sent James, 'young Bremner' (Krauss, 261), to London to study guitar with Geminiani. Robert published *Instructions for the Guitar*, probably written by James, in 1758. James studied violin in Naples, with the society's support, and then in 1763 moved to Philadelphia, where he taught harpsichord, flute, and guitar, initiated subscription concerts (perhaps modelled on Edinburgh's), and became a friend of Francis Hopkinson, a signer of the American Declaration of Independence, who was considered the 'country's first native composer' (ibid., 261). James died around 1780, presumably in Philadelphia. Meanwhile, Robert became an agent for the Edinburgh Musical Society, travelling to London and Dublin searching for talented musicians and singers for the society's concerts. In 1761 he was shrewd enough to publish the first orchestral pieces in the Mannheim style by a British composer, 6 Overtures, Op. 1, by Thomas Erskine, sixth earl of Kellie, which later had an American première in James's Philadelphia concerts (1765).

Leaving a manager in his Edinburgh shop, 'at the sign of the Golden Harp', opposite Blackfriars Wynd, Robert Bremner moved to London in 1762, where he probably lived over his premises 'At the Harp and Hautboy, opposite Somerset House in the Strand' (Glen). There he re-issued Kellie's works and published *A Plan for Teaching a Croud* (1762), 'an instruction manual describing how to start parish choirs from scratch in a country town' (Johnson, *Music and Society*, 179).

As well as continuing his successful dance music series, including reprints of earlier Scottish compositions and collections, Bremner's London publications included English and Italian operas, English, Scots, and Masonic songs, and a wide range of other instrumental music. As a music dealer and collector, he astutely purchased the most extensive and important collection of music by William Byrd, John Bull, Orlando Gibbons, and others, now known as the Fitzwilliam virginal book (Cambridge University Library).

Bremner was no doubt well-respected and well-to-do by the time of his death on 12 May 1789 at his home in Kensington Gore. According to Johnson his 'stock, plates and copyrights were bought by Preston and Son, who described their purchase as "not only the most extensive, but also the most valuable list of works ever exhibited in this kingdom"' (Johnson, 'Bremner', 187). In his will Bremner left the greatest part of his estate to his daughter, Ellen, while his two sons, Charles and James, were left £761 13s. 1d. each.

MARY ANNE ALBURGER

Sources M. A. Alburger, *Scottish fiddlers and their music* (1983); repr. (1996) · G. S. Emmerson, *A social history of Scottish dance* (1972) · J. Glen, *The Glen collection of Scottish dance music*, 2 (1895) · C. Gore, *The fiddle music index* (1995) · D. Johnson, *Music and society in lowland Scotland in the eighteenth century* (1972) · [D. Johnson], 'Robert Bremner', *Music printing and publishing*, ed. D. W. Krummel and S. Sadie (1990), 187 · F. Kidson, *British music publishers* (1900) · A. M. Krauss, 'James

Bremner, Alexander Reinagle and the influence of the Edinburgh Musical Society on Philadelphia', *Scotland in America in the age of the Enlightenment*, ed. R. Sher and J. R. Smitten (1990) · *GM*, 1st ser., 59 (1789), 471 · old parish registers, Church of Scotland, Edinburgh · will, PRO, PROB 11/1180, fols. 34*v*–36*v*

Wealth at death at least £3046 12*s*. 5*d*.; greater part of estate to daughter; £761 13*s*. 1*d*. each to his sons: will, PRO, PROB 11/1180, fols. 34*v*–36*v*

Bremner, William John [Billy] (1942–1997), footballer and football manager, was born in Stirling on 9 December 1942, and was adopted by James Lobban Bremner, a coalman, and his wife, Bridget Bessie Newlands, on 18 February 1943. He was educated locally at Catholic schools: St Mary's primary and St Modan's secondary. His selection as a Scottish schoolboy international footballer attracted the attention of leading Scottish and English clubs, but he signed for the then struggling English first division club Leeds United in 1958. Despite making his first team début at seventeen in January 1960, he was at first extremely homesick, and the Leeds manager, Don Revie, eventually drove to Stirling to involve Bremner's girlfriend Helen McKay Vick (Vicky; *b*. 1942/3) in his efforts to hold the player. Gradually Bremner settled in Yorkshire, aided by his increasing success on the field and his marriage to Vicky on 14 November 1962.

Originally an outside right, Bremner became the fulcrum of the Leeds United midfield in the 1960s. Only 5 feet 5½ inches tall and weighing less than 10 stone, Bremner was nevertheless an extremely fierce tackler, highly energetic, and had a natural flair for organization and leadership. However, although he enjoyed much success, captaining Leeds to the league championship in 1969 and 1974, the FA cup in 1972, and the League cup and the Inter City Fairs cup in 1968, the club frequently failed to win major honours. Bremner's receipt of the footballer of the year award in 1970 was scant compensation for a season that saw Leeds win no trophy after being poised to win three. His autobiography, *You Get Nowt for Being Second* (1969), was perhaps titled more presciently than he realized.

Bremner made his début for Scotland's under-23 side in February 1964 and won his first full cap the following May. He captained Scotland in the world cup finals of 1974 and eventually won fifty-four caps, the last against Denmark in 1975. The total would have been more but for an incident over a Copenhagen nightclub bill which resulted in Bremner and four others being banned for life from the national side. Bremner's punishment (generally regarded as harsh) was only one of the more extreme among the controversies that punctuated his career. Revie's Leeds side took to new levels the gamesmanship that had become a marked feature of English football from the later 1950s, and Bremner's aggressive, hard-tackling style and willingness to harangue and dispute with referees to some degree typified the club's approach. Moreover, as journalists short of inspiration never tired of claiming, his temperament matched his red hair. Under Revie's influence Bremner became more self-disciplined, but he could never quite turn the other cheek. This was most famously displayed in the Charity Shield match in August

William John Bremner (1942–1997), by unknown photographer, 1965

1974 when he and Liverpool's Kevin Keegan were the first British players sent off at Wembley stadium. A brawl, which Bremner did not start, followed by a lengthy argument with the referee, earned them their dismissals, at which point they pulled off their shirts and threw them on the pitch. It is unfortunate that football folklore often focuses on the more distasteful aspects of Bremner's game. His passing ability was exceptional and he was especially adept at the disguised pass, drawing players onto him before dispatching the ball at the last moment and not always to the most likely places. He was also a useful goal scorer, scoring ninety football league goals in 586 games for Leeds.

Bremner left Leeds for Hull City in 1976, and played there for two seasons until a series of injuries effectively forced his retirement. In November 1978 he moved into football management, enjoying two spells with fourth division Doncaster Rovers between 1978 and 1985 (he played occasionally during this period) and from 1989 to 1991. He also managed Leeds from 1985 to 1988. Like many former players, his record off the pitch was far more modest than on it, though he piloted Doncaster to promotion from the fourth division in 1981 and again in 1984. His spell at Leeds coincided with a difficult period in the club's history and he was not alone in failing to reinvigorate it. After his resignation from Doncaster in November 1991 he spent the rest of his life as a media pundit and highly successful after-dinner speaker.

Bremner is remembered by many as easy-going and humorous. He and Vicky had a son, Billy junior, and two daughters, Donna and Amanda, and the couple remained happily together until his death at the Montagu Hospital, Mexborough, on 7 December 1997 from a heart attack following pneumonia. His funeral, prior to cremation at the Rose Hill crematorium in Cantley, was held at St Mary's Church, Edlington, near Doncaster, four days later. An iconic figure among Leeds fans, who admired not only his footballing skills but also his transparent affection for the club, he was subsequently memorialized by a statue erected outside Leeds's Elland Road ground.

DAVE RUSSELL

Sources B. Bale, *Bremner! the legend of Billy Bremner* (1998) · B. Bremner, *You get nowt for being second* (1969) · *The Times* (8 Dec 1997) · *The Independent* (8 Dec 1997) · *The Scotsman* (8 Dec 1997) · adopted children register, General Register Office for Scotland, Edinburgh · m. cert. · d. cert. · *The Guardian* (8 Dec 1997) · *Daily Telegraph* (8 Dec 1997)
Likenesses photographs, 1960–c.1975, Hult. Arch. [*see illus.*] · F. Siegelman, statue, 1999, Elland Road football ground, Leeds · portraits, repro. in Bale, *Bremner!* · portraits, repro. in Bremner, *You get nowt*
Wealth at death under £180,000: probate, 1998, *CGPLA Eng. & Wales* (1998)

Brenan, Beaumont (*d.* 1761), poet and playwright, was possibly a Roman Catholic, given his surname, which would explain why such a literary young man did not attend university. Baker's *Biographica dramatica* states that Brenan was a limner, although there is no other evidence to support this claim. Brenan became a close friend and literary associate of Edmund Burke when Burke was at Trinity College, Dublin. They seem to have been introduced by Richard Shackleton, son of Burke's schoolmaster at Ballitore, co. Kildare.

Burke's 'Hints for an essay on the drama' praises Brenan's *The Lawsuit* as a model comedy and describes the play, now lost, as concerning an iniquitous suit and 'low necessitous lawyers of bad character and profligates of desperate fortune'. Burke failed to get the play published by subscription in 1747. His *Punch's Petition*, addressed to Thomas Sheridan, manager of Smock Alley Theatre, sold hundreds of copies but was unsuccessful in persuading Sheridan to stage the play.

Henceforth, Sheridan was a target for the anger of the two young men. Burke wrote in March 1747 that Brenan 'has lately publishd a Thing called Fleckno's Ghost' (*Correspondence*, 1.88), but no copy has been traced. It was perhaps reworked or republished as *The Stage, or, Coronation of King Tom: a Satyr* (1753), which is a mock panegyric on Sheridan, modelled on Dryden's *Mac Flecknoe*. Brenan also contributed to Burke's weekly newspaper, *The Reformer* (January–April 1748), which took the reformation of the Dublin stage as its starting point in the reformation of manners and political morals in Ireland.

Brenan's verse *Congratulatory Letter from one Poet to another, on the Divorcement of his Wife* (1747) is a salacious satire on Matthew Pilkington's separation from his wife, Laetitia: it incorporates an imitation of the ribald tale (seventh day, novel 2) in Boccaccio's *Decameron*. Annexed to the *Congratulatory Letter* is a misogynist ballad, *The Female Combatants*, said to be based on a physical fight between Anne, Lady Prendergast, and a Mrs Phipps in 1745.

In 1748 Brenan contributed a poem to Mary Goddard's *Poems on Several Occasions*. Entitled 'An Answer to the Foregoing', it is a squib on the Virgilian pretensions of the preceding poem in the collection which was written by Burke. Mrs Goddard addresses young Brenan in a poem entitled 'To Mr B— on his Saying that he wou'd not be Content with a Lady's Heart without her Person' and with teasing flattery remarks that Brenan's 'superior charms' are those 'That captivate the soul'.

Brenan's poem 'To the Memory of Dr Swift' was prefixed to Sarah Cotter's Dublin edition of John Hawkesworth's *Life of Swift* in 1755. Brenan's best work, a bright and engaging farce called *The Painter's Breakfast*, was published in the following year. Probably inspired by Samuel Foote's *Taste*, Brenan's one-act 'dramatic Satyr' is similar to his *Lawsuit* in that there are no redeeming characters: he focuses on the cynical tricks of art dealers and the pomposity and greed of connoisseurs.

Brenan left Dublin for London in January 1758 and died there, unmarried, in the summer of 1761. Burke wrote to Richard Shackleton to tell him that Brenan died, 'after a very long and painful illness, in which however, he was exposed to no want, and which he bore with constancy. Sure he was a man of the first rate Genius, thrown away and lost to the world' (*Correspondence*, 1.142–3).

KATHERINE O'DONNELL

Sources *The correspondence of Edmund Burke*, ed. T. W. Copeland and others, 10 vols. (1958–78) · A. C. Elias, jun., 'Male hormones and women's wit: the sex appeal of Mary Goddard and Laetitia Pilkington', *Swift Studies*, 9 (1994), 5–16 · A. P. I. Samuels, *The early life, correspondence and writings of the Rt. Hon. Edmund Burke, LL. D.* (1923)
Wealth at death financial straits widely known; bankrupt: F. McLynn, *The Jacobites* (1985), 82

Brenan, Edward FitzGerald [Gerald] (**1894–1987**), writer and Hispanic scholar, was born on 7 April 1894 at Sliema, Malta, the elder son (there were no daughters) of Hugh Brenan, subaltern in the Royal Irish Rifles, and his wife, Helen, daughter of Sir Ogilvie Graham, cotton and linen merchant. Gerald, as he was always known, spent the first seven years of his childhood either travelling with the regiment in South Africa and India, or living in the family home of the Grahams, Larchfield, near Belfast. However, in 1901 Hugh Brenan became almost stone deaf as a result of malaria, and had to leave the army. Gerald was a precocious, imaginative little boy, and devoted to his mother, who stimulated his love of books and his interest in history, travel, and especially botany. He won an exhibition to Radley College, where he was extremely unhappy, and was awarded the Scott essay prize every year.

In obedience to his father's wishes, Brenan passed into Sandhurst. Detesting this prospect, at seventeen he concocted and carried out a wildly romantic scheme to escape with an older friend, a donkey, and very little money, and walk to Asia. His friend got no further than Venice, but Brenan plodded on alone, braving wolves and snowstorms until he gave up in the Balkans, after having

Edward FitzGerald Brenan (1894–1987), by Dora Carrington, 1921

covered over 1500 miles. His parents were relieved at the return of the prodigal, and—a year later—the outbreak of the First World War temporarily settled his future. He was commissioned into the 5th Gloucesters and in due course was sent to France, serving first with the cyclist corps, and later in charge of observation posts, fighting at Ypres, Passchendaele, and the Somme, and gaining the MC (1918) and the Croix de Guerre. It was in the army that he met Ralph Partridge and made the greatest friendship of his life, lasting as it did until Partridge's death in 1960, despite a violent breach over an affair with Partridge's first wife, Dora *Carrington.

Demobilized in 1919, Brenan was eager to get away from England, and acquire the education he felt Radley had failed to supply. With little equipment except his war gratuity and some 2000 books in various languages, including the classics, he embarked for Spain, thinking his war gratuity would last longer there, and rented a little house in the village of Yegen on the beautiful slopes of the Sierra Nevada. Here he began life in his adopted country, devoting himself to reading, walking immense distances in the mountains, and writing quantities of long and brilliant letters. He considered himself a 'writer' from the first, though he never finished his projected life of St Teresa of Avila, and his first publication was a picaresque novel called *Jack Robinson* written under the pseudonym George Beaton (1933), which received élitist rather than wide acclaim.

During his visits to London, Brenan made many literary friends, and when in Spain he was visited by Lytton Strachey, Virginia Woolf, Bertrand Russell, Roger Fry, David Garnett, and V. S. Pritchett, with their consorts. At his best a brilliant and amusing talker, Brenan's character was full of contradictions: he had a great capacity for prolonged and concentrated study as well as outstanding intelligence and originality in the interpretation of its results; he would often work far into the night, but he might collapse many times in a month with what he called 'flu'. *Jack Robinson* was followed by an unceasing output until the book of aphorisms, *Thoughts in a Dry Season: a Miscellany* (1978), in his eighties. *The Spanish Labyrinth* (1943), a brilliantly penetrating study of the history of modern Spain, and *The Literature of the Spanish People* (1951) were much admired in academic circles, while Brenan's knowledge of Spain took a form designed to appeal to the general reader in *The Face of Spain* (1950) and *South from Granada* (1957). The latter was one of his most successful and often reprinted books. Two volumes of autobiography, *A Life of One's Own* and *Personal Record*, followed in 1962 and 1974; he also wrote two more novels and a life of St John of the Cross, *St John of the Cross: his Life and Poetry* (1973).

As a young man Brenan was tall, sparely built, and agile; he had straight fair hair and small, nearly black eyes set wide apart in a face that was expressive and charming rather than good looking. He kept his agility until his seventies. In comparison with all his intellectual activity his emotional life ran an uneasy course. His love affair with Dora Carrington was far the most serious in his life, producing as it did an enormous two-way correspondence, some ecstasy, and considerable unhappiness on both sides. Otherwise he was obsessed by sex, and inhibited by fears of impotence. A stream of prostitutes, hippies, and peasant girls occupied his agitated thoughts and feelings and directed his travels. In 1930, while in Dorset, he met the American poet and novelist (Elisabeth) Gamel Woolsey who was then involved with the literary Powys family, especially Llewelyn. She was the daughter of William Walton Woolsey, plantation owner, of South Carolina. She and Brenan drifted into a relationship, and although their temperaments differed greatly—between his nervous excitability and her dreamy melancholy—they grew very close. In 1931 they went through a pseudo-marriage in Rome, ratified later in London. Gamel died of cancer in 1968. Brenan had one child, a daughter, Miranda, whose mother was Juliana Pellegrino, an unmarried girl from Yegen village. She was born in 1931 and later legally adopted by her father and Gamel, who took her to England to be educated. She died of cancer in 1980.

After the end of Franco's regime most of Brenan's books were translated, and he became a hero in Spain, receiving the Pablo Iglesias award. He was also appointed CBE (1982). In 1970 Brenan moved inland to a smaller house built to his own design, and here he spent his last seventeen years, while his eyesight and health gradually declined. He was cared for by Lynda Price and her husband, Lars Pranger. In 1984 the burden of his rapidly declining state led to his consenting to be taken by Lars to a home in Pinner, near London, to the great indignation of his Spanish admirers. This resulted in an extraordinary and much publicized sequel when two members of the

Junta de Andalucia flew to London, kidnapped Brenan, and took him back to Alhaurin, where they arranged for him to be nursed and cared for at his home. He died there on 19 January 1987.   FRANCES PARTRIDGE, rev.

Sources X. Fielding, ed., *Best of friends: the Brenan–Partridge letters* (1986) · J. Gathorne-Hardy, *The interior castle: a life of Gerald Brenan* (1992) · personal knowledge (1996) · *CGPLA Eng. & Wales* (1987)
Archives Ransom HRC, corresp. and literary papers | CUL, letters, mainly to Sir Samuel Hoare · CUL, letters to Viscount Templewood and others · King's AC Cam., letters to W. J. H. Sprott · McMaster University, Hamilton, Ontario, letters to Bertrand Russell · U. Sussex, corresp. with Virginia Woolf · U. Sussex, corresp. with Leonard Woolf
Likenesses D. Carrington, oils, 1921, NPG [*see illus.*] · J. Hope-Johnstone, two photographs, c.1922, NPG · photograph, c.1924, Hult. Arch. · D. Carrington, oils (as a young man)
Wealth at death £1504: probate, 2 Dec 1987, *CGPLA Eng. & Wales*

Brenan, John (b. 1625, d. in or after 1692), Roman Catholic archbishop of Cashel, was born in Kilkenny, the son of a merchant in the city, and of the stock of the landed gentry family of O Brenan of Uí Duach to the north of Kilkenny. The name of his mother has not been preserved. No details have survived of his early life or schooling, but in his youth the Roman Catholics in places such as Kilkenny could maintain schools because they still retained their land and property. On 12 February 1647 he sailed from Waterford harbour for Rome under the tutelage of Pierfrancesco Scarampi, sent as papal envoy to the Irish confederate Catholics in 1643. Another young Irishman who sailed with him was Oliver Plunket, the future archbishop of Armagh. He and John Brenan became lifelong friends. When they arrived in Rome on 15 June they applied for admission to the Irish College there, but they had to wait for a year until places became vacant. Both proved to be brilliant students at the Jesuit Collegio Romano, and were ordained priests at the end of their course. The date of Brenan's ordination has not been located, but it is reasonable to infer that he was ordained on the same day as Oliver Plunket, 1 January 1654. At this date Ireland had been conquered by the army of the English Commonwealth, and there was almost universal confiscation of Roman Catholics' property and sharp persecution of their religion. It was impossible for priests to return to Ireland, and Brenan continued his studies for two or three years and secured his doctorate in theology. Both he and Oliver Plunket found employment in Rome as teachers of philosophy and theology in the missionary college of *propaganda fide*.

With the Restoration in 1660 religious persecution was relaxed in Ireland, but very little confiscated property was restored. The Roman Catholic church began cautiously to reorganize its mission. It was the end of the decade before it was judged politic to appoint bishops. Oliver Plunket was appointed archbishop of Armagh on 4 July 1669 and John Brenan bishop of Waterford and Lismore on 6 May 1671. He was consecrated bishop in Rome on 6 September, and had arrived in Ireland before the end of November. Here a practical compromise seemed to be emerging in a situation where the great majority were Roman Catholics, for the most part dispossessed and existing in breach of the law. Two factors governed the situation in practice.

The first was government policy, which could and did fluctuate quite sharply in response to the political exigencies of the moment. Brenan arrived in 1671 at a benign period with John, first Baron Berkeley of Stratton, as lord lieutenant. Archbishop Plunket was able to introduce Brenan to the lord lieutenant, who assured him of his goodwill. The second factor was the attitude of the local authorities and magnates. Brenan's diocese included the whole of co. Waterford and the southern portion of co. Tipperary. Waterford, and more particularly Waterford city, was heavily protestantized, and though he was received by the Church of Ireland bishop and from time to time noted kindnesses from individual ministers the general atmosphere was hostile. In co. Tipperary, on the other hand, numbers of Roman Catholics had been restored to their estates, owing the favour to the fact that they were close relatives of James Butler, duke of Ormond, lord lieutenant during the 1660s. The great Catholic Butler houses of Kilcash and Rehill could at times provide refuge for Bishop Brenan. Organization of his diocese was therefore possible, but never easy.

The situation deteriorated suddenly with a proclamation on 27 October 1673 banishing all bishops. Some left, but Brenan went north to Archbishop Plunket, where they went into hiding together in conditions of considerable hardship. In a few years the persecution had passed, and Oliver Plunket as primate conducted a visitation of the ecclesiastical province of Cashel. The outcome was the appointment of Brenan as archbishop of Cashel on 26 February 1677. He retained the administration of Waterford and Lismore because the metropolitan see was too poor to support him. In September 1678 the Popish Plot erupted, during which his lifelong friend Archbishop Oliver Plunket was put to death on 1 July 1681. But already Titus Oates had lost all credibility and the storm was beginning to subside.

A complete change came with the accession of James II in 1685. On 6 October, Brenan was able to convoke a synod of his ecclesiastical province, which tried once again to lay down the pattern of the Counter Reformation church in what now seemed very favourable conditions. Two years later he was able to report that it was now possible to practise the Roman Catholic religion freely and publicly, and that churches were being built and schools opened, even though there had as yet been no repeal of the laws and the great poverty of the people limited what they could do. His own poverty had been alleviated by the pension of £200 a year granted to him by the king, but fortunes were again completely reversed when William of Orange was invited to England, and James fled first to France and then to Ireland. He left for France again after his defeat at the battle of the Boyne on 1 July 1690, and though the war continued the cause was lost. That Bishop Brenan was active in public affairs is clear from the fact that he was one of the commissioners appointed to discuss terms for the final Jacobite surrender on 25 September 1691. The discussions ended on 28 September, and the treaty of Limerick was signed on 3 October. Brenan did not live long enough to see its unhappy outcome. His last extant letter is dated

20 September 1692, from the Butler mansion at Rehill, and it was probably there that he died not long afterwards. He was buried in the old churchyard nearby at Tubrid.

PATRICK J. CORISH

Sources P. Power, *A bishop of the penal times* (1932) · J. Linchaeo [J. Lynch], *De praesulibus Hiberniae*, ed. J. F. O'Doherty, 2 vols., IMC (1944) · L. F. Renehan, *Collections on Irish church history*, ed. D. McCarthy, 2 vols. (1861–74), vol. 1 · W. Carrigan, *The history and antiquities of the diocese of Ossory*, 4 (1905) · P. F. Moran, *Memoir of … Oliver Plunket*, 2nd edn (1895) · *The letters of St Oliver Plunkett*, ed. J. Hanly (1979) · B. Millett, ed., 'Calendar of volume 3 (1672–5) of the *Scrittore riferite nei congressi, Irlanda* in Propaganda archives [pt 1]', *Collectanea Hibernica*, 18–19 (1976–7), 40–71 · B. Millett, ed., 'Calendar of volume 3 (1672–5) of the *Scrittore riferite nei congressi, Irlanda* in Propaganda archives [pt 2]', *Collectanea Hibernica*, 21–22 (1979–80), 7–81 · J. Hanly, 'Records of the Irish College Rome under Jesuit administration', *Archivium Hibernicum*, 27 (1964)

Archives Sacra Congregazione di Propaganda Fide, Rome

Brenan, John (1768?–1830), physician and satirist, was born at Ballaghide, co. Carlow, the youngest of six children. Little is known about his parents, who were Roman Catholic and possessed some property. Brenan contributed poetry to *The Sentimental and Masonic Magazine*, published by John Jones of Grafton Street, Dublin, between 1792 and 1795. He is reputed to have graduated as a doctor of medicine in Glasgow, and subsequently established a practice in Dublin about 1800. Widdess notes that he was commonly known as Turpentine Brenan. This was due to his belief in the curative powers of turpentine, which he developed while treating cases of puerperal fever with the substance in Dublin in 1812. Brenan set out his ideas in 1814 in a pamphlet entitled *Thoughts on puerperal fever and its cure by spirits of turpentine, illustrated by cases in the lying-in hospital, Dublin; also, cases of inflammation and spasm cured by the internal and external exhibition of that medicine*. Although his methods were ignored by his Dublin colleagues they were adopted with success by doctors in the rest of Ireland and Britain.

Brenan was an associate of Walter Cox, to whose publication, the *Irish Magazine*, he contributed many articles and verses. A former member of United Irishmen, Cox began the production of his magazine in 1808. In 1812 he was tried in Dublin for publishing an article in favour of a repeal of the union between Great Britain and Ireland and was imprisoned for twelve months. During this time Brenan quarrelled with Cox and started his own magazine known as the *Milesian Magazine*, or the *Irish Monthly Gleaner*, in which he regularly attacked his former associate. The first issue was produced in 1812 and it ran at irregular intervals until 1825. Cox regularly referred to Brenan as the Wrestling Doctor, scurrilously describing his bouts. A typical entry read:

> The Wrestling Doctor will superintend a wrestling match on the North Strand on Sunday, and expects the attendance of his friends. There will be no interruption from General Suds, as the Doctor has a licence for breaking shins, and the Sabbath, from the major. (*Irish Magazine*, 1812, 104)

Brenan also became embroiled in a long-running dispute with the Royal College of Physicians of Ireland. The college resisted the attempts of a number of Scottish-trained doctors, including Brenan, to become licentiates.

Brenan attacked the college for its stance in a pamphlet he published in 1813 entitled *Essay on child-bed fever, with remarks on it, as it appeared in the lying-in hospital of Dublin, in January 1813*. He continued his dispute with the college in the pages of the *Milesian Magazine*, where he satirized many of its members. Brenan also used the magazine to attack persons agitating for Catholic emancipation. It was claimed by Madden, in the second appendix to his book *The United Irishmen, their Lives and Times* (1858), that Brenan secretly received a government pension for this work. Brenan died in Dublin in July 1830.

KARL MAGEE

Sources DNB · J. D. H. Widdess, *A history of the Royal College of Physicians of Ireland, 1654–1963* (1963) · R. R. Madden, *The United Irishmen: their lives and times*, 2nd edn, 2nd ser. (1858), appx · J. T. Gilbert, *A history of the city of Dublin*, 3 (1861) · D. J. Hickey and J. E. Doherty, *A dictionary of Irish history* (1980) · R. J. Hayes, ed., *Manuscript sources for the history of Irish civilisation*, 11 vols. (1965) · Royal College of Physicians of Ireland, Dublin, Kirkpatrick archive

Archives Gilbert Library, Dublin, Gilbert collection, MS 286 · Royal College of Physicians of Ireland, Dublin, Kirkpatrick archive

Brenchley, Julius Lucius (1816–1873), traveller and author, born at Kingsley House, Maidstone, on 30 November 1816, was the son of John Brenchley of Maidstone and Mary Ann, daughter and coheir of Thomas Coare of Middlesex. His mother's family was of French extraction, and her mother was a daughter of Edward Savage of Rocksavage, Cheshire. Brenchley was educated at the grammar school at Maidstone, subsequently entering St John's College, Cambridge, where he graduated BA in 1840. He was ordained in 1841. In 1843, after proceeding MA, he became curate at Holy Trinity Church, Maidstone. Subsequently he held a curacy at Shoreham, Kent.

In 1845 Brenchley left England to travel on the continent with his father. After the latter's death in Paris in 1847, Brenchley travelled alone. In 1849 he visited the United States, where for some time he lived among the indigenous peoples, before, in 1850, travelling to the Pacific coast. In the Hawaiian Islands, he met the naturalist Jules Remy, who in 1892 published an account of their experiences there. Brenchley and Remy then went to California and thence to Utah, publishing a joint account entitled *A Journey to Great Salt-Lake City* (2 vols., 1861). In 1856 the travellers visited Panama and Ecuador, Peru and Chile; and in 1857 they were again in the United States.

In 1858 and 1859 Brenchley explored Algeria, Morocco, Spain, and Sicily and in 1862–3 he went east to India and Ceylon, and thence to China, Mongolia, and Japan. He then visited Australia, and in 1864 travelled to New Zealand, with Herbert Meade, where his help in bringing the Maori to submission was acknowledged by Sir George Grey, the governor. Brenchley then sailed among the islands of the south Pacific and published an account of his cruise in *Jottings during the Cruise of HMS Curaçao among the South Sea Islands in 1865* (1873). The ethnographical objects collected during the voyage were exhibited at Sydney, and a catalogue of them published there in 1865.

Shortly afterwards Brenchley went to Shanghai, and

made a second journey through China and Mongolia, reaching the little-known steppes of Siberia, which he traversed in the winter of 1866–7 on sledges. Having crossed the Ural Mountains he reached Moscow and St Petersburg in January 1867. He afterwards travelled extensively in central Europe, finally reaching Paris when the Prussians were threatening it in 1870. He returned to England and settled down at Milgate House, Bearsted, near Maidstone, but because of ill health moved to Folkestone in 1872, where he died on 24 February 1873. He was buried in the family vault at All Saints, Maidstone.

Brenchley bequeathed the bulk of his collections in ethnography and natural history, and his oriental objects, paintings, and library to the town of Maidstone, with an endowment for their preservation. They are installed in the museum there, of which Brenchley's close friend, William James Lightfoot, was the curator between 1865 and 1875. The collections are large and their diversity reflects Brenchley's eclecticism and the extent of his travels. Together they form an unusually fine collection for a local museum.
F. V. James, *rev.* Elizabeth Baigent

Sources Maidstone Museum and Art Gallery, Kent, Brenchley MSS · *CGPLA Eng. & Wales* (1873) · *BL cat.* · Venn, *Alum. Cant.* · private information (2004)
Archives CKS, journals and papers
Likenesses J. Durham, marble bust, 1873, Maidstone Museum and Art Gallery, Kent · W. C. Dobson, oils, Maidstone Museum and Art Gallery, Kent
Wealth at death under £120,000: probate, 15 March 1873, *CGPLA Eng. & Wales*

Brenchley, Winifred Elsie (1883–1953), agricultural botanist, was born on 10 August 1883 in London, the only child of William Brenchley, a Camberwell schoolmaster who was once mayor of the borough, and Elizabeth Beckett. She was educated at James Allen's Girls' School in Dulwich, at Swanley Horticultural College, and at University College, London, studying under Francis Oliver (1864–1951), who became a lifelong friend. In 1906, she went to Rothamsted Experimental Station, Harpenden, Hertfordshire, as holder of the Gilchrist studentship for university women; in the following year she joined the permanent staff there as head of the botanical section (later botany department). She was the first woman scientist to be appointed at any agricultural institute in this country, and her arrival apparently caused some consternation among the Rothamsted establishment. Many years later it was reported that the widow of one of the founders (Sir Henry Gilbert) had declared, 'that woman had better not take tea with all those men—she will have her tea with me' (private information). However, Brenchley did take tea with the men and before long her abilities put her on level terms with the best of them. She was awarded her DSc in 1911 and was made a fellow of University College in 1914.

In her early years at Rothamsted, Brenchley improved the technique for growing plants in water culture to a stage where it became a useful scientific tool. With this technique, she came very close to discovering the essential role of copper and zinc in plant nutrition, as her book

Inorganic Plant Poisons and Stimulants (1914, revised 1927) shows. However, careful scientist as she was, in those days it was just not possible to reduce copper and zinc concentrations in water culture to levels low enough to restrict plant growth.

Brenchley's book *Weeds of Farmland* (1920) was the first comprehensive scientific study of weeds in this country, relating weed distribution to soil type. She showed that the seeds of certain arable weeds could retain their viability in soil for upwards of fifty years; her studies of rates of change in weed seed populations make her Britain's first quantitative weed ecologist. The last edition of her book with H. C. Long, *Suppression of Weeds by Fertilizers and Chemicals* (1949), was published just as the new selective organic weedkillers were being taken up by farmers, replacing inorganic horrors like sodium arsenite; no one was more aware of the need for less toxic and more selective herbicides than Brenchley. Another book, *Manuring of Grass Land for Hay* (1924), contains her published work on how lime and fertilizers affect the botanical composition of grasslands—still a lively topic with ecologists. A bound copy of her collected papers (fifty-two in all) is in Rothamsted Library; her meticulously kept notebooks and a photograph of her at work are in the Rothamsted archives.

Brenchley was appointed OBE in 1948, the year of her retirement. She was a fellow of the Linnean Society and the Royal Entomological Society.

Aunt Winnie—as she was known behind her back—could be great fun at the right time, but once at work, with her hearing aid switched off (childhood measles had left her partially deaf), even directors hesitated to disturb her. Just and fair, she insisted that credit should go to whoever did the research, however junior or senior. Her principal hobby was gardening, as befits a botanist, but she also collected stamps, harvesting them from her many friends around the world. She was interested in insects and learned much about them from her good friend Augustus Imms (1880–1949), an entomologist of distinction then working at Rothamsted. She never married.

With retirement, Brenchley returned to her garden and allotment with unrestrained vigour. She started to bring together the mountain of unpublished observations in her research notebooks but not long afterwards suffered a devastating stroke, from which she never recovered. She died at her home, 10 Clarence Road, Harpenden, Hertfordshire, on 27 October 1953. Talented botanist as she was, she is best remembered as the first woman in this country to break into the all male preserves of agricultural science.
D. S. Jenkinson

Sources E. J. Russell, *A history of agricultural science in Great Britain, 1620–1954* (1966) · *The Times* (28 Oct 1953) · *Nature*, 172 (1953), 936 · *Annals of Applied Biology*, 41 (1954), 368 · E. Grey, *Rothamsted Experimental Station: reminiscences, tales, and anecdotes of the laboratories, staff, and experimental fields, 1872–1922* (privately printed, Harpenden, [1922]) · private information (2004) [J. Thurston] · *Who's who among living authors of older nations*, 1 (1921–32) · *CGPLA Eng. & Wales* (1954)

Archives Rothamsted Experimental Station, Harpenden, notebooks

Likenesses photograph, Rothamsted Experimental Station, Harpenden

Wealth at death £11,076 15s. 6d.: probate, 15 April 1954, CGPLA Eng. & Wales

Brendan mac Nemainn (d. 565/573). See under Meath, saints of (act. c.400–c.900).

Brendan of Clonfert (d. 577). See under Connacht, saints of (act. c.400–c.800).

Brennan, Joseph (1887–1976), civil servant in Ireland, was born on 18 November 1887 in Bandon, co. Cork, one of seven children of Joseph Brennan (c.1861–1948), a wealthy merchant, and his wife, Mary Hickey, also of co. Cork. After the local national school, he went to the Jesuit boarding-school Clongowes Wood College and from there to University College, Dublin. He transferred to Christ's College, Cambridge, in 1909 where he obtained first-class degrees in classics. After Cambridge he competed successfully for a first-division clerkship in the civil service. His first appointment was in London but he agreed before long to accept a place in the chief secretary's office in Dublin Castle and took up duty there on 1 June 1912. On 25 September 1918 he married Evelyn, daughter of James Simcox, a merchant, of Douglas, co. Cork. They had one son and two daughters.

Working in Dublin Castle became increasingly disagreeable after 1916, and by 1920 Brennan was considering leaving the service. However, he found a fulfilling, if dangerous, outlet for his patriotism in clandestine briefing of Michael Collins in 1921 on the economic and financial aspects of the treaty negotiations. In all, he served for forty-one years as an Irish official of exceptional ability and tenacious purpose, preoccupied with economy and integrity. His name is often coupled with that of his friend and colleague for many years, James J. McElligott: their contribution to establishing the respectability and viability of the new state was outstanding. McElligott had taken part in the Easter rising but both men were silent throughout their lives on their 'subversive' activities.

Brennan became, in April 1923, secretary of the department of finance of the Irish Free State. He personally laid down the principles and practices of sound financial administration for the new state. Its first national loan in 1923 was a phenomenal success. Another significant achievement was the establishment of commissions to guarantee quality and impartiality in public service appointments. Retrenchment zeal in 1924 lopped 1s. off the old-age pension of 10s., cut teachers' salaries, and lengthened the working day of civil servants. Income tax, however, was reduced from 25 per cent in 1924 to 15 per cent in 1926. The ultimate financial settlement with Britain in 1926 benefited from Brennan's negotiating toughness. Differences of personality and outlook between him and his minister, Ernest Blythe, had, however, so developed by 1927 that the two men were no longer even on speaking terms. Brennan resigned from the civil service but accepted office as first chairman of the new Currency Commission.

While with the Currency Commission Brennan chaired a commission of inquiry into the public service (1932–5) and the major Banking Commission (1934–8). When the Central Bank was established in 1943 to replace the Currency Commission, he was appointed its first governor. His ten-year governorship of the Central Bank saw no move to exercise any of its functions other than publishing cautionary advice to the government. He was told of his reappointment only on the day his seven-year term of office expired and was the victim of insensitivity when, under strain midway through his second term (April 1953), his offer to resign was immediately accepted. His relations with government had been deteriorating over many years. The critical and conservative elements in his character had become more pronounced, overlaying the earlier creativity and constructiveness and increasing his distrust of the profligate propensities of governments.

Though essentially a private rather than a gregarious person—indeed, judged by his staff to be aloof—Brennan enjoyed long walks and skiing, was a keen golfer, and a regular theatregoer, as well as being active in social charities. In retirement he lived quietly in Dublin, exercising remote control over the extensive west Cork businesses inherited from his father. A story is told of instructions being sought from him on the telephone as to what should be done with a horse that lay dead in a mill yard (Ó Broin, 168). He died at his home, Clancool, Shrewsbury Road, Dublin, on 3 March 1976, and was buried on 5 March.   T. K. WHITAKER

Sources L. Ó Broin, *No man's man: a biographical memoir of Joseph Brennan* (1982) · R. Fanning, *The Irish department of finance, 1922–58* (1978) · J. J. Lee, *Ireland 1912–1985, politics and society* (1989) · M. Moynihan, *Currency and central banking in Ireland, 1922–60* (1975) · T. K. Whitaker, *Interests* (1983) · m. cert. · personal knowledge (2004)

Archives NA Ire., Department of Finance files · NL Ire., papers

Wealth at death £302,682: probate, 1 July 1976, CGPLA Éire

Brennan, Louis Philip (1852–1932), mechanical engineer, the son of Thomas Brennan, a hardware merchant, and his wife, Bridget McDonnell, was born at Castlebar, co. Mayo, on 28 January 1852, and baptized Luis on 2 April. While still a boy he was taken to Australia, and it was when he was living in Melbourne as a watchmaker that he devised the dirigible torpedo for coast defence for which his name is chiefly known.

The invention was brought to the notice of the British government in 1880 by Commodore J. C. Wilson, and Brennan was invited to go to England. He was provided with facilities on the Medway for the development of the weapon, receiving an annual grant of £1000 with a preliminary award of £5000. In 1885 the torpedo was adopted by the government, which, in November 1886, purchased the exclusive rights for over £100,000. This figure was criticized as being excessive, but the commission which recommended the payment justified it on the ground that it was important not to allow the device to pass into the hands of other countries. In 1887 Brennan was appointed superintendent of the government factory at Gillingham,

Kent, established for the manufacture of the torpedo, and he held that position until 1896, subsequently acting, until 1907, as consulting engineer. His torpedo had two screws, revolving in opposite directions, and drums mounted on each propeller shaft were wound with wires the ends of which were connected with a high-speed engine on shore. Steering was effected by varying the rate at which the wires were unwound from one or other of the drums by the engine, so varying the relative speed of rotation of the screws.

After the torpedo Brennan turned his attention to a monorail system of transport, with self-propelled vehicles travelling on a single rail, or even a tightly stretched cable, and maintained upright by a high-speed gyrostat rotating in a vacuum. He showed a model of this arrangement at a conversazione of the Royal Society in 1907 and later carried out trials with full-scale equipment. The monorail was used by the public at the Japan–British exhibition at White City, London, in 1910 but the system did not come into practical use.

During the First World War Brennan was employed in the munitions inventions department of the Ministry of Munitions, and from 1919 to 1926 he worked for the Air Ministry at the Royal Aircraft Establishment, Farnborough, Hampshire, on the development of helicopters. He later developed a gyroscopically balanced automobile. He was appointed CB in 1892 and elected an honorary member of the Royal Engineers Institute in 1906, and he was a founder member of the National Academy of Ireland (1922). He married, in 1892, Anna Mary (d. 1931), daughter of Michael Quinn, of Castlebar; they had one son and two daughters. Following a car accident, Brennan died at the Clinique Florimont, Montreux, Switzerland, on 17 January 1932. He was buried at Kensal Green Roman Catholic cemetery, London, on 26 January 1932.

H. M. ROSS, rev. JOHN BOSNELL

Sources Nature, 129 (1932), 227–8 · The Times (21 Jan 1932) · The Times (26 Jan 1932) · Engineering (29 Jan 1932) · N. Tomlinson, Louis Brennan: inventor extraordinaire (1980) · [R. E. Wilkes], Louis Brennan, 1: Dirigible torpedo [1973] [Gillingham Public Libraries, no. 5] · R. Graham, 'Brennan: his helicopter and other inventions', Aeronautical Journal, 77 (1973), 74–82 · CGPLA Eng. & Wales (1932)
Archives Gillingham Public Libraries, Kent · Medway Archives and Local Studies Centre, Rochester, Kent, corresp. relating to helicopter design
Likenesses photograph, Kent County Library, Gillingham
Wealth at death £2275 10s. 10d.: probate, 4 March 1932, CGPLA Eng. & Wales

Brennan, Michael [Mícheál] (1896–1986), Irish revolutionary and general, was born on 2 February 1896 at Gortgarraun, near Meelick, co. Clare, the youngest of three rebel sons of Patrick Brennan, a tenant farmer (1865–1901), and Mary (1862/3–1939), daughter of Michael Clancy from Rathurd, co. Limerick. His father's early death from tuberculosis left Mary Brennan in charge of the substantial family farm of 62 acres near Meelick, just north-west of Limerick.

Like his brothers, Patrick (1892–1986) and Austin Joseph (1894–1983), and other fatherless revolutionaries in the making such as Michael Collins, Harry Boland, and Eamon

De Valera, Michael Brennan was politically precocious. He was only fifteen (having just left St Munchin's College, Limerick) when sworn into the Limerick circle of the Irish Republican Brotherhood (IRB) by Patrick, whose friend Seán MacDermott had secured the supreme council's dispensation. At the same age Austin had become secretary of the United Irish League in Meelick, being co-opted two years later to the Limerick board of guardians after growing a beard to prove the requisite maturity. While Patrick worked in London as a junior clerk like his friend Michael Collins, Michael and Austin helped launch Limerick's Irish Volunteers in November 1913. After briefly studying wireless telegraphy in Dublin, Michael returned to Limerick at MacDermott's suggestion to organize and train companies of the volunteers in counties Limerick and Clare. Along with Austin he joined the dissident minority after John Redmond's appeal to the volunteers to serve in the First World War, forming a signalling section for the Limerick battalion and acting as an instructor in the absence of experienced drill sergeants. He was twice arrested before the Easter rising and briefly imprisoned for inciting the volunteers to shoot if ordered to surrender their arms. As North Munster representative on the supreme council Brennan was already an influential and militant republican organizer, intimate with those plotting an insurrection in Dublin and central to the network of conspirators around Limerick.

The military fiasco of 1916 left Brennan disillusioned with the Dublin leadership and resolved to follow his own nose in quest of the republic. Instructed by the IRB to 'hold the roads leading into Limerick from Clare', he was not told 'whether I was to prevent people getting in or getting out' (Brennan, The War in Clare, 11). The outcome, as in most districts outside Dublin, was that no rising occurred in counties Limerick or Clare. After this faltering start Brennan's revolutionary career was a minor epic of daring and ingenuity, chronicled in his unpretentiously revealing memoir submitted to the Bureau of Military History in 1954 but unpublished until 1980. Between 1916 and 1918 he spent five spells in detention, amounting to two and a half years. An autograph book from Reading gaol in 1916 teems with affectionate inscriptions and cartoons depicting a dapper daredevil dispensing hospitality, hilarity, and wisdom to acolytes visiting his cell. In Mountjoy gaol his request for a concertina was indignantly rejected by the governor, who spluttered that 'musical instruments are obviously out of place in prison' (Fitzpatrick, 126). His levity masked implacable determination: during internment at Fron-goch after the rising he had inscribed another autograph book with the dictum (ascribed to Admiral Lord Fisher) that 'when you go to war, hit first, hit hard and hit anywhere' (Seán O'Mahony, Frongoch: University of Revolution, 1987, 80). Prominent among the hunger strikers demanding 'political status' at Cork, Mountjoy, and Dundalk, he showed the instincts of a fighter rather than a politician. While briefly at liberty in June 1917, after absconding from non-custodial internment in Yorkshire, he declined nomination by Sinn Féin for East Clare, in the by-election that was to launch the political career of Eamon De Valera.

After release from Belfast gaol on Christmas eve 1918 Brennan determined to put Fisher's principles into effect and to avoid rearrest by going on the run. He immediately became commandant of the new East Clare brigade, following the removal of his brother Patrick from the county command after a dispute with the chief of staff, Richard Mulcahy. Within a year Michael too had been sacked after redirecting payments intended for old-age pensioners to the purchase of weapons in Dublin, so spoiling the black market for other units. Duly replaced by Austin, Brennan went on to lead the nascent 'flying column', an improvised unit of a dozen or so armed outlaws whose success encouraged Mulcahy to instruct all brigades to establish 'active service units'. In mid-1921 Brennan was assigned the daunting task of co-ordinating and controlling the unruly volunteer bands scattered throughout co. Clare and southern co. Galway, becoming commandant of the new 1st western division. His supremacy in republican co. Clare seemed unassailable, despite simmering resentment in the less efficient mid- and west co. Clare brigades, and recurrent clashes with Collins and Mulcahy.

Brennan's dominance owed more to his exploits and panache than his fraternal connections, though the clandestine camaraderie of the IRB was to influence his decisions at several critical moments. With his quick wit, curly black hair, sharp eyes, and small but nimble frame, Brennan epitomized the resourceful and chivalrous boy hero exalted by the Fianna Éireann, the republican scout movement through which he had been introduced to the IRB. An ingenious guerrilla fighter, he participated in set pieces such as the rescue of Seán Hogan at Knocklong (May 1919), the storming of Kilmallock barracks (May 1920), and the ambush at Cratloe (January 1921). He evaded rearrest after 1918 but was severely wounded while attacking two policemen at O'Briensbridge in September 1920. Under his leadership the co. Clare volunteers became almost as formidable as those in Cork and Tipperary, and Brennan's missionary influence introduced the guerrilla campaign to once quiescent districts in west co. Clare and co. Galway. His enterprise extended to local government, and in June 1920 he became Sinn Féin's surprisingly punctilious chairman of the Clare county council. It was Brennan who showed that by cunning and opportunism the republicans could maintain local services even after repudiating the crown, a policy taken up by Dáil Éireann and later applied generally. His zeal in repairing by day the roads which his own forces were destroying by night earned him grudging admiration from the gentry, whose castles he occasionally commandeered for council meetings. Though never a deputy in Dáil Éireann he had become a major force in Irish republicanism well before signature of the Anglo-Irish treaty in December 1921.

Brennan played a crucial part in outmanoeuvring those opposed to the treaty, having allied himself with Collins and Mulcahy against De Valera and the Cork-centred opposition within the IRB. His influence in co. Clare

defused active resistance, and his almost bloodless occupation of Limerick, following a truce with the local republicans just after the outbreak of civil war, gave the provisional government an invaluable stronghold which helped confine and isolate the dissident 'republic of Munster'. Brennan relished the fact that Limerick had been secured by bluff, the irregulars being persuaded that disguised water-pipes were Lewis guns. His evident desire for compromise with republicans raised suspicion among his own colleagues in the national army, but Brennan avoided implication with either of the clandestine factions purged after the mutiny of March 1924. He took over the southern command in February 1924, becoming adjutant-general in October 1925, inspector-general of the defence forces in October 1928, and chief of staff in October 1931. By November 1926 Brennan had already acquired the reputation of an 'iron disciplinarian', for which he was admired by a British military observer who found him of 'much more than average ability … He does not drink, and is not very sociable' (Captain N. J. Chamberlain MSS, King's, Lond.). Like many another boy fighter, he had lost his sparkle during the civil war.

Brennan presided over drastic retrenchments in the army, quelling Seán Mac Eoin's challenge by excluding serving officers from the National Defence Association in November 1930. He rejected Eoin O'Duffy's proposal to collaborate in a *coup d'état* against the incoming Fianna Fáil government in 1932, so securing the rather unexpected survival of parliamentary democracy. Thereafter Brennan relentlessly professionalized what remained of the army while warning the government of its incapacity to defend Ireland against invasion. In 1936 he sardonically advised the executive council to seek assistance from the War Office, counsel put into effect during the 'emergency' known elsewhere as the Second World War. The army's capacity, and Brennan's organizational skills, were further tested in 1938 by the transfer of the treaty ports from British to Irish control. De Valera's decision to retain him, while dismissing O'Duffy as police commissioner, testified to Brennan's reputation as a fair-minded and loyal servant of the state. This was confirmed by his unprecedented reappointment as chief of staff in 1934 and 1937.

On 14 April 1926, in the university church on St Stephen's Green, Brennan had married (Bridget) May (1898–1956), Queensland-born daughter of Thomas Conheady from Donaghmore, co. Limerick. The celebrant was Bishop Michael Fogarty of Killaloe, De Valera's relentless antagonist in co. Clare and a key supporter of the treaty settlement. The Brennans and their growing family (Miriam, Sheila, and Alin Patrick, born respectively in 1929, 1931, and 1932) lived rather grandly through the 1930s in the former private secretary's lodge in the Phoenix Park. Despite Brennan's growing aloofness a steady stream of politicians and socialites visited the lodge to view the army's man of destiny. In a striking sketch by Seán Keating, an austere and unsmiling figure of authority is depicted in the elaborate ceremonial uniform with which Brennan had been presented in April 1937. Within three years Brennan's reputation for efficiency was to be irreparably tarnished by an embarrassingly unresisted raid on the Magazine Fort, from which the IRA removed most of the army's ammunition in thirteen trucks. This stunt, worthy of Brennan in his prime, caused De Valera to secure his premature retirement as chief of staff in January 1940. Having declined demotion to the Curragh command Brennan was promoted to lieutenant-general but removed from office 'in the public interest' (cabinet minutes, 22 Jan 1940). At the age of forty-three, after twenty-six years as a volunteer and soldier, he faced half a lifetime of anticlimax.

The cabinet had cushioned the blow by appointing Brennan to the office of public works as chief superintendent of divisions, a sedentary sinecure which he detested. Having acquired Simmonscourt House in Ballsbridge for a pittance (some £3500), he settled into prosperous middle age. After May's death on 10 July 1956 from cancer of the colon, soon followed by his retirement from the civil service, Brennan's habitual reticence subsided into reclusion, in the leafy bayside surroundings of South Hill, Killiney. By 1972 he was virtually housebound, apart from walks with his ferocious German Shepherd dog, occasional meetings with Patrick, and annual reunions with the cattily cantankerous Ernest Blythe. Historians were infrequent visitors, courteously if guardedly received by a revolutionary survivor who did not allow rancour to distort his recollections.

The family farm, maintained by Brennan's mother and sister Margaret despite the burning of their house as a 'reprisal' in 1920, had passed to Austin after the widow's death in 1939. Austin, also a retired army officer who (unlike Michael) had been prominent in O'Duffy's Blueshirts, stood unsuccessfully for County Clare as a Fine Gael candidate in 1948 and eventually retired to Dublin. Patrick's public career had ended prematurely, upon his departure from the Dáil in 1923, following a turbulent term in 1922 as assistant commissioner of the civic guard, and a brief period commanding the 1st western division against the irregulars. While still superintendent of the Oireachtas (parliamentary) staff Patrick betrayed his ideological sympathies by presenting a blackthorn to Hitler for his fiftieth birthday on 20 April 1939. Thereafter, he devoted himself to promoting German-Irish friendship and tourism, before retreating into misanthropy in co. Westmeath. Michael, attended by a devoted housekeeper and visited regularly by his daughter Miriam, lingered on until 24 October 1986, when he succumbed to multiple disorders of the heart and other organs at his home, South Hill, Killiney Hill Road, Killiney, co. Dublin. After an impressive series of Catholic obsequies he was buried on 28 October in Dean's Grange cemetery with full military honours to the sounds of gunfire, the 'Dead march' from Handel's *Saul*, and a Celtic lament. His net estate was valued for probate at more than £126,000, of which £80,000 was attributable to the house and £16,000 to its furnishings. Brennan's obituary in *The Times* caught the essence of his career in its headline: 'Poacher turned gamekeeper'.

DAVID FITZPATRICK

Sources M. Brennan, *The war in Clare* (1980) · D. Fitzpatrick, *Politics and Irish life, 1913–1921: provincial experience of war and revolution*, new edn (1998) · *Irish Times* (25 Oct 1986) · *Irish Times* (27–8 Oct 1986) · *Irish Times* (29 Oct 1986) · *Irish Times* (8 Nov 1986) · *The Times* (25 Oct 1986) · M. Brennan, MSS autograph book, Reading, 1916, priv. coll. · MSS records of general prisons board; cabinet minutes; census schedules for 1901, 1911, NA Ire. · J. P. Duggan, *A history of the Irish army* (1991) · C. Younger, *Ireland's civil war* (1968) · MSS revision books, co. Clare, Valuation Office, Dublin · private information (2004) [Michael Brennan; A. Brennan; Miriam Brennan; contemporaries and friends] · b. cert. · d. cert. · d. cert. [Mary Brennan]
Archives Army Archives, Dublin, papers relating to first western division and south-western command · NRA, priv. coll., family MSS | NA Ire., MSS records of general prisons board · University College, Dublin, Mulcahy papers
Likenesses S. Milroy, cartoon, 1916, priv. coll. · S. Keating, portrait, c.1937, priv. coll.
Wealth at death £130,948.56—gross; £126,186.71—net: probate, 12 Jan 1987, probate registry, Four Courts, Dublin

Brennan, Robert (1881–1964), Irish republican and diplomatist, was born in John's Gate Street, Wexford, on 22 July 1881, one of five children of Robert Brennan, a victualler and cattle dealer, and his wife, Bridget, *née* Kearney, shopkeeper. After completing local schooling by the Christian Brothers in 1898, he began his career with the Wexford county surveyor and attended technical schools in the evenings, later qualifying through the Royal University, Dublin. About 1906 Brennan was one of the founders of a Gaelic League branch in Wexford and served as a teacher in it and other nearby branches at a modest salary. Afterwards he was a founder member of a branch of Sinn Féin in Wexford. Subsequently Brennan was sworn into the Irish Republican Brotherhood by Seán T. O'Kelly, later president of Ireland. He served as county secretary of both Sinn Féin and the Irish Republican Brotherhood. In 1909 Brennan resigned his post as assistant county surveyor and a month later married Una, with whom he had a son and three daughters; in the same year he went to work for the *Enniscorthy Echo* and was Wexford correspondent for the *Irish Times*. According to his autobiography, Brennan wrote over 100 short detective stories in three years around this time, most being published in the magazine *Ireland's Own*. He also unsuccessfully tried farming a 10 acre holding.

During Easter week in 1916 Brennan was quartermaster of the Wexford brigade of the Irish Volunteers that held Enniscorthy until Patrick Pearse, provisional president of the Irish republic, from Dublin ordered it to surrender. He was sentenced to death, but this was commuted to five years' penal servitude and he was sent to Dartmoor in England, where he was incarcerated with about sixty republican prisoners, including Eamon De Valera. While in Dartmoor he petitioned unsuccessfully for stationery to allow him to write fiction. He was later removed with the other Irish convicts to Lewes prison. On his release under the general amnesty of June 1917, he returned to Ireland and was active in the reorganizations of the Irish Volunteers and Sinn Féin. In the following year he was appointed head of the Sinn Féin department of publicity, assisting the anti-conscription campaign by writing the preface to De Valera's pamphlet *Ireland's Case Against Conscription*

(1918). As Sinn Féin looked forward to the post-war general election, Brennan became the party's director of elections. On 20 November 1918 he was again arrested and was interned without charge in Gloucester prison. After some three months he was released on parole.

During 1919 and 1920 Brennan helped organize the Sinn Féin administrative, publicity, and diplomatic effort, becoming under-secretary in the department of external affairs for the Dáil (the underground government) between February 1921 and January 1922. He assisted with publishing the *Irish Bulletin* and in 1922 helped to organize the Irish race conference held in Paris. Being opposed to the Anglo-Irish treaty of December 1921, Brennan, a close associate of De Valera, acted as director of publicity for the republican forces during the civil war (1922–3). When De Valera made preparations to found a newspaper, the *Irish Press*, in 1931 Brennan was its secretary and then its first general manager until 1934, when he joined the diplomatic service. De Valera defended this as a re-engagement, since Brennan had been 'in the service of Ireland in Republican days … he was Under-Secretary of the Department of External Affairs … actually head of that Department' (Keatinge, 140). In February 1934 he was appointed secretary of the Irish legation in Washington, where he acted as chargé d'affaires between March and August 1938 and then as minister-plenipotentiary until early 1947. As a confidant of De Valera, he was the ideal person to explain Ireland's neutrality during the war to a sceptical American state department and to the Roosevelt administration. His efforts, if generally successful, were at times hampered by concern that anti-British sentiment led to a pro-Nazi attitude in the Irish government. Some of his colleagues, notably Frank Aiken, alienated the American president. Later he wrote about this period for the *Irish Press*, notably in 'Wartime mission', published on 15 May 1958. During his years in the United States he took a keen interest in furthering the links between Irish-Americans and Ireland, and in December 1945 he actively sought their support for an end to partition.

On his return to Ireland in 1947, Brennan was seconded from the department of external affairs to become director of broadcasting in Radio Éireann from March 1947 to August 1948. He was a director of the Irish News Agency when it was established in 1950 and was also an active writer. He wrote plays and short stories and published a collection of prose poems. His plays, *Bystander* and *Good Night, Mr O'Donnell*, were produced in Ireland and England. Brennan's detective novels, *The Toledo Dagger* (1927) and *The Man who Walked Like a Dancer* (1951), enjoyed substantial popularity. An autobiography, *Allegiance* (1950), covers the years through the civil war, but is imprecise about dates. Brennan died in Dublin on 12 November 1964, having been predeceased on 3 August 1958 by his wife. After a funeral mass at St Paul's Retreat, Mount Argus, he was interred in Mount Jerome cemetery.   ALAN O'DAY

Sources R. Brennan, *Allegiance* (1950) • *Irish Times* (13 Nov 1964) • *Irish Press* (13 Nov 1964) • R. Brennan, 'Wartime mission', *Irish Press* (15 May 1958) • P. Keatinge, *The formation of Irish foreign policy* (1973) • T. D. Davis, *Dublin's American policy: Irish-American diplomatic relations, 1945–1952* (1998) • A. Mitchell, *Revolutionary government in Ireland* (1995) • P. O'Farrell, *Who's who in the Irish war of independence and civil war* (1997) • Earl of Longford and T. P. O'Neill, *Eamon de Valera* (1970) • b. cert. • H. Boylan, *A dictionary of Irish biography*, 3rd edn (1998)
Archives NL Ire., MSS | University College, Dublin, Eamon De Valera MSS
Likenesses photograph, repro. in Brennan, *Allegiance*
Wealth at death £3768: probate, 30 March 1965, *CGPLA Éire*

Brent, Charlotte (1734–1802), singer, was born in London on 17 December 1734, a daughter of the fencing master Charles Brent (1692/3–1770) and his wife, Catharine. She was a pupil of Thomas Augustine *Arne and went to Dublin with him and his wife in 1755, making her stage début at the Smock Alley Theatre in Arne's *Eliza* on 29 November. She appeared in his *Rosamond* and *Comus*, sang between the acts, and played Laura in *The Chaplet* and Polly in *The Beggar's Opera*. On 25 May 1756 she sang in Arne's *Alfred* and shortly afterwards she and Arne returned to London, leaving Mrs Arne in Dublin. Charlotte Brent, who by now was almost certainly Arne's mistress as well as his pupil, made a few appearances singing his music in London during the next three years. David Garrick refused Arne's request to employ her at Drury Lane, claiming that music was, at best, only pickle to his roast beef. Arne is said to have replied, 'Davy, your beef shall be well pickled before I have done' (Baker, 1.11), and in autumn 1759 Charlotte drew crowds to Covent Garden Theatre as Polly in *The Beggar's Opera*, with the tenor John Beard as Macheath. A correspondent to the *Theatrical Review* (1763) was distressed to find the ballad airs 'trill'd, sustinuto'd, ad libitinis'd' (p. 48), but audiences were enthusiastic and there were thirty-seven performances in thirty-eight nights. Charlotte Brent was plain and no actress but she remained the star soprano singer at Covent Garden for eleven years. She created Sally in Arne's afterpiece *Thomas and Sally* (28 November 1760) and Mandane in his opera *Artaxerxes* (2 February 1762), with airs crowded with 'all the Italian divisions and difficulties which had ever been heard at the opera' (Burney, *Hist. mus.*, 4.673). In 1760 Beard became the manager of Covent Garden and staged a series of new English operas with music selected and arranged by Arne or Samuel Arnold and with Charlotte Brent as the heroine. These included *Love in a Village* (Isaac Bickerstaff, 8 December 1762), *The Guardian Outwitted* (Arne, 12 December 1764), *The Maid of the Mill* (Bickerstaffe, 31 January 1765), *The Summer's Tale* (Richard Cumberland, 6 December 1765), and *Tom Jones* (Joseph Reed, 14 January 1769). In the summer she sang at Vauxhall, Ranelagh, or Marylebone gardens, at the Three Choirs festival in 1765–7, and in oratorios at York in 1769.

On 16 October 1766, to Arne's scorn, Charlotte married the violinist Thomas *Pinto (bap. 1728, d. 1783), a talented but lazy musician who made heavy losses from his involvement in Marylebone Gardens in 1769. Between April 1769 and March 1770 four children of Thomas and Charlotte Pinto were buried, including twin sons born on 12 February 1770. Her father died that August. The Pintos left for Edinburgh, possibly to escape creditors, and Sylas Neville heard Charlotte there in January 1772, 'grown so ugly that it is necessary to shut one's eyes to enjoy her singing' (*Diary*, 148). In 1773 they moved to Dublin, where Thomas Snagg encountered 'the ruins of the once celebrated Miss Brent' (Snagg, 93). After her husband's death in Dublin in December 1782 Charlotte returned to London, where she lived with Pinto's daughter from his first marriage and taught her musically gifted step-grandson, George Frederick Pinto. The Royal Society of Musicians could not give her a pension, because Pinto had been expelled for non-payment of his subscriptions. *The Beggar's Opera* was staged for her benefit at the Haymarket Theatre on 15 March 1785, when she sang her last Polly, for it is unlikely that she appeared in *The Beggar's Opera* mounted for her benefit in 1786. The oboist W. T. Parke provided the echo for her in 'Sweet Echo' (from Arne's *Comus*) on 22 April 1785, and remembered that her voice 'possessed the remains of those qualities for which it had been so much celebrated,—power, flexibility and sweetness' (Parke, 1.57). Four days later she appeared for the last time, singing Mandane's celebrated aria 'The soldier tired' from *Artaxerxes*. She died at Vauxhall Walk, Lambeth, on 10 April 1802 and was buried five days later at St Margaret's, Westminster.

OLIVE BALDWIN and THELMA WILSON

Sources G. W. Stone, ed., *The London stage, 1660–1800*, pt 4: *1747–1776* (1962) • C. B. Hogan, ed., *The London stage, 1660–1800*, pt 5: *1776–1800* (1968) • parish registers of St Anne, Soho; St Paul, Covent Garden; St Mary-le-Strand; and St Margaret, Westminster • B. Boydell, *A Dublin musical calendar, 1700–1760* (Dublin, 1988) • T. J. Walsh, *Opera in Dublin, 1705–1797: the social scene* (1973) • D. E. Baker, *Biographia dramatica, or, A companion to the playhouse*, rev. I. Reed, new edn, rev. S. Jones, 1 (1812) • *Theatrical Review* (1763) • Burney, *Hist. mus.*, vol. 4 • *The diary of Sylas Neville, 1767–1788*, ed. B. Cozens-Hardy (1950) • T. Snagg, *Recollections of occurrences* (1951) • W. T. Parke, *Musical memoirs*, 1 (1830) • 'A parallel between Mrs. Vincent and Miss Brent', *British Magazine* (1760), 348–50 • M. Sands, *The eighteenth-century pleasure gardens of Marylebone, 1737–1777* (1987) • D. Lysons and others, *Origin and progress of the meeting of the three choirs of Gloucester, Worcester and Hereford* (1895) • T. Wilkinson, *The wandering patentee, or, A history of the Yorkshire theatres from 1770 to the present time*, 4 vols. (1795) • *Recollections of R. J. S. Stevens: an organist in Georgian London*, ed. M. Argent (1992) • F. Gentleman, *The dramatic censor, or, Critical companion*, 2 vols. (1770), vol. 2 • S. Klima and others, eds., *Memoirs of Dr. Charles Burney, 1726–1769* (1988) • *The Times* (14 April 1802) • *European Magazine and London Review*, 41 (1802) • 'Memoir of George Frederick Pinto', *The Harmonicon*, 6 (1828), 215–16 • *The Euterpeiad* [Boston, USA] (21 July 1821)
Likenesses line engraving, watch-paper (as Sally, with John Beard, in Arne's and Bickerstaffe's *Thomas and Sally*), BM

Brent, John (1808–1882), antiquary and author, was born at Rotherhithe on 21 August 1808, the eldest son of John Brent, a shipbuilder, who moved to Canterbury about 1821, became mayor of the city on three occasions, and was deputy lieutenant for the county. His mother was Susannah, third daughter of the Revd Sampson Kingsford, of Sturry, near Canterbury. In his early days Brent was a miller, but he later became clerk of the Canterbury board of guardians and superintendent registrar. On the formation of the Canterbury and East Kent Permanent Benefit Building Society he was elected secretary, an office he held until his death.

Brent entered politics at an early age, and spoke as a whig at public meetings in Canterbury and other parts of east Kent in support of the Reform Bill of 1832. For many years he occupied a seat on Canterbury council and he was elected an alderman, but he resigned in 1871 when he became city treasurer, a post he held for about seven years.

Brent was well known for his many humanitarian activities: he was a member of the Anti-Slavery Society and became local secretary of the Polish Association when the vicious suppression of an insurrection in Poland brought many refugees to Britain. He was also an anti-vivisectionist and an active member of many other philanthropic movements. With these activities went a keen interest in the history of Canterbury and Kent. He became a fellow of the Society of Antiquaries in April 1853, and was also a member of the British Archaeological Association and the Kent Archaeological Society. His contributions to antiquarian literature are mostly to be found in the various publications of these societies. He carried out a number of archaeological excavations in Kent, particularly in the Saxon cemeteries of Sarre and Stowting, and received high praise for his research and discoveries there. His *Catalogue of the Antiquities in the Canterbury Museum*, of which he was an honorary curator, appeared in 1875.

In 1855 Brent was asked to revise Felix Summerly's *Handbook for Canterbury*, and in 1860 appeared his own well-received book on the city, *Canterbury in the Olden Time*, which was an enlarged version of a paper originally published in the *Journal of the British Archaeological Association* and which appeared as a companion volume to the *Handbook*. He was also an accomplished novelist and poet: he published at least three novels, including *The Sea Wolf* (1834) and *Ellie Forestere* (1850), and six books of verse, although most of these were originally published anonymously. Two of his volumes of verse are on Polish themes. A collected edition of his poems in two volumes appeared in 1884. Tales, poems, and miscellaneous items by Brent are also to be found in various periodicals of the time.

Brent married Eliza Ann, née Hounsell (1846/7–1878), the daughter of a west of England surgeon: they had no children. A Unitarian for most of his life, during the last few years he attended Church of England services. Brent died of heart disease at his house, 8 Dane John Grove, Canterbury, on 23 April 1882.

GORDON GOODWIN, rev. SHIRLEY BURGOYNE BLACK

Sources *The Times* (29 April 1882) • *Kentish Gazette* (25 April 1882) • *Kentish Chronicle* (29 April 1882) • *Journal of the British Archaeological Association*, 38 (1882), 235–6 • C. R. Smith, *Retrospections, social and archaeological*, 1 (1883), 9, 159–61, 303–7 • d. cert. [Eliza Ann Brent] • *CGPLA Eng. & Wales* (1882)
Archives U. Edin. L., letters to James Orchard Halliwell-Phillipps
Wealth at death £1010 6s. 7d.: probate, 13 May 1882, *CGPLA Eng. & Wales*

Brent, Margaret (c.1601–c.1671), colonist and proprietary agent in America, was born in England, the eldest daughter of Catholic gentry parents, Richard Brent (1573–1652) of the manor of Lark Stoke and Admington in Gloucestershire, and his wife, Elizabeth, daughter of Giles Reed and Katherine Grevill. Her early life is obscure, but she arrived in Maryland—a colony of which her cousin, Cecil Calvert, second Baron Baltimore, was proprietor—in 1638 with a sister and two brothers, Mary, Fulke, and Giles. Unmarried and hence legally able to own and manage property, she established herself as a substantial landowner and businesswoman, capable of managing her affairs without male assistance.

Margaret Brent's business and diplomatic skills proved crucial to the survival of Maryland after a parliament-backed force raided the Catholic-led colony in 1645. The Catholic governor, Leonard Calvert, fled to Virginia, and at his return with soldiers late in 1646 he found Maryland in shambles, most of its former inhabitants gone. On 9 June 1647 he died, naming Margaret Brent his executor with instructions to pay his debts. These included the soldiers' wages, which he had pledged, if necessary, to pay himself or from the estate of his elder brother, the absentee proprietor, Lord Baltimore. However, the deceased governor's available assets were insufficient. Brent kept pacifying soldiers ready to mutiny. Finally, on 3 January 1648, with no time to gain the proprietor's consent, the provincial court made her his attorney-in-fact—replacing Calvert, who had had that power—so that she could sell Baltimore's cattle immediately.

At this point, Margaret Brent made the move for which she is most famous. On 21 January, perhaps in hopes of avoiding a sale without Baltimore's direct authorization, she asked admission to the assembly with two votes, one for herself and one as the proprietor's attorney. She well knew that without her persuasion the assembly would not vote taxes to pay soldiers whom Calvert had promised to pay himself. In an age when women, queens excepted, did not participate directly in political life, Governor Thomas Green refused. Of necessity, Brent then began the sale, thereby averting a crisis that could have destroyed the colony and its experiment in religious freedom.

The Maryland assembly expressed well the nature of Margaret Brent's achievement. 'We do Verily Believe', they wrote to Lord Baltimore,

> [your estate] was better for the Collonys safety at that time in her hands then in any mans else … for the Soldiers would never have treated any other with … Civility and respect. … She rather deserved favour and thanks from your Honour for her so much Concurring to the publick safety then to be justly liable to … bitter invectives. (Browne and others, 1.239)

The men of her place and time would not give her the vote, but they openly acknowledged that her leadership and civilizing talents had been of crucial importance to the 'publick safety'.

In England, Baltimore was outraged at this appropriation of his property. By 1651 his wrath had driven Margaret and Mary Brent to join their brother Giles—also suffering the proprietor's strong disfavour—in northern Virginia. There, at their plantation called Peace in Stafford county, Margaret Brent died about 1671, possessed of 2700 acres of land.

Some have interpreted Margaret Brent as an early suffragette. This she was not. Well born, exceptionally able, and entrusted with a heavy responsibility, she undoubtedly felt entitled to participate in making decisions necessary to rescue the colony; but nothing indicates a belief that women generally should have the vote. Nevertheless, her act had future consequences when twentieth-century Americans discovered her story and used it to forward the history of women. LOIS GREEN CARR

Sources W. H. Browne and others, eds., *Archives of Maryland*, vols. 1–4, 10, 41 (1883–1922), vols. 1, 3–4, 10, 41 · *Genealogies of Virginia families from the 'Virginia Magazine of History and Biography'*, 1 (Baltimore, 1981), 233–7, 272–3, 286, 291–3, 303, 320–21, 328–30 · MSS, Maryland State Archives, Annapolis, Maryland, patents 1:24, 31–3; 3:112; 6:26–7; 11:282–3 · D. M. French, *The Brent family: Carroll families of Maryland* (Alexandria, VA, 1981) · A. Loker, 'Margaret Brent: attorney, adventurer, and suffragette', *Chronicles of St Mary's*, 46 (1998), 317–31 · J. C. Spruill, 'Mistress Margaret Brent, spinster', *Maryland Historical Magazine*, 29 (1934), 259–68 · B. E. Steiner, 'The Catholic Brents of colonial Virginia: an instance of practical toleration', *Virginia Magazine of History and Biography*, 70 (1962), 387–409
Wealth at death 1000 acres at Kent Island in Maryland; 2700 acres in Virginia; livestock; six silver spoons; land rights in Maryland not worth much: will, *Genealogies of Virginia families*, vol. 1, pp. 229–30, 320–21

Brent, Sir Nathanael (1573/4–1652), ecclesiastical lawyer and college head, was one of twelve children and the fifth son of Anker Brent (d. 1598) of Little Wolford, Warwickshire, and of his wife, Elizabeth, daughter of John Prat of Chipping Camden, Gloucestershire. Chosen in 1589 postmaster (scholar) of Merton College, Oxford, he matriculated on 13 November 1590, aged sixteen. After graduating BA on 20 June 1593 he was admitted fellow of Merton on 9 October 1594, and confirmed on 9 October 1595. Brent proceeded MA on 31 October 1598. In 1603–4 Brent was deputy to the senior proctor of the university, William Laud then being junior proctor. On 15 April 1607 he himself was elected senior proctor. Due to a shortage of senior jurists, Brent was dispensed in July 1609 to participate in law exercises at the act but he did not proceed to a degree. From 1605 to 1613 he was subwarden of Merton and effectively governed for the frequently absent warden, Sir Henry Savile, supervising his refurnishing of the college library and building of the Fellows' Quadrangle.

The college rewarded Brent in April 1612 with a lifetime lease of the tithes of Burmington and in August with £15 per annum for travel abroad. He left for France on 5 May 1613, acting as tutor to Lord Cromwell. In Venice he attached himself to Sir Dudley Carleton's embassy, initially as steward to Lady Carleton, Sir Henry Savile's stepdaughter. In 1615 he was arrested by the Spanish authorities on a visit to Milan, but swiftly released. He eventually replaced Isaac Wake as Carleton's secretary, and in 1616 transferred with his patron to The Hague, where he was for a time left in charge during an ambassadorial absence. Later that year Carleton unsuccessfully proposed Brent, who had returned to England, for appointment as secretary of Ireland. For more than a year Brent sought promotion in London, appealing through Savile's cousin, Sir

Richard Beaumont, to Sir Edward Villiers, the marquess of Buckingham's brother. Powerful patronage eventually came from Archbishop George Abbot, who, advised by the renegade archbishop of Spalato, Antonio De Dominis, sent him back to Venice in 1618 to smuggle out Paolo Sarpi's Italian history of the Council of Trent. This was published by De Dominis in 1619, and by Brent in translation in 1620 as *The Historie of the Councel of Trent*, with dedications to King James and Abbot.

Although a long-term absentee, and, as he wrote of Oxford in 1621, 'an absolute stranger to that Israel' (Bodl. Oxf., MS Add., C. 259, fol. 32r), Brent had been senior fellow of Merton since 1614. When Savile died on 19 February 1622, Brent rushed into residence, and was the fellows' preferred candidate to succeed as warden at an election on 21 February. Despite the late candidature of Sir Isaac Wake, promoted by Prince Charles, the visitor, Archbishop Abbot, appointed Brent, who on 20 March assumed the wardenship. Shortly afterwards Brent surrendered the Burmington tithes to Subwarden Simonson, who had doubtless aided his election and whom he maintained in office for several years. With dispensations from convocation, Brent took his BCL and DCL degrees together on 11 October 1623. On 20 February 1626 he married Martha (*d.* 1650/51), daughter of the late Bishop Robert *Abbot of Salisbury and niece of the archbishop. Their eldest son, George, was born about 1627; two other sons and two daughters survived their father. As warden Brent actively defended Merton's property interests and effected improvements in college buildings, including enlargement of the library, the fitting of a gallery to the warden's lodgings in 1626, and the decoration and paving with marble of the chapel choir after 1634. The number of fellows increased considerably, reaching a historic high in the mid-1630s.

Meanwhile, perhaps in an attempt to prove his loyalty in the context of the conversion of some cousins to Catholicism, he undertook at Abbot's urging an edition of a work by Francis Mason in defence of Anglican orders, published in 1625 as *Vindiciae ecclesiae Anglicanae*, with a dedication by the editor to King James. Under archiepiscopal patronage he was already developing a career as a church lawyer. Admitted to practise in the court of arches on 23 October 1624 (although he did not enter Doctors' Commons until 26 April 1637), he also became commissary of the Canterbury diocese, master of the faculties, and vicargeneral to Abbot, jointly with Sir Thomas Ridley, from 10 December 1628 and alone from 9 February 1629. As Abbot's influence declined, Brent benefited from another patron in his former diplomatic chief, Sir Dudley Carleton (*d.* 1632), secretary of state and Viscount Dorchester from 1628. He was knighted at Woodstock on 23 August 1629 and afterwards entertained at Merton first the French and Dutch ambassadors and then, by Dorchester's influence, the king and queen.

William Laud, as Abbot's successor at Canterbury from 1633, was initially suspicious of his inherited vicargeneral, but Brent soon gained his confidence, being in the visitation of the southern province between 1634 and 1637 the chief visible agent of the implementation of the Laudian programme. It was Brent who presided over the inculcation of canonical practices, ordered clergy to use only the prayer book catechism and encouraged them to read the Book of Sports, although he later claimed that he was unenthusiastic about the order for receiving communion at the altar rail and thus enforced it only sparingly. When, as chancellor, Laud brought the king and queen to Oxford in 1636 Brent, pronounced an 'honest man' by his archbishop (PRO, SP 16/330/17), presented Prince Rupert for the MA degree. However, his long absences from Merton exacerbated internal tensions, and gave the hostile senior fellow, Peter Turner, Laud's most trusted Oxford agent, an opportunity to undermine Brent's flourishing career. In 1637 Brent and his subwarden, Alexander Fisher, were accused by fellows of financial irregularities such as maladministration and extravagance. Despite efforts by Brent and Fisher to impede their investigations, commissioners appointed by Laud to visit the college found that the warden had indeed been negligent about discipline and, more seriously, that he had granted irregular leases to the detriment of the house and the benefit of himself and friends. In April 1638 Gilbert Sheldon, one of the commissioners, wrote to Laud that Brent would have great need of mercy and after a hearing at Lambeth from 2 to 4 October Laud noted, 'the Warden appeared very foul' (*The Works of … William Laud*, ed. J. Bliss and W. Scott, 7 vols., 1847–60, 3.230). The visitation continued until the Long Parliament, but the archbishop took no action against Brent, possibly in part because an important commissioner, Richard Baylie, president of St John's College and husband of Laud's niece, was sympathetic to Brent's plight.

None the less, all understanding between Laud and Brent was destroyed. By 1640 the warden had aligned himself with Laud's enemy, and successor as chancellor of the university from 1641, Philip Herbert, earl of Pembroke. It was probably with the backing of Pembroke and certainly with that of the anti-Laudian college heads John Prideaux and Paul Hood that Brent unsuccessfully sought election to parliament for the university in 1640. Although suspect in parliament for exercise of ecclesiastical jurisdiction, and even threatened with impeachment for his condemnation of John Bastwick, Brent stayed afloat thanks to powerful friends, such as the earls of Northumberland and Essex, Sir Benjamin Rudyerd, and Michael Oldisworth. He may have flirted with claiming the visitorship of Merton for Archbishop John Williams of York. Brent avoided commitment in the protestation returns of early 1642 by absence from college. By June 1642 Pembroke had determined to make him, a layman and therefore capable in parliament's eyes of exercising jurisdiction, vicechancellor (albeit under certain conditions) but royal intervention forced a climb-down. About three months later Brent left Oxford for London and was soon committed against the king.

In 1643 Brent was appointed by parliament a licenser for books on legal and other matters and in the year that followed there was 'no man more ready to impeach Laud at his trial' (Wood, *History and Antiquities*, 2.615) by providing hostile evidence of popish disposition and of tyrannical interference at Merton. On 25 June 1644 parliament appointed him to a committee for raising money and forces in Oxfordshire. Later that year, on 4 November, he was named by parliamentary ordinance to head the prerogative court of Canterbury, a position he filled until death. He was soon acting as provost marshal for the parliamentary forces and on 16 August 1644 was appointed a commissioner for courts martial. By 1644 Brent was advising parliamentary committees on admiralty matters and treaties, and acting as judge in the high court of admiralty. On 3 April 1646 he was appointed to a court martial for London, Westminster, and the lines of communication.

Brent was by now a wealthy man: in 1644 the committee for advance of money assessed him at £500, with estates in Northumberland, Warwickshire, Berkshire, and Oxfordshire. However, on 24 January 1645 the king ejected Brent from his wardenship for joining the rebels, acting in judicial capacity for parliamentary forces, and abandoning office, and appointed in his place his own physician, Dr William Harvey, who was admitted on 9 April.

With the surrender of Oxford in July 1646 and Harvey's withdrawal, Brent simply came back. On 1 May 1647, with Pembroke restored to the chancellorship, parliament commissioned him to head visitors appointed to reform the university. Lampooning the chancellor's formal entry into Oxford on 11 April 1648 Thomas Winyard singled out Brent, 'the courteous Knight of the bald pate', as one of Pembroke's leading supporters (*An Owle at Athens*, 1648, 5).

Merton, used as the visitors' base and dominated by Brent, had an unusually high proportion of submissions in 1648, probably because the warden made easy terms for docile royalists. Anthony Wood, despite recalcitrance, was countenanced by Brent's favour to his mother, and in April 1650 was given a remunerative sinecure as Bible clerk. Even this failed to win over the loyalist Mertonian antiquary who was horrified by the warden's sacrilegious removal of chapel hangings for use in his bedchamber.

Merton was briefly restored to a measure of self-government. By August 1649, however, Brent had lost control of the visitors, from whose activities he gradually withdrew, and in February 1651 he appealed to the parliamentary committee against visitatorial interference. It seems that he also refused the engagement. He resigned the wardenship on 27 November 1651. The tragic death of his eldest son in a duel in France about 1649, and perhaps that of his wife which occurred about this time or shortly after, must have taken their toll.

Brent retired to a house in Aldersgate Street, Little Britain, London, where he died on 6 November 1652. He was buried beside his late wife in the church of St Bartholomew-the-Less on 17 November. A eulogistic Latin epitaph by John Sictor, a Bohemian exile who had been helped by Brent, was printed. Brent's will, dated 4 November 1652 and proved 29 April 1653, manifests his standing as a man of property. He confirmed a gift of the manors of Clapcot and Rush Court near Wallingford, Berkshire,

granted to his elder surviving son, Basil, on his recent marriage. Dr Richard Corbett, husband of Brent's elder daughter, Mary, was made executor and entrusted with two younger children. He was also forgiven his debts and left a lease of the rectories of Embleton and Ponteland, Northumberland, which Brent held from Merton College in the name of another, and about which questions had been asked at the visitation. The remainder of a lease from Eton College of the rectory of Long Compton, Warwickshire, was given to Brent's younger son, Nathaniel, who also received houses in Fleet Street and Temple Bar, London. An unmarried second daughter, Anne, was left £2500. Brent bequeathed most of his library to Corbett, and the residue of his estate to Basil.

Brent was a man of talent but it is hard to dissent from Anthony Wood's hostile assessment that, 'minding wealth and the settling of a family more than generous actions' (Wood, *Ath. Oxon.*, 2.316), he had done far less for his college than had his predecessor. Brent had turned on the church and bishops after defending them in print and building his career on them: the warden was a 'weathercock' (Wood, *History and Antiquities*, 2.615).

A. J. HEGARTY

Sources Merton College register, Merton Oxf. · J. M. Fletcher, ed., *Registrum annalium collegii Mertonensis, 1567–1603*, OHS, new ser., 24 (1976) · Wood, *Ath. Oxon.*, new edn, 2.316; 3.333–6 · *The life and times of Anthony Wood*, ed. A. Clark, 1, OHS, 19 (1891), 144, 147, 162–3; 2, OHS, 21 (1892), 368–9 · W. B. Chilton, 'The Brent family', *Virginia Magazine of History and Biography*, 12–22 (1904–14) · A. Wood, *The history and antiquities of the University of Oxford*, ed. J. Gutch, 2 (1796), 502, 614–15 · *Reg. Oxf.*, 2/1.248; 2/2.181, 294; 2/3.177 · J. Sictor, 'Epitaphium', Bodl. Oxf., MS Wood 429 (7) [one sheet, printed] · Bodl. Oxf., MS Add. C. 259, fols. 25r–26r, 27r–28r, 32r–v, 47r–v · Bodl. Oxf., MS Bodley 659 · Abbot register, LPL, II, fols. 234v–236r, 236v–237r · M. Burrows, ed., *The register of the visitors of the University of Oxford, from AD 1647 to AD 1658*, CS, new ser., 29 (1881), lxi, cix, 257, 328 · C. H. Firth and R. S. Rait, eds., *Acts and ordinances of the interregnum, 1642–1660*, 1 (1911), 186, 456, 486, 498, 564–6, 842 · BL, MS Stow 176, fol. 122r · J. W. Stoye, *English travellers abroad, 1604–1667* (1952) · parish register, London, St Bartholomew-the-Less, 17 Nov 1652, GL [burial] · parish register, London, St Stephen Coleman Street, 20 Feb 1626, GL, MS 4449/1 [marriage]

Archives Bodl. Oxf., corresp., MS Bodley 659

Wealth at death confirmation of manors of Clapcot and Rushcourt, remainder of lease on Long Compton rectory, and residue of estate to elder son; houses in Fleet Street and Temple Bar, plus £50 at the age of sixteen to younger son; lease of Embleton and Ponteland to son-in-law, whose debts were forgiven; £50 at the age of sixteen and further £2500 to younger daughter; £10 each to servants; 20 nobles to poor of parish; £4 to poor of Long Compton; £20 to bishop of Rochester; £10 to his wife: will, PRO, PROB 11/229, fol. 222; Chilton, 'Brent family', 316–18

Brentford. For this title name *see* Ruthven, Patrick, earl of Forth and earl of Brentford (*d.* 1651); Hicks, William Joynson-, first Viscount Brentford (1865–1932).

Brenton, Edward Pelham (1774–1839), naval officer and naval historian, the second son of Rear-Admiral Jahleel Brenton (1729–1802) and his wife, Henrietta, daughter of Joseph Cowley of Wolverhampton, and younger brother of Vice-Admiral Sir Jahleel *Brenton, was born in Rhode Island on 20 July 1774. He entered the navy in November

1788, and, after serving in the East Indies and in the Channel Fleet, was made lieutenant on 27 May 1795, and served in the North Sea, on the Newfoundland station, and in the West Indies. On 29 April 1802 he was made commander. He married, on 29 March 1803, Margaret Diana, daughter of General Thomas Cox, and they had a large family. On the renewal of the war in 1803 he was appointed to command the *Merlin*, and employed in the blockade of the north coast of France. On 16 December 1803 he succeeded in a brave attempt to destroy the frigate *Shannon*, which had got on shore near Cape Barfleur, and had been taken possession of by the French. In January 1805 he was appointed to the brig *Amaranthe*, in which he cruised with some success in the North Sea; and in 1808 he was sent to the West Indies, where, for his distinguished bravery in the attack on a small French squadron under the batteries of St Pierre of Martinique, he was advanced to post rank, his commission being dated back to 13 December 1808, the day of the action. Anticipating his promotion, the admiral, Sir Alexander Cochrane, had appointed him acting captain of the *Pompée* (74 guns), bearing the broad pennant of Commodore Cockburn, under whose immediate command he served with the brigade of seamen landed for the capture of Martinique. He afterwards returned to Europe, with the commodore, in the *Belleisle*, in charge of the garrison, who, according to the capitulation, were to be taken to France and there exchanged. As, however, the French government refused to restore an equivalent number of British, the prisoners, numbering some 2400, were taken to Portsmouth and detained there until the end of the war. Brenton was afterwards employed in convoy service, and in August 1810 was appointed to command the frigate *Spartan*, in succession to his brother Jahleel. In 1811 the *Spartan* was sent to North America, and continued there during most of the Anglo-American war, but met with no opportunity of distinguished service. She returned to England in the autumn of 1813, when Brenton went on half-pay; nor did he ever serve again, with the exception of a few months in the summer of 1815, when he acted as flag-captain to Rear-Admiral Sir Benjamin Hallowell.

Brenton then turned to writing, publishing in 1823 his *Naval History of Great Britain from the Year 1783 to 1822* (5 vols.), and in 1838 the *Life and Correspondence of John, Earl of St. Vincent* (2 vols.). As an officer of rank, who had been actively employed during the period of his history, his opportunities of gaining information were almost unequalled; but he seems to have been incapable of sifting his evidence, and to have been guided more by prejudice than judgement. The plan of his work is good, but the execution feeble, and its authority as to matter of fact is often slender. His public disagreement with the other historian of the navy in the French wars, William James, was based on very different politics (Brenton being a whig and James a tory), as well as matters of fact and the merit of a civilian commentator on the service. He also published pamphlets and took an active, and latterly an absorbing, part in the promotion of temperance societies, in the establishment and conduct of the Society for the Relief of

Shipwrecked Mariners, and more especially of the Children's Friend Society, the intention of which was, in many respects, better than the results. These activities provoked harsh criticism of him, which he felt severely, and which embittered his last years. He died suddenly, at York Street, Gloucester Place, London, on 6 April 1839. Among the mourners at his funeral on 13 April 1839, at Marylebone church, where he was buried, were one hundred boys of the Children's Friend Society, the senior boy bearing the flag presented by Mrs Brenton, hung with black crape.

J. K. LAUGHTON, rev. ANDREW LAMBERT

Sources W. James, *The naval history of Great Britain, from the declaration of war by France, in February 1793, to the accession of George IV, in January 1820*, [2nd edn], 6 vols. (1826) · J. Marshall, *Royal naval biography*, suppl. 1 (1827), 411–27 · J. Brenton, *Memoir of Captain Edward Pelham Brenton* (1842) · review, QR, 62 (1838), 424–52 · GM, 2nd ser., 11 (1839), 659

Archives Yale U., Beinecke L., corresp. relating to his naval history of Great Britain

Likenesses Franklin, engraving, repro. in E. P. Brenton, *Naval history* (1837) · line and stipple engraving (after Franklin), BM, NPG; repro. in E. P. Brenton, *Naval history* (1837)

Brenton, Sir Jahleel, first baronet (1770–1844), naval officer, was born on 22 August 1770 in Rhode Island, North America, the eldest of the ten children of Rear-Admiral Jahleel Brenton (1729–1802) and his wife, Henrietta, daughter of Joseph Cowley of Wolverhampton and his wife, Penelope Pelham. The family, which had originally emigrated to America in the seventeenth century, returned to Britain in 1780, during the American War of Independence, as Brenton's father, then a commander in the Royal Navy, was a loyalist.

Early life and naval service Brenton first attended a school at Enfield, but in 1781 entered the armed ship *Queen* under his father's command, and moved with him to the *Termagant* until 1783. For the next two years he was at a school in Chelsea for the sons of naval officers, and thereafter joined his family in France until 1787. On their return Brenton again entered the navy, and served two years at Nova Scotia. When he returned to England in 1789 he saw no hope of employment and, having passed his lieutenant's examination in March 1790, he accepted a commission in the Swedish navy. On 9 July 1790 he took part in the battle of Svenskund between the Russian and Swedish navies then disputing Baltic supremacy.

Brenton was promoted to the rank of lieutenant in the Royal Navy on 20 November 1790 and returned to England, where he was appointed second lieutenant of the troop ship *Assurance*, bound for Halifax. But while at Rochester, pressing deserters, he was arrested and temporarily imprisoned by the mayor. Subsequently he was appointed first lieutenant of the *Speedy*, pursuing smugglers until the sloop was paid off in 1791. Two years' service on the Newfoundland station between 1792 and 1794 was followed by embarking the remnants of the British army from Flanders in the *Sybil*. The extreme cold and fatigue of this service forced him to seek sick-leave at the end of 1795. On his recovery he was appointed to a Mediterranean-bound store-ship. He protested to the Admiralty at this seeming humiliation and again, on reaching the Mediterranean, to Admiral Jervis, who appointed him first lieutenant of the *Gibraltar*. This reflected Jervis's stated policy of promoting the sons of naval officers, whom he regarded as 'children of the service' (Raikes, 64). Nevertheless, the appointment was no sinecure. The *Gibraltar*'s officers were riven with factions. Introducing Brenton, Captain John Packenham appealed to them to 'bury the hatchet and be friends' (ibid., 65) and Jervis attributed the subsequent improvement in feeling to Brenton's influence. As a result, when the *Gibraltar* was disabled in a gale and sent home for repair, Brenton was temporarily placed in the *Barfleur*, in which he served at the battle of Cape St Vincent and of which he was then promoted first lieutenant. In August 1797 he removed first to the flagship the *Ville de Paris* and then to acting command of the *Speedy* at Lisbon in September 1798, confirmed on 3 July 1799. His actions against enemy gunboats several times in 1799 won Admiralty approval and promotion to post rank on 25 April 1800, when he was appointed temporarily to the prize *Généreux*, and gave up the command of the *Speedy* to Lord Cochrane. Although the *Généreux* was undermanned and damaged by a gale, Brenton got her to sea in May to join the blockade of Genoa. On 1 January 1801 he was appointed to the *Caesar*, as flag-captain to Sir James Saumarez, and played an important part in the battle of Algeciras on 6 July. Through the exceptional exertions of his enthusiastic crew, Brenton repaired the *Caesar*'s serious battle damage and enabled her to take part in the subsequent brilliant defeat of the Franco-Spanish squadron in the straits on 12 July 1801. He continued in the *Caesar*, after the peace, until March 1802, when he obtained leave to return to England. He had long been engaged to Isabella Stewart, the daughter of Anthony Stewart of Maryland. A loyalist family, the Stewarts moved to Nova Scotia in 1783. Although Brenton met Miss Stewart in 1788, he promised his father he would not marry until he achieved post rank. Now, after arriving in England on 7 April 1802, he married her on 19 April, and they spent the succeeding months at their home in Bath.

War service and captivity, 1803–1815 In March 1803 Brenton was appointed to the frigate *Minerve*, but had only just joined her when he was severely concussed by a block falling on his head, which compelled him to go on shore. He resumed the command in June, but in his first cruise, having chased some vessels in towards Cherbourg in a thick fog, the ship ran aground under the guns of the heaviest batteries on 2 July 1803. After sustaining their fire, and that of two gunboats, for ten hours, and failing to get her off, Brenton was compelled to surrender. This early French success was announced in the Brussels theatre by Napoleon himself, who ascribed it to the gunboats, and as a result the captured *Minerve* was renamed *La Canonière*. The whole ship's company were made prisoners of war, and Brenton and his officers were marched to the French prison depot of Verdun, approximately 600 miles away. Despite giving their parole not to escape, they had a numerous armed escort. At Caen, Brenton protested to the district commander, who expressed contemptuous ignorance of what Brenton's parole meant. He indignantly replied 'It is, with a British officer, stronger than any prison you have in France' (Raikes, 159). His honourable conduct and thoughtfulness for his fellow prisoners gradually improved harsh conditions, on the march and at Verdun, and when he became senior British officer there he extended this care to British prisoners at other depots in north-eastern France.

As the exchange of prisoners had broken down, Brenton asked permission for his family to join him at Verdun. M. Decrès, minister of marine, arranged a passport and on 28 April 1805 Brenton's sister, wife, and eldest son, John Jervis Brenton (b. 19 Jan 1803), arrived there. Considerable relaxation of the rules governing prisoners of war was sometimes allowed on both sides to officers who gave their parole not to escape. Brenton, whose health was indifferent, received permission to spend the winter of 1805 at Tours. The family proceeded via Epernay, where they toured the champagne cellars of Messrs Moët, and at Meux on 4 November they heard the news of Trafalgar from the local innkeeper. Brenton's second child, Frances Isabella, was born at Tours on 15 January 1806 and in a letter to his wife in 1810, Brenton recalled this period as the happiest of his life and 'always present in my recollection' (Raikes, 389). Here in December 1806 Brenton heard of his exchange for Captain Infernet of the *Intrepide*, a nephew of Marshal Masséna, taken prisoner at Trafalgar with his ten-year-old son.

Brenton arrived in England on 29 December 1806 and was tried for the loss of the *Minerve*, on 7 February 1807; he was honourably acquitted and immediately appointed to the *Spartan*, a new frigate of 32 guns, which he joined on 10 February for the Mediterranean.

At first Admiral Collingwood received Brenton coolly. The loss of the *Minerve* may have led him to believe Brenton rash. The more recent loss, off Lisbon, of a transport convoyed by the *Spartan* and the heavy casualties she suffered on 14 May 1807 in an ill-judged attack on an enemy polacre off Nice, led to a court of inquiry into Brenton's conduct. Although he was acquitted, Collingwood, that most careful and economical of commanders with men and stores, expressed himself dissatisfied with the verdict and Brenton spent the remainder of that year cruising off Toulon, attempting to redeem his reputation.

In September 1808 the *Spartan* joined the *Impérieuse* (Captain Cochrane), which was successfully attacking merchant vessels in the Bay of Rosas and French positions on the Spanish coast. From there, between October and the spring of 1809, Brenton cruised in the eastern Mediterranean. In early April, after conveying the British and Spanish ambassadors from Malta to Trieste, *en route* for Vienna, he took command of a small squadron of three frigates, *Amphion*, *Thames*, and *Mercury*, and drove the French out of Pesaro on 23 April. On 12 May, in co-operation with Austrian troops, he forced the surrender of the French garrison on the Croatian island of Lussin, and in early October of French garrisons on the Ionian islands of Zante, Cephalonia, and Cerigo. These successes caused Collingwood to commend Brenton's zeal and talents to the Admiralty, declaring that at Lussin 'he undertook and accomplished a service which would have established a reputation had he never had another opportunity' (Raikes, 365).

In May 1810, while cruising in company with the *Success* (32 guns), Brenton chased a small French squadron into Naples. This consisted of the frigate *Cérès*, of superior force to the *Spartan*, the frigate *Fama* (28 guns), a brig, and a cutter. Brenton, feeling certain that the French ships would not come out in the face of two frigates, dispatched the *Success* to the southward, and on the morning of 3 May stood back towards Naples, hoping to tempt the enemy to come out. They had anticipated his wish, and having taken on board an additional 400 soldiers and been joined by seven gunboats, they met the *Spartan* in the very entrance of the bay, about midway between Ischia and Capri. The action that ensued was extremely bloody. The *Spartan*'s broadsides created havoc on the crowded decks of the French ships, while the heavy fire of the gunboats inflicted losses of ten killed and twenty-two wounded on the *Spartan*. Brenton himself was badly wounded in the hip by a grapeshot, and during the latter part of the fight the *Spartan* was commanded by her first lieutenant, G. W. Willes. The brig was captured, but the *Spartan*'s rigging was so damaged she could not prevent the *Cérès* and *Fama* from getting under some batteries in Baia Bay. Willes was deservedly promoted for his conduct, and Captain Brenton's bravery, his tactical skill, and the severity of his wound won him sympathy and admiration. Yet his judgement had been at fault, since the French had already determined to engage him, independently of the *Success*'s absence. The patriotic fund at Lloyd's voted him a sword, worth 100 guineas, and the king of the Two Sicilies presented him with the grand cross of St Ferdinand on 10 May 1810. Brenton was made a baronet on 3 November 1812 and a KCB on 2 January 1815.

Latter years, 1815–1844 On 4 May 1810 Brenton learned of his appointment as commander of the Adriatic squadron, which he was too ill to accept. His wound compelled him to return to England in the *Spartan*. For nearly two years he was on shore, suffering much pain, aggravated by the loss of all his property by the failure of his agents, and by the loss of a prize appeal which left him in debt to the extent of £3000. His friends paid this debt, and a pension of £300, in compensation for his wound, helped relieve the financial anxiety. Yet he had to give up his home at Bath, and move to the London area, where he took lodgings in Paddington. In March 1812, partially recovered, he accepted the command of the *Stirling Castle* (74 guns) in the channel; but he soon resigned the appointment, feeling his health was too poor for active service. Towards the close of 1813 he was appointed commissioner of the dockyard at Port Mahon, and on the abolition of that establishment at the peace he was sent on 1 January 1815 to the Cape of Good Hope in the same capacity. His wife died there on 29 July 1817 after a long illness, and a month later, on 27 August, Brenton's eldest son died at Hyde Abbey School, after being ill a short time. Brenton's heir was now his son Lancelot Charles Lee (*b*. 18 Feb 1807). Named after a fellow

prisoner of Brenton at Verdun, whose father had been warden of Winchester College, he took his degree at Oxford but later became a nonconformist minister. He died without an heir in 1862, and the baronetcy became extinct.

The establishment at the Cape was reduced on the death of Napoleon in 1821, and Brenton returned to England on 1 January 1822. On 9 October he married his cousin Harriet Mary Brenton (*d*. 1863), the youngest daughter of James Brenton of Halifax, Nova Scotia. A daughter, Harriet Mary, was born on 16 January 1824. In later life she wrote a collection of naval stories for children, *Evenings with Grandpapa* (1860), adapted from those told her by her father and based on his experiences. For some time Brenton had the temporary command of the royal yacht, and from November 1829 until the summer of 1830, of the guardship *Donegal* at Sheerness. He attained his flag as rear-admiral of the Blue on 22 July 1830, and on the death of Captain Browell, was appointed lieutenant-governor of Greenwich Hospital in September 1831, at a salary of £800 a year. Here he found old shipmates from the *Spartan*, who welcomed him with 'Here we are, sir, laid up together in Greenwich tier' (Raikes, 639). In course of seniority he would have been included in the promotion on Queen Victoria's coronation, and have been made a vice-admiral of the White. This was incompatible, however, with his office at Greenwich and the rank was held in abeyance, although it was given him, with his original seniority, on his retirement on 1 July 1840. After his retirement Brenton lived first at Casterton, Westmorland, but his health was poor; he suffered increasingly severe attacks of gout and moved to the midlands, where he lived at Elford House, near Lichfield, and finally at 28 Lansdowne Place, Leamington Spa, which was then being developed as a fashionable spa by Henry Jephson. Here Brenton died, of 'general debility', on 21 April 1844.

Brenton was tory in his loyalty to the crown and, earlier, to the younger Pitt, but religion was a greater influence than politics on his life. He was a serious-minded but cheerful man, a regular reader of the Bible and John Newton's letters. In later life he was a friend of William Wilberforce. One of the witnesses to his will in 1840 was the philanthropic clergyman the Revd William Carus-Wilson of Casterton, founder, in 1824, of a school for the daughters of poor clergy made notorious in *Jane Eyre* as Lowood Institution. A sabbatarian but not a Tractarian, Brenton was one of a new breed of early nineteenth-century naval officers whose piety could produce active philanthropy but could also lead to gloomy introspection; in retirement he expressed guilt at entering the Swedish service in 1790, 'led away by the idea of distinction and eminence' (Raikes, 40).

Throughout his life Brenton spent time and energy on the work of religious and charitable organizations. At Verdun he persuaded the authorities to permit the use of a building as a chapel with regular services and temporarily established a school for the boy prisoners there. At Greenwich he reorganized the naval school and established libraries for the pensioners. During his active career, and in retirement, he developed his interest in the conditions of merchant seamen. His brother Edward Pelham *Brenton shared these interests, and together they formed a society for the relief of shipwrecked sailors, and investigated the problems of juvenile delinquency.

To promote these subjects Brenton wrote a number of books and pamphlets: *An Appeal to the British Nation on Behalf of her Sailors* (1838), *The Hope of the Navy, or, The True Source of Discipline and Efficiency* (1839), and *Remarks on the Importance of our Coast Fisheries etc.* (1843). A *Memoir of Captain Edward Pelham Brenton* (1842) commemorated his brother's literary achievements and their shared interests.

An active and zealous officer, whose training of his crews in ship-handling and gunnery illustrates the increasing professionalism of naval officers, Brenton lacked the opportunities to make an outstanding naval career. In a letter of 1844 to O'Byrne, he described the surrender of the *Minerve* as the most important event of his life. His imprisonment certainly interrupted his career at a crucial point, and ill health as a result of wounds prevented later active service at an equally important period. Yet his employment after 1815 marks the esteem in which he was held by the Admiralty, and his lieutenant-governorship of Greenwich Hospital suitably crowned a useful career.

Brenton once said he felt his courage was not natural but acquired; that on going into action he felt anxious until the first shot was fired, although from that moment he thought of nothing but the battle. He could appear rash, yet his impetuous action off Naples in 1810 was similar to Philip Broke's challenge to Lawrence of the *Chesapeake* in 1813. On going into action against the *Cérès*, Brenton's surgeon and friend Williamson declared 'Now sir, here is victory or Westminster Abbey for you' (Raikes, 401), a Nelsonian quotation: many officers in this period were inspired to emulate Nelson, who had often appeared reckless. Brenton's reactions, typical of his time, were none the less genuine, both in their youthful spirit of emulation and in his later reprobation of them when age and ill health had brought reflection.   P. K. CRIMMIN

Sources J. Marshall, *Royal naval biography*, 2/1 (1824) • O'Byrne, *Naval biog. dict.*, [2nd edn] • BL, Add. MS 38040, fols. 243–9 • D. Syrett and R. L. DiNardo, *The commissioned sea officers of the Royal Navy, 1660–1815*, rev. edn, Occasional Publications of the Navy RS, 1 (1994) • H. Raikes, ed., *Memoir of the life of Vice Admiral Sir Jahleel Brenton*, new edn, ed. L. C. L. Brenton (1855) • M. Lewis, *Napoleon and his British captives* (1962) • Burke, *Gen. GB* • Burke, *Peerage* • W. Stockdale, *The present peerage of the UK* (1820) • R. Brown, *The baronetage for 1844* (1844) • d. cert.
Archives BL, books, pamphlets • Courtauld Inst., Witt Library, collection of his drawings, incl. battle of Algeciras, various views at Cape of Good Hope, HMS *Rochefort* (1815), battle of St Vincent • PRO, corresp., and papers as commissioned at Simonstown, ADM 7/2–6 | BL, papers of Sir Hudson Lowe, Add. MSS 20139, fol. 91; 20233, fol. 6; 20189, fol. 187; 20190, fol. 241 • BL, corresp. with Sir T. Martin, Add. MS 41394, fols. 143–8; fols. 284–6 • BL, replies to O'Byrne's enquiries 1844, Add. MS 38040, fols. 243–9
Likenesses Smith of Barbadoes?, miniature, NMM • drawing (copy), NMM; repro. in Raikes, ed., *Memoir*, frontispiece
Wealth at death everything to wife: will, PRO, PROB 11/1998

Brereley, John. *See* Anderton, James (1557–1613).

Brereley, Roger (*bap.* 1586, *d.* 1637), Church of England clergyman and separatist leader, was born in Marland, then a hamlet in the parish of Rochdale, and baptized in the parish church on 7 August 1586. His father, Thomas Brereley, and his grandfather Roger Brereley were farmers, and in 1626 Roger himself was still in possession of a close in Castleton, in the manor of Rochdale, which had belonged to his grandfather.

Almost nothing is known of Brereley's early life and career. It seems probable that he attended the grammar school in Rochdale, which had been founded by Archbishop Matthew Parker in 1565. It is also likely that Rochdale was at the time an outpost of Lancashire puritanism. Richard Midgley and his son Joseph Midgley, who successively ministered to the parish from 1561 until 1607, were both repeatedly in trouble for nonconformity; in 1607 the younger Midgley was deprived of his benefice during Archbishop John Bancroft's campaign against clerical nonconformity. The influence of the Midgleys may account for Brereley's early religious proclivities, for later in life Brereley himself suggested that in his younger days he had been '[b]y some good fellows, tearm'd a Puritan' (Brereley, appendix, 3). He did not apparently receive any formal university training. By 1615 he had abandoned the mainstream puritanism of his youth, only to emerge as a charismatic preacher and spiritual leader, whose teachings were widely regarded by his fellow clergymen as erroneous, perhaps even heretical. At an unknown date before 1618 he married Anne, and he was perhaps the Roger Brearley who married Anne Hardman in September 1615 at St Mary, Bury, Lancashire.

In 1615 he and an associate named Richard Tennant were in trouble with the authorities for having preached without licence at the West Riding village of Gisburn; Brereley was further accused of baptizing a child there without using the sign of the cross. By this time he also appears to have been serving as curate to the chapelry of nearby Grindleton (Waddington parish), for in the same visitation he was accused of failing to read the Book of Common Prayer there and of having neglected to receive the holy communion at his parish church. He apparently conformed and was absolved, but in September 1616 he found himself before the York high commission on a much more serious set of charges. In that month various articles were produced against him, along with a schedule of fifty propositions, in which Brereley and his followers were accused of a broad range of doctrinal errors. Some of these accusations smacked of nonconformist extremism, as when it was claimed that 'what church or chappell hath within it a surplisse, crosse or such like, there will the lord never reveale himself either to preacher or people'. More typical were allegations suggesting a mystical form of piety, in which traditional puritan ideas of assurance and regeneration were seized, embellished, and in certain respects distorted to produce a mode of religiosity stressing the transformative effects of grace and the exalted state of believers.

Thus, Brereley and his followers had allegedly argued that 'after a man hath assurance of the forgiveness of his sinnes, he can never doubt again', and that 'The christian assured can never committ a gross sinne'. These allegedly powerful effects of divine grace were apparently taken to emanate from the intimate union that Brereley posited between believers and Christ: 'A man humbled in his soule for sinne ought not to putt upp any prayer to god in the name of christ, till by faith he is assured that christ dwells in him'; in a similar vein, he had allegedly taught that 'a christian may have more then faith, and more then assurance, for he may have god himself'. As for Brereley himself, it was claimed that his followers had dubbed him 'the Angell of England and the onlie one of a thousand', hinting at the intensely charismatic, even prophetic, role that the minister played within the movement that had grown up around him (Sippell, 50–52). Brereley's high commission case dragged on for over a year, drawing in dozens of witnesses; for part of this period Brereley was imprisoned. In the end he made a full declaration of his conformity, and in September 1617 he was restored to his spiritual function and excused court costs.

Yet this did not end Brereley's career as a charismatic preacher and he remained for several years at Waddington, where his daughter Ales (Alice) and son Thomas were baptized in August 1618 and August 1620 respectively. In his diary Nicholas Assheton claimed that on 18 April 1618 one John Swinglehurst had been buried in the parish of Waddington: 'he dyed distract: he was a great follower of Brereley'. Similarly, in 1619 it was alleged by the churchwardens of the puritan parish of Giggleswick that 'many goe to Grindleton and neglect their own parish church' (Marchant, 40). Meanwhile, Brereley appears to have won followers among the clergy, including not only the aforementioned Richard Tennant (rector of Burnsall from 1619 and vicar of Kettlewell from 1632), but also one William Boyes, who was presented from Kirkby Moorside in 1620 for erroneous opinions and for holding conventicles. By 1623 Brereley had moved on to become curate of St Andrew, Kildwick in Craven, also in Yorkshire; here two more of his children, Maria and Roger, were baptized in 1627 and 1630.

Other ministers who may have been influenced by Brereley were Peter Shaw, a notorious antinomian preacher first in the north and later in London; Robert Towne, who likewise began his clerical career in Yorkshire before appearing in the capital in the later 1620s; and William Aglin or Eglin, an obscure minister who was called as a witness in Brereley's first high commission trial and who later wrote a long verse tribute to Brereley upon the latter's death, describing his own conversion to Brereley's form of mystical religiosity. Word of Brereley's ministry and his talents appears to have spread quickly. By the early 1620s his ideas seem to have been creeping into Lancashire, for at some point before 1621 antinomian manuscripts began circulating in that county. There likewise survives a pastoral letter from Brereley to a follower in Newcastle, suggesting that his influence was not limited to the region straddling the Yorkshire–Lancashire border. Indeed, while suffering from a crisis of conscience at Cambridge in the mid-1620s, Thomas Shepard, later a celebrated patriarch of the Massachusetts Bay colony, heard tales of Brereley's ministry and resolved to travel to Grindleton to seek spiritual assistance. It was presumably during these years, as word of his ministry and following spread, that the label 'Grindletonian' came into common usage.

In spite of his popularity as an eccentric, enthusiastic, and possibly unorthodox preacher, Brereley was not, however, completely cut off from the puritan community at large. Thus, at some point before 1623, he still felt able to participate in the Halifax exercise, a puritan-dominated institution that centred on the figure of Dr John Favour, the nonconformist vicar of Halifax (also, paradoxically enough, a chaplain to Archbishop Tobie Matthew and an active member of the York high commission). Participation in such intra-puritan conferences eventually placed Brereley in jeopardy again. It was apparently as a result of such meetings that in April–May 1627, he, Tennant, and Boyes were once again summoned before the high commissioners. Although no articles or answers survive for this case, it seems that they were charged together with other puritan clergymen for having participated in informal clerical debates; in the course of the investigation, however, the accusation once again emerged that Tennant held opinions 'tending to the sect called Grindletonians and deeply suspected of Familisme' (Marchant, 46). Both Brereley and Tennant were likewise forced to provide lists of people who had attended their conventicles, while Boyes, now curate of Goathland, was compelled to give over a bond 'for the reformation of the errors' of which he had been accused (ibid., 47). Brereley was inhibited from preaching at any location other than Kildwick (perhaps suggesting that he had been doing so elsewhere), and he remained under censure until August 1628, when once again he was restored to his full spiritual functions, presumably after making yet another submission to the court.

In 1631 Brereley finally received a settled living within the church when he was presented to the rectory of Burnley, Lancashire. Kildwick, however, appears to have continued as a centre of Grindletonianism, for in 1634 his old curacy was filled by John Webster, who was quickly won over to Grindletonianism before going on to a career as a parliamentary army chaplain and a noted writer. In June 1637 Brereley died, survived by his wife, Anne, as well as at least three children, Thomas, Anne, and Abel (bap. 15 Dec 1633) and possibly also Alice. He was buried in Burnley church on 13 June. To judge from Aglin's funereal verses, Brereley's passing was greeted with a sense of deep mourning among his admirers, attesting to the powerful hold this charismatic minister exercised over many of his listeners.

Brereley's religious thought places him squarely within the 'antinomian' subculture that was developing at the edges of the puritan community during the first decades of the seventeenth century. Like other contemporaries accused of antinomianism, such as John Eaton and John

Traske, he appears to have objected to the overweening legalism of his puritan brethren, an objection that led him to downgrade the role of the law in the lives of believers. Yet he also appears to have been influenced by various mystical traditions emanating from outside the mainstream protestant tradition. The most important of these was the tradition associated with the *Theologia Germanica*, that famed work of medieval mysticism that had been published by Martin Luther on the eve of the Reformation, only to be rejected as a dangerous work of blasphemy by later reformers. Brereley reportedly translated the *Theologia* into English, a translation which seems to have circulated in London in the years before the civil war, eventually providing the basis for the edition published by the notorious antinomian Giles Randall in 1646. Yet hostile observers often claimed that Brereley's debt to unorthodox works of mysticism was greater still; as his 1627 high commission case reveals, he and his followers were habitually accused of flirting with the ideas of Hendrik Niclaes, the messianic founder of the Family of Love. In a Paul's Cross sermon of 1627, for instance, the London preacher Stephen Denison denounced those he called 'Grindltonian Familists' (S. Denison, *The White Wolfe*, 1627), while Thomas Shepard likewise suggested a connection between Grindleton and the Familists with whom he consorted during his period of spiritual malaise.

Modern scholars have found little to substantiate these claims in Brereley's own sermons and poems, which were published posthumously, probably by an obscure admirer named Josiah Collier. Brereley's writings appear to have circulated fairly widely in manuscript after his death; fragments of his work, together with selected poems and tracts by Collier, now survive in at least two separate archives (LPL, MS 3461 and Chetham's Library, MS A. 2. 24). Collier's collection of Brereley's sermons, cobbled together from 'head-notes', presumably as recorded by a listener, were first published in Edinburgh in 1670 under the title *A Bundle of Soul-Convincing, Directing and Comforting Truths*. In 1677 another edition appeared in London, this time with an appendix of Brereley's religious poetry. These works seem to reveal a temperament very different from that described by his enemies. Far from emerging as an enthusiastic crypto-Familist firebrand, the Brereley that takes shape from his own sermon notes seems a rather unpolemical, even uncontroversial figure. While the influence of the *Theologia Germanica* is felt throughout, his sermons contain few of the allegorical exuberances or hints of perfectionism characteristic of Hendrik Niclaes or his Familist followers. Rather, at least as revealed in his sermons, Brereley's mystical interests seem to have played themselves out within a broader context of strenuous, reformed protestantism. Thus, he consistently foregrounded the utter sinfulness of humanity, the sheer inability of humans to do any good of themselves, and the absolute necessity of Christ's extrinsic righteousness in the process of salvation. Brereley consistently reminded his listeners that to be saved people needed to suffer together with Christ, abasing themselves, allowing their own wills and works to die through divine grace, and in this manner to come into conformity with God's will.

None of this on its own was particularly controversial or heterodox, and were Brereley's sermons our only evidence concerning Grindletonianism it would be difficult to see why and how so many people saw him and his followers as dangerous heretics. Yet the writings of Collier and Aglin suggest that Brereley's private teachings were rather more radical than his public sermons would suggest. Collier, for instance, leaves no doubt that the Grindletonians were arguing that true believers were free of the commanding power of the moral law—the hallmark of theological antinomianism. Indeed, at least some of his followers, including the minister Aglin, took Brereley to be preaching an evangel of perfection, in which believers were brought by virtue of their union with Christ to a state of prelapsarian sinlessness. As Aglin described Brereley's ministry:

> He opened that misterye hye
> of Christ in power of the deitye
> his power in man, mans power brought to nought
> god all in all, this depth he ever sought
> the soule with Christ in unitye to dwell
> the sinfull poyson thereby to expell,
> the first estate of Innocence to finde
> by changeing quallytye of soule and minde
> by powerfull actions of the persons three
> the eye of man clearly the sonne to see
> whereby in that great fount the saints weare washt
> their sinfull soules weare with it all bedasht
> till puer and white, and of another dye
> they weare againe conformed perfectly
> into that Image of the light and then
> stood up again perfect and liveing men,
> from death redeemed and from hell set free.
> (LPL, MS 3461, pp. 245–6)

Thus, despite Brereley's own studiously moderate public pronouncements, and despite his protestations of orthodoxy, it seems beyond doubt that some of his earliest and most devout followers understood him as dispensing a message in which true believers were brought to a state of prelapsarian perfection, an opinion generally associated with Hendrik Niclaes and his Family of Love. Whether Brereley and his followers understood themselves to be Familists, they were most certainly propounding a message that was entirely out of step with the predominant mode of puritan piety of the time. Their own form of religiosity is probably best understood as a species of antinomianism, an alloy of standard reformed divinity blended with more exotic mystical traditions imported from continental religious radicals.

The importance of Brereley's theology is difficult to assess. Indirectly he surely played an important role in creating an underground antinomian community in pre-civil-war England, and from this perspective it might be argued that he played an important, albeit intangible, role in the evolution of the radical sectarian puritanism that would burn through the country during the 1640s and 1650s in the persons of men such as Henry Denne, William Erbury, and John Saltmarsh. Yet some observers, both contemporary and modern, have argued for a more direct connection between Grindleton and civil-war radical religion. Drawing attention to the startling geographical overlap between areas of Grindletonian activity and areas of early Quaker penetration, certain commentators have seen in Grindletonianism a sort of seedbed in which the earliest Friends were able to plant their message. This view is not without foundation: indeed, the elderly William Boyes, once a follower of Brereley, welcomed George Fox in the early 1650s, while another ex-Grindletonian, Thomas Barcroft of Colne, wrote a pastoral letter to his old co-religionists seeking to persuade them to join ranks with the Friends. Nevertheless, the idea of a substantial Grindletonian contribution to the early Quaker movement remains largely speculative. It seems clear, for instance, that some veteran Grindletonians, Collier among them, clung to their old ways long after Quakerism had firmly established itself in northern England. Nevertheless, it is safe to conclude that at least obliquely, Brereley and his followers exerted a major, if not direct, influence upon the development of the mid-seventeenth-century religious scene, helping to forge a theological antinomianism that would have important political and social consequences during the tumultuous years of the civil war and interregnum. DAVID R. COMO

Sources R. Brereley, *A bundle of soul-convincing, directing and comforting truths* (1677) · D. Como, *Blown by the spirit: puritanism and emergence of an antinomian underground in pre-civil war England* [forthcoming] · R. Marchant, *The puritans and the church courts in the diocese of York, 1560–1642* (1960) · *DNB* · J. Darling, 'The Grindletonians: Roger Brierley, John Webster, Robert Towne', PhD diss., Columbia University, 1988 · Grindletonian MSS, Chetham's Library, Manchester, MS A. 2. 24 · Grindletonian MSS, LPL, MS 3461 · notes on Brereley, Chetham's Library, Manchester, Lancashire MSS C. 6. 21, p. 6; C. 6. 27, p. 31 · BL, Add. MS 4933B, fols. 163v–164v · T. Sippell, *Zur Vorgeschichte des Quaekertüms* (1920), 50–52 · T. Barcroft, letters, RS Friends, Lond., Swarthmore MS 351 · K. Fincham, *Prelate as pastor: the episcopate of James I* (1990), 323 · IGI
Archives LPL, sermons, MS 3461 | Chetham's Library, Manchester, MS A. 2. 24

Brereton [*née* Hughes], **Jane** (1685–1740), poet, was born at Bryn Gruffydd near Mold in Flintshire, the younger daughter of Thomas Hughes and his wife, Ann Jones. Her father educated her at home, so that by the time of his death in 1701 she had 'already discovered a peculiar genius for poetry' ('Account', ii). On 29 January 1711 she married Thomas *Brereton (1690/91–1722), at that time a commoner of Brasenose College, and the only son of a major in the army who had fought under the duke of Marlborough and left Thomas a large fortune. They had two sons, Thomas and John, who both died in infancy, and two daughters, Lucy (the elder) and Charlotte. After Oxford, Thomas pursued a literary career in London, publishing verse and plays and a periodical (*The Critick*) in 1718, while Jane also published some occasional verses (*The Fifth Ode of the Fourth Book of Horace, Imitated* in 1716 and *An Expostulatory Epistle to Sir Richard Steele upon the Death of Mr Addison* in 1720). Domestically, however, their life was turbulent: Brereton soon squandered his fortune, despite his wife's household economy, and revealed an ugly temper: 'his

first fit of passion, after their marriage, was like a thunderclap to her' (ibid., vi).

About 1721 Jane Brereton took her daughters to live in Wales, risking censure for having separated from her husband. He obtained a position in the customs office at Parkgate, near Chester; in February 1722 he was returning across the estuary to Chester from visiting his family when he was drowned by the incoming tide. Soon after this Jane Brereton moved to Wrexham in Denbighshire, for the sake of her daughters' education. There she became part of a genteel female social group, and addressed a number of poems to various members of this circle. In general, she eschewed publication, although *Merlin: a Poem* was published as a quarto pamphlet in 1735 (dedicated to Queen Caroline, the poem engages with the modish myth of Merlin, who becomes a mouthpiece for some fulsome praise of the house of Brunswick); and from 1734 onwards she published some verse in the *Gentleman's Magazine* under the pseudonym Melissa. This provoked some humorous verse ripostes from a certain Fido, whom Brereton discovered (only after his death by suicide) to be Thomas Beach, a wine merchant and a Wrexham acquaintance of hers who had encouraged her writing. Apparently to console Brereton for the loss of this literary friendship, Edward Cave, the editor of the *Gentleman's Magazine*, put her in touch with Elizabeth Carter: they corresponded from 1738 onwards. However, Jane Brereton died at Wrexham on 7 August 1740, after a five-week attack of 'the gravel' ('Account', vii). She was buried on 10 August 1740 in Wrexham church. She was survived by her daughters: Lucy went to live in Cork with Jane Brereton's brother Thomas, a successful brewer, while Charlotte went to live in Essex and herself wrote poems.

Probably for the benefit of her daughters, proposals for printing Jane Brereton's *Poems on Several Occasions* were published in 1741 and 1742; subscribers included Elizabeth Carter and John Cleland, and the volume eventually appeared in 1744, with a valuable 'Account of the life of Mrs Brereton', almost certainly written by Charlotte. The 'Account' plays down her literary career ('writing was her darling entertainment, and was to her a relaxation from her cares'; 'Account', xii), and emphasizes her exemplary qualities as wife, mother, widow, and Christian. Brereton's body of poetry displays a flair for tactful occasional writing, and represents a transitional moment in women's writing in the eighteenth century, a moment at which being a published writer while retaining respectability was becoming a real possibility.

KATHERINE TURNER

Sources [C. Brereton], 'An account of the life of Mrs Brereton', in *Poems on several occasions: by Mrs Jane Brereton, with letters to her friends, and an account of her life* (1744) · R. Lonsdale, ed., *Eighteenth-century women poets: an Oxford anthology* (1989), 78–9
Archives Flintshire RO, Hawarden, letters

Brereton, John (b. 1571/2?, d. in or after 1619?), travel writer, is thought by modern scholars to have been the third of four sons of Cuthbert Brereton of Norwich who was educated at Norwich School and was admitted pensioner of Gonville and Caius College, Cambridge, aged seventeen on 17 January 1589; a scholar of the college until 1596, he graduated BA in 1593 and proceeded MA in 1596. This John Brereton was ordained deacon and priest in Norwich in 1598 and became curate of Lawshall, Suffolk, and in 1619 rector of Brightwell, Suffolk. An East Anglian origin would fit well with the known origins of others on the voyage which made Brereton's name in 1602. In the *Dictionary of National Biography* by contrast John Brereton the voyager was assumed to be of the Brereton family of Brereton, Cheshire, and a relative of Sir William Brereton (1604–1661), who had an interest in the settlement of New England, being granted land on Massachusetts Bay in 1629 and settling tenants there. Venn likewise uncompromisingly states that the Suffolk John Brereton is not the voyager.

Whatever his origins and subsequent life Brereton the voyager comes to notice in 1602 when he joined Bartholomew Gosnold, Bartholomew Gilbert, Gabriel Archer, and others to make the first English attempts to settle in what since 1616 has been known as New England. Thirty-two men left Falmouth in a small barque, the *Concord*, on 26 March 1602, reaching New England by May and returning to Exmouth on 23 July that year. (A full account of the voyage is given in the article on Bartholomew Gosnold.) Brereton's role in the voyage, according to Quinn and Quinn (1983), was to act as recorder and chaplain. The manuscript of his journal, now lost, formed the basis of published accounts which appeared in 1602 and 1603.

When the voyagers returned to England they found themselves in trouble with Sir Walter Ralegh. His patent of 25 March 1584 gave him a monopoly on English voyages to North America, apart from Newfoundland, but he had known nothing of Gosnold's voyage in advance and was very exercised when the party returned with a cargo of goods similar to those which he himself was trying to sell. He reached an accommodation with the voyagers, however, whereby an account of the 1602 voyage was to be published in an effort to draw more settlers to North America and revive the colonization plans set back by earlier unsuccessful attempts at settlement. Brereton's journal was chosen for this account and was edited for publication by an unknown hand, which the Quinns suggest might be that of Thomas Harriot, the mathematician who did much work for Ralegh. It was first published in 1602 as *A Briefe Relation of the Description of Elizabeth's Ile*, and was dedicated to Ralegh. The first printing was soon exhausted and a second larger edition entitled *A Brief and True Relation of the Discovery of the North Part of Virginia*, dated 1602, appeared either that year or probably in 1603. The second edition is more clearly designed as propaganda for future voyages and indeed Gosnold's second voyage was already being planned at its publication. Brereton's journal, as edited, offers an attractive picture of New England, and his accuracy and attention to detail in describing the flora and fauna, and the people the voyagers encountered, lend credibility and interest to the description. Brereton was struck by the abundance of natural resources, particularly by comparison with his homeland. He was 'ravished at the beauty and delicacie of this sweet soile' and described 'such things as God & Nature hath bestowed on these places, in comparison whereof, the most fertil part of al England is (of it selfe) but barren' (Quinn and Quinn, 152).

Brereton's was the first published account of a voyage to New England with the exception of a letter written by Giovanni da Verrazzano after his 1524 voyage, which was published in Italian in 1556. It alerted people in England to the possibility of settling in New England and building there a prosperous and free life. It painted a rosier picture of New England than was strictly accurate, though this was probably not deliberate deceit but a reflection of the fact that early voyagers neither experienced nor anticipated the severity of New England winters. Brereton's appraisal of New England as a favourable place for colonization proved accurate, and helped shape future colonization.

ELIZABETH BAIGENT

Sources D. B. Quinn and A. M. Quinn, eds., *The English New England voyages, 1602–1608*, Hakluyt Society, 2nd ser., 161 (1983) · W. F. Gookin and P. L. Barbour, *Bartholomew Gosnold: discoverer and planter* (1963) · Venn, *Alum. Cant.* · DNB

Brereton, Joseph Lloyd (1822–1901), educational reformer, was born on 19 October 1822 at Little Massingham rectory, Norfolk, the third son of eleven children of Charles David Brereton (1790–1868), for forty-seven years rector of Little Massingham, and his wife, Frances (d. 1880), daughter of Joseph Wilson of Highbury Hill, Middlesex, and Stowlangtoft Hall, Suffolk. In the 1820s C. D. Brereton wrote important pamphlets on poor law and agricultural questions. Brereton was educated at Islington proprietary school under John Jackson, afterwards bishop of London, and at Rugby School (1838–41) under Thomas Arnold. He gained a scholarship at University College, Oxford, in 1842, obtained the Newdigate Prize in 1844 for a poem on the battle of the Nile, and graduated BA in 1846 and MA in 1857. He took holy orders and held curacies at St Edmund's, Norwich, St Martin-in-the-Fields, London, and St James's, Paddington (1847–50). On 25 June 1852 he married Frances, daughter of William Martin, rector of Staverton, Devon. From 1852 to 1867 he was rector of West Buckland, Devon, and from 1867 until his death rector of Little Massingham, in succession to his father. An energetic and attractive man, Brereton was highly successful at West Buckland, compiling two parochial yearbooks, founding the Barnstaple Farmers' Club in 1854, initiating an annual agricultural show, and helping to bring the railway from Taunton to Barnstaple. In Norfolk his similar efforts led to the King's Lynn and Fakenham railway.

Brereton averred that 'reverence and affection for Dr Arnold' (*Lynn Advertiser*, 9 Nov 1895) guided him in life. From Arnold he took his broad churchmanship and his concern for middle-class education, though he differed from him in distrusting the state as an agency of reform. Another lasting influence was his father's vision of a paternalist rural polity controlled by squire and parson. In his most detailed work, *County Education* (1874), Brereton asserted that the supervision of middle-class schools should be transferred from the state to a network of agencies dominated by universities and county notables; he seemed unaware that any feasible alternative to centralism would lie with popularly elected bodies. Ideas formed in discussions in the 1850s with his close friend Viscount Ebrington (later the third Earl Fortescue) led Brereton to advocate financing middle-class schools with private capital bearing fixed interest, a common Victorian expedient. This scheme led in 1858 to the founding in West Buckland of Devon county school, a boarding-school intended for the sons of 'the midmost man in England', the tenant farmer with between 200 and 300 acres. In the early years enrolment was high, farmers' sons and Devon being strongly represented; the maximum permitted dividend was paid, 5 per cent. In the 1850s 'proprietary' finance seemed the best means available owing to the moribund state of grammar school endowments. By the 1870s, however, these were being revitalized by the endowed schools' commissioners, and therefore inhibited the raising of capital for Brereton's second venture, the Norfolk county school, opened in 1872. Brereton adhered still to the commercial principle, but his proposals for creating a partnership between private and endowment capital, set out in *County Education*, scarcely met the practical difficulties. The agricultural depression that began in 1879 also hit the schools; the one in Devon survived with difficulty, but the one in Norfolk had to close in 1891. Nevertheless, there was enough potential in the county school idea to inspire the founders of schools at Barnard Castle, Framlingham, and Cranleigh, and these, like West Buckland School, still thrived in the late twentieth century. In recognition of his efforts for county education Brereton was made prebendary of Exeter Cathedral in 1858.

Problems also dogged Brereton's last venture, the Graduated County Schools Association, formed in 1884 on proprietary principles to foster girls' schooling. Nine schools, located in an area between Darlington, Blackheath, and Taunton, were founded by the association or were transferred to it by their owners. But unity was nominal, and not fruitful. Brereton's judgement was impaired by injuries suffered in a railway accident in 1882. Chronically impecunious, he confused his own money and the association's, a suspect episode that aggravated underlying weaknesses; the association was forced into liquidation in 1887.

Brereton's biggest single enterprise, Cavendish College, Cambridge, bore the family name of its largest investor, the seventh duke of Devonshire. After some years in temporary premises, the college moved to new buildings in 1877. Not a Cambridge college in the strict sense but a hostel for non-collegiate students, Cavendish was planned to benefit boys excluded from the usual route to a Cambridge degree by the expense of a traditional college. A frugal life in a college might cost £150 a year in the 1870s; a Cavendish education cost about £110 inclusive, and its academic year was longer. But the college lacked a hall and a proper kitchen, and a very narrow bed was patented for its tiny bedrooms. Remoteness from university life was also a drawback, Cavendish being a mile from the city centre where traditional colleges clustered. In contrast, 'noncoll.' students might live in comfortable lodgings in the town on £80 a year. After initial recruitment of matriculants who were mostly from professional families (and similar in background to many other Cambridge students, though younger), the college failed to make its mark. In 1887 a restructured company (that much to his chagrin excluded Brereton) tried to cope with mounting debt and lack of amenity, but Cavendish had to close in 1892, and was sold in 1894 to Homerton College which still occupied the buildings a century later.

Brereton's wife died on 13 May 1891; of their family of five sons and six daughters, three boys became noncollegiate students at Cambridge. Brereton himself died at Little Massingham, Norfolk, on 15 August 1901, and was buried in the churchyard there. PETER SEARBY

Sources P. Searby, 'A failure at Cambridge: Cavendish College, 1877–1892', *Proceedings of the Cambridge Antiquarian Society*, 72 (1982–3) · P. Searby, 'Joseph Lloyd Brereton and the education of the Victorian middle class', *Journal of Educational Administration and History*, 11 (1979) · J. R. de S. Honey, *Tom Brown's universe: the development of the Victorian public school* (1977) · D. I. Allsobrook, *Schools for the shires: the reform of middle-class education in mid-Victorian England* (1986) · Venn, *Alum. Cant.* · *DNB* · *CGPLA Eng. & Wales* (1902)

Archives Homerton College, Cambridge · Norfolk RO

Likenesses G. Richmond, portrait, 1868, West Buckland School, Barnstaple, Devon · E. B. Stephens, statue, West Buckland School, Barnstaple, Devon · D. Wilkie; formerly at Stowlangtoft Hall, Suff., 1912 · memorial, St Andrew's Church, Little Massingham, Norfolk

Wealth at death £4144 16s. 2d.: probate, 14 Jan 1902, *CGPLA Eng. & Wales*

Brereton, Owen Salusbury (1715–1798), antiquary, was born in London and baptized Owen Brereton, the son of Thomas Brereton (d. 1756), of Chester, and his first wife, Mary, daughter of Brigadier-General Henry Trelawny, of Whitley, Devon. His father's second wife was Catherine, daughter and heir of Salusbury Lloyd (d. 1734), MP for Flint Boroughs, through whom his father inherited Shotwick Park in Cheshire, whereupon he changed his surname to Salusbury. Owen Brereton was educated at Westminster School from 1725 to 1734, and matriculated from Trinity College, Cambridge, in December 1734. He was elected a scholar in 1735 but did not graduate. He was called to the bar from Lincoln's Inn in 1738 and subsequently practised on the Welsh circuit. He held the post of a lottery commissioner in 1738 and in September was appointed recorder of Liverpool, an office he retained until his death. When he tried to resign in 1796, he was asked by the corporation to remain and a deputy was appointed to relieve him of the pressure of his duties.

On 13 December 1755 Brereton married Catherine (bap. 1722, d. 1800), daughter of William Whitmore (d. 1725), MP, of Lower Slaughter, Gloucestershire, and Apley, Shropshire, and Elizabeth Pope. They had five children, all of whom died young. Brereton succeeded to Shotwick and other estates in Cheshire, Denbighshire, and Flintshire on his father's death in 1756 and added Salusbury to his name. He decided against succeeding his father as MP for Liverpool, and many years elapsed before he entered parliament in 1775, as MP for Ilchester. He was appointed constable of Flint Castle in return for supporting Lord North, but made no mark in the Commons and stepped down in 1780.

Salusbury Brereton became a member of the Society of Arts in 1762, and was vice-president from 1765 to 1798, rendering great service to the society. He was elected a fellow of the Society of Antiquaries in 1763 and was vice-president from 1773. He was also a fellow of the Royal Society, a bencher and treasurer of Lincoln's Inn, and keeper of the black book. He had one paper published in the *Philosophical Transactions* (1781) and several published in *Archaeologia*. His paper on the Brereton church window (*Archaeologia*, 9, 1786, 368) was said by Ormerod in his *History of Cheshire* (1882, 2.573) to have contained several inaccuracies.

Salusbury Brereton collapsed while on his way to the races at Egham and subsequently died at his home at Park Street, Windsor, on 8 September 1798. He was buried in St George's Chapel, Windsor, on 22 September. Following the death of his widow on 10 May 1800 his estates were left in trust to Charles Trelawny, on condition that he take the name Brereton.   C. W. SUTTON, *rev.* J. A. MARCHAND

Sources L. B. Namier, 'Salusbury Brereton, Owen', HoP, *Commons, 1754–90* · *GM*, 1st ser., 68 (1798), 816 · *GM*, 1st ser., 70 (1800), 491 · *Corrections and additions to the Dictionary of National Biography*, Institute of Historical Research (1966) · J. Evans, *A history of the Society of Antiquaries* (1956) · J. Brooke, 'Salusbury (formerly Brereton), Thomas', HoP, *Commons, 1754–90* · Venn, *Alum. Cant.* · IGI · will, PRO, PROB 11/1312, sig. 584

Likenesses J. Barry, group portrait, oils (*The Society for the Encouragement of Arts*), RSA · W. Evans, stipple (after miniature), BM, NPG · silhouette, BM

Wealth at death estates in Cheshire, Chester, Flintshire, and Denbighshire left to widow: will, PRO, PROB 11/1312, fols. 117r–118v

Brereton, Priscilla. *See* Kemble, Priscilla (1758–1845).

Brereton, Thomas (1690/91–1722), writer, was born in Cheshire or Flintshire, the son of Major Thomas Brereton (*d.* in or before 1712) of Northop, Flintshire, a protestant convert and soldier in the army of the duke of Marlborough, and was descended from the family of Brereton of Brereton, Cheshire. Major Brereton died before his son reached his majority. Educated at the Free School, Chester, and the boarding-school in Chester of Mr Denis, a French refugee, Brereton matriculated from Brasenose College, Oxford, on 16 April 1709, aged eighteen (BA, 14 October 1712); he remained a member of the college until 7 August 1718. On 29 January 1711 he married Jane Hughes [see Brereton, Jane (1685–1740)], of Flintshire, also a poet, with whom he had two sons, who died in infancy, and two daughters. The younger, Charlotte, is presumably the author of 'An account of the life of Mrs. Brereton' (*Poems on Several Occasions: by Mrs. Jane Brereton*, 1744), the primary source for his life.

At Oxford, Brereton showed a penchant for verse satire, publishing *Charnock's Remains* (1713; revised as *Charnock Junior*, 1719), a satire on the Jacobite conspirator Robert Charnock and a parody of John Dryden's *MacFlecknoe*. An admirer of French classical drama, Brereton produced the first English translation of Racine's *Esther*, titled *Esther, or,*

Faith triumphant, a sacred tragedy in rhyme … translated with improvements from Racine (1715). Another play, 'Sir John Oldcastle' (1717?), based on Corneille's *Polyeucte*, has not survived; and two other plays, begun by 1719, were not completed.

Brereton turned social, political, and literary commentator in a series of lively weekly essays, *The Critick* (22 numbers, Mondays, 6 January–2 June 1718; published in one volume, 1719), the 'first serial that deliberately set out to be a critical publication in the modern sense' (Graham, 100). Had he lived, it is likely that he would have been numbered among the writers satirized by Alexander Pope. Politics, however, are lacking in *A Day's Journey from the Vale of Evesham to Oxford* (1717?), an evocative, humorous, pre-Romantic poem, dedicated to his Welsh friend and fellow poet Nehemiah Griffith. This, his only personal poem, contains autobiographical glimpses, including the admission that he was myopic.

Left a considerable inheritance, Brereton was 'so much a fine Gentleman that he soon ran out most of his Fortune' (Brereton, iv), forcing his wife to a strict economy, which he himself praised. Their domestic life was further strained by Brereton's impetuous nature and changeable temper; 'yet he would sometimes, in a handsome Manner, acknowledge his Fault, and seem so sensible, that any, who did not know him too well, would have imagined him secure against a Relapse' (ibid., vi). Jane Brereton was compelled at last to separate from him, retiring to Wales with their daughters about 1721.

Financial exigency spurred Brereton, a whig and staunch anti-Catholic, to seek opportunities for preferment under the new Hanoverian regime. On a visit to Paris he came to the notice of the English ambassador, the earl of Stair, who recommended him to the duke of Marlborough as the son of one of Marlborough's old soldiers. Through the influence of the earl of Sunderland he obtained a customs post at Parkgate, near Chester, about 1721.

Political disputation indirectly led to Brereton's death. His intimate friend and kinsman Thomas Brereton (afterwards Salusbury) of Shotwick Park, later an MP for Liverpool and tool of Sir Robert Walpole (*Egmont Diary*), was then opposing the powerful Sir Richard Grosvenor in the Chester election. At his instigation Brereton wrote 'a Sort of Libel', in which 'he gave himself such a Loose as to come within the Power of the Law' (Brereton, v). In February 1722, to evade arrest, Brereton, a strong swimmer, abandoned his horse in a fatal attempt to swim the Saltney estuary as the tide was coming in (the night before, he had visited his family). His body was recovered by his friends and interred at Shotwick Chapel, near Parkgate, Chester, overlooking the River Dee.   PAGE LIFE

Sources [G. Jacob], *The poetical register, or, The lives and characters of the English dramatick poets*, 2 vols. (1719–20) · J. Brereton, *Poems on several occasions: by Mrs. Jane Brereton, with letters to her friends, and an account of her life* (1744) · HoP, *Commons, 1715–54* · [C. B. Heberden], ed., *Brasenose College register, 1509–1909*, 1, OHS, 55 (1909), 286 · D. E. Baker, *Biographia dramatica, or, A companion to the playhouse*, rev. I. Reed, new edn, rev. S. Jones, 3 vols. in 4 (1812) · G. Ormerod, *The history of the county palatine and city of Chester*, 2nd edn, ed. T. Helsby,

3 vols. (1882) · D. F. Canfield, *Corneille and Racine in England* (1904); repr. (New York, 1966) · W. J. Graham, *English literary periodicals* (1930) · *Manuscripts of the earl of Egmont: diary of Viscount Percival, afterwards first earl of Egmont*, 3 vols., HMC, 63 (1920–23), vol. 1, pp. 85–7 · D. F. Foxon, ed., *English verse, 1701–1750: a catalogue of separately printed poems with notes on contemporary collected editions*, 2 vols. (1975)

Wealth at death squandered inheritance

Brereton, Thomas (1782–1832), army officer, was born in King's county, Ireland, on 4 May 1782. He went as a volunteer to the West Indies with his uncle Captain Coghlan in 1797, and received his commission as ensign in the 8th West India regiment in 1798; he was promoted lieutenant in 1800 and captain in 1804. Apart from a short period of service in Jersey in 1803–4, he seems to have stayed in the West Indies until 1813, acting for a time as brigade major to his relative Major-General Robert Brereton, lieutenant-governor of St Lucia. He was present at the capture of Martinique in 1809 and of Guadeloupe in 1810. He was invalided to England in 1813. In 1814 he was appointed lieutenant-governor of Senegal and Goree and the next year was made lieutenant-colonel of the Royal African Corps. In December 1816 he was again invalided to England. He was appointed to a command on the frontier of the Cape Colony in 1818, visited England in 1819, and commanded the Cape Town garrison until 1823. In the meantime, he had exchanged into the 53rd regiment, into the Royal York rangers in 1820, and into the 49th regiment in 1821. On his final return to England he was appointed inspecting field officer of the Bristol recruiting district from 1823. He married in London, before 1826, Olivia, daughter of Hamilton Ross, formerly of the 81st regiment and then a merchant at the Cape. She died on 14 January 1829. They had two daughters, born in 1826 and 1828.

As senior officer in the district, Brereton had command of the troops quartered in the neighbourhood of Bristol at the outbreak of the reform riots there in October 1831. The recorder of Bristol, Sir Charles Wetherell, a vigorous opponent of parliamentary reform, refused to be dissuaded from visiting the city and two troops of the 14th light dragoons and one of the 3rd dragoons were sent to Bristol after a request from the magistrates, who expected trouble. On 29 October a crowd gathered to meet Wetherell and showered him and the mayor, Charles Pinney, with abuse and stones. They retreated, pursued by the crowd, to the mansion house, from where, after appealing to the crowd to disperse, Pinney read the Riot Act. The meagre force of constables which the magistrates had been able to assemble failed to deal with the crowd and at 6 p.m. the 3rd dragoons arrived, led by Brereton. They were cheered and Brereton moved among the people, persuading them to disperse. At 9 p.m. the 14th light dragoons, known as the 'bloody blues', arrived, to jeers from the crowd, who jostled them roughly. At midnight, after the crowd had begun to attack the council house, the troops charged, dispersing the crowd using the flat of the sword, though one youth was shot in a skirmish. At 7 a.m. the next day the crowd reassembled, to be met by the 14th, who provoked so much opposition that Brereton withdrew them and replaced them with the 3rd. As the 14th retreated they fired at those who followed them. Brereton returned to the square and to cheers told the crowd that there would be no more firing and that he had sent the 14th out of the town. The crowd grew less violent, but did not disperse. Instead groups broke away to attack the Bridewell and New gaol, releasing prisoners and firing the buildings. Twenty soldiers from the 3rd arrived, were cheered, reputedly cheered back, and, to most people's astonishment, rode off. The crowd went on to attack toll houses, Gloucester county gaol, Lawford's Gate lockup, and the bishop's palace, and completed their destruction of the mansion house. The customs house, excise office, and many other houses in Queen Square were then destroyed. The destruction continued throughout the night with no check. At 5 a.m. on 31 October Brereton returned with troops and began to disperse the crowd, but it was the actions of the 14th under Major Beckwith and the Bedminster yeomanry who were largely responsible for clearing the streets. Official figures suggested twelve killed and ninety-four injured: a more recent suggestion is that as many as 250 were killed or injured (Harrison, 288–9).

After a military commission had investigated Brereton's conduct he was court-martialled at Bristol on 9 January 1832. Eleven serious charges were brought against him, but on the fifth day the trial was stopped by the news that he had shot himself in his bed early that morning at Redfield Lodge, Lawrence Hill, Bristol. The verdict at the inquest was that 'he died from a pistol-wound, inflicted on himself while under a fit of temporary derangement'. He was buried on 16 January at Clifton church, near to his wife.

The story of the riot has been told many times but, depending as it does on sometimes conflicting eyewitness accounts and conjecture about discussions in closed sessions of the mayor and magistrates, it is impossible to establish the facts beyond all doubt. Contemporary commentators and even more recent ones such as Babington (1990) accuse Brereton of being irresponsible, foolish, and even mad. Others, notably Harrison (1988), while conceding that he misjudged the situation, stress the humane motives which held him back from using force and point to the very considerable loss of life which occurred when the troops were sent in in earnest. Similarly, older accounts and Babington tell of an orgy of destruction, but other modern writers stress that attack was, until the end, reserved for the property of the corporation and other despised figures or institutions, such as the bishop and the customs and excise offices. Contemporary accounts speak of the mob, egged on by outsiders, committing unprecedented outrages. Modern accounts stress that the crowd were locals, whose actions received some tacit approval from wealthier Bristolians, who largely refused to act as special constables to clear the streets. One notable factor which has aroused little comment is the vast quantity of alcohol that was available from the bonded warehouses and wine cellars of the houses in Queen Square sacked by the crowd. Perhaps it was this more than anything else that tipped the disturbance from being a good-humoured, if vigorous protest, according to customary rules, to a frightening and uncontrolled outbreak.

It seems clear that Brereton was at the least irresolute, but, with few troops, vacillating civil authorities, and a citizenry unwilling to defend a council they regarded as motivated chiefly by self-interest, he was heavily circumscribed. A more general difficulty was the extent to which the military authorities were empowered to act without unequivocal instruction from the civil powers. Brereton was aware throughout of this difficulty, which was emphasized later when the soldier who had shot and killed the youth in the fray was tried for manslaughter. There has been general agreement among historians that Brereton's conduct in the riot pointed to the need for an effective civil police force, but the ratepayers of Bristol opposed the establishment of such a force after the riot and, when one was set up in 1836, its recruits were almost wholly from outside the city. On balance Brereton's conduct in the riot, though hardly heroic, was possibly no more reprehensible than that of those who hounded him to suicide. ELIZABETH BAIGENT

Sources M. Harrison, *Crowds and history* (1988) · S. Thomas, *The Bristol riots* (1974) · *Trial of Charles Pinney, Esq., in the court of King's Bench* (1832) · A. Bonner, 'Catholics and the Bristol riots of 1831', *The Month*, 160 (1932), 426–33 · A. Babbington, *Military intervention in Britain* (1990) · B. Howell, *The police in late Victorian Bristol* (1989) · *GM*, 1st ser., 102/1 (1832), 84–5

Brereton, Sir William (*d.* 1541?), lord justice of Ireland, was the eldest son of Sir Andrew Brereton of Brereton, Cheshire, and Agnes, daughter of Robert Legh of Adlington in the same county. William was knighted before 1523 and served on several local commissions. He married, first, Alice, daughter of Sir John Savage; they had one son, William, who predeceased his father and whose son and namesake was Sir William's heir. His second wife was Eleanor, daughter of Sir Ralph Brereton of Ipstone; they had three sons and five daughters.

In October 1534 Brereton and the lord deputy, Sir William Skeffington, sailed from Graycott for Ireland and Brereton, his son John, and 500 troops eventually landed at Howth. Believing that Thomas Fitzgerald was about to besiege Drogheda, on 18 October Skeffington and Brereton set out for the town, where they remained for seven days before returning to Dublin. On 15 November, Brereton accompanied Skeffington to Trim where Fitzgerald's forces were defeated. In early January 1535 Brereton and other military commanders were stationed at Newcastle Lyons and various strategic outposts in south-west Dublin, and he remained there until the summer of 1535. From these outposts Brereton led several attacks on towns which were Geraldine strongholds. On 6 March, in an attack mounted near Naas, his troops were involved in killing 100 of Fitzgerald's galloglass. He participated in the siege of Maynooth Castle: on 23 March he scaled the walls of the castle, cried 'St George St George', and advanced his standard on the top of one of the turrets to signal the capture of the fortress.

By June 1535 Brereton was a member of the Irish council. In July he yielded Rathangan Castle to the forces of Lord Thomas and O'Connor, and in early August he participated in a campaign against Fitzgerald's forces in Allen. At the end of August he was party to an indenture with the O'Dunnes of Oregan. During this summer Skeffington learned that Fitzgerald had resorted to Munster. Lord Leonard Grey, Brereton, and others were dispatched, and engaged in several fruitless skirmishes with the Geraldine forces. Partly upon Brereton's recommendation, Grey negotiated with Fitzgerald and eventually secured his surrender in August. Brereton subsequently returned to England where he was appointed deputy chamberlain of Chester. In early October 1536 he was engaged in levying 250 archers to travel to Ireland. In late October and early November 1539 he sent a retinue to Ireland. Although hampered by the fact that he had broken his leg in two places as a result of a fall from his horse, on 4 November he accompanied the remainder of his forces to Ireland. Sir William was present on a campaign in Dundalk in the early months of 1540, though his son John had to act as his substitute owing to his incapacitated condition.

On 1 April 1540 Brereton was appointed lord justice of Ireland following Lord Leonard Grey's removal. He held this office from 2 May to about 12 August 1540 when the newly appointed lord deputy, Sir Antony St Leger, arrived in Ireland. On 12 May he negotiated a peace with O'Neill. During his term as lord justice Brereton assembled an army, bolstered by approximately 2000 residents of the pale, to defend the colony from the forces of the Geraldine league. In the event, the Gaelic forces dispersed but Brereton pursued O'Connor into Offaly, forcing the latter to hand over his son Cnogher as security for his father's compliance. Brereton was soon after promoted lord high marshal of Ireland. Late in 1540 Brereton was sent to take the submission of James FitzJohn, earl of Desmond, but died *en route*, at Kilkenny. Certain sources state that he died in December 1540 but his burial date of 4 February 1541 makes this unlikely. He was buried in the choir of St Canice's Cathedral, Kilkenny. MARY ANN LYONS

Sources *LP Henry VIII*, vols. 7–9, 14/2–16 · *LP Henry VIII*, vols. 2/3, 3/3 · G. Ormerod, *The history of the county palatine and city of Chester*, 2nd edn, ed. T. Helsby, 2–3 (1882) · J. S. Brewer and W. Bullen, eds., *Calendar of the Carew manuscripts*, 1: 1515–1574, PRO (1867) · *CSP Ire.*, 1509–73 · *Holinshed's chronicles of England, Scotland and Ireland*, ed. H. Ellis, 6 (1808) · B. Burke, *A genealogical history of the dormant, abeyant, forfeited and extinct peerages of the British empire*, new edn (1883) · *The Irish fiants of the Tudor sovereigns*, 4 vols. (1994) · J. Morrin, ed., *Calendar of the patent and close rolls of chancery in Ireland, of the reigns of Henry VIII, Edward VI, Mary, and Elizabeth*, 1 (1861) · R. Lascelles, ed., *Liber munerum publicorum Hiberniae … or, The establishments of Ireland*, 2 vols. [1824–30] · R. Cox, *Hibernia Anglicana, or, The history of Ireland from the conquest thereof by the English to the present time*, 1 (1689) · J. L. J. Hughes, ed., *Patentee officers in Ireland, 1173–1826, including high sheriffs, 1661–1684 and 1761–1816*, IMC (1960) · T. W. Moody and others, eds., *A new history of Ireland*, 9: *Maps, genealogies, lists* (1984) · L. McCorristine, *The revolt of Silken Thomas: a challenge to Henry VIII* (1987) · S. G. Ellis, *Tudor frontiers and noble power: the making of the British state* (1995) · B. Bradshaw, *The Irish constitutional revolution of the sixteenth century* (1979) · S. G. Ellis, *Ireland in the age of the Tudors* (1998)

Brereton, William (*c*.1487×90–1536), courtier and administrator, was the sixth of the nine sons of Sir Randolph Brereton (*d.* 1530) of Malpas, chamberlain of the county palatine of Cheshire, and Eleanor, daughter of Piers Dutton of Halton. Sir Randolph's family must be distinguished from that of his distant relative Sir William Brereton of Brereton, who died, probably in 1541, as lord high marshal of Ireland. As Sir Randolph settled an income on his sixth son in 1508, William was probably then approaching adulthood or even already of age; if so he was born *c*.1487×90. Sir Randolph was a figure at court, as well as in Cheshire. He was a knight of the body and after the 1513 campaign was made a knight banneret. This record allowed him to place four of his sons at court, and the parliamentarian general Sir William Brereton of Handforth (1604–1661) was the grandson of Urian, the youngest of these.

Nothing is known of Brereton's early career, but Wolsey claimed that he had assisted his progress. By 1521 he was at court and by 1524 at the latest a groom of the privy chamber. There he appears to have attached himself to Henry Norris, the groom of the stool, but little is known of his privy chamber service, although he may have acted as a witness to Henry's marriage to Anne Boleyn early in 1533. The major public task Brereton is known to have undertaken was collecting signatures in June 1530 for the petition to the pope from the notables of England.

Thanks to his standing at court and assisted initially by his father's status in Cheshire, Brereton had by 1530–31 amassed thirty-six crown grants, making him the dominant royal servant in Cheshire and north Wales. At the same time the grant of the dissolved abbey of Lesnes in Kent had given him a *pied-à-terre* near the court. His gross income from crown sources was in excess of £1000 a year; grants and annuities from private persons and from monasteries increased this to almost £1300. Brereton also farmed and traded, with special interests in cattle, horses, deer, and sheep. The horses and sheep were disposed of in London, and he may have supplied the court directly as he did with wood when granted the farm of the manor of Finchley during the minority of William Compton's heir. His net overall income was *c*.£800 a year, and he was able to lend significant amounts to other courtiers.

This precision about Brereton's activities is possible because his papers have substantially survived, making him one of the best documented men of his rank and time. Although no longer consolidated, the material includes letters, accounts, and business documents, and is principally important for the light it throws on the English commerce in royal offices. Unlike the French crown, Tudor monarchs did not sell places direct, but the Brereton material shows that once obtained, these were traded like any other asset. The archive also shows initial grants being obtained by pressure on the king and bargaining with his officers, and how courtiers schemed against each other; the letters about Brereton's struggle with Sir Ralph Egerton over the royal park of Shotwick-on-Dee are particularly revealing.

Royal favour to Brereton reached a peak in 1529 and 1530. First he benefited from the disgrace of the Savages of Rocksavage. This great Cheshire family had contributed significantly to victory at Bosworth, but the death in 1507 of Thomas Savage, archbishop of York, removed protection for a high-handed use of local prestige and influence, and in 1516 the Savages fell foul of Wolsey. When Sir John Savage the younger (Thomas Savage's great-nephew) failed to keep up payments on the resulting fine, the family estates were sequestered and granted to Brereton to farm. Within months even this was eclipsed. Sir John died and in 1529 Brereton married his widow, Elizabeth, the daughter of Charles Somerset, earl of Worcester, and Henry VIII's cousin. Lady Elizabeth would have been a 'king's widow', and, given her father's relationship with the royal family, Henry must have approved of or even promoted the match. To cap this, William was appointed to succeed his father as chamberlain of Chester.

Brereton benefited from the consequences of Savage 'over-mighty' behaviour, but he equally used his local influence with a high hand. He dominated the local monasteries to his advantage, notably Valle Crucis in Denbighshire and the Cheshire houses of Vale Royal, Norton, and St Werburgh. He exploited the constitutional distinctiveness of Cheshire to block Thomas Cromwell and he was accused of covering up, even encouraging, lawless behaviour in the marcher lordships where he was steward—Chirk and Bromfield and Yale—and of holding 'grett porte and solemnites' at Holt Castle (PRO, SP 1/85, fols. 57–8), the strategic key to north Wales which had notoriously been the base of the traitor Sir William Stanley. The most nefarious episode was the judicial murder of John ap Gruffith Eyton, his former deputy, whom Brereton accused of complicity in the killing of a Brereton retainer. He sent him to London under armed escort, but Eyton retaliated with complaints to Star Chamber about Brereton's 'mayntenaunce of murderers, theves and misruled persons and bering of ill factes and dedes' (PRO, STAC 2/14/194, 195). According to Ellis Gruffydd, Eyton was acquitted, but was then tricked by Brereton and rearrested. Whether that story is true or not, Eyton was certainly in prison at Holt Castle in July 1534, and Rowland Lee reported to Cromwell that 'it is the comon noysse that the gentilman hee brought downe shall dye if hee may' (PRO, SP 1/85, fols. 57–8). Gruffydd claimed that Brereton rigged a trial and had Eyton hanged before his local supporters could rally.

The significance of the Eyton episode is twofold, first in relation to Thomas Cromwell's increasing concern with the lawless state of the marcher lordships. Not only was pressure stepped up against Brereton's management of the marches, but royal policy shifted from controlling marcher lordships to abolishing them. Second, the Eyton episode explains the riddle of an innocent Brereton's being arrested on 4 May 1536, accused of committing adultery with Anne Boleyn, tried and condemned on 12 May, and beheaded on the 17th. He was buried that day at St Peter ad Vincula, Tower Green.

That Brereton was innocent in respect of Anne is beyond question. His detention two days after the queen's arrest shows that there was nothing against him before the panic of May week began—Anne, indeed, showed no response to his arrival in the Tower. As a courtier he was not in the front rank. He was significantly older than the rest and did not belong to Anne's close circle—Wyatt, who did, noted that 'common voice doth not so sore thee rue' and described William as 'one that least I knew' (Wyatt, cxlix). The indictment gave four specimen dates for his alleged offences, but on two of these at least Anne was not at the location claimed. In private, but when his arrest was imminent, Brereton protested his innocence to a former schoolfriend, George Constantine; he pleaded not guilty at his trial and made this clear on the scaffold so, as Constantine put it, 'if he were gyltie, I say therefore that he dyed worst of them all' (Amyot, 65). His wife (no novice at court) always treasured 'the laste token' he sent her (Ches. & Chester ALSS, DCH/E294).

Brereton was not, however, innocent over John Eyton, and when George Cavendish, who knew him, wrote a speech in which William laments his execution, he has him ignore the allegation of adultery entirely.

> God of his justice, foreseeing my malice,
> For my busy rigour would punish me of right,
> Ministered unto Eyton, by colour of justice—
> A shame to speak, more shame it is to write:
> A gentleman born, that through my might
> So shamefully was hanged upon a gallows tree,
> Only of old rancour that rooted was in me.
>
> Lo, here is th'end of murder and tyranny!
> Lo, here is th'end of envious affection!
> Lo, here is th'end of false conspiracy!
> Lo, here is th'end of false detection
> Done to the innocent by cruel correction!
> Although in office I thought myself strong,
> Yet here is mine end for ministering wrong.
> (Cavendish, 34–5)

Involving Brereton in the charges against Anne allowed Cromwell to get rid of a potential obstacle to his plans for Wales and achieve some retribution for Eyton, as well as add one more to the parade of the queen's 'lovers'. That Brereton's involvement in Anne's fate was fortuitous is strongly suggested by the behaviour of Elizabeth I. By rewarding the Norris family she tacitly acknowledged Sir Henry's defence of her mother's reputation; William Brereton's two sons got nothing. Henry, the elder (probably the king's godson), died without issue, but the second, Thomas, survived as a minor Cheshire gentleman, while his son John became mayor of Chester in 1623.

E. W. IVES

Sources Letters and accounts of Wm. Brereton, ed. E. W. Ives, Lancashire and Cheshire RS, 116 (1976) • E. W. Ives, 'Court and county palatine', Transactions of the History Society of Lancashire and Cheshire, 123 (1972), 1–38 • E. W. Ives, 'The fall of Anne Boleyn reconsidered', EngHR, 107 (1992), 651–64 • E. W. Ives, 'Faction at the court of Henry VIII', History, 57 (1972), 169–88 • E. W. Ives, 'Patronage at the court of Henry VIII', Bulletin of the John Rylands Library, 52 (1970), 365–9 • PRO, state papers, Henry VIII, general series, SP 1/85, fols. 57–8 • star chamber proceedings, PRO, Henry VIII, STAC 2/14/194, 195 • T. Amyot, 'Memorial from George Constantine', Archaeologica, 23 (1831), 65 • [T. Wyatt], Collected Poems, ed. J. Daalder (1975) • G. Cavendish, Life of Wolsey, ed. S. W. Singer (1825), 34–5 • Ches. & Chester ALSS, DCH/ E294 • T. Thornton, Cheshire and the Tudor state (2000) • PRO, special collections, rentals and surveys, portfolios, SC 12/23/51 • PRO, state papers domestic, supplementary, SP 46/162, fols. 236–7

Archives BL, Stowe MSS • PRO, various classes

Wealth at death £1236 12s. 6¼d. income: PRO, SC 12/23/51, fols. 295–302, in Letters, ed. Ives, 266–71

Brereton, Sir William, first baronet (1604–1661), parliamentarian army officer, was born on 13 September 1604 and baptized in the Manchester collegiate church two weeks later. He was the eldest son of William Brereton (1584–1610) of Handforth, and Margaret Holland (1585–1609), daughter of Richard Holland of Denton. His parents died when he was six, leaving him the heir to several Cheshire manors, at least one advowson, and property in and around Chester which had once belonged to the Sisters of St Mary, and which was still known as 'the Nuns'. Brereton's ancestors had acquired church properties as a result of a close association with the court of Henry VIII (but one of them, also named William Brereton, had been executed as a supposed lover of Anne Boleyn).

Early life In all, Brereton inherited perhaps 3000 acres of land. In 1621, just after his sixteenth birthday, he matriculated at Brasenose College, Oxford; he remained there for almost three years without taking a degree, and went on to attend Gray's Inn in 1623–4. He was a ward of Sir George Booth of Dunham Massey, *custos rotulorum* of Cheshire, and in 1623, at the age of nineteen, was married to Booth's fourth daughter, Susanna, with whom he had two sons and two daughters. After her death in 1637 he married in 1641 a wealthy Staffordshire widow, Cicely Mytton (d. 1649), daughter of William Skeffington of Fisherwick, Leicestershire, with whom he had two more daughters and through whom he doubled his land holding.

In the 1620s and 1630s Brereton emerged as a vigorous and active businessman and magistrate. He was an inveterate traveller, and the journals of his travels in the Netherlands, Ireland, and Scotland are among the best surviving from this period; they display a lively interest in agriculture, architecture, food, and public religion. But he also seems to have travelled to the Spanish Netherlands, to Paris, and perhaps to Italy (a passport having been issued him in 1637). He may well have planned an expedition every summer. He acquired property in New England in 1629 and settled tenants there; and he tried to acquire property in Ireland. He was a pioneer in estate management, especially in a commercially successful duck decoy he constructed in Saltney marshes near Chester in 1631 (the source of much litigation with his neighbours). He was also involved in a series of disputes with the city of Chester over the exemption of his former monastic properties from city jurisdiction. He was not afraid of confrontation. He was the most active of all Cheshire JPs from 1625 to 1641, attending more than eighty per cent of all sessions (only one other JP managed above forty per cent) and signing more than twice as many documents addressed to the clerk of the peace as any other JP; and he was an assiduous deputy lieutenant.

In 1627 Brereton acquired a baronetcy through the good

Sir William Brereton, first baronet (1604–1661), by unknown engraver, pubd 1647

offices of the duke of Buckingham, in exchange for maintaining 30 foot soldiers in Ireland for three years. He did not resist Charles I's prerogative taxes, but he recorded privately his dislike of royal policy, especially over religious matters. He stood for parliament in 1625 but lost after agreeing to abide by a drawing of lots among the candidates. He was, however, returned unopposed in 1628, though there is no evidence that he spoke in either session of the parliament. He stood again in both the elections of 1640 and was returned after bitter contests on both occasions. He quickly became a noted supporter of godly reformation in the Long Parliament, sitting on the committees considering the reform or abolition of the court of high commission, investigating the activities of Bishops Wren and Piers, and on the Bill against Scandalous Ministers; and he ensured that the Cheshire puritans circulated and presented a petition for reform of the church roots and branches. He himself was one of those who favoured not a reform of the established church but its abolition and a fresh start. He played little part in the debates on the reform of secular institutions.

Civil war In the winter of 1641–2 the Commons dispatched Brereton to Cheshire to supervise the transportation of men, money, and supplies to put down the Catholic rising in Ireland (he himself invested £1000 in the expedition), and in the summer of 1642 he was sent down to implement the militia ordinance there. He tried to seize Chester in the high summer of 1642 but was rebuffed and limped back to London. On his return in January 1643 with 500 men he joined up with 2000 volunteers recruited by five

prominent gentlemen and he then moved resolutely but not very competently to clear most of southern and eastern Cheshire of royalists, to garrison the market towns (other than royalist Chester), and to set up his headquarters in Nantwich. Acting on parliamentarian ordinances of 9 January and 15 March 1643 (greatly strengthened by further ordinances of 26 March and 7 May 1644) which appointed him commander-in-chief of all the forces serving in Cheshire and gave him unusually sweeping powers to raise the resources to sustain a war effort in and around the county, he waged an aggressive and relentless war throughout the north midlands. At different times he took his troops into each of the seven counties that are contiguous with Cheshire and led joint operations with local commanders there. Lack of clarity in the ordinances under which he served often led to clashes with commanders and committeemen in neighbouring counties, and demands from the gentry of Cheshire that he concentrate on affairs within, not outside, the county, but he was determined to follow a broader strategic vision; and in return for his assistance to others, he was able to call on troops from north Wales, Shropshire, and along the Pennine spine to assist him in Cheshire.

Late in 1643 the seizure of a large supply of royalist ordnance and ammunition sent back from Ireland gave Brereton the ability to strike against the bridge and fort guarding a key crossing-point over the Dee at Farndon and Holt and to overrun north Wales. This success brought Cheshire to the front of royalist concerns, and 4000 men were sent from Oxford to strengthen Chester, while 8000 troops from the English expeditionary force in Ireland were transported back to Chester. His position was saved only by a daring and generous 120-mile march through thick snow by Fairfax and his Yorkshire forces which resulted in the first unequivocal parliamentarian victory of the war at Nantwich (25 January 1644). This was a crucial victory, and Brereton's courage and imagination on the field were recognized by Fairfax, who commanded the combined force on the day, and was rewarded with a Roman-style triumph through the streets of London.

In 1645 Brereton seems to have devised a series of high-profile military provocations to lure the king's army to Cheshire where it was to be destroyed by an allied force made up of the Scots, the New Model Army, and the various brigades of north midlanders. It almost happened, but at the last minute Rupert swerved south not north from Staffordshire, only to be defeated at Naseby. Thereafter Brereton's overwhelming interest was in the siege of Chester, undertaken semi-continuously from autumn 1644 to February 1646. He had been exempted from the self-denying ordinance in February 1645 to complete this great work, but was recalled when it had not been completed by June. However, after Sydenham Poyntz's victory over the king and the relieving royalist army at Rowton Heath (September 1645), Brereton was reinstated and he completed the work, negotiating the surrender which finally took place in early February 1646. He remained in arms for the mopping up operation, taking great pleasure in destroying the spire of Lichfield Cathedral with play of cannon: 'it was erected in ressemblance of the Pope's triple Crown and if so its fall may be ominous and prognostic of another downfall' (Birmingham Reference Library, MS 595611, pp. 250–51).

Brereton was in arms continuously for 52 months from January 1642 except for two periods (of two and four months' duration) in parliament in 1644 and 1645. Otherwise he executed his command with 'notable sobriety and indefatigable industry' (Clarendon, *Hist. rebellion*, 2.471). He was involved in more than thirty engagements in which blood was shed, he stormed eleven garrisoned towns, and was on six battlefields in which more than 2000 men were engaged—Middlewich and Hopton Heath (March 1643), Middlewich (December 1643), Nantwich (January 1644), Montgomery (September 1644), and Stow-in-the-Wold (March 1646).

Five letter books from the last eighteen months of the war—some 2000 letters in all—have survived from what was probably an even larger collection, and they are one of the most important sources for understanding the military, administrative, and political dynamics of civil-war parliamentarianism. They reveal the deep fissures within the movement throughout the north and west midlands, and at Westminster, for Brereton was a close ally of the 'war party' in the Long Parliament, and especially of lords Saye and Wharton, and Oliver St John and Henry Vane. Among the agents who worked to secure his interests and those of his army was his fellow Cestrian and rising lawyer John Bradshaw who was, in the mid-1640s, judge of the London sheriff's court and a solicitor attached to the committee for sequestrations (the body which handled the confiscated land of all convicted royalists).

Later years With the end of the first civil war Brereton moved back to Westminster. He was lavishly rewarded for his victories, receiving Eccleshall Castle and, more importantly, using his arrears of pay to acquire the archbishop of Canterbury's palace at Croydon, which he made his home until his death in 1661. In 1646 and 1648 he took the side of the army grandees in all the great political crises and he sat on important executive committees, including the committee of the army and the indemnity committee; but he absented himself without permission for several months in 1647, for which he was heavily fined by the Commons. He did not take his seat in the Rump Parliament until after the regicide, and though named as one of the king's judges, he did not sit at the trial or sign the death warrant, though at his trial in 1660 Hugh Peters (who knew Brereton well) claimed that he had seen him urging Cromwell in December 1648 to establish a high court (*An Exact and Impartiall Accompt of the Indictment … of 29 Persons*, 1661, 167, 248).

Brereton was an occasional attender of parliament in 1649, but a more frequent one in each of 1650, 1651, and 1652, and he was elected to the council of state in each of the last two years of the Rump, though given the forty-first and last place. Little is known of his role there. He had withdrawn from all his Cheshire offices and he did not become active as a JP or commissioner in Surrey. He was in Cheshire at the time of the 1654 parliamentary election

and he ran in 1656 in opposition to the slate of candidates put up by Major-General Bridge. When the Rump was restored in 1659 he took his seat, but took little part in its proceedings. At the Restoration his palace at Croydon was returned to Archbishop Juxon, but he appears to have been allowed to stay on as a tenant, for he died there on 7 April 1661 and his burial is recorded in the parish register there.

Brereton was a strong puritan, but his letters lack Cromwell's biblical rhetoric and Prynne's apocalyptical fervour. Like Cromwell, he knew—in religion and in politics—what he would not have but not what he would have; but in Brereton this induced after 1646 an increasing lethargy and indecision. Success in war led on to the home comforts of peace: it was said that he had 'such a prodigious stomach' that he had converted the chapel of the palace at Croydon into a kitchen (*The Mysteries of the Good Old Cause*, 1659, 3); and his insistence in August 1646 on being given Eccleshall Castle as a reward for all he had achieved led to a debate so heated that Sir John Clotworthy suggested that a ballot box be brought into the Commons so that the issue could be settled by secret vote (Kishlansky, 137).

Yet in the 1630s Brereton was the epitome of a puritan magistrate: stern paternalism and vigorous self-improvement; and for four years of civil war he was a tireless warrior and administrator, putting the wider needs of his cause above the convenience and narrow self-interest of his own county and his own homelands. With the king defeated, puritans at one another's throats, and old friendships rubbed raw by the contingencies of war, he lost his way. The final decade of his life was devoted to retaining the trappings of power and showed his lack of stomach for a new campaign to perfect the godly commonwealth.   JOHN MORRILL

Sources *The letter books of Sir William Brereton*, ed. R. N. Dore, 2 vols., Lancashire and Cheshire RS, 123, 128 (1984–90) · R. N. Dore, 'The early life of Sir William Brereton', *Transactions of the Lancashire and Cheshire Antiquarian Society*, 63 (1952–3), 1–26 · R. N. Dore, *The civil wars in Cheshire* (1966) · J. S. Morrill, *Cheshire, 1630–1660: county government and society during the English revolution* (1974) · J. S. Morrill, 'Sir William Brereton and England's wars of religion', *Journal of British Studies*, 24 (1985), 311–32 · J. S. Morrill, 'Parliamentary representation', *VCH Cheshire*, 1.101–8 · J. P. Earwaker, *East Cheshire: past and present, or, A history of the hundred of Macclesfield*, 1 (1877), 250–64 · B. Worden, *The Rump Parliament, 1648–1653* (1974) · R. P. Stearns, *The strenuous puritan: Hugh Peter, 1598–1660* (1954) · M. A. Kishlansky, *The rise of the New Model Army* (1979) · W. Brereton, *Travels in Holland, the United Provinces, England, Scotland, and Ireland, 1634–5*, ed. E. Hawkins, Chetham Society, 1 (1844) · J. E. Auden, 'Sir Jerome Zankey (or Sankey), of Balderton Hall, co. Salop, and of Coolmore, co. Tipperary', *Transactions of the Shropshire Archaeological Society*, 50 (1939–40), 171–8 · K. S. Bottigheimer, *English money and Irish land* (1971) · P. J. Pinckney, 'The Cheshire election of 1656', *Bulletin of the John Rylands University Library*, 49 (1966–7), 387–426 · G. P. Higgins, 'County government and society in Cheshire, c.1590–1640', MA diss., U. Lpool, 1973 · M. Wanklyn, 'Landed society and allegiance in Cheshire and Shropshire in the first civil war', PhD diss., University of Manchester, 1976 · *JHC*, 1–7 (1547–1659) · *The manuscripts of his grace the duke of Portland*, 10 vols., HMC, 29 (1891–1931) · T. Malbon and E. Burghall, *Memorials of the civil war in Cheshire and the adjacent counties*, ed. J. Hall, Lancashire and Cheshire RS, 19 (1889) · *An exact and* *impartiall accompt of the indictment … of 29 persons* (1661) · Birm. CL, MS 595611

Archives Birm. CL, letter-book relating to military operations, MS 595611 · BL, papers and corresp., Add. MSS 11331–11333 · Bodl. Oxf., letters · Ches. & Chester ALSS | BL, Aston MSS, Add. MSS 36913–36914 · BL, Randle Holmes MSS, Harley MSS 1943–2174 · Bodl. Oxf., Lenthall MSS

Likenesses R. Cooper, engraving, AM Oxf., Sutherland collection · G. Glover, line engraving, BM · engraving, repro. in J. Ricraft, *A survey of England's champions* (1647) [*see illus.*] · line engraving, BM, NPG; repro. in J. Vicars, *England's worthies* (1647) · portrait, Grosvenor Museum, Chester

Wealth at death approx. £1000 p.a.: Dore, 'Early life'

Brereton, William, third Baron Brereton of Leighlin (*bap.* 1631, *d.* 1680), politician and natural philosopher, was baptized on 4 May 1631 at Brereton, Cheshire, the eldest son of William Brereton, second Baron Brereton (1611–1664), and his wife, Lady Elizabeth (*d.* 1687), daughter of George *Goring, first earl of Norwich. The barony was a Jacobean Irish creation, referring to Leighlin, co. Carlow, bestowed on Brereton's grandfather in 1624. The family was quietly royalist during the civil war but Brereton and his parents were taken prisoner when the parliamentary forces in Staffordshire captured Biddulph Hall in 1644. Lord Goring sent Brereton in 1646 to the Low Countries to study under the mathematician John Pell, a friend of Lord Brereton, at the Breda Academy, from where he returned in 1652, a competent mathematician and algebraist. On 11 November 1657 he married, apparently against his father's wishes, Frances (*d.* 1680), daughter of Francis *Willoughby, fifth Baron Willoughby. Three sons were born: only the eldest, John (1659–1718), and the youngest, Francis (*d.* 1722), survived to adulthood.

Brereton was a close friend of Samuel Hartlib and his circle (Hartlib's son Clodius was his physician) and a patron of many literary and scientific undertakings. While abroad he had been in the company of Thomas Hobbes and Sir Charles Cavendish. He frequented the scientific gatherings at Gresham College in 1658 that preceded the formation of the Royal Society, of which he was a founder member and active participant. His interests encompassed the reproduction of language, chemistry, and many aspects of agriculture. He was fascinated by London's new Turkish coffee house, whose exotic drink was for the first time available in Britain. At the Royal Society he sat on the georgics (agriculture) and mechanics committees. After Hartlib's death in penury in 1662 Brereton purchased the two trunks containing his papers and transported them to Cheshire, where John Worthington arranged them into some kind of order.

Elected to represent Newton, Lancashire, in Richard Cromwell's parliament in 1659, and in 1660 the seat of Bossiney, Brereton voted with the Presbyterian opposition. He made no speeches in parliament but was elected to the chair of the public accounts commission (1667–70), and was a gentleman of the privy chamber from 1673 until his death. Financial hardship dogged Brereton for much of his life: he was obliged to alienate the barony of Malpas to compensate for his family's support of the royalist cause, his wife brought little or no portion, and even after

inheriting the title in 1664 he was in very straitened circumstances. His father-in-law drowned in Barbados in 1666, and his wife's inheritance was not paid out until 1674.

His acquaintances held Brereton in high regard. John Aubrey, who had known him since his return from Breda, could not 'mention this Noble Lord but with a great deale of Passion, for a more virtuous person (besides his great learning) I never knew' (*Brief Lives*, 232). To Hartlib he was 'really a noble gentlemen, & of a much enlarged spirit to the good of mankind' (*Diary and Correspondence of Dr John Worthington*, 1.188). Samuel Pepys, having met him at Lady Carteret's dining table, judged him to be 'a very sober and serious, able man'; after dinner Brereton went to the organ and 'played a verse very handsomely' (Pepys, 8.10–11). He was an excellent musician and a good composer. In 1666 John Worthington sent him a polyphon (a kind of harpsichord) together with a book of lessons.

Brereton died in Westminster on 17 March 1680, and was buried on 19 March at St Martin-in-the-Fields, Westminster. His wife died in September the same year, and was also buried at St Martin-in-the-Fields. The title passed to his son John, who married but died childless, then to Francis, who died unmarried in 1722, whereupon it became extinct.   ANITA MCCONNELL

Sources M. Greengrass, M. Leslie, and T. Raylor, eds., *Samuel Hartlib and universal reformation: studies in intellectual communication* (1994), 4–7 · M. Hunter, *The Royal Society and its fellows, 1660–1700: the morphology of an early scientific institution* (1982) · *The diary and correspondence of Dr John Worthington*, ed. J. Crossley and R. C. Christie, 2 vols. in 3, Chetham Society, 13, 36, 114 (1847–86) · G. Ormerod, *The history of the county palatine and city of Chester*, 2nd edn, ed. T. Helsby, 3 (1882), 86, 89 · T. Malbon and E. Burghall, *Memorials of the civil war in Cheshire and the adjacent counties*, ed. J. Hall, Lancashire and Cheshire RS, 19 (1889), 122 · HoP, *Commons, 1660–90* · *Aubrey's Brief lives*, ed. O. L. Dick (1949); pbk edn (1992), 231–2 · GEC, *Peerage*, new edn · Evelyn, *Diary*, 3.218, 232, 488 · Pepys, *Diary*, 8.10–11

Brereton, Sir William (1789–1864), army officer, was born at Bath on 29 December 1789. He was descended from the ancient Cheshire family of Brereton of Brereton Hall, through its Irish branch, the Breretons of Carrigslaney, co. Carlow. He was a son of Major Robert Brereton, who fought at Culloden, and younger half-brother of Major-General Robert Brereton of New Abbey, co. Kildare (formerly of 30th and 63rd regiments), and lieutenant-governor of St Lucia, who died in 1818.

Brereton entered the Royal Military Academy, Woolwich, in 1803, and passed out in May 1805 as a second lieutenant, Royal Artillery. He served in the Peninsular and Waterloo campaigns from December 1809 to June 1815, including the defence of Cadiz, where he commanded the guns at Fort Matagorda and was wounded, the battle of Barossa, the Burgos retreat, the battles of Vitoria and the Pyrenees, the siege of San Sebastian, where he was temporarily attached to the breaching batteries, and the battles of Orthez, Toulouse, Quatre Bras, and Waterloo. For most of this period he was a subaltern of the famous troop of the Royal Horse Artillery commanded by Major Norman Ramsay, with which he was severely wounded at

Waterloo. He became a second captain in 1816, and was placed on half pay in 1817.

Brereton was brought on full pay in 1823, and, after a quarter of a century of further varied service at home and in the colonies (KH 1837, CB July 1838), was sent to China, where he was second in command under General d'Aguilar in the expedition to the Bogue (Humen) and at the capture of Canton (Guangzhou) in 1848. During the early part of the Crimean War, Brereton, then on the strength of the horse artillery brigade at Woolwich, was present with the Black Sea Fleet as a guest on board HMS *Britannia*, flagship of his relative, Vice-Admiral Sir J. D. Dundas, and directed the fire of her rockets in the attack on the Sevastopol forts on 17 October 1854. He became major-general in December 1854 and KCB in June 1861. For a short period he was chief of the Irish constabulary, and in April 1864 was made colonel-commandant of the Royal Artillery. He wrote a brief narrative, *The British Fleet in the Black Sea* (privately printed, 1857?). Promoted lieutenant-general a few days before, Brereton died at his home, 3E The Albany, Piccadilly, London, on 27 July 1864. By his will he left £1000, of which the interest was to be applied in perpetuity to encouraging cricket among artillery NCOs at Woolwich.

H. M. Chichester, *rev.* James Lunt

Sources F. Dwarns, 'Observations upon the history of one of the old Cheshire families', *Archaeologia*, 33 (1849), 63–83, esp. 55–83 · J. Lodge, *The peerage of Ireland*, rev. M. Archdall, rev. edn, 2 (1789), 251 · Burke, *Gen. GB* · *Hart's Army List* · J. Kane, *List of officers of the royal regiment of artillery from 1716*, rev. edn (1869) · F. Duncan, ed., *History of the royal regiment of artillery*, 2 vols. (1873) · W. Brereton, 'Memoirs translated from the new work of General Paixhans entitled *Constitution militaire de la France*', *Minutes of the Proceedings of the Royal Artillery Institution*, 124–34 · *Annual Register* (1864) · *ILN* (6 Aug 1864), 154 · *ILN* (17 Sept 1864), 299 · Officers Records, royal artillery, MOD Central Library, 2, fol. 170 · Boase, *Mod. Eng. biog.* · *GM*, 3rd ser., 17 (1864), 526

Wealth at death under £25,000: probate, 16 Aug 1864, *CGPLA Eng. & Wales*

Brerewood, Edward (*c.*1565–1613), antiquary and mathematician, was one of three surviving children born to Robert Brerewood (*c.*1532–1601) of Chester, and his wife, Elizabeth, daughter of Thomas Horton of Chester. Although illiterate, Robert Brerewood was a prosperous dealer in skins who also manufactured leather goods and dealt in timber and wool. He was three times mayor of Chester, and at his death left considerable wealth and property. His eldest son, John (*c.*1561–1599), was apprenticed to his father and inherited the business; his son was Sir Robert *Brerewood (1588–1654), judge. It is not known which school Edward Brerewood attended, but he matriculated at Brasenose College, Oxford, in 1581 aged about sixteen. He gained a reputation for assiduous scholarship, graduating BA in February 1587 and proceeding MA in July 1590. He then migrated to St Mary Hall, and on 26 September 1592, when Queen Elizabeth was at Oxford, he replied at a disputation in natural philosophy. Perhaps he lacked a patron, for it was related, 'being candidate for a fellowship, he lost it without loss of credit, for where preferment goes more by favour than merit, the rejected have more honour than the elected' (Fuller, *Worthies*, 190).

When Sir Thomas Gresham's foundation came into being in London, Brerewood was one of six graduates from Oxford and Cambridge who were recruited in 1596 as professors of the new Gresham College; his inaugural lecture as professor of astronomy was delivered at the end of 1597. Brerewood seems to have retained his reputation for scholarship largely undiluted by any commerce with students or colleagues, although 'always ready in private conference or writing to advise those who sought his counsel' (Wood, *Ath. Oxon.*, 2.139). He was a member of the Elizabethan Society of Antiquaries, but otherwise 'led a retired and private course of life, delighting with profound speculations, and the diligent searching out of hidden verities' (ibid.). From these labours he composed a great many treatises, on logic, and on a diversity of subjects connected with the languages and religion of oriental Christians. In 1611 'pens were brandished betwixt [Nicholas] Byfield and Brerewood about the keeping of the sabbath, Brerewood maintaining that Byfield [a Chester preacher] exacted more strictness than God enjoined' (Fuller, 294). He died in London on 4 November 1613, and was buried on the 8th in St Helen, Bishopsgate.

Brerewood published nothing during his lifetime, bequeathing his large and valuable library and his manuscripts to his nephew Robert, who saw many of them into print. A study of ancient coins, *De ponderibus et pretiis veterum nummorum* (1614), was later inserted in the apparatus of Brian Walton's *Biblia polyglotta* and the *Critici sacri*. *Enquiries touching the diversities of languages and religions through the chief parts of the world* (1614) went through several editions, being translated into French in 1640 and into Latin. *Elementae logicae* (1614) was followed by *Tractatus quidam logici* (1628), the latter and other short works, together with Brerewood's commentaries on Aristotle's ethics, being published in Oxford over the years by Thomas Sixesmith, fellow of Brasenose College.

Thompson Cooper, *rev.* Anita McConnell

Sources J. Ward, *The lives of the professors of Gresham College* (1740), 74–6 · *Brief lives, chiefly of contemporaries, set down by John Aubrey, between the years 1669 and 1696*, ed. A. Clark, 1 (1898), 122 · D. M. Woodward, 'Robert Brerewood: an Elizabethan master craftsman', *Cheshire Round*, 1/9 (1968), 311–16 · *GM*, 1st ser., 61 (1791), 714–16 · Wood, *Ath. Oxon.*, new edn, 2.139 · Wood, *Ath. Oxon.: Fasti* (1815), 236, 251 · parish register, St Helen, Bishopsgate, London, 8 Nov 1613 [burial] · Fuller, *Worthies* (1840), 1.294–5 · will, PRO, PROB 11/122, sig. 98

Brerewood, Sir Robert (1588–1654), judge, was born in Chester, the son of John Brerewood (*c.*1561–1599), sheriff of that city, and his wife, Mary (*d.* 1592), daughter of Thomas Parry of Nannerch, Flintshire. In 1605 he was sent to Oxford, where, in October 1607, he matriculated at Brasenose College. He spent two years at Brasenose, having also in 1607 been admitted to Middle Temple, London.

Brerewood's uncle Edward *Brerewood (*c.*1565–1613), professor of astronomy at Gresham College, bequeathed his large and valuable library and his many unpublished treatises to Robert, who saw several of them into print with admirable dispatch, writing a large and learned preface to Edward's *Enquiries touching the diversities of languages and religions through the chief parts of the world* (1614). Brerewood was called to the bar in November 1615. Three years later he was appointed on the king's recommendation as clerk of the prentice (town clerk) at Chester. In 1624 he farmed out this office in order to devote more time to his legal practice, and when the city's council discovered in February 1627 that the assembly's orders and the returns for jurors for gaol delivery were defective he was called on to resign. Brerewood and his clerk were also accused of disrespect for the mayor and JPs. The post of clerk of the prentice was a personal one, and after the matter had been referred to the privy council Brerewood admitted that he had been absent from his duties and duly resigned. In 1628 the mayor twice proposed that he be elected onto the city council but the assembly rejected him, and his election took place only in 1633.

Brerewood was twice married: his first wife was Anne (1600–1630), daughter of Sir Randall Mainwaring (d. 1632) of Over Peover, Cheshire; their first child, John (1616–1701), another son, and two daughters survived childhood, three others did not. His second wife was Catherine (d. 1692), daughter of Sir Richard Lea of Lea and Dernhall, Cheshire. Of their seven children, three sons and two daughters survived childhood and benefited considerably under the terms of his will.

In 1637 Brerewood was appointed JP for Anglesey, Caernarfon, and Merioneth, and a judge in north Wales. In 1638 he was Lent reader at Middle Temple; in April 1639 the city of Chester elected him as an alderman and its recorder. A staunch royalist, he became serjeant-at-law in 1640, and the following year serjeant-at-law to the queen. He was MP for Chester in the Short Parliament. He was knighted in 1643, and raised to the bench on 31 January 1644, being sworn in by the king at Oxford. Though he continued to sit until the end of the civil war, he never sat in Westminster Hall, and after the execution of Charles I he retired into private life, devoting himself to the agricultural improvement of his estates. He owned a manuscript account of Middle Temple which was extensively used by Dugdale in his *Origines juridiciales* and much later presented to Middle Temple. He died on 8 September 1654, and was buried the following day in the church of St Mary on the Hill, Chester.   ANITA McCONNELL

Sources J. B. Williamson, ed., *The Middle Temple bench book*, 2nd edn, 1 (1937) · Foss, *Judges* · Wood, *Ath. Oxon.*, new edn, 2.140 · J. Hutchinson, ed., *A catalogue of notable Middle Templars: with brief biographical notices* (1902), 36 · M. J. Groombridge, ed., *Calendar of Chester city council minutes, 1603–1642*, Lancashire and Cheshire RS, 106 (1956) · will, PRO, PROB 11/259, sig. 383 · J. P. Earwaker, *History of the church and parish of St Mary on the Hill, Chester* (1898) · J. P. Rylands, ed., *Cheshire and Lancashire funeral certificates, AD 1600 to 1678*, Lancashire and Cheshire RS, 6 (1882), 38 · will, PRO, PROB 11/259
Archives Middle Temple, London, MSS
Wealth at death rich: will, PRO, PROB 11/259, sig. 383

Brerewood, Thomas (d. **1748**), poet, was the son of Thomas Brerewood of Horton, Buckinghamshire, and grandson of Sir Robert *Brerewood the judge. Brerewood

lived at Place House, Horton, near Windsor, an Elizabethan mansion modernized by his father, and died unmarried in 1748. Some pieces of poetry by him, notably a sequence of risqué pastoral songs on the seasons (in 1744, 1746, and 1754), were printed in the *Gentleman's Magazine. Galfred and Juetta, or, The Road of Nature: a Tale in Three Cantos*, 'written nearly forty years ago' was published in 1772: in octosyllabic couplets, it is full of coarse rustic humour on drunkenness and fornication.

THOMPSON COOPER, *rev.* W. B. HUTCHINGS

Sources G. Lipscomb, *The history and antiquities of the county of Buckingham*, 4 vols. (1831–47) · C. P., letter to editor, *GM*, 1st ser., 61 (1791), 713–16
Archives Middle Temple, London, MSS

Bresal mac Ségéni (d. **801**). *See under* Iona, abbots of (act. 563–927).

Bressan, Peter [*formerly* Pierre Jaillard] (**1663–1731**), musical instrument maker, was born Pierre Jaillard in Bourg-en-Bresse, France, on 27 May 1663, the son of Claude Jaillard (d. 1667), carrier, and his wife, Philibert (d. 1694), daughter of Louis Mercier, joiner. Bressan probably received his early education at the Jesuit-run college in Bourg. On 13 May 1678 he was apprenticed to Jean Boysser, master turner of Bourg, for two years. He then probably undertook some (further) training in woodwind instrument making as well as performing in Paris from one of the Hotteterres. Jaillard settled in England about 1688. His name doubtless proving awkward for English tongues, he began calling himself Peter Bressan, signifying 'from Bresse'. He was one of five oboists who went to Holland with William III in April 1691, but did not join the royal musical establishment.

About 1702 Bressan lodged with Claude Mignon, a French apothecary, in Duchy House, Duchy Lane, Somerset House Yard, London, part of the estate of the duchy of Lancaster, whose red rose (in stylized form) became part of Bressan's maker's mark. The house was situated by Somerset watergate stairs, a main thoroughfare from the Thames. Upon Mignon's death (1714) Bressan took over his lease. About 1703 Bressan married Mignon's daughter Mary Margaret (d. 1738), a sponsor of exhibitions, and he lived happily with her until his change of fortune, when he experienced domestic strife. According to several witnesses in the suit he filed against her in 1721–4, she had a tempestuous disposition, threatening his life, concealing money, and incurring large debts. She confessed to marrying him 'only because he was in a way of getting a great deal of money' (Byrne, 'More on Bressan', 105). Witnesses described Bressan as industrious, sober, and good-tempered. He became a denizen on 12 September 1723. Yet in 1730 he left his wife and fled to Tournai in Flanders, where he died on 21 April 1731, probably at the house of the celebrated woodwind player François la Riche. Bressan's death abroad, his debts, and his marital difficulties complicated the settlement of his will.

James Talbot chose to give measurements for five instruments by Bressan—flute, treble, and tenor oboe, and tenor and bass recorder—showing that Bressan's reputation for woodwind instrument making had already been established. In 1721 he testified that he had acquired fame and fortune 'in making of musicall instruments and particularly of flutes [recorders]' (Byrne, 'More on Bressan', 102), but since 1715 his trade had fallen off sharply. His great success with the gentleman amateur market for almost thirty years presumably accounts for the survival of no fewer than forty-eight of his recorders—far more than from any other early maker. They are prized among modern players for their mellow, vibrant, and slightly 'edgy' timbre and flexible playing technique; some fifty modern makers have produced copies of one or more sizes. Three of Bressan's flutes have also survived, unfortunately not in their original condition, but no oboes or bassoons.   DAVID LASOCKI

Sources M. Byrne, 'Pierre Jaillard, Peter Bressan', *Galpin Society Journal*, 36 (1983), 2–28 · M. Byrne, 'More on Bressan', *Galpin Society Journal*, 37 (1984), 102–11 · A. Baines, 'James Talbot's manuscript (Christ Church Library, music MS 1187): wind instruments', *Galpin Society Journal*, 1 (1948), 9–26 · P. Young, *4900 historical woodwind instruments* (1993) · A. Ashbee and D. Lasocki, eds., *A biographical dictionary of English court musicians, 1485–1714*, 2 vols. (1998)
Wealth at death possessions valued at £36 5s. 4d.; also shares and annuities: Byrne, 'Pierre Jaillard', 16–17, 25–8

Bressey, Sir Charles Herbert (1874–1951), civil engineer, was born at Wanstead, Essex, on 3 January 1874, the son of John Thomas Bressey, architect, and his wife, Mary Elizabeth Farrow. He was educated at Forest School, Walthamstow, and at Bremen and Rouen, before becoming articled to his father in 1891. He became partner to his father in 1896, and on the latter's retirement continued his practice in the City of London. He also succeeded his father as surveyor to Wanstead urban district council. In 1902 he married Lily Margaret Francis, daughter of Francis Charles Hill, merchant, of Wanstead. They made their home at 3 Fernbank, Church Road, Buckhurst Hill, where they raised two sons.

By the outbreak of the First World War, Bressey had many years' experience of surveying and civil engineering work and he was commissioned in the Royal Engineers, dealing particularly with military roads. He served in France and Flanders and rose to the rank of lieutenant-colonel. He was mentioned in dispatches, appointed OBE, and made a chevalier of the Légion d'honneur. In 1916 he became a staff officer of the roads directorate in France, and for the latter part of the war he served with Sir Henry Maybury under Sir Eric Geddes. Immediately after the war he served for a short time as a member of the inter-allied commission, Rhine province communications, based near Cologne. On the formation of the Ministry of Transport in 1919 he was invited to become the first divisional road engineer for London by Maybury, the director-general of roads. In 1921 Bressey succeeded J. S. Killick as chief engineer for roads. When Maybury retired at the end of 1928 he was succeeded by Bressey. The post of director-general was abolished and Bressey retained the title of chief engineer.

A sound practical engineer, Bressey had the misfortune,

perhaps, to be overshadowed by Maybury's brilliance. His most impressive achievement was the highway development survey of Greater London. This survey, intended to determine highway requirements for the next thirty years, was ordered by Leslie Hore-Belisha, the minister of transport. Bressey was seconded to the work, acting as engineer in charge from 1935 to 1938. Sir Edwin Lutyens was appointed as consultant to help Bressey in his task. Bressey went to great lengths to ensure his report formed a comprehensive treatment of the subject. He toured the continent, and consulted widely with local authorities, professional bodies, and other interested parties. His report was issued in 1938 and featured novel techniques in its preparation—aerial surveys and photography, journey-time studies to measure delays, and an original and destination survey of traffic to the docks. The report was well received but the outbreak of war in the following year precluded any action, although its references to schemes such as orbital roads, the improvement of communications to docklands, and major motorways radiating from the metropolis, featured in many subsequent planning reports on Greater London.

Bressey retired in January 1938, following completion of his report. In the following year (1938–9) he was the president of the Chartered Surveyors' Institution and of the Junior Institution of Engineers. He was chairman of the road engineering industry committee and of the British Standards Institution and an honorary member of the Institution of Royal Engineers. He was also a member of the Town Planning Institute, the Chartered Institute of Transport, and the institutions of Municipal and of Highway Engineers. He served on the council of the Institute of Professional Civil Servants. He was appointed a CBE in 1924, a CB in 1930, and knighted in 1935. He was awarded the honorary degree of DSc (Eng.) by London University in 1938 for his London roads survey. He died in the Knaresborough Nursing Home, Sawbridgeworth, Hertfordshire, on 14 April 1951, of cerebral haemorrhage and arteriosclerosis.   ALEX SAMUELS, rev. MIKE CHRIMES

Sources *The Engineer* (20 April 1951), 514–15 · *RICS Journal*, 30 (June 1951), 964–5 · *Journal* [Junior Institution of Engineers], 61 (1950–51), 364–5 · *Engineering* (20 April 1951), 473 · *The Journal* [Institution of Highway Engineers], 2 (1951), 8 · m. cert. · d. cert. · CGPLA Eng. & Wales (1951) · *The Engineer* (20 April 1951), 514
Archives PRO, Ministry of Transport records
Likenesses W. Stoneman, photograph, 1940, NPG · Lafayette, photograph, repro. in *Engineering*, 473 · photograph, repro. in *The Engineer*, 514
Wealth at death £16,924 0s. 10d.: probate, 8 Sept 1951, CGPLA Eng. & Wales

Bresslau, Marcus Hyman (1807/8–1864), newspaper editor, was born in Hamburg, possibly with the Hebrew forenames Mordecai Chaim, to Jewish parents of whom nothing is known. He migrated to London in his youth. He had evidently received a traditional Jewish education, but at the same time had inculcated the ideas of the *Haskalah* (the Jewish enlightenment), which since the late eighteenth century had been influencing sections of continental Jewry. A keen and able Hebraist, Bresslau was employed for some time from 1834 as *baal kora* (reader of the law) at the Western Synagogue, St Alban's Place, Haymarket, London, and occasionally delivered sermons; he then taught Hebrew at the Westminster Jews' Free School and went on to tutor privately. As a follower of the *Haskalah* he was intent on extending Hebrew far beyond its time-honoured, restricted role as the language of Jewish prayer into a revived and vibrant vehicle for literary expression, linguistic exploration, and a cultural renaissance of the Jewish people. Accordingly, he became associated with the *Hebrew Review and Magazine of Rabbinical Literature*, which ran from 1834 to 1836. It was founded and edited by Morris J. Raphall (1798–1868), then employed as secretary to Chief Rabbi Solomon Hirschell; Raphall later became, in turn, minister of the Birmingham Hebrew congregation and a renowned and controversial rabbi in New York.

Bresslau's collaboration on this production familiarized him with the essentials of journalism. In October 1844 he was appointed editor of the recently relaunched *Jewish Chronicle* by that newspaper's new proprietor, Joseph Mitchell (d. 1854). Unlike the rival *Voice of Jacob*, which it soon eclipsed, the *Jewish Chronicle* under these two men provided a platform for all viewpoints within the Anglo-Jewish community. Yet they had a definite agenda of their own. They sought to undermine the fledgeling Reform movement by urging an appropriately offensive response by the Orthodox authorities: they robustly campaigned for certain limited modifications to the traditional liturgy and ritual, which would enhance Orthodox Judaism's appeal to the modern Jew and thereby reduce the inroads being made by Reform Judaism. They sought an outward-looking Orthodox rabbinate, as well versed in secular as in Jewish learning, and therefore equipped to deal with the challenges of the wider society. In an approach reminiscent of that of followers of the *Haskalah*, demanding an end to discrimination and disabilities in institutionally antisemitic continental lands, they believed that Anglo-Jewry must demonstrate that it deserved the parliamentary emancipation to which it laid claim. Bresslau and Mitchell, therefore, vigorously promoted self-improvement for the Jewish masses, including the implementation of a more effective system of communal poor relief.

Popular education was especially close to the hearts of both men. They applauded and publicized the Jews' and General Literary and Scientific Institution, opened at Sussex Hall, Leadenhall Street, City, in January 1845. Their paper reported in detail the annual general meetings of Jewish schools and other worthy communal initiatives. No doubt partly to encourage others to donate, they regularly published lists of financial contributors to those institutions, who always included a not insignificant number of non-Jewish well-wishers in keeping with the liberal spirit of the day. As a fluent German-speaker who knew continental Jewish sources well, Bresslau performed sterling service in extracting items of interest from Jewish newspapers on the continent, including speeches by fighters for Jewish emancipation, translating them, and reproducing them in the *Jewish Chronicle*.

Bresslau was by nature peevish and argumentative, and despite a broad commonality of aim his relations with Mitchell were often strained. In July 1848 he relinquished the editorship following a dispute, but resumed duties two months later. He remained for approximately two years, resigning again about October 1850. In January 1853 another communal newspaper, the *Hebrew Observer*, was founded, edited by Abraham Benisch (1811–1878), who had apparently helped to edit some issues of the defunct *Voice of Jacob*. A letter from Bresslau appeared the following month, and thenceforward he regularly contributed articles, being thereby drawn into close association with Benisch, who bought the new paper in 1854. On Mitchell's death that same year Bresslau resumed the editorship of the *Jewish Chronicle*. It was clear that the Jewish community could not support two publications, and after their merger (officially as the *Jewish Chronicle and Hebrew Observer*) in February 1855 Benisch became the editor.

For reasons now unknown, and evidently puzzling to his associates, Bresslau turned down several offers of employment within the Jewish community. He made a valiant but abortive attempt to revive the *Hebrew Review*. Described by a contemporary as 'a ready scribe and to some extent also the Hebrew poet of the community' he produced a Hebrew grammar and a Hebrew dictionary, and translated various Hebrew manuscripts in the Bodleian Library. He composed a Hebrew version of the national anthem. Although only middle-aged, he showed increasing signs of infirmity, and was presented with several hundred pounds raised by public subscription within the Jewish community in recognition of a literary career which had flourished for over three decades. He is also believed to have been granted a small pension by a kind-hearted admirer. Slipping increasingly into ill health and obscurity, he died 'among strangers' at the German Hospital, Dalston, on 15 May 1864, of heart disease and dropsy. His age on the death certificate was given as fifty-six, and his occupation as 'professor of languages'. He never married, and appears to have left no immediate family.

HILARY L. RUBINSTEIN

Sources *Jewish Chronicle* (20 May 1864) · D. Cesarani, *The Jewish Chronicle and Anglo-Jewry, 1841–1991* (1994) · *The Jewish Chronicle, 1841–1941: a century of newspaper history*, Jewish Chronicle (1949) · J. M. Shaftesley, 'Dr Abraham Benisch as newspaper editor', *Transactions of the Jewish Historical Society of England*, 21 (1968) · A. Barnett, *The Western Synagogue through two centuries (1761–1961)* (1961) · J. M. Shaftesley, ed., *Remember the days: essays on Anglo-Jewish history presented to Cecil Roth* (1966) · d. cert.
Wealth at death Died indigent, reliant on charity

Bressler, Moses. *See* Hart, Moses (1675–1756), *under* Hart, Aaron (1670–1756).

Breteuil, Robert de [Robert ès Blanchmains, Robert the Whitehanded, Robert de Beaumont], **third earl of Leicester** (c.1130–1190), magnate, was the only son of *Robert, second earl of Leicester (d. 1168), justiciar, and Amice, daughter of Ralph de Gael. His parents married c.1121, and he was born after a number of elder sisters. The first charter of his father he attested was that which founded Leicester Abbey about 1139, when he may have been around ten years old. His education was committed to Hugh Barre, later archdeacon of Leicester, although apart from mention of his tutor, there is no evidence of his literacy other than some surviving items of correspondence.

Robert is first known to have taken an active part in events in spring 1153 at Bristol. Duke Henry made a confirmation to him, independently from that to his father, of the honours of Breteuil and Pacy-sur-Eure. Charter evidence places him at Winchester in November 1153, which implies that he followed the duke on campaign that summer. After 1154 he seems to have spent much of his time in charge of the Leicester lands in Normandy. By 1159 he had received from the king the marriage of Petronilla de *Grandmesnil (d. 1212), daughter and heir of Guillaume, lord of Grandmesnil, which increased his commitment to the duchy. He issued ten charters during the late 1150s and 1160s, which reveal that he had the resources to form his own large lay and clerical household. The seal he used before his father's death demonstrates that he had taken the surname de Breteuil. This has some significance in that it reveals him stressing his descent from William fitz Osbern, no doubt to assist his dealings with his Norman tenants: the other name by which he is known, Robert ès Blanchmains ('the Whitehanded'), is not attested before the fourteenth century. In March 1163 he witnessed the treaty of Dover for Henry II and in 1164 he was in Normandy, making a grant for an infant son, buried at the priory of Le Désert. He succeeded his father as earl of Leicester in April 1168, when he must already have been approaching middle age. He was the executor of his father's last testament, a duty he admitted later to have discharged negligently.

Robert seems to have made little impact on the court of Henry II, and his close identification with Normandy may have caused him to gravitate towards the clique of Norman magnates who favoured Henry the Young King, which had as its leader his first cousin, Robert (II), count of Meulan (d. c.1210). When the Young King and his brothers allied with Louis VII of France against their father in April 1173, the earl joined them. In Normandy his secession to France was so rapid as to leave his castles there unprepared to resist, and they quickly fell to Henry II. In July 1173 a royal army sought to take Leicester, but was only able to take the town not the castle. In September 1173 the earl was present at the conference at Gisors between Henry II and his sons. He is recorded as losing his temper and at the end of the conference making as if to draw his sword and strike the old king, until restrained by those standing around him. Immediately after this conference Robert, at the instigation of Louis VII, travelled to Flanders, recruited a large force of Flemish and Hollander mercenaries, and sailed to England.

Robert landed on the coast of Suffolk at Orwell on 26 September and joined forces with Hugh (I) Bigod at Framlingham Castle. After a few days spent extorting money from the surrounding area, the earl made an attempt on the borough of Dunwich, but was driven back. An attempt by Bigod against Ipswich was apparently more successful.

At length, needing to link up with the midland insurgents, Robert headed west and besieged the castle at Haughley, between Framlingham and Bury St Edmunds, which surrendered after four days. By this time local royalists had had time to concentrate, and he found his way westward barred at Bury by a large force. Baffled, he returned to Framlingham, until the arrival of Richard de Lucy, the justiciar, and Humphrey (III) de Bohun at Bury compelled him to try to break out of East Anglia. On 16 October at Fornham, near Bury St Edmunds, the royal force of 300 knights along with local levies and the earls of Gloucester, Arundel, and Cornwall, and their military households offered battle. A first assault by local knights led by Walter fitz Robert was repulsed, but the earl's mercenaries proved unable to deal with the knights of the royal household under Humphrey de Bohun and broke, leaving the earl, his wife, and his cousin, Hugues de Châteauneuf, to be captured. The Flemings were routed across the countryside and slaughtered.

The earl and countess of Leicester were initially sent to Portchester Castle, from where they were sent to face Henry II in Normandy. The earl returned with the court to England late in June 1174, and in July he witnessed the surrender of the castles of Leicester, Mountsorrel, and Groby by his constables to the king. In August he was taken back to Normandy and imprisoned with the other leading rebels, first at Caen and then Falaise. In 1176, in the meantime, the earl's castles at Leicester and Groby were razed, while Mountsorrel in England and Pacy-sur-Eure in Normandy were retained by the king as his own. In January 1177 the earl's lands were returned to him, but the only castle left to him seems to have been Breteuil, his Norman centre. In March and September 1177 Robert appeared at court, but not thereafter. He went on pilgrimage to Jerusalem in 1179 and may not have returned until at least 1181, when his lands and heir were recorded as in the king's hands. War between Henry II and his sons broke out again in 1183, and the earl and countess were arrested and held separately in the castles of Salisbury and Bedford. The pair were released in the course of 1184, before September.

After 1183 Robert was particularly attached to Count Richard, with whom he took the cross in 1188, and when Richard succeeded to the throne in 1189 the earl had restored to him all that he had lost under Henry II. He carried a sword at the king's coronation and accompanied the king's progress around England and into Normandy in 1190. When the third crusade began, the earl travelled overland separately from the king, with whom his son and heir, Robert de *Breteuil (d. 1204), voyaged. Robert died at Durazzo, in 1190, probably at the end of August. He was buried in Leicester Abbey. He was survived by his wife until 1212. He had three sons, William de Breteuil (who predeceased him in 1189), Robert, who succeeded him as earl, and *Roger, who was elected bishop of St Andrews in 1189. He also had several daughters; *Amice [see under Breteuil, Robert de, fourth earl of Leicester] married first Simon de Montfort the younger, count of Évreux, and second William des Barres the elder; Margaret married Saer de Quincy (d. 1219); Hawise entered the priory of Nuneaton as a nun, and another daughter, Petronilla, is mentioned in the obituary of Lyre Abbey. The earl made no religious foundations of his own, but generously patronized those founded by his ancestors and those also within the areas where he was powerful. DAVID CROUCH

Sources R. Howlett, ed., *Chronicles of the reigns of Stephen, Henry II, and Richard I*, 4, Rolls Series, 82 (1889) · *Jordan Fantosme's chronicle*, ed. and trans. R. C. Johnston (1981) · W. Stubbs, ed., *Gesta regis Henrici secundi Benedicti abbatis: the chronicle of the reigns of Henry II and Richard I, AD 1169–1192*, 2 vols., Rolls Series, 49 (1867) · Cartulary of Le Désert, Archives Départementales de l'Eure, G164 · Cartulary of Lyre, Marquise de Mathan MSS · *Reg. RAN*, vol. 3 · Pipe rolls · GEC, *Peerage*

Breteuil, Robert de, fourth earl of Leicester (d. 1204), magnate, was the second son of Robert de *Breteuil, third earl of Leicester (c.1130–1190), and Petronilla de *Grandmesnil (d. 1212), daughter of Guillaume de Grandmesnil. *Roger, bishop of St Andrews, was his brother.

Early career and crusade Robert's parents married between 1154 and 1159 and he was born after an elder brother, William. The two boys were closely associated as they grew up with the aristocratic circle in opposition to Henry II of which their father was a leader. William and Robert de Breteuil are frequently to be found together in their father's charters before 1189 and are also to be found associated with the household of their cousin, Robert, count of Meulan. The elder brother, William, died (as a leper according to later legend) at some time in 1189, after the accession of King Richard (for he witnessed some of his father's numerous acts settling affairs before his departure for the Holy Land), and possibly on 23 November 1189, if he was the 'Willelmus de Bretoil', whose obit was celebrated at Lyre Abbey on that day. At this point Robert de Breteuil became heir. During the period before his departure in 1190 on the third crusade he was associated with John, count of Mortain (the future king), in acts transacted at Burford, Clipstone, and Canterbury, but crossed to Normandy and was with his father at the royal court at Verneuil on 2 January 1190.

Unlike his father, who took a separate route, the younger Robert de Breteuil seems to have travelled to the Holy Land with the king, and was with Richard at Messina when news reached the king of the death of Earl Robert (III) at Durazzo on 31 August or 1 September 1190. The king invested Robert (IV) with the earldom in Sicily on 2 February 1191. The new earl arrived with the king's fleet at Acre on 8 June 1191, and he was one of the leaders of the assault on the town on 11 July. He fought at the battle of Arsuf on 7 September. He was dispatched with the count of St Pol by the king on 6 November to assist an ambushed party of templars at Ibn-Ibrak, himself rescuing several knights by the force of his onset and winning considerable celebrity through his energy and skill in arms. In December, when attempting to rescue three knights of his household from a large party of Turks outside the camp at Ramlah, he was himself surrounded with his knights, including his chief tenant, Arnold du Bois of Thorpe Arnold. He was rescued in turn by his Norman cousin, Robert de Neubourg, and

then brought to safety by a party of the royal household, in the meantime having been nearly drowned in a river and having had two horses killed under him, but none the less bringing out his company intact. He attested a charter of the king at Jaffa on 10 January 1192. His was the second banner displayed above the walls of Deir al-Bela when it was stormed on 22 May 1192. On 17 June 1192 he commanded a party which fought off a Saracen attack against a Christian caravan near Ramlah, racing ahead and hurling the first Turk he encountered to the ground in the sight of the army. His force drove the Turks into an abrupt rout. On 24 June he fought alongside the king in the capture of a Saracen supply column at al-Khuweilfe. He was with the king in a fleet which relieved Jaffa on 29 July, and on 5 August was one of those ten knights who thwarted an attempt to kidnap the king in his tent at Jaffa, and was saved by the king when he was thrown from his horse. Thereafter his movements cannot be traced, but he is likely to have sailed for home in September or October 1192 after a distinguished crusade which seems to have earned him a European reputation and King Richard's long-lasting goodwill.

Royal service in England and France Earl Robert next appears in March 1193 as lately returned from crusade and taking responsibility for the defence of Normandy against the king of France, Philip Augustus (d. 1223). In 1194, on 15 June, he and his household were captured in a skirmish with Philip's forces near Gournay while on an incautious mission out of Rouen to harry the king's withdrawal from Normandy. He was imprisoned at Étampes for over a year, and only secured his release after delivering to Philip his castle and lordship of Pacy-sur-Eure on the Norman frontier. He gained his freedom in or soon after February 1196. In the summers of 1197 and 1198 he is to be found campaigning with King Richard, and he was with the king in March 1199 just before the fatal assault on Châluz. He was a firm supporter of John's succession to the throne—the two men had been associated while John was count of Mortain. He acted as steward in John's coronation on 27 May 1199, claiming and exercising the office conceded to his grandfather by Henry II in 1153. In the period of the first few years of John's reign his influence at court was regarded as paramount, as the life of St Hugh, bishop of Lincoln, the earl's enemy, records. He fought in Normandy for John as hard as he had fought for Richard, naturally perhaps, as he was one of the greatest magnates in the duchy and had much to lose. Because of this, it appears that John was willing to reward him handsomely for his continuing good service. In September 1203 he was granted all Richmondshire in north-west Yorkshire: a major addition to his English estates. The fall of Normandy hit him harder than any other Anglo-Norman magnate. In April 1204 he was sent with William Marshal, earl of Pembroke (d. 1219), to negotiate with King Philip. While in France he and Earl William also took advantage of the opportunity to open up the possibility that they might retain their Norman honours, despite the Capetian conquest. For a large fine the two earls were given a year to think the matter over. Earl William fell into royal disfavour when news of this reached King John, but there is no indication that Earl Robert did; indeed he was granted in September 1204 the substantial English lands of the Norman branch of the Harcourt family, and lands of other Normans, presumably as some compensation for his Norman losses.

Death, patronage, and reputation Earl Robert never had to make the decision about doing homage to King Philip, for he died on 20 or 21 October 1204, when probably only in his forties. The report in the life of St Hugh of Lincoln that he died a leper is most likely to be a calumny. He left no children with his wife, Loretta de *Briouze, daughter of William (III) de *Briouze, who may well have been a child bride. He was buried in the choir of the Augustinian abbey of Leicester in November. His lands were divided between his two sisters. The elder, Amice [see below], carried to the Montfort family the town of Leicester and the comital title. The younger, Margaret, carried half the old earldom, focused on Brackley, Northamptonshire, to her husband, Saer de *Quincy (d. 1219), and it formed the endowment for his earldom of Winchester. Countess Loretta survived her husband by many decades, becoming a much respected recluse at Hackington, near Canterbury, about February 1221, and dying after 1266.

Earl Robert was moderately generous to the houses within his advocacy in England and Normandy but founded no new ones, although he did constitute the two small Leicestershire priories of Ulverscroft and Charley as cells of his Norman abbey of St Evroult. He further endowed his family's foundations at Lyre and St Evroult in Normandy, and Leicester and Nuneaton in England. His most notable grant was a substantial deathbed endowment at Anstey, Leicestershire, to Leicester Abbey for his burial. He issued a number of privileges to the borough of Leicester. There is little evidence that Earl Robert much exerted himself to form any powerful political connection in England: he was in any case in the Holy Land and France for much of the time he held his earldom. He did, however, form a strong link with his Leicestershire magnate neighbours, the d'Aubigné family of Belvoir, and also maintained ascendancy over some leading Leicestershire knightly families, notably those of Du Bois, Astley, Martinwast, and Cranford. He was able to use his influence at court to local effect. In this way he was able to secure for good the former episcopal manor of Knighton, outside the walls of Leicester, from the bishop of Lincoln—allegedly by the favouritism of King John. There was something in his career which raised him, like William Marshal, above the run of magnates. He was a man of international reputation, whose military exploits were much talked of. He was clearly a formidable warrior and commander, and a natural confidant and companion of princes. That, and the wide spread of his possessions from the Tees to the Eure, meant that his natural sphere was in that shifting world of high politics which in his day spanned the entire Plantagenet empire. He was the last of the great cross-channel Norman magnates, and it is perhaps fitting that his death coincided with the final collapse of the Anglo-Norman realm.

Countess Amice and succession to the earldom of Leicester The title of Leicester was carried on through the Franco-Norman family of Montfort. Robert de Breteuil's elder sister, **Amice**, countess of Rochefort and *suo jure* countess of Leicester (d. 1215), ultimately carried the earldom's chief seat of Leicester and half its English lands to the family of her husband, Simon de Montfort, lord of Montfort-en-Yvelines (alias Montfort l'Aumary) and Rochefort in the marchlands between Normandy and Paris. The dates of Countess Amice's marriage to this Simon, son of Simon de Montfort, count of Évreux and lord of Montfort (d. 1181), are unknown, but it had certainly ended by 1188, when she was already married to her second husband, William des Barres the elder, whom Rigord calls in that year by right of his wife 'Guillelmus de Barris comes de Rupeforti'. Countess Amice had two sons by the Montfort marriage, another Simon, the future crusader against the Albigensians, and a younger son called Guy. She also had a daughter, Petronilla (d. 1216). Following her husband's death and with her children as minors, according to the French custom, Amice carried her husband's lands and title to her second husband, the French curial knight, William des Barres, sometimes called count of Rochefort. This seems to have been the self-chosen comital style adopted by the younger branch of the Montfort family, for before 1190 Amice's father refers to her as 'comitissa Roceforti'. This would be because the sons of Simon, count of Évreux, split his comital dignity: Amaury, the elder, had taken the title of Évreux, and Simon, the younger, had taken the title of Rochefort (from one of the family's principal possessions in Yvelines). Amice was also known as 'lady of Montfort' in a charter she issued late in 1189, making a grant for the soul of her late brother, William de Breteuil. Late in 1204 or early in 1205, she was prompt to sell her claim on the Leicester lordship of Breteuil in Normandy to King Philip Augustus in return for the castle of St Leger in the area of Yvelines. However, she was markedly keen to maintain her claims on her share of the Leicester inheritance in England. She used the title 'countess of Leicester' several times following her brother's death in 1204. The cathedral of Chartres had a grant from her as 'countess of Leicester and lady of Montfort' dated 1206, and Wareham Priory once possessed a deed issued by her as 'countess of Leicester' which dated to the period 1212–15. An entry on the close roll for 1206 also referred to her as 'the countess of Montfort'. Her eldest son, Simon de Montfort, came to England in 1205 or 1206 in pursuit of the Leicester inheritance, and in 1207 it was at last decided by inquisition what her half of the earldom was to be, although in fact the Montfort inheritance was given to a succession of keepers answering to the exchequer until 1231. All that Amice can be proved to have enjoyed in England after 1204 was her marriage portion from the lands of the earldom of Leicester at Shapwick and Winterborne, Dorset, where she made confirmations to the ancestral abbey of Lyre. It is probable that Countess Amice lived most, if not all, of her adult life in France. She died on 3 September 1215, and was buried at the abbey of Hautes-Bruyères in Yvelines. The lands of the earldom of Leicester were promptly granted by King John to the earl of Chester with whom they remained until 1231. None the less, Amice's son Simon de Montfort (d. 1218) and his elder son, Amaury de Montfort (d. 1241), maintained their claim to Leicester, both occasionally styling themselves 'count of Montfort and Leicester', until Henry III recognized the right of Amice's grandson, Amaury's younger brother Simon de *Montfort (d. 1265), in 1231. Amice had by her second marriage a further son, William des Barres, the younger, but confusion between the father and son makes it impossible to say whether Amice was outlived by her second husband.

DAVID CROUCH

Sources register of Leicester Abbey, Bodl. Oxf., MS Laud misc. 625 · BL, Add. MS 16975, fol. 7r · BL, Harley MS Ch. 83 A 26 · Coll. Leber, Bibliothèque Municipale, Rouen, cart. 4, no. 142 · W. Stubbs, ed., *Gesta regis Henrici secundi Benedicti abbatis: the chronicle of the reigns of Henry II and Richard I, AD 1169–1192*, 2 vols., Rolls Series, 49 (1867) · L. Landon, *The itinerary of King Richard I*, PRSoc., new ser., 13 (1935) · M. Bateson and others, eds., *Records of the borough of Leicester*, 7 vols. (1899–1974) · J. C. Atkinson and J. Brownbill, eds., *The coucher book of Furness Abbey*, 2 vols. in 6, Chetham Society, new ser., 9, 11, 14, 74, 76, 78 (1886–1919) · *Œuvres de Rigord et de Guillaume le Breton, historiens de Philippe-Auguste*, ed. H. F. Delaborde, 1 (Paris, 1882) · GEC, *Peerage* · BL, Cotton MS Otho B.xiv, fols. 35r, 62v · J. H. Round, ed., *Calendar of documents preserved in France, illustrative of the history of Great Britain and Ireland* (1899) · *Knighton's chronicle, 1337–1396*, ed. and trans. G. H. Martin, OMT (1995) [Lat. orig., *Chronica de eventibus Angliae a tempore regis Edgari usque mortem regis Ricardi Secundi*, with parallel Eng. text]

Breteuil, Roger de [Roger fitz William], **earl of Hereford** (*fl.* 1071–1087), magnate and rebel, was the second son of Earl *William fitz Osbern (d. 1071) and Adelize de Tosny. When William fitz Osbern died, William I gave Roger his father's English manors and made him earl of Hereford, a more circumscribed title than his father had enjoyed. Although all his father's English property fell to him, perhaps with additions, and although he was able to pursue his father's aggression in south Wales with some success, the new earl chafed at his limited opportunities and found the encroachment of royal sheriffs on his lands intolerable.

In 1075, at the wedding feast of his sister Emma, Earl Roger was drawn into a conspiracy against the king by his new brother-in-law, *Ralph de Gael. The youthful Roger prepared for rebellion in Herefordshire, but the king's men captured him before he could cross the Severn. Archbishop Lanfranc tried first to dissuade him from open defiance, then to intervene on his behalf, and finally begged him to show contrition; but all in vain, and at Christmas 1075 Earl Roger's lands were confiscated and he was sentenced to life imprisonment. On his deathbed in 1087 William I offered release to any of his prisoners who promised to keep the peace, but for whatever reason Roger remained incarcerated until his own death at an unknown date. His sons Reynold and Roger were in the service of Henry I but never recovered their lost inheritance.

C. P. LEWIS

Sources Ordericus Vitalis, *Eccl. hist.* · *The letters of Lanfranc, archbishop of Canterbury*, ed. and trans. H. Clover and M. Gibson, OMT (1979), nos. 31–3 · A. Farley, ed., *Domesday Book*, 2 vols. (1783) · GEC, *Peerage*, new edn, 6.449–50

Bretherton, James (*c.*1730–1806), engraver and printseller, may have been born about 1730 and must have married his wife, Sarah (*fl.* 1762–1773), by about 1755, since his son Charles (d. 1783) was signing prints in 1770. Nothing is known of his early life. He was settled in Cambridge by 1762, when the first of three more children, Elizabeth, Mary, and Bartholomew, was born, and by 1765 he was established as a drawing-master in Green Street. From this address he published landscapes of his own composition and prints calculated to demonstrate his ability to imitate the style of various masters: etchings and drypoints after Dürer, Giovanni Battista Piazzetta, and Carlo Maratta (1768), Rembrandt (1769 and 1770), and Godfried Schalken (1769). He also published similar prints by his precocious son Charles, the 'young man' recommended by Thomas Gray to Horace Walpole as an engraver for volume four of *Anecdotes of Painting*. Bretherton was a talented copyist, and his fifteen imitations of Rembrandt, notably *The Three Trees* (1770) and *Landscape with a Cottage and Haybarn* (1769?), are still considered 'extremely deceptive' (D'Oench, 84).

Most drawing-masters of the period taught caricature, and so it was probably as a result of having instructed them that Bretherton became the principal engraver or publisher of the amateur caricaturists Thomas Orde, William Henry Bunbury, Edward Topham (all students at the university), and Michael Tyson, fellow of Corpus Christi College. This Cambridge connection also yielded commissions for portraits of academics, reproductions of paintings, and antiquarian subjects such as the window of King's College chapel (1776), as well as introductions to the portrait collectors Horace Walpole and Joseph Gulston.

On 13 April 1771 Bretherton announced that he would very shortly leave Cambridge for the capital. He exhibited his etchings of Samuel Cooper's miniatures of Oliver Cromwell and Prince Rupert with the Society of Artists in 1771 and an etching after Bunbury in 1772. In his new shop—at no. 134 in the fashionable New Bond Street—Bretherton set up as a printseller, and in 1775 he issued a printed catalogue of his stock. This was overwhelmingly dominated, numerically speaking, by portraits, although Bretherton also sold 'historical prints', 'original etchings', mezzotints, and his own prints. He launched his business in 1772 by publishing twenty-five of his own etchings with drypoint after Bunbury; he eventually issued eighty-five plates after this highly fashionable artist. Bunbury must have been Bretherton's most valuable property, but he also had a stake in the work of Sir Joshua Reynolds (having acquired many of James Watson's plates) and he published portraits by other contemporary artists, such as Gainsborough's *Viscount Howe* (1778). He and his son also engraved (and in some cases published) caricatures by James Sayers, while some anonymous designs may have been entirely their own work.

Bretherton had retired from a long, stable, and apparently successful career in business by 31 January 1799, when a sale of his 'extensive and valuable stock of Antient and Modern Prints' was held by James Christie. His death 'at an advanced age' at his house in Michael's Grove, Brompton, was announced in May 1806 in the *Gentleman's Magazine*. Among many other places, his prints are in the British Museum, London; the Fitzwilliam Museum, Cambridge; the Lewis Walpole Library, Connecticut; and Gainsborough's house at Sudbury, Suffolk.

TIMOTHY CLAYTON

Sources T. Clayton and J. Riely, catalogue raisonné of prints after Henry Bunbury, priv. coll. • Walpole, *Corr.*, 1.313, 360, 386n.; 5.75n.; 14.188–9; 33.401n.; 35.628–30; 43.92, 331 • J. Venn, ed., *The register of St Michael's parish, Cambridge* (1891) • *GM*, 1st ser., 76 (1806), 484 • *Cambridge Chronicle and Journal* (3 May 1767) • *Cambridge Chronicle and Journal* (25 June 1768) • *Cambridge Chronicle and Journal* (3 June 1769) • *Cambridge Chronicle and Journal* (1 July 1769) • *Cambridge Chronicle and Journal* (1 Dec 1770) • *Cambridge Chronicle and Journal* (26 Jan 1771) • *Cambridge Chronicle and Journal* (13 April 1771) • private information (2004) [David McKitterick] • J. Bretherton, *Catalogue of prints for 1775* (1775) • *A catalogue of the extensive and valuable stock of antient and modern prints … of Mr James Bretherton, drawing master and printseller of no. 134 New Bond Street, retiring from business, 31 January 1799 and following days* (1799) [Christies catalogue] • E. D'Oench, '"A madness to have his prints": Rembrandt and Georgian taste, 1720–1800', in C. White, D. Alexander, and E. D'Oench, *Rembrandt in eighteenth century England* (1983), 73–81, 84 [exhibition catalogue, Yale U. CBA] • T. Clayton, *The English print, 1688–1802* (1997), 214–15 • G. Goodwin, *British mezzotinters: Thomas Watson, James Watson, Elizabeth Judkinns* (1904)

Bretherton, Russell Frederick (1906–1991), civil servant and entomologist, was born on 3 February 1906 at Belgrave House, Belgrave Road, Gloucester, the only son of the marriage of Frederick Hawkins Bretherton (1852–1945), solicitor, and Gertrude, *née* Wing (1864–1952). He had three half-sisters and four half-brothers from his father's earlier marriage. He was a history scholar at Clifton College from 1917 to 1923 before entering Wadham College, Oxford, where he took firsts in modern history (1926) and philosophy, politics, and economics (1928) and won the Webb Medley scholarship for up-and-coming economists. Elected a fellow of Wadham in 1928, he tutored in economics and modern history until 1939; he was a university research lecturer from 1936 to 1939. From this period came his *Public Investment and the Trade Cycle*, written with F. A. Burchardt and S. G. Rutherford, published in 1941 and correspondingly overshadowed by war. Meanwhile on 31 December 1930 he had married Jocelyn Nina Mathews (1904–1990), daughter of Henry Montague Segundo Mathews, colonial official in Burma. They had met at Oxford, where she had been a history student at Somerville College. Together they had three sons and one daughter.

In 1939 Bretherton was drafted into the Ministry of Supply as a temporary civil servant. By 1946 he was an under-secretary in charge of the raw materials department in the Board of Trade, which brought him into contact with a former pupil, Harold Wilson, president of the Board of Trade from 1947 to 1951. With growing family commitments he decided to forsake academe and become an established civil servant, a transition far from automatic. Seconded to the economic section of the cabinet office in 1949, he was at the centre of the sterling crisis that provoked the devaluation of the pound. From 1951 to 1954 he was at the Ministry of Materials, coping with dislocations of supply arising from the Korean War and its aftermath. He was back at the Board of Trade, as under-secretary, from 1954 to 1961. He was made a CB in 1951.

Thus far Bretherton's was the worthy but unremarkable career of a distinguished public servant. However, he was marked out by history for his conspicuous role in Britain's troubled economic relations with Europe. He had experience of European diplomacy and negotiation from his work with the Organization for European Economic Co-operation (from 1947) and the North Atlantic Treaty Organization (from 1949). Throughout it was United Kingdom policy to ensure that national sovereignty was upheld. The six countries that in 1951 instituted the European Coal and Steel Community chose a different path. In 1955 they met at Messina to consider the creation of a common market. Having appointed a committee under Paul-Henri Spaak to flesh out their plan the six invited Britain to participate. Bretherton was the British choice, as a 'representative', not a delegate. The other six countries were represented by ministers rather than officials, and Bretherton later recalled his surprise at being addressed as 'Your excellency'. He soon found himself in an invidious position. 'If we take an active part in trying to guide the final propositions', he reported, 'it will be difficult to avoid later on the presumption that we are, in some sense, committed to the result' (Young, 89). In August the mutual aid committee instructed him 'not to imply, in saying that certain features of the proposals would make it very difficult for the UK to join, that we would join if our points were met' (ibid., 90).

Of what happened next records and recollections are confused. Bretherton's withdrawal from the Spaak committee in November 1955 later saw him demonized as the brains behind another of Britain's aversions to joining in European construction. In truth, as a professional he complied with the instructions that his political master, Peter Thorneycroft, gave him and that flowed from the collective decisions of the government: to co-operate, to be helpful, but to enter into no commitment. When this isolated him in the committee, and when Spaak ruled that only those who were committed to an economic community could continue as committee members, Bretherton's attendance served no further purpose. According to Jean-François Deniau, a member of the French delegation, writing twenty years after the event, Bretherton walked out of the Spaak committee after delivering scathing comments on the unreality of the treaty which was being discussed and its unacceptability to Britain. This version of events is at odds with Bretherton's own recollection. In his words 'We were thrown out' (Charlton, 191). Thorneycroft bestowed on him the highest praise: 'He was a keen European and one of the most brilliant officials I've ever had the pleasure of working with' (ibid., 182). After the event Bretherton reflected that opposing the customs union of the six amounted to a missed opportunity. 'If we had been able to say that we agreed in principle, we could have got whatever kind of Common Market we wanted. I have no doubt of that at all' (ibid., 184).

When Britain reacted to the creation of the EEC by instigating the European Free Trade Association, Bretherton was again in the thick of it. He regarded the EFTA as a second best and would have endorsed his permanent secretary's later dismissal of the organization as one born of 'common funk'. He remained at the Board of Trade until 1961, the year of Britain's first, unsuccessful application to join the European Communities. He moved to the Treasury in that year, again as under-secretary, and finally retired in 1968.

There was another noteworthy Bretherton: the walker, hill climber, and lepidopterist. He possessed one of the finest collections of butterflies in the country, and named for his wife a hitherto undetected daylight flying moth, *Zygaena lonicerae jocelynni*. His 'List of the microlepidoptera and pyralidina of north west Surrey' was meticulous. He contributed copiously to the *Journal of the Royal Entomological Society*—an article was on his typewriter at the time of his death.

Bretherton died of a heart attack on 11 January 1991 at the Royal Surrey County Hospital, Guildford. He was cremated, and his ashes were placed in the churchyard at Bramley, Surrey, where he had lived since 1963. He was not a believer, but the local church had been part of his social life. He was survived by his four children, his wife, Jocelyn, having died in 1990. His study of British economic policy, *The Control of Demand, 1958–1964*, was published posthumously by the Institute of Contemporary British History in 1999.   WILLIAM NICOLL

Sources M. Charlton, *The price of victory* (1983) · H. Young, *This blessed plot* (1998) · P.-H. Spaak, *Combats inachevés* (1969) · J.-F. Deniau, *L'Europe interdite* (1977) · R. Denman, *Missed chances* (1996) · R. Mayne and J. Pinder, *Federal union* (1990) · M. Camps, *Britain and the European Community, 1955–1963* (1964) · R. Holland, *The pursuit of greatness* (1991) · *WWW*, 1991–5 · personal knowledge (2004) · private information (2004) [James Bretherton, son] · b. cert. · m. cert. · d. cert.

Archives SOUND BBC Radio 3, 'The price of victory', 9 programmes x 60 mins., 1982

Wealth at death £532,944: probate, 9 April 1991, *CGPLA Eng. & Wales*

Bretland, Joseph (1742–1819), Presbyterian minister and schoolmaster, was born on 22 May 1742 at Exeter, the youngest son of Joseph Bretland (*bap.* 1706, *d.* 1791), a tradesman in that city and a dissenter, and his wife, whose maiden name was Mills and forename probably Mary (1701/2–1784). Educated at Exeter grammar school, he was first employed in a counting-house in 1757, but left shortly after to prepare to train for the ministry with William West and John Turner. He entered Exeter Theological Academy in 1761, under Micaijah Towgood, Samuel Merivale, and John Hogg, and left in 1766, having proved an outstanding student. He spent his whole life in Exeter in the service of dissent, in particular of Unitarianism, and education. From 1770 to 1772 he was minister at the Mint Meeting-House, and on leaving opened a school to teach

the classics, which he successfully maintained until 1790. Previously he assisted in the school run by Revd Joseph Twining.

Bretland's tenure at the Mint was short because he was a theological pioneer.

> It is pretty well known that nearly half a century ago, he declared, from the pulpit of the Mint meeting house, his belief in the Unity, and the simple humanity of our Lord Jesus Christ, and he stood alone as the preacher of this doctrine in the West of England—these religious principles he maintained to the last.   (Kennaway, 1.x)

However changing times and beliefs meant that in 1789 he returned to the ministry at the Mint, resigning in 1793 over a nice point of principle respecting the liturgy used by the congregation which he had prepared himself. In 1794 he was invited to become minister at George's Presbyterian Meeting in Exeter, with the assertive Unitarian Timothy Kenrick as joint pastor. This ministry included the Bow Meeting, which refused to accept the Unitarianism of Bretland; the congregation was at a very low ebb and the chapel closed the same year. Bretland resigned from George's Meeting in June 1797 following a dispute over the number of ministers being employed, some members wanting to take up his earlier offer to retire if the financial position required it.

Bretland now gave up the ministry, but continued to be widely recognized as a leading scholar among the radical dissenters. Joseph Priestley, for example, asked him to revise his *Rudiments of English Grammar*, 'being confident that you who have been several years in the practice of teaching it, must be much better qualified to improve it than I should now be' (J. Priestley to J. Bretland, *Works of Joseph Priestley*, 23.13).

Bretland had for some time sought with Towgood, Hogg, and Kenrick to reopen the Exeter Theological Academy. In 1785 a proposal to achieve this came to nothing, but, with the expiry of the academy at Hackney, the scheme was revived in 1799 and the third Exeter Academy was formed. Students were for both the ministry and commercial life, with Bretland teaching his speciality, mathematics, as well as geography, globes, general grammar, oratory, and history. Bretland's presence as tutor was an attraction underlined by the invitation to him in 1798 to become theological professor at Manchester New College, which he declined. The academy was open to students of any denomination, no assent to articles of faith was required, and any place of worship could be attended.

After the closure of the academy in March 1805, following Kenrick's death, Bretland retired into private life. His wife, Sarah Moffatt (*d.* 1804), whom he had married at All Hallows on the Walls, Exeter, on 17 August 1795, had died the previous year. He died at his home in Exeter on 8 July 1819 and was buried on 15 July 1819, his funeral conducted by Revd James Manning. 'In morals, in theology, in metaphysics, and in biblical criticism, his learning was profound, his judgment solid and acute, and his integrity inflexible and unimpeached' (Jervis, 445).

ALAN RUSTON

Sources W. B. Kennaway, *Memoir, with sermons, of Bretland*, 2 vols. (1820) · A. Brockett, *Nonconformity in Exeter, 1650–1875* (1962), 140–59 · [J. Jervis], *Monthly Repository*, 14 (1819), 445 · J. Murch, *A history of the Presbyterian and General Baptist churches in the west of England* (1835), 402–3, 445–8 · *Monthly Repository*, 14 (1819), 473–5, 494, 559–60 · *The theological and miscellaneous works of Joseph Priestley*, ed. J. T. Rutt, 23 (1824), 13 · J. W. Ashley Smith, *The birth of modern education: the contribution of the dissenting academies, 1660–1800* (1954), 179 · *IGI* · 'The Kenrick letters', *Transactions of the Unitarian Historical Society*, 3/4 (1923–6), 388–9 · H. McLachlan, *The Unitarian movement in the religious life of England: its contribution to thought and learning, 1700–1900* (1934), 92–4 · *DNB* · will, PRO, PROB 11/1618/308
Archives Harris Man. Oxf., commentary, notes, and paraphrases on Greek New Testament; papers
Likenesses Thomson, stipple, pubd 1820, NPG; repro. in Kennaway, *Memoir … of Bretland*, vol. 1, frontispiece
Wealth at death over £2000: will, 1819, PRO, PROB 11/1618/308

Bretnor, Thomas (1570/71–1618), astrologer and medical practitioner, was born in Bakewell, Derbyshire, and went to London about 1604, settling in the parish of St Sepulchre. Though he appears not to have attended university, he was fluent in Latin, French, and Spanish, and became a well-known figure in Jacobean London. Bretnor published a series of almanacs for the years 1607 to 1619, in which he advertised as a teacher of arithmetic, geometry, and astronomy, and practitioner of physick. He vigorously defended the truth of astrology against critics such as John Chamber (1546–1604), citing scripture and continental as well as English authorities. Against those who claimed that astrology undermined free will and God's sovereignty, he insisted that no study did more to inspire religious devotion and awe at the majesty of the creation, and that the stars functioned by God's permission, like other secondary causes.

Bretnor's almanacs gave detailed weather forecasts and farming, dietary, and medical advice, and listed 'good' (lucky) and 'evil' days for the year ahead. These features and the semi-proverbial aphorisms scattered throughout the text help to explain his popularity and fame. He is mentioned by name by Ben Jonson and Thomas Middleton. Middleton claimed, in a masque, that the country

> farmer will not cast his seed i' the ground
> Before he looks in Bretnor; there he finds
> Some word which he hugs happily, as *Ply the Box*,
> *Make hay betimes.*
> (Middleton, 7.211)

Jonson's allusion, in *The Divell is an Asse* (I. ii) suggests that Bretnor had succeeded Edward Gresham as the leading compiler of the period.

In 1612 a rival compiler, John Keene, denounced Bretnor as vain and ignorant, claiming that his clients came 'for the most part out of the lewdest places' (Keene), but this attack was wide of the mark. Bretnor was no charlatan. His mathematical skills included land and quantity surveying, map-making, and navigation. He was a friend of many of the leading mathematicians of the day, including Edmund Gunter, professor of astronomy at Gresham College, Aaron Rathborne, the surveyor, Arthur Hopton, and Elias Allen, William Pratt, John Thompson, and Thomas Clay of Reigate, all makers of mathematical instruments. In his almanacs Bretnor publicized their inventions, and

drew attention to new mathematical books such as a translation of Napier's work on logarithms, Rathborne's *The Surveyor*, and Mark Ridley's *Magneticall Animadversions*. Bretnor was also innovative on matters astronomical, as an early, consistent, and pugnacious champion of Copernican theories. In his medical practice he favoured chemical medicines, and admired Paracelsus. In 1618 he published *Opiologa*, a treatise on the medicinal use of opium and the preparation of laudanum. The work had been compiled by the Italian émigré physician Angelo Sala, and published in French at The Hague in 1614, with a dedication to the estates-general. Bretnor translated and expanded the text, and added a preface. He described himself as 'M. M.' ('Master of medicine') and dedicated the piece to his friends the physicians D[r Thomas] Bonham and Nicholas Carter.

Very little is known of Bretnor's personal life. His expertise in modern languages and medicine raises the possibility that he may have studied medicine on the continent at one stage in his career. In the almanacs for 1612–14 he gave his address as near the Holborn Conduit, and in 1615 as Cow Lane, near Smithfield. By 1617 he had moved to Cranbrook, Kent. In the preface to the edition for 1618 he stated that he had intended to stop compiling almanacs because of ill health, but felt compelled to refute recent attacks on astrology and the folly of the new 'Christian Almanacs' (by Richard Allestree and Gervase Dauncy), which he dismissed as ignorant and worthless.

Bretnor died in 1618, in the parish of St Sepulchre, London; letters of administration were granted on 17 November. An almanac for 1619, published under his name, was probably completed by another hand. Bretnor's publications have a moralistic and evangelical flavour but say little on contemporary political affairs. His main interests lay in the latest scientific trends, and despite his popular appeal it is clear that he moved in the most respected mathematical circles of his day. 'Ezekiel Bretnor', who issued almanacs for 1629–30 calculated for Colchester, was probably a pseudonym used by a compiler hoping to capitalize on a name still famous.   BERNARD CAPP

Sources B. S. Capp, *Astrology and the popular press: English almanacs, 1500–1800* (1979) · E. G. R. Taylor, *The mathematical practitioners of Tudor and Stuart England* (1954) · F. R. Johnson, *Astronomical thought in Renaissance England* (1937), 250–53 · J. Keene, *An new almanacke and prognostication for the yeare … 1612* [1612], sig. B2–2v · T. Middleton, 'The Inner Temple masque', *The works of Thomas Middleton*, ed. A. H. Bullen, 7 (1886), 211 · B. Jonson, *The divell is an asse* (1641) · T. Bretnor, deposition, 1611, GL, MS 9065 A/4, fols. 55v–56

Breton, Adela Catherine (1849–1923), archaeologist, was born on 31 December 1849 in England, the daughter of William Breton (1799–1887), naval officer, and Elizabeth d'Arch (1820–1874), who married in 1844 and had in addition to Adela a younger son, Harry. When she was very young the family settled at 15 Camden Crescent, Bath. Her family life was happy and her first journeys were made with them to the continent. Nothing is known of her education, but her work suggests she must have had some artistic training. By 1887 her parents were dead and her brother married, and soon after this her serious travelling

Adela Catherine Breton (1849–1923), by unknown photographer [with her manservant Pablo Solorio]

began. Her first trip to Mexico was in 1894, after which she is reputed to have asked the noted archaeologist of the Maya region, Alfred Percival Maudslay, if there were some work she could do there. His suggestion that she copy paintings and bas-reliefs which were showing serious wear marked a turning point in her life. In 1900 she went to Chichén Itzá on the then very remote Yucatán peninsula, and from then until her death she travelled widely in Central and South America, Egypt, Australia, Japan, and Fiji. Her primary field of interest was Mexico and she made thirteen trips there between 1900 and 1908, travelling with her loyal Indian guide, Pablo Solorio, making detailed scale drawings and water-colours of archaeological sites. She was critical of photography which she felt distorted the scale of monuments and could give no information about colour. An accomplished linguist, she also copied important manuscripts, maps, and codices.

Arthritis began to affect her archaeological work, but it stimulated rather than halted her travels, as she sought as much as possible to avoid damp British winters. Like other women travellers, her journeys marked escape from ill health as well as from the social constraints of home, and she exclaimed during a period of illness, 'If I could have Pablo & the horses, an outdoor life & tortillas I should soon be better' (Giles and Stewart, 43). She maintained her home in Bath, but lived in England only when obliged to for family reasons, such as the death of her brother's wife and then of his only daughter. She began to publish her work and corresponded with leading Americanists throughout the world, and joined the work of learned societies, contributing to congresses and publications. She was not always easy to work with: Edward Thompson,

United States consul and archaeologist, described her as 'a ladylike person, but full of whims, complaints and prejudices' (Giles and Stewart, 19). All, however, were agreed that her drawings were not the sketches of a dilettante traveller, but the meticulous records of a dedicated scholar. She died at the Hotel Pomeroy, Bridgetown, Barbados, on 13 June 1923 on her way home from a conference in Rio de Janiero. She left her houseful of artefacts, notes, and paintings to the Bristol Museum.

In her lifetime Adela Breton was a respected member of the small, international group of scholars who laid the foundations of Maya archaeology. By the 1960s, however, she was almost forgotten, as archaeology turned to new scientific methods and techniques. As interest rekindled in fine art and monumental architecture at the end of the twentieth century, the value of her work was again realized, not least because some of what she so painstakingly recorded had since disappeared or been damaged beyond repair. ELIZABETH BAIGENT

Sources S. Giles and J. Stewart, *The art of ruins* (1989) · E. N. Fallaize, *Man*, 23 (1923), 125 · *CGPLA Eng. & Wales* (1923)
Archives Bristol City Museum and Art Gallery | Harvard U., Peabody Museum of Archaeology and Ethnology, Bowditch, Tozzer MSS · Harvard U.
Likenesses double portrait, photograph, University of Bristol, department of archaeology [*see illus.*] · photograph, repro. in Giles and Stewart, *Art of ruins*, frontispiece
Wealth at death £27,368 9s. 8d.: administration with will, 23 Nov 1923, *CGPLA Eng. & Wales*

Breton [Briton], **Guillaume le** (*fl.* 1249), Franciscan friar and theologian, was believed by Leland to be English on the strength of his name, while Bale declared that he was a Welshman who died at Grimsby in 1356. The latter was followed by Pits, while Tanner quotes Leland verbatim, but makes a contribution of his own by confusing the friar with the early thirteenth-century author of the *Philippidos*, an account of the exploits of King Philip Augustus. There seems to be no reason to doubt that Guillaume was a Frenchman from Brittany, and he is firmly placed in the middle of the thirteenth century by his fellow Franciscan, the Italian chronicler Salimbene de Adam, who records meeting Guillaume at Vienne and Lyons in 1249, and remarks on his small stature and short temper, though he also praises Guillaume's learning. It is also possible that Guillaume was identical with the Magister Guillelmus Brito recorded as rector of the University of Paris in 1304, though the likely commonness of the name precludes certainty.

Guillaume le Breton wrote a number of theological works, of which the most important was his *Expositiones vocabulorum Biblie*, usually known simply as *Summa Britonis*. A dictionary of difficult words from the text of the Vulgate, containing some 2500 entries, the *Summa* is largely a compilation from classical, patristic, and medieval Latin writers, who are often cited verbatim. Roger Bacon knew it by 1272, though he did not think much of it, criticizing it as full of mistakes. Nevertheless, the *Summa* circulated widely. In 1284 John Pecham ordered that it should be among the reference books that Merton College, Oxford, was to keep available for consultation, chained to a table, and the English Dominican Robert Holcot used it in his lectures on the Wisdom of Solomon, of *c*.1335. About 130 manuscripts survive. It was printed under the name of Henricus de Hassia, in or about 1475, but received a modern edition only in 1975. Guillaume also wrote an *Expositio in prologos Biblie*, a commentary on St Jerome's prologues to the various books of the Bible, which was several times printed in early editions of the *Postillae* of Nicholas de Lyre, and a treatise in verse on Greek and Hebrew words; a collection of his sermons, recorded in 1304, has not survived.   HENRY SUMMERSON

Sources *Summa Britonis: sive Guillelmi Britonis Expositiones vocabulorum Biblie*, ed. L. W. Daly and B. H. Daly, 2 vols. (1975) • F. Stegmüller, ed., *Repertorium biblicum medii aevi*, 2 (Madrid, 1950), 401–10 • [*Cronica fratris Salimbene de Adam ordinis Minorum*], ed. O. Holder-Egger, MGH Scriptores [folio], 32 (Hanover, 1905–13), 233 • *Commentarii de scriptoribus Britannicis, auctore Joanne Lelando*, ed. A. Hall, 2 (1709), 356–7 • J. Pits, *Relationum historicarum de rebus Anglicis*, ed. [W. Bishop] (Paris, 1619), 481 • Tanner, *Bibl. Brit.-Hib.*, 128 • B. Smalley, *English friars and antiquity in the early fourteenth century* (1960), 152

Breton [Bretun], **John le** [John Brito] (*d.* 1275), justice and bishop of Hereford, was chosen bishop from among the canons of Hereford in January 1269 and was consecrated on 2 June of that year. On his death in 1275 certain chronicles describe him as an 'expert in English laws, who had written a book about them called *le Bretoun*'. The bishop could not in fact have written *Britton* in the version in which it has survived, because this third full-scale treatise on English law to survive (along with *Bracton* and *Fleta*) from the thirteenth century refers to statutes made up to fifteen years after his death, and the question is why he should have been credited with its authorship. John Selden argued in the seventeenth century that the bishop had been confused with the contemporary judge Henry of Bracton, the supposed author of the great treatise *De legibus et consuetudinibus Angliae*, of which the untitled *Britton* might be regarded as a condensation. Selden observed that the words attributing the book to John le Breton do not appear in most of the annals recording the bishop's death, and believed that they were a much later interpolation 'by some smatterer' in those few manuscripts of the *Flores historiarum* in which they do appear.

But the attribution is also made in the *Annals of Six Reigns*, written *c*.1320 by Nicholas Trevet, who was about seventeen when Breton died, and whose father was a justice on eyre between 1268 and 1272. Moreover, *Britton* is quite unlike *Bracton* in important respects. It is the first legal treatise in the French of the knightly families who ruled the shires rather than the Latin of the clerks of the king's household, and it is a practical work, omitting *Bracton*'s Romanist jurisprudence. *Britton* passes over the first hundred or so folios of *Bracton* on the nature and theoretical divisions of law, and begins with a description of the various sorts of justices, of the duties of coroners, and of the way eyres are held—material which is presented in a form that suggests the particular concerns of an official administering the king's justice in the shires. This is a strong pointer to the bishop, for he can be identified with the 'John le Breton, clerk' who was sheriff of Hereford from

May 1254 to April 1257, and also with the John le Breton who appears in June 1257 as the Lord Edward's constable of Abergavenny and bailiff of that honour.

In October 1259 this John le Breton was granted protection as he went beyond seas on business for the king and his son Edward. By the spring or early summer of 1260 he was keeper of the Lord Edward's wardrobe, and after the prince's quarrel with Roger Leyburn he succeeded to the latter's office of steward, in which capacity he was appointed in November 1261 to reinforce and victual Edward's castles throughout England and Wales. In Trinity term he is recorded as owing £120, partly from his time at Edward's wardrobe. Against this debt the memoranda roll notes that 'the bishop of Hereford should be written to', which suggests that John was already one of the canons introduced by the notorious Bishop Peter d'Aigueblanche, a past keeper of the king's wardrobe. For the next three years of baronial conflict, during which the Savoyard bishop and his canons were a target of the adherents of Simon de Montfort, John le Breton disappears from sight. Then in September 1265, a few weeks after the battle of Evesham, he received a royal protection, and in the following July he was granted £40 a year at the exchequer on his appointment as a justice of the king's bench. As a justice he could have drawn on his previous experience as both sheriff of Hereford and the Lord Edward's steward, which had included commissions to hear disputes between marcher barons and to hold inquiries as far afield as Oxfordshire and Berkshire. Between January and September 1268, John le Breton was also a justice on eyre in Yorkshire, but he was not at the next session in that circuit at Nottingham in November, and his election as bishop in January 1269 brought his career as a justice to an end.

John le Breton must have been one of the most senior of the former servants of Edward who received protections in July 1273 as they went beyond seas to meet the new king, Edward I, returning from crusade. But he is not listed among the bishops at Edward's coronation in September 1274, and he was dead by 12 May 1275, when a keeper of the bishopric of Hereford was ordered to seize and value the goods of the late Bishop John, 'who was bound to the king in divers debts at the day of his death'. The memoranda roll for 1275 shows that the debts went back twenty years to his service as constable of Abergavenny. Thomas Wykes gives the death of John 'dictus Brito', bishop of Hereford, prominence immediately after an account of Edward's 'famous and solemn' first parliament at Westminster in which the king is described as setting out to restore the laws of the country to their proper state, 'by the counsel of his loyal vassals and experts in the law'. The Statute of Westminster I was indeed the effective beginning of a great stream of parliamentary legislation, which was much concerned with local administration. It may be that this juxtaposition of events is the trivial source of the association of John, bishop of Hereford, with Edward's law-making, and hence with *Britton*, which is presented as a royal enactment of the laws of the land, revised as the king decided with the assent of his council. But John's unusual combination of experience as sheriff, constable, justice, and bishop makes it plausible that he was involved in the devising of a project of legislative reform which he did not live to carry forward.

ALAN HARDING

Sources Chancery records · Ann. mon., 4.219, 263 · H. R. Luard, ed., Flores historiarum, 3 vols., Rolls Series, 95 (1890), vol. 2, p. 480; vol. 3, p. 46 · N. Trevet, Annales sex regum Angliae, 1135–1307, ed. T. Hog, EHS, 6 (1845), 247 · F. M. Nichols, ed. and trans., Britton, 2 vols. (1865) · Joannis Seldeni ad Fletam dissertatio (1647); repr. with additions D. Ogg (1925), 11–19 · private information (2004) · PRO, Queen's Remembrancer's Memoranda Rolls, E159/50, m. 10 · PRO, Lord Treasurer's Remembrancer's Memoranda Rolls, E368/36, m. 14d, 22, 22d · D. Crook, Records of the general eyre, Public Record Office Handbooks, 20 (1982) · H. G. Richardson, ed., 'The coronation of Edward I', BIHR, 15 (1937–8), 94–9

Breton [Britton], **Nicholas** (1554/5–c.1626), poet, was the son of William Breton (d. 1559), businessman, and Elizabeth, daughter of John Bacon of Bury St Edmunds. The poet was descended from a branch of the Breton family settled from at least the fourteenth century at Layer Breton in Essex (Grosart, ix–xii). His grandfather William Breton (d. 1499) had resided at Colchester and his father moved to London and grew wealthy through trade. William's 'capitall mansion house' was in Red Cross Street, in the parish of St Giles Cripplegate, and he owned properties in other parts of London, besides land in Essex and Lincolnshire. When William Breton made his will on 12 February 1558 (Grosart, xii–xvii) he had living two sons, Richard (b. 1550) and Nicholas, and three daughters, Thamar, Anne, and Mary. Nicholas was born in 1554 or 1555, since the will of Roger Poole of the Boar's Head, Cheapside, was witnessed by Nicholas in 1609, when he gave his age as fifty-four (Robertson, xii).

Early years William Breton died on 12 January 1559 and under the terms of his will Nicholas was left 'all that my manor of Burgh in the Marshe [near Wainfleet] with th'appurtennances in the Countie of Lyncoln … And all those my landes and Tenements in Wykes in the Countie of Essex called nelmes' (Grosart, 1.xiv), along with £40 and various family items. William's widow, Elizabeth, was to use the rents from the properties willed to Nicholas for his maintenance and to have the use of the household stuff until he was twenty-four, 'provyded always and uppon condicion that my saied wif do not mary after my deceasse' (ibid., 1.xiii). Despite this clause, within three months of William Breton's death, Elizabeth had married Edward Boyes of Nonnington in Kent. In the event of his widow's remarriage, William Breton had specified that his father-in-law, John Bacon, and Lawrence Eresbie of Louth should act as administrators of the estate. But both of these individuals seem to have died in 1559 or 1560 and Edward Boyes apparently then wrested control of the Breton children's inheritance.

Elizabeth clearly regretted her rapid union with Boyes and on 23 November 1561 at Christ Church Greyfriars she married the poet George *Gascoigne, even though she was still legally Boyes's wife. On 30 September 1562, as Henry Machyn excitedly recorded in his diary,

> the same day at night between viii and ix was a great fray in Redcrosse Street between two gentlemen and their men for

they did marry one woman and divers were hurt; these were there names Master Boysse and Master Gaskyn gentlemen! (Robertson, xiv)

Chancery proceedings had already been initiated to adjudicate over Elizabeth's complex marital position and, by an order issued the day after the affray in Red Cross Street, both Boyes and Gascoigne were forbidden from having any contact with Elizabeth. The Breton children brought a bill against Boyes on 24 November 1566 and it seems that the court ruled in favour of Gascoigne.

In due course Elizabeth gained her divorce from Boyes and was granted a licence to marry Gascoigne again, probably in late 1566. In November 1566 Gascoigne joined with Elizabeth and her children in a prosecution of their case to recover property from Boyes. The task of looking after the interests of the Breton children then fell to the executors of John Bacon's will, his brother and his son (both called George) and Thomas Andrewes. Following the delayed inquisition post mortem from March to October 1567, Gascoigne and his wife, Elizabeth, were summoned in 1568 to the Guildhall for a lord mayor's enquiry into the Breton children's property. This resulted on 17 February 1569 in the wardship of Richard Breton being granted to Gascoigne, who himself may have later unscrupulously appropriated revenues due to the Breton children to solve his own financial dilemmas (Robertson, xvi).

After their marriages Gascoigne and his wife, Elizabeth, lived variously in Red Cross Street, at the manor of Willington, and in Cardington (both in Bedfordshire), and in Walthamstow. The Breton children, including Nicholas, probably lived with their mother and their stepfather, who died on 7 October 1577. Nothing is known about Nicholas's early schooling, although he may have attended Oxford University since Richard Madox recorded in his diary (14 March 1582): 'I dyned w^t Mr Carlil at his brother Hudson's who is governowr of Anwerp … Ther was Mr Brytten, once of Oriel Colledge, wch made wyts wel. He speaketh the Italian wel' (Robertson, xviii). Breton's name has not been traced in any university records, although The Pilgrimage to Paradise (1592) was printed at Oxford and contains an address 'To the Gentlemen students and scholars of Oxforde'.

Early career By 20 February 1577 Breton was residing in London since his verse miscellany, A Floorish upon Fancie [including The Toyes of an Idle Head] (1577), is signed on that date as from his 'Chamber in Holborne'. Other poems probably written between the period 1575 and 1577 reached print in A Smale Handfull of Fragrant Flowers (1575), dedicated to Lady Douglas Sheffield; and The Workes of a Young Wit (1577). It is also possible that The Passionate Shepheard (1604) collected together some of Breton's verses from a much earlier period. Predictably, the influence of Gascoigne's by then outdated style of versifying—heavily dependent upon laboured alliterative effects and narrative prose links between poems—is evident in some of Breton's early writings, as well as that of Gascoigne's close friend, George Whetstone, who also then resided in Holborn. Nevertheless, Breton's early works persuaded George Puttenham to list his name among 'another crew of courtly makers … who have written excellently well' in *The Arte of English Poesie* (1589). As his reputation as a poet grew, Breton's song, 'Phillida and Coridon', was considered worthy of inclusion in *The honorable entertainement gieven to the queenes majestie in progresse, at Elvetham in Hampshire* (1591). In this early phase of his writing career, Breton also produced a collection of five prose discourses, *The Wil of Wit*, although the earliest surviving copy is now the 1597 edition (see Robertson, xli).

After the second edition of *A Floorish* (1582) no published work by Breton is known until a prose romance, *The Historie of … Don Federigo di Terra Nuova* (1590), set in Portugal but perhaps adapted from an Italian source and dedicated to Richard Blount, again from Breton's 'Chamber in Holborne'. Breton later dedicated his *Melancholike Humours* (1600) to Thomas Blunt and *The Honour of Valour* (1605) to Charles Blount, Lord Mountjoy and earl of Devon, although Richard Blount's exact relationship to these individuals (if any) remains uncertain. Breton's other substantial attempt at prose romance, *The Strange Fortunes of Two Excellent Princes* (1600), dedicated to John Linewray of the royal ordinance office, may also have been developed from an Italian original.

It is possible that Breton had spent some time abroad during this period. Madox's reference in March 1582 to Breton has sometimes been interpreted as describing a meeting in Antwerp but it is now known that Madox was back in England by that date. Breton should be also differentiated from the Captain Nicholas Breton (*d.* 1624) of Tamworth, who served in the Low Countries in 1586, and to whose wife, Anne, Breton dedicated his *Old Mad-Cappes New Gally-Mawfrey* (1602). Breton clearly had a working command of Italian (although it cannot be assumed from this that he ever visited Italy) and some of his later prose works, such as *A Dialogue … between Three Phylosophers* (1603), dedicated to John Linewray, are based on Italian sources. *A Merrie Dialogue betwixt the Taker and Mistaker* (1603, repr. 1635 as *A Mad World my Masters*) was dedicated to the Italian scholar John Florio; and in the preface to *Auspicante Jehova* (1597) Breton describes himself as 'having passed some partes of the world, and beholding the stately pallaces of divers princes'. On 14 January 1593 Breton married Anne Sutton at the church of St Giles Cripplegate and the parish registers reveal some details of their children: Anne (*b.* 1601), Mary (*d.* 1603), Henry (1603–5), Edward (*b.* 1606), and Matilda (1607–25).

The 1590s: *The Phoenix Nest* and the countess of Pembroke's patronage Following his contributions to *The Phoenix Nest* (1593), Breton was listed among England's most distinguished poets in William Covell's *Polimanteia* (1595); and in Francis Meres's *Palladis tamia* (1598) he was named as an excellent lyric poet. *Englands Helicon* (1600) included several of his poems and he was also commended in John Bodenham's *Belvedere* (1600). Ben Jonson was prevailed upon to contribute a commendatory verse to Breton's *Melancholike Humours* (1600). Similarly, Breton very occasionally contributed such verses to the publications of other writers, including John Taylor's *The Sculler* (1612). Breton's poems also appeared in some of the major printed miscellanies of the period. On 3 May 1591 Richard Jones entered a collection published as *Brittons Bowre of Delights* (1591), even though only about ten of its verses can be attributed with any confidence to Breton. In his preface to *The Pilgrimage to Paradise* (1592), Breton complained that the *Bowre* contained 'many thinges of other mens mingled with a few of mine'. A corrupt version of one of the poems attributed to Breton in *Brittons Bowre* opened the half-sheet folio collection of ballads, *The Shepheards Delight* (*c.*1617).

In the verse miscellany *The Phoenix Nest* (1593), five poems were attributed to 'N. B. Gent.'. *The Arbor of Amorous Devices* (1597) contained ten poems possibly by Breton and *Englands Helicon* (1600) printed eight of Breton's poems. Such printed publications also prompted some individuals to copy poems attributed to Breton into their own manuscript commonplace books, as is the case in BL, Add. MS 34064, once owned by Anthony Babington of Warrington, which contains other poems possibly by Breton; and Bodl. Oxf., MS Rawl. poet. 85, a miscellany attributed to Sir John Finett (1571–1641). Five poems (dated 1 June 1616–17 October 1617) are attributed to Breton in Bodl. Oxf., MS Tanner 169, the commonplace book of Sir Stephen Powle of Blackmore, Essex, who received the dedication of Breton's *The Court and Country* (1618). Various musical settings of Breton's poems in manuscript are noted by Beal (Beal, 1.4.14).

During the early 1590s Breton was keen to cultivate aristocratic patronage, most notably that of Mary Herbert, countess of Pembroke, the sister of Sir Philip Sidney. Although, as already noted, Breton repudiated much of *Brittons Bowre* (1591), he firmly acknowledged the elegy on Sidney, 'Amoris lachrimae', as his own. The volume in which this repudiation was made, *The Pilgrimage to Paradise, Joyned with the Countess of Pembroke's Love* (1592), was dedicated to the countess with a claim that he had in some way benefited from 'the hand of your honour'. Two years previously, the earl of Pembroke had written a letter in support of 'Brittan a schoolmaster' (BL, Harleian MS 6995, fol. 35, August 1590). Thomas Nashe had also sought the countess's patronage through his dedication to her of an unauthorized edition of Sidney's *Astrophil and Stella* (1591) and his mockery of *Brittons Bowre* (in the preface to his edition of Sidney's sonnets) may have been prompted by a growing rivalry with Breton for the countess's interest. The manuscript version of *The Passions of the Spirit* (1599, entered in the Stationers' register, 30 May 1594) was probably also written at this period. *The Passions* was formerly attributed to the countess of Pembroke. (See Plymouth Public Library MS, ed. J. O. Halliwell-Phillipps, 1853, and BL, Sloane MS 1303, ed. N. G. B., 1862.)

In 1597 Breton dedicated *Wits Trenchmour* to the countess's kinsman, William Herbert of Redcastle, Montgomeryshire; and in the same year his *Auspicante Jehova, Maries exercise* was addressed to her. Breton sometimes linked Mary Herbert's name with that of Mary Magdalen (see Robertson, lxiii) and he may have had her in mind when he composed the devotional treatise *Marie Magdalens Love: a Solemne Passion of the Soules Love* (1595; *A Solemne*

Passion was later reprinted separately). In a possibly autobiographical passage of *Wits Trenchmour*, Breton describes the lavish hospitality and earnest tone of religious devotion at an unnamed great house (possibly the countess's seat, Wilton House) and how a certain gentleman had lost the favour of a great lady. The reasons given for this alienation are either obscure or euphemistic, ranging from 'the deceitfull working of the envious', 'the desert of his owne unworthinesse', the consequences of 'a little idle busines', and (most mysteriously of all) a fall on a 'cold snowy day' into 'a Saw-pitte'. They have been interpreted as signifying either Breton's 'over-indulgence in wine' (Grosart, xxviii) or a tactless dedication by the stationer Thomas Este of *The Passions of the Spirit* in the printed version to Mrs Mary Houghton (Brennan, 'Nicholas Breton's Passions'). Whatever the circumstances of this falling out, by 1601 Breton again felt himself in a position to dedicate to the countess *A Divine Poeme, Divided into Two Partes: the Ravisht Soule and the Blessed Weeper*, gratefully acknowledging her 'bountifull undeserved goodnesse'.

Further pursuit of patronage Although a voluminous writer in both prose and verse, no firm biographical information is known about Breton's life after 1590, other than that which may be tentatively surmised from the dedications prefacing his works. He sought to cultivate the favour of a wide range of patrons, including James I, members of the nobility (Robert Cecil, earl of Salisbury; Charles Blount, Lord Mountjoy and earl of Devon; Ludovick Stuart, duke of Lennox; Dudley, Lord North; and Lady Sara Hastings), and prominent court figures (Sir Francis Bacon and John Linewray, master surveyor of the royal ordinance), as well as prosperous figures from London (Sir William Rider, lord mayor of London; Sir Thomas Lake, a clerk of his majesty's signet; and John Cradocke Cutler who lived at Temple Bar) and the county middle classes (Griffith Pen of Buckinghamshire; Maximilian Dallison of Kent; James Dackham of Steepleton, Dorset; Sir John Crooke of Buckinghamshire; and Sir Gilbert Houghton of Lancashire), with a special emphasis upon Essex dignitaries (Thomas Gardner of Boreham; Sir Stephen Powle of Blackmore; and Sir Mark Ive of Rivers Hall). It is likely, of course, that Breton came across many of these provincial figures during their visits to London rather than in their home counties. He also sometimes addressed works to the children of wealthy parents (Thomas Roe, 'sonne to the Lady Bartley at Stoke' and Mary Gate, daughter of Sir Henry Gate of Seamer, Yorkshire), and, very occasionally, to a fellow writer (Humphrey King, the author of *An Halfe-Penny-Worth of Wit*, who also received the dedication of Thomas Nashe's *Lenten Stuffe* in 1599). A six-line poem by Breton was even appended to an engraving of Lucy, countess of Bedford, by Simon van de Passe (Robertson, frontispiece). But no evidence remains of any material rewards or preferments gained from these addresses, even though Breton sometimes thanked the recipients of his dedications for some unspecified 'undeserved kindness' (Edward Conquest) and 'undeserved favours' (Thomas Blunt).

After 1600: verse satires and devotional verse After 1600 Breton's range as a writer was considerable, although much of his prodigious output may have been penned largely as a means of eking out a modest living since he is not known to have occupied any official post or salaried position. Certainly, his works published during the reign of James I proliferate in references to the penury and unpredictable conditions of writers:

> For let him bragge, and brave it as he list,
> The Poets is a poore profession.
> (N. Breton, *No Whippinge*, 1601, sig. A7r)

His verse satires gained considerable popularity during the first two decades of the seventeenth century, with passing references to their fashionable appeal in Rowland's *Tis Merrie when Gossips Meete* (1602), Dekker's *The Guls Horn-Booke* (1609), and Beaumont and Fletcher's *Wit without Money* (1614). As a satirist, Breton was a skilled, opportunistic writer, for example, rapidly concocting in 1601 his *No Whipping, nor Tripping: but a Kinde Friendly Snippinge* as a retort to John Weever's *The Whipping of the Satyre*, published earlier in that year. Most popular of all were his *Pasquil* series of 1600, including *Pasquils Mad-Cappe* (in two parts), *Pasquils Passe, and Passeth not, Pasquils Mistresse*, and *Melancholike Humours* (originally 'Pasquilles, swullen humours'). The fact that no less than four different stationers (Bushell, Johnes, Smithicke, and Fisher) published these satires, suggests that Breton was probably hawking his manuscripts from stationer to stationer as they were completed.

Breton also specialized in the compilation of collections of popular verse aphorisms and maxims. *The Mothers Blessing* (1602), dedicated to Thomas Roe, contained a generous helping of such commonplace wisdoms; and possibly intended as a companion piece to this collection, *Honest Counsaile: a Merrie Fitte of a Poeticall Furie* (1605), dedicated to James Dackham of Steepleton, Dorset, offered wise paternal advice to a son. Another such volume, *A True Description of Unthankfulnesse* (1602), was dedicated as a 'token of my thankfulnes' to Mary Gate, daughter of Sir Henry Gate of Seamer, Yorkshire. Similar kinds of advice, but pitched at a rather higher social level, were dispensed in *A Murmurer* (1607), dedicated to the privy council and focused specifically upon the various manifestations of ingratitude towards the king and the nobility.

Breton usually reserved the dedications of his manuals of devotional verse for the highest echelons of court and city society. In addition to those works dedicated to the countess of Pembroke, *The Soules Heavenly Exercise* (1601) was dedicated to Sir William Rider, lord mayor of London. This volume may have elicited some form of personal support for Breton since some seven years later he addressed a devotional prose tract, *Divine Considerations of the Soule* (1608), to Sir Thomas Lake, who was Rider's son-in-law. *An Excellent Poeme, upon the Longing of a Blessed Heart* (1601), was addressed to Dudley, Lord North, who also received from Breton an autograph manuscript collection, 'Auspicante Jehovah: auxilium memoriae liber' (Yale University Library, MS 394), of three prose dialogues, probably compiled at about the same period. *The Passion of a Discontented Minde*

(1601), although lacking a dedication, seems to be closely related in both sentiment and subject matter to *An Excellent Poeme* (see Robertson, cxcii–xcviii). His most popular manual of devotional verse, *The Soules Harmony* (eleven editions, 1602–76), was offered to Lady Sara Hastings as a tribute to her 'zealous love to divine studies'. The culmination of this phase of Breton's writing came with *The Soules Immortall Crowne* (1605), dedicated to James I. (A presentation manuscript of this work has also survived, BL, Royal MS 18.A.LVII.)

In 1605 Breton, ever the opportunist, saw the exposure of the Gunpowder Plot as a means of bringing himself to the attention of the royal circle. Just as the details of the plot became publicly known, he dutifully expressed his outrage at the conspiracy in verse, 'An Invective Against Treason' (BL, Royal MS 17.C.XXXIV), which was later published as *The Hate of Treason* (1616), both versions being dedicated to Ludovick Stuart, duke of Lennox, a favourite of James I. Breton also dedicated a short collection of verses, *The Honour of Valour* (1605), to Charles Blount, Lord Mountjoy and earl of Devon, timed to coincide with his appointment in November 1605 as general of the force assembled to repress any possible rebellion triggered by the exposure of the plot. Later in the reign, Breton also cobbled together (probably for the purpose of drawing attention to himself at court) two conventionally anti-Machiavellian verse tracts: *The Uncasing of Machivils Instructions to his Sonne* (1613) and *Machivells Dogge* (1617), with twenty stanzas offering a prayer for the king's safety silently lifted from his own *I would, and would not* (1614).

Prose writing In conjunction with these inventive attempts to cultivate favour at court through his poetry, Breton increasingly viewed prose as the most productive (and presumably lucrative) medium through which to maintain his popular image as a witty and wry social commentator. Apart from his devotional works, which were always finely tuned to the introspective and heavily morbid spirituality of the period, Breton's real skill as a prose writer lay in the production of light but entertaining miscellanies of popular aphorisms, social observations, and pithy nuggets of popular wisdom. The ephemeral nature of such publications is indicated by the fact that the earliest surviving edition of *The Figure of Foure* (entered in the Stationers' register in 1597), dedicated to Thomas Gardner of Boreham, dates from 1631; while that of *The Figure of Foure: the Second Part* (entered in 1614) dates from 1626. These two collections were the precursors in both content and popularity to an even more successful volume, *Wits Private Wealth, Stored with Choice Commodities to Content the Minde*, dedicated to Sir John Crooke of Buckinghamshire, which went through twelve editions between 1607 and 1670. But probably the most popular and long-lasting of such prose works was Breton's epistolary collection of lively anecdotes, quips, proverbs, and jests, *A Poste with a Packet of Madde Letters*, dedicated to Maximilian Dallison of Kent, which was reprinted many times between 1602 and 1685. Aiming at a similar market, Breton also churned out three anthologies of proverbial wisdom: *Crossing of Proverbs* (two parts, both 1616) and *Soothing of Proverbs* (1626).

Such collections were of little literary value and by the middle of the second decade of the seventeenth century it seems as though Breton had 'outlived his reputation as a writer, and was forced to do hackwork for booksellers in his latter years' (Robertson, xxxi).

Breton excelled at two other forms of popular prose composition: dialogues between travellers about life's vicissitudes, such as *Grimellos Fortunes* (1604), *I Pray you be not Angrie: a Pleasant and Merry Dialogue, between Two Travellers* (1605), and *An Olde Mans Lesson, and a Young Man's Love* (1605); and what may be loosely described as essays in the Theophrastan character style. His first attempt at this latter form, *Fantasticks: Serving for a Perpetuall Prognostication*, dedicated to Sir Mark Ive, has as its earliest known edition a 1626 copy (although it was entered in 1604). A more substantial work, *Characters upon Essaies Morall, and Divine*, was published in 1615 with a hopefully fulsome dedication praising Sir Francis Bacon's skill in essay writing. It is not known whether this volume elicited any response from Sir Francis Bacon and in the following year another collection of Breton's essays, *The Good and the Badde* (1616), was dedicated to a rather less distinguished personage, Sir Gilbert Houghton of Lancashire.

Breton's authorship of his printed works was usually indicated by either his full name or initials, although the 'Epistle Dedicatory' of *Pasquils Mistresse* (1600) was signed Salochin Treboun (an imperfect anagram of Nicholas Breton) and the preface to *The Passionate Shepheard* was signed Bonerto. 'Auspicante Jehova' (Yale MS 394) is entirely in Breton's own hand, as is the dedication to the duke of Lennox of 'An Invective Against Treason' (BL, Royal MS 17.C.XXXIV). He also penned a brief inscription in the autograph album of Captain Francis Segar (Hunt. L., HM 743, fol. 86). Contrary to the assertions in Robertson (cx, cxii, and cxv), the manuscripts of 'The soules immortall crowne' (BL, Royal MS 18.A.LVII) and the 'Elogy of Queen Elizabeth' (BL, Harleian MS 6207, fols. 14–22), along with the text of 'An Invective Against Treason', are *not* autograph. Works doubtfully attributed to Breton are considered by Robertson (cxxxviii–clv). Breton's last published work, *Strange Newes out of Divers Countries*, appeared in 1622 and in July and August of the same year three other now lost, or never published, books attributed to Breton ('Nay then by Nicholas Bretton', 'Nothinge by Nicholas Bretton', and 'Oddes, or, All the World to Nothing, by N. B.') were entered in the Stationers' register. The date of his death is unknown, although when his daughter, Matilda, was buried on 27 July 1625, the parish register does not refer to her father as deceased.

MICHAEL G. BRENNAN

Sources A. B. Grosart, introduction, in *The works in verse and prose of Nicholas Breton*, ed. A. B. Grosart, 1 (1879), ix–lxxvi · J. Robertson, 'Introduction', in *Poems by Nicholas Breton*, ed. J. Robertson (1952), xi–clix · P. Beal, *Index of English literary manuscripts*, ed. P. J. Croft and others, 1/1 (1980) · *DNB* · M. G. Brennan, 'Nicholas Breton', *The Cambridge bibliography of English literature*, ed. D. Sedge, 3rd edn, 3 [forthcoming] · M. G. Brennan, 'Nicholas Breton's *The passions of the spirit* and the countess of Pembroke', *Review of English Studies*, new ser., 38 (1987), 221–5 · M. P. Hannay, *Philip's phoenix: Mary Sidney, countess* of Pembroke (1990) • STC, 1475–1640 • Wing, STC • A. F. Marotti, *Manuscript, print, and the English Renaissance lyric* (1995) • BL, Harleian MS 6995, fol. 35 • Francis Segar [autograph album], Hunt. L., HM 743

Brett [*née* Mason], **Anne** [*other married name* Anne Gerard, countess of Macclesfield] (**1667/8–1753**), courtier, was born in Shropshire, the younger daughter of Sir Richard Mason of Shropshire, clerk comptroller in the royal household. At the age of fifteen, on 18 June 1683, she married Charles *Gerard, Viscount Brandon (*c*.1659–1701), nine years her senior. The marriage, a stormy one, lasted for about two and a half years and ended in a separation that remained in force until their divorce in 1698. In 1694, on the death of the earl of Macclesfield, her husband inherited the title and she became the countess of Macclesfield. During the separation she had two illegitimate children, Anne and Richard Savage, with Richard *Savage, the fourth Earl Rivers (*c*.1654–1712). Anne was born in 1695 and Richard two years later. Despite her efforts to conceal the births—she wore a mask while giving birth to her son—rumours reached her husband. The earl accused his wife of adultery, a trial ensued, but before it came to an end a bill of divorce was introduced on 15 January 1698. The poet Richard *Savage, friend of Dr Johnson, later claimed to be this illegitimate son. Anne herself never publicly recognized his claim and always maintained that both children had died in infancy. Modern opinion is divided on the validity of his claim.

Anne's fortune, some £12,000 to £25,000, was returned to her on her divorce and she became a lady-in-waiting to Princess Anne. Two years later she married **Henry Brett** (**1677/8–1724**), politician, a friend of Colley Cibber. They had one daughter, Anna (or Anne) Margharetta [*see below*].

The son of Henry Brett, gentleman, of Oxford, Henry Brett matriculated at Balliol College, Oxford, on 3 January 1693, aged fifteen, as of Sandywell Park, Gloucestershire, but did not proceed to a degree, instead entering the Middle Temple as a student in 1695. Colley Cibber wrote that Brett 'so little followed the Law there, that his Neglect of it, made the Law (like some of his fair and frail Admirers) very often follow *him*' (Cibber, 201). Brett had gone backstage after a performance of Cibber's *Love's Last Shift* in 1696 and had offered to buy the extravagant wig that Cibber wore in the play. They became lifelong friends. Sir Thomas Skipwith, shareholder in the Theatre Royal, Drury Lane, a friend of Cibber's, introduced Brett to the countess of Macclesfield. Cibber, whose loan of a clean shirt allowed Brett to present himself to the countess, states that 'in about ten Days he marry'd the Lady' in 1700 (ibid., 205).

Between 1701 and 1708 Brett was three times elected tory MP for Bishop's Castle, Shropshire, and during the same period, in 1705, was given the rank of lieutenant-colonel of a regiment of foot raised by Sir Charles Hotham. He gave that up within a year. Some time thereafter he became a member of Joseph Addison's little Senate, a circle of men of letters which met at Will's Coffee House and later at Button's. If Brett is the Colonel Rambler of *Tatler*, no. 7, he would have known Richard Steele, and presumably Addison and others, as early as 1709, the date

of Steele's *Tatler*. By 1713 he was a particular friend of Addison, who in a letter to Ambrose Philips, another member of the little Senate, wrote in November 1713, 'Pray give my most H. Service to all friends and particularly to Col. Brett' (*Letters*, 282).

Cibber describes Brett as having 'an uncommon Share of Social Wit, and a handsome Person, with a sanguine Bloom in his Complexion' (Cibber, 201). The famous scene in Cibber's *The Careless Husband* where Lady Easy finds her husband asleep in an armchair while their maid sleeps in another beside him was said to have been based on a similar incident between the Bretts. However, as Cibber read each scene of the play to the Bretts as soon as it was finished, this is perhaps unlikely. James Boswell described how Cibber 'had so high an opinion of her taste and judgment as to genteel life and manners, that he submitted every scene of his "Careless Husband" to Mrs. Brett's revisal and correction' (Boswell, *Life*, 1.174 n. 2). Colonel Brett died suddenly in 1724. At some time shortly after his marriage Sir Thomas Skipwith had given him his shares in the Drury Lane Theatre. In his will, dated 14 September 1724 and proved two days later, Brett left all his real and personal property to his wife, except for his lottery tickets, the proceeds of which, if they were to draw prizes, were to be divided between his wife and his sister Miller.

The Bretts' daughter, Anna Margharetta [**Anna Margharetta Leman** (1704?–1743)] allegedly became a mistress of George I shortly after her father's death. However, the story seems to have originated with Horace Walpole, and there is no earlier evidence for Anna Brett being thought of as the king's mistress. She is described by Horace Walpole as 'very handsome, but dark enough by her eyes, complexion and hair for a Spanish beauty. … When his Majesty shoud return to England a countess's coronet was to have rewarded the young Ladys compliance, & marked her secondary rank' to the duchess of Kendal. Walpole further writes:

> Miss Brett, when the King set out, ordered a door to be broken out of her apartment into the royal garden. Anne, the eldest of the Princesses [daughters of the prince of Wales], offended at that freedom, & not chusing such a companion in her walks, ordered the door to be walled up again. Miss Brett, as imperiously reversed that command. The King died suddenly, & the empire of the new Mistress, & her promised coronet vanished. (*Reminiscences*, 31–2)

The incident, according to George's twentieth-century biographer Ragnhild Hatton, 'hardly bears the interpretation [Walpole] put on it' (Hatton, 135). She later married Sir William Leman (*d*. 1741), and died in 1743.

Anne Brett survived her husband by nearly thirty years and her daughter by ten. She died on 11 October 1753 at her home in Old Bond Street, London.   ARTHUR SHERBO

Sources Foster, *Alum. Oxon.* • C. Cibber, *An apology for the life of Colley Cibber*, new edn, ed. B. R. S. Fone (1968) • Boswell, *Life* • H. Koon, *Colley Cibber: a biography* (1986) • *The letters of Joseph Addison*, ed. W. Graham (1941) • *Reminiscences written by Mr Horace Walpole in 1788*, ed. P. Toynbee (1924) • R. Holmes, *Dr Johnson and Mr Savage* (1993) • *DNB* • R. Hatton, *George I: elector and king* (1978)

Brett, Arthur (*d. c*.1677), poet, was the son of John Brett of Middlesex. Having been a scholar of Westminster School, he proceeded to Christ Church, Oxford, in 1653. He graduated BA in February 1657 and MA in 1659. He was one of the *terrae filii* in the act of 1661, 'at which time', Anthony Wood sniffs, 'he shew'd himself sufficiently ridiculous' (Wood, *Ath. Oxon.*, 3.1144). Wood had an equally low opinion of his serious verse: Brett's published work includes a poem *The Restauration* (1660), *Threnodia* (1660), a meditation on the death of Henry, duke of Gloucester, and *The Book of Job, in Lyrick Verse* (1661). Having taken orders, he became the rector of Templeton, Devon, in 1662, returning to Christ Church four years later to preach a controversial sermon which alluded to the dean and several of the canons. In May 1670 he became the vicar of Market Lavington, Wiltshire, but he resigned his living shortly afterwards and went to London. There he fell into poverty, and began to beg in the streets. It was in this condition that Wood met him by chance in 1675, the same year that Brett composed a ten-line verse-letter to Sir Joseph Williamson, inviting the secretary of state to sponsor him; the following year he sent a further, macaronic study and recalled with gratitude 'the handfull of money which you were pleased to allott mee' (*CSP dom.*, 1660–85, SP 29/382/29). He died in his mother's house in the Strand about 1677 and was buried, Wood supposes, in the churchyard of St Clement's in the Strand.   JONATHAN PRITCHARD

Sources Wood, *Ath. Oxon.*, new edn, 3.1144 • Wood, *Ath. Oxon.: Fasti* (1820), 192, 220 • *The life and times of Anthony Wood*, ed. A. Clark, 2, OHS, 21 (1892), 92–3, 563 • *CSP dom.*, 1660–85 • A. B. Z. W. [A. Brett], *A demonstration how the Latin tongue may be learn't with far greater ease and speed than commonly it is* (1669) • J. Welch, *The list of the queen's scholars of St Peter's College, Westminster*, ed. [C. B. Phillimore], new edn (1852), 141–2 • *Old Westminsters*, 1.119 • *DNB*

Brett, Dorothy Eugenie (1883–1977), painter, was born on 10 November 1883 at 2 Tilney Street, Mayfair, London, the third of the four children of Reginald Baliol *Brett (1852–1930), Liberal MP for Penryn and Falmouth (1880–85), and his wife, Eleanor (Nellie) Frances Weston (*c*.1862–1940), daughter of Sylvain Van de Weyer, Belgian ambassador to the court of St James. Her father succeeded as second Viscount Esher in 1899. His role as unofficial adviser to the royal court dominated her childhood, and she attended dancing classes with Queen Victoria's grandchildren. In 1902 complications from an operation for appendicitis left her battling with increasing deafness, and she was an unsuccessful débutante in 1903.

Brett attended the Slade School of Fine Art (1910–16), where she became known simply as Brett, developed a close, platonic relationship with Professor Frederick (Nutty) Brown, and won first prize for figure painting in 1914. She became friends with her fellow students Dora Carrington and Mark Gertler, the latter executing a controversial portrait of Brett in 1915 (exh. New English Art Club, 1915). Concentrating on portrait and figure painting, Brett exhibited with the New English Art Club (1914–16) and the Grosvenor Gallery (1921–2), developing the bold, simplified style that makes *War Widows* (exh. New English Art Club, 1916, no. 297) one of her most successful

early compositions. She struggled unsuccessfully, however, to depict the flamboyant hostess Lady Ottoline Morrell (1916–19), for whom she developed one of a series of 'crushes'. Ottoline described Brett as 'a slim, pretty young woman, looking much younger than she really was. She had a Joe Chamberlain nose, a peach-like complexion, rather a rabbit mouth and no chin' (*Ottoline at Garsington*, 52). Ottoline put Brett up at her Garsington home (1916–19) and provided her with a studio ('the Monastery', later shared with Mark Gertler). Here she formed friendships with the writer Katherine Mansfield and her husband, the critic John Middleton Murry (whose lover she briefly became *c*.1922), and the novelist Aldous Huxley, who portrayed her as Jenny Mullion in *Crome Yellow* (1921) and Beatrice Gilray in *Point Counter Point* (1928).

Introduced to the writer D. H. Lawrence and his German wife, Frieda, in 1915, Brett moved with them to Taos, New Mexico, in 1924 (naturalized 1938), becoming devoted to Lawrence, and living near Frieda and the hostess Mabel Dodge Luhan (and often quarrelling with them) after Lawrence's death. In a letter of 12 December 1915 to Lady Ottoline Morrell, Lawrence described Brett as 'one of the "sisters" of this life' (*Selected Letters*, 111) and fictionalized her as Hilda Blessington in *The Boy in the Bush* (1924), Dollie Urquhart in 'The Princess' (*St Mawr*, 1925), and Miss James in 'The Last Laugh', written in 1925 and published in *The Woman who Rode Away* (1928). Brett's portrait of Lawrence (1925) is in the National Portrait Gallery, London, and her memoir of their relationship, *Lawrence and Brett: a Friendship*, was published in 1933.

In Taos, Brett produced her most successful works, large canvases based on the life and ceremonies of the Pueblo Indians, which, alongside her friendship with Lawrence, brought her fame in her last years, but despite a small family legacy she was always impecunious. Retrospectives of work were held at the American British Gallery, New York (1950), and the Taos Gallery of Contemporary Art (1980). Two of her Taos paintings are in the Tate collection; other examples of her work are in the Harry Ransom Humanities Research Center, University of Texas at Austin, and the Yale Center for British Art, New Haven, Connecticut. Brett was admitted to hospital in Taos suffering from lung congestion shortly before her ninety-fourth birthday. She died there on 27 August 1977, and her ashes were later scattered on the Red Rocks below Mount Lobo in Taos.

SARAH MACDOUGALL

Sources S. Hignett, *Brett: from Bloomsbury to New Mexico, a biography* (1984) • M. Luhan, *Some letters concerning D. H. Lawrence* (1978) • *Mark Gertler: selected letters*, ed. N. Carrington (1965) • D. Ellis, *D. H. Lawrence: dying game, 1922–1930* (1998) • *The selected letters of D. H. Lawrence*, ed. J. T. Boulton (1997) • *Ottoline at Garsington: memoirs of Lady Ottoline Morrell, 1915–1918*, ed. R. Gathorne-Hardy (1974) • M. Seymour, *Ottoline Morrell: life on the grand scale* (1992) • J. Byrne, *A genius for living: a biography of Frieda Lawrence* (1995) • F. Spalding, *20th century painters and sculptors* (1990), vol. 6 of *Dictionary of British art* • G. M. Waters, *Dictionary of British artists, working 1900-1950* (1975) • C. M. Bach, *Picturesque images from Taos and Santa Fe* (1975) [exhibition catalogue, Denver Art Museum] • G. Elinor, 'Dorothy Brett's paintings: from Bloomsbury to Taos', *Woman's Art Journal*, 12 (1991–

2), 9–14 • C. Petteys, *Dictionary of women artists: an international dictionary of women artists born before 1900* (1985)
Archives U. Texas, collection | McMaster University, Hamilton, Ontario, Mills Memorial Library, Bertrand Russell collection • priv. coll., corresp. [copies, Tate collection, Mark Gertler collection] • priv. coll., letters to S. S. Koteliansky • U. Cal., Berkeley, Bancroft Library, corresp. with Una Jeffers • U. Texas, Ottoline Morrell and Spud Johnson collections • University of Cincinnati, Ohio, D. H. Lawrence, Frieda Lawrence, and John Middleton Murry letters • Yale U., corresp. with Mabel Dodge Luhan • Watlington, Oxfordshire, Esher family archives
Likenesses K. Barnard, oils, 1888, repro. in Hignett, *Brett* • M. Gertler, oils, 1914–15; formerly priv. coll. • M. Gertler, pencil drawing, *c*.1914–1915, priv. coll. • O. Morrell, photographs, 1916–19, U. Texas; repro. in Hignett, *Brett* • A. Guevara, oils, 1920–21, repro. in Hignett, *Brett* • D. E. Brett, self-portrait, pencil, 1924, repro. in Hignett, *Brett* • D. E. Brett, group portrait, oils, 1958 (*Lawrence's Three Fates*), repro. in Hignett, *Brett*

Brett, Edwin John (1828–1895), journal editor and publisher, was born in White Horse Lane, Canterbury, the son of Thomas Brett (*c*.1777–1867), British army officer, and his wife, Mary. At fourteen he was apprenticed to a watchmaker, but soon moved to London, where he worked as an artist-engraver. By the age of sixteen he was engraving for Henry Vizetelly's *Pictorial Times*.

Brett joined a radical Chartist circle that included Feargus O'Connor and George Augustus Sala, the latter friendship continuing until his death. He was present at the Kennington Common Chartist demonstration on 10 April 1848, and later claimed that its failure was decisive in his later shift towards mainstream politics. On 4 January 1849 he married Eliza (1832–1893), daughter of Henry Archer, a Clerkenwell butcher. Brett found a valuable professional mentor in Herbert Ingram, publisher and Liberal MP, but his proposed take-over of the editorship of the *Illustrated Inventor* was thwarted on 8 September 1860 when Ingram drowned in Lake Michigan.

Brett gained his first editorship in 1864, presiding over Edward Harrison's *English Girl's Journal and Ladies' Magazine* with William Emmett. When it folded the following year they parted acrimoniously, and went into competition with each other in the expanding market for boys' periodicals. Brett then joined the Newsagents' Publishing Company (NPC) at 147 Fleet Street, and inaugurated an era of astonishing success with a series of best-selling periodicals. With aggressive marketing and shrewd identification of his target readership, he garnered profits that only his lack of interest in bookkeeping prevent historians from estimating. Under his management the NPC developed a new sub-genre in 'penny-dreadful' fiction that placed juvenile heroes in tales of sensational brutality. These publications came under attack for their glamorization of highwaymen and housebreakers.

By 1866 this success had allowed Brett to found *Boys of England* at 173 Fleet Street, a weekly whose blend of thrilling fiction and factual articles enjoyed popularity until its closure in 1899. It adopted a somewhat spurious moral tone, repackaging lurid narratives within the dignifying context of imperial heroism. Articles exhorted boys to participate in outdoor games and surrender their pocket money to the journal's lifeboat subscription fund (Brett

named the vessel after himself). By January 1868 the periodical had proved popular enough for him to target a slightly older readership with *Young Men of Great Britain* (1868–72), a 'healthy, moral, instructive and amusing companion for every age'. Brett became agony uncle to thousands of boys who sought his advice on broken voices, bad breath, and the propriety of using tinted writing paper. He eventually gave the paper its own etiquette column.

As 173 Fleet Street became 'The Boys of England Office', Brett nurtured a new respectability. He found homes for several street orphans, helping them to honest careers. The prestige of his papers was further enhanced when he took advantage of the bankruptcy of the adventure novelist Captain Mayne Reid, signing him as a regular contributor and saving the author from ruin.

During the 1870s Brett expanded into other markets, overseeing the production of popular romantic fictions under such titles as *Wedding Bells* (1870–79) and *Something to Read* (1881–99). His *English Ladies' Novelettes* (1891–2) became the *Princesses' Novelettes*, which survived until 1904. By this time Brett was dividing his time between two residences, Burleigh House, at 342 Camden Road, and Oaklands, on the Isle of Thanet. Financial success allowed him to indulge his passion for arms and armour, and over thirty years he acquired nearly a thousand items of militaria. After the death of Eliza Brett on 30 May 1893, he occupied himself with the collection, for which he published a lavishly illustrated catalogue in 1894. This formed the basis of the Christies catalogue when he began to sell the collection at auction on 18 March 1895. After a long illness Brett died at Burleigh House on 15 December 1895, leaving an estate worth £76,538 to his nine children. The majority of his publishing empire was left to his eldest sons, Edwin Charles and Edgar Percy, who continued to manage its titles until the business collapsed in 1909. Brett was buried in the family vault in Highgate cemetery on 19 December 1895.

MATTHEW SWEET

Sources *Biograph and Review*, 4 (1880), 456–61 • 'Mr Edwin John Brett', *Boys of England* (29 Jan 1892) • J. Springhall, '"A life story for the people?" Edwin J. Brett and the London "low-life" penny dreadfuls of the 1860s', *Victorian Studies*, 33 (1989–90), 223–46 • *ILN* (8 Feb 1896) • m. cert. • d. cert. • J. Sutherland, 'Edward J. Brett', *The Stanford companion to Victorian fiction* (1989) • Boase, *Mod. Eng. biog.* • Poll of the Freemen and Electors who voted at the election of the two members to represent the city of Canterbury in Parliament, 1865–7
Archives Bodl. Oxf., Pettingell, John Johnson MSS, collection of Newsagents' Publishing Company penny dreadfuls
Likenesses engraving, 1891, repro. in *Moonshine* (12 May 1891)
Wealth at death £76,538 9*s*. 6*d*.: probate, 28 Jan 1896, *CGPLA Eng. & Wales*

Brett, Henry (1677/8–1724). *See under* Brett, Anne (1667/8–1753).

Brett, John (*d*. 1785), naval officer, was probably the son or near relative of Captain Timothy Brett, with whom he went to sea as captain's servant in the sloop *Ferret* about 1722. He followed Timothy Brett to the *Deal Castle* in May 1727, and to the *William and Mary* yacht in the following November. On 2 March 1734 he was promoted lieutenant and in 1740 commanded the sloop *Grampus* in the Mediterranean. On 25 March 1741 he was posted into the *Roebuck* (40 guns) by Vice-Admiral Nicholas Haddock, whom he brought home a passenger, invalided, in May 1742; Brett was appointed to the *Anglesea* in November 1742, and in April 1744 moved to the *Sunderland* (60 guns).

On 6 January 1745 the *Sunderland*, in company with the *Captain*, *Hampton Court*, and *Dreadnought*, fell in with, but did not capture, the two French ships *Neptune* and *Fleuron*. The *Sunderland* was afterwards sent out to join Commodore Peter Warren at Cape Breton, and took part in the operations which resulted in the capture of Louisburg. In 1755 Brett commanded the *Chichester* in the squadron sent under Rear-Admiral Francis Holburne to reinforce Vice-Admiral Edward Boscawen on the coast of North America. On 19 May 1756 he was appointed to the *St George*, and on 1 June ordered to turn over to the *Namur*. Three days later Brett was promoted rear-admiral of the white; however, he refused to take up the commission, and it was accordingly cancelled. Brett's explanation for this refusal was given privately to Lord Anson, but no reason for it appears on record, and from this time Brett lived in retirement, occupying himself, to some extent, in literary pursuits.

Between 1777 and 1779 Brett published *Translations of Father Feyjoo's Discourses* (4 vols.) and in 1780 *Essays or Discourses Selected from the Works of Feyjoo*. In 1772 he corresponded with Wilkes, equating himself with the latter as 'a friend of liberty'. His correspondence also refers to his wife and children, about whom no further details are known. By seniority he was promoted admiral on 29 January 1770. He died in 1785.

J. K. LAUGHTON, *rev.* ROGER MORRISS

Sources correspondence between J. Cleveland and George Rodney, 1 June 1756; Henry Osborne to Admiralty Secretary 13 June 1756, PRO, ADM 30/20/6; 1/922 · *GM*, 1st ser., 51 (1781), 34 · *GM*, 1st ser., 55 (1785), 323 · J. Charnock, ed., *Biographia navalis*, 5 (1797), 67 · D. A. Baugh, ed., *Naval administration, 1715–1750*, Navy RS, 120 (1977) · 'Boscawen's letters to his wife, 1755–1756', ed. P. K. Kemp, *The naval miscellany*, ed. C. Lloyd, 4, Navy RS, 92 (1952), 163–256

Brett, John (1831–1902), landscape and marine painter, was born at Bletchingley, Surrey, on 8 December 1831, the son of Captain Charles Curtis Brett (1789–1865), an army veterinarian attached to the 12th lancers, and Ann Pilbean (b. 1808/9). As a boy he studied drawing in Dublin, to which city his father was posted. He abandoned thoughts of joining the army, and instead in 1851 became a pupil of the painter James Duffield Harding in London and also took lessons from Richard Redgrave. In winter 1852–3 Brett was introduced to the Pre-Raphaelite painter William Holman Hunt in the house of the poet Coventry Patmore, and soon afterwards entered the Royal Academy Schools. His early artistic inclination was recorded in a diary entry for 18 May 1853:

> I am going on fast towards Preraphaelitism—Millais and Hunt are truly fine fellows. I greatly admire and honor them—Have resolved in future to go through severe course of training and close childlike study of nature. In short to follow their steps. (Cordingly, 'Stonebreaker', 141)

Brett made his professional début at the Royal Academy in 1856, exhibiting a portrait of Mrs Coventry Patmore along with two other portraits, while in the following year his genre subject *Faces in the Fire* (known from early photographs) was shown at the Academy. During the second half of the 1850s he became a familiar figure on the fringe of the Pre-Raphaelite circle, exhibiting with them and in 1858 joining the Hogarth Club. Among the fine portrait drawings that Brett made of fellow Pre-Raphaelite artists are one of Arthur Hughes, of 1858 (NPG) and another of Alexander Munro, of 1861 (priv. coll.). Over a period of about two years, from 1856, Brett seems to have been romantically inclined towards the poet Christina Rossetti, and it is possible that he sought to marry her but was rejected. An unfinished portrait of Christina Rossetti made by Brett in 1857 survives in the collection of a descendant of the artist.

If Brett began with figurative subjects and portraits, landscape painting was also in his thoughts in the mid-1850s. The fourth volume of Ruskin's *Modern Painters* (subtitled 'Of mountain beauty') was issued in April 1856; Brett was so struck by what he read that he 'rushed off to Switzerland in obedience to a passion that possessed me and wd listen to no hindering remonstrance' (Cordingly, 'Life of John Brett', 128), as he described in a diary entry for December of the year. There in the Bernese Oberland he met the Yorkshire-born painter John William Inchbold, who was working on a mountain subject entitled *The Jungfrau, from the Wengern Alps*. Brett was deeply impressed by Inchbold's meticulous technique and by his search for a way to describe the alpine landscape as informatively and with as much scientific accuracy as possible. Thus he recorded in his diary how, 'there and then [I] saw that I had never painted in my life, but only fooled and slopped, and thenceforward attempted in a reasonable way to paint all I could see' (Staley, *Pre-Raphaelite Landscape*, 124–5). Brett's *Glacier of Rosenlaui* (Tate collection), the immediate outcome of this trip and exhibited at the Royal Academy in 1857, shows a great mass of ice and snow, an eroded mountainside crested by five fir trees (which provide a sole indication of scale in the composition), and in the foreground boulders of granite and gneiss deposited as moraines by the flow of ice. The painting reveals Brett's awareness of scientific theory about the action of glaciers, notably the pioneering work of the Swiss geologist Louis Agassiz, whose *Études sur les glaciers* was published in 1840. *Glacier of Rosenlaui*, which remained unsold after the Royal Academy exhibition of 1857, and a watercolour entitled *Wetterhorn, Wellhorn, and Eiger, Canton of Berne* (priv. coll.), also of 1856, were lent to the exhibition of British paintings and drawings that travelled in the United States in 1857–8. In Boston these two works were seen and approved as accurate accounts of mountain structure by Louis Agassiz himself, as was described in a letter from the organizer to the art critic William Michael Rossetti: 'Professor Agassiz gives unqualified praise to Brett's two pictures of the glacier and the two horns. His authority here is absolute, and praise from him will I hope secure the sale of the pictures' (*Selected Letters of William Michael Rossetti*, ed. R. Peattie, Pennsylvania, 1990, 88 n. 4).

Brett's next work—*The Stonebreaker* (Walker Art Gallery, Liverpool)—which he painted back in England in the summer of 1857, was a rustic genre subject replete with a complex pattern of moral, social, and religious inferences. A boy is seen engaged in the arduous labour of smashing flints into small fragments with a hammer. The open landscape beyond, painted from nature at Norbury Park in Surrey, is serenely beautiful but seems to offer no consolation to the young labourer. A milestone in the foreground of the composition indicates that London is a mere 23 miles distant, but again the boy seems unaware of a larger world beyond. A blasted tree, with a bullfinch perched in the uppermost branch of a single healthy stem, is seen on the right side of the composition. Various pencil sketches for *The Stonebreaker* bear inscriptions such as 'outside Eden' and 'the Wilderness of this World', thus indicating Brett's purpose in representing a figure painting symbolical of man's fall. The painting was badly hung at the 1858 Royal Academy, and most of those who commented on it perceived it as a documentary account of rustic life in a landscape setting. Ruskin, for example, writing of it in *Academy Notes*, felt that 'in some points of precision it goes beyond anything the Pre-Raphaelites have done yet'. He went on: 'I know no such thistle-down, no such chalk hills, and elm-trees, no such natural pieces of far-away clouds, in any of their works' (Ruskin, *Works*, 1903–12, 14.171).

Ruskin took Brett up, believing him to have the technical skill and personal compliance to be able to fulfil his latest ideas about landscape painting. The alpine subject *Val d'Aosta* (priv. coll.) represents a westward view from the Château St Pierre near Villeneuve along the valley of the River Dora Baltea, with Mont Paramont in the distance, and seems to have been painted in response to Ruskin's plea that Brett should look for grander and more majestic scenery than the 'Surrey downs and railway-traversed vales'. Ruskin visited Brett while he was working on the painting, subjecting him to intensive instruction in his own principles of landscape painting. Given Ruskin's involvement in the gestation of the painting, Brett was understandably disconcerted when Ruskin responded equivocally to it when it was shown at the Royal Academy in 1859. In *Academy Notes* the critic expressed himself pleased that 'any simple-minded, quietly-living person, indisposed towards railway stations or crowded inns' might find out from the picture 'what a Piedmontese valley is like in July', but went on to criticize the work on the grounds that it was mechanical and lacked evidence of the artist's feeling for nature, and finally described it as 'Mirror's work, not man's' (Ruskin, *Works*, 1903–12, 14.235–7). Even so, Ruskin bought *Val d'Aosta* in 1859—perhaps out of sympathy for an artist whose commercial prospects, at least on that occasion, he had so gravely damaged—and in fact he owned the painting until his death.

Brett continued to paint figurative subjects, notably *The Hedger* (priv. coll.) of 1860—which follows in line of succession to *The Stonebreaker*—and on one occasion a large costume piece in a medieval setting entitled *Warwick Castle*, which was a critical failure but a commercial success—

being bought by Thomas Plint for £420—when it was exhibited at the Royal Academy in 1861. Ruskin, however, sought to persuade Brett to devote himself to pure landscape, mocking 'that ridiculous Pre-Raphaelite love of painting people with purple cheeks and red noses by way of being in the sun' (Hickox and Payne, 110), and upbraiding him for having 'lost no end of time by that accursed fit of hankering after being a figure painter, that took you' (ibid.).

During the first half of the 1860s Brett made a series of long visits to various European destinations. In 1861 he visited the Alps again, staying at Champéry near the Lake of Geneva and painting a watercolour entitled *Mountains of St Gingough* (FM Cam.). He travelled on from Switzerland to Florence, where he stayed during winter 1861–2 and where he painted a watercolour of the Ponte Vecchio, which was later purchased by the critic's father and art collector, John James Ruskin. He returned to Florence in 1862–3, a sojourn that led to the extraordinary city view *Florence from Bellosguardo* (Tate collection), which was scandalously rejected by the selection committee of the 1863 Royal Academy, but which was much admired when Brett subsequently exhibited it in his own studio and promptly sold to the financier and National Gallery trustee Lord Overstone. The winters of 1863–4 and 1864–5 Brett spent in the south of Italy, painting watercolour and oil views of the coast near Capri and Sorrento. While abroad Brett painted what was perhaps his last figurative subject, a work entitled *Lady with a Dove* (Tate collection), which was a portrait of one Madame Loeser, a woman with whom Brett was romantically involved. Later in the decade he painted in the Thames valley, as witnessed by his *River Scene, Near Goring-on-Thames* (Whitworth Art Gallery, Manchester) of 1865. In 1868 he made a series of watercolours of the harbour at Great Yarmouth. It is noticeable that a feeling of detachment is increasingly found in these drawings of the 1860s, in which the landscape is often seen across a barrier of water with a concomitant sense of remoteness. Occasional oils, such as *Massa, Bay of Naples* (Herron Museum of Art, Indianapolis) of 1864, display the same characteristics. Increasingly Brett saw painting purely as a means of recording meteorological and atmospheric effects, rather than a landscape where there was evidence of human activities.

Brett was clearly a man of powerful intellect. Ruskin quoted a remark of Brett's in the fifth volume of *Modern Painters* (1860), describing him as 'one of my keenest-minded friends' (Ruskin, *Works*, 1903–12, 7.360). However, a breach later occurred between Brett and Ruskin when the two men argued about a point of science. In 1865 the latter had had cause to write to D. G. Rossetti (who had himself taken to complaining about Brett):

> I will associate with no man who does not more or less accept my own estimate of myself. For instance, Brett told me, a year ago, that a statement of mine respecting a scientific matter (which I knew à fond before he was born) was 'bosh.' I told him in return he was a fool; he left the house, and I will not see him again 'until he is wiser'. (ibid., 36.493–4)

Brett was particularly interested in astronomy, and from a young age had made astronomical observations. In 1870 he joined an expedition to Sicily to observe a solar eclipse, and in the following year he was elected to the Royal Astronomical Society, regularly publishing accounts of his observations thereafter and making careful drawings of lunar craters. He seems to have drawn the conclusion that if the origin and construction of the physical world were to be understood in scientific terms, biblical explanations were redundant. Thus in the course of the 1860s the Christian faith that he had previously embraced seems to have been undermined.

About 1870 Brett met, and later married, Mary Ann Howcroft, with whom he had seven children. At this later stage in his career he turned almost exclusively to coastal and marine subjects, often on a large scale. Two paintings shown in 1871 at the Royal Academy—*The British Channel Seen from the Dorsetshire Cliffs* (Tate collection) and *Etna from the Heights of Taormina* (Mappin Art Gallery, Sheffield), the former consisting entirely of a view of sea and sky, the latter including sea, coast, and distant mountain—seem to mark the pattern of his later exhibits. Brett owned a succession of sailing boats, and on occasions made oil sketches and notations of the scenery as observed from these vessels. These sketches, generally of a double-square format, provided the basis of large-scale oil compositions of the same proportions, painted in the studio during the winter months. In 1886 he staged an exhibition entitled 'Three Months on the Scottish Coast' at the Fine Art Society in London. In a foreword to the catalogue he stated that the works exhibited—forty-six sketches and three small paintings—represented a season's work, and that each sketch was the outcome of a single session of about 3 hours and therefore was intended to capture whatever particular effect of light was to be observed on that occasion. Brett stated that for him a sketch was 'the painting of a single observation unadulterated, comprising whatever happens to occur at the time, and as much of it as circumstances allow to be recorded at one sitting' (Brett, 'The commentaries', 8). Of the process by which the sketches were translated into studio pictures, Brett seems to have prided himself on the efficiency and speed of his manufacture, and in anticipation of any criticism that the resulting works had become impersonal and lacking in feeling he concluded that 'sentiment in landscape is chiefly dependent on meteorology' (ibid., 10).

Brett was for a period in the 1880s a successful and admired artist (although the last years of his life witnessed a dramatic decline in his commercial prospects). In 1880 *Britannia's Realm* (Tate collection) was bought by the trustees of the Chantrey bequest. The following year Brett was elected as an associate of the Royal Academy. Brett always kept a place to live and a studio in London: in the 1850s he shared lodgings with his elder sister Rosa *Brett (1829–1882)—herself a painter—and brother Edwin in Camden Town, close to the Rossetti family in Albany Street. From 1859 to 1869 he lived in Pump Court in the Temple. Later addresses from which he sent works to exhibitions were in the area to the north of Oxford Street

around Cavendish Square, and from 1873 to 1892 he kept a studio at 38 Harley Street. About 1877 he built for himself, in Keswick Road, Putney, a curious bungalow, fitted with central heating and asphalt floors (to prevent noise and vibration), piped rainwater to every bedroom, and an equatorial telescope mounted on the roof. In 1888 he commenced a larger house on Putney Heath, at the junction of West Hill and Kingston Road, called Daisyfield. This was arranged on an open plan, with all spaces connecting with a central top-lit gallery. There he lived with his family until his death on 7 January 1902; his wife survived him. Daisyfield and the Keswick Road bungalow were both later demolished. CHRISTOPHER NEWALL

Sources 'Artists' houses', *Art Journal*, new ser., 2 (1882), 57–8 · J. Brett, 'The commentaries', *Three months on the Scottish coast: a series of sketches and pictures painted during the summer of the present year* (1886) [exhibition catalogue, Fine Art Society, London] · J. Brett, 'Landscapes at the National Gallery', *Fortnightly Review*, 63 (1895), 623–39 · M. Girouard, 'An open plan in the 1880s', *Country Life* (29 March 1962), 720–22 · A. Staley, *The Pre-Raphaelite landscape* (1973), chap. 10 · A. Staley, 'Some water-colours by John Brett', *Burlington Magazine*, 115 (Feb 1973), 88–93 · P. J. Brett, 'Portraits by pen and camera: John Brett's work as seen by Beatrix Potter', *Country Life* (27 Sept 1979), 948–9 · M. Pointon, 'Geology and landscape painting in nineteenth-century England', *Images of the earth: essays in the history of the environmental sciences*, ed. L. J. Jordanova and R. S. Porter (1979), 87–108 · D. Cordingly, 'The stonebreaker: an examination of the landscape in a painting by John Brett', *Burlington Magazine*, 124 (March 1982), 141–5 · K. Bendiner, 'John Brett's The glacier of Rosenlaui', *Art Journal* (autumn 1984), 241–8 · K. Bendiner, *An introduction to Victorian painting* (New Haven, 1985) · M. Hickox, 'John Brett and the Rossettis', *Journal of Pre-Raphaelite Studies*, 5/2 (1985), 105–10 · J. Marsh, *Christina Rossetti* (1994) · M. Hickox, 'John Brett's The stonebreaker', *Review of the Pre-Raphaelite Society*, 4/1 (1996), 13–23 · M. Hickox, 'The Royal Academy's rejection of Brett's Florence', *Review of the Pre-Raphaelite Society*, 3/1 (1995), 10–16 · M. Hickox, 'The unpublished correspondence of Ruskin and Brett', *Ruskin Gazette* [edited by O. E. Madden] (1995), 1–25 · M. Hickox and C. Payne, 'Sermons in stones: John Brett's stonebreaker', *Re-framing the Pre-Raphaelites* (1996), 99–114 · M. Hickox, 'John Brett's portraits', *Review of the Pre-Raphaelite Society*, 4/1 (1996), 13–19 · P. McEvansoneya, 'More light on the Royal Academy's rejection of Brett's Florence', *Review of the Pre-Raphaelite Society*, 4/1 (1996), 19–23 · D. Cordingly, 'The life of John Brett: painter of Pre-Raphaelite landscapes and seascapes', PhD diss., U. Sussex, 1983 · M. Hickox, 'John Brett and Ruskin', *Burlington Magazine*, 138 (Aug 1996), 521–6 · A. Sumner, ed., *John Brett: a Pre-Raphaelite on the shores of Wales* (2001) [exhibition catalogue, NMG Wales, 14 Aug–25 Nov 2001] · d. cert. · D. A. Lewis, 'Pondered vision: the art and life of John Brett, A.R.A., 1830–1902', PhD diss., Indiana University, 1986 · CGPLA Eng. & Wales (1902)

Archives NMM, sketchbooks | RAS, letters to Royal Astronomical Society

Likenesses J. Brett, self-portrait, 1883, Aberdeen Art Gallery · T. S. Lee, bust, 1890, Art Workers' Guild, London · photograph, NPG

Wealth at death £6289 15s.: resworn probate, CGPLA Eng. & Wales (1902)

Brett, John Watkins (1805–1863), art collector and telegraph engineer, was born in Bristol, one of at least seven children of William Brett, cabinet-maker. By the age of twelve his enthusiasm for the fine arts was so great that his parents put him under the tuition of Mintorn, a Bristol artist, with whom he remained until the age of twenty-one, although by then he was himself teaching drawing and watercolouring. In 1830 he took a house at Clifton, intending to establish his artistic career. His speciality at this time was the painting of miniatures on ivory, but his tastes were already universal, and he visited some of the most celebrated galleries on the continent, where he studied and sketched many of the old masters. His future as an artist seemed assured, but in 1831, a few days before the Bristol riots, a fire broke out which destroyed his own accumulated works, as well as rare items which he had acquired. After this disaster he abandoned painting for the study and collection of old masters, and shortly afterwards travelled to the United States with a collection of fine paintings, where he remained for a few years before returning to London in 1842, living at first in Regent's Park before taking up permanent residence at 2 Hanover Square. Here he amassed a wide-ranging collection of fine art and pictures, some of which he loaned to art exhibitions held in Manchester, at the South Kensington Museum, and at the Royal Institution of British Architects.

The invention of the electric telegraph caught Brett's attention and, even in its early days, he had a vision of a future when telegraph lines would stretch beyond the land, and bring all parts of the globe into almost instant communication. His first consideration of submarine telegraphs arose from a conversation early in 1845 with his brother Jacob, who had some talent for mechanics. Since telegraph cables could be laid under ground, why not under water, and if under water, why not across the ocean bed? In the same year Jacob Brett registered a company for uniting Europe and America by telegraph, but the project was considered too risky, and failed to attract public support. The brothers' more modest offer to the British government to link Dublin Castle with Downing Street was also declined. Their application to the French government for a concession to lay a cable between Dover and Calais was granted in 1847. Brett sold a large number of paintings at Christies in April that year, which raised £6788 towards the capital needed, but the project did not progress fast enough to meet the stipulated time limit and was abandoned. A successful cable was laid in 1850 under a new agreement, but was severed by a fisherman after the exchange of only a few messages.

Brett finally established a permanent link in September 1851, and followed this with further submarine cables all over the world. He published *On the origin and progress of the oceanic telegraph, with a few brief facts and opinions of the press* in 1858, and contributed several papers on the same subject to the Institution of Civil Engineers, of which he was a member. He was confident that Britain and America would one day be connected by telegraph, and in 1856 he helped to found and finance the Atlantic Telegraph Company which laid the first transatlantic cable. Owing to inadequate preparation this failed after a few weeks, and Brett unfortunately did not live to see the successful cable of 1866. He died in the lunatic asylum at Coton Hill, Staffordshire, on 3 December 1863, aged only fifty-eight, and was buried in the family vault in the churchyard of Westbury-on-Trym, near Bristol. He never married. His obituarist in the Royal Geographical Society wrote of him,

> It is rare to find a highly cultivated taste for the fine arts combined with such an enterprising mind, yet such was eminently the case with Mr Brett, as proved by his choice and varied collection of works of art. (*Proceedings*, 188)

Under the terms of his will, this extensive collection was put on sale at Christies from 5 to 18 April 1864, and raised some £14,500. Brett bequeathed his estate, valued at under £40,000, to various missionary societies.

ROGER BRIDGMAN

Sources C. Bright, *Submarine telegraphs: their history, construction, and working* (1898) · G. R. M. Garratt, *One hundred years of submarine cables* (1950) · *Journal of the Society of Arts*, 12 (1863–4), 158 · *Proceedings* [Royal Geographical Society], 8 (1863–4), 188 · *N&Q*, 3rd ser., 8 (1865), 203 · *The Times* (1 April 1864), 550 · sale catalogue (1847) [Christies, 23 Mar – 4 April 1847] · sale catalogue (1864) [Christies, 5–18 April 1864] · Catalogue of the Ronalds Library, Inst. EE · will of J. W. Brett, *CPR* · *DNB*

Archives Inst. EE, Archives, business papers and corresp.

Likenesses photograph, repro. in A. Williams, *Telegraphy and telephony* (1928)

Wealth at death under £40,000: probate, 29 Jan 1864, *CGPLA Eng. & Wales*

Brett, Sir Peircy (1709–1781), naval officer, was the son of Peircy Brett, a master in the navy and subsequently master attendant at Sheerness and Chatham dockyards. After serving as a volunteer and midshipman he was promoted to the rank of lieutenant on 6 December 1734 and appointed to the *Falkland* with Captain the Hon. Fitzroy Lee, with whom he remained until July 1738, when he was appointed to the *Adventure*. A few months later he was moved to the *Gloucester*, one of the ships which sailed under Commodore George Anson for the Pacific in September 1740.

On 18 February 1741 Brett was transferred to Anson's own ship, the *Centurion*, as second lieutenant, and in this capacity he commanded the landing party which sacked and burned the town of Paita on 13 November 1741. After the capture of the Spanish treasure ship *Nuestra Señora de Covadonga*, and following the promotion of Philip Saumarez, Brett became first lieutenant, and Anson appointed him captain of the *Centurion* on 30 September 1743, when the commodore left the ship on his visit to Canton. On the arrival of the *Centurion* in England the Admiralty refused to confirm this promotion, though they gave Brett a new commission as captain dated the day the ship anchored at Spithead. However, on 29 December 1744 the original commission was confirmed under a new Admiralty of which Anson was a member.

In April 1745 Brett was appointed to command the *Lion* (60 guns) in the channel. On 9 July off Ushant he fell in with the French ship *Elisabeth* (64 guns), a king's ship, nominally in private employ, but actually convoying the small frigate on board which Prince Charles Edward was taking passage to Scotland. The *Lion* and *Elisabeth* fought from 5 p.m. until 9 p.m., by which time the *Lion* was a wreck, with 45 killed and 107 wounded out of a complement of 400; and the *Elisabeth* was too badly damaged to continue her voyage. Although the frigate escaped to land Prince Charles in Scotland, his cause was much hampered because stores, arms, and money for his intended campaign were on board the *Elisabeth*.

In January 1745 Brett married Henrietta Colby (*d.* 1788), daughter of the clerk of the cheque at Chatham. They had two sons who died in infancy and one daughter, Henrietta, who later married Admiral Sir George Bowyer.

Early in 1747 Brett was appointed to the *Yarmouth* (64 guns), which he commanded in the action off Cape Finisterre on 3 May; that summer he was temporarily superseded by Captain Saunders; but he was reappointed in the autumn, and continued in the same ship until the end of 1750, during the latter part of which time the *Yarmouth* was guardship at Chatham.

In 1752 Brett was appointed to the yacht *Royal Caroline*, and in the following January, having taken the king over to Germany, he was knighted. In February 1754 he was one of a commission appointed to examine the condition of the port of Harwich, which was found to be silting up. He continued in command of the *Royal Caroline* until the end of 1757, and in January 1758 was appointed to the *Norfolk* as commodore in the Downs. During Anson's cruise off Brest in the summer of 1758 he acted as first captain of the *Royal George*, in a capacity since known as captain of the fleet. Afterwards he returned to the *Norfolk* and the Downs, and held that command until December 1761, during which period, in the summer of 1759, he was employed on a commission for examining the coasts of Essex, Kent, and Sussex, with a view to their defence against an enemy landing, upon which he made a report dated 15 June 1759. Early in 1762 he was sent out to the Mediterranean as second in command; soon afterwards he was promoted rear-admiral. He came home the following year and did not serve again at sea, though he was a lord commissioner of the Admiralty (1766–70) under Sir Edward Hawke. He was MP for Queenborough from 1754 to 1774. A supporter of the Grenville and Rockingham administration, he moved into opposition with the return of Lord Chatham as prime minister in 1766. He became a vice-admiral of the blue on 18 October and of the white on 24 October 1770, and admiral on 29 January 1778. He died on 14 October 1781 and was buried in a vault in Beckenham church in Kent; a tablet to his memory is in the church. Lady Brett survived her husband for only a few years; she died in August 1788, aged eighty-one, and was buried in the same vault in Beckenham church.   J. K. LAUGHTON, *rev.* ROGER MORRISS

Sources J. Charnock, ed., *Biographia navalis*, 5 (1797), 239 · *GM*, 1st ser., 51 (1781), 517, 623 · G. Williams, ed., *Documents relating to Anson's voyage round the world, 1740–1744*, Navy RS, 109 (1967) · J. Brooke, 'Brett, Sir Peircy', HoP, *Commons*
Archives NMM, letterbooks
Likenesses J. S. Müller, line engraving, BM, NPG; repro. in T. Smollett, *History of England* (1757)

Brett, Reginald Baliol, second Viscount Esher (1852–1930), courtier, was born on 30 June 1852 at 19 Prince's Terrace, Kensington, London, the eldest of three children of William Baliol *Brett, first Viscount Esher (1815–1899), barrister and later master of the rolls, and his wife, Eugénie (1814–1904), a Frenchwoman, daughter of Louis Mayer and a stepdaughter of Colonel John *Gurwood

Reginald Baliol Brett, second Viscount Esher (1852–1930), by Glyn Philpot, 1922

(1790–1845), the editor of Wellington's dispatches. The Bretts had been small squires, but they had no fixed estate. W. B. Brett acquired a moderate fortune at the bar, became a Conservative MP, solicitor-general, and in 1885 was ennobled by Lord Salisbury.

School and university Reginald Brett went to preparatory school at Cheam in 1863 and to Eton College in 1865. His five years at Eton were among the most important in his life. The political and romantic friendships he developed there influenced his later career and personality. They rendered Eton a lost golden age that he looked back upon with longing, nostalgia, and regret. His most influential master there, William Johnson (1823–1892), encouraged adolescent homoeroticism and historical study of heroic statesmen. Later, in 1872, Johnson had to resign from Eton, reportedly because of a scandal with a boy. He changed his surname to Cory, married, and lived in retirement, but Brett remained loyal and later published a memoir of him, *Ionicus* (1923).

Brett went to Trinity College, Cambridge, in 1870 (BA 1875, MA 1879, hon. LLD 1914). He soon met William Harcourt, then a barrister and Cambridge law professor, but later a leading Liberal politician. Harcourt let Brett occupy his rooms at Trinity. Brett's father was a Conservative, but influenced by Harcourt and a new Cambridge friend, son of the queen's former private secretary, Albert Grey, Brett became a Liberal, though he was perhaps most attracted by the style of the aristocratic whigs. He was admitted to the Middle Temple in April 1873 and called to the bar in 1881, but never practised as a lawyer.

Early career and marriage Late in 1877, on Harcourt's advice, Lord Hartington appointed Brett one of his private secretaries, starting in January 1878, which put him at the centre of Liberal politics. Brett wrote well and Hartington frequently used him as a speechwriter in their seven years together. Brett was Liberal MP for Penryn and Falmouth from 1880 to 1885. In November 1885 he unsuccessfully contested Plymouth, and he never again stood for elective office. The House of Commons was not his *milieu*. A private life in which he continued to have romantic relations with other men made him wary of publicity and of prominent office all his life. Working behind the scenes and in roles he tailored for himself suited him best.

On 24 September 1879 Brett married in Winkfield church Eleanor (Nellie) Frances Weston Van de Weyer (d. 7 February 1940), third and youngest daughter of Sylvain Van de Weyer, the Belgian ambassador. They had two sons, two daughters, and a happy marriage, despite Brett's male friends, or perhaps because his wife acknowledged and welcomed them. The Van de Weyers were friends of the queen and the newly-weds' move in 1884 to Orchard Lea, near Windsor, strengthened the connection. Association with the royal family was to be the key to much of Brett's later political influence and power. Among his varied friends were A. J. Balfour, Major-General Charles George Gordon—whom he greatly admired and whose death in January 1885 much affected him—and W. T. Stead. In 1884 he was secretly involved, with 'Jackie' Fisher and H. O. Arnold-Forster, in Stead's 'The Truth about the Navy' campaign.

After his parliamentary defeat in 1885 Brett resigned his post with Hartington. In the next ten years he wrote *Footprints of Statesmen during the Eighteenth Century in Britain* (1892) and *The Yoke of Empire, Sketches of the Queen's Prime Ministers* (1896). He raced horses, entertained, and decorated his house. None of this was enough to satisfy his ambitions. When his Eton contemporary Lord Rosebery became prime minister in 1894 and offered him the permanent secretaryship of the office of works in 1895, Brett accepted.

Monarchy The office of works was responsible for maintenance and decoration of state buildings, including royal palaces. Brett had installed a lift for Queen Victoria at Windsor Castle. He accompanied her to Kensington Palace and pushed her wheelchair around the rooms she had inhabited as a child. He also cultivated the prince of Wales, who asked him to serve on the committee to organize the diamond jubilee. Brett loved the theatre. He also agreed with Joseph Chamberlain's aim of closer imperial economic and defence unity. Under Brett's influence the diamond jubilee of 1897 was showier, more triumphal, and more imperial than previous London ceremonies. The jubilee organizers also persuaded the queen to drive south

of the river through Kennington. They were attempting to bring the monarchy into closer contact with both the empire abroad and the newly enfranchised working classes at home.

When the queen died in January 1901 Lord Esher, as Brett became on his father's death in May 1899, was the one to whom others turned for precedents for her funeral. He also played a prominent part on the committee which planned Edward VII's coronation, and on another which created a memorial to Queen Victoria by reconstructing the Mall as a processional route from Admiralty Arch to the statuary group in front of Buckingham Palace. These efforts led the monarchy to acquire a new reputation for ceremonial.

Esher also promoted the monarchy's role in politics. Edward VII gave him rooms at Windsor Castle and superintendence of the archives. He used these, and his friendship with the king's private secretary Francis Knollys, to inform and advise the king. He provided examples from Queen Victoria's papers to show that the sovereign had been better informed in the previous reign and to advocate that ministers submit more official business to the king for review.

Closely connected was Esher's editing of the queen's letters in collaboration with A. C. Benson. The first three volumes, *The Letters of Queen Victoria, 1837–1861*, were published in 1907. Another six volumes were edited by G. E. Buckle, on Esher's lines. Esher intended the *Letters* to show that the queen had been well informed and influenced policy. He also wanted to reveal the queen's character, to put her in a heroic light, and to make the *Letters* widely accessible. The *Letters* were a work of selection and were meant as a monument to her. He also edited two volumes on her youth, *The Girlhood of Queen Victoria* (1912), and published an essay on Edward VII after his death in 1910. He retained close links to George V and his private secretary, Lord Stamfordham, though of the sovereigns he served he was closest to Edward. He was appointed constable and governor of Windsor Castle in 1928, posts then normally reserved for royalty. Although formerly a Liberal, and from 1886 a Liberal Unionist, he was essentially a conservative who wanted the monarch to retain influence in an increasingly democratic constitution; however, he remained friendly with Liberals, especially Rosebery and John Morley. Although he increased the prestige of the monarchy's ceremonial and helped retain the monarch's right to be informed, he could not prevent the continued dwindling of the monarchy's political influence.

Army From his Eton schooldays Esher was interested in military history, and as private secretary to Hartington when secretary of state for war and chairman of the Hartington commission (1888–1890) he became concerned with defence reform. The commission recommended War Office reorganization with a board approximately on the Admiralty model, abolition of the commander-in-chief, and a general staff: these were not implemented. However, in the early years of the twentieth century the situation became favourable for Esher and the reforms he wanted, essentially those of the Hartington commission.

Edward VII, to whom he was confidant and adviser, became king; his friend Balfour became prime minister; and the South African War created a strong public and parliamentary demand for army reform. In November 1900 St John Brodrick (later earl of Midleton; 1856–1942) became secretary for war and Esher offered himself as permanent under-secretary at the War Office, hoping to influence policy. Brodrick refused, and thereafter opposed Esher's interference, including his attempts to have Roberts sacked from the command-in-chief. Later in his memoirs Brodrick wrote that Esher had 'power without responsibility' and that this 'usurpation of power by an outsider' caused 'endless contretemps' (Brodrick, 157, 149–50).

Esher was a member of the royal commission on the war in South Africa (the Elgin commission, 1902). Its report (1903) made no substantive reform recommendations but Esher dissented, advocating a War Office board. In September 1903 Balfour invited Esher to be war secretary, but he refused. He wrote to his son that he did not want to 'sacrifice all independence, all liberty of action … for a position which adds nothing to that which I now occupy' (Hamer, 224). Balfour appointed H. O. Arnold-Forster (1855–1909). He proposed major army reorganization, which provoked strong opposition and against which Esher intrigued. Arnold-Forster condemned Esher's 'constant interference' by 'an unauthorised and irresponsible person' (ibid., 226), blamed him for the rejection of the proposals, and never forgave him. Meanwhile, in 1903 at Esher's suggestion, Balfour appointed the War Office reconstitution committee (the Esher committee): Esher (chairman), Sir John Fisher, and Sir George Sydenham Clarke, 'all being root-and-branch reformers' (Clarke, 175). Its reports (1904) proposed radical War Office reorganization: abolition of the commander-in-chief and establishment of an army board and general staff. It also recommended a permanent secretariat for the committee of imperial defence (CID). Moreover the Esher committee insisted that 'new practices demand new men' (ibid., 236) and that the 'old gang' of Roberts and others must be replaced. Balfour rapidly implemented the War Office reform, and new men, mostly those favoured by Esher and his colleagues, were appointed. The War Office reform was crucial, introducing 'a functional structure designed to prepare the army for war' (Gooch, 'Boer war', 47). From 1905 Esher was a permanent member of the CID.

From 1905 to 1912 R. B. Haldane was secretary for war. Esher became his confidant and adviser, chaired his unofficial Territorial Army committee (1906)—nicknamed the Duma—and supported his reforms. Esher believed compulsory service ultimately necessary but politically unfeasible until the Territorial Force (TF) had been tried. He supported the TF and was chairman (1909–13) and later president (1912–21) of the London County Territorial Force Association. On the CID and its subcommittees he had an active role in defence planning. In 1909, for example, he unsuccessfully proposed, contrary to the rival War Office and Admiralty strategies for possible war with Germany, a strategy of naval blockades and raids, with a token land force to assist the French.

During the First World War, Esher served in France liaising informally between French and British generals. He spoke excellent French and perhaps because his mother was French he understood the French better than most. He also reported to his cabinet and court friends on the problems of the British staff officers. His role was not well defined and inspired the jealousy of the British ambassador. There had been similar protests in the newspapers about his 'irresponsible' influence before the war. While some distrusted him, others confided in him as a useful conduit to those in high office. Kitchener, Haig, Asquith, Balfour, Stamfordham, and George V regarded him as contributing to the war effort.

Retirement After the war Esher and his wife spent much time in Scotland. Although his parents had lived relatively modestly in London and at a small country place Esher used his paternal inheritance, about £130,000, to acquire houses in Mayfair, Windsor, and Perthshire. He also profited from his brief association (1901–4) with the City financier Ernest Cassel. Cassel was a crony of Edward VII who hired Esher to look after his interests in Egypt and America at a salary of £5000 a year and 10 per cent of the firm's profits.

In retirement Esher's activities were mainly literary. He had already published compilations of his journalism: *Today and Tomorrow* (1910) and *The Influence of King Edward* (1914). He published *After the War* (1918), a slim volume dedicated to Robert Smillie (1857–1940), the trade union leader, which argued against too radical reform of institutions, like the crown, of which leftist politicians were critical. He also wrote *The Tragedy of Lord Kitchener* (1921), describing Kitchener's flaws; some reviewers alleged that it was unfair and disloyal. In his autobiographical essays, *Cloud Capp'd Towers* (1927), Esher criticized Lytton Strachey and others for mocking the Victorians. At the end of his life he declared himself out of sympathy with the temper of the times.

Although on good terms with his wife at the end of his life, Esher did not have affectionate relationships with three of his four children. Neither Oliver (later third Lord Esher) nor Sylvia, who married the future raja of Sarawak, nor Dorothy *Brett, a painter who moved to New Mexico, felt they had been fairly treated by their father. Esher was unusually close to Maurice, his second son, with whom he had a passionate relationship, especially while the boy was at Eton. In later life Maurice bore his father no grudge, married actress Zena *Dare, and began editing his father's papers; after Maurice's death Oliver completed the project.

Esher died in the dressing room of his London house, 2 Tilney Street, Mayfair, on 22 January 1930 while preparing to meet a male protégé for lunch at Brooks's. He was buried in the family vault in the graveyard of the Esher parish church. He was succeeded by his elder son, Oliver Sylvain Baliol Brett (1881–1963).

Esher was intelligent, able, and arrogant, with a gift for friendship; an effective and adaptable organizer, negotiator, intermediary, and manipulator. He was an enigma to contemporaries and has puzzled historians. A controversial *éminence grise*, functioning largely behind closed doors and through others, his own achievement is difficult to assess. Edward VII liked and relied on Esher. As a result, Esher aroused the contempt and suspicion traditionally felt for courtiers and royal favourites. Some distrusted him as an irresponsible, devious intriguer who plotted, leaked confidential information, and interfered unconstitutionally in affairs of state. Some persons also distrusted his financial role and associates. Sir Charles Brooke, the raja of Sarawak, opposed the marriage of his heir, Vyner, to Esher's daughter Sylvia because he suspected a plutocratic plot, involving Esher, to exploit Sarawak. However, although Esher did not originate the defence reforms, his role in defence reform and planning contributed to British preparedness in 1914 and victory in 1918. Moreover the monarchy's success as a national and imperial symbol was partly due to his stage-management of its most prominent ceremonies.   WILLIAM M. KUHN

Sources J. Lees-Milne, *The enigmatic Edwardian: the life of Reginald, 2nd Viscount Esher* (1986) · P. Fraser, *Lord Esher: a political biography* (1973) · S. Heffer, *Power and place: the political consequences of King Edward VII* (1998) · Viscount Esher [R. B. B. Esher], *Cloud-capp'd towers* (1927) · W. M. Kuhn, *Democratic royalism* (1996) · *Journals and letters of Reginald, Viscount Esher*, ed. M. V. Brett and Oliver, Viscount Esher, 4 vols. (1934–8) · Venn, *Alum. Cant.* · GEC, *Peerage* · Burke, *Peerage* (1999) · W. S. Hamer, *The British army: civil–military relations, 1885–1905* (1970) · E. M. Spiers, *Haldane: an army reformer* (1980) · J. Gooch, *The plans of war: the general staff and British military strategy, c.1900–1916* (1974) · H. Strachan, *The politics of the British army* (1997) · W. St J. Brodrick, *Records and reactions, 1856–1939* (1939) · R. Williams, *Defending the empire: the conservative party and British defence policy, 1899–1915* (1991) · P. Smith, ed., *Government and the armed forces in Britain, 1856–1990* (1996) · J. Gooch, 'Britain and the Boer War', *The aftermath of defeat: societies, armed forces and the challenge of recovery*, ed. G. J. Andreopoulos and H. E. Selesky (1994), 40–58 · L. S. Amery, *My political life, 1: England before the storm* (1953) · Lord Sydenham of Combe [G. S. Clarke], *My working life* (1927) · R. F. MacKay, *Fisher of Kilverstone* (1973) · R. F. Mackay, *Balfour: intellectual statesman* (1985) · *CGPLA Eng. & Wales* (1930)

Archives CAC Cam., corresp. and papers · Royal Arch. | BL, corresp. with Arthur James Balfour, Add. MSS 49718–49719 · BL, corresp. with H. O. Arnold-Foster, Add. MS 50309, *passim* · BL, letters to Lord Gladstone, Add. MSS 46048–46086 · BL, corresp. with Lord Ripon, Add. MS 43544 · BL, corresp. with J. A. Spender, Add. MSS 46391–46392 · BL OIOC, letters to Lord Curzon, MSS Eur. F 111–112 · Bodl. Oxf., letters to H. H. Asquith; corresp. with Geoffrey Dawson; letters to Lewis Harcourt; corresp. with Lord Kimberley; corresp. with J. S. Sanders · CAC Cam., corresp. with Lord Randolph Churchill; letters to Lord Fisher; letters to W. T. Stead · Chatsworth House, Derbyshire, letters to eighth duke of Devonshire · CUL, corresp. with Lord Hardinge · HLRO, letters to David Lloyd George; corresp. with John St Loe Strachey · Houghton Hall, King's Lynn, letters to Sir Philip Sassoon · IWM, corresp. with H. A. Gwynne; corresp. with Sir Henry Wilson; papers relating to South African War Commission, etc. · JRL, letters to *Manchester Guardian* · NA Scot., corresp. with A. J. Balfour · NAM, letters to Earl Roberts · NL Scot., letters to Douglas Haig; corresp. with Lord Haldane; corresp. with Lord Rosebery · NL Wales, corresp. with Thomas Jones · NRA Scotland, priv. coll., corresp. with Sir John Ewart · PRO, corresp. with Lord Kitchener, PRO 30/57; WO 159 · Ransom HRC, letters · U. Birm. L., corresp. with Joseph Chamberlain · UCL, letters to Sir Francis Galton

Likenesses J. Storey, oils, *c.*1885 · E. Brock, oils, *c.*1905 · W. Strang, chalk drawing, 1907, Royal Collection · G. Philpot, oils, 1922, priv. coll. [*see illus.*] · W. Stoneman, photograph, 1923, NPG

Wealth at death £40,686 3s. 1d.: probate, 10 April 1930, *CGPLA Eng. & Wales*

Brett, Richard (1567/8–1637). *See under* Authorized Version of the Bible, translators of the (*act.* 1604–1611).

Brett, Robert (1808–1874), surgeon, was born on 11 September 1808, probably at or near Luton. As soon as he was old enough, he entered St George's Hospital, London, as a medical pupil, and passed his examinations, both as MRCSE and LSAL, in 1830. He then probably filled some hospital posts, and certainly married. At this time he wished to take holy orders and go abroad as a missionary, but he was dissuaded from such a step, and continued the practice of his profession. On the death of his wife he became an assistant to Samuel Reynolds, a surgeon at Stoke Newington, whose sister he married; he was Reynolds's partner for fourteen years. He had at least one daughter. He continued to practise at Stoke Newington until his death from heart disease and lung congestion on 3 February 1874.

Brett was an energetic Tractarian and an acquaintance of many of the leaders of the movement. It was his initiative that encouraged A. J. Beresford Hope to establish St Augustine's College, Canterbury. He was a member of W. E. Gladstone's lay fraternity, The Engagement. He founded the Guild of St Luke, a group of doctors and surgeons who co-operated with the clergy. He was active in church building at Stoke Newington and was a member of the first church union, being at his death a vice-president of the English Church Union. Brett published sixteen devotional books, mostly for use in hospitals or sick rooms. His funeral at Tottenham cemetery on 7 February 1874 was notable for the number of Tractarians who attended.   JOHN ASHTON, *rev.* H. C. G. MATTHEW

Sources Gladstone, *Diaries* · C. Matthew, 'Gladstone, evangelicalism and "the Engagement"', *Revival and religion since 1700: essays for John Walsh*, ed. J. Garnett and C. Matthew (1993), 111–26 · private information (1885)

Archives PL, corresp. with Archbishop Tait

Wealth at death under £3000: probate, 19 Feb 1874, *CGPLA Eng. & Wales*

Brett, Rosa [*pseud.* Rosarius] (1829–1882), painter, was born on 7 December 1829 and baptized at St George's, Camberwell, Surrey, on 26 March 1830, the eldest of the five children of Captain Charles Curtis Brett (1789–1865), veterinary surgeon in the 12th lancers, and his wife, Ann, *née* Pilbean (b. 1808/9), of Tonbridge, Kent. The artist John *Brett (1831–1902) was her brother.

Rosa Brett's childhood was peripatetic. Between 1833 and 1840 her father was stationed at various locations between Manchester and the south coast of England, from 1841 to 1843 in Ireland (Dublin and Dundalk), and it was not until 1846—after further postings in Manchester, Nottingham, and Coventry—that the family finally settled in the Maidstone area of Kent (Mrs Brett's birthplace), where Charles Brett remained permanently based in the cavalry depot. During the 1850s they occupied various addresses on the north-eastern outskirts of Maidstone—at Penenden Heath, then on the Boxley Road, and from 1858 to 1860 at Lynchfield House, Detling.

It is not known whether Brett received art instruction but by December 1850 she was sufficiently proficient to sell a drawing. She was very close to her brother, John Brett, and frequently worked with him, even after his entry into the Royal Academy Schools in 1853. The influence on her brother of the landscape painter J. D. Harding (they met in January 1851), who encouraged working outdoors directly from nature and the scientific study of natural subject matter, and the inspiration of John Ruskin (first read by John Brett in 1852) undoubtedly filtered through to Rosa also. Both sketched in the Vale of Boxley and on the chalk hills of the north downs, trees being a favourite subject: *Birch Tree in our Lawn* (1852; exh. Maas Gallery, London, 1991) is typical of her meticulous approach. Rosa Brett suffered from recurrent illness in the 1850s and her visits to Folkestone in 1852 and to Belgium for four months in 1855 (both of which produced outdoor sketches) may well have been undertaken for health reasons. In 1858, the year in which John Brett's *The Stonebreaker* appeared at the Royal Academy, Rosa exhibited *The Hayloft* (photograph Courtauld Inst., Witt Library), an indoor scene of a cat on hay, at both the Royal Academy—where it received praise from the Pre-Raphaelites—and the Liverpool Academy. The picture was submitted from a Dublin address under the pseudonym Rosarius, a name she retained for exhibiting purposes until 1862.

In 1860 the Brett family moved to Barming Heath, a village on the western side of Maidstone, and from 1861 until *c*.1870 occupied 45 Tonbridge Road in Maidstone itself. Throughout the 1860s and 1870s—they moved again, to Fant in the early 1870s and further afield, to Rochester, about 1875—Brett continued to produce landscapes, in oil and watercolour: *In the Artist's Garden* (*c*.1859–60; exh. 'Pre-Raphaelite Women Artists', Manchester City Art Gallery, 1997), *Heathland* (1879; ex Sothebys, 12 November 1992), *They Toil not neither do they Spin* (1879; ex Sothebys, 12 November 1992), and *Study of a Turnip Field* (exh. 'Landscape in Britain', Tate Gallery, 1973) were all executed in oil. She also painted buildings, with a Ruskinian attention to detail, examples being *Detling Church* (1858; ex Sothebys, Belgravia, 18 April 1978) and *The Old House at Farleigh* (1862; exh. 'Pre-Raphaelite Women Artists', Manchester City Art Gallery, 1997), a few portraits (chiefly of her family), and, increasingly, natural still lifes of plants and small animals, such as *A Thrush in a Horse Chestnut Tree* (exh. Liverpool Academy, 1860), *Thistles* (exh. RA, 1861), *The Field-Mice at Home* (exh. RA, 1867), and *Starling and Bluetit* (exh. RA, 1876). Occasional figure subjects include a richly coloured oil of two ladies in a garden (1864; ex Sothebys, 19 June 1984), one of them holding a lily, which recalls early work by Millais. Brett's paintings were not often shown: she exhibited nine at the Royal Academy (1858–81), four in Liverpool (1858–72), one in Manchester (1867), and two with the Society of Lady Artists (1880, 1881). Her sketchbooks, however (two of which are in the National Maritime Museum, Greenwich), and works in private collections testify to considerable industry. She remained close to her brother, John, with whom she spent occasional holidays in Wales and in 1867 visited the notorious Georgina

Weldon in Beaumaris on the Isle of Anglesey; her last exhibits, in 1880 and 1881, were submitted from his studio at 38 Harley Street in London. In his diary, John described Rosa affectionately as 'ardent, impulsive and unbendable' (entry dated 25 Dec 1858; Cordingly, 5). Brett died, unmarried, at Caterham, Surrey, on 31 January 1882.

CHARLOTTE YELDHAM

Sources P. Gerrish Nunn, 'Rosa Brett, Pre-Raphaelite', *Burlington Magazine*, 126 (1984), 630–34 [incl. list of works] · D. Cordingly, 'The life of John Brett: painter of Pre-Raphaelite landscapes and seascapes', PhD diss., U. Sussex, 1983 · *Pre-Raphaelite women artists* (1997) [exhibition catalogue, Manchester City Art Gallery] · *John Ruskin and his circle* (1991) [exhibition catalogue, Maas Gallery, London] · J. Soden and C. Baile de Laperrière, eds., *The Society of Women Artists exhibitors, 1855–1996*, 4 vols. (1996) · Graves, *RA exhibitors* · E. Morris and E. Roberts, *The Liverpool Academy and other exhibitions of contemporary art in Liverpool, 1774–1867* (1998) · exhibition catalogue (1867) [Royal Manchester Institution] · artist's file, archive material, Courtauld Inst., Witt Library · d. cert.
Archives NMM, sketchbooks

Brett, Thomas (1667–1744), bishop of the nonjuring Church of England, was born on 3 September 1667 at Betteshanger, near Sandwich, Kent, the son of Thomas Brett (1640–1695) and Letitia Boys (1644–1731). He was educated at the Wye grammar school, under John Paris and Samuel Pratt (afterwards dean of Rochester), from 1674 until his admission to Queens' College, Cambridge, on 20 March 1684. Recalled home by his father in 1687 he returned to school, and moved to Corpus Christi College, Cambridge, on 17 January 1690. He received an LLB from Corpus Christi (1690) and an LLD from Queens' College (1697). Ordained deacon on 21 December 1690, he held the curacy at Folkestone before being ordained to the priesthood on 20 September 1691. He was chosen as lecturer at Islington on 4 October 1691, and there began his conversion from whig principles to tory and high-church principles.

After the death of his father Brett moved in May 1696 to Spring Grove at his mother's request. There he took the cure of Great Chart, Kent, and married Bridget Toke (1677–1765), daughter of Sir Nicholas Toke, on 22 September 1696; they had twelve children. In 1697 he moved to Wye, Kent, before becoming the rector at Betteshanger on the death of his uncle, Thomas Boys, in 1703. On 12 April 1705 Thomas Tenison, archbishop of Canterbury, made him rector of Ruckinge, and allowed him to hold the vicarage of Chislet 'in sequestration'.

Having earlier taken the oaths without scruple, the trial of Sacheverell in 1710 convinced Brett never to take the oaths again. His growing attachment to the exiled monarchy did not prevent him from preaching twice before Queen Anne (1711 and 1713). John Sharp, archbishop of York, had issued the second invitation while Brett was under censure by Archbishop Tenison for his sermon on the remission of sins. That sermon, which exhibited a high view of sacerdotal absolution, was preached in three London churches in the autumn of 1711. The published version led to further attacks in convocation on 22 February 1712. The proposed censure was dropped, apparently at the behest of Francis Atterbury, prolocutor of the lower house of the convocation of Canterbury. In another politically related work, *The Review of the Lutheran Principles* (1714), Brett called into question the validity of Lutheran orders and sacraments, which was important as the new king was Lutheran. On the accession of George I, Brett declined to take the oaths, resigned his livings, and was received into communion by the nonjuring bishop George Hickes. Following his conversion, he led a small congregation that met in his house. In 1716 he was presented to the assizes for keeping a conventicle, but was cleared by an act of indemnity and continued to lead his congregation. His secession from the church led to charges of popery, which he responded to in *Dr Brett's Vindication of himself* (1715), where he dismissed the charges and claimed to hold to the primitive church.

Brett and Henry Gandy were consecrated as bishops by Jeremy Collier, Nathaniel Spinckes, and Samuel Hawes on 25 January 1716 at Scroops Court, Holborn, London. That year the nonjurors began discussions with the Greek bishop of Thebes, Arsenius, then in London concerning a concordat with the Eastern church. The bishops prepared a document, which they sent with Arsenius to the Russian tsar, Peter the Great, and by him to the Eastern patriarchs. The discussions continued until Peter's death in 1725. Brett also joined Collier in proposing a return to the first liturgy of Edward VI (1549), which they deemed closer to the primitive liturgies. He defended his position in his *Tradition Necessary to Explain and Interpret the Holy Scriptures* (1718). Brett and Thomas Deacon then created a new liturgy in accordance with their principles. This led to a schism within the nonjuror church over the restoration of four usages: the oblation, invocation of the Holy Spirit, prayers for the dead, and the mixed chalice. After the death of Jeremy Collier in 1726, Brett became the primus for the usager party. In that capacity he later sought to heal the schism; with the help of nonusager bishop George Smith of Durham, he drew up a concordat that was signed in April and May 1732, thus ending the schism, though a significant number on both sides continued to maintain their separation.

Brett remained active in the nonjuror movement until his death, though after 1737 he did not travel far from his home at Spring Grove. A prodigious writer, Brett's liturgical works included *The Christian Altar and Sacrifice* (1713), *Collection of the Principal Liturgies, used by the Christian Church in the Celebration of the Holy Eucharist* (1720), and *Some Remarks on Dr. Waterland's Review of the Doctrine of the Eucharist* (1736). The latter work challenged Daniel Waterland's refusal to use the language of material sacrifice in the eucharist, though Waterland recognized that the liturgy had sacrificial implications. He defended the independence of the church from the state in *The Independency of the Church upon the State as to its Pure Spiritual Powers* (1717), and the divine foundations of the episcopacy in *The Divine Right of the Episcopacy* (1718). Brett contributed several works in support of Roger Laurence in the lay baptism controversy, including *An Enquiry into the Judgement and Practice of the Primitive Church* and *The Extent of Christ's Commission to Baptize* (both 1712). He also published a collection of six sermons in 1715, which included his controversial sermon 'On remission of sins'. Brett died at Spring Grove on 5 March 1744 and was interred in the family vault at Wye, Kent. He was survived by his wife, who died on 7 March 1765, and their son Nicholas (1713–1776), a nonjuring Church of England priest and chaplain to Sir Robert Cotton of Steeple Gidding, Huntingtonshire.

ROBERT D. CORNWALL

Sources Nichols, *Lit. anecdotes*, 1.407–10 · Venn, *Alum. Cant.*, 1/1.211 · H. Broxap, *The later nonjurors* (1924) · R. Cornwall, *Visible and apostolic: the constitution of the church in high Anglican and non-juror thought* (1993) · W. Kennett, *A letter about a motion in convocation* (1712) · T. Lathbury, *A history of the nonjurors* (1845) · S. Runciman, 'The British nonjurors and the Russian church', *The ecumenical world of Orthodox civilization*, ed. T. E. Bird and A. Blane (1974), 155–61 · R. Cornwall, 'Advocacy of the independence of the church from the state in eighteenth century England', *Enlightenment and Dissent*, 12 (1993), 12–27 · J. H. Overton, *The nonjurors: their lives, principles, and writings* (New York, 1903)
Archives Bodl. Oxf., corresp. and papers · LPL, corresp., papers, and sermons · priv. coll., MSS | BL, papers relating to Wye College, Add. MSS 5514–5515 · NL Scot., letters to Archibald Campbell

Brett, William Baliol, first Viscount Esher (1815–1899), judge, was born on 13 August 1815 at the rectory, Lenham, Kent, the second son of the Revd Joseph George Brett (d. 20 May 1852), of Ranelagh, Chelsea, who was for many years the incumbent of Hanover Chapel, Regent Street, and his wife, Dorothy, daughter of George Best of Chilston Park, Kent. Brett was educated at Westminster School and at Gonville and Caius College, Cambridge. While at Cambridge he distinguished himself as a rower, being part of the crew which defeated Oxford in the first annual boat race, in 1839. He graduated BA (senior optime) in 1840, and received his MA in 1845.

Admitted to Lincoln's Inn on 30 April 1839, and called to the bar on 29 January 1846, Brett rapidly built up an extensive commercial and marine practice on the northern circuit, and was a successful practitioner in the court of passage at Liverpool and the court of Admiralty at Westminster. He also had a considerable bankruptcy practice, and for a time he was revising barrister for a Liverpool district. Solid and practical rather than obviously brilliant, he was a fluent speaker who was highly popular with juries. On 3 April 1850 he married Eugénie Mayer (1814–1904), only daughter of Louis Mayer, and stepdaughter of Colonel Gurwood CB. He became a queen's counsel in 1860 and a bencher in 1861.

An ardent tory (as he styled himself), who favoured moderate extension of the franchise, Brett contested the seat of Rochdale on the death of Richard Cobden in April 1865, unsurprisingly losing to Cobden's friend Thomas Bayley Potter. In the following year he contested Helston in Cornwall. The two candidates receiving the same number of votes, the mayor declared Brett's opponent returned; Brett successfully petitioned the Commons against this decision, thereby gaining the seat for himself in July 1866. In parliament, his experience as a revising barrister made him very useful to the government in committee on franchise questions. He also contributed to the legislation conferring Admiralty jurisdiction on the county courts. On 10 February 1868 he was appointed solicitor-general, in which capacity he prosecuted various Fenians over the Clerkenwell prison explosion.

On 24 August 1868 Brett was appointed a justice of the court of common pleas; his judgment in the gas stokers' case in 1872, imprisoning the stokers, effectively overturned the Liberal government's trade union legislation. On the fusion of the superior courts in 1875, he became initially a justice of the Common Pleas Division, then (on 27 October 1876) a justice of appeal. Eventually, on 3 April 1883, he became master of the rolls, in succession to George Jessel. He was created Baron Esher of Esher in Surrey on 24 July 1885. In many ways a common-law traditionalist, he thought highly of juries, which he directed genially but forcefully. In criminal matters he opposed Bramwell's attempt to allow defendants and their spouses to give evidence. He was, however, in favour of a court of criminal appeal. In matters of civil law too he was very much the traditionalist, speaking against equitable innovations in common-law procedure—though he noted on more than one occasion that the two were not as different as had sometimes been suggested. He was by no means incapable of handling technical issues, but had little patience for them. His brusque and direct manner—a characteristic utterance being that law was not a science but rather the practical application of right and wrong— was regarded by some as the epitome of good sense, and by others as alarmingly simplistic. His manner in court to members of the public, whether jurors or not, was open and friendly, and indeed many barristers thought that he played too much to the gallery. With the bar he was a much sterner figure, disdainful of over-technical approaches, contemptuous of the convention that he should pretend to know nothing that had not been proved in evidence, and often descending into mere rudeness or bullying. He was not active in the Lords, speaking only on technical legal questions, and being responsible for only one piece of legislation, the Solicitors Act of 1888, which tightened discipline over solicitors.

Though a commanding figure at the time, Brett left comparatively few judgments of significance in later years. His greatest displays of erudition were in the criminal law, notably his judgment in *Prince* (1875) and his (dissenting) judgment in *Keyn* (1876). His minority judgment in *Heaven* v. *Pender* (1883), though of little impact then, can now be seen as a precursor to Lord Atkin's famous opinion in *Donoghue* v. *Stevenson* (1932), and thus to prefigure the flowering of the tort of negligence in the twentieth century.

Brett retired in 1897, and received the title Viscount Esher on 11 November of that year. He died at his town house, 6 Ennismore Gardens, Kensington, London, on 24 May 1899. His remains were interred in the family vault at Moor Place, Esher, the seat of his younger brother; in Esher churchyard there is an elaborate monument. He

was succeeded by his elder son, Reginald Baliol *Brett. A younger son, Lieutenant Eugène Leopold Brett, had died on 8 December 1882 of fever contracted in Egypt.

STEVE HEDLEY

Sources Law Times (10 May 1902) · Law Journal (23 Oct 1897) · Solicitors' Journal, 43 (1898–9), 505–6 · H. D. Ward, A romance of the 19th century (1923) · DNB · M. C. Curthoys, 'Trade union legislation 1871–6', DPhil diss., U. Oxf., 1988
Archives CAC Cam., corresp. with second Lord Esher · U. Birm., corresp. with Joseph Chamberlain
Likenesses Lock & Whitfield, woodburytype, NPG; repro. in T. Cooper, Men of mark: a gallery of contemporary portraits (1877), pl. 31 · effigy on monument, Esher churchyard, Surrey, Esher family vault · oils, Gon. & Caius Cam. · photograph, carte-de-visite, NPG
Wealth at death £82,726 9s. 2d.: resworn probate, March 1900, CGPLA Eng. & Wales (1899)

Brettargh, Katharine. *See* Brettergh, Katherine (1579–1601).

Brettell, Jacob (1793–1862), Unitarian minister and poet, was born at Sutton in Ashfield, Nottinghamshire, on 16 April 1793, the only son of Jacob Brettell (d. 1810) and his second wife, Anne Cates (d. 1817), the widow of a Mr Sudbury of Fakenham, Norfolk. The elder Brettell, whose own father had preached as an Independent and then as a Calvinistic Methodist, became a Calvinistic preacher at seventeen and eventually settled in Sutton in 1788, where he renounced Calvinism and in 1791 opened a separate meeting-house. In 1795 he became assistant to Jeremiah Gill, minister of the 'presbyterian or independent' chapel at Gainsborough, becoming sole pastor on Gill's death in 1796. Brettell, who also kept a school, died on 19 March 1810.

The younger Brettell had entered Manchester College, York, in 1809; after his father's death a public subscription, aided by the vicar of Gainsborough, allowed him to remain there until 1814. In July of that year he became minister to the congregation at Cockey Moor chapel in Ainsworth, Lancashire, which had been seriously divided when the previous minister, Joseph Bealey (1756–1813), moved from Arianism to Unitarianism. The Unitarian majority prevailed in appointing Brettell, who was committed to the humanity of Christ, but his early departure for Rotherham in September 1816 may be explained by continuing congregational differences. He remained at Rotherham until his retirement in June 1859. The chapel was almost completely rebuilt in 1841.

Brettell is described as a good scholar and an effective public speaker, though the length of one sermon at mid-century, while much admired by one elderly member, provoked a younger hearer (Blazeby, 178–9) to some rueful reflections on the sermon's text John, 7: 46, 'Never man spake like this man'. A strong liberal, as is evidenced by the dedication of his major poetical work to Viscount Milton, later the fifth Earl Fitzwilliam, Brettell took an active part in the anti-corn law agitation and was an intimate friend of Ebenezer Elliott (1781–1849), the corn law rhymer, whose poetry he improved through his criticism. Dedicated to religious liberty, Brettell opened his chapel in 1847 to Joseph Barker (1806–1875), at that point a Chartist whom the magistrates had refused to allow to speak in the court house, and continued to invite him to speak, as did his successor William Blazeby (1832–1908).

On 29 December 1815 Brettell had married Martha (d. 1864), daughter of James Morris of Bolton; they had two daughters and four sons. The two youngest sons, seriously disabled, led a precarious existence as proprietors of a stationery shop and were a source of deep concern to their father. The younger, Francis, died aged thirty-eight in 1868, and the elder married a daughter of Robert Shenton (1805?–1889), the Apostle of the Peak, who ministered to several small Unitarian congregations in Derbyshire. Brettell continued to live in Rotherham after his retirement, a rather old-fashioned figure. In his later years he suffered from 'softening of the brain', and died on 12 January 1862 at Rotherham. He was never well off, and no personal estate is recorded.

Brettell's best-known poem is the partly autobiographical *The Country Minister*, its couplets modelled on Goldsmith and Crabbe, published in 1821 and revised and expanded in 1825 and 1827. He had originally intended to write on the evils of ministerial poverty (his initial salary at Rotherham was £46), but friends pointed out a possible awkwardness in Goldsmith's reference in *The Deserted Village* to a village preacher 'passing rich with forty pounds a year', and Brettell expanded his vision to the daily round of ministerial life. In 1826 he brought out *Sketches in Verse, from the Historical Books of the Old Testament*. He was a prolific writer of hymns, some of which, altered not always to their advantage, appeared in Unitarian hymnals. He contributed hundreds of religious, political, and patriotic pieces to the *Christian Reformer*, the *Sheffield Iris*, the *Wolverhampton Herald*, and other periodicals.

His eldest son, **Jacob Charles Cates Brettell** (1817–1867), lawyer, born on 6 March 1817 at Rotherham, began to study for the ministry at Manchester College, York. He subsequently became a Roman Catholic, and emigrated to the United States, where he was successively classical tutor in New York, minister of a German church, and a successful member of the bar in Virginia and Texas. He died at Owensville, Texas, on 17 January 1867.

R. K. WEBB

Sources W. Blazeby, *Rotherham old meeting house and its ministers…* (1906) · *DNB* · parish register, Ainsworth, Cockey Moor chapel, Lancs. RO, UAi7 · d. cert. · register of births, 6 March 1817, Rotherham chapel, Yorkshire [J. C. C. Brettell] · letters [Morris Brettell], 18 Feb–11 March 1885, JRL, Alexander Gordon MSS, GOR 1/67

Brettell, Jacob Charles Cates (1817–1867). *See under* Brettell, Jacob (1793–1862).

Brettergh [*née* Bruen], **Katherine** (1579–1601), exemplar of godly life, was born in February 1579, the daughter of John Bruen (1510–1587), and his wife, Dorothy Holford, at Bruen Stapleford, Cheshire, and was baptized there on 13 February. Only eight years old when her father died, her short life was dominated by her illustrious elder brother, the godly gentleman John *Bruen, who had care of Katherine and ten of her siblings, bringing them up in an atmosphere of strict household discipline and rigorous religious observance. About 1599 Katherine married another of the self-professed godly, William Brettergh (b. c.1571), of Brettergh Holt, near Liverpool, with whom she had one child, Anne. The two shared an extraordinarily pious lifestyle at Little Woolton in Childwall, Lancashire, reading at least eight chapters of the Bible every day and hearing two sermons on Sundays whenever possible, and she appears to have stiffened his resolve in withstanding the hostility, mockery, and harassment of the parish's strong Roman Catholic minority, organized by a local seminary priest, Thurstan Hunt, and the lord of the manors of Speke and Garston, Edward Norris. In turn, William Brettergh's attempt as high constable of West Derby hundred to apprehend recusants within the parishes of Huyton and Childwall in May 1600 provoked not only a full-scale riot but the maiming of Brettergh's cattle on two separate occasions over the following months.

However, it is Katherine's premature and agonizing death rather than her short life which brought her most fame, and which provoked the biographies that provide virtually all the evidence of her godly lifestyle. At the age of twenty-two she succumbed to an unknown illness, and on her deathbed suffered from a terrible crisis of faith, during which she raged against God's unmercifulness and threw her Bible repeatedly to the floor. She died on 31 May 1601. Her agonies formed the centrepiece of a polemical account of her embattled life appended to the two sermons preached by William Harrison and William Leigh at her funeral in Childwall church on 3 June 1601, published together in 1602 as *Death's Advantage Little Regarded*, of which five editions had appeared by 1617 and a further two by 1641. Harrison in particular attempted to explain her deathbed anguish as the consequence of a diabolical assault on her virtue rather than a providential punishment for sin and hypocrisy. As a result her death became not only a gigantic struggle between God and Satan for her soul, but also, through a pamphlet exchange (of which the Catholic side has unfortunately not survived), a furious debate between Romanists and puritans over which religion could promise the more merciful death. From this perspective the conspicuous absence of any reference to Katherine's deathbed crisis in William Hinde's elaborate biography of her older brother, published in 1641, seems striking, perhaps even deliberately evasive.

Katherine's husband's second marriage, to Anne Hyde of Urmston, took place at Stockport on 5 August 1602, though the union was less characterized by puritan self-discipline than might be expected. Their son, Nehemiah, was renowned for his drunkenness and fought on the royalist side in the civil war.

STEVE HINDLE

Sources W. Harrison and W. Leigh, *Death's advantage little regarded, and The soules solace against sorrow … whereunto is annexed, the Christian life and godly death of the said gentlewoman*, 1st–5th edns (1602–17); later edns as *The Christian life and death, of Mistris Katherin Brettergh* (1634–) [later edns as *The Christian life and death of Mistris Katherin Brettergh* (1641–)] · W. Hinde, *A faithful remonstrance of the holy life and happy death of John Bruen of Bruen Stapleford* (1641) · G. Ormerod, *The history of the county palatine and city of Chester*, 2nd edn, ed. T. Helsby, 2 (1882), 320–22 · PRO, STAC 5/A8/31 · PRO, SP

12/275/102, 115 • PRO, SP 12/304/20 • *VCH Lancashire*, 3.119 • R. G. Dottie, 'The recusant riots at Childwall in May 1600: a reappraisal', *Seventeenth-century Lancashire: essays presented to J. J. Bagley*, ed. J. I. Kermode and C. B. Phillips (1983), 1–28 • B. W. Quintrell, 'Government in perspective: Lancashire and the privy council, 1570–1640', *Transactions of the Historic Society of Lancashire and Cheshire*, 131 (1981), 35–62 • P. Collinson, '"A magazine of religious patterns": an Erasmian topic transposed in English protestantism', *Godly people: essays in English protestantism and puritanism* (1983), 499–525 • R. N. Watson, *The rest is silence: death as annihilation in the English renaissance* (1994), 306–15 • R. C. Richardson, *Puritanism in north-west England: a regional study of the diocese of Chester to 1642* (1972)

Likenesses line engraving, BM, NPG; repro. in S. Clarke, *The marrow of ecclesiastical history* (1650) • portrait, repro. in Harrison and Leigh, *Death's advantage little regarded*

Brettingham, Matthew, the elder (1699–1769), architect, was born in Norwich, the son of Lancelot Brettingham (1664–1727) and his wife, Elizabeth Hillwell (*d.* 1729), of the parish of St Giles. Lancelot Brettingham was called a mason in the city poll-book recording the parliamentary election of 1714. Both Matthew and his elder brother Robert were apprenticed, as bricklayers, to their father and, having served their time, both brothers were made freemen of the city of Norwich on 3 May 1719.

Matthew Brettingham's transition from builder and craftsman to architect was gradual. Pivotal to this process was his appointment in 1734, at an annual salary of £50, as clerk of works for the building of Holkham Hall on the north Norfolk coast, a large Palladian mansion based on the designs of William Kent with a major input of ideas from the patron, Thomas Coke, earl of Leicester. Brettingham's work at Holkham, which included the design of a number of structures in the park and was to extend over a score of years, earned him the respect and friendship of his employer and provided him with contacts which were to prove critical in the development of his career. His public work at this time, all within the bounds of Norfolk, included: the construction, in 1741, of Lenwade Bridge across the River Wensum; the rebuilding of the nave and crossing of St Margaret's Church in King's Lynn, damaged by the collapse of the spire in 1742; the raising of the new shire hall at Norwich Castle in 1747–9 and, over the same period, repairs to the castle itself; and repairs to Norwich Cathedral. Brettingham received a number of commissions for the design and remodelling of country houses in the 1740s which were initially confined to the county of Norfolk: the halls at Hanworth, Heydon, Honingham, and Langley were altered, while the hall at Gunton was an entirely new structure.

The outward extension of Brettingham's country-house practice in the late 1740s coincided, more or less, with his increasing presence in London which, as his surviving account books show, from 1747 and for most of the next two decades, was the centre of his activity. His first major London commission was, appropriately, the building of Norfolk House in St James's Square for Edward Howard, ninth duke of Norfolk. Other work followed in St James's Square, Piccadilly, and Pall Mall. Engravings for the house in Pall Mall, raised in 1761–3 for Edward Augustus, duke of York, appeared in volume 4 of *Vitruvius Britannicus*, published in 1767. Brettingham's country-house work in these years included alterations to Goodwood, in Sussex (1750), Marble Hill, Twickenham (1750–51), Euston Hall, Suffolk (1750–56), Moor Park, Hertfordshire (1751–4), Petworth House, Sussex (1751–63), Wortley Hall, Yorkshire (1757–9), Wakefield Lodge, Northamptonshire (1759), Benacre House, Suffolk (1762–4), and Packington Hall, Warwickshire (1766–9).

Brettingham's architecture has been described as an unexciting, if dignified, variety of Palladianism. His practice was, however, successful, and the secret of his success was his ability to adapt the grander ideas of others to the purposes of his clients, confining himself to a limited number of design themes. His corner-towered scheme for Langley was, essentially, a restatement of the same theme at Holkham; the minimal Palladianism of Norfolk House, the façade of which was no more than blank walling relieved only by door- and window-cases and a parapet, a continuation of the minimalist treatment he had observed at Hanworth and which he himself had followed earlier at Gunton. Having encountered difficulties in obtaining ashlar, the earl of Leicester settled for the facing of Holkham Hall with white brick: Brettingham was to repeat the use of white brick at Gunton and again at Norfolk House, arranging, for Norfolk House, for the bricks to be made at Holkham and brought to London. Brettingham's forays into Gothic and his use of round arches, as in the nave arcades of St Margaret's, King's Lynn, and the galleried exterior of the shire hall in Norwich, indicate the approach of an engineer rather than an antiquary and are now seen as outlandish. It was towards the end of his working life, in 1761, that Brettingham published *The Plans, Elevations and Sections of Holkham in Norfolk*, with his own name inscribed on the plates as 'architect'. Critics, from Horace Walpole onwards, have assumed that Brettingham was claiming the credit for Kent's designs but he himself may have used the inscription, legitimately from his view, to indicate his status as executive architect and draughtsman.

Matthew Brettingham died in his own house in the Norwich parish of St Augustine on 19 August 1769 and, as epitaphs in the parish church state, is buried in a vault at the east end of the north aisle, alongside his wife, Martha Bunn (*c.*1697–1783), whom he had married on 17 May 1721; their resting places are close to those of two of their sons, Matthew *Brettingham the younger (1725–1803) and Robert Brettingham. Nine children were born to him and his wife and all those for whom baptismal records have been identified were baptized in the church of St Augustine.

ROBIN LUCAS

Sources epitaphs of Matthew Brettingham and family, St Augustine's, Norwich • will of Matthew Brettingham the elder, PRO, PROB 11/951, sig. 300 • account books of Matthew Brettingham the elder, 1747–64, PRO, C 108/362 • L. Schmidt, *Thomas Coke, 1st earl of Leicester: an eighteenth-century amateur architect* (1980) • D. E. H. James, 'Matthew Brettingham and the county of Norfolk', *Norfolk Archaeology*, 33 (1962–5), 345–50 • D. E. H. James, 'Matthew Brettingham's account book', *Norfolk Archaeology*, 35 (1970–73), 170–82 • C. Hiskey, 'The building of Holkham Hall: newly discovered letters', *Architectural History*, 40 (1997), 144–58 • W. Brettingham, *De*

Brettenham and Brettingham: an English family history (1971) • Colvin, *Archs.* • S. J. Wearing, *Georgian Norwich: its builders* (1926) • P. Millican, *The freemen of Norwich, 1714–52: a transcript of the third register*, Norfolk RS, 23 (1952) • IGI
Archives PRO, account books, C 108/362 | Norfolk RO, Norfolk Quarter Sessions, order books and bills submitted
Likenesses J. T. Heinz, oils, RIBA • portrait, RIBA
Wealth at death real estate in Saint Clement outside Saint Augustine's Gates (Norwich) left to wife; annuity of £70 left to son; lands left to sons in Weston Longville, the rents of which were to be assigned to the support of his unmarried daughters: will, PRO, PROB 11/951, sig. 300, 1769

Brettingham, Matthew, the younger (1725–1803), architect, was probably born in Norwich, the eldest of the nine children of Martha Bunn (*c*.1697–1783) and the architect Matthew *Brettingham the elder (1699–1769). His father was from 1734 executant architect of Holkham Hall, Norfolk, and designer of the garden buildings there for Thomas Coke, later earl of Leicester (1697–1759). It was under his father that Matthew the younger first learned the practice of architecture. In August 1747 he was sent, aged twenty-two, to Italy to further his architectural studies, and arrived in Rome on 14 November. Lord Leicester evidently not only contributed substantially to the travel and maintenance costs but also had sufficient confidence in the younger Brettingham's judgement to entrust him with considerable sums of money with which to purchase statues and pictures on behalf of himself, Lord Dartmouth, and others to be shipped back, some of them for resale, to Britain. In April 1748 Brettingham and the architects and architectural draughtsmen James Stuart and Nicholas Revett, accompanied by the recently arrived Scottish painter Gavin Hamilton, walked from Rome to Naples and back. By 1751 Brettingham was sharing the Palazzo Zuccari in Rome with Joshua Reynolds, Thomas Patch, Joseph Wilton, and other artists.

In Italy, Brettingham was mainly occupied with arranging for moulds to be made from the best antique decorations and statues in the principal Roman collections and elsewhere, from which unlimited copies could be cast in Britain. He envisaged casts as the central feature of a proposed academy of design, long discussed in London, for which he made several grand designs. The scheme came to nothing, but subsequently, in 1758, the duke of Richmond opened a cast room at his house in Whitehall under Wilton's direction. Brettingham's sales of casts were similarly unsuccessful, and most of them went to houses where his father was architect. Some went to Holkham, Kedleston Hall, Derbyshire, and Petworth House, Sussex. Several of the paintings he acquired, including copies of Raphael, went to the duke of Northumberland's new gallery at Northumberland House in London, and two landscapes by Claude went to Holkham. Brettingham's time in Italy was highly lucrative, though many dealers and artists, perhaps envious, considered him grasping and, as Robert Adam wrote from Rome to his brother James in 1755 a year after Brettingham's departure, 'his genius [was] much inferior to his fortune' (Kenworthy-Browne, 47).

After returning to Britain via Germany and the Netherlands in 1754, Brettingham spent some years deputizing, chiefly at Holkham, for his father, whose architectural practice was flourishing. He later bought statues for Charles Wyndham, second earl of Egremont (1710–1763), a member of the Society of Dilettanti, for the sculpture gallery at Petworth. On the earl's appointment in the spring of 1761 as plenipotentiary to the congress of Augsburg to arrange terms of peace with France, Brettingham accompanied him to Germany to supervise his accommodation. Under the patronage of Lord North, whom he had met in Rome, Brettingham hoped to succeed Henry Flitcroft as comptroller of the works, but George III was determined in 1769 to appoint William Chambers to the post. As a consolation North appointed Brettingham president of the board of greencloth, and subsequently to the comparatively lucrative sinecure of deputy collector of the Cinque Port duties.

Brettingham's income from these posts freed him from the need to practise architecture extensively. He made numerous designs—some in an English Palladian style, others in which a dome motif recurs—for constructing new or remodelling existing buildings, but most remained unexecuted. There are drawings by him at Lincoln's Inn, the RIBA drawings collection, and Sir John Soane's Museum. His only independent commission seems to have been for alterations in the neo-classical style, including a domed hall, to the early seventeenth-century Charlton Park, Wiltshire (1772–6), for Henry Howard, twelfth earl of Suffolk (*d*. 1779), but even these remained unfinished into the nineteenth century. At Petworth he converted the state bedroom into the White Library (1774–6) for Lord Egremont. On this evidence Brettingham barely qualifies as an architect. He was, however, good at organizing and negotiating on behalf of patrons. Through his dealing he helped to disseminate examples of neo-classical sculpture in Britain and the course of his career in Italy presaged in many respects the experiences of several aspiring architects later in the eighteenth century, notably those of Charles Heathcote Tatham.

Brettingham lived in Norwich, where he was made a freeman of the city in 1769. He died at his home there on 18 March 1803.   RICHARD RIDDELL

Sources Colvin, *Archs.* • J. Kenworthy-Browne, 'Matthew Brettingham's Rome account book, 1747–1754', *Walpole Society*, 49 (1983), 37–132 • J. Fleming, *Robert Adam and his circle in Edinburgh and Rome* (1962), 161, 258, 342, 352 • J. Ingamells, ed., *A dictionary of British and Irish travellers in Italy, 1701–1800* (1997) • S. J. Wearing, *Georgian Norwich: its builders* (1926), 4–5 • Nichols, *Illustrations*, 3.725 • H. A. Wyndham, *A family history*, 2: *1688–1837: the Wyndhams of Somerset, Sussex and Wiltshire* (1950), 141, 169 • L. Lewis, *Connoisseurs and secret agents in eighteenth-century Rome* (1961), 151–4 • Farington, *Diary*, 1462 [4 Dec 1800] • C. W. James, *Chief Justice Coke: his family and descendants at Holkham* (1929), 286–9 • *East Anglian*, 2 (1866), 131–2 • *Catalogue of the drawings collection of the Royal Institute of British Architects: B* (1972), 102–6
Archives Bodl. Oxf., corresp. and papers, incl. family papers, MS Eng. misc. c. 504 • Cumbria AS, Carlisle, plans and elevations • Holkham Hall, Norfolk, account of works of art bought at Rome, MS 744 • Lincoln's Inn, London • RIBA BAL, designs, sketches, and sketchbooks • Sir John Soane's Museum, London, 4D | NRA, priv.

coll., accounts, letters to Charles Wyndham, poem with biographical information
Wealth at death see will, PRO; Colvin, *Archs.*

Brettingham, Robert William Furze (*c*.1750–1820), architect, was the son of Michael Savary Furs and his wife, the daughter of Matthew *Brettingham the elder (1699–1769). At some point before enrolling at the Royal Academy as a student of architecture in 1775 he adopted his maternal grandfather's surname, 'supposing that professionally it might be of service to him' (Colvin, *Archs.*, 159). In 1778 he travelled to Italy with the young John Soane, passing through Paris *en route* for Rome. It was there that he first met the Dorset landowner Henry Bankes, for whom he later made alterations to Kingston Lacy, near Wimborne, Dorset (1784–9). He returned to Britain in 1782 and in the following year exhibited three drawings at the Royal Academy. He exhibited again at the academy in 1790 and 1799. After setting up practice his first notable appointment came in 1790, when he succeeded William Blackburn as architect of several prisons, including Downpatrick gaol, co. Down, Ireland (1789–96), Northampton county gaol (1791–4), and Reading county gaol (1793–4). In 1792 he moved to 42 (now 9) Berkeley Square and later added a 'fine room' at the rear of the house.

Brettingham was an original member of the Architects' Club, founded in 1791, together with William Chambers, Robert Adam, John Soane, James Wyatt, and S. P. Cockerell, and further consolidated his position within the architectural establishment when appointed resident clerk in the office of works in 1794, a post he held until 1805, when he retired. Despite these advancements, on 4 November 1799 he failed to be elected as an associate of the Royal Academy in the face of strong competition from J. M. W. Turner, George Garrard, George Byfield, and Thomas Hardwick. In 1800 he married Mary Smith, the widow of Samuel Smith, a banker and MP for Ilchester and Worcester, at St George's, Hanover Square. The marriage brought a 'good fortune' (Colvin, *Archs.*, 159). In 1801 he moved to his wife's house at 32 Grosvenor Place. In 1803 he took legal action against Sir John Sebright, for whom he had built a library at 19 Curzon Street in 1802, claiming unpaid professional charges, but lost. John Soane interceded in this dispute, suggesting a compromise that was not taken up. By the time of this lawsuit it appears that Brettingham had ceased practising. His known London projects include alterations at 91 Pall Mall for the first marquess of Buckingham (1785–6); three houses on the south side of Little Dean's Yard, Westminster (1789); 21 St James's Square, for the fifth duke of Leeds (1791–5; completed by John Soane); and a house in Baker Street (1792). Elsewhere he carried out alterations at Longleat House, Wiltshire, for the first marquess of Bath (*c*.1790), enlarged Taplow Lodge, Buckinghamshire, for John Fryer (*c*.1795), and was probably responsible for the single-storey outer wings at Waldershare Park, Kent, for the earl of Guilford (*c*.1802). He designed Duke Street Bridge over the River Kennet in Reading (1787–8), Great Marlow Bridge (over the River Thames), Buckinghamshire (1790), and made alterations and repairs to Saffron Walden church, Essex (1790–

92). He also produced a design for refitting the choir at Downpatrick Cathedral, co. Down (1795), and designed a Temple of Concord for the fourth Lord Howard de Walden at Audley End, Essex (1790).

Surviving drawings of interiors designed for Kingston Lacy show that Brettingham's style belongs to the neo-classical *œuvre* of James Wyatt and Robert Adam. His most noteworthy pupil was George Smith. There is a portrait of Brettingham by George Dance in the British Museum. He died in 1820 at Petersham and in his will he left his house in Cumberland Street and its contents to his wife along with his property in Dean's Yard, Westminster. He left 35 Baker Street and rents in Baker and Paddington streets to his stepdaughter Miss Elizabeth Smith.

WILLIAM PALIN

Sources Colvin, *Archs.* · [W. Papworth], ed., *The dictionary of architecture*, 11 vols. (1853–92) · *DNB* · will, PRO, PROB 11/1636 · W. Brettingham, *The Brettingham family of Norfolk* (1969) · Farington, *Diary* · A. T. Bolton, *The portrait of John Soane* (1969) · W. T. Whitley, *Artists and their friends in England, 1700–1799*, 2 vols. (1928), vol. 2 · G. Darley, *John Soane: an accidental romantic* (2000) · A. Cleminson, 'Christmas at Kingston Lacy. Lady Frances Bankes's ball of 1791', *Apollo*, 134 (Dec 1991), 405–9 · P. de la Ruffinière du Prey, *The making of an architect* (1982) · letter to Soane, 22 Dec 1798, Sir John Soane's Museum, Archives, I.B.12.2; letter to Soane, 25 Nov 1795, Sir John Soane's Museum, Archives, I.B.13.3; design for 21 St James's Square, *c*.1799–1800, Sir John Soane's Museum, 38/7/6–38/7/7, 38/7/10
Archives Sir John Soane's Museum, London, letters and drawings
Likenesses G. Dance, portrait, BM

Breval, John Durant (1680/81–1738), writer, was the only son among the four surviving children of a French immigrant, Francis Durant de Brevall (*d.* 1707), and his wife, Susanna (*d.* in or after 1707). De Brevall was described in 1669 as 'heretofore Preacher to the Queen-Mother' (Henrietta Maria), and probably came to England soon after the Restoration as one of the Roman Catholic clergy of her chapel at Somerset House. In 1666 or 1667 he converted to protestantism, and in 1671 he was described as chaplain to Charles II and a minister of the French church in the Savoy. During the visit of Prince William of Orange to England in 1670 he pronounced his church's official welcome (in French, published in translation in 1671), and preached to him on the text 'Sois fidele jusques à la mort, et je te donneray la couronne de vie' ('be thou faithful unto death, and I will give thee a crown of life'; Revelation 2: 10); he later published the sermon with a dedication playing on the prince's presumed interest in the subject 'd'une *Couronne*, et des moyens legitimes qui la font infailliblement acquerir' ('of a crown, and of the legitimate means that infallibly bring about its acquisition'). In 1674 (according to Nichols, *Lit. anecdotes*, 1.254) he became a prebendary of Westminster Abbey.

John Breval was educated at Westminster School and was admitted a pensioner at Trinity College, Cambridge, in 1697, aged sixteen, in which year he began his career as advocate of protestant whig ideology by contributing to the university's *Gratulatio* on the peace of Ryswick. In Breval's contortedly Virgilian Latin verse, William III is hailed as a new Brutus and a new Augustus, bringer both of liberty and of peace. Breval became a scholar in 1698, took his BA degree in 1701, was elected a fellow of Trinity in 1703, and took his MA degree in 1704. Although his father had anticipated that he might take holy orders, in 1708 he was expelled from the fellowship in circumstances obscured by the developing controversy between the master of Trinity, Richard Bentley, and dissident fellows. It is alleged that Breval was involved with a married woman in Berkshire, assaulted her husband, and ignored a summons to answer the charge of assault. According to his supporters, however, 'he only beat the Husband for his ill usage to his Wife, which was very frequent. … He was known to be a sort of Romantick Platonick Lover' (Miller, 81). According to Bentley's biographer, Monk, Breval 'some years afterwards, asserted upon oath his innocence of the adulterous intercourse imputed to him' (Monk, 1.217). According to Miller, when the senior fellows objected that there was no evidence of adultery and that the college might be sued, Bentley 'barbarously and insolently reply'd, *Never fear that, his Father died as poor as he could p—s*, and that *they were all Beggers*' (Miller, 81). Miller further reported, as hearsay, 'some bickerings between his Father and Dr. *Bentley*, which happen'd once at *Westminster*, which was never forgiven, but reveng'd upon the Son soon after his Father's Death' (ibid., 80), while Monk cites his action as an instance of Bentley's unconstitutional high-handedness. Monk also reports a charge against Breval of 'gambling with young men of the College, and winning their money' (Monk, 1.217). Another of the dissident fellows paraphrases a letter from Breval to the effect that '*Except* Dr. *Bentley* had actually *cut my Throat*, he cou'd not have us'd me in a *more barbarous manner*' (Blomer, 76). In 1713 Breval enlisted as lieutenant in Pearce's (5th) regiment of foot, but a third-hand report by Nichols, ultimately derived from Breval's friend Samuel Gale, is the only authority for the tradition that Marlborough promoted him and 'employed him in divers negotiations with several German Princes' (Nichols, *Lit. anecdotes*, 1.255). Although his right to be called 'Captain' was later defended by his bookseller, Edmund Curll (Curll, 24), no such promotion has been confirmed, and Breval seems to have left the army shortly after his commission was renewed in 1715.

Breval then became a professional writer of verse and stage entertainments, and became involved, to the detriment of his reputation, in Curll's marketing ploys. Curll invented the fictitious author Joseph Gay (often rendered simply as 'Mr. Gay'), intending his works to be mistaken for those of John Gay, and Breval was the principal—but not the only—writer to assume the disguise. Pope originally drafted the phantom poet episode in book 2 of the *Dunciad* as a satire on this fraud at his friend's expense, and he preserved slighter allusions in published versions (*Alexander Pope: The Dunciad*, ed. V. Rumbold, 151, 163). Particularly offensive to Pope among the 'Joseph Gay' publications was Breval's *The Confederates* (1717), an attack on John Gay's ill-fated farce *Three Hours after Marriage* (incorporating contributions from Pope and John Arbuthnot). *The Confederates* presents Pope's hunchbacked form in a crude

caricature on its title; he is described by the prologue as 'In *Form*, a *Monkey*; but for *Spite*, a *Toad*', and his part in the collaboration is consistently exaggerated. Breval's various attacks on Pope are not simply venal, but have a strong political charge: Pope's Catholic and tory associations were anathema to Breval's brand of whig protestantism.

Breval's verse in these years is a technically competent but conceptually unambitious commercial product, adept in capitalizing on simple discursive structures, social and political stereotypes, smutty suggestiveness, and easy targets for topical satire. *The Art of Dress: a Poem* (1717), for example—which, according to Curll, 'Mr. *Pope* read over in Manuscript, and approv'd' (Curll, 26)—revisits several topics highlighted in such successful publications as *The Tatler* and *The Rape of the Lock*. The dedication explains that 'Female DRESS, though touch'd upon lightly in Many excellent Pieces, has not, that I know of, ever been wholly the Subject of One', which probably indicates something of Breval's method of scanning the market for likely openings, but the crudity of his commentary on gender relations and the casualness of his episodic structure betray the shallowness of the project. The speaker hints effectively at the prurient motives of 'Canting *Puritans*':

> Of ev'ry Ornament they strip'd the Fair,
> And hid their Bubbies with Paternal Care

and fantasizes their 'Attempts … to Preach the *Smock* away':

> For *Smocks*, so near the Flesh, were Carnal, plain,
> Too like the *Surplice*, and of course Profane.

He unabashedly advises on hygiene:

> Take, gentle Creatures, take a Friend's Advice,
> In polishing your Teeth be wond'rous nice

and:

> How plain soe'er your DRESS, be thoroughly clean,
> Nor let the *Smock* be foul, because unseen.

Far from moralizing against the vanity of fashion, he reflects that

> 'Tis no small Task the true *Genteel* to hit
> And shun the Censure of the Park or Pit.

Some of his advice is interestingly adjusted to the minutiae of contemporary modes.

As time went on, however, Breval developed more seriously the whig protestant commitment whose corollary was the anti-Catholic and anti-Irish strain so noticeable in his early publications—see, for example, the descriptive poem *Calpe, or, Gibraltar* (1708 on title, actually 1717), the polemical drama criticism *A Compleat Key to the Non-Juror* (1718), and the comedy *The Play is the Plot* (1718; reworked in 1727 as *The Strolers*). The poem *Henry and Minerva* (1729) praises Henry VIII as reformer and patron of learning and the arts, and the carefully documented *History of the House of Nassau* (1734), strategically dedicated to Anne, the princess royal, on her engagement to the prince of Orange, celebrates William III and his ancestors.

Meanwhile, Breval had from about 1720 taken on the role of travelling tutor, experience which underlay his later celebrity as a travel writer. In 1726 he published by subscription two folio volumes of *Remarks on Several Parts* of Europe (1726), describing himself as 'late Fellow of Trinity College in Cambridge'. The dedicatee, who had himself travelled with Breval, is George Cholmondeley, styled Viscount Malpas (later third earl of Cholmondeley, and by this time married to Sir Robert Walpole's daughter). The prince of Wales heads a subscription list in which the nobility is well represented, and, though Walpole is the only patron to take two copies, the range of political and cultural figures (including several from Pope's circle) shows that support for the project was by no means confined to a particular political or literary faction. Two further volumes of *Remarks* were published in 1738 with a dedication to Charles Lennox, second duke of Richmond and Lennox (grandson of Charles II and a staunch supporter of Walpole), 'in whose *Virtuoso-Parties* abroad I had sometimes the Honour to make one'. Breval, now described simply as 'Author of the Former *Remarks*', introduces his work with increased assurance: he asserts that his experience extends well beyond the beaten track; he focuses explicitly on 'the Investigation of *Antiquity*' as 'my principal Aim throughout'; and he makes a particular pitch for the connoisseur market by undertaking 'to lessen the Trouble which young *Dilettanti* often meet with Abroad in their *Virtuoso* Pursuits', offering as preamble an outline history of the appreciation of the fine arts in Europe.

This last phase of Breval's career may be alluded to in the figure of the travelling tutor who addresses Dulness in book 4 of Pope's *Dunciad in Four Books* (*Alexander Pope: The Dunciad*, ed. V. Rumbold, 310–11). Horace Walpole claimed that the eloping nun in *Dunciad*, IV, also alluded to Breval's adventures, and that he later married her (ibid., 317). On his death in Paris in 1738 Breval was commemorated as 'Author of several Volumes of Travels' (*London Magazine*). Nichols's account suggests a considerable recuperation of reputation over the years: 'the celebrated traveller' who died 'universally beloved' stands in striking contrast with the scandals of Breval's former life (Nichols, *Lit. anecdotes*, 1.255).   VALERIE RUMBOLD

Sources *The autobiography of Sir John Bramston*, ed. [Lord Braybrooke], CS, 32 (1845), 157 · Venn, *Alum. Cant.*, 1/1 · C. Dalton, ed., *English army lists and commission registers, 1661–1714*, 6 (1904), 231–2 · R. Bentley, *The present state of Trinity College in Cambridg* [*sic*] (1710), 29–31 · E. Miller, *Some remarks upon a letter entituled 'The present state of Trinity College in Cambridge': written by Richard Bentley* (1710), 80–81 · T. Blomer, *A full view of Dr Bentley's letter to the Lord Bishop of Ely* (1710), 76 · Nichols, *Lit. anecdotes*, 1.241, 254–5, 368 · J. H. Monk, *The life of Richard Bentley, DD*, 2nd edn, 1 (1833), 216–18 · [E. Curll], *The Curliad: a hypercritic upon the Dunciad variorum, with a farther key to the new characters* (1729) · A. Pope, *The Dunciad*, ed. J. Sutherland (1943), vol. 5 of *The Twickenham edition of the poems of Alexander Pope*, ed. J. Butt (1939–69); 3rd edn [in 1 vol.] (1963); repr. (1965) · A. Pope, *The Dunciad in four books*, ed. V. Rumbold (1999) · *London Magazine*, 7 (1738), 49 · will, PRO, PROB 499, fols. 276v–277r [Francis Durant de Brevall, father]

Brevint, Daniel (*bap.* 1616, *d.* 1695), dean of Lincoln and theologian, was baptized on 11 May 1616 in the parish of St John's on the island of Jersey, the son of Daniel Brevint (1573–1651) and Elisabeth Le Sebirel (*d.* 1631). He was the third consecutive protestant clergyman in his family. His grandfather, Cosme Brevint (1520–1605), was a strong

Huguenot who studied in Geneva where he met John Calvin, and, after ordination as a Reformed minister, served at Sark from 1570 to his death. His father studied at the protestant University of Saumur and served as pastor of St John's from 1604 until his death; he only reluctantly accepted the prayer book when it was imposed in Jersey in 1623.

Daniel Brevint the younger followed his father to Saumur, where he graduated MA in 1634, after which he worked as a private tutor in Poitou. When Charles I founded three fellowships at Oxford in 1636 for Channel Islanders, Daniel was chosen from Jersey, and went up to Jesus College in the following year, only having his Saumur MA incorporated on 12 October 1638 after the vice-chancellor had overruled Archbishop William Laud's objections. He remained at Oxford until 1648, when he was deprived of his fellowship by the parliamentary commissioners; this resulted from his holding a fellowship endowed by the crown, or (more likely) because his theological and political views had now diverged from his French Reformed roots. On return to Jersey, he became pastor of Grouville, in which capacity he preached in French at St Helier before the future Charles II and his brother the duke of York on 25 November 1649. He travelled to France at least twice during this period, probably because of action by the parliamentary forces. Exactly when he was ordained as a Reformed pastor is not clear; it could have been before he went up to Oxford in 1637 but 1648, the year of his appointment to Grouville, is more probable. He took a further theological and political step in 1651, when on Trinity Sunday—a day earmarked for ordinations in the prayer book—he was ordained deacon and priest at the same time by Bishop Thomas Sydserf in Paris. This took place in the private chapel of Sir Richard Browne alongside his fellow islander Jean Durel. Sydserf had fled his Scottish diocese of Galloway during the civil war. In his diary John Evelyn refers to Sydserf alluding to 'the poor Church of England's affliction' in the service, and recounts that John Cosin, also in exile, preached the sermon (*Diary of John Evelyn*, 3.9). Brevint returned to Grouville, but was back in France in late 1652, where he served a protestant congregation in Compiègne, and made further contacts with Huguenot notables; these included the marshal de Turenne, one of the most influential men in France, and Charlotte de Caumont, his wife, to whose household he served as chaplain. As a monarchist, ordained as a Church of England priest, he returned to England with Charles II in 1660, and officiated at the French chapel of the Savoy. But on 17 December of that year he succeeded Cosin as prebendary of Durham and rector of Brancepeth on the latter's appointment as bishop of Durham. He was made DD of Oxford by royal decree on 27 February 1662. He subsequently became dean of Lincoln on 7 January 1682, on the death of another prominent royalist, Michael Honywood. He died at the deanery, Lincoln, on Sunday, 5 May 1695 and was buried in the choir of the cathedral.

In 1643 Brevint had married Anne De Carteret, daughter of Sir Philippe De *Carteret, bailiff and lieutenant-governor of Jersey. They had one daughter, Charlotte, named after Charlotte de Turenne; she was baptized in the French Reformed church at Charenton, outside Paris, in 1663, a sign of the religious roots of both sides of the family. Anne Brevint died at Lincoln on 9 November 1708.

Brevint's writings include both the polemical, like *Missale Romanum, or, The Depth and Mystery of Roman Mass* (1672), and the devotional and systematic, like *The Christian Sacrament and Sacrifice* (1673). The former, as its title suggests, is an attack on the Roman Catholic understanding of the mass: 'This mass-oblation, which by its strange presupposal contradicts both sense and reason … affronts the express words of holy Scripture' (Brevint, 141). The latter, on the other hand, breathes a different atmosphere: 'The Sacrament instituted by Christ at the eve of his passion, which St Paul calls the Lord's Supper is, without controversy, one of the greatest mysteries of godliness, and the most solemn festival of the Christian religion' (ibid., 3). He is clearly influenced by two theologians from the end of the preceding century, the Anglican Richard Hooker, whose writings would have been familiar to him in his Oxford days, and the French Reformed Philippe du Plessis-Mornay, who had helped to establish the university at Saumur. There are also signs of influence from his near contemporary Jeremy Taylor. *Christian Sacrament and Sacrifice* can be said to demonstrate the importance of seventeenth-century Anglican theology as a nuanced development of the Reformation, being biblically based, historical in inspiration, and devotional in application (each chapter usually ends with a prayer). When John and Charles Wesley produced their *Hymns on the Lord's Supper* in 1745, they reissued an abbreviated version on this work, showing its impact on their hymnody. Brevint was admired by subsequent Anglican theologians and continues to be studied today. KENNETH W. STEVENSON

Sources J. A. Masservy, 'Notice sur la famille Brevint', *Société Jersiaise*, 7 (1914), 35–44 • G. R. Balleine, *A biographical dictionary of Jersey*, [1] [1948], 48–50 • D. Wilkins, ed., *Concilia Magnae Britanniae et Hiberniae*, 4 (1737), 534 • J. Walker, *An attempt towards recovering an account of the numbers and sufferings of the clergy of the Church of England*, pt 2 (1714), 120 • *The diary of John Evelyn*, 25 June 1651 • *The works of the most reverend father in God, William Laud*, 5, ed. J. Bliss (1853), 140, 170 • private information (2004) [B. Allen, Jesus College, Oxford] • D. Brevint, *The Christian sacrament and sacrifice*, new edn (1847) • K. Stevenson, *Covenant of grace renewed: a vision of the eucharist in the seventeenth century* (1994), 98–109 • J. E. Rattenbury, *The eucharistic hymns of John and Charles Wesley* (1948) • PRO, PROB 11/485, fol. 199r–v
Archives Bibliothèque Nationale, Paris, Manuscrits Conrat XIV, sermons and unedited MSS • Durham Cathedral, Hunter MSS, private coresp.
Wealth at death see will, PRO, PROB 11/485, fol. 199r–v

Brewer, Anthony (*fl.* 1607–1617), playwright, wrote the pseudo-history play *The Love-Sick King*, nominally set in Saxon England but freely mixing events and characters from different centuries. The main plot concerns King Canute of Denmark, who appears at the beginning of the play after England's King Ethelred is killed by invading Danes. Canute courts a nun named Cartesmunda, eventually winning her love. But his infatuation distracts him

from the doings of the new English king, Alured (the historical Alfred the Great), who kills Canute's sister and joins with the king of Scotland to raise an army which moves south to Newcastle. There they are welcomed by Roger Thornton, a rich merchant of the Dick Whittington type and an actual historical personage who lived about 1400, three centuries after Canute. Alured and Canute eventually meet in battle, during which Canute accidentally stabs Cartesmunda to death and is taken prisoner by Thornton. King Alured then graciously allows Canute to return to Denmark.

The Love-Sick King was printed in 1655 with an attribution to 'Anth. Brewer, Gent.' and was performed in 1680 under the title of 'The Perjured Nun'. However, the play's deferential treatment of Scotland and Denmark, along with specific references noted by Swaen and Dodds, indicate that it was written during the reign of James I. Thornton sings an adaptation of a song in Beaumont's and Fletcher's *The Knight of the Burning Pestle* (written 1607), another version of which appears in Thomas Heywood's *The Rape of Lucrece* (1608). The Canute–Cartesmunda plot closely parallels William Barksted's *Hiren, or, The Faire Greeke* (1611), and the play as a whole is heavily indebted to John Speed's *History of the Empire of Great Britaine*. This and other evidence seems to indicate a date about 1611–12, but Dodds argues that Brewer's play was written in 1617 when King James visited Newcastle. The play may have been written at the earlier date and later revised for a specific occasion. Brewer drew numerous incidents and details for his play from *Edmund Ironside* (written *c*.1590), in which Canute is also a central character, and William Haughton's *Grim the Collier of Croydon* (written 1600, printed 1662). He has been mistakenly identified as the author of *Lingua* and *The Merry Devil of Edmonton*, among other plays.

The identity of the Anthony Brewer who wrote this play is uncertain. In the manuscript play 'The Two Noble Ladies' (BL, Egerton MS 1994) 'Anth Brew:' is noted in the margin as a minor actor, and Dodds suggests that this is the playwright Anthony Brewer. This suggestion is intriguing but not very helpful, since the company and exact date of 'The Two Noble Ladies' are unknown. Numerous Anthony Brewers were baptized in England between 1560 and 1600, but none can be identified with the playwright. On 27 October 1615 Antony Brewer of Oxfordshire, aged thirteen, matriculated from Oriel College, Oxford (Foster, *Alum. Oxon.*, 177), but he was probably too young to be the playwright. DAVID KATHMAN

Sources A. E. H. Swaen, 'Introduction', *Anthony Brewer's 'The love-sick king'* (1907), v–xiv • A. E. H. Swaen, 'The date of Brewer's "Love-sick king"', *Modern Language Review*, 4 (1908–9), 87–8 • M. H. Dodds, '"Edmund Ironside" and "The love-sick king"', *Modern Language Review*, 19 (1924), 158–68 • G. E. Bentley, *The Jacobean and Caroline stage*, 7 vols. (1941–68), vol. 3, pp. 42–5 • Foster, *Alum. Oxon.* • R. W. Dent, 'The love-sick king: Turk turned Dane', *Modern Language Review*, 56 (1961), 555–7 • R. Martin, 'Sources for *The love-sick king*', '*Edmund Ironside*' and Anthony Brewer's 'The love-sick king' (1991), 171–89

Brewer, Cecil Claude (1871–1918), architect, was born on 12 December 1871 at 9 Endsleigh Street, Bloomsbury, London, the youngest child of Alfred Brewer, an upholsterer, and his wife, Anne Heal. He was educated at a private school in Elstree, Hertfordshire, and at Clifton College. In 1890 he was articled for three years to the London architect F. T. Baggallay. He also studied at the Architectural Association, of which he remained an active member, and at the Royal Academy Schools. In 1894 he joined the office of Robert Weir Schultz in Gray's Inn; it was perhaps through Schultz that he was introduced to a circle of architects around W. R. Lethaby who talked of architecture, in the language of the arts and crafts movement, as reasonable building. Much of Brewer's career was spent among these colleagues, and he admired Lethaby all his life. But his sense of what constituted reasonable building changed with time.

In the early 1890s Brewer was living at University Hall in Gordon Square, Bloomsbury, a settlement devoted to work among the poor. The architect **Arnold Dunbar Smith** (1866–1933), born in London on 2 December 1866, the son of Joseph Smith, a leather merchant, and Elizabeth Margaret Mason, was also a resident, and he too was studying at the Royal Academy. In 1895 he and Brewer won a limited competition for the design of a new building for the settlement in Tavistock Place, Bloomsbury. The Passmore Edwards Settlement (later Mary Ward House) was built in 1896–7 in the inventive yet reticent vernacular style which Lethaby and others used for middle-class houses in the country. Applied here for the first time to a public building in London, it had a striking and appropriate freshness, the influence of which can be felt in the work of other young progressive architects in Britain, including Charles Rennie Mackintosh. Following this success Smith and Brewer went into practice together.

The two partners were very different. Brewer was electric, urbane, interested in ideas, a fragile figure with a permanently boyish face. He could work feverishly, but had a weak heart and was never far from physical collapse. Smith was shy, composed, and precise. Perhaps because of these differences, they could collaborate closely. Theirs was not a large practice, and for a dozen years or so their work consisted mainly of houses in the home counties and East Anglia. Thanks perhaps to their settlement connections, progressive intellectuals and social reformers figured rather largely among their clientele. In 1899, for instance, they built Heath Cottage, Oxshott, Surrey, for Bernard and Helen Bosanquet, and in 1907 a small house in Haslemere, Surrey, for Adelaide Anderson, the first head of the women's branch of the factory inspectorate. The houses themselves were designed after the model of English domestic architecture of the sixteenth to eighteenth centuries, as was usual then, but treated with a mixture of freedom and severity typical of the Lethaby circle. In some of them, small complex spaces were cleverly articulated with English classical details, as if Wren had been asked to fit out a ship's cabin.

On 25 May 1904 Brewer married Irene MacDonald (1857–1939), a daughter of George MacDonald, the novelist. They were introduced by her cousin the architect Frank Troup, who was one of Brewer's Gray's Inn circle. They lived at first in Gray's Inn; when Smith and Brewer moved their office to 6 Queen Square, Bloomsbury, in 1914, the Brewers moved there too.

In 1910 Smith and Brewer won the competition for the design of the National Museum of Wales at Cathays Park in Cardiff. This complex, monumental classical building was a new departure for the practice. Reasonable building it might be, but not in the homely sense of the arts and crafts movement. A friend wrote of Brewer, 'in later years he inclined more and more to the larger view of architecture as a matter of fine planning, ordered massing and intellectual expression' (*Architectural Association Journal*, 34, 1918, 27). Such a view had been gaining ground in England since about 1905, inspired by French theory and American practice in the classical tradition. In 1911 Brewer went to the United States to study museum design. On his return the competition design was revised in the light of his admiration for American classical work, particularly the entrance hall of the Metropolitan Museum of Art in New York and the work of McKim, Mead, and White. The building of the museum was interrupted by the war, so that Brewer never saw the design carried out; the same was true of the firm's designs of 1914–15 for extensions to the Fitzwilliam Museum in Cambridge.

Brewer's last major work was the rebuilding and enlargement, in 1914–16, of part of Heals furniture shop in Tottenham Court Road, London (Ambrose Heal, the furniture designer and manufacturer, was Brewer's cousin). A commercial, steel-framed building, it was as much a departure from their earlier work as the museum in Cardiff and, until it was unhappily extended by Sir Edward Maufe in 1937, its subtle, stripped classical façade was one of the best-proportioned and most expressive modern shop-fronts in London. Brewer was also a founder of the Design and Industries Association, set up in 1915 to bring good design to bear on industry as the Deutscher Werkbund had done in Germany, and as the arts and crafts movement in Britain had failed to do. Brewer was an enthusiast for Germany, and would pester his friends with preaching and photographs of the latest German work. In its early years the association was run from 6 Queen Square and he acted as joint secretary until 1918, despite failing health.

In March 1916 the doctors told Brewer that the condition of his heart was worsening, and from that date he and Irene spent more time at Town End Farm, Radnage, near Stokenchurch in Buckinghamshire. Though very much a Londoner, he took to the Chilterns. His invalid's couch was fitted with a drawing-board; in one of his last letters, he wrote 'I am designing, mostly in my head, a great church upon a hill' (Brewer to Hope Bagenal, 21 July 1918, RIBA). Cecil Brewer died at Town End Farm, Radnage, on 10 August 1918, aged forty-six, and was cremated at Golders Green on 14 August. The practice continued in his partner's hands until 1933. The National Museum of Wales was partly completed under Smith's supervision, and the designs for the Fitzwilliam Museum were carried out as the Marlay (1924) and Courtauld (1931) galleries. Smith designed other university buildings in Cambridge, and also in Newcastle. On 11 August 1911 he married Clara

Ellen Dean (*d.* 1944), becoming stepfather to the folklorist Margaret Josephine Dean-*Smith (1899–1997). He died on 7 December 1933 at his home, Pine Court, 4 Gervis Road, Bournemouth..   ALAN CRAWFORD

Sources B. Blackwood, 'Smith and Brewer', *Catalogue of the drawings collection of the Royal Institute of British Architects: S*, ed. M. Richardson (1976), 82–5 · H. M. Fletcher, 'The work of Smith and Brewer', *RIBA Journal*, 42 (1934–5), 629–47 · B. Blackwood, 'Smith and Brewer', *The dictionary of art*, ed. J. Turner (1996) · 'The work of Smith and Brewer', *ArchR*, 27 (1910), 327–40 · H. Bagenal, 'Some notes on the late Cecil C. Brewer', *Architectural Association Journal*, 38 (1922), 112–14 · A. Forty, 'The Mary Ward settlement', *Architects' Journal*, 190 (1989), 28–49 · C. C. Brewer, 'American museum buildings', *RIBA Journal*, 20 (1912–13), 365–403 · *Architectural Association Journal*, 34 (1918), 25–7 · W. R. Lethaby, 'Cecil Claude Brewer', *RIBA Journal*, 25 (1917–18), 246–7 · *The Times* (11 Dec 1933) · letters to Harry Peach, 1914–18, RIBA BAL, Peach MSS · N. Pevsner, 'Patient progress three: the DIA', *Studies in Art, Architecture and Design*, 2 (1968), 227–76 · b. cert. · b. cert. [Arnold Dunbar Smith] · m. cert. · d. cert. · d. cert. [Arnold Dunbar Smith] · *Building News*, 115 (1918), 135 · A. S. Gray, *Edwardian architecture: a biographical dictionary* (1985), 333 [Arnold Dunbar Smith] · C. Brewer, letter to H. Bagenal, 21 July 1918, RIBA BAL

Archives RIBA BAL, MSS | Col. U., Avery Architectural and Fine Arts Library, Goodhue MSS, drawings, and archives, letters between Brewer and Bertram Grosvenor Goodhue · RIBA BAL, corresp. mainly with H. H. Peach

Likenesses photograph, Art Workers' Guild, London · photograph (Arnold Dunbar Smith), repro. in Fletcher, 'The work of Arnold Dunbar Smith and Cecil Brewer', 628

Wealth at death £8905 14s. 10d.: probate, 18 Dec 1918, *CGPLA Eng. & Wales* · £17,328 0s. 1d.—Arnold Dunbar Smith: probate, 8 Jan 1934, *CGPLA Eng. & Wales*

Brewer, Ebenezer Cobham (1810–1897), educationist and lexicographer, was born in Russell Square, Bloomsbury, London, on 2 May 1810, the third of the eleven surviving children of John Sherren Brewer (1775/6–1848), a Norwich schoolmaster, and his second wife, Elizabeth, daughter of Robert Kitton of Norwich. His brothers William, Robert Kitton, and John Sherren *Brewer (1809–1879) were all highly gifted. He was educated by his father and in 1832 entered Trinity Hall, Cambridge, where he took his BA in civil law in 1836, LLB in 1839, and LLD in 1844. He was ordained in 1838.

After graduating Brewer taught in his father's school at Mile End, near Norwich, but his lifelong educational contribution was a range of simple and comprehensive textbooks in catechetical form. His pioneering and best-selling *Guide to the Scientific Knowledge of Things Familiar*, first published about 1841, made his name. His *Poetical Chronology* (1847) remains interesting for its skilful use of mnemonic devices. He was then headmaster of Mile End School (renamed King's College School) but by 1852 had moved to Paris, where he lived until 1858. On 5 July 1856 he married Ellen Mary (1831/2–1878), eldest daughter of the Revd Francis Tebbutt of Hove, Sussex. By 1859 they were living in Bloomsbury, London, where their two daughters, Ellen Maria Elizabeth and Amy Mary, were born, and his outpouring of textbooks in arts and science subjects continued unabated.

Brewer's most enduring work was his *Dictionary of Phrase and Fable* (1870). Substantially revised by him in 1895, it has

Ebenezer Cobham Brewer (1810–1897), by George Burnett Esam, *c.*1895

seen many new versions since. Planned as the first part of a trilogy, the distillation of a lifetime's reading, it was followed by his acclaimed *Reader's Handbook* (1880) and *Historic Note-Book* (1890). His *Dictionary of Miracles* (1884) interestingly reveals his mature approach to history and ties in with polemic ripostes he wrote in 1871, under the pseudonym Julian, to a lecture series sponsored by the Christian Evidence Society. These and other pamphlets contrast oddly with his conventionally religious works, but have some affinity with a late pamphlet in his own name, *Constance Naden and hylo-Idealism: a Critical Study* (1891).

Brewer had moved to Westbourne Park, near Paddington, London, by the late 1860s, and he subsequently settled in the village of Lavant, near Chichester, in Sussex. After his wife's death in 1878 he made his home with his eldest daughter in Nottinghamshire, first at Ruddington, where his son-in-law was vicar, and from 1884 at Edwinstowe. He continued in vigour until he suffered a stroke on 27 February 1897. He died at the vicarage in Edwinstowe on 6 March 1897 and was buried on 10 March at the village's parish church.   ANN MARGARET RIDLER

Sources Brewer family papers, Norfolk RO · R. K. Brewer, *The battle fought, or, A short memoir of the Rev. Dr. R. K. Brewer* (1876) · census return for 14 Bernard Street, Bloomsbury, London, 1861 · *Men of the time* (1884) · 'A grand old lexicographer at home: an interview with the Rev. Dr. Brewer', *Westminster Gazette* (1895) [cutting, Norfolk RO, Brewer family MSS] · *Daily Graphic* (9 March 1897) · E. C. Brewer, *Poetical chronology* (1847), title page · E. C. Brewer, *Introduction to science*, 2nd edn (1848), title page · E. C. Brewer, 'Preface', in E. C. Brewer, *Constance Naden and hylo-idealism: a critical study* (1891), annotated by R. Lewins MD · J. R. Tanner, ed., *Historical register of the University of Cambridge … to the year 1910* (1917) · C. B. Jewson, 'The Brewer family', *Eastern Daily Press* (12 Oct 1948) · C. B. Jewson, *Simon Wilkin of Norwich* (1979), 91–2 · W. White, *History, gazetteer, and directory of Norfolk*, 2nd edn (1845) · *The Post Office London directory* (1861); (1863); (1865) · P. M. C. Hayman, 'Memoir', in E. C. Brewer, *Dictionary of phrase and fable*, 1870; centenary edn (1970) · Crockford (1884) · Crockford (1897) · *CGPLA Eng. & Wales* (1897) · m. cert.

Archives Norfolk RO

Likenesses G. B. Esam, photograph, *c.*1895, NPG, Norfolk RO [*see illus.*] · A. C. Brewer, portrait (in old age), priv. coll.; repro. in Brewer, *Dictionary of phrase and fable*

Wealth at death £1623 16s. 10d.: probate, 10 April 1897, *CGPLA Eng. & Wales*

Brewer, George (*bap.* 1766), writer, was baptized on 6 November 1766 at St Martin-in-the-Fields, Westminster, the son of John Brewer, well known as a connoisseur of art, and his wife, Rosamond. In his youth he served as a midshipman under Lord Hugh Seymour, Rowland Cotton, and others and visited America, India, China, and Scandinavia. In 1791 he was made a lieutenant in the Swedish navy. Afterwards abandoning the sea, he read for law in London, and established himself as an attorney.

While he was still in the navy, Brewer wrote *The History of Tom Weston* (1791), a novel in the style of Fielding's *Tom Jones* (1749). He also published *Maxims of Gallantry* in 1793, but his first real appeal to the public was a comedy, *How to be Happy*, acted at the Haymarket in August 1794. After three nights, 'owing to the shaft of malevolence', this comedy was withdrawn, and it was never printed. In 1795 Brewer wrote *The Motto, or, The History of Bill Woodcock* (2 vols.), and in 1796 *Bannian Day*, a musical entertainment in two acts which was published and performed at the Haymarket in the same year for seven or eight nights, though but 'a poor piece'. In 1799 *The Man in the Moon*, in one act, attributed to Brewer, was announced for the opening night of the season at the Haymarket, but its production was evaded, and it disappeared from the bills.

In 1800 Brewer published a pamphlet entitled *The Rights of the Poor*, dedicated to 'Men who have great power, by one without any', which received copious notice in the *Gentleman's Magazine* (1st ser., 70, 1800, 1168 ff.). He was writing at this time also in the *European Magazine*, and his contributions included 'Siamese Tales' and 'Tales of the 12 Soubahs of Indostan', and some essays, advertised as after the manner of Goldsmith, which were collected and published by subscription in 1806 as *Hours of Leisure, or, Essays and Characteristics*. In the prefatory address, he alludes to his life as being 'misplaced or displaced' and altogether luckless. In 1808 Brewer produced another two-volume tale, *The Witch of Ravensworth*, and about the same time he published *The Juvenile Lavater*, stories for the young to illustrate Le Brun's *Passions*, which bears no date, but of which there were two or more issues, with slightly varying title-pages. A periodical, *The Town*, was attempted by Brewer after this but had a short existence.

Some sources claim that Brewer also wrote *The Law of Creditor and Debtor*, but there is no trace of this work in the *English Short Title Catalogue*. The date of Brewer's death is unknown. JENNETT HUMPHREYS, rev. REBECCA MILLS

Sources [J. Watkins and F. Shoberl], *A biographical dictionary of the living authors of Great Britain and Ireland* (1816) · G. Brewer, 'Introduction', *Hours of leisure, or, Essays and characteristics* (1806), xii–xvi · D. E. Baker, *Biographia dramatica, or, A companion to the playhouse*, rev. I. Reed, new edn, rev. S. Jones, 1/1 (1812), 67; 2 (1812), 48, 311 · Watt, *Bibl. Brit.*, 1.149 · Genest, *Eng. stage*, 7.275 · IGI

Brewer, Sir (Alfred) Herbert (1865–1928), organist and composer, the eldest son of Alfred Brewer, hotel proprietor, of Gloucester, and his wife, Cordelia Dyer, was born on 21 June 1865 at Gloucester. For three years, from 1877 to 1880, he was a chorister at the cathedral under Dr Charles Harford Lloyd, with whom he began his musical studies alongside George Robertson Sinclair, Lloyd's assistant. He then passed on to his earliest organistships, first at St Catherine's Church, then at St Mary-de-Crypt, ending this early Gloucester phase in 1882. Except for that part of the following year, 1883, during which Brewer held the first open organ scholarship ever given at the Royal College of Music in London (where he studied under Walter Parratt, Frederick Bridge, and Charles Villiers Stanford), he was in Oxford from 1882 until 1885. There he succeeded Parratt as organist at St Giles's Church, and was, in addition, for two years organ scholar at Exeter College, where he matriculated in 1884. Despite ill health, those Oxford days were rich in experience for him: new music helped with new friendships to further his development.

In 1885 Brewer was appointed to the organistship of Bristol Cathedral on the dismissal of George Riseley by the dean and chapter. However, Riseley won his case before the chancellor of the diocese and was reinstated; Brewer was forced to give up his employment. Fortunately a more useful and permanent post came soon after with his appointment in 1886 to St Michael's, Coventry (afterwards Coventry Cathedral). For six years there he did his purely church work brilliantly; he characteristically rebuilt the organ (with the help of Henry Willis), and he reorganized the Coventry Choral Society. Then and there—as elsewhere later—he showed eagerness to improve upon things as he found them. Tonbridge School next felt the stimulus of his presence, during the years (1892–6) in which he was director of music there. There, too, he rebuilt the organ. In 1894 he married Ethel Mary, daughter of Henry William Bruton, of Gloucester; they had two sons and a daughter.

In 1897 Brewer was to have competed to succeed W. T. Best as organist of Liverpool town hall, but he withdrew in the hope that he would be appointed at Gloucester Cathedral (after Charles Lee Williams's resignation in December 1896). On his appointment at Gloucester, Brewer took over the post on 15 December, eagerly welcoming the return to his native city and to the cathedral, well known for its standards of organ playing and, under Lloyd and Williams, of choir training. In each sphere Brewer succeeded. He was an able church musician and choir trainer, while his abilities as an organist, both as performer and accompanist, benefited from his studies with Lloyd and Parratt. A succession of illustrious pupils—among them Ivor Gurney, Herbert Howells, Ivor Novello, John Dykes Bower, R. Tustin Baker, and Herbert Sumsion, who succeeded him at Gloucester—attest to his reputation as a teacher, while his founding of the Gloucestershire Orchestral Society (from 1905) allowed him to exercise his capabilities as a conductor.

Brewer increasingly used the platform of the Gloucester Three Choirs festival as an outlet for his interests in contemporary music, an attribute that set him apart from his colleagues at Worcester (Ivor Atkins) and Hereford (George Robertson Sinclair). Encouraged by the success of the 1898 festival, which featured the up-and-coming Coleridge Taylor's ballade in A minor and Verdi's *Four Sacred Pieces*, he was increasingly progressive with his choice of repertory. Besides new works by Parry and Elgar, which included the première of the violin concerto in 1910, he was keen to promote the younger generation of British composers such as Vaughan Williams, Holst, Bliss, Goossens, W. H. Bell, and Walford Davies. Indeed by 1925 no fewer than thirty-four native composers were represented at the festival. Contemporary continental works—such as the closing scene of Strauss's *Salome*, Skryabin's *Poème de l'extase*, and Sibelius's *Luonnotar*, op. 70—were also included.

As a composer Brewer was industrious and he touched upon many different styles. *Emmaus* (1901), orchestrated by Elgar, and *The Holy Innocents* (1904) were 'oratorios of a seriousness and scope less well suited either to his inclinations or his abilities. At the other extreme his songs often went dangerously far in concession to popularity' (*DNB*). But between these diverse styles there was another, far more native to him. It is found charmingly expressed in the *Three Elizabethan Pastorals* (1906), in *Summer Sports* (1910), in the song-cycle *Jillian of Berry* (1921), and in *A Sprig of Shamrock* (1921), while his setting of the evening canticles in D (1927) is still sung.

Brewer was elected a fellow of the Royal College of Organists in 1895 and he became an honorary RAM in 1906. He received the Dublin MusB in 1897 and the Canterbury MusD in 1905. He was widely known as an examiner and adjudicator. He was city high sheriff of Gloucester for the year 1922–3, and he was knighted in 1926. He died at his home, Miller's Green, Palace Yard, Gloucester, after an illness of only a few hours, on 1 March 1928.

JEREMY DIBBLE

Sources DNB · A. H. Brewer, *Memories of choirs and cloisters: fifty years of music* (1931) · A. N. Boden, *Three Choirs: a history of the festival* (1992) · W. Shaw, *The Three Choirs festival* (1954) · C. L. Williams, *Annals of the Three Choirs of Gloucester, Hereford and Worcester: continuation of history and progress from 1894–1922* (1922) · E. Fellowes, *Memoirs of an amateur musician* (1946) · *Gloucester Journal* (3 March 1928)
Archives Gloucester Cathedral, Three Choirs archive · Gloucester Public Library
Likenesses photographs, Gloucester Public Library, Brewer collection · photographs, Gloucester Cathedral, Three Choirs archive
Wealth at death £20,737 13s. 5d.: probate, 18 April 1928, CGPLA Eng. & Wales

Brewer, James Norris (*fl.* 1799–1830), novelist and topographer, was the eldest son of a merchant of London. He married the daughter of a gentleman at Clapham. He wrote many romances which have been long forgotten, ranging from *A Winter's Tale, a Romance* (1799), and *Secrets Made Public* (1808), through some four others to *Sir Gilbert Easterling, a Romance* (1813).

In 1807 Brewer published *Some Thoughts on the Present State of the English Peasantry*. His topographical writings began with *A descriptive and historical account of various palaces and public buildings, English and foreign; with biographical notices of their founders or builders, and other eminent persons* in 1810. The best are his contributions to *The Beauties of England and Wales*, which include *Oxfordshire* (1813), *Warwickshire* (1814), and *Middlesex* (1816). He dealt with actors in *Histrionic topography, or, The birthplaces, residences, and funeral monuments of the most distinguished actors* (1818).

Brewer was a contributor to the *Universal*, *Monthly*, and *Gentleman's* magazines. Nothing is recorded of his death.

JOHN D. HAIGH

Sources DNB · [J. Watkins and F. Shoberl], *A biographical dictionary of the living authors of Great Britain and Ireland* (1816) · Watt, *Bibl. Brit.* · *Monthly Review*, new ser., 58 (1809), 217
Archives TCD, letters to William Shaw Mason

Brewer, Jehoiada (*c.*1752–1817), Independent preacher, was probably born in Newport, Monmouthshire. He was apprenticed to a currier at Bristol but, influenced by a minister of the Countess of Huntingdon's Connexion, trained for the ministry at Trevecca College and, upon leaving, took to preaching in the villages around Bath. Afterwards he preached with remarkable popularity throughout Monmouthshire. Intending to enter the established church he applied for ordination, but was refused by the bishop of Llandaff.

Brewer persisted in preaching, in spite of the fact that he was not ordained, and from 1780 to 1783 was settled at Rodborough in Gloucestershire. He afterwards proved a popular minister at Sheffield, where he spent thirteen years from 1783 to 1796 before settling in 1796 at Birmingham, first as minister at Carr's Lane Chapel and then, from 1802, at a chapel in Livery Street, where he attracted a large congregation. At the time of his death a new and spacious chapel was being built for him in Steelhouse Lane.

According to John Angel James, who knew him personally, Brewer was a 'very striking and popular preacher' (Sibree and Caston, 179). His literary output, however, was meagre, and his only published work of any note was the hymn 'Hail sovereign love, that first began'. He died in Birmingham on 24 August 1817 and was buried in the grounds adjoining the new chapel in Steelhouse Lane.

J. H. THORPE, *rev.* M. J. MERCER

Sources C. Surman, index, DWL · J. Sibree and M. Caston, *Independency in Warwickshire* (1855) · J. A. James, *An account of the rise and present state of the various denominations of nonconformists in Birmingham* (1849) · E. H. Rowland, *A biographical dictionary of eminent Welshmen who flourished from 1700 to 1900* (privately printed, Wrexham, 1907) · J. Julian, ed., *A dictionary of hymnology*, rev. edn (1907); repr. in 2 vols. (1957) · W. Haylock, *Brief history of Queen Street Congregational Church, Sheffield* (1933)
Likenesses Ridley, stipple, NPG; repro. in *Evangelical Magazine* (1799) · H. Wyatt, oils, NMG Wales · stipple, NPG; repro. in *Christian's Magazine* (1791)

Brewer, John [name in religion Bede] (1742–1822), Benedictine monk, was born on 9 March 1742 at Ribbleton Lodge, Preston, Lancashire, the son of Henry Brewer of Newton-cum-Scales. He had at least one brother and sister, since Anselm Brewer and Father Edward Slater, monks of Ampleforth, were his nephews. In 1757 he became a monk, taking the name of Bede, in the English monastery of St Laurence's in the little town of Dieulouard in eastern France. Here he took solemn vows in 1758—it was not at all unusual at that time to be so young—and after some years there he was ordained. He was sent to Paris to study at the Sorbonne some time before 1763 (he defended theses there in July of that year) and in 1771 he became chaplain to the English Benedictine nuns in Paris. Here he eventually took his doctorate at the Sorbonne on 13 April 1774, being placed first in a year or class of eighty-three. At the same time he prepared a second edition of *Principia religionis naturalis et revelatae* (1774) by the Irish scholar Luke Joseph Hooke, who was perhaps his supervisor. Hooke's letter to Brewer forms the work's 'Preface', and in it Brewer is referred to as a 'wisest and dear friend'. Hooke's own edition was published in 1752–4: it had a long life, much of it being included by J. P. Migne in his *Theologiae Cursus* of 1838. Brewer added chapters to the *Principia* on papal primacy, conciliar authority, and bishops' powers, which reveal liberal and Gallican sympathies and show also in his friendship with, and support for, his fellow monk Cuthbert Wilks, who was involved with Brewer's blue books in the 'Cisalpine stirs'. Some of their letters were published in 1799.

After further study, in 1776 Brewer was sent, like many of the other English Benedictine monks of his own and later centuries, to a mission in England, first briefly at Cheam in Surrey and then at Bath. In Bath he built a new chapel, thus incurring a debt of £800, so that his superior, the southern provincial, was anxious to move him to the northern province. While they were arguing about the accounts the anti-Catholic riots associated with the name of Lord George Gordon broke out, and the new chapel (and perhaps with it the accounts) was burnt down. 'Dr Brewer being pursued through several streets by the mob', says Allanson, 'and refused admittance into two of the principal Inns of the town was at last admitted into another called the Grey-Hound and escaped by a back door' (Allanson). It is said, however, that the landlord of the White Horse lent him a horse. He afterwards brought an action against the hundred of Bath for neglect of duty in not suppressing the ravages of the mob, and damages were awarded to the amount of £3735.

Brewer then moved to Woolton near Liverpool, which remained his base thereafter. Here he founded a school for boys, and in 1795 gave refuge to the nuns from Cambrai. He was made titular prior of Rochester (1794) and then of Canterbury (1802); he was president of the congregation from 1799 until his death. His determination showed in secondary disputes arising out of the clashes between Cuthbert Wilks and Bishop Walmsley over the oath of allegiance. It was his firmness and energy—he remarked that weak government was no government at all—that brought about the collapse of Abbot Maurus Heatley's attempt to take the English community at Lamspringe in Germany out of the congregation; this won him much praise, and shortly afterwards he rescued what he could from the community and school there on its secularization by the Prussian government in 1803. This last action enabled him to strengthen greatly the remnants of the English monastery at Dieulouard, near Nancy, seized by the French in October 1793, which he re-established at

Ampleforth, Yorkshire, in 1802 and, with the Lamspringe pupils, he established the school there in April 1803. He continued to support the Ampleforth foundation and about 1812 he built with his own money (which the monk missioners of the time of necessity were allowed to keep) the large north wing of the new college, which was only replaced in 1985.

It was under Brewer's presidency that the English community of St Edmund's, Paris, France, virtually destroyed by the French Revolution, was re-established in the former St Gregory's Monastery at Douai, near Lille. These monks had been expelled in 1793, but by 1814 had established themselves at Downside. The present Douai Abbey at Woolhampton, Berkshire, came from the refounded St Edmund's after the French expulsion of 1903. For the last three years of his life Brewer lived at Ampleforth to support the then young Prior Laurence Burgess, where his observant religious life greatly impressed contemporaries, among them his biographer Allanson: he was always first into the chapel before the night office, was regular in choir, and he spent a lot of time on local pastoral work. After a stroke, and some disagreement with Prior Burgess, he returned to Woolton, where he died on 18 April 1822, and was buried in Liverpool at St Peter's, Seel Street.

ANSELM CRAMER

Sources [J. B. Brewer], *Deo juvante et auspice Die-para theses ex universa philosophia publice propugnabit Joannes Beda Brewer ... julii ... 1763* (Paris, 1763) · J. B. Brewer, *Theses* (1766) · L. J. Hooke, *Principia religionis naturalis et revelatae* (1774) · *Copy of the sentence given by the Rev. Doctor Brewer on the appeal made to him by the Rev. Doctor Wilkes; and of the correspondence relating thereunto* (1799) · A. Allanson, *Biography of the English Benedictines* (1999) · Gillow, *Lit. biog. hist.*, 1.291–2 · B. Green, 'Bede Brewer: the founder of Ampleforth', *Ampleforth Journal*, 84 (1979), 134–8 · G. Scott, *Gothic rage undone: English monks in the age of Enlightenment* (1992), chap. 8 · T. O'Connor, *An Irish theologian in Enlightenment France: Luke Joseph Hooke, 1714–96* (1995), 102–3 · F. Blom and others, *English Catholic books, 1701–1800: a bibliography* (1996)

Archives Ampleforth Abbey, corresp. · Archives du Nord, Lille, letters and MS copy of *Natural religion* | Downside Abbey, near Bath, Birt collection, corresp.

Brewer, John Sherren (1809–1879), historian, was born in Norwich on 13 March 1809, the eldest son of a schoolmaster of the same name (*d.* 1848), and his wife, Elizabeth. The family reputedly came originally from Kent, and the elder Brewer was a biblical scholar, who as an adult had become a Baptist. However, the son does not appear to have shared these convictions, and matriculated at Queen's College, Oxford, in 1827 without any recorded objection on either side. However nominal had been his original Anglicanism, while at Oxford, Brewer became strongly influenced by the Tractarian movement, and took holy orders in 1837. Meanwhile he had taken a first in *literae humaniores* in 1833, and proceeded MA in 1835. Although he already had some reputation as a scholar, and a man of wide reading, an early marriage about 1834 precluded his appointment to a college fellowship. For about four years he supported himself as a private tutor, and during that time published an edition of Aristotle's *Nicomachean Ethics* (1836). On taking orders he moved to London, and was at once appointed to the distinctly unacademic post of chaplain to the workhouse of the united parishes of St Giles-in-the-Fields and St George's, Bloomsbury. Although he seems to have thrown himself into this work with enthusiasm, his incumbency was brief, and an intended promotion to the cure of a new church in the neighbourhood did not take place. This appears to have been the result of disagreements arising from his Tractarian convictions, and he was to hold no further cure until two years before his death.

Meanwhile the editorial labours which were to occupy most of Brewer's working life had already commenced. While still at Oxford he had been engaged by the record commission to draw up a catalogue of the manuscripts in some of the college libraries, and after giving up his chaplaincy he was employed for a time in a similar capacity at the British Museum. The interval, however, was a short one, and in 1839 he was appointed to a lectureship in classical literature at the newly established King's College, London. With the flexibility typical of a small institution at that time, he soon found himself teaching English literature and history as well as classics, and his editorial labours quickly reflected this mixture: Goodman's *Court of King James I* (2 vols., 1839); Cosin's *History of Popish Transubstantiation* (1840); Field's *Book of the Church* (1843); and Fuller's *Church History* (1845). F. D. Maurice had been appointed to the chair of English in 1840, and for over a decade the two men worked closely together, although not always in complete harmony. When Maurice left in 1853, Brewer succeeded him in the chair. By this time he already had a substantial reputation as an editor of historical texts, and an established position in London academic life. So it is not surprising that when the master of the rolls, Sir John Romilly, was seeking a director for a major new editorial project in 1856 Brewer should have been approached. The project was the *Letters and Papers, Foreign and Domestic, of the Reign of Henry VIII*. Brewer had no particular training in the history of the period, or indeed any training at all beyond his classical first degree, but he was a widely read and experienced scholar. On 22 October 1856 he wrote to the master of the rolls 'I could place at your disposal six hours every day, with the exception of two hours four days a week during term time at King's College …'. No one seems to have found this somewhat minimal attitude to his teaching responsibilities at all reprehensible. When in 1865 he added the chair of history to that of English, it apparently made no inroads upon his editorial labours.

It was several years before the first volume of the *Letters and Papers* appeared, partly because Brewer found the task more difficult than he had anticipated, on account of the scattered nature of the collections which he had to use, and partly because he continued to edit other texts. The chronicle of Battle Abbey (*Chronicon monasterii de Bello*) appeared in 1846, and Gerald of Wales's *De instructione principum* in the same year. Between 1858 and 1861, when he was already engaged with Henry VIII, he also edited no fewer than three other volumes for the Rolls Series; the *Monumenta fransiscana* in 1858, the *Opera inedita* of Roger Bacon in 1859, and the complete works of Gerald of Wales in 1861. In one respect only do the *Letters and Papers* appear to have changed his life. From about 1854 to 1860 he had also written extensively for the daily newspapers on a variety of topics, and was even for a short while editor of *The Standard*. This second (or third) career he abandoned as Henry VIII became more demanding, apart from a few vociferous protests on the subject of Irish church disestablishment.

Brewer's style of editing was hardly rigorous by modern standards, and his perfect command of Latin meant that the presentation of medieval texts required little labour. However the *Letters and Papers* were part catalogue, part calendar, and the work of preparation was far more arduous and exacting. Towards the end of his life he was being paid for this work at the not inconsiderable rate of £200 a year, but it was money hard earned. The nature of the edition required him to be selective, not in respect of which documents to include, for the ambition was to be comprehensive, but in respect of which passages to reproduce, which to paraphrase, and which to omit. Even had his knowledge been deeper, his decisions would have been open to challenge, but the work remains his great achievement and has never been superseded. The first volume appeared in 1862, and Brewer was wholly responsible for the first four volumes, as well as for the editorial policy of the project. In 1870 an anxious clerk at the record office reported that he had been paid in full for volume five, which was less than half complete, and had received one quarter's advance for volume six, which he had not yet started. He continued to work on the project right up to his death, but with decreasing application, and volumes five and six both appear to have been completed by James Gairdner, who was first his assistant, then his associate, and finally his successor. It was Gairdner who ultimately did most of the work, completing the project in twenty-one volumes not long before his own death. Brewer continued to take on and discharge new editorial projects to the end of his life: *A Calendar of the Carew MSS … at Lambeth* (with W. Bullen) appeared between 1867 and 1873, and the register of Malmesbury Abbey (for the Rolls Series) in 1879. He retired from his chair at King's in 1877, and was given the crown living of Toppesfield in Essex. There he took his pastoral duties all too seriously, undermined his health, and died at the rectory on 16 February 1879. His wife, Fanny Aurelia, survived him. He was buried at Toppesfield.

John Brewer's qualities were in a sense both admired and recognized. His lectures to the working men's college were remembered with gratitude, and he was frequently consulted by the staff of the record office, where he was particularly friendly with the deputy keeper Sir Thomas Hardy. Lord Romilly appointed him both reader and preacher at the rolls. On the other hand he received no formal mark of recognition, academic or otherwise, and when he died *The Times* did not even carry an obituary. By comparison with his editorial labours, his original work was slight. By far the most substantial was contained in the introductions to the first four volumes of the *Letters and Papers*, which were separately republished by Gairdner after his death, in 1884. Apart from that, he was responsible for an elementary atlas of history and geography (1865), two defences of the Athanasian creed (1871 and 1872), and *The Students' Hume* (1878). It was only after his death that his status as a professor of English literature was reflected in a collection of his *English Studies*, edited by Henry Wace (1881). In spite of his clerical status and classical background, Brewer was no amateur in the fields of medieval or early modern history. He was a professional scholar, in every sense of those words, and left an enduring legacy, both in the *Letters and Papers* and also in his contributions to the Rolls Series. If his vocation as a priest was frustrated, it was to the benefit of posterity.

DAVID LOADES

Sources Foster, *Alum. Oxon.* · H. Wace, 'Preface', in J. S. Brewer, *English studies* (1881) · P. Levine, *The amateur and the professional: antiquarians, historians and archaeologists in Victorian England* (1986) · DNB · E. Searle, ed., *The chronicle of Battle Abbey*, OMT (1980), 20 · d. cert. · *CGPLA Eng. & Wales* (1879) · IGI
Archives PRO, corresp. relating to *The letters and papers*, 1.24, 1.35; 37.24
Wealth at death under £3000: probate, 15 March 1879, *CGPLA Eng. & Wales*

Brewer, Samuel (*bap.* **1669**, *d.* **1743**?), botanist, was baptized on 8 March 1669, at Trowbridge, Wiltshire, the fourth of the five sons of William Brewer (1625/6–1707) of Trowbridge, described in Aubrey's *Natural History of Wiltshire* as operating 'the greatest trade for Medleys of any clothier in England', and his wife, Abigail, formerly Strode. Unlike most clothiers William Brewer was a tory and hence became the first clothier JP in Wiltshire. Little is known of Samuel Brewer's early life apart from an interest in natural history. A surviving account of his journey, 'Adversariorum hodoeporicum', shows that in 1691 he undertook a journey from Yorkshire to London in order to meet famous people and to examine the best collections of living plants and books. After this tour, Brewer returned to Kendal before walking home to Dockray in Cumberland. The analysis of Brewer's diary of this event, compiled by H. A. Hyde in 1930, shows that the circumstances of Brewer's own account do not accord with the widely held belief that he was engaged in the woollen trade at Trowbridge; Hyde suggests that he may, even by this date, have been involved in the same trade in Kendal. In 1699 Brewer married Elizabeth, daughter of James Bennett, a wealthy Salisbury merchant. At this time he lived in a house near the rectory in Trowbridge, which had formerly been part of the Hungerford family estate. After the death of their father in 1707, the two eldest Brewers inherited the extensive estates in Trowbridge and surrounding areas; of the three younger sons, one was a merchant in China and the second a clergyman, and Samuel inherited the business, including the Dutch looms, the materials of trade, and £150 which was to go towards the considerable sum of money he owed his father's estate. There is scant information about his career as a clothier, but the suggestion that he went bankrupt seems unfounded. Indeed he must have been well regarded by the western clothiers as he was chosen to represent their opposition to the Mixed Broadcloth Bill in 1714. While on

this business, he was assaulted in the court of request by William Day, a woollen draper of the Strand. Brewer petitioned the Lords for protection and Day was reprimanded. In the altercation, Day claimed that Brewer was a rascal, and printed false information suggesting that he, Day, had been responsible for a pamphlet or broadsheet stating the clothiers' case. Little is known relating to this period of Brewer's life. According to MS Sloane 4053.30, he suffered 'great loss by fire, bad debts, some thousands by a partner and being barred by an elder brother and other relations from three or four considerable estates by unjustly cutting of entail'. The same manuscript also refers to his loss of £20,000 earned by the 'sweate of his braines'.

Brewer devoted most of his spare time to plant collecting, discovering a number of species that were incorporated by Johan Dillenius in the third edition of Ray's *Synopsis*, published in 1724. It is believed that by this time he had given up the wool trade. In 1726 he accompanied Dillenius to the Mendips, through Bristol into north Wales and Anglesey. During this period he regularly sent samples of dried plants to Dillenius, helping to clarify several botanical disputes. In the autumn of 1727 Brewer moved to Yorkshire, living initially at Bingley and later at North Bierley, near Bradford, close to his patron, Dr Richard Richardson. The loss of his private income and family friction at this time gave a morbid tone to his correspondence. This was compounded by a disagreement with Dillenius concerning the return of Brewer's plant samples gathered on the Welsh trip. Brewer had a small house at North Bierley and devoted most of his time to the culture of plants; he was at some time head gardener to the duke of Beaufort at Badminton. He died at North Bierley, probably in 1743, and was buried near to the east wall of the old Cleckheaton chapel.

Brewer received limited recognition during his lifetime, his reputation being based posthumously on his achievements as a collector of plants, insects and shrubs. The botanical genus *Breweria* was named in his honour. He had discovered a species of rock rose native to north Wales, which was subsequently named *Helianthemum breweri*. An exotic, naturally weeping spruce originating from the high mountains of Oregon was named *Picea breweriana* after him. Although he had spent the last years of his life working on a text, 'The botanical guide', it was never completed. In 1928, a manuscript of 107 pages by Brewer on the cultivation of auriculas and carnations came into the hands of Edward Heron Allen of Selsey Bill, Sussex, a successful grower of auriculas. Allen made a copy which was found in a second-hand bookshop in 1954 by Dr R. Newton. According to the note in the flyleaf, the original manuscript had been undertaken by Samuel Brewer's son from his father's first draft, at the request of the Revd George Harbin, with whom Brewer had been associated. Newton subsequently published the section, covering pages 72 to 86, relating to auriculas.

JOHN MARTIN

Sources J. de L. Mann, *The cloth industry in the west of England from 1640 to 1880* (1971); repr. (1987) · T. B. Flower, 'A biographical notice of Samuel Brewer the botanist, AD 1670', *Wiltshire Archaeological and Natural History Magazine*, 18 (1879), 71–80 · R. Pulteney, *Historical and* biographical sketches of the progress of botany in England, 2 vols. (1790) · M. McGarvie and J. H. Harvey, 'The Revd. George Harbin and his memories of gardening, 1716–1723', *Garden History*, 11/1 (1983), 6–36, esp. 10–11 · *VCH Wiltshire*, vol. 7 · K. Rogers, *The book of Trowbridge: a history* (1984) · H. A. Hyde, 'Samuel Brewer's diary: a chapter in the history of botanical exploration of north Wales', *Report of the Botanical Society and Exchange Club of the British Isles*, 9 (1929–31), suppl. (1930) · *DNB* · S. Brewer to Sir Hans Sloane, BL, Sloane MS 4053.30

Archives Knowsley Hall Library, near Preston, Lancashire, account of a journey to north Wales · NHM, botanical diary and corresp. [botanical diary: copy] · NMG Wales, account of a journey to north Wales · RBG Kew, account of a journey home from Yorkshire to London · U. Oxf., Taylor Institution, diary | BL, letters to Sir Hans Sloane, Sloane MSS 4050–4054, 4076, *passim*

Brewer, Thomas [T. B.] (*fl.* **1605–1640**), writer, of whose life no biographical details are known, was the author of miscellaneous tracts in prose and verse. The first of his literary works, a prose tract entitled *The life and death of the merry devill of Edmonton, with the pleasant prancks of Smug the smith, Sir John and mine host of the George about the stealing of venison*, appeared in 1631. This piece was written and probably printed at a much earlier date for on 5 April 1608 'a booke called the lyfe and deathe of the Merry Devill of Edmonton, &c., by T. B.' was entered in the Stationers' register. Brewer's text, reprinted in 1657, related 'the many excellent jeasts' (Brewer, sig. [A4] ll. 2–3) of Peter Fabell and the trickery orchestrated by Smug the Smith and was doubtless influenced by the popular anonymous drama *The Merry Devill of Edmonton*, which was reissued five times between 1608 and 1631 and was acted at the court, the Globe, and the Cockpit. William Rowley, Thomas Dekker, and John Ford's collaborative *The Witch of Edmonton* (1658) also drew on this connection with the earlier play:

The town of Edmonton hath lent the stage
A Devil and a Witch, both in an age.
To make comparisons it were uncivil
Between so even a pair, a Witch and Devil.
('Prologue', ll. 1–4)

In 1624 Brewer published a small collection of satirical verses under the title of *A Knot of Fooles*; this was reprinted in 1658. The stanzas to the reader are signed 'Tho. Brewer'; they are followed by a dialogue between fools of various sorts. The body of the work consists of satirical couplets, under separate titles, on the vices of the day.

Brewer's next verses were inspired by a series of plague outbreaks in London. *The Weeping Lady, or, London Like Ninivie in Sack-Cloth* was printed in 1625. It was dedicated to Walter Leigh, swordbearer to the lord mayor of London. On the title-page is a woodcut representing a preacher addressing a crowd from Paul's Cross; a scroll issuing from his mouth bears the inscription, 'Lorde, have mercy on us. Weepe, fast, and pray'. The address to the public emphasized that the author's intentions were clearly of a reforming nature and that he hoped, above all, to stimulate awareness of God's infinite mercies. Each page, both at top and bottom, has a mourning border of deep black. Allusions are made to the return of Charles I from Spain and the arrival of Henrietta Maria but the most striking part of the tract is a description of the flight of citizens

from the metropolis and of the sufferings that they underwent in their attempts to reach a place of safety.

Two other tracts by Brewer, relating to the plague, were published by H. Gosson in 1636. *Lord have Mercy upon Us: the World, a Sea, a Pest-House* explores the insecurities, instabilities, and dangers of the human world, again written from a viewpoint sensitive to the voracity of sin:

punishment is the companion of sinne … That it is thus, we see though not till we see it, to repent it: so bedazeled we are with the beauty, lustre and splendor that is spread by the world over sinne and high-handed offences.   (sig. A2r)

The second tract was entitled *A Dialogue betwixt a Cittizen and a Poore Countrey-Man and his Wife*.

Brewer's remaining works retained an interest in contemporary themes, relating the gruesome events surrounding the murders committed by Jane Hattersley (*The Bloudy Mother*, 1610) and the development of the Overbury affair. *Mistress Turner's repentance, who, about the poysoning of the Ho. knight Sir Thomas Overbury, was executed the fourteenth day of November last* (1615) was attributed to Brewer by Robert Lemon in *Catalogue of a collection of printed broadsides in the possession of the Society of Antiquaries of London* (1866).

In 1605 Brewer contributed *A New Ballad, Composed in Commendation of the Societie or Companie of the Porters*, and in 1647 this was followed by *The Brewers Plea*. His municipal celebrations culminated in 1656 in *London's Triumph*, a descriptive pamphlet of the extravagant lord mayor's show for that year.

Brewer's commendatory verses head the sequence introducing John Taylor's *Works* (1630) and in Thomas Heywood's *Exemplary Lives and Memorable Acts of Nine of the most Worthy Women of the World* (1640). All three poets composed verses which preface *The Phoenix of these Late Times* (1637), a curious and brief work detailing the hermetic life of Henry Welsby.   ELIZABETH HARESNAPE

Sources T. Brewer, *The life and death of the merry devill of Edmonton* (1631) · T. Corser, *Collectanea Anglo-poetica, or, A … catalogue of a … collection of early English poetry*, 3, Chetham Society, 71 (1867), 105–7 · Arber, *Regs. Stationers*, 3.374 (165) · R. Lemon, ed., *Catalogue of a collection of broadsides in possession of the Society of Antiquaries of London* (1866), 45 · F. W. Fairholt, *Early English poetry, ballads and popular literature of the middle ages* (1843–4), 10, pt 1, 64; pt 2, 277–82 · P. Corbin and D. Sedge, *Three Jacobean witchcraft plays* (1986), 20–21 · G. Wickham, *Early English stages, 1300–1660*, 2 (1959–81), 2.81 · *STC, 1475–1640* · *DNB*

Brewer, Thomas (1611–*c.*1660), musician and composer, was the son of Thomas Brewer, a poulterer, and his wife, True. He was born in London, where his parents lived in the parish of Christchurch, Newgate Street, and was educated at Christ's Hospital. He was admitted there on 9 December 1614 at the age of three, and learned the viol from the school music master. On this instrument he became a celebrated performer. On 20 June 1626 he was discharged from the school by his mother and by Thomas Warner, to whom he became apprenticed. From 1638 Brewer was 'song-school-master' at Christ's Hospital, but he was dismissed in 1641 because he had married, which was forbidden by his contract there; he was also accused of various misdemeanours. The post of music master was paid for by the deed of Robert Dow, which provided only for an unmarried master: this was by no means unusual, and dismissals on similar grounds were common at Christ's Hospital and other schools and colleges.

Brewer then became a resident musician in the household of Sir Hamon L'Estrange (1583–1684) in Hunstanton, Norfolk. Brewer is first recorded there in 1636 as teacher of the bass viol to the younger son, Roger L'Estrange (1616–1704), who became a very accomplished player; if the dates are right, he must have been an adult pupil. The composer John Jenkins was another resident musician in this cultivated household, and Brewer also met and worked with Henry and William Lawes, Francis Quarles, and John (Jack) Wilson. Sir Nicholas L'Estrange recorded this anecdote about Brewer:

> Thom[as] Brewer, my Mus[ical] Servant, through his Pronenesse to good-Fellowshippe, having attaind to a very Rich and Rubicund Nose; being reproved by a Friend for his too frequent use of strong Drinkes and Sacke; as very Pernicious to that Distemper and Inflammation in his Nose. Nay—Faith, sayes he, if it will not endure sack, it's no Nose for me.

The picture of him that emerges is of a lively and irrepressible personality.

Brewer composed both instrumental and vocal music, including six fantasias for four viols, seven catches, six songs, twenty-eight airs for four parts, and two psalm settings written for the choir of Christ's Hospital to perform on Easter Monday and Tuesday. Some of the viol fantasias have written-out organ parts, as do those of Jenkins and Lawes. The manuscript sources for Brewer and Jenkins are often linked, and Brewer may be identifiable with 'Hand B' in the L'Estrange manuscripts. Meyer notes that Brewer's viol fantasias tend towards a simplified, homophonic style, and *The New Oxford History of Music* comments that they 'avoided the problematic and profound'. However, his vocal music has attracted praise. His best-known composition is 'Turn, Amaryllis, to thy swain', a glee which was reprinted numerous times. Spink considers that Brewer's songs reveal deep feeling and that his religious song 'O that mine eyes could melt', a meditation on the passion, is 'thoroughly counter-reformation', suggesting 'Italian sympathies'. It was among several songs by Brewer chosen for the *Musical Companion* (1667) of John Playford, who selected it as an example of an English song which could be performed in the way described in his *Directions for Singing after the Italian Manner*. Another partsong by Brewer also included was *Gloria tribuatur Deo*.

Brewer is thought to have died *c.*1660. While Meyer claims that Brewer was in favour at the Restoration court, he gives no source for this. He may have been the father of Thomas Brewer (*d.* 1690), from whom a line of American migrants later traced its descent.　　　　JULIA GASPER

Sources private information (2004) [Rhona Mitchell, Christ's Hospital museum and archives] · *New Grove* · A. Ashbee and P. Holman, *John Jenkins and his times: studies in English consort music* (1996) · I. Spink, *English song from Dowland to Purcell* (1974) · I. Spink, ed., *English songs, 1625–1660*, Musica Britannica, 33 (1971); 2nd edn (1977) · P. S. Willetts, 'Sir Nicholas Le Strange and John Jenkins', *Music and Letters*, 42 (1961), 30–43 · G. Abraham, ed., *The new Oxford history of music* (1968); repr. (1998) · E. H. Meyer, *Early English chamber music from the middle ages to Purcell* (1946); E. H. Meyer and D. Poulton, revs. (1982) · P. M. Young, *A history of British music* (1967) · *DNB*

Brewer [Briwerre]**, William** (*d.* 1226), administrator and justice, was the son of Henry Brewer, a royal forester of Bere, Hampshire. It seems that it was in Hampshire that this family originated: William's grandfather, also a William Brewer, held lands outside the west gate of Winchester. The family's interests, however, probably extended outside the bounds of this county, since William's grandfather founded the nunnery of Polsloe, Devon, and William himself married Beatrice de Valle (*d.* before 1220), allegedly the sometime mistress of Reginald, earl of Cornwall (*d.* 1175) and father of Henry fitz Count (*d.* 1221), who brought with her the manor of Colton, Somerset. Anyone looking for an instance of the exemplary royal servant of the middle ages could hardly do better than to examine the life of William Brewer. Aptly described by one modern writer as a 'die-hard Angevin', his career, spanning fifty years, was a model of loyalty and usefulness. He served four Angevin kings, among them King John, who is reported to have attributed to Brewer the ability to know his master's mind; it was John, above all, who made Brewer extraordinarily wealthy, and by the time of his death he was the master of some sixty knights' fees focused in the south-west, with a newly created *caput* at Bridgwater, Somerset. The roots of this vast fortune, however, lay in the reigns of John's predecessors, Henry II and Richard I.

William Brewer began his career as forester of Bere in succession to his father, Henry, and by 1179 had become sheriff of Devon. In 1185 he was made custodian of the barony of Bampton, following the flight from England of Fulk Paynel (*d.* 1208). This barony was to provide one of the many lucrative matches Brewer made for his children, when he married his daughter, Alice, to Fulk Paynel's son and heir, William. At about the same time Brewer was also appointed warden of the Cornish tin mines. It was under Richard I, however, that William Brewer broke into the heart of royal administration, though quite how he brought himself to Richard's attention is not at all clear. From the earliest moments of the reign Brewer was associated as a lesser justice with the two justiciars appointed by Richard to run England during his absence on crusade. He remained loyal to the king throughout Richard's absence, both on crusade and in captivity, and was present at Worms when the terms of Richard's ransom were agreed on 29 June 1193. It was also during Richard's reign that Brewer began his career in the exchequer, where he was to prove most useful to his Angevin masters. Painter, in his study of King John, thought that attendance at the exchequer was 'an unwelcome burden' for William Brewer (Painter, 72), but this can hardly have been so, since he made himself indispensable in this department and became renowned for his financial acumen. He sat at the exchequer throughout John's reign, and during the minority of Henry III he took an important role in the revitalization of royal finances following the chaos created by the civil war.

Like all Angevin administrators, Brewer was able to turn

his hand to most tasks assigned to him. He sat as a justice on the king's bench in the reigns of both Richard and John, and he can be found in the court of *coram rege* witnessing fines throughout John's reign. He was sheriff of a mass of counties, sometimes holding several at once, and was obviously extremely—and unwelcomely—efficient, since the men of Cornwall, Dorset, and Somerset all paid to have someone other than William Brewer appointed as their sheriff, a request that John would no doubt have seen as a tribute to his choice of servant. During the interdict Brewer's knowledge of John's wishes, which must have owed much to the fact that he was constantly in attendance on the king, made him the ideal person to negotiate with the pope's legates at Dover in 1209, and John showed further confidence in his servant by appointing him to be present at the election of no fewer than eight bishops. During the minority of Henry III Brewer took a position in government only marginally below the main players in that drama. He was among the council that advised William (I) Marshal, and after the Marshal's resignation, on 9 April 1219, Brewer was one of the second tier of ministers supporting the triumvirate of Hubert de Burgh (d. 1243), Peter des Roches (d. 1238), and Pandulf (d. 1226), which, in the early 1220s, directed the affairs of the realm. He can mostly be found answering to Hubert de Burgh. By 1223 he was high enough in the minority government to be personally addressed by Pope Honorius III (r. 1216–27) in letters demanding that Henry be given 'free disposition' of his kingdom.

Brewer benefited enormously from the competence and constancy of his service. He had the odd setback—as in 1209 when he was removed from his many shrievalties—but, like others who lost their offices in this year, he was soon back in harness. His *caput* at Bridgwater had been acquired from Fulk Paynel in 1199 as his reward for bringing Fulk back into royal favour. Rewards came thick and fast under John: for example, in 1203 he received fourteen knights' fees in Cornwall; in March 1204 he acquired the twenty-three and three-quarters knights' fees that made up the barony of Horsley, Derbyshire; and in April the same year he gained the honour of Lavendon, Buckinghamshire. In addition, Brewer was granted numerous markets, fairs, and boroughs on his lands, as well as pardons for his debts to the king, and, like other royal servants, he also enjoyed many custodies of castles and wardships of heirs.

Not surprisingly, given Brewer's close association with John, many great barons were prepared to pay highly for his intercession on their behalf with the king. John gave Brewer permission to build a castle (which he seems to have built) on Fulk Paynel's former manor of Bridgwater, relinquished to Brewer in 1199, along with two other castles (which he seems not to have built), one in Devon and the other in Hampshire. Paynel was also persuaded to give up many other manors for Brewer's good offices with the king. William Ferrers gave him the manor of Blisworth, Northamptonshire, a grant that looked to Ralph V. Turner 'suspiciously like a bribe' (Turner, 81). And even a great man in Brewer's own preferred locality, like Henry

de la Pomeroy, lord of the Devon barony of Berry Pomeroy, who was obviously high in royal favour and, moreover, was one of John's household knights, felt the need to grant the manor of Bradworthy to Brewer in order to have him on his side.

Painter memorably summed up Brewer's achievement in constructing his own substantial barony: 'it required consistent loyalty and usefulness to the crown combined with a lack of squeamishness in acquiring demesne and fees. William Brewer was well supplied with these qualifications' (Painter, 73). They made him a man to be feared. In 1211 he was numbered by Roger of Wendover among King John's evil counsellors, and he certainly made the most of John's favour, which enabled him to override other people's hereditary property rights, intimidate opponents, and extort favours. Not surprisingly, he retained a high regard for royal authority, and in 1223 spoke out against the confirmation of Magna Carta and the charter of the forest, declaring that 'the liberties you seek should not rightfully be observed, since they were extorted by violence' (Paris, *Chron.*, 3.76). One of his objectives, assiduously promoted, was to make provision for his children. Brewer had two sons and five daughters, all of whom received marriages that brought considerable profit. His eldest son, Richard, was given the manor of Odcombe, Somerset, which Brewer extracted from Walter Croc and John de Longchamp, who had been competing for it. Richard also received some estates from his father in Wiltshire, Derbyshire, and Nottinghamshire. On Richard's death, about 1215, these lands reverted to Brewer. The latter's second son and eventual heir, William Brewer, was married to Johanna de Revières, daughter of William de Revières, earl of Devon. Like his father, the younger William Brewer enjoyed a career as a royal administrator: he was a forest justice in 1219; a collector of tallages in Northumberland and Cumberland in 1223; sheriff of Northumberland and custodian of Newcastle in 1223–4; and sheriff of Devon in 1224–5. When this William died childless in 1232, his heirs were the descendants of his sisters Graecia, Isabella, and Johanna, together with his surviving sisters Alice and Margery, who divided the inheritance equally.

As he had for his sons, William Brewer found profitable marriages for all his daughters: Graecia married Reginald de Briouze of Kington, Herefordshire; Isabella married first a son of Fulbert of Dover, who was a ward of her father, and second Baldwin Wake of Bourne, Lincolnshire; Johanna married another of her father's wards, William de Percy (d. 1245), lord of Topcliffe, Yorkshire; Alice married first Reginald de Mohun of Dunster, Somerset, and second William Paynel of Bampton; and Margery married first William de la Ferté, second Eudo de Dammartin, and third Geoffrey de Say of West Greenwich, Kent.

Perhaps the best indication of William Brewer's wealth is his many benefactions to the church. Whether through feelings of guilt or a desire to demonstrate his newly acquired wealth to his peers and neighbours, Brewer was more than conventionally generous to the church. He founded no fewer than three new houses: in 1196 he established a Premonstratensian house at Torre, Devon; in 1201 he endowed an Augustinian house at Mottisfont, Hampshire; and in 1201, in imitation of King John, he founded the Cistercian abbey of Dunkeswell, Devon, where in 1226 he was to be buried in the habit of a Cistercian monk below the high altar. In addition to these foundations Brewer also made donations to established churches, such as the 4000 marks he covenanted to the templars at Acre for the use of his nephew, William *Brewer (d. 1244), bishop of Exeter, during a pilgrimage to the Holy Land, a journey the bishop undertook in 1227. He also gave a gold chalice to Worcester Cathedral for its rededication in 1217, sent two silver chalices to Prémontré in France, and founded a hospital at Bridgwater, Somerset.

William Brewer died on 24 November 1226, after a career like that of many of those relatively lowly men who flourished in royal service under the Angevin kings. By dint of hard work and considerable skill, not to mention the ruthless exploitation of the advantages that his position brought him, he made his way up the slippery ladder of royal service until 'he was one of the half dozen or so men closest to the centre of power in England' (Turner, 71).   S. D. CHURCH

Sources R. V. Turner, 'William Briwerre', in R. V. Turner, Men raised from the dust: administrative service and upward mobility in Angevin England (1988), 71–90 · S. Painter, The reign of King John (1949) · I. J. Sanders, English baronies: a study of their origin and descent, 1086–1327 (1960) · D. A. Carpenter, The minority of Henry III (1990) · G. Oliver, Monasticon diocesis Exoniensis (1846) · D. Seymour, Torre Abbey (1977) · Paris, Chron.

Brewer, William (d. 1244), bishop of Exeter, was a nephew and protégé of the baron William *Brewer, an important royal servant with considerable territorial interests and frequent employment in Devon; nothing is known of either his parentage or his education. Through his namesake's influence Brewer obtained, in the vacancy after Bishop Henry Marshal's death in 1206, the episcopal church of Braunton (1208) and the cathedral precentorship; and in the vacancy after Bishop Simon's death (September 1223), when the baron was royal custodian of the bishopric, Brewer was quickly elected to the see and was consecrated on 21 April 1224. No one thought him learned, but his promotion was not considered scandalous.

Brewer assumed office towards the close of Henry III's turbulent minority and was caught up in the new spirit of liberty in English society sparked off in 1215 by Magna Carta. His cathedral chapter, dissatisfied with its archaic constitution and lack of an elective head, had probably made reform a precondition of his election, and within two years he agreed to the creation of the offices of an elective dean and a chancellor, endowed the deanery, and increased the revenues of the other dignitaries, the vicarschoral, and the common fund, all at the expense of the episcopal estate. He sanctioned the building of a chapter house and started to erect a new palace. He agreed not to confirm or alienate in perpetuity any churches or lands without the consent of the dean and chapter. And he issued in a synod the first comprehensive set of statutes

for his diocese. These owed much to those promulgated at Salisbury. He also granted charters of liberties to the boroughs he founded at Crediton and Penryn.

Hardly had Brewer been consecrated than Henry III ordered him to take custody of the rebel Falkes de Bréauté's castle at Plympton; and he would have taken it by storm had not his troops demurred. His creation of a semi-independent capitular government at Exeter increased his own freedom. In the summer of 1227, making use of the 4000 marks of silver bequeathed to him in 1226 by his uncle, the baron, he sailed from Brindisi with his friend Peter des Roches, bishop of Winchester, for the Holy Land, where the two played an important part in its affairs both before and after the arrival of the emperor Frederick II on his belated crusade. In March 1228 Brewer visited Jerusalem, liberated by the emperor, and, since his presence is not noted at Exeter before April 1231, he probably then accompanied des Roches on his leisurely return through Italy and France, engaged in diplomatic business. Back in England, he carried out some diplomatic missions for Henry III: in 1234, again with des Roches, treating for peace with Louis IX of France; in 1235 conducting Henry's sister, Isabella, to her marriage with the emperor at Worms in July; and early in 1236 again negotiating in France. In January 1241 he crossed the channel with the departing papal legate, Otto, bound for Gregory IX's (abortive) general council at Rome. He reached Pontigny by 24 March. Before October 1231 he was constructing with the king's help a deer park at Faringdon, parcel of his chapelry of Bosham, and royal gifts of deer, venison, and timber were regular until August 1237.

The man of action was also pious. Brewer was devoted to the Virgin Mary and founded at Crediton a hermitage dedicated to her. He was generous to religious houses and interested in indulgences. He fostered the religious services in his cathedral, and was remembered as the greatest donor of vestments and ornaments to the cathedral treasury; his anniversary service was awarded the exceptional use of eight candles. Brewer requested permission to resign, and on 15 December 1244 Pope Innocent IV ordered the new bishop of Winchester to receive his resignation; but he had already died, on 24 November. The chronicler Matthew Paris noted that he was remarkable for his good character, noble birth, and ability, perhaps an understatement of his virtues.   FRANK BARLOW

Sources F. Barlow, ed., Exeter, 1186–1257, English Episcopal Acta, 12 (1996) · F. M. Powicke and C. R. Cheney, eds., Councils and synods with other documents relating to the English church, 1205–1313, 1 (1964) · Rogeri de Wendover liber qui dicitur flores historiarum, ed. H. G. Hewlett, 3 vols., Rolls Series, [84] (1886–9) · Paris, Chron. · Matthaei Parisiensis, monachi Sancti Albani, Historia Anglorum, sive … Historia minor, ed. F. Madden, 3 vols., Rolls Series, 44 (1886–9) · Chancery records
Archives Devon RO · Exeter Cathedral, dean and chapter library

Brewster, Abraham (1796–1874), judge, was born in April 1796, the son of William Bagenal Brewster of Ballinulta, co. Wicklow, and his wife, Mary, née Bates. He went to school at Kilkenny College and entered Trinity College, Dublin, in 1812; he obtained his BA in 1817 and his MA in

1847. He was called to the English bar in 1817 and to the Irish bar in 1819; he then worked the Leinster circuit, soon acquiring the reputation of a sound lawyer and a powerful speaker. Brewster took silk on 13 July 1835.

Politically, Brewster was a Conservative, and despite charges of Orangeism by Daniel O'Connell he was appointed legal adviser to the lord lieutenant of Ireland on 10 October 1841. He was also solicitor-general of Ireland between 2 February and 16 July 1846. By the influence of his friend Sir James Graham, first lord of the Admiralty, he was attorney-general of Ireland from 10 January 1853 until the fall of the Aberdeen ministry on 10 February 1855. In 1819 Brewster married Mary Ann, *née* Gray, of co. Carlow. They had a son, William, and a daughter, Elizabeth, both of whom died before their parents. Mary died in 1862.

Brewster was well known as a great equity and criminal lawyer. He became a privy councillor in 1853 and, after his resignation as attorney-general in 1855, he was involved in several important cases, including the Mountgarrett case in 1854, the Carden abduction case in 1854, the Yelverton case in 1861, the Egmont will case in 1863, the marquess of Donegal's ejectment action, and *Fitzgerald v. Fitzgerald*. Brewster succeeded Francis Blackburne (1782–1867) as lord justice of appeal in Ireland in the Derby ministry (July 1866) and as lord chancellor of Ireland (March 1867). As lord chancellor he sat in his court for the last time on 17 December 1868, when Disraeli's government resigned, and he afterwards withdrew from public life. Only three or four judgments delivered by him, either in the appellate court or the court of chancery, were printed. He died at his residence, 26 Merrion Square South, Dublin, on 26 July 1874, and was buried at Tullow, co. Carlow, on 30 July. A portrait by Frank Reynolds hangs in the hall of the King's Inns, Dublin.   G. C. BOASE, *rev.* SINÉAD AGNEW

Sources O. J. Burke, *The history of the lord chancellors of Ireland from AD 1186 to AD 1874* (1879) · F. E. Ball, *The judges in Ireland, 1221–1921*, 2 vols. (1926) · Ward, *Men of the reign* · Boase, *Mod. Eng. biog.* · *ILN* (1874)
Archives PRO NIre., Hamilton MSS, corresp. with Lord Abercorn · Sheff. Arch., corresp. with Earl Fitzwilliam · U. Nott., Pelham MSS, corresp. with duke of Newcastle
Likenesses F. Reynolds, oils, King's Inns, Dublin
Wealth at death under £140,000 (in England and Ireland): probate, 24 Sept 1874, *CGPLA Ire.* · under £50,000 (in England): probate, 24 Sept 1874, *CGPLA Eng. & Wales*

Brewster, Sir David (1781–1868), natural philosopher and academic administrator, was born on 11 December 1781 in a house in the Canongate, Jedburgh, second son and third of the six children of James Brewster (*c.*1735–1815), rector of Jedburgh grammar school, and his wife, Margaret (1753–1790), only daughter of James Key and Grisel Scott of Dundee. James Brewster had been educated at the University of Aberdeen, and subsequently taught at Dundee grammar school before being appointed rector at Jedburgh in 1771. In 1775 he married Margaret Key; she died, aged thirty-seven, soon after the birth and death of their sixth child, when David Brewster was only nine. The remaining four brothers were brought up largely by their sister Grisel, and were all educated for careers in the Church of Scotland: James (1777–1847), later minister at

Sir David Brewster (1781–1868), by David Octavius Hill and Robert Adamson, 1843

Craig, Ferryden, near Montrose; David; George (1784–1855), minister at Scoonie, Fife; and Patrick *Brewster (1788–1859), minister at the abbey church, Paisley.

Education, marriage, and early career Young David's formative years in Jedburgh, outside school, were spent in company which helped to direct his intellectual interests towards scientific and literary pursuits. The local minister, Dr Thomas Somerville, a scholar and author, made the young man his literary assistant, so that Brewster acquired early the skills in language, writing, and editing which later became his livelihood. Although not a studious boy he read avidly his father's undergraduate notes on physical science. He constructed his first telescope at the age of ten, under the guidance of a local ploughwright and amateur astronomer, James Veitch (1771–1838) of Inchbonny, near Jedburgh. Their friendship lasted until Veitch's death, despite Brewster leaving Jedburgh grammar school, in 1794, aged twelve, to attend Edinburgh University. He corresponded with his mentor, Veitch, on scientific and religious topics throughout the time he was there until he graduated in 1800 as MA. Brewster then remained in Edinburgh and its vicinity, working as a tutor and journalist. He had begun contributing to the *Edinburgh Magazine* in 1799 and became its editor in 1802 after its amalgamation with the *Scots Magazine* until about 1807. He began experimenting in optics at about the same time. His first scientific paper was accepted in 1806. His daughter's biography asserts that at this period he still had every intention of following a career in the established church, and, licensed to preach in 1804, Brewster undertook pastoral duties in and around Edinburgh. However, it soon became apparent that he found public speaking such a stressful ordeal—on one occasion, he fainted at a dinner party when invited to say grace—that he was obliged to turn his attention to other methods of earning an income. He was an unsuccessful candidate for the chair of mathematics at the University of Edinburgh in 1805, and again for that at the University of St Andrews in 1807, but as university teaching then was solely by lecture, he must have come to realize that this avenue was similarly closed to him. Fortunately, in 1808 he was invited to become editor of a new publishing venture: the *Edinburgh Encyclopaedia*.

The appointment was something of a mixed blessing, involving the commissioning of major articles from often recalcitrant and difficult contributors and ultimately producing much of the work himself, under legal threats from the publishers. The *Encyclopaedia* appeared volume by volume at increasingly uneven intervals, and it was not until 1830 that the entire work was available. However, the positive side to this endeavour was that it provided Brewster with an income, and kept him in touch with a network of scientists and scholars across Europe and North America. But the inadequacy of this income is shown by Brewster's simultaneous contribution of articles to this encyclopaedia's main rival, the *Encyclopaedia Britannica*, which at this period was still being produced and published in Edinburgh. He contributed articles to the fourth (1810), fifth (1817), and sixth (1820–23) editions, and more extensively to the seventh (1827–42) and eighth (1853–60) editions.

Brewster was married on 31 July 1810 in Edinburgh to Juliet Macpherson (c.1776–1850), younger daughter and the youngest of four illegitimate children of James *Macpherson (1736–1796), of Belleville, near Kingussie, the alleged translator of ancient poetry by Ossian. They had four sons and a daughter, Margaret Maria Gordon, *née* Brewster (1823–1907), who wrote the sympathetic but largely domestic biography which remains the major contemporary source for Brewster's life.

Journalism and writing In 1819, with the mineralogist Robert Jameson, Brewster became joint editor of the *Edinburgh Philosophical Journal*, but this was not a success, partly because of the editors' incompatibility; from 1826 the *Edinburgh New Philosophical Journal* was run under Jameson's sole editorship. Meanwhile Brewster managed to persuade another publisher to launch a rival imprint edited by himself, entitled the *Edinburgh Journal of Science*. This survived until 1832, read in particular for its strong views on the alleged decline of science in Britain. Then it was acquired by the printer and publisher Richard Taylor of London, who owned the long established *Philosophical Magazine*, and Brewster became one of the three, later four, editors of the *London and Edinburgh* (later *London, Edinburgh and Dublin*) *Philosophical Magazine*, a position he held until his death. His review articles, ranging over a huge variety of subjects, appeared in many periodicals of the day: the *Edinburgh Review*, the *Quarterly Review*, *Fraser's Magazine*, the *Witness*, the *Weekly Instructor*, *Good Words*, the

Monthly Chronicle, and others. Brewster's friendship with the Evangelical minister Thomas Chalmers led to his association with the *North British Review*, founded in 1844, and to which he submitted seventy-five articles, many of which were longer, and submitted later, than the editors wished; however, his vigorous prose was always worth reading for its visual style and vibrant language.

Brewster's reputation as a historian of science has perhaps outlived reputations he earned in other fields, yet even this accolade is not straightforward. His writing—as opposed to his journalism and editing—generally falls into the later part of his career, after 1830. However, he often prefaced his review and encyclopaedia articles with historical information, placing his writing within context. Even his optical work was occasionally given a historical introduction, particularly that which was written to appeal to a general audience, such as his *Treatise on Optics* in *Dr Lardner's Cabinet Cyclopaedia* (1831).

The title of his *Martyrs of Science: Lives of Galileo, Tycho Brahe and Kepler* (1841) amused his family, who observed that there were no martyrs in it. But Tycho and Kepler suffered treatment similar to Brewster's own: lack of support from the state in undertaking internationally important scientific work. However, Brewster was unable to sympathize with Galileo's recantation and failure to grasp the martyr's crown of death for his scientific beliefs, and this evangelical fervour was to emerge again in his work on Isaac Newton.

A lifelong interest in the person who had shaped the scientific framework in which he worked led Brewster to write a short and popular *Life of Sir Isaac Newton* (1831), which was well received. In his self-appointed role as Newton's defender, his *Memoirs of the Life, Writings and Discoveries of Sir Isaac Newton* (1855) was deeply researched and written as a vindication against the charges of insanity and immorality levelled by J. B. Biot in 1822 and again in Francis Baily's *Life of Flamsteed* (1835). In 1837 Brewster was able to gain access to the Portsmouth Collection of manuscripts, which contains many Newton letters which had not previously been consulted. However, although able to refute both Biot and Baily with newly discovered correspondence, he encountered unexpected and upsetting evidence: Newton was deeply involved in alchemical literature and experimentation, and his religious beliefs were extremely unorthodox.

Despite these traumatic discoveries—which essentially negated the purpose behind his historical biography—Brewster attempted to synthesize his findings. His biography of Newton, which remained the best available until 1980, managed to include all the problems of the enigmatic figure of Newton for the first time, and attempted to solve them in the light of Brewster's own times. The work is remarkable as much for the insights it gives about Brewster, as it is for information about Newton.

University life After leaving Edinburgh University in 1800 Brewster seemed by inclination unsuited for a career which involved public speaking; even so, he applied for university posts on a number of occasions, which, had he been successful, would have ensured a steady income on which he could support his growing family. The first such occasion was in 1805, and again in 1807; the third—and possibly most bruising occasion—was in 1833, when he put himself forward as a candidate for the chair of natural philosophy at Edinburgh, only to find that his young protégé James David Forbes had rallied support through the British Association (of which Brewster was a founder), and was also backed by Edinburgh town council which was still formal patron of the university and controlled most professorial appointments.

It was not until 1838 that Brewster obtained the security he must have craved with a non-teaching post at the University of St Andrews; but, characteristically, he made of this sinecure a rod to beat his own back. Politically Brewster was a reform whig, and his connection especially with the career politician Henry Brougham, later lord chancellor, influenced his life in a number of ways. The pair had met at university and Brougham had apparently suggested that the young Brewster should start to conduct experiments in optics as early as 1798. Later Brougham was to ensure that Brewster received a government pension of £100 per annum, increased in 1836 to £300 a year, and it was Brougham who assisted in the founding of the British Association and paved the way towards Brewster's knighthood. Through political influence two of Brewster's sons became officials in the Indian Civil Service, and it was the government which appointed Brewster to the principalship of the United Colleges of St Leonard and St Salvator at the University of St Andrews in 1838.

There he attempted to turn the slumbering and somewhat corrupt university into a dynamic college to teach and promote science, and naturally met resistance. There was a very earnest attempt to deprive Brewster of his post by showing that he was a religious dissenter; but, as he was an elder of the Free Church and not a minister he had signed the Act of Protest but not the Deed of Demission, and so could not be ousted. In 1859, again through Brougham's influence, he was elected principal and vice-chancellor of the University of Edinburgh, and in that office presided when Brougham was installed as chancellor of the university. He retained the post until his death.

Although he was appointed to a university position so late in life Brewster became involved in the reform of the Scottish universities—an act of parliament was passed only in 1858, although hearings had been heard over three decades before various royal commissions set up to investigate effectiveness of the running of the universities. His attempts to introduce science into the curriculum in a more vigorous way than was already represented in the general arts degree (which required both mathematics and natural philosophy) was only moderately successful. The real campaign for scientific and technological university education was to be fought in the next generation. In any case, Brewster's own campaign for state support of a scientific career was in terms of those models which he had seen on the continent, that of an academy or institute for researchers, not one where such valuable work had to be snatched between teaching classes of boisterous students.

Optics and vision During his lifetime Brewster was regarded by contemporaries as one of the pre-eminent international scientific figures, yet after his death his reputation rapidly sank into oblivion. He made a number of significant contributions to science, where, despite his broader interests which often figured in his journalism, his efforts remained focused on optics. His initial interest in astronomy and instrumentation was demonstrated by the contents of his first major scientific publication, *A Treatise on New Philosophical Instruments* (1813), the latter part of which was devoted to his measurements of the refractive and dispersive powers of almost 200 substances in his pursuit of improvements to achromatic instruments.

In 1808 Étienne Malus discovered the polarization of light by transmission. Brewster had investigated these effects independently, but, cut off from French research by the Napoleonic wars, he learned of Malus's work only just before its publication. This knowledge, combined with his own recent discoveries in polarization, pushed Brewster's focus of interest from instrumentation into optical theory, and for the next fifteen to twenty years he energetically pursued four related fields of research in this area. First, he followed the line that successive polarization by refraction through a pile of glass plates, which he concluded was a constant, ought to allow both the investigation of the form and structure of crystals, and indeed, the nature of light itself. Second, he searched for a general law of polarization—the law which now bears his name—finding that the index of refraction of the reflecting medium is the tangent of the angle of polarization. Third, he studied metallic reflection, concluding that light was elliptically polarized, and deduced laws which predicted quantities and angles of polarization of light. His fourth research field created the new fields of optical mineralogy and photoelasticity. His experiments in 1813 on the structure of topaz led to the unexpected discovery of its two optical axes, and by 1819 Brewster had classified hundreds of minerals and crystals into their optical categories by painstaking experiment. While undertaking this project, he also discovered that heat and pressure could alter the doubly refracting structures of minerals and crystals and again, he deduced the general laws which enabled these phenomena to be predicted. Still searching for ways to improve instrumentation, Brewster undertook an extensive investigation of absorption spectroscopy. Adding a further 1600 dark lines to Fraunhofer's 354, these researches led him to reinterpret the colours of the spectrum, disagreeing with Newton's deductions, yet reaffirming an emission theory of light. He never fully accepted the undulatory theory of light because he felt that it did not explain all the phenomena.

In the 1830s his intensive and energetic youthful researches changed direction, and he devoted more research time to applications of optics and the physiology of vision. His experiments on the structure of the eye helped to lay the foundations of modern biophysics, while in his work on subjective visual phenomena he made important discoveries, but these were subsequently overshadowed. Brewster was very much an experimentalist rather than a theorist. He deplored the lack of state patronage in supporting scientific research; but on a number of occasions he successfully persuaded societies and universities to supply him with the equipment with which he could do his work. Because he never fully accepted the wave theory of light and because he outlived most of his scientific contemporaries, Brewster found his experimental work marginalized towards the end of his life. Much of the valuable work he did was subsequently not attributed to him, something he would have found hard to take.

Instruments and photography The first part of Brewster's *Treatise* described improvements to precision instruments and new devices; although some of these remained proposals, others were subjected to careful technical development. An example of the latter was his attempt to increase the resolving power of microscope objectives by using jewel (instead of glass) lenses, capitalizing on the high refractive index and low dispersive power of optical minerals. These lenses proved successful but extremely expensive, and eventually the problem was resolved by a different route with the introduction of the cheaper Wollaston lens, and ultimately with the design of effective achromatic lenses.

The invention which he claimed and defended for most of his life was a type of zonal lens built up from annular rings and described as his polyzonal lens, which is now called a Fresnel lens after the independent development of such a lens by one of his principal French rivals. Lenses of this type could be made of very large aperture, and they came to some prominence when they were developed by Augustin Fresnel for use in French lighthouses about 1820. Brewster had first investigated lenses of this type in 1812, and by 1820 was urging the Northern Lighthouse Board to adopt the system. In 1823 he published an account of his illumination system, and this led to a series of successful experiments ten years later. However, the dispute over the priority of invention kept Brewster in print over the years, until at least 1860.

Brewster was involved in photography from its very beginnings: he stayed with William Henry Fox Talbot in 1836, and although Talbot did not publish his findings until 1839 Brewster was sent examples of his work from an early stage: 'my father's connexion with photography and photographers might well furnish a chapter of his life in competent hands', his daughter wrote (Gordon, 162–3). Indeed, Brewster's correspondence with Talbot meant that St Andrews was the first place outside England that the calotype was practised, and it was on Brewster's advice that Talbot did not patent his invention outside England. However, although Brewster collected photographic prints and wrote fairly extensively on the subject he does not appear to have had sufficient time to practise the new photographic art much himself.

Brewster's name is connected principally with the invention of two optical devices: the stereoscope and the kaleidoscope. The stereoscope, a device connected with Brewster's work on the physiology of vision, was invented by Charles Wheatstone in 1832 in order to investigate binocular vision. Because this was before the invention of photography, special three-dimensional pictures had to be drawn, and the device was really only used in an experimental capacity, although later Wheatstone declared that Talbot and Henry Collen, another early calotype pioneer, had supplied photographic prints for his instrument. It was not until 1849 that Brewster read two papers—one concerning his lenticular stereoscope, the other his binocular camera—and the following year he took the prototype with him to France, where he showed it to the Parisian opticians François Soleil and his son-in-law Jules Duboscq. They constructed a stereoscopic viewer, together with some daguerreotype photographs produced in a rudimentary stereoscopic camera, which they displayed at the Great Exhibition in London in 1851. 'The stereoscope', wrote Brewster, 'attracted the particular attention of the Queen, and M. Soleil executed a beautiful instrument which was presented to Her Majesty in his name by Sir David Brewster' (Brewster, 177). With royal patronage the device could not fail commercially, and there was an insatiable demand over the next few years. However, as with the lighthouse lenses, Brewster was again caught up in a priority dispute, on this occasion conducted in the correspondence columns of *The Times*, with Wheatstone. Sir John Herschel summarized the dispute succinctly thus: 'Wheatstone invented the stereoscope; Brewster invented a way of looking at stereoscopic pictures' (Wade, 36).

The kaleidoscope is a primarily a toy which uses simple principles of reflection noticed by Brewster when experimenting in 1816; but it was observed even by his contemporaries that these principles had been known since antiquity. In a manner which was to become something of a pattern, Brewster defended his brainchild in print, then mustered supporters to his aid: a series of articles appeared over the years in encyclopaedias and journals, summarized by the grand *Treatise on the Kaleidoscope* (1858). In this case he had rashly gone to the expense of obtaining a patent for protecting the manufacture of the kaleidoscope, which was negated when the enthusiasm of the London instrument maker to whom he entrusted the prototype led to the principles of the device becoming known. Instantly, the expensively produced brass tube was copied, and he wrote to his wife: 'had I managed my patent rightly, I would have made one hundred thousand pounds by it!' (Gordon, 97). It appears to have been the first instance of a national fashionable craze, and an indication that consumers could create markets overnight in a newly industrialized society.

Scientific associations and societies Brewster was involved in setting up a number of societies throughout his life, and although his primary motive for this was often to further his belief in the cause of scientific knowledge, frequently he tried to use such a body as a forum for his own ends. In 1821 Brewster became closely involved in the setting up of two new Edinburgh organizations: the Society of Arts (later the Royal Scottish Society of Arts), to promote and reward Scottish inventions; and the Edinburgh School of Arts, the first of the wave of mechanics' institutes which were to be set up all over the United Kingdom during the next decade or so. Both of these were successful enterprises, although Brewster's impetuous behaviour led to his rapid dissociation from the latter, while pressure of work meant that his involvement with the former became more remote over the years.

Brewster was able to set up large-scale associations of far-flung scientific researchers, because of the contacts he had made through his editorial work, and through his travels to London and on the continent. His standing in science was such that others were glad to be associated with him, and his considerable personal charm must have also helped. His most successful enterprise—although within a few years it had turned against him—was the British Association for the Advancement of Science, which held its first meeting at York in 1831.

By arguing that there was a probable decline of science in England, as opposed to its rise in Europe, Brewster successfully attracted influential people to the association's first meeting, but he did little to organize it. Many of the Cambridge scientists stayed away, alienated by Brewster's declinist attitude. In 1832 the association met at Oxford, where Brewster presented a report on optics and was awarded an honorary degree; he was also the association's vice-president and sat on its council. However, in 1833 it all began to go horribly wrong when Forbes was supported by the association in his successful bid for the Edinburgh chair. At the association's 1833 meeting, held in Cambridge, the supporters of the wave theory of light (and thus opponents of Brewster) moved into the attack, and a new report on optics was commissioned. Although he was later to become its president at the Edinburgh meeting in 1850, Brewster remained disappointed that his brainchild had not fulfilled its early promise, and that it had become a creature of the establishment rather than a lobbying forum able to affect government policy, especially in scientific matters.

Brewster was also involved in the foundation of other societies. For example, on his removal to St Andrews in 1838, he set up the St Andrews Literary and Philosophical Society. This might have remained as obscure as many other literary and philosophical societies, except that it was at this venue that Talbot's calotypes were first displayed, sent to Brewster through the post, stimulating important early photographic work in Scotland. It was Brewster who introduced to each other David Octavius Hill and Robert Adamson, whose partnership was so influential to early photography. Mrs Gordon also mentions Brewster's presidency of the Peace Congress in 1851, and in 1862 the Inventors' Institute chose him as their first president.

Historical significance Brewster's standing in science was perhaps at its greatest during the earlier part of his lifetime when his support of an unmodified Newtonian theory of light could still be seen as a tenable position. However, with time, other bright young men superseded him.

He was first seriously threatened by his own protégé James David Forbes, who was the successful candidate for the natural philosophy chair at Edinburgh in opposition to Brewster, and whose work on the nature of heat did much to extend understanding of the electromagnetic spectrum. In due course he was overshadowed in stature by Forbes's protégé, James Clerk Maxwell, who was to produce original and far-reaching ideas in the same field. Brewster's real contribution was the measurement of the optical properties of hundreds of crystals in an attempt to classify and understand their structures: the unglamorous donkey work of science.

Brewster's influence in scientific instrumentation for measurement and observation was fourfold: he improved many devices which already existed; he invented others, of which the kaleidoscope and the lenticular stereoscope are the most famous; his position as a major figure in optical research enabled him to wield influence in areas such as patent law reform and involved him in jury work at the Great Exhibition in 1851 and again at the Paris Exhibition of 1855; and in turn this involved him in the active patronage of instrument makers in the United Kingdom.

Brewster's scientific papers totalled 299 items. But perhaps more influential on a wider audience (which may never have read any of that enormous output of scientific work) were his more popular books, articles, and reviews, many of which were anonymous. Together with his papers, these have been estimated to number about 1240. For historians of photography Brewster has come to be seen as the catalyst who enabled Talbot's process to be used in Scotland in a patent free environment.

Scientific honours were awarded to Brewster from an early age: in 1807 he was made honorary LLD by the University of Aberdeen and honorary MA by Cambridge University. In 1808 he was elected fellow of the Royal Society of Edinburgh, of which he was its general secretary from 1819 to 1828, and president from 1864 until his death. He was awarded its Keith medal twice. In 1815 he was elected fellow of the Royal Society and won its Copley medal; subsequently he won the Rumford medal in 1818 and one of the royal medals in 1830, each for discoveries connected with his work in polarization of light. Brewster became a member of the Institution of Civil Engineers in 1820 and a member of the Royal Irish Academy in 1822. In 1831 he was created a knight of the Royal Guelphic Order by William IV, and the following year he was made honorary DCL by the University of Oxford. Awards also flowed in from abroad. In 1816 the French Institute awarded him a cash prize and in 1825 made him a corresponding member; in 1849 he was made one of only eight foreign associates of the Académie des Sciences, in succession to the Swedish chemist Jakob Berzelius. He was made a corresponding member of—among others—the royal societies of St Petersburg, Berlin, Brussels, Copenhagen, Stockholm, and Vienna; to these scientific honours the king of Prussia added the order of merit in 1847, and the French Emperor Napoleon III, the cross of the Légion d'honneur in 1855.

Brewster married Jane Kirk Purnell (*b*. 1827) in Nice on

27 March 1857. She was the second daughter of Thomas Purnell of Scarborough. They had a daughter. Sir David Brewster died of pneumonia and bronchitis on 10 February 1868, at Allerly, the house he had built outside Melrose, in the Scottish borders. He was buried in the cemetery at Melrose Abbey, beside his first wife and second son. He was survived by his second wife.

A. D. MORRISON-LOW

Sources M. M. Gordon, *The home life of Sir David Brewster* (1869) • A. D. Morrison-Low and J. R. R. Christie, eds., *Martyr of science: Sir David Brewster, 1781–1868* [Edinburgh 1981] (1984) [incl. bibliography] • N. J. Wade, ed., *Brewster and Wheatstone on vision* (1983) [incl. Royal Society obit.] • A. D. Morrison-Low and A. D. C. Simpson, 'A new dimension: a context for photography before 1860', *Light from the dark room: a celebration of Scottish photography*, ed. S. Stevenson (1995) • *Proceedings of the Royal Society of Edinburgh*, 6 (1866–9), 282–4 • *The Scotsman* (11 Feb 1868) [biographical sketch] • E. W. Morse, 'Brewster, David', *DSB*, 2.451–4 • R. S. Westfall, 'Introduction', in D. Brewster, *Memoirs of the life, writings and discoveries of Sir Isaac Newton* (1965), vol. 1, ix–xlv • A. D. C. Simpson, 'François Soleil, Andrew Ross and William Cookson: the Fresnel lens applied', *Bulletin of the Scientific Instrument Society*, 41 (1994), 16–19 • P. D. Sherman, *Colour vision in the nineteenth century: the Young-Helmholz-Maxwell theory* (1981) • H. J. Steffens, 'The tenacity of Newtonian optics in England: David Brewster, the last champion', *The development of Newtonian optics in England* (1977), 137–51 • J. G. Burke, 'The concepts of crystal symmetry', *Origins of the science of crystals* (1966), 147–75 • G. Smith, *Disciples of light: photographs in the Brewster album* (1990) • A. D. C. Simpson, 'Brewster's Society of Arts and the pantograph dispute', *Book of the Old Edinburgh Club*, new ser., 1 (1991), 47–73 • T. N. Clarke, A. D. Morrison-Low, and A. D. C. Simpson, *Brass and glass: scientific instrument making workshops in Scotland* (1989) • [D. Brewster], 'Binocular vision and the stereoscope', *North British Review*, 17 (1852), 177 • D. Brewster and others, eds., *The Edinburgh encyclopaedia*, 18 vols. (1813); facs. edn with introduction by R. Yeo (1999)
Archives Hunt. L., letters • J. Paul Getty Museum, California, album • NL Scot., corresp.; letters • NRA Scotland, priv. coll., papers • U. Edin. L., corresp. • U. St Andr. L., corresp. and MSS relating to university administration • UCL, letters to the Society for the Diffusion of Useful Knowledge | BL, corresp. with Charles Babbage, Add. MSS 37182–37200, *passim* • BL, letters to Macvey Napier, Add. MSS 34612–34624, *passim* • Bodl. Oxf., letters to Stephen Rigaud • CUL, letters to Sir George Stokes • ICL, letters to Lord Playfair • NL Scot., corresp. with Blackwoods • NL Scot., letters to Alexander Fraser • NL Scot., letters to John Lee • NL Scot., letters to William Lizars • NRA Scotland, priv. coll., letters to James Veitch • RS, corresp. with Sir John Herschel • Sci. Mus., letters to Fox Talbot • Trinity Cam., letters to William Whewell • U. Edin. L., letters to Thomas Chalmers • U. Newcastle, Robinson L., corresp. with Sir Walter Trevelyan • U. St Andr. L., corresp. with James Forbes • UCL, letters to Lord Brougham
Likenesses W. Bewick, chalk drawing, 1824, Scot. NPG • W. Holl, stipple, 1832 (after H. Raeburn), BM, NPG; repro. in W. Jerdan, *National portrait gallery* (1832) • D. O. Hill and R. Adamson, photograph, 1843, NPG [*see illus.*] • J. Wilson, oils, 1852, U. Glas. • R. Lehmann, crayon drawing, 1857, BM • C. G. Lewis, engraving, pubd 1863–4 (*The intellect and valour of Great Britain*; after T. J. Barker), BM, NPG • J. Watson-Gordon, oils, 1864, NPG • N. Macbeth, oils, *c.*1869, Royal Society, Edinburgh • W. Brodie, statue, 1871, U. Edin. • D. O. Hill, photographs, Scot. NPG • D. O. Hill, photographs, NPG • D. Maclise, group portrait, lithograph (*The Fraserians*), BM; repro. in *Fraser's Magazine* (1835) • D. Maclise, lithograph, NPG; repro. in *Fraser's Magazine* (1832) • D. Maclise, pencil studies, V&A • D. Maclise, pencil study, V&A • Wighton, oils, U. Edin. • lithograph (after D. Maclise), NPG
Wealth at death £6600 6s. 4d.: confirmation, 1 April 1868, NA Scot., SC62/44/45/781–823

Brewster, Sir Francis (d. 1704/5), merchant and writer on trade, was born to unknown parents, possibly from co. Kerry or co. Westmeath, where he later certainly owned land. He is first recorded in 1671, when he was accused of illegally exporting timber and wool to Amsterdam. He was a citizen and alderman of Dublin, and served as lord mayor in 1674–5. At an unknown date he was knighted.

Whiggish in his politics, Brewster was elected MP for Tuam in 1692. In the short-lived Irish parliament that followed he was one of the leading advocates of the claim that the Commons had the sole right to raise money. His stance earned him the sobriquet of an 'English' troublemaker from the lord lieutenant, Henry, Viscount Sidney, suggesting that it was known that Brewster had close associations with English politicians. This was confirmed by Brewster's central role in the presentation of evidence about abuses in Ireland to the English parliament in February 1693. Brewster's involvement with the Irish opposition ceased in 1695 when the whig Henry, Lord Capell (or Capel), was made lord deputy as part of a negotiated compromise between the Irish government and the 1692 opposition. Following his re-election for Tuam in 1695 Brewster acted in the government's interest, earning himself praise from Capell for his endeavours in promoting government business in the Commons. However, Brewster also supported the attempted impeachment of the lord chancellor, Sir Charles Porter. In 1697 Brewster acted as a witness before the English Board of Trade in relation to the Irish woollen export issue. In 1699 he was appointed by the English parliament as one of seven commissioners to inquire into the Irish forfeitures. The commissioners disagreed among themselves, with three of them, including Brewster, refusing to sign the final report, which they believed to be 'false and ill-grounded in several particulars' (Tindal, 399). In 1703 Brewster was elected MP for Doneraile.

Brewster was the author of *Essays in Trade and Navigation, in Five Parts* (1695). Only the first part, which included evidence of his opposition to the new Bank of England, was published. In 1702 he issued *New Essays on Trade*, and the anonymous book *A Discourse Concerning Ireland and the Different Interests Thereof* (1698), relating to the woollen issue, has also been ascribed to him. He died at some point between March 1704 and February 1705. Brewster appears to have had a son, William, although by 1733 the Brewster estate in co. Kerry was in the possession of Nathaniel Bland.

C. I. McGRATH

Sources BL, Harley MS 4892, fols. 127–90 [information to House of Commons] • NA Ire., MS M.1854, fol. 12 [rent roll of Brewster's estate] • NL Ire., MS D.9778 [conveyance of lands] • *JHC*, 26–55 (1753–1800) • N. Tindal, *The continuation of Mr Rapin de Thoyras's 'History of England'*, 2nd edn, 1 (1751) • J. I. McGuire, 'The Irish parliament of 1692', *Penal era and golden age: essays in Irish history, 1690–1800*, ed. T. Bartlett and D. W. Hayton (1979), 1–31 • *CSP dom., 1695, with addenda, 1689–95* • *Report on the manuscripts of his grace the duke of Buccleuch and Queensberry … preserved at Montagu House*, 3 vols. in 4, HMC, 45 (1899–1926), vol. 2 • *Report on the manuscripts of the marquis of Downshire*, 6 vols. in 7, HMC, 75 (1924–95), vol. 1 • *Report on the manuscripts of Allan George Finch*, 5 vols., HMC, 71 (1913–2003), vol. 2 • *The manuscripts of the House of Lords*, new ser., 12 vols. (1900–77), vol. 4 • J. G. Simms, *The Williamite confiscation in Ireland, 1690–1703*

(1956) • C. I. McGrath, 'Securing the protestant interest: policy, politics and parliament in Ireland in the aftermath of the Glorious Revolution, 1690–1695', MA diss., University College Dublin, 1991 • T. G. Doyle, 'Parliament and politics in Williamite Ireland, 1690–1703', MA diss., University College Dublin, 1992 • P. Kelly, 'The Irish Woollen Export Prohibition Act of 1699: Kearney revisited', *Irish Economic and Social History*, 7 (1980), 22–44 • C. Rose, *England in the 1690s: revolution, religion and war* (1999)

Archives BL, evidence supplied to parliament, Harley MS 4892, fols. 127–92

Wealth at death £672—total annual rent roll: NA Ire., MS M.1854, fol. 12

Brewster, John (1754–1842), Church of England clergyman and antiquary, the son of the Revd Richard Brewster (c.1719–1772), vicar of Heighington in co. Durham, and Isabella Baxter (c.1726–1797), was born on 18 January 1754 in Pilgrim Street, Newcastle upon Tyne. He was educated at Newcastle grammar school under the Revd Hugh Moises, and at Lincoln College, Oxford, where he matriculated in 1772, graduated BA probably in 1775 and MA in 1778. He was appointed curate of Stockton-on-Tees in 1776, and became a lecturer there in 1777. In 1791 he was presented to the vicarage at Greatham, co. Durham, where, on 16 June 1791, he married Frances Robinson (d. 1818), youngest daughter of Leonard Robinson, a Stockton merchant, and Priscilla Consett of Bradford. Their son, John, was baptized at Greatham on 2 August 1792 and succeeded Brewster as vicar of Greatham in 1818. In 1799 Brewster became vicar of Stockton through the patronage of Bishop Shute Barrington, who afterwards successively preferred him to the rectories of Redmarshall in 1805, Boldon in 1809, and Egglescliffe in 1814. According to Robert Surtees, Brewster was 'long and justly respected for the exemplary discharge of his parochial duties' (Surtees, 3.319).

Brewster never professed himself an antiquary, but the chief work for which he is now remembered is his *Parochial History and Antiquities of Stockton-upon-Tees*, published in quarto at Stockton in 1796. A second and enlarged edition was printed in 1829 in response to the considerable changes that had taken place in the town. The history is enlivened by Brewster's own reflections on the modern state of the town and the manners and morals of its inhabitants, whose reformation was always a matter close to his heart. Surtees acknowledged Brewster's assistance in supplying information for his own county history of Durham.

Brewster was a keen supporter of efforts to increase the provision of churches among the labouring classes. At Greatham, where he had found the church in a dilapidated state, he organized its reconstruction and in subsequent years lent his enthusiastic support to the Church Building Society, preaching a series of sermons in aid of that fund published under the title *A sketch of the history of the churches in England, applied to the purposes of the Society for Promoting the Building and Enlargement of Churches and Chapels* (1818). Between 1790 and 1823 he published seventeen books and pamphlets, most of which were sermons or devotional works, including a memoir of his former schoolmaster at Newcastle grammar school, Hugh

Moises, which was reprinted in Nichols's *Illustrations of Literature*. Brewster died at Egglescliffe, co. Durham, on 28 November 1842.   C. W. SUTTON, *rev.* R. H. SWEET

Sources R. Surtees, *The history and antiquities of the county palatine of Durham*, 3 (1823), 139–40 • Nichols, *Illustrations*, vol. 5 • R. Welford, *Men of mark 'twixt Tyne and Tweed*, 3 vols. (1895) • *GM*, 2nd ser., 19 (1843), 325, 538–9 • IGI • Foster, *Alum. Oxon.*

Archives Bucks. RLSS, corresp. with J. L. Dayrell

Likenesses W. B., stipple, pubd in or before 1827 (after J. C.), BM • J. Burnet, line engraving (after J. Ramsay), BM

Brewster, Patrick (1788–1859), Church of Scotland minister and political activist, was born at Jedburgh on 20 December 1788, the youngest of the four sons of James Brewster (c.1735–1815), rector of Jedburgh grammar school, and his wife, Margaret Key (1753–1790). He was the younger brother of Sir David *Brewster (1781–1868). Brewster wished to be a soldier, but his father had destined all his sons for the ministry. After the necessary theological studies at the University of Edinburgh, Brewster was licensed as a probationer by the presbytery of Fordoun on 26 March 1817. In the following August he was presented to the second charge of the abbey church of Paisley by the marquess of Abercorn. On 10 April 1818 he was ordained to this charge, which he continued to hold until his death. He had not been long at Paisley when he married Frances Anne, the daughter of Colonel Edward Stafford of Mayne in Ireland, on 19 January 1820. They had three daughters and two sons. Frances Brewster died in June 1831, and Brewster married again on 4 February 1834. His second wife was Mary, daughter of James Smith, his predecessor at Paisley. Between 1835 and 1846 they had five sons and two daughters. The second Mrs Brewster outlived her husband, dying in Hanover in May 1888.

The plight of the impoverished hand-loom weavers of Paisley first directed Brewster's attention to social issues. His political views became explicitly radical and, by the late 1830s, he was a prominent member of the Chartist movement, with a reputation for public oratory. In 1838 he attended a Chartist convention at Calton Hill in Edinburgh, and was responsible for the adoption of the Edinburgh resolutions, which condemned the use of physical force to promote the cause. However, he failed to win election to the national convention of Chartists, and despite an appearance on the same platform as Feargus O'Connor (1796–1855) in 1839 his vehement commitment to moral force alone lost him rank and file support. By 1841 he was turning to Joseph Sturge's Complete Suffrage Union, in the hope of a rapprochement between the two movements that would promote moral-force views. Ironically, just as Brewster was being sidelined within the Chartist movement, the Paisley presbytery, which had for some time been concerned by his political activities, chose to proceed against him. The immediate cause was his decision to preach on the rights of the poor at a Chartist church in Glasgow in 1841. After some preliminary actions a libel was served at the instance of the marquess of Abercorn and other heritors of the abbey parish in February 1843, but it was subsequently cancelled in December in the changed circumstances of the Disruption. Brewster's opinions were unchanged: he published *The Seven Chartist and Military Discourses* (1843), in which he maintained that Christian churches had always opposed unjust rulers and should oppose the present tyranny of capitalism. At the Disruption he refused to join the Free Church because of what he perceived as Chalmers's opposition to political activism on behalf of the poor. He was also convinced that the new Free Church would, in fact, give a congregation less real freedom in the choice of a minister than the established one.

During his career Brewster supported other radical causes more acceptable to his social peers: he advocated the abolition of the slave trade, temperance (he was president of the Paisley Total Abstinence Society in the 1840s and 1850s), poor-law reform (in 1841 he founded the Society for the Protection of the Destitute Poor in Paisley), and a national system of education. In the 1840s he was a strong supporter of the Anti-Corn Law League. Although once a strong advocate of Catholic emancipation, he subsequently became anti-Catholic after his daughter's conversion to Rome: his antipathy was apparent in a publication provoked by the Crimean War, *The Perils and Duties of the War: European Freedom and Popish Conspiracy* (1854). He died at his home at Craigie Linn, near Paisley, on 26 March 1859. His popularity earned him a public funeral, and, in 1863, a monument was raised to his memory in Paisley cemetery by public subscription.

Brewster's passionate conviction that religion and politics were inseparable—he argued that 'The Bible is full of politics'—and his almost Marxist recognition of working-class alienation within a capitalist state make him an outstanding and unusual figure among the establishment clergy of mid-nineteenth-century Scotland. His breadth of vision and analysis contrasts starkly with the more traditional social remedies of most of his clerical contemporaries, who supported nothing more radical than Chalmers's 'godly commonwealth'.

ROSEMARY MITCHELL

Sources S. Mechie, *The church and Scottish social development, 1780–1870* (1960), 100–18 • H. T. Blethen, 'Brewster, Patrick', *BDMBR*, vol. 2 • *Fasti Scot.*, 3.169–70 • A. Wilson, *The chartist movement in Scotland* (1970) • L. C. Wright, *Scottish chartism* (1953) • D. C. Smith, *Passive obedience and prophetic protest: social criticism in the Scottish church, 1830–1945* (1987), 175 • W. H. Marwick, 'Social heretics in the Scottish churches', *Records of the Scottish Church History Society*, 11 (1951–3), 227–39 • J. Christodoulou, 'The Glasgow universalist church and Scottish radicalism from the French Revolution to chartism: a theology of liberation', *JEH*, 43/4 (1992), 618
Likenesses J. G. Mossman, statue, 1863, Paisley cemetery
Wealth at death £337 10s. 4¼d.: inventory, 25 Dec 1859, NA Scot., SC 58/42/26/130

Brewster, Thomas (*b.* 1705), physician and translator, was born on 18 September 1705 in Eardisland, Herefordshire, the son of Benjamin Brewster (*bap.* 1674), and his wife, Anne Whittington. He was educated at Merchant Taylors' School, and was admitted to St John's College, Oxford, in 1724. He graduated BA in 1727, MA in 1732, and BM and DM in 1738. He was also elected a fellow of his college.

In 1733 he published a translation, the 'Second Satire of Persius', in English verse by itself, in order, as he says in the preface, 'to save himself the Trouble of employing more Time upon so difficult an Author, if this should fail of giving Satisfaction'. The third and fourth satires were published together in 1742, the fifth and sixth appeared separately in the same year, and the six satires were issued in a single volume in 1751.

Edward Owen praised Brewster's translation, noting the poet's 'uncommon delicacy of ear' and 'perfect knowledge of his author'. Some indication of Brewster's easy, lively style is given by his translation of Persius, *Satires*, i.96–7:

> M. What of these Lines, Sir … if you can't admire 'um,
> Grant me, at least, they equal *Arma Virum*.
> Nay *Virgil*'s sure, are spungier still than these;
> *His* empty Lines! like Limbs of dodder'd Trees,
> Puft up with fungous, fat excrescencies!

After leaving the university Brewster practised medicine at Bath. Henry Fielding paid his compliments in his 1743 *Miscellanies*, both to the physician, whom he terms the 'glory of his art' ('To Miss H—and at Bath') and to the translator. In his 'Essay on conversation' in that volume, Fielding quotes from Brewster's translation of Persius, which he describes as 'thus excellently rendered by the late ingenious translator of that obscure author'. Despite the ambiguous phrasing, it seems that Brewster was still alive: he was one of the subscribers to *Miscellanies*, and it is very probable that he was the Dr Brewster mentioned at the end of *Tom Jones* (1749) as being in attendance on the philosopher Square during his last illness at Bath (Fielding, xviii, 4). It is not known when Brewster died, although the phrasing of the address to the second edition of Persius in 1751 suggests that he was still alive then, and in 1757 his name is found in the list of subscribers to Sarah Fielding's *Lives of Cleopatra and Octavia*.

ALFRED GOODWIN, *rev.* SARAH ANNES BROWN

Sources Foster, *Alum. Oxon.* • Mrs E. P. Hart, ed., *Merchant Taylors' School register, 1561–1934*, 2 vols. (1936) • M. J. Simmonds, *Merchant Taylors' fellows of St John's College, Oxford* (1930) • E. Owen, *Translation of Juvenal* (1785) • *IGI* • H. Fielding, *The history of Tom Jones, a foundling*, ed. M. C. Battestin and F. Bowers, 2 vols. (1974), vol. 1, pp. xviii, 4 • *DNB*
Archives BL, letters to John Wilkes, Add. MSS 30867, 30875, *passim*

Brewster, William (1566/7–1644), separatist leader, was born, probably in Scrooby, Nottinghamshire, the son of William Brewster (*d.* 1590), from 1575 bailiff to the archbishop of York, and his probable first wife, Mary (*d.* 1567?), daughter of William Smythe and widow of John Simkinson. He entered Peterhouse, Cambridge, on 3 December 1580 (the same day as the later separatist John Penry), but did not graduate. In 1583 he became a secretary of William Davison, Elizabeth's ambassador to the Netherlands in 1584 and 1585–6 and assistant to the secretary of state, Francis Walsingham, until his disgrace following the execution of Mary queen of Scots in 1587. Brewster proved 'so discreet and faithful that he [Davison] trusted him above all others' (Bradford, 325).

Withdrawing from court to Scrooby (a stop on the Great North Road), Brewster succeeded his father in 1590 as Archbishop Sandys's bailiff-receiver, and about 1594 was appointed postmaster, supervising local distribution, relays of horses, and entertainment of travellers. By 1593 he had married Mary (claims for both Wentworth and Wyrrall as her surname have been rejected), with whom he had six children, those born after 1600 bearing such puritan names as Patience, Fear, Love, and Wrestling. The family occupied part of the palatial archiepiscopal manor house. Brewster was zealous 'in promoting and furthering religion … by procuring of good preachers' (some of whom favoured separatism) and by large financial contributions (Bradford, 235–6). In 1606 Richard Clyfton's company of separatists (among them the young William Bradford) began meeting in Brewster's house, where John Robinson soon joined them.

Threats of persecution led to plans to escape to Holland. Their first attempt, in 1607, largely financed by Brewster, was betrayed by their ship's captain. Brewster was one of seven imprisoned at Boston before being bound over to the assizes. The second attempt, from the Humber in the summer of 1608, partially evaded pursuit, and eventually the refugees reassembled in Amsterdam. In 1609 they moved to Leiden, where he was elected ruling elder. Impoverished, he supported his family by teaching English to Danish and German university students, adapting the rules of Latin grammar. In 1616, with the help of Edward Winslow, he started printing separatist and proscribed texts on a press in Koorsteeg (Choir Alley). In 1617 and 1619 he visited England to negotiate with Sir Edwin Sandys for a land grant and permission to settle in Virginia. He and John Robinson co-signed the seven articles which disingenuously concealed their church's separatism. In 1619 complaints from James I led to Dutch investigation of his publications. He fled to England and lay low until embarking with his family on the *Mayflower*. As ruling elder he was the religious leader of the pilgrims when they finally set sail from Plymouth in September 1620.

In the absence of long-settled or competent ministers in Plymouth plantation Brewster, the non-graduate elder, preached, taught, prayed, catechized, and disciplined the congregation. His plain sermons were 'very moving and stirring of affections' and his prayers were capable of 'ripping up the heart and conscience before God' (Bradford, 327–8). His library contained nearly 400 Latin and English books valued at £43. Though the only gentleman pilgrim, he was modest, tactful, frugal, and 'peaceable' (Bradford, 326). In 1627 he became one of the undertakers who assumed Plymouth's debt of £1800 to London investors. Though the elder was disbarred from civil office, the governor, William Bradford, consulted him 'in all weighty affairs' (ibid., 327). Despite many reverses of personal and plantation fortunes, he maintained a cheerful good humour and lived to a healthy old age. He died at Duxbury, Massachusetts, on 10 April 1644. His personal estate totalled £150, including 'a red cap, a white cap, a quilted cap, a lace cap, a violet coat and a pair of green drawers' (Willison, 8). His 110 acre farm in his later home of Duxbury was divided between his two surviving sons, Jonathan and Love. ROGER THOMPSON

Sources W. Bradford, *Of Plymouth Plantation, 1620–1647*, ed. S. E. Morison (1952); repr. (1953) · R. G. Usher, 'Brewster, William', *DAB* · R. C. Anderson, ed., *The great migration begins: immigrants to New England, 1620–1633*, 1 (Boston, MA, 1995), 227–30 · J. G. Hunt, 'Mother of William Brewster', *New England Historical and Genealogical Register*, 124 (1970), 250–54 · G. D. Langdon, *Pilgrim colony: a history of New Plymouth, 1620–1691* (1966) · H. M. Dexter and M. Dexter, *The England and Holland of the pilgrims* (1906) · G. F. Willison, *Saints and strangers* (1945) · *DNB*

Wealth at death moveable estate £150; 110 acres at Duxbury and land in Plymouth: Anderson, *The great migration*, 1.228

Brewtnall, Edward Frederick (1846–1902), watercolour painter, was born in 1 Crane Court, St Dunstan's parish, London, on 13 October 1846, the eldest son of Edward Brewtnall (1818–1892), headmaster of the People's College, Warrington, Lancashire, and subsequently editor of the *Warrington Guardian*, and his wife, Elizabeth Susanna. Like Luke Fildes and Henry Woods, he studied at Warrington School of Art under J. Christmas Thompson. In 1867 his father moved to London, and Brewtnall, after having worked in a cotton mill, attended the South Kensington School of Art. He began his career as an illustrator for *The Graphic*. He exhibited a watercolour, *Post Time*, with the Society of British Artists in 1868, and in 1875 was elected an associate of the Old Watercolour Society, becoming a full member in 1883. In total he exhibited some 217 pictures with the society. His watercolours generally sold for between £35 and £65, but the highest recorded price for any of his drawings is £189 in 1884 (for *Blue Beard's Wife*). His usual signature was E. F. Brewtnall.

Many of Brewtnall's pictures were romantic or fanciful in character, such as his large oil *The Sleeping Beauty* (Warrington Museum and Art Gallery) or the watercolour *The Spirit of the Genii* (Royal Watercolour Society diploma collection). His work also included landscapes, such as his two drawings in the Victoria and Albert Museum in London, *At Cley-Next-the-Sea, Norfolk* and *Near St Mawgan, Cornwall*, and genre pictures, of which *Where Next* (priv. coll.) is a good example. One contemporary, in a review of the Royal Watercolour Society's winter exhibition, praised him as 'a fine colourist' with 'a poetic fancy' (*Morning Post*, 2 Dec 1891); it was also remarked that he was clearly an admirer of Albert Goodwin, a fellow member of the society. Brewtnall served on the society's council for many years, and he was also a member of both the Society of British Artists (from 1882 to 1886) and the Society of Oil Painters. Of the eighteen pictures he exhibited with the Royal Academy, most were in oils. According to Marcus Huish, his later work showed signs of decline. Just after Brewtnall's death, Huish opined that the artist 'missed by very little being a great artist. … [however] especially in his more important work, he was too entirely fascinated by colour and composition, to the neglect of draughtsmanship, the necessity for which he was apt to overlook' (Huish, 88–9).

On 17 September 1884 Brewtnall married Ellen Faraday, with whom he had three daughters. He moved house quite frequently within London, though from 1885 to 1889 he lived at Westcott, near Dorking, Surrey; his last address was 32 Fairfax Road, Bedford Park, Chiswick, Middlesex, where he died on 13 November 1902. He was buried in the old churchyard, Chiswick. His wife survived him, but died shortly afterwards.   SIMON FENWICK

Sources DNB · Bankside Gallery, London, Royal Watercolour Society MSS · M. B. Huish, British water-colour art (1904) · Warrington Guardian (7 May 1892) · Graves, RA exhibitors · Wood, Vic. painters, 3rd edn · CGPLA Eng. & Wales (1903) · b. cert. · d. cert. · Morning Post (11 Nov 1902) · private information (2004) [family]
Archives Bankside Gallery, London, Royal Watercolour Society MSS
Likenesses likeness, repro. in Year's Art (1890)
Wealth at death £701 19s.: administration, 17 Feb 1903, CGPLA Eng. & Wales

Brian Bóruma [Brian Boru] (c.941–1014), high-king of Ireland, was born at Kincora, Killaloe, the son of Cennétig (d. 951), king of Dál Cais, king of Tuadmumu (Thomond, in north Munster), and rígdamna Caisil, 'royal heir to', or merely, 'the material of a king of', Cashel or Munster. His mother was Bé Binn, daughter of Aurchad mac Murchada, king of Uí Briúin Seóla in west Connacht (d. 945), which may account for the occurrence of the name Brian, hitherto very rare, among the latter family. He was nicknamed Bóruma (Anglicized as Boru) from the Old Irish bóruma, 'of the cattle tribute', or perhaps 'of Béal Bóruma', a fort north of Killaloe in Clare.

Brian Bóruma had at least four wives (all from the northern half of Ireland, Leth Cuinn), probably not without some degree of overlap. The first was Mór, daughter of Edend mac Cléirig, of the weak south Connacht dynasty of Uí Fiachrach Aidne: they had three sons (all of whom died childless), Murchad (d. 1014), Conchobar, and Flann. He later famously married Gormlaith (d. 1030), daughter of Murchad mac Finn, king of Leinster (r. 966–72), with whom he had his son Donnchad (d. 1064); she had previously been the wife of Óláfr Cuarán (Olaf Sihtricson) of Dublin, being mother of his son Sihtric Silkenbeard, and was later married to Máel Sechnaill mac Domnaill of the southern Uí Néill, high-king before and after Brian. Another of Brian's wives was Echrad, daughter of Carlus mac Ailella of the obscure sept of Uí Áeda Odba in the territory of the southern Uí Néill; this may have been a device to win friends there at Máel Sechnaill's expense, and is significant only because she bore Brian's son Tadc, from whom the later Uí Briain of Munster were descended. The final known wife was Dubchoblaig (d. 1009), daughter of Cathal mac Conchobair, king of Connacht, though it is doubtful if she was the mother of his sixth son, Domnall (d. 1010). Brian also had at least three daughters: Sadb (d. 1048); Sláine, the name (according to the Welsh text Historia Gruffud vab Kenan) of the daughter who is known to have married Sihtric Silkenbeard, son of her erstwhile stepmother; and Bé Binn, who married Flaithbertach Ua Néill, king of the northern Uí Néill (d. 1036).

Dynastic origins Brian's early ancestors were the Déisi (literally, 'the vassalry') whose lands stretched from Waterford, through south Tipperary, to Limerick, the branch in the latter area acquiring the name In Déis Bec ('the little Déis'), and subsequently splitting into two groups, In Déis Deiscirt ('the southern Déis'), and In Déis Tuaiscirt ('the

northern Déis') to which Brian belonged, and which by the mid-eighth century had gained political dominance in east Clare. They later adopted the dynastic name Dál Cais (literally, 'the share of Cas'), first recorded in 934 (Annals of Inisfallen), about seven years before Brian's birth, just when their fortunes were undergoing a remarkable leap forward, at the expense of the Eóganachta. This latter group of related dynasties, all theoretically descended from Eógan Már, son of Ailill Ólomm, formerly dominated Munster from Cashel, but their irregular succession pattern, and subjection to repeated Uí Néill pressure, allowed space for Dál Cais expansion; the latter even produced a patently false pedigree concealing their Déisi origins and claiming descent from a brother of Eógan Már, Cormac Cass (not to be confused with their eponym, Cas[s] son of Conall Echlúath, who would have lived some six generations later), thereby giving them a position of collateral equality with the Eóganachta.

Brian belonged to a lineage of Dál Cais known as Uí Thairdelbaig, whose eponym allegedly lived seven generations after the apical Cas and seven before Brian. During this period a rival lineage, Clann Óengusso, monopolized the kingship and Uí Thairdelbaig (first mentioned only in the tripartite life of Patrick, c.900) did not manage to oust them until 934, under the leadership of Brian's obscure grandfather, Lorcán, son of Lachtna, and then his father, Cennétig, first noted in the annals in his own right in 944. They may have been helped by an alliance with the Uí Néill, whose high-king, Donnchad Donn mac Flainn (r. 919–44), took, as one of his wives, Cennétig's daughter, Órlaith, the first of Brian's siblings to appear in the historical record. Donnchad had her put to death in 941 for adultery with his own son, indicating the high-king's indifference to Dál Cais reaction, and, perhaps, their continuing lack of status, though he would hardly have chosen to form a marriage alliance unless they were already in the ascendant.

War and dynasty in tenth-century Munster Dál Cais, under Brian's father, were heavily defeated by the Eóganachta in the battle of Mag Dúine in 944. One annal calls it a victory over Tuadmumu (Ann. Ulster), the first record of the name in the annals, probably reflecting a new division of power between Dál Cais in the north and the various Eóganachta lineages elsewhere in the province. According to the Uí Thairdelbaig genealogy, those killed in the battle included Finn and Dub, two of Brian's eleven brothers, though only eight are there named (another two, Flann and Conchobar, Brian's only full brothers, are recorded in the Banshenchas). Two more of Brian's brothers, Echthigern and Donncuan—whose son Céilechar died as abbot of Terryglass (Tír dá Glas) in 1008—were killed in 950 when the new high-king, Congalach mac Máele Mithig of Brega, campaigned in Munster, presumably in an attempt to halt their continued expansion. Brian's father, Cennétig, died in 951, and the titles bestowed on him by his obituarists indicate the status he had won. He was apparently succeeded by Brian's brother Lachtna, who was killed within two years and is not given a royal style in his obit.

Another of Brian's brothers now succeeded; this was

Mathgamain, who by 959 was acting as commander of the men of Munster and is described in the annals in 967 as 'king of Cashel' (*Ann. Ulster*), the first member of Dál Cais to win the title, and perhaps the first non-Eóganachta king of the province in five centuries. Mathgamain also gained control over the Norse settlement at Limerick, when he defeated them in the battle of Sulchóit (near Limerick Junction) in 967, the first real battle in which Brian, now in his mid-twenties, distinguished himself, according to the early twelfth-century tract known as *Cogad Gaedel re Gallaib* ('The war of the Irish with the foreigners'). Indeed, this source would have them ruling jointly:

> There were then governing and ruling this tribe two stout, able, valiant pillars, two fierce, lacerating, magnificent heroes, two gates of battle, two poles of combat, two spreading trees of shelter, two spears of victory and readiness, of hospitality and munificence, of heart and strength, of friendship and liveliness, the most eminent of the west of Europe, viz., Mathgamain and Brian, the two sons of Cennétig. (*Cogadh Gaedhel re Gallaibh*, 57–9)

King of Munster However, the Norse of Limerick were instrumental in Mathgamain's downfall, being party to his capture in 976 by the king of Uí Fidgente in west Limerick, who handed him over to his most prominent challenger, Máel Muad mac Brain of Eóganacht Raithlind, who killed him. Only at this point, at perhaps thirty-five years of age, does Brian emerge fully into the light of history. As the *Cogad* puts it: 'he was not a stone in the place of an egg; and he was not a wisp in the place of a club; but he was a hero in place of a hero; and he was valour after valour' (*Cogadh Gaedhel re Gallaibh*, 101), and his actions in the aftermath of Mathgamain's murder indicate that he had been, rather rarely among Irish dynastic siblings, a loyal lieutenant during his brother's life, and was now an energetic and shrewd avenger. He began, in 977, with an assault upon Limerick, and when its king, Ívarr, fled to the monastic site on Scattery Island, Brian, according to the annals of Tigernach, profaned the sanctuary of St Senan and slew Ívarr and his two sons. The annals of Inisfallen report that he then led a punitive raid on Uí Fidgente. In the course of a military career spanning five decades, Brian fought relatively few major battles (though the *Cogad*, with conventional exaggeration, estimates twenty-five victories over the Norse alone), but his first vital encounter was the battle of Belach Lechta in 978, a contest for the kingship of Munster between Dál Cais and the Eóganachta, led by Máel Muad mac Brain. The latter was defeated and killed, and Brian emerged victorious. According to the annals of Ulster and the annals of the four masters, Máel Muad was at least 'king of Desmumu' (Desmond, in south Munster), if not 'king of Cashel' (*Annals of Inisfallen*), but with his death that honour passed unchallenged to Brian, and he forced home the point by immediately rounding again on Uí Fidgente and the Limerick Norse.

Little of substance is known of Brian's activities over the next four years, but in 982 the Munster army raided the important buffer kingdom of Osraige that separated them from Leinster. If not an unqualified success, it was enough to demonstrate that Brian now represented a threat to the other provincial rulers. Not surprisingly, therefore, it evoked a response from the new Uí Néill high-king, Máel Sechnaill mac Domnaill, who brought the army of Leth Cuinn south to Thomond, and broke down the tree of Mag Adair. Since this stood on the Dál Cais inauguration site, the act was designed, presumably, to deny Brian's royal pretensions; but it was entirely without effect, since Brian harried Osraige in the following year and gained hostages as a sign of its submission. If the annals of Inisfallen are to be believed on the point, which seems doubtful, he also obtained the hostages of Leinster. Furthermore, he brought a large fleet up the Shannon to attack Connacht, though some of his followers were slain there, including Máel Sechnaill, son of Brian's influential uncle Coscrach (two grandsons of the latter, Cathal Mac Maine (d. 1013) and Coscrach Mac Aingid (d. 1040), were later abbots of Killaloe). Then he sent his 'officials' overland into Uí Briúin Bréifne, again, though, with mixed results. In 983 he was once more in Osraige and took its king captive, before going on to devastate Leinster. He also reached Waterford and exchanged hostages with its Hiberno-Norse rulers, 'as a guarantee of both providing a hosting to attack Dublin' (*Annals of Inisfallen*, s.a. 984), though this does not seem to have materialized.

For the rest of the 980s Brian remained in a strong position. When the Déisi of south-east Munster made off with 300 of his cows in 985, he harried their king as far as Waterford, and was later active in western Mide (Westmeath). Although internal opposition manifested itself in the following year, in the person of his nephew, Áed, son of Mathgamain, Brian imprisoned him—the action, apparently, of a merciful ruler, since when Áed died in 1011 he bore the prestigious title of *rígdamna Caisil*. In 987 Brian stamped his authority over Desmond and took hostages from the churches of Lismore, Cork, and Emly, 'as a guarantee of the banishment of robbers and lawless people therefrom' (*Annals of Inisfallen*, s.a. 987). He manipulated the church by appointing his brother Marcán abbot of Emly in 989, and by the time the latter died, in 1010, he was 'head of the clergy of Munster' and abbot of Killaloe, Terryglass, and Inishcaltra. In 988 Brian launched his most ambitious campaign yet. He put 300 boats on Lough Ree, including the Waterford fleet, and harried Mide, going in person to Uisnech, a site of long-standing symbolic as well as contemporary political importance, being the royal site of Clann Cholmáin, the branch of the southern Uí Néill to which the high-king, Máel Sechnaill mac Domnaill, belonged. Brian then sent a detachment of twenty-five boats to Connacht but these suffered a reverse, the dead including Dúnlang mac Duib Dá Boirenn, head of the now subservient Eóganacht Raithlind.

King of southern Ireland The 990s began unfavourably for Brian with the battle of Carn Fordroma, his first major encounter with the high-king, in which the latter routed the forces of Thomond and killed 600 men, including the king of Múscraige Tíre. When Brian ventured out of Munster in 991, to invade Leinster, he again seems to have fared badly and lost another of his subordinates, the *rígdamna* of Osraige. The campaigns of 992 were no better.

While Máel Sechnaill was hosting in Connacht, Brian—called *Bóruma* for the first time by an annalist, though this may be a later interpolation—brought armies from Munster and Connacht and went as far as Lough Ennell, at the heart of Clann Cholmáin territory, but retreated 'like a runaway' (*Annals of Tigernach*, s.a. 992). The tide may, however, have begun to turn in Brian's favour at this point. In 993 his fleet was on Lough Ree, his forces raiding overland as far north as Bréifne. Máel Sechnaill again responded by invading Munster; he burned Nenagh, ravaged the province, and defeated the Munster army. Perhaps conscious of his vulnerability, Brian began a major building programme in 995, erecting fortresses at Cashel, on an island in Lough Gur, at Singland near Limerick, and elsewhere. His base secure, he went north in 996 and killed 300 of Máel Sechnaill's men in Westmeath, and also appeared in Leinster, where, at Mag nAilbe, in Carlow, he obtained the hostages of Uí Chennselaig, from the south of the province, and of the kings of the Liffey plain. Brian now controlled most if not all of Leth Moga, the southern half of Ireland, and had therefore achieved for Dál Cais a new position of eminence. It was a status which Máel Sechnaill seems to have felt compelled to acknowledge. In 997 Brian and the princes of Munster sailed to Port Dá Chaineóc, near Clonfert, and there reached an agreement with Máel Sechnaill to divide Ireland between them: the latter abandoned the centuries-old Uí Néill claim to overlordship of the entire country and became master of Leth Cuinn alone, and, as a sign of Brian's overlordship of Leth Moga, Máel Sechnaill gave him the hostages of Leinster and Dublin. This was the high point of Brian's career to date, though, in reality, it may have owed as much to Máel Sechnaill's weakness as to Brian's strength.

Their partnership was a real one. When Brian went to Athlone in the next year and obtained the hostages of Connacht, part of Leth Cuinn, he handed them over to Máel Sechnaill (*Annals of Inisfallen*). Other sources say that they went together to Connacht and won its hostages, and then took those of Dublin (*Chronicum Scotorum*), and that both then separately attended to their respective spheres of influence, Máel Sechnaill ravaging Connacht and Brian ravaging Leinster (*Ann. Ulster*). The hostility in Leinster to Brian's overlordship necessitated his going north, late in 999, to Glenn Máma (near Newcastle Lyons, co. Dublin), where the Hiberno-Norse and the Leinstermen assembled to attack him, forcing him to commit his armies to a pitched battle, something he seems generally to have avoided. But his enemies' forces were slaughtered and Glenn Máma must stand out as one of his greatest victories. It enabled him to march on Dublin, where he spent a week, departing laden with gold, silver, and captives. He banished Sihtric Silkenbeard, who unsuccessfully sought refuge in Ulaid, but was eventually forced to hand over hostages to Brian, who thereupon restored him to his fortress.

At this point, Brian and Máel Sechnaill went together to Connacht to re-assert control there; but recent events had demonstrated that Brian was now the stronger and the year 1000 witnessed what the annals of Tigernach call Brian's 'first turning against Máel Sechnaill the Great, through treachery' (*Annals of Tigernach*, s.a. 1000). He gathered together the forces of Osraige, Leinster, and Dublin, and those of south Connacht in Leth Cuinn, and proceeded as far as Tara. A party of Dublin horsemen advanced further into the plain of Mag Breg, but were set upon and slaughtered by Máel Sechnaill. Brian then moved to Ferta Nemed, near Moynalty, but 'returned without battle, without ravaging, without red fire' (ibid.). The annals of Ulster add that this was done 'by the Lord's insistence', implying that his revolt against Máel Sechnaill, and incursion into the very heartland of the southern Uí Néill, was by no means universally appreciated. When the Munster army appeared there again a year later, they were forced to abandon their prey and suffered 'a slaughter of heads' (*Ann. Ulster; Annals of Tigernach*), but Máel Sechnaill seems now to have grasped the extent of his weakness and in 1001 joined with Cathal mac Conchobair, king of Connacht, and, it is said, 'all Leth Cuinn', in building a great barrier across the Shannon at Athlone 'against the men of Munster' (*Annals of Inisfallen*, s.a. 1001). This, however, seems to have proved a pointless exercise.

The high-kingship of Ireland The almost cryptic accounts of the following year's events tell no more than that Brian appeared at Athlone (the annals of the four masters with, perhaps, a measure of seventeenth-century wishful thinking, have Dublin), and took the hostages of Connacht and Mide. Clearly this was an event of momentous importance. Brian had obtained the submission of the Uí Néill high-king, overturned a convention that was several centuries old, and was now entitled, if he could enforce his claim throughout Leth Cuinn, to assume the title of high-king of Ireland. And yet the whole affair is curiously understated in the sources. Perhaps contemporary writers, who can hardly have failed to appreciate the sea change which had just occurred, played down its significance out of sheer bias, or regarded it as a temporary aberration. Whatever the explanation, it surely cannot be that modern observers have invested the event with a spurious significance. Brian did end the Uí Néill monopoly of the high-kingship. In a sense, he ended the very concept of the high-kingship as it had evolved under them, since, though Máel Sechnaill mac Domnaill recovered it after Brian's death, the title remained in abeyance for a full half-century after his own demise in 1022. When attempts were then made to revive the office, under Brian's descendants rather than the now considerably weakened Uí Néill, what emerged was the sometimes quite hollow concept of a *rí Érenn co fressabra*, literally 'king of Ireland with opposition'.

There seems, therefore, little reason to cast doubt on the generally accepted view that Brian Bóruma earned himself a truly exceptional place among Irish kings. The compiler of the great twelfth-century corpus of genealogies in Oxford, Bodleian Library, MS Rawlinson B 502, in his list of the kings of Ireland of the Christian era, states that there was not a single one of them who was not of the Uí Néill, except for Brian and the remarkable Báetán mac Cairill, king of Ulaid (*r.* 572–81), adding 'Sed tamen alii Baetan non numerant inter magnos reges' ('But others do not count Báetán among the high-kings'; *Corpus genealogiarum Hiberniae*, 124). The list, in fact, ends with Brian, and he is given a reign of twelve years, commencing, therefore, with the events of 1002. The significance of those events became immediately apparent. Brian set about making a reality of his claim by taking north the army of Munster, Leinster, Waterford, and Dublin, and, from Leth Cuinn, Connacht and the forces of his new subordinate, Máel Sechnaill. They marched to Dundalk, to obtain the submission of Ulaid and the Cenél nEógain branch of the northern Uí Néill, but failed to gain it and declared a truce. It was another two years before Brian again set out to achieve his goal, partly perhaps because he was busy in Leinster in 1003, where he deposed the reigning Uí Dúnchada king and set up in his stead an Uí Fáeláin rival. When he did launch a new campaign in 1004, with the intention of traversing the north, he found his path blocked by the Cenél nEógain army at Trácht Eothaile, a strand near Ballysadare, in Sligo.

Although now approaching his mid-sixties, Brian persisted in his ambitions. The various accounts of his 1005 expedition contradict each other in some respects, but it was evidently his most elaborate campaign yet. His impressive host was made up of 'the royalty of Ireland' (*Ann. Ulster*) or, more precisely, 'the men of Ireland, both foreigners [Hiberno-Norse] and Irish from south of Slíab Fúait', in south Armagh (*Annals of Inisfallen*). They marched through Mide, staying one night in Tailtiu (presumably because of its symbolism as site of the *óenach* or assembly of the kings of Tara), and thence to Armagh, where Brian stayed a week and camped (surely again conscious of symbolism) at Emain Macha, Ulster's ancient capital. From there Brian proceeded to Rathmore in Ulaid, 'to obtain the hostages of Cenél Conaill and Cenél nEógain' (*Annals of Inisfallen*, s.a. 1005). Although one source states that he indeed returned home 'bringing the pledges of the men of Ireland' (*Ann. Ulster*), another has it that he won only the pledges of the Ulaid lineages of Dál nAraidi and Dál Fiatach (*AFM*), and even the encomiastic *Cogad* is clear that Cenél Conaill did not submit.

While at Armagh Brian 'left twenty ounces of gold on Patrick's altar' (*Ann. Ulster*, s.a. 1005). The early ninth-century Book of Armagh, with its collection of early Patrician texts and statements of Armagh's primatial claims, was apparently produced for inspection by Brian's *anmchara* ('confessor', literally, 'soul-friend'), Máel Suthain (d. 1031); he then entered an inscription into the book acknowledging Armagh's ecclesiastical supremacy over all Ireland, which concludes: 'I, Calvus Perennis [a Latinization of Máel Suthain], have written this in the presence of Brian, emperor of the Irish [*imperatoris Scotorum*], and what I have written he has determined for all the kings of Cashel' (*Liber Ardmachanus*, fol. 16v). This title is unique in Irish history, and may reflect, Aubrey Gwynn has argued, the adoption less than a decade earlier by Otto III of the title *imperator Romanorum* (emperor of the Romans) in place of the earlier *imperator Romanus* (Roman

emperor), or, as has elsewhere been suggested, the influence of the grandiloquent contemporary styles of the royal house of Wessex (Flanagan, 179). Whatever the background, it was an important break with precedent, and an insight into Brian's ambition and sense of his own status.

The pursuit of stability Brian's achievements to date should not, however, be exaggerated. This is the only known instance in which he used the title 'emperor of the Irish', and there is no evidence that he brought any new ideas to the role, or planned to exercise a more intensive overlordship than the Uí Néill had. Indeed, the events of the next few years, while testimony to the awesome energy of a man now heading towards his seventies, also indicate the weakness of his regime and the extent to which its stability depended on his own physical presence. In 1006 Brian again mustered an army of all the province kings south of Slíab Fúait (those to the north being still recalcitrant). From Connacht he crossed the Erne at Assaroe and journeyed through the north, then crossed the Bann near Camus, into Antrim, and headed back south by Louth, through the territories of Cenél Conaill, Cenél nEógain, Ulaid, Airgialla, and Conailli Muirthemne; and everywhere he went he was granted 'the full demand of the community of Patrick and of his successor [the abbot of Armagh]' (*Ann. Ulster*, s.a. 1006). Here Brian was acting as patron of Armagh, the high-king, appropriately, enforcing payment of taxes to his newly adopted ecclesiastical capital. But within a year Flaithbertach Ua Néill of Cenél nEógain had invaded his traditional enemies in Ulaid, forcing Brian to return again to Armagh to recover the hostages of Ulaid from him. This stabilized the situation for two years, but by 1010 Flaithbertach had become enough of a nuisance for Brian to feel compelled to journey to Armagh, in his seventieth year, where 'Ua Néill gave to Brian his demand in full, and Brian brought Ua Néill's hostages to Cenn Corad [Kincora]', a hill overlooking the Shannon at Killaloe where Brian had his royal residence (*Annals of Inisfallen*, s.a. 1010). The version preserved in the annals of Ulster is that Brian came to Claenloch, near Slíab Fúait, 'and took the pledges of Leth Cuinn' (*Ann. Ulster*, s.a. 1010).

Clearly Brian was now in command, but no sooner had he quelled Cenél nEógain than their rivals, Cenél Conaill, became restive. Brian went north with 'a great muster of the men of Ireland', his age showing perhaps in that command was taken by his sons Domnall (who died peacefully that same year) and Murchad (active as early as 1000, according to the material collected in the *Cogad*), joined by Flaithbertach Ua Néill. While Brian and Máel Sechnaill mac Domnaill remained in a naval camp at Enach Duib on the upper Shannon, their armies harried Cenél Conaill and carried off much booty to Munster. Although Brian returned to Kincora, Cenél Conaill had not been fully subdued. Later that year, therefore, Brian led a hosting northwards by land and sea, forcing its king, Máel Ruanaid Ua Maíl Doraid, to return with him to Kincora, where he accepted a large stipend from Brian as a sign of his inferior status, 'and made complete submission to him' (*Annals of Inisfallen*, s.a. 1011). At this juncture Brian had reached the apogee of his power, though he went north again in 1012, as far as Mag Muirtheimne in Louth, but only, as the annals of Ulster assert, to secure immunity from lay exactions for Armagh's subject churches. Apart from this, he seems to have spent the year strengthening his fortresses at Kincora and its hinterland, and may well have had thoughts of retirement.

Crisis and death At this point, however, the power structure which Brian had laboriously built up began to crumble. The first crack in the edifice was not an assault on Brian at all, but the successful expedition by Flaithbertach Ua Néill (having already imposed himself on Cenél Conaill and Ulaid) to Kells in 1013, where Máel Sechnaill was forced to abandon the field to him. Although this was ostensibly a contest for paramountcy between the northern and southern Uí Néill, Máel Sechnaill's evident weakness possibly encouraged others to test him, since the army of Mide fought a major battle at this point with the men of Leinster and Dublin (at Drinan, in the north of what is now co. Dublin), in which Máel Sechnaill lost 150 men, including his son. The Dublin forces then provoked Brian by launching a naval expedition, admittedly unsuccessfully, around the south coast, and Brian spent from 9 September until Christmas 1013 attacking them in Osraige and Leinster (the *Cogad* has him besieging Dublin) but 'he did not bring about a peace' (*Annals of Inisfallen*, s.a. 1013). Meanwhile his son Murchad led an army from Glendalough to Kilmainham, within sight of Dublin, burning the country and taking booty and captives, but again without restoring the peace.

The inevitable consequence of this revolt was Brian's attempt to force Leinster and Dublin back into submission. The *Cogad*, in fact, claims that 'messengers went from Máel Sechlainn [*sic*] to Brian, to complain of this, namely, that his territory was plundered and his sons killed, and praying him not to permit the foreigners and the Leinstermen … to come all together against him' (*Cogadh Gaedhel re Gallaibh*, 149), and this culminated in the famous battle fought at Clontarf on Good Friday 23 April 1014. It was a bloody affair, the Dublin and Leinster armies being reinforced by troops from Man and the western and northern isles while Brian had only the support of the south Connacht armies of Uí Maine and Uí Fiachrach Aidne, Máel Sechnaill mac Domnaill having held aloof. Nevertheless, they won the day, although Brian himself was killed. The *Cogad* appears to borrow a motif from Asser's life of Alfred when it portrays the elderly and saintly King Brian, while praying in his tent, being brutally assassinated in the hour of victory by the fleeing viking leader, Bróðir. There is no hint of this in contemporary accounts, though they do report that after the battle the body of Brian, 'high-king of the Irish of Ireland and of the foreigners [the Hiberno-Norse] and of the Britons', along with that of his son Murchad, was brought ceremoniously to Armagh by its abbot and clergy, and there waked for twelve nights, before being buried in a new tomb (*Ann. Ulster*, s.a. 1014).

Assessment and reputation Later traditions embellished the account of Brian's death in other ways, for instance, by making his former wife Gormlaith (mother of Sihtric Silkenbeard of Dublin, and sister of Máel Mórda of Leinster) into the stereotypical female villain of the piece; but more especially by casting the affair as a climactic confrontation between the Irish and the Norse, in which the Irish triumphed, but with the tragic loss of their hero. The trend among modern scholars is to challenge the notion of Clontarf as the epic denouement of the conflict between the Irish and the viking invader, and to see the occasion more as an attempt by the king of Munster, and claimant to the high-kingship of Ireland, to gain the submission of the errant king of Leinster, with the Hiberno-Norse of Dublin playing a secondary role. There is much to be said in favour of this interpretation, though one has to be wary of turning tradition too violently on its head. The contemporary annals of Inisfallen and the annals of Ulster lay heavy emphasis on the foreign composition of Brian's opposition and clearly do not perceive Clontarf as a run-of-the-mill assertion of Munster hegemony over Leinster.

The fact, too, that Brian and the battle inspired writers in the Scandinavian world (most notably the author(s) of *Njáls saga*), makes it more than that, and the story is also told in detail in, for instance, the Welsh *Brutiau*. In Ireland, by the early twelfth century, in the *Cogad* and elsewhere, the battle was portrayed in terms that come close to explicit nationalism, and Brian himself assumed messianic proportions. A poem, written soon after the English invasion, ends:

> From the time Brian was slain, foreigners did not inhabit Ireland until the present day, with the arrival of the Earl [Richard de Clare, Strongbow]; from the day the Earl came, a fleet of foreigners comes every year, until, alas, they have taken Ireland in general. When will Brian's like come [again], north or south, east or west, a man to save the Irish from anguish, as he alone saved [them]? (Simms, 59)

Something about the battle and its hero has never failed to hold the imagination of the Irish nation and it seems that Clontarf will remain an important landmark. As it was Brian Bóruma's ultimate victory (however Pyrrhic) over his opponents, it can be said with justification that his career ended in glory, that he broke the Uí Néill monopoly of the high-kingship, and thereby shaped the course of Irish history for the next 150 years. He was succeeded by his son Donnchad (d. 1064), then in turn by the latter's more successful nephew, Tairdelbach mac Taidc (d. 1086) and by the latter's son, Muirchertach (d. 1119), the family by then sporting with pride the surname Ua Briain.

SEÁN DUFFY

Sources S. Mac Airt, ed. and trans., *The annals of Inisfallen* (1951) · *Ann. Ulster* · W. Stokes, ed., 'The annals of Tigernach [8 pts]', *Revue Celtique*, 16 (1895), 374–419; 17 (1896), 6–33, 119–263, 337–420; 18 (1897), 9–59, 150–97, 267–303, 374–91; pubd sep. (1993) · *AFM* · W. M. Hennessy, ed. and trans., *Chronicum Scotorum: a chronicle of Irish affairs*, Rolls Series, 46 (1866) · D. Murphy, ed., *The annals of Clonmacnoise*, trans. C. Mageoghagan (1896); facs. edn (1993) · M. C. Dobbs, ed. and trans., 'The Ban-shenchus [3 pts]', *Revue Celtique*, 47 (1930), 283–339; 48 (1931), 163–234; 49 (1932), 437–89 · M. A. O'Brien, ed., *Corpus genealogiarum Hiberniae* (Dublin, 1962) · J. H.

Todd, ed. and trans., *Cogadh Gaedhel re Gallaibh / The war of the Gaedhil with the Gaill*, Rolls Series, 48 (1867) · M. Magnusson and H. Palsson, trans., *Njal's saga* (1976) · *Liber Ardmachanus: the Book of Armagh*, ed. J. Gwyn (1913) · W. Stokes, ed. and trans., *The tripartite life of Patrick, with other documents relating to that saint*, 2 vols., Rolls Series, 89 (1887) · *Historia Gruffud vab Kenan / Gyda rhagymadrodd a nodiadau gan*, ed. D. S. Evans (1977) · T. Jones, ed. and trans., *Brut y tywysogyon, or, The chronicle of the princes: Red Book of Hergest* (1955) · *Asser's Life of King Alfred: together with the 'Annals of Saint Neots' erroneously ascribed to Asser*, ed. W. H. Stevenson (1904); repr. with a supplementary article by D. Whitelock (1959) · J. V. Kelleher, 'The rise of Dál Cais', *North Munster studies*, ed. E. Rynne (1967), 230–41 · J. Ryan, 'Brian Boruma, king of Ireland', *North Munster studies*, ed. E. Rynne (1967), 355–74 · J. Ryan, 'The battle of Clontarf', *Journal of the Royal Society of Antiquaries of Ireland*, 7th ser., 8 (1938), 1–50 · A. J. Goedheer, *Irish and Norse traditions about the battle of Clontarf* (1938) · D. Ó Corráin, *Ireland before the Normans* (1972), 111–31 · M. T. Flanagan, *Irish society, Anglo-Norman settlers, Angevin kingship: interactions in Ireland in the late twelfth century* (1989) · A. Gwynn, 'Brian in Armagh (1005)', *Seanchas Ardmhacha*, 9 (1978–9), 35–50 · K. Simms, 'The battle of Dysart O'Dea', *Dál gCais*, 5 (1979), 59–66

Brian fitz Count (*c*.1090–*c*.1149), magnate, was the son of Alan (IV) Fergant, duke of Brittany.

Background and marriage Brian was most likely illegitimate, for his mother's name is not recorded, and he is not known to have held any land by inheritance. He became a great landowner under Henry I, and one of his most intimate counsellors. In the early 1140s, when embroiled in the civil war of Stephen's reign, he would look back to 'the good and golden days' of Henry I, describing himself as a man 'whom good king Henry brought up and to whom he gave arms and an honour' (Davis, 303). The honour was that of Wallingford, which he had acquired by his marriage before 1119 to Matilda, lady of Wallingford, who was the heir of Miles Crispin. Matilda's parentage is a matter of continuing scholarly discussion. The earliest contribution to this was made by a local jury in 1183, who stated that Matilda was daughter of Robert (I) d'Oilly (*d. c*.1093) and wife of Miles Crispin (*d.* 1107). This would make Matilda a mature lady at the time of her second marriage, and an elderly one when she died; and some later historians suggest Matilda was the daughter of Miles Crispin; but the jurors, some of whom would have known Matilda, may be thought the best witnesses. In addition to Wallingford, also by 1119, Brian had control of the lordship of Abergavenny and Upper Gwent. In the pipe roll of 1129/30 he is shown as having exemptions from geld on 720 hides of land, in eleven counties, and owning a town house in Southwark. He himself rendered account for the borough of Wallingford, and for the office and part of the land of Nigel d'Oilly. The office may have been the constableship previously in the d'Oilly family, for Brian fitz Count attested as constable shortly thereafter.

Early career and Stephen's accession Brian fitz Count is first recorded at Westbourne in Sussex probably in 1114, when he was a member of the royal household about to cross over to Normandy. It was, however, only after 1125 that he was regularly at court, in the last decade of Henry I's life witnessing over forty of his charters, the majority of them in Normandy. It was a decade dominated politically by Henry's attempt to provide for the succession. Brian was

at Woodstock and at Rockingham in the autumn of 1126 immediately after the Empress Matilda (*d.* 1167) returned from Germany; and in the same year Waleran, count of Meulan, was transferred to his custody at Wallingford. He may be presumed to have been at Windsor on 1 January 1127 when the empress was designated as Henry's 'lawful successor' (Malmesbury, 3); and he and Robert, earl of Gloucester (*d.* 1147), then accompanied the empress to Rouen in May 1127 for her betrothal to Geoffrey, count of Anjou. The same two trusted counsellors were responsible for a special audit of the treasury during the financial year 1128/9. In the years 1129 and 1130 Brian was with the king in England and in Normandy. In February 1131 he occurs at Rouen as constable, while in the summer of that year he was at Arques, and a charter addressed to him and the vicomte of Arques suggests that he may then have had control of that castle. In September 1131 he was present at an important meeting of the royal court at Northampton, at which oaths in support of the empress's succession were again sworn. He crossed with the king to Normandy in the summer of 1133, and attested several charters at Rouen in 1134. He saw at first hand the conflict that then developed, in consequence of the demand made by the empress and her husband that the king transfer castles as security for the succession, which he refused them. In the late summer of 1135 Henry was at Argentan, and strengthened its defences; an attestation of Brian there may date from this time.

This conflict provides a part of the context which allowed Stephen of Blois, count of Mortain and Boulogne, to claim the English crown after Henry's death on 1 December 1135. Brian fitz Count cannot have welcomed this development, but initially he went along with it. He was at Stephen's Easter court in late March 1136, and early in April at Oxford when the charter of liberties was issued, by which time Robert, earl of Gloucester, had also come to terms with the king. It may have been at Wallingford that Robert joined the royal court as it travelled along the Thames valley. Both Brian and Robert, as marcher lords, were confronted by the threat posed by the Welsh resurgence after Henry's death. Brian accompanied Richard de Clare when he rode through Abergavenny to Cardigan, but (according to Gerald of Wales) Richard ignored his advice and sent him back, riding alone into an ambush in which he was killed on 15 April 1136. Brian also attested for Stephen at Hereford, in two charters probably dating from May 1138. At this time many of the marcher lords rebelled against Stephen, following the lead of Robert of Gloucester, but Brian is not mentioned among them.

Adherence to the empress It was only when the empress landed in the autumn of 1139 that Brian fitz Count declared for her. He was then at Wallingford. Robert of Gloucester left the empress outside Arundel and set out for Bristol; and Brian is described by William of Malmesbury as meeting him half way, which might have been at Marlborough. Stephen turned immediately to attack Wallingford, but this 'impregnable castle' (*Gesta Stephani*, 91) held out until it was relieved by Miles of Gloucester. Brian is next noted in March 1141, after Stephen had been captured at the battle of Lincoln, as one of those who swore in support of the promises made by the empress to Henry de Blois, bishop of Winchester (*d.* 1171), the papal legate, after which she was received as *domina Anglorum* ('lady of England'; Malmesbury, *Historia novella*, 47). He would retain a very clear memory of this event. The empress's charters, supported by the chronicles, show that for the remainder of a particularly eventful year Brian was continually at her side. In June he was with her at St Albans, when she came to terms with the Londoners; then at Westminster, where she issued the first of her charters to Geoffrey de Mandeville; and then in July, after the Londoners had driven her out, at Oxford, where Miles of Gloucester (*d.* 1143) was made earl of Hereford. Brian followed the empress to Winchester early in September, but she was driven out from here also. In the retreat from Winchester, Robert, earl of Gloucester, was captured, but the empress escaped to Devizes accompanied by Brian, by which—says the *Gesta Stephani*—they 'gained … a title to boundless fame, since as their affection for each other had before been unbroken, so even in adversity … they were in no wise divided' (p. 135). A charter of Miles, earl of Hereford, precisely dated to the last week of September, suggests that Brian and the empress next moved to Gloucester. The empress then sought to establish a base at Oxford, and Brian was with her there at times in 1142, but she was besieged by Stephen's forces in the castle, and at the end of December in that year she made her escape to Wallingford; thereafter, until she withdrew from England in 1148, she was based at Devizes.

Defence of the Angevin cause The retreat of the Angevin party, back to its original bases in the west country, left the castle of Wallingford exposed, and Brian was tied down to its defence. He resigned his marcher lordships. Having no son of his own, he in effect adopted Walter, the second son of Miles of Gloucester, giving him Grosmont possibly even before 1139 (for the grant was confirmed by Stephen). To Miles himself he resigned Abergavenny, to hold of him in return for the service of three knights. It became difficult even to provision Wallingford garrison. Seeking to defend the detention of goods bound for the fair at Winchester, probably in September 1142, Brian said that he had lost control of the lands which Henry I had given him. 'As a result I am in the greatest distress and am not harvesting one acre of corn from the land which he gave me' (Davis, 302).

Brian was writing in response to a curt letter from Henry, bishop of Winchester, reproaching him for supporting the empress, and threatening that he would shortly be numbered 'amongst the unfaithful men of England' (Davis, 301). Brian sent the bishop a lengthy and passionate defence of his integrity. It was not lack of faith but simple necessity that now led him and his men to self-help: 'neither I nor my men are doing this for money or fief or land, but because of your command the lawfulness of myself and my men'. The command had been given at Winchester in April 1141:

> you yourself who are a prelate of holy church have ordered me to adhere to the daughter of king Henry your uncle, and

to help her to acquire that which is hers by right but which has been taken from her by force.   (Davis, 301)

He called as witnesses no fewer than fifty-three prelates and magnates who had been there, whom he seems to have been able to list from memory. Henry of Winchester, who had heard much in this vein, had told Brian not to look back: 'remember the wife of Lot' (ibid., 301). In response, Brian brushed Lot's wife aside, and looked back to the first crusade. A further list of great men followed, starting with the bishop's father, 'who obeyed the pope's command and left so much behind, who by assault and force of arms conquered Jerusalem like good knights, and established there a good and lawful king by the name of Godfrey'. Stephen most certainly was not 'a good and lawful king' (ibid., 301). The demonstration of why this was so was provided by Gilbert Foliot, then abbot of Gloucester, in response to a letter from Brian. This letter (of *c*.1143) does not survive, but it must have been long—*librum edidisti* ('you have written a book'; *Letters and Charters*, 61, no. 26)—and the courtesies of correspondence led the abbot to pick up some of its themes in his preamble. Here was the reference to the good and golden days of Henry I, now turned to base metal. Here had been a fuller biography, for that king had 'brought you up from boyhood, educated you, knighted you, enriched you' (ibid.). It was quite understandable, granted what had come after, that those days lived vividly in Brian's memory. Now he was sustaining the empress's cause, 'not just with arms but with the grace and truth of eloquence' (ibid.). The abbot then turned to business. Brian had proposed that everything that had belonged to King Henry was by right (*iure*) owed to his legitimate daughter. Gilbert was prepared to show that this was so by divine, natural, and human law; and this he did at some length. In these few letters, survivals from an active pamphlet warfare, can be seen fully articulated the case for the Angevin succession, a decade before it would be realized. In an age when the biographies even of prominent laymen are difficult to construct, the fragments of autobiography which come from Brian fitz Count have a particular value.

Later career and reputation After 1142 references to Brian fitz Count are sparse and most often at second hand. When William Martel, one of Stephen's leading lieutenants, was captured at the battle of Wilton in 1143, he was sent as prisoner to Wallingford, where according to Matthew Paris he was placed in *cloere Brien* (Brian's dungeon), specially constructed for him (Paris, 2.174). In 1146 Stephen was joined by Ranulf (II), earl of Chester (*d.* 1153), in a further direct assault on Wallingford; but this too failed. Relations between the garrison of Wallingford and the men of the bishop of Winchester continued on a war footing: one of Brian's knights captured the bishop's castle at Meredon (in Hursley, Hampshire), but it was recaptured with the king's help.

Brian 'the son of the count' never became an earl. It is noteworthy that in his letter to Henry of Winchester he gives the title earl to only one of the many creations after 1135, either of Stephen or the empress, which suggests a patrician disdain for new titles. There are signs, however, that in the Angevin camp a distinctive honorific was created for him, since William of Malmesbury describes him as 'marchio de Walingeford', which could equally well be translated 'marcher' or 'marquess'; it was given as a title to later lords of Wallingford. A further sign of the esteem in which he was held was the grant (*c*.1144) by the empress to Reading Abbey of the royal demesne manor of Blewbury in Berkshire, 'for the love and loyal service of Brian fitz Count, which he has rendered me' (*Reg. RAN*, 3, no. 703); and her son Henry, in 1147 or 1149, confirmed the grant and associated himself with the sentiments. A letter of David, king of Scots, addressing Brian alongside the abbot and convent of Reading, shows that he was viewed as closely associated with the house which Henry I had founded and in which he was buried. Matilda of Wallingford, Brian's wife, maintained a close relationship with the abbey of Bec, granting it the two manors of Ogbourne in Wiltshire which became the centre of their estate in England. The last of her confirmations was issued at Bec in 1150 or 1151; and since Brian was neither present nor mentioned in it, he may be presumed to have died. The gap in the evidence concerning his last days was filled by later tradition. The Abergavenny chronicle stated that he had gone on crusade, but this is unlikely. The memory of the shire was that both he and his wife entered religion, and this is more probable. The quiet end became the man. Brian fitz Count was born illegitimate, and died childless. The distractions and the commitments of family are missing in his career, and this as much as temperament must account for what is distinctive in it. In his day he was a great man, but in his heart he remained always the household knight of Henry I. The love (*amor*) of which he wrote so frequently, and that he lavished on Henry's daughter, was neither carnal nor platonic but rather the very essence of chivalric loyalty and integrity.

EDMUND KING

Sources *Reg. RAN*, vols. 2–3 · M. Chibnall, *The Empress Matilda* (1991) · K. R. Potter and R. H. C. Davis, eds., *Gesta Stephani*, OMT (1976) · *Letters and charters of Gilbert Foliot*, ed. A. Morey and others (1967) · H. W. C. Davis, 'Henry of Blois and Brian fitz-Count', *EngHR*, 25 (1910), 297–303 · *Pipe rolls*, 31 Henry I · M. Chibnall, ed., *Select documents of the English lands of the abbey of Bec*, CS, 3rd ser., 73 (1951) · William of Malmesbury, *Historia novella: the contemporary history*, ed. E. King, trans. K. R. Potter, OMT (1998) · C. W. Hollister, *Monarchy, magnates, and institutions in the Anglo-Norman world* (1986) · D. Crouch, *The image of aristocracy in Britain, 1000–1300* (1992) · K. S. B. Keats-Rohan, 'The devolution of the honour of Wallingford, 1066–1148', *Oxoniensia*, 54 (1989), 311–18 · B. R. Kemp, ed., *Reading Abbey cartularies*, 2 vols., CS, 4th ser., 31, 33 (1986–7) · J. A. Green, *The government of England under Henry I* (1986) · Paris, *Chron.* · GEC, *Peerage*

Brian, Guy, Baron Brian (*c*.1310–1390), soldier and diplomat, was the son and heir of Sir Guy Brian of Torbryan, Devon, and an unknown mother. He is first recorded during Edward III's Scottish campaign of 1327, when he was present at the surprise attack on the English by the earl of Douglas. By July 1330 he was a squire of the king's household. Brian served on the Scottish campaign of 1337 and on the Flemish campaign of 1339, and was appointed governor of St Briavel's Castle, Gloucestershire, and warden of the Forest of Dean, in 1341. His rise in royal favour is shown by an order of May 1347 that he should hasten to the king at Calais in expectation of an attack by the French. However, Brian was more than a soldier, for on the resignation of Chancellor John Offord in 1349, he was entrusted with the temporary custody of the great seal. In December 1349 he served at Calais as the king's standard-bearer against the French, a task that earned him an annuity of 200 marks.

On 25 November 1350 Brian was summoned to parliament by personal writ; he continued to receive writs of summons until his death. He is thus considered to have become Lord Brian. He was made a knight-banneret in 1355 when he received royal licence to purchase lands to the value of £200 for the better support of his dignity. In 1353 he served as a commissioner to negotiate with the count of Flanders for the observance of the truce, as an ambassador to the French court for a peace treaty, and as an ambassador to the pope. He was again in Scotland in 1356, and in May 1357, styled 'Lord of Walwyn's Castle and one of the king's counsellors' (*RotS*, 1.784), he helped to negotiate a truce. He also served as steward of the royal household between 1359 and 1361, and as chamberlain in 1370. In 1360 he was again engaged in fighting and negotiating in France. When Edward III returned to England Brian was one of four entrusted with the custody of Calais, and, in October, he was one of a group including the prince of Wales who swore to the fulfilment of the peace. In 1361 he was again dispatched to the papal court. Upon the death of Sir John Chandos in 1370, he was made a knight of the Garter; his plate of arms (replaced or refurbished in the reign of Henry V) survives in stall K 11 of Windsor Castle chapel. He campaigned in France in 1369 and against the Scots in 1370.

Brian acted as the king's spokesman in parliament in 1372, and in 1373 and 1376 he was one of the lords selected to discuss business with the Commons. The Good Parliament appointed him to the council of nine that it established to advise the king. A man of talent and integrity, Brian's services were valued. He was appointed a feoffee of the duchy of Lancaster, and was one of John of Gaunt's executors. He was also named as an executor by Gaunt's son, Henry Bolingbroke, and by Isabella, countess of Bedford (*d*. 1379), Thomas Beauchamp, earl of Warwick (*d*. 1369), and Sir Walter Manny (*d*. 1372). Yet in spite of his ties to John of Gaunt, it was Lord Brian (and Lord Fitzwalter) who in 1377 informed the Londoners that the marshal, Henry Percy, was illegally holding a prisoner in his London house, thereby provoking a riot aimed at John of Gaunt and Percy, who were attempting to extend the marshal's jurisdiction in London. Dining together, the two had to flee for their lives.

Brian was often involved in the keeping of the seas. He served as admiral of the fleet for westward parts, and he was commissioned as late as 1382 to arrange shipping for Joan, duchess of Brittany. After 1367 he was less active at court, but he remained a valued soldier. His accounts for the Plymouth muster for the 1375 Breton campaign survive. Brian was to command his own retinue in the French expedition, which was aborted by Edward III's death. He did serve in Ireland in 1380 with the earl of March, and was a commissioner of array in Devon as late as 1385. He remained active on local commissions in Devon, Dorset, and Somerset until his death. He was a chamber knight in Richard II's household, but a very inactive one.

Guy, Lord Brian, died on 17 April 1390. He was reputed to have been ninety, but this is probably exaggerated. In 1330 he was described as being of full age, and in 1349 (when litigating against his own father over Walwayn Castle in Pembrokeshire) as 'being thirty years old and more' (*CIPM*, 9, no. 333). He was buried in Tewkesbury Abbey. His tomb survives, with an effigy which now lacks its left arm. Inquisitions post mortem for Brian exist for Devon, Somerset, and Dorset, but they are not informative about the value of his estates. He had established a chantry for four chaplains at the chapel of St Mary on his manor of Slapton, Devon. His first wife may have been Ann or Alice, daughter of William Holway. He then married Elizabeth, widow of Hugh Despenser and daughter of William *Montagu, the first earl of Salisbury. With his first wife Brian had a daughter, Elizabeth, and with his second at least three sons, Guy, William, and Philip. His coheirs were the daughters of his eldest son, Guy.   JAMES L. GILLESPIE

Sources G. F. Beltz, *Memorials of the most noble order of the Garter* (1841) · T. Moore, *History of Devon*, 2 (1831) · GEC, *Peerage* · C. A. Stothard and J. Hewitt, *The monumental effigies of Great Britain*, new edn (1876) · N. H. Nicolas, *History of the orders of knighthood of the British empire*, 2 (1842) · *Œuvres de Froissart: chroniques*, ed. K. de Lettenhove, 25 vols. (Brussels, 1867–77) · A. Goodman, *John of Gaunt: the exercise of princely power in fourteenth-century Europe* (1992) · C. Given-Wilson, *The royal household and the king's affinity: service, politics and finance in England, 1360–1413* (1986) · [T. Walsingham], *Chronicon Angliae, ab anno Domini 1328 usque ad annum 1388*, ed. E. M. Thompson, Rolls Series, 64 (1874) · A. F. O'D. Alexander, 'The war with France in 1377', *BIHR*, 12 (1934–5), 190–92 · *Chancery records* · PRO, E 101/33/33 · *CIPM*, vol. 3, s.a. 1384–92

Likenesses tomb effigy, Tewkesbury Abbey; repro. in Stothard, *Monumental effigies*

Wealth at death exact sum unknown: *CIPM*, 1384–92

Brian, (William) Havergal (1876–1972), composer, was born in Dresden, Staffordshire, on 29 January 1876, the eldest survivor of the seven sons (four of whom died in infancy) and one daughter of Benjamin Brian, a potter's turner, and his wife, Martha, daughter of James Watson. He was educated at the local infants' school and at St James's School, Longton, which had a strong musical tradition. His formal education ceased at the age of twelve: he had already shown musical talent, as a chorister and on violin, cello, and piano—and while trying a variety of trades (carpenter's apprentice, railway office boy, clerk, and buyer for a timber firm) he attempted to become a professional musician. He trained with a reactionary but thorough local music teacher, Theophilus Hemmings, and began to gain some reputation as a fine church organist (it was at this time that he assumed the name Havergal, probably after the hymn composer W. H. Havergal). At the 1896 Staffordshire triennial festival he heard Beethoven's ninth symphony and the première of a contemporary English work, *King Olaf*, by Edward Elgar—and, fortified by encouragement from Elgar, he resolved to become a composer.

The years 1906–12 saw Brian resident in Stoke-on-Trent and recognized as a promising figure among British composers of the younger generation, with his choral compositions becoming staple fare as test-pieces in competitions and his early cantatas and orchestral works produced to critical acclaim at various festivals. He was also active as a critic; consorted with leading musicians—Elgar, Frederick Delius, Thomas Beecham, Ernest Newman, Henry Wood, and especially Granville Bantock, who became a close and lifelong friend; and was supported by the patronage of the pottery magnate Herbert Minton Robinson. This palmy period was shattered by the breakup of his first marriage in 1913, and for the next fourteen years Brian struggled to make ends meet in London, Birmingham, and Sussex, producing hack-work and occasional journalism. On the outbreak of war he joined the Honourable Artillery Company as a private, but was invalided out in 1915 (having not served abroad) and worked first in the audit office of the Canadian forces contingent, listing the effects of men killed in action, and later as a clerk in munitions for Vickers Ltd in Birmingham. After the war he was a music copyist for various publishers. The price of this hectic and unsettled life was professional obscurity: his early music dropped out of the repertory, even though in the meantime he had developed considerably, composing two works of extraordinary brilliance—the satirical anti-war opera *The Tigers* (1917–19) and the huge first symphony, the 'Gothic' (1919–27), for gigantic choral and orchestral forces.

Brian moved back to London in 1927, and his position stabilized when he became assistant editor of the journal *Musical Opinion*, a post he held until 1939. In these years, as well as producing copious and acute journalism, he continued to write a series of large-scale symphonies (nos. 2–5), but hardly any of his post-1912 music was performed: he was virtually a forgotten composer. During the Second World War he was awarded a civil-list pension and worked as a clerk for the Ministry of Supply, remaining in the civil service until retirement in 1948. From that latter date—possibly partly as a result of the publication of a short biography by Reginald Nettel, *Ordeal by Music: the Strange Experience of Havergal Brian* (1945)—began an extraordinary Indian summer of creativity which produced a vast body of music including four operas and twenty-seven more symphonies (twenty-one of these after the age of eighty). Largely owing to the efforts of the composer and producer Robert Simpson, Brian's works began to be broadcast by the BBC, beginning with his eighth symphony in 1954, and there was a revival of interest in his music—gradual at first but much accelerated by a performance of the 'Gothic' at the Royal Albert Hall in 1966 to mark the composer's ninetieth birthday. The army of performers included 500 singers, 50 brass, 16 percussionists, and 30 woodwind players.

Brian was twice married. In 1899 he married Isabel Alice,

daughter of George Dalton Priestley, painter and decorator; they had four sons (one died in infancy) and a daughter. After his first wife died he married in 1933 Hilda Mary (*d.* 1980), daughter of Creswell Hayward, decorator of china and other pottery; previously they had had three daughters and two sons.

In 1958 Brian moved from Harrow (where he had spent the previous twenty years) to Shoreham by Sea, Sussex. Manchester University conferred on him the honorary degree of doctor of music in 1967; the following year he moved into a council flat on Shoreham beach, and he composed his last works there. In July 1972 he received the accolade of composer of the year from the Composers' Guild of Great Britain.

Physically a small man, of impassive and unassuming mien, his conversation richly flavoured by the Potteries accent he never lost, Brian dedicated his life to music with the utmost tenacity of a sardonic, idiosyncratic, and deeply original mind. His knowledge of past and contemporary music was more encyclopaedic than that of practically any of his contemporaries, and he was deeply stirred by nature, by Gothic architecture, and Romantic literature—he taught himself German, French, and Italian. Despite his humble origins and lack of worldly success he did not regard himself as socially or artistically disadvantaged, and the early termination of his formal education left him free to follow his own interests to the furthest degree.

Though in his early years Brian wrote many songs and partsongs, as well as some instrumental music, after the age of fifty he concentrated almost exclusively on music-drama and works for large orchestra. Several of these pieces remain unperformed, and his largest—a cantata setting of Shelley's *Prometheus Unbound* (1937–44)—is lost, a fate which has overtaken several earlier scores. His music developed from the stylistic basis of the late Romantics (Berlioz, Wagner, Elgar, and Strauss), but a pronounced streak of scepticism led him to question the heroic assumptions of these masters and to counterbalance their harmonic opulence with a muscular, 'objective' polyphony inspired by the example of Bach and Handel, searching development of motivic cells, and ironic juxtapositions of highly contrasted and mutually subversive kinds of music. While his works are generally tonal, therefore, their argument is elliptical, rejecting carefully formalized solutions in favour of open-ended procedures that continually undercut the listener's expectations. It is not comfortable (though it can be inspiring) music to listen to; it is also extremely difficult to play without extensive rehearsal, and few of his symphonies have yet been performed to a standard sufficiently high to project their substance with the force it deserves. Nevertheless, the 'Brian revival' proved no temporary phenomenon; a gradual realization grew that he was one of the most important British composers of the twentieth century. He died on 28 November 1972 at Southlands Hospital, Shoreham, as a result of complications following a fall outside his home. His youngest child, a daughter, predeceased him by seven months. MALCOLM MACDONALD, *rev.*

Sources K. Eastaugh, *Havergal Brian: the making of a composer* (1976) · R. Nettel, *Havergal Brian and his music* (1976) · M. MacDonald, *The symphonies of Havergal Brian*, 3 vols. (1974–83) · personal knowledge (1986) · H. Cole, 'Brian, Havergal', *New Grove*

Archives BL, autograph scores and sketches, Add. MSS 51056–51065, 54212–54213, 54337 · Keele University, papers | BL, letters to Ernest Newman, MS Dep. 2001/06 · JRL, letters to *Manchester Guardian* · McMaster University, Hamilton, Ontario, letters to Granville Bantock, etc. | SOUND BL NSA, 'Talk about Havergal Brian', BBC Radio 3, 15 Aug 1971, M4124W · BL NSA, ' Havergal Brian's Gothic symphony', B8428/10 · BL NSA, *Talking about music*, 188, 1LP0201381 S2 BD3 BBC TRANSC · BL NSA, *Talking about music*, 204, 1LP0202045 S2 BD2 BBC TRANSC · BL NSA, documentary recordings

Likenesses J. Goldblatt, three photographs, *c.*1970, NPG

Briand, Jean-Olivier (1715–1794), Roman Catholic bishop of Quebec, was born on 23 January 1715 at St Éloi in the parish of Plérin in the diocese of St Brieuc in Brittany, France, the eldest of the five or six children of François Briand (1688–1745), a peasant farmer, and his wife, Jeanne Burel (1689–1768). Educated by his uncle, Jean-Joseph Briand, Jean-Olivier set his sights on the priesthood at an early age. He studied at the seminary of St Brieuc and was ordained a priest on 16 March 1739. After practising his ministry for two years he consented, along with René-Jean Allenou of Lavillangevin, to a request from Henri-Marie Dubreil de Pontbriand, recently named bishop of Quebec, to become a missionary in Canada.

All three arrived at Quebec on 29 August 1741. Soon named de Pontbriand's secretary and confidant, Briand went unnoticed in his early ministry, his shyness being such that he could not preach. He was none the less well informed about the situation of the Canadian church and its administration, to which he now dedicated himself.

In the following decade, with de Pontbriand ill, Briand was named vicar-general of the district of Quebec before the bishop withdrew to Montreal in the company of the French army defeated at the Plains of Abraham in September 1759. The bishop's death in June of the following year, coupled with the capitulation of the country signed in September, left the diocese entirely in the hands of the diocesan chapter. Seven vicars-general—three in Canada, three in remote territories (Acadia, Illinois, Louisiana and Mississippi), and one in France—shared its administration. Briand, while directing the district of Quebec, was at the same time designated the head of the vicars-general.

To the British, Briand adopted a moderate attitude, proving conciliatory on the unessential and firm on the essential. With relations between church and state founded on the words of Paul to the Romans (13: 1–7), Roman Catholics in Canada were requested to show the same degree of obedience to George III as they had done to Louis XV. Briand permitted the governor, James Murray, to interfere in certain religious affairs and finally agreed to replace the name of the French king with that of the British in the canon of the mass. In return he expected the British to support the ecclesiastical authorities as a just exchange between two distinct jurisdictions. Following the signing of the treaty of Paris in 1763, Briand ordered the singing of the Te Deum in all parishes in his district in thanksgiving for the restoration of peace.

The fourth article of the peace treaty granted Canadian residents the freedom to practise Roman Catholicism 'inasmuch as the laws of Great Britain allow it'. After many interventions, the secretary of state, Lord Wyndham, sanctioned the possible election of a bishop by the chapter of canons of Quebec. With foreign Catholic priests forbidden from entering British North America, a bishop was necessary to ordain Canadian priests. Assisted by Governor Murray, Briand was chosen by the chapter in September 1764 and departed for London with an election attestation and a letter of introduction for Rome.

Briand was delayed in London for thirteen months until December 1765, when he left for France with assurances that the British authorities would not prevent his return to Canada. On 21 January 1766 he was ordained bishop of Quebec in the oratory of the castle of Suresne, near Paris, by the bishop of Blois, Charles-Gilbert Demay de Termont. Passing through London on his return to Canada, the new bishop swore allegiance to George III and declared his satisfaction with the official title of superintendent of the Roman Catholic church in Canada. The crowd that welcomed him on his arrival in Quebec represented the 65,000 diocesans scattered over the vast territory of North America.

In Paris, Briand had obtained the authorization from Rome to choose his own coadjutor *cum futura successione* in an attempt to avoid a repeat of the problems he had experienced before his own ordination. In Quebec Briand's powers and proposal were accepted by the new governor, Guy Carleton, and on 12 July 1772 the ordination of Louis-Philippe Mariauchau d'Esgby ensured the Roman Catholic episcopal succession in the country.

During 1767–8 and 1771–3 Briand made pastoral visits to the whole of his diocese. Despite a series of difficulties—among them the reduction of presbyteral staff, cases of debauchery and mixed marriages, and bitter opposition to the pastors and the bishop over church building and the payment of tithes—Briand remained tranquil and enthusiastic. He learned to speak in public and, though he often expressed himself in a rather harsh manner, he succeeded in settling problems, notably the rebuilding of Quebec's Notre Dame Church after its bombardment in 1759.

Further efforts to achieve reconciliation after war came in June 1774 in the form of the British government's Quebec Act. The British had seen the crucial importance of the geographical position of Quebec in North America and the necessity of ensuring the loyalty of French Canadians in the face of American independence. In response they re-established French civil laws (repealed in 1764) and granted Roman Catholics access to public office without the requirement to swear the test oath, along with freedom in the practice of religion (though they remained subject to the supremacy of George III) and the right of pastors to collect tithes. Bishop Briand was delighted by news of British concessions and had no difficulty in writing a pastoral letter of 22 May 1775 in which he urged his fellow Catholics to obey the government in Westminster.

Briand's episcopacy included few brilliant evangelizing activities, *The Little Catechism in Use in the Diocese of Quebec*

(1777), written by Montgolfier, marking the culmination of religious instruction in his pastorate. For the remainder of the time Briand was content to keep the zeal of his priests alive when they exchanged letters ordinarily about canonical or administrative problems. Anxious to provide for the needs of the population (over 112,000 inhabitants in 1784), he founded fifteen new parishes. In later years Briand suffered increasingly from sciatica and possibly from gout. On 29 November 1784 he resigned in favour of the ordination of a younger bishop, and thereafter he lived modestly at the seminary at Quebec. Briand died on 25 June 1794, aged seventy-nine, and was buried two days later in Quebec city.   LUCIEN LEMIEUX

Sources L. Lemieux, *Les XVIIIe et XIXe siècles: les années difficiles (1760–1839)* (Montreal, 1989), vol. 2/1 of *Histoire du catholicisme québécois*, ed. N. Voisine (1984–) · A. Vachon, 'Briand, Jean-Olivier', *DCB*, vol. 4 · L. Lemieux, *Établissement de la première province ecclésiastique au Canada, 1783–1844* (Montreal, 1968) · *Madements, lettres pastorales et circulaires des évêques de Québec*, 2 (Québec, 1888) · A. Shortt and A. G. Doughty, eds., *Documents relatifs à l'histoire constitutionnelle du Canada, 1759–91*, 2nd edn, 2 vols. (Ottawa, 1921) · PRO, CO 42, 24 (1761–3) · Evêques de Québec, 1, Archives de l'Archevêché de Québec, Quebec, Quebec CL, IV

Archives Archives de l'Archevêché de Québec, Quebec

Brian-na-Samhthach. See O'Rourke, Brian Oge (*c.*1569–1604), *under* O'Rourke, Sir Brian (*d.* 1591).

Briant, Alexander [St Alexander Briant] (**1556–1581**), Roman Catholic priest and martyr, was born in Somerset or Dorset. He was admitted to Hart Hall, Oxford, in Lent term 1574 and proceeded to Balliol College, Oxford. His tutors included the future Jesuits Richard Holtby and Robert Persons; they drew him towards Catholicism, so that he quit the university and entered the seminary at Douai on 11 August 1577. His training foreshortened 'on account of his singular learning and virtue' (Foley, 4.346), he was ordained priest at Cambrai on 29 March 1578, arrived in Rheims on 8 April, and was sent by William Allen with twenty other priests on the mission to England on 3 August 1579.

Back in England, Briant renewed his affiliation with Persons by converting the latter's father to the Roman Catholic faith. In March 1581 he was arrested at a bookseller's in London, more or less by accident, since his pursuers had a warrant for Robert Persons. Even so, in arresting Briant the authorities were apprehending both an admirer and a close associate of the Jesuit, who described him as his 'disciple and … pupil' (Foley, 4.346). A pattern of systematic abuse characterized the treatment of the arrested priest: he was robbed of his valuables and sent to the Counter prison with orders to be kept starved. Before 25 March he was sent to the Tower and repeatedly tortured—'racked more than the rest' (ibid., 353)—in order to get him to reveal his contacts with Persons. Indeed Briant's connections with Persons were fully maintained, for the young priest paid his mentor the high compliment of applying through him for admission into Persons's Jesuit order. His interrogators focused closely on the dangerously destabilizing political implications of the Catholic priestly mission of which he was part—his supposed involvement in Romanist conspiracy in England or Ireland, links with Mary, queen of Scots, and so on. Briant's confession in the Tower dated 6 May 1581 indicated a less than loyal political profile, for he was 'content to affirm that the Queen is his sovereign lady', but would not 'affirm that she is so lawfully' (ibid., 349).

When Briant and his priest companions went on 15 or 16 November 1581 to their arraignment in queen's bench the charge had all to do with militant and conspiratorial politics in the style of Allen and Persons: an alleged international plot based on Rheims, Rome, Florence, and Madrid, 'death and final destruction' of the queen, invasion, and sedition (Foley, 4.359). It was the crown's fear of Roman Catholic treason that led to its great show trials of Jesuits and seminarians in the autumn of 1581, including the conviction and execution of the Jesuit Edmund Campion, followed by the barbarously clumsy execution by hanging, drawing, and quartering of Briant, now received into the Society of Jesus, at Tyburn in London on 1 December 1581. In 1970 Briant was canonized by Pope Paul VI as one of the forty Catholic martyrs of England and Wales.

THOMPSON COOPER, rev. MICHAEL MULLETT

Sources H. Foley, ed., *Records of the English province of the Society of Jesus*, 4 (1878) · Wood, *Ath. Oxon.*, new edn, 1.479 · R. Challoner, *Martyrs of the Catholic faith: memoirs of missionary priests and other Catholics of both sexes that have suffered death in England on religious accounts from the year 1577 to 1684*, [new edn], 1 (1878) · Gillow, *Lit. biog. hist.*, vol. 1 · P. McGrath, *Papists and puritans under Elizabeth I* (1967) · F. Edwards, *Robert Persons: the biography of an Elizabethan Jesuit, 1546–1610* (1995) · G. Anstruther, *The seminary priests*, 1 (1969) · T. M. McCoog, *English and Welsh Jesuits, 1555–1650*, 1, Catholic RS, 74 (1994) · D. H. Farmer, *The Oxford dictionary of saints* (1978)
Archives Shrops. RRC, philosophical notes
Likenesses portrait, c.1581, repro. in Foley, *Records of the English province of the Society of Jesus*, facing p. 347 · line engraving, BM, NPG

Brice, Andrew (1692–1773), printer, was born in Exeter on 21 August 1692, the son of Andrew Brice, shoemaker. His parents originally intended him to become a dissenting minister but his father was too poor to support his studies and he was apprenticed at the age of seventeen to the Exeter printer Joseph Bliss, from whom he absconded by enlisting in the army. He married Sarah Leach on 26 May 1713 and, to support his family, he set himself up as a printer about 1714 with only one size of type.

In 1717 Brice established *The Postmaster*, a newspaper which continued under a variety of names until after his death. He was soon in trouble with the authorities, being summonsed for printing the proceedings of the House of Commons in November 1718. He pleaded guilty, and was reprimanded and discharged. He was also involved in several grant infringement cases in this period. In 1727 Brice ran a campaign in his newspaper, then entitled *Brice's Weekly Journal*, to improve prison conditions in Exeter. In 1730, after an expensive lawsuit by Thomas Glanville, the keeper of St Thomas's prison, he was confined to his house to avoid arrest for debt and during this time composed a lengthy poem in blank verse entitled *Freedom; a Poem, Written in Time of Recess from the Claws of Bailiffs* (1730) which also presented his case. In 1737 he wrote *The Mobiad*,

a mock heroic account of a city election, although this was not published until 1770. Brice also published *The Agreeable Gallimaufry, or, Matchless Medley*, much of whose contents came from his fertile pen. The early dialect work *An Exmoor Scolding* has also been attributed to him, the first part appearing in his newspaper of 2 June 1727. Brice briefly established the first press in Truro in 1742 but soon returned to his 'beloved native Exeter (from which no endeavours have prevail'd to take me away' (*Mobiad*, xviii). In 1743 he took his daughter Sarah Brice into partnership and they traded as Andrew and Sarah Brice until 1746. It is claimed in the *Universal Magazine* that more women were trained as printers in his office than in almost any office in England, it being common to see three or four at work.

Brice was a strong supporter of the theatre, conniving at the players' illegal performances which masqueraded as concerts of music by selling papers of brick dust under the name of tooth powder at the same price as would have been charged for theatre tickets. Brice also wrote several prologues for plays which were performed in Exeter, and even appeared in comic roles when required. When in 1745 the theatre was closed and converted into a chapel for the Methodists, Brice published a poem, *The Play-House-Church, or, New Actors of Devotion*. His style of writing abounded in newly coined words, which became known as Bricisms, and his speech, behaviour, and dress were so remarkable that he was the inspiration for the character Lord Ogelby which Thomas King introduced in *The Clandestine Marriage*. Brice's first wife had died in 1730 and in 1747 he married Hannah Seager of St Kerrian, Exeter, who died in 1763.

In 1759 Brice issued his largest work, *The Grand Gazetteer*, a large folio in two columns with 1446 pages originally published in forty-four monthly parts and completed in 1755. The sheets were also reissued in two volumes in London in 1759 with the title *A Universal Geographical Dictionary*. This work, one of the most comprehensive gazetteers of the century, involved Brice in expending more than £100 in the acquisition of works of reference and it includes an extensive and lively account of Exeter. In 1763 his journeyman William Andrews and his apprentice Robert Trewman quarrelled with their irascible master and left to establish the *Exeter Mercury*. In 1769 he took the printer Barnabas Thorn into partnership and retired in his favour to a house on the outskirts of the city on condition of receiving 2 guineas every Monday morning. After his death in Exeter on 7 November 1773 Brice's remains were conveyed to the Apollo Room at the New Inn where they lay in state for several days, a fee of 1s. being charged for admission to defray the expenses of his burial. This took place in St Bartholomew's churchyard, Exeter, on 14 November. Brice was a prominent freemason and some 200 members of the brotherhood accompanied his corpse during the funeral.

IAN MAXTED

Sources T. N. Brushfield, 'Andrew Brice and the early Exeter newspaper press', *Report and Transactions of the Devonshire Association*, 20 (1888), 163–214 · *Universal Magazine of Knowledge and Pleasure*, 79 (1781), 281–3 · G. Oliver, 'Biographies of Exonians', *Trewman's Exeter Flying Post* (1849), 7 · R. Polwhele, *The history of Cornwall*,

7 vols. (1803–8), vol. 5, pp. 87–90 · *Western Antiquary*, 4 (1885), 196 · *Western Antiquary*, 5 (1885), 164 · *GM*, 1st ser., 43 (1773), 582 · T. N. Brushfield, 'Who wrote the "Exmoor scolding and courtship"?', *Report and Transactions of the Devonshire Association*, 20 (1888), 400–09 · I. Maxted, *The Devon book trades: a biographical dictionary* (1991), 42–3 · C. H. Timperley, *Encyclopaedia of literary and typographical anecdote*, 2nd edn (1842), 729–31 · Nichols, *Lit. anecdotes*, 3.686, 718 · J. Davidson, *Bibliotheca Devoniensis* (1852), 26, 127–8 · R. M. Wiles, *Freshest advice: early provincial newspapers in England* (1965) · H. R. Plomer and others, *A dictionary of the printers and booksellers who were at work in England, Scotland, and Ireland from 1668 to 1725* (1922) · I. Maxted, 'Andrew Brice, printer of Exeter: an agreeable biographical gallimaufry', *Lives in print* (2002), 83–110
Likenesses Jehner, mezzotint, 1781 · R. Woodman, line engraving, 1784 (after Mrs Jackson), BM · Lency, line engraving, 1794 (after Mrs Jackson) · line engraving (after Mrs Jackson), repro. in *Universal Magazine*

Brice, Edmund (*fl.* 1648–1696), translator and schoolmaster, was admitted to Jesus College, Oxford, on or before 27 October 1648. He matriculated on 12 March 1649 and graduated BA on 12 July 1650. On 2 January 1651 Brice was by order of the committee for reformation of the university constituted a fellow of All Souls College in the place of Dr Wainwright. His appointment was opposed by the visitors of Oxford University, who had put one Mr Osborne into the vacancy. Writing on 17 January to the committee at London the visitors acknowledged that Brice was 'a gentleman wee all respect', adding the proviso that they 'would be glad to accomodate him in any thinge that may not be to the prejudice of others' (Burrows, 320). Eager for compromise the visitors eventually resolved the dispute in May 1651 when a further vacancy at All Souls enabled both Brice and Osborne to be made fellows of the college.

According to Richard Roach's account, while at All Souls, Brice and a companion heard a sermon at the university church 'preached in great Power' by John Pordage (1607–1681), rector of Bradfield, Berkshire. Together with his companion, Thomas Bromley (1630–1691), Brice went to 'Discourse' with Pordage. It was said that the pair 'received Such a Satisfactory Acc[oun]t' from Pordage 'that they Immediate[ly] Joyned themselves' to his 'Little Society, & Continued among 'em to their Dying Day' (Bodl. Oxf., MS Rawl. D 833, fol. 63*v*). The 'Little Society' to which Roach referred was Pordage's 'Family, who live together in Community, and pretend to hold visible and sensible Communion with Angles, whom they sometime see, and sometime smell' (*Reliquiae Baxterianae*, 1.77). How long Brice spent at Bradfield in the company of Pordage and his 'Family' is unknown, though battels receipts indicate that he retained his fellowship at All Souls until about December 1660.

On 24 April 1669 Brice subscribed as a schoolmaster to the Thirty-Nine Articles and was licensed to instruct boys in (Latin) grammar in the diocese of London. In later life he translated Theodore Mundanus's epistolary response to Edmund Dickinson 'concerning the Quintessence of the Philosophers', doubtless from the published Latin text of the letter (Oxford, 1686). This translation survives in manuscript. Brice also translated, as 'The center of nature concentrated, or, Ali Puli his tractate of the regenerated salt of nature' (BL, Sloane MS 487), a work ascribed to Ali

Puli, purportedly an 'Asian moor' who 'left the Mahumetan, & receaved the Christian Faith' (ibid., fol. 1*v*). His translation was printed for J. Harris at the Harrow in Little Britain, London, in 1696 under the title *Centrum Naturae Concentratum, or, The Salt of Nature Regenerated*. It seems that Brice used a Dutch text published in 1694, though it should be noted that in 1682 Johann Otto Helbig had completed a German version of the treatise (supposedly derived from a Portuguese translation of Puli's Arabic original). The title page of *Centrum Naturae Concentratum* described Brice as 'a Lover of the Hermetick Science' and in his preface to the reader Brice declared that 'the highest wisedom consists in this, for Man to know himself, because in him God has placed his Eternal Word, by which all things were made and are upheld' (Pili, p. 3). The date of Edmund Brice's death is unknown. His name is inscribed on the flyleaf of a copy of Jakob Boehme's *Aurora, that is, the Day-Spring* (1656). This book passed into the hands of Caleb Gilman, a founding member of the Philadelphian Society. ARIEL HESSAYON

Sources M. Burrows, ed., *The register of the visitors of the University of Oxford, from AD 1647 to AD 1658*, CS, new ser., 29 (1881) · Bodl. Oxf., MS Rawl. D. 833, fol. 63*v* · A. Pili [A. Puli], *Centrum naturae concentratum, or, The salt of nature regenerated*, trans. E. Brice (1696) · BL, Sloane MS 487 · *The epistles of Ali Puli*, trans. J. W. Hamilton-Jones (1951) · 'Theodorus Mundanus his letter to Dr. Dickenson', BL, Sloane MS 3762, fols. 32*r*–63*v* · E. Dickinson, *Epistola Edmundi Dickinson* (1686) · A. Hessayon, 'Gold tried in the fire': the prophet Theaurau John Tany and the puritan revolution [forthcoming] · N. Thune, *The Behmenists and the Philadelphians: a contribution to the study of English mysticism in the 17th and 18th centuries* (1948) · *Reliquiae Baxterianae, or, Mr Richard Baxter's narrative of the most memorable passages of his life and times*, ed. M. Sylvester, 1 vol. in 3 pts (1696), pt 1, p. 77

Brice, Edward (1568/9–1636), protestant minister, is usually supposed to have been from Airth, Stirlingshire, though nothing is known of his background or early life. He graduated from the University of Edinburgh in August 1593, so he probably entered the university in 1589. On 30 December 1595 he was inaugurated to the parish of Bothkenner in Stirlingshire. He was translated to the living of Drymen, near Glasgow, by James VI on 22 May 1602, and admitted by the presbytery of Dumbarton on 30 September. At the synod of Glasgow on 18 August 1607 he was one of two ministers who objected to the appointment of Archbishop Spottiswood as permanent moderator, a move which would have created an episcopate within the presbyterian structure, but he 'would never condescend but spoke publicly about it in bitter terms' (*Historical Works of Balfour*, 2.22). This is sometimes seen as giving rise to persecution of Brice by Spottiswood on religious grounds, but this is unlikely, since it was not referred to by Brice's more radical presbyterian friends, such as Robert Blair, who were concerned to chronicle such episodes of persecution. It is more likely that personal tensions between Spottiswood and Brice were to blame when, on 23 December 1613, Brice was deposed from his living by Spottiswood and the presbytery of Glasgow for alleged adultery.

Brice may already have been in Ireland by this time. According to the inscription on his gravestone he was admitted to the living of Templecorran (or Broadisland) by

Bishop Echlin of Down and Connor in 1613. In September 1619 he became prebendary of Kilroot, in the cathedral chapter of Connor. According to the returns of the royal visitation of 1622 Brice served the cures of Templecorran, Kilroot, and Ballycarry. These appointments may have been the result of the intervention of the local landlord, William Edmondston of Dunreath, in Stirlingshire. Edmondston, who probably came from the same part of Stirlingshire as Brice, had acquired the property in which these parishes lay in 1609.

Brice is usually assumed to have been the first presbyterian minister in Ulster. It was not unusual to find presbyterians of Scottish origin holding Church of Ireland livings before the 1630s. Similarity in theological outlook and shortage of ministers in Ulster made such an accommodation possible. However it is difficult to define in what sense Brice was a presbyterian. It is unlikely that he established presbyterian structures, such as the kirk session, in his parish. He certainly did not belong to the radical wing of presbyterianism which emerged in Ulster from the mid-1620s under the leadership of Robert Blair. In 1630, for instance, he was invited to preach at a presbyterian-style communion service at Templepatrick but obstinately refused. After the sermon he declared to the preacher, Robert Blair, 'of a truth the Lord was with you', to which Blair replied, 'Sir, God forgive you for your backsliding' (*Life of Robert Blair*, 85–6). However he did have presbyterian sympathies, and in 1629 he was assisted at Broadisland by an English presbyterian preacher, Henry Calvert (or Colwart), who had come to Ireland before 1625. Calvert was maintained as Brice's assistant by Lady Edmondston of Dunreath, the wife of the local landlord. In June 1630 Calvert became minister at Oldstone, in co. Antrim, in succession to James Glendining.

By the late 1620s Brice was described as 'a godly aged minister' by the co. Down presbyterian minister John Livingstone (*Brief Historical Relation*, 82) and as 'ancient' by Robert Blair (*Life of Robert Blair*, 75). His advanced age, combined with his moderate religious stance, may explain why in 1632 Brice was left alone when the Ulster presbyterian ministers who held Church of Ireland livings at Larne and Templepatrick were deprived for failing to subscribe to the canons. However, the appointment of the more Laudian-inclined Henry Leslie as bishop of Down and Connor in 1635 saw a more concerted effort made against those among the Church of Ireland clergy who had presbyterian sympathies. At Leslie's primary visitation of his diocese, held at Lisburn in July 1636, he required subscription to the recently passed 1634 canons by the clergy of the diocese. Five, including Brice, refused to subscribe. A private conference was held in the hope of finding an accommodation, but no compromise could be reached. On 12 August 1636 the five were silenced by the bishop. According to Brice's gravestone in the parish church he died in Ballycarry at the age of sixty-seven later the same year. He had two sons and two daughters, but nothing is known of his wife. RAYMOND GILLESPIE

Sources *The life of Mr Robert Blair … containing his autobiography*, ed. T. M'Crie, Wodrow Society, 11 (1848) · *A brief historical relation of the life of Mr John Livingstone*, ed. T. Houston (1845) · J. B. Leslie, ed., *Clergy of Connor: from Patrician times to the present day* (1993) · *Fasti Scot.*, new edn · J. S. Reid and W. D. Killen, *History of the Presbyterian church in Ireland*, new edn, 3 vols. (1867) · *The historical works of Sir James Balfour*, ed. J. Haig, 4 vols. (1824–5)

Brice, Thomas (1535/6–1570/71), martyrologist, was born in the hamlet of Billericay, Essex. His father's name was probably John Bryce. Nothing else is known about his early life until Mary's reign, when he is recorded by Foxe as having smuggled heretical books from Wesel into Kent and London, narrowly evading arrest. He was ordained a deacon on 25 April 1560, when he was said to be aged twenty-four, and ordained a priest on 4 June. Six days later, on 10 June 1560, Brice married Joanne Browne. By the end of that year he was serving as the curate of Ramsden Bellhouse (a village about 2 miles from Billericay) for an absentee rector. Brice would dedicate his poem, the *Compendious Regester*, to William Parr, marquess of Northampton, whose mansion was in close proximity to the Ramsden Bellhouse parish church. It is likely that Brice had led a protestant congregation in Ramsden Bellhouse in Mary's reign (this would explain both his subsequent rectorship and his rapid preferment); Northampton may well have sheltered Brice during this period. Brice was collated rector of the parish of Little Burstead (which included Billericay) on 11 February 1561. In a register of churchwardens' presentments, compiled in June 1565, Brice is described as preaching sermons in parishes throughout the area.

Despite his heroism in Mary's reign and his pastoral zeal, Brice is remembered solely for his poem, *A Compendious Regester in Metre*, which was published in the first half of 1559. This work, consisting of seventy-eight six-line stanzas, lists the Marian martyrs in order of the dates of their executions, and ends with a paean to Elizabeth. The *Compendious Regester* has little poetic merit, and it has been overshadowed as a source of information on the martyrs by John Foxe's magisterial *Acts and Monuments*. Nevertheless, Brice's poem is not without interest. In a very few cases, Brice provides the name of a martyr unmentioned by Foxe. More important, Foxe used Brice's work in his own research, although sometimes with less than happy results. Indeed, Brice was probably of more use to Foxe as an oral informant. The stories of his own 'miraculous' escapes during Mary's reign demonstrate that he communicated with Foxe. It would be surprising if Foxe did not draw on Brice's knowledge of underground protestantism in Mary's reign.

The *Compendious Regester* was clearly aimed at a popular audience; Brice expresses the hope that his work will make the names of the martyrs widely known because it is in verse, which is easier to understand, and also inexpensive. Moreover, Brice's list of the martyrs is remarkably egalitarian; men and women are all commemorated as martyrs for the gospel regardless of rank, status, education, and gender. In fact Brice makes a point of listing the humble occupations of his martyrs. Brice's inclusive approach to martyrology would not be without its influence on Foxe. Brice became a pioneer in the propagation of edifying literature cast in the form of unsophisticated, easily assimilated verse. A verse composition entitled *Against Filthy Writing, and suchlike Delighting* was published in 1562; a single copy exists in the Huntington Library, San Marino. But nothing survives of two other books, apparently also in didactic verse, which are assigned to Brice in the Stationers' register. The *Compendious Regester* was reprinted in 1599. In 1570 John Allde received a licence to print 'An Epitaphe on Mr. Brice' (Arber, *Regs. Stationers*, 1.359); this was very probably Thomas Brice, who was certainly dead by 10 April 1571, when a successor was collated to his living at Little Burstead. THOMAS S. FREEMAN

Sources T. Brice, *A compendious register in metre* (1599) · J. Foxe, *The second volume of the ecclesiasticall history, conteyning the acts and monuments of martyrs*, 2nd edn (1570) · GL, MS 9535/13 · CCC Cam., MS 122 · Essex RO, MS D/AEV 1 · Essex RO, MS D/P 139 · Arber, *Regs. Stationers*, vol. 1 · F. G. Emmison, ed., *Essex wills*, 1: *1558–1565* (1982), no. 486 · J. W. Martin, 'Sidelights on Foxe's account of the Marian martyrs', *Religious radicals in Tudor England* (1989), 171–8

Brickdale, Sir Charles Fortescue- (1857–1944), barrister and land registrar, was born on 1 March 1857 at 41 Victoria Street, Westminster, London, the oldest of the five children of Matthew Inglett Brickdale (1817–1894), barrister and sometime radical lawyer, and of Sarah Anna (1833/4–1909), daughter of Judge Edward Lloyd. At the time of Charles's birth the family name was Brickdale, and it was not until the Edwardian period that he and his siblings adopted the double-barrelled form. His sister, (Mary) Eleanor Fortescue-*Brickdale (1872–1945), achieved fame as a painter and stained-glass artist, and his brother, J. M. Fortescue-Brickdale (1869–1921), was a physician of some note.

Brickdale was educated at Westminster School and Christ Church, Oxford, where he also attended the Ruskin School of Drawing and learned proficiency in drawing and etching. Following in his father's footsteps, he was called to the bar in 1883 from Lincoln's Inn and specialized in land law. He acquired his credentials as a land reformer with a short book published in 1886, *Registration of Title to Land and how to Establish it without Cost or Compulsion*. The Land Registry, set up under an act of 1862 to register and secure title to land and thus ease property transfers, the costs, complexities, and delays of which were a national scandal, had up to that time proved to be a failure. The system was a voluntary one; it was strongly opposed by conveyancing lawyers and a mere three thousand or so titles had been registered. Brickdale pointed to the success of the Australian and Prussian systems of land registration, and argued that the key was to accept that registered land would offer not 'indefeasible' but 'guaranteed' title.

In 1888 Brickdale was appointed by the lord chancellor, Lord Halsbury, as assisting barrister at the Land Registry. From this time on, as a result of his energy and thoroughness, the thrust of its activities changed. Under Halsbury's protection, Brickdale took advantage of the strong agitation of the period for land reform, notably the controversies arising from the Irish land question and the campaigns of the American Henry George (1839–1897) and his English followers for the taxation of land values, to press consistently for the compulsory registration of land as the key to practical progress. After much lobbying and extensive study of the German and Austrian systems of registration and other foreign modes of tenure, Brickdale achieved this goal in the shape of the Land Transfer Act, 1897.

The conversion of a voluntary system into a compulsory one in the teeth of continued opposition from lawyers proved a formidable task, and in the event was achieved only gradually, beginning from 1899; a critical date was the extension of registration to the City of London in 1902. Brickdale was rewarded for his persistence by being appointed chief registrar in 1900, a post he held until he retired in 1923. He was the butt of fierce criticism from the Law Society, and the costs and workings of the Land Registry were among the issues investigated by the royal commission on land reform conceded by the Liberal government in 1908–9. In the event Brickdale managed to turn the radicalism of the moment to advantage. In 1910 he secured Lloyd George's promise of a new 'Domesday office' which would combine the Land Registry with the Ordnance Survey and the valuation department of the Inland Revenue.

The Liberal land-reforming tide then receded, and R. B. Haldane as lord chancellor proved less amenable to Brickdale's ambitions than had been expected. What had in effect become a competition over conveyancing between the Land Registry and the solicitors came to an end through the compromise of the Law of Property Bill (1922), enacted only in 1925 after Brickdale's retirement. However, during his period of office he had transformed a failure into a respected, revenue-earning department of government, housed in a handsome, purpose-built headquarters on the south side of Lincoln's Inn Fields. Brickdale himself in 1900 supplied the initial sketches for the Land Registry building, in a Jacobean style blending in with Lincoln's Inn. It was carried out by the office of works in 1903–5 and 1912–13, the latter phase housing also the Inland Revenue's land valuers.

Brickdale was typical of the more highly educated reformers of his period, earnest, single-minded, cultivated, but stubborn. In 1888 he married Mabel Beatrice Gibbs (d. 1944), daughter of George Louis Gibbs of the merchant banking firm Anthony Gibbs & Sons; they had two sons. Most of his many publications concerned land transfer and registration; he also edited the recollections of his brother-in-law, the soldier Sir Henry Hallam Parr, in 1917. He received a knighthood in 1911. He died at Gorse Corner, Townsend Drive, St Albans, on 20 September 1944 from heart disease and senile decay and was buried at East Sheen. ANDREW SAINT

Sources A. Offer, *Property and politics, 1870–1914* (1981) · A. Offer, 'The origins of the law of property acts, 1910–25', *Modern Law Review*, 40 (Sept 1977), 505–22 · *WWW* · *Land registry centenary, 1862–1962* (1962) · G. L. Taylor, *Centenary exhibition of works by Eleanor Fortescue-Brickdale, 1872–1945* (1972), introduction [exhibition catalogue, AM Oxf., 1 Dec 1972–7 Jan 1973] · PRO, WORK 12/147, 149 · b. cert. · d. cert.

Archives priv. coll. | PRO, LAR classes and LCO classes

Likenesses E. Fortescue-Brickdale, portrait, 1924, HM Land Registry

Wealth at death £3909 9s. 1d.: probate, 29 Jan 1945, *CGPLA Eng. & Wales*

Brickdale, (Mary) Eleanor Fortescue- (1872–1945), artist, daughter of Matthew Inglett Brickdale (1817–1894), a barrister of Lincoln's Inn, and his wife, Sarah Anna Lloyd (1833/4–1909), daughter of Judge Edward John Lloyd QC, of the Bristol county court, was born on 25 January 1872 at her parents' house, Birchamp Villa, Beulah Hill, Upper Norwood, Surrey. She had two older brothers, Charles Fortescue-*Brickdale (1857–1944) and John, who had distinguished careers in the law and medicine respectively, and an older sister, Kate. From the age of seventeen she studied at the Crystal Palace School of Art, London, and then at the Royal Academy Schools, to which she gained admission on her third attempt. The crowning achievement of her career at the schools came in 1897 when she won a £40 prize for a design for a mural decoration. In the following year she published her first illustrations, line drawings for Joseph Arthur Gibbs's *A Cotswold Village* (1898). She made her public début as an oil painter at the Royal Academy exhibition of 1899 and continued to show an oil there each year until 1908, after which her contributions were less regular; the last appeared in 1932. In 1901 the Dowdeswell Galleries mounted an exhibition of forty-five of her watercolours under the title 'Such stuff as dreams are made of!'. The exhibition was widely reviewed and critics recognized her artistic debts to Dante Gabriel Rossetti, William Holman Hunt, and other artists of the Pre-Raphaelite circle, as well as to her friend and fellow 'Neo-Pre-Raphaelite', John Byam Shaw. In the same year Eleanor Fortescue-Brickdale was elected an associate of the Royal Society of Painters in Water Colours, where she was to exhibit regularly for the rest of her career, and in 1902 she became the first woman member of the Institute of Painters in Oils. Also in 1902 she exhibited most of the watercolours from the Dowdeswell exhibition, along with some oils and drawings, at Leighton House, in London. By this date she had taken a studio at 11 Holland Park Road, nearly opposite Leighton House, which she kept until the building was damaged by enemy action in the Second World War.

Eleanor Fortescue-Brickdale never married, and from 1903 to 1943 she lived with her sister, Kate, who was also unmarried, at 23 Elsham Road, Shepherd's Bush. She travelled often to the continent and was clearly influenced by the fifteenth- and early sixteenth-century art which she saw on visits to Italy. There were further exhibitions of her works at Leighton House in 1904, with a catalogue containing appreciative remarks by George Frederic Watts, and at Dowdeswell's in 1905 and 1909. She continued her illustrative work, which from about 1905 consisted of both line drawings and watercolours made for reproduction as half-tone colour plates. In 1911 two editions of Tennyson's *Idylls of the King* (de luxe and popular) were published with illustrations from her watercolours while the originals were on show in another of her one-woman exhibitions, this time at the Leicester Galleries. From that year she taught in the art school in Kensington founded by Byam Shaw. During the First World War she designed posters for various government departments, and after the war more than twenty commemorative stained-glass windows (1914–38), as well as a memorial in York Minster to the 6th (King's Own Yorkshire) light infantry (unveiled 1921). She was elected a full member of the Royal Society of Painters in Water Colours in 1919. A further one-woman exhibition at the Leicester Galleries in 1920 was a showcase for her watercolour illustrations to *Eleanor Fortescue-Brickdale's Golden Book of Famous Women*, published the previous year. After 1923 she suffered intermittent ill health and failing eyesight, and in 1938 she had a stroke. She died in Fulham Hospital, London, on 10 March 1945 and was buried in Brompton cemetery.   MALCOLM WARNER

Sources G. L. Taylor, *Centenary exhibition of works by Eleanor Fortescue-Brickdale, 1872–1945* (1972) [exhibition catalogue, AM Oxf., 1 Dec 1972–7 Jan 1973] · J. Christian, ed., *The last Romantics: the Romantic tradition in British art* (1989), 130–31 [exhibition catalogue, Barbican Art Gallery, London, 9 Feb – 9 April 1989] · Burke, *Gen. GB* (1972) · d. cert.
Likenesses photograph, c.1920, repro. in Taylor, *Centenary exhibition*, fig. 2 · J. Byam Shaw, pastel, repro. in *The Queen* (30 July 1904), 195
Wealth at death £3546 10s. 8d.: administration with will, 16 Oct 1945, *CGPLA Eng. & Wales*

Bricmore, H. (*d.* 1382?), logician, is alleged by the early seventeenth-century Scottish writer Thomas Dempster to have been a Scot, a canon of Holyrood Abbey, Edinburgh, though elsewhere it is asserted that he was an Englishman. Dempster states that Bricmore had been sent to Oxford by a decree of the Council of Vienne (1311–12) and that he died in England in 1382. The authority quoted for the details of his death seems, however, to have been misunderstood. Sixteenth-century antiquaries record his authorship of several logical texts used in the Oxford faculty of arts. There survive in Oxford and in the Vatican, attributed to him, various commentaries on the works of Boethius and Aristotle, and also a collection of logical notes. These notes, which are found in association with the writings of Duns Scotus and Walter Burley, appear to indicate little development from the logical arguments prevalent in Oxford and Paris in the preceding century.

JOHN M. FLETCHER

Sources Emden, *Oxf.*, 1.262–3 · T. Dempster, *Historia ecclesiastica gentis Scotorum* (Bologna, 1627), xvi, 100–01 · P. O. Lewry, 'Grammar, logic and rhetoric, 1220–1320', *Hist. U. Oxf.* 1: *Early Oxf. schools*, 401–33

Bridei mac Maelchon. *See* Brude mac Maelchon (*d. c.*586).

Bridei son of Beli. *See* Brude mac Bile (*d.* 693).

Bridell, Frederick Lee (*bap.* 1830, *d.* 1863), landscape painter, was baptized William Frederick Bridell (the name Lee was added before 1854) at St Mary's Church, Southampton, Hampshire, on 5 December 1830. He was the son of John Bridell, a carpenter living at Houndwell Place, Southampton. His father wanted him to go into the building trade, but the boy preferred art, and 'was drawing avidly from his ninth year' (Sweetman, 'Romantic landscape', 142). When he was fifteen he compromised with his father and became a house painter; he also began to write verse and paint portraits about this time. An early portrait of his friend Henry Rose probably dates from 1848 (Southampton Art Gallery). 'Tight but competent, it is distinguished by an almost immaculate paint surface, bearing out Rose's testimony that from his early years Bridell gave careful study to pigments and their durability' (ibid.).

Bridell's work attracted the attention of Edwin Holder, a picture dealer visiting Southampton, who, in 1848, offered him a five-year contract to copy old master paintings throughout England; the finished paintings belonged to Holder. This arrangement gave Bridell the opportunity to study painting techniques and the works of great artists, and was the only form of art education he ever had, but it was restrictive and his work did not become widely known. He was interested principally in landscape painting. In 1851, when he was living in Maidenhead, Berkshire, he exhibited his first picture at the Royal Academy: *A Bit in Berkshire*. In 1853 his contract with Holder was renewed on condition that he be sent to the continent. After a short stay in Paris he established himself in Munich, where he formed friendships with Karl Theodor von Piloty and other eminent painters. Here he developed an appreciation for alpine landscapes, perfected his technique, painted, and exhibited several pictures highly commended by the German critics; he sent one, *Kaiserspitze* (*Wild Emperor Mountains*), to the Royal Academy in 1856. In 1857 he returned to England and unsuccessfully sought release from his contract. His first important work, *Sunset on the Atlantic, as Seen from the Bill of Portland Lighthouses*, was exhibited at Liverpool in November of that year, and excited great admiration for the effective treatment of sea and sky. Bridell exhibited ten paintings at the Liverpool Academy between 1856 and 1862, and three at the Liverpool Society of Fine Arts; he also exhibited at the Royal Manchester Institution between 1857 and 1866. In London he exhibited at the Royal Academy again in 1858 and 1860–62 and at the British Institution in 1856–7 and 1860–63, and exhibited two pictures at the Society (later Royal Society) of British Artists in 1851.

In 1858 Bridell was living in Southampton and working on a number of commissions for the shipping magnate J. H. Wolff, including his *Temple of Love*, an ideal composition painted in emulation of J. M. W. Turner. In the autumn he toured the Rhine valley and Italy. In Rome he painted *The Coliseum at Rome by Moonlight* (1858–9; Southampton City Art Gallery), his most impressive work, which was exhibited at the Royal Academy in 1860 and the International Exhibition of 1862. It was intended to be the final piece in a series of poetical landscapes illustrating the rise, greatness, and decline of imperial Rome, but the rest of the series were never painted.

In February 1859, in Rome, Bridell married Eliza Florance (1823/4–1903) [see Fox, Eliza Florance Bridell-], the daughter of the Unitarian minister William Johnson *Fox and an artist of distinguished talent, but Bridell's health failed almost immediately afterwards. He returned to England and freed himself from his contract by means of a heavy payment in money and pictures. He spent his time in London, Hampshire, and Derbyshire, as well as on the continent. In 1860 he was again in Italy, where he made sketches for numerous landscapes and painted almost obsessively; *The Woods of Sweet Chestnut above Varenna, Lake Como* (1860; Tate collection; sketch, Southampton Art Gallery) is from this period. Although he seemed to have had every prospect of a brilliant career, his health worsened. He continued to paint until within six months of his death, on 20 August 1863, at his home, 8 Victoria Road, Kensington, London, at the age of thirty-two, when he finally succumbed to tuberculosis. He was buried at Brompton cemetery.

Notwithstanding his youth and the obstacles created by impaired health and unfavourable circumstances, Bridell had already proved himself 'a great master of landscape and an honour to the English school' (Wornum, 544–5). His art had gone counter to the tendencies of his day. While his contemporaries, under Pre-Raphaelite influences, inclined more and more to the minute and realistic, Bridell, inspired by Turner, was broad, ample, and imaginative. His work was bold and rapid and full of rich colour. He aimed especially at conveying the feeling of a landscape. Sunrise and sunset, mist and moonshine, combinations of light and shade in general were his favourite effects. 'In his painting of skies and clouds in particular', wrote Sir Theodore Martin in his obituary, 'Mr. Bridell seems to us to occupy a place among British artists only second to Turner' (Martin, 12). His principal patron was J. H. Wolff, who formed a Bridell gallery at Bevois Mount House, Southampton; this was subsequently sold at auction through Christies on 26 February 1864 for nearly £4000. Bridell also enjoyed the patronage of Josiah Radcliffe, Martin, John Platt, and other collectors. Many of the artist's works were assembled in the early twentieth century by W. Burrough Hill; these now form the core of the collection at Southampton Art Gallery.

RICHARD GARNETT, *rev.* ARIANNE BURNETTE

Sources J. Sweetman, 'F. L. Bridell and the Romantic landscape', *Apollo*, 100 (1974), 142–5 · J. Sweetman, 'Bridell, Frederick (Lee)', *The dictionary of art*, ed. J. Turner (1996) · [T. Martin], *Art Journal*, 26 (1864), 12 · R. N. Wornum, *Epochs of painting* (1864) · [E. Ogborn], *Southampton Art Gallery collection* (1981) · *Concise catalogue of the Tate Gallery collection*, 9th edn (1991) · Graves, *RA exhibitors* · E. Morris and E. Roberts, *The Liverpool Academy and other exhibitions of contemporary art in Liverpool, 1774–1867* (1998) · Graves, *Brit. Inst.* · J. Johnson, ed., *Works exhibited at the Royal Society of British Artists, 1824–1893, and the New English Art Club, 1888–1917*, 2 vols. (1975) · Redgrave, *Artists* · Wood, *Vic. painters*, 3rd edn · *CGPLA Eng. & Wales* (1863)
Likenesses E. Bridell-Fox, portrait, exh. RA 1859 · E. Bridell-Fox, portrait; exh. Liverpool Institution of Fine Arts, 1864
Wealth at death under £1500: will, 22 Oct 1863, *CGPLA Eng. & Wales*

Brideoake, Ralph (*bap.* 1613, *d.* 1678), bishop of Chichester, was the eldest surviving son of Richard Brideoake (Briddock) of Cheetham Hill, Manchester, and his wife, Cicely Boardman. He was baptized at Manchester on 31

January 1613 and probably educated at the town's grammar school. He was admitted to Brasenose College, Oxford, on 15 July 1630, matriculating on 9 December 1630 and graduating BA on 9 July 1634.

From this point onwards Brideoake's life was punctuated by moments of good fortune and the assiduous courting of influential patrons. His academic performance impressed Robert Pinck, warden of New College, who appointed him pro-chaplain of the college. When Charles I visited the university in 1636 Brideoake was made MA by royal letters, and for a time he harboured ambitions of becoming a court poet. He addressed some verses to the dramatist Thomas Randolph and later wrote two elegies on the death of 'Master Ben Jonson'. In 1638 he penned some Latin and English verses for the celebratory *Musarum Oxoniensium charisteria pro regina Maria recens e nixus laboriosi discrimine recepta* (1638). However, his failure to gain access to court was remedied by his appointment as curate to John Brikenden in Wytham, near Oxford. While there he somehow became a corrector for the press and in 1638 edited a work by Thomas Jackson, president of Corpus Christi College. Brideoake's editing so pleased Jackson that he offered him the high mastership of Manchester grammar school, of which he was patron.

Once back in Manchester, Brideoake quickly found a new patron in Lord Strange (later seventh earl of Derby) and became chaplain at Lathom House. The outbreak of hostilities in Manchester in July 1642 soon forced men to take sides, and Brideoake chose to remain within the Derby household. He was present during the sieges of Lathom House in 1644–5 and for his loyalty was rewarded with the living of Standish, Lancashire. From 1646 and throughout the 1650s he was typical of men who, naturally royalist in sympathy, accommodated themselves to successive parliamentary regimes. When the earl of Derby was captured in 1651 Brideoake travelled to London to plead with William Lenthall for his patron's life. Although nothing could halt Derby's execution, Lenthall was impressed enough by Brideoake that he made him his chaplain and later preacher of the rolls, despite several complaints. Brideoake attended Lenthall's deathbed in 1662 and heard and recorded his penitence for his sins of rebellion. Through the patronage of Lenthall, he also acquired in the mid-1650s the vicarage and rectory of Witney, Oxfordshire, which he retained until August 1663.

Within Manchester, despite facing sequestration, Brideoake skilfully forged relations with moderate parliamentarians. He was elected an elder in Manchester's presbyterian classis in 1647 and became a friend of the scholar John Worthington. In March 1649 he was a mediator in negotiations with the philanthropist Humphrey Chetham regarding the vacant college house, which later became the site of Chetham's Hospital. The relationship became close and Brideoake wrote a preface to Nicholas Mosley's *Natural and Divine Contemplation of … the Soul of Man* (1653), which was dedicated to Chetham. In 1654 he was among the electors of Manchester's first MP, Charles Worsley, and was confirmed in his living at Standish,

although this was subsequently disputed. His reconciliation with the protectorate was completed on 14 March 1659, when he was appointed a 'trier' for the ordination of presbyterian ministers. About 1660, however, Brideoake returned to Gray's Inn, Middlesex, and married Mary Saltonstall, daughter of Sir Richard Saltonstall of Ockendon, Essex. They had three surviving sons and settled at Isleworth, Middlesex.

At the Restoration, Brideoake quickly conformed to the new religious mood, and his service during the wars recommended him to Charles II. From 1660 until his death he sought and acquired a wide range of preferments. He became a chaplain to the king, and was created prebendary of Windsor on 28 July 1660, and DD on 2 August 1660. He was also installed as minister at St Bartholomew by the Exchange, London, on 8 September 1660, which in 1662 he offered to Richard Heyricke in exchange for his wardenship of Manchester collegiate church. The swap did not take place, and in the years following the great fire, when the church and all but three houses were burnt down, Brideoake clashed with the vestry over claims to parish property. One meeting which Brideoake summoned in 1673 ended acrimoniously, when 'by sume wordes that did Arise the vestrey was dismist!' (Freshfield, 113). He retained links with Manchester and on 25 February 1661 was elected a feoffee of the grammar school. He continued to seek preferment and in September 1667 was appointed dean of Salisbury. By 1670 his income from Standish and St Bartholomew's alone was £589 per annum.

On 9 March 1675, probably through the venal duchess of Portsmouth, Brideoake was made bishop of Chichester and was allowed to hold *in commendam* his livings at Windsor and Standish. Such wealth was offset by a mixed reputation for preaching. Although Anthony Wood praised his efforts in 'outvying in labour and vigilancy any of the godly brethren' (Wood, *Ath. Oxon.*, 4.860), his enthusiasm was not shared by either the Manchester minister Henry Newcome or John Evelyn, who heard Brideoake preach on 5 March 1676 and declared his text 'a very meane discourse for a bishop' (Evelyn, 4.85). Nevertheless, in his last years he remained active in Chichester diocese and his labours there probably contributed to his eventual demise. It was perhaps fitting that in 1677, shortly before his death, he erected a monument to his first patron, Robert Pinck, in New College chapel. He died suddenly on 5 October 1678 while on a diocesan visitation, and was buried in Bray's Chapel, Windsor, where an alabaster monument erected by his widow covered his grave.

S. J. GUSCOTT

Sources Wood, *Ath. Oxon.*, new edn, 4.859–61 · *The life and times of Anthony Wood*, ed. A. Clark, 1, OHS, 19 (1891), 328; 2, OHS, 21 (1892), 304, 417, 420; 3, OHS, 26 (1894), 22 · *Walker rev.* · Evelyn, *Diary*, 4.29–30, 61, 85 · J. Spurr, *The Restoration Church of England, 1646–1689* (1991), 176–7 · *DNB* · A. A. Mumford, *The Manchester grammar school, 1515–1915* (1919), 56, 74 · *CSP dom.*, 1655; 1660–61; 1673–6; 1678 · records of Manchester grammar school, Man. CL, M516 · episcopal registers, W. Sussex RO, Ep.I/1/10, fols. 2–15 · W. A. Shaw, ed., *Minutes of the Manchester presbyterian classis*, 1, Chetham Society, 20 (1890), 15 · Foster, *Alum. Oxon.*, 1500–1714 [Raphe Brideoake] · *The* *registers of the cathedral church of Manchester*, 1 (1908), 184 [introduction by E. Axon] • E. Freshfield, ed., *The vestry minute books of the parish of St. Bartholomew Exchange in the City of London, 1567–1676* (privately printed, London, 1890) • [C. B. Heberden], ed., *Brasenose College register, 1509–1909*, 1, OHS, 55 (1909), 160

Archives W. Sussex RO, episcopal registers, Ep.I/1/10, fols. 2–15 | Man. CL, Manchester grammar school records, M516

Likenesses W. Bird, marble effigy on monument, 1678, St George's Chapel, Windsor; repro. in S. M. Bond, ed., *The monuments of St George's Chapel* (1958), 24

Wealth at death £599 p. a. from Standish parish tithes, St Bartholomew's parish, bishopric of Chichester, and prebend of Windsor (1670): Spurr, *The Restoration Church of England*, 176–7; administration, 1678, PRO, PROB 6/53, fol. 102r; Ches. & Chester ALSS, WCW 1699

Bridge, Ann. *See* O'Malley, Mary Dolling, Lady O'Malley (1889–1974).

Bridge, Bewick (1767–1833), mathematician, was born at Linton, Cambridgeshire, and received his education at Peterhouse, Cambridge, where he later became a fellow. He graduated BA as senior wrangler in 1790, MA in 1793, and BD in 1811, and was proctor in 1800. After serving as professor of mathematics in the East India Company's college at Haileybury, near Hertford (1806–16), he was presented to the vicarage of Cherry Hinton, near Cambridge, by Peterhouse in 1816.

Bridge, who was elected a fellow of the Royal Society in 1812, published mathematical works mainly between 1810 and 1821. He first produced books of lectures on algebra and trigonometry, which soon led to the publication of two volumes of *Mathematical Lectures* (1810 and 1811). He wrote textbooks on mechanics, algebra, trigonometry, and the solution of various families of algebraic equations. After leaving Peterhouse for Cherry Hinton, his prodigious output of books gradually ceased. Bridge was active in promoting philanthropic causes, and was especially involved with the Cambridge Savings Bank and with efforts for the relief of the poverty-stricken Vaudois of the Piedmont valleys. He died at Cherry Hinton on 15 May 1833. THOMPSON COOPER, rev. JULIA TOMPSON

Sources GM, 1st ser., 103/2 (1833), 88 • Venn, *Alum. Cant.* • [J. Watkins and F. Shoberl], *A biographical dictionary of the living authors of Great Britain and Ireland* (1816)

Bridge, Sir Cyprian Arthur George (1839–1924), naval officer, was born on 13 March 1839, at St John's, Newfoundland, the eldest son of Thomas Finch Hobday Bridge (b. c.1812), rector (afterwards archdeacon) of St John's, Newfoundland, and his wife, Sarah Christiana, daughter of John Dunscomb, an aide-de-camp to the governor of Newfoundland. On his father's side Bridge was descended from a Flemish family settled in England in the twelfth century, and among his immediate predecessors he had associations with the sea service: two of his grandfather's brothers served in the navy, one of them under Rodney; his grandfather was a midshipman in the East India Company's and the Admiralty's packet services; his father was prevented only by short sight from adopting a sea life, and became chaplain to Admiral Sir Thomas John Cochrane, governor of Newfoundland.

Bridge went to England first in 1851, with a nomination for the navy given by Admiral Cochrane. He was sent to school at Walthamstow House, passed, in January 1853, the entrance examination for the navy—then a very simple test—and was appointed to the paddle wheel sloop *Medea*, 850 tons, and, later, to the flagship *Cumberland* on the North American station. Early in 1854 he was transferred to the corvette *Brisk*, under Commander Beauchamp Seymour (afterwards Lord Alcester), and in her was sent into northern waters on the 1856 outbreak of war with Russia; he was present at the operations in the White Sea of the squadron under Sir Erasmus Ommanney.

In 1855 Bridge passed for midshipman, having served two years as cadet; he was still under sixteen years of age, but had been in three ships, had served on foreign stations, and had seen war service. He was next appointed to the *Pelorus*, again under Seymour, for service in the East Indies. He took part in operations at Rangoon which continued for some years after the Second Anglo-Burmese War, and in the Bay of Bengal and the Red Sea made acquaintance with the old Indian navy, shortly afterwards dissolved; he was a constant advocate of its resuscitation as a fighting force in later years. He became a mate in 1858, and a lieutenant in 1859, aged twenty. Having passed the necessary examinations he joined the *Algiers*, line of battle ship, and in her served in the Mediterranean under Sir William Fanshawe Martin, whom later he described as the greatest flag officer since the Napoleonic wars and an abler man than Lord St Vincent. His period of service in the *Algiers* was uneventful but highly instructive, for Admiral Martin conducted a continuous investigation into fleet evolutions and the tactics of battle. After three years in the Mediterranean, Bridge served successively in the *Hawke* on the Irish station, and the *Fawn* (1864–7) in the West Indies.

Being now of eight years' standing as a lieutenant, Bridge went to the *Excellent* in order to qualify in gunnery; he did not, however, serve as a gunnery specialist, for he was invited by Sir Alfred Ryder, second in command of the Channel Fleet (1868–9), to act as his flag-lieutenant. In April 1869, at the age of thirty, he was promoted to commander. He had now seen sixteen years of service, mostly at sea. In later life he contrasted the sea service of his younger days with that of more recent times.

> In the third quarter of the nineteenth century most officers and men were at sea from 250 to 300 days out of the 365. In the last quarter … there were not many officers and men who had been in blue water for 90 days in the year.

The importance of service at sea and of acquiring the habit of taking responsibility and risks were deeply impressed upon him. A service which has to take the risks of war must not, he considered, be nurtured delicately in peace; he, when in command, never shrank from taking such risks.

After his promotion Bridge was appointed to the *Caledonia* in the Mediterranean. Two years of service in her were followed by a year in the gunnery ship *Cambridge*, a year in the *Implacable*, and two and a half years in the *Audacious*, flagship of Admiral Ryder in China.

After returning to England, Bridge married, in 1877,

Eleanor, daughter of George Thornhill of the Indian Civil Service; there were no children of the marriage. In September 1877, with eight years' service as a commander, but not yet of command, he was promoted to captain. Four years on half pay followed.

During 1878 and 1879 Bridge served on Admiralty and War Office committees on heavy guns, on armour plates and projectiles, and on explosives; for six months in 1881 he was a member of the ordnance committee. He was then offered command of the *Espiègle*, on the Australian station. In that appointment he was deputy commissioner for the Western Pacific, and made a series of reports on conditions in the islands which displayed the breadth of his mind and the acuteness of his perception. A note from the Admiralty hydrographic department in September 1884 remarked: 'The *Espiègle* sends us more information than any other dozen ships.'

Bridge returned from Australia in September 1885. After six months on half pay he was appointed to command the *Colossus*, the latest type of battleship, and while serving in her prepared and submitted to the Admiralty a scheme for the mobilization of the navy. He vacated this command in 1888, and in 1889 was made director of the recently established intelligence department at the Admiralty. This department fulfilled, within limits, the functions of a naval staff, an institution to which Bridge in his later years was much opposed, holding the view that a staff of the military type was not adapted to the needs of sea service. After fourteen and a half years in the rank of captain, Bridge reached flag rank in 1892. In June 1893 he chaired the preliminary meeting which led to the establishment of the Navy Records Society. On leaving the Admiralty in August 1894 he was highly complimented by Lord George Hamilton, the first lord, on his stable and well thought out work as director of naval intelligence.

In November 1894 Bridge hoisted his flag as commander-in-chief of the Australian squadron. He held the command, with his flag on board the *Orlando*, until 1898. He was promoted vice-admiral in 1898, and was created KCB in 1899, but he had no further command until April 1901 when he was appointed commander-in-chief in China. During the period of his command the Anglo-Japanese treaty was concluded (1902); Bridge's tact, ability, and firmness were important contributions to the successful issue of the negotiations. He strongly opposed the plan of establishing a permanent naval base at Weihaiwei, which had come into British hands in 1898, after the Sino-Japanese War. In a paper, 'The supply and communications of a fleet', which he read at the Hong Kong United Service Institution in 1902, he demonstrated that the quantity of stores needed by a squadron in those waters was too great to be maintained in peacetime, and that therefore, whether a permanent base were established or not, a chain of supplies would be needed. Flying bases, he explained, had always had to be maintained and were almost certain to be in better positions for strategical needs than permanent bases erected in peace. This reasoning appears to have been accepted by the Admiralty.

Bridge reached the rank of admiral in 1903 and was promoted GCB. He remained in command in China until the spring of 1904, when he returned to England. He retired, having reached the age limit, on 15 March 1904.

Bridge served as an assessor on the international commission of inquiry into the Dogger Bank incident (October 1904), and as a member of the Mesopotamia commission of inquiry appointed in August 1916. During the First World War he maintained an optimistic attitude, and wrote many letters to the press rebuking pessimism and criticism of British action at sea. His belief that control of the sea was synonymous with control of communications strengthened the argument of those who claimed that as long as Jellicoe enjoyed the latter there was no need to seek the complete destruction of the German fleet. In the controversy which arose after the war concerning the size of fighting ships, Bridge was a strenuous advocate of a reduction in their size.

Bridge was widely read in many languages. He read Latin, French, German, and Swedish with facility and was acquainted with Italian and Spanish. His study of war began early and continued throughout his life. It covered a wide period of modern history and thought and was by no means confined to naval affairs—one of his earliest papers was 'Memoirs of the marquis of Pombal' (*Edinburgh Review*, July 1872). The result of his wide reading was that his opinions were founded on a broad basis of recorded experience. This gave him at once clear vision and a consistency of view which never amounted to tenacious adherence to his own opinions. With beliefs rooted in history and principles distilled from experience, and with a desire to arrive at truth only through honest investigation, Bridge disliked profoundly a naval policy which, in his view, not only conflicted with reason and experience but also suppressed all attempts at discussion. This, in his words, was a 'dictatorship of the materialate', meaning thereby a dictation of naval policy by men of a school of thought the dominating idea of which was the possession of instruments of war more powerful than those of any possible opponent—in short, the subordination of the strategical factor to the material. Naval architecture, Bridge held, should be 'the handmaid of tactics', and his views on shipbuilding policy were to a great extent compressed within two short objective paragraphs:

> Have the smallest fleet that can do the work which you want it to do: not the biggest that you can cajole or force the taxpayers into granting the money for. (*Current History*, March 1921)

> Build the smallest and least costly ships that can play their part in war: not the biggest that naval architects and engineers are able to design and build. (ibid.)

These views inevitably made Bridge an opponent of Fisher's construction of HMS *Dreadnought*, the all big gun warship. The ship may have represented a significant advance in naval technology but Bridge regarded it as actually harmful to British interests. The new ships were far more costly and the result was that the British could afford to build fewer of them. This meant less, not more security. Bridge, by 1904, had other problems with Fisher and regretted the impending departure of what he considered the forthrightness and honesty represented by Fisher's predecessor, Admiral Lord Walter Kerr. Bridge had not forsaken the battleship itself, however, and in 1914 he was one of those who criticized Admiral Percy Scott for what he regarded as an exaggeration when Scott asserted that the submarine had driven the battleship from the seas. Bridge at this time was inclined to underestimate the role of the submarine in war, largely because neither the Russians nor the Japanese had made use of them in the Russo-Japanese War.

Bridge's political outlook was, conformably to his sentiments, Liberal. His was one of the names proposed for a peerage in the Parliament Bill crisis of 1911. In 1910 Asquith spoke of him as one of the country's most distinguished admirals, 'a man absolutely detached from the various conflicting schools of the navy'. His social gifts were considerable. Very courteous, he was both a good listener and a good talker with a ready and sometimes caustic wit. He sought information at all times and was quick to discern those who possessed it.

Besides numerous contributions to the daily press Bridge wrote, from 1872 to 1923, many articles on tactics, strategy, and naval policy in the reviews. His books were *The Art of Naval Warfare* (1907), *Sea Power and other Studies* (1910), and *Some Recollections* (1918). He also edited a *History of the Russian Fleet during the Reign of Peter the Great by a Contemporary Englishman, 1724* (Navy Records Society, 1899), and wrote an important Admiralty paper, *British Port Defence Policy* (1901). Bridge died at Coombe Pines (a house he had built for himself), Coombe Warren, Kingston Hill, Surrey, on 16 August 1924 and was buried at Putney Vale cemetery four days later. His correspondence and journals were deposited at the National Maritime Museum, Greenwich.   H. W. RICHMOND, *rev.* PAUL G. HALPERN

Sources C. Bridge, *Some recollections* (1918) · private information (1937) · personal knowledge (1937) · A. J. Marder, *From the Dreadnought to Scapa Flow: the Royal Navy in the Fisher era, 1904–1919*, 5 vols. (1961–70) · *The Times* (18 Aug 1924) · *The Times* (21 Aug 1924) · A. J. Marder, *The anatomy of British sea power*, American edn (1940) · *Navy Records Society, 1893–1993: a note on the first one hundred years*, Navy RS (1993) · D. M. Schurman, *The education of a navy: the development of British naval strategic thought, 1867–1914* (1965) · *WWW, 1916–28* · Foster, *Alum. Oxon.*

Archives NMM, letterbooks, journals, and corresp. | BL, corresp. with Sir E. T. H. Hutton, Add. MSS 50094, 50097, *passim* · King's AC Cam., letters to Oscar Browning · NL Scot., letters to Blackwoods · NMM, corresp. with Sir Julian Corbett · UCL, letters to Sir Francis Galton · UCL, letters to David Hannay

Likenesses photograph, repro. in *The Times* (18 Aug 1924)

Wealth at death £18,485 7s. 2d.: resworn probate, 4 Nov 1924, *CGPLA Eng. & Wales*

Bridge, Frank (1879–1941), composer and conductor, was born on 26 February 1879 at 7 North Road, Brighton, the tenth of twelve children of William Henry Bridge (1845–1928) and the first of the three children from his third marriage, to Elizabeth Warbrick (1846–1899). Frank's father was a printer who in middle age gave up his job as a master lithographer to become a violin teacher and theatre orchestra conductor. As a child Frank, like all the younger children, became involved in family music-making. His brother William (1883–1956) was to become a professional cellist.

Frank Bridge received his first violin lessons from his father. When he was twelve he continued his studies at the Brighton School of Music. He played in his father's music-hall orchestra, occasionally conducting and arranging music. In 1896, aged seventeen, Bridge was enrolled as a violin and piano student at the Royal College of Music, London. There were harmony and ensemble classes to attend as well, but it was not until 1899 that his creative ambitions were recognized. He won a foundation scholarship, which enabled him to remain at the college for another four years to study composition with Sir Charles Stanford. Stanford put all his students through a strict regime of counterpoint, a grounding which Bridge later described in a letter to family friend Marjorie Fass, in June 1918, as being like drinking 'water through a straw instead of glaxo and bovril' (Hindmarsh, 103). It served him well, however, and he began to compose with true seriousness of purpose in 1900. His early chamber works—a piano trio, a string quartet (for which he was awarded the Sullivan prize), a string quintet, and a piano quartet—were all given first performances in the college. A humorous *Scherzo Phantastick* (1901) and an elegant *Valse-intermezzo* (1902), both for strings, showed more imaginative promise. Bridge left the college in April 1903, with a glowing report: his violin playing was described as 'very good', his ensemble playing 'most excellent', and his composition 'great' (private information). He received the Tagore gold medal for the most generally deserving pupil.

Bridge made his mark in London's musical life first as a string player. He belonged to several theatre orchestras. He played in the orchestra of the Royal Philharmonic Society and in Henry Wood's Queen's Hall Orchestra. However, he found his natural métier in chamber music. He became second violinist of the Grimson Quartet, and having taken up the viola during his college years he found himself the viola player in the Motto Quartet and in his own English Quartet, which he and three fellow students had formed in 1903. In November 1906 Bridge was invited to play the second viola part in the Brahms sextet no. 2 with the famous Joachim Quartet. A year later the English Quartet became regular participants in the recitals of the prestigious Classical Concerts Society. Through his friendship with the society's founder, the German-born businessman Edward Speyer (1838–1934), Bridge met and performed with some of the leading musicians of the day, including Pablo Casals, Artur Rubinstein, Gabriel Fauré, and Maurice Ravel. The English Quartet returned almost weekly to the Royal College of Music to coach and play chamber music, and made regular visits to Oxford University for the same purpose. Bridge remained the guiding force and inspiration behind the English Quartet until the early 1920s.

The Grimson and English quartets both gave first performances of Bridge's chamber music, most notably the *Three Idylls* and the first version of the piano quintet. However, Bridge's reputation as a composer was established through competition successes and orchestral perform-ances. In September 1905 his *Phantasie* in F minor for string quartet won second prize in the first W. W. Cobbett musical competition. The *Phantasie* in C minor for piano trio won the first prize in the third competition in 1907, and the *Phantasie* in F♯ minor was commissioned by W. W. Cobbett in 1910. Bridge's string quartet in E minor received a 'mention d'honneur' from the Accademica Fil-harmonica, Bologna. In 1911 Bridge was one of the leading young British composers invited to contribute music for a 'pageant of London', in celebration of the coronation of George V. Henry Wood became a champion of Bridge's music, conducting the première of Bridge's symphonic poem *Isabella* at a Queen's Hall Promenade Concert in 1907 and following this with the first of many performances of Bridge's most popular work, the suite *The Sea*, on 24 Sep-tember 1912.

The years 1903–12 were the most prolific of Bridge's car-eer, when he was writing fluent, romantic music, later described by his future pupil Benjamin Britten as 'grateful to listen to and to play' (Britten, 'A tribute'). On 2 Septem-ber 1908 Bridge married Ethel Elmore Sinclair (1881–1961), an Australian violinist and fellow student at the Royal Col-lege of Music. Thereafter he wrote less but gradually began to enrich his musical style through the influence of such composers as Debussy and Ravel, whose music he played, and Skryabin and Berg, whose music was begin-ning to be heard in Britain. The string quartet in G minor (1915) and cello sonata (1913–17) offer the clearest evidence of this process of transition.

The First World War cast long and deep shadows over Bridge's life and music. Many of his friends and colleagues were killed in action, including Thomas Morris, first vio-linist in the English String Quartet, and his fellow com-poser Ernest Farrar, to whose memory Bridge later dedi-cated his piano sonata. His *Lament* for strings was com-posed in memory of a young family friend who was drowned when the *Lusitania* was sunk in 1915. Bridge held pacifist views, and in other orchestral works, like the sec-ond of the *Two Poems* for orchestra, his message was one of hope in a world torn by violence: 'How beautiful a delight to make the world joyous! The song should never be silent, the dancer never still, the laugh should sound like water that runs for ever' (from *The Story of my Heart* by Richard Jefferies, quoted at the top of the score). Bridge's reputa-tion was at its height during these years. His publishers were anxious to publish all the short pieces he could pro-duce, so Bridge allowed many of his early songs and short salon pieces to appear in print, as well as new works. He was conscious, however, of being labelled 'the viola player who composes', and in his letters to friends he referred to his wish to play less and to concentrate on composing and conducting.

Bridge had made a favourable impression as a student, and was often invited to conduct his own music. In 1905 he directed repertory rehearsals for the New Symphony Orchestra. He began to establish himself professionally in 1910, when he directed the first of two seasons of opera at the Savoy Theatre. Henry Wood, who admired Bridge's conducting as much as his music, regularly invited Bridge to conduct his own music at the Queen's Hall Promenade Concerts. In November 1913 Bridge conducted a season of opera at Covent Garden. There were also concerts of popu-lar classics and choral music at the Royal Albert Hall, but rarely a complete concert at the Queen's Hall. Bridge was much in demand as last-minute deputy for an indisposed maestro, and although his musicianship was such that he always acquitted himself well on these occasions, he even-tually found the label 'ambulance conductor' as frustrat-ing as 'the viola player who composes'. During the 1930s he was a frequent guest conductor for BBC studio broad-casts.

Bridge set the highest standards for himself, and expected those around him to be of a like mind. Writing in an obituary of Bridge in 1941, Ivor James, a lifelong friend and the cellist of the English String Quartet, considered that his reputation as a conductor would have been higher 'but for his blunt honesty, he being quite unable to restrain himself from saying exactly what was in his mind'. Bridge's ambition, as he wrote to Edward Speyer in 1916, was to be conductor of 'a decent orchestra' which would 'devote a serious amount of time to rehearsing and knowing upside-down every blessed thing it performs in public' (private information). His only permanent appointment was as the principal conductor of the Aud-rey Melville Orchestra. This was an orchestra of amateur musicians, with professional stiffening, which gave con-certs in many of the poorer areas of London.

As a composer, Bridge desired above all to give his 'musical faculty full reign to create … to get my mind cleared of all obstacles' (F. Bridge to E. S. Coolidge, 7 Dec 1923, Library of Congress, Washington, DC). He found this hard to achieve at first. A slump in sheet music sales forced him back to teaching, and like his father before him Bridge found himself teaching the violin two days a week at schools in Kent and Surrey. Then in May 1922 he was introduced to the American millionaire and musical patron Elizabeth Sprague Coolidge. She befriended Bridge and his wife and, appreciative of his financial and creative problems, offered to help. In the following autumn Bridge was one of the featured composers at Mrs Coolidge's Berk-shire Festival of Chamber Music in Massachusetts. This visit was followed by a conducting tour, which Mrs Cool-idge arranged at Bridge's request. He conducted the lead-ing symphony orchestras in Cleveland, Boston, Detroit, and New York in works of his own. Towards the end of his three-month stay, Mrs Coolidge offered Bridge permanent financial assistance in the form of an annual stipend from her Coolidge Foundation Fund. Bridge's acceptance freed him from the need to play and teach and gave him all the time he wanted to broaden his creative horizons.

Bridge returned to a new home, specially built in the Sussex hamlet of Friston, near Eastbourne. It was there, over the next ten years, that he produced a series of rad-ical chamber and orchestral works, which are considered to be his finest achievements. The piano sonata was com-pleted within three months of his return. There followed a third string quartet (1927), a piano trio (1929)—his chamber music masterpiece—and a violin sonata (1932), all dedicated to Mrs Coolidge and premièred at her music festivals in Europe and the USA. In the orchestral field, Bridge completed four adventurous works, none of which received a warm initial critical reception: *Enter Spring* (1927), *There is a Willow Grows Aslant a Brook* (1927), *Oration* (*Concerto elegiaco* for cello and orchestra, 1930), and *Phantasm* (rhapsody for piano and orchestra, 1931).

Bridge composed very little between 1932 and 1936. The Wall Street crash had caused Mrs Coolidge to reduce her activities, and Bridge's latest music made little headway in London. In the 1930s, and more particularly as the Second World War approached, he spent much more of his time in his Sussex cottage, entertaining friends and young musicians, among whom the young Benjamin Britten, who came to Bridge for a series of lessons as a schoolboy, became his 'young friend, pupil and quasi adopted son' (F. Bridge to E. S. Coolidge, 4 July 1939, Library of Congress, Washington, DC). In October 1936 Bridge suffered a serious heart attack. After six months' convalescence, he resumed some of his conducting activities and began to take up composition once more, in what was to be a late flowering of creativity. These last works, which included a fourth string quartet (1938), *Divertimenti* for wind quartet (1934–8), and the overture *Rebus* (1940), are more optimistic in character and classical in concept than the more introspective music he had composed ten years earlier.

As a young man Bridge enjoyed tennis, was widely read, and maintained a wide circle of like-minded artistic friends. He loved the Sussex countryside, particularly driving around the South Downs. On the afternoon of 10 January 1941, while repairing his car, Bridge was taken ill, and he died peacefully at his home, Friston Field, Friston, East Dean, near Eastbourne, later that evening; after cremation his ashes were interred beside the church at East Dean. His widow, Ethel, survived him, and for the next twenty years until she died did what she could to keep interest in Bridge's music alive. But it was largely through the commitment of Benjamin Britten, and subsequently through the efforts of the estate of Frank Bridge, with its music committee administered by the Royal College of Music, London, that Bridge's true stature as one of the most accomplished and original composers of his generation came to be recognized.　　　　PAUL HINDMARSH

Sources P. Hindmarsh, *Frank Bridge: a thematic catalogue* (1983) · T. Bray, *Frank Bridge: a life in brief* (2000) · I. James, *RCM Magazine*, 37/1 (1941), 21 · B. Britten, BBC broadcast, 1947 · B. Britten, *Bridge centenary festival brochure* (1979) · B. Britten, 'A tribute to Frank Bridge', *Composer*, 19 (1966), 2 · F. Bridge, letters to E. S. Coolidge, L. Cong., manuscript division · private information (2004) · A. Payne, 'Bridge, Frank', *New Grove*, online edn · A. Payne and L. Foreman, *Frank Bridge* (1976) · A. Payne, *Frank Bridge: radical and conservative* (1984)

Archives Boosey and Hawkes plc, London · Britten–Pears Library, Aldeburgh, Suffolk, MSS | Britten–Pears Library, Aldeburgh, letters to Britten and Fass · L. Cong., letters to Coolidge | SOUND BL NSA, oral history interview · BL NSA, performance recordings · BL NSA, 'Peter Pears on Frank Bridge', 1970, T461R · BL NSA, *Talking about music*, 79, 1LP0151928 S1 BD1 BBC TRANSC · BL NSA, *Talking about music*, 230, 1LP0203100 S2 BD2 BBC TRANSC

Likenesses H. Lambert, photogravure, *c.*1922, NPG · plaster death mask, 1941, Royal College of Music, London · M. Forss, pencil sketches, Royal College of Music, London · photographs, Royal College of Music, London

Wealth at death £8101 9s. 0d.: probate, 30 April 1941, CGPLA Eng. & Wales

Bridge, Sir (John) Frederick (1844–1924), organist and composer, was born on 5 December 1844 at Oldbury, Worcestershire, the eldest son of John Bridge, of Oldbury, and his wife, Rebecca Cox. After moving to Rochester, John Bridge was appointed a vicar-choral at the cathedral. Frederick, at the age of six, was admitted probationer and began his education at the cathedral school. He remained in the choir until 1859, and was trained by John Larkins Hopkins, the cathedral organist, to whom he was later articled.

While still an apprentice, Bridge was appointed organist of Shorne church, near Gravesend, about 1860, and of St Nicholas's Church, Strood, near Rochester, in 1861. He studied composition under John Goss for four years (1863–7). In 1865, at the end of his apprenticeship, he was appointed organist of Holy Trinity Church, Windsor, where he was influenced and encouraged by George Job Elvey, organist of St George's Chapel, Windsor. Mrs Oliphant, the author, who came to live at Windsor in 1866, also became interested in him, urging him to compose and in many ways preparing him for his career. In addition he formed a friendship with John Stainer, which was later marked by the marriage of Bridge's younger daughter to Stainer's son, Edward. From 1865 Bridge gave lessons at the lower school at Eton College. He studied hard, and became a fellow of the Royal College of Organists in 1867, but at about the same time he competed unsuccessfully for the position of organist at Queen's College, Oxford. He graduated with the external degree of BMus from Oxford in 1868 and DMus in 1874.

In 1869, aged only twenty-four, Bridge was appointed organist of Manchester Cathedral, and by 1872 had joined the teaching staff at Owens College. Chiefly because of his enthusiasm, the standard of the cathedral music was improved, and his friend Sir William Houldsworth presented a new organ to the cathedral.

In 1875 Bridge was appointed permanent deputy organist of Westminster Abbey on the retirement of James Turle from active work; he succeeded to the full post on Turle's death in 1882. During Bridge's tenure the organ there was greatly enlarged and modernized, befitting the splendid ceremonies whose music he directed. He reformed many unsound traditions in the choir, such as life-tenure of posts as vicars-choral and inadequate rehearsal of boys and men together. The services soon became renowned through his marked gifts as a trainer of boys' voices. Outstanding incidents in his work at the abbey were the direction of the music at Queen Victoria's jubilee (1887), the Purcell commemoration (1895), Edward VII's coronation (conductor-in-chief, 1902), the Orlando Gibbons commemoration, which he instigated (1907), the national memorial service on the occasion of King Edward's

Sir (John) Frederick Bridge (1844–1924), by Elliott & Fry

Musicians' Company, and became master in 1892. From 1917 to 1921 he was president of the Musical Association. As conductor of the Royal Choral Society from 1896 to 1922 he was successful and popular, and he was the first conductor to include Bach's Mass in B minor in the society's repertory.

Bridge composed much church and choral music, including festival cantatas and oratorios, and music for royal occasions. He edited the music for the coronations of Edward VII (1902) and George V (1911). He also wrote and edited many carols, and was musical editor of the *Westminster Abbey Hymn-Book* and the *Wesleyan Hymn-Book*; his long experience of the needs of a congregation ensured the wide acceptance of these hymns, although by the end of the twentieth century most of his music was rarely performed. Bridge's primers on musical subjects such as strict counterpoint became standard works in their time, while his autobiography, *A Westminster Pilgrim* (1918), was widely known and esteemed.

Bridge was warmly regarded by his friends in many walks of life. His sympathy for musicians who were not well off found expression in the Organists' Benevolent League, which he founded in 1909.

Bridge was knighted in 1897, and created MVO in 1902 and CVO in 1911. He was awarded honorary degrees from the universities of Durham (MA, 1905) and Toronto (MusD, 1908). He was married three times: first, in 1872, to Constance Ellen (*d.* 1879), the daughter of John Lines Moore, of Hoxne, Suffolk; second, in 1883, to Helen Mary Flora (*d.* 1906), the daughter of Edward Amphlett, of Horsley, Staffordshire; and third, in 1914, to Marjory Wedgwood (*d.* 1929), the daughter of Reginald Wood, of Bignall End, Staffordshire. From his first marriage he had a son and a daughter, and from his second a daughter. He died at his home, Littlington Tower, the Cloisters, Westminster Abbey, on 18 March 1924. His funeral took place at Glass, Aberdeenshire, where he was then buried, on 21 March.

W. G. ALCOCK, *rev.* JUDITH BLEZZARD

Sources G. Warrack, 'Bridge, Sir John Frederick', *New Grove* · *The Times* (19 March 1924), 16 · P. A. Scholes, *The mirror of music, 1844–1944: a century of musical life in Britain as reflected in the pages of the Musical Times*, 2 vols. (1947) · L. Baillie and R. Balchin, eds., *The catalogue of printed music in the British Library to 1980*, 62 vols. (1981–7), vol. 8, pp. 178–90 · J. F. Bridge, *A Westminster pilgrim* (1918) · private information (1937) · personal knowledge (1937) · *The Times* (24 March 1924)

Archives Bodl. Oxf., letters to T. W. Bourne

Likenesses Elliott & Fry, photograph, NPG [*see illus.*] · Spy [L. Ward], chromolithograph caricature, NPG; repro. in *VF* (14 April 1904) · photograph, repro. in *The Times*, 18 · photograph, repro. in Scholes, ed., *Mirror of music*, facing p. 584 · print on process block, BM; repro. in *MT* (1907)

Wealth at death £10,455 0s. 3d.: probate, 8 May 1924, *CGPLA Eng. & Wales*

funeral (1910), the Samuel Sebastian Wesley commemoration (1910), George V's coronation (conductor-in-chief, 1911), and the reinauguration of Henry VII's chapel as the chapel of the Order of the Bath (1913). From 1898 his assistant was the outstanding organist Walter Galpin Alcock.

In 1876 Bridge was appointed professor of organ at the National Training School for Music, and on the opening of the Royal College of Music in 1883, on the nomination of the prince of Wales, he was appointed professor of harmony and counterpoint. He retained this post until his death. In 1890 he was elected Gresham professor of music at Gresham College, London. Because of his persuasive style and apt illustrations, his lectures drew large audiences. His antiquarian sympathies naturally influenced his choice of subjects, and he was a notable contributor to the revival of early English music. He devoted enthusiastic research to the music of Richard Dering, Henry Purcell, and others, and corrected many inaccuracies previously accepted. In 1899 he sought to restore Handel's instrumentation in performances of *Messiah*, avoiding the use of additional instruments characteristic of nineteenth-century performances. His course of lectures at the Royal Institution in 1903 on 'The musical references in Pepys's Diary' was well received, and he was prominent in the formation of the Pepys dining club in 1903. In the same year he was appointed King Edward professor of music at London University. He was for many years a member of the

Bridge, John (1755–1834), jeweller, was born in Piddletrenthide, Dorset, on 21 January 1755, the eldest son of Thomas Bridge (*d.* 1792) and his wife, Mary (*d.* 1779). Following in the footsteps of his future partner, Philip Rundell, he was apprenticed in 1769 to the jeweller William Rogers of Bath. His apprenticeship over, Bridge migrated to London about 1776, where he was employed as a shopman by Pickett and Rundell, goldsmiths and jewellers, at the Golden Salmon, Ludgate Hill. William Pickett, the senior partner, retired from business in February 1786, and Philip Rundell, by then in sole control, invited Bridge in December 1787 to join him in a partnership; thereafter the firm continued as Rundell and Bridge. The two partners, so different in character that they were respectively known by their employees as 'Oil' (Bridge) and 'Vinegar', worked tirelessly to place the business at the forefront of their trade. By 1805, when the firm had become Rundell, Bridge, and Rundell, Joseph Nightingale wrote that it exceeded 'all others in the British Empire, if not in the whole world, for the value of its contents'.

Bridge was described as 'mild and affable in his deportment, possessing great equality of temper, and a very engaging suavity of manners'. It is said that in 1789 he was introduced to George III by a wealthy cousin, also called John Bridge, who shared the monarch's interest in farming. The jeweller so pleased the king and other members of the royal family that Rundell and Bridge received many fresh orders. Their growing success was then assured.

Bridge remained a partner in the firm until his death. He never married. Towards the end of his life he bought Wood House with its estate at Wood Lane, Shepherd's Bush, where he lived with two cousins, Amelia and Maria Bridge. He died on 9 April 1834 at the Manor House, Piddletrenthide, and was buried in the family vault in the local churchyard. In the aisle of the church a carved stone tablet with a portrait profile of John Bridge in marble was erected 'by his surviving relatives in testimony of their grateful and affectionate remembrance'.

JOHN CULME, rev.

Sources Memoirs of the late Philip Rundell, Esq...by a gentleman many years connected with the firm (1827) • S. Bury, 'The lengthening shadow of Rundell's [pts 1–3]', The Connoisseur, 161 (1966), 79–85, 152–8, 218–22 • J. Culme, Nineteenth century silver (1977) • A. G. Grimwade, London goldsmiths, 1697–1837: their marks and lives, from the original registers at Goldsmiths' Hall, 3rd edn (1990), 448–9, 738 • A. Pike, Piddletrenthide: the village and the church (1977) • G. Fox, History of Rundell, Bridge and Rundell, 1843, Harvard U., Baker Library, Mss: 597 1843
Likenesses carved marble tablet, Piddletrenthide church, Dorset
Wealth at death £400,000: will, 22 May 1834

Bridge, Sir John (1824–1900), police magistrate, was born on 21 April 1824, the only son of John H. Bridge of Finchley, Middlesex. At Oxford, where he matriculated from Trinity College on 10 March 1842, he graduated BA with a first class in mathematics in 1846, and proceeded MA in 1849. On 10 April 1844 he was admitted student at the Inner Temple, where he was called to the bar on 25 January 1850. He practised with some success on the home circuit. In 1857 he married his cousin Ada Louisa, daughter of George Bridge of Merton, Surrey.

In 1872 Bridge accepted the post of police magistrate at Hammersmith, where, as afterwards at Westminster (1880–81) and Southwark (1882–6), he performed the laborious duties of subordinate office with conscientiousness and discretion. Moving to Bow Street in 1887 he succeeded Sir James Ingham in 1890 as chief metropolitan magistrate, being at the same time knighted. During his tenure of this office he committed for trial several offenders, prominent among them Oscar Wilde (5 April 1895), Jabez Balfour, the fraudulent director of the Liberator Building Society, on his extradition by the Argentine republic (16 April 1895), and L. S. Jameson and his associates in the Transvaal raid (15 June 1896). He retired from the bench early in 1900, and on 26 April in the same year died at his home, 50 Inverness Terrace, London. He was buried at Headley, Surrey, where he had a home. His wife died on 1 March 1901.

J. M. RIGG, rev. CATHERINE PEASE-WATKIN

Sources Foster, Alum. Oxon. • J. Foster, Men-at-the-bar: a biographical hand-list of the members of the various inns of court, 2nd edn (1885) • The honours register of the University of Oxford: completed to 1883 (1883) • Royal Kalendar (1872) • Royal Kalendar (1880) • Royal Kalendar (1882) • Royal Kalendar (1891) • Annual Register (1894), 5 • Annual Register (1895), 19, 25 • Annual Register (1896), 33 • The Times (28 April 1900) • Law Times (5 May 1900) • CGPLA Eng. & Wales (1900)
Likenesses Spy [L. Ward], chromolithograph caricature, NPG; repro. in VF (25 April 1891)
Wealth at death £66,384 13s. 9d.: probate, 6 July 1900, CGPLA Eng. & Wales

Bridge, (Stephen Henry) Peter (1925–1982), theatre producer, was born at Wimbledon, Surrey, on 5 May 1925, the only son and eldest child of Stephen Henry Howard Bridge (d. 1943), stockbroker, of Wimbledon, and his wife, Ella Mary Twine (d. 1940). He was educated at Tyttenhanger Lodge, Seaford, Sussex, and at Bryanston School, Dorset, which he left at sixteen, his mother and sister having been killed by enemy action in 1940. His father died in 1943. He was an actor before joining the RAF. Apart from landing at Normandy six days after D-day, he served in Burma in photographic intelligence and as personal assistant to the air officer commanding Hong Kong, where he ended as air aide-de-camp to the governor. Demobilized, Bridge worked for Lord Tedder as assistant manager of the RAF Malcolm clubs, but a love of theatre turned him to show business and in his early twenties he managed a tour of Diana Morgan's family comedy *Set to Partners*, which reached the Embassy, Swiss Cottage, as *Rain before Seven* in 1949. He co-produced Val Gielgud's *Party Manners* (Embassy, 1950). Neither play transferred.

In 1948 Bridge married Roslyn Mary, daughter of Douglas Seymour Foster, of independent means. They had three sons, of whom Andrew became a distinguished lighting designer. With a young wife and children to support, Bridge became assistant manager to Alec Clunes at the Arts Theatre Club, then rated as a small national theatre. He was also appointed manager of the Winter Garden Theatre when Clunes hoped it would become a second auditorium to the Arts, and he co-presented Christopher Fry's *The Firstborn*. When the Winter Garden venture failed, Bridge joined the ticket agency Keith Prowse to scour the provinces for plays to transfer to London (1953–5). With the advent of independent television he then became director of sport for Associated Television (ATV), and as one of the country's six professional lawn-tennis referees (not to be confused with umpires) he produced ITV coverage of Wimbledon for two years. But the call of the theatre persisted, and in 1957—when great changes were imminent in the British theatre after *Look Back in Anger*—Bridge returned to the fold as an independent manager. Stars, he used to say, filled theatres, not upstart writers, hence his reputation for polished, bland revivals of Wilde, Shaw, Galsworthy, Coward, and Priestley, acted by the famous.

In fact Bridge was interested in new writers as long as they were not assertively intellectual. One such writer was Alan Ayckbourn. It was a notice in *The Stage*, the profession's weekly paper, of *Standing Room Only* (1961), about a bus load of passengers in a futuristic London traffic jam, that caught Bridge's eye. 'Will no management drive this bus into Shaftesbury Avenue?' asked the reviewer, a member of the Scarborough company (Watson, 61). Bridge was intrigued. He left London immediately for Yorkshire—not that the play reached London—but having bought it Bridge also bought a London bus, assuring Ayckbourn that success lay in the casting. Impressed by Bridge's tall, dark presence, genial self-assurance, and tendency to chain smoke, Ayckbourn kept on revising the play to suit various stars until it became unrecognizable. Eventually Bridge took another Ayckbourn piece to London, *Mr What-not* (1964), a frail whimsical comedy conducted mainly in mime, that failed but caught the fancy of Mrs Michael Hordern, whose husband starred in Ayckbourn's first West End hit, *Relatively Speaking* (1967). When his second was bound for London, *How the Other Half Loves* (1970), Bridge brought in Robert Morley to head the company. In summing up Bridge, a fashionable play agent called him 'a sweet, kind but talentless man, and as a manager rather pre-war: honourable and endearing but lacking in discrimination and in the belief that authors were as important, or more so, than stars' (Watson, 147).

Bridge had already brought to London a dozen other non-classical dramatists after Rosemary Anne Sisson's *The Queen and the Welshman*, with which he returned to management (Lyric, Hammersmith, 1957). Among them were a smash hit board-room drama, *Any Other Business* (1958); a well-received American trial-play, *Inherit the Wind* (1960); a lively West End revue, *On the Bright Side*; a whodunit, *Guilty Party* (1961); an unknown play by Tennessee Williams, *Period of Adjustment* (1962); and an Irish adaptation from James Joyce, *Stephen D* (1963). He also produced *Say Who You Are* by Keith Waterhouse and Willis Hall (1965); Danny La Rue in *Come Spy with Me*; a new British musical, *Strike a Light*; a thriller, *Wait until Dark*; and, from Oxford, Aleksey Arbuzov's *The Promise*, with Judi Dench and Ian McKellen, long before they became stars. He also produced remarkable new plays such as Giles Cooper's *Happy Family*; Peter Terson's *Zigger-Zagger*; Robert Shaw's *The Man in the Glass Booth* (1967); and the relatively daring homosexual comedy, Mart Crowley's *The Boys in the Band* (1969).

A tireless traveller in search of theatrical talent, Bridge rarely missed an Edinburgh or Dublin festival, a Sunday night try-out, or a rumoured masterpiece on the fringe.

His shows were not definable, but they suited middle-class, middle-aged, middlebrow audiences. The 1960s were his decade. In 1967 he had three West End openings within a fortnight. He slowed down a little in the 1970s. His last production was of Priestley's *Dangerous Corner* (1981), another all-star affair. What distinguished Bridge from other managers was his heart-felt, star-struck delight in theatre, especially its glamour. He was popular with actors and authors because, unlike other managers, he liked and respected them. Whether or not they shared his enthusiasm, he would telephone at all hours from all places with tidings of new projects, gossip, and box-office figures. Among his idols whom he was proud to engage were Jack Hulbert and Cicely Courtneidge, Eric Portman, Roger Livesey, Margaret Lockwood, Celia Johnson, Margaret Rawlings, Michael Denison, and Dulcie Gray. Few other managers could so serenely allow the so-called new wave of British drama to pass them by. Bridge died at his home, 15 Claremont Road, Highgate, London, on 24 November 1982.   ERIC SHORTER

Sources I. Herbert, ed., *Who's who in the theatre*, 16th edn (1977) • I. Watson, *Conversations with Alan Ayckbourn* (1981) • C. Chambers, *Peggy: the life of Margaret Ramsay, play agent* (1997) • personal knowledge (2004) • *DNB* • CGPLA Eng. & Wales (1983)
Wealth at death under £25,000: probate, 26 May 1983, CGPLA Eng. & Wales

Bridge [Bridges], **Richard** (*d.* 1758), organ builder, was born in London. He trained with John Harris, son of Renatus Harris, and worked at times in collaboration with the elder John Byfield and the younger Abraham Jordan. Some writers have also associated him with Thomas Griffin, who provided organs to churches on lease, but this has been questioned. On 29 December 1720 Bridge married Esther (or Hesther) Brown at St James's Church, Clerkenwell, London; in 1748 he was living in Hand Court, Holborn. He died in London on 7 June 1758, and was succeeded in business by George England, who himself retired in 1766, passing the firm to his brother John. One of the brothers (according to tradition George, but now thought to have been John) married Bridge's daughter.

Twenty-one instruments can be reliably ascribed to Bridge; at least ten of his organ cases survive, but only one instrument retains most of the original pipework, chests, and mechanisms. This is his *magnum opus* at Christ Church, Spitalfields, London, opened on 25 March 1735. Erected at a cost of £600, it contained thirty-three stops when new and was then the largest parish church organ in England. The organ at St Leonard, Shoreditch (1754), also contains a significant quantity of Bridge's pipework; little is known to survive elsewhere. Bridge worked mainly in and around London; in addition to the above instruments he built organs for St Luke, Chelsea (probably in collaboration with Jordan, *c.*1720), St James's, Clerkenwell (1730), St Bartholomew-the-Great, Smithfield (with Byfield, opened 31 October 1731), St George, Ratcliffe Highway (1733), St Luke, Old Street (with Jordan, 1733), the hall of the Worshipful Company of Parish Clerks (1737), Spa Fields Chapel, Clerkenwell (1740), St Anne, Limehouse (1741), Chelsea Old Church (All Saints') (1746), St Andrew,

Enfield (1752), Eltham parish church (date unknown), and Vauxhall Gardens (with Byfield, date unknown). Outside London, he built the organ at St Philip, Birmingham (1715?), St Nicholas's parish church and St George's chapel of ease, Great Yarmouth (both with Byfield and Jordan, opened 20 December 1733 and 14 February 1734 respectively), and Faversham parish church (1753–4). A chamber organ by him was later moved to Farnham parish church. Two instruments were exported to America, for Trinity Church, Newport, Rhode Island (1733), and King's Chapel, Boston, Massachusetts (1756). Bridge carried out repairs or rebuilding at St Giles Cripplegate (1735), Exeter Cathedral (with or on behalf of Jordan, 1742), Worcester Cathedral (1752), and Canterbury Cathedral (1753). The organs at Woolwich parish church (1741 or later) and Cuper's Gardens, Lambeth, may also have been his work.

DAVID BURCHELL

Sources J. Boeringer, *Organa Britannica*, 3 vols. (1983–9), 1.93–7, and entries on individual organs (alphabetical by county) • *New Grove* • S. Bicknell, *The history of the English organ* (1996), 162–8, 179, 190, 200 • B. Owen, 'Colonial organs: being an account of some early English instruments exported to the eastern United States', *Journal of the British Institute of Organ Studies*, 3 (1979), 92–107 • M. Goetze, *St Helen Bishopsgate 1743 Thomas Griffin organ*, Harley Foundation Technical Reports, 12 (1997), 2 • N. M. Plumley, *The organs of the city of London* (1996), 49, 71–3, 205 • B. B. Edmonds, 'John Loosemore', *Journal of the British Institute of Organ Studies*, 5 (1981), 23–32 • J. L. Speller, 'The organ case in Holsworthy church, Devon', *Journal of the British Institute of Organ Studies*, 2 (1978), 126–7 • D. Dawe, *Organists of the City of London, 1666–1850* (1983), 43 • C. W. Pearce, *Notes on English organs of the period 1800–1810* (1912), 49 • C. F. A. Williams, *The story of the organ* (1903), 217 • R. Russell, 'The organ at Christ Church Spitalfields', *The Organ*, 19 (1939–40), 112–17

Bridge, Thomas William (1848–1909), zoologist, was born at 4 Easy Row, Birmingham, on 5 November 1848, the eldest son of Thomas Bridge, a boot- and shoemaker, and Lucy, daughter of Thomas Crosbee, both of Birmingham. After attending the Moseley School he studied science at the Midland Institute, Birmingham. In November 1869 he went to Cambridge as private assistant to John Willis Clark, then director of the University Museum of Zoology. He matriculated in 1871, and two years later entered Trinity College as a foundation scholar. While an undergraduate he was appointed university demonstrator in comparative anatomy (for which post he was nominated by Alfred Newton). He came out first in the second class of the natural science tripos of 1875, and graduated BA in 1876 and MA in 1880. Following his graduation in 1876, he spent six months at the zoological station at Naples. The result of this journey was a paper entitled 'Pori abdominales of Vertebrata'. On returning to Cambridge he resumed his post as demonstrator.

In February 1879 Bridge was elected professor of zoology at the Royal College of Science for Ireland. After a year he returned to Birmingham to take up the post of professor of biology at the newly founded Mason College (later Birmingham University). Subsequently the chair was divided into a botanical and a zoological professorship, and Bridge held the latter appointment until his death. Both as teacher and organizer, he contributed

much to the success of the institution, and was for a time secretary, vice-chair, and later chairman of the academic board. He devoted himself unstintingly to the welfare of his college and department.

As an investigator Bridge was distinguished for his researches into the anatomy of fish, and in particular for his work upon the swim-bladder and the auditory organ in the Siluridae. He contributed a paper on the subject to the Royal Society in 1889 and to the society's *Philosophical Transactions* in 1893. His article 'Fishes' in the *Cambridge Natural History* (vol. 7, 1904) is another example of his careful, lucid, and accurate method.

Bridge held the post of vice-president of the Birmingham Natural History Society and of the Birmingham Philosophical Society. He was also first president of the merged societies in 1894. He was made ScD at Cambridge in 1896 and MSc by Birmingham University in 1901, and elected FRS in 1903. He died on 29 June 1909, unmarried, at his home, Ferndale, Oakfield Road, in Selly Park, Northfield, King's Norton, Worcestershire.

F. W. GAMBLE, *rev.* YOLANDA FOOTE

Sources S. F. H., *PRS*, 82B (1909–10), vii–x • *Birmingham Daily Post* (1 July 1909) • *WWW* • Venn, *Alum. Cant.* • b. cert. • d. cert. • *Nature*, 81 (1909), 42–3
Wealth at death £2354 14s. 8d.: probate, 16 Sept 1909, CGPLA Eng. & Wales

Bridge, William (1600/01–1671), Independent minister, was born in Cambridgeshire. He was admitted as a sizar at Emmanuel College, Cambridge, on 7 June 1619, graduated BA in 1623, proceeded MA in 1626, and became a fellow of the college. While a student at Cambridge he and Jeremiah Burroughs attended John Rogers's lectures at Dedham, Essex. On 23 December 1627 he was ordained a priest in the Church of England. As a lecturer at Saffron Walden, Essex, beginning in 1629 he did not wear the surplice and hood, claiming this freedom on the grounds that he had not been licensed by the bishop, though he conformed after he was licensed on 1 January 1631. He may have lectured at Colchester before accepting the living of St Peter Hungate, Norwich, from the Norfolk trustees, who were acting on the advice of London puritans, in December 1631. On 12 April 1632 he was licensed as curate and lecturer at St George Tombland, Norwich. Bridge married at least twice: the mother of his daughter Hannah, baptized at St George's on 20 March 1633 or 1634, was probably Susannah, with whom he later baptized two children at Yarmouth.

With the approval of the congregation and Richard Corbet, bishop of Norwich, Bridge organized a combination lectureship at St George's, utilizing puritan ministers in East Anglia such as Burroughs and William Greenhill, which freed him to lecture at St Andrew's, Norwich. For attacking Arminians and espousing a limited atonement he was cited before the consistory court in 1634 and temporarily suspended by Corbet. The nonconformist Edward Wale served as his curate in 1635. During his campaign against nonconformity Matthew Wren, the new bishop of Norwich, deprived Bridge in 1636, prompting the latter's supporters to petition the king on the grounds that Wren was undermining the local economy. Bridge refused to reply to the charges against him, rejected the chancellor's authority to sentence him, and was excommunicated.

By 13 May 1636 Bridge had settled at Rotterdam. Informed of this development by William Laud, Charles I responded that they were well rid of him. In Rotterdam, Bridge joined the English church to which Hugh Peter had ministered, renounced his ordination, and was chosen co-pastor with John Ward, who reordained him. The congregation became embroiled in a controversy over prophesying, which Sidrach Simpson favoured, whereas Bridge approved only the questioning of ministers after sermons on weekdays. Simpson left the church, and Ward, who had opposed Bridge and incurred dissatisfaction by preaching old sermons, was deposed in January 1639. Burroughs replaced him. In the meantime, Bridge had written to Norwich councilmen in 1637 criticizing episcopal polity, and his congregation dispatched members to Norwich and Great Yarmouth to help establish Independent congregations. On 10 May 1639 Leiden University admitted him *honoris gratia*. His sermon on Numbers 10: 35, preached on 16 May 1640 against the background of the Scottish crisis and published as *The True Souldiers Convoy* (Rotterdam, 1640), warned that God would awaken from his apparent slumber and scatter his enemies.

In early 1641 Bridge returned to England, and some time prior to 6 April he preached a sermon on Revelation 14: 8, published as *Babylons Downfall* (1641), to the House of Commons, urging public officials to destroy Catholicism and popish remnants and to appoint fast days. At St Margaret's, New Fish Street Hill, London, early the following year he called for increased attention to Ireland and explained that God permitted his children to suffer before destroying his enemies (*Two Sermons*, 1642). Addressing those who had been or might be driven from their homes in *A Sermon Containing some Comfortable Directions* (1642), he anticipated the approach of war, and in *A Sermon Preached unto the Volunties of … Norwich and … Great Yarmouth* (1642) he called for courage in battling 'a vaunting, bragging, boasting Cavalierisme' (p. 6). When Henry Ferne condemned parliament's supporters as rebels, Bridge retorted in *The Wounded Conscience Cured* (1642), asserting the right of subjects to defend themselves and of parliament to declare what the law is. In May 1643 he contributed to *A True Relation of a Great Victory* (1643), praising discipline in the army. That summer he again responded to Ferne in *The Truth of the Times Vindicated* (1643), acknowledging that civil war is the worst form of conflict but insisting that truth must be defended. In a fast sermon to the House of Commons, he called for an '*exactnesse of Reformation*', noting that other nations were watching England (*A Sermon Preached … Novemb. 29. 1643*, 1643, A4r). Having accepted a position as town preacher at Yarmouth in 1642, he organized an Independent church, signed its covenant on 28 June 1643, and formally became its pastor on 9 September. The following day he and Susannah baptized a son, Samuel, at the church; their daughter Sarah was baptized there on 25 January 1646.

In the Westminster assembly, to which he had been appointed for Cumberland on 25 April 1642, Bridge was one of the 'dissenting brethren' and a co-author, with Burroughs, Simpson, Thomas Goodwin, and Philip Nye, of *An Apologeticall Narration* (1643) espousing congregational polity. Thomas Edwards retorted in *Antapologia* (1644), which includes Bridge's 1637 letter to friends in Norwich. In *The Loyall Convert* (1644) Bridge published annotations on Francis Quarles's *The Loyall Convert* (1643), denouncing 'service-book men' who refused to uphold the solemn league and covenant. In a sermon to the House of Lords on 28 October 1646, published as *The Saints Hiding-Place* (1647), he proclaimed that God was still angry with England because its divisions as well as its sins continued, the end of the war notwithstanding. He was active in the London area, succeeding Burroughs as lecturer at Stepney and Simpson at St Margaret's, New Fish Street Hill, both in 1646, and accepting a third lectureship, at All Hallows, Staining, in 1647. To the House of Commons on 5 November 1647 he held out hope for the future of the three kingdoms (*England Saved*, 1648), and following the New Model Army's victory in Wales he preached to the Commons on 17 May 1648 about Christ's imminent return (*Christs Coming Opened*, 1648). He also subscribed the *Reasons of the Dissenting Brethren* (1648) against presbyterian polity.

Further testimony to Bridge's prominence came with the publication of his works in three volumes in 1649, including an epistle by Greenhill, John Yates, and William Adderley. He preached before the lord mayor of London on 22 July 1649 (*Grace and Love beyond Gifts*, 1649) and subsequently at Whitehall, for which the council of state paid him 20 marks on 20 December 1649. Responding to sectarian criticism, he defended the sacraments in *A Vindication of Ordinances* (1650). On 30 July 1651 parliament awarded him an annual stipend of £100, to be paid from impropriated tithes, and it consulted him about augmenting clerical salaries. With Simpson, Nye, and others Bridge petitioned parliament in February 1652 against Socinianism, and the following year he advised Oliver Cromwell on the selection of members for the Nominated Assembly. Another edition of his works, *Twelve Several Books*, appeared in 1654, the year he was appointed an assistant to the Norfolk commission. In 1655 he served on the commission considering the readmission of Jews to England. His *Scripture-Light, the Most Sure Light* (1656), three sermons on 2 Peter 1: 19, elicited a response from the Quaker George Whitehead, *The Law and Light Within* (1656?). An expanded edition of Bridge's works, *Twentyone Several Books*, was published in 1657, indicating a healthy market for his writings. He attended the Savoy conference in 1658, and late the following year worked with other Independents in a failed attempt to persuade George Monck to remain loyal to the Good Old Cause.

In addition to his commitments in the London area, Bridge served his church at Yarmouth. He co-operated with the presbyterian John Brinsley, whose congregation met in the nave of the parish church while Bridge's worshipped in the chancel. He supported Brinsley when efforts were made to oust him, and he contributed an epistle to Brinsley's *Gospel-Marrow* (1659). In ministering to his congregation, which included William Burton, governor of Yarmouth, he was assisted by John Tillinghast (1651–2) and Job Tookey.

Following the Restoration, Bridge and Tookey were ejected in 1661. By 1663 Bridge had moved to Clapham, Surrey, where he ministered to an Independent church. In June he narrowly avoided arrest at a London conventicle. As the plague ravaged London he wrote an exposition of Psalm 91, *The Righteous Man's Habitation* (1665), offering hope of divine protection. Note-takers provided the texts for *Christ and the Covenant* (1667), a series of ten sermons, and *The Sinfulnesse of Sinne* (1667). *Seasonable Truths in Evil-Times* (1668), nine sermons preached in the London area, included one that explicated the repression of nonconformists as part of God's design to test his children. With the help of funds raised by congregationalists and presbyterians, Bridge returned to Yarmouth in late December 1667 or early the ensuing year, attracting substantial audiences and inspiring dissenters to oppose the established church openly. At the Norfolk quarter sessions in January 1669 he admitted having held conventicles and violating the Five Mile Act, whereupon Lord Townshend, after ordering him not to come within 5 miles of Yarmouth, released him. He retired to Clapham, where he died at age seventy on 12 March 1671 and was buried three days later. His will, dated 6 August 1669 and proved on 4 April 1671, bequeathed £300 and his library, apart from publishable manuscripts, to his son Samuel, a graduate of Pembroke College, Cambridge (BA, 1664; MA, 1667), and a minister in the Church of England. Bridge was also survived by his second wife, Margaret (*d.* 1675), who had been the widow of John Arnold, merchant and bailiff of Yarmouth, by his two daughters, Hannah, wife of the Congregationalist minister Richard Lawrence, and Sarah, wife of John Copeman, and by a stepson, John Arnold, and three stepdaughters, one of whom had married Captain Thomas Ravens, alderman of Yarmouth, in whose house Bridge's congregation met in the late 1660s.

Bridge's posthumously published works include *The Freeness of the Grace and Love of God* (1671), seven sermons with a preface by J. O. (not John Owen, as he himself attests in an epistle to Joseph Caryl's *Nature and Principles of Love*, 1673), and *Bridge's Remains* (1673), a collection of eight sermons, seven of which were prepared for the press by Bridge before his demise. An elegy to Bridge is prefixed to *The Life and Death of Henry Jessey* (1671). Interest in his works continued long past his death, as reflected by the countess of Huntingdon's endorsement of his *Seven Sermons* (1789) and the publication of his works in 1845.

RICHARD L. GREAVES

Sources *Calamy rev.*, 74 · *CSP dom.*, 1649–50, 447; 1655–6, 23; 1658–9, 75; 1667–8, 88, 145, 277; 1668–9, 11, 77, 95, 99–100, 159–60, 278; 1670, 512; 1671–2, 533 · K. W. Shipps, 'Lay patronage of East Anglian puritan clerics in pre-revolutionary England', PhD diss., Yale U., 1971 · Venn, *Alum. Cant.* · K. L. Springer, *Dutch puritanism: a history of English and Scottish churches of the Netherlands in the sixteenth and seventeenth centuries* (1982) · G. F. Nuttall, *Visible saints: the congregational way, 1640–1660* (1957) · *JHC*, 2 (1640–42), 545 · F. Peck, ed., *Desiderata curiosa*, new edn, 2 vols. in 1 (1779) · C. Holmes, *The eastern association in the English civil war* (1974) · P. S. Seaver, *The puritan lectureships: the politics of religious dissent, 1560–1662* (1970) · *The works of the most reverend father in God, William Laud*, 5/2, ed. J. Bliss (1853), 340 · J. Browne, *A history of Congregationalism and memorials of the churches in Norfolk and Suffolk* (1877) · PRO, PROB 11/335, sig. 45 · *IGI* [parish registers of St George Tombland, Norwich, and of the Independent Church, Great Yarmouth]

Archives BL, Harley MS 3784, fol. 55 · Bodl. Oxf., Tanner MS 68, fols. 8, 79 · Bodl. Oxf., Tanner MS 314, fol. 155v · Essex RO, Chelmsford, MS D/ACA/47, fols. 70v, 161v · GL, MS 1175/1, fol. 83v · GL, MS 4956/3, pp. 122, 127 · LMA, MS DL/C/343, fol. 102 · Norfolk RO, MS CON/2/3a, fol. 3 · PRO, State Papers, 29/225, 230, 236, 247, 249, 250, 254, 258, 280, 308

Likenesses J. Caldwell, line engraving, NPG · W. Sherwin, line engraving, BM, NPG · W. Sherwin, portrait, repro. in *The works of the Rev. William Bridge*, 1 (1845) · portrait, DWL · portrait, repro. in Bridge, *Bridge's Remains* (1673)

Wealth at death £540 plus four annuities worth 20s. p.a.: will, PRO, PROB 11/335, sig. 45

Bridgeman [*née* Parker]**, Dame Caroline Beatrix**, Viscountess Bridgeman (1873–1961), political activist and churchwoman, was born on 30 June 1873, the third of five children and eldest daughter of the Hon. Cecil Thomas Parker (1845–1931), son of the sixth earl of Macclesfield and land agent for the duke of Westminster, and his wife, Rosamund Esther Harriet Longley (1843/4–1936), daughter of Charles Thomas Longley, archbishop of Canterbury from 1862 until 1868. Educated privately she worked as a school manager in London's East End and for the Charity Organization Society before marrying William Clive *Bridgeman (1864–1935) on 30 April 1895. They had three sons (including Sir Maurice Richard *Bridgeman and Robert Clive *Bridgeman), each of whom went on to distinguished public and private careers, and lived at Leigh Manor, near Minsterley, Shropshire, where she enjoyed landscaping the garden.

Six weeks after marrying, Caroline Bridgeman assisted her husband with his parliamentary campaign for Mid Derbyshire, and although he lost, the campaign launched a durable political partnership. In 1904 Caroline Bridgeman formed one of the country's first women's unionist associations in Oswestry (for which her husband became MP in 1906), and by 1918 it was one of the largest such associations in the country. Nationally she was active with the British women's covenant committee (opposing Irish home rule) and the Women's Unionist Tariff Reform Association. Once women were enfranchised in 1918 the latter became formally affiliated with the Conservative Party as the Women's Unionist Organization (WUO), which Caroline Bridgeman chaired after obtaining a guarantee of control over all non-financial matters. She urged women to be broad-minded and join political parties rather than feminist societies; and the success of parties, particularly the Conservatives, at attracting women members helps somewhat to account for the decline of women's groups in the 1920s. The admiration which she commanded within the party strengthened the WUO's position, and its effectiveness contributed to the party's later success with women voters. She was a good committee worker and eloquent speaker, who laced her speeches with humour, yet was reserved and rarely at ease with individuals. Most of her close friends were men, as women often found her critical nature intimidating, and the tenants at Leigh regarded her with respect rather than affection. An attractive woman, her erect posture made her appear taller than she was, and she had simple tastes, preferring buses to taxis, though she later permitted herself the luxury of one of Britain's first television sets.

Bridgeman's contributions to the Conservative Party were recognized with a DBE in 1924. Later that year, when her husband became first lord of the Admiralty, the attendant spousal duties forced her to resign from the WUO leadership. Yet she was not away from the party for long, and in May 1926 she was elected to a one-year term as chair of the central council of the National Union of Conservative and Unionist Associations, making her the first woman to hold such a position in any party. She sought a greater role for women in policy making and in 1927 she introduced the requirement that at least one of the four party conference delegates from each constituency was a woman. Within a few years women formed over one third of all delegates. In 1928, when her husband announced his intention to retire as an MP, there was some suggestion that she should stand in his place. However, she regarded her political role as adjunct to his and simultaneously withdrew from politics. Thirty years later, when the first life peeresses were being selected for nomination to the House of Lords, her name was suggested within the party as a possibility, but by 1958 she was too old to embark on a parliamentary career.

However, Viscountess Bridgeman (as she was styled from 1929, when her husband was created a peer) did have interests outside politics. As the granddaughter of an archbishop (and sister of a bishop of Pretoria, Wilfrid Parker) it was perhaps unsurprising that her non-political energies were devoted to the Church of England. Between 1925 and 1960 she was a member of the house of laity, serving as vice-chair from 1942 until 1947. She believed that the church assembly had to foster directly the nation's spiritual life, and encouraged this with her tireless promotion of religious education and improved clerical pay. The church's survival depended on maintaining a community of believers, she submitted, and this could be accomplished only through religious education, and more particularly by promoting denominational schools. Similarly, increased stipends and pensions for the clergy and their dependants were necessary for sustainable clerical recruitment, and she argued forcefully and successfully for better allowances. These issues demanded the church's highest attention, even if it required short-term economizing on church building and physical improvements. She was the only woman member of the archbishops' commission which sat between 1930 and 1935 to consider the relationship between church and state, following parliament's rejection of the prayer book measure. (Her husband, who shared an ecclesiastical background, had unsuccessfully sponsored the measure in the House of Commons in 1927.)

Church colleagues hoped that Caroline Bridgeman would promote religious broadcasting after her appointment as a BBC governor in 1935 in succession to her husband, who had died that August. During her four years on the board she monitored carefully the progress of religious broadcasts, but warned against making them too sentimental and maintained that the church should concentrate on the medium of print, since broadcasting had only an emotional appeal and could not make as lasting an impact. In addition to this work she chaired the Florence Nightingale Hospital for Gentlewomen for fifteen years and, during the First World War, the Shropshire women's war agriculture committee and the selection committee of London land workers. She also served on the royal commission on London squares in 1927 and was appointed a magistrate in 1934. While she regarded the church as her life's main cause, the path she charted in politics led the way for other women, particularly those who preferred established parties over feminist societies as outlets for public activity. She died on 26 December 1961.

DUNCAN SUTHERLAND

Sources *The Times* (28 Dec 1961) · *The Times* (1 March 1962) · *Daily Telegraph* (28 Dec 1961) · *Church Times* (5 Jan 1962) · 'Our new chairman', *Home and Politics* (April 1926) · N. McCrillis, *The British conservative party in the age of universal suffrage* (1998) · G. E. Maguire, *Conservative women* (1998) · *The modernisation of conservative politics: the diaries and letters of William Bridgeman, 1904–1935*, ed. P. Williamson (1988) · *Record of Proceedings* [Church Assembly] (1925–60) · private information (2004) [granddaughter] · B. Brooke, letter to Oliver Poole, 25 June 1958, Bodl. Oxf., Conservative Party archive, CCO 60/4/32 · *Church Times* (31 May 1935) · Burke, *Peerage* · *WW* · *CGPLA Eng. & Wales* (1962)

Archives Shrops. RRC, corresp., diaries, and papers | FILM British Pathé, London, news footage

Wealth at death £23,714 19s. 0d.: probate, 20 Feb 1962, *CGPLA Eng. & Wales*

Bridgeman [Bridgman], **Charles** (d. 1738), landscape gardener, was possibly of East Anglian origin. Nothing is known of his parentage or education, although there is some speculation that his father might also have been a gardener (Willis, *Bridgeman*, 2002). He is first recorded by the inscription 'Bridgman Descript' in the cartouche of an accomplished plan of the grounds of Blenheim Palace, Oxfordshire, dated 1709; the quality of this drawing would seem to indicate some architectural training. On 2 May 1717, at Gray's Inn Chapel, he married Sarah Mist (d. 1743/4), the daughter of John Mist, a paviour from St Anne's parish in Westminster and a friend of Bridgeman's from the board of works. The Bridgemans had seven children, four of whom survived infancy (Charles, Sarah, Elizabeth, and Ann).

Innovator and royal gardener Bridgeman was a key figure in the evolution of the English landscape garden, which, as *le jardin anglais*, *der englische Garten*, or *il giardino inglese*, swept through eighteenth-century Europe. As such, he played a crucial role in the transition from the geometric layouts of English estates in the later 1600s and early 1700s, epitomized by the work of George London and Henry Wise, to the freer designs of William Kent and Lancelot 'Capability' Brown. London died in 1714, and in 1716 Wise entered into partnership with Joseph Carpenter, one of several men—Bridgeman perhaps among them—who had helped Wise to run Brompton Park nurseries, for 'the ordering and keeping of all His Majesty's Gardens' (Willis, *Bridgeman*, 33). On Carpenter's death in 1726 Bridgeman succeeded as Wise's collaborator, and on Wise's retirement in 1728, following the accession of George II and Queen Caroline the previous year, Bridgeman became sole royal gardener.

In Horace Walpole's opinion, expressed in *The History of Modern Taste in Gardening* (first published in 1780), Bridgeman was 'the next fashionable designer of gardens' after London and Wise. For although Bridgeman still 'adhered much to straight walks with high clipped hedges', he had 'many detached thoughts, that strongly indicate the dawn of modern taste'. Notable among these were his introduction at Richmond of 'cultivated fields, and even morsels of a forest appearance', and his use of the 'simple enchantment' of the ha-ha so that 'nature was taken into the plan' and each step 'pointed out new beauties and inspired new ideas' (Willis, *Bridgeman*, 18–19). The ha-ha consisted of a ditch and sunken retaining wall which divided the garden proper from the surrounding landscape and kept livestock visible but separate from the area close to the house. It removed the need for an enclosing boundary wall and was described by Walpole as the 'capital stroke, the leading step to all that has followed' (ibid., 19). The ha-ha may owe its origin to fortifications, and its use in England was also promoted by the garden writer and theorist Stephen Switzer and by John James, who illustrated one in his *The Theory and Practice of Gardening* (1712), a book based on A. J. Dézallier d'Argenville's *La théorie et la pratique du jardinage* (1709). The impact of the ha-ha was decisive. 'How rich, how gay, how picturesque the face of the country!', Walpole exclaimed in his *Modern Taste in Gardening*: 'The demolition of walls laying open each improvement, every journey is made through a succession of pictures' (Willis, *Bridgeman*, 19).

The features of Bridgeman's designs, both for official and private clients, are demonstrated in the collection of his drawings in the Bodleian Library (MS Gough drawings A3 and A4). Plans in ink, pencil, and watercolour predominate, ranging from simple surveys of Wimpole in Cambridgeshire (c.1720–1724) to highly elaborate presentation drawings for Eastbury, Dorset (c.1723), and Amesbury, Wiltshire (1738). Displayed in these plans are all the formal, transitional, and progressive characteristics of Bridgeman's layouts: the formal—seen in parterres, kitchen gardens, avenues, and rectilinear, round, or octagonal lakes or ponds; the transitional—in lawns, mounts, amphitheatres, statues, garden buildings, and irregular *cabinets*; the progressive—in the use of ha-has, rides, and walks to exploit key vantage points. As Bridgeman fused these diverse elements, the final impression of the gardens rested upon their context and his exploration of the *genius loci*. His designs also depended increasingly upon allusions to literary, historical, and mythological subjects and the promotion of the virtues of country life, leading to that 'Farm-like Way of Gardening' advocated by Switzer in his *Ichnographia rustica* (appendix to vol. 3, 1742). This in turn may have prompted the *fermes ornées* found on estates such as Dawley in Middlesex, where Bridgeman may have assisted Henry St John, first Viscount Bolingbroke, from about 1723.

Bridgeman was able to combine work on such private landscapes with his official post as royal gardener; the extent of his duties at the various royal gardens was laid out in documents of 1726 and 1728 now in the Public Record Office at Kew and reproduced in Willis, *Bridgeman*, 151–5. He even published *A Report of the Present State of the Great Level of the Fens* in 1725 (reissued 1766). Strictly speaking, the royal gardener did not form part of the establishment of the office of works, but, in effect, between 1728 and 1738 Bridgeman was in charge of the royal gardens and parks at Hampton Court, St James's Park, Windsor, and Hyde Park and Kensington Gardens (where he was responsible for creating the Round Pond and the Serpentine). More significantly, in the 1730s Bridgeman assisted Queen Caroline in laying out Richmond Gardens, where William Kent designed several buildings, notably the Hermitage, which contained busts by Rysbrack and Guelfi, and Merlin's Cave, a thatched gothic building which contained three pairs of wax figures. The effect was idiosyncratic. The eccentricities of the queen's gardening came to be used as a political pawn and were the subject of widespread derision in such journals as Bolingbroke's *The Craftsman*. Visitors found the impression bucolic: when he visited Richmond in 1733, Sir John Clerk of Penicuik (1676–1755), foreshadowing Walpole's comments on Bridgeman's activities there (in *Modern Taste in Gardening*), recorded in his travel diary on 15 May the 'fields of corn' which had been introduced chiefly 'for the benefite of the game' (NA Scot., Clerk MSS, GD 18/2110). Most of Bridgeman's work in the royal gardens, however, consisted of preserving the existing layout rather than initiating new and adventurous schemes, and Hampton Court and Windsor retained their formality.

For private clients, the most rigid of Bridgeman's designs was at Eastbury, for the Dodington family, illustrated in the third volume of Colin Campbell's *Vitruvius Britannicus* of 1725. Elsewhere he could be much more adventurous, as when employed in the 1720s by Richard Lumley, second earl of Scarbrough, at Lumley Castle in co. Durham, or by Thomas Pelham-Holles, fourth duke of Newcastle, at Claremont in Surrey. At Claremont, Bridgeman's amphitheatre has been restored by the National Trust to his design published in Switzer's *General System of Hydrostaticks and Hydraulicks* of 1729. Bridgeman was employed at Rousham House in Oxfordshire in the 1720s and 1730s by the Dormer family. Here his work was once again linked to that of Kent, who was altering the existing

Jacobean mansion, in its exploitation of the pictorial qualities of an exquisite site.

Stowe The most magnificent of these private estates was Stowe in Buckinghamshire, the seat of Richard Temple, first Viscount Cobham, and the most celebrated English landscape garden of the day. Bridgeman began to work there shortly after 1713, variously alongside Vanbrugh, James Gibbs, Kent, and Henry Flitcroft. However, it was Bridgeman who laid out and planned the whole garden; a bird's-eye view (*c*.1720) of the proposed layout of the grounds is in the Bodleian Library, Oxford. Numerous poems attest to Stowe's glories, the most famous being Gilbert West's *Stowe, the Gardens of the Right Honourable Richard, Lord Viscount Cobham*, published in London in 1732 and dedicated to Alexander Pope. In 1733–4 Bridgeman commissioned Jacques Rigaud to draw fifteen perspective views of Stowe, which, engraved by Rigaud and Bernard Baron, were duly published by Bridgeman's widow, Sarah, in 1739, the year after her husband's death. No other English garden of the period has such remarkable visual documentation. Accompanying the views was an unsigned plan of the layout, locating the planting and buildings and providing a comprehensive display of the features described by West. Here may be seen a remarkable fusion of formal, transitional, and progressive elements within a cohesive and dramatic layout, with rides, walks, ha-has, regular and irregular planting, waterscape, and numerous temples and garden features—many of them embodying personal, literary, historical, and mythological themes. Guidebooks to Stowe multiplied, Bernard Seeley's *Descriptions of … Stowe* prominent among them. All told, Stowe became a supreme reflection of the Cobham family motto *Templa quam delecta*, and travellers, including Thomas Jefferson, third president of the United States, hastened to look and admire. One of the earliest French publications promoting the English style in France was the poem *Les charmes de Stow*—dated 1748, and similar to William Gilpin's *A Dialogue upon the Gardens … at Stowe* of the same year—which serves as a reminder that to many Frenchmen Stowe was *ne plus ultra*: not for nothing were Rigaud's and Baron's views of Stowe titled in both French and English.

The adventurous ideas found at Stowe must have stemmed in part, at least, from Lord Cobham, but they also reflect Bridgeman's own friendship and collaboration with architects (notably Vanbrugh, Gibbs, and Kent), writers (such as Pope and Matthew Prior), and painters (such as John Wootton, Philip Mercier, and Sir James Thornhill). Bridgeman's election to the exclusive Society of the Virtuosi of St Luke in 1726 was only one indication of his wide friendships and the esteem in which he was held. Pope admired Bridgeman's Stowe: the *Epistle to Richard Boyle, Earl of Burlington* included the line 'Lo! Bridgman comes, and floats them with a lake', a tribute paid in the first three editions, all dated 1731 ('Cobham' was substituted for 'Bridgeman' in later editions to appease Kent and the new taste). Indeed, the royal gardener may have assisted with the poet's garden at Twickenham.

Although only one individual portrait of Bridgeman survives (attributed to William Hogarth, and in the Vancouver Art Gallery), he does appear in several group paintings, including *A Conversation of Virtuosi … at the Kings Arms* (also known as *A Club of Artists*), attributed to Gawen Hamilton (*c*.1735; NPG), and *An Assembly of Virtuosi* (*c*.1730), also attributed to Hamilton (unfinished, AM Oxf.). In these paintings Bridgeman is set among fellow artists and kindred spirits such as Kent, Gibbs, Wootton, J. M. Rysbrack, and Michael Dahl, whose friendships would have ensured that he was well conversant with the progressive thinking of the day. Bridgeman was also represented in the second plate (*The Levee*) of *A Rake's Progress* by Hogarth (1734–5; Sir John Soane's Museum, London), in which he is tempting the rake to waste his substance on gardening.

Death and posthumous reputation Apart from spells in official residences at Hampton Court and Kensington Palace, Bridgeman lived from 1723 until his death at 19 Broad Street (later 54 Broadwick Street) in Westminster. A three-storey house of red stock brick, with handsome interior panelling and plasterwork, it was one of several terraces built by his brother-in-law John Mist. Larger, but not dissimilar in character, was 8 Henrietta Street (later 11 Henrietta Place, demolished in 1956), designed by James Gibbs as part of Lord Harley's Marylebone estate, which Bridgeman leased from 1725 but never seems to have occupied. Late in life, about 1736, he purchased The Bell inn at Stilton in Huntingdonshire. He died on 19 July 1738 at his official house in Kensington 'Of a Dropsy' (Boyer, 94), and was buried on 22 July at St James's Church, Piccadilly. Within weeks of his death he was succeeded by Samuel Milward at St James's Park and Kensington, George Lowe at Hampton Court, John Kent at Windsor and Newmarket, and the Thomas Greenings, father and son, at Richmond. This division of responsibilities ended the concept of a single royal gardener which had begun in England in 1666 with Charles II's appointment of John Rose (*c*.1621–1677).

It is impossible to ascertain Bridgeman's wealth on his death. The bequests in his will of 6 July 1738 (reproduced in Willis, *Bridgeman*, 169–70) include The Bell inn at Stilton and the leasehold on his house at 8 Henrietta Street to his widow, Sarah, subject to conditions, and £2000 each to his daughters Sarah, Elizabeth, and Ann. Although the 'residue or surplus' was left to Mrs Bridgeman, she was soon appealing to George II (in a petition of 1738) for 'his Majestys Royal Compassion', as she and her family had been left 'in very narrow Circumstances' (ibid., 168). She also pleaded for money from Sarah, duchess of Marlborough, probably for work by her husband at Wimbledon, but this was of no avail, partly because, as the duchess claimed when writing to her, some of those 'who are no Enemies to [her], and know [her] Circumstances, that they are good' (BL, Add. MS 61478).

When Bridgeman died in 1738 his place at Stowe was taken by Capability Brown, who had travelled south from Northumberland. It was a symbolic moment in the history of the English landscape garden. The revolution in England was all but won, and in 1755 the journal *The World* could only note its positive delight at 'the rapid progress of this happy enthusiasm' (no. 118, 3 April 1755). In due course Brown moved so far beyond the most advanced ideas of Bridgeman and Kent that Sir William Chambers could write that Brown's landscapes 'differ very little from common fields, so closely is nature copied in most of them' (W. Chambers, *A Dissertation on Oriental Gardening*, 1772, v). PETER WILLIS

Sources P. Willis, *Charles Bridgeman and the English landscape garden* (1977) · P. Willis, *Charles Bridgeman and the English landscape garden. Reprinted with supplementary plates and a catalogue of additional documents, drawings and attributions* (privately printed, Newcastle upon Tyne, 2002) · P. Willis, 'From desert to Eden: Charles Bridgeman's "capital stroke"', *Burlington Magazine*, 115 (1973), 150–55 · P. Willis, 'The gardener and the painter: a new attribution to Hogarth', *Apollo*, 95 (1972), 30–33 · D. Jacques, 'The grand manner: changing style in garden design, 1660–1735', PhD diss., U. Lond., 1999 · [J. Rigaud], *Stowe Gardens in Buckinghamshire, laid out by Mr Bridgeman, delineated in a large plan, and fifteen perspective views. Drawn on the spot by Mons. Rigaud, now reprinted. To which is added an account of the original publication and descriptive notes to each view by George B. Clarke*, repr. (1987) · G. B. Clarke, ed., *Descriptions of Lord Cobham's gardens at Stowe (1700–1750)*, Buckinghamshire RS, 26 (1990) · J. Roberts, *Royal landscape: the gardens and parks of Windsor* (1997) · A. Boyer, *The political state of Great Britain*, 56 (1738), 94 · burial register, St James's Piccadilly · Boyd's marriage index, 1701–25, Society of Genealogists
Archives BL, Add. MSS 2235, 5842, 15776, 18238–18248, 22926, 23076, 33085, 34733, 38488A, 39167B, 47030, 51345 · Hunt. L., Stowe papers · PRO, papers of the Board of Works, works 1/1, 1/2, 3/2, 4/1–4/8, 5/56–5/59, 5/104, 5/105, 5/141, 5/150, 6/8, 6/15, 6/16, 6/114, 6/184/4, 16/2/8, 16/3/1, 16/39/1 · U. Durham L., Willis papers
Likenesses attrib. G. Hamilton, unfinished group portrait, oils, *c*.1730 (*An assembly of virtuosi*), AM Oxf. · W. Hogarth, painting, oils, 1734–5 (*A rake's progress*), Sir John Soane's Museum, London · attrib. G. Hamilton, group portrait, oils, *c*.1735 (*A conversation of virtuosi … at the Kings Arms*), NPG · W. Hogarth, group portrait, oils, *c*.1735 (*An assembly of artists*), AM Oxf. · M. Dahl, portrait · W. Hogarth, group portrait, engraving (*A rake's progress*), BL · attrib. W. Hogarth, oils, Vancouver Art Gallery, Canada · J. Thornhill, pencil, probably priv. coll.
Wealth at death exact sum unknown: Willis, *Charles Bridgeman*, 161–7, 169–70; will, PRO, PROB 11/731 [Sarah Bridgeman]; inventory, PRO, PROB 3/37/95; will, PRO, PROB 11/692

Bridgeman, Sir Francis Charles Bridgeman (1848–1929), naval officer, was born Francis Charles Bridgeman-Simpson at Babworth, Nottinghamshire, on 7 December 1848. He was the fourth son of the Revd William Bridgeman Simpson (1813–1895), rector of Babworth (who was nephew of Orlando Bridgeman, first earl of Bradford), and his wife, Lady Frances Laura Fitzwilliam (1813–1887), daughter of Charles William, fifth Earl Fitzwilliam. He resumed the family name of Bridgeman in 1896. He entered the *Britannia* as a naval cadet in 1862, and after serving as midshipman in the Pacific and the Channel fleets, in 1868 went for nearly four years to the *Blanche* on the Australian station, being promoted sub-lieutenant in 1869. Bridgeman was promoted lieutenant in 1873, and, having taken up gunnery, served for nearly four years on the China station in the *Encounter* as gunnery lieutenant: while doing the same duty in the *Temeraire* in the Mediterranean he was promoted commander in 1884. In this rank he served in the *Triumph*, Sir Michael Culme-Seymour's flagship in the Pacific, from 1885 to 1888, and afterwards

in the gunnery training ship *Excellent* until he was promoted captain in 1890. In 1889 he married Emily Charlotte (1842–1922), daughter of Thomas Shiffner, of Westergate, Sussex; they had no children.

Bridgeman's first ten years as captain were mainly employed as flag captain to Culme-Seymour in the Channel Fleet and the Mediterranean, and at Portsmouth. In October 1900 he went on half pay until January 1903, when he commissioned the *Drake* and joined Admiral W. H. Fawkes's cruiser squadron. In August of that year he was promoted rear-admiral; he hoisted his flag as second in command to Lord Charles Beresford in the Channel Fleet for a year in June 1904, and in 1906 he again served as second in command to Beresford, this time in the Mediterranean Fleet. In March 1907, having reached the rank of vice-admiral, he was selected as commander-in-chief of the newly formed Home Fleet, and held this command for two years with his flag in the new battleship *Dreadnought*. From 1910 until March 1911 he was second sea lord at the Admiralty under Reginald McKenna. He then returned as admiral to the command of the Home Fleet; but in December of the same year he came back to the Admiralty as first sea lord under Winston Churchill, on the retirement of Admiral Sir Arthur Wilson. Twelve months later he resigned. On his resignation he was promoted GCB, having been created KCVO in 1907 and KCB in 1908, and promoted GCVO in 1911. In another year he had reached the age limit of his rank and was placed on the retired list. On leaving the Admiralty he went to live at Copgrove Hall, Burton Leonard, near Harrogate, his country seat, and rarely went to London except to attend court functions in his capacity as vice-admiral of the United Kingdom, to which he was appointed in 1920 in succession to his old chief, Sir Michael Culme-Seymour.

Bridgeman was a man of singularly handsome presence, and a fine sea officer with a great knowledge of the service. He was a strong supporter of the naval reforms and strategic schemes of Lord Fisher, and gave him loyal and valuable support in the formation of the Home Fleet originally created out of the reserve divisions at the home ports. When Bridgeman returned to its command in March 1911, it had been combined with the Channel Fleet, and he did fine work in organizing and training it for the duties which it was later to fulfil with the Grand Fleet during the First World War.

Bridgeman had had no previous administrative experience at the Admiralty before he became second sea lord, but he was regarded as a man of sound judgement and commanded confidence in the fleet. When Churchill became first lord and reconstituted the Board of Admiralty, he chose Bridgeman as his first sea lord. Bridgeman was a loyal supporter of Churchill in his plans for the constitution of a naval war staff. Nevertheless he soon became annoyed at Churchill's methods, such as sending signals to the fleet without the authority of the board and circulating peremptory orders to the other sea lords. Churchill, in turn, after a year apparently found Bridgeman unsatisfactory and used his poor health as an excuse to require his resignation. He loyally accepted the decision, but the form in which it was communicated to him caused much resentment, and was the subject of an acrimonious debate in the House of Commons.

Bridgeman was popular in his home county of Yorkshire, and after his retirement devoted himself to the pursuits of a country squire. After the war he was chairman of the divisional council for demobilization and resettlement in the Yorkshire and east midlands areas. He died at Nassau in the Bahamas on 17 February 1929; his burial took place at St Michael and All Angels, Copgrove, on 4 March 1929.   V. W. BADDELEY, rev. PAUL G. HALPERN

Sources The Times (19 Feb 1929) · admiralty records, 1937, PRO · Hansard 5C (1912) · S. Roskill, Churchill and the admirals (1977) · A. J. Marder, From the Dreadnought to Scapa Flow: the Royal Navy in the Fisher era, 1904–1919, 5 vols. (1961–70), vol. 1 · R. S. Churchill, Winston S. Churchill, 2: Young statesman, 1901–1914 (1967) · P. Gretton, Former naval person: Winston Churchill and the Royal Navy (1968); repr. (New York, 1969) · N. A. Lambert, 'Admiral Sir Francis Bridgeman-Bridgeman', The first sea lords: from Fisher to Mountbatten, ed. M. H. Murfett (1995), 55–74 · S. Ross, Admiral Sir Francis Bridgeman: the life and times of an officer and a gentleman (1998)

Archives IWM, papers | IWM, Loch MSS · NMM, corresp. with Sir Julian Corbett · Sheff. Arch., diaries of Orlando Bridgeman-Simpson

Likenesses E. Moore, portrait, NPG; repro. in Marder, Road to war

Wealth at death £138,354 5s. 11d.: probate, 31 July 1929, CGPLA Eng. & Wales

Bridgeman, Henry (1615–1682), bishop of Sodor and Man, was born at Peterborough on 22 October 1615, the third of the five sons of John *Bridgeman (bap. 1577, d. 1652), then first prebendary of the cathedral there (where Henry was baptized three days later at the consecration of the new font), and his wife, Elizabeth Helyar (d. 1636), daughter of William Helyar, archdeacon of Barnstaple and canon of Exeter Cathedral. In 1619 his father became bishop of Chester, a position which he held until his death, albeit spending his last years in inevitable retirement during the eclipse of the Church of England.

Henry Bridgeman matriculated from Oriel College, Oxford, in October 1629. After graduating BA on 20 October 1632 he was elected a fellow of Brasenose College in the following year (6 December 1633), and proceeded MA on 16 June 1635. He resigned his fellowship in July 1639 to take up the rectory of Barrow, Cheshire (to which he was admitted on 16 December 1639). Three weeks later, on 6 January 1640, he was appointed rector of Bangor Is-coed, Flintshire, on the resignation of his father. The following year, in February 1641, he married Catherine Lever (d. 1678?), daughter of William Lever of Kersal, near Manchester, with whom he had three daughters. Bridgeman's benefices were sequestrated during the civil war: Barrow in 1643, probably on grounds of pluralism, and Bangor in 1646, perhaps as the result of his royalist sympathies. He apparently served as a chaplain to James, seventh earl of Derby, reportedly being present at the earl's execution at Bolton on 16 October 1651. In 1648, when the appointment had no effective meaning, he was appointed archdeacon of Richmond in the diocese of Chester.

At the Restoration, Bridgeman was created DD at the University of Oxford. Resigning from the archdeaconry of Richmond, he was appointed dean of Chester on 13 July 1660 through the intercession of the dowager countess of Derby and in addition regained the rectories of Barrow and Bangor after petitioning the House of Lords for restitution on 23 June. He also became prebendary of Stillingfleet in York Minster (30 July) and vicar of Plemstall, Cheshire, in 1661, the latter a living in the gift of his eldest brother, Sir Orlando *Bridgeman.

Bridgeman displayed a reluctance to persecute nonconformists, possibly reflecting the influence of both his father, who as bishop had shown considerable moderation in the treatment of his puritan clergy, and of his godly mother; his overall position was anti-Arminian. Prior to his sequestration from Bangor he had installed Robert Fogg as curate, an appointment of which the committee for plundered ministers plainly approved as Fogg was granted the living on 1 July 1646. With Bridgeman's return Fogg remained as curate in Bangor, despite being offered £80 to leave, but was finally removed following the Act of Uniformity in 1662. Bridgeman nevertheless continued to procrastinate when it came to enforcing Anglican strictures in the parish, at first allowing the distinguished nonconformist Philip Henry (ordained 16 September 1657) to remain unmolested at Worthenbury, a chapelry of Bangor. In May 1661 Henry even offered to surrender part of his stipend and take a subordinate post to his designated successor, Richard Hilton, but the son of the nonconformist's patron and Henry's former pupil, Roger Puleston, was determined to have him removed. Puleston eventually persuaded Bridgeman to proclaim Henry's discharge 'before a Rable' on 24 October 1661 (Diaries and Letters, 98). During the decade after the Restoration, Bridgeman lived mainly in Chester, where, Henry recorded in December 1661, he was then 'busy in repairing the Deanes house, as if hee were to live in it for ever' (Diaries and Letters, 102).

In 1671 Bridgeman was nominated as bishop of Sodor and Man on the translation of Isaac Barrow to St Asaph and was consecrated on 1 October. He continued to hold his deanery in commendam and in 1672 became sinecure rector of Llanrwst, Denbighshire. Bridgeman appears to have spent little time in the Isle of Man, yet showed interest in the welfare of the diocese. He continued to pursue the educational policies of his predecessor, fostering the academic school established by Barrow at Castletown in 1668. He purchased Rushen Abbey as a site for the school, although it was never located there. With Barrow he established a trust to pay for a teacher at the school. Bridgeman also donated a chalice to German parish church. He presided over diocesan business in person on several occasions in 1675, 1678–80, and at a convocation of Manx clergy in 1680. Following the death of his first wife Bridgeman married, on 22 January 1679 at Bishopscourt in the Isle of Man, Margaret Nowell, née Litherland, the widow of Henry Nowell, a former governor of the island, with whom he had one daughter. He died in Chester, at the deanery, on 15 May 1682 and was buried without memorial in Chester Cathedral.   J. R. DICKINSON

Sources DNB · T. S. Ball, *Church plate of the city of Chester* (1907) · *The history of the cathedral church at Chester* (1793) · Foster, *Alum. Oxon.* · *Diaries and letters of Philip Henry*, ed. M. H. Lee (1882) · A. W. Moore, *A history of the Isle of Man*, 2 vols. (1900); repr. (1977) · J. Addy, 'The life and administration of the archdeaconry of Richmond, 1541–1836', MA diss., U. Leeds, 1963 · Peterborough Cathedral registers, Peterborough Cathedral [baptisms] · Malew parish registers, 1678–9, Manx Museum Library, microfilm PR 19 [marriages] · W. Ferguson Irvine, ed., *Marriage licences granted within the archdeaconry of Chester in the diocese of Chester, 1639–1644*, 4 (1911) · episcopal wills, 1672–5, Manx Museum Library, microfilm EW 21 · *Calendar of the manuscripts of the marquess of Ormonde*, new ser., 8 vols., HMC, 36 (1902–20), vol. 4 · [C. B. Heberden], ed., *Brasenose College register, 1509–1909*, 2 vols., OHS, 55 (1909) · W. Dugdale, *The visitation of the county palatine of Lancaster, made in the year 1664–5*, ed. F. R. Raines, 2, Chetham Society, 85 (1872), 186 · J. P. Earwaker, *An index to the wills and inventories … at Chester, from A. D. 1660 to 1680*, Lancashire and Cheshire RS, 15 (1887) · J. Bridgeman, journal, Staffs. RO

Bridgeman, John (*bap.* 1577, *d.* 1652), bishop of Chester, was baptized at St Petrock, Exeter, on 2 November 1577, the son of Thomas Bridgeman (*d.* 1627), merchant, of Greenway, Devon. He matriculated sizar from Peterhouse, Cambridge, in 1593 and graduated BA in 1597. In 1599 he was elected a fellow of Magdalene College and the following year he proceeded MA, incorporating his degrees into the University of Oxford on 23 February 1597 and 4 July 1600 respectively. On 12 July 1601 he was ordained deacon and priest at Peterborough Cathedral. On 13 April 1605 he was collated to the cathedral's first prebend and on 28 October 1609 he was appointed cathedral receiver.

On 28 April 1606 Bridgeman married at Dunchideock, Devon, Elizabeth (*d.* 1636), daughter of William Helyar, archdeacon of Barnstaple, and it is possible that her interest in puritan preachers such as John Angier (who prayed with her during her illness) influenced Bridgeman's toleration of such divines for the next two decades. The couple had five surviving sons, including Sir Orlando *Bridgeman (1609–1674) and Henry *Bridgeman (1615–1682). In 1610 Bridgeman was instituted to the vicarage of Bexhill in Sussex; he returned to Cambridge in 1612 to take his DD. Appointed a royal chaplain in 1613, his gravitation through the orbit of the court drew him into the earl of Northampton's clientèle. Bridgeman praised the crypto-Catholic earl for influencing Bishop William Cotton of Exeter to bestow on him in 1613 canonical office at Exeter Cathedral (from whence he was soon elected to a residentiary position). In 1615 Bridgeman joined Bishop Thomas Dove of Peterborough for the consecration of the cathedral's new font. Commissioned at Bridgeman's personal expense, it was used for the baptism of his son once the consecration was concluded. The previous year Bridgeman had been appointed Peterborough's cathedral treasurer. His career was marked by his efforts to recover for the church from 'sacrilegious ravens' (Lincs. Arch., MS Cor.M/2, fol. 58) dilapidated revenues such as the advowson of Allerton church, Lincolnshire, which he alleged had been appropriated through underhand dealing by a Peterborough prebendary.

In 1616, through the king's patronage, Bridgeman succeeded Edward Fleetwood in the rich parsonage of Wigan, and on 15 June that year he gained a prebend at Lichfield Cathedral and resigned his stall at Peterborough. On 15 March 1617 he joined the king's entourage to Scotland, and it was in his capacity as royal chaplain that he would have seen the latest styles of ecclesiastical art and architecture exemplified in the royal chapels at Windsor, Whitehall, and Holyroodhouse, which may have influenced his future ecclesiological investments. Bridgeman was among the ten 'English doctors' who during the Scottish visitation shocked the iconomach William Cowper, dean of the Scottish Chapel Royal, when they instructed the Scottish clergy on the king's theological justification for using images and fine ornaments for decorating the chapel. On 3 May 1618 Bridgeman was offered the deanery of Windsor, but he had to forgo it when the renegade archbishop of Spalato, Marco de Dominis, reminded the forgetful James I that it had already been promised to him. Bridgeman therefore focused his attention directly upon Wigan. This rich benefice brought him the rights and titles due to the lord of Wigan manor, and the parson quickly dismayed his neighbours by reasserting the lay and spiritual authority of these offices for the first time since the Elizabethan Reformation and then calling upon the privy council to help silence local protest against what was seen as a reactionary encroachment.

On 7 March 1619 Bridgeman was nominated bishop of Chester; he was consecrated on 7 May at St Benet Paul's Wharf, London. This appointment reflected crown policy of enlightening areas strongly affected by Catholic recusancy and by puritanism by placing experienced clergy in leading positions in the north. Thus Bridgeman retained Wigan and, from 1621 to 1640, the rectory of Bangor, *in commendam* with the bishopric in order to concentrate his evangelical attentions upon Lancastrian recusants. This policy continued until the translation of Richard Neile to the archbishopric of York in 1632, following which he was obliged to attend to his episcopal duties. Yet Bridgeman was by no means negligent of the cathedral. He conducted his first cathedral visitation in 1619, ordering residential canons to wear 'comlie apparell', care for their 'scholastical habits', and maintain the condition of church ornaments through proper allocation of fabric revenues (Ches. & Chester ALSS, EDA 3/1, fol. 254). His intermittent attendance at court in 1620 gave him the reputation of 'an excellent pulpit man' (*Chamberlain Letters*, 2.161) and he was occasionally on the lookout for promising clerics to edify his flock through preaching.

Bridgeman's real interest between 1620 and 1623, however, was the beautification of Wigan All Saints. Long before the Laudian vision of the 'beauty of holiness' became prominent, he installed new stained-glass windows and a private chapel for his devotions. Thereafter he re-edified the church completely, restoring the old chancel and building an additional new one. One of his finest investments was the commission of a Mortlake tapestry dorsal, which stretched across the east end of the new chancel. Based on a Raphael cartoon, it portrayed the death of Aninas, who was an infamous despoiler of the early church (Acts 5: 1–6) and whose actions were equated by contemporaries with puritanism and the lay impropriation and destruction of church property. Once Archbishop William Laud and his circle were in the ascendant, and the drive for order and beauty in worship was fully under way, Bridgeman demonstrated much sympathy with it. He donated £20 towards the new chapel at Peterhouse, whose 'scandalous images' prompted William Dowsing's iconoclastic fury the following decade, and his consecration sermons during the 1630s threatened the destruction of those who would 'violate a Temple of God' (Ches. & Chester ALSS, EDA 3/1, fols. 244r–246r).

Yet Bishop Bridgeman's confidence that he was improving the prospects of his children and placing the church's financial resources on a surer footing for his successors was soon put to the test when his conduct became subject to the scrutiny of a royal commission in 1633. This was a result of complaints to the privy council that he had embezzled fines taken for commuting penances. James Martin, the plaintiff, was once one of the king's preachers in the north-west and had been deprived of his living in Preston by Bridgeman in 1623. Charges of *praemunire* led to prosecution in and out of the court of high commission and to intense scrutiny of the bishop's financial affairs. Unique among the Caroline bishops in being treated this way, Bridgeman was ultimately fined and lost control of the king's preachers. There is no evidence that the local gentry came to his aid at this time, which possibly reflected their alienation consequent to the successes of his litigious activity. If this was not enough for one year, Bridgeman had also to face staunch criticism from Archbishop Richard Neile. Neile's metropolitical report to the king deplored lax conformity in Chester diocese and, notwithstanding Bridgeman's own liturgical tastes, the poor quality of worship in the cathedral, especially infrequent use of the litany and employment of prayers 'never appoynted or authorised to be added to the Publick service'. His principal grievance was that Bridgeman was pursuing a policy ostensibly designed to curtail popery 'least that by carrying a severer hand upon the Puritans then they had power to carry upon the Papists, the Popish party might take heart and opinion of Favor' (Bridgeman, *Wigan*, 369–71).

From 1634 Bridgeman's policies, under the supervision of his new vicar-general, Edmund Mainwaring, began to reflect those of the leaders of the Caroline church. Churchwardens were instructed to erect railed altars and arrange seats 'chancelwise' thereby laying emphasis on the sanctity of the eastern regions of churches in his charge (BL, Harley MS 2103, fol. 29; Ches. & Chester ALSS, P65/8/1). In 1637 Bridgeman reintroduced stained glass to Chester Cathedral, 'with the story of the Annunciation, Nativity, circumcision, Presentation &c. of our Saviour', 'raised the steps [of] the altar', 'gilded the organs … and ordered a new sett of pipes' (Ches. & Chester ALSS, 3/1, fol. 131). A point of significant controversy was the erection of an altar in the cathedral in 1635. According to William Prynne, this was an old *mensa* recovered from its burial

under Edward VI or Elizabeth. Locals interpreted this policy as proof of how 'he prudently applyeth himself to the times, and acteth his part accordingly' (John Ley, *A Letter (Against the Erection of an Altar Written June 29 1635)*, 1641, 16). Yet to maintain his position in the Caroline church it could be argued that Bridgeman had little choice. His subsequent career involved a careful balancing act between the interests of the local gentry and Laudian clergy. In 1638 squabbles between the cathedral clergy and gentry over seating rights in the cathedral were compounded by the punishment of godly citizens for their entertainment of the puritan controversialist Prynne (whose prison carriage passed through Chester) and inflamed by the Scottish covenanters' rebellion against English ecclesiastical policy. Archbishop Neile, who stood by the cathedral clergy zealously, did not share Bridgeman's sensitivity to the situation. Only the intervention of a nervous Laud with letters from the king helped the bishop pull the clergy into line and realize the gentry's wishes to reassert their secular power in the cathedral by carrying swords and occupying prestigious seating, thus postponing the nightmare of violent disorder. Bridgeman was doubtless assisted by the fact that his eldest son, Orlando, became vice-chamberlain of Chester in 1638 and steward of the liberties of Archbishop Laud in 1639.

Bridgeman was personally absent from both sessions of convocation in 1640–41, and thus escaped impeachment for involvement in the ecclesiastical canons. In August 1642, with his son, he headed a group of local dignitaries who took Chester for the king. Subsequently divested of his cathedral, and sequestered from his rectory at Wigan in 1643, he retired to his son's property at Moreton, Shropshire. He died in 1652, probably on 11 November, at Moreton Hall and was buried at Kinnerley church (for which a date of 11 November is also given). His most significant surviving works are his three ledgers, respectively for his cathedral church (compiled by his servants), Wigan church and manor, and his personal account book. Together they are a remarkable testament to his litigious successes and ecclesiastical investments, which demonstrate the fruits of his financial acumen destined for a future that was not to be.   PETER DAVID YORKE

Sources G. T. O. Bridgeman, *The history of the church and manor of Wigan, in the county of Lancaster*, 2, Chetham Society, new ser., 16 (1889) · G. T. O. B. [G. T. O. Bridgeman], 'Bishop Bridgeman', *Palatine Note-Book*, 3 (1883), 1–12 · P. D. Yorke, 'Bishop John Bridgeman and the "Beauty of holiness"' [forthcoming] · account book, Staffs. RO, MS D 1287/3/1 · ledger, Wigan Archives Service, Leigh, D/D–A–13/1 · Ches. & Chester ALSS, Bridgeman cathedral MSS, EDA 3/1 · W. Quintrell, 'Lancashire ills, the king's will, and the troubling of Bishop Bridgeman', *Transactions of the Historic Society of Lancashire and Cheshire*, 132 (1982), 67–102 · K. Fincham, *Prelate as pastor: the episcopate of James I* (1990) · J. Davies, *The Caroline captivity of the church: Charles I and the remoulding of Anglicanism, 1625–1641* (1992) · J. Wickham Legg, ed., *English orders for consecrating churches in the seventeenth century*, HBS, 41 (1911) · F. Gastrell, *Notita Cestriensis, or, Historical notices of the diocese of Chester*, ed. F. R. Raines, 1–2/1, Chetham Society, 8, 19 (1845–9) · S. Lunton, *The history of the church of Peterburgh* (1686) · *The Chamberlain letters*, ed. E. M. Thomson, another edn (New York, 1966) · *Reg. Oxf.*, 2/1 · Venn, *Alum. Cant.* · *Walker rev.* · Wood, *Ath. Oxon.: Fasti* (1815), 1.286 · IGI

Archives Bolton Central Library, estate register, financial and other papers, Bolton central ledger · Ches. & Chester ALSS, Bridgeman cathedral MSS · Ches. & Chester ALSS, ledger · Derbys. RO, ledger · Staffs. RO, corresp., notebooks, and papers
Likenesses attrib. C. Johnson, oils, Weston Park, Shropshire · P. van Somer, oils, Weston Park, Shropshire · oils, Bishop's House, Chester

Bridgeman, Sir Maurice Richard (1904–1980), oil industrialist, was born at 13 Mansfield Street, Marylebone, London, on 26 January 1904, the third son of William Clive *Bridgeman (1864–1935), a Conservative politician who was created Viscount Bridgeman in 1929, and his wife, Caroline Beatrix *Bridgeman (1873–1961), a political activist and churchwoman, and elder daughter of the Hon. Cecil Thomas Parker. Robert Clive *Bridgeman was his elder brother. Both parents were of aristocratic birth, W. C. Bridgeman's grandfather being the second earl of Bradford and his wife's grandfather being the sixth earl of Macclesfield.

Maurice Bridgeman was educated at Eton College, where he was captain of the Oppidans, captain of the eleven, and president of Pop. He followed in his father's footsteps in going to Trinity College, Cambridge, but where the father had been a classical scholar the son read science and, despite his considerable intellectual ability, left without taking a degree. Eager to join the world of commerce and industry, in 1926 he accepted an offer of employment (at a salary of £5 a week, then the best on offer) with the Anglo-Persian Oil Company (renamed the Anglo-Iranian Oil Company in 1935 and the British Petroleum Company in 1954). At that time the company (established in 1909) owned the concession for oil exploration and production in most of Persia and was expanding its operations rapidly.

Bridgeman's first assignment was to accompany as secretary the deputy chairman, Sir John Cadman, to Persia for the shah's coronation. Afterwards he was posted to Persia and spent some time there before recurrent jaundice forced his return to Britannic House, the company's head office in London. In 1933 he married Diana Mary Erica Wilson (d. 1979), younger daughter of Humphrey Minto Wilson. The Bridgemans had a family of four daughters.

Luck and coincidence, Bridgeman said, had twice played an important role in his career, firstly in 1926 when he deputized for Cadman's usual secretary, and secondly in 1934 when he was unexpectedly sent to take charge of the company's New York office. Both appointments brought him, early in his corporate life, close to the centre of events and power. He served in New York for three years and the knowledge of and contacts in the American oil industry that he acquired then were to be immensely useful.

The government controlled the oil industry during the Second World War and from 1939 to 1946 Bridgeman occupied a succession of government posts: in 1939 he was petroleum adviser to the Ministry of Economic Warfare; he was assistant secretary in the petroleum department and joint secretary to the Oil Control Board from 1940 to 1942;

Sir Maurice Richard Bridgeman (1904–1980), by Bassano, 1949

a two-year spell as petroleum adviser to the government of India followed; and finally he served from 1944 to 1946 as principal assistant secretary to the petroleum division of the Ministry of Fuel and Power. He was honoured in 1946 when he was made CBE.

Resuming his career with the company after the war, in 1952 Bridgeman was appointed managing director of the company's exploration subsidiary, D'Arcy Exploration Company. He was thus in a most significant position at a critical time in the company's affairs when, in 1951, it lost its concessionary position in Iran, forcing a radical review of the direction of exploration effort. Bridgeman believed that the company must diversify its sources of oil and he was instrumental in directing exploration to other areas, resulting in discoveries in Libya, Nigeria, the North Sea, and Alaska.

Bridgeman was appointed to the main board of British Petroleum (BP) in 1956; he became deputy chairman in 1957 and chairman in July 1960. During his nine years as chairman the company made considerable progress in diversifying its activities, a strategy close to Bridgeman's heart. BP had started to manufacture chemicals in a joint venture with the Distillers Company soon after the end of the war, and in 1967 it bought out Distillers's share; British Petroleum Chemicals then became a wholly owned subsidiary, the second largest chemicals business in the UK. The company also discovered and developed a process which converted oil to protein, forming the basis for a nutrition business. In the USA it began the negotiations which would lead to a considerable presence for BP in that continent, through the acquisition of the Standard Oil Company of Ohio (Sohio)—completed in the time of Bridgeman's successor.

Bridgeman was a consistent and fierce critic of British governments' taxation policies *vis-à-vis* both the oil companies and the individual. His aloof manner concealed a keen business sense and he was a tough negotiator. He travelled widely throughout the 1960s, visiting all parts of the company regularly; his kindliness and concern for people won him great respect. Bridgeman's commitment to BP, however, left him little time to pursue his other interests of fishing, gardening, shooting, ornithology, and the arts. Moreover, he considered the chairmanship of BP to be a full-time job and took on relatively few other responsibilities. His long-term interest in the Middle East was reflected in his membership of the Advisory Council on Middle East Trade from 1958 to 1963 and in his acting as president of the Middle East Association from 1956 to 1976. He was chairman of the public appeal to fund the creation of Fitzwilliam College, Cambridge, in 1962, and the college made him an honorary fellow in 1967; Leeds University made him an honorary LLD in 1969.

Bridgeman was knighted in 1964; he was made a knight of St John in 1961, a knight grand cross of the Italian Republic in 1966, and grand officer, order of Orange Nassau, in 1968. He received the Iranian order of Homayun in 1968 and the Cadman memorial medal in 1969. He retired from BP in 1969 and spent the next two years as a member of the Industrial Reorganization Corporation. After suffering from Parkinson's disease Sir Maurice Bridgeman died of heart failure on 18 June 1980 at 4 Lansdowne Crescent, Kensington, London.   JUDY SLINN

Sources R. W. Ferrier, 'Bridgeman, Sir Maurice Richard', *DBB* · J. Gearing, interview with Sir M. Bridgeman in *BP Shield*, Feb 1969, BP Archive, University of Warwick · C. Tugendhat, 'Bridgeman of BP', *Financial Times* (18 June 1969) · *The Times* (19 June 1980) · *WWW* · obituary, *BP Shield*, July 1980, BP Archive, University of Warwick · *WWBMP* · b. cert. · d. cert.
Archives University of Warwick, BP Archive, business papers and letters etc.
Likenesses Bassano, photographs, 1949, NPG [*see illus.*] · photographs, University of Warwick, BP Archive
Wealth at death £343,212: probate, 4 Sept 1980, *CGPLA Eng. & Wales*

Bridgeman, Sir Orlando (1609–1674), judge, was born in Exeter on 30 January 1609, the eldest of the five surviving sons of Dr John *Bridgeman (*bap.* 1577, *d.* 1652), chaplain to James I and later bishop of Chester, and his wife, Elizabeth (*d.* 1636), daughter of Dr William Helyar, archdeacon of Barnstaple. Two of Bridgeman's brothers, Dove (1610–1637) and Henry *Bridgeman (1615–1682), went into the church, the latter becoming bishop of Sodor and Man in 1671. Another, James (*b.* 1618), was knighted and the youngest, Richard (*b.* 1621), after having apprenticed in London, earned his living as a merchant in Amsterdam.

Education and parliamentary career Bridgeman's early education in Greek and Latin was under his father's direction and by the age of eleven he was being tutored in Hebrew

Sir Orlando Bridgeman (1609–1674), by William Faithorne the elder, pubd 1671

by a schoolmaster. By then he had already matriculated at Queens' College, Cambridge (1619), but he later moved to Magdalene, where he took his BA in 1623. The following year, at the age of fifteen, he was awarded the MA, *filius nobilis*, and was elected a fellow of Magdalene, although his father would not let him accept the fellowship on the grounds that these should be reserved for men of more modest means.

Bridgeman married on 30 January 1628 Judith (*d.* 1644), eldest daughter and eventual heir of John Kynaston, of Morton, Shropshire. They had one son, John, born on 16 August 1631, from whose line the earl of Bradford (*b.* 1947) is descended. Having been admitted to the Inner Temple in November 1624, Bridgeman was called to the bar on 10 February 1632 and in a short time his career and his reputation in the law were to advance rapidly, probably by virtue of both his legal ability and his personal connections. In 1638, while still in his twenties, he was made vice-chamberlain of Chester; the following year he became steward of the liberties of Archbishop Laud; and in 1640 was appointed attorney of the court of wards and made solicitor-general to the prince of Wales. He was also granted the reversion of the office of keeper of the writs and rolls in common pleas.

In 1640 Bridgeman was returned to both the Short and Long parliaments for Wigan, the borough of his father's former rectory. There he emerged as a committed and outspoken royalist. A supporter of Laudian innovations in the church, he defended the right of the clergy to make new canons, insisting that in so doing they were exercising the ecclesiastical jurisdiction of the crown and could not therefore be guilty of treason or *praemunire*. Although he joined the unanimous vote of the House of Commons to impeach the earl of Strafford, he was later to be one of the conspicuous fifty-nine 'Straffordians' who were denounced in London and Westminster as 'enemies to their country' for opposing the earl's attainder for treason (Clarendon, *History*, 1.327). Arguing against the bill, Bridgeman distinguished between two kinds of evidence, one necessary to prove a crime and the other required for treason. He would return to these early concerns for the definition and limits of treason when, in 1660, he presided at the trial of the regicides.

The civil war and interregnum Bridgeman left parliament for Cheshire in June 1642 and when civil war began in August he and his father, the bishop, at the head of a group of city leaders, lawyers, and courtiers, took control of Chester for the king. In several contemporary accounts Bridgeman, who had effectively assumed the governance of the city, was deprecated for being an outsider 'who had never done any service there' (BL, Add. MS 36913) and for exercising his rule so imperiously that the citizens were offended at his 'usurpations' (*Unfaithfulnesse of the Cavaliers*). Clarendon, however, regarded Bridgeman as

a lawyer of very good estimation; who not only informed them of their duties, and encouraged them in it, but upon his credit and estate, both which were very good, supplied them with whatsoever was necessary for their defence. (Clarendon, *History*, 2.511)

Perhaps more important was Bridgeman's being faulted for concentrating on the protection of the city of Chester to the detriment of the defence of the county at large, in particular for his alleged 'timorousnesse pretending danger of the Citty where none was' (BL, Add. MS 36913). This criticism was compounded by his leading role in negotiating the attempted pacification of Cheshire in the failed treaty of Bunbury (23 December 1642). The treaty, which called for the demilitarization of the county, was condemned by some royalists for allegedly allowing Sir William Brereton and his parliamentary forces in Cheshire to pass unopposed into Shropshire provided that they committed no hostile act in Cheshire.

Whether or not Bridgeman was overbearing in his control of the city of Chester and insufficiently aggressive in his defence of the county of Cheshire, there appears to be no question about his active commitment to the royalist cause. Throughout 1643 he co-ordinated important local intelligence for the conduct of the war, provided ordnance and munitions to neighbouring royalists, and was principally instrumental in arranging food, clothing, and money for the duke of Ormond and his royalist army sent from Ireland in November. Despite protesting at one point that 'I am so turmoyled here that I scarce know what to write or what to doe' (Phillips, 6.289), Bridgeman appears to have handled his responsibilities with considerable

efficiency and skill. He was knighted soon thereafter (17 November 1643), sat in the Oxford parliament of 1644, and was one of the king's commissioners at the failed treaty of Uxbridge in 1645. In the Uxbridge negotiations he reasserted the royalist position as a matter of law that control of the militia was vested in the king, although in matters of the church he was prepared to make concessions to Presbyterianism, much to the dismay of Charles I. According to Hyde, Bridgeman

was a Man of excellent Parts, and honestly inclined … but if it were not safe for him to be steady … He would at last be drawn to yield to any Thing, He should be powerfully pressed to do. (*Life of … Clarendon*, 1.176)

Bridgeman continued in Oxford until the surrender of the city in June 1646, when he retired first to Shropshire and then to the environs of London. His first wife, Judith, had died at Oxford on 12 June 1644, and in 1647 he married Dorothy (d. 1697), daughter and coheir of Dr John Saunders, provost of Oriel College, Oxford, and the widow of George Craddock of Caverswall Castle, Staffordshire. They had two sons, Orlando (1649–1701) and Francis (b. 1656?), and a daughter, Charlotte. After the first civil war and throughout the interregnum he was not permitted to appear at the bar, but he practised instead as a conveyancer and chamber counsel. In 1647 he drew the deed that led to the *Duke of Norfolk's case* and the establishment of the modern rule against perpetuities. It was also during this time, by his skilful use of the strict settlement to protect dynastic estates from alienation or forfeiture, that he established his reputation as 'the father of modern conveyancers' (Holdsworth, *Eng. law*, 6.605). Much of this conveyancing work was in support of his royalist friends; yet by the testimony of Thomas Page Johnson, his clerk, even Bridgeman's enemies did not regard their estates as secure without his advice. The majority of his own estate, however, was unprotected in fee simple and he was obliged to compound for his royalism, his fine being fixed first at £2246 17s. 2d., and upon further petition reduced to £1986 5s. 9d. Although Bridgeman is no longer credited as the inventor of the strict settlement (Bonfield, 60–69), his singularly influential book of conveyancing precedents remains a critical guide to the instruments and workings of seventeenth-century land law. First published in 1682, *Bridgeman's Conveyances* had gone through five editions by 1725.

Bridgeman, having made his peace with the Commonwealth, lived quietly during the 1650s, but although cautious by nature he seems at the same time to have been working under cover for the return of the monarchy. When in 1660 he was installed by Lord Chancellor Clarendon as chief justice of the common pleas and his many services to Charles I were recounted, Clarendon went on to remark how Bridgeman 'had served his Majestie that now is, during his exile by giving him constant information, intelligence & advice' (BL, Hargrave MS 55), thereby lending credence to Ludlow's later assertion that

Sir Orlando Bridgman … upon his submission to Cromwel had been permitted to practise the law in a private manner, and under that colour had served both as spy and agent for his master.   (*Memoirs of Edmund Ludlow*, 2.303)

The Restoration Bridgeman did not reappear as a public figure until the spring of 1660 when he emerged as one of the leading members of the king's party in meetings to arrange Charles II's return to England, and he was at that time elected a bencher of the Inner Temple. As a mark of his legal reputation and his favour with the restored monarchy he was in rapid succession made a serjeant-at-law (31 May), lord chief baron of the court of exchequer (2 June), and a baronet (7 June), but it was as presiding judge in the trials of the regicides in October of that year that he came to national political prominence. The outcome of these show trials was never in doubt. The twenty-nine men arraigned on a charge of high treason under the statute of 25 Edward III were certain to be found guilty of compassing and imagining the king's death, but the predictable outcome of the trial in no way detracted from Bridgeman's rulings and conduct of the proceedings, which at all times were legally and judicially correct. He emphasized repeatedly and with justification that the defendants were being tried strictly according to the known law. In his opening speech to the grand jury he insisted that if the king 'will try a man for his father's death, you see he will try them by the laws. The law is the rule and square of his actions' (*State trials*, 5.991). Yet, notwithstanding the care with which he explicated and applied the law of treason, over time Bridgeman would come to be more closely associated with his sharply worded dictum of non-resistance: 'no authority, no single person, no community of persons, not the people collectively, or representatively, have any coercive power over the king of England' (ibid., 989). The trials ended on 19 October, and three days later Bridgeman was appointed chief justice of the court of common pleas.

Bridgeman's tenure on common pleas, lasting nearly seven years, enhanced his eminence for learning and integrity and added a further reputation for punctilious attention to statutory construction. Underscored by the statement attributed to him derisively by Roger North that it would be a violation of Magna Carta to move the common pleas a few feet back from the door of the court in order to avoid a draft (North, 97), this reputation for legal exactitude was none the less well deserved. In the abortive attempt to impeach Clarendon in 1663 it was Bridgeman who drafted the unanimous opinion of the judges that the charges did not constitute high treason. Making the point that the security of the people lay in narrowing and not enlarging the reach of 25 Edward III, Bridgeman acknowledged that it was 'an offence to bring the king into contempt, or to endeavour to alien the peoples affections from him; but yet', he asserted, 'it is not treason' (Stowe MS 302). And in *Benyon* v. *Evelyn* (1664) he ruled that the Statute of Limitations did not run against a plaintiff who refused to use the courts during the time of the 'usurpation', even though parliament was later to confirm the judgments rendered in those courts. As Samuel Carter said of Bridgeman's arguments, they provided 'an exact anatomy of the case, and a dextrous piercing into

the very bowels of it' (Carter, preface). Bridgeman's own *Reports* was edited from the Hargrave manuscripts and published by S. Bannister in 1823.

When in August 1667 Clarendon finally fell, the great seal was given to Bridgeman as lord keeper, although he did not surrender the office of chief justice until May 1668. Granting that Bridgeman had no significant political standing, the work of hearing writs of error and administering justice upon appeal, being much of the burden of the Restoration House of Lords, may have suggested his appointment. By this time he had also acquired considerable experience on the woolsack, substituting for Clarendon during the chancellor's frequent illnesses. Pepys commended Bridgeman as 'mighty able' and observed that he was 'the man of the whole nation that is best spoken of and will please most people' (Pepys, 8.410, 421). Yet despite his professional skill and personal integrity Bridgeman's success as lord keeper was limited. As an equity judge he was sometimes criticized for relying upon precedent and sticking too closely to common law rules, so much so that Burnet asserted that Bridgeman 'never seemed to apprehend what equity was' (*Burnet's History*, 171). Later Roger North accused him of being 'timorous to an Impotence' and of wanting to please everyone, with the result that chancery ran 'out of Order into Delays, and endless Motions in Causes' (North, 88).

As a politician striving for balance Bridgeman fared no better. Although generally sympathetic to dissenters he was criticized for being inconsistent and ineffective in securing their relief. In 1672 he recommended pardons for Quakers who were imprisoned for holding to their principles, yet eight years earlier while presiding at the Hertford assizes he had rigorously enforced the Conventicle Act against them. In 1667–8 Bridgeman was instrumental in the negotiations and proceedings for a bill of comprehension and he even favoured a scheme of indulgence provided that it did not extend to Catholics, but when both comprehension and indulgence failed he was among those faulted for an insufficient commitment to seeing them succeed. This perception was underscored in March 1672 when he refused to affix the great seal to the king's declaration of indulgence that extended widespread relief to dissenters and a limited toleration to Catholics.

Dismissal and death By 1670 Bridgeman's political stature was conspicuously in decline. In the intrigues surrounding the treaty of Dover he had been set up to make the case before parliament for money to support the triple alliance, while being kept ignorant of the king's secret diplomacy for a French alliance, and by 1671 Buckingham and Ashley were conspiring to replace Bridgeman with the earl of Anglesey. Finally in November 1672 he was abruptly dismissed with an annual pension of £2000. In addition to having refused to seal the declaration of indulgence, Bridgeman had more recently baulked at enjoining suits against bankers who were seeking protection from their creditors because of the government's stop of the exchequer. It is also likely that five months earlier, in a move certain to incur the king's displeasure, he had refused to seal a commission for martial law on the grounds that it violated the petition of right. Yet whatever the proximate cause of his dismissal, his documented resistance to government policies in the 1670s would appear to belie both North's opinion of him as 'timorous to an impotence' and Clarendon's lament that Bridgeman was 'drawn to yield to any thing he should be powerfully pressed to do'. Less problematic was the issue of Bridgeman's precarious health, it having been reliably reported that his 'frequent sicknesse and not attending businesse was become a great grievance to the people' (BL, Add. MS 21948, fol. 427v). Charles II, therefore, was not being altogether disingenuous when he told the lord keeper 'that, in consideration of his great indisposition of body, he had thought fit to free him from that troublesome imployment' (Thompson, 1.101).

Bridgeman had for some time suffered from gout and he became progressively infirm, being often confined to bed at his houses in Teddington, Middlesex, or at Essex Court in the Strand, London. He died at Teddington on 25 June 1674 and was buried in the parish church, St Mary with St Alban, where there is a large plaque erected to his memory and a mid-twentieth-century window featuring his likeness. By his will, dated 19 February 1674, Bridgeman left £3000, most of his personal property, and a life tenancy of his Essex Court house to his wife, Dorothy. To his son Orlando he devised his estates in Cheshire and Flintshire as well as his Essex Court house after Dorothy's death. He left his house and lands at Teddington to his son Francis; £6000 to his daughter, Charlotte; and the residue of his personal estate to John, his eldest son and executor, for whom he had previously provided. Expressing regret that none of his three sons had followed him into the practice of law, Bridgeman willed his manuscripts and law books to his son John, 'hoping that some one of his sonnes will betake himself to that honorable profession'. Bridgeman's reports, spanning his time as chief justice of the common pleas, are in the British Library (BL, Hargrave MSS 55–58). As to his personal papers, there are notebooks and letters relating to Bridgeman family and public affairs in the Staffordshire Record Office, and some miscellaneous correspondence at Longleat.   HOWARD NENNER

Sources E. R. O. Bridgeman and C. G. O. Bridgeman, 'The sequestration papers of Sir Orlando Bridgeman', *Transactions of the Shropshire Archaeological and Natural History Society*, 3rd ser., 2 (1902), 1–64 · GEC, *Peerage*, new edn · T. Carte, *Life of Ormonde*, 3 vols. (1735–6) · E. Hyde, earl of Clarendon, *The history of the rebellion and civil wars in England*, 7 vols. (1849) · *State trials* · W. Phillips, 'The Ottley papers relating to the civil war [pts 1–2]', *Transactions of the Shropshire Archaeological and Natural History Society*, 2nd ser., 6 (1894), 27–78; 2nd ser., 7 (1895), 241–360 · Pepys, *Diary* · *The life of Edward, earl of Clarendon ... written by himself*, 3rd edn, 3 vols. (1761) · BL, Add. MS 21948 · BL, Add. MS 36913, fols. 122–6, pt 3, items 4 and 7 · BL, Hargrave MS 55 · BL, Stowe MS 302 · *The unfaithfulnesse of the cavaliers and commissioners of array in keeping their covenants* (1643) [Thomason tract E 84(37)] · L. Bonfield, *Marriage settlements, 1601–1740: the adoption of the strict settlement* (1983) · R. North, *The life of the Right Honourable Francis North, baron of Guilford* (1742) · S. C. [S. Carter], ed., *Reports of several special cases argued and resolved in the court of common pleas ... in the time when Sir Orlando Bridgman sate chief justice there* (1688) · S. Bannister, ed., *Reports of judgments delivered by Sir Orlando Bridgman, when chief justice of the common pleas, from Mich. 1660 to Trin. 1667* (1823) · E. M. Thompson, ed., *Correspondence of the family of Hatton, 2 vols., CS*, new ser., 22–3 (1878) · M. Jansson, ed., *Two diaries of the Long Parliament* (1984) · J. S. Morrill, *Cheshire, 1630–1660: county government and society during the English revolution* (1974) · *The journal of Sir Simonds D'Ewes from the beginning of the Long Parliament to the opening of the trial of the earl of Strafford*, ed. W. Notestein (1923) · *Bishop Burnet's History of his own time*, new edn, 2 vols. (1838) · *The memoirs of Edmund Ludlow*, ed. C. H. Firth, 2 vols. (1894) · Venn, *Alum. Cant.* · Foss, *Judges* · Holdsworth, *Eng. law*

Archives Longleat House, Warminster, Wiltshire, corresp. and related material · Staffs. RO, corresp. relating to family and public affairs, notebooks, and penalties imposed on him and on John Bridgeman | BL, Hargrave MSS

Likenesses W. Faithorne the elder, line engraving, pubd 1671, BM, NPG [*see illus.*] · J. M. Wright, oils, 1671, Inner Temple, London · P. Borsselaer, oils, Weston Park, Shropshire · J. Riley, portrait, repro. in Bridgeman and Bridgeman, 'The sequestration papers of Sir Orlando Bridgeman' · portrait, Magd. Cam., Pepys Library; repro. in O. Bridgeman, *Conveyances* (1682), frontispiece · portrait (after P. Borsselaer), Chirk Castle and Gardens, Wrexham

Wealth at death considerable: will

Bridgeman, Robert Clive, second Viscount Bridgeman

(1896–1982), army officer, was born at 89 Harley Street, London, on 1 April 1896, the eldest son of the Conservative politician, William Clive *Bridgeman (1864–1935), who was created Viscount Bridgeman in 1929, and his wife, Caroline Beatrix *Bridgeman, *née* Parker (1873–1961). Sir Maurice Richard *Bridgeman was his younger brother. He was educated at Eton College (*c*.1910–1913), and the Royal Military College, Sandhurst (1913–14), and commissioned in the rifle brigade in 1914. Without any natural aptitude for games, and deprived of maternal affection, Robert displayed gaucheness as a young man and was always quiet and unassuming. His intelligence and practical administrative abilities were evident from an early age and, but for the war, he would probably have gone to Cambridge. He served in France from 1915 to 1918, won the Military Cross, and was fortunate to miss the March 1918 offensive by the Germans in which his battalion (the 3rd) suffered heavy losses. As a promising regular officer he survived the post-war contraction of the rifle brigade, and by 1922 he was a captain and adjutant of the 2nd battalion. He graduated from the Staff College, Camberley, and served as brigade major to the 7th infantry brigade (1932–4), and at the War Office as a brevet lieutenant-colonel (1935–7).

Bridgeman succeeded his father as second viscount in 1935, having married Mary Kathleen Lane-Fox (1905/6–1981), daughter of George Lane-Fox, Baron Bingley, on 12 June 1930. He reluctantly left the army in 1937 in order to earn more money for the maintenance of the family estate and his three daughters. Sigismund Warburg proved a useful contact for him to begin the second career in banking which he would resume after 1945.

On the outbreak of war in September 1939 Bridgeman was selected by his former Staff College instructor, Major-General Henry Pownall, to be a member of the small, harmonious, and efficient headquarters staff of the field force in France. When the German offensive began on 10 May 1940, Lord Gort, the commander-in-chief, left his main headquarters in Arras for a succession of advanced command posts. Though only a lieutenant-colonel nominally responsible for staff duties, Bridgeman virtually ran

Robert Clive Bridgeman, second Viscount Bridgeman (1896–1982), by Lafayette, 1930

the headquarters comprising some 250 officers. As the terrible prospect of allied disintegration loomed, with the probable encirclement of the field force, Gort entrusted Bridgeman with preparing the plans for a retreat to the channel coast; and when the fateful decision was taken, on 25 May, Bridgeman was given a key role, under the command of General Sir Ronald Adam, in organizing the defences around Dunkirk. For his excellent work there he was awarded a DSO, and on returning to England he helped Gort prepare his dispatches. Though a man of equable temperament and not prone to harbour grievances, Bridgeman never forgave Churchill for what he regarded as the unnecessary sacrifice of the rifle brigade at Calais.

For the remainder of the war Bridgeman served with the rank of major-general, as deputy director and director-general of the Home Guard and the Territorial Army (1941–4), and as deputy adjutant-general (1944–5). Despite the ceaseless travel and some difficult political issues—such as the introduction of compulsion in 1942, to which he was opposed—Bridgeman was a tremendous success in a job described as 'somewhere between that of a labour relations expert and a professional politician' (Mackenzie, 178). In the judgement of the historian of the Home Guard, Bridgeman was:

an infinitely patient listener who smoked a pipe and spoke with a disarming honesty and conciliatory manner [and] managed the difficult task of making those he talked and corresponded with in the Home Guard feel that he understood and cared about their point of view. He could

publicly sing the praises of the force in lyrical terms … at the same time realistically coping with periodic forays by the prime minister into directorate affairs and dealing with Whitehall bureaucrats who did not always understand that the Home Guard could be coaxed and cajoled but never ordered about. (ibid., 178–9)

So valuable was Bridgeman's role as the link between the War Office and the Home Guard that only as the latter was approaching stand-down was he transferred to the post of deputy adjutant-general. There his main concern was that the impressive improvements in army welfare should be preserved for the post-war army. In a memorandum in June 1945 he argued that 'Army welfare has come to stay … it is an indispensable factor in maintaining morale and … without it the modern soldier cannot be enabled to reproduce in his Army life conditions which, in his estimation, are sufficiently civilised to be tolerable' ('The army welfare services after the war', DAG/A, 16 June 1945, PRO, WO32/14569).

After the war Bridgeman was briefly a front-bench Conservative spokesman on defence in the House of Lords, and resumed his pre-war interest in the Army Cadet Force, becoming colonel of the 4th Territorial Army battalion of the King's Shropshire light infantry. But the great bulk of his time and energy was devoted to local government in Shropshire where he was a JP, alderman of the county council (1951–74), and HM lieutenant of the county (1951–69). In peace, as in war, he proved himself a first-class administrator of absolute integrity. To the end of his life he remained courteous, incisive, and co-operative with a lucid style and a prodigious memory. Forty years after the traumatic events of May 1940 he could still captivate audiences with his total recall of his part in decisions which had affected Britain's survival in the war. Bridgeman died from lung cancer on 17 November 1982 at his home, Leigh Manor, Minsterley, Shropshire. He was succeeded as third viscount by his nephew.   BRIAN BOND

Sources WW · WWW · *The Times* (18 Nov 1982) · J. R. Colville, *Men of valour: Field Marshal Lord Gort VC* (1972) · *Chief of staff: the diaries of Lieutenant-General Sir Henry Pownall*, ed. B. Bond, 1 (1972) · S. P. Mackenzie, *The home guard* (1995) · private information (2004) · personal knowledge (2004) · War Office papers, PRO · Viscount Bridgeman [R. C. Bridgeman], 'The home guard', *Journal of the Royal United Service Institution*, 87 (1942), 140–49 · Burke, *Peerage* (1939) · GEC, *Peerage* · b. cert. · m. cert. · d. cert.
Archives King's Lond., Liddell Hart C., military papers · Shrops. RRC, corresp. | King's Lond., Liddell Hart C., corresp. with Sir B.H. Liddell Hart | SOUND IWM SA, oral history interview
Likenesses Lafayette, photograph, 1930, NPG [*see illus.*] · E. Kennington, pastels, *c*.1943, priv. coll.
Wealth at death £455,244: probate, 13 April 1983, *CGPLA Eng. & Wales*

Bridgeman [*née* Weld-Forester], **Selina Louisa**, **countess of Bradford** (1819–1894), correspondent of Benjamin Disraeli, was the seventh and youngest child of Cecil, first Baron Forester (1767–1828), MP and landowner, and his wife, *née* Lady Katherine Manners (1779–1829), second daughter of the fourth duke of Rutland. On 10 April 1844 she married Orlando George Charles Bridgeman, Viscount Newport (1819–1898), sporting peer and Conservative MP for South Shropshire, 1842–65. Benjamin Disraeli

Selina Louisa Bridgeman, countess of Bradford (1819–1894), by Edward Clifford, 1876

described him in 1843 as 'very agreeable, a shrewd, tall, fair, unaffected, very young man' (*Disraeli Letters*, 4.1307); he succeeded his father as third earl of Bradford in 1865, living at Weston Park, Weston under Lizard, in Staffordshire. They had four children, two sons and two daughters.

Selina Bradford was a leader of society, 'not cultured in the usual sense, but with much mother-wit, a *grande dame*, yet a fine lady too' (Paget, 1.127). She first met Disraeli in the 1840s. 'Somehow [Disraeli] is a man I cannot respect', she wrote in 1849 (Bradford, 308). Not until nearly a quarter of a century later did they become intimate. In July 1873, at a dinner party given by Lady Augusta Sturt, Selina Bradford captivated the 68-year-old Conservative leader, whose elderly wife had died a few months earlier. Disraeli was soon besotted, beginning an epistolary romance not only with Selina Bradford but also with her sister Anne *Stanhope, countess of Chesterfield. Within a few weeks 'Dear Lady Bradford' had become 'Dearest Lady Bradford'; such was his ardour that in September, staying at Weston, he broke the habit of a lifetime and rode to hounds (not a successful venture), and by November he was writing her passionate love letters. In 1874 when Disraeli became prime minister, he appointed Bradford master of the horse. 'Selina', he wrote, 'will ride in Royal Carriages, head the line even in an entree and gallop over all Her Majesty's lieges' (*Letters … to Lady Bradford*, 1.54). As prime minister, his life revolved to an astonishing extent around the need to write to Selina or the chance of seeing her; he was plunged into deepest gloom by her silences and elated by a meeting. 'I live for Power and the affections', he declared,

and he observed somewhat wistfully that 'there is no greater misfortune than to have a heart that will not grow old' (*Letters … to Lady Bradford*, 1.57, 73). In May 1875 he proposed to Anne Chesterfield, who was a widow and available, in order to be closer to Selina, who was neither (wisely Anne Chesterfield refused). The thousand or so letters that Disraeli wrote to Selina Bradford leave no doubt as to the depth of his affection for her, though he perhaps used letter-writing as a vehicle for the fantasy which was so necessary to his existence. Selina Bradford, however, was outwardly cold and detached. None of her letters has survived, but Disraeli complained that her cold demeanour belied her letters, and hints survive that she reciprocated his feelings. 'Have confidence in me, believe in me, believe that I am true—oh, how true', she wrote on one occasion (Bradford, 309), and she was evidently nervous lest her letters be seen by her family, which may explain why, unlike Disraeli's, they were destroyed. Selina Bradford died at Weston Park on 25 November 1894, after a lengthy illness. She was buried in Weston under Lizard.

JANE RIDLEY

Sources *Letters of Disraeli to Lady Bradford and Lady Chesterfield*, ed. marquis of Zetland, 2 vols. (1929) · S. Bradford, *Disraeli* (1982) · *Benjamin Disraeli letters*, ed. J. A. W. Gunn and others (1982–), vol. 4 · W. Paget, *In my tower*, 2 vols. (1924) · GEC, *Peerage*
Archives Staffs. RO
Likenesses E. Clifford, portrait, 1876, Weston Park, Shropshire [*see illus.*] · Cruikshank, engraving (after miniature by Thorburn), NPG · F. Grant, engraving (after oil painting by F. Grant), NPG · engraving (after E. Clifford, 1876), NPG
Wealth at death £12,850 12s. 7d.: probate, 6 March 1895, *CGPLA Eng. & Wales*

Bridgeman, William (1645/6–1699), government official, was born in Amsterdam as the only son of Richard Bridgeman (b. 1621) of Combs Hall, Suffolk, himself the eighth son of John *Bridgeman, bishop of Chester (bap. 1577, d. 1652). At the time of William's birth his father was a merchant and agent for the East India Company in Amsterdam. His mother was Catherine, daughter of William Watson, a fellow merchant of Amsterdam. The foreign-born Bridgeman was naturalized in 1657. Bridgeman was educated at Westminster School in 1656 and on 17 December 1662, aged sixteen, he matriculated at Queen's College, Oxford. In 1674 Bridgeman married Diana Vernatti (1653–1707) who was of Italian origin and whose father, Peter Vernatti, was to be briefly caught up in the Popish Plot in 1678. According to John Evelyn, who knew the couple intimately, among her other talents Diana had an 'extraordinary skill and dexterity' at the guitar (Evelyn, 4.360). William and Diana had three children: Orlando (1680–1731), MP for Ipswich in 1713, who as the only male heir of William Bridgeman inherited his property at Combs in Suffolk in 1699; William (b. 1684), who died in infancy; and Catherine (d. 1742).

Bridgeman's official life as an administrator in the later Stuart government began in 1667 when he entered the office of the secretary of state, Lord Arlington. His post as personal secretary to Arlington, in succession to William Godolphin, appears to have been the result of the patronage of his uncle Sir Orlando *Bridgeman (1609–1674), then lord keeper. In office William proved an able and capable subordinate, although noted on occasion as being rather too keen to stand upon his dignity. His friend John Evelyn claimed that Bridgeman was a 'very industrious and usefull man' and 'a very ingenious person' (Evelyn, 5.325; 4.197). In 1674 Bridgeman transferred his services to Sir Joseph Williamson and in 1679 he became under-secretary to Robert Spencer, second earl of Sunderland.

In the popular mind at least, Bridgeman was most closely associated with Sunderland. It was the rise of Sunderland which confirmed Bridgeman in the role of a professional civil servant of some note. Sunderland, as had Arlington, disliked routine administration and was content to leave this to Bridgeman, who was described in the 1690s as an 'indefatigable secretary-to-all-turns' ('A French conquest', 10.490). Although the term under-secretary was not in much use at that time, it aptly describes Bridgeman's functions and he appears to have learned much from his service in the expanding and increasingly professional secretariat. As a result of his close association with Sunderland, Bridgeman's career suffered in 1680 when he was removed from office during the Exclusion crisis with the fall of his patron. Sunderland's return to power in 1683 saw Bridgeman once again reappointed as under-secretary in January 1683, seeming to confirm his status as Sunderland's client.

In the reign of James II Bridgeman proved more active on the public scene. A clerk-extraordinary of the privy council in 1676–85, he was appointed a clerk of the privy council from 1685 to December 1688 (and again in 1693 until his death). He had in any case been busily acquiring social and business positions in the usual outlets for a person of his social rank. He was a justice of the peace for Middlesex (1677–89), for Westminster (1678–89), and for both counties from 1689 to his death. He acquired his residences in Pall Mall and at Combs Hall in Suffolk and he was elected a fellow of the Royal Society on 18 December 1680. He was master of the Clothworkers' Company in 1686–7. He was also to become chairman of the Charitable Adventure in 1699. Politically, Bridgeman was active for the court as a member of parliament for Bramber in 1685 in the only parliament of James's reign. In 1688 he assisted Sunderland by preparing the lists of court candidates for the abortive second parliament of that year. On 17 November 1688 he was called upon to witness the will of James II, and from November to December 1688 he briefly served Charles, second earl of Middleton, again as under-secretary.

After the revolution of 1688 Bridgeman was singled out for questioning about his activities for the former regime, including his part in various *quo warranto* proceedings, as well as about the ecclesiastical commission on which he served as registrar from 1687 to October 1688. His interrogation by the Commons on 4 December 1689 illustrates an excellent civil servant's ability to equivocate, as well as his selective memory: he apparently saw nothing, knew nothing, and did nothing in equal measure—he even 'forgot' that Sunderland had been a member of the commission

and claimed 'I was indisposed in my health, and remember no more' (Grey, 9.339–41; *JHL*, 14.388).

As a man useful to all turns, however, Bridgeman's past was no worse than many others' at that time and it in turn was soon forgotten. Ailesbury tells the tale in his 'Memoirs' of Bridgeman's worth as an under-secretary to the earl of Shrewsbury in 1689–90, when the latter told him that 'Mr William Bridgeman … read all the letters and reported to him the material contents on which he drew what moves were requisite, and then [Shrewsbury only] set his name to them' (*Memoirs of … Ailesbury*, 1.247–8). However, although this story was true of Bridgeman's attitude to his masters in general, in that he was remarkably efficient, the appointment is not supported by any other evidence. Bridgeman was appointed as an under-secretary to Henry Sydney in December 1690. Secretary Trenchard kept him in office from March 1693 until July 1694 and because of the secretary of state's illness it seems Bridgeman did most of the work.

In August 1694 having spent over a quarter of a century in the secretariat in one form or another Bridgeman was appointed secretary to the Admiralty in order to deal with the crisis there. Bridgeman immediately brought the organizational abilities he had acquired in the secretariat to bear on a confused and somewhat dated naval administration. As the senior administrative official in the Admiralty his gift for restructuring the business of the office enabled him to supervise what one naval historian of the period has called the greatest advance in naval administration since Pepys's work there in the 1680s (Ehrman, 559). The new classification of office business and records was the result of Bridgeman's efforts and William III 'believing him very fitt for the employment' gave him his favour, doubtless appreciating Bridgeman's efficiency in the face of an increasingly difficult war (BL, Add. MS 37992, fol. 56). Using administrative methods carried over from the secretary of state's office the work of the office was divided and subdivided, records were regularly kept, staffing was reorganized, and a system of administration established.

While Bridgeman had administrative ability, in reality he had little knowledge of naval matters. Despite his innovations the actual burden of office proved too heavy for one man. The 'continuall round of Business', as well as the claims of Admiral Russell for his particular client, Josiah Burchett, brought in Burchett to hold the office of secretary jointly with Bridgeman from September 1694 (BL, Lansdowne MS 1152B (II), fol. 266). For some time Bridgeman remained the senior man in the partnership and it was not until the autumn of 1695 that Burchett began to take his share of the work there. Thereafter Bridgeman's increasing ill health in the last two years of the war and his frequent absences from the office began to shift the balance of power and after the peace of Rijswick in 1697 he virtually ceased to act as secretary. He left the post in June 1698 and in the following year he died on 10 May.

Bridgeman's exceptional capacity for hard work within the later Stuart administration marks him out as a notable figure in the administrative revolution of the later seventeenth century. He became one of the first of the professional 'civil servants', establishing routines and administrative precedents, particularly in the Admiralty, which were to last well into the eighteenth century and even beyond.   ALAN MARSHALL

Sources E. R. O. Bridgeman and C. G. O. Bridgeman, eds., 'History of the manor and parish of Weston-under-Lizard in the county of Stafford', *Collections for a history of Staffordshire*, William Salt Archaeological Society, new ser., 2 (1899), 236–8 · J. Ehrman, *The navy in the war of William III, 1689–1697* (1953), 558–9 · J. P. Kenyon, *Robert Spencer, earl of Sunderland, 1641–1702* (1958) · Evelyn, *Diary* · 'A French conquest neither desirable or practicable', *A collection of scarce and valuable tracts … Lord Somers*, ed. W. Scott, 2nd edn, 10 (1813) · F. M. G. Evans, *The principal secretary of state: a survey of the office from 1558 to 1680* (1923) · W. D. Christie, ed., *Letters addressed from London to Sir Joseph Williamson*, 2 vols., CS, new ser., 8–9 (1874) · A. Marshall, 'Sir Joseph Williamson and the conduct of administration in Restoration England', *Historical Research*, 69 (1996), 18–41 · J. C. Sainty, ed., *Officials of the secretaries of state, 1660–1782* (1973) · A. Grey, ed., *Debates of the House of Commons, from the year 1667 to the year 1694*, new edn, 9 (1769), 339–41 · JHL, 14 (1685–91), 388 · Foster, *Alum. Oxon.* · *Memoirs of Thomas, earl of Ailesbury*, ed. W. E. Buckley, 2 vols., Roxburghe Club, 122 (1890) · BL, Add. MS 37992, fol. 56 · BL, Lansdowne MS 1152B (II), fol. 266 · HoP, *Commons, 1660–90* · J. C. Sainty, ed., *Admiralty officials, 1660–1870* (1975)
Archives BL, Lansdowne MS 1152, papers · PRO, SP | BL, letters to Lord Essex, Stowe MSS 202–205 · CKS, letters to Alexander Stanhope · Hunt. L., letters to Sir Cloudesley Shovell

Bridgeman, William Clive, first Viscount Bridgeman (1864–1935), politician, was born on 31 December 1864 at 89 Harley Street, London, the only surviving child of the Revd John Robert Orlando Bridgeman (1831–1897), third son of the second earl of Bradford and rector of the family living at Weston under Lizard, Staffordshire, and his wife, (Marianne) Caroline (1841–1930), only child of the Ven. William Clive, great-nephew of Lord Clive of India and archdeacon of Montgomery. He was educated at a preparatory school in Malvern, at Eton College (1877–84), where he became captain of Oppidans, and then at Trinity College, Cambridge, where he graduated as thirteenth classic in 1887. He was a lifelong Etonian: he briefly worked as an assistant master at the school, and that his sons each succeeded him there as captain of Oppidans and that he was himself elected an Eton fellow in 1929 were sources of great personal satisfaction. Another early and enduring involvement was in cricket: a member of his school and university elevens (he gained a blue in 1887), he became a considerable 'gentleman' cricketer and played for county sides (Shropshire and Staffordshire), I Zingari, and the MCC, of which he was elected a committee member and, in 1931, president.

Bridgeman established himself as a country gentleman on a Clive family estate at Leigh, near Minsterley, Shropshire, but also prepared himself for a career in politics, in which he continued his family's attachment to the Conservative Party. He was assistant private secretary to the colonial secretary, the first Viscount Knutsford, in 1889–92, and to the chancellor of the exchequer, Sir Michael Hicks Beach (later Earl St Aldwyn), in 1895–7. On 30 April 1895 he married Caroline Beatrix [see Bridgeman, Dame Caroline Beatrix (1873–1961)], elder daughter of Cecil Parker, land agent to the duke of Westminster. She was a strong force behind her husband's career, and from the 1920s had a distinguished public career of her own.

During a long search for a parliamentary seat, Bridgeman was active in London politics as chairman of the Marylebone Conservative Association and a member of the London school board from 1897 to 1904, and of London county council in 1904. After three unsuccessful contests in various constituencies, he became Conservative MP for the northern (Oswestry) division of Shropshire from 1906 to 1929.

Bridgeman's political rise remained slow, but this was not for want of commitment and significant activity. Adhering to the Disraelian tradition of social reform, to unionism, and to closer imperial unity—a belief deepened by a world tour in 1892–3—he first became prominent as an activist in Joseph Chamberlain's tariff reform campaign and as a critic of Balfour's party leadership. As an Anglican lay churchman he also participated in movements to defend church schools and to resist Welsh church disestablishment. After becoming an opposition whip in 1911 he helped organize the bitter division-lobby warfare against the peacetime Liberal government, and as a government whip in the Asquith coalition government of May 1915 he worked hard—despite his own misgivings about cabinet vacillation—to hold the Unionist parliamentary party together amid successive crises over the Dardanelles, conscription, and Ireland. During 1916 he was additionally assistant director of the war trade department. In Lloyd George's coalition governments he became parliamentary secretary successively at the newly created Ministry of Labour (December 1916–January 1919) and at the Board of Trade (January 1919–August 1920), and then the inaugural secretary of the new mines department (August 1920–October 1922). In these posts, and from membership of the archbishops' committee on industrial relations (1917–18), he acquired that contempt for strike leaders and doctrinaire socialists yet admiration for moderate, 'patriotic' trade unionists which characterized Conservative Party leaders in the mid-1920s.

Participation in the 1922 Conservative undersecretaries' revolt against the coalition leadership propelled Bridgeman to the political front rank. As home secretary in the Conservative governments, October 1922–January 1924, he achieved notoriety for refusing to reprieve Edith Thompson from execution after the Thompson–Bywaters murder case, and for deporting over 100 Irish Republican Army suspects, an action ruled illegal by the criminal court of appeal and for which he had to obtain an act of indemnity. With similar resolution, as first lord of the Admiralty, November 1924–June 1929, he upheld naval effectiveness and morale in the face of disarmament opinion and successive economy drives by the chancellor of the exchequer, Winston Churchill. He ordered resumed construction of the Singapore base and in the 'cruiser crisis' of July 1925 he successfully wielded a resignation threat to obtain the building of new warships. As leader of the British delegation at the 1927 Geneva naval disarmament conference he resisted American claims to 'parity' in cruisers, which in reality threatened a relative weakening of the British navy, even though this resulted in the failure of the conference and a marked deterioration in Anglo-American relations.

Bridgeman was of short stature, rosy-faced, and slow of speech, yet this appearance of a simple country squire was misleading. He had varied and respected political experience, exemplified by his joining the inner group of cabinet advisers during the coal dispute and general strike in 1925–6. His manifest sincerity, common sense, directness, and social ease made him widely admired in the House of Commons, a quality which persuaded the archbishops in December 1927 that he could best introduce the measure for a revised prayer book there—though on this occasion he badly miscalculated, and could not prevent the measure's defeat. Through the 1920s he was the closest cabinet friend of Stanley Baldwin and contributed to the tone of Baldwinite Conservatism, with its emphasis upon moral seriousness and social reconciliation. In May 1923 he canvassed notables for Baldwin's appointment as prime minister, in the autumn supported his adoption of protection, and in December encouraged him to remain leader after his general election defeat. He similarly supported Baldwin in adversity after the Conservative government's 1929 election defeat, and in a dramatic intervention in March 1931 helped persuade him to withdraw his resignation as party leader.

Bridgeman retired from the House of Commons at the 1929 general election. He was created a viscount in June of that year, and found new outlets for his commitment to public service. In 1930 he led a British Legion inquiry into its organization and finance. During 1932 he chaired a committee of inquiry on the Post Office, became chairman of the standing committee of the Church of England's National Society (responsible for administering church schools), and was appointed to the BBC board of governors. In March 1935 he succeeded J. H. Whitley as chairman of the BBC, but his tenure was too short to leave any mark. He was also a Shropshire JP and deputy lieutenant, a privy councillor (1920), an elder brother of Trinity House (1928), honorary LLD of Cambridge University (1930), and a long-serving chairman of the governors of Shrewsbury School. Bridgeman died at home at Leigh Manor, near Minsterley, on 14 August 1935, and was buried in the churchyard of the nearby village of Hope. The Bridgemans had three eminent sons: Robert Clive *Bridgeman, the second viscount, had a distinguished army career and became lord lieutenant of Shropshire; Geoffrey John Orlando Bridgeman (1898–1974) was a leading eye surgeon; and Sir Maurice Richard *Bridgeman was a senior civil servant and later chairman of British Petroleum.   PHILIP WILLIAMSON

Sources *The modernisation of conservative politics: the diaries and letters of William Bridgeman, 1904–1935*, ed. P. Williamson (1988) • R. C. Bridgeman, 'Life of William Bridgeman', Shrops. RRC, Bridgeman papers • *The Times* (15 Aug 1935)
Archives CAC Cam., copies of naval policy correspondence and Geneva diary, taken from the Shrewsbury collection • Shrops. RRC, corresp., diaries, and papers | Bodl. Oxf., corresp. with G. Dawson • Bodl. Oxf., corresp. with third earl of Selborne • CAC

Cam., Winston Churchill MSS • CUL, S. Baldwin MSS • HLRO, corresp. with Andrew Bonar Law • HLRO, corresp. with J. C. C. Davidson • Lpool RO, corresp. with seventeenth earl of Derby • Mitchell L., Glas., Glasgow City Archives, letters to Sir John Stirling-Maxwell • NMM, corresp. with Dame Katherine Furse • PRO, files of Ministry of Labour, Board of Trade, Home Office, Admiralty • U. Birm. L., Neville Chamberlain MSS • W. Sussex RO, L. Maxse MSS | FILM BFI NFTVA, news footage
Likenesses drawing, repro. in *ILN* (1 Aug 1925)
Wealth at death £62,913 6s. 0d.: probate, 21 Oct 1935, *CGPLA Eng. & Wales*

Bridges. *See also* Brydges.

Bridges, Charles (1794–1869), Church of England clergyman, was born on 24 March 1794 at Northampton, the fourth son of John Bridges (1756–1833), captain of an East Indiaman, and his wife, Margaretta Anna, daughter of the Revd Robert Cooke of Boxted, Essex. He was educated at Queens' College, Cambridge, and proceeded BA in 1818 and MA in 1831. He was ordained deacon in 1817 and priest in 1818. In 1823 he was presented to the vicarage of Old Newton, near Stowmarket. In 1849 he was nominated vicar of Weymouth, where he remained until failing health forced him in 1856 to withdraw to the quieter parish of Hinton Martell, Dorset. He was presented to the latter living by Lord Shaftesbury. On 25 April 1821 Bridges married Harriet Torlesse (d. 1878) at Ipswich. They had four children who survived infancy, two sons, including John Henry *Bridges, positivist and medical administrator, and two daughters. Bridges was a prominent member of the evangelical party in the church, and author of many popular devotional and theological treatises. His works included several devotional biographies, as well as tracts and books on ecclesiastical controversies. Notable among these were *An Exposition of Psalm CXIX* (1827) and *The Christian Ministry* (1830), the standard evangelical handbook on its subject of its day. Bridges died on 2 April 1869 at Hinton Martell rectory. A small selection from Bridges' correspondence was published in the year after his death under the title *Letters to a Friend*.

RONALD BAYNE, *rev.* I. T. FOSTER

Sources Venn, *Alum. Cant.* • J. Foster, *The peerage, baronetage, and knightage of the British empire for 1883*, 2 [1883] • *Christian Observer* (1869), 471–5 • *The Record* (5 April 1869) • *The Guardian* (7 April 1869) • Allibone, *Dict.* • Boase, *Mod. Eng. biog.*
Likenesses J. H. Lynch, lithograph (after S. Laurence), NPG
Wealth at death under £12,000: probate, 7 Sept 1869, *CGPLA Eng. & Wales*

Bridges, Daisy Caroline (1894–1972), nursing administrator, was born on 7 April 1894, the daughter of John Henry Bridges JP (1852–1925), and his wife, Edith Isabella Trillon (d. 1907) of Ewell, Surrey. Educated at Heathfield School, Ascot, and Cheltenham Ladies' College, she trained as a nurse at the Nightingale school, St Thomas's Hospital, London, between 1919 and 1923, after serving in the British Red Cross throughout the First World War, when she was mentioned in dispatches. On qualifying as a state registered nurse Daisy Bridges enrolled for midwifery training at the Radcliffe Infirmary, Oxford, and stayed on as a staff midwife until she returned to St Thomas's in 1925. A decade of advancement there as ward sister, office sister, home sister, and night superintendent was followed by her enrolment in 1936 for a course in hospital and nursing administration with the Florence Nightingale International Foundation, an educational body established only two years earlier. Her completion of the course in 1937 led to a Rockefeller fellowship for a year's study of nursing education in Canada and the USA. She returned in 1938, taking up a post as resident tutor with the foundation.

After the foundation's activities went into abeyance on the outbreak of the Second World War, Daisy Bridges served in France, Egypt, and India with the Queen Alexandra's Imperial Military Nursing Service, and in 1943 was awarded the Royal Red Cross for service in the Middle East. Her retirement from military nursing in 1945 with the rank of principal matron coincided with the reconstruction of the international nursing movement to which she now returned. With the kudos of her wartime distinction she served on the Ministry of Health's postwar working party on nurses' recruitment and training, and was president of the National Council of Nurses of Great Britain and Ireland in 1947–8. But she early re-established her connection with the foundation, taking responsibility in 1946 for initiating a review of its organization and functions, working in co-operation with the International Council of Nurses, which was later to incorporate the foundation.

The council had promoted nursing organizations' international co-operation since 1899. Towards the end of 1947 its headquarters was re-established in London, and Daisy Bridges, having led delegations to its early post-war meetings and to its 1947 congress, became its general secretary in 1948. Her first year's overseas travel set the pattern for her whole period of office. Visits to Austria, the Netherlands, Geneva, Paris, and Stockholm were followed by reports in 1949. By now the council was linked to UNESCO and UNICEF; the next five years included congresses in Brazil and Istanbul, agreement on an international code of nursing ethics, and exchange programmes for nurses to extend their studies abroad. There was co-operation with the WHO and with other international bodies. The late 1950s saw Daisy Bridges in Thailand, Japan, Hong Kong, and South Africa; she was taken by American military air transport to visit hospitals, health centres, and children's homes in Korea. The council's expansion under her guidance is indicated by the numbers of national nursing associations represented at its proceedings: fifty-eight by the 1960s as against twenty-one at its 1951 congress.

Daisy Bridges retired from the council in 1961. Her contribution to international nursing was acknowledged in the awards of the Coronation Medal and the Florence Nightingale Medal in 1953; full recognition came with her CBE in 1954. She became a fellow of the Royal Society of Health in 1959: an unexpected honour, according to her, as she did not see her work as directly appropriate to it. Her comment was made in a note to the Queen's Institute of District Nursing, on whose council she had served since 1951. The inclusion of district nursing as part of the National Health Service, from 1948, meant that the Queen's Institute had lost its long-standing function of co-ordinating voluntary agencies' district nursing and was forging a new role for itself. Daisy Bridges' connection with the Queen's Institute continued for at least eight years after she left the council, and was mostly concerned with enabling overseas nurses to gain experience of district nursing in Britain and with British district nurses' assistance in other countries' training courses. The scraps of correspondence that survive in the institute's records testify to a friendly, unpretentious, and co-operative practicality that accords with colleagues' reminiscences of Daisy Bridges' St Thomas's days, which were published in the *Nursing Times* when she retired from the council. Her lasting memorial, however, is her *History of the International Council of Nurses, 1899–1964*, completed in her retirement and published in 1967. She died, unmarried, in St George's Hospital, London, on 29 November 1972; *The Times*'s notice that there were to be 'no flowers, no mourning' at her funeral at St Paul's, Knightsbridge, on 4 December 1972 was fully consistent with the image of a fulfilled lifetime.   ENID FOX

Sources *Nursing Times* (28 April 1961) · *The Times* (1 Dec 1972) · *The Times* (18 Jan 1973) · D. C. Bridges, *A history of the International Council of Nurses, 1899–1964* (1967) · Wellcome L., Queen's Nursing Institute archives · *WWW* · A. Crawford and others, eds., *The Europa biographical dictionary of British women* (1983) · d. cert. · census returns for Ewell, 1891
Archives Wellcome L., Queen's Nursing Institute archives
Wealth at death £13,994: probate, 25 May 1973, *CGPLA Eng. & Wales*

Bridges, Edward Ettingdene, first Baron Bridges (1892–1969), civil servant, was born at Yattendon Manor, Berkshire, on 4 August 1892. He was the third of the three children and only son of Robert Seymour *Bridges (1844–1930), poet laureate from 1913 to 1930, and his wife, (Mary) Monica (1863–1949), daughter of the architect Alfred *Waterhouse.

Family, education, and war service Both Bridges' maternal grandparents were from long-established Quaker families; Bridges, however, grew up as a member of the Church of England. His early years in the family homes at Yattendon and later at Boars Hill, near Oxford, were greatly influenced by his family background. Although Robert Bridges qualified in medicine, and for some time practised it, he and his wife had sufficient private income to enable him to spend all his time on literature, writing poetry and essays, and compiling the Yattendon hymnal (published as *The Small Hymn-Book: the Word-Book of the Yattendon Hymnal*, 1899); the family homes were full of books. The whole family was also keen on listening to and making music; Edward Bridges played the clarinet well when young.

Bridges' early education was far from happy. In 1902, at the age of ten, he went to Horris Hill, near Newbury, but he disliked the school and did not do particularly well. He left for Eton College in 1906 without getting a scholarship. At Eton, where he was much happier, he received a

Edward Ettingdene Bridges, first Baron Bridges (1892–1969), by Walter Stoneman, 1940

records that on 21 August 1915 Second Lieutenant Bridges joined the battalion in the trenches at Hebuterne: the conditions were appalling and in the winter of 1915–16 there was 2 to 4 feet of water in the trenches. He became lieutenant in May 1916 and later was promoted to captain and adjutant. He was awarded the Military Cross in January 1917. On 2 March 1917, when serving in the front line opposite La Maisonette, Herbecourt, he was severely wounded by a bullet which shattered both bones in his right arm; he carried a fragment of the bullet in his arm for the rest of his life. He returned to England, where, in November 1917, a medical board decided that he was sufficiently fit to be assigned to clerical work for a period of not less than six months. According to John Winnifrith, the Treasury heard (because its officials had many links with Oxford) that:

> Bridges, who had established his reputation at Oxford as a man with a first-class brain and a highly ordered way of thinking and expressing his thoughts, was available and persuaded the War Office to let him come to the Department. (Winnifrith, 39–40)

Clerical duties in the Treasury were thought to be just the job for an adjutant, and Bridges consequently became a temporary administrative assistant from 11 December 1917. He soon made his mark and when the medical board in March 1918 pronounced him fit for home service the chancellor of the exchequer, as well as Treasury officials, pleaded to be allowed to keep him until he was fit for overseas service. On 29 October 1918 he was passed fit for active service again, though there is some doubt about whether he actually reached his battalion, then serving at the front line in Italy, before hostilities ceased.

Early years in the civil service After the war Bridges competed in the reconstruction competition for what were then called class I clerkships in the civil service; but before the results were known the Treasury re-employed him for just over two months from 6 November 1918, as a temporary administrative assistant. His first significant assignment was to be secretary to the committee on the remuneration of scientific and technical officers. Sir Malcolm Ramsay, the controller of establishments, wrote to the civil service commissioners that because of the special aptitude and promise he had shown during his temporary appointment, he should be permanently assigned to the Treasury as an assistant principal. As a result of his success in the competition and the request from the Treasury, his established appointment in the Treasury dated from 12 January 1919. After only eighteen months he was promoted to principal, in June 1920. In 1922 he married Katherine (Kitty) Dianthe Farrer (1896–1986), daughter of Thomas Cecil Farrer, the second Baron Farrer, the son of T. H. Farrer who had been permanent secretary to the Board of Trade. They had two sons and two daughters, and lived at Goodman's Furze, Headley, Surrey.

The next fourteen years, 'of the utmost value and significance in his later career' (Winnifrith, 40), were spent in establishment work, mainly involving the scrutiny and control of the numbers, grading, and conditions of service in government departments: from 1927 to 1934 he

grounding in the classics, but here also he was not particularly successful academically. Nevertheless, he was so influenced by his history tutor, C. H. K. Marten, who later became provost of Eton, that he decided to become a history specialist. Bridges recorded that from Marten he learned a great deal 'about how to get inside a subject, how to order his thoughts and how to set them out in an orderly convincing way' (Winnifrith, 39). Largely because of Marten's teaching, Bridges won a history demyship at Magdalen College, Oxford, where he went in 1911. There, he started to read Greats (*literae humaniores*) with the object of taking his degree in two and a half years, going on to read modern history in the next eighteen months, and then trying for a prize fellowship. He was awarded a first in Greats in July 1914 but, owing to the war, he never read history. In 1919 and 1920 Bridges took the All Souls prize fellowship examination. This led to the award of an All Souls fellowship in 1920—a prize fellowship with no prescribed duties except attending college meetings. His proposed course of study, approved by the college on 29 October 1921, was the development of English administration from 1855 to 1906. He held this fellowship simultaneously with his post in the Treasury until 1927 (and became a fellow of All Souls again from 1954). He always felt that he had a historical bent of mind and he developed this interest, in reading and writing, whenever he had the time and opportunity.

In September 1914 Bridges, as a cadet in the Officers' Training Corps, was called for service with the 4th battalion Oxfordshire and Buckinghamshire light infantry. He was on active service in France with the 145th brigade from March 1915 to March 1917. The battalion war diary was deputy establishment officer of the Treasury. From May 1933 to April 1934, however, he served in a division responsible not only for the establishments but also for the functional expenditure of the common service departments: the Post Office, Stationery Office, Office of Works, and others. He served as secretary to a number of important committees, including three royal commissions; and from 1926 he was the official side secretary to the National Whitley Council. For a time he was also attached to the estimates committee of the House of Commons. Then, for four years from 1934, when he became assistant secretary, he was primarily concerned with rearmament because he was put in charge of the division responsible for the pay and conditions of service of the three armed services. His main role in the Treasury at that time, when he was one of the 'original minds at the official level' (Peden, 23) and had responsibility for detailed supervision of defence programmes, was to contribute to advice to the chancellor on how much finance could be found for defence. This was a major responsibility of vital national importance.

This period gave Bridges valuable insights and experience of the conditions of service in government departments, but probably his most valuable insights into the problems and personalities of the civil service were gained when he was secretary to the (Tomlin) royal commission on the civil service, from 1929 to 1931. His skill in committee work was especially important in the rearmament period, when defence expenditure was being discussed in cabinet and cabinet committees, and many briefs were prepared for the chancellor of the exchequer. Bridges also sat as the Treasury representative on the committee of imperial defence. His capacity for hard work and his drafting abilities were widely recognized and he acquired, according to Winnifrith, 'a great and completely deserved reputation for the skill with which he was able to assimilate the sense of any proposition and to single out the points which the Chancellor should take' (Winnifrith, 43).

Secretary to the cabinet and the Second World War Bridges was promoted to principal assistant secretary in January 1937, and when Sir Maurice Hankey retired in 1938, Sir Warren Fisher, then head of the home civil service, recommended him for appointment as secretary to the cabinet. Neville Chamberlain approved and he began his new duties on 1 August 1938. His formal title was secretary to the cabinet and permanent secretary of the combined offices of the cabinet, committee of imperial defence, Economic Advisory Council, and minister for the co-ordination of defence. He was assisted by two deputies: Sir Rupert Howarth, who was clerk to the privy council and deputy secretary to the cabinet, and Colonel H. L. (later Lord) Ismay, secretary to the committee of imperial defence, who was promoted to the rank of major-general in 1939. Bridges was appointed at a critical time: war seemed inevitable and the machinery for government in time of war, already in draft, had to be scrutinized and brought up to date. Some of the correspondents who wrote to him when his appointment was announced recognized it as the most important post in the kingdom (or

even, as Professor George Catlin suggested, in the empire). Margery Fry, Bridges' cousin, showed particular insight into his personality and standards as well as into the nature of the position when she wrote to him: 'the mere fact of your presence in the room will make it harder for ignoble decisions to be taken' (Chapman, 9).

Bridges' personal qualities were immediately called upon in a number of ways because he was appointed to his position from outside the existing cabinet office staff, and there was considerable antipathy to changes in its procedure and organization. Bridges gave Ismay responsibility for the activities of the military side and for co-ordinating the plans and intelligence of the services and supply ministries under the chiefs of staff, and he focused his own attention on the civil and political side of the work. At the outbreak of war, the war cabinet office moved from Richmond Terrace to specially fortified rooms in Great George Street where officials slept and worked—these rooms were later made into a museum. Under Bridges the offices of the war cabinet became the centre of the war effort, manned day and night. It was a remarkably successful combination of civil and military personnel, and much of the team spirit that emerged was directly inspired by Bridges personally.

Bridges was responsible for recording the deliberations of the war cabinet and its committees; he did this in a new compact style, by taking notes and then marshalling the arguments, usually without attributing them, and finally drawing conclusions. He also briefed Winston Churchill, the prime minister, on the handling of business. It was his primary responsibility to ensure that the machinery of government was well prepared and always ready to respond to the prime minister. Consequently he acquired an immensely important position in the government machine, and was always being consulted by those making or contributing to decisions. Indeed, much of his time was spent in consultations to ensure that departments were ready with all the information necessary for decisions. At the same time Bridges was heavily involved with detailed planning for the reconstruction period after the war: he designed the organization to do this and chose the officials for it. In addition, because of his interest in history, he was determined that the war histories of the Second World War should not suffer the fate of the histories of the First World War (which were still not complete).

There were four ways in which Bridges' personal qualities enabled him to become an outstanding leader of the cabinet office. First, he demonstrated selfless energy, dedication to his work, and infectious enthusiasm. Consequently he was an inspiration and encouragement to others, and his example was an asset in keeping up morale in the cabinet office. Second, he appointed or influenced the appointment of staff to key positions: here, his experience of establishment work in the Treasury was very useful. Third, he brought together a wide variety of people—serving officers, scientists, politicians, and civil servants—and encouraged them to work together. He did this through his unrivalled knowledge of the machinery of government, his openness and honesty in the presentation of argument, his skill in the formulation of questions for discussion, and his capacity for giving himself wholeheartedly to the problems of the moment. Fourth, Bridges was always being called upon to deal with new problems and challenges such as the submarine menace, the growing information on the new German weapons (the V1s and V2s), and the post-war administration of German-occupied territory. He, with other cabinet office staff, attended both the Yalta and the Potsdam conferences, and while Bridges was in charge of the cabinet office it acquired something of an international reputation, and its practices and procedures became models for such new international organizations as the OECD, NATO, and the United Nations. Above all, Bridges was able to work well with Churchill and meet his demands—a role that was by no means easy. Churchill, in particular, appreciated Bridges' abilities and, in *Their Finest Hour*, wrote enthusiastically of the important part he had played in the war effort.

Head of the civil service When Sir Richard Hopkins retired in 1945 from his post as permanent secretary to the Treasury and head of the civil service, Churchill faced a difficulty. Bridges was the obvious person for the appointment but Churchill did not want to lose his services as secretary to the cabinet. A temporary measure was therefore agreed, whereby Bridges continued as secretary to the cabinet, with the assistance of Norman Brook (later Lord Normanbrook) as an additional secretary, but Bridges simultaneously became permanent secretary to the Treasury and head of the civil service. After the 1945 general election Clement Attlee, the new prime minister, decided that Bridges should concentrate on his Treasury position and the headship of the civil service, which he did for eleven years until his retirement in 1956. People who worked with Bridges during the war always spoke and wrote in high praise of the important contribution he then made to public service. It may, however, be argued that his post-war public service, particularly as head of the civil service—a position of potential power and enormous influence—was even more important, and his legacy in that role has proved to be of longer lasting significance.

As head of the civil service Bridges demonstrated a combination of his personal beliefs and interests, and built upon his practical experience of life. He did good works discreetly, in a style consistent with the Quaker influence from his maternal family background. He possessed an enormously strict morality which guided his own behaviour and influenced the many others who had contact with him. It was a morality embodying high ideals, and if someone had behaved badly it could be applied with a degree of ruthlessness. Winnifrith wrote that Bridges operated by example rather than precept; 'he gave few directions but all concerned knew what they had to do' (Winnifrith, 53). Sir William Armstrong, in his obituary, referred to Bridges' 'very fundamental honesty', and his confident and masterly control of difficult situations inspired great loyalty from his colleagues (Armstrong). Sir

Ian Jacob, who served under Ismay in the war cabinet secretariat, wrote to Lady Bridges on Bridges' death, 'we would all have done anything he asked of us', and Sir Walter Adams, director of the London School of Economics, wrote: 'My admiration and affection for him are akin to worship' (Chapman, 14).

Bridges' standards and beliefs were especially applied when he was engaged in defending the civil service. Often public attacks on the service were rebutted by people in authority with replies that had been personally planned and prepared by Bridges. He did not himself become a controversial public figure in this role but, without denouncing criticism with attitudes of self-righteousness, he ensured that the civil service never went undefended. Moreover, he personally contributed a great deal to what has been published on aspects of civil service work. Writing from his own experience he would patiently explain how government officials went about their work. For example, he gave important lectures which were subsequently published, including *Treasury Control* and *The Elements of any British Budget*. His most important publication was, however, his Rede lecture in 1950, *Portrait of a Profession*, which both explained and argued the case for the generalist administrator in the civil service. This lecture, more than anything else written by Bridges or others, helped fuel public debate and criticism about the nature of the British civil service that had been developed since the mid-nineteenth century. In particular, the civil service was stunningly criticized by Thomas Balogh in his essay 'The apotheosis of the dilettante' (1959). The debate continued and led in 1966 to the creation of the Fulton committee on the civil service.

After his retirement Bridges wrote the most significant book in the New Whitehall Series, a series of books which he had influenced in their approach many years earlier: *The Treasury*, published in 1964. In addition it is remarkable that, for such a private person determined to avoid public attention in any controversial sense, he could be easily persuaded to broadcast, especially on overseas services. For example, he contributed to the 'This I believe' series which, in 1953 and 1954, claimed to be 'the most listened to programme in the United States', was 'broadcast around the world daily in six languages', and also had a 9.5 million weekly circulation through syndication to newspapers. One of Bridges' most time-consuming activities as head of the civil service concerned personnel work, or establishment work as it was generally called in the civil service. He played the key role in deciding promotions to senior posts in the civil service when there was no formal selection committee to make recommendations to the highest positions. He also had clear views on such matters as training in the civil service and, in particular, on implementing the recommendations of the Assheton committee on training, which reported in 1944.

After the publication in 1954 of Sir William Clark's report on the highly controversial Crichel Down case, Bridges took the unusual step of writing to all civil servants telling them to 'read and take to heart' the comments made by the internal committee of officials which had considered the future of the civil servants implicated in the case. He quoted from the famous report of the 1928 inquiry, chaired by his predecessor Sir Warren Fisher, into the irregularities revealed by the Francs case, and ended his circular: 'It will do no harm if each of us goes over the ground himself, and makes sure there is nothing amiss' (Chapman, 305).

Bridges was probably one of the two greatest civil servants of the twentieth century. His high standards of integrity and some of the specific details of his achievements have already been mentioned, but it was through his patient and unassuming leadership that the civil service achieved in practice Warren Fisher's vision of a single service regardless of department. After his death there was a continuing debate about civil service reform—much of it critical of the traditional approach he was thought to represent. At the end of the twentieth century, however, following changes associated with the approaches of the 'new public management', especially the devolution of authority and the consequent breakup of the unified civil service, regrets were expressed for the passing of some of the values Bridges represented and for which he, on occasions, argued so strongly.

Retirement Bridges had a very active and enjoyable retirement. After he was raised to the peerage in 1957 he joined the cross benches, contributing to such debates as the one in 1963 on the Robbins report on higher education. From 1954 he was again a fellow of All Souls College, Oxford, and took an active part in deliberations about its future role. Early in 1957 he was appointed chairman of the National Institute for Research into Nuclear Energy. From 1957 to 1968 he was chairman of the Fine Arts Commission. From 1959 to 1967 he was chairman of the British Council. He was also chairman of the committee on training in public administration for overseas countries, which reported in 1963. He became chancellor of Reading University in 1959, chairman of the Oxford Historic Buildings Fund from its inception in 1957, and a trustee of the Pilgrim Trust in 1955 and its chairman from 1965 to 1968. He was chairman for many years of the local committees for the National Trust properties near his home at Headley Heath and on Box Hill, Surrey. He was also active on behalf of the Royal Institute of Public Administration, regarding it as a great honour when he became president in 1958, and serving until 1968.

Bridges was awarded many honours and distinctions. In 1952 he was given the rare honour, for a non-scientist, of election to a fellowship of the Royal Society. He was knighted in 1939, appointed GCB in 1944 and GCVO in 1946, sworn of the privy council in 1953, raised to the peerage in 1957, and appointed knight of the Garter in 1965. He received honorary degrees from the universities of Oxford, Cambridge, London, Bristol, Leicester, Liverpool, Reading, and Hong Kong. He was elected a fellow of Eton in 1945, and an honorary fellow of Magdalen College, Oxford, in 1946, of the London School of Economics (where he was chairman of the court from 1957 to 1968), and of the Royal Institution of British Architects.

Edward Bridges died following a heart attack on the

heights of Winterfold Heath on 27 August 1969: only his wife was with him at the time—they had gone to enjoy the view over the North Downs which he loved so much. His ashes were buried under the churchyard cross at Yattendon. He was succeeded by his elder son, Thomas Edward (b. 1927).   RICHARD A. CHAPMAN

Sources R. A. Chapman, *Ethics in the British civil service* (1988) · J. Winnifrith, *Memoirs FRS*, 16 (1970), 37–56 · PRO · E. Bridges, *Portrait of a profession* (1950) · T. Balogh, 'The apotheosis of the dilettante', *The establishment*, ed. H. Thomas (1959) · G. C. Peden, *British rearmament and the treasury, 1932–1939* (1979) · R. A. Chapman and J. R. Greenaway, *The dynamics of administrative reform* (1980) · J. M. Lee, *Reviewing the machinery of government, 1942–1952* (privately printed, London, 1977) · *The Robert Hall diaries, 1947–53*, ed. A. Cairncross, 1 (1989) · A. Seldon, *Churchill's Indian summer: the conservative government, 1951–55* (1981) · *The civil service: reports of the committee, 1966–68*, 1 (1968) [Fulton Report] · W. Armstrong, 'Edward Bridges, 1892–1969', *Public Administration*, 48 (1970), 1–2 · private information (2004) [present Lord Bridges] · WWW

Archives Bodl. Oxf., MSS, corresp. relating to his father's papers | BL, letters to Albert Mansbridge, Add. MS 65253 · Bodl. Oxf., corresp. with Clement Attlee; corresp. with Lord Monckton; corresp. with third earl of Selborne · CUL, corresp. with Sir Samuel Hoare · Nuffield Oxf., Lindemann MSS, corresp. with Lord Cherwell · PRO, Cabinet MSS, corresp. and MSS, CAB 127/259–81, 326–327; CAB 134, T215, T273

Likenesses W. Stoneman, photograph, 1940, NPG [*see illus.*] · A. Gwynne-Jones, oils, 1962, U. Reading

Wealth at death £90,427: English probate resealed in Hong Kong, 10 April 1970, *CGPLA Eng. & Wales* (1969)

Bridges, John (1535/6–1618), bishop of Oxford, is said to have been born in London, but cousinship claimed with the Raleghs, and the early patronage of Francis Russell, second earl of Bedford, suggest he came from Devon. At Michaelmas 1554 he matriculated pensioner of Peterhouse, Cambridge, migrating in 1556 to Pembroke as fellow. In 1557 he graduated BA, being placed first in seniority. He then spent three or four years in Italy supported by Bedford, and subsequently translated three books of Machiavelli's discourses from Italian. He decided not to publish them after hearing the author denounced in a Paul's Cross sermon. In 1560 he proceeded MA at Cambridge and on 24 November was ordained deacon by Bishop Richard Cox in Ely Cathedral. One of this name was collated to the rectory of Paglesham, Essex, on 7 September 1562. It was certainly the future bishop who on 21 December 1562 was collated by Archbishop Parker to the vicarage of Herne, Kent, which he resigned by 5 September 1590.

In 1563 Bridges delivered an oration to welcome the queen to Pembroke, and about this time was at court, where he was helped by Bedford in overcoming his 'bashfull nature and slacknesse of speach towarde [his] superiors' (Bridges, *Sacro-sanctum Novum Testamentum*, sig. a. 2). By grace of 2 July 1564 he proceeded BTh. On 13 August 1565 he was collated by Bishop Horne to a canonry in Winchester Cathedral, to which he was installed on 19 August. On 10 May 1566 he was collated to the rectory of Brightwell, Berkshire, which was also in the bishop of Winchester's gift, and in the same year acquired the Hampshire rectory of Bishop's Waltham. On 3 June 1571 he preached at Paul's Cross a racy denunciation of popery and a defence of the central protestant doctrine of justification by faith, subsequently printed with a dedication to Sir William Cecil as chancellor of Cambridge University (STC 3736). In 1572 he became vicar of Cheriton, Hampshire, and also published a translation of the homilies on the Acts of the Apostles by the Zürich reformer Rudolph Gwalther and dedicated it to Bedford (STC 25013). In the following year he published his own *Supremacie of Christian Princes* (STC 3737), a reply to the Catholic writers Thomas Stapleton and Nicholas Sander. He proceeded DTh at Cambridge by grace of 3 June 1575.

On 13 December 1577 the queen nominated Bridges dean of Salisbury; he was elected on 3 January 1578 and installed by proxy the following day. On 21 February he was admitted to the formality of residence by virtue of the annexed prebend of Heytesbury. He lived at Salisbury for the next quarter of a century, and must have been married by or soon after his arrival there. In 1581 John Aylmer, bishop of London, named him among divines who might prepare a refutation of the Jesuit Edmund Campion's *Ten Reasons*. In the following April he was one of those whom the privy council suggested for a conference with the Romanists. In 1584 he preached against the puritan manifesto *A Briefe and Plaine Declaration*, also known as the *Learned Discourse*, written some years earlier by William Fulke and now published by Robert Waldegrave. Bridges' counter-arguments, first articulated at Paul's Cross, were developed into the massive defence of the established church which he published three years later. Meanwhile he had other concerns. In March 1585 he petitioned the privy council to be exempted from a charge of £12 10s. levied on his Winchester canonry to furnish half a mounted lancer. He claimed that he had already been assessed for three such persons out of his deanery, from which £140 of his £210 annual income went in tax. His total income from all benefices was not above £320, of which more than half (£166) was taken from him. More particularly, for the Christmas quarter he had paid £45 and would receive £47, leaving only 40s. to 'entertayn' above 1000 poor householders and generally maintain hospitality in his own household (PRO, SP 12/187, no. 56). Whether the council was impressed by any of this is not recorded.

Bridges' chief service to the nation was not, however, to be measured in halves of lancers or mince pies by the thousand, but in the 1400 pages of his *Defence of the Government Established in the Church of England* (1587; STC 3734), in which he set out to answer the presbyterian opponents of the religious settlement, and in particular the *Learned Discourse* and Theodore Beza's *Judgement of a most Learned Man from beyond the Seas* as published in translation c.1580. Archbishop Whitgift saw the book in proof, and commended it as unanswerable, though contemporary critics doubted whether the archbishop had truly thought its publication worthwhile. Bridges took issue with the presbyterian claim that their case was grounded in scripture— 'when we come to seeke for the words, wee can never find them' (Bridges, *Defence*, 1289). He also questioned the usefulness of the primitive church as a model for the present, suggesting it was not as pure as his opponents supposed.

Nevertheless he tried to be sympathetic, calling his opponents brothers, and acknowledging Calvin to be an excellent man though not a binding authority. While never claiming it was the only model for a reformed church, he set out the scriptural basis for episcopacy, and emphasized the distinction between *ordo* and *officio* to refute the argument for ministry by congregational election. But, fatally, he invited his adversaries to document their allegations of negligence and bribery in the Elizabethan hierarchy, a challenge that has been identified as the spur to the Marprelate controversy. Before that, however, there came two learned replies: Dudley Fenner's *Defence of the Godlie Ministers* (1587), confining its attention to Bridges' preface, and *A Defence of the Ecclesiasticall Discipline* (1588), probably the work of Walter Travers, and a thoroughgoing restatement of Thomas Cartwright's original presbyterian formulation. The length and ponderous style of Bridges' work were consistently criticized as much as its content. He had followed the common but dangerous academic practice of rehearsing his opponents' arguments verbatim in order to refute them; they cheerfully welcomed this additional publicity, while begging him to 'leave perverting of playne sentences, and to reason pithelie and syllogisticallie out of Gods worde' (Fenner, 150).

In the scurrilous pamphleteering that followed, the sharp wit of his opponents found a soft target in the dean of Salisbury. The first two tracts from the Marprelate press were headed *Oh Read Over D. John Bridges for it is a Worthy Worke* (1588; STC 17453–4). Bridges was lambasted as a neo-papist, a traitor, a non-resident, a card player, and a swearer of oaths, a Cambridge clown with the brains of a woodcock. Even the price of his book (7s.) was ridiculed. While all this was deliberately offensive, it was also amusing and at least partially accurate (Bridges was clearly a shameless pluralist). Allusions to his unfulfilled hopes of a bishopric may well have been accurate. But the debate touched rock-bottom when John Penry opined that Bridges 'hath wallowed him selfe all his life in Romuli fece' (McGinn, 73). The dean did not respond to his critics, and later commentators on the Marprelate controversy have shown him little sympathy. In 1908 William Pierce could make fun of his 'long wearisome periods and his mazy style' (Pierce, 143), and Scott Pearson in 1925 contrasted the 'clear and pointed exposition' of the *Learned Discourse* with Bridges' 'diffuse and wearisome tome' (Pearson, 273).

Meanwhile an ugly relationship was developing at Salisbury between Bridges and the cathedral organist, the elder John Farrant, who in 1572 had married Bridges' niece Margaret Andras. She had frequently complained to her uncle about the 'unbecoming manner' in which her husband treated her. Bridges eventually rebuked Farrant in front of the assembled chapter, and Farrant, regarding this as unwarranted public interference in his domestic affairs, spoke abusively of the dean. Matters came to a head during evensong on 5 February 1592, when Farrant left the cathedral during the Magnificat and confronted the dean in his study, drawing a knife on him and threatening to cut his throat. A scuffle followed, in which the dean's gown was torn, but further violence was avoided when a chorister whom Farrant had brought with him contrived a diversion. Bridges was then able to lock himself in his bedroom. Farrant returned to the cathedral in time to take part in the anthem, but had understandably absconded when the chapter sent for him a few days later. He duly lost his position.

Despite having been so literally at the sharp end of a matrimonial dispute, Bridges was undeterred and made what must have been his second marriage on 30 October following at Mitcham, Surrey, to Jane Davey. On 6 March 1593 he was admitted to Gray's Inn. In 1598 he received the vicarage of Broughton, Hampshire. He had long been the queen's chaplain—in 1599 he described himself as her 'ancientest' (*Salisbury MSS*, 9.143)—and on 19 May he was reappointed by James I. Nevertheless he is not known to have preached at court in either reign. His opponents had smugly noted that the *Defence* had not brought him a bishopric, and it may well be that he was 'not the type of man to carry out the policy of Elizabeth and Whitgift' (Pierce, 140n.). Promotion eventually came on 21 December 1603 when James nominated him to the bishopric of Oxford. He was elected on 4 January 1604 and on 12 February he was consecrated at Lambeth by Whitgift, the bishops of London, Rochester, Durham, and Chichester assisting. He was now sixty-eight, the oldest of James's bishops on appointment, and his elevation must have been more a personal honour than an indication of royal policy. The see of Oxford was ill-endowed, vacant since 1592 and poorly served before that. Bridges was allowed to keep his vicarage of Cheriton and (until 1611) his Winchester canonry *in commendam*.

Unlike most of his few predecessors Bridges did reside in his diocese, and was active in procuring terriers of parishes; otherwise he left business to his chancellor. There are no extant visitation articles or injunctions from his episcopate, the impact of which seems to have been minimal. His successor's efforts to foster the rite of confirmation suggest that Bridges rarely administered it. His scholarly work, however, continued. Since at least 1599 he had been busy with a rendering of the gospels into Latin hexameters; this he published in 1604, with a dedication to the king, as *Sacro-sanctum Novum Testamentum ... translatum* (STC 3735). That year he attended the Hampton Court conference. On 30 August 1605, during the king's visit to Oxford, he was made MA there, although he could more properly have been incorporated DTh. On 13 May 1610 he once more preached at Paul's Cross. In the parliament of 1614 Bridges supported the bill for Sabbath observance, proposing one additional clause forbidding all commerce and another against the 'great abuse' prevalent in London of arresting men on their way to and from church (*Hastings MSS*, 4.279). As with all else in that parliament, no legislation resulted. Bridges' final years were inactive. In 1615 Archbishop Abbot unkindly commented that his brother of Oxford was 'old and knewe not what hee said or did' (PRO, SP 14/80, no. 113, p. 122). Bridges died

at the bishop's residence of Marsh Baldon, Oxfordshire, on 26 March 1618, and was buried there. He had a son William (*c*.1579–1624) whom he appointed archdeacon of Oxford in 1614. In the absence of a will, little can otherwise be said of the bishop's family.　　　　　C. S. KNIGHTON

Sources Venn, *Alum. Cant.*, 1.215 · J. Venn, ed., *Grace book Δ* (1910), 117, 141, 177, 283 · T. A. Walker, *A biographical register of Peterhouse men*, 1 (1927), 179 · Foster, *Alum. Oxon., 1500–1714*, 1.181 · *Fasti Angl., 1541–1857*, [Canterbury], 93 · *Fasti Angl., 1541–1857*, [Salisbury], 6, 96 · *Fasti Angl., 1541–1857*, [Bristol], 75, 84 · PRO, state papers domestic, Elizabeth I, SP 12/187, no. 56 [*CSP domestic, 1581–90*, 31] · PRO, state papers domestic, James I, SP 14/80, no. 113 [repr. in *Camden miscellany, XXIX*, p. 339] · D. H. Robertson, *Sarum Close: a history of the life and education of the cathedral choristers for 700 years* (1938), 147, 149–53 · K. Fincham, *Prelate as pastor: the episcopate of James I* (1990), 10, 19–20, 54, 62, 126, 188 n. 59, 305, 310 · M. MacLure, *Register of sermons preached at Paul's Cross, 1534–1642*, rev. J. C. Boswell and P. Pauls (1989), 51–2, 64, 95 · *Report on the manuscripts of the late Reginald Rawdon Hastings*, 4 vols., HMC, 78 (1928–47), vol. 4, pp. 279, 284 · *Calendar of the manuscripts of the most hon. the marquis of Salisbury*, 24 vols., HMC, 9 (1883–1976), vol. 9, pp. 143–4; vol. 15, p. 224 · A. F. Scott Pearson, *Thomas Cartwright and Elizabethan puritanism* (1925), 272–3, 279, 281 · D. J. McGinn, *John Penry and the Marprelate controversy* (1966), 42–7, 70, 73, 121 · W. Pierce, *An historical introduction to the Marprelate tracts* (1908), 139–44 · D. Fenner, *A defence of the godlie ministers, against the slaunders of D. Bridges* (1587) · 'John Howson's answer to Archbishop Abbot's accusations at his "trial" before James I', ed. N. W. S. Cranfield and K. Fincham, *Camden miscellany, XXIX*, CS, 4th ser., 34 (1987), esp. 339 · *Parochial collections made by Anthony à Wood and Richard Rawlinson*, ed. F. N. Davis, 1, Oxfordshire RS, 2 (1920), 15 · J. Bridges, *A defence of the government established in the Church of England for ecclesiasticall matters* (1587) · J. Bridges, *Sacro-sanctum Novum Testamentum in hexametros versos translatum* (1604)

Archives Oxon. RO, register as bishop of Oxford, MS Oxf. dioc. papers c. 264

Bridges, John (*bap.* 1666, *d.* 1724), county historian, was baptized at Binfield, Berkshire, on 24 June 1666. He was the eldest of the twelve children of John Bridges (1642–1712), squire of Barton Seagrave in Northamptonshire, and his wife, Elizabeth (1642–1712), daughter of William Trumbull. After two years at Trinity College, Oxford (1683–4), which he left without taking a degree, he was admitted to the Middle Temple on 23 April 1684; he was called to the bar on 22 May 1691. He moved to Lincoln's Inn in 1716, and became a bencher in 1719; his address there was 6 New Square.

On 8 August 1695 Bridges was appointed agent and solicitor to the customs. There can be little doubt that he got the job through the influence of his uncle the tory politician Sir William Trumbull, who had been made secretary of state on 3 May of that year. From 11 January 1712 he was a commissioner of customs and from 24 November 1714 to 24 November 1715 receiver-general of excise. He inherited the Barton Seagrave estate on the death of his father and so from 1713 had both a London and a Northamptonshire house. The Barton estate brought in £460 per annum, enough to make him financially independent and able to resign from a position which his surviving letters to his uncle show he was finding increasingly onerous.

John Bridges (*bap.* **1666**, *d.* **1724**), by George Vertue, 1726 (after Sir Godfrey Kneller, 1706)

During his period as a government official Bridges achieved an established place for himself in the intellectual life of the capital and was personally acquainted with most of the leading people of learning of his day. On 7 April 1708 he was elected a fellow of the Royal Society; in 1712 and 1715 he was voted on to the council. In common with many contemporary figures, he was well known as a collector of fine books, and possessed a large library containing works relating mainly to the history and antiquities of Great Britain. It was the formation of this collection which brought him into contact with the Oxford antiquary Thomas Hearne, whose *Diary* affords glimpses of Bridges' generally affable nature and bookish interests. It is in this source that there is the first indication of his intention in the summer of 1718 to engage in serious research into the history of Northamptonshire.

Bridges was no innovator in the writing of county history. The general plan of his *History*, with its division of the county into hundreds and parishes, and his emphasis on the descent of estates from the medieval period, indicates an intention to model the work on Sir William Dugdale's *Antiquities of Warwickshire* (1656), but ideas derived from more recent antiquaries can also be discerned. What distinguished Bridges from others in the field was his willingness to set up and pay for a team of research assistants of very high quality and his ability to assemble in six years almost the whole of the material required for an acceptable county history.

Bridges employed a series of copyists, notably William Slyford, to work through Northamptonshire material in public repositories and private collections. He made use of William Taylor, a local schoolmaster, to copy monumental inscriptions and to compile basic topographical information on a parochial basis, using a systematic questionnaire derived from one devised by Browne Willis. He employed the Flemish artist Peter Tillemans to produce topographical drawings; these were to have been engraved by Andrew Motte, mathematician and translator of Sir Isaac Newton's *Mathematical Principles of Natural Philosophy*. He used Thomas Eayre (1691–1758), bellfounder of Kettering, to make an up-to-date county map to accompany the *History*, as well as maps of the main towns of Northamptonshire. He engaged in extensive correspondence with other learned people in Northamptonshire, mainly members of the clergy, and spent the summer months of the years 1718–22 in touring the county, often accompanied by Slyford, making topographical notes.

The project attracted considerable attention and was widely applauded by contemporaries. On 24 June 1718 Bridges was elected a fellow of the reconstituted Society of Antiquaries of London, and he became a vice-president in 1723 and 1724; he was a frequent exhibitor of antiquities at meetings. But before the *History* could be completed, he died, on 16 March 1724 at Lincoln's Inn. His health had been poor and his correspondence is full of references to colds, the ague, the colic, and gout, but Hearne's *Diary* shows that the real cause of Bridges' death was syphilis. He was buried at Barton Seagrave on 25 March.

Bridges never married and under the terms of his will his property was divided among his brothers; the library was sold. The materials collected for the *History* were to be kept by the eldest, William, with the intention that they would eventually be made over to someone considered fit to bring the project to a conclusion. They consisted of some forty-nine volumes and portfolios of notes and transcripts together with the accumulated drawings and plans made by Tillemans and others. Bridges had prepared indexes to these materials and was in the process of ordering the information they contained parish by parish, according to a standardized scheme, noting omissions, clear evidence that work had begun on the preparatory phases of writing the *History*.

It was not until 1735 that the project was revived, but difficulties with money and in securing a suitable editor meant that the complete *History and Antiquities of Northamptonshire* did not appear until 1791, under the editorship of Peter Whalley. Although Whalley did not use all the material Bridges had accumulated, it is clear that a great deal of what Bridges actually wrote in his manuscript notes is incorporated in the final edition, which at the end of the twentieth century was still the only complete county history of Northamptonshire to have been published.   A. E. BROWN

Sources A. Brown and G. Foard, *The making of a county history: John Bridges' Northamptonshire* (1994) · *Remarks and collections of Thomas Hearne*, ed. C. E. Doble and others, 11 vols., OHS, 2, 7, 13, 34, 42–3, 48, 50, 65, 67, 72 (1885–1921), vols. 4–10 · *Northamptonshire Notes and Queries*, 1 (1886), 110–12 · monumental inscription, Barton Seagrave church, Northamptonshire · B. A. Bailey, ed., *Northamptonshire in the early eighteenth century: the drawings of Peter Tillemans and others*, Northamptonshire RS, 39 (1996)
Archives BL, Add. MS 32467 · BL, Northamptonshire collection, Add. MSS 32118–32122, 32467 · Bodl. Oxf., Northamptonshire collection | BL, corresp. with Sir William Trumbull · Bodl. Oxf., letters to Thomas Hearne
Likenesses G. Vertue, line engraving, 1726 (after G. Kneller, 1706), BM, NPG [*see illus.*] · G. Vertue, line engraving (after G. Kneller), repro. in J. Bridges, *The history and antiquities of Northamptonshire*, ed. P. Whalley (1791), frontispiece

Bridges, John Henry (1832–1906), positivist and medical administrator, was born on 11 October 1832 at the vicarage, Old Newton, Suffolk. Slight, fair-haired, and fine-featured, he was the third of five children of the Revd Charles *Bridges (1794–1869), a well-known evangelical, and his wife, Harriet (*d.* 1878), daughter of the Revd Charles Martin Torlesse and his wife, Catherine. Raised in the strictest puritan piety, he attended preparatory schools in Suffolk and entered Rugby School in August 1845; he left as head boy in 1851, steeped in the Coleridgean and Wordsworthian enthusiasms that then pervaded the school. He won a scholarship to Wadham College and at Oxford established a reputation for wide reading and independent thinking—perhaps too independent for the examiners, who gave him a third class in the final examination in *literae humaniores* in 1854, though one of them acknowledged he was 'the ablest man in' (Liveing, 57). He was president of the Oxford Union. Oriel College elected him to a fellowship in 1855 on the strength of his Arnold history prize essay on 'The Jews in Europe in the Middle Ages', which was published in *Oxford Essays* (1857).

At Wadham, Bridges made lifelong friends with two other undergraduates, E. S. Beesly and Frederic Harrison, who were to become, with their college tutor Richard Congreve, the nucleus of the positivist movement in Britain. After Congreve openly avowed himself a disciple of Auguste Comte in 1854, Bridges was the first of his students to commit himself, subscribing to the Positivist Society in Paris in 1856 and attending Comte's funeral in 1857. In accordance with Comte's prescription that aspirants to the positive priesthood study medicine, Bridges trained at St George's Hospital, London, 1856–9, graduated BMed at Oxford in 1859, and was admitted member of the Royal College of Physicians in 1860. While in training he lodged with John Chapman, editor of the *Westminster Review*, at whose house he mixed with such leaders of British intellectual radicalism as G. H. Lewes, George Eliot, and Herbert Spencer.

Bridges married his cousin Susan Torlesse on 7 February 1860, amid the emotional turmoil occasioned in both clerical evangelical families by his unconcealed religious heterodoxy. To escape this the couple immediately emigrated to Australia, but Bridges' wife died of typhoid fever shortly after their arrival in Melbourne. He returned,

assuaging his grief by translating Comte's *General View of Positivism* during the voyage home. He settled in Bradford, where he was appointed physician to the infirmary in 1861. His deep religiosity and altruism found new channels in serving the labouring people of northern England. During the cotton famine he joined local radicals in denouncing the inability of the poor law to cope with the massive unemployment. He conducted private sanitary surveys and lectured audiences both professional and popular on public health.

Bridges' zeal and talents were recognized by his profession, which elected him FRCP in 1867, and by the government, which appointed him factory inspector for north Yorkshire in 1869. In 1870 he was appointed a metropolitan medical inspector to the Local Government Board. He held this position until he retired in November 1892, his health seriously impaired by years of strenuous efforts to enforce his high standards of duty on the various London poor-law boards, and the schools and infirmaries under their authority. Among his particular causes were the containment of smallpox, the eradication of infant ophthalmia, and the promotion of women as poor-law guardians and nurses and teachers. These activities fell within the maternal sphere as defined by positivism. By contrast he opposed women's employment in factories or entering politics.

On 1 June 1869 Bridges married another cousin, Mary Alice Hadwen, the nineteen-year-old daughter of George Hadwen, a Halifax silk manufacturer, and his wife, Georgina. He had long been close to the Hadwens, and had given them a strong sympathy for positivism. The marriage was a breach of Comte's doctrine of perpetual widow(er)hood, however, and strained relations with Congreve, the ordained head of British positivism, who had regarded Bridges as his truest disciple. Bridges had applied in 1864 to Comte's successor, Pierre Laffitte, for the sacrament of destination. In 1865 he published his translation of the *General View of Positivism*, and in 1866 a defence of Comte in response to J. S. Mill's critique. As British public interest in Comte's ideas crested in the late 1860s, he participated in positivist propagandizing in the *Fortnightly Review*, *Commonwealth*, and *Bradford Review*, though less combatively than Beesly and less fluently than Harrison. He was active in the London Positivist Society founded by Congreve in 1867 and its Chapel Street school, but, like Beesly and Harrison, broke with Congreve in the schism of 1878 and was appointed president of the London Positivist Committee; he resigned that office to Harrison in 1880.

Bridges wrote a third of the biographical entries in the *New Calendar of Great Men*, and a hundred articles for the *Positivist Review* between 1893 and 1906, on doctrinal and scientific issues and current events. Like his fellow positivists, he was passionately anti-imperialist, pro-Irish home rule, and an ardent Francophile. He made an important contribution to fostering the new discipline of sociology, and was a founding member of the Sociological Society (1903).

Perhaps Bridges' best writing was historical, in

extended essays on French, Irish, and Chinese history. His published lectures on *France under Richelieu and Colbert* (1866) moved S. R. Gardiner to lament that a great historian was lost to the Local Government Board. Unfortunately what was intended to be his masterpiece, his edition of Roger Bacon's *Opus majus* (1897), had serious scholarly deficiencies and was withdrawn by the Clarendon Press in the face of severely critical reviews. Bridges reissued the text in 1900 with corrections but the event clouded his retirement, as did financial pressures and uncertain health. He died at 2 Woodbury Park Gardens, Tunbridge Wells, on 15 June 1906, in a mentally disturbed state after a bicycle accident; he was buried at St Barnabas, Tunbridge Wells, according to the directions of his wife, an Anglican. Offended, his positivist friends declined to attend but held their own memorial, attended by 200, at South Place in London. Bridges was remembered as somewhat shy in public, but a brilliant conversationalist. Childless, he was deeply loved by several of his nieces, on whom his learning and kindness left a deep impression, testified to by their published memoirs of him.

CHRISTOPHER A. KENT

Sources S. Liveing, *A nineteenth century teacher: John Henry Bridges, MB, FRCP* (1926) · F. H. Torlesse, *Some account of John Henry Bridges and his family* (1912) · *Recollections of John Henry Bridges, M.B.* (1908) · J. E. Mac Gee, *A crusade for humanity: the history of organized positivism in England* (1931) · C. Kent, *Brains and numbers: élitism, Comtism and democracy in mid-Victorian England* (1978) · M. S. Vogeler, *Frederic Harrison: the vocations of a positivist* (1984) · T. R. Wright, *The religion of humanity: the impact of Comtean positivism on Victorian Britain* (1986) · R. Harrison, *Before the socialists: studies in labour and politics, 1861–1881* (1965) · *CGPLA Eng. & Wales* (1906) · *DNB*
Archives BL, corresp. with R. Congreve, Add. MSS 45227–45228 · BLPES, corresp. with Frederic Harrison · Maison d'Auguste Comte, Paris, letters to Pierre Laffitte, Charles Jeannolle, and others · UCL, E. S. Beesly MSS
Likenesses F. Yates, oils, 1904, RCP Lond.
Wealth at death £5153 2s. 11d.: probate, 13 July 1906, *CGPLA Eng. & Wales*

Bridges, (Stephen) Lucas (1874–1949). *See under* Bridges, Thomas (c.1842–1898).

Bridges, (Mary) Monica (1863–1949). *See under* Bridges, Robert Seymour (1844–1930).

Bridges, Noah (*fl.* 1643–1662), stenographer and mathematician, was educated at Balliol College, Oxford, and acted as clerk of the parliament which sat in that city in 1643 and 1644. He was created bachelor of civil law on 17 June 1646, 'being at that time esteemed a most faithful subject to his majesty' (Wood, 94). He was in attendance on Charles I during most of his imprisonment, particularly at Newcastle and the Isle of Wight. The king granted Bridges the office of clerk of the House of Commons, but the appointment failed to pass the great seal because of the surrender of Oxford. It appears that the king also promised him the post of comptroller, teller, and weigher of the mint. After the Restoration he vainly endeavoured to obtain the grant of these offices with survivorship to his son Japhet. For several years he kept a school at Putney, where he was living in 1660.

Bridges was the author of two arithmetics and a text on shorthand writing and cryptography. *Vulgar Arithmetique* (1653) is unusual for its brevity and its use of the modern method of division. This was followed by *Stenographie and Cryptographie, or, The Arts of Short and Secret Writing* (1659), an extremely scarce work, dedicated to Sir Orlando Bridgeman. The address to the reader is dated 'March 18/59 the first of the four last months of 13 yeares squandered in the Valley of Fortune'. A second edition appeared in 1662. Bridges' second arithmetic, *Lux mercatoris, Arithmetick Natural and Decimal*, appeared in 1661.

THOMPSON COOPER, rev. H. K. HIGTON

Sources *CSP dom.*, 1652–3; 1660–62 · Foster, *Alum. Oxon.* · Wood, *Ath. Oxon.: Fasti* (1815) · W. T. Lowndes, *The bibliographer's manual of English literature*, ed. H. G. Bohn, [new edn], 6 vols. (1864)
Likenesses D. Loggan, engraving, 1661, repro. in N. Bridges, *Lux mercatoris* (1661) · S. Cooper, watercolour miniature, 1666, Institut Néerlandais, Paris, Fondation Custodia · W. Faithorne, line print, BM; repro. in N. Bridges, *Vulgar arithmetique* (1653)

Bridges, Robert Seymour (1844–1930), poet, was born at Walmer, Kent, on 23 October 1844, the fourth son and eighth child of John Thomas Bridges (1805–1853) and Harriett Elizabeth Affleck (1807–1897), third daughter of the Revd Sir Robert Affleck of Dalham, Suffolk.

Ancestry and early years The Bridges family had been yeoman farmers in the Isle of Thanet since the sixteenth century, but John Thomas Bridges, who inherited the property in the late 1820s, did not want to farm and moved his young family to Walmer, where in 1832 he purchased Roseland, a house with some 6 acres of land perched on a height from which it was possible to look down to the sea and Walmer Castle, one of the coastal forts built by Henry VIII and a residence of the duke of Wellington in his capacity as lord warden of the Cinque Ports. There were several military bases in the area and two of Robert's elder brothers were to enter the forces. Robert's early years were spent in a happy family with Puseyite religious belief, music, and games in the large garden or on the rolling countryside around Upper Walmer or its pebbly beach. The importance of these formative experiences is celebrated in poems such as 'The Summer-House on the Mound' and Bridges' memoir of Digby Mackworth Dolben, both of which show his ability to evoke a range of sensory impressions, remembered with astounding precision. It is this capacity to create vivid lines and images that is Bridges' main strength as a poet.

In 1853 Robert faced the first of many tragedies in his life. After a short illness his beloved father died at the early age of forty-seven. The following year his mother married the eminent churchman John Edward Nassau *Molesworth (1790–1877), vicar of Rochdale in Lancashire, sold the family property, and moved her family to Rochdale. Robert was sent to Eton College, a school which his eldest brother, John Affleck Bridges (1832–1924), had attended. He was a good but not top student and his love of music, games, and mild pranks meant that he fitted in easily. He began lifelong friendships with Lionel Muirhead, who was a fine artist, the musician Hubert Parry, and V. S. S. Coles,

Robert Seymour Bridges (1844–1930), by Frederick Hollyer, 1888

who later became principal of Pusey House in Oxford. Fascinated by language, Bridges wrote poems, exchanging criticism with his 'cousin' Digby Mackworth Dolben until, comparing his efforts with those of the great literary figures, he despaired and wrote very little for a number of years. In 1860 his brother George (b. 1836) died; he had been a lieutenant aboard the royal yacht and had married the novelist Samuel Butler's sister Harriet in 1859.

Bridges' years at Corpus Christi College, Oxford (1863–7), were a continuation of his classical education, with leisure time given to music and sport where he was a distinguished oarsman. Among the friends he made at Oxford were William Sanday (later Lady Margaret professor of divinity) and the poet Gerard Manley *Hopkins. He belonged to the ascetic, high Anglican Brotherhood of the Holy Trinity. But Oxford was entering a period of considerable change and his religious certainty was undermined by Darwinian debate and German higher criticism. The role religion was to play in his adult life was also altered in 1866 by the death of his younger brother, Edward (b. 1846), who had always had delicate health but with whom Robert had been hoping to live an informally religious life in which he would look after him. The drowning in July 1867

of Dolben, who was very devout, broke another of the religious ties of his youth.

Medical studies and practice On leaving Oxford, from which he graduated with a second class in *literae humaniores*, Bridges travelled in the Middle East, partly to test his religious beliefs. He was away from January to June 1868 and returned to find that his elder sister, Harriett Plow (1837–1869), was dying after a murderous attack in which her husband and new-born baby had been killed. Bridges, who like his elder brothers was expected to choose a career, decided on medicine. He spent eight months in Germany learning German, the language of many scientific papers at the time, and then in 1869 registered as a student at St Bartholomew's Hospital, London. The explosion in scientific knowledge of the time was transforming medical training and making it more structured and rigorous. (Bridges later described it as the age of the microscope.) He balanced his heavy medical load with leisure spent with artistic friends, among whom at this period were Samuel Butler, the publication of whose *Erewhon* (1872) he offered to help finance; Harry Ellis Wooldridge, later Slade professor of fine art; John Stainer, who became university professor of music at Oxford; and Robert Bateman, a painter on the fringes of the Pre-Raphaelite group. Bridges joined the Savile Club in 1872, getting to know Edmund Gosse, Philip Rathbone, and the architect Alfred *Waterhouse (1830–1905). In 1873 he published his first volume of poems, which gives hints of the crises through which he had been passing in lyrics such as 'In my most serious thoughts o' wakeful nights' and 'In that dark time'. Most of the poems were written in 1872–3. It was a review of this volume by Andrew Lang that first made Hopkins aware that Bridges wrote verse.

Bridges failed his final medical examinations in 1873 and, unable to retake the papers immediately, spent six months in Italy with Muirhead, Wooldridge, and the Rathbones, who were collectors of art. He learned Italian and as much about Italian art as he could. He then spent July 1874 studying medicine in Dublin. Re-examined in December of that year, he obtained his MB and became a house physician to Dr Patrick Black at St Bartholomew's Hospital. In 1876 he published *The Growth of Love: a Poem in Twenty-Four Sonnets*, the oblique account of a love affair. The identity of the woman is unknown and he later expanded the volume, adding to its range of subjects and, unfortunately, altering its verb forms and pronouns away from current English. Early in 1876 he spent two extremely busy months working in the Hôpital de la Pitié in Paris. He saw as much French theatre as he could squeeze into his schedule, an experience which heavily influenced the plays he later wrote. It was a year in which he was elected a member of the Royal College of Physicians but also grieved over the illness and death of his youngest sister, Julia (b. 1841), who was a Sister of Mercy and who died from tuberculosis.

Bridges' next medical appointment was as a casualty physician at Bart's, an account of which he published in 1878. The physicians were placed under immense pressure, expected each morning to diagnose the ailments of

150 patients in under two hours. Bridges was exceptionally conscientious, spending significantly more time on each case. In the year he saw nearly 31,000 patients in the casualty ward. In 1878, in addition, he became outpatients' physician at the Hospital for Sick Children, Great Ormond Street, and assistant physician at the Royal Northern Hospital, Islington, giving some 50,000 consultations. The publication of his report on the casualty department of Bart's, in which he was critical of its organization for physicians and patients, probably explains his not being offered any further appointments there. He transferred his efforts to the other two hospitals, becoming full physician responsible for the training of some of the medical students at the Royal Northern. Edward Thompson, a friend in Bridges' last years, later remarked that he had never known anyone as sensitive as Bridges to others' physical suffering (Thompson, 7). Bridges also published in 1879 and 1880 two volumes of poetry which contain some of his finest lyrics, including his experiments in sprung rhythm in 'London Snow', 'The Voice of Nature', and 'On a Dead Child'.

In June 1881 Bridges developed pneumonia. He took more than a year to recover and, looked after by Muirhead, spent much of the winter in southern Italy. The long recuperation gave him time to rethink his priorities. The deaths of so many of his siblings meant that he now had a greater share of the family wealth. When his mother, to whom he was devoted, had been widowed again in 1877, he had made a home for her with him in London, and their combined income meant that he no longer needed to earn a salary. In addition, as he later recorded, he had a poor memory and was badly worried by the strain on it at a time when doctors were not yet allowed to specialize and were even expected to remember the recipes for the drugs they prescribed. Since the volumes of poetry he had published had met with an encouraging response, he resolved to give up medicine and spend his time writing.

First writings, marriage, and literary friendships In August 1882 Bridges and his mother moved to a manor house in the village of Yattendon, near Newbury, Berkshire. The next two decades were ones of great productivity. He wrote eight plays, a masque (*Prometheus the Firegiver*), a translation of Apuleius's *Eros and Psyche*, a revolutionary study of Milton's prosody, and more volumes of lyric poems. He collaborated with various musicians, including Hubert Parry and Charles Villiers Stanford, and, with Harry Ellis Wooldridge, produced *The Small Hymn-Book: the Word-Book of the Yattendon Hymnal* (1899), which was important in the reform of English hymnody and the resuscitation of Elizabethan music.

These were also years of great personal happiness. On 3 September 1884 Bridges married (Mary) Monica Waterhouse (1863–1949), the architect's elder daughter, who was some twenty years his junior. The couple had three children: Elizabeth (1887–1977), Margaret (1889–1926), and Edward Ettingdene *Bridges, first Baron Bridges (1892–1969), secretary to the cabinet. It was to be an exceptionally successful partnership with shared interests, most especially in music and calligraphy. In 1903 Monica

and Margaret contracted tuberculosis and for some years the family spent periods living near sanatoriums where the mother and daughter were institutionalized, as well as nine months in Switzerland in 1905–6. In 1907, with money left them by Alfred Waterhouse, the Bridgeses built Chilswell on Boars Hill, near Oxford.

Through Monica, Bridges came to know her cousin Roger Fry, who was the first of several prominent members of a younger generation with whom Bridges was to become acquainted. They included W. B. Yeats, Ezra Pound, Henry Newbolt, Mary Coleridge, Robert Graves, Virginia Woolf, and E. M. Forster, though, despite Bridges' friendliness, only Newbolt and Mary Coleridge seem to have been at ease with him and few publicly acknowledged his assistance or their admiration for his poetry. The friendship with another young man, W. J. Stone, the son of a former master at Eton, prompted Bridges to try writing English verse using classical quantitative metres. He translated parts of the *Aeneid* and wrote two long discursive epistles and a number of lyrics. The first of the epistles, 'Wintry Delights', and the lyric 'Johannes Milton, senex' are attractive examples of the method.

In 1909 Bridges published the first of several editions with memoirs of friends. This was *Poems by the Late Rev. Dr. Richard Watson Dixon*, whose friendship he had made through Hopkins. The second was *The Poems of Digby Mackworth Dolben* (1911). When he turned for a second time to *The Poems of Gerard Manley Hopkins* (1918)—his first attempt having been shortly after Hopkins's death in 1889— Bridges unfortunately found that his feelings were too complex for a biographical memoir and he wrote instead a critical introduction and, most unusually for a contemporary poet at the time, explanatory notes to the poems. He later composed a memoir to accompany *The Collected Papers of Henry Bradley* (1928) and an introduction to *A Selection from the Letters of Sir Walter Raleigh, 1880–1922* (1928). The memoirs were subsequently republished as *Three Friends* and are masterpieces of their kind: vivid, informative, and beautifully written. His other prose works included *Collected Essays* (10 vols., 1927–36) on a range of topics from the writing of poetry, Shakespeare, the relation of words and music, and an important study of John Keats, to shorter pieces which had been published from 1919 to 1930 in the Tracts of the Society of Pure English, an organization of which he was a founder member. These included one on English pronunciation for early use by the BBC.

The poet laureateship and *The Testament of Beauty* In 1912 Oxford University Press published Bridges' *Poetical Works, Excluding the Eight Dramas* in the Oxford Standard Poets series. He was one of only two living poets to be included in the series, and the honour was based in part on the facts that his naturalistic handling of rhythm was influencing younger writers and that the demand for his *Shorter Poems* had necessitated their reprinting four times in five years. *Poetical Works* sold 27,000 copies in its first year alone, a popularity that led to Bridges' being offered the poet laureateship a year later when Rudyard Kipling refused it. Had he known the sort of poem 'written to order' the post would entail in the First World War, he might not have accepted (and might well not have been asked). His main poetic interest in 1913 was in developing a prosody appropriate to modern subjects that was independent of traditional rhythm and rhyme but, unlike free verse, was able to play off poetic units against syntactic ones. His experiments centred on syllabics, which he developed simultaneously with and independently of the American poet Marianne Moore. The strengths and variety of which the metre is capable can be seen in *New Verse* (1925) and *The Testament of Beauty* (1929).

Bridges' contribution to the war effort included belonging to 'Godley's army', a regiment of Oxford citizens past military age. The better war poems he wrote can be found in *'October' and other Poems* and *New Verse*. He also compiled *The Spirit of Man*, a very popular anthology of poetry and prose extracts for soldiers and civilians. His son Edward was posted to the western front in the autumn of 1915 and, shortly after the Bridges' home was gutted by fire, was repatriated wounded in February 1917. Fearful of the long-term effect of what he saw as the vengeful nature of the treaty of Versailles, Bridges was a vocal advocate of the League of Nations. His political role gave him more contact with Americans than he had had previously and in 1924 he accepted an invitation from the University of Michigan to spend three months there talking to groups of students, including delivering a fascinating lecture to the medical school on his own medical experience.

In 1926 Bridges' daughter Margaret died, and he and his wife were devastated. Urged by Monica, he tinkered with a poem he had begun two years earlier. Then, after a break, he returned to it and spent the next three years writing what became *The Testament of Beauty*, the longest of his poems. It is a discursive work, setting out his understanding of man's nature, spiced with scenes and incidents from his experience and reading. When Oxford University Press published it, just in time for Bridges' eighty-fifth birthday in 1929, they were unprepared for its success. Printings could scarcely keep up with demand, and by 1946 it had sold over 70,000 copies. On 3 June 1929 Bridges was awarded the Order of Merit, which was the last of a list of distinctions that included an honorary fellowship of Corpus Christi College, Oxford, an honorary DLitt from Oxford University, honorary LLDs from St Andrews, Harvard, and Michigan universities, a fellowship of the Royal College of Physicians, and an honorary fellowship of the Royal Society of Medicine.

Bridges' health was failing, undermined by cancer and its complications. He died at his home, Chilswell, on 21 April 1930 and was buried at Yattendon. The poet Henry Newbolt, who wrote the obituary for *The Times* (22 April), spoke of his

> great stature and fine proportions, a leonine head, deep eyes, expressive lips, and a full-toned voice, made more effective by a slight hesitation in his speech. His extraordinary personal charm was, however, due to something deeper than these; it lay in the transparent sincerity with which every word and motion expressed the whole of his character, its greatness and its scarcely less memorable littlenesses. His childlike delight in his own powers and personal advantages,

his boyish love of brusque personal encounters, his naïve pleasure in the beauty of his own guests and the intellectual eminence of his own friends and relations—none would have wished these away. … Behind them was always visible the strength of a towering and many-sided nature, at once aristocratic and unconventional, virile and affectionate, fearlessly inquiring and profoundly religious.

(Mary) Monica Bridges [*née* Waterhouse] (1863–1949) was born at Barcombe Cottage, Victoria Park, Manchester, on 31 August 1863. Her early years were spent at the beautiful estate of Fox Hill, near Reading. The Waterhouses were devout and musical and Monica became a competent pianist and composer. Her mother Elizabeth, *née* Hodgkin (1834–1918), was a Quaker but joined the Church of England a few years after her marriage. She taught the children painting and handicrafts and encouraged them to share her love of poetry.

In 1878 Alfred Waterhouse bought the Yattendon estate near Newbury and built there a home for his family into which they moved in April 1881. The Waterhouses were the local squires of the village of Yattendon, building a well, equipping a reading-room and lending library, and running evening classes. In the late 1870s, when Monica first met Robert Bridges, she was no more than fifteen or sixteen.

Despite suffering a number of serious illnesses, Monica was Bridges' partner in many of his artistic projects. These ranged from music to modifications of spelling with a set of phonetic founts based on Anglo-Saxon letters, and development of typeface, especially the Fell types of the early sixteenth century which the Bridges brought back into press use by choosing them for the *Yattendon Hymnal* (1895–9). She helped Harry Ellis Wooldridge to provide Palestrinal harmonization for nearly eighty plainsong melodies used in the hymnal. She also became an expert calligrapher, publishing *A New Handwriting for Teachers* (1899), which was influential in establishing an italic hand in schools, and helping with a tract on handwriting (*S. P. E. Tract XXIII*). Bridges placed great trust in her literary judgement, not letting his work out of his hands until she had seen it. She transcribed the pages of *The Testament of Beauty* as he wrote it between 1924 and 1929 and Bridges instructed the Oxford University Press to rely on her judgement should he die before it were published. In 1927 Monica began to edit small volumes of Bridges' collected essays, partly as an experiment in his extended alphabet. After his death she guided the series to completion in 1936.

From its inception in 1919, Monica participated in meetings of the committee of the Society for Pure English, for which Bridges had written a number of his essays. She collaborated with him on some tracts under the shared pseudonym Matthew Barnes, did much of the secretarial work in the early 1920s, and on Bridges' death became a full member of the committee. Logan Pearsall Smith paid tribute to her 'enthusiastic interest' and 'clear and fine judgement'. Monica remained at Chilswell until 1943, when a bomb damaged it, and she then rented a room from a neighbour. By the time Chilswell could be repaired she was too frail to live there and moved to a rest home in south London run by the Misses Alexander. She died on 9 November 1949 and was buried with Robert Bridges at Yattendon. The family's monument there to Monica and her husband reads 'In omnibus operibus eius adjutrix'.

CATHERINE PHILLIPS

Sources C. Phillips, *Robert Bridges: a biography* (1992) · *The selected letters of Robert Bridges*, ed. D. E. Stanford, 2 vols. (1983–4) · H. Newbolt, *The Times* (22 April 1930) · *The Times* (May 1930) · *The Times* (31 July 1930) · *DNB* · E. Thompson, *Robert Bridges, 1844–1930* (1944) · d. certs. [Robert Seymour Bridges; Mary Monica Bridges] · L. P. Smith, 'Robert Bridges and the S. P. E.', *S. P. E. Tract*, 35 (1931), 481–502 · private information (2004) [Bridges family]
Archives Bodl. Oxf., MSS, corresp., and literary letters, corresp., and MSS | BL, corresp. with Samuel Butler, Sir Sidney Cockerell, Norman MacColl, E. W. Scripture, Charles Wood · BL, corresp. with George Bernard Shaw, Add. MS 50529 · BL, letters to G. K. Chesterton, Add. MS 73235 · Bodl. Oxf., corresp. with Henry Bradley; letters to A. H. Bullen; corresp. with Samuel Butler; letters to Bertram Dobell; letters to Alfred Fairbank; letters to H. A. L. Fisher; letters to Edmund Gosse; letters to J. W. MacKail; letters to Harold Minto; letters to Gilbert Murray; letters to Henry Newbolt; letters to Logan Pearsall Smith; letters to E. J. Thompson; corresp. with W. B. Yeats · Bodl. Oxf., letters to Lascelles Abercrombie; letters to A. C. Benson · CUL, letters to F. J. H. Jenkinson · Duke U., Perkins L., letters to Edmund Gosse · Harvard U., Houghton L., letters to Sir William Rothenstein · King's AC Cam., letters to E. M. Forster · King's AC Cam., letters to Roger Fry [incl. copies] · RCP Lond., letters to Sir Thomas Barlow; letters to Samuel Gee · Royal College of Music, London, letters to C. V. Stanford · Somerville College, Oxford, letters to Percy Withers · Trinity Cam., corresp. with R. C. Trevelyan · U. Reading L., letters to George Bell & Sons; letters to Sir Hubert Parry and Lord Arthur Ponsonby · Wellcome L., letters to Sir Thomas Barlow and Lady Barlow · Worcester College, Oxford, letters to C. H. O. Daniel
Likenesses F. Hollyer, sepia photogravure, 1888, NPG [*see illus.*] · C. W. Furse, oils, 1893, Eton, Marken Library; repro. in D. E. Stanford, *In the classic mode: the achievement of Robert Bridges* (1978) · W. Rothenstein, lithograph, 1897, BM, NPG · W. Strang, etching, 1898, BM, NPG; repro. in Stanford, ed., *Selected letters of Robert Bridges*, vol. 1 · W. Strang, gold-point engraving, 1898, NPG · W. Richmond, oils, 1911 · Mrs M. G. Perkins, photogravure, 1913, NPG; repro. in *Testament of beauty* (1929) · W. Rothenstein, pencil drawing, 1916, Eton · T. Spicer-Simson, incised plasticine medallion, 1922, NPG · W. Stroud, two photographs, 1923, NPG · M. Beerbohm, caricature, 1924 (*The old and young self*), AM Oxf. · O. Morrell, photograph, 1924, repro. in D. E. Stanford, *In the classic mode: the achievement of Robert Bridges* (1978) · O. Morrell, photograph, 1924, NPG · A. L. Coburn, photogravure, NPG; repro. in *Men of mark* (1913) · W. Rothenstein, drawings, repro. in *English portraits* (1897) · W. Rothenstein, drawings, repro. in *Twenty-four portraits* (1920) · W. Rothenstein, drawings, repro. in *The portrait drawings of W. Rothenstein, 1899–1925* (1926) · photograph, repro. in A. H. Miles, ed., *The poets and poetry of the century*, 8: *Robert Bridges and contemporary poets* (1893), frontispiece · photographs, priv. coll.; repro. in Phillips, *Robert Bridges*
Wealth at death £6928 10s. 6d.: probate, 26 July 1930, CGPLA Eng. & Wales

Bridges, Thomas (*b.* 1710?, *d.* in or after **1775**), playwright and novelist, was a native of Hull, in which town his father was a physician of some repute. Thomas Bridges was a wine merchant, and a partner in the banking firm of Sell, Bridges, and Blunt, which failed in Hull in 1759. In 1762 Bridges produced, under the pseudonym of Caustic Barebones, *A Travestie of Homer*, in two volumes, which achieved some popularity for its spirited versification and pointed humour. This was reprinted in 1764 and in an

enlarged form in 1767, 1770, and 1797. He also wrote *The Battle of the Genii* (1765), burlesquing, in a poem in three cantos, Milton's description in *Paradise Lost* of the fight with the rebel angels. *The Battle of the Genii* was for some time attributed to Francis Grose, the antiquary.

Bridges' only novel, *The Adventures of a Bank-Note* (2 vols., 1770), capitalized on the success of Charles Johnstones's *Chrysal, or, The Adventures of a Guinea* (1760–65), an immensely popular work which went through perhaps twenty editions by 1800. It seems likely that Bridges turned to writing this type of novel (in which an inanimate object or animal takes on the role of a 'hero') owing to its popular appeal. There are definite signs of haste in the composition of the novel as, for example, at the close of volume 1 where a Sternian-type intervention is introduced by the author in order to explain the reason for the lack of continuance of a plot line (see Tompkins, 341). Tompkins describes *The Adventures of a Bank-Note* as being a 'crude and vigorous picaresque' but also insists that Bridges should not 'be classed as a bad writer' and points to the fact that the novel was successful enough to induce the author to add two more volumes to it in 1771 (Tompkins, 20, 341). In volume 3 there is a noticeable mixing of picaresque with sensibility in the character of Mr Villiers, whose tearful outpourings accord with the sentiments of Mackenzie's hero in *The Man of Feeling* (1771) (Tompkins, 95; Bateson, *Bibliography*, 355). A decade after the novel was first published, the *Critical Review* was still inveighing against this type of fiction (December 1781).

To the stage Bridges contributed *Dido*, a comic opera in two acts with music by James Hook, which was produced at the Haymarket on 24 July 1771 and printed the same year. The comic opera concludes with Dido attempting to hang herself with her own garter but being saved by Iarbas whom she agrees to marry (*The London Stage, 1660–1800*, 8.1558). His next play, *The Dutchman*, was also produced at the Haymarket, on 21 August 1775 and thereafter on 23 and 25 August, and on 8 September (ibid., 8.1903, 1904). The play is a musical entertainment in two acts with the music written by Hook and with the addition of dance which changed with the productions (on 21 August, 'The Merry Lasses'; 23 August, 'Tambourine Dance'; 25 August, 'The Medley'). The play was printed in the same year.

JOSEPH KNIGHT, rev. GAIL BAYLIS

Sources J. M. S. Tompkins, *The popular novel in England, 1770–1800* (1932) · *Critical Review*, 52 (1781) · F. W. Bateson, *The Cambridge bibliography of English literature*, 2 (1940) · G. W. Stone, ed., *The London stage, 1660–1800*, pt 4: *1747–1776* (1962) · *N&Q*, 12th ser., 12 (1923)
Likenesses C. J. Smith, double portrait, line print (with Laurence Sterne), BM; repro. in T. F. Dibdin, *Bibliographical tour in England and Scotland* (1838)

Bridges, Thomas (*c.*1842–1898), dictionary compiler, missionary, and sheep farmer, was found abandoned, perhaps on a bridge near Bristol, aged about two and a half, and taken to an orphanage, the name of which remains unknown. He was adopted by the Revd George Pakenham Despard, master of a private school in Stapleton, Bristol, and later secretary of the Patagonian Missionary Society. The aim of the society was to establish a mission among the indigenous Yámana, or Yaghan, people of the Beagle Channel area of southern Tierra del Fuego. Earlier attempts to establish a mission had failed. In 1833 Robert Fitzroy repatriated to Tierra del Fuego the Fuegians that he had taken on his first voyage, with the intention of leaving one, Jemmy Button, in the care of Richard Matthews, who hoped to establish a mission on the island. The terrified Matthews soon re-embarked on the *Beagle*. A second attempt was made in 1850, by Allen Gardiner and six companions, who starved to death in 1851. In 1856 Despard, a close friend of Gardiner and now mission superintendent, travelled to Keppel Island, in the Falklands, taking his family with him. An attempt to establish a settlement on Tierra del Fuego in 1859 ended in the massacre of the missionaries by the Yámana. Bridges had been left behind on Keppel because of his youth. Despard, who had stayed behind to deal with administrative matters, resigned and returned to England, leaving the young Bridges temporarily in charge of the mission. With the help of the Yámana who had been settled by Despard on Keppel, Bridges set about compiling a dictionary of their language. On his arrival, in January 1863, Despard's successor, the Revd W. H. Stirling, found Bridges proficient in Yámana and studying its intricate grammar system. In that year they travelled together to Tierra del Fuego, to find that measles had killed many of the Yámana. In 1867 they founded a settlement in Ushuaia ('inner harbour to the west'), a large natural harbour on the northern shore of the Beagle Channel.

Recalled to England in the following year by the Patagonian Missionary Society (now renamed the South American Missionary Society), Bridges was ordained deacon. While lecturing in Bristol in 1869 he met and married Mary Ann Varder (1842–1922), a teacher from Harbeton, Devon, and almost immediately set sail for the Falklands. With their nine-month-old daughter they left Keppel in 1871 to settle permanently in Ushuaia. There Bridges acted as judge and peacemaker to the Yámana, whom he named Yaghan after their word for the Murray Narrows, the geographical centre of their land. In 1884, as visitors to Tierra del Fuego increased, another outbreak of disease struck Ushuaia, killing over half the native population. Bridges urged the missionary society to obtain land away from encroaching civilization for the Yaghan to settle on, but they declined on the grounds that a mission should confine itself to evangelical work. Disillusioned, and with a growing family, Bridges abandoned his missionary work and obtained a lease on land some 40 miles east of Ushuaia. In 1887 the family moved there and began rearing sheep brought over from the Falklands on a farm named Harbeton after Mary's birthplace in Devon.

Early in 1898 the *Belgica*, carrying an expedition to the South Pole, ran aground near Harbeton. On board was Dr Frederick A. Cook, the American explorer, who persuaded Bridges that he could arrange publication of his Yámana–English dictionary. Bridges had continued his work on the dictionary with enthusiasm:

> Incredible though it may appear, the language of one of the poorest tribes of men, without any literature, without poetry, song, history or science, may yet through the nature of its structure and its necessities have a list of words and a style of structure surpassing that of other tribes far above them in the arts and comforts of life. My dictionary of Yaghan has One Thousand and Eighty One pages, each averaging 30 words, which multiplied make thirty-two thousand four hundred and thirty words.   (T. Bridges, xvii)

Cook arranged to pick up the manuscript on his return from Antarctica. In the meantime Bridges sailed with a cargo of timber for sale in Buenos Aires, but fell ill in Bahía Blanca during the return journey and was transferred to the British Hospital in Buenos Aires, where he died, of stomach cancer, on 15 July 1898. He was buried in the city's Chacarita cemetery. On his return Cook carried off the manuscript, the fruit of some thirty years' work by Bridges, together with a collection of papers relating to the Yámana language. News later reached the Bridges family that the Observatoire Royal Belgique was printing the dictionary under the authorship of Cook, with a statement in small print that Thomas Bridges had been 'instrumental in collecting the words' (L. Bridges, 534).

(Stephen) Lucas Bridges (1874–1949), writer and sheep farmer, was born on 31 December 1874 at Ushuaia, the third of Thomas Bridges' six children. On hearing of Cook's appropriation of his father's work Bridges travelled to Belgium in 1910 and convinced M. Lequent, curator of the observatoire, that the order of names on the cover should be reversed, with the authorship going to Thomas Bridges 'while at the foot it was to be stated in small type that Dr. Frederick A. Cook had brought the work to the notice of the Observatoire Royal' (L. Bridges, 534). With the outbreak of the First World War, in 1914 the manuscript of the dictionary disappeared until, fifteen years later, the family received a letter from Dr Ferdinand Hestermann, professor at the University of Münster, informing them that he had the manuscript. Hestermann transcribed the dictionary into the anthropos phonetic system and in 1933 it was privately printed at Mödling, in Austria, in a limited edition of 300 copies. The Bridges family wanted the manuscript donated to the British Museum, but on the outbreak of the Second World War both Hestermann and the manuscript disappeared. At the end of the war both were rediscovered, Hestermann having hidden the manuscript in a kitchen cupboard. It was presented to the British Museum on 9 January 1946.

During its early years Harbeton farm was visited by a small party of Haush, or Manekenk. Their numbers reduced to around sixty, the Haush had been gradually forced further into the swamps and marshes of southeastern Tierra del Fuego by the Selk'nam, or Ona. In 1894 Bridges made contact with the Selk'nam, feared nomadic hunters who roamed over the steppes of northern and central Tierra del Fuego and were the last Patagonian tribe to come into contact with Europeans. The discovery of gold in 1881 and the establishment of large sheep farms over most of their territory led to conflicts in which the poorly armed Selk'nam suffered heavy loss of life. Many more died from disease and despair in the missions established by the Salesians on Dawson Island and Tierra del Fuego. Bridges befriended the survivors, who had been forced into the inhospitable mountains of southern Tierra del Fuego, learned to speak their language, and accompanied them on trips hunting guanaco (a close relative of the alpaca) and witnessed their religious ceremonies. As pressure on their hunting grounds increased the Selk'nam asked Bridges to establish a farm on the Atlantic coast where they could spend the winter safe from the sheep farmers and miners. In 1907 he obtained a lease to land on the east coast, which he named Viamonte, where he provided shelter and work for some of the Selk'nam.

Falsifying his age, Bridges joined the Royal Field Artillery in 1914 and saw action in the third battle of Ypres, at Passchendaele. While on leave in 1917 he met and married Jannette McLeod Jardine (b. 1890), with whom he had three children. After the war he leased land in an area between the Devuli and Sabi rivers from the Chartered Company of Southern Rhodesia. News of the murder of a farm manager and mounting financial losses in a joint venture brought him back to Patagonia, this time to the remote Rio Baker region of mainland Chile. After suffering several minor heart attacks Bridges retired to Buenos Aires and wrote his autobiography, *Uttermost Part of the Earth* (1948). He died in Buenos Aires, of a heart attack, on 4 April 1949; he was buried in the city's Chacarita cemetery. Harbeton and Viamonte are still owned by direct descendants of Thomas Bridges.

In 1850 there were four distinct groups of natives living in Tierra del Fuego and its adjacent archipelago, each with its own language and customs and together numbering at least 10,000. Archaeological evidence suggests that they had been there for over 10,000 years. By the beginning of the twentieth century they were down to a few hundred, and a century later only a handful of old people survived, their languages and traditions forgotten. The Bridges' efforts did not alter their fate, but Thomas's dictionary stands as a record of the Yámana language, while Lucas's autobiography records the customs and way of life of his friends the Selk'nam.   JAMES PIGGOT

Sources T. Bridges, *Yámana–English dictionary* (1933); repr. (1987) · L. Bridges, *Uttermost part of the earth* (1948); repr. (1987) · C. McEwan, L. A. Borrero, and A. Prieto, eds., *Patagonia: natural history, prehistory and ethnography at the uttermost end of the earth* (1997) · C. Darwin, *The voyage of the Beagle* (1997) · private information (2004) [N. Goodall] · 'Patagonian missionary Rev. George Despard', *Lenton Times*, 7 (1992), 16–18 · N. Hazlewood, *Savage: the life and times of Jemmy Button* (2000)
Archives BL, 'Dictionary of the Yamana or Yaghan language', Add. MSS 46177–46180 | SOUND BBC WAC, recorded talks
Likenesses photograph, repro. in Bridges, *Yámana–English dictionary*, frontispiece

Bridges, Sir (George) Tom Molesworth (1871–1939), army officer, was born on 20 August 1871 at Park Farm, Eltham, Kent, the third son of Major Thomas Walker Bridges (the elder brother of the poet laureate Robert *Bridges) and his wife, Mary Anne Philippi. After schooling at Newton Abbot College and the Royal Military Academy, Woolwich, Tom Bridges joined his father's regiment, the Royal Artillery, in 1892. After service in India and Nyasaland he saw active service with the Imperial light horse

in the Second South African War between 1899 and 1901. In this war he received the first of many war wounds. Blessed with a fine physique and iron constitution, he made a rapid recovery. He raised and commanded another irregular cavalry unit, the tribal horse, in the operations against the mullah in Somaliland between 1902 and 1904, when he was again severely wounded. For this service he was awarded the DSO.

Bridges attended the Staff College, Camberley, between 1905 and 1906, before joining the German section of the War Office military intelligence directorate in 1907. In the same year, on 14 November, he married Janet Florence Marshall (1867/8–1937), the widow of W. G. Marshall and daughter of Graham Menzies of Haliburton House, Coupar Angus, Perthshire. They had one daughter, Alvilde Lees-*Milne (1909–1994) [see under Milne, (George) James Henry Lees-]. In 1908 Bridges became chief instructor at the Cavalry School at Netheravon. Seeking more rapid advancement in the army, Bridges transferred to the 4th dragoon guards with the rank of major in 1909. His most important peacetime appointment was that of military attaché to the Low Countries and Scandinavia between 1910 and 1914. In 1912 he acted as the go-between when the chief of the Imperial General Staff, Field Marshal Sir John French, approached the Belgian general staff in an attempt to initiate joint strategic planning for Anglo-Belgian military co-operation in a future European war. Although unsuccessful in this task, the links Bridges established with the Belgian and British authorities were to influence his career when war broke out on the continent in 1914.

During the First World War, Bridges demonstrated his varied talents as both a field commander and liaison officer. On the outbreak of war he went with his regiment to France. The squadron which he commanded was the first unit of the British expeditionary force (BEF) to actively engage the Germans, at Soignes on 22 August. Bridges soon proved himself an inspiring leader of men. The incident at St Quentin on 27 August, in which he rallied two demoralized battalions with a tin whistle and drum purchased in a toy shop, has become part of the mythology of the British army's retreat from Mons. But Sir John French, commanding the BEF, soon called on Bridges' expertise in dealing with the Belgian military. When the Belgian fortress of Antwerp was besieged in early October, Bridges was flown to the city to provide intelligence on the situation there for British headquarters. Bridges remained as Sir John French's liaison officer with the Belgian army until the end of 1915. In this capacity he provided the British commander-in-chief with important intelligence of the Belgian army's operational capabilities.

In December 1915 Bridges was appointed to command the 19th division of the New Army. He was promoted to the rank of major-general in July 1916. Bridges devoted his energy to turning a mediocre division which had received a bloody baptism of fire in the September 1915 Loos offensive into an efficient and well-led fighting formation. He purged the senior officers and set about training the men to a high pitch of efficiency. Being in reserve on the opening day of the battle of the Somme the division escaped the heavy casualties sustained in that disastrous assault. Under its capable and inspirational commander it subsequently acquitted itself well in the many small consolidating attacks around La Boiselle in early July which followed the failure of the main assault.

Following America's entry into the war in April 1917 Bridges' experience in inter-allied liaison was again called upon, and he was seconded to the allied mission to the United States. He returned in time to lead his division in the battle of the Menin road ridge, being severely wounded on 20 September 1917. The loss of a leg did little to restrict Bridges' activities. He recovered quickly and, after briefly taking over the trench warfare department of his close friend Winston Churchill's Ministry of Munitions, was sent back to Washington by the prime minister, David Lloyd George, as head of a new British military mission, with the principal objective of urging the speedy dispatch of American reinforcements to the western front. Under Bridges' influence the Americans reorganized their trooping arrangements and the flow of reinforcements across the Atlantic increased threefold.

On returning to London, Bridges was appointed to head another liaison mission, to the allied armies in Salonika. After the war Bridges continued to serve as 'Head Housemaid to the Near East' (Bridges, 279), keeping the peacemakers in Paris informed of the turbulent situation in the Balkans and the Black Sea. In 1920 he was responsible for the evacuation of the British mission and the remains of General Denikin's White Army from Novorossiysk. His last active service was with the Greek forces fighting the Turks in Asia Minor.

Not being fit enough to accept a command in India, Bridges retired from the army in 1922 with the rank of lieutenant-general. After this Bridges was appointed to the governorship of South Australia, a largely ceremonial post which he held until 1927, and in which he was able to pursue his interests in sport, painting (he had studied at the Slade School of Fine Art, London), and natural history. A staunch conservative, Bridges emphasized the dangers of Bolshevism and the benefits of immigration in his public pronouncements. He was popular with former servicemen, and though he had difficulties with the Labor administrations in Australia of 1924–7, these problems were generally kept from the limelight. He was much decorated for his war and post-war service; he was mentioned in dispatches nine times, awarded numerous foreign decorations, and appointed CMG (1915), CB (1918), KCMG (1919), and KCB (1925).

Bridges devoted his final retirement to painting and writing. He published a volume of memoirs, *Alarms and Excursions*, in 1938, and, posthumously, an anthology of writings on Englishness, *Word from England*, in 1940. He died at 12 Dyke Road, Brighton, on 26 November 1939.

WILLIAM PHILPOTT

Sources T. Bridges, *Alarms and excursions: reminiscences of a soldier* (1938) · E. Wyrall, *The history of the 19th division, 1914–18* [1932] · L. Macdonald, *1914* (1987) · W. J. Philpott, *Anglo-French relations and strategy on the western front, 1914–18* (1996) · W. J. Philpott, 'The strategic ideas of Sir John French', *Journal of Strategic Studies*, 12/4 (1989), 458–78 · J. E. Edmonds, ed., *Military operations, France and Belgium*, 14 vols., History of the Great War (1922–48) · private papers of Sir John French, IWM · *WWW* · *The Times* (27 Nov 1939) · *DNB* · Burke, *Peerage* (1939) · *AusDB* · m. cert. · *CGPLA Eng. & Wales* (1942)

Archives IWM, corresp. with Sir Henry Wilson

Likenesses F. Dodd, charcoal and watercolour drawing, 1918, IWM · W. Stoneman, photograph, 1918, NPG

Wealth at death £1110 0s. 3d.: probate, 1 Oct 1942, *CGPLA Eng. & Wales*

Bridges, Sir William Throsby (1861–1915), army officer, was born on 18 February 1861, at Elm Bank Cottage, Eldon Street, Greenock, Renfrewshire, where his father, Captain William Wilson Somerset Bridges RN (1831–1889), was then stationed. Of an Essex family, Captain Bridges married Mary Hill Throsby (1837–1914), daughter of Charles Throsby, of Moss Vale, New South Wales. Their son William was educated at a school in Ryde, Isle of Wight, at the Royal Naval School, New Cross (1871–2), at Trinity College School, Port Hope, Ontario (his father having retired to Canada), and at the Royal Military College, Kingston, Ontario (1877–9). While he was at the military college his parents moved suddenly to Moss Vale, New South Wales, after a bank collapse. William left the college without completing his course, joined his parents in Australia, and became an assistant inspector of roads and bridges.

In 1885 Bridges obtained a lieutenancy in the New South Wales permanent artillery and was posted to the Middle Head forts at Sydney. He married on 10 October 1885 Edith Lilian (1862–1926), daughter of Alfred Dawson Francis, of Moruya, New South Wales; they had two sons and two daughters. He attended courses in England and by 1893 had become chief instructor at the New South Wales School of Gunnery and colonial firemaster. In 1898 and 1902 Bridges undertook delicate spying missions for the War Office in German Samoa and French New Caledonia. Bridges saw special service as a major in the Second South African War and was present at the relief of Kimberley and the battles of Paardeberg and Driefontein before succumbing to enteric fever in May 1900.

On his return to Australia Bridges joined the headquarters staff and served successively as assistant quartermaster-general (1902); chief of intelligence (1905); chief of the general staff and Australian representative on the Imperial General Staff in London (1909); founder commandant, Royal Military College, Duntroon (1910); and inspector-general of the commonwealth military forces (1914). He was promoted lieutenant-colonel in 1902, colonel in 1906, and brigadier-general in 1910, and was created CMG in 1909. A superb staff officer, Bridges was more than anyone else responsible for the structure and planning of the new post-Federation Australian army and the mobilization plans which he himself eventually executed in 1914. With characteristic thoroughness he visited military schools in America, Belgium, Britain, Canada, France, and Germany before establishing the new military college at Duntroon.

At the outbreak of war in 1914 Bridges was selected to command the 1st Australian Imperial Force (AIF) (a name he chose and which strongly reflected his sentiments), with the rank of major-general. He took the AIF to Egypt, trained it, and then commanded the 1st Australian division on the Gallipoli peninsula, where he was mortally wounded by a sniper on 15 May 1915. He died at sea, three days later, on a hospital ship. His body was taken back to Australia and interred in the grounds of the military college at Duntroon on 3 September.

Bridges was gazetted KCB on 17 May 1915, the notice appearing four days after his death. He was tall, thin, and loose-limbed, with a stoop at the shoulders which proclaimed him a student; a slow but deep thinker; so shy that he appeared to be dour and brusque in manner, a trait productive of a like nervousness in his subordinates; somewhat intolerant of opposition; a man of singularly few words; never one to seek for favours; always quietly efficient. The successful establishment of the Royal Military College, Duntroon, and the 1st AIF may be seen as his outstanding achievements.

C. V. OWEN, rev. CARL BRIDGE

Sources C. D. Coulthard-Clark, *A heritage of spirit: a biography of Major-General Sir William Throsby Bridges* (1979) · *The Times* (24 May 1915) · 'Bridges, Sir William Throsby', *AusDB*, 7.408–11 · C. D. Coulthard-Clark, 'Major-General Sir William Bridges: Australia's first commander', *The commanders*, ed. D. M. Horner (1984) · J. Mordike, *An army for a nation: a history of Australian military developments, 1880–1914* (1992) · P. Dennis and others, *The Oxford companion to Australian military history* (1995)
Archives Australian War Memorial, Canberra, MSS · IWM, Gallipoli diary · NRA, priv. coll., diaries | IWM, Lord Birdwood MSS · King's Lond., Sir Ian Hamilton MSS · NL Aus., Sir Edward Hutton MSS · NL Aus., corresp. with Viscount Novar
Likenesses F. Rodway, oils, 1919, Art Gallery of New South Wales, Sydney, Australia · photographs, Australian War Memorial, Canberra

Bridgetower, George Augustus Polgreen (1780–1860), violinist, was apparently born on 29 February 1780 (though some authorities give 11 October 1779) at Biała in Poland. He was the son of an African father, who went by the names of John Frederick or Friedrich de August Bridgetower and who was a page to Prince Esterházy, and a Polish mother, Maria or Mary Ann (d. 1807). A child prodigy, Bridgetower made his performing début, aged nine, at the Concert Spirituel in Paris on 13 April 1789. He and his father were in England during the same year, and the young violinist performed at Windsor before George III. His first London appearance took place at one of the Lenten oratorio performances at Drury Lane Theatre on 19 February 1790, when he played a concerto between the first and second parts of Handel's *Messiah*. He was attended by his father, who is reported to have been irresponsible with money, and who was known in London as 'the Abyssinian Prince'; on this occasion he was dressed in extravagant Turkish robes. It is probable that this very well-received performance attracted the attention of the prince of Wales, for on 2 June following, Bridgetower and Franz Clement, a Viennese violinist of about his own age (for whom Beethoven later wrote his violin concerto), gave a benefit concert at the Hanover Square Rooms under the prince's patronage. At this concert the two boys (with Ware and F. Attwood) played a quartet by Ignace Joseph Pleyel. The celebrated Abbé Vogler was among the audience.

Bridgetower's principal master, under the patronage of the prince, was François Hippolyte Barthélémon, though he is also said to have studied the violin under Giovanni Giornovichi and composition with Thomas Attwood and possibly with Haydn. On 15 April 1791 he played in the violin section at one of the Haydn–Salomon concerts in London, and at the Handel commemoration at Westminster Abbey in the same year he and Hummel, dressed in scarlet coats, sat on each side of Joah Bates at the organ, pulling out the stops. In 1792 he played in several of the oratorios at the King's Theatre under Thomas Linley's management (24 February to 30 March), and on 28 May he played a concerto by Viotti at a concert given by Barthélémon, at which Haydn also performed. He took part in a concert given by the prince of Wales in aid of the distressed Spitalfields weavers in 1794. On 6 November 1794 he played a concerto in the style of Viotti for a benefit in Salisbury.

Bridgetower was for a time one of the first violinists in the prince of Wales's private band at the Brighton Pavilion, but in 1802 he obtained leave to visit his mother, who lived in Dresden with another son (a cellist), and to go to the baths at Karlsbad and Teplitz. At Dresden he gave concerts on 24 July 1802 and 18 March 1803, which were so successful that, having obtained an extension of leave, he went to Vienna in April 1803. Here, on account of his stylish playing and his eminent patron, he was received with great cordiality, and was introduced by Prince Lichnowsky to Beethoven, who earlier that year had begun sketching the first two movements of what was to become the 'Kreutzer' sonata. This work was first performed at a concert given by Bridgetower at the Augarten-Halle in Vienna on 24 May 1803, Beethoven himself playing the piano part. The sonata was barely finished in time for the première, as the piano part of the first movement was only sketched, and Bridgetower was required to read the violin part of the second movement from Beethoven's manuscript. The performance and the work itself delighted the audience, which included Prince Esterházy, Count Razumovsky, and the British ambassador.

A copy of the sonata, formerly belonging to Bridgetower, contains a memorandum of an alteration he introduced in the violin part (imitating the passage work of the piano in the first movement), which so pleased Beethoven that he jumped up exclaiming, 'Noch einmal, mein lieber Bursch!' ('Once more, my dear fellow!'). There is little doubt that the sonata was originally intended to be dedicated to him, as the original manuscript includes the inscription 'Sonata mulattica composta per il mulatto Brischdauer, gran pazzo e' compositore mulattico' ('Mulatto sonata composed for the mulatto Bridgetower, great fool and mulatto composer'). But before he left Vienna he had a quarrel with Beethoven about some love affair which caused the composer to alter the inscription and dedicate the work instead to the eminent French violinist Rodolphe Kreutzer.

After his visit to Vienna, Bridgetower returned to England via Dresden. On 23 May 1805 he gave a concert under the patronage of the prince of Wales, in the New Rooms, Hanover Square (the programme also refers to an F. Bridgetower, a cellist, possibly the violinist's brother). He was elected to the Royal Society of Musicians in London on 4 October 1807, and in June 1811 he took the degree of BMus at Cambridge, where his name was entered at Trinity Hall. His exercise on the occasion was an anthem to words by F. A. Rawdon, which was performed with full orchestra and chorus at Great St Mary's Church on 30 June 1811. During this period Bridgetower taught the piano, and in 1812 published a small piano work entitled *Diatonica armonica*, which was dedicated to his pupils. He was involved in the Philharmonic Society's first season in 1813. Records show that he was married at the time of being readmitted to the society on 6 November 1819; his wife's maiden name was probably Drake. After this it becomes more difficult to determine his activities and movements. He appears to have spent much time abroad, especially in Rome and Paris, making occasional visits to Britain (1843 and 1846) before eventually settling in England. His compositions, which include songs and chamber works for strings, are secondary to the excellence and prominence he achieved as a violinist.

An account of Bridgetower's appearance given in his passport (Dresden, 27 July 1803) describes him as 'of medium height, clean shaven, swarthy complexion, dark brown hair, brown eyes, and straight, rather broad nose'. His character was described by contemporaries as melancholy and discontented. He died on 29 February 1860 in Peckham, London, and was buried at Kensal Green cemetery. W. B. SQUIRE, *rev.* DAVID J. GOLBY

Sources F. G. Edwards, 'George P. Bridgetower and the Kreutzer sonata', *MT*, 49 (1908), 302–8 · B. Matthews, 'George Polgreen Bridgetower', *Music Review*, 29 (1968), 20–26 · *The letters of Beethoven*, ed. and trans. E. Anderson (1961), 90 ff. · A. W. Thayer, *Thayer's life of Beethoven*, rev. E. Forbes, 1 (1964), 331–3 · M. Campbell, *The great violinists* (1980), 27 · G. Grove, 'Bridgetower, George (Augustus) Polgreen', *New Grove* · H. Riemann, *Opern-Handbuch: … ein notwendiges Supplement zu jedem Musiklexicon* (1887)
Likenesses H. Edridge, drawing, repro. in D. Gill, ed., *The book of the violin* (1984), 112 · H. Edridge, pencil and watercolour drawing, BM
Wealth at death under £1000: probate, 3 July 1860, Edwards, 'George P. Bridgetower'; *CGPLA Eng. & Wales*

Bridgett, Thomas Edward (1829–1899), Roman Catholic priest and historian, was born at Derby on 20 January 1829, in a house attached to the mill owned by his father, a silk manufacturer. He was the third son of the seven children of Joseph Bridgett and his wife, Mary Gregson. His father had been brought up a Baptist, while his mother's background was Unitarian. From the age of eight, Bridgett was educated at the Mill Hill School, near Hendon, which was an Independent establishment; he found Sunday worship there very dismal. In 1839, two years after his family had moved to Colney Hatch, he was sent to a school kept by a Swiss master at Worksop in Nottinghamshire and, in 1843, to Tonbridge School, where he experienced a religious awakening and was baptized on 20 March 1845. His

father died in 1846, but the family had enough money to send Bridgett to Cambridge, where he entered St John's College in October 1847. Here he was attracted in turn by the high church and broad church parties. The works of Kenelm Digby and the sermons that he heard J. H. Newman preach in London led to his conversion to Roman Catholicism. He was received into the church by Father Stanton at the Brompton Oratory, and was conditionally baptized on 12 June 1850.

Shortly afterwards Bridgett determined to enter the Redemptorist order: he began his noviciate at St Trond in Belgium, before continuing his studies at Willem in the Netherlands, where he remained for five years. He was professed in October 1851 and ordained on 4 August 1856, after which he returned to England to join the Redemptorist house of St Mary at Clapham. He remained there until May 1862, when he was appointed consultor to the Limerick House, where he was subsequently rector. Here he established a branch of the Confraternity of the Holy Family in 1868, during a successful men's mission. His later years (from 1874) were spent mainly at the Clapham house, where he was several times rector and where he wrote many of his publications. He was also rector of the St Joseph's House of Studies at Teignmouth in 1893–4. In the course of his life, he conducted some 80 missions and over 150 retreats. He died at St Mary's House, Clapham, on 17 February 1899, probably of cancer.

Bridgett's first work was *The Ritual of the New Testament* (1873), in which he explained the development of ideas which led to his conversion. He was better known, however, for his historical works, particularly his biographies of John Fisher (1888) and Thomas More (1891). Although Bridgett did not question More's sanctity, he was painstaking in his research, reading all of More's works and many manuscripts in the Public Record Office. The result was a biography which conveyed the variety of More's activities, and dealt ably with his theological writings; it has been called 'the first and best of the modern biographies' (Marius, xix). Bridgett also wrote an original study of English devotion to the Virgin Mary entitled *Our Lady's Dowry* (1875), a ponderous *History of the Holy Eucharist* (1881), and an exposé of anti-Catholic historical fallacies, *Blunders and Forgeries* (1890). His work had a tendency to become a mere compilation of facts, and he rarely ventured beyond printed primary sources, but his scrupulous revision of aspects of sixteenth-century English history establishes him as a modest disciple of John Lingard.
A. F. POLLARD, *rev.* ROSEMARY MITCHELL

Sources C. Ryder, *The life of Thomas Edward Bridgett* (1906) · R. Marius, *Thomas More: a biography* (1984) · *The Eagle*, 20 (1899), 577–84 · *The Times* (20 Feb 1899)
Likenesses photographs, repro. in Ryder, *Life of Thomas Edward Bridgett*

Bridgewater. For this title name *see* Egerton, John, first earl of Bridgewater (1579–1649); Egerton, Frances, countess of Bridgewater (1583–1636); Egerton, John, second earl of Bridgewater (1623–1686); Egerton, Elizabeth, countess of Bridgewater (1626–1663); Egerton, John, third earl of Bridgewater (1646–1701); Egerton, Francis, third duke of

Bridgewater (1736–1803); Egerton, Francis Henry, eighth earl of Bridgewater (1756–1829).

Bridgewater, John (*b. c.*1532, *d.* in or after **1596**), college head and Roman Catholic exile, is of uncertain origins. Dodd mentioned that he may have claimed to be a Welshman or may have been born in Yorkshire. The *Dictionary of National Biography* described him as having been born of a good family in Somerset. He was a student at Hart Hall, and then Brasenose College, Oxford; he graduated MA in 1556. He was ordained in the same year. Even though he was a Marian priest he must have taken the Elizabethan oath of supremacy to enter into possession of his subsequent benefices and to participate in the convocation of 1562. On 23 January 1560 he was presented by the queen to the archdeaconry of Rochester. He was admitted to the rectory of Wootton Courtney, Somerset, on 1 May 1562 and in 1563 was a prebendary of Bristol, holding the third stall. A member of convocation, he subscribed to the Thirty-Nine Articles of 1562–3. But he voted against the six articles which would have abolished all saints' days, the sign of the cross in baptism, the obligation to kneel when receiving the communion, the use of all vestments but the surplice, and the use of organs, and which would have had the minister face the congregation during the service at which he officiated. The proposal failed by one vote.

The earl of Leicester, usually seen as a supporter of the godly, whom Bridgewater served as a domestic chaplain in London, nominated him as rector of Lincoln College, Oxford, confirmed by the college on 14 April 1563. The former rector, Francis Babington, whom Leicester had nominated three years earlier, had been deprived for his adherence to the old faith. Bridgewater became master of St Katherine's Hospital near Bedminster on 28 November 1570. In 1574, however, he either resigned his benefices for conscience's sake or was deprived. He arrived at the English College at Douai with some of his students from Oxford in the same year, although the Douai diaries give the date of his arrival as 26 December 1575 and under that date describe him as 'the most famous John Bridgewater … recently of the queen's hall and enjoying many ample benefices' (*Diaries of the English College*, 99). There is no evidence to explain how he spent his exile on the continent. Wood reports rumours that late in life he became a Jesuit. Not only is there no record of his entering the Society of Jesus, but he associated with Catholic exiles such as William Gifford and Charles Paget known for their opposition to the political programme of Robert Persons. In 1596 he refused to sign a petition in favour of the English Jesuits then criticized for their governance of the English College in Rome and their treatment of the secular clergy. Nothing is known of his death.

Two works formerly attributed to Bridgewater, *Confutatio virulentae disputationis theologicae* (1589) and *Concertatio ecclesiae catholicae in Anglia adversus Calvinopapistas et puritanos* (1583), were in fact written by the English Jesuit John Gibbons. Milward believes that Bridgewater did edit the second edition of the *Concertatio* (1589)

because he realized the volume's importance for publicizing throughout Europe the suffering endured by the English Catholics. None the less there is no real evidence that he was the editor. JOHN J. LaROCCA

Sources T. F. Knox and others, eds., *The first and second diaries of the English College, Douay* (1878) · A. Wood, *The history and antiquities of the colleges and halls in the University of Oxford*, ed. J. Gutch (1786) · Gillow, *Lit. biog. hist.* · P. Hughes, *The Reformation in England*, 3 (1954) · P. Williams, 'Elizabethan Oxford: state, church and university', *Hist. U. Oxf. 3: Colleg. univ.*, 397–440 · D. M. Rogers, introduction, in [J. Gibbons and J. Fenn], *Concertatio ecclesiae catholicae in Anglia adversus Calvinopapistas et puritanos* (1970) · C. Dodd [H. Tootell], *The church history of England, from the year 1500, to the year 1688*, 3 vols. (1737–42) · *Fasti Angl.* (Hardy) · Wood, *Ath. Oxon.*, new edn · P. Milward, *Religious controversies of the Elizabethan age* (1977)

Bridgman, Charles. *See* Bridgeman, Charles (*d.* 1738).

Bridgman, Richard Whalley (**1761/2–1820**), legal writer, of whose early life little is known, was an attorney, and acted as one of the clerks of the Grocers' Company. He wrote a number of abridgements of the law. His unfinished *Thesaurus juridicus, containing the Decisions of the Several Courts of Equity, … Systematically Digested from the Revolution to 1798* (2 vols., 1799–1800) was a digest of equity cases, together with some revenue cases. *An Analytical Digested Index of the Reported Cases in the Several Courts of Equity* (2 vols., 1805) reached a third edition in 1822, under the editorship of his son, R. O. Bridgman. His *Short View of Legal Bibliography, containing some Critical Observations on the Authority of the Reporters and other Law Writers* (1807) became a widely used work of reference. A number of other works, published between 1804 and 1817, were also intended to provide an accessible synthesis of aspects of the law. Bridgman died at Bath on 16 November 1820.

C. W. SUTTON, *rev.* JONATHAN HARRIS

Sources *N&Q*, 6th ser., 11 (1885), 12–14 · *GM*, 1st ser., 90/2 (1820), 477 · Watt, *Bibl. Brit.*, 1.150 · W. Reed, *Bibliotheca nova legum Angliae, or, A complete catalogue of law books* (1809), 6–7, 304 · Holdsworth, *Eng. law*, 12.172; 13.443, 472

Bridie, James. *See* Mavor, Osborne Henry (1888–1951).

Bridlington, Robert of [Robert the Scribe] (*fl.* **1147–1160**), prior of Bridlington and theologian, was a canon regular and the fourth prior of Bridlington Priory in Yorkshire, one of the larger and wealthier English houses of Augustinian canons. He became prior about 1147, and may have resigned his office before his death, perhaps in 1159; Leland reports that he was buried in the cloister before the doors of the chapter house, his tomb bearing the inscription 'Robertus cognomento Scriba quartus prior' (a copy of the *Epitaphium Rob. prioris de Bridlington* is found in BL, Cotton MS Vespasian E. vii 16). His epithet of 'Scribe' derived from his many writings, some of which were seen by Leland in the library at Bridlington. He may, however, have sometimes been confused with his contemporary, Robert of Cricklade, prior of St Frideswide's Priory, Oxford—another Augustinian house.

Robert of Bridlington's principal works were biblical commentary and exegesis, and those attributed to him include: *Expositio in Pentateuchum*, including *Post collectam quæstionum de operibus sex dierum* (Oxford, Trinity College,

MS 70); *Super prophetas duodecim minores*, including *Teste beato Jeronimo* (Oxford, St John's College, MS 46, which has an ex-libris and belonged to the Cistercian abbey at Byland); and *Expositio in cantica canticorum* (Oxford, Balliol College, MS 19). In York Minster, MS 9, there is a copy of *Frater Robertus In cantica*, and Leland maintained that he saw a copy of Robert's commentary on the epistles of St Paul at Queens' College, Cambridge. The following works in the Bodleian Library have been ascribed to him: *Expositio super psalmos Davidis* (*sic*), including *A quibusdam fratribus diu rogatus* (Bodl. Oxf., MS Laud misc. 454, associated with 'Robertus prior' and thus possibly Robert of Cricklade); *Prophetiæ* (Bodl. Oxf., MS Bodley 623, Summary Catalogue 2157, containing at fol. 91v the inscription 'Robertus scriba doctor Bridlington'); commentaries on the Apocalypse (Bodl. Oxf., MS Bodley 864, but possibly by Robert of Cricklade, and Bodl. Oxf., MS Bodley 1636); and part of a collection of *vaticinia* (prophecies) (Bodl. Oxf., MS Arch. Selden B. 8). In the British Library are commentaries on Exodus (BL, Royal MS 3 B. iv) and on the psalter (BL, Royal MS 3 B. xi). Some of his biblical commentaries may have been commissioned by Abbot Gervase of Louth Park, the Cistercian house in Lincolnshire, which may help to explain the *Super prophetas* from Byland.

Smalley considered him a 'compiler' in a conservative theological tradition but referred to substantial extracts from the commentary on St Paul by Master Lambert of Utrecht, with quotations from Anselm of Laon, which occur in a compilation by Robert which had considerable popularity in the twelfth century, and which thus illustrates Robert's contact with the continent. The *Colloquium magistri et discipuli in regula beati Augustini de vita clericorum* has been hesitantly associated with him, but, as J. C. Dickinson remarked, its parochial nature is perhaps inconsistent with Robert's wider connections with continental Europe. This treatise, an intensely practical work noteworthy for its efforts to strike a balance between worldliness and puritanism in its recommendations for religious life, became the main exposition for observances by English Augustinian canons.   DAVID POSTLES

Sources D. Knowles, C. N. L. Brooke, and V. C. M. London, eds., *The heads of religious houses, England and Wales*, 1: *940–1216* (1972), 154 · J. Burton, *Monastic and religious orders in Britain, 1000–1300* (1994), 165, 188, 202, 208, 296–7 [esp. 202, 208] · Robert of Bridlington, *The Bridlington dialogue: an exposition of the rule of St Augustine for the life of the clergy* (1960) · J. C. Dickinson, *The origins of the Austin canons and their introduction into England* (1950), 66, 120, 189 [esp. 66] · B. Smalley, *The study of the Bible in the middle ages*, rev. edn (1984), 51, 60–61, 369 · F. Madan and H. H. E. Craster, *A summary catalogue of Western manuscripts in the Bodleian Library at Oxford*, 2/1 (1922), 155, 235, 520, 609 · A. G. Watson, ed., *Medieval libraries of Great Britain: a list of surviving books … supplement to the second edition*, Royal Historical Society Guides and Handbooks, 15 (1987) · N. R. Ker, ed., *Medieval libraries of Great Britain: a list of surviving books*, 2nd edn, Royal Historical Society Guides and Handbooks, 3 (1964), 23 · R. W. Hunt, ed., *A summary catalogue of Western manuscripts in the Bodleian Library at Oxford*, 1 (1953) · R. A. B. Mynors, *Catalogue of the manuscripts of Balliol College, Oxford* (1963), 13 · J. S. Purvis, 'The priorate of Robert the Scribe', appended to B. Smalley, 'Gilbertus Universalis, bishop of London', *Recherches de Théologie Ancienne et Médiévale*, 7 (1935), 250–51 · W. Ullmann, 'A forgotten dispute at Bridlington Priory and its canonistic setting', *Yorkshire Archaeological Journal*, 37 (1948–51), 456–73, esp. 466 · *Index of manuscripts in the British Library*, 8 (1985), 364–71 · T. Smith, *Catalogue of the manuscripts in the Cottonian Library, 1696 / Catalogus librorum manuscriptorum bibliothecae Cottonianae*, ed. C. G. C. Tite (1696); repr. (1984), 117 · M. R. James, *The western manuscripts in the library of Trinity College, Cambridge: a descriptive catalogue*, 4 vols. (1900–04), vol. 3, p. 341 [note by Gale on Robert of Bridlington] · H. O. Coxe, ed., *Catalogus codicum MSS qui in collegiis aulisque Oxoniensibus hodie adservantur*, 2 vols. (1852); facs. edn under title *Catalogue of the manuscripts in the Oxford colleges* (1972), vol. 1, p. 5 · *DNB*

Archives Balliol Oxf., MS 19 · BL, Royal MSS 3 B.iv, 3 B.xi · Bodl. Oxf., MS Arch. Selden B.8; MSS Bodley 623, 864, 1636; MS Laud misc. 454 · St John's College, Oxford, MS 46 · Trinity College, Oxford, MS 70 · York Minster, MS 9

Bridport. For this title name *see* Hood, Alexander, Viscount Bridport (1726–1814).

Bridport, Giles of (*d.* 1262), bishop of Salisbury, was a native of the town in Dorset from which he took his name. He had become archdeacon of Berkshire by 1238, and it is under this title that he is recorded at Oxford in 1252; he may also have studied at Paris. He was still archdeacon in 1253, when he was elected as dean of Wells. Following the death of William of York, in January 1256, Bridport was elected by the canons of Salisbury as their bishop, and the king made no objection to their choice. His consecration was delayed until 1257, however, because of the royal embassy to Rome he undertook in June 1256, with the abbot of Westminster and Rustand the messenger, concerning the money the pope claimed in return for the gift of the Sicilian crown: Bridport took advantage of this to obtain papal documents allowing him to keep the revenues of his former offices. The three men returned in early 1257, reaching England only with some difficulty due to the hostility of the French.

The new bishop was consecrated on 11 March 1257 by the archbishop of Canterbury and the bishops of Worcester, Norwich, and Bath. One of Bridport's first actions was to provide the lead to roof the new cathedral at Salisbury, and he ensured that this church's dedication, on 30 September 1258, was a large-scale affair, conducted in the presence of the king and queen, and many bishops. Although he was involved in the political events of the late 1250s and early 1260s—he was one of the council of twenty-four in 1258, and was chosen by the king to arbitrate between him and the barons in 1261—Bishop Bridport did not abandon his diocesan duties. He produced a set of diocesan statutes, and the unusual illustrations in a copy of the book of Revelation which he gave to Abingdon Abbey during these years, with their emphasis on the authority of the church, and more especially on the pastoral and disciplinary functions of bishops, give striking visual expression to the concerns of an English bishop active in church reform. In 1262, the year of his death, he claimed the right to act as visitor for the cathedral church; however, the canons' protests that by the constitution of St Osmund visitation of the canons belonged to the dean led him to renounce any claim to jurisdiction over them on 4 October 1262. He also demonstrated his concern for education by founding the De Vaux College, the 'domus de

Valle scholarum', in the same year. With its provision for two chaplains and twenty poor scholars, who were to study the scriptures and liberal arts under the wardenship of a cathedral canon, Bridport's foundation was the first university college in England, two years before the earliest Oxford college. Bridport died on or about 13 December 1262 and was buried in the cathedral on the south side of the choir, in a chantry he had founded in the chapel of St Mary Magdalen where his tomb remains.

PHILIPPA HOSKIN

Sources J. M. J. Fletcher, 'Bishop Giles of Bridport, 1257–62', *Wilts. Arch. and Nat. Hist. Magazine*, 46 (1932–4), 625–36 · Paris, *Chron.*, 5.57a–g · *Ann. mon.*, 36a–e · *Fasti Angl., 1066–1300*, [Lincoln] · *Fasti Angl., 1066–1300*, [Salisbury] · F. M. Powicke and C. R. Cheney, eds., *Councils and synods with other documents relating to the English church, 1205–1313*, 1 (1964), 637–50 · *VCH Wiltshire*, vol. 3 · H. Anstey, ed., *Munimenta academica*, 1, Rolls Series, 50 (1868) · S. Lewis, 'Giles de Bridport and the Abingdon apocalypse', *England in the thirteenth century* [Harlaxton 1984], ed. W. M. Ormrod (1985) · M. E. Roberts, 'The tomb of Giles de Bridport', *Salisbury Cathedral Art Bulletin*, 65 (1983)
Likenesses effigy on a monument, 1262, Salisbury Cathedral, Wiltshire

Bridson, (Douglas) Geoffrey (1910–1980), writer and radio broadcaster, was born on 21 August 1910 at Heaton Norris, near Stockport, the only child of John Douglas Bridson, a Manx shipping manager, of Stockport, and his wife, Marion (1883/4–1967), daughter of Josiah Barlow, of Rawtenstall, and his wife, Marion Bowker, *née* Ruthven. His parents soon moved to Lytham St Anne's, where he attended King Edward VII School (1920–27), matriculating brilliantly at an early age.

In 1927 Bridson and his mother went back to Manchester, already, as he later described it, 'the waning capital of a grimly autonomous Northern republic'. He soon relieved a routine office job with the Sun Insurance Company by contributing both verse and criticism to local and national publications. Bridson's poems of social protest, written during the depression while he was still under twenty-one, caught the eye of Ezra Pound, the American poet. They also brought him to the notice of E. A. F. (Archie) Harding, the talented BBC programme director in Manchester whose Marxist views had caused Sir John Reith to remove him from being a features producer in London.

Bridson began to contribute programmes for Harding and found they shared a crusading passion for the radio feature as an organ of social change. In 1935 he abandoned freelancing and joined the BBC staff. An early Bridson programme, and the BBC's first verse feature, was *The March of the '45* (1936), an account of the Jacobite rising. It was broadcast eight times in the UK, overseas on BBC transcription service, and again on Radio 4 on 27 August 1989; it has been heard by an estimated audience of 100 million around the world. His radio output was prolific: in twenty-five years over 800 documentaries, plays, and feature programmes carried the imprint of D. G. Bridson. 400 had recorded repeats. Some, such as *Aaron's Field* (1939) and *Steel* (1937), became microphone classics. On 10 November 1934 he had married Vera (1909–1963), the fabric designer daughter of Harry Richardson, an antiquarian bookseller. Twins, Hermione Cicely (*d.* 1987) and Gavin Douglas Ruthven, were born to them on 12 February 1936, but the marriage did not survive the war.

From 1939 to 1945 broadcasts to America about the British war effort occupied most of Bridson's time. He moved from Manchester to London in 1941 to become overseas features editor until 1943, when he crossed the Atlantic for the first time to act as guest producer with the New York office. Here he rapidly made friends with folk-singers such as Burl Ives and Alan Lomax, as well as Josh White and other black musicians leading the struggle against segregation. Much later he was to produce (with Langston Hughes) *The Negro in America* (1964), a series of nineteen separate shows broadcast on the Third Programme, which vividly recalled the developments of a dramatic decade.

After VE-day Bridson travelled the world widely for the BBC, including work as a guest writer and producer for the SABC in South Africa in 1947, and for the ABC in Australia and the NZBS in New Zealand in 1948. Growing up before the cautious days of pre-recorded radio, he approached the developing technology of his profession with zest. He was the first British producer to exploit the use of magnetic tape recording, with equipment captured from the Germans in Norway.

Bridson's limited experience in television was less successful but he was the natural choice for BBC television to send as its adviser—and indeed watch-dog—for the American documentary series *The Valiant Years* based on Sir Winston Churchill's memoirs. The BBC had taken an option on the American series, but was profoundly depressed by the quality of the first scripts and considered cutting its losses. Bridson helped reshape the programmes into an acceptable and moreover popular series. This assignment, due to last six months, in fact kept Bridson in New York for a year. It followed immediately upon his second marriage, on 9 April 1960, to Joyce Thirlaway Rowe (1915/16–1989), the BBC's first radio publicity officer. She was the daughter of Claude Harold Rowe, an antiques dealer in London who was a direct descendant of Nicholas Rowe, poet laureate. Her good nature tolerated the year-long separation with equanimity. Geoffrey and Joyce Bridson's Highgate home became a convivial London meeting place for poets, actors, and writers. Bridson was a short, neat man with red hair and an imperial beard; a courteous host and a witty raconteur. He loved books and collected them with discrimination. He had a well-stocked cellar and a well-stocked mind.

From 1964 to 1967 Bridson was programme editor for arts, sciences, and documentaries (sound). Much of the most distinguished writing of his career was produced for the Third Programme. Its transformation into Radio 3 made him unhappy, as did the eventual winding up of the once outstanding features department, of which he had become the assistant head. His autobiography, *Prospero and Ariel: the Rise and Fall of Radio. A Personal Recollection*

(1971), reflected this malaise. Other publications by Bridson include *Aaron's Field* (1943); *The Christmas Child*, a collection of poems for reading aloud (1950); *The Quest of Gilgamesh* (1972); and *The Filibuster: a Study of the Political Ideas of Wyndham Lewis* (1972).

After Bridson retired from the BBC in May 1969 he adapted and dramatized French and English novels, which continued to be broadcast in the domestic and external services of the BBC long after he died of leukaemia at the Royal Free Hospital in Hampstead, London, on 19 October 1980. His wife outlived him by nine years. In the memories of his contemporaries, many of Bridson's distinguished contributions to a largely ephemeral art similarly survived him.　　　　　LEONARD MIALL, *rev.*

Sources *Daily Telegraph* (22 Oct 1980) · *Daily Telegraph* (11 Aug 1981) · *The Times* (21 Oct 1980) · *The Times* (24 Oct 1980) · W. Vaughan-Thomas, funeral address, 24 Oct 1980 · *They did it first*, Radio 4 feature, 26 Oct 1981 · F. Watson, 'D. G. Bridson, 1910–1980', *Radio Writers' Newsletter* [Society of Authors] (May 1981), 19–20 · D. G. Bridson, *Prospero and Ariel: the rise and fall of radio* (1971) · m. certs. · d. cert. · personal knowledge (1986) · *CGPLA Eng. & Wales* (1981) · M. Crozier, 'The poet who joined the BBC', *The Guardian* (17 June 1960), 9 · K. Whitehead, *The Third Programme: a literary history* (1989) · private information (2004) [G. D. R. Bridson]
Archives BBC WAC, corresp. · Indiana University, Bloomington, Lilly Library, Broadcasting Archive, corresp. and papers · U. Sussex, collection, handmade volumes of photos of Western paintings, annotated | JRL, letters to Michael Schmidt | SOUND BL NSA, recording of conversation between D. G. B. and Conrad Aiken (1968), recording of *The negro in America*
Likenesses E. Levy, red chalk drawing, 1930–39, priv. coll. · M. Ayrton, pen and wash drawing, 1969, Whitworth Gallery, Manchester · M. Ayrton, pen and wash drawing, 1969, Indiana University, Bloomington, Lilly Library · M. Ayrton, portrait, 1969, U. Sussex
Wealth at death £48,638: probate, 14 Jan 1981, *CGPLA Eng. & Wales*

Bridson, Thomas Ridgway (*bap.* **1795**, *d.* **1863**), cotton bleacher, was baptized on 12 July 1795 at Horwich, Lancashire, the eldest son of Paul Bridson, merchant and banker of the Isle of Man, and his wife, Mary, daughter of Thomas Ridgway, of Wallsuches, Horwich, near Bolton. Bridson was educated at Ormskirk, presumably at the town's grammar school, after which he secured employment at Wallsuches bleachworks, then under the proprietorship of his uncles Joseph Ridgway and Thomas Ridgway (the younger). At the age of twenty-three he became a partner in the concern, which, by 1824, was trading as Thomas Ridgway & Nephew, Joseph having retired. In 1832 he left the partnership and set up on his own account, taking over Lever Bank bleachworks. This was situated on the River Irwell at Little Lever, a few miles to the south-east of Bolton, and had previously been acquired by the partnership. He also took over a bleachworks at Chorley Street, Little Bolton.

The trade boom of the mid-1830s doubtless helped Bridson's business to prosper, as did his various bleaching and dyeing patents. These included the 'elastic' finishing process, dating from about 1840, and an improved washing machine, patented in 1855. He granted licences for others to use these advances, thereby bolstering the funds

he had available for investment, though he also had to fight costly legal battles against patent infringements.

Bridson played a full part in the civic as well as the business life of Bolton. In 1840, in his capacity as borough reeve of Great Bolton, and in the company of his counterpart for the adjoining township of Little Bolton, he visited London to present Queen Victoria with an address of congratulation from Bolton's loyal inhabitants on her marriage to Prince Albert. Following Bolton's incorporation as a borough in 1842, he was elected as a member of the town council and, at its first meeting, was appointed to the watch committee. In 1845 he became a borough magistrate and two years later borough mayor. These were troubled times as Chartist agitation reached its peak, but, none the less, Bridson is credited with able management of town affairs, receiving the thanks of the home secretary and even the offer of a knighthood, which he declined. In 1849 he stood unsuccessfully as a Conservative candidate for Bolton, a trial concerning his patent rights apparently proving too great a distraction. He was not, though, a gifted speaker, preferring to express himself in writing.

Bridson also took a keen interest in education. From 1847 to 1850 he was president of Bolton's Mechanics' Institute, helping to meet its liabilities during the economic downturn in 1848. Additionally, he served on the corporation's library and museum committee.

In 1854 Bridson retired from business and moved to Southport. Here, too, he took a keen interest in community life, acting as treasurer for the dispensary and becoming involved with the Strangers' Charity or Convalescent Hospital, the Athenaeum, and the Co-operative Stores. He was also appointed as *ex officio* member of the Ormskirk board of poor-law guardians, as well as of Southport improvement commissioners, and, in 1855, a county magistrate. For many years he was associated with freemasonry, holding high office. He was married to Sarah, daughter of the Revd Henry Matthews. They had five daughters and five sons, eight of whom survived their father.

Bridson died of heart disease at his home, Mornington House, Southport, on 24 January 1863. Amid a great deal of public mourning, a measure of the esteem in which he was held, his body was taken by special train to Bolton, and then by hearse to Holy Trinity Church, Horwich, where it was interred in the family vault.

J. GEOFFREY TIMMINS

Sources A. J. Sykes, *Concerning the bleaching industry* (1925) · S. H. Higgins, *A history of bleaching* (1924) · *Bolton Chronicle* (31 Jan 1863) · *Southport Visiter* (27 Jan 1863) · *Southport Visiter* (30 Jan 1863) · E. Baines, *History, directory and gazetteer of the county palatine of Lancaster*, 1 (1824) · 6 inches to the mile ordnance survey map, 1840x49, sheet 95 · *CGPLA Eng. & Wales* (1863)
Likenesses portrait, repro. in Sykes, *Concerning the bleaching industry*, p. 63
Wealth at death under £60,000: probate, 13 March 1863, *CGPLA Eng. & Wales*

Briercliffe, John (*bap.* **1618**, *d.* **1682**), antiquary, was baptized on 29 August 1618 in Halifax, the eldest in the family of three sons and a daughter of Edmond Briercliffe (*d.*

1639), clerk to John Favour, preacher and physician, and his first wife, Hester, daughter of Michael Bentley. Edmond Briercliffe, who may have acted as locum to Favour, had been bequeathed Favour's copy of Clever's *Physicke*. This, together with Hester's inheritance of income from local estates in 1625, may have persuaded him to apprentice John to an apothecary following his education at Halifax Free Grammar School.

A convinced puritan, Briercliffe took up arms for the parliamentary side in the early 1640s, and when the royalists gained the upper hand he fled on 3 July 1643 into Lancashire. There he met his future wife, Dorothy (d. 1687), daughter of Richard Meadowcroft of Smethurst, near Bury. The date of their marriage is uncertain, but they went back to Halifax on 9 February 1644 when the royalists left, settling in a house on the main street where a son and six, possibly seven, daughters were born. Their son, John (d. 1709), also became an apothecary and married Hannah Ramsden, with whom he had a son, also John (d. 1713), and four other children. The short time between the deaths of these two Johns has led some biographers to compress the family into two generations.

Briercliffe, who held office in the town, made various collections relating to Halifax. Such interests were unusual among puritans and parliamentarians, antiquaries being generally royalist and even Roman Catholic by persuasion. His *Surveye of the Housings and Lands within the Towneshippe of Halifax* (1648) was said to be among the books belonging to the parish church which he enumerated in 1651. He was the first to compile a list of the persons beheaded on the Halifax town gibbet between 1541 and 1650 under an ancient law permitting the townspeople to execute those found guilty of serious crimes. In his *Vicaria Leodiensis* (1724) Ralph Thoresby refers to his catalogue of the vicars of Halifax and to inscriptions under their arms painted on tables in the library of that church (p. 68). Briercliffe died in Halifax on 4 December 1682, having been ill of a fever for fourteen days, and was buried on 7 December in Halifax church, where his wife too was later interred.　　　ANITA McCONNELL

Sources J. Watson, *The history and antiquities of the parish of Halifax, in Yorkshire* (1775), 454–9 · T. W. Hanson, 'John Brearcliffe, the antiquary', *Transactions of the Halifax Antiquarian Society* (1907), 213b–241b · T. W. Hanson, 'John Brearcliffe, the antiquary: the gibbet law book', *Transactions of the Halifax Antiquarian Society* (1908), 321–48

Brierley, Benjamin (1825–1896), writer, was born at The Rocks, Failsworth, near Manchester, on 26 June 1825, the son of James Brierley (b. 1795), hand-loom weaver, and his wife, Esther Whitehead (d. 1854). He learned to read from his mother and then at a village school, which he had to leave before he was six, when his parents, who were very poor, removed to the neighbouring village of Hollinwood. He developed a passion for reading, helped by the Sunday schools and night schools he attended. He was set to work as a bobbin-winder, and soon afterwards sent into a factory as a 'piecer'; the manager there lent him numbers of *The Pickwick Papers*. Later he became a hand-loom weaver, and ultimately a silk-warper.

On returning to Failsworth, when he was only fifteen, Brierley and some other youths formed a mutual improvement society, which developed into the Failsworth Mechanics' Institution. In his study of Burns, Byron, and other poets he was encouraged by an uncle, Richard Taylor, also poor but with strong intellectual tastes. Some of his earliest literary efforts appeared with the help of the poet Elijah Ridings in the *Oddfellows' Magazine* and the *Manchester Spectator*. In the latter journal in 1856 his charming series entitled A Day's Out appeared, and it was well received by the public. In the autumn of 1854 Brierley's mother died of cancer, and on 29 April 1855 he married Esther Booth (b. 1833/4) of Bowles. They had only one child, a daughter, Annie (d. 1875).

Brierley's first articles were separately published in 1857 with the original title, and in 1859 under the title *A Summer Day in Daisy Nook: a Sketch of Lancashire Life and Character*. In 1863 he abandoned silk-warping and became sub-editor of the *Oldham Times*. In the following year he spent six months in London on journalistic work. Having returned to Manchester he completed his first long story, *The Layrock of Langleyside* (1864), and with Edwin Waugh and other friends founded the Manchester Literary Club. In 1863 he produced his *Chronicles of Waverlow*, and two volumes of *Tales and Sketches of Lancastrian Life*.

In April 1869 Brierley began the publication of *Ben Brierley's Journal*, first as a monthly and afterwards as a weekly magazine. The fifth number sold 13,000 copies. He continued to edit this until December 1891, when it ceased to appear.

Although not a ready speaker, Brierley was an effective reader from his own works, and his services at public entertainments were in great demand. From his youth he had a passion for amateur theatricals, and involved friends in plays of his own composition, and once in *Othello*. This later led him to dramatize and act in several of his own stories, notably *Layrock of Langleyside* at the Manchester Theatre Royal.

In 1875 Brierley was elected a member of the Manchester city council, and served six years. In 1880 he paid a short visit to America, and in 1884 a longer one, and embodied his impressions in his *Ab-o'th'-Yate in America*. He had the misfortune in 1884 to lose a great part of his savings through the failure of a building society. A public subscription was raised for his relief, and on 16 March 1885 he was presented with £650. A few years afterwards, when his health failed, a grant of £150 from the royal bounty fund was obtained for him. A further testimonial and the sum of £356 were presented to him on 29 October 1892.

Brierley died at his home, 17 Hall Street, Moston, Manchester, on 18 January 1896, and was buried at Harpurhey cemetery. On 30 April 1898 John Cassidy's statue in his honour, raised by public subscription, was unveiled at Queen's Park, Manchester, by George Milner, president of the Manchester Literary Club.

Brierley's autobiography, *Home Memories*, was published in 1886; it complemented his *Collected Works*, which had appeared in eight volumes between 1882 and 1886. In all of his writings Brierley endeavoured 'to rescue the Lancashire character from the erroneous conceptions of Tim Bobbin' (Brierley, *Home Memories*, 88–9). His works long retained their great popularity throughout the county. They are written largely in the dialect of south Lancashire, and with their rich humour and unforced pathos they provide a valuable picture of the life of working-class people in the period 1825–90.

C. W. SUTTON, *rev.* JOHN D. HAIGH

Sources B. Brierley, *Home memories and recollections of a life* (1887) · J. Dronsfield, 'Preface', in B. Brierley and J. Dronsfield, *Ab-o'th'-Yate sketches* (1896), 1.v–xxv · *Ben Brierley's Journal* (28 Nov 1874) · *Manchester City News* (21 March 1885) · *Manchester City News* (25 Jan 1896) · *Manchester City News* (7 May 1898) · *Manchester Guardian* (29 Oct 1892) · *Manchester Guardian* (20 Jan 1896) · *Manchester Guardian* (2 May 1898) · *Manchester Courier* (20 Jan 1896) · *Papers of the Manchester Literary Club*, 22 (1896), 487 · m. cert. · d. cert. · CGPLA Eng. & Wales (1896)
Archives Man. CL, Manchester Archives and Local Studies, MSS
Likenesses J. Cassidy, statue, c.1898, Queen's Park, Manchester · G. Perkins, oils, Failsworth Liberal club, Lancashire · photograph, repro. in Dronsfield, ed., *Ab-o'th'-Yate sketches*, frontispiece
Wealth at death £432 5s. 1d.: probate, 24 March 1896, CGPLA Eng. & Wales

Brierly, James Leslie (1881–1955), international lawyer, was born in Huddersfield on 9 September 1881, the eldest son of Sydney Herbert Brierly, woollen manufacturer, and his wife, Emily Sykes. He was educated at Charterhouse; then as a scholar of Brasenose College, Oxford, where he gained a first in classical moderations (1902), a second in *literae humaniores* (1904), and a first in jurisprudence (1905), and won a senior Hulme scholarship. In 1906 he gained a certificate of honour in the final examinations for the bar and a seven-year prize fellowship at All Souls College. The following year he was called to the bar at Lincoln's Inn, and entered the chambers of F. H. Maugham.

In 1913 Brierly was elected to a fellowship in law at Trinity College, Oxford, but in 1914 he joined the Wiltshire regiment as a second lieutenant. He served in the adjutant-general's department in the War Office, then as deputy assistant adjutant-general with the army of the Black Sea, reached the rank of brevet major, and was appointed OBE (1919). He married in 1920 Ada Ellen Amelia (d. 1966), who was the daughter of John Christopher Foreman, merchant, and was twice mentioned in dispatches when serving as a nurse with the army of the Black Sea in 1919. They had one son.

In 1920 Brierly was appointed professor of law at Manchester, where he played a valuable part in restarting the law faculty. In 1922, on the death of Sir Erle Richards, he was elected Chichele professor of international law and diplomacy at Oxford, and returned to All Souls. His inaugural lecture, published in the *British Year Book of International Law* for 1924, was devoted to the shortcomings of international law. In this lecture, characteristic of his whole approach to international law, he examined the stresses to which the legal system is subject in the international community by reason of the absence of adequate procedures for bringing about peaceful change.

Brierly's best-known work, *The Law of Nations*, was written for 'students and for laymen anxious to learn something of the part played by law in the relations between States' (6th edn, p. vii). First published in 1928, it set out with admirable clarity and precision the main principles of the law of peace. In its own genre it was a masterpiece and won wide popularity, being translated into four foreign languages. It showed that Brierly possessed in high degree the qualities of judgement, vision, and scholarship which would have enabled him to write a work of major importance. But this was not forthcoming, for, first-rate technician though he was, the absorbing interest of international law for him was the role that it could play in promoting international peace and human welfare rather than its detailed rules. The lectures given by him at the Hague Academy in the same year, and published in volume 23 of the *Recueil des cours* (1923) under the title 'Le fondement du caractère obligatoire du droit international', contain a brilliantly clear study of the different theories concerning the basis of the obligatory force of international law. He pointed out the damaging effect of some traditional postulates such as the doctrine of the fundamental rights of states, questioning their absolute validity and advocating that relief from them should be sought in a resurgence of natural law. A second course of lectures, given in 1936 and published in volume 58 of the *Recueil des cours* (1936) under the title 'Règles générales du droit de la paix', was based on his *Law of Nations* but was more critical and reflective. His last book, *The Outlook for International Law*, written in 1944, when people tended to regard international law as a bankrupt system, seeks to draw up a balance sheet of the values and limitations of law in the relations between sovereign states, and contains a penetrating analysis of the problems arising from the so-called 'vital interests' of states. Brierly also published numerous articles in learned journals, several appearing in the *British Year Book of International Law*, of which he was editor from 1929 to 1936. Twenty-eight of these articles, covering a large variety of topics, were reprinted, together with his first Hague lectures, in a posthumous volume entitled *The Basis of Obligation in International Law* (1958). In addition, he was responsible in 1911 for the scholarly translation of Richard Zouche's *Juris et judicii fecialis explicatio*, published in the Carnegie series of Classics of International Law. And he joined with Sir John Miles in editing several editions of Sir William Anson's *Principles of the Law of Contract*, and in compiling a casebook on that branch of English law.

After retiring from his Oxford chair in 1947 Brierly was Montague Burton professor of international relations at Edinburgh from 1948 to 1951. His contribution was not confined to the academic field. He was a member of the League of Nations committees on the codification of international law and on the port of Danzig. During the Italo-Abyssinian dispute he acted as legal adviser to the emperor of Abyssinia, accompanying him in 1938 to the critical session of the league assembly. In 1948 he was elected an original member of the United Nations International Law Commission, being its rapporteur for the law of treaties in 1949–50 and chairman of the commission in 1951.

Brierly also had a high sense of social obligation which led him to undertake many public duties in his own country. At Oxford he served on the university's council and chest and from 1923 to 1950 was a delegate of the university press. Taking a keen interest in the emancipation of women, he served on the councils of Somerville and St Hilda's colleges. A justice of the peace for the city from 1932 to 1955, he discharged his duties with ability and humanity. He was chairman of the Oxford court of referees, of the national service hardship committee, and of four local trade boards, and a member of the Agricultural Wages Board. He served on a number of government committees, including, during the Second World War, the advisory committee established under defence regulation 18B. He was appointed CBE in 1946. His deep humanity also led him to many acts of kindness to those in misfortune. Many a refugee from the two world wars, from the Spanish Civil War, and from Hitler found in him an unselfish friend ready to give them personal help and to work in their interest.

Brierly was a DCL of Oxford (1931), and honorary doctorates were conferred upon him by the universities of Oslo (1946), Chicago (1948), and Manchester (1953). In 1929 he was elected an associate of the Institute of International Law and in 1937 a full member. Brierly died at his home, 6 Brookside, Headington, Oxford, on 20 December 1955.

HUMPHREY WALDOCK, rev.

Sources The Times (22 Dec 1955) · Manchester Guardian (22 Dec 1955) · Oxford Mail (22 Dec 1955) · H. Lauterpacht, 'Brierly's contribution to international law', British Year Book of International Law, 32 (1955–6), 1–20 · private information (1971) · WWW · J. L. Brierly, The law of nations, 6th edn (1963) · CGPLA Eng. & Wales (1956) · F. H. Lawson, The Oxford law school, 1850–1965 (1968)

Archives Bodl. Oxf., Society for Protection of Science and Learning, MSS

Likenesses photograph, repro. in British Year Book of International Law, frontispiece

Wealth at death £40,651 13s. 9d.: probate, 9 April 1956, CGPLA Eng. & Wales

Brierly, Sir Oswald Walters (1817–1894), marine painter and naval engineer, was born at Chester on 19 May 1817, the son of Dr Thomas Brierly (d. in or before 1872), a physician and amateur artist. After schooling in Chester, he became a pupil at Henry Sass's academy, Bloomsbury, London, and later studied naval architecture, rigging, and navigation at Plymouth. At the Royal Academy in 1839 he exhibited two drawings of British men-of-war. In 1841 he joined Benjamin Boyd as staff artist on a voyage round the world in the topsail schooner Wanderer.

On reaching Sydney in July 1842, Boyd settled in New South Wales, supervised Boydtown, a new settlement, and engaged Brierly as manager of a fleet of whaling ships. A cape nearby was named Brierly Point after the artist, as was an island among the hundred surveyed in the Louisiade archipelago. By 1848 Boyd's business had failed and Brierly joined Captain Owen Stanley on two Admiralty surveying expeditions, to the Barrier Reef, and to the Louisiade archipelago and the south coast of New Guinea.

Sir Oswald Walters Brierly (1817–1894), by unknown engraver, pubd 1887

Throughout these dangerous expeditions (on one occasion Brierly was kidnapped) he sketched and wrote journals, now deposited in the Mitchell Library, Sydney. In 1848, at Stanley's house at Sydney, Brierly painted what was probably the first mural in Australia—a view of HMS Rattlesnake. Stanley died unexpectedly in March 1850 and Brierly transferred to HMS Maeander under Captain Henry Keppel. They sailed from New Zealand, on 10 June 1850, and along the coasts of Chile, Peru, and Mexico, reaching Spithead on 29 July 1851. Elected an FRGS, Brierly's account of the visit of HMS Maeander to Tongatabu in the Friendly Islands was published in the society's Journal (1852). On 26 August 1851 he married a Quaker, Sarah Fry (d. 1870), the daughter of Edmund Fry, a bookseller.

In 1854, at the outbreak of the Crimean War, Brierly joined Keppel as artist–observer on the man-of-war HMS St John d'Acre in the allied Baltic fleet. Retained by the Illustrated London News to sketch the actions (reproduced from 25 March 1854), Brierly was one of the earliest naval war artists commissioned by a newspaper. In 1855 he accompanied Keppel, in HMS Rodney, to the Black Sea and Sea of Azov; during this voyage he was often under enemy fire, and was subsequently awarded the Baltic and Crimean medals. His work illustrates the transition from the steam frigates of 1837 to the great steam fleet of 1854 (Roget, 'Sir Oswald Brierly', 129–34). His obituary in the Illustrated London News notes that his sketches, full of spirit, caught the public eye, and that after the Crimean War he 'found himself in possession of the notoriety which he had long sought and always appreciated. He was essentially self-assertive, but genial and kindly withal' (22 Dec 1894, 770).

Queen Victoria commissioned two views of the naval review held at Spithead in April 1856, seen from the royal yacht Victoria and Albert—the first of over 150 works by Brierly which became part of the Royal Collection. In 1864 he sailed to Norway in Count Gleichen's ship, HMS Racoon, in which Prince Alfred was serving. In February 1867 Brierly was invited to join the prince (created duke of Edinburgh in May 1866) on his appointment to command

HMS *Galatea* on a journey round the world. An attempted assassination of the duke near Sydney cut short the voyage and they returned to England in June 1868. Brierly illustrated *The Cruise of HMS Galatea*, an account of the voyage published by the ship's chaplain, the Revd John Milner, in 1869. At the South Kensington Museum in London in 1872 the trophies from the duke's journeys of 1867–71 were exhibited, along with thirty-seven watercolours by Brierly. In 1869 Brierly joined the expedition of the prince of Wales up the Nile and to Constantinople, the Crimea, and Greece. Brierly later depicted yachts at Cowes, on the Isle of Wight, and the Royal Thames Yacht Club jubilee race (1887) for the prince. He succeeded J. C. Schetky as marine painter to the queen in 1874, and also became marine painter to the Royal Yacht Squadron; he was knighted in 1885.

Brierly drew his subjects in pencil, or occasionally pen and ink, and used either a slight colour wash or occasionally elaborate watercolour. He exhibited ten paintings at the Royal Academy between 1839 and 1871; he also showed 192 works at the Royal Society of Painters in Water Colours, to which he was elected an associate in 1872 and a member in 1880. He travelled to Italy, especially Venice, in 1874 and 1882. Brierly's later work (often lithographed) includes many history pictures, especially views of the Armada. In 1881 he was appointed curator of the Painted Hall at Greenwich. A retrospective exhibition was held at the Pall Mall Gallery, 57 Pall Mall, London, from April to July 1887. The main collections of his works are held in the National Maritime Museum, Greenwich, and the Mitchell Library and the Art Gallery of New South Wales in Sydney.

On 25 June 1872 Brierly married Louise Marie Aimée Flore Huard, daughter of Louis Alexis Huard, an artist. Before his second wife's death in 1893, Brierly was already an invalid; he died on 14 December 1894 at his home, 24 Ladbroke Crescent, Notting Hill, London. His daughter, Emma, wrote that the interest that Queen Victoria had always taken in his work had been 'one of the happiest memories that remained with him and cheered him to the very last' (correspondence, 19 Dec 1894, Royal Archives, Windsor Castle, PP Vic 11140).   DELIA MILLAR

Sources J. L. Roget, 'Her majesty's marine painter: Sir Oswald Brierly', *Art Journal*, new ser., 7 (1887), 129–34 · *The Times* (17 Dec 1894) · *The Athenaeum* (22 Dec 1894), 868–9 · *The Academy* (22 Dec 1894), 542 · *ILN* (22 Dec 1894) · J. Milner and O. W. Brierly, *The cruise of HMS Galatea* (1869) · D. Millar, *The Victorian watercolours and drawings in the collection of her majesty the queen*, 2 vols. (1995) [nos. 334–491] · M. Basset, *Behind the picture: HMS Rattlesnake's Australia–New Guinea cruise, 1846 to 1850* (1966) · *Sir Oswald Walters Brierly: sailing ships and ports of the seven seas* (1982) [exhibition catalogue, Hunter Museum of Art, Chattanooga, TN, 4 April - 30 May 1982] · *Loan exhibition of works by Sir Oswald Brierly* (1887) [exhibition catalogue, Pall Mall Gallery, London, 1887] · *The cruise of H. R. H. the duke of Edinburgh K.G. round the world in H.M.S. 'Galatea'* (1872) [exhibition catalogue, South Kensington Museum, London; with handlist: *A guide to the works of art and science, collected by Capt. HRH the duke of Edinburgh, during his five year cruise round the world on HMS Galatea, 1867–71*] · J. L. Roget, *A history of the 'Old Water-Colour' Society*, 2 vols. (1891) · *DNB* · *AusDB* · E. H. H. Archibald, *Dictionary of sea painters* (1980) · O. W. Brierly, 'Brief geographical sketch of the Friendly Islands, with an account of the visit of HMS Maeander, Capt. the Hon.

Henry Keppel, to the island of Tongatabu, June 1850', *Journal of the Royal Geographical Society*, 22 (1852), 97–118 · H. Keppel, *A visit to the Indian archipelago in HM ship Maeander* (1853) · m. certs. · *CGPLA Eng. & Wales* (1895) · Graves, *RA exhibitors*
Archives Mitchell L., NSW, MSS · Royal Arch., corresp. · Royal Collection
Likenesses N. Daly, portrait, repro. in H. Keppel, *A sailor's life*, 2 (1899), 156 · Elliott & Fry, photograph, repro. in *Sir Oswald Walters Brierly*, fig. 1 · F. Needham, drawing (of Brierly drawing on board HMS *Galatea*, 1867–8), Royal Collection; repro. in Millar, *Victorian watercolours*, vol. 2, p. 652 · wood-engraving, repro. in *Art Journal* (1887), 133 [see illus.] · wood-engraving, repro. in *ILN* (22 Dec 1894), 770 · wood-engraving, NPG; repro. in *ILN* (2 Jan 1886)
Wealth at death £634 10s. 2d.: probate, 21 Jan 1895, *CGPLA Eng. & Wales*

Briggs, Henry (*bap.* 1561, *d.* 1631), mathematician, was born at Daisy Bank in the township of Warley, near Halifax, Yorkshire, and baptized on 23 February 1561 at St John's Church, Halifax, the son of Thomas Briggs, farmer, and his wife, Isabel Beste. Mary Briggs, who was probably either his sister or half-sister (Isabel Beste seems to have been Thomas Briggs's second wife), was baptized on 28 October 1557, and Richard Briggs, who matriculated from St John's College, Cambridge, in 1577 or 1578, was possibly his brother. The family lived at Daisy Bank, Warley. After attending grammar school locally Briggs matriculated on 15 March 1578 from St John's College, Cambridge, and as a founder's scholar of the county of Yorkshire on 5 November 1579. He graduated BA in 1581 or 1582, MA in 1585, and on 29 March 1588 was admitted an Ashton fellow of the county of Yorkshire. Subsequently he was appointed topicus sublector (9 July 1591) and mathematicus examiner (7 July 1592), which implies that he lectured in mathematics, and, on 8 September 1592, to the Linacre lectureship in physic.

According to Hallowes, Briggs allied himself to the strong puritan faction then in St John's College. His political and religious stance is indicated in three petitions that he supported during his time in Cambridge. In early March 1597 he became professor of geometry in the newly founded Gresham College in London, at £50 per annum. His work on astronomy, geography, and navigation (subjects which the new college aimed to improve) began with *A Table to Find the Height of the Pole* (1602), and *Tables for the Improvement of Navigation* (1610). The latter included closely calculated tables for the declination of the sun between 1608 and 1612. Briggs's association with Cambridge nevertheless continued after he took up the Gresham post, and he seems to have had a prominent position in the administration of the affairs of his old college. A letter of March 1600 shows him participating, on behalf of St John's, in a discussion with the fellows of Trinity over the planned enclosure of the Backs. Although not formally elected as one of the eight governing senior fellows, his signature on a college decree of 24 February 1602 indicates that he was considered as such.

In 1609 Briggs became acquainted with James Ussher, later archbishop of Armagh. Two of Briggs's letters to him survive. One, of August 1610, dealt with the possibility of an anonymous publication in England of a manuscript written by the Calvinist Ussher (presumably of some political and religious sensitivity). Among other things, it included a discussion of eclipses with the comment that Johannes Kepler had confused all with his unconventional approach to the laws of planetary motion. Briggs also sought to become personally acquainted with other prominent mathematicians of the day. In a second letter, of 10 March 1616, having encountered John Napier's *Mirifici logarithmorum canonis descriptio* (1614), he informed Ussher that

> Napper [elsewhere spelt Neper or Naper], Lord of Markinston, hath set my Head and Hands a Work, with his new and admirable Logarithms. I hope to see him this Summer if it please God, for I never saw Book which pleased me better, or made me more wonder. (Parr, 36)

This encounter determined the course of his future life and he was lecturing on Napier's logarithms at Gresham College as early as 1615.

Logarithms simplified the astronomical and navigational calculations central to the research programme at Gresham College by enabling multiplication of two many-digit numbers to be performed by addition of their corresponding logarithms. A feature of Napier's original definition was that logarithms were what has become known as 'hyperbolic' (for their base was approximately $\frac{1}{e}$), so that as the numbers increased their corresponding logarithms decreased. Thus the logarithm of 1 was about 161,000,000 and the logarithm of 10,000,000 was zero. Napier indicated in an 'Admonitio' on the last leaf of some copies of the book that he was developing a simpler definition.

Briggs now wrote to Napier suggesting that it would be more convenient to work in steps of 10. Thus the logarithm of 10,000,000 (the value commonly taken for the 'whole sine', i.e. the sine of 90° or the radius, R, of the circle in relation to which the trigonometric sine and cosine were then defined as lengths) would remain zero, but the logarithm of $^8/_{10}$ (i.e. of sine 5° 44′ 21″) would be equal to 10,000,000,000; he calculated numerical values on this basis, and in the summer of 1615 went to visit Napier in Edinburgh. During his one-month stay, and a second visit in the summer of 1616, Briggs and Napier agreed on a redefinition suggested by Napier (presumably that already hinted at in his 'Admonitio') which gave logarithms increasing as the corresponding number increased, namely, log 1 = 0 and log R = 10,000,000,000. In his *Rabdologia* (1617) Napier declared that Briggs and he had developed a better method for logarithms, whose manner and use they hoped to publish, but poor health compelled him to leave these extensive calculations to other learned men, especially Henry Briggs, his most highly esteemed friend. Briggs and Napier were, however, dissimilar in nature, Briggs being opposed to astrology, and a severe Presbyterian.

In a letter of 6 December 1617 Henry Bourgchier informed James Ussher that soon after Napier's death on 4 April 1617, Briggs's *Logarithmorum chilias prima* (undated) had been published in London. Briggs had replaced log R = 10,000,000,000 with log 10 = 1, thus producing logarithms

to base 10. The work consisted of sixteen pages each containing 67 numbers, the base 10 logarithms of 1 to 1000 calculated to fourteen decimal places. From 501 the 4th order differences relating to the seventh decimal place are given for interpolation. Only one copy of this, the first base 10 logarithm table, is extant. The English translation, *The First Chiliad of Logarithmes*, is also undated, but was probably issued in 1626.

Briggs undoubtedly computed the first base 10 logarithms. Controversy over what part Napier played in formulating the theory seems to have sprung from the fact that the 'Admonitio' was absent from several copies of Napier's *Descriptio*. This controversy was later fuelled by remarks about Napier's role made by the mathematician Charles Hutton, though these were in turn challenged by Napier's descendant Mark Napier when he published Napier's early treatise as *De arte logistica* in 1839. Today it is clear that the friendly relations between John Napier and Henry Briggs remained unbroken up to the end, and this friendship explains the inclusion of important sections written by Briggs in the English translation of Napier, *Description* (1616), in the *Rabdologia*, and in the *Mirifici logarithmorum canonis constructio* (1619). While Justus Bürgi is credited as an independent inventor of logarithms, Briggs is acknowledged as the creator of one of the most useful systems for mathematics (without having had any knowledge of power notation in the twentieth-century sense). On the continent the contributions of Napier and Briggs have generally been met with greater acclaim than those of Bürgi, Adriaan Vlacq, or Henry Gellibrand. Briggs's tables simplified the otherwise laborious computations involving multiplication and division of numbers to several decimal places, which had led the great European astronomers to fear that greater exactness in trigonometry was unattainable as it demanded impracticably arduous calculations.

In 1619 Briggs was appointed to the professorship of geometry in Oxford, newly established by Henry Saville, and on 8 January 1620 he took up the position at a salary of £150 a year. He lived in Merton College and was incorporated MA on 7 July 1620. After seven years' untiring computation his chief work, *Arithmetica logarithmica* (1624), appeared, containing the logarithms of the numbers 1 to 20,000 and 90,001 to 100,000, calculated to fourteen decimal places, with their complete differences. In it he explained at length his method of calculation which was based on the axiom 'Logarithmi sunt numeri qui proportionalibus adiuncti aequales servant differentias' ('Logarithms are numbers that, proportional parts co-ordinated, create equal differences'). From first principles he calculated to thirty-two decimal places the values of 10, $\sqrt{10}$, $2^2\sqrt{10}$, $2^3\sqrt{10}$, ... $2^{54}\sqrt{10}$, together with the corresponding forty-decimal place logarithms (1, $\frac{1}{2}$, $\frac{1}{2}^2$, $\frac{1}{2}^3$, ... $\frac{1}{2}^{54}$). These enabled him to find close-meshed starting values from which he could interpolate using nth order differences (derived recursively) to obtain the intervening logarithms. In deriving the differences Briggs formulated, in anticipation of Newton, the first four terms of the binomial expansion $(1 + x)^{1/2}$. His notation has peculiarities, thus 5^{9321} stands for the decimal fraction $5.9321/10000$ and l(3)8 stands for $^{3}\sqrt{8}$. Briggs coined the terms 'mantissa' for the decimal part of the logarithm, and 'characteristic' for the whole number; moreover he assisted with terminology for John Minsheu's multilingual *Ductor in linguas* (1617) in this period of consolidation of the western European literary languages.

Although Briggs was busily employed in calculating the remaining logarithms (for 20,001 to 90,000), it was Adriaan Vlacq who completed the work, publishing logarithms to ten decimal places for all the numbers between 1 and 100,000 in a second edition of *Arithmetica logarithmica* (1628). An English edition, *Logarithmicall arithmetike*, was published in London in 1631. After Briggs's death Henry Gellibrand published as *Trigonometria Britannica* (1633) two volumes of Briggs's posthumous works. Briggs also published *Lucubrationes et annotationes in opera postuma J. Neperi* (1619), and *Euclidis elementorum vi libri priores* (1620), the author being identified only as H. B. Since 28 April 1619 Briggs had been auditor for the Virginia Company and this was the origin of his publication of *A Treatise of the Northwest Passage to the South Sea* (1622), which has a map ascribed to him. A group of islands there was subsequently named 'Brigges his Mathematickes' by Luke Fox though the name fell out of use. In *Mathematica ab antiquis minus cognita* (1630) Briggs summarized the more important mathematical inventions up to that time. Four additional treatises dealing principally with geometry remained unpublished.

Briggs died on 26 January 1631 in Merton College, Oxford. The entry in the college register shows the high reputation he enjoyed. At his interment on 29 January 1631, William Sellar conducted the service and Hugh Cressy gave the funeral oration. Briggs was buried in the choir of Merton College chapel with a gravestone bearing only his name and a lozenge. His will of 16 November 1629 was proved on 11 February 1631 by Jeremy and Miles Briggs, his executors. No known portrait of him survives. Briggs was regarded by contemporaries as an upright, extraordinary individual: 'beyond all praise, too famous for any panegyric … worthy, therefore to receive our infinite thanks which are beyond calculation even by your own logarithms', wrote Isaac Barrow (Hallowes, 86). He had taken an active part in the society of his day; indeed Hill judged his role as 'contact and public relations man' (Hill, 38) to outweigh his importance as a mathematician.

WOLFGANG KAUNZNER

Sources D. M. Hallowes, 'Henry Briggs, mathematician', *Halifax Antiquarian Society* (1961), 79–92 · private information (2004) [M. G. Underwood] · J. Ward, *The lives of the professors of Gresham College* (1740) · T. Smith, 'Vitae quorundam eruditissimorum et illustrium virorum', trans. J. T. Foxell, in A. J. Thompson, *Logarithmetica Britannica*, 1 (1952) · *Biographia Britannica, or, The lives of the most eminent persons who have flourished in Great Britain and Ireland*, 2 (1748) · R. Parr, ed., *The life of the most reverend father in God, James Usher … with a collection of three hundred letters* (1686) · C. Hill, *Intellectual origins of the English revolution* (1965) · H. S. Carslaw, 'The discovery of logarithms by Napier', *Mathematical Gazette*, 8 (1915–16), 76–84, 115–19 · 'Briggs, Henry', 'Logarithm', 'Napier, John', 'Table, mathematical', *Encyclopaedia Britannica*, 11th edn (1910–11) · D. T. Whiteside, 'Patterns of mathematical thought in the later seventeenth century', *Archive for History of Exact Sciences*, 1 (1960–62), 179–388 · D. T. Whiteside, 'Henry Briggs: the binomial theorem anticipated', *Mathematical Gazette*, 45 (1961), 9–12 · parish register (baptism), Halifax, St John, 23 Feb 1561

Archives Bodl. Oxf., MS Bodley 313 · Bodl. Oxf., MS Birch 4395 · Pulkowo Observatory, Kepler MSS, vol. 11, fols. 269–72 [Johannes Kepler, *Gesammelte Werke*, 18 (1959), 220–29]

Briggs, Henry Perronet (1791–1844), antiquary and subject painter, was born at Walworth, London, the son of John Hobart Briggs (*bap.* 1760), who held a lucrative position in the Post Office, and his wife, Mary, *née* Oldham. He was named after his great-grandfather the Methodist minister Vincent Perronet (1693–1785) whose daughter Elizabeth married in 1748 William Briggs of the Custom House. He was also second cousin to the painter John Opie's wife, Amelia, whose portrait he painted and exhibited at the Royal Academy in 1831. His father had intended him for a commercial career but Briggs showed an early love for art. While Briggs was at Epping Academy in 1805 a Thomas Squire (presumably his mentor) sent two well-executed drawings of Epping church by him at the age of fourteen to the *Gentleman's Magazine* which were engraved and illustrated in the magazine in 1806 together with a letter about the artist: 'the juvenile efforts of a rising young genius. H. P. Briggs of this academy' (76, part 1, 312–13). At the age of nineteen, on 26 February 1811 he entered as a student at the Royal Academy Schools, and in 1813 went to Cambridge where he painted portraits of several college members including one of H. Goodridge of Trinity College (later exhibited at the Royal Academy).

Briggs settled in London, exhibiting two portraits at the Royal Academy in 1814 from a Soho address. By 1818 he turned his attention mainly to historical and Shakespearian scenes of which he exhibited nineteen at the British Institution from 1819 to 1830. In 1823 the directors of the institution awarded him £100 for the Shakespearian scenes he exhibited that year, and in 1827 his large painting *George III presenting the sword to Earl Howe on board the Queen Charlotte, 1794* was purchased by the directors for 500 guineas and they subsequently donated it to Greenwich Hospital.

In 1825 Briggs was elected an associate of the Royal Academy, gaining that honour before Landseer with whom he co-operated on *The ladies Charlotte, Augusta and Katherine Scott, great-grandchildren of the Lord Chancellor Eldon with his favourite dog 'Pincher' a German spaniel. The dog by E. Landseer esq. R.A.*, exhibited at the Royal Academy in 1840. His cousin Amelia Opie (*née* Alderson) related that for some of his juvenile sitters she tucked barley balls into the pocket of her dress, one of these being tossed into the child's lap at intervals to keep its gaze focused expectantly in the direction of the artist.

On 7 August 1830 Briggs married a near relative, Elizabeth Alderson (*d. c.*1840) at St Marylebone, Middlesex.

On the death of Northcote, Briggs was elected Royal Academician in 1832, and from this date devoted himself almost entirely to portraiture. In 1834 his portrait was painted during a visit to London by Carl Christian Vogel (1788–1868). As Baron Briggs he was placed first by W. M. Thackeray in his 'List of best Victorian painters' in *Fraser's Magazine* (1838). About two years later his wife died of tuberculosis. Also infected, he made his will on 16 January 1844 and died two days later on 18 January at his home at 33 Bruton Street, London. He left a son, Henry, who died young, and a daughter, Elizabeth Amelia (*d.* 1912), who married the Revd James Haslewood Carr MA (1831–1915). His will proved in London on 24 February 1844 mentions his sister Catherine Briggs and names his brother-in-law Thomas John Alderson. His pupils included John Birch, Thomas Brigstocke, Thomas Brooks, Thomas Frank Dicksee, Father Edward Mackey, and Edward Opie.

Up to the time of his death Briggs continued to paint portraits, four of which were exhibited posthumously at the Royal Academy in 1844. His studio sale was held at Christies on 25–27 April 1844.

W. W. WROTH, rev. MERVYN CUTTEN

Sources Graves, *RA exhibitors* • Graves, *Brit. Inst.* • B. Stewart and M. Cutten, *The dictionary of portrait painters in Britain up to 1920* (1997) • Graves, *Artists* • T. Squire, letter, *GM*, 1st ser., 76 (1806), 312–13 • *Art Union*, 6 (1844), 62 • *The Athenaeum* (27 Jan 1844), 90–91 • A. Earland, *John Opie and his circle* (1911), 208 • S. C. Hutchison, 'The Royal Academy Schools, 1768–1830', *Walpole Society*, 38 (1960–62), 123–91, esp. 166 • G. Popp and H. Valentine, *Royal Academy of Arts directory of membership: from the foundation in 1768 to 1995, including honorary members* (1996) • d. cert. • R. Ormond, *Early Victorian portraits*, 2 vols. (1973) • Wood, *Vic. painters*, 3rd edn • *IGI*
Likenesses C. C. Vogel, drawing, 1834, Staatliche Kunstsammlungen, Dresden • J. D. Harding, portrait, *c.*1840, NPG • H. P. Briggs, self-portrait, oils, Uffizi Gallery, Florence
Wealth at death exact sum unknown: will, proved 24 Feb 1844

Briggs, James Alexander (1871–1961). *See under* Briggs, William (1839–1919).

Briggs, John (1785–1875), army officer in the East India Company, eldest child of James Briggs (*d. c.*1830), of Scottish descent, physician-general of Madras, and his first wife, Martha (*d. c.*1788), daughter of John Bryan Pybus, of the Madras civil service, was born at Madras on 18 September 1785. Educated at Dr Winter's school, Ormond Street, London, and at Eton College (1794–9), he later wrote, 'I benefited little by my public school education … I was very often flogged' (Bell, 8). He entered the 15th Madras native infantry in July 1801. He took part in both the nineteenth-century Anglo-Maratha wars, serving in the campaign which ended that eventful struggle as a political officer under Sir John Malcolm, whom he had previously accompanied on his mission to Persia in 1810. On 3 September 1811 Briggs married Jane (*d.* 1870), youngest daughter of John Dodson of the London custom house. They had two sons, who died in early boyhood, and three daughters.

Briggs was one of Mountstuart Elphinstone's assistants in the Deccan, subsequently served in Khandesh, and succeeded Captain Grant Duff as resident at Satara from 1823 to 1827, after which, in 1831, he was appointed senior member of the board of commissioners for the government of Mysore when its administration was assumed by

the British owing to the maharaja's misrule. This appointment by the governor-general, Lord William Bentinck, was not agreeable to the government of Madras, and after a somewhat stormy tenure, lasting barely a year, Briggs resigned in September 1832, and was transferred to the residency of Nagpur, where he remained until 1835, when he left India for ever. He was promoted colonel of the 13th Madras native infantry (1836), major-general (1838), lieutenant-general (1851), and general (6 February 1861).

After his return to England, entitled by his ownership of India stock to membership of the court of proprietors of the East India Company, Briggs was there prominent in the discussion of Indian affairs and for several years a leader of the ineffectual opposition. He opposed the government of India, and especially Dalhousie's annexation policy. However, unlike other reformers, he opposed transfer of the company's remaining powers to the crown. In 1836 he proposed a scheme to the president of the Board of Control for establishing military colleges in India to train Indian officers' sons as officers in Indian infantry regiments; but it came to nothing. He was an active member of the Anti-Corn Law League, and as a Liberal and free trader contested Exeter in April 1844 and July 1845. He was a good Persian scholar, and translated a work by Ferishta as *Mohammadan Power in India*, and the *Siyar-al-Mutákhirin*, which recorded the decline of the Mughal power. He wrote an essay on the land tax of India (1830), and in *Letters Addressed to a Young Person in India* (1828) he discussed various questions for the conduct of young Indian officers, civil and military, and especially their treatment of Indians. He published in 1856 a small book entitled *India and Europe Compared*, restating his views on the Indian land tax, advocating greater opportunities for educated Indians in government service, and warning of Sepoy disaffection.

In November 1838 Briggs was elected FRS for his achievement in oriental literature. Overweight, Briggs for a year (1864–5) followed Banting's diet system, losing 46 lb in weight and 10 inches in girth, and, he claimed, improving his health. He died at his residence, Bridge Lodge, Clayton, Burgess Hill, Sussex (where he had lived his last twenty years), on 27 April 1875.

A. J. ARBUTHNOT, rev. ROGER T. STEARN

Sources E. Bell, *Memoir of General John Briggs* (1885) • *Allen's Indian Mail* (1875) • J. Briggs, *Letters addressed to a young person in India* (1828) • T. A. Heathcote, *The military in British India: the development of British land forces in south Asia, 1600–1947* (1995) • N. McCord, *The Anti-Corn Law League, 1838–46*, 2nd edn (1968) • Boase, *Mod. Eng. biog.* • *CGPLA Eng. & Wales* (1875)
Archives Bodl. Oxf., corresp., literary MSS, and papers | BL OIOC, letters to Mountstuart Elphinstone, MS Eur. F 87–89
Likenesses portrait, repro. in Bell, *Memoir of General John Briggs*
Wealth at death under £35,000: probate, 10 May 1875, *CGPLA Eng. & Wales*

Briggs, John (1788–1861), vicar apostolic of the Yorkshire district and Roman Catholic bishop of Beverley, was born in Manchester on 20 May 1788. He was educated first at Sedgley Park, near Wolverhampton, and then, in 1804, began his theological studies at St Cuthbert's College, Ushaw. He was ordained priest in 1814 but remained at

Ushaw as a professor until 1818, during which time the future Cardinal Wiseman was one of his pupils. He was then sent as a mission priest to Chester where he remained until his recall to Ushaw as president in 1833. While at Chester he fostered the vocation of a young altar server and then contributed towards his education at Ushaw and Rome. The boy, Thomas Grant, later became bishop of Southwark. Briggs remained president of Ushaw until 1836, despite being appointed coadjutor bishop in the northern district later in 1833. In 1836 he succeeded Penswick as vicar apostolic of the northern district and when this area was divided in two in 1840 Briggs became vicar apostolic of the Yorkshire district. Ten years later, on the restoration of the Catholic hierarchy by Pius IX, Briggs was appointed bishop of Beverley.

Although the oldest of the newly appointed diocesan bishops, and often in ill health, Briggs lived out his motto 'Non recuso laborem' (I do not refuse the work). He played an important role in calming fears of 'papal aggression' and reconciling the people of Yorkshire to the restoration of the hierarchy. He built churches, invited religious orders to Yorkshire, set up new diocesan organizations, and laid down guidelines for priests in his *Admonitions and Exhortations* (1853) which were to survive and to be used as a model by other bishops for many years. A tall, imposing figure with flowing white hair, the bishop seems to have been much loved by priests and people in the diocese, where he was known as 'the late Dr Briggs' because his unwillingness to cut short conversations frequently made him late for appointments. Briggs also played a part in the wider church. He was held in high regard by the Irish because of his efforts to alleviate distress in Ireland during the famine years by personally begging for aid throughout England. He exchanged letters with Newman; Pagani dedicated his *Life of the Rev. Aloysius Gentili* (1851) to Briggs; Pius IX honoured him by creating him a count of the Holy Roman empire, a domestic prelate, and an assistant at the pontifical throne.

As his health deteriorated Briggs resisted attempts to supply him with a coadjutor, but on 7 November 1860 increasing infirmity forced him to resign. Two months later, on 4 January 1861, the bishop died at his house in York, aged seventy-two. Thomas Grant said his requiem mass and on 10 January Briggs was buried at St Leonard's Church at Hazlewood, near Tadcaster, where mass had been said without interruption since its foundation by Sir William Vavasour in 1286. The bishop was described in his obituary as 'a favourite of men of all creeds and parties' (*Hull Advertiser*).　　　　　　JENNIFER F. SUPPLE-GREEN

Sources Briggs letters, Leeds Roman Catholic Diocesan Archives · *Hull Advertiser* (12 Jan 1861), 4–5 · W. M. Brady, *The episcopal succession in England, Scotland, and Ireland, AD 1400 to 1875*, 3 (1877), 396–8 · D. Milburn, *A history of Ushaw College* (1964), 127–30 · J. F. Supple-Green, *The Catholic revival in Yorkshire, 1850–1900* (1990), 15–24
Archives Hexham and Newcastle Diocesan Archives, corresp. mainly relating to mission funds · Leeds Roman Catholic Diocesan Archives, corresp. and papers · Northumbd RO, Hexham RC Diocese MSS · Ushaw College, Durham, corresp. and papers · Westm. DA

Likenesses J. M'Elheran, coloured lithograph, 1851, NPG · oils, bishop's house, Leeds
Wealth at death under £7000: probate, 18 Feb 1861, CGPLA Eng. & Wales

Briggs, John (1862–1902), cricketer, was born at Lord Street, Sutton in Ashfield, Nottinghamshire, on 3 October 1862, the son of James Briggs (1837/8–1899), a stocking framer and knitter, and his wife, Ellen Banner. His father played cricket as a professional and was good enough to get an obituary notice in *Wisden*. His elder brother Joseph (1860–1902) made six appearances for Nottinghamshire in 1888. The family moved to Lancashire and Briggs made his début for the county in 1879, when only sixteen. Primarily selected for his outstanding fielding abilities (usually in the covers), he soon developed as an attacking batsman. On 14 July 1885 he married Alice (b. 1863/4), daughter of John Burgess, a labourer. Three days later he made 186 against Surrey—the highest score of his career. In the same year his bowling began to be of value and from 1887 onwards he regularly took over 100 wickets in a season.

Yet it was purely as a batsman that Briggs made his test début against Australia at Adelaide in 1884 and later in the series he scored 121 at Melbourne. It was 'as grand a display of batting as ever was seen', wrote Arthur Shrewsbury, his captain (Shaw and Shrewsbury, 102). He appeared thirty-three times for England (1884–99), and W. G. Grace declared that 'no England representative side would be complete without him' (W. G. Grace, *Cricket*, 1891, 288). Among outstanding bowling performances were eleven wickets for 74 against Australia at Lord's in 1886, fifteen for 28, all in one day, against South Africa at Cape Town in 1889, and a hat-trick against Australia at Sydney in 1892. He was the first bowler to secure 100 test wickets. He also had a share in England's spectacular defeat of Australia at Sydney in 1894. England, forced to follow on, secured victory by 10 runs through the combined efforts of Briggs and Robert Peel.

Briggs was a slow left-arm bowler with an easy action, spinning the ball both ways and varying his flight. He had a well-concealed quicker delivery. He and Peel of Yorkshire were an outstanding pair in the England side, with Wilfred Rhodes ready to replace them. Rhodes made his début for England in the same year (1899) in which Briggs played his last test.

The circumstances of this were sad. For some years Briggs had suffered from epilepsy. After the end of play on the first day of the test against Australia at Leeds in 1899 he had a severe fit when at 'a place of amusement with his fellow professionals' (*Wisden*, 1900, 69). There followed some months in Cheadle Asylum, though he returned to have a highly successful season for Lancashire in 1900. Once again he took over 100 wickets, including all ten for 55, in the dismissal of Worcestershire for 106. He also batted 'with an amount of consistency he had not often equalled' (*Wisden*, 1901, 29). But his recovery was short-lived and he was sent back to Cheadle Asylum, where he died on 11 January 1902. In his career he had scored 14,092 runs (average 18.27) and taken 2221 wickets (average 15.95).

At 5 feet 6 inches, Briggs was known as The Boy or The Midget. He was the most popular Lancashire player of his day and contemporaries were unanimous in praising his good humour and cheerfulness—important qualities in one who made the long round trip to play in Australia on six occasions, a record subsequently equalled by Lord Cowdrey. Despite the sadness at the end, Briggs fared better than many a nineteenth-century professional cricketer. His benefit match at Old Trafford during Whitsun holiday 1894, although spoilt by the weather, raised over £1000 and enabled him to open a shop in Manchester. His wife survived him.   GERALD M. D. HOWAT

Sources Wisden (1880–1903) · H. Turner, The life of John Briggs (1902) · Cricket Field (12 May 1894), 58 · Cricket (26 Feb 1885), 81 · A. Shaw and A. Shrewsbury, Shaw & Shrewsbury's team in Australia, 1884–85 (1885) · P. Bailey, P. Thorn, and P. Wynne-Thomas, Who's who of cricketers, rev. edn (1993) · C. Martin-Jenkins, World cricketers: a biographical dictionary (1996) · b. cert. · m. cert. · DNB · CGPLA Eng. & Wales (1902)
Likenesses E. Hawkins, photograph, 1888, repro. in Wisden (1889) · T. W. Thomas, photograph, 1894, repro. in Cricket Field
Wealth at death £103 12s. 6d.: probate, 7 May 1902, CGPLA Eng. & Wales

Briggs, John Joseph (1819–1876), naturalist and writer on country life, was born on 6 March 1819 at King's Newton, near Melbourne, Derbyshire, the son of John Briggs, farmer, and his wife, Mary Briggs. His parents were cousins, and they lived on the farm at King's Newton on which his father had been born, and which had belonged to their family for three centuries. In 1828 Briggs was sent to the boarding-school run by the topographer and antiquary Thomas Rossel Potter at Wymeswold, Leicestershire. In 1833 he moved on and was taught privately by a Revd Solomon Saxon, of Darley Vale, Derbyshire. In 1834 he was apprenticed to William Bemrose of Derby, founder of the printing firm of Bemrose & Sons.

As a result of his weak health Briggs gave up printing about 1840 and returned to the family occupation of farming. On the farm he kept careful meteorological and natural history records for thirty years. These diaries were the basis for the regular 'Naturalists' column' which he originated in 1855 in The Field (weekly, founded 1853), and which brought him into correspondence with many of the leading naturalists of his time. He also published material in The Zoologist, The Critic, The Reliquary, The Sun, the Derby Reporter, and the Leicestershire Guardian. His reports tended towards picturesque descriptions of nature, and also contained sketches of places and objects in the midland counties that were of antiquarian or archaeological interest.

In 1869 Briggs married Hannah Soar of Chellaston, near Derby. Among his works are an illustrated history of the village of Melbourne, as well as more general histories of Derbyshire and Leicestershire. He also wrote The Peacock at Rowsley (1869), a gossiping book about fishing and country life at the junction of the Wye and Derwent rivers. His main books were all published by his former employer, Bemrose & Sons. Many of his observations on natural history, as well as a projected book, Worthies of Derbyshire, remain unpublished. His plan, announced towards the

end of his life, to published his extensive naturalist's diaries, also failed to come to fruition. He died at the family farm at King's Newton on 23 March 1876. His wife, a son, and three daughters survived him.

JOHN WESTBY-GIBSON, rev. ALEXANDER GOLDBLOOM

Sources The Reliquary, 17 (1876), 49–54 · personal knowledge (1885) · Boase, Mod. Eng. biog.
Archives Derbys. RO, corresp. and papers; Derbyshire natural history; diaries; literary papers; nature notes
Wealth at death under £5000: probate, 13 June 1877, CGPLA Eng. & Wales

Briggs, Sir John Thomas (1781–1865), naval administrator, son of William Briggs, of an old Norfolk family, a direct descendant of the physician William *Briggs (c.1650–1704), and, in a collateral line, of the mathematician Henry *Briggs (bap. 1561, d. 1631), was born in London on 4 June 1781. He entered early into the civil service of the Navy Board in 1796 and in 1806 at the age of twenty-five was appointed secretary to the 'commission for revising and digesting the civil affairs of the navy', under the presidency of Lord Barham, in which capacity he helped to compile the voluminous reports issued by the commission, 1806–9. He married in 1807 Frances (1782/3–1873), daughter of Thomas Lewis, merchant, formerly of Cadiz. When the work of the commission was ended, Briggs was appointed assistant secretary of the victualling board, a post which he held until in 1830 he was selected by Sir James Graham, then first lord of the Admiralty, as his private secretary; but was shortly afterwards advanced to be commissioner and accountant-general of the victualling board. That board was abolished in 1832, and Briggs was appointed accountant-general of the navy. He held this office for the next twenty-two years, during which term many and important improvements were made in the system of accounts, notably double-entry bookkeeping, in the framing of the naval estimates, in the method of paying the seamen, and, more especially, in enabling them to remit part of their pay to their wives and families. On 26 February 1851 Briggs was knighted in acknowledgement of his long and efficient departmental service, from which he retired in February 1854. Briggs made a major, sustained contribution to the modernization of naval administration between 1809 and 1854. He published several pamphlets on naval administration. He died at his home, 4 Royal Crescent, Brighton, Sussex, on 3 February 1865. His wife survived him, and died aged ninety, on 24 December 1873. His eldest son, Sir John Henry Briggs (1808–1897), was born on 19 April 1808, educated at Westminster, and was an Admiralty civil servant from 1826 and chief clerk from 1865. He retired in March 1870 and was knighted on 23 June 1870. He married first Amelia, daughter of L. Hopkinson, and secondly, in 1889, Elizabeth, daughter of James Gruar. He wrote Naval Administrations, 1827 to 1892 (edited by Lady Briggs, 1897). He died at his home, 6 Elm Park Road, South Kensington, London, on 26 February 1897.   J. K. LAUGHTON, rev. ANDREW LAMBERT

Sources J. M. Collinge, Navy Board officials, 1660–1832 (1978) · J. C. Sainty, ed., Admiralty officials, 1660–1870 (1975) · R. Morriss, The royal dockyards during the revolutionary and Napoleonic wars (1983) · J. H.

Briggs, *Naval administrations, 1827 to 1892: the experience of 65 years*, ed. Lady Briggs (1897) • R. V. Hamilton, *Naval administration* (1896) • *GM*, 3rd ser., 18 (1865), 395 • *Morning Post* (8 Feb 1865) • *Morning Post* [3 Jan ?] • *Daily Telegraph* (6 Jan 1874) • private information (1885) [Sir J. H. Briggs] • *Dod's Peerage* (1858) • Boase, *Mod. Eng. biog.* • *CGPLA Eng. & Wales* (1865) • *WWW*, 1897–1915

Archives BL, letters to Sir Charles Napier, Add. MSS 40028–40030 • NMM, letters to Lord Melville

Wealth at death under £6000: probate, 31 March 1865, *CGPLA Eng. & Wales*

Briggs, Katharine Mary (1898–1980), writer and folklorist, was born on 8 November 1898 at 102 Fellows Road, Hampstead, eldest daughter of Ernest Edward Briggs (1866–1913) and his wife, Mary Cooper (1867–1956). Her father belonged to a wealthy Unitarian family in Yorkshire, engaged in mining, banking, and various industrial enterprises; he made an unconventional but happy marriage with a farmer's daughter. After a serious illness at sixteen he had given up a career in the family firm for the Slade School of Art, and become a distinguished landscape painter. When Katharine was twelve they moved from London to a beautiful house, Dalbeathie, built by Ernest above the River Tay near Dunkeld, Perthshire. It was filled with books and pictures, and a constant stream of guests, mostly artists and writers, came to stay.

Katharine and her two sisters, Winifred and Elspeth, had an idyllic childhood, and she gained her love of folktales, local traditions, and storytelling from an early age, encouraged by her father. But he died when she was fourteen, and they were left somewhat isolated. Katharine went to school (Lansdowne House) in Edinburgh and then to Oxford to read English at Lady Margaret Hall, taking her degree in 1921. She returned to Dalbeathie to devote herself to her family, and the sisters worked at writing and art, Winifred producing some of their work on a small printing press. Katharine and Elspeth collected rare books on the seventeenth century, and wrote historical novels. They worked with Guides and Brownies, and Katharine became interested in story-telling, mimes, and plays for children, and invited Guide and Brownie leaders and others to the house for dramatic work. She developed a touring company called the Summer Players, rehearsing at Dalbeathie and giving performances in remote places far from theatres. Her own plays, along with ballads and folk-songs, were included in the repertory. In 1939 the family bought a house in the Cotswolds as a more accessible centre, but the outbreak of war changed everything.

Evacuees came to Dalbeathie, which Winifred ran almost single-handed, while Elspeth trained as a draughtsman in London, and Katharine shocked her friends by joining the Women's Auxiliary Air Force in 1941 as an ordinary recruit. She worked as a nursing orderly, a great contrast to the privileged existence she had led hitherto, but she gained from contacts with a wider world, and made many friends. She attained the rank of lance air corporal, and as time went on she was able to organize plays and entertainments, write poems, and plan books.

After the war she moved into the Barn House in Burford and set about making it habitable, while planning to do research in seventeenth-century literature at Oxford. She

had become fascinated by the rich variety of fairy characters when working with Brownies, and had written a small book, *The Personnel of Fairyland*, published in 1953. Ethel Seaton, her sympathetic and inspiring supervisor, encouraged her to work on beliefs in the supernatural in seventeenth-century literature, and she achieved her doctorate in 1952. After her mother's death in 1956 Dalbeathie was sold, and Elspeth and Winifred moved to the Barn House.

Once more they took up dramatic work, with memorable Shakespeare productions in their garden, and plays in Burford church; Katharine had now become a loyal member of the Church of England. She had support from Faith Spachman (later Sharp), a gifted musician; they tried to establish an arts centre, but had to be satisfied with the rebuilding of the parish hall.

Katharine's work at Oxford resulted in two important books, *The Anatomy of Puck: an Examination of Fairy Beliefs among Shakespeare's Contemporaries and Successors* (1959) and *Pale Hecate's Team* (1961), on magic and witchcraft. She also published *Hobberdy Dick* (1955), a delightful tale for children set in the Cotswolds in Tudor times with a household brownie as the main character, and *Kate Crackernuts* (1963), a powerful and moving story of witchcraft based on a folktale, begun during the war. *The Fairies in Tradition and Literature* (1967) dealt with recent fairy traditions, and included a list of fairy beings, as did the earlier *Personnel of Fairyland*; out of these her enormously popular *Dictionary of Fairies* (1976) developed. But for ten years she was working on a more ambitious project, a *Dictionary of English Folktales*, in four massive volumes; the manuscript was duly delivered to Routledge and Kegan Paul on the appointed day, and published in 1970–71. Katharine was elected to the council of the London Folklore Society in 1961, and was an extremely successful president from 1967 to 1970, doing much to rebuild the society at a crucial time in its history.

Now, however, Katharine's life had become difficult. Two accidents left her seriously lame; Elspeth, to whom she was devoted, had died in 1961, and Winifred in 1966, and she could no longer manage alone. Then in 1975, when staying with a relative in Dover, she made a new friend in Katharine Law, and moved to St Margaret's Bay to live with her and Dr Carol Duff. She was nursed back to health and her remaining years were filled with happy activities. She made visits to America, where she was immensely popular, proved an excellent broadcaster, and published several popular books on folk-tales and fairy lore, while her work was translated into various languages including Japanese. Katharine was a woman of great charm, making friends everywhere and holding audiences enthralled by her story-telling. Her life was full and serene until her sudden death at her home, Southolme, Sea View Road, St Margaret's Bay, on 15 October 1980. Her ashes were buried at the church of St John the Baptist, Burford. Her portrait, painted by John Ward, was exhibited that year at the Royal Academy. The Folklore Society sponsors an annual Katharine Briggs lecture, while the Katharine Briggs Club, an interdisciplinary group, holds regular meetings and conferences. The Katharine Briggs Trust is now being set up to promote publication and research. HILDA ELLIS DAVIDSON

Sources H. R. E. Davidson, *Katharine Briggs: story-teller* (1986) · U. Leeds, Brotherton L., Briggs MSS · *CGPLA Eng. & Wales* (1981) · private information (2004) [Evelyn Goshawk]
Archives U. Leeds, MSS relating to Briggs family · U. Leeds, Brotherton L., papers relating to her studies on folklore
Likenesses J. Ward, portrait, exh. RA 1980
Wealth at death £9750: probate, 29 April 1981, *CGPLA Eng. & Wales* · £236,618: further grant, 30 April 1981, *CGPLA Eng. & Wales*

Briggs, Richard (*fl.* 1788), writer on cookery, was for many years at the Globe tavern, Fleet Street; the White Hart, Holborn; and the Temple Coffee House, Fleet Street, London. His book, *The English Art of Cookery*, was first published in 1788 and by 1798 it had gone into several editions in England, Ireland, and America. Its name was changed to *The New Art of Cookery* for the subsequent American editions.

Briggs's book was aimed at housekeepers and has been described as 'largely a plagiarisation or, more charitably, a competent revision and enlargement' of John Farley's *The London Art of Cookery* of 1783 (Mennell, 99). However, Briggs's work reveals considerable improvements over Farley's. Cooking times, methods, and quantities of ingredients are often clarified and Briggs includes a wider range of foods—notably fish and vegetables. Interestingly he broke new ground by including recipes for fish rarely mentioned in eighteenth-century cookery books, such as 'To Boil John-a-Dore', a simple recipe remarkably similar to one favoured by James Quin, the actor renowned for his predilection for this fish (Davidson, 81). Although the book was predominantly about English food there were none the less German, Spanish, West Indian, Italian, Dutch, French, and Jewish influences in the recipes. Some were adapted and others are identical with recipes found in Hannah Glasse's *The Art of Cookery* (1747) and Elizabeth Raffald's *The Experienced English Housekeeper* (1769). Both writers were major sources for *The London Art of Cookery*, and Briggs selected additional recipes not found in Farley's book.

Little is known of Briggs, but in the preface to his book he revealed that he was 'one whose Habits of Life have been active, and not studious'. This may account for the unusual spelling of occasional words, for example 'Gou de Vou' for Godiveau, 'Peregoe' for Perigueux, and 'Hollybert' for the now obsolete hollybut (halibut), as well as 'John-a-Dore' already mentioned. FIONA LUCRAFT

Sources R. Briggs, *The English art of cookery*, 3rd edn (1794) · V. Maclean, *A short-title catalogue of household and cookery books published in the English tongue, 1701–1800* (1981) · K. Bitting, *Gastronomic bibliography* (1981) · B. Lillywhite, *London coffee houses* (1963) · A. Davidson, *North Atlantic seafood* (1986) · S. Mennell, *All manners of food: eating and taste in England and France from the middle ages to the present* (1985)

Briggs, William (*c.*1650–1704), physician and oculist, born at Norwich, was the second of the seven sons (there was one daughter) of Elizabeth Aldrige and Augustine Briggs (*c.*1618–1684). The family was prominent in Norwich; Augustine Briggs served as alderman and mayor, and was

William Briggs (*c.*1650–1704), by John Faber junior, 1738 (after Robert White, 1697)

MP for the city on four occasions. William Briggs entered Corpus Christi College, Cambridge, in 1663, under the care of Thomas Tenison, later archbishop of Canterbury. Briggs received his BA in 1667 and his MA in 1670. He then began to study medicine, was incorporated at Oxford in October 1670, and attended lectures of Vieussens at Montpellier, under the patronage of Ralph Montagu, then ambassador to France. Interestingly, there may have been an earlier connection between the Briggs family and Montpellier medicine: in 1659 the physician Thomas Sydenham accompanied 'Mr. Briggs' (possibly William Briggs's older brother, Robert, professor of law at Gresham College) to Montpellier, where Sydenham studied with the physician Charles Barbeyrac (Payne, 90–91).

In 1676 Briggs published an anatomy of the eye, *Ophthalmographia*, dedicating it to his Montpellier patron, Montagu. The following year, Briggs received his MD at Cambridge. He was elected fellow of the Royal College of Physicians in 1682, later serving as censor in 1685, 1686, and 1692. On moving to London, he was appointed physician to St Thomas's Hospital in 1682. He became known for treating difficult eye diseases. In 1682 the first part of his 'Theory of vision' was published by Robert Hooke (*Philosophical Collections*, no. 6, p. 167). The second part was published in *Philosophical Transactions* in 1683. In 1684 Martin Lister, physician and natural philosopher, then serving on the council of the Royal Society, proposed Briggs for membership of that body; this nomination evidently failed (Hunter, 58). Despite this, Briggs's 'Theory of vision' attracted the attention of Isaac Newton, who supported the publication of a Latin translation of it in 1685. In the preface Newton acknowledged the benefit he had received from Briggs's anatomical skill.

Briggs's work on vision and the anatomy of the eye reflects the emphasis on experimental science and comparative anatomy that emerged at Cambridge out of the work of William Harvey and his disciples earlier in the century. Briggs contributed to the understanding of the role of the optic nerve in vision, suggesting that the fibres of the optic nerve (rising from two protuberances of the thalami optici) were more concerned with vision than either the cornea, the humours, or the retina, as others had held. He maintained that the fibres of the retina convey vibrations to the papilla of the eye and from there to the optic nerve. He also hypothesized that the superior fibres in each thalamus had the greater tension and the inferior the lesser—concluding that the tension on the two sides must be compatible for proper vision.

In 1687 a second edition of Briggs's *Ophthalmographia* was published; this was a reprint of the first edition, containing no new illustrations. Briggs was removed from his position at St Thomas's Hospital in 1696, blaming a rival physician for this dismissal. That same year he became physician-in-ordinary to William III and served for five years. Briggs never obtained the payment promised him for these services, and early in the reign of Queen Anne he begged for consideration in regard to a hospital appointment.

Briggs died at Town Malling, Kent, on 4 September 1704, and was buried there on 11 September. He left three children from his marriage to Hannah, daughter of Edmund Hobart of Holt, Norfolk: Mary, wife of Thomas Bromfield, of London; Henry, chaplain to George II, and rector of Holt, who erected a cenotaph to his father's memory in Holt church in 1737; and Hannah, wife of Dennis Martin, of Loose, Kent.   BARBARA BEIGUN KAPLAN

Sources R. R. James, ed., *Studies in the history of ophthalmology in England prior to the year 1800* (1933), 74–83 · Munk, *Roll* · M. Hunter, *The Royal Society and its fellows, 1660–1700: the morphology of an early scientific institution* (1982), 9, 58 · J. F. Payne, *Thomas Sydenham* (1900), 90–91 · Venn, *Alum. Cant.* · C. Webster, *The great instauration: science, medicine and reform, 1626–1660* (1975), 315–16 · *DNB* · HoP, *Commons*
Archives RCS Eng. · Royal Society of Medicine, London
Likenesses J. Faber junior, mezzotint, 1738 (after R. White, 1697), NPG [*see illus.*]

Briggs, William (1839–1919), chemical manufacturer, was born at East Retford, Nottinghamshire, on 25 March 1839, the eldest son of William Briggs, stage-coach proprietor, and his wife, Jemima, née Bennett. He attended the King Edward VI Grammar School in Retford, then, aged fifteen, went to Chesterfield to work for a telegraph company. He was transferred to Edinburgh in 1858, but a year later left the telegraph service and moved to Greenock to become an apprentice in a chemical works, probably that of John Poynter & Sons, which had a reputation for generating the strong smells that wafted over the town. Leaving Greenock in 1860, he joined the British Asphalte Company in Glasgow, then the most important centre of the chemical industry in Scotland. He rose to become assistant manager

at the company's Port Dundas works and in his spare time attended chemistry classes at Anderson's College. Having acquired a modest amount of capital, and with the assurance of further financial backing from his future brother-in-law, Archibald Smith, Briggs moved to Arbroath in 1865 to open a coal-tar distillation plant and asphalt works. Briggs married Jane Smith on 13 September 1866; they had three sons, William, James, and Archibald.

Arbroath was already a prosperous centre for the manufacture of linen textiles and sailcloth. Timber, pitch, and tar from the Baltic and North America, some of which was used in the local shipbuilding industry, were unloaded in its harbour. Although there was no coal in the immediate vicinity, it could readily be transported by sea from the Fife or Lothian coalfields. Moreover, Briggs contracted the local gas company to supply its waste tar, from which a wide range of products could be derived. Briggs's products were mainly used in the construction industry. He also imported, from Germany, France, and Italy, mastic rock asphalt to be laid on foundations, floors, and roofs, including those of farm buildings. Although Briggs displayed considerable energy and enterprise, the firm chiefly benefited from the Victorian building boom, notably the rapid expansion of the city of Dundee, where factory and housing construction proceeded apace during the second half of the nineteenth century. From modest beginnings the firm diversified its product range and grew to be one of the most important of its kind in the east of Scotland.

Briggs expanded the firm beyond Arbroath and in 1890 shifted its centre of operations to Dundee, opening subsidiary works at Kirkcaldy and at Ladybank in Fife. In addition to its trade in coal-tar products, the firm also manufactured and applied bituminous anti-corrosive compounds to iron and steel structures, especially in the shipbuilding industry; here again, given the rapid expansion of steel shipbuilding on the Clyde and elsewhere, Briggs was well placed to exploit the market for his specialized products. He also took a keen interest in the manufacture and use of concrete, on which he published a study in 1891. In 1900 the firm became a limited company with Briggs as managing director.

Briggs clearly had great skill and energy and built up a very successful enterprise in the chemical and related industries. Apart from his business interests, he was an enthusiastic amateur scientist, was actively involved in Liberal politics, and was a member of churches in Greenock, Glasgow, Arbroath, Dundee, and Pitlochry, where he served for over forty years as a sabbath school superintendent. His teaching services for the church were recognized by his appointment as a director of the Scottish National Sabbath School Union. Briggs retired in 1907 to Pitlochry, where he built a handsome villa, Torrdarach, and spent his time in church and philanthropic work. He died there on 9 May 1919, and was buried on the 12th in Arbroath. His wife had predeceased him. His estate was valued at £14,451, a sum which suggests that the bulk of his assets had earlier been transferred to other members of his family.

The company expanded rapidly under the management

of his sons, and in particular William Briggs (1869–1961) and **James Alexander Briggs** (1871–1961), who was born at Arbroath on 18 July 1871 and educated at Arbroath high school. The brothers greatly increased the number of depots and agencies for the firm's products in major seaports at home and abroad, and formed or acquired associated companies in Germany, the Netherlands, the United States, and elsewhere. For thirteen years before the First World War, William looked after the firm's interests in Germany, supplying anti-corrosives to the shipbuilding industry. However, the firm's main driving force, after he became managing director on his father's retirement, was James. In the inter-war years he oversaw the company's greatest increase in productive capacity. Before 1930 bitumen had been imported from North America, but such was the demand for the company's products that an oil distillation and bitumen plant, the Camperdown refinery, was built near Dundee harbour. The products included diesel oil, lubricating oils, and various grades of bitumen. Clearly aware of the market potential of new developments in road transport, Briggs also initiated the manufacture of tarmacadam. As a result of these initiatives, the bulk of the company's work came from road-making products, although construction materials, such as roofing felts, damp courses, and electrical insulation compounds, remained important. Until his retirement from the chairmanship of the company in 1947, James Briggs headed one of the largest and most successful producers of road-making and construction materials in the United Kingdom. He died at 30 Farington Street, Dundee, on 12 May 1961, his wife, Lizzie Jane Logan Yule, having predeceased him.   IAN DONNACHIE

Sources *Arbroath Herald* (16 May 1919) · J. M. Jackson, ed., *The third statistical account of Scotland*, 25: *The city of Dundee* (1979) · C. W. Munn, 'Briggs, James Alexander', *DSBB* · Scottish Advertisers, *The history of Dundee* (1960), 129–33 · newspaper files, Central Library, Dundee · Watt Library, Greenock · Nynas UK AB, Dundee · d. cert. · d. cert. [James Alexander Briggs]

Archives NA Scot., dissolved company files · Nynas UK AB, Dundee, Briggs Oil records

Likenesses portrait, Nynas UK AB, Dundee

Wealth at death £14,451 1s. 11d.: NA Scot., SC 49/32/37

Brigham, Nicholas (*d.* 1558), administrator and antiquary, is of unknown origins. The date and place of his birth are unrecorded, and there is no evidence, Anthony Wood's surmises notwithstanding, that his family was associated with Caversham in Oxfordshire before his elder brother Anthony acquired property there about 1540. Nor are there any records to associate him with Hart Hall, Oxford, as Wood also suggests, and it seems more likely that he was educated at Cambridge, where one Nicholas Brigham (or Burtham) graduated BCL in 1522–3. Wood states that he studied at the inns of court, but his name is not found in any of the extant registers. It is possible that, like his fellow antiquary John Leland, Brigham was a member of the household of Thomas Howard, duke of Norfolk. Certainly, beginning in 1554 he acted as agent for the financial affairs of the duke, who had died in the same year, for which his annual salary was £13 6s. 8d. On 26 June 1544 Brigham was granted the reversion of the office of

exchequer teller by Richard Warner, whose daughter Margaret he had married. He succeeded as fourth and most junior teller in 1545, and held the position of teller for the rest of his life, becoming first teller in 1555.

After Mary's accession in 1553, Brigham's financial responsibilities increased, and in 1556 he was put in charge of money arising from the sale of crown land. In 1558 he became principal receiver of the loan raised in the city of London. In May of this same year he was rewarded with a £50 annuity, which in August was extended to his wife in survivorship. In late 1558, probably in December, Brigham died, at Westminster according to John Bale, but there is no record of the exact date and he did not leave a written will, only a verbal statement in his wife's favour. His only child, Rachael, predeceased him in 1557. Brigham appears to have been scrupulously honest, in spite of the financial temptations of his office—he had the right to use crown money in his custody between reception and disbursal—and his executors had no difficulty balancing his exchequer account after his death. The so-called 'Dudley conspiracy' against Queen Mary in 1556 had among its ramifications a plot to rob the exchequer, in which Margaret Brigham was perhaps unwittingly involved, but Brigham emerged from the situation unscathed. In 1559 Margaret married William Hunnis, who may have been associated with the conspiracy, and with whom she was rumoured to have been intimate in 1556. She died in the year of her second marriage, and Hunnis, who acted as her executor, was thus considered to have control over Brigham's estate.

Brigham, who was described by the 1556 conspirator John Dethicke as 'trusty and true' (SP 11/7, fols. 8–9), appears to have been conservative in his religion as well as in his financial dealings, and he came to his greatest prominence in Mary's reign. His friends did, however, include religious radicals, John Bale praising him as 'Anglicarum antiquitatum amator maximus' (Bale, *Cat.*, 1.718). Bale credits him with a historical work entitled *De venationibus rerum memorabilium* and memoirs or *Res quotidianae*, as well as poetry. Of the poetry all that survives is a four-line epitaph to Chaucer, which was composed for the marble monument to Chaucer which Brigham erected in Westminster Abbey in 1555 or 1556. Although the prose works are both now lost, Bale cites the *De venationibus*, described as a 'magnus liber', as his source of information about a number of medieval authors and texts, some unattested elsewhere. These include Asser, Ralph of Coggeshall, Frithegod of Brioude, John Gower, Lawrence Cunde, Ralph Strode, Robert Balsac, Domesday Book, and *Mum and Soothsayer* (although the incipit quoted actually derives from *Richard the Redeless*).

Brigham is known to modern scholarship primarily as a collector of medieval manuscripts and, as the monument to Chaucer suggests, he was interested in vernacular materials as well as Latin texts: *Mum and Soothsayer*, for example, Thomas Hoccleve's *Regiment of Princes*, and the writings of John Gower. From Sir Ralph Copinger (*d.* 1550/51) he borrowed a copy of *Piers Plowman*. In his letter to Matthew Parker, Bale states that, like those of Robert Talbot, Brigham's executors had 'many noble antiquytees' (Graham and Watson, 25), and Brigham is the single most quoted source in the *Index Britanniae scriptorum*. Although a concerted effort to trace manuscripts owned or consulted by Brigham might yield significant results, to date very few have been identified: Lambeth Palace Library, MS 1106, and BL, MS Harley 1620 (copies of the *Flores historiarum*), Cambridge, Gonville and Caius College, MS 153/203 (Ailred of Rievaulx's life of Edward the Confessor), perhaps BL, MS Cotton Claudius A.i (Frithegod's *Breviloquium vitae beati Wilfridi*), Claudius B.vii, fols. 114–94 (a chronicle of England from 1189 to 1204), and Cleopatra A.i (a history of Britain to 1298).   JAMES P. CARLEY

Sources J. Alsop, 'Nicholas Brigham (d. 1558), scholar, antiquary, and crown servant', *Sixteenth Century Journal*, 12 (1981), 49–67 • Emden, *Oxf.*, 4.70 • Bale, *Index* • Bale, *Cat.*, 1.718 • *The recovery of the past in early Elizabethan England: documents by John Bale and John Joscelyn from the circle of Matthew Parker*, ed. T. Graham and A. G. Watson (1998) • Wood, *Ath. Oxon.*, new edn, 1.309–10 • M. McKisack, *Medieval history in the Tudor age* (1971), 68 • state papers domestic, Mary, and Philip and Mary, PRO, SP 11/7, fols. 8–9

Brighouse, Harold (1882–1958), playwright and novelist, was born at Inglewood, 25 Ellesmere Avenue, Eccles, Salford, on 26 July 1882, the eldest child of John Southworth Brighouse (1844/5–1917), manager in a cotton-spinning firm, and Charlotte Amelia Harrison (1853/4–1909), a schoolteacher and headmistress. He and his sister Hilda (*b.* 1884) were technically illegitimate: his father had married Charlotte Harrison, his deceased first wife's sister, in an unrecognized ceremony in Montreux in 1881. Brighouse was educated at Clarendon Road school, Eccles, before winning a scholarship to Manchester grammar school. He left there at the age of seventeen to work as a textile buyer in a shipping merchant's office. In 1900 he attended a summer season of plays by F. R. Benson's company at Manchester's Royal Theatre, which kindled his interest in drama. In 1902 he went to London to set up an office for his firm, and became a regular West End theatregoer. As a 'gallery first nighter' he met Emily Lynes (*b.* 1876/7), a photographer's assistant, and they married in Lillington, near Leamington Spa, on 7 February 1907. They had one daughter, Barbara. After a promotion at work Brighouse returned to Manchester, but in 1908 became a writer.

Brighouse was fortunate that his writing career coincided with the contemporary development of the regional repertory movement. Some of his early plays were produced in Glasgow and Liverpool, but in particular he benefited from the strong support Annie Horniman, and her first producer Ben Iden Payne, gave to original writing at the Gaiety Theatre in Manchester from 1908 onwards. His first play to be produced by them was *The Doorway* in 1909, though *Lonesome Like* was the first to be written. Together with Stanley Houghton and Allan Monkhouse, Brighouse formed a triumvirate of talented local dramatists at the Gaiety who wrote plays commonly, but not exclusively, with a Lancashire setting. *Hobson's*

Harold Brighouse (1882–1958), by unknown photographer

Choice (1916), a three-act play, proved to be his major success. In 1915 Payne was in America, so the play was first produced in New York in November that year. The first English production was on 22 June 1916 at the Apollo Theatre in London, where it ran for 246 performances. It became the source of a successful film directed by David Lean (1953), starring Charles Laughton, Brenda de Banzie, and John Mills. It was also in 1964 the acclaimed fifth production of the new National Theatre at the Old Vic, London, directed by John Dexter with Michael Redgrave, Joan Plowright, and Frank Findlay in the key roles. *Hobson's Choice* continues to be widely performed, and is a recurring item on school syllabuses, in the early twenty-first century.

As early as 1915 Payne referred to Brighouse as a 'prolific' writer, and certainly between 1908 and 1930 Brighouse wrote extensively over a wide field including drama, fiction, and journalism. Much of his drama consisted of one-act pieces or 'curtain raisers'. A selection of his best (*The Northerners*, *Zak*, and *The Game*) were published as *Three Lancashire Plays* in 1920. These revealed the northern realism with which Brighouse is normally associated, but during these years he also wrote such plays as *The Oak Settle* (1911) and *Maid of France* (1917), which are very different in setting and tone. The novel for which he had most affection was *Hepplestalls* (1922), which traces the rise of a Lancashire mill-owning family through the nineteenth century.

In the later stages of the First World War, Brighouse was recruited into the nascent RAF and employed in propaganda work. In 1919 he and his wife moved permanently from Manchester to London to a house at 67 Parliament Hill, Hampstead. He became a keen member of the Dramatists' Club, and during the 1920s he associated with many of the literary figures of the time, having a particular friendship with Frank and Veronica Vernon. In 1927 he was in polite dispute with John Galsworthy and George Bernard Shaw over royalties. They were generous in their attitude to royalties from amateur dramatic societies, but Brighouse had to point out that less eminent playwrights could not afford such largesse. During this decade he responded to the burgeoning dramatic societies of the Village Drama League and the Women's Institute with such anthologies as *Plays for the Meadow and Plays for the Lawn* (1921) and *Open Air Plays* (1926), which were light, even fey, compositions, far removed from the realism of *Hobson's Choice*. He served as chairman of the Authors' Society dramatic committee from 1930 to 1931.

After 1931 Brighouse never wrote a full-length play. In his autobiography, *What I Have Had* (1953), he writes that he 'wilted' and speaks of a 'domestic tragedy' (possibly concerning his wife's health) which continued for twenty years and discouraged him from writing. In 1939 he even 'faded out' from the Dramatists' Club, surprised to find that fellow members were supporting censorship. Nevertheless he could claim that by 1953 his work had appeared in more than seventy anthologies, and that 1947 had been a 'peak year' for productions of his 'pet' play, *Lonesome Like*. From 1913 until 1949 he was also a regular and proud contributor of reviews and miscellaneous pieces to the *Manchester Guardian*, and for many years he was an adviser to French's, the drama publisher. Brighouse collapsed in the Strand, London, on Friday 25 July 1958, on the eve of his seventy-sixth birthday, and died on the same day in Charing Cross Hospital. He was cremated in London at a private ceremony on 30 July.

BRIAN CHARLES HOLLINGWORTH

Sources H. Brighouse, *What I have had* (1953) · M. Hawkins-Dady, *Playwrights* (1994), vol. 2 of *International dictionary of theatre* · H. Brighouse, *Hobson's choice* (1916) · A. Nicoll, *English drama, 1900–1930* (1973) · W. Baghouse, 'The work of Harold Brighouse', *Papers of the Manchester Literary Club*, 58 (1932), 108–21 · H. Brighouse, *Three Lancashire plays* (1920) · J. Goodby, *Harold Brighouse, 'Hobson's choice': notes* (1988) · G. Rowell and A. Jackson, *The repertory movement* (1984) · d. cert. · b. cert. · private information (2004)
Archives Salford Museum and Art Gallery, Salford Local History Library | JRL, Basil Dean Archive; A. N. Monkhouse MSS
Likenesses photographs, Salford Museum and Art Gallery, Salford Local History Library [*see illus.*]
Wealth at death £14,471 3s. 2d.: probate, 29 Oct 1958, CGPLA Eng. & Wales

Bright, Sir **Charles Tilston** (1832–1888), telegraph engineer, was born at Wanstead, Essex, on 8 June 1832, the third and youngest son of Brailsford Bright, a manufacturing chemist, and his wife, Emma Charlotte, the daughter of Edward Tilston. He was educated at the Merchant Taylors' School (1840–1847) but was unable to attend university as his father's income became uncertain. He and his elder

Sir Charles Tilston Bright (1832–1888), by unknown photographer, pubd 1907–9

brother therefore took employment with the Electric Telegraph Company, which had been formed to exploit the patents held by Cooke and Wheatstone. In 1852 he joined the Magnetic Telegraph Company (an amalgamation), of which his brother became the manager. For this company he laid many telegraph lines between and within London, Manchester, Liverpool, and other cities, showing much initiative in organizing the mechanical work that was needed. He also laid a six-wire cable between Port Patrick, Scotland, and Donaghadee, Ireland; it was only the third sea cable laid, and the first in deep water.

Bright experimented with transmission of telegraph signals over long distances by connecting a number of London-to-Manchester lines end to end, and showed that a circuit 2000 miles long was usable. He and his brother held wide-ranging patents on telegraphy; their inventions were mechanical rather than electrical, although applied to electrical uses. An unusual one was the 'teredo tape' for submarine cables, an abrasive layer used to blunt the teeth of teredo worms trying to bore into a cable.

Bright's most widely known achievement was the laying of the first Atlantic telegraph in 1858, between Valentia (on the west coast of Ireland) and Newfoundland. The history of this cable has been told many times; Bright himself described it in 1887. It was planned in 1856, and a company was formed to construct and operate it. The capital was subscribed quickly, chiefly from the British side. Professor William Thomson (later Lord Kelvin) was one of the directors, and the company's electrician was E. O. W. Whitehouse. In late 1856 Bright was appointed engineer-in-chief to the company, but he was too late to influence the design of the cable, which he thought to have too small a conductor. The governments of Great Britain and the USA each lent a large ship for the laying operation, which began in June 1857 from the Irish terminal. However, the control of the cable as the ship rose and fell in the waves was inadequate; the cable broke, and could not be retrieved from the deep water at about 300 miles out. For a second attempt, in 1858, Bright had redesigned the brakes on the laying gear, and new cable had been made to replace what had been lost. This time the laying began, as Bright had wished, in mid-Atlantic; thus the most difficult part of the work was done first, and more attempts could be made if the first failed. Another advantage was that the laying would be complete in half the time, reducing the risk of interruption by bad weather. Several attempts failed almost immediately, but on two occasions several hundred miles were laid before the cable broke. The ships then returned to Plymouth, but Bright obtained reluctant agreement to try once more. This time the laying began on 29 July, and the two ships arrived at their respective destinations on 5 August. The main cable was connected to the shore ends and the instruments installed by 13 August. Bright's achievement was rewarded by a knighthood; he was only twenty-six.

The cable was never brought into full commercial use. The company had hoped to work it with normal telegraph instruments rather than the more sensitive ones that Thomson had designed, and the cable was probably damaged by the use of unduly high voltages to do so; but it is also likely that the cable was already imperfect when laid, for the many failures had used up the new cable, and much of what was laid was that remaining from the 1857 work, which had lain in a dockyard all through the winter and had been several times loaded and unloaded. The cable failed in October, but it had served to demonstrate that long undersea cables could be laid and used. Some of the messages had demonstrated the value, in both human and commercial terms, of quick communications between one continent and another.

Bright left the Magnetic Telegraph Company in 1860, although he continued to be a consultant to them. He went into partnership with Latimer Clark as a consulting engineer, and took charge of much cable-laying in the Mediterranean and in the Persian Gulf. In 1868 he laid a cable from Key West, Florida, to Cuba, and between then and 1871 laid thousands of miles of cable in the West Indies. This work was difficult because of the abrupt changes of sea depth encountered, and because it was an unhealthy area, in which his crews suffered badly from infectious diseases. In 1871 Bright himself was so weak from malaria that he had to abandon his work and return to England; he laid no more cables, and was in uncertain health for the rest of his life.

Bright's most enduring achievement, although it is largely unrecognized, arose from his proposal in 1861, jointly with Clark, that the British Association (BA) should specify a system of electrical units. The suggested units were to have names such as 'volt' and 'ohmad', derived from the names of scientists (this was a new idea), and were to be used with prefixes indicating ratios of 1000 (not 10 as in the metric system). The suggestions were improved by Thomson, Clerk Maxwell, and others, on behalf of the BA; but the idea for names, and the ratios of 1000, were adopted, and both survive in the international system of units.

In 1869 Bright broke off his partnership with Clark, in the mistaken belief that the large companies formed to build and operate telegraph systems would rely on the skills of their own staffs rather than use independent consultants. He turned to mining for lead and copper. He and his brother had already mined copper without commercial success in the south of France (1862–5), in the Hartz Mountains (1864), and in Somerset (1865–7). From 1873 they successfully mined copper in Serbia, but in 1876 war broke out there, and eventually they had to abandon the mines. In this period Bright was becoming less active in telegraphy, although he patented a telegraphic fire-alarm system in 1876.

In 1865–8 Bright had been MP for Greenwich, a cable-making town, as an independent Liberal, and he was active in seeking changes in the Telegraph Purchase and Regulations Act of 1868, by which all inland telegraphs were acquired by the Post Office. He became a member of the Institution of Civil Engineers in 1862, and of the Society of Telegraph Engineers on its foundation in 1871; he was president of the latter in 1886, just before it became the Institution of Electrical Engineers. He was one of the British delegates to the Paris Exhibition of 1881, and for his services was made a member of the French Légion d'honneur. He wrote little for publication, but sometimes delivered lectures which were then printed. He did, however, assemble a large collection of published information related to telegraphy in a series of scrapbooks, which were continued by his son, and were later transferred to the Institution of Electrical Engineers.

On 11 May 1853 Bright married Hannah Barrick, the daughter of John Taylor, a merchant of Hull. They had three daughters, of whom Beatrice became a well-known portrait painter, and three sons, of whom Charles became a telegraph engineer and wrote an authoritative treatise on telegraph cables.

Bright was described as genial and clubbable, generous to the point of extravagance. His main interests outside telegraphy were shooting and fishing. Although he earned a good income in his younger days, he did not accumulate savings, and in his later years moved several times into successively less expensive houses (to 20 Bolton Gardens, Kensington; then to Philbeach Gardens), and shortly after his death his widow moved again, to West Cromwell Road, Kensington. He died suddenly, of apoplexy, at his brother's house, Goldie Leigh, Abbey Wood, near Erith, Kent, on 3 May 1888, and was buried in the family vault at Chiswick on 7 May.   A. C. LYNCH

Sources E. B. Bright and C. Bright, *The life story of the late Sir Charles Tilston Bright*, 2 vols. (1899?) · C. Bright, *The life story of Sir Charles Tilston Bright*, rev. and abridged edn (1910) · *The Electrician* (9 Nov 1861), 3–4 · m. cert. · d. cert.
Archives Inst. EE, letter-book and corresp. relating to West Indies and Panama telegraph · Inst. EE, 'Telegraph notes'
Likenesses photograph, pubd 1907–9, NPG [*see illus.*] · Count Gleichen, marble bust, repro. in Bright, *Life story of Sir Charles Tilston Bright*; plaster cast of bust, Inst. EE · engraving, repro. in Bright, *Life story of Sir Charles Tilston Bright* · wood-engraving, NPG; repro. in *ILN* (4 Sept 1858)
Wealth at death £1274: probate, 15 July 1888, *CGPLA Eng. & Wales*

Bright [*married name* Knatchbull], **Dora Estella** (1862–1951), composer and pianist, was born on 16 August 1862

at 375 Glossop Road, Ecclesall Bierlow, Yorkshire, the daughter of a merchant's clerk, Augustus Bright, and his wife, Katherine Coveney Pitt. In February 1881 she entered the Royal Academy of Music, where she studied piano and composition and won many important prizes, including in 1888 the first Charles Lucas prize for composition to be awarded to a woman. During her student years Bright gave many public performances as a pianist, often of her own works. Among these were *Variations on an Original Theme of Sir G. A. Macfarren*, for two pianos (1888; published, 1894), and her first piano concerto, a fluent and attractive work, which she performed in 1888 at a Royal Academy concert in St James's Hall and at the Covent Garden Promenade Concerts. Further performances of this work followed in 1889 and 1891. The score is one of the few manuscripts by Bright to survive.

In 1889, already established as a successful pianist and composer, Bright left the Royal Academy. In that year she started an annual series of piano recitals and chamber concerts which became widely acknowledged for their adventurous programming of new British music. Her own songs, piano pieces, and chamber works were being published by such firms as Ashdown, Elkin, Novello, and Stanley Lucas, Weber & Co. She also wrote a considerable amount of orchestral music, including a fantasia for piano and orchestra, which she performed in May 1892 at the notoriously conservative and prestigious Philharmonic Society. This was the first orchestral work by a woman to be played by the society since the performance of Maria Milanollo's violin concerto in 1845.

On 22 March 1892 Bright married the landowner and Crimean veteran Captain Wyndham Knatchbull. After her marriage she curtailed her performing career somewhat but continued to compose, and she established an amateur dramatic and operatic society at her home at Babington, near Bath, in Somerset. Bright's involvement with theatrical music can be dated from 1893, when she wrote the incidental music for Seymour Hicks and Laurence Irving's *Uncle Silas* at the Shaftesbury Theatre in London. In the first decade of the twentieth century she established a fruitful artistic relationship with the dancer Adeline Genée, who had danced the title role in the first professional performance of Bright's ballet *The Dryad* in 1907 and for whom Bright composed several ballets, among then *La camargo* (1912) and *A Dancer's Adventure* (1915). She also took further composition lessons with Maurice Moszkowski in Paris, and it was probably while there that she composed her *Variations* for piano and orchestra (1910). Other orchestral works from the early twentieth century include a *Concertstück* for six drums and orchestra (1915?) and a *Suite bretonne* for flute and orchestra (1917).

After the First World War records of performances or publications by Bright became much less frequent. She appears to have turned instead to music journalism, and in the 1940s she worked as the radio critic for *Musical Opinion*. Her reviews of the BBC's output are deeply critical of most contemporary music. Bright was a dynamic and charismatic musician, widely acclaimed as a leading pianist and composer in the 1880s and 1890s. Letters written by her close friend and fellow Royal Academy student Ethel Boyce depict a fun-loving woman who loved the opera and giving parties, including one where her appearance as Carmen in a short red dress was regarded as 'rather too daring'. Despite her earlier championing of new music, by the end of her life she was unable to appreciate radical developments in the musical world and her own pioneering contributions, as both pianist and composer, were almost entirely forgotten. She died of cerebral thrombosis on 16 November 1951 at her home in Babington.

SOPHIE FULLER

Sources S. Fuller, 'Women composers during the British musical renaissance, 1880–1918', PhD diss., U. Lond., 1998 • S. Fuller, 'Dora Bright', *The Pandora guide to women composers: Britain and the United States, 1629 – present* (1994) • 'Lady instrumentalists: Miss Dora Bright', *Strand Musical Magazine*, 3 (1896), 157 • D. Bright, 'What has happened to music?', *Musical Opinion*, 65 (1941–2), 37–8 • *Royal Academy of Music Magazine* (Jan 1952) • *The Times* (23 Nov 1951) • *The Times* (29 Nov 1951) • *The Times* (4 Dec 1951) • H. Saxe-Wyndham and G. L'Epine, *Who's who in music*, 2nd edn (1915), 29 • I. Guest, *Adeline Genée: a lifetime of ballet under six reigns* (1958) • Royal Academy of Music Archives • letters from Ethel Boyce to Harland Chaldecott, Chertsey Museum, Harland Chaldecott papers, D 2463 • b. cert. • m. cert. • d. cert. • S. Banfield, 'Lehmann, Liza', *The new Grove dictionary of women composers*, ed. J. A. Sadie and R. Samuel (1994), 275–7

Likenesses photograph, repro. in 'Lady instrumentalists: Miss Dora Bright', 157

Bright, Gerald Walcan- [*performing name* Geraldo] (1904–1974), band leader, was born in Islington, north London, on 10 August 1904, the twin son (there were also three daughters) of Isaac Walcan-Bright, master tailor, and his wife, Frances Feldman. Like his brother, Sidney, he was musical from an early age. He started to learn the piano when he was five and he continued his training at the Royal Academy of Music, after attending the Hugh Middleton Central School at Islington. His first professional engagement was as a relief pianist accompanying silent films at a cinema in the Old Kent Road. His first band was formed in 1924 to play at the Metropole in Blackpool, but recognition came for him during the five years he spent as musical director at the Hotel Majestic, St Anne's-on-Sea. His band broadcast from the hotel three times a week and became the most popular dance orchestra in the north of England.

In 1929 Bright disbanded the orchestra and went to South America, where he spent some time in Argentina and Brazil studying Latin-American rhythms. He returned to London and formed his Gaucho Tango orchestra, which started playing at the Savoy Hotel in August 1930. He remained there for ten successful years. During this time he changed his stage name from Gerald Bright to Geraldo. He made his first recordings in 1930 with the orchestra, which gave more than 2000 broadcasts from the Savoy. In 1933 they appeared at the royal command performance. In September that year he formed a new orchestra for the Savoy, widening his repertory to include dance music and changing his signature tune from 'Lady of Spain' to 'I bring you sweet music' (it later became 'Hello again'). This orchestra made brief appearances in the films *Lilies of the Field* (1930) and *Ten-Minute Alibi* and played the whole score for *Brewster's Millions* (1935). At one time during the 1930s Geraldo was leading four bands and employing more than 200 musicians.

At the outbreak of the Second World War Geraldo was appointed supervisor of the bands division of the Entertainments National Service Association and director of bands for the BBC. Broadcasting several times a week in such programmes as *Tip-Top Tunes*, *Over to You*, and *Dancing Through*, Geraldo's orchestra became the most popular in Britain. His wartime band was more orientated towards jazz and swing than his groups of the 1930s—it included such men as trombonist Ted Heath, trumpeter Leslie Jiver Hutchinson, and clarinettist Nat Temple, who all led their own orchestras later. Geraldo took the orchestra to entertain the troops in the Middle East, north Africa, and Europe, covering nearly 20,000 miles and twice crash-landing (in Italy and Gibraltar).

After the war Geraldo ran several orchestras, the largest comprising seventy-five musicians, but he became more interested in the business side of music, supplying orchestras for liners (including those of the Cunard Line), dance-halls, theatres, and restaurants. His own orchestra continued to broadcast, and he was the first bandleader to appear on British television when it reopened after the war. He was a founder director of Harlech Television and, for a while, musical director of Scottish Television. In the early days of independent television (ITV) he appeared in a long-running television series called *Gerry's Inn*.

Although his public appearances diminished, Geraldo returned for a series of nostalgic concerts at the Royal Festival Hall from 1969, which led to a television series recalling the era of swing music. He was still recording in the 1970s. His last public appearance was at a concert in Eastbourne a few weeks before his death.

Geraldo was of medium height, sturdily built, with dark brown hair and brown eyes. He was always immaculately dressed and his voice had a slight cockney accent. He loved classical music but firmly believed in the value of dance music. When Malcolm Sargent criticized dance music in 1942 Geraldo said that he would conduct Sargent's orchestra in any piece of classical music if Sargent would conduct Geraldo's orchestra in a piece of swing music. Sargent refused the challenge.

Geraldo married Alice Plumb in 1948 and they were divorced in 1965, when he married Marya, daughter of Leopold Detsinyi, a Hungarian textile manufacturer. He died on 4 May 1974 of a heart attack while on holiday with his wife in Vevey, Switzerland.   TONY AUGARDE, *rev.*

Sources *The Times* (6 May 1974) · *The Times* (20 May 1974) · *The Guardian* (6 May 1974) · J. Vedey, *Band leader* (1950) · A. McCarthy, *The dance band era* (1971) · *CGPLA Eng. & Wales* (1975)

Wealth at death £120,640: administration with will, 11 Feb 1975, *CGPLA Eng. & Wales*

Bright, Henry (1715–1777), merchant, was born on 21 March 1715 at Brockbury, Worcestershire, the second of the six children of Henry Bright (1692–1726), a landed gentleman, and his wife, Mary, *née* Hill (1692–1780). Young Henry moved to Bristol, where he was apprenticed to

Richard Meyler, a hooper, in 1731. This marked the beginning of a long period of business interaction between the Bright and Meyler families. Bright and Meyler established a West India mercantile business in the late 1730s. Bright was sent as the firm's supercargo to St Kitts and then served as its agent in Jamaica, where he built up a successful trade in sugar, slaves, provisions, and dry goods. After his return to Bristol, on 27 September 1746 he married his partner's daughter, Sarah Meyler (1720–1769), the heir to Ham Green, a fine country house on the Somerset side of the Bristol Avon. They brought up one child.

Bright returned to Jamaica for the period 1748–51, after which he came home for good. During this final spell in the Caribbean he arranged sugar consignments for Meyler and was active in the slave trade, especially the illegal traffic with the Spanish American market. He was the managing agent of twenty-one slave voyages between 1749 and 1766, and was a member of the Company of Merchants Trading to Africa in 1755. With Meyler he continued to run a mercantile house in Jamaica with two branches, one in Kingston, the other in Savanna la Mar.

By the 1760s the Brights and the Meylers went their separate ways in terms of West India trade. Bright, ill with gout, retired in 1775. But he ensured the continuity of his merchant house by putting his son Richard into partnership with his nephew Lowbridge Bright. By the time of the American War of Independence the Brights had established an important provincial trading dynasty: they were known to be men of large fortune, and their merchant house was considered to be in higher credit than any other West India concern in England.

Bright's West India trading was supplemented by other business activities. He was a shipowner and partner in various privateering ventures during the Seven Years' War. In Jamaica he owned land in St Catherine's parish with his brother Francis, took out a mortgage on Cabarita plantation in Westmorland parish, and owned properties in Kingston. He became a member of the Harford Bank, one of the earliest banks established in Bristol.

Bright played an active role in local politics in Bristol. He served on the Bristol common council from 1753 until 1777, being appointed sheriff in 1753 and mayor in 1771. He was an active whig at general elections. In 1767 he became a member of the Society of Merchant Venturers, the most prestigious mercantile body in Bristol, on payment of a fine. He was a member of the Congregational meeting at Castle Green, Bristol. Although he lived mainly in a town house at 28 Queen Square, one of the most fashionable residences for Bristol merchants, and at Ham Green, he also owned land at Welland Court, Worcestershire, and in Colwall and Coddington parishes, Herefordshire. Bright died at Bristol on 25 November 1777 and was buried at St Nicholas's Church in the city on 29 November. He is reputed to have left a fortune worth £50,000, a substantial amount for a provincial merchant of the time.

KENNETH MORGAN

Sources University of Melbourne, Bright family papers · K. Morgan, 'Bristol West India merchants in the eighteenth century', *TRHS*, 6th ser., 3 (1993), 185–208 · J. Hunter, *Familiae minorum*

gentium, ed. J. W. Clay, 1, Harleian Society, 37 (1894), 135–6 · J. W. Damer Powell, *Bristol privateers and ships of war* (1930) · C. H. Cave, *A history of banking in Bristol from 1750 to 1899* (privately printed, Bristol, 1899) · BL, Add. MS 12436 · PRO, CO 142/31 · Bristol RO, Bright MSS · G. Baillie, *Interesting letters addressed to Evan Baillie esq. of Bristol, merchant, member of parliament for that great city, and colonel of the Bristol volunteers* (1809) · D. Richardson, ed., *Bristol, Africa and the eighteenth-century slave trade to America*, 3: *The years of decline, 1746–1769*, Bristol RS, 42 (1991) · H. A. Bright, *The Brights of Colwall* (1875) · apprenticeship lists, Bristol RO · will, PRO, PROB 11/1053, sig. 235 **Archives** Bristol RO, MSS [microfilm] · University of Melbourne, family papers | U. Mich., Clements L., Bristol shipping account books **Likenesses** portrait, repro. in Cave, *History of banking in Bristol*, 91 **Wealth at death** approx. £50,000: J. Latimer, *Annals of Bristol in the eighteenth century* (1893), 462

Bright, Henry (1810?–1873), watercolour painter, was born in Saxmundham in Suffolk, third son and probably youngest of the nine children of Jerome Bright (1770–1846), a clockmaker and jeweller, and his wife, Susannah Denny (*c*.1771–1842). Bright's date of birth is uncertain: the most likely date is 5 June 1810, although both his death certificate and gravestone state that he was fifty-nine when he died. The Bright family attended the Congregational chapel at Rendham near Saxmundham where there is a family vault. After school in Saxmundham (supposedly Mr Farrow's School for Young Gentlemen), Bright was apprenticed to a chemist in Woodbridge. He then moved to Norwich to work for a chemist and soda water manufacturer, Paul Squires, who introduced Bright into the local artistic circles where he must have met artists such as John Sell Cotman and John Berney Crome. Determined to become an artist himself, he persuaded his parents to let him transfer his indentures to the painter Alfred Stannard.

On 8 May 1833 Bright married Eliza Brightly (1813/14–1848) in Saxmundham parish church; they had two sons who died in childhood and two daughters. In 1836 the family moved to London where he lived for twenty years, in Paddington and subsequently at Grove Cottage in Great Ealing. Bright began exhibiting at the British Institution and the Liverpool Academy in 1836, and from 1839 to 1845 he was a member of the New Society of Painters in Water Colours, where he showed thirty-eight drawings before his resignation; Queen Victoria purchased his *Entrance to an Old Prussian Town* from the 1844 exhibition. Between 1843 and 1850 Bright exhibited nine oils at the Royal Academy, but failed to be elected to the academy when he stood in 1847. He was also a member of the Graphic Society from 1847 to 1853. His circle of friends included David Cox, Samuel Prout, Henry Jutsum, and James Duffield Harding—an important influence artistically—who eventually passed on to Bright his considerable teaching practice. Bright earned up to £2000 per annum from his many royal and aristocratic pupils; they included the landgravine of Hesse-Homburg and the Grand Duchess Marie of Russia (whom Bright once carried on his back across a swollen stream at Brodick Castle on the Isle of Arran). As well as publishing chromolithographs and drawing books, such was his reputation that he gave his name to

Bright's Superior Coloured Crayons and his testimonials included Winsor and Newton's Moist Water Colours.

Bright was a natural draughtsman and his watercolours—typically of open skies and landscapes—have considerable freedom, freshness, and richness of colour; he also made many drawings in chalk or pastel of old and picturesque buildings. In 1861 Bright wrote, 'as Flatou [a dealer] says, "They *smell* 'em now" when they buy. The days of "suggestive art" *only* are past, elaborate finish is looked for' (Allthorpe-Guyton, 30). Although it was exceptionally successful in its time, Martin Hardie regarded Bright's work as 'lurid and theatrical' and displaying 'dexterity rather than poetic feeling' (Hardie, 2.70). Examples include *Sunset River Yare* and *Old Mill, Moonlight* (Norwich Castle Museum); his drawings—usually signed H. Bright—can also be found in the Victoria and Albert Museum and the British Museum. Some of his work was done in collaboration with other artists, including Sir Francis Grant and both Charles and Edwin Landseer.

A photograph of Bright aged thirty-one shows an apparently stout man with a full face and black tangled hair. He suffered from ill health and there is a suggestion of restlessness about his life: much of his surviving correspondence is written from hotels. As well as making sketching tours within the British Isles, his exhibited works indicate visits to the Netherlands, France, Germany, and Prussia. He remained active in East Anglia, however, and was vice-president of the Suffolk Fine Art Association. By October 1870 Bright had returned to Ipswich to live at the house of his niece at 22 Anglesea Road, where he died after months of illness on 21 September 1873; he was buried in Ipswich cemetery. At the time of his death he was said to have enough commissions to last him for ten or twelve years. A studio sale was held by Christie, Manson, and Woods on 22 May 1874.　　　　　SIMON FENWICK

Sources M. Allthorpe-Guyton, *Henry Bright, 1810–1873* (1986) · F. G. Roe, *Henry Bright of the Norwich school* (1920) · M. Hardie, *Water-colour painting in Britain*, ed. D. Snelgrove, J. Mayne, and B. Taylor, 2nd edn, 3 vols. [1967–8] · C. Reeve, *Home and away* (1998) [exhibition catalogue, Bury Museum, 1998] · IGI **Archives** Hove Central Library · Norwich Castle Museum **Likenesses** C. J. Fox, photograph, *c*.1841, repro. in Allthorpe-Guyton, *Henry Bright* · engraving, repro. in Reeve, *Home and away* · wood-engraving (after photograph by Elliott & Fry), NPG; repro. in *ILN* (25 Oct 1873)

Bright, Henry Arthur (1830–1884), author and merchant, was born in Liverpool on 9 February 1830, the eldest son of Samuel Bright JP (1799–1870) and Elizabeth Anne, eldest daughter of the Liverpool banker Hugh Jones. The Brights, a long-established and well-respected family of Bristol merchants, traced their ancestry to Nathaniel Bright of Worcester (1493–1564) and still held the manor of Brockbury in Herefordshire purchased by his grandson.

Bright was educated at Rugby School and at Trinity College, Cambridge (1847–51). Although not attracted to the academic studies of Cambridge, he availed himself to the full of opportunities for meeting interesting people and for participating in the affairs of the union. He qualified for his degree, but as a Unitarian would not subscribe to the Thirty-Nine Articles of the Church of England (as then required) and was thus unable to graduate. After the Test Act was repealed (1856), he and his close friend and relative, James Heywood, were in 1857 the first dissenters to graduate at Cambridge. In 1861 he married Mary Elizabeth, the daughter of Samuel Thompson of Thingwall, Cheshire. They had three sons and two daughters.

On leaving Cambridge, Bright was made a partner in his father's firm of Gibbs, Bright & Co. Samuel Bright had initiated an Australian packet-ship service, the Eagle Line, using auxiliary screw steamers. Brunel's famous *Great Britain*, then still the largest ship in the world, was purchased very cheaply and converted first into a four-master, later a three-master, with auxiliary steam, and she was followed by the purpose-built *Royal Charter* of 1856. Their low thermal efficiency made them expensive vessels to operate, but in the days of the Australian gold rush their short passage times made them highly successful. Trade soon began to slacken, however, and the wreck of the *Royal Charter* in 1859 dealt the firm a blow from which it never fully recovered.

Bright seems to have been no more cut out for the shipowning life than he was for the academic life of Cambridge. The best that his anonymous memorialist could say of his business activities was that 'the value of his literary faculties in the letter-writing branch of the office was duly appreciated' (*Henry Bright*, 7), implying that he was not in the front line of entrepreneurial innovation. He was keenly involved in the campaign which sought to outlaw 'crimping' (the practice of recruiting sailors by entrapment) and the physical abuse of sailors at sea, which suggests he was a sensitive man, ill at ease in a harsh business.

While visiting the USA in 1852 Bright first met the American writer Nathaniel Hawthorne (1804–1864). It was to prove a significant meeting for the young Bright, who turned with increasing devotion and success to literature, a process assisted and encouraged by Hawthorne's arrival as American consul in Liverpool the following year. It was a symbiotic relationship in which Hawthorne provided the intellectual stimulation Bright lacked in his everyday life and received in return an entrée to the mercantile élite of Liverpool. It was through Bright that Hawthorne was invited to the celebratory *déjeuners* for the recommissioning of the *Great Britain* and the launch of the *Royal Charter*. A close and constant friendship between the two was broken only by Hawthorne's death and Bright was frequently mentioned in Hawthorne's notebooks.

It was through Hawthorne that Bright learned about the brutalities inflicted on American sailors, some of whom were seriously, occasionally fatally, injured by ships' officers in the name of discipline. Bright's humane attitude was reflected in his election as chairman of the Sailors' Home in Canning Place in Liverpool in 1867 and 1877. He was credited with securing the opening of a dispensary in the Custom House arcade, opposite the Sailors' Home, in 1877, and with opening a second home, in Luton Street, the following year.

From 1871 until his death Bright wrote for *The Athenaeum*. He was also a contributor to the Unitarian newspaper *The Enquirer* from 1856 to 1860, and later wrote pieces for the *Christian Reformer* and *Christian Life*. He was involved in a number of societies, including the Roxburghe Club, which published his edition of poems from Sir Kenelm Digby's papers, and the Philobiblon Society, which published his edition of some previously unpublished letters of Coleridge. He also wrote the first account of the Glenriddell manuscript of the poems of Robert Burns (*Athenaeum*, 1 Aug 1874). His paper on the history of the Warrington Academy, an important dissenting institution (*Transactions of the Historic Society of Lancashire and Cheshire*, 2, 1859), was a noteworthy piece based on original documents in his possession. He also published a history of his family, *The Brights of Colwall* (1872). His only well-known book, *A Year in a Lancashire Garden* (1879), was republished in 1989 as *A Year in a Victorian Garden*.

Bright was a significant figure in literary circles in Liverpool, and was described in 1893 as 'a man of rare talent, culture and refinement' (Orchard, 201). In 1882 his health began to deteriorate. After the fashion of the time, he tried the effect of a milder climate, staying for a while in the south of France and spending a winter in Bournemouth. In spring 1884 he returned to Liverpool and died at his home, Ashfield, Knotty Ash, near Liverpool, on 5 May 1884. He was buried at Knotty Ash, and was survived by his wife.

ADRIAN JARVIS

Sources [R. M. Milnes], *Henry Bright: in memoriam* (1884) · *The Times* (10 May 1884) · *The Athenaeum* (10 May 1884), 599–600 · N. Hawthorne, *The English notebooks*, ed. R. Stewart (1941) · H. A. Bright, *A year in a Victorian garden*, ed. F. Perry (1989) · B. G. Orchard, *Liverpool's legion of honour* (1893) · M. K. Stammers, *The passage makers* (1978) · Venn, *Alum. Cant.* · Boase, *Mod. Eng. biog.* · CGPLA Eng. & Wales (1884)

Archives Trinity Cam.

Likenesses portrait, repro. in Bright, *Year in a Victorian garden*, frontispiece

Wealth at death £45,552 0s. 4d.: probate, 2 July 1884, CGPLA Eng. & Wales

Bright, Herbert Christian Bankole- (1883–1958), medical practitioner and politician in Sierra Leone, was born of Sierra Leonean parents on 23 August 1883 at Okrika (later in Nigeria), the son of Jacob Galba Bright (1843–1910), businessman, and his wife, Laetitia, *née* Williams (d. June 1893). Bankole-Bright's was a prominent Krio (Creole) family, something of which he was inordinately proud. Educated at the Wesleyan Boys' High School, Freetown (1898–1904), and Edinburgh University (1905–10), where he qualified as a doctor in 1910, he set up in private medical practice in Freetown. In November 1911 he married Addah Maude, daughter of T. Colenso Bishop, a former legislative council member. They had four children.

Increasingly Bankie, as he was known, became concerned with politics and from 1918 to 1925 edited his own newspaper, *The Aurora*. He supported the pan-African West African Congress of British West Africa, attended the inaugural meeting in Accra in 1920, and kept the Sierra Leone branch going intermittently until 1939. He was also active in setting up the West African Students' Union in London in 1925.

In 1925 three elected members were added to the Sierra Leone legislative council. Bankole-Bright was one, and in alliance with Ernest Beoku-Betts, a successful lawyer (the 'Double-Bs', they were called), he mounted persistent challenges to the government. He was a fearsome orator, uttering his lengthy tirades in a roaring voice; when the governor told him to moderate it he flatly refused. But the council had retained its official majority, so the government could always outvote them. Vainly they demanded legislation to end racial discrimination in government service and promoted workmen's compensation, extension of the franchise, and other popular causes. They deplored the gulf the government deliberately maintained between the Sierra Leone colony and protectorate, and enraged the government by publicly supporting a railway strike in 1926.

In 1937 Beoku-Betts left politics for a legal appointment. Then in 1939 the political scene changed dramatically after the outspoken radical Isaac Theophilus Akuna Wallace-Johnson (1894–1965) returned to Freetown and established his Youth League. His fiery, populist rhetoric eclipsed Bankole-Bright, whom he ridiculed publicly as a silly old diehard. This was more than a man filled with family pride who disdained his social inferiors could possibly tolerate. When the government introduced bills to restrict civil liberties, aimed at Wallace-Johnson and the Youth League—bills Bankole-Bright would normally have strenuously opposed—he voted for them, thus alienating his supporters. He resigned his seat and left politics.

Over the next ten years government policy began moving towards decolonization. Colonial rule in Sierra Leone was based on the 'divide and rule' principle of rigidly separating the coastal colony with its small Krio population from the rest of the country, which was administered as a protectorate where the people were deliberately held down within a static political system that denied them opportunities of education and social advancement. When a new constitution was proposed the Krios felt their interests must be safeguarded. For a century and a half they had been British subjects, at first favoured by the colonial government then, for half a century, excluded from promotion on grounds of race. Now they felt they had a right to undertake the responsibilities of government they had been denied.

Colonial Office and government had long detested the Krios. When a new constitution was drawn up in 1947 it gave an overwhelming balance of power to the protectorate. A Krio group, the National Council of Sierra Leone, led by Bankole-Bright, protested against it vociferously. But in 1951 it was introduced and the results of the first general election made it possible for a protectorate-based party, the Sierra Leone People's Party, led by Dr Milton Margai, to take power. He and Bankole-Bright each obdurately refused any serious compromise, and henceforth the National Council of Sierra Leone, as the opposition party in the legislature, carried on a petty, obstructive 'policy of obnoxiousness', as Bankole-Bright's biographer has called

it (Wyse, 161). In 1957 the council lost all its seats, Bankole-Bright's included.

Bankole-Bright was an alarming figure. His huge, ungainly stature, protuberant eyes, and arrogant, bullying manner made him a frightening opponent. His private life was notoriously disreputable. On allegedly medical grounds he took charge of his dying father in 1910 and made him sign a will in favour of him and his brother instead of his stepmother (who successfully contested it in the courts). He was constantly involved in lawsuits, some involving sexual scandals, pursuing his cases implacably and vindictively. So when he died in somewhat reduced circumstances on 14 December 1958 at Garrison Street, Freetown, the fulsome obituary tributes were tempered with sighs of relief. He was buried in Freetown.

CHRISTOPHER FYFE

Sources A. J. G. Wyse, *H. C. Bankole Bright and politics in colonial Sierra Leone, 1919–1958* (1990) • L. H. Ofosu-Appiah, ed., *The encyclopaedia Africana dictionary of African biography, 2: Sierra Leone, Zaire* (1979) • *Sierra Leone Weekly News* (14 Dec 1912) • C. P. Foray, *Historical dictionary of Sierra Leone* (1977)
Likenesses photograph, repro. in *Encyclopaedia Africana*, 2.41

Bright, Jacob (1821–1899), politician, was born on 26 May 1821 at Green Bank, Conkeyshaw, Rochdale, the fourth son in the family of eleven children of Jacob Bright (1775–1851) and his wife, Martha Wood (1788/9–1830). John *Bright (1811–1889) was his elder brother, and Priscilla *McLaren (1815–1906) was his elder sister. Jacob senior had built up a cotton spinning business at Fieldhouse, near Rochdale. Jacob junior adopted neither his father's strict Quakerism, though he attended the Friends' school at York (1834–7), nor his strongly patriarchal outlook. Following an unsuccessful venture into trade, he joined the family business in 1842 and with his brother Thomas gradually took over its management. He took a particular interest in the Fieldhouse School, which was built in 1840 and sponsored by the Bright family. He took a distinctly radical stance by supporting Chartism, the Rochdale People's Institute (founded 1849), and the incorporation of Rochdale as a borough. As a member of its first town council, he learned the cut and thrust of party politics, and was elected the first mayor of the town in December 1856. On 13 September 1855 he married Ursula (1835–1915), daughter of Joseph Mellor, a Liverpool merchant also of Quaker background. Ursula Mellor *Bright shared many of his causes. They had a daughter, Esther, and two sons.

In the late 1850s the family moved to Manchester, where Bright developed his commercial interests, not only in cotton spinning and carpets, but also in pioneering the introduction of the linotype machine into Britain. He continued his radical activities, demanding a wide extension of the parliamentary franchise to both men and women. After unsuccessfully contesting the Manchester seat in July 1865, he was elected an MP for the city in November 1867, and in the same year took the chair at a meeting from which arose the Manchester Society for Women's Suffrage. When J. S. Mill lost his Commons seat in 1868, Bright became leader of the suffragists in parliament, and took charge of the Women's Disabilities Removals Bill. In

1870 he and Sir Charles Dilke introduced what was the first women's suffrage bill. Although the bills to extend the parliamentary suffrage to women all failed during the early 1870s, Bright achieved one success by carrying an amendment, suggested by Lydia Becker, to what became the Municipal Corporations Act of 1869, which enabled women householders to vote in municipal elections.

Bright was also active in the married women's property campaign, in and out of parliament: he sponsored one bill in 1869 (which led to a very limited act in 1870) and another in 1872. His tireless work for this cause led to the successful acts of 1881 (Scotland) and 1882 (England). The Brights were involved in the campaign to repeal the Contagious Diseases Acts, as founder members of the Ladies' National Association, and did not share the view that this agitation was a danger to the suffrage cause. He lost his seat in February 1874, and after his return in February 1876 introduced his last bill in the Commons on women's suffrage in 1878. During the subsequent debates within the women's suffrage movement, he held out for the full franchise demand, including married women, rather than the more limited enfranchisement of widows and single women.

Jacob Bright never courted his constituents and tried them sorely, particularly on the Irish question. Gladstone's Coercion Act of 1881 had strong Liberal support but Bright's libertarian principles meant that he opposed it at every stage. A speech to his constituents won them over. In the Commons he only spoke when strictly necessary, and was terse and to the point. His wife published an edited collection of his speeches in 1885. When he stood for the new constituency of Manchester south-west in the general election of November 1885 he lost his parliamentary seat, but he was elected there as a Gladstonian Liberal in July 1886. He stood down in July 1895.

Ursula Bright confessed that her husband had a vein of intolerance in political matters: 'He could not quite believe in the goodness of a Tory, though his incredulity vanished when he met an opponent in private life' (*Rochdale Observer*, 15 Nov 1899). Women's suffrage was his obsession: 'He brought it into all his speeches, much to the annoyance and even dismay of some of his staunchest supporters. "Jacob is at it again!" some really affectionate friend would whisper; and it was true. He was always "at it"' (*Manchester Guardian*).

Jacob Bright was overshadowed by his brother John, who took a different view of women's suffrage and of marriage; his sister Priscilla commented that John 'could *never* bear women to assist themselves' (Robbins, 219, 233). John disliked the campaign centred on the Contagious Diseases Acts, though he voted for repeal. Jacob was described as 'more delicate-looking than his brother, of slighter build, does not wear a coat of Quaker cut, and has a thick beard and moustache … His features are sharper and his eye is keener than that of his brother' (J. E. Ritchie, *British Senators*, 1869, 132). Although he never sought office or recognition, Bright was sworn of the privy council in June 1894 and it gave him pleasure to be 'Rt Hon.'. Despite ill health, he remained chairman of the family firm in Rochdale.

Bright died on 7 November 1899 at his home, Nunn's Acre, Goring-on-Thames, Oxfordshire, and was cremated three days later at Woking, without a funeral service. The memorial gathering at Nunn's Acre a few days later consisted of leaders of all shades of the suffragist movement. In a resolution the central committee of the Society for Women's Suffrage summed up his signal contribution. 'Jacob Bright was not only one of the earliest parliamentary leaders of the women's suffrage movement but throughout the whole of his political career one of its most constant and more courageous champions' (*Englishwoman's Review*).   ALAN RUSTON

Sources *Manchester Guardian* (9 Nov 1899) · *Rochdale Observer* (11 Nov 1899) · *Rochdale Observer* (15 Nov 1899) · *Rochdale Observer* (18 Nov 1899) · *The Times* (9 Nov 1899) · *Englishwoman's Review*, 31 (1900), 60–62 · O. Banks, *The biographical dictionary of British feminists*, 1 (1985) · N. J. Gossman, 'Bright, Jacob', BDMBR, vol. 3, pt 1 · C. Rover, *Women's suffrage and party politics in Britain, 1866–1914* (1916), 56, 211, 218–19 · G. M. Trevelyan, *The life of John Bright* (1913), 22–3, 85, 100–01, 106 · K. Robbins, *John Bright* (1979), 5, 118 · S. S. Holton, *Suffrage days: stories from the women's suffrage movement* (1996)

Likenesses F. C. Gould, group portrait, sketch, 1894, repro. in J. L. Hammond and B. Hammond, *Life of James Stansfield* (1932) · Spy [L. Ward], chromolithograph caricature, NPG; repro. in *VF* (5 May 1877) · photograph, repro. in Robbins, *John Bright*, pl. 7b · portrait, repro. in *Lancashire leaders* (1895) · portrait, repro. in *St Stephen's Review* (3 Oct 1891)

Wealth at death £5499 6s. 1d.: probate, 3 Jan 1900, CGPLA Eng. & Wales

Bright, James Franck (1832–1920), college head, was born in Westminster, London, on 29 May 1832, the third son of Richard *Bright (1789–1858), MD, the discoverer of the true causes and nature of 'Bright's disease'. His mother, his father's second wife, was Elizabeth, daughter of Captain Benjamin Follett, of Topsham, Devon, and sister of Sir William Webb *Follett. In 1844 Bright went to Rugby School, which was then under the headmastership of Archibald Tait, the future archbishop of Canterbury, and still inspired with the traditions of Dr Arnold. There he made some lifelong friendships, notably with George Joachim Goschen, Thomas Jex-Blake, and Horace Davey. In 1851 he went up to University College, Oxford, then under the mastership of Dr Frederick Plumptre, and in December 1854 obtained a first class in the recently created school of law and modern history. He had originally intended to follow his father's profession of medicine, but finally decided to take holy orders. He was ordained deacon in 1856 and priest in 1876, and became BD and DD in 1884.

Meanwhile Bright had been offered a temporary post as a junior master at Marlborough College. The headmaster, Dr George Cotton, was so well pleased with his work that in 1855 he promoted him to the mastership of the modern school, which had just been started. Bright left an account of the school when Cotton was appointed headmaster in 1852. 'It was', he wrote, 'in a very bad state: there was a great deal of bullying of a severe character; one boy, for instance, was periodically half-hanged; another tall ruffian used to take a small boy into Savernake forest, and, giving him twelve yards' start, proceeded to pot him with a pistol.' There was also a strong hostility to the masters.

The arrangement of the school buildings lent itself to disorder—immense dormitories and schoolrooms in which certain privileged boys were allowed to sit out of school hours, where they cooked illicit meals, but where it was nearly impossible to read or study; and an enormous big-school room, the scene of all sorts of pranks and bullying, into which all the unprivileged were crowded. Something had been done by Cotton with the help of E. S. Beesly and other masters before the arrival of Bright, who at once joined the reformers. He was specially successful in improving the relations between the masters and the boys, in reorganizing the schoolrooms, and in introducing changes after the model of his old school, Rugby. Finding that there was a deficiency of suitable books on English history for boys, Bright also began his *English History for the Use of Public Schools* (5 vols., 1875–1904). In 1860 he opened Preshute House, the first private house to be established at Marlborough, and in 1864 married Emmeline Theresa, daughter of the Revd Edmund Dawe Wickham (1810–1894), vicar of Holmwood, Surrey. The Harrow schoolmaster Reginald Bosworth *Smith was his brother-in-law. At Marlborough he remained to see the great prosperity of the school under the new headmaster, George Granville Bradley, appointed in 1858.

Bradley's departure from Marlborough to University College, Oxford, in 1870 was a great loss to Bright, but it was the death of his wife in 1871 which finally induced him to abandon his school work. She was a very clever, lively woman, who had been of the greatest assistance to him and to whom he was deeply attached. There were, moreover, four daughters to bring up. In 1872, therefore, he retired, intending to devote himself to literary work, and especially to the completion of the second volume of his *History of England*; but in 1873 Bradley offered him the post of lecturer in modern history at University College, with the promise of a fellowship, while Balliol and New College also agreed to add him to their staffs.

When Bright took up his new post (he was elected a fellow in 1874) the condition of University College was not very satisfactory. Undergraduate numbers were in decline and relations between them and the tutors were by no means friendly. Among other insubordinate student practices in fashion was that of locking up the dons in their rooms. In time, however, Bradley's reforms had due effect, and in the revival of the prosperity of the college the new numbers whom he added to his staff, especially Bright and Samuel Henry Butcher, gave him valuable assistance.

Bright's character well fitted him for the work of conciliating the undergraduates. He possessed a genuine sympathy for every form of wholesome energy, physical and intellectual, and was ever ready with encouragement and advice. In the university Bright took a prominent part in establishing the new honours school of modern history, for which he was frequently an examiner and a member of the faculty board in its early years. He was active in the establishment of inter-collegiate lectures in history open to all members of the university. Bright's own lectures, more particularly those on foreign history during the eighteenth century, were well attended, and were appreciated for their breadth of treatment.

So invaluable had been Bright's work as a tutor, and for some time as dean of the college, that, when Bradley was appointed to the deanery of Westminster in 1881, Bright was elected to succeed him as master. His election, however, took place only after the scientist T. H. Huxley declined to be nominated a candidate. Henceforth he devoted most of his time to the general administration of the college and to university work, while he spent his leisure moments in completing his *History of England*. In the improvement of the college he was materially assisted by his great friend Arthur Dendy, bursar of the college, R. W. Macan, who succeeded him as master, and H. M. Burge, eventually bishop of Oxford, his son-in-law. He took a leading part in the conversion of 'the hall' and no. 90 High Street into the Durham buildings, in the extension of the dining hall, and in the restoration of its fine hammer-beam roof. On his retirement from the mastership he appropriated his pension to the assistance of poor students of his college, and in his will left £2500 for the same purpose. In 1890 he was shot and wounded by a woman aggrieved that she had been jilted by a fellow of the college in favour of one of Bright's daughters. He recovered and continued to play an active part in college and university administration.

Bright was an active member of the hebdomadal council of the university, where he was identified with liberal causes. He strenuously supported the proposal, not adopted until 1920, to throw open the theological degrees to others than members of the Church of England. He was president of the Association for Promoting the Education of Women in Oxford (1883–9), and supported proposals to allow women to take degrees. He also took an active part in municipal affairs, and was a member of the city council from 1897 to 1901. He initiated the experiment of a technical school and presented a site in St Clement's for the purpose. He was also treasurer of the Radcliffe Infirmary (1883–93).

Bright felt deeply the death (1905) of his sister-in-law, Julia Isabella Wickham, who had controlled his house and helped him in his literary work since his wife's death, and in the following year he resigned his mastership. He retired to Hollow Hill, a house belonging to William Carr, of Ditchingham Hall, Norfolk, who was educated at Marlborough and University College, and married Bright's eldest daughter, Margaret, in 1886. Here Bright took a leading part in county work as JP and poor law guardian. He died at Ditchingham Hall on 22 October 1920.

A. H. JOHNSON, rev. M. C. CURTHOYS

Sources *The Times* (25 Oct 1920) · J. Foster, *Oxford men and their colleges* (1893) · private information (1927) · personal knowledge (1927) · *Hist. U. Oxf.*, vols. 6–7 · *CGPLA Eng. & Wales* (1921)

Archives University College, Oxford | King's Cam., Oscar Browning MSS

Likenesses Hills & Saunders, photograph, *c.*1892, repro. in Foster, *Oxford men and their colleges*, facing p. 27 · G. Reid, oils, University College, Oxford

Wealth at death £59,412 9s. 10d.: probate, 5 April 1921, *CGPLA Eng. & Wales*

Bright, Sir John, baronet (*bap.* 1619, *d.* 1688), parliamentarian officer and landowner, was baptized on 14 October 1619, the third but only surviving son of Stephen Bright (1583–1642), of Carbrook, Yorkshire, and his first wife, Joan Westby (*d.* 1633), daughter of George Westby of Whaley, Derbyshire. Bright came from humble origins. His grandfather was a yeoman farmer and one of his great-uncles a husbandman. The family's rise in wealth and status during the early seventeenth century was largely the work of Bright's father, who used the profits from his office as bailiff of the earls of Arundel in the Sheffield area to help purchase lands worth about £600 a year.

Having been admitted to Gray's Inn on 18 June 1639, John Bright had returned to Yorkshire by early 1642 and soon emerged as a leading figure among the West Riding parliamentarians. Early in 1643 he raised soldiers for the defence of Sheffield against the royalists and received a captain's commission from Ferdinando, Lord Fairfax. About May 1643 he was made a colonel under Fairfax and, though young, 'grew very valiant and prudent, and had his officers and soldiers under good conduct' (Ritson, 102–3). Bright fought at several major engagements including the battles of Adwalton Moor (June 1643), Nantwich (January 1644), and Marston Moor (July 1644). He showed particular bravery during the royalists' recapture of Pontefract Castle in March 1645; mounted on a white charger and drawing heavy fire, he was the last parliamentarian to quit the field. He ended the war covered in glory and as military governor of Sheffield and York. By the outbreak of the second civil war he was a colonel in the northern brigade under his brother-in-law and friend, Colonel John Lambert. Bright fought alongside Lambert in the battle of Preston (August 1648) and acted as his second-in-command at the siege of Pontefract Castle during the winter of 1648–9. In contrast to Lambert, Bright was opposed to the regicide, and writing to his friend Adam Baynes in October 1649 declared himself ready to quit his employments rather than take the oath of engagement (BL, Add. MS 21418, fol. 100). In July 1650, while his regiment was at Newcastle preparing for the invasion of Scotland, Bright resigned his commission 'upon some little discontent' over Cromwell's refusal to grant him leave (Ritson, 127). This 'little discontent' was probably a pretext to hide his much larger discontent at the proposed war against the Scots and Charles II, which was the issue over which Thomas, Lord Fairfax, had resigned his command a few weeks earlier. Nevertheless Bright accepted a militia colonelcy from the Rump Parliament to help repel the Scottish invasion of 1651. He remained in good odour with Cromwell and Lambert, who offered him a regiment in the regular army in 1654, but Bright refused. On 12 July 1654 he was returned for the West Riding to the first Cromwellian parliament. However, his parliamentary career was cut short on 15 November by his appointment as sheriff of Yorkshire. Trusted by Cromwell, he served as governor of Hull (1655–8) and helped Major-General Robert Lilburne suppress the Yorkshire royalist uprising of 1655. In the elections to Richard Cromwell's parliament in 1659 he supported the candidacy of Lambert at Pontefract, and

in August he led his Yorkshire militia regiment to Lambert's assistance against Sir George Booth. Bright probably welcomed the Restoration and was created a baronet on 16 July 1660. He seems to have devoted himself largely to private affairs after 1660, although he did serve as a deputy lieutenant and a militia colonel during the Restoration period.

Like his father, Bright was a ruthless operator in the Yorkshire land-market. His estate almost tripled in value between 1642 and 1660, much of this expansion apparently driven by his shrewd exploitation of the profits of military office and his privileged position as one of the West Riding's leading administrators. His most significant purchase came in 1653, when he acquired the forfeited manor of Badsworth (for £8600), which became his principal residence. After 1660 most of his income derived from rent receipts, money-lending, and marriage portions. Bright married four times. He married first, about 1645, Catherine Lister, daughter of Sir Richard Hawksworth, who died in January 1663. Secondly, about 1665, he married Elizabeth Norcliffe (*b.* 1623/4), daughter of Sir Thomas Norcliffe, who died aged fifty on 26 June 1674. In July 1682 he married Susanna Vane (*b.* 1658/9), daughter of Sir Thomas Liddell, second baronet, and widow of Thomas Vane, who died in November 1682. Fourthly Bright married on 7 June 1683 Susannah Wharton (1650/51–1737), daughter of Michael Wharton. Bright's 'mettle' in venturing 'upon girls' was noted: his last two wives were some forty and thirty years younger than him (Roebuck, 219). According to report, he had 'thirteen or fourteen thousand pounds by his wives', his last wife alone netting him £5000 (Roebuck, 219). At his death his estate was worth £3210 a year. Although he attended Anglican church services, he employed the ejected presbyterian ministers Matthew Sylvester and Jeremy Wheat as his domestic chaplains. He died on 13 September 1688 and was buried with great pomp in the chancel of Badsworth church on 21 September. His only surviving child was Catherine, the daughter of his first wife.   DAVID SCOTT

Sources Sheff. Arch., Bright MSS, Wentworth Woodhouse muniments · BL, Baynes correspondence, Add. MSS 21417–21427 · J. Hunter, *Hallamshire: the history and topography of the parish of Sheffield in the county of York*, new edn, ed. A. Gatty (1869) · P. Roebuck, *Yorkshire baronets, 1640–1760* (1980) · J. Ritson, ed., *Memoirs of Captain John Hodgson* (1806) · *Dugdale's visitation of Yorkshire, with additions*, ed. J. W. Clay, 3 vols. (1899–1917) · G. Fox, *The three sieges of Pontefract Castle* (1987) · HoP, *Commons* [draft] · *JHC*, 7 (1651–9) · *Calamy rev.* · *CSP dom.*, 1644; 1651; 1655–6; 1667–8 · Thurloe, *State papers*, vol. 6 · Notts. Arch., Savile correspondence, DDSR 221/96/17

Archives Bodl. Oxf., corresp. and extracts from deeds owned by him · HLRO, main papers, 15 Feb 1642, 6 June 1642 · Sheff. Arch., Wentworth Woodhouse muniments, corresp. and papers · Sheff. Arch., Wentworth Woodhouse muniments, deeds | BL, Baynes corresp., Add. MSS 21417–21427 · Notts. Arch., Savile corresp., DDSR 221/96/17

Wealth at death £3210 p.a.—estate: Roebuck, *Yorkshire baronets*

Bright, John (1780/81–1870), physician, was the fourth son of Paul Bright (*d.* 1804), of Inkersall, Derbyshire. He was educated at Wadham College, Oxford, where he matriculated on 13 December 1797, aged sixteen. He graduated

BA (1801), MA (1804), BM (1806), and DM (1808). He commenced medical practice at Birmingham, being appointed physician to the general hospital there in 1810, but relinquished the office the following year and soon after moved to London. Bright was admitted a candidate of the Royal College of Physicians in 1808 and was elected a fellow in 1809. He was censor in 1813, 1822, 1833, and 1840; Harveian orator in 1830; *consilarius* in 1839; and named elect in 1839.

Appointed physician to the Westminster Hospital in 1823, Bright officiated in that capacity (alongside Sir George Tuthill, who was concurrently physician to Bethlem Hospital) until his resignation in 1843, subsequently serving as consulting physician until 1870. During the 1830s he was known as an advocate of the controversial Brunonian approach to medicine (the treatment of disease mostly by alcohol and opium, according to whether the condition was classified as sthenic or asthenic). He was dubious about the utility of the approach of the French 'solidists', who emphasized the findings of post-mortem pathological examinations. Partly as a result, he took little interest in dissection and was rather sceptical about the benefits of modern medicaments. A physician in the classical mould, he was an accomplished Greek and Latin scholar, distinguished more for this by some colleagues and obituarists than for his contributions to medicine. He was characterized as humorous, imaginative, and well-mannered, but was censured in the medical press for his neglect of his teaching responsibilities.

Bright's other major professional profile was in the visitation of lunatics. Clearly a physician with good connections in society, besides being influential at the Royal College of Physicians, he was appointed by the college as one of the commissioners for regulating madhouses; he became secretary to the commissioners in 1825. Bright was twice called to give evidence before the select committee on pauper lunatics, whose report framed the consolidating English Lunacy Act of 1828, and his evidence confirmed how inadequate previous visitation had been. He presented his own suggestions for reform to the committee and some of his proposals, such as that two medical signatures be required for a certificate of lunacy, directly anticipated the provisions of the subsequent lunacy legislation. From 1828 to 1845 Bright served as one of five new metropolitan commissioners in lunacy. However, most medical professionals regarded the commission's powers as inadequate and its composition as severely compromised, ten laymen also serving as commissioners. Its relatively lax licensing of private madhouses and its self-satisfied reports confirm that its effectiveness was sorely limited. Bright was attacked in the pages of *The Lancet* as negligent, incompetent, and ignorant about medical science and insanity. His reputation was damaged further in the 1840s with the publication of criticisms made by John Perceval, a patient he had visited, who became an active lunacy reformer and a founder of the Alleged Lunatics' Friend Society. Bright also served for a time, from 1 September 1836, as a lord chancellor's visitor in lunacy.

An ample private income, and the sum of £1 an hour for

his work as a commissioner, meant that Bright was relatively free from professional anxieties, and consequently he practised very little medicine and did not deign to venture into print. He was married to Elizabeth (Eliza) Mynors, with whom he had two sons, John Edward Bright (b. 1810/11), barrister, and Mynors *Bright (1817–1883), literary scholar. Bright died at his address at 19 Manchester Square, London, on 1 February 1870; neither the *British Medical Journal* nor the *Journal of Mental Science* noticed his death. He was survived by his two sons.

JONATHAN ANDREWS

Sources *The Lancet* (12 Feb 1870), 250 · 'Select committee on pauper lunatics and lunatic asylums in the county of Middlesex', *Parl. papers* (1826–7), 6.41–9; 62–3; 155–9, no. 557 · T. Irving, 'Westminster Hospital: glance at its medical officers', *The Lancet* (24 April 1830), 125–8, esp. 126 · J. Langdon-Davis, *Westminster Hospital: two centuries of voluntary service, 1719–1948* (1952), 78–9 · Munk, *Roll* · A. Scull, C. MacKenzie, and N. Hervey, *Masters of Bedlam: the transformation of the mad-doctoring trade* (1996), 216 · J. Perceval, *A letter to the secretary of state for the home department, upon the unjust and pettifogging conduct of the metropolitan commissioners on lunacy, in the case of a gentleman, lately under their surveillance* (1844), 5–6, 14 · *The Lancet* (27 Oct 1838), 201 · *The Lancet* (19 Sept 1840), 931 · *The Lancet* (8 July 1843), 533 · *The Lancet* (12 Sept 1846), 294–5 · *The Lancet* (10 Oct 1846), 401–3 · *The Lancet* (4 Oct 1862), 373 · N. Hervey, 'A slavish bowing down: the lunacy commission and the psychiatric profession, 1845–60', *The anatomy of madness: essays in the history of psychiatry*, ed. W. F. Bynum, R. Porter, and M. Shepherd, 2 (1985), 98–131, esp. 100 · A. Scull, *The most solitary of afflictions: madness and society in Britain, 1700–1900* (1993), 200 and note 122 · D. J. Mellett, *Bureaucracy and mental illness: the commissioners in lunacy, 1845–90', Medical History*, 25 (1981), 221–50, esp. 223–4 · *CGPLA Eng. & Wales* (1870) · Foster, *Alum. Oxon.* · N. Hervey, 'Advocacy or folly: the Alleged Lunatics' Friend Society, 1845–63', *Medical History*, 30 (1986), 245–75
Likenesses Elliott & Fry, photograph, Wellcome L. · H. J. Whitlock, photograph, Wellcome L.
Wealth at death under £10,000: probate, 2 March 1870, *CGPLA Eng. & Wales*

Bright, John (1811–1889), politician, was born at Green Bank, Rochdale, Lancashire, on 16 November 1811, the second son of Jacob Bright (1775–1851) and Martha Bright, *née* Wood (1788/9–1830). Jacob Bright came originally from Coventry, to where his Quaker ancestors had migrated from Wiltshire in the early eighteenth century, but he settled in Rochdale in 1802, becoming a bookkeeper to John and William Holme, the cotton spinners. He married Sophia Holme, his employers' sister, but she died in May 1806, and he married Martha Wood in 1809. They had seven sons and four daughters among whom were Jacob *Bright and Priscilla Bright [see McLaren, Priscilla Bright]. John Bright became the eldest when their first child died in 1814.

Early life, education, and travels John Bright attended a variety of schools between 1820 and 1827. Initially he was educated locally, at the Townhead School in Rochdale. Then in the summer of 1821 he went to a school at Pendarth, near Warrington, and in the following year he moved to the Friends' school at Ackworth, near Pontefract, which his father had attended. He objected to the severe regime at Ackworth, however, and his father withdrew him in 1823 and sent him instead to a school in York

John Bright (1811–1889), by Rupert Potter, 1879

run by William Simpson (later Bootham School). Of all his schools John Bright enjoyed this one most, and later said he learned more here in two years than anywhere else. But his delicate health suffered in York and so in 1825 he was moved again, this time to a healthier environment, to a school in Newton in Bowland, near Clitheroe in Lancashire, where he remained for eighteen months, during which time he took up fishing. Jacob Bright had established his own business in 1823. The firm prospered and expanded during the 1820s and 1830s. On leaving school, John Bright joined the firm, and worked in the warehouse and office. In 1839 Jacob Bright retired and his sons took over the running of the business.

John Bright's schooling in politics began in 1830. He was reputed to have taken a lively interest in Henry 'Orator' Hunt's election at Preston in 1830, and scrawled, it is claimed, 'Hunt for ever' on the walls of the mill at Green Bank. But it was in the temperance movement and in the local literary and philosophical society that Bright initially took a small part in public life. His first speeches were delivered during 1830 in local chapels in support of temperance, and he and others founded the Rochdale Juvenile Temperance Band. In 1833 he helped establish the Rochdale Literary and Philosophical Society. Bright spoke regularly at the society's debates, and although discussion of party politics and religion was barred, he led motions against the monarchy, and against popular amusements and capital punishment. Bright's own preferred leisure activity was cricket, although he averaged only 6 in the 1833 season.

In 1832 Bright visited Ireland; he sailed from Liverpool to Dublin, visited Belfast, and returned via Glasgow. In June of the following year he travelled to the continent for the first time; he spent a month in Belgium and followed the Rhine through Germany and back to Rotterdam. After falling ill, and being fearful of the cholera epidemic, Bright cut short this trip. Three years later he undertook a much longer tour, embarking from Liverpool in August 1836 and spending eight months travelling with James King across the Mediterranean to Greece, Beirut, Jerusalem, and Egypt (where he fell ill with a fever); he returned by road via Italy and France, visiting Pompeii, Rome during the carnival, and Florence. Bright viewed much of the Mediterranean in a Byronic haze. He enjoyed Greece, but disliked Turkey, finding it plague-ridden and despotic, and he thought it of no consequence if Russia were to take over Constantinople. He found Jerusalem too ornate.

Rochdale politics, 1835–1840 In the mid-1830s Bright began to make a name for himself in local politics. In 1836, in what was considered a bold move, he took on one of the leaders of the factory movement, the Oldham MP John Fielden, attacking his influential *The Curse of the Factory System*. Bright produced a pamphlet which replied to Fielden's *Curse*. In it he agreed that there was a need to reduce the hours worked by children, but he thought parliamentary legislation would be ineffective, in so far as factory masters would evade the law. But Bright also used his reply to criticize Fielden's hostility to foreign trade, arguing that repeal of the corn laws was the best way to help factory workers. At the same time Bright was drawn into local electoral politics. Along with his father in 1834 he was a founder member of the Rochdale Reform Association, one of the first local electoral registration associations in the country. And in January 1837, anticipating a general election, Bright published anonymously a pamphlet, *To the Radical Reformers of the Borough of Rochdale*, in which he warned of the revival of toryism both at Westminster and locally, where the church party was gaining strength over the church rates issue, using the influence of the drink trade to win support. Bright's attack on the tories focused in particular on their wish to repeal the new poor law, a measure that he felt deserved a fair trial.

Bright was a keen supporter of better educational provision, and it was in this context that he first met Richard Cobden, when he invited him in 1837 to speak on the issue in Rochdale. Bright also played a leading role in the opposition to the setting of a church rate in Rochdale. This local controversy, which attracted a great deal of national attention, was partly inspired by the arrival in 1840 of J. E. N. Molesworth as local vicar. Molesworth, a forthright supporter of the principle of church rates, made his views known locally and also at public meetings elsewhere in the country. Bright's family had themselves suffered from distraint for non-payment of rates (Bright's father had been levied with twenty-one warrants). Bright became one of the main leaders of the Religious Freedom Society, established to fight the setting of the rate. The struggle reached a climax in July 1840, when, at a meeting held in the churchyard of St Chad's, Bright and Molesworth climbed onto tombstones to deliver their speeches. Bright proposed that no rate be set—the vicar's own income could be used to support the church—and he looked forward to the time when 'a State Church will be unknown in England', and when the church would depend 'upon her own resources, upon the zeal of her people, upon the truthfulness of her principles, and upon the blessings of her spiritual head' (Smith, 52). Although the anti-church rate party narrowly won the vote at this meeting, at a subsequent poll the decision was reversed. The church rate controversy continued in Rochdale for many years. In 1842, for example, Bright contributed to the *Vicar's Lantern*, a periodical published in reply to one produced by Molesworth entitled *Common Sense*. In one article Bright denied Molesworth's claim that the church was based on prescription: 'custom without truth', he wrote, 'is but agedness of error' (Robertson, 104).

Husband and widower By the late 1830s, as well as being an influential businessman, Bright had earned a formidable reputation as a leader of political dissent in Rochdale. Not surprisingly, when the Anti-Corn Law Association was formed in Manchester in October 1838 he joined and contributed money to its appeal for funds. At the beginning of February 1839 he addressed an anti-cornlaw meeting in Rochdale (a meeting at which Chartists defeated the anti-cornlaw motion). But Bright's growing public reputation caused him a great deal of private anguish, as his increasing involvement in politics threatened to draw him away from both Quaker principles and Quaker society. Matters came to a head in 1838–9, after he met Elizabeth Priestman (*d.* 1841) from Newcastle at the Quaker meeting at Ackworth. Bright wanted to marry Elizabeth, but the Priestman family were worried by Bright's political notoriety and probably also by his laxity over smoking and consumption of alcohol. During 1839 Bright did his best to placate the Priestman family: he gave up cigars, made very few public speeches, and commenced building a marital home—One Ash in Rochdale. Bright and Elizabeth Priestman were married in November 1839; they honeymooned in the Lake District; and a daughter, Helen, the future mother of Hilda *Clark, physician and humanitarian aid worker, was born in October 1840. Elizabeth Bright shortly after the birth showed the symptoms of the tuberculosis of which she soon died. Between caring for his wife and daughter, Bright resumed his public persona. Invited by Cobden, he addressed anti-cornlaw meetings in Bolton and Manchester, and in January 1840 became the treasurer of the Rochdale branch of the Anti-Corn Law League. However, Bright's full commitment to the league came only when Elizabeth died in September 1841. Cobden implored Bright to overcome his grief by absorption in the work of the league, and this he did, leaving his daughter in the care of his sister Priscilla.

The Anti-Corn Law League, and the Commons Bright threw himself into the league's campaign within months of his wife's death. In December 1841 he was sent by the league to speak in Ireland, in February 1842 he joined deputations which held interviews with various ministers, pleading for a change in government policy, and in the same month he gave his first speech in London, addressing a league delegate conference at the Crown and Anchor tavern. As economic conditions worsened in 1842, Bright voiced the growing dissatisfaction of manufacturing opinion. He presented petitions opposing the reintroduction of the income tax, talked of linking free trade to the extension of the suffrage, and contemplated a campaign of factory closure in March 1842. However the 'plug' plots and widespread Chartist agitation during the summer of 1842 curbed his militancy. Bright's own employees supported the general strike of 11 August 1842. He called on them to avoid violence, and several days later issued an *Address to the Working Men of Rochdale* in which he insisted that 'neither Act of Parliament nor act of a multitude can keep up wages', and that although the principles of the Charter would be granted eventually, this would only be when the electorate was convinced, and in the meantime people had to work in order to live.

From late 1842 onwards Bright's influence within the league grew, and his national reputation began to supersede his parochial fame (in 1843 he was still known in the national press as 'Mr Bright of Rochdale'). Although he has often been seen simply as Cobden's lieutenant, Bright in fact brought to the league a new vigour and direction at a time when the campaign was beginning to falter. Bright brought over a great deal of dissenter support to the league. He was far more open than Cobden to the idea of including parliamentary reform with the demand for corn law repeal, and thought that the league might join its programme to that of the Complete Suffrage Union. Above all, Bright infused the league's operations with a sense of energy and optimism. He was a tireless public speaker, and one of the principal contributors to the league's *Anti-Corn Law Circular*. Unlike the more sceptical Cobden, Bright seems never to have despaired at the league's changing fortunes—he always believed that the league would succeed because of the justice of its cause.

During the late autumn and winter of 1842 Bright joined Cobden and other league speakers in an expansion of the league's operations in the midlands, north-east, and Scotland. But by 1843 he was beginning to think that more could be achieved from within parliament, and by influencing metropolitan opinion. By then the league had decided to contest all by-elections and in March 1843, almost at the last moment, Bright decided to fight the seat of the city of Durham. He lost the contest at the beginning of April, but his supporters brought a petition against his opponent, Lord Dungannon. Dungannon was unseated for bribery, and when another election contest took place in July, Bright again contested the seat and was this time successful. He took his seat in the House of Commons on 28 July, and delivered his maiden speech ten days later, supporting William Ewart's motion in favour of a reduction of import duties.

Bright made a fairly immediate impact in parliament, not least because of his relative youth—it was unusual for someone of his provincial manufacturing background to be in parliament aged only thirty-one. His Quaker allegiance drew less comment. The *Illustrated London News* observed that Bright's 'dress is rather more *recherché* than that of the Friends of a generation back, differing but slightly from the ordinary costume of the day' (7 Nov 1843, 228). Although his deceased wife's family feared that, in becoming an MP, Bright was joining a 'club', Bright did manage to keep parliament and his Quakerism separate. During the 1840s and 1850s in particular, when in London he avoided the social circles which enveloped parliament, and regularly attended Quaker meetings at Devonshire House in Bishopsgate. Within the Commons, Bright and Cobden soon developed a troublesome double-act, with Cobden usually speaking first, quietly presenting the financial aspects of a topic, and then Bright speaking later in the debate, tearing into his opponents' speeches, often in a personalized fashion. Bright's raw, abrasive style drew the attention of the parliamentary reporters, but did not endear him to other MPs.

In 1844–5 the league began to change its strategy, and concentrate more on exposing the poor condition of the rural population. This was partly tactical, in order to win over a wider range of opinion. But it was also in response to the fact that in parliament Bright and Cobden were both coming under increasing attack from supporters of factory legislation—notably Lord Ashley—as poor employers. In March 1844 Bright countered Ashley's charge that conditions were so bad in the factories, by calling into question the reliability of Ashley's information, and by comparing the terrible plight of the rural labourer with that of the factory worker. Bright drew on examples derived from information he had collected while on speaking tours in north-east England, lowland Scotland, and southern England during the autumn and winter of 1843–4. In March 1844 Bright supported Cobden's motion for a select committee to inquire into the effects of protection on tenant farmers and their labourers. William Gladstone challenged Bright and Cobden over whether they would suspend discussion of the issue in parliament until such a committee reported; Bright replied that they would. Bright himself mounted an attack on the game laws, which allowed landowners to preserve game for hunting, despite the damage done to tenants' crops. On 27 February 1845 Bright moved for the appointment of a select committee to inquire into the working of the laws, and this was granted, but in the event the committee's report made little impact. Bright tried to steer the committee towards a consideration of the whole working of the landlord–tenant relationship, and the following year, at his own expense, Bright published an abstract of the evidence heard by the committee, and wrote a preface addressed to the farmers of the country, but all to no avail. In March 1848 Bright's bill to repeal the game laws was unsuccessful.

In April 1845 Bright opposed Sir Robert Peel's proposal to augment the grant to Maynooth College in Ireland. Cobden in fact supported the measure—a rare moment of disagreement between the two men. Bright not only disapproved of the general principle of state endowment, but he also thought that the Maynooth grant was a form of 'hush money', a 'sop' given to the Catholic priests to dampen down wider Irish discontent. By the end of 1845, however, it was clear that famine in Ireland demanded a change in ministerial policy. Bright welcomed Lord John Russell's indication of his support for repeal, and following the announcement of the early recall of parliament in the new year of 1846, the league intensified its campaign, pressing for unconditional total repeal. At a meeting at Covent Garden in the middle of December 1845 Bright spoke of the threatening character of public agitation, and warned of the dangers of the ministry ignoring the calls for repeal.

On 27 January 1846 Peel publicly proposed corn law repeal, and the following day Bright spoke in support of Peel's decision. In the same session Bright was unsuccessful in his opposition to the Ten Hours Factory Bill, introduced by Lord Ashley in January and given a second reading in May. But the league felt vindicated by corn law repeal—Bright saw the struggle as a victory for the manufacturing north over the south. Throughout the summer of 1846 huge public celebrations were held in Manchester, Durham, and Rochdale. At Rochdale on 8 July a procession 12,000 strong paraded through the streets, carrying at its head alongside a tiny loaf a 60lb loaf inscribed with 'Cobden' and 'Bright' on its sides. A public subscription totalling £5000 was raised for Bright and was used to present him with 1200 books in a specially built bookcase, carved with the emblems of free trade.

MP for Manchester, and second marriage In the longer term, the impact of corn law repeal on Bright's political career was more complicated. In Manchester many Liberals wanted either Bright or Cobden to stand as candidate for parliament, and Bright was rather annoyed that Cobden, away on the continent, procrastinated over withdrawing his name in favour of Bright's. Eventually, in October 1846, Bright was invited by the Manchester Reform Association to stand, and he accepted. But more moderate Liberal opinion in Manchester remained opposed to Bright, and preferred a whig or Peelite candidate. However, as the parliamentary session of 1847 unfolded, the unpopularity of the religious policy of the former and current ministries continued. Bright's resolute opposition to Lord John Russell's education scheme, and to the proposal to create a bishopric in Manchester, secured support from a large section of the Manchester electorate, and at the end of July 1847 he and Thomas Milner Gibson were returned unopposed. At the election hustings Bright was denounced by some of the crowd for his continued opposition to factory legislation.

Not for the first time, the new turns in Bright's political career also threatened to upset his private life. In June 1847 he married Margaret Elizabeth Leatham (known as Elizabeth; d. 1878), the daughter of a deceased wealthy

Wakefield banker, William Leatham, and his wife, Margaret. Like the Priestmans, the Leathams were concerned by Bright's devotion to public affairs and feared that his becoming MP for Manchester would increase rather than lessen the problem. In the event the marriage went ahead, and seven children were born between 1848 and 1863. Elizabeth Bright remained in Rochdale, and during the 1850s and early 1860s Bright endeavoured to be at home as much as possible.

In the late 1840s and early 1850s Bright became one of the most prolific public speakers inside and outside parliament. Like many other radicals, he saw corn law repeal as the commencement rather than the conclusion of an era of reform, and he looked to the whigs under Russell as the natural party of progress and change. However, unlike Cobden, who now put financial reform and peace in Europe ahead of most other political considerations, Bright concentrated on a wide range of issues.

Radical causes Of these the most important issue was parliamentary reform. Bright gave immediate support to Joseph Hume's reform proposals in 1848, declaring just over a week after the Chartist demonstration in April that the existing system of 500,000 electors garrisoned by 5 million others required overhauling. In parliament he also gave consistent support to motions in favour of the ballot. At the end of 1848 Bright joined with the leading radical reformers in what became the National Parliamentary and Financial Reform Association, and he also supported his local freehold land society, which helped create 40s. freehold votes in Lancashire. Bright saw the redistribution of seats as the key to parliamentary reform, but in the aftermath of Chartism many deduced from his rhetoric that he also had radical plans for the extension of the suffrage. At the end of 1851 Bright made it clear that he did not support manhood suffrage, but rather sought a suffrage based on payment of rates and subject to a twelve-month residency qualification. When Russell brought forward a reform bill in 1852 and again in 1854, Bright criticized what he saw as Russell's attempt to dodge the question of the suffrage by creating the so-called 'fancy franchises' and the minority clause; Bright called this latter plan 'something like making the last in the race the winner' (*Hansard 3*, 130, 16 Feb 1854, col. 735).

After 1847 Bright also became prominently associated with Indian affairs. Concerned by the diminishing supply of cotton from the southern states of America, and convinced that the days of cotton plantation slavery were numbered, Bright—along with other leading Lancashire merchants, manufacturers, and MPs—looked to India as an alternative source of cotton supply. In 1848 he chaired a select committee on the subject, and in 1850, backed by the Manchester chamber of commerce (though without the support of the East India Company), Bright and his colleagues funded an unofficial mission of inquiry to India. Taking the view that the East India Company stood in the way of effective development of India's commercial resources, Bright opposed renewal of the company's charter in June 1853, and called for the government of India to be made more accountable to parliament, and for settlement and colonization in India to be encouraged.

Bright's reputation as one of the foremost spokesmen of religious dissent grew at mid-century. In parliament he supported Jewish emancipation, abolition of church rates, and the ending of religious tests in the ancient universities: in May 1853 he told the Commons that 'if this country had been governed upon the principles prevalent in the Universities, it would have remained Roman Catholic in religion, and Austrian in politics to this day' (*Hansard 3*, 127, 26 May 1853, col. 639). He was horrified by the anti-Catholic reaction of 1851, although in assuming it was simply a 'Cockney' panic he perhaps underestimated its salience. Along with other radicals he opposed Russell's Ecclesiastical Titles Bill, arguing that religious doctrine could not be the basis of citizenship.

Reform of Ireland and political alliances After 1847 Bright remained faithful to the cause of free trade, opposing the sugar duties and supporting the newspaper tax repeal movement. Like Cobden he continued to advocate the reform of landed society—he was a member of select committees on county government and on the condition of tenant farmers, although these achieved little. But after 1847 the main focus of Bright's campaign for land reform became Ireland. As early as 1843 Bright had told the Durham electorate that the source of discontent in Ireland lay in 'an absentee aristocracy and an alien Church'. Unlike many of his contemporaries, including Cobden, Bright did not despair of the capacity of the Irish for self-improvement. He pointed to America as an example of what industrious Irish emigrants could achieve in the right environment, and his first pronouncements on Irish reform were directed to this end, calling for something like freedom of religion combined with free trade in land. In December 1847 Bright set out his proposed reforms to the Commons, which included the sale of encumbered estates. He also wanted to see the transfer of the funds of the Church of Ireland to the Catholic, protestant, and Presbyterian churches. At the same time in 1847–8 Bright gave his support to the Russell government's security measures in Ireland (with the exception of the Crown and Government Security Bill of April 1848, which included the British mainland as well), and, in April 1849, along with most of the other members of the select committee on the Irish poor laws, he opposed the use of British poor law funds for the support of the Irish poor.

Bright only began to develop a deeper awareness of the Irish problem in the summer of 1849, when he visited the province for a month, and appreciated more fully that Irish economic problems could not be simply remedied by free trade in land. He interviewed over sixty people, and from this and from taking copious notes from the 1845 report of the Devon commission on land occupation in Ireland, realized that the insecurity of tenanted land was a fundamental obstacle to the development of a landed middle class in Ireland. In November 1849 he wrote to Russell, urging him to support tenant-right and to end the law of entail, and by June 1850 he had prepared his own tenant-right bill, although he deferred this, giving his support to a similar bill proposed by William Sharman Crawford. In October 1852 Bright again visited Ireland, trying to gain the adhesion of the southern Tenant League to Sharman Crawford's schemes.

In identifying himself so publicly, and so stridently, with Irish reform and with parliamentary reform Bright alarmed most of the whigs. He in turn despaired over their hesitancy and caution, and their propensity to make political capital out of scares such as the Don Pacifico incident and the papal aggression. By the early 1850s Bright was beginning to believe that better political leadership would be forthcoming from the Peelites, and in November 1852 he even began corresponding with Benjamin Disraeli. When Lord Aberdeen formed his coalition ministry in December 1852, Bright was disappointed not to be offered a post. Bright's radicalism—especially over Ireland, Lord Palmerston's foreign policy, and the papal aggression—was also beginning to alienate some of his more moderate constituents in Manchester. However, he remained secure as MP for Manchester. In 1851 he turned down the opportunity to stand as candidate for Rochdale, and against the backdrop of the revival of the protectionist cry, both he and Milner Gibson were returned unopposed in 1852.

Although disappointed not to be included in the coalition administration, Bright did at least believe that the presence of Peelites and Sir William Molesworth in the cabinet boded well for peace in Europe. Bright himself was reluctant to get too involved as tensions between France and Britain grew, and Russia continued to encroach upon the Black Sea and Turkey. In October 1853 he refused an invitation to attend a meeting in Manchester to denounce Russian actions; but he was equally hesitant over speaking at the Edinburgh peace conference in the same month, and went there only after pressure was put on him by his brother-in-law Duncan McLaren. At Edinburgh Bright spoke on the same platform as Admiral Sir Charles Napier. But this appearance aside, Bright spent most of the winter of 1853–4 concentrating on parliamentary reform, speaking at Sheffield and Manchester on this in January, and placing his hopes for peace in the Aberdeen cabinet's negotiations.

The Crimean War By March 1854 it was clear that a British declaration of war against Russia was inevitable. Bright accepted this, but was alarmed at the mood of levity and lack of solemnity which appeared to surround the decision to go to war, a mood manifest at a Reform Club dinner given by Lord Palmerston and other ministers to Napier before his departure to the Baltic. In the Commons Bright objected to the proceedings at the dinner, provoking a sarcastic reply from Palmerston in which he referred to Bright as 'the hon. and reverend gentleman'. But Bright was careful to ground his opposition to the war in diplomatic analysis, rather than simply reverting to humanitarian pacifism. When war was finally declared at the end of March, he criticized the decision, pointing out that the balance of power argument could not apply to Turkey.

Although he remained relatively quiet, Bright's unpopularity grew throughout the summer and autumn of 1854. He was burnt in effigy in Manchester, and his name became synonymous with 'unEnglish', commerce-obsessed pacifism. Tennyson caricatured him in *Maud* as

> This broad-brimm'd hawker of holy things,
> Whose ear is cramm'd with his cotton, and rings.

In such an atmosphere Bright was convinced that reason would not prevail: '[t]he country is drunk just now, and will hear nothing against its passion', he confided to his diary at the beginning of November (*Diaries*, 4 Nov 1854, 178). But his constituents forced his hand, when in October Absalom Watkin wrote to him, inviting him to attend a meeting in Manchester in aid of the Patriotic Fund, and to use the occasion to 'state the conclusive reasons for [his] condemnation of the war'. Bright replied in a long letter, which was published simultaneously on 4 November in the *Manchester Examiner and Times* and in the London *Times*, and, to the anger of his critics, later in the *St Petersburg Journal*. In the letter Bright reiterated his opposition to the war, criticized Watkin for claiming that the war was morally justifiable, and asserted his right to hold views that were independent of his constituents. Bright subsequently attended the meeting in Manchester, but was unable to get a hearing.

Back in Westminster, some parliamentary opinion was beginning to doubt the wisdom of the government's direction of the war. Bright capitalized on this, delivering a powerful speech on 22 December against the Enlistment of Foreigners Bill, and in the following February, once the Aberdeen cabinet had resigned, he urged Palmerston to give his backing to Russell's peace mission to Vienna. At 1 a.m. on 23 February, labouring under a heavy cold, Bright delivered one of the most moving speeches he ever gave in the House of Commons. He lamented the losses that the nation had sustained, losses felt even in parliament itself: '[t]he Angel of Death has been abroad throughout the land; you may almost hear the beating of his wings' (*Hansard 3*, 136, 23 Feb 1855, col. 1761). Bright kept up the pressure on Palmerston throughout the spring, offering the prime minister a curious bargain by which he promised not to speak in the Commons again for the next fifteen years if the government ended the war. Eventually, Russell's mission came to little, and during June and July Bright attacked Palmerston for undermining Russell's negotiating hand.

Nervous breakdown and convalescence These speeches in parliament proved to be Bright's last public appearance for some time. In the middle of January 1856, shortly after the birth of his sixth child, Bright suffered a nervous breakdown which left him physically incapacitated—as he later described his condition he 'could neither read, write, nor converse for more than a few minutes'—and kept him out of public life for over two years. The breakdown was undoubtedly brought on by the stress he endured as the leading opponent of the government during the war, but the mental strain of being separated from home and a sense of religious crisis may also have played a part. He sought rest and recuperation, first at a hydropathic establishment in the Yorkshire dales before travelling to Scotland where he fished for salmon and stayed with friends such as the family of Edward Ellice sen. He spent much of the autumn of 1856 in Llandudno in north Wales, and then in November travelled to the Mediterranean; he stayed in Algiers, Italy, and Nice (where he met the empress of Russia) before returning to Rome in January 1857, where he remained for two months. He headed homewards via Turin and Switzerland, and reached Britain in June.

In his absence Manchester opinion continued to turn against Bright. In November 1856 he actually offered to resign as MP on account of his ill health, but a meeting in the city in the new year requested him to stay on. When an election was called in March, following Palmerston's defeat over the bombardment of Canton (Guangzhou), Bright again offered to stand down, leaving it up to local Liberals to decide whether his name should go forward. They did, and Bright issued an address from Rome, but it proved a mistake. Although Cobden spoke on his behalf, both Bright and Milner Gibson were defeated, with Sir John Potter (whom Bright called a 'vain man who ate and dined his way to a knighthood') and James Aspinall Turner elected in their places. Bright's fractious decade as MP for Manchester was finally at an end.

Return to politics and parliamentary reform Within months of his defeat at Manchester, Bright's name was being linked with various constituency vacancies, including Rochdale. During the summer he was asked to stand at Birmingham. He initially refused, suggesting instead that Cobden or Milner Gibson be approached, but the Liberal committee in Birmingham insisted on a candidate who was closely identified with parliamentary reform. Bright's unopposed election took place as news of the Indian mutiny continued to come through, and Bright was careful to signal to his new constituents that he supported the suppression of the mutiny, although in private he castigated the folly and misrule which had now met with retribution.

Leaner and fitter, Bright returned to the House of Commons at the beginning of February 1858, and shortly afterwards seconded Milner Gibson's motion on the Conspiracy to Murder Bill, introduced following the attempted assassination of Napoleon III. When he was defeated on this motion, Palmerston resigned office, and Lord Derby formed a new administration. Bright urged Gladstone, to whom he had grown closer, not to join Derby's cabinet. Like its predecessor, the Derby government became preoccupied with the reform of Indian government, and Bright played a central role in the discussions in parliament. Indeed, some of Derby's proposed reforms, such as the composition of the new council for India, were included to conciliate Bright. Bright welcomed the transfer of power from the East India Company to the British government, but wanted to go further, and called for greater decentralization through the creation of five separate presidencies.

By the summer of 1858 Bright was contemplating a return to public speaking for the first time in over two years. In February he had given public support to the call for the renewal of the campaign for parliamentary reform, calling for a major redrawing of the electoral map. 'The franchise itself', he pointed out, 'gives no real power, unless accompanied by the right of all the possessors of it to elect something like an equal number of representatives' (*Public Letters*, 51). At the end of October he delivered two speeches to his Birmingham constituents. In the first speech on parliamentary reform, which was widely covered in the national press, he appealed to the Liberal Party to ignore the peerage and reassert its traditional commitment to reform, based above all on the redistribution of seats. In his second speech, given to a banquet two days later, Bright attacked interventionist foreign policy, which he characterized as 'a gigantic system of outdoor relief for the aristocracy' (Bright, *Speeches*, 2.382). Bright was criticized by some for wanting to 'Americanize' British institutions, but most agreed that he was setting the pace in the reform campaign. During the following winter Bright gave a series of speeches in London, the north-west, and Scotland supporting parliamentary reform, while behind the scenes he attempted to reach agreement with Lord John Russell over reform measures. This failed and at Bradford in the new year Bright unveiled his own reform bill, which included a ratepayer franchise in the boroughs, £10 rental franchise in the counties, the secret ballot, and a massive redistribution of seats.

Disraeli introduced the government's own reform bill on 20 February, and Bright, Russell, and most of the rest of the Liberal Party united in their opposition to it. The Conservative administration was dissolved at the end of March, with both Palmerston and Russell hinting that a future Liberal government would support a reform measure. In April Bright was re-elected at Birmingham. Lord Derby's government resigned soon after the new parliament met, and Bright and Cobden became pivotal in the machinations surrounding the formation of the new administration. At a public meeting of the Liberal Party at Willis's Rooms on 6 June Bright pledged himself to follow Palmerston's and Russell's leadership if they committed themselves to parliamentary reform. His attack on the peerage still fresh, Bright was not offered a place in the new cabinet, although Cobden was. (He declined.)

The Liberal Party and the American Civil War With the Liberal Party reunited under the ageing Palmerston, in the early 1860s Bright became a figurehead for a variety of reform issues and pressure groups. Some of these were familiar. He resumed his role as a prominent spokesman for dissent, supporting the Liberation Society and its campaign to abolish church rates, pointing out on several occasions that Wales and Scotland furnished examples of how the church might flourish if state support was withdrawn. Bright remained a supporter of temperance, although he thought that alcohol consumption would be best regulated by municipal licences rather than a permissive bill, as many zealous temperance campaigners wished. Bright also returned to the attack on indirect taxation, calling in a speech to the Financial Reform Association at Liverpool in December 1859 for the complete abolition of duties, except on wine, spirits, and tobacco, and for a fixed income tax to be brought in instead. Bright's commitment to fiscal reform was partly inspired by Gladstone's chancellorship of the exchequer, and partly by Cobden's part in the negotiation of the Anglo-French commercial treaty—negotiations which Bright supported resolutely in the Commons throughout 1860. But Bright also saw fiscal reform as a means to other ends. He wanted to curb the power of the Lords, whose obstruction over the repeal of the paper duty in May 1860 he found particularly unconstitutional. Bright also kept up pressure on the cabinet over parliamentary reform—bills were shelved in 1860 and 1861—and in this respect he became more radical, tending to talk less about the redistribution of seats and more about the need for parliament to represent working-class interests. Bright's support for land reform continued afresh as well, and led him into controversy in December 1863, when *The Times* accused both Cobden and Bright of wanting to redistribute the land of the rich among the poor.

Bright's public and parliamentary appearances were fairly restricted during 1861, but the growing concern within Britain over the American Civil War brought him back to his old crusading self. Initially reluctant to get involved in an issue of war, Bright was stirred into action by the economic distress in Lancashire brought on by the severance of the cotton supply (his own firm went onto short time), and by the talk of war between Britain and the Union which followed the *Trent* affair. Bright was also alarmed by the expressions of support for the Southern Confederacy which he heard in some quarters, including Cobden, Gladstone, and his fellow Birmingham MP William Scholefield. In speeches in Rochdale, Birmingham, and London during 1862–3 he argued that the southern states were fighting for the maintenance of slavery, not independence, and that emancipated labour would lead to a better cotton supply. In June 1863 Bright opposed Roebuck's motion in the Commons calling for the recognition of the Confederacy. Throughout the war Bright corresponded with the leading politicians of the north, especially Charles Sumner, and more than anyone else in Britain he was responsible for a positive image of the north (he called it a 'lifeboat' for the downtrodden of Europe) and of Lincoln. Bright's reputation soared in the United States: his portrait was hung in Lincoln's presidential offices, a tree was named after him in California, two small editions of his speeches were published in New York in 1862 and one in Boston in 1865, and countless invitations called on him to visit the country.

The end of the American Civil War marked a turning point in Bright's life. Younger generations of advanced Liberals—in particular, positivists, Oxford academics such as J. E. T. Rogers, and the trade-union-led Reform League—looked to Bright for radical leadership. Lord Palmerston's death in October 1865 was the signal for the revival of the parliamentary reform movement, and

Bright was expected to play a major part. There were also private reasons for an even greater involvement in public affairs. The year 1864–5 was one of sadness for Bright: his son Leonard died on 8 November 1864 aged five, Cobden died on 2 April 1865, and Bright's brother-in-law and close political ally Samuel Lucas died two weeks later. As with his first wife's death, Bright buried his grief by absorption in public affairs and began to spend less time at home in Rochdale.

Parliamentary reform, 1865–1868 Bright was re-elected at Birmingham in July 1865, and his name was mooted by Gladstone when Russell formed his cabinet later in the year, but W. E. Forster was preferred instead. During 1865 Bright was an active supporter of the campaign to try Governor Eyre for the execution of Jamaican rebels, and he also counselled moderation over treatment of Fenian conspirators. On 12 March 1866 Gladstone introduced the government's reform bill. This prompted the opposition of some of the Liberal Party—principally Robert Lowe and Edward Horsman—and on the following night Bright attacked them, comparing them to refugees in the 'cave of Adullam' (*Hansard 3*, 182, 13 March 1866, col. 219). In June 1866 Russell's government faltered over the Reform Bill. Bright urged them to dissolve and call an election, but instead they resigned and widespread public agitation ensued. Bright now stood firmly with the radical movement outside parliament, defending the right of the Reform League to hold a meeting in Hyde Park in July, the meeting having been previously prohibited by Lord Derby's new government. From August through to December, Bright undertook an arduous speech campaign, comparable to those of the Anti-Corn Law League days, all the time putting further pressure on the government so as to make parliamentary reform irresistible. At Birmingham at the end of August he told his audience that the object of reform was 'to restore the British constitution in all its fulness, with all its freedom, to the British people' (Bright, *Speeches*, 2.198), and later in the year he warned of the dangers of withholding change, comparing the impending catastrophe to the eruption of Etna or Vesuvius.

Bright's prominence at the head of the reform campaign made him the target of criticism. The Adullamites mounted an assault on his reputation as a factory master (this was refuted by Bright's own employees at a meeting in January 1867), the *Fortnightly Review* carried an attack (later retracted), and at the beginning of February he received a note threatening his assassination. As well as campaigning in public, Bright wrote to Disraeli in private, urging him towards reform. Disraeli introduced the Conservatives' reform bill on 18 March, and during its long-drawn-out second reading Bright criticized its limitations, both inside and outside parliament. Finally, in August an amended bill was passed, which included the clause for the representation of minorities. Bright objected to this, but in most other respects he thought the bill was a mirror of his own proposals of 1859.

Although exhausted by the reform campaign, Bright's attention was also fixed upon Ireland by agrarian discontent and Fenian conspiracies. He had spoken in Dublin in

July 1866, and he returned to Ireland in July 1868, as well as addressing Irish affairs in some of his speeches in England during the spring. Bright supported the union, compared Ireland to the situation of the American colonists, and called for lenient treatment of the Fenian prisoners. As ever he backed extensive land reform, advocating the breakup and sale of large estates (especially those of absentee peers) to existing tenants in order 'to make the Irish farmer attached to the soil by tie of ownership rather than by … the necessity to have a holding in land that he may live' (*Public Letters*, 139). Bright and Gladstone were in constant communication over Irish affairs and other matters, and during the election campaign that followed the dissolution of parliament in November, Bright was careful not to say anything that committed the Liberals to a specific Irish policy.

In and out of the cabinet, 1868–1880 During the summer of 1868 Bright was already talked of as a cabinet minister-elect, and following Lord Derby's resignation he was invited to what he called 'a sort of Opposition Cabinet Meeting'. Widely tipped to become secretary of state for India, he was indeed offered this post by Gladstone in December, but declined the position on the grounds of its being a burdensome office, and one associated with the military establishment. Instead, he accepted the presidency of the Board of Trade, glad to join the cabinet, not least because it would mean fewer speeches. Impeccably dressed (including a pair of white bridal gloves, which he was advised to remove), Bright was sworn in at Windsor, and came away feeling respect for the queen, 'a Monarch whom Monarchy has not spoiled' (*Diaries*, 337).

Bright's first spell in cabinet was fairly short, as at the beginning of 1870 he was cut down by a recurrence of his Crimean War nervous illness. During 1869 he supported Gladstone's proposed disestablishment of the Church of Ireland, and was particularly critical of possible opposition from the Lords. In a public letter in June he warned that if they remained out of harmony with the nation they might 'meet with accidents not pleasant for them to think of' (*Public Letters*, 146–7). He also pressured the cabinet to include an extra clause in the Irish Land Bill to provide state aid for tenant land purchase. This became known as the 'Bright clause'. But apart from this Bright took little part in either the general legislation of the government, or in the running of his own department. Indeed, his absence from the consultation leading to the Elementary Education Bill was regretted by several leading nonconformists, and later (much to Forster's discomfort) by Bright himself. At the beginning of August 1870 Bright wrote a letter of resignation to Gladstone, which he then withdrew. Troubled not only by ill health, but also by the government's unwillingness to concede Russia's Black Sea claims, Bright sent another letter of resignation to Gladstone in November, and this was made public on 20 December, the sole stated grounds for his resignation being his ill health. Bright did not reappear in parliament until April 1872, and he resisted Gladstone's pleas to rejoin the cabinet until August 1873, when he became chancellor of the duchy of Lancaster (an office he had once opposed).

Bright did not speak in parliament at all between August 1869 and February 1875, and confined himself to addressing the public through letters to newspapers. In his absence, advanced Liberalism moved in a more radical direction, and Bright's public letters in these years attest to his refusal to move as quickly. He opposed the enfranchisement of women, believing it would strengthen toryism and priestcraft; he was unsympathetic to the demands of the temperance movement; and he was opposed to working-men parliamentary candidates, and also to the rise of the mandate and caucus system. In his one major public speech in these years, given to his Birmingham constituents in October 1873, Bright declared that '[t]he history of the last forty years of this country … is mainly a history of the conquests of freedom … For me the final chapter is now writing' (*Public Addresses*, 213). He was increasingly viewed as an elder statesman within the Liberal Party, and he now looked the part with his heavier gait and silvery white hair. Although he regained his seat, the Liberals were defeated in the 1874 general election, Gladstone resigned, and at the meeting held in February 1875 to elect a leader, Bright presided and, somewhat ironically, the whig Lord Hartington was chosen.

Bright did return to the public platform during the political crisis over the Eastern question in 1876–8, but even then he did so with some reluctance. He spoke out against Disraeli's support for the Ottoman empire and, as on previous occasions, he argued that the problem of the Eastern question stemmed from the flaws contained in the 1856 treaty of Paris, and it was to the revision of that treaty that he looked for a remedy. Such caution and mellowing on his part were thought by many to have sapped Gladstone's campaign against the Bulgarian atrocities. However, Bright did strike a more strident note, calling for strict neutrality when it seemed as though Disraeli was going to involve Britain in war against Russia, and later in 1878–9, in Afghanistan and Egypt. In the midst of all this in May 1878 Bright's wife died of apoplexy, and, although their relationship had been a rather distant one, he went into severe depression, suffering from 'desolation' at his loss.

Back in cabinet, resignation, home rule, and death Disraeli's government was defeated in the general election of March 1880 and Bright, returned unopposed for Birmingham, was made chancellor of the duchy of Lancaster once again, although with a reduced workload. On the opening of parliament Bright became involved in the controversy over Charles Bradlaugh's wish to affirm rather than take the oath, but most of his time during the next few years was taken up with Irish affairs. Out of necessity, Bright supported the suspension of habeas corpus in January 1881, but was pleased with the Land Bill which was given a second reading in May. Indeed, Bright was convinced that this act, building on the Irish legislation of Gladstone's first ministry, provided the basis of a peaceful settlement. In July 1882 Bright resigned from the cabinet, following the bombardment of Alexandria, and from then on he took a more independent stance on Irish policy. As he had done publicly since the mid-1860s, he defended the union, arguing that two separate assemblies would be the source of confusion and mischief. Above all, Bright denigrated the parliamentary tactics of Charles Stewart Parnell and other nationalist MPs. He accused them of sympathizing with criminal acts in Ireland, and of destroying a moderate programme of land reform by insisting on the appropriation of land from its present owners in the province.

Bright notched up two anniversaries in 1883—forty years in the Commons and twenty-five years as MP for Birmingham—and in June 500,000 people lined the streets of Birmingham to celebrate the occasion. Bright remained obdurate in his old radicalism. He opposed the new vogue for land nationalization and resisted the campaign to include proportional representation in the new franchise bill. On the question of parliamentary reform, he wanted to curb the Lords' power of veto, especially when they threw out the Franchise Bill of 1884, with Lord Salisbury justifying their action by referring to Bright's 1859 declaration that the redistribution of seats was more important than the extension of the franchise.

In 1885 Bright was returned for the new constituency of Birmingham Central, beating off the challenge of Lord Randolph Churchill. Despite pressure from his family, from fellow MPs, and from Gladstone himself, Bright opposed home rule for Ireland when Gladstone made it his policy in 1886. In March 1886 the two had a long discussion on the issue, and to his usual objections to a Dublin parliament and to what he saw as capitulating to the Parnellites, Bright now added 'the views and feelings of the Protestant and loyal portion of the people' (*Diaries*, 536). At his unopposed election at the beginning of July 1886 Bright stated that he could not follow Gladstone simply because he was party leader, and later suggested that only Gladstone's personal authority gave home rule any credence. The disagreement with Gladstone caused Bright much personal anguish, and he refused to play a more public role in the growing division within the Liberal Party, although reports of his views dominated the press during the summer and gave encouragement to the unionists.

Bright hardly appeared in public after 1886, but honours continued to come his way. Oxford awarded him an honorary DCL in 1886, Mrs Humphry Ward asked to write his biography, and a new but ill-fated university was named after him in Wichita, Kansas. In August 1887 he gave what turned out to be his last speech at a dinner in Greenwich given to Lord Hartington. By the following summer he was suffering from lung congestion, and to this became added diabetes and chronic nephritis. Bright died aged seventy-seven on 27 March 1889 in his home, One Ash, and after a quiet ceremony three days later was buried in the graveyard of the Friends' meeting-house in Rochdale. On the same day a funeral service was held at Westminster Abbey.

Bright in perspective   Long before he died Bright was already the subject of much political hagiography. Three major biographies were published before his death (at least one of which he revised himself), and a substantial and enduring collection of his speeches was published in 1869, at the height of his public career. Inevitably, his historical reputation has tended to rest on the earlier part of his career: his nonconformism, the Anti-Corn Law League years, his lonely opposition to the Crimean War, and his leadership of the reform movement in the mid-1860s. Such a focus is not without justification—Bright himself often expressed the view that all that was most formative in British Liberalism had occurred between 1830 and 1870—but it is a view that obscures some of the complexities of Bright's politics. Bright's religion too was complicated. Rather than providing him with a public vocation, his Quakerism often served to remind him of a private world he had forsaken. Tenniel's depiction of Bright (in cartoons in *Punch*) wearing a broad-brimmed Quaker hat and an eye-glass neatly captures this ambiguity. (A similarly double-edged caricature was Anthony Trollope's salmon-fishing radical in the Palliser series of political novels.)

On some major political issues Bright shifted ground. Over parliamentary reform, his views on the order of priority between redistribution of seats and franchise extension did change, and like Gladstone, he only really embraced the working-class radical movement in the 1860s. Over Ireland he grew more moderate on the question of land reform, and less tolerant towards Catholic nationalism. Where he might have been expected to change his views, on the other hand, he held firm, resisting calls for state intervention at the height of the agricultural depression and during the land nationalization fervour of the mid-1880s. But Bright was consistent in two main areas, which coloured virtually all his thinking: his hostility to the peerage, and to the established church. When nineteenth-century Liberalism required a whipping-post, it was usually one of these parts of the established order which fulfilled the role, and there was no more effective orator than Bright in denouncing them.

Bright was the most effective radical speaker of the Victorian years, and although his diaries and his voluminous correspondence fill out the picture somewhat, his life and his views, as his contemporaries always suggested, are still to be found in the many addresses and impromptu speeches that he gave. He was a compulsive speaker, a master of extemporization, usually only requiring a few hastily written notes to give him his cue.

In time Bright became something of a national hero. Suspected of being a *nouveau riche* in the 1840s, by the 1860s he was being celebrated as 'honest' John Bright, a man whose humble origins vouchsafed his authenticity as a leader of the working class. Just as Gladstone's career is a microcosm of British political life in nineteenth-century Britain, so Bright's public life, stretching from the local church rate battles of the mid-1830s to the home-rule crisis fifty years later, is a distillation of all that was brilliant and all that was complex in nineteenth-century British radicalism.

MILES TAYLOR

Sources J. Bright, *Speeches on questions of public policy*, ed. J. E. T. Rogers, 2 vols. (1869) · *Public addresses by John Bright*, ed. J. E. T. Rogers (1879) · *Public letters of John Bright*, ed. H. J. Leech (1885) · *The diaries of John Bright*, ed. R. A. J. Walling [1930] · J. McGilchrist, *The life of John Bright, MP* (1868) · W. Robertson, *The life and times of the Right Hon. John Bright* (1877) · G. B. Smith, *The life and speeches of the Right Hon. John Bright*, 2 vols. (1881–2) · R. B. O'Brien, *John Bright* (1910) · G. M. Trevelyan, *The life of John Bright* (1913) · J. T. Mills, *John Bright and the Quakers*, 2 vols. (1935) · H. Ausubel, *John Bright: Victorian reformer* (1966) · D. Read, *Cobden and Bright: a Victorian political partnership* (1967) · J. L. Sturgis, *John Bright and the empire* (1969) · K. Robbins, *John Bright* (1979) · M. Taylor, *The decline of British radicalism, 1847–1860* (1995) · Gladstone, *Diaries*
Archives BL, corresp. and papers, Add. MSS 43383–43392 · Duke U., papers · Hunt. L. · Princeton University, New Jersey, letters · priv. coll. · Rochdale Museum, corresp. · RS Friends, Lond., letters · Swarthmore College, Philadelphia, Friends Historical Library, corresp. and papers · U. Birm. L., letters · University of Bristol Library, corresp. | Birm. CL, letters to William Harris · BL, letters to Richard Congreve, Add. MS 45241 · BL, letter to Lord Cranbrook, Add. MS 62537 · BL, corresp. with W. E. Gladstone, Add. MSS 44112–44113 · BL, letter to Arthur Hargreaves, Add. MS 62079 · BL, letters to William Hargreaves, Add. MS 62079 · BL, corresp. with W. H. Northy, Add. MS 44877 · BL, letters to Charles Sturge, Add. MS 64130 · BL, letter to H. Y. Thompson, Add. MS 63520 · BL, letters to Charles Wilson, Add. MS 60539 · Bodl. Oxf., letters to Benjamin Disraeli; letters to Lord Kimberley; letters to J. E. Thorold Rogers · Dorset RO, letters to Henry Calcraft · Duke U., Perkins L., letters to Thomas Tomasson · Holyoake House, Manchester, Co-operative Union archive, letters to G. J. Holyoake · Lancs. RO, letters to William Bright · Man. CL, Manchester Archives and Local Studies, letters to T. B. Potter; letters to J. B. Smith; letters to George Wilson · NL Scot., corresp. with Edward Ellice; letters to Lord McLaren · PRO, corresp. with Lord Granville, PRO 30/29 · PRO, corresp. with Lord John Russell, PRO 30/22 · Trinity Cam., letters to Lord Houghton · Tyne and Wear Archives Service, Newcastle upon Tyne, letters to Joseph Cowen · U. Birm. L., corresp. with Joseph Chamberlain; letters to R. W. Dale · U. Durham L., letters to John Henderson · UCL, letters to Margaret Bright · W. Sussex RO, corresp. with Richard Cobden
Likenesses C. A. Duval, portrait, 1843, priv. coll. · S. W. Reynolds junior, mixed-method engraving, pubd 1843 (after C. A. Duval), BM, NPG · S. Bellin, group portrait, mixed-method engraving, pubd 1850 (*The Anti-Corn Law League*; after J. R. Herbert, 1847), BM, NPG · H. Daumier, caricatures, lithographs, c.1856, NPG; repro. in *Le Charivari* · G. Cruikshank, group portrait, oils, 1860 (*Bright reform bomb*), Palace of Westminster, London · G. Fagnani, oils, 1865, New York chamber of commerce, New York · G. Fagnani, oils, 1865, Union League Club, New York · C. Lucy, oils, 1869, V&A · J. Adams-Acton, marble bust, c.1870, National Liberal Club, London · L. Dickinson, oils, 1874, Reform Club, London · W. Theed, marble statue?, c.1877, Manchester City Hall · W. W. Ouless, oils, 1879, NPG · R. Potter, photograph, 1879, NPG [*see illus.*] · J. E. Boehm, plaster bust, 1881, National Liberal Club, London · T. O. Barlow, mezzotint, pubd 1882 (after J. E. Millais), BM, NPG · F. Holl, oils, 1882, City Museum and Art Gallery, Birmingham · E. Crowe, oils, 1883, Reform Club, London · S. P. Hall, pencil sketch, 1887, NPG · F. Holl, oils, 1887, Reform Club, London · A. B. Joy, marble statue on monument, 1891, Albert Square, Manchester · W. H. Thornycroft, bronze statue, 1891, Rochdale · A. B. Joy, marble statue, 1892, City Museum and Art Gallery, Birmingham · A. Gilbert, statue, 1896, National Liberal Club, London · Ape [C. Pellegrini], caricatures, prints, BM, NPG · Bassano, cabinet photograph, NPG · J. Doyle, caricatures, drawings, BM · R. Fowler, oils (after J. E. Millais, 1880), Palace of Westminster, London · H. Furniss, caricatures, pen-and-ink drawings, NPG · J. Phillip, group portrait, oils (*The House of Commons, 1860*), Palace of Westminster, London · F. Sargent, pencil drawing, NPG · carte-de-visite, NPG · marble bust, Lady Lever Art Gallery, Port Sunlight

Wealth at death £86,289 1s. 7d.: resworn probate, June 1890, CGPLA Eng. & Wales (1889)

Bright, Mynors (1817–1883), literary scholar, was born in Cambridge, and baptized on 29 March 1817 at Eccleshall, Stafford, the son of John *Bright (1780/81–1870), physician, and his wife, Elizabeth (Eliza), *née* Mynors. He was educated at Shrewsbury School, and entered Magdalene College, Cambridge, on 3 July 1835. He was a senior optime in mathematics, and took a second class in classics. He proceeded BA in 1840 and MA in 1843, and was ordained priest in 1844. He became foundation fellow, tutor, and eventually president of Magdalene (1853–73), and was chosen proctor in 1853.

Bright is known chiefly for his work on the manuscripts of Samuel Pepys's diary. Magdalene College had been bequeathed a set of important papers by Pepys in 1724, including six volumes in an almost indecipherable shorthand. About 1820 the Hon. Revd George Neville, assisted by his relative Lord Grenville, deputed John Smith, an undergraduate of St John's, to decipher these volumes. The resultant 9325 page manuscript was then edited (very imperfectly) by Lord Braybrooke, who published a selection comprising roughly a quarter of the whole in 1825 (3rd edn, 1848–9).

Bright resolved to decipher the diary afresh, and realized, unlike Smith, that Thomas Shelton's *Tachygraphy* (a copy of which had been in Pepys's library) was the system of shorthand that Pepys had used. Taking an interleaved copy of a Braybrooke edition, he made corrections and additions, and printed a fuller edition between 1875 and 1879, which included some seven-tenths of the original.

In 1873, owing to ill health, Bright retired from Magdalene and moved to London. He became paralysed about 1880, and died at his home, 23 Sussex Place, Regent's Park, on 23 February 1883. He never married. He bequeathed part of the income from his Pepys edition to Magdalene College. H. B. Wheatley re-edited Bright's transcript, with additions, in ten volumes, from 1893 to 1899, but it remained for the twentieth-century editor Robert Latham to add those passages which Bright had regarded as unprintable.

JOHN D. HAIGH

Sources M. Bright, preface, in *Diary and correspondence of Samuel Pepys*, ed. R. Braybrooke and M. Bright, 6 vols. (1875–9), vol. 1, pp. vii–x · M. Bright, preface, in *Diary and correspondence of Samuel Pepys*, ed. R. Braybrooke and M. Bright, 6 vols. (1875–9), vol. 2, p. viii · R. D. Altick, *The scholar adventurers* (1966), 208–9 · Venn, *Alum. Cant.* · R. Latham, introduction, in *The illustrated Pepys: extracts from the diary*, ed. R. Latham (1978), 12–13 · Crockford (1882) · *BL cat.*, 42.386 · *Fasti Angl.* (Hardy), 3.635 · *The Academy* (3 March 1883), 151–2 · *The Athenaeum* (3 March 1883), 280 [18??] · *DNB* · *IGI* · Boase, *Mod. Eng. biog.*
Archives Magd. Cam., Pepys collection
Likenesses L. Dickinson, oils, Magd. Cam.
Wealth at death £36,859 18s. 5d.: probate, 19 March 1883, CGPLA Eng. & Wales

Bright, Richard (1789–1858), physician, was born at 29 Queen Square, Bristol, on 28 September 1789, the third son of dissenters Richard Bright (1754–1840) and his wife, Sarah, *née* Heywood (d. 1827). Wealthy merchants and

Richard Bright (1789–1858), by Maull & Polyblank

bankers, the family were descended from the Brights of Brockbury, Herefordshire.

Education and early career, 1795–1814 Bright's early years were spent in the family home at Ham Green, near Bristol. In 1795 he joined his elder brothers at Dr John Prior Estlin's school, St Michael's Hill, Bristol, where he met his lifelong friend Henry Holland, with whom he shared a developing interest in natural phenomena, particularly the gathering of geological specimens. In 1805 Bright was sent to Exeter to be tutored by the Revd Lant Carpenter. His determination to pursue a career in medicine greatly concerned his father, who considered it too demanding a profession, but after some discussion with his son he concluded in a letter to Carpenter that the decision was 'founded on a serious and deliberate preference rather than as the result of some accidental influence' (Berry and Mackenzie, 31).

Bright enrolled at Edinburgh University in 1808, lodging at 21 Hill Street with the Revd Robert Morehead of the Episcopalian church, who, it was hoped, might persuade him to abandon medicine in favour of the ministry. Premedical studies in the sciences and humanities were required at Edinburgh University and thus Bright attended lectures on political economy with Professor Dugald Stewart, mathematics with Sir John Leslie, and natural philosophy with Professor John Playfair, whose lectures further stimulated his geological interests. With the award of his first degree Bright commenced his medical studies in 1809. He enrolled for a course of lectures in chemistry with Charles Hope, anatomy with Alexander

Monro tertius, and medicine with Andrew Duncan. A medical student's life was relentlessly demanding and the conscientious Bright found scant time for leisure pursuits. However, in 1810, together with his old friend Henry Holland, he accompanied Sir George Steuart Mackenzie of Coul on an expedition to Iceland to undertake mineralogical research and to assess the theories of Werner and Hutton relating to the origins of the earth's crust. The party left Leith on 18 April 1810 bound for Stromness, where they took passage in the *Elba* to Reykjavík. In his *Travels in the Island of Iceland* (1811) Mackenzie wrote:

> Mr. Bright has made the most of the materials we had time to collect for an account of the Zoology and Botany of Iceland. To him we are indebted for the preservation of the plants we gathered and indeed for by far the greatest part of the collection. (G. S. Mackenzie, *Travels in the Island of Iceland*, 1811, preface)

Bright returned to Bristol much changed from the untested youth who had gone up to Edinburgh in 1808. His parents now saw in him a 'philosophical equanimity' which they believed would sustain him in the future demands of an exacting profession.

In October 1810 Bright recommenced his medical studies at Guy's Hospital, London, as physician's clerk to William Babington. He lodged with Richard Stocker, the apothecary, whose job it was to assess all presenting patients, and from him Bright at last gained some experience of practical medicine, learning to cup and apply poultices, leeches, and blistering agents. Guy's and St Thomas's were linked for teaching purposes as the United Hospitals. Bright attended medical lectures given by Babington and Curry, and studied chemistry and natural philosophy with Alexander Marcet and William Allen, midwifery and physiology with John Haighton, and surgery with Henry Cline and the renowned Sir Astley Cooper. The last clearly inspired Bright's interest in morbid anatomy and led him to recognize its importance in the understanding of disease. Bright used his skill as a draughtsman to record the appearance of normal and diseased organs. It was in 1811 that he first drew a granular kidney. He was a meticulous observer, able to capture the minutest detail in the capillary web of a sectioned organ just as he would note the veining in mineralogical specimens, or the angle of a shadow in artistic representations. Bright's keenness and dedication was soon noticed and a favourable report from Stocker persuaded Benjamin Harrison, Guy's Hospital treasurer, that he was sufficiently qualified to dispense drugs and other medical preparations. In December 1810 he was honoured with election to Guy's Physical Society. He presented his inaugural paper on bloodletting which he considered was often used to excess. Again leisure pursuits were limited but Bright did attend meetings of the Geological Society of London to which he presented his geological collection made in the Liverpool area and around Bristol and also duplicates of specimens collected during the Icelandic expedition. In November 1811 he read a paper on the geology of his native city.

In 1812 Bright returned to Edinburgh to complete his

MD. He was again fortunate in having excellent tutors such as Dr Gregory, renowned for his purging powders, Dr Rutherford, Dr Home, Dr Thompson, and again Andrew Duncan, now lecturing in medical jurisprudence. He had some notable contemporaries, for example Thomas Addison, with whom he later worked at Guy's. He also met many interesting people from other disciplines, such as Francis Jeffery, advocate and founder of the *Edinburgh Review*, who remained a lifelong friend. While at that time people from the arts and sciences mingled freely and exchanged ideas, there remained, even in Edinburgh, a very real dichotomy between medicine and surgery although this was less marked than elsewhere. This was a source of concern to Bright who wrote to his father: 'it is quite impossible to draw the line between them so much do they run into and depend upon each other' (Berry and Mackenzie, 70). It was time now for Bright to consider the various options open to him on completion of his MD, one possibility being the position of house surgeon at the Lock Hospital, Westminster. Bright graduated MD in 1813 with a dissertation on contagious erysipelas, a subject suggested as a result of 'some instances of apparent contagia which occurred under [his] observation at Guy's'. His application to the Lock Hospital was successful but, having a year to wait before taking up his post, he decided to join his brother Henry at Peterhouse, Cambridge, intending to graduate from there also. But finding that the curriculum did not meet his requirements and that the library was inferior to that at Edinburgh he left after one term and on the advice of James Laird he commenced work at Dr Bateman's public dispensary in Carey Street, London, in January 1814. Here Bright gained firsthand experience of the powerful influence of poverty on the health of the nation. The severe winter of 1814 led to epidemics of bronchitis and pneumonia. In a vain attempt to alleviate the patients' suffering he administered oxygen using a pig's bladder rather than a cylinder.

Continental tours, 1814–1818 By mid-February 1814 a growing wanderlust had Bright in its grip. He wished to visit the continent 'on account of the real information [he would] obtain and still more on account of the Ideal Value which others [would] bestow upon that information' (Berry and Mackenzie, 78). He also thought it desirable 'as the means of acquiring the languages of these countries' and 'on account of the general expansion of mind and the delightful remembrances' to be gained. Here we see many facets of his character revealed: the keen professional, the linguist, the intellectual, the romantic, and the artist, which together produced a man of undisputed achievement.

Bright's tour began in the Netherlands with a visit to the renowned medical faculty at Leiden. He then travelled through Belgium and Germany, and so to Berlin where he saw something of the neurological practice of Horn and the clinics of Hufeland. He also met Dr Klaproth, the chemist, and saw Blumenbach's fine collection of skulls. He was anxious not to miss the congress in Vienna and decided to winter there. The account of that sojourn and his subsequent travels in Hungary provide the fascinating text of his book *Travels from Vienna through lower Hungary with some remarks on the state of Vienna during the congress in the year 1814* (1818). The book includes some delightful sketches made by the author during his travels. He was fortunate to meet Johann Peter Franck, the sole survivor of the famous Vienna school of medicine, long the stronghold of Boerhaave's doctrines of clinical observation. He was fascinated by his visits to the general hospital where 'the medical lectures of Hildenbrand, the instruction of Beer and the surgical practices of Rust and Kern, afford[ed] great attractions' (Berry and Mackenzie, 89). He was delighted by the city's fine art collection. In Hungary Bright found much to interest him: the social life, the baths, the Gypsies, while the gold and silver mines of Schemnitz and Kremnitz appealed to the amateur geologist. He was impressed by the university hospital at Pest where lectures were still delivered in Latin. He stayed with Count Festetics at his castle in Keszthely, which carries a memorial plaque commemorating his visit. On his return journey to England he learned of Wellington's great victory and naturally joined the multitude visiting Waterloo. He was much moved by the suffering he witnessed and quickly became involved with caring for the wounded.

On his return to London, Bright worked for a short time at the dispensary, then commenced work at the Lock Hospital caring for syphilitic patients. In December 1816 he was made licentiate of the Royal College of Physicians. The following February his friend James Laird recommended him for a post at the London Fever Hospital, which he accepted. Again he witnessed the terrible effects of poverty and during the winter typhus epidemic he too succumbed to the disease and went home to Bristol to recuperate. In the summer of 1818 he made a further visit to Europe, spending some time in Paris and fulfilling an earlier ambition to see a little practice there. He was beginning to suspect a link between dropsy and the function of the kidney and the established practice on the continent of post-mortem examination yielded an abundance of material for him to study. He studied chest diseases with Laënnec and met Rayer, who was similarly interested in pathology and whose later work on the kidney acknowledged the importance of Bright's findings.

At Guy's Hospital, 1820–1844 Bright returned to London much stimulated by all that he had seen and learned. He was keen both to develop his interest in pathology and also to teach, feeling that he had much to contribute in both areas. About 1820 he took out a lease on 14 Bloomsbury Square. He was elected a fellow of the Royal Society; a little later in the year he was surprised and delighted to learn that he had been appointed to the prestigious post of assistant physician to Guy's Hospital with particular responsibility for Laird's patients. On the latter's retirement in 1824 he was appointed full physician and felt himself as such 'to be placed at the pinnacle of the profession' (Berry and Mackenzie, 116). He shared Dr Cholmeley's lectureship in practical medicine.

October 1825 saw the opening of the new medical school building at Guy's with Bright's name in the prospectus as full lecturer in theory and practice of medicine.

He was innovative in his teaching. He took his students into the wards, encouraging them to obtain specimens of blood and urine that were later to be carefully examined, analysed, and described. This led in time to the concept of the specialist unit or ward for renal patients. Two more new names appeared on the prospectus—Thomas Addison and Thomas Hodgkin—both Edinburgh graduates who shared Bright's views on the role and duties of the physician. Bright and Addison later collaborated in the writing of a medical textbook entitled *Elements of the Practice of Medicine* (1839), in which there is one of the best descriptions of acute appendicitis. They were both excellent teachers albeit that Addison was considered the more charismatic of the two. Bright was again innovative in requiring his students to develop delicacy in the handling of patients, saying, 'the touch of a blind man is your duty to acquire' (Berry and Mackenzie, 203).

On 14 August 1822 Bright married Dr Benjamin Guy *Babington's daughter Martha Lyndon Babington. They shared a brief year of happiness before her death in December 1823 five days after the birth of their son William Richard. In the ensuing years he found some consolation in his work and in membership of the newly formed Athenaeum. He spent as much as six hours a day at Guy's. His research and the writing up of cases was all-absorbing but he did find some relaxation in the company of Elizabeth Follett, sister of Sir William Webb *Follett. The couple married on 27 July 1826 and had seven children, six of whom survived to adulthood, including James Franck *Bright. A growing family required a larger house and in 1831 they moved to 11 Savile Row, where Bright lived until his death in 1858.

Bright's most important and influential research is undoubtedly represented in his two-volume major work, the *Reports of medical cases selected with a view of illustrating the symptoms and cure of diseases by a reference to morbid anatomy*. The first volume (1827) contained the famous renal work and the second (1831) dealt mainly with diseases of the brain and nervous system. These works brought Bright international acclaim and later the eponymous recognition. Charles Wells and John Blackall had both come close to an accurate description of renal disease, bringing together the triad of dropsies, albuminuria, and kidney derangement, but it was Bright's work which provided the necessary links in the chain of indisputable symptoms and manifestations definitively attributable to impaired renal function, that is, the early clinico-pathological classification of nephritis. John Bostock contributed invaluable observations on the chemical properties of the urines examined, laying the foundations of clinical biochemistry in renal medicine. Some points in Bright's work were contested by the Irish physician Robert Graves, while the Edinburgh physician Robert Christison later confirmed Bright's findings. Of his many papers, the most original is considered to be that on abdominal diseases entitled 'Cases and observations connected with diseases of the pancreas and duodenum' describing fatty stools and glycosuria in pancreatic disease (*Medico-Chirurgical Transactions*, 1833, 18).

The 1830s brought many honours. Bright was elected a fellow of the Royal College of Physicians in 1832 and was Goulstonian lecturer the following year. In 1837 he was appointed physician-extraordinary to Queen Victoria. That same year Bright delivered the Lumleian lecture on 'Disorders of the brain' to the college, where he was censor in 1836 and 1839. One of the greatest honours he received was from his continental colleagues when in July 1838 he was awarded the Monthyon medal jointly with Pierre-François Olive Rayer and Martin Solon for their work on diseases of the kidney—'a previously little known disease but now recognized under the name "maladie de Bright, albuminuria or albuminous nephritis"' (Berry and Mackenzie, 212). During his working life he was made an honorary member of most European medical societies and in 1848 was elected associate member of the Société de Biologie of Paris of which Rayer was president. In 1853 Bright received an honorary DCL from Oxford University.

Private practice and final years, 1844–1858 In 1844 Bright retired from Guy's and entered full-time private practice. An attack of gallstones in 1842 had left him fatigued and he had to reduce his workload. His many private patients included Lord Macaulay, the historian and whig MP, Lord and Lady Jeffrey, Isambard Kingdom Brunel, and the poet Tennyson. He also treated Dr John Snow and, like him, was a founder member of the Epidemiological Society founded by Benjamin Guy Babington in 1850. By this date Bright was surprised to discover that his annual income had increased to £6000.

The final years of Bright's life brought increasing ill health which necessitated periods of rest and convalescence. He spent time painting and fishing in Argyll and at Tennyson's house on the Isle of Wight. In 1857 he undertook his last holiday in Europe but by the following January he was suffering from severe angina. He died on 16 December 1858 and post-mortem examination showed that death resulted from calcific congenital bicuspid aortic valve disease, a diagnosis which Bright had suspected some eight years earlier. He was buried in Kensal Green cemetery; a memorial plaque to Bright was put up in his parish church, St James's, Piccadilly. His wife survived him.

In the Bright oration delivered at Guy's Hospital in 1927 W. S. Thayer paid tribute to Bright's personal qualities and compared him with Laënnec, adding that although not brilliant 'Bright showed a steadfastness of purpose, and an equanimity … rarer and more precious than mere brilliancy' (Berry and Mackenzie, 236). Bright was also a good husband and father and clearly his warm, generous nature endeared him to all who shared his life in whatever capacity. In the opinion of his colleague and friend George Hilaro Barlow not only had Bright advanced the knowledge of renal disease but he had also achieved a 'greater revolution in [the] habits of thought and methods of investigating morbid phenomena and tracing aetiology of disease' as a whole. DIANA BERRY

Sources D. Berry and C. Mackenzie, *Richard Bright, 1789–1858* (1992) • P. Bright, *Dr. Richard Bright, 1789–1858* (1983) • W. S. Thayer,

'Richard Bright', The Bright oration, delivered at Guy's Hospital, 1927 · J. S. Cameron, 'A historical review', *The nephrotic syndrome*, ed. J. S. Cameron and R. J. Glasscock (1988) · *The Lancet* (25 Dec 1858), 665 · Munk, *Roll* · S. J. Peitzman, 'Bright's disease and Bright's generation: towards exact medicine at Guy's Hospital', *Bulletin of the History of Medicine*, 55 (1981), 307–21 · Bristol RO, microfilms F45–F48

Archives Guy's Hospital, London, Wills Library · Norfolk RO, corresp. · RCP Lond., drawings and case notes · Royal College of Physicians of Edinburgh, corresp. and MSS · University of Melbourne, corresp. with his father **Likenesses** F. R. Say, oils, 1860; replica, RCP Lond. · W. Behnes, marble bust, RCP Lond.; presented in 1871 · Maull & Polyblank, photograph, NPG [*see illus.*] · daguerreotype, RCP Lond. · portrait (as a child with mother, Sarah Bright), Ditchingham Hall, Norfolk; repro. in Berry and Mackenzie, *Richard Bright* **Wealth at death** under £50,000: probate, 9 Feb 1859, *CGPLA Eng. & Wales*

Bright, Timothy (1549/50–1615), physician and writer on shorthand, was the son of William Bright (*d.* 1592), possibly the William Bright who was mayor of Cambridge in 1571. Sheffield, Yorkshire, has been given as his birthplace, but Bright himself stated that he was born and educated in Cambridge (*Hygieina*, sig. A5v). On 21 May 1561, aged eleven, he matriculated as sub-sizar at Trinity College, Cambridge. He began his residence in 1564 under the tutelage of Vincent Skinner MA, was admitted scholar on 18 April 1567, and graduated BA in 1568. Bright left Trinity without taking his MA after Michaelmas 1570 and presumably studied medicine on the continent.

Bright was in Paris on Sunday 24 August 1572, the outbreak of the St Bartholomew's day massacre, when he and other foreign protestants, including the young Philip Sidney, found refuge in the house of English ambassador Sir Francis Walsingham, 'a very sanctuarie', he later wrote, for those who otherwise would have 'all tasted of the rage of that furious Tragedy, had not your honour shrowded them'. Writing of the event sixteen years later, he said that it was still '(as ever it will bee) fresh with mee in memory' ('Dedication' to *An Abridgement of the 'Booke of Acts and Monumentes of the Church'*, 1589). Besides impressing on his mind an indelible sense of horror, the event undoubtedly buttressed his protestant beliefs and encouraged his strong nationalism; moreover, it left him in grateful debt for the 'especiall protection' afforded him by the cultivated and powerful Walsingham.

Bright probably continued his medical studies in Europe, possibly in Italy and Germany, before returning to Cambridge. He graduated MB in 1574, was licentiate of medicine in 1575, and graduated MD in 1579, by which time he was married and living in the parish of St Mary-the-Great, Cambridge. On 13 July 1578 his son Timothy had been baptized, the first of four sons and three daughters born to him and his wife, Margaret, by 1588. Bright's first work, *A Treatise: Wherein is Declared the Sufficiencie of English Medicines* (1580), was a 'piece of medical nationalism' (Keynes, 3), in which Bright extolled the native English pharmacopoeia—herb, flower, fruit, vegetable, and animal (including the virtues of decocted frogs). He composed a two-part treatise, dedicated to university chancellor Lord Burghley, on health and cure of disease: *Hygieina* (1582), its preface indicating that Bright lectured at Cambridge; and *Medicinae therapeuticae* (1583). *In physicam Gulielmi Adolphi Scribonii* (1584) reveals that Bright's medical theories owed much to Galen and Greek philosophy. His dedication to Sir Philip Sidney, Sir Francis Walsingham's son-in-law, was dated from Ipswich, Suffolk, where Bright was apparently living.

In February 1585 letters from Walsingham and his brother-in-law Sir Walter Mildmay, among others, secured Bright's appointment to the prestigious post of chief physician to the Royal Hospital of St Bartholomew, London, against the nomination by the College of Physicians of the highly qualified Henry Wootton. Bright assumed the post about a month later, at a salary of 40s., an allowance of wood and coal, and a house on the Christ's Hospital side of St Bartholomew's. On 1 October he was one of seven attesters of the statutes of Emmanuel College, Cambridge, founded by Mildmay, who resided in the parish of St Bartholomew-the-Great. On 10 November 1587 he was sentenced *in absentia* by the College of Physicians to be incarcerated in Fleet prison (presumably because he had practised in the city of London without their licence). The sentence was never carried out but, charged repeatedly by the hospital's governors in 1590 and 1591 with dereliction of duty, Bright was dismissed and ordered to leave by Michaelmas (29 September) 1591.

While neglecting his patients at St Bartholomew's Hospital, Bright authored the two works for which he is remembered. In *A Treatise of Melancholie* (Vautrollier, 1586), addressed 'To his melancholicke friend: M', he explored the interdependence of mind (synonymous with soul) and body, and 'what the difference is betwixt natural melancholie, and that heavy hande of God upon the afflicted conscience' (sig. *3v). To 'comfort them in that estate most comfortles', he offered 'advise of phisicke helpe: what diet, what medicine, and what other remedie is meete for persons oppressed with melancholie feare, & that kind of heavinesse of hart' (sig. *4r). Only months before, he and his wife, Margaret, had suffered the death of one of their children. His metaphysical *Treatise*—'an important historical document for the psychiatrist and for the practitioner of psycho-somatic medicine' (Keynes, 8)—influenced Robert Burton's more famous *The Anatomy of Melancholy* (1621), and was probably known to Shakespeare, whose *Hamlet* echoes Bright's language (Jordan-Smith; O'Sullivan).

Bright's other significant work, a landmark in the history of shorthand, was *Characterie: an Arte of Shorte, Swifte, and Secrete Writing by Character* (1588). Shorthand was known to the Romans, and other shorthand systems were doubtless used and taught by 1588, but Bright was the first to publish his 'invention … altogether of English yeeld' (sig. A4v). He dedicated 'this new sprong ympe' (sig. A5v) to Elizabeth I, who on 26 July 1588 (one day after the struggle off the Isle of Wight between the English fleet and the Spanish Armada) granted him a special royal patent forbidding others for fifteen years to teach or publish his or any rival shorthand system 'not before this tyme comonly knowen & used by any other our subjects' (Carlton, *Bright*,

72). The patent, ironically, impeded the development of modern shorthand. Although Bright's system contained an alphabet, neither it nor the system of Peter Bales (*The Writing Schoolemaster*, 1590) was alphabetic in the orthographic sense that letters could be joined, like that of John Willis (*The Art of Stenographie*, 1602).

Bright's ingenious but cumbersome system was written vertically, top to bottom, resembling Chinese or cryptograms. His 'characterie' (meaning the expression of thoughts by symbols or characters) consisted of 537 'charactericall' words that had to be memorized. It employed eighteen vertical symbols, each representing a letter (or letter group) of the alphabet. To each alphabetical letter one of twelve appendages (hooks, lines, loops) was added to indicate particular words beginning with that letter. Each word thus formed could be written in three other positions (horizontally or sloping left or right) so that forty-eight words might theoretically be formed from each alphabetical letter. By using small alphabetic letters, dots, ticks, and lines in various positions to each of the 537 'charactericall' words, the writer could indicate synonyms, antonyms, negatives, plurals, and noun and verb endings. Arbitrary symbols served for 'particles' (common words such as articles, conjunctions, and prepositions).

The inherent difficulties of the system and its unsuitability for reproducing verbatim speech have been noted (Gibbs; Lewis; Pitman; Matthews, 'Peter Bales'), yet it was probably practised with facility by some and certainly by one: the first known female shorthand writer, Jane Seager, a lady of the court, presented to Queen Elizabeth in 1589 *The Divine Prophecies of the Ten Sibills*, composed in both longhand and Bright's 'Charactery'. One 'A. S.' and John Lewys purported to take down in 'Characterie' and publish sermons by Stephen Egerton (1589) and Henry Smith (1590) respectively. Whether the term referred to Bright's system or had more generic use is admittedly uncertain. According to the *Oxford English Dictionary*, Bright's was the first use of 'characterie', a word found in Shakespeare. Bright's system has long been of interest to Shakespearian scholars who believe that Elizabethan shorthand may play a role in solving the editorial problems of the so-called 'bad quartos' (textual differences between the early quarto editions and the 1623 first folio).

Bright's 'tender plant, yong & strange' (*Characterie*, sig. A4v) metamorphosed over several years. On 30 March 1586 Vincent Skinner, Bright's Cambridge tutor, wrote to his friend Michael Hicks, a confidential secretary to Lord Burghley, seeking Bright's introduction to Burghley's son Robert Cecil for the reason that he 'hath enterprised a matter of rare noveltie and effected it' (Carlton, *Bright*, 60). He enclosed Bright's own shorthand transcription of *St. Paul's Epistle to Titus* written in a system differing considerably from that of 1588. Bright, he suggested, might 'do as much for you as Mr. Babingtons Barber had done in a lyke case of using his art and faculty by requitall' (ibid., 61), an allusion perhaps to the cryptographic correspondence between Anthony Babington and Mary, queen of Scots,

deciphered by Walsingham and his agents. The following year, in 1587, Bright submitted to William Davison, secretary to Queen Elizabeth, a manuscript titled *De clandestino scripto methodica tractatio*—his translation, undertaken at Davison's request, of two sections of *De furtivis literarum notis, vulgo de ziferis* (1563), a Latin work on cryptography by Giovanni Battista della Porta, a copy of which had been sent to him by Lord Burghley through Davison. Bright was thus performing service for the Elizabethan intelligence network; he may also have served in some capacity as physician to one or more of his several patrons.

Shortly afterwards Bright published yet another work, an abridgement of John Foxe's popular book of martyrs. Cheaper and one-quarter the length of the original, it may have had wider circulation. His dedication suggests that Bright had received financial support from Walsingham, but his patrons were in decline: Davison had fallen from power, Mildmay died on 31 May 1589, and Walsingham died on 6 April 1590. Before his sacking from St Bartholomew's Hospital, however, Dr Timothy Bright had acquired a new vocation, that of cleric. On 5 July 1591 he was instituted to the rectory of Methley, near Wakefield, West Riding, Yorkshire, and on 30 December 1594 to that of Barwick in Elmet, 12 miles from Methley. He held these lucrative livings, valued at almost £26 and £34 respectively, in plurality. He had been preferred but apparently not instituted to the rectory of Stanford Rivers, near Ongar, Essex, on 19 July 1590. All three were in the gift of the chancellor of the duchy of Lancaster, who from 1587 until his death had been Walsingham. On 24 August 1592, the twentieth anniversary of the St Bartholomew's day massacre, Bright buried his father, William, at Methley. Only the three eldest of his seven children (Timothy, Titus, and Elizabeth) survived to adulthood.

Five days after his institution at Methley, Bright signed a pact with John Savile, lord of the manor, agreeing that if he resigned the living he would inform Savile and, by implication, support Savile's new nominee. Methley parishioners complained that Bright refused to accept customary tithes and failed to fulfil his own customary duties, such as:

> yearlie to finde a bull and a boare & also att his owne charge to fynde & carie to the church of metheley two loads of strawe to be there employed in the pues or stals of the church which he refuseth. (Carlton, *Bright*, 135)

As he had shirked his medical offices at St Bartholomew's in favour of authorship, shorthand, and cryptography, so he now neglected his 'Trowblesom prishioners' (ibid., 138). In 1593 Savile charged that Bright 'is a Phisicon and continually practiseth the same' and that 'his practice of Phisicke draweth him upon hollidaies to leave his charge destitute' (Hall, 33). He visited and evidently intended to write a treatise about the mineral springs at Harrogate; and his early work on English *materia medica* was reissued in 1615 with the addition of an extensive catalogue of medicines. While he evidently 'cared more for the fleece than the flock' (Carlton, *Bright*, 147), there was at Barwick 'an old tradition that he knew not his own oxen but desired his steward to buy such as those were in the field not understanding 'em to be his own' (Colman, 66).

Timothy Bright's will, dated 9 August 1615, suggests a man of culture and erudition, a lover of books and music, a linguist and accomplished musician. To his brother William, public preacher of St Mary's, Shrewsbury, he bequeathed books, his theorbo (a kind of lute) with its case, and the Irish harp 'which I most usuallye played upon'. He was buried at St Mary's, Shrewsbury, on 6 September 1615. His wife, Margaret, executor of his will proved at York on 13 November, was buried with him at St Mary's on 9 February 1620. Bright's motto was 'Ingenio, arte, manu' ('By ability, by art, by hand'). To English literature he left an unexpected legacy, being, through his son Timothy, the great-great-grandfather of dramatist William Congreve.   PAGE LIFE

Sources W. J. Carlton, *Timothe Bright, doctor of phisicke: a memoir of 'The father of modern shorthand'* (1911) · W. J. Carlton, 'An unrecorded manuscript by Dr Timothy Bright', *N&Q*, 209 (1964), 463–5 · G. Keynes, *Dr. Timothie Bright, 1550–1615: a survey of his life with a bibliography of his writings*, Wellcome Historical Medical Library, new ser., 1 (1962) · H. A. Hall, 'Dr. Timothy Bright: some troubles of an Elizabethan rector', *Publications of the Thoresby Society*, 15 (1905–9), 30–37 · W. J. Carlton, *Bibliotheca Pepysiana*, 4: *Shorthand books* (1940), 1–6 · E. Pocknell, 'Timothy Bright's, or the first English, shorthand, 1588', *Shorthand: a Scientific and Literary Magazine*, 2 (1884), 126–32 · will, York consistory court, 31, fol. 180 (13 Nov 1615) · [W. Brown], 'The will of Timothy Bright, MD, rector of Methley and Barwick-in-Elmet, 1615', *Yorkshire Archaeological Journal*, 17 (1902–3), 50–54 · F. S. Colman, *A history of the parish of Barwick-in-Elmet, in the county of York*, Publications of the Thoresby Society, 17 (1908), 65–6; repr. (1967) · *Documents relating to the university and colleges of Cambridge*, Cambridge University Commission, 3 (1852), 483–523 · M. Doran, 'Manuscript notes in the Bodleian copy of Bright's *Characterie*', *The Library*, 4th ser., 16 (1935–6), 418–24 · M. I. O'Sullivan, '*Hamlet* and Dr. Timothy Bright', *Publications of the Modern Language Association of America*, 41 (1926), 667–79 · P. Jordan-Smith, *Bibliographia Burtoniana: a study of Robert Burton's 'The anatomy of melancholy', with a bibliography of Burton's writings* (1931) · W. Matthews, 'Shorthand and the bad Shakespeare quartos', *Modern Language Review*, 27 (1932), 243–62 · W. Matthews, 'A postscript to "Shorthand and the bad Shakespeare quartos"', *Modern Language Review*, 28 (1933), 8 · W. Matthews, 'Peter Bales, Timothy Bright and William Shakespeare', *Journal of English and Germanic Philology*, 34 (1935), 483–510 · M. Förster, 'Shakespeare and shorthand', *Philological Quarterly*, 16 (1937), 1–29 · A. Davidson, '"Some by stenography"? Stationers, shorthand, and the early Shakespearean quartos', *Papers of the Bibliographical Society of America*, 90 (1996), 417–49 · K. Brown and D. C. Haskell, *The shorthand collection in the New York Public Library* (1935) [bibliography of Bright and Shakespeare shorthand controversy] · P. Gibbs, *An historical account of compendious and swift writing* (1736), 36–8, 42 · J. H. Lewis, *An historical account of the rise and progress of short hand* (privately printed, London, c.1825), 37–41 · I. Pitman, *The history of shorthand*, 3rd edn (1891), 7–10 · *IGI* · W. J. Carlton, 'Charactery', *N&Q*, 213 (1968), 366–7

Archives BL, presentation copy to Elizabeth I of J. Seager's *The divine prophecies of the ten Sibills upon the birthe of our Saviour Christ in his characterie*, Add. MS 10037 · BL, signature of attestation of statutes of Emmanuel College, Cambridge, Sloane MS 1739 · Bodl. Oxf., *De clandestino scripto methodica tractatio a Timotheo Brighto Cantabrigiensi ex secondo & tertio libro Johannis Baptistæ Portæ Neapolitani, De furtivis literarum notis, ad honoratissimum virtum, & serenissimae reginae Elizabethae a secretis D. Guliel. Davisonum*, Western MS 9804 · PRO, bills of privy signet, signet bill 1488, July A, 30 Elizabeth · PRO, patent roll, 30 Elizabeth, part 12 · PRO, petition to

J. Puckering relating to litigation of Methley parishioners, chancery proceedings, 34 Elizabeth, M.m. 13, no. 16

Wealth at death solvent: will, 9 Aug 1615, proved 13 Nov 1615, York consistory court, 31, fol. 180 · in financial difficulties: daughter-in-law's will, Carlton, *Timothe Bright*, 167; J. Hunter, *Chorus vatum anglicanorum*, 4 (1848), 360 · held two of most valuable livings in Yorkshire (Methley, fifth in value; Barwick, third); Methley living (1591) yielded £25 8s. 11d. without tithes: *N&Q*, 4th ser., 5 (1875), 430 · Methley yielded £25 8s. 6½d.: Moore, *History*, vol. 2, p. 440 · Barwick in Elmet (1594) yielded £33 12s. 6d. without tithes: Carlton, *Timothe Bright*, 144; Moore, *History*, vol. 2, p. 440 · in 1595 two benefices equal to value in 1911 of £500, exclusive of tithes: Carlton, *Timothe Bright*, 167

Bright, Ursula Mellor (1835–1915), campaigner for women's rights, was born on 5 July 1835, daughter of Joseph Mellor, a Liverpool merchant. It appears that her mother was a daughter of John Pennington of Hindley, Lancashire. Certainly Frederick Pennington, the Liberal MP and supporter of many women's causes, and Thomas Thomasson, the philanthropist, who had married another daughter of John Pennington, were her uncles. Her father and her brother, J. P. Mellor, were generous supporters of women's suffrage societies. Although nothing is known of her education, she was brought up in a milieu that gave importance to educating daughters. Her own daughter noted that she was 'a strong generous soul, very direct, simple as a child in some ways, yet with a keen brain and fine judgment' (Bright, *Ancient One*, 7) and that she was an excellent chess player.

The Mellors were in touch with many like-minded families. In the 1840s Ursula's cousins, Martha and Alice Mellor, are recorded as discussing women's suffrage with Priscilla Bright (later McLaren) in Rochdale, and on 13 September 1855, in Acomb parish church, Ursula Mellor married Jacob *Bright (1821–1899), then working with the family firm, John Bright & Brothers. The Brights lived at Alderley Edge, in Cheshire, moving in 1867, after Jacob's election as Liberal MP for Manchester, to 31 St James's Place, London, during the parliamentary session. Two sons died in early childhood, within a fortnight of each other, of diphtheria. Two more sons were born and, in 1868, a daughter, Esther.

The Brights shared 'radical Liberal' views and were particularly concerned with advancing the woman's cause. Esther remarked in her memoirs that they were a family of reformers. In 1870 they became founder members of the Ladies' National Association, pressing for the repeal of the Contagious Diseases Acts. Ursula Mellor Bright was a member of the executive committee of the Married Women's Property Committee for its entire duration (1868–82) and its treasurer (1874–82). The passing of the 1882 Married Women's Property Act was acknowledged to have been due to her efforts. Elizabeth Cady Stanton noted 'for ten consecutive years she gave her special attention to this bill … was unwearied in her efforts, in rolling up petitions, scattering tracts, holding meetings' (Biggs, 872). As a counterpoint, Elizabeth Wolstenholme Elmy, who had worked jointly with her on that campaign, wrote disparagingly in 1889 of Mrs Bright's lack of business sense and her inability to 'take suggestions from those who know' (BL, Add. MS 47449, fol. 46). Elizabeth Wolstenholme Elmy was by then, however, no friend.

In 1866 Ursula Bright signed the petition in favour of women's suffrage presented to parliament by John Stuart Mill; she was a member of the first Women's Suffrage Society, formed in Manchester in 1867. She continued to work for the society and its London-based sister until, in 1890, at the insistence of the Pankhursts, although to the disgust of Elizabeth Wolstenholme Elmy, who thought she gave undue support to Gladstone, she was made honorary secretary of the Women's Franchise League. Unlike the main National Society for Women's Suffrage, the league was concerned to support the enfranchisement of married women as well as of widows and spinsters. Her work with the league resulted in the inclusion in the Local Government Act of 1894 of the right of married women to all local franchises. The Brights were certainly keen home-rulers but Ursula's lifelong commitment to the Liberals may not have been as great as Elizabeth Wolstenholme Elmy surmised. Mrs Pankhurst recorded that when, in 1894, she joined the Independent Labour Party, Ursula Bright offered to do so herself. She was dissuaded; it would have meant a break with so many old friends.

Ursula Bright was interested in the abolition of the House of Lords, opposed compulsory vaccination, and had a wide circle of friends, both artistic and political, on both sides of the Atlantic. In the 1890s she was a member of the revising committee for Elizabeth Cady Stanton's *The Woman's Bible* and became increasingly interested in theosophy; she was already a vegetarian. After Jacob Bright's death in 1899, Annie Besant, on her visits to England, lived with Ursula and Esther. The latter remarked that her mother did not always agree with Annie Besant, but in 1898 gave £3000 to the Theosophical headquarters in northern India. Ursula Bright died on 12 March 1915 at her home at 82 Drayton Gardens, Kensington, London. Having taken no part in the more colourful twentieth-century agitation for the vote, being severely incapacitated by osteoarthritis, her earlier strenuous political efforts received scarcely a mention from obituarists.

ELIZABETH CRAWFORD

Sources E. Bright, *The ancient one* (1927) · E. Bright, *Old memories and letters of Annie Besant* (1936) · *Speeches of Jacob Bright*, ed. Mrs J. Bright (1885) · BL, Elizabeth Wolstenholme Elmy MSS, Add. MSS 47449–47452 · C. A. Biggs, 'Great Britain', *History of woman suffrage*, ed. E. C. Stanton, S. B. Anthony, and M. J. Gage, 3 (1886), 833–94 · S. S. Holton, *Suffrage days: stories from the women's suffrage movement* (1996) · m. cert. · d. cert.

Wealth at death £5848 3s. 2d.: probate, 4 June 1915, CGPLA Eng. & Wales

Bright, William (1824–1901), church historian, born at Doncaster on 14 December 1824, was the only son of William Bright, town clerk of Doncaster, Yorkshire, and Mary Ann Branson. He was sent first to a preparatory school at Southwell, and then, in 1837, to Rugby School, where he reached the sixth form at the time of Thomas Arnold's death. Having gained a scholarship at University College, Oxford, he matriculated on 20 March 1843; he graduated BA in 1846, obtaining first-class honours in classics, and

William Bright (1824–1901), by Gillman & Co.

proceeded MA in 1849. He was awarded the Johnson theological scholarship in 1847, and the Ellerton prize for theological essays in 1848. He was ordained deacon in 1848 and priest in 1850.

Elected fellow of University College in 1847, Bright retained his fellowship until 1868. He became tutor of his college in 1848, but in 1851 accepted the theological tutorship at Trinity College, Glenalmond, under the wardenship of Charles Wordsworth, later bishop of St Andrews. The Scottish bishops also appointed him to the Bell lectureship in ecclesiastical history, an office that entailed the custodianship of a mass of important documents pertaining to the church history of Great Britain, which had been accumulated by the founder for the use of his lecturer. Bright was thus encouraged to pursue the historical studies to which he came to devote his energies. In 1858 the bishop of Glasgow, Walter John Trower, procured Bright's ejection from both the Glenalmond tutorship and the Bell lectureship on the grounds of his Tractarian opinions on the church settlement of Henry VIII. Bright protested in a pamphlet, *A Statement of the Facts as to Certain Proceedings of the Bishop of Glasgow* (1858). Later on, the injustice of the proceedings was acknowledged, and he was made an honorary canon of Cumbrae Cathedral, an office which he held from 1865 to 1893.

After returning to Oxford in 1858, Bright resumed his tutorship at University College in 1859, and became a colleague of Pusey and Liddon. He was appointed in 1868 regius professor of ecclesiastical history at Oxford and canon of Christ Church in succession to H. L. Mansel, and in 1869 was made DD. In his new office he proved himself industrious. His 'Sylva', his set of manuscript notebooks of matter bearing on lectures from 1870 to 1880, amounts to over sixty large and methodical volumes. He was a most forceful lecturer, full of contagious energy and quirky humour. He preached effectively in the university church and the cathedral, and was always ready to help any Oxford clergyman by giving a sermon, or taking the chair at church meetings. Anxious to make provision for the rapidly growing suburbs of Oxford, he earnestly advocated, and liberally contributed to, the building of the fine church of St Margaret in north Oxford. He was proctor in convocation for the chapter of Christ Church from 1878; examining chaplain to Edward King, bishop of Lincoln, from 1885; and subdean of Christ Church from 1895. He died unmarried at Christ Church on 6 March 1901, and was buried in the Christ Church portion of Osney cemetery, Oxford.

Bright's works of history focus mainly on the early church and the church fathers. They include several sets of published lectures: *A History of the Church, AD 313–451* (1860; 5th edn, 1888); *Chapters of Early Church History* (1878; 3rd edn, 1897); *The Roman See in the Early Church* (1896); and the two-volume *The Age of the Fathers*, posthumously published in 1903. In addition, he published a large number of sermons, devotional works, and tracts, such as *Faith and Hope*, a collection of readings (1864); *The Incarnation as a Motive Power* (1889); and (jointly with Peter Goldsmith Medd) *Liber precum publicarum* (1865), a Latin version of the Anglican liturgy. Bright was well known as a hymn writer and was author of 'We know thee who thou art, Lord Jesus, Mary's son', 'And now, O father, mindful of the love', and the evening hymn 'And now the wants are told'. His *Hymns and other Poems* was published in 1866 and again in 1874.

ANDREW CLARK, rev. MYFANWY LLOYD

Sources *Letters of William Bright, D.D.*, ed. B. J. Kidd (1903) · S. R. Driver, 'Canon Bright: an appreciation', *Oxford Magazine* (13 March 1901), 276–7 · *The Times* (7 March 1901) · *Oxford Times* (9 March 1901) · P. Schaff and S. M. Jackson, *Encyclopedia of living divines and Christian workers of all denominations in Europe and America: being a supplement to Schaff-Herzog encyclopedia of religious knowledge* (1887) · S. L. Ollard, *A short history of the Oxford Movement* (1915) · O. Chadwick, *The spirit of the Oxford Movement: Tractarian essays* (1990) · *Men and women of the time* (1899)

Archives Bodl. Oxf., corresp., diaries, notebooks, and papers etc. · LPL, corresp. · Mitchell L., Glas., notanda | Birmingham Oratory, letters to J. H. Newman · Bodl. Oxf., letters to Basil Harwood · Pusey Oxf., letters to E. B. Pusey · University of Dundee, letters to Alexander Forbes · University of Dundee, letters to sixth earl of Glasgow

Likenesses Gillman & Co., photograph, repro. in *Letters of William Bright*, ed. Kidd [see illus.]

Wealth at death £58,210 18s. 4d.: resworn probate, July 1902, CGPLA Eng. & Wales (1901)

Brightman, Frank Edward (1856–1932), liturgical scholar, was born at Bristol on 18 June 1856, the second of the three sons of Charles Brightman, a master shoemaker of Bristol, and his wife, Emma, daughter of Isaac Brown. Educated at Bristol grammar school, he won a scholarship to University College, Oxford, in 1875. After being awarded a first class in mathematical moderations (1876) and a second class in classical moderations (1877), *literae humaniores* (1879), and theology (1880), he won in 1882 both a Denyer and Johnson theological scholarship and the Hall-Houghton senior Septuagint prize (BA 1879, MA 1882). He was ordained deacon in 1884 and priest in 1885, after having been appointed in 1884 as one of the original librarians of Pusey House, Oxford, an office which he held until the year after his election to a fellowship at Magdalen in 1902.

Brightman was one of the most learned of the group of liturgical scholars, including Percy Dearmer (1867–1936), W. H. Frere (1863–1938), and Edmund Bishop (1846–1917), who were active in England at the turn of the century. While most concentrated on the study of Latin liturgies, Brightman was generally associated with the liturgies of the Eastern Christian churches: his amplification of C. E. Hammond's *Liturgies, Eastern and Western* did not go beyond the first volume on Eastern liturgies, published in 1896. Despite the breadth of his erudition Brightman wrote little, a circumstance partly attributable to the generous assistance which he gave his students. Moreover, from 1904 to 1932 he devoted much time and effort to joint editorship of the *Journal of Theological Studies*. He also acted as an adviser to the leaders of the Church of England, and in the controversy over Anglican orders he was consulted in the compilation of the reply to the bull *Apostolicae curae* (1896). His essay 'The terms of communion and the ministration of the sacraments in early times' (published in *Essays on the Early History of the Church and the Ministry*, edited by H. B. Swete, 1918) displayed a depth and range of scholarship such as no other liturgical scholar then alive could have provided. Brightman also edited Lancelot Andrewes's *Preces privatae* (1903) and *Manual of the Sick* (1909), and produced a monumental work in two volumes, *The English Rite* (1915), a synopsis in which he set out the sources of the Book of Common Prayer and the changes made from 1549 to 1662. This, and his book on the oriental liturgies, remain standard works. During debates on the revision of the prayer book in 1927 a devastating article from his pen in the *Church Quarterly Review* influenced church opinion against the proposed book. He was critical of almost every change in the book: 'Among the new contents of the book I seem to have noticed three things, and perhaps only three, which are of real distinction.'

Brightman was a short man, who walked with his head bent as if avoiding notice, but his finely domed head, ascetic face, and grave but kindly eyes marked him out. He was very shrewd, and his rare sermons were made deeply arresting by their moral earnestness. Despite his preoccupation with liturgy his churchmanship was not extreme in external ritualistic matters, being more of an old-fashioned high-church variety than that of the fully developed Anglo-Catholic Darwell Stone (1859–1941), his successor as librarian at Pusey House. He detested publicity, but honours came to him nevertheless. Bishop Edward King collated him in 1902 to a prebend in Lincoln Minster; the University of Louvain conferred upon him the honorary degree of DPhil in 1909, and the University of Durham that of DD in 1914. In 1926 he was elected a fellow of the British Academy. Shy and reticent with strangers, he attracted a wide range of undergraduates, who soon forgot in his rooms the disorder of the books as they listened to his conversation, touched with irony and humour. He died unmarried in his college rooms on 31 March 1932, and was buried in Holywell cemetery, Oxford, on 4 April 1932.

S. L. OLLARD, rev. DONALD GRAY

Sources *The Times* (1 April 1932) • H. N. Bate, 'Frank Edward Brightman', *PBA*, 19 (1933), 345–50 • *Oxford Times* (8 April 1932) • *WWW* • F. L. Cross, *Darwell Stone, churchman and counsellor* [1943] • G. J. Cuming, *A history of Anglican liturgy*, 2nd edn (1982) • b. cert. • B. Nichols, 'F. E. Brightman', *They shaped our worship*, ed. C. Irvine, Alcuin Club Collection, 75 (1998), 35–41
Archives LPL, corresp. with William Bishop and Arthur Cayley Headlam
Likenesses W. Stoneman, photograph, 1930, NPG
Wealth at death £6552 5s. 8d.: probate, 26 May 1932, *CGPLA Eng. & Wales*

Brightman, Thomas (1562–1607), Church of England clergyman and presbyterian controversialist, was born in Nottingham. Nothing is known about his parents. On 21 February 1577 he was admitted a pensioner of Queens' College, Cambridge, where he matriculated in 1578. Having graduated BA in 1581, he proceeded MA and became a fellow in 1584. Some time in his Cambridge career Brightman associated himself with presbyterian dissent, joining a small group of radical dons which held meetings in the late 1580s. He signed one of the two petitions on behalf of Francis Johnson in 1589 and debated issues of church reform with George Meriton, a fellow of Queens' from 1589 and later dean of York. Although he denounced separatism as well as the tactics of Martin Marprelate, he may have subscribed the Book of Discipline, and was an outright nonconformist and a critic of episcopacy and the religion of the prayer book. None the less, Brightman proceeded BD in 1591. In 1592, upon William Whitaker's recommendation, Sir John Osborne gave him the rectory of Hawnes, Bedfordshire, where he remained for the rest of his life under Osborne's continuing patronage and protection. There he took a semi-separatist position in the subscription controversy sparked by the canons of 1604. Citing his 'bitter invectives against the ecclesiastical government and governors', the bishop of Lincoln suspended him the same year (*Salisbury MSS*, 330), and for a time he was harboured in the Osborne home.

Meanwhile, although the presbyterian movement had been defeated by about 1590, Brightman made continued zealous and innovative attempts to renew the stricken cause through his writings. His theology of redemption, exemplified in *The Arte of Self-Deniall* (1646), sketched familiar disciplinary and ascetic ideals of the godly, but his main interest and distinction lay elsewhere. The only presbyterian of the time to frame theology on a grand scale, he incorporated the movement's arguments and hopes into a sweeping vision of history and eschatology.

That vision was set forth in three Latin works which remained unpublished in his lifetime. His masterpiece was *Apocalypsis apocalypseos*, which came to 717 pages in the first edition, published at Frankfurt in 1609. An English translation appeared in 1611 and went through four editions to 1644. Additional elaborations appeared in short Latin commentaries on Canticles and portions of the book of Daniel published in one volume at Basel in 1614 and in separate English translations in 1644, although none of his work was published in England until 1641.

Drawing upon the ideas of John Bale, John Foxe, and many other interpreters of Christian history and prophecy, Brightman had a particular interest in the tradition of eschatological interpretation stemming from Joachim of Fiore. He devised an elaborate synthesis that was at once primitivist, historicist, and millennial. Its governing norm was the primitive apostolic church, in which Brightman, like all English presbyterians, identified the order of elected officers and consistorial discipline partially realized in his own time in Reformed churches abroad. Departure from it was the cause of all historic ills of the Christian movement and the essential fault of the Roman Antichrist; return to it was the script for the future written in the pages of the book of Daniel, the Song of Solomon, and, supremely, the book of Revelation. After a steep decline from the age of Constantine through centuries of progressive Catholic apostasy, the true church had begun, in the age of John Wyclif, a process of recovery, which had risen to near completion in contemporary Geneva, France, Scotland, and other Reformed centres. In that process England had played an eminent part. Properly deciphered, the book of Revelation's prophetic code gave prominent roles to John Wyclif, Henry VIII, Thomas Cromwell, Thomas Cranmer, Elizabeth I, and William Cecil. Like Cecil, with his harsh measures against invading Jesuit missionaries in the 1580s, each had given a blow to the Antichrist and advanced the apostolic recovery. Yet much remained to be done. The episcopal government, formal liturgy, and lax discipline of the national church embodied a stubbornly arrested early phase of restoration. To spur the land anew into the path of reform, Brightman argued that the way back to apostolicity was also an exhilarating trek forward to an earthly New Jerusalem. Laying claim to special divine inspiration, he redrew the map of the future. He foresaw not a near and sudden end to history at judgment day, but a continuing spiral of events which moved towards the overthrow of the Catholic church about 1650, the conversion of the Jews, and the dawn of a lengthy period of peace, plenty, and religious fulfilment centred upon a restored apostolic church. Thus the whole process of history was advancing toward a global presbyterian utopia.

Through his advocacy of this concept, Brightman became England's first major millennial theorist and a large influence upon eschatological speculation in both Old and New England in the seventeenth century. Near the end of his life, with undimmed puritan conviction, he strove in an exchange of letters to persuade Laurence Chaderton, head of Emmanuel College, Cambridge, that the use of the surplice and hood in the college chapel were impure remnants of Antichrist. On 24 August 1607 he died suddenly not far from home while riding in a coach with his patron. He had never married. He was buried on the day of his death in the church at Hawnes; Edward Bulkely, rector of Odell, in the same county, preached his funeral sermon.   THEODORE DWIGHT BOZEMAN

Sources Cooper, *Ath. Cantab.*, vol. 2 · K. R. Firth, *The apocalyptic tradition in Reformation Britain, 1530–1645* (1979) · M. Reeves, 'History and eschatology: medieval and early protestant thought in some English and Scottish writings', *Medievalia et Humanistica*, new ser., 4 (1973), 99–124 · H. C. Porter, *Reformation and reaction in Tudor Cambridge* (1958) · *DNB* · *Calendar of the manuscripts of the most hon. the marquess of Salisbury*, 16, HMC, 9 (1933) · P. Lake, *Moderate puritans and the Elizabethan church* (1982) · F. Osborne, *The works of Francis Osborne*, 8th edn (1682) · T. Brightman, to L. Chaderton, 10 Jan 1605, LPL, MS 2550, fol. 176r

Archives LPL, letter to L. Chaderton, MS 2550, fol. 176r

Likenesses engraving, repro. in T. Brightman, *Apocalypsis apocalypseos* (1609) · line engraving, BM, NPG; repro. in T. Brightman, *The revelation of Saint John, illustrated with analysis and scholions* (Amsterdam, 1644)

Brighton, Albert George [Peter] (1900–1988), palaeontologist and curator, was born on 29 December 1900 at 13 Conyers Road, Streatham, London, the son of George Freeston Brighton, gardener, and his wife, Susan Alice Jayne. He was educated at St Leonard's School, Streatham, and Westminster City School, before gaining a scholarship to read natural sciences at Christ's College, Cambridge. Despite showing considerable early promise of a first, and becoming joint winner of the Wiltshire prize for geology and mineralogy, Bertie, or Peter as he was best-known, graduated from Cambridge with a second-class degree in 1922. There he remained, committed to a career in palaeontology, and eventually began a doctorate which he did not complete. Brighton's first paper, on cretaceous echinoids from Nigeria, was published in 1925. Over the next decade his rate of publication steadily decreased as his palaeontological interests found a new direction, curation. He continued to lecture on fossil echinoids and nurtured many notable research students, but it is for his pioneering curatorial work on the fossil collections of the university's Sedgwick Museum that he is most widely known.

In the late 1920s the Sedgwick Museum remained much as it had been at the end of the nineteenth century, inaccessible, disorganized, and largely neglected. Owen Thomas Jones (1878–1967), who was elected Woodwardian professor of geology in 1930, immediately sought to resurrect its fortunes and appointed Brighton, who was a keen voluntary worker at the museum, to the post of curator in 1931 (the year in which, on 18 June, Brighton married Edith May, daughter of John Martin, accountant). Brighton estimated the museum then held half a million uncurated specimens, most only documented by the label tablets to which they were attached. The collection became his life's work as he slaved tirelessly at its identification, cataloguing, and arrangement. His preoccupation with these tasks perhaps reflected his largely unambitious and reclusive nature, and his obsessively ordered lifestyle. In the early years he also maintained correspondence with academics around the world but was happy to delegate these duties on the appointment of an assistant in 1954.

Brighton was autocratic and donnish, and he imposed rigour and methodology, qualities manifest in his indexes and in the 'shelf catalogues' which he developed as physical specimen databases. In a career spanning thirty-seven years he curated 375,000 specimens, and in so doing probably processed three times that number. The Sedgwick collections were transformed into a fully functioning modern palaeontological museum, which also now held a large collection of notebooks, maps, and annotated monographs chronicling its history. Brighton's selfless

Albert George Brighton (1900–1988), by unknown photographer [centre, in fedora]

dedication had produced an unusually data-rich resource which became the basis for pioneering work on the computerization of museum records, work he encouraged and which was ultimately to influence such developments nationally. On his retirement in 1968 Brighton left the museum without ceremony, seldom to return.

Though he lacked social graces Brighton was a cultivated man: he was extremely well read, a fine artist, an accomplished pianist, and a lover of the cigarette. Edith by contrast was very sociable, even charismatic, and their elegant house on Parkers Piece became something of a haven for the fashionable of Cambridge in the post-war years. Both were keen letter writers. Together, diminutive and eccentric, they were a perfect match. Peter Brighton died of emphysema at Langdon House, Scotland Road, Chesterton, Cambridgeshire, on 9 April 1988, and was cremated in Cambridge on 14 April; Edith survived him, dying on 22 September 1994. Brighton's personal memorial was a collection so perfectly curated that those who effortlessly used it failed to realize or credit the labour that had been involved. In 1992, the Geological Curators' Group (GCG), a specialist group of the Geological Society of London, instituted a medal in Brighton's honour. The aims of the GCG mirrored those of Brighton; the A. G. Brighton medal now celebrates those who, in the Brighton mould, have made an outstanding contribution to geology through the interpretation and preservation of geological material in museums.   SIMON J. KNELL

Sources private information (2004) · D. Price, 'A life of dedication: A. G. Brighton (1900–1988) and the Sedgwick Museum, Cambridge', *Geological Curator*, 5 (1988–94), 95–9 · D. Price and R. G. Clements, 'The A. G. Brighton medal', *Geological Curator*, 5 (1988–94), 331–4 · D. Price, 'Collections and collectors of note, 39: the Sedgwick Museum, Cambridge', *Geological Curator*, 3 (1981–3), 28–35 · R. B. Rickards, 'The physical basis of palaeontological curating', *Special Papers in Palaeontology*, 23 (1979), 75–86 · *The Times* (12 April 1988) · b. cert. · m. cert. · *CGPLA Eng. & Wales* (1988)
Archives U. Cam., Sedgwick Museum of Earth Sciences
Likenesses photographs, c.1922–1968, priv. coll. · photograph, 1931, U. Cam., Sedgwick Museum of Earth Sciences · R. B. Rickards, photograph, 1978, repro. in Price, 'A life of dedication', cover, p. 98 · photograph, U. Cam., Sedgwick Museum of Earth Sciences · photograph, priv. coll. [*see illus.*]
Wealth at death under £70,000: probate, 11 July 1988, *CGPLA Eng. & Wales*

Brightwell, (Cecilia) Lucy (1811–1875), etcher and author, was born at Thorpe, near Norwich, on 27 February 1811, the eldest child of Thomas Brightwell (1787–1868), a solicitor and amateur microscopist, and mayor of Norwich in 1837, and his first wife, Mary Snell (1788–1815), the daughter of William Wilkin Wilkin of Costessey, near Norwich, and his wife, Cecilia Lucy. Known as Lucy Brightwell, she lived for most of her life in the family home at 3 Surrey Street, Norwich. The family was nonconformist and closely connected with the natural history, literary, and artistic circles of Norwich. Lucy studied etching under John Sell Cotman and became a skilful copyist of etchings by old masters, including Rembrandt and Dürer. So exact were her copies that experts were unable to distinguish her copy of Rembrandt's *Landscape with a Cottage and Hay Barn, 1641* from the original. She exhibited her etchings only once at the Norfolk and Norwich Art Union, in 1839. Her own landscape compositions from nature, some of which are dated between 1842 and 1848, are less successful. She is known to have produced at least thirty-five etchings. Several are signed with initials CLB and two with a monogram. An almost complete set of etchings and thirty-two of the copper plates are in Norwich Castle Museum and Art Gallery.

The devoted companion of her father, Lucy Brightwell assisted him with his various interests. In 1848, when he produced for private distribution 100 copies of *Sketch of a Fauna infusoria for East Norfolk*, she spent long periods studying specimens under a powerful microscope to make drawings for the illustrations. These she transferred to lithographs, and later she hand coloured many of the plates in the individual books. A deeply religious woman, her own writings 'tended to the religious and moral, as well as the mental improvement of the young' (*Norwich Mercury*, 1 May 1875). She produced more than twenty, mainly biographical, works between 1854 and 1857, some published by the Religious Tract Society. Her first and most significant publication was *Memorials of the Life of Amelia Opie Selected and Arranged from her Letters and Diaries and other Manuscripts* (1854). Mrs Opie was a family friend, and Thomas Brightwell acted as her executor. Following the death of her father in 1868, Lucy Brightwell wrote 'out of the abundance of the heart' *Memorials of the Life of Mr Brightwell of Norwich* (1869), for private circulation. She was described by Carlyle, whom she met in 1848, as 'a very amiable looking artistic lady' (*Diary*, 327), and in 1849 she noted 'Was weighed—weight 9 stone 10 lbs. measured in height. 5 feet 4 inches & ½' (*Diary*, 24 March 1849). By 1864 she experienced the first signs of cataract which eventually led to blindness. She never married, but in 1869, at the age of fifty-eight, she received a proposal of marriage from the recently widowed author George *Borrow. He and his family were close friends of Lucy Brightwell, and it was believed that she would have accepted had not her brother strongly opposed (Fraser, 109). In 1874 Lucy Brightwell was 'Attacked … by disease of the brain [and] sank after eight months of severe suffering' (*Norwich Mercury*, 1 May 1875). She died on 17 April 1875 at her home in Surrey Street and was buried on 22 April at the Rosary cemetery, Norwich.   NORMA WATT

Sources *Norwich Mercury* (1 May 1875) · A. Fraser, 'Lucy Brightwell', *George Borrow Bulletin*, 15 (1998), 41–54 · A. Fraser, 'George Borrow and Lucy Brightwell', *N&Q*, 220 (1975), 109–11 · C. B. Jewson, *Simon Wilkin of Norwich* (1979) · C. L. Brightwell, *Memorials of the life of Mr Brightwell of Norwich* (1869) · *CGPLA Eng. & Wales* (1875) · C. L. Brightwell, diary, Norfolk RO
Archives Norfolk RO, diary | Hispanic Society of America, New York, George Borrow MSS
Likenesses J. R. Sawyer, photograph, c.1860–1869, Norfolk Studies Library, Norwich
Wealth at death under £6000: probate, 21 July 1875, *CGPLA Eng. & Wales*

Brightwen [*née* Elder], **Eliza** (1830–1906), naturalist and writer, was born on 30 October 1830 at Banff, Scotland, the fourth child of George and Margaret Elder. Following the death of her mother in 1837 she was adopted by her uncle,

Alexander Elder, one of the founders of the publishing house of Smith, Elder & Co. He had no children, and Eliza Elder was brought up in his country houses, Sparrow Hall, Streatham, and Thornbury Park, near Stamford Hill. On 5 June 1855 she married George Brightwen (1820–1883), a businessman. They settled in Stanmore, Middlesex, where Eliza Brightwen lived for the remainder of her life.

From childhood on Elder had a deep interest in natural history, a pursuit that she was well able to exercise during her childhood, roaming the grounds of her uncle's estates and reading from among the thousands of books in his library. As she said of herself, 'the early lessons of Natural History kept me constantly wondering and asking "the reason why"' (*Eliza Brightwen*, 7). Although her expertise stemmed primarily from her keen powers of observation, developed over years of nature study, throughout those years Elder also experimented scientifically, developing cultures and dissecting specimens. She also sketched and produced finished watercolours of natural objects. All of these enterprises further enhanced her exceptional powers of observation.

After marriage Eliza Brightwen enjoyed similar study at The Grove, Stanmore, a home which offered her lakes, woods, and a large garden. There she kept copious notes on its birds, plants, and animals and developed a menagerie which she observed closely. About 1872 her nervous system broke down completely, but, by her sixtieth year, she recovered sufficiently to begin assembling her work for publication. The literary result was *Wild Nature Won by Kindness* (1890), an unqualified success, which made her one of the most popular natural history writers of her day. This was followed by: *More about Wild Nature* (1892); *Inmates of my House and Garden* (1895); *Glimpses into Plant Life* (1898); *Rambles with Nature Students* (1899); and *Quiet Hours with Nature* (1903). During this period she remained at Stanmore and carried on a wide correspondence about natural history, much of which came about through enquiries from her readers.

Eliza Brightwen believed in educating the public about animal preservation. She opposed falconry, she wrote pamphlets and essays deploring the use of feathers for the trimming of human clothing, she rescued animals, and she lectured in local schools about bird trapping and the destruction of nestlings. In part her concern for other species came from her observations of animal species, and in part it stemmed from her evangelical religion. To her mind, creation was 'all out of order for a time' (*Eliza Brightwen*, 131) because of humanity's fall, and humans had inappropriate responses to animals as a result. In addition to her books on nature she wrote two religious books, *Practical Thoughts on Bible Study* (1871) and *Side Lights on the Bible* (1901).

In her later years, Eliza Brightwen rarely left her beloved estate, where she died on 5 May 1906. She was buried in the Stanmore churchyard. Another volume of natural history writing, *Last Hours with Nature*, was published posthumously in 1908, and fragments of an autobiography, introduced by her nephew, Edmund Gosse, were entitled *Eliza Brightwen: the Life and Thoughts of a Naturalist*

and published in 1909. Eliza Brightwen declined an entry in *Who's Who*, and reportedly sent the *Who's Who* form to a friend, filled in as follows:

> *Name and title*: 'A lover of Nature, protector of everything in fur and feathers.'
> *Educated at*: 'The shrine of Nature by no end of clever teachers.'
> *Academical distinctions*: 'Dame Nature does not bestow outward and visible honours, but she gives keen eyes, sharpened wits and ever-increasing pleasure.'
> *Recreations*: 'Searching for beetles and everything that flies and hops.'
> *Address*: 'At home everywhere in the world of Nature.'
> (*Eliza Brightwen*, xxx–xxxi)

BARBARA T. GATES

Sources *Eliza Brightwen: the life and thoughts of a naturalist*, ed. W. H. Chesson (1909) · m. cert. · d. cert. **Likenesses** P. Bigland, portrait, 1902 · portrait, repro. in E. Brightwen, *More about wild nature* (1892), frontispiece · print (after P. Bigland, 1902), repro. in Chesson, ed., *Eliza Brightwen* **Wealth at death** £9027 6s. 5d.: probate, 26 June 1906, *CGPLA Eng. & Wales*

Briginshaw, Richard William, Baron Briginshaw (1908–1992), trade union leader, was born on 15 May 1908 at 183 Mayall Road, Brixton, London, the first son of Richard Briginshaw, newspaper worker, and his wife, Alice Jubilee, *née* Coates. He was educated at Stuart School, Brixton. Although his background was classic working class and he left elementary school at fourteen to take a job as a printer's devil, his early days were not poverty stricken: his father had a comparatively well-paid and secure job as a printer with Odhams Press. Even so there was a great deal of poverty in homes close to the Briginshaw family and in later years Briginshaw (Dick or Briggie, as he was universally known) vividly recalled the ambience of his childhood in Brixton—children at his school without boots, often without food, widespread poverty because of unemployment, and a depression that was to colour and determine his political thinking and the course of his life.

Briginshaw's father encouraged him to read and through night school and his own ambitious drive he studied economics and law in his spare time, and eventually earned a diploma from University College, London. At the same time he worked his way from job to job as a trainee in the machine rooms of Fleet Street, not as a skilled compositor but as a machine hand. He found work in virtually every machine room in Fleet Street and as he moved from newspaper to newspaper he quickly acquired a reputation as an articulate union advocate. On 15 November 1931 he married Catherine Morritt (1910/11–1989), daughter of Harry Morritt, a Covent Garden porter. They had three sons.

In 1938 Briginshaw was elected assistant secretary of the London machine branch of the National Society of Operative Printers and Assistants (NATSOPA), one of the most influential units in the union. He became the youngest official in the union. His election to secretary of the branch seemed to be a virtual formality—a post that would have put him in line for the top job as the union's general secretary, then occupied by George Isaacs, later

Richard William Briginshaw, Baron Briginshaw (1908–1992), by W. Harrison

minister of labour in Attlee's government. But Briginshaw was already deeply radicalized and had joined the Communist Party. He was a leading organizer of the Printers' Anti-Fascist Movement, which Isaacs and the NATSOPA executive steadfastly refused to recognize. To the union hierarchy this was a communist 'front' organization and beyond the fringe of acceptability. They ordered Briginshaw to withdraw from it. He refused and was dismissed from his union post. The period that followed was frequently a hard struggle for Briginshaw but he refused to yield to the union's anti-communist policy. He volunteered for the army shortly after the outbreak of the Second World War and was finally called up in 1941. He served in India, the Middle East, and western Europe, several times refusing a commission on the grounds of wanting to remain among the rank-and-file as an ordinary soldier.

Briginshaw returned to civilian life at the end of 1945, with no job prospect in the union and the need to return to any Fleet Street machine room that would employ him. By then he had joined the Labour Party, though he remained firmly on the left, and his relationship with the right-wing union establishment was still abrasive. Yet by 1948 he had re-established himself and was elected again as assistant secretary of the London machine branch. From then his rise was rapid. In 1949 he was elected a national officer of NATSOPA and in 1951 he was elected

general secretary—succeeding (after a brief interregnum) his old foe George Isaacs, who had held on to his union post despite being a minister in the Attlee cabinet. Briginshaw remained general secretary until his retirement at the end of 1974.

Briginshaw's twenty-three years as leader of the strongest print union in the country was a remarkable stint by any standards. His awkward, often almost disdainful, style brought him more enemies from among the other print union leaders than from among the newspaper barons themselves. Even his political friends on the left found him a difficult ally, since he was often more cavalier with them than with political opponents—or with employers, some of whom became close enough to be regarded, almost, as friends. He often found himself alongside strange bedfellows, including Lord Beaverbrook, with whom he formed an 'unholy alliance'—as his critics claimed—during the campaign opposing Britain's entry into the Common Market. Briginshaw regularly wrote feature articles for all the Express group, denouncing the government negotiations, and when Britain eventually joined the community he became a joint founder of the Get Britain Out campaign. In 1969 his support for Rupert Murdoch was a substantial factor in Murdoch's acquisition of *The Sun* (the former *Daily Herald*), which had been put on the market by the International Publishing Corporation. To the fury of his fellow print union leaders he made clear his preference for Murdoch over Robert Maxwell as a potential purchaser of the paper, on the grounds that Murdoch was a better guarantor of job security and higher wages for his members.

Briginshaw's reputation in the print industry was that of a tough negotiator and a ruthless, albeit extremely shrewd, campaigner for his members. He symbolized the uncompromising attitude of print workers in their demands for higher wages, job protection, and the closed shop. Yet he was also a modernizer and foresaw much of what was to transform the newspaper and print industry long before Murdoch performed his dramatic switch to Wapping. He predicted the revolution in print technology and privately admitted that the 'gravy train' would hit the buffers before long. He always wanted one big union for the printing industry rather than a multitude of smaller, specialized craft unions. In 1966 he took a big step along that road by bringing about a merger between NATSOPA and the National Union of Printing, Bookbinding, and Paper Workers, to form the Society of Graphical and Allied Trades (SOGAT). Nevertheless, the two sections soon fell apart amid bitter recriminations, and remerged only after Briginshaw's retirement. He was a formidable opponent of all attempts at an incomes policy—whether operated by Conservative or Labour governments. He resigned from the Labour Party in 1968 because he disagreed with the Wilson government's introduction of a statutory pay policy, though he soon rejoined. His membership of the TUC general council (1965–75) was less significant than it might have been, considering his seniority as a union leader, and he was never a member of the TUC's 'inner circle'. His constant opposition to TUC policy on incomes, and indeed to any co-operation with government that might limit trade union freedom, left him always on the margin of influence.

Briginshaw caused a mild sensation by accepting a life peerage as Baron Briginshaw of Southwark when he retired at the end of 1974. A year later he published *Abolish the House of Lords*—denouncing the House of Lords as 'a creaking anachronism' (*The Independent*, 31 March 1992). He served on the council of the Advisory, Conciliation and Arbitration Service (ACAS) from 1974 to 1976, and was a member of the British Overseas Trade Board (1975–7) and the board of the British National Oil Corporation (1976–9). He was a member of the court of Cranfield Institute of Technology and served for six years as a governor of Dulwich College. His retirement was marred by allegations of malpractice following the discovery that union funds had been moved into Swiss bank accounts in the wake of trade-union legislation by the Heath government in 1971. Members of the NATSOPA section of the merged union took legal action against Briginshaw and three colleagues, accusing them of misapplying funds. He was finally cleared of all charges in 1982, when he made it clear that his actions had been wholly concerned with protecting union funds against possible seizure under Heath's new legislation.

Briginshaw was a tall, powerfully built, handsome man, whose healthy bronzed appearance often persuaded his critics that he had just returned from holiday. As he grew older his carefully coiffed silver-grey hair crowned a strong, bespectacled face. His wife, Catherine, died in 1989, but by then he had formed relationships with several women and had one son with Kathleen Maybin and a son and daughter with his secretary and personal assistant, Joan Wing. He died at the Mayday Hospital, Croydon, on 26 March 1992, of a perforated duodenal ulcer. He was survived by his six children.   GEOFFREY GOODMAN

Sources *Annual Report* [Trades Union Congress] (1968), 598–9, 601 · *Annual Report* [Trades Union Congress] (1970), 552, 636 · *Annual Report* [Trades Union Congress] (1971–4) [speeches] · *The Times* (28 March 1992) · *The Independent* (31 March 1992) · *The Independent* (6 April 1992) · *WWW* · personal knowledge (2004) · private information (2004) · b. cert. · m. cert. · d. cert.
Likenesses photograph, 1970, repro. in *The Independent* (31 March 1992) · W. Harrison, photograph, News International Syndication, London [*see illus.*]

Brigit [St Brigit, Brigid] (439/452–524/526), patron saint of Kildare, is the only native Irish saint to enjoy a widespread cult in all the Celtic countries. About the events of her life little can be said, since the earliest sources come from more than a century after her supposed death, on 1 February in either 524 or 526, and were in any case interested in miracle stories rather than biographical detail. Her early cult is, however, among the most influential and the most interesting of any saint in Ireland or Britain.

The cult and lives The early texts in Brigit's hagiographical 'dossier'—ranging from the seventh to the early ninth century—contain different perceptions of her natural clientele. At one end of the spectrum, she was a pan-Irish saint, enjoying local support in all the provinces of the island; at the other end, she was the saint of her own people, the Fothairt, settled mainly in Leinster but with outposts elsewhere. The Fothairt were never, in the historical period, a leading power even in Leinster, let alone anywhere else; indeed, their particular pride was that Brigit belonged to them. Even within Leinster different texts emphasized different themes: the life by Cogitosus (*c*.675) was written by a champion of her principal church, Kildare; there, so the life claimed, she lay enshrined, alongside her episcopal helper, Bishop **Conláid** [Conláed, Condlaed] (*d*. 518/520). On the other hand, the *Vita prima*, which powerful arguments would date earlier than Cogitosus, is more interested in Brigit's relationship with the people of her father, Dubthach, the branches of the Fothairt settled on the north-western frontier of Leinster. The same is true of the ninth-century vernacular life, *Bethu Brigte*, which is related to, but not dependent on, the *Vita prima*; both probably drew on a lost life of the mid-seventh century. These local affiliations were to be enduring: Brigit has remained to this day the patron saint of Kildare, but her cult has continued to be vigorous around Croghan Hill in Offaly, which is mentioned in *Bethu Brigte* and was close to the home of her father.

One of the most interesting aspects of the hagiography of Brigit is, therefore, its variety, rooted in particular places and enjoying different audiences. Cogitosus's life was addressed initially to the bishop and other educated clerics within the double monastery of Kildare and then to their equivalents in the other major churches; to meet the expectations of such a readership it had to be, and is, a polished piece of writing; the *Vita prima* probably envisaged a wider readership and was appropriately written in a simpler style reminiscent of the gospels. Again, Cogitosus's life includes a startling claim to archiepiscopal status for Kildare, thus challenging the other major churches of Ireland; the *Vita prima* avoids the controversies of high ecclesiastical politics.

For Cogitosus, therefore, Conláid was important as the first archbishop; a different aspect of his character is implied by the genealogies of the saints, according to which he was 'Conláed the devout, son of Cormac', and belonged to the Dál Messin Corp (Ó Riain, §252). 'Devout' (*cráibdech*) is a term bestowed on persons of acknowledged sanctity; the Dál Messin Corp, in the days of the genealogists, was a second-ranking political force around the modern town of Wicklow, although in Conláid's time they had been one of the leading powers of Leinster. Conláid was also remembered in the genealogies of the saints as Brigit's craftsman, *cerd*. An element of conscious stylization is implicit in the statement that there were 'three chief craftsmen of Ireland, namely Tassach for Patrick and Conláed for Brigit and Daig for Ciarán, and these three were bishops' (Ó Riain, §82.1).

One possible source of Brigit's status as one of the three principal saints of Ireland (together with Patrick and Columba) is that she may have supplanted a pre-Christian goddess, also known as Brigit. 'Cormac's glossary' (*Sanas Cormaic*, composed *c*.900) has an entry on the name Brigit according to which it stood for 'a female poet, the daughter of the Dagda', and as 'a goddess whom the poets used to worship' (*Sanas Cormaic*, ed. Meyer, no. 150). It then mentions two other Brigits, sisters of the first, who were attached to other crafts, of the doctor and the smith, all being daughters of the Dagda, the 'Good God'. The Christian nun may have taken over some of the characteristics and some of the cult sites of her predecessor; Kildare may have been one such site. It may be significant that when her father sold his slave woman, Broicsech, who was then carrying Brigit in her womb, Broicsech went first to a poet and then to a druid; moreover, when her father wanted to marry Brigit to a suitor, the person envisaged was another Dubthach, Dubthach maccu Lugair, who was, in hagiography, the representative of the poets. Her feast day, 1 February, coincides with the pre-Christian festival of Imbolc, marking the beginning of spring. It has been thought, therefore, that Brigit, the Christian nun, a 'second Mary' as she is described in the early, probably seventh-century, poem *Huait a meic hui Moguirni* ('By you, O Moccu Moguirni'), might be nothing more than the pre-Christian goddess of poets thinly disguised as a Christian saint.

Yet there are good reasons for distinguishing between the two and thus for attributing an independent reality to the Christian saint. First, the nun had a notably undistinguished family background. True, her father, Dubthach, was described as a nobleman in the early lives; and Cogitosus allows his readers to think that her mother, Broicsech, was also of noble birth. The *Vita prima*, however, and *Bethu Brigte* declare outright that Broicsech was a slave and conceived Brigit as a result of adulterous intercourse with her master. This is crucial, since, as the child of a slave woman, Brigit herself was born into servile status, although she, and then her mother, were soon to be freed. Second, it seems unlikely that, if a goddess should have been transformed into a nun, she would have been attributed to the Fothairt rather than to a more powerful people. In Wales, moreover, there was a clear distinction between the name of the goddess (preserved in the river name Braint) and that of the saint, namely Braid, as in the place name Llansanffraid ('the church of St Brigit'). Braid was an early medieval borrowing from Irish, showing that the saint's cult was Irish in origin, while the cult of the goddess was pan-Celtic and thus native within Wales.

Place among Irish saints In their hagiography the three principal saints of Ireland had, as befitted their diverse origins, markedly different personae. Columba, the saint of royal blood, was identified from the start with his kindred, the Uí Néill, the leading royal dynasty of Ireland; their position of eminence had recently been gained by violent conquest. It was easier for his influence and later his cult to transcend his kindred in Britain rather than in his native Ireland. Patrick was the outsider, the British missionary, who could be made into the voice of Christianity in judgment upon kings. Because he acquired this authority, he—and thus his principal church, Armagh—was soon embroiled in dynastic politics. Brigit, however, stood apart from kings, not just because she was a woman,

but because as a former slave girl, she could speak for those who suffered at the hands of the powerful. The most direct comparison is between the hagiographies of Patrick and Brigit, partly because the texts themselves may have influenced each other in the seventh century, partly because they brought Patrick and Brigit into a direct personal relationship. At least one major ecclesiastical figure of the mid-seventh century, Ultán of Ardbraccan, Meath, appears to have been interested in the hagiography of Brigit as well as of Patrick; according to the Middle Irish saints' genealogies, Brigit's mother, Broicsech, belonged to his people, Dál Conchobuir.

The differences appear in the character of the miracles the saints are said to perform. Patrick (that is, in his late seventh-century guise; the original Patrick was very different) is the saint who defeats the *magi*, the druids, of the pagan king; he is also the saint who by his blessings and curses decrees the fates of dynasties; the habitat of this Patrick is thus as much the royal household as the church. Brigit, on the other hand, never dictates the course of dynastic politics. Her power is expressed in 'helping miracles', healings, feeding the hungry, and rescuing the weak from violence. The contrast can be seen most directly in the different treatments of a single theme, the conflict between two branches of the Uí Néill, Cenél Coirpri and the descendants of Conall Cremthainne, for control of the midlands. In Tírechán's *Collectanea*, Patrick intervenes directly: he curses Coirpre and mingles with his curse a prophecy of the decline of his lineage; he then goes on to bless Conall Cremthainne and so grants him hegemony over his brothers. Tírechán was here playing the tune of a contemporary high-king of Ireland, Fínsnechtae Fledach, who ruled between 675 and 695. The *Vita prima* has Brigit intervene in the same quarrel, but she does so in order to save the rivals from each other, not to give one of them the victory. Her concern is to avert violence, not to legitimize anyone's triumph.

The mode of action is as different as the objective: Patrick acts as an Irish Samuel, taking kingship from Coirpre and his descendants, confronting proud kings in their own halls and places of assembly. Brigit, on the other hand, is sought out by the rival brothers, approached on the open road, and she saves each of them from the other. Whereas Patrick deals in the ambitions of kings, Brigit reacts to their fears. When Conall Cremthainne's childless queen sought Brigit's prayers so that she might have a child, Brigit only communicated with her through a nun. The latter asked Brigit: 'Why is it you don't ask the Lord for the queen to have a son, whereas you often ask him on behalf of the wives of the common folk?' And Brigit said:

> Because all the common folk are servants and they all call upon their Father, but the sons of kings are serpents and sons of blood and sons of death apart from a few who are chosen by God. But since the queen entreats us, go and tell her, 'There will be offspring but it will be offspring that sheds blood and will be an accursed stock and will hold sway for many years.' And so it was. (Connolly, 'Vita prima', §62)

The 'accursed stock' so roundly condemned by Brigit was the southern Uí Néill, rulers of the midlands, recipients of

Patrick's blessing. Yet Brigit's attitude was not expressed in the language of political rivalries: although a Leinster saint might be expected to defend the interests of the province against its principal enemies—and later Brigit was given precisely this role—here she condemns the most powerful kings of the day from the standpoint of the common people, not just of Leinster but of all Ireland. When she did go to Tailtiu, the site of the great royal assembly presided over by the high-king, she went to give her aid to a synod hearing a false accusation of rape brought against one of Patrick's bishops, Brón; she was not willing to meddle in the affairs of princes.

For Brigit's actions, the determining model was more often the New rather than the Old Testament. Most of her miracles are humble affairs for people of low rank and poor circumstances. Unlike Patrick, she has a concern for animals, dogs, and wolves; so too does Columba, but significantly his concern was for a bird that had been driven by the wind from his native kingdom, ruled by his kinsmen, Cenél Conaill. Whether or not there is any historical truth in the claim that she was a slave by birth—something which cannot be known—she was certainly presented by the *Vita prima* and *Bethu Brigte* as a saint for the poor. Nor was she a saint only for the Irish: the cult reflected in the Welsh place names is already suggested by a story in both the *Vita prima* and *Bethu Brigte* according to which two blind Britons came to her guided by a young leper belonging to her own people, the Fothairt. They complained, 'You have healed the infirm of your own people and you neglect the healing of foreigners. But at least heal our boy who is of your own people' (*Bethu Brigte*, ed. Ó hAodha, §27). In response to their plea, Brigit healed both the boy of his leprosy and the Britons of their blindness: as Christ began with the Jews but extended his teaching and his miracles to Samaritans and Gentiles, so Brigit might begin with the Fothairt but she came to be a saint also for the Britons.

Brigit's origins in context In the *Vita prima* and *Bethu Brigte*, Brigit first began to transcend her father's people, the Fothairt, precisely because she was a slave child, the daughter of a slave woman. Dubthach's patrimony is said by *Bethu Brigte* to have been 'in the two plains of the Uí Fhailgi', a reference to *Tuath dá Maige* ('the people of the two plains'). The area inhabited by this people is best indicated by the medieval ecclesiastical deanery of Tothmoy; it included Cróchan Breg hÉle (Croghan Hill) and some or all of the lands of the Fothairt Airbrech, to the east of Croghan Hill, which extended as far as the church of another nun, Rígnach (Cell Rígnaige, Kilrainy). Although the genealogies distinguish Brigit's own paternal lineage within the Fothairt, the Uí Bresail, from the Fothairt Airbrech, the latter were neighbours and some branches of the Uí Bresail lived among the Fothairt Airbrech. The Uí Fhailgi were one of the leading royal dynasties of Leinster: they, therefore, were the overlords and the various neighbouring Fothairt were their clients.

All these lands lay immediately on the Leinster side of the frontier with Mide, one of the territories of the Uí Néill. Moreover, in spite of the political dividing line,

ecclesiastically there were strong links between Brigit's homeland and Mag Tulach, the adjacent client kingdom within Mide. It was there that Brigit was veiled as a nun; moreover, one of her episcopal allies, Mac Caille, who participated in her veiling, was associated both with Croghan Hill, within Leinster, and with Mag Tulach, within Mide. For Tírechán, writing in the late seventh century in praise of Patrick, Mag Tulach was one of Brigit's territories. The later ruling kindred of Mag Tulach claimed to be descended from a late sixth-century king of Leinster, Brandub mac Echach. Even within Mide, therefore, her cult went with Leinster connections.

The beginning of Brigit's life according to the *Vita prima* was played out against the background of the jealousy felt by Dubthach's wife towards Broicsech, her husband's slave woman and concubine. The wife brought pressure on Dubthach to sell Broicsech to someone from another country. In telling this story, the *Vita prima* uses the model of Abraham, Sarah, and his Egyptian slave woman, Hagar, adopting for its own use the words of Sarah, 'Cast out this bondwoman and her son: for the son of this bondwoman shall not be heir with my son, even with Isaac' (Genesis 21: 10). Yet it reverses the implications of the Genesis story, for it includes a prophecy that the descendants of the wife would serve the offspring of the slave woman. As Hagar was driven out into the desert, so Broicsech was sold to a poet from the lands of the Uí Néill. She was subsequently sold on to a druid, in whose household Brigit was born, either in 439 or in 452, according to different annalists' guesses. This druid was to prove crucial for Brigit's early life. His paternal lineage was in Munster, in the northern Munster kingdom of Uaithne Tíre according to *Bethu Brigte*; his mother's family came from Connacht, while he himself was then resident in the north of Ireland. In this way Brigit made her first journey, from Leinster to the lands of the southern Uí Néill, then to the north, and on to Connacht and Munster. This journey has been seen as an assertion of ecclesiastical lordship, a theory supported by the statement made by the infant Brigit in Connacht, 'This will be mine; this will be mine' (Connolly, 'Vita prima', §11). Yet there are clear differences between Brigit's journey and the circuit around northern Ireland made by Patrick, according to Tírechán. Part of the journey was made by Brigit when she was still in her mother's womb; moreover, whereas Patrick's circuit went sunwise, *deisel*, Brigit's went widdershins, *tuaithbiul*. Because of her association with a poet and a druid, her journeyings were more directly linked with the circuits of poets and other 'people of art' than with the circuits of kings. Brigit's journeys were hagiographical conventions that, in this instance, expressed connections and alliances more often than lordship. Later she was made to visit Armagh and Downpatrick, two pre-eminent Patrician sites. This can hardly have been because the hagiographer wished to claim that they belonged to Brigit. It is much more likely that behind the visit to Armagh lay the fact that a branch of the Fothairt was settled nearby.

Another difference between Brigit's first journey and

Patrick's circuit is in the attitudes expressed to druids. Patrick consistently opposed and defeated druids, perceived as the embodiment of Irish paganism. The druid of Munster parentage who bought Brigit's mother, Broicsech, is treated much more gently. The ambiguities are well brought out by an anecdote concerning their stay in the druid's Munster home. Brigit had difficulty eating:

> Observing this the druid carefully investigated the cause of the nausea, and when he discovered it, said, 'I am unclean, but this girl is filled with the Holy Spirit. She can't endure my food.' Thereupon he chose a white cow and set it aside for the girl, and a certain Christian woman, a very God-fearing virgin, used to milk the cow and the girl used to drink the cow's milk and not vomit it up as her stomach had been healed.   (Connolly, 'Vita prima', §11)

The druid, though unclean, was perceptive and concerned. He was also responsible for liberating both Brigit and her mother, and almost in the act of liberating his slaves he was himself liberated from paganism. By contrast, Brigit's father is less kindly treated: having sold his slave woman, she was eventually restored to him by the druid as a free woman; Dubthach then decided to sell Brigit into slavery, because of her habit of giving everything to the poor. When that had been averted, he put her under pressure to accept marriage; and when she had avoided that outcome, she left for the lands of the Uí Néill to take the veil.

Brigit and Kildare None of the lives explains how Brigit acquired what became her principal church, Kildare. This lay a short distance beyond Uí Fhailgi territory, at the furthest remove from Brigit's home near Croghan Hill. Kildare remained, for several centuries, a double house: it had both bishops (later often replaced by abbots) and abbesses; the latter appear to have normally been of the Fothairt, while the bishops or abbots sometimes came from the ruling families of Leinster. The abbess was the heir of Brigit; the close bond was emphasized by the story that her immediate successor, **Dar Lugdach** (*d.* 525/527), died one year to the day after Brigit's own death; just as Columba's successor, Baíthéne, died a year to the day after Columba, and thus came to have the same feast day as his predecessor, so too Dar Lugdach's feast day was 1 February. Although Baíthéne was also Columba's close kinsman, there is no information about Dar Lugdach's descent, and she is not included in the list of Fothairt saints. Her cult was effectively subsumed in that of Brigit—something not entirely true of Baíthéne.

Kildare was also an important centre of scholarship, which helped to make it the most important church of northern Leinster; moreover, Mag Lifi, the plain of the Liffey, on the western edge of which Kildare is situated, was the principal centre of power in the whole province of Leinster. Kildare thus became the pre-eminent church of the province. In Irish law, a church of such importance conferred a status on its head equivalent to that of a bishop. The abbess of Kildare, the heir of Brigit, was thus far and away the most important woman in Ireland. Abbesses of Kildare were the only women whose obits were often recorded in the annals, more frequently commemorated even than queens of Tara.

In the late seventh century Kildare was especially open to English and continental influence. In the period after it had embraced the Roman Easter (probably in the 630s) and before Armagh followed suit (probably in the 680s), Kildare had the opportunity to take the leadership of the Roman party within the Irish church. Cogitosus's life of Brigit was principally written to further this ambition. Its depiction of the shrines of Brigit and Conlaíd within the church of Kildare is the earliest evidence for the elevation and enshrinement of relics in Ireland. This practice, already popular for more than a century in Francia, was also spreading in England in the late seventh century, as illustrated by the translation and enshrinement of Cuthbert's body in 697. The exact date of Cogitosus's life is uncertain, but his text may well be the earliest evidence for the practice in either Ireland or Britain. As in Cuthbert's case, so also in Brigit's: this enhancement of the visible status of the saint had a background of ecclesiastical politics. Cogitosus's life consists of a series of largely humble, down-to-earth miracle stories related to those in the last section of the *Vita prima*, but these are framed by two major political statements. The passage on the two shrines comes at the end; at the beginning there is a preface in which it is asserted that Kildare is the see of an archbishop whose authority extends over the whole island. In Irish terms, this was a novel assertion soon to be countered by Armagh's claim to such an island-wide archiepiscopal status in the *Liber angeli* ('Book of the angel'). The model for such claims is likely to be the authority given to Theodore, archbishop of Canterbury, by Pope Vitalian: from 669 until 735 the archbishops of Canterbury were entitled 'archbishops of the island of Britain'. Kildare, therefore, was the quickest of all Irish churches to react to developments on the continent and in England. Yet its ambitions were never to be realized: Armagh, threatened by Kildare and by Northumbrian power, itself adopted the Roman Easter, whereupon the prestige of Patrick as the apostle of Ireland, to which the *Vita prima* of Brigit is one of the earlier and more eloquent (because independent) witnesses, gave Armagh a decisive advantage. In the twelfth-century reorganization of the Irish church, Kildare became the see of a diocese for north-west Leinster, but it was the nearby Hiberno-Norse city of Dublin that became the seat of an archbishopric.

Significance of the cult Yet this relative decline of her main church made very little difference to the strength of Brigit's cult, since its true power did not lie in the sphere of high politics. This is shown by its popularity among Irishmen in Francia in the ninth century: such circles as that around Sedulius Scottus spread her cult on the continent. Even in Cogitosus's life, once the reader turns away from the grand statements at the beginning and the end, the humbler Brigit is easy to see in such anecdotes as that recounting a gift of pigs from southern Leinster. The donor came himself to Kildare, but asked that Brigit's men be sent to his distant farm to collect the pigs. When these men had reached the watershed dividing northern from southern Leinster, they were met by the pigs, guided along the road by wolves that had come from Mag Fea to the south. According to the Middle Irish notes on Broccán's hymn to Brigit, the man's farm was in the Fothairt territory at the south-east tip of Leinster; Mag Fea, mentioned by Cogitosus, was another Fothairt kingdom in south-central Leinster. The background to the story, therefore, appears to be the right of a major church, attached to a particular dynastic group, to collect gifts from the people of that group's territories. The pigs were just such gifts collected from the lands of the Fothairt. Elsewhere wolves were usually symbols for the dedicated violence of 'the sons of death' deplored by Brigit; that, 'out of the utmost respect for blessed Brigit' (Cogitosus, cap. 19), these wolves rounded up and drove these pigs along the road demonstrated the power of the holy over non-human as well as human violence, the power of holiness to transform the world into peaceful harmony. Her cult thus expressed a faith in an interventionist God, prepared to change the natural order of events in the world, in human holiness as the expression of the divine will, and thus in an alliance between such an interventionist God and a human saint to push the world back towards a peaceful order lost when Adam and Eve were expelled from the Garden of Eden.   T. M. CHARLES-EDWARDS

Sources S. Connolly, trans., 'Vita prima sanctae Brigidae', *Journal of the Royal Society of Antiquaries of Ireland*, 119 (1989), 14–49 · Cogitosus, 'Vita sanctae Brigidae', trans. S. Connolly and J.-M. Picard, *Journal of the Royal Society of Antiquaries of Ireland*, 117 (1987), 11–27 · *Bethu Brigte*, ed. and trans. D. Ó hAodha (1978) · R. I. Best and H. J. Lawlor, eds., *The martyrology of Tallaght*, HBS, 68 (1931) · M. A. O'Brien, ed., *Corpus genealogiarum Hiberniae* (Dublin, 1962), 84 (126 a 27–9) [subdivisions on the page] · P. Ó Riain, ed., *Corpus genealogiarum sanctorum Hiberniae* (Dublin, 1985) · Cormac mac Cuilennáin, *Sanas Cormaic: an old-Irish glossary*, ed. K. Meyer (1912), vol. 4 of *Anecdota from Irish manuscripts*, ed. O. J. Bergin and others (1907–13), 15 · J. J. O'Meara, ed., 'Giraldus Cambrensis in topographia Hibernie: the text of the first recension', *Proceedings of the Royal Irish Academy*, 52C (1948–50), 113–78 [Gerald of Wales, *Topographia Hiberniae*, at chaps. 67–72, 77] · M. A. O'Brien, ed., *Corpus genealogiarum Hiberniae* (Dublin, 1962), 79–81 [*Huait a meic hui Moguirni*] · 'Brigit bé bithmaith', *Thesaurus Palaeohibernicus*, ed. W. Stokes and J. Strachan, 2 (1903), 325–6, esp. 325-49 · 'Ní car Brigit búadach bith', *Thesaurus Palaeohibernicus*, ed. W. Stokes and J. Strachan, 2 (1903), 327–49 · *Hail Brigit*, ed. K. Meyer (1912) [corrected in *Zeitschrift für Celtische Philologie*, 8 (1912), 600] · 'Liber angeli', *The Patrician texts in the Book of Armagh*, ed. L. Bieler, Scriptores Latini Hiberniae, 10 (1979), 184–91, esp. 190 [§32] · M. Esposito, 'On the early Latin lives of St Brigid of Kildare', *Hermathena*, 49 (1935), 120–65, esp. 125–6 [Rheims prologue]; repr. in M. Esposito, *Latin learning in mediaeval Ireland*, ed. M. Lapidge (1988), chap. 7 · C. Plummer, 'A tentative catalogue of Irish hagiography', *Miscellanea hagiographica Hibernica*, Subsidia Hagiographica, 15 (Brussels, 1925), nos. 11–13, 83, 86–8, 202–3, 219 · M. Lapidge and R. Sharpe, *A bibliography of Celtic-Latin literature, 400–1200* (1985), 84, 102–3, 110, 120, 124–5, 220 · J. F. Kenney, *The sources for the early history of Ireland* (1929), 356–64 (nos. 147–56) · F. Ó Briain, 'Brigitana', *Zeitschrift für Celtische Philologie*, 36 (1978), 112–37 · R. Sharpe, 'Vitae s. Brigitae: the oldest texts', *Peritia*, 1 (1982), 81–106 · K. McCone, 'Brigit in the seventh century: a saint with three lives?', *Peritia*, 1 (1982), 107–45 · C. Stancliffe, 'The miracle stories in seventh-century Irish saints' lives', *Le septième siècle: changements et continuités*, ed. J. Fontaine and J. N. Hillgarth (1992), 87–111 · D. N. Kissane, 'Vita metrica sanctae Brigidae: a critical edition with introduction, commentary and indexes', *Proceedings of the Royal Irish Academy*, 77C (1977), 57–192 · 'Vita quarta', *Medieval Irish saints' lives: an introduction to Vitae sanctorum Hiberniae*, ed. R. Sharpe (1991), 139–208 · Donatus, bishop of Fiesole, Life of St Brigit, 9th cent., Biblioteca Medicea Laurenziana, Florence, Conv. Soppr. 266 pt 1 · Donatus, bishop of Fiesole, Life of St Brigit, 9th cent., Biblioteca Nazionale Centrale, Florence, Conv. Soppr. c. 4 1791 · Donatus, bishop of Fiesole, Life of St Brigit, 9th cent., Biblioteca Casanatense, Rome, 726 · *Félire Óengusso Céli Dé / The martyrology of Oengus the Culdee*, ed. W. Stokes, HBS, 29 (1905); repr. (1984) · *Félire húi Gormáin / The martyrology of Gorman*, ed. and trans. W. Stokes, HBS, 9 (1895) · M. O'Clery, *The martyrology of Donegal: a calendar of the saints of Ireland*, ed. J. H. Todd and W. Reeves, trans. J. O'Donovan (1864) · *Ann. Ulster* · W. M. Hennessy, ed. and trans., *Chronicum Scotorum: a chronicle of Irish affairs*, Rolls Series, 46 (1866) · Lord Killanin and M. V. Duignan, *The Shell guide to Ireland*, 2nd edn (1967)

Brigstocke, Thomas (1809–1881), portrait painter, born at 61 King Street, Carmarthen, on 17 April 1809, was the third son of David Brigstocke, a tradesman in that town, and his wife, Mary. At the age of sixteen he entered Henry Sass's academy at 6 Charlotte Street, Bloomsbury, London. He won two silver medals from the Society of Arts, studied at the Royal Academy, and was subsequently a pupil of Henry Perronet Briggs and John Prescott Knight. He spent between eight and ten years studying in Paris and Italy, forming a Welsh-speaking clique in Rome with the painter Penry Williams and the sculptor John Gibson. He made copies from old masters, including Raphael's *Transfiguration* in the Vatican; on the advice of the painter William Collins, the copy was purchased for Christ Church, Albany Street, London.

In 1847 Brigstocke went to Egypt, where he stayed for sixteen months; here he was commissioned by the Egyptian ruler, Mehmet Ali, to paint portraits of him and his family. Later he also painted a portrait of Mehmet Ali for the Oriental Club in London (exh. RA, 1849). Between 1842 and 1865 he exhibited sixteen works at the Royal Academy and two at the British Institution. His first painting to appear at the academy was a literary and oriental subject, *The Reverie of Alnaschar* (exh. RA, 1842), but the great majority of his works were portraits. Many of his sitters had Eastern connections: he painted General Sir William Nott with Kandahar, Afghanistan, in the background (exh. RA, 1845); the Revd Dr Wolff, recently returned from Bukhara in central Asia (exh. RA, 1846); Captain Gotteau of the Madras infantry in the costume of a Lebanon sheikh (exh. RA, 1849); and Jung Bahadoor, prime minister of Nepal and ambassador to England (exh. RA, 1858). He also painted and exhibited portraits of members of leading Welsh families, including Miss Conway Griffith of Anglesey (exh. RA, 1865). Examples of his works are found in private and public collections in Britain, including the National Portrait Gallery, London, and Llanelli town hall, Carmarthenshire; some were engraved.

Brigstocke married a widow, Mrs Cridland, who predeceased him, as did too their only child. He died on 11 March 1881 at his home, 53 Welbeck Street, Cavendish Square, London, and was buried at Kensal Green cemetery.

L. A. FAGAN, *rev.* KENNETH BENDINER

Sources *DWB* · Graves, *RA exhibitors* · Bryan, *Painters* (1866) · E. Rowan, *Art in Wales: an illustrated history, 1850–1980* (1985), 20, 26 · *CGPLA Eng. & Wales* (1881)

Wealth at death £80 4s. 6d.: probate, 30 June 1881, *CGPLA Eng. & Wales*

Brihtnoth. *See* Byrhtnoth (d. 991).

Brihtwald. *See* Berhtwald (c.650–731).

Brihtwold (d. 1045), abbot of Glastonbury and bishop of Ramsbury, had been a monk and then abbot at Glastonbury, and was made eighth bishop of Ramsbury in either 995 or 1005. Although he presided over the see for at least forty years, Brihtwold remained so great a patron of Glastonbury that William of Malmesbury accused him of despoiling his diocese for the abbey. Brihtwold's estates, including one granted to him by King Æthelred, must have provided a reasonable income, but there is evidence that he dilapidated the cathedral church at Ramsbury. His successor Herman complained of the poverty of his seat, and eventually moved it to Salisbury. The near-contemporary life of King Edward relates a vision which Brihtwold had at Glastonbury, in the reign of Cnut, of Edward the Confessor being crowned by St Peter and granted a life of celibacy. Brihtwold died on 22 April 1045 and was buried in Glastonbury.

W. R. W. STEPHENS, *rev.* MARIOS COSTAMBEYS

Sources *ASC*, s.a. 1006, 1045 [texts E, C] · *AS chart.*, S 934 · F. Barlow, ed. and trans., *The life of King Edward who rests at Westminster* (1962) · F. Barlow, *The English church, 1000–1066: a history of the later Anglo-Saxon church*, 2nd edn (1979) · *Willelmi Malmesbiriensis monachi de gestis pontificum Anglorum libri quinque*, ed. N. E. S. A. Hamilton, Rolls Series, 52 (1870)

Wealth at death four manors in Wiltshire and a large estate at Sonning, Berkshire: Barlow, *The English church*, 221

Brill, Kenneth Henry (1911–1991), social worker, was born on 13 April 1911 at 28 Rectory Road, Barnes, Surrey, the elder of the two sons of Percy Henry Archelaus Thomas Brill (1881–1918), schoolteacher, and his wife, Charlotte Emily, *née* Crisp (1882–1940), also a schoolteacher and later headmistress of Kilve School, Somerset. Brill, brought up by his mother after his father died in the First World War, was educated at Bristol grammar school, which he left, aged sixteen, after an undistinguished school career. After a time as a trainee surveyor in Somerset he moved to London, where he lived in an East End settlement. There he became involved in the parish of a radical Anglican priest, St John Beverley Groser, and joined campaigns to support the Jarrow marchers, to fight slum landlords, and to challenge Mosley's Blackshirts. This radicalism was reinforced when he met Jessica Atkinson (1915–1990), daughter of Frederick Atkinson, commercial traveller; they married on 21 August 1938 and shared a lifelong commitment to Christianity, socialism, and (later) social work. They had one daughter, Judi. Meanwhile Brill trained at the London School of Economics as a probation officer and psychiatric social worker but the Second World War interrupted his social work career. He volunteered for the Royal Air Force and served as a flight sergeant and navigator (one who frequently found it difficult to follow the map, he confessed).

After the war Brill worked for MIND (the National Association for Mental Health) while serving as a Labour councillor in Haringey. The creation of children's departments in 1948 offered him an opportunity to bring together his commitment to children, his organizing ability, and his vision of a better future in the role of children's officer. His first appointment was in Croydon, after which he moved to Devon, where he worked for thirteen years; his final post as children's officer was in Barnet. Children's departments were an organizational response to the vulnerability and potential for abuse of a virtually unregulated foster care system. The drive that Brill brought to his successive appointments was founded on the needs of children as individuals, not cases. His pioneering approach saw a dramatic reduction in the numbers of children in residential care. The emphasis of all the departments in which he worked was switched to family support. Initially Brill could seem austere and distant; his concern for detail and his meticulous drafting sharply differentiated him from those social workers whose concern for humanity outran their concern for organization and order. As secretary of the Association of Children's Officers for seventeen years he used his great organizational skills to the benefit of a national body. The association supported the development of a unified social work profession, which came into being with the Local Authority Social Services Act of 1970.

The British Association of Social Workers (BASW) was established as a professional association in 1970. Brill was a logical choice for the first general secretary and brought a natural authority to the role as well as a rich knowledge of the history of the fledgeling profession. He succeeded in welding together a number of disparate professional groups. During his time as general secretary BASW was at its zenith, with over 1000 members attending its annual general meetings. The pressures of the job were immense, with a demanding membership, fast developing social services, and (latterly) daily commuting from London to Birmingham, where the association decided to relocate— a decision fully supported by Brill despite the personal consequences. Throughout this period his drive and energy seemed inexhaustible. Then, at the age of sixty-three, when his contemporaries were pursuing retirement activities, he startled the social work world by returning to Barnet as director of social services. He took on the post during a strike and characteristically led from the top by personally undertaking emergency duty out of hours.

Conventional retirement was never likely to appeal to Brill. He served as clerk to the Council of National Voluntary Child Care Organisations, edited the newsletter of the Devon branch of BASW, was active in his parish council and in local organizations, and registered for a PhD at the University of Birmingham. The subject of his study was the development of children's services from the Curtis report of 1946 to the Children Act of 1989. Despite failing health he completed his thesis and received his doctorate in Birmingham two days before his death, at his home, Dunns Cottage, Cheriton Fitzpaine, Devon, on 16

December 1991. He was survived by his daughter, his wife having died in the previous year. He was buried at Cheriton Fitzpaine on 2 January 1992. In the course of a long and active working life Brill helped to shape the new profession of social work. His commitment to quality in child care was an inspiration to those who knew and worked with him.   TERRY BAMFORD

Sources *The Guardian* (3 Dec 1970) · *Community Care* (4 Sept 1974) · *Community Care* (2 Jan 1992) · Gordon Halliday, funeral address, 2 Jan 1992 · *The Times* (23 Dec 1991) · b. cert. · m. cert. · d. cert. · personal knowledge (2004) · private information (2004) [Judi Brill, daughter] · *CGPLA Eng. & Wales* (1992)
Likenesses photograph, repro. in *The Times*
Wealth at death under £125,000: probate, 4 March 1992, *CGPLA Eng. & Wales*

Brimelow, Thomas, Baron Brimelow (1915–1995), diplomatist, was born on 25 October 1915 at 94 Sale Road, Tyldesley, Lancashire, the second of three sons of William Brimelow (*b*. 1885), a cotton yarn salesman and later cotton mill director, and his wife, Hannah, *née* Smith (*b*. 1890), a teacher. Early on he showed that combination of hard work and high intellect which was to mark his whole career: the elementary school in New Mills led to the county secondary school, a state scholarship to Oriel College, Oxford, and a first in modern languages in 1936. Brimelow's father had travelled widely for his firm and Brimelow, an ambitious lad who had won fellowships which gave him a year in Paris and a year studying Russian in Riga, decided on the consular service. He took first place in the 1938 examination. So, in October 1938, an apple-cheeked young man with an engaging smile who needed 'a bit of polish and slightly wider knowledge of the world to become very useful' (private information), he went as a probationary vice-consul to Danzig, deciphering telegrams, helping with the accounts, and serving at the counter. Here, as Europe moved to war, he acquired first-hand experience of totalitarian bullying which must have served him well when, as the Germans moved into Danzig, he went as vice-consul to Riga, in November 1939. A year later, as the USSR moved into Latvia, Brimelow, still only twenty-four, earned praise for his work in closing down the legation.

After a spell in New York, Brimelow was posted in June 1942 as third secretary and vice-consul in Moscow, where he spent the remainder of the war and began to acquire that personal experience of the workings of the Soviet state which was to make him, throughout most of the cold war, the acknowledged authority on the interpretation of Soviet policy and the formulation of the British response. He returned to Britain in the early summer of 1945, and, on 19 May 1945, married Jean Ethel (Jeanie) Cull (1917–1993), a clerical officer in the Home Office, and daughter of John William Underwood Cull, a coach trimmer, of Glasgow. They had two daughters.

Brimelow served in the Foreign Office from June 1945, and was officially appointed there in September 1945. He was promoted first secretary in November 1946. He served as first secretary (commercial) and consul at Havana from April 1948 to October 1951, when he returned to Moscow

as first secretary until September 1954. He was made an OBE in the same year. There then followed two years in Ankara as counsellor (commercial) before Brimelow returned to the Foreign Office as head of the northern department, in August 1956. He was made a CMG in 1959. From 1960 to 1963 he served as counsellor in Washington, before again returning to Moscow as minister, until 1966. He was ambassador to Poland from August 1966 to March 1969, deputy under-secretary of state at the Foreign and Commonwealth Office until November 1973, and permanent under-secretary of state and head of the diplomatic service until November 1975, when he retired. He was promoted KCMG in 1968 and GCMG in 1975, and made a life peer, as Baron Brimelow of Tyldesley, in 1976. He took the Labour whip.

Brimelow's command of the Russian language and his understanding both of the Russian character and of the Soviet system were legendary. Some saw him as the toughest of the cold warriors. Tough he was and having, as he said, 'been brought up under Stalin' (*The Independent*, 4 Aug 1995), he had no illusions. But his policy was essentially that of George Kennan: 'Stand up to them, but not aggressively and let the hand of time do its work' (G. F. Kennan, *Memoirs, 1925–50*, 1967). In 1964, when it was hoped that, in its own interest, the USSR might move away from confrontation, Brimelow argued that the ideology of class conflict was pulling the cartload of Soviet interests in the wrong direction. One day the cart would wear out the horse. British policy should look towards that day, but the horse was not yet dead and the leadership was neither willing nor able to cut the harness. Unyielding in his hatred of the Soviet system, he still worked for better relations and opposed any policy designed to promote instability within the Soviet empire. He was content to wait another two decades until the horse fell terminally sick and Russia cut itself free.

In 1971, as deputy under-secretary of state, Brimelow advised on the mass expulsion of Soviet intelligence agents, but there was no truth to the suggestion that he was himself a member of the intelligence service. As deputy and later as permanent under-secretary his responsibility was much wider than the Soviet area. He was in a key position for the run-up to British membership of the EC and the first two years of membership. As head of the service he never forgot the well-being of its most junior members.

On retirement, while adding modern and ancient Greek to his linguistic repertoire, Brimelow took on the chairmanship of the Occupational Pensions Board (1978–82) and served for two years as a member of the European parliament (1977–8). Having mastered the complexities of agricultural finance, he used this knowledge to good effect in the House of Lords. A major retirement project was to research the repatriation of Soviet citizens at the end of the war. He had dealt with this as a junior in the northern department and, angered by unfair and inaccurate public comment, he worked with Brigadier Anthony Cowgill and Christopher Booker on a detailed study of the forced repatriation of Cossacks and Yugoslavs from

Austria. This was published as *The Repatriations from Austria in 1945*, in 1980. Brimelow's separate history of the whole affair was, sadly, never published.

Brimelow's life was marked by an untiring devotion to the task in hand, a care for his fellows, and modesty in success. Never one for public display, his kindness was never superficial. Mild, inscrutable, and gentle in manner, he was logical and precise in analysis and exposition, ruthless in his demolition of muddled argument, and wide in his range of interests. From first to last he remained a rather private man, deeply devoted to his wife Jean and to their two daughters. His wife's death in 1993, after months of distressing illness, affected him deeply. He died at his home, 12 West Hill Court, Millfield Lane, Highgate, Camden, London, on 2 August 1995, of bronchopneumonia and myeloid leukaemia; his body was cremated. He was survived by his two daughters. CURTIS KEEBLE

Sources PRO, Foreign Office records · personal knowledge (2004) · private information (2004) · *Hansard 5L* (1984), 455.1015 · P. Barton, *Baltic countdown* (1984) · A. Cowgill, T. Brimelow, and C. Booker, *The repatriations from Austria in 1945* (1980) · N. Tolstoy, *Victims of Yalta* (1977) · N. Bethell, *The last secret* (1974) · *The Times* (5 Aug 1995) · *The Independent* (4 Aug 1995) · Burke, *Peerage* · *WWW*, 1991–5 · b. cert. · m. cert. · d. cert.
Archives CAC Cam., typescript interview · PRO, FCO records | U. Birm. L., corresp. with Lord Avon
Likenesses photograph, repro. in *The Times* · photograph, repro. in *The Independent*
Wealth at death £123,168: probate, 1 Nov 1995, *CGPLA Eng. & Wales*

Brimley, George (1819–1857), essayist and librarian, was born at Cambridge on 29 December 1819, the son of Augustine Gutteridge Brimley. From the age of eleven to sixteen he was educated at a school in Totteridge, Hertfordshire, then from 1838 at Trinity College, Cambridge, where in 1841 he was elected a scholar. He obtained his BA in 1842, and was made MA in 1845. Although the state of his health prevented him from obtaining a college fellowship, he was known to possess ability, and he was appointed college librarian on 4 June 1845, an office he held until a few weeks before his death. Physical weakness prevented the sustained effort necessary for the production of any important work; but for the last six years of his life he contributed to the press. Most of his writings appeared in *The Spectator* or in *Fraser's Magazine*, the only one to which his name was attached being an essay on Tennyson's poems, published in the *Cambridge Essays, contributed by Members of the University* of 1855. He died, unmarried, at Park Terrace, St Andrew the Great, Cambridge, on 29 May 1857. A selection of his essays was made after his death and published with a prefatory memoir by W. G. Clark, then fellow and tutor of Trinity. This volume contains reviews of a large number of Brimley's contemporaries, including Wordsworth, Carlyle, Thackeray, and Dickens. Brimley enjoyed a nineteenth-century reputation as a shrewd and impartial judge of contemporary literature. Though considerate in his criticism of friends and fellow writers, Brimley none the less 'never hesitated to state

what he believed to be right' (Clark, viii–ix). Sir Arthur Helps paid tribute to Brimley as 'one of the finest critics' of his day (ibid., xi).

E. S. SHUCKBURGH, rev. CHARLES BRAYNE

Sources W. G. Clark, 'Memoir', in *Essays by the late George Brimley MA*, ed. W. G. Clark (1858) · private information (1885) · Venn, *Alum. Cant.* · *GM*, 3rd ser., 3 (1857), 101 · d. cert.
Likenesses E. Radclyffe, engraving, repro. in Clark, ed., *Essays by the late George Brimley*, frontispiece

Brind, Sir James (1808–1888), army officer in the East India Company service, son of Walter Brind, ribbon manufacturer and silk merchant of Paternoster Row, London, was born in London on 10 July 1808. After training at Addiscombe College (1825–6), he became second lieutenant, Bengal artillery, on 3 July 1827. He was promoted first lieutenant (15 October 1833), brevet captain (3 July 1842), captain (3 July 1845), brevet major (20 June 1854), major (26 June 1856), lieutenant-colonel (18 August 1858), brevet colonel (26 April 1859), colonel (18 February 1861), major-general (1 June 1867), lieutenant-general and general (1 October 1877), and colonel-commandant, Royal Artillery (3 October 1877).

Brind arrived in India on 14 August 1827, and was sent to the upper provinces. On 28 February 1834 he was posted to the 7th company, 6th battalion Bengal artillery. After being attached for some three years to the revenue survey he was appointed adjutant to the 5th battalion of artillery on 13 April 1840, and division adjutant to the artillery at Agra and Mathura in July 1842. Ill health compelled him to resign the adjutancy in November 1843, and he went home on furlough in 1844. In August 1854 Brind commanded the artillery of the field force under Colonel Sydney J. Cotton against the Mohmands of the Kabul River; he was mentioned in dispatches, and awarded a brevet majority.

Brind was commanding a battery at Jullundur in June 1857 when the troops there mutinied. From Jullundur he went to the siege of Delhi, where he commanded the foot artillery of the Delhi field force, and from the time when the siege batteries were ready until the assault on 14 September 1857 he commanded no. 1 siege battery ('Brind's battery'): five 18-pounder guns, one 8-inch howitzer, and four 24-pounder guns. Vigilant, Brind seemed never to sleep. He used to lie in the battery reading his Bible, until the enemy opened fire, when he would spring into action. Careful of his men, he exposed himself unhesitatingly to danger. It was said by another Delhi veteran, 'Talk of Victoria Crosses; if Brind had his due he would be covered with them from head to foot' (Vibart, 422). On 20 September Brind commanded the force of artillery and infantry which attacked and carried the Jama Masjid. On the following day, as soon as the city of Delhi was completely captured, the difficult task was allotted to him of ensuring the safety of the gateways. He earned high praise: Sir Charles Reid wrote of him, 'A finer soldier I never saw', and Roberts called him 'the bravest of the brave' (Roberts, 120).

From December 1857 to March 1858 Brind commanded a light column in the Muzaffarnagar. In April 1858 he commanded the artillery of the force under Brigadier-General Robert Walpole, was present at the unsuccessful attack on Fort Ruiya on 15 April, and at the defeat of the rebels at Aliganj on the 22nd, after which the column joined the commander-in-chief. Brind commanded the artillery brigade in the march through Rohilkhand, and at the battle of Bareilly (5 May) and the capture of that city. He was employed in clearing it of rebels on that and the following day. In October 1858 Brind commanded the artillery of Colonel Colin Troup's force in Oudh, and took part in the actions of Madaipur (19 October) and Rasalpur (25 October), the capture of Mitaoli (9 November), and the affair of Aliganj (17 November). He commanded a light column on the following day in pursuit of the rebels, and defeated them near Mehudi, capturing nine guns, after which he rejoined Troup and moved by Talegaon via Biswan, where Firoz Shah was posted, and took part in the action of 1 December. The column then moved north, driving the remaining rebels towards Nepal and terminating the campaign.

For his mutiny services Brind was mentioned in dispatches, made a CB, military division, on 24 March 1858, and received the thanks of government and a brevet colonelcy. He afterwards served for some years in the North-Western Provinces as inspector-general of artillery with the rank of brigadier-general. He was promoted KCB, military division, on 2 June 1869. From 26 December 1873 to the end of 1878 he commanded the Sirhind division, Bengal army; he then retired with a pension and returned to England. He was made GCB on 24 May 1884.

Brind was five times married: first, on 20 April 1833, to Jane (Joanna), daughter of Captain Joseph Conway Waller, who died on 29 December 1849; second, on 11 September 1852, to Mary Georgiana (d. 2 March 1854), daughter of Benjamin Carter and niece of Admiral Carter; third, on 24 October 1861, to Georgina (d. 1862), daughter of Henry George Philips, vicar of Mildenhall; fourth, in 1864, to Jane (d. 6 Nov 1868), daughter of the Revd Daniel Henry Maunsell of Balbriggan, co. Dublin; and last, in 1873, to Eleanor Elizabeth Lumley, daughter of the Revd Henry Thomas Burne of Grittleton, Wiltshire, who survived him and died in March 1924. He died at Ticehurst, Sussex, on 3 August 1888. **R. H. VETCH, rev. ROGER T. STEARN**

Sources *The Times* (6 Aug 1888) · V. C. P. Hodson, *List of officers of the Bengal army, 1758–1834*, 4 vols. (1927–47) · *Army List* · F. W. Stubbs, ed., *History of the organization, equipment, and war services of the regiment of Bengal artillery*, 1–2 (1877) · H. M. Vibart, *Addiscombe: its heroes and men of note* (1894) · J. W. Kaye, *A history of the Sepoy War in India, 1857–1858*, 9th edn, 3 vols. (1880) · G. B. Malleson, *History of the Indian mutiny, 1857–1858: commencing from the close of the second volume of Sir John Kaye's History of the Sepoy War*, 3 vols. (1878–80) · C. Hibbert, *The great mutiny, India, 1857* (1978) · T. A. Heathcote, *The military in British India: the development of British land forces in south Asia, 1600–1947* (1995) · *Dod's Peerage* (1878) · Boase, *Mod. Eng. biog.* · Lord Roberts [F. S. Roberts], *Forty-one years in India*, 31st edn (1900) · *CGPLA Eng. & Wales* (1888)

Wealth at death £5135 15s. 2d.: probate, 23 Nov 1888, *CGPLA Eng. & Wales*

Brind, Sir (Eric James) Patrick (1892–1963), naval officer, was born at Paignton on 12 May 1892, the third son of Colonel Edward Agincourt Brind of the 88th Connaught Rangers, and his wife, Florence Lund. Brind's father settled in Dorchester after retiring from the army.

Brind entered the Royal Navy as a cadet in 1905, passing through the Royal Naval College at Osborne and Dartmouth before joining his first seagoing ship as a midshipman on 5 September 1909. In May 1916, as a young lieutenant, he was at the battle of Jutland in the new 15 inch battleship *Malaya* which suffered damage. Brind married, in 1918, Eileen Margaret (d. 1940), daughter of the Revd Josiah Marling Apperly, rector of Tonge, Sittingbourne, Kent: they had one daughter, born in 1919.

Early promotion to commander on 30 June 1927 indicated that Brind was well thought of, and this was further substantiated when he was promoted captain on 31 December 1933, at the age of forty-one, at a time when the number of promotions had been much reduced. Brind's appointment to the Admiralty tactical division in May 1934 gave further indication of a promising future, and offered scope for his insistence that the new aircraft-carriers of the Formidable class should be fitted with armoured flight decks, an indispensable benefit in the war that followed.

As a captain, Brind commanded the cruiser *Orion*, and later the cruiser *Birmingham*. He took the latter to Tsingtao (Qingdao) in 1939, at a time when China and Japan were at war, to investigate the arrest of a British merchant ship by the Japanese. He called on the Japanese admiral and announced his intention of rescuing the British ship despite the presence of Japanese heavy cruisers and a carrier, and the threat to blow the *Birmingham* out of the water. Brind insisted on the release of the merchant ship and sailed the next day, escorting her to safety. In December 1940 Brind became chief of staff to Admiral John Tovey, commander-in-chief, Home Fleet, and was thus involved in the long chase and the destruction of the *Bismarck* on 27 May 1941. He was created CBE for his part in the action.

Having been promoted rear-admiral on 6 February 1942, Brind was appointed assistant chief of naval staff in May 1942, and served in the Admiralty until August 1944, taking a large part in the planning for operation Neptune (the Normandy landings). In July 1944 he was made CB in recognition of this work. From October 1944 until January 1946 Brind had command of a squadron of ships of the British Pacific Fleet, and was engaged in offensive operations in the long task of defeating the Japanese. He was present at the conclusion of the war with the Japanese in August 1945 and attended the act of surrender in Tokyo.

Brind was promoted vice-admiral on 16 October 1945, and was advanced to KCB in June 1946. In October 1946 he was appointed president of the Royal Naval College at Greenwich, and held this appointment until he assumed the naval command as commander-in-chief, Far East station, in January 1949. He retained the latter, perhaps his most important job, until 1951, the year in which he was created GBE. He was promoted full admiral on 20 March 1949. It was in 1949 that the *Amethyst* was held hostage by communists 150 miles up the Yangtze (Yangzi) River for three months. Realizing that negotiations were fruitless, Brind turned a blind eye to official policy, and initiated and organized the *Amethyst*'s spectacular withdrawal from the Yangtze—a triumphant success.

When the Korean War broke out in June 1950, Brind was ready to oppose the North Korean assault. He at once ordered his ships to be placed under American command, without waiting to learn the official policy. The whole area was in turmoil, with communist aggression in China and Korea, the threat to Taiwan, an emergency in Malaya, and piracy. A false move might have had major international repercussions, but Brind, who was on the spot, seemed instinctively to sense the right moves. With a sizeable fleet involved in continuous operations 2000 miles from its main base, Brind had to improvise rapidly. Thanks to enthusiastic support his efforts were highly successful. His staff officer operations, Captain P. Dickens, thought that Brind's performance at this time was the peak of his career: 'To his patience, charm, and kindness I would add an indefatigable capacity for work, and a sense of duty, directed towards God and what he believed to be right' (private information). Brind's final appointment was as commander-in-chief, allied forces northern Europe (1951 to 1953), a new NATO command. He retired in 1953 and was succeeded in the NATO appointment by his deputy, General Sir Robert Mansergh.

Brind's first wife died in 1940. In 1948 he married Edith Gordon (d. 1979), daughter of William Duncan Lowe, writer to the signet, Edinburgh, and widow of Rear-Admiral H. E. C. Blagrove who was lost in the sinking of the *Royal Oak* in 1939. Brind was known throughout the navy as 'Daddy'. When his secretary, Captain S. A. B. Morant, was asked about the derivation of the nickname, he replied that doubtless it was because he had white hair, a paternal air, and was one of the kindest and most charming men one could ever hope to meet. His widow said that the nickname was given to him when he was a lieutenant doing courses. His hair was prematurely white and he had a benign appearance.

Brind died on 4 October 1963 at his home, Lye Green Forge, Withyham, near Crowborough, at the age of seventy-one. His memorial in Withyham church has the appropriate inscription: 'Write me as one that loves his fellow men'.   S. W. C. PACK, rev.

Sources *The Times* (5 Sept 1963) · *The Times* (10 Sept 1963) · private information (1981) · *WWW* · S. W. Roskill, *The war at sea, 1939–1945*, 3 vols. in 4 (1954–61) · M. H. Murfett, *Hostage on the Yangtze: Britain, China and the Amethyst crisis of 1949* (1991) · *CGPLA Eng. & Wales* (1964)
Archives King's Lond., Liddell Hart C., papers | FILM IWM FVA, actuality footage · IWM FVA, documentary footage
Likenesses photograph, 1946 (with military commanders), Hult. Arch.
Wealth at death £46,655: probate, 10 March 1964, *CGPLA Eng. & Wales*

Brind, Richard (d. **1718**), organist and music teacher, was the son of Richard Brind and an unknown mother. He was educated as a chorister, and later admitted as a probationer vicar-choral, at St Paul's Cathedral, where he

remained, succeeding Jeremiah Clarke as organist in 1708. He held this post for the rest of his life.

Brind was active as a teacher and composer, and is chiefly remembered for his pupil Maurice Greene. He was a minor composer of sacred vocal music, which included two thanksgiving anthems, now lost, which are mentioned in Sir John Hawkins's *General History of the Science and Practice of Music* (1776). None of his music survives in the partbooks at St Paul's, although five anthems in William Croft's *Divine Harmony* (1712) are attributed to him. His contemporaries considered him 'no very celebrated performer'. Brind died in London in 1718 and was buried on 18 March in St Gregory's vault in the cathedral. He seems to have been unmarried, and his will was proved on 7 April by his father.   DAVID S. KNIGHT

Sources H. W. Shaw, *The succession of organists of the Chapel Royal and the cathedrals of England and Wales from c.1538* (1991) · D. Dawe, *Organists of the City of London, 1666–1850* (1983) · PRO, PROB 6/94, fol. 66r · J. Hawkins, *A general history of the science and practice of music*, 5 vols. (1776) · I. Spink, *Restoration cathedral music, 1660–1714* (1995) · *DNB*

Brindley, James (1716–1772), civil engineer, was born at Tunstead in the parish of Wormhill in Derbyshire, the eldest of seven children of James Brindley (c.1684–1769/70), yeoman, and his wife, Susannah Bradbury (c.1695–1779). The couple had married in Chesterfield on 25 June 1716. About 1726 the family moved to a farm at Low Hill near Leek in Staffordshire owned by Richard Bowman, a brother of Brindley's grandmother. The family inherited this farm on Richard's death in December 1727.

Nothing is definitely known of Brindley's education, but although he was literate some of the spelling in his rough notebooks is phonetic. From an early age he showed an interest in mechanical work, and at the age of seventeen began a seven-year apprenticeship with Abraham Bennett, a millwright and wheelwright at Sutton near Macclesfield. At first he was regarded as a bungler by Bennett, but he was to become Bennett's right-hand man after his work on a silk mill at Macclesfield, and at a paper mill at Wildboarclough, where he saved the firm's professional reputation after Bennett's own bungling meant that the machinery he was installing there would not work properly. Brindley remained with Bennett after his apprenticeship ended, running the business until his employer's death in 1742.

Brindley then moved back to Mill Street, Leek, and set up as a millwright on his own account, building a reputation for good workmanship and an ability to suggest improvements to machinery, gaining the nickname 'the Schemer'. His business thrived, and in 1750 he set up a second workshop at Burslem, in property leased from the Wedgwood family. During the next decade he worked on several water and wind mills, including Leek corn mill (subsequently a Brindley museum); he installed several atmospheric engines and in 1758 patented a minor and ultimately unsuccessful improvement to their boiler design (no. 730); and he attracted attention for a drainage scheme at the Wet Earth colliery at Clifton near Manchester. Here Brindley took water from the River Irwell

James Brindley (1716–1772), by Francis Parsons, 1770

through an underground tunnel over 800 yards long that ran under the river to drive an overshot wheel, which pumped out the mine. This success emphasized Brindley's engineering skills and his understanding of hydraulic problems.

On 8 December 1765 Brindley married Anne Henshall, aged nineteen, the daughter of a close associate, John Henshall of Newchapel, land surveyor, at Wolstanton. They set up home at Turnhurst, and had two daughters, Susannah and Anne. Brindley may also have had a natural son, John Bennett, the son of Mary Bennett, baptized at Burslem on 31 August 1760. It is part of the Bennett family tradition that John was the great-great-grandfather of the novelist Arnold Bennett.

Brindley became involved in canal construction, the activity for which he is now best known, towards the end of the 1750s. Early in 1758 his reputation was such that he was hired to survey a canal to link Liverpool and the Mersey with the potteries and the Trent. Although construction did not begin until 1766, this survey, and his work at Clifton, made him an obvious choice to the duke of Bridgewater for his scheme to bring coal out of his mines at Worsley by water, and then transport it by canal to Salford. Argument has arisen about Brindley's exact responsibility for the Bridgewater Canal, the first arterial canal in England. Many contemporaries, his first biographer, Samuel Smiles, and some modern historians give Brindley the credit, but other modern historians argue that John Gilbert, the duke of Bridgewater's estate steward, played the major role. Bridgewater and Gilbert had been planning the canal since 1757, obtaining an act in March 1759.

It was only then that Brindley was brought in to make a detailed survey of the route.

It seems probable that it was Brindley who suggested a radical change in the intended route, to carry it across the Irwell by aqueduct and into Manchester, as such a route could more easily link up with his proposed Trent and Mersey Canal. Brindley's notebooks show that between July and October 1759 he spent forty-six days surveying this canal, working on an atmospheric engine at Coalbrookdale at the same time; that he was employed on the construction of the canal until it opened in 1761; and that he then surveyed and began constructing the extension to Preston Brook and the Mersey, although he was to disagree and part company with the duke before this extension was completed. He also played an important role in convincing parliament of the viability of the scheme. Brindley was not an employee of the duke, but a consultant responsible to Gilbert, who was the duke's manager. Gilbert did play an important role in planning and constructing the canal, as did the duke, but Brindley was a major contributor to the success of a scheme which did so much to intensify interest in canal construction in this country, and it was to be Brindley who became a major canal engineer, while Gilbert remained in his lucrative post as the duke's estate steward.

During the last fourteen years of his life Brindley emerged as the man who gave shape to the English canal network, working on a number himself and training many of the engineers who completed the task of constructing the network. Before being hired by the duke, Brindley had propounded ideas for a 'Grand Cross', a series of canals to link the four main river estuaries, the Mersey, Trent, Thames, and Severn. The success of the Bridgewater Canal encouraged separate groups of investors to revise and implement Brindley's vision, and Brindley was to be employed as the principal engineer by all these groups, on the Trent and Mersey Canal, the Coventry Canal, the Oxford Canal, and the Staffordshire and Worcestershire Canal. Brindley was employed as the principal engineer on over ten canals in all, including the Birmingham Canal, the Droitwich Canal, the Chesterfield Canal, and the Huddersfield Broad Canal. Several other canal companies, including the Leeds and Liverpool, employed Brindley as a consulting engineer for advice about a specific problem or to check the suggestions of other engineers. In all there are at least twenty-three canal schemes in which he was involved, only five of which were not implemented. These last included a proposed canal from Lichfield to the Trent and a proposed Stockton and Darlington Canal, which was later to emerge as the early famous railway, while in 1770 he surveyed the Thames, favouring a canal from Sonning to Mortlake as the best option, but also making proposals to improve the existing river navigation.

Most of Brindley's canals were narrow, contour-hugging canals, as opposed to the wide cut and fill built Bridgewater Canal, but there were economic and technical constraints that determined Brindley's style of construction. Many of his canals were later substantially shortened by the use of the embankments and cuttings he had eschewed, but the finance was never available to widen them. The narrow width of the canal network that Brindley shaped was to be a disadvantage later, but at the time they were built they were a substantial improvement to the transport system. Brindley's work also pioneered the development of canal aqueducts and tunnels, especially famous being the Barton aqueduct on the Bridgewater Canal and Harecastle Tunnel on the Trent and Mersey Canal, the first transport tunnel to be started in Britain.

During these same years Brindley continued to work on mills and atmospheric engines; he became a partner in his brother John's pottery works at Burslem; and, in 1760, in partnership with brother John, his future brother-in-law Hugh Henshall, and John and Thomas Gilbert, he purchased the Turnhurst estate in Staffordshire, including the Golden Hill colliery. The partners built underground canals to bring coal out of the mines into the Harecastle Tunnel on the Trent and Mersey Canal. To accomplish all these projects Brindley overworked, but he also had a large staff of assistants, who were installed on some canals as resident engineers reporting to Brindley while he worked elsewhere, not without some criticism from the companies concerned. The most famous of his assistants was Robert Whitworth senior, but Thomas Dadford and his sons, Hugh Henshall, and Samuel Simcock were also important. These engineers who learned their trade under Brindley's supervision were to complete the canals he had started, for only a few had been finished before his death; but they were also to build many new canals and thus extend Brindley's influence on the development of the English canal system long after his death.

For at least eight years before his death Brindley suffered from diabetes, and his incessant work strained his health. In 1772 he got soaked to the skin while surveying a branch canal from Etruria to Froghall and his condition worsened after being put up in a damp bed at a local inn. After an illness of some duration he died at home at Turnhurst, Staffordshire, on 27 September 1772 at the age of fifty-six, and on 30 September he was buried at Newchapel. His memorial inscription described him as an engineer. On 30 December 1775, Brindley's widow, Anne, married Robert Williamson, a potter, and they had seven children. Williamson died in 1799, and Anne remained a widow until her death at the age of seventy-nine in 1826.

K. R. FAIRCLOUGH

Sources C. T. G. Boucher, *James Brindley, engineer, 1716–1772* (1968) · S. Smiles, *Lives of the engineers*, 1 (1862) · diaries and notebooks, Inst. CE, Brindley papers · A. G. Banks and R. B. Schofield, *Brindley at Wet Earth colliery: an engineering study* (1968) · H. Malet, *Bridgewater: the canal duke, 1736–1803* (1977) · P. Lead, *Agents of revolution: John and Thomas Gilbert, entrepreneurs* (1989) · K. M. Evans, *James Brindley canal engineer: a new perspective with particular reference to his family background* (1997) · J. Phillips, *A general history of inland navigation*, 5th edn (1805) · P. Adams, ed., *Burslem parish registers*, 3 vols. (1913), 1.269 · P. Adams, ed., *Wolstanton parish registers*, 2 vols. (1914), 1.368 · parish register, Newchapel, Staffordshire, 30 Sept 1772 [burial] · Bodl. Oxf., MS Top. Staffordshire c.1, fol. 44

Archives Birm. CL, diaries · Inst. CE, diaries | Bodl. Oxf., MS Top. Staffordshire, c.1, fol. 44

Likenesses F. Parsons, oils, 1770, NPG [*see illus.*] · R. Dunkarton, mezzotint (after F. Parsons), BM, NPG · F. Parsons, oils, Inst. CE · F. Parsons, portrait, repro. in Boucher, *James Brindley, engineer*, frontispiece · portrait, Josiah Wedgwood & Sons Ltd

Wealth at death approx. £7000: Evans, *James Brindley*

Brine, James (1813–1902). *See under* Tolpuddle Martyrs (*act.* 1834–c.1845).

Brine, John (1703–1765), Baptist minister, was born at Kettering, the son of a cobbler. Owing to the poverty of his parents he had scarcely any school education, and when still young was sent to work in the staple manufactory of his town. Converted by the preaching of John Gill, he became a baptized member of the church at Kettering. While at Kettering he married Anne Moore (d. 1745), daughter of the Revd John Moore, a Baptist minister of Northampton who had been a fellow evangelist with David Crosley and William Mitchell in the Pennines area. Brine's conversion had stimulated a desire for learning, and Moore supplied the young man with a copy of Hutter's Hebrew Bible. Anne Brine died on 11 August 1745, and in 1750 Brine published *Some account of the choice experiences of Mrs Anne Brine, as written by herself, and collected out of her letters*. After some time he married again; his new wife's name was Mary (1698–1784).

Brine was recognized as a preaching minister by his church at Kettering, and about 1726 was called to be pastor of the Baptist church in Coventry. There he remained until about 1730, when he succeeded William Morton as pastor of the congregation at Currier's Hall, Cripplegate, London. From his arrival he became an active member of the group of London ministers known as the Baptist Board. He was for a time one of the Wednesday evening lecturers in Great Eastcheap, and also preached in his turn at the Lord's Day Evening Lecture in Devonshire Square. Physically of short stature, he had a low voice. He was generally reputed a high Calvinist and a supralapsarian. He was called by many people an antinomian, even though his personal life was exemplary. His Calvinism led him to oppose other Calvinists who thought that unconverted people had a moral responsibility to hear and respond to the gospel. His teaching elevated the initiative of God in salvation, to the extent of believing that God adopted and justified the elect even before their own experience of faith. Preachers therefore had no right to 'offer' Christ to their hearers, as this challenged the sovereign actions of God. John Gill thought Brine had shown 'great understanding, clear light and sound judgement in the doctrines of the gospel' (Gill, 1.591–2). Of his many printed works, *A treatise on various subjects: controversial tracts against Bragge, Johnson, Tindal, Jackson, Eltringham and others* (2 vols.) was reprinted in 1750, 1757, and 1766.

Brine lived for many years in Bridgewater Square, London, but during his last illness he took lodgings at Kingsland, in London, where he died on 24 February 1765. He was buried in Bunhill Fields. He left positive orders that no funeral sermon should be preached for him; however, his intimate friend Dr John Gill preached a sermon upon the occasion to his own congregation, which was afterwards published, but contains no express reference to Brine.

Very significant in his lifetime, Brine's theological influence waned towards the end of the eighteenth century as a new evangelical Calvinism made his tenets unfashionable. In 1813 James Upton published a revised edition of the *Treatise*, together with some sermons, and *Choice Experiences of Mrs A. Brine*, as well as a life of Brine previously printed by Walter Wilson.   S. L. COPSON

Sources W. Wilson, *The history and antiquities of the dissenting churches and meeting houses in London, Westminster and Southwark*, 4 vols. (1808–14), vol. 2 · J. Ivimey, *A history of the English Baptists*, 4 vols. (1811–30), vol. 3 · J. A. Jones, ed., *Bunhill memorials* (1849) · J. Gill, *Sermons and tracts* (1773) · *DNB*

Brink, Charles Oscar [*formerly* Karl Oskar Levy] (1907–1994), classical scholar, was born on 13 March 1907 at Pybalstrasse 14, Charlottenburg, Germany, the elder of two sons of Arthur Levy (1874–1941), lawyer, and his wife, Elise (1879–1956), daughter of Oskar Misch, businessman, of Deutsch Wilmersdorf. His parents and grandparents were citizens of the German empire who professed the Jewish faith. He himself joined the Lutheran evangelical church in early 1931, and changed his surname to Brink on 31 August of that year. He was educated at the Lessing Gymnasium in Wedding, a working-class district of Berlin where his father practised law, and in 1925 entered the philosophical faculty of the University of Berlin. He attached himself to Werner Jaeger and spent some months of 1928 studying in Oxford with Jaeger's British friend W. D. Ross. He obtained his doctorate in 1933 with a thesis entitled 'Stil und Form der pseudaristotelischen *Magna moralia*', still highly regarded sixty years later among students of Aristotle and his school. For the next five years he held a post at the *Thesaurus linguae Latinae* in Munich, financed by the Rockefeller Foundation.

Brink went to England in 1938 through the efforts of W. D. Ross and spent four not altogether happy years on the staff of the *Oxford Latin Dictionary*. He was interned between June and October of 1940 among those refugees 'about whom there must be some doubt'. The following year he took over his friend C. G. Hardie's teaching at Magdalen College. Although he was now a stateless person, in April 1942 he was accepted in marriage by Daphne Hope Harvey (*b*. 1918), physiotherapist, daughter of Godfrey Eric Harvey, civil servant in India and historian of Burma. They had three sons, Adrian Charles (*b*. 1944), Denis Hope (*b*. 1946), and Stephen Arthur Godfrey (*b*. 1950). From 1943 to 1948 he was senior classics master at Magdalen College School. Naturalization came in 1947. An article on Callimachus and Praxiphanes published in the *Classical Quarterly* in 1946 enhanced his scholarly reputation, and in 1948 he obtained a post in the department of humanities in the University of St Andrews. In 1951 he was appointed to the chair of Latin in the University of Liverpool and in 1954, his reputation having been further enhanced by the publication of several articles about the Roman historian Tacitus, he was appointed to the Kennedy chair of Latin in the University of Cambridge, which he held until his retirement in 1974.

Election to a professorial fellowship of Gonville and Caius College in 1955 brought him into a bitter quarrel about what course the college's life should take in the future. He failed narrowly to become master in 1959 and remained leader of a faction with distinctive policies through the masterships of Nevill Mott and Joseph Needham. He supported a scheme which took shape in the late 1960s of setting up a co-educational adjunct of the college. This proved to be the seed of the independent Robinson College, which received its royal charter in 1985. Brink had been a member of the board of trustees from 1973 and the board's chairman from 1975. His failure to persuade Sir David Robinson to endow the new institution with funds earmarked for academic research disappointed him gravely.

When in 1959 the University of Cambridge moved to drop knowledge of Latin from among its requirements for matriculation, Brink assumed, a little hesitantly, the leadership of a campaign of opposition. This campaign failed, and he turned his political skills towards an effort to guide the changes he saw as inevitable in the classical curricula of English schools and universities in such a way as to preserve as much as possible of a genuine understanding of Latin literature. He helped to found the Joint Association of Classical Teachers in 1963 and was one of those behind the Cambridge schools classics project, which began work in 1965 with the support of the Nuffield Foundation on a new manual for teaching the elements of Latin, based on contemporary linguistic theory. From 1965 to 1969 he chaired the classics committee of the Schools Council. The curricular changes which actually came to be made pleased him little.

In 1963 Brink published *Horace on Poetry. I. Prolegomena to the Literary Epistles*, which addressed the old issues of the structure of the *Epistle to the Pisos* and the poet's debt to Neoptolemus of Parium and the peripatetic tradition of theorizing about literature. Opinions among reviewers about Brink's handling of these issues were divided, and personal enemies exploited some of the disagreements expressed. The high quality of the massive commentary on the *Epistle to the Pisos* which Brink published eight years later surprised many who had hitherto tended to dismiss him as no more than an academic politician. The third and final volume of the trilogy, a commentary of similar proportions on the *Epistles to Augustus and Florus*, came out in 1982 and stilled all doubt about his scholarly stature. The deep knowledge of the whole tradition of Horatian scholarship evinced by the three volumes received more appreciation abroad than in England, and it was out of a course of lectures delivered at the Scuola Normale Superiore in Pisa that sprang *English Classical Scholarship: Historical Reflections on Bentley, Porson, and Housman* (1986).

Brink stayed away from Germany for nearly thirty years. His interest in the language of Horace's poems took him back to Munich in December 1966 for a visit to the archive of the *Thesaurus linguae Latinae*. He joined the international commission in charge of the dictionary in 1967 as the British delegate, and became the commission's president in 1989. He was to be invited to serve a second five-year term the day he died.

Brink had a strong and imposing physique which he

looked after carefully. A natural feeling for rhythm and harmony and a courteous manner impressed even the uncouth. His views on society and politics were conservative, but never predictably so. He combined a rationalizing philosophical outlook with a profound religiousness, and from 1942 remained a communicant member of the Church of England. He died on 2 March 1994 in Addenbrooke's Hospital, Cambridge, some days after suffering a heart attack in his college rooms. His ashes were interred in St Giles's cemetery on 11 April. He was survived by his wife.   H. D. JOCELYN

Sources *The Times* (8 March 1994) · *The Independent* (13 March 1994) · *The Independent* (26 March 1994) · *The Guardian* (19 March 1994) · *The Guardian* (24 March 1994) · *Daily Telegraph* (12 April 1994) · J. Diggle, R. Duncan-Jones, and J. Lewis, *The Caian* (1993–4), 86–94 · H. D. Jocelyn, *Liverpool Classical Monthly*, 19 (1994), 37–55 · H. D. Jocelyn, *Gnomon*, 67 (1995), 650–55 · E. Vogt, *Jahrbuch der Bayerischen Akademie der Wissenschaften* (1995), 260–64 · H. D. Jocelyn, 'Charles Oscar Brink, 1907–1994', *PBA*, 94 (1997), 317–54 · H. D. Jocelyn, 'Brink, C. O.', *Enciclopedia Oraziana III* (1998), 142–5 · personal knowledge (2004) · private information (2004)
Archives Gon. & Caius Cam., files relating to his post at the college | Bodl. Oxf., Society for the Protection of Science and Learning, MSS
Likenesses photograph, 1933–7, priv. coll. · D. Brink, photograph, 1964, repro. in *Gnomon*, following p. 652 · D. Brink, photograph, 1964, repro. in Jocelyn, 'Charles Oscar Brink', following p. 318 · photograph, 1981, repro. in *Cambridge Daily News* (29 May 1981) · M. Taylor, oils, 1986, Robinson College, Cambridge · G. Orlandi, photograph, 1987, priv. coll.
Wealth at death £139,732: probate, 25 May 1994, *CGPLA Eng. & Wales*

Brinkley, John (1766/7–1835), mathematician and astronomer, was born, probably in December 1766 but possibly in January 1767, in Woodbridge, Suffolk, and was baptized there on 31 January 1767. His father was John Toler, a vintner, and his maternal grandfather was John Brinkley, a butcher. His mother, Sarah Brinkley, married a James Boulter in 1770. He graduated as senior wrangler and Smith's prizeman at Gonville and Caius College, Cambridge, in 1788 and was a fellow of Caius from 1788 to 1790. It appears that his fees at Cambridge were paid by a donor, who may have been his last tutor, the Revd Tilney of Harleston, Northamptonshire, who recognized his scholarly talents and prepared him for entry to Cambridge. He was ordained deacon in Ely Cathedral in 1790 and priest in Lincoln Cathedral in 1791. Probably in 1792 he married Esther Weld, the daughter of Matthew Weld of Dublin. They had two sons, John and Matthew, and fifteen grandchildren are recorded; one son was ordained in the Church of Ireland and the other was for a time a vicar choral.

Brinkley was, during 1787 and 1788, an assistant to the astronomer royal, Nevil Maskelyne, at Greenwich. At the age of twenty-four he was appointed as Andrews' professor in succession to the first holder, Revd Henry Ussher (d. 1790), who had survived only five years in post. Ussher had planned the building and instrumental equipment of the Dunsink observatory in 1783–5 in collaboration with Maskelyne, and, after consultation with Maskelyne, the board of Trinity College, Dublin, chose Brinkley in preference to existing fellows of the college who sought to obtain the appointment—but only after the provost, John Hely Hutchinson, had exercised his veto. Realizing that strong measures were necessary, Hutchinson not only consulted Maskelyne as to the best person he could recommend, but succeeded within a few years in having the Andrews' professor recognized as royal astronomer of Ireland by letters patent of George III in 1792.

It was intended that the Andrews' professor should convey to his students the achievement of 'natural philosophy' in reducing the elaborate representation of planetary motions of the Ptolemaic system to a system described by a few simple equations of motion and an equation for the force of gravity. Brinkley, as the first royal astronomer of Ireland, fulfilled the role by being a distinguished scientist as well as an inspiring teacher. It is likely that his *Elements of Plane Astronomy* of 1808 was the first English-language textbook for teaching astronomy in universities; in Dublin it went through several revisions up to the end of the nineteenth century as a standard Trinity College text.

Brinkley's work in astronomy was in mathematical methods, including a pioneering application of Gauss's method of least squares to reduction of observational data. He derived new values for fundamental astronomical quantities, including aberration, nutation, and precession, published in 1819, and it was for the first theory of the motion of lunar perigee, published in 1818, that he was awarded the Cunningham medal of the Royal Irish Academy in 1817. He had also produced, in 1814, a definitive account of refraction by the earth's atmosphere.

Delivery of Jesse Ramsden's long-awaited 8 foot vertical circle, completed after his death by his successor Matthew Berge, was finally made in 1808. Brinkley thereupon set out on what he intended to be his life's work—the determination of the parallax of a star, or the direct observation of the distance to one or more of the nearest stars. He concentrated his work on some fifteen bright stars, and in due course he settled on four, alpha Cygni, alpha Lyrae, alpha Bootis, and alpha Aquilae, as having shown a parallax of near to 1 arc-second (in the case of the first three) and of 2.7 arc-seconds (in the case of alpha Aquilae). Throughout the course of this work, and at its conclusion, John Pond at Greenwich steadfastly maintained that the observed parallaxes were spurious, basing his ultimate opinion on results from instruments fixed to a meridian 'wall', each one to observe just one star round the year, as far as possible. This was one of the most celebrated controversies in observational astronomy of that time and it was concluded by a verdict clearly against Brinkley, in spite of the care with which he had reduced his observations. The cause of Brinkley's failure has been recognized to lie in his instrument, which was not suited to the task in that it was larger than other similar circles and had no special refinement in its adjustments. In fact these stars are far too distant to show parallax. However, Brinkley is generally credited with having paid great attention to the methods used in deriving parallax from observations, and the later success of others benefited from his jeopardized attempts.

Finding his salary as a professor of astronomy inadequate for his needs, Brinkley sought and obtained preferment in the Church of Ireland to the extent that he became a recognized authority on ecclesiastical law. After holding several sinecures he was appointed bishop of Cloyne, in co. Cork, in 1826, an unusual attainment for a man born out of wedlock.

Brinkley was made a fellow of the Royal Society of London in 1803 and received its Copley medal in 1824. He was president of the Royal Irish Academy from 1822 to 1835 and of the Astronomical Society of London from 1831 to 1833, which office he held at the time of the granting of the royal charter in 1831, when it became the Royal Astronomical Society. Brinkley had a gentle and peaceable character and his reluctant dispute with Pond was carried through without rancour. His humble origin was, for its time, unusual for a man of his eminence. He died at Leeson Street, Dublin, on 14 September 1835, and was buried in Trinity College chapel.   P. A. WAYMAN

Sources *Abstracts of the Papers Printed in the Philosophical Transactions of the Royal Society of London*, 3 (1830–37), 354 · *Monthly Notices of the Astronomical Society of London*, 3 (1833–6), 148 · R. S. Ball, *Great astronomers* (1895) · *Comptes Rendus Hebdomadaires des Séances de l'Académie des Sciences*, 1 (1835), 212 · *DNB* · S. M. P. McKenna, 'Brinkley, John', *DSB* · 'Report of the council of the society to the sixteenth annual general meeting, February 12 1836', *Memoirs of the Royal Astronomical Society*, 9 (1836), 281 · P. A. Wayman, *Dunsink observatory, 1785–1985: a bicentennial history* (1987) · W. M. Brady, *Clerical and parochial records of Cork, Cloyne, and Ross*, 3 (1864), 130 · J. B. Leslie, *Clogher clergy and parishes* (1929), 47 · Venn, *Alum. Cant.* · private information (2004)

Archives Denbighshire RO, Ruthin, family and other corresp. · Dunsink observatory, Dublin · TCD, corresp. and papers | Hunt. L., letters to Sir Francis Beaufort · RS, corresp. with Sir William Herschel

Likenesses M. Cregan, oils, c.1827 · J. Hogan, relief on marble monument, TCD · effigy on memorial tablet, TCD · oils, Gon. & Caius Cam. · portrait (as president of Royal Irish Academy), Royal Irish Acad.

Brinkley, Richard (*fl.* 1355–1375), Franciscan friar, theologian, and philosopher, was for a long time mistakenly referred to as Walter Brinkley. Nothing is known of his early life, except that he joined his order in Oxford. Brinkley's philosophical and theological ideas circulated at the University of Paris and Prague University, and were discussed at Prague in connection with those of the mid-fourteenth-century Oxford philosopher Richard Billingham. But though mentioned by W. Senko in connection with an anonymous list of celebrated doctors of Prague University, he is not listed at all in Josef Tříška's catalogue of pre-Hussite Prague University students and scholars. Brinkley's works have only recently been rediscovered, and are just beginning to be discussed by contemporary medievalists. In fact, to date only part 5, chapters 6–10, the tract *De significato propositionis* of his *Summa nova de logica* (so called by Thomas Rossy, a late fourteenth-century Franciscan) and *De obligationes* from part 7 have been critically edited.

Thus far what is known of Brinkley's philosophical views is that he defended a version of metaphysical 'realism', with respect to the ontological status of universals,

against the prevailing nominalist views of the day. He defended a perspectivist theory of intellectual cognition, against direct intuitive cognition theories, such as those defended by Albert von Sachsen, William Ockham, or Duns Scotus. Brinkley likewise maintained a variety of reism with respect to the ontological status of the referent of an entire proposition, similar to that of André Neufchâteau, sharply criticizing the propositional views of Richard Billingham, William Bermingham, and Richard Feribrigge. Brinkley also held the views that the referent of the phrase 'God's existence' (*Deum esse*) is identical with the referent of the term 'God' (*Deum*), and that the ways God acts internally (*ad intra*), when understood adverbially, are the same as when he acts externally (*ad extra*). Brinkley's only complete surviving work, the *Summa nova de logica* (composed between 1355 and 1365), exists in two manuscripts: Prague University Library, ČR. III. A. 11 (olim 396), fols. 31–104; and Leipzig University Library, MS 1360, fols. 1–105. There also exists a portion of his *Summa*, namely the tract *De insolubilibus*, in BL, Harley MS 3243; and portions of his *Lectura in libros sententiarum, inc: utrum per aliquam disciplinam vel scientiam*, in Paris, Bibliothèque Nationale, Lat. 16535, fols. 123r–129r, and Lat. 16408, fols. 40r–42r. Brinkley's other two known works, his *Determinationes, inc: sit aliqua conclusio theologiae* and his *Distinctiones scholasticae, inc: ad sciendam primam originem et finalem*, both seem to be lost. Brinkley exerted some influence on the theological writings of Heinrich Totting of Oyta, Dionysius the Carthusian, Johann Hiltalingen of Basel, Jean de Ripa, Pietro de Candia, Guglielmo Centueri da Cremona, and possibly the logical writings of John Wyclif.

MICHAEL J. FITZGERALD

Sources G. Gal and R. Wood, 'Richard Brinkley and his *Summa logicae*', *Franciscan Studies*, new ser., 40 (1980), 59–101 · *Richard Brinkley's theory of sentential reference*, ed. and trans. M. J. Fitzgerald (Leiden and New York, 1987) [Engl. and Lat. text] · Emden, *Oxf.*, 1.267–8 · A. G. Little, *The Grey friars in Oxford*, OHS, 20 (1892), 223 · J. Bale, *Illustrium Maioris Britannie scriptorum … summarium* (1548) · Bale, *Cat.*, 2.52 · J. Pits, *Relationum historicarum de rebus Anglicis*, ed. [W. Bishop] (Paris, 1619), 395 · J. H. Sbaralea, *Supplementum … ad scriptores … S. Francisci*, 3 vols. (Rome, 1908–36), 196 · L. Waddingus [L. Wadding], *Scriptores ordinis minorum*, [new edn] (1906), 102 · [Bonifacius a Ceva], *Firmamenta trium ordinum beatissimi patris nostri Francisci* (Paris, 1512) · W. Senko, 'Niezana lista autorow scholastucz nych z polowy XV. W. W rekopisie wroclawskiej Biblioteki Universy-teckiej', *Materialy i Studia Zakludu Historii Filozofii Starozytnej i Sredniowiecznej*, 7 (1967), 136–40, esp. 140, n. 42 · J. Tříška, *Zivotopisny Slovnik predhusitske 'Praszke' Univerzity, 1348–1409* (Prague, 1981) · *Richard Brinkley's Obligationes: a late fourteenth century treatise on the logic of disputation*, ed. G. A. Wilson and P. V. Spade (Münster, 1995) [Lat. text with Engl. commentary]

Archives Bibliothèque Nationale, Paris, MSS Lat. 16535, fols. 123r–129r; Lat. 16408, fols. 40r–42r · BL, Harley MS 3243 · Leipzig University Library, MS 1360, fols. 1–105 · Prague University Library, ČR.III.A.11 (olim 396)

Brinklow [Brinkelow], **Henry** [*pseud.* Roderyck or Roderigo Mors] (*d.* 1545/6), polemicist, was apparently the eldest of nine children of Robert Brinklow, a farmer of Kintbury, Berkshire (*d.* 1543), and his wife, Sibyl or Isabell Butler (*d.* in or before 1545). He became a mercer and a citizen of London, and, like many London mercers, favoured evangelical reform. He had a hand in electing the reformer

Sebastian Harris as chaplain to the Mercers' Company, and his business partners included known evangelicals. He stood surety for the reformist preacher Robert Wisdom when Wisdom was imprisoned in 1543. Brinklow's will of 20 June 1545 uses vigorously protestant language; he also left £5 to 'the godly learned men … that wt goddes worde doo fight ayenst Antechrist and his membres', and prescribed for himself a funeral without ceremony, even threatening to disinherit his wife if she wore mourning for him (PRO, PROB 11/31, fols. 158v–159r). His estate was as robust as his faith; he expected to leave over £350. He was dead by 20 January 1546, leaving a widow, Margery (d. 1557), and a son, John.

This was Brinklow's public face. Only in the 1550s did John Bale reveal the secret: that Brinklow was Roderyck (Roderigo) Mors, the author of a number of vitriolic polemics printed from 1542 onwards. He concealed his identity by having his works printed abroad, and by claiming to be an exiled former Franciscan. Bishop Gardiner realized Mors was a pseudonym, but believed George Joye to be the true author. Brinklow wrote two polemics which survive, a third which is lost, and he may also be the author of *A Supplication of the Poore Commons*, printed in 1546. The known works went through at least eight editions between them: an excerpt from *The Complaynt of Roderyck Mors* (1542) was reprinted as late as 1641. His *Lamentacion of a Christian* (1542) was publicly burnt in London in 1546; Gardiner called it a 'most abhominable booke' (*Letters*, ed. Muller, 163). Brinklow was certainly one of the most outspoken evangelicals of his time. He demanded that all remnants of traditional religion be swept away, urging particularly that the 'forcked cappes', the bishops, be stripped of their power.

Unlike most reformers, Brinklow was willing openly to criticize Henry VIII's ambivalent commitment to the evangelical cause, and to defy 'the .xiii. artycle of our crede added of late, that what so ever the parlament doth, must nedys be well done'. His religious programme shaded into a manifesto for wholesale social reform. He called for reform of rents, enclosures, wardships, and of the heresy and treason laws; for a stipendiary bar and judiciary; and for the two houses of parliament to be merged. He reviled the monasteries but condemned the royal seizure of their lands: 'the fatte Swyne onely were greased, but the poare Shepe to whom that thing belonged had least' (Brinklow, *Complaynt*, sig. D5v, *Lamentacion*, sigs. B5v, D8r). He also put forward a programme for full-scale redistribution of ecclesiastical wealth. His writing is clear, vigorous, and pungent, and his presence in London gave it an immediacy which exiled polemicists could not match.

ALEC RYRIE

Sources PRO, PROB 11/29, fol. 189r–v; 11/31, fols. 158r–159v; 11/33, fol. 42v • Bale, *Index* • PRO, SP 1/213, fol. 131r • *The letters of Stephen Gardiner*, ed. J. A. Muller (1933), 160–63 • S. Brigden, *London and the Reformation* (1989) • *STC, 1475–1640* • J. Foxe, *Actes and monuments* (1563), 574 • GL, MS 9531/12, fol. 45r–v • J. Strype, *Ecclesiastic memorials*, 1/1 (1822), 608–21 • J. M. Cowper, ed., *H. Brinklow's 'Complaynt of Roderyck Mors'*, EETS, extra ser., 22 (1874)

Wealth at death approx. £350–£400; bequeathed £109 13s. 4d cash; £7 debt remitted; £3 6s 8d. in jewellery; household effects: will, 20 June 1545, PRO, PROB 11/31, fols. 158r–159v

Brinknell, Thomas (c.1470–1539), schoolmaster and theologian, originated in the diocese of Coventry and Lichfield, and studied the arts course at Lincoln College, Oxford, during the 1490s, gaining an MA degree by 1495. On leaving Oxford he began a lifelong vocation as a grammar-school master. His first post was at Magdalen College School, Wainfleet, Lincolnshire, an appointment in the gift of Richard Mayew, president of Magdalen College, Oxford. Brinknell is first mentioned teaching the school at Michaelmas 1495, and was ordained priest while working there, three years later. His work was valued enough for him to be promoted, probably between Michaelmas 1501 and Michaelmas 1502, to the headmastership of Magdalen College's other, more important, grammar school in Oxford. He taught in this post until about Christmas 1507, as well as studying theology in the university, graduating BTh in 1501 and DTh in 1508. In 1505 he acted as an examining chaplain in an ordination held by Mayew, now bishop of Hereford, in the college chapel. His third teaching appointment was as master of St John's Hospital, Banbury, Oxfordshire, beginning in 1511. This hospital had been turned into a grammar school, with the master as teacher, by William Smith, bishop of Lincoln, in 1501, with the aim of making it a first-rate foundation. His initial appointee was John Stanbridge, the well-known writer of school textbooks, who was allowed to increase the basic stipend of £12 by holding other benefices. After Stanbridge died in 1510, Smith secured Brinknell's services, ensuring that he too was rewarded in dignity and stipend by the additional grant of the canonry and prebend of Marston St Lawrence in Lincoln Cathedral, worth a further £12.

Brinknell remained in charge of the Banbury school until at least 1535 and probably until his death. His reputation as a theologian also involved him in work outside his classroom. When Cardinal Wolsey endowed a theological lectureship at Oxford University in 1519, Brinknell was the first occupant and held the post for at least two years. In 1521 he was nominated by the university convocation as one of four scholars to attend a conference, called by Wolsey, to consider the doctrines of Luther, and he was subsequently one of a group of Oxford scholars who wrote individual refutations of them, though his contribution was not the one regarded as the best by the university or forwarded to Wolsey. Later, in 1531, his name appears in a list of theologians living outside the universities who might be consulted about the king's divorce. He played no major role, however, in either the controversies or events of the Reformation, and died in 1539, probably in the spring of that year.

NICHOLAS ORME

Sources Emden, *Oxf.*, 1.268 • N. Orme, *Education in early Tudor England: Magdalen College Oxford and its school, 1480–1540* (1998) • W. T. Mitchell, ed., *Epistolae academicae, 1508–1596*, OHS, new ser., 26 (1980), 91, 112, 114, 380

Brinsley, John (*fl.* 1581–1624), schoolmaster and writer on education, matriculated as sizar from Christ's College,

Cambridge, in March 1581, and graduated BA in 1585 and MA in 1588. Of his youth and concerning his parents no information remains. He was curate at Kegworth, Leicestershire, in 1591, and at Ashby-de-la-Zouch, Leicestershire, in 1601. From 1600 he was also master of Ashby School, chosen by the third earl of Huntingdon, the principal benefactor. Brinsley's contemporary as vicar was the puritan Arthur Hildersham. In April 1598 Brinsley married Barbara Hall, born in Ashby in September 1578, and sister of Joseph *Hall, later bishop of Norwich. Their son, John *Brinsley (1600–1665), attended Emmanuel College, Cambridge, and was also a puritan minister and author. Brinsley enjoyed wide patronage: the Hastings family; William Cavendish, Baron Cavendish of Hardwick; Edward Denny, Baron Denny of Waltham; Robert Johnson, archdeacon of Leicester and school founder; and possibly Sir John Harper.

According to his pupil William Lilly, the astrologer, Brinsley was 'very severe in his life and conversation' and a 'strict puritan' (Lilly, 12). At James I's accession he signed the diocesan petition calling for religious reform. In 1604 Brinsley was cited for ceremonial offences and suspended from his curacy. Most of his publications appeared while he was at Ashby. They included translations of Cicero, Ovid, Virgil, Cato, and Corderius, as well as *Pueriles confabulatiunculae* (1617) and *Sententiae pueriles* (1612); a devotional tract (*The True Watch and Rule of Life*, 1606, fourth part, 1624), grammar texts (*The Posing of the Parts*, 1612; *Stanbrigii embryon relimatun, seu, Vocabularium metricum*, 1614); a detailed manual for country schoolmasters (*Ludus literarius, or, The Grammar Schoole* 1612); and an abbreviated and more general version (*A Consolation for our Grammar Schooles*, 1622). He regarded publication as part of his 'holy & warrantable' calling (Brinsley, *Consolation*, 17–19).

Brinsley's educational views were an amalgam of the ideas of recent continental and English educators and his own classroom experience, aided by surveys of schoolmasters, results of 'yearely trialls' (Brinsley, *Consolation*, 22) of his methods in other schools, and criticism of pre-publication drafts, notably by Laurence Chaderton. He even invited criticism from readers. His work, intended for the 'meaner & ruder' (ibid., 26) country schools, reflected both a pragmatic approach and a strong religious consciousness. Reacting to parental concern over preparation for employment, Brinsley suggested starting school at the age of five and emphasized, quite uncommonly, continuing skill and practice in the vernacular. Brinsley also stressed numeracy, recommending Recorde's work and the founding of 'cyphering' schools. Practical advice included instructions on making a pen and on selecting a style of handwriting, and perhaps the earliest English mention of chalk and a board or table. Competition— 'contention for praise'—should be an important motivator (Brinsley, *Ludus literarius*, 50). Generally following humanist views of discipline Brinsley suggested moderate correction, in graduated form from reproof to sparing use of the rod. Incorrigible children should be removed from the school. To facilitate greater command of Latin

and Greek, Brinsley recommended 'grammatical translation', which involved translating sentences first in their grammatical order and only then addressing stylistic issues. This method would maintain facility in English while assisting adults in recovering lost ability in Latin. Brinsley also favoured disputations on grammar. His suggestions of classical texts were commonplace; of contemporary writers, he praised Ramus, Corderius, Coote, and Stockwood. Brinsley left logic to the universities, but did recommend Talon (or Butler's edition) for rhetoric.

Learning could be the 'sweetest pleasure' (Brinsley, *Consolation*, 3), even the 'chiefest glory of a Nation' (Brinsley, *Ludus literarius*, sig. 3), but only if it were godly. Brinsley's apocalyptic evangelicalism interpreted England's recent political 'deliverances' as setting the stage for the 'glorie of this last succeeding age' including dramatic educational changes (Brinsley, *Consolation*, 51). This required Christianity for the 'poore Indians' of Virginia and, for the 'rudest Welch and Irish', a knowledge of English to reduce them to civility and political obedience (ibid., A3v, 46–7, 78). Against the admirable vigilance of Jesuit schoolmasters, grammar schools, particularly in 'barbarous countries', would prove protestantism's chief hope. Since a teacher's labour was 'next unto the worke and charge of the holy Ministery' (Brinsley, *Ludus literarius*, 253–4), schoolmasters had to be models not only of learning but also of godliness and good behaviour. Daily Bible reading and catechizing (through William Perkins as well as Nowell), and the nonconformist Paget's history of the Bible would provide a foundation for attendance at Sunday sermons.

In September 1617 Brinsley and his wife were both cited to ecclesiastical court. 'Persecuted by the bishop's officers', according to Lilly (Lilly, 12–13), Brinsley lost his schoolmaster's job in 1617. In the same year he was licensed to teach grammar in St Ethelburgh, London, and throughout the whole diocese. He was last certainly known to be alive with the publication of the fourth part of *The True Watch and Rule of Life* in 1624. Andrew Willet called Brinsley an 'excellent Preacher', conformist, and controversialist (Willet, sig. 3v). JOHN MORGAN

Sources CUL, MS Dd. IX. 14 (C), fols. 46v–51 · act books of correction courts, Leics. RO, MS 1 D 41/13/44, fol. 51v · court book, 1602–9, Lincs. Arch., MS Cj. 14, fols. 67, 74v · BL, Add. MS 8978, fols. 1, 107ff, 116 · IGI · LMA, MS DL/C/341, fol. 47v · Venn, *Alum. Cant.* · J. Peile, *Biographical register of Christ's College, 1505–1905, and of the earlier foundation, God's House, 1448–1505*, ed. [J. A. Venn], 1 (1910) · C. W. Foster, ed., *The state of the church in the reigns of Elizabeth and James I*, Lincoln RS, 23 (1926) · W. Lilly, *Mr William Lilly's history of his life and times*, another edn (1826) · L. Fox, *A county grammar school: a history of Ashby-de-la-Zouch through four centuries, 1567 to 1967* (1967) · F. Watson, *English grammar schools to 1660: their curriculum and practice* (1908) · CUL, Add. MS 6730, fol. 87 · act books of correction courts, Leics. RO, MS 1 D 41/13/50, fols. 15ff, 138v · BL, Add. MS 5863, fol. 65 · W. Scott, *The story of Ashby-de-la-Zouch* (1907) · A. Willet, *An harmonie upon the First booke of Samuel* (1614) · J. Morgan, *Godly learning: puritan attitudes towards reason, learning, and education, 1560–1640* (1986) · R. O'Day, *Education and society, 1500–1800: the social foundations of education in early modern Britain* (1982) · J. Brinsley, *A consolation for our grammar schooles* (1622) · J. Brinsley, *Ludus literarius, or, The grammar schoole* (1612) · J. Brinsley, *The posing of the parts* (1612)

Brinsley, John (1600–1665), clergyman and ejected minister, was born at Ashby-de-la-Zouch, Leicestershire, the son of John *Brinsley (*fl.* 1581–1624), the renowned puritan schoolmaster at Ashby, and his wife, Barbara (*b.* 1578), who was a sister of Joseph *Hall, later bishop of Norwich. He was educated at his father's school, then from the age of thirteen at Emmanuel College, Cambridge, where he matriculated in 1615, graduated BA in 1620 and proceeded MA in 1623. In 1618 he took a break from his studies to act as secretary to his uncle, Dr Hall, at the Synod of Dort.

Brinsley devoted most of his career to providing a moderate puritan ministry to the godly of Great Yarmouth. He was ordained in the diocese of London in 1623 and his first living was at Prestons, near Chelmsford, Essex. In April 1625 he was invited to Yarmouth by a group of puritan aldermen to fill one of the two lectureships attached to the parish church of St Nicholas, and in the summer endeared himself to local inhabitants by remaining at his post when plague broke out in the town. However, he quickly became embroiled in a dispute between Yarmouth corporation and Bishop Samuel Harsnett and the dean and chapter of Norwich over the right to present to the town living. In February 1627, after a chancery hearing before Archbishop George Abbot, he was ordered to vacate the lectureship.

Brinsley stayed on in the town as preacher attached to the Dutch chapel. In 1629 he married Elizabeth, daughter of Edward Owner, MP for Yarmouth and a leading member of its oligarchy of puritan merchants. Through the patronage of Sir John Wentworth he was also appointed to the nearby living at Somerleyton, Suffolk, and here, through the 1630s, the Brinsleys had several children, including John, Ralph, and Deborah. When Wentworth established a new lectureship at Lound, about 1630, Brinsley became its principal preacher. In 1631 the new bishop of Norwich, Francis White, was persuaded by Brinsley's puritan allies to license him as town lecturer, but this was opposed by an anti-puritan faction among the town's governors and also by the Norwich dean and chapter. The issue was eventually resolved at a hearing before the privy council in March 1632. The king took the chair and, after some prefatory remarks about the dangers of puritan subversion, barred Brinsley from preaching in Yarmouth, ordered that the Dutch chapel be closed, and imprisoned four of the puritan aldermen. Despite these restrictions Brinsley continued to minister to the townsmen, with large numbers travelling to Lound to hear him preach.

During the 1640s and 1650s Brinsley's concerns were those of a typical member of the new orthodox Calvinist ecclesiastical establishment. In 1641 Great Yarmouth corporation reclaimed its right to nominate the town's two ministers and by 1644 Brinsley was reinstated in his old living at St Nicholas's, with a free house and a stipend of £100 a year. He remained there until his ejection in 1662. During this period he was a staunch presbyterian, in 1644 preaching in support of the solemn league and covenant, and signing the Norfolk attestation of 1648 which supported the Westminster assembly presbyterian stance on church government. He may initially have been caught up in the quarrels between presbyterians and Independents in Great Yarmouth in the 1640s, but he quickly came to realize that the main threat for orthodox Calvinists lay elsewhere.

In a letter which was later published in Thomas Edwards's *Gangraena*, Brinsley described how in mid-1645 he was assailed in his own house by Anabaptists and antinomians who refused to accept the authority of the Christian magistrate (Edwards, 2.161). He responded by publishing a sermon denouncing 'that spreading gangrene of Anabaptism which unless timely prevented may prove fatall to the whole body of this church' (*The Doctrine and Practice of Paedobaptisme*, 1645, preface). This was followed by a stream of further publications between the mid-1640s and mid-1650s in which he sought to provide an 'antidote' against the 'dangerous and damnable errours … broken in upon us'—for example, *A Looking Glass for Good Women* (1645), *Standstill, or, A Bridle for the Times* (1647), and *An Antidote Against the Poisonous Weeds of Heretical Blasphemies* (1650). At the same time, apparently conscious of the need for orthodox divines to unite against radical challenges, Brinsley developed a notably close relationship with his Independent counterpart in Great Yarmouth, William Bridge. In a 1646 sermon he made conciliatory remarks about Independency in a New England context and insisted that the real danger came from those who separated from the church 'by forsaking communion with it' (*The Arraignment of the Present Schism*, 1646, preface). In 1650 he and Bridge reached an amicable agreement whereby the huge parish church of St Nicholas was divided into two, by bricking off the north chancel, so that both could hold services simultaneously, and when Brinsley was suspended from his living by the council of state in 1651, for refusing to take the engagement, Bridge successfully petitioned for his reinstatement.

After 1660 Brinsley made strenuous efforts to come to terms with the restored monarchy. He published a number of sermons in which he bent over backwards to demonstrate his loyalty to the king, together with others in which he sought to console his congregation over the dramatic turn of events—for example *The Drinking of the Bitter Cup* (1660), *Prayer and Praise* (1661), *The Christians Cabala* (1662), and *Aqua coelestis, or, A Soveraigne Cordial* (1663). Edmund Calamy suggests that during this period he was 'tempted with offers of preferment' (Calamy, 2.477–8). In 1662, according to a local informant, he was willing to subscribe under the terms of the Act of Uniformity, but was persuaded against doing so by his presbyterian congregation, who promised him a pension of £80 a year for life. He continued to minister in Great Yarmouth from his ejection in 1662 until his death on 22 January 1665; he was buried on 25 January in the parish church of St Nicholas. Thirty-four of his works survive in print, published between 1631 and 1663.

RICHARD CUST

Sources *Calamy rev.*, 75 · E. Calamy, ed., *An abridgement of Mr. Baxter's history of his life and times, with an account of the ministers, &c., who were ejected after the Restoration of King Charles II*, 2nd edn, 2 vols.

(1713), vol. 2, pp. 477–80 · R. Cust, 'Anti-puritanism and urban politics: Charles I and Great Yarmouth', *HJ*, 35 (1992), 1–26 · K. W.
Shipps, 'Lay patronage of East Anglian puritan clerics in pre-
revolutionary England', PhD diss., Yale U., 1971, 216–40 · H. Swin-
den, *The history and antiquities of the ancient burgh of Great Yarmouth*,
ed. J. Ives (1772), 837–49 · C. J. Palmer, *The history of Great Yarmouth*
(1856), 158–73 · T. Edwards, *Gangraena, or, A catalogue and discovery of
many of the errours, heresies, blasphemies and pernicious practices of the
sectaries of this time*, 2 (1646), 161–2 · *STC, 1475–1640* · Wing, *STC* ·
P. Gauci, *Politics and society in Great Yarmouth, 1660–1722* (1996) · *CSP
dom.*, 1667–8, 186
Archives Norfolk RO, Great Yarmouth corporation archives

Brinsmead, John (1814–1908), piano manufacturer, was
born on 13 October 1814 at West Gifford, Devon, the son of
a small farmer and lime-burner. He had left school by 1826
and at the age of thirteen was apprenticed for seven years
as a cabinet-maker in Torrington, Devon. As his more famous forerunner, John Broadwood, had done in 1761, Brinsmead set out for London in 1835, walking the whole way.
After a year as a journeyman piano case maker, he had
saved sufficient capital in 1836 to set up his own piano
making business in partnership with his elder brother
Henry (*d.* 1880) on the top floor of 35 Windmill Street, off
Tottenham Court Road. This was not a fruitful relationship, however, and by 1837 John Brinsmead was running
his own firm with the help of one man and a boy, moving
in 1841 to Charlotte Street, and in 1863 to Wigmore
Street.

In the last quarter of the nineteenth century, Brinsmead
introduced and patented several improvements in the
piano. Aware of the need for active advertisement and
marketing of his products, which he exported as far afield
as Australia, he showed them, often with success, at the
various international exhibitions. In 1878, following the
display of his instruments at the Paris Exhibition, he was
awarded the French Légion d'honneur. He had also by
then been noted in the *Royal Blue Book*, and in 1884 his biography was recorded in *Fortunes Made in Business: a Series of
Original Sketches*. The name of his wife is not known, but he
had at least two sons and a daughter.

Such acclaim had its reward in the mounting sales of
Brinsmead pianos, which by the turn of the century
resulted in the firm becoming a limited company, employing more than 200 men, and producing more pianos per
year than the Broadwood company. The firm had also
acquired the smaller piano making business set up in
Rathbone Place by John Brinsmead's brother and former
partner, Henry. Opinion is still divided on whether at this
time the quality of the Brinsmead piano was better than
the Broadwood, but it seems that there was little to choose
between them. John Brinsmead died on 17 February 1908
at his home, 16 Albert Road, Regent's Park, London. The
firm thereafter was in the hands of Brinsmead's eldest
son, Thomas, who 'demonstrated both acute xenophobia
and puritanical attitudes towards his workers' (Ord-
Hume, 54–5). Because of these qualities and his inflexibil-
ity, the business declined, and after the First World War, in
January 1920, in the face of mounting competition,
general industrial unrest, a shortage of skilled labour, and
poor management, the firm went bankrupt. The firm of

John Brinsmead (1814–1908), by Reinhold Thiele

Cramer subsequently acquired the business, and pianos
were once more made under the company name of John
Brinsmead Ltd, production continuing until 1960. In that
year the business was taken over by Kemble Pianos, later
Yamaha-Kemble, which produced pianos with the brand
name of Brinsmead.   CHARLES MOULD

Sources C. Ehrlich, 'Brinsmead, John', *DBB* · E. Brinsmead, *The
history of the pianoforte* (1889) · C. Ehrlich, *The piano: a history* (1976) ·
[J. Hogg], ed., *Fortunes made in business: a series of original sketches*, 3
vols. (1884–7) · M. Cranmer, 'Brinsmead, John', *New Grove* ·
A. W. J. G. Ord-Hume, 'Brinsmead, John, 1814–1908', *Encyclopedia of
keyboard instruments*, ed. R. Palmieri, 1 (1994), 54–5 · *CGPLA Eng. &
Wales* (1908) · d. cert.
Likenesses R. Thiele, NPG [*see illus.*]
Wealth at death £46,127 18s. 5d.: probate, 22 April 1908, *CGPLA
Eng. & Wales*

Brinson, Peter Neilson (1920–1995), writer and lecturer
on dance, was born on 6 March 1920 at Sea View Villa,
North Parade, Llandudno, the son of Harold Neilson Brinson, a major in the King's Liverpool regiment and cotton
broker, and his wife, Vera Mabel Mathison. He was educated at Denstone College, Staffordshire, before going up
to Keble College, Oxford, in 1938. During the Second
World War, which interrupted his studies, he joined the
Royal Artillery and achieved the rank of captain. He
served as tank commander with General Montgomery at
El Alamein. After the war Brinson went back to Oxford and
took a first in philosophy, politics, and economics in 1948.
In that year he joined the London Film Centre as scriptwriter and research director. During this time he became

actively involved with classical ballet. In 1952 he wrote and produced *The Black Swan*, featuring the Covent Garden stars Beryl Gray and John Field, the first ballet film to use the new techniques of stereoscope. In the same year he began as a freelance writer on dance for *The Times* and for specialist dance magazines. In 1954 he was appointed as the first editor of the magazine *Films and Filming*. He wrote widely on the arts and was also invited to give a series of extramural lectures on dance for the universities of Oxford, Cambridge, and London.

In 1963 Brinson published *The Choreographic Art* with Peggy van Praag, who later became director of the Australian Ballet. In 1964 he established Ballet for All, a touring programme of the Royal Ballet. Working with a small group of dancers and then actors, he criss-crossed the British Isles presenting penetrating introductions to some of the most popular works. As deviser, writer, and presenter he gave thousands of adults and children their first experience of the power and appeal of ballet. Though rooted in ballet, he quickly recognized and embraced the importance of contemporary dance, particularly in the work of Martha Graham. Brinson developed a strong association with the work of the London School of Contemporary Dance and its founder, Robin Howard. His driving vision was always of a unified, national dance culture in which all forms of dance were valued and provided for.

In 1968 Brinson was appointed director of the Royal Academy of Dancing in London and in 1972 director of the UK and Commonwealth branch of the Calouste Gulbenkian Foundation. During the next ten years he took a leading role in promoting national and international initiatives in the arts, education, and community development. Through strategic funding of people and projects, initiating national commissions, and related research and publications he was at the epicentre of innovation in each of these areas.

Brinson had great powers of synthesis and overview and was in constant demand to chair commissions, to give keynote addresses, to lead inquiries, and to moderate conferences and symposia. Through the Gulbenkian Foundation he wrote or contributed to seminal works on the arts and public policy. These included *Dance Education and Training* (1980) and *The Arts Britain Ignores* (1980), as well as *The Economic Situation of the Visual Artist* and *The Arts in Schools: Principles, Practice and Provision*. He chaired the dance board of the Council for National Academic Awards, prepared reports for Commonwealth governments, and accepted academic appointments at York University, Toronto, as adjunct professor of dance, and at Goldsmiths' College, London.

Through his work Brinson helped gain respectability for dance in education, both as a practical discipline and as a subject of serious study. He was instrumental in establishing a chair of dance studies at the University of Surrey, the first of its type in the United Kingdom. He was uniquely qualified to fill this position but his role in creating it effectively disqualified him. In 1982 he left the Gulbenkian Foundation to become head of postgraduate studies at the Laban Centre at Goldsmiths' College, University of

London, to advise and influence new generations of dance scholars.

Brinson travelled ceaselessly throughout the world, promoting and supporting the development of dance and dance education. He developed particularly close ties with Australia, Canada, Ireland, and Hong Kong. In 1992 he was awarded the Digital Dance award for services to dance education and training. With typical grace he donated the prize money to a pilot scheme for a national dancers' injury and health scheme.

Brinson was a tall, slim man with an elegant bearing who was often taken to be fifteen or twenty years younger than he was. He shared much of his adult life with his devoted partner Werdon Douglas Anglin. They lived and worked together for twenty years, residing for much of that time in their welcoming, book-lined home in Stockwell, south London. Always charming and engaging, Brinson listened intently and spoke with a calm authority, his conversation often interrupted by a gentle, self-conscious laugh. He was a man of fine sensibilities and taste, not least in wine. His favoured aperitif was a cocktail of dry sherry and dry white wine, known to many in his circle as a Brinson.

In 1988 Peter Brinson was diagnosed as suffering from myelofibrosis. He faced the disease with strength and persistence, outliving considerably the early forecasts of his doctors. The illness required regular and lengthy blood transfusions. Typically, he came to value these as positive times when he could work and write without the interruption of meetings or telephone calls. He died at Trinity Hospice, Clapham, London, on 7 April 1995, and was cremated. During his lifetime he was in turn a film-maker, journalist, academic, and social entrepreneur. Brinson excelled in all these roles and brought to them a consistent passion for the arts, for social justice, and for equality. In particular, he played a leading role in transforming the nature and status of dance education in Britain and in many other parts of the world.   KEN ROBINSON

Sources *Dance Research: Journal of the Society for Dance Research*, 15/1 (1997), 1–55 [Peter Brinson memorial issue] · *Dance Theatre Journal* (summer 1995) · *The Independent* (8 April 1995) · *The Times* (18 April 1995) · *The Guardian* (8 April 1995) · *Times Educational Supplement* (April 1995) · b. cert. · d. cert. · personal knowledge (2004) · private information (2004) · P. Bassett, 'Peter Brinson: a bibliography', *Dance Research*, 15/1 (1997), 49–55 · *CGPLA Eng. & Wales* (1995)
Archives Goldsmiths' College, London, Laban Centre
Likenesses A. Crickmay, photograph, repro. in *Dance Research*, 5
Wealth at death under £125,000: probate, 30 June 1995, *CGPLA Eng. & Wales*

Brinton, Thomas (d. 1389), bishop of Rochester, took his name from Brinton in Norfolk. His parentage is unknown, but was probably humble. Having become a Benedictine monk in Norwich Cathedral priory he probably studied at Cambridge in 1352–3, before continuing his education at Oxford, where he incepted as a doctor of canon law from Gloucester College in 1363–4. A member of the papal household by 1362, on 31 January 1364 he was appointed proctor of the English Benedictines at the curia, while on 25 November 1366 he was described as a papal penitentiary and nuncio. He seems to have been in England about this time, but soon returned to the curia at Avignon, before accompanying Urban V during the pope's stay in Rome from 1367 to 1370. Internal evidence suggests that four of his surviving sermons were preached during these years of papal service, at either Avignon or Rome. He was also involved in the foundation of the English Hospice in the latter city.

On 31 January 1373 Brinton was made bishop of Rochester by papal provision, and consecrated at Avignon on 6 February. The see was one often bestowed on favoured preachers: its small size reduced the administrative burden on its occupant, while its position gave easy access to London and the court. Brinton played his part in government business. He was a trier of petitions in parliament seven times between 1376 and 1380. In the Good Parliament of 1376 he was one of four bishops selected to advise the Commons (at the latter's request), and in the following year was among the lords and prelates chosen to consult with the Commons for the good of the realm. In 1379, 1380, and 1381 he was named to commissions to examine the king's revenues, while in 1380 he also went on an embassy to negotiate with the French at Calais. Brinton was clearly respected for his integrity—in 1381 the rebellious peasants are reported to have asked him to present their grievances to the king. In May 1382 he attended the 'earthquake council' at the London Blackfriars, where Wyclif was condemned, undoubtedly with Brinton's approval—in his sermons he denounces Wyclif and his followers as false prophets. But although he was nominated to the peace commission for Kent in December that year, thereafter he disappears almost entirely from government records, undoubtedly owing to the failure of his health—every year from 1382 until his death sickness led to his being replaced by the prior of Rochester in his cathedral's Maundy Thursday ceremonies.

Brinton made his will at his manor of Trottescliffe on 29 April 1389. In a document that suggests that he had only limited means, he made bequests to Norwich Priory and Brinton church, to a number of kinsmen (but no brother or sister), and to members of a modest-sized household. At Rochester he left 6s. 8d. to each monk for prayers for his soul, and gave two vestments to the cathedral. He named John, third Baron Cobham, to whose collegiate foundation at Cobham he had been a benefactor, as overseer of his will, and bequeathed him £10. He died five days later, on 4 May. He had requested burial in the lady chapel of his cathedral, but is commemorated only by the indent of a memorial brass in the north aisle.

Brinton's most important legacy was his collection of 105 sermons (originally 108), surviving in Harley MS 3760 in the British Library—without much doubt 'the book of my sermons' which constituted another bequest to Rochester Cathedral. Published in a scholarly edition by M. A. Devlin in 1954, they do much to explain Brinton's contemporary renown as a preacher. The address he gave in London on 17 July 1377, the day after Richard II's coronation, is commended by the city's *Liber custumarum* as likely to please God, and reported in detail by Thomas Walsingham. Brinton clearly expected the clergy to be learned and to use their learning in the pulpit. His own sermons—preserved in Latin, though many will have been originally delivered in English or French—draw on a wide range of sources to proclaim a fundamentally conservative social message, albeit one with potentially radical implications. Though accepting the traditional divisions of society, he repeatedly stresses the interdependence of rich and poor, and outspokenly denounces the wealthy and powerful, whether lay or ecclesiastical, who fail to meet their responsibilities and whose pride, greed, and sloth impoverish their inferiors and drive them to desperation and crime. He attacks the corruption of the court of the end of Edward III's reign, and makes clear (and hostile) reference to the king's mistress Alice Perrers. But Brinton is no revolutionary, for he expresses horror at the peasants' revolt, and in his pursuit of justice and social harmony looks back to the fairly recent past, the days of Edward, the Black Prince, before moral decline brought military disaster, before 'God who used to be English withdrew from us' (*Sermons*, 47). Many of his sermons are primarily concerned with religious and theological issues; others illuminate a conscientious bishop's perceptions of a period of social and political strain.

HENRY SUMMERSON

Sources *The sermons of Thomas Brinton, bishop of Rochester, 1373–1389*, ed. M. A. Devlin, 2 vols., CS, 3rd ser., 85–6 (1954) · *Chancery records* · J. Greatrex, *Biographical register of the English cathedral priories of the province of Canterbury* (1997), 487–8 · Emden, *Oxf.*, 1.268–9 · W. A. Pantin, ed., *Documents illustrating the activities of the general and provincial chapters of the English black monks*, 3, CS, 3rd ser., 54 (1937) · *RotP*, vols. 2–3 · [T. Walsingham], *Chronicon Angliae, ab anno Domini 1328 usque ad annum 1388*, ed. E. M. Thompson, Rolls Series, 64 (1874) · [T. Netter], *Fasciculi zizaniorum magistri Johannis Wyclif cum tritico*, ed. W. W. Shirley, Rolls Series, 5 (1858) · F. S. Haydon, ed., *Eulogium historiarum sive temporis*, 3 vols., Rolls Series, 9 (1858), vol. 3 · H. T. Riley, ed., *Munimenta Gildhallae Londoniensis*, 3 vols. in 4, Rolls Series, 12 (1859–62) · M. A. Devlin, 'Bishop Thomas Brinton and his sermons', *Speculum*, 14 (1939), 324–44 · D. Knowles [M. C. Knowles], *The religious orders in England*, 2 (1955) · H. L. Spencer, *English preaching in the late middle ages* (1993) · W. J. Brandt, 'Remarks on Bishop Thomas Brinton's authorship of the sermons in MS Harley 3760', *Mediaeval Studies*, 21 (1959), 291–6 · F. A. Gasquet, 'A forgotten English preacher', *The Old English Bible and other essays*, 2nd edn (1908), 54–86 · M. Harvey, 'Preaching in the curia: some sermons by Thomas Brinton', *Archivum Historiae Pontificiae*, 33 (1995), 299–301 · G. R. Owst, *Preaching in medieval England* (1926) · G. R. Owst, *Literature and pulpit in medieval England*, 2nd edn (1966) · W. A. Pantin, *The English church in the fourteenth century* (1955) · R. M. Haines, 'Social, political, and religious impressions from some late medieval sermon collections', *Ecclesia Anglicana* (1989), 201–21
Archives BL, Harley MS 3760
Wealth at death wealth not great: will, *Sermons*, ed. Devlin, vol. 2, pp. 503–4

Brinton, William (1823–1867), physician, was born at Kidderminster on 20 November 1823, the fourth child and second son of Henry Brinton (1796–1857), chairman of Brinton's Limited, the town's oldest firm of carpet manufacturers, and his wife, Martha Eliza (1792–1869), the daughter of John Gardiner of Dublin. After education at private schools he was apprenticed at seventeen to Thomas Thursfield, a long-established surgeon of Kidderminster with an extensive practice. As pupil and assistant he attended to his arduous duties in an exemplary fashion. At the end of three years, though articled for the customary term of five years, Brinton was encouraged to matriculate at London University in order to start medical studies at King's College, where he was a student of extraordinary industry. He became senior scholar and gained every distinction for which he tried before graduating MB in 1847 and MD the following year. In 1849 he became a member of the Royal College of Physicians and was elected FRCP in 1854.

After holding the post of medical tutor for two years at King's College, Brinton was appointed lecturer in forensic medicine and co-lecturer in physiology at St Thomas's Hospital. Between 1852 and 1860 he combined these appointments with the duties of a physician at the Royal Free Hospital; he was first introduced to the Royal Free Hospital by Thomas Wakley, with whom he had a close friendship. In 1860 he became sole lecturer in physiology at St Thomas's, where he was also elected physician. As a teacher with graphic powers of illustration and unhesitating flow of language Brinton was in his day unsurpassed. He also had a remarkable dexterity with drawing, a talent he used in the illustration of his books. He had an iron will and high ambitions. He was bitterly disappointed in 1853 to be runner-up rather than the successful candidate chosen to succeed Robert Bentley Todd as professor of physiology at King's College. Brinton married, on 27 July 1854, Mary Danvers (1830–1891), the daughter of Frederick Dawes Danvers, clerk to the duchy of Lancaster, and sister of Emily, Viscountess Hambleden. They lived in Brook Street, Grosvenor Square, London, first at no. 20, and later moving to a larger and more convenient house, no. 24. There were six children of the marriage.

In his choice of the physiology and pathology of the gastrointestinal tract as interesting and rewarding subjects for special study and research Brinton was ahead of his time. In 1848, only five years after entering university, he submitted a paper on *Contributions to the Physiology of the Alimentary Canal* to the Royal Society. He was an accurate clinical observer and lucid commentator. His book *On the Pathology, Symptoms, and Treatment of Ulcer of the Stomach* (1857) was the first complete treatise on that subject to appear in English. Among his original descriptions was that of linitis plastica, known for a time as Brinton's disease. He noted the efficacy of a bismuth preparation for treating gastric ulcer. In *Lectures on the Diseases of the Stomach* (1859) he described correlations between clinical observations on numerous patients and subsequent post-mortem findings. Brinton concluded that dyspepsia was not a single and substantive disease, but rather a group of symptoms caused by a variety of ailments, and he predicted that the term would 'undergo successive subtractions … into special maladies' eventually resulting in 'the removal of this term from our nosology' (W. Brinton, *Diseases of the Stomach*, 2nd edn, 1865, 254). In the absence of any pathological basis for an affection often referred to in general literature as well as in medical books as 'gout in the stomach' (ibid., 291), he argued successfully against the existence of this hypothetical malady. His book *On Food and its Digestion,*

being an Introduction to Dietetics (1861), which was based on lectures he gave in physiology at St Thomas's Hospital, provided a clear account of existing knowledge. Intestinal obstruction was the subject of his Croonian lectures to the Royal College of Physicians in 1859; the book with this title was edited by his friend Dr Thomas Buzzard, and was published posthumously. In addition to Brinton's extensive writings on gastrointestinal subjects he wrote a short treatise, *On the Medical Selection of Lives for Assurance* (1856). His involvement in methodical studies of disease at the bedside combined with his intuitive flair for making quick and accurate diagnoses meant that he soon developed a large and demanding practice as a physician. For recreation he loved mountaineering, spending his annual holidays alone in the Tyrol, where he had a reputation for achieving feats of great physical endurance. In 1862 he contributed two accounts of his excursions to the journal of the Alpine Club, *Peaks, Passes and Glaciers*. Brinton was elected FRS in 1864. During the last three years of his life Brinton suffered from symptoms of progressive renal impairment, but continued with his busy professional commitments until shortly before his death at his home, 24 Brook Street, London, on 17 January 1867, aged only forty-three. He was buried at Kensal Green cemetery.

NORMAN MOORE, rev. D. D. GIBBS

Sources T. Buzzard, 'Memoir of William Brinton', *The Lancet* (26 Jan 1867), 129–31 · *BMJ* (26 Jan 1867), 95–6 · Munk, *Roll* · D. Gibbs, 'The demon of dyspepsia: some nineteenth-century perceptions of disordered digestion', *Gastroenterology in Britain—historical essays*, ed. W. E. Bynum, Wellcome Institute for the History of Medicine, Occasional Publications, no. 3 (1997) · W. Brinton, *Lectures on diseases of the stomach* (1857) · private information (2004) [family] · *IGI*

Likenesses E. Armstrong, oils, *c*.1864, RCP Lond.

Wealth at death under £20,000: probate, 15 Feb 1867, *CGPLA Eng. & Wales*

Briot, Nicholas (1579–1646), coin- and seal-engraver and medallist, was born at Damblein in Bassigny, duchy of Bar, France, the son of Didier Briot, merchant. Between 1606 and 1625 he was engraver-general at the Paris mint, where he experimented with machinery for striking coins, a subject which was to dominate his thinking for the rest of his life. Having set out his proposals in 1615 in a treatise entitled 'Raisons, moyens, et propositions pour faire toutes les monnaies du royaume', in 1617 he engaged in a trial with the traditional moneyers who struck by hand. Briot proposed using 'a single man, to turn out more blanks in one day, than twenty ordinary workers using the hammer could do; and similarly to coin more pieces in one day than ten hand moneyers could fashion' (Sellwood, 108–9). Given both gold and silver to work on, he did his best, producing pattern pieces which today are extremely rare, but in the end he could not match the production performance of the time-honoured processes and, notwithstanding the support of King Louis XIII, failed to transform the minting process.

Frustrated by this, constantly under attack for his dereliction of duty by also working as engraver-general for the duke of Lorraine between 1611 and 1624, 'and pressed hard by his creditors, Briot fled to England in 1625' (*DNB*), where he sought and obtained the patronage of Charles

I. In April 1626 a payment to him of £100 was authorized for making pieces of largesse; then, on 16 December 1628, he was made a free denizen with monopolistic rights at £250 a year to draw and engrave the royal effigy. On 22 January 1634 he was appointed outside the establishment (that is to say, the normally accredited staff of mint officials) chief engraver of the mint, at £50 a year, a sum which in fact he drew from 25 December 1632 to 25 December 1646, the year of his death. During this time he produced, in his own workshop in the Tower, in addition to his engraving work, two small issues of coins: the first, in 1631–2, totalled 26 lb 11 oz in gold and 221 lb 4 oz in silver; the second, in 1638–9, was only in silver, 930 lb 1 oz in all. These coins were distinctive because not only did they carry Briot's own mark—a B, or a B with a flower or anchor—but they were struck by machinery, the larger ones in a rocker press, the smaller ones in a screw press. Although Briot never succeeded in his aim of ensuring that all English coins were struck by machinery rather than the hammer, he made a vital contribution in that transition; indeed, it may be conjectured that, but for him, the entire mechanization of the mint under Charles II would not have come as surely and as quickly as it did.

Briot also made an important contribution to the Scottish coinage. In 1632 he was sent north to issue copper pence and twopences. In the event, no pence were struck but twopences, or turners as they were known, were, in large quantities. The use of cylinder presses meant that these were the first Scottish coins to be made by machinery rather than by the hammer. In 1635 he was made master of the mint in Edinburgh, and in 1637 he introduced mechanized coin production using both screw and rocker presses. In the same year his office was renewed, with the difference that in future he was to hold it jointly with his son-in-law, John Falconer.

Having lost control of the Tower mint in London in 1642, Charles I planned to establish mints at Shrewsbury and York, and it was to York that Briot was summoned. Unfortunately for all concerned, his equipment was seized on board ship off Scarborough on 15 July, and there was a delay of some months before coining actually began, probably in January 1643. Once again he used cylinder presses, but this time the coins were in silver and this thus became 'the only instance of this method being used in Britain for the production of a precious metal coinage' (Besly, 'York mint', 214). His widow was subsequently to claim that Briot also did some work for the Oxford mint, but there only the hammer was employed.

Briot's medallic work was never his main concern. In France his principal pieces were executed in 1610 for the coronation of Louis XIII while in England, notwithstanding his medals to mark the English coronation of Charles I in 1626 and the Scottish coronation in 1633, his outstanding works were the *Dominion of the Sea* medal (1630), the *Return to London* (1633), the *Prince of Wales* (1638), and *Peace or War* (1643). Although Briot also produced seals in both France and England, it was the English seals, notably the great seal, which were the more important.

Briot's will was written in the parish of St Martin-in-the-Fields, London, on 22 December 1646 and it was at that church, after presumably dying in London, that he was buried on 25 December. He was twice married, first to Pauline Nisse (d. 1608), and second, in 1611, to Esther Petau, who survived him. She was subsequently paid £258 10s. for his coinage equipment, and in 1662 she petitioned the government for £3000 which she claimed was owing to her husband at the time of his death.

C. E. CHALLIS

Sources M. Jones, 'Nicolas Briot', *The Medal*, 12 (1988), 4–9 · E. Besly, 'Rotary coining in Britain', *Metallurgy in numismatics*, ed. M. M. Archibald and M. R. Cowell, vol. 3, Royal Numismatic Society, Special Publication 24 (1993), 118–27 · E. Besly, 'The York mint of Charles I', *British Numismatic Society*, 54 (1984), 210–41 · L. Forrer, *Biographical dictionary of medallists*, 1 (1904) · H. Farquhar, 'Nicholas Briot and the civil war', *Numismatic Chronicle*, 4th ser., 14 (1914), 169–235 · H. Symonds, 'English mint engravers of the Tudor and Stuart periods', *Numismatic Chronicle*, 4th ser., 13 (1913), 349–77 · H. Symonds, 'Charles I: the trials of the pyx, the mint-marks and the mint accounts', *Numismatic Chronicle*, 4th ser., 10 (1910), 388–97 · C. E. Challis, ed., *A new history of the royal mint* (1992) · C. E. Challis, 'Mint officials and moneyers of the Stuart period', *British Numismatic Journal*, 59 (1989), 157–97 · R. B. K. Stevenson, 'The "sterling" turners of Charles I, 1632–9', *British Numismatic Journal*, 29 (1959), 128–51 · D. Sellwood, 'The trial of Nicholas Briot', *British Numismatic Journal*, 56 (1986), 108–23 · M. Mazerolle, 'Nicolas Briot', *Revue Belge de Numismatique*, 60 (1904), 191–203 · DNB
Archives Archives Nationales, Paris | PRO, state papers domestic, etc.

Briouze, Giles de (c.1170–1215), bishop of Hereford, was one of the oldest among the sixteen children born to William (III) de *Briouze (d. 1211), and his wife, Matilda de St Valéry (d. 1210). Loretta de *Briouze was his sister. William held numerous lordships in Normandy, England, and Wales, notably in Brecon and Upper Gwent in the southern Welsh marches. It is likely that William and Matilda married before 1170 and that Giles was born in or around that year. It is not known how or where he was educated, though it is conceivable that he received some of his schooling from one of his father's clerks, Master Hugh de Mapenore, whom he later made dean of Hereford.

The bishopric of Hereford fell vacant on the death of William de Vere on Christmas eve 1198, and an attempt by Hereford Cathedral chapter to elect Walter Map (d. 1209/10) as his successor in 1199 was thwarted by the death of Richard I. At the start of John's reign William de Briouze was high in the king's favour; in addition to other benefits, John bestowed the bishopric of Hereford early in 1200 on William's son Giles to increase the family's standing in the Welsh marches yet further. Giles was consecrated on 24 September 1200 in St Catherine's Chapel at Westminster, and during his first four years as bishop he continued to receive signs of John's favour, including the grant of an annual fair at Lydbury North in 1201 and the right to take sixteen deer in the forest of Malvern in 1204.

Briouze was an active and efficient diocesan. Nearly fifty of his episcopal *acta* survive, and although most of these, as would be expected, are charters requested by beneficiaries, many of them show knowledge of and interest in canon law. To support him in his administration Briouze employed at any one time about four clerks with the title *magister*, in addition to chaplains and junior clerks. One of the *magistri* was Walter Map's nephew Philip. In addition to his duties as diocesan, Briouze was fairly often appointed to act as papal judge-delegate. The cases included the dispute between the priories of Llanthony Prima (Llanthony in Wales) and Llanthony Secunda (Lanthony by Gloucester) over the division between the two houses of their widely scattered properties and of their rights and their muniments. Briouze, acting with two fellow bishops, Mauger of Worcester (*d.* 1212) and Eustace of Ely (*d.* 1215), attempted to settle this dispute in 1205.

As bishop of Hereford, however, Briouze was also a marcher lord, and through this and his family connections was drawn into Welsh border politics. He was involved in the dispute between his family and Gwenwynwyn of Powys (*d.* 1216?), settled by King John in August 1204. Then, late in 1206, King John began to take action against the hitherto loyal William de Briouze, and in 1208 he appointed his mercenary captain, Gerard d'Athée (*d.* 1213), sheriff of Herefordshire, the better to threaten William's lordship in Brecon and Giles's own position as bishop of Hereford. In late April and early May 1208 Briouze seems to have been forced to travel with John, presumably as surety for his father's good conduct. Later in May he fled to France, where he formed part of a group of English exiles seeking the support of King Philip Augustus against John. It is likely that Briouze, whose feelings against John must have been further embittered by his treatment of his mother and eldest brother, who were starved to death in Windsor Castle in 1210, assisted Llywelyn ab Iorwerth (*d.* 1240) to make his treaty of alliance with Philip Augustus in 1212. In order to support himself in France, Briouze seems to have offered his services to French bishops as a substitute: in May 1210 he dedicated a chapel at St Riquier at the request of Bishop Richard of Amiens.

After John had made terms with the papacy in May 1213 Briouze, with the other exiled bishops, returned to England. John visited Hereford late in 1213 and granted him seisin of the manor of Tetbury, and when John left Hereford, Briouze accompanied him to Guildford. Early in 1214, however, John ordered Briouze and three other bishops to keep the peace. Briouze's main grievance was that his family's lands were being withheld from his young nephews, the sons of his eldest brother, William. Negotiations between the two parties broke down in May, after which John gave Briouze's Gloucestershire lands to Henry fitz Count (*d.* 1222). During the summer Briouze joined the baronial opposition to John, and he and Llywelyn ab Iorwerth won the support of all the inhabitants of the marches except Hugh de Mortimer, whose castle of Cwm Aran in Maelienydd they razed. Peace was made in October by the papal legate Nicolò of Tusculum, at a council held at Wigmore.

Once more, Briouze returned to John's entourage, accompanying his ruler to Worcester in December and to London in January. However, his sympathies must certainly have been with the other side, and it was probably his influence that led to the inclusion of a clause condemning Gerard d'Athée in Magna Carta. Following Llywelyn's seizure of Shrewsbury on 17 May 1215, Briouze rose in rebellion and he and his brother Reginald took possession of their family's castles in Brecon, Giles himself capturing Brecon, Hay, Radnor, Builth, and Blaenllyfni. On 21 October Briouze agreed to pay a fine of 9000 marks to John in return for the restoration of his lands, castles, and the custody of his nephews, but before the necessary arrangements could be made Briouze died on 17 November at Worcester. He was buried in Hereford Cathedral, where his tomb was marked by an effigy in the late thirteenth century.   JULIA BARROW

Sources *Chancery records* (RC) · Llanthony cartulary A2, PRO, Chancery, Masters' Exhibits, C115 K1/6681, fols. 247v–248 · Bibliothèque Nationale, Paris, MS fr. 12036, 34–5 · R. W. Banks, ed., 'Cartularium prioratus s. Johannis evang. de Brecon', *Archaeologia Cambrensis*, 4th ser., 14 (1883), 18–49, 137–68, 221–36, 274–311, esp. 35 · J. Barrow, ed., *Hereford, 1079–1234*, English Episcopal Acta, 7 (1993), 45–6, 59–60, 81–100, 106–7, 112–13, 181–224, 304, 317–19 · Dugdale, *Monasticon*, new edn, 6.350 · J. H. Round, ed., *Calendar of documents preserved in France, illustrative of the history of Great Britain and Ireland* (1899), 461 · S. Painter, *The reign of King John* (1949), 43–4, 123, 206, 240–41, 275 · F. M. Powicke, 'Loretta, countess of Leicester', *Historical essays in honour of James Tait*, ed. J. G. Edwards, V. H. Galbraith, and E. F. Jacob (1933), 247–72, esp. 248, 271–2 · P. Lindley, 'Retrospective effigies, the past and lies', *Medieval art, architecture and archaeology in Hereford*, ed. D. Whitehead, British Archaeological Association Conference Transactions, 15 (1995), 114 · *Fasti Angl., 1066–1300*, [Hereford], 5, 151
Likenesses effigy, *c.*1295, Hereford Cathedral

Briouze, Loretta de, countess of Leicester (*d.* in or after 1266), noblewoman and recluse, was one of the children of William (III) de *Briouze (*d.* 1211) and Matilda de St Valéry (*d.* 1210). Her father was a great man in the Anglo-Welsh marches, and four of her five sisters who survived into adulthood married Welsh or marcher lords; notably Matilda married *Gruffudd ap Rhys, the son and heir of *Rhys ap Gruffudd, the Lord Rhys of Deheubarth, about 1197. Moreover her brother Reginald in 1215 married Gwladus, the daughter of *Llywelyn ab Iorwerth, as his second wife. But Loretta herself married Robert de *Breteuil, earl of Leicester (*d.* 1204), in 1196, and for her marriage portion received the manor of Tawstock near Barnstaple. Her early life was thus at the centre of the Norman-Angevin political world. Her husband was a powerful earl and a hero of the crusades, her family well connected. Following her husband's death, and after much discussion, she received dower lands in Hampshire, Berkshire, and Dorset to the value of £140 per annum in 1205.

The decline and fall of the family of Briouze, a process which began at the end of 1207 and led to the starving to death of Loretta's mother and brother William in Windsor Castle in 1210, and to the death of her father as a political refugee in France in 1211, fundamentally affected Loretta's security and well-being. In November 1207 she was obliged to promise not to marry again without the king's consent, and probably withdrew to France shortly afterwards; her lands were taken into the king's hand. By 1214 she was back in England, and once more promised not to remarry without royal licence, thereby recovering her confiscated estates. She subsequently gave land at Tawstock to the sisters of the order of St John at Buckland Sororum, Somerset. By early in 1221, however, Loretta had taken steps that served to secure her future, in the one way that was open to her; probably acting under the influence of Archbishop Stephen Langton, she took a vow of chastity, and became a recluse at Hackington, near Canterbury. Her preparations had begun no later than 20 June 1219, when she granted her dower lands for three years to the bishop of Winchester and Philip d'Aubigny. The rent was probably intended to finance her anchorage, in which she may well have been attended by two female attendants and certainly retained a manservant.

Loretta's sister Annora had become a recluse at Iffley by 1232. Two members of one family therefore entered upon a not uncommon path for powerful aristocratic women, one which allowed them to retain some control over the direction of their own affairs, as well as to pursue fashionable religious ideas. Loretta's retirement did not preclude her using her influence for the poor and needy; for instance, she might obtain a pardon for a man who had killed by misadventure. And she acted to help the establishment of the Franciscan order in England, being described in the treatise *De adventu Fratrum Minorum* as cherishing the friars as a mother does her children. A story in a thirteenth-century French manuscript suggests that she felt a particular devotion to the Virgin Mary. But even in the last years of her long life she might still be called upon to become involved in national politics, albeit indirectly. On 29 April 1265 Simon de Montfort asked her to help resolve an issue of constitutional significance concerning the 'rights and liberties' of the stewardship of England—an office once held by Loretta's husband, and now exercised by Montfort himself. It is not known how, or even whether, she replied. Loretta de Briouze died on 4 March, either in 1266 or shortly afterwards, and was buried in the church of St Stephen, Hackington.

SUSAN M. JOHNS

Sources F. M. Powicke, 'Loretta, countess of Leicester', *Historical essays in honour of James Tait*, ed. J. G. Edwards, V. H. Galbraith, and E. F. Jacob (1933), 247–72 · GEC, *Peerage*, new edn, 7.533–7 · *Fratris Thomae vulgo dicti de Eccleston tractatus de adventu Fratrum Minorum in Angliam*, ed. A. G. Little (1951)

Briouze [Braose], **Philip de** (d. before 1201), soldier, was the son of Philip de Briouze (d. 1134×55). Along with his brother, William (II) de Briouze, lord of Bramber, Sussex, he accompanied Henry II to Ireland in 1171–2, and was assigned by Henry to the garrison at Wexford. In 1177 he received a speculative grant of the kingdom of Limerick, the area of Thomond in north Munster. His attempt in that year to take possession failed after the citizens of Limerick, expecting the Anglo-Norman forces to storm the walls successfully, set the town on fire. The kingdom was to be granted to his nephew, William (III) de *Briouze, lord of Bramber, by King John on 12 January 1201.

J. H. ROUND, rev. M. T. FLANAGAN

Sources Giraldus Cambrensis, *Expugnatio Hibernica / The conquest of Ireland*, ed. and trans. A. B. Scott and F. X. Martin (1978), 104–5, 178–9, 184–7 · W. Stubbs, ed., *Gesta regis Henrici secundi Benedicti*

abbatis: the chronicle of the reigns of Henry II and Richard I, AD 1169–1192, 2 vols., Rolls Series, 49 (1867), 1.163, 172–3 · *Chronica magistri Rogeri de Hovedene*, ed. W. Stubbs, 2, Rolls Series, 51 (1869), 135 · T. D. Hardy, ed., *Rotuli chartarum in Turri Londinensi asservati*, RC, 36 (1837)

Briouze [Braose], **William (III) de** (d. 1211), magnate, was a landholder of the Welsh and Irish marches, whose friendship with King John won him rich rewards, but whose dramatic fall from favour and relentless pursuit by John contributed to baronial distrust and fear of the king.

Norman origins The name derives from Briouze-St Gervais, near Argentin, where William held his ancestors' three fees until the loss of Normandy in 1203–4. William (III) was the son of William (II) de Briouze and Bertha, daughter and coheir of Miles of Gloucester, earl of Hereford (d. 1143). William the Conqueror had granted the castle and rape of Bramber, Sussex, to William (III)'s great-grandfather, whose son Philip de Briouze (d. 1134×55) took the Welsh lordships of Radnor and Builth before the end of the eleventh century; Philip also acquired a claim to the baronies of Totnes and Barnstaple, Devon, through his marriage to Aenor, daughter of Juhel of Totnes. Philip's son, William (II) de Briouze (d. 1192/3), held in addition to his patrimony the lordship of half of Barnstaple, acquired through his mother, coheir to the barony. In 1158 he had offered the king a fine of 1000 marks for twenty-eight knights' fees as his mother's share of her inheritance, and when he died he still owed £430. William (II)'s marriage brought him the lordships of Brecon and Abergavenny on the southern Welsh marches as his wife's share after the deaths of her two brothers. William (II) de Briouze concentrated his energies on his Welsh marcher lands, serving Henry II as sheriff of Herefordshire, 1173–5. The marriage of his daughter Sibyl to William de Ferrers, earl of Derby (d. 1190), indicates the status that the Briouze family enjoyed.

William (III) de Briouze married Matilda (d. 1210), the daughter of Bernard de St Valéry, lord of Beckley, Oxfordshire. He continued to add to his family's holdings until he held as fiefs or custodies 325 knights' fees and sixteen castles in England, Wales, and Ireland, reaping a yearly income of over £800. He lacked only the title of earl to denote his ranking among the greatest magnates. By 1194 he had gained the barony of Kington, Herefordshire, which Adam de Port had forfeited to the crown in 1171. Port had offered a £200 fine, never paid, to regain his lands, and somehow the barony's twenty-two or twenty-three knights' fees passed into Briouze's hands. Meanwhile another Adam of Port (d. 1213), baron of Basing, Hampshire, who also traced his ancestry to the Domesday lord of Kington, married Sibyl, widow of the earl of Derby, and apparently an arrangement was made whereby he would hold a portion of Kington as a fief of his wife's brother William. In 1195 Briouze made an agreement with Oliver de Tracy, who had a claim to the barony of Barnstaple through his mother, sister of Briouze's grandmother Aenor. Tracy acknowledged Briouze as lord of Barnstaple, and he held his half as Briouze's tenant, receiving in return for his agreement an annual payment of £20. Briouze also enjoyed temporary custodies; as early as 1190, before his father's death, he offered 1000 marks for custody of the land and heir of Gilbert of Monmouth, who came of age in 1205.

Servant to Richard I and King John Briouze's career in the king's service began under Richard I; he served as sheriff of Herefordshire almost continuously from 1191, when he replaced Henry de Longchamp, brother of the fallen chancellor, until removed by King John in October 1200; and he participated in the general eyre of 1194/5, sitting as a justice in Staffordshire. Throughout Richard's reign he was active in defending and extending England's frontier against the Welsh. In 1190 a royal writ allowed him to spend over half his 1000 mark fine for custody of the barony of Monmouth, fortifying three castles at Carmarthen, Swansea, and Llawhaden against Welsh attack. In July 1198 the Welsh besieged him at Painscastle or Maud's Castle, lying to the south of Radnor and Builth, until he was rescued by Geoffrey fitz Peter, the justiciar, who routed the Welsh in battle on 13 August. During Richard I's reign Briouze served in the king's army in Normandy in 1194, and he was again with the king on the continent in the spring of 1199. He was at Châlus on 5 April 1199, the day before Richard received his fatal wound.

Briouze played an important part in winning John's acceptance over his nephew Arthur, count of Brittany, as heir to the kingdom of England; in John's early years he became an almost constant companion of the king, one of the most frequent witnesses to his charters. Briouze continued to play an important role in Welsh matters under John. He seems to have watched over Walter de Lacy's Welsh marcher barony, while Walter, his son-in-law, occupied in Ireland with his honour of Meath, looked out in turn for his father-in-law's Irish interests. In July 1207 Briouze took custody of the Lacy castle at Ludlow, Shropshire. John encouraged his expansion of territory in both Wales and Ireland as a counterbalance to William (I) Marshal's power in those regions, and he showered favours on him; for example, he named Briouze's second son bishop of Hereford in 1200. Under King John, Briouze continued to add to his holdings. In 1200 the king granted him all the lands that he could conquer from his Welsh enemies to increase the size of his barony of Radnor. Briouze continued to hold custodies under John, and in 1202 won wardship of the heir to the barony of Salwarpe, Shropshire, and to the Welsh marcher lordships of Glamorgan and Gower. The next year he took control of the barony of Great Torrington, Devon, and during the interdict he held two priories for the king. Also in 1203 the king granted Briouze additional Welsh territory, Gower with the castle of Swansea, and, in Herefordshire, the castle and manor of Kington. The following year John granted him the Surrey estates of Alan Trenchemer, a famous sea captain. In 1206 a lawsuit awarded him the barony of Totnes; the tenant, Henry de Nonant, recognized Briouze as his lord and held his part of it as a fief. William paid generously for this judgment: he offered the king £100 to have the case heard before him, also a gift of 300 cows, 30 bulls, and 10 horses for expediting the plea, and 700 marks 'if it indeed

should be won' (*Rotuli de oblatis et finibus*, 45). The same year Briouze offered a fine of 800 marks plus a number of horses and hunting dogs for having the three Welsh castles at Grosmont, Skenfrith, and Whitecastle in Gwent, holding them by the service of two knights.

Under John, Briouze expanded his holdings into Ireland. Henry II had granted Philip de Briouze, his grandfather, the honour of Limerick, but Philip had never acted to take possession of it. In January 1201 John regranted Limerick to Briouze as a fee of sixty knights in exchange for an offering of 5000 marks payable at 500 marks annually; excluded from the grant were the city of Limerick and the fees of William de Burgh. Later, however, Briouze received custody of the city of Limerick as well, holding it at a farm of 100 marks.

King John's confidence lost In September 1202 the king forgave all debts that William (II) de Briouze had owed to Henry II and that Briouze himself owed to Richard I; the following spring Briouze was forgiven a £50 debt to Jewish moneylenders, and in 1204 the king pardoned him of £825 owed for his son's marriage to a coheir of the Limesy barony. None the less he continued to accumulate new debts, most notably his fine of 500 marks for Limerick; and like most barons, he made little attempt to pay off his promises made to the king for favours. In 1210 he still owed £2865 of his fine for Limerick and £350 for three Welsh castles, plus assorted debts as several years' farm from the city of Limerick. These large crown debts made him vulnerable, should the king decide to demand full payment, subjecting him to the law of the exchequer: once John viewed Briouze as an over-mighty subject whose power posed a threat to royal authority, his debts could provide the means for bringing him to heel. Meiler fitz Henry, justiciar in Ireland until 1208, was encouraging the king's suspicion of Briouze.

The king evidently had a reason beyond debt collection for his mounting distrust of Briouze, however, and that was the latter's knowledge of circumstances surrounding the death of the king's nephew, Arthur of Brittany, his rival for the Angevin inheritance. When Briouze's wife, Matilda, made an indiscreet statement about John's murder of young Arthur in 1208 and refused to hand over her eldest son to the king as a hostage out of fear for his life, John could no longer trust in her husband's silence. Briouze was almost certainly with John at Rouen at the time of Arthur's disappearance from the Tower in early April 1203, and he may even have encouraged John to end the boy's life. Two sources for young Arthur's death, the annals of Margam Abbey in Glamorgan and the *Philippide* of Guillaume le Breton, reflect information supplied to the authors by Briouze; he had close ties to Margam Abbey, and its annals supply the fullest account of any chronicle of Arthur's death. Whatever the king's motive, he began to move toward Briouze's destruction in 1208, and in 1212 he released a letter, addressed 'to all who may read it', describing and justifying his actions. This royal statement, attested by a dozen great men, sought to present the pursuit of Briouze and his family as within the letter of the law, as 'according to the custom of England and the law of the exchequer' (Rymer, *Foedera*, 1, i.107–8), because of his supposed resistance to paying in full his fine of 500 marks for Limerick and the farm of the city of Limerick. It claimed that Briouze had unlawfully removed chattels from his lands in England before they could be distrained for debt. Also, as part of the royal harassment of the family, Briouze's eldest son was amerced 300 marks for forest offences in 1208. In the spring Briouze's wife and other relatives asked the king for a meeting; they met at Hereford, where William surrendered his marcher castles of Hay, Brecon, and Radnor, mortgaged his English lands, and surrendered hostages. The king's letter claimed that once the castles were in royal hands, Briouze and two of his sons attacked them and, failing to take them, carried the warfare into Herefordshire, burning half the town of Leominster. Some time during the summer Briouze was summoned to court, but excused himself on account of illness.

Arrests and death Once the Briouzes turned to violence their fate was sealed, and John ordered the family's arrest. Briouze, his wife, and two of their sons—William (IV) and Reginald—fled to Ireland. Soon after proclamation of the interdict on England in the spring of 1208, a third son, Giles, bishop of Hereford, left the kingdom for France. Early in 1209 Briouze took refuge with William Marshal, whose quarrel with King John had led him to retire to his Irish honour of Leinster. When the Irish justiciar commanded that Briouze be surrendered to him, the Marshal disingenuously declared that he had merely given shelter to 'his lord' (*Histoire de Guillaume le Maréchal*, 2.147), knowing nothing of the king's quarrel with Briouze. After three weeks, he escorted his visitors to their kinsmen, Walter de Lacy and his brother Hugh, in Meath. According to John's letter Hugh de Lacy promised that William de Briouze would make satisfaction to the king, and that if he did not, then he would no longer give him refuge in Ireland. Briouze then went to John in Wales, where the king was gathering forces for his invasion of Ireland. Sheltering of the fugitive William de Briouze by the Anglo-Norman lords in Ireland had been a major factor in John's preparation of his Irish expedition for the summer of 1210. Briouze offered 40,000 marks for the king's goodwill, but John refused the fine unless his wife, Matilda de St Valéry, was turned over to him. In a two-month campaign the king crushed most of his Anglo-Norman opposition in Ireland. He expropriated William de Briouze's lands and those of the Lacy brothers for having sheltered him; he did not seize the property of William Marshal, who had also given refuge to Briouze, but demanded hostages from him. Matilda and William (IV) de Briouze, her eldest son, fled from Carrickfergus Castle in Ulster to Scotland in company with the Lacys; there they fell into the hands of a Scottish lord, Duncan of Carrick, who handed them over to the English king. Matilda renewed her husband's offer to John of 40,000 marks, and in September 1210 William met the king at Bristol, where he accepted the arrangement. No baron could possibly have raised such a huge

fine, and when Matilda admitted that she and her husband could not pay, John proceeded to have William outlawed by the ancient process in the county court. William de Briouze fled to France to join his son Giles, already in exile there; it was probably then that the French court learned the details of Arthur of Brittany's death.

Briouze died at Corbeil outside Paris on 4 September 1211, and was buried in the abbey of St Victoire at Paris. Stephen Langton, in the city awaiting settlement of the Canterbury succession crisis, is said to have assisted at the funeral. John had had Briouze's wife and eldest son imprisoned at either Windsor or Corfe Castle, where they were deliberately starved to death, dying before the end of 1210. John's hounding of this family exposed his cruelty to the English barons, and his equating the harsh law of the exchequer with English custom heightened their fears of his arbitrary rule.

Children and decline of the Briouzes William de Briouze and his wife, Matilda, had at least four sons and five daughters. William (IV), their eldest son, died in 1210 imprisoned with his mother. He had married Matilda, daughter of Richard de Clare, earl of Hertford, and they had four sons, who remained imprisoned in Corfe Castle until 1218. Briouze's second son, Giles de *Briouze, was elected bishop of Hereford in September 1200 and died in November 1215. During the baronial rebellion against King John, he and his younger brother Reginald allied with the prince of north Wales, Llywelyn ab Iorwerth, in order to recover their family's lost lands. Giles was reconciled with King John shortly before his death, however, and on 21 October 1215 the king granted him his father's confiscated lands in return for a fine of an unspecified amount. Giles's death the next month left Briouze's third son, Reginald (*d.* 1227/8), as head of the family; he had gained possession of his father's lands by May 1216. He married first Graecia, daughter of William Brewer, a powerful figure in south-western England and one of John's closest counsellors; his second marriage was in 1215 to Gwladus, daughter of Llywelyn ab Iorwerth, cementing his alliance with the Welsh leader. In 1219 Reginald was sued by the widow of William (IV) de Briouze and her eldest son, John, recently freed from prison. John had gained possession of Bramber and some minor Briouze holdings, and he was seeking the family's possessions on the Welsh marches, but Reginald held on to all of them except Gower. A fourth son of William (III) de Briouze and Matilda de St Valéry, John, married Mabel de Limesy, widow of Hugh Bardolf and coheir to the barony of Cavendish, Suffolk; his father offered the king £1000 in 1203 for the marriage. Briouze married two of his daughters to other Welsh marcher lords. Margaret married Walter de Lacy, lord of Weobley, Herefordshire, and of Meath, Ireland, and Annora married Hugh (III) de Mortimer, baron of Wigmore, Herefordshire. A third daughter, Matilda or Maud, married Gruffudd ap Rhys (*d.* 1201), the son of the Lord Rhys of Deheubarth, while Loretta de *Briouze married Robert de *Breteuil, fourth earl of Leicester. In 1210 Annora was taken prisoner with her mother and eldest brother, but King John ordered her release on 27 October

1214 at the request of the papal legate. Possibly John felt some remorse for his harrying of the Briouzes, for a few days before his death, he authorized Margaret to found a religious house for the souls of her father, mother, and brother. The Briouze name faded from history in the early 1230s. William (V) de Briouze, son of Reginald, was hanged by Prince Llywelyn in 1230, leaving four daughters as coheirs, and John, son of William (IV), died without heirs in 1232. RALPH V. TURNER

Sources Chancery records · Pipe rolls · *Chronica magistri Rogeri de Hovedene*, ed. W. Stubbs, 4 vols., Rolls Series, 51 (1868–71) · *Ann. mon.*, vol. 1 · *Rogeri de Wendover liber qui dicitur flores historiarum*, ed. H. G. Hewlett, 3 vols., Rolls Series, [84] (1886–9) · H. S. Sweetman and G. F. Handcock, eds., *Calendar of documents relating to Ireland*, 5 vols., PRO (1875–86), vol. 1 · D. Walker, *Medieval Wales* (1990) · GEC, *Peerage* · I. J. Sanders, *English baronies: a study of their origin and descent, 1086–1327* (1960) · I. W. Rowlands, 'William de Braose and the lordship of Brecon', *BBCS*, 30 (1982–3), 122–33 · P. Meyer, ed., *L'histoire de Guillaume le Maréchal*, 3 vols. (Paris, 1891–1901) · Rymer, *Foedera* · T. D. Hardy, ed., *Rotuli de oblatis et finibus*, RC (1835) · F. M. Powicke, 'Loretta, countess of Leicester', *Historical essays in honour of James Tait*, ed. J. G. Edwards, V. H. Galbraith, and E. F. Jacob (1933), 247–72

Brisbane, Sir Charles (1769?–1829), naval officer, fourth but eldest surviving son of Admiral John Brisbane (d. 10 Dec 1807) and brother of Sir James *Brisbane (1774–1826), was in 1779 entered on board the *Alcide*, commanded by his father, was present at the defeat of the Spanish fleet off Cape St Vincent, and at the relief of Gibraltar in January 1780, and afterwards in the West Indies. At the end of 1781 he was placed on board the *Hercules* with Captain Savage, and was present in the action of Dominica on 12 April 1782, where he was badly wounded by a splinter. He continued serving during the peace, and after the Spanish armament in 1790 was promoted to the rank of lieutenant on 22 November. In 1793 he was in the frigate *Meleager*, in which he went out to the Mediterranean, and was actively employed on shore at Toulon, and afterwards in Corsica, both at San Fiorenzo and at the siege of Bastia, under the immediate orders of Nelson, and like him lost an eye after a severe wound in the head inflicted by the small fragments of an iron shot. He afterwards served for a short time in the *Britannia*, bearing the flag of Lord Hood, by whom he was specially promoted to the command of the sloop *Tarleton* on 1 July 1794; he served in her during the remainder of that and the following year in the squadron acting in the Gulf of Genoa, under the immediate orders of Nelson.

In the autumn of 1795 Brisbane was sent from Gibraltar to convoy two troopships to Barbados. On his way thither he fell in with a Dutch squadron. Finding the Dutch were bound for the Cape, he set aside his orders, and his initiative led to the capture of the Dutch ships on 18 August 1796. His action received official approval and he was promoted to the command of one of the captured vessels. But he had previously, on 22 July, been promoted by Sir John Jervis, the commander-in-chief in the Mediterranean, under whose orders he had sailed, and he also received the thanks of the Admiralty. He continued on the Cape station

in command of the frigate *Oiseau*, and was in her at St Helena when a dangerous mutiny broke out on board. This was quelled by his firm measures, and he was shortly afterwards recalled to the Cape to take command of the *Tremendous*, Rear-Admiral Pringle's flagship, which was also threatened with extreme danger by the mutinous spirit on board. In the course of 1798 he returned to England with Pringle in the frigate *Crescent* and in 1801 was appointed to the frigate *Doris*, one of the squadron off Brest, under Admiral Cornwallis. During the short peace he commanded the frigate *Trent* and the *Sanspareil* in the West Indies. He was afterwards moved into the *Goliath*, in which on his way home he was nearly lost in a hurricane.

In 1805 Brisbane was appointed to the frigate *Arethusa*, which he took to the West Indies. Early in 1806 he had the misfortune to run the ship ashore among the Colorados Rocks, near the north-west end of Cuba, and she was refloated only by throwing all her guns overboard. In this defenceless condition she fell in with a Spanish line-of-battle ship off Havana; but the Spanish captain, ignorant of the *Arethusa*'s weakness, did not consider his vessel a match for even a 38-gun frigate, and ran in under the guns of the Moro Castle. Having refitted at Jamaica, the *Arethusa* was again off Havana in August, and on the 23rd, in company with the *Anson* (44 guns), captured the Spanish frigate *Pomona*, anchored near a battery mounting eleven 36-pounders, and supported by ten gunboats. The gunboats were all destroyed and the battery blown up, apparently by some accident to the furnaces for heating shot, by which the *Arethusa* had been set on fire, but without any serious consequences, though she had two men killed, and thirty-two, including Captain Brisbane, wounded.

On 1 January 1807 Brisbane, still in the *Arethusa*, with three other frigates, having been sent off Curaçao, reduced all the forts and captured the island without serious difficulty or loss. The fortifications, both by position and armament, were exceedingly strong, but the Dutch were unprepared for a vigorous assault, and were, it was surmised, still sleeping off the effects of a new year's eve carousal, when, at dawn, the British squadron sailed into the harbour. For this success Brisbane was knighted in 1807, and he, as well as the other three captains, received a gold medal. He continued in command of the *Arethusa* until near the end of 1808, when he was transferred to the *Blake* (74 guns), but was almost immediately afterwards appointed governor of St Vincent, which office he held, without any further sea service, until his death. On 2 January 1815 he was nominated a KCB, and he attained his flag rank on 12 August 1819. He had married Sarah, daughter of Sir James Patey of Reading, and left several children. He died on St Vincent in December 1829. Brisbane was an officer of genuine ability—his initiative and resource marked him out from the majority of his contemporaries.

J. K. LAUGHTON, rev. ANDREW LAMBERT

Sources A. C. Burns, *History of the British West Indies* (1954) · *GM*, 1st ser., 100/1 (1830) · J. Marshall, *Royal naval biography*, 1/2 (1823), 730–43 · J. Ralfe, *The naval biography of Great Britain*, 4 vols. (1828)

Archives NRA Scotland, priv. coll., corresp. and MSS, incl. duplicate dispatches and memorials from St Vincent

Likenesses H. R. Cook, stipple, pubd 1808 (after J. Northcote), NPG · H. R. Cook, lithograph, repro. in Clowes, 5 (1900), 236 · W. Greatbach, engraving, repro. in James, *Naval history*, 4 (1837), 352 · J. Northcote, oils, Scot. NPG · J. Northcote, portrait, repro. in Clowes, 5 (1900), 236 · J. Northcote, portrait, repro. in James, *Naval history*, 4 (1837), 352

Brisbane, Sir James (1774–1826), naval officer, fifth son of Admiral John Brisbane (d. 10 Dec 1807) and brother of Rear-Admiral Sir Charles *Brisbane, entered the navy in 1787 on board the *Culloden*. After serving in various ships he was transferred to the *Queen Charlotte*, bearing the flag of Lord Howe, to whom he acted as signal-midshipman in the battle of 1 June 1794. He was made lieutenant on 23 September 1794, and served at the capture of the Cape of Good Hope. He was afterwards moved into the *Monarch*, Sir George Elphinstone's flagship, and was present in her at the capture of the Dutch squadron in Saldanha Bay on 18 August 1796. Sir George promoted Brisbane into one of the prizes, and soon afterwards moved him into the frigate *Daphne*, in command of which he returned to England. The promotion, however, was not confirmed until 27 May 1797. For the next four years he was on half pay. He married in 1800 the only daughter of Mr John Ventham, and they had one son and two daughters.

In 1801 Brisbane was appointed to the command of the sloop *Cruiser*, attached to the Baltic fleet under Sir Hyde Parker. He was more particularly attached to the division under Nelson, and on the nights of 30 and 31 March 1801 was in charge of the work of sounding and buoying the channels approaching Copenhagen. For these services he was promoted to post rank on 2 April 1801, and in the latter part of the year commanded the *Saturn* as flag-captain to Rear-Admiral Totty until the admiral's death, when the ship was paid off. From 1803 to 1805 he commanded the sea fencibles of Kent, and in 1807 the frigate *Alcmene* on the coast of Ireland and in the channel. In 1808 he was appointed to the *Belle Poule*, a 38-gun frigate, and was ordered by Lord Collingwood to take command of the squadron blockading Corfu. While so employed he captured, on 15 February 1809, the French frigate *Var*, which had tried to break the blockade. He was afterwards engaged in the capture of the Ionian Islands and the establishment of the septinsular republic. He continued in the Adriatic until the summer of 1811, capturing or destroying several of the enemy's small cruisers, and he repeatedly engaged with their batteries on different parts of the coast. In September 1812 Brisbane was appointed to the *Pembroke* in the Channel Fleet, and the following summer was again sent to the Mediterranean, where he was actively employed. In 1815 he again served in the Mediterranean, and in 1816 was Lord Exmouth's flag captain aboard the *Queen Charlotte* for the expedition against Algiers. After the bombardment on 27 August 1816 he was sent home with dispatches, and on 2 October was knighted. He had already been made a CB in June 1815. In 1825 he was appointed commander-in-chief in the East Indies with the local rank of commodore; he arrived there in time to direct the concluding operations of the First Anglo-Burmese War, for

which he was officially thanked by the governor-general in council. His health, however, had suffered severely, and he never fully recovered. He lingered for some months, and died at Penang, Malaya, on 19 December 1826. Brisbane was an officer of great experience in coastal bombardment, power projection and, latterly, riverine warfare.   J. K. Laughton, *rev.* Andrew Lambert

Sources D. Pope, *The great gamble: Nelson at Copenhagen* (1972) · C. N. Parkinson, *Edward Pellew, Viscount Exmouth, admiral of the red* (1934) · G. S. Graham, *Great Britain in the Indian Ocean: a study of maritime enterprise, 1810–1850* (1967) · J. Marshall, *Royal naval biography*, 2/1 (1824), 400 · W. James, *The naval history of Great Britain, from the declaration of war by France in 1793, to the accession of George IV*, [5th edn], 6 vols. (1859–60) · *GM*, 1st ser., 97/2 (1827)

Brisbane, John (c.1720–1776?), physician, was born in Scotland and graduated MD at Edinburgh in 1750. He became a licentiate of the Royal College of Physicians in 1766 and held the post of physician to the Middlesex Hospital, London, from 1758 until 1773, when he was superseded for being absent without leave. His name disappears from the college list in 1776. He was the author of *Select Cases in the Practice of Medicine* (1772) and *Anatomy of Painting: with an Introduction Giving a Short View of Picturesque Anatomy* (1769). This work contains the six *Tables* of Albinus, the *Anatomy* of Celsus, with notes, and the *Physiology* of Cicero.

[Anon.], *rev.* Caroline Overy

Sources Munk, *Roll* · I. Graef, 'John Brisbane, MD', *Diabetes*, 6 (1957), 196–202 · S. C. Lawrence, *Charitable knowledge: hospital pupils and practitioners in eighteenth-century London* (1996) · P. J. Wallis and R. V. Wallis, *Eighteenth century medics*, 2nd edn (1988)

Likenesses portrait, repro. in Graef, 'John Brisbane, MD', cover

Brisbane, Sir Thomas Makdougall, baronet (1773–1860), colonial governor and astronomer, was born at Brisbane House, Largs, Ayrshire, on 23 July 1773, the eldest son of Thomas Brisbane (1720?–1812) and his wife, Eleanor, daughter of Sir William Bruce of Stenhouse, Stirlingshire. Their second child, Mary, died unmarried at Bathgate, Somerset, on 31 March 1855; their youngest, Michael (1777–1802/3), followed his uncle Michael Bruce to India where he became a writer to the East India Company and died in Bombay. Thomas was educated at home, then at the University of Edinburgh, after which the brothers boarded at the technical school of Robert Thomson in Kensington.

Military career Thomas Brisbane became an ensign in the 38th foot on 9 April 1789, and accompanied his regiment to Ireland in 1790. There he became acquainted with Arthur Wellesley, future duke of Wellington. He advanced to lieutenant on 30 July 1791, left Dublin on securing a captaincy in an independent company of foot on 12 April 1793, and transferred to the 53rd foot on 1 January 1794 when he was already serving in the duke of York's expeditionary force to Flanders. He had been wounded at Famars on 18 May 1793, thus missing an engagement four days afterwards, but later that year fought at Dunkirk. In 1794–5 he was in action at Valenciennes, Nieuwpoort, Tournai, and during the retreat to Bremen. He returned to England with the 53rd in May 1795, was promoted major on 5 August, and in October went with the regiment to

Barbados. He took part in the capture of St Lucia and Trinidad, the suppression of civil disorder on St Vincent, and the failed invasion of Puerto Rico before returning home on sick leave in 1798. Two years later he sailed for Jamaica, having been appointed lieutenant-colonel in the 69th foot on 4 April 1800, but left on sick leave once more in 1803. When the 69th was ordered to India in September 1805 Brisbane chose instead to go on half pay, because of his health, in the York rangers.

Brisbane remained in the York rangers until 1814, though he was promoted colonel in the army on 25 July 1810. After eighteen months as an assistant adjutant-general in the Peninsula, in 1812 he took command of the 1st brigade of Lieutenant-General Thomas Picton's 3rd division, with the rank of brigadier-general. He spent part of the winter of 1812–13 in England on leave, returning to lead the brigade at the battles of Vitoria, the Pyrenees, Nivelle, Nive, Orthez, and Toulouse, where he was again wounded. He advanced to major-general on 4 June 1813, and, for his services in the Peninsula, received a gold cross with one clasp for Vitoria, the Pyrenees, Nivelle, Orthez, and Toulouse, and the silver war medal with one clasp for the Nive. Appointed KCB in 1814, he reached Canada with reinforcements in time to command a brigade during General Sir George Prevost's abortive attack on the American stronghold of Plattsburgh, on Lake Champlain, in September. He thus missed the battle of Waterloo but commanded a brigade, and for some time a division, in the army of occupation in France, and returned to Scotland when that force was withdrawn in 1818. On 15 November 1819 he married Anna Maria (1786–1862), daughter and heir of Sir Henry Hay Makdougall, baronet, in 1826 adding her maiden name to his. Their first child, Isabella Maria (1820–1849), was born at Glentoul, near Cork, and died at Brisbane.

Governor of New South Wales, 1821–1825 In November 1820, on the duke of Wellington's advice, Brisbane was appointed governor of New South Wales and the dependent territory of Van Diemen's Land, and on 1 December 1821 he succeeded Major-General Lachlan Macquarie. Macquarie had concentrated on raising the moral standard of the colony's inhabitants by building schools and churches, encouraging Bible societies, and seeking to educate Aborigines. He relied heavily on former convicts ('emancipists'), many of whom he had pardoned: scarcely one person in thirty of the population, when Brisbane replaced Macquarie, was a non-convict immigrant. Landowners dismissed Macquarie's policies as 'absurd and mischievous' (Fitzpatrick, 118) and alleged that emancipists fooled him into granting them land and power through a show of false piety. Brisbane, therefore, inherited serious problems and was further constrained by the British government's determination either to relocate convicts in remote settlements or to assign them as labourers to farms in outlying districts. Voluntary immigration from Britain was to be encouraged and land grants to former convicts discontinued. Controversially, in keeping with this required change of emphasis, Brisbane looked primarily to free immigrants (as distinct from former convicts) for support, not least because legislative and judicial changes initiated from London brought fundamental division between the established wealthy landowners, poorer settlers, and the emancipists. Brisbane fostered cultivation of the vine, sugar-cane, and tobacco plant, as well as horse-breeding and the rearing of sheep and cattle in the hinterland. He also sponsored exploration beyond the borders of the colony.

Fear of French intrusion, coupled with a desire to expand trade with south-east Asia, led to the creation of a settlement on Melville Island, off Australia's north coast, which failed to survive. Under his auspices, in probing northwards from Sydney along the coast for the site of a new penal settlement, John Oxley discovered a river which he named Brisbane and on which the capital of Queensland, bearing that name, would be built. However, Brisbane offended vested interests in allowing a free press. The Scots Presbyterian minister John Dunmore Lang wrote a damning critique of Brisbane's governorship in his *Historical and statistical account of New South Wales*, describing him as 'a man of the very best intentions … but … constitutionally disinclined to business' (Lang, 149). While he was 'brave even to heroism on the field of battle' Lang found him 'destitute of that decision of character … necessary to insure pre-eminence in the field of the world' (Lang, 150). Undoubtedly, the finances of the colony were unsatisfactorily managed and the colonial government often on the point of bankruptcy. The emancipists, whose influence had been undermined by Brisbane, and the landowners, who resented the rising economic power of new settlers, denounced him to London, though there was no direct evidence of deliberate malpractice on his part. At worst, he had been naïve. None the less, he was recalled to England after precisely four years, on 1 December 1825. Strangely, but possibly indicative of his lack of political awareness, he attended a public dinner arranged for him by leading emancipists before leaving the colony, which had grown from 23,000 to 36,000 inhabitants during his tenure of office. Two children were born to him and his wife during his governorship: Eleanor Australia (1823–1852), who died at Ventnor, Isle of Wight, and Thomas Australius (1824–1849) who died at Gibraltar. Their last child, Henry, was born at sea in 1826 on the way home from Rio and died at Milford Haven two months later.

Brisbane had, meanwhile, been promoted lieutenant-general on 27 May 1825, and on 16 December 1826 he was appointed colonel of the 34th foot, a position he held until his death in 1860. As colonel, he inspected the regiment in Dublin on 21 June 1844, addressing 'the men in a most soldier-like and impressive manner' (Cannon, 34), provided dinner for all non-commissioned ranks and their families at his own expense, and remarked most favourably on the condition of the regimental hospital and the boys' and girls' school. Four days later he similarly gave a dinner for the officers at which he contrasted the state of the present army with that of the one that he had joined in the previous century. It was now 'more scientific … better educated … more sober' (ibid., 97), and the officers, largely due to the establishment of the Royal Military College at Sandhurst, professionally more competent. Specifically, he was delighted to discover that 85 per cent of the men in the 34th were literate. Recalling that his father had fought alongside the regiment at Culloden as the earl of Home's aide-de-camp, he underlined both the moral courage of the British soldier in action and 'his humanity after the battle' (ibid., 98).

Astronomy and geophysics After his vessel was nearly shipwrecked due to the captain's miscalculation on the way back from Jamaica in 1798, Brisbane had decided to improve his understanding of navigation, buying books and seeking tuition, purchasing the best instruments, and thereafter always carrying a pocket sextant, chronometer, and artificial horizon. In 1808 he built Brisbane Observatory, a stone structure some distance from Brisbane House in Largs. It had three clocks, several instruments by Troughton, including his 2 foot mural circle, the first of its kind, and which served as the model for the 6 foot circle installed at Greenwich Observatory. The equatorial and a journeyman clock were in an adjacent room. Brisbane rose daily at first light to make observations and on occasion observed throughout the night. During the Peninsular War he took regular observations with a pocket sextant, prompting Wellington to remark that he 'kept the time of the army' (*DNB*). Brisbane is alleged to have exclaimed, from heights overlooking the battlefield of Vitoria: 'Ah, what a glorious place for an observatory' (ibid.). In 1816 he was unanimously elected a corresponding member of the Institut de France, though less for his scientific prowess than for having prevented violation of its premises by a detachment of allied troops. During the occupation of France the duke of Wellington asked him to compute a table for determining time from the altitudes of heavenly bodies, for the benefit of the army; he was also asked to draw up a comparison of English weights and measures with those of France as the British army was being supplied to French standards. Both tables were printed in 1818 at the army HQ press in Cambrai.

Brisbane had taken with him to New South Wales his Troughton transit and mural circle and these were installed in an observatory built at his expense, pending the arrival of new instruments; he also employed Karl Rümker and James Dunlop as his assistants.

Within eight months most of the eighteenth-century French astronomer Lacaille's 10,000 stars had, for the first time, been reviewed; and on 2 June 1822 Encke's comet had been sighted on its first predicted return. Brisbane himself observed the winter solstice of 1822 and, on 3 November 1822, the transit of Mercury. Details of this were published in *Philosophical Transactions* (1829) and by William Richardson of the Royal Greenwich Observatory, at the behest of the Admiralty, in *A catalogue of 7,385 stars, chiefly in the southern hemisphere, prepared from observations made 1822–6 at the observatory at Paramatta* (1835). Unfortunately the value of this so-called 'Brisbane Catalogue' was lessened by errors due to instrumental defects. None the less, Brisbane's ability and commitment were not in

doubt, and on 8 February 1828 he received the gold medal of the Astronomical Society. In presenting the award, Sir John Herschel praised his 'noble and disinterested example' and described him as 'the founder of Australian science' (Herschel, 60). Soon after Brisbane left New South Wales, control of the Paramatta observatory passed to the colonial government. It was demolished in 1855 and an obelisk erected on the site in 1880.

After returning from Australia, Brisbane built Makerstoun Observatory in 1826 and installed a Troughton transit and an equatorial by Troughton and Simms. When the British government agreed to take part in Gauss's Geomagnetic Union, which brought many countries together for co-ordinated observations throughout one year, Brisbane built and fitted out an adjacent magnetic observatory in 1841 (for many years thereafter the only one in Scotland). He employed a series of assistants, including James Dunlop, John Allan Broun, later director of Trivandrum Observatory, John Welsh, later superintendent of Kew Observatory, and Alexander Hogg, who was still in post at Brisbane's death. The original nature of his achievements at Makerstoun brought him the Royal Society of Edinburgh's Keith medal in 1848. He had been a member of the Royal Society of London since 1810, even earlier having joined the Astronomical Society, of which he was elected a vice-president in 1827. He became an honorary member of the Royal Irish Academy, and he presided over the 1834 meeting of the British Association for the Advancement of Science in Edinburgh. In 1833 he succeeded Sir Walter Scott as president of the Royal Society of Edinburgh, holding that office until he died. He endowed a Royal Society medal for the encouragement of scientific study, known as the 'Brisbane Biennial', and another medal to be awarded by the Scottish Society of Arts.

Final years Much of Brisbane's later life was occupied with philanthropic works at Largs. He improved the town's drainage and endowed a parish school and an educational establishment, the Brisbane Academy. He was made GCH (1831), was created a baronet (1836), was made GCB (1837), and was promoted general on 23 November 1841. He estimated that, during his military service, he 'crossed the tropics twelve times, the equinoxial line twice, and circumnavigated the globe, besides having been in America and other parts of the world' (Cannon, 100). Honorary degrees were conferred on him by Oxford (1832), Cambridge (1833), and Edinburgh (1834). Acknowledged not only as a respected scientist and philanthropist but as a practising Christian, Brisbane died, on 27 January 1860, at Brisbane House, in the same room in which he had been born almost eighty-seven years earlier. Sir Thomas was buried on 3 February in the old churchyard at Largs, as were three of his children, and later his wife.

JOHN SWEETMAN and ANITA MCCONNELL

Sources T. M. Brisbane, *Reminiscences of Sir Thomas Makdougall Brisbane* (1860) · J. D. Heydon, 'Brisbane, Sir Thomas Makdougall', *AusDB* · Burke, *Gen. GB* · Burke, *Peerage* · W. Rogerson, *Historical records of the 53rd, Shropshire, regiment … from 1755 down to 1889* [1891] · R. Cannon, ed., *Historical record of the thirty-fourth, or the Cumberland regiment of foot* (1844) · A. Bryson, memoir, *Transactions of the*

Royal Society of Edinburgh, 22 (1861), 589 · *Proceedings of the Royal Society*, 11 (1860–62), iii–vii [obit.] · J. F. W. Herschel, *Monthly Notices, Astronomical Society*, 1 (1827–8), 54–60 [Address when delivering the medals, 1828] · J. D. Lang, 'Brisbane's governorship', *An historical and statistical account of New South Wales*, 2 vols. (1834) [Chapter 6] · B. Fitzpatrick, *The Australian people, 1788–1945* (1946)

Archives Bodl. Oxf., corresp. and papers · Mitchell L., Glas., corresp. and accounts · Mitchell L., NSW, corresp., letter-books, and papers · NL Aus., corresp. and papers · NL Scot., corresp. and papers · NRA Scotland, priv. coll., corresp.; corresp. relating to astronomy · RAS, corresp. and papers · U. Mich., Clements L., corresp., reports, and papers | Derby Central Library, Matlock, letters to Sir Robert Wilmot-Horton · Mitchell L., Glas., letters to Hugh Crawford · U. St Andr. L., corresp. with James Forbes
Likenesses J. Watson-Gordon, oils, 1848, Royal Society, Edinburgh · J. Watson-Gordon, pencil sketch, Scot. NPG
Wealth at death £11,802 4s. 8d.: 1860

Briscoe, Arthur John Reginald Trevor (1873–1943), engraver and marine artist, was born on 25 February 1873 at Mount Pleasant, Oxton, Birkenhead, Cheshire, the eldest son of John Briscoe (d. 1893), a prominent Liverpool businessman and senior partner in the cotton-broking firm of Briscoe, Fox & Partners, and his wife, Eliza Ann Trevor, whose father was proprietor of the *Chester Chronicle*. Educated at Shrewsbury School, Briscoe demonstrated an aptitude for drawing which had been evident from early childhood. After leaving school he accompanied his father on a world tour and on his return announced that he wanted to be an artist. Arrangements were made for him to go to the Slade School of Fine Art, where he studied under Professor Frederick Brown. On completing his studies at the Slade he spent eighteen months at the Académie Julian in Paris, where he started etching in Pre-Raphaelite style, but this practice was brought to a halt when he temporarily ran out of funds and was obliged to sell his press.

Briscoe returned to London, where he produced black and white images, under the Burne-Jones influence. Soon afterwards he was commissioned to illustrate an edition of Keats (his favourite poet) and the fairy tales of Hans Christian Andersen. Although a cartoonist of great ability, Briscoe never felt the need to establish himself as an illustrator. He had a comfortable allowance, was not ambitious, and had no wish to raise his prices to wealthier clients.

Abandoning French styles, Briscoe became interested in the work of Philip Wilson Steer (1860–1942). Also a Birkenhead man, Steer had been painting in Essex and this influence led Briscoe to Malden and Heybridge basin, where he obtained lodgings and a studio, making local friends who were interested in small-boat sailing. Briscoe designed and built his own flat-bottomed dinghy and was a founding member of the Blackwater Sailing Club. About 1899 he bought a 3 ton cutter, the *Doris*, in which he sailed around the Essex coast.

On 19 March 1901 Briscoe married Mabel Grace Sarah (1881/2–1969), eldest child of Samuel Shawyer, an Indian mutiny veteran; their son William was born in 1903. The family generally spent eight or nine months of the year aboard the yacht, sailing to Calais, along the Belgian coast, and through the Dutch waterways; when abroad Briscoe

was constantly sketching and painting in watercolours and oils. He excelled as a marine artist, his sketches being evocative of the last days of square-rigged sailing ships, Dutch craft, the coast of East Anglia, and nautical activity. Influenced by Vermeer, the Van der Veldes, and also by Mesdag, Mauve, and Breitner, he had studied his subjects intensively, filling his sketchbooks with details of rigging, barges, and steamers, all with the intention of understanding the workmanship involved. As a result he combined technical accuracy with aesthetically pleasing and balanced effects, and his work remains unsurpassed.

In 1906 Briscoe held a one-man show of thirty-five watercolours, called 'Round the North Sea and Zuyder Zee', at the Modern Gallery in Bond Street, London. It was a great success and established his reputation. Other exhibitions followed at the Leicester Square Galleries, London, and elsewhere. Briscoe wrote and illustrated *A Handbook on Sailing* (1908) under the pseudonym Clove Hitch, the name he frequently used in the yachting press. Later in that year he took delivery of a yacht named the *Golden Vanity*. He often took this yacht in to the Dutch canals, and his sketchbooks are filled with drawings of scenes from these parts.

In 1910 Briscoe's mother financed the building at West Mersea of Buzzon, a house with a studio. When the First World War broke out, Briscoe was offered a commission in the navy. He enlisted in the Royal Naval Volunteer Reserve auxiliary patrol as lieutenant, and joined his ship on 31 December 1914. The immediate post-war period was spent cruising to and around the Netherlands in the *Golden Vanity*, but about this time Briscoe came across several unused copperplates from his days in Paris and began etching. In 1923 James McBey saw these plates and took them to London, where he printed them on his press. Briscoe started etching seriously, his activities coinciding with the etching revival, which he witnessed at its peak and then saw slump.

In 1926 Briscoe made a superb scale model of the *Cutty Sark*, a vessel which appears intermittently throughout his sketchbooks. He was divorced in that year, and in May 1927 married Alice Conyers Baker (d. 1942), leasing a small studio flat in Notting Hill, London. In August he and Alice cruised to the Netherlands and were joined at Rotterdam by Harold Dickens, who published his etchings. The *Golden Vanity* was sold in 1929 and the couple moved to Lansdowne House in Holland Park, London, where Briscoe devoted his energies to etching and painting. He and Alice spent long summer holidays at St Mawes and he also had an 18 foot lugger built, named the *Liberty*. Sketchbooks during his cruise aboard the *Alastor*, in 1929 or 1930, are full of sketches and colour washes detailing the trip, and are rich with vignettes of polar bears, nude sketches of Alice, and various other details.

In the early 1930s Briscoe's mother died and he came into a considerable inheritance. He had never liked London and bought a house in Walton on the Naze. He added a large studio, had the *Liberty* brought over from St Mawes, and in 1934 settled in.

When the Second World War broke out, Briscoe tried to

rejoin the Royal Naval Volunteer Reserve but at sixty-six he had to be content with being an ARP warden. Early in 1940 he suffered a stroke, and he and Alice went to the Berry Head Hotel in Brixham, overlooking Tor Bay, where in former days he had loved to sketch the sailing trawler fleet. Alice died in 1942, and Briscoe moved into a private hotel, Broomfield Lodge, Broomfield Road, Chelmsford, near where his son was living. He died there on 27 April 1943 and was buried in Broomfield church.

CHANTAL SERHAN

Sources A. A. Hurst, *Arthur Briscoe—marine artist: his life and work* (1974) · J. Laver, *A complete catalogue of the etchings and drypoints of Arthur Briscoe* (1930) · W. Sheridan, ed., *Catalogue of sketches in the Briscoe collection* (1980) [Science Museum Library pictorial collection] · M. C. Salaman, 'The etchings of Arthur Briscoe', *The Studio*, 91 (1926), 90–93 · M. C. Salaman, *Arthur Briscoe*, Modern Masters of Etchings, 23 (1930) · J. Laver, 'The etchings of Arthur Briscoe', *Bookman's Journal*, 13 (1925–6), 165–9 · H. Wright, 'Arthur Briscoe: a chronological list of his later etchings', *Print Collectors' Quarterly*, 26 (1939), 97–103 · *Catalogue of water-colours square rigged and fore and aft by Arthur Briscoe*, Fine Art Society (1926) · *Collection of paintings, watercolours and prints by Arthur Briscoe* (1984) [sale catalogue, Christies, 19 Nov 1984] · *The Times* (30 April 1943), 7d · b. cert. · m. cert. [Mabel Shawyer] · d. cert.

Archives BM · NMM · Sci. Mus. · V&A

Briscoe, John (*d.* 1697), merchant and projector, is described in many records as a merchant, although little is known of his trading activities. He was apprenticed to a member of the London Salters' Company, although his name does not appear in that company's serving registers. He may have been the John Briscoe of St Antholin, London, citizen and salter, who, aged about twenty-six, married Elizabeth Carre of St Botolph, Aldgate, on 19 December 1676.

On 15 April 1685 Briscoe petitioned 'for letters patent for the sole use and benefit of a new invention for making sizing and whitening all sorts of writing, printing and other paper' (*CSP dom.*, 1685, 130). The following year he, with others, petitioned for a charter as

> at vast expense of money and time they have brought to perfection the finest sorts of writing and printing paper by the making whereof not only will thousands be employed and brought up to industry and art, but vast sums of money will be kept in the country which are now daily sent abroad to pay for imported paper. (ibid., 1686–7, 167)

They were incorporated as the Governor and Company of White Paper Makers, and in the mid-eighteenth century it was acknowledged that 'Mr Brisco & Co. … improved the paper made greatly' (Coleman, 76).

Briscoe was involved in the establishment of a number of other companies. In 1691 he became the deputy governor of a 'new corporation for the setting the poor at Work, by a joint stock throughout England' called the Royal Corporation in England (*CSP dom.*, 1690–91, 422). Also in this year he became an assistant in the Company of Copper Miners in England for the melting down, refining, and purifying of copper ore, was involved in the incorporation of a company to establish a linen manufacture in Scotland, and became the deputy governor of the Company of Merchant Adventurers trading to the north-west part of America.

In 1694 Briscoe published *A Discourse on the Late Funds*, in which he criticized existing funds and set forth the details of his proposed land bank to be founded upon the subscriptions of land by copyholders and freeholders. He proposed the issuing of bills of credit 'being a new Species of Money, and to all Intents and Purposes as useful as Money' (Briscoe, *A Discourse on the Late Funds of the Million Act, Lottery Act, and Bank of England*, 1694, 30). Despite having his plans rejected by a Commons committee in 1695 Briscoe opened the books for subscription to the National Land Bank on 11 June 1695. With the initial target of £100,000 in land subscriptions met, a meeting was held on 10 September to establish a committee for the bank. Many failed to pay their initial instalments, and consequently the bank did very little business in the early months. At this time Briscoe's proposals to lend the government much needed money to finance the war led to a collaboration with the founders of the Land Bank at Exeter Exchange, John Asgill and Nicholas Barbon. Despite opposition, particularly from the Bank of England, the two banks were incorporated by act of parliament as the Governor and Company of the National Land Bank of England to lend the government over £2.5 million at 7 per cent interest. Subscription books were opened at the end of May 1696 but very little was subscribed, and on 11 June one contemporary observed that the 'land bank makes but little progress' (Luttrell, 4.71). The failure of this scheme has been attributed not only to the shortage of coin in this year, and the financial climate more generally, but also to 'public opinion' which appeared 'to have been against the venture' (Horsefield, 207). Both banks, however, continued separately, with Briscoe's holding meetings until at least July 1696. John Briscoe died on 13 February 1697 and in his will, proved in the prerogative court of Canterbury on 24 March, he left property in the county of Hertford to his son, John, and his London property to his daughter, Elizabeth.

NATASHA GLAISYER

Sources J. K. Horsefield, *British monetary experiments, 1650–1710* (1960) · *CSP dom.*, 1685–7; 1690–91 · D. C. Coleman, *The British paper industry, 1495–1860* (1965) · W. R. Scott, *The constitution and finance of English, Scottish and Irish joint-stock companies to 1720*, 2 (1911) · J. L. Chester and J. Foster, eds., *London marriage licences, 1521–1869* (1887) · N. Luttrell, *A brief historical relation of state affairs from September 1678 to April 1714*, 4 (1857) · private information (2004) [K. George, Salters' Company] · will, PRO, PROB 11/437, sig. 48 · *Report on manuscripts in various collections*, 8 vols., HMC, 55 (1901–14), vol. 6

Archives NL Scot., 'A scheme for a national land-bank', MS Adv. 31.1.7, fol. 104 | GL, minutes of the national land-bank, GL MS 61

Briscoe, John Potter (1848–1926), librarian, was born at Lever Bridge, Tonge with Haulgh, near Bolton, Lancashire, on 20 July 1848, the eldest son of John Daly Briscoe, a schoolmaster, and his wife, Mary Elizabeth Scowcroft. He was educated at his father's school and was a teacher there from 1862 until 1866, when he was appointed assistant librarian in Bolton Public Library. Three years later, at twenty-one, he became chief librarian of Nottingham Public Library, a post he held for forty-seven years. He was twice married, first to Elizabeth Baxter of Bolton, then to Sophia Wallis of Nottingham.

Briscoe was an original member of the Library Association of the United Kingdom (established in 1877), a member of its council from 1881 to 1891, and a vice-president from 1891 to 1920. He further served the association as a summer school lecturer and enthusiastically supported its annual conferences, which he addressed frequently. In 1890 he helped to form the North Midlands Library Association, serving as its first president.

As a leading figure in the early development of professional librarianship, Briscoe wrote extensively on a variety of issues, especially those associated with promoting library services and extending them into society, to people who, because of their social or personal circumstances, made little use of them. His philosophy was that libraries should serve all, irrespective of class distinction or an individual's intellectual or physical limitations. He thus decried, for example, the lack of books for blind people in public libraries. He believed librarians had part of the missionary spirit in them and should not spare themselves in working for the common good. Public libraries, in particular, he held, had an important role to play in furthering education and assisting personal progress, enabling people to become good workers and worthy citizens.

Briscoe's contribution to the development of the library service in Nottingham was notable. After 1869, under his energetic leadership, the book stock of the central library expanded rapidly, a reference department was opened, and a system of branch reading rooms was put in place. In 1881 the central library moved into new premises. The town had been late in adopting the Public Library Acts, and at first lagged far behind industrial towns of comparable size; by the turn of the century, however, he had transformed Nottingham's library service into one of the country's leading library authorities.

One of the most striking features of this transformation was Briscoe's pioneering work in providing library services to children. He initiated the first separate children's service (for seven- to fourteen-year-olds) in the country. The Nottingham Library for Boys and Girls, comprising a stock of 3000 volumes and staffed by a dedicated female assistant, was opened in 1882 with the help of a £500 donation from Samuel Morley, the hosiery manufacturer. Briscoe hoped to encourage reading among children by offering books that were well written, professionally printed, and attractively illustrated. Although he insisted that the material made available to children should be morally correct, it was not his intention to indoctrinate his younger readers according to a narrow moral code. Rather, his aim was to excite the imaginations of the young, so school textbooks were excluded from the children's library.

In 1890 Briscoe pioneered a series of half-hour talks to the public about books and writers, designed to assist people in their selection of books and encourage reading. For similar reasons he supported the idea of the reading circle (as operated by the National Home Reading Union, often in collaboration with public libraries), in which the public actively participated by reading and discussing

selected works. His enthusiasm for talks and circles was derived from his belief that the increasingly hurried pace of life was resulting in too much light and scrappy reading, and that it was the duty of the librarian to counter the effects of a bustling age by guiding people to more advanced and contemplative, but equally pleasurable, literature.

Briscoe praised the work that public libraries began to undertake towards the end of the nineteenth century in acting as agents for the government's emigrants' information service, which aimed to advise those—especially the poor and ignorant—on matters that would protect them from the fraud, exploitation, and hardship that often accompanied the search for a new life in the colonies.

Briscoe was said to be a bookman born. He founded a local literary society, the Nottingham Sette of Odde Volumes, and was a member of the council of the Thoroton Society. His literary and scholarly interests were first and foremost in the field of local history. For many years he edited the local history column in the *Nottingham Weekly Guardian*. His extensive writings on Nottinghamshire history included *Bypaths of Nottinghamshire History* (1905), *A Concise History of Nottingham Castle* (1899), *Old Nottinghamshire* (2 vols., 1881–4), *Chapters of Nottinghamshire History* (1908), *Nottinghamshire and Derbyshire at the Opening of the Twentieth Century* (1901), *Nottinghamshire Facts and Fancies* (1876), *A Popular History of Nottingham* (1893), *Contributions to a Bibliography of Hosiery and Lace* (1896), and *Stories about the Midlands* (1883). From 1892 he edited six volumes of *Nottinghamshire and Derbyshire Notes and Queries*.

Beyond antiquarianism, Briscoe's literary interests were eclectic. He designed and edited The Bibelots (1899–1907), a series of twenty-nine midget reprints of English classics. His *Gleanings from God's Acre* (1883) included a collection of epitaphs and Samuel Johnson's essay on the subject. He also published *Tudor and Stuart Love Songs* (1902). Aside from his literary endeavours, his recreations included gardening and photography.

At first glance, Briscoe's scholarly pursuits confirm the stereotype that emerged in the twentieth century of the librarian as a genteel, socially detached, literary recluse. However, in Briscoe's case this image is undermined by his active engagement in civil society, and the social and civic life of Nottingham in particular. His work and interests were furthered by intimate and dutiful associations with local citizens, bodies, and organizations. He was a staunch supporter of the temperance movement and for a number of years edited the *Midland Temperance Record*. Like many librarians of his time he was involved in freemasonry, his enthusiasm for the practice illustrated by his writings on the subject, which included *Notes on Early Freemasonry in Nottingham* (1924) and, for private circulation, 'Notes on some masonic degrees' (1924).

Briscoe was forced to retire as librarian at Nottingham, owing to ill health, in 1916. On his retirement he was honoured with the position of consulting city librarian. He was succeeded as librarian by his only son, Walter Alwyn Briscoe (1878–1934), like his father a leading advocate of library publicity and promotion. Hampered in later life by hardening of the arteries, Briscoe eventually suffered a serious cerebral haemorrhage and died at his home, 38 Addison Street, Nottingham, on 7 January 1926, having given over sixty years of service and support to libraries, local government, and a variety of reforming issues.

ALISTAIR BLACK

Sources 'Personalities of the past, V: John Potter Briscoe', *Librarian and Book World*, 30/9 (May 1941), 164–5 · J. Minto, *A history of the public library movement in Great Britain and Ireland* (1932), 304–6 · L. S. Jast, *Library Association Record*, 28 (1926), 5–6 · *WWW* · b. cert. · d. cert. · J. L. Thornton, *Selected readings in the history of librarianship* (1966), 191–3 · A. Black, *A new history of the English public library: social and intellectual contexts, 1850–1914* (1996) · T. Kelly, *A history of public libraries in Great Britain, 1845–1975* (1977), 38–9, 53, 79–80, 100, 149, 201 · A. Ellis, *Library services for young people in England and Wales, 1830–1970* (1971), 12, 15, 16, 17, 20, 24, 35 · *CGPLA Eng. & Wales* (1926) · J. P. Briscoe, 'Libraries for the young', *Library Chronicle*, 3 (1886) · J. P. Briscoe, 'Libraries for the blind', *Library Chronicle*, 4 (1887) · J. P. Briscoe, 'Half-hour talks about books with library readers', *The Library*, 7 (1895) · J. P. Briscoe, 'How to extend the library movement', *The Library*, 8 (1896) · J. P. Briscoe, 'Public libraries and emigration', *Library Association Record*, 1 (1899) · J. P. Briscoe, 'Libraries and reading circles', *Library Association Record*, 5 (1903)
Archives Nottingham Central Library, documents
Likenesses photographs, Nottingham Central Library
Wealth at death £1345 7s. 8d.: probate, 9 March 1926, *CGPLA Eng. & Wales*

Brise, Sir Evelyn John Ruggles- (1857–1935), prison administrator and founder of the Borstal system, was born on 6 December 1857 at Spains Hall, Finchingfield, Essex, the second son of Sir Samuel Brise Ruggles-Brise (1825–1899) and his wife, Marianne Weyland, fourth daughter of Sir Edward Bowyer Smith, tenth baronet, of Hill Hall, Essex. There were three other sons and seven daughters. Sir Samuel, a landowner, was Conservative member of parliament for East Essex from 1868 to 1884.

As a small boy Evelyn received early morning lessons in Latin and Greek from his father. His classical education continued at a private school near Hitchin, Hertfordshire, where hunger drove him to steal peas from neighbouring fields. His older brother, Archie, was already at Eton College; when Evelyn went there on a scholarship, there was some resentment:

> They said, 'His brother is a bloody Oppidan and President of Pop so we'll jolly well take it out of him.' And they tore the gown off my back … and beat me and treated me as badly as they could. (Leslie, 20)

His recollection of Eton (1869–76), despite scholastic and sporting achievements, was one of 'barbarism and savagery', and it left him with a lifelong hatred of patrician tories.

At Balliol College, Oxford, Ruggles-Brise worked hard and got a second class in moderations (1877), and a first in Greats (1880), and played in the cricket eleven. In 1880 he was placed sixth in the competitive examination for the civil service. His father spoke to the Liberal home secretary, Sir William Harcourt, who offered Ruggles-Brise a post; he became a Home Office clerk in 1880. From 1883 to 1891 he was principal private secretary to four home secretaries—Harcourt, Sir Richard Cross, H. C. E. Childers, and Henry Matthews. During this period of his life Ruggles-

Brise lived frugally in rooms, dined out most nights, and later told his second wife that as a second son he did not feel welcome at Spains Hall.

In 1892 Henry Matthews appointed Ruggles-Brise commissioner of prisons for England and Wales. He was not the choice of the commission chairman, Sir Edmund du Cane, royal engineer and architect of Wormwood Scrubs. Over thirty years he had perfected a system of penal discipline based on silence, hard labour, and progressive stages, and was an autocratic administrator. Ruggles-Brise crossed him once by daring to criticize a favoured underling—'I cannot remember that he ever spoke to me again' (Leslie, 87).

Press criticism of Sir Edmund reached such a pitch that in 1894 the home secretary, H. H. Asquith, appointed a committee of inquiry under Herbert Gladstone. The committee reported in 1895 that prisoners had been 'treated too much as a hopeless or worthless element in the community' ('Departmental committee on prisons', 7). Reform, they proposed, was henceforth to rank alongside deterrence as one of the objects of the English prison system. They wanted special provision for young offenders, who ought to be kept out of prison for as long as possible, and for incorrigible repeat offenders, who ought to be kept in for as long as possible. These concerns were central for penal administrators—how to confine prisoners with economy, but with humanity, and without further corrupting beginners in crime. Du Cane had solved the problem with rigid discipline. The Gladstone committee sought to move the system in the direction of reform. Both tendencies saw 'classification' as the key to containment without contamination.

Sir Edmund, too ill to give evidence to the committee, resigned his post. Asquith appointed Ruggles-Brise, then thirty-seven, chairman of the Prison Commission to usher in a new dispensation. But despite his personal radicalism he remained a generally cautious administrator, resisting pressure to create an independent prison inspectorate and to abolish corporal punishment. Perhaps the most important feature of the 1898 Prison Act was the power it gave home secretaries to amend prison rules without primary legislation. Ruggles-Brise used it to abolish the treadwheel and the crank.

The innovation which made Ruggles-Brise's reputation followed a trip to the United States in 1897 to look at the Elmira Reformatory, run by the ebullient Zebulon Brockway. The 'Borstal' experiment—separate provision for a 'juvenile-adult' class of prisoners aged sixteen to twenty-one—began in Bedford prison in 1900, but took its name from the prison at Borstal, near Rochester, Kent, where the prisoners were housed from 1901. The regime combined rigorous discipline, drill, and physical exercise, to allay public anxiety about mollycoddling, with trade training, to meet the ambitions of the Gladstone committee, and an aftercare system run by middle-class volunteers initially recruited by Ruggles-Brise at a dinner party. Great success was claimed for the first prisoner-trainees—a high proportion finding work and a low proportion being reconvicted. The scheme was placed on a statutory footing by the Prevention of Crime Act of 1908.

'Borstal' entered the language as a byword for 'enlightened' work with young criminals, and its fame went round the world. Under the active supervision of prison commissioner Alexander Paterson in the 1920s, an extraordinary era ensued in which Arnoldian public school values were grafted onto the penal treatment of working-class youth. Like other 'progressive' penal innovations, Borstal eventually succumbed to the pressures of numbers, inappropriate allocation, declining success rates, lowered staff morale, and the subversive influence of the inmate subculture. However, according to its admirers, the Borstal experiment called forth a flowering of idealism unparalleled in English prison history—an influence on staff that endured long after the institutions themselves had lost sight of their origins.

The first impression people had of Ruggles-Brise was one of aloofness, but his intelligence and humanity soon emerged; one prison governor described him as 'an absolute sahib' (Rich, 19). He had many friends, few of them intimate, and they were amazed when 'the confirmed bachelor' married on 3 September 1914 Jessie Philippa, daughter of Robert Russell Carew and widow of Francis Robert Stonor, fourth Baron Camoys (1856–1897). She died on 29 November 1928, and he remarried on 6 June 1933; his new wife was Sheelah Maud Emily, daughter of Captain the Hon. Francis Algernon James Chichester, and widow of Essex Edgeworth Reade; she survived Ruggles-Brise. She kept an extensive diary of her conversations with him and he also dictated a short autobiography. A partridge-shooting country gentleman who professed 'socialism', he called himself a pagan and despised 'toadyism'. He had no ear for music, no eye for fine art; but books were his passion. Hugo's *Les misérables* greatly influenced his commitment to social justice. He was instrumental in allowing Oscar Wilde to have the paper and pencils with which he wrote *De Profundis* in Reading gaol. During Winston Churchill's brief but lively occupancy of the Home Office (1910–11), he did battle with dramatist John Galsworthy over separate confinement.

Evelyn Ruggles-Brise was made CB in 1899 and KCB in 1902. He wrote *The English Prison System* (1921), a lucid history; *Prison Reform at Home and Abroad* (1924); and pamphlets, reports, and contributions to international crime congresses. He died of throat cancer at Ridings Copse, Peaslake, Surrey, on 18 August 1935, and was buried at Finchingfield. He was the very model of a Victorian public servant: classically educated, socially well connected, liberal, humanitarian, imbued with an almost monastic sense of service, disinterested in the best sense of the word, administratively prudent—and the instigator of an internationally significant departure in the institutional treatment of young criminals. PHILIP PRIESTLEY

Sources S. Leslie, *Sir Evelyn Ruggles-Brise* (1938) · L. Radzinowicz and R. Hood, *A history of English criminal law and its administration from 1750*, 5: *The emergence of penal policy in Victorian and Edwardian England* (1986) · R. Hood, *Borstal re-assembled* (1965) · E. Ruggles-Brise, *The English prison system* (1921) · M. Benny, *Low company* (1937) · Boase, *Mod. Eng. biog.* · *The Eton register*, 4 (privately printed, Eton, 1907) · I. Elliott, ed., *The Balliol College register, 1833–1933*, 2nd edn (privately printed, Oxford, 1934) · C. E. F. Rich, *Recollections of a prison governor* (1932) · 'Departmental committee on prisons', *Parl. papers* (1895), vol. 56, C. 7702 · Burke, *Peerage* (1967) · *CGPLA Eng. & Wales* (1935)
Archives Essex RO | BL, corresp. with Lord Gladstone, Add. MSS 46056–46084 · Bodl. Oxf., corresp. with Sir William Harcourt
Likenesses W. Stoneman, photograph, 1918, NPG · Bassano, photograph, NPG · Spy [L. Ward], caricature, NPG; repro. in *VF* (10 Feb 1910)
Wealth at death £4710 7s. 9d.: probate, 28 Oct 1935, *CGPLA Eng. & Wales*

Bristol. For this title name *see* Digby, John, first earl of Bristol (1580–1653); Digby, George, second earl of Bristol (1612–1677); Hervey, John, first earl of Bristol (1665–1751); Chudleigh, Elizabeth [Elizabeth Hervey, countess of Bristol] (c.1720–1788); Hervey, George William, second earl of Bristol (1721–1775); Hervey, Augustus John, third earl of Bristol (1724–1779); Hervey, Frederick Augustus, fourth earl of Bristol (1730–1803); Hervey, Frederick William John Augustus, seventh marquess of Bristol (1954–1999).

Bristol, Ralph of (d. 1232), bishop of Kildare, was a native of Bristol, but settled in Dublin. He first appears in the records as the clerk of William Piro, bishop of Glendalough from 1192 to 1212. Before 1200 he was appointed first treasurer of St Patrick's Cathedral, Dublin, by Archbishop Henry of London. His name, sometimes with the title 'magister', occurs as a witness to many charters of this archbishop.

In 1223 Ralph was consecrated bishop of Kildare, where his episcopacy began a succession of English and Anglo-Irish bishops which was maintained until the end of the fifteenth century. As bishop of Kildare he was involved in a dispute with William (II) Marshal over advowsons, the outcome of which is unknown. Ralph was one of the churchmen deputed by Henry of London, as archbishop of Dublin, to collect witness depositions and material relating to the sanctity and miracles of Lorcán Ó Tuathail (Laurence O'Toole) before that saint's canonization. The results of this inquiry were sent in letters, with the archbishop's seal, to Eu in Normandy, whose canons wrote the first life of Laurence. According to James Ware, Ralph granted a fourteen day indulgence to the abbey of Glastonbury. The construction of Kildare Cathedral was begun during his episcopacy. He died on 24 August 1232.

C. L. KINGSFORD, *rev.* MARGARET MURPHY

Sources N. B. White, ed., *The Dignitas decani of St Patrick's Cathedral, Dublin*, IMC (1957) · J. T. Gilbert, ed., *Chartularies of St Mary's Abbey, Dublin: with the register of its house at Dunbrody and annals of Ireland*, 2 vols., Rolls Series, 80 (1884) · M. P. Sheehy, ed., *Pontificia Hibernica: medieval papal chancery documents concerning Ireland, 640–1261*, 2 vols. (1962–5) · H. S. Sweetman and G. F. Handcock, eds., *Calendar of documents relating to Ireland*, 5 vols., PRO (1875–86) · *The whole works of Sir James Ware concerning Ireland*, ed. and trans. W. Harris, rev. edn, 2 vols. in 3 (1764) · J. T. Gilbert, ed., *Register of the abbey of St Thomas, Dublin*, Rolls Series, 94 (1889) · E. St J. Brooks, ed., *Register of the hospital of S. John without the New Gate, Dublin* (1936) · M. F. Roche, 'The Latin lives of St Laurence of Dublin', PhD diss., University College Dublin, 1981

Bristow, Edmund (1787–1876), painter, was born on 1 April 1787 and baptized on 6 April at Clewer, Berkshire, the son of James Bristow, a heraldic painter, and his wife, Ann, *née* Rolls (d. 1846). He spent all his life in the vicinity of Windsor and Eton. Bristow attended Ward's school in Peascod Street, Windsor, leaving at the age of twelve; he had no formal art training but at an early age he was patronized by the Princess Elizabeth, the duke of Clarence (afterwards William IV), and others. His paintings, in the Morland tradition and often on a small scale, ranged from still-lifes, interiors, and aspects of rural life to portraits of well-known local characters. His animal paintings were popular; the Royal Collection includes several examples in this genre, such as *Beauty with a Spaniel* (1821) and *The Farrier's Shop* (1845). His *Monkey Pugilists* was purchased by Henry Ingalton of Eton who acquired several of his works. His painting *Cat's Paw* is said to have been the inspiration for Landseer's work of the same subject. In 1809 he exhibited at the Royal Academy *Smith Shoeing a Horse*, the first of twelve of his works to be shown there; he was also an occasional exhibitor at both the British Institution and the Society of British Artists, Suffolk Street, until 1838.

Bristow was a man of independent eccentric views, would not work to order, and on occasion, as when Baroness Burdett Coutts visited his studio, refused to sell even his finished productions. Engravings of a few of his works, such as *Sportsmen Refreshing* (1816) and *Pheasant Shooting* (1816), were published in the *Sporting Magazine* and elsewhere.

After the death of his mother in 1846, Bristow continued to live in Eton with his sister. He died there, unmarried, on 12 February 1876, at the age of eighty-nine. He was buried on 19 February in Eton cemetery. Although he is said to have been a kind-hearted and entertaining companion, he died in such total obscurity that the writer of his obituary in the *Art Journal* could find nothing to say about him. After his death the contents of his studio were sold by auction. Examples of his work are in the Royal Collection; Nottingham Art Gallery; Ferens Art Gallery, Hull; and Leicester Art Gallery.   WALTER HEPWORTH, *rev.* SARA SOWERBY

Sources *Windsor & Eton Express* (19 Feb 1876) · *Art Journal*, 38 (1876), 148 · *The exhibition of the Royal Academy* (1905) [exhibition catalogue] · *Catalogue of the British Institute* (1908) · J. Johnson, ed., *Works exhibited at the Royal Society of British Artists, 1824–1893, and the New English Art Club, 1888–1917*, 2 vols. (1975) · W. Gilbey, *Animal painters of England*, 3 vols. (1900–11) · S. Mitchell, *The dictionary of British equestrian artists* (1985) · Wood, *Vic. painters*, 2nd edn · O. Millar, *The Victorian pictures in the collection of her majesty the queen*, 2 vols. (1992) · Bryan, *Painters* · M. A. Wingfield, *A dictionary of sporting artists, 1650–1990* (1992) · Redgrave, *Artists* · S. H. Pavière, *A dictionary of British sporting painters* (1965) · W. S. Sparrow, *Angling in British art through five centuries: prints, pictures, books* (1923) · J. Maas, *Victorian painters* (1969) · *CGPLA Eng. & Wales* (1876)
Wealth at death under £4000: probate, 16 March 1876, *CGPLA Eng. & Wales*

Bristow, Henry William (1817–1889), geologist, was born on 17 May 1817 in London, the son of Major-General Henry Bristow (1786–1874), a member of a Wiltshire family, and his wife, Elizabeth Atchorne (d. 1850) of High Wycombe. He was educated at Fortescue House, Twickenham, and at King's College, London, where he studied in the departments of civil engineering and science applied to the arts and manufactures. He joined the staff of the Geological Survey in 1842 as an assistant geologist and was set to work mapping the strata of Radnorshire. He was transferred to Wincanton in 1845, and worked his way through Somerset and Dorset, reaching Swanage, on the coast, in 1851. The strain of constant fieldwork led to a breakdown in Bristow's health, which was then restored by a month's travel on the continent. In 1852 he started work on the Isle of Wight with Edward Forbes which resulted in his *Geology of the Isle of Wight* (1862).

Bristow was highly regarded as a field surveyor, being promoted to geologist in 1847 and district surveyor in 1867. He was offered geological postings to New South Wales, India, and Tasmania at different times, but always chose to remain in England. He married, on 22 October 1863, Eliza Harrison, second daughter of David Harrison, a London solicitor. They had two sons and two daughters.

In the 1860s Bristow surveyed parts of Berkshire and Hampshire with W. Whitaker, and made a detailed study of the Rhaetic beds in England and Wales. He also spent time in the Museum of Practical Geology in London, working on a catalogue of rock specimens. In his spare time he wrote the *Glossary of Mineralogy* (1861), and translated and edited *The World before the Deluge* (1867) from the work by L. Figuier, and *Underground Life* (1869) by L. Simonin. He was elected fellow of the Geological Society in 1843 and FRS in 1862, was an honorary member of sundry societies, and was appointed to the order of SS Maurizio e Lazzaro. His separate papers are few in number—about eight—and throughout his life he suffered from deafness, which prevented him from taking part in the business of societies. The high point of his survey career came in 1872 when he succeeded A. C. Ramsay as senior director for England and Wales. He retired from the survey in July 1888 and died on 14 June 1889 at his home, 103 Knatchbull Road, Camberwell. He was survived by his wife and children.

JOHN C. THACKRAY

Sources *Geological Magazine*, new ser., 3rd decade, 6 (1889), 381–4 · W. T. Blanford, presidential address, *Quarterly Journal of the Geological Society*, 46 (1890), 44–5 · *Nature*, 39 (1888–9), 206–7 · J. F. Kirkaldy, 'William Topley and *The geology of the weald*', *Proceedings of the Geologists' Association*, 86 (1975), 373–88 · L. C. Sanders, *Celebrities of the century: being a dictionary of men and women of the nineteenth century* (1887) · *CGPLA Eng. & Wales* (1889) · *DNB* · IGI
Archives BGS, letter-book, memoranda, notebooks, and official corresp. | ICL, letters to Sir Andrew Ramsay
Likenesses cartes-de-visite, c.1870, GS Lond. · cartes-de-visite, BGS
Wealth at death £872 19s. 11d.: probate, 11 July 1889, *CGPLA Eng. & Wales*

Bristow, Richard (1538–1581), Roman Catholic priest, was born in Worcester, the son of Jane Bristow. He was schooled in grammar by Roger Goulbourne. He then passed to Oxford University where he matriculated from Exeter College in 1555, graduated BA on 17 April 1559, and proceeded MA on 26 June 1562. He was a student of Christ Church in 1565. One of his companions at this time was Edmund Campion, the future martyr, and they were known as 'the two brightest men at the university' (Gillow, *Lit. biog. hist.*, 300). Perhaps for this reason they were chosen to participate in the public disputation held before Queen Elizabeth on 3 September 1566, with great applause. Bristow's fellowship of Exeter the following year was obtained through the interest of Sir William Petre. However, Petre later withdrew his support after Bristow's controversy with Dr Laurence Humphrey: Bristow attacked Humphrey on certain points of religion, showing all too clearly his own Catholic tendencies.

Bristow left Oxford in 1568 and sought refuge in Flanders among a group of Oxford men who were gathering, first at Louvain, then at Douai, around William Allen. Allen recognized his abilities, and Bristow soon became his invaluable assistant as Allen set about the founding of his new college at Douai. Bristow continued with his own studies as well as teaching at the college. He was awarded his STD by the University of Douai on 2 August 1575. He had been ordained to the priesthood (the first of those enrolled at the college to be so) at Brussels on 21 March 1573, having been granted a dispensation in 1571 to be ordained (presumably to the diaconate) *defectu natalium*. Giving his age as thirty-two, the dispensation explains that his father married his mother, Jane, without the certainty that his first wife was dead, there thus being a possibility of Richard's illegitimacy.

As well as being a close collaborator with Allen in the administration of the college and being prefect of studies there, Bristow was responsible, with Gregory Martin, for much of the translation of the Douai–Rheims Bible, the great enterprise of the exiles to render the Vulgate into English for the use of Catholics in England. When the college was temporarily removed to Rheims, Allen placed it under Bristow's care. Such was his reputation that in 1579 the rebellious students at the English College in Rome said that Dr Bristow was the only really fit Englishman they would accept as their governor, but that he was so busy at Rheims that they knew he could not be spared. In 1574 Bristow published *A Brief Treatise of Divers Plain and Sure Ways*, often known as 'Bristow's motives'. This was compiled at Allen's express wish and used much material from Allen's own *Articles*. It immediately became rare and sought after, since 367 copies were intercepted by the English authorities. The government seized upon the 'Motives' as a useful weapon in its continuing assault on the incoming seminary priests, and it is specifically referred to in the fifth of the 'bloody questions', where it is described as commending and confirming Pius V's bull *Regnans in excelsis* encouraging the deposition of Elizabeth. These questions, first used at the trial of Edmund Campion and others in 1581, marked the intensification of a policy of portraying all Catholic priests as disloyal to the queen. The fifth question, by specifically referring to the works of Bristow and his contemporary Sanders, sought to use a work of theology for political purposes. It moved the issue from condemning a man for what he had done to demanding that he incriminate himself by answering hypothetical questions as to what he might do.

Bristow's many labours affected his health and he contracted consumption. Advised to return to the English climate, he left Douai on 23 September 1581 and found lodgings with the Bellamy family at Harrow on the Hill, Middlesex. The circumstances of his death are somewhat confused. However, there does appear to be evidence that Bristow was arrested and arraigned with his old friend Campion and others on 14 November. Bristow gave as his reason for returning to England the relief of his poor widowed mother. The Douai diary records his death in London on 14 October 1581, but the entry seems to be a later insertion after the news had arrived, though in the same hand. It would not have been impossible to have confused the months. Anstruther concludes that 'Bristow died in prison on 14th November 1581 between arraignment and indictment' and that 'natural death robbed us of a martyr' (Anstruther, 53). Gillow comments: 'His death was a general loss to the cause as well as to the College at Douay, for, according to the character given to him in its records, he might rival Allen in prudence, Stapleton in acumen, Campion in eloquence, Wright in theology, and Martin in languages' (Gillow, *Lit. biog. hist.*, 301).

PETER E. B. HARRIS

Sources G. Anstruther, *The seminary priests*, 1 (1969) · Gillow, *Lit. biog. hist.*, vol. 1 · A. C. Southern, *Elizabethan recusant prose, 1559–1582* (1950) · P. Holmes, *Resistance and compromise: the political thought of the Elizabethan Catholics* (1982) · T. F. Knox and others, eds., *The first and second diaries of the English College, Douay* (1878) · P. Milward, *Religious controversies of the Elizabethan age* (1977) · P. McGrath, 'The bloody questions reconsidered', *Recusant History*, 20 (1990–91), 305–19 · D. A. Bellenger, ed., *English and Welsh priests, 1558–1800* (1984) · A. Gasquet, *A history of the venerable English College, Rome* (1920) · G. E. Phillips, *The extinction of the ancient hierarchy* (1905) · P. Hughes, *The Reformation in England*, rev. edn, 3 vols. in 1 (1963)

Bristowe, John Syer (1827–1895), physician, was born in Camberwell, Surrey, on 19 January 1827, the eldest son of John Syer Bristowe, a medical practitioner in Camberwell, and his wife, Mary, *née* Chesshyre. He was educated at Enfield and King's College schools, and, from 1846, St Thomas's Hospital, where he won many prizes, including the highest distinction, the treasurer's gold medal. In 1849 he became a member of the Royal College of Surgeons of England and licentiate of the Society of Apothecaries. He graduated MB, London, in 1850 with medals in surgery, anatomy, and materia medica, and MD, London, in 1852. Bristowe was appointed house surgeon at St Thomas's Hospital in 1849. A range of appointments followed there: curator of the museum and pathologist (1850), assistant physician (1854), lectureships in botany (1859), materia medica (1860), general anatomy and physiology (1865), pathology (1870), and medicine (1876), and full physician (1860). Bristowe married, on 9 October 1856, Miriam Isabella, eldest surviving daughter of Joseph P. Stearns of Dulwich. They had five sons and five daughters. Bristowe held many important offices in the Royal College of Physicians and became FRS in 1881. At various times he held the presidencies of the Pathological Society of London, the Neurological Society, the Medical Society of London, the Society of Medical Officers of Health, the Hospital

Association, and the metropolitan counties' branch of the British Medical Association.

In his lifetime Bristowe's reputation rested on his powers of description, his diagnostic acumen—'slow but very sure … perhaps in consequence of his very exceptional pathological experience … diagnosis in doubtful cases was postponed, and an expectant attitude was maintained' (Newsholme, 35)—and his textbook, *The Theory and Practice of Medicine* (1876), which went through seven editions before 1890. It 'displayed throughout the extent to which chemistry, microscopy, cellular pathology, and bacteriology had been the key sciences for clinical medicine of his lifetime' (Bynum, 140). A therapeutic nihilist, his favourite prescription for most diseases was 'Inf. Gent. Co.' which, he said, was a bitter tonic, nearly as good, though not so nice, as a glass of beer. Parsons recounts the anecdote that at the bedside of a woman who had lost her voice but was very garrulous in a whisper, Bristowe wrote something thought, at last, to be a prescription. It read:

Through grief the Lady lost her voice
Her grief remains. Her friends rejoice.
(Parsons, 3.215)

In hospital lore he was famous for diagnosing tabes dorsalis in the assistant surgeon, W. W. Wagstaffe, after observing his gait along the hospital corridor, and for doodling and drawing on committee papers and patients' records.

Bristowe's reputation now rests largely on his public health work, primarily as a member of the privy council medical department in the 1860s, but also as medical officer of health for Camberwell from 1856 to 1895. The former was a group of doctors led by the council's medical officer, John Simon. Commitment to the sanitary cause led to an outraged secretary to the Treasury describing their activities as 'unlimited missionary action' (Lambert, 314). Bristowe's appointment was part time and temporary, paying 3 guineas a day with expenses. He acted as a 'shoe-leather' epidemiologist, preparing detailed reports on fever in Calstock (1861), Whitehaven (1863), Grantham (1864), and Debenham (1864). All contributed to the medical department's policy to 'shock localities with incontrovertible proof of sanitary neglect' (Lambert, 432). His 'Report on the manufactures in which phosphorus is produced or employed, and on the health of the persons engaged on them' (1862) and 'Inquiry whether the rag trade is of influence in spreading infections of disease' (1865) were part of the department's major investigation at this time into occupational health—'the most meticulous and comprehensive survey of the sanitary condition of labour so far undertaken directly by English government' (Lambert, 331). The phosphorus inquiry was concerned largely with jaw necrosis in matchmakers. He visited fifty-seven matchmaking establishments in London, Norwich, Bristol, Manchester, Newcastle, Nottingham, Liverpool, Birmingham, Leeds, and Leicester. Through personal enquiries and the literature he discovered fifty-six cases of jaw disease. He examined seventeen himself. In his inquiry into the rag trade he tested the hypothesis that smallpox in country districts had its origins in the rag departments of paper mills. After visiting a dozen rag merchants, a score of marine store dealers, a factory handling challies (cotton and wool rags from dresses), and eighty-six paper mills from Devon to Lancashire he concluded that smallpox was rarely contracted from rags.

Bristowe's most substantial report, on the hospitals of the United Kingdom, was conducted in 1863 jointly with Timothy Holmes, surgeon at St George's Hospital, London. It was commissioned after the debate between Simon and Florence Nightingale and others about the site for the new St Thomas's Hospital. Simon considered that it should remain in the metropolis and be located on the banks of the Thames, a particularly unhealthy location according to Miss Nightingale. Simon prevailed. The Bristowe–Holmes report supported him: 'we have been led irresistibly to the conclusion, that the chief cause of all the differences, real and apparent, which exist between different hospitals, is to be found in the constitution of the hospital itself'. Location was deemed less important. In its preparation Bristowe and Holmes together visited thirty-seven hospitals in England, six in Scotland, and two in Paris, and by himself Bristowe inspected a further thirty-three, thirteen in Ireland. The 280-page report 'forms a milestone in the literature of the nineteenth century hospital' (Taylor, 27). It describes buildings and internal arrangements in detail and analyses surgical operations and their mortality, providing a comprehensive picture of events just before the introduction of antisepsis. Bristowe retired from St Thomas's Hospital in 1892. He died on 20 August 1895, at Dixton vicarage, Monmouth, and was buried at Norwood cemetery, London. He was survived by his wife.　　T. H. PENNINGTON

Sources W. M. O., 'In memoriam—John Syer Bristowe', *St Thomas's Hospital Reports*, new ser., 23 (1896), xvii–xxv • *DNB* • F. G. Parsons, *The history of St Thomas's Hospital*, 3 (1936) • A. Newsholme, *Fifty years in public health: the years preceding 1909* (1935) • R. Lambert, *Sir John Simon, 1816–1904, and English social administration* (1963) • A. Wilkinson, 'The beginnings of disease control in London: the work of the medical officers of health in 3 parishes, 1850–1990', DPhil diss., U. Oxf., 1981 • Reports of the Medical Officer of the Privy Council, 1860–65 • J. Taylor, *Hospital and asylum architecture in England* (1991) • W. F. Bynum, *Science and the practice of medicine in the nineteenth century* (1994) • Transactions of the Pathological Society of London [membership lists] • m. cert. • d. cert.

Likenesses photograph, 1893, repro. in *St. Thomas's Hospital Reports* • photograph, before 1893, repro. in Newsholme, *Fifty years in public health* • A. Wyon, bronze medal, 1895 • B. M. Bristowe, oils, St Thomas's Hospital, London • wood-engraving (after photograph by Jerrard), NPG; repro. in *ILN* (31 Aug 1895)

Wealth at death £16,119 6s. 4d.: probate, 16 Sept 1895, *CGPLA Eng. & Wales*

Brit, Walter. See Bryt, Walter (*fl.* 14th cent.).

Britannia (*fl.* 1st–21st cent.), allegory of a nation, emblem of empire, and patriotic icon, is by origin a child of Rome, representing an outpost of the Roman empire. Her earliest known appearances did not augur well for her future: rock reliefs at Aphrodisias in south-west Turkey, dating to the middle of the first century AD, illustrate the conquest of Britain with scenes of the emperor Claudius (*r.* AD 41–

Britannia (*fl.* 1st–21st cent.), by Jan Roettier, 1667 [reverse]

54) overpowering a distraught Britannia. Dressed as an Amazon, one breast bared, she is forced to the ground as Claudius grabs her hair and raises his arm to strike her. However, in the following century she was shown in a more positive light on coins of the emperor Hadrian (*r.* AD 117–138), as part of a series minted in Rome personifying the territories of the empire.

This was Britannia's first portrayal on currency, laying the foundation for a long tradition in the future. As with her sister provinces, she is named by the inscription on the coin. Seated on rocks which are perhaps indicative of Hadrian's projected wall, she leans her bare head on her hand and is armed with a spear and large shield with a spike in the centre. Some commentators have interpreted her bowed head as sorrow at her subjugation, but in Hadrian's view of empire his regions were not slaves but faithful satellites, and Britannia appears on the coins to be vigilant, armed, and secure on her rocky ground, characteristics which remain central to her being. She is also distinguished by native British features such as her tunic and breeches and the spiked shield, in contrast to the classical drapery of the other personifications. Some coins of Antoninus Pius (*r.* AD 138–161), Hadrian's successor, seem to show her downcast and dejected, acknowledgement perhaps of Rome's aggression in crushing native uprisings, but this is not typical—generally she maintains her watchful stance. One attractive coin design even anticipates Britannia's later role as ruler of an empire: she is seated on a globe above the sea, relaxing against her shield, resting her right foot on the globe and swinging her left above the waves. Later, one of the coins minted in London for the usurper Carausius (*r.* AD 287–293) provided a positive interpretation of his rebellion in Britain by depicting a standing Britannia welcoming him as emperor, with the inscription 'Expectate Veni' ('Come O expected one'). In the eighteenth century the pedestal of an ancient statue with a Latin dedication to Britannia was

apparently discovered in York. Unfortunately the statue itself had disappeared and with only the impression of the feet remaining, there is no record of how she was depicted. The base, too, is now lost; however, if genuine, this is the only epigraphic reference from Roman Britain to the person of Britannia.

These early sightings of Britannia have been associated with the Celtic deity Brigantia, seen in a stone relief from a Roman site in Dumfriesshire, but her lineage may be traced even further back to the Greek goddess Pallas Athene, warrior-queen, guardian, and giver of wise counsel, qualities subsequently ascribed to the Roman goddess Minerva. In later manifestations Britannia is frequently shown with Athene's warrior attributes—crested helmet, breastplate, spear, and shield, but she is also often bareheaded, holding an olive branch, a reminder of the belief that Athene gave the first olive tree to her city, a source of food and symbol of peace. Often Britannia is summoned to be the champion of heroes, protector of cities, and keeper of the nation's conscience, ever reflecting the polarity of Athene's nature: action and contemplation, strength and compassion. More rarely, she may reveal her wilder aspect, with gorgon's head, or hint at the archetypal female, mysterious source of fertility and nourishment.

Early modern renaissance After her first appearance in the Roman world, Britannia did not re-emerge until the late sixteenth century. In the highly symbolic frontispiece of his *General and Rare Memorials portraying the Perfect Art of Navigation* (1577) John Dee included a small figure of Britannia kneeling by the shore beseeching Elizabeth I, seated in a ship, to protect her empire by strengthening her navy. Here Britannia is clearly in thrall to her glorious monarch, but later images may be seen as a legacy of the Elizabethan age, a period of renaissance inspiring classical ideals, national expansion, and naval triumph, exemplified by the defeat of the Spanish Armada. Elizabeth's long rule may also have encouraged representation of the nation by a female figure after her death. The union of the crowns (1603) by which James VI and I proclaimed himself king of Great Britain may have inspired new expressions of national imagery, among them the union flag which first appeared in 1606. Some early seventeenth-century manifestations of Britannia referred back to her Roman origins, but made it clear that she now assumed a position of authority. Thus in 1607 the title-page of William Camden's *Britain, or, A chorographicall description of the most flourishing kingdomes, England, Scotland and Ireland* showed a small figure of Britannia similar to that on Roman coins, bareheaded, with tunic and spiked shield, while beneath her figures of Ceres and Neptune point to her dominion over land and sea—earlier and later editions were adorned simply with emblems or heraldic devices. In 1612 Henry Peacham's book of emblems, *Minerva Britannia, or, A garden of heroical devises*, showed her standing on a shore repelling a Roman ship (emblem 208): the accompanying verse describes how once she was a Roman captive, 'with haire dishevel'd and in mournfull wise', but now Rome stands in awe of her.

Despite James's personal union of the two kingdoms, regions of Britain retained distinct identities, and both then and in succeeding centuries Britannia served to depict England alone as well as the whole of Britain. In *Britannia's Pastorals* (1616) William Browne's Devon shepherd singing 'What need I tune the swains of Thessaly? … Thus, dear Britannia, will I sing of thee' may well be praising England, while the lord mayor's show of 1628 featured Britannia as 'a Mother's Counsel', supported by pillars to represent the united realms of York and Lancaster. The same distinction is explicit in the splendid figure adorning the title-page of Michael Drayton's *Poly Olbion* in 1612, her robe formed of a topographical map of England reminiscent of that on which Elizabeth I stands in the Ditchley portrait: though some may see her as Britannia, Drayton's work is concerned only with England and Wales, and he names the figure Albion.

Ruler of the waves Later in the seventeenth century John Roettier began a long tradition of medallic art featuring Britannia as the guardian of her kingdom. His medals celebrating naval victories and the peace of Breda between England and the Netherlands in 1667 depicted Britannia seated at the foot of a rock, surveying her fleets at sea; in one she is crowned with laurel by two genii. This association drew on the myth that Neptune had surrendered his sovereignty of the sea to Britannia, who in succeeding centuries has since been regularly portrayed seated by the shore, admiring her navy, guiding sea-borne trade, and above all holding a trident, even when standing on dry land. She may even appear exuberantly riding the waves in a shell chariot drawn by sea horses, sometimes indeed with Neptune as her companion. Here again is a link with Athene, believed in Greek myth to have built the first ship. In 1672 Britannia received official status, being placed on the back of copper coins of Charles II. Designed by Roettier, the coins were clearly derived from Roman prototypes, showing Britannia seated on a globe, with spear and shield, but her profile resembles that on the medals, which was reputed, not least from a reference by Samuel Pepys, to be that of the king's alleged mistress, Frances Teresa *Stuart, later the duchess of Lennox and Richmond. Opinion has since been divided as to whether the similarity was intentional, though certainly the features and hairstyle of the Britannia bear comparison with Roettier's elegant bust of Stuart on a portrait medal. In 1694 the newly founded Bank of England chose Britannia for its seal and placed her on all its notes, sitting gazing on a 'bank of mony'. Given this date, before the union of the Scottish and English parliaments in 1707, and the role of the bank in financing English concerns (the Bank of Scotland was founded in 1695), this is perhaps another instance of Britannia representing England rather than a wider Britain. However, from these beginnings Britannia became a constant feature on money, so consolidating her role in daily life as a symbol of authority.

In the eighteenth century Britannia combined her official role with less formal public appearances as she was swept up in the fervour of popular nationalism, rousingly articulated in Thomas Arne's setting of James *Thomson's song 'Rule Britannia', published in 1740. In medals, prints, and broadsheets she was invoked as mentor to the sovereign and the British people, victorious wager of war, and patron of resulting peace and prosperity. On a glorious medal by Thomas Pingo jun. to mark George III's accession in 1760 she serenades king and country, playing a tambourine while her sons and daughters, the children of the land, dance round an oak tree. Throughout succeeding reigns, Britannia's allegiance to the throne continued on commemorative medals showing her attending royal coronations, marriages, births, and deaths. But her protection also extended to her subjects, their welfare and their duty: a print of 1756 entitled *The acceptable fast, or, Britannia's maternal call to her children to deep humiliation, repentance and amendment in heart and life* shows her with arms outstretched, extolling moral virtue to all classes of society.

But such virtue was not always practised, even by those in positions of power, and political satire often revealed Britannia beaten and abused, helpless against her enemies. In such cases she may have evoked the defeated majesty of the monarch or the vulnerability of citizens, becoming an emotive vehicle for political protest. Failure to address foreign threats provoked much anger: in *Britannia: a Poem*, written in 1727 and published two years later, James Thomson described her as the queen of nations, despairing as her feeble sons failed to keep the Spanish at bay, in contrast to earlier naval strength:

> Bare was her throbbing bosom to the gale
> That hoarse, and hollow, from the bleak surge blew.

A print of 1757 depicted her tied down and mutilated by the French army, while its title, *A View of the Assassination of the Lady of John Bull*, united her with another popular patriotic figure of the age. In 1776 a print entitled *The Parricide* attacked the radical John Wilkes, shown encouraging the rebellious colonies in America in the form of a Native American woman threatening Britannia with a tomahawk and knife. At home, the domestic violence of internal politics was no less frightful: a print parodying Poussin's *Martyrdom of St Erasmus* displays Britannia's half-naked body on a table, her mouth stretched in a grimace of horror as she is dismembered by the cut and thrust of corrupt politicians.

Typically, however, Britannia's breast remained sternly encased in armour as she urged her troops to victory. As early as 1682 the Royal Navy gave the name Britannia to a gunship; in 1707 Queen Anne granted the regiment of English line infantry ultimately known as the Royal Norfolk regiment a figure of Britannia for their badge, in recognition of their bravery at the battle of Almanza during the War of the Spanish Succession. Winning further glory during the Peninsular War, the regiment became known as 'the Holy Boys' reputedly from the Spaniards' rather surprising assumption that Britannia with her helmet, trident, and shield—and, admittedly, an olive branch—was the Virgin Mary. In 1716 the decorative artist James Thornhill's ceiling for the Great Hall in Blenheim Palace commemorated victory over the French with Britannia about to crown the duke of Marlborough with laurel, while admiring his battle plans. During the 1750s she appeared on a series of medals marking successful actions, such as that of James Wolfe in Quebec, and in the 1790s she celebrated Nelson's naval triumphs. A medal by Conrad Küchler for the victories of 1798 shows her seated among trophies of war, holding a small figure of victory in the tradition of classical iconography, while a drawing by Philip James de Loutherbourg places her next to George III, with the British lion fiercely defending his shores as the sun breaks through the clouds. It may be no coincidence that on his new 'cartwheel' copper coinage of 1797 Matthew Boulton depicted her ruling the seas, holding a trident rather than a spear, with waves around her and a ship in the distance. Just as she gloried in Nelson's conquests, so Britannia shared the nation's sorrow at his death at Trafalgar in 1805. Thus James Gillray drew Nelson leaning against a weeping Britannia without her helmet, while broadsides described her tears for a darling son, her hero now at rest. Indeed, the growing cult of popular hero-worship gave her a spiritual role as the embodiment of national consciousness and mourning. In 1852, on a medal for the death of the duke of Wellington, she is draped in mourning, leaning her head on her right hand and attended by her lion, symbol of bravery. In this role Britannia reached beyond official duty to convey the emotions of the people: for example, when Queen Caroline died in 1821, having been reviled by her husband and the government, the public's sympathy was expressed in commemorative pieces such as a glazed dish showing Britannia seated sadly by a sarcophagus with the legend 'To the Memory of Caroline, the injured and persecuted Queen of Great Britain'.

Imperial icon Above all, however, the nineteenth-century Britannia presided over a nation made richer by the rewards of trade and empire. Her capitalist function as protector of commerce is exemplified by her many appearances on the nation's money. On Bank of England notes her pile of coins had been transformed into a beehive, traditional emblem of industry, while on the notes issued by many hundreds of local banks serving towns across Britain she performed a variety of functions. Usually she is shown with plumed helmet, breastplate, and trident or spear, with a shield bearing the union flag; she was also sometimes accompanied by a lion lying watchfully at her feet. On other occasions she stood alone, next to a landmark of the town, or was the central figure in an elegant triumvirate with Scotia and Hibernia—a composition pointing up the ambiguity that on some occasions she represents only England. In lending her authority to these private banks, Britannia bestowed upon them desirable classical qualities of wisdom and prudence; she also echoed Athene's role as goddess of the city, thus assuming civic responsibilities as well as her national duties. But there is evidence too of a wider ambition, the expansion of overseas trade and colonization: banks based in coastal towns, and even some that were not, frequently depicted her surrounded by cargo with a background of ships at sea. In the colonies themselves, images of Britannia

emphasized British imperial supremacy. On notes for Ceylon in the late 1840s she gestures towards an elephant, palm trees, and the sea symbolizing her territory, while for the Bank of Bengal she accepts the fruits of empire from a cornucopia offered up by a kneeling Indian woman. From 1840 similar imagery was adopted for colonial postage: though William Mulready's postal stationery boasting Britannia and her lion directing commerce to all the peoples of the empire was ridiculed and soon withdrawn, vignettes of Britannia with bales of sugar were adopted for stamps in Mauritius, Trinidad, and Barbados, with variations spreading to other colonies.

Later images show that the influence of empire was just as strongly felt within Britain. In *Britannia and her Boys* by G. Durand, printed in *The Graphic* in 1885, Britannia stands aloft in her chariot, her long hair streaming as she brandishes the union flag above the 'boys', who surround her—soldiers drawn from every corner of her lands, Sikh turbans marching with Scottish tartans. A year later, a map of the world by the writer on imperial defence J. C. R. Colomb showed her seated on a globe supported by Atlas, gazing down on the peoples and creatures of her empire. By the turn of the century popular sentiment was infused with passion for empire: she appeared on postcards in regal pose, next to patriotic verses, and, in a rare moment of sensuality, adorned a programme of the Empire Theatre in a clinging gown, her hair tumbling loose from her helmet. Inside theatres, the contralto Clara *Butt thrilled audiences by dressing as Britannia for her performances of 'Land of Hope and Glory', a practice later adopted by others at the last night of the Proms. At the Devonshire House ball to celebrate Victoria's diamond jubilee in 1897 Edith Amelia, Lady Wolverhampton, attended as Britannia, another splendid indication that Britannia had so successfully represented her people that they now personified her.

Twentieth century and beyond The First World War aroused Britannia's martial character, evident in her defiant stance on treasury 10s. notes and her helmeted head on national savings stamps. But it awakened sorrow, too, for E. Carter Preston's design for the 800,000 memorial plaques given to the next of kin of all who died in the First World War carried the most poignant and personal image of Britannia in mourning. Her lion beside her, she walks with head bowed, her face sombre, holding out a wreath to honour the fallen. In contrast, during the Second World War, Russell Flint's Britannia for a war savings card was a haughty creature, hand on thigh as she stamped contemptuously on a crumpled Nazi flag. An imperial and naval theme lingered on high-value postage stamps depicting Britannia surging through the waves in a chariot drawn by sea horses, a powerful design reintroduced in 1990 to commemorate the introduction of the Penny Black postage in 1840. A new £10 stamp in 1993 reverted to the stern profile of a classical seated figure, but brought her up to date with a bust size conforming to the national average of 36B.

In 1951 the festival of Britain had as its symbol a helmeted profile of Britannia surmounting the points of a compass to represent Britain's contribution to civilization, but with the waning of empire and the weakening of British commercial supremacy Britannia's role in national life diminished in the second half of the twentieth century. She reappears with every burst of popular patriotism: thus a medal commemorating Britain's first referendum on joining the European Union showed a bareheaded figure sitting on a little globe above a map of Europe—as with the empire, so may Europe be viewed comfortably from a superior vantage point; and during the Falklands War in 1982 Britannia as bringer of victory was invoked on medals and commemorative plate.

Politics too may generate contemporary versions of earlier imagery, such as the newspaper cartoons and souvenirs marking the Conservatives' three consecutive terms with images of Margaret Thatcher as Britannia in a smart blue suit and high heels. In daily life at the start of the twenty-first century Britannia lived on in the name of institutions and businesses, from the once royal yacht to, appropriately, an archaeological journal, a building society, and even a removal firm, which depicts her seated in classical style on the side of its vans. However, at a time when formality is out of fashion, her chivalrous dignity does not sit easily with the youth culture known as 'cool Britannia', but which by its very nature limits her appearance to traditional contexts, such as currency. On coins she has changed little, though on modern Bank of England notes she has moved through different fashions, from the serene sculptured head of the late 1950s to the demure child Britannia, modelled on the daughter of the artist, Reynolds Stone. Most recent issues have reverted to the mid-nineteenth-century incarnation by Daniel Maclise, a peaceable seated figure, bareheaded and holding an olive branch. Sometimes she takes the form of a reflective foil security feature, now offering practical as well as symbolic guardianship of the nation's wealth—even allegories, it seems, must work.

Over two millennia Britannia has matured from allegory of a province to spirit of a nation, variously characterized as subdued or martial, triumphant or compassionate, contemporary or timelessly dignified. Yet as globalization spreads and debate continues on the nature of 'Britishness', or whether such an identity even exists, it remains to be seen what part Britannia may play in her country's future. VIRGINIA HEWITT

Sources M. Dresser, 'Britannia', *Patriotism: the making and unmaking of British national identity*, vol. 3, ed. R. Samuel, *National fictions* (1989), 26–49 · *Britannia depicta: quality, value and security*, National Postal Museum (1993) · H. Mattingly, *Nerva to Hadrian*, reprint (1976), vol. 3 of *Coins of the Roman empire in the British Museum* · H. Mattingley, *Antoninus Pius* (1968), vol. 4 of *Coins of the Roman empire in the British Museum* · P. H. Webb, *Probus to Diocletian*, ed. H. Mattingly and E. A. Sydenham (1933), vol. 5/2 of *The Roman imperial coinage*, ed. H. Mattingly and others (1923–94) · J. M. C. Toynbee, *The Hadrianic school: a chapter in the history of Greek art* (1974) · M. Henig, 'Britannia', *Lexicon Iconographicum Mythologiae Classicae*, 3/1 (1983), 167–9; 3/2 (1983), 140–42 · K. T. Erim, 'A new relief showing Claudius and Britannia from Aphrodisias', *Britannia*, 13 (1982), 277–81 · *GM*, 1st ser., 10 (1740), 189 · H. Peacham, *Minerva Britannia, or, A garden of heroical devises* (1612) · M. Drayton, *Poly Olbion* (1612) ·

J. Thomson, *Britannia: a poem* (1729) · W. Browne, 'Britannia's pastorals', in R. Anderson, *A complete edition of the poets of Great Britain*, 4 (1793), 253–343 · F. A. Yates, *Astraea: the imperial theme in the sixteenth century* (1977) · R. Strong, *Gloriana, the portraits of Queen Elizabeth I* (1987) · H. A. Atherton, *Political prints in the age of Hogarth. A study of the ideographic representation of politics* (1974) · L. Brown, *British historical medals, 1760–1970*, vol. 1 (1980); vol. 2 (1987); vol. 3 (1995) · L. L. Gordon, *British battles and medals*, 4th edn (1971) · C. Eimer, *British commemorative medals and their values* (1987) · C. Eimer, *The Pingo family and medal-making in 18th century Britain* (1998) · C. W. Peck, *English copper, tin and bronze coins in the British Museum, 1558–1958*, 2nd edn (1970) · T. J. Edwards, *Regimental badges* (1953) · J. S. Farmer, *Regimental records* (1901) · V. H. Hewitt and J. M. Keyworth, *As good as gold: 300 years of British bank note design* (1987) · V. Hewitt, 'A distant view: imagery and imagination in the paper currency of the British empire, 1800–1960', *Nation-states and money. The past, present and future of national currencies*, ed. E. Gilbert and E. Helleiner (1999), 97–116 · J. Barnes, 'Letter from London. Real Britannia', *New Yorker* (12 April 1993), 36–42

Likenesses J. Roettier, gold medal (reverse), 1667, BM, George III, Eng. med. 87 [*see illus.*]

Brito, Ranulf [Ranulf le Breton] (d. **1246**), administrator and ecclesiastic, first appears in royal records in 1221 as a clerk of Hubert de Burgh. Throughout his career, his fortunes were to remain closely attached to those of his patron. As treasurer of the king's chamber, Brito accompanied the king's expedition to Brittany in 1230, but in the following year he was summarily dismissed from his offices and ordered to depart from the realm, a casualty of the factional infighting between Hubert de Burgh and the bishop of Winchester, Peter des Roches. Although de Burgh was quickly able to restore Brito to royal favour, in July 1232 des Roches exiled him from the realm and confiscated his secular property, probably because Brito, like de Burgh, was suspected of involvement in the anti-Roman riots that had occurred a few months earlier. Other grievances had also arisen against Brito. He had been active in acquiring properties during his time at court, and at Chalfont St Giles, Buckinghamshire, his acquisitions brought him into conflict both with the templars and with Missenden Abbey. He also seems to have been suspected of forest offences, including unauthorized assarting. In late September 1232 Brito promised the king a fine of £1000 to have his grace and the restoration of his lands. In 1234, however, he was still attempting to secure the complete return of his property.

Despite his retirement, in 1239 Brito again fell foul of the king's wrath. As they had certainly been in 1232, his problems in 1239 may have been connected with the renewed hostilities that erupted in that year between King Henry and Hubert de Burgh. In the latter year a former royal messenger and convicted felon became an approver and accused Brito of treason. At the king's command, the mayor of London thereupon dragged him from his house near St Paul's and placed him in chains in the Tower of London. This violation of clerical immunity brought a general sentence of excommunication upon all offenders from the dean and chapter of St Paul's (where Brito was a canon, having held the prebend of Caddington Major since 1228) and an interdict upon the cathedral church, which the bishop of London threatened to extend to the entire city if Brito was not immediately set free. The king yielded, and Brito was released. Soon afterwards the approver confessed the falsity of his accusations and was hanged. But Brito's relations with the king remained uneasy, and over the years that followed his ecclesiastical revenues were sequestered to force payment of the remainder of his 1232 fine. He died suddenly, in 1246, reportedly of apoplexy while watching a game of dice, with approximately £600 of his fine still owing. His heir was his brother and fellow royal official William le Breton.   ROBERT C. STACEY

Sources *Chancery records* · *Pipe rolls* · D. A. Carpenter, 'The fall of Hubert de Burgh', *Journal of British Studies*, 19/2 (1979–80), 1–17 · Paris, *Chron.* · C. A. F. Meekings, 'Justices of the Jews, 1216–68: a provisional list', *BIHR*, 28 (1955), 173–88 · *Fasti Angl., 1066–1300*, [St Paul's, London], 33 · N. Vincent, *Peter des Roches: an alien in English politics, 1205–38*, Cambridge Studies in Medieval Life and Thought, 4th ser., 31 (1996)

Briton, William. *See* Breton, Guillaume le (*fl.* 1249).

Brittain, Sir Henry Ernest [Harry] (1873–1974), journalist and politician, was born on 24 December 1873 at Storth Oaks, Ranmoor, near Sheffield, Yorkshire, the oldest surviving child in the family of two sons and three daughters (one daughter died in infancy) of William Henry Brittain (1835–1922), twice mayor of Sheffield, and twice master cutler, and his wife, Frances, daughter of J. J. Mellor of Prestbury, Cheshire. He was educated at Repton School and Worcester College, Oxford, where he was awarded a third-class degree in jurisprudence in 1896. After a year's training in the family steel business in Sheffield, he moved to London, where he was called to the bar at the Inner Temple in 1897, but he never practised.

Brittain's first job was as private secretary to Sir William Ingram, managing director of the *Illustrated London News*, leaving to work for C. Arthur Pearson, founder of the *Daily Express*, when Pearson acquired *The Standard* and the *Evening Standard* in 1902. In 1905 he married Alida Luisa (1883–1943), only daughter of Sir Robert Harvey of Dundridge, Devon, and his French wife. Alida, a Roman Catholic, had been born in Chile, where her father had made his fortune in the nitrate trade. A composer and a fine harpist, she was created DBE in 1928 for her political activities. They had one son and one daughter.

Inspired by his first visit to the United States in 1902, Brittain joined a group of American journalists and lawyers in London who were discussing the idea of founding a society that would bring Americans and Englishmen together to promote Anglo-American good fellowship. When the Pilgrims Society was formed in July 1902, Brittain was appointed honorary secretary. The Pilgrims Society of the United States was founded in New York in January 1903, with membership of one automatically entailing membership of the other. Harry Brittain was in his element as he built up the membership list, and invited distinguished guests to dinners, and soon he was the effective head of the organization. With a dinner in 1905 to welcome the new American ambassador, Whitelaw Reid, to Britain, the Pilgrims established the tradition that the first public speech made by an incoming American ambassador would be to the Pilgrims. Harry Brittain became

chairman in 1913, and after he resigned in 1919 he was elected a vice-president.

When Arthur Pearson was appointed chairman of the new Tariff Reform League by Joseph Chamberlain in July 1903, Brittain helped him to organize it. The Liberal landslide in the 1906 general election put an end to the league. In 1907, however, while visiting Canada as a member of a Board of Trade delegation, Brittain had the idea of organizing a meeting of the editors and owners of newspapers from all parts of the empire. He devoted the next two years to winning support for the first Imperial Press Conference, which took place in London in 1909, with fifty-five overseas representatives and over twenty British newspapermen. One permanent result of the conference was the formation of the Empire Press Union (from 1950, the Commonwealth Press Union).

With the outbreak of the First World War, Brittain was sent by Lord Grey on a mission to the United States in May 1915 representing the Royal Colonial Institute; he sailed on the last voyage of the *Lusitania* before it was torpedoed by the Germans. In 1917 he spent five months as director of the intelligence branch of the national service department. After the entry of the United States into the war, Brittain mobilized the Pilgrims Society to establish the American Officers' Club.

Harry Brittain was knighted in 1918 and successfully fought the 1918 'coupon' election as Unionist candidate for the new constituency of Acton, serving as MP until his defeat in the 1929 general election. He steered a private member's bill for the protection of wild singing birds through parliament in 1925, and he was on the committee of the Empire Parliamentary Association. During the 1930s he busied himself with his numerous committees: he was, for example, on the committee of the Oxford Society, founded in 1932 along the lines of an American alumni association, and he took on the responsibility of tracing Oxford University graduates in the United States and the empire.

At the beginning of the Second World War, Brittain hoped for a job in the United States on an Anglo-American committee, but when this failed to materialize he became vice-chairman of a government hospitality committee for American servicemen, set up in 1942. Together with the chairman, Sir Edward Grigg, he started the Churchill Club, and organized the Oxford leave courses at Balliol College. He also joined the panel of the Anglo-American Brains Trust, touring British army camps.

Sir Harry Brittain was a superb organizer, attending to every detail, and he loved committees: he was a member of the British Peace Centenary Committee from 1912 to 1914, president of the British International Association of Journalists in 1920–1922, representative of the British Olympic Association at the winter games in Chamonix in 1924, a founder member of the British Travel Association in 1929, and a vice-president of the English-Speaking Union. Although he was not universally popular, he was very gregarious, a member of the Bath and Carlton clubs, and a well-known public figure, always with a carnation in his buttonhole (the 'Sir Harry Brittain' carnation won an award at the 1938 Chelsea flower show). He also loved travel, and claimed to have visited every country in Europe except Albania, and every state in the United States. He was a fine sportsman, excelling especially at tennis, skiing, and shooting, and enjoying golf. He was also a prolific writer: his books include *To Verdun from the Somme* (1917); *The ABC of the BBC: the Romance of British Wireless* (1932); a history of the first forty years of the Pilgrims Society, *Pilgrim Partners* (1942); and two volumes of autobiography, *Pilgrims and Pioneers* (1945) and *Happy Pilgrimage* (1949).

In 1961 Brittain remarried. His second wife was Muriel Lesley (1905–1994), daughter of H. Leslie Dixon; she had been his private secretary since the mid-1950s. He remained active to the very end of his long life, and, as Lord Astor said at his memorial service, he never lost his 'boyish enthusiasm'. Elected Pilgrim emeritus in 1971, he resigned the chairmanship of the Pilgrims' membership committee in 1972 at the age of ninety-eight, and was guest of honour at the seventieth anniversary dinner on 25 January 1972. The last Pilgrims function he attended was only a few weeks before his death, on 9 July 1974 at his London home, 88 St James's Street, SW1. He was buried on 12 July at Randalls Park, Leatherhead, Surrey.

ANNE PIMLOTT BAKER

Sources H. Brittain, *Pilgrims and pioneers* (1945) • H. Brittain, *Happy pilgrimage* (1949) • H. Brittain, *Pilgrim partners* (1942) • archives of the Pilgrims Society of Great Britain, Allington Castle, Maidstone, Kent • A. Harvie, *Those glittering years* (1980) • *The Times* (10 July 1974) • *WWW* • Harry Brittain's collection of newspaper cuttings, Worcester College, Oxford • papers, Institute of Commonwealth Studies, London

Archives BLPES, papers | archives of the Pilgrims Society of Great Britain, Allington Castle, Maidstone, Kent • BL, corresp. with Lord Northcliffe, Add. MS 62166 • Bodl. Oxf., corresp. with A. L. Goodhart

Likenesses W. Orpen, portrait, c.1911, probably Carlton Club; repro. in Brittain, *Pilgrims and pioneers*, frontispiece

Wealth at death £70,968: probate, 20 Aug 1974, CGPLA Eng. & Wales

Brittain, Sir Herbert (1894–1961), civil servant, was born in Preston, Lancashire, on 3 July 1894, son of the Revd John Hicks Brittain, a teacher, and his wife, Martha Elizabeth Gration. He was educated at Rochdale secondary school and Manchester University, where he graduated BSc with second-class honours in mathematics in 1915. He served in the Royal Field Artillery (1915–19), reaching the rank of major, and was twice mentioned in dispatches. He entered the civil service in 1919, going straight into the Treasury, where he spent his entire career. On 26 May 1920 he married Annie Crabtree (b. 1894/5), with whom he had one son and one daughter.

Of Brittain's first ten years in the Treasury, no less than eight were spent as private secretary, first to Basil Blackett, the first controller of the Treasury finance department, and then to successive financial secretaries. This latter post was rather routine and dull, but was the focal point of contact between the Treasury and parliament. Brittain used these years to become the acknowledged authority on supply procedure and wrote the standard

Treasury manual on the subject, *The British Budgetary System* (1959). In the first half of the 1930s he worked as one of the two principals in external finance, but returned to home finance in 1937 on promotion to the rank of assistant secretary and appointment as the Treasury officer of accounts. This official advises Whitehall on public accounting practice and is the standing Treasury representative before the public accounts committee and, thus, the main channel of communication between the executive and parliament.

On promotion to the rank of third secretary in 1942, Brittain added important additional duties in managing the wartime borrowing programme. In this area he struggled to absorb the advice of the economist and statesman John Maynard Keynes, who was brought into the Treasury in 1940 to range freely over wartime monetary and fiscal policies. Like Keynes, Brittain sought to minimize the cost of wartime borrowing and ensure that the maturity dates of government loans were spread evenly, but he resisted the Keynesian approach of using the Treasury's borrowing and spending after the war as a powerful tool of peacetime macroeconomic management. As a result Brittain—in some ways the very embodiment of the Treasury attitudes that Keynes had confronted during the inter-war years—received some very public humiliations from Keynes's acerbic tongue.

Brittain was indeed much less comfortable in the post-war Treasury than he had been in the 1930s. But he was not alone in finding it difficult to cope with the Treasury's much more exposed post-war position. It was not until the later 1950s that the Treasury's structures and leading personalities were really appropriate to its expanded roles in Whitehall and national economic management. Brittain strove to come to terms with the new demands but had the misfortune to be transferred back to overseas finance shortly before the devaluation of 1949, which created intense friction between Treasury officials and the Labour Party's economic ministers. He also subsequently played an important part in the Robot scheme to float sterling, which poisoned relations within the Treasury until the later 1950s. His conscientiousness carried him through these difficult times, and he was rewarded in 1953 by promotion to second secretary in charge of home finance and supply expenditure, his area of strength. After retirement in 1957 he took on a number of boardroom posts in industry and finance, and produced his book on the British budgetary system. He was appointed CB in 1941, KBE in 1944, and KCB in 1955.

Despite spending his career in London, Brittain remained a Lancastrian in speech and outlook, and epitomized the very Lancastrian virtues of mental toughness, practical good sense, and a conscientious approach to work. He was a dark, small, rather round and neat man—not unlike his handwriting—who was a diffident speaker and not always a success in conferences and meetings. His effectiveness as a civil servant came, first, from his mastery of the facts and his ability to anticipate and circumvent snags, and second from his ability as a draftsman. His minutes and memoranda were invariably economical and businesslike but were also carefully tailored to specific needs. He knew, for example, that the wartime chancellor of the exchequer, Sir Kingsley Wood, had been a preacher and liked biblical references in his speeches, and Brittain duly included them. He also had a talent for impersonation that was not entirely in keeping with the rest of his character. He died in St George's Hospital, Westminster, London, on 6 September 1961; his wife survived him.

ALAN BOOTH

Sources *The Times* (8 Sept 1961) · treasury registered files, PRO · G. C. Peden, *The treasury and British public policy, 1906–1959* (2000) · *The Robert Hall diaries*, ed. A. Cairncross, 2 vols. (1989–91) · *British Imperial Calendar and Civil Service List* · CGPLA Eng. & Wales (1961) · b. cert. · m. cert. · d. cert.
Likenesses photograph, repro. in *The Times*
Wealth at death £4425 13s. 7d.: probate, 21 Nov 1961, CGPLA Eng. & Wales

Brittain, Thomas (1806–1884), naturalist, was born in Sheffield on 2 January 1806. After receiving his education at a private school he followed a career as a professional accountant. Throughout his life, however, he pursued an active amateur interest in natural science and especially, after 1834 when he obtained his first microscope, in microscopy.

Brittain moved about 1842 to Manchester, where he remained for the rest of his life. There he took a leading role in local scientific societies. In December 1858 he was one of the promoters of a Manchester Microscopical Society, which ultimately became a section of the Manchester Literary and Philosophical Society. When a second Manchester Microscopical Society—a more popular association—was established in 1879, he repeatedly held the office of vice-president, and, in 1882, president. For many years he lectured on various subjects of natural science to a great number of the mechanics' institutes and similar bodies. He made frequent contributions to the *Manchester City News*, *Unitarian Herald*, and other papers on matters of scientific interest. He was also involved in an unsuccessful attempt to establish a Manchester aquarium, and had a short experience, from 1858 to 1860, of municipal work. On 4 October 1883 he was presented with an address at the Manchester Athenaeum to mark his retirement, which was due to failing health and advancing years. He died on 23 January 1884 at his home, 3 Lodge Avenue, Urmston, near Manchester, and was buried two days later in Ardwick cemetery. He was married, with children, but no details of his wife are known.

Brittain's published works include a collection of songs, a manual on how to win at whist, a pamphlet guide to the Manchester aquarium, and a volume entitled *Micro-Fungi, when and where to Find them* which, in spite of some obvious defects, was said to have been of considerable use to local students. It was arranged in order of the months of the year and first appeared in the *Northern Microscopist*. While Brittain did not make any claim to be a discoverer, he was a clear and animated speaker and did much to popularize the taste for natural history in and around Manchester.

W. E. A. AXON, *rev.* GILES HUDSON

Sources Desmond, *Botanists*, rev. edn, 101 · *Manchester Guardian* (24 Jan 1884) · *Transactions of the Liverpool Botanical Society*, 1 (1909), 62 · *Gardeners' Chronicle*, new ser., 21 (1884), 155 · personal knowledge (1885) · CGPLA Eng. & Wales (1884)
Archives Yorkshire Museum, plants
Likenesses London Stereoscopic Co., photomezzotype photograph, repro. in *Transactions of the Manchester Microscopical Society* (1891), frontispiece
Wealth at death £197 4s. 5d.: probate, 4 March 1884, CGPLA Eng. & Wales

Brittain [married name Catlin], **Vera Mary** (1893–1970), writer, was born on 29 December 1893 at Atherstone House, Sidmouth Avenue, Newcastle under Lyme, Staffordshire, the elder of the two children of (Thomas) Arthur Brittain (1864–1935), a paper manufacturer, and his wife, Edith Mary, née Bervon (1868–1948), daughter of John Bervon, a musician and church organist. In 1895 the Brittains moved from Newcastle under Lyme to the manufacturing town of Macclesfield, Cheshire. Vera's brother, Edward Harold Brittain (1895–1918), was born on 30 November 1895. As they grew up, tended by a governess and servants, in an environment of Conservative middle-class values, close supervision, and comparative isolation, brother and sister formed a companionship that was to be a dominant force in Vera's life. Her main vocation was established early: 'As a child I wrote because it was as natural to me to write as to breathe, and before I could write I invented stories' (V. Brittain, *On Becoming a Writer*, 1947, 172).

Early years of a feminist The Brittains moved again in 1905 to Buxton, Derbyshire, 10 miles away, in the Peak District. In that fashionable spa resort town, the Brittains lived in a large house, High Leigh, for two years; then an even larger house, Melrose, near the park. While she enjoyed physical activities like tennis, and walking in the country surrounding Buxton, Vera felt suffocated by the town's smug provincial mores and rigid social life. Pretty and diminutive, with dark hair and striking violet eyes, she was lively, highly intelligent, and ambitious. Shy, but also demanding and volatile, she repeatedly clashed with her conventionally patriarchal father and rejected her mother's acceptance of the traditional female roles of subservient wife and housekeeper. Her calmer brother gave her support and advice through this stormy period; but his companionship was diminished by educational separation. After two years at the Grange School in Buxton, Vera was sent to boarding-school in 1907. She was fortunate to be sent to St Monica's, a recently established girls' school in Kingswood, Surrey, that offered a solid, well-rounded education rather than stressing purely social 'feminine' attainments. She went there because one of the school's two principals was an aunt, Florence Bervon. The other, Louise Heath-Jones, the school's formidable founder, exerted a powerful influence, as did Edith Fry, a teacher who strongly encouraged Brittain's literary talent and ambition. Her younger, less intellectual brother was sent to Uppingham School in 1908.

Back in Buxton during 1912 and 1913 Brittain attended a course of Oxford University extension lectures given by

Vera Mary Brittain (1893–1970), by Howard Coster, 1936

the historian John Marriott, who encouraged her academic ambition. Inspired also by a nearby vicar, Joseph Ward, and his socialist ideals, Brittain set about qualifying herself for admission to one of the recently established women's colleges at Oxford. Coaching at a local crammer enabled her to pass the university and college entrance examinations, and she was awarded a Somerville College exhibition to study English literature. By then she had met Edward's closest schoolfriend, Roland Leighton, elder son of the two popular novelists Robert Leighton and Marie Connor Leighton, and brother of the artist Clare Leighton. Vera was impressed by Roland's intellectual and literary brilliance; and their relationship deepened when he introduced her to Olive Schreiner's *The Story of an African Farm* and informed her that she strongly resembled the novel's feminist heroine, Lyndall.

War and pacifism When war broke out in August 1914 Edward and Roland, together with their close friend Victor Richardson, immediately applied for commissions in the British army. While Edward had to wait until 1916 for his commission, and Victor's hopes were postponed by a severe illness, Roland was dispatched to the western front as an officer in the 7th Worcestershire regiment early in 1915. He and Vera corresponded frequently and voluminously. They had now declared their love; and that August, during his first leave, became engaged. By the end of her first year at Somerville (1914–15) she decided it was her duty to abandon her academic career to serve her country. During the long summer vacation she worked at the Devonshire Hospital, Buxton, as a nursing assistant, tending wounded soldiers; then applied to join the voluntary aid detachment (VAD) as a nurse and in November 1915 was

posted to the First London General Hospital at Camberwell, London. On 27 December she learned that Roland had been killed by a sniper. He was the first of the four young men close to her whom the war destroyed.

The second, Geoffrey Thurlow, had become Edward's closest friend while the two were training in England. Vera's friendship with him burgeoned after he was invalided home from France in March 1916. She was still nursing at Camberwell when Edward arrived at the hospital, wounded on the first day of the battle of the Somme, 1 July 1916. (He was awarded the Military Cross later that year.) In September she was sent to Malta. There she heard of Geoffrey's death in April 1917, just two weeks after Victor Richardson (who helped sustain Vera in the months after Roland's death) was badly wounded in the battle of Vimy Ridge. Learning that Victor was blind, she decided to return to England, intending to marry him and devote herself to his comfort; but he died two weeks after her arrival in May 1917.

Brittain now requested VAD service in France and was sent to 24 General Hospital, Étaples; but her hope of seeing Edward in France was frustrated. In November his regiment, the 11th Sherwood Foresters, was abruptly transferred to the Austrian–Italian front. Nursing gassed German prisoners strengthened Vera's evolving pacifism. During the final German offensive of the war, a period of strain and danger for the hospital, Vera was summoned home to look after her parents. Resentfully she obeyed, and she was in her parents' flat in Kensington when a telegram arrived to inform them that Edward had been killed on 15 June 1918.

After such traumatic losses, rebuilding her life was a severe challenge: Brittain returned to nursing, in a London hospital, so as to continue tending her parents; but writing was her main source of psychological strength. In August 1918 *Verses of a V.A.D.* was published. She also struggled to write a novel based on her nursing experiences in France, with a heroine who reflected an admired matron, Faith Moulson. Her fiction continued to be both autobiographical and earnestly moral. She had kept a 'reflective record' of her life for many years and this diary, itself an important literary and historical work, became a resource for her later writing. Sharp observation, unvarnished truth, and a potent direct style make Brittain's diaries, as well as *Testament of Youth* (which was largely based on her First World War diary), together with her best journalism and letters, arguably her highest achievement as a writer, though she yearned throughout her career for acclaim as a novelist.

In October 1919 Brittain returned to Somerville College, now to read modern history, in order, as she explained in *Testament of Youth*, 'to understand how the whole calamity [of the war] had happened, to know why it had been possible for me and my contemporaries, through our own ignorance and others' ingenuity, to be used, hypnotised and slaughtered' (V. Brittain, *Testament of Youth*, 1978 edn, 471). She was close to a breakdown, and her first encounters with the fellow student who was soon her closest friend, Winifred Holtby, were competitive and resentful.

But their similar northern origins, service in the war, and literary and social ambitions, together with 'opposite' temperaments and appearance, drew them into a lasting partnership which to some extent replaced Brittain's lost comradeship with Edward. Leaving Oxford for London in 1921 with second-class degrees, the two young women set up a joint household whose influence on their personal lives and their careers was entirely positive. In that period they encouraged and helped each other constantly while establishing successful parallel careers as journalists, lecturers, social activists, and novelists.

Holtby's and Brittain's journalism and lecturing centred in advancing the causes they both held dear: feminism, socialism, and the achievement of peace. They wrote prolifically for left-wing journals like Lady Rhondda's *Time and Tide*, lectured for the League of Nations, advocated in both articles and lectures the feminist agenda of the Six Point Group, and travelled together in post-war Europe observing and commenting on political and social realities. Brittain's first novel brought her notoriety as well as praise: melodramatic and naïve, *The Dark Tide* (1923) was seen as an attack on Somerville College. Her second novel, *Not without Honour* (1924), drew extensively on her early entries in her 'reflective record', lightly fictionalizing the relationship between the adolescent Vera and the Revd Joseph Ward, and attacking Buxton and its parochial values. Both novels attempted to connect feminist, socialist, and pacifist themes; these were synthesized much more effectively in her third novel, *Honourable Estate*.

Marriage and fame On 27 June 1925 Brittain married George Edward Gordon Catlin (1896–1979). He was a very young political scientist with socialist ideals who served briefly in the army as the war ended, read history at New College, Oxford, and then, after lecturing at Sheffield University, became a professor at Cornell University, Ithaca, New York. After honeymooning in Europe, they settled in Ithaca. Vera quickly reacted against the isolation and petty routine of a 'university wife', pining for her vivid London life and its literary opportunities. To save the marriage Catlin agreed to a future of alternating separation (while he taught at Cornell) and family life (when he returned for the summer to London). Despite marital and other complications flowing from this 'semi-detached marriage', they did succeed, at first together with Winifred Holtby, in creating a family home in which they could find contentment and fulfil their common urges to write, entertain, and converse.

Their first child, John Edward Brittain-Catlin (1927–1987), was born on 19 December 1927. In that same month Brittain completed a book based on a series of articles, *Women's Work in Modern England* (1928), and went on to publish a short satirical jab at conventional marriage, *Halcyon* (1929). Her resumed career as a journalist had prospered, with regular publication of articles and reviews, but she felt impelled to publish her war memories and struggled intermittently to find a suitable mode. By the time her second child, Shirley Vivian (who became the MP Shirley Williams), was born on 27 July 1930, Brittain had found that mode in autobiographical books like Robert Graves's

Goodbye to All That, recently published to popular acclaim. *Testament of Youth: an Autobiographical Study of the Years 1900–1925* (1933) was a best-seller on publication and earned Vera Brittain instant international fame. Based on her diary and research notes, it quoted poems and letters by Roland Leighton and others, to represent both personal and collective experience. The book argued strongly and realistically for peace, in the face of the coming war, while respecting the bravery of those who had sacrificed their lives in the First World War. The book was dedicated to Roland Leighton and Edward Brittain. During the period between the great international success of *Testament of Youth* and the outbreak of the Second World War, she twice completed exhausting and highly successful lecture tours in the United States, where she made several close friends.

In 1935 Brittain's father committed suicide; and then Winifred Holtby—who had kept her severe illness secret for two years while concentrating on completing *South Riding*, her last and finest novel—died in a London nursing home. Grief-stricken, Vera Brittain struggled to complete her own finest novel, *Honourable Estate: a Novel of Transition* (1936)—long, ambitious, feminist, pacifist, a family saga based on the recent history of the Brittain and Catlin families. It greatly disturbed George for it drew particularly on the diary of his mother, who had abandoned son and husband. Meanwhile Brittain's onerous tasks as Holtby's literary executor were extended into the writing of *Testament of Friendship: the Story of Winifred Holtby* (1940), which she completed on the eve of the outbreak of war.

In 1938, under the influence of Canon Dick Sheppard, Brittain proclaimed herself a pacifist and joined his Peace Pledge Union (PPU) as a sponsor. During the Second World War she held firmly to pacifist principles, working unceasingly to help prepare a peaceful future. She inaugurated a biweekly *Letter to Peace-Lovers* and, with only secretarial help, produced and disseminated it throughout the war. She also published two books which put the pacifist's case: *England's Hour: an Autobiography, 1939–41* (1941) and *Humiliation with Honour* (1942). Two campaigns dominated her committee work and journalism: against the blockade of German ports and against the mass bombing of German cities. She published *'One of these little ones …': a Plea of Parents and Others for Europe's Children* in 1943 and *Seed of Chaos: What Mass Bombing Really Means* in 1944—the latter, when published in reduced form in the USA, provoked a furore which, Brittain was convinced, subsequently diminished her reputation and sales there. News that an atom bomb had been dropped on Hiroshima in August 1945 justified her worst forebodings about war's destructiveness for civilians. She was now—having spent all the war in England, most of it in London—exhausted and close to a breakdown. She later learned that her name was among those listed in the Gestapo's notorious 'black book'.

Later years and reputation Her final two novels, *Account Rendered* (1945) and *Born 1925: a Novel of Youth* (1948), were both essentially anti-war works; they were based, respectively, on the experiences of a doctor, Leonard Lockhart, whose murder trial Brittain had attended (he had been traumatized by his experience in the First World War), and of Dick Sheppard, the priest who had converted her to full pacifism. Neither of these novels achieved the success for which Brittain had hoped, and she turned away from fiction. Among the numerous biographies and historical studies she published in her last years are *Testament of Experience: an Autobiographical Story of the Years 1925–1950* (1957), *Lady into Woman: a History of Women from Victoria to Elizabeth II* (1960), *Women at Oxford: a Fragment of History* (1960), *Pethick-Lawrence: a Portrait* (1963), *The Rebel Passion: a Short History of some Pioneer Peacemakers* (1964) and *Radclyffe Hall: a Case of Obscenity?* (1968).

Almost to the end Vera Brittain was a prolific writer and indefatigable activist. She continued her work for the PPU and similar organizations, now greatly sought after for delegations, committees, public speeches. She was chairman of the PPU, chairman of the *Peace News* board, became an active member of the Campaign for Nuclear Disarmament, and supported the Committee of 100. After the Second World War she fulfilled old ambitions in visiting India (1949) and South Africa (1960), with their potent reminders of Mahatma Gandhi and Winifred Holtby respectively. Seen by the establishment as a rebel and outsider (her wartime pacifist activism had included public attacks on Winston Churchill's personality and leadership), she feared her reputation had hurt even her husband's political aspirations in the Labour Party, of which she was a long-time member. There were honours, like election as fellow of the Royal Society of Literature and an honorary doctorate from Mills College, California, in 1946, but not the high national recognition her achievements appear to have deserved. However, in her later years she greatly enjoyed the pleasures of her private life—friendship and family (she now had grandchildren); and to the church of St Martin-in-the-Fields, Trafalgar Square, London, of which Dick Sheppard had been rector, she gave strong support. It was while walking there to give a talk in November 1966 that she fell—an accident that initiated the slow decline that ended in her death on 29 March 1970 in a nursing home at 15 Oakwood Road, Wimbledon, London. In accordance with her last wishes, Vera Brittain's ashes were scattered over Edward's grave at the cemetery of Granezza on the Asiago plateau, Italy, in September 1970.

Vera Brittain's life was dedicated above all to furthering two noble causes, pacifism and feminism, and to an intense yearning to fulfil her literary talent and ambition. *Testament of Youth* has been translated into many languages and was adapted for television by Elaine Morgan in 1979, following the republication of the memoir by Virago the previous year. Both helped to secure a place for *Testament of Youth* in the canon of First World War literature. The publication in 1981 of Brittain's First World War diary as *Chronicle of Youth* further illuminated her experiences, while the vitality of Brittain's and Holtby's journalism was vividly documented in *Testament of a Generation*, published in 1985. Shortly before his death in 1987 John Brittain-Catlin completed the final draft of his memoir, *Family Quartet*, which

in part chronicled his often tempestuous relationship with his mother. Both he and Shirley—whom Brittain called 'my brilliant and beloved' daughter (Berry and Bostridge, 510)—were ultimately much closer to their father than their mother. Her dedication to causes and her career as writer often made her seem remote. As a boy John called his mother, disparagingly, 'the novelist' (J. Catlin, *Family Quartet*, 1987, 1). He also comments that—slim, diminutive, pretty—'she looked young for her age until she was nearing fifty' (ibid., 3), and was always carefully and fashionably groomed; the perceived discrepancy between this attractive, 'conventional' appearance and her very unconventional opinions and behaviour occasioned uneasiness and sometimes hostility.

The centenary of Brittain's birth (1993) was celebrated with an international conference at McMaster University and commemorated in London with a plaque, unveiled by Shirley Williams, in the Dick Sheppard Memorial Chapel at St Martin-in-the-Fields. Her reputation as First World War, feminist, and pacifist icon shows no signs of diminishing, and she continues to be the focus of research with her papers in McMaster University Library, Hamilton, Ontario, being much consulted. In 1995 the Imperial War Museum published a facsimile edition of *Verses of a V.A.D.*, while two fine biographies were also published in the mid-1990s: *Vera Brittain: a Life* (1995) by Paul Berry and Mark Bostridge, and *Vera Brittain: a Feminist Life* (1996) by Deborah Gorham. In 1998 a selection of letters by Brittain and her four young friends who died in the First World War appeared as *Letters of a Lost Generation*, edited by Alan Bishop and Mark Bostridge, while two of her novels, *The Dark Tide* and *Honourable Estate*, have been reissued in paperback. Her achievement as a pacifist is also attracting renewed attention. It seems clear that Vera Brittain's social, political, and literary importance, very well acknowledged now, some thirty years after her death, will continue to grow.

ALAN BISHOP

Sources McMaster University Library, Hamilton, Ontario, William Ready Division of Archives and Research Collections, Vera Brittain archive · P. Berry and M. Bostridge, *Vera Brittain: a life* (1995) · b. cert. · m. cert. · d. cert.
Archives Bodl. Oxf., Indian notebooks · McMaster University Library, Hamilton, Ontario, William Ready Division of Archives and Research Collections, corresp., journals, and papers · NRA, corresp. and papers | BL, letters to J. Brunius, Add. MS 61893 · Commonwealth Collection, Bradford, corresp. with Hugh Brock · Hull Central Library, corresp. with Winifred Holtby · University of Cape Town, corresp. with W. G. Ballinger
Likenesses photograph, *c*.1918, Hult. Arch. · W. Rothenstein, oils, *c*.1930–1939, priv. coll. · H. Coster, photograph, 1936, NPG [*see illus.*] · K. Hulton and M. Magee, group photograph, 1949, Hult. Arch. · M. Gerson, photograph, 1954, NPG · group photograph, 1961, Hult. Arch.
Wealth at death £27,796: probate, 24 July 1970, *CGPLA Eng. & Wales*

Brittany, Eleanor of. *See* Eleanor of Brittany (1275–1342).

Brittany, John of, first earl of Richmond (1266?–1334), magnate and administrator, was the second son of John (II), duke of Brittany (d. 1305), and Beatrice (d. 1275), second daughter of *Henry III and *Eleanor of Provence, who married in 1260. Probably born in 1266, he was brought up in England with Henry, son of Edward I, who died in October 1274, and passed his life exclusively in the service of the English crown. As a young man he took part in tournaments, but his military talents were modest. In October 1294 his first independent command was as joint leader of the vanguard of an army sent to Guyenne, recently overrun by the French. Some towns along the Gironde were retaken, but John failed before Bordeaux. After this he made Rions, near Cadillac, his base but retreated ignominiously when the French attacked at Easter 1295. He remained in Guyenne until again defeated, along with Henry de Lacy, earl of Lincoln, at Bellegarde in January 1297. He nevertheless continued to enjoy Edward I's favour, and was treated almost as a son. Probably present at the battle of Falkirk (22 July 1298), in August 1299 John was granted £1000 p.a. In 1300 he took part in the siege of Caerlaverock, was summoned to parliament by writ on 24 May 1305, and finally promoted in October 1306, by a king notoriously miserly with honours, earl of Richmond in succession to his father and in preference to his elder brother, Arthur (II), duke of Brittany (d. 1312), with whom his relations were frequently prickly.

John's later services to the English crown were chiefly administrative. Although modern historians tend to judge him harshly as a political nonentity, he gained a contemporary reputation as a skilful and trustworthy mediator. His diplomatic abilities, already revealed by negotiations with Foix and Castile in 1294–5, led Edward I to appoint him 'Guardian of the land' of Scotland on 15 October 1305, and he held a parliament at Scone, where the main business was legal reform, before accompanying Prince Edward on embassy to France in March 1307. Shortly after his accession Edward II named him keeper of Scotland again in September 1307, and confirmed this in January 1308. An embassy to the pope on behalf of Gaveston followed in March 1309, and in March 1310, as relations between Edward II and his opponents worsened, John was named one of the *lords ordainer. Another embassy to France followed when he was joint leader with John, bishop of Norwich, of the English delegation at the Process of Périgueux (April–May 1311). Afterwards he continued to serve in Guyenne before returning to England, where, with the earls of Pembroke and Gloucester, he attempted to reconcile the king and his opponents (1312–13). In May 1313 he sailed with Edward II and Isabella to France and enjoyed hospitality at the French royal court before returning to open parliament in July in advance of the king's arrival. He remained close to Edward in increasingly difficult days and was frequently employed on conciliar business, for example, opening parliament again at Lincoln in January 1316, appointed to commissions of reform and a guarantor of the treaty of Leake in August 1318.

John once more accompanied the king and queen to France in June 1320 and went again to treat with the Scots in February 1321. He was among those urging the exile of the Despensers and helped besiege Lord Badlesmere in Leeds Castle, Kent, in October 1321, but agreed to the Despensers' return in November. Before the Boroughbridge campaign he was sent to treat with the Mortimers but was present when Thomas of Lancaster was condemned at Pontefract on 22 March 1322. While covering the retreat of Edward II from an abortive Scottish campaign in October 1322, he was captured by the Scots at Byland with Henry de Sully. He was a prisoner until the summer of 1324 when he was ransomed for 14,000 marks. Shortly after his release he went on embassy again to France in November 1324, visited Scotland for the same purpose in February 1325, and returned to France in March. John now aligned himself for the first time openly with opposition to the king, and in early 1326 his lands in England were seized, and he proceeded to Guyenne as lieutenant of Prince Edward. With the successful coup of Isabella and Mortimer his lands in England were restored on Christmas day 1326, but he remained abroad, treating again with the French in February. He does not seem to have returned again to England but spent his declining years in France, excused from parliament and military expeditions; he demised his English lands to Mary, countess of Pembroke, in return for £1800 p.a. shortly before his death. When he died, unmarried, on 17 January 1334, he was buried in the church of the Franciscans at Nantes and his nephew, John (III), duke of Brittany (1312–1341), was confirmed as earl of Richmond. MICHAEL JONES

Sources GEC, Peerage · I. Lubimenko, Jean de Bretagne, comte de Richmond: sa vie et son activité en Angleterre, en Ecosse et en France, 1266–1334 (1908) · J. R. S. Phillips, Aymer de Valence, earl of Pembroke, 1307–1324: baronial politics in the reign of Edward II (1972) · M. Prestwich, Edward I (1988) · P. Chaplais, Piers Gaveston: Edward II's adoptive brother (1994) · G. P. Cuttino, English diplomatic administration, 1259–1339, 2nd edn (1971) · N. Fryde, The tyranny and fall of Edward II, 1321–1326 (1979) · H. Johnstone, 'The wardrobe and household of Henry, son of Edward I', Bulletin of the John Rylands University Library, 7 (1922–3), 384–420 · Rymer, Foedera, 2.873–4 · Dom G. A. Lobineau, Histoire de Bretagne, 1 (1707), 270

Wealth at death £1800 p.a. value of Earldom of Richmond in 1333: Rymer, Foedera

Britten, (Edward) Benjamin, Baron Britten (1913–1976), composer, was born on 22 November 1913 in Lowestoft, Suffolk, the youngest of the four children (two sons and two daughters) of Robert Victor Britten (1878–1934), a dental surgeon, and his wife, Edith Rhoda (1874–1937), the daughter of Henry William Hockey, king's messenger at the Home Office in London. After her marriage Britten's mother proved herself to be an active amateur singer and pianist, and she became the secretary of the Lowestoft Choral Society. There was much music-making in the home, where her younger son participated as accompanist, and sometimes as a composer, in events that on occasion took the shape of musical soirées, attended by family and friends.

Early influences There can be no doubt that his mother was the dominant influence on Britten's early years. The child's first musical experiences would have been hearing his mother sing, and it cannot be altogether accidental that song, in its broadest sense, and more specifically the relationship of words to music—their colour, their

(Edward) Benjamin Britten, Baron Britten (1913–1976), by Sir Cecil Beaton

rhythm—was to form so large a part of the *œuvre* he created in his maturity. This was a reason, too, no doubt, for his eventual choice of an aspiring and gifted young tenor, Peter Neville Luard *Pears (1910–1986), as his lifelong companion, about whose voice a close friend from the Lowestoft years remarked that it recalled in character the voice of his mother. While recognizing the importance of the maternal influence it would be a mistake to exaggerate it. Some of Britten's most remarkable compositions are to be found among his chamber music and his orchestral works, and while it is certainly true that songs are prominent among his earliest compositions, so too are numerous string quartets, many sonatas for piano, and a by no means inconsiderable array of attempts at large-scale orchestral works. One must be ever wary in Britten's case of drawing too strict parallels between life and art. His prodigious musical gifts, which declared themselves at an astonishingly early age—a legitimate and meaningful parallel here with Mozart and Mendelssohn—undoubtedly in themselves would have constituted a prime influence, in particular his exploration of the absolutely basic materials of music—scales, triads, and so forth—at the keyboard. It was his mother who gave him his first music lessons, but in 1921 she was succeeded by a local piano teacher, Ethel Astle. It is prudent to remember that Britten's childhood prowess at the keyboard meant that in his very early youth his musical career (if there were to be one) was probably envisaged as that of a successful pianist. The commitment to composing came later, though it

is highly likely that the boy himself had already made the decision significantly in advance of the rest of his family. From the age of thirteen or fourteen his unusual compositional gift and creative ambition were recognized, and his mother in particular was active in drawing attention to them. A key work here among Britten's juvenilia is the sequence of *Quatre chansons françaises* (1928) for high voice and orchestra, dedicated 'To Mr & Mrs R. V. Britten on the twenty-seventh anniversary of their wedding'.

There can be no doubt that Britten's mother cherished and nourished the extraordinary talents of her youngest child as the years progressed. It is perhaps less easy to reach so clear-cut a conclusion about his relationship with his father, who could be inflexible and a shade daunting and was perhaps more anxious than his wife about his son's future. This may have created a certain tension between them, but what should be recalled is Britten's note in his diary after his father's death in 1934—'A great man with one of the finest minds I have ever come across & what a father!' (*Letters*, 1.334)—and Mr Britten's salute to his son in a letter in 1933, on hearing news of a rehearsal of his op. 3, *A Boy was Born* (1933), the work that was one of Britten's early choral masterpieces: 'Hearty congratulations! over and over again and also envy & jealousy ... Go on my son. Your very loving & admiring Pop' (ibid., 1.310). 'Envy and jealousy': a strange choice of words! The work in fact was dedicated 'To my Father'. Of the Brittens' other children, two girls, Barbara and Elizabeth (Beth), and a boy (Britten's elder brother, Robert), it was only Robert who showed a specific musical talent: he played the violin. In temperament and character Robert was perhaps closer to his father. There was never an easy relationship between the two brothers, but it was for Robert and the school of which he was headmaster that Britten wrote his *Friday Afternoons*, op. 7 (1935), one of the first of his works for children's voices. Neither of the two sisters had pronounced musical abilities. Barbara, the elder, became a health visitor and settled down in life with a woman companion, while Beth married and wrote a vivid and valuable memoir of family life in Lowestoft after her brother's death. Britten maintained affectionate relationships with both sisters and especially with Beth's children, though her problematic temperament was to cause him much anxiety and stress in later years. His closest relatives, however, were of fundamental importance to the evolution and character of his first steps in composition. After all, they were his first patrons and performers, and many of his juvenilia were written for their use.

In 1923 Britten entered South Lodge preparatory school, Lowestoft, and began viola lessons with Audrey Alston. The viola was not only to be Britten's own instrument for the rest of his life but also the string instrument to which he assigned some of his most expressive and intimate inspirations, for example *Lachrymae*, op. 48, for viola and piano (later arranged for viola and string orchestra), and the prominent solo role as the 'voice' of the suffering Apprentice in the great orchestral passacaglia from *Peter Grimes*, op. 33. His prodigious talent for music—he passed grade eight of the Associated Board piano examination at the age of twelve—did not affect his conventional school success: he was academically bright, was an excellent and enthusiastic sportsman—he was vice-captain of the cricket team and in 1955, when describing his schooldays, made special mention of his love for the game—and became head boy in 1927. It has long been assumed that these preparatory school years were largely happy and unclouded. But Eric *Crozier, the librettist of *Albert Herring*, one of the original founders of the Aldeburgh Festival in 1948, and a close collaborator of Britten and Pears in many similar and related activities, left a personal memoir in which he claimed that Britten had told him that he had been 'raped' by 'a teacher' at school. The fact of Crozier's claim has to be recorded. But one has to add that if true, it seems remarkable that there has been no shred of supporting evidence from quarters closer to Britten than Crozier—Peter Pears, for example, who after Britten's death often referred to his companion's 'idyllic' childhood; and Pears was never uncomfortable in discussing with friends his and his partner's homosexuality. It seems scarcely conceivable that Britten would not have mentioned this incident to Pears, or, if he did, that Pears would not have said a word about it to anyone before he himself died. A classic instance this, one might think, of what Brian Vickers has named 'surmise *ex silentio*'.

What is established is the fuss that attended Britten's leaving his prep school, caused by an essay in which he argued against hunting, thus revealing his budding pacifist and humanist convictions. The choice of Gresham's School, Holt (in Norfolk)—at the height of its reputation as a 'progressive' public school—reflected his parents' desire to find an environment that would accommodate his views and neither stifle nor disparage his musical gifts. Whatever its merits, Gresham's was not altogether a happy experience: the music teaching and activities—his diaries make frequent caustic references to performances by his teachers—fell far below his expectations and standards. 'So you are the boy who likes Stravinsky!' (Beth Britten, *My Brother*, 27) was the unpromising welcome he had from Walter Greatorex, the music master, about whom Britten confided to his mother that 'no two notes were together' in what Greatorex himself played on the piano, with 'a gripping touch, and terrible tone' (*Letters*, 1.30). None the less, it was during these years that Britten's own creative gift underwent expansion and exploration: the juvenilia of the period clearly show him attempting in work after work to establish a language, a style, that could form a basis for the future. The process at the time would have been largely unconscious. In retrospect, however, the most overtly 'experimental' period in Britten's compositional life can be seen to have belonged, paradoxically, to his schooldays. In the two *Portraits* for strings he composed at this time the span of his linguistic explorations may be heard, the first pressing hard at and beyond the limits of strict tonality, the second a self-portrait (a solo viola takes the lead) conceived in a reflective, almost pastoral mode. In short, the music from his school years reveals far more about the evolution of the composer Britten was to become than his school reports.

First compositions That his gift was technically so advanced by the time he left Gresham's was not exclusively Britten's own doing. A very large debt was owed to the teaching of the composer Frank Bridge, whom he had first met in 1927. From Bridge he acquired the integrity of his technique, his professionalism, and his awareness of the 'new' music in Europe, Berg's in particular. Bridge was himself a viola player and a pacifist—reasons for an immediate sympathy between master and pupil—and Britten was to regard him as his 'musical conscience' throughout his creative life. In 1930 Britten won an open scholarship to the Royal College of Music, London. At Bridge's insistence he studied with another composer, John Ireland, while continuing at the college his piano lessons with Arthur Benjamin (1893–1960), having previously studied the piano, for about a year, with Harold Samuel (1879–1937). Britten was an industrious, conscientious, and ambitious student, twice winning the Ernest Farrar composition prize (1931 and 1933) and funds (though not the award) from the Mendelssohn scholarship; but in general the college years seemed to duplicate the musical discouragement, frustrations, and disappointments that he had encountered at Gresham's. There is no doubt that his precocity proved a heavy burden for the youth to carry; in the eyes and ears of many, his prolific creativity gave rise to deep-seated suspicions of shallow 'cleverness'— 'too clever by half' was an attitude that pervaded much opinion and commentary from this period. Worst of all, there was little recognition at the college of his compositional achievements in terms of performance. What was heard—two works in all—was badly played. 'I have never heard such an appalling row!' he remarked of the rehearsals of his *Sinfonietta*, op. 1 (*Letters*, 1.276). Britten had a very long memory, and the impact of this débâcle stayed with him to the end of his life. It was in fact his life outside the college—London's music, including the famous Macnaghten-Lemare concerts, as well as cinemas and theatres—that gave him the enlarged horizons that influenced his development.

John Grierson, the innovative head of the General Post Office film unit, employed Britten—on the recommendation of the college—to write some film music, and he soon became in effect the unit's resident composer and music editor. He found himself in sympathy with the pronouncedly leftish social and political preoccupations of the unit and significantly assisted in the development of the documentary film. In 1935 began his collaboration with W. H. Auden (1907–1973), then working for the unit as script writer and occasional director, on two of the most memorable of British documentary films, *Coal Face* (1935) and *Night Mail* (1936). The scores that Britten wrote for these films make a highly original contribution to the history of music for the cinema. Each employed only tiny resources, but his exploitation of them introduced all manner of innovations, some of which foreshadow the techniques and modification of materials associated with the much later development of *musique concrète*, but to precisely reverse effect; Britten, that is, achieves miracles of *realistic* sound out of his electronic manipulation and treatment of his assembly of eccentric 'instruments'. The percussion ensemble assembled for *Coal Face* included 'blocks of wood, chains, rewinders, cups of water, etc., etc.'—'entirely experimental stuff', as Britten himself described it. He was to compose a more conventionally conceived score for the only full-length feature film in which he was involved: this was *Love from a Stranger* (1937), starring Ann Harding and Basil Rathbone. Film, thereafter, claimed relatively little of his attention, though out of his last contribution to this field—*Instruments of the Orchestra* (1945)—was born a work, *The Young Person's Guide to the Orchestra*, which has influenced generations of the young persons for whom it was written—both to edify and to entertain, as Britten's dedication characteristically puts it—as well as winning a permanent place in the orchestral repertory worldwide.

Of enduring importance, clearly, for the composer of opera that Britten was to become was the experience he gained in the film studio of the pacing and characterization of dramatic events, reinforced by participation in Rupert Doone's famous thirties theatrical venture, the Group Theatre, for which he wrote much incidental music. Among the most celebrated Group Theatre productions were two collaborative dramas by Auden and Christopher Isherwood (1904-1986), *The Ascent of F6* (1937) and *On the Frontier* (1938), for both of which Britten wrote substantial musical numbers. It was during these years that Auden's profound influence on Britten was at its height. He was not only hugely to widen the composer's literary and above all poetic interests but he also, in his role as apostle incarnate of bohemianism, blew away any vestiges of provinciality still clinging to Britten, who about this time was probably beginning to acknowledge and accept his homosexual nature. It seems likely that Britten found it difficult, or was reluctant, to commit himself physically in sexual relationships. Auden in this context was an ever-present and minatory counsellor; as he wrote himself in 1938, 'It's better to sleep two than single; it's better to be happy'—advice that Britten was ready to accept, but not before he had found the right partner.

To all this activity in the film studio and theatre, and for radio—collectively amounting to an *œuvre* in its own right, one not only of specific period interest but, more importantly, a direct product of what were then new communication technologies (film, radio)—Britten was strangely indifferent in later years. What gave him satisfaction, undoubtedly, was the fulfilment it permitted him of entering full-time employment as a composer without any transitional intermission. But in tandem, of course, with this rich mass of incidental music—among British composers of Britten's generation, without precedent—and in some cases preceding it, there was a steady flow of key works destined for the concert hall. Among these were the *Sinfonietta*, his op. 1 (1932), an early manifestation of his preference for chamber-like instrumental textures and proportions; *A Boy was Born* (1933), the virtuosic choral demands of which continue to present a challenge to performers even though the century in which it was written has come to an end; and *Variations on a Theme of Frank Bridge*

(1937), for string orchestra, in which his innovative exploitation of the strings and mastery of variation form—each variation was in fact a portrait of his revered teacher, a programme that Britten kept hidden—won him international recognition at the Salzburg Festival of 1937. Even earlier successes outside England had been at International Society for Contemporary Music festivals at Florence (1934) and Barcelona (1936).

To 1936 belongs the first of Britten's orchestral song cycles, *Our Hunting Fathers*, one of the major fruits of his friendship and collaboration with Auden, who devised its text. The virtuoso instrumental textures of this brilliant work guarantee it a special place in the history and evolution of British orchestral music, and the same can be said of Britten's phenomenally challenging vocal writing. This was indeed a young man's music, taking no account of the performing skills available to him or the prevailing—and conservative—musical culture of the time. (It is scarcely to be believed that this was the first orchestral music of his own making that Britten had actually heard to date.) Furthermore—and one thinks back to the rebellious prep school essay on hunting—the work was fired by his and his poet companion's impassioned reaction both to the Spanish Civil War, then at its height, and to the threat of European fascism, and by his own extravagantly burgeoning genius. It was no accident that the image of the hunt is central to the concluding song, a setting of words by Thomas Ravenscroft entitled 'Dance of Death'. This erupts finally in a frenzied interlude for orchestra alone of Bergian intensity, and the last words to be heard after the tumult has subsided are just two: 'German, Jew'. The work met with total incomprehension at its première at Norwich, on 25 September 1936, after a chaotic rehearsal with the London Philharmonic Orchestra of the day; its members simply could not believe that the young composer's intentions should be taken seriously. It was nearly fourteen years or so before the work was heard again. It is now recognized as one of the very few major statements about the history and politics of the thirties made before the war by a British composer, not just a document of the times but a fierce condemnation of them.

North America Despite some indications at least of an eventual career of high achievement, Britten, with the singer Peter Pears, left England for North America in May 1939, going first to Canada and then to New York. Various factors influenced this decision: the worsening political situation; the success Britten's former teacher, Frank Bridge, had enjoyed in the United States; the persuasive examples of Auden and Isherwood, who had already emigrated; loosening family ties (his father had died in 1934, his mother in 1937); discouraging reviews of his music in the English press; often inadequate performance standards; and, from 1937, the growth of his friendship with Pears. Undoubtedly too, Pears as an aspiring singer, and Britten as an ambitious young composer, on the threshold of his career and in search of new stimulus and new channels for his creativity, had it in mind to assess for themselves what the New World might have to offer.

It was in fact in Grand Rapids in June 1939 that Britten made the unreserved physical commitment to Pears, the liberation to which Auden for so long had been prompting Britten in poems addressed to him. It proved to be an exemplary relationship, both personal—their mutual passion survived until the very end of Britten's life—and musical: 'Peter Pears accompanied by Benjamin Britten' developed into one of the most distinguished and celebrated voice and piano duos of the century. Their *Winterreise* (Schubert) and *Dichterliebe* (Schumann), for example, were but two classical masterpieces their performances of which were unique examples of re-creation and renewal. It was during these American years that Britten wrote his first cycle for Pears, the famous *Seven Sonnets of Michelangelo*, the first of the long sustained stream of works conceived for Pears's voice and, not less, his astonishing ability not just to articulate words but to use them to colour the pitches of which they formed an integral and, above all, musical part. It was the beginning too of Britten's significant interest in and revival of Purcell: his realizations of Purcell's vocal music were motivated by his developing a recital repertory, in which Pears was his partner (as were his folk-song arrangements). On the other hand, the American period marked the end of Britten's career as a solo pianist. The United States première of his piano concerto, which he gave in 1940 in Chicago, was effectively his last public appearance in a solo role in the concert hall; thereafter he was heard only in chamber music and vocal music, almost always with very close musical colleagues.

For two and three-quarter years Britten and Pears lived mainly on Long Island, at Amityville, where they shared the family home and life of Dr William Mayer and his wife, Elizabeth (1884–1970), the latter a friend too of Auden, with whom she later made a translation of Goethe's *Italienische Reise*. They moved briefly in 1940 to a house in Brooklyn, 7 Middagh Street, which was to enjoy fame for its literary and musical associations and a bohemian lifestyle, over which Auden presided as proxy landlord. This was not much to their taste, and they spent the summer of 1941 at Escondido, California. As it happened, Britten suffered a serious composing block—as he remembered it, a 'complete incapacity' to work—towards the end of his sojourn in North America, but despite this the list of works completed or composed is impressive: it includes *Les illuminations* (it was Auden who had earlier introduced Britten to Rimbaud); the first string quartet; *Sinfonia da requiem*, given its first performance by the New York Philharmonic under John Barbirolli; and *Diversions*, for piano (left hand) and orchestra, commissioned by Paul Wittgenstein, the brother of the philosopher Ludwig Wittgenstein. The *Sinfonia* had been preceded by the first performance at Carnegie Hall of the violin concerto.

Serious attention, without doubt, was beginning to be paid to Britten's music in the USA, and a further bid, of a particularly significant kind, was made in a unique collaboration from this period, the composition of *Paul Bunyan*, an operetta, so-called, based on the famous American folk-hero. Auden wrote an inimitably brilliant and witty libretto, in turn funny and profoundly moving, while Britten, with the exercise of comparable skills, ingeniously and inventively explored the language and styles of popular American music, including country music (such as the narrator's ballads accompanied by guitar). Britten and Auden even had an eye on the ear of Broadway, though ultimately the work received its first production by a semi-professional company on the campus of Columbia University, New York, on 5 May 1941. It was a flop, generally derided by local critics. Britten and Auden contemplated revisions, but the process was halted by the composer's return to England; moreover, his experience of working with Auden on the operetta had begun to indicate that all was not altogether plain sailing as far as future collaborations were concerned—and such at length proved to be the case. But nothing can take away from the importance of the operetta as Britten's very first full-length work for the stage. At the end of his life he revised it himself and would doubtless have been gratified, if surprised, by the success it has since enjoyed, above all its triumphant revival in New York—and on Broadway!—at the New York City Opera in 1998.

Peter Grimes While in California in 1941, Britten and Pears's attention had been drawn to George Crabbe's *The Borough* by an article by E. M. Forster in *The Listener*, and in particular to that part of Crabbe's poem entitled 'Peter Grimes'. This led to the composition of Britten's first opera proper of the same title, with a libretto based on Crabbe by Montagu Slater, an old friend and collaborator from Britten's pre-war activities in the left-wing theatre. In the meantime, and an indication of the heightening of Britten's profile in America, Serge Koussevitsky had conducted the *Sinfonia da requiem* in Boston and was clearly impressed by the composer's potential, perhaps especially his sense of the dramatic. As a result, the Koussevitsky Foundation commissioned Britten to write his new opera, and substantial thought was given to the project before Britten and Pears's return to England in March 1942. It was a return motivated by anxiety at wartime separation from friends and relatives and a profound sense of deracination on Britten's part, further deepened by his chance encounter with Crabbe's narratives, rooted as they were in Britten's own Suffolk. When the Second World War had broken out in September 1939, Britten and Pears were advised officially not to attempt a return, and it was not until March 1942 that they succeeded in making the perilous crossing of the Atlantic from Halifax, Nova Scotia, to Liverpool. During the journey Britten worked away at completing his setting of Auden's *Hymn to St. Cecilia*. Despite the claustrophobic below-deck circumstances of a wartime crossing, what emerged was an unaccompanied choral work celebrating music and creativity, remarkable for its technical perfection and the innocent radiance of its inspirations, a reminder of what C major still had to offer. Yet another choral work was also done: *A Ceremony of Carols*, for treble voices and harp, destined to become one of the best loved and most widely performed of Britten's choral works and one in which for the first time on so elaborate a scale he employed boys' voices (the precedents here were *Friday Afternoons* and the suite of Rossini arrangements originally written as the soundtrack for an animated silhouette film of Lotte Reiniger's and later, in revised form, to win fame in the concert hall as the *Soirées musicales* of 1936). Thereafter, works for children or works which included children as performers occupied increasing space in Britten's output, among them the miniature opera *The Little Sweep*, from *Let's make an Opera* (1949), *Noye's Fludde* (1958), a setting of the Chester miracle play that was also a major step along the road to the church parables of the 1960s, *The Golden Vanity* (1966), and *Children's Crusade* (1969). In this category, special mention has to be made of *The Turn of the Screw*, the chamber opera of 1954, in which the crucial role of Miles is allotted to a treble.

In the première of that opera the role of Miles was undertaken by David Hemmings, with whom, it has been reliably suggested, Britten became 'infatuated', although it seems that Hemmings at the time was unaware of this. Hemmings himself, who later became a celebrated stage and screen actor, has described the infatuation in terms that might well be realistically applied to all of Britten's relationships with boys: 'In all of the time that I spent with him he *never* abused that trust' (BBC2, 13 Aug 1994). Interestingly enough, Michael Crawford, a well-known actor and stage personality whose career, like that of Hemmings, owes much to his early encouragement by Britten (having had roles in both *The Little Sweep* and *Noye's Fludde*), wrote in his autobiography (1999):

> I cannot say enough about the kindness of that great man … [He] was the pre-eminent British composer of his time and he had a wonderful patience and affinity with young people. He loved music, and loved youngsters caring about music. (Crawford, 43)

There can be no doubt that young boys—'thin-as-a-board juveniles … sexless and innocent', as Auden put it in a famous letter to Britten in 1942—made a powerful sexual appeal to Britten, and much discussion of this predilection followed in the wake of his death. It is probably unrealistic to suggest that Hemmings's and Crawford's should be accepted as the last words on a topic that since Britten's death has consumed far too much space and time and generated an excess of speculation. But at least a plea can be entered for a sense of proportion; the meaning and significance of Britten's works, prodigious in quantity and diversity, should be sought in themselves alone, not in some supposed explanatory parallel between life and art.

When back in England, Britten and Pears registered as conscientious objectors. Both men held strong pacifist convictions of long standing. Pears was successful on making his first appearance before the tribunal. Britten, however, was not granted the unconditional exemption he sought, and appealed. The first statement of his position he made to the tribunal is of fundamental importance to the understanding of his pacifist philosophy; in addition it throws light on the much-debated topic of his specifically 'religious' beliefs. In fact, Britten informed the tribunal first time round that he did not believe in the divinity of Christ and had not attended church during the preceding five years. He spelt out, in his written submission, that 'The whole of my life has been devoted to a life of creation (being by profession a composer) and I cannot take part in acts of destruction' (*Letters*, 2.1046). This clearly defined principle not only had immediate consequences for his day-to-day musical activities but was to surface prominently in his creative thinking in the years ahead. On appeal, he was granted exemption on the condition that he gave concerts with Pears for the wartime Council for the Encouragement of Music and the Arts (CEMA). Already on the Atlantic crossing Britten had shown the preoccupation with English word-setting that characterized much of his music for the rest of his life, a pronounced thrust that was to mark the works that were composed between 1942 and 1945. Two of them, his second song cycle for voice and orchestra, the *Serenade* (1943) for tenor, horn, and strings, and the opera *Peter Grimes* (1945), brought Britten to the forefront of public and critical attention. In particular, the opera established an unprecedented international reputation for a British composer and constituted the memorable and indeed monumental first step in the creation of a national tradition of opera. The momentum generated by *Grimes* continues even as the twenty-first century begins. The *Serenade*, with its *two* virtuoso soloists, one vocal, one instrumental, was a magical exercise in nocturnal imagery and matching sonorities, supremely lyrical but executed with a challenging technical sophistication. The work was almost immediately recognized as the masterpiece it is. Typically, in a letter written even before the première, Britten described it as 'not important stuff, but quite pleasant, I think' (*Letters*, 2.1144). *Grimes*, too, of course, has its lyrical moments, but the *Serenade* would hardly have prepared anyone for the savagery of *Grimes*, its dramatic power and the skill with which Britten managed the very large vocal and orchestral forces involved. While it is perfectly true, as is often said, that in the opera Britten reaffirms his Suffolk roots, perhaps more importantly it remains a work in which he unequivocally asserts his *European* roots. He had by no means put behind him the European stylizations embodied by such crucial works as *Les illuminations*, the Michelangelo sonnets, and *Sinfonia da requiem*. It is indeed the symphonies of Mahler, Alban Berg's *Wozzeck*, and Shostakovich's *Lady Macbeth of the Mtsensk District* that stand behind, but do not overshadow, *Grimes*. Indeed, the last act of Britten's opera contains a 'mad' scene, a phenomenal recapitulatory cadenza virtually for the solo voice alone, which must count as one of the most audacious concepts in twentieth-century opera.

Grimes is exceptional too in that its narrative is tightly focused on the outsider, the nonconformist, the social reject. Philip Brett, in his pioneering study of the work, has drawn attention to the parallel that can be drawn here with Britten's own experience as a homosexual in an often virulently homophobic society. It is undoubtedly a painfully relevant point, but of course it is the power of Britten as an artist that he can universalize his theme and make it directly meaningful to humanity at large. The Europeanism of the opera's style was surely an additional factor that helped establish the work on an international scale. One notes, however, the peculiar irony of so bleak and pessimistic a work being given its première at Sadler's Wells Theatre on 7 June 1945, at the very time that the allies were celebrating their military triumph in Europe. (The paradox only emphasizes that one of Britten's distinguishing features was his pessimism.) Furthermore, this was a work composed by a pacifist, whose beliefs, sexuality, and absence in the USA had not only been the subject of hostile comment but at one stage were the preoccupation of a dissenting group at the theatre, who threatened the opera's launch and succeeded in preventing its immediate revival at the Wells—sorry proof of the discouraging parochialism still prevalent in post-war English musical culture.

All this makes of quite special significance the tour of the German concentration camps in which Britten, very much on his insistence, accompanied, both musically (at the piano) and personally, the remarkable violinist Yehudi Menuhin. This harrowing experience left its mark on the music written immediately in its aftermath, in particular the sometimes distraught settings of the *Holy Sonnets* of John Donne (op. 35). As Menuhin himself later observed, Britten clearly felt the need to experience at first hand the suffering that war had brought to his fellow humans and from which his unshakeable pacifist convictions had excluded him. There can be no doubt that the *War Requiem*, composed in 1961 for the reconsecration of Coventry Cathedral, a work that perhaps exceeded even *Grimes* in the impact it made virtually worldwide, also reflected the horror and compassion generated by the tour of the camps; but it should also be remembered that while this was, as it had to be, a unique experience, compositionally speaking there had preceded it, from the 1930s onwards, a significant quantity of music in which Britten had unequivocally demonstrated his resistance to and condemnation of acts of war and personal violence. Thus it is that the *War Requiem*, which so captured the public imagination and mood of the 1960s that it became virtually an icon of the period, perhaps particularly for the younger generations, was in fact not something new but the consummation of a long-established creative ideology. Nor was it an end: the requiem was succeeded until the time of Britten's death by works of diverse character, in all of which in some way or another was expressed his preoccupation with violence, among them *Voices for Today*, commissioned by the United Nations for its twenty-fifth anniversary in 1965, and which led to the memorable meeting in New York the following year between the composer and the then secretary-general of the UN, U Thant. In 1970, in this same context, Britten undertook what proved to be his penultimate opera, *Owen Wingrave*, after a story by Henry James. He had many times been asked to consider an opera for television. It was altogether characteristic of him that, when the BBC finally secured a positive response, he seized the opportunity to exploit the

mass medium for the first time to challenge the conventions and traditions of militarism, especially that form of it rooted in dynasties. On its first transmission in 1971, the opera was seen and heard in at least thirteen countries, a global mass audience to match the mass medium for which the work was conceived. After its launch, the work was occasionally performed in the theatre, but it was not until 2001 that a new film was made for television by Channel 4. The advances in film technology since the première were imaginatively explored to make the opera's anti-militarist message clear and meaningful to television audiences in the new century.

Chamber opera Both *Wingrave* and its successor, *Death in Venice* (1973), amply illumine Britten's late style and the many innovations he had introduced into the musical theatre spanning three decades of prodigious fertility. Post-*Grimes* his operas continually explored new paths. Already, in 1946, as a result of an invitation from John Christie, he had composed *The Rape of Lucretia*, commissioned to reopen post-war Glyndebourne. What was startlingly new here was the concept of chamber opera—opera wanting nothing in the virtuosity demanded of the singers and players but involving relatively slender forces (a maximum instrumental ensemble of thirteen players). *Lucretia* took as its theme ravaged innocence, to which Britten returned again and again in his œuvre, in many guises and contrasting genres. His second chamber opera, *Albert Herring*, looked at innocence from quite another angle. The opera's protagonist, Albert, has to free himself from his domineering mother—not only free himself, indeed, but *find* himself. That voyage of self-discovery had certainly been part of Britten's own experience and profoundly enriches the humane comedy of *Herring*. The serious underside of the opera, already anticipated in the second half of act II, breaks surface at the end of act III, the great threnody in which the supposed death of the absent Albert is mourned—an audacious dénouement that was widely misunderstood and misinterpreted when the work was first heard. The last of the trinity of chamber operas was an arrangement—'realization', to use Britten's own term—of John Gay's *The Beggar's Opera*, a coruscatingly brilliant exercise in digging out the totally unexpected from what were often 'traditional' tunes, often by contrapuntal means, canon especially. Here, as also in his many folk-song arrangements for voice and piano or orchestra, Britten, by treating the melodies as if he had composed them himself, succeeds in creating a work wholly in his own musical image. This is an opera which remains much underestimated. Its dazzling counterpoint alone secures it a special place in the evolution of Britten's compositional techniques.

The new concept of chamber opera was an idea—better, an ideal—that Britten had thought out even before *Grimes*, and one should not think that its materialization was, *au fond*, other than the development of a powerful creative preference. None the less, there were other factors involved that had long-term consequences with regard to the character and dissemination of Britten's own works and, above all, their authentic performance; in addition there was a serious ambition to detach himself from the ethos of 'grand opera' and create a format that would make opera more accessible to the public at large, especially by means of touring. Thus the foundation of the English Opera Group with a group of close colleagues in 1947 represented an intricate combination of aesthetic, economic, and socio-political motivations. *Herring*, the second of the three chamber operas to be played at Glyndebourne, was in fact the first of the works to be launched under the banner of the new company. Thereafter, with only very occasional exceptions, Britten's musico-theatrical works were written for and first performed by the group. However, it was not Britten's works alone that were the group's preoccupation. Fundamental to the ambition and aesthetic of the organization was the systematic commissioning—and subsequent touring, at home and abroad—of new chamber operas from both established and aspiring composers, among them Lennox Berkeley, Harrison Birtwistle, Gordon Crosse, Thea Musgrave, Arthur Oldham, William Walton, and Malcolm Williamson. This was a brave and serious attempt to discover new talent and give body to the new tradition of English opera initiated by *Grimes* in an economically viable format that might win new audiences in locations which in the past had had no opportunity to experience opera. There was a further intention that must not be overlooked, with once again very long-term consequences for Britten's own development and for musical culture in Britain during the latter half of the twentieth century. He had always found it congenial to create and himself perform in the context of close collaborations with friends. The formation of the English Opera Group meant that the design, stage direction, and vocal and instrumental resources were all undertaken by colleagues from whom Britten might expect sympathy for, and comprehension of, his artistic aims; it also provided the capacity to meet his undeniably stringent demands. Having secured, in the shape of the English Opera Group, the ideal means of achieving his own vision of opera, Britten took a further momentous step in 1948 with the creation of the Aldeburgh Festival. This in turn secured the platform on which performances, at their best of an incomparably creative character, would be given and addressed to an audience rooted in East Anglia. There is no reason to doubt the sincerity of Britten's feeling for the region in which he was born or his commitment to the community—Aldeburgh—in which he lived and worked for most of his life. The founding of the festival speaks for itself. On the other hand, what had begun as a sometimes emphatically local venture rapidly developed into a unique national artistic annual event, and by the time of Britten's death it had for years commanded international attention.

The nexus represented by the group and festival was in fact the result of the interaction between Britten's activities as a creator and a performer. In both areas he was the generating force, which is not to underestimate or undervalue the massive contribution of Peter Pears and, at a later stage, of Imogen Holst, the daughter of Gustav Holst. The attention paid internationally to the festival of course derived in large measure from the constant flow of new works by Britten that were first heard there; while it was the festival which enabled Britten to introduce to Aldeburgh audiences a quite astonishing collective of international performers of the highest calibre. Janet Baker, Heather Harper, Dietrich Fischer-Dieskau, Sviatoslav Richter, Mstislav Rostropovich, Murray Perahia, Julian Bream, the Amadeus Quartet, and Galina Vishnevskaya were only a few, the majority of whom remained firm friends until the end of Britten's life. It was some of these artists whose gifts and personalities in turn stimulated Britten to write new works for them. Thus was the flow of creativity sustained by a kind of amalgam of all the areas in which Britten, with his chosen team of collaborators, was active. The next inevitable step—again something that he had had in mind for a long period—was to build the concert hall which, together with the Suffolk churches already conscripted, would accommodate festival performances. These were not only of his own music and that of his contemporaries, but of the great legacy of the past—Bach, Dowland, Purcell, Haydn, Mozart, Schubert, Mendelssohn, Schumann, Mahler, for example—performances which, since the composer's death, have rightly come to be assessed as one of the musical phenomena for which the twentieth-century musical scene will be remembered, such was the intense identification with whichever composer Britten was re-creating, whether he sat at the keyboard or stood on the podium. Supremely endowed as he was as a pianist, he could without any doubt have been among the world's top-class public virtuosos; but, like Melville's Bartleby, he 'preferred not to'.

It was a feature of Britten's compositional method that he would sometimes comprehensively explore a musico-theatrical format that he had himself established in a sequence of works, as in the case of the ground-breaking trinity of chamber operas, composed between 1946 and 1948, and, later, in the composition of the three church parables in the 1960s. But even where the format imposed a certain unity of method, this did not result in any lack of diversity in the character of the individual works, each of which occupies strikingly different worlds of feeling and *mise en scène*. (In a different example of the genre altogether, the five *Canticles*, composed between 1947 and 1974, demonstrate what diversity Britten could achieve even while respecting the basic concept.)

When *The Beggar's Opera* (1948) was succeeded by *Billy Budd* (1951; revised, 1960) and *Gloriana* (1953), both of which operas involved very large resources, large choruses in particular, and both of which were composed for first performance at Covent Garden, it might have been concluded that the genre of chamber opera had been abandoned. In 1954, however, there followed at the festival of contemporary music in Venice the first performance of *The Turn of the Screw*, a work which can properly be regarded not only as the summit of Britten's chamber opera concept but as one of his greatest masterpieces for the musical theatre. It is, above all, distinguished for its unique form—a theme and variations for orchestra which enclose the sixteen scenes of the opera and culminate in a passacaglia (another form which Britten made peculiarly his own; among his principal sources were Purcell, Berg, and Shostakovich). The tightness of the form is matched by the economy of means and an unfaltering pacing of the drama. It was in the *Screw* too, for the first time, that there emerged explicitly and audibly Britten's growing preoccupation with the ordering and organization of all twelve pitches of the chromatic scale, though there had been intimations of this in *Billy Budd*, some three years earlier. While Schoenberg was indubitably an influence, in the *Screw* this shows up principally at the horizontal (that is, the thematic) level, not the vertical (accompanimental) level. (As a youth, it should be remembered, Britten had much admired certain of Schoenberg's works and had even himself played Schoenberg's *Sechs kleine Klavierstücke*, op. 11, at one of his mother's soirées—a 'modern music' evening—when still a schoolboy. This Lowestoft première on 30 April 1930 would surely have come as something of a surprise to Mrs Britten's guests.) Thereafter, what can be described as 'twelve-note propositions' recurred with increasing frequency, complexity, and weight in Britten's music to the end of his life. However, there was never any adherence to the strict serial system as conceived by Schoenberg or any systematic abandonment of tonality, which, for Britten, as he himself vowed, was absolutely fundamental and indispensable to his own creativity; he could not envisage composing without it.

Heterophony Thus it is that the *Screw* must occupy a special place in any account of the evolution of Britten's musical language, one which throughout his life (and his commitment to tonality apart) was notably eclectic in character and non-ideological in spirit. What he chose as materials or means of organization, he made his own. This flexibility proved a notable resource for the operas, and in particular those which succeeded the chamber operas of the 1940s: *Billy Budd*, *Gloriana*, *A Midsummer Night's Dream* (1960), *Owen Wingrave* (1970), and, finally, *Death in Venice* (1973). The very diversity of the dramas and the changing landscapes, seascapes, and cityscapes in which they are located called for music of an exceptional versatility. Britten's inventiveness and imagination rose to the challenge; his, indeed, was a language which, to the very end of his life, was in a continuous process of accumulating fresh vocabulary. On occasion these made a covert appearance in advance of their later patent materialization. *Billy Budd* is a case in point. Despite the fact that the work might be said to be dedicated to re-energizing the power and image of the triad—one of the basic building-blocks of music across four centuries—it also employed at a critical moment in the evolution of the drama a type of polyphony—heterophony, often the simultaneous combination of different rhythmic versions of the same melody—that played a conspicuous role in his later music, not only for the theatre but also for the concert hall; indeed, it was to constitute the distinguishing feature of Britten's final period of composition. The accrual of this specific technique marks one of the most important developments in the evolution of Britten's composing and is intimately tied in with the events of his

life. It was in fact during his wartime sojourn in the United States that Britten met the Canadian-born composer, pianist, and scholar Colin McPhee (1901–1964). McPhee it was who had studied the indigenous music of Bali and its orchestra—the gamelan—and soon after they had first met in 1939 he introduced Britten to examples of Balinese ceremonial music arranged (by McPhee) for two pianos. (A historic recording of this exists, made by McPhee and Britten in New York, probably in 1941.) Although Britten seems not to have betrayed to McPhee much immediate enthusiasm for Balinese music, clearly the experience made a profound impression on him: the first audible stirrings of it are to be found in the prologue to *Paul Bunyan*, when the chorus observes that the moon is 'turning blue', and Britten had to come up with comparably distinctive and arresting music. In short, there began the incorporation of a new vocabulary, and the techniques to make it explicit, into works composed by Britten after *Peter Grimes* (for example, the 'Sunday Morning' interlude, or the explosion of heterophony in *Billy Budd* (Vere's C minor aria in act II)). But, fascinatingly, it was not until 1957, and the first performance by the Royal Ballet at Covent Garden of the full-length ballet *The Prince of the Pagodas* (Pagodaland, as the ballet has it, was, of course, Bali), with choreography by John Cranko, that public and critical attention was drawn to the oriental dimension that forms so prominent a part of the score, the longest orchestral score in fact Britten was ever to compose. Part of it was a large independent percussion orchestra—Britten's version of the gamelan—in which audiences were regaled with brilliant transcriptions for Western instruments of music that Britten himself had heard on his momentous visit to Bali (he was on a world tour with Peter Pears) in 1956: 'about as complicated as Schönberg' (Cooke, *Britten and the Far East*, 70), he wrote when assessing its technique in a letter to Imogen Holst from the island.

When this extraordinary work was first heard, its overt links with and references to the Orient were regarded as a probable one-off day trip to a highly decorative, exotic world of sound. But this assumption was confounded when, eight years later, Britten composed and brought to first performance (in 1964, again with the English Opera Group, again at the Aldeburgh Festival) the first of his three parables for church performance, *Curlew River*, even though, in retrospect, significant foreshadowings and parallels may be found in *Noye's Fludde* and even earlier in *St Nicolas*, the quasi-dramatic church cantata of 1948. But what was peculiar to *Curlew River* was its Japanese roots. A visit to Japan had immediately followed the visit to Bali (on this same round-the-world excursion Britten and Pears had also been in Yugoslavia, Turkey, and Pakistan, and had then continued their tour in Singapore, Indonesia, Japan, Macao, Thailand, India, and Ceylon), and it was in Tokyo, in February 1956, that Britten attended a performance of the ancient and famous Noh play *Sumidagawa* ('The Sumida River'). Britten was overwhelmed by the drama, the ritualistic, idealized action, and the music, a form of recitation accompanied by a very small instrumental on-stage ensemble. Although Britten himself declared, typically, that it was never his intention to attempt an authentic replica in any sense of Noh, a well-known Japanese composer declared that he was astonished at Britten's absorption in so short a time of so much identifiable detail taken from Japanese sources; and it was not only Noh drama that was at the heart of *Curlew River* but also Britten's encounter with *Gagaku*, the ancient traditional court music of Japan. It is true, of course, that Britten relocated his version of Noh in the medieval English mystery play (compare *Noye's Fludde*), but what should be borne in mind is that Noh itself might be meaningfully compared with the liturgical drama of the middle ages; both genres run in chronological parallel. What, however, is of central importance to comprehend with regard to *Curlew River* and its successors, *The Burning Fiery Furnace* (1966) and *The Prodigal Son* (1968), is the acquisition and deployment of new techniques—heterophony, above all—culled from Britten's encounters with musics from non-Western cultures, an example of the process of absorption and accumulation by which he constantly renewed his musical language.

This radical new path makes it possible to present Britten as the most important twentieth-century Western composer substantially to incorporate non-Western techniques into his own compositional practice, and it can be traced back to the early 1940s and the accident of his meeting with McPhee in Amityville, New York. It could be argued indeed that there is sufficient evidence in works preceding the encounter with McPhee to make it logical—predictable even—that the techniques he absorbed on Bali and in Japan should have made so powerful a creative appeal. In other words, there was an established predisposition to succumb to what he heard. Thus it was that the new techniques and new sonorities he brought home with him as part of his creative baggage continued to play an often dominant role in much of Britten's final music, in works as contrasted as *Death in Venice*, where Bali and the gamelan surface prominently to characterize the Tadzio of Thomas Mann's imagination and the athletics of the children on the beach, and the late song cycle *The Poet's Echo* (1965), settings of Pushkin (in the original Russian) composed for Galina Vishnevskaya and Mstislav Rostropovich. The song cycle belongs unequivocally to the wholly European tradition of song cycles for voice and piano established by Britten's great predecessors and memorably sustained by him from his first cycle, the Michelangelo sonnets of 1940, until his last, *Who are these Children?*, of 1969. Analysis, however, reveals that the Pushkin settings, though they may wear a European face, are serviced technically by heterophony, the principal form of polyphony in south-east Asia and the Orient.

This unique interaction between East and West, which secures for Britten a quite singular place in the history of twentieth-century music, is perhaps best exemplified in his penultimate opera, *Owen Wingrave* (1970), where Owen's climactic apostrophe to peace is delivered over the rotation of twelve triads spanning the twelve pitches of the chromatic scale in simultaneous combination with an independent percussion ensemble, the heterophonic texture of which provides a horizontal, gamelan-like complement to the vertical conflation of the triads. Thus, to articulate the universal need for and importance of peace, Britten unites sonorous images and techniques drawn from cultures of East and West without detriment to their distinctiveness. There is no other moment quite like this in European music of the past century.

Orchestral and other works It is easy, because of the scope, stature, and sheer volume of the operas, and the wealth of vocal music of all kinds, to pay insufficient attention to the many works Britten wrote in other, specifically non-vocal genres. Even in his schooldays and early youth Britten had composed no fewer than six string quartets, one of which (in D) he was to revive and revise in 1974. These were the predecessors of the three masterly string quartets, the first composed in 1941 in the United States; the second in 1945, in celebration of the 250th anniversary of Purcell's death; the third in 1975, at the very end of his life. Fascinatingly, this late-style work ends with a passacaglia which incorporates materials from *Death in Venice*. The quartet's finale was itself written in Venice. Britten heard a run-through of the piece by the Amadeus Quartet in the library of the Red House in Aldeburgh on 28 September 1976, but he died before the première at the Snape Maltings on 19 December.

Many of the orchestral works have established themselves in the concert repertory both at home and overseas, among them the early *Simple Symphony* (1934, and less simple than its title would suggest); the *Variations on a Theme of Frank Bridge* for string orchestra (1937); and the *Young Person's Guide to the Orchestra* (1946), subtitled 'Variations and Fugue on a Theme of Henry Purcell'. Britten had composed his piano concerto—his only work in this genre—in 1938; in August that year he appeared as soloist in its première at a Promenade Concert under Henry Wood. In 1939 there followed the violin concerto, again to remain a solitary example of its kind, which received its first performance in New York in 1940; and it was there, in 1941, that the *Sinfonia da requiem* was first performed, having been completed in the preceding year. These three major orchestral works form a virtual trinity united in their response, albeit diverse in degree and musical character, to the political anxieties of the time which had already erupted with such extraordinary vehemence in the orchestral song cycle *Our Hunting Fathers* (1936). What is encountered here is a teasing but highly significant creative paradox: that while public recognition of Britten's works involving orchestra was established only well after the première of *Peter Grimes*, it was in those very works that the orchestral mastery which was to win the enthusiasm of the opera's first audiences had been prepared and demonstrated. Ironically enough, the consequence of Britten's developing relationship with the orchestra was the creation of a four-movement suite from the opera—the *Four Sea Interludes*—that soon became the best known of Britten's orchestral music, which says something about the symphonic scale of his thinking in the opera. (In later years his orchestral works were to enjoy an independence that is entirely their own right.)

Although Britten never made use of 'symphony' as a title without qualifying or descriptive additions, two large-scale works, the *Spring Symphony*, for solo voices, chorus, boy's choir, and orchestra (1949), and the *Symphony for Cello and Orchestra* (1964), belong to a symphonic tradition created largely by Mahler, by whom Britten was much influenced; he was among that composer's earliest admirers in England, in the mid-1930s. The *Spring Symphony*, for instance, incorporates vocal forms and the matching resources to realize them—including cantata, orchestral song, and a choral finale—that, until the advent of Mahler (with the profoundly influential exception of Beethoven), had been excluded from the concept of symphony proper. The *Symphony for Cello and Orchestra* on the other hand, composed in 1963 and inspired by the peculiar genius of Mstislav Rostropovich, must rank among the most important of Britten's purely instrumental works. It shows a mastery of the narrative form Mahler had bequeathed to composers of symphonies in the twentieth century, proceeding as it does from darkness to light in a sequence of movements which, while never failing to exploit the virtuosity of the soloist, demonstrably make up a symphony, not a concerto. The soloist is the vehicle by means of which the symphonic drama is enacted. The proof the *Cello Symphony* offers of Britten's ability to think and create in purely instrumental terms on so exceptional a scale gives cause for much regret that he did not more often turn to the genre of the symphony. This same work was also undoubtedly indebted to that other inheritor of Mahler's potent legacy, Dmitry Shostakovich (1906–1975). An extraordinarily close friendship grew up between Shostakovich and Britten, particularly towards the end of their lives. The immense admiration each felt for the other is amply documented, not least in Britten's dedication to Shostakovich of the third of his church parables, *The Prodigal Son* (1968), and Shostakovich's dedication to Britten of his symphony no. 14, the first performance of which outside of Russia was entrusted by the composer to his British friend and colleague at the Aldeburgh Festival of 1970. It is in this symphony that Shostakovich memorably avows his bond with Britten in his setting of Küchelbecker's 'O Delvig, Delvig!', a text which celebrates the freedom an artist should enjoy as of right and reminds us that 'inspired deeds and sweet song are alike immortal!'.

An earlier and very important friendship was with Michael Tippett (1905–1998), with whom Britten was particularly close after his return from the United States to England at war, where Tippett too was a notably steadfast pacifist. There was much mutual admiration and shared musical ideals, activities, and ambitions at this time, when the pairing of Britten and Tippett was often used to identify the cutting edge of a perceived renaissance in English music. Other prominent composer friends included Lennox Berkeley (1903–1989) and William Walton (1902–1982), though the latter seemed to find it difficult to accept (or enjoy) the success of his younger colleague.

From 1947 Britten lived in the small coastal town of Aldeburgh in Suffolk, first in a house facing the sea on Crag Path, then in the Red House, on Golf Lane, where he died in 1976. In February 1970, however, as a consequence of the ever-increasing pressures on the Red House—which had become the headquarters of Britten's public and private lives—he and Pears, after a long search, purchased a 'retreat', an old farmhouse in a markedly remote location in rural Suffolk, to which they made two important additions, a big music room conceived by the same architect, Peter Collymore, who had designed the library adjoining the Red House, completed in 1980, and perhaps even more importantly a studio, located in the farthest corner of the land, modelled, it must have been, on the 'composing house' that was a vital adjunct to Mahler's creativity. This Horham studio secured the calm and isolation essential to Britten's composing, which the constant busyness of the Red House put at risk; and it was here that much of Britten's late music was composed, including his last opera, *Death in Venice*, the première of which he heard, at least in part, on the radio at Horham, where he was convalescing after his heart surgery in 1972. There had been no intention of altogether parting company with the Red House but undoubtedly in the longer term he and Pears had thought of Horham, with its spectacular land- and cloudscapes, and a tiny open air swimming pool, as a possible ultimate home. In the event, while both men enjoyed some happy and fruitful times there, the collapse in Britten's health put paid to their occasional residence. It was from Horham, indeed, that Britten made his last journey to the Red House before his death. Britten was held in public, indeed national, esteem throughout the final decades of his life, and his music never lost its grip on both public attention and affection. In the sixties and seventies, however, there was a discernible cooling off in responses to his music, especially among the younger generations of composers, many of whom had previously adopted him as a role model. Britten was undoubtedly aware of and pained by this adverse swing in opinion; but the fashion to dismiss him, not only at home but also abroad, was not of long duration. Since his death there has been global recognition of his status as one of the most important composers of the century. A quite different kind of negative response—the only one of its kind during the years of Britten's creative maturity—was generated by the première of *Gloriana*, the opera he wrote to celebrate the coronation of Elizabeth II and first performed at the Royal Opera House, Covent Garden, on 8 June 1953. The royal gala that launched the opera proved to be a difficult, sceptical occasion, with an audience made up largely of diplomats, courtiers, and politicians whose first interest was not music. This might have been foreseen. What was not was the seizing of the opportunity to give the composer a robust dressing-down: many voices were raised to suggest that Britten had overreached himself, had pushed his luck too far, and somehow not composed a work worthy of the event it purported to honour; by some indeed it was considered an affront to the monarch. The fracas that ensued deserves (brief) attention for the reason that it was perhaps the only occasion in Britten's later life when there bubbled to the surface clear intimations of resentment and envy of his success that had long been around but had hitherto lacked a point of ignition. Undoubtedly too the row was fuelled, albeit more covertly, by other long-standing sources of hostility: his pacifist convictions and, above all, his homosexuality. The strong vein of homophobia in British culture, particularly in the post-war years, can never be disregarded when tracing the trajectory of Britten's life. It would be absurd to pretend that the life and the art were otherwise than complex. But psychobiography and the most extreme of gender studies apart, there is one conjunction of Britten's life and art that can be simply stated: his life *was* his music; he had no other, and it is a serious error of judgement to read the art as if it were somehow an autobiographical account of the life.

Almost the only interruptions that Britten permitted to his compositional activity were those generated by his partnering of Peter Pears, both at home and overseas, and the demands made by the Aldeburgh Festival and the English Opera Group, especially when, as was often the case, one of his own operas—a new one, or an important revival—was involved. There were occasional bouts of ill health, but in general he had the energy and physical stamina to fulfil his creative programme; as is well known, he was a keen and formidably accomplished tennis player; he swam, he ate and drank moderately, and he did not smoke. Long walks, which accompanied the exercise of his creative imagination, were part of his daily routine. There were, to be sure, what might be described as psychosomatic illnesses; it cannot have been entirely accidental that these set-backs seemed specifically to affect his ability physically to use pencil and manuscript paper. But these blocks, though real enough—and painful— were rare (the works in question, some of them among the most important he was to write, eventually got done), and it was not until the very last years of his life that he succumbed to a serious illness of the heart that had its origins in early childhood. But even this crisis in his health, for so it proved to be, did not stop—dam—his determination to compose. Against the advice of his doctors he refused to undergo the necessary surgery until he had put the finishing touches to *Death in Venice*. After open-heart surgery, which was only partially successful, and during which he suffered a minor stroke—one of the major consequences of which was that he was no longer able to play the piano (his right arm and hand were affected)—he continued to compose. Among the works created against the odds in this final phase were the *Suite on English Folk Tunes*, 'A Time there was ...' (his last orchestral work), the dramatic cantata *Phaedra* (for Janet Baker), and, for the Amadeus String Quartet, the third quartet—works which showed no diminution in the power of his creativity, though all were touched, inevitably, by his consciousness of impending mortality.

Significance For all his fame and worldwide recognition, Britten remained a truly modest man. Though it may seem strange to those who were not close to him, and

were yet fully aware of the prodigious gifts with which he was endowed, he felt inwardly insecure and uncertain that he was as good a composer as so many told him he was. As Peter Pears once observed, Britten would never have ranked himself alongside his great classical predecessors: it was just that he knew he was better at what he did than most of his contemporaries, perhaps especially those at home. Since his death the world seems to have taken a more positive view than the composer's own. There followed a significant increase in the number of performances of his works instead of the customary decline. But his self-assessment was typical of the unsparing standards by which he judged himself, and which often he seems not to have noticed that he had achieved or exceeded. In this sense, his insecurity may be said to have contributed to his eventual mastery. He was always wanting to do better still. As he remarked in an interview in 1964, 'I haven't yet reached the simplicity I should like in my music, and I am enormously aware that I haven't yet come up to the technical standards Bridge set me.'

Generous in spirit (though frugal in his habits), kind, courteous, compassionate, genial in his everyday dealings with the everyday world—all these qualities might with truth serve any attempt at describing his personality. He was, it is true, conspicuously reserved in public manner, but when travelling at home or abroad with close friends or taking part in quasi-family outings—picnicking was a much favoured and much enjoyed pursuit—he could be very good company: warm, observant, amused, and amusing, his habitually attendant anxieties in temporary suspense. Watching cricket with Pears, sometimes with binoculars, was another relaxation, especially when the two men were on tour and a convenient window overlooking the ground afforded them the opportunity. Perhaps it was only in later years, when he seemed to become ever more conscious of the world's pain and ills, that liberating laughter was less often heard from him. On the other hand, manifestations of ironic comedy made a powerful appeal, hence no doubt his own (serious!) comedy in music, *Albert Herring*, and his long-standing enthusiasm for the classic Marx Brothers films. But, as was inevitable, given the complexities of his creative character and his multiple activities and responsibilities, relationships were sometimes less tranquil with those associates who found themselves working alongside him, especially in the field of management and administration. Here, in particular, there was often a legacy of unhappiness and ruptured friendship. Needless hurt was sometimes inflicted, and there was much talk during Britten's lifetime and after his death of betrayal, disloyalty, deceit, and the ditching of old colleagues. This may, in retrospect, seem somewhat exaggerated and unrealistic. The world of the arts has ever been high-voltage territory, and it is scarcely surprising that the history of Aldeburgh, its festival, and the English Opera Group should vouchsafe its fair share of rows and ructions. At the height of crises of this kind, mention was often made of 'sacrifices'. Britten was undeniably ruthless when it came to professional standards or the achieving of a creative vision or ambition, when he would absolutely not be thwarted. But what has to be remembered in this context is Britten's sacrifice of himself to the often killing demands his own creativity made of him.

Britten was awarded many prizes, awards, and distinctions. He kept his decorations, so he claimed, in a drawer nearby his socks and handkerchiefs. He was created Companion of Honour in 1953; was admitted to the Order of Merit in 1965; and was created Baron Britten of Aldeburgh in the county of Suffolk in 1976, the first time a life peerage had been bestowed on a British composer. His acceptance of this honour puzzled some of his closest friends, to one of whom he remarked, 'Will you ever speak to me again?' Influential here, without doubt, was his growing sense of physical isolation at Aldeburgh, a consequence of his increasing ill health, and a sense too of no longer being at the centre of British musical life which he had dominated for more than thirty years. He received honorary doctorates from Cambridge (1959), Oxford (1963), and nine other British universities, and was an honorary fellow or member of many colleges and institutions. Among his many prizes and awards were the Coolidge medal (1941), the Hanseatic Goethe prize (1961), the first Aspen award (1964), the Wihuri-Sibelius prize (1965), the Ravel prize (1974), and the Mozart medal (1976). His executors were approached with a request for his burial in Westminster Abbey, but he had declared a preference for Aldeburgh parish church; the abbey, however, was home to a thanksgiving service which took place on 10 March 1977, attended by an overflowing congregation. (A memorial stone was laid in the north choir aisle of the abbey in 1978.) Britten was unsentimental about death, a convinced humanist rather than a believer. On 4 December 1976 he died without fear in his bedroom at the Red House, his home, with his nurse, Rita Thomson, by him, and in the arms of his lifelong companion, Peter Pears. The burial took place on 7 December. Both men now lie side by side in the graveyard of the parish church, within sight and sound of the sea.　　　　　　　DONALD MITCHELL

Sources B. Britten, *My brother Benjamin* (1987) · P. Brett, 'Britten, (Edward) Benjamin', *New Grove*, 2nd edn · *Letters from a life: selected letters and diaries of Benjamin Britten, 1923–1945*, ed. D. Mitchell and P. Reed, rev. edn, 2 vols. (1998) · D. Mitchell and J. Evans, eds., *Pictures from a life, 1913–1976* (1978) · D. Mitchell, *Britten and Auden in the thirties: the year 1936* (1981); new edn (2000) · P. Evans, *The music of Benjamin Britten* (1979); rev. edn (1996) · C. Palmer, ed., *The Britten companion* (1984) · M. Cooke, ed., *The Cambridge companion to Benjamin Britten* (1999) · M. Cooke, ed., *Britten and the Far East* (1998) · H. Carpenter, *Benjamin Britten: a biography* (1992) · D. Mitchell and H. Keller, *Benjamin Britten: a commentary on his works from a group of specialists* (1952) · E. W. White, *Benjamin Britten: his life and operas*, 2nd edn (1983) · P. Banks, ed., *Benjamin Britten: a catalogue of the published works* (1999) · personal knowledge (2004) · private information (2004) · *CGPLA Eng. & Wales* (1977) · M. Crawford, *Parcel arrived safely: tied with string: my autobiography* (1999) · K. Mitchell, 'Edinburgh diary 1968', *On Mahler and Britten*, ed. P. Reed (1995) · D. Matthews, *Britten* (2003)

Archives Britten–Pears Library, Aldeburgh, music MSS, diaries, letters, concert programmes, press cuttings, posters, photographs · Merton Oxf., letters · U. Southampton L., MSS | Bodl. Oxf., letters to Boosey and Hawkes · NPG, Britten–Pears photographic collection · Tate collection, corresp. with Lord Clark · W. Sussex RO, letters to Walter Hussey | FILM BBC WAC · BFI NFTVA, 'Benjamin Britten the hidden heart', Channel 4, 29 July 2001 · BFI NFTVA, documentary footage · BFI NFTVA, home footage · BFI NFTVA, performance footage · BFI NFTVA, *South Bank show*, LWT, 6 April 1980 · Britten–Pears Library, Aldeburgh | SOUND BL NSA, 'Aspects of Britten' (parts 3 and 4), 1995, H5379/2, H5379/3 · BL NSA, 'Benjamin Britten: the early years' (Parts 1 to 3), BBC Radio 3, April 1980, T2986 BWC1, T2997 BW, T3017 BWC1 · BL NSA, 'Britten and Pears in the USA', BBC Radio 3, 3 Dec 1996, H8224/1 · BL NSA, 'Britten's apprenticeship', (parts 1 to 4), 1995, H6157/4, H6181/3, H6235/2, H6231/1 · BL NSA, 'Britten's radio music', (Parts 1 and 3), 1995, H6231/1, H6272/1 · BL NSA, 'Company of heaven', B4377/02 · BL NSA, current affairs recording · BL NSA, documentary recordings · BL NSA, 'Interview', 25 May 1956, T9346 BW/W08/W08 S2 C5 · BL NSA, 'Interview', 30 May 1957, T9340 BW W04/W04 S2 C1 · BL NSA, *Mining the archive*, BBC Radio 3, 29 Nov 1996, H8092/2 · BL NSA, 'My dear Grace…', 1995, H6366/3 · BL NSA, oral history interview · BL NSA, performance recordings · BL NSA, 'Performing Britten' (parts 1 to 3), Nov 1999, 1CDR0000921BD1, 1CDR0000924BD1, 1CDR0000931BD1 · BL NSA, 'Battle of Britten: young Apollo', B977/2 · BL NSA, 'Reminiscences of Britten', 1994, H4475/2 · BL NSA, 'The six ages of Britten', 1973, T679W BD1 · BL NSA, 'Turning point', BBC Radio 3, 3 March 1997 · BL NSA, *Vintage years*, H1267/02 · Britten–Pears Library, Aldeburgh

Likenesses K. Green, double portrait, oils, 1943 (with Peter Pears), NPG; repro. in Mitchell and Evans, eds., *Pictures from a life*, pl. 231 · K. Green, oils, 1943, Britten–Pears Library, Aldeburgh; repro. in P. Banks, ed., *The making of 'Peter Grimes'* (1996) · H. Lamb, oils, 1945, Britten–Pears Library, Aldeburgh; repro. in Mitchell and Evans, eds., *Pictures from a life*, pl. 234 · M. Austria, group portrait, photograph, 1948, NPG; *see illus. in* Crozier, Eric John (1914–1994) · G. Ehrlich, plaster cast for bronze head, 1951, NPG · Y. Karsh, two bromide prints, 1954, NPG · M. Potter, oils, 1959, repro. in Mitchell and Evans, eds., *Pictures from a life* · oils, 1975, Britten–Pears Library, Aldeburgh · C. Beaton, photograph, NPG [*see illus.*] · photographs, Britten–Pears Library, Aldeburgh · photographs, NPG · photographs, Hult. Arch.

Wealth at death £1,664,714: probate, 5 Sept 1977, *CGPLA Eng. & Wales*

Britten, James (1846–1924), botanist and Roman Catholic propagandist, was born on 3 May 1846 at 18 Shawfield Street, Chelsea, London, the son of James Alexander Britten, bookseller, and his wife, Mary Ann (*née* Shepard). His father was a prominent active member of the local community, and Britten Street was named after him. Educated privately, by the age of ten Britten had become interested in plants, aided by Anne Pratt's *Flowering Plants of Great Britain* (1855). Intending a medical career he spent four years from 1846 onwards with a doctor at High Wycombe, Buckinghamshire, but in 1869 abandoned medicine for botany and was appointed a junior assistant in the herbarium at the Royal Botanic Gardens, Kew, where he was befriended and encouraged by Daniel Oliver. He had already (1863) contributed a note on plants found near Kew Bridge and while at Kew prepared an account of the *Crassulaceae* for Oliver's *Flora of Tropical Africa* (1871).

In 1871 Britten moved to the department of botany at the British Museum, where he worked until he retired in 1909. His interest in field botany led to publications on the plants of Buckinghamshire (especially those of High Wycombe) and other counties. Undoubtedly his major task, appreciated by amateur and professional botanists alike, was editing the *Journal of Botany, British and Foreign*

James Britten (1846–1924), by Maull & Fox, 1906

early Cape botanists and collectors' in the *Journal of Linnean Society–Botany*, (45, 1920, 29–51) reveals his detailed knowledge of botanical history.

About 1867 Britten entered the Roman Catholic church and served it thereafter with ardour and industry; he was for some years honorary secretary of the Catholic Truth Society, wrote some of its polemical publications, and bequeathed most of his estate to Roman Catholic charities. Described as 'the most active Catholic layman' (Rendle, 340), he received the knighthood of St Gregory in 1897 and was promoted to knight commander in 1917. He died suddenly on 8 October 1924 in Bedford Street, London, and was buried at Isleworth cemetery, near his home in Brentford. He never married.

Britten had a ready wit and keen sense of humour, possessed a strong visual memory, held very firm views sometimes virulently expressed, and was appreciated for his scholarship and willingness to share his knowledge. The botanical names *Brittenia* Cogniaux (1890) and *Jamesbrittenia* O. Kuntze (1841) commemorate him.

WILLIAM T. STEARN

Sources A. B. Rendle, *Journal of Botany, British and Foreign*, 62 (1924), 339–43 [incl. list of publications] · B. D. J. [B. D. Jackson], *Proceedings of the Linnean Society of London*, 137th session (1924–5), 64–6 · C. H. Wright, letter, 16 March 1933, RBG Kew · *The Times* (10 Oct 1924) · *The Times* (8 Dec 1924) · b. cert. · *CGPLA Eng. & Wales* (1924)
Archives NHM, corresp. relating to *Biographical index of botanists* · RBG Kew, biographical notes relating to Merionethshire
Likenesses Maull & Fox, photograph, 1906, Linn. Soc. [*see illus.*] · photograph, *c.*1922, repro. in Rendle, *Journal of Botany*, facing p. 339
Wealth at death £21,980 17s. 7d.: probate, 1 Dec 1924, *CGPLA Eng. & Wales*

from 1879 until his death in 1924. This became the esteemed and convenient medium for the publication of records of British plants, descriptions of new species, obituaries, and articles on botanical bibliography (which particularly interested Britten—a bookman in the broadest sense). Britten's editorial notes and reviews were entertaining, critical, and sometimes caustic. The management of the Royal Botanic Gardens, Kew, with its ambition to absorb the department of botany, British Museum (Natural History), was a frequent target for witty attacks. Thiselton-Dyer considered one so libellous that he threatened a lawsuit, and to avoid this Britten agreed to make a large donation to a charity. He gave it to Richmond Hospital whose grateful governors, ignorant of the reason for his donation, made him a privileged life governor, to his lasting amusement.

Editing the *Journal of Botany* for forty-five years was only a part of Britten's activities. Between 1879 and 1891 he published in parts a well-illustrated pteridological work, *European Ferns*. *A Dictionary of English Plant Names* (in collaboration with Robert Holland, 1878–81), and, in collaboration with George Simmonds Boulger, *A Biographical Index of British and Irish Botanists* (1891). He was also responsible for the publication of a reprint (1892) of Turner's *The Names of Herbes* (1549) and of *Illustrations of Australian plants collected in 1790 during Captain Cook's voyage … by Sir Joseph Banks and Dr Daniel Solander* (1900–05). His paper, 'Some

Britton, James Nimmo (1908–1994), educationist, was born on 5 May 1908 in Scarborough, Yorkshire, the second of the four children of James Nimmo Britton (1873–1945), Baptist minister, and his wife, Elsie Clare (1884–1956), daughter of the Revd William Slater, Baptist minister in Lincoln. His father, who had converted to the Baptist faith as a young man, was noted as a great preacher and an outstanding evangelist in his several ministries. The children followed different paths: James in education, his elder sister, Clare, in social work and child therapy, his brother, Karl, as a professor of philosophy, and his younger sister, Elizabeth, as an art teacher. Britton's early education was at schools in Clapham (1912–17), followed by the Strand School, Brixton (1917–22) and Southend-on-Sea high school, Essex (1922–6). He read English at University College, London (1926–9), having gained the Campbell Clarke entrance scholarship. He then trained as a teacher, unusually for a graduate at that time, taking the diploma in education course at the London Day Training College (1929–30), which was shortly to become the University of London's Institute of Education (1932), the beginning of a long association.

Britton had written his own grammar book for schools, *English on the Anvil*, by 1934. His alert but also intimate voice, with its apparently effortless manner of simplifying complex material, was heard here, speaking directly to pupils. He was, from 1930 to 1933, assistant master for both physical education and English in the Woodhouse School, Finchley, and, from 1933 to 1938, senior English master and senior assistant master (1937) at the Harrow Weald county grammar school. Relationships with his lifelong colleagues Nancy Martin and Harold Rosen began in these productive teaching years, the triumvirate of Jimmy, Nancy, and 'Johnny' later becoming well known to English teachers.

Britton left teaching for publishing, and worked as education editor for John Murray, from 1938 to 1953. He served in the Royal Air Force from 1940 to 1946, attaining the rank of wing commander, was awarded the Greek Air Force cross for service in the Crete campaign, and was mentioned three times in dispatches. Returning to John Murray's but looking for a move to teacher training, he completed an MA, and for his dissertation made a subtle experimental study of response to poetry. Briefly lecturer in education at Birmingham College of Arts and Crafts (1953–54), he was appointed head of English at the Institute of Education in 1954, from a field of forty candidates.

Britton spoke once of his faith in 'quiet processes' and 'small circles', and these words apply to the collaborative enquiry which gathered round him in the years that followed. He had helped to found the London Association for the Teaching of English in 1947, and in study groups, and also at the institute, he constructed a rationale for English teaching which steadily grew in influence. His work was made distinctive, as Nancy Martin noted, by its quality of 'attention' and by its 'synthesising mode' (Lightfoot and Martin), and by the breadth of thinking that he brought to language. He remained head of the English department in the Institute of Education until 1970, and was then Goldsmiths' professor of education (1970–75). He directed influential research into the development of writing abilities (1968–73), and was a member of the committee of inquiry into the reading and the use of English (the Bullock committee) from 1972 to 1975, where his hand was clearly recognizable in the report. He wrote the classic *Language and Learning* (1970), his major work. His delicate explorations of talking, reading, and writing put teachers' work in touch with thought about the human mind.

Britton edited several international collections, and in retirement brought out *Prospect and Retrospect* (1982), a volume of his own essays. He received the David H. Russell award for distinguished research in English teaching from the American Council of Teachers of English in 1977, and in the same year an honorary doctorate from the University of Calgary. He was still writing just before his death. His later work included *Record and Recall* (1988), a memoir of a war episode in Crete; a volume of poems, *The Flight-Path of my Words* (1994); and *Literature in its Place* (1993), which was as sharp and vigorous as anything written earlier.

Britton married Muriel Robertson (1909–1990), artist and art teacher at Harrow Weald, in 1938, and he shared a life with Robert, as she was known, for more than fifty years. They had two daughters: Celia, a linguist and French scholar, and Alison, a potter. Family times were spent in their house in Hatch End, Middlesex, and at their much-loved cottage in Padstow, Cornwall. In later years the Brittons moved to a flat in Hampstead, London. Robert died in 1990. Britton died, from a stroke, at the Royal Free Hospital, Hampstead, on 28 February 1994; he was cremated on 4 March at Golders Green crematorium, London.   TONY BURGESS

Sources J. S. Kanter, ed., *Face to face with Clare Winnicott: her life and legacy* [forthcoming] · J. Britton, *The flight-path of my words: poems, 1940–1992* (1994) · J. Britton, *Record and recall: a Cretan memoir* (1988) · M. Lightfoot and N. Martin, eds., *The word for teaching is learning: essays for James Britton* (1988) · *The Guardian* (3 March 1994) · *The Independent* (10 March 1994) · *The Times* (18 March 1994) · personal knowledge (2004) · private information (2004)

Archives U. Lond., Institute of Education, personal library and papers |FILM film made by BBC, Horizon programme, On Reading (c. 1975), includes interview and commentary by Britton

Likenesses photograph, 1941, repro. in Britton, *Record and recall* · photograph, c.1985, repro. in *The Guardian* · photograph, repro. in *The Times* · photograph, repro. in *The Independent*

Wealth at death £512,835: administration with will, 31 May 1994, *CGPLA Eng. & Wales*

Britton, John (1771–1857), antiquary and topographer, was born on 7 July 1771 at Kington St Michael, near Chippenham, Wiltshire, the son of Henry Britton, a small farmer, maltster, baker, and village shopkeeper, and his wife, Anne Hillier. His mother died young, having reared ten children, of whom John was the fourth and the eldest son. When he left school at thirteen to help in the family shop he knew little except the alphabet and the Bible, and when he left Wiltshire for London in 1787 he had never seen a newspaper or a dictionary. As a penniless apprentice he spent five years in the cellar of the Jerusalem tavern, Clerkenwell, corking and bottling, and secretly studying by candlelight. It was in a Clerkenwell bookshop in 1789 that he first met Edward Wedlake Brayley. From this chance encounter stemmed a topographical partnership lasting sixty-five years; its first fruits were *The Beauties of Wiltshire* (2 vols., 1801). During the mid-1790s Britton had been living on the fringes of the theatrical world, working as a solicitor's clerk by day, singing and reciting dramatic monologues by night. From this period stem his earliest publications, notably *Sheridan and Kotzebue: the Enterprising Adventures of Pizarro* (1799).

In 1800 the publishers Vernor and Hood suggested to Britton that he undertake a topographical survey of the whole country, a six-volume compilation appearing in monthly instalments over three years. In the event *The Beauties of England and Wales* ran to twenty-seven bound volumes and took twenty years to complete. The names of Britton and Brayley alternately precede each other on the title-pages of the first six volumes: *Bedfordshire, Berkshire and Buckinghamshire* (1801), *Cambridgeshire, Cheshire and Cornwall* (1801), *Cumberland and Derbyshire* (1802), *Devon and Dorset* (1803), *Durham, Essex and Gloucestershire* (1803), and *Hampshire, Isle of Wight and Herefordshire* (1805). The labour of preparing the letterpress fell largely to Brayley. Britton was responsible for some of the historical commentaries and for most of the travelling, correspondence, collection of historical materials, and the direction of draughtsmen

John Britton (1771–1857), by John Wood, 1845

Britton's direction: Samuel Prout and Frederick Mackenzie, John and Henry Le Keux, Edward Blore, George Cattermole, R. W. Billings, and Henry Shaw.

Britton's rapidly growing knowledge of antiquities, as well as his quest for higher standards of illustration, had been restricted by the cursory format of *The Beauties*. His next series, the *Architectural Antiquities of Great Britain*, set out to exhibit 'specimens of the various styles' of medieval architecture by 'correct delineations and accurate accounts ... drawn and engraved with scrupulous accuracy' and by 'enlarged representations of particular parts and ornaments, with ground plans etc.'. His publishers, Messrs Longman and Taylor, were co-operative. His engravers, notably Smith, Roffe, Rawle, Woolnoth, and the Le Keux brothers, were supremely competent. His list of 'scientific artists' was dazzling: Prout, Nash, Alexander, Hearne, Wyatville, Porden, Wilkins, Cotman, Buckler, Gandy, Wild, Westall, Dayes, Fielding, West, Turner, Shee, Repton, Blore, and Mackenzie. The result was possibly Britton's most successful undertaking and certainly his most profitable. The first four volumes appeared fairly quickly, in 1807, 1809, 1812, and 1814. A fifth, *A Chronological History and Graphic Illustrations of Christian Architecture in England*, appeared in 1827. This has been described as 'the first attempt at a *coherent history* of English Gothic' (P. Frankl, *The Gothic*, 1960, 498). Its preparation involved a formidable amount of research, and Britton understandably decided to reduce his labours thereafter—from twelve or fourteen hours a day to a mere six or eight. In fact he was by that date scarcely halfway through another multiple work, which turned out to be his *magnum opus*, the *Cathedral Antiquities of England*.

Britton was the first to attempt a complete survey of English cathedrals since Browne Willis (1727–42). Carter's series (1797–1801), sponsored by the Society of Antiquaries, had proved abortive; Storer's *Cathedrals* (1812) had been popular but inadequate. Only two masters held the field: Bentham's *Ely* (1771) and Milner's *Winchester* (1793). A few cathedrals were already well documented but none had previously been subjected to measured plans, sections, and geometrical elevations. Britton's series moreover was superbly produced by Charles Whittingham's Chiswick Press. The resulting fourteen volumes—published between 1814 and 1835—can claim a place 'among the greatest ... glories of British book design' (R. McLean, *Victorian Book Design*, 1963, 2–6). But the volumes for Rochester, Durham, Chichester, Chester, Carlisle, Ely, and Lincoln never appeared. A technical revolution—the substitution of steel engraving for copperplate—made the series uncompetitive. Not to be outdone Britton thereupon switched to the new medium, producing a number of money-spinning volumes with mass-produced steel engravings, notably *Bath and Bristol* (1829), and *Modern Athens* (1829)—the definitive panorama of classical Edinburgh. There was still a market for lavish publications on the lines of his earlier *Fonthill* (1823) but the superlative plates of *Cassiobury* (1837), *Toddington* (1841), *Windsor* (1842), and *London and Birmingham Railway* (1838–9) all depended

and engravers. Responsibility thereafter was more distinct. *Hertfordshire, Huntingdonshire and Kent* (1808) went to Brayley; *Lancashire, Leicestershire and Lincolnshire* (1807) went to Britton. Scarcely had Brayley begun *London, Middlesex and Westminster* than he fell foul of Hood's successor, John Harris. Of the first five volumes on the metropolis (1810–16) Brayley contributed two before giving way to Joseph Nightingale and J. N. Brewer. Meanwhile some of the work prepared by Brewer was completed by the Revd J. Evans as *Monmouthshire, Norfolk and Northamptonshire* (1810). Then came *Northumberland and Nottinghamshire*, by the Revd J. Hodgson and F. C. Laird; *Oxfordshire and Rutland* (1813) by Brewer; and *Staffordshire* (1813) and *Shropshire and Somerset* by Nightingale. *Yorkshire* (1812) was farmed out to John Bigland, *Suffolk, Surrey and Sussex* (1813) to Frederick Shoberl, *Warwickshire* (1814) to Brewer, *North Wales* (1812) to Evans, and *South Wales* (1815) to Thomas Rees. Britton completed *Wiltshire* in 1814 and in the same year joined with Brewer, Hodgson, and Laird to finish *Worcestershire and Westmorland*. Finally Brewer added an introductory volume containing a historical survey of British antiquities, a formidable bibliography, and an exposé of the quarrels that had punctuated the whole work. The cost of production (some £50,000) had been enormous; the labour involved was heroic. For the first five volumes alone the two authors travelled 3500 miles, often on foot; between 8 June and 20 September 1800 they walked 1350 miles. Britton was the organizing genius throughout. In the crowded field of English topography there had been nothing so comprehensive since Camden's *Magna Britannia* (1720–31); Grose and Gough had been relatively selective. In addition a whole school of artists and engravers had grown up under on private subsidies, to say nothing of his classic description of Sir John Soane's collection, *The Union of Architecture, Sculpture and Painting* (1827).

Towards the end of his career Britton faced criticism as well as bankruptcy. When his *Dictionary of the Architecture and Archaeology of the Middle Ages* appeared in 1831–8 it seemed already outdated. But among his later works was one that satisfied creditors as well as critics, making a profit of £1400: *Specimens of Gothic Architecture* (2 vols., 1820–25). It was Britton's energy as editor, and his experience as publisher, that guaranteed the success of *Specimens*, as much as the drawings by A. C. Pugin and the documentation by E. J. Willson. Britton and Pugin co-operated again, with equal success, in *The Public Buildings of London* (2 vols., 1825) and *The Architectural Antiquities of Normandy* (1825–8). In subsequent years *Memoirs of the Tower of London* (1830) and *The Ancient Palace and Late Houses of Parliament at Westminster* (1834–6) saw Britton once again productively in harness with his old partner E. W. Brayley. The *Gentleman's Magazine* christened them 'the Castor and Pollux of Topographers' (*GM*, 1st ser., 101/2, 1831, 47).

During the last twelve years of his life Britton published little apart from his rambling two-volume *Autobiography* (1850, 1857); this included an exhaustive list of works compiled by his secretary T. E. Jones. His first wife—whom he married in 1802 and to whom he was devoted—died in 1848. After his second marriage—to his late wife's niece Ellen, in 1849—he was so short of money that he had to resign his membership of the Society of Antiquaries. Disraeli came to the rescue with a civil-list pension of £75 in 1852. Apart from his literary achievements Britton merited this award on grounds of public service. As adviser to the Royal Literary Fund for forty years he dealt with 1200 applications for relief. As a member of the Art Union committee he was regularly involved in the management of funds and distribution of prizes. Waltham Cross, Stratford church, and St Mary Redcliffe, Bristol, all owed their restoration to his efforts. For many years he campaigned for governmental protection of ancient monuments, and he was one of the keenest supporters of the future Royal Institute of British Architects. (Appropriately he was made honorary fellow in 1835; its council organized the Britton testimonial in 1845, attended his funeral at Norwood cemetery in 1857, and later installed an elaborate brass in his memory at Salisbury Cathedral.)

John Britton died of bronchitis at his home, 17 Burton Street, St Pancras, London, on 2 January 1857. There is an early portrait of him in the *European Magazine* for 1828 and later likenesses in the *Autobiography* showing him in his study at his home, near Tavistock Square. In fifty years he was responsible for more than 100 publications. He never avoided controversy: he even tried to elucidate the origin of Stonehenge, the identity of Junius, and the authorship of Shakespeare's plays. As a draughtsman and designer he was undistinguished, but as editor, publisher, and publicist his influence on the development of the Gothic revival ranks with that of A. W. Pugin and John Ruskin. His energy was stupendous but he seldom made a profit; what spurred him on was the status and prestige attached to

learning. Charles Knight remembered him as 'kind-hearted … indefatigable, good-tempered, self-satisfied, pushing and puffing' (Knight, *Passages of a Working Life*, 1864, 1.31; 2.307; 3.43). His ambitions as a scholar far outran his talents. But architectural historians have reason to be grateful to the man who William Beckford called 'that highly ridiculous, highly impertinent Britton, the Cathedral fellow' (B. Alexander, ed., *Life at Fonthill, 1807–22*, 1957, 228–9, 21 Oct 1817).

Britton had no children by either of his marriages. His second wife, Ellen, survived him. His library and collection of prints and drawings was dispersed soon after his death.   J. MORDAUNT CROOK

Sources J. Britton, *Autobiography*, 2 vols. (1850); (1857) [with a full list of works by T. E. Jones; London Library copy with MS additions by Charles Ellis] · J. Mordaunt Crook, 'John Britton and the genesis of the Gothic revival', *Concerning architecture*, ed. J. Summerson (1968) · M. D. Wyatt, *R.I.B.A reports and papers* (1856–7), 57 · *The Builder*, 15 (1857), 22–5 · *GM*, 3rd ser., 2 (1857), 191 · *The Ecclesiologist*, 18 (1857), 70 · will, PRO, PROB 11/2245, sig. 90 · *IGI* · J. Britton and E. W. Brayley, *The beauties of England and Wales*, 18 vols. in 25 (1801–16)

Archives Bodl. Oxf., authorial copy of 'Rights of literature', incl. notes and additional papers · Bodl. Oxf., corresp. and papers relating to Dulwich Picture Gallery, and authorship of the letters of Junius · Boston PL, corresp. · CUL, notes and papers, incl. biographical collections and annotated printed works · U. Edin. L., corresp. | Bodl. Oxf., corresp. with William Beckford · Bodl. Oxf., MSS Dom. D. 87 and Eng. Misc. d. 222 · Bodl. Oxf., corresp. with Sir Thomas Phillipps · Devizes Museum, Wiltshire Archaeological and Natural History Society, MS catalogue of Wiltshire collection · Devizes Museum, Wiltshire Archaeological and Natural History Society, corresp. with William Cunnington and his family, and others · Devizes Museum, Wiltshire Archaeological and Natural History Society, corresp. with J. E. Jackson · DWL, letters to Henry Crabb Robinson · Herefs. RO, letters to Thomas Bird · Lpool RO, corresp. with Matthew Gregson · Soane Museum, London, Soane corresp. · U. Edin. L., letters to James Halliwell-Phillipps · W. Sussex RO, letters to the duke of Richmond · Yale U., Beinecke L., index to Wiltshire sketches

Likenesses J. Thomson, stipple, pubd 1828 (after J. Wood), BM, NPG · W. Brockedon, chalk drawing, 1831, NPG · S. Williams, line engraving, pubd 1841 (after bust by W. Scoular), NPG · J. Wood, oils, 1845, NPG [*see illus.*] · J. H. le Keux, mezzotint (after photograph by Claudet), BM · J. Thomson, stipple (after T. Uwins), BM, NPG; repro. in *European Magazine* (1820) · portrait, repro. in *European Magazine*, 77 (1828) · portrait, repro. in Britton, *Autobiography*

Britton, Thomas (1644–1714), concert promoter, book collector, and coal merchant, was born on 14 January 1644 at Rushden near Higham Ferrers, Northamptonshire. He migrated to London where he apprenticed himself to a 'small-coal' (slack-coal, or charcoal) merchant near St John the Baptist's Street in Clerkenwell. When his time was up his master gave him a monetary inducement to go elsewhere. However, after a period in his native county, he returned and established a rival business in a stable which he turned into a house on the corner of Jerusalem Passage in Aylesbury Street, Clerkenwell. Britton's business flourished to the extent that by 1678 he was in a position to establish the weekly concert series, patronized by an elevated acquaintanceship, for which he is chiefly remembered. By the 1690s he was paying rates on two buildings

Thomas Britton (1644–1714), by John Wollaston, 1703

and renting another, and was elected a highways' surveyor for Clerkenwell. Britton continued to work in the small-coal trade until his death, although he might have retired on the proceeds of this and of his dealings in rare books.

Britton's concerts took place in a long narrow room above his coal store with a ceiling so low that 'a tall man could but just stand upright in it' (Hawkins, 790), reached by a difficult exterior staircase, and attracted the rich and famous to these unglamorous surroundings, initially by their novelty, subsequently perhaps by their cult status. Sir Roger L'Estrange, press censor and pamphleteer, helped inaugurate the series on the viol, evidence that Britton already moved in elevated circles, particularly as a result of his bibliophile activities. Thus, in 1694 (coincidentally the year in which Samuel Pepys noted his expertise in Tudor liturgical music) Britton sent for auction 'a curious collection of books in divinity, history, physick and chimistry' together with 'an extraordinary collection of manuscripts in Latin and English' (*The Library of Mr Tho. Britton, Smallcoal-Man*, title-page).

Britton may have made the transition from tradesman to savant after making the acquaintance of a Clerkenwell neighbour, Theophilus Garencières, who found in him an apt, enthusiastic, and original pupil in the science of chemistry. He constructed 'a moving Elaboratory' which so impressed a friend of Garencières that he paid Britton a handsome fee to construct one for him on his Welsh estate. They also shared an interest in esoteric knowledge as Garencières was the translator of Nostradamus and Britton was an admirer of Rosacrucian ideas. However, it

is likely that Britton was valued more widely for his knowledge of books in general and of the book trade. Thus the bibliophiles Robert Harley, earl of Oxford, the duke of Devonshire, and the earls of Pembroke, Winchilsea, and Sunderland encouraged his conversation on their book hunting expeditions in the City on winter Saturday afternoons. Similarly, Britton is said to have sold a collection to Lord Somers—which formed the basis for the Somers Tracts published in 1748–52—for a very large sum.

Britton's concert series was the longest-lasting of several established in the late seventeenth century, and, in this respect particularly, one of the most important. Here Handel once played the organ (though it had only five stops), and J. C. Pepusch the harpsichord. Significantly, the British Library has a 'Sonata by Mr Pepusch, called Small coal' (Johnstone and Fiske, 443, n. 45). However, Hawkins's statement that Handel played there in 1711 has not received subsequent corroboration. Yet the list of other players was respectable enough: they included the musicians John Banister, Matthew Dubourg, Philip Hart, and Abel Whichelo, and keen amateurs like Sir Roger l'Estrange, the poet John Hughes, the excise officer Henry Needler, and the portrait painter J. Wollaston. Britton himself played the viol da gamba—opinions vary, however, about his musical ability. What is not in doubt is how extensive was his music collection—which must have provided the basis of the programmes, some engraved, but much 'pricked with his own Hand (very neatly and accurately)' (*Remarks*, 103)—nor how impressive was his collection of instruments including a fine guitar, dulcimer, harpsichord, virginal, viols, and numerous rare violins. Thus when Ralph Thorseby and his party 'called at Mr Britton's' in 1712, Thorseby believed they 'heard a noble concert of music, vocal and instrumental, the best in town' (*Diary*, 111–12). The balance of evidence is that Britton provided these concerts 'for his own entertainment, and that of the gentry, &c., gratis', rather than charging a subscription, and 'most foreigners of distinction' visited them occasionally, 'for the fancy of it' (ibid.). The celebrated beauty the duchess of Queensberry is another known to have ascended the ladder-like stairs of Britton's 'House … not much higher than a Canary Pipe, … [with] the Window of … [its] State Room … very little bigger than the Bunghole of a Cask' (Ward, 299–306).

Britton was 'a short, thickset man' who appears to have had a frank countenance and 'a sprightly temper' (*Remarks*, 104). He clearly had the means and capacity to inspire the loyalty from musicians which sustained his concerts for nearly four decades. However, stories of his mixing briefly with high aristocrats while still dressed in his blue smock and with the coal sack he had been carrying about the streets, suggest that he may have been tolerated as a colourful and humble 'character' as well as valued for his knowledge. Britton was painted twice by J. Wollaston. The first portrait showed him in his smock, with a coal measure in his hands, the second tuning a harpsichord.

Britton's death was supposed to have been occasioned by a trick played upon him by one of his genteel 'friends', a

Middlesex magistrate, who knew Britton was very superstitious and employed a ventriloquist to assume the voice of God—commanding him to his knees. The terror felt by the now elderly Britton sent him into an immediate and fatal decline and he died a few days later, on 27 September 1714. His funeral was attended 'in a very solemn and decent manner by a great Concourse of people' (*Remarks*, 104) and he was buried on 1 October in the churchyard of St James's, Clerkenwell. He left a widow, about whom nothing is known, his literary and musical collections which were sold at auction, and an enduring reputation.

DOUGLAS A. REID

Sources *Remarks and collections of Thomas Hearne*, ed. C. E. Doble and others, 5, OHS, 42 (1901) • J. Hawkins, *A general history of the science and practice of music*, 2 (1776); repr. (1963) • C. Price, 'The smallcoal cult', *MT*, 119 (1978), 1032–4 • Rimbault, 'Thomas Britton', Grove, *Dict. mus.* • H. D. Johnstone and R. Fiske, eds., *Music in Britain: the eighteenth century* (1990), vol. 4 of *The Blackwell history of music in Britain*, ed. I. Spink (1988–95) • *DNB* • *The diary of Ralph Thoresby*, ed. J. Taylor, 2 (1830) • E. Ward, *A compleat and humorous account of all the remarkable clubs in the Cities of London and Westminster* (1745) • J. Bullord, *The library of Mr Tho. Britton, smallcoal-man* (1694) [sale catalogue, London, 1 Nov 1694]
Likenesses J. Wollaston, oils, 1703, NPG [*see illus.*] • Maddocks, engraving (after J. Wollaston), repro. in Caulfield, *Remarkable persons* • J. Simon, mezzotint (after J. Wollaston) • J. Wollaston, line engraving (after C. Grignion), NPG • portrait, repro. in *London Magazine* (Feb 1777)
Wealth at death see will, GL, cited without details, Price, 'Smallcoal cult'

Broackes, Sir Nigel (1934–1999), financier and industrialist, was born at One Ash, Church Lane, Wakefield, Yorkshire, on 21 July 1934, the son of Donald Broackes (*d.* 1943), a solicitor, and his wife, Nancy Rowland Tansley. His father died while serving in the army in 1943, leaving an estate of just £38. His mother was denied a war pension because her husband had died of natural causes, and the memory of her having to scrape a living as a young widow left a profound impression on her son. His paternal grandfather, however, was comfortably off, but had fallen out with his son. When he died he left £28,000 in trust for his grandson, with the income to be used to support his widowed daughter-in-law and to pay school fees. Nigel was sent at first to Brambletye School in Sussex and then to Stowe School.

After leaving Stowe at sixteen Broackes went to work for Stewart and Hughman, a small firm of Lloyds underwriters, before doing his national service from 1951 to 1953 in the 3rd hussars. At Stewart and Hughman he quickly discovered an aptitude for understanding corporate accounts. After leaving the army he returned to the firm but was soon disillusioned and decided to go into business on his own. He quickly lost the whole of his inheritance in three unsuccessful and diverse ventures in house conversion, hire purchase, and tool making. In the process he came to the conclusion that London's many bomb-sites were ripe for development. He worked for a short spell with Collins and Collins, a West End estate agent, to learn something of the trade, and through a stockbroking friend of his mother made contact with potential financial backers. His first large-scale venture was to develop the corner site of Half Moon Street and Piccadilly, and then, through Eastern International, a small finance company, he bought up other potentially very profitable sites. At the same time he began to invest in 'unexplored sleepy concerns which had maintained a Rip Van Winkle posture since, during, or even before, the war' (Broackes, 57). In 1956 he married Joyce Edith Horne, *née* Skidmore (*d.* 1993). They had two sons and one daughter.

In 1961 Victor *Matthews, a builder from the East End who had been contracts manager with the well-known firm of Trollope and Colls and was now in business on his own, won a contract from Broackes to convert a block of flats. The two became firm friends, and were a perfect foil for each other. Matthews was hard-nosed and at home on the shop floor, while Broackes was urbane and cultivated, with a sharp eye to the balance sheet. Broackes was so successful that Eastern International was renamed Trafalgar House (previously the name of a subsidiary) and was launched on the stock exchange in July 1963. The company was capitalized at £1.6 million, of which Broackes himself held twenty-one per cent. He was determined, however, on diversification to protect his enterprise from the cyclical fluctuations of the property market. Accordingly in 1964 Trafalgar House took a forty-nine per cent stake in Matthews's construction company, Bridge Walker, with an option over the remainder of the capital. Victor Matthews became a member of the Trafalgar House board and Eric Parker, an accountant, joined to become finance director in 1969. Broackes and Matthews pursued an aggressive takeover strategy, winning control of a number of hotel, property development, and technically advanced building businesses, including Trollope and Colls and the Ideal Building Corporation. Long before branding became a popular concept, their strategy was to buy businesses with familiar names which had fallen on hard times and develop their potential. They failed in an ambitious attempt, in conjunction with Commercial Union, to acquire Metropolitan Estates in 1970, but succeeded in a well-timed bid for the shipping company Cunard the following year. Trafalgar House acquired assets of some £40 million for an investment of £26 million. Many commentators who were sceptical about the ability of Broackes and Matthews to manage a shipping company were surprised by the speed and efficiency with which it was assimilated.

With more than 260 companies under his wing, Broackes was now well known, and on 3 January 1972, along with Jim Slater and Jacob Rothschild, he was entertained at Chequers by the prime minister, Edward Heath. He later recalled with the benefit of hindsight that Heath 'wanted to encourage an investment boom with an abundance of easy credit' (Broackes, 221). Broackes emerged almost unscathed from the ensuing financial crisis which engulfed many of his contemporaries, perhaps because, unlike them, he was not an asset-stripper. He, Matthews, and Parker were more determined than ever to broaden the base of their corporate empire. They were able to take advantage of the crisis in the London property market by acquiring the Ritz Hotel for less than £2 million in 1975.

Within fifteen years it was valued at over £140 million. There was concern among financial commentators, bruised by the experience of the secondary banking crisis when conglomerates such as Slater Walker collapsed, that Trafalgar House lacked a clear acquisition strategy. This impression was confirmed in 1977 when Matthews persuaded Broackes to buy Express Newspapers, which since Lord Beaverbrook's death thirteen years earlier had lacked direction. Matthews quickly became obsessed by newsprint, while Broackes was happy to take a back seat. This allowed him to accept the offer in 1979 from the newly elected prime minister Margaret Thatcher of the chairmanship of the nascent London Docklands Development Corporation (LDDC). He was no stranger to public service, having been involved in charitable housing trusts and chairing the Ship and Marine Technology Requirements Board. He at once recognized the development potential of the derelict wharves so close to the city. He became as absorbed with LDDC as Matthews was with Fleet Street. In that year Broackes published an autobiography giving a very frank account of his successes and failures. In the few references to Matthews he mentioned his pessimistic turn of mind. This led to a sharp rejoinder from Matthews, who unfairly accused Broackes of 'idling his time away in the South of France' (*The Independent*, 5 Oct 1999) where he had a house in the Alpes-Maritimes.

Despite this friction Express Newspapers made a remarkable recovery under the Trafalgar House umbrella and was floated off in 1982 as a separate company, Fleet Holdings, with Matthews as chairman. Bereft of Matthews's support, Broackes now had to devote more time to Trafalgar House. In 1984 he gave up the chairmanship of LDDC at the end of his first five-year term. He had overseen the construction of thousands of badly needed homes and had laid the foundation of what became the City airport and the Docklands Light Railway. He was rewarded with a knighthood. In the previous year he had failed in a bid for P. & O. There followed a series of disastrous acquisitions in an attempt to build Trafalgar House's presence in the offshore oil industry and in shipbuilding and engineering, in the belief that the two went together as property development and construction had done in the 1960s. John Brown's and Davy International may once have enjoyed a worldwide reputation, but by the 1980s their problems were deep-seated and they lacked assets which could be easily developed. Likewise Broackes's ambitious proposal of a bridge and tunnel link across the English Channel lacked immediate credibility and failed to prevail against the proposed tunnel that was finally built, though as it turned out this cost vastly more than had been projected in Broackes's plan. Unlike the managers of P. & O., Broackes and Eric Parker, who had succeeded Matthews as chief executive, did not appreciate the growing demand for cruises and as a result did not order new tonnage. The last straw for investors was the takeover in 1991 of the Scott Lithgow shipyard on the Clyde with a drilling rig under construction. Unknown to Broackes, the management had lacked both the skills and the know-how to undertake such a complex contract, and

Trafalgar House incurred enormous losses. There were suggestions that 'eccentric accounting practices' (*The Independent*, 5 Oct 1999) had been adopted to disguise the extent of the problem. In the following year Hong Kong Land acquired a controlling stake in the group and ousted Broackes as chairman.

When he retired Broackes continued his habit of spending weekends at Checkendon Court, near Henley, and weekdays in London. Away from his desk he was fond of music and was an accomplished silversmith. This had earned him the chairmanship of the Crafts Council from 1991 to 1997, in which he delighted. Although he enjoyed the trappings of wealth, his homes and his yachts, he was at heart a family man. After his much loved wife, Joyce, died in 1993, he became more reclusive, but he remained a moving force in the Goldsmiths Company and an influential trustee of the National Maritime Museum. He died on 29 September 1999 at his London home, 41 Chelsea Square, Chelsea. He set high standards for both himself and his family, wishing to excel in everything he did. Though supportive of Margaret Thatcher, he was perhaps more of a one-nation Conservative. In contrast to the business activities of many of his contemporaries, much of what he achieved survived under the umbrella of Kvaerner, which ultimately acquired Trafalgar House.

MICHAEL S. MOSS

Sources N. Broackes, *A growing concern* (1979) · F. E. Hyde, *Cunard and the north Atlantic, 1946–73* (1975) · *The Times* (1 Oct 1999) · *The Guardian* (5 Oct 1999) · *The Independent* (5 Oct 1999) · *The Scotsman* (5 Oct 1999) · WWW · private information (2004) [Justin Broackes, son; Victoria Beverley, daughter]
Likenesses N. Broackes, portrait, oils, c.1952, priv. coll. · photograph, 1977, repro. in *The Times* · P. Benning, portrait, oils, c.1985, priv. coll. · S. Adler, photograph, repro. in *The Guardian* · R. Fisher, sculpture, priv. coll. · photograph, repro. in *Daily Telegraph* · photograph, repro. in *The Independent* · photograph, repro. in *The Scotsman*
Wealth at death £16,170,313—gross; £16,127,898—net: probate, 14 Feb 2000, CGPLA Eng. & Wales

Broad, Sir Charles Noel Frank (1882–1976), army officer, was born at Lahore on 29 December 1882, the only child of Major Charles Herbert Broad, 5th fusiliers, and his wife, Ann Paul. He was educated at Wellington College, Berkshire, and Pembroke College, Cambridge, but did not take a degree. After serving in the Second South African War as a private in the militia he was commissioned into the Royal Artillery in 1905. He went to the Staff College, Camberley, in 1914 and eventually went to France as a brigade-major in the late summer of 1915. In the Somme campaign of 1916 he was chief staff officer (as a major) to General H. C. C. Uniacke, an outstanding gunner, who was major-general Royal Artillery in the Fifth Army. He was appointed to the DSO in 1917, and received the Croix de Guerre and Légion d'honneur. In 1915 he married Lillian Mary, daughter of Edwin Mackintosh, who worked in shipping; they had one daughter.

Broad's proven ability was recognized by his appointment as artillery instructor at the Staff College in 1919 where his students included four future chiefs of the Imperial General Staff. Four years later he transferred to the newly established Royal Tank Corps (RTC), and during the next decade he made his chief contribution to the profession as an exponent of mechanization and armoured warfare. Broad's talents were at once recognized by his appointment as commandant of the tank gunnery school at Lulworth, and in 1925 he succeeded another brilliant newcomer to the corps, George Mackintosh Lindsay, as chief instructor at the tank corps central school. Here he contributed to the first tactical manual for armoured forces and developed the medium tank, equipped with anti-tank gun and machine-guns and designed to fire on the move.

During the years 1927–31, which witnessed the climax of British experiments with mechanized forces, Broad served in the staff duties section of the general staff at the War Office responsible for organizing for war. In 1929 he drafted what was to become a famous manual—*Mechanised and Armoured Formations*—popularly known in the army as the 'purple primer' from the colour of its covers. Although progressive in tone, Broad's manual skilfully avoided the extremism and polemics which characterized much of the literature on mechanization. He stressed the superiority of armoured forces over infantry in power, mobility, and endurance; moreover he made the revolutionary suggestion that armoured forces might keep up advances of 30 to 50 miles a day for nearly a week—a feat which was achieved by Germany's Panzer divisions in the early campaigns of the Second World War. General Heinz Guderian later acknowledged Broad's influence on his thinking, though it should be noted that the infantry component of the Panzer divisions was much stronger than Broad had recommended.

In 1931 Broad, now a brigadier, was given a wonderful opportunity to try out his ideas as commander of the experimental 1st brigade RTC. According to the expert on tank warfare Basil Liddell Hart those trials on Salisbury Plain were 'the most influential tactical experiments in the British Army since Sir John Moore's training of the Light Brigade at Shorncliffe Camp' (Liddell Hart, 1.179) during the Napoleonic wars. Broad demonstrated that his units, composed of medium and light tanks, could play a more adventurous role than close co-operation with slow-moving infantry. He proved that tank formations could be controlled while manoeuvring over difficult terrain by a combination of flags and radio telephony. These trials lent support to the proposition that only mechanized armoured forces could be manoeuvred under the intense fire to be expected on the modern battlefield. Unfortunately Broad's 'five year plan' for the creation of four permanent armoured brigades was shelved owing to the financial crisis and the resignation of the Labour government in 1931. The momentum generated by Broad and his colleagues such as Lindsay, Sir F. A. Pile, and P. C. S. Hobart was lost, and six years elapsed before mechanization began in earnest in 1937.

This proved to be Broad's last direct connection with mechanization, though he remained deeply interested in the subject for the rest of his life. He became major-general in 1936. In 1937 he made an excellent impression on the new secretary of state for war, Leslie Hore-Belisha, but was given only the dead-end job of major-general in charge of administration at Aldershot. Since the main duty there was to organize the annual tattoo this was a scandalous waste of expertise. Whether there was an actual conspiracy at the War Office against Broad and the other tank pioneers is uncertain; but there was evidently a feeling in the military hierarchy that they should not be conspicuously rewarded in competition with sound but conservative officers of equivalent rank. Broad had not helped his prospects by a contretemps with the chief of the Imperial General Staff, Viscount Gort (Liddell Hart, 2.35).

On the outbreak of war in 1939 Broad was promoted to the Aldershot command, and in the following year he was made lieutenant-general and general officer commanding-in-chief, Eastern army, India, where he worked hard to modernize the Indian army under the threat of a Japanese invasion. He was appointed CB in 1938 and KCB in 1941 and retired in the following year on reaching retirement age, though he continued to be colonel commandant of the RTC until 1948. Broad's first wife died in 1942, and in 1944 he married Diana Myrtle, younger daughter of Colonel Philip Robert Bald, of Barton Lodge, Cerne Abbas; they had three sons (one deceased) and one daughter.

Slight of stature and generally mild of manner, Broad occasionally showed impatience with slower-minded senior officers. Several of his peers rated him an outstanding officer but one also mentioned his occasional want of tact. Perhaps it was this flaw which caused his estrangement from Gort over a trivial misunderstanding. Broad was sometimes depressed by the lack of funds for new equipment and realistic training, and also felt that the army was bedevilled by cliques. In later years he was apt to reproach himself for lacking the crusading zeal of a Joan of Arc, but it is hard to see that he could have made more of his brief opportunities in comparatively junior positions. Indeed his reputation is assured as a shrewd and balanced theoretician of armoured warfare in the years when Britain led the world in its tank manuals and field exercises. Broad died at Beaminster, Dorset, on 23 March 1976.

BRIAN BOND, *rev.*

Sources B. H. Liddell Hart, *The memoirs of Captain Liddell Hart*, 2 vols. (1965) · K. Macksey, *The tank pioneers* (1981) · private information (1986) · *The Times* (24 March 1976) · B. Bond, *British military policy between the two world wars* (1980) · R. H. Larson, *The British army and the theory of armored warfare, 1918–1940* (1984) · J. P. Harris and F. N. Toase, eds., *Armoured warfare* (1990) · *WWW* · *CGPLA Eng. & Wales* (1976)

Archives King's Lond., letters relating to the destruction of his papers | King's Lond., corresp. with Sir B. H. Liddell Hart

Likenesses I. J. Courtney, portrait, 1979, Royal Tank headquarters, London

Wealth at death £23,963: probate, 21 July 1976, *CGPLA Eng. & Wales*

Broad, Charlie Dunbar (1887–1971), philosopher, was born at Harlesden, Middlesex, on 30 December 1887, the only child of Charles Stephen Broad, wine merchant, of an old family of Bristol builders, and his wife, Emily

Gomme. Broad was brought up in quietly comfortable circumstances and in an environment of elderly relatives of varying degrees of eccentricity; he was relieved from the need to work by a modest family trust. He was at Dulwich College from 1900 to 1906 when A. H. Gilkes was headmaster. Having moved from the 'engineering side' to the 'science side' of the school, he won a science scholarship to Trinity College, Cambridge, and went up there in 1906. At that time, he says of himself, he adhered to a 'smug and thin rationalism' under the influence of the writings of H. G. Wells and other advanced thinkers of the age. An interest in philosophy had been awoken at school by reading Schopenhauer. In 1908 he got a first in part one of the natural sciences tripos, but, doubting his chances of doing first-class work in science, turned to philosophy.

That decision was justified in 1910 by Broad's achievement of first-class honours, with special distinction in 'moral science'. His main teachers were J. M. E. McTaggart and the logician W. E. Johnson. He also had some contact with Bertrand Russell, the philosopher to whom technically he was closest, sharing Russell's conviction that science is very substantially inconsistent with common sense and more worthy of belief than common sense, and with G. E. Moore. It was the early and largely shared doctrines of these two major philosophers that he was to elaborate and to defend, despite Laodicean protestations, throughout his career.

In 1911 Broad was elected a fellow of Trinity on the basis of a dissertation that was published in an improved form in 1914 as *Perception, Physics, and Reality*. From 1911 to 1920 he was at the University of St Andrews, first as assistant to G. F. Stout, then as lecturer at the Dundee part of the university. During the war he gave some time to work at a neighbouring munitions factory. In 1920 he succeeded C. Lloyd Morgan as professor at Bristol, and he returned to Trinity in 1923 to succeed McTaggart in his teaching post there. For the rest of his life he continued to live in Trinity, for most of the time in rooms once inhabited by Newton. From 1933 until his retirement in 1953 he was Knightbridge professor of moral philosophy, in succession to W. R. Sorley.

As a philosopher Broad, as he was the first to admit, had little in the way of new ideas to contribute to philosophy. If anything, indeed, he was inclined to exaggerate both his uncreativeness and the rapidity with which he lost any real interest in the subject. In fact, he was a creditable specimen of what Locke claimed to be, namely an 'underlabourer' for whom it is 'ambition enough to be employed ... in clearing the ground a little and removing some of the rubbish'. In a long series of books on a wide range of philosophical topics he explored the interests and doctrines of Russell with much greater care and thoroughness than Russell, and those of Moore without Moore's repetition and exasperating slowness.

The Lockean account of perceptual knowledge, as a rather precarious inference from private 'sensa' to public objects endowed with only a few of the qualities commonly ascribed to them, was developed at length in Broad's dissertation. It reappears as part of a general account of the philosophy of science, taking account of recent developments in science, in *Scientific Thought* (1923) and as part of a comprehensive philosophy of mind in his Tarner lectures, *The Mind and its Place in Nature* (1925). Here for the first time appears a discussion of the psychical research to which he was to devote much of his energy. In 1927 he brought out the second and less abstract volume of his teacher McTaggart's *The Nature of Existence*, still in draft at its author's death. In 1934 *Five Types of Ethical Theory* gave careful, sometimes idiosyncratic accounts of some major moral philosophers. Broad's main work in the 1930s was his *Examination of McTaggart's Philosophy* (vol. 1, 1933; vol. 2, 1938), the largest and most impressive of his works, in which he gave enormously fair, even if ultimately negative, consideration to what was for him an ideal example of the kind of speculative philosophy that he believed to be possible in principle over and above the analytic or critical philosophy orthodox in his time.

Broad's later works were essay collections—*Ethics and the History of Philosophy* (1952) and *Religion, Philosophy and Psychical Research* (1953)—*Lectures on Psychical Research* (1962), and posthumously published lecture series on Leibniz and Kant. He had several honorary degrees, including both a LittD and ScD from Cambridge, and was elected FBA in 1926.

Broad was a conspicuous example of the traditional bachelor don of his epoch. Boyhood interests in railways and the Nordic world, particularly the latter, persisted into later life. In 1946 he made his first trip out of Britain to Scandinavia, and found the young men of Sweden a source of profound delight from that time forward. In the Second World War he served as junior bursar of his college and acquitted himself well. He did not visit America until the academic year following his retirement, 1953–4, when he lectured at Michigan and the University of California at Los Angeles. He was a conscientious supervisor of his pupils but a dull lecturer, dictating matter already written out. He claimed to have lost all interest in philosophy by the time he became professor in 1933, but that is belied by the amplitude and seriousness of the work he continued to produce at least until the end of the 1930s. The sour retrospection more probably reflects his resentment at the fashionable obsession with Ludwig Wittgenstein, who returned to Cambridge in 1929 and soon stole any fire Broad may have had.

In appearance Broad was short, a little stocky, and bald from an early age. In later life he resembled nothing so much as a very senior warrant officer in the Royal Army Service Corps, with his rigidly set face and darting, suspicious eyes. He died in his rooms in Trinity College, Cambridge, on 11 March 1971.   ANTHONY QUINTON, *rev.*

Sources C. D. Broad, 'Autobiography', *The philosophy of C. D. Broad*, ed. P. A. Schlipp (1959) · K. Britton, 'Charlie Dunbar Broad, 1889–1971', *PBA*, 64 (1978), 289–310

Archives Trinity Cam., record books of dreams, personal accounts | CUL, letters to G. E. Moore

Likenesses W. Stoneman, photograph, 1930, NPG · R. Spear, chalk drawing, 1948, Trinity Cam.

Wealth at death £92,957: probate, 16 June 1971, *CGPLA Eng. & Wales*

Broad, Mary Aylett (1860–1942), headmistress, was born on 13 December 1860 at Brunswick Lodge, Wandsworth Road, Kennington, London, the eldest of twelve children, seven of whom survived (three boys and four girls), of Arthur Broad, a mercantile clerk, and his wife, Sarah Ann West. The family had a strong tradition of religious and philanthropic work, Mary's paternal grandfather having given up his prosperous London business to become a Baptist minister. Unusually for the period her father believed that all his daughters should have a boarding-school education, and at the age of eleven Mary was sent to Carlton House, a boarding-school in Melbourn in Cambridgeshire. In 1876 she became a pupil at the newly founded Wandsworth high school and in 1878 passed the Oxford local examination. From September that year she taught at a private school in Gipsy Hill, and then in two other small schools.

But Mary Broad was ambitious to have a school of her own that would teach a curriculum such as the new high schools were offering, and on 29 October 1885 set out with her friend Miss Thresher to '"a very nice little place near Christchurch" called Bournemouth' (*Jubilee Book*, 19) to search for a suitable school to buy. They found one in Bradburne Road where the proprietor was about to be married, and in January 1886 it opened under its new ownership with thirty girls. Early pupils remembered Mary Broad's enthusiasm and high spirits, and how she joined the fourth form for Latin and maths—subjects which she had never studied in her own schooldays. In 1889 Miss Thresher, who had been responsible for the organization and finance, left to get married, and the school became Mary Broad's sole responsibility.

Mary Broad had always admired North London Collegiate School which Frances Buss had founded in 1850, and hoped that her own private venture could become a public school like it. But Miss Buss warned her not to put her school under the control of a body of governors until she had herself built the sort of buildings she wanted, otherwise 'you will wait many years for them' (*Jubilee Book*, 28). But by 1898 the strain was too much for her and she handed over the school—which then became Bournemouth high school—to the Winchester diocesan trustees. (Though brought up a nonconformist she had joined the Church of England soon after she came to Bournemouth.) The original trustees persuaded her to accept the guarantee of a pension when she retired, but as this meant the school would have to forgo an increased grant from the Board of Education, she renounced the pension in 1902. Eventually she agreed to accept an annuity in exchange for the freehold of one of the houses that then made up the school.

Mary Broad's generosity was always unstinted; her favourite maxim was: 'The glory of life is to love, not to be loved; to give, not to get; to serve, not to be served' (*Jubilee Book*, 73). And she was light-hearted; unlike North London Collegiate in Miss Buss's time, Bournemouth high school was run with a lot of laughter and only two rules: 'No talking on the stairs' and 'Keep to the right' (ibid., 41). She was an excellent mimic with a keen sense of humour, who gloried in jokes about herself. When she saw a caricature of herself, very broad in the beam and clad in her shapeless old cardigan, she ordered that prints should be sold for the building fund. Many of the best-known girls' boarding-schools grew from tiny beginnings out of the vision of a dedicated founder. The big day schools, however, were usually born out of corporate effort, so that Mary Broad's achievement must be reckoned to approach that of Frances Buss.

Mary Broad had aged early and in 1924 retired, first to a house in Bournemouth and latterly to Wallington, Surrey, where she had once taught. Here she interested herself in the Girl Guides and in the local schools. Miss Buss's prophecy had been correct; the school did not have its own purpose-built premises until ten years after Mary Broad left. She laid the foundation-stone of what was later to be known as Talbot Heath in December 1933, and was present when it was formally opened by William Temple, archbishop of Canterbury, in 1935. Characteristically she refused to buy any new clothes for this occasion. Though she came down to Bournemouth at the outbreak of war, Mary soon returned to Wallington, where she died at her home, 34 Grosvenor Road, on 13 July 1942. She was buried in Wallington.   GILLIAN AVERY

Sources *The Jubilee book: Bournemouth high school, Talbot Heath, 1886–1946* (1946) · b. cert.
Likenesses Debenham & Gould Ltd, photograph, 1922, repro. in *Jubilee book*, frontispiece · J. Gunn, portrait, 1936
Wealth at death £4418 14s. 9d.: probate, 1942, CGPLA Eng. & Wales

Broadbent, Donald Eric (1926–1993), psychologist, was born on 6 May 1926 at 361 Station Road, Yardley, Birmingham, the youngest of the three children of Herbert Arthur Broadbent (b. c.1890), accountant, and his wife, Hannah Elizabeth (Margie) Williams (1893–1965), a secretary before her marriage. Although born in Birmingham he resolutely identified himself as Welsh, partly on grounds of ancestry but also because he spent much of his childhood there. His father worked as a sales manager for a multinational company. Although from a poor background he advanced rapidly, and the family was briefly affluent. But at the start of the Second World War he parted from both the company and the family, and Donald never saw him again. His mother 'was determined', wrote Broadbent:

> that never, under any circumstances would I later be handicapped in dealing with people who had a heavier ballast of educational advantage. So instead of getting me to the best schooling she could afford, she made up her mind with sublime arrogance as to which she thought was the best school in the country, and that was were I went: Winchester.

His exhibition was not sufficient to cover all the fees, but his father's pension fund and the school made up the difference. He was steered towards classics by the school, with an assurance that he could follow it up with science. He did not feel at home with history, classics, or later the physical sciences. Already at school he developed an interest in social 'real world' problems. The question of which

Donald Eric Broadbent (1926–1993), by unknown photographer

career to pursue was cut short, apparently with some relief, by the imminence of military service.

Long fascinated by flying, Broadbent joined the Royal Air Force in 1944. He was first sent to Cambridge for a short engineering course, and later that year went into the RAF proper. In 1945 he sailed on the *Aquitania* to New York for flying training in the USA. His experience there had several important spin-offs. He became aware of the practical problems of equipment design in relation to human usage. He recounted how in the AT6, a plane with two identical levers close together under the seat, 'with monotonous regularity one or another of my colleagues would pull the wrong lever and drop an expensive airplane onto its belly in the middle of the field'. He also noted the difficulty of reading instruments. A second spin-off was that his training put him in contact with students, and he discovered that psychology was a respectable subject in America. He had also been greatly impressed by the personnel selection battery used by the RAF, which had a concrete and practical quality untouched by his formal studies, and used the 'progressive matrices test' when asked for an assessment of some airmen while still in the RAF.

On returning to Cambridge, to the surprise and suspicion of the admission committee at Pembroke College, Broadbent announced his determination to study psychology, despite the college's urging him to read chemistry. The college eventually relented and Broadbent joined Sir Frederick Bartlett's department. Bartlett had been actively involved in wartime research on human performance under various demanding, stressful conditions, and this was a context into which Broadbent fitted easily. Bartlett instilled a philosophy that psychological principles should derive from real-life situations whenever possible: that data should determine theory, rather than theory being used to search for data. Thirty years later Broadbent still found this approach 'sound and vital'. A major influence in the department was the brilliant young Kenneth Craik, who died in a tragic accident just before Broadbent arrived, but the intellectual interest in 'cybernetic' control systems was clearly established. The department was

poor—there was only one copy of the standard textbook (Woodworth's *Experimental Psychology*), for which students queued up on a rota—but there was an air of excitement over these new developments, and a gifted group of staff and colleagues, including Alan Welford, G. C. Grindley, J. T. MacCurdy, R. H. Thouless, and Derek Russell Davis.

Broadbent graduated with a first-class degree in moral science in 1949, and on 23 June that year he married his childhood sweetheart, Margaret Elizabeth (Peg; *b*. 1924), daughter of Frederick Holden Wright, a proprietor. They had two daughters (one of whom died in a traffic accident in 1979). He remained in Cambridge after his marriage, having secured a post with the Medical Research Council's Applied Psychology Unit (APU) in Cambridge, of which Bartlett was director, studying the effects of noise on performance, for the Royal Navy. Broadbent remained at the APU in Cambridge for the next twenty-five years, during which time he developed his highly influential approach.

It was a natural experimental move for Broadbent to study the effects of noise using 'vigilance tasks', such as radar watching and other repetitive monitoring demands, as these had been a long-standing interest in the unit. Fortunately he was also able to study less boring tasks, such as air traffic control systems, in which listeners characteristically are confronted with a multitude of signals arriving more or less simultaneously, but can react only to a limited subset. This led him to pursue fresh developments in communication engineering and control theory, and he began to formulate models of systems that showed 'attentional selection' in the context of information theory. The topic of attention, which had remained fallow for many years, was thus reinstated but in information-theoretic terms. Experimental work led Broadbent into the area of short-term memory, from which emerged a model that postulated a limited capacity for input and storage of information. He proposed a selective filtering device located early in the nervous system, preceded by a temporary buffer store. These and other ideas were put together in his book *Perception and Communication*, first published in 1958, which quickly became recognized as a turning point both for him and for the field. In it was planted the germ for a fully flowering growth widely labelled 'cognitive psychology'. Information processing analyses cast in 'box-and-arrow' flow charts became commonplace over the next thirty-five years.

In the same year as the publication of *Perception and Communication*, the directorship of the APU became vacant, and the Medical Research Council displayed courageous judgement in appointing Broadbent to the post at the relatively young age of thirty-two. The appointment came as a relief to him as until then he had held no tenured post. By this time the APU was one of the largest psychology laboratories in Europe, with a well-developed arrangement with the Royal Navy (which also supplied not only equipment but also many of the human subjects for experiments) and with government departments. The period of Broadbent's directorship from 1958 to 1974 was one of consolidation and development, and the pursuit of interactions with a wide range of potential 'customers', helped by two assistant directors, R. Conrad and E. B. Poulton. Broadbent's own burden was greatly eased by his acquiring, for the first time, a graduate assistant, Margaret Hope Pattison Gregory (b. 1929), who was an active and invaluable collaborator for the rest of his career. She was the daughter of the Revd Romney Moncrief Pattison Muir. She and Broadbent married on 11 November 1972, their first marriages both having ended in divorce.

While director of the APU Broadbent devoted a very large amount of time to promoting psychology, appearing regularly on radio and television. He also foresaw the practical relevance of cognitive psychology to the imminent computer age. Despite heavy administrative burdens in the late 1960s he sat on numerous national committees. But the very size of the APU meant that a great deal of political organization was required, especially when outstations were opened in Oxford, Sussex, and another location in Cambridge. Broadbent was increasingly weighed down—perhaps even marginalized—in the organization he had so successfully shaped and nourished. As he ruefully remarked, his colleagues began to apologize when they asked to discuss a scientific point with him, but never apologized if they wanted to raise an administrative matter. 'They saw administration as my job now, on which I *ought* to spend time.' In 1971 he gave the Medical Research Council three years' notice of his intention to resign, and in 1974 he moved to the Oxford department of experimental psychology as a member of external MRC staff.

In Oxford the Broadbents gathered around them an active and varied team of research students and post-doctoral collaborators, pursued further developments on the relationship between attention and memory, and initiated new lines of work, such as on the effects of stress and anxiety on the health of industrial workers (in which Broadbent collaborated with psychiatric colleagues), and on implicit learning in complex situations. Despite his reluctance to pursue a university career (he spoke with a touch of pride of the fact that he had never held a university post), he devoted himself to academic and university life with energy and aplomb. He was, in many ways, a more active and donnish member of the university than many of its own appointees. He accepted a fellowship at Wolfson College (he had been a fellow of Pembroke College, Cambridge, from 1965 to 1974), chaired the faculty board, sat on many committees, helped with the university campaign, and gave numerous seminars. He also sat on several national committees, and fostered collaborative research links with groups in Germany and Belgium.

Broadbent injected a 'paradigm shift' into both academic and applied psychology, which continued to permeate wide reaches of both domains. His own breadth of interest was such that he excluded absolutely nothing as a proper subject for study, provided that it was soundly based on empirical observation. He gave encouragement from his prestigious position to groups and areas of research from which others shied away, such as personality research, aptitude assessment, and the study of mood and emotional assessment. He was a perspicacious role model. Paradoxically, although he was adamant about his credentials and commitment to applied psychology, his own contribution may well be considered that of a theoretician, or at least a paradigm maker, a provider of a general theoretical framework, and a brilliant analyst and synthesizer.

Personally Broadbent appeared as something of a contrast with the all-embracing nature of his intellectual interests. He was a very private person, inscrutable in his personal interactions with colleagues. He once told a former colleague at the APU that he wished he could engage in small talk, but did not know how. He had a puritanical streak, acknowledged and attributed by him to the rigours of his Welsh childhood, which made his judgement on ethical issues invaluable, sound, and trusted. Many were puzzled by his commitment to camping holidays even at a very mature age. He is said to have eschewed the use of taxis if there was any possibility of using public transport, even on arrival after a long transatlantic flight. He continued his solitary walks, especially in the Welsh hills—where, fittingly, his ashes were ultimately scattered. His seriousness about moral matters no doubt made it more painful for him when he was led to renounce his Christian faith, deeply and strongly held well into middle age, after the death of his daughter as an innocent victim of a road accident in October 1979. One feature of his personality universally commented upon by students and colleagues was his generosity. He was never too busy to speak, listen, or write to people, absorbing each topic or problem and then devoting himself to a full and serious answer. He rarely, if ever, put anyone down—at most he would produce only a quizzical expression or a muted chuckle.

Broadbent was elected a fellow of the Royal Society in 1968, and a foreign associate of the US National Academy of Science in 1971. He was appointed CBE in 1974. He received nine honorary doctorates. He died suddenly and unexpectedly of heart failure at his daughter's home, 31 Narbeth Drive, Aylesbury, Buckinghamshire, on 10 April 1993. He was survived by her and by his second wife, Margaret. He was cremated at Oxford crematorium on 20 April 1993.

LAWRENCE WEISKRANTZ

Sources L. Weiskrantz, *Memoirs FRS*, 40 (1994), 33–42 · 'D. E. Broadbent', *The history of psychology in autobiography*, ed. G. Lindzey, 8 (1981) · *The Independent* (16 April 1993) · *The Times* (21 April 1993) · *WWW*, 1991–5 · personal knowledge (2004) · private information (2004) · b. cert. · m. cert. · d. cert.
Archives SOUND BL NSA, performance recordings · recorded talks for Open University
Likenesses N. Chmiel, photograph, 1990?, U. Oxf., department of experimental psychology; repro. in *The Independent* · photograph, 1991, NPG · P. Fitzgerald, oils, 1993, priv. coll. · photograph, repro. in *The Times* · photograph, priv. coll. [see illus.]
Wealth at death under £125,000: probate, 1993

Broadbent, Sir Ewen (1924–1993), civil servant, was born at 23 Vesta Road, Brockley, London, on 9 August 1924, the only child of the Revd Wilfred Broadbent (1880–1945), Baptist minister, and his Scottish wife, Mary, *née* Ewen (1890–1972). He attended King Edward VI School, Nuneaton, where he was an almost precocious schoolboy, excelling at languages and games, and was head boy and captain of cricket. In 1942 he moved on to St John's College, Cambridge, to read modern languages, but in 1943 war interrupted his studies. He joined the Gordon Highlanders, in which he rose to the rank of captain, and saw service in Egypt and Norway. He returned to Cambridge in 1947 and graduated in 1949 with a distinction in oral German.

After leaving Cambridge, Broadbent took the home civil service and the Foreign Office examinations. He was in the top three of both. He joined the Air Ministry as an assistant principal in 1949. He rapidly made his mark and after being private secretary to two official members of the Air Council he was private secretary to three successive secretaries of state for air, from 1955 to 1959. These were difficult times—the Suez crisis, spiralling costs of equipment, and much argument both within the Air Ministry and among the three services. Broadbent maintained a steady hand and earned widespread respect. In 1959 he was promoted assistant secretary and in 1961 he was dispatched to Cyprus as deputy chief officer of the recently established British sovereign base areas, becoming chief officer in 1964. He established an administration which stood the test of time remarkably well. After returning to Whitehall in 1965 he was private secretary to the secretary of state for defence, Denis Healey, from 1967 to 1968, and spent eighteen months deeply involved in the contentious arguments of the time, particularly those concerning the withdrawal of British forces from the Far East.

In January 1969 Broadbent became an assistant undersecretary, but soon after disaster struck. He was rushed to hospital following a heart attack and suffered another heart attack after leaving intensive care. It was a measure of the man that he returned to work in the autumn of 1969 and in 1972 became deputy under-secretary of state (air) with a seat on the air force board. It had become increasingly apparent that Broadbent had a particular talent for management and organization, coupled with the ability to persuade people to do what he wanted. Hence in 1975 he became deputy under-secretary of state (civilian management) for the whole of the Ministry of Defence. In 1982 he became second permanent under-secretary of state with a seat on each of the three service boards, which were primarily concerned with the organization and management of their services. For nearly a decade he took pride of place in bringing about changes in management and organization. He was firm but fair. One yardstick of his success was that during this period the number of civilian employees in the Ministry of Defence was reduced by about 25 per cent. Broadbent oversaw and managed these changes with great skill, and rightly earned the respect of the trade unions. He tackled the thorny question of reorganizing the Ministry of Defence police and placing them on a statutory footing. He was deeply involved in implementing the reforms that Michael Heseltine introduced soon after he became secretary of state for defence in 1983.

Broadbent was renowned for his immense ability to bring about change without too much bloodshed. He was a fine judge of what was possible, but with a strong bias for moving forward. His skills in dealing with people had no doubt been honed by his six private secretary appointments. His determination and courage were exemplified by his success in rising to the highest ranks of his service, despite his illness in 1969. His character was perhaps the result of his Scottish ancestry and of his being a son of the manse. He was by any standards a first-class administrator. His benign and gentle appearance belied his effectiveness. He had an ironic sense of humour and a generally quizzical approach, and much enjoyed the company of his many friends.

Following his retirement Broadbent was in much demand. He was vice-chairman of the Council of the Royal United Service Institute for which he wrote a book, *The Military and Government*, published in 1988; vice-chairman of the Farnborough Aerospace Development Foundation and of the Carroll Foundation, which endowed the chair of Irish history at Hertford College, Oxford; chairman of International Military Services; and an enthusiastic trustee of the Royal Air Force Museum. He was also as a trustee deeply involved in seeking to recover the missing millions from the Daily Mirror pension fund. Perhaps closest to his heart was his chairmanship of the Council of Voluntary Welfare Work from 1985, and from 1988 of Look Ahead—the latter dedicated to providing temporary homes in south London for single homeless people, and training them for jobs. In both these active appointments he felt he was partly redeeming a debt to those less fortunate than himself.

Broadbent was a fine sportsman all his life. In his earlier days he played much squash and cricket. He later concentrated on golf and found time to be captain of his club and write its centennial history. He was appointed CMG in 1965, CB in 1973, and KCB in 1984. On 3 February 1951 he married Barbara David (*b*. 1919), then a squadron leader in the Women's Royal Air Force. They had one son. Broadbent died of a heart attack on Hampstead golf course on 27 February 1993; his remains were cremated at Breakspear crematorium, Ruislip, Middlesex, on 4 March. He was survived by his wife and son.   FRANK COOPER

Sources personal knowledge (2004) · private information (2004) [Lady Broadbent and others] · *The Times* (4 March 1993) · *Daily Telegraph* · *The Independent* (4 March 1993) · b. cert. · m. cert. · d. cert. · WWW · F. Cooper, address at memorial service, 2 April 1993, priv. coll.

Likenesses photograph, repro. in *The Times*

Wealth at death £395,993: probate, 12 July 1993, *CGPLA Eng. & Wales*

Broadbent, Thomas Biggin (1793–1817). *See under* Broadbent, William (1755–1827).

Broadbent, William (1755–1827), Unitarian minister, was born on 28 August 1755, the son of William and Elizabeth Broadbent. He was educated for the ministry at Daventry Academy from 1777 to 1782, first under Thomas Robins, who resigned the divinity chair in June 1781 from loss of voice, and then under Thomas Belsham. Broadbent became classical tutor to the academy in August 1782, and in January 1784 exchanged this appointment for that of tutor in mathematics, natural philosophy, and logic. Belsham resigned the divinity chair in June 1789, having become a Unitarian, and the academy was moved in November to Northampton. Broadbent continued to act as tutor until the end of 1791, when he became minister at Warrington, taking out his licence on 18 January 1792.

Like many of his fellow students at Daventry, Broadbent believed in the exercise of reason and private judgement, and had probably arrived at the limited view of Christ's divinity known as Arianism. At Warrington he re-examined his theological convictions and, becoming a Unitarian of the Belsham school, succeeded in taking nearly all his congregation with him. Broadbent kept up a close friendship with Belsham. Biblical exegesis was Broadbent's favourite study, and textual interpretation played a prominent part in his preaching. He resigned his Warrington charge in the spring of 1822 on the grounds of poor health and depression after the death of his son. He died at Latchford, near Warrington, on 1 December 1827, and was buried in the Warrington chapel on 6 December.

Broadbent and his wife, Rebecca, had one child, **Thomas Biggin Broadbent** (1793–1817), also a Unitarian. He was born at Warrington on 17 March 1793 and entered the University of Glasgow in November 1809. After graduating MA in April 1813 he became classical tutor in the short-lived Unitarian academy at Hackney, an office he filled until 1816, preaching impressively, latterly at Prince's Street Chapel, Westminster, during a vacancy. He resigned his London work, however, and returned to Warrington to undertake ministerial training as his father's assistant. He prepared for the press, in 1816, part (1 and 2 Corinthians, 1 Timothy, and Titus) of Belsham's *Epistles of Paul the Apostle* (1822). Broadbent also edited the fourth edition (1817) of the *Improved Version of the New Testament*, originally published in 1808 under Belsham's superintendence. Two of his sermons, published posthumously in 1817, reached a second edition. Broadbent died, unmarried, of apoplexy on 9 November 1817 at Latchford, near Warrington. At the time of his death he was engaged to Helen Bourn (1797–1871) of Manchester, who subsequently married Thomas Martineau (*d.* 1824) and Edward *Tagart (1804–1858).

ALEXANDER GORDON, *rev.* R. K. WEBB

Sources *Monthly Repository*, new ser., 2 (1828), 59 · J. Williams, *Memoirs of the late Reverend Thomas Belsham* (1833) · H. McLachlan, *English education under the Test Acts: being the history of the nonconformist academies, 1662–1820* (1931), 162–5 · *Monthly Repository*, 12 (1817), 690–91 · T. Belsham, *Monthly Repository*, 13 (1818), 1–4 · W. I. Addison, ed., *The matriculation albums of the University of Glasgow from 1728 to 1858* (1913) · register of baptisms, Sankey Street Chapel, Warrington [T. B. Broadbent], 13 May 1793 · private information (2004) [Revd Ann Peart]

Likenesses J. Partridge?, engraving (T. B. Broadbent; after miniature), repro. in *Monthly Repository* (1818); copy, Central Library, Warrington

Broadbent, Sir William Henry, first baronet (1835–1907), physician, was born at Lindley, near Huddersfield, Yorkshire, on 23 January 1835, the eldest surviving of the seven children of John Broadbent (1796–1880), woollen

Sir William Henry Broadbent, first baronet (1835–1907), by Bassano, 1898

manufacturer and Wesleyan Sunday school superintendent, and his wife, Esther, *née* Butterworth (*d.* 1879). After education from 1840 to 1845 at a local day school at Longwood Edge, Yorkshire, to which the family had moved in 1837, and as a weekly boarder at Huddersfield College (1845–50), he left school to enter his father's business. Finding manufacturing uncongenial he was apprenticed to a Manchester doctor in 1852. While studying for the University of London examinations at Owens College, Manchester, and the Manchester Royal School of Medicine he won prizes in anatomy, physiology, surgery, medicine, chemistry, materia medica, botany, midwifery, and ophthalmology. He won the gold medals in anatomy, physiology, and chemistry for his first MB examinations in 1856, and qualified as member of the Royal College of Surgeons and licentiate of the Society of Apothecaries in 1857. After working as a clinical dresser and clerk at Manchester Royal Infirmary, he failed to secure the post of house surgeon at Manchester Royal Infirmary or Lancaster Infirmary in 1857 and this prompted him to study at the École de Médecine, Paris. Living with the protestant pastor Armand Delille he acquired a love of French culture and fluency in the French language. After returning to England in 1858 he was awarded first-class honours in medicine and the gold medal for obstetrics in the University of London final MB.

Broadbent was appointed obstetrics officer at St Mary's Hospital, London, in December 1858. His appointment in October 1859 as resident medical officer and apothecary at

St Mary's, despite strong opposition within the honorary staff, allowed him to move from specialist work with the diseases of women and children to more general medicine and a study of respiratory diseases. He was appointed pathologist, museum curator, and lecturer in physiology and zoology at St Mary's Hospital medical school in 1860, and lecturer in comparative anatomy in 1861. Having taken his MD degree in 1860, the year in which he left the Wesleyan Methodists to join the Church of England, he began to establish a private practice at 23 Upper Seymour Street, London. He supplemented his small income from this source by coaching resident students. Honorary appointments as physician to the London Fever Hospital from 1860 to 1879 and as physician to the Western General Dispensary in 1863 brought prestige without income. In 1861 he considered but rejected a well-paid professorship in anatomy and physiology at Melbourne University, Australia. Sir William Osler considered his career advancement to be an exemplar for all medical students: 'for years he lived the self-denying life of the true student ... such distinguished success was won by a man who came to London without friends' (W. Osler, St Mary's Hospital introductory address, *St Mary's Hospital Gazette*, November 1907, 97). Broadbent married Eliza, daughter of John Harpin of Holmfirth, Yorkshire, on 5 August 1863. They had two sons, both of whom became medically qualified, and three daughters.

In 1865 Broadbent was elected as physician to outpatients at St Mary's Hospital against strong competition, though he found canvassing distasteful and more expensive than anticipated. He was promoted to physician in charge of in-patients in 1871 and lecturer in medicine. He remained on the active staff of St Mary's until 1896, five years longer than the statutory twenty years on the senior staff by special resolution of the board of management, and was then elected consulting physician. From 1877 to 1884 Broadbent allied himself with the house officers and older unqualified nurses at St Mary's in opposition to the efforts of the matron, Rachel Williams, a protégée of Florence Nightingale, to introduce modern nursing reforms, eventually forcing the resignation of Williams whom he perceived as a personal enemy. He was popular personally with the medical students but was too innately shy to be a good teacher of undergraduate medicine, though his teaching was sound and practical rather than abstract and academic (*St Mary's Hospital Gazette*, 79). His common sense advice to students when diagnosing chest diseases was that 'What you do not hear is often more important than what you do hear' (Broadbent, *Life*, 230).

Broadbent early became an expert in neurology. In 1866 he published papers on an investigation into sensorimotor ganglia and the association of nerve nuclei, considered in 1907 by Hughlings Jackson to be outstanding in the advancement of neurology (*BMJ*, 180). In it he advanced the theory known as Broadbent's hypothesis which attempted to explain the unequal distribution of paralysis in the face, body, arm, and leg and why some associated muscles are immune from paralysis in cases of hemiplegia, a neurological disease in which one side of

the body is paralysed. He also studied aphasia, a disorder of language caused by disease in one of the brain hemispheres, suggesting theories as to how the brain formulated thought and speech. His interest in nervous diseases was also reflected in studies of the pathology of chorea (a jerky involuntary movement of the limbs), syphilis, spinal paraplegia, and the effects of alcohol on the nervous system.

Broadbent also became an authority on heart disease. His 1887 Croonian lectures at the Royal College of Physicians on the pulse formed the basis of his book *The Pulse* (1890). His 1884 Harveian lectures before the Harveian Society on prognosis in valvular disease of the heart and his Lumleian lectures on prognosis in structural diseases of the heart to the Royal College of Physicians in 1891 were drawn upon in his *Heart Disease* (1897), written in collaboration with his elder son, John Broadbent.

Broadbent's work was also concerned with the scientific application of therapeutics to clinical practice. At the beginning of his career, he gained a reputation in the treatment of cancer, believing that he could alleviate it with injections of acetic acid into the tumour. However, his failure to effect lasting improvements and his fear of being seen as a cancer specialist caused him to stop using this treatment by 1870. He also wrote on the application of chemical principles to the explanation of the effects of remedies and poisons. Attention was also paid to the treatment of typhoid fever, the subject of his 1894 Cavendish lecture to the West London Medico-Chirurgical Society, for which he recommended careful dieting, nursing, and hydrotherapy.

A member of the Royal College of Physicians from 1861 Broadbent became a fellow in 1861, an examiner in 1876–7 and 1883–4, and senior censor in 1895. He was runner-up in the 1896 elections for the presidency of the college. He was an active member of the British Medical Benevolent Society as secretary (1864–72), treasurer (1872–1900) and president (1900). He served as president of the Harveian (1875), Medical (1881), Clinical (1887), and Neurological (1896) societies. He was supportive of the medical education of women, serving on the council of the newly established London School of Medicine for Women at the Royal Free Hospital in 1874. He was an examiner in medicine to London (1883) and Cambridge (1888) universities. Broadbent was a founder of the Imperial Cancer Fund, for which he served as vice-president, and was also made consulting physician to the New Hospital for Women and the Victoria Hospital for Sick Children in 1896. He was elected fellow of the Royal Society in 1897. Honorary degrees were awarded to him by the universities of Edinburgh (1898), St Andrews (1899), Leeds (1904), Montreal (1906), and Toronto (1906). He was an honorary member of many foreign medical societies. As chief organizer and first president of the Entente Cordiale Médicale in 1904, he was invested with the grand cross and insignia of a commander of the Légion d'honneur.

In later life Broadbent gave his support to public movements for the cure and prevention of diseases. In 1881 he was appointed to the royal commission on fever hospitals.

In 1892 he established and funded a district nurse at Longwood, Yorkshire, which after his death was continued by the subscriptions of the local workmen it was intended to benefit. He became chairman of the organizing committee for promoting the formation of the National Association for the Prevention of Consumption, aiming at public education on the avoidance of tuberculosis, in 1898. He then served as chairman of the organizing council of the British Congress on Tuberculosis, which met in London in July 1901. He chaired the advisory committee appointed by Edward VII in 1901 to plan King Edward VII's Sanatorium at Midhurst, to which he was subsequently appointed consulting physician and also to the King Edward VII Hospital for Officers, London. He also supported schemes for colonies for epileptics and for the promotion of temperance and public hygiene.

Increasing public success diverted Broadbent's attention from clinical research to practice. Secure in his position at St Mary's, Broadbent was free to extend his consultant practice, mainly among the aristocracy, and, as he became more affluent, he moved from Upper Seymour Street to a larger house at 34 Seymour Street in 1872, and finally to 84 Brook Street in 1892. By 1880 he had an annual income of £3400, and in 1891 he earned over £13,000 and was able to turn away more patients than he could treat. He would see poorer patients without a fee only at the request of the doctor making the referral. In 1890 he treated Lady Rosebery for typhoid fever and in November 1891 was called in when Prince George of Wales contracted typhoid fever. He was again summoned to Sandringham in January 1892 during the fatal illness of the duke of Clarence, subsequently being appointed physician-in-ordinary to the prince of Wales in February 1892 as a mark of appreciation for having attended both princes during their illnesses. Ever an advocate for St Mary's Hospital, he persuaded the duke of York to become president of the hospital and the prince of Wales to allow a new wing, for which funds were being sought, to be named as a memorial to the late duke of Clarence. A baronetcy was awarded in 1893 on the occasion of the marriage of the duke of York, and in 1898 Broadbent was appointed physician-extraordinary to Queen Victoria. In 1901 he was appointed physician-in-ordinary to Edward VII and the prince of Wales and made KCVO.

In appearance Broadbent was stocky, robust, and bespectacled. A keen mountaineer, swimmer, and oarsman, he would bathe in the Thames and Serpentine even when they were iced over in winter. In politics he had Liberal sympathies and admired William Gladstone as much as he loathed Benjamin Disraeli. Despite his Francophile tastes he supported Prussia during the Franco-Prussian War, even considering going off to the war with an ambulance, but later came to distrust the German empire after visiting Alsace-Lorraine in 1873. Noted for his abrupt, blunt, and outspoken manner Broadbent could also be cheery, simple, and unaffected when it suited him, prompting the French physician Professor Huchard to describe him as universally loved and respected. His businesslike bedside manner inspired confidence and he was

considered one of the ablest clinical observers of his time. His colleague at St Mary's, the surgeon Edmund Owen, considered him stubborn and quick to form a prejudice. He died of influenza at his London home on 10 July 1907 and was buried at Wendover, Buckinghamshire, where he owned a small country house, on 13 July. The baronetcy passed to his son Sir John Broadbent (1865–1946), physician.　　　　　　　　　　　　　　　KEVIN BROWN

Sources M. E. Broadbent, *Life of Sir William Broadbent* (1909) · *The writings of Sir William Broadbent*, ed. W. Broadbent (1908) · *The Lancet* (13 July 1907) · *BMJ* (20 July 1907) · *St Mary's Hospital Gazette*, 13 (July 1907) · *The Practitioner*, 80 (1907), 448 · H. A. Caley, 'Sir William Broadbent's retirement from the senior physiciancy', *St Mary's Hospital Gazette*, 2 (June 1896), 83–7 · minute books of board of governors of St Mary's Hospital, 1865–96, St Mary's Hospital Archives, London, SM/AD 1/9–19; SM/AD 2/1–2 · minute books of medical committee of St Mary's Hospital, 1865–96, St Mary's Hospital Archives, London, SM/AD 13/1–4 · Z. Cope, *A hundred years of nursing* (1955), 73–89

Archives RCP Lond., papers relative to illnesses of the royal family | NL Scot., corresp. with Lord Rosebery

Likenesses photograph, *c*.1896, repro. in *BMJ* · Bassano, four negatives, 1898, NPG [*see illus.*] · Scholderer, portrait, priv. coll. · Spy [L. Ward], caricature, chromolithograph, Wellcome L., NPG; repro. in *VF* (30 Oct 1902)

Wealth at death £88,139 1*s*. 11*d*.: resworn probate, 26 July 1907, *CGPLA Eng. & Wales*

Broadfoot, George (1807–1845), army officer in the East India Company, was born at Kirkwall, Orkney, the eldest surviving son of the Revd William Broadfoot, from a west Yorkshire family and minister of the Kirkwall Secession Church, 1798–1817, and his wife, Helen, *née* Sutherland (1783–1839), of Orkney. In 1817 they moved to London, where William Broadfoot was minister of Oxenden Chapel. George Broadfoot was educated at various day schools and privately. In 1825 he obtained a cadetship in the East India Company service and sailed for India.

Broadfoot entered the Madras army as an ensign in January 1826, and served with the 34th native infantry. From 1833 to 1838 he was away from India on furlough. He travelled on the continent, studied his profession, and in 1836–7 was orderly officer at the East India Company's military seminary, Addiscombe College, where he also studied fortification. In 1838 he returned to India and served in the commissariat department of the Madras army. In 1840, when a captain, during the British-Indian occupation of Afghanistan, he was posted to Shah Shuja's army and raised a regiment of sappers from heterogeneous recruits including Gurkhas. He marched them to Kabul, escorting the women and some of the treasure of Shah Shuja and another Afghan chief, by bravery and bluff, through mutinous Sikh soldiery in the troubled Punjab. At Kabul in 1841 he, on his own initiative and despite official discouragement, procured tools for his sappers, forcing the hostile Kabul smiths to make them. His sappers were attached to Major-General Sir Robert Sale's brigade, and with it fought their way to Gandamak, Broadfoot distinguishing himself in action: he was mentioned in dispatches.

In November 1841 Sale's brigade occupied Jalalabad, then remained there besieged by Afghan forces. Broadfoot became garrison engineer and supervised the repair and improvement of the dilapidated fortifications: his tools were crucial. The garrison fought off attacks, but the situation was dangerous and uncertain. Elphinstone and Pottinger at Kabul ordered Sale to evacuate Jalalabad. Sale, brave but indecisive, in January 1842 held a council of war, called by Captain Henry Havelock their 'jackdaw Parliament' (Marshman, 100). Sale and the political agent Captain George Macgregor favoured evacuation, and were supported by the majority of officers present. Only Broadfoot, vehemently, spoke against this, and only Captain Oldfield voted with him (though his friend Havelock, present as a member of the general's staff and voteless, agreed with him). However, later the majority changed their views and in February a council of war voted, contrary to Sale and Macgregor, against evacuation: 'and thus the firmness of one man, and he nearly the junior in the council of war, preserved his country's arms from suffering another deep and disgraceful blow' (Durand, 400). Broadfoot continued active in the defence, and on a sortie in March was severely wounded. In April Major-General George Pollock's army relieved Jalalabad. Broadfoot had been 'the real hero of Jalalabad' (Macrory, 271). He accompanied Pollock's army, and distinguished himself in the actions at Mamu Khel, Jagdalak, and Tezin. In October he was promoted brevet major and made a CB.

Lord Ellenborough, the governor-general, admired the 'illustrious garrison' of Jalalabad and especially favoured Broadfoot, whom in 1842 he appointed his aide-de-camp, and then commissioner of the Tenasserim provinces, Burma. Broadfoot was sent as a reformer, to eliminate corruption and improve relations with the Burmese kingdom. He was partially successful, but his health suffered from his wound and the climate, and, also hoping for war service, in December 1843 he requested a transfer. In 1844 Sir Henry Hardinge, the new governor-general, appointed him his agent for the north-western frontier: an important position when war with the Sikhs seemed likely. He reported on the Punjab situation, negotiated with the Sikhs and, when war seemed imminent, gathered supplies for the army. In December 1845 the Sikhs invaded British territory. Broadfoot served on Hardinge's staff and was at the battles of Mudki and Ferozeshahr. At the latter, on 21 December, he was killed, shot through the heart. After his death he was praised by Hardinge—who wrote that he was 'as brave as he was able in every branch of the political and military service' (Broadfoot, 399)—and by Havelock and others. Over his grave at Ferozepore his friend Colin Mackenzie had placed a stone inscribed 'the foremost man in India'. John Clark Marshman wrote that 'in the annals of British India ... there is no name more illustrious than that of George Broadfoot' (Marshman, 86). Broadfoot was survived by a brother, Alexander, and two unmarried sisters. Two brothers, William (1810–1841), 1st European regiment, and James Sutherland (1816–1840), Bengal Engineers, had been killed in the Anglo-Afghan War.

A. J. ARBUTHNOT, rev. ROGER T. STEARN

Sources W. Broadfoot, *The career of Major George Broadfoot ... in Afghanistan and the Punjab* (1888) · J. C. Marshman, *Memoirs of Major-*

General Sir Henry Havelock, new edn (1891) · private information (2004) · G. R. Gleig, *Sale's brigade in Afghanistan: with an account of the seisure and defence of Jellalabad* (1846) · J. W. Kaye, *History of the war in Afghanistan*, 2 vols. (1851) · P. Macrory, *Signal catastrophe: the story of a disastrous retreat from Kabul, 1842* (1966); repr. as *Kabul catastrophe* (1986) · H. M. Durand, *The First Afghan War and its causes* (1879) · J. A. Norris, *The First Afghan War, 1838–1842* (1967) · *Annual Register* (1845) · H. Mackenzie, *Storms and sunshine of a soldier's life*, 2 vols. (1884) · *The letters of the first Viscount Hardinge of Lahore ... 1844–1847*, ed. B. S. Singh, CS, 4th ser., 32 (1986)

Archives BL, corresp. and papers, Add. MSS 40127–40131 | BL OIOC, corresp. with Henry Lawrence, MSS Eur. F 85

Likenesses drawing (later reconstruction), repro. in Broadfoot, *Career of Major George Broadfoot*, frontispiece

Broadhead, William (1815–1879), trade unionist and publican, was born at Whirlow, near Sheffield, in September 1815. As a boy he worked with his father, who was a foreman in a saw-grinding workshop in Garden Street in Sheffield. On leaving his father, he worked for a time as a saw grinder at Stacey Wheel in the Loxley valley. At about that time, he married Mary Jane Wildgoose; they had nine children. Still employed as a saw grinder, he then became landlord of The Bridge inn at Owlerton.

Sheffield was then the leading saw-making centre in England—indeed in the world. Like many of the edge-tool trades, saw manufacture was a highly skilled, arduous, and sometimes dangerous occupation, conducted by a highly unionized workforce, which sometimes resorted to terrorism to enforce union membership. Broadhead emerged as a union leader in the late 1840s, having shown his sympathy with his more extreme fellow workers by supporting them (it is said out of his own pocket) in court. About 1848 he became secretary of the saw grinders' union. This was a small body—with about 190 members in 1867—but within five years under Broadhead its workers contributed £9000 to sick and unemployed members. The union's power was also demonstrated in other ways: under Broadhead's secret direction, it began a series of 'rattenings' (the removal of the driving-bands from machines), 'outrages' (bombings and shootings), and more straightforward acts of intimidation (such as the sending of 'Mary Ann' or threatening letters). By the mid-1850s, Broadhead was a publican at The Greyhound inn in Gibraltar Street; after the mid-1860s he ran the Royal George Hotel in Carver Street. These became the headquarters of the saw grinders' union, over which Broadhead's control was said to be dictatorial.

In the 1850s and early 1860s, Broadhead's strong-arm tactics became increasingly daring: they included a fatal shooting and various attempts to blow up non-union factories. Broadhead was widely suspected of being the instigator, but he always employed henchmen to conduct the outrages and was quick to protest his innocence. After an attempt was made to blow up a house in New Hereford Street in October 1866, for example, he wrote a letter to the press offering a reward to bring the 'dastards to justice' (though he pointedly refused to sympathize with the victims) (*Sheffield Daily Telegraph*, 12 Oct 1866). However, this proved an outrage too far. Local opposition to

Broadhead's activities was growing, particularly in the Sheffield newspapers, where the editor of the *Sheffield Daily Telegraph*, William Leng, led a campaign against Broadhead. With trade unionism very much in the public eye, reports of another Sheffield outrage became the subject of a national debate.

In early 1867 a royal commission of inquiry into trade unions was set up, with special powers to report separately on the Sheffield outrages. The hearings, lasting daily for almost five weeks between June and July 1867, excited great interest in Sheffield. Broadhead was questioned closely and at first 'carried himself with confident air, flourishing his gold eyeglass and patronising the proceedings of the court' (*Sheffield and Rotherham Independent*, 17 March 1879). But immunity certificates were offered to his accomplices, who in dramatic fashion broke down under questioning. Their testimony, which confirmed their secretary's role as instigator of the outrages, undermined Broadhead's position. Eventually, he too confessed and admitted instigating a murder and at least a dozen other outrages. His certificate of immunity protected him from a court sentence, and the saw grinders' union supported him and refused to expel him. But general public disdain, combined with the refusal of the local authorities to renew his publican's licence, led to his emigration to America in 1869, his passage paid for by a workers' subscription. Unable to settle in America, Broadhead returned to Sheffield in the following year, by then a broken man.

Some contemporaries believed that Broadhead had 'considerable natural ability, and his crimes were due, not to a malicious disposition, but to a grievously mistaken view of the interests of his trade and the duty he owed to it' (*Sheffield and Rotherham Independent*, 17 March 1879). However, there was widespread support for the kind of violent and illegal trade union sanctions favoured by Broadhead and other union leaders, as a counterbalance to an unjust industrial system. For this reason, rattenings did not die out in 1867, but continued until the old type of trade society declined later in the century.

Broadhead survived for a time as a symbol of Sheffield's old and robust style of trade unionism. In his final years, he opened a grocer's shop in Meadow Street, but after 1876 suffered a series of strokes that steadily incapacitated him. He died at his home, 114 Meadow Street, Sheffield, on 15 March 1879 and was buried in All Saints' parish churchyard, Ecclesall, on 20 March. He was survived by his wife. Broadhead was depicted as Grotait in Charles Reade's novel *Put yourself in his Place* (1870).

GEOFFREY TWEEDALE

Sources *Sheffield Daily Telegraph* (17 March 1879) · *Sheffield Daily Telegraph* (12 Oct 1866) · *Sheffield and Rotherham Independent* (17 March 1879) · S. Pollard, *A history of labour in Sheffield* (1959) · 'Sheffield outrages inquiry: report presented to the trades unions commissioners', *Parl. papers* (1867), 32.397, no. 3952-I; repr. with introduction by S. Pollard as *The Sheffield outrages* (1971) · J. H. Stainton, *The making of Sheffield, 1865–1914* (1924) · V. L. Melton, 'Trade unionism and the Sheffield outrages', *Sheffield Museums Information Sheet*, 6 (1975) · d. cert.

Broadhurst, Sir Edward Tootal, baronet (1858–1922), cotton manufacturer, was born on 19 August 1858 at Bury Old Road, Broughton, near Manchester, the second son of Henry Tootal Broadhurst (1822–1896), cotton manufacturer, and his first wife, Mary Margaret, *née* Brooks. He attended Dr Hungerford's Eagle House School at Wimbledon, and Winchester College, and joined the family firm in 1876. Charlotte Jane (*b.* 1861/2), the youngest daughter of the prominent Hyde cotton manufacturer Thomas Ashton, became Broadhurst's wife on 18 June 1887. They had no children.

Edward Tootal Broadhurst was a third-generation cotton manufacturer. Such men, particularly those with experience of Winchester or other élite establishments, are often accused of preferring the grouse moor to the counting house. It cannot be denied that Broadhurst shot grouse and lived in a manor house, but he was also a conscientious worker who took good care of his fortune.

Broadhurst's father, together with Henry and Joseph Lee, and Robert Scott, were business partners who later formed a limited company, Tootal Broadhurst Lee (Tootals). Tootals was a vertically integrated firm, combining spinning and power-loom weaving, at a time when there was a tendency for firms to specialize in a single process. A further distinctive feature was Tootals's marketing network, including offices and warehouses in Bradford, Belfast, and Paris, and agencies further afield. Tootals employed about 5000 workers in 1887, and operated 172,000 spindles and 3500 looms, making it the third largest vertically integrated cotton firm in Lancashire.

Broadhurst's main responsibility during the 1880s and 1890s was for the financial side of the business, leaving management of the mills to Harold Lee, son of Henry Lee. The 1890s were difficult times for the cotton industry because of growing overseas competition. Chairmanship of the finance committee passed to Broadhurst in 1900, and he represented the firm on the board of the British Northrop Loom Company, which made advanced American 'automatic' looms, and on the council of the British Cotton Growing Association. Improved trade boosted the firm's profits in the early 1900s. Following a weavers' strike, Broadhurst replaced Harold Lee as chairman of the company in 1907, but retained a conciliatory style and continued to work from a very modest office. His strategy was to concentrate production in the best mills: Sunnyside at Bolton, and Ten Acres and Hemming Works near Manchester. Sunnyside was converted from steam to electric power in 1912, and two new weaving sheds were built. The First World War, and the boom of 1918–20, brought Tootals even higher profits.

In 1919, the market value of Tootals's shares was £1,700,000. Using this measure, Tootals ranked fourteenth among textile producers in the UK, and one hundred and fifteenth among all British industrial enterprises.

Sir Edward Tootal Broadhurst, baronet (1858–1922), by unknown photographer

Tootals was among the top ten firms in the Lancashire cotton industry, although it was much smaller than the largest combines, such as the Fine Cotton Spinners' and Doublers' Association, which had been created by merger at the end of the Victorian period. It would be fair to say that, under Broadhurst's leadership, the company held its own by the standards of the time.

Broadhurst was a moderately important political figure in Lancashire, especially in the Manchester North West constituency. He was president of the Prestwich Conservative Association. During the 1900s, as an ardent free-trader, he found himself at odds with the protectionist stance of the Conservative Party. Broadhurst believed that the introduction of a tariff would be disastrous, because other countries would retaliate against Britain's export industries, including cotton. Broadhurst chaired Manchester's Free Trade League, and the Manchester Free Trade Unionist Association, and was a member of the Unionist Free Trade Club. In 1906 he defied his party in order to campaign for the Liberal candidate in Manchester North West, Winston Churchill. Broadhurst chaired an election meeting for Churchill, and gave him a rousing introduction: 'For Free Trade or against it! There is no halfway house for timid retaliators to shelter in' (Churchill,

116). He served as high sheriff of Lancashire in 1906–7. At the 1908 election he supported Churchill again, and was one of the 'Mugwump Millionaires' abused by the Conservative candidate for betraying the party. Declining to allow his name to be put forward as a rebel Conservative candidate in 1908, Broadhurst began to realize that the next election would be about more than free trade versus protection. He deplored the radicalism of Lloyd George and the new Liberals, and feared that they would reduce the country to socialism, or worse. At the first 1910 election Broadhurst promised to vote conservative, but could not bring himself to take an active part in the campaign. Between 1910 and 1912 Broadhurst suffered lengthy bouts of nervous illness.

In 1914 Broadhurst and other businessmen formed a committee which raised the Manchester City battalions (Manchester Pals), a volunteer formation including staff from offices, warehouses, and mills. He contributed £1000 to the cost of equipment and uniforms. In 1917 he was appointed to the Cotton Control Board, which rationed the dwindling supply of cotton by placing restrictions on the operation of machinery. Firms working on government orders were given permission to run more machinery for longer hours. Tootals was caught red-handed in October 1918, working flat out on normal civilian orders, while claiming to be engaged on war contracts.

Despite this violation, Broadhurst received a baronetcy for his war work in 1918. An Anglican by persuasion, he was involved in the usual round of good works: he was president of an orphan school, a governor of the Whitworth Institute, chairman of the Manchester and Salford Lifeboat Fund, and member of the council of Manchester University. He sat on committees to find work for ex-servicemen after the war, and gave Manchester some playing fields, as a thank-offering for victory and a tribute to Manchester's contribution to the war.

Broadhurst's home was the Manor House, North Rode, Congleton, in rural Cheshire; he died of cancer at 9 Hyde Terrace, Leeds, on 2 February 1922. He was survived by his wife.   JOHN SINGLETON

Sources M. W. Dupree, 'Broadhurst, Sir Edward Tootal', *DBB* · A. D. Chandler, *Scale and scope* (1990) · P. F. Clarke, *Lancashire and the new liberalism* (1971) · R. S. Churchill, *Winston S. Churchill*, 2: *Young statesman, 1901–1914* (1967) · H. D. Henderson, *The cotton control board* (1922) · R. A. Hempel, *Unionists divided* (1972) · P. Simkins, *Kitchener's army: the raising of the new armies, 1914–16* (1988) · J. Singleton, 'The cotton industry and the British war effort, 1914–1918', *Economic History Review*, 2nd ser., 47 (1994), 601–18 · b. cert. · m. cert. · d. cert. · *CGPLA Eng. & Wales* (1922)

Likenesses photograph, Whitworth Art Gallery, Manchester [*see illus.*]

Wealth at death £149,902 10s. 1d.: probate, 3 April 1922, *CGPLA Eng. & Wales*

Broadhurst, Sir Harry (1905–1995), air force officer, was born on 28 October 1905 at 4 Warrant Officers' Quarters, Blackdown Barracks, Frimley, Surrey, the son of Colour Sergeant Henry Broadhurst, South Lancashire regiment, and his wife, Amelia Louisa, *née* Patterson.

Educated at Portsmouth grammar school (1915–22),

Harry Broadhurst was initially an articled pupil to a surveyor. He also served in the Territorial Army, with the Hampshire heavy brigade, from May 1925 to October 1926 when he was seconded to the RAF on appointment to a short service commission. He did his flying training with 11 squadron, gaining his wings in August 1927 and continuing to serve with the squadron, which was sent to India in 1928. Equipped with Wapitis and then Harts, it had a peace-keeping role on the north-west frontier.

On 19 October 1929 he married Doris Kathleen French at St Thomas's Cathedral, Bombay, and in the 1931 birthday honours was mentioned in dispatches. Later that year he was posted back to the UK, to join 41 fighter squadron, newly equipped with Bristol Bulldogs. He came top in the annual air firing competitions and at the 1932–3 Hendon air displays performed solo aerobatics.

During 1933 Broadhurst started training as a flying-boat pilot, but was removed from the course and sent to another Bulldog squadron, 19. Ten months later he was posted overseas again—to 4 flying training school, Isma'iliyyah, Egypt, as chief ground instructor from November 1936 (having been awarded a permanent commission) to July 1937. By now a squadron leader, he had been awarded the AFC in the 1937 new year honours. Then for four months he served at headquarters 2 bomber group, and in 1938 completed the staff college course. At the end of that year he was posted to command 111 fighter squadron, which had been the first to be equipped with Hawker Hurricanes.

Broadhurst, who was known as Broady, earned his reputation as a fighter leader early in the Second World War, at squadron, group, and station level. Awarded the DFC in January 1940, he was on the staff of 11 group, served with the British expeditionary force air component in France, then successively commanded Coltishall, Wittering, and Hornchurch during the battle of Britain. From March 1941, when he was mentioned in dispatches, to July when he was awarded the DSO (with bar in December), to September 1942 when he received a bar to his DFC, his outstanding courage, leadership, and skill were recognized.

In October 1942 Broadhurst was posted to air headquarters, western desert, initially as senior air staff officer with the acting rank of air vice-marshal. Then on 1 February 1943, when the Eighth Army was about to enter Tunisia, he succeeded Air Vice-Marshal 'Maori' Coningham in command of the desert air force. When the Eighth Army was halted at the Mareth line in March 1943 it was Broadhurst's brilliant handling of his fighter bombers in low-level attacks which broke axis resistance and earned him the epithet 'another commander in the Coningham manner: bold, original, creative'.

Broadhurst continued as air officer commanding the desert air force during the allied invasions of Sicily and Italy, then was posted back to the UK to participate in planning for operation Overlord, the landings in Normandy. As air officer commanding 83 group he set up his headquarters there four days after D-day (6 June), side by side with that of his army opposite number, Lieutenant-General Miles Dempsey, who commanded the British Second Army.

Broadhurst's squadrons of ground-attack fighters, equipped with the formidable rocket-firing Typhoons, played a crucial role in supporting the Second Army's advance; and when the Luftwaffe introduced Me 262 jet fighters with their speed and height advantages, he countered them by means of standing patrols near their airfields. In April 1944 he was honoured by the Americans with the Legion of Merit, and in August was made CB; then in July 1945 he became 'Sir Harry' with the KBE, and in the 1946 new year honours was mentioned in dispatches. His first marriage having been dissolved in 1945, he married on 13 May 1946 Jean Elizabeth Townley (1914–2001).

Broadhurst's wartime reputation as a successful air commander led to increasingly senior appointments during the cold war period: as air officer administration, Fighter Command (1945–6) and air officer commanding, 61 (eastern reserve) group (1946–8). In 1949 he took the Imperial Defence College course and the following year was posted to the British air forces of occupation (BAFO) as senior air staff officer. This appointment continued into 1952 when BAFO was renamed second Tactical Air Force—of which, after a spell as assistant chief of the air staff (operations), he was made commander-in-chief in December 1953.

Broadhurst returned to the UK in January 1956 to be air officer commanding-in-chief, Bomber Command, which was re-equipping with V-bombers and atomic weapons, assuming command shortly before the Avro Vulcan entered service. In one of these delta-winged aircraft he led Tasman flight, a most successful visit to Australia and New Zealand, in September 1956. While returning to London's Heathrow airport for a VIP reception on 1 October, Broadhurst was flying as co-pilot when, in poor visibility, the Vulcan struck the ground about 700 yards short of the runway. Its undercarriage was torn off and its trailing-edge control surfaces damaged. The captain, Squadron Leader D. R. Howard, applied full power: the aircraft climbed steeply but he found it to be uncontrollable so gave the order to eject. He and Broadhurst did so; the Vulcan stalled and crashed, killing the three rear-crew members and an Avro technical representative.

Broadhurst re-energized Bomber Command, bringing it into the jet age and introducing a fighter-type mentality: he served there until May 1959 when he took up his last appointment, as commander, allied air forces, central Europe. An air chief marshal from February 1957, he was placed on the retired list in March 1961, then joined A. V. Roe & Co. Ltd—makers of the Vulcan and the Blue Steel stand-off bomb—as managing director. He was also a director of Hawker Siddeley Aviation (1961–76), and a director of the Hawker Siddeley Group (1968–76), and president of the Society of British Aerospace Companies (1974–5). He finally retired in 1976, his buccaneering spirit finding an outlet in sailing his 7 ton Bermuda cutter from Chichester harbour near his home at Birdham, Sussex.

Broadhurst personified the fighting spirit of the RAF,

serving with distinction in the battle of Britain, the Mediterranean campaigns, the liberation of Europe, and in high commands during the cold war. He died at Westhampnett Nursing Home, Chichester, on 29 August 1995 in his ninetieth year. His second wife, Jean Elizabeth, survived him by six years: she died in a Chichester nursing home on 21 October 2001. HUMPHREY WYNN

Sources b. cert. · RAF record of service · H.Broadhurst and head of the air historical branch (RAF), Group Captain E. B. Haslam, interview, 28 Oct 1976 · *The Times* (1 Sept 1995) · *The Independent* (1 Sept 1995) · K. Cross, *Straight and level* (1993) · J. E. Johnson, *Full circle: the story of air fighting* (1964) · A. Brookes, *V Force: the history of Britain's airborne deterrent* (1962) · H. Wynn, *The RAF strategic nuclear deterrent forces: their origins, roles and deployment, 1946–1969, a documentary history* (1994) · personal knowledge (2004) · *WWW* · *CGPLA Eng. & Wales* (1995) · m. cert. · d. cert.

Archives SOUND RAF Bentley Priory, Stanmore, Middlesex, Air Historical Branch, oral history interview, 28 Oct 1976

Likenesses photographs, repro. in *The Times*

Wealth at death £181,028: probate, 1995

Broadhurst, Henry (1840–1911), trade unionist and politician, was born at Littlemore, Oxfordshire, on 13 April 1840, the fourth son and youngest of the twelve children of Thomas Broadhurst, stonemason, and his wife, Sarah. He was educated at a village school near Littlemore, and at the age of twelve he left to do miscellaneous jobs about the village, and soon afterwards was regularly employed by its blacksmith.

In 1853 Broadhurst was apprenticed to his father's trade in Oxford, and was soon working as a stonemason in Buckingham and Banbury. Trade depression in the late 1850s forced him to travel the country in search of work. In 1858–9 he tramped 1200 miles in the south of England without finding employment. At Portsmouth he attempted to enlist in the army, but was rejected as being too short. In 1860 he married Eliza (*d.* 1905), a seamstress, daughter of Edward Olley of Norwich. They had no children. In 1865 he moved to London, and shortly afterwards was employed by the contractor who was building the clock tower and adjoining corridor of the houses of parliament.

Broadhurst became involved in the reform and other radical movements of the time. When in 1872 an agitation for increased pay in the London building trade came to a head with the employers locking out their men, Broadhurst was elected chairman of the masons' committee and was its chief spokesman. The result of the dispute was an immediate increase of pay by a halfpenny per hour, a reduction of hours by four per week in summer, and a full half-holiday on Saturdays. Following this, Broadhurst became a full-time official in the Stonemasons' Union. He worked to change the structure and role of the union, with increased powers being given to the central executive and superannuation and unemployment benefits being offered for the first time to its staff.

In 1872 Broadhurst became the union's delegate to the Trades Union Congress (TUC), and was elected a member of the parliamentary committee. The role of this committee was to monitor laws affecting labour and to campaign for amendments as necessary. Broadhurst took a leading

Henry Broadhurst (1840–1911), by Olive Edis

role in the agitation on the conspiracy and master and servant laws, and other issues. In 1873 he was elected secretary of the Labour Representation League, formed to send trade unionists to parliament. That year he unsuccessfully sought election to the London school board for Greenwich. Workmen had been candidates for parliament before the league's days, but in 1874 it produced the first list of Labour candidates at any election and succeeded in returning two of them, Alexander MacDonald for Stafford and Thomas Burt for Morpeth. Broadhurst himself stood for High Wycombe on a day's notice, but polled only 113 votes.

In 1875 the TUC elected Broadhurst secretary of the parliamentary committee. Among the reforms supported by the committee were extension of the franchise, improvements to the Employers and Workmen Act and the Factory Act, new merchant shipping and employers' liability bills, and the abolition of property qualifications for office on local governing bodies—the first subject on which Broadhurst had to draft a bill (1876). The committee chiefly engaged in the direct parliamentary lobbying of ministers and other leading politicians. Broadhurst was also the secretary of the workmen's committee of the Eastern Question Association, which condemned the conduct of the Turks in Bulgaria (1875–1880), and this brought him into contact with W. E. Gladstone. He also promoted international trade union conferences, like that in Paris in 1883, which were forerunners of the International Socialist congresses.

After the general election of 1874 the Labour Representation League gradually collapsed. Broadhurst became increasingly associated with the Liberal Party, and in 1878 was chosen one of the two Liberal candidates for Stoke-on-Trent. He was elected easily to the seat in 1880. In the House of Commons Broadhurst supported employers' liability bills—upon which he made his maiden speech—and proposed amendments to factory legislation. Broadhurst successfully pioneered proposals in 1884 for the appointment of working men as justices of the peace, and for the inclusion of a fair wages clause in government contracts. He also investigated the employment conditions of women and children in the heavy industries of the Black Country (and produced in the House of Commons in 1883 one of the nail-making machines to illustrate his speech on the subject). But a bill he proposed to ban girls under fourteen from working in nail- and chain-making failed to be supported. His income throughout this period was limited to the £150 a year he received as secretary of the TUC parliamentary committee, from which he had to pay for clerical help at his office. He claimed that he could only afford clothes made by his wife.

From 1882 Broadhurst took an active interest in leasehold enfranchisement, and wrote journal articles and one book (co-authored by Sir Robert Reid) on this issue. He was appointed a member of the royal commission on the housing of the working classes in 1884. In 1882 he was offered an assistant factory inspectorship, and in 1884 an inspectorship of canal boats, but declined both.

Broadhurst, as secretary of the TUC parliamentary committee, continued to be a leading campaigner for extension of the franchise. At the election which followed the Franchise and Redistribution Acts of 1885, Broadhurst declined to contest either of the new Pottery constituencies, into which Stoke-on-Trent had been divided, and stood for and won the Bordesley division of Birmingham. On the formation of Gladstone's Liberal ministry in February 1886 he accepted office as under-secretary in the Home department, the first working man to be appointed a government minister (Gladstone's attempt to reduce the post's remuneration consequently seemed bizarre). This appointment necessitated Broadhurst's resignation of the secretaryship of the parliamentary committee. The queen agreed to excuse him from attending levees, and he was the first minister to whom such permission was granted.

In the election following the collapse of the Liberal government in the autumn, Broadhurst moved from the Bordesley seat, as Birmingham was now a unionist stronghold, and contested West Nottingham, which he won. In September 1886 he was again elected secretary of the TUC parliamentary committee. Broadhurst had begun to come under attack from others within the trade union movement for insufficiently supporting in parliament the interests of labour. Resentment towards him was greatly increased by his opposition to the legal enforcement of the eight-hour day. The most notable criticism came from Keir Hardie at the 1887 and 1889 Trades Union Congresses, largely over Broadhurst's ownership of shares in J. T. Brunner's chemical firm, his failure to question in parliament the death of a worker at the firm, and, in general, his support for a Liberal Party heavily influenced by employers. Broadhurst was able to deflect these attacks and retain the support of delegates. But at the 1890 congress his position on the eight-hour day was defeated, and new members for the parliamentary committee were imposed upon him. Following this, Broadhurst resigned as secretary of the committee, claiming ill health. He also moved that year from London to Cromer on the Norfolk coast.

In 1892 Broadhurst was appointed a member of the royal commission on the aged poor, and submitted a minority report advocating pensions for the aged. He was defeated in the 1892 election following the withdrawal of support by the miners in his West Nottingham seat, and also in an 1893 by-election in Grimsby because, he claimed, of the opposition of the Independent Labour Party and other sections of the labour movement. In 1894 he won a seat in Leicester in a by-election, and retained this until his retirement in 1906, continuing as a leading member of the small group of 'Lib-Labs' in parliament.

Outspoken, and with a strong voice, Broadhurst was a powerful figure in the labour movement at the time of its initial attempts to gain political representation. After his retirement he became involved in local affairs in Norfolk, and was an alderman and justice of the peace. Broadhurst died at his home, Trent Cottage, Cromer, on 11 October 1911. He was buried at Overstrand, near Cromer, on 14 October. J. R. MacDonald, rev. Marc Brodie

Sources H. Broadhurst, *Henry Broadhurst, MP: the story of his life from a stonemason's bench to the treasury bench* (1901) • *The Times* (12 Oct 1911) • *The Times* (16 Oct 1911) • *DLB* • J. Shepherd, 'Labour and parliament: the lib-labs as the first working-class MPs, 1885–1906', *Currents of radicalism: popular radicalism, organised labour, and party politics in Britain, 1850–1914*, ed. E. F. Biagini and A. J. Reid (1991), 187–213 • *WWW* • Gladstone, *Diaries*

Archives BLPES, political corresp. and papers • London Metropolitan University, TUC collections, papers | Bishopgate Institute, London, letters to George Howell • BL, corresp. with W. E. Gladstone, Add. MSS 44456–44524, *passim* • Bodl. Oxf., corresp. with Lord Kimberley

Likenesses O. Edis, photograph, NPG [*see illus.*] • bust, probably Leicester Art Gallery • cartoon, repro. in Broadhurst, *Henry Broadhurst, MP*, 223 • photograph, repro. in Broadhurst, *Henry Broadhurst, MP*, frontispiece

Wealth at death £6962 6s. 2d.: probate, 8 Dec 1911, CGPLA Eng. & Wales

Broadhurst, Mary Adelaide (1857/8–1928), agricultural reformer and radical, was the daughter of William Broadhurst, a city councillor in Manchester. Very little is known of her early life except that, having completed an MA degree at London University, she was one of the pioneers who attempted to organize physical science laboratories in girls' secondary schools. She played a similar role in allied educational movements.

In conjunction with Margaret Farquharson, Mary Broadhurst was one of the founders of the National Political League (NPL) in 1911, and served as its president until her death in 1928. One of the organization's principal aims was to promote agricultural settlements, whereby trainees could learn poultry farming and other similar tasks on a co-operative basis. Its schemes were, however, specifically intended to provide employment for the professional middle-class women who were unable to find alternative sources of suitable work, and who largely made up the membership of the NPL. This programme was accompanied by the formation of the National Land Council. Its other members included Muriel, Countess De La Warr, Lady Willoughby de Broke, Emily Hobhouse, Margaret Farquharson, Walter Coates (committee of Vacant Land Cultivation Society), Professor S. J. Chapman, and R. E. Prothero (Lord Ernle).

Despite strenuous efforts to popularize its work, the National Land Council under Mary Broadhurst's leadership achieved very little in a practical sense during the First World War. Indeed in 1916, in a report from Sir Sydney Olivier, secretary to the Board of Agriculture and Fisheries, it was concluded that organizations like the NPL were of little real value. Olivier particularly criticized the NPL for pursuing its objectives through (unspecified) 'mischievous' methods. The role played by the NPL, and also by the Women's Legion, was eventually terminated by the Board of Agriculture and Fisheries on the grounds of inefficiency. Confirmation of the lack of practical achievements is also evident in the group's few surviving records at the Imperial War Museum.

After the war the NPL was one of many organizations to instigate a national campaign against what contemporaries regarded as the communist menace. It had links with a number of other right-wing organizations. During Broadhurst's time as president the league was also, according to contemporary accounts, actively involved in the promotion of Anglo-Arab friendship with particular reference to the development of the Arab states. The aim was to prevent the spread of Bolshevist intrigues in the Middle East. At the time of her death Mary Broadhurst was working for British control over the wealth of the Dead Sea, an issue which she considered to be the key to the peaceful development of the Middle East.

Mary Broadhurst never married, and died in a nursing home at 99 Cromwell Road, South Kensington, London, on 8 December 1928. There was a private funeral at Brockwood three days later. Best known as the president of the National Political League, she was an active and energetic proponent of rather grandiose schemes for the agricultural employment of women; and most of these failed to reach fruition. JOHN MARTIN

Sources The Times (8–10 Dec 1928) · The Times (15 Dec 1928) · WWW · S. White, 'Ideological and political control: the sociology of anti-Bolshevism in Britain, 1918–20', Scottish Labour History Society, 9 (June 1975) · IWM, National Political League papers · P. Horn, Rural life in England in the First World War (1984) · A. Marwick, Women at war, 1914–18 (1977) · S. Olivier, 'Minutes on the further employment of women in agriculture', c.Oct 1916, MAF 59/1 · d. cert. · P. King, Women rule the plot: the story of the 100 year fight to establish women's place in farm and garden (1999)

Archives IWM, Land IV National Political League folder

Likenesses photographs, IWM

Wealth at death £296: administration, 1 Aug 1929, CGPLA Eng. & Wales

Broadhurst, Robert (1859/60–1948), pan-African nationalist leader, was born probably in Sierra Leone, the son of a Manchester merchant, John S. Broadhurst, who had a business there; his mother, whose name is unknown, was from Sierra Leone. He was sent to Britain to be educated at Nantwich, in Cheshire, about 1869; seven years later he returned to Sierra Leone. Back in England in 1905 he worked for the family firm, Broadhurst & Sons in Manchester, until 1909, when the company vanishes from the Manchester directories and Robert Broadhurst is no longer listed as residing at St Anne's-on-Sea, a salubrious area. In 1912 Broadhurst is reported in the Sierre Leone Weekly News as a cocoa merchant. From 1916 to 1918 he worked as an agent for the Niger Company in Jos and Lokoja, and then as a general merchant in Freetown and Conakry. By 1936, when West Africa noted him as a 'senior commercial agent', he had been a UK resident for some years, with offices in the City.

In Britain Broadhurst became involved in black politics, and in 1911 he attended the Universal Races Congress, an apolitical gathering sponsored by philanthropists. He was a founder member of the African Progress Union (APU) and its first secretary from 1918 to 1921, and he remained on the union's executive committee until the APU's demise in 1925. The APU was a political organization formed to 'promote the social and economic welfare of Africans in the world' (Gold Coast Leader). It protested, for example, against the restoration of African colonies to Germany in 1918, and at the end of the First World War asked that the 'principle of self-determination for weaker races … will be applied to the African colonies' and that an 'African adviser' should be included in the British peace treaty delegation (Greene). The APU protested against the lack of protection offered by the police during the anti-black riots in Liverpool in 1919, against the 'flogging and shooting of natives in British East Africa' (Manchester Guardian) in 1923, and in 1921 announced its intention to set up a hostel for Africans who were experiencing racial discrimination in their attempts to find lodgings.

Broadhurst was also an active member of the West African Students Union and was involved in the many protests regarding the Italian invasion of Abyssinia in 1935. The breadth of his political involvement is demonstrated by his service with two organizations that were under the aegis of the socialist anti-imperialist activist George Padmore: he was treasurer of the International African Service Bureau from its formation in 1937 and president of the first Pan-African Federation. Broadhurst is noted in the press as attending a variety of political and welfare functions organized by black people; his lack of sectarianism and overwhelming desire to aid and support his people is also proved by his membership of the London branch of the Universal Negro Improvement Association, created by Marcus Garvey.

Broadhurst was also involved internationally. Through the APU he was in contact with members of the National Congress of British West Africa, both by correspondence and also in person, when the congress delegates visited Britain in 1920–21 seeking constitutional and electoral reforms. Other delegations supported by Broadhurst in his capacity as APU secretary were those from South Africa in Britain in 1919, petitioning the king for 'Freedom, Liberty, Justice and Fairplay' and representation at the peace conference, and Nigerian nationalists Herbert Macaulay and Chief Oluwa, pressing land claims. He was also in touch with other west African nationalist and commercial interests: for example he was associated with the West African Co-Operative Producers Ltd, started by Gold Coaster W. Tete-Ansa, and with the delegates of the Aborigines' Rights Protection Society of the Gold Coast visiting Britain in 1935–6. Through letters to west African papers such as *The Aurora* of Freetown he informed west Africans of events in Britain of relevance to them.

In 1921 he was the 'English' secretary for the Pan-African Congress organized by W. E. B. DuBois, whom he had met at the 1911 congress in London; he is noted as attending with his daughter, who would have been one of the few women present. The congress's demands included an end to expropriation of land by 'the unrestrained greed of invested capital', and local government for 'backward groups, deliberately rising to complete self-government'. He also attended the Paris sessions of the 1921 congress. However, neither he nor other prominent west Africans in Britain attended the 1923 congress, which met in London and Lisbon, perhaps as a result of disagreements that had arisen in 1921 with the congress's organizer.

From about 1939 until 1948 Broadhurst was vice-consul for the Republic of Liberia in London. How he obtained this position is not known. He was still active in his eighties, and was part of the delegation that in 1944 met Walter White, the American civil rights leader and official of the National Association for the Advancement of Colored People. In 1945 he attended the Pan-African Congress in Manchester as Liberia's representative. Robert Broadhurst died, aged eighty-eight, in Hackney Hospital on 10 December 1948. His funeral took place in Hampstead parish church; his son, also a merchant, is noted as having attended.

Nnamdi Azikiwe, future president of Nigeria, recalled in his memoirs that in 1934, as he was about to leave London, Robert Broadhurst 'blessed me and wished me godspeed and prayed that God might guide me in my humble efforts to serve Africa' (Azikiwe, 212). He described Broadhurst as 'an elderly gentleman of African descent … mentally virile and very progressive in his ideas' (ibid.). That Broadhurst certainly was; some four years before his death his erstwhile colleague in 1930s London, I. T. A. Wallace Johnson, later a political leader in Sierra Leone, called him 'the Grand Old Man of African nationalism' (*African Standard*).   MARIKA SHERWOOD

Sources J. Greene, 'The African Progress Union of London, 1918–1925', seminar paper, 5 Feb 1991 [delivered at the Institute of Commonwealth Studies, London] · J. A. Langley, *Pan-Africanism and nationalism in west Africa, 1900–1945: a study in ideology and social classes* (1973), 246, 251–3 · N. Azikiwe, *My odyssey* (1970), 212 · *West Africa* (1936–) · *Gold Coast Leader* (20 April 1921) · *West India Committee Circular* (31 Oct 1918) · *African Telegraph* (Jan×Feb 1919) · *African Standard*

(19 May 1944) · *Manchester Guardian* (7 Nov 1923) · *The Aurora* (1921) [Freetown] · d. cert.

Broadingham, Elizabeth (*d.* 1776), murderer, lived in Flamborough, near York, with her husband, John Broadingham, a convicted smuggler. No information about her exists before her trial. During her husband's confinement in York Castle, Elizabeth took up residence with one Thomas Aikney. The two continued the adulterous relationship and moved to Lincolnshire after Elizabeth's husband was released from prison. Elizabeth allegedly proposed the idea of killing her husband to Aikney on several occasions, often getting him intoxicated first. Aikney initially refused to entertain her murderous plan, suggesting that they simply elope, but at length capitulated to her repeated requests. To effect the deed Broadingham returned to her husband's home, ostensibly to reconcile their marriage, while Aikney found lodgings close by. On the night of 13 February 1776, eight days after returning to her husband, Broadingham roused him from his sleep, claiming there was someone knocking at the door. Her husband, suspecting perhaps it was one of his fellow smugglers seeking refuge, answered the door, whereupon Aikney attacked him with a knife. Broadingham was stabbed in the thigh and then suffered a gash across his abdomen so deep that Aikney, either accidentally or by design, left the knife in his victim's body. At their trial at the York assizes, the principal evidence against Aikney and Broadingham was the knife, identified as belonging to Aikney. Both of the accused were convicted of the crime and, despite Broadingham's being only a conspirator, both were executed on 20 March 1776. Broadingham was convicted of petit or petty treason, for which the punishment was burning to death; she was one of the last women to receive this sentence before the practice was abolished in 1790 (30 Geo. III, c. 48). On the execution day she was drawn upon a sledge from York Castle to Tyburn, near York, where she was strangled and her body burnt at the stake. According to one report, at the place of execution Broadingham 'did not discover the least signs of contrition and behaved as at her trial' denying her role in the murder 'with a degree of boldness and unconcern, that shocked all who saw her' (*Newcastle Journal*). Aikney was hanged for murder and his body sent to Leeds for dissection.   GREG T. SMITH

Sources B. Laurie, *The Newgate calendar, or, Malefactors' bloody register* (1932), 908–10 · *Annual Register* (1776), 138 · *Newcastle Journal* (23 March 1776)

Broadwood, Henry Fowler (1811–1893), piano manufacturer, was born in London in June 1811, the fifth child of James Shudi Broadwood (1772–1851), piano manufacturer, and his second wife, Margaret Schaw Stewart (1778–1849). The founder of the firm was his grandfather, John *Broadwood (1732–1812), whose eldest son, James Shudi Broadwood, together with his half-brother, Thomas Broadwood (1786–1861), from 1812 carried on and developed the business. John Broadwood had been a pioneer in the development and popularization of the piano, both in the 'square' form and in the more traditionally shaped 'grand' form, in

Henry Fowler Broadwood (1811–1893), by unknown photographer, *c*.1861

the last quarter of the eighteenth century. James Shudi Broadwood and Thomas Broadwood continued this development into the early nineteenth century with such success that by 1840 the company was one of the twelve largest employers of labour in London, with the factory at Horseferry Road, Westminster, producing 3000 instruments a year at its peak.

Henry Fowler Broadwood had not expected to take over the firm, since he had two older brothers, the sons of their father's first marriage to Sophia Bridget Colville. However, the eldest son, John (1798–1864), took holy orders and became a scholar and collector of folk-songs, and the second son died before he could take any active part in the firm. Henry Fowler, talented at sport in his youth, was educated at Harrow School and at Heidelberg. He matriculated at St John's College, Oxford, but a few months later was admitted to Trinity College, Cambridge (on 24 May 1830), though it would appear that he did not take a degree. In 1840 he married Juliana Maria Birch (1816–1898), daughter of Wyrley Birch, gentleman. They had two sons and nine daughters, one of whom was Lucy Etheldred *Broadwood, the musician and folk-song collector. In 1861, when his uncle Thomas Broadwood died, Henry Fowler Broadwood became a partner in the firm, and he then took charge of the business until his death.

In 1862 Broadwood contributed a particularly valuable document to the study of the harpsichord in England: *Some notes made by J. S. Broadwood, 1838, with observations and elucidations by H. F. Broadwood*. In the section concerning the harpsichord he quotes from his father that: 'Tabel, a

Fleming, who had learned his business in the house of the successor of Ruckers, at Antwerp, was, it is believed, the first person who made harpsichords in London, where he resided between 1680 and 1720.' Although Broadwood was quoting an earlier document, from 1838, it seems that either this was never published or that copies of it are extremely rare, as are copies of the 1862 pamphlet. In fact Broadwood was wrong in stating that Tabel was the first person to make harpsichords in London, but the significance of the observation concerning him is to show how his harpsichords (on which those of Burkat Shudi and Jacob Kirkman were clearly based) were derived from the Flemish school of the Couchets, and through them, the famous Ruckers family. The 1862 pamphlet is also very useful for the study of the early piano in England, and is particularly relevant to the study of Broadwood pianos.

Despite the excellence of Broadwood pianos, which brought about a great demand for them in both home and export markets (Broadwood pianos were used by Beethoven, Chopin, and Mendelssohn, and there are numerous examples of their use by the British royal family), under Henry Fowler Broadwood the firm did not move with the times. It is thought that he was sceptical of the abilities of British founders to make reliable castings and was therefore reluctant to use the single cast-iron frame and the technique of overstringing, both of which were adopted by his competitors and are still universally employed in piano design. Accordingly the fortunes of the firm declined, and though members of the family accumulated considerable personal wealth it was only through the intervention of C. E. Heath, brother of Ada Randolph Heath, the wife of Broadwood's younger son Henry John Tschudi Broadwood (1856–1911), that the firm received the financial help which restored its stability; it was then reformed with the name John Broadwood & Sons Ltd. Pianos bearing this name were still being made under licence by Whelpdale, Maxwell, and Codd in the late 1990s.

Broadwood died on 8 July 1893 at Lyne House, Newdigate, Surrey, on the country estate bought by his father in 1799. His wife survived him. CHARLES MOULD

Sources D. Wainwright, 'Broadwood, Henry Fowler', *DBB* · G. Dodd, 'Piano-forte manufacture', *British manufactures*, 4 (1845), 145–65 · C. Ehrlich, *The piano: a history* (1976) · D. Wainwright, *Broadwood by appointment: a history* (1982) · R. Palmieri, ed., *Encyclopedia of keyboard instruments* (1994) · D. H. Boalch, *Makers of the harpsichord and clavichord, 1440–1840*, ed. C. Mould, 3rd edn (1995) · *Some notes made by J. S. Broadwood, 1838, with observations and elucidations by H. F. Broadwood* (1862) · Boase, *Mod. Eng. biog.* · *CGPLA Eng. & Wales* (1893) · d. cert.

Archives Surrey HC, corresp.

Likenesses photograph, *c*.1861, Broadwood Trust; copyprint, NPG [*see illus.*] · photograph (aged fifty), repro. in Wainwright, *Broadwood by appointment*, 190

Wealth at death £84,550—personal estate: 8 July 1893, Wainwright, 'Broadwood, Henry Fowler' · £80,830 5*s.*: probate, 25 Nov 1893, *CGPLA Eng. & Wales*

Broadwood, John (1732–1812), harpsichord and piano manufacturer, was born on 6 October 1732 at Oldhamstocks, near Cockburnspath, Berwickshire, Scotland, the

John Broadwood (1732–1812), by William Say, pubd 1812 (after John Harrison junior)

eldest son of James Broadwood (1696–1774) and his wife, Margaret Purves (1698–1799). He came from an old family of Northumbrian yeomen who in the sixteenth century owned land near Hexham but who by the eighteenth century had moved into Scotland. Broadwood, having learned cabinet-making from his father, is often said to have walked from Scotland to London to seek his fortune, equipped only with a half-crown in his pocket. However, it seems more likely that he also carried with him letters of introduction from the local laird, Sir John Hall of Douglass, and that these enabled him, in September 1761, to obtain a position as an apprentice to Burkhardt Tschudi (1702–1773), one of the most successful makers of harpsichords in London.

Tschudi had Anglicized his name to Burkat *Shudi, and it was in this form that he signed his instruments. In 1718 he moved to London and worked with Herman Tabel as an apprentice; Tabel had received a training from the famous firm of Ruckers, Antwerp, whose instruments were, and still are, universally acclaimed. Tabel's surviving harpsichord shows many of the characteristics of the Antwerp school, and not surprisingly Shudi's harpsichords are very similar in their case construction and layout. In their outer decoration, however, instruments by Ruckers are invariably painted, whereas Shudi harpsichords have plain wooden cases with veneered panels surrounded by stringing and cross-banding in the same restrained style as much good quality eighteenth-century English furniture. It is interesting that even by the end of the eighteenth century English grand pianos, whose cases had to withstand a much greater string tension, still retained an internal structure similar to the harpsichords of the same period.

Evidently the young Broadwood soon gained favour with Shudi, and was trusted with some of the most exacting work which would affect the tonal character of the instruments. In 1765, when Broadwood was only four years into his apprenticeship, Frederick the Great commissioned Shudi to make harpsichords for his new palace at Potsdam. A published affidavit of the period runs as follows:

> The greatest part of the work of the said Harpsichords was done by … Andrew Clark and John Broadwood, under the direction of their said master Burkat Shudi; and particularly … John Broadwood remembers his having glewed up the sounding boards of all the said Harpsichords, and his having assisted his said master Burkat Shudi, in putting the sounding-board (after [he] had wrought and finished the same under the immediate direction of … Burkat Shudi), into the first of the said Harpsichords sold to his Prussian Majesty. (Russell, 169)

In 1769 Broadwood married Shudi's daughter Barbara (1749–1776), and, presumably having successfully completed his apprenticeship, in 1770 he was taken into partnership by his father-in-law. In March of the following year Shudi retired to a house in Charlotte Street, not far from the Pulteney Street and Bride Street premises where the instruments were made and which in the same year he leased to Broadwood for £50 per annum. Shudi died on 19 August 1773.

Three manuscripts preserved in the Bodleian Library, Oxford, shed much light on Broadwood's activities. MS Eng. misc. b. 107, entitled on the spine 'Journal', and MS Eng. misc. e. 663, untitled, but containing much information on John Broadwood's personal financial dealings, demonstrate that he was involved in at least four branches of the harpsichord business. These included the making of harpsichords; selling harpsichords at home and abroad; hiring harpsichords for domestic and concert use; and tuning and regulating instruments (which Broadwood carried out on an extensive scale). Finally he also sold a variety of other musical instruments. Beyond this, however, the personal account book shows that he was also, like his rival Jacob Kirkman, involved in moneylending, advancing mortgages on property, and even dealing in shipping.

Barbara's role in the business is revealed in the third manuscript, 'Barbara Broadwood's Account Book' (MS Eng. misc. c. 529). This contains a delightful hotchpotch of domestic accounts, a list of her husband's clothes, a business diary, timetables of the departures of carriers' wagons from London to the provinces, and shopping lists; these are interspersed with graffiti which look as if they had been drawn by a child and include pictures of candles, and also included are the initials 'IB' [Iohannes Broadwood], and some as yet unexplained items. The domestic accounts are particularly engaging, containing such items as 'A Bullox Heart—1s 2d', 'Potetys—2d', 'Mengling [mangling]—3d', and 'Spary Grace [asparagus]—1s 3d'. There are also tantalizing accounts of various transactions between a group of wives, among whose names, apart from Mrs Broadwood, are those of several spouses of harpsichord and piano makers; and names of other musicians of the London circle are recognizable. The entry is headed 'Five pieces of handkerchief' and against the names are sums which are all multiples of 3s. 6d., but there are no suggestions as to what this might refer to. Perhaps of greater importance, and probably not in Barbara's hand, are continuation entries from the 'Journal', which list the main transactions involving the sale of harpsichords and pianos. From this there is little doubt that among his clients Broadwood numbered many wealthy and influential people at home and abroad. The 'Journal' also shows very clearly the decrease in the popularity of the harpsichord which was rapidly being replaced by an increasing demand for the piano.

In 1761 a former employee of Shudi's, Johann Christoph Zumpe, had left to set up his own business, and it may be that Broadwood had replaced Zumpe as an apprentice in Shudi's workshop. Zumpe was particularly successful in popularizing small square pianos, and this example must have fired Broadwood with enthusiasm to tap this growing market and to experiment with the development of the grand piano, particularly with regard to the action. According to the definitive study of Broadwood, the following story was passed down from John Broadwood to his son James Shudi Broadwood, and was thus given by James's son:

> John Broadwood, then with his apprentice Stodart, in the employ of Burckhardt Shudi, used to go of an evening to Jermyn-street, to assist Backers in bringing his mechanism to perfection. This was the case, and hence the dying man recommended the further care of his invention to his friend John Broadwood. (Wainwright, 41–2)

In his will Shudi left to Broadwood the rights in the 'Venetian swell' (a device for varying the volume of the harpsichord), provided that he paid Shudi's young son (also named Burkat) an annuity of £40. After Shudi's death Broadwood continued in partnership with the young Burkat Shudi (b. 1737). Despite the fact that Broadwood was the senior partner in the firm, the instruments continued to be signed (as they had since 1770), 'Burkat Shudi et Johannes Broadwood', and this is borne out by the earliest surviving instrument signed in this style, dated 1770. The latest surviving harpsichord which is known to bear both their names is dated 1791, which is surprising: Burkat Shudi junior lived until 1803, but Broadwood had carried on the direction of the firm alone from 1782.

Barbara Shudi died at the early age of twenty-seven, in 1776, and Broadwood was left with three children to bring up. However, five years later, in 1781, Mary Kitson became his second wife, and they had a further six children between 1782 and 1793. In 1795 Broadwood took his son James Shudi Broadwood (1772–1851) into partnership, making the firm John Broadwood & Son (by this time devoted wholly to the pianoforte); and when another son, Thomas, entered the partnership in 1807, it became John Broadwood & Sons.

In the eighteenth century many attempts were made to 'improve' the harpsichord. Shudi's Venetian swell was one of many attempts, but it was one which remained in favour until the effective demise of the harpsichord at the end of the century. Improvement upon the fragile and somewhat brittle nature of bird quill as a material for the plucking of the strings occupied many people, including Francis Hopkinson, a lawyer of Philadelphia, who in 1780 devised his improved method of quilling the harpsichord, whereby a small metal staple was added to the quill to give it greater stability. In 1783 and 1784 Hopkinson read papers on the subject to the Philosophical Society of Philadelphia, and mentioned therein the instrument made for him by 'Shudi and Broadwood', though judging from the date Broadwood must have built the instrument himself. Broadwood, however, does not seem to have incorporated Hopkinson's improvements in any of the instruments made for the general public, preferring increasingly to use leather plectra for one rank of jacks, though quill was never completely replaced. Leather was used almost certainly to give a variety of tonal capability to the harpsichord, not to increase the durability of the plectra. It is noteworthy that the 'Journal' shows evidence of older instruments being taken back to the workshop so that leather plectra might be fitted to one row of jacks which were formerly quilled.

Broadwood's instruments were of the finest quality, and ranked with those of Jacob Kirkman as the epitome of harpsichord building. Both single- and double-manual instruments were made, and those writing on the harpsichord today still accept as true the oft-quoted words of Frank Hubbard, written in 1965, on the subject of English harpsichords:

> Although these almost mass-produced harpsichords did not have as musical a disposition as their French contemporaries, it is possible that they represent the culmination of the harpsichord-maker's art. For sheer magnificence of tone, reedy trebles and sonorous basses, no other harpsichords ever matched them. (Wainwright, 162)

As Broadwood's business and family increased, he needed more space. Accordingly in 1787 he took a lease of twenty-one years on a house in the country, as his family described it, though it could hardly be described as now: no. 14 Kensington Gore, London, which cost £25 per year. Broadwood also leased the adjoining house, no. 15, for £10 per year. The latter was smaller but had a longer garden; this ran down to the market gardens and had an open view at the back over the village of Brompton. The Royal College of Art later stood on the site.

The performance of the king's birthday ode at St James's Palace was an annual event, for which before 1793 Broadwoods always hired out a harpsichord; after this date, however, the harpsichord was sent and used for the rehearsal, but it was replaced by a pianoforte for the performance. Significantly, the harpsichord was never used again for this event. The latest extant Broadwood harpsichord is dated in the same year—1793—and is the only harpsichord signed by Broadwood alone: 'Johannes Broadwood Londini Fecit 1793'.

It is thought that the last harpsichord to be made by a British maker is an extant instrument of 1800 by Jacob

Kirkman, though Carl Engel (without quoting his source of information) states that the last instrument was made in Kirkman's workshop in 1809; it is very probable that Broadwood had turned exclusively to piano making by the middle of the last decade of the eighteenth century. Broadwood played a prominent part in the affairs of his firm until his death, in mid-July 1812; by then in his eightieth year, he suffered a stroke while dining with his son Thomas in Great Pulteney Street. He died the following day, on 17 July 1812. CHARLES MOULD

Sources D. Wainwright, *Broadwood by appointment: a history* (1982) · M. N. Clinkscale, *Makers of the piano, 1700–1820* (1993) · R. Palmieri, ed., *Encyclopedia of keyboard instruments* (1994) · R. Russell, *The harpsichord and clavichord*, 2nd edn (1959) · Surrey RO, Broadwood Archive · D. H. Boalch, *Makers of the harpsichord and clavichord, 1440–1840*, ed. C. Mould, 3rd edn (1995)

Archives Bodl. Oxf., account books, MSS Eng. misc. c. 529, b. 107, and e. 663 · Surrey HC, corresp.

Likenesses W. Say, mezzotint, pubd 1812 (after J. Harrison junior), BM, NPG [*see illus.*] · portrait, repro. in Wainwright, *Broadwood by appointment*, 59

Broadwood, Lucy Etheldred (1858–1929), musician and folk-song collector, was born on 9 August 1858 at Pavilion House, Melrose, Scotland, the youngest of the eleven children of Henry Fowler *Broadwood (1811–1893), piano manufacturer, and his wife, Juliana Maria, *née* Birch (1816–1898). She was the great-granddaughter of John Broadwood (1732–1812) who founded the piano firm which bears his name. In April 1864, the family moved into the Broadwood country mansion at Lyne, on the Surrey–Sussex border near Rusper, where Lucy Broadwood's childhood and early youth were spent, with occasional visits to London where the family retained a house. Educated privately, she possessed literary, artistic, and musical abilities, which she developed in her adult life. She remained at Lyne until 1894, when she moved with her widowed mother to London. In February 1899 she took a flat in Victoria Street, sharing it from December of that year until 1920 with her niece, Barbara Craster. She then moved into a flat in Drayton Gardens, South Kensington.

Lucy Broadwood's interest in folk-song was inspired partly by her uncle John Broadwood (1798–1864), who in 1843 published a collection of folk-songs titled *Old English Songs*, which was edited and reissued as *Sussex Songs* in 1890 with the tunes reharmonized by H. F. Birch Reynardson and with additional songs collected by Lucy Broadwood. In her youth she had been fascinated by the carols sung by the Sussex 'tipteers' or mummers when they visited Lyne at Christmas-time. Encouraged to cast the net wider, she continued to build up her connections with other collectors such as Sabine Baring-Gould (1834–1924), travelling with him to Cornwall to collect songs. In 1893 she published the influential *English County Songs* with the music critic and writer John Alexander Fuller Maitland (1856–1936), a relative and a close friend throughout her life.

Lucy Broadwood was a gifted singer and pianist, a keen concert goer, and a participant in numerous amateur concerts. By 1885 she was a regular singer in concerts given in London by various philanthropic organizations. She was from 1884 to 1888 a pupil of the singer William Shakespeare (1849–1931) and continued to be associated with him in her participation in private and charity concerts. Throughout the 1890s she performed with some success a number of the folk-songs she herself had collected, as well as some songs of her own composition. She was also involved in the early-music movement as a performer and editor. She met Arnold Dolmetsch (1858–1940) in late 1893 and in 1895 she was invited by him to sing at his private concert of viol, harpsichord, and lute music; she declined a further invitation to perform publicly. In the same year she was invited by William Barclay-Squire to edit some

Lucy Etheldred Broadwood (1858–1929), by unknown photographer, 1901

Purcell songs for the Purcell Society, of which she became a member in 1896. She eventually edited Purcell's opera *Amphytrion* for the society. Much of her interest in early music was fostered by the writer on musical instruments Alfred James Hipkins (1826–1903), who had been associated with the family firm from 1840 and was in many ways her mentor.

In 1898 Lucy Broadwood was one of the 110 founder members of the Folksong Society, and was a member of its first committee which was made up of established musicians, such as Ralph Vaughan Williams, and committed amateurs. In 1904 she became honorary secretary, patching together divisions within the society and applying high standards of editing with colleagues Frank Kidson, Anne Gilchrist, Fuller Maitland, and Cecil Sharp; she became honorary editor in 1908. Although the arrival of Cecil Sharp early in 1904 precipitated reform in the society, there were later tensions in the relationship, and by 1911 Lucy Broadwood clearly resented his autocratic approach. Sharp left the society to found the English Folk Dance Society in 1912; the two were amalgamated in 1931.

Like Sharp, Lucy Broadwood spent much time noting down folk-songs from older people living in isolated villages. Beginning in Sussex, one of her most famous sources of songs was Henry Burstow, who was sixty-eight years old in 1893 when she first heard him. By 1902, when with the support of Frank Kidson she published the songs in the *Journal of the Folksong Society*, she was able to boast that England did indeed have indigenous folk music. In 1905 the Royal Musical Association expressed interest in her work, which resulted in a paper, 'On the collecting of English folk-song', in which she gave copious information about her sources and experience. Her article on Irish music ('Songs from County Waterford, Ireland', *Journal of the Folksong Society*, 3, 1907–8) documents the contribution of Michael and Bridget Geary, and her phonograph recordings of songs collected in Scotland in 1908 are held on loan by the National Sound Archive (British Library). Percy Grainger, inspired by her RMA lecture, joined the Folksong Society in 1905 and shortly afterwards proselytized for the use of the phonograph when collecting songs, a controversial idea at the time. Lucy Broadwood also wrote the introduction to Frances Tolmie's collection of Scottish songs published in the *Journal* in 1911, providing notes on Gaelic scales.

Although devoted to folk-song, Lucy Broadwood maintained close contacts with the musical establishment and gave lavish musical parties for pianists such as Fanny Davies (1861–1934) and the Brazilian Guiomar Novaës (1896–1979). From 1915 she also supported Belgian musicians and was patron and friend of the composer, violinist, and pianist Juliette Folville (1870–1946). She was always in demand as an adjudicator of singing in provincial music festivals and was long associated with Vaughan Williams's Leith Hill Music Festival. In 1916 and 1917 she collaborated with L. E. Walter, harmonizing a selection of nursery rhymes. In 1921 she published simple musical settings for Lewis Carroll's poetry in *Alice in Wonderland* and *Through the Looking-Glass*. By this time she had experienced some financial difficulty and considerable domestic disruption as she moved out of her flat and sold much of her furniture. Despite these setbacks she remained fairly active up to her death and succeeded Lord Tennyson as president of the Folksong Society in December 1928. She died suddenly on 22 August 1929 while attending a music festival in Dropmore, near Canterbury, and was buried in Rusper church.

Photographs of Lucy Broadwood reveal a handsome, slightly severe-looking woman. Her friend Mary Venables wrote of her determination to remain single and of her sense of humour mingled with seriousness. She was well read, wrote poetry, and enjoyed fine art. Her voice as a singer was evidently small but pleasant; this no doubt aided her in her collection and performance of folk-song. Health problems plagued her throughout her life, particularly lumbago and throat ailments. As a collector and editor she was untiring and her careful and sincere approach set a standard for others to emulate. As a musician she was an important link between the musical establishment and the burgeoning folk-song revival. The latter especially underwent significant change after her death in both social and musical terms, but owed her much for its secure and genuine foundation. DOROTHY DE VAL

Sources L. E. Broadwood, 'On the collecting of English folk-song', *Proceedings of the Musical Association*, 31 (1904–5), 89–109 • M. Dean-Smith, ed., 'Letters to Lucy Broadwood', *Journal of the English Folk Dance and Song Society*, 9/5 (1964), 233–68 • E. Bassin, 'Lucy Broadwood, 1858–1929: her contribution to the collection and study of Gaelic traditional song', *Scottish Studies*, 9 (1965), 145–52 • D. Wainwright, *Broadwood by appointment: a history* (1982) • J. A. Fuller, *Monthly Musical Record*, 59 (1929), 296–7 • *Journal of the Folksong Society*, 8 (1929), 168–9 • private information (2004)

Archives BL, annotations relating to folk-song, Add. MS 50887 • Surrey HC, corresp. and papers • Surrey HC, diaries and notebooks • Surrey HC, corresp. re. music, folksong • Vaughan Williams Memorial Library, London, financial and domestic papers, notes, photographs, publishers' corresp., sketches, etc. | Cecil Sharp House, London, English Folk Dance and Song Society collection, corresp. with Sharp, folk-songs, journals from her library, etc. • U. Aberdeen L., letters to A. J. Keith • Vaughan Williams Memorial Library, London, corresp. with Cecil Sharp | SOUND BL NSA, performance recording, 1907, C37/1535–1579

Likenesses photograph, 1901, NPG [*see illus.*] • M. Craster, group portraits, photographs (with family and friends), Surrey HC • G. Peel, group portraits, photographs (with family and friends), Surrey HC

Wealth at death £8949 3s. 4d.: probate, 27 Sept 1929, *CGPLA Eng. & Wales*

Brocas, Sir Bernard (c.1330–1395), soldier and administrator, was a younger son of Sir John Brocas (d. 1365) of Clewer and Windsor, Berkshire, and his first wife, Margaret (d. in or before 1366); his father's family was of Gascon descent. Although the deaths of two intermediate heirs would eventually make him his father's successor, as a younger son Bernard at first made his way as a soldier, starting with the Crécy campaign of 1346, and later fighting in other parts of France, notably Brittany, in Scotland, and in Spain. By 1354 he had been knighted. He joined the retinue of Henry, duke of Lancaster, accompanying him on an embassy to Avignon in 1354, and serving under him in Brittany in 1356; he may have fought at Poitiers in the same year. By February 1358 Duke Henry had granted him an annuity of £20 for life. Shortly after Henry's death in 1361 Edward III granted Brocas an annuity of £40; he became a royal chamber knight, and remained in the king's service thereafter. He probably fought in Spain in 1367. In 1376 he was granted the custody of Corfe Castle, Dorset, but surrendered it shortly afterwards, apparently in exchange for Odiham Castle, Hampshire.

Between 1377 and 1379 Brocas was captain of Calais, a post that led to his being involved in important diplomatic negotiations with France. In 1382–3 he was sheriff of Wiltshire, while in 1385 he accompanied Richard II on the latter's Scottish campaign. Probably in 1387 he became chamberlain to the queen. His position at court did not jeopardize his career at the time of the Merciless Parliament of 1388, and he retained his offices. In 1391 he acted as the king's attorney, and following Queen Anne's death in 1394 was granted a further annuity of £40 for his good service to her. He was clearly possessed of considerable diplomatic skills—on good terms with John of Gaunt, duke of Lancaster, he was also a close friend for many years of Gaunt's enemy William Wykeham, bishop of Winchester.

Brocas married three times. His first wife, whom he married before 1349, was Agnes Vavasour, of an influential Yorkshire family; he divorced Agnes in 1360 and married Mary Roches, the widow of Sir John Boarhunt, who brought him eight manors in Hampshire and one in Dorset, and also the hereditary office of master of the king's buckhounds. Finally, between December 1380 and May 1382, he made his third marriage, to Katherine Plaunk, the sister of Lady Elizabeth Clinton; Katherine outlived Brocas, dying in 1398. This marriage brought him manors in Wiltshire and Leicestershire. His landed acquisitions, and particularly those that resulted from his second marriage, along with the problems he encountered in securing his inheritance in Berkshire, had the effect of making him predominantly a Hampshire landowner. Consequently it was the latter county that he represented in parliament in 1369, 1371, 1373, 1380 (twice), 1386, 1393, and 1395. He also sat for Wiltshire in 1391. Beaurepaire, north of Basingstoke, became his principal residence, and he was a substantial benefactor to Southwick Priory (where he founded a chantry) and Titchfield Abbey. Brocas died on 20 September 1395, and was buried in Westminster Abbey, near the royal tombs.

Brocas was succeeded by his son and heir, another **Sir Bernard Brocas** (c.1354–1400), who was said to be aged about forty-one at his father's death, and so must have been the son of the latter's first marriage. Styled an esquire in February 1385, the younger Bernard had been knighted by 1390. He inherited most of his mother's estates, and also the office of master of the king's buckhounds, and he was among the knights retained by Richard II. He also appears to have acted as a feoffee for William Scrope, earl of Wiltshire, one of Richard's principal ministers. He may not have been assiduous in attending the court (surviving documents record him most often in

Hampshire, where he was appointed a JP in 1396), but he showed his loyalty to Richard II after the latter's deposition, taking part in the 'Epiphany rising' of 1400 against Henry IV. Tried and condemned for treason at the Tower of London on 4 February, on the following day he was obliged to walk to Tyburn and was there beheaded (hanged, according to the *Brut*). He was buried in the church of the London Greyfriars. Some time before 1380 he had married Joan (d. 1429), daughter of Sir Thomas Midelton. They had five children. The family was not treated vindictively by Henry IV; Joan was allowed her husband's goods, for the payment of his debts, and also her own dower, as early as 15 February 1400, and her elder son, William, was granted possession of his father's estates (valued at 200 marks per annum) on 16 November following.

HENRY SUMMERSON

Sources L. S. Woodger, 'Brocas, Sir Bernard', HoP, *Commons, 1386–1421*, 2.359–62 · J. S. Roskell and L. S. Woodger, 'Brocas, William', HoP, *Commons, 1386–1421*, 2.363–4 · B. Williams, ed., *Chronicque de la traïson et mort de Richart Deux, roy Dengleterre*, EHS, 9 (1846), 101–2, 258–60 · F. W. D. Brie, ed., *The Brut*, EETS, 2 (1908), 136 · *The chronicle of Adam Usk, 1377–1421*, ed. and trans. C. Given-Wilson, OMT (1997), 88–9 · M. Burrows, *The family of Brocas of Beaurepaire*, 2 vols. (1886) · W. P. Baildon and W. Clay, eds., *Inquisitions post mortem relating to Yorkshire*, Yorkshire Archaeological Society, 59 (1918), 3n. · *Chancery records* · C. Given-Wilson, *The royal household and the king's affinity: service, politics and finance in England, 1360–1413* (1986), 224–5 · CPR, 1401–5, 474 · CClR, 1389–92, 173 · CIPM, 17, no. 583

Likenesses C. A. Stothard, line print, 1810 (after tomb effigy), NPG · tomb effigy, Westminster Abbey, London

Wealth at death value of estates was £133 6s. 8d. p.a.—Bernard Brocas (c.1354–1400): CPR, 1401–5, 474

Brocas, Sir Bernard (c.1354–1400). *See under* Brocas, Sir Bernard (c.1330–1395).

Broccoli, Albert Romolo [Cubby] (1909–1996), film producer, was born on 5 April 1909 in Hoyt Avenue, Long Island, New York, the son of Giovanni Broccoli (c.1870–c.1932), a labourer, and his wife, Cristina, née Vence (c.1884–1965), a former cook to H. N. Marvin, whose Biograph company had discovered the pioneer director D. W. Griffith. His parents had emigrated from Calabria. An uncle reputedly imported the first broccoli seeds to America, and as a boy Broccoli frequently helped him on his farm in Long Island. He was educated at Rye Free State Elementary School and at New York City College, where he studied journalism.

Having abandoned his studies to farm land in Florida's Okeechobee region Broccoli joined his cousin Pat De Cicco in Hollywood in 1934. Having been briefly employed at a beauty parlour and a jeweller's he became a production assistant at Twentieth Century Fox. Settling into Tinseltown society he married and divorced Joan Blondell's sister Gloria (1910–1986), also an actress, in the early 1940s, during which time he also became friends with tycoon Howard Hughes, who appointed him Jane Russell's chaperon during the shooting of *The Outlaw* (1943). Cubby Broccoli (who was nicknamed after the cartoon character Abie Kabibble) made further useful contacts

Albert Romolo Broccoli (1909–1996), by unknown photographer, c.1975

while serving as entertainments officer for the US Navy's eleventh district, which assisted his rise at Charles K. Feldman's Famous Artists talent agency after the war.

In 1951 Broccoli received his first production credit, alongside De Cicco and Irving Allen, on *Avalanche*. Forming Warwick Films with Allen, he relocated to Britain and embarked on a series of pictures with Alan Ladd—*The Red Beret* (1953), *Hell below Zero*, and *The Black Knight* (both 1954)—even heading the second unit for the middle film's mission to Antarctica. In all he co-produced nineteen features with Allen, the most accomplished being *Cockleshell Heroes* (1955) and *The Trials of Oscar Wilde* (1960). However, following the failure of their Eros distribution company the partnership was dissolved in 1960. Broccoli's private life was equally tumultuous in this period. He had married singer Buddy Clark's widow, Nedra, in December 1951. But in 1958, just two years after the birth of their daughter Tina, Nedra died of bladder cancer. In June the following year Broccoli married the actress Dana Wilson (who had a son, Michael, from a previous marriage) in Las Vegas, with Cary Grant as his best man. Their daughter, Barbara, was born in 1960.

Broccoli had contemplated adapting the spy thrillers of Ian Fleming in the late 1950s but it was only after he went into partnership with Canadian producer Harry Saltzman that James Bond finally reached the screen. Sean Connery was cast as 007 in *Dr No* (1962), and an unexpected phenomenon was born. Laced with sex, designer violence, and exotic locations the series epitomized 1960s chic and tapped into the international fascination with 'swinging London'. It earned Eon Productions the chance to handle the Beatles' first film, *A Hard Day's Night*. But, because of Saltzman's links with Bob Hope the company made the forgettable *Call me Bwana* (1963) instead.

Nevertheless Eon was on a roll, with each successive Bond outperforming the last at the box office. However, Connery was becoming increasingly worried about typecasting and, following *From Russia with Love* (1963), *Goldfinger* (1964), *Thunderball* (1965), and *You Only Live Twice* (1967), he quit the series and Australian model George Lazenby

was drafted in for *On Her Majesty's Secret Service* (1969). Broccoli was also keen to try something new and, in 1968, produced the children's musical *Chitty Chitty Bang Bang*, from a Fleming story. He and Connery briefly reunited for *Diamonds are Forever* (1971) before finally parting in an atmosphere of mutual mistrust and grudging admiration.

Although 007's distribution company, United Artists, wanted Clint Eastwood, Eon gave Roger Moore the licence to kill in *Live and Let Die* (1973). But the film was more notable for the growing feud between Broccoli and Saltzman, which resulted in an acrimonious split after *The Man with the Golden Gun* (1974). The episode typified Broccoli's ruthless approach to business, his ready sense of grievance, and his tendency to vilify his adversaries—characteristics that tempered the geniality of his autobiography, *When the Snow Melts* (1998). Yet there was no denying his energy and his commitment to the Bond franchise. In 1977 he renegotiated his deal with United Artists to ensure creative control over the series, while sharing the financial risk. Consequently he took sole producer credit on all but one of Moore's remaining outings: *The Spy who Loved me* (1977), *Moonraker* (1979), *For your Eyes Only* (1981), *Octopussy* (1983), and *A View to a Kill* (1985). The latter saw his stepson, Michael G. Wilson, come on board as both co-producer and co-scenarist (with Richard Maibaum).

The recipient of the prestigious Irving G. Thalberg award in 1982, Broccoli was appointed honorary OBE in February 1987, while in France he was created a commander of the order of arts and letters. By then Timothy Dalton had assumed the mantle of 007 but neither *The Living Daylights* (1987) nor *License to Kill* (1989) were particularly successful, and critics began to doubt whether Bond had a place in the world of special-effects blockbusters and high-concept adventures. Yet Broccoli was sufficiently alert to the character's continuing popularity to fall out with yet another business partner, this time MGM/UA, over video and television rights to the series in 1991.

Michael G. Wilson and Barbara Broccoli supervised the Pierce Brosnan entry, *Golden Eye* (1995), which was billed as 'Presented by Albert R. Broccoli'. However, it proved to be Broccoli's last involvement with the Bond series, as he died of cardiac problems in Beverly Hills, California, on 27 June 1996, by which time, reportedly, half the world's population had seen a Bond movie. He was buried in Hollywood's legendary resting place, Forest Lawn, on 1 July 1996. He was survived by his wife, two daughters, and stepson.

DAVID PARKINSON

Sources C. Broccoli, *When the snow melts* (1998) · A. Lane and P. Simpson, *The Bond files* (1998) · E. Katz, *The film encyclopedia*, 3rd edn (New York, 1998) · www.uk.imdb.com, Jan 2001 · *The Times* (29 June 1996) · *The Independent* (29 June 1996)

Archives FILM BFI NFTVA, 'The world of James Bond: a tribute to Cubby Broccoli', ITV, 18 Aug 1996

Likenesses photograph, c.1975, Hult. Arch. [*see illus.*] · photograph, c.1976, repro. in *The Independent* · photograph, repro. in *The Times*

Brochfael Ysgithrog [Brochfael ap Cyngen] (*supp. fl.* **6th cent.**), king of Powys, enjoys a reputation enhanced by his son *Tysilio, the saint of Meifod. A poem ascribed to

Taliesin is in praise of another son, *Cynan Garwyn. A cycle of verses put into the mouth of Heledd, perhaps of the ninth century, describes Powys as 'the land of Brochfael'. In the twelfth century Cynddelw's poem in praise of Tysilio celebrates the generosity of his father, although a late Breton version of Tysilio's life portrays Brochfael as hostile to the monastic vocation of his son. Brochfael is mentioned in the life of another major saint, Beuno, whose origins were believed to be in Powys although his main church was Clynnog in Gwynedd. Brochfael's son Mawn is said in the life to have given Aberriw to Beuno 'for his own soul and that of his father'.

There are, however, major chronological and genealogical difficulties in surviving accounts of early Powys: first, there are two conceptions of the origins of the royal dynasty, one claiming descent from Vortigern, the other descent from Cadell Ddyrnllug, a man said to have been raised to the kingship from humble origins by St Germanus; second, while Brochfael's grandson Selyf ap Cynan is identified with the Selyf said by the *Annales Cambriae* to have died in 613, apparently at the battle of Chester against Æthelfrith of Northumbria, Brochfael's son Tysilio is said to have fought, before he became a monk, at the battle of Cogwy in 642 (identified with Bede's 'Maserfelth', at which Oswald of Northumbria was killed). The Brochfael said by Bede to have been appointed to guard the monks of Bangor Is-coed at the battle of Chester may have been another member of the dynasty and thus a kinsman of the king, Selyf ap Cynan ap Brochfael. The dynasty was clearly prone to repeating names. For what they are worth, the marriage connections of the family suggest a sixth-century date for Brochfael: his mother is given in *De situ Brecheiniauc* as Tudglyd, daughter of *Brychan; one of her other children is named as Sanand, wife of Maelgwn, king of Gwynedd (d. 549). Tudglyd is described as the wife of Cyngen, who is also named as Brochfael's father in the Harleian genealogies. Brochfael's own wife is said to have been Arddun, or Garddun, daughter of *Pabo Post Prydain. The Brochfael whose obit is given in the *Annales Cambriae* under the year 662, may have been yet another member of the dynasty; the addition by MS 'B' of the epithet Escithrauc (a form of Ysgithrog, meaning 'the Tusked') shows that the scribe identified this later Brochfael with the father of Tysilio, but he is likely to be mistaken. By the twelfth century, at least, Brochfael was part of the canonical early history of Powys, connected with other heroic kings and saints. The ninth-century Pillar of Elise shows a variant version of the foundation legend of Powys already in existence; it may originally have mentioned Brochfael Ysgithrog (as well as his descendant and namesake, Brochfael ab Elise), but the inscription was already partly illegible in the late sixteenth century when Edward Lhuyd made the first transcript.

T. M. CHARLES-EDWARDS

Sources I. Williams, ed., *Canu Llywarch Hen* (1935), no. 11, stanza 37c · P. C. Bartrum, ed., *Early Welsh genealogical tracts* (1966) · *The poems of Taliesin*, ed. I. Williams, trans. J. C. Williams (1968), no. 1 · A. W. Wade-Evans, ed. and trans., *Vitae sanctorum Britanniae et genealogiae* (1944) · E. Phillimore, ed., 'The *Annales Cambriae* and Old Welsh genealogies', *Y Cymmrodor*, 9 (1888), 141–83 [version A], 152–69 [A version] · J. Williams ab Ithel, ed., *Annales Cambriae*, Rolls Series, 20 (1860) [B and C versions, with A] · Bede, *Hist. eccl.*, 2.2 · M. Richards, *Welsh administrative and territorial units* (1969)

Brock family (*per. c.*1895–1960), illustrators and painters, came to prominence with **Charles Edmund Brock** (1870–1938). Born in London on 5 February 1870, the son of Edmund Brock (1841–1921), a scholar in medieval and oriental languages and a reader at the Cambridge University Press, and his wife, Mary Ann Louise, *née* Pegram (1836–1914), he was the eldest of a large family of which two other sons were also to make their living from their art. **Richard Henry Brock** (*b.* early 1870s), landscape painter, was also born in London, before the family moved to Cambridge where Thomas Alfred Brock, mathematician, was born, followed by **Henry Matthew Brock** (1875–1960) on 11 July 1875.

H. M. Brock, as he was to sign his work, described himself as an illustrator and watercolour artist. From 1895 until the outbreak of the First World War, Charles and Harry, as he was known to the family, were in the front rank of British book and magazine illustrators, with Charles also becoming established as a portrait painter. In order to avoid confusion with the unrelated homonymous portrait painter who was the son of the sculptor Sir Thomas Brock, Charles dropped his second forename in signing his work. His initial training was largely in the studio of the Cambridge sculptor Henry Wiles. Charles Brock came to public notice as an illustrator in the 'black and white' school led by Hugh Thomson with 130 pen drawings for Thomas Hood's *Humorous Poems*, published in Macmillan's attractive Cranford series in 1893. His wash drawings for the Tyneside publisher Walter Scott, who brought out *The Humour of Germany* and *The Humour of America* in that year, made less impact. In 1894 Macmillan printed a further 100 of Charles's pen drawings in an edition of Swift's *Gulliver's Travels*, also in the Cranford series. In the following year Macmillan published Galt's *Annals of the Parish* and Jane Austen's *Pride and Prejudice*, both in its Illustrated Standard Novels series. By this time, Charles was in great demand and was working for other publishers, including Service and Paton, who published his illustrations to Scott's *Ivanhoe* (1897) and Goldsmith's *Vicar of Wakefield* (1898). A high point of his work for Macmillan came in 1896 with a two-volume edition of Charles Kingsley's *Westward Ho!*.

The same publisher also brought H. M. Brock to prominence with Captain Marryat's stories, *Jacob Faithful* and *Japhet in Search of a Father*, both issued in the Illustrated Standard Novels series in 1895. In the following year Harry produced over 100 pen drawings for Cassell's edition of W. M. Thackeray's *Ballads and Songs* and in 1898 illustrated Elizabeth Gaskell's *Cranford* for Service and Paton. Later reprints of this title carried colour plates from his watercolours. In 1898 he illustrated *Scenes of Child Life*, by Lady Frazer. This was the first of a number of school texts in French to be illustrated by H. M. Brock, Siepmann's *Primary French Course* following in 1902 and H. F. Collins's

French Course for Schools in 1929–30, all published by Macmillan. Harry's pen drawings, which were much more forceful than those of his brother, gave a convincing, if imaginary, picture of French life. In 1928, when the opportunity to illustrate standard novels was almost non-existent, Harry painted thirty-two watercolours for G. Bell & Sons' *New French Picture Cards*, published to accompany textbooks by Marc Ceppi. Before the end of the First World War, the brothers contributed to *Punch*, and over seventy articles and stories in the *Strand Magazine* carried their illustrations.

Both Harry and Charles Brock benefited greatly from their introduction to the fledgeling London publisher J. M. Dent, for whom they jointly provided watercolour drawings for a set of Jane Austen's novels in 1898. Both were attracted to the architecture, furniture, and costume of the later eighteenth and early nineteenth centuries and set about gathering period artefacts for their studio, which they shared with Richard, although his interests did not lie in period illustration. Notable examples of Charles's work are the watercolours he provided for Dent's English Idylls series (1904–9) and English Essayists series, where his pen drawings are to be found in two volumes of Lamb's *Essays of Elia*. Harry's major contribution to this series was in the three-volume *Breakfast Table* essays of Oliver Wendell Holmes of 1902, which led to a series of well-known posters for Chivers, the Cambridgeshire jam manufacturers. He also provided the drawings for *Essays of Leigh Hunt* and *Essays of Douglas Jerrold* (both 1903), and *Sir Roger de Coverley and other Papers from The Spectator* (1905). The strength of Harry's drawing is particularly obvious in W. E. Mallett's *Introduction to Old English Furniture*, issued by Newnes in 1906.

Because of their versatility and willingness to take on such a wide variety of work, it is believed that the Brocks did not command the respect publishers accorded Arthur Rackham and Edmund Dulac, who were much less prolific. As a result, they did not have the opportunity to work on the lavish picture books issued by such publishers as Heinemann and Hodder and Stoughton between the turn of the century and 1914. Charles's best opportunity was to contribute coloured illustrations for Sampson Low's boxed, limited issues of Blackmore's *Lorna Doone* (1910) and three of Jeffrey Farnol's popular historical novels. Harry's finest colour work came in the large-format books of fairy tales published in 1913 and 1914 by Frederick Warne. Unlike his brothers, Richard Brock illustrated few standard novels. His work was published in such annuals as *The Prize* and *Chatterbox* and, in general, restricted to the illustration of children's stories, where his drawings appear weak when compared with those of Harry, who illustrated the popular school stories of Desmond Coke.

Much of the Brock brothers' later income came from uninspiring periodicals, children's annuals and the cheap 'budget' books sold in chain stores. Charles was also in demand in Cambridge as a portrait painter specializing in college and local dignitaries, and Richard apparently made a modest income from paintings, mainly in oils, of the local landscape. Both Charles and Harry were interested in the theatre: with Russell Flint, Charles illustrated *The Mikado* (1928) and *The Yeomen of the Guard* (1929), while Harry produced posters for the D'Oyly Carte Company and large coloured illustrations which appeared in the Christmas numbers of *The Graphic*, *Holly Leaves*, and *The Sphere*. He also provided a large number of attractive watercolour drawings of Gilbert and Sullivan characters for cigarette cards issued by John Player & Sons in 1925 and 1926.

The depressed years of the 1930s severely curtailed the market for illustration. Richard illustrated girls' stories for Blackie & Sons while Charles provided watercolours for Harrap's handsome editions of Charles Dickens's *Pickwick Papers*, *Christmas Tales*, *Nicholas Nickleby*, and *Martin Chuzzlewit* (1930–32). His best work of this period is in Annie and Eliza Keary's *The Heroes of Asgard* (1930) and Mrs Molesworth's *The Cuckoo Clock* (1931), both published by Macmillan. Charles provided spirited colour work for the book jackets of Jeffrey Farnol's novels, a task subsequently taken over by Harry after 1938. All three brothers exhibited at the Royal Academy and also at the Royal Institute of Painters in Water Colours, Harry being elected to the Royal Institute in 1906 and Charles in 1908. Charles, who had married Annie Dudley Smith, died in Cambridge on 28 February 1938. The couple had no children. Harry Brock died in Cambridge on 21 July 1960, survived by his widow, the former Doris Joan Pegram, and his children Margaret, Joan, and Bevis. It is not known where or when Richard died.

IAN ROGERSON

Sources C. M. Kelly, *The Brocks* (1975) · I. Rogerson, *The Brocks* (1985) · *WWW* [Charles Brock] · *WWW*, 1951–60 [Henry Matthew Brock] · S. Houfe, *The dictionary of British book illustrators and caricaturists, 1800–1914*, rev. edn (1981) · *Cambridge Independent Press* (4 March 1938) [Charles Brock] · *CGPLA Eng. & Wales* (1938) [Charles Brock]
Archives BL, corresp. with Macmillans, Add. MS 55235 · PRO NIre., letters to Lady Londonderry · U. Reading, Lester Corrall collection of H. M. Brock
Wealth at death £2457 18s. 3d.—Charles Brock: administration with will, 6 May 1938, *CGPLA Eng. & Wales*

Brock, Alan Francis Clutton- (1904–1976), art critic, was born in Weybridge, Surrey, on 8 October 1904, the son of Arthur Clutton-*Brock (1868–1924) and his wife, Evelyn Alice Vernon-Harcourt. His father was a barrister who forsook law to write on art and literature, regularly contributing articles to *The Times*, a path his son was to follow; his mother was an artist. His parents moved to Farncombe Lodge, Godalming, Surrey, and later they resided at the Red House, Godalming, a fine early Edwin Lutyens house. Clutton-Brock entered Eton College as a king's scholar in April 1919, and left in summer 1923 after winning a Fielder exhibition to King's College, Cambridge. At Eton he won several prizes for art and English verse, becoming a protégé of the classicist Andrew Gow, who encouraged his interest in painting; they met again at Cambridge, when Gow became a fellow and tutor at Trinity College in 1925. Clutton-Brock abandoned classics for the English tripos, in which he achieved a first in 1926. He proceeded MA in 1956. He painted pastiches of the Italian masters from the trecento to Titian on the large panels in the set occupied by a fellow (Richard Braithwaite) in the Gibbs building (later obliterated), and affected bohemian habits such as that of drinking brandy for 'elevenses'.

In 1927 Clutton-Brock married Shelagh Archer, whom he had met as a Newnham College undergraduate, and they settled in London, where they lived 'among beautiful objects and chaos overlaid with dust and cobwebs' (King's College annual report). Shelagh died in a road accident in 1936, leaving him with a daughter and a son; the son died of polio in South Africa during the Second World War.

Although Clutton-Brock studied for a while at Westminster School of Art (*c.*1926/7) and exhibited at the London Group, also holding some one-man shows, his charming oil landscapes, much influenced by Constable and French impressionism, did not establish his reputation; but he soon made his mark as a writer on joining *The Times* in 1930 and contributing to the *Times Literary Supplement*. Widely read and gifted, he produced prose that was always elegant and finely turned. He published a few popular books: *Italian Painting* (1930), *Introduction to French Painting* (1932), and a short life of William Blake (1933); a detective novel, *Murder at Liberty Hall* (1941); and for R. H. Wilenski's Faber Library, jointly with Adrian Stokes, *Cézanne* (2 vols.) in 1947–55.

During the Second World War Clutton-Brock served in intelligence with the Royal Air Force volunteer reserve Bomber Command. He had married again in 1936; his second wife was Barbara Foy Mitchell, with whom he had another daughter, and they lived for a while at Hadleigh, Suffolk. He became art critic of *The Times* in winter 1945, remaining there until 1955, the year he was elected for three years as Slade professor of fine art at Cambridge. He also served as a trustee of the National Gallery. On the death of a cousin, Mrs Whitmore-Jones, in 1955, he inherited Chastleton House, Oxfordshire, a fine but plain early seventeenth-century manor house, where the Clutton-Brocks were hospitable and lived well but in some domestic disorder.

As befitted a Cambridge man, Clutton-Brock was greatly influenced by Roger Fry, a family friend, and his lucid introduction to the exhibition catalogue for the Duncan Grant retrospective, held at the Tate Gallery in 1959, reflects both his allegiances and his critical objectivity. Witty and charming, Clutton-Brock could be trenchant:

> The story of its [the 'Post-Impressionist Exhibition' of 1910] reception has often been told, but it is still impossible to read any account of the indignation it provoked without being startled, more especially by the ferocity of cultivated and experienced critics who might have been expected to view these pictures with the indulgence they had been trained to give to the crudities of Cimabue. (Introduction, *Duncan Grant*, 1959)

In 1975 he suffered the first of two strokes which led to his death on 18 December 1976 at Chastleton House. He was buried on 22 December, probably at St Mary's, Chastleton.   DENNIS FARR

Sources private information (2004) · *Annual Report of the Council* [King's College, Cambridge] (1977) · *The Times* (21 Dec 1976) · *The Times* (20 Dec 1976) · J. J. Withers, *A register of admissions to King's College, Cambridge, 1797–1925* (1929), 570 · R. H. Bulmer and L. P. Wilkinson, eds., *A register of admissions KCC, 1919–1958* (1963), 52 · *WWW, 1971–80* · *WW* (1972)

Wealth at death £87,058: probate, 4 July 1977, *CGPLA Eng. & Wales*

Brock, Arthur Clutton- (1868–1924), essayist and journalist, was born at Weybridge, Surrey, on 23 March 1868, the third son of John Alan Clutton-Brock, a banker, and his wife, Mary Alice, daughter of the Revd H. J. Hill. After attending Summerfields, Oxford, he went to Eton College with a scholarship in 1882; he then proceeded in 1887 to New College, Oxford. At Eton, where he won an English verse prize with an ode in the manner of Shelley, and still more at Oxford, Clutton-Brock developed his love of literature and art, and the wit of his conversation and the brilliance of his circle at the university were acknowledged by all who knew him. He obtained third classes in classical honour moderations (1889) and in *literae humaniores* (1891). On leaving Oxford he was apprenticed for a short time in a stockbroker's office, but was called to the bar by the Inner Temple in 1895, and practised for some years. Meanwhile his natural bent for writing revealed itself in a number of early essays and poems, some of which were printed in a posthumous collection, *The Miracle of Love and other Poems* (1926).

In 1903 Clutton-Brock married Evelyn Alice, daughter of Leveson Francis Vernon-*Harcourt, civil engineer, and settled down to a life of regular literary and critical work. From 1904 to 1906 he was literary editor of *The Speaker* and a frequent contributor to the *Times Literary Supplement*. This latter paper, which was founded in 1902, owed to him much of its early success and wide reputation; indeed, its editor went so far as to say that Clutton-Brock 'made it'. After being art critic on *The Tribune* and the *Morning Post* for a short time, in 1908 Clutton-Brock joined, as art critic, the staff of *The Times*, for which he wrote on many other subjects as well, ranging from gardening to religion, for the rest of his life. In 1909, at the age of forty-one, he wrote his first important book, which was also considered his best, *Shelley, the Man and the Poet* (materially revised in 1923). He also contributed an introduction to *The Poems of Percy Bysshe Shelley* (ed. C. D. Locock, 2 vols., 1911). Clutton-Brock combined a serious appreciation of Shelley's poetry with a sober survey of Shelley's life in a way which antagonized the poet's more devoted followers.

The profound joy which Clutton-Brock took in his own daily work led him to accept William Morris's aesthetic approach to socialism, and in 1909 he joined the Fabian Society. When the First World War broke out he had just completed an appreciation of Morris for the Home University Library. The war wrought a considerable, if not a radical, change in his outlook, making him less of an aesthete and more of a moralist. In a series of articles in the *Times Literary Supplement* (republished as *Thoughts on the War*, 2 vols., 1914–15; see also *The Ultimate Belief*, 1916) Clutton-Brock preached against turning patriotism into a religion, as he alleged the Germans had done. His outlook became more definitely Christian, and in articles and

Arthur Clutton-Brock (1868–1924), by Sir William Rothenstein, 1919

books from 1917 onwards he professed a religion of love, laughter, and beauty which, had he lived longer, might have established him as a religious philosopher. He continued to produce a series of essays on art, literature, and life, written more for pleasure than for profit, which represent his mature thought and culture. While he repudiated the criticism of art in terms of morals which he found in men like Ruskin and Tolstoy, yet art, literature, religion, and politics were indissolubly linked in his philosophy of life. Thus his earlier interest in Morris's socialism led, in later years, to an active involvement in the Farncombe Labour Party.

In his *Studies in Christianity* (1918) religion had given Clutton-Brock 'a buoyantly happy mood', but in 1919 he told his wife that 'he felt he had attained his religious optimism too easily', and at the time of his death he was still seeking a constructive philosophy of life. Hence his *Essays on Religion*, posthumously published in 1926, have been described by B. H. Streeter, in the introduction, as 'an unfinished torso'. But although his work in this field thus remained imperfect, Clutton-Brock was placed by his contemporaries in the group of first-rate essayists which England produced in the first quarter of the twentieth century.

After three years of intermittent illness Clutton-Brock, died at his home, the Red House, Godalming, on 8 January 1924, leaving his widow and three sons, among them the art critic Alan Francis Clutton-*Brock (1904–1976). It was reported that his final act was to direct his physician's attention to the beauty of an iris.

M. P. ASHLEY, *rev.* ANNETTE PEACH

Sources *The Times* (9 Jan 1924) • J. L. H., 'Arthur Clutton Brock, 1868–1924', *TLS* (17 Jan 1924), 37 • [W. E. Barnes], 'The kingdom of heaven', *TLS* (22 May 1919), 276 • [E. de Selincourt], 'Clutton-Brock's poetry', *TLS* (1 April 1926), 246 • R. Beum, ed., *Modern British essayists: first series*, DLitB, 98 (1990), 69–73 [incl. bibliography] • A. Clutton-Brock, *The miracle of love* (1926) [introduction by Evelyn Clutton-Brock] • *The Observer* (13 Jan 1924) • W. Rothenstein, *Twenty-four portraits* (1920) • D. L. Murray, *London Mercury*, 9 (1923–4), 512–20 • J. L. Hammond, introduction, in A. Clutton-Brock, *Essays on life* (1925) • *CGPLA Eng. & Wales* (1924)
Archives U. Glas. L., letters to D. S. MacColl
Likenesses W. Rothenstein, pencil drawing, 1916, NPG • W. Rothenstein, chalk drawing, 1919, Tate collection [*see illus.*] • W. Rothenstein, drawing, repro. in Rothenstein, *Twenty-four portraits*
Wealth at death £2647 10s. 3d.: administration with will, 16 Feb 1924, *CGPLA Eng. & Wales*

Brock, Charles Edmund (1870–1938). *See under* Brock family (*per. c.*1895–1960).

Brock, Daniel de Lisle (1762–1842), judge, was born, probably in Guernsey, on 10 December 1762, the third son in a family of fourteen children of John Brock (*d.* 1777) of St Peter's, Guernsey, who had been a midshipman in the Royal Navy, and his wife, Elizabeth, *née* de Lisle, daughter of a former lieutenant-bailiff of the island. His brothers included Isaac *Brock, army officer. The Brock family was originally English but had been established in Guernsey since the sixteenth century.

After such schooling as the island afforded in those days, Brock was placed at Alderney under the tuition of M. Vallat, a Swiss pastor, afterwards rector of St Peter-in-the-Wood, Guernsey, and subsequently at a school at Richmond, Surrey. He was taken away at the age of fourteen, however, to accompany his ailing father to France, where the latter died at Dinan. He spent about twelve months visiting the Mediterranean, Switzerland, and France, in 1785–6. In 1798 he was elected a jurat of the royal court of Guernsey, and from this point on his name is intimately associated with the island's history.

On four separate occasions, between 1804 and 1810, Brock was deputed by the states and royal court of Guernsey to represent them in London, in respect of certain measures affecting the trade and ancient privileges of the island. In 1821 he was appointed bailiff, or chief magistrate, of the island, and soon after was again dispatched to London, to protest, which he did with success, against the extension to Guernsey of the corn law. In 1832, when the right of the inhabitants to be tried in their own courts was threatened by a proposed extension of the power of writs of habeas corpus to the island, Brock and Charles de Jersey, king's procureur, were sent to London to oppose the measure, and did so with success. Three years later Brock was once more dispatched to London at the head of a deputation to protest against the proposed withdrawal of the right of the Channel Islands to export corn to England free of duty. As a result of the deputation, a select committee of the House of Commons was appointed to inquire into the subject, and the bill was subsequently withdrawn. On this occasion the states of Jersey presented Brock with a service of plate valued at £100, and his portrait was placed in the royal court house of Guernsey. Brock was married and had two children, a son, who became a captain in the 20th foot, and a daughter. He died in Guernsey on 24 September 1842 and was given a public funeral, in recognition of his long and valued services to his native island.

H. M. CHICHESTER, *rev.* CATHERINE PEASE-WATKIN

Sources *The life and correspondence of major-general Sir Isaac Brock*, ed. F. B. Tupper, 2nd edn (1847), appx B · J. Jacob, *Annals of some of the British Norman isles constituting the bailiwick of Guernsey* (1830)
Likenesses portrait, royal courthouse, Guernsey

Brock, Dame (Madeline) Dorothy (1886–1969), headmistress, was born on 18 November 1886 at 496 Caledonian Road, Islington, London, second daughter and youngest of three children of George William Frederick Brock, commercial clerk, and his wife, Eliza Jane Wilkins. Sir Laurence George Brock (1879–1949), chairman of the Board of Control (1928–45), was her elder brother. The family moved about 1891 to the house at Bromley, Kent, which remained its base for more than half a century. The household she grew up in was happy and hospitable, prominent in the local Congregational church and liberal in outlook. The daughters attended Bromley high school, founded by the Girls' Public Day School Company, from which Dorothy, supported by a Kent county scholarship, entered Girton College, Cambridge, in 1904 to read classics. She spent six blissful years there, progressing via a first class in the tripos (1907) to a Pfeiffer research studentship (1909–10) and a seat, albeit lowly, at the Girton high table. Cambridge degrees being closed to women she took her BA (1907) at Trinity College, Dublin. Her dissertation on the Latin author Fronto, which earned her a Dublin LittD, was subsequently published (1912). A brilliant pianist, she was the mainstay of college concerts, as also of more frivolous occasions, and made many lasting friendships. She remained deeply attached to Girton and later on represented the old students on its governing body.

In 1910, realizing perhaps that a life of pure scholarship would not satisfy her human interests, Dorothy Brock joined the staff of the King Edward VI High School for Girls, Birmingham, where she discovered her true vocation. In January 1918, just turned thirty-one (and the youngest of fifty applicants), she became headmistress of the Mary Datchelor, an endowed girls' grammar school supported and managed by the Clothworkers' Company which from its site at Camberwell in south London served a lively clientele consisting in roughly equal proportions of fee-payers, with at best moderate means, and scholarship-holders from the elementary schools. Here Dorothy Brock was content to stay, declining attractive invitations to move elsewhere, until she retired in 1950. She made the school famous: for its scholarly attainments, achieved in part by unconventional teaching methods; for the variety of careers it opened to its pupils, in industry, commerce, and social service, as well as more

Dame (Madeline) Dorothy Brock (1886–1969), by Bassano, 1947

traditional occupations such as nursing (she was a member of two inquiries into nurse training, the Lancet commission, 1931, and the government-appointed Athlone committee, 1937); and most markedly for its all-pervasive music. She was alert to the ever-narrowing gap between schooldays and adulthood, signalized politically in 1928 by the lowering of the voting age for women to twenty-one, and in her benign conduct of the school she linked freedom with responsibility.

Dorothy Brock quickly made her mark in the Association of Headmistresses (AHM), of which she was chairman, 1927–9, and president, 1933–5, and was the first woman to chair the Joint Committee of Four Secondary Associations, 1935–7. Her management of meetings was relaxed yet businesslike, allowing scope for disagreements which 'left no sting' (*M. Dorothy Brock*, 24). She made her début on the national educational scene in 1919 as a member of the committee appointed by the prime minister to inquire into the position of classics in the educational system; in 1930 she became the first woman vice-president of the Classical Association. She was a member from 1931 to 1940 of the Board of Education's consultative committee on secondary education and hence contributed to the Spens report (1939); she served a long stint on the Secondary Schools Examination Council (1937–51); and she was a member of the committee on public schools which produced the Fleming report in 1944. Her presence on such bodies was made doubly valuable (and doubly onerous) by the general sparsity of women members and she seized every opportunity to promote awareness in government circles of girls' schools and their achievements.

Still at the height of her powers in 1939, Dorothy Brock grappled successfully with the many problems attendant on the evacuation of her school first to Kent and then to Llanelli in south Wales. During the post-war years before her retirement she played a leading part in the negotiations which secured voluntary aided status for the Mary Datchelor under the 1944 Education Act and in 1947 became nationally famous as the first serving headmistress to be advanced to DBE (she was appointed OBE in 1929). She frankly enjoyed her honours, which included the freedoms of the Clothworkers' Company and City of London (1936) and borough of Camberwell (1950) and an honorary LLM from London University (1947).

Dorothy Brock retired with her greatly beloved sister Elsie, who also never married, to Whitstable in Kent, where seabathing long formed part of their daily routine. As well as involving herself in local affairs, she was for many years a director of the University of London Press, overseeing in particular its output of school books. She died after a long illness on 31 December 1969, at Barham Nursing Home, Barham, eager to the last for news of the Mary Datchelor and perhaps unaware that its future within the evolving comprehensive system was precarious; it eventually closed in 1981. A memorial service was held on 20 February 1970 at St Martin-in-the-Fields, London.

Dorothy Brock was witty, eloquent, and handsome, dressing with a casual elegance which enhanced her feminine charm. Her interest in people of all sorts was unfeigned and she was an unfailing source of kindly, practical advice, backed by a moral authority made all the greater by the lightness of her touch. Normally high-spirited, she had her bleak moments, discernible only to the most observant. In good times and bad she was sustained, latterly as an Anglican, by a deeply held Christian faith.　　　　　　JANET SONDHEIMER

Sources M. Dorothy Brock, 1886–1969 (1970) · R. N. Pearse, ed., The story of the Mary Datchelor School, 1877–1977, new edn (1977) · M. D. Brock, 'The girls' school', Schools in England, ed. J. Dover Wilson (1928), 138–61 · M. D. Brock, 'The creed of a head mistress', The head mistress speaks (1937), 35–56 · private information (2004) · b. cert. · d. cert.
Likenesses H. Knight, oils, 1937, Clothworkers' Hall, Dunster Court, Mincing Lane, London; repro. in M. Dorothy Brock · Bassano, photograph, 1947, NPG [see illus.] · M. Codner, oils, 1950, Clothworkers' Hall, Dunster Court, Mincing Lane, London; repro. in M. Dorothy Brock · M. Donnington, bronze bust, Clothworkers' Hall, Dunster Court, Mincing Lane, London
Wealth at death £15,757: probate, 28 April 1970, CGPLA Eng. & Wales

Brock, (Arthur) Guy Clutton- (1906–1995), agriculturist and political activist, was born on 5 April 1906 at Lake View, Green Lane, Ruislip, Middlesex, the son of Henry Alan Clutton-Brock, stockbroker, and his wife, Rosa Gertrude Eleanor, née Bowles. He was educated at Rugby School and, from 1924 to 1927, at Magdalene College, Cambridge, where he read history. At one point he contemplated ordination and went briefly to Ripon Hall, Oxford, but he took up boys' club work instead, first at Cambridge House and then at Rugby House. He entered the borstal service in 1933, and in 1936 became principal probation officer for the Metropolitan Police court district. Meanwhile, on 14 April 1934 he married Francys Mary (Molly) Allen (b. 1911/12), daughter of John Nelson Allen, merchant. They had one daughter, Sarah (Sally).

A convinced pacifist, Clutton-Brock worked during the Second World War as head of the Oxford House settlement in Bethnal Green, establishing a training community centre. In 1944 he was appointed by the Allied Control Commission for Germany to direct relief for starving and homeless young people, and in 1946 he continued this work with Christian Reconstruction in Europe. He became convinced that the young needed direct contact with the land. He returned to England in 1947 to work as an agricultural labourer and market gardener.

In 1949 Clutton-Brock was invited to go to St Faith's Mission, near Rusape, Southern Rhodesia, where the Anglican mission farm was run down and threatened with a government take-over. His experience of agriculture had been as a labourer rather than as a manager. He did not run St Faith's farm as an agri-business. Instead he set up a non-racial co-operative farm. He summoned the men back from migrant labour in the towns. One of them, John Mutasa, became the farm manager. Much to the horror of the district commissioner and local white people, Clutton-Brock and his wife became part of a vibrant non-racial community. She set up a clinic for disabled children. He organized a debating society and invited politicians, chiefs, bishops, and professors to address weekend conferences. Ideas bubbled at St Faith's, and the young leaders of the emerging African nationalist movement came to the conferences and stayed on to talk with Clutton-Brock. He helped draft the constitution of the Southern Rhodesian African National Congress (ANC) and joined it when it was established in September 1957.

Clutton-Brock's personality was very attractive to young nationalists such as George Nyandoro, Robert Chikerema, and Robert Mugabe. He was wise rather than clever; humble but sure of what he believed; supportive without ever wanting to take a lead. He was absolutely trusted, respected, and revered. The Rhodesian regime, however, could not understand the motives of anyone who worked with Africans on terms of equality. In March 1959 the ANC was banned and 500 of its leaders and members were detained, Guy Clutton-Brock among them. He spent a month in prison, and on release became chairman of the Southern Rhodesia Detainees Legal Aid and Welfare Committee. Also in 1959 he published Dawn in Nyasaland and Facing 1960 in Central Africa, in both of which he set out his belief in multi-racialism.

In 1960, supported by the African Development Trust, Clutton-Brock went to Botswana and began a co-operative there. He also helped in the establishment of the Bamangwato Development Association. But Southern Rhodesia had become his home and he returned in 1964. By this time the nationalist parties had been banned and leaders like Robert Mugabe and Joshua Nkomo were in prison or restriction. Clutton-Brock kept the spirit of collaborative nationalism alive by inspiring another co-operative at Cold Comfort Farm, in a designated 'European' area only 8 miles from the Rhodesian capital, Salisbury. Young nationalists like Didymus Mutasa—later speaker of the Zimbabwe parliament—gained leadership experience at Cold Comfort. The daughter co-operative farm at Nyafaru on the north-eastern border with Mozambique brought Clutton-Brock into contact with Chief Rekayi Tangwena and his people, who were resisting eviction from their land. He became a major supporter and publicist for the Tangwena, publishing *Rekayi Tangwena: Let Tangwena be* in 1969. (Later, in 1975, Robert Mugabe escaped into Mozambique to join the guerrilla war by way of the Nyafaru co-operative.)

These activities became intolerable to the Smith regime and in January 1971 the Cold Comfort Society was declared illegal. Didymus Mutasa was imprisoned, and spent two years in detention without trial. Clutton-Brock was declared a prohibited immigrant. He and his wife were deported to Britain, where they settled in a farm labourer's cottage in north Wales. They led a simple life there but Clutton-Brock maintained a vast correspondence with Rhodesians both inside the country and in Mozambique. The leaders of all Rhodesia's many nationalist parties trusted him. He lobbied the British government and raised funds for relief in Mozambique. After Rhodesia's independence in 1980 as Zimbabwe the Clutton-Brocks decided not to return, other than for a brief visit, believing that they were now too old to be able to contribute. But Clutton-Brock continued to command respect from Zimbabwe's new leaders, and he became president of the Britain–Zimbabwe Society. He died on 29 January 1995 at Wynne's Parc Nursing Home, Brookhouse Road, Denbigh, of bronchopneumonia, and was survived by his wife and daughter. He was rapidly declared a Zimbabwean national hero and after cremation his ashes were taken to Harare and scattered at Heroes Acre (making him the only white man so honoured). The Zimbabwean government also honoured him by instituting the Guy Clutton-Brock scholarship, for a Zimbabwean student studying at Magdalene College, Cambridge.   TERENCE O. RANGER

Sources G. Clutton-Brock, *Cold Comfort Farm Society* (1970) · G. Clutton-Brock, *Cold Comfort confronted* (1972) · *G. Clutton-Brock and M. Clutton-Brock: reminiscences from their family and friends on the occasion of Guy's eightieth birthday* (1987) · *The Times* (2 Feb 1995) · *The Independent* (16 Feb 1995) · WWW · b. cert. · m. cert. · d. cert.
Likenesses photograph, repro. in *The Times* · photograph, repro. in *The Independent*
Wealth at death under £125,000: probate, 25 July 1995, *CGPLA Eng. & Wales*

Brock, Henry Matthew (1875–1960). *See under* Brock family (*per. c.*1895–1960).

Brock, Sir Isaac (1769–1812), army officer, was born in Guernsey on 6 October 1769, the eighth son of John Brock (*d.* 1777) of St Peter's, Guernsey, and his wife, Elizabeth, *née* de Lisle. In his youth he was an accomplished swimmer and boxer, reputedly precocious yet gentle by nature. At the age of ten he went to school in Southampton, and then moved to Rotterdam for tuition with a French pastor. On 2 March 1785 he became an ensign in the 8th foot by purchase, advancing to lieutenant on 5 March 1789 while the regiment was stationed in southern England. On 16 December 1790 he further advanced to captain, apparently after raising men for an independent company, and shortly afterwards he went on half pay, though no record

of this appears in the *Army List* from which his name is absent in 1791. Undoubtedly, though, on 15 June 1791 he secured a captaincy in the 49th foot, with which he would complete his professional career and life. He joined the regiment in the West Indies, serving in Jamaica and then in San Domingo. In 1793 he sailed to England on sick leave and undertook recruiting duties until the 49th returned three years later. He purchased a majority in the regiment on 24 June 1795, and the junior lieutenant-colonelcy on 25 October 1797, assuming effective command in the absence of the senior lieutenant-colonel Frederick Keppel, whom he formally succeeded on 22 March 1798. The 49th had returned from the West Indies in a poor state, but he worked hard to improve its efficiency.

Under Brock the 49th served in Major-General John Moore's brigade with the duke of York's expedition to The Helder in the Netherlands in 1799, taking part in the battle of Egmont-op-Zee. Brock led the regiment and acted as second-in-command for the whole military contingent during Admiral Sir Hyde Parker's expedition to Denmark in March–July 1801. He was present on the *Ganges* when Vice-Admiral Lord Nelson bombarded the batteries of Copenhagen into submission. Brock insisted that his soldiers stay on deck during this action, firing small arms and assisting the naval gunners when required. Neither he nor any of the 49th went ashore, but the regiment did provide a guard of honour in ceremonial dress when Rear-Admiral Thomas Graves was invested with the Order of the Bath by Nelson on the quarter-deck of the *St George*. On 25 August 1802 Brock and the 49th arrived in Canada. Initially stationed in Montreal, he moved to York (Toronto) in 1803 and sent a detachment of the 49th to guard Fort George on the Niagara River—the border with the United States. He soon proved a firm, but just, regimental commander, mindful of his men's welfare but disinclined rigorously to enforce petty regulations. On serious issues, however, he acted decisively. When a planned mutiny was uncovered at Fort George, he took personal control, sent the ringleaders for court martial, and swiftly restored discipline.

Brock returned home on leave in 1805 and was promoted colonel on 30 October, but hastened back to Canada early the following year when war with the United States seemed imminent. He stayed in Quebec until 1810, then assumed command of all troops in Upper Canada. Subsequently he acquired civil responsibilities as lieutenant-governor of the province. In this new capacity he established a reputation for administrative competence and fairness, especially gaining the confidence of the Shawnee Indian leader Tecumseh. Promoted major-general on 4 June 1811, Brock was so concerned about the continuing American threat that he persuaded the governor to delay sending the 41st and 49th regiments back to England. Even so, there were only four regular regiments (with a total of 1450 men) to guard 1000 miles of frontier. His caution was justified, as the United States declared war on 23 June 1812 and General Hull invaded Upper Canada with a body of American militia on 12 July. Hull soon withdrew into Detroit, however, where Brock boldly attacked him with 350 British regulars, 600 Canadian militia, and 400 untrained volunteers to force his surrender on 16 August 1812. When the enemy captured two brigs under the guns of Fort Erie, Brock summarily replaced the garrison commander. He was appointed KB on 10 October 1812, as Major-General van Rensselaer with another 6000 Americans sought to cross the Niagara River and advance on Montreal. Part of this force attacked Queenstown, held by the flank companies of the 49th and the York volunteer militia, during the night of 12–13 October. Sensing the crucial nature of this assault, Brock rode the 5 miles from Fort George, arriving on the scene at daybreak, 13 October, to discover that a party of invaders had scaled a narrow path to dominating heights and captured a British 18-pounder gun. Quickly realizing the inherent danger, he led an uphill counter-attack but was mortally wounded in the right breast by a rifleman, who picked him out in his full dress. His last words were: 'Never mind me—push on the York volunteers' (*DNB*).

Brock's body was carried into Queenstown, and then to Fort George, where, with that of Lieutenant-Colonel McDonell, his Canadian militia aide-de-camp who also fell on 13 October, it was interred in a bastion, which Brock had himself designed. In his memory, the 49th sought to purchase a portrait of its late commanding officer, but a suitable one could not be found. The House of Commons voted £1575 for a public monument to be placed in the south transept of St Paul's Cathedral in London; and pensions of £200 were awarded to his four surviving brothers, together with a grant of land in Upper Canada, as Brock had died unmarried. Precisely twelve years after his death, on 13 October 1824, the bodies of Brock and McDonell were reburied in a vault on Queenstown heights, where they had both been killed. Over the vault was erected a monumental Etruscan column with an internal, winding staircase, for which the provincial legislature had voted £3000. The monument was blown up by a disaffected Irishman on Good Friday 1840. At an open-air meeting held beside the ruin on 30 July 1841, presided over by the lieutenant-governor and attended by some 8000 people, it was agreed to replace the monument at public expense, and £5000 was duly allocated for that purpose. The new monument, placed on the original site, comprised a column surmounted by a statue of Brock and was set within 40 acres of ornamental grounds with entrance gates bearing the Brock arms. The York Rifles placed a stained-glass window in the memorial church in Queenstown, and his name was also commemorated in the township of Brockville, Ontario, on the St Lawrence River. Brock was 6 feet 2 inches tall, energetic, and erect though a trifle portly, and with a pleasant disposition and dislike of ostentation, characteristics that had been discernible since his boyhood in Guernsey.   JOHN SWEETMAN

Sources Army List · F. Myatt, *The royal Berkshire regiment* (1968) · F. L. Petrie, *The royal Berkshire regiment*, 1 (1925) · R. Cannon, ed., *Historical record of the eighth, or the king's regiment of foot* (1844) · *DNB*
Archives NA Canada, corresp. and military papers · Quebec Citadel Museum, diary
Likenesses J. W. L. Forster, oils, parliament buildings, Toronto, Canada · portrait, repro. in Myatt, *Royal Berkshire regiment*, 32

Brock, John (1834–1916), chemical manufacturer, was born on 25 August 1834 in Manchester, the younger of two children of William Brock of Nantwich, Cheshire. He was educated privately and later sent to Chorlton Hall School. Brock's career started with Crosfield and Shanks, chemical manufacturers, in St Helens, where after ten years he had risen to be manager. He left this firm in 1867, to enter into partnership with Edward Sullivan, James Sievwright, and John Crossley. On 1 September 1867 the partnership (Sullivan & Co.) acquired a 24 acre site. The British Alkali Works, or Brock's Works as it became known, with Brock as managing partner, was soon erected. It was the last sizeable chemical concern established in the canal region of Widnes, and its main product was soda ash from the Leblanc cycle. In conjunction with the works manager, Brock devised several improvements for the manufacture of bleaching powder.

Brock married twice, both marriages being childless. His first wife was Elizabeth Wilson (1835–1877); his second was Sarah Mowle (1855–1929), whom he married after the death of Elizabeth. In 1875–6 Brock gave evidence to a royal commission investigating the working of the 1863 and 1874 Alkali Acts. He was appointed a justice of the peace for Lancashire in 1881. His greatest influence came in 1883 when he was instrumental in establishing the Lancashire Bleaching Powder Manufacturers' Association. Under Brock's chairmanship this organization unsuccessfully attempted to regulate the market in bleaching powder by establishing quotas for its members and a fixed price for the sale of their products, and by intervening directly in the market to maintain that fixed price.

Problems within the Leblanc industry were patently clear by the end of the 1880s, and Brock strongly supported calls made by Sullivan for a closer union of the alkali manufacturers and more defensive measures to protect the Leblanc manufacturers from competitors using the more efficient Solvay process. Brock was influential in the brief negotiations that led to the formation of the United Alkali Company (UAC), which was the first industrial amalgamation of its kind, save perhaps the Salt Union formed in 1888. The UAC was incorporated in February 1891 with Brock as chairman, and pioneering rationalization brought brief initial success. Profits peaked in 1892 and thereafter declined rapidly, due in part to American tariff barriers. The UAC fought back by establishing a factory in Michigan (1897) which was run by the North American Chemical Company, of which Brock was president, but this venture failed to improve the fortunes of the company. He retired as chairman of the UAC in 1913. Thirteen years later the company was amalgamated with three others to form Imperial Chemical Industries. Brock was also vice-chairman of the Power and Gas Corporation Ltd (established 1901) and a director of Holywell–Halkyn Mining and Tunnel Company Ltd.

Brock was a man of few words and fixed opinions, a strict but effective disciplinarian, handsome in appearance, dignified, and always well groomed. He retired to Colwyn Bay, moving to The Cedars, Hoole Road, Hoole,

Chester, eighteen months before his death on 20 February 1916, which followed a short illness. His funeral was on 24 February at All Saints' Church, Hoole, followed by his interment at Christ Church, Colwyn Bay. Brock's sole beneficiary was his wife, Sarah.

ROBERT DAVIDSON, JR

Sources D. W. F. Hardie, *A history of the chemical industry in Widnes* (1950) · notes on Brock and Sullivan, British Alkali Works, Widnes, Ches. & Chester ALSS, MS D/3075/2 · K. Warren, *Chemical foundations: the alkali industry in Britain to 1926* (1980) · *Chemical Trade Journal* (4 March 1916) · *Chester Chronicle* (26 Feb 1916) · *Chester Courant* (23 Feb 1916) · W. J. Reader, *Imperial Chemical Industries, a history*, 1 (1970) · J. M. Cohen, *The life of Ludwig Mond* (1956) · d. cert.

Archives Ches. & Chester ALSS, United Alkali Company MSS · Ches. & Chester ALSS, MS D/3075/2

Likenesses photograph, 1888 (after portrait), Ches. & Chester ALSS · portrait, repro. in Hardie, *History of the chemical industry*

Wealth at death £13,428 13*s*.: Ches. & Chester ALSS, MS D/3075/2

Brock, Sir Osmond de Beauvoir (1869–1947), naval officer, was born at Plymouth on 5 January 1869, the eldest son and second of the six children of Commander Osmond de Beauvoir Brock RN, of Guernsey, and his wife, Lucretia Jenkins, daughter of Henry Clark, of Clifton, Bristol. Brock entered the Royal Navy in January 1882, and after leaving the *Britannia* served as a midshipman in masted ships for three and a half years. While in the *Raleigh* he was awarded the Royal Humane Society's certificate on vellum for saving a stoker from drowning in Simon's Bay. In his sub-lieutenant's courses he gained the maximum award of seniority, and was promoted to lieutenant in February 1889 at the age of twenty. He specialized in gunnery and served as gunnery officer in the *Cambrian*, and then for five years in the flagship of the commander-in-chief, Mediterranean.

Promoted to commander on 1 January 1900, Brock became executive officer of the *Repulse* in the channel, and afterwards of the *Renown*, the flagship in the Mediterranean of Sir John Fisher. In 1903 he commanded the *Alacrity* in China and was promoted to captain on 1 January 1904. He was flag captain to Lord Charles Beresford in the Mediterranean and later to Sir Berkeley Milne in the Home Fleet. Between sea appointments he served at the Admiralty as assistant director of naval intelligence and as assistant director of naval mobilization.

In 1913 Brock commissioned the new battle cruiser *Princess Royal* and joined the flag of David Beatty. He fought his ship successfully at the battles of Heligoland bight and the Dogger Bank, becoming Beatty's flag captain while the *Lion* was being repaired. He was promoted to rear-admiral on 5 March 1915 and given command of the 1st battle squadron with his flag in the *Princess Royal*. He followed in the wake of Beatty's flagship throughout the battle of Jutland, and when her wireless was shot away became responsible for passing on all Beatty's signals and reports. He was two years older than Beatty, but they saw eye to eye in all naval matters and were close friends. So when Beatty became commander-in-chief of the Grand Fleet, he naturally selected Brock to be his chief of staff. It was a wise choice: the studious and intellectual Brock was the ideal

Sir Osmond de Beauvoir Brock (1869–1947), by Walter Stoneman, 1934

complement. Beatty said of him in a letter: 'O. de B. has developed a tremendous capacity for work and is perfectly excellent, clear as a bell, and is of the very greatest assistance'. Brock was promoted to vice-admiral in 1919 and accompanied Beatty to the Admiralty as deputy chief of the naval staff. He became commander-in-chief of the Mediterranean Fleet in April 1922, and held the appointment for three years. His firm attitude to the Turks, after they had driven the Greeks out of Anatolia, was commended by the first lord of the Admiralty in the House of Commons in 1923. He was promoted to admiral in July 1924 and in 1926 hoisted his flag as commander-in-chief, Portsmouth. Three years later he was promoted to admiral of the fleet, and was placed on the retired list on 31 July 1934.

Brock married in 1917 Irene Catherine Wake (1889–1939), daughter of Vice-Admiral Sir Baldwin Wake Walker, second baronet, granddaughter of Admiral Sir Baldwin Wake Walker, and widow of Captain Philip Francklin who was killed at the battle of Coronel. They had one daughter. Brock was appointed CB (1915), KCB (1919), GCB (1929), CMG (1916), KCMG (1918), and KCVO (1917); he received the honorary degree of DCL from the University of Oxford in 1929; he was a commander of the Légion d'honneur and held a number of other foreign decorations.

A man of great tact and charm of manner Brock possessed a humility which endeared him to those with whom he was closely associated. He was brilliantly clever and a tremendous reader. His analytical brain was ever active, and his knowledge ranged over a wide field from art to nuclear theory. He was more interested in things than in people, but he was generous, tolerant, and a great example. Although he paid great attention to detail, he never lost sight of the principles governing a problem, and his judgement was sound. He died at his home, St Anns, Links Road, Winchester, on 14 October 1947.

W. S. CHALMERS, *rev.*

Sources *The Times* (15 Oct 1947) · *WWW* · private information (1959) · Burke, *Peerage* (1980) · S. W. Roskill, *Admiral of the fleet Earl Beatty: the last naval hero, an intimate biography* (1980) · *CGPLA Eng. & Wales* (1948)
Archives BL, corresp. with Lord Keyes | FILM IWM FVA, actuality footage
Likenesses W. Stoneman, photographs, 1913–34, NPG [*see illus.*] · F. Dodd, charcoal and watercolour drawing, 1917, IWM · A. S. Cope, group portrait, oils, 1921 (*Naval officers of World War I, 1914–18*), NPG
Wealth at death £21,512 4s. 1d.: probate, 17 Jan 1948, *CGPLA Eng. & Wales*

Brock, Richard Henry (*b.* **early 1870s**). *See under* Brock family (*per. c.*1895–1960).

Brock, Russell Claude, Baron Brock (1903–1980), surgeon, was born on 24 October 1903 at 840 Old Kent Road, London, the second of six sons and fourth of eight children of Herbert Brock, a master photographer, and his wife, Elvina, daughter of James Carman, of Hinderclay, Walsham-le-Willows, Suffolk. He was educated at Haselridge Road School, Clapham, and at Christ's Hospital, Horsham. An accident in the school laboratory, resulting in severe burns to his face and hands, may well have inspired his interest in medicine and he entered Guy's Hospital medical school in 1921 with an arts scholarship. After an outstanding undergraduate career he qualified LRCP and MRCS in 1926, and graduated MB, BS (Lond.), with honours and distinction in medicine, surgery, and anatomy in 1927. In the same year he married Germaine Louise (*d.* 1978), daughter of Léon Jacques Ladavèze, of Paris, a gentleman of independent means. They had three daughters.

Following resident appointments at Guy's Brock was appointed demonstrator in anatomy and in pathology, and passed the final FRCS examination in 1929. Elected to a Rockefeller travelling fellowship in 1929–30, he worked in the surgical department of Evarts Graham at St Louis, Missouri, and there developed a lifelong interest in thoracic surgery. On returning to Guy's he became surgical registrar and tutor in 1932 and was appointed research fellow of the Association of Surgeons of Great Britain and Ireland. He won the Jacksonian prize of the Royal College of Surgeons in 1935 and was elected a Hunterian professor in 1938.

Brock's more senior posts began with appointment as consultant thoracic surgeon to the London county council (1935–46) and surgeon to the Ministry of Pensions at Roehampton Hospital (1936–45). From 1936 to 1968 he was appointed surgeon to Guy's and the Brompton hospitals. During the Second World War he was also thoracic surgeon and regional adviser in thoracic surgery to the Emergency Medical Service in the Guy's region. Following the war cardiac surgery, and especially operations on the open heart, was developing apace. Brock played a major part in pioneering the surgical relief of mitral stenosis and of other valvular lesions of the heart. His introduction of the technique to correct pulmonary artery stenosis and right ventricular outflow tract obstruction in the beating heart was inspired by exchange professorships between himself and Dr Alfred Blalock of Johns Hopkins Hospital, Baltimore. Thereafter Brock, when not the initiator, was ever to the fore of new developments in this fast-expanding field of surgery. This came to overshadow some of his earlier contributions to lung surgery, the basis for which had been described in his own classical publication on the anatomy of the bronchial tree in 1946.

Brock was an outstanding diagnostician, a conscientious teacher, and meticulous in the care of his patients. He gave great service to the Royal College of Surgeons, serving on its council from 1949 to 1967 and being an active member or chairman of many of its standing committees. He was vice-president in 1956–8 and president in 1963–6. He gave the Bradshaw lecture in 1957 and the Hunterian oration in 1961. He was knighted in 1954 and elevated to a life peerage in 1965. On retirement from his hospital appointments in 1968 he continued in private practice for a while, and he also became director of a newly formed department of surgical sciences at the Royal College of Surgeons which had been set up during his presidency. Subsequent alterations to this department caused him much upset and disappointment.

Brock's medical awards and honours were numerous. He was president of the Thoracic Society of Great Britain and Ireland in 1952; and of the Society of Cardiovascular and Thoracic Surgeons of Great Britain and Ireland, and also of the Medical Society of London in 1958. An elected fellow of the Royal College of Physicians in 1965, he had become an honorary fellow of the American College of Surgeons in 1949; the Brazilian College in 1952; the Australasian College in 1958; the Royal College of Surgeons in Ireland in 1965; and the Royal College of Physicians and Surgeons of Canada and the Royal College of Surgeons of Edinburgh in 1966. He was honorary fellow or member of a number of surgical societies abroad, as well as the recipient of many foreign and domestic prizes and gold medals. He received the highly prestigious international Gardiner award for 1960–61, and was appointed Lister medallist and orator in 1967. He also received honorary degrees from the universities of Hamburg (1962), Leeds (1965), Cambridge (1968), and Guelph and Munich (both 1972).

Having been appointed assistant editor of the Guy's Hospital reports before his election to the senior staff, Brock was editor from 1939 to 1960. Thenceforward he contributed a stream of important papers on cardiac and thoracic surgery to medical and surgical journals and textbooks. He was the author of several important books: *The Anatomy of the Bronchial Tree* (1946), *Lung Abscess* (1952), *The Life and Work of Astley Cooper* (1952), and *The Anatomy of Congenital Pulmonary Stenosis* (1957).

Brock could be a difficult person to get to know and to some he seemed excessively fussy and meticulous. But he was a man of total dedication and integrity who gave unswerving support to those of his juniors who shared his own very high standards. His students were taught with firmness and courtesy. He was a shy, kindly man who could often seem brusque, particularly in the operating theatre. Outside his professional work he had considerable knowledge of old furniture and prints, and of history, including medical history. Less well known was his interest in private medicine: he served on the governing body of Private Patients Plan and was chairman (1967–77) before becoming its president. He was responsible for the discovery and restoration at Guy's of an eighteenth-century operating theatre on the site of the old St Thomas's Hospital.

After his first wife's death in 1978, Brock married in 1979 Chrissie Palmer Jones, his secretary, daughter of John Alfred Jones, secretary to a colliery. Brock died in Guy's Hospital on 3 September 1980.

REGINALD MURLEY, *rev.* TOM TREASURE

Sources *The Times* (5 Sept 1980) · *The Times* (12 Sept 1980) · *BMJ* (20 Sept 1980) · *The Lancet* (13 Sept 1980) · personal knowledge (1986) · private information (1986)
Archives RCS Eng., surgical notes
Likenesses C. Sancha, portrait, RCS Eng.
Wealth at death £92,607: probate, 29 Sept 1980, *CGPLA Eng. & Wales*

Brock, Sir Thomas (1847–1922), sculptor, was born on 1 March 1847 at Worcester, the only son of William Brock, a builder and decorator, and his wife, Catherine, daughter of William Marshall. He was educated at the Government School of Design, Worcester, and then served an apprenticeship in modelling at the Worcester Royal Porcelain Works. In 1866 he became a pupil in the London studio of John Henry Foley, a leading mid-nineteenth-century sculptor. The following year he entered the Royal Academy Schools in London where, in 1869, he won a gold medal for his sculpture *Hercules Strangling Antaeus* (priv. coll.). In that year he married Mary Hannah (d. 1927), the only child of Richard Sumner of Nottingham; the couple had eight children.

When Foley suddenly died in 1874, Brock undertook the completion of most of his unfinished commissions. The most important of these were the 42 foot high monument to Daniel O'Connell (1866–83, O'Connell Street, Dublin; another version, 1886–90, St Patrick's Cathedral, Melbourne), and the 15 foot seated bronze figure of Prince Albert, the central figure of the Albert Memorial (1874–6, Kensington Gardens, London). Brock's success in completing work led to many commissions for public monuments in his own right, so that by the time of the death of Sir Edgar Boehm in 1890, he led the field in official sculpture. Unlike Boehm, however, Brock also successfully tackled imaginative, 'ideal' sculpture. One example which received acclaim at the Royal Academy was *A Moment of Peril* (1880, Tate collection), which portrayed an American Indian on horseback, threatened by a giant snake. In its theme, its realism, and its vigour, it owes much to Frederic Leighton's *Athlete Wrestling with a Python* (1877, Tate collection), a seminal work of the New Sculpture, which Brock

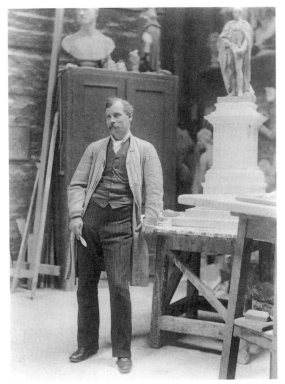

Sir Thomas Brock (1847–1922), by Ralph W. Robinson, 1889

had helped to cast. More typical of Brock's *œuvre* were the portrait statue monuments to Robert Raikes (1880) and Sir Bartle Frere (1888), both in the Embankment Gardens, Westminster, London. In 1883 he was elected to associate membership of the Royal Academy, which was followed by full membership in 1891.

In the latter year Brock was commissioned to design the new coinage effigy of Queen Victoria. His replacement of Boehm's 'small crown' with a tiara, a more prominent veil, and a shorter neck, resulted in an image of greater dignity and equal realism. It received widespread praise, with *The Times* claiming 'The likeness is good, and, as was to be expected from so scholarly a sculptor as Mr. Brock, the modelling is excellent' (31 Jan 1893). An equally successful work of this period but on a far larger scale was his monument to his close friend Leighton (1896–1902, St Paul's Cathedral, London). The recumbent effigy of the artist is flanked on either side by mourning figures representing Painting and Sculpture. This equality seems surprising, as Leighton was far more prolific as a painter than as a sculptor. However, his influence on a generation of sculptors including Brock, Alfred Gilbert, Hamo Thornycroft, and Harry Bates was such that Brock's tribute is entirely appropriate. The monument caused M. H. Spielmann to enthuse: 'In proportion, in harmony of line … in conception, in detail, in decoration, in spirit, it is not very far from perfect' (Spielmann, 26).

Brock's most significant provincial commission was for the massive bronze equestrian statue of Edward, the Black Prince (1896–1903), in City Square, Leeds. Although it shows some dependence on precedents from the Renaissance and on Emmanuel Fremiet's more recent *Joan of Arc* (1874, place des Pyramides, Paris), the statue is careful in its detailing and powerful in its impact. It perfectly symbolizes the democratic, patriotic, and civic aspirations of its patron, T. Walter Harding, lord mayor of Leeds in 1898–9. *The Black Prince*, together with such ideal works as *The Genius of Poetry* (1889–91, Carlsberg Museum, Valby, Denmark) and *Eve* (1898, Tate collection), reflects Brock's transition from the robust realism of Foley to the greater stylistic and psychological complexity of the New Sculpture.

The work which dominated Brock's later career was the Queen Victoria Memorial (1901–24, The Mall, London). Unusually, no competition was held to choose the sculptor. Brock's appointment came at the invitation of the memorial committee and reflected the fact that no other living sculptor had produced more portraits of the queen. The memorial was envisaged as part of an ambitious civic scheme, designed by Aston Webb, involving the transformation of the Mall into a grand processional route adorned with sculptural groups. This was only partially realized, whereas Brock's memorial was executed much as he had intended, giving it unexpected dominance. The memorial consists of a 24 foot high marble statue of the enthroned queen, surrounded by groups representing Truth, Justice, and Motherhood. These are surmounted by a gilt-bronze figure of Victory, supported by Courage and Constancy. Around the rim and at the outer corners are further large-scale allegorical groups. When George V unveiled the memorial in May 1911, he was so pleased with the result that in an impromptu gesture he demanded a sword and knighted Brock on the spot. Although most sculptures for the memorial were completed by 1914, the final groups on the surrounding plinths were not placed in position until 1924, two years after Brock's death.

Opinions have always differed over the merits of the Queen Victoria Memorial. From the outset, what was regarded as its allegorical pomposity aroused critical hostility. More recently, in *The New Sculpture* (1983), Susan Beattie castigated the memorial for being derivative, citing works by Alfred Stevens, Jules Dalou, and Alfred Gilbert as obvious precursors. Yet Brock can be equally admired for intelligent eclecticism in his use of these sources. Moreover, the sculptures have a fine sense of rhythm and proportion, and the imperial panache of the ensemble is undeniable. Aston Webb alluded to these qualities in his tribute to Brock as an artist 'highly sensitive to beauty of proportion, form and design and endowed with a keen insight into character, this being combined with great technical skill, which made him in every way a master of his craft' (*The Builder*, 8 Sept 1922).

Among Brock's later works are the monuments to Sir Henry Irving (1910, Irving Street, London), Captain James Cook (1914, Pall Mall, London), and Richard John Seddon (1911–15, parliamentary buildings, Wellington, New Zealand). He received numerous honours besides his knighthood, including an honorary doctorate from the University of Oxford (1909) and honorary memberships of the

Royal Institute of British Architects, the Royal Society of Arts, and the Société des Artistes Français. In 1905, the year after its foundation, he was appointed founder president of the Society of British Sculptors. His studio assistants included Henry Fehr and Francis Derwent Wood.

Thomas Brock died at 4 Dorset Square, London, on 22 August 1922 and was buried in Mayfield, Sussex. He was survived by his wife. Since his death his art historical reputation has dwindled so considerably that he has been dubbed 'London's forgotten sculptor' (Sankey, 61). His qualities of intelligence, punctuality, consistency, care, courteousness, and cost-effectiveness count for little when the product is considered reactionary and academic. He has paid dearly for fitting so well into his age.

MARK STOCKER

Sources J. A. Sankey, 'London's forgotten sculptor', *ILN* (Dec 1985), 61–4 · M. H. Spielmann, *British sculpture and sculptors of to-day* (1901), 25–33 · B. Read, *Victorian sculpture* (1982) · E. Darby and M. Darby, 'The nation's memorial to Queen Victoria', *Country Life*, 164 (1978), 1647–50 · B. Read and A. Kader, *Leighton and his sculptural legacy: British sculpture, 1875–1930* (1996) [exhibition catalogue, Matthiesen Gallery, London, 8 Feb – 22 March 1996] · J. Blackwood, *London's immortals: the complete outdoor commemorative statues* (1989) · J. Darke, *The monument guide to England and Wales* (1991) · M. Stocker, 'A great man and a great imperialist: Sir Thomas Brock's statue of Richard John Seddon', *Sculpture Journal*, 1 (1997), 45–51 · M. Stocker, 'The coinage of 1893', *British Numismatic Journal*, 66 (1996), 67–86 · B. Lewis, 'The Black Prince in City Square', *Leeds Art Calendar*, 84 (1979), 21–8 · S. Beattie, *The New Sculpture* (1983) · E. Gosse, 'The new sculpture, 1879–1894 [pt 2, 4]', *Art Journal*, new ser., 14 (1894), 200–03, 306–11, esp. 202 · S. Jones and others, eds., *Frederic Leighton, 1830–1896* (1996) [exhibition catalogue, RA, 15 Feb – 21 April 1996] · *DNB* · M. Stocker, 'Brock, Sir Thomas', *The dictionary of art*, ed. J. Turner (1996) · B. Read and P. Ward-Jackson, eds., *Archive 4: 18th and 19th century sculpture in the British Isles*, Courtauld Institute illustration archives (1976–), pt 7: *London* (1978) · J. Sankey, 'Thomas Brock and the Albert Memorial', *Sculpture Journal*, 3 (1999), 87–92 · *CGPLA Eng. & Wales* (1922) · *WWW · The Connoisseur*, 64 (1922), 121–2 · Graves, *RA exhibitors*

Archives Civic Museum, Dublin · Henry Moore Institute, Leeds · NL NZ · PRO, Mint 7/48 · V&A NAL, biography | CUL, letters to Lord Stamfordham and H. Baker · V&A NAL, letters to Lord Alverstone

Likenesses T. B. Wirgman, oils, c.1888, Aberdeen Art Gallery · R. W. Robinson, photograph, 1889, NPG [*see illus.*] · Russell & Sons, photograph, after 1901, NPG · photograph, 1903, repro. in *Black and white guide to the Royal Academy and the New Gallery* (1903) · H. von Herkomer, oils, 1908 (*The council of the Royal Academy*), Tate collection · R. Cleaver, group portrait, pen-and-ink drawing (*Hanging committee, Royal Academy, 1892*), NPG · Maull & Fox, photograph, NPG · Spy [L. Ward], cartoon, NPG; repro. in *VF* (21 Sept 1905)

Wealth at death £83,555 16s. 8d.: probate, 17 Oct 1922, *CGPLA Eng. & Wales*

Brock, William (1807–1875), Baptist minister, was born on 14 February 1807 at Honiton, Devon, the eldest of the three children of William Brock, brazier and ironmonger, and his wife, Ann, daughter of Thomas Alsop, pastor of the Baptist church at Prescot, Devon. William had one surviving brother and one sister. His father died, after a period of incapacity, in 1811, leaving the family dependent on the charity of relatives. William was educated first at Culmstock, and afterwards as a free scholar at Honiton grammar school. He was persecuted by the other boys on account of his tradesman father and dissenting religion.

Interest from a small legacy enabled him to attend a Mr Trenow's school for a few months, and his desire for learning was rekindled. In 1819 he spent a term under the guidance of the Revd Charles Sharp at Bradninch, near Exeter.

In 1820, aged thirteen, Brock was apprenticed to a watchmaker at Sidmouth, where he remained for seven years, often suffering on account of his religious beliefs, although they had not yet coalesced into convictions. After his apprenticeship he worked for two years as a journeyman watchmaker in Hertford. It was during this period, under the guidance of a local Baptist lay preacher, that Brock espoused specifically Baptist principles. He was baptized at Highgate Baptist Church in 1829. He entered Stepney College (now Regent's Park College) in 1830 and stayed until 1833, having been offered pastorates before his studies were completed. He accepted the call of the congregation of St Mary's Baptist Church, Norwich, in 1833. He had a tempestuous relationship with the church, resigning in 1838 over the issue of closed communion: Brock strongly supported open communion, that is, the opening of the communion table to all Christians, not only those baptized as believers. His church merely reappointed him their minister. Brock was prominent among Norwich church leaders for his outspoken denunciations of slavery, church rates, the corn laws, and bribery at elections. He was particularly interested in the work of the Anti-State Church Association and gave it his support. In 1835, while convalescing after an illness, he met and married Mary Bliss (d. 1872) of Shortwood, Gloucestershire.

In 1847 an eye disease was diagnosed, and Brock temporarily moved to London for treatment. He was advised to leave Norwich permanently for the sake of his health. At this time Samuel Morton Peto was building his showcase Bloomsbury Chapel and was looking for a minister to fill it. He invited his friend Brock to undertake the difficult task of building up a new church on the principles of open communion. Brock accepted in 1848 and remained at the church for over twenty years. An energetic preacher and organizer, Brock presided over the diverse agencies of the church, including a domestic mission to St Giles-in-the-Fields. He instituted the popular midsummer morning sermons for young men and women (collected and published in 1872).

He lectured widely in London and in 1859 delivered a sermon in the Britannia Theatre, at a time when the movement for theatre preaching was still young. Although opposed to the Crimean War and a member of the Peace Society, Brock published a memoir of the life of the Baptist general Sir Henry Havelock in 1857, which had an enormous circulation. He endured some bitter criticism from within and without the denomination for his portrayal of the 'Christian soldier'.

In 1865 Brock helped to form the London Baptist Association, and was elected its first president. In the following year he visited the United States, and on his return entered into the ritualist controversy. In 1869 Brock was elected to the presidency of the Baptist Union of Great Britain and Ireland. In September 1872 he resigned his post at Bloomsbury Chapel; his wife died a few days before he preached his farewell sermon, and one of his two daughters had died in childbirth in January of the same year. After three years spent in active retirement, Brock died from an attack of bronchitis at St Leonards on 13 November 1875; he was buried in Abney Park cemetery. The elder of his two sons, William Brock (1836–1919), was minister of Heath Street Chapel, Hampstead.

Many of Brock's addresses were on religious and political topics, and these sermons and lectures comprise the bulk of his published works. The best known are: *Sacramental Religion Subversive of Vital Christianity* (1850), *Three Sermons about the Sabbath* (1853), *Mercantile Morality, a Lecture* (1856), *The Wrong and the Right Place of Christian Baptism* (1866), and *The Christian Citizen's Duty in the Forthcoming Election* (1868). Harvard College conferred on him an honorary DD in 1860. G. B. Smith, *rev.* L. E. Lauer

Sources E. C. Starr, ed., *A Baptist bibliography*, 3 (1953), 155–8 · 'Memoirs of Baptist ministers deceased', *Baptist Hand-Book* (1876), 338–41 · G. W. M'Cree, *William Brock, D.D.* (1876) · C. M. Birrell, *The life of William Brock, D.D.* (1878) · F. Bowers, *Called to the city: three ministers of Bloomsbury* (1989)
Likenesses portrait, 1854, Regent's Park College, London · J. R. Dicksee, lithograph, BM · J. R. Dicksee, stipple, NPG · B. R. Haydon, group portrait, oils (*The Anti-Slavery Society Convention*, 1840), NPG · stipple, NPG · wood-engraving (after photograph by London Stereoscopic Co.), NPG; repro. in *ILN* (27 Nov 1875)
Wealth at death under £6000: probate, 4 Dec 1875, *CGPLA Eng. & Wales*

Brock, William John (1818?–1863), religious writer, was the eldest son of John Brock of Portman Square, London. He was educated at Magdalen Hall, Oxford, and obtained the degree of BA in 1852, and MA in 1861. After taking orders he entered the church as curate of St George's, Barnsley, in 1847, and was ordained deacon in 1852, and priest the following year. He left Barnsley in 1856 to become incumbent of Hayfield, Derbyshire, where he remained until his death. Brock was married, possibly in 1845; his wife, Anne, survived him. He died at Hayfield on 27 April 1863 and was buried there. His written works included *Wayside Verses* (1847), a volume of poetry celebrating the beauty of nature, and *Twenty-Seven Sermons* (1855), which ran to a second edition.

Jennett Humphreys, *rev.* Sarah Brolly

Sources *GM*, 3rd ser., 14 (1863), 801 · Foster, *Alum. Oxon.* · Crockford (1860) · Allibone, *Dict.* · *CGPLA Eng. & Wales* (1863)
Wealth at death under £300: probate, 7 Aug 1863, *CGPLA Eng. & Wales*

Brockedon, William (1787–1854), painter, writer, and inventor, was born on 13 October 1787 in Totnes, Devon, and baptized there on 12 November, the only child of Philip Brockedon (d. 1802), watchmaker, and his wife, Mary (d. 1837). Brockedon was educated at a private school in Totnes, but acquired his knowledge of science and mechanics from his father. At fourteen he took over the running of the watchmaking business for almost twelve months owing to his father's illness, and after the latter's death in September 1802 he spent six months perfecting his skills with a watch manufacturer in London, before returning to Totnes to carry on the family business for a further five years.

Early years In 1809 Brockedon's artistic, as opposed to mechanical, talents attracted interest from two local patrons, the Revd (later Archdeacon) J. A. Froude and A. H. Holdsworth, MP for Dartmouth and governor of the castle there; with their support he was able to go to London to study at the Royal Academy Schools and to pursue a new career as a painter. He exhibited at the Royal Academy from 1812, at first showing mostly portraits, but from 1817 he began to exhibit a series of ambitious large-scale religious subjects at the British Institution. The first of these was *The Judgement of Daniel*, which after its showing in London was also exhibited in Totnes and Exeter, and was presented by the artist in 1817 to the Devon magistrates at Exeter Castle (Exeter crown court). In the following year at the British Institution his exhibits included a sketch for a proposed altarpiece for Exeter Cathedral 34 feet in length by 20 in height, *St Peter's Repentance*, and *Christ Raising the Widow's Son at Nain*, for which he was awarded a prize of 100 guineas by the directors of the British Institution. Both were exhibited again in Exeter later in the same year; the altarpiece itself, unsurprisingly, was never realized, but Brockedon gave the *Christ Raising the Widow's Son* to Dartmouth parish church (*in situ*) in gratitude to Holdsworth. Later, in 1824, he presented another painting, *Christ in the Garden*, previously exhibited in Totnes in 1817, London in 1818, and Plymouth in 1820, to the parish church at Dartington (*in situ*) as a mark of respect to Froude. In making these presentations, as well as honouring his early patrons, Brockedon contrived to sidestep the problem faced by other aspiring history painters of a lack of demand for works of this type.

Travels in Europe Brockedon made his first trip to Europe in 1815, visiting France and Belgium. Following his marriage to Miss Elizabeth Graham (*d.* 1829) in 1821, he travelled to Italy, spending the winter in Rome, where he painted *The Vision of Zechariah*. The picture was exhibited in April and May 1822 at the Pantheon in Rome, and in London at the British Institution in 1823; he was subsequently elected to the academies of Florence and Rome and, as convention required, presented a self-portrait to the Florentine academy (Uffizi Gallery, Florence), as his fellow Devonians Sir Joshua Reynolds and James Northcote had before him. A son, Philip North, was born in Florence on 27 April 1822. Although he continued to exhibit the occasional religious picture, he increasingly turned to more modestly scaled historical and genre subjects, many of them on currently fashionable Italian themes, such as *Pifferari* (exh. RA, 1824) and *La Bella Fornarina Observing the Progress of her Portrait in Raphael's Study* (exh. British Institution, 1824). However, he became better known as a topographical landscape artist with a particular interest in the scenery of the Alps, and from the late 1820s onwards his work circulated more by means of engraving and illustrated books than through public exhibitions.

Brockedon's interest in the Alps began with his crossing of the Simplon in 1821 *en route* for Italy and his return by the Brenner Pass the following year. In July 1824, with Clarkson Stanfield as travelling companion, he made the first of a series of summer excursions; initially the project was conceived as a contribution to the debate about the route followed by Hannibal, but it broadened into a systematic exploration of all the alpine crossings. Other journeys were made in 1825, 1826, 1828, and 1829—the last as a way of seeking consolation after the loss of his wife in childbirth on 23 July that year. By his own estimate, Brockedon had crossed the Alps nearly sixty times by thirty different routes. The outcome was *Illustrations of the passes of the Alps by which Italy communicates with France, Switzerland, and Germany*, consisting of ninety-six engravings with descriptive commentaries issued in twelve parts between 1827 and 1829, and published in two well-received volumes in 1828 and 1829. This was followed by *Journals of excursions in the Alps, the Pennine, Graian, Cottian, Rhetian, Lepontine, and Bernese* (1833), an expanded narrative, without illustrations, of the excursions of 1824 and 1825. In summer 1837 he retraced the heroic journey by which Henri Arnaud led the defiant Waldensians back to their native valleys in Savoy in August 1689, and this formed the basis of the illustrations he contributed to William Beattie's *The Waldenses, or, Protestant Valleys of Piedmont, Dauphiny and the Ban de la Roche* (1838). Brockedon also wrote the sections dealing with Savoy and the Alps for Murray's *Handbook for Travellers in Switzerland* (1838).

In the 1830s and 1840s Brockedon consolidated his position among a group of travel artists and writers working for the burgeoning market for annuals and illustrated books. He compiled the text which accompanied *Finden's Illustrations of the Life and Works of Lord Byron* (3 vols., 1833–4), the production of which delayed another work he was editing for William and Edward Finden, the *Illustrated Road Book from London to Naples*; it eventually appeared in 1835, with engravings after his own designs and those by Samuel Prout and Stanfield. He produced the majority of the illustrations and wrote the descriptions in *Italy, Classical, Historical and Picturesque* (1842–4), dedicated to Prince Albert and claiming to be the fullest pictorial survey of Italy yet attempted. In 1846 he contributed the historical descriptions to the volume on Egypt and Nubia of David Roberts's *The Holy Land*.

Inventions Brockedon never lost his early aptitude for scientific and mechanical pursuits, and he applied for patents for several of his inventions, none of them connecting with his career as an artist, though the earliest might still relate to his initial training as a watchmaker. This was in September 1819, when he invented an improved method of wire-drawing which involved drawing the wire through a hole defined by diamonds or other gemstones in order to maintain a precise diameter. In 1831 he patented with Sampson Mordan an improved writing pen with an oblique slit in the nib. In 1838 came the first of a series of his patents relating to new applications of indiarubber, the potential of which was only just coming to be realized; he proposed using it with a combination of other materials such as felt as a substitute for corks and bungs, and he followed this in 1840 and 1842 with patents for further improvements in the same direction, involving the manufacture of fibrous materials coated in indiarubber for the cores of stoppers. In April 1843 he patented improvements in the manufacture of wadding for firearms, and in December that same year improvements in the manufacture of pills and medicated lozenges, and in preparing and treating black lead by solidifying granulated forms under pressure. It was widely believed among contemporaries that this last process was of direct benefit to artists, in that its application made it possible to produce much better pencils.

Further patents in 1844, 1846, and 1847 show that Brockedon remained interested in the applications of indiarubber or gutta-percha in liquefied form to waterproof roofs and fabrics and to improve buoys and buoyancy in boats. These, and his earlier inventions in the field, led to his becoming involved with the Manchester firm of Charles Mackintosh & Co., in which he became a partner in 1845. The patent of 1844 also referred to covering valves used in 'propelling by atmospheric pressure', which may have been prompted by Brunel's experiments in atmospheric propulsion on the Exeter and South Devon Railway, floated in the same year. Another patent of 1847 proposes burning gas instead of solid fuel to heat rooms and apartments, with the gas ignited over pumice-stone in a fireplace to give the appearance of a real fire. His last patent, in 1851, deals with applications of vulcanized indiarubber or gutta-percha in surgery, for example in plugging gunshot wounds, or in relieving the bowels or urinary organs by means of vessels activated by an air pump. The final line of the patent noted that this arrangement might also be applied to the milking of cows.

Later years Brockedon helped to form the Royal Geographical Society in 1830: he was a member of its first council and was elected a fellow in 1831. He was elected a member of the Athenaeum on 12 June 1830, and on 18 December 1834 a fellow of the Royal Society. He also founded the Graphic, an art society, in 1833. The full extent of his intellectual interests and associations becomes apparent from the pages of two volumes he compiled as an inheritance for his son of portrait drawings in pencil, each accompanied by an autograph letter from the sitter, and which he referred to as 'Philip's book of his father's friends' (letter from Henry Hopley White to the artist, NPG, Heinz Archive). These 104 drawings constitute an informal record of his great contemporaries, and range over the worlds of art, literature, geography, and science in which Brockedon himself had moved. The series begins in 1823 and continues until July 1849, but the son for whom it was intended, at that time a promising pupil of Brunel, died of consumption on 13 November 1849 aged only twenty-seven. The albums passed instead to Brockedon's daughter Elizabeth, and were bequeathed to the National Gallery by her son in 1926. The drawings were formally transferred to the National Portrait Gallery in 1994.

Brockedon married Anna Maria, widow of Captain Farwell of Totnes, on 8 May 1839; there were no children by this second marriage. His health declined after the loss of his son; he suffered from gallstones for several years and finally succumbed to an attack of jaundice. He died on 29 August 1854 at his home—29 Devonshire Street, Queen Square, Bloomsbury, London—and was buried at St George the Martyr, Hunter Street, Brunswick Square, Bloomsbury on 2 September. His second wife survived him. Examples of his work are held in the British Museum and the Victoria and Albert Museum, London.

NICHOLAS ALFREY

Sources DNB · Blewitt's panorama of Torquay: a descriptive and historical sketch of the district comprised between the Dart and the Teign (1832), 271–4 · patent office abstracts · G. Pycroft, Art in Devonshire (1883) · R. Ormond, Early Victorian portraits, 1 (1973), 554–6 · Graves, Brit. Inst. · Graves, RA exhibitors · 'Cunningham's town and table talk', ILN (2 Sept 1854), 206 · E. Windeatt, Transactions of Devonshire Association of Literature, Science and Art, 9, 243–9 · Trewman's Exeter Flying Post (23 April 1817) · Trewman's Exeter Flying Post (24 July 1817) · Trewman's Exeter Flying Post (30 July 1818) · Trewman's Exeter Flying Post (10 June 1824) · Exeter Gazette (18 Nov 1854) · d. cert. · IGI · will, PRO, PROB 11/2201, sig. 890 · D. Robertson, Sir Charles Eastlake and the Victorian art world (Princeton, 1978) · J. Hamilton, 'Artists, scientists and events', Fields of influence: conjunctions of artists and scientists, 1815–1860, ed. J. Hamilton (2001)

Archives Devon RO · Exeter Central Library, west country studies library · John Murray, London · NPG · NPG, letters · RGS · V&A, 2962–1876; 318–1887; 179–1889

Likenesses W. Brockedon, self-portrait, 1822, Uffizi Gallery, Florence; repro. in Burlington Magazine (Sept 1971), 562 · C. Turner, mezzotint, exh. RA 1833, BM · engraving, 1835 (after Turner) · W. Newton, miniature, exh. RA 1853 · C. Stanfield, pencil and coloured chalk drawing, NPG

Wealth at death owned house in Devon and house in London; pictures; books; drawings; prints; articles of vertu; left several bequests of money, some of thousands of pounds, to several people apart from family: will, PRO, PROB 11/2201, sig. 890

Brockett, John Trotter (bap. 1788, d. 1842), antiquary, was baptized on 21 September 1788 at Witton Gilbert, co. Durham. His father, another John Brockett (1764–1827), was deputy protonotary in the courts of Durham and a skilled mathematician; his mother was Frances Sophia Trotter (bap. 1770, d. 1833). In his childhood his parents moved to Gateshead, and he was educated at the school of the Unitarian minister William Turner (1761–1859) of Newcastle. Having trained in the law, he was admitted an attorney, and practised for many years at Newcastle in the mayor's and sheriff's courts, dealing reliably with tenures and conveyancing. His wife, Isabella (d. 1865), whom he married on 26 February 1814, was the eldest daughter of John Bell, a merchant. His brother William Henry Brockett was a Newcastle merchant, a principal proprietor of the Gateshead Observer, secretary of the Gateshead dispensary, and a prominent local politician.

Brockett was a keen numismatist and was also interested in antiquities and philology. He built up considerable collections of books, coins, and medals, and when in 1823 he offered some of them for sale by auction at Sothebys, the sale of the latter two collections lasted ten days and raised £1760; the book sale lasted fourteen days and raised £4260. In 1818 Brockett published Hints on the Propriety of Establishing a Typographical Society in Newcastle, which led to the foundation of such a society, and initiated the production of an interesting series of privately printed tracts at Newcastle, to which he himself contributed four tractates. In the same year, 1818, he also published *An enquiry into the question whether the freeholders of the town and county of Newcastle-upon-Tyne are entitled to vote for members of parliament for the county of Northumberland*, and in 1825 the first edition of his *Glossary of North Country Words in Use* appeared. The manuscript collections for this valuable work were not originally intended for publication, and passed into the library of John George Lambton, afterwards Lord Durham, but he agreed to their publication. A much revised second edition was published in 1829; a third was in preparation at the time of the author's death, and was published, under the editorship of his son W. E. Brockett, in 1846. Brockett also compiled a list of seventeenth-century tradesmen's tokens in the collections of the Society of Antiquaries of Newcastle upon Tyne, arranged according to counties and published by that society in 1854. Memoirs by him of the engravers Thomas and John Bewick prefaced the 1820 edition of Thomas Bewick's *Select Fables*. In 1882 a *Glossographia Anglicana*, from a manuscript left by Brockett, was privately printed by the Newcastle Typographical Society as part of the so-called 'Sette of odd volumes', with a biographical sketch of the author by Frederick Bloomer of Newcastle.

Brockett was a member of the Newcastle Literary and Philosophical Society, and served as a member of its committee of management, and later as a trustee and secretary from 1837 until his death. He was a founder member of the Society of Antiquaries of Newcastle upon Tyne, itself an offshoot of the previous society, and served on its council. He was elected a fellow of the Society of Antiquaries of London about 1822. He died at his home, 14 Albion Place, Newcastle, on 12 October 1842, leaving two sons and a daughter. C. W. SUTTON, *rev.* C. M. FRASER

Sources R. Welford, *Men of mark 'twixt Tyne and Tweed*, 1 (1895), 390–6 · 'Biographies of contributors to the society's literature', *Archaeologia Aeliana*, 3rd ser., 10 (1913), 116–19 · J. Fenwick, *Biographical sketch of … John Trotter Brockett* (1843) [grangerized copies, Newcastle Central Library] · N. McCord, 'Gateshead politics in the age of reform', *Northern History*, 4 (1969), 167–83, esp. 168–72
Archives Northumbd RO, memoranda, NRO 93 (ZAN M13/C1)
Likenesses W. Collard, engraving, 1824 (after drawing by W. Nicholson), repro. in *Glossary*, 3rd edn (1846), frontispiece · Sprague & Co., photograph, repro. in *Archaeologia Aeliana*, 11, 2nd ser. (1886), pl. 14

Brockhurst, Gerald Leslie (1890–1978), painter and printmaker, was born on 31 October 1890 in the Edgbaston district of Birmingham, and registered as the son of Arthur Brockhurst, a coal merchant: the various mythologies surrounding his early life established a pattern of lifelong ambiguities and energetic self-promotion. By 1901 he was registered at the Birmingham School of Art, where his precocious talent won him a place at the Royal Academy Schools, which he entered in 1907. Here, among other awards, he won the gold medal and travelling scholarship, the latter enabling him to visit Paris and Italy where he studied the art of the fifteenth-century Italian painters and more specifically the work of Piero della Francesca, Botticelli, and Leonardo da Vinci. Their influence was to

be central to the evolution of his own artistic development. In 1914 he married his first wife, Anaïs, *née* Folin, a Frenchwoman whose distinctive features provided the inspiration for many of his early portraits (such as *Ranunculus*, 1914, Sheffield City Art Galleries). From 1915 to 1919 Brockhurst and Anaïs lived in Ireland, where they were introduced by Oliver St John Gogarty to Augustus John and his circle. In 1919 the first significant exhibition of Brockhurst's work was held at the Chenil Galleries in London, where he returned to live in that year. Contemporary reviews of the exhibition spoke of his art as giving 'an edge to forms which vision does not experience' (*Vogue*, 15 April 1919). This 'edge' was to characterize the best of all his subsequent work.

It was during the 1920s and 1930s that Brockhurst established himself first as a printmaker of outstanding virtuosity and second as one of the most original and successful portrait painters of his generation. Both printmaking and portraiture were notoriously over-subscribed in the inter-war years but, concentrating almost exclusively on female portraits and frequently using his wife as his model, he produced a large body of memorable etchings throughout the 1920s, often repeating the image in pencil and oil. An example of this process is his exceptional male portrait of Henry Rushbury (1927, Carnegie Museum of Art, Pittsburgh, Pennsylvania). By 1930, while still pursuing printmaking, he had turned increasingly to painting, establishing for himself a role as a portraitist of rare power and vision. Working with a new model, Kathleen Woodward (whom he met when she was sixteen, and renamed Dorette, and who later became his second wife after he and his first wife divorced in 1940), he was inspired to create some of his most highly charged images, as, for example, the etching *Adolescence* (1932) and the painting *Dorette* (1933, Harris Museum and Art Gallery, Preston). Later sitters included the actresses Merle Oberon (exh. RA, 1937; priv. coll.) and Marlene Dietrich (exh. RA, 1939; priv. coll.) and the duchess of Windsor (1939, National Portrait Gallery, London).

In 1939, at the height of his career, Brockhurst moved to the United States, where he remained for the rest of his life, living first in New York city and later in New Jersey. Although he continued to paint and undertook many commissions, he never again attained that powerful combination of technical prowess and psychological intensity which characterized the etched and painted work of his earlier career. Brockhurst died on 4 May 1978 in Franklin Lakes, New Jersey, where he and Dorette had made their home. ANNE L. GOODCHILD

Sources A. Goodchild, *A dream of fair women: an exhibition of the work of Gerald Leslie Brockhurst RA (1890–1978), painter and etcher* (1986) [exhibition catalogue, Sheffield, Birmingham and NPG, Dec 1986–May 1987] · H. Stokes, 'The etchings of G. L. Brockhurst', *Print Collector's Quarterly*, 11 (1924), 409–24 · H. J. Wright, 'Catalogue of the etchings of G. L. Brockhurst', *Print Collector's Quarterly*, 22 (1935), 62–77 · *Vogue* (April 1919) · M. F. Symmes, 'Gerald Leslie Brockhurst's portraits of Henry Rushbury', *Print Review*, 17 (1983), 51–62
Likenesses H. Todd, photograph, 1 Feb 1937, Hult. Arch. · photographs, 1937–9, Hult. Arch. · H. Coster, photographs, c.1938, NPG ·

photograph, 1947, NPG · G. L. Brockhurst, self-portrait, chalk, 1949, priv. coll. · Kirby, drawing, Chelsea arts club

Brockie, Donald Andrew [name in religion Marianus]

(1687–1755), Benedictine monk and historian, was born at Edinburgh on 2 December 1687, the son of George Brockie, a protestant, and Isabel (née Farquharson), a Catholic. The family moved to Arbroath, where George, a lawyer, was notary public and clerk of regality, and became a Catholic before his death in 1708. Brockie was brought up in the Catholic faith and, having completed his schooling at Aberdeen grammar school and entered Aberdeen University, went in 1705 to the Scots abbey at Regensburg.

In 1707 Brockie received the monastic habit, taking the religious name Marianus, and on 25 February 1708 made his vows. He studied philosophy with the Franciscans in Regensburg, thereby becoming interested in the Franciscan theologian John Duns Scotus; he then studied theology at St Emmeran in Regensburg and became acquainted with the Maurists' historical work. In 1713 he was ordained priest.

Brockie's early academic career was meteoric. Already he had published *Scotus a Scoto propugnatus* (1711), asserting Scotus's Scottish origin. Sent in 1711 to complete his theological studies at Erfurt University, he graduated master of theology in 1714 and began to teach philosophy. In 1717 he published an introduction to logic, *Ars philosophiae loquendi*, was made professor and assessor in the faculty of philosophy, defended his doctoral thesis, 'De charactere sacramentali', and graduated doctor of theology. Then in 1719 the Regensburg abbot appointed him prior of the Scots monastery in Erfurt.

Almost at once Brockie took part in the Jansenist controversy by publishing *Examen theologicum doctrinae Quesnellianae* (1720), in which he vigorously attacked both the leading Jansenists and their chief opponents, the Jesuits. In the ensuing dispute with the local Jesuits Brockie, supported by the university (where Scottish Benedictines traditionally held the chair of philosophy), emerged victorious. He was, however, disputatious by temperament and continued to engage in strife in various quarters, until in 1727 his abbot removed him from Erfurt and sent him to the Scottish mission.

Little is known of Brockie's twelve years in Scotland. He was stationed initially in Strathavon in the north-east, and in 1731 he took six boys to the Scots seminary in Regensburg. Having returned to Scotland, he is recorded in 1734 and 1736 as working in Edinburgh. Finally in 1739 he took five boys to Regensburg, and this time, his health being impaired, he remained there.

The rest of Brockie's life was spent in compiling two very large and ambitious works. Having agreed to edit an enlarged edition of L. Holstenius's *Codex regularum*, he set to work and was eminently successful. The result was an edition in six large folio volumes, published posthumously at Augsburg in 1759, of the extant rules of religious orders. The first volume was his scholarly edition of Holstenius's work; the remaining five were his work alone.

Simultaneously with this, Brockie was preparing a second major work, a comprehensive Scottish *Monasticon*. He had investigated the monastic archives in Regensburg and Erfurt, and while in Edinburgh had worked on the collections in the Advocates' Library. A prospectus of the three projected volumes was printed in 1752 and a fair copy of his script was made by a fellow monk, but the work was never published.

Brockie died at the Scots abbey, Regensburg, on 2 December 1755, having been prior for about four years. He has never been given adequate credit for his lion's share of the *Codex regularum* and has received blame rather than credit for his *Monasticon*. It is clear that he accepted dubious or spurious documents uncritically, that he made judgements according to his prejudices, and that he altered the text of some documents. Nevertheless the *Monasticon* contains much valuable material and later writers have used it, though sometimes with unhappy results. Brockie to this day remains something of an enigma.   MARK DILWORTH

Sources L. Hammermayer, 'Marianus Brockie und Oliver Legipont', *Studien und Mitteilungen zur Geschichte des Benediktinerordens*, 71 (1961), 69–121 · H. Docherty, 'The Brockie forgeries', *Innes Review*, 16 (1965), 79–127 · M. Dilworth, 'The Brockie forgeries', *Innes Review*, 16 (1965), 220–21 · J. F. S. Gordon, ed., *The Catholic church in Scotland* (1874) · P. J. Anderson, ed., *Records of the Scots colleges at Douai, Rome, Madrid, Valladolid and Ratisbon*, New Spalding Club, 30 (1906) · H. Flachenecker, *Schottenklöster / Irische Benediktinerkonvente im hochmittelalterlichen Deutschland* (1995) · *Rotula*, Munich University Library [death notice]
Archives Scottish Catholic Archives, Edinburgh

Brockington, Sir William Allport

(1871–1959), educational administrator, was born at 62 Constitution Hill, Birmingham, on 18 June 1871, the son of Thomas Alfred Brockington (d. in or before 1898), a gold beater, and his wife, Fanny Allport. Educated at King Edward VI Grammar School, Birmingham, and Mason College, he graduated BA as a London University external candidate with first-class honours in English in 1890, taking an MA in 1893.

After spending the next seven years lecturing at Mason College, Brockington went as principal to the Victoria Institute, Worcester, in 1898, marrying Jessie Mac Geoch (1869/70–1951), daughter of Alexander Mac Geoch, a draper, on 23 August in the same year. In 1903 he was appointed director of education for Leicestershire county council where he stayed for the next forty-four years, becoming, in the process, one of the most distinguished county education officers of the first half of the twentieth century.

Brockington's first task when the new local education authority (LEA), created by the 1902 Education Act, came into being on 1 July 1903 was to centralize the education administration previously undertaken by numerous school boards. Accordingly, by 1915, this had been concentrated in the county education offices with a staff of thirty-eight of whom Brockington was to remain both the only graduate and the only former teacher until his retirement. He next addressed the problem of numerous, small, voluntary church elementary schools inherited by the new authority, replacing them with council schools whenever possible. Nevertheless, in 1915, there were still 189 church schools and only 74 council schools in the county.

In 1917, however, the wartime shortage of teachers gave Brockington the opportunity to begin the restructuring of the county's elementary schools. Showing remarkable diplomacy, he convinced the managers of the church school in the village of Enderby of the wisdom of admitting all the children over eleven, while the council school admitted the juniors, anticipating by a decade the kind of reorganization advocated by the Hadow report of 1926. This policy of 'beheading' schools, despite considerable opposition, was vigorously pursued in the inter-war period, in the process of which the county became a pioneer of what later became the secondary modern school.

A plethora of small, uneconomic grammar schools provided a third problem, prompting Brockington to compensate for the authority's lack of Edward VI foundations by creating Edward VII schools at Coalville, Melton Mowbray, and Market Harborough under LEA control. Moreover, suspecting that those children whose families could not pay fees were a source of hitherto untapped ability, he introduced in 1919 a general secondary schools selection examination, taken by all children at eleven, which revealed the need for many more scholarships. Accordingly, despite adverse economic conditions, he managed to keep the number of scholarships fluctuating between 300 and 400 until fees were abolished in 1944. The resultant expansion in the secondary school population, meanwhile, drew all the grammar schools, except the two at Loughborough which remained independent, into the control of the LEA.

In 1914, aged forty-three, Brockington was rejected for military service, serving instead in the Territorial Army, which was fortunate because it enabled him to play a crucial role in launching a most remarkable educational development. In 1915 Herbert Schofield's appointment as principal of Loughborough Technical Institute, established largely on Brockington's initiative in 1909, coincided with an urgent demand for munitions. Seizing their opportunity, Brockington, Schofield, and Alderman Bumpus, chairman of the governors, by personally guaranteeing £1000, secured the establishment of an 'instructional factory' in which the Ministry of Munitions invested buildings and machinery worth £150,000, all of which were transferred to the LEA at the end of the war. Thus began the principle of 'training on production' which quickly gave Loughborough a national and later an international reputation and the distinction of being the prototype of the colleges of advanced technology designated in 1955.

In 1924 Sir Robert Martin became chairman of both the county council and the education committee, forming, with Schofield and Brockington, a powerful triumvirate intent on expanding the Loughborough concept. Accordingly in 1930 the teacher training college for physical education, art, and craft was added to the embryo campus. By the time Brockington retired in 1947 the constituent components of what was later to become the University of Loughborough were all flourishing.

Brockington, meanwhile, had become a national figure. Serving on the Burnham committee on teachers' salaries from 1919 to 1944, he was a member of the consultative committee to the Board of Education from 1926 until 1944, participating in the production of two Hadow reports, *The Primary School* (1931) and *Infant and Nursery Schools* (1933), and the Spens report, *Secondary Education* (1938), of which he drafted the chapter on administrative problems. He also served on the Secondary Schools Examination Council which produced the Norwood report of 1943. Appointed OBE in 1917, he was made a CBE in 1928, but although he was sixty-five in 1936 his continuing vigour and non-pensionable post left retirement out of the question. Consequently, having previously served as president of the Association of Directors and Secretaries for Education, he was still able to hold the office of honorary secretary of the authorities' panels from 1944 until 1947.

A most humane and approachable individual, Brockington regarded administrative minutiae with disdain. A stickler for economy, he was his own inspector-cum-adviser. As a result it was the local HM inspector, S. C. Mason, who fed into the office much of the information needed for the development plan established by the county following the 1944 Education Act, and duly succeeded him as director in 1947. Brockington, who was knighted in 1946, died at 3 Owls Road, Boscombe, Bournemouth, on 14 February 1959, his successor having just inaugurated the 'Leicestershire plan' of comprehensive education, the foundation for which Brockington had laid.

DONALD K. JONES

Sources M. Seaborne, 'Sir William Brockington, director of education for Leicestershire, 1903–1947', *Leicestershire Archaeological and Historical Society Transactions*, 43 (1967–8), 45–59 · R. H. Holt, *Leicestershire Archaeological and Historical Society Transactions*, 43 (1967–8), 57–8 · M. Seaborne, 'William Brockington, director of education for Leicestershire, 1903–1947', *Education in Leicestershire, 1540–1940*, ed. B. Simon (1968), 195–224 · H. C. Dent, 'Legend of urbanity and tact', *Education* (9 Jan 1976), 35 · b. cert. · m. cert. · d. cert. · S. Mason, *Education* (9 Jan 1976), 35

Archives BL, corresp. with Albert Mansbridge, Add. MSS 65257A–65258

Likenesses photograph (aged fifty), repro. in *Transactions of the Leicestershire Archaeological and Historical Society*, facing p. 46 · photograph (aged about seventy-four), repro. in *Transactions of the Leicestershire Archaeological and Historical Society*, facing p. 47 · photograph (after retirement), repro. in B. Simon, ed., *Education in Leicestershire, 1540–1940* (1968), facing p. 208

Wealth at death £8172 1s. 5d.: probate, 29 June 1959, *CGPLA Eng. & Wales*

Brocklesby, Edward (1524/5–1573/4), Church of England clergyman, was the youngest of three surviving sons of Robert Brocklesby of Glentworth, Lincolnshire (d. 1553) and his first wife (née Cusforthe). He was educated at Eton College and King's College, Cambridge, matriculating on 13 August 1542 at the age of seventeen. A fellow from 1545, he graduated BA in 1547 and proceeded MA in 1550.

Brocklesby clearly became a protestant, for he relinquished his fellowship in 1555 and on 9 June 1558 was granted citizenship of Emden, whose exile community during Mary I's reign included Nicholas Bullingham, former archdeacon and future bishop of Lincoln. In the interim he had married—his daughter Sara was herself married by 1573—and had perhaps also become engaged in secret protestant activities in Marian England, like his exact contemporary Robert Cole, fellow of King's from 1545 to 1551.

Nothing is known of Brocklesby's first wife, and he probably returned to England a widower. Although instituted vicar of Congresbury, Somerset, on 1 June 1560 he quickly gravitated to London, and in late 1561, as minister of the vacant parish of St Nicholas Olave, was described in a report to Matthew Parker, archbishop of Canterbury, as unmarried, learned, but non-resident, and living in the household of Edmund Guest, bishop of Rochester. Since Guest had been vice-provost of King's during his residence, Brocklesby perhaps went to London as one of Guest's private chaplains. In October 1562 he received letters of sequestration as curate of St Nicholas Olave.

Brocklesby's brother Richard was among those who stood surety for Bullingham's first fruits as bishop of Lincoln (1560), and in 1563 he was himself nominated by Bullingham to the vicarage of Hemel Hempstead, Hertfordshire. He was soon embroiled in the campaign waged by the Oxford heads Thomas Sampson, dean of Christ Church, and Laurence Humphrey, president of Magdalen, against Archbishop Parker's drive for clerical conformity. Since this was originally confined to Oxford, Cambridge, and London, Brocklesby would hardly have attracted attention had he simply withdrawn to rural Hertfordshire. He was thus perhaps one of the 'four other' London clergy examined by Parker on 3 March 1565 along with Sampson and Humphrey, since on 8 May he was arraigned before the ecclesiastical commissioners at Lambeth. The case was heard by Parker, bishops Guest and Edmund Grindal of London, Sir Ambrose Cave, and William Drury. When the use of the surplice was demanded Brocklesby resolutely refused. He was thereupon deprived of Hemel Hempstead, thus becoming the first official casualty of the vestiarian controversy—'the first put out of his living for the surplice' (Peel, 1.52). Sampson was deprived of Christ Church at about this time, but his successor, Thomas Godwin, was not appointed until 26 May.

In March 1566 Parker suspended thirty-seven London ministers who repudiated the surplice and square cap. Those refusing to conform within three months faced deprivation, but by royal warrant of 1 July 1566 were granted the right to sue for the cancellation of any remaining instalments of first fruits where these had not already fallen due. Brocklesby managed to take advantage of this warrant, appearing before the barons of the exchequer at Easter 1568 with letters testimonial from Parker rehearsing the circumstances of his deprivation three years earlier, and drawn up at that time. He and his sureties were duly discharged of their obligations for Hemel Hempstead's first fruits.

In 1568 or 1569 Brocklesby was instituted rector of Branston, Lincolnshire, on the presentation of Christopher Wray, the future lord chief justice, who had married the widow of Brocklesby's eldest brother, Robert (d. 1557). In 1571 he was collated by Bullingham to the prebend of Sexaginta Solidorum in Lincoln Cathedral. He died in possession of both preferments.

In his will, dated 9 December 1573, Brocklesby left detailed bequests to his son Nathaniel, his unmarried daughters Rebecca and Elizabeth, and a married daughter, Sara Standeburne. Nathaniel, a minor, and Brocklesby's (unnamed) second wife were appointed executors. He died, at Branston or Lincoln, within weeks. Probate was granted to his (still unnamed) wife on 2 April 1574, power being reserved to Nathaniel until his majority.

BRETT USHER

Sources exchequer, first fruits and tenths office, plea rolls, PRO, E337/5, no. 100 · B. Usher, 'Edward Brocklesby: "the first put out of his living for the surplice"', *From Cranmer to Davidson: a Church of England miscellany*, ed. S. Taylor (1999), 47–68 · S. T. Bindoff, 'Wray, Christopher', HoP, *Commons, 1558–1603*, 3.653–4 · A. R. Maddison, ed., *Lincolnshire pedigrees*, 4 vols., Harleian Society, 50–52, 55 (1902–6) · A. Pettegree, *Marian protestantism: six studies* (1996) · A. Peel, ed., *The seconde parte of a register*, 2 vols. (1915) · CCC Cam., MS 122, 94–5 · will, Lincs. Arch., will register 1574 i, fols. 11r–12v

Wealth at death only household goods and books: will, Lincs. Arch., register 1574 i, fols. 11r.–12v

Brocklesby, Richard (1634/5–1714), theologian and non-juring Church of England clergyman, was born at Tealby, Lincolnshire, the son of George Brocklesby, yeoman. After attending Caistor grammar school Brocklesby entered Sidney Sussex College, Cambridge, as a sizar on 19 October 1652, aged seventeen, graduating BA in 1657 and MA in 1660. He became rector of Folkingham, Lincolnshire, at some point between 1662 and 1674. Little of substance is known of his tenure at Folkingham. Brocklesby was apparently not a Jacobite, but declined to take the 1702 oath of abjuration. He was deprived of his living on 10 November 1702, and moved to Stamford, where he devoted his time to theological studies.

Brocklesby is mainly distinguished for the theological treatise he composed and published while in retirement at Stamford. This folio volume of some 1082 pages appeared in 1706 as *An explication of the gospel-theism and the divinity of the Christian religion. Containing the true account of the system of the universe, and of the Christian Trinity*. Despite the fact that Brocklesby is described on the title-page as a 'Christian Trinitarian', the theology explicated in this ponderous work is heterodox with respect to the Trinity. The idiosyncratic contents of the volume are replete with material culled from sources ranging from patristic and medieval theology to travel accounts and secular literature. His familiarity with the works of sixteenth- and seventeenth-century antitrinitarians is revealed through his allusions to the theology of Fausto Sozzini and the Racovian catechism, along with quotations from the Hungarian unitarian György Enyedi, the Socinian Johann Crell, and the English unitarian tracts of the 1690s. Curiously Brocklesby claims no direct knowledge of the sixteenth-century antitrinitarian Michael Servetus.

Keen to steer between the Charybdis of contemporary unitarianism and the Scylla of what he terms 'Scholastic Trinitarianism', Brocklesby's Christology contains both heterodox and orthodox elements. While he rejects both the eternal generation and the pre-existence of the Son, and forcefully repudiates the Athanasian trinitology of three co-equal and co-eternal persons, he affirms Christ's consubstantiality with God the Father. The position at which he arrived can perhaps best be described as a species of monarchianism in which the Father has supremacy as almighty God. Agreeing with antitrinitarian writers that the scholastic Trinity at first sight appears 'monstrous, contrary to Reason and common Sense' (Brocklesby, 1037), Brocklesby looks askance at the orthodox trinitarian characterization of their doctrine as a mystery, labelling scholastic theology as 'a Mist of Darkness' (Brocklesby, 1043). His 'Christian Trinity' embodies a combination of Christ's status as Messiah and the Unity of God, which he characterizes as the chief articles of Christianity and Judaism respectively. Thus, for Brocklesby the Father is 'the one sole Person of the Almighty God', with Christ and the Holy Spirit partaking in the godhead in so far as they belong to the imperial estate of the Father, whose deity alone is underived and absolute. Yet this is not strictly dynamic monarchianism (defined as a belief that Christ was a man endowed with divine power and not himself divine), as Brocklesby affirms not only this unity within the divine imperial rule, but also some essential unity between Father, Son, and Holy Spirit. Moreover, in conscious contradistinction to Socinianism, Christ is not a creature. Brocklesby's theology points to both a narrow sense of God as the Father and a broader sense in which the godhead constitutes the three persons in the divine imperial estate.

In the conclusion to *Gospel-Theism* Brocklesby reveals eirenic motivations in his belief that his Christian Trinity will lead to the peace and unity of the church. For him both unitarianism and the orthodox trinitology are hindrances to faith; with respect to the latter, he even goes so far as to speak of the contradictions of the scholastic Trinity having been 'exploded' by Jews and Muslims, suggesting that the orthodox view is a stumbling block to the other monotheistic religions as well. The heterodox contents of this work notwithstanding, Brocklesby's *Gospel-Theism* initiated no storm of controversy. This is no doubt due in large part to the volume's innocuous title, and the fact that the contents are rendered partially obscure by a meandering text punctuated with eccentric neologisms.

Brocklesby was not, however, without some influence. It may be significant that Thomas Emlyn, later a prominent antitrinitarian, attended Brocklesby's church at Folkingham between 1674 and 1678. Some material from *Gospel-Theism*—with the distinctive theology expunged—was reworked by John Maxwell, prebendary of Connor, and published in the 1727 English edition of Richard Cumberland's *Treatise of the Laws of Nature*. But Brocklesby's most important theological legacy is seen in the career of William Whiston, who affirms that the *Gospel-Theism* was an important inspiration in his conversion to a form of Arianism about 1706 (Whiston, *An Historical Preface to Primitive Christianity Reviv'd*, 4–5). In 1713, by which time his antitrinitarianism was a notorious public heresy, Whiston was advertising the availability of Brocklesby's *Gospel-Theism* in his London 'Primitive Library' (*Daily Courant*, 28 Jan 1713). This, even though Whiston's Arian Christology affirmed the pre-existence of Christ, and denied the consubstantiality of God and Christ and the eternal generation of the Son. Whatever the precise nature of Whiston's theological debts to Brocklesby, there was a perception as late as 1727 that the former was guilty of 'stealing' ideas from the latter (Whiston, *Mr Henley's Letters*, 10).

Brocklesby died at Stamford in 1714, probably in February, and was buried in the church at Folkingham. He left his Stamford house and substantial properties in Lincolnshire and Huntingdonshire. The intended disbursements of his will help fill out his character. Brocklesby, who never married, appointed his collateral descendants to administer from the rents of his properties the founding and maintenance of schools at Folkingham and Kirkby-on-Bain in Lincolnshire and Pidley in Huntingdonshire for teaching poor children 'their Catechism and to read the holy Bible' (will, fol. 185r). Proceeds from the sale of a farm in Lincolnshire were to be devoted to 'the Propagation of the Gospel in the Eastern parts' (will, fol. 185v), or, if this failed, £300 was to be used for the purchase and distribution of bibles in Lincolnshire, Nottinghamshire, Leicestershire, Northamptonshire, and Huntingdonshire. Brocklesby left £150 for the restoration of the parish church of Wilsthorpe, Lincolnshire; £150 each was also given to the communities of French and Dutch protestant refugees. To this was added £10 each for eight named dissenting ministers. If it is reasonable to assume that the £10 Brocklesby originally left to Whiston signals some initial sympathy for the latter's cause, the annulment of this bequest in a codicil of 30 January 1714 may point to some sort of disaffection with Whiston on Brocklesby's part. Personal contact between the two men is possible either in London, or during a trip Whiston made to Stamford in 1709.

Brocklesby also left libraries in both London and Stamford. The first of these was left to be sold by Brocklesby's printer, John Heptinstall, and the schoolmaster of Stamford, William Turner. The second was sold by auction and the catalogue reveals a considerable collection of works on history, philology, and theology, with the latter category including many antitrinitarian publications, among them Johann Völkel's *De vera religione*, Johann Crell's *De uno Deo*, and the Racovian catechism.

Richard Brocklesby was a man of eirenic temperament whose will confirms his missionary spirit, biblicist piety, and Christian charity. His heterodox theological *magnum opus*, little read on its release and now obscure, nevertheless contributed in a small but important way to the theological ferment within and without the Church of England during the early eighteenth century.

STEPHEN D. SNOBELEN

Sources DNB · R. Brocklesby, *An explication of the gospel-theism* (1706) · will, PRO, PROB 11/541, sig. 154, fols. 185r–189v · H. J. McLachlan, *Socinianism in seventeenth-century England* (1951) · W. Whiston, *An historical preface to primitive Christianity reviv'd* (1711) · W. Whiston, *Mr Henley's letters and advertisements* (1727) · *Daily Courant* (1713) · Venn, *Alum. Cant.* · J. C. Findon, 'The nonjurors and the Church of England, 1689–1716', DPhil diss., U. Oxf., 1978

Brocklesby, Richard (1722–1797), physician, was the only son of Richard Brocklesby (d. c.1763), of Cork, and his wife, Mary Alloway, of Minehead, Somerset, in which town Brocklesby was born on 11 August 1722. He received his early education in his father's house and, as both parents were Quakers, he was sent at the age of twelve to a Quaker school at Ballitore, co. Kildare. Edmund Burke became a pupil there during Brocklesby's final year, and despite the difference in their ages the two boys established a friendship that proved to be lifelong. In 1742 Brocklesby began studying medicine in Edinburgh, but before completing his course he transferred to Leiden, so as to avoid the anti-Jacobite feelings in London which might prevent an Edinburgh graduate from practising in the metropolis. On 28 June 1745 Brocklesby gained his MD with his thesis, 'De saliva sana et morbosa'.

Brocklesby's first practice was in Broad Street, near Bishopsgate, in the City of London; to support him during the difficult years before he could earn an adequate income, his father made him an annual allowance of £150. To gain some publicity he wrote *An essay concerning the mortality … among horned cattle in several parts of Europe and chiefly about London* (1746). The epidemic was a matter of widespread concern, and as Brocklesby had witnessed its devastating results while in the Netherlands, his essay was opportune. He advocated the burial of the infected carcasses in deep graves. Prudently he dedicated his essay to Richard Mead, the most influential physician in London. During the next few months Brocklesby sent four articles to the Royal Society (of which Mead was a fellow), and these in due course appeared in the society's *Philosophical Transactions*. Two of them were concerned with certain poisons and their effects on humans and animals; a third gave an account of the author's experiments to analyse the various types of salts; the fourth described his efforts to prove that fish can hear and make sounds. Mead was impressed by Brocklesby's talents and in February 1747 proposed him for membership of the Royal Society; he was elected later in the month. Another article dated June 1755 described his experiments on various animals which demonstrated that the nerves transmitting pain were separate from those serving motor functions.

In 1749 Brocklesby published a book entitled *Reflections on Antient and Modern Musick with the Application to the Care of Disease*. In it he described many of the ways that music was used in the ancient world to affect the emotions, especially its use as therapy—a function that in his opinion ought to be revived. His abilities as both writer and practitioner were by now recognized, and in April 1751 he was admitted licentiate of the Royal College of Physicians. Three years later he was awarded an honorary MD from Dublin and a similar degree from Cambridge. His election

as fellow of the Royal College of Physicians followed in June 1756. He delivered the Harveian oration in 1760.

In 1758 Brocklesby was appointed physician to the army and served in Germany during the Seven Years' War. His experiences there provided the material for his most important work, *Oeconomical and medical observations … from 1758 to 1763 inclusive tending to the improvement of military hospitals and to the care of camp diseases incident to soldiers* (1764). Brocklesby observed that army surgeons were poorly equipped to deal with the majority of soldiers' illnesses, which were medical, not surgical, cases; thus it was important that a medical officer should be a qualified physician. At that time there were very few barracks, most of them badly designed: Brocklesby believed that barracks of a good quality would help troops to stay healthy by promoting personal cleanliness, physical activity, and regular meals. On the Isle of Wight he had noticed that men suffering from wounds or diseases were more likely to survive in sheds open to fresh air than in poorly ventilated houses requisitioned by the army as hospitals. His continuing interest in the health of soldiers led in March 1794 to his appointment as physician-general to the ordnance.

Brocklesby had moved to a new house in Norfolk Street, off the Strand, London, in 1763 and lived there for the rest of his life with an unmarried sister as his housekeeper. On the death of his father he inherited £600 a year and this sum, added to his fees from his many patients and his half-pay from the army, gave him an ample income. Part of this he spent on hospitality to his friends, who appreciated his sociability and his conversational powers. But he was also noted for his many charitable acts: he raised a subscription for Captain William Coram, who had spent all his money on establishing the Foundling Hospital, and among his patients there were several widows who received free treatment and financial support. Brocklesby had intended to leave his friend Edmund Burke a legacy of £1000 in his will, but in fact gave it to him as an 'instant present' in 1788, as at that time Burke had no official pension (*Correspondence of Edmund Burke*, 406).

In politics Brocklesby was a whig, like his patient John Wilkes, whom he had known since their days at Leiden, and his friend the duke of Richmond. Brocklesby's most famous patient was Samuel Johnson, whom he attended from June 1783 until Johnson's death eighteen months later. They became close friends, although Johnson was a difficult patient, prone to self-treatment and to violent criticisms of his doctor's methods. With his usual generosity Brocklesby offered to accommodate Johnson in his own more spacious house, and on another occasion, to finance a trip to the continent. Johnson as an orthodox Christian was deeply worried by Brocklesby's 'speculative views' on religion and tried to persuade him of the importance of Christian faith (Boswell, *Life*, 4.414). But these efforts were ineffective and Brocklesby remained a deist.

After Johnson's death Brocklesby kept in touch with members of the Johnson circle and attended the meetings of the Essex Head club which he and Johnson had founded. He maintained his busy practice and devoted much time to the education of his brilliant great-nephew Thomas *Young (1773–1829), who described him as 'somewhat querulous in temper and exacting in claims to respect … although liberal in great things he was somewhat parsimonious in small' (Peacock, 124). According to the *Gentleman's Magazine*, 'the Doctor had one son, a private pupil to Mr Wakefield after he quitted the academy at Hackney' (*GM*, 1132–3).

Brocklesby's portrait by John Copley has been lost, but an engraving shows a middle-aged man dressed in Quaker style in black with white cuffs, his expression alert and good-humoured. Brocklesby died suddenly at home in Norfolk Street, London, on 11 December 1797, very soon after the death of Edmund Burke. His own death may have been hastened by a visit to Beaconsfield to offer condolences to his friend's widow; he died within hours of his return to London. He was buried in St Clement Danes Church on 18 December. He bequeathed his house, furniture, library, and pictures with £10,000 to Thomas Young; his Irish estates were left to his nephew Mr Beeby.

ERNEST HEBERDEN

Sources W. S. Curran, 'Dr Brocklesby of London', *Journal of the History of Medicine and Allied Sciences*, 17 (1962), 509–21 · H. A. L. Howell, 'Richard Brocklesby', *Journal of Royal Army Medical Corps*, 17 (1911), 115–22 · A. Rees and others, *The cyclopaedia, or, Universal dictionary of arts, sciences, and literature*, 45 vols. (1819–20) · Boswell, *Life*, 4.176, 254, 338n.2, 414 · 'Memoirs of the late Richard Brocklesby', *European Magazine and London Review*, 33 (1798), 291–6 · Munk, *Roll* · T. H. Bishop, 'Richard Brocklesby', *Medical Bookman and Historian*, 1/12 (Dec 1947), 17–19 · *GM*, 1st ser., 67 (1797), 1132–3 · R. W. Innes Smith, *English-speaking students of medicine at the University of Leyden* (1932), 32 · G. Peacock, *Life of Thomas Young* (1855), 124 · *The correspondence of Edmund Burke*, 5, ed. H. Furber and P. J. Marshall (1965), 406 · *DNB*
Archives RS
Likenesses G. Dance, drawing, 1795, BM · W. Daniell, soft-ground etching, 1795 (after G. Dance), RCP Lond. · W. Ridley, stipple, 1798 (after J. S. Copley), BM, NPG (destroyed during the Second World War); repro. in *European Magazine* (1798) · J. S. Copley, chalk drawing, Metropolitan Museum of Art, New York · J. S. Copley, group portrait, oils (*The collapse of the earl of Chatham in the House of Lords, 7 July 1778*), Tate collection
Wealth at death over £30,000 in bequests and value of Irish estates: Rees and others, *Cyclopaedia*

Brockman [*née* Bunce], **Ann**, **Lady Brockman** (d. 1660), writer on medicine, was the daughter of Simon Bunce of Linstead and Dorothy, daughter of William Grimsdiche. Her date of birth is unknown, as are details of her early life. She married Sir William Brockman of Newington, Kent, on 28 May 1616, and they had seven children. Her first son, Henry, died 'aged four years and eight months' on 13 September 1622 (according to his sepulchre in Newington church). One other child (Helen) died young, but five survived into adulthood: Martha, Anne, James, Helen, and Margery. The loss of their first child evidently affected the parents most deeply, since he was the only one given a sepulchre in the local church. Sir William Brockman was lord of the manor of Beachborough, owning Cheriton manor as well.

In 1638 Ann Brockman began 'A book of receits'. She titled, dated, and signed the frontispiece, and the book was evidently used as her household and estate medicine book. The handwriting is a clear italic, with later additions in different inks. Included among the recipes are ones for 'a thin coff', 'the coff of the lungs', 'an excellent water for the stock', 'a tetter or ring worm', 'the payne in the head', and 'the payne in the back' (fol. 3). Her index shows the range and kinds of diseases she treated, and some of the methods: aching backs, ague, 'bath, for any smelling', sore breasts, bruises, burns, conception, convulsions, dropsy, eyes, headache, impostumes, itch, hypochondria, measles, melancholy, mouth sores, palsy, piles, plague (a late entry), purging, rupture, plasters, pox, running sores, salve, scalds, sleep, spleen, stones, sweating, syrup of vinegar, tobacco salve, toothache, sore throat, water, worms, wounds. The breadth of ailments, from simple aches and pains to more severe illnesses such as plague, suggests that she may have been treating a large household and its surrounding villagers. The recipes do not suggest the need for a physician—although her recipe for a purgation is 'of Doctor Merton' (fol. 3)—but they show that she provided traditional herbal recipes and treatment.

During the civil war Brockman's husband fought on the king's side, and was imprisoned twice: once in 1642, and again in 1648 after he was captured for his key role at the siege of Maidstone. On both occasions Ann Brockman petitioned for his release, personally writing the first petition on 7 February 1643 but merely signing that of 1648. In 1643 she says she is worried about 'the preservation of his health, which I fear may be in some danger through the multitude of prisoners committed lately to that place' (Brockman, 'The humble petition', fol. 4), while in 1648 the writer of the petition says that it is her health that is suffering. Active petitioning of committees for prisoners was commonly performed by wives of imprisoned cavaliers during the civil war, but Ann's words illustrate her personal love and concern for her husband and her sense of responsibility in his absence. Her husband's letters on taxation and the provision of militia during the civil war occasionally refer to her knowledge of their estate, suggesting her role as partner with him in managing it.

During her husband's lifetime Brockman had some personal control of land and money: a bond of £100 to her is included in the Drake-Brockman papers in the British Library. After her husband's death in 1654, their son James inherited his lands and title. However, Ann continued to manage some lands and money as her dower, which James paid from the estate until her death in 1660. In the years between 1656 and 1660 she received about £130 annually for 'her lady days rent', and a similar amount at Michaelmas, some from 'her 5 acres of meadow' (BL, Add. MS 45206, fol. 5). Ann Brockman died on 29 November 1660 and is buried at Newington church. Given that she married in 1616, she must have been at least sixty.

KATE AUGHTERSON

Sources D. H. Drake-Brockman, *Record of the Brockman and Drake-Brockman families* (1936) · A. Brockman, 'A book of receits', BL, Add. MS 45197 · A. Brockman, 'To the noble committee for prisoners', BL, Add. MS 42618, fol. 9 · J. Brockman, 'Accounts', BL, Add. MS 45206, fols. 3–12 · A. Brockman, 'The humble petition', BL, Add. MS

42618, fol. 4 · A. Everitt, *The community of Kent and the great rebellion, 1640–60* (1973) · E. Hasted, *The history and topographical survey of the county of Kent*, 2 (1782)
Archives BL, Drake-Brockman papers
Wealth at death some wealth annually; perhaps just a dower: Brockman, 'Accounts', 1656–60

Brockway, (Archibald) Fenner, Baron Brockway (1888–1988), politician and campaigner, was born on 1 November 1888 in Calcutta, the only son and eldest of three children of the Revd William George Brockway, London Missionary Society missionary, and his wife, Frances Elizabeth, daughter of William Abbey. His mother died when he was fourteen. Educated at the School for the Sons of Missionaries at Blackheath, he became a journalist. He moved from Liberalism to the Independent Labour Party (ILP) and by 1912 was editor of the ILP newspaper, the *Labour Leader*. Still in his twenties, he worked closely with leading figures on the British left.

Brockway played a heroic role in the ILP's opposition to the war of 1914–18, as a journalist, and then through the No-Conscription Fellowship as an opponent of military conscription. On four occasions he was sentenced to gaol—the last time in July 1917 to two years' hard labour. When released in April 1919, he had served a total of twenty-eight months, the last eight in solitary confinement. His war record increased his status in several sections of the labour movement, and in the election of 1929 he was returned as the Labour member for East Leyton. In 1919 he became editor of *India* and joint secretary of the British committee of the Indian National Congress. From 1926 to 1929 he was editor of the *New Leader*, the renamed organ of the ILP, of which he had become organizing secretary in 1922.

Brockway's continuing involvement in the ILP section of the wider Labour Party made him an increasingly controversial figure. From 1926 the ILP moved to the left under the leadership of James Maxton, and called for 'socialism in our time', a radicalization backed enthusiastically by Brockway. With the 1929 Labour government proving helpless in the face of rocketing unemployment, Brockway was prominent among a small group of ILP rebel members. This small section of left-wingers refused to accept the party's disciplinary guidelines, and were denied endorsement for the 1931 election. Like most Labour MPs, Brockway lost his seat. The dispute over discipline was symbolic for many of a much more fundamental division over policy. In July 1932, with Brockway in the chair, the ILP voted to disaffiliate from the Labour Party.

There followed the most radical period of Brockway's career as he sought to articulate a socialism distinct from the pragmatism of Labour and the Stalinism of the Communist Party. But the ILP's membership dwindled, and it was squeezed between its rivals. The Spanish Civil War modified his pacifism and deepened his suspicion of the Communist Party. In 1937 he visited Spain and observed the repression of the ILP's Spanish equivalent by the Communist Party. During the Second World War, he felt cross-pressured between his distaste for militarism and his thorough antipathy to fascism. In wartime by-elections he

(Archibald) Fenner Brockway, Baron Brockway (1888–1988), by Bassano, 1930

argued for socialism as a means of ending the war. After Labour's 1945 electoral success, he decided that the ILP offered no distinctive way forward and rejoined the Labour Party. From 1942 to 1947 he was chairman of the British Centre for Colonial Freedom, and in 1945 he helped establish the Congress of Peoples against Imperialism.

In February 1950 Brockway returned to the Commons as the member for Eton and Slough. He remained firmly on the left, participating in the faction centred around Aneurin Bevan, but his radicalism was always tempered by a concern not to reproduce what he had come to see as the disastrous split of 1932. His strong anti-militarism was expressed in his involvement with the Campaign for Nuclear Disarmament. His principal fame came from his championing of anti-colonial movements. His interest in Indian independence had been long-standing, and from 1950 he began to visit Africa regularly. Some called him the member for Africa and he knew several of the first generation post-independence African leaders. From 1954 he was chairman of the Movement for Colonial Freedom. His anti-colonialism was reflected in a thorough opposition to racism in Britain. In nine successive sessions he introduced bills into the Commons aimed at outlawing discrimination. Ironically, when the 1964 Labour government embarked on such legislation, Brockway had just lost his parliamentary seat. The margin was eleven votes and some commentators ascribed his defeat to the race issue. Despite misgivings, he accepted a life peerage

(1964), and campaigned for his causes within the traditionalism of the upper house. His radicalism remained vibrant in his new environment. Brockway was a prolific writer, of books, pamphlets, and articles. These included four volumes of autobiography and major studies of two ILP contemporaries, Fred Jowett (*Socialism over Sixty Years*, 1946) and Alfred Salter (*Bermondsey Story*, 1949). In 1914 he married Lilla, daughter of the Revd William Harvey-Smith. They had four daughters, two of whom predeceased him (1941 and 1974). As Brockway acknowledged later, the marriage was not a success, and he had several, often short-lived, affairs in the inter-war years. After a divorce in 1945, in 1946 he married Edith Violet, daughter of Archibald Herbert King, electrician; they had one son. Both his wives shared many of his political views.

Many found Brockway to be highly principled and warmly sympathetic. His style inherited something of his missionary background, and his socialist politics owed much to a broader tradition of English radicalism; a statue in London's Red Lion Square (1985) depicts him addressing a crowd, arm aloft. Not an intellectual, he was yet an independent thinker. Born in the age of Gladstone, he died in the age of Thatcher on 28 April 1988, at Watford General Hospital, Hertfordshire.　　　DAVID HOWELL, rev.

Sources *The Guardian* (29 April 1988) · *The Times* (30 April 1988) · *The Independent* (2 May 1988) · F. Brockway, *Inside the left* (1942) · F. Brockway, *Outside the right* (1963) · F. Brockway, *Towards tomorrow* (1977) · F. Brockway, *98 not out* (1986) · *CGPLA Eng. & Wales* (1988) **Archives** BLPES, corresp. with the Independent Labour Party · Bodl. RH, corresp. relating to colonial questions · CAC Cam., papers · Labour History Archive and Study Centre, Manchester, papers | International Institut voor Sociale Geschiedenis, Amsterdam, corresp. with Dora Russell · McMaster University, Hamilton, Ontario, corresp. with Bertrand Russell **Likenesses** Bassano, photograph, 1930, NPG [*see illus.*] · photographs, 1933–70, Hult. Arch. · R. Hutchings, photograph, 9 June 1984, Hult. Arch. · statue, bronze, 1985, Red Lion Square, London **Wealth at death** under £70,000: probate, 16 Sept 1988, *CGPLA Eng. & Wales*

Brocky, Charles [*formerly* Károly] (1807–1855), painter, was born in Temesvár, Hungary, on 22 May 1807. His mother died when he was a young boy, about 1814, and Brocky and his father joined the family of his sister, whose husband managed a company of travelling actors; Brocky's father became the hairdresser for the theatrical group. Brocky worked in a cook's shop and as a barber's assistant before travelling to Vienna in 1823 with the small financial support his aunt could provide. He studied at the Akademie der Bildenden Künste until 1832, where he specialized in miniatures and portraits, gaining the patronage of Princess de Mousleard, the aunt of the emperor of Austria. Despite this early success biographies emphasize the many privations Brocky endured to obtain his artistic training.

In 1837 Brocky travelled to Paris and Italy to study old master paintings. While in Paris he met Hugh Andrew Johnstone Munro, a Scottish aristocrat who invited him to London in 1838. Through Munro, Brocky made the acquaintance of the influential art dealer Dominic Colnaghi. In that same year Brocky exhibited for the first time

at both the Royal Academy and the British Institution, a practice he would continue throughout his career. He became known for his portraiture, for example *Mrs Norman Wilkinson* (National Gallery of Hungary, Budapest), and he attracted many prominent sitters, including Queen Victoria. In the 1840s Brocky travelled to Germany and Italy, completing many watercolour studies. He returned to Vienna, residing there in 1845–6 before settling permanently in London, where he was known as Charles.

Brocky worked in both oils and watercolours, as in his *Girl Reading by a Window* (1850; V&A). In the 1850s he moved beyond portraiture and literary scenes to address mythological motifs, such as *The Nymph* (National Gallery of Hungary, Budapest), exhibited at the Royal Academy in 1850. In that same year he painted his *Self-Portrait* (National Gallery of Hungary, Budapest). In 1854 Brocky was elected a member of the New Society of Painters in Water Colours. He maintained close ties with the Hungarian community in London, and his only known history painting, now destroyed, was *Granting a Charter to Hungary* (1851). As his friend and biographer Norman Wilkinson noted, 'Brocky's diffidence prevented him from appreciating himself as an artist, but he never ceased to pride himself upon having been born a Hungarian' (Wilkinson, 38). Brocky died, unmarried, in London on 8 July 1855 of liver problems. His estate, including his own art work, was auctioned by Christie and Manson on 2 August 1855. He was buried at Kensal Green cemetery, London. The Victoria and Albert Museum in London and the National Gallery of Hungary in Budapest hold a number of Brocky's works.

MORNA O'NEILL

Sources N. Wilkinson, *Sketch of the life of Charles Brocky the artist* (1870) · K. Gellér, 'Brocky, Károly [Charles]', *The dictionary of art*, ed. J. Turner (1996) · Redgrave, *Artists* · *Catalogue of water colour paintings by British artists and foreigners working in Great Britain*, V&A, rev. edn (1927), 52–3 · Thieme & Becker, *Allgemeines Lexikon*, 37.40–41 · Wood, *Vic. painters*, 3rd edn **Likenesses** K. Brocky, self-portrait, 1850, National Gallery of Hungary, Budapest

Brodbelt [*née* Penoyre], **Anne** (1751–1827), letter writer and social observer, was born on 1 January 1751 at Spanish Town, Jamaica, one of two children of Thomas Penoyre (1722–1766), physician, and his wife, Sarah, daughter of Thomas Gardner of Spanish Town. The Penoyres were descended from the landed family of Penoyre of the Moor, of Clifford, Herefordshire, and were originally of Welsh extraction.

Nothing is known of Anne Penoyre's life or of her education prior to her marriage, at Spanish Town on 1 January 1770, to the physician Francis Rigby Brodbelt (1746–1795), son of Daniel Brodbelt and Anna Maria Rigby, both of Spanish Town. Anne and Francis Brodbelt established their own household at Spanish Town, where Dr Brodbelt provided medical care to wealthy plantation-owning families and also served as physician to the Spanish Town gaol. They had three children: Francis (1771–1827), Ann (1774–1828), and Jane (1779–1856). Because Dr Brodbelt was 'passionately desirous that his daughters should be well educated and thoroughly accomplished' (*Letters*, 15), in 1788 he decided that Ann and Jane should be enrolled at English boarding-schools, in order that they might attain the genteel education that was unavailable to them in Jamaica, owing to the lack of educational institutions in the island. They settled on the boarding-school kept by the author Eliza Fenwick at Flint House in Greenwich.

Over the course of the following decade Anne Brodbelt wrote dozens of lengthy and news-filled letters to her daughters, particularly to Jane, and it is upon these letters, later edited and published by her descendant Geraldine Mozley, that her posthumous literary reputation is based. Written between 1788 and 1796, they offer a vivid picture of the experiences of the plantation gentry in colonial Jamaica, and depict Anglo-Jamaicans enjoying a pleasant and relaxed mode of life modelled upon English norms of genteel behaviour, yet at the same time being constantly aware of the potential threats posed to this lifestyle by epidemic disease and by slave revolt. Anne Brodbelt describes in one letter a celebration of the absent Jane's birthday, at which

> all the Negroes made a dance in the Evening, and gave us a great deal of Singing and most of their Songs ended with success and happiness to My Lady Jane: the evening they concluded with three Huzzas and your health in a bowl of Grog. (*Letters*, 38)

In stark contrast she informs Jane in a subsequent letter that 'an Insurrection had broke out upon the Maroon Negroes … in consequence of which we have lost several Brave officers and men in the Militia, as well as in the regular troops' (ibid., 119). Her letters describe the lavish 'amusements at the King's House during the Sessions' in the Jamaican capital, attended by 'those who are fond of dancing and dress' (ibid., 95), but also describe the ravages of yellow fever, whose 'uncommon Mortality' (ibid., 90) kept her in almost perpetual mourning for friends and family members who succumbed to the disease. She wrote with wit and verve, the subjects of discussion in her letters ranging beyond family news and social life to include her opinions about local politics and the progress of the revolution in France.

Anne Brodbelt remained in Jamaica for several years after her husband's sudden death on 9 December 1795. In 1798 she sailed for England, where she was reunited with her now adult children. She lived at Chudleigh, Devon, for a number of years but later moved to Bath, home to many West Indian absentee landowners, where she resided at 12 Beaufort Buildings East. She died at Bath on 6 September 1827 and was buried on 13 September in the family plot of the Penoyres of the Moor, in the churchyard at Clifford, Herefordshire. Her letters to Jane and Ann have remained in the possession of her descendants, and excerpts from them were edited, annotated, and published in 1938 by her great-great-granddaughter Geraldine Mozley.

NATALIE ZACEK

Sources *Letters to Jane from Jamaica, 1788–1796*, ed. G. Mozley (1938) · K. E. Ingram, *Jamaica*, World Bibliographical Series, 45 (1984) · K. E. Ingram, *Sources of Jamaican History*, 2 vols. (1976) · E. Brathwaite, *The development of Creole society in Jamaica, 1770–1820* (1971) · *Lady Nugent's journal: Jamaica one hundred years ago*, ed. F. Cundall (1907) · A. Mackenzie-Grieve, *The great accomplishment* (1953) · 'Bibliography for researchers of Jamaican genealogy and history', www.sephardim.org/jamgen/index.html, 20 Feb 2001
Archives priv. coll., letters to daughter Jane
Likenesses oils, *c*.1768, priv. coll. · N. Plimer, miniature, 1790, priv. coll. · Mrs Beetham, silhouette, *c*.1791, priv. coll.; repro. in Mozley, ed., *Letters to Jane from Jamaica* · J. Miers, silhouette, priv. coll.

Broderick, John (1924–1989), writer, was born on 30 July 1924 at the family home in Connaught Street, Athlone, Westmeath, Ireland, the only surviving child of John Broderick, owner of a large and successful bakery business, and his wife, Mary Kate, formerly Golden. When his father died in 1927 his mother continued the business, and in 1936 married the bakery manager. Broderick's childhood was materially comfortable, but, as he claimed in later life, less so emotionally and educationally—he attended six nursery and primary day schools in Athlone, including the Marist Brothers' school at the age of eleven. Nevertheless, he wrote and spoke in later life with evident fondness for the Athlone of his youth:

> There are so many memories. Ass carts in Connaught Street and herds of sheep on the Batteries. An old fashioned gramophone in Walsh's out of which, after some strenuous winding, the voice of John McCormack would float through a horn. The slow tramp of four police feet on the street at night. (Murtagh, 11)

From 1936 to 1941 Broderick was a boarder in schools in Sligo and Ballmasloe.

Aged seventeen Broderick planned to take his place in the family business, but, instead, the continuing financial success of the bakery enabled him to travel extensively throughout Europe, during which time he became passionately fond of Paris. In 1944 he moved with his mother to The Willows, a large, handsome house on the canal bank in Athlone, but in the early 1950s he lived in Paris for several years. He travelled throughout Europe during this time and published travel articles in the *Irish Times*, which were also broadcast on Radio Éireann. He was an excellent travel writer: atmospheric, evocative, and informative, and many of those who admired his travel writing, including Patrick Murray in the journal *Éire–Ireland*, thought that it was in this area of writing that he truly excelled.

In 1962 Broderick moved with his mother to The Moorings, a very large house with extensive grounds. Throughout the 1960s and 1970s he contributed critical essays and reviews to the *Irish Times* and the *Irish Independent* and reviewed new novels and collections of short stories for the journal *Hibernia*. The range of his literary interests was extraordinary; he wrote thoughtful, well-informed, and judicious reviews of the work of writers as diverse as Greene, Updike, Giraudoux, Boll, Sagan, and Gorky, while his prolific output was equally remarkable, particularly for a man wealthy enough not to need to work for a living. However, perhaps because of his financial independence, Broderick could be acerbic in reviews and interviews when discussing indigenous authors, and over the years he managed to offend numerous Irish writers; a much publicized feud with Edna O'Brien, for example, carried on for many years, although the pair were eventually reconciled.

The Pilgrimage, Broderick's first novel, was published in 1961, and is set primarily in a small town in the Irish provinces. Although the principal characters are sexually active when away, they are deeply religious in their home town, where they are preparing to go on the parish pilgrimage to Lourdes, and the novel is driven by the conflict between the sacred and the profane, a dynamic that was to become a characteristic feature of Broderick's Irish novels. *The Pilgrimage* was instantly banned in Ireland by the board of censorship for its descriptions of heterosexual activity, the suggestion of homosexuality, and a final chapter which was construed as blasphemous. *The Pilgrimage* was published (as *The Chameleons*) to a modest but respectful response in America, but was considerably more successful in France, where Broderick had befriended the Paris-based, flamboyantly homosexual writer Julien Green a decade previously. Broderick, himself homosexual, and Green were lifelong friends and when *The Pilgrimage* was republished in France in 1991, Green provided an introduction.

Broderick then published three novels in quick succession: *The Fugitives* (1962), *Don Juaneen* (1963), and *The Waking of Willie Ryan* (1965), but his career as a novelist, which had resulted in his election to the Irish Academy of Letters in 1968, seemed to have ended when his habitual heavy drinking, which hitherto he had kept under control, degenerated into alcoholism. Over the next six years Broderick wrote nothing and almost drank himself to death. He emerged alive from this dark period, however, and in 1973 he published *An Apology for Roses*, his biggest commercial success. He wrote seven more novels, including *London Irish* (1979), *The Flood* (1987), and *The Irish Magdalene* (1991), which was completed by his publishers after his death. His first five novels were published in America, and almost all of them were translated into French. In 1975 Broderick received the Irish Academy literature award. He also wrote several radio plays, including the very successful *The Enemies of Rome*, which was broadcast by Radio Éireann in 1980. Broderick's favourite, and most successful, fictional setting is small-town Ireland, often recognizably Athlone. His claustrophobic, Catholic communities seethe with gossip, much of it malicious, but Broderick, a practising Catholic for most of his life, is even-handed in his depictions of Catholicism: he invariably suggests that its rituals provide security and spiritual sustenance, but he is equally alert to the ways in which such comfort vitiates independent thought. His mother died in 1974 and Broderick lived alone in the family home until 1981, when he moved to a Georgian terraced house in Russell Street, Bath. John Broderick died at his last home, 8 The Vineyards, Bath, on 28 May 1989. Despite his move to England, he remained deeply attached to Athlone and his books, records, and papers form a special collection in Athlone Library. In May 1999 the Rotary Club of Athlone organized the first John Broderick weekend, marking the tenth anniversary of his death; during this event a new street was named in his honour. In May 2002 a second John Broderick weekend took place, which attracted a number of speakers from around the world.   KEVIN McCARRON

Sources *The Independent* (2 June 1989) · H. Murtagh, ed., *Irish midland studies: essays in commemoration of N. W. English* (1980) · M. Kingston, 'John Broderick: an Athlone author in search of a European home' [unpublished paper given on behalf of the Association for the study of Anglo-Irish literature, Bath, 2000] · E. Maher, *Crosscurrents and confluences: echoes of religion in twentieth-century fiction* (2000) · b. cert. · d. cert.
Archives Athlone Library, Westmeath, Republic of Ireland
Wealth at death £178,122: probate, 22 Dec 1989, *CGPLA Eng. & Wales*

Broderip, Edmund (*bap.* 1727, *d.* 1779). *See under* Broderip, William (1683–1727).

Broderip [*née* Hood], **Frances Freeling** (1830–1878), children's writer, second daughter of Thomas *Hood (1799–1845), poet, and his wife, Jane Reynolds (1791–1846), was born at Winchmore Hill, Middlesex. She was named after her godfather, her father's friend Sir Francis Freeling, the secretary to the General Post Office. Little is known of her life before her marriage on 10 September 1849 to the Revd John Somerville Broderip (1814–1866), son of Edward Broderip (*d.* 1847) of Cossington Manor, Somerset, and his wife, Grace Dory, daughter of Benjamin Greenhill. John Somerville Broderip was born at Wells, Somerset, educated at Eton College and at Balliol College, Oxford (BA 1837, MA 1839), and became rector of Cossington in 1844. The couple had four daughters.

In 1857 Frances Broderip commenced her literary career with the publication of *Wayside Fancies*. She became a prolific author of stories for children. *The Academy* termed her publications, which included *Tiny Tadpole, and other Tales* (1862), *My Grandmother's Budget Stories* (1863), *Mamma's Morning Gossips* (1866), and *Tales of the Toys Told by themselves* (1869), the 'offspring of a tender fancy and a cultivated mind' (*The Academy*, 450).

Frances Broderip also collaborated with her brother Tom *Hood (1835–1874) on several works. He provided illustrations for *Funny Fables for Little Folks* (1860), *Fairyland, or, Recreations for the rising generation by T and J Hood and their son and daughter* (1861), *Merry Songs for Little Voices* (1865), and *Excursion into Puzzledom* (1879).

In 1860 Frances Broderip and her brother edited *Memorials of Thomas Hood*, and in 1869 she selected and published the *Early Poems and Sketches* of her father. She and her brother also published in a collected form *The Works of T. Hood* (10 vols., 1869–73). Frances Broderip died at her home, Ivy Bank, Ladies Bay, Walton in Gordano, Somerset, on 3 November 1878, and was buried on 9 November in St Mary's churchyard, Walton by Clevedon.

G. C. BOASE, *rev.* VICTORIA MILLAR

Sources *The Academy* (9 Nov 1878), 450 · *GM*, 4th ser., 2 (1866), 769 · F. F. Broderip, *Memorials of Thomas Hood*, 2 vols. (1860) · *CGPLA Eng. & Wales* (1879)
Wealth at death under £1500: probate, 6 Feb 1879, *CGPLA Eng. & Wales*

Broderip, Francis Fane (*c.*1750–1807). *See under* Broderip, William (1683–1727).

Broderip, John (1719–1770). *See under* Broderip, William (1683–1727).

Broderip, Robert (*c*.1758–1808). *See under* Broderip, William (1683–1727).

Broderip, William (1683–1727), organist and composer, was born on 10 July 1683, the son of Adrian Broderip. He held several posts at Wells Cathedral, initially as vicar-choral from 1701 and then as sub-treasurer from 1706. He was paid a salary of 40s. per annum, as well as additional fees for some of his duties, and was expected to take responsibility for the care of the cathedral plate, altar linen, vestments, and candlesticks, and to provide wax for sealing leases and bread and wine for communion. On 2 January 1713 he was appointed cathedral organist, and three years later he also became master of the choristers, posts that he held until his death. As a composer he is known for the 1713 anthem 'God is our hope and strength', written in celebration of the peace of Utrecht, and for a verse morning and evening service, both of them included by Thomas Tudway in the last volume of his important manuscript collection of services and anthems (BL, Harleian MS 7342). A single chant by Broderip survives in the library of Christ Church, Oxford. By Christmas 1726 he was unable to play the organ due to illness; he died in Wells on 31 January 1727 and was buried in the nave of the cathedral. He was survived by his wife, Martha (*d*. 1773), and ten children.

Several other Broderips are known to have been engaged in provincial musical activity during the eighteenth century, particularly in the west country, and most, if not all, of them were descended from William. His son **John Broderip** (1719–1770) published a small amount of sacred choral music—two sets of anthems (*c*.1747 and *c*.1750) and a collection of *Psalms, Hymns and Spiritual Songs* (1769), and he was organist at Minehead, Somerset, in 1740. He became a vicar-choral at Wells in the same year, and was organist and master of the choristers at the cathedral from 1741 until his death. He was buried in Wells on 30 December 1770. Another of William's sons, **Edmund Broderip** (*bap*. 1727, *d*. 1779), was a pupil of Francesco Geminiani and Joseph Kelway, and was organist at St James's Church, Bristol, from 1746, and at the mayor's chapel there from 1764. He played organ concertos in Salisbury in 1756 and at the opening in 1757 of the new organ in the Bristol assembly rooms in Princes Street, where he was a frequent performer. He was a teacher of the young Wesley brothers, Samuel and Charles, and also a friend of the poet Thomas Chatterton, who in January 1769 published a poem entitled 'On Mr Broderip's Excellent Performance on the Organ'. The two later fell out, however, apparently following Chatterton's expulsion from the organ loft for irksome behaviour, and subsequently Chatterton became openly critical of Broderip, most severely so in his poem 'Kew Gardens':

> While Broderip's hum-drum symphonies of flats
> Rival the harmony of midnight cats,

> What charms has music, when great Broderip sweats
> To torture sound to what his brother sets!
> (Padgett-Chandler, 799)

Among William Broderip's grandchildren, John's son **Robert Broderip** (*c*.1758–1808) played the organ in Bristol at the mayor's chapel and at St Michael's Church. He composed a number of keyboard works, including a *galant* concerto, several voluntaries, and a set of didactic lessons with instructions for novices, as well as a set of violin sonatas and some vocal music, none of which is of particular importance. He died in Church Lane, Bristol, on 14 May 1808. **Francis Fane Broderip** (*c*.1750–1807), music publisher, was probably also a son of John Broderip, and thus the brother of Robert. From 1775 he worked in the London firm Longman, Lukey, and Broderip, which made musical instruments and printed and sold music at 26 Cheapside. After Lukey's departure the following year the company was known as Longman and Broderip, and as such it became one of the most enterprising music publishers in the country, boasting an extensive and wide-ranging catalogue of works by English and foreign composers, including the 'London' symphonies of Haydn. Additional premises were acquired at 13 Haymarket in 1782, and in September 1789 further shops at Margate and Brighthelmstone (Brighton) for the sale of instruments were advertised. However, the business later succumbed to bankruptcy, and the partnership was dissolved in 1798. Broderip continued to trade at the Haymarket site with C. Wilkinson, as Broderip and Wilkinson, until his death at his home on Upper Fitzroy Street on 18 February 1807. He was survived by his wife, of whom no details are known other than that she died on 9 June 1807 in Upper Fitzroy Street.   PETER LYNAN

Sources I. Spink, *Restoration cathedral music, 1660–1714* (1995), 360 • *New Grove* • H. W. Shaw, *The succession of organists of the Chapel Royal and the cathedrals of England and Wales from c.1538* (1991), 289 • D. E. Padgett-Chandler, 'Thomas Chatterton and music', *MT*, 111 (1970), 799–800 • C. Humphries and W. C. Smith, *Music publishing in the British Isles, from the beginning until the middle of the nineteenth century: a dictionary of engravers, printers, publishers, and music sellers*, 2nd edn (1970) • D. J. Reid, 'Some festival programmes of the eighteenth and nineteenth centuries [pt 1]', *Royal Musical Association Research Chronicle*, 5 (1965), 51–79 • *GM*, 1st ser., 77 (1807), 190, 597 • *GM*, 1st ser., 78 (1808), 559

Broderip, William John (1789–1859), lawyer and naturalist, was born on 21 November 1789 at Bristol, the eldest son of William Broderip, surgeon. After being educated at the Revd Samuel Seyer's school in his native city, he matriculated at Oriel College, Oxford, in 1807 and graduated BA in 1812. While at college he found time to attend the anatomical lectures of Sir Christopher Pegge, and the chemical and mineralogical lectures of John Kidd. After completing his university education, he entered the Inner Temple, and began studying in the chambers of the then well-known Godfrey Sykes, where he had as contemporaries Sir John Patteson and Sir John Taylor Coleridge. He was called to the bar at Lincoln's Inn on 12 May 1817, when he joined the western circuit, and shortly after, in conjunction with Peregrine Bingham, began reporting in the court of common pleas. These reports were published in three volumes between 1820 and 1822. In 1822 Broderip accepted from Lord Sidmouth the appointment of magistrate at the Thames police court. He held this office until 1846, when he was transferred to the Westminster court, where he remained for ten years. He was compelled by deafness to resign, having obtained a high reputation for his good sense and humanity. In 1824 he edited the fourth edition of R. Callis's work on the Statute of Sewers, which, with its combination of antiquarian and strict legal learning, was exactly suited to his taste and talent. He was elected bencher of Gray's Inn on 30 January 1850 and treasurer on 29 January 1851, and was given care of its library.

Throughout his life Broderip was an enthusiastic collector of natural objects. His conchological collection was unrivalled, and many foreign professors inspected the treasures which were accumulated in his chambers in Gray's Inn. This collection was ultimately purchased by the British Museum. He was elected a fellow of the Linnean Society in 1824, of the Geological Society in 1825, and of the Royal Society on 14 February 1828. In co-operation with Sir Stamford Raffles he was instrumental in the formation of the Zoological Society in 1826 and was one of the original fellows. He was secretary of the Geological Society for some time, and performed the arduous duties of that office with Roderick Murchison until 1830. To the *Transactions* of this society he contributed numerous papers, but most of his original writings on molluscs are to be found in the *Proceedings and Transactions of the Zoological Society*. Broderip's descriptions of animal habits were graphic. His 'Account of the manners of a tame beaver', published in the *Gardens and Menagerie of the Zoological Society*, is a prime example of his tact as an observer and power as a writer. He published extensively on zoological matters. His contributions to the *New Monthly Magazine* and to *Fraser's Magazine* were collected in the volumes entitled *Zoological Recreations* (1847) and *Leaves from the Note-Book of a Naturalist* (1852). He wrote zoological articles in the *Penny Cyclopaedia*, including all the articles relating to mammals, birds, reptiles, crustacea, and molluscs. His last publication, 'On the shark', appeared in *Fraser's Magazine* in March 1859. Broderip died in his chambers, 2 Raymond Buildings, Gray's Inn, London, on 27 February 1859. He was unmarried.

G. C. BOASE, rev. CATHERINE PEASE-WATKIN

Sources *Law Magazine*, new ser., 8 (1859–60), 174–8 • Foster, *Alum. Oxon.* • *Proceedings of the Linnean Society of London* (1858–1959), xx–xxv • *ILN* (14 Nov 1846), 317 • *ILN* (8 March 1856), 253 • L. Berger, *Broderip, William John, ancien magistrat, naturaliste, littérateur* (1856)
Archives NMG Wales, commonplace book | BL, letters to Charles Babbage, Add. MSS 37188–37198, *passim* • GS Lond., letters to Roderick Impey Murchison • Linn. Soc., letters to William Swainson • NA Scot., corresp. with Sir Charles Augustus Murray • NHM, letters; corresp. with Richard Owen and William Clift
Likenesses wood-engraving, NPG; repro. in *ILN* (8 March 1856)
Wealth at death under £8000: resworn probate, Jan 1862, *CGPLA Eng. & Wales* (1859)

Brodetsky, Selig (1888–1954), mathematician and Zionist leader, was born on 5 July 1888 at Olviopol, a small town in Ukraine 100 miles north of Odessa, the second son among

the thirteen children of Akiva Brodetsky (1864–1942), a synagogue official, and his wife, Adel Prober (1864–1926). The family emigrated in 1893 and settled in the East End of London. Brodetsky recalled how his mother escorted her four children across the Ukrainian-German border, preventing discovery by stifling with a kerchief the crying of the infant she was carrying. The normal difficulties of life for a poor immigrant family were compounded by Akiva's failure to find steady employment with a living wage. From 1894 to 1900 Selig attended the Jews' Free School in Whitechapel, from where he won a scholarship to the Central Foundation School, Cowper Street, in the City of London. His academic potential showed itself when he headed the 1902 list of London County Council intermediate scholarship winners, and in 1905 he won a mathematical scholarship to Trinity College, Cambridge. His success in being bracketed senior wrangler in the 1908 mathematical tripos caused a minor national sensation. Newspaper editorials noted that if the Aliens Act restricting immigration had been passed earlier the Brodetsky family would have been barred. Later he was awarded the Isaac Newton studentship to work in the Cambridge observatory. In 1912 he went to Leipzig where he took his PhD for a thesis on gravitation.

Brodetsky's first academic appointment was as lecturer in applied mathematics at Bristol University. During the First World War, besides sharing a full heavy teaching load with the lecturer in pure mathematics, he was mathematical adviser to a firm specializing in the construction of optical instruments such as submarine periscopes, and collaborated with Professor G. H. Bryan of University College, Bangor, on mathematical aeronautics. His pioneering book, *Mathematical Principles of the Aeroplane*, was published in 1921, following his 1920 text *A First Course in Nomography*.

On 13 January 1919 Brodetsky married Mania (1890–1969), daughter of Paul Berenblum, from Białystok and Antwerp. There was a son, Paul (1924–1979), later on the staff of Ruskin College, Oxford, a daughter, Adèle (Mrs Kitrick), and four grandsons. In 1920 he moved to Leeds as reader in applied mathematics, becoming professor in 1924, and succeeding his colleague W. P. Milne as head of the mathematics department in 1946 until his retirement in 1948. He continued his academic research into aeronautics and fluid mechanics. In 1927 he published a life of Sir Isaac Newton, which appeared simultaneously with the Newton bicentenary celebrations in which he took a leading part, and which included a pilgrimage to Newton's birthplace. His successful popular book *The Meaning of Mathematics* appeared in 1929.

Already at Cambridge Brodetsky had established the pattern of dividing his time between academic work and public service, especially but by no means exclusively for the Jewish community and the Zionist movement. While at Leeds he was active in the affairs of the League of Nations Union (later the United Nations Association) and of the Association of University Teachers. In 1928 he became a member of the World Zionist Executive and head of its political department in London. In 1940 he became president of the Board of Deputies of British Jews, the lay head of British Jewry. His election symbolized a democratic revolution, with the communal leadership being taken over from the old-established families by the descendants of the late nineteenth-century immigration. It also demonstrated that Zionism, towards which much of the establishment had been indifferent or hostile, had now the support of the majority of the community, undoubtedly owing to the traumatic events of the Nazi era and the Second World War.

Brodetsky achieved his crowning ambition when in 1949 he was elected president of the Hebrew University of Jerusalem, a year after the foundation of the state of Israel. However, there appeared to be differing views as to the role of the presidency, which under his predecessor, Judah Magnes, had become semi-honorific, whereas Brodetsky viewed the post as analogous to that of a British vice-chancellor rather than to that of a chancellor. Many of the reforms of the university administration which he advocated were subsequently put into effect but, tragically, the continuing controversies led to a breakdown in his health. After a massive heart attack in 1950, he returned to London in 1951, resigned from the presidency effective in 1952, and devoted his remaining few years to the writing of his memoirs. He died at his home, 8 Brompton Lodge, 9–11 Cromwell Road, London, on 18 May 1954, and was buried at Willesden Jewish cemetery, London, two days later. He was survived by his wife. His public work was recalled thirty years on in a meeting called by Lord Weidenfeld at the House of Lords. Streets were named after him on the Hebrew University campus and in Tel Aviv. A Brodetsky House was attached to Tel Aviv University, a Brodetsky School was established in Leeds, and a Brodetsky House at the Jews' Free School.

LEON MESTEL

Sources S. Brodetsky, *Memoirs: from ghetto to Israel* (1960) · *Reminiscences and letters of Sir Robert Ball*, ed. W. V. Ball (1915) · private information (2004) [Mrs Kitrick, daughter]
Archives U. Southampton L., corresp. and papers | Bodl. Oxf., corresp. relating to Society for Protection of Science and Learning · Central Zionist Archives, Jerusalem, corresp. relating to Hebrew University · LMA, papers as president of board of deputies of British Jews · U. Leeds, Brotherton L., corresp. relating to Leeds academic assistance committee · U. Southampton L., corresp. with James Parkes
Likenesses group portrait, photograph, 2 Nov 1949, Hult. Arch. · J. Epstein, bust, probably Hebrew University, Jerusalem · J. Kramer, oils, U. Leeds
Wealth at death £3679 11s. 3d.: probate, 4 Nov 1954, CGPLA Eng. & Wales

Brodie [Brody], **Alexander, of Brodie, Lord Brodie** (1617–1680), politician and judge, was born on 25 July 1617, the eldest of the four children of David Brodie of Brodie (1586–1632) and his wife, Katherine (d. c.1664), daughter of Thomas Dunbar of Grange, dean of Moray. In 1628 he was sent to England where he remained until 1632. He was further educated at St Andrews and at King's College, Aberdeen (1632–3), but did not take a degree. He married Elizabeth (d. 1640), eldest daughter of Sir Robert Innes of Innes and widow of John Urquhart of Craigston, on 28 October

1635, and they had two children, Grissel (b. 1636) and James (1637–1708). On 19 May 1636 he was served heir to his father.

Brodie was appointed a justice of the peace for Aberdeen about 8 December 1636 and in September 1638 was appointed a commissioner to enforce subscription to the king's covenant in Elgin and Forres. He was, however, a strong presbyterian and in December 1640 was among a party which vandalized two paintings in, and part of the structure of, Elgin Cathedral. On 5 July 1642 he was appointed a commissioner for the apprehension of Jesuits and seminary priests in the areas of Banff, Elgin, Forres, and Nairn. A shire commissioner for Elgin from 1643, he was to serve on several of the parliamentary and other administrative bodies of the covenanting regime in the following years. He was a member of the committee of estates (1643, 1645, 1647, 1649), the committee for the protection of religion (July 1643), the committee of war for Elgin, Nairn, and Inverness (August 1643, July 1644, February 1649) and for Elgin and Forres (1648), the committee of excise (January 1644), the visitation of the University of Aberdeen (1645, 1649), and the commission for plantation of kirks (1649). His property was devastated by Montrose's royalist forces in 1645, the burning of his writs resulting in his petitioning parliament in August of that year to be secured from loss. The petition was granted, and the barony of Brodie was ratified to him by parliament in 1647.

On 6 March 1649 Brodie was appointed by the ruling kirk party a commissioner to negotiate with the exiled Charles II at The Hague. Though Charles's agreement to their terms was not obtained, Brodie was commended for his services on his return to Scotland. With the removal from office of those who had lent support to the engagement, he was appointed an ordinary lord of session, as Lord Brodie, on 22 June 1649, and nominated a senator of the college of justice 'Notwithstanding of many reasons offered be him in the Contrair' (APS, 6(2).436). In February to March 1650 he was again nominated, by both kirk and state, to treat with the king, acting as one of the 'uncompromising extremists' (Stevenson, 157) among the commissioners. He joined the other state commissioners in inviting Charles to Scotland despite his failure to subscribe the terms presented to him (presumably signing on a ruling requiring unanimity), but opposed the invitation as a representative of the kirk. In June 1650, with the king already embarked for Scotland, Brodie was among the commissioners who insisted on securing further concessions. Back in Scotland, he served on the committee appointed to further purge the army of those deemed insufficiently committed to the cause, and was named commissary-general. He was among those who strove to keep Charles from the army lest his popularity overshadow the cause of the covenants. Unsurprisingly he was one of the individuals considered for capture in an unsuccessful plot directed by royalist associates of the king in October 1650.

With the Cromwellian conquest of Scotland, the English Commonwealth seemed eager to entice Brodie into serving the new regime. He was among those cited to London by Cromwell, on 17 June 1653, to discuss a union of Scotland and England. He avoided the citation, as he then also avoided taking his seat after nomination to the Barebone's Parliament later in the year. In August 1654 he was one of those entrusted to ensure, for the area north of Forfarshire, that only 'Godly and able men' (*APS*, 6(2).831–2) be admitted to the ministry and to educational posts. He was appointed a burgess of Glasgow in September 1655. He was again made a justice of the peace in October 1655 despite his reluctance to take an oath acknowledging the protectorate. Pressed to resume his seat as a judge, he declined until January 1658, only to be dismissed at the Restoration. He was excepted from the indemnity and fined £4800 Scots in 1662 though he had not yet been repaid the money he had advanced the king in 1650, a debt the Scottish parliament agreed to honour in 1661. Though opposed to the restoration of episcopacy, he resolved 'to be as submissive, and obedient, and peaceable as any' (*Diary*, ed. Laing, xlix) and thereafter resided mostly at Brodie. He died on 17 April 1680 and was succeeded by his son. Surviving portions of his diary, concerned with 'daily religious experiences and meditations, interspected with occasional notices of public occurrences' (*Diary*, ed. Laing, xi) were published in 1740 and 1863.   ALISON G. MUIR

Sources *The diary of Alexander Brodie of Brodie … and of his son James Brodie*, ed. D. Laing, Spalding Club, 33 (1863) • *APS*, 1643–69 • M. D. Young, ed., *The parliaments of Scotland: burgh and shire commissioners*, 1 (1992), 68–9 • G. Brunton and D. Haig, *An historical account of the senators of the college of justice, from its institution in MDXXXII* (1832), 343–4 • G. Bain, *Lord Brodie: his life and times, 1617–80* (1904) • *Reg. PCS*, 2nd ser., 6.349; 7.77, 289 • *Reg. PCS*, 3rd ser., 2.49, 5.340 • *CSP dom.*, 1650, p. 157; 1655, p. 126; 1655–6, p. 296; 1656–7, p. 10 • J. Nicoll, *A diary of public transactions and other occurrences, chiefly in Scotland, from January 1650 to June 1667*, ed. D. Laing, Bannatyne Club, 52 (1836), 109, 111–12, 210 • J. Spalding, *The history of the troubles and memorable transactions in Scotland and England: from 1624 to 1645*, ed. J. Skene, 1, Bannatyne Club, 25 (1828), 286 • L. Shaw, *The history of the province of Moray* (1775), 105–7 • Burke, *Gen. GB* (1965–72) • D. Stevenson, *Revolution and counter-revolution in Scotland, 1644–1651*, Royal Historical Society Studies in History, 4 (1977) • J. R. Young, *The Scottish parliament, 1639–1661: a political and constitutional analysis* (1996) • *DNB*

Brodie, Alexander, of Brodie (1697–1754), politician, was born on 17 August 1697, the second son of George Brodie MP (*d*. 1715), of Brodie and Aslick, Elgin, and his wife, Emilia, the fifth daughter and coheir of James Brodie of Elgin. He was educated at Marischal College, Aberdeen, where he matriculated in 1710, and, it is believed, at Leiden, where he may have matriculated in 1719.

Brodie was descended from an ancient Elginshire family with a long-established interest in politics, his father and grandfather both having represented local seats in parliament. In 1720 he succeeded his brother James (1695–1720), both as laird of Brodie and as MP for Elginshire (James had been returned at a by-election in January 1720, but died the following October). Alexander held the seat without opposition for over twenty years, from 29 December 1720 to 25 May 1741. On 3 September 1724 he married Mary Sleigh (1704–1760), the daughter of Major Samuel Sleigh of the 16th foot; they had a son, Alexander (1741–1759), and a daughter, Emilia (*b*. 1730).

Brodie was a loyal government supporter and was rewarded by appointment as lord Lyon king of arms by a commission of 6 July 1727, with a salary of £300 a year. He was the first lord Lyon of the Hanoverian dynasty, and his appointment took place under exceptional circumstances, since his predecessor, Sir Alexander Erskine, had been deep in Jacobite intrigues and the office of lord Lyon was viewed as a centre of Jacobite sympathies. In addition, everything Scottish was viewed from London with suspicion bordering on hatred: Brodie's commission was the first made without reference to Scottish sources and the first not to carry the hitherto customary knighthood. Brodie nevertheless adopted the title lord Lyon king of arms and the prefix 'honourable' and maintained the right to walk in the coronation procession of George II. Despite the necessity to be resident in London for a large part of the year to carry out his parliamentary duties, Brodie took an active interest in the business of the Lyon court. He is said to have enforced the laws of arms with vigour and impartiality, and even such exalted offenders as the earl and countess of Wemyss suffered deletion and removal of bogus arms which they had created. Matriculation of arms and the heraldic and genealogical business of the Lyon court seems to have been conducted with understanding and appreciation under his direction.

Brodie was politically attached to Lord Ilay, Walpole's election manager for Scotland, to the extent of 'giving himself the airs of being my Lord Ilay's minister in the north' (Fraser, 1.379). During intrigues surrounding the 1734 general election he came into conflict with several neighbouring influential landowners, including Lord Lovat, with whom he quarrelled violently in January 1733. According to Lovat, Brodie:

> abus'd me, threaten'd me and insulted me … He first accus'd me sillily that I and all the Frasers had made a league with Culodin against Grant … Then he threatened me, and told me he would blow me up with the Earle of Ilay. I told him that he and all the Brodies on earth joined to all the divels in hell could not blow me up with the Earle of Ilay … I own my temper was much try'd … but bless God, providence stiffled my passion, that I did not send the mad fool to hell as he deserv'd. (Lovat to Sir James Grant, 23 Jan 1733, Fraser, 1.379)

Brodie then set out to gain control of Nairnshire, but the candidate he put up at a by-election in 1735 was unsuccessful.

In 1741 Brodie was forced to surrender his Elginshire seat to Sir Ludovick Grant, but he was brought in for Caithness by his nephew George Sinclair of Ulbster, its hereditary sheriff. Brodie was a government informer, and at the time of his death he was receiving a secret-service pension of £300 per year. After the Jacobite rising of 1745 he reported to the duke of Newcastle that the earl of Sutherland had been harbouring a prominent rebel. It was also said that he had helped to procure evidence against Lord Lovat, observing that 'it will be of the greatest service to the family of Lovat to have the old man beheaded, which would save the son' (BL, Add. MS 32709, fol. 389). The next year he reported to Newcastle the landing of a Jacobite agent by a French privateer on the west coast of the highlands. He took a hard line over the Highland Dress Bill in 1746, dismissing the doubts of those who felt it should not apply to clans who had taken the government's side during the rising and saying that this 'would not do; the thing must be general or could have no effect' (Brodie to Duncan Forbes, 1 July 1746, Warrand, 5.112–13).

However, Brodie could show compassion and magnanimity. A number of heralds and other officers on his staff in the Lyon office declared on the side of the Jacobites during the rising, but Brodie used his influence to save them from government vengeance—including, in one instance, obtaining for one of the clerks a pardon from sentence of death; in 1749 he secured the restoration of their salaries.

In the 1747 parliament, in which Caithness was not represented, Brodie sat for Inverness burghs under a scheme drawn up by Henry Pelham to prevent contests between government supporters in Scotland. He died of a heart complaint in London on 9 March 1754. His body was embalmed and carried north for burial at Dyke, close to the family seat at Brodie House.   ANDREW M. LANG

Sources J. M. Simpson, 'Brodie, Alexander', HoP, *Commons, 1715–54* · T. Innes, *The Brodie family: Alexander Brodie of Brodie, 1697–1754* (1930) · J. Foster, *Members of parliament, Scotland … 1357–1882*, 2nd edn (privately printed, London, 1882) · Burke, *Gen. GB* (1972) · *Scots Magazine*, 16 (1754), 109 · *History of the family of Brodie of Brodie* (1881) · W. Brodie, *The genealogy of the Brodie family* (1862) · W. Fraser, ed., *The chiefs of Grant*, 3 vols. (1883) · G. Menary, *The life and letters of Duncan Forbes of Culloden* (1936) · D. Warrand, ed., *More Culloden papers*, 5 vols. (1923–30)
Likenesses portrait, Brodie Castle, Moray

Brodie, Alexander

Brodie, Alexander (1829/30–1867), sculptor, was born at 8 Virginia Street, Aberdeen, the youngest of the three sons of John Brodie (1786/7–1865), shipmaster and merchant seaman, of Banff and Aberdeen, and his wife, Mary Walker (1786?–1846). While serving an apprenticeship as a brass-finisher in the foundry of Messrs Blaikie Bros. in Aberdeen, he attracted the attention of Sheriff Watson of Aberdeen, an influential early benefactor of his elder brother, the sculptor William *Brodie (1815–1881). Watson's patronage enabled Alexander Brodie to move to Edinburgh, where he attended the Trustees' Academy from 1850 to 1852 and worked concurrently in his brother's studio. In 1852, having gained a special prize for ornamental design, he made his public début as an independent sculptor by exhibiting portrait medallions at the Royal Scottish Academy. Following his readmission to the Trustees' Academy as a student of Robert Scott Lauder in 1855, he secured the highest prize for modelling from the antique in 1856.

By this time Brodie had already shown 'great promise of outstripping his brother in the race for fame', as William Brodie's obituarist later commented (*Daily Free Press*, 31 Oct 1881). In 1858 he returned permanently to Aberdeen and worked from a studio in Bothwell's Court, Justice Street, and, by 1865, from 56 Loch Street. In addition to his considerable practice in bust portraiture in marble, he

specialized in graveyard monuments, typified by the William Copland monument (1863) in St Nicholas's churchyard, Aberdeen, and the memorial obelisk to his own parents (1865) in St Clement's churchyard, Footdee, Aberdeen. His abiding interest in ideal and narrative sculpture was confirmed by his submission of *Oenone* to the International Exhibition of 1862 in London. Of his other recorded groups in marble, *Mercury* (1862) is at Bowood House, Wiltshire, *The Mitherless Lassie* and *Cupid and Mask* were exhibited at the Royal Academy in 1864, and *Highland Mary* (undated) is in Aberdeen Art Gallery.

Brodie's return to Aberdeen initiated a series of commissions for public sculpture, all financed by subscription and of major regional significance. Modelled in plaster in 1858, his memorial statue of the Revd Charles Gordon of St Peter's Roman Catholic chapel in Justice Street was cut in granite by Alexander MacDonald (resited on the façade of Nelson Street School). In 1862 his monument to the fifth duke of Richmond was unveiled on the Square in Huntly, Aberdeenshire. Two years later he was unanimously selected as the sculptor for the Aberdeen statue of Queen Victoria, commissioned as a pendant to Baron Marochetti's bronze of the prince consort and executed in Sicilian marble in 1866 from sittings at Balmoral. The distinctively Scottish character of the statue evolved by royal command, a plaid of royal Stewart tartan being substituted for court robes. Originally positioned at the junction of Union Street and St Nicholas Street, the monument was removed indoors in 1888 and was later placed in Aberdeen city chambers. A related bust, begun in 1865, was completed in 1867 after the sculptor's death by his brother William (versions at Windsor, Balmoral, and the Scottish National Portrait Gallery, Edinburgh).

By May 1867 Brodie had accumulated over three years' work in his studio. His recent exertions apparently precipitated a sudden mental collapse, resulting in his suicide at his residence, 6 Garvock Street, on 30 May. He was unmarried. He was buried in St Clement's churchyard, Footdee, Aberdeen, probably on 3 June.

HELEN E. SMAILES

Sources G. M. Fraser, 'William and Alexander Brodie, sculptors', *Scottish Notes and Queries*, 3rd ser., 1 (1923), 4–7, 20–21, 35–6, 49–51, 65–8 · R. L. Woodward, 'Nineteenth century Scottish sculpture', PhD diss., U. Edin., 1979, vol. 3, pp. 17–20 · 'The Aberdeen statue of the queen', *Aberdeen Free Press* (21 Sept 1866) · *The Scotsman* (31 May 1867), 3 · *Aberdeen Journal* (5 June 1867) · J. Stark, *Priest Gordon of Aberdeen* (1909), xiv, 131 · *Wiltshire*, Pevsner (1963) · statutory register of deaths, Aberdeen, St Nicholas's parish, 1867, no. 504 (168/1) · memorial, St Clement's churchyard, Footdee, Aberdeen · School of Design (Trustees' Academy) Edinburgh, ledger of students, 1848–56, NA Scot., NG 2/1/4 · C. B. de Laperriere, ed., *The Royal Scottish Academy exhibitors, 1826–1990*, 4 vols. (1991), vol. 1, p. 178
Likenesses J. Bisset, photograph, after 1858, priv. coll.; repro. in Fraser, 'William and Alexander Brodie', 33
Wealth at death £352 1s. 6d.—personal estate, incl. stock-in-trade, Bothwell's Court, Aberdeen: inventory, 1867, NA Scot., SC 1/36/61/3

Brodie, Sir Benjamin Collins

Brodie, Sir Benjamin Collins, first baronet (1783–1862), physiologist and surgeon, was born on 8 June 1783 at Winterslow, Wiltshire, the fourth child and third son of Peter Bellinger Brodie (1742–1804), rector of the parish, and his

Sir Benjamin Collins Brodie, first baronet (1783–1862), by Maull & Polyblank, late 1850s

wife, Sarah (1755–1847), daughter of Benjamin *Collins, a banker and printer in Salisbury. He received his early education from his father, who had been educated at Charterhouse School and Worcester College, Oxford, and who was of Scottish descent, related to the Brodies of Brodie. When he went up to London at the age of eighteen to enter the medical profession Brodie found that he was better educated than other medical students. Brodie began anatomical studies by attending the lectures of John Abernethy at St Bartholomew's Hospital, and in 1801 and 1802 those of James Wilson at the Hunterian school in Great Windmill Street. He learned pharmacy in the shop of William Clifton, a licentiate of the Society of Apothecaries, in Little Newport Street. At this time he became a close friend of the surgeon William Lawrence and he was joint secretary with Henry Ellis of a student academical society which had moved from Oxford to London and to which many future eminent writers and lawyers belonged.

In the spring of 1803 Brodie entered St George's Hospital as a surgical pupil of Everard Home; he was appointed house surgeon in May 1805, and afterwards demonstrator to the anatomical school. He was admitted MRCS on 18 October 1805. When his term of office had expired he assisted Home in his private operations and in his researches on comparative anatomy with William Clift at the Hunterian Museum in the College of Surgeons. In later life Brodie spiritedly defended Home against the accusation that his publications were plagiarized from those of his (Home's) brother-in-law, John Hunter. In 1808

he was elected a member of the Society for the Improvement of Medical and Chirurgical Knowledge, a club limited to twelve members, founded by John Hunter and George Fordyce in 1793 and dissolved in 1818. Brodie's study of anatomy also continued at the Great Windmill Street School, where he demonstrated jointly with Wilson until 1812. From 1808 until 1830 he also delivered an annual course of surgical lectures at the school. He was elected assistant surgeon to St George's Hospital in 1808, and was made senior surgeon in 1822, holding the post until 1840, when he resigned to make way for a younger man. In 1809 he began private practice, taking a house in Sackville Street, Piccadilly, for the purpose.

Brodie's career embraced physiology, surgery, psychology, and membership of Britain's medical clerisy. Between 1808 and 1825 he was an active member with Home, Humphry Davy, William Brande, William Babington, and others of the Royal Society's select dining club, the Assistant Society for the Improvement of Animal Chemistry. The club encouraged Brodie's physiological interests, which challenged the prevailing theory that had been established by Lavoisier of the purely chemical origin of animal heat. In vivisections that destroyed an animal's brain while respiration and heartbeat were maintained artificially Brodie showed that the animal's temperature plummeted. Moreover, if the brain was desensitized by poisons such as tobacco smoke, alcohol, or curare, and then allowed to recover, the animal's power of generating heat also returned. Later investigators, including Claude Bernard, supposed that Brodie had shown animal heat to be under nervous control; but, as a committed empiricist, he merely drew the conclusion that a chemical explanation of animal heat was insufficient. These factual experiments, which also included a demonstration of the control of gastric secretion by the vagus nerve, were reported to the Royal Society (to which he was elected on 15 February 1810) in the form of five papers and a Croonian lecture between 1810 and 1814. Greatly impressed, the Royal Society awarded him the Copley medal in 1811, making him its youngest ever recipient.

Brodie's unremitting devotion to intensive study, lecturing, and experimenting without any break told seriously upon his health, and he had a breakdown in 1815. This was one reason why he withdrew from physiological investigations where, in any case, he lacked the theoretical and speculative cast of mind needed to make a great investigator. Another reason was his marriage in 1816 to Anne (1797–1861), the daughter of Baker John *Sellon (1762–1835), a sergeant-at-law. Of their four children, a son, Sir Benjamin Collins *Brodie (1817–1880), became a distinguished chemist, and their daughter Maria Eliza (d. 1863) was the mother of Joseph Charles Hoare, bishop of Victoria, Hong Kong. It was at this juncture that Brodie decided on humanitarian grounds to devote himself to surgery, a field he rather despised for requiring little intellectual accomplishment (Works, 143). While not devoid of manual skill and proving an efficient operator, his particular forte was diagnosis, aided by his vigorous practice of keeping detailed case notes. When he was a house surgeon his interest had been aroused by a case of spontaneous dislocation of the hip. This led him to study other cases of diseases of the joints, and in 1813 he published a pathological paper in the *Medico-Chirurgical Transactions* that became the basis of a major treatise on orthopaedics, *Diseases of the Joints* (1818). This important and influential text, which skilfully analysed case histories, and aimed to teach surgeons how to preserve limbs that might otherwise have been amputated, went through five editions, and was translated into several languages. It included descriptions of hysterical pseudo-fracture of the spine, and the first clinical description of ankylosing spondylitis. In the fifth edition (1850) he identified Brodie's disease, a chronic synovitis in which an affected joint undergoes a pulpy degeneration. He was often adventurous in trying out new surgical procedures (though slow to adopt anaesthesia after its introduction in 1847). For example, in a paper on varicose veins of the legs, published in the *Medico-Chirurgical Transactions* in 1816, he described the first subcutaneous operation on record; in 1828 he devised a technique for trephining the tibia for chronic inflammation (Brodie's abscess); in 1835 he pioneered a technique for correction of abnormalities in the anal sphincter (Brodie's pile); and in 1840 he identified a particular form of breast tumour (Brodie's tumour). Case histories collected for his student lectures formed the basis of two other influential texts, *Diseases of the Urinary Organs* (1832) and *Local Nervous Diseases* (1837). Brodie disliked lithotomy and was quick to adopt the French procedure of lithotrity, in which a stone is crushed in the bladder. Despite such texts on particular subjects, Brodie avoided specialization and always saw himself as a general surgeon. This was exemplified in his *Lectures Illustrative of Various Subjects in Pathology and Surgery* (1846). These lectures recorded the first description of claudication in man, as opposed to horses, and Brodie's test for valvular damage in the veins. All of his papers were collected posthumously for publication in 1865. This contains a shrewdly written autobiography that he produced for family consumption in 1855.

A theist and anti-materialist, Brodie was profoundly interested in metaphysical questions. In 1854 he published an anonymous volume of *Psychological Enquiries*, a series of essays in dialogue form among a country gentleman, a doctor, and a lawyer. Much influenced by Davy's posthumous *Consolations in Travel* (1830), the essays were intended to illustrate for the general reader the mutual relations of physical organization and mental faculties. In 1862 a second series followed, to which he put his name. Although by then he had accepted the theory of evolution, these well-meaning, but turgid, dialogues were concerned with unfashionable topics such as dualism, natural theology, and the problem of pain and immortality. They made little impact on Brodie's contemporaries, who found Herbert Spencer's psychological and evolutionary writings more exciting.

Brodie had reached the pinnacle of the medical profession by 1819 when he moved to Savile Row. His time was fully occupied with hospital duties, lecturing, lucrative practice, consultancies, and chairmanships, and by the 1830s he was earning £10,000 p.a. As general practitioners began to clamour for institutional reforms, he was perceived as a member of the conservative medical establishment. A Foxite whig politically, and a close family friend of the third Lord Holland, Brodie did see the need for some reforms, providing they preserved a hierarchical division of labour between hospital consultants and general practitioners. He firmly believed that its moral, religious, and scientific education and leadership should distinguish the élite of the medical profession. He therefore strongly supported the foundation of the *London Medical Gazette* in 1827 to counter Thomas Wakley's assertions in *The Lancet* that hospital surgeons and the council of the Royal College of Surgeons were corrupt. Unflinching against quackery, he was instrumental in bringing the empiric St John Long to justice for manslaughter, and his clinical evidence in the witness box was effective against the poisoner Dr William Palmer in 1856. From 1819 to 1823 he was professor of comparative anatomy and physiology at the Royal College of Surgeons, and he delivered four courses of lectures on the anatomy and physiology of the heart and lungs (including comments on death by drowning, strangulation, and hanging), the organs of digestion, and the nervous system. The lectures show that, while he had not lost the knack of animal experimentation, he ignored the French and German work on comparative anatomy that was currently exciting the more radical general practitioners. While he held this office he was summoned to attend George IV, and assisted at an operation for the removal of a tumour from the king's scalp. He became the king's personal surgeon in 1828, attending him during his final illness in 1830. When William IV succeeded to the throne Brodie was made sergeant-surgeon (1832), a post he continued under Queen Victoria. He was made a baronet in 1834 and bought Broome Park, Betchworth, Surrey, as his family seat in 1837, in which year he travelled to France for the first time. He was president of the Royal Medical and Chirurgical Society (1839), where he introduced discussions at meetings. In 1844 he was elected president of the Royal College of Surgeons, having been for many years examiner and member of the council, and having introduced important improvements into the system of examinations and the structure of its hitherto self-perpetuating council. Together with Joseph Henry Green and John Simon he was closely involved in the complex negotiations that led to the Medical Act of 1858; while this met some of the demands of general practitioners, it satisfyingly kept power in traditional hands. He thoroughly disapproved of homoeopathy and of unlicensed practice, and saw the necessity for a regulatory body such as the General Medical Council, whose first president he became in 1858. In the same year he became the first surgeon to be elected president of the Royal Society, but resigned in 1861 when failing eyesight caused by untreatable cataracts interfered with the discharge of his duties. Brodie was a member of the Institute of France, the Academy of Medicine of Paris, and the Royal Academy of Sciences of Stockholm. The University of Oxford conferred upon him the degree of DCL in 1855. He died at Broome Park on 21 October 1862 from a shoulder tumour brought on by a riding accident in 1834, and was buried in Betchworth churchyard.

Brodie's writing and lecturing were concise, but purely observational. As a surgeon he was a successful operator, distinguished for coolness and knowledge, a steady hand, and a quick eye; but the prevention of disease was in his opinion of greater significance than operative surgery, and his strength was diagnosis. An accurate observer, his memory was very retentive, and he was never at a loss for some previous case that threw light upon the knotty points in a consultation. He was 'small but strongly built, vigorous and brusque, with keen grey eyes and fine expressive features' (Le Fanu, 43). He was a committed Christian all of his life, memorably declaring upon his deathbed that despite his pain, 'after all, God is very good' (Holmes, 199).

W. H. BROCK

Sources The works of the late Sir Benjamin C. Brodie, ed. C. Hawkins, 1 (1865) · H. W. Acland, Biographical sketch of Sir Benjamin Brodie (1864) [offprinted from PRS, 12 (1863), xlii–lvi] · T. Holmes, Sir Benjamin Collins Brodie (1898) · W. R. Le Fanu, 'Sir Benjamin Brodie', Notes and Records of the Royal Society, 19 (1964), 42–52 · J. Goodfield, 'Brodie, Benjamin Collins', DSB, 2.482–4 · K. B. Thomas, 'Benjamin Brodie, physiologist', Medical History, 8 (1964), 286–91 · N. G. Coley, 'The Animal Chemistry Club', Notes and Records of the Royal Society, 22 (1967), 173–85 · F. H. Garrison and L. T. Morton, A medical bibliography, 4th edn (1983) · A. Desmond, The politics of evolution: morphology, medicine and reform in radical London (1989) · DNB · P. J. Wallis and R. V. Wallis, Eighteenth century medics, 2nd edn (1988)
Archives Bodl. Oxf., Radcliffe Science Library, corresp. · CUL, corresp. · RCP Lond., corresp. and papers · RCS Eng., papers · Royal Institution of Great Britain, London, letters · St George's Hospital, London, medical school, corresp. and papers · University of Leicester, corresp. · Wellcome L. | BL, letters to Charles Babbage, Add. MSS 37188–37189, passim · BL, corresp. with Sir Robert Peel, Add. MSS 40390–40601, passim · Bodl. Oxf., letters to Sir Henry Wentworth Acland · RS, corresp. with Sir John Herschel · RS, letters to Sir John Lubbock · UCL, letters to William Sharpey · Yale U., Beinecke L., letters to T. J. Pettigrew
Likenesses C. Turner, mezzotint, pubd 1821 (after J. J. Halls), BM, Wellcome L. · H. Heath, etching, 1830, Wellcome L. · W. Behnes, plaster bust, 1835, Oxf. U. Mus. NH · W. Wyon, bronze medal, 1841, RCS Eng. · Maull & Polyblank, albumen print, 1856–9, NPG [see illus.] · G. F. Watts, portrait, 1860, repro. in Holmes, Sir Benjamin Collins Brodie · H. Weekes, marble bust, 1863, RCS Eng. · A. Thompson, oils, 1873 (after G. F. Watts), RS · J. Brain, stipple and line engraving (after H. Room), NPG, Wellcome L. · F. Chantrey, pencil drawing, NPG · D. J. Pound, stipple and line engraving (after Maull & Polyblank), NPG, Wellcome L.; repro. in Illustrated News of the World · wood-engraving (after Smyth), Wellcome L.
Wealth at death under £18,000: probate, 11 March 1863, CGPLA Eng. & Wales

Brodie, Sir Benjamin Collins, second baronet (1817–1880), chemist, was born in Sackville Street, Piccadilly, London, on 5 February 1817, the eldest son of Sir Benjamin Collins *Brodie (1783–1862), surgeon, and his wife, Anne Sellon (1797–1861). At the age of eleven he went to Harrow School from where he won a classics scholarship to Gonville and Caius College, Cambridge. However, his father, preferring him to be educated as a commoner, sent him to Balliol College, Oxford, in 1835, where his interests turned away from classics to mathematics. Brodie graduated BA

in 1838, but because of his agnosticism and refusal to assent to the Thirty-Nine Articles, he was unable until 1860 to obtain the MA degree essential for a respectable academic career at Oxford. For some time after graduation Brodie trained for the bar at Lincoln's Inn in the chambers of his uncle, Peter Brodie. In 1844, finding that he disliked the law, he decided to study chemistry with Justus Liebig at Giessen, where he was awarded a doctorate in 1850 for the analysis of beeswax. This work, for which he was elected a fellow of the Royal Society (1849) and awarded its royal medal (1850), proved the existence of solid alcohols that were homologous with known alcohols, and had important implications for the understanding of animal metabolism.

Following his return to London in 1845, and for the following decade, Brodie worked in his own private laboratory near Regent's Park, where he taught chemistry to his intimate friend and later Oxford colleague, Nevil Story Maskelyne. In April 1848, Brodie married Philothea Margaret Vincent (d. 27 Jan 1882), daughter of John Vincent Thompson, a sergeant-at-law. There were six children.

Brodie's early chemical work was an attempt to reconcile Berzelian electrochemical dualism with newer ideas concerning the multi-atomicity of certain elements. He was intensely interested in allotropy, which he believed to be due to the arrangement and charge of the particles making up an element. By 1850 Brodie had established himself as a leading experimental and theoretical chemist. From 1850 to 1856 he was secretary of the Chemical Society, and while its president (1859–61) was one of the British delegates to the conference on atomic weights in Karlsruhe. During the 1850s he published fundamental experimental studies of the allotropic modifications of sulphur, phosphorus, and carbon. He discovered that iodine catalysed the conversion of yellow into red phosphorus, and that pure graphite, when treated with potassium chlorate, formed a crystalline graphitic acid, which he speculated might contain a graphite radical, graphon $[(Gr)_4]$. His process for the purification of graphite, which he patented, proved of considerable technical value.

In 1855, despite some opposition from theological fellows, Brodie was elected to the Aldrichian chair of chemistry at Oxford, where he did much to gain recognition for chemistry as an academic study, as well as proper laboratory facilities for its teaching. He also took a leading part in the campaign for university reform. In 1865, three years after he succeeded to his father's baronetcy, Brodie's chair was renamed the Wayneflete, but because of his marriage no college fellowship was ever offered to him. He resigned from the chair in 1872 because of ill health, and retired to a magnificent house on the top of Box Hill in Surrey. In the same year he published a paper on the action of electricity on oxygen which confirmed suggestions that the ozone molecule was triatomic, and introduced the well-known apparatus for the preparation of ozone, 'Brodie's ozonizer'.

Brodie's most remarkable theoretical achievement was his sustained opposition to Dalton's atomic theory. In

1866 he published a 'calculus of chemical operations' which introduced Greek symbols for standardized volumes of the chemical elements to replace the roman alphabet (Berzelian) symbols that contemporary chemists used to represent atomic weights. Besides its revolutionary symbolism, the calculus also demanded an appreciation of George Boole's algebraic logic. Few contemporary chemists were able to follow Brodie's reasoning and what principally interested them was its implication that elements such as chlorine might be compounds. Brodie's 'ideal chemistry', as he called it, stimulated a great deal of fruitful controversy in the 1860s and 1870s, as well as spectroscopic observations, but it ultimately foundered because of his inability to account for the phenomenon of stereoisomerism—something that was brilliantly elucidated by Le Bel and Van't Hoff using the theory of chemical structure based upon an atomic theory of matter.

Brodie died at Torquay on 24 November 1880 from rheumatic fever, with the calculus on which he had spent twenty years of his life uncompleted. He was buried in Betchworth churchyard, Surrey. W. H. BROCK

Sources *JCS*, 39 (1881), 182–5 • W. V. Farrar, 'Sir B. C. Brodie and his calculus of chemical operations', *Chymia*, 9 (1964), 181–200 • W. H. Brock, ed., *The atomic debates: Brodie and the rejection of the atomic theory* (1967) • Burke, *Peerage* • D. C. Goodman, 'Brodie, Benjamin Collins', *DSB* • W. H. Brock, 'The Newdigate prize in 1837: Stanley and Brodie', *N&Q*, 213 (1968), 412–13 • V. Morton, *Oxford rebels: the life and friends of Nevil Story Maskelyne, 1823–1911* (1987) • W. R. Ward, *Victorian Oxford* (1965) • *DNB* • personal knowledge (2004)
Archives MHS Oxf., corresp., notebooks, and papers • University of Leicester Library, corresp. and papers | Bodl. Oxf., corresp. with H. H. Vaughan • CUL, letters to Sir George Stokes • LUL, A. de Morgan collection • RCP Lond., letters to Sir James Alderson • Trinity Cam., corresp. with William Whewell
Likenesses photograph, *c*.1875, repro. in Brock, ed., *Atomic debates*, frontispiece • J. Brain, engraving (after H. Room), RS • Maull & Co., portrait, RS
Wealth at death under £30,000: probate, 4 March 1881, *CGPLA Eng. & Wales*

Brodie, David (1707?–1787), naval officer, was born in Scotland, and went to sea at the age of twelve. An apprentice on the *James of Banff* merchantman for three-and-a-half years, and later master of the *Margarett*, he also served for some years in naval vessels before passing his lieutenant's examination on 8 February 1734. He was commissioned on 5 October 1736, and served under Vernon at Porto Bello in 1739, and at Cartagena in 1741.

Brodie was made master and commander first, on 3 May 1743, of the *Terror*, and then of the sloop *Merlin* (10 guns) in the West Indies, and for about four years he was repeatedly engaged with French and Spanish cruisers and privateers, twenty-one of which he captured and brought in. In one of these encounters he lost his right arm. Early in 1747 Rear-Admiral Knowles appointed him acting captain of the *Canterbury* (58 guns); and in 1748, after the capture of Port Louis, he moved to the *Strafford* (60 guns). In this ship he was present at the unsuccessful attempt on Santiago, and had a distinguished share in the battle off Havana on 1 October 1748, when the one prize of victory, the *Conquistador* (64 guns), struck to the *Strafford*. In the courts martial

which followed Brodie gave evidence in support of Admiral Sir Charles Knowles.

In 1750 Brodie was compelled to approach the Admiralty, representing himself as incapacitated from further service, and praying for some mark of the royal favour. In 1753 he presented another and stronger petition to the same effect, as a result of which he was granted a pension. Nevertheless in 1762, on the declaration of war with Spain, he applied to the Admiralty for a command. His application was not accepted, and accordingly when, in 1778, his seniority seemed to entitle him to flag rank, he was passed over as not having served 'during the last war'. On 5 March 1787 Brodie's claims were brought up in the House of Commons, and he was represented as a much-injured man, deprived of the promotion to which he was justly entitled. His case helped to establish the principle that captains too old or infirm to serve when they reached the top of the seniority list, be placed on a separate, superannuated list, with a pension of 10 shillings per day.

Brodie died 'one of the oldest captains in the royal navy' (*GM*, 742), at his home in Bath, on 30 July 1787, and was buried there in the abbey church.

J. K. LAUGHTON, *rev.* RANDOLPH COCK

Sources register of commissions and warrants, PRO, ADM6/15,16 • lieutenants' passing certificates, 1713–45, PRO, ADM107/3, fol. 230 • J. Charnock, ed., *Biographia navalis*, 6 vols. (1794–8) • W. L. Clowes, *The Royal Navy: a history from the earliest times to the present*, 7 vols. (1897–1903), vol. 3, pp. 344–7 • *Naval Chronicle*, 3 (1800) • *GM*, 1st ser., 57 (1787), 742

Brodie, Deacon. *See* Brodie, William (1746–1788).

Brodie, George (1786?–1867), historian, was born in Chesterhill, near Dalkeith, Edinburghshire, where his father, William Brodie, was a substantial farmer and agricultural improver. Educated at the high school and the University of Edinburgh, he became in 1811 a member of the Faculty of Advocates. He seems to have done little at the bar. He was an ardent whig, and his political creed partly inspired the one work by which he is known, his *History of the British empire from the accession of Charles the First to the Restoration, with an introduction tracing the progress of society and of the constitution from the feudal times to the opening of the history, and including a particular examination of Mr. Hume's statements relative to the character of the English government*. The 'statements' which Brodie undertook to refute were chiefly those in which Hume found precedents for the claims of the Stuarts in the action of the Tudor sovereigns. Brodie's history was by far the most elaborate assault on the Stuarts and their apologists, especially Hume and Clarendon, and the most thoroughgoing vindication of the puritans, that had then appeared. It was not of high historical value but is of interest in the context of Scottish historiography.

In the Scottish campaign for the first Reform Bill, Brodie presided at a vast gathering of Edinburgh working people held on Arthur's Seat in November 1831 against the rejection of the bill by the peers. In 1836 he was appointed historiographer of Scotland, on Melbourne's recommendation, with a salary of £180 a year. The appointment did not prove a stimulus to publication, though in 1866 Brodie issued a second edition of his history. Besides it, Brodie published an edition of Stair's *Institutions of the Law of Scotland*, adding a commentary and a supplement on mercantile law. Lord Cockburn said of it and him: 'His edition of Stair is a deep and difficult legal book. His style is bad, and his method not good' (*Journal of Henry Cockburn*, 2.113). Brodie was also the author of a pamphlet, *Strictures on the Appellate Jurisdiction of the House of Lords* (1856).

Brodie and his wife, Rachel (*née* Robertson), moved to London, first to Rio Lodge, Randolph Road, Maida Vale, and then to Percy House, Randolph Road, Maida Hill, where, on 22 January 1867, Brodie died. His wife survived him.

FRANCIS ESPINASSE, *rev.* H. C. G. MATTHEW

Sources *The Scotsman* (31 Jan 1867) · *GM*, 4th ser., 3 (1867) · Boase, *Mod. Eng. biog.* · *Journal of Henry Cockburn: being a continuation of the 'Memorials of his time', 1831–1854*, 2 vols. (1874) · *CGPLA Eng. & Wales* (1867)
Wealth at death under £4000: probate, 5 March 1867, *CGPLA Eng. & Wales*

Brodie, Sir Israel (1895–1979), chief rabbi, was born at Newcastle upon Tyne on 10 May 1895 as the second son and second of the five children (one daughter; a son died in infancy) of Aaron Uri Brodie (originally Braude or Broide), a sales representative who had immigrated from Kovno, and his wife, Sheina Maggid, whose surname derived from her father's occupation as a popular preacher in Lithuania (Tsemach Isaac, 'the Tsemach maggid'). His schooling at Rutherford College, Newcastle upon Tyne, was supplemented by Jewish instruction, and in 1912 he entered University College, London, and simultaneously Jews' College, London, to prepare for a career in the Jewish ministry. A first-class BA (1915) in Hebrew, Arabic, and Syriac qualified him for research, and he proceeded to Balliol College, Oxford, in 1916 to work for a BLitt (completed in 1921) on the origins of Karaism (medieval Jewish sectaries). He served from 1917 to 1919 as a chaplain on the western front. He returned to Balliol in 1919–20. Formal rabbinical training followed, with ordination in 1923 and practical experience in congregational and youth work in the East End of London under the guidance of J. F. Stern. He was in these years also much influenced by the impressive Jewish club leadership of Basil Henriques and by Herbert Loewe at Oxford, who involved him in Jewish adult education and introduced him to the study circle of Claude Montefiore.

In 1923 Brodie went to Melbourne, Australia, to succeed Joseph Abrahams as rabbi and to take charge of the Jewish ecclesiastical court of Victoria. He was the first minister to visit all the continent's Jewish communities, thereby contributing to a Jewish federal cohesion. He returned to Balliol in 1937 as an advanced student. In 1939 he joined the staff of Jews' College as tutor and lecturer in homiletics—an appropriate assignment since he was an impressive speaker. But the Second World War took him back to chaplaincy work in France, and he was among the last to be evacuated from Dunkirk. Service in the Middle East with the Royal Air Force prepared him to succeed as senior Jewish chaplain in 1944. He returned to Jews' College briefly as its principal in 1946, and in that year he married

Sir Israel Brodie (1895–1979), by Michael Wallach

Fanny Levine, whom he had known years before as a teacher in Jewish classes: her father, Jacob Levine, was a Hebrew teacher. There were no children. The same year saw the death of Chief Rabbi J. H. Hertz, to whom Brodie was an obviously eligible successor, and he was appointed to the office in 1948: in 1965 he became the first incumbent to retire. Distinctions followed: the presidency of Jews' College, a fellowship (1950) of University College, London, an honorary DCL from Durham University and DD from Yeshiva University, New York, and in 1969 appointment as KBE. A collection of essays presented to him on his seventieth birthday edited by H. J. Zimmels, J. Rabbinowitz, and I. Finestein, appeared in 1967.

Brodie's courteous manner contrasted with the masterful personality of Hertz, whose public statements had sometimes embarrassed the lay leadership. An attempt was made to impose on Brodie a consultative committee; but, while declaring willingness to consult, he made it clear that he would make his own decisions on all matters. The availability of air travel meant that his tenure would be very different from that of Hertz, and his achievements are best compartmentalized geographically.

Australian experience familiarized Brodie with the situation of Jewish outposts, their educational problems and risks of erosion. He visited the antipodes, and also quite frequently South Africa, even after it left the Commonwealth, and he tried to attract ministerial trainees to Jews' College. In 1957, as a contribution towards reconstruction of the pitiful remnants of European Jewry, Brodie convened what became a standing conference of European rabbis, the limitations of which were, however, implicit in its restriction to Orthodox representatives, whose following by then constituted minorities within the European Jewish pattern; and the sort of topics that it was prepared to discuss were largely matters of detail.

Brodie had always been a Zionist. He visited Israel frequently, and once declared his willingness to subordinate his Halakhic (jurisprudential) responsibilities to a central authority in Jerusalem should one ever emerge, although he must have known that this was unlikely. He supported not only the secular Hebrew University of Jerusalem but also the creation of the religiously articulated Bar Ilan University, where a chair was named in his honour. At home he worked hard to advance Jewish education. He secured purpose-built premises for Jews' College, he supported the movement to create Jewish day schools, and concerned himself with the reorganization of part-time Jewish education, while ruling that children whose mothers were not Jewish by birth or Orthodox conversion must be excluded from synagogue classes. He fought a rearguard action, in the face of enthusiasm for all things Israeli, against the introduction in the Ashkenazi synagogues under his jurisdiction of the Israeli (broadly Sephardi) pronunciation of Hebrew. The emergence of the state of Israel stimulated significant reversion towards traditionalism and greater use of Hebrew in prayer among the Progressive (non-Orthodox) congregations; but because of the movement's self-determination in matters involving Jewish status, Brodie maintained an aloofness from it no less distant, if less fulminating, than his predecessor's.

The greatest crisis of Brodie's incumbency made national headlines of a domestic Jewish issue. Rabbi Louis Jacobs, a lecturer at Jews' College and an impressive preacher, had in popular writings acknowledged the view that if reason is considered God-given, issues of biblical fundamentalism, criticism, and modern science should not be evaded in the pulpit and restricted to muted discussion by mature Jewish minds only. Jacobs was passed over for the principalship of Jews' College; and in 1963 his former congregation purported to re-engage him as minister, despite Brodie's withholding his requisite approval. The attempt was blocked as unconstitutional. Brodie, sensitive to views of rabbis on his own ecclesiastical court whose education had been entirely Talmudic, and concerned at what was regarded as an implicit threat to the authority for Jewish observance, found himself driven into making a statement about intellectualism and authentic Jewish tradition that upset some Jewish intellectuals (including rabbis). His main scholarly work was the publication (1962–7) of the *Etz hayyim* of Jacob of London, a thirteenth-century compendium of Jewish liturgy, ceremonial, and law.

Brodie's tenure of the chief rabbinate, itself otherwise unremarkable, reflected changed conditions: the wane of Anglo-Jewish, as of British, influence, and the rise of Israel as the renewed centre of gravity for post-Hitlerian Jewry. The chief rabbinate, safeguarded by act of parliament, represented the hub of a nineteenth-century Anglo-Jewish solidarity that no longer corresponded to the statistical facts of Jewish observance and intermarriage, but it nevertheless remained entrenched by Anglo-Jewish conservatism. Within its framework, any attempt to transcend separatisms (save where Israel's security and fundraising for Israel were concerned) would have required a character capable of riding out any storm, which Brodie did not possess. As a gentleman, a representative figure of dignity in bearing, as a well-liked chaplain to the forces, and by his devotion to what he considered his duty, he handed on intact to his successor an office of potential leadership, and retained the broad loyalty of some English-born Jews who might otherwise have lapsed. Brodie died in London on 13 February 1979 and was buried at Willesden Jewish cemetery.　　RAPHAEL LOEWE, *rev.*

Sources *CGPLA Eng. & Wales* (1979) · *Jewish Chronicle* (16 Feb 1979) · personal knowledge (1986) · H. J. Zimmels, J. Rabbinowitz, and I. Finestein, eds., *Essays presented to … Israel Brodie*, 2 vols. (1967) **Archives** LMA, corresp. and papers · U. Southampton L., journals and papers | U. Southampton, Anglo-Jewish archive, pressmark 206 **Likenesses** M. Wallach, photograph, priv. coll. [*see illus.*] · portrait, repro. in Zimmels, Rabbinowitz, and Finestein, eds., *Essays*, vol. 1 **Wealth at death** £21,049: probate, 29 May 1979, *CGPLA Eng. & Wales*

Brodie, Peter Bellinger (1778–1854), lawyer, was born at Winterslow, Wiltshire, on 20 August 1778, the eldest son of the Revd Peter Bellinger Brodie (1742–1804), rector of Winterslow, and his wife, Sarah (1755–1847), third daughter of Benjamin *Collins of Milford, Salisbury. One of his brothers was Sir Benjamin Collins *Brodie, first baronet, an eminent surgeon. Brodie chose the law as a profession and, because of an asthmatic complaint from which he suffered, he devoted himself to conveyancing. At first he became a pupil of Charles Butler the Roman Catholic lawyer. After practising for some years, he was called to the bar at the Inner Temple on 5 May 1815. He soon obtained a considerable share of business, and it increased so as to place him in a few years among the most eminent conveyancers of the time. One of the drafts that established his reputation was that of the Rock Life Assurance Company (1806), which became a model of its kind. In 1829 he drew up the charter of King's College, London.

Brodie was married twice: first, on 16 March 1810, to Elizabeth Mary (d. 1823), daughter of Sutton Thomas Wood of Oxford; second, on 1 June 1826, to Susan Mary (d. 1870), daughter of John Morgan. There were several sons. The eldest, Peter Bellinger *Brodie (1815–1897), was a well-known geologist.

Brodie's name is intimately connected with the history of law amendment. A leading member of the real property commission from 1828, Brodie drew up the part of its first report (May 1829) that dealt with fines and recoveries. He also drew up the portion of the report of June 1830 relating to the probate of wills, and the section of the third report (May 1832) relating to copyhold and ancient demesne. Soon after the presentation of the first report, it was determined to bring in bills founded on its recommendations; Brodie prepared the most important of these, a bill for abolishing fines and recoveries, which was brought in at the end of the parliamentary session in 1830 and which became law in 1838. The preparation of his part of the reports, and especially of the bills, almost deprived Brodie of his private business for a while, but he gradually recovered his practice. He wrote *A treatise on a tax on successions to real as well as personal property, and the removal of the house-tax, as substitutes for the income-tax, and on burdens on land and restrictions on commerce and loans of money* (1850). Brodie died at his residence, 49 Lincoln's Inn Fields, London, on 8 September 1854.

G. C. BOASE, *rev.* BETH F. WOOD

Sources J. F. Waller, ed., *The imperial dictionary of universal biography*, 3 vols. (1857–63) · *Law Review*, 21 (1854–5), 348–54 · Boase, *Mod. Eng. biog.* · *DNB*

Brodie, Peter Bellinger (1815–1897), Church of England clergyman and geologist, was born on 27 January 1815 at 49 Lincoln's Inn Fields, London, the first child of Peter Bellinger *Brodie (1778–1854), barrister, and his first wife, Elizabeth Mary (*d.* 1823), daughter of Sutton Thomas Wood, agriculturist, of Oxford. Early interested in natural history, Brodie regularly attended meetings of the Geological Society of London in Somerset House, enjoying 'the many intellectual combats between the geological giants of those days' (Brodie, *Quarterly Journal of the Geological Society*, 1887, 33). He was a frequent visitor at the Royal College of Surgeons, with which his uncle, Sir Benjamin Collins Brodie, was closely connected. William Clift, curator of its museum, proposed Brodie as fellow of the Geological Society of London; he was elected on 23 January 1834. In the same year he was admitted pensioner at Emmanuel College, Cambridge, where his interest in geology continued alongside his degree studies. He attended lectures in geology by Adam Sedgwick (1785–1873), accompanied him on field excursions, and assisted him in his museum. Sedgwick remained his friend and mentor, and encouraged him to continue his research. He was awarded his BA degree in 1838 and MA in 1842.

Brodie was ordained deacon at Salisbury Cathedral on 23 December 1838 and ordained priest on 22 December the following year. He was elected curate to the Revd Francis Baker (1773–1840), rector of Wylye, Wiltshire, in 1838, and between 1840 and 1853 he worked in Buckinghamshire, Gloucestershire, and Warwickshire. His final move was to Rowington, Warwickshire, in 1853, when he was instituted vicar of St Lawrence's Church.

Brodie performed his clerical duties conscientiously. He raised funds for a new school in Rowington, for a major restoration of the church, and for the building of a mission chapel in an outlying hamlet. Probably on 1 July 1841 he married Isabella Octavia (1821–1896), daughter of the Revd Francis Baker; they had one daughter and five sons. Isabella died on 17 November 1896, and a stained-glass window in Rowington church was dedicated to her by the Worcestershire Diocesan Girls' Friendly Society, for whom she was a founder worker.

Wherever he worked and lived Brodie continued his geological researches. His work was acknowledged by many leading geologists, not only in their publications but also by the numerous species which they named for him. He published over a hundred papers, and his book *The Fossil Insects of the Secondary Rocks of England* (1845) was the first treatise on this subject. In 1887 he was awarded the Murchison medal by the Geological Society of London. In 1853 he became a member of the thriving Warwickshire Natural History and Archaeological Society and a year later he founded its field club. He was active in every aspect of the society's work—leading field trips, writing papers, serving on committees, and donating hundreds of fossils to the museum.

Brodie was described as a genial man who infected people with his enthusiasm and energy. His parishioners held him in high regard and affection, and they dedicated two memorial stained-glass windows to him in Rowington church. He died at home on 1 November 1897, and was buried alongside his wife and two of his sons in Rowington churchyard on 5 November. In a letter to the Warwickshire Natural History Society, after Brodie's death, Charles Lapworth (1842–1920) wrote:

> we of the younger generation of geologists look up to Mr Brodie as one of the fathers of our science … not only does palaeontological geology owe a deep debt of gratitude to Mr Brodie, but stratigraphical geologists have cause to be equally grateful.   (Lapworth, *In Memoriam*, 13–14)

Specimens from his huge fossil collection—at one time he had about 25,000 specimens—are to be found in museums throughout the country. After his death large numbers of specimens were sold to the British Museum, and to the University of Vienna.

MARGARET GREEN

Sources P. B. Brodie, *The fossil insects of the Secondary rocks of England* (1845) · J. W. Judd, 'Award of the Murchison medal', *Quarterly Journal of the Geological Society*, 43 (1887), 31–3 · *Proceedings of the Warwickshire Naturalists' and Archaeologists' Field Club* (1900), 46–53 [list of papers] · C. Lapworth, *In memoriam: the Rev. Peter Bellinger Brodie*, pamphlet, 1898, Warks. CRO, C.920BRO.(P) · H. B. Woodward, 'Eminent living geologists: the Rev. P. B. Brodie', *Geological Magazine*, new ser., 4th decade, 4 (1897), 481–5 · W. Whitaker, *Quarterly Journal of the Geological Society*, 54 (1898), lxvii–lxxii · *Proceedings of the Warwickshire Naturalists' and Archaeologists' Field Club* [Warwickshire Museum] (1853–98) · *Reports of Warwickshire Natural History and Archaeological Society* [Warwickshire Museum] (1853–98) · parish records, Rowington, Warks. CRO [births, marriages, deaths] · parish register, Warks. CRO, DR 716/1 [burial], nos. 650, 670 · parish register (baptism), 19 May 1815, St Giles-in-the-Fields, London · E. Lodge, *Peerage, baronetage, knightage and companionage of the British empire*, 81st edn, 3 vols. (1912) · tombstone, St Lawrence's churchyard, Rowington, Warwickshire · Geological Society election certificate, no. 1000, 1834, GS Lond. · *Autobiography of the late Sir Benjamin C. Brodie*, ed. B. C. B. [B. C. Brodie], 2nd edn (1865) · Crockford · admissions register, Emmanuel College Library, Cambridge · *Warwick Advertiser* (Nov 1897)

Archives Bath Museum, deposits from fossil collection · Birmingham Museums and Art Gallery, deposits from fossil collection · BM, palaeontology department · GS Lond., deposits from fossil collection · Jermyn Street Museum, deposits from fossil collection · Leeds Museum, deposits from fossil collection · Leicester Museum, deposits from fossil collection · NHM, deposits from fossil collection · Oxf. U. Mus. NH, deposits from fossil collection · U. Newcastle, Hancock Museum, deposits from fossil collection · University of Vienna, deposits from fossil collection · Warwickshire Museum, deposits from fossil collection · Warwickshire Museum, MS notes on papers in the *Quarterly Journal of the Geological*

Society of London | Oxf. U. Mus. NH, Hope Library, Buckland collection · Oxf. U. Mus. NH, letters to J.O. Westwood relating to his work on fossil insects · Warks. CRO, Warwickshire Natural History and Archaeological Society archive · Wilts. & Swindon RO, diocesan records, MS submitted to the diocesan registry in connection with ordination as deacon

Likenesses photograph, *c*.1845, GS Lond. · marble bust, *c*.1896, Warwickshire Museum · Graham, photograph, repro. in *Proceedings of the Warwickshire Naturalists' and Archaeologists' Field Club* (1896)

Wealth at death £1246 19*s*. 7*d*.: probate, 14 June 1898, *CGPLA Eng. & Wales*

Brodie, William [*known as* Deacon Brodie] (**1746–1788**), local politician and thief, was probably born at Brodie's Close, Lawnmarket, Edinburgh, the eldest of eleven children of Francis Brodie (*d. c*.1787), a prominent and prosperous local cabinet-maker or wright, whose family had been members of the Moray gentry, and his wife, Cicel. He was educated at Edinburgh high school and in 1756 entered his father's business, though he proved a reluctant apprentice, harbouring a desire to enter the navy and to fight in the Seven Years' War. Brodie was always of a somewhat fantastical and romantic nature. His character was much influenced by performances of John Gay's *The Beggar's Opera* (1728), which he watched at Edinburgh's new playhouse, the Theatre Royal. Gay's story of a confident and disrespectful criminal underworld provided Brodie with an attractive model of adulthood at odds with his own highly respectful profession. In 1781 Francis Brodie fell ill, and William succeeded him as deacon, or leader, of the wrights, then the largest of the town's incorporated trades, and thus gained an influential and lucrative position on the unelected city council, which controlled many aspects of Edinburgh's civic life.

By the mid-1780s rumours were beginning to surface about Brodie's abuse of this position, and in particular about his alleged role in the escape from the Tolbooth of the son of a Grassmarket stabler convicted of murder. Brodie's reputation also suffered with stories of his keeping, Macheath-style, two mistresses, Jean Watt and Anne Grant of Cant's Close, Edinburgh, with whom he had several illegitimate children. In August 1786 Brodie embarked on a series of burglaries, assisted by members of a criminal gang composed of acquaintances made during his frequent visits to the cockpits behind the Grassmarket. Among his targets were the bankers of the Royal Exchange, from whom he took £800 (he later returned his share of the money); several goldsmiths on Parliament Close; a Leith grocer, who lost over 3 hundredweight of tea in August 1787; and on 30 October the university library, from where the college mace was taken. A further burglary on a silk shop in the High Street early in 1788 prompted the intervention of the lord advocate, Ilay Campbell of Succour, who proposed a pardon for members of the gang who turned king's evidence. The offer initially produced no results, though at the same time the increasingly disreputable Brodie received unfavourable publicity over his involvement with the town's cardsharps, after a dispute with James Hamilton, master of the

Edinburgh chimney sweeps. None the less he was still considered of sufficiently good character to be chosen as a juror on a murder trial in February 1788.

Brodie's eventual downfall came about as a result of a failed burglary on the town's excise office on 8 March. Several days later an informer disclosed the identities of certain gang members with connections to Brodie, who now emerged as the instigator of the recent crime wave. Suspecting imminent arrest, on 12 March Brodie fled Edinburgh for London and then, by June, the Netherlands, with the intention of sailing to New York. However, his delayed departure gave the authorities time to have him extradited to Edinburgh (where he arrived on 17 July) to stand trial alongside an accomplice, the Cowgate grocer George Smith, who had since confessed to his, and confirmed Brodie's, involvement in burgling the excise office.

At his trial, which began in August 1788, Brodie was represented by Henry Erskine, the dean of faculty and brother of the earl of Buchan, and John Clerk of Eldin. Their whig sympathies, though not shared by Brodie, prompted a defence which took the form of an appeal against English tory intrusions, personified by the activities of Pitt's representative in Scotland, Henry Dundas. Accusations of interference were especially prominent with regard to the position of the chief prosecution witness, John Brown (also known as Humphrey Moore), the former gang member who had turned king's evidence in March. Since Brown had himself been previously convicted in an English court, his evidence was deemed inadmissible without a royal pardon. This was duly secured by Dundas's prosecutors, and subsequently upheld by the presiding judge, Lord Braxfield, despite claims of injustice from Brodie's defence counsel. Brown's testimony was sufficient to establish Smith's and Brodie's involvement in the crime, and resulted in a sentence of hanging to be carried out at the Tolbooth gallows on 1 October.

In the aftermath of the case the bookseller William Creech, Brodie's former colleague on the town council and a member of his jury, published a highly moralistic and commercially successful *Account of the Trial*, which attributed Brodie's fall to his passion for gaming and loose women. Brodie himself was sanguine of the chances of a reprieve and petitioned Dundas for his sentence to be commuted to transportation. Even when this attempt failed he remained confident that—in the manner of Macheath—he would cheat death with the help of a steel collar to mitigate the effect of a shortened hangman's rope, followed by rescue by his friends. In fact, the shortened rope was detected and restored, and, despite furious efforts to revive him after the event, Brodie died from hanging on 1 October. From the quack's premises in Cowgate to which Brodie had first been taken, the body was then removed, and may have been buried in a churchyard near the town's George Square. However, his impudence did live on in the form of a spoof in which he bequeathed his bad qualities to his fellow town councillors and the lord provost.

Memories of Brodie's criminal activity, rumours of his

possible survival, and most significantly a fascination with a life lived both in respectable and underworld society were maintained by local folklore. It was this story of dualism which interested the young Edinburgh resident Robert Louis Stevenson, who wrote an early, and now lost, play on the subject which he later developed into an unsuccessful London drama, *Deacon Brodie, or, The Double Life* (1879). Stevenson followed this a decade later with his more accomplished and celebrated novel of the escape from personality, *Dr Jekyll and Mr Hyde*. In time the mythology which grew up around Deacon Brodie also did much to transform him from an immoral criminal to a colourful, spirited rogue, subsequently claimed as an ancestor by Miss Jean Brodie in Muriel Spark's eponymous novel.

JOHN SIBBALD GIBSON

Sources DNB · W. Rougheath, *The trial of Deacon Brodie* (1900) · W. Creech, *An account of the trial of William Brodie and George Smith* (1788) · A. Morison, *The trial of William Brodie, wright and cabinet-maker in Edinburgh* (1788) · J. S. Gibson, *Deacon Brodie: father of Jekyll and Hyde* (1977) · P. MacKenzie, *Reminiscences of Glasgow and the west of Scotland*, 3 vols. (1865–8) · *The anecdotes and egotisms of Henry Mackenzie, 1745–1831*, ed. H. W. Thompson (1927) · R. Chambers, *Traditions of Edinburgh*, 2 vols. (1825) · *Letters to Charles Baxter*, ed. J. De Lancey Ferguson (1956) · J. E. Steuart, *Robert Louis Stevenson*, 2 vols. (1924)

Archives NL Scot., papers, MS 3284
Likenesses J. Kay, caricature, etching, 1788, NPG · J. Haldane, caricature, etching, NPG · J. Kay, double portrait, caricature, etching (with George Smith; *The first interview* in 1786), BM

Brodie, William (1815–1881), sculptor, was born in Banff on 22 January 1815, and baptized on 10 February 1815 at Banff, the oldest of the three sons of John Brodie (1786/7–1865), shipmaster and merchant seaman of Banff and Aberdeen, and his wife, Mary Walker (1786?–1846). The sculptor Alexander *Brodie (1829/30–1867) was his brother. About 1821 the family settled in Aberdeen where, after serving an apprenticeship, William Brodie was employed as a plumber at the Broadford works. On 12 June 1841 he married Helen Chisholm (1817–1886), an amateur painter, by whom he had four children including the sculptor Mary Brodie, Lady Gowans (d. 1911). Evening tuition at the mechanics' institute in Aberdeen enabled Brodie to acquire considerable proficiency in modelling portrait medallions and miniature busts in wax or lead and induced a fascination with phrenology which was to inform his mature practice as a portrait sculptor. Additional instruction in drawing was allegedly provided by George Washington Wilson. Between 1846 and 1850, at the combined instigation of Sheriff William Watson and John Hill Burton, Brodie attended the Trustees' Academy in Edinburgh where, in 1848, he gained the highest premiums for modelling from the life and from the antique and, from 1847, exhibited annually at the Royal Scottish Academy.

About 1852 Hill Burton introduced Brodie to James Buchanan (1785–1857), the Glasgow merchant and founder of the Buchanan Institution, for whom, in 1860, he designed an architectural monument in the Dean cemetery, Edinburgh, incorporating an undated marble bust (another reduced version is in the Merchants' Hall, Glasgow). Financed by Buchanan, he spent the following year in Rome, immersing himself in the study of the antique and exploring his aptitude for ideal statuary in the studio of Laurence MacDonald. Executed under MacDonald's guidance, Brodie's marble group *Corinna, the Lyric Muse* was exhibited to acclaim at the Royal Scottish Academy in 1855 (a related marble bust, originating from the Buchanan collection, is at Bonskeid House, Pitlochry) and reproduced in Copeland Parian ware in 1856. This commercial exploitation of Brodie's first major ideal group and the adoption of the porcelain statuette as a prize by the Royal Association for the Promotion of the Fine Arts in Scotland set a precedent for similar promotions of *Penelephon, the Beggar Maid* (1867) and *Ruth* (1873; full-scale marble, 1872, in Aberdeen Art Gallery).

Brodie's election to associate membership of the Royal Scottish Academy in 1852 testified to his dexterous cultivation of Edinburgh society and, in particular, the legal élite through the intermediary of his Aberdonian mentors. Following his return to Edinburgh in 1854, he was to gain national recognition—despite vigorous competition from Sir John Steell—as one of the most proficient and prolific British exponents of bust portraiture in the liberally classicizing tradition of Sir Francis Chantrey. (Brodie is extensively represented in the collections of the University of Edinburgh; New College; the Faculty of Advocates; and the Scottish National Portrait Gallery, Edinburgh, which holds a version of his 1859 bust of Hill Burton.) His range also encompassed large-scale portrait reliefs, a genre modified and perpetuated by his most distinguished pupil, James Pittendrigh Macgillivray.

Initiated during the late 1850s, the private patronage of the Kinnaird family was subsequently extended to monumental commissions for marble statues of Lady Frances Kinnaird, widow of the ninth baron, and Lady Olivia Kinnaird (recumbent effigy, 1871; both at Rossie Priory, Perthshire). In the public domain the success of Brodie's first venture—a posthumous marble statue of Lord Cockburn for the Faculty of Advocates at Parliament House, Edinburgh—prompted further prestigious commissions including the freestone monument to Prince Albert in Perth (1864), marble figures of John Graham-Gilbert (1870; Glasgow Art Gallery) and Sir David Brewster (1877; University of Edinburgh), and, most notably, the seated bronze monuments to Thomas Graham (1871; George Square, Glasgow) and Sir James Young Simpson (1877; Princes Street Gardens, Edinburgh).

Of Brodie's later narrative works, the small commemorative bronze effigy *Greyfriars Bobby* (integrated into a drinking fountain commissioned by Baroness Angela Burdett-Coutts for the city of Edinburgh in 1871 and sited on George IV Bridge) has attained international popular celebrity. During the same period Brodie was engaged on a series of freestone figures illustrative of the Waverley novels for the second phase of the sculptural embellishment of the Scott monument on Princes Street, Edinburgh. Of these, the statuette of Amy Robsart (1871) was also rendered in marble (Tweeddale Museum, Chambers Institute, Peebles).

Brodie's commissions for the Scott monument were included among his final exhibits at the Royal Scottish Academy in 1881. On 30 October 1881 he succumbed to heart disease and oedema of the lungs at his principal residence, Douglas Lodge in Merchiston Place, Edinburgh. He was buried in the Dean cemetery, for which he himself had executed a number of memorials, on 5 November. A major sale of his studio equipment and stock-in-trade was conducted by Dowell's of Edinburgh on 16, 17, and 19 December 1881. An oil portrait of Brodie of 1875 by Alexander Rhind who was formerly his pupil and then for thirty years his assistant, was in a Scottish private collection.

HELEN E. SMAILES

Sources G. M. Fraser, 'William and Alexander Brodie, sculptors', *Scottish Notes and Queries*, 3rd ser., 1 (1923), 4–7, 20–21, 35–6, 49–51, 65–8 • R. L. Woodward, 'Nineteenth century Scottish sculpture', PhD diss., U. Edin., 1979, vol. 1, pp. 72–5; vol. 3, pp. 21–9 • NL Scot., Brodie MSS, Acc. 8093 • *Catalogue of the valuable collection of works of art, sculpture, paintings, library etc. belonging to the estate of the late William Brodie … to be sold by auction by Mr Dowell* (16–19 Dec 1881) • *The Scotsman* (31 Oct 1881) • *Edinburgh Courant* (31 Oct 1881) • *Aberdeen Journal* (1 Nov 1881) • *Daily Free Press* (31 Oct 1881) • *Quiz* (4 Nov 1881) • *The Scotsman* (5 Nov 1881) • correspondence, NL Scot., Burton MS 9395, fols. 63, 75 • [J. Colston], *History of the Scott monument, Edinburgh* (1881), 99–102 • Trustees' Academy, Edinburgh, ledger of students, 1848–56, NA Scot., NG2/1/4 • J. P. Macgillivray, letter to G. M. Fraser on Brodie's career, 30 Oct 1922, NL Scot., Macgillivray MS Dep. 349, no. 115 • P. Atterbury, ed., *The Parian phenomenon* (1989), 45, 132, 134, 260; figs. 497, 508, 510, 516, 614 • C. B. de Laperriere, ed., *The Royal Scottish Academy exhibitors, 1826–1990*, 4 vols. (1991), vol. 1, pp. 179–84 • R. Billcliffe, ed., *The Royal Glasgow Institute of the Fine Arts, 1861–1989: a dictionary of exhibitors at the annual exhibitions*, 4 vols. (1990–92), vol. 1, pp. 171–2 • D. McAra, *Sir James Gowans: romantic rationalist* (1975), 22–3 and illustrations • inventory, sheriff court, Edinburgh, 5 Dec 1881, NA Scot., SC 70/1/211, 94–108 • additional inventory, sheriff court, Edinburgh, 1 Sept 1882, NA Scot., SC 70/1/217, 1–7 • bap. reg. Scot. • d. reg. Scot. • m. reg. Scot.

Archives NL Scot., MSS; corresp. | *The Scotsman* offices, Edinburgh, archives, John Ritchie Findlay diaries • Edinburgh City Archives, Edinburgh town council minute book, SL 7/1/305 • NA Scot., minute books of the Royal Association for the Promotion of the Fine Arts in Scotland • NL Scot., John Hill Burton MSS 9394, 9395 • Perth and Kinross council, archives, Kinnaird MSS

Likenesses J. G. Tunny, photograph, c.1854, Royal Scot. Acad. • J. Phillip, oils, 1859, Royal Scot. Acad. • A. Rhind, oils, 1875 • Nesbitt & Lothian, carte-de-visite, NPG • J. Phillip, oils, Aberdeen Art Gallery • photographs, NL Scot.

Wealth at death £9732 0s. 8d.: confirmation, 8 Dec 1881, CCI • £2508 4s. 10d.: additional estate, 1 Sept 1882, CCI

Brodribb, Charles William (1878–1945), journalist and poet, was born in London on 11 June 1878, the elder son of Arthur Aikin Brodribb (b. 1849/50), journalist and for many years director of the parliamentary reporting staff of *The Times*, and his wife, Dinah Alice, daughter of William Crook, a Wiltshire farmer. He was distantly related to Sir Henry Irving, the actor, whose original name was Brodribb; and his father's half-brother was W. J. Brodribb, translator of the writings of Tacitus. Through his paternal great-grandmother he was a great-great-grandson of Gilbert Wakefield, the classical scholar, and he was also a collateral descendant of the writer Mrs A. L. Barbauld, *née* Aikin.

Brodribb was a scholar at St Paul's School, London, and at Trinity College, Oxford. After taking honours in classical moderations (1899) and a third class in *literae humaniores* (1901), he went to Germany for further study and subsequently was appointed a temporary assistant master at St Paul's. He joined the editorial staff of *The Times* in April 1904 and remained in its service for the rest of his life. He began as a sub-editor but soon became one of the editor's secretaries, and just before the First World War he was appointed an assistant editor and a special writer for *The Times* and its *Literary Supplement*. His influence on the paper, and therefore on educated opinion in England, was very considerable. In 1923 he married Sylvia Corrie, the second daughter of Perceval Charles Woolston MRCVS; they had one son.

Although Brodribb's classical scholarship did not bring him the highest academic distinctions, it remained throughout his life his primary interest, which was reflected in the columns of *The Times*, in scholarly articles in *Notes and Queries* and the *Classical Review*, and in his concern for good English. London and its antiquities, especially St Paul's Cathedral, claimed from him a loving attention. His knowledge of English literature was wide, but he was particularly at home in the periods of Milton, Pope, and Johnson. His *Pope: his Friendships and his Poetry* was published in 1925. Brodribb's verse was characterized by its precision and strength in lightness, and its epigrammatic wit; patriotism and love of scholarship are its abiding themes. His translation of Virgil's *Georgics* into English hexameter appeared in 1928, and a selection of his poems with an introduction by Edmund Blunden was published posthumously in 1946.

During the Second World War, Brodribb was chiefly responsible for the series of daily quotations in *The Times* under the heading 'Old and true' (collected edition 1945), which brought encouragement to many, and for *The Times Broadsheets for the Services* (collected edition 1948). A Unitarian, he was a good churchman and churchwarden of St Bride's, Fleet Street. Brodribb died at his brother's home at Chapel Row, Bucklebury Common, Bradfield, near Reading, Berkshire, on 21 June 1945.

DEREK HUDSON, rev. SAYONI BASU

Sources *The Times* (22 June 1945) • E. C. Blunden, introduction, in C. W. Brodribb, *Poems* (1946) • CGPLA Eng. & Wales (1945)

Archives News Int. RO, papers

Likenesses M. Bone, sketch, United University Club, London • photograph, repro. in C. W. Brodribb, *Poems* (1946), frontispiece

Wealth at death £10,317 11s. 5d.: probate, 1 Nov 1945, CGPLA Eng. & Wales

Brodribb, William Jackson (*bap.* 1829, *d.* 1905), translator, only son of William Perrin Brodribb MRCS, and his first wife, Maria Louisa Jackson, was baptized at the Independent Chapel, Warminster, on 1 March 1829. On his father's removal to a practice in Bloomsbury Square, he was educated first at a neighbouring private school and afterwards at King's College, London. From King's College he was elected in 1848 to a classical scholarship at St John's College, Cambridge. In 1852 he was bracketed sixth in the classical tripos, was a junior optime in the mathematical tripos, and graduated BA. Elected a fellow of his college in 1856, he was ordained as a priest of the Church of England in 1858, and was presented in 1860 to the college living of Wootton Rivers, Wiltshire. This preferment he held for life.

Devoted to classical study, Brodribb joined his cousin, Alfred John Church (1829–1912), in translating the works of Tacitus: the *History* appeared in 1862, *Germania* and *Agricola* in 1868, the *Annals* in 1876, and *De oratoribus* in 1877. The work was competent and gained general recognition. The two translators also edited the Latin text of *Germania* and *Agricola* in 1869, and of select letters of Pliny in 1871; a translation of Livy, books 21–4, followed in 1883. His other works were: 'Demosthenes' in *Ancient Classics for English Readers* (1877), *A Short History of Constantinople* (1879), in collaboration with Sir Walter Besant, and classical contributions to the *Encyclopaedia Britannica* and scholarly periodicals.

In 1880 Brodribb married Elizabeth Sarah Juliana, only daughter of David Llewellyn, vicar of Easton Royal, Wiltshire, but was left a widower, without children, in 1894. He died at his rectory on 24 September 1905, and was buried in the churchyard.

A. A. BRODRIBB, *rev.* M. C. CURTHOYS

Sources private information (1912) · Venn, *Alum. Cant.* · CGPLA Eng. & Wales (1905)

Wealth at death £4339 14s. 6d.: probate, 4 Dec 1905, CGPLA Eng. & Wales

Brodrick, Sir Alan (1623–1680), royalist conspirator and politician, was born on 28 July 1623, the eldest of the ten children of Sir Thomas Brodrick (d. 1642), military administrator, and his wife, Katherine (d. 1678), daughter of Robert Nicholas of Manningford Bruce, Wiltshire. Brodrick's mother's connections to the Nicholas, St John, and Villiers families were to be highly significant for his career. He matriculated from Magdalen Hall, Oxford, in November 1639, and was admitted to Gray's Inn in May 1642. Though not in arms during the civil war Brodrick's sympathies were royalist. He was called to the bar in May 1648, but his failure to take the covenant prevented him from taking up a legal practice. Instead, he went abroad. He was in France about 1650–51, and then spent three years in Italy. For fourteen months he was laid up with an illness before returning to England. But at some stage in 1656 he became involved with the association of royalist conspirators known as the Sealed Knot.

Brodrick met one of the Sealed Knot's leading members, Sir Richard Willys, in Italy, but he was related to another, Edward Villiers, as well as to the principal co-ordinator of royalist conspiracy from exile, Sir Edward Hyde. From November 1656 Brodrick acted as the Knot's regular correspondent with Hyde. The Knot was notoriously cautious in its views on the practicability of royalist insurrection, and by 1659 found that more eager advocates of action—especially Viscount Mordaunt—were beginning to encroach on its role. Despite Hyde's efforts to get them to co-operate the rivalry between Mordaunt and the Knot became intense and destructive, and there developed between the viscount and Brodrick (who in mid-1659 was

trying to put together his own group of young conspirators based around Oxfordshire, Gloucester, Warwick, and the north) an extreme antipathy. Brodrick believed that he was the victim of a campaign of character assassination, with it being spread about that he was a Catholic, a drunkard, and had been sacked from his role with the Knot. The Knot's credibility was wrecked, though, by the revelation in July 1659, shortly before a planned rising with presbyterians was due to take place, that Willys had co-operated with the state authorities and betrayed royalist plans. Brodrick's arrest and committal to the Tower of London on 31 July, just before a planned rising, was attributable to Willys's betrayal, but he found the apostasy of an old associate and friend hard to credit. He managed to secure his release by suing for a writ of habeas corpus at the beginning of November. With Hyde urging royalists to secure election to the Convention Parliament, Brodrick found a seat at Orford in Suffolk in April 1660, and became a central figure in the management of the royalist interest in the Commons, conveying to other supporters the tactics adopted at regular meetings with Geoffrey Palmer and the earl of Southampton.

After the Restoration, Brodrick was assimilated into the circle of Hyde (from 1661 earl of Clarendon). In reward for his services in August 1660 he was knighted and appointed surveyor-general for Ireland (where his brother, a successful career soldier, had settled) for life, although it took some months to wrest the office away from the incumbent, Sir Adam Loftus. At first he exercised it by a deputy while he continued to help in managing the Cavalier Parliament (in which he sat again for Orford), but early in 1661 he was appointed one of the commissioners for executing the king's November 1660 settlement of the land claims in Ireland; he obtained a grant of the confiscated estates of two regicides; and he secured a seat in the Irish House of Commons, for Dungarvan. He left London to carry out his duties in Ireland shortly after the end of the parliamentary session in July 1661.

After the passage by the Irish parliament of a new land settlement in 1663 Brodrick was appointed, in May of that year, to replace Henry Coventry as one of the commissioners for executing it—the court of claims. But not only was Brodrick regarded (even by his patron, Clarendon, who distanced himself from the appointment) as lacking in judicial detachment; he was also widely seen as a man on the make, and was the least popular of the commissioners in Ireland: in September 1663 it was reported that three of the commissioners were for the king, three for the English interest, and 'one for himself, vizt: Brodrick' (*CSP Ire.*, 1663–5, 231). Brodrick's own interest was centred on gaining compensation for his grant of forfeited land, lost when all regicides' lands were granted instead to the duke of York. He secured it in early 1663. When the Act of Explanation was passed in 1665 to iron out some of the many difficulties in the land settlement, Brodrick—to some dismay among the protestant gentry—was appointed to the new court of claims.

Despite his involvement in Ireland, Brodrick remained active in English politics. In the 1665 and 1666–7 sessions of parliament he worked—ultimately unsuccessfully—to resist the Irish Cattle Bill, hampered by the indecision and disagreement at court about how far to take its opposition. The role of Brodrick together with his cousin Sir Allen Apsley as Clarendon's henchmen became notorious and was lampooned in the anonymous 'Clarendon's housewarming' of 1667, and in Marvell's *Last Instructions to a Painter*. While in London Brodrick also helped to oversee the construction work at Clarendon's new house in Piccadilly. But Clarendon's dismissal at the end of August 1667 removed his principal patron and largely ended his involvement with government affairs in England. Brodrick defended Clarendon against the impeachment launched in October, but himself came under some threat as Irish protestant interests challenged the activities of the court of claims in the English parliament early in 1668. By 1669 the work of the court of claims was over. Free of government office and profoundly upset by the fate of his old patron, he maintained his close contact with the Hyde family, and adopted their hostility to the earl of Danby and his administration. Brodrick's withdrawal from much political life was linked to an increasing piety which (given his rakish reputation) made him something of a catch for the clergy. The preacher at his funeral warmly commended it: '(how late soever he set out) yet when he once began the course, he made such large and nimble steps Heaven-ward, that he outstrip'd the ordinary Passenger that had begun long before' (Resbury, 13–14). He died on 25 November 1680 at Wandsworth in Surrey and was buried there on 3 December. Brodrick never married, and left most of his estate to his brother's family in Ireland, forming the basis of the wealth of the viscounts Midleton in the eighteenth century.

PAUL SEAWARD

Sources Surrey HC, Brodrick (Midleton) papers, MS 1248/1 · Bodl. Oxf., Clarendon MSS · Bodl. Oxf., MSS Carte · *Calendar of the Clarendon state papers preserved in the Bodleian Library*, ed. O. Ogle and others, 5 vols. (1869–1970) · CSP Ire., 1660–69 · M. W. Helms and P. Watson, 'Brodrick, Allen', HoP, Commons, 1660–90, 1.721–4 · D. Underdown, *Royalist conspiracy in England, 1649–1660* (1960) · N. Resbury, *A sermon preach'd at the funeral of Sir Alan Broderick* (1680) · *The correspondence of Henry Hyde, earl of Clarendon, and of his brother Laurence Hyde, earl of Rochester*, ed. S. W. Singer, 2 vols. (1828) · *Calendar of the manuscripts of the marquess of Ormonde*, new ser., 8 vols., HMC, 36 (1902–20) · *Collins peerage of England: genealogical, biographical and historical*, ed. E. Brydges, 9 vols. (1812), vol. 9 · CSP dom., 1625–6, 572 · 'Broderick genealogy', *Miscellanea Genealogica et Heraldica*, new ser., 2 (1877), 359–70, esp. 364 · J. Foster, *The register of admissions to Gray's Inn, 1521–1889, together with the register of marriages in Gray's Inn chapel, 1695–1754* (privately printed, London, 1889) · R. J. Fletcher, ed., *The pension book of Gray's Inn*, 1 (1901) · VCH Surrey, 4 · 'Genealogical notes and queries', *Miscellanea Genealogica et Heraldica*, 4th ser., 3 (1908–9), 137–41, esp. 137–9
Archives Surrey HC, Brodrick (Midleton) MSS | Bodl. Oxf., Carte MSS · Bodl. Oxf., Clarendon MSS
Likenesses oils, 1660?, repro. in R. Ollard, *Clarendon and his friends* (1987)
Wealth at death bequests of 410 guineas; plus £50; land in Wandsworth and Ireland left to nephew with payments of £180 p.a. charged on it to others: will, 'Genealogical notes and queries', 137–9

Brodrick, Alan, first Viscount Midleton (1655/6–1728), politician and lord chancellor of Ireland, was the second son of St John Brodrick (*d.* 1712) of Ballyannan, near Midleton, co. Cork, and his wife, Alice, daughter of Laurence Clayton of Mallow in the same county. The Brodricks, who hailed from Surrey and retained estates and close connections there, were Cromwellian arrivals. Brodrick's father had received a substantial grant of property in co. Cork in 1653, which he expanded after the Restoration, when his eldest brother, Alan, was a commissioner for settling the affairs of Ireland. All St John's children were put to the law: Alan attended Magdalen College, Oxford, matriculating on 3 May 1672 aged sixteen, and the Middle Temple, from where he was called to the bar in May 1678. He married his first wife, Catherine, daughter of Redmond Barry of Rathcormack, co. Cork, and Mary Boyle of Castle Lyons, with whom he had a son, St John (*c.*1685–1728), and a daughter.

At the revolution of 1688 the Brodricks fled to England, and were attainted by James II's Irish parliament. Alan was prominent among the Irish exiles in London who pressed for a prompt reconquest. After returning in 1690, he was given office as second serjeant, but became dissatisfied with the Dublin administration, especially over the treaty of Limerick, which he felt was too favourable to the Jacobites. When the Irish parliament met in 1692, Brodrick, who sat for Cork, where he was recorder, was one of the foremost critics of government, despite being an officeholder himself. He was also vocal in asserting the claim of the Irish House of Commons to a 'sole right' in initiating supply legislation. He did not, however, join in attempts to raise the grievances of Ireland at Westminster. When the whig Lord Capell was appointed lord deputy of Ireland and sought a settlement with opposition, Brodrick was promoted to Irish solicitor-general. In 1693 he married, by a licence of 16 October, his second wife, Lucy (*d.* 1703), third daughter of a neighbouring landowner, Sir Peter Courthope of Little Island; they had two sons and a daughter.

Brodrick and his brother Thomas became the mainstays of the court party under Capell and succeeding governors. They were themselves identified as whigs, distinguished by their virulent hatred of 'popery' and insistence on the enactment of penal laws against Catholics. Brodrick did not take an active part in the 'patriotic' agitation against the English Woollen Act of 1699 and forfeitures resumption of 1700, though he made no secret of his resentment at this interference in Irish affairs. The appointment of the tory Lord Rochester as lord lieutenant in 1700 briefly threatened his position as solicitor-general, but he was still in post when Rochester was replaced in 1703 by an Irish tory, the duke of Ormond. Ormond kept Brodrick at a distance, but to begin with did nothing to alienate him. In the new parliament which met in 1703 Brodrick was chosen speaker of the Commons, with Ormond's approval. His response, however, was to lead the opposition in the first session, in the winter of 1703–4, promoting inquiries and resolutions which he knew would embarrass the viceroy. As soon as the session was over Ormond had him removed.

Brodrick returned to office when Ormond was succeeded by the moderate Lord Pembroke in 1707. High-church pamphleteers assumed that the ministry now wished to repeal the sacramental test in Ireland, and that Brodrick had hatched the scheme. In fact, his commitment was lukewarm: he had little sympathy for dissenters, especially Ulster presbyterians, and regarded the campaign for repeal as a threat to his party's popularity. He showed only a superficial interest in Pembroke's indirect proposal to the Irish parliament to consider repeal, and retreated as soon as it became clear that most MPs were opposed. More important were the debates on supply, in which the two parties in Ireland competed to show who could be the more useful to government. The difficulty for Brodrick was that in previous sessions he had taken up a 'patriotic' stance which he was now obliged to modify. His former insistence that the parliamentary 'additional' supply be given for only one year at a time caused him particular difficulties, which continued into the viceroyalty of the whig Lord Wharton, in 1709, for whom Brodrick was indisputably the chief parliamentary manager. Before Wharton's second parliamentary session Brodrick was preferred, in May 1710, to the place of chief justice of queen's bench in Ireland. However, the political pendulum swung again in the autumn of 1710, and Ormond was restored. Brodrick's tenure as chief justice lasted only until Ormond arrived in Dublin in 1711. Out in the cold for two years, he was able to return to the Irish House of Commons at the 1713 election, held under the lord lieutenancy of the duke of Shrewsbury, and to resume the parliamentary leadership of his party. Chosen again as speaker, in a contest with a court-sponsored tory candidate, he presided over a session marked by vicious party conflict, in which the whigs controlled proceedings in the lower house and did all they could to obstruct government business.

Following the accession of George I, Brodrick was made lord chancellor of Ireland in October 1714, and in April 1715 was raised to the Irish peerage as Baron Brodrick. He soon discovered, however, that the dignity and authority of his new office was not matched by political influence. The patronage directly at his disposal was limited, especially in comparison with that enjoyed by his most important rival among the Irish whigs, his successor as speaker, William Conolly (the chief commissioner of the revenue). Moreover, in taking the chancellorship Brodrick had left the Commons, where the all-important debates on supply took place. His restiveness was apparent in the first session of the new Irish parliament, in 1715–16, when his eldest son, St John, and the rest of the family connection, voted against the ministry on several issues, most notably over the proposed relief for dissenters. Brodrick excused himself at the castle on the grounds that he could not control his son. Cynical contemporaries doubted this explanation, but it is confirmed to some extent by Brodrick's own correspondence (always allowing for the fact that he assumed that his letters would be opened by political enemies in the Dublin post office). On 1 December 1716 Brodrick embarked on his third marriage, to Anne (1657/8–1748), widow of Michael Hill and the daughter and eventual heir of Sir John *Trevor, speaker of the English House of Commons. This last marriage was childless.

The appointment of a distant connection, the duke of Bolton, as viceroy in 1717 temporarily raised Brodrick's spirits, and he behaved as if he were Bolton's parliamentary 'undertaker'. Promotion in the peerage to Viscount Midleton on 15 August 1717 was a public recognition of his status. But rivalry with Conolly continued, and an unsuccessful attempt to exclude the speaker from the commission of lords justices appointed on Bolton's return to England seriously weakened Midleton's position. He blamed the English chief minister, Lord Sunderland. A visit to Westminster in 1718, to take up his seat in the British House of Commons (for Midhurst), may have enabled Midleton to begin an intrigue with Sunderland's enemies, Walpole and Townshend. Already his resignation was considered imminent. But he did not break openly with the ministry until 1719, when he refused to support Sunderland's Peerage Bill. His papers include a detailed defence of his position, which some historians have taken at face value. As far as Sunderland was concerned, Midleton was now on borrowed time. During the ensuing parliamentary session in Ireland in 1719, St John Brodrick led an opposition alliance against Bolton, focusing on yet another proposal to repeal the test, although Midleton himself conspicuously defended the ministry, and English interests generally, in the continuing storm over the case of *Annesley* v. *Sherlock*, and the issue of the appellate jurisdiction of the Irish House of Lords.

Midleton was saved from dismissal in 1720 by the return to government in England of Walpole and Townshend. He did not care for Bolton's replacement, the duke of Grafton, and was suspicious when Grafton flattered him. Fearing that the viceroy was in Conolly's pocket, Midleton began another intrigue in England, opening a line of communication with Walpole's rival, Lord Carteret. When popular fury was aroused against Wood's halfpence, Midleton expressed himself against the patent, and obstructed the viceroy's efforts to force the acceptance of the coin. In return Grafton tacitly supported attacks on Midleton in the Commons. However, Midleton was careful not to identify himself publicly with opposition. Although he had private meetings with Swift during the controversy, he refused the dedication to a collection of pamphlets on the halfpence, and advocated the prosecution of the author of the *Drapier's Letters*. Walpole's solution to the political crisis was to replace Grafton with Carteret, who was forced to choose between Midleton and Conolly as his Irish manager. Soon Midleton found himself excluded from the new viceroy's confidence. Required to support the continuance of the halfpence, he resigned in April 1725. He went into opposition, but after one parliamentary session left the leadership of his faction to St John. He died at his seat at Ballyannan, and was buried at Midleton on 29 August 1728. St John had predeceased him by six months, and his titles passed to a younger son and namesake. But his political heir, as leader of the 'Munster Squadron' in the Irish parliament, and eventually speaker of the Commons, was St John's erstwhile political lieutenant, Henry Boyle, later Lord Shannon.

Although personally ambitious and opportunistic, Midleton was certainly not unprincipled. Throughout his political career he could be described as a whig, even though, for tactical reasons, his supporters co-operated with tories in opposition after 1715. He was committed to the revolution settlement and protestant succession, and determined to prevent any possibility of a Catholic resurgence. But at the same time he shared Anglican prejudices against dissent, and his failure to endorse the repeal of the test after 1715 was consistent with reservations he had always expressed privately. Where his integrity might have been challenged was on constitutional questions. In 1692, and again in 1703–5, he took up 'patriotic' grievances only to compromise them on taking office: over the 'sole right' in 1692–5, and annual subsidies in 1703–9. In each case he covered himself to some extent by securing concessions from government. Subsequently, in his opposition to the claims made by the Irish House of Lords in *Annesley v. Sherlock*, and in his attitude to Wood's halfpence, he appeared to be letting down the patriot cause. Undoubtedly there was an element of political calculation in his conduct, but a broadly consistent position may be constructed: while seeking to advance Irish interests, he was acutely conscious of the limitations of 'patriotism', and of the underlying dependence of Irish protestants on the English connection.   D. W. HAYTON

Sources Surrey HC, Midleton MSS 1248/1–7 · W. Coxe, *Memoirs of the life and administration of Sir Robert Walpole, earl of Orford*, 2 (1798), 170–219, 346–439 · PRO, SP 63/366–90 · BL, Add. MSS 61633–61636, 61652 · GEC, *Peerage*, new edn, 8.701–2 · R. R. Sedgwick, 'Brodrick, Alan', HoP, *Commons, 1715–54* · *CSP dom.*, 1689–1704 · W. Troost, 'William III and the treaty of Limerick, 1691–1697', Doctor in de Lettern diss., University of Leiden, 1983 · D. W. Hayton, 'Ireland and the English ministers, 1707–16', DPhil diss., U. Oxf., 1975 · P. McNally, *Parties, patriots and undertakers: parliamentary politics in early Hanoverian Ireland* (1997) · S. J. Connolly, *Religion, law, and power: the making of protestant Ireland, 1660–1760* (1992) · D. W. Hayton, 'British whig ministers and the Irish question, 1714–25', *Hanoverian Britain and empire: essays in memory of Philip Lawson*, ed. S. Taylor, R. Connors, and C. Jones (1998), 37–64

Archives Surrey HC, papers | BL, Blenheim MSS, Add. MSS 61633–61636, 61652 · NL Ire., letters to Jane Bonnell

Likenesses G. Kneller, oils, priv. coll.

Brodrick, Cuthbert (1821–1905), architect, was born on 1 December 1821 at Summergangs, Hull, the sixth son of the ten children of John Brodrick, shipowner and merchant, and his wife, Hannah Foster. Both families had been employed for several generations in maritime activities on the Yorkshire coast. The young man grew up in Hull, then one of the chief ports in the United Kingdom. He was educated there, at first privately and then at Kingston College. On 4 January 1837 he was articled to Henry Francis Lockwood (1811–1878), who had set up in practice in 1834 in the town, where his best work, such as Trinity House

Chapel (1839–43), was neo-classical in style and an obvious influence on the young Brodrick, who was quick to reveal his talents as a draughtsman. In this respect he probably benefited from the presence of Thomas Allom (1804–1872), the noted topographical and architectural artist, who was a junior partner of Lockwood's for a short time *c.*1841–1843. In 1839 Brodrick was awarded a silver medal for his measured drawings of the elaborate fourteenth-century Percy tomb in Beverley Minster, Yorkshire.

After completing his articles, Brodrick had a year's tour of buildings in England, France, and Italy; there is no record of a companion on his travels. After his return to Hull in 1845 he set up in practice there on his own account and secured a number of minor commissions; but in November 1852 he was appointed architect for the Hull Royal Institution, an impressive public building of which the main façade was a Corinthian colonnaded screen based on the late seventeenth-century east front of the Louvre, Paris. The institution was the starting point of his design for Leeds town hall, which he won in open competition in 1853. This extended the colonnaded screen treatment to the whole building, in which can be identified the influence of the bourse in Paris (built from the designs of J. T. Brongniart, 1739–1813) and of Sir John Vanbrugh's 'heroic' architecture. It is 'the most considerable public monument built just after the mid-century' (Hitchcock, *Nineteenth and Twentieth Centuries*, 158), with its great domed tower that was an addition to the original design but quickly became a *sine qua non* for other municipal palaces. The town hall was a model for several other public buildings, for example the town halls at Bolton (1866–73), Portsmouth (1886–90), Morley, Yorkshire (1895), and Durban, Natal (1883–5), and Parliament House, Melbourne, in Australia (1856).

In 1856 Brodrick was awarded a silver medal in the prestigious international competition for Lille Cathedral, and he had begun to enter contests for public buildings in London and the major towns. In 1857 he was placed fifth for his design for a new War Office in Whitehall, which *The Builder* noted as having strong points of resemblance to Leeds town hall, his first major building, which became an *idée fixe* that haunted him. Its heavy columnar mass was there again in his designs submitted in 1866 in a limited competition for remodelling and enlarging the National Gallery in Trafalgar Square. The elliptical Leeds corn exchange (1860–62), in some ways his finest work because of the unity of design and relationship between decoration, form, and function, owed its inspiration to the eighteenth-century Halle au Blé, Paris, but its interpretation is Brodrick's. Other buildings he designed in Leeds are the mechanics' institute (1860–66), warehouses in King Street (1862), and Headingley Hill Congregational Church (1864).

In Hull, his native town, Brodrick won the competition for a new town hall in 1861, but he was not successful in the competitions for Preston town hall (1853), Manchester assize courts (1859), Liverpool Royal Exchange (1863), the Natural History Museum, South Kensington (1864), Bolton town hall (1865), Hull Dock offices (1866), Manchester

Royal Exchange (1866), the National Gallery (1866), and Manchester town hall (1866). Although the elemental form of Leeds town hall could sometimes be discerned in these designs, Brodrick used both Gothic and Second Empire eclectic styles as alternatives to the classical columnar. He even used a Moorish style for the Oriental Baths in Leeds (1864), and what *The Builder* called 'a mixture of Hindoo and Mohammedan' (29 Sept 1866, 724) for a vast custom house in Bombay, which was commissioned but not built.

It was in the Second Empire style that Brodrick designed his last major success, the Grand Hotel, Scarborough (1862–7). Rising high above the town on its prominent site, this huge hotel with 300 bedrooms and impressive public rooms symbolized the wealthy West Riding on holiday, just as Leeds town hall is the apotheosis of local government and culture. The colourful brick and stone façades burst out at the top into mansarded pavilion roofs, domes, *œil-de-bœuf* windows, caryatids, and pediments, all reminiscent of the new Louvre, Paris, and creating what Henry-Russell Hitchcock called 'the climax of English Second Empire' (Hitchcock, *Early Victorian Architecture*, 1.213). Inside, its staircase is a modified version of that in the Paris Opéra, and the decoration in the rooms was Parisian-inspired.

Brodrick remained in practice in Leeds (and in London, where he had opened an office in 1863) until about 1870, and he occasionally exhibited at the Royal Academy. He was elected a fellow of the Royal Institute of British Architects in 1860, and a member of its council in 1874, although by that time he was living in France. In England he had led a bachelor life in lodgings and clubs, but in 1876 he bought a house at Le Vésinet, Seine-et-Oise, a *ville-parc* laid out on picturesque English lines. On 7 May 1885 he made a late marriage to Margaret Chatham, *née* Barber (*c*.1814–1888), a widow. After her death at Le Vésinet he is believed to have moved away from the town, but nothing more is known of him until around 1899, when he rented a house, La Colline, Gorey, Jersey, where he died on 2 March 1905. He was buried in St Martin's churchyard, near Gorey.   DEREK LINSTRUM

Sources D. Linstrum, *Towers and colonnades: the architecture of Cuthbert Brodrick* (1999) · D. Linstrum, 'Cuthbert Brodrick: an interpretation of a Victorian architect', *Journal of the Royal Society of Arts*, 119 (1970–71), 72–88 · D. Linstrum, *West Yorkshire: architects and architecture* (1978) · D. Harbron, 'Cuthbert Brodrick, or, Cabbages at Salona', *ArchR*, 79 (1936), 33–5 · T. B. Wilson, *Two Leeds architects* (1937) · H. R. Hitchcock, *Early Victorian architecture in Britain*, 2 vols. (1954) · H. R. Hitchcock, *Architecture: nineteenth and twentieth centuries* (1958) · *Catalogue of the drawings collection of the Royal Institute of British Architects: B* (1972), 101–11 · *The Builder*, 10–28 (1852–70) · m. cert. · census, 1876 · census returns, 1881 · census, 1886 · parish register (baptism), Hull, Holy Trinity, 7 Oct 1822

Archives W. Yorks. AS

Likenesses photograph, priv. coll. · self-portrait, repro. in Harbron, 'Cuthbert Brodrick'

Wealth at death £7490 9s. 1d.: probate, 17 April 1905, CGPLA Eng. & Wales

Brodrick, George Charles (1831–1903), college head, was born on 5 May 1831 at the rectory, Castle Rising, Norfolk, the second of four sons and five children of William John Brodrick (1798–1870), clergyman and seventh Viscount Midleton (1863–70), and his second wife (and first cousin), Harriet (1804–1893), daughter of George Brodrick, fourth Viscount Midleton. His paternal grandfather was archbishop of Cashel; his father, 'the most consistently devout Christian and the most perfect gentleman that I have ever known' (Brodrick, 2), was rector of Bath (1839–54), chaplain to the queen (1847), canon of Wells (1855), and dean of Exeter (1861–7). Brodrick followed his father's evangelical creed, and in 1850 matriculated as a commoner at his father's former Oxford college, Balliol, after schooling with his elder brother at Eton (1843–8). A fellow of Eton from 1887, Brodrick acknowledged 'the spell of Eton traditions and sentiment', yet argued that 'Eton might have been a far better training-ground of character and intellect than it was' (ibid., 42). His health collapsed there while striving for the Newcastle scholarship; but, following a recuperative voyage to India, at Balliol he proved a thoroughbred in examinations, taking firsts in moderations (1852), *literae humaniores* (1853), and law and history (1854), and the chancellor's English essay and Arnold essay prizes (1855). Jowett was influential as a tutor, and Brodrick extolled the institution of long vacation reading parties, when dons and select undergraduates exercised together and 'discussed every subject, human and divine' (ibid., 87). Brodrick was a president of the Oxford Union and also co-founder of a mutual improvement society: this, known as the Essay Society, involved debating theories of government and ethics in the company of such as Bryce, Dicey, Goschen, and Frederic Harrison. Disappointment in fellowship examinations at Balliol and Oriel was overlaid by success at Merton in 1855. This was in open competition, although one aged life fellow, who resided in Bath in term time and admired Brodrick's father, made a surprising intervention, declaring he had come to vote for Brodrick 'whatever might be the result of the examination' (ibid., 112). Brodrick spent a year as a probationary fellow before moving to London to read for the bar. He was called to the bar at Lincoln's Inn (1859), having taken the degree of LLB at London University (1858).

The western circuit, on which he practised (1859–62), Brodrick found genial but intellectually unstimulating, and after his chancellor's essay, 'Representative government in ancient and modern times', was read by the editor of *The Times*, Delane, he accepted invitations to contribute reviews and leaders. Between 1860 and 1873, though never on the permanent staff, Brodrick wrote about 1600 leading articles for *The Times* covering most topics, home and abroad, though he was largely kept off the American Civil War because of his declared sympathy with the Union cause. Suitably impressed by his own versatility, he liked to think that he was 'doing the work of an unrecognised statesman, and exercising a greater influence on public opinion than any politician, except a very few in the foremost rank' (Brodrick, 141). The Brodrick family was tory in politics, but from 1852 Brodrick emerged as 'a decided, though moderate, Liberal'. He contributed to *Essays on Reform* (1867), the celebrated symposium of liberal-minded Oxbridge dons who were seeking a partnership with provincial nonconformist political leaders in pressing for the abolition of religious tests at the ancient universities while refuting the predictions of Robert Lowe that franchise extension would vitiate good government. Brodrick shared Lowe's utilitarian principles but applied them more to the economy than to politics: however efficient in pursuit of 'the happiness of the people at large' a government was, Brodrick thought, its objectives were unattainable while it excluded the mass of people from representation. Popular government would furnish them with 'moral training' in 'the duties of citizenship'. The remainder of Brodrick's life witnessed a retreat from this optimism to the point where, in *Memories and Impressions* (1900), he fully recanted, acknowledging that Lowe was right to prophesy that 'men of ability and professing high principles would not scruple to flatter the prejudices, pander to the passions, and inflame the class antipathies of voters whom they might have educated, for the sake of winning their support' (ibid., 223).

In 1867 Brodrick supposed that he and his fellow essayists would constitute the next governing generation in high politics. He was disappointed in this too: the voters of Woodstock (in 1868 and 1874) and Monmouthshire (in 1880) rejected his representations. At the 1874 contest of Woodstock, Brodrick lost to the Marlborough interest, personified by Lord Randolph Churchill who, as well as being 'restrained by few scruples, and by little respect for others' (Brodrick, 156), was a former undergraduate of Merton. Brodrick's sole supporter among the country gentlemen was Sir Henry Dashwood; otherwise, he appealed to the agricultural labourers, newly unionized by Joseph Arch, and the workforce of Godden's glove manufacture in the borough. But he was 'no advocate of socialistic measures, nor will I be party to an agitation whereby class may be set against class'. Brodrick maintained his reputation as a reformer by a study of local government, published by the Cobden Club (1875), which 'contemplated a reconstruction of local institutions from the parish and township upwards, instead of one beginning with County Councils, working downwards, and ending with Parish Councils' (ibid., 195); he also addressed the land question, culminating in *English Land and English Landlords* (1881), which advocated greater owner-occupancy through revision of the systems of tenure, especially of the law and customs of entail and primogeniture. Polemical writing brought Brodrick no nearer his ambition of playing a practical part in government, nor did personal connection, extensive though that was; challenged to estimate the private houses in the four home counties in which he had stayed, he counted some 400, and he could claim as friends thirteen of the fifteen members of Gladstone's first cabinet, the closest being Goschen. This conjunction was strengthened through the men's mistrust of weak-minded philanthropic measures, conceived in ignorance of political economy—as Brodrick termed it: 'the sinister alliance of Ritualism and Socialism' (ibid., 344). Above all, they rued Gladstone's demagogy and Irish land and home-rule policies. Two-thirds of the Brodrick estate of 9580 acres was in co. Cork (the rest

was in Surrey), but it was not from narrow familial interest that Brodrick opposed home rule, rather from an imperial and even Irish standpoint, arguing that Irish progress and freedom were better guaranteed by preserving the Union. Together with A. V. Dicey, Brodrick led the Liberal Unionist cause in Oxford, speechifying and pamphleteering.

This was Brodrick's last sustained political engagement. On 17 February 1881 he had become warden of Merton, succeeding the nonagenarian Dr Bullock Marsham, in occupation since 1826. This was distinct second best to high political office, though Brodrick was consolingly reminded that, while cabinet ministers were numerous and MPs legion, there was only one warden of Merton. Roseate recollections of Brodrick's twenty-two years' headship glide over the strong views he expressed on major issues of academic policy: his keen defence of the college system; his condemnation of the failure to frame an organic relationship between tutors and the new classes of university professor and reader; and his admonitions about the trend towards academic specialism, riding on the back of the endowment of research and the promotion of the natural sciences. The last question involved Brodrick in a fierce exchange with the Linacre professor of comparative anatomy, E. Ray Lankester, who resigned his professorial fellowship at Merton in 1898. Brodrick wrote slightingly about the 'hypercritical and unpractical spirit' of academics, 'the legislative imbecility of the University', and 'the inherent incapacity of Academical politicians to construct anything that will last' (Brodrick, 365–7). Holding these views, it was unsurprising he turned down the vice-chancellorship (1898), though he served on the visitatorial board and as a curator of the Indian Institute and delegate of the Common University Fund. He also represented the university as alderman on the Oxford city council (1889–92), following the precepts of T. H. Green in seeking harmony between town and gown. He had previously pursued the same course as a co-opted member of the London school board (1877–9), steering between the board school and voluntary school factions. He was also an assiduous county magistrate but, while admiring the ethic which inspired people to undertake unpaid service on umpteen public bodies, conceding, too, their aggregate useful result, Brodrick never found it attractive and believed 'it is generally carried on with an enormous waste of time and energy'.

A frustrated politician and ultimately ineffectual, if prodigious, tract writer, Brodrick reserved his greatest role to the last, and this was Brodrick of Merton. The college's archives, dating from the thirteenth century, excited his scholarship. Brodrick's copy of his *Memorials of Merton College* (1885) survives, containing a profusion of marginalia in his fine bold handwriting and conveying additional information which testifies to his continued passion for the history of the college. A bachelor, he was a generous host. He could afford it: at his death he left effects probated at £141,090. But he was inveterately sociable and his visitors' book records the procession of illustrious Victorians through the warden's lodgings and at college high table: statesmen, senior permanent officials, ecclesiastics and lawyers, artists and scientists, writers and critics. Nor was Brodrick exclusive in his invitations: a viceroy of India might be seated next to an ordinary undergraduate, though doubtless to their mutual incomprehension. Brodrick's pastimes included riding: he journeyed about the country by horse whenever he could, rode daily in Rotten Row when staying in his Mount Street and (from 1893) Pall Mall London apartments, and exercised over Boars Hill when in Oxford. Favourite, however, was 'talkin''—Brodrick retained the old aristocratic style of speech, and, though his stamina was sometimes dismaying, his period charm and kindliness were memorable. So was his appearance: reddish whiskers, tall and thin, and with protruding teeth which earned him the nickname Curius Dentatus, used alike by undergraduates and Henry James, a guest in 1884. The sartorial code, too, was antiquated: a tailcoat of old-fashioned cut with top hat for the day, and always full evening dress for dinner. He died on 8 November 1903 in the warden's lodgings, a month after resigning the wardenship, and was buried at Peper Harow, Surrey, the seat of the Midleton family.   PHILIP WALLER

Sources G. C. Brodrick, *Memories and impressions, 1831–1900* (1900) · C. Harvie, *The lights of liberalism* (1976) · A. J. Engel, *From clergyman to don* (1983) · GEC, *Peerage* · *CGPLA Eng. & Wales* (1903)
Archives Merton Oxf., papers · NL Ire., corresp. and literary papers | News Int. RO, papers as leader writer for *The Times*
Likenesses M. Beerbohm, two caricatures, 1890, probably Merton Oxf. · M. Beerbohm, study for a statue, 1891?, Merton Oxf. · W. Carter, oils, 1899, Merton Oxf. · R. Macbeth, oils, 1899, Merton Oxf. · Spy [L. Ward], cartoon, NPG; repro. in *VF* (30 Aug 1884)
Wealth at death £141,090 1s. 2d.: probate, 8 Dec 1903, *CGPLA Eng. & Wales*

Brodrick, James Patrick (1891–1973), Jesuit and author, was born on 26 July 1891 in Kingsland, Athenry, co. Galway, the son of Peter Broderick (d. 1900), building contractor and small landowner, and his wife, Julia Rushe. Both parents were Irish. His father died in 1900 and Julia moved to Dublin where James went to school at the O'Brien Institute in Dublin for five years. He moved to London and found his life's vocation after admission to the Jesuit noviciate at Roehampton on 1 February 1910. His training was not easy, as he suffered from bad health, which was to plague him all his life. He also had a critical and well-read mind, and did not find it easy to mix with more robust youths, but he persevered. After first vows on 2 February 1912 and the juniorate for academic studies, he went to teach at St Michael's College, Leeds, in May 1912. From 1913 until 1922 he was engaged in philosophical and theological studies at St Mary's Hall, Stonyhurst, and St Beuno's College, near St Asaph. He proceeded MA from London in 1919 and was ordained priest on 23 September 1923.

On ending formal studies, in 1924 Brodrick joined the Farm Street community in London as a writer for *The Month*. Less than happy to produce 'ephemeral articles or book reviews on demand about all and sundry' (Crehan), he was already engaged in larger interests. After the tertianship, the last phase of Jesuit training, in 1927 he returned to Farm Street. *The Life and Work of Blessed Robert Bellarmine, 1541 to 1621*, appeared in two volumes in 1928. This was revised and reissued as one volume in 1961. His *Times* obituarist later provided an apt comment for all his works.

> Brodrick's writing was not the result of original research but he was more than a popular writer. He brought his own sense of history to bear on the findings of scholarship ... Then with all the gifts of an Irish-born raconteur, he would draw a living and gripping story out of the mass of documentation ... rescuing the early Jesuit saints from the apologists and hagiographers and subjecting them to historical criticism. (*The Times*, 28 Aug 1973)

He could be critical of fellow Jesuits, praising A. Astrain's seven-volume history of the Spanish Jesuits (1902–1925) as one of the best of the Jesuit histories, but attacking H. Fouqueray's account of the Jesuits in France (published 1910–25): 'Fouqueray gets too indignant and is all out to defend the French Jesuits no matter what they were up to', he wrote. 'Also he is confoundedly dull. Astrain is lively and very honest' (Provincial Archives, 48/1/16/6).

On 25 January 1928 Brodrick underwent two surgical operations, one severe. After convalescence he returned to Farm Street on 27 March and was professed of four vows in the society on 2 February 1929. On 29 May 1931, after another bout of ill health and specialist treatment at Freiburg im Breisgau, he returned in improved health on 10 August 1931. A few months later he fractured a thigh bone, but serious intestinal problems were diagnosed in April 1934. Remarkably, none of this held up *The Economic Morals of the Jesuits*, which appeared in the year of tribulation, 1934, or his monumental life of Saint Peter Canisius, published in 1935.

Brodrick spent the first part of the war in London. After the blitz of 1940 he moved to Stonyhurst. During the war the students of the English College, Rome, settled at St Mary's Hall there. From 1941 Brodrick became their spiritual father, returning to Farm Street in January 1947. Two important works belong to this period, *The Origin of the Jesuits*, of 1940, and *The Progress of the Jesuits*, 1946. A projected full-scale life of St Ignatius never materialized but a life of St Francis Xavier appeared in 1952. In 1956 *The Pilgrim Years* was offered as the first—and only—part of a life of St Ignatius. Brodrick's last historical work before the heart attack in 1967 which ended his working life was the booklet of 1965, *Galileo, the Man, his Work, his Misfortune*.

Brodrick was a man of profound spirituality and he manifested this side in broadcasts, articles, booklets, and personal contacts. Antonia White was quoted as saying, 'I had a wonderful afternoon with him and I've never met a better and kinder priest. He comforted me so much in every way, even about my perpetual doubts' (Provincial Archives, 48/1/16/3). From 1968 his last years were spent in the Bon Secours Nursing Home at Wokingham, where he died on 28 August 1973. His funeral took place from Farm Street on 5 September; he was buried at Kensal Green cemetery.   FRANCIS EDWARDS

Sources Curricula vitarum, Curia SJ, Farm Street, London · J. Crehan, *Letters and Notices*, 79 (1974), 237–44 · Archives of the British Province of the Society of Jesus, London, 48/1/16/1–7 · *The Times* (28 Aug 1973)

Archives Archives of the British Province of the Society of Jesus, London
Likenesses photographs, Archives of the British Province of the Society of Jesus, London, Box 31/A–B

Brodrick, Mary (1858–1933), archaeologist, was born at 18 Navarino Terrace, Dalston Lane, Hackney, London, on 5 April 1858, the daughter of Thomas Brodrick (d. c.1875), solicitor, and his wife, Mary Smith Haviside. Thomas Brodrick was in practice in London and in Salisbury, Wiltshire. Little is known about her early years, though in 1881 she was lodging in Hove, Sussex.

Brodrick's first visit to Egypt was probably made in 1888, when she was thirty, apparently so that she could avoid the English winter. Her first journey up the Nile was in a party with one of the Nile inspectors. Occupied by the British in 1882, Egypt had become a popular destination owing to the excursions arranged by Thomas Cook and the interest stimulated by Amelia Edwards's *A Thousand Miles up the Nile* (1877). Edwards was keen to develop British archaeological work in Egypt, and her enthusiasm brought about the foundation of the Egypt Exploration Fund in 1882.

Brodrick was inspired to study Egyptology, but found it almost impossible to do so in London. As a result she looked to Paris, determined to study at the Sorbonne under Professor Gaston Camille Charles Maspero (1846–1916), who had served as the director-general of the Egyptian antiquities service (1881–6). He was not immediately sympathetic, reputedly saying, 'But we don't take little girls here' (*Egypt Papers*, vii–viii). At Maspero's suggestion she approached Joseph Ernest Renan (1823–1892) at the Collège de France, who was equally reluctant to allow her to attend lectures: 'I have never taught a woman in my life, and I never will!' (ibid., viii).

Maspero, however, raised Brodrick's case with the council of the Sorbonne, and as a result she was permitted to attend lectures at both the Sorbonne and the Collège de France. She studied Egyptology with Maspero, Eugène Charles Revillout (1843–1913), professor of demotic, Coptic, and Egyptian law at the École du Louvre, and Paul Pierret (1837–1916), curator at the Louvre. Renan, who had undertaken archaeological work in the Lebanon at the prompting of Napoleon III, taught her Hebrew, 'Semitic archaeology', and Roman law and history. Maspero wrote to Amelia Edwards in spring 1888 about Brodrick's attendance at his lectures. Although the other students were not immediately accepting of her, in one instance pouring ink down her back, she was able to make lifelong friends during her time in Paris. These included a number of Egyptologists: Georges Legrain (1865–1917), Émile Chassinat (1868–1948), Georges Aaron Bénédite (1857–1926), and Philippe Virey (1853–1922). William N. Groff (1857–1901), the American Egyptologist, extended hospitality to Brodrick, permitting her to work at his parents' home in Paris.

Brodrick returned to London and enrolled at the women's hall of residence, College Hall, Byng Place, London, in order to pursue her study of archaeology and in particular Egyptology. She was trained by some of the key figures in British Egyptology. Records at University College, London, show that she was a fee-paying student for the 1890–91 session under Reginald Stuart Poole (1832–1895). She enrolled under Flinders Petrie, whose chair in Egyptology had been endowed through Amelia Edwards's bequest, for the 1893–4 and 1894–5 sessions, and continued as a student at University College, London until 1906.

Brodrick had developed close links with the British Museum, perhaps from winter 1888 (*Egypt Papers*, xv), working with Peter le Page Renouf, keeper of the department of oriental antiquities at the British Museum, whom she recalled giving her a hieroglyphic inscription to read: 'I took it back humiliated and told Renouf that I could make nothing of it. The old man looked up with a charming smile and said: "Neither can I," and added that he had given it to me to see if I had any grit' (ibid., ix). She also acknowledged the influence of Alexander Stuart Murray, an early member of the Egypt Exploration Society's committee, who had excavated at Tanis.

Brodrick was permitted 'to deliver two courses of lectures and one set of Demonstration Classes on Roman Antiquities at the British Museum' (*Egypt Papers*, ix). Although it has been claimed that Brodrick was the first woman to fulfil this role, she was following in the footsteps of other women. These included Jane E. Harrison, who had lectured on Greek art and archaeology in the British Museum during the 1880s, and Margaret Harkness and Helen Mary Beloe (Lady Tirard; 1854–1943), who lectured to groups of women at the British Museum to support the Egypt Exploration Fund (1884–6).

At this time there were few Egyptological textbooks in English. Brodrick was one of several women, including Kate Griffith (d. 1902), Anna Anderson Morton (1876–1961), and Lady Tirard, who prepared a series of revisions of key Egyptological works and translated them into English. Among Brodrick's translations were *Egypt under the Pharaohs: a History Derived Entirely from the Monuments* (1891) and *Outlines of Ancient Egyptian History* (1890), from the works of Heinrich Ferdinand Karl Brugsch and François Auguste Ferdinand Mariette respectively.

The Egypt Exploration Fund, renamed Egypt Exploration Society in 1887, had received support in North America from its earliest days from the Revd William Copley Winslow of Boston, Massachusetts. In the face of growing criticism, in particular from Cope Whitehouse, the society had sought to strengthen its position, and Amelia Edwards herself made a lecture tour in 1889 and 1890. Brodrick served as English honorary secretary in the United States of America for the society. In July 1893 her work in America was acknowledged by the award of a University of Kansas PhD degree by the College of the Sisters of Bethany, Topeka, an Episcopalian foundation. She was also elected a member of the advisory council and of the committee of philology and literary archaeology at the Columbian International Exposition (c.1898).

From 1894 to 1896 Brodrick held a Pfeiffer fellowship awarded by the council of College Hall. She continued to lecture at the British Museum, and travelled in Italy,

Greece, and Egypt. Brodrick was invited to revise Murray's *Handbook for Egypt* (1895), and then to prepare a new expanded edition to include the Sudan, *A Handbook for Travellers in Lower and Upper Egypt* (10th edn, 1900). After her fellowship expired, she worked in Egypt (1897–1908) under Maspero, now the director-general of Egyptian antiquities. This was a fruitful period for Egyptology, which saw the opening of the Cairo Museum of Antiquities (1902). There was also a growing number of British women actively involved in Egyptology. Among them were Kate Bradbury (d. 1902), the companion of Amelia Edwards, who married F. L. Griffith in 1896; Emily Paterson, Edwards's secretary, and subsequently the secretary of the Egypt Exploration Fund; Margaret Alice Murray; and Margaret Benson, who travelled in Egypt between 1894 and 1900, and excavated at the temple of Mut at Thebes with Janet Agnes Gourlay (1863–1912).

Brodrick was particularly active, collaborating with Renouf on *The life and confession of Asenath: the daughter of Pentephres of Heliopolis, narrating how the all-beautiful Joseph took her to wife* (1900), a study based on 'the Greek version of the Armenian MS. in the Abbey of Beauvais'. She collaborated with Anna Anderson Morton, who had also studied Egyptology at University College, publishing a study of the tomb of Pepi-Ankh near Sharuna in the *Proceedings of the Society of Biblical Archaeology* (1899) as a result of a brief visit in 1896. Brodrick and Morton then produced *A Concise Dictionary of Egyptian Archaeology: a Handbook for Students and Travellers* (1902), which appeared in five editions. By 1906 the *Daily Mail* could report, 'Miss Brodrick is perhaps the greatest lady Egyptologist of the day' (*Daily Mail*, 26 Nov 1906; *Egypt Papers*, xv).

Brodrick's winters were often spent on a *dahabiyeh* on the Nile, 'with my own crest embroidered pennant flying' (*Egypt Papers*, ix). She was frequently joined by parties which included other archaeologists, artists, and government officials. In March 1890 the American Charles Edwin Wilbour came across her in an all-women party ('no white man with them') on the *Gameeleh*, a steel-hulled *dahabiyeh* ('one of the prettiest and fastest … on the river'; Sayce, 260) sometimes used by the Assyriologist Archibald H. Sayce (*Travels in Egypt*, 564). Brodrick recalled one incident at Luxor, when grave-robbers smuggled a mummy onto her *dahabiyeh*, at night and against her wishes, so that Maspero would not find it. Brodrick also kept in touch with Petrie, visiting him, for example, at the Egypt Exploration Society excavation at Dendera in winter 1897–8.

Brodrick was an active member of the Society of Biblical Archaeology, and was a committee member of the Egypt Exploration Society. She was closely involved with the Society for the Preservation of the Monuments of Ancient Egypt, a body first convened in August 1888 by the painter Edward Poynter. Poynter forwarded one of Brodrick's letters to *The Times*; in it she made a report of some of the problems faced in Egypt, noting, 'I caught two Egyptian soldiers in the act of cutting their names on the entrance of Aboo Simbel' (letter of 4 July 1890). Her observations had no doubt been made in the spring tour of that year mentioned by Wilbour.

Brodrick was also involved with British society in Egypt. A contemporary newspaper cutting noted: 'Miss Brodrick holds very strong views on the lasting benefit done to Egypt by the British occupation and, in common with all who really know Egypt, asserts that if British rule were withdrawn the result would be utter chaos' (*Egypt Papers*, xv). Her memoirs give brief glimpses of her Cairo circle. In 1901 or 1902 she attended the luncheon in Cairo to discuss the plan by Cecil Rhodes to connect Cape Town and Cairo by railway and boat. She also made a visit to Khartoum, where she apparently took the 'salute' at the Gordon memorial service (1913–14).

Brodrick's interests were not confined to Egypt, and her earlier training in the archaeology of the Near East brought about an invitation to prepare the Murray's *Handbook for Travellers in Syria and Palestine* (1903). Lectures on Christian themes were published as a book, *The Trial and Crucifixion of Jesus Christ of Nazareth* (1908). She lectured widely in Cairo, England, Scotland, and Italy. Her friend and executor Eversley Chaning Robinson (d. 1949), the wife of Sir Arnold Percy Robinson (1879–1960), wrote that when Brodrick spoke:

> People, places, things rose again as the lecturer described them with punctilious accuracy, clearness, humour and insight into character. The dry bones of the past awoke again to life as she caught their spirit and clothed them with imagination, tempered by patient historical research. (*Egypt Papers*, xii)

One of her last lectures was on the discovery of the tomb of Tutankhamen in November 1922. Her excitement was clear: 'The intense interest lies in this, that here for the first time we have the complete equipment of a royal tomb made and decorated at the moment of the highest point of Egyptian art—and perfect' (ibid., 67). A selection of Brodrick's lectures and newspaper articles were republished in a volume, *Egypt* (1938), edited by Eversley Robinson.

Brodrick received several recognitions for her work as an Egyptologist. In 1896 she was elected a life member of the Bibliothèque Nationale in Paris, as well as a life member of College Hall, London. In 1899 she was elected a life member of the Comité de la Société Française d'Égyptologie. In 1913 she was made a dame of grace of the order of St John of Jerusalem. She was elected an honorary fellow of the Royal Geographical Society (1916) and an honorary fellow of the American Geographical Society (1925).

Brodrick was grateful for the support given by College Hall and University College, London. In 1913 she made a modest donation to the appeal set up to purchase Petrie's Egyptian collection. In 1924 she established the Mary Brodrick prize in geography at University College (since 1964 the Brodrick–Parry prize). In 1929, when College Hall was expanding, she gave a generous donation towards the new building. Indeed she bequeathed her archaeological library to College Hall; in 1964 the Egyptological volumes were placed on loan with the Edwards Library at University College, London. Her contribution to College Hall was acknowledged by Dr Louisa Macdonald, in an address in

London in November 1933: 'It is not only as a benefactor that we commemorate her, she was among the most distinguished that belonged to us. She was one of the best-known pioneer women Egyptologists' (*Egypt Papers*, xiv).

In her later years May (as she was known to friends) Brodrick resided at the Villa Primavera in Bordighera, Italy, where there was a sizeable English community. She died at Stoneycrest, Hindhead, Surrey, on 13 July 1933. She never married. An appreciation in *The Times* (22 July 1933) noted her 'fine head and brow, with its upstanding short white hair, keen eyes, and vivid smile, the spare form always clothed in black'. It also described her as 'one of the kindest, wisest, most generous and true of friends'.

DAVID GILL

Sources *The Times* (22 July 1933) · *Egypt: papers and lectures by the late Mary Brodrick*, ed. E. Robinson (1938) · W. R. Dawson and E. P. Uphill, *Who was who in Egyptology*, 3rd edn, rev. M. L. Bierbrier (1995) · R. M. Janssen and J. Janssen, 'Excavating in the Petrie Museum', *Studies on ancient Egypt in honour of H. S. Smith*, ed. A. Leahy and J. Tait (1999), 151–6 · W. R. Dawson, 'Letters from Maspero to Amelia Edwards', *Journal of Egyptian Archaeology*, 33 (1947), 66–89, esp. p. 86 · *Travels in Egypt (December 1880 to May 1891): letters of Charles Edwin Wilbour*, ed. J. Capart (Brooklyn, 1936) · R. M. Janssen, *The first hundred years: Egyptology at University College London, 1892–1992* (1992) · T. G. H. James, ed., *Excavating in Egypt: the Egyptian Exploration Society, 1882–1982* (1982) · M. S. Drower, *Flinders Petrie: a life in archaeology*, 2nd edn (Madison, 1995) · A. H. Sayce, *Reminiscences* (1923) · A. M. Copping, *The story of College Hall* (1974) · b. cert.
Archives UCL, Edwards Library, books · UCL, Petrie Museum of Egyptian Archaeology, antiquities
Likenesses N. Fulcher, portrait, priv. coll.
Wealth at death £46,352 6s. 8d.: probate, 21 Aug 1933, *CGPLA Eng. & Wales*

Brodrick, (William) St John Fremantle, first earl of Midleton (1856–1942), politician, was born in London on 14 December 1856, the eldest of the three sons of William Brodrick, later eighth Viscount Midleton (*d.* 1907), and his wife, Augusta Mary, third daughter of Sir Thomas Francis Fremantle, later first Baron Cottesloe and his wife, Lady Augusta Henrietta, *née* Scott. He was a nephew of G. C. Brodrick. Until 1870, when his father succeeded to the title, Brodrick was taught strictly but affectionately to fit himself for hard work. He was, however, a worker by disposition. He was educated at Eton College, where his greatest friend was Alfred Lyttelton, and at Balliol College, Oxford, where he obtained a second class in modern history and was president of the Oxford Union in 1878. After taking his degree he soon made himself financially independent as his father had desired, beginning with journalism and later making a much more profitable and a permanent connection with telegraphic cable companies.

In 1880 Brodrick entered the House of Commons as a Conservative, unopposed for West Surrey: from 1885 to 1906 he represented the Guildford division. The acute Irish problem at once seized his attention in the house. He disapproved of the neglectful conduct of many Irish landowners; he did not forget that the principal part of the fortune which he was destined to inherit was derived from Midleton in co. Cork. But the unusual knowledge of Irish affairs which he acquired, and which was commended by Gladstone, by no means shook his conviction (until the

war of 1914–18 brought new conditions) that the well-being of Ireland depended upon kindly and intelligent rule by England. His first office was that of financial secretary to the War Office (1886–92). It was he who in opposition during the Liberal government of 1892–5 discovered the deficiency of ammunition for the army and inspired the 'cordite' motion which caused the fall of Rosebery's government. In 1895 he became under-secretary of state for war, and in 1898 under-secretary for foreign affairs. He was sworn of the privy council in 1897.

Such experience amply prepared Brodrick for his appointment as secretary of state for war after the election of 1900. Brodrick played some part in the establishment of the committee of imperial defence (largely A. J. Balfour's achievement) in 1902. Brodrick did not believe that the Second South African War had exposed serious malfunctioning in the army, and he was a staunch defender of the Cardwell system of 1870–72, and he attempted to reform it by renovating it. He also wanted a stronger home army, organized in six corps, three of which would be ready to serve as an expeditionary force—the first plan which took account of Britain's increasingly continental orientation. Poor planning in detail and difficult relations with many of his senior officers meant that little of Brodrick's plan was achieved. The Elgin and Norfolk royal commissions and the Esher committee on War Office reconstruction suggested very different reforms—an army board, on the model of the Admiralty—and Brodrick was left stranded. However, he introduced a new forage cap for the guards which came to bear his name. Lord Esher advised Brodrick in August 1903 to resign; he did not, but Balfour took advantage of the ministerial reshuffle consequent upon the cabinet crisis in September 1903 over tariff reform to remove him from the War Office. Still in the cabinet, he was an effective counter-force to his successor, H. O. Arnold-Forster, who attempted to replace Brodrick's reform programme with his own, the consequence being that the Unionists went out of office with little to show in the way of army reform despite the high priority they claimed to give to it.

From 9 October 1903 to 11 December 1905 Brodrick was secretary of state for India. He was pitched almost immediately into the controversy over the partition of Bengal, already under consideration. This led to a major quarrel with his schoolfriend G. N. *Curzon, now, as Lord Curzon, viceroy of India. They also strongly disagreed on frontier policy with respect to Afghanistan and Tibet. Curzon sent his plan for partition on 2 February 1905. Brodrick tried to encourage Curzon to put forward a more limited proposal—a commissioner for parts of Bengal—but on 9 June he agreed to Curzon's plan, though warning him of its likely explosive consequences. Partition was announced on 19 July and executed on 16 October 1905, shortly before Brodrick resigned with the rest of Balfour's government.

At the same time, Brodrick was under pressure from Kitchener to force on Curzon strengthening of the commander-in-chief's authority in India. Brodrick offered compromise but, in a subsidiary row over a military appointment, Curzon resigned. Rows with Curzon blighted Brodrick's secretaryship. In his pamphlet, *Relations of Lord Curzon as Viceroy of India with the British Government, 1902–5*, which he privately published in June 1926 (a year after Curzon's death), with a note that it was 'seen and approved by the Earl of Balfour, June 1926', he took the view that Curzon had been nervously exhausted, 'as early as 1902 … almost at the end of his tether'.

At the general election of 1906 Brodrick was defeated and in 1907 he succeeded his father as ninth Viscount Midleton, taking up residence at Peper Harow, near Godalming. He now had more time to attend to Ireland and he became leader of the southern unionists. The most important event in this connection was his part in 1917 in trying to arrange through the Irish convention a settlement between north and south. The aim was a united, autonomous Ireland 'within the British Empire' with adequate safeguards for unionist minorities. The first flush of general enthusiasm soon faded into the old suspicions and enmities. It was widely thought that Midleton overestimated the likelihood that Ulstermen would subject their intense loyalty to the union to conditions under which, as they believed, they could hardly maintain it. After the breakdown of the convention Lloyd George pressed Midleton to accept the lord lieutenancy of Ireland; but Midleton declined when he learned that he would have to support a double policy of 'autonomy and conscription', in which he profoundly disbelieved. On 4 July 1921 he attended a conference in Dublin, at De Valera's invitation, and was subsequently able to persuade Lloyd George to agree to a truce, pending discussions, which he proceeded to negotiate in consultation with Sir Nevil Macready. But Midleton considered the subsequent settlement a 'lamentable conclusion' and thereafter took no further part in Irish affairs.

In politics Midleton was notable for his sincerity; he would join with zest in fair political stratagem, but never in intrigue. His long experience of men and affairs left him with an unexpected simplicity which was very attractive to his friends but which meant that he was ill equipped to deal with the Curzon affair.

Midleton was twice married: first, in 1880, to Hilda Charteris (*d*. 1901), daughter of Lord Elcho, later eighth earl of Wemyss and sixth earl of March, with whom he had one son and four daughters; and second, in 1903, to Madeleine Cecilia Carlyle, elder daughter of Colonel John Constantine Stanley, Grenadier Guards, with whom he had two sons, who were both killed in action at Salerno (1943). He was an alderman of the London county council from 1907 to 1913; was appointed KP in 1916; was advanced to an earldom by Lloyd George in 1920; and received the honorary degree of LLD from Trinity College, Dublin, in 1922. He died at Peper Harow on 13 February 1942.

J. B. ATKINS, *rev.* H. C. G. MATTHEW

Sources *The Times* (16 Feb 1942) · Earl of Midleton [W. St J. F. Brodrick], *Ireland* (1932) · Earl of Midleton [W. St J. F. Brodrick], *Records and reactions, 1856–1939* (1939) · N. Goradia, *Lord Curzon: the last of the British moghuls* (1993) · F. Pakenham, *Peace by ordeal* (1935) · E. M. Spiers, *Haldane: an army reformer* (1980) · B. W. Cox and M. Prevezer, 'The Brodrick cap', *Journal of the Society for Army Historical Research*, 60 (1982), 213–25 · L. J. Satre, 'St John Brodrick and army reform,

1901–1903', *Journal of British Studies*, 15/2 (1975–6), 117–39 · P. Magnus, *King Edward the Seventh* (1964)

Archives PRO, corresp. and papers, PRO 30/67 | BL, corresp. with H. O. Arnold-Foster, Add. MSS 50311, 50314, 50325, 50347, *passim* · BL, corresp. with Arthur James Balfour, Add. MSS 49720–49721, *passim* · BL, corresp. with J. H. Bernard, Add. MS 52781 · BL, corresp. with Lord Curzon, Add. MSS 50072–50077 · BL, corresp. with Sir E. T. H. Hutton, Add. MS 50085, *passim* · BL, corresp. with G. D. Ramsay, Add. MS 46448 · BL OIOC, corresp. with Lord Ampthill, MS Eur. E 233 · BL OIOC, letters to Arthur Godley, MS Eur. F 102 · BL OIOC, letters to John Morley, MS Eur. D 555 · BL OIOC, letters to H. E. Richards, MS Eur. F 122 · Bodl. Oxf., letters to Hebert Asquith; letters to Margot Asquith; letters to Lady Milner; corresp. with Lord Selborne · Bodl. Oxf., corresp. with A. J. Balfour etc. · Herts. ALS, letters to Lady Desborough · HLRO, corresp. with Andrew Bonar Law; corresp. with David Lloyd George; corresp. with John St Loe Strachey · King's AC Cam., letters to Oscar Browning · Lpool RO, corresp. with Lord Derby · NA Scot., corresp. with A. J. Balfour and G. W. Balfour; corresp. with Phillip Kerr; corresp. with Lord Minto · NAM, letters to Lord Roberts · NL Ire., letters to J. Redmond · Plunkett Foundation for Cooperative Studies, Oxford, corresp. with Sir Horace Plunkett · U. Birm. L., letters to Austen Chamberlain and Joseph Chamberlain

Likenesses B. Stone, photograph, 1902, NPG · Russell, photogravure, 1911, NPG · W. Stoneman, photograph, 1921, NPG · W. Carter, oils, county hall, Kingston upon Thames, Surrey · B. Partridge, caricature, pen-and-ink cartoon, NPG; repro. in *Punch* (29 Jan 1902) · attrib. Russell, photograph, NPG · Spy [L. Ward], chromolithograph caricature, NPG; repro. in *VF* (18 July 1801)

Wealth at death £68,590 further grant: 1943, CGPLA Eng. & Wales

Brodrick, Thomas (1704–1769), naval officer, was the only son of William Brodrick, attorney-general of Jamaica and later judge of king's bench in Ireland, a kinsman of Viscount Midleton. He entered the navy as a volunteer per order in 1722 in the *Mermaid*, and served in several ships until he passed for lieutenant on 10 January 1728, and was appointed to the *Rye* next day. Later he served in the *Nassau* and then the *Gosport* against the Salé pirates and in the Mediterranean. Subsequently he was in the *Diamond* and *Strafford* before joining the *Burford*, Edward Vernon's flagship in the West Indies. He commanded the landing party which stormed the Castillo de Fierro. In recompense for his brilliant conduct Vernon promoted him to the command of the fireship *Cumberland*, in which in 1741 he took part in the expedition to Cartagena. On 25 March he was promoted captain of the frigate *Shoreham*; he continued actively employed, often on detached duties, during the rest of that campaign, and afterwards in the expedition to Cuba. After other service he returned to England in March 1743. In July he was appointed to the *Phoenix* and in January the following year he was sent in the *Phoenix* to reconnoitre Brest. Early in 1745 he was appointed to the *Exeter* (60 guns), in the channel squadron, and in March he served in the *Dreadnought*, which was sent out to the Leeward Islands, and continued there protecting trade until after the peace in 1748. In May 1756 Brodrick was sent out to the Mediterranean in command of reinforcements for Admiral John Byng, whom he joined at Gibraltar just before the admiral was ordered home under arrest. He had in the meantime (4 June 1756) been advanced to be rear-admiral, in which rank he served under Sir Edward Hawke until towards the close of the year, when the fleet returned home. In January 1757 he was a member of the court martial on Byng; he was afterwards, with his flag in the *Namur*, third in command in the expedition against Rochefort in which he reconnoitred the site of the proposed landing.

Early in 1758 Brodrick was appointed second in command in the Mediterranean, with his flag on board the *Prince George* (90 guns). On 13 April, being then off Ushant, the *Prince George* caught fire with the loss of 550 lives. The admiral himself was picked up by a merchant ship's boat, after he had been swimming for about an hour. Brodrick and the survivors of his ship's company were taken by the frigate *Glasgow* to Gibraltar, where he hoisted his flag in the *St George*. On 14 February 1759 he was promoted vice-admiral, and shortly afterwards he was superseded by Admiral Edward Boscawen, under whom he commanded during the blockade of Toulon, and in the action of 18–19 August, culminating in the burning or capture of the French ships in Lagos Bay. When Boscawen returned to England Brodrick continued to blockade the remaining ships of the French force at Cadiz so closely that they were ridiculed even by their Spanish allies. They are said to have stuck up a notice in some such terms as 'For sale, eight French men-of-war. For particulars apply to Vice-Admiral Brodrick'. The French ships did not stir out until the passage was cleared for them by a gale, which compelled the blockading squadron to put into Gibraltar. Brodrick returned to England in February 1760 and had no further employment. His marriage (*c*.1735) to Mary Robins (*d*. 1760), daughter of Benjamin Robins, produced four daughters and a son, of whom only the latter, Edward, survived him. Brodrick seems to have been hardy, as shown by his survival after the burning of the *Prince George*, and competent, from his selection for detached work. On the other hand the crew of the *Dreadnought* complained of their treatment, while his vanity was commented upon by Boscawen. In some sources he is named 'Broderick', by which he is often found in official records, but he signed 'Brodrick'. The family seat was at Peper Harow, near Godalming, where he seems to have resided at times, but in his will he is 'of Sackville Street, St James'. He died from cancer on 1 January 1769.

J. K. Laughton, rev. A. W. H. Pearsall

Sources DNB · H. W. Richmond, *The navy in the war of 1739–48*, 3 vols. (1920) · *The Vernon papers*, ed. B. McL. Ranft, Navy RS, 99 (1958) · J. S. Corbett, *England in the Seven Years' War*, new edn, 2 vols. (1992) · 'Boscawen's letters to his wife, 1755–1756', ed. P. K. Kemp, *The naval miscellany*, ed. C. Lloyd, 4, Navy RS, 92 (1952), 163–256 · R. Beatson, *Naval and military memoirs of Great Britain*, 3 vols. (1790) · J. Charnock, ed., *Biographia navalis*, 6 vols. (1794–8) · Burke, *Peerage* (1890) · *GM*, 1st ser., 39 (1769), 54 · logs, PRO, ADM 51/194, 605, 729, 903, 944 · muster books, PRO, ADM 36/3210, 3441 · pay books, PRO, ADM 33/303, 361 · letters, PRO, ADM 1/1484 · journal, PRO, ADM 50/3

Brodum, William (*fl.* 1767–1824), quack, claimed to have been born in Mecklenburg-Strelitz, Germany, the son of Abraham and Caroline Brodum. This was thrown into doubt in 1805 by an article in the *Medical and Physical Journal* which stated that his real name was, in fact, Issachar Cohen, that he had been born in Copenhagen, and that he

William Brodum (*fl.* 1767–1824), by Ezekiel Abraham Ezekiel, pubd 1797 (after G. Barry)

had made his living by selling ribbons on the street before arriving in London at the age of twenty. After working for a time as a street seller on Tower Hill, in 1787 he began an association with a Dr Lamert, a purveyor of patent medicines, who employed him to do odd jobs. It was alleged that Cohen then adopted the name of Williams, and he was credited by Lamert as 'a smart active youth, very loquacious, and of sonorous lungs' (Ietros, 67), and sent by him to Kent to sell his 'Switzer's balsam' and other remedies. John Corry's *Detection of Quackery* (1802) gives an entirely different account of the start of Brodum's career and states that he attended Dr Bossy, another huckster of medicines, 'in the quality of a footman' when he toured England. Corry also quotes a statement by Brodum in his *Guide to Old Age* that 'There is no other person of the name of Brodum in England'. He probably made the name up, possibly as a Latinized version of the Polish Jewish surname Broda. On 15 January 1791 he was awarded an MD degree by Marischal College, Aberdeen, on the recommendation of doctors Saunders and Leo. Marischal College required no examination, and, providing the college's fees were paid, the recommendation of two doctors of medicine was deemed sufficient.

In 1795 Brodum published his *Guide to Old Age, or, A Cure for the Indiscretions of Youth*, in two volumes, dedicated to George III. This booklet was a puff for his two preparations: the nervous cordial, which he recommended for consumption, debility, and menstrual problems; and the botanical syrup, which he claimed would cure scurvy, scrofula, leprosy, cancer, and venereal disease. It could also be mixed with white lead and olive oil and painted on scrofulous skin. Both preparations were sold in bottles of various sizes for 5*s*. 5*d*., 11*s*. 6*d*., or £1 2*s*. 0*d*. and could be bought from agents in Philadelphia and the English provinces or from Brodum's house at 9 Albany Street, Blackfriars Road, London. His claims were supported by many testimonials from named persons and by a copy of his doctoral diploma from Marischal College. The book went into four editions, each with a freshly engraved portrait of its author. It also claimed to have been translated into Italian, French, and Spanish.

Brodum was then summoned before the president and censors of the Royal College of Physicians for practising medicine without their licence. He claimed that he was merely selling medicines for which he held a royal patent. The president said that the college had no objection to that, but he should not accept consultation fees and must remove the brass plate from his house which described him as Dr Brodum. He refused to do so, pointing out that he held a doctorate in medicine from Marischal College, which he had purchased with a recommendation from a member of their college. The college of physicians took no further action. The medical faculty of Marischal College sought counsel's opinion as to whether they could cancel his doctoral degree, because of his notorious and impudent quackery and the immoral tendency of many passages in his various publications. Solicitor-General Blair advised them that they had no power to do so and pointedly suggested that they should make 'the case of Dr Brodum a lesson of caution and circumspection to themselves for the future in the bestowing of Academical honours' (Anderson, 2.133–4).

Because Brodum was rich and a doctor of medicine, in 1798 he was elected a steward for a fund-raising banquet organized by Abraham Goldsmid to establish a free school for the education of the children of the Jewish poor. Then Goldsmid discovered that on 28 June 1798 Brodum had been naturalized, for which he had professed his adherence to the protestant religion. Since he had thus publicly renounced Judaism, he was dismissed from office in this Jewish charity. Brodum then sold his pharmaceutical business to one Anthony Daffy Swinton, with whom he was caricatured in 1811.

When Brodum made his will in 1824, he styled himself De Brodum and was living at 21 Great Coram Street, London. He left money to four charities in Copenhagen, where he owned property, as well as to the Westminster Hospital and to the Foundling Hospital, London. He and his wife, Cecilia, had no surviving children and his heirs were nephews and great-nephews in Copenhagen and Hamburg. In his will he complains that a promise made by the prime minister of Denmark, Count Moltke, to confer certain honours on him had not been confirmed by the king of Denmark. He therefore revoked an undertaking he had made to leave his estate in Denmark to six Danish charities, three to be nominated by the king and three by himself. However, the 'De' suggests that he had acquired noble status there.

Brodum's *Guide to Old Age* is a shameless marketing exercise. It shows that Brodum was aware of the discovery that orange or lemon juice cured scurvy, and it is probable that his botanical syrup contained some fruit juice. It

was chiefly the old formula of the decoction of woods, consisting of sassafras, guaiacum, and a few other articles, which he procured from Mr Chamberlin, an eminent chemist in Fleet Street. The decoction [was] well edulcorated with sugar of molasses.   (Ietros, 71)

Nothing else in the book suggests any knowledge of medicine. His other publications were *By his Majesty's Royal Letters Patent: Dr Brodum's Nervous Cordial, and Botanical Syrup* (1808) and *A Medical Essay on the Nature, Cause, and Cure of Coughs* (1814).   EDGAR SAMUEL

Sources will, PRO, PROB 11/1693 · W. Brodum, *Guide to old age, or, A cure for the indiscretions of youth*, 2 vols. (1795–1802) · *Fasti academiae Mariscallanae Aberdonensis: selections from the records of the Marischal College and University, MDXCIII–MDCCCLX*, 2, ed. P. J. Anderson, New Spalding Club, 18 (1898), 2 · S. S. Levin, 'The origins of the Jews' Free School', *Transactions of the Jewish Historical Society of England*, 19 (1955–9), 97–114 · C. J. S. Thompson, *The quacks of old London* (1928) · A. Rubens, *Anglo-Jewish portraits* (1935) · A. Rubens, *A Jewish iconography*, rev. edn (1981) · W. A. Shaw, ed., *Letters of denization and acts of naturalization for aliens in England and Ireland, 1701–1800*, 2, Huguenot Society of London, 27 (1923) · Ietros, 'Of quacks and empiricism', *Medical and Physical Journal*, 13 (1805), 66–75 · J. Corry, *Detection of quackery* (1802)

Likenesses I. G. Walken, engraving, 1 July 1795 (after bust by S. Polack), repro. in Brodum, *Guide to old age*, frontispiece · E. A. Ezekiel, engraving, pubd 1797 (after a miniature by G. Barry), Wellcome L. [see illus.] · J. Chapman, engraving, 1802 (after R. Collins), repro. in Brodum, *Guide to old age* · portrait, Wellcome L.

Wealth at death property in Copenhagen; bequests to four charities in Copenhagen and to the Westminster Hospital, London: will, PRO, PROB 11/1693

Brodzky, Horace Asher (1885–1969), artist and writer, was born on 30 January 1885 in Pakington Street, Kew, a suburb of Melbourne, Australia, the second of the seven children of Maurice Brodzky (1847–1919), journalist and publisher, and Florence Leon (1860–1958), daughter of Szymanski Leon and his wife, Selina Asher. His parents were both Jewish. The name Brodzky means 'of Brody', a small town in western Ukraine, though the nomadic wanderings of the family took them through much of Europe before, and after, reaching Australia. It was a peripatetic existence: in 1904 the Brodzkys sailed for the United States, and four years later they migrated to England.

Horace Brodzky showed artistic talent from an early age. His art education was haphazard and included two short spells in the drawing class at the National Gallery of Victoria in Melbourne (1901 and 1904) and a brief period in London at the City and Guilds Art School (1911). He dated the real beginning of his artistic career to his arrival in Britain and the determination to learn all he could from others. He taught himself enough to be selected as one of the artists representing Britain at the Venice Biennale of 1912—the first Australian to do so.

As a visual artist Brodzky worked chiefly in three media: painting, drawing, and printmaking. His early work in oils—dramatic, strongly coloured, and structured—reveals a number of influences, chief among them that of David Bomberg and Mark Gertler. Walter Sickert encouraged him, and it is possible that he looked at Frank Brangwyn's work. The one great source of inspiration which he himself always claimed was Piero della Francesca.

Brodzky's portraits of Jacob Epstein and Jacob Kramer (both 1915, priv. coll.) and Eugene O'Neill (c.1920) show that he was a good character draughtsman, but his nude studies are often uninspiring. He would have done well to concentrate his energies on the telling masses of the lino-cut, for it was in this medium that he excelled. He made forty-four in all, mostly between 1912 and 1919, all of which are bold powerful designs of stark black and white contrasts. As regards other kinds of prints, he made a handful of woodcuts in 1912 and again in 1921, and he produced some sixty-two etchings. Many examples of his prints are in the British Museum, London.

The biggest event in Brodzky's life was his friendship with the sculptor Henri Gaudier-Brzeska, whom he met in January 1912 and with whom he became close friends. His 1933 biography of Gaudier is by far the most substantial book he wrote. (His two others were short descriptive texts on Jules Pascin and on Gaudier's drawings, both published in 1946.) According to Brodzky, Ezra Pound in his book *Gaudier-Brzeska: a Memoir* (1916) misunderstood Gaudier's sculptural ideas. Brodzky always stressed Gaudier's emotional and human strengths, whereas Pound, he felt, encouraged a purely intellectual reading of the work which distorted its humanism and led to a form of spiritual decadence. Although Brodzky was no great stylist, his pen portrait is very readable, vigorously anecdotal, and entertaining. For a man who spent his life largely in the shadow of Gaudier, and whose subsequent reputation has similarly suffered, he was remarkably even-handed and generous in his judgements.

Brodzky was slight in build, but striking. He stooped, as if under the weight of his noble head. (When Gaudier did Brodzky's bust, the head was appropriately larger than life-size.) He had a love of music, and of good food and drink, though he could rarely afford to indulge himself. His was a life of chronic hardship and little success, with too much energy spent as a jobbing artist painting stage decorations or designing book jackets. While in New York for the second time (1915–23) he married, in 1919, Bertha Greenfield (1899–1982), a nanny. The couple had three sons, but the marriage broke down in 1934 after the family had moved to London. From 1948 until 1962 Brodzky was art editor of the *Antique Dealer and Collector's Guide*, a magazine founded by his brother Vivian. He lived long enough to see a modest revival of interest in his work and died on 11 February 1969 in London. ANDREW LAMBIRTH

Sources H. R. Lew, *Brodzky* (1987) · F. Spalding, *Horace Brodzky* (1989) · J. Laver, *40 drawings by Horace Brodzky* (1935) · H. Brodzky, *Henri Gaudier-Brzeska* (1933) · H. Brodzky, *Pascin* (1946) · H. Brodzky, *Gaudier-Brzeska drawings* (1946) · H. S. Ede, *Savage Messiah*, 2nd edn (1971) · R. Cole, *Gaudier-Brzeska: artist and myth* (1995) · M. Parkin, *The Café Royalists* (1972) · F. Carey, *Avant-garde British printmaking, 1914–1960* (1990) · *CGPLA Eng. & Wales* (1969)

Archives AM Oxf. · Arts Council · Birmingham Museums and Art Gallery · BM · FM Cam. · IWM · Leeds City Art Gallery · Museum of Modern Art, New York · National Gallery of New South Wales, Sydney · State Library of Victoria, Melbourne, Latrobe Library · Tate collection, papers incl. corresp., etching plates, lino blocks, and photographs · Tel Aviv Museum · V&A | National Archives of Australia, Canberra, Michael Cannon collection | SOUND BL NSA, documentary recordings

Likenesses H. Gaudier-Brzeska, bronze bust, 1913, Bristol City Museum and Art Gallery · H. Gaudier-Brzeska, pastel drawing, 1914, repro. in *Mercury Gallery Catalogue* (1991) · N. Hamnett, oils, *c*.1915, Southampton Art Gallery · H. Gaudier-Brzeska, drypoint drawing, repro. in Brodsky, *Henri Gaudier-Brzeska*, 157 · H. Gaudier-

Brzeska, pen drawing, repro. in Brodsky, *Henri Gaudier-Brzeska*, 23 · H. Gaudier-Brzeska, pen drawing, repro. in Brodsky, *Henri Gaudier-Brzeska*, 65 · self-portrait, linocut, V&A

Wealth at death £7977: probate, 15 May 1969, *CGPLA Eng. & Wales*

Brogan, Sir Denis William (1900–1974), historian, was born on 11 August 1900 in Glasgow, the eldest of the four sons of Denis Brogan, a master tailor, and his second wife, Elizabeth Toner. His father, a native of co. Donegal, had briefly lived in the USA and Brogan grew up in a home responsive to the politics of both Ireland and America. Educated at Rutherglen Academy, Glasgow University (MA, 1923), and Balliol College, Oxford, where he obtained a first class in history in 1925, he was guided towards the USA by Samuel Eliot Morison, then visiting Harmsworth professor at Oxford. A year at Harvard on a Rockefeller research fellowship established the study of the American past and the American present as the ruling passion of his life.

On his return from the USA, after a brief period on the staff of *The Times*, Brogan was appointed in 1928 as lecturer in history at University College, London, and in 1930 as lecturer in politics at the London School of Economics. He was married in 1931 to Olwen Phillis Frances, an archaeologist, daughter of William Kendall, medical practitioner. They had three sons and a daughter.

The literary product of these years was his best-known book, *The American Political System* (1933). Appearing at a turning point both in American national development and in British awareness of the United States, its freshness, pungency, wit, and zest rediscovered America for a generation of British readers and profoundly influenced the perception of American politics in both academic and non-academic circles. The book's emphasis was on the actualities of the political process, made vivid by personal observation, a brilliant if teasing allusiveness, and an astonishing breadth of reading in both contemporary and historical literature. *An Introduction to American Politics* (1954) had the same qualities; it was indeed a comprehensively revised and rewritten version.

In 1934 Brogan left London for Oxford, as fellow and tutor at Corpus Christi College. There he expanded his academic interests to take in the study of France, with a brio, a range, and an intimacy analogous to his study of the USA. The impressive first-fruit of this was *The Development of Modern France, 1870–1939* (1940; revised edition, 1870–1959, 1967), over twice the length of *The American Political System*, and packed with detail. Here for the first time, in English or French, the complex phenomena of modern French politics, at home and abroad, are reduced to a comprehensible narrative that does justice to economic and social factors but keeps the individual, from peasant to president, at the heart of the story. The tone is affectionate, but free of illusion, vivacious and sharp-edged. A later study, *The French Nation from Napoleon to Pétain, 1814–1940* (1957), is marked on a smaller scale by the same characteristics.

To fit a figure like Brogan into the machine of the Second World War was never easy. He began in the foreign

Sir Denis William Brogan (1900–1974), by Howard Coster, 1940s

research and press service, moved briefly to the American division of the Ministry of Information, was then for a short time with the political warfare executive, but finally found his niche with the overseas services of the BBC. Perhaps one should rather say 'niches' because Brogan's exuberant energies overflowed from the European service to the North American service; in each capacity his role was that of an intelligence officer, providing background information and policy guidance from his diverse and capacious store of contemporary and historical knowledge. Thrown off, almost, amid these taxing labours was *The English People: Impressions and Observations* (1943), characteristically precise, yet wide-ranging and shrewd, an essay in presenting the distinctive features of the English way of life by 'a foreigner of a kind'. *The American Problem* (1944) was a series of loosely linked essays on the evolution of modern America, which discharges an analogous function from west to east.

In the spring of 1939 Brogan had been elected to the professorship of political science at Cambridge and to a fellowship at Peterhouse and to this he returned at the war's end. His approach to his chair was that of a liberal, a pragmatist, and a historically minded student of institutions. Sceptical of systems, suspicious alike of sociological and philosophical abstractions, he warned in his inaugural lecture, published as *The Study of Politics* (1946), against imposing on his subject 'a degree of abstractness or bogus neutrality that it cannot stand'. His lectures, delivered with a minimum of notes, regrettably do not survive, but

some of the fruits of his approach can be gathered from *The Price of Revolution* (1951).

For a historian and an Americanist it was regrettable that Brogan produced no study of the American past on a scale comparable to *The Development of Modern France*. His *Abraham Lincoln* (1935, revised 1974, posthumously) is a miniature, albeit a classic one. *The Era of Franklin D. Roosevelt* (1950, published in Britain as *Roosevelt and the New Deal*, 1952) is a useful, balanced, compact treatment curiously lacking in its author's individual touch. *American Aspects* (1964), which reprints a number of historical and political articles, including the classic 'The illusion of American omnipotence', has far more of Brogan's range and historical penetration about it. The fact is, however, that the student who would glean all that Brogan has to offer would have to search the pages, particularly the review pages, of a host of journals, but in particular the *Times Literary Supplement*, where his fecund genius, particularly in his later years, found a more natural outlet.

Brogan retired from his chair in 1968 and died in Cambridge on 5 January 1974. In addition to many honorary doctorates from France and the United States, he was an honorary LLD of Glasgow (1946) and an honorary DLitt of Oxford (1969). He was an honorary fellow of Peterhouse and Corpus Christi colleges, Cambridge, and became a fellow of the British Academy in 1955. He was knighted in 1963.

H. G. NICHOLAS, *rev.*

Sources H. G. Nicholas, 'Sir Denis William Brogan, 1900–1974', *PBA*, 62 (1976), 399–410 · personal knowledge (1986) · private information (1986) · *CGPLA Eng. & Wales* (1974)
Archives IWM, papers | JRL, letters to *Manchester Guardian* · King's Lond., corresp. with Sir B. H. Liddell Hart
Likenesses H. Coster, photograph, 1940–49, NPG [*see illus.*] · W. Stoneman, photograph, 1955, NPG · H. Coster, photographs, NPG
Wealth at death £17,711: probate, 9 May 1974, *CGPLA Eng. & Wales*

Brograve, Sir John (*bap.* **1538**, *d.* **1613**), lawyer, was the son of Richard Brograve of Kelsey's in Kent and Jane Sayers, and was baptized on 27 October 1538 in St Mildred Poultry, in the city of London. After studying at St John's College, Cambridge, in 1554, he proceeded a year or two later to Gray's Inn and was called to the bar in 1560. In 1572 he was appointed reader of Barnard's Inn. His Gray's Inn reading, in the summer of 1576, was on the jointure provisions of the Statute of Uses; it survives in manuscript, and a version was printed in 1648. Shortly afterwards he was described as 'very lerned, pore, smaly practised, worthie of greate practise' (PRO, SP 12/111/27). Someone must have paid heed, for in 1580 he was appointed to the lucrative post of attorney-general of the duchy of Lancaster, an office which he held until his death. It was doubtless because of his business rather than his poverty that he resisted the call to give a second reading, and obtained a perpetual discharge in 1589; he nevertheless served thrice as treasurer of Gray's Inn. His office also explains his election to parliament four times under Elizabeth I as member for the duchy boroughs of Preston and Boroughbridge, and he came to be regarded as one of the leading lawyers in the House of Commons. He was knighted in 1603.

Brograve had settled in Hertfordshire by 1579, when he was added to the commission of the peace, and he later served as *custos rotulorum* for that county. At an unknown date he married Margaret (*d.* 1603), the daughter of Simeon Steward of Lakenheath, Suffolk. He established his seat at Hamells, in the parish of Braughing, where he built 'a fair brick house … situated upon a dry hill where is a pleasant prospect to the east' (Chauncy, 226). He died on 11 September 1613, and was buried in Braughing church, where there is a wall monument. He had three sons and two daughters. The principal estates in Hertfordshire were entailed on the eldest son, Simeon (*d.* 1639), who is commemorated by a monument at Braughing. An estate in Essex, with a lump sum of £1200, was left to the second son, John (*d.* 1625). The third son, Charles, predeceased his father in 1602. All three sons were members of Gray's Inn, Simeon and John becoming ancients. Simeon's grandson, Sir Thomas Brograve (*d.* 1670), was created a baronet in 1663.

J. H. Baker

Sources HoP, *Commons, 1558–1603*, 1.487–8 • R. J. Fletcher, ed., *The pension book of Gray's Inn*, 2 vols. (1901–10) • R. Somerville, *History of the duchy of Lancaster, 1265–1603* (1953), 409 • J. Foster, *Register of admissions to Gray's Inn, 1521–1881* (privately printed, London, 1887), 103–4 • Venn, *Alum. Cant.* • H. Chauncy, *The historical antiquities of Hertfordshire* (1700), 226–8 • J. E. Cussans, *History of Hertfordshire*, 1 (1870), 195 • J. Dyer, *Three learned readings* (1648), 69–97 • BL, Harley MS 829, fols. 29–39v • VCH *Hertfordshire*, 3.313 • PRO, SP 12/111/27 • monumental inscription, Braughing church

Brok, Laurence del (*c.*1210–1274), lawyer and justice, was probably born in or before 1210 in Buckinghamshire. His first appearance in the records is in 1231, when he was appointed to act as an attorney in a Buckinghamshire case. By the late 1230s he had become one of a small group of professional lawyers practising in the common bench in Westminster. Such men spoke in court on behalf of litigants and also stood surety for them when required. They also performed similar functions for litigants in the eyre when the common bench was not in session.

In 1247 Laurence del Brok became the first professional lawyer to be retained by the king. Thereafter he received an annual salary of £20 each year until 1262, and can be traced acting for the king in litigation until 1263. The main focus of his activity on the king's behalf during this period was the court of king's bench, but he can be found speaking for the king in the common bench as well. It is unclear whether or not he also continued acting for other litigants. From 1250 onwards he received a number of *ad hoc* commissions to act as a royal justice, and was regularly commissioned to act as a gaol delivery justice at Newgate and elsewhere. He sat as one of the justices of king's bench in Easter term 1271, but never became a regular justice of the court.

Laurence del Brok began acquiring property on a small scale in 1236, and over the course of his lifetime he spent well over £1000 on property acquisitions. The inquisition post mortem held after his death shows him in possession of lands worth over £60 a year. These are probably undervalued. Moreover the inquisition excludes both holdings in Middlesex that he had passed to his younger son in 1271, and the lands he is known to have acquired in Oxfordshire and Cambridgeshire, and which are later found in the possession of his family. How the acquisitions were financed is less clear. He is known to have been in receipt of pensions from at least three institutional clients (the abbeys of Glastonbury and Ramsey and the priory of Durham), and probably received similar pensions from many other individuals and institutions. At the very end of his life there was also a suggestion that he was in receipt of bribes for the release of prisoners at Newgate, though this allegation seems not to have been proved.

Brok's first wife was Millicent, daughter of Robert Malet. He married her in 1242 or 1243, and she was the mother of his eldest son and heir, Hugh. He had married his second wife, Maud, by no later than Michaelmas term 1245. Maud was the mother of his second son, William. Laurence del Brok probably died a few days before 25 December 1274.

Paul Brand, *rev.*

Sources king's bench, curia regis rolls, PRO, KB26 • court of common pleas, feet of fines, PRO, CP 25/1 • *Curia regis rolls preserved in the Public Record Office* (1922–), vols. 16–18 • Chancery records • G. O. Sayles, ed., *Select cases in the court of king's bench*, 5, SeldS, 76 (1958) • *CIPM*, 2, no. 110 • P. A. Brand, *The origins of the English legal profession* (1992)

Wealth at death £60 p.a. from lands: *CIPM*

Broke, Arthur. *See* Brooke, Arthur (*d.* 1563).

Broke [Brooke], **Sir Arthur de Capell** [*formerly* Arthur Supple], **second baronet** (1791–1858), geographer, was born in Bolton Street, Mayfair, Westminster, on 22 October 1791. His family was originally from Cheshire. He was the elder son of Sir Richard de Capell Brooke (1758–1829) and Mary (*d.* 1846), only child and heir of Major-General Richard Worge; they also had four daughters. Arthur's father was the first baronet and in 1797 had adopted the name of Brooke in accordance with his uncle's will and in addition changed his first surname from Supple to de Capell by royal licence. Arthur was educated at Magdalen College, Oxford, where he graduated BA on 20 May 1813 and MA on 5 June 1816. On 27 November 1829 he succeeded his father in the title and estates. He used the older spelling of his family name, Broke. He joined the army, rising to the rank of major in 1846. Much of his early life was spent in foreign travel, especially in Scandinavia. In 1823 he published *Travels through Sweden, Norway and Finmark to the North Pole … in 1820* which was followed by *A Winter in Lapland and Sweden* (1827). *Winter sketches in Lapland … intended to exhibit a complete view of the mode of travelling with reindeer* (1827) contained much entertaining incident, topographical and ethnographical detail, splendid illustrations, and a fine map. However, Broke's intention of describing the Swedish peasantry, which might have been of more lasting value, was not realized. It is for his Scandinavian works that he is chiefly remembered, but he also published a minor work *Sketches in Spain and Morocco* (1837).

Broke was an original member of the Travellers' Club,

but in 1827, feeling strongly that many of the newly elected members had little interest in foreign travel, he founded the Raleigh Club, of which he was for many years president. It attracted many of the most distinguished travellers and geographers of the day and had both geographical and convivial aims. In 1830 some members, with Broke's apparent approval, set up a Geographical Society, which later became the Royal Geographical Society. In 1854 the Raleigh Club became the Geographical Club which was very closely connected to the Royal Geographical Society. Broke was thus intimately connected with the establishment and success of the main geographical institutions in the country. He was a fellow of the Royal Geographical Society and of the Royal Society. In his later years he took an active interest in temperance and in various charitable and religious causes. He died at Oakley Hall, Great Oakley, Northamptonshire, on 6 December 1858. He and Elizabeth Zilpah, widow of J. J. Eyre of Endcliffe, near Sheffield, had married on 18 December 1851, but had had no children, so Broke was succeeded by his brother William. Sir Roderick Murchison described him as 'of retiring and unostentatious habits', with no desire to participate in public life, yet with 'all the spirit of an adventurous traveller' (*Journal of the Royal Geographical Society*, 1859). He was in fact deputy lieutenant and later sheriff of his home county of Northamptonshire, but seems to have been equally or more at ease in a Finnish sauna or treating his Raleigh Club friends to dine on reindeer.

ELIZABETH BAIGENT

Sources C. R. Markham, *Some account of the Geographical Club*, 6th edn (1905) · *Journal of the Royal Geographical Society*, 29 (1859), cxxviii · *The Royal Geographical Society: its foundation and history* (1939) · C. R. Markham, *The fifty years' work of the Royal Geographical Society* (1881) · H. R. Mill, *The record of the Royal Geographical Society, 1830–1930* (1930) · Burke, *Peerage*
Archives Northants. RO | RGS, Raleigh Club MSS
Likenesses print, repro. in Broke (1827)
Wealth at death under £14,000: probate, 2 Feb 1859, *CGPLA Eng. & Wales*

Broke, Sir Philip Bowes Vere, first baronet (1776–1841), naval officer, of an old Suffolk family, the eldest son of Philip Bowes Broke (1749–1801) and his wife, Elizabeth, *née* Beaumont (d. 25 June 1822), was born at Broke Hall, near Ipswich, on 9 September 1776. As a young child he wanted to go to sea, and aged twelve was entered at the Royal Naval College, Portsmouth Dockyard, from which, in June 1792, he was appointed to the sloop *Bulldog*, under Captain George Hope. In August 1793, he followed Hope to the *Éclair*, then in the Mediterranean, and afterwards at the occupation of Toulon and the siege of Bastia. In May 1794 he was discharged into the *Romulus*, and was present when Lord Hood chased the French fleet into Golfe Jouan (11 June 1794), and in the action off Toulon (13–14 March 1795). In June he was appointed to the *Britannia*, flagship of the commander-in-chief, was in her in the engagement off Toulon on 13 July 1795, and on the 18th was appointed third lieutenant of the frigate *Southampton*, under Captain Macnamara. During the next eighteen months the *Southampton* was actively employed on the coast of Italy, often with the squadron under Nelson, and was with the fleet in

Sir Philip Bowes Vere Broke, first baronet (1776–1841), by Charles Turner, pubd 1816 (after Samuel Lane, exh. RA 1814)

the action off Cape St Vincent on 14 February 1797. In the following June she was sent home and paid off. Broke was almost immediately appointed to the frigate *Amelia* in the Channel Fleet, and in her was present at the defeat and capture of the French squadron on the north coast of Ireland on 12 October 1798. On 2 January 1799 he was made commander and appointed to the brig *Falcon*, from which a few months later he was transferred to the sloop *Shark*, attached to the North Sea Fleet, under Lord Duncan, and employed mostly on convoys. On 14 February 1801 he was promoted captain, after which he was four years unemployed.

Broke's father died shortly after his promotion, and on 25 November 1802 he married Sarah Louisa (d. 1843), daughter of Sir William Middleton, baronet. When the war resumed he immediately applied for a ship, but without success, until in April 1805 he was appointed to the frigate *Druid*, which he commanded in the channel and on the coast of Ireland for the next sixteen months. On 31 August 1806 he was appointed to the *Shannon*, a fine 38-gun frigate, carrying 18-pounders on her main deck and 32-pounder carronades on quarter-deck and forecastle. During the summer of 1807 she was employed on the coast of Spitsbergen, protecting the whalers, and in December was with the squadron at the capture of Madeira. During the greater part of 1808 she was cruising in the Bay of Biscay, and on the night of 10–11 November 1808, attracted by the sound of the firing, she arrived on the scene of action in time to witness the capture of the French *Thétis* by the *Amethyst*, Captain Michael Seymour— a capture which this unfortunate arrival of the *Shannon*, as well as of the line-of-battle ship *Triumph*, deprived of some of its brilliance. The *Shannon* afterwards towed the prize to Plymouth, but Broke, in recognition that the capture was due to the *Amethyst* alone, obtained the agreement of the *Shannon*'s officers and ship's company to forgo their claim to the prize money. As the *Triumph*'s claim, however, was maintained, the *Shannon*'s generous offer was declined. The next two years were passed in similar service, cruising from Plymouth, off Brest, and in the Bay of Biscay; it was not until June 1811 that she was ordered to refit for foreign service. At the beginning of August she sailed for Halifax, Nova Scotia, where she arrived on 24 September. The relations between Britain and the United States were even then severely strained, and on 18 June 1812 war was declared.

For the next year the *Shannon* cruised, without opportunity for important service. Broke realized the need to keep the ship in fighting trim, a necessity which the successes of the previous twenty years had tempted some of his contemporaries to ignore. At great pecuniary loss to himself and the ship's company, he carried out a resolution to make no prizes which would entail sending away prize crews, and so weakening his force, and most of the ships captured were therefore burnt. He took extraordinary pains to train his men, especially in gunnery. While the custom then was never to cast the guns loose except for action, Broke introduced systematic training, and every day in the week, except Saturday, the men, either by watches or all together, were exercised at quarters and in firing at a target, so that they attained an unprecedented proficiency. Such was the reputation of the *Shannon*, that many ships arriving on the station fresh from England brought out orders to exchange a certain number of men with the *Shannon*, so that they too might receive the benefit of the new system. In May 1813 the *Shannon* was cruising off Boston, watching the US frigate *Chesapeake*. On 1 June a spectacular battle between the two ships took place within sight of Boston. The *Shannon* quickly overwhelmed the *Chesapeake*. Broke, calling out 'Follow me who can!', sprang on board the latter, followed by some fifty or sixty of his men. The struggle was short. The Americans, bewildered and panic-stricken, were beaten below without much difficulty. Broke was seriously wounded on the head by a cutlass blow; but within fifteen minutes from the first gun being fired by the *Shannon* the *Chesapeake*'s colours were hauled down, and the British colours hoisted.

The apparently easy capture of the *Chesapeake*, a ship of the same nominal force, but larger, with more men and a heavier armament than the *Shannon*, created a sensation in America and in Britain. The success of the engagement (which made Broke famous) was due to his care, forethought, and skill, much more than to that exuberant courage which caught the popular fancy. As Mahon observed: 'no more thoroughly efficient ship of her class had been seen in the British Navy during the twenty years' war with France' (Mahan, 2.133). Honours and congratulations were showered upon him. He was made a baronet on 2 November 1813, and KCB on 3 January 1815; but, with the exception of taking the *Shannon* home in the autumn of 1813, his brilliant exploit was the end of his active service. He became in course of seniority a rear-admiral on 22 July 1830. The terrible wound on the head had left him subject to nervous pains, which were much aggravated by a severe fall from his horse on 8 August 1820; his health was far from robust, and his sufferings were at times intense; he died at Bayley's Hotel, Berkeley Square, London, on 2 January 1841 during a series of operations to relieve the pressure on his brain caused by his injuries. His remains were taken to Broke Hall, and interred on 9 January in the parish church of Nacton, near Ipswich. He had a numerous family, many of whom died young. The eldest son, who succeeded to the baronetcy, died unmarried in 1855; the fourth son had no children, and at his death the title became extinct.

Broke's success, and the advocacy of those who emulated him, including Sir Samuel Pechell and Sir Howard Douglas, laid the foundation of modern naval gunnery as a profession requiring skill, training, and service. He was the worthy victor of the finest single ship action in the history of naval warfare under sail. His training methods, professionalism, and commitment reversed the trend of American victories, restored national pride, and laid the foundation for the post-war navy. That his success rested on a solid educational base has too often been ignored.

J. K. LAUGHTON, *rev.* ANDREW LAMBERT

Sources P. Padfield, *Broke and the Shannon* (1968) · A. T. Mahan, *Sea power in its relation to the war of 1812* (1905) · A. D. Lambert, *The last sailing battlefleet: maintaining naval mastery, 1815–1850* (1991) · *GM*, 2nd ser., 16 (1841), 91–3 · Burke, *Peerage* (1879) · J. G. Brighton, ed., *Admiral Sir P. V. B. Broke* (1866) · private information (1885)
Archives Suffolk RO, Ipswich, corresp., diaries, and papers | NMM, letters to his wife
Likenesses H. R. Cook, stipple, pubd 1814 (after G. Engleheart), BM · C. Turner, engraving, pubd 1816 (after S. Lane, exh. RA 1814), BM [*see illus.*] · T. Blood, stipple, BM, NPG; repro. in *Naval Chronicle* (1815) · W. Greatbach, engraving, repro. in *Outlook*, 70 (1902), 327 · S. Lane, portrait, repro. in Mahan, *Sea power in its relation to the war of 1812*, 134 · engraving, repro. in *Harper's Magazine*, 24 (1862), 173 · oils (after S. Lane, *c.*1814), NMM

Broke, Sir Richard (*d.* 1529), judge, was the fourth son of Thomas Broke of Leighton, Cheshire. Though descended of an old Cheshire family, he has been confused with John Broke or Brook (*d.* 1522) of Bristol and the Middle Temple, subsequently king's serjeant-at-law, whose son Sir David Brook became chief baron of the exchequer. In fact they were unrelated, and Richard Broke was a member of Gray's Inn. Manuscript evidence shows that he spoke frequently at learning exercises in Gray's Inn, including Edmund Dudley's reading in 1496, and attended them regularly even after becoming a serjeant. His own second reading, given in the early 1500s, was on Magna Carta, and a discussion of villeinage on that occasion is reported by Spelman. He is mentioned in the first decade of the sixteenth century practising in chancery and Star Chamber, and his clients included the duke of Buckingham. He married, before 1495, Anne, daughter of William and Jane Ledes of Sussex, and settled at first in that county, which was well represented in Gray's Inn. In 1495 he is found acting with Edmund Dudley as a feoffee for John Covert, and he was a justice of the peace for Sussex from 1498 until 1509. In 1514 he obtained from his son-in-law George Fastolf the manor of Nacton in Suffolk, and this became his principal seat; he subsequently acquired at least nine other Suffolk manors, which are listed in his will.

Much of Broke's professional life was connected with the city of London. As early as 1502 he succeeded Dudley in the judicial office of under-sheriff, from which he was promoted in 1510 to be recorder. In the latter year he was created serjeant-at-law, at the same time as John Broke, although he had been given royal permission (as recorder) to refuse the degree if he wished. He continued as recorder until 1520, and served twice in the parliaments of 1512 and 1515 as member for the city. Even after 1520 he remained closely in touch with London affairs as an informal adviser, and in his will mentioned as his 'entier and harty frendes' both his successor, William Shelley, and Shelley's successor, John Baker, whom he made overseers.

In 1520 Broke was appointed a puisne justice of the common pleas and knighted. He was translated to the exchequer as chief baron on 4 January 1526, and remained there until his death in 1529. Throughout this period he was commissioned as a justice of assize on the Norfolk circuit. His death doubtless occurred between 6 May, when he wrote his will, and 12 May, when his successor was appointed.

In 1526 Broke had rebuilt the manor house at Nacton, called Cow Hall (later Broke Hall), which was enlarged and altered in 1767. The Brokes remained at Broke Hall until 1855, their descendants in the female line continuing still longer. The chief baron also had a house in the parish of St Thomas the Apostle, London, leased without rent from the earl of Northumberland, which was occupied at the time of his death by Alderman Spencer. A portrait at Broke Hall, and later at Shrubland Park, was said to represent the chief baron, but is in fact a Jacobean judge. Broke's eldest son, Robert (b. 1495), became an ancient of Gray's Inn in 1534. A descendant, Sir Robert Broke (d. 1694), was created a baronet in 1661 but the title expired on his death. Another baronetcy was conferred in 1813 on a still later descendant, Admiral Sir Philip Bowes Vere *Broke. Sir Richard's will also mentions four daughters, Bridget (the wife of George Fastolf), Cecile, Elizabeth Fouleshurst, and Margaret, who was to marry William Whorwood (d. 1545), attorney-general to Henry VIII.   J. H. BAKER

Sources HoP, Commons, 1509–58, 1.503–4 · Foss, Judges, 5.138–40 · W. A. Copinger, The manors of Suffolk, 7 vols. (1905–11), vol. 3, pp. 67–9 · E. W. Ives, The common lawyers of pre-Reformation England (1983), 453–4 · C. Rawcliffe, The Staffords, earls of Stafford and dukes of Buckingham, 1394–1521, Cambridge Studies in Medieval Life and Thought, 3rd ser., 11 (1978), 227–8 · will, PRO, PROB 11/23, sig. 3 · The reports of Sir John Spelman, ed. J. H. Baker, 2 vols., SeldS, 93–4 (1977–8), vol. 1, pp. 144, 224 · Sainty, Judges, 72, 94 · Bodl. Oxf., MS Rawl. C. 705 · BL, Harley MS 5103

Broke, Sir Robert (d. 1558), judge and legal writer, was probably born in the first decade of the sixteenth century. He was the eldest son of Thomas Broke of Claverley, Shropshire, and Margaret, daughter of Humphrey Grosvenor of Farmcote in the same county. He is doubtless the 'Robertus Broke de Strond Inne' whose name is written in an early copy of Littleton now in Cambridge University Library. From Strand Inn he was admitted to the Middle Temple some time between 1525 and 1528, and he studied pleading in the office of John Jenour, the protonotary. On becoming a bencher in 1542, he read on the Statute of Limitations of 1540; this reading circulated in manuscript and was printed in 1647. His second reading, in 1551, was on pleas of the crown (taking chapter 18 of Magna Carta as the text) and this also circulated in different versions before a text reached the press in 1641. Like Sir Richard Broke, to whom he was not related, he began his judicial career in the service of the city of London, which appointed him common serjeant in 1536 on the recommendation of the king and queen; the explanation for this mark of royal favour is unknown. He was promoted to the recordership in 1545 and over the next ten years was returned to five parliaments as member for the city, serving as speaker in 1554. These offices did not preclude private practice, and his signature is found on bills in chancery in the 1530s and 1540s. He was also during this period deputy chief steward for the duchy of Lancaster in the north parts, and was created a serjeant-at-law at the general call of 1552.

On 8 October 1554 Broke was appointed chief justice of the common pleas, and he was knighted the following January. A number of his judgments are reported by Dyer, including his opinion in 1555 that gold and silver mines belonged to the queen by virtue of the prerogative; Dyer wrote that he did not believe Broke when he said he had 'seen a book' to that effect (Reports, ed. Baker, 15). In 1557 Broke fell out with his brethren when he named his second wife's brother, Thomas Gatacre of the Middle Temple, as chief protonotary. The puisne judges rejected Gatacre as unsuitably qualified, but Broke's second nominee, William Wheteley, was allowed to take office despite the puisnes' preference for another candidate. Broke was evidently sympathetic to the Marian religious regime, and was indeed described as a zealous Catholic. As it happens, the latest reported case in his Abridgement concerned the procedure for burning heretics in 1555. Had he survived he would doubtless have suffered the ignominy of replacement, but in the event he died a month before the queen, on 5 or 6 September 1558, while visiting friends at Patshull in Staffordshire. He was buried in Claverley church, where there is an alabaster monument bearing his effigy in judicial robes, with a collar of SS and roses and a pendent crucifix, lying between his two wives.

Broke is remembered in the legal profession chiefly for *La graunde abridgement*, which was published posthumously in 1573 by Richard Tottell, and reprinted in smaller format in 1576 and 1586. (Supposed earlier editions of 1568 and 1570 are ghosts.) This was more ambitious even than Fitzherbert's *Graunde Abridgement*, containing over 20,000 entries digested under a wider range of titles, and had useful marginal notes guiding the reader more readily to the contents. Contemporaries found it easier to use than Fitzherbert, and it is still a valuable reference tool. Although the abridgement was primarily derived from the medieval year-books, Broke added a number of cases from his own observation, some statutes and other sources, and even a few extracts from readings in the inns of court. The contemporary cases, though only briefly noted, may be considered as original law reports. They were extracted by Richard Bellewe and published separately, in a chronological rearrangement, as *Ascuns Novell Cases* (1578), an enterprise which placed Broke among the canonical-law reporters; the volume was reprinted several times, most recently in 1873. A different version of the cases, in alphabetical order, was published in English translation (as *Some New Cases*) by John March in 1651; this was reprinted in *The English Reports* in 1907. Broke gave to his colleague Sir Anthony Browne 'a greate written booke of presidentes', which Browne bequeathed to Robert Mordaunt; these precedents were probably entries of pleading, reflecting Broke's clerical training, rather than reports or abridged cases.

Of the two wives portrayed on Broke's tomb, the first was Anne, daughter of Nicholas Waring of Shrewsbury, and widow of Nicholas Hurleston (*d.* 1531), clerk of the green cloth, who married Broke in the mid-1530s. Anne gave birth to his eldest son, John (*d.* 1598), who was to represent Bridgnorth in the parliaments of 1558 and 1563, and at least three other children. Anne having died, in 1544 Broke married as his second wife Dorothy, daughter of William Gatacre of Gatacre, Shropshire, and with her had at least five sons and four daughters. In his will Broke asked Dorothy to be contented with a third part of his money and movables, 'because wee have many children to advance'. The inscription on his monument stated that there were seventeen in all, from the two marriages, though presumably not all of them survived infancy. To each unmarried daughter he left a portion of £160, 'so that they kepe them selfes good women and doe marry with suche persons as shalbe meete to have suche portion by reason of their landes, lerninge, office, feate of merchandise or such like'. His youngest sons were to be maintained until sufficiently learned in reading and writing, and in Latin, or until apprenticed or able to help themselves. The sixth son, Ralph, joined Clement's Inn and the Middle Temple; but none of the sons seems to have been called to the bar.

Broke described himself in his will as 'of London', where by 1547 he had a house in Warwick Lane, off Newgate Street, in the parish of St Gregory. He also had a country home in Putney. However, he retained his paternal estates in Shropshire, selling his house called Spicer's Hall

in Claverley on acquiring the monastic manor of Madeley from the crown in 1544. Madeley became the principal seat of his eldest son and descendants.   J. H. BAKER

Sources HoP, *Commons, 1509–58*, 1.504–6 · P. Winfield, *Chief sources of English legal history* (1925), 232–8 · J. Cowley, *Abridgements* (1932), xlix–li · J. H. Baker and J. S. Ringrose, *A catalogue of English legal manuscripts in Cambridge University Library* (1996), 299–300 · *Reports from the lost notebooks of Sir James Dyer*, ed. J. H. Baker, 1, SeldS, 109 (1994), esp. 14–15 · will, PRO, PROB 11/41, sig. 54 · will, PRO, PROB 11/49, sig. 20 [Sir Anthony Browne] · BL, Cotton MS Nero C.i, fol. 42v · inquisition post mortem, PRO, C 142/121/155 · PRO, CP 40/1064, m 559 d · ownership inscription, CUL, Inc. 3.J.3.2 · C. H. Hopwood, ed., *Middle Temple records*, 1: *1501–1603* (1904) · R. Somerville, *History of the duchy of Lancaster, 1265–1603* (1953), 427 · Emden, *Cam.*, 73 · J. Dyer, *Cy ensuont ascuns nouel cases* (1585) · W. Dugdale, *Origines juridiciales, or, Historical memorials of the English laws*, 3rd edn (1680), 225, 329 · *CPR, 1547–8*, 153 · R. Tresswell and A. Vincent, *The visitation of Shropshire, taken in the year 1623*, ed. G. Grazebrook and J. P. Rylands, 1, Harleian Society, 28 (1889)
Likenesses alabaster effigy on monument, *c.*1558, Claverley, Shropshire

Broke, Thomas (*b. c.*1513, *d.* in or after **1555**), religious radical and member of parliament, was possibly the younger son of Thomas Brooke (or Cobham) of Reculver, Kent, or of Edward Broke of Aspall, Kent. His name was far from uncommon, and establishing his identity poses some difficulties. He was clearly not the Thomas Broke of Glastonbury who died in 1537 nor the Thomas Broke appointed a fellow of Pembroke College, Cambridge, in 1536; it is also unlikely that he was the Thomas Broke who captained a royal ship, the *Swepestake*, in 1543. His early life is obscure, and though he is known to have married, the identity of his wife is unrecorded, but from the early 1530s he was a gentleman usher of the king's chamber and clearly had influential patrons at court, including several gentlemen of the privy chamber. They probably helped him obtain a position in the Calais garrison and a lease of the lands lately held in Calais by the attainted Edward Thwaytes in 1534. By 1538 he was working as Edmund Peyton's deputy as customer at the Lanterngate in Calais, and was also an alderman of Calais.

It is, however, as a religious radical that Broke is best known. He was a member of the circle of proponents of the 'new religion' that enjoyed the patronage of Thomas Cromwell. Broke corresponded regularly with Cromwell, and the latter's accounts between 1537 and 1540 contain a number of payments to one Thomas Broke 'for things done' (*LP Henry VIII*, 14/2, no. 782). In August 1538 Broke petitioned Cromwell for the reversion of William, Lord Sandes's receivership of Guînes. Although he was not successful, the following November Cromwell acquired for him the reversion of Peyton's office of customer. However, the two related issues of Cromwell's influence over patronage in Calais and religion stirred disquiet among the Calais council, led by the deputy, Lord Lisle. Many of those whom Cromwell had promoted for office in Calais were outspoken religious reformers, and the controversy they provoked threatened the peace and stability of the town.

In April 1539 Broke was returned by the mayor and aldermen of Calais to sit in parliament. Despite warnings from his patron, Broke openly attacked the religiously conservative Six Articles Bill. When parliament rose on 28 June he stayed in London to support his fellow members of the Calais garrison who were accused of sacramentarian heresy (denying the real presence of Christ in the eucharist), being committed to the Fleet for his trouble. On 4 August, however, Cromwell obtained for him a royal pardon. On his return to Calais the attacks by the Calais council on him, and on other religious reformers and clients of Cromwell, continued. In March 1540 the council reported him for eating meat in Lent to the commissioners empowered to investigate heresy and unrest in Calais. He was also accused of fraud as deputy customer at the Lanterngate. That these attacks were directed against Cromwell, as well as the religious reformers in Calais, is shown by the tirade of charges levelled against Henry Palmer, the bailiff of Guînes, 'a man who my Lord Privy Seal favoureth with all his life' (Lisle Letters, 5.1192). As a result of the commissioners' findings Broke and twelve others were committed to the Tower of London.

Broke survived the fall of his patron in April 1540 and reappeared in September 1543, as paymaster of the king's works at Dover harbour; in November 1545 he was appointed receiver of the lordships of Marke and Oye, just outside Calais. His rehabilitation may have been due to support from George Brooke, Lord Cobham, the deputy of Calais and also, if Thomas was indeed connected with the Brokes of Aspall, a kinsman. In October 1547, at the instigation of Cobham, Broke was returned as MP for the Calais council. His religious sensibilities, however, continued to cause him trouble: in 1550 he was reputed as one of the leading sacramentarians in Kent, and in November 1552 was again committed to the Fleet, possibly on religious grounds. He was released towards the end of 1554 but in the following year another commission sent to Calais to enquire into heresy there ordered that Broke should be discharged of all his offices. The date of his death is unknown.

The nature of Broke's religious beliefs, and in particular his opinions on the doctrine of transubstantiation, are readily apparent from his extant works as a theologian. He was the author of *Certeyn meditacions and things to be had in remembraunce ... by every Christian before he receive the sacrament of the body and bloude of Christ* (1548). Although temperate in its language, it is unambiguous in its denial of transubstantiation. He clearly became an admirer of John Calvin, translating into English his *De vita* as *Of the Life and Conversacion of a Christian Man* (1549) and printing *The Forme of Common Praiers used in the Churches of Geneva* (1550). He also claimed to have prepared a translation from Calvin's *Institutio*, but no copy of this survives. His final printed work was *A Reply to a Libell Cast Abroad in Defence of D. Ed. Boner, by T. Brooke* (n.d.). Broke probably developed his ideas by contact with the reforming communities of Geneva and Zürich. He visited the protestant communities in Europe at least once: in a letter written towards the end of 1549 the English merchant William Quick told Calvin that, despite the fall of the duke of Somerset, he had been assured that the new religion would prosper in England.

His informant was Thomas Broke, whom he had met in Italy along with Broke's two sons, possibly Arthur Broke, translator of 'Romeus and Juliet', and Thomas Broke the younger.

DAVID GRUMMITT

Sources HoP, *Commons, 1509–58* · D. I. Grummitt, 'Calais, 1485–1547: a study in early Tudor politics and government', PhD diss., U. Lond., 1997 · M. St C. Byrne, ed., *The Lisle letters*, 6 vols. (1981) · *LP Henry VIII*, 14/2, no. 782 · *DNB* · Broke to Cromwell, PRO, SP 1/95, fols. 178–9, SP 1/96, fols. 82, 146, SP 1/135, fols. 110–13, SP 1/143, fols. 166–7, SP 1/153, fols. 11–12 · Broke to Lisle, PRO, SP 3/2, nos. 45, 47 · R. Peter and J.-F. Gilmont, *Bibliotheca Calviniana: les oeuvres de Jean Calvin publiées au XVIe siècle*, 1 (Geneva, 1991) · F. Hyman, 'Calvin's work in translation', *Calvinism in Europe, 1540–1620*, ed. A. Pettegree, A. Duke, and G. Lewis (1994), 90–91

Archives PRO, Lisle MSS, letters to Arthur, Lord Lisle, SP 3/2, no. 47; SP 3/2, no. 45 · PRO, state papers, domestic, Henry VIII to Thomas Cromwell, SP 1/95, fols. 178–9; SP 1/96, fol. 82; SP 1/96, fol. 146; SP 1/135, fols. 110–13; SP 1/143, fols. 166–7; SP 1/153, fols. 11–12

Broker, Nicholas (d. 1426), coppersmith, was, with his fellow craftsman **Godfrey Prest** (*fl.* 1395–1399), a citizen of London. In April 1395 the two men were awarded the contract for the gilt bronze effigies of Richard II and Queen Anne for their tomb in Westminster Abbey. The marble parts were supplied by Master Henry Yevele (d. 1400) and Stephen Lote, also of London, and this division of labour had also occurred in the manufacture of earlier tombs at Westminster, by William Torel and the royal master masons in the 1290s. The contract negotiated between Broker and Prest, the king, and his treasurer, states that the effigies and other metal components of the tomb were to be made according to a royally approved cartoon supplied to Broker and Prest. The contract is extremely detailed, specifying all aspects of the effigies, canopies, heraldry, and inscriptions. The effigies were to be portrait likenesses, an early documented instance. The work, costing about £700, was to be completed by Michaelmas 1397, and was undertaken in two houses on Wood Street, London, hired for the four years 1395–9. Broker and Prest were rewarded for the casting and gilding in two instalments between 1397 and 1399 and were also supplied with drink. The tomb of Richard and Anne is one of the best-documented tombs produced in medieval England. Cast in separate components, the effigies, canopywork, and daintily engraved surfaces demonstrate the remarkable refinement of taste at Richard's court. Nothing else is known of the careers of the two men, but it is possible that they were also involved in the manufacture of monumental brasses. Broker's will of 1424, enrolled in 1426 (and suggesting that he died in that year, in London), notes that he left a property in the parish of St Benedict West near Pauleswharf, London, for the foundation of a chantry for himself and others.

PAUL BINSKI

Sources Rymer, *Foedera*, 1st edn, 7.795–8 · F. Devon, ed. and trans., *Issues of the exchequer: being payments made out of his majesty's revenue, from King Henry III to King Henry VI inclusive*, RC (1837), 263 · A. P. Stanley, 'On an examination of the tombs of Richard II and Henry II in Westminster Abbey', *Archaeologia*, 45 (1880), 309–27 · R. R. Sharpe, ed., *Calendar of wills proved and enrolled in the court of husting, London, AD 1258 – AD 1688*, 2 (1890), 440 · J. H. Harvey, 'The Wilton diptych, a re-examination', *Archaeologia*, 98 (1961), 1–28, esp. 8 · R. Brown, H. M. Colvin, and A. J. Taylor, eds., *The history of the king's works*, 1 (1963), 487–8 · J. Alexander and P. Binski, eds., *Age of* *chivalry: art in Plantagenet England, 1200–1400* (1987), no. 446 [exhibition catalogue, RA]

Brokesby, Francis (1637–1714), nonjuring Church of England clergyman, son of Obadiah Brokesby (*d.* 1696), 'a gentleman of independent fortune', of Stoke Golding, Leicestershire, and his wife, Elizabeth (*d.* 1683), daughter of James Pratt of Wellingborough, Northamptonshire, was born at Stoke Golding on 29 September 1637. As all the nine children of his grandfather Francis received scriptural names, it is probable that he came from puritan stock. His family enjoyed some eminence in their parish; 'the name of *Brokesby* [was] written over the church porch' and, at the end of the eighteenth century, the antiquary John Nichols was still able to distinguish 'an old mural monument … almost devoured by time and moss … [with] the family name and date 1604' (Nichols, *The History, and Antiquities of Hinckley*, 1782, 175). Francis was admitted to Trinity College, Cambridge, in 1652, graduating BA in 1656 and proceeding MA in 1659. He was elected to a fellowship there in 1658 and proceeded BD in 1666. A poem on the eucharist, stylistically indebted to both George Herbert and Richard Crashaw and declaring his unworthiness before God, is suggestive of Brokesby's humility and ardent piety at this time. He apparently took orders early; he succeeded to a college living, the rectory of Hatfield Broad Oak in Essex, in the place of its ejected rector, John Warren, who remained on good terms with the new incumbent and came to hear him preach—a circumstance which perhaps encouraged the emphasis on the reconciliation of dissenters common in Brokesby's writings.

In 1670 Brokesby became rector of Rowley, in the East Riding of Yorkshire, a living Thomas Hearne estimated to be worth £200. Soon afterwards he married Isabella (*d.* 1699), daughter of a Mr Wood of Kingston upon Hull. From this period dates a series of Latin memoranda of both spiritual and more mundane domestic reflections, comprising a sort of journal, the original now apparently lost, from which Nichols published a representative selection. The diary offers *inter alia* a record of the clergy's battle to recover tithes, with Brokesby variously offering thanksgiving for the successful conclusion of a suit and on another occasion pledging to donate half his tithes to the poor should a case be won. About 1675 Brokesby's first son, Francis, was born, but he did not survive childhood. A second son, Richard (*b.* c.1678), later settled in business in Liverpool. Of the Brokesbys' four daughters, both Jane, who married a local merchant, and Anne, 'a notorious and furious Jacobite', moved north with their brother. Dorothy, the second daughter, married Samuel Parr, vicar of Hinckley, and was the grandmother of Dr Samuel Parr, the celebrated Greek scholar (Nichols, *Leicester*, 742). High tory and even Jacobite associations continued in this line until the eve of the nineteenth century, when Sarah Anne, a great-granddaughter of Dorothy, who had married into the Watkin Wynn dynasty, had her daughter baptized Christine Sobieska, an allusion to James Francis Edward Stuart's Polish consort.

The exclusion crisis prompted Brokesby's first publication, the plangent and self-explanatory pamphlet, *A persuasive to reformation and union as the best security against the designs of our popish enemies* (1680). Here he attested his belief in a Roman Catholic conspiracy, urging nonconformist 'Brethren of the Separation' to return to the national church and 'keep the unity of the Spirit in the bond of Peace' (p. 18). Brokesby's claim, that their schism was based on matters indifferent and therefore unjustifiable, voiced an Anglican commonplace, but one which would prove a principal theme of his writings and be of particular significance in his estimation of the causes, consequences, and eventual resolution of the schism which followed the revolution settlement.

Like many high-churchmen who had earlier assailed popery and stoutly defended the Anglican establishment, Brokesby was unable to take the oath of allegiance to William and Mary, considering that he was still conscientiously bound by a precedent and higher oath to King James. He explained his position in a letter to a friend shortly after the revolution: 'Was king James dead, I could, not withstanding the presence of the Prince of Wales, swear allegiance to King William and Queen Mary, because in possession, and the other claim dubious', a cryptic and eclectic formula, incorporating *de jure* and *de facto* considerations, yet one entirely characteristic of the times (Nichols, *Leicester*, 740). The material consequences of Brokesby's scruples were poignantly recorded in a letter of August 1690 from Isabella to her sister lamenting that 'We are now cutting down our corn, for we cannot sell it' (ibid., 737). The family now retired to its modest patrimony in Stoke Golding, though for some time after the revolution Brokesby lived in London in the household of Lady Fanbourne, and, according to Nichols, in Yorkshire.

The issues of allegiance and communion were further complicated after February 1691, when the offices of those clergy who had failed to comply with the oaths were filled with new incumbents. Henry Dodwell, who had resigned his post as Camden professor of history at Oxford, led the vanguard in asserting the schismatical implications of the new appointments to the episcopate. These arguments, collectively distinguished as 'the Church point', led Brokesby to worship separately, at first at Hinckley then, following the death of his wife in 1699, principally in the little society of nonjurors established by the generosity of his distant kinsman Francis Cherry, at Shottesbrooke in Berkshire. Here he enjoyed the fellowship of Robert Nelson, whom he helped compile his magisterial survey of the Anglican calendar, and Dodwell, whose erudition informed his own research and as whose amanuensis he served after the latter's sight began to fail. During this period he corresponded with Thomas Hearne on antiquarian interests and contributed to his work on John Leland. In 1706, following the death of Mr Smith, he became chaplain to Cherry's household.

In 1701 appeared Brokesby's *Of Education*, a prescriptive examination of both schools and universities which recalled Renaissance thinking in its earnest commendation of the study of horsemanship and navigation. Its prefatory 'Letter of advice to a young gentleman' was surprisingly eclectic in its suggested reading, with Gilbert Burnet's *History of the Reformation* commended alongside more predicable tory staples. Its nonjuring provenance was apparent in a suggestive aside on the illustrious record of the anonymous addressee's forebears, 'excepting the Conqueror's and his Son's Reign, then probably opprest, because they asserted their just Rights, or would not violate their Consciences, by submitting to any thing contrary to their Duty' (p. 187). In 1708 Brokesby published *Some Proposals towards the Propagation of the Gospel in our American Plantations*, dedicated to Nelson. The principal aim of the work, which he acknowledged was indebted to Dodwell's conversations with Morgan Godwin, was 'to Encourage and Promote the erecting and establishing Episcopal Sees in our Foreign Plantations' (p. 28). The text was replete with typographical errors. In the Bodleian Library's autograph corrected version Brokesby tenders a poignant apology, referring to 'urgent occasions' which had taken him away from the press, an oblique allusion to the death of his singularly unfortunate son in Virginia, soon after the successful resolution of an incident in which one of his ships had been taken by pirates.

Since he considered an objection to the propriety of the state prayers insufficient grounds for their continued separation, one consequence of the argument expounded by Dodwell was that the nonjurors should return to the national communion following the death or resignation of the last surviving ejected bishop. According to this line of thought, the schism had been initiated by the new incumbents filling the episcopal sees of unwillingly and illegitimately deprived prelates; they could only be considered intruders so long as the previous occupants asserted their claims. With their demise or the decision to waive their claims there could be no objections to accepting the authority of their successors. Wisely, Dodwell chose to rehearse his arguments fully before the event, in a series of pamphlets, beginning with *The Case in View* (1705). With the death of William Lloyd, bishop of Norwich, and the immediate resignation of Thomas Ken from the see of Bath and Wells in January 1710, the circumstances of Dodwell's conjectures were realized, an occasion marked by his further exposition, *The Case in View now in Fact*. Writing on Dodwell's behalf to a wavering correspondent in March, Brokesby asserts, 'We are here satisfied the Schism is at an End, where there is no Altar against Altar, nor any other Bishops but *Suffragan* to require our Subjection. And therefore we go all to Church' (Marshall, appx 6, xviii). The term 'suffragan' referred to Archbishop Sancroft's clandestine decision to concur in the consecration of George Hickes, dean of Worcester, in order to perpetuate a nonjuring episcopacy, the announcement of which was initially met with scepticism by the Shottesbrooke community and subsequently with a robust critique of its validity and significance. Over the next three years an animated correspondence with unknown nonjurors who felt obliged to perpetuate the separation continued, in which Brokesby retailed counter-arguments, principally of Dodwell's making, to

those of George Hickes's party. In a letter of 1712, written on the ailing Cherry's behalf, Brokesby counters a significant objection to returning to the church—that all bishops created after the deprivation were, by their implicit assent to the filling of the contended episcopal sees, culpable in schism—with the argument that 'the *Intruders* were the *Principal Schismaticks*, and the *Ante-Revolution* Bishops accidentally only, and by *Contagion*' (Marshall, appx 12, xlix). This correspondence, first published posthumously in an appendix to Nathaniel Marshall's rebuttal of Hickes, was an early and influential contribution to what became the Bangorian controversy.

Once reconciled to the established church, Brokesby returned with renewed vigour to the labour of commending its society to nonconformists. His *chef d'œuvre*, *An History of the Government of the Primitive Church* (1712), was dedicated to Cherry, whose library had furnished the materials of his research. Its principal aim was to demonstrate the ubiquity of episcopal government in the early church, thereby countering presbyterian historiography, with 'a chief Regard to what *Blondel* has written against Episcopacy; his Book being the great Armoury from which other Adversaries have borrowed their weapons' (p. xliv). Brokesby acknowledged John Potter's definitive work on the subject but proffered the modest hope that his treatise would appeal to those who would 'not be at the Pains to read so large a Book … yet … need to have their Notions of Church-Government rectified' (p. iv). His preliminary dissertation returned to the theme of his exclusion crisis thesis—the reconciliation of dissenters with the established church—promising 'a serious and affectionate *Perswasive*' (p. xxxiv). The dissertation proved popular and was separately republished in 1714 as the baldly titled *The divine right of church government by bishops … [with] a perswasive to dissenters to return to the communion of the Church of England*.

Following Dodwell's death in 1711, Brokesby dedicated his last years to a compendious survey of his mentor's formidable body of writings. The passing of Cherry two years later caused him great distress, but enabled him to compose a fitting memorial to Cherry's generosity and piety, with the incorporation of a full account of the Shottesbrooke community in his biography. Published posthumously in 1715, *The Life of Mr Henry Dodwell; with an Account of his Works* was largely an erudite epitome of its subject's writings which acknowledged its indebtedness to the method of its dedicatee, Nelson, in his biography of Bishop Bull. In the preface Brokesby requested his readers' indulgence, hoping 'the Defects will admit of an Excuse in an Author in the Seventy seventh Year of his Age'. Hearne regretted its appearance, claiming the labour was beyond Brokesby's modest gifts, but the unusual degree of pique that he displayed is suspicious, given his own declared wish to have been Dodwell's memorialist.

Any appraisal of Brokesby's character must be largely drawn from the variously unpromising sources of his writings, which are seldom personally revealing, and the terse and, latterly, grudging memoranda of Hearne. In his writings Brokesby's humility and modesty are everywhere apparent, especially in his generous acknowledgement of the role of friends in assisting his researches. It is thus perhaps unsurprising that no likeness of this most retiring of men should be known to the rich engraved record of the nonjurors. In his endeavour to reconcile nonconformists to the established church Brokesby gave repeatedly forceful expression to the orthodox or high view of ecclesiology while avoiding the satirical sallies which frequently call into doubt the sincerity of such enterprise by his peers. The entries in his diary reveal a faith closer in affinity to Caroline Arminianism than to Restoration latitude. He died at Hinckley and was buried at Stoke Golding on 24 October 1714. In his will he appointed Samuel Parr his executor, confessing himself 'sensible that my personal estate will not pay my debt and legacies' (Nichols, *Leicester*, 741–2). He requested that small patrimonies in Yorkshire be sold in order to raise £400 he pledged to his unmarried daughter, Anne. As well as distributing sums to the poor of Rowley and Hinckley, Parr was requested to manage the mortgaged estate at Stoke which, on reversion, was to be shared between Brokesby's three daughters. **D. A. BRUNTON**

Sources J. Nichols, *The history and antiquities of the county of Leicester*, 4 (1807–11) · *Remarks and collections of Thomas Hearne*, ed. C. E. Doble and others, 11 vols., OHS, 2, 7, 13, 34, 42–3, 48, 50, 65, 67, 72 (1885–1921) · N. Marshall, *Defence of our constitution in church and state* (1717) · F. Brokesby, *The life of Mr Henry Dodwell* (1715) · T. Lathbury, *A history of the nonjurors* (1845) · Nichols, *Illustrations*, 4.117 · *GM*, 1st ser., 69 (1799), 458–9 · *DNB* · J. C. Findon, 'The nonjurors and the Church of England, 1689–1716', DPhil diss., U. Oxf., 1978 · Venn, *Alum. Cant.*

Wealth at death approx. £400: will, Nichols, *History and antiquities*, 741–2

Bromby, Charles Hamilton (1843–1904). *See under* Bromby, Charles Henry (1814–1907).

Bromby, Charles Henry (1814–1907), bishop of Tasmania, born at Hull on 11 July 1814, was the son of John Healey Bromby, vicar of Holy Trinity, Hull, and his wife, Jane, *née* Amis. He entered Uppingham School in August 1829, became captain of the school in 1833, and left it with an exhibition in October 1833. Elected to a scholarship at St John's College, Cambridge, he graduated BA as junior optime and with a third class in the classical tripos in 1837; he proceeded MA in 1840 and DD in 1864. Ordained deacon in 1838 and priest in 1839, he was licensed in 1838 to the curacy of Chesterfield. On 9 July 1839 he married Mary Ann (d. 1885), daughter of Dr William Bodley and sister of G. F. *Bodley, the architect. In 1839 Bromby was appointed headmaster of Stepney grammar school and in 1843 he became vicar of St Paul's, Cheltenham, and first principal of the Cheltenham Training College for School Teachers, which he organized with marked success. He was also one of the founders of the Ladies' College, Cheltenham, and he helped to form a large working men's club, one of the first institutions of its kind. He edited the influential *Papers for the Schoolmaster*, strongly contesting Robert Lowe's 'revised code' of 1862.

On the resignation of Francis Russell Nixon in 1864, Bromby was appointed by the crown to the bishopric of Tasmania, being the last colonial prelate appointed by letters patent. He was consecrated in Canterbury Cathedral on 29 June 1864. Bromby worked for eighteen years in the colony. He managed with tact and skill the financial reorganization of the church on its disestablishment in Tasmania, and it was largely owing to his influence that a commutation act was passed, which supplied the church with the nucleus of the diocesan church fund. He took an active part in the movement which led to the formation in 1872 of a general synod of the dioceses of Australia and Tasmania, and in 1874 he saw a cathedral—planned by his brother-in-law G. F. Bodley—for the diocese consecrated at Hobart. A high-churchman, and opposed to Erastianism, Bromby enjoyed the general confidence of the colonists. Advancing years led him to resign in 1882.

After returning to England, Bromby was, from 1882 to 1887, assistant bishop in the diocese of Lichfield and rector of Shrawardine with Montford, Shropshire. He resigned the living in 1887 on appointment as warden of St John's Hospital, Lichfield, but remained assistant bishop until 1891. He then filled a similar office in the diocese of Bath and Wells until 1900. Bromby died at All Saints' vicarage, Clifton, Bristol, on 14 April 1907. A son and a daughter survived him. A Bishop Bromby memorial studentship was founded by the synod of Tasmania in 1910. Bromby published three pamphlets on education, in 1861, 1862, and 1895. His first son, Henry Bodley Bromby (1840–1911), received promotion in the Australian church from his father.

Bromby's second son, **Charles Hamilton Bromby** (1843–1904), born on 17 June 1843 and educated at Cheltenham College, matriculated at St Edmund Hall, Oxford, on 3 May 1862, and graduated BA (New Inn Hall) in 1867. He was called to the bar at the Inner Temple on 18 November 1867. After joining the New South Wales bar and practising in Tasmania, he became a member of the executive council and was attorney-general of Tasmania (1876–8). He then returned to England, and practised at the English bar. Of artistic temperament and a keen student of Italian literature, he published a translation, with introduction and notes, of Dante's *Quaestio de aqua et terra* (1897). Bromby died on 24 July 1904, at 50 Weymouth Street, London, and was survived by his wife, Mary Ellen. After his death there appeared *Alkibiades, a Tale of the Great Athenian War* (1905), edited by Mary Hamilton Bromby.

A. R. BUCKLAND, *rev.* H. C. G. MATTHEW

Sources F. S. A. Lowndes, *Bishops of the day: a biographical dictionary of the archbishops and bishops of the Church of England* (1897) · J. P. Graham, ed., *Uppingham School roll, 1824–1913* (1914) · E. Stock, *The history of the Church Missionary Society: its environment, its men and its work*, 4 vols. (1899–1916) · H. H. Condon, 'Bromby, Charles Henry', *AusDB*, vol. 3 · *CGPLA Eng. & Wales* (1904)

Archives LPL, corresp. with A. C. Tait

Likenesses W. Walker & Sons, carte-de-visite, NPG · print, NPG · wood-engraving, NPG; repro. in *ILN* (8 Oct 1864)

Wealth at death £5374 4s. 8d.: probate, 16 July 1907, *CGPLA Eng. & Wales* · £2856 7s. 1d.—Charles Hamilton Bromby: probate, 11 Nov 1904, *CGPLA Eng. & Wales*

Brome, Adam (*d.* 1332), administrator and first founder of Oriel College, Oxford, was probably the son of Thomas of Brome, who took his name from Brome near Eye in Suffolk; according to the inquisition held after the death of Edmund, earl of Cornwall, in 1300, Adam Brome then held a modest inheritance of half a knight's fee. He may have come into the king's service through the good offices of the locally prominent d'Avilers family, or through his proximity to the centre of Earl Edmund's honour of Eye. There is no evidence of any university education. He appears first as a collector of food supplies in Dorset in 1297, and was in Ireland on unspecified service in April 1298 (from November 1299 he was in charge of the assize of corn and wine). Also in 1299 he is recorded as leading troops from Yorkshire to Carlisle for a campaign in Scotland. In 1305 he was an auditor of the accounts of the papal tenth, and in 1312 an assessor of tallage in the midlands. For part of this period (1306–29) he was a clerk of chancery. After 1311 he was appointed to various judicial offices: as a justice of assize, a commissioner of oyer and terminer, and a justice to deal with offences against the wool customs. He remained in favour at Westminster after the fall of Edward II, being summoned as a chancery clerk to attend the Lincoln parliament of September 1327, and acting in an unspecified role for the king in October 1329.

For these services Brome received modest rewards. Having been ordained priest on 2 March 1301, three weeks later he was admitted as rector of Wyck Rissington, Gloucestershire. He became master of God's House, Dunwich, in 1306, briefly rector of Bridford, Devon (1311–12), Handsworth, Yorkshire (1313–16), and of St Creed, Cornwall (1314), chancellor of Durham *sede vacante* (1311 and 1316–17), archdeacon of Stow in the diocese of Lincoln (1320), and more substantially prebendary of Bathwick in Wherwell Abbey, Hampshire (1314–20), rector of St Mary's, Oxford (1320–26), warden of St Bartholomew's Hospital, Oxford (1326–32), and rector of a moiety of Eckington, Derbyshire (1328–32). These were normal emoluments for a royal servant of middling rank, and they indicate the limits of his capacity to rise in the king's favour.

Brome distinguished himself from his colleagues by his project of founding in Oxford 'a certain college of scholars studying various disciplines in honour of the Virgin' (*Oriel College Records*, 1). The college was to consist of a provost and ten fellows. His precise intentions are unclear, but as rector of St Mary's he had already become involved in university business, and although he modelled his statutes on those of Merton College (1274), he specifically directed the fellows to study in the higher faculties. It is likely that he had in mind as the fellows' future occupation both service to the crown and ecclesiastical duties; if so, he might have seen as recent precedents Exeter College in Oxford, founded by Walter Stapeldon (*d.* 1326), bishop of Exeter and later treasurer of England, and the King's Hall in Cambridge. To this end he obtained a licence in mortmain to acquire a property in Oxford on 20 April 1324, and purchased for the college Perilous Hall in the parish of St Mary Magdalen, and Tackley's Inn in his own, as well as

the advowson of Aberford, Yorkshire. Before the end of 1325 his intentions were altered; he transferred the property he had acquired to Edward II, who granted it to the college in a charter, together with the advowson of St Mary's, and appointed Brome its provost on 21 January 1326. The king therefore became the founder of the new college, and his successor Edward III, besides confirming the charter, gave the reversion of La Oriole, a large house in Shidyerd Street (now Oriel Square), from which the college took its commonly used name, in May 1329. Brome, unusually among founders of colleges, made no provision for his kindred (none of whom are known) and showed no bias to his countrymen; Oriel came to be the least regional of Oxford colleges. He remained provost until his death in college on 16 June 1332. He was buried in his chapel on the north side of St Mary's, where his tomb (from which the memorial brass has been removed) remains. In his will he made a bequest of two Oxford properties to Richard Overton, a scholar who was probably his agent in endowing the college: both properties passed to Oriel shortly afterwards. JEREMY CATTO

Sources *Chancery records* · *CEPR letters*, 2.197 · special collections, ancient petitions, PRO, SC8/4567 · 'Registrum palatinum Dunelmense': the register of Richard de Kellawe, lord palatine and bishop of Durham, ed. T. D. Hardy, 4 vols., Rolls Series, 62 (1873–8), vol. 4, pp. 76–7, 80, 82, 324 · C. L. Shadwell and H. E. Salter, *Oriel College records*, OHS, 85 (1926), 1–19, 86–8, 119–21, 164–5, 274, 290–92, 485–9 · *Statutes of the colleges of Oxford*, 3 vols. (1853), pt 5 · H. E. Salter, ed., *Munimenta civitatis Oxonie*, OHS, 71 (1920), 35–6, 38, 49, 261–2 · F. M. Powicke, 'More notes on Adam de Brome', *Oriel Record* (1941), 135–9 · Emden, *Oxf.* · Tout, *Admin. hist.*, 2.144 (n.2)

Brome, Alexander (1620–1666), poet and lawyer, was born in the parish of Evershot, Dorset, the eldest son of the seven children of John Brome and his wife, about whom little is known. Henry *Brome (*d.* 1681), the London bookseller, was a younger brother. Brome was educated at the free grammar school in the parish of West Milton, Dorset, and probably had a private tutor as well. No evidence exists that he received a university education. He went to London about 1640 to pursue a career in the law, serving first as a law clerk of Robert Henley, master of the court of king's bench, then becoming a master about 1652. He was granted admission to Gray's Inn in 1648 and to Lincoln's Inn in 1659. In 1660 he received permission to enrol pleas in king's bench in his own name. From 1659 he also served as an attorney of the lord mayor's court.

About 1650 Brome married Martha Whitaker, *née* Hull, widow of Thomas Whitaker, a bookseller. The Bromes had five children, as well as Martha Brome's three daughters from her first marriage. From 1661 Brome and his family lived in London in the parish of St Stephen Walbrook.

Though he was a successful attorney, Brome's claim to fame derives from his avocation as poet. Between 1640 and 1660 Brome composed over 200 poems, including love poems in the cavalier mode, satires attacking the enemies of the king and, later, the Commonwealth government, drinking songs in the Anacreontic tradition, an assortment of occasional poems, translations of epigrams from the Greek and Latin, and other translations. Some of these poems were printed anonymously, while others appeared

Alexander Brome (1620–1666), by A. Hertocks, pubd 1661

as dedications or in poetical miscellanies. Brome also published in 1654 his only play, *The Cunning Lovers*, and two editions of *Five New Playes* (1653 and 1654) by Richard Brome (no relation). The publication in 1661 of Brome's own collected poems, *Songs and other Poems*, which contained commendatory verses by Izaak Walton, was a fitting climax to his work as poet. He published a corrected and enlarged edition in 1664. To this edition are prefixed a prose commendatory letter signed 'R. B.' (probably the initials of Richard Braithwaite), additional verses by Charles Steynings and Valentine Oldis, and a prose letter signed 'H. T.' (revised to the initials 'R. B.', for Ralph Bathurst, in the 1668 edition). Among the new poems in this edition are an epistle 'To his Friend Thomas Stanley, Esq., on his Odes', and 'Cromwell's Panegyrick'. A third edition appeared posthumously in 1668 containing a few new poems and with elegies by Charles Cotton and Richard Newcourt. Brome also collected, edited, and published in 1666 existing translations of *The Poems of Horace*, translating twenty-five poems himself. Posthumous editions followed in 1671 and 1680. Commendatory poems by Brome are prefixed to the first folio edition of Beaumont and Fletcher's works (1647), and to the second edition of Walton's *Angler* (1655).

Stylistically, Brome's poetry showed the transition from the metaphysical mode of the first half of the century to the neoclassical mode of the second half. Contemporaries praised his poetry for its plainness and avoidance of far-fetched metaphors and strong lines. As a love poet, Brome showed an affinity in his poems with the work of other cavalier poets. He frequently tested the conventional and stereotyped views about love, and like other cavaliers revealed an increase in psychological awareness. Brome's drinking songs earned him the title of the English Anacreon. These and his poems in praise of the retired life appealed to many cavaliers during the interregnum. As a political satirist, Brome most often heaped ridicule on the king's enemies and later on the low-born who attained power over their social 'betters'. Wedgwood's comment that Brome's poems reflected most clearly from 1640 until after the Restoration the changing moods of the typical cavalier is an apt summation of his work (Wedgwood, 86).

Brome died on 30 June 1666 in the parish of St Stephen Walbrook, having made his will the previous day. Bequests in his will of money and lands to his wife and various members of his family indicated that at his death Brome was a man of substantial means. He was buried at St Stephen Walbrook on 4 July. ROMAN R. DUBINSKI

Sources *Alexander Brome: poems*, ed. R. R. Dubinski, 2 vols. (1982) • J. L. Brooks, 'Alexander Brome: his life and works', PhD diss., Harvard U., 1932 • copy of Alexander Brome's will, PRO • E. Phillips, *Theatrum poetarum, or, A compleat collection of the poets, especially the most eminent of all ages* (1675) • W. Winstanley, *The lives of the most famous English poets* (1687) • G. Langbaine, *An account of the English dramatick poets* (1691) • G. E. Bentley, *The Jacobean and Caroline stage*, 7 vols. (1941–68), vols. 1, 3 • J. Foster, *The register of admissions to Gray's Inn, 1521–1889, together with the register of marriages in Gray's Inn chapel, 1695–1754* (privately printed, London, 1889) • W. P. Baildon, ed., *The records of the Honorable Society of Lincoln's Inn: admissions*, 1 (1896) • H. R. Plomer and others, *A dictionary of the booksellers and printers who were at work in England, Scotland, and Ireland from 1641 to 1667* (1907) • W. B. Bannerman and W. B. Bannerman, jun., eds., *The registers of St Stephen's, Walbrook, and of St Benet Sherehog, London*, 1, Harleian Society, register section, 49 (1919) • R. Newcourt, *Repertorium ecclesiasticum parochiale Londinense*, 2 (1710) • P. W. Thomas, *Sir John Berkenhead* (1969) • C. V. Wedgwood, *Poetry and politics under the Stuarts* (1960) • R. A. Anselment, *Loyalist resolve: patient fortitude in the English civil war* (1988) • H. R. Richmond, *The school of love* (1964) • E. Miner, *The metaphysical mode from Donne to Cowley* (1969) • E. Miner, *The cavalier mode from Jonson to Cotton* (1971) • E. Miner, *The restoration mode from Milton to Dryden* (1974) • *DNB*

Likenesses A. Hertocks, engraving, Hunt. L.; repro. in A. Brome, *Songs and other poems* (1661) [*see illus.*] • A. Hertocks, engraving, repro. in A. Brome, *Songs and other poems*, 2nd edn (1664), insert; held at Hunt. L. • D. Loggan, line engraving, BM, NPG; repro. in A. Brome, *Songs and other poems*, 2nd edn (1664)

Wealth at death substantial; bequeathed £115 cash; lands in Dorset were to be sold to provide £500 marriage portions for each surviving daughter; lands in Somerset and residue of estate to go to wife, and after her decease to son: will, PRO

Brome, Henry (*d.* 1681), bookseller, was born probably in the early 1620s in Evershot, Dorset, perhaps the second of at least seven children of John Brome, of whom the eldest was Alexander *Brome, the poet. The father was styled as a gentleman when Alexander was admitted to Gray's Inn in 1648, although confirmation of this family status has not been found. Henry Brome probably went to the local school, but at some point during the next twenty years the family moved to nearby West Milton, Dorset, as that was the paternal address given when, on 2 October 1646, Henry Brome was apprenticed to John Allen of the London

Haberdashers' Company for seven years. He was freed on 14 October 1653. He followed his brother Alexander's example in marrying a bookseller's widow: by 27 September 1658 he had 'lately married' Joanna (d. 1684), widow of Francis Leach (Stationers' Company, court book D, fol. 36r). On 22 May 1664, the Bromes' first child was born, a son, Charles, and on 28 April 1668, they baptized their second, a daughter, Allet.

Henry Brome's name first appears on an imprint in 1656, with his shop at the sign of the Hand in St Paul's Churchyard; in 1658 he moved just to the north, at the Gun in Ivy Lane, where he remained until 1665. He was one of only a few booksellers who had been apprenticed to members of the Haberdashers' Company, from whom he may have gained special experience in auctioneering and making inventories—skills that Brome was later called upon to use. In marrying Leach's widow, Brome did not gain Leach's bookshop as that went to Leach's son Thomas, but he did secure from Leach an association with the royalist author Roger L'Estrange which was to prove long and productive. In 1659 he was already selling the work of L'Estrange's brother Hamon, and during the winter and spring of 1660 he was helping to publish, anonymously, the prolific Roger, who later recalled of his many royalist works on the eve of the Restoration that 'honest Harry Brome got them printed too, to his very great Hazzard' (L'Estrange, 31). Especially in 1659–62 and again after 1678, L'Estrange benefited greatly from Brome's support of his energetic pamphleteering as well as his later journal *The Observator*, which Brome published in the last months of his life in 1681. In 1680–81 L'Estrange accounted for almost half the titles the busy Brome had in print, and the two were very closely associated in satirical attacks at this date, such as *A Dialogue betwixt H.B.'s. Ghost, and his Dear Author R.L.S.* (1681).

Including L'Estrange's many publications and republications, Brome's list averaged about twenty new titles a year, with the highest number appearing in the year before his death, when the lapsing of the so-called Licensing Act and the exclusion crisis had much increased pamphleteering. Controversial works aside, his list is marked by a preponderance of religious, scientific, and literary titles, reflecting the work and the tastes of his clientele, who seem to have included many of 'the most important figures in the political, social, religious and intellectual life of Restoration England' (Mandelbrote, 74). Having left Ivy Lane early in 1666 for premises in Little Britain (first at the Dial, and then at the Star), Brome returned in 1669 to an address closer to St Paul's, where his shop at the sign of the Gun in Ludgate Street flourished, with the family living upstairs. On 2 October 1678, Brome applied (along with the bookseller Richard Chiswell the elder) and was admitted gratis to the freedom of the Stationers' Company. He was formally freed on 4 November and the next year was chosen as one of the company's renter wardens. Brome's prosperous business seems to have served its customers as something of a library. Brome was said to have given considerable support to L'Estrange, and his estate, less debts and charges, was valued at his death at £2785. He died at Ludgate Street about 11 May 1681.

After Brome's death his wife, Joanna, took over the business until her own death late in May 1684, just before their son Charles reached his majority. Subject to prosecution in October 1681 for publishing a too controversial issue of *The Observator*, she was able to get her case transferred to the king's bench; again in 1683, she was presented to the London sessions, this time for printing *The Observator* without licence, but that publication continued uninterrupted nevertheless. She had been accused of improper relations with L'Estrange, but he was notorious for his ways with printers' wives. She was styled 'rich and proud' in the correspondence of a disgruntled client (Raine MSS, G. Hickes to T. Comber, 17 Jan 1684) and came to marry her daughter Allet to Alexander Davenant, brother of Charles, with a portion of £3000. Charles Brome, who was freed by patrimony on 10 June 1684, kept up the business at the Gun in Ludgate Street. His publishing list recalls that of his father but later displayed Jacobite tendencies. In 1705 Dunton described him as 'a Genteel Man in his Garb, a Prudent Man in his Actions, and thriving Man in his Shop' (Dunton, 300). His last imprints are dated 1711–12.

NICHOLAS VON MALTZAHN

Sources Wing, *STC*, vol. 4 · C. Nelson and M. Seccombe, *British newspapers and periodicals, 1641–1700* (1987) · J. L. Brooks, 'Alexander Brome: his life and works', PhD diss., Harvard U., 1932 · *Alexander Brome: poems*, ed. R. R. Dubinski, 2 vols. (1982) · T. C. Faulkner, 'The publishing history of Sir Roger L'Estrange's *Observator*', *Papers of the Bibliographical Society of America*, 73 (1979), 89–93 · N. von Maltzahn, *Milton's History of Britain* (1991) · private information (2004) [M. Treadwell, Trent University, Canada] · Stationers' Company, Stationers' Hall, London, court book D · G. Mandelbrote, 'From the warehouse to the counting-house', *A genius for letters*, ed. R. Myers and M. Harris (1995), 49–84 · R. L'Estrange, *Discovery upon discovery* (1680) · D. F. McKenzie, ed., *Stationers' Company apprentices*, [2]: *1641–1700* (1974) · J. Dunton, *The life and errors of John Dunton ... written by himself* (1705), 328, 349 · Durham Cath. CL, Raine MSS, vol. 33 · L. Hotson, *Commonwealth and Restoration stage* (1928)
Wealth at death £2785 8s. 8¾d.: CLRO, orphans inventory, common serjeants' book 4, fols. 174, 206, 28 March 1682, and then augmented

Brome, James (1651/2–1719), Church of England clergyman and travel writer, was born in Cambridge, the son of William Brome. He was educated at Newark School until 1663, then at King Edward VI Free Grammar School, Bury St Edmunds, being admitted sizar at Christ's College, Cambridge, with an annual exhibition of £5. He graduated BA in 1670/71, MA in 1677. Ordained priest in 1673, he was appointed vicar of Newington, near Hythe, Kent, in 1674 and additionally rector of Cheriton in 1679, holding both appointments until his death. His marriage, aged twenty-six, at Canterbury Cathedral on 27 June 1677 to Priscilla Johnson of Canterbury brought them four children: Margaret (b. 1678), James (b. 1679), William (b. 1682), and Priscilla (b. 1684).

Brome first ventured into print with two fast sermons, delivered on 13 November 1678 and 11 April 1679 and published together as *The Famine of the Word Threatened to Israel and God's Call to Weeping and to Mourning* (1679). Dedicated to his 'most honoured Friend and patron' James Brockman, and his wife, Lucy, these fiercely anti-Catholic works called England to repentance and to unity in the face of popish and Jesuit plotting to reimpose a 'Romish yoke'. With her clergy unappreciated and herself the subject of 'unjust prejudices', the Church of England, established in purity by God's providence, was in danger of subversion by sin, wreckers, and dissension from within.

Brome's edition of the *Treatise of the Roman Ports and Forts in Kent* (1693), left in manuscript by the antiquary William Somner (1598–1669), was dedicated to Henry, Viscount Sidney. When Sidney, by this time earl of Romsey, was on 1 June 1694 installed as warden of the Cinque Ports, Brome, as chaplain to the institution, preached the sermon. *A Sermon at St Mary's Church in Dover* (1694) celebrated the righteous magistrate in general and the heroic King William in particular, and called on subjects to do their duty without complaint.

The *Historical Account of Mr R. Rogers's Three Years' Travels over England and Wales* (1694) was later admitted to be by Brome; in the preface to his own *Travels over England, Scotland and Wales* (1700) Brome claimed that it had only recently come to his notice that his own *Travels* had been brought out in an imperfect form under Rogers's name. A second edition was published in 1707. The book was allegedly written for the two eldest sons of van Ackar, a Dutch merchant, whom Brome had encountered on their travels. It seems unlikely however that Brome had ever ventured far beyond his own library, since each place receives only a brief historical summary, with the notable exception of Cambridge, where Christ's College receives a true description extending over several pages. The *Dictionary of National Biography*'s attribution of *Travels through Portugal, Spain and Italy* (1712) to Brome is now discounted. Brome died in 1719, the exact date and his place of burial being unknown.

ANITA McCONNELL and VIVIENNE LARMINIE

Sources E. Hasted, *The history and topographical survey of the county of Kent*, 3 (1790), 392, 399 · Venn, *Alum. Cant.* · *N&Q*, 3rd ser., 3 (1863), 49 · S. H. A. H. [S. H. A. Hervey], *Biographical list of boys educated at King Edward VI Free Grammar School, Bury St Edmunds, from 1550 to 1900* (1908)

Brome, Richard (*c*.1590–1652), playwright, is of unknown birth and parentage. It has been suggested that he came from Cornwall, since his plays make several detailed allusions to the county and preserve one of the few surviving scraps of Middle Cornish speech, but this necessarily remains speculative (Jonson, *Magnetic Lady*, 220–22). There is no clear evidence concerning his date of birth. On the basis of the prologue to *The Court Beggar* (1640), which refers to 'the poet full of age and care' (Brome, 1.184), scholars have adopted *c*.1590 as a plausible birth date but it could well have been significantly earlier. Though three Richard Bromes born *c*.1589–90 have been found in legal and baptismal records, it is impossible to know whether any was the dramatist (Kaufmann, 175). The only certainties are that Brome's background was humble and that much of his early life was spent as a servant, working in

Reader, lo heere thou wilt two faces finde,
One of the body, t'other of the Minde- ;
This by the Graver so, that with much strife
Wee thinke Brome dead, hee's drawne so to the life
That by's owne pen's done so ingeinously
That who reads it, must thinke hee nere shall dy.
                                                    A·B·
            T. Croße sculp̃it.

Richard Brome (*c*.1590–1652), by Thomas Cross, pubd 1653

London for the poet and dramatist Ben Jonson. His posthumous editor Alexander Brome (who was not a relative) said 'Poor he came into th' world and poor went out' (Brome, 2.vii–viii) and compared him to authors like Aesop or Plautus, who were born into slavery or worked in mean occupations (ibid., xvii).

Association with Jonson Brome is first named in Ben Jonson's *Bartholomew Fair* (1614). In the induction the stage keeper at the Hope playhouse in Southwark warns that the play is too clever but lowers his voice 'lest the poet hear me, or his man, Master Brome, behind the arras' (*Ben Jonson*, 6.13). In 1632 Jonson described Brome as 'my old faithful servant, and, by his continued virtue, my loving friend', calling him Dick and praising his 'faithful parts' (ibid., 8.409). Though the precise dates of his employment are unknown Brome spent some time with Jonson; since Jonson calls his service a 'prenticeship' at least seven years seem to be implied. He would have worked at Jonson's house in Blackfriars, although the poet's household was not stable, for he was away in 1612–13 and 1618–19 and for one five-year period was lodging nearby with his patron,

Esmé Stuart, Seigneur d'Aubigny. None the less as Jonson's 'man' Brome would have seen a remarkable literary circle; Jonson maintained friendships with aristocrats, scholars, and poets and liked to think of his house as a place where his friends would find intellectual stimulus mixed with conviviality.

It seems likely that Brome sometimes acted as Jonson's literary factotum. The only half-facetious pretence that he was backstage at the first performance of *Bartholomew Fair* suggests that he negotiated between poet and actors, and other allusions to Jonson's 'man'—though not necessarily referring to Brome—exemplify literary tasks that he could have performed. In 1607 and 1608 'Mr Johnson's man' was paid for transcribing parts for dramatic entertainments commissioned from Jonson by the Merchant Taylors' Company and the earl of Salisbury (Guildhall Library, Merchant Taylors' accounts, vol. 9, p. 17; Hatfield House, bills, 35/1a). Another task appears in Jonson's epigram 'Inviting a Friend to Supper' (c.1610), which promises a visitor an evening of conviviality at which:

> my man
> Shall read a piece of Virgil, Tacitus,
> Livy, or of some better book to us,
> Of which we'll speak our minds amidst our meat.
> (*Ben Jonson*, 8.65)

Even if Brome was not in Jonson's employ as early as this, such remarks suggest the kinds of duties the poet required. Yet Brome's day-to-day tasks were clearly very menial. When in 1629 Jonson was piqued that Brome's play 'The Lovesick Maid' succeeded just as his own *The New Inn* failed he wrote verses accusing the audience of preferring 'Brome's sweepings' before 'the best ordered meal' (ibid., 6.493). The pun on Brome's name (which was pronounced Broom) satirizes the offending play as a leftover dropped by the master and reminds Brome of his place—to ensure Jonson's domestic tidiness. In his prefatory verses for the collected plays of Beaumont and Fletcher (1647) Brome called himself an 'old serving-creature' or a porter holding the gate for his betters.

Inevitably Brome later found it hard to avoid writing in Jonson's shadow. Many of his plays borrow Jonsonian plot motifs, and eccentric 'humours' characters were always part of his dramaturgy. Perhaps Jonson gave him some literary training, as he did to another protégé, the actor Nathan Field, who studied Horace and Martial with him. Jonson's verses to Brome praise him for learning well

> those comic laws
> Which I, your master, first did teach the age
> (*Ben Jonson*, 8.409)

and Brome's friend John Hall wrote in 1652 that 'by great Jonson [you] were made free o'th'trade' (Brome, 3.347). But while Brome absorbed Jonson's methods his drama drew on a deliberately wide range of models, and too much focus on his employer eclipses the equally formative influence of other playwrights. With their citizen heroes, scepticism about courtiers, and ironically moralistic endings his comedies are as much Middletonian as Jonsonian, while in verses praising *The Northern Lass* Thomas Dekker enthusiastically claimed Brome as his

'son' (ibid., 3.xi). At the height of his career Brome's closest professional links were with Thomas Heywood, with whom he co-authored three plays, but rather than identifying self-consciously with any literary school he preferred to represent himself (somewhat misleadingly) as a simple, conscientious craftsman, writing plays notable for 'mirth and sense' (ibid., 1.104). The tone of his prologues and epilogues was always studiously self-deprecatory, and the friends with whom he exchanged commendatory verses were men like Shakerley Marmion, Robert Chamberlain, John Tatham, Thomas Jordan, and Thomas Nabbes—minor poets, miscellanists, and jobbing playwrights scraping a living at the lower end of the literary marketplace (Butler, 185–90). He liked to describe himself as a

> plain poet, who cannot forget
> His wonted modesty
> (ibid., 2.86)

and 'never spilt ink, except in comedy' (Bentley, 3.54).

Early dramatic career At some time during the 1620s Brome moved into theatre on his own account. In 1623 a now lost play, 'A Fault in Friendship', 'by Young Johnson, and Brome', was licensed for the Prince's Men, who were performing at the Curtain, one of London's amphitheatre playhouses at the popular end of the market. Nothing more is known of this play, nor of 'Young Johnson', who was apparently unrelated to the poet. Brome next surfaces in 1628, on a list of the Queen of Bohemia's players sworn as grooms of the chamber (Bentley, 1.188). This was a troupe of strolling actors who appear intermittently in provincial records and whose leaders had earlier been members of Lady Elizabeth's Men. This evidence is generally thought too slight to establish that Brome followed an early career as a player, though since the affairs of the Prince's and Lady Elizabeth's Men often intersected it is possible that his connection was long-standing. It has been conjectured that Brome and George Chapman wrote their lost play 'Christianetta, or, Marriage and Hanging Go by Destiny' for the Prince's Men (ibid., 3.59). A link with either company would account for Brome's friendship with Dekker, who wrote for both.

Brome's writing career took off in 1629, when he achieved two big successes with London's premier company, the King's Men: 'The Lovesick Maid, or, The Honour of Young Ladies' (licensed on 9 February) and *The Northern Lass* (first acted on 29 July, published in 1632). 'The Lovesick Maid' is lost but it was so popular that the company made the master of the revels an *ex gratia* payment of £2 and Jonson, smarting from the recent failure of *The New Inn*, was provoked into lampooning the audience's taste. *The Northern Lass* was equally successful. This first surviving play is a characteristically involved comedy with frenetically complicated plotting among three interlinked city families. Brome borrows many Jonsonian motifs but gives them a typically subversive twist; no sooner has the courtier Sir Philip Luckless married the city widow Mrs Fitchow than they discover their incompatibility, and the rest of the play details their stratagems for tricking each other into divorce. Brome populates this anti-romantic plot with a gallery of fantastic comic types—the foolish magistrate, witty servant, idiotic younger brother, bragging tutor, and cunning whore—but anchors it emotionally in the person of the country lass, Constance, who runs mad for love after a single encounter with Sir Philip, expressing her sorrows in a string of melancholy ballads. As in most Brome plays, though matters end well pragmatism prevails over idealism; unwanted liaisons are avoided but the play draws back from endorsing marriage as an easy solution to anyone's problems. This happy combination of farce and sentiment proved attractive, and the central character was much admired; the prologue to T. B.'s *The Country Girl* (1632?) praised 'that brave blithe girl' and she was celebrated in several ballads (Bentley, 3.6, 83). *The Northern Lass* became Brome's first publication, printed in 1632 with a fanfare of commendatory verses and a dedication to Richard Holford, a Cheshire gentleman residing in London.

In the following years Brome wrote at least two, possibly three more plays for the King's Men: *The Novella* (1632, published 1653), *The Late Lancashire Witches* (July 1634, published 1634; co-authored with Heywood), and, perhaps, *The Queen's Exchange* (usually dated *c*.1631, though conceivably later; published 1657). But with his popular and satirical bent he was not a natural King's Men dramatist; as the stiffly romantic formulae of *The Novella* suggest he may have been uncomfortable with the styles prevailing at the exclusive Blackfriars theatre. By contrast *The Late Lancashire Witches*—with its scenes depicting a world turned hilariously upside down by old women's magical powers—was written for the Globe, the company's outdoor playhouse, where his carnivalesque comedy was more at home. This subject was topical, for the witchcraft trials it depicted were still *sub judice*; indeed someone gave the authors access to confidential documents, perhaps hoping their play would influence the court's judgment. As for that fantastic and eventful Anglo-Saxon tragicomedy *The Queen's Exchange*, since the King's Men connection was not asserted until 1655 it could well have belonged to some other company. With its sensational plot, jokes about flattering courtiers, and disparaging treatment of a queen who sets private desires above her country's laws, *The Queen's Exchange* seems unlike standard Blackfriars fare and closer to the popular, politically subversive comedies that Brome wrote later in the decade. Certainly by January 1634 he had become temporarily settled with the Prince's Men at the rather downmarket Red Bull playhouse in Clerkenwell.

During these years Brome had probably been working with several companies as a jobbing dramatist. Possibly some of his lost plays and collaborations with Heywood belong to this period, such as 'The Apprentice's Prize' and 'The Life and Death of Sir Martin Skink, with the Wars of the Low Countries' (titles that sound most suited to the plebeian amphitheatres). Of his surviving plays it has been suggested that *The City Wit* (1629–30?, published 1653) was written for the new boys' troupe, the King's Revels, at the Salisbury Court playhouse in Whitefriars (Bentley, 3.60). A farcical intrigue similar to *The Northern*

Lass, this has many parts for women or boys and features songs, disguises, and parodic humour well calculated for the talents of youthful actors. It is also socially combative, for its hero, Crazy, is a small citizen bankrupted by gentlemen who owe him money and harassed by a domineering wife. The plot charts his ingenious revenges and culminates with a typical Bromean apocalypse that somehow manages to be both moralistic and anarchic. *The New Exchange* (*c*.1632?, published 1658) is difficult to place chronologically but its over-burdened plot and throng of Jonsonian and Middletonian eccentrics suggest that it too was an early play. Much the most considerable of Brome's early plays is *The Weeding of Covent Garden* (*c*.1633, published 1658), the auspices of which are unknown (it is often linked to the Blackfriars but with little evidence). This virtually plotless satire, called a 'facetious comedy' on its title-page, presents a multi-faceted panorama of London's newly fashionable West End and the various social types who frequent it. Brome's Covent Garden is full of swaggering cavaliers and fanatical puritans, and while he satirizes their rampant individualism they also seem intended as symptomatic of failures of authority in contemporary society at large. If the play's social ideal is a wise paternalism it cannot be found in the fathers and magistrates who try to police this suburb, for their whimsical unpredictability is the underlying source of Covent Garden's problems. This panoramic style, depicting familiar environments and anatomizing society's problems in a playful but incisive manner, would become a hallmark of Brome's drama.

Salisbury Court plays In 1635 Brome began what should have been a more settled period as house dramatist at the Salisbury Court, a fashionable indoor theatre competing directly with the Blackfriars. He was first approached by the manager, Richard Gunnell, in early 1634, while at the Red Bull, and signed a three-year contract in July 1635, undertaking to write exclusively for the theatre and to supply three plays a year for 15*s*. a week plus one day's profits on each play. This is the only such formal contract that we know of from the pre-civil war period. Other dramatists must have had comparable agreements but Brome's is the only one of which details survive and is further unusual in binding the playwright to work exclusively for a single theatre. Unfortunately the security it promised did not last. Brome wrote two plays for the Salisbury Court, *The Sparagus Garden* (1635, published 1640), which he later claimed earned them £1000, and *The Queen and Concubine* (probably 1636 according to Butler, 42, published 1659), but in April 1636 the London theatres were closed by plague and they remained shut until October 1637. Brome's salary dried up and he turned to Christopher Beeston, manager of the Cockpit theatre in Drury Lane, who in August 1636 advanced him £6 on promise of a play. This prompted the Salisbury Court to offer him a new interim salary but this too stopped and he again resorted to Beeston. Eventually the master of the revels, Sir Henry Herbert, negotiated a compromise between playwright and company, and once the theatres reopened Brome served out his contract, albeit ending several plays in arrears. In August 1638 he was offered a new contract, for seven years at 20s. a week and with a requirement to supply the plays still owing. But relations with the company continued to sour and in April 1639 he finally abandoned them for the Cockpit, now under Beeston's son William, which was rapidly consolidating its reputation as, after the Blackfriars, London's second theatre. The Salisbury Court players were outraged and commenced a legal action for breach of contract. More woundingly they attacked Brome from their stage, reviving Thomas Goffe's *The Careless Shepherdess* with a specially composed induction ridiculing some of the plays that he had written for them—an assault to which Brome replied in the epilogue to his *The Court Beggar* (1640).

In his plays for the Salisbury Court, Brome had continued to develop his popular, satirical, and contemporary vein but with an increasing astringency and political edge. His most characteristic work is seen in the four comedies, *The Sparagus Garden* (1635), *The English Moor* (1637, published 1658), *The Damoiselle* (1637–8, published 1653), and *The Antipodes* (1638, published 1640). All of these display his well-calculated mix of farce, fantasy, melodrama, and sentiment, their topical and quasi-realistic London settings being a notch below the fashionable urban society presented in the plays of James Shirley. The first three are similar in form, for each presents a series of parallel actions that seem to proceed independently of each other but turn out to be intricately interlocked. They centre emotionally on the stories of young amorous couples, whose desire to marry for love gets blocked by the confusions of an urban milieu thronged with cranky gentlemen, calculating citizens, untrustworthy gallants, and greedy usurers, whose eccentricities provide most of the entertainment. Generally the lovers' difficulties are resolved by the discovery of siblings forgotten or neglected by their parents so that it typically turns out to be the fathers who are symbolically to blame for the plays' problems. This generational emphasis recalls the comedies of Thomas Middleton but Brome's plots focus less on contests over individual inheritance than on the recovery of a collective social health. The children's frustrations are traced to paternal folly or incompetence, and each plot saves the younger generation by forcing the older to reform, giving the plays a markedly progressive edge. In the later plays this reforming structure is extended into a more overtly political preoccupation with social wrongs. In *The Damoiselle* the fathers are mixed up with extortion and legal chicanery, allowing Brome to imply that his characters' wrongs are generic to the financial and legal systems in which they get entangled. In *The Antipodes*, his most ambitious play, a clan of sexually frustrated Londoners are cured by the performance of a play set in a fantasy Anti-London that provocatively inverts all the hierarchies of the normal world, thereby linking the recovery of psychic health to the cure of social deformities. Normal service is eventually resumed but the play leaves open the question of whether London or Anti-London is to be preferred.

This political edge was even sharper in Brome's other Salisbury Court plays, the parody tragicomedies *The Queen and Concubine* (1636) and *The Lovesick Court* (1638 according to Bawcutt, 202; published 1658). These are fantastic, pseudo-historical tales, set in a notionally remote Sicily and Thessaly, that obliquely but pointedly evoke some of the constitutional anxieties posed by King Charles's personal rule. In *The Queen and Concubine* the Sicilian king puts away his queen and her supporters for love of a concubine, who promptly plunges his rule into chaos through her tyrannical and self-serving behaviour. In a fantasy ending the state is saved by the loyalty to the old ways of the king's rustic subjects and those courtiers he cast into disfavour, while the play's most ridiculed figure is the courtier whose slavish obedience to the crown now seems quite misplaced. In *The Lovesick Court* business is similarly disrupted by the inability of the princess to choose between the two aristocratic brothers who are her suitors and their equally absurd unwillingness to damage their friendship by advancing their own private claims. Once again the aristocrats seem incapable of managing their own affairs and the court has to be protected against itself by the rural peasantry, who prevent the ambitious courtier Stratocles from using the power vacuum to seize rule for himself. It is difficult not to read these plays, with their combative themes and ironical handling of romantic motifs, as offering a critical perspective on the court, both politically and in terms of Whitehall's theatrical tastes.

Cockpit plays At William Beeston's Cockpit, with its varied repertoire of old and new, popular and sophisticated, Brome finally joined a theatre where he seemed at home. Only three plays survive from his post-1638 work but this was still an eventful period. Beeston revived *The Northern Lass* and may have restaged *The City Wit* and *The Weeding of Covent Garden*, each of which have revival prologues; meanwhile in 1639 Brome oversaw the publication of John Fletcher's *The Night Walker*, a play from the Cockpit repertory. The following year he published two of his Salisbury Court plays, dedicating *The Sparagus Garden* to the earl of Newcastle and *The Antipodes* to the earl of Hertford; he also wrote verses praising Newcastle's play *The Variety* and presented Hertford with a manuscript of *The English Moor*. These aristocratic connections are straws in the wind and signs of Brome's increasingly politicized outlook. Newcastle, though a courtier, was disenchanted with what he saw as Caroline Whitehall's Frenchified tendencies, and Hertford was widely perceived as a court critic, an associate of the earl of Essex, and an enthusiast for parliament. In Brome's later prologues his animosity towards the centre comes out strongly both on professional and ideological grounds. The prologue to *The Antipodes* ridicules the ostentatious but empty 'love and honour' drama produced by the new breed of amateur gentleman-playwrights such as William Davenant, Sir John Suckling, and Thomas Killigrew, whose plays were in vogue and were beginning to damage the livelihood of established playwrights like Brome. *The Damoiselle*'s prologue transparently attacks Davenant's laureate pretensions and distinguishes Brome from

> those, whose towering muses scale the throne
> Of kings.
> (Brome, 1.377)

A Mad Couple Well Matched begins by pouring scorn on 'the compliments, the trips and dances' of fashionable plays (Brome, 1.x).

The implications of Brome's dedications are writ large in the events of 4 May 1640, when Beeston was arrested and the theatre closed down for three days for having performed an unlicensed play that included satirical allusions to the king's recent, and disastrous, military campaign against the Scots. Almost certainly this was Brome's *The Court Beggar* (published 1653), which includes a character transparently lampooning Suckling, whose battlefield conduct had been notoriously incompetent. Suckling was an enemy for being one of the most prominent of the courtly amateurs, who had recently published his tragicomedy *Aglaura* in an ostentatiously expensive folio. Brome's prologue ridiculed the 'new strain of wit', 'love-toys', and 'gaudy scenes' enjoyed by upmarket audiences, and he derided *Aglaura* in a separate poem: 'Never did I see … so little in so much' (Brome, 1.184, 2.175). However, the play also extended its attack to strictly political targets, in the title character Mendicant, who is satirized for his begging of projects, monopolies, and other favours typical of the financial exigencies to which Caroline courtiers resorted. In the spectacular final scene the monopolist enters decked with the symbols of his patents; these are pulled from him and his 'projectors' are thrust out—and all this at a moment when Charles's first parliament for eleven years, from which great changes were hoped, was newly in session. Brome himself seems to have escaped questioning but it is little wonder that Beeston was removed as the company's governor and replaced with Davenant as a safer pair of hands.

Brome's other Cockpit plays are equally remarkable. *A Mad Couple Well Matched* (1638–9, published in *Five New Plays*, 1653) is one of the period's most radical re-examinations of sexual relations within the gentry household and tilts at a series of sacred cows via the careers of the rake, Careless, his aunt, Lady Thrivewell, and his uncle's mistress, Alicia Saleware. Though Careless's gentility allows his promiscuity to be condoned he still emerges as a rather unpleasant, self-serving individual. As for the women, Alicia is punished for adultery but Lady Thrivewell acts with an independence that undermines orthodox assumptions about female behaviour. As in other Brome plays, a framework of traditional values (in this case the sexual double standard) remains but all its inner assumptions are unsettled. This tendency is even more apparent in *A Jovial Crew, or The Merry Beggars* (1641, published 1652), Brome's last surviving and best play. Written after Davenant's fall and Beeston's return as manager, this comedy charts the adventures of a group of genteel lovers who, bored with the inexplicable melancholy of their parent Oldrents, resolve to discover what life is

like among the beggars. But, faced with the reality of the beggars' world, their naïve expectations about finding a world free from everyday responsibilities quickly collapse. A fantasy ending guarantees a happy outcome but the whole adventure returns them, chastened, to their ordinary lives, and the beggars perform a masque that predicts ominously how the country, city, and court, if they are cudgelled by the soldier, will be overcome by the beggar. The lovers' flight from their cares resonates with current apprehensions about the political future of the nation, and although the play expresses nostalgia for old ways it presents little grounds for supposing either that traditional society is perfect or that it is likely to last. It ends in a kind of political agnosticism, fearful about events to come but equally disenchanted with the past.

Final years and reputation Brome's playwrighting career ended abruptly on 2 September 1642, when the London theatres were closed by parliament, not to reopen for eighteen years. Appropriately enough *A Jovial Crew* was playing at the Cockpit on the day that the order was made but the closure was catastrophic for its author. He disappears immediately from the record, not to re-emerge until the publication of his commendatory poem in the 1647 Beaumont and Fletcher folio. Possibly he was sustained in the intervening years by the generosity of patrons. In 1649 he was the editor responsible for *Lachrymae musarum*, a collection of elegies on the death of Henry, Lord Hastings, and in 1652 *A Jovial Crew* was printed with a dedication to Sir Thomas Stanley, who befriended James Shirley, Richard Lovelace, and others. However, it seems clear that Brome ended his life in poverty, for on 25 March 1650 he entered the Charterhouse, a charitable institution in London, where he remained until his death on 24 September 1652. Two collections of his plays were edited by Alexander Brome, in 1653 and 1659, but it is a melancholy end for a writer who, in the lawsuit with the Salisbury Court, had at last begun to call himself a 'gentleman'.

Brome has since experienced much neglect. His comedy has often seemed too directly reflective of topical matters to be worth retrieving and his frankness over sexual matters did not recommend him to the early Victorian editors who did so much to recover the work of his contemporaries. Yet his fertile strain of fantasy kept some plays alive well into the eighteenth century. *The Northern Lass* was revived after the Restoration and was reprinted in 1663, 1684, 1706, and 1717. Aphra Behn adapted *A Mad Couple Well Matched* as *The Debauchee* (1677), and *The City Wit* and *The Court Beggar* were pillaged for George Powell's *A Very Good Wife* (1693). The most enduring of all has been *A Jovial Crew*. Pepys saw it four times and in the eighteenth century it was scarcely off the boards, especially after being remade in 1731 into a light-hearted ballad opera, with upwards of sixty musical numbers. The Royal Shakespeare Company revived it successfully in 1992, in an adaptation by Stephen Jeffreys, and *The Antipodes* was revived at the Globe in 2000.

Modern scholarship has been slow to recognize Brome's importance but he is now increasingly regarded as the last major dramatist to emerge before the playhouses closed.

His writing is all the more significant for bridging the élite and popular traditions, and for going against the grain of the courtly idealism or genteel good manners that prevailed in the plays of his politer contemporaries. His work kept older and socially inclusive dramatic modes current to the very end of the theatrical Renaissance, and his drama's playful ironies, sceptical questioning, and overt (if inconsistent) radicalism ensured that these traditional forms were handled with an unpredictable subversiveness and sophistication. His achievement was to ensure that the English Renaissance drama remained challenging and provocative down to its latest historical moment.   MARTIN BUTLER

Sources R. Brome, *Dramatic works*, ed. J. Pearson, 3 vols. (1873) · R. J. Kaufmann, *Richard Brome, Caroline playwright* (1961) · G. E. Bentley, *The Jacobean and Caroline stage*, 7 vols. (1941–68) · A. Haaker, 'The plague, the theatre and the poet', *Renaissance Drama*, new ser., 1 (1968), 283–306 · R. C. Evans, 'Richard Brome's death', *N&Q*, 234 (1989), 351 · M. Butler, *Theatre and crisis, 1632–1642* (1984) · *Ben Jonson*, ed. C. H. Herford, P. Simpson, and E. M. Simpson, 11 vols. (1925–52) · H. Berry, 'The Globe bewitched and *El hombre fiel*', *Medieval and Renaissance Drama in England*, 1 (1984), 211–30 · A. Gurr, *The Shakespearian playing companies* (1996) · B. Jonson, *The magnetic lady*, ed. P. Happe (2000) · *The control and censorship of Caroline drama: the records of Sir Henry Herbert, master of the revels, 1623–73*, ed. N. W. Bawcutt (1996) · A. Thaler, 'Was Richard Brome an actor?', *Modern Language Notes*, 36 (1921), 88–91

Likenesses T. Cross, line engraving, BM, NPG; repro. in R. Brome, *Five new playes* (1653) [*see illus.*] · pen-and-ink drawing (after engraving), NPG

Brome, Thomas (d. c.1380), Carmelite friar, joined that order in London and studied at Cambridge, being ordained acolyte on 28 March 1338. On 15 April 1353 he obtained a papal indulgence to choose his own confessor, and in 1358 he incepted as DTh at Oxford. He then taught in the Carmelite studium in London, where he was prior for a time. At the provincial chapter in Cambridge in 1362 Brome was elected provincial, a position he held for the next seventeen years. He travelled abroad on the order's business, attending general chapters, and, on 10 October 1375, he was at the papal court in Avignon, together with another English Carmelite, Thomas Maldon (d. 1404). Brome was outstanding for his reforming zeal and John Bale, referring to lost provincial records, writes that:

> he revived many forgotten customs of the holy fathers to their original purity. He was a great lover of chastity and so had a keen devotion to St John the Evangelist and St Edward the Confessor, erecting statues of them in all the houses. When he visited a community, his first concern was the chapel in order to improve and expand the liturgy. All saw him as a model of the true contemplative and an exemplary religious. A visit from him brought health to the sick and joy to the faithful. (BL, Harley MS 3838, fols. 78–78v)

Brome resigned from his office in 1379 and retired to the Carmeline house in London where he died and was buried, probably the following year. Four works by him are recorded: the lectures he gave at Oxford when he incepted, a commentary on St Paul's epistle to the Romans, a collection of sermons, and a work on the scriptures. None survives, although Leland saw a copy of the Oxford lectures in the Carmelite house in London, in 1533–4.   RICHARD COPSEY

Sources J. Bale, Bodl. Oxf., MS Bodley 73 (SC 27635), fols. 3, 40, 51, 80v, 118, 133, 205 · J. Bale, Bodl. Oxf., MS Selden supra 41, fol. 170 · J. Bale, BL, Harley MS 3838, fols. 78–78v · *CEPR letters*, 3.505 · B. de Cathaneis, ed., *Speculum ordinis fratrum Carmelitarum* (Venice, 1507), 83v · J. Bale, *Illustrium Maioris Britannie scriptorum … summarium* (1548), fol. 163 · Bale, *Cat.*, 1.486 · Emden, *Oxf.*, 1.275 · Emden, *Cam.*, 95–6 · *Commentarii de scriptoribus Britannicis, auctore Joanne Lelando*, ed. A. Hall, 2 (1709), 375

Bromfield, Edmund de. *See* Bramfield, Edmund (d. 1393).

Bromfield, William (bap. 1713, d. 1792), surgeon, the son of Thomas Bromfield, a physician, and his wife, Mary, daughter of William *Briggs (c.1650–1704), was born in New North Street, Holborn, London, and baptized at St Andrew's, Holborn, on 30 July 1713. He had a brother, James (d. 1790), and a sister, Hannah. Bromfield was introduced into surgery by John Ranby and by 1736 he was married to Irene Heriot, living in Fetherstone Buildings, Holborn, and practising surgery. There were at least two children from this marriage: William Heriot (bap. 1736, d. 1762), who became a physician, and Charles (bap. 1748, d. 1784), who followed his father into surgery. In 1735 Bromfield was lecturing in anatomy and the following year published *Syllabus anatomicus*. He was appointed demonstrator of anatomy at Barber–Surgeons' Hall in 1744. He is also known to have bought the anatomical collections of Francis Sandys, which he later sold to William Hunter for £200.

Bromfield had become a governor of St George's Hospital, London, in 1743 and went on to be appointed surgeon there a year later. He held the post until 1780. In 1746 he was the principal actor in the founding of the Lock Hospital, which opened in July that year, with Bromfield serving as its surgeon until 1769. Some years later, along with Martin Madan, he organized a performance of an old comedy, *The City Match*, altered for the occasion by Bromfield himself, in order to raise funds for the hospital.

Bromfield held a number of other posts: he was appointed surgeon to Prince Frederick in 1745 and to the queen's household in 1769. At the Company of Surgeons he was made a member of the court of assistants (1760), the court of examiners (1768), and senior warden (1768).

Bromfield married for a second time in 1758, his wife being Anne Grover; there were no children from this marriage. Bromfield was a successful but not a particularly gifted surgeon. His writings are unexceptional and, like many eighteenth-century medical practitioners, he managed to get involved in a minor pamphlet war—his own was fought with George Aylett in 1759. He moved to Conduit Street in 1745 before settling for a time at Chelsea Park. His claim to the title of baronet has been shown to have been unfounded (Peachey). Bromfield died at his home in Conduit Street, and was buried on 24 November 1792. In his will he directed that all his property, except for his house and furniture at Conduit Street, be sold and the proceeds invested to provide an annuity of £200 to his friend Mrs Catriona Ryley, of St James's Place. He also left her some jewels and a portrait of his deceased wife, Anne.

To his friend, the surgeon John Griffiths, he left £1000, his surgical instruments, and manuscripts, together with his collection of medicinal recipes.   MICHAEL BEVAN

Sources G. C. Peachey, 'William Bromfield, 1713–1792', *Proceedings of the Royal Society of Medicine*, 8 (1914–15), 103–25 [section of the history of medicine] · *GM*, 1st ser., 62 (1792), 1062, 1158 · S. C. Lawrence, *Charitable knowledge: hospital pupils and practitioners in eighteenth-century London* (1996) · IGI
Likenesses B. Vandergucht, mezzotint, pubd 1777 (after J. R. Smith), BM, NPG · D. Orme, coloured engraving, 1792 (after R. Cosway), Wellcome L. · Coates, portrait, repro. in Peachey, 'William Bromfield, 1713–1792' · R. Cosway, portrait, repro. in Peachey, 'William Bromfield, 1713–1792' · B. Vandergucht, portrait, repro. in Peachey, 'William Bromfield, 1713–1792'
Wealth at death £1000 to John Griffiths; all property, except house and furniture in Conduit Street, to be sold to provide £200 annuity for Mrs Catriona Ryley

Bromfield, William Arnold (1801–1851), botanist, was born on 4 July 1801 at Boldre, New Forest, Hampshire, the only son of John Arnold Bromfield (c.1770–1801), priest, formerly of New College, Oxford. He was the grandson of Robert Bromfield (d. 1786), physician and fellow of the Royal Society. His father died in his first year and he was educated under Dr Knox of Tonbridge School, Dr Nicholas of Ealing, and the Revd Mr Phipps of Warwickshire. He entered Glasgow University in 1821 and took his degree in medicine in 1823. However, he had independent means and did not need to make a living from medicine. During his undergraduate years he became interested in botany, and made an excursion into the Scottish highlands in search of plants.

Bromfield was a versatile traveller. After leaving Scotland in 1826, he toured Germany, Italy, and France, returning to England in 1830. His mother died shortly afterwards and he lived with his sister at Hastings and Southampton, before finally settling at Ryde, Isle of Wight, in 1836. During this period he published many observations on Hampshire plants in *The Phytologist*, and began collecting materials for his (posthumous) *Flora Vectensis* (ed. Sir W. J. Hooker and T. B. Salter, 1856), which, despite fourteen years' labour, he never considered ready for publication. In 1842 he botanized for some weeks in Ireland, and in January 1844 he began a six-month tour of the West Indies, spending most of his time in Trinidad and in Jamaica. Two years later he visited North America, contributing some remarks on its climate and its plants to *Hooker's Journal of Botany* (1848–9). In September 1850 he embarked for the East, and spent some time in Egypt, ascending the Nile as far as Khartoum, which he described as a region of dust, dirt, and barbarism. After two of his companions succumbed to illness and died, he returned to Cairo in June 1851, travelled on to Syria, visited Jerusalem, and ended up in Damascus. Although he had originally planned to leave Constantinople for Southampton in September 1851, his last letter was sent from Beirut on 22 September. He arrived in Damascus in early October, only to fall ill with typhus. He died at Damascus on 9 October 1851, and was buried at the Christian burial-ground there.

Bromfield's letters from Egypt and Syria were printed for private circulation in 1856. He was regarded as a zealous naturalist and belonged to the Botanical Society of London. After his death his collections from Egypt and Syria were sent to Kew, and some of them were shared out among his scientific friends. The seeds were divided between Kew Gardens and a Mr Lawrence of the Isle of Wight. His herbarium passed into the possession of the Isle of Wight Philosophical Society, but his flora of Hampshire was never published.

B. D. JACKSON, rev. P. E. KELL

Sources *Proceedings of the Linnean Society of London*, 2 (1848–55), 182–3 · *Hooker's Journal of Botany and Kew Garden Miscellany*, 3 (1851), 373–82 · *GM*, 2nd ser., 36 (1851), 666 · F. Townsend, *Flora of Hampshire* (1883) · *Catalogue of scientific papers*, Royal Society, 1 (1867), 644 · W. A. Bromfield, preface, *Flora Vectensis*, ed. W. J. Hooker and T. B. Salter (1856) · Foster, *Alum. Oxon.* · Munk, *Roll* · Desmond, *Botanists*, rev. edn
Archives Carisbrooke Castle, Isle of Wight, Isle of Wight Philosophical Society archives · RBG Kew, corresp. and papers | RBG Kew, letters to Sir W. Hooker
Likenesses R. J. Lane, engraving on stone? (after drawing by Knowles), repro. in Bromfield, *Flora Vectensis*, frontispiece · R. J. Lane, lithograph (after Knowles), NPG · portrait, RBG Kew · portrait, Carnegie Mellon University, Pittsburgh, Pennsylvania, Hunt Institute

Bromhall, Andrew (bap. 1608, d. 1662), clergyman and ejected minister, was the son of Richard Bromhall of Shrewsbury and was baptized on 17 June 1608 at St Mary's Church in that town. On 25 January 1628 he matriculated as a commoner at Balliol College, Oxford, graduating BA on 26 January 1628 and MA on 1 June 1630. On 22 September 1633 he was ordained a deacon in the diocese of Wells. For the next few years the whereabouts of his ministry are unknown, but on 20 December 1638 he was instituted to the rectory of Athelhampton and on 2 April the following year added to this the rectory of Burleston. Bromhall held both these Dorset livings in 1642, when he signed the protestation. By an order of 10 June 1645 Matthew Osbourn, an MA and a founding fellow of Wadham College, Oxford, was sequestered from the rectory of Maiden Newton, having deserted his parish and returned to Oxford to join the royalists there; probably soon afterwards Bromhall was instituted to the valuable living, rated in 1650 at £130 per annum, with the glebe estimated at a further £50 per annum. As early as 7 January 1647 he was acting as a trier of other ministers under the authority of the Dorset standing committee.

It is not known when Bromhall married, but his wife, Frances, gave birth to at least two children, Richard and Frances, baptized at Maiden Newton on 27 September 1656 and 1 April 1659 respectively. After the Restoration, Osbourn, the sequestered rector, was restored, but there is no record of Bromhall's prior ejection. A note in the parish register recalls of the two men:

> Mr Osborne, MA who was unjustly turned out by the Rumpish Triers, and afterwards restored by the hand of providence. Mr Brumhall his base and unworthy successor, put in by that scandalous party and turned out by God Almighty. (Hutchins, 2.689)

If this is taken to mean that Bromhall died before his

removal could be effected by human agency, it is not quite accurate, for the record of his will describes him as 'late of Stoke Newington' (PRO, PROB 11/309, fol. 48). Evidently he had already left Dorset before he died, and moved to the environs of London. Thus it is quite possible, as Edmund Calamy suggested, that Bromhall preached the undated sermon 'How is hypocrisy discoverable and curable' (which was printed in Samuel Annesley's edition of *The Morning-Exercise at Cripple-Gate*, 1664) after the Restoration, while an unattached minister in London. But he did not preach at Cripplegate after the Act of Uniformity came into force, for the will is dated 25 August 1662, the day after the ejections of St Bartholomew's day. In his nuncupative will, the report of witnesses of the words he spoke from his deathbed, Bromhall left all his goods to his wife, Frances. He died very shortly after, probably closer to 25 August than to 30 September, when the will was proved by his widow.   STEPHEN WRIGHT

Sources Calamy rev. • Foster, *Alum. Oxon.* • J. Hutchins, *The history and antiquities of the county of Dorset*, 3rd edn, ed. W. Shipp and J. W. Hodson, 2 (1863) • C. H. Mayo, ed., *The minute books of the Dorset standing committee* (1902) • will, PRO, PROB 11/309, fol. 48 [quire 113] • S. Annesley, ed., *The morning-exercise at Cripple-gate*, [2nd edn] (1664)

Bromhead, Sir Edward Thomas Ffrench, second baronet

Bromhead, Sir Edward Thomas Ffrench, second baronet (1789–1855), mathematician and landowner, was born in Dublin on 26 March 1789, the eldest of three sons (there were no daughters) of General Gonville Bromhead (1758–1822) of Thurlby, Lincolnshire, who was created baronet in 1806, and his wife, Jane (d. 1837), youngest daughter of Sir Charles Ffrench, baronet. After schooling in Halifax and two years at Glasgow University he entered Gonville and Caius College, Cambridge, in June 1808.

Bromhead won the college mathematical prize in 1809 and graduated BA in 1812. He left Cambridge the following year, not having sat the mathematical tripos because of his delicate health, and became a barrister of the Inner Temple. In 1817 he was elected to a fellowship of the Royal Society, in whose *Philosophical Transactions* his sole mathematical paper, 'On the fluents of irrational functions', had appeared in 1816. He succeeded to the baronetcy in 1822 and spent the remainder of his life as a leading public figure in Lincoln, of which he became high steward, and its county.

Bromhead was a key figure in the renaissance of English mathematics brought about by the efforts of a generation of Cambridge mathematicians which included Sir John Herschel, George Peacock, and Charles Babbage. The Analytical Society, their pressure group for reform, was Bromhead's suggestion, mooted at a gathering in his lodgings in 1812, and he read a paper, 'On notation', at its first meeting. The prime object of the society was to secure the adoption of the continental, or Leibnizian, notation for the calculus, in preference to the Newtonian notation then used in England, and thereby to open English mathematics to the eighteenth-century continental developments. Bromhead was the link between the society and

Robert Woodhouse, a fellow of Caius who in 1803 had published the first book in England employing the continental notation, *Principles of Analytical Calculation*. When Bromhead contributed the article 'Differential calculus' to the 1819 supplement to the *Encyclopaedia Britannica* he emphasized Woodhouse's influence.

Bromhead rendered further service to mathematics through his support of two outstanding self-taught mathematicians from the east midlands, George Green and George Boole. Bromhead was a subscriber to Green's first memoir, published in 1828, and the contact led to Green's visiting Thurlby Hall and eventually to his career as a Caius undergraduate and fellow. Bromhead was active in communicating Green's later memoirs to the Cambridge Philosophical Society and the Royal Society of Edinburgh (of which Bromhead had been elected a fellow in 1823). George Boole's father had been curator of the Lincoln Mechanics' Institute when Bromhead was president, and the connection led to the latter's support and encouragement for the younger Boole, to whom he lent mathematical books.

Bromhead was shrewd in his advice and generous in his support. Kindness and humour shine through his letters. He combined the best English traditions of amateur science and patronage by the landed gentry, to the great benefit of mathematics. Always of weak constitution, he suffered progressively from blindness in his last years, and died, a bachelor, on 14 March 1855 at Thurlby Hall, Thurlby. His brother, Sir Edmund de Gonville Bromhead (1791–1870), succeeded as third baronet.

A. W. F. EDWARDS, rev.

Sources D. Phillips, *George Green: his academic career* (1976) • A. Hyman, *Charles Babbage: pioneer of the computer* (1982); repr. (1984) • D. MacHale, *George Boole, his life and work* (1985) • D. M. Cannell, *George Green: mathematician and physicist, 1793–1841* (1993) • J. Venn and others, eds., *Biographical history of Gonville and Caius College*, 8 vols. (1897–1998) • private information (1993) • d. cert. • M. Cannell, 'Sir Edward Ffrench Bromhead, 1789–1855', *The Caian* (1995–6), 126–35

Archives BL, letters to Charles Babbage, Add. MSS 37182–37185, *passim* • U. Edin. L., letters to James Halliwell-Phillipps

Bromley, Sir Edward

Bromley, Sir Edward (bap. 1563, d. 1626), judge, was probably born in the parish of Worfield, Shropshire, where he was baptized on 17 October 1563, the second son of Sir George Bromley (c.1526–1589) of Hallon in Worfield, Shropshire, chief justice of Chester and *custos rotulorum* of Shropshire, and his wife, Joan (1532/3–1606), daughter and heir of John Waverton of Worfield. Educated at Shrewsbury School, Bromley was admitted to the Inner Temple, of which his father had been treasurer, on 23 November 1580, shortly after the appointment as lord chancellor of his uncle, Sir Thomas Bromley, also a member of the Inner Temple. In 1586 he was returned to parliament for the borough of Bridgnorth, Shropshire, where by 1583 his father was recorder, and for which his uncle Sir Thomas Bromley had sat in 1558. Bromley continued to sit for Bridgnorth until becoming a judge, 'making no mark on the proceedings of the House' (Jones, 489), and in the last years of his life was recorder of the borough. On 18 April 1593 he married Margaret (d. 1657), daughter and heir of Nicholas

Lowe of Tymore, in the parish of Enville, Staffordshire. They had no children.

Bromley was called to the bar on 5 July 1590 and became a bencher of the Inner Temple on 19 May 1603. He was Lent reader in 1606, and acted frequently as an auditor of the steward's accounts. A justice of the peace in Shropshire by 1596, he became recorder of Much Wenlock, Shropshire, in 1607. In the following year he was temporarily appointed surveyor of lands in the south parts of the duchy of Lancaster, in hope of which office he had written to Sir Michael Hicks, secretary to Robert Cecil, earl of Salisbury, in July 1607. In 1614 he was reappointed to the surveyorship for life, with the succession in his kinsman Thomas Bromley, and by 1619 was recorder of Shrewsbury. Mr Baron Heron of the court of exchequer died in July 1609. Chosen as his successor, Bromley was created serjeant-at-law on 5 February 1610, and appointed a baron of the exchequer on the following day, the letter writer John Chamberlain noting the appointment as that of 'one Bromley, an obscure lawyer of the Inner Temple' (*Letters of John Chamberlain*, 1.296).

Bromley was knighted on 26 February 1610. He rode the northern circuit as a justice of assize between 1610 and 1618, and the midland circuit from 1618 until 1626. In 1611 he was one of those judges, named to the high commission by reworded letters patent, whom Sir Edward Coke led in refusing to sit or to take the oath as commissioners. In July and August 1612 Bromley presided with Mr Baron Altham over the trials at the York and Lancaster assizes of twenty alleged witches, eleven of whom were condemned to death. A report of the trials by Thomas Potts, a clerk at the assizes, commissioned by the judges and revised and corrected by Bromley, was published in 1613. In 1616 Bromley was among the judges who heard the *Case of Commendams* in spite of the attorney-general's letters demanding postponement of the trial, and who, abandoning the position of the chief justice, Sir Edward Coke, subsequently conceded a royal power to require prior consultation. In 1619, as recorder of Shrewsbury, Bromley was among those to whom the privy council delegated consideration of part of the long-running dispute between the drapers and mercers of Shrewsbury over control of the Welsh cloth trade. Bromley died on 2 June 1626, leaving his wife and John Bromley, grandson of his cousin Sir Henry Bromley of Holt, Worcestershire, as executors of his will, the overseers of which included 'my beloved friends and brethren' (will, PROB 11/150, sig. 128) Sir John Denham, baron of the exchequer, and Sir Richard Hutton, justice of the common pleas. Bromley's lands were devised to John Bromley, and his goods to his wife for life, together with bequests to his servants, and to the poor of the Shropshire towns of Bridgnorth, Much Wenlock, Sheriffhales, Shrewsbury, and Worfield. A substantial monument to Bromley and his wife was erected in St Peter's Church, Worfield, where he was buried on 12 June 1626.   N. G. JONES

Sources W. J. Jones, 'Bromley, Edward', HoP, *Commons, 1558–1603* · parish register, Worfield, St Peter's Church, 1562, Shrops.

RRC, P 314/A/1/1 · R. Tresswell and A. Vincent, *The visitation of Shropshire, taken in the year 1623*, ed. G. Grazebrook and J. P. Rylands, 1, Harleian Society, 28 (1889) · F. A. Inderwick and R. A. Roberts, eds., *A calendar of the Inner Temple records*, 1 (1896); 2 (1898) · will, PRO, PROB 11/150, sig. 128 · will, PRO, PROB 11/264 [Lady Bromley], sig. 196 · Foss, *Judges* · Sainty, *Judges* · J. Randall, *Worfield and its townships* (1887) · Baker, *Serjeants* · E. Calvert, ed., *Shrewsbury School regestum scholarium, 1562–1635: admittances and readmittances* [1892] · W. R. Williams, ed., *Official lists of the duchy and county palatine of Lancaster* (1901) · H. Owen and J. B. Blakeway, *A history of Shrewsbury*, 1 (1825) · J. S. Cockburn, *A history of English assizes, 1558–1714* (1972) · Borough of Bridgnorth, Third Great Leet Book, 1586–1684, Shrops. RRC, BB/F/1/1/3 · BL, Lansdowne MS 90 · *The letters of John Chamberlain*, ed. N. E. McClure, 1 (1939) · T. Potts, *The wonderfull discoverie of witches in the countie of Lancaster* (1613) · W. A. Shaw, *The knights of England*, 2 (1906) · memorial, St Peter's Church, Worfield, Shropshire
Likenesses effigy on monument, St Peter's Church, Worfield, Shropshire

Bromley, Henry. *See* Wilson, Anthony (1750?–1814?).

Bromley, James (1800–1838). *See under* Bromley, William (*bap.* 1769, *d.* 1842).

Bromley, John (*bap.* 1653, *d.* 1718), translator, was baptized on 5 June 1653 at St Julian's, Shrewsbury, the son of John Bromley, a burgess of the town, and his wife, Isabell. His father had been appointed to a parochial committee in 1647, when the town was in parliamentary hands. On 9 December 1663 Bromley entered Shrewsbury School, and on 29 March 1671 he was admitted as a pensioner to Magdalene College, Cambridge. He was licensed to preach by the bishop of London on 16 May 1677, and having graduated BA was appointed rector of Hadleigh, Essex, on 19 January 1680.

Bromley's incumbency was characterized by strife. Having sued his predecessor's widow for dilapidations in 1681 he aroused parish grievances by 1686 when he was presented by the grand jury for neglecting to maintain ditching and a gate. By 1687 he had become a Roman Catholic, though he retained his living, and on 25 February 1687 he was authorized by James II to keep schools, which authorization discharged him both from parochial duties and from canonical obedience. Following the revolution he was charged with 'not residing upon his said rectory for about three years last and for being a reputed papist' (Guildhall Library, LDR 9531/18, fol. 77v), and he was deprived of his living on 6 May 1689. According to the Catholic priest and historian Charles Dodd, having been a corrector of the press in the king's printing house Bromley ran a boarding-school in Bloomsbury, supposedly taught the poet Alexander Pope, and travelled abroad with pupils.

Dodd identified Bromley as the translator of *The Catechism for the Curats, Compos'd by the Decree of the Council of Trent* (1687), which a later translator of the catechism described as 'so unfaithful and even ludicrously absurd that it must be regarded rather as a burlesque than a translation of the decrees' (Gillow, *Lit. biog. hist.*, 1.310). Translation of *The Canons and Decrees of the Council of Trent* (1687) has also been attributed to him.

He was married to Mary Prichard (*d.* 1724), perhaps the daughter of Thomas Pritchard, a goldsmith in Drury Lane,

London. They had no surviving children. He returned to Shropshire and died at Madeley on 10 January 1718. He was buried at Madeley the next day.   ANDREW STARKIE

Sources C. Dodd [H. Tootell], *The church history of England, from the year 1500, to the year 1688*, 3 (1742), 459 · subscriptions books, bishop's register, GL, London diocesan MSS, 9540/2, fol. 7; 9540/3, fol. 14v; 9531/17, fol. 59v; 9531/18, fols. 77v–78 · *CSP dom.*, 1686–7, 374 [citing PRO, SP 44/337, pp. 205–9] · administration, PRO, PROB 6/94, fol. 72r; PROB 6/100, fol. 217r · Gillow, *Lit. biog. hist.*, 1.310 · *Transactions of the Shropshire Archaeological and Natural History Society*, 10 (1887), 289 · index to quarter sessions records, court in session: sessions roll epiphany 1686, presentments by grand jury, Essex RO, Q/SR 449/1 · W. Chaffers, *Gilda Aurifabrorum* (1899), 178 · Venn, *Alum. Cant.* · parish register, Shropshire, Madeley, 11 Jan 1718, Shrops. RRC [burial] · W. Kinsella, ed., *Shropshire parish registers: Roman Catholic registers*, Shropshire Parish Register Society (1913), with introduction by H. F. J. Vaughan · J. E. Auden, *Shrewsbury School register, 1636–1664* (1917), 67

Bromley, John (1876–1945), trade unionist, was born on 16 July 1876 at Haston Grove, Hadnall, Shropshire, the son of Charles Alfred Bromley, a dyer, and his wife, Martha Helen, *née* Wellings. He attended the local board school, followed by an upper grade church school until he was twelve. Straitened home circumstances then compelled him to work part-time, first as a country postboy at 4s. a week, then as a chemist's errand-boy, and finally on W. H. Smith & Sons' bookstall at Shrewsbury Station. This led to a job at the age of fourteen as an engine cleaner with the Great Western Railway (GWR) at 6s. a week.

John Bromley (1876–1945), by Walter Stoneman, 1930

Between August 1892 and March 1896 Bromley was employed as a spare main line fireman. Promotion to the grade of regular fireman entitled him to join the Associated Society of Locomotive Engineers and Firemen (ASLEF). He was subsequently active in the union branches around Shrewsbury, becoming secretary of the branch at Worcester; when he moved to Southall in London he served as secretary of the branch there also. On 6 March 1901 Bromley married Ann Hill (1880–1953) at Holy Trinity Church, Shrewsbury.

During the years down to 1905, when the GWR registered him as a driver, Bromley learned to appreciate the value of his skill and the need to defend its craft status against the claims of other railway workers. He attended the union's triennial conferences in 1903, 1906, and 1909 and was elected by national ballot in 1909 to be union organizer for the north of England, based at Manchester. From 1908 he represented ASLEF on the sectional conciliation board. When Albert Fox, ASLEF general secretary, resigned through ill health, Bromley was chosen by a clear majority to succeed him in October 1914. One of his major tasks in this role was to defend the craft status of his members from encroachment by the Amalgamated Society of Railway Servants. By virtue of both his office and his industrial experience, Bromley was appointed to the advisory committee of the Ministry of Transport during the war years of government direction of railways, 1914–18.

In domestic industrial policy Bromley achieved renown through his pursuit of a maximum eight-hour day for footplatemen. In August 1917 ASLEF gave notice of an official strike with this objective. During the war years, 1914–18, the rival union, the National Union of Railwaymen (NUR), negotiated flat-rate wage increases for all railway workers; but this eroded the differentials enjoyed by ASLEF members. In the event the government prohibited the strike under the terms of the Munitions Act of 1915; but Bromley secured from Albert Stanley, the president of the Board of Trade, a promise that the matter would be settled within a month of the end of the war. He kept Stanley to his promise, the formal agreement being signed by ASLEF's leaders on 2 December 1918, a few days before a similar agreement was reached with the NUR. In the following year he negotiated with the railway executive committee full standardization of locomotivemen's wages and conditions of service. These agreements proved to be an important boost to the morale of the craft union and helped secure its continuing independence from the much larger industrial union.

Bromley was a member of the Independent Labour Party (ILP) in the early post-war years. In the election of December 1918 he stood unsuccessfully as Labour candidate for Leeds North East. At Barrow in Furness in the general elections of 1922 and 1923 he came much nearer to success, and was elected there in 1924, gaining more than half the votes cast. He retained his seat in 1929 but resigned before the general election of 1931.

In 1921 the seventeen-member parliamentary committee of the TUC was replaced by a thirty-six-member general council, and John Bromley formed part of the new, and more left-wing, membership. He resigned his membership of the executive committee of the Labour Party after a year, however, to concentrate on the problems of trade unions nationally and internationally. In 1924 he was a member of the first TUC delegation to the Soviet Union. He nevertheless continued to defend his union's interests and between 20 and 29 January 1924 led a national strike of locomotivemen against the worsening of working conditions proposed by the national wages board.

On his retirement from his post as general secretary of the union in 1936 Bromley and his wife moved to Liskeard in Cornwall. He died from a cerebral haemorrhage at his home there, Mon Repos, Barras Cross, on 7 September 1945 and was cremated at Efford, Plymouth, on 11 September. His wife survived him by eight years.

PHILIP S. BAGWELL

Sources *Locomotive Journal* (Oct 1945) · P. Collick, funeral oration, 11 Sept 1945, Associated Society of Locomotive Engineers and Firemen archives, 9 Arkwright Road, London [delivered at Plymouth] · H. A. Clegg, A. Fox, and A. F. Thompson, *A history of British trade unions since 1889*, 2 (1985) · J. R. Raynes, *Engines and men* (1921) · N. McKillop, *The lighted flame: a history of the Associated Society of Locomotive Engineers and Firemen* (1950) · C. J. Wrigley, *Lloyd George and the challenge of labour: the post-war coalition, 1918–1922* (1990) · A. Briggs and J. Saville, eds., *Essays in labour history, 1918–1939* (1977) · J. T. Ward and W. H. Fraser, *Workers and employers* (1980), chap. 9 · G. A. Phillips, *The general strike: the politics of industrial conflict* (1976) · M. Morris, *The general strike* (1976) · private information (2004) · *CGPLA Eng. & Wales* (1946) · b. cert. · m. cert. · d. cert.
Archives U. Warwick Mod. RC | Associated Society of Locomotive Engineers and Firemen, London, archives · Trades Union Congress, London
Likenesses W. Stoneman, photograph, 1930, NPG [*see illus.*] · portrait, repro. in McKillop, *Lighted flame*, facing p. 98
Wealth at death £5540 15s. 5d.: probate, 12 Jan 1946, CGPLA Eng. & Wales

Bromley, Sir Richard Madox (1813–1865), civil servant, was born on 11 June 1813, the second son of Samuel Bromley (d. 1835), surgeon of the Royal Navy, and his wife, Mary, daughter of Tristram Maries Madox of Greenwich. He was educated at Lewisham grammar school, and in 1829 entered the Admiralty department of the civil service. His efficiency in procuring supplies for the troops quartered in London during the Reform Bill crisis of 1831–2 brought him to the notice of his superiors. He married on 6 July 1843 Clara, daughter of Robert Moser, a partner in the Crawshay ironworks, south Wales.

In 1846 Bromley was appointed by Lord Auckland to visit the dockyards on a confidential mission to investigate their economic management, shortly after which he was named accountant to the Burgoyne commission on the Irish famine. The system of accounting which he introduced to the famine relief commission achieved savings to the exchequer amounting to £½ million, which were favourably commented on in parliament. This success led to his appointment by Lord John Russell in June 1848 as secretary to the commission for auditing the public accounts. He introduced improvements to the department, including an examination for new appointments to weed out incompetent nominees. He was frequently

employed by successive prime ministers on special commissions of inquiry into public departments, including that appointed in 1849 for a revision of the dockyards, and that of 1853 on the contract packet system. In 1854 he was nominated CB. In February 1854, on the outbreak of war with Russia, he was appointed accountant-general of the navy, and was knighted on 6 September 1858. Ill health forced his retirement on 31 March 1863, when he was appointed a commissioner of Greenwich Hospital.

Although Bromley wished to raise the standard of recruits to the civil service, and was anxious to introduce promotion by merit, he doubted the benefits of the Northcote–Trevelyan proposals in 1853 to introduce open competition aimed at attracting university graduates.

> I have been bred in the Civil Service, having passed through the various gradations of a clerk career, without any interest or in any way seeking it, to the highest appointment in the department in which I commenced my career

he reflected in August 1854 (*Papers Relating to the Reorganisation of the Civil Service*, 1855, 52). Bromley died at 113 Marina, St Leonards, Sussex, on 30 November 1865, and was survived by his wife.

M. C. CURTHOYS

Sources *GM*, 4th ser., 1 (1866), 277–8 · *GM*, 2nd ser., 20 (1843), 312 · Boase, *Mod. Eng. biog.* · Walford, *County families* · [T. T. Shore], ed., *Cassell's biographical dictionary* (1867–9) · *DNB*
Archives BL, corresp. with Lord Halifax, Add. MS 49585, *passim* · Bodl. Oxf., letters to Benjamin Disraeli
Wealth at death under £4000: probate, 24 Jan 1866, CGPLA Eng. & Wales

Bromley, Sir Thomas (d. 1555), judge, was born about the end of the fifteenth century. He was the second son of Roger Bromley of Mitley, Shropshire, and Jane, daughter of Thomas Jennings of Church Pulverbatch. He was a cousin of George Bromley (d. 1534) of Hodnet, bencher of the Inner Temple and recorder of Shrewsbury. Thomas Bromley joined the Inner Temple about 1515, was temporarily put out of commons in 1519 for 'evilly behaving' himself, but was called to the bar soon afterwards and to the bench in 1533. His one and only reading was on the statute of 11 Hen. VII, c. 20, concerning the wrongful alienation by widows of their dower land. By 1526 he had married Isabel, the daughter of Richard Lyster of Rowten; some pedigrees indicate that he was previously married to Elizabeth, the daughter of John Dodd. Bromley was active in the affairs of the borough of Shrewsbury, and became its recorder in 1532; he was also a justice of the peace for Shropshire from 1536. As early as 1537 he was recommended by Bishop Rowland Lee for the chief justiceship of Chester, as 'right well learned', though he was not appointed. He also practised in London, appearing in the duchy chamber as early as 1528, and signing several bills in chancery in Wolsey's time. In 1529 he served in parliament for an unknown constituency.

Bromley took the coif in 1540, and was immediately appointed one of the king's serjeants. He gained judicial experience as a commissioner on the Oxford assize circuit, which he exchanged for the Norfolk in 1542. He became a puisne justice of the king's bench in 1544, was knighted in 1546, and as an executor of Henry VIII was made a member of the regency council in 1547. On the deathbed of Edward VI he was forced to consent to the settlement of the crown on Lady Jane Grey, despite his prior advice that it would be illegal, but he managed to avoid witnessing the instrument. Notwithstanding this, on 4 October 1553 Queen Mary promoted him to be her first chief justice of the queen's bench, having decided not to reappoint Sir Roger Cholmeley. He presided over a number of treason trials after Wyatt's rebellion in 1554, and found himself in disfavour for his conduct of the trial of Nicholas Throckmorton, whose acquittal by the jury was greeted by rapturous shouting in Westminster Hall. His conduct was hardly lenient by modern standards, for Throckmorton, though given a greater freedom of speech than was usual, was denied a witness and the sight of a statute on which he relied. Holinshed also reported that Bromley's summing up was defective, 'either for want of memory or good will', and had to be corrected by the prisoner himself. Though not removed from office, he did not long endure the queen's displeasure, dying on 15 May 1555.

Bromley built up a substantial estate in Shropshire, partly from monastic land, and established himself at or near Wroxeter. He was buried in Wroxeter church, where there are effigies of himself, in judicial robes (coloured red, with green facings) and collar of SS, and of his wife, Isabel, who survived him. The marginal inscription describes him as 'lord chyffe justes of Englond also beyng on of the executors to the kyng of most famous memorye Henry the eyght'. Bromley and his wife, Isabel, had only one child, Margaret, who married Sir Richard Newport (d. 1570), MP and member of the Inner Temple, who was also buried at Wroxeter; from them were descended the earls of Bradford of the first creation (1694–1762). By his will, made in 1552, the chief justice left a piece of gold to Sir Rowland Hill (d. 1561), lately lord mayor of London, 'for a token of a remembraunce for the olde love and amytie betwene him and me nowe by this my decease ended'. Among other bequests to collateral relatives, he left an annuity of 40s. to his cousin Sir Thomas Bromley, son of George Bromley, 'provided alwaies that the saide Thomas Bromeley do apply the studdy of the lawes of this realme'; this namesake, a student of the Inner Temple, rose to be lord chancellor. J. H. BAKER

Sources HoP, Commons, 1509–58, 1.508–10; 2.359–60; 3.16–17 • F. A. Inderwick and R. A. Roberts, eds., A calendar of the Inner Temple records, 1 (1896) • LP Henry VIII, 12/2, no. 770 • Sainty, Judges • BL, Lansdowne MSS 1119, 1133 • H. Owen and J. B. Blakeway, A history of Shrewsbury, 1 (1825), 538 • PRO, DL 5/5, fol. 357v [counsel in requests] • inquisition post mortem, PRO, C 142/104/94 • R. Tresswell and A. Vincent, The visitation of Shropshire, taken in the year 1623, ed. G. Grazebrook and J. P. Rylands, 1, Harleian Society, 28 (1889)

Likenesses alabaster effigy on monument, c.1555, Claverley, Shropshire

Wealth at death a piece of gold to Sir Rowland Hill; an annuity of 40s. to Sir Thomas Bromley

Bromley, Sir Thomas (c.1530–1587), lord chancellor, was a younger son of George Bromley (d. 1545) of Hodnet, Shropshire, and his wife, Jane (b. c.1505), daughter of Sir Thomas

Sir Thomas Bromley (c.1530–1587), by unknown artist, 1585

Lacon of Willey, Shropshire. His was a legal family: his father was a bencher of the Inner Temple, as were his uncle Sir Thomas Bromley (d. 1555), chief justice of the king's bench, and his brother George, chief justice of Chester, whose son Edward Bromley became a baron of the exchequer in the time of James I.

Early career and marriage Bromley was admitted to Clifford's Inn in 1547. He subsequently entered the Inner Temple, probably in the early 1550s. A studious young man, who as lord chancellor was to remind new serjeants-at-law to 'leave a time for study or else learning would decay' (Baker, Serjeants, 312), he was appointed an auditor of the steward of the inn in 1555, and by 1557, in which year he was an auditor for the treasurer, he possessed a copy of the manuscript law reports of John Caryll, which was referred to at a meeting of the assize judges in Trinity term 1557. In the following year he was returned to parliament for Bridgnorth, Shropshire, a local family borough, and in 1559 was MP for Wigan, Lancashire, perhaps through the influence of the Gerrard family. By 1560 he had married Elizabeth (b. c.1540), daughter of Sir Adrian Fortescue of Shirburn, Oxfordshire, who survived him. Their eldest son, Henry, knighted in 1592, was MP for Plymouth, Shropshire, and Worcestershire, sheriff of Worcestershire, and gentleman of the privy chamber of James I. Thomas Bromley and his wife had three other sons and four daughters, who received with Henry the dedication of The Right Rule of Christian Chastitie (1580), compiled by their tutor William Hergest. Bromley was returned to parliament again in 1563, this time for Guildford, Surrey, under the patronage of Henry Fitzalan, earl of Arundel, to whom he was to be executor. Again auditor for the treasurer in the Inner Temple in 1564, and attendant on the reader in 1565, in autumn 1566 Bromley was himself reader of the Inner Temple, giving four lectures on the Statutes of Attaints. In the same year he was appointed recorder of London. Returned to parliament for the city of London in 1566, he chose instead to continue to sit for Guildford, and in the session of 1566 was a member of a legal committee and of the succession committee.

Solicitor-general Bromley was retained by Lord Hunsdon, and patronized by William Cecil, and his advancement now came quickly: on 14 March 1569 he was appointed solicitor-general in succession to Richard Onslow, a fellow member of the Inner Temple with whom Bromley had pleaded in *Lucy* v. *Walwyn* (1561), a leading contract case. In 1570 Bromley sat in the north as a commissioner to try the rebels of 1569, and was to be embarrassed by the accusation that he had assisted his kinsman, the attainted rebel Richard Dacres of Aikton, Cumberland. In 1571 Bromley played a leading role as solicitor-general in the trial for treason of Thomas Howard, duke of Norfolk, speaking after Nicholas Barham, queen's serjeant, and the attorney-general, Gilbert Gerrard. In the following year he was among the commissioners sent to Sheffield to lay charges before Mary, queen of Scots, and among those who examined John Leslie, bishop of Ross, in the Tower. In 1573 his second reading in the Inner Temple, for Lent 1574, was postponed to avoid a conflict with his parliamentary duties, and in November 1573 he was elected treasurer of the inn, his term of office being extended for a further year in November 1575. In 1574 he was one of the committees appointed to arbitrate a dispute between the university and city of Oxford. Though he was never created serjeant-at-law, Bromley's practice in the queen's bench and in chancery flourished. As early as 1560 he had been of counsel to Richard Bertie and his wife, Katharine, dowager duchess of Suffolk, in a chancery action for breach of trust against Walter Herenden of Gray's Inn, later reported as a leading case. His success in practice was due, it was said, to his habit of screening cases carefully before proceeding, a method that he recommended to the new serjeants in 1580, urging them to pay special attention to the honesty of the causes that they accepted and not to take on more work than they could manage. Success in practice enabled Bromley to buy land in Shropshire and elsewhere, including an estate at Holt, Worcestershire.

Lord chancellor Close to Edward de Vere, earl of Oxford, Sir William Cordell, master of the rolls, Lord Hunsdon, and others, as solicitor-general Bromley came to overshadow the attorney-general, Gilbert Gerrard. It was not, therefore, unexpected that when the long-serving Lord Keeper Bacon died in February 1579 Bromley should replace him, taking the title of lord chancellor, which had been denied to Bacon, despite his abilities, perhaps on account of his humble background. Passed over for the great seal, Gerrard was knighted, and appointed master of the rolls in 1581. Bromley took up office on 26 April 1579,

though his appointment had been heralded on 11 March 1579 by his admission to the privy council. He was knighted in May 1579. Mendoza, the Spanish ambassador, reported that the earl of Leicester and Sir Christopher Hatton had pushed Bromley forward as chancellor to gain a supporter for the Alençon marriage, Bromley having promised them both large pensions should he obtain the place. Whatever the truth of this, and Leicester's public support for the Alençon marriage was not to last, the new chancellor was at once embroiled in the question of the queen's marriage, changing his view with the majority of the council, and pleading his inexperience in such affairs, being new to his post, when confronted by Elizabeth with his variation.

In 1581 Bromley's judgment was much commended by the Commons when he refused to issue a writ for the election of another burgess to replace the Stafford member accused of felony, who should, he said, remain a member of the house until convicted. The recipient in 1581 of a substantial gift of plate from Francis Drake, newly returned from his circumnavigation, in the Trinity term of that year, 'having no real reason to be there at all' (Simpson, 33), Bromley gave his opinion in favour of the defendant at a meeting of the judges at York House to discuss the case of *Wolfe* v. *Shelley*. Out of the eventual decision arose the 'rule in *Shelley's case*', long a leading doctrine in English real-property law, though the political background of the case is plain: the queen had directed Bromley to assemble the judges, and while Richard Shelley, lessor of the unsuccessful plaintiff, had been imprisoned in 1580 for his 'obstinacye in Poperye' (*APC*, 12, 1580–81, 153), the defendant, Henry Shelley, had been brought up in the reformed religion. Bromley was none the less capable of a degree of judicial independence, as he demonstrated in 1582 in the affair of Thomas Knyvett, a gentleman of the privy chamber and his distant kinsman by marriage, who had killed one of the earl of Oxford's men. Warned by the vice-chamberlain, Sir Christopher Hatton, that 'it is very necessary you take care to please the Queen in this case' (Nicolas, 256), Bromley responded that though he had not expressly refused the request for a special commission to try Knyvett, he would not grant such a commission until he had heard further from Knyvett or his counsel, that such a commission would not help Knyvett, who would remain liable to an appeal of felony, and that following the coroner's verdict of self-defence the pleading of Knyvett's pardon in private could easily be arranged.

In 1582 Bromley was consulted by the queen upon the proposals conveyed by the French ambassador concerning the Alençon marriage, and in the same year his influence in his native county was demonstrated in his support for Oswestry, Shropshire, in preventing a movement of the market for Welsh cloth back into Wales, and in resisting the town of Chester's petition to the privy council that it be granted the staple for Welsh cottons. It was believed that Bromley's intercession with the queen had been crucial, and the corporation of Shrewsbury voted him 20 marks for a piece of plate in recompense of his goodwill. Recompense from another quarter was embodied in 1580 in a licence to import Irish wool, in 1585 in the grant of the farm of the office of aulnage, and in 1586 in a crown grant of the manor of Wick Episcopi, Worcestershire. In 1585 came appointment as deputy chancellor of the University of Oxford in place of Leicester, about to depart upon campaign to the Netherlands.

In June of the same year Henry Percy, earl of Northumberland, who was implicated in the Throckmorton plot, and who knew that his fellow conspirator William Shelley, related to the parties in *Wolfe* v. *Shelley*, must confess under torture, was found dead in his rooms in the Tower. A member of the consequent commission of inquiry, Bromley set out the government's case that the earl had committed suicide. In 1586 Bromley took part in the first examination of Anthony Babington, who had plotted to assassinate the queen, and in the same year presided over the commission sent to Fotheringhay to try Mary, queen of Scots, for her complicity in the Babington plot, presiding again in Star Chamber when the guilty verdict was pronounced. A new parliament was summoned, as Burghley put it, 'to make the burden better borne and the world abroad better satisfied' (Neale, *Elizabeth I and her Parliaments, 1584–1601*, 104). Bromley told the two houses that they had been summoned not to make laws or to vote subsidies, but to advise the queen as to one of the conspirators 'that, by due course of law, had received her sentence' (ibid., 106), and subsequently, with the speaker, presented to the queen the petition of both houses for Mary's death. Bromley applied the great seal to Mary's death warrant in early February 1587, but, it is said, the strain of the business was beginning to tell, and he soon took to his bed. When parliament met again later the same month Sir Edmund Anderson, chief justice of the common pleas, was appointed to act in place of the absent Bromley, who died in London, at York House, early in the morning of 12 April 1587. He was buried in Westminster Abbey on 2 May, where a monument was erected in St Paul's chapel, leaving his eldest son, Henry, as his executor and the principal beneficiary of his will.

'Something of a disappointment' Bromley's rise was rapid, and his success spectacular even in a successful legal family. A member of the inner ring of Elizabeth's government, though in 1586 he still could not read 'one half line' of her handwriting (Neale, *Elizabeth I and her Parliaments, 1584–1601*, 132), and compliant in matters of state, he 'acted a bloody part against Mary queen of Scots' (Nicolas, 595), accounts of which are prominent in the historiography. But as the Knyvett affair demonstrates, in lesser matters Bromley was not incapable of taking an independent line, and in 1582 was prepared to write to the earl of Derby and the bishop of Chester in support of his sister, the recusant Lady Egerton of Radley, expressing his regard for her and urging persuasion by gentle means. As an equity judge he faced, as he saw himself, a difficult task in succeeding Lord Keeper Bacon, 'one of the greatest of English judges' (Jones, 32), and his tenure of the great seal can be seen as 'something of a disappointment' (ibid., 39). He pronounced only two chancery orders of importance, both in 1581, one concerned with bail, the other with the

examination of exemplifications, and if his opening and closing speeches in the House of Lords are a guide he perhaps lacked eloquence on the bench. But he supervised acceptance of the work of his greater predecessor, and disappointment should not be exaggerated. A cautious chancellor, who was said never to intervene in a case heard at law without first consulting the judges, he received praise from many, and Coke took him to have had a 'great and profound knowledge and judgment in the law' (*Wolfe* v. *Shelley*, 1581). To him were dedicated Thomas Churchyard's *A Pleasaunte Laborinth called Churchyardes Chance* (1580), William Fleetwood's table to the later year-books, first published in 1579, and Bartholomew Chamberlaine's sermon preached before the privy council in 1580.

N. G. JONES

Sources HoP, *Commons, 1558–1603*, vol. 1 · W. J. Jones, *The Elizabethan court of chancery* (1967), 32, 36–9, 60 · *CSP dom.*, *1581–94* · APC, *1571–5, 1578–81* · M. A. S. Hume, ed., *Calendar of letters and state papers relating to English affairs, preserved principally in the archives of Simancas*, 4 vols., PRO (1892–9), *1568–86* · *State trials*, 1.957ff., 1173ff. · R. Tresswell and A. Vincent, *The visitation of Shropshire, taken in the year 1623*, ed. G. Grazebrook and J. P. Rylands, 1, Harleian Society, 28 (1889), 78 · will, PRO, PROB 11/70, sig. 18 · J. Campbell, *Lives of the lord chancellors*, 4th edn, 10 vols. (1856–7), vol. 2 · F. A. Inderwick and R. A. Roberts, eds., *A calendar of the Inner Temple records*, 1 (1896) · CPR, *1563–84* · T. Nash, *Collections for the history of Worcestershire*, 1 (1781), 594–5 · D. Lloyd, *State worthies*, ed. C. Whitworth, 2 vols. (1766), vol. 1, p. 497 · S. D'Ewes, ed., *The journals of all the parliaments during the reign of Queen Elizabeth, both of the House of Lords and House of Commons* (1682), 122, 283 · F. Peck, ed., *Desiderata curiosa*, new edn, 2 vols. in 1 (1779), 117, 122 · N. H. Nicolas, *Memoirs of the life and times of Sir Christopher Hatton* (1847), 256, 258, 263 · J. E. Neale, *Elizabeth I and her parliaments*, 1: *1559–1581* (1953), 376 · J. E. Neale, *Elizabeth I and her parliaments*, 2: *1584–1601* (1957), 25, 104, 106, 132, 190 · E. St J. Brooks, *Sir Christopher Hatton* (1946), 65, 90–91, 128, 171, 247, 288, 332 · *Calendar of the manuscripts of the most hon. the marquis of Salisbury*, 2, HMC, 9 (1888), 16, 19, 273 · *The manuscripts of Shrewsbury and Coventry corporations*, HMC, 47 (1899), 23 · T. C. Mendenhall, *The Shrewsbury drapers and the Welsh wool trade in the XVI and XVII centuries* (1953), 33, 135 · Baker, *Serjeants* · A. W. B. Simpson, *Leading cases in the common law* (1995) · BL, Stowe MS 586, fol. 76r · *Wolfe* v. *Shelley*, 1 Coke Report 106a, 76 ER 238 [CD-ROM]

Archives BL, letters, Egerton MS 2173

Likenesses alabaster sculpture on monument, c.1579, Westminster Abbey, London, St Paul's chapel · oils, 1585, priv. coll. [*see illus.*] · J. Cole, engraving, repro. in J. Dart, *Westmonasterium, or, The history and antiquities of the abbey church of St Peters Westminster*, 1, 178 · engraving (after painting, priv. coll.), Inner Temple, London · line engraving, BM; repro. in T. Nash, *Collections of the history and antiquities of Worcestershire* (1781) · line engraving with pink wash (after engraving), BM; repro. in J. Thane, ed., *British Autography* (1819), pl. 46 · painted panel; Christies, 3 June 1977, lot 135 · painting; formerly at Davenport House, Shropshire, 1831 · portrait (after painted panel), Harvard U., law school

Bromley, Thomas (*bap.* 1630, *d.* 1691), mystical writer, was baptized on 1 February 1630 in the parish of St Michael Bedwardine, Worcester, a younger son of Henry Bromley (*d.* 1647) of Upton upon Severn, Worcestershire, a descendant of Sir Thomas *Bromley, Elizabethan lord chancellor, and Mary (*d.* 1658), daughter of Sir William Ligon of Madresfield. According to his biographer, 'in his younger years' he was 'religiously educated' (Bromley, 3). Admitted as a commoner of Oriel College, Oxford, in June 1650, he matriculated on 22 November. How long he remained there is unknown, though battels receipts indicate that about April 1652 he migrated to All Souls College. According to Richard Roach's account, while at Oxford Bromley and a companion heard a sermon at the university church 'preached in great Power' by John Pordage (1607–1681), rector of Bradfield, Berkshire (Bodl. Oxf., MS Rawl. D. 833, fol. 63v). Together with his companion, Edmund Brice, fellow of All Souls, Bromley spoke with Pordage and was deeply satisfied with what he heard. About April 1654 he left Oxford 'when he was to have beene elected fellow of All Soules … according to the statutes of the house as kinsman to the founder'. At the election day he went to join Pordage's community at Bradfield, 'and never returned to Oxford againe' (Nicolson, 279).

About three weeks before his departure Bromley preached a sermon on Acts 14: 22, 'That we must through much tribulation enter into the kingdom of God'; some years later his elder brother Henry Bromley (1626–1667) believed that Thomas had expected 'to draw wisdome out of a clearer fountaine, and to be call'd by God to preach the Gospell' (Nicolson, 279). Bromley's mother, Mary, 'a sober, pious Woman', did not prove so understanding, and prevailed upon her son to pass on his writings to Richard Baxter, who deemed 'that their Guide differed much from the Scripture'. Baxter found Bromley to be of 'a very good Disposition, aspiring after the highest Spiritual State, and thinking that visible Communion with Angels was it, he much expected it, and profest in some measure to have attained it'. None the less, Baxter perceived that Bromley was 'a young, raw Scholar of some Fryar whom he understood not', and in a letter intended for Bromley dated 30 May 1654 he attempted to confute some of Bromley's opinions, attacking 'Diabolicall Delusory Apparitions' and a dependence on spirits and voices. Some years later Baxter was again to write against Pordage 'and his Family, who live together in Community, and pretend to hold visible and sensible Communion with Angels, whom they sometime see, and sometime smell' (*Reliquiae Baxterianae*, 1.78; Baxter, *Worlds of Spirits*, 176; DWL, MS Baxter Treatises, III 67, fol. 302r).

On 5 October 1654 John Pordage was brought before the commissioners for ejecting of scandalous ministers for the county of Berkshire, nominally to be tried on charges of blasphemy, although others, it seems, cast covetous glances at the lucrative living of Bradfield. During these proceedings it appears that Bromley conceded to having seen a vision of a woman's guardian angel 'in her morning coat'. Pordage was found guilty 'of denying the Deity of Christ' and ejected from his living on 8 December 1654, though he continued to live at Bradfield (Fowler, 102, 116; J. Pordage, *Innocencie Appearing through the Dark Mists of Pretended Guilt*, 1655, 1, 3). It seems that Bromley, 'his chief Proselyte' and companion, remained with him (Baxter, *Worlds of Spirits*, 176). In 1655 Thomas Bromley published *The Way to the Sabbath of Rest*, a mystical treatise heavily influenced by the writings of Jakob Boehme, which Richard Baxter judged to be a 'most clean and moderate piece' of doctrine (Baxter, *Key for Catholicks*, 331). This work was to be translated into Dutch, German, and Swedish.

Bromley appears to have spent many years at Bradfield in the company of Pordage and his 'family'. In the fire of London he lost 'about [£30] worth of books, most Greeke and Hebrew', and an edition of the polyglot Bible (Nicolson, 279). In the episcopal returns of 1669 he was suspected, along with Pordage, of holding a conventicle at Bradfield. Bromley was also a correspondent of Viscount Conway, and for several years, despite illness and infirmity, he solicited money from Conway which he distributed charitably among the poor of London and the surrounding countryside. By November 1670 Bromley had returned to Upton upon Severn. From Upton he corresponded with Anne, Viscountess Conway, visiting her on occasion at her country seat at Ragley, Warwickshire. It was at Ragley that Bromley made the acquaintance of the Cambridge Platonist, Henry More, and of Franciscus Mercurius van Helmont. Bromley was also written to in 1680 by Richard Baxter, who outlined for him his judgement on the nature of free will. All the while, it seems that Thomas Bromley maintained contact with John Pordage and his community; he was bequeathed money for a mourning ring by Pordage in his will, and commended a Behmenistic work called *A Fountain of Gardens* by Jane Lead, who was to found the Philadelphian Society.

Bromley's last years appear to have been spent at Upton. He died on Easter Monday, 13 April 1691, and was buried at Upton on 15 April. His estate was administered by his niece, Elizabeth. Some months after his death his library, containing works on the apocalypse, Socinianism, atheism, heresy, and Jakob Boehme, was auctioned. Bromley also left several works in manuscript, some of which were published in the eighteenth century.

ARIEL HESSAYON

Sources T. Bromley, *The way to the sabbath of rest* (1710) • Bodl. Oxf., MS Rawl. D. 833, fols. 63–64 [R. Roach, 'Account'] • *The Conway letters: the correspondence of Anne, Viscountess Conway, Henry More, and their friends, 1642–1684*, ed. M. H. Nicolson, rev. edn, ed. S. Hutton (1992), 272, 278–80, 365–6, 370 • *Reliquiae Baxterianae, or, Mr Richard Baxter's narrative of the most memorable passages of his life and times*, ed. M. Sylvester, 1 vol. in 3 pts (1696), pt 1, p. 78 • R. Baxter, *The certainty of the worlds of spirits* (1691), 176 • DWL, MS Baxter Treatises, III 67, fols. 302–9 • [C. Fowler], *Daemonium meridianum: Satan at noon* (1655), 102, 116 • R. Baxter, *A key for Catholicks* (1659), 331 • N. Thune, *The Behmenists and the Philadelphians: a contribution to the study of English mysticism in the 17th and 18th centuries* (1948), 51–5 • A. Hessayon, 'Gold tried in the fire': the prophet Theaurau John Tany and the puritan revolution [forthcoming] • G. F. Nuttall, 'James Nayler: a fresh approach', *Journal of the Friends' Historical Society*, suppl. 26 (1954), 3–6 • C. L. Shadwell, ed., *Registrum Orielense*, 1 (1893), 261
Archives BL, 'A sermon from Mount Olivet', MS Sloane 2569, fols. 78–9 • Bodl. Oxf., 'A discourse of visions and other dispensations called extraordinary', MS Rawl. C. 372
Wealth at death library auctioned after death

Bromley, Valentine Walter (1848–1877), painter, son of William Bromley, the engraver and associate of the Royal Academy, was born in London on 14 February 1848. Under the instruction of his father he displayed a facility for invention coupled with rapid execution. At the age of nineteen Bromley was elected an associate of the Institute of Painters in Water Colours; he also belonged to the Society of British Artists. He worked regularly for the *Illustrated London News* as art correspondent, and in 1875 he illustrated the American travels of the fourth earl of Dunraven, entitled *The Great Divide* (1876), having accompanied him on his tour. He died unexpectedly from an attack of smallpox on 30 April 1877 at his home, Fallowes Green, Harpenden, Hertfordshire; his picture *The Fairy King* was then on show at the Royal Academy exhibition and he had just undertaken an important series of illustrations of Shakespeare (for the firm of Cassell, Petter, and Galpin) and the Bible (for the *Illustrated London News*). A widower, he had married for a second time less than a year before, on 7 June 1876. His second wife was Ida Mary, an artist and writer on art, and daughter of John Forbes-Robertson. Bromley's picture *Troilus and Cressida* (owned by the publishers Virtue & Co., London) was engraved for the *Art Journal* for 1873, and his portrait of an Indian chief is held in the Anschutz collection, Denver.

RICHARD GARNETT, *rev.* CHLOE JOHNSON

Sources *Art Journal*, 39 (1877), 205 · *Art Journal*, 35 (1873), 358 · *The Athenaeum* (5 May 1877), 585 · Bénézit, *Dict.*, 3rd edn · Wood, *Vic. painters*, 3rd edn · m. cert.
Likenesses wood-engraving, NPG; repro. in *ILN* (19 May 1877)
Wealth at death under £600: probate, 18 June 1877, *CGPLA Eng. & Wales*

Bromley, William (*bap.* 1663, *d.* 1732), politician, was descended from an old Staffordshire family whose ancestry extended back to King John's reign. He was the eldest son of Sir William Bromley (*d.* 1682), and was born at his father's seat at Baginton, Warwickshire, where he was baptized on 31 August 1663. His mother was Ursula, the daughter of Thomas, first Baron Leigh of Stoneleigh, Warwickshire. After matriculating at Christ Church, Oxford, in 1679, he proceeded to the degree of BA in July 1681, and in 1683 was entered at the Middle Temple. He inherited his father's estates in 1682 and, despite his youth, soon became a conscientious and active figure among the Warwickshire gentry. His first wife, Catherine, the daughter of Sir John Clobery of Winchester, whom he had married by 1685, died in childbirth in 1688, and he shortly afterwards embarked on a tour of France and Italy, thereby missing the events of the revolution. On 21 November 1689 he married Trevor (or Trever; *d.* *c.*1691), the daughter of Samuel Fortrey of the parish of St Giles-in-the-Fields, but she too died a little later without surviving children, and by 1692 he had married his third wife, Cecilia (*d.* before 1698), the daughter of Sir William Swan, first baronet, of Southfleet, Kent.

Bromley's political career began in 1690, when, as a tory, he was elected knight of the shire for his county. Though he took little part in proceedings during his first years in the Commons, he aligned himself with the 'country' opponents of the ministry. He courted controversy, however, in 1692 with his travel memoirs, *Remarks on the Grand Tour of France and Italy*, in which distinctly pro-Catholic and pro-Jacobite nuances could be detected, including a reference to the king and queen as prince and princess of Orange, and he was forced to withdraw all unsold copies.

Like many tories at the time he found great difficulty in reconciling himself to the Williamite regime, and on several occasions in the earlier 1690s he strongly refuted arguments that William III had obtained his crown by right of conquest. However, country leaders soon came to esteem him for his strong tory prejudices, not least his unswerving devotion to the Church of England, his stand against governmental corruption, and his dedication to the detailed work of the house, particularly in committee. It was not for any originality of purpose that Bromley rose in stature among the backbench squires, but for his great personal integrity. In 1696 his growing prominence in the Commons was recognized in his election to the commission of public accounts, but in February, in the wake of the Fenwick conspiracy, the plot to assassinate William III, Bromley's refusal, along with eighty other high-church tories, to take 'the association' acknowledging William as 'rightful and lawful king', incapacitated him from serving, preventing him from fulfilling Robert Harley's hopes that he would play a central part in stepping up country opposition to the ministry. Then, as later, his relations with Harley were complicated by an inability to reconcile himself to Harley's political manipulativeness. Bromley's potentially disloyal stand in 1696 precluded any chance of his readoption as MP for Warwickshire at the 1698 election, and he remained out of parliament until Oxford University, a bastion of high-church toryism, chose him at a by-election in March 1701. The university created him DCL in August 1702. In the meantime he had been married a fourth time, in January 1698, to Elizabeth, the daughter of Ralph, Lord Stawell.

During the early years of Queen Anne's reign Bromley played an increasingly conspicuous role in the tory-dominated House of Commons, but did not endear himself to the ministry. During the years 1702–5 he held the chair of the committee of privileges and elections, and he was a commissioner of public accounts from 1702 until 1704. More significantly, he championed the campaign of the high-church tories in the lower house against 'occasional conformity' by dissenters, a practice which he denounced as an 'abominable hypocrisy', and he promoted bills to outlaw it in 1702, 1703, and 1704. These efforts, which the ministry scuppered, and his part in the establishment of 'Queen Anne's bounty' to subsidize impoverished clerical livings, won him universal praise from high-church tory MPs, who now looked to him as their chieftain. After his unanimous re-election at Oxford in 1705 he failed in a strenuous party contest for the speaker's chair, his opponents having resurrected his *Grand Tour* as evidence of possible Jacobite leanings. Over the next few years, Bromley, with Sir Thomas Hanmer, ably led the high-church tories in opposition, and, guided by his mentor, the Anglican peer Lord Nottingham, judiciously resisted overtures from both Lord Godolphin and, after 1708, Harley, each of whom stood to benefit from the accession of strength that his political group would bring to their respective factions.

The impeachment of Dr Sacheverell in 1710, which Bromley was instrumental in turning to tory advantage by pressing for the trial to be held publicly in Westminster Hall, was followed later in the year by the appointment of a tory administration under Harley and a landslide tory victory at the polls. Bromley was unanimously elected speaker, a result which Harley actively encouraged, recognizing that Bromley's extensive connections and acquaintanceships among the backbench tory squires, and the respect he commanded among them, would enable him to control a house now heavily populated with tories. Initially, Bromley continued to doubt Harley's commitment to high-church tory goals, but his attitude softened amid the huge wave of loyalty and support towards the minister prompted by Guiscard's assassination attempt in March 1711. In August 1713 Harley, now Lord Treasurer Oxford, appointed Bromley to the openly political role of secretary of state in the northern department so that he could exert greater rein over the increasingly fractious tories. For as long as he could he avoided taking sides in the mounting conflict between Oxford and Bolingbroke and in the tense political atmosphere did his utmost to sustain tory unity. In the final months of the queen's life, however, he drifted more and more towards Bolingbroke, sensing that Oxford's days in power were numbered, but oblivious to the fact that Bolingbroke had no intention of including him in any new ministry he might be asked to lead. In September 1714, after the accession of George I, Bromley was duly removed from office. He declined a compensatory tellership of the exchequer as being a place of profit and not of public service.

Bromley remained MP for Oxford University up to his death, and in 1714 became a trustee of the considerable bequest to the university made by his friend Dr John Radcliffe. Until the early 1720s he led the tories in their opposition to the whig administrations, but his health, which was never in good repair, eventually curtailed his activities. It has been supposed that he was a Jacobite in the last phase of his political career, but there is no firm evidence for such an assertion; indeed, he regarded Jacobitism as a harmful influence on tory unity. He died 'unexpectedly' at his New Bond Street lodgings on 13 February 1732 and was buried at Baginton. His estate passed to his eldest surviving son, William *Bromley (by his fourth wife), while to his three younger children he left portions amounting to £18,000. He expressed regret in his will that his final marriage had proved unhappy.   A. A. HANHAM

Sources 'Bromley, William', HoP, Commons · DNB
Archives BL, collection of journals and other papers relating to parliament, Add. MSS 36824–36868 · JRL, letters and papers · Keele University Library, papers relating to public revenue · U. Leeds, Brotherton L., letter-books as secretary of state for the northern department [copies] | BL, letters to duke of Ormond, Add. MS 63093 · BL, letters to Lord Oxford, Add. MS 70287 · Warks. CRO, letters to Sir John Mordaunt
Likenesses attrib. J. Closterman, oils, 1710, Christ Church Oxf. · M. Dahl, oils, c.1712, Examination Schools, Oxford · J. Smith, mezzotint (after M. Dahl), BM, NPG
Wealth at death left Baginton and £18,000 to younger children: 'Bromley, William', HoP, Commons

Bromley, William (bap. 1699, d. 1737), politician, was the second son of William *Bromley (bap. 1663, d. 1732) and

his wife, Elizabeth Stawell. He was admitted on the foundation at Westminster in 1714, at the age of fifteen, and matriculated at Christ Church, Oxford, on 27 February 1717; he was also a member of Oriel College, Oxford, where he was awarded a DCL on 19 May 1732. In 1721 he engaged on a European tour, during which he paid his respects to the Old Pretender in France. On 2 July 1724 Bromley married Lucy Throckmorton, the daughter and heir of Clement Throckmorton of Haseley, Warwickshire. According to the first earl of Egmont's diaries, the marriage, which produced two sons and one daughter, was not successful, resulting in his wife's adultery and Bromley's heavy drinking (cited in HoP, Commons).

Bromley was elected member of parliament for Fowey, Cornwall, in 1725 and for Warwick in 1727. Although he was politically inactive before his father's death, he later emerged as a critic of Walpole's government. On 13 March 1734 he was put forward by the party opposed to Walpole to move the repeal of the Septennial Act. Parliament was dissolved soon after, and Bromley was returned at Warwick before losing his seat on petition. He was elected in February 1737, on the death of George Clarke, to represent the University of Oxford, which his father had served as MP from 1702 to 1732. He died on 12 March 1737 of a 'pleuretic fever' which, according to Egmont, was partly induced by his alcoholism.

[ANON.], rev. PHILIP CARTER

Sources S. Matthews, 'Bromley, William', HoP, Commons · Foster, Alum. Oxon. · GM, 1st ser., 7 (1737), 125, 189 · An exact account of the poll, as it stood between the Honourable Mr Trevor and Wm. Bromley, esq. [1737] · Hist. U. Oxf. 5: 18th-cent. Oxf. · Old Westminsters
Likenesses oils, Examination Schools, Oxford

Bromley, William (bap. 1769, d. 1842), engraver, was baptized on 4 August 1769 at Carisbrooke, Isle of Wight, the second son of John Bromley and his wife, Sarah, née Glede. Bromley was apprenticed to an engraver named Wooding in London, and began exhibiting at the Royal Academy in 1786 and at the Society of Artists in 1790. Initially Bromley exhibited sketches and paintings of literary and biblical subjects, such as Christ Washing his Disciples' Feet (exh. RA, 1786), but his major output throughout his career was his line, and occasionally mezzotint and steel, engravings. He was the first of a large family of engravers.

Bromley found early employment working for booksellers: in 1791 he engraved two plates after Samuel de Wilde for volume 6 of Bell's British Theatre. Soon after, he engraved the work of Fuseli, Opie, Smirke, and Northcote for Robert Bowyer's monumental edition of David Hume's History of England (1792–1806). Several examples of impressions from engraved plates are in the Fine Arts Museum of San Francisco. In 1799 he produced engravings for Thomas Macklin's Bible and Milton's Paradise Lost. In the same year he personally published his hand-coloured engravings of Shakespeare's Seven Ages of Man after Thomas Stothard (Fine Arts Museum of San Francisco). Bromley also engraved numerous single prints, for instance in 1803 an engraving with T. Landseer after Smirke's Victors of the Nile.

During and after the Napoleonic wars Bromley was employed to engrave several commemorative paintings, such as A. W. Devis's *Death of Nelson* (NMM) in 1812, Thomas Lawrence's portrait *Arthur Wellesley, First Duke of Wellington* (Royal Collection) in 1818, and Luke Clennell's *Charge of the Life Guards at the Battle of Waterloo* in 1821. In 1819 Bromley was elected an associate engraver of the Royal Academy, and also a member of the Accademia di San Luca, Rome.

In 1822 Bromley began exhibiting engravings of the Elgin marbles. These were made for the trustees of the British Museum after Henry Corbould's drawings, several of which are in the British Museum. Bromley continued to exhibit his engravings of the marbles nearly every year until 1835. During this period, while he lived at London addresses in Brompton and Pimlico, he also exhibited three further portraits after Lawrence, then the president of the Royal Academy, *Countess Lieven* ('finished etching', exh. RA, 1823; original painting, Tate collection), *The Late Sir Henry Englefield* (exh. RA, 1825), and *John Abernethy* (exh. RA, 1828). Bromley continued to produce engravings for books, executing a rare steel-engraving after Sir Joshua Reynolds's portrait of Horace Walpole for the latter's *Anecdotes of Painting* (1826–8).

Bromley's second son, John Charles Bromley (*d.* 1839), was baptized in London on 27 July 1795 at St Luke's, Chelsea, when his mother's name, Ann, was recorded in the register. He was the first of William Bromley's sons to achieve reputation as an engraver, engraving plates for *River Scenery* after Turner and Girtin in 1826 and exhibiting at the Royal Academy in 1827 and 1829. In 1830 J. C. Bromley engraved *The Trial of Lord William Russell* (priv. coll.) after Sir George Hayter, and in 1837 he published his mezzotint of Haydon's *The Reform Banquet* (NPG), a copy of which is in the Guildhall collection. Bromley's third son, **James Bromley** (1800–1838), is best remembered as the engraver of several of Hayter's portraits of prominent public figures. These included a mezzotint of *Queen Victoria when Princess*, which was published by Colnaghi on 1 November 1834, and reissued upon Victoria's accession in 1837. He also engraved Hayter's *Victoria, Duchess of Kent* (Royal Collection) and *Lord John Russell Holding the Reform Bill* in 1836.

William Bromley survived both James (who died in London, unmarried, on 12 December 1838) and John Charles (who died of water on the chest on 3 April 1839, leaving a large family). In his later years he lived at numerous London addresses and continued to exhibit at the Royal Academy. In 1834 he made engravings of antiquities for the Dilettanti Society, and between 1836 and 1842 he exhibited engravings of the Townley marbles, for example, *Ceres Crowned as Isis* (exh. RA, 1839). He also made engravings of British antiquities which appeared in *The Publications of the Antiquarian Etching Club*, 5 vols. (1849–54). Bromley died on 24 November 1842. He is said to have also been the father of Frederick Bromley (*fl.* 1832–1870), who engraved works after Daniel Maclise, J. P. Knight, and Charles and Edwin Landseer, although Redgrave suggests that Frederick was the son of John Charles Bromley. William Bromley has also been unconvincingly named as the father of Clough

William Bromley (*b.* 1850, *d.* after 1904), a London-based illustrator, engraver, and contributor to the *English Illustrated Magazine*. M. G. SULLIVAN

Sources R. K. Engen, *Dictionary of Victorian engravers, print publishers and their works* (1979) · Redgrave, *Artists* · J. Turner, ed., *The dictionary of art*, 34 vols. (1996) · Graves, *Soc. Artists* · Graves, *RA exhibitors* · Bryan, *Painters* (1930) · DNB · W. Sandby, *The history of the Royal Academy of Arts*, 2 vols. (1862); facs. edn (1970) · parish register, Carisbrooke St Mary, Isle of Wight, Newport RO · O. Millar, *The Victorian pictures in the collection of her majesty the queen*, 2 vols. (1992) · R. K. Engen, *Dictionary of Victorian wood engravers* (1985) · B. Hunnisett, *A dictionary of British steel engravers* (1980) · J. Home, *Douglas: a tragedy* (1791), vol. 6 of *Bell's British Theatre*, ed. J. Bell · T. S. R. Boase, 'Macklin and Bowyer', *Journal of the Warburg and Courtauld Institutes*, 26 (1963), 148–77 · *The publications of the Antiquarian Etching Club*, 5 vols. (1849–54) · IGI

Brompton, John (*fl.* 1436–*c.*1464), abbot of Jervaulx and supposed chronicler, was educated at Oxford, and was elected abbot of the Cistercian foundation of Jervaulx, Yorkshire, in 1436, holding that office until *c.*1464. He was claimed as the author of a very substantial chronicle, printed in Twysden's *Decem scriptores* of 1652, but the only medieval association of Brompton and the chronicle is the claim in one of the two surviving manuscripts that the book was procured for Jervaulx by him, and it is very unlikely that he was its author. The chronicle is written on a considerable scale, but even so it does not represent all the compiler intended. In his preface he proposes to continue from Geoffrey of Monmouth's *Historia regum Britanniae*, to give an account of English history from the arrival of St Augustine to the reign of Edward I. However, in both manuscripts the work ends abruptly at the beginning of John's reign. Nevertheless, the work proceeds on a grand scale, to give an account of the conversion of England, and of the reigns of the Anglo-Saxon kings, through the conquest, with increasing weight being given to each successive Norman king. It is clear that the work as it stands was written in the fourteenth century. The latest event mentioned in the text occurs in a genealogy of the kings of Scotland, which records the marriage of David II in 1328. However, the apparent use of the second recension (the so-called AB text) of Higden's *Polychronicon* suggests powerfully that it was written after 1340. There are a number of occasions on which the compiler anticipates later events, but none of these takes the text beyond the early to mid-fourteenth century. It has also been argued that, since Richard the Lionheart is never styled Richard I, the work was probably written before the accession of Richard II in 1377.

The personality of the chronicle's author is peculiarly difficult to discern because the work is almost entirely compiled from earlier sources. These include the work of Walter of Guisborough, Henry of Huntingdon, a Latin *Brut*, the *Quadripartitus*, and Benedict of Peterborough as major sources, and to a lesser extent, William of Malmesbury, John of Worcester, William of Newburgh, Geoffrey of Monmouth, Bede, and various hagiographical works. Some of these are to be expected in this type of work, but the special interest in the laws of the Anglo-Saxon and early Norman kings is the most distinctive characteristic of the work. In general the geographical focus of the work appears to be twofold. On the one hand there is mention throughout the work of events involving the Scots and northern England. On the other there is a special concern with East Anglia, particularly with the area around Bury St Edmunds. It is conceivable that these are remnants of an earlier compilation, but the interests of the compiler appear more generalized than marked. On occasion interpolations from universal histories are made, but the overall preoccupation remains insular. Although it has been claimed that it was written for a secular patron, the work reveals close and detailed acquaintance with a wider range of works than was to be found in any but the best-stocked library, and no special interest in epic deeds or in any particular family (except perhaps the Scottish royal family). The date, authorship, and even the purpose of the work are still largely undetermined. It contains very little information that cannot be found in other sources, although scholars in early modern England drew on it heavily. Its enduring interest is as an antiquarian historical enterprise of great learning, extraordinary diligence, and remarkable ambition, which has been described as representing 'the most ambitious attempt in fourteenth century England to write a sustained account of the British past' (Taylor, 109).   V. J. GOODMAN

Sources R. Twysden, ed., *Historiæ Anglicanæ scriptores X* (1652), 725–1284 · J. Taylor, *English historical literature in the fourteenth century* (1987), 19–20, 108–09 · *The Universal Chronicle of Ranulph Higden*, ed. J. Taylor (1966), 23, 143–4 · T. D. Hardy, *Descriptive catalogue of materials relating to the history of Great Britain and Ireland*, 2, Rolls Series, 26 (1865), 539–41 · M. R. James, *A descriptive catalogue of the manuscripts in the library of Corpus Christi College, Cambridge*, 1 (1909), 183–4 · A. Gransden, *Historical writing in England*, 2 (1982), 56–7, 359, n. 103 · A. F. Sutton and L. Visser-Fuchs, 'Richard III's books [pt 6]', *The Ricardian*, 8 (1988), 104–19 · F. Liebermann, *Quadripartitus, ein englisches Rechtsbuch von 1114* (Halle, 1892), 70–75 · F. Liebermann, ed., *Die Gesetze der Angelsachsen*, 1 (Halle, 1898), xix–xx; 3 (1916), 308–10 · L. Keeler, *Geoffrey of Monmouth and the late Latin chroniclers, 1300–1500* (1946), 20–23 · Emden, *Oxf.*, 1.277

Archives BL, Cotton MS Tiberius c.xiii · CCC Cam., MS 96

Brompton, Richard (*c*.1734/5–1783), portrait painter, was of unknown origins but he evidently possessed sufficient means to study under Benjamin Wilson and in 1757 to travel to Rome, where he studied under Anton Raphael Mengs during the years 1758 and 1759. He remained in Italy until 1767, working in Venice (8 January 1763–August 1764), Parma, Bologna, and Rome (September 1764–January 1766), being elected *accademico di merito* at the Accademia di Santa Luca in Rome on 17 November and receiving his diploma in person on 5 January 1766.

Brompton's talents were quickly recognized. He was patronized in Italy by Horace Mann, Lord Ossory (whose portrait he painted), and Lord Northampton, ambassador-extraordinary to Venice in 1762–3, who invited the artist to join him there. After Northampton's departure for England, Brompton remained in the city. When the duke of York and his retinue arrived for the feast of the ascension at the end of May 1764, Brompton was engaged to paint a conversation group of the royal party and also to make copies. He complained to the actor David Garrick, who was then in Venice, about the difficulty of obtaining payment for the original and copies, whereupon Garrick lent him £80 to be paid in instalments. Brompton disregarded the terms of the loan, replying truculently and ungratefully to Garrick's reproaches, behaviour which seems to have been a constant and unfortunate aspect of his character. When the picture was exhibited at the Society of Artists in 1767 it established his reputation as a portraitist and has since remained in the Royal Collection.

Brompton continued in royal favour; in 1771 he painted full lengths of the prince of Wales in the robes of the Garter and his brother Prince Frederick in the robes of the Bath (both Royal Collection), both engraved by J. Saunders. At the same time he was painting William Pitt, first earl of Chatham, in his peer's robes. In 1772 the portrait was presented to Philip, second earl of Stanhope, and after being on show in the artist's studio at Greenwich was hung at Chevening, Kent, where it has since remained (copy in National Portrait Gallery, London; engraved by J. K. Sherwin and also by E. Fisher).

In October 1773 when Brompton was at Wilton House, Wiltshire, restoring (and, according to Waagen, ruining) the Van Dyck of *Philip, Earl of Pembroke, and his Family*, he learned that he had been elected a member of the Society of Artists, of which he became president in 1777 (Waagen, 3.153). He exhibited with them in 1767, 1773–4, 1776–7, and lastly in 1780 (by which time he was probably in Russia), when he showed portraits of John Smart, his fellow member, and Admiral Charles Saunders KB (Greenwich Hospital Collection, Greenwich, National Maritime Museum, London) among others. He also exhibited at the Free Society in 1768–9, and at the Royal Academy in 1772 as 'Professor, Roman Academy'. According to Henry Angelo, Brompton collaborated with David Morier on equestrian portraits, painting the figures while the Swiss artist dealt with the horses.

Between 1777 and 1778 Brompton was imprisoned for debt. In his *Diary* Joseph Farington noted that:

> [Brompton] married at Oxford ... His wife went to Russia & carried with Her a picture which he had painted of the great Lord Chatham & some other works, & exhibited them to the Empress Catherine, & represented that the Artist was confined in prison in England for debts of £600 or £1000. The Empress ordered the debts to be paid & that he shd. come to Russia upon an establishment viz: to be pd. £600 a year & *for His works*.   (Farington, *Diary*, 2244)

More probably this resulted from the recommendation of Baron Dimsdale and Sir James Harris, ambassador at St Petersburg. Brompton arrived at St Petersburg late in 1779 and is known to have painted there a mythological work on the exploits of Achilles for Prince Potyomkin. His charming portrait of Prince Aleksandr Kurakin, signed 'R. Brompton pinx. 1781' (Tretyakov Gallery, Moscow), which depicts the prince standing at ease in a park-like landscape, marks a change in his style towards a relaxed informality and also represents an innovation in Russian portraiture. In addition, he made a portrait of Countess Branitskaya (*c*.1781), *The Grand Duke Constantine as a Child* (*c*.1780; Pavlovsk Palace, St Petersburg), *The Grand Dukes Alexander and Constantine* (1781; Hermitage Museum, St

Petersburg), and two portraits of Catherine, one bust-length (also in the Hermitage Museum) and the other full-length, probably unfinished and now in a poor state (Pavlovsk Palace).

Jeremy Bentham, who described Brompton as a 'harum-scarum ingenious sort of an artist' (*Correspondence of Jeremy Bentham*, 2.512), stated that he had married a Miss Yalden. There is no record of his marriage to Ann Yalden, nor of a possible earlier one, although a daughter, Frances Percy, married the Revd London King Pitt, chaplain to the English factory, St Petersburg, in 1798 and after his death in 1813 became the Empress Mother Maria Fedorovna's constant companion. Three children were born to Brompton and his wife in St Petersburg: two daughters died in 1782 but a son, Alexander Constantine, born in that same year, survived. On 1 January 1783 os Brompton died at Tsarskoye Selo, near St Petersburg, of 'gniloy goryachki' ('putrid fever'). Brompton died, as he had lived, in debt, owing 5000 roubles, which the empress alleviated with the gift of half a year's salary, and Potyomkin with 1000 roubles. He was buried in Tsarskoye Selo.　　ALAN BIRD

Sources J. Ingamells, ed., *A dictionary of British and Irish travellers in Italy, 1701–1800* (1997) · W. T. Whitley, *Artists and their friends in England, 1700–1799*, 2 vols. (1928) · O. Millar, *The later Georgian pictures in the collection of her majesty the queen*, 2 vols. (1969) · PRO, Hoare (Pitt) MSS, 30/70 · G. F. Waagen, *Treasures of art in Great Britain*, 3 vols. (1854) · RA, Society of Artists MSS · Farington, *Diary*, vol. 16 · *Proceedings of the Russian Historical Society of Moscow University* [*Chteniya v Imperatorskom obshestviye istorii i drevnostei rossiiskikh pri Moskovskom universitetiye*], 4 (1891), 65 · E. P. Renne, 'Pictures by Brompton in the Hermitage', *West European Art of the XVIII Century: Publications and Research Articles* ['*Kartiny Bromptona u Ermitzhe*', *Zapadnoevropeiskoe iskusstvo XVIII veka: publikatsii i issledovaniia*] (1987) · *The correspondence of Jeremy Bentham*, ed. T. Sprigge and others, [11 vols.] (1968–), in *The collected works of Jeremy Bentham* · K. V. Malinovski, *Notes by Jacob von Stahlin on the fine arts in Russia* (1990), 1.92 [*Zapiski Iakova Shtelina ob iziashchnykh v Rossii*] · registers of the church attached to the English factory, St Petersburg, Russia, GL, MS 11, 192B, fol. 261 · B. Allen and L. Dukelskaya, eds., *British art treasures from the Russian imperial collections in the Hermitage* (1996) [exhibition catalogue, Yale U. CBA, 5 Oct 1996 – 5 Jan 1997] · L. A. Dukelskaya and E. P. Renne, *British painting, sixteenth to nineteenth centuries* (1990), vol. 13 of *The Hermitage catalogue of western European painting* (1983–)
Wealth at death he owed 5000 roubles

Bromsgrove, Richard (d. 1434), abbot of Evesham, doubtless took his name from Bromsgrove in Worcestershire. He probably studied at Gloucester College, Oxford. A bachelor of canon law, he was infirmarer of Evesham Abbey at the time of his election as abbot of that house on 6 December 1418. He was blessed on 21 December in Bengeworth church, near Evesham, by William Barrow (d. 1429), bishop-elect of Bangor and chancellor of Oxford University, and installed on Christmas eve. Soon after election he received a personal letter of felicitation from Thomas Langley (d. 1437), bishop of Durham and chancellor of England. In or after 1425 Abbot Bromsgrove was a chaplain to Richard, duke of York (d. 1460). The abbot was summoned regularly to parliament and served as a local commissioner for royal loans. Under Abbot Richard the

Evesham *Gesta abbatum* were continued from 1379 to 1418, and a register of his acts was begun, but Evesham was censured by the Benedictine provincial chapter in 1423 and 1426 for failing to send its quota of students to Oxford.

Richard Bromsgrove's known writings are *De fraterne correctione canonice excercenda* (extracts in BL, Cotton MS, Titus C. ix, fol. 32v) and a letter of congratulation of *c*.1424 to Roger Pershore, the new abbot of Malmesbury (fol. 30), which borrows material from Bishop Langley's similar letter to Bromsgrove. According to the Evesham *Successio abbatum* Bromsgrove died on 10 May 1435, but the year was in fact 1434. He was buried in the abbey's lady chapel, at the altar step.　　D. C. COX

Sources Bromsgrove's register, BL, Cotton MS, Titus C. ix, fols. 1–38 · The Evesham *Successio abbatum*, Bibliothèque Royale, Brussels, MS. 7965, fol. 133 · *Chancery records* · W. A. Pantin, ed., *Documents illustrating the activities of … the English black monks, 1215–1540*, 3 vols., CS, 3rd ser., 45, 47, 54 (1931–7), vol. 2, pp. 151–2, 172 · *Reports … touching the dignity of a peer of the realm*, House of Lords, 4 (1829), 843–92 · W. D. Macray, ed., *Chronicon abbatiae de Evesham, ad annum 1418*, Rolls Series, 29 (1863) · *CPR, 1429–36*, 444
Archives BL, Cotton MS, Titus C. ix, fols. 1–38

Bromyard [Bromyarde], **John** (d. *c*.1352), Dominican friar and preacher, was of obscure origins, and nothing certain is known of his education except that it must have included advanced study of canon law. He spent most of his working life in the newly established Dominican priory at Hereford, in which diocese he was licenced to hear confessions in 1326; his licence was transferred to another friar in 1352, probably after Bromyard's death. John Bromyard was the author of handbooks for preachers, comprising nine works (five of which are lost) totalling probably well over 2 million words, which had a marked influence on homiletic literature in the later middle ages. The pragmatic intent of all his literary work is illustrated by his providing each of his books with a detailed alphabetical index and an efficient system of cross-reference, at a time when it was still a relative novelty for an author to index his own works. Bromyard's first book, the *Tractatus iuris canonici et civilis* (also known as the *Opus trivium*), attempted to displace frivolous material such as animal lore and exotic stories from the pulpit, and replace it with the solid moral doctrine of canon law—perhaps a reaction to the nascent humanism of the 'classicizing' friars such as Nicholas Trevet (d. 1328).

Although the *Tractatus*, which was printed at Mainz about 1473, and again at Lyons in 1500, was his most successful work in the middle ages, Bromyard is now best known for the expanded version that he made of the *Tractatus*, the massive alphabetical encyclopaedia of preaching lore, the *Summa praedicantium*, which occupied him up to his last years. In it he shows a less austere sense of the preacher's office, and includes sermon material of every description. Although not an original thinker, Bromyard was a venomous and effective critic of abuses and vanities in all areas of ecclesiastical and secular life. The *Summa praedicantium* remained popular during the sixteenth century and after. It was first printed by

A. Koberger at Nuremberg in 1485, and other editions followed, the most widely circulated being that of Arcangelus Ritius at Venice in 1586. As late as 1614 Hieronymus Verdussen published an edition at Antwerp, which he reissued in 1627 under the title *Promptuarium concionatorum*. In modern times its value as a source for medieval social history, as well as for the development of sermon literature, came to be appreciated primarily through the work of G. R. Owst. Until 1953 Bromyard the Dominican preacher was generally confused with a younger namesake, also a Hereford Dominican, who was chancellor of Cambridge University in 1382.

PETER BINKLEY

Sources P. Binkley, 'John Bromyard and the Hereford Dominicans', *Centres of learning: learning and location in pre-modern Europe and the Near East*, ed. J. W. Drijvers and A. A. MacDonald (1995), 255–64 · L. E. Boyle, 'The date of the *Summa praedicantium* of John Bromyard', *Speculum*, 48 (1973), 553–7; repr. in L. E. Boyle, *Pastoral care, clerical education and canon law, 1200–1400* (1981) · Emden, *Oxf.* · G. R. Owst, *Literature and pulpit in medieval England*, 2nd edn (1961) · J.-T. Welter, *L'exemplum dans la littérature religieuse et didactique du moyen âge* (Paris, 1927)

Brón mac Icni (*d.* 512). *See under* Connacht, saints of (*act.* c.400–c.800).

Brónach (*fl.* 5th–6th cent.?). *See under* Ulster, saints of (*act.* c.400–c.650).

Bronckorst, Arnold (*fl.* 1565–1586), painter, was active in both England and Scotland. The earliest record of him is a payment for a portrait of Sir Henry Sidney, probably a miniature (1565/6). A full-sized portrait of William Cecil, Lord Burghley (Hatfield House, Hertfordshire), is signed with initials and dated 1573, the same year in which he painted an *Andromeda* for Queen Elizabeth's office of the revels. In 1578 he added a fuller signature to a portrait of Oliver St John, Lord St John of Bletso (priv. coll.), and the spelling of his surname there is the one that has been preferred, though other records use a wide variety of forms: Bronckhorst, van Bronckhorst, van Brounckhorst, van Brounckhurst, and Brunkhurst. There is also some uncertainty about his forename. One of the latest contemporary records, which describes him as a Dutch painter living in the Langbourne ward of London in 1583, calls him Arthur rather than Arnold. This form is also used by Stephen Atkinson in his history of gold-mining in Scotland, written in 1619 with the assistance of the miniaturist Nicholas Hilliard (c.1547–1619), with whom Bronckorst had been associated. However, the most copious records, those written during Bronckorst's sojourn in Scotland, all use the form Arnold.

In Scotland Bronckorst is first recorded in April 1580, when he was paid by the treasury for a number of portraits. His original purpose in travelling to Scotland, however, appears to have been to prospect for gold on behalf of Hilliard and another Netherlandish painter, Cornelius de Vos, who may have been his cousin. The excavations at Crawford Muir, in Lanarkshire, were initially successful but at some later stage he fell foul of the regent, James Douglas, fourth earl of Morton, over the export of the gold-bearing materials that had been produced. This

forced him to seek employment at court as provider of 'all the small and great pictures' for the young James VI. This lifetime office was granted on 19 September 1581 and his fees were paid regularly until Martinmas 1583. However, by the following term, Whitsun 1584, he had been replaced as painter-in-ordinary by Adrian Vanson, who was part of the Netherlandish community living in Edinburgh.

In the mid-1580s, when Bronckorst had resettled in London, there are records of a wife, Sara, and the baptism of three children—Sara, Michael, and, in 1586, William—at St Nicholas Acons, Lombard Street.

Only a few paintings can be attributed to Bronckorst with a reasonable degree of certainty. In addition to those mentioned there are portraits of James VI as a child, holding a hawk, and of the earl of Morton, with whom Bronckorst had clashed, which are almost certainly his work (both Scottish National Portrait Gallery, Edinburgh).

DUNCAN THOMSON

Sources D. Thomson, *Painting in Scotland, 1570–1650* (1975) [exhibition catalogue, Scot. NPG, 21 Aug – 21 Sept 1975] · S. Atkinson, *The discoverie and historie of the gold mynes in Scotland, written in the year 1619* (1825) · M. Edmond, *Hilliard and Oliver* (1983) · *Return of the aliens dwelling in the city and suburbs of London*, 10 (1900), pt 2 · E. Auerbach, *Tudor artists* (1954) · E. Auerbach, *Nicholas Hilliard* (1961) · R. Strong, *The English icon* (1969) · accounts of the treasurer of Scotland, NA Scot., E 21/61, fol. 19, 43; E 21/62, fol. 162v; E 21/63, fol. 46, 95; E 22/6, fol. 97v, 134, 184; E 23/5/6 · register of the privy seal, NA Scot., PS 1/47, fol. 40 · M. R. Apted and S. Hannabuss, eds., *Painters in Scotland, 1301–1700: a biographical dictionary*, Scottish RS, new ser., 7 (Edinburgh, 1978)
Archives NA Scot., accounts of the treasurer of Scotland, E 21/61, E 21/62, E 21/63, E 22/6, E 23/5/6 · NA Scot., register of the privy seal, PS 1/47

Bronescombe, Walter of [Walter de Exonia] (c.1220–1280), bishop of Exeter, was born in Exeter; of his parentage nothing is known. He was trained at university, no doubt at Oxford, appears to have obtained his first benefice *in commendam* (Coningsby, Lincolnshire) in 1243, and, probably having been attached to the *familia* of William of Raleigh, bishop of Winchester (*d.* 1250), was archdeacon of Surrey by 1245. Between 1245 and 1257 he obtained dispensations to hold several benefices in plurality, which included the rectory of Farnham, annexed to the archdeaconry of Surrey, the rectory of East Clandon in Surrey, the chapel of Bloxworth in Dorset, and a prebend in the king's free chapel of St Nicholas at Wallingford Castle.

During the same period Bronescombe clearly became involved in royal service, for in 1250 he acted for Henry III at the papal curia in securing the confirmation of the highly controversial election to the bishopric of Winchester of Aymer de Lusignan (*d.* 1260), the king's half-brother; in the following year he was appointed to be the king's proctor at the papal curia. Favour with the king was combined with papal favour, for he was styled papal chaplain by 1250. By 1254 he was a canon of Exeter Cathedral, and became chancellor of the cathedral soon afterwards. His election as bishop of Exeter on 23 February 1258 was apparently undisputed. Royal assent was given on 3 March, and the temporalities were restored on the 6th.

Along with the new bishops of Norwich and Coventry and Lichfield, Bronescombe was ordained priest on 9 March and consecrated as bishop on 10 March by the archbishop of Canterbury, Boniface of Savoy (d. 1270). He was enthroned in Exeter Cathedral on 14 April.

In common with most bishops in the thirteenth century, especially those with university training, Bronescombe did not combine his ecclesiastical duties with a high office of state. Even so, he continued in royal service, acting from time to time as royal negotiator and adviser, notably at times of crisis. He gives the strong impression of having been practical and conciliatory, a man who inspired confidence in those with whom he had dealings. He was already in Paris on the king's business during July 1258, and early in 1263 he was one of Henry III's proctors in the French king's court. In these years he was one of a few markedly royalist bishops among a generally Montfortian episcopate.

Between 1263 and 1265 Bronescombe was much involved in treating for peace at home between the king and his barons. When peace came he was one of the committee of six who, having co-opted a further six, devised the settlement: the dictum of Kenilworth of 31 October 1266. On 11 December 1272 he transferred the spiritualities of the see of Canterbury to the new archbishop, Robert Kilwardby (d. 1279), and on the following day was the only bishop recorded as present in London at an important declaration concerning royal rights in respect of the pope's provision of Kilwardby. With the bishop of Winchester he presented Kilwardby with his pallium in May 1273, and immediately set out for Burgundy, to meet Edward I on his return from crusade. He rejoined Edward in Gascony in the autumn, and baptized Edward's son Alfonso, born at Bayonne on 24 November. He then attended the general council at Lyons from May to July 1274, returning to England for Edward's coronation on 19 August. Scarcely any evidence survives to shed light on his particular role during these various activities, but he was clearly a staunch and respected supporter of both Henry III and Edward I.

Bronescombe's diocesan work can be studied in much more detail, for his register is the first extant episcopal register for the diocese of Exeter, and probably in fact the first to be compiled. It reveals a vigorous and conscientious bishop, active in visiting, and often rededicating, the churches of his large diocese. He restored and augmented the collegiate church of Crediton, and founded and endowed another college on a large scale at Glasney in Cornwall, near Penryn, consecrating the church on 27 March 1267; eight years later he endowed a chantry there. In 1268, and again in 1275, he issued statutes for his cathedral church, as he also did for his collegiate foundation at Glasney. Bronescombe is remembered also for his work on the manor house at Bishop's Clyst, where he founded or refounded the chapel and dedicated it to St Gabriel, to whom he had a special devotion. During his last years he was involved in a bitter and ramified dispute with Edmund, earl of Cornwall (d. 1300), in the defence of ecclesiastical rights following the encroachments of the earl and his agents. It was during these years, too, that an eastern extension was begun to Exeter Cathedral, with the addition of a square-ended lady chapel with flanking chapels. From this important beginning a major new project of rebuilding developed, which eventually embraced the whole cathedral. The chapel on the south side of the lady chapel was St Gabriel's chapel, and here on 20 July 1280 the bishop ordained a chantry, where he chose to be buried. Bronescombe died in Bishopsteignton on 22 July 1280, and on his tomb, under the northern arch of his chantry chapel, was placed an impressive monumental effigy, notable for its flowing drapery. An elaborate canopy was added in the fifteenth century.

J. H. DENTON, rev.

Sources O. F. Robinson, ed., *The register of Walter Bronescombe, bishop of Exeter, 1258–1280*, 1, CYS, 82 (1995) · F. C. Hingeston-Randolph, ed., *The register of Walter Bronescombe*, 1 (1889) · A. Baudrillart and others, eds., *Dictionnaire d'histoire et de géographie ecclésiastiques*, [27 vols.] (Paris, 1912–) · Emden, *Oxf.*, 1.279 · *Ann. mon.*, vols. 1–4 · *Chancery records* · A. M. Erskine, ed. and trans., *The accounts of the fabric of Exeter Cathedral, 1279–1353*, 2 vols., Devon and Cornwall RS, new ser., 24, 26 (1981–3) · *Les registres d'Innocent IV*, ed. E. Berger, 4 vols. (Paris, 1884–1921) · J. Whetter, *The history of Glasney College* (1988)
Likenesses tomb effigy, Exeter Cathedral [*see illus.*]

Bronowski, Jacob (1908–1974), mathematician, poet, and humanist, was born on 18 January 1908 in Łódź, Poland, the first of the three children of Abram Bronowski, haberdasher, and his wife, Celia Flatto. During the First World

Walter of Bronescombe (c.1220–1280), tomb effigy

Jacob Bronowski (1908–1974), by unknown photographer

War the family lived in Germany, and in 1920 they moved to England. Bronowski subsequently attended the Central Foundation School in London and Jesus College, Cambridge. He studied mathematics at Cambridge, achieving a first class in part one of the mathematical tripos (1928), becoming a wrangler in part two (1930), and earning a doctorate in 1933 (the same year he became a naturalized British subject). Besides his work in algebraic geometry, topology, statistics, and mathematical aspects of biology, Bronowski's intellectual interests already had expanded to include philosophy and literature, particularly poetry. This led to his first major work, *The Poet's Defence* (1939), in which he wrestled with the relationship between the truth of poetry and that of science. It marked the real beginning of his attempts to 'create a philosophy for the twentieth century which [is] … all of one piece' (Bronowski, 15). He continued to develop this theme in his study of the poetry of William Blake, published in 1944. His friendship with poets Laura Riding and Robert Graves induced Bronowski to try his own hand at poetry, a practice he continued throughout his life. He published little of his poetry, but each year his Christmas card to friends and family featured one of his pieces.

Bronowski left Cambridge in 1934 to take up a lectureship at the University College of Hull. In 1941 he married Rita Coblentz, the sculptor Rita Colin; they later had four daughters. By 1942 Bronowski was recruited to the war effort, in his case pioneering the field of operational research methods. As scientific deputy to the British joint chiefs of staff mission to Japan in 1945 he applied these

methods to write a report, *Effects of the Atomic bombs at Hiroshima and Nagasaki*. He extended this approach to government research on industrial problems, becoming director of the coal research establishment of the National Coal Board of Great Britain in 1950. From 1959 to 1963 Bronowski served as director-general of process development, when he elaborated his research into smokeless fuel. During this time he acted as a consultant to UNESCO (1948) in Paris and as Carnegie visiting professor at the Massachusetts Institute of Technology (1953). Especially significant to his future work in popularizing science, Bronowski began to work as a commentator for the British Broadcasting Corporation. There (particularly in a series called *The Brains Trust*) he displayed remarkable talent for explaining and conveying scientific concepts to a lay audience.

To chronicle Bronowski's posts and achievements, however, scarcely captures the eclectic intellectual interests that powered his most enduring contributions. Bronowski saw art and science, the 'two cultures', as 'twin expressions of the human imagination' (Wren, 91). During his Cambridge years he had sought to understand literature as a form of universal knowledge. Bronowski gradually turned from poetry to science as revelatory of imagination, 'a shift of emphasis rather than a shift of position' (ibid.). It was perhaps his wrestling with the betrayal of human values exemplified by the holocaust and the atomic bombing of Japan that caused Bronowski to reverse his earlier views about the value-transcendent quality of imaginative thought.

The last twenty years of Bronowski's life were dedicated to developing the theme of the humanistic dimensions of science. In his *Science and Human Values* of 1956 (derived from his lectures at Massachusetts Institute of Technology in 1953), Bronowski argued that civilization's failures were associated with an arrogant faith in the panacea of value free science unshaped by its social environment. Only an ethical code built on 'truth, trust and freedom to dissent' (Wren, 92) permitted the scientific imagination to flourish. Contemporaries have identified this work as initiating the two cultures debate, and C. P. Snow himself acknowledges Bronowski's contributions in *The Two Cultures: and a Second Look* (1963).

In 1964 Bronowski emigrated to the United States to become senior fellow at the Salk Institute for Biological Studies in San Diego, California, and later director of its council for biology in human affairs (1970). There he researched the topic of human specificity, which he understood as the attempt to define the unique biological and behavioural characteristics of the human species. This work, which emphasized the special role of imagination for explaining human nature, served as the basis for the thirteen-part BBC television series *The Ascent of Man* (1973). The series was broadly intended by the BBC to present the development of science to a lay audience in much the way that Kenneth Clark's *Civilisation* had done for art. Written in July 1969, the shooting of the series took over two years to complete and led to Bronowski's visiting some thirty countries. First broadcast in 1973, it enthralled many from academic and non-academic back-grounds alike, and won Bronowski the Royal Television Society's silver medal for outstanding creative achievement.

Honours and distinctions recognized Bronowksi's contributions to the humanities and science. He was an honorary fellow of Jesus College, Cambridge (1967), a foreign honorary member of the American Academy of Arts and Sciences (1960), and a fellow of the Royal Society of Literature. He delivered a number of distinguished lectures, including the Silliman lectures at Yale University (1967), the Bampton lectures at Columbia (1969), and the Mellon lectures at the National Gallery of Art in Washington, DC. His own words best sum up the unity of purpose behind his undertakings:

> All that I have written, though it has seemed to me so different from year to year, turns to the same centre: the uniqueness of man that grows out of his struggle (and his gift) to understand both nature and himself. (Biographical sketch from the Bronowski MSS)

Bruno, as he was known to his friends, was widely considered a warm and vibrant man—a liberal with a strong belief in humanity and the power of education. A meeting with him was 'a powerful tonic which left one feeling intellectually and emotionally stimulated and enhanced' (E. Roll and F. Roll, *The Times*, 11 Sept 1974). None the less, when considering human folly, or weighing public acclaim against his own opinion of an individual's true worth, he could be bitingly sardonic (ibid.). He died of a heart attack on 22 August 1974 at East Hampton, Long Island, New York. He was survived by his wife.

SUSAN SHEETS-PYENSON

Sources DNB · D. Wren, 'Bronowski, Jacob', *Thinkers of the twentieth century: a biographical, bibliographical and critical dictionary*, ed. E. Devine (1983), 96–7 · *The Times* (23 Aug 1974) · *The Times* (11 Sept 1974) · *New York Times* (23 Aug 1974) · 'Bronowski, Jacob', *Encyclopaedia Britannica*, 2 (1989) · University of Toronto, Thomas Fisher Rare Book Library, Bronowski MSS · WWW · J. Bronowski, *The ascent of man* (1973)
Archives University of Toronto, Thomas Fisher Rare Book Library, literary MSS and papers | Rice University, Houston, Texas, Woodson Research Center, corresp. with Sir Julian Huxley
Likenesses photograph, NPG [*see illus.*]

Brontë, Anne [*pseud.* Acton Bell] (1820–1849), novelist and poet, was born on 17 January 1820 at the parsonage in Market Street, Thornton, near Bradford, Yorkshire, the sixth and youngest child of the Revd Patrick *Brontë (1777–1861) and his wife, Maria (1783–1821), daughter of Thomas Branwell of Penzance and his wife, Anne. Patrick Brontë, born in Emdale, co. Down, Ireland, graduated BA from St John's College, Cambridge, in 1806 and was ordained an Anglican priest in December 1807. Four curacies preceded his appointment in 1815 to Thornton, where Anne was baptized on 25 March 1820. Her siblings were Maria (1814–1825), Elizabeth (1815–1825), Charlotte *Brontë (1816–1855), (Patrick) Branwell *Brontë (1817–1848), and Emily Jane *Brontë (1818–1848). By 20 April 1820 the family had moved to the moorland parish of Haworth, of which Patrick Brontë had been appointed perpetual curate.

After their mother's death on 15 September 1821 the Brontë children were cared for by their aunt Elizabeth Branwell (1776–1842). The early deaths of Anne's elder sisters Maria on 6 May 1825 and Elizabeth on 15 June 1825 perhaps increased the family's protective care for the delicate Anne. She was not sent to the Clergy Daughters' School at Cowan Bridge (the fearsome 'Lowood' of Charlotte Brontë's *Jane Eyre*) but was educated at home by her aunt and her father until mid-1832, when Charlotte Brontë began to teach her younger sisters. Anne and her inseparable companion Emily acquired considerable linguistic skills, developed their talent for music, and invented a secret, exotic, imaginary land—Gondal. No prose stories of Gondal survive, but some twenty-three of Anne's poems describe the loves and griefs of its romantic heroes and heroines. They reflect the sisters' delight in oriental tales and the works of Scott and Thomas Moore. Anne and Emily, like Charlotte and Branwell Brontë in their Angrian saga, chronicled the violent feuds, treacheries, and imprisonments of warrior kings and tragic queens; but while Angria had been virtually abandoned in 1839, new volumes of the Gondal saga were still being written as late as 1845.

In July 1835 Charlotte Brontë became a teacher at Margaret Wooler's school at Roe Head, Mirfield. Their father wanted to keep Anne at home for another year, but Emily, who had accompanied Charlotte as a pupil, longed for freedom and rapidly declined in health. Anne replaced her at Roe Head from October 1835, until in December 1837 she too became 'wretchedly ill', suffering from pain and difficult—probably asthmatic—breathing, and perhaps also from gastric fever (*Letters of Charlotte Brontë*, 1.173–5). Charlotte took Anne home, where she gradually recovered. Charlotte returned to the school early in 1838 and continued teaching there when it was moved to Heald's House, Dewsbury Moor, in that year. Anne may also have returned at that time. She was a quiet, diligent pupil, earning a prize for good conduct, and developing her talents for languages and drawing.

Anne was the most attractive looking of the Brontë sisters. A friend of the family, Ellen Nussey, described 'dear gentle Anne' as she appeared in 1833: 'Her hair was a very pretty light brown and fell on her neck in graceful curls. She had lovely violet blue eyes, fine pencilled eye-brows, a clear, almost transparent complexion' ('Reminiscences of Charlotte Brontë', *Letters of Charlotte Brontë*, 1.598). The publisher George Smith recalled Anne as 'a gentle, quiet, rather subdued person, by no means pretty yet of a pleasing appearance. Her manner was curiously expressive of a wish for protection and encouragement' (Huxley, 60). Charlotte Brontë's pencil drawing of Anne dated 17 April 1833 was identified as an excellent likeness, while two of her watercolours (*c.*1833 and 17 June 1834) and Branwell Brontë's oil painting of his sisters (now in the National Portrait Gallery) show Anne's attractive colouring.

Anne Brontë had an affectionate nature and inspired affection in others. On 20 January 1842 Charlotte described the young curate William Weightman sitting opposite Anne in church, sighing softly '& looking out of the corners of his eyes to win her attention—& Anne is so quiet, her look so downcast' (*Letters of Charlotte Brontë*, 1.279). Anne's poem 'I will not mourn thee, lovely one', written in December 1842 after Weightman's death, shows her trying to control her grief for the loss of one whose 'angel smile … Could my fond heart rejoice'. In the end Anne also won the hearts of two of her pupils, the wayward and difficult Robinson girls. Mild and reticent as she seemed, she possessed an extraordinary heroism of endurance.

Anne Brontë's work as a governess began on 8 April 1839, when she insisted on going alone to Blake Hall, Mirfield, where she was to teach Joshua Cunliffe Ingham and Mary Ingham, the eldest children of Joshua Ingham and his wife, Mary. Like the eponymous heroine of her novel *Agnes Grey*, Anne found her pupils spoilt little dunces whom she was not allowed to punish. She endured the 'struggle of life-wearing exertion' to keep the children in decent order until the end of the year, when her employment at Blake Hall ceased—probably by her employers' decision (*Letters of Charlotte Brontë*, 1.210).

Anne next became a governess in the family of the Revd Edmund Robinson and his wife, Lydia, *née* Gisborne, at Thorp Green Hall, Little Ouseburn, near York. She probably arrived on or about 8 May 1840, and remained until June 1845. Her pupils were Lydia Mary, Elizabeth Lydia (Bessy), and Mary, and she may have taught Latin to Edmund. Agnes Grey's time at Horton Lodge is partly based on Anne's experiences at Thorp Green, while her descriptions of the 'broad, bright bay' of A— recall Anne's delight in Scarborough, where she accompanied the family during their summer holidays. Anne had much to endure in the Robinson household. In her diary paper for 30 July 1841 Anne recorded that she disliked her situation and wished to change it for another, and Emily in her paper sent 'from far an exhortation of courage courage! to exiled and harassed Anne wishing she was here'. Charlotte thought of her as a 'patient, persecuted stranger— amongst people … grossly insolent, proud & tyrannical' (*Letters of Charlotte Brontë*, 1.264, 263, 267).

Anne's return to Thorp Green at the Robinsons' urgent request in January 1842 was perhaps a victory of conscience over inclination, for her poem 'In memory of a happy day in February' shows her rejoicing in God's glory shining 'throughout the moral world'. Her faith was to be tested by the death of William Weightman from cholera on 6 September 1842 and the painful death of Elizabeth Branwell on 29 October 1842. Materially, Anne benefited by her aunt's bequest of a quarter-share of effects which were valued at under £1500. She bought books and drawing materials, and continued to study Latin and German, for she and her sisters intended ultimately to set up their own school.

Meanwhile, Branwell Brontë became tutor to the young Edmund Robinson in January 1843. A year later he and Anne were still 'wonderously valued in their situation' (*Letters of Charlotte Brontë*, 1.342). But according to Branwell, Mrs Robinson soon became 'damnably too fond' of him, and inspired an 'attachment' on his part, leading to 'reciprocations … little looked for' and, apparently, to Mr Robinson's discovery of an affair. He abruptly dismissed Branwell in July 1845 for conduct 'bad beyond expression' (ibid., 399–414; Barker, 455–77). Anne may not have realized the full extent of the alleged affair, but she left Thorp Green on or just after 11 June 1845, and recorded in her diary paper for 31 July that she had 'had some very unpleasant and undreamt of experience of human nature' (*Letters of Charlotte Brontë*, 1.410). Anne, witnessing with pain and revulsion Branwell's descent into increasingly heavy drinking and drug taking, grieved over his wasted talent and his moral and spiritual degeneration. In her preface to the second edition of *The Tenant of Wildfell Hall* she defended her realistic presentation of 'vice and vicious characters' as the best method of warning inexperienced youth to avoid the 'snares and pitfalls of life'.

Branwell's behaviour led his sisters finally to abandon their plan for a school at the parsonage. But in the autumn of 1845 Charlotte discovered a manuscript volume of verse in Emily's handwriting, and with difficulty persuaded her that it should be published. Anne quietly produced some of her own poems, and by about 22 May 1846 Aylott and Jones had published, at the authors' expense, *Poems* by Currer, Ellis, and Acton Bell—nineteen by Currer (Charlotte), twenty-one each by Ellis (Emily) and Acton (Anne). Although only two copies of the first issue were sold, *The Critic* and *The Athenaeum* reviewed it favourably on 4 July, and the volume was reissued by Smith, Elder & Co. in 1848. *Fraser's Magazine* published Anne's poem 'The three guides' in August and her hymn beginning:

> Believe not those who say
> The upward path is smooth

in December that year.

Soon after 27 June 1846 the Brontë sisters began to offer to various publishers three novels: Anne's *Agnes Grey*, Emily's *Wuthering Heights*, and Charlotte's *The Professor*, the last of which was rejected by all. The other two, accepted by Thomas Cautley Newby by July 1847, were not published until December, after the outstanding success of Charlotte's *Jane Eyre* in October convinced Newby that any works by the 'Bells' would be a profitable venture. In *Agnes Grey* Anne Brontë describes the tribulations of a governess, shrewdly portrays her worldly employers and spoilt pupils, and contrasts the miseries of a mercenary marriage with the happiness of Agnes and her ideal clergyman, Edward Weston. Modern critics see *Agnes Grey* as an effective exposure of the threat to woman's integrity and independence posed by a corrupt and materialistic society. At the time, though praised for its minute observation, the novel (like those of the other Bells) was criticized for its concern with the eccentric and unpleasant, and accused of exaggeration in parts 'carefully copied from the life', as Anne was to recall in the preface to the second edition of her next novel.

Undeterred by such criticisms, Anne Brontë courageously depicted in *The Tenant of Wildfell Hall* a wife who leaves her debauched and adulterous husband in order to protect her young son, and who earns her living as an artist, returning only to nurse her husband—now an ungrateful and peevish invalid—in the hope that he will seek and receive God's mercy. Before Newby published the novel in June 1848, he informed an American publisher that it was the latest work of Currer Bell. Since Smith, Elder & Co., the publishers of Jane Eyre, had arranged that Harper & Brothers should publish the first American edition of Currer Bell's next work, George Smith demanded an explanation. Charlotte and Anne made their hasty 'pop visit' to London from 8 to 12 July, astonishing Smith by identifying themselves as two of the famous Bells, and confronting Newby with his chicanery. On the day they arrived in London, The Spectator admitted the power of Acton Bell's novel, but condemned the writer's 'morbid love for the coarse, not to say the brutal' (21, 662–3). The book sold well, despite or because of such criticism. Today it is seen as an innovative and radical expression of feminist values, challenging the then current ideal of woman as an 'angel in the house', submissive to her lot as her husband's chattel.

Anne Brontë felt harsh reviews keenly, and must have been especially depressed by allegations that the revolting details of the novel made it unfit to be read, in spite of its unimpeachable moral and religious purpose. For Anne, the need to pursue and to guide others into the difficult upward path of Christian faith was paramount. Her religious poems, eloquent in their self-analysis and exhortation, include the well-known hymn, 'My God! O let me call thee mine!' Her last and most moving poem,

A dreadful darkness closes in
On my bewildered mind

was written in January 1849, when she knew she was mortally ill. It moves from that torturing darkness to a prayer for patience, fortitude, and hope. Anne was supported by her belief in the doctrine of universal salvation, which she had cherished from her childhood.

After Branwell Brontë's death on 24 September 1848 and Emily's on 19 December, symptoms of pulmonary tuberculosis became evident in Anne's declining health. As courageous as her sister but more amenable, she accepted medical help and wished strongly for recovery. Her journey to Scarborough in May 1849 in the company of Charlotte and of Ellen Nussey was undertaken in the hope of improvement; but on 28 May Anne Brontë died at their lodging at 2 St Nicholas Cliff, Scarborough—with almost her last breath saying she was happy, and thanking God that 'death was come, and come so gently' (Wise and Symington, 2.337). Her funeral took place at Christ Church, Scarborough, on 30 May, and she was buried in St Mary's churchyard on Castle Hill, Scarborough, the same day.

MARGARET SMITH

Sources The letters of Charlotte Brontë, ed. M. Smith, 2 vols. (1995–2000), vol. 1 • J. Barker, The Brontës (1994) • C. Brontë, 'A biographical notice of the authors ... and a preface', Wuthering Heights and Agnes Grey, by Ellis and Acton Bell, ed. C. Bell (1850), [vii]–xvi, [471]–3, 490–91 • A. Brontë, Agnes Grey, ed. H. Marsden and R. Inglesfield, Clarendon edn (1988) • A. Brontë, The tenant of Wildfell Hall, ed. H. Rosengarten, Clarendon edn (1992) • E. Chitham, ed., The poems of Anne Brontë: a new text and commentary (1979) • parish register, Old Bell Chapel, Thornton, Yorkshire, 1813–27 [baptism] • d. cert. • manuscript diary of Elizabeth Firth of Kipping House, Thornton, University of Sheffield • T. J. Wise and J. A. Symington, eds., The Brontës: their lives, friendships and correspondence, 4 vols. (1932) • E. C. Gaskell, The life of Charlotte Brontë (1857) • [L. Huxley], The house of Smith Elder (1923) • E. Chitham, A life of Anne Brontë (1991) • C. Alexander and J. Sellars, The art of the Brontës (1995) • M. Allott, ed., The Brontës: the critical heritage (1974) • G. A. Yablon and J. R. Turner, A Brontë bibliography (1978) • M. H. Frawley, Anne Brontë (1996) • A. J. Drewery, 'The tenant of Wildfell Hall: a woman's place?', Brontë Society Transactions, 19 (1998), 251–60

Archives BL, papers • Brontë Parsonage Museum, Haworth, West Yorkshire, collection • Hunt. L., papers • Morgan L., papers • NYPL, papers • Princeton University, New Jersey, papers • Ransom HRC, papers

Likenesses C. Brontë, pencil drawing, 1833, Brontë Parsonage Museum, Haworth, West Yorkshire • C. Brontë, watercolour drawing, c.1833, priv. coll.; [on loan to Brontë Parsonage Museum, Haworth, West Yorkshire] • B. Brontë, group portrait, oils, c.1834 (The Brontë sisters), NPG; see illus. in Brontë, Charlotte (1816–1855) • B. Brontë, group portrait, oils, c.1834 ('The gun group') • C. Brontë, watercolour drawing, 1834, Brontë Parsonage Museum, Haworth, West Yorkshire • C. Brontë, pencil, c.1835 (Anne Brontë?), repro. in A. Brontë, The tenant of Wildfell Hall, Thornton edn (1907), frontispiece • E. Brontë, pen-and-ink sketch in diary paper, 1837, Brontë Parsonage Museum, Haworth, West Yorkshire • photograph and pencil tracings (after B. Brontë, 'The gun group'), Brontë Parsonage Museum, Haworth, West Yorkshire • portraits, repro. in Alexander and Sellars, Art of the Brontës

Wealth at death under £600; incl. quarter-share of aunt's estate of under £1500; salary of £40 p.a. during employment at Thorp Green; £50 received from publisher Newby for The tenant of Wildfell Hall; legacy of £200 from godmother; plus unspecified funds: administration, Borth. Inst.

Brontë, (Patrick) Branwell (1817–1848), writer and painter, was born on 26 June 1817 at Thornton in the West Riding of Yorkshire, the fourth of six children of the Revd Patrick *Brontë (1777–1861), Church of England clergyman, and Maria Branwell (1783–1821), daughter of Thomas and Anne Branwell of Penzance. In April 1820, having accepted the position of perpetual curate, Patrick Brontë moved his family—Maria (1814–1825), Elizabeth (1815–1825), Charlotte *Brontë (1816–1855), Branwell, Emily Jane *Brontë (1818–1848), and Anne *Brontë (1820–1849)—to Haworth, where his wife died in September 1821.

Branwell was educated at home by his father. Like his sisters, he read widely from an early age, being particularly fond of Blackwood's Magazine, especially the 'Noctes Ambrosianae'. After the deaths of their mother in 1821 and their two eldest sisters in 1825, he and his remaining sisters, stimulated by their reading, began to make up and act out plays. These 'Young Men' plays, under the leadership of Charlotte and Branwell, evolved into the complex saga of the imaginary Glasstown confederacy, situated in the Asante country of west Africa.

Brontë's earliest known piece of writing dates from March 1827, but with the production in January 1829 of his Magazine, which quickly became Branwell's Blackwood's Magazine, he revealed his literary aspirations—preeminently as poet, but also as dramatist, critic, historian, conversationalist, editor, and publisher—in short as the man of letters he saw exemplified by Christopher North and James Hogg in the 'Noctes Ambrosianae'. Between 1835 and 1842 Brontë wrote six times to Blackwood's, offering his services and samples of his poetry, and in December 1835 putting himself forward to replace the late James

(Patrick) Branwell Brontë (1817–1848), self-portrait, c.1840

Hogg. Most of his hundreds of manuscript pages up to the end of 1837, chronicling events and activities in Glasstown, and later in Angria, were works 'published' in Glasstown (later Verdopolis); in 1832 he embarked on the first manuscript volume of his 'collected' poems, to be followed by others in 1835 and 1837. In his competitive/collaborative chronicling of the worlds of Glasstown and Angria with Charlotte, Brontë's particular interest lay in the politics, civil wars, and military campaigns that led to the emergence of Arthur Wellesley, Marquis of Douro and Duke of Zamorna (Charlotte's hero), and Alexander Percy, earl of Northangerland (Brontë's protagonist); to the creation in 1834 of the kingdom of Angria, with Zamorna as king and Percy as his premier and father-in-law; and to their subsequent self-destructive rivalry.

Meanwhile, and probably as early as 1834, Brontë was also receiving instruction in painting from the portrait painter William Robinson. It was about 1834 that he completed his portrait of the Brontë sisters, having painted over the original representation of himself in the portrait. Although he drafted a letter in 1835 seeking admission to the Royal Academy, recent evidence suggests that the letter was never sent and that Brontë never made the infamous trip to London described by earlier biographers (Barker, 226–31). In July 1838 he set up as a portrait painter in Bradford, but the venture was unsuccessful, and his career as painter came to an end. In the course of it, however, he had made numerous literary and artistic acquaintances, including the sculptor J. B. Leyland and his brother Francis, both of whom remained Brontë's lifelong friends.

In June 1839 Brontë embarked on a review of the classics with his father to prepare for employment as a tutor. On 1 January 1840 he took up a position in the home of Robert Postlethwaite in Broughton in Furness. Proximity to the Lake District inspired a return to literary activity. In April 1840 he sent a long poem and his translations of five of Horace's *Odes* to Thomas De Quincey at Dove Cottage, Grasmere. Five days later he sent another poem and two translations to Hartley Coleridge at Nab Cottage, Rydal Water, to solicit his opinion on whether it would 'be possible to obtain remuneration for translations … such as these' (Barker, 333). A visit to Nab Cottage on 1 May, at Coleridge's invitation, encouraged Brontë to undertake a complete translation of book I of the *Odes*, which Coleridge promised to read on completion. Despite his dismissal as tutor, Brontë sent the completed translations to Coleridge in June 1840. Because the translations were of a high quality and would probably have found a ready market (Barker, 336), it is unfortunate that Coleridge never completed the very positive and encouraging reply he began to draft in November–December 1840.

In October 1840 Brontë was employed as assistant clerk-in-charge at Sowerby Bridge on the new Leeds and Manchester Railway, and promoted to clerk-in-charge at Luddenden Foot on 1 April 1841. Contrary to the traditional view of Brontë's dissipation during this employment, the proximity to the literary and artistic circles of Halifax, which included not only the Leyland brothers, but also poets such as William Dearden, John Nicholson, and Thomas Crossley, provided new impetus for literary activity. Within a month of his promotion, Brontë published his first poem, 'Heaven and Earth', in the *Halifax Guardian*. Despite being dismissed from his railway post in March 1842 because of a discrepancy in the accounts for which he was held responsible, though not suspected of theft or fraud, by the end of 1842 Brontë published seven further poems and an article on Thomas Bewick in *The Guardian*, eight in the *Bradford Herald* (six of which appeared simultaneously in *The Guardian*), and one in the *Leeds Intelligencer*, all but one under the pseudonym 'Northangerland'. Publication in *The Guardian* was no mean achievement; the paper was proud of the original poetry it featured and the high standards it set. Brontë also tried *Blackwell's* once more, unsuccessfully, and sent lines to Caroline Bowles, James and Harriet Martineau, and Leigh Hunt for criticism and advice.

Employed as tutor with the Robinsons at Thorp Green, near York, from January 1843 to July 1845, Brontë continued to write, publishing two more poems in *The Guardian* in 1845, four in the *Yorkshire Gazette* (one a repeat from the *Bradford Herald*), and commencing work on a novel, never completed.

After his dismissal from Thorp Green because of an affair with Mrs Robinson, and the subsequent realization in 1846, on the death of her husband, that she had no intention of marrying him, Brontë declined into chronic alcoholism, opiates, and debt. His behaviour after his dismissal from Thorp Green caused the family much distress, embarrassment, and on the part of Charlotte, bitterness over talent wasted (Barker, 568–9). Yet even in his decline Brontë published two further poems in *The Guardian*, in 1846 and 1847 respectively. He died at Haworth parsonage on 24 September 1848, most likely of tuberculosis aggravated by delirium tremens (Barker, 564, 569), although his death certificate gives the cause as 'chronic bronchitis-marasmus'. He was buried in the family vault on 28 September, having much more nearly realized his literary aspirations than has been traditionally acknowledged.

VICTOR A. NEUFELDT

Sources J. Barker, *The Brontës* (1994) · V. A. Neufeldt, *A bibliography of the manuscripts of Patrick Branwell Brontë* (1993) · V. A. Neufeldt, *The poems of Patrick Branwell Brontë* (1990) · *The works of Patrick Branwell Brontë*, ed. V. A. Neufeldt, 2 vols. (1997–9)
Archives Brontë Parsonage Museum, Haworth, West Yorkshire, corresp. and literary papers · Harvard U., Houghton L., letters and literary MSS · Ransom HRC · U. Leeds, Brotherton L. | NYPL, Berg collection · Princeton University, New Jersey, Taylor collection
Likenesses P. B. Brontë, self-portrait, drawing, *c.*1840, Brontë Parsonage Museum, Haworth, Yorkshire [*see illus.*]

Brontë [*married name* Nicholls], **Charlotte** [*pseud.* Currer Bell] **(1816–1855)**, novelist, was born on 21 April 1816 at the parsonage, Market Street, Thornton, near Bradford, Yorkshire, the third of the six children of the Revd Patrick *Brontë (1777–1861) and his wife, Maria, *née* Branwell (1783–1821). Her siblings were Maria Brontë (1814–1825), Elizabeth Brontë (1815–1825), (Patrick) Branwell *Brontë (1817–1848), Emily Jane *Brontë (1818–1848), and Anne *Brontë (1820–1849).

Early years and education On 20 April 1820 the Brontë family moved to the bleak moorland village of Haworth, where Patrick Brontë was appointed perpetual curate, a rapid rise for a man who had been born in an Irish crofter's cottage. Intent on upward mobility, Charlotte's father had evinced remarkable cleverness and determination in educating himself, studying for a degree at St John's College, Cambridge, and patiently making a career as an evangelical Anglican. An eccentric and something of a hypochondriac, Patrick Brontë was not the irascible, neglectful father of Brontë legend. He encouraged his children to explore the moors and to take an interest in natural history, habits which provided them with a deep love of nature and a sense of personal freedom. His liberal Wordsworthian attitude towards education, his enlightened toryism, his passion for politics and military campaigns, his enthusiasm for the duke of Wellington, and love of poetry and the classics are all reflected in Charlotte's juvenilia. Her strongest loyalty throughout life was to her father, although she grew to disagree with some of his religious and political views.

Charlotte regretted that she knew so little of her mother, the small sprightly woman who had called her future husband 'my dear saucy Pat' (Wise and Symington, 1.20), and who had not only delighted in the romantic tales of the *Lady's Magazine* but had also written an essay for publication entitled 'The advantages of poverty in religious concerns'. At Haworth, Maria Branwell Brontë grew

Charlotte Brontë (1816–1855), by Branwell Brontë, *c.*1834 [*The Brontë Sisters*: Charlotte (right), Anne (left), and Emily (centre)]

steadily weaker from an illness caused by rapid childbearing; she was said to have cancer, but more recently gynaecologists have suggested chronic pelvic sepsis together with increasing anaemia as more likely (*Transactions of the Brontë Society*, 16, 1972, 2.102). Primitive gynaecological knowledge and lack of funds for further treatment (Patrick Brontë's salary was only about £200 per annum) led to her slow and painful death on 15 September 1821.

Elizabeth Branwell (1776–1842) reluctantly agreed to leave her beloved Cornwall and care for her sister's children and household for, as it transpired, the rest of her life. She was financially independent and, like her sister Maria, she was lively and well read. She would tease guests by offering them a pinch of her snuff and could 'tilt arguments against Mr Brontë without fear' (*Transactions of the Brontë Society*, 2, 1899, 10.75). She disliked the cold Yorkshire moors and probably resented the authoritarian role she had to play in the Brontë household as guardian of five children and educator of three young girls. There is no evidence for the accusations of harsh discipline and Calvinistic tyranny that biographers have levelled against Aunt Branwell; she was a Wesleyan Methodist who attended Patrick Brontë's Anglican services. Charlotte and Emily seem to have felt gratitude rather than love for her, but Branwell and Anne were genuinely attached to their aunt. Her independence of mind and perseverance in uncongenial circumstances provided the Brontë sisters with a model of a strong woman whose sense of duty had directed her own path in life.

From an early age Charlotte Brontë was keenly aware that, lacking her aunt's financial independence, she must earn her own living. Her hypersensitivity to her perceived lack of physical charm gave her little faith in the 'marriage market', and she realized that she must rely on her own fortitude and cultivate what talents she had. Self-improvement became a driving force. She was naturally studious and quickly seized every educational opportunity. At eight she was described as 'Altogether clever for her age but know[ing] nothing systematically' (Barker, 129). But it was not simply useful knowledge that she sought; as a girl of twelve she was keen to cultivate a discerning mind and refine her taste in art: 'She picked up every scrap of information concerning painting, sculpture, poetry, music, etc., as if it were gold' (Wise and Symington, 1.92). It was only with great reluctance that her early ambitions to be first an artist, then a poet, were abandoned for the more typical middle-class female occupation of governess.

Charlotte's first experience of institutional schooling was brief and traumatic. In September 1824 she and Emily followed their two older sisters to the Clergy Daughters' School at Cowan Bridge in Lancashire, established in 1823 by the Revd William Carus Wilson (the prototype for Mr Brocklehurst in *Jane Eyre*, 1847). In early 1825 typhoid fever combined with the harsh regime and poor food at the school led to a number of deaths. Maria, already desperately ill, was brought home on 14 February and died on 6 May. After Elizabeth was also sent home ill on 31 May, Patrick Brontë speedily fetched his younger daughters back to Haworth two weeks before Elizabeth's death on 15 June. Both Maria and Elizabeth died of pulmonary tuberculosis. Charlotte's distress and her bitterness towards the school are immortalized in the portrayal of Lowood School in *Jane Eyre*.

The memory of Maria Brontë, who had been both mother and moral guide to the young Charlotte, inspired the depiction of Helen Burns in *Jane Eyre*. Now Charlotte felt that she must assume the mothering role left by her talented and selfless sister. It was a duty that weighed heavily on Charlotte's shoulders for the remainder of her life, constantly conflicting with her feverish creativity and ambition. At six, fired by the descriptions of the celestial city in *Pilgrim's Progress*, she had set off towards Bradford in the hope of reaching her dream city, but was found and was returned home by an anxious servant before she reached the outskirts of her own village (Reid, 24–6). This early thwarted escapade prefigures the constant sense of unfulfilled desire and ambition that burdened Charlotte throughout her life; the quiet exterior of her devotion to family and duty masked 'a truculent spirit' (*Shirley*, vol. 1, chap. 4) beneath its placidity, and produced in her novels and their heroines a poignant ambiguity and passionate frustration towards life. Her novels embody her search for truth in art and for personal integrity in the face of 'this world's desolate and boundless deluge' (Alexander, *Early Writings*, 243).

For the next five and a half years Charlotte was educated at home. Aunt Branwell taught her nieces their letters, needlework, and a little French, while Patrick Brontë gave Branwell (and later his sisters) lessons in the classics. The children also learned to draw and paint, taking occasional lessons from John Bradley, founder member of the Keighley Mechanics' Institute, and possibly from Thomas Plummer, son of the master of the Keighley Free Grammar School. The gendered nature of their art lessons is evident in Charlotte's earliest letter written to her father when she was thirteen and staying with relatives: 'Branwell has taken two sketches from nature, & Emily, Anne, & myself have likewise each of us drawn a piece from some views of the lakes which Mr Fennell brought with him from Westmoreland' (23 Sept 1829, *Letters of Charlotte Brontë*, 1.105).

Early reading and writing Illustrated books seized the imagination of Charlotte Brontë in much the same way as Thomas Bewick's *History of British Birds* impressed both image and word on the mind of the young Jane Eyre. They provided solace, escape, and inspiration. Charlotte not only copied the engravings in such works but also modelled the format, content, and style of her early writing on the books and magazines that she read. Unlike most middle-class Victorian households, there was little censorship of reading in the Brontë parsonage. The Bible was staple fare; yet Patrick Brontë also encouraged an eclectic diet of Homer, Virgil, Shakespeare, Bunyan, Milton, Pope, Johnson, Gibbon, Cowper, Burns, Wordsworth, Coleridge, Scott, Southey, and Byron. He borrowed scientific and travel books from the Keighley Mechanics' Institute Library, and more contemporary works from local circulating libraries. His children devoured local newspapers and especially the tory monthly *Blackwood's Edinburgh Magazine*—'the most able periodical there is', the twelve-year-old Charlotte announced (*Edition of the Early Writings*, ed. Alexander, 1.4)—relishing discussion on the political or religious controversies of the day. Such precocious reading combined with more typical childhood favourites like Aesop's *Fables*, *Arabian Nights*, and *Gulliver's Travels* to produce the rich texture of allusion that is so characteristic of Charlotte Brontë's writing.

Reading and discussion fuelled the Brontë children's play and led to dramatic enactments of historical and imaginary events, often woven around the characters of their toy soldiers. One favourite set of twelve soldiers, given to Branwell in June 1826 and known as the 'Young Men', led to the documentation of the 'plays' and to the Glasstown saga, the story of an imaginary African kingdom colonized by British heroes. These creative adventures were pursued with intense passion and led to partnerships and rivalry. Charlotte and Branwell dominated their younger sisters and vied for control over the narration and direction of the saga. No manuscripts by Emily or Anne relating to the Glasstown saga survive; their first reference to any 'play' is in an 1834 diary note by Emily mentioning their later Gondal saga. Charlotte first recorded the 'plays' in 'The history of the year', March 1829, and wrote her first 'Romantic Tale' the following month, beginning her long literary apprenticeship. (Her earliest extant manuscript, a tiny illustrated story for her sister Anne, is undated and was written at least a year earlier.)

The quantity of Charlotte Brontë's early writings

amounts to more than all her later published novels; and Branwell's output is similar. As she and Branwell wrote miniature magazines, poems, histories, reviews, and novelettes for and about the Young Men, the Glasstown saga gradually took shape. They documented the adventures in love and war of their favourite characters, and described their families, friends, and enemies. In doing so, they traced the fortunes of a federation of nations centred on the capital city of Verdopolis (originally the Great Glasstown) and on the rivalry between Alexander Percy, Lord Northangerland (Branwell's hero and *alter ego*), and the Marquis of Douro, Duke of Zamorna, and King of Angria (Charlotte's hero, the son of Wellington). Charlotte and Branwell wrote prolifically, modelling their characters on eminent political, military, or historical figures such as Wellington, Napoleon, Mary, queen of Scots, or Mme de Staël, or on characters from Scott's novels or Byron's poems. Old geography books, accounts of African exploration, picturesque plates, and their own moorland walks provided a mix of British and exotic landscapes. The adventures they created reflect contemporary colonial expansion, Gothic tales of the supernatural, romantic intrigues, political gossip and scandal.

The Brontë children's manuscripts were originally only a few inches square to match the size of the toy soldiers; they were hand-sewn to look like books and written in a minuscule handwriting to suggest print. The tiny size of their writing meant that the content of the young Brontës' imaginary world remained a secret from the eyes of adults and strangers. This shared activity cemented what Mr Brontë called 'a little society amongst themselves' (*Transactions of the Brontë Society* 8, 1833, 43.92) that fostered creativity and emotional security. Whenever Charlotte or her sisters were away from Haworth (and by implication removed from their creative and spiritual sustenance), they languished both physically and psychologically.

Schooling at Roe Head and artistic endeavours On 17 January 1831 Charlotte Brontë went to Margaret Wooler's school at Roe Head, Mirfield, near Dewsbury, 15 miles from Haworth. There she met the two young women who became her lifelong friends and correspondents: the conscientious, calm, religious Ellen Nussey who fulfilled Charlotte's dutiful self and need for affection, and the fiercely independent Mary *Taylor (1817–1893), the 'Rose Yorke' of *Shirley*) whose radical views on politics, women, and religion fuelled Charlotte's ambitious and rebellious nature. Both described Charlotte's acute awareness of her short stature and plain bespectacled appearance, her shyness among strangers, and, ever aware that she was an object of expense to those at home, her diligence in her studies. When she left, Charlotte carried off the silver medal for achievement and the prize for French.

After only eighteen months Charlotte returned home to share her new knowledge with her sisters. Judging from the quantity and lively content of her creative activity over the next three years, this seems to have been the happiest period of Charlotte's life. Together with her family

she read, studied, taught, wrote letters to schoolfriends and wandered the moors. She spent hours meticulously copying engravings and teaching her sisters the same exercises in delineating eyes, ears, noses, and classical heads that she had learned at school. Above all, she resumed her writing and the Glasstown saga prospered. In Charlotte's absence, Emily and Anne had formed their own imaginary realm of Gondal, and Branwell had launched a republican rebellion in Verdopolis, the combined Paris, London, and Babylon of their African federation. Charlotte quickly negotiated a peace and an intense literary partnership developed between the two siblings which lasted until 1837 (after which Charlotte relied less on her brother's vigorous plot making). The centre of interest moved to the new kingdom of Angria and the political and sexual fortunes of Zamorna and his new wife, Mary Percy. As Charlotte's interest in Byron gradually replaced her fascination for Scott, her writing reflected both her fixation with her hero and her ambivalence towards her own and her heroines' adoration of him.

Charlotte also drew her Angrian heroes and heroines, often modelling them on illustrations of society beauties, on Finden's engravings of Byron's heroines, or even on local Haworth personalities. Her descriptions of Angrian scenes reflect, in particular, the engravings of John Martin's illustrations for the Bible: his paintings of the ancient world and its cataclysmic events and his picturesque scenes of the Garden of Eden. Early practice and knowledge of the visual arts profoundly influenced Charlotte Brontë's mature writing, especially her close observation of character and scene, her sensitivity to colour, her fondness for the vignette, her method of analysing a scene as if it were a painting, and her passionate adherence to drawing verbal pictures 'from the life' (*The Professor*, chap. 12). G. H. Lewes praised *Jane Eyre* for its wordpainting: 'The pictures stand out distinctly before you: they are pictures, and not mere bits of "fine writing"' (Allott, 55).

The majority of Charlotte Brontë's 180 surviving illustrations are detailed copies in pencil, ink, or watercolour made from engravings in drawing manuals, books, or annuals. Her meticulous study and duplication of plates is reflected in Lucy Snowe's drawing in *Villette* (vol. 3, chap. 35), a practice that Charlotte later recognized as an exercise in skill rather than truth in art. Nevertheless this was the contemporary method by which women should acquire the 'accomplishment' of painting and Charlotte's diligence was exemplary. Her ambition was not simply for ladylike accomplishment, although she never progressed to oil-painting as her brother did. At least until the age of twenty she aspired to a career in art, possibly that of a miniaturist, which would have accommodated her problem of extreme short-sightedness. Such an ambition, however, was impossible; professional training was denied to her because scarce family funds had to be reserved for Branwell's studio at Bradford, and his private lessons from eminent local painter William Robertson. Although two of her picturesque scenes were accepted for the 1834 summer exhibition of the Royal Northern Society for the Encouragement of the Fine Arts, in Leeds (Alexander and Sellars, 52), her drawing was destined to be confined within the bounds of the schoolroom.

Teaching at Roe Head On 29 July 1835 Charlotte Brontë returned to the Roe Head school as a teacher, as Miss Wooler had offered free education for one of Charlotte's sisters in return for her services. Emily accompanied her as a pupil but within three months was physically ill with homesickness and was replaced by Anne, who proved more adaptable. Charlotte remained in Miss Wooler's employment for three and a half years, moving with the school to Heald's House, Dewsbury Moor, early in 1838 and finally resigning in December that year.

Charlotte's second stay at Roe Head was marked by an increasing disjunction between her inner and outer worlds, between her urge to indulge her creative life and her sense of duty. Her Roe Head journal records her misery and frustration with her enclosed conventional life:

> The thought came over me: am I to spend all the best part of my life in this wretched bondage, forcibly suppressing my rage at the idleness, the apathy and the hyperbolical and most asinine stupidity of those fatheaded oafs, and on compulsion assuming an air of kindness, patience and assiduity? (Alexander, 'Roe Head', 413)

She lamented the 'divine, silent, unseen land of thought' denied her by the drudgery of her situation. Moments of 'divine leisure' acted like opium to whirl her away to Angria and relief; their interruption by some unsuspecting pupil was akin to physical violence: 'I thought I should have vomited' (ibid., 413).

When she had been a pupil, Charlotte's dream world had provided solace and escape; now that she was mentally and emotionally starved it took possession of her hungry imagination. She herself was shocked by her obsession with Zamorna and his Angrian kingdom; he was her idol, her 'mental King' (Alexander, *Early Writings*, 142). Racked with guilt about the morality of Angria and her self-indulgence, she came close to confiding the fantasies of her emerging sexuality to Ellen Nussey, who could respond only with a conventional piety that exacerbated Charlotte's sense of sinfulness. Her 'bright, darling dream' had become an 'infernal world' that manifested itself externally in religious crisis. At the same time, Charlotte transferred her desperate need for love onto Ellen, to whom she now wrote in the tone of a lover, deploring her unworthiness and morbid sensibility: 'If you knew my thoughts; the dreams that absorb me; and the fiery imagination that at times eats me up and makes me feel Society as it is, wretched insipid you would pity and I dare say despise me' (*Letters of Charlotte Brontë*, 144). She feared that in her obsession for Ellen (as for Zamorna) she was in danger 'of losing sight of the *Creator* in idolatry of the *creature*' (ibid., 164), a phrase she later recast to characterize Jane Eyre's fear of obsession with Rochester.

Torn as she was between the conflicting claims of imagination and reality, Charlotte Brontë never wavered from the determination to make something of herself. During her Christmas holiday of 1836 she wrote to the poet laureate Robert Southey, sending copies of her verses, speaking of her ambition 'to be for ever known' as a poet, and asking for his judgement. His advice against the dangers of habitual day-dreams which produce 'a distempered state of mind' echoed her own fears, and his discouragement of her writing for publication might have crushed a lesser spirit: 'Literature cannot be the business of a woman's life: & it ought not to be' (*Letters of Charlotte Brontë*, 166–7). Southey expressed the conventional Victorian censure against women writers, an opinion which only increased Charlotte's frustration at the limits put on women's capacity to earn both a living *and* distinction. Yet she was grateful for his acknowledgement that she possessed 'the faculty of Verse' and her reply carefully notes that he did not actually forbid her to write so long as she did not neglect 'real duties' (ibid., 168). On the basis of such justification, and despite the continuing grind of teaching, she produced over sixty poems and six substantial novelettes (the latter written during holidays) in the two years before she left Miss Wooler's school at the end of 1838—a 'shattered wretch' (ibid., 178).

'Governess drudgery', farewell to Angria, and plans for a school At home Charlotte gradually recovered her sense of equilibrium. Her letters show a new self-assurance and a more balanced affection for Ellen Nussey. There is a positive exuberance in her comments on the visits of her father's new curate, the flirtatious and handsome William Weightman, whose portrait she drew with skill and feeling (Alexander and Sellars, 254–5).

Charlotte Brontë's writing at this time demonstrates a new maturity, and a greater reliance on her own experience. Although she continued to use a male narrator, his character was altered, to that of the sardonic Charles Townshend. Elizabeth Hastings, the governess heroine of 'Henry Hastings' (February–March 1839), can be seen as a prototype of Jane Eyre, and Zamorna's seduction of his ward, Caroline, in 'Caroline Vernon' (July–December 1839) is viewed with cynicism rather than excitement; Zamorna is no longer the heart-throb, but simply an old Byronic roué preying on romantic innocence. These last two novelettes mark the end of Charlotte's overt involvement in the Angrian saga. Although she was to write numerous fragments over the next few years, and although Angria continued to provide material for future characterization, scene, and theme, she made a distinct move towards artistic independence from both her brother and her private world.

Publication was now Charlotte Brontë's aim. In December 1840 she sent one of her post-Angrian drafts, probably the fragmentary 'Ashworth' (Alexander, *Early Writings*, 203–9), to Hartley Coleridge for judgement. His censure of her 'Richardsonian Concern' stung, but failed to suppress her literary ambition. She justified her proliferation of characters as part of her creative process, a world produced 'out of one's own brain', peopled with inhabitants with whom she conversed daily. The habits of her Angrian apprenticeship were to remain in place throughout her literary career.

In the first six months of 1839 Charlotte refused two proposals of marriage, the first from the Revd Henry Nussey, Ellen's brother; the second from the Revd James Bryce, an Irishman whom she barely knew. Her decision to refuse Henry Nussey (whose style of proposal is echoed in that of St John Rivers in *Jane Eyre*) was brave and honest, since despite the fact that his support would relieve the need to provide her own living, Charlotte did not love him. She remained convinced of the need for self-respect and saw no reason why this should be denied to unmarried women: 'there is no more respectable character on this earth than an u[n]married woman who makes her own way through life quietly pers[e]veringly' (*Letters of Charlotte Brontë*, 448).

In May 1839 Charlotte took the temporary post of governess to the Sidgwick family at Stonegappe, Lothersdale, near Skipton, and soon found that the 'governess drudgery' at Roe Head was as nothing compared to the trials of being a private governess. In particular the position was an affront to her sense of pride in her own worth and in her intellectual superiority to her employers. She felt humiliated as an inferior and an outsider, expected to teach and dress unruly children, do the household mending in her spare evenings, and (like Jane Eyre) subdue her internal rebellion and make herself invisible in society: 'I see now more clearly than I have ever done before that a private governess has no existence, is not considered as a living and rational being except as connected with the wearisome duties she has to fulfil' (*Letters of Charlotte Brontë*, 191). By 19 June 1839 she had left the Sidgwicks' employment.

In March 1841 Charlotte again tried to reconcile herself to the inevitable: she became governess to the Whites of Upperwood House, Rawdon, near Leeds. By December she was home again, but her situation had been happier partly because of future plans now being made by the Brontë sisters. They intended to open their own school, either at Haworth, or in the East Riding of Yorkshire, which Charlotte had visited with Ellen on her first trip to the seaside in September 1839. There was also the tempting prospect of taking over Miss Wooler's school, which would still allow Charlotte to retain some control over her own life. But the offer was finally rejected in favour of further education on the continent.

Impatient of restraint, Charlotte longed for 'wings' (*Letters of Charlotte Brontë*, 266). She was acutely conscious of talents unexercised and a thirst for knowledge unquenched. Her friend Mary Taylor was already studying in Brussels; the school project would simply be postponed so that Charlotte and Emily could improve their languages and attract more pupils. Aunt Branwell agreed to provide the finance, and the 25-year-old Charlotte was ecstatic at the prospect of becoming a pupil again.

Brussels On 8 February 1842 Charlotte and Emily, accompanied by their father, set out for Brussels, staying in London for three days *en route*. Charlotte's impressions of London, the model for her Babylonian Verdopolis, are reflected in Lucy Snowe's narration in *Villette* when her spirit 'shook its always-fettered wings half loose' as if she were 'at last about to taste life' (chap. 6). The sisters enrolled at the Pensionnat Heger, 32 rue d'Isabelle, Brussels, initially for six months, but they were subsequently invited to stay on, Charlotte to teach English and Emily music in lieu of fees. The Hegers were impressed by the Brontës' application and remarkable progress. Charlotte was inspired by Constantin Heger's innovative teaching of French literature, and by his lessons in composition and literary analysis, which taught her to exercise control over her material and style. She became devoted to this fascinating master, cultured yet choleric, autocratic yet kind. She was less impressed by her dull schoolfellows, who were younger than Emily and herself and uninterested in intellectual pursuits.

Charlotte's studies were cut short by Aunt Elizabeth Branwell's death at the end of October; the sisters failed to arrive home in time for her funeral. Their homecoming was overshadowed by death: William Weightman had died of cholera in early September and Martha Taylor, the lively younger sister of Mary, had died in Brussels, also of cholera, a few weeks before Aunt Branwell. The sisters each received a legacy of £300 from their aunt. Emily was relieved to be able to stay at home and resume her role as housekeeper; Anne returned to her post as governess to the Robinson family of Thorp Green, taking Branwell with her as tutor to the Robinsons' son; and Charlotte returned alone to Brussels on 27 January 1843 as both teacher and pupil. She was soon confronted by a loneliness that dampened her buoyant spirits since she was too timid to accept the Hegers' invitation to join them in their private sitting-room. Mary Taylor had left Brussels, and there was, of course, no substitute for Emily's companionship. Furthermore she felt isolated as a protestant foreigner in a Roman Catholic country.

Charlotte grew increasingly dependent on the company of Constantin Heger, to whom she taught English in exchange for French lessons. She returned his kind gifts of French books and his genuine enthusiasm for her intellectual progress with a hero-worship that bordered on obsession. Mme Heger, an astute woman, became correspondingly more remote and less kind. When Charlotte was alone during the long summer vacation, her isolation and mental torture became too much: she wandered the streets and once, finding herself in the Catholic cathedral of Ste Gudule, vehement protestant though she was, had an overwhelming need to make confession. She later used this situation to powerful effect in *Villette*. By the end of the year Charlotte—'shaken' in mind and heart—had decided to return home to Haworth. Nevertheless her Brussels experience had been one of personal and professional growth, and it furnished her with significant material for her later novels, especially *The Professor* and *Villette*.

A renewal of the old plan to open a school for girls at the parsonage failed to attract pupils and was abandoned. Haworth was no longer a happy place for Charlotte. She was depressed by M. Heger's failure to respond to her letters and by Mary Taylor's departure for New Zealand. Patrick Brontë's sight was failing fast and he needed assistance. After Anne resigned her post at Thorp Green in June

1845 Charlotte gained some relief in a three-week visit to Ellen Nussey who was staying at Hathersage in Derbyshire. There she met the Eyre family and saw their ancestral home, North Lees Hall, where a mad woman was once kept in an upper room. On her return in late July she was confronted by a further trial: Branwell had been dismissed from his post for conduct 'bad beyond expression', having been discovered in an affair with Mrs Robinson (*Letters of Charlotte Brontë*, 412). Unlike Charlotte, Branwell indulged his misery and became a strain on the family, resorting to the alcohol and opium that were to lead to his rapid decline.

Charlotte's own torment of unrequited love remained a secret from her family; it manifested itself in the headaches and 'sickliness' she suffered throughout the rest of her life whenever she was depressed or under stress. Her burning need for some sign of recognition from her old master is revealed in the few surviving examples of the many passionate letters she wrote to him. Almost seventy years later these letters (now in the British Library) were published in *The Times* for 29 July 1913, one of the saddest records of 'a consuming sentiment burning down self-respect and self-restraint' (*Letters of Charlotte Brontë*, 63–4).

Publication of Poems (1846) by Currer, Ellis, and Acton Bell
Charlotte Brontë eventually alleviated her depression through writing and through the prospect of authorship. In September 1845 she made her famous discovery of one of Emily's notebooks of poetry, and persuaded her very secretive sister that they merited publication. Together with Anne the sisters made a selection of their verses, removed Angrian and Gondal references and polished the poems for publication. They chose pseudonyms designed to avoid criticism based on gender. *Poems* by Currer, Ellis, and Acton Bell appeared in May 1846, published by Aylott and Jones at the authors' expense (£31 10s. paid from their aunt's legacy). Only two copies were sold, yet several favourable reviews and the satisfaction of seeing their work in print provided the stimulus needed for the sisters to pursue their ambitions as authors. For Charlotte especially it acted as an antidote to her grief at M. Heger's silence, and to her disappointment over Branwell's deteriorating behaviour.

Meanwhile the Brontë sisters had been reworking and expanding earlier prose drafts into novels designed to reach a wider audience. Charlotte Brontë completed *The Professor* (27 June), transforming her Brussels experience into an exploration of a happier teacher–pupil relationship; Emily Brontë wrote *Wuthering Heights*, recasting much of the material from her Gondal saga; and Anne Brontë wrote *Agnes Grey*, based on her life as a governess. Together the three manuscripts were hawked around various publishers for a year and a half, always travelling in the same reused wrapper that betrayed the signs of previous rejection. Finally in July 1847 *Wuthering Heights* and *Agnes Grey* were accepted for publication by Thomas Cautley Newby. But *The Professor* suffered repeated rejection. The novel had been a calculated reaction against the imaginative excesses of Angria: Charlotte had turned from 'that burning clime … to a cooler region where the

dawn breaks grey and sober' ('Farewell to Angria', 1839), and the resulting suppression of her imaginative and poetic energy was not a happy one. *The Professor* was never published in Charlotte Brontë's lifetime, although she often returned to her first novel during her literary career, in an effort to revive what she referred to as her 'idiot child'. The firm of Smith, Elder & Co. (who finally published *The Professor* on 6 June 1857) had sent encouraging comments with the return of her first manuscript; so it was to them that she now offered a work of 'more vivid interest' (*Letters of Charlotte Brontë*, 535), begun in Manchester where Charlotte had attended her father during his cataract operation in August 1846.

Jane Eyre (1847) *Jane Eyre: an Autobiography*, 'edited by Currer Bell', was enthusiastically received, was published in three volumes on 19 October 1847, and became one of the year's best-sellers. Speculation was rife about the identity of the author and whether or not it was the work of a woman. The story of the abused orphan child whose sense of injustice and self-worth leads through rebellion and containment to a liberation of the spirit, was both inspirational and threatening for Victorian readers who saw the novel as a potent form of moral and social commentary. *Jane Eyre*'s plea for the equality of all before God, and for spiritual affinity in marriage, was radical. Some critics saw the relationship between Jane and Rochester as improper, and an influential review by Elizabeth Rigby (later Lady Eastlake) in the *Quarterly Review* (December 1848) condemned the novel as 'pre-eminently an anti-Christian composition' and, if by a woman, the work of an immoral one who has 'long forfeited the society of her own sex' (E. Rigby, 'Vanity Fair and Jane Eyre', QR, 84, 1848, 173–4).

All Charlotte Brontë's heroines were seen by many contemporary readers as 'unfeminine' in their displays of deep feeling and independent expression. Jane Eyre's impassioned individualism and personal acts of rebellion against authority and social convention were seen as vigorous and powerfully original, but also as alarmingly analogous to political ferment of the time. Rigby and other guardians of public morality saw the novel as subversive:

> We do not hesitate to say that the tone of mind and thought which has overthrown authority and violated every code human and divine abroad, and fostered Chartism and rebellion at home, is the same which has also written *Jane Eyre*.   (QR, 84, 1848, 173)

Yet the powerful romance of *Jane Eyre* caught the imagination of readers. The 'grey and sober' character of the rejected *Professor* had been replaced by a more sensational story, more imaginative writing, and more sustained suspense. Material was still drawn from Charlotte Brontë's own experience—early schooling at Cowan Bridge, childhood memories of fairy tale and early reading, employment as a governess, local houses and tales of mad women immured in attics, her unrequited love for Monsieur Heger, and the like—but this material was transformed by a colourful and intricate pattern of contrasting character and imagery, and unified by the consciousness of the narrator heroine. Her 'autobiographical' technique allowed her to expand social conceptions of reality to include emotion and imagination. By emphasizing the importance of a balance between reason and passion in Jane's journey towards social and spiritual maturity, Charlotte Brontë created a *Bildungsroman* focused not only on the individual's negotiation of the external world but on the well-being of one's interior life. The reader is apprised of Jane's internal world through the use of biblical, literary, and pictorial allusion, through fairy tale, dream, and myth. The poetic use of natural imagery (of fire and ice, and the moon), in particular, enables psychological states to be externalized. Thus the more melodramatic and Gothic elements of the novel are woven into the realistic narrative of an entirely credible character who engages the reader both intellectually and emotionally. This fusion between romance and realism is hailed as Charlotte Brontë's major contribution to the form of the novel.

By January 1848 a second revised edition of *Jane Eyre* had appeared, dedicated to Thackeray; a third edition followed in April, with a note stating that this was the only novel Currer Bell had written. Newby had finally published *Wuthering Heights* and *Agnes Grey* by early December 1847, rushing to capitalize on the success of *Jane Eyre*, whose author was obviously related to Ellis and Acton Bell. He then embarked on a clever but unscrupulous advertising campaign to confuse the identity of the three Bell 'brothers', suggesting that the novels—including Anne's *Tenant of Wildfell Hall* (June 1848)—were the work of one person. Charlotte and Anne travelled to London to confront Newby with his lies and to allay the concerns of Smith, Elder & Co., by proving their separate identities. They were given a warm welcome by George Smith and his reader William Smith Williams, and taken to the opera, the Royal Academy, and the National Gallery.

Family tragedy and the writing of Shirley (1849) Charlotte Brontë's first taste of literary celebrity soon paled beside an onslaught of family tragedy. She later confided to Smith Williams:

> A year ago—had a prophet warned me how I should stand in June 1849—how stripped and bereaved—had he foretold the autumn, the winter, the spring of sickness and suffering to be gone through—I should have thought—this can never be endured.   (Wise and Symington, 2.340)

On her return from London Charlotte had begun the first volume of her next novel, *Shirley*; but within a month it was laid aside as first Branwell died, followed by Emily and Anne in rapid succession.

Branwell's lack of self-discipline was obvious to Charlotte from an early age, yet she shared her family's hopes that the sacrifices made for this favoured and talented son might bring their reward. However, the burden of family expectation and an inability to persevere with routine meant that Branwell was unable to settle to a career. The grandiose expectations of his Angrian world paralysed his humble efforts in the real world: he failed as a portrait painter, a railway clerk, and a tutor. He never made the long-planned trip to London to enter the schools of the Royal Academy of Art. He died aged thirty-one of chronic bronchitis on 24 September 1848, his constitution ravaged by addiction to alcohol and opiates.

Twentieth-century biographers have complained of Charlotte's lack of sympathy for her debauched brother, overlooking the fact that, of all the family, her expectations and disappointment may have been the greatest. The most ambitious of her siblings, she conspired in exaggerating Branwell's capabilities, vicariously seeking through him the professional fulfilment she could not achieve as a daughter. The severity of her bitterness at the dissipation of his talents suggests that she suffered a sense of bereavement long before Branwell actually died. For her his death was a mercy; she felt only pity for his wasted life.

The day of Branwell's funeral was the last time that Emily left the parsonage. She caught a cold, grew rapidly weaker and—refusing to consult a doctor despite Charlotte's desperate pleas—died with relentless stoicism on 19 December 1848, of pulmonary tuberculosis, aged thirty. Almost immediately Charlotte recognized the same symptoms of tuberculosis in Anne. In May 1849, she and Ellen Nussey took Anne to her beloved sea at Scarborough with hopes of restoring her health, but within the month Anne too was dead, at the age of twenty-nine. Charlotte was now left desolate. She had lost not only two beloved sisters but her sole support for her literary endeavours. Together the three Brontës had discussed their plots, style, and characters; Charlotte felt lonely and vulnerable in what was now a 'silent workshop of [her] own brain' (Wise and Symington, 3.21). Yet, as always, she persevered, completing *Shirley* by the end of August, grateful that she had had an occupation and the courage to pursue it.

Shirley celebrates the need perceived by Charlotte Brontë for activity in women's lives, and their right to self-respecting work. In this book, published in three volumes on 26 October 1849 by Smith, Elder, Charlotte abandoned the directly personal female voice of *Jane Eyre* and adopted a more authoritative, often satirical, third-person narrator in order to challenge the reader's assumptions about women's nature and education, and about contemporary interpretations of religious and political controversy. The novel examines the lives of Shirley Keeldar (based in part on Emily) and Caroline Helstone, two women of contrasting natures and ambition, against a broad socio-historical perspective at the time of the Luddite riots in the West Riding of Yorkshire (1811–12). Keen to avoid the 'passion, and stimulus, and melodrama' (*Shirley*, chap. 1) for which she had been criticized in *Jane Eyre*, Charlotte Brontë began her novel with a realist manifesto promising 'something as unromantic as Monday morning'. She intended *Shirley* to be a mid-century 'condition of England' novel, commenting by analogy with the Luddite period, on industrial unrest in the 1840s, on the struggles of the Chartists, and on dissatisfaction with the government, and with a church split by sectarian controversy. Her more urgent agenda, however, was articulated in her letter to Smith Williams, on 12 May 1848: 'I often wish to say something about the "condition of women" question'

(Wise and Symington, 2.215–16). The resultant split between the novel's social and political preoccupations and its exploration of the personal lives of the two heroines has been viewed by many readers as a basic flaw in its structure.

Nevertheless, *Shirley* has maintained its status as a socio-historical novel. As with all of Charlotte Brontë's novels, the text is rich in literary and religious allusion; despite reservations about 'Yorkshire roughness' and a lack of 'good taste' (Allott, 165), contemporary critics praised the work for its cleverness and power. The identity of Currer Bell was again an issue and readers had a field day identifying not only the presumed 'female' author but also the thinly disguised models for many of her characters and places. G. H. Lewes, with whom Charlotte Brontë had corresponded after his positive review of *Jane Eyre*, attacked *Shirley* for its 'over-masculine vigour' and the 'intolerable rudeness' of all her characters (p. 163), provoking her celebrated outburst: 'I can be on my guard against my enemies, but God deliver me from my friends!' (Wise and Symington, 3.67).

Loneliness and literary celebrity Literary success became Charlotte Brontë's passport to 'the society of clever people'. Ironically, her acute shyness made this long-standing ambition a trial as much as a blessing. In November 1849 she went to London to stay with George Smith and his mother, fulfilling another ambition to see the works of artists she had admired since childhood and to meet her literary hero William Makepeace Thackeray. She had been mortified to learn (January 1848) that her dedication of the second edition of *Jane Eyre*, meant as a compliment to Thackeray, had caused him to be the butt of malicious gossip. She had been unaware of the parallel between Thackeray's marriage to a wife who was now insane and incarcerated, and that of Mr Rochester. Thus her dedication to the author of *Vanity Fair*, whose heroine was also a governess, lent further credence to the speculation that Currer Bell had been a governess in Thackeray's family. Although Thackeray had been magnanimous, thanking her for 'the greatest compliment I have ever received in my life' (Wise and Symington, 2.183), the ordeal of finally meeting him at the Smiths' dinner party (4 December 1849) left her too nervous to eat and awed into silence. By comparison, her visit to Harriet Martineau, an equally formidable figure, was a relief. While in London, Charlotte also attended a Turner exhibition at the National Gallery, saw William Charles Macready acting in *Macbeth* and *Othello*, and visited the new houses of parliament.

Charlotte stayed with the Smiths again in May 1850, visiting the Royal Academy and the opera, dining with Thackeray, seeing her childhood hero the duke of Wellington, and having her portrait drawn by George Richmond, the celebrated society artist. In July she met the Smiths in Edinburgh, and the following month stayed with Sir James Kay Shuttleworth near Windermere, where she met Elizabeth Gaskell, her future biographer. In May 1851 Charlotte made a further visit to London where she visited the Great Exhibition three times, and

saw the actress Rachel (whom she recreated as Vashti in *Villette*) perform twice. With George Smith (and under the assumed names of Mr and Miss Fraser) she went to a phrenologist to have her character read. On her final visit (January 1853) Charlotte was determined to see the 'real' life of London—the prisons, the hospitals, the Bank of England, and the stock exchange. Fame and its attendant social exposure, however, took its toll. Charlotte could never be at ease among strangers and her constitution was far from robust. Without her sisters to share the success, literary fame had lost much of its lustre.

Harriet Martineau was impressed by Charlotte Brontë's powerful intellect and her physical appearance, describing her as 'the smallest creature I had ever seen (except at a fair) and her eyes blazed'. Charlotte was proud of her large hazel eyes, but was acutely conscious of defects in the rest of her features. Contemporaries noted her 'excessive anxiety about her personal appearance' and her 'quaint old-fashioned look' (Wise and Symington, 3.52). Having her portrait drawn by Richmond was a nerve-racking ordeal, so much so that when the artist mistook her unfashionable hairpiece for padding for her hat and asked her to remove it, Charlotte was reduced to tears of embarrassment (Barker, 644). Her paralysing shyness prevented her from shining on social occasions. Thackeray remembered 'the trembling little frame, the little hand, the great honest eyes' (Wise and Symington, 3.46) and he admired her ability to spy out 'arrogance or affectation, with extraordinary keenness of vision', but the dinner party that he held for her on 2 June 1850 was a notorious failure: instead of the brilliant conversation his company expected, they were ignored by the guest of honour who spent most of the evening in a corner talking to the governess. Apparently Thackeray sneaked off to his club, leaving his guests to entertain themselves (ibid., 50).

One bonus of success, however, was an increase in correspondence and contact with a variety of new people once Charlotte had returned to Haworth. W. S. Williams at Smith, Elder had been her literary and personal confidant for a number of years, and she now corresponded with writers and critics like G. H. Lewes, Sydney Dobell, and Julia Kavanagh. She formed a genuine friendship with Elizabeth Gaskell, staying with her in Manchester (April 1853), and with the formidable Harriet Martineau, with whom she stayed at Ambleside (December 1850). She refused a proposal of marriage from James Taylor, an employee of Smith, Elder, but wished him well when he left to establish the firm in India. Letters and gifts of books from her publishers kept Charlotte in touch with the literary scene and provided a retreat from the loneliness of the parsonage at Haworth and the uninvited attentions of visitors curious to meet Currer Bell.

On 10 December 1850 Charlotte Brontë's edition of *Wuthering Heights* and *Agnes Grey* appeared, now published by Smith, Elder, and prefaced with a 'Biographical notice' (*Wuthering Heights*, ed. Marsden and Jack, 435–44). She found the writing of the latter painful but was determined to perform this 'sacred duty' to counter all erroneous conjectures about her sisters' identities and their characters and to justify the so-called 'coarseness' of their writing. In doing so, she became her sisters' interpreter to the world, accounting for the 'eccentricities' and the 'secret power and fire' of Emily's writing by recourse to a theory of Romantic genius: 'the writer who possesses the creative gift owns something of which he is not always master'. She explained that Anne, reserved and long-suffering, was driven by honesty not to 'varnish, soften or conceal'. Thus the myth of the Brontë sisters, untutored in the ways of the world but impelled by a sense of truth and writing purely 'from the impulse of nature, the dictates of intuition', was established, to be further propagated by future critics and biographers.

Charlotte Brontë's role as editor of her sisters' works is surprisingly inconsistent with her wish to honour their integrity. She added a selection of their poems to the new 1850 edition, 'improving' the original texts not only by removing all reference to the imaginary world of Gondal, but also by altering words and adding lines that often changed the meaning and tone of the original. Modern writers have censured such intervention in the text, and they have criticized her for her faint praise of *Agnes Grey* and her dismissal of the choice of subject of *The Tenant of Wildfell Hall* as 'an entire mistake'. Charlotte Brontë certainly believed that there were certain subjects not suitable for novelistic treatment, and she refused to allow the republication of *The Tenant*, arguing that the subject was incongruous with her sister's nature and that Anne Brontë had persevered with the work only out of a morbid sense of duty to portray debauchery realistically as a warning to others.

Villette, marriage, and death Charlotte Brontë was now under constant pressure from her publishers and her proud father to produce another novel. She found the writing of *Villette* therapeutic but difficult. In this novel, published on 28 January 1853, Charlotte returned to her forte: the female autobiographical mode of narration. An older Lucy Snowe, made cold and duplicitous by adversity, tells the story of her experience as an English teacher in a girls' school in Villette (Brussels); of her suppressed attraction to the handsome English doctor, John Graham Bretton (based on George Smith, Charlotte's young publisher); and of her fascination and love for Monsieur Paul Emanuel, a despotic little professor (based on Constantin Heger). Charlotte's last novel reflects her maturity as both writer and woman. The sophistication of the style is revealed in the way Lucy's narration repeatedly traps and encloses the reader in false assumptions, reflecting the disturbing effects that social repression has had on Lucy herself. Her deception and unreliability are part of the self-protective facade that Charlotte saw as a necessity for a woman's survival in society. Violent metaphors define the repression of self: Lucy knocks on the head her longings to escape her present existence, 'driving a nail through [her] temples'; but they are only 'transiently stunned, and at intervals would turn on the nail with a rebellious wrench' (chap. 12). Through Lucy Snowe, the author expressed the bitterness of her resentment at having to live 'a buried life'.

Critical response to *Villette* was favourable, but the cynical tone did not go unremarked. Despite Charlotte Brontë's efforts to subdue emotion in the novel, Matthew Arnold found nothing but 'hunger, rebellion and rage' in the mind of its author (Allott, 201). Charlotte was deeply hurt that her friend Harriet Martineau found the book 'intolerably painful' and resented the writer's dwelling on the need to be loved (ibid., 172). As previously, with G. H. Lewes's review of *Shirley*, Charlotte felt both personally and professionally betrayed by a friend; her correspondence with Martineau ceased, but the rupture did not prevent Martineau from paying a warm tribute to Charlotte in her obituary notice. Charlotte was disappointed too by the financial returns from a publisher she trusted. Smith, Elder offered her only £500 for the manuscript of *Villette* (*Transactions of the Brontë Society*, 18, 1982, 92.113), the same price she had received for each of her earlier novels, compared to Elizabeth Gaskell's £2000 for her last novel from the same publisher. Charlotte Brontë's total literary earnings were only about £1500.

In the last years of her life Charlotte achieved a personal happiness that had for so long escaped her. Arthur Bell Nicholls (1819–1906), her father's curate for seven years, had been quietly developing a passionate attachment to her, yet Charlotte was shocked when he suddenly proposed marriage. Patrick Brontë was furious and Nicholls left the parish. Although Nicholls had made little impression on Charlotte, except as a model for one of the more competent curates in *Shirley*, she was now moved by his obvious love for her, by his distress, and by her own embarrassment at the cruel hostility of her father. A secret correspondence led to their engagement and to Nicholls's return to Haworth. They were married in Haworth church on 29 June 1854, spent their honeymoon in Ireland where Charlotte met the uncle and aunt who had raised Nicholls, and returned to Haworth parsonage to look after Patrick Brontë.

Charlotte's letters clearly reveal her genuine happiness, despite the difficulties of adjusting to a reduced independence. In the months before her marriage, she had begun the introductory chapters of a new novel, 'Emma'; now this was abandoned for a new found pleasure in domesticity. Her late found happiness, however, was not to last. Weakened by excessive morning sickness in the early stages of pregnancy, Charlotte caught a chill and died on 31 March 1855, less than a year after her marriage. She was buried four days later in the family vault beneath the aisle of Haworth parish church. Her death certificate records 'phthisis' (tuberculosis) but Dr Philip Rhodes, following Gaskell's description, diagnoses *hyperemesis gravidarum* (severe vomiting in pregnancy; *Transactions of the Brontë Society*, 16, 1971, 2.106–8), a judgement now generally accepted but disputed by J. Maynard (Maynard, 218–24).

The pursuit of truth When she first chose a male pseudonym, Charlotte Brontë had only a vague idea that women writers were looked on with prejudice. She was shocked to find that even her mode of thinking was viewed by critics as 'unfeminine'. Her unconventional upbringing and her religious training had bred in her a tenacious commitment to truth. Her whole being rose up in rebellion against the need to dissemble: the strain of disguising her loathing of teaching, of living in other people's houses, of being unable to admit (even to herself) her love for a married man, had produced in her not only mental torment but periodic bouts of migraine and intense depression that she referred to as 'the tyranny of Hypochondria' (*Letters of Charlotte Brontë*, 505), a phrase she also used in *Jane Eyre*. When she had applied herself to a conventional mode of learning, as in her diligent reproduction of engravings, her imagination had been stultified and her artistic ambitions thwarted. She told her publishers (September 1848):

> Unless I have something of my own to say, and a way of my own to say it in, I have no business to publish. Unless I can look beyond the greatest Masters, and study Nature herself, I have no right to paint. Unless I can have the courage to use the language of Truth in preference to the jargon of Conventionality, I ought to be silent.   (Wise and Symington, 2.255)

The pursuit of truth became the guiding principle in Charlotte Brontë's literary career. Her novels are not only a statement of the position of women in the mid-nineteenth century, but also a timeless plea for the intellectual worth of women, for their financial independence and equality in marriage, for the right to express their passionate selves, and for a religious commitment to truth in life and art. Thackeray paid tribute to 'that intrepid outspeaker and champion of truth, that eager, impetuous redresser of wrong' when he published Charlotte's last fragmentary sketch, 'Emma', in the newly founded *Cornhill Magazine* (April 1860).

Posthumous reputation and historical significance   Charlotte Brontë was one of the most distinguished novelists of her time, projecting through her heroines the strength of women's intellect and sexuality, as well as her own struggle for integrity and self-sufficiency. Her writing gave a new authority to the female voice in fiction. In the years immediately following her death, Elizabeth Gaskell's biography of her friend (*The Life of Charlotte Brontë*, 1857) did much to stress her reputation for courage and integrity. Gaskell had known her only in the last sad years of her life and had been struck by her quiet survival in a life marred by a wastrel brother, a harsh father, and the deaths of her sisters: 'the wonder to me is how she can have kept heart and power alive in her life of desolation' (*The Letters of Mrs Gaskell*, ed. J. A. V. Chapple and A. Pollard, 1966, 10–12). Using her novelistic skills and building on Charlotte Brontë's own construction of her sisters as romantic heroines (in the 'Biographical notice'), Gaskell portrayed her subject as a long-suffering daughter whose tragic life had been directed by duty and stoicism. The biography was a monumental success, moderating negative judgements about Charlotte's unwomanly writing and establishing a mythology about the Brontës' lives for over a century.

Subsequent decades proved less kind to Charlotte Brontë as an artist. By the end of the century her novels were seen as emotionally subjective and intellectually inferior because, as Leslie Stephen put it, her novels are simply 'the study of her life'. Stephen was replying to Swinburne's 'unfashionable' claims for 'the genius of Charlotte Brontë' (in a 'Note' in *Cornhill*, December 1877), and his influential judgement shaped the view held by critics in the first half of the twentieth century, namely that Charlotte Brontë is an author with a powerful imagination who wrote in a 'surging flood of self-revelation' but who is a failure as a 'craftsman' (Lord David Cecil, *Early Victorian Novelists*, 1934). Even with the advent of the new criticism in the 1940s and 1950s, which severed biography from the text, her work was still judged to be lacking in 'formal unity'. In 1948 she was excluded from F. R. Leavis's 'great tradition' of English novelists.

In the last thirty years, however, critics have rehabilitated Charlotte Brontë's reputation by an examination of both the artistry and the socio-historical context of her work. Feminist criticism, in particular, has reorientated debate about the importance of her novels, arguing that earlier values of unity and rationality are no longer unquestioned indicators of literary merit. The passion and rebellion in Charlotte Brontë's writing are now seen as inspirational, and recent critical studies emphasize her intellectual engagement with political, religious, social, and artistic controversies of her time. Her juvenilia, now fully recovered and edited, are seen as a revealing source of her literary apprenticeship and as an indication of her early reading. The later 'juvenile' manuscripts are accomplished novelettes in their own right and are now used in schools to provide inspiration for young writers. Twentieth-century critics prize *Villette* for its sophisticated narration and ambiguity, but *Jane Eyre* has maintained its appeal as Charlotte Brontë's most popular novel.

Jane Eyre has always been something of a literary phenomenon. The tale of the little governess, 'disconnected, poor, and plain', whose strength of spirit and intellect fortifies her in her pilgrimage towards self-respect and true love, has had a powerful appeal for a variety of international audiences. The novel has been rediscovered by new generations of readers and translated into many languages. It has been reworked for stage, film, ballet, opera, and television. Artists like Edmund Dulac (1905 and 1922) have been inspired to illustrate the novels. Film-makers from Orson Welles (1944) to Franco Zeffirelli (1996) have reinterpreted the characters. Writers such as Daphne Du Maurier (*Rebecca*, 1938) and Jean Rhys (*Wide Sargasso Sea*, 1966) have found inspiration for their own novels in *Jane Eyre*; and the passionate internal struggle of the heroine in Jane Campion's film *The Piano* (1993) owes much to Jane Eyre's pursuit of self-sufficiency and love in the face of a stultifying convention. *Jane Eyre* itself has been interpreted not only in the context of women's liberation but (with a concentration on Jane's 'other'—the imprisoned wife, Bertha) in terms of sexual and racial repression. Each successive generation has found its own concerns and cultural values in Charlotte Brontë's classic novel.

CHRISTINE ALEXANDER

Sources The letters of Charlotte Brontë, with a selection of letters by family and friends, ed. M. Smith, vol. 1, 1829–1847 (1995) · T. J. Wise and J. A. Symington, eds., The Brontës: their lives, friendships and correspondence, 4 vols. (1932) · C. Brontë, Jane Eyre, ed. J. Jack and M. Smith, Clarendon edition, 1 (1969) · C. Brontë, Shirley, ed. H. Rosengarten and M. Smith, Clarendon edition, 3 (1979) · C. Brontë, Villette, ed. H. Rosengarten and M. Smith, Clarendon edition, 4 (1984) · C. Brontë, The professor, ed. M. Smith and H. Rosengarten, Clarendon edition, 5 (1987) · E. Brontë, Wuthering Heights, ed. H. Marsden and I. Jack, Clarendon edition (1976) · E. C. Gaskell, The life of Charlotte Brontë, 2 vols. (1857) · E. C. Gaskell, The life of Charlotte Brontë, ed. A. Shelston, 2 vols. (1975) · C. Brontë and E. J. Brontë, The Belgian essays: a critical edition, ed. and trans. S. Lonoff (1996) · C. Alexander and J. Sellars, The art of the Brontës (1994) [incl. catalogue of art work] · An edition of the early writings of Charlotte Brontë, ed. C. Alexander, 3 vols. (1987–91) · C. Alexander, The early writings of Charlotte Brontë (1983) · J. Barker, The Brontës (1995) · C. Alexander, A bibliography of the manuscripts of Charlotte Brontë (1982) · M. Allott, ed., The Brontës: the critical heritage (1974) · E. McNees, ed., The Brontë sisters: critical assessments, 4 vols. (1996) · J. Maynard, Charlotte Brontë and sexuality (1984) · P. Nestor, Charlotte Brontë (1987) · W. Reid, Charlotte Brontë: a monograph (1877) · C. Alexander, 'Charlotte Brontë at Roe Head', Jane Eyre, ed. R. J. Dunn, 2nd edn, Norton Critical edition (1987) [includes text of The Roe Head Journal] · W. Gérin, Charlotte Brontë: the evolution of genius (1967) · J. Stevens, Mary Taylor, friend of Charlotte Brontë: letters from New Zealand and elsewhere (1972) · T. Winnifrith, The Brontës and their background: romance and reality (1973) · M. Peters, Unquiet soul: a biography of Charlotte Brontë (1975) · H. Moglen, Charlotte Brontë: the self conceived (1976) · L. Gordon, Charlotte Brontë: a passionate life (1994) · A. C. Swinburne, A note on Charlotte Brontë (1877)

Archives BL, letters to G. H. Lewes, Add. MS 39763 · Brontë Parsonage Museum, Haworth, West Yorkshire, collection · FM Cam., papers · Harvard U., Houghton L., letters and literary MSS · Hunt. L., corresp. and literary MSS · JRL, papers · King's School, Canterbury, papers · Lancs. RO, letters to Lady Kay-Shuttleworth · NL Scot., papers · NRA, priv. coll., papers · NYPL · Princeton University, New Jersey, corresp. and literary MSS · Ransom HRC, papers · Rutgers University, papers · State University of New York, Buffalo, papers · U. Birm. L., corresp. with Harriet Martineau · U. Leeds, Brotherton L., papers · University of Missouri, Columbia, papers · Wellesley College, Massachusetts · Yale U., papers | Morgan L., Bonnell collection, family papers

Likenesses B. Brontë, group portrait, oils, c.1834 (The Brontë sisters), NPG [see illus.] · G. Richmond, coloured chalk drawing, 1850, NPG · photograph, c.1879, Brontë Parsonage Museum, Haworth, West Yorkshire · E. Walker, glass negative, NPG

Wealth at death approx. £2000: letters, esp. to George Smith, 18 April 1854, Brontë Society Transactions, 18, pt 92 (1982), 113

Brontë, Emily Jane [pseud. Ellis Bell] (1818–1848), novelist and poet, was born on 30 July 1818 at the parsonage in Market Street, Thornton, near Bradford, the fifth of the six children of the Revd Patrick *Brontë (1777–1861) and his wife, Maria (1783–1821), daughter of Thomas Branwell, a merchant of Penzance, and his wife, Anne. Patrick Brontë, the son of a poor tenant farmer, had left his native Ireland in 1802 to take up a sizarship at St John's College, Cambridge, and, after graduating, was ordained into the Church of England. In 1812 he met Maria Branwell who had left Cornwall to assist her uncle and aunt in the running of Woodhouse Grove School, Rawdon, near Bradford. They married in the same year and had six children: Maria (1814–1825), Elizabeth (1815–1825), Charlotte *Brontë (1816–1855), (Patrick) Branwell *Brontë (1817–1848), Emily Jane (1818–1848), and Anne *Brontë (1820–1849). With so large a family and no income except his

small salary and his wife's even smaller annuity, Patrick faced constant financial problems. In 1820 he accepted preferment to Haworth, a small industrial township surrounded by moorland, some 12 miles away from Bradford. The post offered him an increase in salary, security of tenure, and a larger parsonage house in which his family could live rent-free. Before her second birthday, therefore, Emily left her birthplace at Thornton for Haworth, which would be her home for the rest of her life and would provide the inspiration for much of her work.

Early years and education In September 1821, eighteen months after the move to Haworth, Mrs Brontë died, and her elder sister Elizabeth Branwell (1776–1842), who had come from Penzance to nurse her, now took up permanent residence with the family. Her determination to enforce habits of 'order, method and neatness in everything' and 'a perfect knowledge of all kinds of household work' (Gaskell, 147) caused many clashes with her nieces, particularly Charlotte, but also instilled a self-discipline for which they were all grateful in later life. Emily, who later took over her aunt's role as housekeeper at the parsonage, was clearly a more apt and willing pupil than her elder sister. Unlike most parsonage daughters, however, the Brontës were not limited to a purely domestic role but were allowed to share their brother's academic lessons with their father, studying not only the Bible but also history, geography, and biography. This in itself was unusual for girls of their age and class but, even more unusually, their father allowed them unlimited and uncensored access to books, periodicals, and newspapers. They exploited this freedom to the full and their reading inspired many of the imaginative games and play-acting which already occupied their leisure hours.

In 1824 the four eldest Brontë girls were sent to the Clergy Daughters' School at Cowan Bridge, a newly opened charitable institution where the daughters of impoverished Anglican clergymen could obtain a formal education at subsidized rates. Conditions at the school were harsh, especially for girls from a relatively comfortable home. Inedible and insufficient food, inadequate heating, and primitive sanitary arrangements, combined with a rigidly disciplinarian regime, caused much suffering. A number of pupils were sent home ill, among them Maria and Elizabeth Brontë, both of whom had contracted tuberculosis. They died, within six weeks of each other, in 1825, and their younger sisters were immediately brought home by their father. While Charlotte never forgot or forgave the school and its founder, whom she blamed for her sisters' deaths, notoriously indicting them in savage portrayals in Jane Eyre (1847), the experience apparently left Emily unscathed. At six she had been the youngest child at Cowan Bridge and this may have afforded her some protection. She certainly enjoyed a privileged status, being remembered affectionately by the superintendent as 'a darling child', 'little petted Em', and 'quite the pet nursling of the school' (Barker, 134).

The four remaining Brontë siblings resumed their education at home under the guidance of their father and Aunt Branwell and threw themselves into their shared passion: the creation of imaginary worlds. The most important, the play of the 'Young Men', was inspired by their father's birthday gift to Branwell of a box of toy soldiers in 1826. It was an indication of their relative roles in the plays that Charlotte chose Wellington and Branwell Bonaparte to be their heroes, while Emily's, 'a Grave Looking ferllow' (Barker, 154), was simply called Gravey and Anne's, Waiting Boy. By 1829 Charlotte and Branwell were recording the adventures of the Young Men in homemade miniature books, a habit they maintained well into adulthood. At what stage Emily and Anne began to do so can only be conjectured, as no complete manuscripts of their prose tales survive. They had already established one independent kingdom, Parrysland, which Charlotte, in 1830, mocked for being mundane and provincial, but the foundation of the most important and long-lasting, Gondal, probably dates from 1833 when Emily was fourteen and Anne thirteen. The creation of Gondal, a large imaginary island in the Pacific, revealed both Emily's determination to break away from the domination of the older children, as well as her greater empathy with her less forceful younger sister.

Ellen Nussey (1817–1897), Charlotte's schoolfriend, visiting Haworth for the first time that year, noted that Emily had now:

> acquired a lithesome graceful figure. She was the tallest person in the house except her Father, her hair which was naturally as beautiful as Charlotte's was in the same unbecoming tight curl and frizz, and there was the same want of complexion. She had very beautiful eyes, kind<ly>, kindling, liquid eyes, sometimes they looked grey, sometimes dark blue but she did not often look at you, she was too reserved. She talked very little, she and Anne were like twins, inseparable companions, and in the very closest sympathy which never had any interruption. (*Letters of Charlotte Brontë*, 1.598)

Ellen's description of Emily is supported by the only two portraits of her known to have survived. The 'Pillar portrait' and the profile portrait, which is a fragment of a larger lost painting known as the 'Gun group', were both painted by Branwell, probably in 1834–5 when he was studying portraiture professionally.

Emily's earliest surviving diary paper, written jointly with Anne on 24 November 1834, gives a cheerful, if chaotic, glimpse of life at the parsonage. 'It is past Twelve o'clock Anne and I have not tid[i]ed ourselv[e]s, done our bed work or done our lessons and we want to go out to play' (Barker, 221). Significantly, it draws no distinction, even by punctuation, between events in the imaginary and real worlds: 'The Gondals are discovering the interior of Gaaldine Sally mosley is washing in the back Kitchin.' Emily's lessons with her aunt and father had now been superseded by lessons from Charlotte, who thus passed on the benefit of her own eighteen months' schooling at Roe Head, Mirfield. Though this was supplemented by instruction in art and music from professional local teachers, Emily's lack of a formal education would make it extremely difficult for her to earn her living in future. When Charlotte returned to Roe Head as a teacher in July 1835, Emily therefore went with her as a pupil, the first

occasion she had left home since Cowan Bridge. This time, however, at seventeen, she was not the youngest but probably much the oldest pupil. With her intense reserve, social awkwardness, and lack of conventional education, it was not surprising that she stood out from the crowd and was miserable. Worst of all, the discipline of the school day and the mind-numbing boredom of rote learning left her little time or energy to indulge in the Gondal fantasy which had become an absolute necessity to her. After only three months at school, she became so ill that her father recalled her to Haworth and her place at Roe Head was taken by the more pliant Anne.

Early writings Emily's experience at school and her separation from Anne, which, apart from holiday intervals, lasted for almost ten years, had two important consequences. Emily seems to have recognized her difference from her peers and decided to reject them, preferring instead to become more intensely self-sufficient and reclusive than before. Perhaps more importantly, because her writing partner and kindred spirit was now far away, she seems to have made a conscious effort to collect her poems, preserve them in writing, and date them, so that they could be shown to Anne whenever she returned. Certainly the earliest surviving dated poems belong to 1836, though she must have been writing poetry earlier. It would be surprising, too, if Emily (and Anne) had not written prose tales about Gondal before this period, though the first reference to one does not occur until the joint diary paper of 26 June 1837 when Emily was then working on her 'Life of A[u]gustus Almeda'.

Unfortunately, and inexplicably, the entire Gondal prose cycle has disappeared. All that survives to indicate its existence are a few passing references in the diary papers and, vitally, Emily's opus of 200 extant poems. Sixty-seven are unquestionably Gondal in origin and between fifty and sixty more have a fictional setting which strongly implies the same inspiration. The status of the rest remains open to doubt, not least because Emily often began a poem with an actual description of the moment of writing before drifting into Gondal composition ('There shines the moon, at noon of night', 'Castle Wood'). Some poems are undoubtedly autobiographical ('Loud without the wind was roaring', 'A little while, a little while') but many more are ambivalent and attempts to categorize them too distinctly should be treated with caution.

Gondal, as revealed through the poems, owes as much to Scotland as to Haworth. Sir Walter Scott, whom Emily had chosen as early as 1827 to be her Chief Man in the Brontë plays of the Islanders, was the paramount influence. His novels and ballads not only provided a landscape setting with which Emily, like her siblings, could identify, but also a host of romantic characters and storylines which they plagiarized and developed. Byron, Wordsworth, and Shakespeare were also major influences, as was the less well-known Scottish poet David Moir, who contributed regularly as Delta to *Blackwood's Magazine*. Even at this early period, when Emily was more attracted to the dramatic, even melodramatic, in her tales of betrayal, revenge, and death, she was already capable of writing with that combination of tender lyricism and deceptive understatement ('Alone I sat the summer day', 'Sleep brings no joy to me') which produced her most powerful poems.

In September 1838 Emily took the startling step of seeking employment as a teacher in a girls' school, Law Hill, near Halifax. 'I have had one letter from her since her departure', Charlotte wrote the following month, 'it gives an appalling account of her duties—Hard labour from six in the morning until near eleven at night. with only one half hour of exercise between—this is slavery I fear she will never stand it' (*Letters of Charlotte Brontë*, 1.182). Emily stood it for six months before falling ill, just as she had done at Roe Head; she returned to Haworth, declaring to her pupils that she preferred the house dog to any of them. It was her first and last attempt to obtain paid employment away from home and, once more, the dutiful Anne took Emily's place as wage earner by becoming a governess herself. Emily remained at home for almost three years. Tabby Aykroyd, the Brontë servant since 1824, had left after complications following a bad fall, so Emily took on many of her household duties, most famously making the bread while reading with her books propped open on the table. She was also, by this time, a proficient pianist, playing the parlour piano 'with precision and brilliancy' (*Letters of Charlotte Brontë*, 1.599), though rarely for anyone outside the family circle. Her love of animals, which had always been held in check by Aunt Branwell, was now indulged with the acquisition of her favourite dog, a huge bull mastiff called Keeper, a pet hawk, a cat, three tame geese, and a wild one.

The arrival in August 1839 of a lively, handsome new curate, the Revd William Weightman, caused much heart-fluttering at the parsonage (and, indeed, in the locality). Only Emily, it seems, remained immune to his charms, earning herself the nickname the Major for defending Charlotte's friend Ellen against Weightman's attentions. This did not prevent her from being a recipient, with her sisters and Ellen, of a set of specially composed and individually dedicated Valentine verses from him—the first any of the girls had ever received. Emily apparently contributed to the Valentine verses the four girls composed in response ('A Rowland for your Oliver'), confirming Ellen's claim that 'Among the curates Mr Weightman was her only exception for any conventional courtesy' (Wise and Symington, 2.274). Apart from Weightman, only Charlotte's friends Ellen Nussey and Mary Taylor seem to have been admitted to any degree of friendship with Emily. Charlotte told Ellen that Emily liked her 'because I never *seemed* to mark her peculiarities and I never pained her by treating her as a peculiar person' (ibid.).

Throughout this period, as her brother and sisters came and went in the search for employment, Emily remained a focal point for the family at home. None of the letters she wrote to her siblings has survived, but incidental references make it clear that she and they corresponded on a fairly regular basis. Her diary paper, written in Anne's absence, on 30 July 1841, is both cheerful and optimistic. 'A

scheme is at present in agitation for setting us up in a school of our own as yet nothing is determined but I hope and trust it may go on and prosper and answer our highest expectations' (Barker, 358). The imaginary world still had her in its grip:

> The Gondalians are at present in a threatening state but there is no open rupture as yet—all the princes and princesses of the [Royal?] royalty are at the palace of Instruction—I have a good many books on hand—but I am sorry to say that as usual I make small progress with any—however I have just made a new regularity paper! and I mean—verb sap—to do great things. (ibid.)

After an immensely productive two years, 1838–9, in which Emily had written exactly a quarter of the poems now extant, her rate of composition had apparently fallen dramatically. It is difficult to see why, given the quality of verse she was producing ('If greif for greif can touch thee', 'In summer's mellow midnight', 'Shall earth no more inspire thee'). It may reflect a temporary preference for prose or it may simply be that Emily herself did not believe that her poems of that period were worth transcribing into the notebooks in which they were preserved.

Whatever the reason for the decline, Emily's life was about to take a dramatic new turn. In pursuit of the idea of setting up their own school, Charlotte had persuaded their aunt to finance a six-month residence for herself and Emily at a school in Brussels. Emily's opinion of the plan is not recorded, but in February 1842 Patrick Brontë escorted his daughters to the Pensionnat Heger, a large boarding-school in the middle of the city. Given her dislike of being thought peculiar, Emily's predicament was particularly harsh. She was not only a protestant and foreigner in a Catholic Belgian school but also, at twenty-four, considerably older than most of her fellow pupils. All the lessons were in French, of which she had no practical knowledge, and she objected strongly to Monsieur Heger's method of teaching, which relied on imitation of classic authors. Nevertheless, she worked hard and won the grudging admiration of her tutor, who rated her genius even higher than Charlotte's.

> Emily had a head for logic, and a capability of argument, unusual in a man, and rare indeed in a woman … Impairing the force of this gift, was her stubborn tenacity of will, which rendered her obtuse to all reasoning where her own wishes, or her own sense of right, was concerned. (Gaskell, 177)

After only nine months in Brussels, Charlotte and Emily were summoned home by the death of Aunt Branwell. Charlotte returned to Brussels in the new year, but Emily remained at home to become the official housekeeper at the parsonage. She picked up the threads of her old life as if nothing had happened, returning to Gondal with a relief that is indicated by the sheer volume of poetry she now produced.

Publications By 1844–5 Emily was at the peak of her poetic powers, writing hauntingly elegiac lyrics in a spare, natural style (for example 'To Imagination', 'Remembrance', 'Anticipation') and preserving them in her fair copy books. It was one of these that Charlotte found in the autumn of 1845.

> I looked it over, and something more than surprise seized me,—a deep conviction that these were not common effusions, not at all like the poetry women generally write. I thought them condensed and terse, vigorous and genuine. To my ear, they had also a peculiar music—wild, melancholy, and elevating. (*Wuthering Heights*, ed. Jack, 357)

Emily was furious that Charlotte had read her poems without her knowledge: it took much patient argument— and the offering by Anne of her own collection—to reconcile her to the discovery and to Charlotte's determination that they should be published. Eventually she gave way and the three sisters began to select poems for publication, taking care to edit out any references which might even suggest their Gondal origins. Emily and Anne each contributed twenty-one poems, Charlotte nineteen. While most of Charlotte's had been written as long ago as 1837, Emily's and Anne's selections were of much more recent date. The two earliest poems Emily included dated back to 1839, but the vast majority, fourteen in all, had been written within the last two years.

The little book, *Poems*, by Currer, Ellis, and Acton Bell (1846), was published pseudonymously by Aylott and Jones of Paternoster Row at the Brontës' own expense from money left to them by Aunt Branwell. It received three favourable reviews, but sold only two copies. Emily, who always referred contemptuously to the 'rhymes', refused to admit disappointment or, more surprisingly, to abandon any thought of future publication. Even before *Poems* was published, she and her sisters had each begun work on a novel which they were determined to sell to a publisher. For the first time in her life, Emily was writing not purely for herself and Anne, but for the public at large. Charlotte and Anne, in *The Professor* and *Agnes Grey*, both made an effort to break away from the spell of the imaginary worlds of their childhood; drawing on their own experiences, in Charlotte's case of the Pensionnat Heger and the master–pupil relationship, in Anne's of being a governess, they both wrote about what they knew, setting their novels firmly in the real world. Emily had no such experience: she had only ever left home three times and never for longer than nine months. Though she could have written a domestic novel, based on parsonage life, she had no wish to do so. She did what she had always done and retreated into Gondal.

Indeed, Emily had never broken away from it. Her last diary paper, written on 31 July 1845, was, as usual, as much about Gondal as the events of the previous four years. The failure of the Brontës' planned school had left her unmoved ('now I dont desire a school at all'); Branwell's dismissal from his post as tutor at Thorp Green and subsequent debauchery merited only a hope that he 'will be better and do better, hereafter' (Barker, 455). Only Gondal could still enthuse her.

> The Gondals still flo[u]rish bright as ever I am at present writing a book on the First Wars—Anne has been writing some articles on this and a book by Henry Sophona—We intend sticking firm by the rascals as long as they delight us which I am glad to say they do at present. (ibid., 453–4)

Anne, significantly, was less enchanted, writing in her paper, 'The Gondals in general are not in first rate playing condition' (ibid., 455). Nevertheless, the two of them, at twenty-seven and twenty-five, had occupied a train journey to York 'our first long Journey by ourselves together' in play-acting Gondal roles (ibid., 450–51).

Wuthering Heights (1847), which Emily began to write less than a year after this incident, was very much a continuation of Gondal. The complex story, weaving together the fate of two generations of the Earnshaws of Wuthering Heights and the Lintons of Thrushcross Grange, is dominated by the powerful, vindictive figure of Heathcliff, who seeks to avenge his ill treatment in his youth by destroying both families and seizing their property. The sole survivor of his generation, he gains his immediate objects, but, tormented by his love for Catherine Earnshaw (who had rejected him to marry Edgar Linton), and longing to be reunited with her in death, he ultimately loses the will to complete his victory by preventing the marriage of the two heirs, Cathy Linton and Hareton Earnshaw. 'I have lost the faculty of enjoying their destruction' he declares, before gladly embracing death himself.

Wuthering Heights is an extraordinary novel, written with a power and passion which baffled and disgusted contemporary critics, who labelled it 'coarse and loathsome' (Barker, 91). Though it is often seen as standing alone in the annals of nineteenth-century fiction, its Gondal antecedents are readily apparent in the striking number of 'similarities of thought, feeling, and verbal expression' (*Wuthering Heights*, ed. Marsden and Jack, 484) with Emily's poems. Catherine's declaration of her love of Heathcliff, for instance, 'If all else perished, and *he* remained, I should still continue to be; and, if all else remained, and he were annihilated, the Universe would turn into a mighty stranger', echoes 'No coward soul is mine', and the famous closing lines of the novel, describing the three graves, are strongly reminiscent of 'The linnet in the rocky dell'. The characters, moorland setting, casual violence, passionate and self-destructive love, and vengeful theme are all typical of Gondal, as is the complete absence of any moral tone or purpose—a quality almost unique in Victorian fiction.

Emily also drew heavily on the sources that had inspired the creation of Gondal. Adopting the philosophy of her favourite poet, Wordsworth, she defied the convention of contemporary fiction writing by choosing characters from 'low and rustic life', believing, with him, that this was where the 'essential passions' and 'elementary feelings' of human nature were under least restraint and could therefore be 'more forcibly communicated' (Wordsworth, 'Preface' to *Lyrical Ballads*, 1802). Walter Scott's influence also permeates the novel, from the opening description of the house at the Heights, which recalls the beginning of *Waverley*, to the scenes set among the uncouth, quarrelsome Earnshaws, who like the Northumberland Osbaldistones of *Rob Roy*, prefer gambling and drinking to the more refined pursuits appropriate to their class. Even the eponymous 'wuthering' of the Heights, which Emily defines as 'a significant provincial adjective, descriptive of the atmospheric tumult to which its station is exposed in stormy weather', is derived from Scottish border ballads, rather than Yorkshire dialect. Nevertheless, *Wuthering Heights* is emphatically a Yorkshire novel, despite the fact that the only explicit reference to the county occurs incidentally, when Linton Heathcliff pours scorn on Hareton's 'frightful Yorkshire pronunciation'. Emily recorded the dialect speech, particularly that of the servant, Joseph, so faithfully that Charlotte later felt obliged to modify it, 'for though—as it stands—it exactly renders the Yorkshire accent to a Yorkshire ear—yet I am sure Southerns must find it unintelligible' (*Letters of Charlotte Brontë*, 2.479).

Emily, like her sisters, found it very difficult to find a publisher for her novel. *Wuthering Heights* and *Agnes Grey* were eventually accepted by Thomas Cautley Newby only on 'terms somewhat impoverishing to the two authors' (*Wuthering Heights*, ed. Jack, 361) who had to contribute £50 towards the cost of publication; Newby undertook to repay this as soon as he had sold enough copies to defray his own expenses. Even then he proved extremely dilatory, being galvanized into action only by the extraordinary success of *Jane Eyre*, published by Smith, Elder & Co. in October 1847. Hoping to cash in on the Bell name, he brought out the books as a three-volume set in December, but, apart from one or two reluctant admissions as to the imaginative power of *Wuthering Heights*, it attracted only hostile and uncomprehending reviews. Sales were apparently not even of an order to justify any payment to either author.

It has been argued, most notably by Winifred Gérin, that the public rejection of Emily's work effectively destroyed her creativity and, ultimately, Emily herself. This is the argument offered to explain the almost complete absence of manuscript material relating to the last two years of her life after the fecundity of the previous years. Charlotte, however, reports that Emily embarked on a second novel, just as she and Anne had done; its existence is supported by a letter from Newby to Emily dated 15 February 1848 urging her to take her time in completing it. The absence of a manuscript of the novel (and of the Gondal prose) can be explained only by a deliberate act of destruction. These were important works by anyone's estimation, yet they, together with Anne's Gondal prose, have disappeared, whereas tiny scraps and fragments of Emily's poetry and ephemera have been preserved. A possible hypothesis is that the prose manuscripts, novel included, were destroyed by Charlotte, who feared that their publication, unlike that of the poetry, might add to the vilification of her sisters' reputation. She later tried to suppress Anne's *The Tenant of Wildfell Hall* (1849) on similar grounds.

Death and posthumous reputation On 24 September 1848 Branwell Brontë died suddenly, the alcoholism of his final years masking the symptoms of the tuberculosis which actually caused his death. At his funeral Emily appeared to catch a cold. All too soon it became apparent that she too was a victim of the disease. She wasted away rapidly and yet, despite her physical weakness, obstinately refused to give up any of her ordinary tasks. Suggestions that she should see a doctor, take medicine, or try homoeopathy were rejected out of hand as different forms of 'quackery'. She died at home, aged thirty, on 19 December 1848 and was buried three days later in the family vault under Haworth church.

The lack of autobiographical material and the difficulty of categorizing her poems has made Emily the subject of much romantic speculation by biographers, most of it unjustified. Her literary reputation, however, has quite rightly undergone a revolution, mainly thanks to A. C. Swinburne, who championed both *Wuthering Heights* and her poetry. *Wuthering Heights* has been staged and filmed many times and remains consistently among the top three best-selling of all classic novels in the English language. JULIET BARKER

Sources J. Barker, *The Brontës: a life in letters* (1997) · *The poems of Emily Brontë*, ed. D. Roper and E. Chitham (1995) · *The letters of Charlotte Brontë*, ed. M. Smith, 2 vols. (1995–2000) · C. Brontë and E. J. Brontë, *The Belgian essays: a critical edition*, ed. and trans. S. Lonoff (1996) · E. C. Gaskell, *The life of Charlotte Brontë*, ed. A. Easson (1996) · T. J. Wise and J. A. Symington, eds., *The Brontës: their lives, friendships, and correspondence*, 4 vols. (1932) · E. Brontë, *Wuthering Heights*, ed. I. Jack (1981) · M. Allott, ed., *The Brontës: the critical heritage* (1974) · W. Gérin, *Emily Brontë* (1971) · E. J. Brontë, *Wuthering Heights*, ed. H. Marsden and I. Jack (1976)

Archives Brontë Parsonage Museum, Haworth, West Yorkshire, papers · Harvard U., Houghton L., letters and literary papers · King's School, Canterbury, papers · Morgan L., papers · NYPL, papers · Swarthmore College, Swarthmore, Pennsylvania, Friends Historical Library, papers | BL, papers, Add. MSS; Ashley MSS · NYPL, papers · Princeton University, New Jersey, Robert H. Taylor collection · U. Texas, papers

Likenesses B. Brontë, group portrait, oils, c.1834 (*The Brontë sisters*), NPG; *see illus. in* Brontë, Charlotte (1816–1855) · B. Brontë, oils, c.1834, NPG · J. Greenwood, tracing, c.1861 (after portrait by B. Brontë, c.1834), Brontë Parsonage Museum, Haworth, West Yorkshire; repro. in *Transactions of the Brontë Society* (1990), 9 · photograph, c.1861 (after portrait by B. Brontë, c.1834), Brontë Parsonage Museum, Haworth, West Yorkshire; repro. in *Transactions of the Brontë Society* (1990), 6

Wealth at death under £450: administration, Borth. Inst.

Brontë [*formerly* Prunty, Brunty], **Patrick** (1777–1861), Church of England clergyman and author, was born at Emdale, co. Down, on 17 March 1777, the eldest of the ten children of Hugh Prunty or Brunty (d. c.1808) and Eleanor McClory (d. 1822). He changed his name to Bronte on entering St John's College, Cambridge, in 1802, and had changed it to Brontë by 1811. It is hard to distinguish fact from legend in discussing the Prunty family. They may have been Gaelic-speaking Catholics; they were certainly humble, and Brontë in later life did not have much contact with them. He was a clever boy who, as a young teacher, attracted the attention of the rector of Drumballyroney, Thomas Tighe, and was sent to Cambridge to prepare for the ministry. He matriculated at St John's College on 3 October 1802, and on 23 April 1806 obtained his degree, maintaining himself from his own savings, the gifts of benefactors, and some exhibitions. Bronte was ordained a deacon on 10 August 1806, and a priest on 21 December 1807.

Bronte's first curacy was at Wethersfield, Essex. Here he

Patrick Brontë (1777–1861), by unknown photographer

fell in love with his landlady's niece, Mary Burder, but received no encouragement from her relatives. In January 1809 he left for Wellington, Shropshire, where he was curate for just under a year before embarking on a series of posts in west Yorkshire, a stronghold of evangelical Christianity. He was at Dewsbury from December 1809 until early 1811, before becoming sole minister at Hartshead. He published several works of poetry, *Winter-Evening Thoughts* (1810) and *Cottage Poems* (1811), which showed sincere piety, but little poetic talent. He later published several tales, including *The Cottage in the Wood* (1815). Brontë's attention was, however, engaged by other than literary matters in these years: during the Luddite outbreaks of 1812 he was a sympathetic observer, despite his life-long tory opinions.

In 1812 Brontë was appointed examiner at the Wesleyan Academy at Woodhouse Grove, and there met Maria Branwell (1783–1821), niece of the headmaster. They were married on 29 December 1812 at Guiseley church. It seems from her letters to him to have been a love match on both sides. A portrait of Brontë as a young man, later acquired by the Brontë Parsonage Museum, shows him as tall and handsome, and he was noted for his vigour.

Brontë's two eldest daughters, Maria and Elizabeth, were born at Hartshead in 1814 and 1815. On 19 May 1815 he took up a new appointment at Thornton, the birthplace of his three famous daughters, Anne *Brontë, Charlotte *Brontë, and Emily Jane *Brontë, and his son, (Patrick) Branwell *Brontë. On 20 April 1820 the Brontës

moved to Haworth. There had been some delays and difficulties about this incumbency. As the perpetual curate, Brontë was in charge of a large if slightly unruly parish; evidence suggests that he was an active and conscientious clergyman. Brontë's appointment seemed to hold much promise for his family, but shortly after their arrival his wife fell ill and died on 15 September 1821.

Brontë seems to have made efforts to remarry, even getting in contact with Mary Burder. Eventually his wife's sister Elizabeth came to live with the family. Anxious to educate his children Brontë sent his four eldest daughters to Cowan Bridge School, but this proved a disaster: Maria and Elizabeth became ill and were brought home to die on 6 May and 15 June 1825. Charlotte Brontë's portrait of Lowood in *Jane Eyre* must owe something to Cowan Bridge, but it is difficult to blame her hard-pressed father for neglect or cruelty. Thereafter the children were mainly educated at home, with Brontë supervising Branwell's schooling and Elizabeth Branwell taking care of the girls.

It was while they were at home that the young Brontës embarked upon their precocious career as authors, writing copiously in prose and verse. Their father had ceased to publish pious poems and fiction, and it is difficult to know the part he played during his children's adolescence. Attempts to find portraits of Brontë in his daughters' novels are probably doomed to failure: it is unlikely that Mr Helstone in *Shirley*, a severe character, neglectful of his niece's welfare, was modelled on Brontë (and the Revd Hammond Roberson has been suggested as the original). The degree to which Brontë—and his own publications—influenced his children's intellectual and literary development is the subject of continued debate, but he certainly encouraged them to read the newspapers and take an interest in politics.

Brontë may well be accused of lacking worldly wisdom in not preparing his children for the social demands of adult life. He did not introduce them to friends, acquaintances, or relatives. His daughters were gauche and ill at ease in company, inadequately prepared in temperament or by training to be teachers or governesses, the only careers open to them. Branwell learnt Greek and Latin from his father, but neither this education nor training as an artist stood him in much stead. On the other hand, Brontë did escort Charlotte and Emily to Belgium in 1842, showing an interest in this attempt to improve their qualifications. Nor was he idle in church affairs, preaching vigorously and speaking out against dissent. Letters to the newspapers and printed copies of his sermons illustrate this aspect of his work.

Elizabeth Branwell died on 29 October 1842, and Emily returned home to look after her father. The next seven years were eventful but sad. In July 1845 Branwell was dismissed in disgrace from his post as tutor to the Robinson family, and took to drink. In 1846 Brontë's eyesight deteriorated, but he was successfully operated on for cataract on 26 August in Manchester; it is said that Charlotte Brontë started writing *Jane Eyre* while attending him. The publication of his daughters' novels at the end of 1847 came as a welcome surprise to Brontë. Tragically, however, Branwell, Emily, and Anne all died within a year; he was left alone with Charlotte. Although pleased with Charlotte's success, Brontë was a demanding parent who did little to alleviate her depression. He objected strongly to her courtship by his curate, Arthur Bell Nicholls, but eventually reconciled himself to the alliance and they were married. No doubt he was motivated by snobbery, and by fear of the danger of childbearing for Charlotte and of loneliness for himself. After Charlotte's death in 1855 he continued to share the parsonage with Nicholls until his own death there from bronchitis on 7 June 1861. He generously assisted Elizabeth Gaskell with her biography of Charlotte, published in 1857, praising it even though it contained several unflattering tales of his eccentricity, based on local gossip. Biographers of the Brontës have been divided in their opinions of him: some portray him as a domestic tyrant, selfish, snobbish, bigoted, and neglectful; others dwell on his lonely and brave struggle to instil right conduct in his children and parishioners, while leaving his daughters the liberty to pursue their own paths. Posterity will undoubtedly give a verdict which lies between the two extremes.   T. J. WINNIFRITH

Sources E. C. Gaskell, *The life of Charlotte Brontë*, 2 vols. (1857) · W. W. Yates, *The father of the Brontës: his life and work at Dewsbury and Hartshead, with a chapter on 'Currer Bell'* (1897) · J. Lock and W. T. Dixon, *A man of sorrow: the life, letters and times of the Rev. Patrick Brontë* (1965) · A. Hopkins, *The father of the Brontës* (1958) · L. Gordon, *Charlotte Brontë: a passionate life* (1994) · J. Barker, *The Brontës* (1994) · d. cert.
Archives Brontë Parsonage Museum, Haworth, West Yorkshire · JRL
Likenesses portrait, *c*.1825, Brontë Parsonage Museum, Haworth, West Yorkshire · photographs (in old age), Brontë Parsonage Museum, Haworth, West Yorkshire · photographs, York Minster Library [*see illus.*]
Wealth at death under £1500: probate, 28 June 1861, *CGPLA Eng. & Wales*

Sir Joseph Guinness Broodbank (1857–1944), by Elliott & Fry

Broodbank, Sir Joseph Guinness (1857–1944), docks administrator and public servant, was born on 15 July 1857 at Poplar, London, the eldest son of Caleb Broodbank, accountant, of Folkestone, and his wife, Sarah, daughter of Captain Thomas Coburn, merchant navy, of Poplar. In 1872 he entered the service of the East and West India Docks Company as a writer at a salary of £30 per annum. Despite this relatively humble beginning—his first address was given as East London Soap Works, Bow—Broodbank rapidly rose through the steep pyramid of the company's staff structure, reaching the rank of chief clerk in 1886, while still in his twenties. In 1882 he moved to Woodford, Essex, where he resided for most of his life. He was married twice: first, in 1883, to Alice (*d*. 1916), daughter of Robert William Reid, wine and fruit importer, of Woodford; and second, in 1917, to Maud Mary (*d*. 1948), daughter of Samuel Barfoot, carpet merchant, of Wanstead, Essex. There were no children from either marriage.

In 1889 Broodbank was appointed secretary to the company, and, on amalgamation with the London and St Katharine Docks Company, in 1901, he became the secretary of the new London and India Docks Company, the largest of the four private docks companies still operating in London. For the next ten years Broodbank was a prime mover in ensuring the smooth transition from the century-old private docks era to a newly-created modern public trust, the Port of London Authority. When the authority came into being in 1909 he played a major role in steering through one of the biggest transfers of assets ever seen in the United Kingdom, when £22 million of property, 15,000 employees, and a 2400-acre estate in east London were passed over by the private companies. Broodbank was appointed a Board of Trade member of the new authority and was elected chairman of the influential dock and warehouse committee, a position he held until 1920, although he retired from direct dock management in 1910.

Broodbank's expert knowledge of dock administration was put to full use during the First World War, when he was one of the chief administrators of the port and transit executive committee, which controlled the work of all the docks and harbours of the United Kingdom throughout the hostilities. It was primarily for these outstanding wartime services that he was knighted in 1917. He was an original member of the traffic diversion committee appointed by the Board of Trade in 1917; he served as technical adviser to the committee of transport of the League of Nations, and as British commercial adviser to the central Rhine committee.

Broodbank retired from his direct association with the

Port of London in 1922, after fifty years' work. A year earlier he had written *A History of the Port of London* (2 vols., 1921), which is still the standard reference book for any serious study of the subject since it is based upon research into the primary archives of the dock companies. His masterful analysis of the complex power struggle that occurred between the government and the entrenched vested interests in the port during the years 1900–10 was based on firsthand experience. His humanitarian side showed itself in his long involvement with the Poplar Hospital for Accidents, of which he was both treasurer and vice-chairman, serving as chairman from 1920 to 1923. In 1918 he became a member of the Food Investigation Board of the Department of Scientific and Industrial Research, and served as its chairman from 1928 to 1934. For twenty years he was responsible for all insurance matters affecting the enclosed docks in London, and in 1916 he became a director of the Employers' Liability Assurance Corporation, being chairman from 1928 to 1934. He was a founder member of the Institute of Transport and became its first honorary treasurer in 1919. He became vice-president in 1921, president in 1923, and was made an honorary member in 1934.

Towards the end of this period Broodbank gradually lost his sight, eventually becoming blind. However, his grasp of affairs and accurate memory remained undimmed, and he continued until his death to be a director of several insurance companies. He died at his last home, Wittle Wick, Chelmsford, Essex, on 14 July 1944, a day before his eighty-seventh birthday.   R. R. ASPINALL

Sources DNB · East and West India Docks Company staff books, Port of London Authority archive · London and India Docks Company staff books, Port of London Authority archive · Port of London Authority board minutes, Port of London Authority archive, 8 · Port of London Authority Dock and Warehouse Committee minutes, Port of London Authority archive · *Port of London Authority Monthly* (Aug 1944) · 'Members of the PLA', photograph album, Port of London Authority archive, 1 · *CGPLA Eng. & Wales* (1944)
Archives Port of London Authority archive, staff books, board minutes, photographs
Likenesses photograph, *c.*1920, Museum of London Docklands Library and Archive · Elliott & Fry, photograph, NPG [*see illus.*] · R. Peacock, oils; in possession of Employers' Liability Assurance Corporation, 1959 · R. Peacock, watercolour; in possession of Employers' Liability Assurance Corporation, 1959
Wealth at death £51,695 7s. 10d.: administration with will, 16 Nov 1944, *CGPLA Eng. & Wales*

Brook, Abraham (*fl.* 1749–1789), bookseller and natural philosopher, of unknown parentage, was the author of *Miscellaneous experiments and remarks on electricity, the air pump, and the barometer, with a description of an electrometer of a new construction* (1789). Brook explained that he had been interested in electrical experiments since 1749, but hitherto had not seen a friction machine that could produce as much electrical power as the one he had constructed after his friend the Revd William Morgan had read Volta's works to him. The said electrometer, which he also described in a paper published in the Royal Society's *Philosophical Transactions* in 1782, was a device to measure quantitatively the repulsive force that these friction machines exerted on a suspended ball, by gearing that suspension to

a pointer on a dial. Brook considered that it would be useful for graduating existing electrometers, such as that of Edward Nairne, one of the leading makers of such apparatus.

Having improved his electrical apparatus, Brook found himself in demand for his 'luminous flasks': these were glass tubes in which a Torricellian vacuum was created over mercury (like the mercury barometer) and which, when rubbed, produced a luminescence. His expertise at boiling mercury to expel the air earned him a commendation in print from William Morgan; he also claimed to have made improvements to air-pumps. Much of Brook's knowledge seems to have come from his wide circle of scientifically minded acquaintants: he twice attended the performances given by James Ferguson, the peripatetic lecturer on science, who was in Norwich in 1769 and again in 1775, and he corresponded with the Revd George Walker FRS, William Morgan, his neighbour the physician William Bewley—the Philosopher of Massingham—and Nairne, with whom he attended meetings at the Royal Society. Nothing is known of Brook's personal life, nor of the date and place of his death.

ROBERT HARRISON, *rev.* ANITA MCCONNELL

Sources A. Brook, *Miscellaneous experiments and remarks on electricity, the air pump, and the barometer, with a description of an electrometer of a new construction* (1789) · J. L. Heilbron, *Electricity in the 17th and 18th centuries: a study of early modern physics* (1979)

Brook, Sir Basil. See Brooke, Sir Basil (1576–1646).

Brook, Benjamin (1776–1848), Independent minister and historian, was born at Nether Thong, near Huddersfield. As a youth he joined the Independent church at Holmfield, under the pastoral care of the Revd Robert Gallond. In 1797 he entered Rotherham Independent college as a student for the ministry. In 1801 he became the first pastor of the Congregational church at Tutbury, Staffordshire. Here he pursued his studies into puritan and nonconformist history and biography, and published the works on which his historical repute chiefly rests. He is agreed to have been more adept in the writing of biography than general history: *The lines of the puritans … from the Reformation under Q. Elizabeth to the Act of Uniformity, in 1662* (1813) is perhaps his best and most frequently cited work.

After resigning his ministerial duties in 1830, from failing health, Brook moved to Birmingham, still continuing his favourite studies and publishing some of their fruits, including his *Memoir of the Life and Writings of Thomas Cartwright* (1845). He was a member of the educational board of Springhill College, opened in August 1838. At the time of his death he was collecting materials for a history of puritans who emigrated to New England. He died at The Lozells, near Birmingham, on 5 January 1848, in his seventy-third year. He is said to have been one of the last who retained among the Congregationalists the old ministerial costume of knee-breeches and black silk stockings.

ALEXANDER GORDON, *rev.* J. M. V. QUINN

Sources *Congregational Year Book* (1848), 214 · J. Bennett, *History of dissenters* (1839), 161 · private information (1885)
Likenesses Freeman, stipple, pubd 1820, NPG

Brook, Charles (1814–1872), cotton spinner and philanthropist, was born on 18 November 1814, in Upperhead Row, Huddersfield, the son of James Brook, of the large banking and cotton-spinning firm of Jonas Brook Brothers, at Meltham, and his wife, Jane. Charles Brook lived with his parents, who in 1831 moved to Thornton Lodge; and following the death of Jonas Brook in 1840 he became partner in the firm, which operated Meltham mills. He took an increasingly active role, becoming adept in mechanics, and making many improvements in the machinery; he also showed remarkable business talents. Brook was bent on promoting the welfare of his 2000 employees. He knew them nearly all by sight, went to see them when ill, and taught their children in the Sunday school, which he superintended for many years. He laid out a park-like retreat, which he himself planned, for his workers at Meltham, and built them a handsome dining-hall and concert room, with a spacious swimming pool underneath. His best-known gift was the convalescent home, outside Huddersfield, where he landscaped the grounds, the whole undertaking costing £40,000. He was constantly erecting or enlarging churches, schools, infirmaries, cottages, curates' houses, and similar institutions in Huddersfield, Meltham, and the district. In 1860 he married Elizabeth, a daughter of John Sunderland Hirst of Huddersfield. At the end of 1864 his nephew joined the firm, and this allowed Brook the freedom for leisure. He spent £67,000 on the acquisition of Enderby Hall, Leicestershire, in 1865, with large estates adjoining, costing £150,000; and he rebuilt Enderby church and the stocking weavers' unsanitary cottages. In politics he was a Conservative. He died at Enderby Hall, of pleurisy, on 10 July 1872, aged fifty-seven. Vast crowds turned out in both Huddersfield and Leicester for his two funerals. He was interred at Enderby church. His wife survived him; but he left no family.

JENNETT HUMPHREYS, rev. ANITA MCCONNELL

Sources *Huddersfield Examiner*, 1471, 1477 · *Huddersfield Weekly News*, 248–9 · *Huddersfield Daily Chronicle*, 1538–9, 1542 · *The Times* (12 July 1872), 12a · *The Warehousemen and Drapers' Trade Journal*, 1 (1872), 263–? · m. cert. · d. cert.
Likenesses S. Howell, portrait, 1882, Huddersfield Convalescent Home · portrait, repro. in *Warehousemen and Drapers' Trade Journal*, facing p. 256
Wealth at death under £250,000: probate, 26 Aug 1872, *CGPLA Eng. & Wales*

Brook [Broke], **Sir David** (c.1498×1500–1559/60), judge, was the third son of John Broke (d. 1522) of Bristol and his wife, Jane, daughter and heir of Richard Americk, sheriff of the same city. His father was a serjeant-at-law, sometime steward of Glastonbury Abbey, and was buried in the church of St Mary Redcliffe with a brass effigy in his serjeant's robes. Although his father was a Middle Templar, David Brook was sent to the Inner Temple. The date of his admission is unknown, but he is mentioned in 1519 and became a bencher in 1535. He served as treasurer of the inn from 1539 to 1542, and gave a second reading in 1540.

Brook married, first, Katherine (d. 1556), daughter of Sir Giles Brydges of Cubberley, and widow of Leonard Poole (d. 1538) of Sapperton. She had been in the service of Henry VIII, who gave her a diamond ring (mentioned in Sir David's will), and was nurse to the future Queen Mary. She was buried at Islington, where there was formerly a monumental brass with her figure and that of Sir David in judicial robes. His second wife, Margaret (d. 1575), whom he married in 1557, was the daughter of Richard Butler of London, and (according to Sir David's will) had forsaken 'a substanciall mariage' for his sake. She had already been married twice, first to Andrew Francis and then to Alderman Robert Chertsey, both of London; and after Sir David's death she achieved a 'substantial marriage' to her fourth husband, Edward North, Baron North of Kirtling (d. 1564). Brook had no children.

Brook was in the employment of his native city as early as 1522, when he acted as deputy for the sheriff of Bristol in the common pleas. From 1529 he served as the city's member of parliament, and from 1540 to 1545 as its recorder; he mentioned in his will a silver-gilt ale cup with the arms of Bristol, presumably a present for his services. He was also a justice of the peace for Gloucestershire from 1531. His private clients included Lord Berkeley. At some time in the 1520s he was committed to the Fleet prison by Wolsey, though the circumstances are obscure. He may have been patronized by Thomas Cromwell, who held the recordership of Bristol before him, though his principal appointments came later. He was a judge in Wales, on the Carmarthen circuit, from 1541 to 1551. In 1547 he became a serjeant-at-law, in 1551 one of the king's serjeants, and on 25 August 1553 chief baron of the exchequer; he was knighted after the coronation in October 1553. His circuit was the home. Lloyd praised his character highly, noting a tradition that he was fond of the precept 'Never do anything by another that you can do by yourself.' His judicial career lasted for most of Mary's reign, and ended with his retirement for reasons unknown. He vacated office before 2 March 1558, when Clement Heigham was appointed, but lived for another year and died between 4 November 1559, when he made a codicil to his will, and 29 January 1560, when the will was proved.

Brook had a house in St Thomas's Street in Bristol, and another at Week in Somerset. In 1554 the queen granted him the manor of Horton, Gloucestershire, which became his principal country residence, and also that of Canonbury, Middlesex. In his will he described himself as of Gloucestershire, leaving his Somerset and Bristol properties to his wife. But he wished to be buried in the church of St Mary Redcliffe, where his father and mother were buried, and he left the church £40 to purchase a silver cross. He left £40 for the marriage of forty poor maidens in Redcliffe Street, and other charitable bequests. To 'the company of serjeants' (probably the Fleet Street inn, where his arms were displayed) he bequeathed a gilt standing cup and cover, 'to thentent the chief justice there for the tyme beinge termelye shall use the same cuppe in the terme to save the psalm of *de profundis* and to praye for my soule and all christen soules'. Another cup was given to his friend John Southcote, later a judge, asking him to assist his wife. He left a number of law books to 'the worshipfull companye of the Inner Temple, to be fixed and made faste in the librarie there for students to looke uppon'; and the residue of his law library was to be shared between his nephew John Walshe (another future judge) and an obscure cousin. By a codicil, written after the Act of Uniformity was passed, he asked for a 'private prayer' to be said at his burial, 'that is to saye the *diriges* yf it maye be suffered'. As overseers he appointed Chief Justice Dyer together with Southcote and Walshe, recently made serjeants, all of them former Middle Templars.

J. H. BAKER

Sources HoP, *Commons, 1509–58*, 1.500–01; 3.21 · Baker, *Serjeants* · Sainty, *Judges* · F. A. Inderwick and R. A. Roberts, eds., *A calendar of the Inner Temple records*, 1 (1896) · will, PRO, PROB 11/43, sig. 10 · D. Lloyd, *State worthies* (1670) · BL, Lansdowne MS 874, fol. 69v [monument at Islington] · W. Dugdale, *Origines juridiciales, or, Historical memorials of the English laws*, 3rd edn (1680), 329 · Foss, *Judges*, 5.358–9 · *LP Henry VIII*, 6, no. 27(66)

Likenesses brass effigy on monument, *c*.1556; formerly at Islington church, Middlesex · N. Charles, sketch of effigy, BL, Lansdowne MS 874, fol. 69v

Brook [*née* Knewstub], **Helen Grace**, **Lady Brook** (1907–1997), advocate of birth control, was born on 12 October 1907 at the Chenil Gallery, 183a Kings Road, Chelsea, London. She was the eldest among the six children of John Knewstub, who ran the gallery, and Helen Harriett Hillier, an Irish artist's model. The gallery exhibited work by Knewstub's brothers-in-law Sir William Orpen and Sir William Rothenstein, as well as artists such as Augustus John and Helen Brook's grandfather Walter Knewstub, who had been a pupil of Dante Gabriel Rossetti.

Helen's mother had converted to Roman Catholicism and sent her daughter to be educated at the Convent of the Holy Child Jesus in Mark Cross, Sussex. Helen loathed the Catholic church and once adult converted to the Church of England. After completing her education at seventeen, Helen had difficulty finding employment and briefly became her father's secretary at the Chenil Gallery. On 10 March 1928 she married (William) George Whitaker (*b*. 1902/3), violinist and leader of the Chenil Chamber Orchestra. In common with many young women of her generation she knew almost nothing about sexual behaviour, and found marriage a great shock. She had little time to adjust, as her first daughter Christine arrived in April 1929, following the failure of the couple's birth-control method, a device called the whirling spray; 'There was a rubber ball at the end, which you filled up with water', she recalled later. 'You put it inside you and squirted it and whirled it round' (*Daily Telegraph*, 7 October 1997). The marriage was dissolved in 1930, as Helen discovered that, rather than being a round of glamorous concerts, life with a musician was 'exceedingly boring'. When Christine was two, Helen departed for Paris to paint, leaving the child for two years with John Knewstub, who was living in Hastings, having separated from Helen's mother. Helen spent about four years in France, keeping company with other English painters including Michael Salaman and Gwen John. Helen's second husband, Ralph Ellis (Robin) Brook (1908–1998), was a very conventional man and her life was

Helen Grace Brook, Lady Brook (1907–1997), by Elisabeth Novick, 1968

very different following their marriage in 1937. Throughout the rest of her life Robin Brook provided his wife with emotional and financial support, and a place within the establishment. He had an illustrious career as a banker, and was appointed OBE in 1945, and a knight in 1974. The couple preferred to forget Helen's previous marriage and divorce, and Christine never felt welcomed by Brook. Helen had two further children, Sara (*b*. 1941) and Diana (*b*. 1943). As was usual for people of their social class, the two girls had nannies, and later went on to Roedean, an exclusive boarding school.

Helen was an ambitious woman with a great deal of energy, which she channelled into voluntary work, joining the increasingly respectable Family Planning Association (FPA) in 1949. She began interviewing clients for the Islington branch in 1952, and became branch chairman eighteen months later. In 1959 the Marie Stopes Memorial Foundation board asked her to take over their nearly moribund clinic in Whitfield Street, London. This meant Helen was no longer bound by the FPA constitution, which forbade the provision of contraception for unmarried women, and a new evening session was quickly filled by female students from the nearby university. This was a radical step in the early 1960s, and the board was not told until eighteen months later, when they agreed that a young persons' advisory centre could be set up. In 1964 the first Brook Advisory Centre for Young People started work. In January 1966 the second centre opened in Walworth, followed by affiliated branches in Birmingham and Cambridge.

The first clinic was a tiny operation, and saw only 564 cases in that first year when more than 63,000 illegitimate births occurred. The Brook clinics were important for helping to legitimize provision of contraception to unmarried women so that they could engage in sexual activity without fear of pregnancy. The double standard had always been dependent upon a proportion of sexually active women covertly engaging in sexual intercourse outside marriage. It was by openly treating this sexual activity as respectable, and deserving of society's support, that Helen Brook contributed to changing sexual mores. Part of her strength lay in the fact that, despite her unconventional past, and her young daughters, she argued that her goal was the prevention of unwanted babies. She believed in female equality, not in women's liberation, and she repeatedly insisted that the clinics did not encourage female promiscuity. The permissiveness that flowered in the late 1960s following the advent of the contraceptive pill shocked her. By the early 1970s the provision of contraception to girls under sixteen had emerged as a controversial issue on which the Brook clinics nevertheless took an uncompromisingly positive stand.

Until losing her sight late in life Helen continued her activities, joining Family Planning Sales in 1972 and acting as chairman from 1974 to 1981. From 1980 she was vice-president of the National Association of Family Planning Nurses, and from 1987 she was vice-president of the national council of the FPA. Helen Brook was a magnetic companion, highly valued by those with whom she worked. Public recognition was slow to arrive and she appreciated her appointment as CBE in 1995. She died of a stroke on 3 October 1997, and was survived by her husband.   HERA COOK

Sources N. Knewstub, obituary, *The Guardian* (7 Oct 1997), 14a–f · H. Cook, *The long sexual revolution* [forthcoming] · *WW* · A. Leathar, *The fight for family planning* (1980) · H. Brook, interview, BL NSA · A. Furedi, obituary, *The Independent* (9 Oct 1997) · *The Times* (7 Oct 1997), 23; (11 Oct 1997) · *Daily Telegraph* (7 Oct 1997) · C. Wrottesley, obituary, *The Scotsman* (7 Oct 1997) · b. cert. · m. certs. · private information (2004) · *CGPLA Eng. & Wales* (1998)
Archives SOUND BL NSA, NLSC collection, Leaders of National Life, interview
Likenesses E. Novick, photograph, 1968, News International Syndication, London [*see illus.*] · N. Sinclair, bromide print, 1992, NPG
Wealth at death £850,728: probate, 17 Feb 1998, *CGPLA Eng. & Wales*

Brook [*née* Brotherton], **Mary** (*c.*1726–1782), writer, was born at Woodstock, Oxfordshire, the daughter of William and Mary Brotherton. The Quaker 'Testimonies' mentions that although her father was a member of the Church of England, Mary was raised a strict Presbyterian under the auspices of an aunt in Warwick ('Testimonies', 251). At an unknown later age she returned to live with her mother at Hook Norton, Oxfordshire. On 18 June 1759 she married

the Quaker Joseph Brook (1720–1790), a wool-stapler, resident in Leighton Buzzard, Bedfordshire, son of Epaphras and Martha Brook from Shepley, Yorkshire. They had two children, Hannah (*b.* 1760) and Mary (1762–1763).

Brook was converted to Quakerism by the preaching of the American preacher Elizabeth Ashbridge (1713–1755), who travelled around Great Britain and Ireland in 1753. The Quaker 'Testimonies' mentions a long conflict of conscience until Brook realized that her fondness of 'Dress and Pleasure' was inconsistent with the life of a true Christian ('Testimonies', 251). Brook became an active minister and, as part of her missionary activities, she visited London and surroundings in 1766, 1771, and 1776, Warwickshire and Northamptonshire in 1768, Oxfordshire in 1770, and York in 1775. A prominent convert, as recorded by B. B. Wiffen in his *Memorial of Richard Thomas How* (1840), was Captain Bradshaw (1734–1809), former sea captain and reading master at Ackworth School ('Notes and queries', 83).

> Testimony notes her as an affectionate Wife, tender Mother, & sincere Friend of Exemplary Life, & conversation.—She was a true and Faithful labourer in spirit for the Resurrection of that divine Life & Power, which is the Crown of all our Religious Assemblies. Her Testimony was living, & sound, delivered in Demonstration of divine authority, like a skilful workwoman, & true Servant of Jesus Christ.   ('Testimonies', 252)

Brook's main religious legacy is her *Reasons for the necessity of silent waiting, in order to the solemn worship of God. To which are added, several quotations from Robert Barclay's Apology* (1774). Brook contests the traditional ceremony of public prayers: 'There is an essential Difference betwixt praying in Reality as the Spirit shall teach us, and praying in Form as Men and Books advise us' (Brook, 9). Instead of mechanically repeating prayers, 'honouring him [God] with the Lips, whilst the Heart is far from him', the true believer should silently meditate and wait for the 'Divine light' to touch his Soul (ibid., 5).

> If the Lord alone can prepare the Heart, stir it up, or incline it towards unfeigned Holiness, how can any Man approach him acceptably till his Heart be prepared by him; and how can he know this Preparation except he wait in Silence to feel it?   (ibid., 1)

Her argument was supported by numerous citations from the scriptures and an appendix with quotations from Robert Barclay's *An apology for the true Christian divinity as the same is held forth by the people called Quakers*.

Brook's pamphlet was exceedingly successful and went through ten editions between 1774 and 1816, two American editions, as well as French and German translations. As late as 1842, as a commentary in the *Irish Friend* of 1 April certifies, Brook's advancement of faith and knowledge through divine revelation was still praised as a meaningful commentary on the holy scripture. The commemorative 'Testimony' from the Quarterly Friends Meeting on 1 April 1783, recapitulating Brook's important contribution to the Society of Friends, was published in the *British Friend* in 1845.

Mary Brook was seized by 'Violent Histericks' at the beginning of 1781, suffered several paralytic strokes, and finally died in Leighton Buzzard on 10 November 1782. She was interred in the Quaker burial-ground at Hogstyend, Buckinghamshire, on 14 November.   NICOLE POHL

Sources [M. Brook], *Reasons for the necessity of silent waiting, in order to the solemn worship of God. To which are added, several quotations from Robert Barclay's Apology. By M.B.* (1774) · 'Testimonies concerning [Quaker] ministers, 1774–1791', RS Friends, Lond., 3.251–4 · Berkshire and Oxfordshire QM marriage digest, 1648–1837, RS Friends, Lond. · digest registers (burials to 1837), RS Friends, Lond. [Buckinghamshire quarterly meeting] · digest registers (births to 1837), RS Friends, Lond. [Buckinghamshire quarterly meeting] · [Y.P.], 'A letter addressed to John Hall', *Irish Friend*, 5 (1 April 1842), 58–9 [extract] · 'Notes and queries', *Journal of the Friends' Historical Society*, 27 (1930), 83 · J. Smith, ed., *A descriptive catalogue of Friends' books*, 1 (1867), 321–3 · 'A testimony concerning Mary Brook from the quarterly meeting for the county of Bucks, held at High Wycombe, the 1st of the 4th month, 1783—signed by 48 Friends', *British Friend*, 3 (1845), 188–9 · 'Women writers among Friends of the seventeenth century and later', *Journal of the Friends' Historical Society*, 10 (1913), 92–5

Archives RS Friends, Lond., 'Testimonies concerning ministers'

Brook, Norman Craven, Baron Normanbrook (1902–1967), civil servant, was born at 18 Cricklade Road, Bristol, on 29 April 1902, the son of Frederick Charles Brook (1867–1937), variously a schoolmaster, inspector of schools, and assessor of taxes, and his wife, Annie Smith (d. 1921). A daughter, Elsie, had been born in 1897. He was educated at Wolverhampton grammar school (1914–21), winning a classics scholarship to Wadham College, Oxford, where he obtained a first in honour moderations (1923) and a second in *literae humaniores* (1925).

Home Office: wartime Whitehall Brook took third place in the examinations for the administrative class of the civil service in 1925, and spent the first thirteen years of his administrative career in the Home Office. In 1929 he married (Ida) Mary, known as Goss (d. 1981), daughter of Edwyn Alfred Goshawk; there were no children. Promotion was slow in inter-war Whitehall, and he did not reach the rank of principal until 1933, and became assistant secretary in 1938. But he had a varied experience of that ministry, serving in the aliens division, the children's branch, the criminal division, as assistant private secretary to two home secretaries (Herbert Samuel and Oliver Stanley), and finally as head of the division dealing with civil emergencies, the 'war book', and defence regulations, where he did important work on war planning.

From early on in the Home Office, Brook was highly rated and seen as certain to rise to the top. Sir John Anderson had been permanent secretary when Brook joined that department, and when—unusually for a civil servant—Anderson entered parliament and became a minister, in 1938, he selected Brook as his key aide and kept him by his side in a succession of vital posts. Thus Brook was principal private secretary to Anderson when, as lord privy seal, he was put in charge of civil defence and air raid precautions, and when (on the outbreak of the Second World War) he became home secretary. From 1940 to 1942, when Anderson was lord president of the council, Brook also headed his small staff and worked closely with

Norman Craven Brook, Baron Normanbrook (1902–1967), by Howard Coster, 1943

him as his personal assistant. Anderson was, in effect, 'home front prime minister', the lord president's committee co-ordinating and directing much of the civil business of wartime government and economic policy. It was here that Brook started to develop his mastery of Whitehall's interdepartmental labyrinth and to perform the sort of role that he was to play for the rest of his career: negotiating and bargaining with departments, striving to minimize the frictions and difficulties at the official level, trying to get some order into tangled discussions, and preparing the ground for ministerial decisions. He excelled at this kind of work and soon caught the eye of Edward Bridges, who picked him as deputy secretary to the cabinet (on the civil side) in March 1942. In this post Brook first came into close contact with Churchill. With planning for the postwar society increasingly becoming the crucial issue on the home front, Brook played a crucial role as secretary of the reconstruction priorities committee from early 1943 and then, from November 1943, as permanent secretary to the Ministry of Reconstruction.

Secretary to the cabinet Brook was one of the outstanding civil servants of the Second World War, his exceptional administrative abilities impressing fellow officials and politicians from both main parties. When Bridges took over as head of the civil service and permanent secretary to the Treasury in February 1945, while remaining cabinet secretary, Brook was appointed to the specially created post of additional secretary to the cabinet (civil). In practice Bridges concentrated on the Treasury and head of the civil service side of his duties, the effective work of arranging and recording the cabinet's business largely being performed by Brook. On 1 January 1947 Brook became secretary to the cabinet in his own right, a post he held for the next sixteen years.

Brook was *the* great technician of cabinet government in mid-twentieth-century Whitehall, managing the cabinet system and organizing its business with extreme thoroughness and care. Brook's Cabinet Office was, compared to the position in later decades, still a small organization, and he had firm views about the need to recruit its staff on the basis of two- to three-year secondments in order to retain the confidence of departments and avoid the impression of a permanent élite at the centre. As cabinet secretary, he played a key role in orchestrating and supervising the cabinet committee system on behalf of his prime ministers. He had very clear ideas about the need for, and the working of, the cabinet committee system, derived from his experience of its operation during the war. Brook was in fact one of the chief architects of the post-1945 extended system of cabinet committees, institutionalizing the striving for consensus inside government. Cabinet committees, he maintained, provided an important means of preserving the collective responsibility of ministers while taking a great deal of weight off the cabinet, keeping its size within practicable limits, shortening cabinet discussion, and preparing the way for decisions. The official files record a constant stream of written advice and face-to-face discussions between him and his premiers about the establishment of committees, their terms of reference, their membership and the appointment of chairmen, and the conduct of their business.

In Brook's day, to a much greater extent than was the case in Whitehall in later decades, there was an elaborate structure of official-level committees 'shadowing' ministerial groups, undertaking preliminary studies, and meeting to go over the ground together before issues were put to ministers. Frequently Brook himself chaired the most important of these official committees.

Burke Trend noted about his predecessor as cabinet secretary:

> To serve the Cabinet and its committees there had to be an effective administrative apparatus, responsible for circulating the relevant papers in good time, for arranging and recording discussions, and for ensuring the prompt and efficient implementation of decisions. The Cabinet Secretariat owed much to the care and time which Brook devoted to these purposes. (*DNB*)

Brook worked to consolidate and codify the practices of the Cabinet Office and the procedure of the cabinet. Notes of guidance were issued to secretaries of committees, for example, setting out the procedures to be followed in ordering the business of committees, circulating papers, briefing chairmen, writing conclusions, and so on. Brook was instrumental in drawing together the directive on *Questions of Procedure for Ministers*, first circulated by Attlee

in 1946, and thereafter regularly updated and expanded by other prime ministers.

Cabinet minutes, Brook insisted, should be brief, impersonal, and decisive, setting out the conclusions reached as clearly as possible so that those departments and ministers who had to take action would know precisely what they had to do. The minutes were 'anonymized' to maintain the principle of collective responsibility. A contemporary profile described Brook as 'a master of minutes, with one of those well-tempered minds which can digest a succession of confused arguments and present them—in his small neat handwriting—in perfect order' (Sampson, 245). Burke Trend recalled:

> He wrote well and easily, but without great colour or emphasis. His prose was lean and muscular; eschewing rhetoric and emotion; and designed to reduce the most heated and confused exchanges to a record of orderly, logical, objective discussion. This was what was required for the efficient dispatch of government business. (*DNB*)

Looking back on Brook's career Burke Trend felt that his role was, in the classic Whitehall mould, 'essentially regulatory, rather than innovative, in character' and involved 'the reconciliation of multiple and differing views rather than the pursuit of a single undivided purpose'. He was not a policy initiator or entrepreneur; 'his natural disposition was that of the co-ordinator', noted Trend, searching for agreement and ironing out interdepartmental differences (*DNB*). He was the quintessential 'back-room man'— the result of his own disposition and temperament, as much as the nature of his work—consistently keeping a low profile and out of the public eye. His great skills were as a smoother of paths and oiler of wheels, and as an unlocker of deadlocks, to which work he brought a deep understanding of the political scene and the working of the government machine; a disciplined, lucid, and dispassionate mind; and an unerring and balanced judgement. He avoided declaring himself a strong adherent of particular lines of action or pushing his own views. Rather, he was the 'supremely effective engine-driver, determined on one thing alone—to hasten the train of government along its appointed track without deviation or accident' (Mallaby, 155).

Prime ministerial adviser and head of the civil service Brook was a personal confidant and adviser to successive prime ministers, and was particularly influential under Churchill and Macmillan. That Churchill was able to continue in office for as long as he did in the 1950s (his stroke in 1953 being kept secret from the public) owed a great deal to Brook's loyal and unflagging service, and the active role he played as cabinet secretary. Churchill trusted Brook implicitly and relied upon him more than on anyone else, politician or official, during his 1951–5 government. Brook advised him on procedure, policy, and even on cabinet appointments, and he was a great steadying influence on the prime minister. He frequently travelled abroad with Churchill for international conferences and high-level talks as, later, he was invariably one of Macmillan's entourage for his overseas trips. Brook was the foremost figure among Macmillan's inner group of advisers and aides after 1957, Macmillan calling him a 'tower of strength' in his diary (H. Macmillan, *Riding the Storm, 1956–1959*, 1971, 188). Brook was said to be more unflappable than Macmillan. They too discussed cabinet appointments and reshuffles (Brook was among those urging the prime minister to sack Selwyn Lloyd in 1962) and Macmillan relied greatly on his advice on a wide range of policy issues and on political matters big and small. The line dividing 'politics' and 'administration' at the top of Whitehall can be something of a grey zone, and it is a moot point how far the extent of Brook's influence and the nature of some of his advice in the Conservative years crossed the conventional boundaries. Traditionalists could say with some justification that at times he seemed to fall into the trap of over-identification with the prime minister and government of the day.

In October 1956, on Bridges' retirement, Brook added to his cabinet secretaryship the job of joint permanent secretary to the Treasury and head of the home civil service. Sir Roger Makins, and later Sir Frank Lee, headed the economic and financial side of the Treasury, with the work on top civil service appointments, civil service management, and the machinery of government falling to Brook. Brook kept out of economic issues, but it was still a tremendous concentration of responsibilities. The combination of roles made Brook the most powerful figure in Whitehall, but it was clear that he found the sheer burden of the work too heavy to carry out the role of head of the civil service as satisfactorily as he would have wished, a problem aggravated by ill health. He was always very accessible to his senior colleagues on the permanent secretaries net, ready with advice and assistance. But he was too tied up with urgent cabinet and prime ministerial business to have the time to devote properly to the task of running the civil service in the way that Bridges had done. He took no great central initiatives and introduced no major reforms in the civil service. Brook himself was well aware of the overload problem, and the Plowden committee on the control of public expenditure was knocking at an open door when, in a secret letter to the chancellor of the exchequer in 1961, it recommended the appointment of a head of the civil service able to give his full-time attention to the management of the service. Brook's retirement at the end of 1962 provided the opportunity to make the change.

The Commonwealth was always very close to Brook's heart. He was secretary to eleven full-scale Commonwealth prime ministers' conferences between 1946 and 1962. He built up a special knowledge of Commonwealth issues and personalities, thought deeply about its long-run development, and acquired many friendships in Commonwealth governments. In 1948–9, when it was uncertain whether an independent and republican India would stay in the Commonwealth, he played a vital role, being sent on a sensitive mission to Canada, Australia, and New Zealand for top-level talks and taking a leading part in policy making inside the British government.

Brook also played a key role at the heart of the machine in the 1956 Suez crisis, as secretary of the ministerial Egypt committee, chairman of the Egypt (official) committee of civil servants, and chairman of the defence (transition) committee of permanent secretaries. By the end he was one of only three civil servants who were fully informed of what was going on, including knowledge of the collusion with Israel and France—but he kept the cabinet minutes 'clean', and after the cease-fire is known to have rounded up and destroyed incriminating documents (private information). Although he had private doubts and misgivings about the Suez expedition (later privately describing it as 'a folly'), he did what he saw as his duty: devising a timetable for the operation for the Egypt committee and working on top secret plans for the administration of Egypt after the overthrow of Nasser. Post-Suez he was fully involved in the Macmillan government's reviews of British overseas and defence policy, culminating in the 1960 'future policy' study (PRO, CAB 134/1929–36).

Intelligence services, the BBC As a long-serving cabinet secretary Brook inevitably had many links with the security and intelligence services. In the early 1950s he was active on the issue of communists in the public service and on the positive vetting issue. He undertook a secret review of the Security Service MI5 for Attlee in 1951 which proposed a major change in the existing arrangements to make the service responsible to the home secretary rather than directly to the prime minister. Later, in 1956, he was instrumental in the appointment of Sir Dick White, then head of MI5, to take charge of MI6 and shake up the Secret Intelligence Service. During the 1963 Profumo affair it emerged that, at MI5's instigation, Brook had in 1961 warned Profumo, then secretary of state for war, about his connections with Stephen Ward because of Ward's association with the Soviet naval attaché, Captain Ivanov. Brook did not pass on this information to Macmillan, but the Denning report (*Parl. papers*, 1962–3, 24, Cmnd 2152) did not support suggestions that he had here gone beyond his province, saying that at that stage neither MI5 nor Brook had any doubts about Profumo and did not know that he and Ivanov were having affairs with Christine Keeler at the same time. Subsequently Brook was appointed as one of the three members of the standing security commission set up by Sir Alec Douglas-Home when he was prime minister.

Brook formally retired from the civil service at the end of December 1962. In May 1964 he became chairman of the BBC, but he was not a great success in that post, partly because of poor health, but also because the job thrust him more into the public eye than he really liked. He did not see himself as a figurehead chairman, and indeed played a leading part in the controversial decision to ban *The War Game*, a brilliant and horrifying film about the aftermath of a nuclear war. He feared it could undermine public support for the deterrent and might be construed as lending BBC support to the Campaign for Nuclear Disarmament. The corporation's financial problems and complaints from both the Conservative government and (after 1964) the Labour government about what they saw as BBC bias made it a difficult time to be at the helm. On the whole, he worked well with Hugh Carleton Greene, the reforming and dynamic but controversial BBC director-general, but there are signs that towards the end he realized that forces of antagonism were building up and that Greene's days were numbered (he was forced out by Brook's successor, Lord Hill).

Discreet, impersonal, politically neutral, highly intelligent, immensely hard-working, devoted to duty—Brook's mastery of the role of a professional British civil servant was complete. He was tall and physically impressive in appearance, with an unhurried and unruffled style. He could seem very formal, 'buttoned-up', and 'official' in his manner, real friendship developing with only a few intimates, though many colleagues point to a quiet, restrained, and dry sense of humour. He lived quietly with his wife in Chelsea, relaxing by playing golf and by practising his hobby of carpentry (he had to endure many jokes about 'cabinet-making'—which had actually been his grandfather's occupation).

Brook was appointed CB in 1942, KCB in 1946, GCB in 1951, and was sworn of the privy council in 1953. He was created Baron Normanbrook in 1963. He was made an honorary fellow of Wadham, his Oxford college, in 1949. He died at his home, 11 The Vale, Chelsea, London, on 15 June 1967, and his title became extinct. He was survived by his wife.   KEVIN THEAKSTON

Sources K. Theakston, *Leadership in Whitehall* (1999), chap. 5 · PRO, cabinet office and prime minister's office files · Bodl. Oxf., MSS Normanbrook · private information (2004) [interviews with former civil servants] · G. Mallaby, *Each in his office* (1972), 49–71 · A. Sampson, *Anatomy of Britain* (1962), 244–6 · *DNB* · P. Hennessy, *Whitehall* (1989) · Burke, *Peerage* (1967) · b. cert. · *CGPLA Eng. & Wales* (1967)
Archives Bodl. Oxf., MSS · PRO, cabinet office papers, corresp. and papers, CAB 127/338-44 | Bodl. Oxf., corresp. with C. Attlee · Nuffield Oxf., corresp. with Lord Cherwell · U. Birm. L., corresp. with Lord Avon | FILM BFI NFTVA, news footage
Likenesses H. Coster, photograph, 1943, NPG [*see illus.*] · group portrait, photograph, 1946, Hult. Arch.
Wealth at death £35,414: probate, 12 Oct 1967, *CGPLA Eng. & Wales*

Brookbank, Joseph. See Brooksbank, Joseph (*b.* 1612/13, *d.* in or after 1660).

Brooke. *See also* Broke, Brook.

Brooke. For this title name *see* individual entries under Brooke; *see also* Greville, Fulke, first Baron Brooke of Beauchamps Court (1554–1628); Greville, Robert, second Baron Brooke of Beauchamps Court (1607–1643).

Brooke, Alan England (1863–1939), biblical scholar and college head, was born at Spring Grove, Middlesex, on 1 September 1863, the youngest of the four sons of Richard England Brooke, an Anglican clergyman, and his wife, Harriet, *née* Hopkins, of Limber Grange, Lincolnshire. The war poet Rupert Brooke was his nephew. He won a scholarship to Eton College and then went, also as a scholar, to King's College, Cambridge, where he graduated BA in 1886 and BD in 1888, having won several university prizes and done well in his examinations. In 1889 he was elected a fellow of King's. Brooke Foss Westcott, regius professor

of divinity at Cambridge, was then at the height of his influence, and he, together with Joseph Armitage Robinson (1858–1933), largely determined the direction of Brooke's future. Brooke was ordained a deacon in 1891 and worked for a few months as curate at Gayton, Northamptonshire, before deciding to return to Cambridge. In the same year he published his first book, an edition of *The Fragments of Heracleon*; this was followed by an edition of *The Commentary of Origen on St. John's Gospel* (2 vols., 1896). In 1901 he married Frances Rachel (*d.* 1919), the daughter of Nicholas John Dunn of St Florence, near Tenby, Pembrokeshire. They had one son.

By 1896 Brooke and Norman McLean had already been commissioned to edit the larger Cambridge edition of the Septuagint; this work was to occupy Brooke for the rest of his life. The first volume of *The Old Testament in Greek* (of which Genesis was published in 1906) was completed in 1917 and the second volume in 1935. The final volume, of which the first part appeared in 1940, shortly after Brooke's death, was never completed, although much of the work had been done. Subsequent discoveries at Qumran greatly reduced the value of this text, however, and removed some of the incentive to complete the project.

From 1894 to 1918 Brooke was dean of King's College and lecturer in divinity at the University of Cambridge. His time was mainly taken up with the Septuagint project and so he published little else; he did, however, bring out a *Critical and Exegetical Commentary on the Johannine Epistles* (1912) which was highly regarded both for its thoroughness and for its spirituality. He was ordained a priest in 1904, was elected Ely professor of divinity at Cambridge in 1916, and in 1918 was appointed a chaplain to the king. In 1926 he was elected provost of King's College (becoming at the same time an honorary canon of Ely) and for seven years during the transitional period after reforms were imposed on the university by a royal commission he was head of the college. He retired from this post in 1933 but continued to work on the Septuagint until he died, at his home, 8 Cranmer Road, Cambridge, on 29 October 1939. He had been elected a fellow of the British Academy in 1934 and in 1939 was awarded what later became known as the Burkitt medal for biblical studies.

A. R. GRAHAM-CAMPBELL, *rev.* GERALD LAW

Sources J. F. Bethune-Baker, 'Alan England Brooke, 1863–1939', *PBA*, 26 (1940), 439–55 · *Cambridge Review* (18 Nov 1939) · *The Times* (31 Oct 1939), 9 · *CGPLA Eng. & Wales* (1940) · private information (1949) · private information (2004)
Archives CUL, papers | King's AC Cam., letters to O. Browning
Likenesses H. Lamb, oils, 1932, King's Cam. · W. Stoneman, photograph, 1934, NPG
Wealth at death £16,226 19s. 10d.: resworn probate, 17 Feb 1940, *CGPLA Eng. & Wales*

Brooke, Alan Francis, first Viscount Alanbrooke (1883–1963), army officer, was born at Bagnères de Bigorre, France, on 23 July 1883, the ninth and youngest child and sixth son of Sir Victor Alexander Brooke, third baronet (1843–1891), of Colebrooke in co. Fermanagh, and his wife, Alice Sophia Bellingham (*d.* 1920), second daughter of Sir

Alan Francis Brooke, first Viscount Alanbrooke (1883–1963), by Yousuf Karsh, 1943

school in Pau, was by some years the youngest of the family, and his father had died when he was eight—he was, by his own account, shy and unsure of himself. He was also delicate and introspective. Nevertheless he passed out of Woolwich well—not high enough to become a royal engineer, but sufficiently well to join a battery of Royal Field Artillery in Ireland and to be earmarked early as a likely candidate for the coveted jacket of the Royal Horse Artillery.

Brooke's first four years of army life were spent in Ireland; then, from 1906, in India where he entered with enthusiasm into every aspect of his profession, caring for his men and his horses and his guns with a meticulous thoroughness and an eye for detail which were his abiding hallmark. He was a noted big-game hunter in India, just as he was a noted race rider there and in Ireland. If early he had thought of himself as uncertain and hesitant, diffidence dissolved in the warmth of regimental life. He became the best of companions, quick-witted and amusing, an excellent draughtsman and caricaturist, and a skilled mimic. He early showed, however, a deep vein of seriousness about both life and his profession which found expression in long letters to the mother he adored. He was highly efficient and incisive, and received outstanding reports at every step. In 1909 he joined N battery, Royal Horse Artillery, in India, and in 1914 he found himself commanding the artillery brigade ammunition column in France.

The First World War saw Brooke's progress from lieutenant to lieutenant-colonel, at all times on the western front and in artillery appointments. In each he shone, and his name as an intelligent, thoughtful, and, in some respects, innovatory, gunner came to stand very high. He was brigade major, Royal Artillery, in the 18th division during the Somme battle, and was credited with the production of the first 'creeping barrage' to ensure that the ground between the enemy's trench lines was covered and the exposure of our advancing infantry to unsilenced machine-gun fire was minimized. Brooke attributed the idea to the French; whatever its provenance it was highly successful and both in the 18th division battles and in the great Canadian attacks of 1917—he was posted as chief artillery staff officer to the Canadian corps in 1917— ground was gained with fewer casualties than in other engagements in the same period. The artillery support in all formations in which Brooke served and where his ideas accordingly prevailed was widely praised and trusted absolutely.

Alan Edward Bellingham, third baronet, of Castle Bellingham in co. Louth. On both sides of the family his roots lay deep in the Irish protestant ascendancy. The first Brooke of Colebrooke, Sir Henry Brooke of Donegal, was the son of an Elizabethan captain of Cheshire origin, and had been rewarded for his part in suppressing the native rising of 1641 by the grant of Colebrooke and 30,000 acres of co. Fermanagh. From that time until Alan Brooke's the natural tastes and aptitudes of the men of the family were for the soldier's life. They fought campaign after campaign, often achieving high rank and distinction in the service of the crown. Twenty-six Brookes of Colebrooke served in the First World War; twenty-seven in the Second World War.

Early military career Alan Brooke was born and brought up at or near Pau in the south of France where his family owned a villa and periodically took a small house in the neighbouring hills in the heat of summer. His mother preferred life at Pau, where there was a flourishing and fashionable English society, excellent hunting and shooting, and an agreeable climate, compared to the rigours of Colebrooke; some consequences of this were that Alan Brooke spoke French—and German—before he spoke English, never underwent a conventional English schooling, and, though he was an excellent horseman, shot, and fisherman, he first entered communal British life on joining the Royal Military Academy at Woolwich at the age of eighteen largely ignorant of the team games and the usual mores of the English schoolboy. From so comparatively solitary an upbringing—he had been to a small local

Military thinking It was natural that Brooke should be selected for the first post-war course at the Staff College at Camberley where he met the best of his contemporaries in the army—men like Viscount Gort, John Dill, Bernard Freyberg, J. F. C. Fuller, and others whose careers or ideas were to coincide with or cross his own. He was an outstanding student and after a few years on the staff of a Northumbrian division of the Territorial Army he was brought back to Camberley as an instructor in 1923. There he distilled his experience of artillery in the recent war and drew lessons which found expression in a series of lectures and published articles. He believed, unequivocally, that firepower dominated movement, which was itself impossible in modern war without the production of massive and effective supporting fire. He also believed that the effect of firepower tended to be underestimated in peacetime, because of the difficulties of simulation, and therefore tended to slip from men's calculations; whereas movements, because they could actually be performed, were practised with inadequate regard to the dominant effect of fire.

This was the period when the British prophets of armoured warfare were singing different songs. They claimed that mechanization would restore mobility to the battlefield, a perception elusive in the First World War, whose opportunities in major tank battles were therefore lost; and that the tank would facilitate deep penetration and great operational movements because it would nullify the tactical stalemate apparently imposed by machine-gun, cannon, and barbed wire. Nevertheless the tank was not yet reliable and its operational effectiveness was probably as much circumscribed by mechanical factors as by unimaginative handling. Brooke pondered the matter deeply. He was initially unconvinced, and he was certainly not one of the pioneers of armoured warfare such as P. C. S. Hobart, G. M. Lindsay, and G. le Q. Martel who looked to Fuller as in some ways their most original mind and to Liddell Hart as their most articulate spokesman. Nevertheless Brooke's ideas moved a great deal between 1926 when he left the Staff College as instructor and 1937 when, to the surprise of some and the displeasure of those who felt that the appointment should go to a tank expert rather than to a gunner, he became the first commander of the mobile division—prototype of the later armoured divisions—on Salisbury Plain.

Meanwhile Brooke went in 1927 as one of the first students to the new Imperial Defence College (IDC), to which he returned in 1932 for two years as an instructor. There he first studied in depth questions of imperial strategy, joint service co-operation, and the higher politico-military direction of war—and of preparations for or prevention of war—with which his life was to be so intimately concerned. He was, by now, a man who inspired no little awe. As at the Staff College, he made a profound impact through the speed and incisiveness of his mind, the clarity and brevity of his speech, and—not least—the gift of friendship, all the more profound because never lightly given. He was a generous and delightful companion to those who got to know him. He was invariably thoughtful and a good listener. He retained his wide interests, his capacity to amuse and for repartee, and his immense knowledge and love of all things connected with nature. Sport, at which he was invariably skilful, had to some extent yielded to ornithology among his loves. He was passionately interested in all sorts of birds, particularly waders; loved photographing them, at which he made himself an expert; and started to collect books and pictures connected therewith. As an ornithologist he has been placed by the highest experts as 'of the very first

rank of non-professionals'. Brooke retained this enthusiasm to the end, and it provided solace in many dark hours of the war which was to come. Brooke was twice married: first, on 28 July 1914, to Jane Mary (d. 1925), the daughter of Colonel John Mercyn Ashdall Carleton Richardson, of Rossfad in co. Fermanagh. They had a daughter and a son. The first Mrs Brooke died tragically after a car accident in which her husband was driving. On 7 December 1929 he married Benita Blanche (d. 1968), daughter of Sir Harold Pelly, fourth baronet, of Gillingham in Dorset, and widow of Sir Thomas Evan Keith Lees, second baronet, of Lytchet Manor. They had a daughter and a son.

Before his time as instructor at the IDC, Brooke, now a brigadier, commanded the school of artillery at Larkhill between 1929 and 1932. He made his usual mark as a meticulous and absolutely determined superior, a man of clear and original ideas, and a dedicated gunner. He commanded an infantry brigade from 1934—a widening experience he greatly enjoyed and was the first to say found highly educative. After a short spell as inspector, Royal Artillery, in the rank of major-general in 1935, he had an equally brief tour as director of military training. It was from that post that he was selected to command the mobile division.

Two contentious issues lay at the heart of policy. First was the principle and the pace of mechanization and the whole future of horsed cavalry. Second was the proper operational employment—and thus the size and shape—of armoured formations. This second question contained another: whether such formations should be virtually 'all tank' or whether the needs of the tactical battle, whatever the scale of the operational movement, would require the combination—and therefore the mobility and the protection—of all arms. Brooke was by now a convinced supporter of rapid mechanization, and his tact and understanding did much to reconcile the sentiment of the dedicated cavalrymen to the stubborn facts of technology. On the operational and tactical issues he stood four-square behind those who believed that future battle would, as before, demand the co-operation of all arms and that therefore all arms must have appropriate equipments in the armoured formations of the future.

From 1938 until shortly before war broke out Brooke was moved to a completely different but no less vital sphere. He was taken from the mobile division, promoted lieutenant-general, and placed in command first of a newly reshaped anti-aircraft corps and then of the whole anti-aircraft command. British air defences were in a state of inadequacy which the European situation and the rate of growth of the Luftwaffe forced upon the government's tardy attention. The first necessity was a sufficiency of fighter aircraft, a requirement supervised by the chief of Fighter Command, Air Marshal Sir Hugh Dowding, alongside whose headquarters Brooke established his own and with whom he developed a warm rapport. Next was the need for a great increase in the number of searchlights and anti-aircraft guns—and the volunteers to man them. A huge expansion was under way, and Brooke had to organize this, to ensure that manning kept pace with production and that organization and operational requirements matched the need of the hour. This was in harmony with RAF doctrine and pursued as fast as money and bureaucracy permitted. Brooke achieved much and laid foundations on which others successfully built for the test to come.

Onset of war In August 1939 Brooke was made commander-in-chief, southern command, and nominated to command the 2nd corps of a British expeditionary force (BEF) on mobilization. It was not long delayed. In September he moved with his largely untrained and ill-equipped corps to France, taking over a part of the line on the Franco-Belgian frontier and, because of the unexpected pause before the Germans attacked in the west, profiting in such a way as to get his corps into as good a shape as conditions permitted. After much debate it had been agreed (plan D) that if the Germans attacked through Belgium and Holland—the repetition of Schlieffen's 'giant wheel' of 1914 which the allies anticipated albeit at a mechanized rate—the allied left wing, including the BEF under Gort, would advance into Belgium and prolong the French Maginot line defences northwards on the line of the Meuse and thence from Namur to Wavre and Antwerp, meeting and following the River Dyle.

From the first Brooke disliked the concept of moving from prepared positions and meeting the German army in open warfare, for which he believed neither the allied left wing's equipment nor its tactical expertise to be adequate. He had two further doubts. He knew the French well, and had not only seen much of them in the First World War but had grown up among them and loved them. He saw enough of them in 1939 now to have profound misgivings about their quality and morale. And though he deeply respected the courage and energetic character which Gort as a leader radiated throughout the army, Brooke did not believe he had the strategic vision required in a commander-in-chief. For his part Gort regarded Brooke as showing pessimism where duty demanded the reverse whether justified or not. The two men were too different to do justice to each other, and throughout the war after Dunkirk Gort felt that Brooke was unfair in his apparent determination to keep him from another field command. Others, including Alexander but not Montgomery (and both were protégés of Brooke), were disposed to feel with Gort on that issue. Brooke was sharp and ruthless in judgements: however, he had what he certainly believed was a sound nose for success.

When the German attack came in May 1940 Brooke's corps took part in the series of withdrawals forced on the BEF by the disintegration of the front in the French sector around Sedan and the rapid advance of the German spearheads. The surrender of the Belgian army soon left his left wing in the air—a gap which he closed by a series of hazardous manoeuvres of great ingenuity and boldness—while in the south the deep flank of the British army had already been bypassed by the virtually unopposed westward advance of the German armoured forces. Gort, on his own initiative and (at the time) contrary to the instructions of the British government, cancelled a joint counter-attack with the French which he rightly saw would be futile and withdrew his army and as many French troops as possible to Dunkirk whence the majority were safely embarked. On 29 May Brooke himself was recalled to England and after a few days' rest was sent to Cherbourg to make contact with General Weygand, who had assumed the supreme command from General Gamelin, and to build a new British army in France on the foundations of the numerous line-of-communication troops between Normandy and the Loire.

Brooke soon saw that any plan to hold an allied bridgehead in Brittany, as was the declared intention, was impracticable for lack of troops. He was also certain that the French lacked the will to continue fighting. He therefore urgently persuaded the British authorities to cancel plans for sending new formations to Europe. Meanwhile he organized the evacuation of the many remaining troops from the various northern and western ports still available. On his second return to England on 19 June he reverted to his previous post at southern command. After a brief interval there, organizing his sector of the English coast against invasion, he became commander-in-chief, home forces.

Invasion was expected daily, and throughout the last two months of 1940 and the early part of 1941, counter-invasion measures and the reorganization and re-equipment of the army were pursued with the greatest energy. Brooke believed that invasion should meet light beach defences, then be dealt with by the strongest and most concentrated counter-attack by mobile troops which could be mounted. Meanwhile, however, the battle for air supremacy, the winning of which Hitler had laid down as a prerequisite for invasion, was won by the Royal Air Force. Operation Sea Lion—the German invasion project—was postponed, and finally abandoned. In June 1941 the German army invaded Russia. British isolation was over.

Head of the army Thereafter it was clear that the function of the British army would be to prepare for overseas operations, a task upon which Brooke had directed increasing emphasis through the early months of 1941. He was untiring in his visits and unsparing in his scrutiny of every part of the expanding army which would soon again, it became clear, be able to resume the offensive. In December the Japanese attacked Pearl Harbor. The axis powers thereafter declared war on America. Japanese forces invaded British possessions or treaty states in Hong Kong and Malaya, and the war became global. In December 1941, also, Brooke became chief of the Imperial General Staff (CIGS) in place of Dill, who had been no match for Winston Churchill. Soon thereafter Brooke became, in addition, chairman of the chiefs of staff committee and effectively the principal strategic adviser to the war cabinet as well as the professional head of the army.

The issue which dominated the early part of Brooke's

tenure of office was to obtain agreement on an allied strategy—co-ordinated between very disparate allies—one of which (the Soviet Union) was unconcealedly hostile and about whose ultimate intentions he had few illusions. The Red Army had been very nearly extinguished by the brilliance and speed of the initial German operations, and great sacrifices by Britain were regarded as imperative to keep Russia combatant. These sacrifices took the form of huge quantities of British and American war *matériel*, and a series of hazardous convoys in northern waters, expensive in ships and casualties with no gratitude from the recipient. Stalin's sole concern was to procure the earliest possible offensive against Germany in the west to take the pressure off Russia—and later to ensure that no western allied theatre of operations would be opened in the Balkans, as this might interfere with long-term Soviet plans when the German tide ultimately ebbed.

With the United States—and in the early years of Brooke's chairmanship the United States had comparatively small forces engaged, and the Americans were not yet the senior partners—the first issue was to agree overall priorities: it was determined that the war against Germany would be treated as paramount. Next, the question of theatres of engagement. Against Germany and Italy the Americans, with some reluctance, were persuaded to co-operate in a Mediterranean campaign, including landings in north Africa, linking up with the British Eighth Army which would take the offensive and advance westwards along the north African coast, and a subsequent invasion of Italy. This strategy inevitably postponed the cross-channel invasion of France which the Americans regarded as the most expeditious route to Germany and to victory. They were persuaded that it could be successfully contemplated only after German strength had been drawn off by a Mediterranean campaign with consequent release of shipping resources, and after the further prosecution of an intensive strategic air offensive.

In the event this strategy was carried out. north Africa was cleared, Italy was invaded and made independent peace, the Anglo-American armies invaded France in June 1944, and Germany capitulated unconditionally eleven months later. Meanwhile the campaign against Japan was conducted by a successful defence of India, followed by a counter-offensive in Burma; and by a maritime and 'island-hopping' Pacific strategy progressively reconquering territory taken by Japanese armies, culminating in Japan's surrender in August 1945 after two atomic bombs had been dropped. All this was accompanied by a savage Russian war of attrition on Germany's eastern front which ultimately bled her white.

If the course of events appeared rational, if not inevitable, in retrospect, at the time they were highly debatable. 1942, Brooke's first year as CIGS, started with allied fortunes at a low ebb. The key to strategy lay in shipping resources and their provision and protection were necessary in support of every existing or projected Anglo-American front. Because of their shortage, offensive plans were inevitably delayed and preliminary steps had to be taken to lessen the strain on and threat to shipping without which even direct defence on land would be inadequate. Meanwhile Japan's entry into the war increasingly menaced the British empire. Hong Kong and Singapore fell, the latter the greatest single blow to the British arms and prestige for centuries. India was directly threatened by land and sea, communications with Asia equally threatened by Japanese maritime concentration in the Indian Ocean. In north Africa there were serious and profoundly disappointing reverses. Promising allied offensives petered out and were turned by the ever-resourceful German command into what too easily appeared triumphs of German boldness and professionalism over British infirmity of purpose and uncertain grasp of the principles of war. In June, Tobruk fell to Rommel's forces. In Russia the Germans advanced to the Volga and invaded the Caucasus. Throughout all this the amount of work Brooke got through astonished his staff, yet he always found time to think, and think ahead.

Turn of the tide Ahead the tide would undoubtedly turn, since the material resources of the western allies and the geographic extent of Russia would, after the first shocks and reverses, overstretch the axis powers. In the summer of 1942 Brooke agreed with Churchill to certain changes in the high command in Egypt which brought Alexander and Montgomery to the direction of affairs in the desert and which immediately preceded the great victory of El Alamein in November. In north Africa in the same month there occurred the allied landings under General Eisenhower which were to culminate in the surrender of the German forces in Africa, the invasion of Sicily and Italy, and Italian capitulation in 1943. In February 1943 the German Sixth Army surrendered at Stalingrad, and the Germans began to extricate their army from the Caucasus so as to contract their front. The long withdrawal in the east had begun.

Brooke had himself been offered high command instead of Alexander. The temptation was sore but he believed, certainly with justice, that he could best serve his country and the allied cause as CIGS and that he must remain in Whitehall.

Meanwhile the battle of the Atlantic was still the overwhelming anxiety of the British government and chiefs of staff. At the conference held with the Americans at Casablanca in February 1943 defeat of the German submarine offensive was agreed as the first allied operational priority, followed by the invasion of Sicily, the clearance of the Mediterranean, and any step which might bring Turkey into the war. Yet another priority was to be the remorseless bombing of Germany, creating a new front in a third dimension.

The first six months of 1943 were probably the most critical in the battle of the Atlantic. By the second half of the year the menace had been largely mastered by a brilliant combination of maritime and aerial operations. By the end of the year the enemy was withdrawing everywhere. For Brooke the year was dominated by inter-allied conferences. Casablanca, Washington in May, Quebec in August, Moscow in October, and Cairo were followed by Tehran at the end of the year. At each of these, hard talking and hard bargaining took place, and at each Brooke's business was to ensure that, from the British point of view, plans were realistic in scope and in timing, that resources matched aspirations, and—not least, and with increasing difficulty—that British strategic and military interests were safeguarded. In all this, and by universal consent, no military man at Churchill's elbow could have been more intelligent, more robust, more zealous, or more loyal.

In 1944 the allied triumphs began which were to end in the total rout of those who had attacked them in 1939 and 1941. France was successfully invaded in June, and by September had been completely liberated. From that point the only serious setbacks were the remarkably (albeit temporarily) successful German offensive in the Ardennes in December 1944, and the allied airborne operation at Arnhem. In May 1945 the German armed forces surrendered unconditionally, and in August so did those of Japan.

In chairing the chiefs of staff committee and in his dealings therein with his naval and RAF colleagues, Brooke combined personal charm and sufficient tact with the vigorous conviction that on no account should there be compromise on essentials except from genuine conviction. If the chiefs could not agree—and he spent long and patient hours seeking honest agreement on the many contentious issues which arose from simultaneous demands on scarce resources—then he was invariably sure that the matter could be resolved only at the political level and by the prime minister himself who should hear all the arguments in the case. He never wavered in this belief and practice, just as he never wavered in his certainty that no 'neutral' military chairman should preside over the chiefs of staff committee, and that the votes should be those and only those of the men personally and individually responsible for the armed services whose chiefs they were (though he supported the concept of a joint commander-in-chief of an operational theatre). Brooke's colleagues during this time as chairman were first Dudley Pound (who died in October 1943), then Andrew Cunningham, first sea lords, and 'Peter' Portal, chief of the air staff; and the system worked the better for the fact that, sharp though professional disagreement often was, these men had deep personal affection for each other. They shared many tastes as well as qualities. Portal like Brooke was a dedicated ornithologist, and like both Brooke and Cunningham, a keen and skilful fisherman.

Relations with Churchill Brooke's chief concerns throughout were to procure and maintain (but only at the appropriate price) sufficient allied harmony to achieve the great design; to ensure that the British army in its various war theatres—Far Eastern, north African, Italian, and northwest European—was properly organized, equipped, reinforced, and, above all, commanded; to achieve consensus in the chiefs of staff committee between the three British services about the right operational policy to follow, particularly over such matters as the appropriate application of air power; and, often above all, to contrive that

Churchill's indispensable and magnificent energies were not misdirected towards unsound and erratic strategic schemes.

In his dealings with the war cabinet, and with Churchill in particular, Brooke succeeded splendidly, though not without many sharp exchanges and a good deal of passing acrimony. He always said exactly what he thought, and, in the face of even the most unremitting determination by Churchill to hear something palatable rather than true, he stuck to his guns. Brooke, as chairman of the committee, was its spokesman on joint matters and it fell to him to enforce in stubborn argument the compulsion of strategic facts upon Churchill's restless genius without losing its astonishing impetus and fertility. Churchill never overruled the chiefs of staff, when united, on a professional matter. He goaded them and girded at their constraints but he respected their robust integrity. Neither Churchill nor Brooke could have done so much without the other—yet each found the other abrasive as well as stimulating and indispensable. That they were able to work together—Brooke wrote of the prime minister as someone whom he 'would not have missed working with for anything on earth' (*The Times*, 18 June 1963); Churchill firmly rejected the idea that he ever contemplated replacing Brooke—was a tribute at once to Churchill's perspicacity and Brooke's strength of mind, character, and physique. It was a high-spirited, high-tempered, exhausting, and astonishingly successful partnership. An indispensable figure in all this was General H. L. (Pug) Ismay, chief staff officer to the minister of defence, capable as few have been of softening obduracy and interpreting strong men to each other.

Achievement Brooke was not an easy man—his brain moved too fast for him to suffer fools gladly and he was impatient, sometimes to a fault, with slower wits than his own. In his dealings with ministers, with colleagues, and with subordinates alike he could appear intolerant. Junior officers were always struck by the considerable awe in which their seniors held the CIGS—the man, not just the office. Clearly they recognized 'Brookie' as the best soldier of them all, straight as a die, uncompromising and unambiguous and entirely devoid of pomposity or self-seeking. In his demanding and abrupt efficiency he knew when to scold, when to encourage, when to protect. He was admired, feared, and liked: perhaps in that order. He became, in particular, the conscience of the army: a dark, incisive, round-shouldered Irish eagle. To those who worked for him he was a tower of strength, a man whose own inner power radiated confidence. All were grateful that he was where he was. Only to his diary, intended for the eyes of his wife alone, did he confide the irritations, anxieties, self-questionings, and uncertainties of a deeply sensitive mind and heart. To all others he was calm, energetic, and indomitable. Those who knew the man rather than just the soldier were to discover an almost unexpected gentleness within the undoubted authority. He had unfailing power to interest and amuse and he was intensely sympathetic to those with whom he had real affinity.

At first Brooke's speed of thought and speech—his abrupt, staccato, and very positive method of expression—led the Americans to regard him with some reserve, in succession to the exceptionally popular and courteous Dill. Soon, however, they appreciated Brooke's worth for what it was: that of a first-class and utterly professional mind. Even the redoubtable Admiral King came to recognize that he was biting on granite. The British and American combined chiefs of staff became a remarkable, indeed unique, example of allied co-operation. With the Russians it was inevitably different. As the war drew closer to its obvious end Russian intransigence grew as their fears receded and their ambitions loomed more naked. Churchill and Brooke saw with unwilling clarity what President Roosevelt and the American chiefs of staff chose to ignore or treat as a distraction: the shape of post-war Europe and the new tyranny by which allied victory would be succeeded.

In his second responsibility, the professional leadership of the British army, Brooke's influence and effectiveness lay largely in his selection of commanders; he delegated to Sir Archibald Nye, vice-chief, much of the running of the general staff in the War Office, concentrating only on major issues and senior personalities. He trusted, and brought to high positions, Alexander, Montgomery, and Slim, among others. They, in turn, respected him as one whose opinion was almost invariably justified in the event and whose word, once given, was law.

After the war Brooke handed over office as soon as could be arranged, ensuring only that Montgomery, his successor, did not appoint his own favourites. He had been promoted field marshal in 1944. Now additional honours were conferred upon him. He became master gunner of St James's Park in 1946, an exacting chancellor of Queen's University, Belfast, in 1949, lord lieutenant of the county of London and constable of the Tower in 1950. At the coronation of Elizabeth II in 1953 he was nominated lord high constable of England and commander of the parade. He was created Baron Alanbrooke of Brookeborough in September 1945 and Viscount Alanbrooke in January 1946. In 1946 too he received the freedom of Belfast and of London.

Alanbrooke had been appointed to the DSO and had received the bar and six mentions in dispatches in the First World War. Having been appointed KCB in 1940, he received the grand cross of both the Bath (1942) and the Royal Victorian Order (1953). In 1946 he was created KG and admitted to the Order of Merit. After giving up active service he became a director of the Midland Bank and numerous companies, engaged in a number of philanthropic activities, and pursued his beloved ornithology. From 1950 to 1954 he was president of the Zoological Society. He died on 17 June 1963 at his Hampshire home, Ferney Close, Hartley Wintney, shortly before his eightieth birthday, and was buried at Hartley Wintney.

Alanbrooke's son from his first marriage became second viscount and died without children. His daughter from his

second marriage had died as a result of a riding accident in 1961, while his son from that marriage, Victor, became third Viscount Alanbrooke in 1972.

D. W. Fraser, *rev.*

Sources D. Fraser, *Alanbrooke* (1982) • King's Lond., Liddell Hart C., Alanbrooke MSS • A. Bryant, *The turn of the tide* (1957) • A. Bryant, *Triumph in the West, 1943–1946* (1959) • *The Economist* (23 Feb 1957) • personal knowledge (1981) • private information (1981) • *CGPLA Eng. & Wales* (1963) • *The Times* (18 June 1963) • Burke, *Peerage* (1999) **Archives** King's Lond., Liddell Hart C., corresp. and papers | CUL, corresp. with Sir Peter Markham Scott • JRL, corresp. with Sir Claude Auchinleck • NHM, letters to David Armitage Bannerman • PRO, corresp. with Sir Henry Maitland Wilson, CAB 127/47 | FILM BFI NFTVA, documentary footage • BFI NFTVA, news footage • IWM FVA, actuality footage • IWM FVA, news footage | SOUND BL NSA, 'The Alanbrooke diaries', 2 June 1957, T8069/01 TR • BL NSA, 'Field-Marshal Viscount Alanbrooke', P 25W 1 G1 **Likenesses** R. G. Eves, oils, 1940, Staff College, Camberley • W. Stoneman, photograph, 1941, NPG • photographs, *c.*1942–1945, Hult. Arch. • Y. Karsh, photograph, 1943, NPG [*see illus.*] • J. Gunn, oils, 1957, Royal Artillery Mess, Woolwich • P. Phillips, oils, 1957, Queen's University, Belfast • J. Pannett, chalk drawing, 1961–3, NPG • O. Birley, portrait, Royal Regiment • H. Coster, photographs, NPG • A. Devas, portrait, Royal Regiment • R. G. Eves, portrait, Hon. Artillery Company, London • J. Gunn, portrait, Royal Regiment • L. Lee, stained-glass memorial window, Royal Military Academy, Sandhurst **Wealth at death** £50,580: probate, 9 Sept 1963, *CGPLA Eng. & Wales*

Brooke [Broke], **Arthur** (*d.* 1563), translator, of whose life very little is known, produced the first known version of the Romeo and Juliet legend in English. His *The tragicall historye of Romeus and Juliet, written first in Italian by Bandell, and nowe in Englishe by Ar. Br.* was first printed on 19 November 1562 by Richard Tottell, with a second edition by the same publisher in 1567. A 'Romeo and Juletta', possibly Brooke's, was licensed on 18 February 1583 (Arber, *Regs. Stationers*), though no edition survives; Richard Robinson brought out an edition in 1587. The influence and popularity of Brooke's work may be gauged from the considerable number of versions of and allusions to the Romeo and Juliet legend by English writers in the decades following its publication, notably Bernard Garter's *The Tragicall and True Historie which Happened betwene Two English Lovers* (1563) and William Painter's 'Romeus and Giuletta' in *The Palace of Pleasure* (1567); most famously, it served as the main source for Shakespeare's play. Brooke's poem, 3020 lines in poulter's measure, is in fact not directly based on Matteo Bandello's *Novelle* (1554) as the title claims, but is an adaptation of Pierre Boaistuau's *Histoires tragiques* (1559), itself derived from Bandello. Brooke refers to 'the same argument lately set foorth, on stage' (Brooke, *Tragicall Historye*, 'To the reader'), which could be evidence for a lost play on Romeo and Juliet of about 1561. Influenced by Chaucer's *Troilus and Criseyde*, Brooke augmented the importance of Fortune in the narrative. He also greatly increased the rhetorical element in the work, and his considerable development of the Nurse's role and character has left a strong imprint on Shakespeare's version. His prefatory material is moralistic and protestant in tone: it accuses the lovers of 'unhonest desire' and disobedience to parental authority, while condemning 'superstitious friers' (ibid., 'To the reader'). The poem itself, however, portrays the lovers sympathetically and presents Friar Laurence as wise, blameless, and saintly (ibid., ll. 1352–480, 2995–3004). The only other surviving work by Brooke, *The agreement of sondry places of scripture, seeming in shew to jarre, serving in stead of commentaryes, not onely for these, but others lyke* (1563), is a translation of an anonymous Huguenot work. In this work Brooke states his intention to produce more protestant apologetics, but the publication was posthumous.

Brooke died on 19 March 1563 in the shipwreck of the *Greyhound* off Rye. The ship, bound for Le Havre, was bearing Sir Thomas Finch, who was to take up the office of knight marshal in France. George Turberville, in an epitaph on Brooke's death, notes that Brooke:

> to foraine Realme was bownd
> … his soveraigne Queene to serve.

Turberville refers to Brooke's authorship of *Romeus and Juliet* and notes that:

> his Vertues were
> As many as his yeares in number few.
> (Turberville, sig. T6v–T7v)

ANDREW KING

Sources Ar. Br. [A. Brooke], *The tragicall historye of Romeus and Juliet* (1562) • A. Brooke, *The agreement of sondry places of scripture* (1563) • G. Turberville, 'An epitaph on the death of Maister Brooke drownde in passing to New Haven', *Epitaphes, epigrams, songs and sonnets* (1567) • *CSP for., 1563*, 338 • R. Pruvost, *Matteo Bandello and Elizabethan fiction* (Paris, 1937), 14–15, 132–3 • P. Boaistuau, *Histoires tragiques, extraictes des oueuvres italiennes de Bandel* (1559) • Arber, *Regs. Stationers*, 2.419 • G. Bullough, ed., *Narrative and dramatic sources of Shakespeare* (1957), 1.274–363 • *The diary of Henry Machyn, citizen and merchant-taylor of London, from AD 1550 to AD 1563*, ed. J. G. Nichols, CS, 42 (1848), 302 • J. Stow and E. Howes, *The annales, or, Generall chronicle of England … unto the ende of the present yeere, 1614* (1615), 654 • J. Levenson, 'Romeo and Juliet before Shakespeare', *Studies in Philology*, 81 (1984), 325–47

Brooke, Sir Arthur (1772–1843), army officer, was the third son of Francis Brooke of Colebrooke, co. Fermanagh, and his wife, Hannah, daughter of Henry Prittie of Dunally, co. Tipperary, and sister of the first Lord Dunally. His elder brother was Sir Henry Brooke (1770–1834), MP for County Fermanagh, who was created a baronet in 1822. Arthur Brooke entered the army as an ensign in the 44th foot on 31 October 1792 and was promoted lieutenant on 26 November 1793. In 1794–5 he served with the 44th in Flanders and during the withdrawal to Bremen. Promoted captain on 19 September 1795, he went in 1796 with Lieutenant-General Sir Ralph Abercromby's army to the West Indies, remaining there until 1797 and taking part in the capture of St Lucia. He then served with the 44th at Gibraltar in 1799 and 1800 and throughout the Egyptian campaign of 1801, being prominent in the actions of 13 and 21 March near Alexandria and, in September, the siege of Cairo.

Having returned with the regiment to Ireland, and then England, Brooke purchased his majority on 26 December 1802, and his lieutenant-colonelcy on 15 June 1804, in the 44th before sailing with it to Malta the following year. When the kingdom of Naples was threatened, the 44th

went to Sicily under Brooke in 1808, and in June 1809 went on to capture the island of Procida in the Bay of Naples. It returned to Messina in August of that year and helped to defeat a French landing nearby in September 1810. Brooke took the regiment back to Malta in August 1811, and went with it from there via Minorca to land in eastern Spain on 3 August 1813 and join Lieutenant-General Lord William Bentinck's force. Promoted colonel on 4 June 1813, he at once took command of the brigade to which his regiment was assigned, and he distinguished himself in every action against Maréchal Suchet, particularly at the combat of Ordal. At the conclusion of the war with Napoleon he was ordered to march his own regiment and certain other ones across southern France to Bordeaux in order to embark for an expedition against the United States; he sailed from the French port in June 1814.

The force, under Major-General Robert Ross, landed near St Benedict on Chesapeake Bay in August and advanced towards Washington, Brooke commanding its 2nd brigade, composed of the 4th and 44th regiments—the former led by his brother, Francis. At Bladensburg, Maryland, on 24 August, superior American forces were routed largely through decisive flank action by Brooke, after which Ross recorded his 'approbation of the spirited conduct of Colonel Brooke, and of his brigade' (Carter, 55). After burning Washington's Capitol and public buildings, in reprisal for American destruction in Canada, the expedition re-embarked at St Benedict and sailed down to the mouth of the Patapsco River, where it was arranged that the troops were to land and advance on Baltimore, while the ships' boats were to force their way up the river to co-operate. In the first skirmish that took place after landing, and before the advance commenced, Ross was killed, and the command now devolved on Brooke. He determined to carry out his predecessor's plan, and although it was reported that Baltimore was defended by 20,000 men, he pushed steadily on to defeat a powerful force of militia on 12 September. He intended to assault the main enemy entrenchments before Baltimore on 13 September, but learned that the anticipated naval co-operation would not be possible because there were sunken ships across the harbour's mouth. A partial retreat on land failed to tempt the defenders from dominating high ground, and Brooke, therefore, re-embarked his men. Shortly afterwards, the fleet sailed for the West Indies, where he was superseded by Major-General John Keane, who delivered to him a most eulogistic dispatch from the commander-in-chief. Nevertheless, the chronicler the Revd G. R. Gleig later criticized Brooke as 'an officer of decided personal courage, but perhaps better calculated to lead a battalion than to guide an army' (Gleig, 96).

At the close of the war Brooke returned to England, became a CB, and was promoted major-general on 12 August 1819, but he never again saw active service. On 22 February 1822 he was nominated governor of Yarmouth (north), receiving an annual allowance of 9s. 6d.—a post he held until its abolition in 1825. Appointed KCB in 1833, he advanced to lieutenant-general on 10 January 1837 and became colonel of the 86th foot on 24 May 1837. He had married Marianne, daughter of the Revd William Sneyd, of Newchurch, Isle of Wight; they had a son and a daughter. He died on 26 July 1843 at his residence in George Street, Portman Square, London.

H. M. STEPHENS, rev. JOHN SWEETMAN

Sources Army List · T. Carter, ed., Historical record of the forty-fourth, or the east Essex regiment of foot (1864) · J. Philippart, ed., The royal military calendar, 3 vols. (1815–16) · GM, 2nd ser., 20 (1843), 556 · Burke, Peerage · G. R. Gleig, The campaigns of the British army at Washington and New Orleans, in the years 1814–1815, 3rd edn (1827)
Archives PRO NIre., autobiography, diary [copies] · Ulster American Folk Park, Camphill, Omagh, expedition diary

Brooke, Arthur (1845–1918), tea merchant, was born in George Street, Ashton under Lyne, Lancashire, on 30 October 1845 to Charles Brooke, tea dealer, and his wife, Jane, née Howard. After an early career in textiles was terminated in 1864 by the 'Cotton Famine', he trained in the wholesale tea firm Peek Brothers and Winch, initially in Liverpool and later in London.

After briefly returning home Brooke opened his first shop at 29 Market Street, Manchester, selling packeted, blended tea, sugar, and coffee, and trading under the name of Brooke, Bond & Co. The name Bond was entirely fictional, being added purely for alliterative effect. He adopted what were then viewed as innovative sales techniques: strictly cash sales, sale weight net of paper wrapping, and aggressive newspaper advertising. Within three years he had opened shops in Liverpool, Leeds, and Bradford, but in 1872 he left these in the hands of a manager and moved to London, opening an office and blending warehouse in Whitechapel High Street, his recently widowed father selling up in Ashton to help him run the business.

Although trade faltered in the late 1870s, leading Brooke to consider emigrating to New Zealand, the following decade witnessed dramatic growth based on supplying packaged, blended tea wholesale to retail grocers. By 1892, when Brooke Bond was converted to a limited liability company with a share capital of £150,000, it was the pace-setter in wholesale packet tea business, although it still retained three retail shops in the north of England. Brooke married Alice Catherine, daughter of William Young, Royal Navy paymaster at Plymouth, on 25 November 1875. They honeymooned in Paris, with Arthur taking the opportunity to visit colour printers to order display cards for his business. The couple lived initially in Stonebridge Park but by 1887 resided in Kensington and had a country house and estate, Leylands, at Wotton near Dorking. They had two daughters and two sons.

Brooke secured his market dominance by becoming 'a careful student of American business methods' (The Grocer, 20 April 1918), visiting America to study distribution methods and sales techniques and appointing an American advertising consultant, John E. Powers, in 1903 at a fee in excess of a director's annual salary. In 1901 'Assam Brooke', as he was sometimes known, established an agency in Calcutta to purchase and blend tea in India which was to develop into a separate company in 1912. By this time his firm was one of the largest tea distributing

Arthur Brooke (1845–1918), by unknown photographer

firms in the world with an extensive domestic and export trade, operating from new premises in Goulston Street, Aldgate, after 1910, and with its own printing and bag-making works in Reading (opened 1902).

Although he retired as director of the company in 1904 and as chairman in 1910 (to be succeeded by his eldest son, Gerald), Brooke continued to retain an active interest in the business, being rumoured to have replied to a request to slow down in his old age, 'Where else could I get eight hours of pleasure so cheaply?' (The Grocer, 20 April 1918). Brooke was also an early advocate of good working conditions, his Times obituary (16 April 1918) describing him as 'a model employer'. He introduced an eight-hour day and bonuses for his employees and supported the principles of co-partnership; his workers were reported to have looked upon him more as a colleague than employer. Brooke was an ardent admirer of W. E. Gladstone, and was regarded as a generous supporter of philanthropic and benevolent institutions, although he did not court publicity.

Brooke died on 13 April 1918 at 61 Hampstead Way, Golders Green, where his daughter Alice lived; the cause of death was recorded as acute tuberculosis and pneumonia. His funeral was at Golders Green on 16 April 1918.

MICHAEL WINSTANLEY

Sources D. Wainwright, Brooke Bond: a hundred years (1970) · D. Wainwright, 'Brooke, Arthur', DBB · The Grocer (20 April 1918) · The Grocer (27 April 1918) · Grocers' Gazette and Provision Trades' News (20 April 1918), 618 · The Times (16 April 1918) · b. cert. · m. cert. · d. cert. · CGPLA Eng. & Wales (1918)
Likenesses photograph, repro. in Wainwright, Brooke Bond, 15 · photograph, Unilever Corporate Archives [see illus.]

Wealth at death £189,584 8s. 3d.: probate, 20 July 1918, *CGPLA Eng. & Wales*

Brooke, Barbara Muriel, Baroness Brooke of Ystrad-fellte (1908–2000). *See under* Brooke, Henry, Baron Brooke of Cumnor (1903–1984).

Brooke [Brook], **Sir Basil** (1576–1646), iron-founder and royalist conspirator, was probably born at Madeley in Shropshire, the eldest son of John Brooke and his wife, Anne, daughter of Francis Shirley of Staunton Harold, Leicestershire. He married Etheldreda Brudenell, daughter of Sir Edmund Brudenell, and together they had a son, Thomas. Brooke was knighted at Highgate on 1 May 1604. His Shropshire estates included Madeley and Wareham Farm with associated coalmines and steelworks, giving him ownership of some of the most important mines in the Coalbrookdale area. He also held Middle in Gloucestershire and North Aston in Oxfordshire and owned a house in Bishop's Court near London. He was a farmer of the Forest of Dean ironworks from 1615 and attempted to manufacture steel under a patent issued to Elliot and Meysey, though the attempt failed and the patent was revoked in 1619.

Brooke was considered one of the leading Roman Catholics in England and was said to have personal connections with both James VI and I and Charles I. With the latter monarch his connections might have been through the queen, to whom he dedicated the devotional work *Entertainments for Lent*, which he had translated from the French of N. Caussin and which was to be republished several times. He also had connections with the earl of Portland. In 1635 he was active in supporting the cause of the Catholic regular clergy against episcopal oversight. During the bishops' wars in 1639–40 he acted as treasurer for contributions raised by English Catholics for Charles I's army. On 27 January 1641 he and others were summoned to the House of Commons, but he fled the capital. In January 1642 he was arrested in York and sent to London to be held in the custody of the sergeant of the House of Commons. In the following August, as civil war broke out, he was moved from the sergeant's custody to the king's bench prison.

Late in 1643 Brooke was implicated in a plot to foment division between the city of London and parliament and thereby to prevent the army of parliament's Scottish allies entering England. The plot was part of Charles I's attempt to win over Londoners by exploiting their grievances and stirring up support for an appeal for peace. Brooke was contacted at the suggestion of Colonel Reade, who had escaped from prison after being arrested in association with the Catholic rising in Ireland. Reade suggested that Brooke be approached with a view to his using his merchant connections to exploit dissatisfaction in the city at the damage being done to trade by the prolongation of war. He planned to drum up support in the citizenry and to stir dissent among the London trained bands through two agents, Thomas Violet, an imprisoned tax defaulter, and Theophilus Riley, London's scoutmaster-

general. The king also wrote to the lord mayor and aldermen assuring them of his commitment to the protestant faith in the hope that they would be induced to declare for peace. His letter was intercepted by the committee of safety and the plot exposed. Charles's apparent willingness to use Catholics as leading figures in intrigues ran counter to simultaneous negotiations which were being established with Independents in the city opposed to the Scottish involvement in the war. On 6 January 1644 Brooke was arrested and imprisoned in the Tower of London by order of the Commons. On 6 May 1645 he was again sent to the king's bench prison until debts by action had been paid.

From 1645 Madeley had been held by the parliamentarian Shropshire county committee as sequestered property, with the ironworks managed by captains Henry Bowdler and Thomas Scott. Brooke was listed as a papist in arms excluded from the general amnesty in parliament's treaty proposals of July 1646, the Newcastle propositions, meaning his estates were to be disposed of according to the wishes of parliament. A series of battles were fought by Madeley tenants and the new grantees of the estate for control of the mines, while some tenants at least briefly took control of the estate as a whole. Brooke died on 31 December 1646 leaving debts of £10,000 on an estate of only £300 per annum and his properties passed to his son Thomas, also classed as a delinquent papist. In 1651 Thomas Brooke secured an allowance of one-fifth of the profits of the property for the benefit of his children, John, Thomas, and Margaret, but forfeited the estate the following year. It was sold to the Leveller John Wildman but seems to have been reacquired by Thomas Brooke soon afterwards.　　　　　　　　　　MARTYN BENNETT

Sources *CSP dom.*, 1642–3 · S. R. Gardiner, *History of the great civil war, 1642–1649*, new edn, 1 (1893); facs. repr. (1987), 269–70 · M. A. E. Green, ed., *Calendar of the proceedings of the committee for compounding … 1643–1660*, 3, PRO (1891), 2231–2 · S. R. Gardiner, ed., *Constitutional documents of the puritan revolution, 1625–1660*, 3rd edn (1906); repr. (1979) · C. O'Riordan, 'Sequestration and social upheaval: Madeley, Shropshire and the English revolution', *West Midland Studies*, 18 (1985), 21–31 · C. O'Riordan, 'Popular exploitation of enemy estates in the English revolution', *History*, new ser., 78 (1993), 183–200 · *N&Q*, 3rd ser., 4 (1863), 81–2, 136 · *DNB*
Likenesses etching, NPG

Brooke, Basil Stanlake, first Viscount Brookeborough (1888–1973), prime minister of Northern Ireland, was born on 9 June 1888 at Colebrooke Park, co. Fermanagh, Ireland, the eldest of five children (three sons and two daughters) of Sir Arthur Douglas Brooke, fourth baronet (1865–1907), of Colebrooke, and his wife, Gertrude Isabella (d. 1918), only daughter of Stanlake Batson, of Horseheath, Cambridgeshire. He succeeded his father as fifth baronet on 27 November 1907. His social class, family background, and co. Fermanagh upbringing exerted a powerful formative influence on him. His family first moved to Ireland from Cheshire in the late sixteenth century and was awarded estates in co. Fermanagh as reward for military service rendered in quelling the 1641 rising.

Basil Stanlake Brooke, first Viscount Brookeborough (1888–1973), by Howard Coster, 1943

Its most prominent characteristic thereafter was its consistent record of military service. Fifty-three of its members served in the two world wars (with Brooke's uncle, Alan Brooke, first Viscount Alanbrooke, the most prominent); twelve sacrificed their lives. In addition, it had a strong tradition of political activism. The Brookes repeatedly served as magistrates, sheriffs, and lord lieutenants within co. Fermanagh and from the eighteenth century intermittently represented the county in parliament. Though they did not think of themselves as other than Irish, when they spoke of standing up for Ireland it meant standing up for the protestants of Ireland. While their participation in the Orange order was generally at a local level, it was almost hereditary in character. Their response to the mounting nationalist challenge which emerged in Ireland during the late nineteenth century was to act uniformly and aggressively in defence of the Union.

Education and early career Brooke's early career broadly conformed to the well-beaten paths trodden by innumerable sons of the Anglo-Irish gentry. After attending private school in southern France (at Pau) he proceeded to Winchester (1901–5), followed by Sandhurst, and then served with the 7th Royal Fusiliers (1908–11) and the 10th hussars in India and South Africa. During these years it was already evident that he fully identified with the defiant Unionism which had characterized the recent history of his family's political involvement. While on leave in

December 1912 he helped inaugurate and organize the Ulster Voluntary Force in co. Fermanagh, and in March 1914 offered to resign his commission and 'return to help the loyalists in Ulster' (Barton, *Brookeborough*, 21). His military service was extended by the outbreak of the First World War. He served throughout the conflict with distinction; he rose to the rank of captain in the hussars, acted as aide-de-camp to General Byng, was mentioned in dispatches, and awarded the Military Cross in 1916 and Croix de Guerre with palm. His experiences on the western front affected him deeply. As a consequence, he lost his religious faith and in early 1916 (before the Easter rising) wrote to his sister of his growing conviction that civil war would be 'worse for Ireland' than home rule (ibid., 25).

In December 1918 Brooke returned to Colebrooke, intent on restoring his neglected estates, having been away from co. Fermanagh for much of the previous twenty-two years. Five months later (on 3 June 1919) he married Cynthia Mary (1897–1970), second daughter and coheir of Captain Charles Warden Sergison, of Cuckfield Park, Sussex. Their relationship was to be tested and strengthened through bereavement and illness. His wife's social competence, unquestioning devotion, resilience, and determination sharpened his ambition and contributed to its fulfilment. The extent of his debt to her he frequently and willingly avowed in public. They had three sons; the eldest and youngest were killed in action during the Second World War, but the second son, John Warden, also a soldier, survived the war and later entered Northern Ireland politics.

Whatever his original intentions, on returning home Brooke was ineluctably drawn once more into the political turmoil which Ireland and Fermanagh were then entering. In June 1920 he organized Fermanagh Vigilance—a small, local, part-time force, designed to counteract the escalating IRA campaign, protect property, and ultimately defend the Union. He decided against calling it the Ulster Volunteer Force in order to encourage Catholic recruitment. Subsequently, he was prominent among those who successfully urged the British government officially to recognize this and other similar organizations which had spontaneously emerged elsewhere in the north. When the Ulster Special Constabulary was established in September 1920 Brooke became Fermanagh county commandant. Almost imperceptibly and certainly unconsciously, through these actions he acquired a reputation and rose to a position of prominence among Ulster unionists. Sir James Craig, Northern Ireland's first prime minister, acknowledged his services by appointing him CBE and offering him a seat in the Northern Ireland Senate. He accepted, but had to relinquish it almost immediately, as the appointment contravened the Government of Ireland Act because he held an office of profit under the crown. Craig described him at the time as 'one of the finest leaders in Ulster today' (Barton, *Brookeborough*, 58). In 1929, Brooke became Unionist MP for the county at Stormont. He accepted the seat from a sense of duty, but also from political ambition; he regarded Colebrooke as 'never enough in itself' (ibid., 15). His thin, wiry frame, with the inevitable cigarette in hand, and clipped, Anglicized accent were to be a feature of Stormont for the next forty years.

Brooke at Stormont From the outset of his political career Brooke addressed public meetings with a frequency to which he was unaccustomed, and generally spoke in moderate tones. But on 12 July 1933 he made a speech which was sectarian in content, and he repeated its main themes several times over the next nine months. In his remarks he admonished audiences 'to employ good protestant lads and lassies' and not Roman Catholics, as they were 'out with all their force and might to destroy the power and constitution of Ulster' (*Fermanagh Times*, 13 July 1933). He also warned of a 'definite plot' whereby southern nationalists would attempt to 'infiltrate' Northern Ireland and subvert its pro-Union majority. The timing of these comments owed much to the strained political context. The formation of de Valera's first Fianna Fáil government in Dublin caused apprehension among unionists, while deepening economic depression threatened the party's unity by accentuating its class divisions. His comments also reflect Brooke's growing disillusionment at the persistent unwillingness of most northern nationalists to recognize Northern Ireland even in the short term. As employer, as politician, and later as minister he was more open-minded in his actual dealings with political opponents than these infamous remarks might suggest; they have unduly coloured subsequent assessments of his career. In mid-1940 he was even prepared to contemplate Irish unity if its attainment would induce de Valera to abandon Éire's neutrality and so possibly ensure the defeat of Nazi Germany.

Brooke's political rise at Stormont was rapid. His progress reflects the dearth of unionist back-bench talent, his relative youth yet considerable experience, extensive social contacts, eagerness to serve, and exceptional personal charm. John MacDermott, a ministerial colleague, said of him that he could have 'sold sand to the Arabs' (interview, 11 May 1979). In May 1929 he was made junior whip and parliamentary secretary at the ministry of finance, and in 1933 became minister of agriculture. At the latter he was knowledgeable, relished the personal contact with farmers afforded by his post, and was supported by civil servants of exceptional quality, who were eager to implement locally the marketing schemes and other radical policy changes then being initiated by Westminster. Though often in later years caricatured as 'a lazy man of limited ability' (*The Autobiography of Terence O'Neill*, 40), as a young politician he quickly acquired a reputation for enterprise, energy, and competence, and his influence and standing within the government rose measurably.

The coming of war was always likely to benefit Brooke's career, enhancing the relevance of his social connections and military background and providing increased scope for his pragmatism and flair for publicity. Craig dissuaded him from returning to full-time military service and, for the first time, he soon began clearly to emerge as a likely future premier. From the outset he demonstrated an unwavering commitment to allied victory. Partly because of his energetic leadership the farmers of Northern Ireland, alone of any region in the United Kingdom, exceeded their tillage quota during 1939–40. His ministerial performance stood out in the context of a Stormont government which in the late 1930s and early 1940s reached unprecedented levels of incompetence and thus attracted increasingly virulent criticism from unionist back-benchers. None the less, Lord Craigavon remained premier and refused to make the cabinet changes which his critics thought necessary.

The Andrews government Craigavon's death (in November 1940) did not presage any substantive improvement in governmental performance. The ageing John Andrews (minister of finance) who succeeded was unsuited to wartime leadership. Critically, he refused to purge the 'old (ministerial) gang', which was reshuffled rather than recast. Brooke became minister of commerce, a small and hitherto ineffectual department widely blamed both by back-benchers and the public for the persistently high levels of local unemployment. There, supported once more by talented officials, he energetically sought more contracts for local firms from mainland supply departments, unashamedly exploiting his contacts at Westminster, while striving to improve the woeful production record of some of the province's leading heavy industries. Such was his success that, by April 1943, regional unemployment had dropped to 19,000, 5 per cent of the insured population (it had been almost 72,000 in November 1940).

Meanwhile, support for the Andrews government was collapsing. In particular, it attracted criticism because of its lack of preparation for the German air raids (April–May 1941), its mishandling of the conscription question later that year, its temporary suspension of Belfast corporation, the steady deterioration in local labour relations, and the perceived inadequacy of its post-war planning. The outcome was a wide-ranging Unionist Party revolt which sought sweeping changes in the composition of both leadership and cabinet. The climax was reached at a meeting of Unionist MPs on 28 April 1943 when, faced with ministerial resignations and a possible party split, Andrews agreed to resign. His miscalculations regarding the strength of opposition led him to attribute his fall to the manipulative skills of his successor, Brooke. However, the evidence suggests otherwise; Brooke had consistently urged Andrews to strengthen his government (offering to resign himself to facilitate the process), had been genuinely surprised by the scale of the crisis, and had made no attempt to exploit the unfolding events. Subsequently, he alone was capable of forming a government commanding a Commons majority, and he was eventually asked to do so by the governor, Lord Abercorn. He immediately appointed a new ministerial team (which included Northern Ireland's first non-Unionist Party government member, H. C. Midgley) and it was broadly successful in achieving its agreed priorities—to bring greater drive to the war effort, devise plans for the post-war years, and maintain the constitution.

Prime minister of Northern Ireland In 1945 Brooke pressed to have national service extended to Northern Ireland in order to lower future unemployment levels, to underline the area's constitutional status within the Union, and also in the hope of attracting Britain's goodwill. Such was his enthusiasm for this proposal that he even suggested increasing state subsidies to local Catholic schools in an attempt to reduce church opposition to it. However, Attlee decided to exclude the six counties from the operation of the National Service Bill in 1946; none the less, Stormont–Westminster relations had meanwhile become markedly closer. This was mainly due to Northern Ireland's cumulative contribution to the war effort— through its provision of goods and agricultural produce, its volunteer recruits, the commercial and strategic role of its ports and bases, and latterly its use as a training ground and launching pad for military offensives. Acting partly from a sense of gratitude the Treasury in 1943 agreed to provide the region with increased financial support to enable it to catch up with social welfare provision elsewhere in the United Kingdom. This Brooke eagerly welcomed, as he was convinced that 'the only chance for the political future of Ulster' was if she became 'so prosperous that the traditional political attitudes are broken down' (B. E. Barton, *Northern Ireland in World War Two*, 130).

The improvement in intergovernmental relations seemed threatened by the British Labour Party's electoral victory (9 July 1945). Brooke subsequently feared the imposition from Westminster of 'very strong socialist measures' combined with pressure on his government to accept Dublin rule (Barton, 'Relations between Westminster and Stormont', 2). None the less he opposed party colleagues who, alarmed by the sweeping economic measures being introduced by UK ministers, urged that Northern Ireland should seek refuge in 'dominion status'. He regarded this option as impracticable given Northern Ireland's financial dependence on Britain. Moreover, his relationship with the Labour leadership soon became surprisingly cordial. Both he and his colleagues broadly welcomed the welfare state legislation, aware not only of the extent of local need, but also that the reforms would widen the gulf in social services between north and south, thus reinforcing partition, and would appeal, in particular, to the protestant working class. In Herbert Morrison's opinion the Stormont ministers behaved throughout like 'moderate socialists' (ibid., 8).

J. A. Costello's decision to withdraw Éire from the empire and create a fully independent 'Republic of Ireland' (with effect from 8 April 1949) provided the unlikely setting for arguably Brooke's foremost political achievement. In the context of Éire's secession and an associated anti-partition campaign he urged that unionists be given reassurance within the text of the Ireland Bill (the Westminster measure ratifying the south's change of status). This Attlee accepted; he included a declaratory clause, stating that Northern Ireland would remain within the Union for as long as a majority at Stormont wished. In fact he had needed little persuading, mainly because he was

advised by a high-level government working party that the province's continued inclusion within the United Kingdom was a vital British strategic interest. Its report continued:

> So far as can be foreseen it will never be to Great Britain's advantage that Northern Ireland should form part of a territory outside His Majesty's jurisdiction. Indeed it seems unlikely that Great Britain would ever be able to agree to this even if the people of Northern Ireland desired it. (Barton, 'Relations between Westminster and Stormont', 12)

Constitutional security, improving welfare services, and economic growth helped ensure that the 1950s and early 1960s were Northern Ireland's most harmonious and promising years; its post-war experience contrasted starkly with the relative stagnation and isolation of the south. Mounting unionist confidence was expressed in the increasing willingness of some party members to consider reform. Meanwhile, the voting behaviour of the minority, its increasing political activism within the six counties, and the ignominious collapse of the IRA campaign of 1956–62 all suggested that it was becoming more reconciled to partition. None the less, there were limits to the level of consensus achieved. Numerous nationalist grievances remained, including the restricted local government franchise and its allegedly gerrymandered electoral boundaries, the religious discrimination practised by public bodies and private firms in the north, and the perceived inadequacy of state funding for Catholic schools.

The Stormont government's failure to initiate fundamental reform was due in large part to Brooke's obsession with unionist unity. He feared a party split which might potentially endanger Northern Ireland's constitutional position. Regarding the minority, his strategy centred throughout on his belief that social reform and economic progress alone would eventually undermine its nationalist aspirations. Thus he failed to support those Liberal Unionists who actively sought accommodation with Catholics by recruiting them into the Unionist Party and were conscious of the changes that had taken place in post-war political and social attitudes. He argued that this was impracticable on political grounds, and noted privately that public 'speeches [on this issue] will only delay matters' (B. E. Barton, *A Pocket History of Ulster*, 1996, 111). From the late 1950s British officials were already warning his government of the 'risk of political disturbance' (ibid., 110) in Newry and Londonderry if religious discrimination was not counteracted. Through his inaction Brooke helped perpetuate the endemic and ultimately fatal sectarian divide in Northern Ireland politics. It is difficult to avoid the conclusion that he failed to rise to that higher level of leadership which does not simply pander to its own supporters but dares to chip away at their prejudices. Brooke was born into the landed gentry and became a soldier by instinct and inclination, but he was driven into politics primarily from conviction—the need to defend and preserve the Union which was then threatened. In his view, during the following decades the threat to its survival persisted and the necessity to defend it therefore did not diminish; this remained his first priority. He himself conceded that he was less 'ecumenical' than others, adding in his own defence, 'it must be remembered that I lived through … the most troubled of times' in Ireland's history (Barton, *Brookeborough*, 234). Though made a viscount in 1952 and later offered an earldom for his services to the state, he never attempted to become a truly national leader with significant cross-community support.

Retirement On 25 March 1963 ill health, old age, and mounting back-bench criticism of his failure to arrest rising unemployment and the drift of unionist voters in Belfast to the Northern Ireland Labour Party impelled Brooke reluctantly to resign as prime minister; he was succeeded by his minister of finance, Captain Terence O'Neill. He retained his seat in parliament until 1968, was created KG in 1965, and developed commercial interests—as chairman of Carreras (Northern Ireland), a director of Devenish Trade, and president of the Northern Ireland Institute of Directors. He was also made an honorary LLD of Queen's University, Belfast. Meanwhile his wife, Cynthia, had served in the Second World War as senior commandant of the Auxiliary Territorial Service, and was created a DBE in 1959. She died in 1970, and the following year Brooke married Sarah Eileen Bell, daughter of Henry Healey, of Belfast, and widow of Cecil Armstrong Calvert FRCS, director of neurosurgery at the Royal Victoria Hospital, Belfast.

Brooke died at home at Colebrooke on 18 August 1973; he was survived by his second wife. He was cremated at Roselawn cemetery, Belfast, three days later, and in deference to his wishes his ashes were scattered on the demesne. He was succeeded in the viscountcy by his only surviving son from his first marriage, John Brooke. It might seem an appropriate as well as a tragic irony that the latter (then minister of state for finance) should have delivered the final speech from the dispatch box at Stormont prior to its suspension by Edward Heath's Conservative government on 28 March 1972. In it he quoted from a poem by Rudyard Kipling entitled 'Ulster', written in 1914, about the time his father's involvement in the political affairs of the province might be said to have begun. It ended with sentiments which Sir Basil fully shared:

Before an empire's eyes the traitor claims his price.
What need of further lies? We are the sacrifice.

BRIAN BARTON

Sources B. Barton, *Brookeborough: the making of a prime minister* (1988) · R. Brooke, *The brimming river* (1961) · W. D. Flackes, *The enduring premier* (1962) · P. Buckland, *A factory of grievances* (1979) · B. E. Barton, 'Relations between Westminster and Stormont during the Attlee premiership', *Irish Political Studies*, 7 (1992), 1–21 · K. Nixon, 'Interviews with Brookeborough', *Sunday News* (Jan–Feb 1968) · *Ulster Year Books* (1926–1960x69) · J. F. Hopkinson, *The Ulster unionist party, 1882–1973* (1973) · Burke, *Peerage* (1970) · T. Hennessey, *A history of Northern Ireland, 1920–1996* (1997) · PRO NIre., Brooke MSS · private information (2004)

Archives PRO NIre., personal and political corresp., diaries, and papers | PRO NIre., Northern Ireland government MSS · PRO NIre., Ulster Unionist Party MSS | FILM BBC · BFI, news footage · PRO NIre., Brooke MSS · Ulster Television, Northern Ireland | SOUND BBC · PRO NIre., Brooke MSS

Likenesses H. Coster, photograph, 1943, NPG [*see illus.*] · W. Stoneman, photograph, 1948, NPG · W. Bird, photograph, 1962, NPG · H. Coster, photographs, NPG

Wealth at death £406,591.83: probate, 5 Dec 1975, CGPLA NIre. · £42,793 in England and Wales: probate, 7 Nov 1973, CGPLA Eng. & Wales

Brooke, Charles (1777–1852), Jesuit, was the son of James Brooke and his wife, Mary, *née* Hoare. He was born at The Mint, part of the old priory of St Nicholas, Exeter, on 8 August 1777. He was educated at the Liège Academy from July 1788, and stayed with the school when it moved to Stonyhurst in 1794; legend has it that he and George Clifford, one of the other four juniors who followed the school to Lancashire, raced each other down the avenue approaching the house for the distinction of being 'first boy' there. He was ordained priest at Maynooth by Archbishop Troy on 13 June 1802, and in September of the following year entered the noviciate of the Society of Jesus at Hodder Place, near Stonyhurst. The Society had been suppressed by Gregory XIV in 1773, but by 1803 the English Jesuits were readmitting members: Brooke, however, was not formally professed until 1818, four years after the official restoration of the Society. He also acted as a professor and prefect of studies at Stonyhurst during this period and helped to reverse the declining academic standards of the college. He was particularly enthusiastic about the study of mathematics. In September 1817 he was appointed to a mission at Clayton, Enfield, where he built a chapel. He became provincial of the Society of Jesus in England on 15 February 1826, and in the spring of 1829 held the first provincial congress of the restored Society at Stonyhurst, where he also opened a new seminary on 30 July 1830. He resigned his post on 28 May 1832, and was subsequently socius to the provincial until 1834. In 1832 he became rector of Stonyhurst seminary, a post which he resigned in June 1838 because of poor health. Afterwards he was rector of the College of St Aloysius but also continued to hold posts at Stonyhurst until September 1845, when he was sent to Exeter to collect information for a continuation of Henry More's *Historia provinciae Anglicanae Societatis Jesu* (1660). The materials which he collected were subsequently used by Henry Foley SJ for his *Records of the English Province of the Society of Jesus* (8 vols., 1870–83). Brooke died at The Mint, Exeter, on 6 October 1852, reputedly in the same room in which he had been born.

THOMPSON COOPER, *rev.* ROSEMARY MITCHELL

Sources G. Oliver, *Collections towards illustrating the biographies of the Scotch, English and Irish members of the Society of Jesus*, 2nd edn (1845) · H. Foley, ed., *Records of the English province of the Society of Jesus*, 7/1 (1882), 88–9 · G. Holt, *The English Jesuits, 1650–1829: a biographical dictionary*, Catholic RS, 70 (1984) · *The Tablet* (16 Oct 1852) · H. Chadwick, *St Omers to Stonyhurst* (1962), 392, 397–8 · T. E. Muir, *Stonyhurst College, 1593–1993* (1992), 81, 86

Archives Archives of the British Province of the Society of Jesus, London, corresp., diaries, historical notes and transcripts

Brooke, Charles (1804–1879), surgeon and inventor of measuring instruments, only son of the mineralogist and businessman Henry James *Brooke (1771–1857), was born on 30 June 1804, in South Lambeth, Surrey. Following an early education in Chiswick he entered Rugby School in

1819 and St John's College, Cambridge, in 1823. He graduated BA in 1827 (as twenty-third wrangler), BM in 1828, and MA in 1853. His medical education was completed at St Bartholomew's Hospital, London; he became a member of the Royal College of Surgeons on 3 September 1834, and a fellow on 26 August 1844. He stayed in London, and after lecturing on surgery at Dermott's School, he soon progressed to surgical appointments at the Metropolitan Free Hospital and then the Westminster Hospital, where he remained until his resignation in 1869. In 1836 he married Mary Anne Sewell (1798/9–1885), with whom he had at least two sons and two daughters.

As a surgeon, Brooke was recognized for his innovative use of the 'bead suture', devised to spread the tension in deep wounds. A master of scientific instrumentation, he was elected a fellow of the Royal Society on 4 March 1847. He belonged to the Meteorological Society and the Royal Microscopical Society, serving as president of the former from 1865 to 1867 and of the latter twice, in 1863–4 and 1873–4. Involved in the management of the Royal Institution, he also served on the council of the Royal Botanical Society, and he was connected with many philanthropic and religious societies, becoming was a very active member of the Victoria Institute and the Christian Medical Association.

Brooke's published papers and lectures were generally oriented towards physics, both mathematical and experimental. His particular forte was the inventing or perfecting of apparatus. Although his analytical papers date back to 1835, when he wrote 'Motion of sound in space', his reputation derived mainly from his publications between 1846 and 1852 about his inventions—self-recording instruments which were adopted at the observatories of Greenwich, Paris, Toronto, and Cambridge, Massachusetts. These consisted of barometers, thermometers, psychrometers, and magnetometers, which automatically registered their variations by means of photography, thus reducing the number of assistants required. Awarded a premium by the government, Brooke also won a council medal from the jurors of the Great Exhibition of 1851. The perfecting of these measuring instruments was described in British Association reports between 1846 and 1849, and in the Royal Society's *Philosophical Transactions* of 1847, 1850, and 1852. By 1852 Brooke was reporting on the automatic temperature compensation of the force magnetometers.

Brooke also studied the theory of the microscope, devising his double nosepiece-changer which allowed two objectives to be interchanged easily by means of a rotating carrier—a device still in use one hundred and fifty years later. He also improved methods of illumination. In his own day he was most widely known for his *Elements of Natural Philosophy*, originally published in 1839 by Golding Bird, who alone had also brought out second and third editions. After Bird's death in 1854, Brooke edited 'a fourth edition, revised and greatly enlarged', and followed it with a fifth edition in 1860. In 1867 he entirely rewrote the work for a sixth edition of 851 pages, prefaced by a protest against a fashionable pantheism. A genial, unassuming,

even reticent man, he died at 6 Brunswick Gardens, Weymouth, on 17 May 1879. His widow died at 3 Gordon Square, London, on 12 February 1885, aged eighty-six.

Brooke's other publications included *The evidence afforded by the order and adaptations in nature to the existence of a God: a Christian evidence lecture* (1872), which was twice reprinted, and *A Synopsis of the Principal Formulae and Results of Pure Mathematics* (1829).

G. C. BOASE, rev. JOHN HEDLEY BROOKE

Sources PRS, 30 (1879–80), i-ii · *Medical Times and Gazette* (31 May 1879), 606 · *Quarterly Journal of the Meteorological Society*, 6 (1879–80), 71 · *Catalogue of scientific papers*, Royal Society, 1 (1867), 653 · *Catalogue of scientific papers*, Royal Society, 7 (1877), 273 · J. Insley, 'Pen portraits of presidents: Charles Brooke, FRS', *Weather*, 53 (1998), 24–6 · G. L'E. Turner, *God bless the microscope!* (1989) · L. S. Pilcher, *The treatment of wounds* (1883), 179–80 · G. L'E. Turner, *The great age of the microscope: the collection of the Royal Microscopical Society through 150 years* (1989), 325 · H. R. Luard, ed., *Graduati Cantabrigienses*, 7th edn (1884), 70 · St John Cam., Biographical archive · C. W. Previté-Orton, *Index to tripos lists, 1748–1910* (1923), 35 [Cambridge] · W. Bulloch, 'Roll of the fellows of the Royal Society', index, RS, vol. 9, p. 193 · Venn, *Alum. Cant.* · will, proved, London, 10 April 1879

Archives RS, corresp. and MSS

Likenesses photograph, Royal Meteorological Society, Reading, Berkshire

Wealth at death under £40,000: probate, 9 June 1879, CGPLA Eng. & Wales

Brooke, Sir Charles Anthoni Johnson (1829–1917), naval officer and second raja of Sarawak, was born at Berrow vicarage, near Burnham, Somerset, on 3 June 1829, the second son of Francis Charles Johnson (1797–1874), from 1825 vicar of White Lackington, and his wife, Emma Frances Brooke (1802–1870), sister of Sir James *Brooke (1803–1868), the first raja of Sarawak. He attended Crewkerne grammar school and joined the Royal Navy in January 1842 as a volunteer first class, serving on the sloop *Wolverine* (captained by his uncle Willes Johnson) for two years and then on *Dido* and *Maeander* under Captain Henry Keppel (1809–1904). He took part in the attacks on the Dayaks of the Batang Lupar in August 1844 (when he was almost killed by a cannon ball) and on the Illanun pirate base at Marudu in August 1845. He considered the navy 'particularly useful as a preparatory school for adventurers … after life aboard ship, any discomforts subsequently experienced are lightly felt' (Crisswell, 2–3).

Brooke served on the China station and in 1852, having been promoted to lieutenant, resigned to join his uncle Raja Sir James Brooke in Sarawak. In 1848 he had changed his name by deed poll to Brooke. Designated *tuan muda* (second in line of succession after his elder brother, John Brooke Johnson, later Brooke, died 1868 aged forty-five), he was appointed resident at Lundu and shortly afterwards to Lingga on the Skrang River where his predecessor had been killed by followers of the Dayak chief Rentap. From then he played a major part in suppressing opposition to Brooke rule. In April and August 1854 and again in 1856 he joined the raja and his forces in expeditions against Rentap and his allies. He had a key role in suppressing, with Dayak and Malay warriors, a rebellion at Kuching (the capital) by Chinese goldminers in February 1857 which threatened to destroy the raja's authority.

In the next two years he mounted three expeditions against Rentap, finally driving him from his fortress on Mount Sadok and into Dutch Borneo. With his fluent command of their language and customs and his outstanding courage and generalship, Brooke won the admiration and loyalty of the Dayaks. His last military action under the raja in 1860 was to attack the Malay town of Muka as part of a strategy to wrest the economically valuable sago-producing areas of the north-eastern coast from Brunei control. In January 1863, after the raja's quarrel with and disinheritance of Brooke's elder brother and the raja's final departure from Sarawak, Brooke was in effective control of the state. In 1866 he published his autobiographical *Ten Years in Sarawak*. The following year the raja's will named him as his successor, and on 3 August 1868 he was proclaimed raja after his uncle's death.

Brooke was short and slim, with piercing grey eyes deep set under bushy brows, and in later life wore a full moustache. Brave, ruthless, decisive, pragmatic, austere, dignified, parsimonious, reserved, and self-sufficient, he was dedicated to Sarawak. He disliked pomp and publicity, and habitually wore a blue serge coat, white duck trousers, and a white topi with a magenta puggaree, the latter reserved to him. Both an English gentleman and an oriental despot, his rule was a benevolent authoritarian paternalism. He continued his uncle's personal style of rule, and was accessible to anyone who wanted to see him. He decided policy and concerned himself with details of administration.

His long reign was marked by further territorial acquisitions from Brunei, 'pacification' of remaining Dayak and other opposition, organization of the administration, economic and technological development, encouragement of Chinese immigration—he stated in 1883, 'without the Chinaman we could do nothing' (*Pall Mall Gazette*, 19 Sept 1883, quoted in *Encyclopaedia Britannica*), and formalization of Sarawak's relations with Britain through a treaty of protection in 1888 (the year Brooke was made GCMG). The treaty secured British protection against foreign aggression and gave Britain control of external relations and defence, while allowing the Brookes internal sovereignty: 'a protected state rather than a protectorate' (Reece, 11). Brooke's relations with the Colonial Office were uneasy. James Brooke had established the sovereign state of Sarawak; Charles extended it to its present borders and made it politically and economically viable. His attempt to take over Brunei and what became North Borneo was thwarted by the British government. He outlawed the slave trade and cautiously ended slavery by 1886, and made progress in reducing traditional Dayak headhunting. Sarawak was not a rich country and Brooke, like his uncle, had neither the desire nor the means to carry out fundamental change. He favoured economic development and wanted European investment, but was determined to prevent exploitation of the country's indigenous inhabitants, and to protect them from speculators and adventurers. His wife wrote that he wanted 'to keep Sarawak for the benefit of its own people, and … from the devastating grasp of money-grabbing syndicates' (Gin,

331). He was suspicious of big companies, disliked large-scale plantations (as in the Dutch East Indies), and refused to allow absentee land-owning. His concerns were strengthened by his awareness of the exploitation in the Congo Independent State: he wrote, 'Congo rules cannot be supported in Sarawak' (Reece, 7). He prevented alienation of native land. He established experimental farms and gardens and encouraged the production of new crops, but with limited success. He encouraged indigenous and Chinese smallholder agriculture and, after initial scepticism, the cultivation of rubber, which had become a major export by the time of the First World War. He allowed a few European plantations, and granted an oil concession to the Anglo-Saxon Petroleum Company, a Shell subsidiary, which struck oil in 1910 and augmented the state's revenues. Telephones and wireless were introduced, roads and a short railway built, and the public debt much reduced. Brooke also founded the Sarawak Museum, and its *Journal* published research on Sarawak. Sarawak became modestly prosperous, but never wealthy. Brooke continued his uncle's taxation policy, taxing the indigenous lightly and gaining a large proportion of revenue from indirect taxation of the Chinese community by farming the government monopolies of opium, gambling, arrack, and pawn shops. In 1867 he wrote that reducing the price of opium would attract more Chinese to settle in Sarawak. Although the farm revenues continued important, their share of the total revenue declined after 1900, while that of import and export duties grew. In 1914 Brooke changed the farm system, increasing direct government involvement. He insisted that his officers be 'gentlemen' and not marry until after ten years' service. He did not object if they became involved with local women, strongly opposing the development of a European élite isolated and alienated from the native people. He criticized the British in India for their isolation from Indians. He held unfashionable views about miscegenation, believing that interbreeding between Dayaks and Chinese would produce a vigorous and intelligent breed of future leaders.

In 1869 Brooke went to England seeking a wealthy wife who would provide an heir. He visited his first cousin Mrs Lily Willes de Windt (*née* Johnson), a wealthy widow. She had inherited a fortune from her French grandmother, Baroness de Windt, and married Captain Clayton Jennings, who took the name de Windt, of Blunsdon Hall, Highworth, Wiltshire. Brooke married quietly at Highworth on 28 October 1869 their daughter Margaret Lili Alice de Windt (*d.* 1936), aged twenty-one, sister of Harry de Windt (1856–1933), the explorer: they had five sons and one daughter. She was tall, fair, good-looking, intelligent, and a talented pianist. She did not find her marriage easy, with Brooke's parsimoniousness and austerities, and his failure to appreciate her talent. They went out to Sarawak in early 1870 and their first three children were born there, only to die of cholera on the return voyage through the Red Sea in September 1873. They subsequently had three more sons, who survived. From the mid-1880s the raja and the rani were estranged and led separate lives. There had been conflict over money matters and her health had never been good in Sarawak. Her last visit there was in 1895 when the raja was not present. Their eldest son, (Charles) Vyner de Windt *Brooke (1874–1963), was declared *raja muda* in 1893, but relations between him and his father became poor. Brooke disliked Vyner's marriage in February 1911 to Sylvia, daughter of Reginald Brett, second Viscount Esher (1852–1930). There was mutual antipathy between Brooke and her. He believed her a bad influence, and she wrote of him, 'now here was a man to make one's flesh creep' (S. Brooke, 125). He distrusted Esher, and suspected a plutocratic conspiracy to exploit Sarawak. By 1912 Brooke was considering replacing Vyner by his brother Bertram, but the conflict was patched up.

Brooke was a Francophile and admirer of Bonaparte. He considered himself a liberal: Gerard Fiennes wrote he was 'a fearful Radical' (Runciman, 227). He disapproved of the Second South African War, and in his pamphlet *Queries: Past and Present* (1907) he criticized arrogant and vainglorious British imperialism and claimed the empire would end about 1950. Despite his stern and ascetic personal style, the raja was an *aficionado* of Italian opera and enjoyed singing badly at dinner parties. He was also widely read in contemporary science and theology as well as English and French literature. At his estate at Cirencester in Gloucestershire, where he latterly spent part of every year, he indulged his favourite pastimes of foxhunting (which in 1912 cost him the sight of one eye) and bird-breeding. Disliking formal ceremony and high society, he was a solitary and detached personality. His treatment of an illegitimate son by a native woman and of his nephew Hope Brooke seemed heartless. Some of his earlier associates, notably Charles Grant, had regarded his replacement of his elder brother as treachery.

Brooke died of 'hypostatic pneumonia' at his English home, Chesterton House, Cirencester, Gloucestershire, on 17 May 1917. His body was embalmed for later burial in Sarawak and placed in a mausoleum, then in 1919 was buried near his uncle at Sheepstor, Devon. There is a memorial to him there and in Kuching opposite the court house that he built. Brooke's achievement in Sarawak—with its isolation, limited natural resources, and adverse geography—stands comparison most favourably with those in contemporary native-ruled states and British colonies. He was succeeded by his eldest surviving son, (Charles) Vyner de Windt Brooke, the third and last raja. The Brooke dynasty, the 'white rajas of Sarawak', ended in 1946 when Sarawak became a crown colony.   R. H. W. REECE

Sources C. Brooke, *Ten years in Sarawak* (1866) · S. Baring-Gould and C. A. Bampfylde, *A history of Sarawak under its two white rajahs, 1839–1908* (1909) · Ranee of Sarawak [M. L. A. Brooke], *My life in Sarawak* (1913) · Ranee Margaret of Sarawak [M. Brooke], *Good morning and good night* (1934) · S. Runciman, *The white rajahs: a history of Sarawak from 1841 to 1946* (1960) · C. N. Crisswell, *Rajah Charles Brooke: monarch of all he surveyed* (1978) · O. K. Gin, *Of free trade and native interests: the Brookes and the economic development of Sarawak, 1841–1941* (1997) · S. Brooke, *Sylvia of Sarawak* (1936) · N. Tarling, *The burthen, the risk and the glory: a biography of Sir James Brooke* (1982) · R. H. W. Reece, *The name of Brooke, the end of white rajah rule in Sarawak* (1982) · *WWW*, 1916–28 · 'Sarawak', *Encyclopaedia Britannica*, 11th edn, 24 (1911) · A. Porter, ed., *The Oxford history of the British empire*, vol. 3 (1999), 384 · N. Tarling, *Britain, the Brookes and Brunei* (1971) · Boase, *Mod. Eng. biog.* · *WWW*, 1929–40 · R. Payne, *The white rajahs of Sarawak* (1986) · *CGPLA Eng. & Wales* (1917)

Archives Bodl. RH, corresp. · Mitchell L., NSW, diary | BL, corresp. with Lady Burdett-Coutts, Add. MS 45283 · Bodl. RH, letters to C. E. A. Ermen · PRO, corresp. with F. Dallas, PRO 30/79

Likenesses Spy [L. Ward], caricature, chromolithograph, NPG; repro. in *VF* (19 Jan 1899) · photograph, repro. in Crisswell, *Rajah Charles Brooke*, frontispiece

Wealth at death £25,065 3s. 2d.: probate, 6 Oct 1917, *CGPLA Eng. & Wales*

Brooke, Charlotte (*c*.1740–1793), writer, was born in Rantavan, co. Cavan, one of the many children of the author Henry *Brooke (*c*.1703–1783) and his wife, Catherine Meares (1712/13–1773), of Meares Court, co. Westmeath, and one of only two, with her brother Arthur, not to predecease her parents. (The number of Charlotte's siblings has been given as twenty-one, possibly an exaggeration owing to the fact that Henry and Catherine Brooke led a joint household with Henry's brother Robert, Robert's wife, Honor, and their children.) The Brooke family was of protestant Anglo-Irish stock, with ties to the Sheridan, Digby, and Fitzgerald families and to the established church; Charlotte, however, was later to follow her mother's Methodist disposition. After an initial, discountenanced desire to go to the stage, Charlotte, who was educated by her father, immersed herself in reading history and literature. She was part of the first generation of the protestant Anglo-Irish settler class who took a positive interest in the Irish language and Gaelic antiquity; her initial interest in Irish language and literature was sparked by hearing it spoken and recited by the labourers in co. Cavan and on the co. Kildare estate where the family moved about 1758. Her first publication was a translation of a poem by the Irish harper Carolan (Toirdhealbhach Ó Cearbhalláin); it appeared in *Historical Memoirs of the Irish Bards* (1786), by the antiquarian Joseph Cooper Walker, who remained a lifelong friend.

Brooke, who appears to have been of a frail physique and a timid and retiring disposition, took care of her father after the death of her mother in 1773, during which time her pietist tendency became more pronounced; meanwhile, the family had moved back to co. Cavan, where a new house called Longfield had been built near the Rantavan estate. The Brookes displayed a costly zeal for the improvement of agriculture and manufacture typical of patriotic Anglo-Irish circles at the time; a few years after her father's death in 1783 Brooke ran into financial difficulties after a model industrial village set up in co. Kildare by her cousin Captain Robert Brooke went bankrupt (1787). Walker and other members of the recently established Royal Irish Academy sought to procure her an income, but Brooke found she had to rely on her pen to make a living.

Brooke's fame rests on the collection of *Reliques of Irish Poetry* (1789), in the preparation and annotation of which she was assisted by Walker and by native Gaelic antiquarians. Its scope followed that of the *Reliques of Ancient English*

Poetry (1765) of Bishop Percy (with whom she corresponded); it played a welcome role in extricating ancient Irish literature from the speculation and obfuscation following James Macpherson's Ossianic forgeries. Brooke's translations used the sentimental and sublime verse style of the day, but the authenticity of her material (which ranged from Ossianic material to more recent, seventeenth-century poems) was pointedly demonstrated by the inclusion of the original texts. Appended to the end is a sample of Brooke's own poetic efforts, based on old Gaelic themes. The main aim of the collection is patriotic: to vindicate the merit of native poetry, to present a fund of literary inspiration to Ireland's literature, and to claim a place for the Gaelic tradition in contemporary British letters.

An edition of her father's collected works in 1792 brought further financial succour, but Brooke (who had meanwhile taken up residence with friends in the hamlet of Cottage, near Longford) died shortly afterwards, on 29 March 1793, of a malignant fever. Her other literary productions are of less importance: a pious educational text, *School for Christians* (1791), and a novel, *Emma, or, The Foundling of the Wood*, published posthumously in 1803. *Reliques of Ancient Irish Poetry* was reissued in 1816.

Brooke's *Reliques* intensified the newly emerging cultural identification of the ruling Anglo-Irish class with Ireland rather than England (among the subscribers figure many of the leading 'patriotic' names in Anglo-Irish learned and political circles); not surprisingly, radical nationalists such as the United Irishmen were in the following decades to take up a cultural Gaelicism indebted to the *Reliques*. But Brooke's work continued to exercise an exemplary function in the field of Irish letters even as the pursuit of national antiquarianism had been rendered politically suspect following the crises of 1798–1800. Throughout the nineteenth and twentieth centuries, bilingual anthologies of older Irish literature have perpetuated her pioneering status and influence.

JOEP LEERSSEN

Sources A. C. Seymour, 'Memoirs of Miss Brooke', *Reliques of Irish Poetry* (1816), iii–cxxviii · E. A. Baker, 'Introduction', in H. Brooke, *The fool of quality* (1906), v–xxxi · L. Davis, 'Birth of the nation: gender and writing in the work of Henry and Charlotte Brooke', *Eighteenth-Century Life*, 18/1 (1994), 27–47 · R. A. Breatnach, 'Two eighteenth-century Irish scholars: Joseph Cooper Walker and Charlotte Brooke', *Studia Hibernica*, 5 (1965), 88–97 · C. H. Wilson, *Brookiana*, 2 vols. (1804) · *DNB*

Archives Royal Irish Acad., corresp.

Brooke, Christopher (*c.*1570–1628), politician and poet, was the son of Robert Brooke (*c.*1531–1599), a wealthy York merchant and alderman, and Jane (*d.* 1604), daughter of Christopher Maltby, a York draper. Robert Brooke was twice lord mayor of York (1582, 1595) and represented the city in the 1584 and 1586 parliaments.

According to Anthony Wood, Brooke attended one of the universities (Wood, *Ath. Oxon.*, new edn, 1813–20, 1.402). It is possible that he studied at Westminster School and Trinity College, Cambridge, like his younger brother, Samuel *Brooke. Christopher entered Lincoln's Inn on 15 March 1587, was called to the bar on 9 June 1594, and formally called to the bench on 11 June 1611. He played an active role in the life of his inn: he was the autumn reader from 1613 to 1614; acted as the expenditor for George Chapman's *Memorable Maske* (1613), jointly produced by Lincoln's Inn and the Middle Temple to celebrate the marriage of Princess Elizabeth; took charge of his inn's contribution to the entertainment at the barriers for Charles's creation as prince of Wales in 1616; was the keeper of the black book from 1620 to 1621; and acted as the inn's treasurer from 1623 to 1624.

Brooke's lifelong friendship with John Donne began in 1592. The two shared chambers, perhaps drawn together by an interest in poetry. Donne addressed a verse epistle and poem, 'The Storm', to Brooke in the mid- to late 1590s. Brooke acted as witness at the secret wedding of Donne and Ann More in December 1601, and Brooke's brother, Samuel, conducted the ceremony. Brooke was committed to the Marshalsea prison for his part in the marriage. He wrote to Sir Thomas Egerton, the lord keeper, on 25 February 1602 complaining that he was kept 'from the sitting at York, where … my profitablest practise lies' and that he was in danger of losing his mother's favour, which 'is the best part of my strenght [*sic*] and meanes of wel doinge' because he was unable to help her with 'her greatest businesses' (Kempe, 338). About 1617 he moved to a house across the street from Donne in Drury Lane, London, and lived there for eleven years until his death. His will left a number of paintings to 'my deere ancient and worthie freind D[o]c[t]or Dunn the Deane Pawles' (*Complete Poems*, 23).

Brooke took a prominent role in a London tavern society, the 'right Worshipfull Fraternitie of Sireniacal Gentlemen', that met at the Mermaid tavern in the first two decades of the seventeenth century. He is among the guests in the Latin poem 'Convivium philosophicum', which celebrates a gathering at the Mitre tavern about 1611 in honour of Thomas Coryate, and he contributed a commendatory verse to *Coryate's Crudities* (1611), republished in the same year as *The Odcombian Banquet*. Brooke, Inigo Jones, Richard Martin, and John Hoskins are identified as the joint authors of the popular satire, 'The censure of a parliament fart', in one copy of the poem (BL, Add. MS 23,339, fol. 17*v*). Brooke's close friends among the 'Sireniacal gentlemen' were fellow members of parliament, Sir Robert Phelips, Richard Martin, John Hoskins, and William Hakewill.

Brooke represented York in the 1604, 1614, 1621, 1624, 1625, and 1626 parliaments. He spoke frequently in the Commons, was active on its committees, and consistently defended rights and privileges of parliament. In James I's first parliament, Brooke spoke against the crown's proposals for the union of the kingdoms. He opposed the crown's case on impositions in the 1610 session and the 1614 'addled' parliament, concluding in 1614 that 'If the King may impose by his absolute power, then no man certain what he has, for it shall be subject to the King's pleasure' (Jansson, 95). After 1610 he was re-elected for York without contest for the rest of his life.

Brooke's earliest known poetic endeavour was the commendatory poem he placed before Michael Drayton's *Legend of Great Cromwell* (1607). Brooke and William Browne were the co-authors of *Two Elegies, Consecrated to … Henry, Prince of Wales* (1613) published by Richard More who went on to include poems by Brooke and Browne in his second edition of *England's Helicon* (1614). In the same year Brooke contributed an eclogue to Browne's *The Shepheard's Pipe* (1614), in which he appeared as the shepherd 'Cuddy', and in this guise reappeared, along with Browne, as one of George Wither's visitors in the Marshalsea prison in *The Shepherd's Hunting* (1615). The efforts of these poets were praised by Richard Brathwaite in his *A Strappado for the Divell* (1615, 23–4). Brooke increasingly saw his poetry in civic terms, as an extension of the counsel he provided in parliament; he published his *The Ghost of Richard the Third* (1614) during the 1614 parliament and used this story of tyranny to illustrate the dangers of a new absolutism. Following the trial of the earl and countess of Somerset for the murder of Sir Thomas Overbury, both Brooke and Browne contributed elegies attacking court corruption to *Sir Thomas Overburie his Wife with New Elegies upon his (now Knowne) Untimely Death* (1616). Brooke's 'polisht lines' received extensive praise from Browne in the second book of his *Britannia's Pastorals* (1616, 37).

Brooke dedicated *The Ghost of Richard the Third* to a fellow Yorkshireman, Sir John Crompton, and his wife, Frances, the daughter of Sir John Crofts. Brooke had a long association with these two families: he produced inscriptions for the tombs of Elizabeth, wife of Charles Crofts (20 December 1597), and Mary, wife of Thomas Crompton.

On 18 December 1619 Brooke married Mary, Lady Jacob (*d.* 1622), the widow of Sir Robert Jacob, the former solicitor general of Ireland, and they had one son, John. Lady Jacob achieved some notoriety for the incivility she displayed towards the Spanish ambassador, Count Gondomar. She died in November 1622. In the 1621 parliament, Brooke took a prominent role in debates and on committees, particularly those involving the prosecution of monopolists, and sought measures to safeguard the Commons' ability to advise on the war (Notestein, *Debates*, 2.494). The next year he published *A Poem on the Late Massacre in Virginia* (1622) which enthusiastically praised George Sandys, the treasurer of the Virginia Company, and seems to have been the company's official lament for the massacre of the colonists. Brooke had joined the Virginia Company in 1609 and remained an active member until its dissolution in 1624. His last recorded poetic work is a funeral poem in memory of Arthur Chichester, earl of Belfast, who died in 1625. Wither supplied a commendatory verse and although it was prepared for the press it was never printed; the provocative tone of Brooke's epistle to the licenser suggests that it may have been suppressed. In the 1626 parliament, Brooke characteristically upheld parliamentary privileges (Ferris, 29–30). This year he was admitted as counsel learned to the council of the north.

Brooke was buried at St Andrew's, Holborn, on 7 February 1628. In his will, drawn up on 8 December 1627, he lamented the poor state of his finances that prevented him from providing for mourning or bequests to his brothers and sisters. None the less, he left a house in Drury Lane, leases of houses and shops in Chancery Lane and Whites Alley, two houses in York, land in Essex, houses and land in Southampton and north Yorkshire, and numerous paintings, some by Italian masters, which he bequeathed to family and friends, such as Donne and Sir Arthur Ingram (*Complete Poems*, 14–23).

A. B. Grosart in 1872 brought out a complete edition of Brooke's poems together with a 'Memorial-introduction' in the Fuller Worthies' Library series. Best-known as a friend of Donne, it is only recently that Brooke has begun to receive attention as a poet in his own right and as a lawyer and committed member of parliament who made a significant contribution to Jacobean parliamentary debates.

MICHELLE O'CALLAGHAN

Sources J. P. Ferris, 'Brooke, Christopher', HoP, *Commons, 1604–29* [draft] · *The complete poems of Christopher Brooke*, ed. A. B. Grosart, *Miscellanies of the Fuller Worthies' Library* (1872) · R. C. Bald, *John Donne: a life*, pbk edn (1986) · M. O'Callaghan, '"Talking politics": tyranny, parliament, and Christopher Brooke's *The ghost of Richard the Third* (1614)', *HJ*, 41 (1998), 97–120 · M. O'Callaghan, *The 'Shepheards nation': Jacobean Spenserians and early Stuart political culture, 1612–1625* (2000) · D. Norbrook, *Poetry and politics in the English Renaissance* (1985) · W. P. Baildon, ed., *The records of the Honorable Society of Lincoln's Inn: the black books*, 2 (1898) · T. Orbison, ed., *The Middle Temple documents relating to George Chapman's 'The memorable masque'* (1983) · M. Jansson, ed., *Proceedings in parliament, 1614 (House of Commons)* (1988) · W. Notestein, F. H. Relf, and H. Simpson, eds., *Commons debates, 1621*, 7 vols. (1935) · B. Galloway, *The union of England and Scotland, 1603–1608* (1986) · A. J. Kempe, *The Loseley manuscripts* (1835) · W. P. Baildon, ed., *The records of the Honorable Society of Lincoln's Inn: admissions*, 2 vols. (1896) · R. H. Skaife, *Catalogue of mayors and bailiffs, lord mayors and sheriffs … of the city of York* (1895) · W. Notestein, *The House of Commons, 1604–1610* (1971)

Wealth at death numerous properties and leases, paintings, and books: will, Brooke, *Complete poems*

Brooke [*née* Colepeper], **Elizabeth**, **Lady Brooke** (1602?–1683), exemplar of godly life, was born in Wigsell, Sussex, the daughter of Thomas Colepeper (*d.* 1613) and his wife, Anne (*d.* 1602), daughter of Sir Stephen Slaney (1524–1609), alderman of London. Her mother died shortly after her birth and was buried on 26 February 1602, so Elizabeth was brought up by her maternal grandmother, Margaret, Lady Slaney (*d.* 1619). About 1620 she married Sir Robert Brooke (*d.* 1646). For the first two years of their marriage the couple boarded in London with Elizabeth's aunt, Mary, Lady Weld. They then moved to Langley, Hertfordshire, and finally settled at Cockfield Hall, Suffolk, Sir Robert's family seat, where Lady Brooke remained until her death. She had seven children, of whom only her daughter Mary survived her. James died in infancy; Anne died in childhood; John died childless in 1651 aged twenty-six; Robert was knighted at Charles II's Restoration and attended parliament in 1660–61, but he died childless, aged thirty-three, in 1669 while travelling in France. Elizabeth and Martha were married with children when they died, Elizabeth aged about twenty-five in 1647 or 1648, and Martha aged about twenty-nine in 1657. The death by

Elizabeth Brooke, Lady Brooke (1602?–1683), by unknown engraver, pubd 1684

drowning of her last surviving son affected Lady Brooke so strongly that friends feared she would die of grief.

Like her brother John *Colepeper (*bap.* 1600, *d.* 1660), created Baron Colepeper in 1644, Lady Brooke was a zealous royalist. She kept a private fast on behalf of Charles I prior to his execution, in the hope that a 'hand from Heaven' might have 'prevented that wickedness'. She told friends that she mourned Charles like a mother, commenting that the 'loss of one of her dearest Children came not nearer to her Heart' (Parkhurst, 68–9). But while conforming to the established church she approved the efforts of those who sought to include dissenters within the Anglican establishment. She supported a number of nonconformist ministers, 'and most earnestly desired to have seen them legally settled in a Publick Ministry' (ibid., 72).

Lady Brooke's piety was stringently applied to all aspects of her life, 'putting Rules upon her Self in all things' (Parkhurst, 52). In addition to a daily routine of personal devotions she supervised the household in twice-daily prayers and weekly catechism, as well as giving spiritual advice when needed. To a maidservant who sought her religious counsel, 'She required her for that time, to forget she was a servant' (ibid., 59). Lady Brooke was also renowned for her hospitality and charity to the neighbouring poor and to indigent ministers.

Lady Brooke was also esteemed for her learning, particularly in theology. Although she never studied Latin, Greek, or Hebrew, she taught herself theology and philosophy by reading biblical commentaries and translations of the classics. According to her biographer she had mastered 'Controversial' as well as practical divinity: 'She could oppose an Atheist by Arguments drawn from Topicks in Natural Theology, and answer the Arguments of Papists, Socinians, Pelagians, &c' (Parkhurst, 48). She left a large number of religious writings, including commentaries on scripture and notes on contemporary theological controversies. None of these has survived, apart from 'Observations, experiences, and rules for practice', printed as an appendix to her funeral sermon.

After a long illness Lady Brooke died on 22 July 1683 at Cockfield Hall, Suffolk, and was buried on 26 July in the parish church at Yoxford. Her funeral sermon, preached by Nathaniel Parkhurst, was published in 1684 with a biography.　　　　　　　　　　　SARA H. MENDELSON

Sources N. Parkhurst, *The faithful and diligent Christian described and exemplified, or, A sermon with some additions preached at the funeral of the Lady Elizabeth Brooke* (1684) · *DNB* · will, PRO, PROB 11/113, sig. 5 [Sir Stephen Slaney] · will, PRO, PROB 11/133, sig. 42 [Margaret, Lady Slaney] · F. Harrison, *Proprietors of the Northern Neck: chapters of Culpeper genealogy* (Richmond, Va.: Old Dominion Press, privately printed, 1926) · Foster, *Alum. Oxon.*
Likenesses line engraving, BM, NPG; repro. in Parkhurst, *The faithful and diligent Christian* [*see illus.*]

Brooke, Emma Frances (1844–1926), novelist, was born on 22 December 1844, at Bollingdon, Macclesfield, Cheshire, daughter of Joseph Brooke, a wealthy industrialist—in later life she described him as a 'capitalist' (Sutherland, 86)—and his wife, Anne, *née* Swindells. On her mother's side she was descended from old yeoman family. Educated at Newnham College, Cambridge, she gave her recreations in *Who's Who* as 'walking, the study of bird life, sitting over the fire with a friend or book, and hearing clever people talk'. In 1879 she moved to London where she became a socialist, joining the Fabian Society at its inception (1884). She studied at the London School of Economics, and published economic analyses of the working conditions of women in Britain and Europe, including *A tabulation of European factory acts, in so far as they relate to the hours of labour, and special regulations for women and children* (1898). She did not marry.

Writing under the curious pseudonym E. Fairfax Byrrne, Brooke published several novels, of which *A Superfluous Woman* (1894) and *Life the Accuser* (1896) attracted most critical attention. In the first, the heroine, married to a syphilitic male, gives birth to 'a poor malformed thing' and is reprimanded by her doctor for the 'crime' of becoming 'a mother by that effete and dissipated race' (*A Superfluous Woman*, 258). She had affinities with eugenic 'new woman' writers such as Sarah Grand, who explored the consequences of degenerate, syphilitic men, arguing that only with premarital chastity for all could the British race be salvaged and improved. In spite of its purported moral intentions, W. T. Stead, editor of the *Pall Mall Gazette*, and vociferous on matters of moral reform, declared *A Superfluous Woman* 'an immoral tale':

> its whole significance lies in the supreme audacity of the authoress. She is so penetrated by a sense of the hideous horror of the fashionable, loveless marriage of a healthy young woman to a *roué* worn out by excess and honeycombed by disease, that she compels her readers to admit that even the unblushing proposal her heroine made to a man who loved her was virtue itself compared with the union which the Church blessed and all the papers chronicled with admiration.   (Stead, 68)

Life the Accuser tells the story of three women: Eliza is too conventional; Rosalie is overly emancipated, and Constantia has an unfaithful husband with whom she stays on account not of duty but sexual desire. Her other novels included *Transition* (1895); *The Confession of Stephen Whapshare* (1898); *The Engrafted Rose* (1900); *The Poet's Child* (1903); *Twins of Skirlaugh Hall* (1903); *Susan Wooed and Susan Won* (1905); *Sir Elyot of the Woods* (1907); *The Story of Hauksgarth Farm* (1909); *The House of Robershaye* (1912).

Writing in *The Ludgate* (1898) on the progress of women under Victoria, Brooke argued that through education women had 'raised the standard of what is expected of them in affairs of the world. Many barriers are broken down, but the test to entrance is always ability to perform.' She added:

> a growing and most remarkable sense of independence is probably to be traced more than anything else to the breakdown of the artificial line of demarcation in games. There is no saying how much women owe to the bicycle! Meanwhile the page on which we read of the progress of women is really the same from which we study the progress of men.   (Brooke and others, 213–14)

Brooke died of old age and cardiac degeneration on 28 November 1926 at the Heath Nursing Home, Weybridge, Surrey. Her novels fell out of fashion, after her death, but late twentieth-century scholarship on the 'new woman' has revived critical interest in her work.

ANGELIQUE RICHARDSON

Sources b. cert. · d. cert. · *WWW* · E. F. Brooke, Iota, S. Grand, and G. Egerton, 'Women in the queen's reign: some notable opinions, illustrated with photographs', *The Ludgate*, 1898, 213–17 · W. T. Stead, 'Book of the month: the novel of the modern woman', *Review of Reviews*, 10 (1894), 64–74 · J. Sutherland, *The Longman companion to Victorian fiction* (1988) · A. Richardson, *Love and eugenics in the late nineteenth century: rational reproduction and the new woman* (2003) · A. Richardson and C. Willis, eds., *The New Woman in fiction and in fact* (2000) · A. L. Ardis, *New Women, new novels: feminism and early modernism* (1990)
Archives UCL, corresp.
Likenesses Elliott & Fry, photograph, repro. in Brooke and others, 'Women in the queen's reign'
Wealth at death £702 1s. 5d.: probate, 1927, *CGPLA Eng. & Wales*

Brooke [née Moore], **Frances** (*bap.* **1724**, *d.* **1789**), writer and playwright, was baptized on 24 January 1724 at Claypole, Lincolnshire, the eldest of three children of Thomas Moore (*bap.* 1699, *d.* 1727), rector of Claypole, and his wife, Mary (*d.* 1738), daughter of the Revd Richard Knowles (*d.* 1722), rector of Hougham and Marston, Lincolnshire, and his wife, Sarah. When Frances was about two years old the

Frances Brooke (*bap.* 1724, *d.* 1789), by Katharine Read, *c.*1771

family, including her sister Catherine (1725–1738), left Claypole for Carlton Scroop, Lincolnshire, where Thomas succeeded his father, Williamson Moore (*d.* 1724), as rector of the parish church. A third daughter was born about six weeks after his death in 1727.

Family life Shortly after her husband's death Mary Moore went with her three daughters to Peterborough to live with her mother and her sister Sarah. Sarah married the Revd Roger Steevens, vicar of Tydd St Mary, Lincolnshire, in 1730. Some time after their mother's death in December 1738 Frances and her surviving sister, Sarah, moved to Tydd St Mary to live with their aunt and uncle.

In an article that first appeared in the *British Magazine and Review* in February 1783 (2, 101–3) the anonymous author stated that Mary Moore was chiefly responsible for Frances's 'most excellent education'. Although Frances did not study Latin, she learned French and Italian, and was introduced to a wide range of English literature. Funds for Frances's career were partly provided by her late father. During her minority his estate gave Frances a share of £35 a year for her 'use and maintenance'. In 1745, however, when she turned twenty-one, it paid her £500. In 1751 and 1752, furthermore, Frances received more money when she sold her share in the properties that she and Sarah had by then inherited from their father. With these relatively modest sums Frances left for London. The exact date of her departure from Tydd St Mary is unknown and, like her sister, she may have spent some time in Tinwell, Rutland, at the home of the Revd Richard Knowles, her maternal uncle. By 1748, however, she was definitely in London.

Where Frances Moore lived and what she did during the

next seven years cannot be ascertained precisely. In 1751 she was living in the parish of St Anne's, Soho, and later spent time in Waltham Holy Cross, Essex, and with her uncle in Tinwell. Throughout this period both she and Sarah regularly visited the Steevenses in Tydd St Mary. By 1755, however, Frances had written poetry as well as a tragedy entitled *Virginia*, which David Garrick 'did not like' and 'would not act' (*Letters*, 2.462). Both Frances and Sarah made the acquaintance of Samuel Johnson. According to Sarah's great-nephew, Johnson visited them soon after the publication of his dictionary in 1755:

> The two ladies paid him due compliments on the occasion. Amongst other topics of praise, they very much commended the omission of all *naughty* words. 'What! my dears! then you have been looking for them?' said Johnson. The ladies, confused at being thus caught, dropped the subject of the dictionary. (Beste, section 3)

Marriage and the *Old Maid* Probably about 1754 Frances married John Brooke (*bap.* 1707?, *d.* 1789), a widower with one daughter. An Anglican clergyman, he had been ordained in 1733 and held several livings in parishes in and near Norwich. Since at least the mid-1740s, however, he had been spending a good deal of time in London. In 1748 he had been appointed the 'afternoon preacher' at Longacre Chapel by the bishop of London, and in the mid-1750s he was assisting at His Majesty's Chapel of the Savoy. By 1755 Frances and John may have already had a daughter who, according to the *British Magazine*, died in infancy. John Moore Brooke, their other child, was born in London on 10 June 1757.

Frances Brooke's first known publication was the *Old Maid*, a weekly periodical that she edited under the pseudonym of 'Mary Singleton, Spinster', and that ran from 15 November 1755 until 24 July 1756. The first number introduced Mary as 'the eldest daughter of an honest country justice' who, 'on the verge of fifty' and still 'an old maid', had determined to give 'to the public the observations' that her 'unemploy'd course of life' had enabled her to make. Frances, who wrote twenty-one of the papers herself, was assisted in the sixteen others by several 'Gentlemen'. They included John Boyle, the earl of Cork and Orrery, whose contributions Frances 'marked L. C.' when she prepared the revised and corrected edition of *The Old Maid* (1764); James Brooke, her brother-in-law; John Brooke; Richard Gifford; and Arthur Murray, who was just beginning his career as an actor.

The *Old Maid* covered a wide variety of subjects, but was particularly concerned with such topics as the education of women, their position in marriage, and their role in public affairs. For example, illustrating her opinion that women had a right to participate in politics, Frances weighed in with an attack on Admiral Byng for behaving 'like a coward' at Minorca in May 1756 (*Old Maid*, 10 July 1756). She was also the chief theatre critic and was responsible for the comment on David Garrick's use of Nahum Tate's 'wretched alteration of *King Lear*', instead of 'Shakspear's excellent original' (*Old Maid*, 13 March 1756), that so distressed Garrick that he was still writing about

Mrs Brooke's 'female Spite' towards him nine years later (*Letters*, 2.462).

Novelist, translator, poet, and playwright Even while she was still producing her periodical, Frances Brooke put together a collection of her compositions, including poems, some of which had already appeared in the *Old Maid*. In her preface to *Virginia, Tragedy, with Odes, Pastorals, and Translations* (1756) she explained that she had decided to have it printed because she had no hope of its ever being staged, two plays already having been presented 'on the same Subject' and 'Mr. Garrick' having declined reading her's' until Samuel Crisp's tragedy of the same name was published, an event that occurred in 1754. Smollett wrote one of the most positive reviews, which concluded: 'we have seen very few modern plays superior to the performance, which is truly moral and poetical, and contains many fine strokes of nature: Nor are the subsequent Pastorals and Odes void of merit and propriety' (*Critical Review*, 1, 1756, 276–9). Although Mrs Brooke's volume was never reprinted, it did merit a 'Tribute of Praise' in the second edition of John Duncombe's poem *The Feminead* (1757). Also included in *Virginia* was an advertisement for 'A poetical translation with notes of *Il Pastor fido*, and other poems. From the original Italian of Signor Battista Guarini'. The collection itself, probably the work on which Frances was collaborating with Richard Gifford in 1756–7, was never issued, however.

Frances Brooke's next publication was an English translation of Marie-Jeanne Riccoboni's *Lettres de milady Juliette Catesby à milady Henriette Campley, son amie*. A sentimental novel written in the epistolary style and set in England, *Catesby* was extremely popular from the time of its first appearance in 1759. Frances's version, however, was possibly even more successful. After its initial publication in 1760, *Letters from Juliet Lady Catesby, to her Friend Lady Henrietta Campley* was issued in new editions in 1760, 1763, 1764, 1769, and 1780. One reason for its success was the quality of Frances's rendering of Riccoboni's novel. In May 1765 Riccoboni asked Garrick if she should encourage Brooke's apparent willingness to translate her other novels. It was in reply to this letter that Garrick told Riccoboni about the *Old Maid* and ordered, 'You will be civil' to Mrs Brooke '& no more' (*Letters*, 2.462).

In her letters to Richard Gifford in the early 1760s Frances Brooke wrote of her need for money and of her various plans for acquiring it. These included getting Garrick to purchase her 'Farce', 'however little' she liked him (Frances Brooke to Richard Gifford, FMS English 1310(7) and 1310(18), Houghton); the negotiations, which were being conducted through her friend Mary Cholmondeley, the sister of the actress Margaret (Peg) Woffington and the wife of the Revd Robert Cholmondeley, evidently did not succeed. The only work by Mrs Brooke that appeared in these years was *The History of Lady Julia Mandeville* (1763). Influenced by such authors as Samuel Richardson, Marie-Jeanne Riccoboni, and probably Jean-Jacques Rousseau, whose *Julie, ou La nouvelle Héloïse* had appeared in 1761, *Lady Julia* was a sentimental novel in the form of a series of letters written by several correspondents. The chief story concerned the unfortunate love affair of Lady Julia Mande-ville and Harry Mandeville, a distant relative, although the courtship and marriage of both Lady Anne Wilmot, a sprightly widow who wrote the most letters in the novel, and her niece are also recounted. Readers and reviewers alike criticized Harry's death in a duel, but the work was generally enthusiastically received. Voltaire, for example, reviewing it in the *Gazette littéraire* (30 May 1764), called *Lady Julia* 'peut-être le meilleur Roman' ('perhaps the best novel') in the epistolary genre that had appeared in England since Richardson's *Clarissa Harlowe* (1747–8) and *Sir Charles Grandison* (1754). By the time this review came out, four English and two Irish editions had been published and the novel was being translated into both French and German. The popularity of *The History of Lady Julia Mande-ville* continued in Europe and North America until well after its author's death.

Canada One topic discussed in these fictional letters of 1762–3 was the need for, and the terms of, ending the war with France. By introducing such a political subject Frances Brooke was reaffirming the rights of women to have views on public affairs. She was also signalling her personal interest in the outcome of the Seven Years' War. Since April 1757, with the possible exception of a few months in 1757–8 when he may have returned to England, her husband had been serving as a chaplain with the British army in such places as Louisbourg, New York, and, finally, Quebec, where he arrived in July 1760. In December of the same year James Murray, the military governor of both the garrison and the district of this occupied territory who had known Brooke for many years, appointed him acting chaplain to the town of Quebec; he was officially commissioned as chaplain to the garrison of Quebec on 28 October 1761. Either Murray or Robert Cholmonde-ley may also have helped to get Brooke awarded the degree of doctor of divinity *honoris causa tantum* from Marischal College, Aberdeen, in February 1763. From the time of his arrival in Quebec, Brooke also acted as 'parish priest to all His Majesty's Protestant subjects in the Government not belonging to particular Regiments' (Fulham papers, 1, 110–13, LPL).

From London, Frances Brooke followed these developments with great interest and increasing hope that not only her husband but also Richard Gifford would receive preferment at Quebec. She also prepared for her own departure for North America. On 4 May 1763 James Murray's wife, who refused to leave for Quebec herself, reported to her mother that 'Mrs Brook' was 'realy a sensable whoman' who did 'not seem to mind the Passage at all' (*Correspondence of Mr. John Collier*, 2.340). Finally, having taken leave of her friends, among them Samuel Johnson, who is said to have called her out from the last of her farewell parties to kiss her goodbye, which he 'did not chuse to do before so much company' (*European Magazine*), Frances, accompanied by her son and her sister, left London for Quebec in early July 1763. They arrived on 5 October, just two days before the proclamation that ended British military rule in Canada and created the colony of Quebec with James Murray as its civilian governor.

With the exception of one trip back to England in 1764–5 Frances Brooke made her home in Quebec for the next four years. She lived in La Maison des Jésuites, a house on the St Lawrence River in Sillery, just outside the town, and as one of the few cultivated Englishwomen in the area she led a busy social life. Nevertheless, her position was not entirely enviable. For example, shortly after their arrival Frances, Sarah, and John all became involved in one of the many quarrels, this one concerning a ball, between the civil and military inhabitants of Quebec. One result was a letter written on 8 January 1764 by James Murray to Brooke urging him to remember his 'Dignity' as a clergyman and to avoid 'engaging in the Idle, very Idle disputes of a Tea Table Conversation' (Murray papers, MG23 GII 1, vol. 2, letter-book 1763–1765, 44–6, National Archives of Canada). Later, on 30 October 1764, Murray, complaining still about Brooke's 'sprightly imagination', added in a letter to Robert Cholmondeley: 'I was in hopes the Ladys would have wrought a change, but on the Contrary they meddle more then he does' (Brooke, *Emily Montague*, xxviii). But even if the Brookes had had less forceful personalities and their social situation had been less difficult, they still would have had problems.

In Quebec, and even for a period in Montreal, John Brooke served his fellow protestants, including those who were not Anglicans. Despite his inadequate knowledge of their language he did his best to convert the French-speaking Roman Catholics to his faith. And he worked on various fronts to establish the Church of England in the province. He was, of course, trying to achieve preferment for himself and extra income for his family; he was also, however, practising what he believed should be the British policy towards its Canadian subjects. In these endeavours his wife ably supported him. In January 1765, for example, Frances presented to the Society for the Propagation of the Gospel in London not only two letters from her husband and a petition from 'The Chief Justice, Civil Officers, Merchants and others of the City and Province of Quebec' (petition to the SPG, 1 Nov 1764, SPG Archives, C/CAN/PRE.6B, United Society for the Propagation of the Gospel Archives) but also a letter of her own. All four documents urged the necessity of the society's appointing two missionaries, one of them Brooke, at Quebec. Mrs Brooke's letter argued the case particularly well as she described the state of the Roman Catholic church in Quebec and pleaded for several items, including an English 'school for boys and another for girls', 'a missionary to the Indians', who admired 'the Church of England "as friendly to Liberty"', and an Anglican 'church with an organ and organist so that the Canadians could have the kind of "music & shew" they are used to' (Brooke, *Emily Montague*, xxxi). Although there was support for the Brookes' position on these matters, the politics of Quebec eventually led both James Murray and Guy Carleton, who succeeded Murray as governor of the province in 1766, to convince the British government that neither Anglicizing nor Anglicanizing was an option in this colony. As a result the Brookes abandoned their Canadian project. Frances, accompanied by her son and John's granddaughter, returned home in late 1767. John stayed on for several months before he too sailed for England, probably in September 1768.

The most important accomplishment of the Brookes in Quebec was Mrs Brooke's *The History of Emily Montague* (1769), which was dedicated to Guy Carleton. She had been writing and revising her second novel for about three years, during which time, a 'subscription' having been collected for its sale at '½ a guinea', she felt 'oblig'd' to expand it from three to four volumes (Frances Brooke to Richard Gifford, 21 May 1771, FMS English 1310(9), Houghton). Like *The History of Lady Julia Mandeville*, this epistolary narrative is related by many correspondents, perhaps the most interesting of whom is the coquette Arabella Fermor, named after the real-life model for Alexander Pope's Belinda in *The Rape of the Lock* (1712). The story recounts the courtship and marriage of several sets of lovers including, most importantly, Ed Rivers, a lieutenant-colonel on half-pay, and the beautiful, but apparently poor, Emily Montague. Such a form was typical of many sentimental novels of the day. Among its distinguishing features, however, is its setting in the colony of Quebec, where Rivers had gone to settle (although, like the Brookes themselves, he and the other main English characters in the novel eventually returned to England), and where he had met Emily. Another distinguishing feature is its comments, reinforcing views already expressed by both Brookes in their letters, on the political, religious, and social characteristics of Britain's recent acquisition.

According to Frances Brooke, this Canadian content, which would make it 'better liked by men than women', was partly responsible for the poor sales; 'a novel to sell shou'd please women because women are the chief readers of novels & perhaps the best judges' (Frances Brooke to James Dodsley, 29 Aug 1770, BL, Add. MS 29747, fol. 68). *Emily Montague* did, however, receive favourable notices. The *Critical Review*, for example, praised its author's 'lively stile', 'happy descriptive talent, characters well-marked', and the 'variety of tender and delicate sentiments on the subjects of love and marriage'. The periodical was also impressed with Mrs Brooke's presentation of Canada 'and the manners of its inhabitants', for in 'her description of these the reader will meet with much amusement, and easily trace in her careless sketches the hand of an artist' (*Critical Review*, 27, 1769, 300–02). *The History of Emily Montague* was also popular. New editions were issued in London in 1777 and 1784, and in the 1790s. Three editions were printed in Ireland: 1769, 1775, and 1786. A German translation of the novel was published in 1769. Two French translations were published in 1770; a third was issued in 1809. A Dutch translation appeared in 1783, and a Swedish, translated 'iFrän Fransyskan' ('from French'), in 1796. In the late eighteenth century the work also became a kind of guidebook for visitors to Quebec.

Later works By the time of the publication of *The History of Emily Montague* Frances Brooke had settled into the patterns that characterized the rest of her life. She moved frequently to various addresses in and near London; in 1769–70 she spent a year in North Ockendon, Essex, where she

met such people as Frances Burney, who described her in 1774 as 'very short & fat, & squints', but added that she had 'the art of shewing Agreeable Ugliness. She is very well bred, & expresses herself with much modesty, upon all subjects.—which in an *Authoress*, a Woman of *known* understanding, is extremely pleasing' (*Early Journals and Letters*, 4–5). Frances watched carefully over the education of her son and composed an oration for him to speak on his leaving St Paul's School in London for Cambridge in 1776. For various reasons—his parishes in Norfolk, her career in London, and even, perhaps, their incompatibility—Frances complained more than once in her letters to Richard Gifford that John spoiled her 'projects' (Frances Brooke to Richard Gifford, after July 1771, FMS English 1310(11), Houghton)—she often lived separately from her husband. Mostly, still in need of money, she kept 'busy' and 'industrious' with a 'close application to business' (Royds, 11).

In the early 1770s Frances Brooke translated two French works: Nicolas-Étienne Framéry's *Mémoires de M. le marquis de S. Forlaix, recueillis dans les lettres de sa famille* (1770), and Claude-François-Xavier Millot's *Elémens de l'histoire d'Angleterre, depuis son origine sous les Romains jusqu'au règne de Georges II* (1769). *Memoirs of the Marquis of St Forlaix* was published in four volumes, the first two in September 1770, and the second two in December of the same year. An Irish edition was also published in 1770. *Elements of the History of England from the Invasion of the Romans to the Reign of George the Second* appeared in four volumes in 1771. Despite Mrs Brooke's statement to Richard Gifford that 'now & then a Gallicism' had 'escaped' her 'from being tired of the task' of translating *Elémens* (Frances Brooke to Richard Gifford, early July 1771, FMS English 1310(5), Houghton), in the accurate and colloquial manner in which they were rendered into English both works showed the benefit of her stay in the French-speaking colony of Quebec.

They also demonstrated other results of Frances's sojourn in North America: her increasing confidence in herself as both a critic and an author, and her willingness to compete actively, even aggressively if need be, in the literary world of London. In her preface to *Memoirs of the Marquis de St. Forlaix*, Mrs Brooke not only criticized several aspects of the novel, its 'high reputation' notwithstanding, but she also offered, albeit 'with diffidence', the 'idea' that 'woman alone can paint with perfect exactness the sentiments of woman' (Framéry, 1. [vii]–xii) and thus claimed for herself and other women authors a unique position as writers of prose fiction. When her translation of Millot's history was pre-empted by the publication of a translation of the same work by William Kenrick, it was Mrs Brooke herself who suggested various ways of 'puffing' her *Elements* and of getting 'the book sellers on [her] side' (Frances Brooke to John Nichols, 23 April 1771, Nichols boxes, Yale U., Beinecke L.). She added material to Millot's notes that clarified and corrected his history, including an inscription from one of the many monuments 'erected' to the memory of Elizabeth I as 'proof of the high esteem' in which this monarch 'was held by her people' (Millot, 3.125). She became so interested in British history, in fact, that she considered composing 'an additional volume' of her own (Frances Brooke to Richard Gifford, July 1771, FMS English 1310(5), Houghton).

Frances Brooke demonstrated her more liberated self most directly in her next published work, *The Excursion* (1777). This novel recounts the story of Maria Villiers and her sister Louisa who, when the narrative opens, live with their uncle in Rutland. Louisa is content to stay in the country, but Maria is determined to leave for London where, with a small inheritance in her pocket and 'a novel, an epic poem, and a tragedy' in her 'portmanteau', she hopes to marry a rich man and climb 'the heights of Parnassus' (Brooke, *Excursion*, 16). Although in the end Maria makes a suitable marriage and sees her tragedy produced, neither event occurs in the city. Her sojourn there, in fact, not only costs her her inheritance and almost her reputation as she becomes involved in the *demi-monde* of gamblers and rakes, but it also fails to bring about the production of her tragedy. With the help of Mr Hammond, a friend of her uncle, her play is offered to Garrick, but he refuses it without reading it, prevaricates about what he has done, and, according to Mr Hammond, thus descends 'to such contemptible arts, with no nobler a view than that of robbing the Dramatic Muse, to whom he owes that fame and those riches, of her little share of the reward' (ibid., 84). Mrs Brooke withdrew this and her other unflattering comments on Garrick, who had died in 1779, in the second edition of her novel issued in 1785, but in 1777 their immediate result was an attempt by Garrick to reign 'confusion' upon her for what he deemed her ill-natured attack (*Private Correspondence*, 2.279–80). Although the *Critical Review* praised *The Excursion* for its 'delicacy of satire … liveliness of imagination … warmth of expression', and 'beautiful variety of colouring' that distinguished 'the former publications' of its 'agreeable writer' (*Critical Review*, 44, 1777, 61–3), the *Monthly Review*, in an assessment attributed to Garrick himself (Nangle), criticized its 'spirit and temper', especially as they were shown in the 'stock of malice' piled upon him (*Monthly Review*, 57, 1777, 141–5). *The Excursion* was published in an Irish edition in 1777, in two French translations, the first issued in 1778 and the second in 1819, and in a German translation, which appeared in 1778. Despite these issues Mrs Brooke's third novel did not become as well known as her other two. It was, nevertheless, the most autobiographical of the three, it was the one in which her ironic voice was most fully developed, and it was the one in which she analysed most directly such social issues as gambling and prostitution as well as the difficulties inherent in the lives of women. In the autumn of 1783, Mrs Brooke negotiated briefly with Frances Burney about their collaboration on a periodical, a possibility that the latter refused, and it was never published.

Throughout the 1770s, despite her translations and her novel, Frances Brooke's main interest remained the theatre. In 1771–2 she laboured hard on drafts of a comic opera; in this she was assisted by Richard Gifford, who sent her several songs, some of which he had given her in the 1750s when they had begun their collaboration (Frances Brooke to Richard Gifford, early July 1771, FMS English

1310(5), Houghton). For its production she negotiated with both George Colman, the manager of the Covent Garden Theatre, and Garrick, who was still in charge of Drury Lane. In July 1772 the latter promised her 'an early answer' (Frances Brooke to Richard Gifford, 21 July 1772, FMS English 1310(10), Houghton), but by late that year the opera had been abandoned. Garrick's apparent refusal of this opera and a misunderstanding between the two over the return of a borrowed book in 1776 were undoubtedly further reasons for the negative opinions that Frances Brooke expressed about him in *The Excursion*. In May 1773, however, Mrs Brooke herself joined the ranks of theatre administrators when she, James Brooke, Mary Ann Yates, the distinguished actress who had become a close friend, and her husband, Richard Yates, purchased the King's Theatre, Haymarket. They ran this establishment until 1778, when they sold it to Thomas Harris and Richard Brinsley Sheridan. It was this experience that finally helped open the London stage to Mrs Brooke's own plays.

Final years In the last decade of her life Frances Brooke finally got the recognition as a playwright that she had sought for so long. From 31 January to 19 February 1781 *The Siege of Sinope*, her tragedy based on Santi's opera *Mitridate a Sinope*, with a prologue by the Revd William Collier and an epilogue by Arthur Murray, was produced ten times at the Theatre Royal, Covent Garden. In early February of the same year it was issued with a preface by Mrs Brooke. There was also an Irish edition published in 1781. Both the production and the publication received mixed reviews. Perhaps the most telling comment on the play was recorded by Hannah More in an anecdote about Samuel Johnson:

> Mrs. B. having repeatedly desired Johnson to look over her new play … before it was acted, he always found means to evade it; at last she pressed him so closely that he actually refused to do it, and told her that she herself … would be able to see if there was anything amiss as well as he could. 'But, sir,', said she, 'I have no time. I have already so many irons in the fire.' 'Why then, Madam,' said he (quite out of patience), 'the best thing I can advise you to do is, to put your tragedy along with your irons.' (Roberts, 1.200–01)

Frances Brooke's next two productions kept her name before the theatre-going public for many years. The first was *Rosina, a Comic Opera, in Two Acts*, which she described in the 'Advertisement' to the first published edition as 'taken from the book of Ruth … the beautiful Episode of Palemon and Lavinia in Thomson's Seasons, and a pleasing Opera of Mons. Favart' and adapted to suit her 'plan' (*Rosina*, 1783, v–vi). With music by William Shield and the libretto by Mrs Brooke—and probably Richard Gifford, since some of the material from the laid aside 1772 work appears to have been included—*Rosina* was first performed at Covent Garden on 31 December 1782. It was immediate and lasting success. According to the *London Stage* (1968, 1, clxxii), it was produced 201 times in the last two decades of the eighteenth century. The second production was *Marian*, another comic opera in two acts about the courtship and marriage of rural couples. First performed at Covent Garden on 22 May 1788, it too had music composed by Shield and a libretto by Mrs Brooke that included other material left over from the earlier collaborations with Gifford. Although it neither played so often nor endured so long as *Rosina*, its reception, according to the *London Chronicle*, was 'in the highest degree flattering', and it promised to be 'a most popular performance' (22–24 May 1788).

By the time of *Marian*'s appearance, both John and Frances Brooke were spending more time in the country, he chiefly in Norfolk, she there and in various other places with her son, who was now an Anglican clergyman, and her sister, who had been widowed in 1786. In 1787 Frances had enough energy to write 'Authentic memoirs of Mrs. Yates', who had died in May 1787, for the *Gentleman's Magazine*, but she was already suffering from the 'very infirm state of health' (Royds, 28) that actually delayed the completion of *Marian*. Her illness, described sometimes as 'a spasmodic complaint' (*London Chronicle*, 29–31 Jan 1789), led to her death on 23 January 1789 at the home of her son in Sleaford, Lincolnshire. Her husband, who had died two days before in Colney, was buried there on 27 January, the same day that Frances was interred at St Denys Church, Sleaford. John Brooke composed the words on the memorial to his mother in this church and also wrote the obituary inserted in the *Gentleman's Magazine* and newspapers.

Reputation For a long time after her death Frances Brooke was chiefly remembered for *Rosina*. In the twentieth century, however, new editions were published of each of her three novels. As a novel of sentiment *The History of Lady Julia Mandeville* was particularly interesting to feminist critics, and as the first Canadian novel *The History of Emily Montague* was frequently studied by critics of this new literature in English. But Mrs Brooke probably deserves a more general encomium, for in her life and in her works she went where few women, especially of her class and education, had gone. She attempted successfully the periodical, the novel, the tragedy, and the comic opera, as well as poetry. In the development of the novel in particular, she was 'an essential link between Richardson on the one hand and Fanny Burney and Jane Austen on the other', and she was 'an interpreter to English fiction of the French novel of sentiment practised by Madame Riccoboni and Rousseau' (Brooke, *Lady Julia Mandeville*, 37). She also set the novel on new paths both in its delineation of North America and in its depiction of the lives of women. Thus, while she was not the extraordinary genius lamented by her son, she was certainly an important author in the canon of eighteenth-century British writers.

MARY JANE EDWARDS

Sources F. Brooke, *The excursion*, ed. P. R. Backscheider and H. D. Cotton (1997) • C.-F.-X. Millot, *Elements of the history of England from the invasion of the Romans to the reign of the George the Second*, trans. F. Brooke, 4 vols. (1771) • 'Anecdotes of Mrs Frances Brooke', *European Magazine and London Review*, 15 (1789), 99–101 • F. Brooke, *The history of Emily Montague*, ed. M. J. Edwards (1985) • F. Brooke, *The history of Lady Julia Mandeville*, ed. E. P. Poole (1930) • *The Old Maid* (15 Nov 1755–24 July 1756) • W. J. Atkin, '"A most ingenious authress": Frances Brooke (1724–1789) and her Lincolnshire connections', *Lincolnshire History and Archaeology*, 32 (1997), 12–20 • H. D. Beste, *Personal and literary memorials* (1829) • *The early journals and letters of Fanny Burney*, ed. L. E. Troide, 2: 1774–1777 (1990) • *Correspondence of Mr. John Collier … and his family, 1716–1780*, ed. C. L. Sayer (1907) • *The autobiography and correspondence of Mary Granville, Mrs Delany*, ed. Lady Llanover, 2nd ser., 1 (1862) • J. Duncombe, *The feminead* (1757) • *La maison des Jésuites*, Les Editions (1995) • *The letters of David Garrick*, ed. D. M. Little and G. M. Kahrl, 3 vols. (1963) • C. B. Hogan, ed., *The London stage, 1660–1800*, pt 5: 1776–1800 (1968) • *The private correspondence of David Garrick*, ed. J. Boaden, 2 (1832) • F. Maseres, ed., *A collection of several commissions, and other public instruments … relating to the state of the province of Quebec in North America* (1966) • W. Roberts, *Memoirs of the life and correspondence of Hannah More*, 3rd edn, 4 vols. (1835), vol. 1 • *British Magazine and Review*, 2 (1783), 101–3 • B. C. Nangle, *The Monthly Review, first series, 1749–1789: indexes of contributors and articles* (1934) • countess of Cork and Orrery [E. C. Boyle], ed., *The Orrery papers*, 2 vols. (1903), vol. 2 • 'Mme Riccoboni's letters to David Hume, David Garrick and Sir Robert Liston, 1764–1783', ed. J. C. Nicholls, *Studies on Voltaire and the Eighteenth Century*, 149 (1976) • E. Royds, ed., *Stubton strong room—stray notes (2nd series): Moore and Knowles families—two sisters* (1928) • *Mrs Simcoe's diary*, ed. M. Q. Innis (1965) • *London Chronicle* (22–4 May 1788) • *London Chronicle* (29–31 Jan 1789) • *The diary of a country parson, 1758–1802, by James Woodforde*, ed. J. Beresford (1978) • F. Brooke, letters, Harvard U., Houghton L., FMS English 1310 • LPL, Fulham papers • letter-book, NA Canada, Murray MSS, GII 1, vol. 2 • United Society for the Propagation of the Gospel Archives, London, SPG archives • Nichols boxes, Yale U., Beinecke L., Osborn shelves • N.-M. Framéry, *Memoirs of the marquis de St. Forlaix*, trans. F. Brooke, 4 vols. (1970)

Archives Harvard U., Houghton L., letters, etc., FMS English 1310 • Northants. RO, Moore family papers | BL, Add. MS 29747, fol. 68 • Harvard U., Houghton L., letters to Richard Gifford and literary MSS • LPL, Fulham papers • NA Canada, Murray MSS, letter-book, GII 1, vol. 2 • NYPL, Berg collection • United Society for the Propagation of the Gospel, London, Society for the Propagation of the Gospel archives • Yale U., Beinecke L., Nichols boxes, Osborn shelves

Likenesses K. Read, portrait, c.1771, NA Canada [see illus.] • M. Bovi, stipple, pubd 1790 (after C. Read), BM

Brooke, George, ninth Baron Cobham (c.1497–1558), soldier and landowner, was the eldest surviving son of Thomas Brooke, eighth Baron Cobham (d. 1529), and his first wife, Dorothy Heydon. He accompanied his father in attending Mary Tudor to her marriage with Louis XII of France in 1514. He returned to France in war in 1522 and served with distinction. He was knighted after the capture of Morlaix at the beginning of July, and led a force of 2000 men in skirmishes round Calais in September. In the court festivities on either side of Christmas 1524 he was prominent in the jousting around 'the castle of libertie' at Greenwich. By 1526 he had married Anne (c.1510–1558), eldest daughter of Edmund, Lord Bray; they had ten sons and four daughters. After succeeding to the barony in 1529 he was among the leaders of Kent society, and was frequently required to escort and entertain state visitors passing along the Dover road. He served as JP for the county and was named to numerous other commissions. He was rewarded with substantial grants of confiscated monastic and collegiate land, notably the site of Cobham College, founded by the third Baron Cobham in 1362.

In spring 1544 Cobham was lieutenant-general for the invasion of Scotland, praised by his commander (Hertford) for his 'ryght honist and paynfull sarvis' (BL, Add. MS 32654, fol. 204r). On 17 June 1544 he was appointed deputy of Calais. There he played a key role in negotiating peace

Brooke Lᵈ Cobham.

George Brooke, ninth Baron Cobham (c.1497–1558), by Hans Holbein the younger

with France and the return of Boulogne. On 24 April 1549 he was nominated knight of the Garter, as which he was installed on 13 December. He was sympathetic to the seizure of power by John Dudley in October (his eldest daughter, Elizabeth, was the second wife of Dudley's close ally the marquess of Northampton), and was rewarded with a place on the privy council from 23 May 1550. By September he had relinquished his post at Calais, and for the rest of Edward VI's reign he was in regular attendance at parliament and the council table. In January 1551, and again in November 1552, he was proposed as lieutenant in Ireland, but was never sent. In December 1551 he was assigned fifty of the mounted 'gendarmes' recently appointed as a security measure.

Cobham supported Dudley's attempted coup after Edward's death; he and Sir John Mason were sent in the name of Queen Jane to explain events to the imperial ambassadors in London, and to deter them from contacting Mary. Following Mary's accession Cobham was pardoned on 11 October 1553; but his loyalty to the new regime was uncertain. When Wyatt raised Kent in January 1554, Cobham was appointed to assist the duke of Norfolk in suppressing the rebellion. Through his mother Wyatt was Cobham's nephew and, despite family discord and disputes over property, looked to his uncle and cousins for support. Cobham joined the royal forces under Norfolk at Gravesend, and warned the duke of the unreliability of the Londoners, but was ignored. Norfolk's forces disintegrated soon afterwards, and Cobham withdrew to his castle at Cooling where, on 30 January, Wyatt gave assault. Cobham claimed to have fought valiantly for seven hours before capitulating to superior strength. In reality (as was at once suspected) his resistance may have been a pretence. Cobham went to Wyatt's camp, which three of his sons also joined, and then 'escaped' to London, where after examination by the council he was imprisoned in the Tower on 2 February.

Cobham was released at the suit of the count of Egmont, one of Charles V's emissaries, on 24 March. He suffered only a fine of £452, and was restored to his place in local, but not national, affairs. During 1554 he attended the arrivals of King Philip and Cardinal Pole. He was appointed to the Kent sewers commission in 1555, and to the heresy commission in the diocese of Canterbury in 1556. He was nevertheless distrusted as a heretic himself and 'of French leanings', in the words of the imperial ambassador Simon Renard (CSP Spain, 1554, 239). His attachment to the reform movement was probably genuine; he received a dedication from Thomas Becon, was on good terms with Archbishop Cranmer, and directed that his funeral be conducted without 'superstitious ceremonye' (PRO, PROB 11/43, fol. 448). He employed protestant tutors for his sons. His character is most pleasantly shown in directions given in 1541 for his eldest son, William *Brooke, later tenth Baron Cobham, who was about to tour Italy. After more conventional moral strictures, he advised him to spend his spare time playing the lute, and not to speak 'too thick' (LP Henry VIII, 16, no. 893).

Cobham died on 29 September 1558 and was buried in Cobham church, where his fine tomb and effigy may be seen. His wife died on 1 November following and was buried on the 26th.

C. S. KNIGHTON

Sources GEC, Peerage, 3.347–8 · LP Henry VIII, 16, nos. 878(60), 893; 19/1, nos. 535, 680, 716, 812(59) · CPR, 1547–8, 79, 85; 1553–4, 35, 36, 437; 1554–5, 110; 1555–7, 24–5, 368 · CSP dom., 1547–53, 274, 290; 1553–8, 25–8, 30, 54, 103 · CSP for., 1547–53 · CSP Spain, 1538–42, 468; 1544, 146; 1550–54; 1554–8, 23 · APC, 1550–52, 56; 1554–6, 83, 345 · The chronicle and political papers of King Edward VI, ed. W. K. Jordan (1966), 25, 30, 31, 47, 52, 100, 124 · J. G. Nichols, ed., The chronicle of Queen Jane, and of two years of Queen Mary, CS, old ser., 48 (1850), 36, 41, 71, 91 · The diary of Henry Machyn, citizen and merchant-taylor of London, from AD 1550 to AD 1563, ed. J. G. Nichols, CS, 42 (1848), 37, 75, 179 · The early works of Thomas Becon, ed. J. Ayre, Parker Society, 2 (1843), 264–8 · J. G. Waller, 'The lords of Cobham, their monuments, and the church [pt 2]', Archaeologia Cantiana, 12 (1878), 113–66 · P. Clark, English provincial society from the Reformation to the revolution: religion, politics and society in Kent, 1500–1640 (1977), 21, 50–51, 95, 105, 421 n. 85, 424 nn. 48, 51, 429 n. 120 · M. A. R. Graves, The House of Lords in the parliaments of Edward VI and Mary I (1981), 23, 225, 263 n. 217 · D. E. Hoak, The king's council in the reign of Edward VI (1976), 54, 62, 136 · H. Miller, Henry VIII and the English nobility (1986), 126, 241, 246 · W. K. Jordan, Edward VI, 1: The young king (1968), 77, 93, 203, 361 · D. M. Loades, Two Tudor conspiracies (1965), 57, 59–62, 82, 254 · D. MacCulloch, Thomas Cranmer: a life (1996) · PRO, PROB 11/43, fols. 447v–453r · Hall's chronicle, ed. H. Ellis (1809) · BL, Add. MS 32654

Archives BL, corresp. as deputy of Calais, Harley MSS

Likenesses H. Holbein the younger, drawing, Royal Collection [see illus.] · effigy on tomb, Cobham

Wealth at death see will, PRO, PROB 11/43, fols. 447v–453r

Brooke, George (1568–1603), conspirator, the youngest son of William *Brooke, tenth Baron Cobham (1527–1597), and his wife, Frances, *née* Newton (d. 1592), was born on the morning of 17 April 1568 at Cobham Hall, Kent. He matriculated from King's College, Cambridge, as a fellow-commoner in 1580 and was created MA in 1586. The family chronicler, Francis Thynne, noted that George had 'by an accidentall chance in his youth some imperfection in one part of his bodie', growing up 'lame and creple', while Geoffrey Whitney in his *Choice of Emblemes* (1586) addressed the young man in an allegory where 'inward vertues' were highlighted over outward show (McKeen, 1.165–6).

Brooke was well provided for by his father and was consequently able to make an advantageous marriage. In 1599 he wedded Elizabeth Burgh (d. c.1637), eldest daughter and coheir of Lord Burgh (d. 1602). They had three children, William (1601–1643), Elizabeth, and Frances. As his brother Henry *Brooke, eleventh Baron Cobham, disclosed under examination in 1603, George subsequently seduced his wife's youngest sister, Frances, who was engaged to his own nephew Francis Coppinger. Dissatisfaction with his wife seems to have been mirrored by a discontent with his portion in life, for the 1590s and early 1600s witnessed a succession of schemes in which Brooke sought out preferments to one ecclesiastical sinecure after another. Despite patronage from two generations of Cecils—Lord Burghley and Brooke's brother-in-law, Sir Robert Cecil—more than one such post eluded him. Frustrated in his designs upon the mastership of St Cross, Winchester, and concerned at the implications of a Stuart succession for a family whose fortunes were founded firmly on the goodwill of the old queen, Brooke embarked upon a particularly inept and fatuous treason.

As conceived by Brooke and his principal associates, the impecunious Catholic squire Sir Griffin Markham and the unstable appellant priest William Watson, this so-called Bye plot had as its objective the kidnapping of King James, the intention being to hold him hostage against an end to persecution of Catholics and a removal of ministers identified with Elizabethan repression. Built upon quite unjustified assumptions of widespread support the scheme foundered long before it was revealed to the authorities. Brooke was arrested and placed in the custody of the bishop of London on 14 July 1603. He was transferred to the Tower five days later ('Journal of Levinus Munck', 244). Well treated there on account of his deformity and his candid revelations, Brooke's deep complicity was nevertheless manifest. His knowledge of a quite separate treason—the so-called Main plot—involving his elder brother and Sir Walter Ralegh, also counted against him. When put on trial at Winchester on 15 November, his vigorous attempts to argue that the king had directed him to investigate these practices also won him censure rather than sympathy. They were certainly the exaggerations of a desperate man. Brooke was found guilty and executed on Winchester Castle Green on 5 December, making, as Cecil reported, 'a patient and constant end' (Nicholls, 826–7).

A likeness of Brooke, the youngest child, was added to the well-known family portrait of the Cobhams which survives in two versions at Longleat and Bolton Abbey. He inherited his father's books, keeping them at the family home at Blackfriars (finding it more convenient than his rented house in Channon Row, Westminster), where they were surveyed by the crown after his arrest. It seems likely that Brooke was the dedicatee in Thomas Weelkes's *Madrigals of 6 Parts* (1600). The verses at the Bodleian Library once attributed to him are the work of George Brooke of Norton, Cheshire.   MARK NICHOLLS

Sources PRO, SP 14/3, 14/4 · PRO, E 178/3521 · Hatfield House, Hertfordshire, Salisbury–Cecil MSS · LPL, MS 3201 · D. McKeen, *A memory of honour: the life of William Brooke, Lord Cobham*, 2 vols. (Salzburg, 1986) · BL, Add. MSS 12514, fols. 56–77v; 37666 · M. Nicholls, 'Treason's reward: the punishment of conspirators in the Bye plot of 1603', *HJ*, 38 (1995), 821–42 · 'The journal of Levinus Munck', ed. H. V. Jones, *EngHR*, 68 (1953), 234–58 · Venn, *Alum. Cant.*

Likenesses portrait, 1560–69 (as a child), Bolton Abbey · portrait (as a child), Longleat, Wiltshire

Brooke, Gustavus Vaughan (1818–1866), actor, was born at 40 Hardwicke Place, Dublin, on 25 April 1818, the eldest of the four surviving children of Gustavus Vaughan Brooke (d. 1827), speculator and inspector of police, and his wife, Frances (d. 1862), the daughter of Matthew Bathurst of Ballinaskea House, co. Meath. He was educated first at Edgeworthstown at a school run by Lovell Edgeworth, and then at an academy in Dublin.

On Easter Tuesday in 1833 Brooke appeared at the Theatre Royal, Dublin, replacing an indisposed Edmund Kean as William Tell. An engagement followed, during which he was billed as 'Master Brooke, the Hibernian Roscius', and played characters such as Virginius, Douglas, and Rolla. He was well received in Limerick, Londonderry, Glasgow, and Edinburgh. His first appearance in London took place at the Victoria Theatre as Virginius, and attracted little attention. Work on the Kent circuit in 1835 was followed by appearances at Glasgow and Kilmarnock in 1836 and Dublin and Sheffield in 1837. He was, by this time, billed as 'G. V. Brooke, tragedian'. At about this time he began a liaison with the actress Marie Duret (d. 1881), who for about ten years 'travelled under his protection and occasionally under the shelter of his name' (Lawrence, 34).

An engagement at Drury Lane with W. C. Macready in 1841 came to nothing when Brooke quarrelled over the parts he was assigned, and he returned to the provinces where he had a growing reputation, and where, in spite of invitations to appear in London, he remained for seven years. He played alongside many celebrated actors, including Helen Faucit, Lester Wallack, Charlotte Custman, and even Macready, and undertook occasional, broadly unsuccessful ventures in management at Ayr and Liverpool. He enjoyed a successful run in Berwick, where he was fêted until Marie Duret attempted suicide for being slighted socially by his admirers.

The height of Brooke's career was marked by his opening at the Olympic, London, on 3 January 1848, as Othello, which excited much interest. During this engagement he appeared as Sir Giles Overreach, Richard III, Shylock,

Virginius, Hamlet, and Brutus, and he created the role of Laurency in *The Lords of Ellingham*, a play by Henry Spicer, the Olympic's manager. Brooke's early promise was not, however, fulfilled: intermittent successes were punctuated by missed opportunities, and imprudence and insobriety led to insolvency. He returned to the provinces, where he was increasingly dilatory in his performances, and was more than once observed to be drunk on stage. In Manchester (where in June 1849 Marie Duret appeared as 'Mrs G. V. Brooke') even his admirers noted the collapse of his voice, brought about by a combination of drink and bronchitis. The following December Marie Duret abandoned him and went to America.

During a Birmingham run, on 17 October 1851, Brooke married Marianne Elizabeth Woolcott Bray (c.1823–c.1860), the daughter of James Bray of New Street, Birmingham, and shortly thereafter he departed for New York. He played Othello at the Broadway Theatre on 15 December 1851 with unqualified success, and toured Philadelphia, Boston, Washington, and Baltimore before undertaking a disastrous management of the Astor Place Opera House, New York, in May 1852. By 1853 he was back in Britain, where he appeared at Drury Lane on 5 September under the management of E. T. Smith to unexpected acclaim. The following year he went to Australia, and was initially successful. He tried another spell of management, with George *Coppin at the Theatre Royal, Melbourne, but, frequently drunk or incapable of performing, he alienated the Australian audiences by an apparently unending series of 'final performances'. On this tour Brooke met the American actress Avonia *Jones (1836–1867), whom he married in Liverpool on 23 February 1863. He had returned to England virtually penniless, and was not well received on his return to the London stage. Provincial and Irish tours could not stave off financial ruin; he again embarked on a series of 'leave-takings' which were becoming absurd, when on 28 December 1865 Avonia Jones saw him and his youngest sister, Fanny, onto the steamer *London*, bound for Australia. The fact that they sailed under assumed names lends credence to the view that Brooke was evading his creditors. A life which bore more traces of farce than of the tragedy in which Brooke specialized ended in grand heroic style when the *London* foundered on 10 January 1866. The shock brought about a fatal heart attack in his sister, and Brooke, who was praised by survivors for his behaviour in the crisis, went down with the ship on 11 January 1866.

K. D. REYNOLDS

Sources W. J. Lawrence, *The life of Gustavus Vaughan Brooke* (1892) · *AusDB* · Hall, *Dramatic ports.* · T. A. Brown, *History of the American stage* (1870) · Adams, *Drama*
Likenesses C. Summers, marble bust, 1869, State Library of Victoria, Australia · Annan & Swan, photogravure, repro. in Lawrence, *Life of Gustavus Vaughan Brooke*, frontispiece · D. J. Pond, stipple and line print (after daguerreotype), NPG · oils (as Shylock), Garr. Club · portraits, Harvard U.

Brooke [Cobham], **Sir Henry** (1537–1592), diplomat, was born on 5 February 1537, the seventh but fifth surviving son of George *Brooke, ninth Baron Cobham (c.1497–

1558), soldier and landowner, and his wife, Anne (c.1510–1558), eldest daughter of Edmund Bray, first Baron Bray, and his wife, Jane. His brothers included William *Brooke, tenth Baron Cobham (1527–1597), and he had four sisters, of whom one died young. He pursued a family eccentricity (or pretension) with unusual determination in using as a surname the family title rather than Brooke.

Education and early career, 1537–1571 Cobham matriculated *impubes* as a pensioner from Trinity College, Cambridge, on 29 September 1547 but did not take a degree and entered the household of the earl of Devonshire—presumably during Edward Courtenay's brief liberty in 1553—where he came to Princess Elizabeth's notice and 'liking' (Birch, 1.17). He was clearly affiliated with Elizabeth's supporters rather than with Mary I's regime and was made gentleman pensioner in 1559, a point from which he then consistently dated self-serving claims of long service to her. Family convention suggests that Cobham might have travelled in his youth. His brothers William and George Brooke (1533–c.1570) went to Italy; another Mr Brooke found in the Veneto in 1555 seems to have been not Cobham but his brother John Brooke (1535–1594), later MP for the family's local seat of Queenborough in Kent (J. Woolfson, *Padua and the Tudors*, 1998, 214). If not before, Cobham learned foreign languages through diplomatic practice. Cobham is, however, a likely candidate for 'the brother of Cobham' who came in August 1559 to assure the Spanish ambassador to London, Alvaro de la Quadra, bishop of Aquila, that 'the affair of the archduke's marriage was in a very good way'. He might even be the 'one of these men called Cobham' whom Quadra reported in March 1562 as implicated in the vague if incriminating intrigues of Margaret Douglas, countess of Lennox, who therefore 'sought an excuse for going to the baths of Liège' (*CSP Spain, 1558–67*, 93, 231). Quadra usually conversed in Italian; Cobham may or may not yet have known much Spanish, but two decades later he could use Italian as a lingua franca with the Turkish envoy in Paris.

Cobham accompanied Sir Thomas Chaloner to Spain in 1561, returning with dispatches later that year—he thought the ambassador insufficiently appreciative of his efforts, particularly in light of his near shipwreck on the Irish coast. He complained that Chaloner had not provided enough money for his expenses, and succeeded in getting it out of the privy council. In 1567 he joined the embassy of Thomas *Radcliffe, third earl of Sussex (1526/7–1583), to pursue the project of an Austrian marriage for the queen. Selection for this embassy may have been influenced by his knowledge of Low German. More importantly, he was connected to Sussex, who stepped in to support as 'a near kinsman of his own' yet another brother, Thomas Brooke (1533–1578), when the Spanish accused him of piracy in 1565 (*CSP Spain, 1558–67*, 455). Sussex's death in June 1583 made Cobham wish, 'God rayse unto me as good and noble a frend' (PRO, SP 78/9/130).

Cobham was sent by Sussex to London in October 1567 to seek further instructions; but the answer that he brought back in December included no religious concessions to Archduke Charles and thus brought the negotiation to an end. Cobham gave a different impression by causing his 'postilion to sound the horn all the way ... crying, "[Long] live Austria and England!"' (*CSP Rome, 1558–71*, 267). Then, acting as a co-envoy, albeit a junior one, he went to see the archduke at Graz in Styria in February 1568. Charles reported to Maximilian II that Cobham agreed he was right not to compromise his faith:

> But he had hoped that I should go to England ... he ... hoped to be able to arrange matters in a manner which would satisfy both me and your majesty ... All that had been said in England about your majesty and my territories was at variance with what he had seen for himself. But he would at his return give them a more truthful relation.

Cobham even offered to 'direct' 'those few who at his advice had bound themselves by oath' so 'that I should see and recognize that he had been my loyal servant and wished always to remain so' (Klarwill, 296–8).

On 19 August 1570 Cobham set out as special ambassador for the Low Countries with messages for the governor, Alvarez de Toledo, duke of Alva, and for Philip II's new queen, Anne of Austria. These proved rather more cordial than recent tense Anglo-Spanish exchanges, and Cobham went on to visit Anne's father, Maximilian, with whom he had an audience on 12 September, at Speyer. Besides appealing to monarchical solidarity against the papal deposition of Elizabeth, Cobham sought to divert the Habsburgs with a token resurrection of the queen's Austrian marriage project. Bertrand de Salignac de La Motte Fénélon, the French ambassador in London, did not believe that 'young Coban' would make more than 'a demonstration', writing sarcastically that after Sussex's failure, 'a young gentleman of no authority, who has scarcely grown his beard ... will achieve even less at this juncture' (Teulet, 3.424–5). Still peripatetic, Cobham passed through France into Spain (20 March to 5 July 1571) to explain English charges against the Spanish ambassador to England, Guerau de Spes, and to explore the idea of restoring a resident ambassador in Spain if the latter were allowed religious freedom, a suggestion that led Gómez Suárez de Figueroa, duke of Feria, to silence Cobham 'for fear he should blurt out some impertinence' (*CSP Spain, 1568–79*, 316). Though he put a brave face on it, he returned dissatisfied in July 1571, opining, 'thynke theys smaule shooes [showers] to be warnyngs of greater storms to cumme, if tymme may fytt them' (PRO, SP 70/118, fol. 2r).

Courtier and county gentleman, 1571–1583 Though Cobham claimed when convenient a need as gentleman pensioner to attend the queen, he established a base in Kentish society after his marriage on 27 January 1573 to Anne (*d.* 1611/12), widow of Walter Haddon and daughter of Sir Henry Sutton of Nottinghamshire. She apparently brought him his main residence at Sutton-at-Hone, Kent, and they had three sons—Calisthenes (1573–1611), who became a soldier and was knighted, John Brooke, later Baron Cobham (1574–1660), and Maximilian (1575/6–1598)—and two daughters, Anne (*b.* c.1577) and Philippa (c.1579–1613).

Cobham had become part of a 'recognizable Elizabethan diplomatic cadre' (Bell, 'Men and their rewards', 208). Rumours of 1572 and 1575 had him receiving the premier diplomatic posting, France. Although his experience of the country had been only in passing, he was sent in 1571 to meet the special French envoy Paul de Foix, in 1572 to meet François de Montmorency, duc de Montmorency, and to escort the French envoys on the royal progress, and in 1577 to Dartmouth in Devon to meet the Marquis d'Haverie. Instead, he finally went back to Spain as special ambassador from 20 June 1575 to 10 January 1576 fortified with a knighthood. He had an audience with Philip on 26 October, despite de Spes's complaint that 'some lord or person of higher position' should have greeted the queen of Spain in 1570 (*CSP Spain, 1567–79*, 273). This coincided with an increase in his diet from £2 per day to £2 10s.

Cobham did stay for some weeks at the Paris embassy with Valentine Dale, who apparently took him on his visits to court. In October near Blaye, in Gascony, he 'was set on' by Huguenots (ironically) 'in a wood', 'with whome we came to the proffer of the pistole, and withstanding then the first brunt we escaped with smaulle inconveniens or losse' (PRO, SP 70/136, fol. 38v). Arriving in Spain, he found there 'little commforte'. He complained that both customs and the Spanish Inquisition insisted on 'visiting my stuffe'. 'So muche more now curious they are become for the respect of religion' that he lacked 'those visitacions whiche the last tyme I found' (PRO, SP 70/135, fol. 248r).

Cobham believed Alva to be favourable towards mitigation of the Spanish Inquisition's scrutiny of Englishmen in Spain. Even so, the negotiations were marred by 'an altercation of some sort', prompting one historian to ask 'why the government felt someone as ill-tempered as he might prove a success in that hostile country' (Bell, 'Men and their rewards', 209, 210). However, with Chaloner and the disastrous John Man dead, and Sir Thomas Chamberlain retired on health grounds, Cobham was probably the candidate with most experience of Spanish negotiations. According to Fénélon, pro-Spanish privy councillors had mooted Cobham's dispatch as early as August 1574—it was no sudden decision. He also believed that, building on the statements of 1571, Cobham might have become resident ambassador if the initial negotiation had been more satisfactory. The papal nuncio claimed credit for his dismissal in January 1576, and Gregory XIII was 'much gratified' (*CSP Rome, 1572–8*, 250). Within a year of his mission, the English were complaining that 'nothing was performed that was promised Sir Henry Cobham at his being last in Spain' (Strype, 2/2.8). Cobham continued to write to the Spanish government personally in an abortive attempt to effect improvement in the treatment of Englishmen there, and to vindicate himself over charges of over-optimism made by the subsequent ambassador, Sir John Smythe. Cobham was allegedly 'much blamed and attacked at court' for misrepresentation (*CSP Spain, 1567–79*, 543).

Cobham remained on the look-out for offices. On the

death of his kinsman Richard Verney, while accompanying him to Spain in 1575, Cobham sought his post of marshal of the king's bench—'the queene's majestie shoulde thearby give me a stocke to stand by in her sarvice, and with that staffe dryve from her a begger' (PRO, SP 70/135, fol. 248r). Soon after returning from Spain, he did become porter of the bag and keeper of the treasury.

On 15 October 1579 Cobham succeeded Sir Amias Paulet as resident ambassador in France on a diet of £3 6s. 8d. per day. He later claimed that the principal secretaries, Sir Francis Walsingham and Thomas Wilson, had 'commaunded … that I should lay asyde all my juste excuses then alleaged of my insufficiency', notably lack of a 'competent yearly lyvyng of my owne, as [other] your majestes mynysters enjoyed' (PRO, SP 78/9/43; 78/9/13). Others impugned his sufficiency in other respects. Cobham perhaps held 'the record for detailed and unassimilated reporting of virtually anything that came to his attention', especially rumours concerning the activities of English Catholic exiles (Bell, 'Men and their rewards', 211). He wished, however, to hear whether his reports were confirmed, 'otherwyse I may be abused, and her majesty's money ill-bestowed' (PRO, SP 78/7/24). Walsingham warned him that the queen was critical of the expense of Cobham's sending so many reports, advising him to reduce the volume somewhat. Moreover, Cobham was not enciphering as he should have been, given that some letters were going astray. Robert Dudley, earl of Leicester, not an intimate of Cobham's though inevitably petitioned by him in his quest for preferment, had already—either helpfully or maliciously—'sent me worde I have very evill intelligence, and that the quene shuld be informed I caryed muche forniture for myself and … my servauntes' (PRO, SP 78/4/72). Cobham continued 'notwithstanding to report what is sent or delivered', though doubtful whether it was 'imployed to any good purpose' (PRO, SP 78/9/109; BL, Cotton MS Otho E. iv, fol. 23r). At least the government did make considerable propaganda use from 1580 of the articles of a purported international Catholic League given to Cobham by John Leslie, former bishop of Ross.

Views of Cobham's French embassy have varied, from grouping him with Elizabethan colleagues with a 'wary distaste for their host country' to finding him 'a particularly effective vehicle for fostering the burgeoning friendship between the two realms' (Leimon and Parker, 1134; Bell, 'Men and their rewards', 211). The second judgement is the more true, but the first still describes Cobham's faults accurately. He regarded Henri III and Catherine de' Medici as unreliable, 'removing princes' (PRO, SP 78/5/80). As for Catherine, 'he trusteth nothinge thatt she says tyll he see yt doone' (PRO, SP 78/4/138). He regarded the half-hearted negotiation combining marriage talks between Elizabeth and François, duc d'Anjou, and Anglo-French alliance against Spain as a lost opportunity because the former were abandoned, effectively scuppering the latter. He was not, however, completely anti-Spanish as a result of his experiences there and recognized the need to play one Catholic power off against another.

Cobham took a different view from Walsingham as to the subordination he owed the secretary of state. It is, however, an extreme picture painted of him by Walsingham's man Nicholas Faunt:

> If heretofore he cared little for me, and such as belong to my master, now he is become so stout and strange … that he hath been at odds with all the honest gentlemen my master favoureth, even to have chased them away; and for those, that yet remain, he hath ever in suspicion and useth these after a strange sort.   (Birch, 1.17–18)

Fundamentally, though, Cobham was too dependent on Walsingham because the secretary was the most likely person to facilitate his recall and for 'the amending of my sillye estate', an obsessive concern (PRO, SP 78/4/4). Even a grant in 1582 worth £2000, when he wanted £3000, tended, in a 'staggringe sorte', to 'have dulled my courage' (PRO, SP 78/7/128). By the end of 1582, he claimed to have 'no more meanes to countenance this place, nor contentment of mynde to indure this trade' (PRO, SP 78/8/53). Unusually, he was joined on his posting by his wife, who, however, wrote to Leicester, 'I lyve a lyfe heere not so muche to my conte[nt] as I trusted I shoulde' (BL, Cotton MS Caligula E. vii, fol. 205r).

Final years, 1583–1592 On 15 September 1583 Cobham was replaced by Sir Edward Stafford, with whom, characteristically, he was reluctant to co-operate. There was, however, a history behind this—Stafford, on a mission concerning the Anjou match, had impugned intelligence provided by William Waad, who was cherished by Cobham. It was logical if petty of Cobham to refuse to brief Stafford on reports which the latter did not value.

Cobham's advance of £500 on departure in 1579 was one of the more generous, his diets of £280 per quarter seem to have been paid regularly, and he received extraordinary sums of at least £1382 over four years. However, by 1583 he claimed to have sold land, leaving him owing over £600 in England and 700 crowns in Paris. A younger son, it is probable that he was 'no loser' by his diplomatic career—but, between pretension and paranoia, he might still have strained his resources, especially while in Paris (Bell, 'Men and their rewards', 113).

In 1587 it was suggested that Cobham join his brother William Brooke in negotiations in the Spanish Netherlands and in 1589 it was proposed that he take a message to James VI. However, he had effectively retired to a country sphere. A JP for Kent by 1573, he became *custos rotulorum* about 1584 and deputy lieutenant in 1588, when he was involved in preparations against the Spanish Armada. He was also active in dealing with recusants in Kent. He returned to parliament, this time as knight of the shire for Kent, in 1586 and 1589 and sat on key committees, including that petitioning for the execution of Mary, queen of Scots, a course he had long advocated. Cobham died intestate and apparently heavily in debt at Sutton-at-Hone on 13 January 1592. Perhaps 'embittered and improvident', nevertheless, even if unable to succeed against the odds in his Spanish missions, he had made a better impression than average for English diplomats in

Austria and France and—difficult though he could be—was clearly regarded as one of the more versatile Elizabethan ambassadors (McKeen, 2.614).   JULIAN LOCK

Sources G. M. Bell, 'Men and their rewards in Elizabethan diplomatic service, 1558-85', PhD diss., U. Cal., Los Angeles, 1974, 3, 33, 38-43, 47, 65ff., 90-98, 108, 113, 131ff., 206-13 · G. M. Bell, 'Elizabethan diplomatic compensation: its nature and variety', *Journal of British Studies*, 20 (1981), 1-25 · HoP, *Commons, 1558-1603*, 1.494-5 · state papers foreign, Elizabeth I, PRO, SP 70 · state papers France, PRO, SP 78 · state papers domestic, Elizabeth I, PRO, SP 12 · state papers domestic additional, Elizabeth I, PRO, SP 15 · Cotton MSS, BL, Caligula E. vii; Galba E. vi; Otho E. iv; Otho E. ix · APC · D. McKeen, *A memory of honour: the life of William Brooke, Lord Cobham*, 2 vols. (1986) · J. G. Nichols, 'Memorials of the family of Cobham', *Collectanea Topographica et Genealogica*, 7 (1841), 320-54 · M. A. S. Hume, ed., *Calendar of letters and state papers relating to English affairs, preserved principally in the archives of Simancas*, 4 vols., PRO (1892-9) · *Correspondance diplomatique de Bertrand de Salignac de la Mothe Fénélon*, ed. A. Teulet, 7 vols., Bannatyne Club, 67 (1838-40) · V. von Klarwill, *Queen Elizabeth and some foreigners; being a series of hitherto unpublished letters from the archives of the Hapsburg family*, trans. T. H. Nash (1928) · *CSP Venice, 1558-80* · *CSP Rome, 1558-78* · T. Birch, *Memoirs of the reign of Queen Elizabeth ... chiefly from the original papers of Anthony Bacon*, 2 vols. (1754), vol. 1, pp. 17-18 · J. Strype, *Annals of the Reformation and establishment of religion ... during Queen Elizabeth's happy reign*, new edn, 4 vols. (1824) · C. Read, *Mr Secretary Walsingham and the policy of Queen Elizabeth*, 3 vols. (1925) · J. G. Retamal-Favereau, 'Anglo-Spanish relations, 1566-72: the mission of Don Guerau de Spes in London, with a preliminary consideration of that of Mr John Man in Madrid', DPhil diss., U. Oxf., 1972 · W. T. MacCaffrey, *Queen Elizabeth and the making of policy, 1572-1588* (1981) · S. Doran, *Monarchy and matrimony: the courtships of Elizabeth I* (1996) · M. Leimon and G. Parker, 'Treason and plot in Elizabethan diplomacy: the "fame of Sir Edward Stafford" reconsidered', *EngHR*, 111 (1996), 1134-58 · GEC, *Peerage* · inquisition post mortem, PRO, C142/735/89 · probate record, PRO, PROB 11/89/45 · parish register, Christ Church, Newgate, 27 January 1573 [marriage] · parish register, St Martin-in-the-Fields, London, 11 January 1612 [burial] · R. G. Lang, ed., *Two Tudor subsidy assessment rolls for the city of London, 1541 and 1581*, London RS, 29 (1993), 133

Archives BL, Cotton MSS, letters to Walsingham, etc. · Hatfield House, Hertfordshire, Cecil papers · PRO, SP 70, SP 78

Wealth at death PRO, C 142/735/89 · professed indebtedness; probate commission to a 'a creditor': probate record, PRO, PROB 11/89/45

Brooke, Henry, eleventh Baron Cobham (1564-1619), conspirator, was born on 22 November 1564 at Cobham Hall, Kent. The second son of William *Brooke, tenth Baron Cobham (1527-1597), and his second wife, Frances Newton (d. 1592), he was the godson of Henry Hastings, earl of Huntingdon, and of Henry Stuart, Lord Darnley, later king of Scotland. Upon the death of his brother Maximilian in France during July 1583 Henry became heir apparent to the barony. He travelled to Paris and the Low Countries in 1586-7, was entered at Gray's Inn by March 1588, and served as MP for Kent, 1588-9, and for Hedon in 1593, before succeeding his father on 6 March 1597. To the chagrin of Robert Devereux, earl of Essex, who had coveted the position, he was also granted his father's principal office, lord warden of the Cinque Ports. He was nominated a knight of the Garter on St George's day 1599.

Throughout the remaining years of her life Queen Elizabeth displayed a genuine affection for the new Lord Cobham, in part a manifestation of the regard in which she had held his loyal and hardworking father, in part a

reflection of the young man's ability to divert and charm. He sumptuously entertained the queen at his London house in Blackfriars on 16 June 1600, and won the hand of the redoubtable Frances Fitzgerald, dowager countess of Kildare (d. 1628) and daughter of Charles Howard, earl of Nottingham. The marriage was contracted on 27 May 1601. This charm, however, failed to captivate Essex, who called Cobham Sir John Falstaff, thought him a 'sycophant' (McKeen, 2.435), and bore him a lifelong grudge. It has likewise been lost on historians ever since. Anthony Weldon, who may have intended charity, described Cobham as 'but one degree from a fool' (A. Weldon, *Court and Character of King James*, 1817, 6), while Thomas Carte, entirely unsympathetic, portrayed him as 'a worthless mortal, without friends, credit or reputation' (T. Carte, *A General History of England*, 4 vols., 1747-55, 3.709). Such judgements are based (and then very selectively) on Cobham's behaviour in 1603, at the crisis of his life, and on surviving contemporary personal descriptions, almost without exception the work of his professed enemies. Prominent among these sources are the letters of Rowland Whyte, county agent of the Sidneys, Kentish neighbours and rivals of the Cobhams, and of Henry Howard, later earl of Northampton, who from motives of personal advancement indulged in the most blatant and exaggerated character assassination during a secret correspondence with James VI before 1603. Still more influential are the bitter comments of Sir Walter Ralegh when, under examination and at his trial, he was led to believe that Cobham had incriminated him in treason.

Cobham's assets, wealth, position, and the monarch's favour, explain a good deal of this hostility. Indeed, when Sir Edward Coke at Ralegh's trial described Cobham as an unwitting tool in Sir Walter's plans the prisoner rejected the interpretation out of hand. 'Whether to favour or to disable my Lord Cobham', he told Coke, 'you speak as you will of him. Yet he is not such a babe as you make him.' (*State trials*, 2.11). Rather more enlightening is another version of Ralegh's outburst: Cobham, he said, 'was as passionate a man as lived ... in his choller he had accused his friends of greater matters than these, and had been sorry for it afterwards' ('The arraignment and conviction of Sir Walter Rawleigh ... coppied by Sir Thomas Overbury', 1648, 13; BL, Harleian MS 39, fol. 283). It was, surely, Cobham's intimacy with the queen that attracted Ralegh, and it was that same intimacy which led a relative political lightweight into murky waters after the queen's death in 1603.

Cobham was at court when the end came. Like other important noblemen outside the privy council—principally his friend Henry Percy, earl of Northumberland, and Lord Thomas Howard—he was involved in the council's deliberations at this time of crisis. He signed the proclamation of King James on 24 March. Thereafter, however, he very rapidly grew disenchanted with the dawning Jacobean age. James gave him a dusty reception on the road to London. Like every other courtier he lived beyond his immediate means, and his debts were by now in excess of

£10,000. Court gossip referred to quarrels with his influential brother-in-law, the secretary, Sir Robert Cecil. While the surviving letters from Cobham among the Cecil papers at Hatfield House suggest a veneer of cordiality, they also show Cobham explicitly recognizing that his day had passed. Very sinister in the light of subsequent disclosures, these letters are full of his plans to travel abroad.

Then, in late June and early July, a plot was discovered in London. Several conspirators had schemed to kidnap King James in order to secure guarantees of toleration for the Catholics of England and the removal of ministers identified with Elizabethan persecution. The ringleaders were William Watson, a mentally unstable Catholic priest prominent among those who opposed the introduction of an archpriest, and Sir Griffin Markham, a Catholic country squire. Another principal participant in this so-called Bye plot was George *Brooke (1568–1603), Cobham's younger brother, and the close family connection inevitably bred suspicions against Cobham himself. Examined on 16 and 17 July Cobham denied any involvement in treason. On 17 July, however, George Brooke admitted that Cobham had known about the Bye. The following day, in a voluntary confession subsequently affirmed before eight privy councillors, Brooke declared that his brother had also been negotiating for the colossal sum of 600,000 crowns from Spain through the good offices of the archduke's envoy, Charles de Ligne, count of Aremberg, 'to assiste and furnishe a second action for the surprise of his majesty' (PRO, SP 14/2/64). This was the first disclosure of what came to be known as the Main plot, a treason which had had as its aim the overthrow and, by implication, the death of King James, and his replacement by Arabella Stuart.

These accusations were duly put to Cobham, who maintained that he had dealt with Aremberg only 'for dogges and amblinge mares and such like thinges' (PRO, SP 14/2/65). He was, nevertheless, committed to the Tower of London. His friend Ralegh had also fallen under suspicion, and Sir Walter, in an effort to display his own loyalty, suggested that Cobham should be questioned more closely on his links with Aremberg. Notified of this on 20 July, Cobham at once flew into a rage, denouncing Ralegh as the sole cause of all his troubles. In so doing he brought Ralegh to a trial for his life; although he retracted these passionate accusations almost at once, the damage had been done. Much later, after Ralegh's conviction as a traitor essentially on the basis of this retracted testimony, Cobham came up with a modified and much more convincing account of Ralegh's treason, a fact that has been substantially lost sight of over the years.

Although revenge and contrition led him into making contradictory statements on Ralegh's complicity, Cobham thereafter never denied his own involvement. As the various Bye plotters were examined, the case against him became ever more convincing. He admitted that he had solicited a large sum of money from Aremberg, anticipating 'generall discontentment' in England and scheming to spend the crowns 'as tyme and occasion was offered'

(PRO, SP 14/2/94). He admitted that his plans for foreign travel were laid with an eye to developing the scheme further, and he admitted knowledge of the Bye plot. In August he could not bring himself to deny that, in a conversation with Brooke, he had looked forward to a day when 'the kinge and his cubbs … were all taken away' (PRO, SP 14/3/16–18, 24).

When all was lost Cobham resolved to remain silent in the face of further questioning. On 7 September the investigating commissioner, Sir William Waad, described him as 'verry much distempered, and very penitent he kept not his first resolutions' (PRO, SP 14/3/63). Instead, the prisoner tried desperately to prepare some form of defence against his trial in a clandestine correspondence with his steward, Richard Mellersh. But the stratagem was discovered, further blighting his prospects.

With plague rife in London the trials of all leading participants in the Bye and Main treasons were held at Winchester during November 1603. George Brooke, Markham, Watson, and others were arraigned on the fifteenth, Ralegh two days later. Although he demanded repeatedly that Cobham should testify in person, and although he exhibited a letter from Cobham which exonerated him, Ralegh was trumped when the prosecution produced another statement by Cobham, accusing Sir Walter afresh. Cobham did not appear. On 25 November he was brought before his peers in the court of the lord high steward. He failed to match Ralegh's bravura performance, showing appropriate submission and much contrition, but making, in the jaundiced view of Dudley Carleton, then a household officer of the earl of Northumberland, 'such a fasting-dayes peece of worke of it that he discredited the place to which he was caled. Never was seene so poore and abject a spirit' (Bodl. Oxf., MS Carte 80, fol. 623v). In an effort to mitigate his offence Cobham tried to argue that although he may have considered acts of treason he had never the slightest intention of putting these thoughts into practice. But with the evidence of his own and so many other confessions laid effectively to his charge by Coke the English nobility rightly found him guilty.

Cobham and the Bye plotters Lord Grey and Sir Griffin Markham escaped execution on the scaffold, thanks to a last minute act of clemency from the king. Ralegh's life was also spared. Thereafter Cobham, Ralegh, and Grey remained in the Tower for many years. Cobham was attainted, and his achievement as KG was taken down and kicked out of St George's Chapel, Windsor, on 16 February 1604. Between writing pathetic appeals to James and Cecil, he devoted his time to study, translating Seneca and amassing a substantial library of more than 1000 volumes to that end; but he was no scholar and the results were meagre. Sick and aged he was permitted to spend the summer of 1617 at Bath, and when the same favour was granted him in the following year, no restriction was placed on his movements. He never again returned to the Tower. He appears to have suffered a stroke, dying impoverished, and 'rather of hunger than any more natural disease' (W. Scott, ed., *Secret History of the Court of James the*

First, 2 vols., 1811, 1.156), in a dingy apartment in the Minories, on 24 January 1619. It is, however, a matter of record that the crown paid him a generous monthly allowance until his death. According to Sir Thomas Wynne he died a Catholic, though this statement apparently lacks corroboration. His wife remained in Cobham Hall until her death in July 1628, having been allowed the house and other Cobham estates for her life by royal grant of 13 May 1604. The couple had no children. MARK NICHOLLS

Sources inventory of Cobham's house at Blackfriars, 1603, PRO, SP E178/3521 · Hatfield House, Hertfordshire, Salisbury–Cecil MSS · GEC, *Peerage* · D. McKeen, *A memory of honour: the life of William Brooke, Lord Cobham*, 2 vols. (1986) · M. Nicholls, 'Two Winchester trials: the prosecution of Henry, Lord Cobham, and Thomas, Lord Grey of Wilton, 1603', *Historical Research*, 68 (1995), 26–48 · M. Nicholls, 'Sir Walter Ralegh's treason: a prosecution document', *EngHR*, 110 (1995), 902–24 · *State trials* · *The letters of John Chamberlain*, ed. N. E. McClure, 2 vols. (1939) · 'The journal of Levinus Munck', ed. H. V. Jones, *EngHR*, 68 (1953), 234–58 · *The diary of John Manningham of the Middle Temple, 1602–1603*, ed. R. P. Sorlien (Hanover, NH, 1976)

Archives Harvard U., law school, terriers of his manors · Hatfield House, Hertfordshire, letters and papers | PRO, state papers, papers · Staffs. RO, corresp. with Sir John Levenson, instructions relating to household and estate, papers regarding forfeited estates

Likenesses group portrait, 1560–69 (as a child; with family); two versions, priv. coll. · R. Peake, portrait, *c*.1600 ('Procession portrait'), Sherborne Castle, Dorset · portrait (Henry Brooke?), priv. coll.; repro. in J. Winton, *Sir Walter Raleigh* (1975), 235

Brooke, Henry (1693x6–1757), schoolmaster, was the son of Anthony Brooke of Heddington, Wiltshire. He was educated at Shareton, Wiltshire, and at Oriel College, Oxford, whence he matriculated on 16 October 1713, possibly aged seventeen. He graduated BA in 1717, was made fellow in 1718, and proceeded MA in 1720. He was appointed high master of Manchester grammar school on 17 September 1727 and was elected a fellow of the collegiate church in Manchester, despite tory opposition. He was presented to the Oriel living of Tortworth, Gloucestershire, in 1730. On 8 January 1732 he married Thomasin Hunt, with whom he had one daughter, Thomasin, who was baptized at the collegiate church in Manchester on 28 October 1734.

Brooke had a chequered career as high master. When he arrived at Manchester there were about 120 pupils in the school, despite the neglect of his predecessor, John Richards. Brooke started a register and began to research into the school's history. His salary was increased to £200, but the number of new pupils began to fall dramatically and in February 1741 the feoffees of the school stopped paying him, on the grounds that he had neglected his duties, and locked him out of the high master's house. This situation appears to have continued for several years, for in June 1743 Brooke's salary was reduced to £10 and he resumed teaching only in 1744. He attempted to defend himself in the prefatory remarks to his end-of-term speech delivered on 13 December 1744 to the feoffees and to the school visitor, the warden of Manchester collegiate church, who was then Samuel Peploe the younger. He admitted that business had forced him to be absent from the school some years earlier and that he had considered

resigning, but argued that he had provided a substitute master with the feoffees' agreement. He pledged that 'now being at free liberty, I shall keep close to the school and the business thereof in person, as I have done for near three years last past, desiring nothing more than the benefit and improvement thereof' (Whatton, 106). Brooke's troubled relations with the feoffees may have been exacerbated by party political divisions, for his whig principles were at odds with the predominantly tory loyalties in Manchester. In the substance of his speech Brooke forcefully demonstrated the continuing importance and benefits of a classical curriculum.

An intake of thirty new boys in 1744–5 must have been welcomed by schoolmaster and feoffees alike but Brooke remained unsalaried until June 1747, when the feoffees paid him an extra £35 each quarter. In October 1747 he was awarded £490 in back pay but his return to his school residence was postponed until the following year. He finally resigned from Manchester grammar school on 21 July 1749 and retired to his living at Tortworth, where he also served as a magistrate.

Brooke published little. Apart from a few sermons and an edition of Demosthenes, published at Oxford in 1721, his principal work was *A Practical Essay Concerning Christian Peaceableness* (1740), which went through several editions. He also wrote a couple of lampoons, 'Lancashire Hob and the Quack Doctor', which were published together with John Collier's *A View of the Lancashire Dialect*. Brooke died on 21 August 1757, possibly aged sixty-three, and was buried at Tortworth church. His wife had predeceased him; he was survived by his daughter, who had married Thomas Maundrell. He bequeathed his library to his successors at Tortworth rectory. W. E. A. AXON, *rev.* S. J. SKEDD

Sources Foster, *Alum. Oxon.* · W. R. Whatton, *The history of Manchester School*, 2 pts (1833–4) · J. Bentley, *Dare to be wise: a history of the Manchester grammar school* (1990) · *Gloucestershire Notes and Queries*, 4 (1890), 95–100 · will, PRO, PROB 11/835, sig. 3 · A. A. Mumford, *The Manchester grammar school, 1515–1915* (1919) · IGI

Brooke, Henry (*c*.1703–1783), writer and playwright, was born in Rantavan, co. Cavan, the second of three sons of the Revd William Brooke (1669–1745) of Rantavan, rector of Moybolgue, Mullagh, Killinkere, Innismagrath, Kildalon, and Lavey, and Lettice Digby, daughter of Simon Digby, bishop of Elphin, and Elizabeth Westenra. The date of Henry's birth is variously given; his immatriculation at Trinity College, Dublin, in 1720 states him to be then 'in his seventeenth year'. Among Henry's earlier teachers was Dr Thomas Sheridan, the friend of Jonathan Swift, and a relation of the Brooke family.

Following his studies in Dublin, Brooke, who at an early age had shown signs of literary talent and of a tender-hearted disposition, was sent to London in 1724 to read law at the Temple. The death of a maternal aunt recalled him to Ireland and saw him appointed guardian over his twelve-year-old cousin Catherine Meares (1712/13–1773), of Meares Court, co. Meath. In the course of his guardianship a love affair developed, and the two young cousins married (clandestinely) some time before 1728. The marriage was to last until Catherine's death in 1773. No fewer than

Henry Brooke (*c.*1703–1783), by Andrew Miller, 1756 (after John Lewis, 1755)

twenty-three children were born, of whom only two, Arthur (captain in the East India Company) and Charlotte *Brooke, were to reach adulthood. Both husband and wife were later described to have been of frail build and pale complexion; two portraits of Henry show a fine-boned high-browed face with large eyes (one with a slight cast).

Brooke returned to London in 1728 to pursue his legal and his literary career. His didactic and religious poem *Universal Beauty* (1735), which established his initial fame, also testified to the increasing sentimentality of his religious feeling which later moved the Brooke household towards Methodism. In 1738 (after having once again returned to London following some seven years' practice as a chamber counsel in Dublin) Brooke published his translation of the first three books of Tasso's *Gerusalemme liberata*.

Brooke's literary bent was primarily sentimental and testified to the cult of tender feeling which began to spread in Europe about the mid-century; however, his writings of the 1740s are mostly conspicuous for their political charge. It was in particular his tragedy *Gustavus Vasa: the Deliverer of his Country* (1739) which propelled him into notoriety. In celebrating the career of the hero who liberated Sweden from Danish rule and was elected Swedish king in 1523, Brooke invoked a familiar icon in Enlightenment political thought—like Wilhelm Tell or William the Silent, men who were praised for their self-sacrificing heroism in defence of their country's liberties. In the political climate of the day, however, the chosen case was politically fraught. Danish and Swedish history had been used by 'Commonwealthsmen' such as Robert Molesworth to illustrate the danger of standing armies against

political liberty; the notion of an elective kingship as glorified in Gustav's career implied a whiggish sympathy for parliamentarian powers against royal prerogative; and in the conflicts of the time, the play was seen as criticism against Sir Robert Walpole and in favour of Frederick, prince of Wales, and the patriot whigs. Accordingly the play was prohibited, but the sale of printed copies was considerable. Matters were only made worse when it was indeed staged in Dublin (outside the English reach of the lord chancellor's prohibition); for in Dublin, where anti-Walpolian feeling was also beginning to run high and patriotism was spreading, the play generated the additional symbolism that Danish-Swedish tensions were interpreted along 'national' English-Irish lines. Later, Brooke's satirical opera *Jack the Giant-Queller* (1748) was to be suppressed after a single performance, likewise on the grounds of its political barbs.

At his wife's prudent behest, Brooke (who had indeed been in close touch with Pope, the prince of Wales, and the patriot whigs) withdrew from the London scene. He took the minor appointment of barrack-master in co. Kildare and occupied himself with occasional literary pursuits, increasingly of an antiquarian nature. Thus he adapted, for Ogle's reworking of the *Canterbury Tales*, the 'Man of Law's Tale'. This penchant for old 'Tales'—again, like Brooke's sentimentalism, a matter of rising fashion in the cultural climate of the day—led to his project of producing a narrative collection of ancient Irish history. For these 'Ogygian tales' he enlisted (or, more precisely, intended to plagiarize) the eminent Gaelic antiquarian Charles O'Conor of Belanagare. The project never went beyond the stage of a prospectus canvassing subscriptions; but as it stands it is one of the earliest indicators of a growing pattern in which native antiquarian lore was beginning to meet with positive interest from the protestant, Anglo-Irish settlers. This pattern was later to culminate in the bilingual anthology *Reliques of Irish Poetry* (1789) by Brooke's daughter Charlotte.

In 1745 Brooke's father died. Brooke moved to his late father's house in co. Cavan, where he led a very numerous joint household with the family of his brother Robert (1710–1784), who had married a cousin, Honor Digby. In the tense months of the Jacobite rising in Scotland, Brooke showed his whiggish, anti-Catholic colours by publishing a number of vehement pamphlets, the *Farmer's Letters*, warning the protestants of Ireland that the country's comparative quietude was but a matter of appearance, and that the disaffected Catholic natives were poised to join the Jacobite cause and rise in a genocidal re-enactment of the 1641 rising. Brooke's scaremongering must be seen against the background of his patriot whiggery, which combined a hatred of political oppression and corruption with a strenuously anti-Catholic protestant stance; a similar attitude is still evinced by his pamphlet *The Spirit of Party* (1754). However, the pamphlets were later an embarrassment both to his feeling and to his political judgement. The Jacobite rising, which in any case produced no upheaval in Ireland, was already collapsing when the pamphlets appeared; Ireland's Catholics had shown great forbearance at this juncture; and later on Brooke, almost in an act of expiation, hired out his pen to the Catholic Committee, feelingly setting forth the disabilities and grievances of Ireland's religious majority (*The Tryal of the Roman Catholics*, 1761).

Owing to financial difficulties, the Brooke family had meanwhile (*c*.1754) been forced to mortgage the Rantavan estate and had moved back from co. Cavan to co. Kildare (Daisy Park, near Sallins, rented from his cousin Digby of Landenstown). Relations with the family of Henry's brother Robert remained close, since Robert had likewise moved to co. Kildare. Among Robert's offspring, Henry's nephews Henry *Brooke (1738–1806) and Robert *Brooke (1744–1811) deserve mention. The former was an important propagandist of Methodism in Ireland, the latter a successful officer in the employ of the East India Company, who founded the industrial village of Prosperous, co. Kildare, helped to pay off the mortgage on the Rantavan estate, and eventually became governor of St Helena.

Brooke's main literary fame came to rest on a novel which he started late in life, *The Fool of Quality* (5 vols., 1766–70). Like Goldsmith's *The Vicar of Wakefield* (1766) or Henry Mackenzie's *The Man of Feeling* (1771), the novel exemplifies a genre which flourished at the time, linked both to Rousseau's *Nouvelle Héloïse* and to Goethe's *Werther*, but also firmly rooted in the British traditions of Francis Hutcheson's benevolent moral philosophy, the patriotic cult of virtue, and the popular genre of the sentimental comedy. Already in 1747 Brooke had added a 'Prologue' to Edward Moore's *The Foundling*, in which he gave the poetics of sentimental narrative in a nutshell:

> He forms Model of a virtuous Soul,
> And gives you more of Moral than of Sport,
> He rather aims to draw the melting Sigh,
> Or steal the pitying Tear from Beauty's Eye;
> To touch the Strings, that humanize our Kind,
> Man's sweetest Strain, the Music of the Mind.

Accordingly, the sentimental novel is episodic in nature and involves, amid a plethora of digressions, a succession of incidents around a main character who is marked by innocence and philanthropy to the point of being 'a child in the drama of the world'. The genre, with its cloying profusion of sympathetic tears, instinctive goodwill, and affecting scenes, was indeed short-lived; but Brooke's novel maintained some posthumous fame as a sentimental variation of the *Pilgrim's Progress*. John Wesley edited a shortened version under the title *Henry, Earl of Moreland* (1781), long a classic among Methodists; a full re-edition of *The Fool of Quality* was brought out in 1859 by Charles Kingsley.

About 1770 Brooke, though successful as the author of *The Fool of Quality*, had lost much of his literary network owing to a quarrel with his erstwhile friend and patron Garrick. The family moved back from co. Kildare to co. Cavan and took up residence in a lodge (Longfield, Anglicized from the Gaelic toponym *Corfoddy*) near the family estate of Rantavan. By this time, Brooke was already showing signs of senile decay; his daughter Charlotte found it

necessary, in her edition of her father's *Poetical Works* (1792), to prune the later portions of *The Fool of Quality* which began to show excessive tendency to rambling digression. Brooke's spirits were wholly broken when his wife, Catherine, died in 1773. He spent the last ten years of his life nursed by his daughter Charlotte and died in Dublin on 10 October 1783. He was buried in his father's old churchyard at Mullagh, co. Cavan, about twelve days later.

While *The Fool of Quality* is now seen at best as a curious example of English sentimentalism, Henry Brooke's continuing interest nowadays is mainly based on his manifold connections with the moral and political life of his times. A representative of the tightly-knit Anglo-Irish class of the mid-eighteenth century and a man of letters trying his hand at various literary genres, he had a sentimentalism which could lead to a positive appreciation of Gaelic folk life and antiquity and to a libertarian defence of patriot principles, while remaining true to a staunchly protestant outlook never wholly free from anti-Catholic reservations. The result of this may seem hybrid and contradictory nowadays, but is probably exemplary of whiggish protestant opinion in a period of tension and transition.   JOEP LEERSSEN

Sources E. A. Baker, 'Introduction', in H. Brooke, *The fool of quality* (1906), v–xxi · H. M. Scurr, 'Henry Brooke', PhD diss., University of Minnesota, 1922 · *DNB* · C. Brooke, 'An account of Henry Brooke, Esq', *The poetical works of Henry Brooke, Esq*, 4 vols., 3rd edn (1792), 1.iii–xix · C. H. Wilson, *Brookiana*, 2 vols. (1804) · L. Davis, 'Birth of the nation: gender and writing in the work of Henry and Charlotte Brooke', *Eighteenth-Century Life*, 18/1 (1994), 27–47 · B. Vickers, 'Introduction', in H. Mackenzie, *The man of feeling* (1967), vii–xxiv
Likenesses A. Miller, engraving, 1756 (after J. Lewis, 1755), NG Ire. [*see illus.*] · J. Armytage, engraving, repro. in H. Brooke, *The fool of quality* (1859) · R. Clamp, stipple (after H. Brooke), BM, NPG; repro. in S. Harding, *Biographical Mirrour* (1793) · etching (after engraving by A. Miller), repro. in *Dublin University Magazine* (1852) · watercolour (after Thurston), repro. in Brooke, 'An account of Henry Brooke, Esq'

Brooke, Henry (1738–1806), history painter, was born in co. Cavan, Ireland, in November 1738 and baptized that month at St Paul's Church, Dublin, one of the five children (there were four sons and one daughter) of Robert Brooke, artist, and his wife, Honor Brooke. His parents were the son and daughter of two brothers who were clergymen of the established church. Brooke's paternal grandfather was the Revd William Brooke of Rantavan, rector of the Union of Mullogh, in the diocese of Kilmore. Brooke was a pious child who was deeply affected by the death of one of his younger brothers. About the age of fifteen he was sent to Dublin to study painting. Four years later he returned to his family and moved with them in 1758 to Killibegs, co. Kildare, about 15 miles from Dublin. On moving to London in 1761 he became an artist of some repute. After periods of dissipation a visit to the Tabernacle at Moorfields led to his adherence to evangelical Christianity. In April 1765 he joined the Methodists, having corresponded with Wesley from 1762. He was later to become Wesley's host during the minister's visit to Dublin. Brooke remained in England until his marriage on 20

April 1767 to Anne Kirchoffer, which took place at St Paul's Church, Dublin. Of their eleven children, their son William Henry *Brooke (1772–1860) became a portrait painter and illustrator. In Dublin he abandoned painting until an unfortunate speculation forced him to resume his original profession.

In 1770 Brooke became a drawing master at Stafford Street, Dublin, and exhibited *The Raising of Lazarus* at the Society of Artists, William Street, Dublin. His work, however, was principally displayed in the decoration of Roman Catholic chapels. In 1776 he sent a mythological painting to the Society of Artists, London. His portrait of his uncle the poet Henry *Brooke (c.1703–1783) was engraved by G. Pye in 1821 for B. W. Procter, *Effigies poeticae* (1824). His cousin, Charlotte *Brooke was the author of *Reliques of Irish Poetry*. Brooke died in Dublin on 6 October 1806. His son-in-law and memoirist, Isaac D'Olier, recorded that Brooke 'was a giant in the spiritual combat, whose strength was daily renewed by his continual waiting upon God' (D'Olier, 147–8).

GORDON GOODWIN, rev. ASIA HAUT

Sources W. G. Strickland, *A dictionary of Irish artists*, 2 vols. (1913) · Redgrave, *Artists* · Bryan, *Painters* · Waterhouse, *18c painters* · F. Lewis, *A dictionary of British historical painters* (1979) · IGI · I. D'Olier, ed., *Memoirs of the life of the late excellent and pious Mr Henry Brooke* (1816)

Brooke, Henry, Baron Brooke of Cumnor (1903–1984), politician, was born at 40 Wellington Square, Oxford, on 9 April 1903, the younger son of (Leonard) Leslie *Brooke (1862–1940), an artist, who was the author and illustrator of numerous children's books, and his wife, Sybil Diana Brooke (1870–1957), daughter of the Revd Stopford Augustus *Brooke. After attending preparatory schools he was educated at Marlborough College and at Balliol College, Oxford (1922–6), where he gained a first in classical moderations (1924) and seconds in mathematical moderations (1924) and *literae humaniores* and was a tutor in philosophy (1926–7). Encouraged by Alexander Dunlop Lindsay, the master of Balliol, he spent a year (1927–8) working in a Quaker settlement for the unemployed in the Rhondda valley. After spending a year on *The Economist* he joined the Conservative Research Department, as a founder member, in 1929 and became its deputy director (1935–7). On 22 April 1933 he married Barbara Muriel Mathews [see below]; they had two sons and two daughters. She was herself a woman of outstanding political acumen.

Brooke was elected to Hampstead borough council in 1936 and Conservative MP for Lewisham West in a by-election of 1938. On 7 May 1940 he made an ardent defence of Chamberlain in the parliamentary debate that brought Churchill to Downing Street. Following Brooke's defeat at Lewisham in 1945 he was recruited as the last deputy chairman of the Southern Railway Company before nationalization (1946–8). He was a member of the church assembly during the 1940s, the Central Housing Advisory Committee (1944–54), and the court of London University (1947). Following election to London county council in 1945 he served as leader of its Conservative group (1945–51). He was returned as Conservative MP for

Hampstead in 1950, but continued to serve on the London county council until 1955 and on Hampstead borough council until 1957.

In 1954 Brooke was appointed to the most influential ministerial post outside the cabinet, financial secretary to the Treasury. 'He is a very virtuous and conscientious man though unfortunately no speaker', the government's economic adviser noted (Cairncross, 2.95). On the formation of the Macmillan administration in 1957 Brooke was promoted to the cabinet as minister of housing and local government, and as minister for Welsh affairs. It fell to him to implement two pieces of legislation enacted in 1956: the Clean Air Act and the more contentious Rent Act. Brooke was transferred in 1961 to the new post of chief secretary to the Treasury (retaining his cabinet status). Public expenditure, the civil service, the universities, and the arts became his responsibilities. To provide him with a salary he was additionally appointed paymaster-general. His hard-working and orthodox character was appreciated in the Treasury, where he helped to prepare some unpopular policies associated with the chancellor of the exchequer, Selwyn Lloyd. By 1962 Harold Evans, the prime minister's public relations adviser, considered him a contender for the premiership: 'he is much more human, much less dour and much less metallic than opinion believes' (Evans, 187).

Macmillan's 'night of the long knives' resulted in Brooke's appointment as home secretary in July 1962. Instead of painstaking work with facts, statistics, and long-term treasury strategies he was plunged into deciding urgent and emotive issues at the Home Office. His declared priorities were to confront the crime wave and to reduce prison overcrowding by a new building programme; but his deliberative pragmatism was ill-suited to his new responsibilities. Brooke's twenty-seven months as home secretary proved peculiarly unsuccessful. He was involved in one rumpus after another, and became widely reviled. His difficulties were aggravated by the stubborn and authoritarian temper of the officials who advised him, and he was unlucky that his difficulties at the Home Office coincided with the heyday of the satire boom. He was pilloried in *Private Eye* and on the television programme *That Was The Week That Was*, which broadcast a biting sketch, on 30 March 1963, 'This is your life, Henry Brooke' (Carpenter, 253).

The first controversy, in July 1962, concerned a deportation order issued against Carmen Bryan, a Jamaican who had been convicted of shoplifting goods valued at £2. Then in August Brooke banned an American Nazi from entering Britain, and was dismayed when the man nevertheless appeared in Gloucestershire. In September came the *cause célèbre* of Dr Robert Soblen, who had been convicted in the USA of spying for Russia, and who slashed his wrists while on an Israeli airliner that then landed in London. The Home Office resolved to hand him to the Americans, although his offence was not covered by the Extradition Act. This controversial decision was forestalled by Soblen's fatal overdose of barbiturates, which somehow reached him in prison. In 1963 Brooke's reputation was further damaged by his handling of the case of Anthony Enahoro, a Nigerian chief detained under the Fugitive Offenders Act of 1881. After five angry parliamentary debates, and bitter criticism that Enahoro had not been granted political asylum, he was returned to Nigeria in May. Meanwhile the hapless Brooke had been further discomfited when the Home Office deported the American comedian Lennie Bruce twice within three days (April 1963).

In March 1963 Brooke met Sir Roger Hollis of MI5 and Sir Joseph Simpson of the Metropolitan Police to discuss rumours surrounding the war minister, John Profumo, whom Brooke's wife later described as 'a man who has sinned against our standards' (*The Times*, 5 Sept 2000). Brooke wished to prevent Profumo's associate Stephen Ward from making disclosures to Labour politicians or journalists, and instigated a wide-ranging police investigation. Ward was arrested on trumpery charges in June and after a show trial committed suicide, like Soblen, with barbiturates.

The state visit of King Paul and Queen Frederica of Greece proved a policing fiasco. After a noisy demonstration (10 July 1963) Brooke fulminated, 'The Queen of England has been booed tonight and I am furious' (Booker, 184). He told his constituents that 'a handful of communists, anarchists, beatniks, and members of the Campaign for Nuclear Disarmament' was destroying Britain's reputation for hospitality. 'The demonstrators were shouting "fascist police" at masses of splendid London policemen who had to be taken off their proper work of fighting crime to … quell their filthy abuse' (*The Times*, 15 July 1963, 7c). In fact, these officers included a mentally ill sergeant from Savile Row police station, Harold Challenor, who planted half a brick on one of those arrested and together with other officers committed perjury to convict demonstrators. Although these improprieties were swiftly revealed, Brooke prevaricated until some of the innocent had endured prison for over a year. It had become evident that he was 'in the wrong job … an almost painfully straightforward man who worries his way ponderously through to his conclusions and then clings to them like grim death' (Watt, 693). His public statements often sounded dreary or petulant, and on such subjects as the Commonwealth Immigration Act were thought by some to be misleading. His unimaginative approach was typified by his insistence that the Royal Philharmonic Orchestra was not entitled to its prefix 'royal'. He opposed all manner of 'sleazy stuff' (*Hansard 5C*, 694, 30 April 1964, 605). Accordingly he declined to reform the criminal laws prohibiting homosexuality and prostitution, despite the recommendations of Sir John Wolfenden's committee. 'Public opinion is not prepared for a change', he declared. 'At this time, when a growing number of people feel free to do anything not specifically condemned by Act, we should be slow to loosen up' (Raison). The latter remark was characteristic of his outlook.

To rally support for the Douglas-Home government before the general election of 1964 Brooke set out to prove that the Conservatives 'mean what we say about helping the young of our country to grow up straight' (Brooke to Sir A. Douglas-Home, 18 Feb 1964, PRO Prem 11/4848). This process began with the Drugs (Prevention of Misuse) Act of 1964, whereby the unauthorized possession of amphetamines became a criminal offence. Informed critics condemned the act as hurried and ill-conceived, and indeed it proved counter-productive: the illicit supply of amphetamines flourished, and they became the most common illicitly used stimulant in Britain for the rest of the twentieth century. Brooke's separate Dangerous Drugs Act of 1964 created a new offence, the cultivation of cannabis, and attempted to target people who permitted cannabis to be consumed on their premises. After drugs Brooke turned to pornography. During June 1964 the Home Office rushed through parliament a new Obscene Publications Act as well as the Malicious Damage Act, directed against mods and rockers.

The Conservatives lost the general election of 1964, and Brooke left office. His unpopularity resulted in a massive swing against him in Hampstead. Subsequently, during the general election of 1966, a concerted campaign from within and without the constituency encompassed his defeat. Some months later, in July, he had the consolation of a life peerage. Previously he had been sworn to the privy council (1955) and been made a Companion of Honour (1964). He was a quiet, friendly, honest, and steadfast man, who was regarded by his detractors as a cruel, deceitful ogre. His gentle, affectionate memoir of his father *Leslie Brooke and Johnny Crow* (1982) belies the public's view of him. Brooke, who latterly suffered from Parkinson's disease, died on 29 March 1984, at home at the Glebe House, Mildenhall, Wiltshire, and was cremated on 2 April.

Brooke's wife, **Barbara Muriel Brooke** [*née* Mathews], Baroness Brooke of Ystradfellte (1908–2000), politician, was born on 14 January 1908 at Llan-wern, Monmouthshire, the youngest child in the family of four daughters and one son of the Revd Alfred Augustus Mathews (1864–1946), Anglican clergyman, and his wife, Ethel Frances (*d.* 1951), daughter of Dr Edward Beynon Evans, of Swansea. She was educated at Queen Anne's School, Caversham, and Gloucester Training College for Domestic Science before teaching in secondary schools. Her marriage, based on shared religious values, was very happy. She was a Hampstead borough councillor from 1948 to 1965, and joint vice-chairman of the Conservative Party Organization from 1954 to 1964, in which post she tried (largely unsuccessfully) to increase the number of women parliamentary candidates. Appointed DBE in 1960 and made a life peer in 1964, in the Lords she was front-bench spokesman on welfare. In 1969 she was elected president of the National Union of Conservative Associations. From 1960 to 1978 she was chairman of the governing body of Godolphin and Latymer School, Hammersmith, and was instrumental in organizing the school's withdrawal from the state sector, in face of the inner London education authority's plans for making it comprehensive in 1977. She was also active on numerous local and national committees. In the 1970s she withdrew from national public life to nurse her husband, but continued active in village affairs at Mildenhall, Wiltshire. She died on 1 September 2000 at Marlborough, Wiltshire, and was survived by her four children. Her elder son, Peter (b. 1934), was a Conservative MP and secretary of state for Northern Ireland (1989–92) and for national heritage (1992–4), while her younger son, Henry (b. 1936), became a lord justice of appeal in 1996, having been knighted in 1988.

RICHARD DAVENPORT-HINES

Sources The Times (30–31 March 1984) · The Times (2 April–3 Feb 1984) · The Times (5 Sept 2000) · DNB · T. Raison, 'Crime is the priority: the new home secretary outlines his approach', New Society (4 Oct 1962), 20 · H. Brooke, Leslie Brooke and Johnny Crow (1982) · R. Davenport-Hines, The pursuit of oblivion (2001) · H. Evans, Downing Street diary (1981) · The Robert Hall diaries, 1954–61, ed. A. Cairncross, 2 (1991) · P. Knightley and C. Kennedy, An affair of state (1987) · D. Watt, 'Brooke's last stand', The Spectator (31 May 1963), 693 · C. Booker, The neophiliacs (1969) · B. Levin, The pendulum years (1970) · R. Bevins, The greasy pole (1965) · J. Ramsden, The winds of change: Macmillan to Heath, 1957–1975 (1996) · D. Frost and C. Booker, 'This is your life, Henry Brooke', That was the week that was, ed. D. Frost and N. Sherrin (1963), 113–14 · H. Carpenter, That was the satire that was (2000) · b. cert. · The Independent (8 Sept 2000) · Burke, Peerage · WW (2000) [Barbara Muriel Brooke]

Archives BL, letters to Albert Mansbridge, Add. MS 65253 · NL Wales, corresp. with Huw T. Edwards · NL Wales, letters to Thomas Iorwerth Ellis · PRO, Home Office papers; Ministry of Housing papers; premier's papers; Treasury papers | FILM BBC WAC · IWM FVA, actuality footage | SOUND BLPES, British Oral Archive of Political and Administrative History, interview, 1980

Wealth at death £194,455: probate, 27 July 1984, CGPLA Eng. & Wales

Brooke, Henry James (1771–1857), crystallographer, was born on 25 May 1771 at Exeter into a family manufacturing broadcloth. After studying for the bar he entered business successively in the Spanish wool trade, South American mining, and as co-founder and secretary of the London Life Assurance Association. Throughout a busy commercial career he seems to have organized his leisure time very efficiently, his initial collecting in natural history and art giving way to scientific endeavour as his mineralogical interest prevailed. In 1809 W. H. Wollaston (1766–1828) had invented the 'reflective' goniometer, which provided a precise tool for the measurement of angles between faces of crystals. Brooke became increasingly respected in the application of this new crystallographic practice, and was elected to the Geological Society in 1815, the Linnean Society in 1818, and to the Royal Society in 1819.

In 1823 Brooke published his Familiar Introduction to Crystallography, a work strongly influenced by the concepts of Haüy, in particular that of a primary form representing the shape of the integrant molecules from which a crystal is built, the primaries being modified by secondary planes formed by omission or addition of rows ('decrements') of molecules. His main innovation was the introduction of spherical trigonometry into the calculation of interfacial angles, a practice whose utility could hardly be appreciated fully until crystal faces came to be plotted as poles on a projection. As the first crystallography textbook in English the Familiar Introduction played a significant part in awakening interest in a science hitherto mainly the preserve of French and German workers; crystal measurement became popular and sales of the Wollaston goniometer were promoted by the instrument maker Cary through a partial reprint of Brooke's work.

Brooke saw crystallography as primarily a determinative tool—allowing the identification of mineral species from the characters of their crystalline forms. In this he preached by example, identifying many 'new' minerals, of which heulandite, monticellite, thomsonite, and whewellite came to be recognized as important species. Brooke also thought that the uniqueness of individual crystal forms could be useful to the chemist, and to this end during the 1820s he embarked on extensive measurements of crystals of artificial salts. The concept of isomorphism, the assumption of identical forms by different chemical compounds, seemed to threaten the utility of this work; Brooke's attack on isomorphism led to a brief brush with the redoubtable Whewell, then (1831) still professor of mineralogy at Cambridge.

The accession to the Cambridge chair in 1832 of Whewell's successor, W. H. Miller, ushered in a new phase of Brooke's scientific career. A strong bond was established between the older and the younger man and a copious correspondence ensued. Even before the 1839 publication of Miller's epic Treatise on Crystallography Brooke was experimenting with the new Cambridge mathematical approach. The appearance then of a rather backward-looking article by Brooke on crystallography in the Encyclopaedia metropolitana (1845), with all the old paraphernalia of primary forms and laws of decrement, seems to have been quite anachronistic; it may have been written a decade earlier. Certainly by the mid-1840s Brooke, now retired from the cares of commercial employment, had revived an older ambition to produce a new edition of the influential An Elementary Introduction to the Knowledge of Mineralogy first published by W. Phillips in 1816. Miller, having agreed to a collaborative venture, came gradually to dominate; the resulting book, published as An Elementary Introduction to Mineralogy in 1852, contains a fulsome disclaimer by Brooke of any substantive role. Miller indeed seems to have provided the lion's share of formal crystallographic exposition and crystal measurements, but Brooke, who wrote most of the mineralogic text and organized the whole, was surely unduly self-effacing in presenting this first mineralogical embrace of the Miller index notation.

Brooke, by 1852 an octogenarian, found failing eyesight and difficulty with writing increasingly restrictive. No longer able to measure crystals himself, he maintained, with the help of his son Charles *Brooke (1804–1879), surgeon and meteorologist, vigorous correspondence with those who could. He read his final work, a substantial and original paper on crystal isomorphism, to the Royal Society in 1856; its publication in the Philosophical Transactions was almost coincidental with his death on 26 June 1857 at his home, 19 Clapham Rise, Lambeth. Nothing is known about Brooke's wife.

GRAHAM CHINNER

Sources J. E. Portlock, *Quarterly Journal of the Geological Society*, 14 (1858), xliv–xlv · H. J. Brooke, *A familiar introduction to crystallography* (1823) · H. J. Brooke and W. H. Miller, *An elementary introduction to mineralogy* (1852) · W. Whewell, 'Report on the present state of mineralogy', *Report of the British Association for the Advancement of Science* (1832) · H. J. Brooke and W. H. Miller, correspondence, U. Cam., department of earth sciences · W. C. Smith, 'Early mineralogy in Great Britain and Ireland', *Bulletin of the British Museum (Natural History)* [Historical Series], 6 (1977–80), 49–74 · P. G. Embrey, introduction, in R. P. Greg and W. G. Lettsom, *Manual of the mineralogy of Great Britain and Ireland* (1977) · d. cert.
Archives U. Cam., department of earth sciences, corresp., mineral collection | U. Cam., department of earth sciences, corresp. with W. H. Miller

Brooke, Henry William (1771/2–1842), civil servant, attended none of the leading schools, nor did he go to university, and his origins and much of his career are shrouded in mystery. For several years he drew a salary as distributor of stamps in Ireland, but it seems unlikely that he was one of the Irish Brookes. He was probably from Kent; at any rate he owned property in Deal and Walmer, and was married at Davington, Kent, on 2 March 1799 to Catherine (1769/70–1825), daughter of the Revd John Tucker, rector of Ringwould, near Walmer. A letter of 1809 refers to their five children.

Brooke's claim to noteworthiness rests on his role in the alien office. Established in 1793 by the Alien Act of that year, the alien office was a branch of the Home Office which ostensibly acted as the administrative centre for the regulation of the conduct of foreigners resident in Britain. In reality, it co-ordinated counter-revolutionary efforts against 'disaffected' Britons as well as suspect foreigners.

The secretiveness of the alien office's work makes it difficult to provide details of Brooke's activities: 'My duties have ever been of the most confidential nature', he wrote to R. B. Jenkinson, second earl of Liverpool, in 1809. Brooke appears to have joined the alien office about 1796, and he was clerk from about 1798 to 1813. He served briefly (1802–3) as acting superintendent, bridging the gap between the departure of Charles Flint and the appointment of John Reeves. Brooke was employed in Manchester, and then in Ireland at the time of the rebellion. After his return to England, he was involved in the interrogation of François Barthélemy, the former French chargé d'affaires in Britain, who fled from France in 1799. Two years later, Brooke was given responsibility for the Kent coast from Dover to Whitstable, with the task of preventing any communication between the French and their English sympathizers. To Lord Liverpool he hinted subsequently at the difficulties in 'serving the ends of Government in such a situation of delicacy with limited Legal powers'.

Ill health obliged Brooke to retire in 1813. His salary at this time was £1000, and upon leaving the service he received a pension of £600 p.a. He devoted his remaining years to Kentish affairs: he was an active local magistrate; he promoted a loyal address to the king from the inhabitants of Walmer in December 1820; and in 1826 he was one of the main subscribers to the enlargement of Walmer church. Brooke died at Walmer on 15 April 1842, aged seventy.   STEPHEN CONWAY, *rev.*

Sources 'Estimates … miscellaneous services for the year ending 31 March 1840', *Parl. papers* (1839), 31.656, no. 142-III · *GM*, 1st ser., 69 (1799), 251 · *GM*, 2nd ser., 17 (1842), 564 · C. R. S. Elvin, *Records of Walmer* (1890) · *Mémoires de Barthélemy*, ed. J. de Dampierre (1914) · R. R. Nelson, *The home office, 1782–1801* (1969) · P. Polden, 'John Reeves', *Journal of Legal History*, 3 (1982), 31–51 · R. Wells, *Insurrection: the British experience, 1795–1803* (1983) · C. W. Chalkin, ed., *Maidstone gaol order book, 1805–1823* (1984) · BL, Liverpool MSS · BL, Peel MSS · d. cert.

Brooke, Humphrey (*bap.* 1618, *d.* 1693), physician and Leveller, was baptized on 29 March 1618 at St Mary Woolnoth, London, the son of Robert Brooke, gentleman, of London. He attended Merchant Taylors' School from 1632 to 1636, and matriculated from St John's College, Oxford, on 12 May 1637, where he graduated BA (1640) and BM (1646). Brooke practised in London from about 1646, by which time he was styling himself gentleman, but lived in the Moorfields home of William *Walwyn, his future father-in-law, from about 1641 until at least 1649. It was almost certainly through Walwyn that he became acquainted with the religious controversialist Clement Writer, who would leave Brooke £5 in his will, and the Levellers and their campaign for greater religious and civil liberty. Brooke is possibly the man of that name who on 14 December 1648 attended the Whitehall debates, the discussions among the Levellers, army, and London clergy on the settlement of the nation through a written constitution, *The Agreement of the People*. After *The Agreement* was abandoned and the Levellers found themselves reviled by the gathered churches and the military government Brooke responded to the attacks in *Walwins Wiles* and the two parts of *The Discoverer* by defending the Levellers, and Walwyn in particular, in *The Charity of Church-Men* and *The Craftsmens Craft* (both 1649). He was not among the Levellers arrested in 1649 for criticizing the new regime, but in the same year Thomas Scott, the Commonwealth's intelligencer, considered him one of the principal Levellers who remained at liberty and questioned him regarding their activities. However, with the disintegration of the Levellers he seems to have turned his energies to his medical career.

On 4 March 1650 Brooke married Elizabeth (*bap.* 1631, *d.* in or before 1667), daughter of William Walwyn and Anne Gundell. In the same year he published *A Conservatory of Health*, in which he offered lay people advice on preserving good health, in language which would enable 'the plain and intelligible conveyance of our minds one to another', spelt out the need for such a book to be available in English, and contrasted his open approach to the dissemination of medical knowledge with that of the more conservative elements of the profession. There is, he said, 'more need of furnishing every man with a Manuall, that might always be ready at hand' (preface). By 1654 he was assisting his father-in-law with his medical interests, whose 'vitae' and aromatic spirits could be purchased from Brooke's house in Duke's Place, Aldgate. Proceeding DM from

Oxford in 1660, the degree was incorporated at Cambridge in 1684. In 1665 Brooke published *Cautionary Tales for Preventing the Sickness*; in the previous year William Bagwell had dedicated his *Sphynx Thebanus with his Oedipus, or, Ingenious Riddles* to Brooke, whom he described as his 'approved good friend and patron' (Wood, *Ath. Oxon.*, 2.221). After the death of his wife Brooke married, by a licence of 27 September 1667, Elizabeth Denton of London; the couple had at least two sons, Humphrey (1667/8–1718) and Benjamin (*bap.* 1674, *d.* in or after 1690). He was elected a fellow of the Royal College of Physicians in 1674 and served as censor in 1675, 1680, 1681, 1684, and 1692; elect, 1697; consiliarius, 1693.

In 1681 Brooke published *The Durable Legacy*, an advice book addressed to his children. He recommended that the boys should look to medicine as a career, for as well as being of constant value, it was 'in the middle region, not too high for the converse of the meanest, not too low for the respect of the greatest'. A sign that he still retained some of his old radical spirit emerged when he advised his sons that if they did not become physicians, they should at least avoid 'being engaged in any thing that is vexatious to the people, I had rather you should be Coblers, than Excise-men, Sergeants, Promoters, Projectors, or any other professions that depends not upon honest business' (p. 156).

Brooke died, worth some £60,000, it is said, on 9 December 1693 in Leadenhall Street, London, and was buried in the church of St Andrew Undershaft. He left three sons, of whom Humphrey followed his father's advice and pursued a career in medicine, and three daughters.

MICHAEL BEVAN and P. R. S. BAKER

Sources Wood, *Ath. Oxon.* · Foster, *Alum. Oxon.* · Munk, *Roll* · H. Brooke, *The charity of church-men, or, A vindication of Mr William Walwyn* (1649) · H. Brooke, *The durable legacy* (1681) · H. Brooke, *Hygieinē, or, A conservatory of health* (1650) · P. R. S. Baker, 'The origins and early history of the Levellers, *c.*1636–*c.*1647', PhD diss., U. Cam. [in preparation] · *The writings of William Walwyn*, ed. J. R. McMichael and B. Taft (1989) · W. Haller and G. Davies, eds., *The Leveller tracts, 1647–1653* (1944) · *The Clarke papers*, ed. C. H. Firth, [new edn], 2 vols. in 1 (1992) · *DNB* · *IGI* · will, PRO, PROB 11/417, fols. 218r–220v · Venn, *Alum. Cant.* · C. H. Firth, 'Thomas Scot's account of his actions as intelligencer during the Commonwealth', *EngHR*, 12 (1897), 116–26

Wealth at death £60,000: Wood, *Ath. Oxon.*

Brooke, Sir James (1803–1868), army officer and first raja of Sarawak, was born at Secrore, a suburb of Benares, India, on 29 April 1803, the second son of Thomas Brooke (1760–1835), chief judge of the East India Company's court at Moorshabad, and his Scottish second wife, Anna Maria (*née* Stuart). He remained in India until the age of twelve when he was sent to stay with his paternal grandmother in Reigate. His only formal schooling was as a boarder at Norwich grammar school, which he hated and ran away from after two or three years. When his parents returned to live in Bath, he joined them there and was placed under the charge of a hapless tutor. He was a spoiled child, shy but wilful. On 11 May 1819, aged sixteen, he entered the service of the East India Company as an ensign attached to

Sir James Brooke (1803–1868), by Sir Francis Grant, 1847

the 2/6th regiment Bengal native infantry, and transferred to 18th native infantry in 1824. Promoted lieutenant in August 1821 and sub-assistant commissary-general in May 1822, he commanded a troop of irregular cavalry in the First Anglo-Burmese War and was seriously wounded in one lung during an action at Rangpur, Assam, on 27 January 1825. He was awarded a wound pension of £70 per annum. There is no truth in the often-repeated story that the wound he suffered in Burma was to the genitals, and it may be significant that during his long recuperation at Bath he was briefly engaged, possibly to the daughter of a Bath clergyman.

Early career Unable to reach India before the expiry of his five years' leave, Brooke resigned his commission and returned home in 1831 on the *Castle Huntley* after visiting China, Penang, Malacca, and Singapore. Presumably about then he had the idea of exploring the Indian archipelago. In 1834 he purchased a brig, the *Findlay*, and made an unsuccessful trading voyage to China. There was reason now to accept what his father had told him earlier: 'about trade you are quite ignorant, and … there is no pursuit for which you are less suited' (Tarling, 15).

After his father died on 12 December 1835, leaving him an unencumbered £30,000, Brooke purchased a schooner of 142 tons which he named the *Royalist*. After a practice voyage in the Mediterranean in late 1836, he sailed on 16 December 1838 for Singapore. In October 1838 he had published a prospectus of his voyage, reflecting the influence of George Windsor Earl's *The Eastern Seas* (1837) and indicating his desire to counter Dutch influence in those areas of the eastern archipelago not divided into clear spheres of influence by the Anglo-Dutch treaty of 1824. His primary focus of interest was Marudu Bay in what is now Sabah, which he saw as one of a string of British settlements linking Singapore with Port Essington in northern Australia. He saw himself as taking up the mantle of Alexander Dalrymple (1737–1808), hydrographer, and Sir Stamford Raffles (1781–1826), the founder of Singapore. The *Royalist* was armed—with six 6-pounders and swivels, flew the white ensign of the Royal Yacht Squadron, and so resembled a small warship.

In Singapore Brooke learned that the profitable antimony trade with Sarawak had been disrupted by a local rebellion against the sultan of Brunei, who exercised sovereignty there in the form of tax-collecting. Entrusted by Governor Bonham of Singapore with the mission of thanking the sultan of Brunei's uncle, Raja Muda Hassim, for his assistance to some shipwrecked British sailors, Brooke was given a warm reception by Hassim when he reached Kuching, the capital, on 15 August 1839. He also received full details of the rebellion which Hassim had been sent to quell when governor Pengiran Mahkota's half-hearted efforts had been unsuccessful. After investigating the coast and visiting the Samarahan and Lundu rivers, where he met the Malays and the Sebuyau Dayaks, he spent the next six months in the Celebes visiting the Bugis kingdoms of Waju and Boni, where he impressed the people with his horsemanship and his accuracy as a marksman. However, he saw no future for himself there.

Raja of Sarawak After a brief spell in Singapore, Brooke returned to Kuching on 29 August 1840 and immediately became embroiled in suppressing the rebellion. With the assistance of his ship's crew, he led Hassim's forces in a rout of the rebel headquarters at Belidah on the Sarawak River. He also interceded with Hassim to spare the lives of the local Malay chiefs who had led the Bidayuh antimony miners in their opposition to Brunei authority. In return for his assistance against the rebels, Hassim had promised Brooke the governorship of Sarawak, a promise Brooke enforced on 24 September 1841 when the *Royalist*'s guns were trained on Hassim's palace. In July 1842 he obtained personal confirmation of his appointment from Sultan Omar Ali of Brunei, and on 18 August 1842 was installed as raja at Kuching in the face of clear hostility from Pengiran Mahkota and his supporters. After the return of Hassim, Mahkota, and their retainers to Brunei, Brooke enlisted the assistance of the Royal Navy in having Hassim installed as the sultan's chief minister in October 1843.

Having secured his sovereign status, Brooke appointed Henry Wise as his London agent to lobby the British government for recognition and to interest potential investors. However, Wise's interest was in forming a large company to exploit Sarawak's much vaunted mineral resources, but Brooke found him impatient and heedless of native interests. In 1848 Wise founded the Eastern Archipelago Company to exploit Sarawak and Labuan, but by the end of that year the two men had fallen out over Wise's unwise financial advice and his unauthorized granting of an antimony concession in Sarawak. In Wise, the raja had made a dangerous enemy.

Influenced by Raffles's *History of Java*, Brooke saw himself as reforming and restoring the corrupt and declining ancient Malay kingdom of Brunei. In Edward Said's terms, he was a romantic 'orientalist'. The code of laws he introduced in Sarawak was based on that of Brunei, tempered by British notions of 'fair play'. Islam was to be respected and Malay was to be the language of government. At the same time Brooke was committed to abolishing practices that offended liberal humanitarian views, such as forced trading, amputation, slavery, and head-hunting. Using the hereditary Malay élite as a second level of authority under his bevy of hand-picked young European officers, he fostered a form of highly personal government consisting largely of the adjudication of disputes and offering the least line of resistance to traditional practices. The polyglot peoples of Sarawak came to refer to it as *perentah* (law and order) rather than *kerajaan* (hierarchically organized power). Brooke's idealistic and reformist stance was transformed by the exercise of power and the constant need to defend it. The raj the man set out to make ended up making the man. Nevertheless, he continued to claim that his government was acting on behalf of native interests, and it was this tradition which continued to be the informing ideology of Brooke rule. Brooke's ability to inspire loyalty and affection among his officers also established a tradition of altruistic service. His economic policy was based on free trade and hostility to middlemen and speculators. Nevertheless his taxation was partly based on monopolies. The indigenous population was lightly taxed, and a large proportion of taxation was from the Chinese community, through the farming of the government monopolies of opium, gambling, and arrack. In 1859 the monopolies contributed 64 per cent of the revenue collected, though normally the proportion was lower.

Campaigns against the Dayaks The territory originally secured by Brooke in July 1842, known at that time as Sarawak Proper, consisted of what is now the first division, the territory from the Samarahan River in the east to Tanjong Datu in the west and inland to the mountain watershed. The remainder of what is now the Malaysian state of Sarawak was under the loose overlordship of the sultan of Brunei and his tax-collectors, including a number of part-Arab sherif who formed alliances with Dayak chiefs in coastal raiding as far as Sumatra. Brooke quickly became involved in putting down this raiding, enlisting the assistance of the Royal Navy through his friendship with Captain Henry Keppel (1809–1904) of HMS *Dido*, whom he met in Penang in early 1843. In June 1843 and again in August 1844 Brooke and Keppel joined forces to attack and destroy the principal Dayak longhouses of the Batang Lupar and Saribas River systems, also putting to flight his principal political opponents, Sherif Sahap and Sherif Mullah, and capturing Pengiran Mahkota. During the second expedition Dayaks under the command of Rentap killed one British officer and the senior Malay chief, Datu Patinggi Ali. However, these events gave the raja effective control over what is now the 2nd division, and this was to be formalized by treaty with the sultan of Brunei in 1853. Much of his success was due to his exploitation of the

Sebuyau and Balau Dayaks' enmity towards the other Dayak tribes and their perception of him as their protector.

The destruction of the pirate base at Marudu by Admiral Sir Thomas Cochrane's fleet in August 1845 meant that coastal raiding by the Illanun of the southern Philippines had been dealt a heavy blow. However, early in 1846 Hassim and Brooke's other allies in Brunei were murdered at the sultan's behest, seriously threatening his plans to reform and manipulate the sultanate to his advantage. In August he accompanied Cochrane on a punitive expedition to Brunei, resulting in the capture of the town and the sultan's cession to Britain of the nearby island of Labuan, which Brooke saw as a strategic base for British shipping and trade.

Governor of Labuan On his return to England in October 1847 Brooke was greeted as a hero and lionized by high society. Made an Oxford DCL in November 1847 and a KCB in April 1848, and with his portrait painted by Sir Francis Grant RA, he quickly became one of the icons of early Victorian imperialism. The publication of his edited Borneo and Celebes journals by Keppel in early 1846 and articles in the *Illustrated London News* had also done much to publicize him. Appointed governor of the new colony of Labuan (November 1847 to February 1856) and consulgeneral for Borneo (July 1847 to August 1855), he nevertheless found it difficult to obtain recognition from the British government of his sovereign status in Sarawak. Eventually he claimed that his authority was derived not from the sultan of Brunei's cession of power to him but from the senior Malay chiefs who collectively conferred it upon him after their rebellion against Brunei. In this spirit he established in 1855 an advisory supreme council with Malay and European representation to meet once a year. From 1841 Brooke was assisted by a Eurasian interpreter, Thomas Williamson, and then by the botanical collector Hugh Low (1824–1905). From 1848 he was assisted and advised by his private secretary, Spenser St John (1825–1910), whose political skills proved invaluable and who later wrote a biography of Brooke.

Continuing his campaign against Dayak raiding, Brooke arranged for Captain Arthur Farquhar's ships to attack the Dayaks of the Saribas once again, resulting in the battle of Beting Marau at the mouth of the Saribas on 31 July 1849, when more than 1000 Dayaks were killed. He also initiated a system of erecting forts on the principal rivers to control the movement of Dayaks and institute a system of government. The first to be built were at Kanowit, Skrang, and Lundu, where his younger nephew, Charles Anthoni Johnson *Brooke (1829–1917), was to be posted on his arrival in 1852. In the meantime he had also encouraged the establishment of an Anglican mission as a means of pacifying the Dayaks in up-river areas. In 1848 the Revd F. T. McDougall and his wife, Harriette, had arrived to head the Borneo mission, establishing a church and a school in Kuching and subsequently organizing a network of mission outposts. In the same year arrived Captain John Brooke Johnson (*d.* 1868, aged forty-five), who in 1848 took the surname Brooke, and was known as Brooke Brooke,

the raja's elder nephew, who was to be trained in government in the expectation of succeeding his uncle.

Although Brooke's duties as governor of Labuan were not very demanding, he was dispatched by the British government in his capacity as consul to Siam in August 1850 to negotiate a new commercial treaty. For once, however, his diplomatic skills were unequal to the task. He was unable to obtain an audience with the king or his chief minister and had to conduct negotiations by letter. When these failed, he foolishly threatened to use the Royal Navy to enforce his requests.

The large sums of prize money claimed through the Singapore naval court by Sir Thomas Cochrane for his action against Illanun raiders and Captain Farquhar for his part at Beting Marau were brought to the attention of parliament and the British public by the radical politicians Richard Cobden—who wrote of Brooke's 'powers of evil' (Morley, 2.55)—and Joseph Hume in 1850, eventually resulting in Lord Aberdeen's appointment of a commission of inquiry in Singapore in 1854. Wise was instrumental in providing much of the damaging evidence. Although Brooke was exonerated of charges of inhumanity and illegality, the experience was humiliating and embittering. Moreover, he had contracted smallpox in May 1853, and the resultant scarring and other complications seem to have caused him serious psychological damage. Contemporaries noted that he was never the same afterwards.

Rebellion in Sarawak Deprived of vital support from the Royal Navy, Brooke's weakened political position was revealed in February 1857 when the 4000 Hakka Chinese goldminers of the Bau *gongsi* (co-operative), led by Liu Shanbang, defied the authority of his magistrates and taxcollectors and descended in force on Kuching to establish a government more sympathetic to their cherished autonomy. In the resulting affray the raja narrowly escaped with his life, and the defeat of the rebels was largely the work of the Borneo Company's steamer and Charles Brooke and his Dayak forces from Lingga. Many hundred Chinese were subsequently killed in their attempt to flee across the border into Dutch Borneo, and some of their heads smoked in the Kuching bazaar.

In 1856 the Borneo Company Ltd had begun operations as the only public company allowed to function in Sarawak. The raja's intention was that it should take over the monopoly of the coal, antimony, sago, and gutta-percha trades and assist the government financially in its own schemes. In the wake of the rebellion he borrowed £5000 from the company for reconstruction, but was furious when it soon called for repayment. The company's coalmine at Sadong had been a costly failure, and the rebellion had resulted in a dearth of Chinese labour for other projects. The debt was eventually paid off by Baroness Burdett-Coutts (1814–1906), the philanthropic millionairess whom the raja had first met in 1848 and who now became his patron and financier. Financial and other anxieties may have prompted the paralytic stroke the raja suffered in England on 21 October 1858.

One heartbreaking casualty of the rebellion had been

the raja's house in Kuching and his extensive library. Largely self-educated, Brooke was widely read in literature and theology and liked to hold court with his intellectual inferiors. Much of his undoubted attraction can be attributed to his erudition and eloquence, but he was essentially an autodidact and a dilettante. A Unitarian by religious persuasion, he was inclined to tease the Anglican bishop and anyone else of orthodox views. Maintaining an interest in natural history, he encouraged the work of Alfred Russel Wallace (1823–1913) and allowed him to use a house at Santubong to write his famous paper on evolution (1855).

Later reverses Brooke's reverses, together with his failure to obtain recognition from the British government and his indebtedness after 1857, led him to offer Sarawak for sale to several European governments in order to recoup his investment. He also stunned his family in 1858 by acknowledging a stable-hand, Reuben George Walker (died May 1874, reportedly aged forty, when the ship *British Admiral* was lost at sea) as his illegitimate son and announcing his intention of taking him out to Sarawak. Whether Reuben was his son, or recognition was to conceal a homosexual relationship, must remain a matter for speculation. The raja was fond of young boys and never married, but early Victorian male behaviour can easily be misinterpreted by later generations. For example, his biographer, Spenser St John, was strongly advised by a friend in 1878 to remove a reference to his kissing the raja on his deathbed as 'too sensational Nelsonic' and likely to cause offence.

The most serious consequence of Brooke's acknowledgement of Reuben and his foreign negotiations was the alienation of his elder nephew, Brooke Brooke, who administered the government during the raja's increasingly extended absences. He saw Reuben as a serious challenge to his inheritance and his uncle as wanting to sell it off. Events came to a head in Singapore in January 1863 when the raja both disinherited and banished Brooke Brooke for defying his authority. After establishing Charles in his place, the raja left Sarawak for the last time on 25 September and returned to England. By this time the British government had finally recognized Sarawak as an independent state, but its finances were still underwritten by Baroness Burdett-Coutts, whom he named as his heir. His close friendship with the eccentric baroness and her companion, Mrs Brown, is another relationship capable of interpretation. He seems to have been a man who was 'able to be the close and intimate friends of women without a tinge of love-making' (Tarling, 7).

The raja's last strategic success in Sarawak had been formally to acquire from the sultan of Brunei in 1862 the Melanau-peopled, sago-producing areas of Muka and Oya to the north of the Rejang River estuary, together with a vast inland area to the Dutch border. The declining demand for antimony and the failure to discover anticipated gold and diamonds had left Sarawak without a staple export. Monopolization of the sago trade with Singapore offered an attractive source of export revenue, and this had been secured in an armed expedition led by his two nephews against Pengiran Nipa of Muka in 1860.

The expedition also disposed of the raja's principal political enemy, the formidable Sherif Masahor, who had been suspected of planning a general native uprising (known as the Malay plot) against the raja and the Dutch for some years.

Retirement and death On his retirement to Burrator, a house he bought following a public subscription in 1859 on the edge of Dartmoor, near the isolated village of Sheepstor in Devon, James lived out his last years in rural seclusion, and was a churchwarden at Sheepstor. Nevertheless, he continued to press the British government to take over Sarawak and to negotiate with foreign governments. Baroness Burdett-Coutts gave up her rights in 1865, enabling James to declare Charles his heir. He achieved some reconciliation with members of his family and former officers alienated by his disinheritance of Brooke Brooke, but did nothing to assist him and his son, Hope Brooke. This contrasted with his generosity towards Reuben and the sons of his Eurasian half-brother, Charles William Brooke, the son of Thomas Brooke and an Indian woman before his marriage to Anna Maria. Charles William had been brought up with the second family, and both James and his sister Emma maintained an affectionate relationship with him. In 1866 Brooke suffered his second stroke, and on 11 June 1868 he died at Burrator after suffering a third stroke two days earlier. He was buried on 17 June at Sheepstor churchyard, Devon. He was commemorated by the Brooke memorial opposite the old court house in Kuching, Sarawak. He was succeeded as raja by his nephew Sir Charles Anthoni Johnson Brooke (1829–1917). Brooke's was a remarkable achievement. A Victorian imperial hero, yet controversial and loathed by some, he founded a state and established a regime which lasted a century, and also influenced the fiction of Kipling, Conrad, and lesser writers. His Sarawak achievement won him fame but no vast fortune: the English probate value of his estate was under £1000.   R. H. W. REECE

Sources H. Keppel, *The expedition to Borneo of H.M.S. Dido*, 2 vols. (1846) • H. Low, *Sarawak* (1848) • G. R. Mundy, *Narrative of events in Borneo and Celebes, down to the occupation of Labuan* (1848) • J. C. Templer, ed., *The private letters of Sir James Brooke*, 3 vols. (1853) • G. Jacob, *The raja of Sarawak*, 2 vols. (1876) • S. St John, *The life of Sir James Brooke, rajah of Sarawak* (1879) • S. Baring-Gould and C. A. Bampfylde, *A history of Sarawak under its two white rajahs, 1839–1908* (1909) • S. Runciman, *The white rajahs: a history of Sarawak from 1841 to 1946* (1960) • N. Tarling, *The burthen, the risk and the glory: a biography of Sir James Brooke* (1982) • Boase, *Mod. Eng. biog.* • V. C. P. Hodson, *List of officers of the Bengal army, 1758–1834*, 1 (1927) • O. K. Gin, *Of free trade and native interests: the Brookes and the economic development of Sarawak, 1841–1941* (1997) • R. Payne, *The white rajahs of Sarawak* (1986) • A. Porter, ed., *The Oxford history of the British empire*, vol. 3 (1999), 378, 381, 384, 454 • J. Morley, *The life of Richard Cobden* (1881) • J. A. Hobson, *Richard Cobden: the international man* (1918) • *CGPLA Eng. & Wales* (1868)

Archives Bodl. RH, corresp. and papers • W. Sussex RO, letters, copies of corresp., memoranda | Alnwick Castle, letters to Henry Drummond • BL, corresp. with Baroness Burdett-Coutts, Add. MSS 45274–45282 • NL Scot., corresp. with Sir Thomas Cochrane • RGS, letters to Royal Geographical Society • U. Durham L., corresp. with third Earl Grey; letters to Maria, Lady Grey

Likenesses F. Grant, oils, 1847, NPG [*see illus.*] • T. Woolner, marble bust, 1858, NPG • G. G. Adams, plaster bust, 1863, NPG • W. J.

Edwards, stipple (after photograph by H. Watkins), NPG · Maull & Polyblank, photograph, NPG · attrib. Maull & Polyblank, photograph, NPG

Wealth at death under £1000: probate, 27 July 1868, *CGPLA Eng. & Wales*

Brooke, (Bernard) Jocelyn (1908–1966), writer and naturalist, was born on 30 November 1908 at 9 Radnor Cliff, Sandgate, Folkestone, Kent, the third child of Henry Brooke, wine merchant, and his wife, May, *née* Turner. Both his parents were English, and were converts to Christian Science. Jocelyn Brooke was brought up in Kent primarily by his nanny, a strict Baptist whom he called Ninnie. A painfully sensitive, precocious child, considered by his family to have weak health, Brooke from a very early age observed his world, the countryside around Folkestone and their summer residence, Ivy Cottage, Bishopsbourne, in the Elham valley. Much younger than his sister, Evelyn, and his brother, Cecil, Brooke seems to have admired and been rather overwhelmed by the gregarious if strictly class-conscious world of his family. He found school a painful experience: life at his preparatory day school was daunting but tolerable. Not so, however, King's School, Canterbury, and he ran away twice in the first two weeks before being sent to the co-educational progressive Bedales School, which seems to have been as good as it could be given that Brooke hated sport and the intrusive environment of boarding-school life. From 1927 he attended Worcester College, Oxford, where he paid to have his first book, *Six Poems*, published in 1928.

After only a year Brooke was sent down from Oxford. He worked in a London bookshop for two years, then joined his father and brother in the wine business, but found that he had no acumen for this or any of the other jobs he worked at and suffered a breakdown of some sort. When the Second World War began he enlisted in the Royal Army Medical Corps (RAMC) and became one of the pox wallahs, those working to treat venereal disease. He was decorated for bravery.

Brooke was restless as a demobbed veteran and soon rejoined the venereal disease branch of the RAMC as a regular: 'Soldiering had become a habit with me' (Brooke, *The Dog at Clambercrown*, 220), he wrote by way of explanation for this rather surprising decision, given his childhood unhappiness at boarding-school. His homosexuality and the orderly anonymity of military life perhaps combined to make the army attractive to Brooke, who was a self-deprecating, extremely private individual; his unsuitability to take over the family business (his brother was killed in action) may well have propelled him away from civilian life.

While Brooke wrote poetry and prose from his schooldays onwards, his next book, *December Spring: Poems*, published by Bodley Head (which became his main publisher), did not appear until 1946. It was followed by *The Military Orchid* (1948), which in addition to receiving critical acclaim (Desmond MacCarthy and Anthony Powell praised it highly) was a sufficient financial success to enable Brooke to buy himself out of the army. He moved to London and became a talks producer for the BBC, but was unhappy in the metropolis. After four months he resigned and moved to the country, eventually settling in an environment familiar from his childhood—Ivy Cottage in Bishopsbourne, which he shared with Ninnie and her husband (who died shortly afterwards).

From this point Brooke wrote full-time and published books of a variety of genres in an astonishingly quick succession (eighteen appeared between 1949 and 1958). They reflect his knowledgeable passions for botany, pyrotechnics, and literature. He was a botanophile from early childhood:

> not content with the English names [of flowers], I memorised many of the Latin and Greek ones as well. Some of these (at the age of 8) I conceitedly incorporated in a school essay. ... The Headmaster read the essay aloud to the school (no wonder I was unpopular). (Brooke, *The Orchid Trilogy*, 23)

He was a founder member of the Kent Trust for Nature Conservation and published two botanical works: *The Wild Orchids of Britain* (1950) and *The Flower in Season* (1952), 'a book about wild flowers for those who like wild flowers' (Brooke, *The Flower in Season*, 11). His only children's novel, *The Wonderful Summer* (1949), includes a detailed description (with diagrams) of how to make fireworks, and the plot revolves around the search for a rare orchid, the Epipogon, by three teenagers in Oxfordshire: a brother and sister and their cousin, Vincent, a mocking self-portrait. This novel is just one aspect of what Anthony Powell aptly described as the 'Brooke myth' (Powell, 3): Brooke's ability to write what has elsewhere been called 'managed autobiography'. Brooke repeatedly drew on his life in the three loosely connected volumes of his trilogy: *The Military Orchid*, *The Mine of Serpents* (1949, named after a type of firework), and *The Goose Cathedral* (1950). In these witty, subtle, deceptively simple works, the narrator records details of the childhood and later life of a young man resembling but not identical to Brooke himself, who is presented as a prototype of his generation and class. The books capture the unfolding of a melancholy, often painfully sensitive male consciousness, an observer who portrays sardonically and with delicate wit a quintessentially English life. His gift lay in evoking life in the inter-war years and in the army with all its idiosyncratic and distinctive elements without creating dated period pieces.

Also on the cusp between autobiography and fiction are the following narratives: *The Scapegoat* (1948)—an excellent portrayal of doomed adolescent angst; *The Passing of a Hero* (1953), in which Brooke wrote in a note that 'all the characters ... including that of the narrator, are ninety per cent fictitious'; *Private View* (1954); *The Dog at Clambercrown* (1955); and *Conventional Weapons* (1961). Brooke's only true novel, *The Image of a Drawn Sword* (1950), is a haunting account of a post-war veteran whose sense of futility is dissolved when he is drawn into a world where fantasy, paranoia, and reality merge with fatal consequences. Brooke's most unusual work is *The Crisis in Bulgaria, or, Ibsen to the Rescue!* (1956), a surrealist pastiche. In addition to his own writing Brooke was a percipient reviewer and wrote critiques of Aldous Huxley, Elizabeth Bowen, Ronald Firbank, and John Betjeman as well as introducing and editing the journals and published works of Denton Welch. His interest in music is shown in his final publication, *The Birth of a Legend: a Reminiscence of Arthur Machen and John Ireland* (1964).

Brooke continued to live at Ivy Cottage after Ninnie's death and was a well-respected albeit solitary figure in Bishopsbourne and the surrounding countryside. Despite his enormous output, he never received due recognition. On 29 October 1966 he was found dead in his cottage of a coronary artery insufficiency due to atherosclerosis. His ashes were scattered at Barham cemetery. A plaque decorated with an orchid on Ivy Cottage commemorates his unassuming yet distinctive achievements:

> Jocelyn Brooke
> 1908–1966
> lived here
> Author & Naturalist.

NATHALIE BLONDEL

Sources A. Powell, 'Introduction', in J. Brooke, *The orchid trilogy* (1981) · J. Brooke, *The dog at Clambercrown* (1990) · J. Brooke, *The flower in season* (1952) · J. Brooke, *The passing of a hero* (1953) · B. Rota, *A checklist of Jocelyn Brooke: his writings together with some appreciations* (1963) · private information (2004) · b. cert. · d. cert.
Archives Ransom HRC, MSS · Washington University, St Louis, Missouri, unpublished autobiographical study and essays
Likenesses Elliott & Fry, photograph, repro. in Brooke, *The orchid trilogy*

Brooke, John (d. 1582), translator, was the son of John Brooke, a member of a family based in Ash-next-Sandwich, Kent, and probable owners of Brooke House in that village. In the foundation charter of 1546, Brooke was appointed a scholar of Trinity College, Cambridge; he earned his BA in 1553–4. At some time Brooke married Magdalen Stoddard of Mottingham; childless, he died in 1582 and was buried in Ash church. Between 1577 and 1582 six translations by Brooke were printed; printers specializing in ephemera, Thomas East and John Charlewood produced two-thirds of these titles.

Nearly all Brooke's pieces were didactic Calvinist or Huguenot tracts, like the second printed English translation of the confession of faith based on the apostles' creed by Jean Garnier, dedicated to Sir William Cecil (1579). In the 1560s Pierre Viret popularized Calvinism in France by writing accessible polemical and pedagogical texts, and Brooke expressed similar goals in England. In addition to the exposition on the Lord's prayer (1582), he also translated another work by Viret, published in 1579 as *Christian Disputations*. Brooke translated the only work by the popular writer Guy de Brès to be printed in English: this was published as *The Staffe of Christian Faith* by John Day in 1577. Brooke's 1579 translation of the famous monster-pamphlets of Melancthon and Luther, rendered as *Of two wonderful popish monsters: to wyt, of a popish asse which was found in Rome in the River Tyber* (1496) *and of a moonkish calfe, calved at Friberge in Misne* (1528) … *witnessed and declared, the one by P. Melancthon, the other by M. Luther*, was also their first

English imprinting. It is unfortunate that without additional evidence it is impossible to know how these translations came to be published; whether the printers, Brooke, or third parties first suggested publication; or even whether Brooke translated the pieces before their appearance in print.

KATHLEEN E. KENNEDY

Sources ESTC · Cooper, *Ath. Cantab.*, vol. 1 · J. R. Planché, *A corner of Kent* (1864)

Brooke, John Charles (1748–1794), herald and antiquary, was born on 27 August 1748 at Fieldhead, in the parish of Silkstone, Yorkshire, the younger son of William Brooke (1706–1755), and his wife, Alice (b. 1718), eldest daughter and coheir of William Mawhood, sometime mayor and alderman of Wakefield; he was the grandson of the Revd Thomas Brooke (1669–1739), rector of Richmond, Yorkshire. He never married. He was apprenticed in 1769 to James Kirkby, an apothecary in Bartlett's Buildings, Holborn, London, but disliked the work and stayed there only two years, seeking instead a position at the College of Arms, having been interested in heraldry since childhood. To secure the good favour of the duke of Norfolk, earl marshal, he drew up a pedigree of the Howard family, by his own account 9 yards long and containing 1000 coats of arms. Following the vacancy at the College of Arms caused by the death of Stephen Martin Leake, Garter king of arms, in March 1773, Brooke was appointed Rouge Croix pursuivant on 1 July 1773. He relinquished that office on being created Somerset herald on 31 January 1778. He served in the office of secretary to the deputy earl marshal from 8 May 1784 until his death. Through the patronage of the duke of Norfolk he was appointed a lieutenant in the militia of the West Riding of Yorkshire, from the duties of which he was not always able to excuse himself. He became free of the Ironmongers' Company of London on 29 April 1772.

Brooke was an industrious herald, solicited for work at every opportunity, and built up a large practice in heraldry and genealogy. An energetic antiquary, he maintained a wide correspondence with similarly minded acquaintances, supplied many with genealogical and heraldic information from the records of the College of Arms, and in return received much from them, in particular drawings of seals. He resided permanently at the College of Arms, and was a frequent and regular attender at meetings of the Society of Antiquaries of which he was elected a fellow on 6 April 1775.

On 3 February 1794 Brooke and his colleague Benjamin Pingo, York herald, were crushed to death at the entrance to the pit of the Little Theatre, in the Haymarket, London, together with fourteen others. He was buried in the church of St Benet Paul's Wharf on 6 February. A monumental tablet was erected there, with an epitaph by his colleague Edmund Lodge, later Clarenceux king of arms, which extolled his piety, judgement, and lack of vanity. Michael Lort regarded him differently, calling him a 'coxcomb' and claimed that early in his career he had been banned from the British Museum for cutting leaves from a manuscript (*N&Q*, 4.130).

Had it not been for his premature death Brooke might in due course have brought several important works to the press. He intended to publish a new edition of Sandford's *Genealogical History of the Kings and Queens of England*; a baronage after Dugdale's method showing the arms of each family, as evidenced by seals; a genealogical history of all the tenants *in capite*, mentioned in Domesday, and where possible their Saxon predecessors. He also planned a history of the West Riding of Yorkshire. His father had inherited the manuscripts of his great-uncle, the Revd John Brooke (d. 1725), rector of High Hoyland, Yorkshire, a collection that had been formed as a foundation for the topography of the western division of that county. Brooke greatly added to this collection by his own researches, and by copying the manuscripts of Jenyngs and Tilleyson. Besides general heraldic and genealogical information Brooke also collected drawings of crosses carved on tombs in the hope of elucidating their stylistic development, and information relating to the etymology of surnames. He contributed to the *Gentleman's Magazine*, signing himself JB, and to *Archaeologia*. He assisted many genealogical and topographical authors, including Sir Richard Worsley, seventh baronet, in his *History of the Isle of Wight* (1781), and Dr T. R. Nash in his *Collections for the History of Worcestershire* (1781). He bequeathed his manuscripts to the College of Arms, but a large part of his correspondence is in the Bodleian Library.   D. V. WHITE

Sources Nichols, *Lit. anecdotes*, 1.681, 684; 3.263; 6.142, 254, 303 · Nichols, *Illustrations*, 6.354–429 · A. Wagner, *Heralds of England: a history of the office and College of Arms* (1967), 407–17 · *N&Q*, 2nd ser., 4 (1857), 130, 138, 160 · *GM*, 1st ser., 64 (1794), 187, 275 · *GM*, 1st ser., 67 (1797), 5 · Coll. Arms, John Charles Brooke MSS · M. Noble, *A history of the College of Arms* (1805), 428–34 · R. G. [R. Gough], *British topography*, [new edn], 2 (1780), 397, 401–2
Archives BL, collection of Yorkshire pedigrees, Add. MS 21184 · Bodl. Oxf., corresp., notebooks, and papers · Coll. Arms, antiquarian, genealogical, and topographical collections · Lincs. Arch., drawings of seals of the lords of the Isle of Wight · Norfolk RO, corresp. · W. Sussex RO, corresp. and papers | Arundel Castle, letters to duke of Norfolk · Bodl. Oxf., corresp. with Richard Gough · East Riding of Yorkshire Archives Service, Beverley, letters to Marmaduke Tunstall · Lincs. Arch., corresp. with Thomas Pownall · U. Leeds, Brotherton L., corresp. with John Wilson
Likenesses E. Bell, mezzotint, pubd 1794 (after T. Maynard), BM, NPG · etching, 1794 (after the earl of Leicester), NPG · T. Milton, engraving (after T. Maynard), repro. in Noble, *History of the College of Arms*
Wealth at death £14,000: Noble, *A history*, 433

Brooke, (Leonard) Leslie (1862–1940), children's writer and illustrator, was born on 24 September 1862 in Birkenhead, near Liverpool, the second of the three children of Leonard Brooke (1825–1885), manufacturer, and his wife Rhoda (1829/30–1915), daughter of Henry Leslie Prentice of Caledon, co. Tyrone. His parents were both Irish. At Birkenhead School Leslie attracted the attention of the headmaster with his drawing. Severe typhoid contracted during a trip to Italy caused partial deafness that made Brooke decide to attend Birkenhead Art School (1880–82) instead of a university. He went on to study in London at St John's Wood Art School (1882–4) and the Royal Academy Art School (1884–8; Armitage medal 1888). Afterwards he began to illustrate books and book covers. When in 1891 he followed Walter Crane as illustrator of Mrs Molesworth's annual children's story-book (for Macmillan) his future blossomed.

On 28 June 1894 Brooke married his cousin Sybil Diana (1870–1957), the daughter of the Revd Stopford Augustus *Brooke. Leonard Stopford was born a year later. Brooke produced *The Nursery Rhyme Book* for Warne, with an introduction and notes by Andrew Lang. It was released for Christmas 1897, 'illustrated by L. Leslie Brooke', the name he chose for publication. The illustrations are full of his trademarks, amusing details and visual puns, the puns often for adults as in 'This little piggy went to market' with humorous newspaper and book titles and a reference to Circe. Edward Lear's *Nonsense Songs* followed. Published in two volumes, *The Pelican Chorus* (1899) and *The Jumblies* (1900), they were eventually combined in 1900.

In September 1899 the family had moved to the village of Harwell near Oxford for Sybil's health. When Brooke decided to write and illustrate a picture-book, Sybil suggested Johnny Crow's garden, a game first begun by his father for his brother Henry and him and carried on by Brooke with his own son, Leonard: the book became a classic. In April 1903 a second son, Henry *Brooke, was born, and *Johnny Crow's Garden* (1903) was dedicated to Brooke's father and both boys. The book has humorous verses and details in each picture. Expressive faces and postures are augmented by subtle touches, again, with some designed to appeal to adults; on the Stork's 'Philosophic Talk' page, one of the books is 'Confuseus', while another is 'Ludovicus Carrollus de Jabberwockibus'.

Brooke next turned to fairy-tales for Warne. *The Story of the Three Little Pigs* and *Tom Thumb* appeared separately, then together in 1904. In 1905 *The Golden Goose* and *The Three Bears*, with its puns ('Tom Bruin's school days', 'The bear truth'), followed; all four were published in one volume, *Golden Goose Book* (1905), considered among his best. Meanwhile, *Johnny Crow's Garden* gained in popularity, and using leftover original rhymes along with old favourites and new creations, Brooke produced a sequel, *Johnny Crow's Party* (1907). Successful again, it assured his reputation. In 1908 the Brookes moved to a house in St John's Wood, London, where he continued to work.

The First World War temporarily halted Brooke's output. His mother died in 1915, and on 25 September 1918 his son Leonard was killed in action. The family moved to Cumnor near Oxford in 1921, building a house. In 1920 another major Brooke work, illustrated nursery rhymes, was published as *Ring o' Roses* (1922), containing his last illustrations of that decade.

A Roundabout Turn by Robert H. Charles (1930) and *Johnny Crow's New Party* (1935) were his last books. Brooke died on 1 May 1940 in the London home, 28 Hollycroft Avenue, Hampstead, to which he and Sybil Brooke had moved in 1933.   MARILYN FAIN APSELOFF

Sources H. Brooke, *Leslie Brooke and Johnny Crow* (1981) [incl. bibliography] · H. P. Williams, 'L. Leslie Brooke', *British children's writers, 1880–1914*, ed. L. M. Zaidman, DLitB, 141 (1994), 50–58 [incl. bibliography] · M. Apseloff, 'L. Leslie Brooke's *Johnny Crow's garden*: the gentle humor of implied stories', *Touchstones*, 3 (1989–90), 21–28 · A. Moore, 'L. Leslie Brooke', *Horn Book*, 17 (May–June 1941), 153–62 · J. C. Stott, *Children's literature from A to Z* (1984) · E. Nesbit, 'The early record', *Horn Book*, 47 (June 1971), 268–74 · W. Whitehead, 'Brooke, L(eonard) Leslie', *Twentieth-century children's writers*, ed. D. L. Kirkpatrick, 124–35 [incl. bibliography] · A. C. Moore, 'Leslie Brooke: Pied Piper of English picture books', *A Horn Book sampler, 1924–48*, ed. N. R. Fryatt (1959), 60–69 · A. C. Moore, 'L. Leslie Brooke', *A Horn Book sampler, 1924–48*, ed. N. R. Fryatt (1959), 63–9 · *The Times* (2 May 1940) · *CGPLA Eng. & Wales* (1940)

Likenesses Leston studio, photograph, 1935 · photograph, 1936, repro. in *Horn Book*, 17 (May 1941), 155 · photograph, 1936, repro. in Brooke, *Leslie Brooke*

Wealth at death £10,728 10s. 1d.: probate, 22 Aug 1940, *CGPLA Eng. & Wales*

Brooke [Brookesmouth], **Ralph** (*c.*1553–1625), herald, was born in London, the son of Geoffrey Brooke, a shoemaker, and his wife, Jane Hyde. By his own account, preserved in the College of Arms, his grandfather was William Brooke of Lancashire; however, Anthony Wagner cites another contemporary account that gives the family name as Brookesmouth, and refers to origins in Wigan; in his lifetime Ralph was often referred to as Brookesmouth as well as Brooke. In 1564 he was admitted to the Merchant Taylors' School, London, where he would have been a younger contemporary of Edmund Spenser and William Harrison. Later he was apprenticed to the Painter–Stainers' Company, where Sampson Camden, the father of his arch-rival William Camden, was an active member; according to the historian Mark Noble, Brooke was made free in 1576.

In 1580 Brooke began a long, profitable, and acrimonious career as a herald when he was made Rouge Croix pursuivant. In spite of his disruptive influence he was elevated in 1592 to York herald, a post he retained until his death. Inadvertently, through unceasing broils with fellow heralds and the earl marshal's office, Brooke had a significant impact on the College of Arms and the earl marshal's court. The College of Arms was in a state of transition during the later part of Elizabeth's reign, and Brooke's vehemence called attention to its internal disarray. He accused his fellow heralds of profiting from false or incorrect arms, of withholding fees due to him, of violent and ungentlemanly behaviour, and of other abuses of office. For example, he challenged the grant of arms made in 1596 by the Garter king of arms William Dethick to John Shakespeare, on the grounds that they resembled too closely those of Lord Mauley. The grant was successfully defended by Dethick and William Camden. Although Brooke was dogged in his assaults on his colleagues, his charges were not entirely without basis, and sometimes struck home—as in 1616, when he orchestrated an elaborate hoax that led Sir William Segar, Dethick's successor as garter, to grant the arms of Aragon and Brabant to Gregory Brandon, the hangman for the City of London. The incident enraged King James and resulted in the earl marshal placing both Brooke and Segar in the Marshalsea.

Brooke himself faced similar charges of abuse of office and misconduct. His behaviour was so belligerent and untoward that it helped to unite the rest of the college. An anonymous document entitled 'Spectacle for purjorers',

apparently signed by six heralds and given to deputies of the earl marshal, outlined Brooke's 'lewd life'. On numerous occasions the college levied fines against Brooke, sent petitions to Lord Burghley objecting to his conduct, and suspended him from its chapter. Between 1588 and 1594 Brooke was frequently forbidden to wear the queen's arms and was denied attendance on Elizabeth, but wilfully defied the lord chamberlain's prohibitions.

The most famous of Brooke's causes, his prolonged attack on William Camden, also served to unite members of the college and added to his paradoxical legacy. Embittered first by Camden's presumption in writing in his *Britannia* about arms and criticizing the work of heralds while having no formal experience or training in the 'mysticall poyntes' of their craft (Brooke, *Discoverie*, A3v), and then by his appointment in 1597 as Clarenceux king of arms, Brooke unleashed his anger in *A discoverie of certaine errours published in print in the much-commended Britannia, 1594, very prejudiciall to the discentes and successions of the auncient nobilitie of this realme* (1599). With a rhetoric that is frequently prurient and sarcastic, Brooke alleges errors in many of Camden's genealogies that, as a result, present 'incestious and unnaturall mariages' (ibid., A2v). According to Brooke the threat of publishing his *Discoverie of certaine errours* moved Camden's friends in the stationers' office to enter his lodgings and partially destroy the work just before its publication, resulting in an imperfect first edition. Brooke sent his rival a copy for comment, and in the 1600 edition of the *Britannia* Camden replied to, and adopted, many of the 'corrections'. Nevertheless, Brooke renewed his attack in *A second discoverie of errours*, which remained unpublished until John Anstis's edition of 1723, which included Camden's responses.

In 1619 Brooke broadened his efforts to correct the 'great hurt and prejudice' being done by 'upstarts and Montebankes' (Brooke, *Catalogue*, A3) to the nobility through inaccurate genealogies, publishing *A catalogue and succession of the kings, princes, dukes, marquesses, earles, and viscounts of this realme of England*, which he enlarged in a second edition in 1622. His persistent belligerence exasperated Augustine Vincent (Windsor herald) and galvanized a number of heralds and others into publishing a counter-attack. In 1622 Vincent, parodying Brooke's original attack on Camden, published *A discoverie of errours in the first edition of the catalogue of nobility, published by Ralfe Brooke, Yorke herald, 1619*. The prefatory material contains numerous personal statements from heralds and scholars, as well as William Jaggard, Brooke's own printer, testifying to Brooke's mischief and Camden's virtues.

The vitriol and debate occasioned by Brooke's conduct and his challenges to Camden's credentials called attention to the professionalization of the herald's office, and ultimately hastened the reform that Camden was fostering. The other major cause that occupied Brooke during the last decade of his life, his challenge to the earl marshal's court or court of chivalry, had a similar effect. Suing the heralds for fees that were allegedly due to him, Brooke filed his suit in chancery, denying that there was such a thing as an earl marshal's court. In 1621 he appeared before the privy council and was committed to the Marshalsea, where he remained for fifteen months before retracting his position and agreeing to have his case heard in the earl marshal's court. The result of his challenge was to reaffirm the existence, authority, and jurisdiction of the office and court of the earl marshal.

According to Wagner, Brooke was twice married. Once described as a vagabond not worth £3, Brooke died presumably in London, on 15 October 1625, wealthy and landed. His acrimonious life evidently extended into the domestic sphere. In his will, drawn up on 20 July 1619, he left 500 marks to his 'eldest' daughter, Mary Dickins, to be paid out of the rents from his London properties. To his 'unkind wife', who survived him, he left a 'third' from the same rents, and to his daughter Tomasin he left £480 and his gold chain. To his 'undutifull sonne' Anthony he left his London lands, subject to various annuities and conditions. He concluded his bequests with a gift of 5 marks 'to my loveing fellowes the officers of armes … to paye for a diner or Supper' (will, PRO, PROB 11/148, fols. 147v–148). He was buried in the church in Reculver, Kent, his grave originally adorned with an effigy depicting him with his heraldic tabard. While the monument has been lost it was often engraved.   WYMAN H. HERENDEEN

Sources A. Wagner, *Heralds of England: a history of the office and College of Arms* (1967) · M. Noble, *A history of the College of Arms* (1805) · Coll. Arms, Arundel 40 · partition book, Coll. Arms, vol. 2 · Star Chamber proceedings, PRO, Elizabeth STAC, 5/B 36/40, 5/B 59/22 · R. Brooke, *A catalogue and succession of the kings, princes, dukes, marquesses, earles, and viscounts of this realme of England* (1619) · R. Brooke, *A discoverie of certaine errours published in print in the much commended Britannia, 1594* (1599) · G. D. Squibb, *The high court of chivalry* (1959) · H. Nicolas, *Life of Augustine Vincent* (1827) · *DNB* · A. Vincent, *A discoverie of errours in the first edition of the catalogue of nobility, published by Ralfe Brooke, Yorke herald, 1619* (1622) · BL, Cotton MS, Faustina E.i · will, PRO, PROB 11/148, sig. 19
Archives BL, historical collections and papers, Harley MSS 810, 834, 886, 888, 891, 897, 1408, 1453, 1567, 3526, 4757 | BL, Cotton MS Faustina E.i · BL, Harley MSS 69, 1107, 4204 · Bodl. Oxf., Smith MS 89
Likenesses line engraving, BM, NPG
Wealth at death considerable property: will, PRO, PROB 11/148, fols. 147v–148

Brooke, Richard (1791–1861), antiquary, was born on 19 July 1791 in Liverpool, the second son of Richard Brooke (1761–1852), a customs officer, and his wife, Mary, daughter of Peter Penny of Knutsford and Liverpool. He practised as a solicitor and notary in Liverpool from 1814. On 17 December 1831 he married Eleanor Elspit, daughter of Alexander Hadden of Bramcote, Nottinghamshire. On the death of his father in 1852, he succeeded to the family estates at Handforth in the parish of Cheadle, as his elder brother had already died.

Brooke devoted his leisure time to investigating the history and antiquities of Cheshire and Liverpool, and certain branches of natural history. One of his favourite occupations was to visit and explore English battlefields, especially those which were the scenes of conflict during the Wars of the Roses. His main objective was to compare the statements of historians with the surviving evidence, and

with the traditions of the neighbourhoods where the battles had been fought. His interest in this line of research began at a comparatively early age during visits to his brother Peter Brooke, who lived near Stoke Field, scene of the battle between Henry VII and John de la Pole, earl of Lincoln, in 1487.

Brooke was elected FSA in 1847, and in 1848 he was a founder member of the Historic Society of Lancashire and Cheshire. He took a great interest in the society, and chaired meetings and read papers on Cheshire and Liverpool history. He joined the Liverpool Literary and Philosophical Society in 1855, and became a member of the society's council in 1860. He read many papers at the meetings of the society, including several on fifteenth-century personalities such as Richard Neville, earl of Warwick, and Margaret of Anjou; these were printed in the society's *Proceedings*. His most important works are *Liverpool as it was during the Last Quarter of the Eighteenth Century, 1775 to 1800* (1853), which included much information derived from his father, and *Visits to Fields of Battle in England in the Fifteenth Century* (1857). He also published *The Office and Practice of a Notary in England* (1847). The historian J. P. Earwaker described Brooke as 'an antiquary of considerable attainments' (Lockett, 180). Brooke died at Liverpool on 14 June 1861, and was buried at Chelford, Cheshire. He was survived by his wife.

C. W. SUTTON, rev. SIMON HARRISON

Sources R. C. Lockett, 'Richard Brooke of Handford vel Handforth, and Liverpool, FSA: some notes concerning his lineage and connections', *Transactions of the Historic Society of Lancashire and Cheshire*, 62 (1910), 175–81 · Boase, *Mod. Eng. biog.*
Wealth at death £30,000: probate, 29 June 1861, CGPLA Eng. & Wales

Brooke, Robert (1744–1811), army officer in the East India Company and colonial governor, was the second son of Robert Brooke (1710–1784), an artist, of Rantavan, co. Cavan, and his wife and cousin, Honor (d. 1800), daughter of Henry Brooke, rector of Kinawley, co. Fermanagh. In 1764 he was commissioned ensign in Ironside's battalion of sepoys (10th) in the East India Company's Bengal army. He was promoted lieutenant on 25 August 1765 and entered on a hard, campaigning life. He took part in the operations against Mir Kasima and Shuja ud-Daula and against the Marathas in northern India in 1764–5. In 1766, when mutiny threatened over Clive's revision of officers' field allowances (the *batta*), he led a detachment to Allahabad to preserve order. With two companies of sepoy grenadiers he was in the force sent by the Bengal government to strengthen Madras in 1767, and served in the subsequent campaigns against Haidar Ali in 1768–9. He was promoted to captain in December 1767 for bravery in the field and returned to Bengal, where, as commander in the province of Kora, in Oudh, he put down a rebellion and assumed the collectorship of the revenues. He was active in suppressing the hill people around Rajmahal, yet treated them with humanity. He also saw service in the Rohilla War in 1774. Brooke's bravery and dedication to duty won him the plaudits of the court of directors. He returned to England in 1775, in which year he married

Anna Maria Wynne, *née* Mapletoft (1754–1824), the widow of William Wynne, a company servant whom she had married in Bengal on 25 August 1770, and the daughter of Robert Mapletoft, chaplain of Fort William, Calcutta; they had two sons and two daughters.

Brooke had inherited some small properties in Ireland and had about £18,000 available for investment, mostly derived from his Kora collectorship. In partnership with a brother and a brother-in-law he established a cotton-spinning factory about 1780 at a site west of Dublin, to which he gave the name Prosperous. He committed both his own and his family's fortune to the project; although he believed that it could be made a commercial success his motive was strongly philanthropic. The Irish parliament, anxious to promote industrial development and attracted by an opportunity to relocate some of Dublin's turbulent artisans outside the city, was ready with grants and loans. He obtained £4000 in direct grants, and in 1784, having claimed to have invested over £40,000, he was granted a £32,000 public loan on the security of his property, subject to an undertaking that over ten years 2000 Dublin artisans would be resettled in Prosperous. In 1785 things began to go wrong. Too much of the investment went into housing, there were labour disputes and marketing problems, Brooke's brother died, anticipated new partners from Manchester were not forthcoming, and the site proved to be unsatisfactory. Finance was no longer readily available, and in 1786 Brooke was declared bankrupt, although he later managed to secure a special discharge. In what was both a self-justification and an essay in rehabilitation he published *A Letter from Mr. Brooke to an Honourable Member of the House of Commons* (1786), a pamphlet in which he detailed his services and reproduced testimonials from those he had served.

The East India Company refused Brooke's request to resume his former rank but immediately afterwards appointed him governor of St Helena, which it administered as a port of call for ships sailing to and from India. He took up the appointment in 1787, when he was promoted to lieutenant-colonel and not long after to colonel. He not only improved the island's military preparedness by strengthening its defences but also ameliorated the lot of the inhabitants. In 1792 he drafted a code of laws designed to limit the powers of the masters of the slave population and to increase that of the magistrates. The company based its own amendments on his draft. He initiated works for a better water supply, encouraged the settlement of former soldiers, and substituted labour for flogging in the garrison. In May and June 1795, in co-operation with the captain of the *Sceptre*, he organized a naval and military expedition to seize the Dutch colony at the Cape of Good Hope before the French could get there. Although it was forestalled by a force from England, Brooke later responded promptly to requests for artillery and cash, which earned him the compliments of the company's directors and Lord Cornwallis. In 1799 he was presented with a sword of honour.

Illness forced Brooke to return home, and he embarked on the *Highland Chief* on 16 March 1801. He retired to Bath, where he died on 25 January 1811. A man of modest abilities, he was energetic, brave, upright, and humane. He was survived by his wife, who died on 26 March 1824.

T. H. BOWYER

Sources DNB · 'Memoir of Governor Brooke', *Asiatic Journal*, new ser., 19 (1836), 181–4; repr. in *Bengal Past and Present*, 7 (1911), 78–82 · P. Gosse, *St. Helena, 1502–1938* (1938) · Burke, *Gen. Ire.* (1958) · D. Dickson, 'Aspects of the rise and decline of the Irish cotton industry', *Comparative aspects of Scottish and Irish economic and social history, 1600–1900*, ed. L. M. Cullen and T. C. Smout (1977), 102–3 · V. C. P. Hodson, *List of officers of the Bengal army, 1758–1834*, 1 (1927) · S. J. Connolly, ed., *The Oxford companion to Irish history* (1998), 465 · Dodwell [E. Dodwell] and Miles [J. S. Miles], eds., *Alphabetical list of the officers of the Indian army: with the dates of their respective promotion, retirement, resignation, or death … from the year 1760 to the year … 1837* (1838) · T. H. Brooke, *History of the island of St. Helena … to the year 1823*, 2nd edn (1824) · J. Warburton, J. Whitelaw, and R. Walsh, *History of the city of Dublin*, 2 (1818)
Archives BL, letters to D. Anderson, Add. MS 45430 · BL, Hastings MS 29133 · University of Witwatersrand, Johannesburg, letters to Lord Macartney
Likenesses coloured miniature, repro. in Gosse, *St Helena, 1502–1938* · miniature, silhouette, repro. in Gosse, *St Helena, 1502–1938*

Brooke, Rupert Chawner (1887–1915), poet, was born on 3 August 1887 at 5 Hillmorton Road, Rugby, Warwickshire, the second of the three sons born to William Parker Brooke (1850–1910), schoolmaster, and his wife, Ruth Mary (*d.* 1930), the daughter of the Revd Charles Cotterill of Stoke-on-Trent. When Rupert was aged three, his mild and scholarly father was promoted from classics tutor to housemaster of School Field at Rugby School. Brooke attended a preparatory school, Hillbrow, as a day boy, 1897–1901, and then proceeded to take his place at Rugby. Home and school thus became the same place, and psychologically this situation may have represented the worst of both worlds: he experienced the sexually sequestered and confusing world of the public school, while simultaneously coping with the emotional intensities generated by a possessive mother and a distantly affectionate father.

In Brooke's adolescence there was a divergence between his conventional achievements and his quietly rebellious romantic and aesthetic interests. He did well at classics and represented both house and school at rugby football and cricket. But at the same time he was writing poems heavily influenced by the poets of the English decadence, and indulging in romantic crushes on other boys. The poems, with their expression of ambivalence towards desire, their feelings of sinfulness and shame, their notions of lost beauty, love, and purity, and their concern with sickness and disease, prefigure the intricate difficulties of Brooke's sexuality in the years that followed.

From 1906 to 1909 Brooke read classics at King's College, Cambridge, but English literature was always his first love. He experienced a difficult first term, and his elder brother died during the Christmas vacation, but despite these setbacks Brooke soon became involved in various Cambridge groups, and was widely acknowledged as a handsome and charismatic figure about the university.

Rupert Chawner Brooke (1887–1915), by Sherril Schell, 1913

Some of the circles in which he moved were predominantly homosexual—Charles Sayle's salon and the exclusive discussion group known as the Apostles—while others (the Fabian Society and the Marlowe Dramatic Society), introduced Brooke to the company of women. Encouraged by friends, he also developed an enthusiasm for long walks, camping, nude bathing, and vegetarianism—a creed which Virginia Woolf christened 'neo-paganism'.

Brooke's public life continued successfully. He acted in various plays, wrote and published poems, and completed his degree. From 1909 to 1912 he lived in Grantchester while he pursued further academic work, concentrating now on Jacobean drama. He won the Charles Oldham Shakespeare prize for an essay on Webster (1909) and the Harness prize for his essay 'Puritanism and the English drama up to 1642', and finally completed a dissertation, entitled 'John Webster and the Elizabethan drama', which won him a fellowship at King's in 1913. These studies were punctuated by various travels in England and on the continent, and a term spent acting as housemaster of School Field at Rugby on the death of his father in 1910. In 1911 he published his first volume of poetry, and in 1912 he helped Edward Marsh to plan the first of his *Georgian Poetry* anthologies.

Despite this parade of achievement, Brooke's private life proceeded from confusion to chaos and crisis. Paradoxically, his emotional and his psychosexual life were ruled by the puritanism which he dissected in his academic writing. To a revulsion from the body he added a deep uncertainty as to the direction of his desires. In 1908

he met and chose to fall 'in love' with Noel Olivier, a fifteen-year-old schoolgirl. This inherently difficult liaison was further complicated by Brooke's deciding in 1909 to lose his virginity with Denham Russell-Smith (1888/9–1912). James Strachey also remained a close friend during this period, although Brooke refused at least two invitations to share his bed. Further chaste entanglements developed in 1910 and 1911 with Katherine (Ka) Laird Cox (1887–1938) and Elisabeth van Rysselberghe (1889/90–1980) respectively.

Brooke's unresolved relationships with Noel and Ka precipitated a nervous breakdown in early 1912, following which he consummated his relationship with Ka. But this led to more misery, and there is some evidence to suggest that Ka bore his stillborn child later that year (Delany, 172). Also during 1912, Brooke was sporadically involved in a tortured and ambivalent relationship with the artist Phyllis Gardner. This liaison foundered when Gardner insisted on the propriety of marriage. Brooke, meanwhile, in late 1912 and 1913, had recommended his complicated dealings with Elisabeth van Rysselberghe and had been attracted to Cathleen Nesbitt. No satisfactory relationship with either woman ensued. As Paul Delany has remarked, Brooke's correspondence at this time is 'sprinkled with coarse and morally repellent attacks on women, homosexuals and Jews' (ibid., 153) that leave no doubt as to the depths of the psychological problems with which he was struggling.

In May 1913 Brooke escaped for a year of travel in which he visited Canada, the United States, and the south seas. This experience resulted in the prose essays collected posthumously as *Letters from America* (1916), and in an affair with a Tahitian woman, Taatamata, who seems to have afforded Brooke some temporary physical satisfaction but little lasting reprieve from his insecurity and paranoia.

On his return to England in June 1914 Brooke's vacillations concerning Cathleen Nesbitt were exacerbated by a developing friendship with Lady Eileen Wellesley. But the outbreak of war saved this situation and Brooke turned his romantic attention away from love towards war. He was given a commission in the Royal Naval division in September and in October was at the siege of Antwerp, but saw little action. Following this experience he wrote the five war sonnets which made him first famous, then infamous when they came to be taken as representative of the supposedly naive patriotism of Brooke's generation. In February 1915 the division sailed for Gallipoli, but Brooke never reached any heroic apotheosis in that ill-fated campaign: he died at sea on 23 April and was buried at Skyros the same day. He is thought to have contracted septicaemia from a mosquito bite. *1914 and other Poems* was published posthumously in 1915, and his *Collected Poems* in 1918.

During his years at Cambridge, influenced by the Jacobean poets and dramatists that he studied, Brooke refined the style of his poetry. The lush extravagance learned from the decadents gave way to a harder-edged diction, metaphor which sometimes tested the boundaries of Edwardian good taste, and a penchant for syllogism. He showed a particular felicity in his use of the sonnet and rhymed octosyllabics. The subject matter of the poems is dominated by conflicts in which youth and innocence are preferred to age and experience, mind is valued above the distrusted body, and the 'eternal' is often aspired to at the expense of the transitory. There is a desire for 'cleanliness' and a shrinking from 'dirt'. It is not difficult to trace the continuities between such concerns and the war sonnets. In the latter, mind triumphs over matter to achieve a youthful and martyred heroism that is eternal; pain, violence, and death are equated with cleanliness and allowed to triumph over erotic love: all this in the name of England.

The war sonnets, and other much-quoted poems, such as 'The Old Vicarage, Grantchester', and 'The Great Lover', together with memoirs which dwelt on Brooke's charm and good looks, created a cultural myth in which the poet—'A young Apollo, golden-haired' in Frances Cornford's famous phrase from the poem 'Youth'—came to symbolize both a golden age of pre-war Edwardian England and the tragedy of willingly martyred youth. Revulsion from the horrors of the First World War, the huge reputation of the trench poets Owen, Sassoon, and Rosenberg, and the general dismissal of Georgian poetry in the 1960s and 1970s created a counter-myth wherein Brooke became politically and poetically unfashionable, though his poems kept their place in anthologies and in public memory: 'The Soldier' (1914), Brooke's elegy to England, was probably the best-known sonnet published in English in the twentieth century. Perhaps now, it is possible to see him and his work from both perspectives as a representative figure of his time, articulating the manifest complexities of Edwardian masculinity.   ADRIAN CAESAR

Sources C. Hassall, *Rupert Brooke: a biography* (1964) · P. Delany, *The neo-pagans: friendship and love in the Rupert Brooke circle* (1987) · J. Lehmann, *Rupert Brooke: his life and his legend* (1980) · A. Caesar, 'Rupert Brooke', *Taking it like a man: suffering, sexuality and the war poets* (1993) · *The letters of Rupert Brooke*, ed. G. Keynes (1968) · P. Harris, ed., *Song of love: the letters of Rupert Brooke and Noel Olivier* (1991) · W. E. Laskowski, *Rupert Brooke* (1994) · S. Hynes, 'Rupert Brooke', *Edwardian occasions: essays on English writing in the early twentieth century* (1972) · G. Bloom, 'The falling house that never falls: Rupert Brooke and literary taste', *British poetry, 1900–1950*, ed. G. Day and B. Docherty (1995) · M. Hastings, *The handsomest young man in England: Rupert Brooke* (1967) · G. Keynes, *A bibliography of Rupert Brooke* (1954) · F. D. Cornford, 'Youth', *Collected poems* (1954) · E. Marsh, 'Memoir', in *The collected poems of Rupert Brooke* (1989)

Archives CUL, corresp. and papers; letters to his mother · Dartmouth College, Hanover, New Hampshire, corresp. and papers, incl. literary MSS · King's AC Cam., corresp., papers, and literary MSS | BL, corresp. with Phyllis Gardner and her mother Mary, Add. MS 74741 · BL, Strachey MSS · CUL, letters to Frances Cornford; letters to Katherine Cox; letters to Hugh Dalton; letters to Geoffrey Fry; letters to Geoffrey Keynes; letters to Jacques Raverat and Gwen Raverat; letters to Charles Sayle; letters to A. F. Scholfield; corresp. with Edward Dent · King's Cam., letters to J. T. Sheppard · NYPL, Berg collection, corresp. with J. Strachey

Likenesses Speight, carte photograph, 1903, NPG · G. A. Dean, carte photograph, 1905, NPG · Scott & Wilkinson, print, 1906, NPG · V. H. Mottram, print, c.1907, NPG · G. Raverat, pencil on paper, 1910, NPG · C. Ewald, oils, 1911, NPG; version, King's Cam. · S. Schell, photographs, c.1913, Hult. Arch., NPG [*see illus.*] · E. Walker, glass positive photograph, 1913 (after S. Schell), NPG · photograph, 1913, NPG · J. H. Thomas, pencil drawing, 1916 (posthumous; after photograph by S. Schell), NPG · H. Thomas and E. Gill, stone memorial plaque, 1919 (after photograph by S. Schell), Rugby School chapel · photograph, NPG · photographs, priv. coll.

Wealth at death £923 10s. 0d.: administration, 29 July 1915, CGPLA Eng. & Wales

Brooke, Samuel (c.1575–1631), college head, was the third son of Robert Brooke (c.1531–1599), merchant and twice lord mayor of York, and his wife, Jane (d. 1604), the daughter of Christopher Maltby of Thornton in Pickering Lythe. He entered Trinity College, Cambridge, as a pensioner about 1592, and was elected to a scholarship in 1593. He graduated BA early in 1595 and proceeded MA in 1598. On 23 December 1599 he was ordained deacon and priest at Peterborough. From 1600 to 1615 he was chaplain of his college. In December 1601 he officiated at the marriage of John Donne, who was a friend of his elder brother Christopher *Brooke and who had unwisely eloped with the daughter of the lieutenant of the Tower; as a result all three young men were briefly imprisoned. Samuel's career proceeded smoothly after this awkward start; in 1607 he took his BD and about 1610 he became a chaplain to Henry, prince of Wales.

While Christopher was becoming known as a poet Samuel Brooke inclined to drama and in the winter of 1611–12 the undergraduates of Trinity first performed his *Adelphe*, a Latin adaptation of Giambattista della Porta's comedy *La Sorella*. On 26 September 1612 Brooke was appointed professor of divinity at Gresham's College, London, on the recommendation of Prince Henry. Following the prince's death later that year Brooke became chaplain to the king. In March 1613 the new heir to the throne, Prince Charles, visited Cambridge with his brother-in-law the elector palatine. *Adelphe* was played before the royal visitors at Trinity on 2 March, followed next evening by the première of Brooke's *Scyros*, again a Latin translation of an Italian original, Guidubaldo Bonarelli's *Filli de Sciro*. The first of these entertainments lasted six hours (through most of which the elector slept), and the second was somewhat longer. Brooke's third play *Melanthe* (for which no source has been identified) was given before James I in Trinity hall on 10 March 1615, and was issued by the university printer on 27 March. Although he seems to have continued to write for the stage, Brooke thereafter concentrated on theological work. In 1615 he proceeded DD and in June 1616 he delivered a dissertation, *De auxilio divinae gratiae*, in which he attacked Calvin and, while claiming not to be his disciple, supported the Dutch theologian Arminius in his rebuttal of the doctrine of predestination.

Brooke then moved to London, and on 1 February 1618 he was admitted to Lincoln's Inn, of which his brother Christopher was a bencher. On 30 June he was instituted to the rectory of St Margaret, Lothbury. That September he sent a dedicatory copy of his *De auxilio* to the earl of Pembroke, whom he had met during the king's visit to Cambridge in 1615. This did not secure publication, but may have led to Brooke's incorporation at Oxford, of which Pembroke was chancellor, on 21 July 1621. On 23

February 1622 the king presented him to the rectory of Hemingford Abbots, Huntingdonshire, of which he had long had promise. In 1627 he exchanged his London rectory for another near Huntingdon, King's Ripton. He had meanwhile become chaplain to Charles I. On 15 July 1628 the king gave him the reversion of the mastership of Trinity, to which he succeeded on 5 September 1629. He then resigned his London chair, and devoted himself to collegiate affairs.

Brooke was increasingly reluctant to serve his turn at court, although aware that the king 'much notes the order and service of his chaplains' (*CSP dom.*, *1629–31*, 128–9). In 1630 he declined to serve as vice-chancellor; he had since April that year been working at a larger tract on the subject of predestination. By 1 December he could report to the chancellor, Bishop William Laud that he had 'found an issue out of that wood and wilderness' which had been unresolved in his previous work (ibid., 396). Laud replied wearily that he would look over the composition if it should not be too long, but doubted Brooke's sanguine claim to have settled an issue which he himself thought 'unmasterable in this life', and warned that the king would not thank him for rekindling the controversy (ibid., 405). Brooke responded (15 December) in terms which the bishop could not have faulted: 'Predestination is the root of Puritanism, and Puritanism the root of all rebellious and disobedient intractableness in Parliament … in the country, nay in the Church itself' (ibid., 411). But the king and Laud had already decreed the discussion closed, and even a supportive voice was unwelcome. In consequence Brooke's tract was never published, and only three of its four projected parts were even completed.

Brooke had long been troubled with calculus (stone in the kidney or bladder), but his death may have been caused by the plague which came to Cambridge in the late summer of 1631. He made his will on 16 September and was dead by the twentieth. He was buried in Trinity chapel. Although he inherited a property in York from his father, his own estate amounted to less than £800, of which the bulk was left to his brothers Arthur and Robert. C. S. KNIGHTON

Sources Wood, *Ath. Oxon.*: *Fasti* (1815), 401–2 · Venn, *Alum. Cant.*, 1/1.277 · *Fasti Angl.* (Hardy), 1.569 · G. Hennessy, *Novum repertorium ecclesiasticum parochiale Londinense, or, London diocesan clergy succession from the earliest time to the year 1898* (1898), 279 · *CSP dom.*, *1628–9*, 211; *1629–31*, 67, 128–9, 384–5, 396, 404–5, 411 · S. Brooke, *Melanthe*, ed. J. S. G. Bolton (1928) · N. Tyacke, *Anti-Calvinists: the rise of English Arminianism, c.1590–1640* (1987), 40, 57 · P. E. McCullough, *Sermons at court: politics and religion in Elizabethan and Jacobean preaching* (1998), 188–9, 197 [incl. CD-ROM] · PRO, PROB 11/160, fol. 239 · N. M. Sutherland, 'Brooke, Robert', HoP, *Commons, 1558–1603* · Borth. Inst., probate register 27, fol. 596

Archives CUL, tracts · Trinity Cam., tract | PRO, letters, SP 16/149, no. 108; 153, nos. 3, 99; 175, no. 69; 176, no. 3; 177, no. 8

Wealth at death £790—the 'substance of his estate': will, PRO, PROB 11/160, fol. 239, proved 20 Sept 1631

Brooke, Stopford Augustus (1832–1916), preacher and writer, was born on 14 November 1832, at Glendoen, near Letterkenny, co. Donegal, the eldest of four sons and four

Stopford Augustus Brooke (1832–1916), by George Frederic Watts, 1871

daughters born to Richard Sinclair Brooke (1802–1882), then curate of the parish, and his wife, Anna (1812?–1903), daughter of Joseph Stopford, the rector of Glendoen. Following Stopford's death in 1833 Richard Brooke took a curacy in Abbeyleix, co. Meath, and in 1836 became chaplain to the Mariners' Church in Kingstown, where he remained until 1862. The elder Brooke was an evangelical, and the deep piety of the household was combined with love of poetry, particularly the romantics of the immediate past.

A sickly child turned handsome and vigorous as a young man, Stopford Brooke was sent in 1847, after some local schooling, to board at the Kidderminster grammar school. Admirably prepared, he entered Trinity College, Dublin, in 1850. He won two prizes, one for divinity, one for English verse, and graduated BA in 1856 and MA in 1858. By the time he entered Trinity he had already begun to question his evangelical inheritance, and one of his earliest articles, in the *Dublin University Magazine*, was a tribute to the Revd Charles Kingsley (1819–1875), whose robust liberal Christianity and social commitment were mirrored in Brooke's career.

Ordained in London on 7 June 1857, Brooke took a curacy at St Matthew's, Marylebone, in an area of extreme deprivation, an experience which fed his sense of social mission; he also taught at the Queen's College, Harley Street, founded by F. D. Maurice (1805–1872) for the education of working men. On 23 March 1858 he married Emma Diana (1831–1874), only daughter of Thomas Wentworth Beaumont (1792–1841), thus uniting a distinguished but straitened Irish clerical family with a wealthy English political dynasty. They had two sons and six daughters. The second son, Graham, died of typhoid fever in 1869, a loss that hastened Mrs Brooke's decline and death. The eldest son, Stopford Wentworth William Brooke (1859–1938), after Winchester College and University College, Oxford, where he graduated in 1881, was Unitarian minister at Clifton from 1883 to 1886 and then was minister at the First Church (Unitarian) in Boston. On his return to England he served as Liberal MP for Bow and Bromley from 1906 to 1910.

In 1859 Brooke moved to St Mary Abbots, Kensington, again as a curate; there his reputation as a brilliant preacher brought him much notice. But he remained restive, while his now firm commitment to the broad-church reduced his mobility. One notable recognition was accorded him. In 1857 he had met Henry King, the publisher, who was casting about for someone to write a biography of F. W. Robertson (1816–1853), whose meteoric rise to fame as a preacher at the proprietary Trinity Chapel in Brighton had been confirmed, particularly among broad-churchmen, by the publication of his sermons in 1855, following his early death. King decided on Brooke and, having gained assent from others, in 1857 offered him the commission, an extraordinary opportunity for an unknown curate of twenty-five.

The next year the princess royal was married to the crown prince of Prussia, leading to the establishment of an English court in the German capital. In 1862 Brooke applied for and was given the post of chaplain to the British embassy in Berlin, where he took up residence in the autumn of 1863, a move that forestalled acceptance of a promising curacy in Hammersmith. The stay in Prussia offered two advantages: a connection through the princess, who much admired him, with the court at Windsor, and time to complete his life of Robertson. Otherwise Berlin proved unappealing, and the family returned to London early in 1865.

The life and letters of Robertson was published that year, to great acclaim, cementing the reputations of both its subject and its author. Brooke preached in the private chapel at Windsor on 23 November 1865 and several times subsequently, and in January 1867 was made a chaplain to the queen. Admiring his preaching and his liberality, Victoria wanted him made a canon of Westminster, but Brooke recalled that Disraeli objected to his politics and Gladstone to his theology; on hearing him preach in Westminster Abbey, Gladstone recorded: 'very noteworthy, a little perilous' (11 June 1876).

By early 1866 Brooke's career had taken on its final form. Against the advice of many friends he accepted the lease of a proprietary chapel in York Street, St James's, where his preaching, begun in mid-April, soon filled the small premises, though the financial return (not of great significance, given his wife's wealth) was minuscule. They took a house in Manchester Square, where he lived almost to the end of his life. Soon after Emma Brooke's death in 1874 the lease on the chapel ended, and a group of his friends secured the lease to the much larger Bedford Chapel in

Bloomsbury, where he began preaching in May 1876 and continued until his retirement in 1895. He was thus assured, as his friends intended, a prominent pulpit, from which he preached to fashionable and enthusiastic audiences, while, as had been the case with Robertson, he could claim a degree of freedom that few ordinary parochial appointments would have allowed. George Bernard Shaw, who was impressed by Brooke's 'cultured suasiveness' in the debating society he chaired at Bedford Chapel, took him as the model for the Revd James Mavor Morell, the Christian socialist clergyman in *Candida* (1893) (Standley, 27–8).

In a remarkable sermon, 'Salt without Savour', preached in Bedford Chapel on 17 October 1880, Brooke announced his withdrawal from the Church of England. The immediate occasion was his inability any longer to accept the miracle of the incarnation, but he had also become disillusioned with the conservative social and political attitudes of an essentially aristocratic church. He had established connections with leading theologians among the Unitarians, notably James Martineau (1805–1900), who joined Brooke's congregation when the Anglican connection was broken, while the young Lawrence Pearsall Jacks (1860–1955), at the beginning of his distinguished career, served as Brooke's assistant in 1887–8 and subsequently married Brooke's daughter Olivia. The Unitarians had welcomed his defection, but he never formally joined their communion, although he sometimes preached in Unitarian churches and after his retirement went on lecture tours under Unitarian auspices.

Brooke's life as a preacher was doubled by his prominent role as writer, lecturer, and literary critic. He was equally devoted to social reform, nature, and the arts, a high mission of his early years that never altered: indeed, when he was told that James Martineau had said of him that he had never grown up, he called it the highest compliment he was ever paid (Jacks, 1.86). He was an omnivorous reader, and if he never reached the originality and breadth of Philip Henry Wicksteed (1844–1927), the great Unitarian minister, social reformer, literary critic, and political economist, he was certainly the superior in talent and reputation of all the other late Victorian ministers who shared his passion for Milton and Shakespeare and the compulsion to share it with their flocks and other contemporaries through lectures.

A course of lectures given at York Street in 1872 and published the next year as *The Theology of the English Poets* dealt with poetry from Cowper to Burns, although fully half the chapters are devoted to Wordsworth. But the book appeared to suggest (to the horror of the orthodox) a parallel canon of revelation, and certainly a sense of inspiration in literature informed Brooke's popular analyses of Milton and Shakespeare, Tennyson and Browning. His *English Literature* (1877), in a series of literature primers edited by the historian J. R. Green (1837–1883), covered the subject from Caedmon to Shelley and Scott (with repeated attention to the theme of Englishness) in 167 pages, a formidable feat of compression which was well received critically and reached printings totalling nearly half a million copies by the time of his death. He was himself a poet; his principal work was a verse drama, *Riquet of the Tuft: a Love Drama* (1880). His sermon 'Art expenditure', given at St James's Chapel and published in 1873 in *Christ in Modern Life*, argues against a narrowly utilitarian and dismissive view of art, and calls for public investment in art and for public collections built up not only from a few merchant fortunes but from the great landed wealth of the country.

Brooke's retirement from Bedford Chapel in 1895, which entailed the closing of the chapel, was dictated by a bout of ill health, though in time he recovered and devoted himself to literary work and lecturing; he also became a painter of considerable skill. In 1911 he built a house, Four Winds, in Cranleigh, Surrey, and retired there fully in 1914. He died at the house on 18 March 1916 of heart failure and underlying diabetes; the death certificate, which listed S. W. W. Brooke as informant, identifies him as a Unitarian minister. His body was cremated on 23 March at Woking crematorium, and the ashes were divided between the Hampstead cemetery, where his wife was buried, and the grounds at Four Winds.

R. K. WEBB

Sources L. P. Jacks, *Life and letters of Stopford Brooke*, 2 vols. (1917) · F. L. Standley, *Stopford Brooke* (1972) · *The Inquirer* (25 March 1916) · *The Inquirer* (1 April 1916) · Gladstone, *Diaries* · Burke, *Gen. GB* (1900) · d. cert.
Archives NL Wales · U. Reading L., letters | BL, corresp. Macmillans, Add. MS 55115 · Castle Howard, North Yorkshire, letters to Rosalind, countess of Carlisle · Harris Man. Oxf., letters to V. D. Davis · Morgan L., letters mainly to William Angus Knight · NL Ire., letters to A. S. Green · NL Wales, letters to M. C. M. Simpson
Likenesses G. F. Watts, oils, 1871, NPG [*see illus.*] · Barraud, photograph, 1889, repro. in *Men and Women of the Day*, 2 (1889) · Beresford, two photographs, 1903–5, NPG · W. Rothenstein, pencil drawing, 1917–18, NPG · Elliott & Fry, carte photograph, NPG · N. S. Kay, photograph, NPG · G. Pilotell, drypoint, BM · W. Rothenstein, pencil drawing, NPG · process print, BM
Wealth at death £10,959 16s. 7d.: probate, 20 May 1916, *CGPLA Eng. & Wales*

Brooke, Sir (Charles) Vyner de Windt (1874–1963), third and last raja of Sarawak, was born on 26 September 1874 at Albemarle Street, London, the eldest son of Sir Charles Anthoni Johnson *Brooke (1829–1917), second raja of Sarawak, and his wife, Margaret Lili Alice de Windt (*d.* 1936) of Blunsdon Hall, Highworth, Wiltshire. Educated at Winchester College, he went on to Magdalene College, Cambridge, where his interests in boxing, horse-racing, and fast cars prevailed over his studies. His first visits to Sarawak were in 1876 as a child, in 1888 with his two younger brothers Bertram and Harry and their tutor Gerard Fiennes, and in 1893 when he was seventeen. In 1891 he was given the title of *raja muda* (heir apparent) by his father and six years later went out as a cadet government officer. Serving first at Simanggang in the second division and then at Muka and Oya in the third division, he was appointed resident in late 1903. In May 1900 he took part in an expedition against the Muruts of the Trusan and in June 1902 helped lead the notorious 'cholera expedition' when one-fifth of 10,000 Dayaks recruited to pacify the rebels of the Ul Ai died of the disease. This experience scarred him for life.

Contrary to her parents' wishes, on 21 February 1911 at St Peter's Church, Cranborne, Brooke married Sylvia, second daughter of Reginald Baliol Brett, second Viscount Esher, and Eleanor Frances Weston. Contrary to his own father's wishes, he took her and her brother Oliver on a visit to Sarawak the following year. This, together with his knowledge of Vyner's gambling debts, his fear that he would hand Sarawak over to British interests, and Sylvia's failure to produce a son, caused Charles seriously to consider disinheriting Vyner in favour of Bertram. Instead, he issued a proclamation in 1912 which established a supervisory Sarawak government commission in London and recognized Bertram as having almost equal status with Vyner. This caused a serious rift between Vyner and his father. After Charles's death and Vyner's proclamation as raja in May 1917, he and Bertram took it in turn to spend half a year in Sarawak as head of state, Vyner always avoiding the English winter. An unwilling raja, he was nevertheless unprepared to hand over the reins to the able and conscientious Bertram. His interest in government was slight and in the resulting power vacuum effective executive control passed first to his brilliant but unstable protégé and adviser, Gerard MacBryan, and then to a group of senior government officers known as the committee of administration. Acute problems brought about by the depression and rubber restriction were left to others to resolve. When the committee's centralizing push caused out-station officers, supported by his nephew Anthony, to rebel against it in April 1939, Vyner appointed him *raja muda* and left him in charge of the government for six months. Subsequently convinced that high office had gone to Anthony's head, he dismissed him but later reinstated him on Bertram's intervention.

Wearying of his role and pressured by the rani and their three daughters, Leonora, Elizabeth, and Valerie, to make a financial settlement and retire to England, Brooke negotiated a secret agreement with the committee of administration in early 1941. This brought him 1 million Sarawak dollars from state funds in return for abandoning most of his prerogative powers and implementing a written constitution. It was duly enacted in September 1941 during the celebration of the centenary of Brooke rule. MacBryan, who was out of favour in the 1930s, had re-emerged in early 1941 to broker the agreement and take charge of the celebrations. Anthony, who had bitterly opposed the constitution as dishonouring Charles's political will, was sent back to England in disgrace.

When the Japanese invaded Sarawak by sea on 16 December 1941, Brooke was on holiday in Australia with MacBryan. On hearing the news the raja flew to Batavia with MacBryan hoping to return to the state but was forced by events to seek sanctuary in Australia. The next two years he spent in Melbourne with MacBryan, who had been held briefly as a suspected Japanese agent in Batavia and then Singapore. Initially critical of the British government's failure to defend Sarawak despite its generous contributions to the war effort, Brooke was pressured into silence. In 1943 he managed to return to London via the

United States and remained there for the rest of the war. Handing over responsibility for Sarawak affairs again to Anthony and reinstating him as *raja muda*, he dismissed him once more in December 1945 when negotiations with the Colonial Office over Sarawak's post-war constitutional arrangements broke down. Entering into direct negotiations with the Colonial Office with MacBryan's assistance, Vyner agreed to cede his sovereignty to the crown on condition that he and his family were left 'no worse off' financially. The Colonial Office had misled him into believing that the war had left a task of reconstruction beyond his means. Nor had he any faith in his nephew Anthony as his successor. He visited Sarawak with the rani briefly in April and May 1946 for the Council Negri debate on the cession bill. His announcement of the cession in February had alienated many of his officers and a substantial section of the Malay population whose agitation surprised and horrified him.

Despite newspaper reports at the time that Brooke had received £1 million from the British government as a quid pro quo for the cession, he received nothing and had to pay tax on his Sarawak pension. Obliged to live in modest circumstances for the rest of his life while supporting Sylvia, he became something of a hermit. He never returned to Sarawak and saw little of his former officers. Towards the end of his life he became reconciled with Bertram, who, together with Anthony, had been disinherited by the cession in 1946. Vyner Brooke died at his flat at 13 Albion Street, Paddington, London, on 9 May 1963, some months before the proclamation of the Federation of Malaysia of which Sarawak then became part. He had been made KCMG in 1928 but the Attlee government declined to elevate him to a baronetcy in recognition of his co-operation over the cession. Sylvia, who had lived for many years in Barbados, died on 11 November 1971. They had kept up a friendly, teasing correspondence to the end. Vyner's portrait was painted by his friend Margaret Noble and is held at Magdalene College, Cambridge, where there is also a stained glass window in his memory. The portrait shows that he had a cast in one eye, something which heightened the inscrutable impression he made on people. Painfully shy in his official role, his carefree and pleasure-loving way of life was in part a reaction to the regime of his ascetic and forbidding father. Loved rather than held in awe by his people, Brooke spoke fluent Malay and Iban and demonstrated an extraordinary ability to remember names and genealogies. He was cremated and his ashes buried in the churchyard at Sheepstor, Devon, alongside his father and great-uncle. R. H. W. REECE

Sources *Sylvia of Sarawak: an autobiography* (1936) · S. Runciman, *The white rajahs* (1960) · R. H. W. Reece, *The name of Brooke: the end of white rajah rule in Sarawak* (1982) · *CGPLA Eng. & Wales* (1963) · d. cert.
Archives Bodl. RH, personal corresp., mainly with his brother | Bodl. RH, letters to G. Gillan; letters to F. Kortright and I. Kortright; letters to C. P. Lowe; corresp. with W. Skrine · PRO, corresp. with F. Dallas, PRO 30/79
Likenesses H. Leslie, silhouette drawing, 1924, NPG · M. Noble, portrait, Magd. Cam.

Wealth at death £29,758 6s. 2d.: probate, 18 Sept 1963, *CGPLA Eng. & Wales* · English probate sealed in Singapore, 12 March 1964, *CGPLA Eng. & Wales*

Brooke, William, tenth Baron Cobham (1527–1597), nobleman and diplomat, was born on 1 November 1527, the eldest of seven surviving sons (there were also four daughters) of George *Brooke, ninth Baron Cobham (*c*.1497–1558), soldier and landowner, and his wife, Anne (*c*.1510–1558), first daughter of Edmund Bray, first Baron Bray, and his wife, Jane. His brothers included the MPs George (*b*. 1533, *d*. in or after 1569), Thomas (1533–1578), John (1535–1594), and Sir Henry *Brooke (1537–1592), the diplomat.

Early years and education, 1527–1558 Though enrolled at Queens' College, Cambridge, between 1542 and 1544 with an exhibition from King's School, Canterbury, William Brooke probably spent most of the time abroad during these years. He was certainly in Padua and the Veneto in 1543 and 1545, supposedly to study civil law, but the Venetian government licensed him to carry arms, noting an inclination to war rather than letters. By 4 June 1535 he was contracted to marry Dorothy (*d*. 1559), daughter of George Neville, third Baron Abergavenny, and his third wife, Mary. They married late in 1545 and had one daughter, Frances Brooke (*b*. 1549), before separating in or before 1553. Dorothy Brooke died at Cobham Hall, Kent, on 22 September 1559 and was buried there on 3 October. William Brooke was enrolled in the Boulogne garrison, then in 1548 was transferred to Calais under his father and knighted on 1 December. He accompanied Sir William Paget on his embassy to Brussels the following year, but after the outbreak of war with France he distinguished himself in a skirmish. That he had been returned as MP for Hythe, Kent, in 1547 was testimony to his father's local, and possibly Paget's national, influence, but he cannot have attended parliament much. Appointed esquire of the body to Edward VI in 1550, the following year Brooke joined the French embassy of William Parr, marquess of Northampton.

The Brookes enjoyed diverse family and political connections. Protestant relatives included Sir William *Cecil (1520/21–1598) and Nicholas Bacon (1510–1579), but they were also related to the Catholic Southwell and Shelley families. Cobham was recruited by John Dudley, earl of Warwick, who added him to the privy council on 23 May 1550. Cobham's daughter Elizabeth (1526–1565) married Warwick's ally Northampton. However, in 1553 Cobham quickly abandoned the Dudley party during the succession crisis. It was therefore typical that the rising of Sir Thomas Wyatt the younger (*b*. in or before 1521, *d*. 1554) in the Brookes' home county of Kent found them attempting to be all things to all people. Cobham retreated before Wyatt into Cooling Castle, Kent, surrendered, and then escaped to London. Sir William Brooke and his brothers George and Thomas remained with the rebels. After the rising proceedings against William and George Brooke were halted following indictment, helped by the intervention of the Nevilles, despite the breakdown of William Brooke's marriage. In 1555 Sir William Brooke was returned to parliament for Rochester, Kent, but made little attempt there to appease Mary I's government.

Tenth Lord Cobham, 1558–1586 Between 1558 and 1559 Brooke's prospects were transformed by the deaths of his father on 29 September 1558, of Sir Thomas Cheyne, lord warden of the Cinque Ports, and of Dorothy Brooke, and by the accession of Elizabeth I. The new peer was appointed by Elizabeth on 18 November 1558 as a special ambassador to take news of Mary's death to Philip II. He had an audience with Philip in Brussels on 9 December and the limited nature of his mission proved a sore disappointment to the king, who was irritated enough not to grant him a pension.

Because of Cheyne's failing health, Cobham took charge of the Cinque Ports. Once appointed lord warden of the Cinque Ports and constable of Dover Castle (16 December 1558), the addition of the lord lieutenantcy in 1559 and the vice-admiralty of Kent gave him much greater dominance in the county than his predecessor. He was JP for Kent from 1558–9 and of the quorum from 1561. These offices were a testimony to Cecil's regard. Possibly Cecil's 'dearest friend', Cobham was certainly to be his most enduring one for the next forty years (Beckingsale, 271). From the start one aspect of political friendship was the helpful use of parliamentary patronage. Queenborough was probably enfranchised for Cobham's benefit, and Rochester was also generally pliable. The county elections from 1586 also mostly went Cobham's way. With some effort the lord warden could get one MP returned out of two in each of the seven Cinque Ports. Control of a dozen seats made him one of the great parliamentary patrons. Despite electoral and financial disputes, economic decline forced the ports into increasing dependence on Cobham: funding of a major reconstruction of Dover harbour was one example of the possible benefits of his patronage.

On 25 February 1560 at Whitehall Palace Cobham married Frances (d. 1592), daughter of Sir John Newton. She was a lady of the bedchamber. The marriage was perhaps fortuitous for both, Frances Brooke being promoted to the rank of lady of the bedchamber, while her personal influence with the queen proved useful to Cobham. Lady Cobham could even tell Elizabeth that François, duc d'Anjou, was too young for her. The couple's children were Maximilian (1560–1583), the twins Elizabeth (1562–1597) and Frances (1562–1615x23), Margaret (1563–1621), Henry *Brooke, eleventh Baron Cobham (1564–1619), William (1565–1597), and George *Brooke (1568–1603).

Cobham's Cinque Ports and Dover offices gave him a critical role at a time of security scares, in gathering intelligence, scrutinizing arrivals from the continent, and handling the disappearance of diplomatic bags. However, when he seized letters from Roberto de Ridolfi in April 1571, according to Cobham 'his ungracious brother Thomas' begged him to keep them from the privy council, 'for he sayd they wold otherwise be the undoyng of the duke of Norfolk and of himself' (Lettenhove, 6.189). Granting this request was a perilous step for Cobham; that he was 'treated with quite astonishing indulgence' has provoked suggestions that he acted with the approval of Cecil, now Lord Burghley, who wanted the continental correspondence to continue to its incriminating destinations (Edwards, 50). A simpler explanation is that Cobham's role in the Ridolfi plot was as accidental as he said and not worth the loss to Burghley of a friend and ally. Rumour went so far as to claim that Cobham had offered

William Brooke, tenth Baron Cobham (1527–1597), attrib. the Master of the Countess of Warwick, 1567 [with his second wife, Frances Newton (right), six of their children, and Frances's sister Johanna (left)]

the Cinque Ports for an invasion, but he escaped with seven months of house arrest with Burghley and a period of political eclipse that included the effective stalling of his election to the Order of the Garter. The Ridolfi plot and Garter episode were warnings that Cobham's friendship towards Thomas Howard, fourth duke of Norfolk, and Henry Fitzalan, twelfth earl of Arundel, was frowned upon.

Persistent reports of Cobham's sympathy for Catholicism were probably attributable to 'undiscriminatingly sanguine agents of Rome' (McKeen, 239). His favoured preachers, such as William Turner, and the dedicators of books to him, such as Thomas Tymme and Arthur Golding, were typically Calvinist, as was his chaplain William Harrison, though another chaplain, Peter Hendley, did tend to Rome. Cobham, however, lacked the religious ambiguity so blatantly shown by Frances Cobham's unhappy marriage to the recusant John Stourton, ninth Baron Stourton. Cobham himself in his last years, according to the life of Magdalene Browne, Viscountess Montague, sought the hand of that devout Catholic widow but this is not evidence of his own faith. It was probably with some care that Cobham was chosen in 1588 to help John Whitgift, archbishop of Canterbury, hunt the author of the Marprelate tracts, although given that the search was concentrated in Surrey and Kent, his selection certainly made sense.

Cobham accompanied Sir Francis Walsingham on the embassy to the Netherlands from 12 June to 7 October 1578. Presumably this was to exercise restraint on behalf of Burghley, but it is an overstatement that 'Lord Cobham was as far towards popery and Spain as Walsingham was towards Geneva and the rebels' (Wilson, 66). He was always willing to defer to Walsingham, the linguist of the party. Elizabeth's over-complicated efforts to balance Spain, France, and the states general doomed their mission: to the last they gave guarantees for loans which the queen would not honour.

Privy councillor and courtier, 1586–1597 Cobham apparently withdrew from London for some years, laying out celebrated gardens at Cobham Hall and in 1584 starting new wings for the medieval house. He was finally nominated to the Order of the Garter on 23 April 1584 and installed on 14 April 1585. He joined the privy council on or before 12 February 1586: according to Thomas Morgan to check Robert Dudley, earl of Leicester, and more radical protestants. Morgan still hoped to persuade Cobham, through his wife, to intercede on behalf of Mary, queen of Scots. However, Cobham was named to try Philip Howard, earl of Arundel, but not Mary. He did join the House of Lords delegations conferring with the House of Commons on the need for Mary's execution, but avoided royal disfavour and was a mainstay of government business in 1587, while his wife offered to help persuade Elizabeth to forgive Burghley for his handling of the Scottish queen's death warrant. Cobham was in high favour. Had Burghley accepted a higher title in 1589, Cobham would have become earl of Suffolk (he claimed descent from the Poles).

Cobham's relations with Leicester deteriorated as he favoured the involvement of Thomas Wilkes and Thomas Sackville, first Lord Buckhurst, in Netherlands affairs. He was also involved in the negotiations initiated by Sir James Croft to try and hold off a Spanish invasion. Between 20 January and 10 August 1588 Cobham was sent with Henry Stanley, fourth earl of Derby, Croft, Dr Valentine Dale, and Dr John Rogers as special ambassadors to Alessandro Farnese, duke of Parma. Whereas Croft went beyond his instructions in trying to negotiate peace by offering concessions, Cobham soon advised the mission's termination. Thus he was unavailable during the Armada crisis; unfortunately at Dover 'they rely so upon my Lord Cobham, that without his warrant they will do nothing' (Laughton, 2.142). Lady Cobham died at Cobham on 17 October 1592 and was buried there. The couple had been very happy together.

By 1592 Cobham had nearly abandoned privy council meetings, but he attended the Greenwich conference with envoys of Henri IV in April 1596 and was seeking to escape the task of taking the Garter over to him when Henry Carey, first Baron Hunsdon, died, and he was appointed lord chamberlain on 8 August. His appointment may have been due to the marriage of Robert *Cecil (1563–1612) to his daughter Elizabeth in 1589. Cobham was identified with the Cecil faction rather than that of Robert Devereux, second earl of Essex. Cecil needed Cobham at court. In his last months Cobham was second only to Cecil in attendance of the privy council. He was 'perhaps the councillor least willing to co-operate in intelligence matters with Essex' (Hammer, 194n.). He resented Essex's insinuations of negligence concerning Spanish activities in the channel, for instance regarding the surprise attack on Calais in 1596, even if their relationship lacked the bitterness which existed between Essex and Lord Henry Brooke, aggravated by the earl's attempt to get the reversion of the Cinque Ports wardenship for the Brookes' Kentish rivals, the Sidneys. However, yet another of Cobham's sons, Sir William Brooke, served under Essex and was his military client.

Cobham's tenure as lord chamberlain from 1596 to 1597 has attracted interest because of his role in supervision of the theatre, even if he hardly had time to make much impact. A 'cloudy legend with which scholars have enveloped Lord Cobham' depends on a largely circular argument involving alleged puritanism and hatred of playhouses, neither of which is demonstrable (Green, 113). Doubtless Cobham insisted that Sir John Oldcastle (an earlier holder of his title) in William Shakespeare's *Henry IV* be renamed Falstaff. Thomas Nashe wrote that the 'state' of the Lord Chamberlain's Men had been 'setled' under Hunsdon (whose son, George Carey, second Baron Hunsdon, rather than his successor in office, took over their patronage) and was 'uncertayne' under Cobham (McKeen, 650). That is the extent of the evidence, except for speculation about later satires; Frank Ford as putative cuckold in *The Merry Wives of Windsor* adopted the pseudonym Brook, perhaps merely suggested by the name Ford itself. Cobham did not object to a theatrical conversion adjoining his Blackfriars house when invited to do so, and in the 1560s he had supported touring players in Kent and his wife's county of Gloucestershire, though he seems to have retrenched after his imprisonment. In more traditional cultural roles he was, according to Harrison, 'an honourable Mecenas of learning, a lover of learned persons, and not inferior in knowledge to anie of the borne nobilitie of England' (Holinshed, 1499).

Cobham's health was in decline, with an 'ague' in the winter of 1596–7 aggravated by the death of his daughter Elizabeth Cecil on 24 January 1597, but he would not relinquish the Cinque Ports wardenship except to his heir. He made his will on 24 February 1597, died at Blackfriars on 6 March, and after a grand funeral procession through north Kent—insisted upon by Burghley despite the will's rejection of 'vanity'—was buried at the church of St Mary Magdalene, Cobham, on 5 April. Besides considerable provision for his younger sons, he made generous provision for the re-edification of his ancestors' dissolved chantry at Cobham as a more acceptable almshouse (Cobham College). This was funded from one of the greatest aristocratic incomes in England, probably over £5000 per annum, though for tax purposes he was allowed never to declare more than a tenth of that. Over a quarter of his rental came from leases extorted by the crown from the sees of Canterbury (including the archbishop's unused Canterbury Palace), Rochester, and York—a high figure, and a testimony of royal favour. With his father's ambiguous connections resolved into close dependence on Elizabeth and the Cecils, Cobham's family seemed securely positioned—unfortunately his sons Henry and George Brooke were to throw this away.   JULIAN LOCK

Sources D. McKeen, A memory of honour: the life of William Brooke, Lord Cobham, 2 vols. (1986) · HoP, Commons, 1509–58, 1.511–13 · R. Holinshed, The first and second volumes of chronicles (1587) [BL 674.I.5–8] · W. Murdin, ed., Collection of state papers ... left by William Cecil, Lord Burghley ... 1572–96 (1759) · Baron Kervyn de Lettenhove [J. M. B. C. Kervyn de Lettenhove] and L. Gilliodts-van Severen, eds., Relations politiques des Pays-Bas et de l'Angleterre sous le règne de Philippe II, 11 vols. (Brussels, 1882–1900) · P. Clark, English provincial society from the Reformation to the revolution: religion, politics, and society in Kent, 1500–1640 (1977) · W. Green, Shakespeare's 'Merry wives of Windsor' (1962) · J. G. Nichols, 'Memorials of the family of Cobham', Collectanea Topographica et Genealogica, 7 (1841), 320–54 · A. Scott Robinson, 'Six wills relating to Cobham Hall', Archaeologia Cantiana, 11 (1877), 199–304 · A. A. Arnold, 'Cobham College', Archaeologia Cantiana, 27 (1905), 64–109 · J. N. McGurk, 'Armada preparations in Kent and arrangements made after the defeat', Archaeologia Cantiana, 85 (1970), 71–93 · L. Stone, The crisis of the aristocracy, 1558–1641 (1965); rev. edn (1979) · Correspondance diplomatique de Bertrand de Salignac de la Mothe Fénélon, ed. A. Teulet, 7 vols., Bannatyne Club, 67 (1838–40) · C. Read, Lord Burghley and Queen Elizabeth (1960) · W. Beckingsale, Burghley: Tudor statesman (1967) · C. Wilson, Queen Elizabeth and the revolt of the Netherlands (1970); 2nd edn (1979) · P. E. J. Hammer, The polarisation of Elizabethan politics: the political career of Robert Devereux, 2nd earl of Essex, 1585–1597 (1999) · J. Woolfson, Padua and the Tudors: English students in Italy, 1485–1603 (1998) · F. Edwards, The marvellous chance: Thomas Howard and the Ridolphi plot (1968) · J. K. Laughton, ed., State papers relating to the defeat of the Spanish Armada, anno 1588, 2 vols., Navy RS, 1–2 (1894) · C. Merton, 'The women who served Queen Mary and Queen Elizabeth: ladies, gentlewomen and maids of the privy chamber, 1553–1603', PhD diss., U. Cam., 1992

Archives BL · CKS, U601 · PRO, corresp., SP 12; SP 15; SP 83 | BL, corresp. with privy council, Stowe MSS 150, 160 · BL, letters to Sir Julius Caesar, Add. MSS 12506–12507 · BL, letters to Sir Francis Walsingham, Add. MS 35841 · BL, diplomatic corresp., Cotton MSS · BL, diplomatic corresp., Harley MSS 286–288 · BL, official corresp., Lansdowne MSS · Folger, corresp. of Cobham and his wife, MS Xd428 · Hatfield House, Hertfordshire, corresp. with William Cecil · Magd. Cam., Pepys Library, letters to Robert Dudley, earl of Leicester · Staffordshire RO, corresp. with Sir John Leveson, D593
Likenesses attrib. Master of the Countess of Warwick, group portrait, oils, 1567, Longleat House, Wiltshire [see illus.]
Wealth at death £3500–£5000 p.a., landed income; over £10,000, rumoured goods: Stone, Crisis of the aristocracy, 487, 760; McKeen, Memory of honour, 123, 690

Brooke, William Henry (1772–1860), portrait painter and illustrator, born possibly in London, was the son of Henry *Brooke (1738–1806), a Dublin painter who moved to London in 1761, and his wife, Anne Kirchoffer. He was also a nephew of Henry Brooke (c.1703–1783), author of The Fool of Quality (5 vols., 1767–70). As a youth he worked briefly in a bank but within a short period became the pupil of the history painter Samuel Drummond. He made rapid progress and soon established himself as a portrait painter, first in Soho and later in the Adelphi, London, and in 1810 he showed his first works at the Royal Academy. However, between 1813 and 1823 he did not exhibit, but in the latter year sent a portrait and two Irish landscapes with figures for exhibition. In 1826 he showed Chastity, and this was to be the final work which he sent to the academy.

In 1812 Brooke began drawing for The Satirist, a monthly publication which changed ownership several times during its short life, expiring finally in 1814. He contributed satirical illustrations to this paper until September 1813, and was then succeeded by George Cruikshank. His drawings for this somewhat obscure periodical seem to have brought him a certain critical appreciation and presumably as a result he was commissioned to illustrate several popular books. Among the more important were Thomas Moore's Irish Melodies (1822); J. Major's edition (1823) of Izaak Walton's The Compleat Angler, for which he supplied some vignettes; T. Keightley's The Mythology of Ancient Greece and Italy (1831); an edition of Jonathan Swift's Gulliver's Travels; Nathaniel Cotton's Visions in Verse for the Entertainment and Instruction of Younger Minds (1786); and Fables in Verse for the Female Sex by E. Moore and his uncle, Henry Brooke (1825). He also drew for William Hone's Every Day Book (1826–7) and W. H. Harrison's The Humorist (1832). Many of his non-humorous designs display a rather winning simplicity and sincerity and the influence of Thomas Stothard is clear. His portraits were evidently popular, as they were frequently engraved. Two of the best-known were of Angelica Catalani, the celebrated soprano, and Catherine, countess of Essex.

Brooke was an associate of the Royal Hibernian Academy in Dublin and exhibited there on several occasions between 1827 and 1846. He died at Chichester, Sussex, on 12 January 1860 and was buried in the churchyard at Westhampnett, Sussex. Examples of his portraiture are in the National Portrait Gallery, London, and Leeds City Art Gallery; some of his watercolours and drawings are in the

British Museum and the Victoria and Albert Museum, London. His engravings, including some woodcuts and etchings, are in the department of prints and drawings of the British Museum.

ERNEST RADFORD, rev. PAUL GOLDMAN

Sources G. Meissner, ed., Allgemeines Künstlerlexikon: die bildenden Künstler aller Zeiten und Völker, [new edn, 34 vols.] (Leipzig and Munich, 1983–) · S. Houfe, The dictionary of 19th century British book illustrators and caricaturists, rev. edn (1996) · M. Bryant and S. Heneage, eds., Dictionary of British cartoonists and caricaturists, 1730–1980 (1994), 194 · Mallalieu, Watercolour artists, 2nd edn, 1.54 · B. Stewart and M. Cutten, The dictionary of portrait painters in Britain up to 1920 (1997) · Engraved Brit. ports., vol. 6 · P. Butler, Three hundred years of Irish watercolours and drawings (1990) · W. G. Strickland, A dictionary of Irish artists, 2 vols. (1913) · CGPLA Eng. & Wales (1860) · IGI
Wealth at death under £600: probate, 25 Feb 1860, CGPLA Eng. & Wales

Brooke, Sir William O'Shaughnessy (1808–1889), doctor and promoter of telegraphy in India, was born William O'Shaughnessy at Limerick in October 1808, the son of Daniel S. O'Shaughnessy of Limerick and his wife, Sara, née Boswell. His uncle was dean of Ennis and his great-uncle Roman Catholic bishop of Killaloe.

O'Shaughnessy graduated MD from Edinburgh University in 1829. In 1831, at the request of the Royal College of Surgeons, London, he made a study of blood samples from cholera patients in Newcastle upon Tyne, concluding that patients in the early stages of cholera should be given copious amounts of tepid water infused with neutral salts. In 1830 and 1831 he also published a series of reviews on the detection of poisons in The Lancet and a translation of Lugol's Essay on the Effects of Iodine in Scrofulous Diseases. It was probably around this time that he married his first wife, Isabella (1805/6–1834); they had at least one child. In August 1833 he joined the Bengal army as an assistant surgeon and shortly after arriving in India was appointed professor of chemistry and medicine at the Calcutta medical college. For a time he was also employed as first assistant in the government's opium factory at Bihar and as physician to Sir Charles Metcalfe.

O'Shaughnessy was a creative and imaginative scientist. In 1837, when it was widely held that India's terrain and climate would defeat electric systems of communication, he laid 30 miles of wire at his own expense to prove that the telegraph would work there. He published his results in the journal of the Asiatic Society, but, at the time, was unable to arouse any official enthusiasm in his experiments. In 1841, in connection with his duties at the medical college, he published a Manual of Chemistry designed to put the latest European practice and laboratory techniques within financial reach of Indian students. He followed this work with The Bengal Dispensatory (1842) and The Bengal Pharmacopoeia (1844), and by 1843 was sufficiently respected by his peers to be elected a fellow of the Royal Society. In the same year he obtained a position in the refinery of the Calcutta mint and while there devised a new, more economical means of parting and refining gold coin. Unhappily, however, the coveted job of assay master

eluded him and by 1849 he was desperate for more lucrative employment. His first wife, Isabella, had died at Calcutta on 30 August 1834, but he had remarried in the following year; his new wife was Margaret, daughter of Francis O'Shaughnessy of Curragh, co. Clare, and by 1849 was father to a large and expensive family.

Aware of Lord Dalhousie's keenness to establish the telegraph in India, O'Shaughnessy asked his principal patron, H. H. Wilson, to bring his 1837 experiments to the attention of the court of directors. Dalhousie leapt at the offer of O'Shaughnessy's experience and in March 1850 authorized him to proceed with an experimental line. In 1852 he succeeded in establishing communication between Calcutta and Diamond Harbour, 80 miles distant, whereupon Dalhousie sent him to London to win the court of directors' approval for an all-India network. Upon his return, Dalhousie appointed him superintendent of electric telegraphs. Work commenced in November 1853. In spite of the lack of trained staff (because of manpower shortages, O'Shaughnessy was forbidden from hiring covenanted civil servants or soldiers), the first telegram from Agra reached Calcutta, 800 miles away, on 24 March 1854. By the following February, Calcutta was linked to Agra, Bombay, Madras, and Attock on the north-west frontier, a remarkable technological feat involving the laying of over 3050 miles of wiring through jungles, across deserts, and over unbridged rivers. Soon after, O'Shaughnessy was to hear both Indians and Britons acknowledge the telegraph as a key factor in Britain's victory over the rebels of 1857.

In 1856 O'Shaughnessy was knighted and in 1859 promoted to surgeon-major. He retired to England in 1861, in which year he assumed by royal licence the additional surname of Brooke. He died at 4 Clarence Parade, Southsea, Portsea, Southampton, on 8 January 1889 and was survived by his third wife, Julia Greenly, daughter of Captain John Sabine of the 23rd Royal Welch Fusiliers.

KATHERINE PRIOR

Sources BL OIOC, Wilson MSS · W. Lee-Warner, The life of the Marquis of Dalhousie, 2 vols. (1904) · D. G. Crawford, ed., Roll of the Indian Medical Service, 1615–1930 (1930) · DNB · Bengal Directory and General Register (1834–61) · surgeons' entrance papers, BL OIOC · ecclesiastical records, BL OIOC · M. Gorman, 'Sir William O'Shaughnessy, Lord Dalhousie, and the establishment of the telegraph system in India', Technology and Culture, 12 (1971), 581–601 · CGPLA Eng. & Wales (1889)
Archives BL OIOC, letters to H. H. Wilson
Wealth at death £5243 6s. 5d.: probate, 6 Feb 1889, CGPLA Eng. & Wales

Brooke, Zachary (1715/16–1788), theologian, was born at Hamerton, Huntingdonshire, and baptized there on 8 February 1716, the son of the Revd Zachary Brooke (1674–1739) and his first wife, Jane Thomas. The name Zachary was to persist in the family; the historian Zachary Nugent *Brooke was the great-great-grandson of the Zachary Brooke born in 1715/16. The latter was educated at Stamford School, Lincolnshire, and admitted sizar of St John's College, Cambridge, on 28 June 1734; he graduated BA in 1737, and proceeded MA in 1741, BD in 1748, and DD in 1753. He was a fellow (1739–65) and tutor (1751–65) of St

John's, and Lady Margaret professor of divinity (1765–88). Meanwhile he was also vicar of Ickleton, Cambridgeshire, from 1744 and rector of Forncett St Mary with St Peter, Norfolk, from 1764. As a royal chaplain from 1758, he delivered sermons of remarkable complacency. In 1748 he published his *Defensio miraculorum*, a brief work of considerable erudition, a response to the scepticism of the theologian Conyers Middleton—and dedicated to the earl of Sandwich. This work called forth several 'letters' in response. In the 1750s Brooke aspired to the mastership of St John's and the Lady Margaret professorship of divinity, both at that time in the hands of John Newcome, thought to be dying. For the mastership his chief rival was W. S. Powell, long a colleague at St John's. But Newcome lingered on until January 1765, and his death was followed by a flurry of intrigue. Brooke had been a supporter of the duke of Newcastle in the 1750s, Powell of Lord Sandwich, Newcastle's chief rival for influence in Cambridge. In 1764–5 Sandwich was involved in a long and unsuccessful attempt to become high steward of the university; and this election muddied the waters in St John's, for it seems to have brought Brooke back into Sandwich's party. When the master of St John's died Powell was able to count on Newcastle's support, Brooke on Sandwich's, and Newcastle was the more powerful. In the event Powell could only be secure of the mastership if he came to an understanding with Brooke; and on 19 January 1765 Brooke was elected to the chair, on 25 January Powell to the mastership. A contemporary described the chair as 'a valuable sinecure' (*GM*, 58.756–7). As was normal at the time Brooke gave no lectures, though he lived in Cambridge and participated in university business. He did Sunday duty at least at Ickleton and probably spent the long vacation at Forncett. On 25 June 1765, aged about 49, he resigned his fellowship and married Susanna (1737–1812), daughter of John Hanchett of Ickleton, who was about 28; they had at least three children. He died at Forncett on 7 August 1788, and was buried at Ickleton church.

C. N. L. BROOKE

Sources R. F. Scott, ed., *Admissions to the College of St John the Evangelist in the University of Cambridge*, 3: *July 1715 – November 1767* (1903), 77, 458–9 · D. A. Winstanley, *The University of Cambridge in the eighteenth century* (1922), esp. 241–66 · *GM*, 1st ser., 35 (1765), 299 · *GM*, 1st ser., 58 (1788), 756–7 · W. Cole, 'Continuation of Mr Baker's history of St John's College in Cambridge', in T. Baker, *History of the college of St John the Evangelist, Cambridge*, ed. J. E. B. Mayor, 2 (1869), 1029–30 · *VCH Cambridgeshire and the Isle of Ely*, 6.236, 243 · P. D. Mundy, 'The Rebecca Powell–Hannah Lightfoot legend', *N&Q*, 194 (1949), 425–6 · private information (2004)
Archives BL, duke of Newcastle archives, Add. MSS 32884 (esp. fol. 92), 32886, 32961, 32963–32965
Likenesses T. Hudson, portrait, St John Cam.

Brooke, Zachary Nugent (1883–1946), historian, was born at Sutton, Surrey, on 1 February 1883, the third child and eldest son of George Brooke, a barrister attached to the Inland Revenue at Somerset House, and his wife, Alice Elizabeth, daughter of the Revd Tresillian George Nicholas, vicar of West Molesey. His father's family had long associations with Cambridge, one of his forebears, Zachary *Brooke (1715/16–1788), having been Lady Margaret

professor of divinity, and on both his father's and his mother's side clerical and scholastic connections were numerous. His mother died when he was four, and the authoritarian character of his father left its mark on the boy for life.

After a school career at Bradfield College, Brooke entered St John's College, Cambridge, as a classical scholar and was placed in the first class of part one of the classical tripos in 1905, but moved over to history, being placed in the first class of part two in 1906. He won the Gladstone and Winchester Reading prizes in 1906, and in 1907 was awarded the Lightfoot scholarship in ecclesiastical history; thenceforward the history of the church in the eleventh and twelfth centuries was the subject of his choice. Elected fellow of Gonville and Caius College in 1908, he remained there for the rest of his life, save for a year's research in Rome in 1911–12, and four years' military service from 1915 to 1919, during which, in 1916, he became a captain.

In 1919 Brooke married Rosa Grace, daughter of the Revd Alfred Herbert Stanton, rector of Hambleden, Henley-on-Thames, who had nursed him when he was invalided home with trench fever during the war. Then for the first time in his life he enjoyed happiness without restraint in a home of his own.

Already heavily burdened with work, Brooke became in 1921 joint editor of the *Cambridge Medieval History*, a task which occupied him for the next fifteen years, bringing him into close and harmonious contact with a contemporary and friendly rival, C. W. Previté-Orton. His own literary work and research inevitably suffered, and he produced only two books, *The English Church and the Papacy* (1931), fruit of the Birkbeck lectures (1929–31), and *A History of Europe, 911–1198* (1938), in its day a standard textbook. He proceeded LittD. in 1932, and was elected FBA in 1940. When at last elected to the chair of medieval history early in 1944, he looked forward to leisure for his own research, but less than three years later, on 7 October 1946, he died suddenly from a heart attack at his home, 19 Wilberforce Road, Cambridge.

Brooke's integrity and simplicity of character, and his sincere piety (he was a devout churchman) were respected by all, but his shy and sensitive nature, concealed under a somewhat brusque exterior, restricted the more intimate manifestations of his personality to his ideally happy home circle, in which his three sons (among them Christopher Nugent Lawrence Brooke, the historian) grew up to share his interests, and to a few friends and pupils to whom he was both generous and intensely loyal. As a scholar he took some of his colour from the austere and exacting standards of post-Acton Cambridge; this, added to the circumstances of his career and a meticulous accuracy which rendered composition toilsome, limited his output, and prevented the production of what might have been a definitive work on the Gregorian reform, but his thankless and unseen work as editor and lecturer did much for the well-being of medieval studies at Cambridge which he had so much at heart.

M. D. KNOWLES, *rev.* H. C. G. MATTHEW

Sources H. M. Cam, 'Zachary Nugent Brooke, 1883–1946', *PBA*, 32 (1946), 381–93 • M. F. J. McDonnell, *The Eagle*, 53 (1948–9), 59–62 • personal knowledge (1959) • *WWW* • *CGPLA Eng. & Wales* (1947) **Archives** Gon. & Caius Cam., diary, research notes **Wealth at death** £10,012 9s. 1d.: probate, 20 Feb 1947, *CGPLA Eng. & Wales*

Brookeborough. For this title name *see* Brooke, Basil Stanlake, first Viscount Brookeborough (1888–1973).

Brookes, Joshua (*bap.* 1754, *d.* 1821), Church of England clergyman, was born at Cheadle Hulme, near Stockport, and baptized on 19 May 1754 at St Mary's, Stockport, the son of Thomas Brookes and his wife, Mary. His father, a shoemaker, who moved soon after his son's birth to Manchester, was disabled and had a violent temper, and was nicknamed Pontius Pilate, but his son cared for him faithfully. Joshua was educated from 21 January 1764 at the Manchester grammar school, where he attracted the notice of the Revd Thomas Aynscough MA, who obtained the aid which, with a school exhibition, enabled Joshua to proceed to Brasenose College, Oxford, where he matriculated on 25 June 1774, graduated BA on 17 June 1778, and proceeded MA on 21 June 1781. He was ordained deacon in 1782, and priest in 1783. He was appointed stipendiary curate of Chorlton chapel in 1782 and perpetual curate in 1789, but was elected chaplain of the Manchester collegiate church on 22 November 1790, a position which he retained until his death.

Brookes acted for a time as assistant master at the grammar school, but was exceedingly unpopular with the boys, who at times ejected him from the schoolroom, struggling and shrieking out at the loudest pitch of an unmelodious voice his uncomplimentary opinions of them as 'blockheads'. He was an excellent scholar, however, and one of his pupils, Joseph Allen, later bishop of Ely, frankly acknowledged that his tuition from Joshua had been the first stepping-stone to the episcopal bench. Brookes was a book collector, though prone to mar his books by inserting tawdry engravings. His memory was prodigious. In his common talk he spoke the broad dialect of the county, and his uncouthness brought him frequently into disputes with the townspeople. He would interrupt the service of the church to administer a rebuke or to box the ears of some unruly boy. A caricature appeared in which he is represented as reading the burial service at a grave and saying, 'And I heard a voice from heaven saying—knock that black imp off the wall!' The artist was prosecuted and fined. Brookes's peculiarities brought him into frequent conflict with his fellow clergymen. His concern was really to uphold the order and authority of church and clergy but, ironically, his eccentricities tended to damage both. He had little sense of the niceties of human relationships. As chaplain of the Manchester collegiate church he baptized, married, and buried more people than any clergyman in the kingdom, for until the division of the immensely large parish in the mid-nineteenth century, all parishioners were entitled to the rites of passage in that church, and these were the chaplains' main duties. Confusions caused by mass weddings were the subject of several Brookes anecdotes. He is described in R. Parkinson's *Old Church Clock* (5th edn, 1880) as the Revd Joseph Rivers, and he appears under his own name in *The Manchester Man* (5th edn, 1882) by Mrs G. Linnaeus Banks, but in *Blackwood's Magazine* for March 1821 appears as the Revd Josiah Streamlet.

In appearance Brookes was diminutive and corpulent; he had bushy, meeting brows, a shrill voice, and spoke rapidly. He was careless and shabby in his dress, except on Sundays, when he was scrupulously clean and neat, dressed in black with ruffles and a three-cornered beaver hat. His general appearance gained him the nickname of the Knave of Clubs, though he was usually styled St Crispin and Jotty Bruks. He shared his house with a formidable housekeeper (to whom he bequeathed the house and most of his money), her 'pert niece', two cats, three pigeons, and (for a time) a monkey.

Apart from signing a petition against the anti-Test Act agitation in 1790 and supporting a Sunday observance society in 1802, Brookes seems to have taken little part in public affairs, though he was a member of the Manchester Literary and Philosophical Society. He died, unmarried, on 11 November 1821 at his home, 11 Long Millgate, Manchester, and was buried on 16 November within the collegiate church.   W. E. A. AXON, rev. HENRY D. RACK

Sources R. Parkinson, *The old church clock*, ed. J. Evans, 5th edn (1880), lxvi–lxx • [C. Wheeler], 'Brief sketch of the Rev. Josiah Streamlet', *Blackwood*, 8 (1820–21), 633–7 • J. F. Smith, ed., *The admission register of the Manchester School, with some notices of the more distinguished scholars*, 1, Chetham Society, 69 (1866), 109–13 • J. Harland, ed., *Collectanea relating to Manchester and its neighbourhood at various periods*, 2, Chetham Society, 72 (1867), 191–4, 200–02, 242–3 • *Aston's Manchester Herald* (20 Nov 1821) • *Manchester Mercury* (23 Feb 1790) • *Manchester Mercury* (29 June 1902) • J. Booker, *A history of the ancient chapels of Didsbury and Chorlton, in Manchester parish*, Chetham Society, 42 (1857), 307–9 • [J. Harland], 'A father and son', in R. Chambers, *The book of days* (1869), 2.568–70 • G. L. Banks, *The Manchester man*, 5th edn (1882), appx 1 • will, proved, 13 Dec 1821, Lancs. RO • appointments at Chorlton chapel and Manchester collegiate church, Ches. & Chester ALSS, 1789, 1790: EDA 1/8/196,222 • register, St Mary's, Stockport, 1754, Man. CL [baptism; microfilm] • Foster, *Alum. Oxon.* • *Manchester Mercury* (13 Nov 1821) • *Manchester Courier* (11 Dec 1866) **Likenesses** E. Scriven, stipple, pubd 1822 (after J. Minasi), BM, NPG; repro. in R. W. Procter, *Memorials of bygone Manchester* (1880), facing p. 143 **Wealth at death** £124 in legacies; 5 guineas in books; bequest of house, furniture, money in funds, and on mortgage to housekeeper: will, Lancs. RO

Brookes, Joshua (1761–1833), anatomist, was born on 24 November 1761. Little is known of his early life. He studied anatomy and surgery in London under William Hunter, William Hewson, Andrew Marshall, and John Sheldon, and for a time attended the practice of Portal and other eminent surgeons at the Hôtel-Dieu in Paris. On his return to London, Brookes began to teach anatomy and form a collection of comparative anatomical material.

From his home in Blenheim Street, Great Marlborough Street, Brookes taught anatomy to approximately 7000 students over a forty-year period. Unlike many other anatomy teachers in London at the time he taught all year round, attracting students from the West End hospitals in the winter and, in the summer, from all the schools as

Joshua Brookes (1761–1833), by Thomas Phillips, 1815

courses were held nowhere else. His lessons consisted both of lectures and dissections. Brookes was generally esteemed to be among the best teachers of practical anatomy in London, having the benefit of original specimens rather than pictures and of possessing a sincere interest in the subject, rather than simply preparing his students for examination.

Brookes developed a means of injecting specimens with nitre, which improved their preservation in hot weather and better reflected their natural colours. For this discovery he was elected FRS in 1819. Brookes was also a fellow of the Linnean Society and of the Zoological Society.

Over the course of thirty years Brookes assembled a vast collection of human and comparative anatomical specimens, including more than 6000 preparations, models, and casts. The museum was crammed into the upper two floors of his house in Blenheim Street. There were more than 3000 specimens of the human body in both the healthy and diseased state preserved in spirits in jars, including heads, limbs, and organs. He also made casts, paintings, and models of uncommon conditions, including an extensive series on the human gravid uterus. His collection included several mummies, one of which he made himself, and a large selection of human crania, as well as the skulls of quadrupeds and birds.

Brookes's brother kept the menagerie in the Exeter Exchange and provided him with many of the subjects for his comparative osteological collection. At the time the comparative material from the Hunterian Museum at the Royal College of Surgeons was in storage, leaving Brookes's as the foremost collection of its kind in London.

His collection as a whole, including both the human and comparative anatomical components, was considered second only to that of John Hunter.

Brookes is said to have been completely devoted to anatomy, spending the whole of his days in the dissecting room. He was an assiduous and demanding teacher but kind and well respected. In his personal habits, however, he was less than fastidious. A contemporary remarked that 'Joshua Brookes was without exception the dirtiest professional person I have ever met with; his good report always preceded him, and his filthy hands begrimed his nose with continual snuff. In his ordinary appearance I really know of no dirty thing with which he could compare—all and every part of him was dirt' (Desmond, 161).

The reasons for Brookes's retirement from teaching are controversial. While one version holds that Brookes retired in 1826 due to ill health caused by the bad air in the dissecting room, a second version suggests a more controversial end to his career. Brookes operated his school outside the auspices of the Royal College of Surgeons, charging only half the fee for an anatomy course that the members of the college council charged. When in 1824 the college decreed that only certificates issued from the universities and London hospitals, or countersigned by London surgeons, were valid, Brookes was deprived of his livelihood. Although professionally respected and considered by some the best anatomist in London, Brookes was shunned by the surgical establishment, perhaps for social as well as financial reasons, and they refused to grant him a seat on the council. He descended into poverty in his old age, ultimately being forced to sell his collection. Brookes's fate was championed as proof of the need for medical reform and he himself supported the formation of the London College of Medicine.

Brookes's collection and premises were put up for auction twice, first in 1828 and again over twenty-three days in 1830. However, the sales never repaid the substantial investment of thirty years' time and £30,000 which Brookes had devoted to assembling it. Brookes's first sale catalogue contains entries for specimens he did not own, included in order to illustrate the complete taxonomic series. The second catalogue is considerably less scholarly, opting for less specific descriptions of the specimens, and was probably not written by Brookes himself.

Brookes died on 10 January 1833 in Great Portland Street, London, where he lived, and was buried in St James's Church, Piccadilly. He left a son who was a surgeon in the Royal Navy. Following Brookes's death a committee was formed to create a memorial to him. The committee was chaired by J. C. Carpue and included several physicians and fellows of the Royal Society. The committee published an engraving and produced a bust of Brookes. Brookes had also been presented with a marble bust of himself in 1826 at the time of his retirement, subscribed for by his pupils.

Brookes's published writings include 'Lectures on the anatomy of the ostrich' (*The Lancet*, vol. 12); *An Address, Delivered at the Anniversary Meeting of the Zoological Club of the Linnean Society* (1828); *Thoughts on the Best Means of Lessening*

the *Destructive Progress of Cholera* (1831); and a description of a new genus of Rodentia (*Transactions of the Linnean Society*, 1829).
P. E. KELL

Sources J. Brookes, *Brookesian Museum* (1828) · *Museum Brookesianum* (1830) · *Memorials of John Flint South*, ed. C. L. Feltoe (1884), 103–6 · 'Joshua Brookes', *The Lancet* (19 Jan 1833), 544 · 'Monument to Joshua Brookes', *The Lancet* (23 Nov 1833), 341 · 'Bust of the late Joshua Brookes', *The Lancet* (2 March 1833), 727 · 'Joshua Brookes: medical reform', *The Lancet* (24 Aug 1833), 722 · *The Lancet* (14 Dec 1833), 454–9 · *DNB* · A. Desmond, *The politics of evolution: morphology, medicine, and reform in radical London* (1989); pbk edn (1992) · *GM*, 1st ser., 103/1 (1833), 184–5
Archives Wellcome L., notes on his lectures; notes taken from his lectures on osteology
Likenesses T. Phillips, oils, 1815, NPG [*see illus.*] · H. Cook, portrait, 1821 (after T. Phillips), repro. in Desmond, *The politics of evolution* · McCarthy, bust, 1833 · W. Ward, mezzotint, pubd 1833 (after B. E. Duppa), NPG · engraving, 1833

Brookes [*née* Emmerton], **Dame Mabel Balcombe** (1890–1975), socialite and charity worker, was born on 15 June 1890 at Raveloe, South Yarra, Melbourne, Australia, the only child of Harry Emmerton (1845–1927), an English born solicitor, and his wife, Alice Mabel Maude (1865–1923), a daughter of Alexander Balcombe. Mabel enjoyed a very privileged upbringing and, while she never lacked any physical comforts, she recalled her childhood years as very lonely. Her attendance at school was limited to a brief spell at a local kindergarten, for she was quickly removed when her mother detected her developing an unladylike accent. After this she was educated at home by her father and a series of governesses. She never fulfilled her father's ambitions of academic brilliance, nor was she ever considered a beauty, but what she lacked in appearance—she was described as short with a large nose—she made up for in personality. Her high spirits, enquiring mind, competitiveness, and determination ensured that she was rarely overlooked.

Much of Mabel's youth revolved around social engagements—encouraged by her father who even built a ballroom at home so she could be launched into society in style. On a trip to London in 1907 as part of a world tour she was presented to Edward VII, even though she was under age to receive such an honour. It was somewhat of a surprise when, at only seventeen, she announced her betrothal to Norman Everard Brookes (1877–1968), the first non-Briton to win the tennis championship at Wimbledon. Norman was almost thirteen years older than Mabel, but their marriage, which took place in St Paul's Anglican Cathedral, Melbourne, on 19 April 1911, was enduring and successful. The couple had three daughters: Cynthia (*b*. 1912), Elaine (*b*. 1913), and Hersey (*b*. 1915).

Marriage brought Mabel even greater social status, due in part to the continuing success of her husband as a rising international tennis star. Up until the outbreak of the First World War in 1914 the couple travelled extensively, mixing with the rich and famous in France, Britain, and the United States of America. Throughout her adult life Mabel mixed with royalty and high society, and numbered among her best-known friends Lord Casey, Sir Winston

Churchill, Lyndon B. Johnson, John Caine, Sir Henry Bolte and Sir Robert Gordon Menzies.

The early war years took Mabel to Cairo, where Norman held the post of commissioner for the Australian branch of the British Red Cross. Here she embarked upon the life of public service which later gained her a reputation as one of the hardest working charity workers in Australia. From 1915, until her return to Melbourne in 1917 (when Norman was posted to Mesopotamia) she devoted herself to organizing rest homes, army nurses' canteens, and concert parties in various districts.

Much of the charitable work which followed was motivated by Mabel's love of children. She served first, in 1918, as a committee member of the (Royal) Children's Hospital, became president of the Children's Frankston Orthopaedic Hospital, the Anglican Babies Home at Frankston and the Society for the Prevention of Cruelty to Children. Other organizations with which she was associated included the Girl Guides Association, the Animal Welfare League, the Institute of Almoners and the Ladies Swimming Association. However, it was her presidency, between 1923 and 1970, of the Queen Victoria Memorial Hospital, a women's hospital staffed by women, that earned her such wide recognition and respect. At the outset of her involvement her father wanted her to confine her charitable activities to the children's hospital, but Mabel was determined to help the women who were struggling so hard to establish a successful hospital. She later described the Queen Victoria as her baby and worked tirelessly and very successfully, often through organizing grand social events, to raise essential funds for its maintenance.

During the Second World War, Mabel turned her residence into a convalescent home for the Red Cross and threw herself into a variety of war work. Among other activities she helped establish a sixty-bed military hospital for servicewomen at the Queen Victoria Hospital, was instrumental in opening a large unit for airmen on leave in Melbourne, acted as an air-raid warden for a time and worked in an ammunitions factory. Less successful were her attempts at establishing a political career: she campaigned vigorously for causes including free education, mental hospital reform, and housing for the poor, but although she gained a lot of public attention she failed to win a seat in either the federal parliament (1943) or the state parliament (1952). Mabel Brookes's outstanding services in charitable welfare and other public spheres, particularly the Queen Victoria Hospital, Melbourne, were recognized in 1933 when she was created CBE and again in June 1955, when she was created DBE in the queen's birthday honours list.

Mabel's childhood passion for reading developed into a second career as an author. Besides writing several works of romantic fiction, she produced two autobiographies as well as an account of Napoleon Bonaparte's relationship with her antecedent, Betsy Balcombe. Her fascination with Napoleon was such that she was ultimately considered to be an authority on him, and her formidable collection of his relics, including a lock of his hair and his death mask, was surpassed only by her vast collection of Australiana.

Mabel Brookes died on 30 April 1975 at South Yarra, Melbourne, Australia and was buried in St Kilda cemetery.

SUSAN L. COHEN

Sources AusDB, 13.265–7 · M. Brookes, Crowded galleries (1956) · M. Brookes, Memoirs (1974) · E. M. Lyons, Amongst the carrion crows (1977), 100–01 · Melbourne Herald (9 June 1955), 22 · The Age [Melbourne] (9 June 1955), 1, 8 · V. Barnes, ed., Modern encyclopaedia of Australia and New Zealand (1964), 188 · Who's Who in Australia, 12th edn (1944), 190 · private information (2004) · G. Swinburne, The Queen Victoria Memorial Hospital: a history (1951) · E. Russell, Bricks or spirit? The Queen Victoria Hospital Melbourne (1997) · WWW, 1961–70, 140 · The Times (30 Sept 1968), 10

Archives NL Aus., catalogue of collection of antique furniture etc., a/NK562.B7S57, ABZ-1373 · NRA, priv. coll., family papers and press cuttings | NL Aus., Brookes MSS, records, series 28 · NL Aus., letters to Herbert Brookes and Ivy Brookes, Brookes MS 1924 series 1, general corresp. items 2822, 2952–2957, 3146–3147, 3158, 3161, 3164–3165, 7540, 7629–7630, 21789, 21814 · NL Aus., Brookes MSS, MS 2979 · NL Aus., material relating to a visit made in June 1957, Kivell MS 4000, folder 20 · NL Aus., corresp. with Sir Robert Menzies, MS 4936, series 1/folder 36, series 2, folders 239, 353, 520, 581, 601, 636, 675, 719, 721, 744, 876, 893

Likenesses W. Dargie, portrait, priv. coll. · C. Pugh, oils, priv. coll.

Wealth at death $308,653: J. Ritchie, ed. AusDB, 13, 1940–80 (1993), 267

Brookes, Richard (*fl.* **1721–1763**), physician and author, has left scant evidence of his life, except numerous compilations and translations on medicine, surgery, natural history, and geography, most of which went through several editions. He was at one time a rural practitioner in Surrey, and at some time before 1762 he travelled in both America and Africa. He was an industrious compiler, especially from the works of continental writers, and his *General Gazeteer* (1762) filled a gap in the market. Brookes's chief writings are: *A History of the Most Remarkable Pestilential Distempers* (1721), *The Art of Angling, Rock and Sea Fishing, with the Natural History of River, Pond, and Sea Fish* (1740), *The General Practice of Physic* (1751), *An Introduction to Physic and Surgery* (2 vols., 1754), and *A ... System of Natural History* (6 vols., 1763). His principal translations are *The Natural History of Chocolate*, from the French of Quélus (2nd edn 1730), and J. B. Duhalde's *History of China* (4 vols., 1736).

G. T. BETTANY, *rev.* CLAIRE L. NUTT

Sources R. Brookes, The art of angling (1740) · R. Brookes, A new and accurate system of natural history (1763)

Brookes, William Penny (1809–1895), surgeon and campaigner for the revival of the Olympic games, was born on 13 August 1809 at 4 Wilmore Street, Much Wenlock, Shropshire, the first of the five children of William Brookes (1776–1830), doctor, and his wife, Mary Doughty (1786–1869). After being apprenticed to a Dr R. Barnett at Stourport in Worcestershire in 1825, Brookes studied at the united hospitals of Guy's and St Thomas's, London, in 1827; it is also known that he went to Padua and to Paris in 1829 to further his studies. Brookes returned to Wenlock in 1831 to take up his father's practice following the latter's death; he was made MRCS in 1831, FRCS in 1870,

William Penny Brookes (1809–1895), by unknown photographer, 1880s

and LSA in 1831. His practice covered a wide rural area of several communities and it is said that he often rode some 70 miles a day to visit his patients.

Brookes was a short, stocky man, his passport stating his height to be 5 feet 2 inches. Nevertheless what he lacked in inches his character made up for in organizational ability, perseverance, energy, and vision. A polymath, Brookes was fluent in French, Greek, and Latin, and was a nationally respected botanist. His many and varied interests, in particular the provision of physical education, were all pursued with relentless enthusiasm. On 18 May 1835 he married Jane Clare Talbot (1811–1885) of Fetters Hall, Tettenhall, Staffordshire, daughter of Thomas Faulkner Talbot and his wife, Jane. At Brookes's death, of his two sons and three daughters only Adeline (1839–1925) survived him; a son, William Brookes (b. 1845), a brilliant student at Oxford, accidentally drowned there in December 1868.

Appointed a justice of the peace and, in 1841, commissioner of roads and taxes, Brookes took an active role in civic life. He was responsible for the refurbishment, in 1849, of the council chamber in Wenlock's beautiful sixteenth-century guildhall, he instigated the building of the corn exchange in the town's high street in 1852, and, ever in touch with progress, he was largely instrumental in bringing gas lighting to the town in 1856 and also the railway, which was officially opened in 1862.

In 1841 Brookes set up the Wenlock Agricultural Reading Society (WARS), an early kind of lending library for working men, which was later accommodated in the reading rooms above the corn exchange. From this society various sections evolved; in particular a class (later called the Olympian Society: WOS) was set up in 1850 to hold annual games 'for literary and fine-art attainments, and for skill and strength in athletic exercise' (W. P. Brookes archives, WOS/1 (1850–76), 135). The games were open to those whom Brookes termed 'every grade of man'. Initially the sports were a mixture of athletic events, old country sports, and a special event to amuse the spectators. On occasion athletes and spectators numbered several thousand, and building on this success Brookes founded the Shropshire Olympian games (1861) and was instrumental in the formation of the National Olympian Society (1865), both of which were hosted by different towns with the host town financing the games. This was a significant new concept; at that time numerous athletic associations were springing up all over the country and the aim of the National Olympian Society was to lay down regulations and to bring some organization to sports associations under one nationally recognized body. Their first games were held at Crystal Palace in 1866 and attracted over 10,000 spectators. The reaction of the 'amateur' sportsmen (principally from the public schools and the universities of Oxford and Cambridge) was swiftly to set up the Amateur Athletic Club (later Association). Anyone could take part in the AAC games but membership of the club was by invitation only. Brookes kept meticulous records relating to the Olympian societies and his other causes, which can now be found in the archives of Wenlock town council.

Although Brookes had a lifelong admiration for Greece and for the Greek ideal of physical fitness there is no evidence that he ever visited that country. His first known contact with Greece was when he sent a prize of £10 to the Zappas Olympian games in Athens in 1859. From this time he intermittently petitioned the Greek government to re-establish Olympic-styled games. The Greek newspaper *The Clio* reported, in June 1881, that 'Dr Brookes, this enthusiastic Philhelline is endeavouring to organise an International Olympian Festival, to be held in Athens' (Coubertin collection). Political unrest prevented this; nevertheless Brookes continued a lively correspondence with the Greek chargé d'affaires in London, I. Genadius.

Brookes's persistent campaign for physical education to be made compulsory in schools brought him into contact with Baron Coubertin, who was researching foreign provision of physical education on behalf of the French government. Following Coubertin's visit to the Wenlock Olympian games in 1890 the two men began a correspondence which lasted until Brookes's death. The young aristocrat referred to the octogenarian Brookes as 'my oldest friend' and, greatly impressed by his lifelong campaign for a revived Olympics with international participation, initially acknowledged Brookes, in the December 1890 edition of *La Revue Athletique*, as the pioneer of modern Olympics: 'If the Olympic Games that Modern Greece has not yet been able to revive still survives today, it is due, not to a Greek, but to Dr W. P. Brookes' (W. P. Brookes archives,

WOS/2 (1877–95), 221). The congress of the Sorbonne was instigated by Coubertin, in 1894, to establish an Olympic revival; Brookes, listed as an honorary member, was unable to attend, through ill health, and died on 10 December 1895 at his home, 4 Wilmore Street, Much Wenlock, four months before the realization of his dream, the first modern Olympics held in Athens, in April 1896. He was buried at the parish church of Much Wenlock on 13 December.   HELEN CLARE CROMARTY

Sources W. P. Brookes, archives, Corn Exchange, Much Wenlock, minute books 1 and 2, 1850–95, Wenlock town council archives · Wenlock Agricultural Reading Society, vols. 1 and 2, 1841–93, Wenlock town council archives, Corn Exchange, Much Wenlock · W. P. Brookes, personal archive, 1841–68 · V. G. Plarr, *Plarr's Lives of the fellows of the Royal College of Surgeons of England*, rev. D'A. Power, 2 vols. (1930) · K. B. Jones, *The Wenlock branch: Wellington to Craven Arms* (1998) · P. Lovesay, *The official centenary history of the Amateur Athletic Association* (1980) · *Bagshaw Directory* (1851), 582 · International Olympic Museum, Lucerne, Switzerland, Coubertin Collection IOC · *Shrewsbury Chronicle* (18 Dec 1868) · M. Furbank, M. Cromarty, and G. McDonald, *William Penny Brookes and the Olympic connection* (1996) · *CGPLA Eng. & Wales* (1896)

Archives International Olympic Museum, Lucerne, Switzerland · Much Wenlock town council, Shropshire, archive incl. herbarium · Shrops. RRC · Wenlock Museum, Much Wenlock, Shropshire

Likenesses photographs, 1880–89, Much Wenlock town council, Shropshire, archive [*see illus.*]

Wealth at death £3896 18s. 4d.: probate, 7 Feb 1896, *CGPLA Eng. & Wales*

Brookfield, Charles Hallam Elton (1857–1913), playwright, was born on 19 May 1857, the third child and second son of William Henry *Brookfield (1809–1874), clergyman and inspector of schools, and his wife, Jane Octavia Elton [see Brookfield, Jane Octavia (1821–1896)], novelist and close friend of Thackeray. From childhood he was accustomed to the company of his parents' literary friends and he inherited his father's gift for mimicry and love for the theatre, creating dramatic diversions with his brother Arthur. From 1871 until 1873 he attended Westminster School and then devoted two years to occasional attendance at lectures at King's College, London, and to dashes across the channel to revel in the techniques of comic actors in the theatres of Paris. He also rubbed shoulders with writers who included Rudyard Kipling and R. L. Stevenson, became a reviewer of novels for *The Examiner*, and began his attachment to London club life when he gained membership of the Savile Club at the age of seventeen. At Trinity College, Cambridge (1875–8), he was prominent in the productions of the Amateur Dramatic Club but went down without taking a degree, distinguished only by the award of the Winchester reading prize. Later photographs show a neat, sleek-haired man with alert eyes; he was described as 'sparkling, debonair and full of stories' (cutting in Brookfield MSS); his gift for repartee and caustic wit ensured great popularity in clubs and social gatherings.

After a short and uncongenial period studying law, Brookfield decided in 1879 to try his luck on the stage in spite of strong opposition from his family, using his friend Henry Kemble (who had never seen him act) as a referee.

He experienced an uneasy start in pantomime and in a touring company, where his health problems became overwhelming for a time, but in 1880 he was invited to join Squire Bancroft's highly successful company in the renovated Haymarket Theatre, London, where he gained many complimentary notices for his performances in supporting roles. He also began writing plays, many translations of, or derivations from, works in French. On 4 December 1884 he married Frances Mary Grogan (1857/8–1926), daughter of William Grogan. She was an actress who used the stage name Ruth Francis. Their only child, Peter (who took the religious name of Paul when he became a monk), was born on 28 June 1888.

On Bancroft's retirement in 1884 Brookfield continued his successful acting career until in 1898 he became very ill and advanced tuberculosis was diagnosed. Periods of convalescence abroad were followed by a financially precarious existence, clouded by ill health, but he remained outwardly cheerful and applied himself to writing and marketing his plays. He converted to Roman Catholicism in 1900, and found peace and enjoyment during visits to Downside Abbey in Somerset, where his son became a pupil in 1901. He was the author of *The Twilight of Love* (1893), *Random Reminiscences* (1902), and, with his wife, of *Mrs Brookfield and her Circle* (1905). He wrote, or co-wrote, many plays, concentrating on farce, revue, and burlesque. A typical product was *Under the Clock*, a spoof Sherlock Holmes story which provoked the wrath of Conan Doyle.

Brookfield's appointment as examiner of plays in 1911 caused an outcry. He had set his face firmly against the New Drama as exemplified by Ibsen and Shaw, and felt an implacable and seemingly obsessive hatred for Oscar Wilde (he had mocked Wilde and *Lady Windermere's Fan* in his play *The Poet and the Puppets* and had helped gather evidence against Wilde in the trial of 1895). Brookfield had also himself been attacked for perceived amorality in his play of 1906, *Dear Old Charlie*. However, he weathered the storm and carried out his duties with aplomb until his death from tuberculosis on 20 October 1913 at his home, 28 Clareville Street, Hereford Square, London. He was buried in the Catholic church at Stratton on the Fosse, Somerset, on 23 October, after a requiem mass on the same day at Brompton Oratory, London. SALLY BEALES

Sources Downside Abbey Library, Stratton on the Fosse, Somerset, Brookfield MSS • C. Brookfield, *Random reminiscences* (1902) • C. H. E. Brookfield and F. M. Brookfield, *Mrs Brookfield and her circle*, 2 vols. (1905) • *The Times* (21 Oct 1913) • *The Times* (23 Oct 1913) • *The Times* (13 Dec 1913) • W. H. Leverton, *Through the box-office window* (1932) • M. Elton, *Annals of the Elton family* (1994) • Charles Brookfield scrapbook, Theatre Museum, London • *WWW* • A. M. Brookfield, *Annals of a chequered life* (1930) • H. Porter, 'Francis Burnand and the early repertoire of the Cambridge ADC', *Cambridge Review* (June 1997) • J. M. Glover, *Jimmy Glover: his book* (1911) • *The truth at last from Charles Hawtrey*, ed. W. S. Maugham (1924)
Archives Downside Abbey Library, Stratton on the Fosse, Somerset, MSS • Theatre Museum, London, scrapbook
Likenesses A. P. F. Ritchie, lithograph, NPG; repro. in *VF* (30 April 1913) • photograph, Downside Abbey, Stratton on the Fosse, Somerset, Brookfield MSS • portrait, repro. in Brookfield, *Random reminiscences*, frontispiece • two photographs, repro. in Leverton, *Through the box-office window*, facing p. 130

Wealth at death £269 18s. 6d.: probate, 9 Dec 1913, CGPLA Eng. & Wales

Brookfield [*née* Elton], **Jane Octavia** (1821–1896), literary hostess and writer, was born on 25 March 1821, at Clifton, near Bristol, the youngest of the eight daughters (there were also five sons) of Sir Charles Abraham *Elton, sixth baronet (1778–1853), of Cleveland Court, near Bristol, and his wife, Sarah Smith (d. 1830). Her father, who had possessed literary inclinations in his youth, was the friend of Lamb and Coleridge and the author of an elegy, 'The Brothers', written after his two eldest sons had drowned in the Bristol Channel, and commended by Southey to Landor. In 1837 the Eltons moved to Southampton. The teenaged Jane, 5 feet 9 inches tall (an immense height for a woman in the Victorian period) and nicknamed Glumdalclitch by her father, was by all accounts of striking appearance. Courted by the newly arrived curate of All Saints' Church, William Henry *Brookfield (1809–1874), she became engaged at the end of 1838. The wedding was delayed for some time while attempts were made to find him a better job. The couple were eventually married, on 18 November 1841, eighteen months after Brookfield's appointment to the curacy of St James's, Piccadilly, London.

The nature of the Brookfields' marriage is open to debate. Twelve years older than his wife, and the son of a Sheffield solicitor, Brookfield was no catch. While Jane's letters to him are lively and agreeably complicit, their early years were characterized by genteel poverty—at one point Brookfield was reduced to sleeping in the church crypt—and Jane spent much of her time billeted on relatives. Subsequently, although Brookfield carved out a modestly successful career for himself as a clergyman (he became an honorary chaplain to the queen) and inspector of schools, he was conscious that he had not lived up to the expectations of his undergraduate days. This, together with his wife's self-confessed 'foolishly blind fondness of being admired', probably contributed to their later difficulties.

Although she maintained an influential literary salon, which included her husband's old college chum Alfred Tennyson, Jane Octavia Brookfield is chiefly remembered for her association with another of his old friends, the novelist William Makepeace Thackeray. The two met for the first time in 1842. Thackeray was initially cautious, as well as preoccupied with the incurable insanity of his own wife, but by the mid-1840s he and the Brookfields were on terms of considerable intimacy: letters and diaries from August 1845 record four visits from Thackeray in the space of a week. Although intense—at any rate on Thackeray's side—the relationship between him and Jane was almost certainly not sexual (there may have been a chaste embrace or two during the course of a joint stay at Clevedon Court, the Elton family's residence, late in 1848); but neither could it be indefinitely sustained. As early as 1847 Thackeray had to apologize for some 'uncouth raptures' (*Letters and Private Papers*, 2.272), of which Brookfield had complained. In January 1849 Jane's cousin, Harry

Hallam, protested at Thackeray's behaviour and effectively warned him off, Thackeray maintaining his innocence. Prolonged by the birth of Jane's first child, Magdalene, in February 1850 and Thackeray's absence abroad, the situation was finally resolved in a flaming three-way argument in September 1851. Here, according to Thackeray, Brookfield 'spoke out like a man', and the affair was resolved. There was a subsequent reconciliation, but the former intimacies were never re-established.

After Thackeray's death in 1863, Jane Octavia Brookfield wrote four indifferent novels, two of which—*Only George* (1866) and *Not too Late* (1868)—have plots reminiscent of the Thackeray–Brookfield triangle. In some ways, however, her chief literary memorial is the contribution to the characters of Amelia Sedley in Thackeray's *Vanity Fair* (1848) and Laura Bell in *Pendennis* (1850). Brookfield, whose health had never been good, died in 1874. Some years before her own death, on 27 November 1896 at 14 Walpole Street, Chelsea, London, his widow caused a minor scandal by publishing some of the Thackeray correspondence in an American magazine. She was survived by her two sons, Arthur Montagu Brookfield (1853–1940) and Charles Hallam Elton *Brookfield (1857–1913). The former wrote several novels and stood for some years as a Unionist MP, then became a successful diplomat; the latter was an actor.   D. J. TAYLOR

Sources C. H. E. Brookfield and F. M. Brookfield, *Mrs Brookfield and her circle* (1906) · *The letters and private papers of William Makepeace Thackeray*, ed. G. N. Ray, 2 (1945) · *The letters and private papers of William Makepeace Thackeray*, ed. G. N. Ray, 3 (1946) · *The letters and private papers of William Makepeace Thackeray*, ed. E. F. Harden, 1 (1994) · G. N. Ray, *Thackeray*, 2 vols. (1955–8), vol. 2 · J. Sutherland, *The Longman companion to Victorian fiction* (1988) · m. cert. · d. cert.
Archives Downside Abbey, Stratton on the Fosse, Somerset
Likenesses attrib. A. C. Sterling, photographs, salt prints, 1847–9, NPG · W. M. Thackeray, pen-and-ink sketch, c.1849–1851, repro. in Ray, ed., *Letters and private papers of William Makepeace Thackeray* (1945) · S. Richmond, oils, 1851, repro. in Brookfield and Brookfield, *Mrs Brookfield*, frontispiece
Wealth at death £1438 3s. 3d.: probate, 15 Jan 1897, CGPLA Eng. & Wales

Brookfield, William Henry (1809–1874), Church of England clergyman, was the son of Charles Brookfield, a solicitor at Sheffield, where he was born on 31 August 1809. He attended Leeds grammar school and in 1827 was articled to a solicitor at Leeds, but he left this position to enter Trinity College, Cambridge, in October 1829 (BA 1833, MA 1836). There he became the friend of Arthur Henry Hallam and Alfred Tennyson, and was familiar with the Apostles (though not one himself). In 1834 he became tutor to George William (later fourth Lord) Lyttelton (1817–1876), with whom he shared an interest in education. In December 1834 he was ordained to the curacy of Maltby in Lincolnshire. He was subsequently curate at Southampton, of St James's, Piccadilly (1840), and from 1841 to 1848 of St Luke's, Berwick Street. In 1841 he married Jane Octavia, the youngest daughter of Sir Charles *Elton of Clevedon Court, Somerset [see Brookfield, Jane Octavia]. Their children included Charles Hallam Elton

*Brookfield (1857–1913), playwright. The wife of Henry Hallam, the historian, was Sir Charles's sister.

In 1848 Brookfield was appointed inspector of schools by Lord Lansdowne. As such, he helped establish criteria for school inspection. He held the post for seventeen years, during part of which time he was morning preacher at Berkeley Chapel, Mayfair. On resigning his inspectorship he became in 1861 rector of Somerby, near Grantham. He was also reader at the Rolls Chapel, and continued to live chiefly in London. In 1860 he was appointed honorary chaplain to the queen, and later chaplain-in-ordinary. He died on 12 July 1874 at 16 Hereford Square, London. Tennyson's moving sonnet, 'To the Rev. W. H. Brookfield', is in the memoir by Lord Lyttelton published in Brookfield's *Sermons* and in C. Ricks's *The Poems of Tennyson in Three Volumes* (1987).

Brookfield was an impressive preacher, and attracted many cultivated hearers. His sermons, which show no particular theological bias, have considerable literary merit. He had an original vein of humour, which made even his reports as a school inspector unusually amusing, and extraordinary powers of elocution and mimicry. He also had the melancholy temperament often associated with humour, and suffered from ill health, which in 1851 necessitated a voyage to Madeira. As a reader he was unsurpassable, and his college friends described his powers of amusing anecdote as astonishing. He lived, with his wife, at the centre of a Cambridge–London circle of literary friends, and had a genius for friendship (though he quarrelled with W. M. Thackeray) and for wit. W. H. Thompson said of him:

> He was by far the most amusing man I ever met, or ever shall meet. It is not likely that I shall ever see again a whole party, all grave and learned men, lying on the floor for the purpose of unrestrained laughter, while one of their numbers poured forth, with a perfectly grave face, a succession of imaginary dialogues between characters real and fictitious, one exceeding the other in humour and drollery. (Brookfield and Brookfield, 1.238)

[ANON.], rev. H. C. G. MATTHEW

Sources W. H. Brookfield, *Sermons*, ed. J. O. Brookfield (1875) · F. M. Brookfield, *The Cambridge Apostles* (1906) · P. Allen, *The Cambridge Apostles: the early years* (1978) · J. S. Hurst, *Education in evolution* (1971) · C. H. E. Brookfield and F. M. Brookfield, *Mrs Brookfield and her circle*, 2 vols. (1905) · *A collection of letters of William Makepeace Thackeray, 1847–1855*, ed. O. Brookfield (1887) · *The letters of Alfred Lord Tennyson*, ed. C. Y. Lang and E. F. Shannon, 1–2 (1982–7) · CGPLA Eng. & Wales (1874) · Venn, *Alum. Cant.*
Likenesses S. Lawrence, oils, repro. in Brookfield and Brookfield, *Mrs Brookfield and her circle*, 2
Wealth at death under £7000: probate, 7 Aug 1874, CGPLA Eng. & Wales

Brooking, Charles (1723–1759), marine painter, 'was bred in some department of the dockyard at Deptford' (Edwards, 5). His father, also Charles Brooking, is believed to have been a house painter who was employed at Greenwich Hospital between 1729 and 1736 and it is possible that Brooking learned the technical side of his trade by assisting his father. The earliest paintings by his hand are two companion panels depicting night scenes. One shows a bomb ketch off a fort and the other depicts a ship on fire and is signed 'C. Brooking, pinxit, aged 17 years'. Nothing else is known of his life until the 1750s, when he emerges from obscurity. At the age of twenty-nine he was commissioned by John Ellis to illustrate *The Natural History of the Corallines*, which was published in 1755. In his introduction to the book Ellis wrote: 'in August 1752, I went to the Island of Sheppey on the Coast of Kent; and took with me Mr Brooking, a celebrated Painter of sea-pieces, to make the proper Drawings for me'.

About this time Brooking was in the hands of an unscrupulous picture dealer near Leicester Square, London, who showed his paintings in the window of his shop but made a practice of removing the artist's signature. Fortunately the quality of the pictures attracted the attention of Taylor White, the treasurer of the Foundling Hospital, who tracked Brooking down and became his patron. In February 1754 he commissioned him to paint for the Foundling Hospital a very large canvas, *The British Fleet at Sea* to match a painting of similar size by Peter Monamy. Brooking completed the work in eighteen days and in June of the same year he was elected a governor and guardian of the hospital. He painted at least three other pictures for Taylor White and his name appears among the list of painters present at a grand dinner held at the Foundling Hospital on 5 November 1757. He died, according to Redgrave 'before his thirty-sixth birthday' (Redgrave, 57) and was buried at St Martin-in-the-Fields on 25 March 1759. He had been ill with tuberculosis but his death was apparently caused by 'injudicious medical advice, given to remove a perpetual headache' (Dayes, 322). His widow and children, who were left in poverty, received the sum of 10 guineas from the profits of the 1761 exhibition of the Society of Artists of Great Britain.

Brooking is generally considered the most gifted of the English marine artists working in the eighteenth century. He was a major influence on Dominic Serres, who knew him well, and his work was admired by Samuel Scott and by Nicholas Pocock, who made copies of his pictures. He depicted ships with an accuracy and an understanding of sail-handling and seamanship which may be explained by Farington's remark that 'he had been much at sea' (Farington, *Diary*, 3.766). His subtle observation of light and atmosphere and the vagaries of the English weather anticipated by many years the achievements of Constable and the English artists of the Romantic movement. Edward Dayes considered that 'his colour was bright and clear, his water pellucid, his manner broad and spirited' (Dayes, 322). He painted a few sea battles but his finest pictures are those portraying becalmed fishing boats in estuaries or ships heeling before a fresh breeze off a distant coast. The largest collections of his paintings are in the National Maritime Museum, London, and in the Yale Center for British Art, Connecticut; the Tate collection has three fine examples, others are at the Ferens Art Gallery, Kingston upon Hull, Yorkshire, and a considerable number are in private collections.　　　DAVID CORDINGLY

Sources C. Sorensen and B. Taylor, *Charles Brooking, 1723–1759: paintings, drawings, and engravings* (1966) [exhibition catalogue, Aldeburgh Festival of Music and the Arts, 9–21 June 1966, and Bristol City Art Gallery, 1–30 July 1966] · E. Edwards, *Anecdotes of painters* (1808); facs. edn (1970) · E. Dayes, *Professional sketches* (1805) · Farington, *Diary* · D. Cordingly, *Marine painting in England, 1700–1900* (1974) · E. H. H. Archibald, *Dictionary of sea painters*, 2nd edn (1989) · Redgrave, *Artists* · D. Joel, *Charles Brooking 1723–1759: and the 18th century marine painters* (2000)

Brooking, Sir Harry Triscott (1864–1944), army officer, was born on 13 January 1864, the son of Lieutenant Arthur Yelverton Brooking (1841–1869) of the Indian army and his wife, Constance (*d.* 1870). He had a sister, Constance Emily. Brooking was educated at Wellington College and the Royal Military College, Sandhurst, from which he was commissioned into the South Wales Borderers on 6 February 1884. The following year he was transferred to the 21st Madras infantry of the Indian army. He remained with this regiment (renamed the 61st pioneers in 1903) for the rest of his regimental career.

The Indian army, at the turn of the century, offered numerous opportunities for active employment and Brooking took full advantage of them. He saw combat in Burma (1888–9), where he was mentioned in dispatches; the Chin hills expedition (1892–4); the north-west frontier (1897); and Tirah (1897–8), where he was present at the actions of Chagru Kotal and Dargai. He also obtained staff experience, becoming deputy assistant adjutant-general for the Madras district in 1898. In 1900 he went to China as deputy assistant quartermaster-general, part of the multinational force dispatched to suppress the Boxer uprising, and was present at the relief of Peking (Beijing). He was again mentioned in dispatches and received the brevet of major. After completing his tour as commanding officer of the 61st pioneers (1906–11) he rejoined the staff. When the First World War broke out he was general staff officer, grade 1, of the 5th (Mhow) division. On 30 November 1889 he had married Amy Agnèse Smith (*d.* 1934), daughter of Albert Smith; they had one daughter.

Brooking's wartime career was spent mainly in Mesopotamia. His command of the 12th Indian brigade (20 September 1915 to 7 May 1916) and, later, the 15th Indian division (from 7 May 1916) demonstrated the qualities of self-reliance, initiative, decision, and resolve which he had absorbed from his experience of frontier warfare. In February 1916 he extricated the advanced detachments of the 12th brigade from Butaniyyah in the face of considerable Arab opposition, afterwards inflicting retribution on the villages of hostile tribes. In September 1916 his successful action as general officer commanding 15th division at al-Sahilan, near Nasiriyyah, probably prevented a serious Arab rising. His greatest achievements, however, came on 28–9 September 1917 at Ramadi where his division captured 3500 Turks, and at Khan Baghdadi on 26–7 March 1918 where his composite 'Brookforce' captured 4000 Turks.

Brooking was a small, slight figure, but a man of great determination and energy. His operational method was characterized by careful preparation, good intelligence, guile, and speed. He excelled at subterfuge and showed a preference for night-time deployments. His victories at

Ramadi and Khan Baghdadi have been described as 'among the most perfectly conceived and conducted minor battles of the whole war' (Anglesey, 144).

Brooking was eight times mentioned in dispatches during the war. He was made CB in 1914, KCB in 1916, KGMG in 1917, and KCSI in 1919. He retired in 1920 and settled to a quiet and private life in Bournemouth with his wife and daughter, Eileen Constance, later Lady Greenway (d. 1963). He died at Marrick, 79 Lansdowne Road, Bournemouth, on 17 January 1944, shortly after his eightieth birthday.

J. M. BOURNE

Sources F. J. Moberly, ed., *The campaign in Mesopotamia, 1914–1918*, 4 vols. (1923–7) · Marquess of Anglesey [G. C. H. V. Paget], *A history of the British cavalry, 1816 to 1919*, 6 (1995) · A. J. Barker, *The neglected war: Mesopotamia, 1914–1918* (1967) · *Army List* · *The Times* · WWW · Burke, *Peerage* (1939) · *Kelly's directory of Hampshire and the Isle of Wight* (1939) · *CGPLA Eng. & Wales* (1944)
Archives FILM IWM FVA, actuality footage
Wealth at death £16,026 11s. 8d.: probate, 1 March 1944, *CGPLA Eng. & Wales*

Brooks, Charles William Shirley (1816–1874), journalist and playwright, was the son of William Brooks, architect, who died on 11 December 1867, aged eighty, and his wife, Elizabeth, the eldest daughter of William Sabine of Islington. He was born at 52 Doughty Street, London, on 29 April 1816; after his early education he was articled, on 24 April 1832, to his uncle, Charles Sabine of Oswestry. He passed the Incorporated Law Society's examination in November 1838, but there is no record of his ever having become a solicitor. From 1848 to 1852 he was parliamentary correspondent for the *Morning Chronicle*. In 1853 the newspaper delegated him to inquire into the questions connected with the subject of labour and the poor in Russia, Syria, and Egypt. His pleasant letters from these countries were afterwards collected and published as *Russians of the South* (1854).

At the start of his writing career, from 1842, Brooks signed his articles for *Ainsworth's Magazine* Charles W. Brooks. His second literary signature was C. Shirley Brooks, and finally he became Shirley Brooks. This early journalism brought him into communication with Harrison Ainsworth, Laman Blanchard, and other well-known men, and he soon became the centre of a group of literary friends, who found pleasure in his wit and social qualities. As a dramatist he frequently achieved considerable success, without, however, once making any ambitious effort—such as, for example, producing a five-act comedy. His first play, *The Creole, or, Love's Fetters*, was produced at the Lyceum on 8 April 1847 to marked applause. A lighter piece, *Anything for a Change*, was staged at the same house on 7 June 1848. Two years later, on 5 August 1850, his two-act drama, *Daughter of the Stars*, was acted at the New Strand Theatre. The exhibition of 1851 occasioned *The exposition: a Scandinavian sketch, containing as much irrelevant matter as possible in one act*, which was produced at the Strand on 28 April in that year. In association with John Oxenford, he supplied to the Olympic, for performance on 26 December 1861, an extravaganza, *Timour the Tartar, or, The Iron Master of Samarkand*. Among his other dramatic pieces may be mentioned *The Guardian Angel*, a farce, *The Lowther Arcade*, *Honours and Tricks*, and *Our New Governess*.

In his earlier days Brooks was a contributor to many of the best periodicals. He was a leader writer on the *Illustrated London News*, for which at a later period he wrote a weekly article entitled 'Nothing in the Papers'. He conducted the *Literary Gazette* (1858–9), and edited *Home News* after the death of Robert Bell in 1867. He supplied three sketches—'The Opera', 'The Coulisse', and 'The Foreign Gentleman'—to a volume edited by Albert Smith, *Gavarni in London* (1849); and in collaboration with Angus B. Reach he published *A Story with a Vengeance* (1852). At thirty-eight years of age he began to assert his claim to consideration as a popular novelist by writing *Aspen Court: a Story of our Own Time*; despite its success he allowed five years to pass before he published his second novel, the *Gordian Knot*, illustrated by J. Tenniel. He published several more novels, including *Sooner or Later*, illustrated by G. Du Maurier (3 vols., 1866–8).

The most important and interesting event in Brooks's life was his connection with *Punch*, which began in 1851 and lasted until his death. He signed his articles 'Epicurus Rotundus'. In 1870 he succeeded Mark Lemon as editor. One of his best-known series of articles was 'The essence of parliament', a style of writing for which he was peculiarly fitted by his previous training with the *Morning Chronicle*, and which created a new genre of witty parliamentary commentary, maintained after Brooks by H. W. Lucy. Brooks had been innovative as a contributor in the 1860s, but he was a 'steady-as-she-goes' editor, and left the journal much as he found it.

Brooks was elected a fellow of the Society of Antiquaries on 14 March 1872. He was always a hard worker, and the four years during which he was editor of *Punch* were no exception to the rule. Death found him in the midst of his books and papers, working cheerfully among his family. Two articles, 'Election epigrams' and 'The situation', were written on his deathbed, and published posthumously. He died at 6 Kent Terrace, Regent's Park, London, on 23 February 1874, and was buried in Kensal Green cemetery on 28 February. His widow, Emily Margaret, daughter of Dr William Walkinshaw of Naparima, Trinidad, was granted a civil-list pension of £100 on 19 June 1876, and died on 14 May 1880.

G. C. BOASE, rev. H. C. G. MATTHEW

Sources G. S. Layard, *A great Punch editor* (1907) · B. Jerrold, 'Shirley Brooks', *GM*, 5th ser., 12 (1874), 561–9 · R. G. G. Price, *A history of Punch* (1957) · DNB
Archives Harvard U., Houghton L., diaries · Hunt. L., corresp. · LUL | Bodl. Oxf., letters to Messrs Bradbury and Evans · U. Leeds, Brotherton L., letters to George Augustus Sala · V&A NAL, letters to W. P. Frith and Mrs Frith
Likenesses Elliott & Fry, carte-de-visite, NPG · Elliott & Fry, photograph, repro. in *ILN* (7 March 1874), 225 · H. N. King of Bath, carte-de-visite, NPG · H. N. O'Neil, group portrait, oils (*Forty-three members in the billiard room of the Garrick Club*), Garr. Club · drawing, repro. in *Cartoon portraits and biographical sketches of men of the day* (1873), facing p. 128 · engraving, repro. in *The Graphic* (7 March 1874), 229 · group portrait, wood-engraving (*Editors of Punch*), BM, NPG; repro. in *ILN* (18 July 1891) · woodcuts (after photograph by Elliott & Fry), NPG

Wealth at death under £6000: probate, 27 April 1874, *CGPLA Eng. & Wales*

Brooks, (William) Collin (1893–1959), journalist, was born at 18 Scotland Road, Stanwix, Carlisle, on 22 December 1893, the second child of William Edward Brooks (1864–1914), a travelling salesman for Lever Brothers, and his wife, Isabella Collin Thomas (1863–1915). Educated at Christchurch Hall School, Southport, Brooks was briefly a trainee accountant before following his father as a commercial traveller. In 1913 he moved into journalism, founding the Manchester Press Agency, which he ran until 1915, when he joined the army. On 8 January 1916 he married Lilian Susanna Marsden (1891–1981), the daughter of Ernest Marsden. They had five children. In February 1916 he left to join his regiment and in July 1916 was commissioned in the machine-gun corps (infantry), 23rd division. He experienced particularly severe fighting on the Italian front with the Austrian breakthrough at Asisgo (June 1918) and the allied crossing of the Piave (October 1918), winning the Military Cross for his actions at Piave.

After demobilization in March 1919 Brooks worked for the weekly *Ways and Means*, *Liverpool Courier*, and *Liverpool Post*, and in 1923 joined the *Yorkshire Post* under Arthur Mann. Relations between the two men were far from cordial and in 1928 he joined Brendan Bracken's *Financial News* as city editor. There he witnessed the guerrilla warfare between the editor, Oscar Hobson, and Bracken, and the financial strictures required to run a paper after the Wall Street crash. After joining the *Sunday Dispatch* in 1934, within a matter of months he met the proprietor, Lord Rothermere, and found himself ushered into the press baron's inner circle. Brooks became a confidant and close friend of the peer, and subsequently ghosted his memoirs, *My Fight to Rearm Britain* (1939) and *Warnings and Predictions* (1939). In September 1935 he accepted the editorship of the *Sunday Dispatch*, but failed to halt the paper's declining circulation, hindered by frequent trips abroad accompanying Rothermere and severe ill health while in Canada in 1937. He relinquished the editorship in November 1937 and after Rothermere's retirement his formal ties with the *Daily Mail* group were severed in 1938.

Politically Brooks was on the right of the Conservative Party. A short period as a lobby correspondent in 1928 had tarnished his vision of parliamentary democracy and he aspired to a vision of hierarchy and aristocratic virtues. Prepared to stand as an independent Conservative in the Norwood by-election of 1935, he willingly assisted Rothermere in his vendetta against Baldwin, and in the late 1930s attacked the critics of Chamberlain's appeasement policy.

In November 1940 Brooks took the editorship of *Truth*. Under his direction the journal questioned the legality of the 18B internment regulations, criticized the Americans, and remained suspicious of the Soviets. Championing these causes led to his being labelled a quisling and a fascist in a parliamentary debate of 1941, an assertion strenuously denied by Brooks and his many Conservative friends. Ironically Brooks had reconciled himself to mainstream Conservatism by this time, helping draft speeches

for the 1922 Committee chairman, Alex Erskine-Hill, and later organizing the Conservative Party front organization Aims of Industry. Brooks retained the editorship and controlling interest in *Truth* until he relinquished control to Staples Press in 1952.

During the war years Brooks's radio broadcasting career began to flourish, as he became a regular fixture either under his own name or as Northcountryman. After 1945 he was a frequent participant on *Any Questions?* and *The Brains Trust*. This firsthand experience of the BBC, and his own distrust of bureaucracy, led him to champion the cause for independent television in his later years.

Brooks was prepared to write about any subject, whether fiction or non-fiction. In all, he produced thirty-nine books between 1914 and his death, some under the pen-name Barnaby Brook. The subjects ranged from legal trials to poetry, and economic punditry to thrillers. All were produced by typing with two fingers on a Corona three-bank typewriter. For him, writing was a means of personal fulfilment as much as economic necessity; his sales figures were never sufficient for his writing to provide a sole source of income.

Standing 5 feet 10 inches tall, with broad shoulders, an upright carriage, and glasses, Brooks dressed semiformally in 'City' clothes mostly with a Savage Club tie. He had a habit of standing with one hand in his back hip pocket while talking. He relished good company and lively debate (both intellectual and trivial). A clubman, variously a member of the Reform, Carlton, Royal Thames Yacht Club, and Savage, he enjoyed a wide circle of friends from political, journalistic, legal, theatrical, and literary circles. His movements, and the gossip and intrigue he collected around Fleet Street and the West End, were recorded in his journal, maintained from 1925 until 1956.

The last years of Brooks's life were marred by Parkinson's disease, which prevented the completion of his memoirs. He died at his home in St George's Court, Gloucester Road, London, on 6 April 1959 and his body was cremated at Mortlake on 12 April.   N. J. CROWSON

Sources Collin Brooks's journals, priv. coll. • *Fleet Street, press barons and politics: the journals of Collin Brooks, 1932–1940*, ed. N. J. Crowson, CS, 5th ser., 11 (1998) • 'Collin Brooks', *The Statist*, 169 (11 April 1959) • private information (2004) [family] • S. Bolton and G. Bolton, *Two lives converge: the dual autobiography of Sybil and Glorney Bolton* (1938) • P. Addison, 'Patriotism under pressure: Lord Rothermere and British foreign policy', *The politics of reappraisal, 1918–1939*, ed. G. Peele and C. Cook (1975) • b. cert. • *CGPLA Eng. & Wales* (1959)
Archives BBC WAC, files • priv. coll., MSS • PRO, war record, WO 339/88414
Likenesses photograph, *c.*1920–1929, repro. in Crowson, ed., *Fleet Street, press barons and politics*, jacket • H. Coster, photographs, 1935, NPG • photograph, *c.*1937, repro. in *The Globe and Mail* [Toronto, Canada] (15 May 1937)
Wealth at death £2063 1s. 1d.: probate, 25 June 1959, *CGPLA Eng. & Wales*

Brooks, David (1802/3–1882). *See under* Rochdale Pioneers (*act.* 1844).

Brooks, Ernest Walter (1863–1955), ancient historian and Syriac scholar, was born in Hambledon, Horndean, Hampshire, on 30 August 1863, the only child of the Revd Walter

Brooks, curate of Hambledon, who died when Ernest was a child, and his wife, Emily Grace, *née* Browning. In September 1876 he went as a king's scholar to Eton College, where, as a pupil of F. St John Thackeray, he achieved an outstanding academic performance (winning numerous prizes, having fifteen pieces of work 'sent up for good', and frequently topping divisions), but it was not altogether a happy time. In November 1878 he was the victim of a particularly nasty practical joke orchestrated by M. R. James which led to a formal complaint being made by Brooks and his stepfather. James had taken a strong dislike to Brooks, describing him as 'not nice and a convenient object for venting one's superfluous energies upon' (Pfaff, 30). While this may have been due to a straightforward clash of personalities (the other collegers in this instance seem to have sided with Brooks), it is possible that it was also influenced by Brooks's close family relationship, via his mother, to the flamboyant historian Oscar Browning, whom James despised, and who had recently been dismissed from his post at Eton.

In October 1883 Brooks entered King's College, Cambridge, as a scholar, and there he again flourished academically. In addition to taking a first class in each part of the classical tripos (1886 and 1887; MA 1890), he was also Bell university scholar (1884) and Carus Greek Testament prizeman (1885). His relationship with Browning (who had taken up residence in King's College in 1876) developed, and after leaving Cambridge he moved to London where, as an independent scholar based at the British Museum, he became involved in researching the Browning family history as well as producing his earliest academic articles. These mostly concentrated on seventh- to ninth-century Byzantine history, and this side of his work eventually culminated in his masterful chapters dealing with the political and military history of the Eastern empire which were published in the *Cambridge Medieval History* (vol. 1, 1911; vol. 2, 1913; and vol. 4, 1923).

Brooks's academic reputation was built, however, upon his specialization in Syriac historical texts. He began with an edition and translation of the short Syriac chronicle of AD 846 (published 1897), and continued with the publication of further Syriac chronicles attributed to authors such as Zacharias Rhetor, James of Edessa, Eliya bar Shinaya, and John of Ephesus (this last was his last major work, published in 1935–6). To these can be added his editions of Syriac hagiographical texts (the lives of various Syrian Orthodox saints by John of Ephesus and others, plus the Syriac version of the life of St George), and of theological texts attributed to Severus of Antioch and Nestorius. He was not always in good health, occasionally suffering from prolonged bouts of insomnia that allowed him to work for only a few hours a day, and yet his output was not only prolific but notable for its learning, conciseness, and lucidity. His editions and translations of Syriac historical texts made them available, often for the first time, to historians of the Eastern empire and of the Near East in general, and so transformed their discipline. Unusually his scholarship won the respect of contemporary scholars not only in the West but also in the Near East

(where his admirers included the Syrian Orthodox patriarch of Antioch, Ignatios Ephrem Barsaum, himself a noted Syriac scholar). His first formal recognition came with the award of an honorary doctorate by the University of Louvain (1927), which was followed (in 1938) by his election as a fellow of the British Academy. The nomination papers for the fellowship simply described him as 'the most distinguished Syriac scholar in England'.

In 1927 Brooks married Ellen Amy, the daughter of Major-General G. B. Mellersh. Shortly afterwards they went to live in Geneva, but on his retirement from active research (he resigned from the British Academy in 1941) they moved to Milford-on-Sea, Hampshire, where he died, at the War Memorial Hospital, on 26 March 1955.

D. G. K. TAYLOR

Sources *WWW, 1951–60* · *Annual Report of the Council* [King's College, Cambridge] (1955) · J. J. Withers, *A register of admissions to King's College, Cambridge, 1797–1925* (1929) · *The Times* (25 April 1955) · Eton, archives · E. W. Brooks, 18 letters, King's AC Cam., Oscar Browning MSS · 1938 nomination papers, British Academy Archives · R. W. Pfaff, *Montague Rhodes James* (1980) · I. E. Barsaum, *Ktobô d-berûlê bdîrê d-ʿl mardût yûlfonê sûryoyê hdîrê* (Qamishli, 1967) · b. cert. · d. cert. · *CGPLA Eng. & Wales* (1955)
Archives King's AC Cam., letters to Oscar Browning
Likenesses photograph, British Academy
Wealth at death £17,766 17s. 8d.: probate, 26 July 1955, *CGPLA Eng. & Wales*

Brooks, Gabriel (c.1704–1741), writing-master, was the son of Gabriel Brooks and his wife, Elizabeth. His father was probably a writing-master working in London between 1670 and 1699. There is little information regarding Gabriel Brooks's life or training except that he was apprenticed to the writing-master Dennis Smith in Castle Street, Southwark. Later in life he kept a day school in Burr Street, Wapping, where, it is assumed, he taught writing. He is principally remembered for the nine pieces of writing which George Bickham engraved for his luxury copybook *The Universal Penman* (1733–41). These homilies on typical subjects such as modesty and idleness, executed in a variety of hands including 'round hand' and 'square text', reveal Brooks's skill in penmanship; composed with modest flourishes they also demonstrate his tendency towards a more ornamental style of writing. The only other recorded example of his work is for a large shop bill for Mr Stanesby jun., a musical instrument maker. According to William Massey's *The Origins & Progress of Letters* (1763), Brooks died in 1741 'aged about 37 years' (Massey, 2.29). In his will, proved that year, Brooks left his property in Maid Lane, in the parish of St Saviour's, Southwark, to his wife, Jane Ann Brooks.

JOHN WESTBY-GIBSON, *rev.* LUCY PELTZ

Sources A. Heal, *The English writing-masters and their copy-books, 1570–1800* (1931) · W. Massey, *The origin and progress of letters: an essay in two parts* (1763) · will, 1741, PRO, PROB 11/710, fols. 15r–15v
Wealth at death property in Southwark to wife: will, 1741, PRO, PROB 11/710, fols. 15r–15v

Brooks, James (1512–1558), bishop of Gloucester, was born in Hampshire in May 1512. Admitted in 1528 to Corpus Christi College, Oxford, as a scholar, he graduated BA on 23 June 1531 and that year was admitted to the fellowship of the college. He proceeded MA on 1 July 1535. Three years later a complaint was made against him and three other fellows that they kept 'the youth of the college from the knowledge of God's Word, resisting against the ordinances for the spread of the gospel and "extirping" of papistical doctrine' (*LP Henry VIII*, 13/2, 218). Brooks proceeded BD in 1544 and DD in 1546, and acquired the Berkshire rectories of East Lockinge in 1545 and East Hendred in 1546. In 1547 he was made master of Balliol College, Oxford, where he seems to have continued until 1555, acting as vice-chancellor of the university for part of 1552. He also served as chaplain and almoner to Stephen Gardiner, bishop of Winchester.

As a faithful supporter of the Church of Rome, Brooks was one of the clerics who played a key role in the restoration of Catholicism during the reign of Mary. He preached at Paul's Cross on 12 November 1553, lamenting the state of religion in England as a result of the advent of protestantism. First printed that year, his sermon was issued again in an expanded version in 1554. Brooks also preached before the queen at St Paul's during Lent 1554. He was consecrated bishop of Gloucester by the bishop of Winchester at St Saviour's, Southwark, on 1 April that year, the see of Canterbury then being vacant. After he became bishop, however, he distinguished himself more by his activities outside the diocese of Gloucester than within it. In the year of his elevation he assisted with the heresy trial of his predecessor, John Hooper. The next year he was one of those commissioned to examine Hugh Latimer and Nicholas Ridley before their executions, and he represented the pope in the examination of Thomas Cranmer. His speech addressed to Cranmer in St Mary's Church, Oxford, on 12 March 1555, and his oration at the close of the former archbishop's examination, were printed, but by the protestant martyrologist John Foxe rather than by English Catholics. In 1555 Brooks was also involved in the heresy trial of John Philpot. Then in 1556 he returned to his own diocese to represent Archbishop Reginald Pole in the metropolitical visitation there. With that notable exception he seems to have relied primarily on his chancellor, John Williams, for the implementation and enforcement of the restoration of Catholicism; Williams personally supervised three of the five burnings of unrepentant protestant heretics in his diocese, including that of Hooper. Brooks was again called to represent Pole in 1557, when he served as one of the visitors to the University of Oxford. In that capacity he ordered the body of the wife of the protestant divine Peter Martyr to be exhumed from sacred ground and reburied in a dunghill. This action prompted John Jewel to describe Brooks as 'a beast of most impure life, and yet more impure conscience' when he wrote to Martyr on 20 March 1559 to tell him of the incident (Robinson, 12).

Brooks died in 1558 between 12 July, when he is mentioned as bishop in diocesan court records, and 20 August, the date of an entry in the bishop's register for the diocese of Gloucester declaring the see vacant owing to the death of the incumbent. His body was allegedly buried in the tomb in Gloucester Cathedral originally built for William Malvern (alias Parker), the last abbot of Gloucester Abbey, but there is no memorial marker.

CAROLINE LITZENBERGER

Sources Gloucester City Library, Hockaday Abstracts, Chronological, 1554–8 · Glos. RO, Gloucester diocesan record, vols. 2a, 11, 13 · J. Foxe, *Acts and monuments*, ed. G. H. Townsend, 8 vols. (1843–9) · H. Latimer, *The sermons and remains of Hugh Latimer*, ed. G. E. Corrie (1845) · *STC, 1475–1640* · D. M. Smith, *Guide to bishops' registers of England and Wales: a survey from the middle ages to the abolition of the episcopacy in 1646*, Royal Historical Society Guides and Handbooks, 11 (1981) · J. Strype, *Annals of the Reformation and establishment of religion … during Queen Elizabeth's happy reign*, new edn, 4 vols. (1824) · J. Strype, *Ecclesiastical memorials*, 3 vols. (1822) · J. Strype, *Memorials of the most reverend father in God, Thomas Cranmer*, ed. P. E. Barnes, new edn, 2 vols. (1853) · D. Verey, *Buildings of England: Gloucestershire*, 2nd edn, 2 vols. (1976) · W. H. Frere and W. P. M. Kennedy, eds., *Visitation articles and injunctions of the period of the Reformation*, 3 vols., Alcuin Club, Collections, 14–16 (1910) · D. Welander, *The history, art and architecture of Gloucester Cathedral* (1991) · A. Wilkins, ed., *Concilia Magnae Britanniae*, 4 vols. (1737) · Wood, *Ath. Oxon.*, new edn · H. Robinson, ed. and trans., *The Zurich letters, comprising the correspondence of several English bishops and others with some of the Helvetian reformers, during the early part of the reign of Queen Elizabeth*, 1, Parker Society, 7 (1842) · Foster, *Alum. Oxon.* · *LP Henry VIII*, vol. 13/2
Archives Glos. RO · Gloucestershire Public Library

Brooks, James (1825–1901), architect, was born at Hatford, Berkshire, on 30 March 1825, the son of John Brooks, a farmer from Hatford who later moved to Wantage, and his wife, *née* Tyrrell. He was educated at Abingdon School, where he showed a precocious interest in agricultural technology, inventing a threshing machine and a new type of ploughshare which became commercially successful. In 1847 he went into the London office of the architect Lewis Stride. He attended T. L. Donaldson's lectures at University College, and in 1849 he enrolled in the Royal Academy Schools. In 1853 he opened his own office at 5 Bloomsbury Square and over the ensuing years he designed several houses and schools in Berkshire and Oxfordshire. He married Emma (d. 1892), daughter of J. Martin of Sandford House, Sandford-on-Thames, Oxfordshire, probably in 1858, and his first son was born in the following year; two more sons and a daughter followed. In 1862 he and his family settled at The Grange, Clissold Crescent, Stoke Newington, London, a red-brick Gothic house built to his own designs.

Brooks's place in the history of architecture derives largely from his London churches. He was a zealous high-churchman and obtained his most significant commissions from like-minded Anglicans, some of whom were fellow worshippers at St Matthias's, Stoke Newington, where he served as churchwarden from 1868 to 1879. His first important church, St Michael's, Mark Street (1863–5), was in the desperately poor parish of Shoreditch in the East End, and he went on to design two more churches in the neighbouring district of Haggerston: St Columba's, Kingsland Road (1868–9), and St Chad's, Nichols Square (1868–9). Other commissions soon followed: St Saviour's, Hoxton (1865–6; dem.), St Andrew's, Plaistow (1867–70), and The Annunciation, Chislehurst (1868–70). With their wide, lofty naves, narrow aisles, raised chancels, and lancet or plate-traceried windows, these noble and beautifully proportioned buildings epitomize the mid-Victorian ideal of the Anglican town church. They were built relatively cheaply, usually of brick, and their unembellished interiors and bulky exteriors have something of the gravity of early Cistercian architecture. Brooks also designed the parsonages and elementary schools which clustered around most of the churches, and in 1870–73 he designed a convent for Anglican nuns next to St Michael's, Shoreditch; its daughter house of St Mary of Nazareth, Edgware, was begun to his designs in 1875, though, like many of his buildings, it was never finished.

There was something of a hiatus in Brooks's career in the 1870s, but in the last twenty years of his life he became one of the most prolific of English church architects. At St John's, Holland Road, Kensington (1872–1910), The Ascension, Lavender Hill, Battersea (1876–98), Holy Innocents', Hammersmith (1887–1901), St Peter and St Paul, Dover (1891–3), and All Hallows, Gospel Oak (1892–1901; completed by Giles Gilbert Scott, 1913–15), and in his competition designs for Liverpool Cathedral (1887; unexecuted), he developed and refined the French-inspired early Gothic style of his earlier churches long after it had gone out of fashion among his younger contemporaries. Except at St Mary's, Hornsey (1888–9), and one or two other churches, he showed little interest in English late Gothic, and his secular buildings, apart from schools and parsonages, are few in number and of negligible interest.

Though less well known than some of his contemporaries, Brooks was one of the most accomplished architects of the Gothic revival. He became a fellow of the Royal Institute of British Architects (RIBA) in 1866, honorary consulting architect to the Incorporated Church Building Society in 1880, and diocesan architect for Canterbury in 1888. In 1881 he joined the RIBA council, became vice-president in 1892, and was awarded the RIBA gold medal in 1895. In 1875 he moved his office to 33–5 Wellington Street, Strand, and in 1892 he took his son and pupil John Martin Brooks into partnership. He took only two other pupils, George Godsall and Alfred Mackmurdo, and of these only Mackmurdo—who set up practice on his own in 1875—made a significant impact on architecture. Though living in London all his professional life, Brooks retained an enthusiasm for rural pursuits, riding to hounds until the age of fifty and shooting until he was sixty. His wife died on 31 August 1892 and he subsequently married his housekeeper, Mary: something which, if his family were to be believed, cost him a knighthood. He died of heart failure at his home, The Grange, Clissold Crescent, Stoke Newington, on 7 October 1901 and was buried three days later in Great Northern London cemetery, Southgate. His son then took over the architectural practice in partnership with George Godsall, and when he died on 24 October 1903 his place was taken by John Standen Adkins, who completed some of Brooks's unfinished buildings.   GEOFFREY TYACK

Sources R. E. Dixon, 'The life and works of James Brooks', PhD diss., Courtauld Inst., 1976 · J. S. Adkins, 'James Brooks: a memoir', *RIBA Journal*, 17 (1909–10), 493–516 · *The Builder*, 81 (1901), 308 · *RIBA Journal*, 2 (1894–5), 553–5 · B. F. L. Clarke, *Church builders of the nineteenth century* (1938) · B. F. L. Clarke, *Parish churches of London* (1966) · G. Stamp and C. Amery, *Victorian buildings of London, 1837–1887: an illustrated guide* (1980) · *CGPLA Eng. & Wales* (1901)

Archives Durham RO, letters relating to work in Wynyard Chapel and Londonderry House

Likenesses photograph, repro. in Adkins, 'James Brooks: a memoir'

Wealth at death £5771 7s.: probate, 4 Dec 1901, *CGPLA Eng. & Wales*

Brooks, John (b. c.1710, d. after 1756), engraver and print publisher, was born in Dublin about 1710, and was admitted to the Dublin Goldsmiths' Corporation as a line engraver in 1736. His earliest known work is an engraved frontispiece to *Odes and Satyrs of Horace*, published by Samuel Fuller at Dublin in 1730. In 1740 he etched a portrait of the actress Margaret Woffington. In the same year he moved to London to learn the technique of mezzotint engraving, possibly with John Faber the younger, some of whose prints he published or republished after his return to Dublin in 1741. In Dublin he established himself as a mezzotint engraver and publisher, in an attempt to break the monopoly of London publishers for the production of mezzotints. He was assisted in particular by Andrew Miller, a London-trained engraver, whom he had persuaded to follow him to Dublin.

Brooks has been described as 'the key figure in Irish engraving' of the 1740s (*Dictionary of Art*), although it was probably Miller, rather than Brooks, who trained the distinguished band of pupils who were later known as the 'Dublin group', and who dominated the production of mezzotints in London from 1750 to 1775; among them were James McArdell, Richard Houston, Richard Purcell, and Charles Spooner. In 1742 Brooks advertised a series of large mezzotint portraits of contemporary notables for publication by subscription; according to W. G. Strickland, of the 100 originally intended prints, only thirty-seven were issued. Among those executed by Brooks himself were, for instance, portraits of William, duke of Devonshire, after James Worsdale (published in 1743), and of William III, after George Kneller (published in 1744). In 1743 Brooks advertised the publication by subscription of eight views of country houses in the vicinity of Dublin; of those, only two etchings, *A North Prospect of Blessington* and *A View of Leixlip and the Waterfall*, appeared. The partial fulfilment of these schemes and Brooks's handing over of his business in 1746 have been attributed to the loss of Miller's vital co-operation when the latter set up on his own about 1744.

In 1746 Brooks, together with McArdell and Houston, emigrated to England and settled in London. From 1746 to 1750 he was recorded as an engraver and publisher at the Strand, but apart from the mezzotint *The Battle of the Boyne*, after Jan Wyck (1746), he seems to have produced very little. It is likely that he had already begun to concentrate on possible applications of transfer printing, a process which he claimed, probably justly, to have invented. He unsuccessfully petitioned for a patent in late 1751 from Birmingham, where he had a workshop and advertised transfer-printed serving trays. Further failed petitions were made in January 1754 and April 1755 from York Place in Battersea. In the summer of 1753 Brooks had become a partner in the York House enamelling manufactory in Battersea, founded that year by Stephen Theodore Janssen, but for financial reasons his partnership probably lasted only a few months. In 1756 he was declared bankrupt, and Strickland, among others, blamed his dissipated habits and bad management for the bankruptcy of Janssen and the closure of the manufactory in the same year. According to the *Allgemeines Künstlerlexikon*, Brooks then lived for a number of years in Dublin; Strickland, however, mentioned his work as a dependent engraver for booksellers in London. It seems that he died on a visit to Chester at an unknown date after 1756.

ANNE PUETZ

Sources DNB · W. G. Strickland, *A dictionary of Irish artists*, 2 vols. (1913) · G. Meissner, ed., *Allgemeines Künstlerlexikon: die bildenden Künstler aller Zeiten und Völker*, [new edn], 14, ed. W. Baumberger and others (Munich, 1996) · D. Alexander, 'The Dublin group: Irish mezzotint engravers in London, 1750–75', *Quarterly Bulletin of the Irish Georgian Society*, 16 (1973), 73–92 · B. Watney, 'Petitions for patents concerning porcelain, glass and enamels with special reference to the great toyshop of Europe"', *Transactions of the English Ceramics Circle*, 6/2 (1996) · R. J. Charleston, 'Battersea, Bilston — or Birmingham? The Ionides gift, and other English enamels', *V&A Museum Bulletin*, 3–4 (1967–8), 1–12 · 'Ireland, painting, and the graphic arts, 1600–1799', *The dictionary of art*, ed. J. Turner (1996) · A. Ray, *Liverpool printed tiles* (1994) · J. C. Smith, *British mezzotint portraits*, 1 (1878), 83–99 · S. Benjamin, 'England enamels', *The dictionary of art*, ed. J. Turner (1996) · F. Cullen, 'McArdell, James', *The dictionary of art*, ed. J. Turner (1996) · J. M. Handley, *18th century English transfer-printed porcelain and enamels: the Joseph M. Handley collection* (Carmel, CA, 1991), 1 · C. Cook, *The life and work of Robert Hancock* (1948), 1

Brooks, Ralph Terence St John- (1884–1963), bacteriologist, was born on 27 October 1884 in Dublin, the third son of Professor Henry St John Brooks (*b*. 1855), medical anatomist, and his wife, Marion Sarah Ohren. Educated at Erasmus Smith's School, he graduated in 1904 from Trinity College, Dublin, with first-class honours in natural science. In his father's footsteps he turned to medicine, hyphenating his surname to emphasize the family connection. He won the Haughton medal and prize in medicine and surgery from Sir Patrick Dun's Hospital (1908), and also gained the qualifications MB, BCh, and BAO.

On 25 May 1912 St John-Brooks married Julia Margaret Gordon (they later had two sons and a daughter). Also in 1912 he moved to the Leeward Islands where he acted as special sanitary investigator for the government. In 1914 he became secretary of the commission for plague investigation in India, working from the Lister Institute of Preventive Medicine in London. During the First World War he served as a captain in the Royal Army Medical Corps, specializing in bacteriology, and developed an interest in the collection and maintenance of representative cultures of various types of bacteria. The basis of such a collection already existed at the Lister Institute; in 1920, augmented by many of St John-Brooks's own isolates, it became the National Collection of Type Cultures (NCTC). The NCTC soon became a national resource of live,

authenticated cultures of microbes for diagnoses, research, and teaching.

St John-Brooks's curatorship of that collection was perhaps his major contribution to science. Expanded to include yeasts and other fungi, and to cover microbes of economic and veterinary as well as medical importance, it became the reference collection on which British microbiology depended for the next thirty years (when it budded off a second collection). When, at the start of the Second World War, the NCTC was hurriedly moved to an outstation of the institute at Elstree there was considerable confusion and many of the live cultures became contaminated, but St John-Brooks had shown considerable foresight: he had prepared two specimens of most of the strains in the collection, sealed in a viable but vacuum dried form. These specimens were recovered and thus saved for posterity.

St John-Brooks was also involved in the naming of type cultures. He served on international nomenclature committees in the 1930s and, in collaboration with North Americans R. E. Buchanan and R. S. Breed, was instrumental in bringing a degree of order to a confused situation by developing a code of bacterial nomenclature which was approved internationally after the Second World War. He also played an important part in organizing the second International Congress of Microbiology (London, 1936) and was president of the third (New York, 1939). He continued his international activities after retiring from the NCTC in 1946. A good-humoured and rather unassuming man, he was noted for his ability to weld independently minded personalities into unanimous and productive committees.

St John-Brooks is especially remembered for his crucial part in founding the Society for General Microbiology. An energetic organizer, he lived near a kindred spirit, dairy microbiologist Dr L. A. Allen. Between them, often during informal visits to each other's houses, they did most of the planning and paperwork which brought Britain's most flourishing microbiological learned society into being in 1945.

St John-Brooks had caught tularaemia, often a lethal disease, from a laboratory specimen in 1923. He recovered, but his health remained precarious and sometimes compelled him to restrict his activities. Serious episodes were two bouts of tuberculosis (1925–7 and 1932–4). Yet he sustained his many microbiological activities with seemingly unimpaired vigour. In this context a friend wrote, 'the gentle wit, which he shared with his wife, lasted him his lifetime' (*The Lancet*, 1115). He enjoyed family life, natural history, and gardening, and in 1950 he retired to his native Dublin, where he died of cancer on 27 April 1963.

JOHN R. POSTGATE

Sources L. A. Allen, *Journal of General Microbiology*, 42 (1966), 165–7 · S. R. Elsden, 'R. St John-Brooks', *Society for General Microbiology Quarterly*, 12/1 (1985), 5–6 · WWW, 1961–70 · *The Lancet* (4 May 1963), 1005 · *The Lancet* (18 May 1963), 1115 · private information (2004) · CGPLA Éire (1963–4)
Likenesses photograph, 1966, repro. in Allen, *Journal*, facing p. 165
Wealth at death £1848: probate, 17 May 1963, CGPLA Éire

Brooks, Robert (1790–1882), businessman and trader, was born in Laceby, Lincolnshire, and baptized there on 5 April 1791 at St Mary's Church, the second son of William Brooks, yeoman farmer at Laceby, and his wife, Ann Ostler. He was apprenticed to the wealthy Hull merchant and shipowner John Barkworth, for whom he travelled as supercargo to Mauritius and India. In 1820 Brooks established his own firm in London. In 1823 he made a trading voyage to Hobart and Sydney aboard his ship *Elizabeth*. This remained his only visit to Australia. He married, on 23 March 1833, Hannah (1801/2–1885), daughter of Joshua Penny, a London wine merchant; they raised five sons and three daughters.

During the 1830s Brooks built up a network of business connections throughout eastern Australia and New Zealand. He soon was one of the largest importers of Australian wool and in 1846 became chairman of the New South Wales and Van Diemen's Land Commercial Association, which regulated the London wool auctions.

Initially Brooks found shipowning a vital element of his colonial trading and he built up a fleet reaching over 5000 tons. After 1850, however, he abandoned his active interest in shipping and only invested in ships directed by business associates. Financing the wool trade and other Australian ventures became his main priority. Brooks was careful to select trusted men like his Sydney agent, Robert Towns (who gave his name to Townsville in Queensland), and Octavius Browne (brother of 'Phiz', Charles Dickens's illustrator) at Melbourne.

In 1855 Brooks took Robert Spence into partnership, styling his firm Robert Brooks & Co. The next year he purchased the estate of Woodcote Park at Epsom, in Surrey, from profits made during the Australian gold rushes and the Crimean War. In the course of the 1860s three of his five sons became partners (the two others joined the church and the army) and the firm remained within the family until its liquidation in 1968. Brooks's prominence, however, rested on much more than developing his private business. He was also active in the corporate sphere. His main interest was the Union Bank of Australia (a forerunner of the Australia and New Zealand Banking Group), of which he was the longest-serving founding director (1837–76). Other directorships included the London Dock Company, the Southern Whale Fishery Company, insurance and mining companies, and several abortive steamshipping ventures, including the Great Eastern Steam Navigation Company. Throughout, Brooks aimed at maintaining a synergetic relationship between companies operating in the Australian trade and the interests of himself and his City colleagues. He ensured that the Union Bank of Australia respected what he regarded as the legitimate field of the private merchant. In the election of 1859 the Conservatives invited him, because of his maritime aura, to contest Weymouth and Melcombe Regis. Despite his opponents accusing him of being an 'auriferous Australian', he represented Weymouth as a back-bencher in the House of Commons until 1868.

From the 1830s to the 1870s Robert Brooks was one of the leaders of the trade between Britain and Australia. His career paralleled the development and spectacular growth of the colonial Australian economy. Brooks was involved in most aspects of the trade: exporting, importing, shipping, finance, banking, and promoting assisted emigration. He helped raise funds for Mrs Caroline Chisholm (1808–1877), 'the emigrant's friend', and was a well-known City figure.

Brooks was meticulous, cautious, and a workaholic. He preferred consensus and co-operation to confrontation and conflict. Determined to succeed in his trade, the boy from Laceby helped make the City the services centre of the world economy. He was a family man with great loyalty to his friends. He had little interest in charities, the arts, or politics. He shunned the limelight and, unlike several of his colleagues, did not receive a knighthood. He died at Woodcote Park on 5 June 1882, leaving his estate largely to his sons, who were also partners, Robert Alexander, Henry, and Herbert.　　　　FRANK BROEZE

Sources F. Broeze, *Mr Brooks and the Australian trade: imperial business in the nineteenth century* (Carlton, Australia, 1993) · F. Broeze, 'Robert Brooks', *Australian financiers*, ed. R. T. Appleyard and C. B. Schedvin (1988), 34–51 · F. Broeze, 'Private enterprise and the peopling of Australia, 1831–1850', *Economic History Review*, 2nd ser., 28 (1982), 582–97 · F. Broeze, 'The view from inside: Robert Brooks and the British connection', *The push from the bush: a bulletin of social history*, 2 (1978), 1–39 · S. J. Butlin, *Australia and New Zealand Bank: the Bank of Australasia and the Union Bank of Australia Limited, 1828–1951* (1961) · F. Broeze, 'Australia, Asia and the Pacific: the maritime world of Robert Towns, 1843–73', *Australian Historical Studies*, 24 (1990–91), 221–38 · B. Dyster, 'The port of Launceston before 1850', *The Great Circle, Journal of the Australian Association for Maritime History*, 3 (1981), 103–24 · 'Select committee of the House of Lords on … the navigation laws', *Parl. papers* (1848), 20/2.110–19, no. 340 [Brooks's testimony] · C. M. Goodridge, *Narrative of a voyage to the south seas, with the shipwreck of the Princess of Wales cutter…* (1832) · *The sales of Australian wool in London: minutes of committee and evidence, London, February 1870* (1870) · d. cert. · Brooks family genealogy, priv. coll. · Dixon pedigrees, Lincs. Arch. · parish register (baptism), St Mary's, Laceby, Lincolnshire, 5 April 1791

Archives NL Aus. · priv. coll. | ANZ Banking Group, Melbourne, Victoria, Australia, archives, Union Bank of Australia MSS · Mitchell L., NSW, Dacre MSS · Mitchell L., NSW, Towns MSS · Port of London Authority, London, Port Authority archives, London Dock Company MSS · PRO, London shipping register, Board of Trade 107–109 [transcripts]

Likenesses silhouette, 1846, priv. coll.; copy, Australia, Melbourne, ANZ Banking Group Archives

Wealth at death £378,887 16s. 9d.: probate, 29 June 1882, *CGPLA Eng. & Wales*

Brooks [*née* Goddard], **(Beatrice) Romaine Mary** (1874–1970), painter and lesbian icon, was born in a hotel in Rome on 1 May 1874, the third of three children of Major Harry Goddard, army officer, and his wife, Ella Waterman (d. 1902), who were both American citizens. Her father was reputed to be an alcoholic, and her parents divorced not long after her birth. Her mother was very rich, having a number of residences in various European countries. Despite this she seems to have spent little time or money on her two daughters, reserving most of her affection for her sickly and unstable son, St Mar; according to Romaine's later account, her mother was extremely cruel both mentally and physically (see Secrest, 15–23). Her education seems to have been haphazard, including a girls' school in

(Beatrice) **Romaine Mary Brooks** (1874–1970), self-portrait, 1923

New Jersey, a convent in Italy, and a finishing school in Geneva. By 1893 she was asserting her independence, first studying singing in Paris, where one of her fellow students was the noted contralto Clara Butt. She also met Alexander Hamilton Phillips, St Mar's doctor, with whom she may have had an affair, and possibly even gave birth to a daughter, but this is extremely uncertain. By 1895 she had extracted a small financial settlement from her mother, and in 1896 went to Rome to study art at the Circolo Artistico and the Scuola Nazionale, where she was the only woman student. She had been drawing and painting since childhood, and from this time she was able to devote most of her time to painting.

In Italy, Romaine Goddard made the acquaintance of a number of expatriates, most of them British. Capri in particular at this time was a haven for wealthy British homosexual men, particularly artists and writers, who were avoiding Britain in the wake of Oscar Wilde's trial, and here from 1899 onward she met such writers as Somerset Maugham and E. F. Benson, as well as John Ellingham Brooks (d. 1929), with whom she struck up a friendship. In 1901 her brother died and her mother summoned her to

Nice. There Mrs Goddard died of diabetes in 1902, leaving a considerable fortune to Romaine. This marked a major change in her life; for example it is at about this time that she began wearing masculine clothing. She married Brooks on Capri on 13 June 1903, thereby incidentally acquiring British citizenship; the marriage seems to have lasted effectively only about a year before Romaine broke off relations with her husband. In September 1904 she went to London, buying a studio in Tite Street, and shortly thereafter took a small studio at St Ives. There she worked on developing what would henceforth be her characteristic austere style, especially her range of greys, blacks, and whites, without apparently any contact with other artists in the town. About this time she also became friendly with Lord Alfred Douglas. In 1905 she moved to Paris, where she soon became involved with the circle around her fellow American, the princesse de Polignac, *née* Winaretta Singer. However, it was not until 1910 that she mounted her first major exhibition at the Galeries Durand-Ruel in Paris, which immediately established her reputation. Gabriele D'Annunzio (with whom she may have had an affair) described her as 'the most profound and wise orchestrator of greys in modern painting' (Secrest, 419), and the critic Robert de Montesquiou called her 'cambrioleur d'âmes' (thief of souls), referring to the perceptiveness of her portraits (Chadwick, 86). In fact, she did not restrict herself to portraits, also painting a number of female nudes of a stylized androgynous type. A favourite model was Ida Rubinstein, sketches for whose portrait she used as the basis of her picture *La France croisée* (1914; Smithsonian Institution, Washington). For this and for the service her art had rendered to France, she was awarded the medal of the Légion d'honneur in 1920.

In 1915 Brooks met another American, the writer and salon hostess Natalie Clifford Barney (1877–1972), who became her partner until 1968. They spent much of the First World War in Paris, although in 1916 Romaine Brooks returned to Italy. She was back in France by the end of the war. About 1921 they made the acquaintance of Radclyffe Hall and Una Troubridge, and Romaine Brooks appeared thinly disguised as Venetia Ford in Hall's novel *The Forge*. Despite her displeasure at this, in 1924 Romaine Brooks painted a portrait of Una Troubridge (Smithsonian Institution, Washington, DC), taking a studio in London for the purpose. The finished portrait was regarded as something of a caricature, and did nothing to improve relationships between the two lesbian couples.

Brooks and Barney collaborated on a novel, *The One who is Legion, or, A. D.'s After-Life*, which was privately printed in London in 1930 with illustrations by Brooks. In 1927 they took two villas in Beauvallon in the south of France which they linked together with a shared dining-room; the resultant house they named Villa Trait d'Union (Hyphen Villa). J. E. Brooks had died in May 1929, and in the mid-1930s Romaine Brooks set about re-establishing her American citizenship. In 1935 she returned to the United States, but was back in Europe by 1939, spending most of the war in or near Florence. After 1945 she rented an apartment in Nice and divided her time between it and the Villa

Gaia (Gay Villa) at Fiesole, near Florence. Her relationship with Natalie Barney grew increasingly fraught over the years, and in 1968 she finally broke off relations on the grounds of her infidelity. Romaine Brooks died at her home, 11 rue des Ponchettes, Nice, on 7 December 1970.

Romaine Brooks' reputation as a painter suffered a sharp decline in the years after the Second World War, but it recovered after her death, especially because of her rediscovery by the lesbian movement in the 1970s. Her reputation as an artist is complemented by the non-heterosexual appeal of her female nudes, by her inclination for a masculine style of dress apparent in her self-portrait (1923; Smithsonian Institution, Washington, DC), and by her position within the well-to-do homosexual circles of France and Britain in the early twentieth century.   DAVID DOUGHAN

Sources M. Secrest, *Between me and life* (1976) · D. Gaze, ed., *Dictionary of women artists*, 2 vols. (1997) · A. Weiss, *Paris was a woman* (1995) · S. Cline, *Radclyffe Hall: a woman called John* (1997) · D. Patmore, 'Passionate friends', *Observer Supplement* (5 Sept 1971) · W. Chadwick, *Amazons in the drawing room: the art of Romaine Brooks* (2000) · P. Dunford, *A biographical dictionary of women artists in Europe and America since 1850* (1990)
Archives Smithsonian Institution, Washington, DC, Archives of American Art, MSS
Likenesses B. R. Brooks, self-portrait, 1923, National Museum of American Art, Washington, DC [*see illus.*] · B. R. M. Brooks, self-portraits, and photographs, repro. in Secrest, *Between me and life* · B. R. M. Brooks, self-portraits, photographs, repro. in Chadwick, *Amazons in the drawing room*

Brooks, Thomas (1608–1680), Independent minister, was probably of a Sussex family, possibly from Lewes, where his cousin Henry Godman was born. He matriculated as pensioner of Emmanuel College, Cambridge, on 7 July 1625, but apparently left the university before graduation. Little is known of his early career. In 1652 he stated that he had been preaching for thirteen years, and mostly in London, but his ministry had been an unsettled one. In the early 1640s he was in the eastern suburb of London, but also preached occasionally at the parish of St Martin Orgar in the City. He became chaplain to the parliamentary fleet and was some years at sea. Chosen in 1648 by the vestry of St Margaret's, New Fish Street Hill, as its minister, he laid down some uncompromising terms for his acceptance of the charge, all of which were Independent in nature. He requested that the parish elders who had been chosen under the presbyterian system should resign, that the godly people of the parish should gather together and own one another's grace in a conference, and that they should receive godly strangers, though differing in opinion, into their church. Furthermore, he declared that he would offer the sacrament only to members of this newly constituted church and baptize only their children. In effect, he was to transform the parochial church into an Independent congregation; as a result the negotiation failed.

During the years 1648–51, Brooks identified himself as preacher of the gospel at St Thomas the Apostle, Queen Street. It was not until March 1652 that, with an order from the committee for plundered ministers, he was finally settled at St Margaret's, New Fish Street Hill. Though confronted with some opposition, he was able to continue his ministry there, and in later years to combine it, until early 1660, with a gathered congregation meeting in the parish church.

Brooks was a steadfast supporter of the Independents and the army. In 1647 and again in 1651 he joined a group of Independent and Baptist churches in issuing two 'declarations', in which among other things they openly espoused the principle of rule by the godly. On 14 November 1648 he preached the funeral sermon of Colonel Thomas Rainsborough and urged the leaders of the army 'to appear for the Saints, to side with the Saints, let the issue be what it will' (*The Glorious Day of the Saints Appearance*, 1648, 15). A month later, after the purge of the Long Parliament by Colonel Thomas Pride, he preached a fast sermon before the House of Commons in which he not only justified the action but exhorted the MPs for the 'execution of justice and judgement' (*Gods Delight in the Progress of the Upright*, 1648, 17). In 1650, after the battle of Dunbar, he appeared before the House of Commons again and preached a thanksgiving sermon on 8 October.

Brooks was one of the Independent ministers that Cromwell called to his residence at the Cockpit in Whitehall in July 1652 for providing godly men to preach the gospel in Ireland, and in early 1655 Cromwell again asked him to be present in an interview with the Fifth Monarchy Men. In October 1659 Brooks joined a group of other Independent leaders in sending a letter to General George Monck in Scotland for mediation of a peace between the two armies, and in April 1660, when General John Desborough contacted congregationalist churches for an uprising in London, he found 'Mr. Brookes is very willing' (*CSP dom.*, 1659–60, 409). In January 1661, however, he joined other congregationalist ministers in issuing a 'renuntiation' against a Fifth-Monarchist insurrection led by Thomas Venner.

In the spectrum of puritan thinkers Brooks may be placed on the radical side of Independency. He always stressed that true religious knowledge must be inward, experimental, and even mystical, not merely external, notional, and formal. However, his writings also show the moderation of Brooks. He unmistakably denounced the antinomians who believed that 'There is no sinne in the Saints, they are under no Law, but that of Spirit, which is all freedome' (*Precious Remedies Against Satans Devices*, 1653, 108). Furthermore, he was clearly opposed to the radical ideas of the Levellers and the Fifth Monarchy Men: 'This Age affords many Church-Levellers, as well as State-Levellers. Some there be, that under the notion of plucking up corrupt Ministers, would pluck up by the very roots, the true Ministry' (*The Unsearchable Riches of Christ*, 1655, 315). Richard Baxter called him a godly orthodox man in 1659.

Brooks was also a scholar. Between 1652 and 1670 he had a prodigious output of sixteen books on Christian devotion and edification, and his books became very popular: *Apples of Gold for Young Men and Women* (1657) reached seventeen editions by 1693. Some of his works were later translated into Gaelic, Welsh, Dutch, and German. After the Restoration, Brooks continued to preach, first in London and then at Tower Wharf and in Moorfields. In 1669 he was one of the lecturers at Hackney, Middlesex, and in 1672 was licensed a congregationalist in Lime Street, London. After his first wife, Martha, died in 1676, he married Patience Cartwright. Brooks died on 27 September 1680, and was buried on 1 October at Bunhill Fields; his funeral sermon was preached by John Reeve. TAI LIU

Sources E. Calamy, ed., *An abridgement of Mr. Baxter's history of his life and times, with an account of the ministers, &c., who were ejected after the Restauration of King Charles II*, 2nd edn. (1713) · *Calamy rev.* · T. Brooks, *Cases considered and resolved* (1653) · St Martin Orgar, churchwardens' accounts; St Margaret, New Fish Street Hill, vestry book, churchwardens' accounts, GL, MS 859/1; MS 1175/1; MS 1176/1 · C. E. Surman, ed., *The register-booke of the fourth classis in the province of London, 1646–59*, 2 vols. in 1, Harleian Society, 82–3 (1953) · *CSP dom., 1651–52; 1659–60; 1671; 1676* · *The Clarke papers*, ed. C. H. Firth, 4 vols., CS, new ser., 49, 54, 61–2 (1891–1901) · *Venn, Alum. Cant.* · G. F. Nuttall, *Visible saints: the congregational way, 1640–1660* (1957) · *Calendar of the correspondence of Richard Baxter*, ed. N. H. Keeble and G. F. Nuttall, 2 vols. (1991) · A. Gordon, ed., *Freedom after ejection: a review (1690–1692) of presbyterian and congregational nonconformity in England and Wales* (1917) · E. C. Mckenzie, *A catalog of British devotional and religious books in German translation from the Reformation to 1750* (1997) · Tai Liu, *Puritan London: a study of religion and society in the City parishes* (1986) · L. F. Salzman, ed., *The town book of Lewes, 1542–1701*, 1 [1946] · J. Reeve, funeral sermon preached 1 Oct 1680 at Bunhill Fields, London

Wealth at death approx. £200 personalty: *Calamy rev.*

Brooksbank, Joseph (*b.* 1612/13, *d.* in or after 1660), Church of England clergyman and author, was the son of George Brookbank of Halifax in the West Riding of Yorkshire. He attended Oxford University, where he matriculated as a commoner at Brasenose College on 20 February 1633, aged twenty, and graduated BA on 9 March 1637. For the next few years nothing is certainly known of him. Brooksbank himself said he was in Oxfordshire in the early part of the civil war, though the information appears in his pamphlet, issued in 1660, in which the author may not have been chiefly interested in factual accuracy: he had been:

> for my loyaltie to your majesties interest, in the just cause of your highness father of ever blessed memory, dragged by the Earl of Essex his army, from Dedington in the county of Oxford (where I was in the way of settlement, therein to have served my God, in my calling the ministry) unto Gloucester, and thence to Newbury fight. (Brooksbank, *Well Tuned Organ*, preface)

Subsequently, claimed the author, he 'suffered abundantly, because I have ever been a servant unto truth, abhorrent unto flattery and sinister policy, and averse unto popularity, which hath caused me hitherto, to be rejected in the world' (ibid.).

The narrative should be treated with suspicion, though there is evidence, in a petition to the king signed by Brooksbank and several other ministers, that he had gone to Ireland but was expelled in 1647. However, his rejection in the world was not so total as to prevent his accepting in 1650 the living of Bradenham, Buckinghamshire, in the place of William Brampton, who had resigned. *The Saints' Imperfection*, dated by George Thomason 19 December

1648, makes no mention of any parish, but Brooksbank was in the area before 6 February 1650, when the London bookseller picked up *Vitis salutaris, or, The Vine of Catechetical Divinity*, for in it Brooksbank, 'preacher of the word', addressed a preface to the godly of neighbouring West Wycombe, where he had been settled for some time. But by 1651, *An English Monosyllabary* reported that its author was 'presbyter and schoolmaster in Vine Court, Holborn'.

Plain, Brief and Pertinent Rules (1654) does not reflect any aversion to flattery and popularity, if its author, 'Jo Brooksbank', by then 'minister and schoolmaster in Jerusalem Court Fleet Street', is indeed the same man, for he addresses an adulatory preface to the lord mayor, Sir Thomas Vyner, a second to the city aldermen, and a third to 'the hopeful and renowned estate of apprentices'. Brooksbank was still at Fleet Street in 1657, when he issued *Orthographia*, which contained a preface to a judge, Hugh Wyndham. His works on pedagogical themes have been described as 'careful and clever' (*DNB*).

Brooksbank had certainly left Bradenham by the time of the installation of William Lardner to the rectory in 1658; Lardner was able to repel the attempt by William Brampton, Brooksbank's predecessor, to regain the living in 1660. In that year, when his pamphlet *The Well Tuned Organ* was issued, Brooksbank was living 'the next door to the Dog and Duck, in George Alley in Shoe Lane, London', where his books could be bought (Brooksbank, *Well Tuned Organ*, 67r). In this pamphlet Brooksbank sought to unravel the question of whether, as its title-page asked, 'instrumental and organical music be lawful in Holy Publick assemblies'. Since the work was dedicated to 'the most pious, gracious and illustrious prince, Charles the second', it will not occasion much surprise that the author found church music perfectly lawful, noting that opponents among 'the unsteady and ignorant but clamorous multitude' were too ready to traduce it as popish: in this they 'wickedly asperse the present practice of his most gracious majesty with impiety and profaneness' (ibid., 1–2).

It is possible that such sentiments eased Brooksbank's passage into new times. There are hints from the preface of *A Breviate*, dated 4 July 1660, that he had experienced difficulties in which Sir Jeremiah Whitchcot had been of recent assistance. The Mr Brooksbank referred to in the diaries of John Worthington, master of Jesus College, appears to have been Abraham Brooksbank, fellow of Christ's College, Cambridge, in 1655–67 and vicar of Bradford. The John Brooksbank admitted sizar at Clare College, Cambridge, in 1653 seems not to have written any of the works here mentioned. Of the author Joseph Brooksbank nothing further is heard after 1660, and in view of the frequency of his publications up to that year, it may be that he died soon afterwards. STEPHEN WRIGHT

Sources *Walker rev.* · *Foster, Alum. Oxon.* · *Wood, Ath. Oxon.*, new edn · [C. B. Heberden], ed., *Brasenose College register, 1509–1909*, 2 vols., OHS, 55 (1909) · J. Brooksbank, *The well tuned organ, or, An exercitation, wherein this question is fully and largely discussed, whether or no instrumental, and organical music be lawful in holy publick assemblies* (1660) · J. Brooksbank, *Plain, brief and pertinent rules, for the judicious* *and artificial syllabication of all English words* (1654) · J. Brooksbank, *A breviate of our king's whole Latin grammar* (1660) · *DNB* · *Diary and correspondence of John Worthington*, ed. J. Crossley, 1, 2/1, Chetham Society, 13, 36 (1847–55) · T. Langley, *The history and antiquities of the hundred of Desborough and deanery of Wycombe, in Buckinghamshire* (1797)

Brooksbank [*née* Soutar]**, Mary Watson** (1897–1978), revolutionary and songwriter, was born on 15 December 1897 at 29 Shiprow, Aberdeen, the only daughter of five children born to Alexander Soutar (1867–1953), dock labourer and founding member of Aberdeen Dockers' Union, and his wife, Roseann Gillan, who worked variously in the fishing industry, as a domestic servant, and as a mill worker. Around 1907 the Soutar family arrived in Dundee by ship from Aberdeen. Mary Soutar's early childhood was marked by poverty and the death of her youngest brother from diphtheria. She left St Andrew's School aged eleven to begin work in the textile industry, but her employment was shortly terminated after a school board investigation. She was then frequently kept from school to look after the younger children, while her mother found employment as a can tramper in another local jute mill. In 1912 she joined her mother in the mill's spinning department to work again as a shifter, and participated in her first industrial dispute. Her early radicalism was founded as much on her involvement in an industry marked by unofficial strikes by women workers, as on her father's collection of labour movement literature. By 1914 she had become a double shifter and, like many other Dundee women, spent her working life moving from mill to mill, and then into casual jobs, including berry picking and factory and shop cleaning, before returning to mill work.

In 1920 Mary Soutar joined the Communist Party, helping to organize lobbies and taking part in the demonstrations for unemployment benefits that culminated in three days of rioting in Dundee in September 1921. A year later she was unemployed, and received three months' training as a domestic servant on a government scheme. She was subsequently sent to Coldstream, Berwick-on-Tweed, as a maid in a hotel, and then moved to work as a domestic in Glasgow, where she attended the last meetings of John Maclean, an activist from the Scottish Labour College. By 1924 she had returned to Dundee, where on 3 October that year she married Ernest Brooksbank (1890/91–1943), a widower, and a journeyman tailor by trade.

Before her expulsion in 1933, Mary Brooksbank was to play a leading role in local Communist Party campaigns, including resisting evictions of rent defaulters and representing the unemployed at labour exchange tribunals. As a result of her political activity her life at this time included periods of imprisonment, lasting variously forty days, three months, and a week. This incarceration provided a further focus for protest that reached beyond the Communist Party and into the wider labour movement, including the Railway Women's Guild in Perth which provided her with meals. During a week under observation in

Perth prison, where her sanity was confirmed, the prison governor even lent her a book on women in politics, and she wrote what was perhaps her first poem, 'Cycling Days' (Brooksbank, *No sae Lang Syne*, 19).

Mary Brooksbank was to play a major part in opposing the introduction of the Means Test. In September 1931, after a number of daily demonstrations protesting the earlier arrest of Communist Party leaders including Bob Stewart, mounted police charged a National Unemployed Workers' Movement rally in the city centre. Mary Brooksbank, one of the speakers, was among those arrested, and subsequently charged with rioting. On her release she formed a branch of the Working Women's Guild, and her other activities included selling the *Daily Worker* and other party literature, picketing the parish council's poorhouse for better conditions, and organizing street demonstrations against the Means Test investigators. In 1932 she was instrumental in launching the guild's 'charter', which included a demand for a reduction in rents. She twice stood in Dundee town council elections as a candidate for the Communist Party, but was not elected.

According to Mary Brooksbank her disillusionment with the Communist Party came after listening to reports from women members who had visited the Soviet Union. She was refused permission to visit Russia, which simply added to her growing suspicions. The very success of the guild seems also to have concerned the party leadership, and accusations of a party within a party were raised. In both her published poetry and her autobiography sharp contrasts are drawn between Leon Trotsky (Brooksbank, *No Sae Lang Syne*, 16) and Joseph Stalin, the 'cook' who 'brewed a sorry stink' (Brooksbank, 'Stalin', *Sidlaw Breezes*, 54). One of her former comrades, Duncan Butchart, who argued for her expulsion, was later to claim in an interview that 'She was no Trotskyist, but she might as well have been one for all the trouble she caused' (interview, priv. coll.).

From an early age Mary Brooksbank had played the violin, appearing in concerts that included a benefit for the Red Cross during the First World War, but it was not until after the Second World War that she gained a reputation as a musician and songwriter. In 1943, during her husband's final illness, she secretly sang in the streets of neighbouring Tayport as a way of supplementing their income. After her husband's death her parents came to live with her, along with her nephew, Frederick Soutar. Around 1948, she gave up waged work to nurse her sick mother, and began to write the poetry and song lyrics that were first published in 1966.

In the 1960s the folk-singer Ewan MacColl, appearing in concert in Dundee, complained of the lack of songs about the city. Mary Brooksbank contacted him, and MacColl was to include a number of her songs in his repertory. Her songs have been recorded by a number of artistes, including MacColl, throughout the world. In the late 1960s and early 1970s Mary Brooksbank performed frequently in television and radio broadcasts in Scotland, as well as in old people's clubs throughout Dundee. In 1971 she wrote a short autobiography, claiming that 'the original manuscript was filched from me by trickery', and that she was unable to retrieve it from 'the possession of an Edinburgh University lecturer'.

Mary Brooksbank's poetry and song lyrics deal not only with working life in the textile mills, on a realistic and often humorous level, but also with social justice, the waste of war (three brothers were killed in the two world wars), political events, women's lives, her love of nature, literary figures, and literature. Her best known, and most quoted, song remains 'Oh, Dear Me' (also called the 'Jute Mill Song'). Often her poems and lyrics are reflective recollections, but almost all her writing contains a dialectical, bitter-sweet appeal. In 'Hoose Prood', for example, Jess, 'the perfect woman', finds no escape from the dirt she spends a lifetime trying to combat, as the last verse of the mocking obituary makes clear:

> For chasin' every speck of dirt,
> Jess never took a minit;
> And noo tae think, whit makes it hurt,
> The criter's happit in it.
> (Brooksbank, *Sidlaw Breezes*, 60)

Mary Brooksbank, the 'wee cheery housewife' (Phillips, introduction to *Sidlaw Breezes*), died at Ninewells Hospital, Dundee, on 16 March 1978. In her will she bequeathed her property to her nephew, Frederick Soutar (whom she may have adopted), with a legacy of £25 to her surviving brother, Edward. In 1980 Dundee district council named a branch library in her honour. Mary Brooksbank remains one of the unrecognized female activists of the inter-war labour movement. Even in Dundee she is celebrated more for her poems and songs than for her political activity. Much of this has to do with her rejection of Stalinism in the 1930s, but the struggles she was involved in, particularly with the Working Women's Guild, have become almost hidden from history. Even after her break with the Communist Party she remained an outspoken critic of officialdom, and continued as an energetic representative of her community up to her death.

GRAHAM R. SMITH

Sources M. Brooksbank, *No sae lang syne: a tale of this city* [1968] · M. Brooksbank, *Sidlaw breezes* (1982) [with an introduction by David Phillips] · interview with Duncan Butchart, priv. coll. · 'New edition of Mary's poems', *Dundee Courier and Advertiser* · *Dundee Courier and Advertiser* (17 March 1978) · Dundee Central Library, Lamb collection, 366 (49) · short biography, University of Dundee, MS 103/38 · B. R. Stewart, *Breaking the fetters* (1967) · b. cert.
Archives University of Dundee, cardboard-covered exercise book of poems, MS 103/38 | Dundee Central Library, Lamb collection
Likenesses photographs, c.1894–1948, repro. in Brooksbank, *Sidlaw breezes*, 89, 90, 92 · D. Phillips, photographs, 1966, repro. in Brooksbank, *Sidlaw breezes*, 93–4

Brooksby [*née* Vaux], **Eleanor** (c.1560–1625), recusant and priest harbourer, was the eldest daughter and second of four children of William *Vaux, third Baron Vaux of Harrowden (1535–1595), and his first wife, Elizabeth (d. 1562), daughter of Sir John *Beaumont of Grace Dieu, Leicestershire, master of the rolls, and his wife, Elizabeth. As a

member of a fervent and prominent Roman Catholic family Eleanor Vaux was educated first at Harrowden under the influence of her older brother's tutor, the Jesuit Edmund Campion. In 1571 the four children of Lord Vaux's first marriage went to live at Grace Dieu with their maternal grandmother, who took on the responsibility for their upbringing.

About 1577 Eleanor married Edward Brooksby of Shoby, Leicestershire. The Brooksbys sheltered Catholic priests, notably the Jesuit Robert Persons. The family's residence at Green Street, East Ham, Essex, was home for a time to a secret recusant printing press. Eleanor Brooksby had two children, William (d. 1606) and Mary (c.1579–1628). Her husband died early in their marriage, in the summer of 1581. Soon afterwards Brooksby adopted her five-year-old first cousin, Frances Burroughs of Burrow on the Hill, Leicestershire, daughter of Maud Burroughs, Eleanor's paternal aunt, who had died in 1581.

Although she was a young widow raising three small children, Eleanor Brooksby became indispensable to the harbouring of recusant priests. She and her unmarried sister Anne *Vaux (bap. 1562, d. in or after 1637) devoted their lives to using their familial connections and wealth in order to establish safe houses for clerics, and they provided significant financial assistance to the Jesuits. In 1586 the Jesuit superior Henry Garnet joined the sisters' household. For two decades Brooksby and Vaux rented many properties for their own use and Garnet's, notably Baddesley Clinton, Warwickshire (1588–92), and White Webbs, Enfield Chase, Middlesex (1600–06).

Fear of discovery necessitated a peripatetic existence. Henry Garnet left a memorable account of how Brooksby coped with the considerable pressures inherent in her dangerous way of life. In his description of a violent search for priests at one of her residences in 1591 he recalled that Brooksby

> was stowed away in a separate hiding place of her own, both to prevent her being torn from her children and carried off to prison, and also because she is rather timid, and finds it difficult to cope with the threats and evil looks of the searchers. (Anstruther, 188)

On that occasion, as on many others, Anne Vaux impersonated her sister, the mistress of the house, in order to relieve Eleanor from having to confront her persecutors. Brooksby's anxieties about punishment for her priest harbouring, however, should not be overstated. Her fears did not dissuade her from continuing to house clerics. Furthermore, she reared a household of committed recusants. Brooksby arranged Catholic marriages for both William and Mary, and in 1597 her cousin Frances Burroughs took her vows as an Augustinian nun at St Ursula's Convent, Louvain. In August 1605 Brooksby participated in an illegal pilgrimage to St Winifred's Well, Holywell. Like her sister she walked barefoot for the last portion of the journey.

Even after the discovery of the Gunpowder Plot, Anne Vaux's temporary imprisonment, and Garnet's execution, Brooksby continued to live as a staunch recusant. In 1615 she took on the responsibility of raising her infant grandson, Edward Thimelby, her daughter Mary's child and the youngest son of the Thimelbys' fourteen offspring. She made William Wright, a priest who lived in her household, responsible for the child's early education, which Edward completed at the English College, Rome, as part of his preparation for the priesthood after her death. In 1625 Brooksby was convicted of recusancy at Leicester Castle and fined £240, which she did not pay. She died of unknown causes later that year.   COLLEEN M. SEGUIN

Sources G. Anstruther, *Vaux of Harrowden: a recusant family* (1953) · P. Caraman, *Henry Garnet, 1555–1606, and the Gunpowder Plot* (1964) · H. Foley, ed., *Records of the English province of the Society of Jesus*, 7 vols. in 8 (1875–83) · M. Hodgetts, *Secret hiding places* (1989) · A. Fraser, *Faith and treason: the story of the Gunpowder Plot* (New York, 1996) · J. Bossy, *The English Catholic community, 1570–1850* (1975) · R. Connelly, *The women of the Catholic resistance: in England, 1540–1680* (1997)

Brookshaw, George (*bap.* **1751**, *d.* **1823**), cabinet-maker and decorative painter, was baptized at St Philip's Church, Birmingham, on 10 July 1751, one of three children of George Brookshaw (*b.* *c.*1722) and his wife, Mary Hawkes (*b.* *c.*1723); his elder brother, the engraver Richard *Brookshaw, was baptized in the same church on 1 January 1749. Nothing is known of his father's occupation or of his own education or training. However, Brookshaw's Birmingham origins and his chosen career suggest a possible early association with the manufacturer Matthew Boulton (1728–1809) and his 'mechanical painting' venture.

By 1777 Brookshaw was living in London, where he set up business as a maker of (almost exclusively) painted furniture—at first in Curzon Street, and from 1782 or 1783 to *c.*1794 at 48 Great Marlborough Street. He adopted a successful decorative formula of painted figurative medallions derived from engravings, largely after Angelica Kauffman, combined with panels of closely observed garden flowers and borders of delicate stylized ornament. This formula was applied not only to movable furniture but also to chimney-pieces in either wood or marble; sometimes the ornament was painted partly on copper panels, mounted on or within the wooden frame. Although lacking strong architectural qualities, Brookshaw's output accorded with a rather feminine expression of neo-classical taste. For a short period in the early 1780s his idiom was favoured by adherents of the refined Anglo-French style promoted by Henry Holland, including William Cavendish, fifth duke of Devonshire, and the prince of Wales—earning him the appellation 'Peintre Ebeniste par Extraordinaire' (inscribed on his bill for a commode supplied to the prince of Wales at Carlton House in 1783). Among his other patrons were Lord Delaval (1781–3), Henry Somerset, fifth duke of Beaufort (1787), William Blathwayt of Dyrham (1791), and Sir Mark Wood of Piercefield Park, Monmouthshire (*c.*1794).

This highly specialized business may have been sustained by capital provided by Brookshaw's wife, Sobieski (*bap.* 1749, *d.* 1811), the daughter of a Birmingham gun maker, William Grice, whom he married on 20 January 1778. At some point they parted company, perhaps in the

mid-1790s when he abruptly abandoned his cabinet-making practice, having probably been forced into bankruptcy; at his death in 1823 he lived with one Elizabeth Stanton, 'who has passed for my wife' (will). For up to a decade (*c.*1794–1804) he lived under an assumed name, G. Brown, earning a living as a teacher of flower-painting and on the proceeds of his first painting manual, *A New Treatise of Flower Painting*, published anonymously in 1797. A 'third' edition by 'G. Brown' was issued in 1799, and the book was eventually reissued under his real name in 1816, followed by various supplementary volumes (on flowers, fruits, and birds) between 1817 and 1819. However, Brookshaw's most important published work, which indeed is of some botanical significance, was his finely illustrated treatise on fruit growing, the *Pomona Britannica*, issued in parts from 1804—when he first resumed his own name—and as a single folio volume in 1812. It was dedicated to his most illustrious former patron, the prince of Wales. But Brookshaw's renown in the botanical world never matched that of his cabinet-making career, and he failed to gain recognition by Sir Joseph Banks, Sir J. E. Smith, and other luminaries of the recently founded Horticultural Society—perhaps in part because of the mystery surrounding his past, which he undoubtedly suppressed deliberately. His last years (1819–23) were spent in obscurity in Twickenham and he died at Greenwich in January or February 1823. He was buried at St Mary's Church, Twickenham, on 6 February 1823 and left the bulk of his small estate (under £450) to his only child, Caroline (by his wife, Sobieski), who died unmarried in 1864.   LUCY WOOD

Sources L. Wood, 'George Brookshaw', *Apollo*, 133 (1991), 301–6, 383–97 · will, proved 20 Feb 1823, LMA · rate books, Out ward, St George, Hanover Square, 1777–83, City Westm. AC · rate books, Great Marlborough Street ward, 1785–94, City Westm. AC · G. Brookshaw, bill to prince of Wales, 1783, Royal Arch., 25051 · general order and new account register no. 4 (1806–23, A-L), fol. 37; ledger 1822–3, BIOUY, fol. 373, Coutts & Co., London, archives · Badminton House, Avon, FML 5/13 (5) · Northumbd RO, Delaval archives, 2DE 34/2/38; 2DE 23/2/17, 21 and unnumbered piece; 2DE 31/2 · Glos. RO, Blathwayt papers, D 1799/A151; D1799/A272; D1799/E258, p. 5; D1799/E265, p. 14 · rate books, 1808–16, Kensington and Chelsea Central Library · rate books, 1819–23, Twickenham Local Studies Library · L. Wood, 'George Brookshaw and his painted furniture', *Partridge Fine Arts PLC: recent acquisitions, 1995*, ed. L. Morton (privately printed, London, 1995), 60–65 [catalogue] · L. Wood, *Catalogue of commodes: Lady Lever Art Gallery* (1994), pp. 239–53, nos. 29–30 · parish register, Birmingham, St Philip, Birm. CL, 10 July 1751 [baptism] · marriage licence, 27 Dec 1748, Lichfield Joint RO, B/C/7 · parish register, Twickenham, St Mary, Twickenham Local Studies Library, 6 Feb 1823 [burial]
Wealth at death under £450; bank balance under £100: will, proved 20 Feb 1823, LMA; ledger 1822–3, BIOUY, fol. 373, Coutts & Co., London, archives

Brookshaw, Richard (*b.* **1748**, *d.* in or after **1779**), mezzotint engraver, was the son of George Brookshaw (*b.* *c.*1722) and his wife, Mary Hawkes (*b.* *c.*1723), and the brother of the cabinet-maker and botanical author and illustrator George *Brookshaw (*bap.* 1751, *d.* 1823). He was born in Birmingham and baptized on 1 January 1749 at St Philip's, Birmingham. Nothing is known of his early life or training, and he is first recorded working as a mezzotint engraver in 1767, in which year he produced two signed prints, one of Elizabeth Chudleigh as Flora and one of a Miss Greenfield. He continued to work for London publishers, producing mezzotint portraits after contemporary artists. He seems to have been employed mostly on producing engraved copies of popular prints by contemporary engravers such as James McArdell and James Watson, apparently in return for very low pay. He also produced a few non-portrait works during this period, including *Lord Grosvenor's Arabian*, after George Stubbs, engraved between 1769 and 1771.

By 1773 Brookshaw had moved to Paris, where he engraved and published a pair of portraits of the French dauphin (later Louis XVI) and Marie-Antoinette. These prints, published in London as well as in Paris, proved very popular, and Brookshaw produced several repetitions of them in various sizes. In Paris he also engraved other mezzotint portraits of members of the French aristocracy, as well as other figures, among them the actor and playwright Samuel Foote (1720–1777), after Francis Cotes. Brookshaw's prints were more successful in Paris than his previous works in England. He is recorded as producing prints in Rouen in 1776 and in Brussels in 1779, and is also said to have gone to Amsterdam at about the same date. Little is known of these movements and it is not known whether he ever returned to England.

Brookshaw was previously said to have worked on the botanical publication *Pomona Britannica*, but this was written and illustrated by his brother George Brookshaw, and there is no evidence that Richard had any association with the publication. Brookshaw's mezzotints are now rare, but examples can be found in the collections of the National Portrait Gallery, the Victoria and Albert Museum, the British Museum, and the Bibliothèque Nationale in Paris.   RUTH COHEN

Sources *DNB* · J. C. Smith, *British mezzotinto portraits*, 1 (1878), 99–105 · R. Portalis and H. Béraldi, *Les graveurs du dix-huitième siècle*, 1 (Paris, 1880), 260–2 · L. Wood, 'George Brookshaw: the case of the vanishing cabinet-maker [pt 1]', *Apollo*, 133 (1991), 301–6 · T. Clayton, 'Mr Warde's Arabian: a new print by George Stubbs?', *Print Quarterly*, 3 (1986), 132 · Thieme & Becker, *Allgemeines Lexikon*, 5.66 · Redgrave, *Artists*, 57 · parish register, St Philip's, Birmingham, 1 Jan 1749 [baptism]

Broom [*née* Livingston], **Christina** [*known as* Mrs Albert Broom] (**1862–1939**), photographer, was born on 28 December 1862 at 8 King's Road, Chelsea, seventh of the eight children of Alexander Livingston (1812–1875), a master bootmaker, and his wife, Margaret, *née* Fair (1826–1884). Both parents were Scottish, her father from Muiravonside, Stirling, and her mother from Edinburgh. Christina was always small, but a sturdy, independent child who enjoyed family holidays at Margate, in Kent, and went to school there, boarding at Miss Searle's Claremont Academy. She excelled in swimming, rifle-shooting, and angling and enjoyed the open air and especially fishing all her life. Margate became a second home, and she joined both Margate and the Dolphins fishing clubs.

On 15 August 1889 Christina Livingston married Albert Edward Broom (1864–1912), who worked in the family ironmongery business at Brompton. They lived with his parents in Cheyne Row, Chelsea, and when Winifred, their only child, was born they moved to Napier Avenue, in Fulham. Albert's sport was cricket and he became captain of Battersea Cricket club. In 1896 he was hit by a cricket ball and suffered serious disablement. At about the same time the family business failed and Albert and Christina invested in a stationery and toy shop in Streatham; Albert's trade card described him as an 'accountant and auditor, specialising in laundry accounts'. By 1903, however, the shop had failed to thrive.

Completely untrained, Christina Broom borrowed a small box camera and experimented. Her first photograph was of the prince and princess of Wales opening the Holborn to Tooting tramway. Then came a portrait of the Derby winner Rock Sand and local street views. In the contemporary craze for postcards these sold well, so she progressed to a larger, secondhand camera, moved her family to Burnfoot Avenue, and began to photograph in earnest. The gas-lit coal cellar became her darkroom; Winifred left school in order to help, mass orders were encouraged, and Christina once printed 1000 postcards overnight. Albert did the neat labelling on the early cards, but his condition worsened and in 1912 he died. Mother and daughter moved again—to 92 Munster Road, Fulham, their final home—and set to work again. Christina became known professionally as Mrs Albert Broom.

While producing postcards Mrs Broom had become an established press photographer, though necessarily of a static kind. In 1904, while getting to know her camera, she had photographed the Scots Guards' sports in Chelsea and had sent copies to their colonel. He approved of these, and from 1904 to 1939, unusually for a woman, Christina Broom became official photographer to the household brigade, with a darkroom in Chelsea barracks. She sold the prints to the soldiers at 2*d.* each, which included an envelope for writing home, and this led Lord Roberts, then commander of the Irish Guards, to pronounce that she had increased recruitment, which had diminished after the Second South African War, and that she should take official army portraits. This she did, mainly of traditional hierarchical groups but also of less formal, off-duty moments. In one, for example, three privates lounge and smoke, while in others soldiers are saying farewell to families before embarkation. From 1904 to 1930 Mrs Broom ran a stall in the royal mews. Although forbidden to do so she attempted to photograph Edward VII's charger Kildare being trained. Reprimanded, she sent in her card to the king; he recognized her name and commanded that she be allowed to take and sell pictures of royal postillions, coachmen, coaches, and the stables. Sadly, unfortunate criticism by her of a customer ended the enterprise.

Because she lived near the Thames, Christina Broom also became the regular photographer of the annual Oxford and Cambridge boat race. Her most memorable pictures, however, are probably those of the women's suffrage movement taken between 1908 and 1913, which comprise a virtually unique record of the less flamboyant moments of their campaign. These include photographs of Emmeline Pethick-Lawrence, Christabel and Sylvia Pankhurst, and Louisa Garrett Anderson in the Women's Sunday procession and meeting in Hyde Park on 21 June 1908, in which a quarter of a million women took part, and of Christabel Pankhurst at the International Suffragette Fair, 1912 (both Museum of London collection).

At an earlier date Mrs Broom had become acquainted with Ernest Brooks, an official photographer to the royal family at Windsor. In 1920 Brooks was disgraced for publishing unsuitable pictures of the young prince of Wales in a 'crossing the line' ceremony but he sold Christina many of his negatives, mainly royal portraits; it is not always evident, therefore, whose negatives she used in producing prints. Brooks also introduced her to David Wilson (1873–1935), a cartoonist, from whom she commissioned political lampoons of subjects that included tariff reform and the Russo-Japanese War, as well as political personalities. These she had reproduced by lithography and contact print and sold as postcards.

Christina Broom continued to flourish throughout the 1920s and 1930s, publishing, for example, in the *Illustrated London News*, *The Tatler*, *The Sphere*, and *Country Life*, and covering most important London events. During the late 1930s she became chronically ill, and on 5 June 1939 she died, at home in Fulham, after a fishing trip at her beloved Margate; she was buried on 9 June in Fulham old cemetery. Considering her tiny stature and the heavy equipment that she and her daughter, her only assistant, had to manage, the consistently high quality of her work is remarkable. In the early 1960s Winifred Broom gave most of her collection of her mother's work to the Imperial War Museum, the National Portrait Gallery, and the Museum of London. Collections of Mrs Broom's glass negatives are held at Maidstone Art Gallery, Kent, the National Museum of Scotland, Edinburgh, and the Royal Maritime Museum, Greenwich. Collections of her prints are also held at the Guards Museum, London; the Gernsheim Collection, University of Texas at Austin, Texas; the Royal Borough of Kensington and Chelsea Local Studies Library; the Hammersmith and Fulham Archive; the National Army Museum; and the Imperial War Museum, London.

SHIRLEY NEALE

Sources photographs, papers, NPG, Heinz Archive and Library · press cuttings, Royal Borough of Kensington and Chelsea, Local Studies Library · press cuttings, Hammersmith and Fulham Library, Hammersmith and Fulham Archive · photographs, papers, IWM · private information (2004) [M. Shillabeer] · V. Williams, *The other observers: women photographers in Britain, 1900 to the present* (1986) · b. cert. · m. cert. · d. cert. · A. Inselmann, ed., *A second look: women photographers of the Gernsheim collection* (Frankfurt am Main, 1993) [exhibition catalogue, Deutscher Werkbund e.V., Frankfurt am Main, 26 Aug – 2 Sept 1993] · *Fulham Gazette* (16 June 1939) · *Fulham Chronicle* (9 June 1939) · J. Frazer, unpublished, undated article, Royal Borough of Kensington and Chelsea, Local Studies Library
Wealth at death £65 18s. 2d.: administration, 23 June 1939, *CGPLA Eng. & Wales*

Broom, Herbert (1815–1882), legal writer, was born at Kidderminster, the eldest son of Herbert Broom, a manufacturer, and his wife, Rebecca, daughter of Richard Watson. He was educated at Lant Carpenter's school in Bristol before entering Trinity College, Cambridge, in 1832, where he graduated BA as forty-first wrangler in 1837, MA in 1854, and LLD in 1864. Broom was admitted to the Inner Temple in April 1837, and after being called to the bar on 20 November 1840 he began to practise on the Oxford circuit. On 26 March 1846, he married Ellen Thornthwaite Thomson, the daughter of John Thomson, a physician of Halifax.

Although his ambitions to become a county court judge were never fulfilled, Broom had a distinguished career as a legal writer and teacher. He was appointed reader of common law in the Inner Temple in 1852 and was professor to the Council of Legal Education in 1873–5. His lectures in these posts formed the foundation of his books. His best-known work was *A Selection of Legal Maxims*, first published in 1845, which reached a fifth edition in 1870 and a tenth in 1939. In 1856 he published *Commentaries on the Common Law, Designed as Introductory to its Study*, which came to be used as a textbook by the Council of Legal Education. In spite of being aimed at students and despite the echoes of Blackstone's work in its title, this book of more than 1000 pages concentrated on the workings of common law in a largely unphilosophical and practical way; and even though it received some criticism it reached a ninth edition in 1896, and was continued as Odger's *Common Law* until 1927. Broom also published, in 1866, *Constitutional Law Viewed in Relation to Common Law and Exemplified by Cases* (2nd edn, 1885), a casebook illustrating the relationship of subjects to the sovereign, to the executive, and to parliament. Besides these, Broom wrote a number of treatises on the practice of the courts, as well as notes of his lectures to students under the title *The Philosophy of Law* (1876). He was also editor of the *Law Magazine and Law Review*, enlisting Brougham's help in attempting to attract a readership beyond the legal profession for this journal. However, the journal did remain primarily specialized.

Broom was also the author of two novels, *The Missing Will* (1877) and *The Unjust Steward* (1879), and had a poem, *Fancy's Dream*, privately published in 1840. In politics, he and his family supported the Liberal cause for many years. Broom died on 2 May 1882 at his residence, The Priory, Orpington, Kent, and was survived by his wife.

MICHAEL LOBBAN

Sources *The Times* (5 May 1882) · *Solicitors' Journal*, 26 (1881–2), 453 · A. W. B. Simpson, ed., *Biographical dictionary of the common law* (1984) · Boase, *Mod. Eng. biog.* · Venn, *Alum. Cant.* · *Law Journal* (23 April 1892), 260 · Holdsworth, *Eng. law*, 15.368, 375 · R. C. J. Cocks, *Sir Henry Maine: a study in Victorian jurisprudence* (1988), 16 · m. cert. · d. cert.
Archives UCL, Brougham MSS
Wealth at death £3139 10s. 10d.: probate, 14 Aug 1882, *CGPLA Eng. & Wales*

Broom, Robert (1866–1951), palaeontologist, was born at 66 Back Sneddon Street, Paisley, Renfrewshire, on 30 November 1866, the third child of John Broom, designer of prints and shawls, and his wife, Agnes Hunter Shearer. His early education was sporadic owing to illness, but in 1879 he entered Hutcheson's Boys' Grammar School, Glasgow. He gained an interest in natural history from his grandfather and from Peter Cameron, a local expert on Hymenoptera. In 1883 he became laboratory assistant to John Ferguson, professor of chemistry at Glasgow University, and also began attending classes at the university. He was contemptuous of Ferguson, but learned botany from F. O. Bower and anatomy from John Cleland. He was attracted to the study of palaeontology by John Young, under-curator of the Hunterian Museum. He gained his BSc in 1887 and then began studying medicine, qualifying MB CM in 1889, and being awarded the William Hunter medal for midwifery.

In 1892 Broom went to join his brother William in north Queensland, Australia. However, he soon moved to New South Wales, supporting himself by practising medicine in several remote towns. He undertook research on the structure of marsupials and monotremes, dealing especially with the organ of Jacobsen and the shoulder girdle. This work formed the basis of Broom's MD thesis, presented to the University of Glasgow in 1895, and of several publications. On 19 November 1893 he married Mary Braid Baillie (d. 1959), to whom he had become engaged shortly before leaving Glasgow. They raised three adopted children. The marriage was stable, despite Broom's many moves and his reputation for flirtation.

In May 1896 Broom and his wife left Australia and spent several months in Britain. Broom's morphological work on Australian mammals had made him interested in their evolutionary origin, and at the British Museum he studied the mammal-like reptiles brought from the Permian rocks of the Karoo region of South Africa. He decided to move to South Africa, with the aim of locating and studying more of these fossils.

Broom sailed to South Africa in January 1897. He supported himself and his wife by practising medicine, again in remote country districts. He worked in Port Nolloth, Port Elizabeth, and then in Pearston, the latter well placed for the discovery of Karoo fossils. In August 1903 he was appointed professor of zoology and geology at Victoria College, Stellenbosch, where he was an unorthodox but successful lecturer. Long vacations were spent collecting fossils, for which purpose he was granted a free railway pass—on the condition that his collections went to the South African Museum in Cape Town. When the pass was withdrawn in 1909, Broom felt himself free to sell fossils to museums abroad—the source of much subsequent friction with the authorities. In 1910 he resigned his chair and visited London and New York, the American Museum of Natural History having a good collection of Permian reptiles from Texas. Broom published important papers describing his South African finds and comparing them with the American specimens. He was also awarded a DSc from Glasgow in 1905 for a thesis on this topic. Broom was an acute observer, and provided careful descriptions of his fossils, often illustrated with his own drawings.

Broom now practised medicine at Springs and at Germiston (both near Johannesburg), collecting and describing fossils in his spare time. In 1913 he gave the Croonian lecture to the Royal Society in London, entitled 'The origin of mammals', and installed a large collection of South African fossils in the American Museum of Natural History. By now he was in regular contact with senior American palaeontologists including Henry Fairfield Osborn, William Diller Matthew, and Samuel Wendel Williston. He also corresponded with the professor of geology at Oxford, William Johnson Sollas. In February 1914 he returned to Britain and did postgraduate medical work in surgery at Glasgow. He was working in the Ear, Nose, and Throat Hospital in London when the First World War broke out. He joined the Royal Army Medical Corps in 1915 but was not sent abroad because of his age. While in London he began collecting paintings of the seventeenth-century Dutch school. He retired after a year and returned to South Africa to practise medicine, eventually settling at Douglas in Transvaal. He continued his fossil-collecting and also worked in physical anthropology, producing descriptions of the various ethnic groups in the region based on skeletons obtained by various (often unorthodox, if not illegal) means.

Broom was elected fellow of the Royal Society in 1920, and served as mayor of Douglas from 1920 to 1924. In 1928 he was awarded the royal medal of the Royal Society, and visited London and New York. In the following year he was awarded the South African Association for the Advancement of Science's gold medal, although he had left the association some years earlier because of friction caused by his selling fossils abroad. However, the award ensured that Broom attended the meeting of the British Association, which took place in South Africa that year and brought many foreign scientists to the country.

About this time Broom began work on books summarizing his views on the origin of mammals and his overall philosophy of evolution. *The Mammal-Like Reptiles of South Africa and the Origin of Mammals* was published in 1932; it provided an overview of the many species he had described and traced the sequence of development from the theriodont reptiles to the primitive mammals. Broom's *The Coming of Man: was it Accident or Design?* appeared in the following year. It presented a philosophy of evolution that was very much a product of the previous century: Broom believed that a supernatural power had guided the main line of evolution toward humankind. All other branches of evolution led to forms too specialized to develop further (this view was taken up in a different context by Julian Huxley, who acknowledged Broom's influence). Broom believed in spiritualism and held that the purpose of evolution was to produce self-conscious souls capable of surviving the death of the body. He also toyed with the Lamarckian theory of the inheritance of acquired characters. He felt that his success in collecting fossils was a sign that he was favoured by higher powers.

In 1934 Broom was appointed curator of fossil vertebrates at the Transvaal Museum, with the active support of Jan Christiaan Smuts—who appreciated Broom's qualities despite his many brushes with the authorities. He now began a new phase of his career in which he was to make major contributions to the study of hominid fossils and human origins. In 1924 he had made the acquaintance of Raymond Dart, who had discovered the first australopithecine fossil at Taung. Broom had been very impressed with the find, and had defended Dart's interpretation of it as an important clue to the origin of humans from apes. Dart in turn helped to smooth relations between Broom and various government departments. From 1936 Broom began actively looking for more hominid fossils and soon found a skull in caves at Sterkfontein, which he named *Plesianthropus*. In 1937 he found a more thickly-built skull nearby, naming it *Paranthropus robustus* (subsequently named *Australopithecus robustus*). During the war years he found an ankle bone of the same species, confirming Dart's view that the australopithecines had walked upright and that bipedalism was the first unique character of the human family, followed only later by the evolution of a larger brain. With G. W. H. Schepers, Broom published an extensive survey, *The South-African Fossil Ape-Men*, in 1946 and a popular account, *Finding the Missing Link*, in 1950. Despite his success, Broom continued to be at loggerheads with the authorities, in this case the Royal Commission on Historical Monuments, over the discovery of fossils. The status of the australopithecines as the earliest members of the human family was soon widely accepted, partly because of Broom's interaction with Wilfrid Le Gros Clark at Oxford. He also corresponded with Arthur Keith, originally a critic of his views on human origins, and with D'Arcy Wentworth Thompson. In 1949 he was awarded the Wollaston medal of the Geological Society of London, following which he undertook an arduous lecture tour of America. Broom was now working with J. T. Robinson on descriptions of hominid fossils, and he was still active in 1950. His health at last began to fail in the following year; he died on 6 April 1951 at his home, 414 Jorissen Street, Pretoria, and was buried at the city's Rebecca Street cemetery four days later. His wife survived him.

PETER J. BOWLER

Sources G. H. Findlay, *Dr Robert Broom, FRS* (1972) · D. M. S. Watson, *Obits. FRS*, 8 (1952–3), 37–70

Archives Transvaal Museum, Pretoria, fossils | NHM, corresp. with W. R. Dawson · U. Birm., E. W. Barnes MSS

Likenesses photographs, 1872–1948, repro. in Findlay, *Dr Robert Broom* · E. Djomba, bronze bust, 1941, National Museum, South Africa

Broome. For this title name *see* Barker, Mary Anne, Lady Barker [Mary Anne Brome, Lady Broome] (1831–1911).

Broome, Arthur MacLoughlin [Arthur Eugenius] (1779–1837), animal welfare campaigner, was born on 18 February 1779 and baptized in Sidbury, Devon, on 28 August 1785. He was apparently the son of Arthur (or Thomas) and Frances Broom. He entered Balliol College in March 1798 and took his BA degree in 1801. Broome was ordained a deacon in 1802 and a priest the following year by the bishop of London. Between 1812 and 1815 he held the curacy at the Kent parishes of Brook and Hinxhill and, from

1816 to 1818, at Cliffe-at-Hoo. In June 1820 he was appointed vicar of St Mary's-Bromley-St Leonard in Middlesex (later Bromley by Bow), but resigned in 1824, presumably to concentrate on his duties as secretary of the newly formed Society for the Prevention of Cruelty to Animals (SPCA).

It is not known how Broome developed his concern for the treatment of animals. In 1822 he published an edited version of Primatt's 1776 essay *The Duty of Mercy and Sin of Cruelty to Brute Animals*, in which he claimed he had 'always felt peculiarly interested' in the subject for its 'moral and religious' implications (Primatt, x). The many editorial comments in the book reveal Broome's interest in the question of whether animals had souls, his fondness for the beauty of nature, and his fear that the practice of cruelty rendered 'human nature proportionably less fit for humanity' (27). The passing of Richard Martin's act to prevent cruelty to cattle in 1822 encouraged Broome to form a society which would enforce the act and promote 'the practice of humanity' (RSPCA, *Prospectus*, 201). In 1823 he stated his intention to donate profits from the sale of the second edition of *The Duty of Mercy* to the as yet nonexistent 'Society for the Prevention of Cruelty to Animals'. In addition he hired an inspector in December 1823 to watch Smithfield market and prosecute offenders against Martin's act.

The society met for the first time on 16 June 1824. In attendance were the well-known MPs Thomas Fowell Buxton, William Wilberforce, and Richard Martin. Broome was elected secretary and the group immediately set to work: in the first twelve months its inspectors procured 149 convictions and numerous tracts were distributed. However, the new society met with 'prejudice and ridicule' and was frequently criticized for attacking pastimes of the lower classes, such as dog-fighting, while leaving upper-class sports, such as fox-hunting, untouched (*Courier*). In addition, the society's finances were suffering. By January 1826 it owed over £168, mostly to printers, and had borrowed over £110 from committee members (more than £80 from Broome himself). As secretary Broome was legally responsible for the debts and hence was imprisoned at king's bench on 27 April 1826. The length of time he spent in gaol is unknown: his absence was noted at an SPCA meeting on 18 May of that year, but he was present at the following meeting on 26 June. By this time his enthusiasm for the society, if not the cause, seems to have diminished: Lewis Gompertz (1784–1861), who had been appointed secretary temporarily during Broome's absence, took over the post completely in 1828 after Broome failed to attend a number of meetings. The committee paid respects to their 'benevolent founder', and Broome remained on the governing committee until 1832; however, he disappears from society records after that time (RSPCA, *Minute Book*, 56). He published a third edition of *The Duty of Mercy* in 1831. His whereabouts between 1832 and 1837 are unknown. He died, probably unmarried, on 16 July 1837 of consumption at 44 Bull Street, Birmingham, and on 21 July was given a pauper's burial there at St Philip's Church (now the Anglican cathedral). There is no mention of his passing in the RSPCA records. The society he founded was granted royal patronage by Queen Victoria in 1840.

MOLLY BAER KRAMER

Sources E. G. Fairholme and W. Pain, *A century of work for animals: the history of the R.S.P.C.A., 1824–1924* (1924) · A. Moss, *Valiant crusade: the history of the RSPCA* (1961) · Royal Society for the Prevention of Cruelty to Animals minute book, 1824–32, Royal Society for the Prevention of Cruelty to Animals Headquarters, Horsham, West Sussex · *Prospectus*, Royal Society for the Prevention of Cruelty to Animals (1824) · 'Diocese of London ordination register', 1675–1809, GL · H. Primatt, *The duty of mercy and the sin of cruelty to brute animals*, ed. [A. Broome] (1822); 2nd edn (1823); another edn (1834) · bishops' transcripts, Sidbury, 1785, Devon RO · admissions register, 1798, Balliol Oxf. · Foster, *Alum. Oxon.* · parish registers, CKS · Bishop's transcripts, CKS · King's Bench Prison Commitments, 1826, PRO, Pris 4/38, 54 · Records of St Philip's Church, Birm. CL · d. cert. · S. Lynam, *Humanity Dick: a biography of Richard Martin, MP, 1754–1834* (1975) · *The Times* (13 June 1824), 3 · *The Courier* (1 July 1825), 4 · King's Bench Prison, Final Discharges, 1827, PRO, Pris 7/46, II

Archives Royal Society for the Prevention of Cruelty to Animals, Horsham, West Sussex, minute books

Broome, Sir Frederick Napier (1842–1896), colonial governor, was born in Canada on 18 November 1842, the eldest son of Frederick Broome, a missionary in Canada and afterwards rector of Kenley in Shropshire, and his wife, Catherine Eleanor (or Elizabeth), the eldest daughter of Lieutenant-Colonel Napier. He was educated at Whitchurch grammar school in Shropshire, and in 1857 emigrated to New Zealand and settled in Canterbury, where he farmed sheep.

On 21 June 1865 Broome married Mary Anne [see Barker, Mary Anne (1831–1911)], the eldest daughter of Walter George Stewart of Jamaica, and the widow of Sir George Robert Barker. In 1869, on account of the harsh climate, they decided to return to London, where they took up writing. In 1868 Broome published *Poems from New Zealand* and in 1869 *The Stranger from Seriphos*. He was almost immediately employed by *The Times* as a general contributor, reviewer, and art critic. He also wrote prose and verse for the *Cornhill Magazine*, *Macmillan's Magazine*, and other periodicals. In 1870 he was appointed secretary of the fund for the completion of St Paul's Cathedral, in 1873 secretary to the royal commission on unseaworthy ships, and in 1875 colonial secretary of Natal, as a member of Sir Garnet (later Viscount) Wolseley's special mission. He was created CMG in 1877. The following year he was appointed colonial secretary of the island of Mauritius, and in 1880 became lieutenant-governor. There he earned the approbation of the home government, as well as the thanks of the South African colonies, by his prompt dispatch of the greater part of the garrison to South Africa after the disaster of Isandlwana.

In 1882 Broome was nominated governor of Western Australia, which was still a crown colony, and he turned his attention to the development of its natural wealth. The first years of his administration saw a rapid extension of railways and telegraphs; he was appointed KCMG in 1884. Increasing prosperity was accompanied by a growing desire for representative government. Broome warmly supported the colonial view, and accompanied his dispatches with urgent recommendations to grant a constitution such as the legislature of the colony requested. In 1889, when the bill was blocked in the home parliament because of difficulties in the transfer of crown lands, Broome went to London with other delegates to urge the matter in person on the Colonial Office. On 21 October 1890 Western Australia received its constitution, and Broome's term of office came to an end. He left the colony amid popular demonstrations of gratitude for his services. He then went to the West Indies, where he was appointed acting governor of Barbados, and afterwards, in 1891, governor of Trinidad. He died in London on 26 November 1896 at his home, 51 Welbeck Street, and was buried at Highgate cemetery on 30 November. His wife survived him.

E. I. CARLYLE, *rev.* LYNN MILNE

Sources *The Times* (28 Nov 1896) · F. K. Crowley, 'Broome, Sir Frederick Napier', *AusDB*, vol. 3

Archives BL, letters to Lord Ripon, Add. MS 43564 · Bodl. Oxf., corresp. with Lord Kimberley

Likenesses wood-engraving (after photograph by Gale), NPG; repro. in *ILN* (12 Dec 1896)

Wealth at death £6424 15s. 5d.: probate, 1 Feb 1897, CGPLA Eng. & Wales

Broome, John Egerton [Jack] (1901–1985), naval officer and illustrator, was born in Seattle, Washington, USA, on 23 February 1901, the younger child and only son of Louis Egerton Broome (1875–1951), an explorer, and his wife, Clara Kathleen Lake (1863–1948). His grandfather was Sir Frederick Napier *Broome (1842–1896). Broome's early years were spent in Alaska, Detroit, and Panama; he went to England in 1908 and was educated at Oakwood School, near Caterham, Surrey. It was decided that a career in the Royal Navy would be suitable for him and 'there were the inevitable exams, selection boards, and then waiting in endless suspense' (private information). Broome entered the Royal Naval College, Osborne, in September 1914 and was rushed through the Royal Naval College, Dartmouth. He left in August 1917 and was appointed a midshipman on the *Colossus*, commanded by Dudley Pound (later first sea lord). Broome watched the surrender of the German high seas fleet from the *Colossus's* foretop.

From 1918 to 1919 Broome was a midshipman on the destroyers *Vivacious* and *Malaya*. Promoted to the acting rank of sub-lieutenant, he served on the *Scimitar*, taking and passing the sub-lieutenants' exam and gaining a certificate 2 in seamanship. He served as a sub-lieutenant on the *Clematis* in 1920 and the *Courageous* in 1922. When he returned to England in October 1922 he entered Trinity Hall, Cambridge, where he became art editor of the magazine *Granta*. Broome left Cambridge in 1923 and, holding the acting rank of lieutenant, was sent on a submarine course. From 1924 to 1937 he spent most of the time serving on and commanding submarines, apart from two brief periods: 1928–9, when he served on the *Tiger*, and 1932–4, when he served as a lieutenant-commander on the *Royal*

Oak. In 1928 Broome married Sybil (*d.* 1963), daughter of Admiral Nicholas; they had a son and a daughter.

Between 1936 and 1938 Broome was an instructor at the RAF Staff College, at the Royal Naval College, Greenwich, and at Andover. At the outbreak of the Second World War he learned that at thirty-eight he was too old to continue serving in submarines. However, he recommissioned the destroyer *Veteran* and served in the western approaches, where he was involved in convoy work under the direction of Admiral Dunbar Naismith, commander-in-chief, western approaches. At the beginning of the Second World War Broome took part in the annual operations at Narvik, Norway, in 1940, and picked up survivors after the aircraft-carrier *Glorious* was sunk. Broome briefly served ashore under Admiral Sir Percy Noble. While working for Noble, Broome helped to implement a scheme whereby escort ships would be formed into reasonably well-balanced groups which trained and worked together under the same commander. Because of his age and experience Broome was appointed senior officer (O), with the *Victorious* serving as the 'father' to miscellaneous escorts. In 1941 he was appointed air liaison officer at Liverpool and was promoted temporarily to captain (D) at the Liverpool base. He was appointed Escort Group 1 in the destroyer *Keppel* at Londonderry in September 1941.

In mid-June 1942 Broome was the senior escort commander for Convoy PQ17, which was composed of thirty-five merchant ships—mainly American—commanded by Commodore J. C. K. Dowding. This convoy sailed from Reykjavík on 27 June 1942 bound for Archangel as Murmansk had been virtually destroyed by German bombing raids. The close escort force commanded by Broome in the *Keppel* joined the convoy three days later on 30 June. On 1 July the destroyers attacked U-boats sighted on the surface and on 4 July the convoy, about 130 miles north-east of Bear Island, was attacked about 7.30 p.m. by German aircraft, some of the bombs falling near the *Keppel* and the American cruiser USS *Wainwright*. Broome remarked that it was the *Wainwright's* 'Fourth of July enthusiasm' as she sped round the convoy firing at the aircraft that was largely the reason the German attack failed (PRO, ADM 234/369, p. 59). A further attack was launched an hour later and the leading aircraft hit the *Navarino* in the middle of the convoy with two torpedoes before crashing in flames just ahead of the *Keppel*. Two other ships were torpedoed, one of which was sunk while the other, a Russian tanker, Broome found 'holed but happy'. Following this attack on the convoy Broome's impression on seeing the resolution displayed by the convoy with its escort was 'provided the ammunition lasted, PQ17 could get anywhere' (ibid., 60).

The Admiralty believed, however, that the *Tirpitz* and other warships were planning to attack the convoy. In the event this fear proved to be tragically unfounded. The first sea lord, Sir Dudley Pound, decided shortly after 9 p.m. that the cruisers must withdraw and the convoy scatter immediately. The decision was relayed to Rear-Admiral Hamilton, in charge of the cruiser force, at 10 p.m. The message was sent to Broome who expected to see the cruisers open fire as the enemy's masts appeared over the horizon. He decided therefore to take the escort destroyers to reinforce the cruisers and ordered the two submarines P165 and P168 to stay with the convoy and to try to attack the enemy while the rest of the escorts sailed independently to Archangel. At 10.15 p.m. on 4 July therefore Broome passed on the order for the convoy to scatter and with his destroyers sailed to join Hamilton. As the escorting destroyers parted Dowding signalled to Broome, 'Many thanks; goodbye and good hunting', to which Broome replied, 'It is a grim business leaving you here' (PRO, ADM 234/369, pp. 63, 67). Broome later described his decision to leave the convoy as the hardest decision he had ever had to make, but in the circumstances it was clearly the right one and his action was later approved by the commander-in-chief, Sir John Tovey, and Rear-Admiral Hamilton. The convoy scattered as ordered, but on 5 July it was attacked by a German aircraft and submarines. Twelve of PQ17's ships were sunk. The attacks continued over the next three days and 23 merchant ships were sunk (10 bombed, 3 torpedoed by aircraft, and 10 by U-boats); only 11 merchant ships reached Russia. For his part in the action Broome was awarded the Distinguished Service Cross early in 1943.

Broome was appointed captain of the escort aircraft-carrier *Avalon* in 1942 and in April 1943 he was appointed captain of the *Begum* in which he served with the Eastern Fleet under Admiral Sir John Somerville. In February 1945 Broome was mentioned in dispatches, as the *Begum* had sunk a Japanese submarine; and in May he was appointed commandant of HMS *Vernon II*, the shore establishment at Portsmouth. Afterwards he was captain of the *Ramillies*.

In 1947 Broome retired from the navy and became editor-in-chief of *Sketch Magazine*, a position he held until 1952. In the 1950s he drew a set of drawings for the Royal Navy signal school which were based on the new NATO phonetic alphabet; and he also drew the 'crossing the line' certificate presented to Princess Elizabeth when she crossed the equator in 1947. In 1969 Broome sued the author David Irving for libellous remarks he had made about him in *The Destruction of Convoy PQ17* and won the case. He was awarded £40,000 in damages and half the costs. The libel law was changed as a result of the case. Broome was the author of five books, including *Make a Signal* (1955) and *Make another Signal* (1973). He also illustrated a further six books between 1936 and 1971 including *Fabulous Admirals* by Geoffrey Lewis (1952). He was the naval adviser on several films including *The Cruel Sea* (1953) and, with Admiral Sir Roy Foster-Brown, wrote the scripts for the television series *The War at Sea* in 1959. He was one of the original members of the Lords Taverners.

Broome and his wife, Sybil, were divorced in 1954, and in the same year he married Joan Featherstonhaugh (*d.* 1996), the daughter of Bernard Crisp. They had no children. Broome moved to Nettlebed, near Henley-on-Thames, in 1960 and played an active part in village life. He died at his home, Gannock Cottage, Nettlebed, on 19 April 1985.

PETER LE FEVRE

Sources private information (2004) · J. Broome, *Convoy is to scatter* (1972) · B. B. Schofield, *The Arctic convoys* (1977) · R. Woodman, *The Arctic convoys, 1941–1945* (1994) · naval staff history of the Second World War, battle summary no. 22, Arctic convoys, 1941–5, PRO, ADM 234/369 · C. Barnett, *Engage the enemy more closely: the Royal Navy in the Second World War* (1991) · *CGPLA Eng. & Wales* (1985) · D. Irving, *The destruction of convoy PQ17* (1969) · S. W. Roskill, *The war at sea, 1939–1945*, 3 vols. in 4 (1954–61)

Archives priv. coll., MSS of autobiographical memoirs | FILM IWM FVA, actuality footage | SOUND priv. coll., recordings

Likenesses photographs, CAC Cam. · photographs, priv. coll.

Wealth at death under £40,000: probate, 25 July 1985, *CGPLA Eng. & Wales*

Broome, Mary Anne. *See* Barker, Mary Anne, Lady Barker (1831–1911).

Broome, William (*bap.* 1689, *d.* 1745), translator and poet, was born at Haslington, Cheshire, and baptized there on 3 May 1689, the son of Randle Broome, a farmer. He was first educated at Eton College, where he was captain of the school until he was eventually sent to St John's College, Cambridge, entering as a subsizar on 3 July 1708 and matriculating as a sizar a week later. He graduated BA in January 1712 and MA in 1716; the degree of LLD was conferred on him when George II visited Cambridge in April 1728. Broome was ordained deacon (in Norwich) on 21 February 1714 and priest (in Ely) on 28 February 1714. He was appointed rector of Oakley Magna, Essex, in 1720 and in 1713 was presented to the rectory of Sturston, Suffolk, by Lord Charles Cornwallis, later the first Earl Cornwallis and baron of Eye, one of his closest friends at Cambridge. In September 1728 Broome resigned Sturston on being presented by the king to the rectory of Pulham, Norfolk, to which Lord Cornwallis added the vicarage of Eye, Norfolk; he retained these appointments until his death. At Sturston on 22 July 1716 he married Elizabeth Clarke, a widow. They had two daughters—Anne (1718–1723), to whose memory he dedicated the ode 'Melancholy' (1723), and a younger one, who also died as a child (1723–1725)—and a son, Charles John (*b.* 1726), who survived Broome by two years. When his son died unmarried, while an undergraduate at Cambridge, Broome's property returned to Lord Cornwallis, 'as a testimony of my gratitude to my great benefactor' (Broome's will, quoted in *Works of Alexander Pope*, 33, n.2).

Shortly after taking his BA at Cambridge—where friends nicknamed him 'the Poet'—Broome recommended himself with a verse translation, in the style of Milton, of books 10 and 11 of the *Iliad*, which was printed in the Pope–Lintot *Miscellany* (1712). He also contributed to the prose translation of the whole poem by John Ozell and William Oldisworth, which appeared in the same year (*The Iliad of Homer ... from the French*, 1712); a verse translation from the Greek followed in 1714. That year marked the beginning of Broome's collaboration with Alexander Pope, to whom he was introduced in the house of Sir John Cotton at Madingley, near Cambridge. Pope had begun his project of an annotated translation of the *Iliad*, to be printed by subscription, in 1712; on 29 November 1714 he assigned Broome the arduous task of making extracts

William Broome (*bap.* 1689, *d.* 1745), by George Vertue, pubd 1727 (after D. Heins, 1725)

from the Homeric scholia of the Byzantine scholar Eustathius, archbishop of Thessalonica; the young John Jortin (1698–1770) was employed as coadjutor in 1718. By December 1718 Broome had completed his notes, to which were added those of John Jortin, and 'An essay on the life ... of Homer' by Thomas Parnell (*The Iliad of Homer*, 6 vols., 1715–20; 2nd edn, 1720).

Broome had by then become acquainted with the poet Elijah Fenton, himself an admirer of Pope and an experienced translator of Homer. According to J. P. Blunt (1707–1734), the two had resolved on translating the *Odyssey* and 'Pope, upon hearing immediately said he would make a third; at last he came to be principal in the work' (Spence, 208); the evidence from Pope's correspondence, however, credits Pope with the initiative. At all events, in 1722 Broome found himself appointed with Fenton as an associate in Pope's translation of the *Odyssey*, which was printed by subscription in 1725–6. Pope took on half of the translation load and the general revision work; Broome translated eight books (2, 6, 8, 11, 12, 16, 18, 23) and was responsible for the notes to the whole poem—a major contribution, for which he was allowed £570 out of the subscription of £4500; Fenton received £200 on account of his four books (1, 4, 19, 20). What Broome resented most bitterly was Pope's attempt to blur the details of the collaboration. In fact Broome had been persuaded to sign a statement to the effect that his share had been the translation of three books and Fenton's the translation of two, to which was added: 'it was our particular request, that our several parts might not be made known to the world till the end of it' (*The Odyssey of Homer*, 1726, 5.226). Pope then, when acknowledging the work of 'those Gentlemen who join'd with me', included a precise reference to this note for the benefit of readers who wished to know 'what assistance I received from them' ('Postscript by Mr Pope', ibid., 5.243). It is significant that there is no evidence left of Broome's work in the surviving manuscript of 'Pope's Odyssey' (BL, Add. MS 4809). Broome was embittered to the extent that in 1726 he was determined to publish a true account of events; Fenton advised him against it.

Relations between Broome and Pope were further compromised by Broome's failure to comment on a couplet circulated by John Henley to publicize the scandal:

Pope came off clean with Homer; but they say
Broome went before, and kindly swept the way.
(Johnson, *Prefaces*, 8.12)

Pope, in response, attacked Broome explicitly in the *Peri Bathous* (1727) and in the *Dunciad* (1728). Broome then had no contact with Pope for seven years. In September 1735 Broome sought to renew their friendship; however, Pope was more concerned about retrieving his letters to Broome. Neither achieved his goal, and correspondence lapsed once more in 1742.

After the Homeric experience Broome collected his original poems and minor translations from Greek and Latin poetry (Hesiod, Apollonius Rhodius, Horace) in a miscellany entitled *Poems on Several Occasions* (1727), introduced by an 'Essay on criticism'; a second edition was dedicated to Lord Charles Townshend (1739). Previously unpublished additions and alterations made by the author in 1743 were included in *The Works of the English Poets, with Prefaces ... by S. Johnson* (vol. 43, 1779). In 1727 Broome proposed to Fenton a translation of Virgil, a 'joint work, something serious' (Spence, 208a), but the project fell through when Fenton died in 1730. In the following year Broome lost another Cambridge friend, Cornelius Ford. The years 1728–39 seem to have witnessed a total interruption of Broome's creative work; a number of poems published between 1728 and 1738 have been attributed to him, with insufficient evidence, including *The Oak and the Dunghill: a Fable* (1728).

Late in life Broome returned to Greek poetry and published, over the pseudonym Charles Chester MD, a verse translation of sixteen 'Anacreontics' in several instalments in the *Gentleman's Magazine* (1739–40); his versions were included in Francis Fawkes's *Works of Anacreon* (1760) and in a collection of French and English translations, *Odes d'Anacréon*, published in Paris in 1835.

As a clergyman Broome published two sermons: *The duty of publick intercession and thanksgiving for princes: a sermon preached ... on the 20th of October, 1722* (1723) and *A sermon preach'd at the assizes in Norwich, August 8th, 1737* (1737); his authorship of the latter was contested by Philip Williams,

president of St John's College, Cambridge (BL, Add. MS 5822, fol. 111).

Broome died of asthma at Bath on 16 November 1745 and was buried in the abbey church. A poem entitled 'On the death of Dr Broome', in Latin and English, appeared in the *Gentleman's Magazine* in January 1746; more than a century later Thomas Worthington Barlow published a *Memoir of William Broome, LL.D.: the associate of Pope in the translation of Homer's Odyssey, with selections from his works* (1855).

ANNA CHAHOUD

Sources *DNB* · D. Bank and others, eds., *British biographical archive* (1984–98), microfiche 1.152.275–98 [microfiche; with index, 2nd edn, 1998] · Venn, *Alum. Cant.* · S. Johnson, *Prefaces, biographical and critical, to the works of the English poets*, 8 (1781), pp. 1–12 · *The works of Alexander Pope*, ed. W. Elwin and W. J. Courthope, 10 vols. (1871–89), vol. 8, pp. 30–183 · J. Spence, *Observations, anecdotes, and characters, of books and men*, ed. J. M. Osborn, new edn, 2 vols. (1966) · *GM*, 1st ser., 9 (1739), 599, 608 · *GM*, 1st ser., 12 (1742), 211 · *GM*, 1st ser., 15 (1745), 614 · *GM*, 1st ser., 16 (1746), 39, 103 · H.-J. Zimmermann, *Alexander Pope's Noten zu Homer* (Heidelberg, 1966) · *The letters of Samuel Johnson*, ed. R. W. Chapman, 3 vols. (1952), nos. 668, 683 · B. Dobrée, *English literature in the early eighteenth century, 1700–1740* (1959), 143, 305, 526, 623 · I. Ehrenpreis, 'The style of sound: the literary value of Pope's versification', *The Augustan milieu*, ed. H. K. Miller, E. Rothstein, and E. S. Rousseau (1970), 234 · A. W. Ward, W. P. Strent, and others, eds., *The Cambridge history of English and American literature* (New York, 1907–21), 9, 18ff.

Archives BL, assignment of copyright of poems with Lintot, Add. MS 38729, fol. 50 | BL, queries sent to Pope on *The Iliad*, Add. MS 4807, fols. 194–9 · BL, letter to E. Cart, Add. MS Extr. 4107, fol. 70b · BL, P. Williams, 'Reasons why Dr Broome cannot be the author of an assize sermon …', Add. MS 5822, fol. 111 · BL, A. Pope, letter to Broome, Add. MS 5860, fol. 58

Likenesses D. Heins, portrait, 1725 · T. Cook, engraving (after D. Heins?), repro. in S. Johnson, *Works of the English poets* (1779) · J.-M. Delattre, engraving (after Heins?), repro. in *The poetical works of Dr. Will Broome*, Bell's edn (1781) · G. Vertue, line engraving (after D. Heins, 1725), BM, NPG; repro. in W. Broome, *Poems on several occasions* (1727) [see illus.]

Wealth at death £44 p.a. bequeathed to Charles Cornwallis: will, *The correspondence of Alexander Pope*, ed. G. W. Sherburn, 5 vols. (1956), 3.33, n.2

Broomfield, Matthew. *See* Brwmffild, Mathau (*fl. c*.1525–*c*.1545).

Brophy, Brigid Antonia [married name Brigid Antonia Levey, Lady Levey] (**1929–1995**), writer and campaigner, was born at 79 Uxbridge Road, Ealing, London, on 12 June 1929, the second child of John *Brophy (1899–1965), a Liverpool-born writer and editor of Irish descent, and his wife, Charis Weare Grundy (1895/6–1975), teacher and novelist. Her mother had been born in Chicago, the daughter of James Grundy, a Scottish archangel (bishop) of the Catholic Apostolic church, but was brought up in Liverpool, and Brigid was baptized into the Anglican church. Because an elder sibling died in infancy before Brigid was born, she was in effect an only child. Her father recognized that she was precocious and encouraged her to read and write from an early age. 'Any ability I have as an adult to write English prose,' she said, 'I learned from him and from reading the masters he directed me to, Bernard Shaw and Evelyn Waugh' (*King of a Rainy Country*, afterword, 276). She was educated at numerous schools, both state and private, including a preparatory school for boys

Brigid Antonia Brophy (1929–1995), by Mark Gerson, 1966

where her mother was head teacher, the Abbey School, Reading, and St Paul's School for Girls, which she left at fifteen. After a spell at Camberwell School of Arts and Crafts and secretarial college, in 1947 she gained a scholarship to St Hugh's College, Oxford, where she read classics but was sent down for unspecified sexual misdemeanours at the end of her fourth term. She began earning her living as a shorthand-typist.

Brophy claimed that she was writing verse dramas at the age of fifteen, but the first book that she published was a volume of short stories, *The Crown Princess*, which appeared in 1953 to highly laudatory notices. She nevertheless expunged the book from her bibliography because, as she put it, 'I can recognize no connection between it and me' ('My first book', 97). In the same year she also published her first novel, *Hackenfeller's Ape*, inspired by hearing the lions roaring when she lived opposite Regent's Park Zoo. It started out as a 'narrative poem on the (alas, still visionary) theme of the liberation of animals' (ibid.), a subject that she was to write about frequently, but it evolved into a short novel, written in two weeks, and won the Cheltenham Literary Festival prize for a first novel. (Iris Murdoch was the runner-up, and subsequently became a close friend.) One result of writing the book, in which someone attempts to prevent an ape from being sent into space, was that Brophy became a vegetarian.

On her twenty-fifth birthday, 12 June 1954, Brophy married Michael Vincent Levey (b. 1927), assistant keeper at the National Gallery, son of Otto Lemuel Herbert Levey, assistant director at the Ministry of Supply. The couple lived at 23 Earls Court Square, London, and had one

daughter. Though both Brophy and Levey came to regard marriage as 'an immoral social institution we ought never to have subscribed to' ('My first book', 98) their own was something that Brophy said she rejoiced in every day. It nevertheless remained distinctly unconventional, accommodating a long period when Brophy was in love with the novelist Maureen Duffy.

Brophy's second novel, *The King of a Rainy Country* (1956), in which a young woman given the author's baptismal name of Susan goes in search of a girl with whom she had been in love at school, is the most straightforwardly autobiographical of her books, although every one of them is steeped in the author's personality and beliefs. Brophy was determinedly experimental as a writer, and each of her novels was different in style and form from its predecessors, but together with her many works of non-fiction these books constitute a highly coherent and distinctive *œuvre*. Her first work of non-fiction was *Black Ship to Hell* (1962), which started out as an attempt to 'psycho-analyse the Greek myth of the Underworld' (p. 19), but ended up as a wide-ranging and characteristically allusive study of 'man as a destructive and, more particularly, self-destructive animal' (p. 13) who can only be saved by a Freudian examination of these impulses. It endeavoured to formulate a morality based on reason rather than religion—Brophy described herself as 'a natural, logical and happy atheist' (*King of a Rainy Country*, afterword, 276). The influence of Freud is discernible in her third novel, *Flesh* (1962), just as her critical study *Mozart the Dramatist* (1964) informs her operatic novel *The Snow Ball*, published in the same year. *The Finishing Touch* (1963), set in the romantic hothouse of a girls' finishing school (the headmistress of which was based on her husband's art-historian colleague Anthony Blunt), is a pastiche of Ronald Firbank, a writer whom she championed in her vast critical work *Prancing Novelist* (1973). The latter book is a dazzlingly speculative and passionately argued investigation of an inventive and neglected writer with whom Brophy clearly identified. (She wrote the book in the same violet ink that Firbank customarily used.) It is subtitled 'A defence of fiction in the form of a critical biography of Ronald Firbank', and in it Brophy argued that 'works of art have and need no justification but themselves' (p. 70) and that 'good fiction is positively and absolutely good' (p. xiii). Fiction—and other writing—that was not good came under attack in *Fifty Works of English and American Literature we could Do Without* (1967), a squib written in collaboration with her husband and their friend Charles Osborne.

Whether or not what writers did was 'useful' Brophy believed that they should be properly paid, and was a driving force behind the campaign to introduce public lending right (PLR), a scheme by which authors were annually paid a kind of royalty, out of government funds, when their books were borrowed from public libraries. The idea had first been posited by her father in 1951, but it was the Writers Action Group, founded by Brophy, Maureen Duffy, Michael Levey, Francis King, and Lettice Cooper in 1972, that overcame the opposition of librarians and through persistent lobbying ensured that PLR came into force by an act of parliament in 1979. (Brophy's *A Guide to Public Lending Right* was published in 1983.) This and other campaigns resulted in Brophy becoming well known as a controversialist during the 1960s, both in print and in broadcasting, and one of her favourite tactics was to pronounce the most heterodox opinions as if they were universal truths. She usefully filled a role similar to that of Gore Vidal in the United States, wittily challenging national complacency and goading her fellow citizens until they were roused from their habitual torpor. She often appeared on the satirical television show *That Was The Week That Was*, and a talk commissioned by BBC radio at the time of the Profumo affair was so scathing about sexual hypocrisy in Britain that the corporation declined to broadcast it. She was a fervent anti-vivisectionist and a campaigner against blood sports (including angling), who allowed her beloved Persian cat, Darius, meat only because felines require a carnivorous diet; she was an outspoken opponent of the campaign against pornography, and wrote a booklet for the Secular Society, *Lord Longford's Threat to Freedom* (1972); and she was an early and articulate supporter of homosexual rights. Her forthright views, and the vigour with which she expressed them, were (she complained) sometimes mistaken for pugnacity. She conceded that her 'Irishly rational tone of voice is infuriating to some readers—or, rather, to some reviewers' (*Prancing Novelist*, 48), but Edward Blishen captured the particular quality of her writing when he observed: 'She has always the gift of a most stirring sort of firmness. It is not the tone of a know-all, it is not remotely bossy; it is, I suppose, basically, the sound that logic makes' (*Reads*, cover).

Brophy's other works of non-fiction include *Don't Never Forget* (1966), a collection of 'views and reviews', two characteristically enthusiastic and idiosyncratic books on Aubrey Beardsley, and *The Prince and the Wild Geese* (1983), in which a series of watercolours by a young Irish woman is used as the basis for an imaginative recreation of the artist's romance with a Russian prince. Brophy's most challenging novel is *In Transit* (1969), a Joycean 'trans-sexual adventure' (cover of 1971 reprint) in which gender, identity, and syntax blur and meld, and which is set, appropriately, in the no-man's-land of an airport. *Palace without Chairs* (1978), subtitled 'a baroque novel', is a subversive, Ruritanian romance, once again influenced by Firbank. Brophy also wrote two plays, one of which, an unorthodox bedroom farce entitled *The Burglar*, was produced unsuccessfully in the West End in 1967; in the following year she published the text with a long and discursive preface in which many of her ideas about drama, writing, and her public reputation are rehearsed. Her one excursion into writing for juveniles, *Pussy Owl* (1976), was read by James Cossins on the popular BBC children's programme *Jackanory* and was subsequently published, with illustrations by Hilary Hayton.

Brophy was quite tall, 'soncy' (as she would put it), with striking blue eyes emphasized by fair hair and very fair skin. She was a stylish dresser, fond of jewellery. In 1983 she was diagnosed as suffering from multiple sclerosis, and gradually became incapacitated. She nevertheless remained resolutely opposed to any medical research involving the use of animals. She continued to write as long as she was physically able, producing two collections of essays and journalism: *Baroque-'n'-Roll* (1987), which includes an account of her illness, and *Reads* (1989). She wrote new introductions and afterwords to reissues of her novels, but none remained in print very long and they even became hard to find in libraries. She remained philosophical about this neglect, remarking of Firbank, but also thinking of herself: 'People are a bit debased about what they expect in fiction. When it isn't there and so much is wittily left out, I think they get confused' (*The Guardian*). Firbank's estimation of his own work—that it was 'aggressive, witty, & unrelenting' (*Prancing Novelist*, 69)—might equally be applied to Brophy.

Brophy eventually became confined to a wheelchair, and Michael Levey, who had become keeper of the National Gallery (and had been knighted in 1981), left his job in order to look after her. In 1991 the Leveys left the flat in the Old Brompton Road where they had lived for twenty-six years and moved to Louth, in Lincolnshire. When she needed full-time professional care Brophy entered the Fir Close Nursing Home, Westgate, Louth, where she died, of pneumonia and multiple sclerosis, on 7 August 1995. She was cremated at Grimsby.

PETER PARKER

Sources *Review of Contemporary Fiction*, 15/3 (1995) • B. Brophy, *The burglar* (1968) • private information (2004) • B. Brophy, 'My first book', *The Author*, 96/4 (1985) • B. Brophy, *Don't never forget* (1966) • B. Brophy, *Prancing novelist* (1973) • B. Brophy, afterword, *The king of a rainy country*, reprint (1990) • B. Brophy, introduction, *The finishing touch*, reprint (1987) • B. Brophy, *Baroque-'n'-roll* (1987) • B. Brophy, *Reads* (1989) • *The Guardian* (14 June 1989) • K. Dick, *Friends and friendship* (1974) • b. cert. • m. cert. • d. cert.
Archives priv. coll. • Ransom HRC
Likenesses M. Gerson, photograph, 1966, NPG [*see illus.*] • J. Bauer, photograph, 1978, priv. coll. • photograph, repro. in 'Review of Contemporary Fiction'

Brophy, John (1899–1965), journalist and novelist, was born on 6 December 1899 at 87 Everton Road, Liverpool, the son of John Brophy, an earthenware dealer, and his wife, Agnes, *née* Bodell. At the age of fourteen, he escaped from a dull adolescence in that city, and joined the army upon the outbreak of the First World War. It was while on infantry service in France and Belgium that he accumulated the information that was to be the basis of much of his writing.

Brophy did not write about the First World War right away. When he was demobbed he returned to Liverpool, took a degree at Liverpool University, and then spent a year at Durham University. On 6 June 1924 he married Charis Weare Grundy (1895/6–1975), the daughter of James Grundy, a clergyman from Chicago. Brophy then took a teaching job in Egypt, but the couple returned to England after two years, Charis Brophy being ill. Brophy found a position writing advertising for a large store in Liverpool and then moved to London to be head copywriter for a leading British advertising firm. He began to take an interest in literature and became the chief reviewer of fiction for the *Daily Telegraph*. He wrote also for *Time and Tide* and for the BBC.

It was Brophy's first novel, however, which truly launched his literary career. *The Bitter End* (1928) was a war novel which featured an attractive semi-autobiographical hero, Donald Foster, who gave voice to the sense of loss and disappointment in England a decade after 'the war to end war'. The novel marked Brophy as an author to watch, particularly in its development of the mixture of nostalgia and anger that was to give a popular appeal to his disillusioned descriptions of the horrors of war.

The Brophys' daughter, Brigid Antonia *Brophy (1929–1995), also a writer, was born in the following year, and Brophy was determined to support his new family as a professional writer. In 1929 he published his second and third novels, *Pluck the Flower* and *Paul Lavelle*, as well as an anthology, *The Soldier's War*. In 1930 he edited, with Eric Partridge, *Songs and Slang of the British Soldier, 1914–1918* (later revised as *The Long Trail*, 1965). Through the 1930s he published at least one novel a year, never equalling his first, and he also wrote *English Prose* (in the How and Why series, 1932), contributed to *The Writer's Desk Book* (1934), and wrote *Ilonka Speaks of Hungary: Personal Impressions and an Interpretation of the National Character* (1936) and *The Five Years* (1936), a rather personal history of the First World War. It was not until 1939 that he had a real success, not with his collection of stories *The Queer Fellow* nor with his novel *The Ridiculous Hat*—both published in that year—but with his fictional life of Shakespeare, *Gentleman of Stratford* (1939).

The Second World War found Brophy editing *John O'London's Weekly* and serving in the Home Guard, for which he wrote handbooks and manuals and, eventually, 'a character study', *Britain's Home Guard* (1945). Brophy came more alive during the war and produced an 'entertainment' called *Solitude Island* (1941) and several action novels well received on both sides of the Atlantic, including *Immortal Sergeant* (1942); *Spear Head* (published in the United States as *Spearhead*, 1943), about commando raids on France and Norway; and *Target Island* (1944), about the brave resistance of Malta. Of these, and in fact of all his work, *Immortal Sergeant* is the best. In 1943 a film was made based on the novel, starring Henry Fonda as Corporal Spence, who rises to the occasion in the Libyan desert war when his sergeant is killed. The film served to enhance Brophy's reputation, which, however, declined after the war.

Brophy's post-war work was more copious than compelling. He collected *Selected Stories* (1946), edited some letters of Sarah Curran (1955), and wrote an introduction to those of Holbrooke Jackson (1960). He also wrote a number of books on art which reflect the keen visual sense shown in his novels: *The Human Face Reconsidered* (1962), recalling his *The Human Face* (1942); *The Face in Western Art* (1963); and *The Face of the Nude* (1965). In addition to a 1964 profile of W. Somerset Maugham written for the British Council, he continued to publish novels such as *City of Departures* (1946), *A Woman from Nowhere* (1946), *Sarah* (1948), *Julian's Way* (1949), *Turn the Key Softly* (1951), *The Prime of Life* (1954), and *The Day they Robbed the Bank of England* (1959). This last

made a successful caper film in 1960, with Peter O'Toole and Aldo Ray. The cinema not only provided Brophy with more money for his passion for old master drawings but made the neat if sometimes sentimental character sketching and swift plotting in his novels known to larger international audiences than those who read his books. John Brophy died at the Royal Waterloo Hospital, Lambeth, London, of heart failure on 12 November 1965; his wife survived him. Brophy's novels were enjoyable, often insightful, well-constructed entertainments, popular in their day. They were translated into sixteen languages and based, in large part, on the personal experience of a sensitive and articulate Englishman of a war-torn century.

LEONARD R. N. ASHLEY

Sources L. R. N. Ashley, 'John Brophy', *DLitB* · J. Brophy, *The mind's eye: a twelve-month journal* (1949) · D. C. Browning, ed., *Everyman's dictionary of literary biography*, 3rd edn (1962) · M. Geismar, review of *Gentleman of Stratford*, *Books* (21 April 1940), 8 · G. Greene, review of *The world went mad*, *The Spectator* (27 July 1934), 144 · L. P. Hartley, review of *The bitter end*, *Saturday Review*, 145 (1928), 568 · [R. D. Charques], 'Commando romance', *TLS* (8 May 1943), 221 · J. P. Walsh, review of *Immortal sergeant*, *Commonweal*, 36 (June 1942), 232 · *WWW*, 1961–70 · b. cert. · d. cert. · m. cert.

Archives Lpool RO, letters | BBC WAC, corresp. with the BBC · Hull Central Library, letters to W. Holtby · JRL, *Guardian* archives, corresp. with *Manchester Guardian* · King's Lond., Liddell Hart C., corresp. with Sir B. H. Liddell Hart · U. Reading, corresp. with Chatto and Windus; corresp. with R. L. Mégroz

Likenesses H. Coster, photograph, NPG

Wealth at death £9399: administration, 29 March 1966, *CGPLA Eng. & Wales*

Brorda [Hildegils] (*d.* 799), magnate, was a Mercian, also known as Hildegils and perhaps of royal birth, who became King Offa's principal counsellor in the 780s and 790s. The name first appears in the witness lists of royal charters in the 760s, and in the 770s was borne by two men, the junior designated *praefectus* ('reeve'), the senior *dux* or *princeps* ('ealdorman' or 'prince'). It was perhaps a family appellation. If so, the family may have been based in the area that is now north-eastern Northamptonshire and the soke of Peterborough. At an uncertain date, perhaps in the late 770s, a Brorda with the title *praefectus* joined with Pusa, the abbot of Medeshamstede (later St Peter's Abbey, Peterborough), in requesting the king to confirm the possessions of the community's dependency of Woking. It may also be significant that in the late 780s or early 790s the *praefectus* Brorda attested a royal confirmation not far away at Irthlingborough in the later county of Northamptonshire; the fact that his only fellow witnesses were the king, the queen, and the local bishop may indicate that Irthlingborough was home territory.

After 780 the witness lists only once contain more than one Brorda. He almost invariably attests land grants at the head of the ealdormen, usually with the designation *princeps*, occasionally with some other title such as *dux* or *praefectus*. Whether he is to be identified with the *praefectus* who was earlier the junior of the two Brordas is unclear. In the 790s, at the very end of Offa's reign, he was occasionally designated *patricius* ('patrician'), a title of especial honour, probably confined to those of royal blood, and perhaps equivalent to chief minister or to the Frankish mayor of the palace.

Brorda seems to have occupied a position of particular prominence during the brief reign of Ecgfrith, Offa's young son and successor (July to December 796), and in the first years of Cenwulf (r. 796–821), who was initially perhaps somewhat insecure since he was only distantly, if at all, related to his immediate predecessors. Almost certainly Brorda, rather than the mysterious Osberht named by William of Malmesbury, was the anonymous *patricius*, *consiliarius* ('counsellor') of the Mercian kingdom (and indeed of the English as a whole), to whom Alcuin sent an important letter in 797. Alcuin's recipient, whom he claimed as a longstanding and loyal friend, was urged to distribute alms and elicit prayers 'through the places conferred on you by God' (*English Historical Documents*, no. 202); to admonish his own king and the Northumbrian king Eardwulf on matters of sexual morality; to encourage the Mercian people as a whole to observe King Offa's good laws; to exhort the bishops and clergy to preach and set a good example to the people; and to require loyalty and right judgement of secular lords. Such responsibilities are what might be expected of an experienced chief minister or head of the royal household at the beginning of a new reign.

Brorda seems to have remained senior ealdorman until his death in 799. By then only he and one other received the designation *princeps*. Alcuin's expectation that Brorda could admonish the Northumbrian king suggests a northern connection which may lie behind the fact that his death in 799 is recorded, most unusually for a Mercian ealdorman, in the northern annals, where he is again accorded the title *princeps*. After 799 the name Brorda disappears from the witness lists. It appears, however, among the kings and *duces* listed on the opening page of the Durham *Liber vitae*. ALAN THACKER

Sources W. de G. Birch, ed., *Cartularium Saxonicum*, 4 vols. (1885–99) · E. Dümmler, ed., *Epistolae Karolini aevi*, MGH Epistolae [quarto], 4 (Berlin, 1895), no. 122 · Symeon of Durham, *Opera*, 2.62 · William of Malmesbury, *Gesta regum Anglorum / The history of the English kings*, ed. and trans. R. A. B. Mynors, R. M. Thomson, and M. Winterbottom, 2 vols., OMT (1998–9) · J. Earle, ed., *Two of the Saxon chronicles parallel: with supplementary extracts from the others*, rev. C. Plummer, 1 (1892), 53 · A. T. Thacker, 'Some terms for noblemen in Anglo-Saxon England, c. 650–900', *Anglo-Saxon Studies in Archaeology and History*, 2 (1981), 201–36 · *AS chart.*, S 144, 1184 · *English historical documents*, 1, ed. D. Whitelock (1955), nos. 3, 202 · [J. Stevenson], ed., *Liber vitae ecclesiae Dunelmensis*, SurtS, 13 (1841) · [A. H. Thompson], ed., *Liber vitae ecclesiae Dunelmensis*, SurtS, 136 (1923)

Broster, Dorothy Kathleen (1877–1950), novelist, was born at Grassendale Park, Garston, near Liverpool, on 2 September 1877, the eldest of the four children of Thomas Mawdsley Broster, shipowner, and his wife, Emily Kathleen, *née* Gething. She was educated privately until she was ten years old; she was then sent to a boarding-school near the coast in Lancashire. When her parents moved to Cheltenham she became, at the age of sixteen, a day girl at Cheltenham Ladies' College, where she was later followed by her two younger sisters, Phyllis and Barbara. She left school when she was nineteen with a scholarship to St Hilda's College, Oxford. She had a lively and intelligent mind and took second-class honours in modern history in 1900, but had to wait until 1920, when the first batch of Oxford women graduates at last were awarded their degrees; she then received her BA and MA simultaneously. At Cheltenham she made a number of friends, but she did not join very actively in the social life and was often seen as a somewhat aloof figure by her juniors. Later, at Oxford, she was known as a worrier, obsessed by the difficulties of daily living, the need to be ready for any and every emergency. Though she had a small circle of admiring friends, she was essentially a very private person and this trait continued throughout her life.

After passing her final examinations, Broster spent the next thirteen years as secretary to the regius professor of modern history at Oxford. During this time she published some poems and her first short story but she seemed to find it difficult to do any sustained work; finally, with the help of one of her college friends, Miss G. W. Taylor, she completed a long historical novel, *Chantemerle*, about the rising in the Vendée after the French Revolution, and this was published in 1911. Two years later, in 1913, they published *The Vision Splendid*, which dealt with the Oxford Movement and the France of Louis Philippe.

At the start of the First World War, Broster registered for war work and found herself, at the end of 1914, nursing wounded Belgian soldiers. She spoke French fairly fluently, so in April 1916 she went to France with the British Red Cross and was stationed in Yvetot, where she cared for wounded French soldiers in an Anglo-American hospital. At new year 1916 she was invalided home with an infection that affected her knee joints; she did not return to France, though she did some further nursing later, in England.

The first novel Broster published as sole author was *Sir Isumbras at the Ford*; this had been started before the war and was finally published in 1918, and reflects her interest in the sea. It was followed by what she thought of as her best book, *The Yellow Poppy* (1920), and her favourite book, *The Wounded Name* (1922). All her early books were set in France and fictionalized various periods of French history, illustrating her continued interest in her earlier academic studies. In 1923, however, she spent five weeks visiting Lochaber in the Scottish highlands and this inspired her to write the trilogy about the Jacobite rising of 1745, for which she is perhaps best remembered: *The Flight of the Heron* (1925), *The Gleam in the North* (1927), and *The Dark Mile* (1929). Because she published as D. K. Broster, she was generally believed to be a man, and a Scotsman at that; she appeared to be somewhat flattered by this and never attempted to put the record straight.

After the war Broster lived for many years in the southeast of England, sharing a house with a friend, Miss G. Schlich. She continued to produce novels at regular intervals; her last, *The Captain's Lady*, was published in

1947. She died on 7 February 1950, of lung cancer, in Bexhill Hospital and was cremated on 13 February at Charing crematorium, Kent.
HILDA D. SPEAR

Sources archives, St Hilda's College, Oxford · archives, Cheltenham Ladies' College · *The Times* (10 Feb 1950) · b. cert. · d. cert. · *CGPLA Eng. & Wales* (1950)
Archives St Hilda's College, Oxford, letters, talks, photographs, MSS
Likenesses photographs, St Hilda's College, Oxford
Wealth at death £67,611 14s. 1d.: probate, 16 May 1950, *CGPLA Eng. & Wales*

Brotherhood, Peter (1838–1902), mechanical engineer, was born on 22 April 1838, the second son of the fourteen children of Rowland Brotherhood (1812–1869), a railway contractor, and his wife, Priscilla, daughter of William Penton, an excise officer. He was born at Maidenhead, Berkshire, where his father was then engaged; later Rowland Brotherhood established an engineering works at Chippenham, Wiltshire, where he was able to field an entire cricket team drawn from his sons. Peter studied applied science at King's College School from 1852 to 1856, underwent practical training in his father's works, and in the Great Western Railway works at Swindon, then, aged twenty-one, entered the drawing-office of Maudslay, Son and Field, Lambeth, the leading marine engineering firm. He married on 19 April 1866 Eliza Pinniger, eldest daughter of James Hunt, a former Indian railways contractor. They had five children, of whom two sons predeceased him.

In 1867 Brotherhood became a partner with G. D. Kittoe, at Compton Street, Clerkenwell. Brotherhood and Kittoe was in business as engineers and millwrights, mainly concerned with brewery machinery, but after Kittoe's retirement in 1871 the firm produced machines and engines of Brotherhood's invention. In 1872 he introduced the Brotherhood engine, a novel design in which three cylinders with single-acting pistons were arranged at angles of 120°, the connecting rods acting on a crankshaft in a central chamber. The engine could be powered by steam, water, or compressed air. Demonstrated at the Agricultural Hall, Islington, and in 1873 at the Vienna exhibition, the Brotherhood engine rapidly gained popularity in Britain and abroad, being licensed for manufacture also in France and being put to a variety of uses. Fitted with compressors of Brotherhood's design, it was used to drive the Whitehead torpedoes coming into service with the British navy and, with modifications, the torpedoes of other navies.

Brotherhood also contributed to the introduction of high-speed engines. The first of this kind, which he designed, constructed, and had under steam within twenty-seven working days, was directly coupled to the dynamo which generated electric light on Queen Victoria's yacht *Victoria and Albert*. Brotherhood had what might be termed a mechanical instinct, which allowed him to evolve sizes and capacities without recourse to formulae or calculations. He insisted on first-rate material and workmanship, and this rule, coupled to his excellent designs, ensured his success. In 1881 his works were transferred to new, larger premises, laid out on the most modern lines, at Belvedere Road, Lambeth, and further expanded in 1896. Here he was able to indulge fully his passion for experiment. Brotherhood was elected an associate member of the Institution of Civil Engineers in 1868, and a full member on 4 February 1879; he was elected a member of the Institution of Mechanical Engineers in 1874, and of the Iron and Steel Institute in 1877.

Brotherhood died at his home, 15 Hyde Park Gardens, Bayswater, London, on 13 October 1902, and was buried at Kensal Green. He was survived by his widow, two daughters, and a son, Stanley (1880–1938), who was general manager of his works and who continued the business.
ANITA MCCONNELL

Sources S. A. Leleux, *Brotherhoods, engineers* (1965) · *Institution of Mechanical Engineers: Proceedings* (1902), 1023–4 · *PICE*, 151 (1902–3), 405–9 · *Engineering* (17 Oct 1902), 515–16 · *CGPLA Eng. & Wales* (1902)
Likenesses photographs, repro. in Leleux, *Brotherhoods, engineers*
Wealth at death £39,223 13s. 3d.: probate, 30 Oct 1902, *CGPLA Eng. & Wales*

Brothers, Richard (1757–1824), self-styled prophet, was born on 25 December 1757 at Placentia, Newfoundland. His father was a gunner, and his family continued to live at Placentia long after Richard was sent as a boy to Woolwich, where he went to school, and from where in 1772 he entered the Royal Navy as a midshipman on board the *Ocean*. In July 1778 he served as a master's mate under Admiral Augustus Keppel in the engagement with the French off Ushant. The next year he was transferred to the *Union* and in 1781 to the *St Albans*, which in June was commissioned for the West Indies. In April 1782 he served under Admiral George Rodney at the decisive battle of the Saints, off Dominica, and in January 1783 he became a lieutenant with seniority. However, in July, a few months before the peace of Versailles, Brothers was discharged at Portsmouth on half pay (£54 p.a.). His movements during the next few years are uncertain. Although he travelled in France, Spain, and Italy, Balleine's conjecture that he visited the New Israel Society at Avignon is 'possible, but very unlikely' (Garrett, 179). On his return to England he married Elizabeth Hasall at Wrenbury, near Nantwich, on 6 June 1786, but by now he appears to have been employed in the mercantile marine and, it was said, he rejoined his ship after the wedding ceremony. Later, on his return, finding his wife living with another man, Brothers moved to London in September 1787.

At this stage Brothers was accustomed to worship either at Long Acre Chapel or at a Baptist chapel in the Adelphi, but there are indications of other religious influences in his life. In addition to his adoption of a vegetarian diet, we may observe Quaker overtones in his beginning to question the rightness of armed service and oath taking, and, a little later, in his insistence on wearing his hat during an interview with the local governors of the poor. In 1790 he decided that he could no longer draw his half-pension as

Richard Brothers (1757–1824), by William Sharp, pubd 1795

its acceptance required an oath that he had not profited from any other form of government employment. Early in 1791 he had a series of visions of the imminent judgment of God on London. Believing that his mission was that of a prophet and that he was a particular object of divine favour, he concluded that it was for his sake that the metropolis was spared. However, having refused to draw his pension, he was soon unable to pay the rent for his lodgings in Dartmouth Street. When his landlady, Mrs Green, who later became one of his followers, complained to the authorities, Brothers was admitted in September to the workhouse, where he had a small room which he was able to furnish with his own items. The workhouse board drew his pension for him and his debts were soon paid, and in February 1792 he took lodgings in Compton Street, Soho. The account, later published as *Anecdotes of Richard Brothers* (1795), by Joseph Moser, a member of the board who regularly visited him, indicates that the prophet was tall and handsome, mild and well bred, and far from being the typical religious enthusiast. He does not seem to have sought or courted an audience, but his apocalyptic perspective aroused interest. In letters to the British authorities he claimed that the French Revolution was a sign of God's judgment, and on 17 May 1792 he was prevented from entering the House of Commons, where he had hoped to explain his conviction that to support the French monarchy was to oppose the will of God.

In September, Brothers was again charged with non-payment of rent and this time he was committed for eight weeks to Newgate prison, where he might have starved had not a poor woman, Isabella Wake, brought him a threepenny loaf of bread each Monday morning. His release was secured only when he authorized, by power of attorney, the collection of his naval pension. Significantly, before signing the document, he struck out the title 'our Sovereign Lord', which he considered blasphemous when referred to George III. The appalling conditions in Newgate may have contributed to his growing conviction that the government rather than the people of Britain was the object of God's wrath. Whereas, in his earlier prophecies, he had compared the metropolis to Babylon on account of the sins of the people, London was now condemned as the capital of the king of England, whom Brothers likened to Belshazzar. On his release in November he briefly contemplated abandoning his prophetic calling and set out for Bristol, with the intention of emigrating, but after walking some 25 miles he felt himself turned about and promptly made his way back to London. From the beginning of 1793 Brothers was living at 57 Paddington Street, Marylebone, and had become seriously preoccupied with the destiny of the Jews and his own calling to be the one who would gather the tribes of Israel and lead them back to Palestine. In this connection he appropriated for himself the titles of Prince and Prophet of the Hebrews and Nephew of the Almighty, claiming descent from King David through James, the brother of Christ. This increasingly philosemitic element in his message may have been related to his growing contacts with members of the Avignon Society such as Peter Woulfe, William Bryan, and John Wright, and Swedenborgians such as William Sharp, whose engraving of Brothers (April 1795) was accompanied by the uncompromising rubric 'Richard Brothers, Prince of the Hebrews: Fully believing this to be the Man whom GOD has appointed, I engrave his likeness'. In 1794, at the expense of his supporter Captain Hanchett, Brothers's two-volume *Revealed Knowledge of the Prophecies and Times* was printed by the bookseller George Riebau who, like Hanchett, remained a faithful follower of Brothers until he died. It is clear from these volumes that when Brothers spoke of Israel he was largely concerned with the ten 'lost tribes', conceived by him as a spiritual community which included many British believers—a significant idea which was later incorporated into the teachings of the British Israelite movement. Brothers envisaged that the tribes of Israel would gather in 1795 in the midst of a world crisis during which George III would yield the throne to Brothers and a great exodus to Palestine would occur. Jerusalem would be rebuilt and the messianic rule of peace would begin in 1798.

Such apocalyptic imaginings might have passed unnoticed, except that they were couched in decidedly revolutionary language at a time when England was engaged in a not very successful war with the French Revolutionary armies. Brothers claimed to have successfully predicted the deaths of Gustavus III of Sweden (assassinated by Johan Ankarström on 29 March 1792) and Louis XVI (guillotined on 21 January 1793). In the context of a bitter winter, serious crop failures, and rising food prices, opposition to the war with France was widespread in 1795 and Brothers's prophecies gained a wide readership. In that year four editions of his *Revealed Knowledge of the Prophecies and Times* were published in London, one in Dublin, eighteen in the United States, and one in Paris. A considerable amount of space was also devoted to Brothers's prophecies in the British press. This was probably because of the vigorous defence of his views by Nathaniel Brassey Halhed, a Sanskrit scholar and member of the House of Commons, 1000 copies of whose *Testimonies to the Authenticity of the Prophecies and Mission of Richard Brothers* (1795) were distributed to his fellow MPs and other 'public personages'. Popular interest in Brothers and his prophecies was reflected in a variety of pamphlets attacking and defending him as well as in cartoons by Cruikshank and Gillray. The latter pictured Brothers, as a revolutionary sansculotte, with Charles James Fox and other opposition leaders in a sack on his back, trampling on the bodies of kings and leading a motley group of followers away from a burning London towards a gallows labelled 'Gate of Jerusalem'. A hostile account, scornfully describing Brothers as 'the Great Prophet of Paddington Street', appeared in *The Times* on 4 March, and the same day he was arrested by two king's messengers armed with a warrant from the duke of Portland. On his own admission, Brothers's examination before a committee of the privy council was courteous, but on 27 March, on medical advice, he was declared insane and confined as a criminal lunatic. According to the *Gentleman's Magazine* the reason for the intervention of the authorities was that Brothers's opinions had 'for several months alarmed and agitated the minds of the people (crowds of whom have resorted to him daily)' (*GM*, 1st ser., 65, 1795, 250). There are definite indications that Brothers's prediction of an earthquake on 4 June (the king's official birthday) was widely known and that many Londoners were apprehensive enough to contemplate leaving the metropolis. On 4 May, with the authorization of the lord chancellor, Brothers was moved to Fisher House, Islington, the private asylum of Samuel Foart Simmons. In 1797 he fell in love with the daughter of an Essex clergyman, Frances Cot, who had been placed in the asylum, but his feelings were not reciprocated and she soon left the institution and married another.

Although in the early years of the nineteenth century Brothers modified his criticism of the authorities and took a more conciliatory tone toward the king and his ministers, he did not entirely adopt the respectable conservatism of his rival Joanna Southcott. In his *Dissertation on the Fall of Eve* (1802) he made clear that he rejected her claims, but in spite of this several of his followers turned to her during Brothers's confinement. Curiously, the most faithful and energetic of his supporters was a Scottish lawyer, John Finlayson, who became active on Brothers's behalf only after his arrest. On learning of the prophet's misfortunes, Finlayson had given up his practice in Edinburgh and moved to London in 1797. At considerable personal expense he published some of Brothers's writings and arranged to have his plans for the New Jerusalem engraved and printed. In his *Revealed Knowledge* Brothers had claimed that, among the hidden Jews in the English

nation, William Pitt was specially marked by God to assist him in his mission, and it was only the prime minister's hostility that led to Brothers's subsequent assessment of him as a persecuting villain. With the death of Pitt in 1806 Finlayson approached the new prime minister, Lord Grenville, and a petition for Brothers's liberation was heard on 14 April before the chancellor Lord Erskine, who ordered his immediate release, though he could not quash the verdict of lunacy, apparently on account of the king's sensitivities in the matter. This meant that Brothers could not draw his half pay, though Finlayson claimed that the chancellor had promised him a government pension of £300 p.a. Ironically it was agreed that Brothers's half pay was to be paid to his wife. For a time Brothers lived with a friendly supporter named Busby, but in 1815 he moved to the Regent's Park home of Finlayson (who had changed his name to Finleyson on Brothers's prompting). During his last years, in addition to pursuing his interest in astronomy which led him to attack the Copernican view of a heliocentric universe, Brothers published *A Correct Account of the Invasion and Conquest of this Island by the Saxons* (1822), of which the object was further to establish the identity of the British with the lost tribes of Israel. He died on 25 January 1824 in Finleyson's house in Upper Baker Street, Marylebone, and was buried in the cemetery in St John's Wood. He died intestate and his widow obtained letters of administration on his estate, but by a chancery order Finleyson prevented her from retaining this right. Finleyson unsuccessfully continued to claim compensation from the government, though in 1830 he obtained the unappropriated balance of Brothers's pay.

TIMOTHY C. F. STUNT

Sources DNB · R. Brothers, *A revealed knowledge of the prophecies and times*, 2 vols. (1795) · J. Moser, *Anecdotes of Richard Brothers, in the years 1791 and 1792 with some thoughts on credulity* (1795) · C. Garrett, *Respectable folly: millenarians and the French Revolution in France and England* (1975), 179–223 · J. F. C. Harrison, *The second coming: popular millenarianism, 1780–1850* (1979), 57–85 · C. Roth, *Nephew of the Almighty* (1933) · G. R. Balleine, *Past finding out: the tragic story of Joanna Southcott and her successors* (1956), 27–36 · J. K. Hopkins, *A woman to deliver her people, Joanna Southcot and English millenarianism in an era of revolution* (1982), 177–86

Likenesses J. Chapman, stipple, pubd 1795, BM · W. Sharp, line engraving, pubd 1795, BM, NPG [*see illus.*] · Barlow, etching (after S. Collings), BM · I. Cruikshank, cartoon · Gillray, cartoon · G. Murray, line engraving (after I. Cruikshank), BM, NPG

Brotherton, Edward (1814–1866), educational reformer, was born at Manchester. He had at least two sisters, Martha and Elizabeth, and a brother, Joseph Hamilton Brotherton, all of whom settled in the United States. Early in life he entered the silk trade, and became a manufacturer. He wrote frequently as 'Libra' and 'Pilgrim' in Swedenborgian periodicals, to which his chief contribution was 'Outlines of my mental history', which appeared in the *Intellectual Repository* for 1849. In 1840 he had taken part in exposing a Mormon elder, James Malone, who claimed to possess a miraculous gift of tongues, and published in 1846 *Mormonism: its Rise and Progress, and the Prophet Joseph Smith*. His pamphlet *Spiritualism, Swedenborg, and the New*

Church (1860), which referred to the claims of the Revd Thomas Lake Harris to a seership similar to that of Swedenborg, identified Brotherton as a disciple of Swedenborg, with a tendency to belief in spiritualistic phenomena.

Foreseeing that the commercial treaty with France (1860) was likely to bring an end to the prosperity of the British silk industry, Brotherton retired and lived on private means with his wife, Elizabeth. They appear to have had no children. He was the editor and writer of the first volume of a monthly periodical, *The Dawn*, published in Manchester in 1861–2. After a year of continental travel he devoted himself to the work of popular education. Early in 1864 the letters of 'E. B.' in the *Manchester Guardian*, which exposed the deficiencies in educational provision for the poor in Manchester and Salford, led to the formation of the Manchester and Salford Education Aid Society, which gave assistance to all parents too poor to pay for the education of their children. Although the society, of which Brotherton was secretary, was well supported, it found, after two years' experience, that its attempts to subsidize the voluntary system were making little impact upon the scale of the problem. When the society's statistics were revealed in 1866, H. A. Bruce described them at a meeting of the Social Science Association as 'the thunderclap' from Manchester. For the society's experience proved that there was no practical alternative to a rate-aided national system of elementary education, and paved the way for the Education Act of 1870. In 1865 Brotherton made a codicil to his will, revoking a bequest he had made in 1861 to establish a school in Manchester, having been 'persuaded that public provision will be made for the education of the children of the poor before many years have elapsed'. In the course of his visitations among the poor he contracted typhus, of which he died, after a few days' illness, at his home in Chester Road, Hulme, Manchester on 23 March 1866. He was buried at the Wesleyan cemetery, Cheetham Hill.

W. E. A. AXON, *rev.* M. C. CURTHOYS

Sources *Manchester Guardian* (March 1866) · *The Recipient* (April 1860) · Boase, *Mod. Eng. biog.* · private information (1885) · S. E. Maltby, *Manchester and the movement for national elementary education, 1800–1870* (1918) · will, Principal Registry of the Family Division, London
Likenesses portrait, Manchester town hall
Wealth at death under £8000: probate, 30 May 1866, *CGPLA Eng. & Wales*

Brotherton, Edward Allen, Baron Brotherton (1856–1930), chemical manufacturer and philanthropist, was born on 1 April 1856 at 2 Tiverton Place, Ardwick Green, Manchester, the eldest of three children of Theophilus Brotherton, a yarn agent, and his wife, Sarah, *née* O'Donnell. His relatives included the educational reformer Edward Brotherton, and Joseph Brotherton, the first MP for Salford. At fourteen he made an abortive attempt to go to sea, returning after two days, when the ship put into Holyhead. He finally left school at the age of fifteen, and worked in a hardware store and as assistant in a chemical

Edward Allen Brotherton, Baron Brotherton (1856–1930), by Sir Benjamin Stone, 1902

laboratory. During this period he also attended Henry Roscoe's evening classes in chemistry at Owens College, Manchester. At the age of nineteen, he obtained a post at a chemical works in Wakefield.

In 1878 Brotherton became a partner in the firm of Dyson Bros. and Brotherton, based in Wakefield, which manufactured ammonium sulphate. Its activities typified Brotherton's approach to business, which, he later suggested, had always been to seek to develop the economic rather than the technical side of the chemical industry. The firm was not technically innovative, aiming rather to exploit the large supplies of ammoniacal liquor produced in the coal-gas industry. It was served by an extensive transportation network, which moved the ammoniacal liquor from gasworks in the surrounding towns to Wakefield, where it was processed on a large scale. Brotherton was both fortunate in business and a shrewd judge of opportunities. During the 1870s Brunner, Mond & Co. was established in Cheshire, manufacturing sodium carbonate by the Solvay process. This process required ammonia, and grew very rapidly late in the nineteenth century, as its product replaced Leblanc soda; Brotherton secured the contract to supply Brunner, Mond. He established other factories, on a similar basis to that at Wakefield, in several major conurbations. In 1881 Dyson Bros. and Brotherton became Brotherton & Co. It exploited other opportunities for the sale of ammonia, supplying the textile industry and becoming associated, through a chance contact between Sir George Beilby and Brotherton, with the Cassel Cyanide Company. This firm extracted gold using potassium cyanide, in the production of which ammonia was employed. Brotherton & Co., meanwhile, expanded into coal-tar distillation, and the treatment of its organic by-products. A range of primary and secondary coal-tar products was manufactured during the First World War—pitch, creosote, naphthalene, anthracene, TNT, and picric acid (an important explosive). Brotherton also purchased the Mersey Chemical Co., which had been German-owned, and extended his interests into the production of both inorganic materials (sulphur dioxide and oleum) and synthetic dyestuffs. His combination of business acumen and relative technical conservatism was highly successful, and in 1902, when his business interests were amalgamated and Brotherton & Co. became a limited company, it was said to be the largest private chemical company in the country. In 1924, on Beilby's death, Brotherton became chairman of Cassel.

Brotherton had many public interests outside his business. He was mayor of Wakefield (1902–3) and Leeds (1913–14), and sat as MP for Wakefield, as a coalition Unionist, from 1902 until 1910, and from 1918 until 1922. But it is as a benefactor of the University of Leeds that he is best remembered, through the university library, and a collection of manuscripts and books which carries his name. His bibliographic interests began in 1922, through the efforts of his niece by marriage, Dorothy Una Ratcliffe, to prevent the export to the USA of a medieval manuscript, the 'Towneley Mysteries', which contained a cycle of plays with Wakefield associations. Characteristically, Brotherton had the manuscript valued, and was unwilling to bid above the valuation when it came up for sale, so that his efforts were unsuccessful. Nevertheless the enterprise led him to begin a collection which eventually included 35,000 books, 400 manuscripts, 4000 deeds, and 30,000 letters, for the administration of which he employed a full-time librarian. Brotherton made a series of large donations to the University of Leeds. He endowed the chair of bacteriology in 1921, and in 1927 donated £100,000 towards the cost of a new university library. One of his last public acts, in June 1930, was to lay the foundation stone of the new library, when he announced that he was leaving his collection of books and manuscripts in trust to the university. When he died, later in the year, his will revealed that he had bequeathed the institution a further £100,000. The Brotherton Library, which was modelled internally on the British Museum reading-room, was completed in 1936. He made numerous other philanthropic donations, including £100,000 for the relief of poverty in Wakefield, as well as contributing £500,000 to the war loan fund.

Brotherton received many honours. In 1923 he was granted the honorary degree of LLD by the University of Leeds. He was honorary colonel of the 15th battalion, the West Yorkshire regiment (the 'Leeds Pals'), which he had raised and equipped, and which was later wiped out on the Somme. He was created baronet in 1918 and Baron Brotherton of Wakefield in 1929. He received the Messel medal of the Society of Chemical Industry, of which he was a founder member, in 1930.

Brotherton was of medium height, with vivid blue eyes and a heavy moustache, which gave him a somewhat Elgarian appearance. He was rarely without a carnation as a buttonhole and grew the blooms himself. He was said to drive a hard bargain, and once claimed never to have had a credit balance at his bankers: he could not sleep if he had, and preferred his banker to have the sleepless nights. In 1882 Brotherton married Jane Brookes, the daughter of the artist and designer Warwick Brookes. She died in childbirth in 1883, the child surviving only briefly. He did not remarry, and it is perhaps unsurprising that his niece described him as a 'lonely, self-contained man'. He chose as his heirs Charles Ratcliffe, his nephew, who later took the name Brotherton, and Dorothy Una Ratcliffe. He lived during his later years at Kirkham Hall, Yorkshire, and Roundhay Hall, Leeds, and died at Kirkham Hall on 21 October 1930. His burial, which was attended, at his stipulation, only by male members of his family, took place at Lawnswood cemetery, Leeds, on 24 October.

JAMES DONNELLY

Sources Lord Brotherton, *Fifty years in the chemical industry* (privately printed, Leeds, [1930]) · D. Cox, 'The Brotherton collection: its beginnings and development', *University of Leeds Review*, 28 (1985–6), 41–60 · *WWW* · *The Times* (22 Oct 1930) · *Yorkshire Post* (22 Oct 1930) · *Yorkshire Post* (23 Oct 1930) · U. Leeds, Brotherton L. · W. Cullen, 'The Brotherton memorial lecture', *Chemistry and Industry* (25 Dec 1948), 487–91 · Bryan, *Painters* (1930)

Archives U. Leeds, Brotherton L. | W. Yorks. AS, Leeds, Symington MSS

Likenesses B. Stone, photograph, 1902, NPG [*see illus.*] · E. Caldwell Spruce, bronze bust, 1914, U. Leeds, Brotherton L. · E. Caldwell Spruce, bronze medallion, 1914, U. Leeds, Brotherton L. · I. Méstrovic, bronze bust, *c*.1916, U. Leeds, Brotherton L. · R. Dick, marble medallion, 1935, U. Leeds, Brotherton L. · photographs, U. Leeds, Brotherton L.

Wealth at death £1,764,529 5*s*. 1*d*.: probate, 20 Nov 1930, *CGPLA Eng. & Wales*

Brotherton, Joseph (1783–1857), Bible Christian minister and politician, was born on 22 May 1783 at Whittington, near Chesterfield, Derbyshire, the son of John Brotherton (*d*. 1809), and his wife, Mary. John Brotherton, a one-time schoolmaster and exciseman, moved his family to Manchester in 1789, and established a cotton and silk mill in the area. Joseph worked with his father, receiving no formal education, and in 1802 he became a partner in the business. John Brotherton died in 1809 and Joseph went into partnership with his cousin William Harvey. He married William's sister, Martha (1781/2–1861), on 13 March 1806, and retired from the business in 1819 at the age of only thirty-six.

This allowed Brotherton to devote more time to his position as minister of the Bible Christian church, of which he had become a member in 1805. He was greatly influenced by William Cowherd, the founder of the sect, and became a minister following the latter's death in 1816. Brotherton was responsible for expanding the church's influence in a number of areas, including a day school for children, evening classes for workers, and the building of a lending library and reading-room. He became noted for philanthropy: in one famous episode he is said to have rescued the daughters of James Hargreaves, inventor of the re-elected five times, on two occasions (1847 and 1852) unopposed. He was a firm believer in economy, retrenchment, and education reforms. Throughout his political career he supported several radical causes: he championed the peace movement; promoted the cause of free, non-denominational elementary education espoused by the National Public Schools Association; opposed the death penalty; and gave full backing for the campaign supporting the abolition of slavery. Brotherton was one of the staunchest supporters of the campaign against the corn laws and he stood firm against all monopolies, especially the East India Company. His first major speech was in support of the 1833 Factory Act, while one of his most famous speeches was in support of the 1847 Ten Hours Act.

Brotherton died suddenly of a heart attack on an omnibus in Manchester on 7 January 1857. His funeral on 14 January was attended by 120 carriages. The procession lasted for two and a half hours. Most of the local shops closed for the day. He was buried at New Barnes municipal cemetery in Salford and in 1858 a statue was built by public subscription in Peel Park. It was inscribed with his famous reply to W. B. Fernand's slighting reference to the fortune that he had amassed in manufacturing, that his wealth was measured 'not so much in the largeness of his means as in the fewness of his wants'. A eulogy of him features in Samuel Smiles's *Self Help* (1859).

PETER SHAPELY

Sources D. F. Schafer, 'Brotherton, Joseph', *BDMBR*, vol. 2 · *WWBMP*, vol. 1 · E. O'Brien, *Eminent Salfordian* (1982) · A. Smith, *Salford sketches* (1976) · *Manchester Guardian*, various cuttings, Salford Local Studies Library · B. Harrison, *Drink and the Victorians: the temperance question in England, 1815–1872* (1971) · *Vegetarian Messenger*, 1 (1849) · *Library Association Record*, 59 (1957) · T. Crostly, *Lancashire poets and other literary sketches* (1897) · *IGI* · Boase, *Mod. Eng. biog.* · *DNB*

Archives Man. CL, Manchester Archives and Local Studies, commonplace book · Salford Archives Centre, scrapbooks | Bolton Central Library, corresp. with Robert Heywood

Likenesses S. W. Reynolds junior, mezzotint, pubd 1836, NPG [*see illus.*] · M. Noble, marble bust, 1856, Gawsworth Hall, Cheshire · M. Noble, lead statue, 1858, Peel Park, Salford · G. Hayter, group portrait, oils (*The House of Commons, 1833*), NPG · Maclure, lithograph, BM, NPG

Joseph Brotherton (1783–1857), by Samuel William Reynolds junior, pubd 1836

spinning jenny, from a life of poverty in Salford. Also, he openly subscribed to a fund for the victims of the Peterloo massacre of 1819. He continued to preach at the church until his death.

Brotherton was also actively involved in local politics and in a number of other voluntary causes. He was an overseer of the poor and a member of the Salford vestry, and in 1820 became a founder of the Manchester chamber of commerce. He also served as a member of the local volunteer corps and as a JP, and conducted a series of lengthy investigations into the Salford charities which led to the exposing of serious corruption and mismanagement. Other causes which he promoted included the incorporation of Salford, which was finally achieved in 1844. He conducted a long campaign in support of libraries and public spaces and was partly responsible for the establishment of Salford Public Library in 1850, which is generally cited as the first municipal free library in the country. His campaign for public spaces led to the establishment of Peel Park in Salford. He was a strong advocate of total abstinence and vegetarianism, two of the causes also promoted by William Cowherd. Brotherton believed that promoting free libraries was a way of offering an alternative to alcohol, and is thought to have written the first teetotal and vegetarian tracts. He was also a founder member and sometime president of the Vegetarian Society, founded in 1847.

Brotherton became Salford's first MP in 1832, and used parliament to promote many of his favoured causes. Although he was never regarded as a great speaker he was

Brotherton [Marshal], **Margaret**, *suo jure* duchess of Norfolk (*c*.1320–1399), magnate, was the eldest daughter and eventually sole heir of *Thomas of Brotherton, first earl of Norfolk (1300–1338), the eldest son of *Edward I from his second marriage, and Alice Hales (*d.* in or before 1330). Margaret married *c*.1335 John, Lord Seagrave (*d.* 1353), and Elizabeth, her second child, was born by 1338. Her eldest child, John, predeceased her. In 1338 she succeeded as coheir, with her sister Alice, to her share of the Brotherton estates, excepting her stepmother's dower—her only brother, Edward, had died in 1337. As a granddaughter of Edward I she received a huge jointure in Seagrave's estates. At some unknown date, possibly in 1350, Margaret set out for Rome in person to secure a divorce. Certainly in that year she was arrested for contravening a royal prohibition on travel. Widowed in April 1353, she remarried, probably in 1354, taking as her husband Sir Walter *Mauny (*c*.1310–1372), marshal of the king's Marshalsea, a long-standing servant of her father, who was over fifty and unmarried. For the couple's failure to secure a marriage licence Margaret's lands were seized, and on 6 June 1354 she and her husband were summoned to explain their contravention of the travel prohibition on 27 October 1350. Margaret was honourably imprisoned in Somerton Castle, Lincolnshire. The Brotherton estates had been restored to the couple on 30 May 1354, but how long Margaret was confined is unclear.

Margaret bore two more children: a son, Thomas, who was drowned in a well at Deptford, and a daughter, Anne, who married John *Hastings, thirteenth earl of Pembroke (d. 1375), and who also predeceased her, dying in 1384. Lord Mauny died in 1372 and for the following twenty-seven years Margaret remained a widow, chiefly preoccupied with the management of her Brotherton and Seagrave lands, to which for a time, in the minority of her Hastings grandson (another John, the fourteenth earl), were added some of the estates of the earls of Pembroke. With her share in her father's property, her Seagrave jointure, and a handsome portion of Lord Mauny's enormous war profits, Margaret was already wealthy when her niece, Joan Ufford, died, leaving no children, in 1375. Joan was the daughter of Margaret's sister, Alice, who married Edward, Lord Montagu, and when her husband, William *Ufford, second earl of Suffolk, died in 1382, the entire Brotherton inheritance was reunited in Margaret's hands. The following year her eldest grandchild and heir, John (IV) Mowbray, earl of Nottingham, died. With a dwindling family, she installed herself at Framlingham Castle, where she seems to have spent most of the rest of her life.

Margaret was an active and resourceful administrator of her property, though sometimes handicapped by problems of distance. In 1371 when the king complained of the neglect of the defences of her Irish lands, she gave the administration to her Pembroke son-in-law. In 1372 she similarly entrusted him with the lordship of Chepstow. Pembroke's death in 1375 forced Margaret to resume control. In 1377 she was ordered to see to Chepstow Castle's defences, and in 1388 she was reminded of her duty to see to the defences of Pembroke Castle, so long as she was its keeper. Between 1373 and 1390 she responded to attacks on her property by requesting commissions of oyer and terminer. In the 1370s there were frequent complaints of her failure to pay the annuities charged on the Hastings properties in her hands. In 1399 her executors were empowered to levy money from the estates to pay her servants, and in 1400 they paid £200 in compensation for oppressions by her and her officials. Margaret had a heightened sense of her own self-importance. She styled herself countess marshal, and by the 1370s the crown was addressing her as Margaret Marshal, even though her father's hereditary office of marshal of England had been granted to others. In 1377 she unsuccessfully claimed a hereditary right to perform the office by deputy at the coronation of Richard II. In 1382 she boldly petitioned the king for 3000 marks still outstanding from Edward I's endowment of her father, an unpaid debt of Edward II due

to her father, and the manor of Hampstead Marshall, which she had first claimed in 1347 and which was anciently annexed to the office of marshal. None of these claims was successful.

As Brotherton's only heir she claimed to be countess of Norfolk in her own right, although neither of her husbands was ever so styled. That the crown accepted the principle is borne out by her elevation from countess to duchess of Norfolk on 29 September 1397, on the same day that her grandson Thomas (I) Mowbray was created duke of Norfolk. Connections with her seem to have been sought and maintained by various members of the nobility, including John of Gaunt, duke of Lancaster, with whom she exchanged new year presents; Henry Bolingbroke, who for a time entrusted her with the upbringing of his son, John; Thomas Beauchamp, earl of Warwick, to whom she had presented a piece of the True Cross formerly belonging to Edward I; and Richard (III) Fitzalan, earl of Arundel, who, though no blood relative, remembered her in his will and called her 'my mother of Norfolk' (*Testamenta vetusta*, 1.130).

Margaret's rather lavish lifestyle is documented in her surviving accounts. Her annual income in the 1390s was almost £3000, though unlike some rich widows of the period she was not a great benefactor of religious houses. One substantial gift was to the Greyfriars, London, where she donated 350 marks for the new choir stalls, and where she chose to be buried. She died on 24 March 1399, at last clearing the way, in theory, for Thomas Mowbray to succeed her. In fact he was by then a political exile, and although he had letters of attorney allowing him to inherit during his absence, these were rescinded four days before the duchess died, and by the summer of 1399 her vast estates were in the hands of Richard II. The first Englishwoman to receive the title of duchess in her own right, Margaret Brotherton provides a striking example of the influence that a long-lived dowager could exert upon the fortunes of her kinsmen.

ROWENA E. ARCHER

Sources Chancery records · PRO · BL, Add Ch. 17208 · Coll. Arms, MS Arundel 49 · W. Sussex RO, Accession 939, II/A/1–17 · R. E. Archer, 'The estates and finances of Margaret of Brotherton, c.1320–1399', *Historical Research*, 60 (1987), 264–80 · F. Blomefield and C. Parkin, *An essay towards a topographical history of the county of Norfolk*, [2nd edn], 11 vols. (1805–10) · J. F. Marsh, *Annals of Chepstow Castle*, ed. J. Maclean (1883) · D. L. Evans, 'Walter de Mauny, sheriff of Merioneth, 1332–72', *Journal of the Merioneth Historical and Record Society*, 4 (1961–4), 194–203 · T. B. Pugh, ed., *The marcher lordships of south Wales, 1415–1536: select documents* (1963) · R. Hawes, *The history of Framlingham*, ed. R. Loder (1798) · G. F. Beltz, *Memorials of the most noble order of the Garter* (1841) · J. I. Catto, 'Religion and the English nobility in the later fourteenth century', *History and imagination: essays in honour of H. R. Trevor-Roper*, ed. H. Lloyd-Jones, V. Pearl, and B. Worden (1981), 43–53 · N. H. Nicolas, ed., *Testamenta vetusta: being illustrations from wills*, 2 vols. (1826) · *CIPM*, 11, no. 306 · C. L. Kingsford, *The Greyfriars of London* (1915)
Likenesses portrait, book of the benefactors of St Albans Abbey, Cotton MS, Nero DVII
Wealth at death £2839—from Segrave and Brotherton lands during 1394–5: Coll. Arms, MS Arundel 49

Brotherton, Sir Thomas William (1785–1868), army officer, the son of William Brotherton, was commissioned ensign without purchase in the Coldstream Guards on 24 January 1800. The following year he took part in the expedition to Egypt. Carrying the regimental colour under fire, he replied to the question, 'How do you feel, sir?' with 'Pretty well, but this is not very pleasant', and observed later: 'I would have died, of course, rather than let it [the colour] go' (Hamilton, 175–6). Brotherton purchased advance to lieutenant and captain (17 July 1801; in later editions of the *Army List*, 27 July), returned to England with the Coldstreams in December, and went on half pay from 25 December 1802. Shortly afterwards he secured a captaincy in the 53rd foot before moving to the 3rd guards as lieutenant and captain (3 December 1803).

Brotherton went to Hanover in November 1805 in Lord Cathcart's force, which soon returned to England without seeing action. Despite his service with Cathcart, Brotherton nominally attended the senior department of the Royal Military Academy from May 1805 to February 1807. In 1807 he transferred to the 6th foot (January), 21st light dragoons (March), and eventually the 14th light dragoons as a captain (4 June). Brotherton served in the Peninsula under Lieutenant-General Sir John Moore (1808–9) and Lieutenant-General Sir Arthur Wellesley (later first duke of Wellington; 1809–14). He fought at Talavera on 28 July 1809 and on the Coa on 24 July 1810. At Fort Concepcion, near Almeida, on 21 July 1810 he helped to delay French attackers long enough for British engineers to blow up the defences, and took part in the battle of Busaco on 27 September 1810. Of the many actions during the ensuing withdrawal towards Torres Vedras he enigmatically wrote that 'the Fourteenth had frequent opportunities of proving their valour' (Oats, 119). On 3 May 1811 he scouted ahead of Wellington's defensive position at Fuentes de Oñoro to engage enemy skirmishers, but during 'a sharp affair' near Sobraol on 14 October he inadvertently incurred a public rebuke from the brigade commander by taking the horse of his orderly, after putting a wounded officer on his own. Nevertheless, Brotherton became a brevet major (28 November 1811), then purchased a majority in the 3rd dragoon guards before exchanging into the 14th light dragoons once more (28 March 1812). During the advance towards Salamanca, in a skirmish on 14 June 1812, Brotherton injured his bridle hand, which temporarily prevented him from playing the fiddle. During a more general encounter on the Guarena River on 18 July he suffered a serious wound in his right side. Officially confined to bed, none the less he contrived to charge with Portuguese cavalry at Salamanca on 22 July and was wounded once more. Brotherton subsequently led his squadron at Vitoria (21 June 1813), during the battle of the Pyrenees (28–30 July 1813), at the Nivelle (10 November 1813), and across the Nive (11 December). Two days later, in his own words, after charging at Hasparren as 'a sort of forlorn hope … belaboured with cuts and thrusts on all sides' (Oats, 178), wounded in the neck, thigh, right side, and 'bottom', he finally surrendered when a blow split his helmet. An exchange was refused, and Brotherton remained a prisoner of war until the peace. After his release he obtained a brevet lieutenant-colonelcy on 19 May 1814. He

later described his time in the Peninsula as 'rough but glorious work' (*Colburn's United Service Magazine*, 1868, pt 1, 437). Strangely, he received no honorary award for his services, although he was appointed CB on 3 February 1817.

Brotherton became a lieutenant-colonel of the 12th lancers (22 October 1820), and went on half pay (24 May 1827), secured command of the 95th foot (15 June 1830), and advanced to colonel (20 July 1830). After returning to half pay (27 September 1831), he rejoined the active list as one of four lieutenant-colonels in the 16th lancers (10 February 1832), having been appointed commandant of the cavalry depot at Maidstone two days previously. Promoted major-general (23 November 1841), assigned to the staff of the northern district (17 August 1842), and having become inspecting-general of cavalry (1 January 1847), in April 1848 he deployed troops in London to deal with anticipated Chartist unrest. Brotherton was nominated colonel of the 15th hussars (18 May 1849), then of the 1st dragoon guards (17 July 1859), advancing to lieutenant-general (11 November 1851) and general (1 April 1860). He was made KCB (5 July 1855) and GCB (28 June 1861). Brotherton married his second wife, Thomasina, daughter of the Revd Walter Hore, at St Peter's Church, Pimlico, on 20 November 1865. He died near Esher on 20 January 1868, at the house of a son from his previous marriage; at his request, men from the 1st dragoon guards carried the coffin at his funeral.

Brotherton's exploits in the Peninsula marked his undoubted bravery and indifference to wounds, which sometimes resulted in lack of sympathy for others. He once dubbed a cornet 'rather a soft sort of fellow', only to find that 'he had good reason to complain, for the piece of shell had buried itself deep in his buttock, and caused his death' (Perrett, 15). A convivial companion and ready raconteur (several of whose anecdotes are printed in Wylly, 159–76), Brotherton did not forget former soldiers like the Coldstream Guards' Sergeant Stuckley, whom he regularly visited at Chelsea. In 1835 Colonel John Fox Burgoyne described him as 'a distinguished cavalry officer' (Wrottesley, 2.469).   JOHN SWEETMAN

Sources *Army List* · L. B. Oats, *Emperor's chambermaids: the story of the 14th/20th king's hussars* (1973) · B. Perrett, *The hawks: a short history of the 14th/20th king's hussars* (1984) · H. B. Hamilton, *Historical record of the 14th (king's) hussars*, 1 (1901) · P. F. Stewart, *The history of the XIIth royal lancers* (1950) · H. Graham, *History of the sixteenth, the queen's, light dragoons (lancers), 1759–1912* (privately printed, Devizes, 1912) · D. Mackinnon, *Origin and services of the Coldstream guards*, 2 (1833) · F. Maurice, *The history of the Scots guards, from the creation of the regiment to the eve of the Great War*, 1 (1934) · H. C. Wylly, *XVth (the king's) hussars, 1759 to 1913* (1914) · G. Wrottesley, *Life and correspondence of Field Marshal Sir John Fox Burgoyne*, 2 (1873) · *Colburn's United Service Magazine*, 1 (1868) · *Dod's Peerage*

Archives Bodl. Oxf., letters to Sir William Napier · NL Scot., letters to Sir George Brown

Wealth at death under £30,000: probate, 2 April 1868, *CGPLA Eng. & Wales*

Brough, Bennett Hooper (1860–1908), mining engineer, born at Clapham on 20 September 1860, was the elder son of John Cargill *Brough (1834–1872), FCS, librarian of the London Institution in Finsbury Circus, and his wife, Mary Elizabeth, *née* Kidd (d. 1867). He was the nephew of Robert

Barnabas *Brough, William *Brough [see under Brough, Robert Barnabas], and Lionel *Brough. His father died when he was twelve, but with the aid of funds raised by friends, Bennett was sent to the City of London School. From there he went in 1878 to the Royal School of Mines, of which he became an associate in 1881. The following year was spent at the Royal Prussian Mining Academy at Clausthal in the Harz. In 1882 Brough was appointed assistant to Sir Warrington W. Smyth, professor of mining at the Royal School of Mines, and in 1886 he started at the school a course in mine surveying, which proved a great success. His Treatise on Mine Surveying, first published in 1888, became a standard textbook, and ran to at least seventeen editions. He was also the author of numerous papers on mining and metallurgy. From 1883 to 1893 he was co-editor of the Journal of the Iron and Steel Institute, and in 1893 became secretary of that institute, a post he held until his death. His services were constantly in demand as abstractor, writer, lecturer, and juror on mining subjects. Brough was elected a fellow of the Geological Society and was on the governing bodies of the Institute of Chemistry, the Chemical Society, and the Institute of Secretaries. He was also a knight of the Swedish order of Vasa.

In 1895 Brough married Barbara Lloyd (whose barrister father had been murdered near Athens in 1870); they had a son and a daughter. On 1 October 1908, while at Middlesbrough for a meeting of the Iron and Steel Institute, Brough was suddenly taken ill; he died at a nursing home, Gresham House, Ellison Place, at Newcastle upon Tyne, two days later, and was buried in the Surbiton and Kingston cemetery. ERNEST CLARKE, rev. ROBERT BROWN

Sources Journal of the Iron and Steel Institute, 78 (1908), 462–3 · D. A. Louis, JCS, 95 (1909), 2202–4 · private information (1912) · G. H. Safford, Who's who in mining and metallurgy (1908)

Wealth at death £3271 6s. 7d.: probate, 2 Dec 1908, CGPLA Eng. & Wales

Brough, John Cargill (1834–1872), science journalist, was born at Pontypool on 11 February 1834, the youngest son of Barnabas Brough (d. 1854), a brewer and wine merchant, and his wife, Frances, née Whiteside. His brothers, William *Brough [see under Brough, Robert Barnabas], Robert Barnabas *Brough, and Lionel *Brough, became well known in literary and dramatic circles, their sense of humour being clearly inherited from their father, who also wrote for the music-halls. In 1839–40 his father gave evidence for the crown at the trial of the Chartist leader John Frost. As a result the family was ostracized and in 1843 moved first to Manchester, where Brough attended the grammar school, and then to London, where his father found work on the Illustrated London News and Brough joined him as an office boy. In 1852 he became a clerk in the audit office of the South Western Railway Company, and began to study science at evening classes in the company's mechanics' institute, of which he became secretary and librarian. Here he also learned the art of popular lecturing.

In 1857, following his marriage to Mary Elizabeth Kidd of Clapham on 24 September 1856, Brough resigned his clerkship to devote himself to freelance journalism, joining his bohemian brothers in the Savage Club and the Grub Street circle described in G. L. M. Strauss's Reminiscences (1882). In 1859 he published a children's book, Fairy Tales of Science. In 1864 he edited and wrote technical articles for Arnold Cooley's Cyclopaedia of Practical Receipts, and contributed to Strauss's English Workshops. In 1860 he had become editor of The Ironmonger and of the Chemist and Druggist. He transformed the latter from a monthly trade journal into a chemical and pharmaceutical journal respected by the scientific community. Brough's growing interest in chemistry inspired him to launch the weekly Laboratory in April 1867 in direct competition with W. Crookes's Chemical News. It was not a commercial success and closed after six months, but its skilful mix of news, comment, and original scientific communications made it a model for Norman Lockyer's Nature two years later.

In 1864 Brough was elected to the Chemical Society, where he became renowned for his sociability and sense of humour. He was the principal poetaster of a group of convivial chemists, the B Club, and with others compiled the comic brochure Exeter Change for the British Association meeting at Exeter in 1869. In 1870 he joined the comedian Thomas Archer in writing the drawing-room comedy An Eligible Situation. For some months in 1869–70 he was a sub-editor for Nature, but rheumatic fever forced his resignation, as well as the abandonment of his two editorships. In 1870, through the kindness of friends, he was appointed lecturer, librarian, and superintendent of the London Institution in Finsbury Circus. His wife died in childbirth in 1867. Brough died of a 'disease of the heart' at Esher on 7 September 1872, leaving his three children, one of whom was the mining engineer Bennett Hooper *Brough, and an adopted orphan nephew and niece destitute. He was buried at Norwood cemetery on 12 September. It was a mark of the affection and high regard in which he was held by his peers that an international appeal to secure the children's education raised £2000. Likened by his contemporaries to Charles Lamb, Brough possessed a shrewd intellect, untapped scientific abilities, and a gentle sense of humour that endeared him to scientific and literary friends alike. W. H. BROCK

Sources Chemist and Druggist (14 Sept 1872), 305–6 · Chemist and Druggist (15 Oct 1872), 340–43 · Berichte der Deutschen Chemischen Gesellschaft, 5 (1872), 885 · G. L. M. Strauss, Reminiscences of an old bohemian, 2 vols. (1882) · W. H. Brock, 'J. C. Brough', Development of scientific publishing in Europe, ed. A. J. Meadows (1980), 115–18 · m. cert. · d. cert.

Likenesses lithograph, repro. in Chemist and Druggist (15 Oct 1872)

Wealth at death died destitute

Brough, Lionel (1836–1909), actor, born at Pontypool, Monmouthshire, on 10 March 1836, was the youngest of the four children (all sons) of Barnabas Brough (d. 1854) and his wife, Frances, née Whiteside. Barnabas Brough was a brewer and wine merchant, of tory principles, who suffered financially through political persecution, and, late in life, wrote plays under the pseudonym of Barnard de

Burgh. Lionel's brothers, William *Brough (1826–1870) [see under Brough, Robert Barnabas], Robert Barnabas *Brough (1828–1860), and John Cargill *Brough (1834–1872), all won some literary distinction.

Brough was educated at Manchester grammar school and at Williams's private academy in London, but when aged about twelve was compelled by the family's impoverishment to start life as an errand-boy in the editorial offices of the *Illustrated London News*. On 26 December 1854 he made his first appearance on the stage, at the Lyceum Theatre under Madame Vestris and Charles Mathews, as Count Carboniferous in his brother William's extravaganza *Prince Pretty Pet and the Butterfly*. Six months later he withdrew from the stage to become assistant publisher to the *Daily Telegraph* on its establishment, and in that position originated the custom of selling newspapers on the streets, by organizing a staff of 240 boys for the purpose. In 1858 he again returned to the theatre, and appeared at the Lyceum under the name Lionel Porter in Robert Brough's extravaganza *The Siege of Troy* and in Falconer's *Francesca*. But he soon left the stage to fill for some three years a commercial position on the staff of the *Morning Star*. On 12 July 1862 he married Margaret Rose Simpson, who was not connected with the theatrical profession. They had four children, Mary, Sydney, Percy, and Margaret, all of whom later took to the stage. Also in 1862 Brough began giving monologue entertainments in the Polytechnic Institution in Regent Street, and the following year he introduced to the provinces the spectral illusion known as 'Pepper's ghost'.

Late in 1863 Brough visited Liverpool with other members of the Savage Club to give a dramatic performance on behalf of the Lancashire famine relief fund. Struck by his abilities, Alexander Henderson, the manager of the local Prince of Wales's Theatre, offered him an engagement. In February 1864 Brough seriously adopted at Liverpool the profession of an actor. He remained at the Prince of Wales's for over two years, and was seen there in May 1865 as the original John Chodd junior in T. W. Robertson's *School* and on Whit Monday 1866 as Castor to the Oenone of Henry Irving in F. C. Burnand's extravaganza *Paris*.

Brough reappeared in London in October 1867, on the opening of the new Queen's Theatre, Long Acre, when he was the original Dard in Charles Reade's *The Double Marriage*. But it was not until the production of H. J. Byron's *Dearer than Life*, in January 1868, that his ability became recognized. His acting as the old reprobate Ben Garner was marked by both power and finish. In October 1869, when Mrs John Wood (Matilda Charlotte Vining) opened the St James's Theatre with a revival of *She Stoops to Conquer*, Brough played Tony Lumpkin for close on 200 nights. Thenceforth he was the accepted representative of the character, which he played in all 777 times. Later at the St James's he gave a droll performance of Paul Pry, which proved popular.

In March 1872 Brough, although he was no trained singer, joined C. T. Fell at the Holborn Theatre to sustain prominent parts in *La vie parisienne* and other light musical pieces. The following August he appeared at Covent Garden in Boucicault and Planché's fantastic spectacle *Babil and Bijou*, an elaborate production which he was engaged to superintend. In April 1873 he became principal low comedian at the Gaiety Theatre under John Hollingshead, but in 1874 he transferred his services to the Globe. At the Charing Cross Theatre (afterwards the Folly and Toole's) in the same year he played the title character in H. B. Farnie's extravaganza *Blue Beard* (originally produced in America), and by his ample comic invention materially contributed to the great success of an indifferent production.

In April 1879 Brough joined the company of Marie Litton at the Imperial Theatre, Westminster, as 'first low comedian', and appeared as Claude Melnotte in Younge's burlesque of *The Lady of Lyons*. Subsequently he gave a number of excellent old comedy characterizations, his Tony Lumpkin and his Croaker in Goldsmith's *The Good-Natured Man* being especially commended. He also appeared as Touchstone in *As You Like It*.

In June 1881 Brough returned to Liverpool, to play Dromio of Ephesus in *The Comedy of Errors* at the Alexandra. In September he appeared at the Theatre Royal, Brighton, as Laurent XVII in the first English performance of Audran's comic opera *La Mascotte*; he played the part in London for the first time in October 1881 at the opening of the new Royal Comedy Theatre. In May 1884 he played Bob Acres in the Haymarket revival of *The Rivals*, and in September he became joint lessee with Willie Edouin of Toole's Theatre (formerly the Folly). The opening bill presented Paulton's burlesque *The Babes*, which, with Brough as Bill Booty, ran for 100 nights. In 1886 Brough went with the Violet Cameron company to America, where he played in *opéra bouffe*. After returning to England early in 1887, he appeared that spring in a round of old comedies with Kate Vaughan at the Opera Comique.

Later Brough paid a visit to South Africa, and performed there in all the principal towns in a repertory of thirty-eight pieces. Following his return to London, he reappeared at the Lyric in October 1890 in Audran's comic opera *La cigale*. In 1894 he joined Herbert Beerbohm Tree's company, with which he remained associated, with slight intermissions, until his death. Among the parts played by him during this period were Picolet in Robert Buchanan's adaptation *A Man's Shadow* (1897), Sir Toby Belch in *Twelfth Night* (1901), and Trinculo in *The Tempest* (1904). On 15 June 1905 his stage jubilee was celebrated at His Majesty's by a testimonial performance in his honour. Here, too, he made his last appearance on the stage, in April 1909, as Moses in *The School for Scandal*.

Brough had little capacity for interpreting character, and obtained his effects mainly by simple drollery. He died on 8 November 1909 at Percy Villa, South Lambeth, where he had lived for a long time. His wife had already died, on 19 May 1901. Only two of his children, Mary and Sydney, survived him. Sydney died in 1911 but Mary Brough went on to have an extensive career on stage and appeared in some films. She died in 1934.

NILANJANA BANERJI

Sources *The Tatler* (10 July 1901) • Adams, *Drama* • C. E. Pascoe, ed., *The dramatic list* (1879); 2nd edn (1880) • E. Reid and H. Compton, eds., *The dramatic peerage* [1891]; rev. edn [1892] • B. Hunt and J. Parker, eds., *The green room book, or, Who's who on the stage* (1906–9) • *Era Almanack and Annual* (1902) • E. D. Cook, *Nights at the play* (1883) • Hall, *Dramatic ports.* • M. Morris, *Essays in theatrical criticism* (1882) • J. Hollingshead, *My lifetime*, 2 vols. (1895) • J. Hollingshead, *Gaiety chronicles* (1898) • personal knowledge (1912) [*DNB*] • private information (1912) • d. cert.

Likenesses Lock & Whitfield, carte-de-visite, *c.*1876, NPG • J. Macbeth, crayon drawing, exh. 1897 • C. Buchel, oils, *c.*1905 (as Verges in *Much ado about nothing*), Museum of London • L. Besche, gouache drawing (as the Commodore), NPG • L. Besche, watercolour drawing, NPG • H. Furniss, caricature, pen-and-ink drawing, NPG • Haines, postcard, NPG • Spy [L. Ward], chromolithograph caricature, NPG; repro. in *VF* (30 March 1905) • St James's Photographic Co., photograph, NPG; repro. in *The Theatre* (1884) • T. C. Turner, photogravure, NPG • caricature, repro. in *Entr'acte* (14 July 1877) • lithograph, NPG • oils (with Toole)

Wealth at death £2572 17*s.* 10*d.*: resworn probate, 15 Jan 1910, *CGPLA Eng. & Wales*

Brough, Peter Royce (1916–1999), ventriloquist, was born Royce Brough on 26 February 1916 at Myrtle Villa, Sterne Street, Hammersmith, London, the son of Arthur Brough, ventriloquist and woollen merchant's buyer, and his wife, Louie Jarram. He came from a family long attached to ventriloquism. It was a hobby for his grandfather, and for his father a part-time business, as Arthur Brough and his dummy, Tim, were well-known figures in the music halls. Although Brough senior never abandoned his day job with Jaeger, he was a master of the ventriloquist's art; and it was his Tim that was used by Michael Redgrave, playing a deranged ventriloquist, in Alberto Cavalcanti's horror film *Dead of Night* (1945).

After leaving school at sixteen Peter Brough (as he was later known) became a junior apprentice at William Whiteleys, the department store. He moved on to work for one of the best tailoring firms in the West End; but he and his father, ambitious commercially, acquired their own clothing shop in Dover Street, and in 1939 set up a flourishing textile agency. In the following year he married Peggy Mary (*b.* 1915/16), daughter of Temple Franklin; they had a son and a daughter. He then served for a short time in the armed forces, before being invalided out with lung trouble.

Brough returned not only to his business interests, but also to his 'act'. He had been coached as a boy by his father, and often practised in front of a big mirror. Being self-employed he was free to perform, and his first serious engagement as a ventriloquist with his dummy, Jimmy, came in December 1938, for a week's music hall at the New Theatre, Oxford. Other performances followed, and he was on the bill of the Golders Green Hippodrome one night when a friend of his, the theatrical agent Walter Ridley, was present. The latter's analysis of his performance was damning: 'Your act is old-fashioned. Your patter is weak. And your dummy—that's atrocious' (Brough, 40).

Realizing that he had to rethink his act, Brough sought a new voice. He later recalled how one came to him while he was walking across Brora Sands in Scotland: 'The thin, cheeky treble of a boy of fourteen or so' (Brough, 42). He and Ridley then sketched out several possible faces for the

dummy; and from these Len Insull, a well-known Streatham craftsman, produced four papier-mâché masks. For £150 a complete figure was then conceived.

The ventriloquist's dummy that emerged was striking: contemporaries commented on its manic eyes, heavy make-up, and garishly striped blazer and scarf. Ted Kavanagh, scriptwriter of *It's That Man Again*, dubbed him Archie Andrews and the name stuck. The new partnership—and the patter—was effective with audiences, and the duo began to be booked with such high-profile performers as Joe Loss and his orchestra, and the Crazy Gang. Their first big break, however, began with a guest appearance on radio. This was in a BBC magazine programme *Navy Mixture*, scripted by Ted Kavanagh and Sid Colin, which had begun in 1943. Brough and Archie were a success and got a regular spot: 'Archie takes the helm'.

The scriptwriters were keen to base a radio comedy programme around Archie, but had to contend with the view of BBC producers that 'Archie would never be strong enough in character to sustain the chief role in a comedy series' (Brough, 64). Yet the idea for such a programme—deceptively simple—was finally sold to the BBC in 1949: 'Archie was a boy—the epitome of mischievous boyhood. Boys go to school. Well, let Archie be educated. So we arrived at the title of our show' (ibid., 78). The producer wrote that 'We see Archie as a boy in his middle teens, naughty but lovable, rather too grown up for his years, especially where the ladies are concerned, and distinctly cheeky' (*The Independent*).

First broadcast on 6 June 1950, *Educating Archie* was a runaway success. The words to the signature tune of the series wonderfully captured the comic spirit:

> We'll be educating Archie
> What a job for anyone
> He's no good at spelling
> He hasn't a clue
> He thinks that three sevens make twenty-two.
> (*The Independent*, 7 June 1999)

Supporting roles were played by a succession of young actors who became stars of television comedy in their own right. Tony Hancock as the teacher memorably let off steam about 'flippin' kids'. Max Bygraves was also hugely popular as Bob, the odd-job man, who had such idiotic, but endearing, catchphrases as 'I've arrived, and to prove it, I'm here' as well as 'That's a good idea—*son*'. Those involved in later series of *Educating Archie* included Hattie Jacques, Harry Secombe, Beryl Reid, Dick Emery, and Gilbert Harding; and in the original series a musical interlude was provided by the thirteen-year-old Julie Andrews.

At the height of its radio success the programme was attracting audiences of 15 million a week, and in October 1950 it won the silver mike, the top variety award, sponsored by the *Daily Mail*. For a time Brough was the BBC's highest-paid entertainer. The format—and Archie—proved surprisingly adaptable, transferring to an independent television series in 1958. The image of Archie, shrewdly managed by Brough, appeared on all kinds of objects—there were even Archie Andrews ice lollipops—

and a children's fan club dedicated to him had over 250,000 members.

The myth of Archie's real existence was also astutely cultivated by Brough, not least in his autobiography, *Educating Archie*, published in 1958. Well-known actresses were happy to pose for photographs of them dancing with Archie; and the Inland Revenue once addressed a tax return to him (no doubt as a joke). Archie's disappearance from the luggage van of a train in October 1951 led to a storm of media speculation. He was eventually found in the left luggage department of King's Cross railway station—suffering, as Brough later recounted, 'from a slight memory loss as to exactly what had happened' (Vox, 112). He could not be recast, as the moulds were destroyed by enemy bombs in the Second World War. Although there only ever was one Archie, he and Brough were reproduced in wax and put on display at Madame Tussaud's.

Archie's broadcasting career finally ended in 1960. Although officially retired, Brough and Archie continued to appear at charity performances, and at special Christmas shows at Windsor Castle (where they were especial favourites of the royal family). Brough nevertheless continued to run his textile interests; and these no doubt benefited from Archie's legacy, as merchandising deals were said to be bringing in at least £5000 a year in the early 1950s. Brough's first marriage had ended in divorce, and he was later married to Elizabeth Chantler (d. 1994), with whom he had another son and a daughter.

Noted for his charm and professionalism, Peter Brough had, like all ventriloquists, to endure carping criticism of his skill in voice projection. No less a figure than Beryl Reid, asked whether she could see his lips moving, rather unkindly replied, 'Only when Archie's talking' (*The Scotsman*, 7 June 1999). Yet in Brough's case it did not really matter, for he was one of those curious creatures, a *radio* ventriloquist; and by giving voice and vigour to Archie Andrews he created one of the great personalities of post-war British radio comedy. He died on 3 June 1999 at Mount Vernon Hospital, Northwood, Hillingdon.

ROBERT BROWN

Sources P. Brough, *Educating Archie* (1953) · V. Vox, *I can see your lips moving: the history of ventriloquism* (1981) · *The Independent* (7 June 1999) · *The Times* (5 June 1999) · *The Scotsman* (7 June 1999) · *Daily Telegraph* (5 June 1999) · S. Connor, *Dumbstruck: a cultural history of ventriloquism* (2000) · b. cert. · m. cert. · d. cert. · CGPLA Eng. & Wales (1999)

Likenesses photographs, Hult. Arch.

Wealth at death under £200,000—gross; under £5000—net: probate, 21 Dec 1999, CGPLA Eng. & Wales

Brough, Robert Barnabas (1828–1860), playwright, journalist, and poet, was born in London on 10 April 1828, one of the four sons of Barnabas Brough (d. 1854), a brewer and wine merchant; his mother, under her maiden name of Frances Whiteside, had gained some popularity as a poet. His brother, **William Brough** (1826–1870), also a playwright, was born on 28 April 1826; the other brothers were John Cargill *Brough (1834–1872), a writer on science, and Lionel *Brough (1836–1909), a comic actor. The family

soon moved to Pontypool in Monmouthshire, and Robert Brough was educated at a private school in Newport; this basic education was later supplemented by his own study, and he acquired knowledge of several languages. In 1843 the family moved to Manchester where Robert began work as a clerk. William Brough, also educated at Newport, had begun his working life as an apprentice to a printer at Brecon.

Robert Brough's literary career began in 1847 when he established a new journal in Liverpool, the *Liverpool Lion*, a local version of *Punch*, for which he produced satiric articles and drawings, and to which his brother William also contributed. In 1848 he collaborated with William in writing their first burlesque play, *The Enchanted Isle*, which was first staged in Liverpool and moved on to the Adelphi in London. Thereafter based in London, Robert quickly made a name for himself writing burlesques for a number of leading theatres. These included *Medea* (1856) and *Masaniello* (1857); among many written in collaboration with William were *The Sphinx* (1849) and *The Last Edition of Ivanhoe* (1850). Robert and William married respectively Elizabeth and Ann Romer; Ann died one year after her marriage, and William Brough subsequently remarried.

In London, Robert Brough's income also came from work for journals. His essays and poems demonstrate his versatility as a writer and parodist. The journals he contributed to included *The Man in the Moon*, *Diogenes*, *Comic Times*, *The Train*, and *Household Words*, and he was for a time Brussels correspondent of the *Sunday Times*. He edited the *Atlas* briefly, and was editor of the *Welcome Guest* from 1859. His translations of poetry, particularly those of Victor Hugo's work, which appeared in *The Train*, were much praised. His incomplete novel, *Marston Lynch*, also first appeared in *The Train*. It was published posthumously in 1860 with a memoir by G. A. Sala. The claim that the work was autobiographical was denied by his brother John Cargill Brough in the *Critic* of August 1860. His other published works included *Shadow and Substance* (1859), illustrated by C. H. Bennett, *Our Miscellany*, with Edmund Yates (1856), *Lady Goodchild's Fairy Ring* (1860), and *Which is Which?* (1860).

While his plays and journalism were admired for their wit and fancy, it was the glimpses of the serious vein in Robert Brough's work that earned him most lasting admiration. Foremost among these were *Songs of the Governing Classes*, published in 1855 during the Crimean War. Ignoring the patriotic fervour of the time, Brough took advantage of the criticism of the handling of the war to launch an attack on the hypocrisy and inadequacy of the ruling class through satiric portraits of fictional aristocratic figures. The book was dedicated to Edward M. Whitty whose satirical essays, *The Governing Classes of Great Britain*, had appeared in 1854. In the preface Brough claimed the inspiration for the work lay in 'a deeply-rooted belief that to the institution of aristocracy in this country ... is mainly attributable all the political injustice ... we have to deplore' (rev. edn, 1890, xi). Edmund Yates (1831–1894), while admiring the poetry, was disturbed by the sentiments, which he considered to be 'dangerous and uncalled for' (Yates, 1.316).

Brough's circle of friends embraced many leading figures among those journalists and dramatists who had struggled up without a university education. In these 'bohemian' circles he was popular for his good-humour and kindness. He was a founder member of the Savage Club (1857) and its president at his death, and involved in many benefit performances to support the families of deceased writers and numerous working-class causes. His health was never strong and the difficulties of an author's life took their toll. He died at 8 Boundary Street, Hulme, near Manchester, on 26 June 1860. William Brough subsequently wrote several more burlesques after his brother's death, in collaboration with Andrew Halliday; he died on 13 March 1870 at his home, 37 Maitland Park Road, Haverstock Hill, London.

Robert Brough had not been able to provide for his widow and three children, but a benefit performance was arranged by the Savage Club, in co-operation with five leading London theatres, to establish a fund for them, with Charles Dickens as a trustee. Brough's daughter Fanny was a popular comic actress.   CYNTHIA DERELI

Sources *DNB* · G. A. Sala, *Welcome Guest*, new ser., 2/44 (1860), 348–50 · E. H. Yates, *Edmund Yates: his recollections and experiences*, 2 vols. (1884) · J. H. Ingram, 'Eliza Cook', *The Victorian poets: the bio-critical introductions to the Victorian poets from A. H. Miles's 'The poets and poetry of the nineteenth century'*, ed. W. E. Fredeman, 1 (New York, 1986), 269–72 · G. L. M. Strauss, *Reminiscences of an old bohemian*, 2 vols. (1882) · *The life and adventures of George Augustus Sala*, 2 vols. (1895); repr. in 1 vol. (1896) · A. Lohrli, ed., *Household Words: a weekly journal conducted by Charles Dickens* (1973) · R. Strauss, *Sala: the portrait of an eminent Victorian* (1942) · *The Critic* (30 June 1860), 797 · *The Critic* (10 March 1860), 300 · *The Critic* (2 June 1860), 682 · *The Critic* (7 July 1860), 5 · *The Critic* (14 July 1860), 37 · *The Critic* (4 Aug 1860), 136 · *The Examiner* (28 July 1860), 470 · d. cert. · *Illustrated Times* (14 July 1860), 27 · *John Bull* (30 June 1860) · *Liverpool Journal* (30 June 1860) · *Liverpool Mail* (30 June 1860), 7 · *Porcupine* (19 March 1870), 497 · *Saturday analyst and leader* (21 July 1860), 677 · *ILN* (6 March 1851), 178

Likenesses H. Watkins, photograph, repro. in G. A. Sala, *Welcome Guest*, 350 · portrait, repro. in R. B. Brough, *The songs of the governing classes* (1890), frontispiece

Wealth at death under £1500—William Brough: probate, 1870

Brough, Robert John Cameron (1872–1905), portrait painter, was born on 20 March 1872 at Garty Cottage, Kilmuir Easter, near Invergordon, the son of Helen Brough, formerly lady's maid to the duchess of Hamilton, and John Cameron, coachman to the Hamiltons. Brough was brought up by maternal relatives on a farm near Aberdeen, and attended school at Ruthrieston until 1884 when he was apprenticed until 1890/1891 as an engraver with Andrew Gibb & Co., Aberdeen. Gibb was a notable architectural draughtsman. Sir George Reid, also formerly an apprentice of Gibb's, later gave Brough access to study his collection of contemporary pictures. Despite working at least fifty-two hours a week, Brough attended evening classes at Gray's School of Art, Aberdeen, from 1885. In 1891 he was accepted by the Royal Scottish Academy life school at Edinburgh, where he won a bursary and two

other awards. His second year there was followed by summer attendance with a fellow pupil, Samuel John Peploe, at the atelier of Rodolphe Julian in Paris where the visiting teachers included Joseph Benjamin Constant, Jean Paul Laurens, and Adolphe William Bougereau.

Although Brough's earliest surviving work is a self-portrait his dashing sketches of Paris streets, rural subjects in Aberdeenshire, Moray, or Brittany, and bathers swimming from rowing boats in small French harbours testify to the variety of his early work. Two commissions in 1892 and 1893 made Brough's name and indicated the direction his later work was to take. William Dallas Ross, afterwards editor of *Black and White*, who had known Brough in Aberdeen, commissioned a portrait of his daughter Mary (McManus Art Gallery, Dundee). Brough's portrait succeeded in catching the young girl in an impatient pose. Her father was so pleased with it that he also sat to Brough. Brough's portrait (National Gallery of Scotland, Edinburgh) shows his patron, in monocle, stiff white shirt and tie, resplendent cloak with exaggerated collar, and an incongruous cigarette, the smoke from which curls and twists slowly above the startled sitter, who assumes an air of sang-froid. A succession of brilliant portraits followed, each a response to the moment. Brough no longer painted quick sketches in the open air, but took the time to produce studio portraits. With a rich palette his brush touches and twists on the canvas with an uncanny simplicity, repeating his sitters' opulent dress and interiors, as in, for example, the portrait of Theodora Crombie (Aberdeen Art Gallery). This and others were painted in Aberdeen, to which he had returned in 1894, contributing also lithographic pictures to the local illustrated journals the *Scottish Figaro* and *Bon Accord*. In 1897 he took an expensive studio in Tite Street, Chelsea, London, near that of Sir John Sargent whose friend and protégé he became. The exhibition of his captivating *Fantasie en folie* (Tate collection) enhanced his reputation. With more and more commissions, however, Brough became careless. But the value of his estate at death—over £9000—is some indication of his success.

In appearance Brough was tall, of regular build, his hair cut conventionally short, suggesting more a banker than an artist. In his self-portrait of 1889 he wears a no-nonsense jacket, collar, and tie, but three years later he is pictured with loose collar and spotted tie, striped jacket and thin waistcoat, spats, and tackety boots. At the height of his success, he wore well-cut clothes including top hats and checked tweeds of his own design. He did not marry, but a daughter born to a friend's wife in London in 1903 was openly acknowledged as his child.

In 1904 Brough travelled to Morocco, where his palette was again turned on landscapes and busy figure scenes. Early the next year he was returning to London from Scotland by a night express when it collided with a Yorkshire mail train in a sudden mist. Badly burned in the consequent fire, he died the next day, 21 January 1905, at the Royal Hospital, Sheffield. He was buried at Old Machar, Aberdeen. Brough's 'style was both powerful and original, uniting simplicity with breadth of treatment ... His portraits are remarkable alike for their richness of colour and virility of draughtsmanship' (*DNB*). W. T. JOHNSTON

Sources E. Pinnington, 'Robert Brough, painter', *Art Journal*, new ser., 18 (1898), 146–9 · *The Times* (23 Jan 1905) · *Dundee Advertiser* (23 Jan 1905) · *The Scotsman* (23 Jan 1905) · *Glasgow Herald* (23 Jan 1905) · *Aberdeen Free Press* (27–8 Jan 1905) · *Exhibition of pictures and sketches by Robert Brough A.R.S.A.* (1907) [exhibition catalogue, Burlington Fine Arts Club, London] · 'Brough, Robert', *Encyclopaedia Britannica*, 11th edn (1910–11) · *DNB* · B. C. Skinner, *Hopetoun House: the Scottish home of the marquess of Linlithgow* (1970), 3 · J. Melville, *Robert Brough ARSA, 1872–1905* (1995) [exhibition catalogue, Aberdeen City Council, Arts & Recreation Division, Aberdeen, 1995] · K. G. Hay, 'Brough, Robert', *The dictionary of art*, ed. J. Turner (1996) · *CGPLA Eng. & Wales* (1905)
Likenesses R. Brough, self-portrait, 1889 · R. Brough, self-portrait, 1892 · J. Cadenhead, pencil drawing, Scot. NPG · W. D. Ross, Royal Scot. Acad. · F. D. Wood, bronze head, Scot. NPG
Wealth at death £9268 14*s.* 11*d.*: confirmation, 8 May 1905, *CCI* · £350 4*s.*: additional estate, 16 March 1906, *CCI* · £250: additional estate, 21 April 1906, *CCI*

Brough, William (d. 1671), dean of Gloucester, whose origins are unknown, matriculated as a pensioner at Christ's College, Cambridge, in July 1613; he graduated BA in 1617 and proceeded MA in 1620 (incorporated at Oxford in 1621) and BD in 1627; he was created DD by royal mandate in 1636 (incorporated at Oxford in 1645). In 1625 he was presented to the rectory of St Michael Cornhill, London, and on 1 February 1639 was installed as a canon of Windsor. The Cornhill parish registers record the baptisms of five daughters and two sons to Brough and his wife, Elizabeth, between February 1629 and November 1638 (of whom one son and one daughter were also buried there in childhood and the other son in his early twenties); a further two daughters were baptized at St George's Chapel, Windsor, in October 1640 and July 1642 respectively.

A supporter of Archbishop Laud and of Arminianism, a royal chaplain, and from January 1642 a chaplain to the protestant members of Queen Henrietta Maria's household, Brough was removed from St Michael Cornhill during the first civil war. According to Anthony Wood and John Walker he fled to Oxford after his house was plundered and his wife and children turned out. His wife reputedly died of grief; if so (and the claim perhaps receives some support from a grant for the maintenance of his family in August 1646 which made no mention of his wife) Brough must have remarried, as his son Edmond was born in 1648 or 1649. When the House of Lords formally sequestered him in March 1643 Brough was reported to have been absent from his parish for a year. He was charged with seldom preaching, with having observed ceremonies, with Arminianism, and with a malignancy towards parliament for its meddling in spiritual matters (singling out for particular blame the lawyers who sat there).

On 17 August 1643, because of 'his Sufferings and Loyalty', the king nominated Brough dean of Gloucester, where he was installed by proxy on 20 November 1644 (Wood, *Ath. Oxon.: Fasti*, 2.85). In 1645 Gilbert Osborne, treasurer of Gloucester Cathedral, sent the cathedral's account book to him and to a fellow canon, Gilbert Sheldon, at Oxford; this meant that the parliamentarian committee of accounts in Gloucester could not calculate rents due to them from the chapter's estates. In March 1647 he compounded with the parliamentarian authorities. During the years of adversity for Anglicanism in the 1650s Brough published three works asserting the spiritual and devotional significance of the services and rites of the Church of England. *Sacred Principles, Services and Soliloquies, or, A Manual of Devotions*, which appeared under the pseudonym of Philo-Christianus, was published in 1650. It went through three further editions in the 1650s and a fifth in 1671, while Rowland Vaughan published a Welsh translation in 1658. The copy in Gloucester Cathedral Library once belonged to John Evelyn. *A Preservative Against the Plague of Schisme* (again published as by Philo-Christianus) followed in 1652 and *The Holy Feasts and Fasts of the Church, with Meditations and Prayers* in 1657.

At the Restoration, Brough was reappointed to his preferments, becoming also rector of Beverston, Gloucestershire, but resigning his living of St Michael Cornhill in 1663. He subscribed to the Act of Uniformity on 18 August 1662. Records at Gloucester reveal both his severity on wrongdoing by cathedral personnel and his compassion on those in need. His coat of arms (with those of the cathedral canons) was painted by John Campion in 1664 on the new organ case. He was also a benefactor of the cathedral library.

In his will, dated 7 May 1671, Brough desired his executors to direct his three surviving children—Edmond, Abigail, and Anne, wife of Nathaniel Stoughton—in such ways as would seem 'most desirable and happy for them' (PRO, PROB 11/336, fol. 367*r*). He was a widower by this time and a man of some wealth with property in Gloucestershire and Middlesex. He proclaimed at length in his will his lifelong commitment to his church:

> I dye a member and sonne of the Church of England as it is established And I pray God it may continue, humbly praising god that by his providence and grace I was borne in itt and understand the excelent frame and constitution of it more perfect then other reformed Churches and more pure and truly primitively Apostolike, then the Romane Churches. (PRO, PROB 11/336, fol. 366*r*)

Brough died at Windsor on 5 July 1671 and was buried two days later at St George's Chapel. At Gloucester Cathedral the bell-ringers were paid 10*s.* 'for Ringeing the great bell at the death of Mr Deane Brough' (dean and chapter account book 3). SUZANNE EWARD

Sources Gloucester Cathedral, chapter act book 1, 1616–87; chapter account book 2, 1634–64; chapter account book 3, 1664–84 · Hockaday abstracts; act books, Glos. RO, Gloucester diocesan records · *CSP dom.*, 1660–61 · Foster, *Alum. Oxon.* · Wood, *Ath. Oxon.*, new edn, 4.801 · Wood, *Ath. Oxon.: Fasti* (1820), 89 · Venn, *Alum. Cant.* · J. Walker, *An attempt towards recovering an account of the numbers and sufferings of the clergy of the Church of England*, 2 pts in 1 (1714), 33, 93, 165 · Walker rev., 43 · J. Le Neve, *Fasti ecclesiae anglicanae* (1716) · *Fasti Angl., 1541–1857*, [Bristol] · S. Bond, ed., *The chapter acts of the dean and canons of Windsor, 1430, 1523–1672* (1966) · S. L. Ollard, *Fasti Wyndesorienses: the deans and canons of Windsor* (privately printed, Windsor, 1950) · E. H. Fellows and E. R. Poyser, eds., *The baptism, marriage, and burial registers of St George's Chapel, Windsor*

(1957) • J. L. Chester, ed., *The parish registers of St Michael, Cornhill, London*, Harleian Society, register section, 7 (1882) • *DNB* • will, PRO, PROB 11/336, sig. 100

Archives Archives and Chapter Library, Windsor Castle, Berkshire, MS book of memoranda

Wealth at death comfortably off; lands and houses to dispose of as well as money and goods: will, PRO, PROB 11/336, sig. 100

Brough, William (1826–1870). *See under* Brough, Robert Barnabas (1828–1860).

Brougham, Henry (*bap.* 1665, *d.* 1696), Church of England clergyman, was one of the twelve children of Henry Brougham of Scales Hall, Cumberland (*c.*1628–1696), sheriff for the county in 1693, and his wife, Mary, the 'fair Miss Slee', daughter of a merchant, William Slee of Carlisle, 'a jovial gentleman' (*DNB*). The young Henry was baptized on 2 March 1665, and his kinsman Sir Daniel Fleming of Rydal (1633–1701) acted as his godfather. On 8 July 1681 Brougham was admitted to Queen's College, Oxford, as a batteler, or child servant, matriculating on 18 July, and was elected a taberdar in February 1685. He graduated BA on 18 March 1686, proceeded MA on 15 June 1689, and was admitted a fellow of the college. At Oxford, Brougham was soon made aware that, though a commoner, it was necessary 'for my credit's sake to live like a gentleman' (*Hist. U. Oxf.* 4: *17th-cent. Oxf.*, 37). He was fortunate to be sent subsidies by Sir Daniel Fleming, and after proceeding MA Brougham's career prospects improved.

On 2 February 1691 Fleming's son George wrote to his father that 'my cousin Browham is chaplin to and lives with the Bishop of Lincoln', Thomas Barlow, and in March he had heard there was 'prospect of other preferment' (Magrath, 2.15, 21). This was duly offered. On 29 September 1691 Brougham was collated, and on the following day was installed prebendary of Asgarby in Lincoln Cathedral. The following month Bishop Barlow died, charging his chaplains, Brougham and William Offley, to look after both his personal property at Buckden, Huntingdonshire, and his own original manuscripts. These were in poor order, Barlow having failed to revise them according to his earlier plan; the bishop seems not to have explicitly forbidden publication, but, when in 1692 Sir Peter Pett issued what he called the bishop's 'Genuine remains', his former chaplains felt bound to protest in print. In *Reflections to a Late Book* they condemned Pett and his collaborator, the vicar of Buckden (where the bishop had died), as 'confederate pedlars' who had published 'for the sake of twenty guineas' (Brougham, epistle dedicatory). Furthermore, they charged, the work as published seriously distorted the bishop's views, notably on toleration for dissenters, and on Socinianism. Its omission of his recommendations of many anti-Socinian works made him seem like a sympathizer, and Brougham listed the omitted references in an appendix.

His ecclesiastical career seem to have taken up most of Brougham's time and he was rarely in Oxford. In March 1693 Fleming asked him to act as tutor for his son Roger. Brougham was very reluctant: 'I must own that I have been very indifferent as to the business of pupilling since I returned from Buckden', especially since the late bishop

of Lincoln had added 'an augmentation to my fellowship' (Magrath, 3.106). Brougham hoped that Fleming would accept another tutor and his own more distant oversight of the young man's welfare. But his godfather would not be denied. Brougham was persuaded to take charge of Roger, who appears to have had little aptitude or inclination for serious study. In February 1694 he was persuaded to take on another Fleming son, James, who seemed a better student. Nevertheless, it appears that Brougham failed to persuade either of his charges to the path of scholarship for very long, or to curb their enthusiasm for excessive spending on food, tobacco, drink, and entertainment. In September 1694 Brougham preached before the assizes at Carlisle and from 1693 to 1695 he acted as pro-proctor for the university. On 26 February 1696 he wrote to Sir Daniel that 'I have been now a fortnight in the country for the benefit of the air, having been under a very bad state of health this half year' (Magrath, 3.266). He died a month later, at ten in the morning of 28 March 1696, aged thirty-one, at William Offley's rectory of Middleton Stoney, Oxfordshire, and was buried in Queen's College chapel, Oxford.   STEPHEN WRIGHT

Sources J. R. Magrath, ed., *The Flemings in Oxford*, 3 vols., OHS, 44, 62, 79 (1903–24) • *Fasti Angl.*, *1541–1857*, [Lincoln] • Wood, *Ath. Oxon.*, new edn, vol. 4 • [H. Brougham and W. Offley], *Reflections to a late book entitled 'The genuine remains of Dr Tho. Barlow' ... falsely pretended to be published from his lordship's original papers* (1694) [Offley wrote the preface] • W. Hutchinson, *The history of the county of Cumberland*, 1 (1794) • J. Nicolson and R. Burn, *The history and antiquities of the counties of Westmorland and Cumberland*, 2 vols. (1777) • will of Thomas Barlow, PRO, PROB 11/407, sig. 215 • grant of administration of Henry Brougham, 22 May 1696, Oxf. UA, chancellor's court • *DNB*

Brougham, Henry Peter, first Baron Brougham and Vaux (1778–1868), lord chancellor, was born on 19 September 1778 at 21 St Andrew's Square, Edinburgh, the eldest son of Henry Brougham (1742–1810), a modest Westmorland squire, and his wife, Eleanor (1750–1839), the daughter of the Revd James Syme and niece of William Robertson, the historian. William *Brougham, second Baron Brougham and Vaux, was his youngest brother. Precociously talented, he was sent at the age of seven to the high school in Edinburgh, where he was taught by the rector, Dr Alexander Adam, passing out as dux (head of the senior class) in 1791. Still too young to enter the university, Brougham spent the next year at the family home, Brougham Hall, Westmorland, where he was taught by a tutor. He matriculated at the University of Edinburgh in 1792, where he read humanity and philosophy, before entering the faculty of law in 1796. Always keen to impress his friends with his nerve, style, and knowledge, in 1792 he formed the Juvenile Literary Society and in 1797 joined the prestigious Speculative Society, which he soon dominated and converted into a whig political debating club. At the same time he developed an interest in experimental science, which would remain with him throughout his life. Before he was nineteen he had published two articles on light in the *Transactions of the Royal Society*, and by the age of twenty-five he had been made a fellow of the Royal Society.

Middlesex jury the gruesome nature of flogging and focused their attention on the real point at issue: freedom of speech. Despite a summing up by Lord Ellenborough in favour of a conviction, the Hunts were acquitted, and Brougham's legal reputation was made. Henceforth, he would never be short of clients, and his income from the northern circuit would not drop below £8000 a year. Because of his politics, however, he was not made a king's counsel until 1827, after unsuccessfully seeking the distinction both after Queen Caroline's death in 1820 and in 1823.

The journalist making his name In 1802 Brougham helped to launch the *Edinburgh Review*, the brainchild of his friends Francis Jeffrey, Francis Horner, and Sydney Smith. Although initially excluded from the management of the journal, he was to dominate its editorial policy for thirty years. He also wrote vast quantities of copy for it, contributing more than 100 articles by 1810. Along with Sydney Smith's, Brougham's iconoclastic, lively, and sometimes abusive style set the controversial tone of the review and ensured its success. His scornful invective on occasion called forth great responses, as when (in 1808) his review of Byron's *Hours of Idleness* prompted the poet to respond with *English Bards and Scotch Reviewers*. However, it could also be unthinkingly destructive. Responsible for most of the scientific reviews in the early numbers, his huge self-confidence led him to pen several satirical and dismissive reviews of significant work. In particular, his savaging of Thomas Young's important works on light and colour resulted in them remaining unsold and unread.

Brougham's influence also served, by 1807, to turn the *Edinburgh Review* into a whig party organ. Perhaps his most politically controversial contribution was the notorious 'Don Cevallos' article, published in October 1808. Though a joint article by Brougham and Jeffrey, this devastating attack on aristocratic government was generally attributed to the former, who had contributed the most inflammatory passages. In any case, it caused a furore, even among the aristocratic leaders of the whigs. Tory readers, including Sir Walter Scott, immediately cancelled their subscriptions, and the earl of Buchan went so far as to kick the offending number out of his home. A rival tory journal, the *Quarterly Review*, was founded, its opening number containing a riposte by Canning.

Brougham continued to write extensively for the *Edinburgh Review*, although by the middle of the 1820s his dominance was being challenged by the stylish prose of Macaulay. Brougham clearly resented his new rival, and in 1830 asserted his power over Macvey Napier, the editor, by forcing him to withdraw his invitation to Macaulay to write a piece on the French Revolution of 1830 so that he himself could write it. It was only in the late 1830s, when he was beginning to become estranged from the whigs, that he stopped writing for the *Edinburgh Review*. Henceforth, much of his prodigious energy for writing was devoted to contributing articles on law reform to the *Law Review* and the *Law Magazine*.

Brougham also maintained close links with the newspaper press, which he sought to cultivate for his personal

Henry Peter Brougham, first Baron Brougham and Vaux (1778–1868), by Sir Thomas Lawrence, 1825

Early years at the bar Brougham was called to the Scottish bar in June 1800, and went directly on the summer circuit. His early experience of life as a lawyer was not a happy one. Although he enjoyed the scope which advocacy gave to his rhetorical skills, and used them daringly to spar with and irritate judges, his showmanship attracted no more than the occasional poor client. Brougham was soon disgusted with law, and resented it for interfering with his politics. He toyed with the idea of seeking a diplomatic post (unsuccessfully applying to Lord Hawkesbury for help) or entering the army, but in the end decided to submit to the 'five years'' dull, unvaried drudgery' required to qualify for the English bar (*Brougham and his Early Friends*, 1.343). In November 1803 he was admitted to Lincoln's Inn, and was called to the bar five years later, having entered the chambers of the special pleader Nicholas Tindal in March 1807. He began to practise on the lucrative northern circuit, where he could dazzle juries with his powers in debate without having to argue too many complex questions of law. Indeed, throughout his career at the bar it was generally agreed that when there was a tricky legal issue to be debated, Brougham would be beaten in the argument. As one attorney put it, 'He strikes hard, Sir, but he strikes wrong' (Bagehot, 3.180). However, his fortune as a barrister was made in 1811, when he defended the Hunt brothers on a charge of seditious libel for reprinting an article from the *Stamford News* in the *Examiner*, which attacked the brutality of flogging in the army. In a passionate and brilliant speech, Brougham impressed on the and party advantage. He organized the whig press campaign in the 1807 election, supplying pamphlets and newspapers all over the country with material, and continued to write copious quantities for the *Morning Chronicle* thereafter. However, his most well-known connection was with *The Times*, edited by his friend Thomas Barnes, and he benefited from ample and enthusiastic coverage of his activities in its columns for many years. Brougham's links with the newspaper were particularly important after 1827, when he first had the prospect of political power. Henceforth, he ensured that Barnes had a continual flow of confidential information, and in return obtained *The Times*'s continuing support for the whigs (and particularly himself), spiced on occasion by criticism of his whig rivals. In the summer of 1834, however, this cosy relationship turned sour, for Brougham fell out with Barnes, partly because of disagreements over political questions (notably the poor law) and partly because the editor felt he had been deceived by Brougham over the latter's attitude towards the earl of Durham. For the next decade *The Times* continued to make merciless attacks on its old ally, deriding him in its columns and portraying him as a drunkard and a madman. It took particular relish in March 1840 in publishing its longest ever book review (over a whole week) of Brougham's translation of *Demosthenes*, which was condemned as 'foul, wallowing, boisterous and unEnglish'.

The politician in search of a seat, 1804–1810 Brougham's first forays into politics revealed a streak of inconsistency which would remain with him throughout his public life. On his arrival in London in 1804, his first political friends came from the abolitionists of the Clapham Sect. He won their attention in particular as a result of his *An Inquiry into the Colonial Policy of the European Powers* (1803), a rambling and somewhat confused work, in which he defended the colonial system but attacked the slave trade. He followed it with a pamphlet, *A Concise Statement of the Question Regarding the Abolition of the Slave Trade*, which was distributed to MPs before the vote on William Wilberforce's Slave Trade Abolition Bill of May 1804. Tory leanings were displayed both in his defence of Pitt's policy towards France in *Colonial Policy* and in his abusive and arrogant attack on Lauderdale's *Enquiry into the Nature and Origin of Public Wealth* in the *Edinburgh Review* of 1804 (which raised a storm of protests from the whigs). They could also be seen in his futile attempt in 1804 to raise a corps of volunteers in Edinburgh at the time of an invasion scare. Indeed, he so convinced Wilberforce of his loyal advocacy of the government's cause that the latter recommended him to Pitt for a diplomatic posting in October 1805, and helped him in the following May to approach Lord Lowther for a Westmorland seat.

By then, however, Brougham had been introduced by Horner into whig circles. He began to attend dinners at Holland House and became a member of the leading whig clubs; and when the whig 'all talents' ministry was set up in January 1806 Brougham wrote a pamphlet, *An Inquiry into the State of the Nation at the Commencement of the Present Administration*, which attacked Pitt's foreign policy and set out a whig programme of reform. However, he was not rewarded with a whig parliamentary seat, though he was (in August 1806) appointed secretary to the mission of Lord Rosslyn and Lord St Vincent to Portugal. The mission proved abortive, and Brougham returned out of pocket, convinced that his absence from England had prevented him acquiring a seat in parliament.

Brougham's brand of whiggism soon proved more radical than the party leaders', and he became increasingly disenchanted with them, disappointed by their timidity in refusing to follow Romilly and Whitbread in denouncing governmental corruption and incompetence. A natural populist, Brougham began to court wider public opinion, and by the beginning of 1808 had succeeded in catching the attention of London and Lancashire merchants with a series of articles attacking the orders in council. The merchants engaged the eloquent barrister as their counsel to present their petitions at the bar of the House of Commons. Brougham's impressive performance here forced the government to lead counter-evidence, and secured his position as an important public figure. With a shortage of effective whig speakers in the Commons, and with Brougham threatening to break with the whig leadership, it was apparent that a seat had to be found for him. Thanks to the intervention of Holland, Grey, and Lauderdale, the duke of Bedford made available the seat of Camelford. Brougham took it up in February 1810, but not before pretending reluctance to give up the prospect of a considerable income at the bar for the seat in parliament he had coveted so long. It was not the last time he would play hard to get.

The member for Camelford, 1810–1812 Once in parliament Brougham demonstrated the political leanings which were at the same time cautious and radical. On the main issues of the day he remained (as he told Holland in 1811) 'an adherent to the true principles of the Whig party and Mr. Fox' (Holland House MSS, BL, Add. MS 51561, fol. 97). On the question of parliamentary reform, he aimed to reduce the influence of placemen rather than to increase the influence of the people, feeling that this would wrest the initiative away from Burdett and the popular radicals. However, on wider humanitarian issues he took a more radical stance, opposing both flogging in the army and solitary confinement in prison. His first great parliamentary speech was on the issue of slavery, and in March 1811 he introduced a bill (which passed) to make it a felony to trade in slaves, which gave a more effective sanction to Wilberforce's measure of 1807. Throughout his life Brougham continued to speak out, in parliament and in public, against the evils of the slave trade and slavery, and he remained proud of his own contribution to the cause of the abolitionists.

In October 1811 Brougham learned that the duke of Bedford was planning to sell the Camelford seat after the dissolution of parliament in 1812. The news came at a frustrating moment, for Brougham had just turned down the offer from Worcester reformers to stand for their city. In these last few months of the parliament Brougham made a much bigger impact than at any point hitherto. Firstly, in January, he attacked the crown's use of the droits of Admiralty, showing that during the period of the war the amount of prize money received by the crown from the sale of confiscated enemy ships had increased dramatically, giving the crown a large fund for jobbery. Although the motion failed without a division, Brougham succeeded in bringing the matter to the public attention, attacking the government, and unsettling the whig leaders.

Secondly, in March 1812 Brougham launched an attack on the orders in council, which he saw as both damaging trade and threatening war with the United States. Ever sensitive to the power of public opinion, Brougham had prepared his ground by writing an article in the *Edinburgh Review*. He then made a motion in the Commons for a committee to look into the matter, and when it was lost urged merchants throughout the country to petition parliament. He was rewarded by the appointment of a committee of the whole house. For six weeks Brougham dominated the inquiry, which he did not allow to be delayed even by the assassination of Spencer Perceval. By June the government relented and lifted the orders in council. This was a heady triumph for Brougham. With the whig opposition weak and divided, he had defeated a strong government single-handed in what he came to regard as his greatest achievement. Throughout the country meetings were held to congratulate Brougham, who was showered with presents of plate as tokens of gratitude.

In search of a seat once more, 1812–1815 At the height of popularity Brougham still faced the problem of having to find a seat for the next election. His mercantile friends in Liverpool were keen for him to stand as their candidate, alongside Creevey. Brougham initially hesitated, and accepted only after Castlereagh had turned down his 'somewhat Quixotic' offer to go to America on behalf of the government to conduct negotiations to end the war caused by the orders in council (Brougham, *Life and Times*, 1.39). The election pitted against each other the greatest political orators of the day, Canning and Brougham. Brougham rose to the occasion, giving 160 speeches in eight days of voting. Nevertheless, Liverpool proved to be a hopeless cause for the champion of the abolitionists, for the influence of the corporation ensured that both whigs would be defeated. With no whig grandee coming to his rescue, Brougham made a last effort to secure election for the Inverkeithing burghs in Fife. It was to no avail, and he remained out of parliament for the next three years in spite of several efforts to find him a seat.

The defeat at Liverpool, which Brougham put down to corruption and to the unwillingness of whig borough-mongers to use their seats to advance the party interest by bringing in men of talent, led him to flirt with the radicals. He had first met Jeremy Bentham at Holland House in 1805, and by the mid-1810s became one of the small circle of men who dined regularly at Bentham's home. Bentham realized, however, that Brougham would never agree with him on political reform. Indeed, a man who

had in his youth said of members of the London Corresponding Society that their 'ignorance and savage barbarity renders them fit only for being tools' was hardly likely to make a comfortable bedfellow for the likes of Major Cartwright (*Brougham and his Early Friends*, 1.33). Indeed, he had in 1812 turned down Cartwright's offer to stand for Middlesex, refusing to support universal suffrage and annual parliaments. Yet in 1814, when his name was put forward for the Westminster seat of Lord Cochrane, Brougham was persuaded by Francis Place to make a public endorsement of Burdett's radical programme of 1809. The event revealed once more how much of an opportunist Brougham could be in seeking personal political advancement, and he failed, in the event, to convince the radicals of his sincerity. Any chance he might have had disappeared when Cochrane was re-elected on a wave of anger at his sentence for a stock exchange fraud.

With little prospect of a return to parliament Brougham fell into one of the bouts of depression and hypochondria from which he suffered periodically from 1801 onwards. He abandoned his legal practice, and retired for several months to Brougham Hall. His psychosomatic illness would keep returning until well into his sixties, and his regular periods of depression and lassitude, matched by periods of intense activity and occasional eccentric behaviour, made some of his friends fear that he might be suffering the affliction of his sister, that of insanity.

Return to the Commons Brougham's health and his spirits took a turn for the better when in July 1815 he was offered the seat of Winchelsea by the earl of Darlington. With the death of Whitbread, and with Romilly ill, he returned as the whigs' most effective debater in the Commons, campaigning tirelessly against the government, arguing for retrenchment, a more liberal foreign policy, and a series of wider reforms. Nevertheless, even at this time Brougham never fully won the trust of his party, for if his ambition was high, his judgement remained poor. His greatest successes came when he appealed to public opinion outside the house; but these successes led him to overestimate his power and importance within the house. His conduct in 1816 is good evidence of this. His attack on the income tax in March, supported by a mountain of petitions organized by Alexander Baring, was a piece of supreme parliamentary skill, and resulted in a humbling defeat for the government. Intoxicated by the victory, he declared (to Francis Place) that he would offer himself to take charge of the government, reform parliament, 'and change the whole of the present ruinous system' (Place MSS, BL, Add. MS 27850, fol. 288). Two days later he undid all the good work with a violent and personal attack on the prince regent, which appalled Ponsonby and Tierney and shocked even Brougham's friend Romilly. Brougham was always attempting to please too many audiences to build up his own political following. His attacks on the prince were bound to delight the radicals, as was his attempt in 1816 to reform the law of libel to allow truth to be a defence in a criminal case. However, his support of the corn laws and his statement in May that the British constitution was never in better shape were aimed more to woo the moderate whigs. The result was that neither fully trusted him.

Brougham crossed the leaders of the whigs once more in 1818 and offended his patron, Darlington, when he decided to stand for his home county of Westmorland. The Lowthers' control of this constituency had not been challenged for forty years. Brougham relished the chance to encourage the freeholders to use their vote against the aristocratic interest, while at the same time forcing the Lowthers to incur great expense. He got little help from the whigs and organized his own campaign, spending much time touring the constituency giving rousing speeches which were reported in the London press. Brougham lost (by 168 votes) but continued to seek election by a popular constituency, failing narrowly to win in Westmorland again in 1820 and 1826.

The queen's attorney-general From 1812 Brougham acted as legal adviser to Princess Caroline, the estranged wife of the regent, in part out of pique at the prince's keeping the whigs out of office, in part in the hope of ingratiating himself with Princess Charlotte, George's heir. In 1813 he had arranged the publication of Caroline's letter to her husband complaining of the restrictions imposed on her seeing her daughter, which won the princess a great deal of public sympathy. In 1814 he counselled the young princess when she broke off her engagement to the prince of Orange, at the same time unsuccessfully urging Caroline to remain in England. By 1819, with the prince keen for a divorce, he negotiated on her behalf with the government. Given the nature of the parties in the dispute, Brougham realized that he needed to use guile to achieve the best result. At the same time Brougham was not averse to using the crisis to bolster his own position, for he sought to attempt to obtain a silk gown from the government. His tactic was to frighten the government by the prospect of Caroline's return, and to deter the latter from returning by the prospect of a trial. The stratagem failed, for after the death of the king Caroline determined to come and claim her title as queen in person. When the government decided to proceed against her with a bill of pains and penalties Brougham, sworn in as her attorney-general in April 1820, led her defence in the House of Lords. His speech, lasting two days, was brilliant, ridiculing the evidence against the queen, coolly analysing the issues, and passionately appealing to their lordships' consciences. So powerful was the speech that Lord Erskine rushed out of the chamber in tears. It had the desired effect: though the Lords gave the bill a second reading, the government took it no further. If Brougham's earlier parliamentary performances had made his name in the Commons and among mercantile communities, this one assured his fame throughout the nation. He received the freedom of numerous cities, and in many parts of the country public houses were renamed the Brougham's Head.

Marriage and family life Brougham married on 1 April 1819. Always slightly uncomfortable in the company of women, he had had occasional affairs, as in 1816, when he had a liaison in Geneva with Caroline Lamb, wife of George Lamb. In 1818 he courted (and was rejected by) Georgiana Pigou, and soon afterwards married a widow, Mary Ann Spalding, daughter of Thomas Eden of Wimbledon and niece of Lord Auckland. She brought with her two children, a house in Mayfair, and an annual income of £1500, but little intellectual stimulation. None of Brougham's friends was told of the marriage, which took place at Coldstream, until well after the event. There was some talk that his marriage was the consequence of an indiscretion, and a daughter (who died in infancy) was born in November. Brougham's wife remained a sickly and nervous woman, particularly after the birth of their second daughter, Eleanor Louise, in October 1822. Totally at sea in polite company, she was rarely invited to Brougham's many dinner parties and remained a recluse in their London home. Her health degenerated progressively, and by the 1840s her hypochondria had developed into total mental breakdown. She died in January 1865. Brougham continued, after his marriage, to have affairs, beginning a liaison with Harriette Wilson, who blackmailed him throughout the late 1820s and early 1830s. He paid up, rather than risk public embarrassment. But Brougham remained devoted to his family throughout his life. He was devastated at the death of Eleanor in 1839, and had her buried in Lincoln's Inn. He supported the legal careers of his brothers James and William (finding them jobs when he was chancellor), and provided for the children and paid the debts of his brother John after his death in 1829.

Reforming education Many of Brougham's greatest achievements were in areas outside the general run of party politics. From the 1810s onwards he began to turn his attention to the need to extend popular education. A member of the Royal Lancasterian Society since 1810, he became a vice-president of the British and Foreign School Society on its formation in 1814. Two years later he told parliament that he wanted to set up a school system with parliament's help, and obtained a committee 'to inquire into the education of the lower orders in the metropolis'. The committee, driven by Brougham's energy, looked at every charity school in London, and revealed the desperate need for improved education as well as the misuse of charitable funds in those schools; in 1818 its remit was extended to all of England and Wales. In the same year he brought in a bill to appoint a commission to investigate all charities in England and Wales. This initiative led to the appointment of the first paid charity commissioners to ensure that charitable bequests were correctly and efficiently applied. It was to take until 1859 for a permanent, powerful set of charity commissioners to be appointed, but they were the fruit of the seed planted by Brougham. However, his efforts to obtain state-supported education, seen in a bill of 1820 to establish parochial schools and again in a bill in 1837, foundered on sectarian religious divisions.

Brougham's greatest contributions to education date from the 1820s. He became involved with Birkbeck's London Mechanics' Institute in 1824 and used his influence to encourage the growth of similar institutes all over the country, organizing in 1825 a series of lectures to be circulated to them. In 1826 he was the moving force behind the foundation of the Society for the Diffusion of Useful Knowledge, set up to publish cheap and accessible works on both scientific and artistic subjects. The idea was not new, for Charles Knight (who became the society's publisher) had planned a similar scheme in 1820; but it was Brougham's energy which made it a success. He wrote the introductory treatise of the society (*Discourse on the Objects, Advantages and Pleasures of Science*, which sold 39,000 copies), and over the next twenty years contributed regularly, taking a constant and active part in supervising, and sometimes editing, the society's publications. Among his other publications for the society was his *Discourse of Natural Theology*, published in 1835. This work displayed both Brougham's highly unorthodox theology and his enthusiasm for popular science, for in it he attempted to show that the truths of religion could be proved by scientific induction. Never an especially religious man, he could easily offend Anglican sensibilities, as he did on one occasion in 1846, in proceedings on a divorce bill in the Lords, when he told a Chinese witness that if she did not speak the truth, then 'her gods' would punish her.

The Society for the Diffusion of Useful Knowledge finally went bankrupt in 1846, largely as a result of Brougham's own decision to start a *Biographical Dictionary*. He remained proud of the society's achievements to the end of his life. In fact, it reflected his social conservatism. As he told Peel in 1842 (when trying to raise funds to rescue it), its tracts on machinery, combination, and capital circulated widely in 1830 in the disturbed areas, while the *Penny Magazine* 'at one time put down a very large proportion of the vile weekly publications which used to abound' (Peel MSS, BL, Add. MS 40482, fol. 7).

Brougham also played a vital part in the establishment of London University in 1826, based on Scottish lines (he was elected lord rector of Glasgow University in 1825). Though the prime mover in the project was Thomas Campbell, it was Brougham who did much of the organizing, and who secured the co-operation of dissenters who were considering setting up a university of their own. He attempted, without success, to obtain a charter for it in parliament, but badgered his friends to buy shares in the scheme and arranged the purchase of land in Gower Street. He also played a strong role in drawing up the curriculum, which he was determined should remain secular. The irreligious nature of the university prompted Anglicans to form the rival King's College; but Brougham made it clear that the two should co-exist peacefully, and in 1836 both colleges joined in the new chartered University of London. Brougham remained president of University College until his death.

Seeking political power, 1827–1830 Throughout the 1820s, when Brougham's unpopularity with the king ensured that he would remain out of office, his political aim had been to divide the liberal tories from the ultras. Despite an initial clash with Canning, whom he accused of 'monstrous truckling' to obtain office (in an incident which

some feared might result in a duel), he gave as much support as he could to Canning's liberal instincts. Brougham's policy—'*anything* to lock the door for ever on Eldon and Co.' (Creevey, 2.114)—finally bore fruit in 1827, on the death of Liverpool, when three whigs joined Canning in a coalition which would keep out the ultras. Lansdowne, Grey, and Althorp had been unwilling to join a coalition as individuals, rather than as a party, and their terms for joining included the appointment of men favourable to Catholic emancipation to the Irish posts in the government. When it seemed that the prospects of a coalition were disappearing Brougham hastily called a meeting at Brooks's, where he inspired a rebellion of whigs which secured Canning the support he needed. The episode soured his relations with the whig leaders, notably Grey, for he was seen to be prepared to sacrifice key whig principles for power, and it effectively ensured that, in March 1830, it would be Althorp who would become whig leader in the Commons. His much-repeated claims to being 'disinterested' in the affair persuaded few; Brougham in fact coveted the attorney-generalship. Instead, he was offered the post of chief baron of the exchequer, which was not quite lucrative enough to tempt Brougham, particularly since it would involve leaving the Commons.

After a subdued period Brougham's political zeal revived with the death of George IV in June 1830, raising his hopes of office. He resigned the Winchelsea seat at the beginning of the year (after the marquess of Cleveland had decided to support Wellington), and was returned by the duke of Devonshire for Knaresborough. However, in the election which followed the death of the king Brougham stood for the county of Yorkshire, largely at the behest of Edward Baines, the editor of the *Leeds Mercury*, supported by dissenters who admired Brougham's anti-slavery stance. During the election he campaigned tirelessly, giving extravagant speeches to large enthusiastic crowds at the same time as arguing cases in the York assizes. His election was a great triumph: Brougham, the outsider, was elected by the richest and most populous county in England without having to spend a penny of his own money. Ever the populist, he regarded it as his proudest moment, stating that he had more pride in representing Yorkshire than he could obtain from any office. For the rest of his life he would refer fondly to his Yorkshire constituents.

During the election Brougham had declared himself in favour of parliamentary reform. Back in parliament he put forward his own reform plan, supported by the whigs. Wellington's response—that the constitution was not capable of improvement—brought down his government and took the whigs into office. The notion that Brougham, at the height of his popularity and power, could easily be accommodated within this government was soon shown to be false. He coveted the mastership of the rolls, but it was considered far too dangerous to give him an irremovable post with a seat in the Commons. Instead, he was affronted by the offer of being made attorney-general. Petulant and unstable, he vowed that he would take no office; but without Brougham the ministry could not stand, and after consultation with the king he was offered the lord chancellorship. He at first refused, but then reluctantly 'agreed to sacrifice independence—and ample income—power—Yorkshire (for I believed not a word of Lord Grey's argument that I might not be re-elected)—and above all I sacrificed the House of Commons to be chancellor for a month' (Melbourne MSS, Box 2, fol. 27). He received the great seal on 22 November 1830 and was ennobled next day.

In government, 1830–1834 Brougham left the Commons with a heavy heart. He would not set foot in the chamber again until 1860, when he listened to Gladstone's budget speech. For the rest of his life he continued to sign his name 'Henry Brougham' or 'H. B.'. For all that, titles were of greater importance to him than he admitted. His vanity impelled him to take the title of Lord Brougham and Vaux, after a barony in fee to which his family claimed descent. This title was a godsend to the wits, who quipped that he should have been dubbed 'vaux et praeterea nihil'. Nor was he averse to fishing for an earldom, 'because our women and especially *my child* have taken a violent fancy to it' (Melbourne MSS, Box 1, fol. 114). In March 1860 the heirless Brougham obtained another patent, with specific remainder to his youngest brother, William.

In the Lords, Brougham played a crucial role in securing the passage of the Reform Bill, although he had no part in its drafting. It was his quick thinking and management of both the king and the Lords which secured the dissolution of parliament in April 1831, after the whigs had lost a key vote in the Commons. He then reputedly coined the slogan of the election: 'The Bill, the whole Bill and nothing but the Bill'. When the bill returned to the Lords in the new parliament, he delivered a speech lasting over three hours, in temperatures of 85° F, ending in the lord chancellor, by now the worse for drink, on his knees, begging the Lords to pass the bill. After its rejection and the prorogation of parliament it was Brougham, convinced that the country was in a revolutionary state, who persuaded the cabinet to secure an early recall so that the momentum for the bill could be maintained. Despite his subsequent disclaimer (in his autobiography), he was in the vanguard of those calling for the king to agree to the creation of between fifty and sixty new peers before the second reading of the Reform Bill in the Lords, a bolder policy than that followed by Grey. The latter's view prevailed, which led to the temporary fall of the government, when (Brougham claimed) the king begged him to stay on to pass a reform measure. With the tories unable to form a ministry Grey returned to office, and the king told the prime minister and Brougham that he would create the necessary peers. The passing of the Reform Bill by the Lords was thereby assured.

On other issues Brougham was a champion of middle-class causes. A committed Malthusian, he took a closer interest in reforming the poor law than any other member of the government—planning his own bill, setting up a royal commission in 1832, monitoring the reports sent in by the assistant commissioners, and then managing the passage of the Poor Law Amendment Act through the Lords in 1834. Consistently hostile to trade unions, in the era of the Tolpuddle martyrs, he considered whether the law could be strengthened to suppress combinations. In government, moreover, he moderated his opinions on some of the causes he had championed, such as slavery (showing little interest in the Slavery Abolition Bill of 1833) and education (opposing the levying of a compulsory rate, which had originally been his idea).

Throughout his tenure of the woolsack, Brougham remained on often uneasy terms with his colleagues. He was seen as a schemer, and as a man unable to resist interfering in other people's business. It was widely believed that he had inspired *The Times*'s attacks in early 1831 on Grey, which accused him of nepotism. More seriously, in June 1834 his clumsy double-dealing over the question of Irish coercion led to Grey's resignation. If many at the time felt that Brougham harboured ambitions to be premier, he saw himself rather in the role of kingmaker. Desperate to remain in office, he sought to bully William IV into retaining the ministry, and credited himself for Melbourne's appointment. His behaviour throughout 1834 was in many ways bizarre. In the summer he went on a tour of Scotland, where he played to the gallery in a series of speeches which enhanced his popularity but offended his political peers (particularly when he upstaged Grey and insulted Durham at a dinner in Edinburgh) and outraged the king, who was not amused by reports of high jinks with the great seal, nor with the chancellor's portraying himself as the king's representative. Many began to comment that the often dishevelled-looking Brougham was not entirely of sound mind. He began to sport tartan trousers, buying enough material to last for the rest of his life, and to shock women at polite dinners by his coarse table manners and crude conversation. His conduct was clearly too much for the king, who dismissed the ministry in November 1834. Brougham hardly helped his chances of a return to office by lecturing the king on the constitutional propriety of dismissing a government with parliamentary support or by returning the great seal in a bag.

Reforming the law If Brougham lacked the subtlety to grasp the finer technicalities of legal doctrine in the courtroom, his political will-power was exactly what was needed to draw attention of parliament and the nation to the chronic state of the legal system. This he first did in February 1828, when he delivered a six-hour speech—the longest ever in the Commons—on law reform, in which he exposed flaws in virtually every area of law (omitting only chancery reform and the criminal law) and staked his claim to be parliament's prime champion of law reform. Brougham's speech struck the perfect note. He showed himself to be committed to a widescale reform of the legal system, while resisting Bentham's iconoclasm. In preparing the speech he had in fact received much guidance (and many manuscripts) from Bentham, who still considered Brougham as the man best placed, after the suicide of Romilly, to advance his projects for codification and the abolition of the common law. However, the speech (prepared with the help of Joseph Parkes) proved a great disappointment to Bentham, who subsequently denounced

Brougham's ideas. The rest of the legal world was more impressed. Brougham's main aim in the speech, as in most of his later reforms, was to make law cheaper and more accessible to the public. The government responded by setting up two royal commissions, into the common law courts and real property. Many of his ideas were not new, but reflected the opinions of the bar, and many were not fully thought out in detail, but required fleshing out and rethinking by lawyers more expert than he. Yet it was Brougham who in effect kick-started the long-delayed movement for reform of the courts, and who ensured that the momentum would be maintained, particularly during his period on the woolsack. Indeed, in 1845 he claimed that fifty-six of the sixty-two defects he had pointed to in the speech had been remedied.

As lord chancellor Brougham had the opportunity to put his ideas into practice. Perhaps his most important achievement was the creation, in 1833, of the judicial committee of the privy council, which ensured that colonial appeals would be heard by professional lawyers. The previous year he had abolished the court of delegates, transferring its jurisdiction to the privy council. Brougham had grand ambitions for this institution. In 1834 he introduced a bill to unite the jurisdiction of the judicial committee and the privy council, which would have created a permanent vice-president of the council and given it jurisdiction over divorce (a power he tried unsuccessfully again to give it in 1845). In 1835 his bill gave the council jurisdiction over patents, and in 1843 he succeeded in extending its authority over ecclesiastical and Admiralty cases. At the same time he regularly attended the sittings of the committee, raising the suspicion in some circles that he was seeking to build a personal judicial empire.

Brougham also sought to reform other institutions. In 1831 he removed bankruptcy from the jurisdiction of the chancery, and set up a separate system of bankruptcy courts to oversee the administration of bankrupts' estates by court-nominated official assignees. In 1833 he attempted to institute a system of local courts (with wide powers of arbitration and power to aid the work of chancery masters), having referred his initial bill of 1830 to the common law commissioners. He introduced this measure again unsuccessfully in 1842, but an act largely based on the proposals of 1833 passed four years later, setting up a new system of county courts. In 1834 he reformed the Old Bailey, extending its jurisdiction to cover all areas within 20 miles of St Paul's Cathedral.

Brougham was also concerned to reform the chancery itself, which was notorious for its abuses, especially after the lengthy tenure of the woolsack by Lord Eldon. Brougham set about abolishing sinecures in the court, substituting fixed salaries for fees, and pruning the court of cases better handled elsewhere (such as bankruptcy and lunacy). In 1834 he introduced a bill to separate the legal and political functions of the lord chancellor, though soon abandoned it. His biggest impact on the chancery, however, was the speed with which he cleared the backlog of cases in the court, ignoring vacations and the customary times of the court. His reputation with the public was enhanced when his achievements were trumpeted in *The Times* and by Sydney Smith. Yet he was less popular with the lawyers. His courtroom manner was brusque, and the lord chancellor often paid little attention to the technical arguments of lawyers, sometimes writing letters or reading proofs of his articles in court, sometimes sleeping. Nor was his legal reasoning—in any case that of a common lawyer—highly regarded, particularly in comparison with his contemporaries Lyndhurst and Sugden.

Brougham's reformist urge also extended to the substantive law. He implemented the reforms recommended by the real property commission, and in 1833 appointed a royal commission on the criminal law to digest all the criminal law into a single code. This he saw as the precursor to the codification of all law. Out of office Brougham remained loyal to this commission: his pressure ensured that a second royal commission was appointed in 1845, and he twice introduced bills based on their reports (in 1844 and 1848) to enact a criminal code.

Into the political wilderness, 1835–1841 Brougham's public career effectively ended in November 1834, although he fought to retain a position by offering to become unpaid chief baron of the exchequer. When the whigs returned to office the great seal was put into commission and Brougham was excluded. He took it badly: 'To be thrown overboard without any one of you having ever had the fairness to say what I am charged with', he wrote to Holland. 'Oh, it is foul! foul! foul!' (Holland House MSS, BL, Add. MS 51563, fol. 147). Melbourne did not mince his words in explaining the reasons for his exclusion: 'you domineered too much, you interfered too much with other departments, you encroached upon the province of the Prime Minister, you worked, as I believe, with the press in a manner unbecoming the dignity of your station, and you formed political views of your own and pursued them by means which were unfair towards your colleagues' (Melbourne MSS, Box 2, fol. 28e).

Although Brougham issued dark threats that he would not be answerable for what '*must* follow' (Holland House MSS, BL, Add. MS 51563, fol. 152), he continued to work with the government, notably in passing the Municipal Corporations Act. However, relations with the whigs were irreparably damaged by the appointment, at the end of 1835, of Sir Charles Pepys as lord chancellor. Brougham was absent from parliament for all of the 1836 session, suffering another bout of illness. When he returned in 1837 he remained on the government benches, although he wasted few chances to snipe at Melbourne, and flirted with both the tories and the radicals. By 1838 his alienation from the whigs was apparent both in his attacks on Durham's handling of the rebellion in Lower Canada and in his publication of his *Collected Speeches*, where he portrayed the whigs as mere place-hunters. The man whose conduct had assured that he would never gain the full confidence of any party now began to attack the party system as a whole, particularly in his *Historical Sketches of Statesmen who Flourished in the Time of George III*, his finest literary work, published in 1839. Nevertheless, he was not a man to bear grudges, and his convivial good nature ensured that his erstwhile enemies were generally reconciled to him sooner or later. Even Melbourne appointed Brougham as his executor.

Despite his fall from power Brougham remained a self-publicist who could not resist seeking attention. However, the attention he received was not always the kind he sought, and by the 1840s he had become a figure of fun, portrayed in endless *Punch* cartoons. He was depicted as Mr Quicksilver in Samuel Warren's novel *Ten Thousand a Year* (1841), having been the model for Foaming Fudge in Disraeli's *Vivian Grey* (1827) and 'the learned friend' in T. L. Peacock's *Crotchet Castle* (1831). In October 1839 reports reached the London press that Brougham had been involved in a coach accident and been killed, and a number of obituaries appeared. It soon transpired that he was alive, and, given that he had written a letter to his family warning them not to be alarmed at rumours of his death, it was soon accepted (despite his strenuous denials) that Brougham had faked his own death, both to boost his popularity and to be able to read his own obituaries. In 1848 he was again the subject of ridicule when he put himself forward as a candidate for election to the French assembly after the revolution against Louis Philippe. Since he was not a citizen, he was informed that he could only stand if he took French—and renounced British—nationality. Brougham's correspondence with the French administration was subsequently published both in France and England, to his public embarrassment. Yet this interest in French politics was no aberration, for in his later years Brougham spent an increasing amount of time in France, where he cultivated friendships with the leading French politicians and thinkers of the day. Indeed, he saw himself as ideally placed to promote friendly relations between the countries. In 1838 (the year of his election to the Institut) he built a château at Cannes, which he first discovered in 1834 and where he would spend every winter. It was largely thanks to Brougham's presence that the town developed into a resort; and the town returned the favour after his death by placing a bust of the great reformer in a square named after him.

On the edge of the woolsack, 1841–1846 From the late 1830s Brougham began to co-operate more with the tories, cultivating friendships with J. W. Croker, Wellington, and Lyndhurst. After 1841 his break with the whigs was complete, and he gave wholehearted support to Peel's administration. Meanwhile, he continued to sit with his former colleagues, though his habit of often taking his place next to the lord chancellor induced Campbell to dub him his 'honourable friend *on the edge of* the Woolsack' (Campbell, 8.525). Brougham's political judgement continued on occasion to be flawed, such as over O'Connell's case, where he privately expressed the view that the lay peers should have overruled the predominantly whig law lords.

Many suspected that Brougham harboured an ambition to succeed Lyndhurst as lord chancellor. In fact, Lyndhurst

sought to accommodate Brougham with judicial appointments on several occasions. In October 1841 he offered the former chancellor the post of paid vice-chancellor, and in April 1844 suggested to Peel that Brougham be made chief baron. The difficulties inherent in accommodating Brougham with a suitable job were revealed in a humiliating episode in 1844. At the beginning of this year he turned down a new post, of vice-president of the judicial committee of the privy council, understanding it to carry the same salary which he would have received as vice-chancellor. Brougham, who had long envisaged that the committee should have a permanent president, then introduced a bill to create a post carrying a salary of £2000, and with an elevated rank, under the impression that he was piloting a bill supported by the government. However, the press seized on the measure as an example of a mercenary Brougham seeking to create a lucrative office for himself. His public embarrassment was crowned when Peel told the Commons that the government had wanted Brougham to take the post, but without a salary. If Brougham's motives were misunderstood, he came out of the episode looking to all the world like a place-hunter.

The transformation by the 1840s in Brougham's approach to politics is seen most clearly in relation to his views on the Anti-Corn Law League and the repeal of the corn laws. The champion of the popular cause in 1832 now attacked the league for appealing directly to the 'mob': its actions in raising money to buy freeholds in order to obtain the franchise for its supporters was as unconstitutional, he told the Lords, as it would be for the crown to issue an unlimited number of patents of peerage. Brougham, the great champion of free trade, condemned what he saw as Peel's folly in giving in to the league. He now strove to keep the Conservatives united at all costs in order to keep the whigs out; when they returned to office he became politically isolated, a free-trader supporting a protectionist party which kept him at an arm's length. In the Lords he remained the defender of the balanced constitution, committed to maintaining the independence and integrity of the upper chamber against encroachment by the Commons, supporting Denman's stance against the Commons in *Stockdale v. Hansard* (1839), and opposing the granting of a life peerage to Wensleydale (1856).

A liberal reformer, 1844–1860 Having lost interest in party politics, Brougham turned to supporting a range of liberal causes, which he explored through a number of pressure groups formed by his friends. In 1844 he founded the Law Amendment Society. Run initially by James Stewart, and subsequently by G. W. Hastings, this society (over which he presided) provided him with material and measures to present before parliament, and kept him in the forefront of law reform. For thirty years he proposed reforms ranging from the structure of the court system to real property law and the law of marriage and divorce. Brougham had an opinion on almost any topic of law reform; but his reputation in this field was a mixed one. When he spoke in sweeping terms, surveying the whole field of law, as in his second great law reform speech in 1848, he was able to capture the public imagination and restore his reputation among his erstwhile critics, *Punch* and *The Times*. Indeed, the latter declared in 1851 that 'The cause of law reform in England for the last forty years can never be disjoined from the name of HENRY BROUGHAM'. However, when he descended to detailed reforms, often suggested by his acolytes in the Law Amendment Society, he got a less favourable reception from his peers.

Brougham could not resist introducing bills on all manner of topics—sometimes doing so in order to provoke the government into passing a measure, sometimes (as with the law of bankruptcy and insolvency in 1844 and 1857–8) because he felt the field was his, and should not be trespassed on by others. Many of his contemporaries (notably Campbell) found Brougham's endless interventions tiresome. None the less, Brougham did introduce some major reforms in his later years (such as the 1842 Insolvent Debtors Act and the act of 1851 allowing parties to suits to testify in the superior courts), and continued to agitate for progressive reforms, such as the appointment of a public prosecutor, the reform of the grand jury, and the creation of a minister of justice.

Brougham also continued to hear cases in the privy council and the House of Lords. Indeed, for two years following the retirement from the woolsack of Cottenham in 1850 Brougham turned himself into a *de facto* lord chancellor, completely dominating the judicial proceedings of the House of Lords. Nevertheless, his reputation as a judge remained blemished. In the 1850 test case of *Hutton* v. *Upfill* Brougham, sitting as single judge in the Lords, overturned the decision of the lords justices, restoring that of his brother, a master in chancery, on a question of shareholder liability. The decision was universally regarded as wrong, and was later overturned by the Lords. Brougham himself was criticized for his proceeding with the case by witnesses before the select committee of 1856 which considered the appellate jurisdiction of the Lords.

In 1857 Brougham presided over the launch of the National Association for the Promotion of Social Science. Although Hastings, rather than Brougham, was the prime mover behind its formation, the latter was essential to its success, given the prestige his name lent to the project, and he continued to be its president until his death. At each congress he gave long speeches, ranging over a vast number of topics, often reminiscing on his past projects and successes, which were reported widely in the press. In 1859 he was elected chancellor of Edinburgh University. Gladstone was rector, and they formed a rather curious friendship in Brougham's later years, Gladstone often wearing 'Broughams' (the black and white check trousers named after the lord chancellor). Even in old age Brougham showed that his taste for showmanship and lack of tact had not deserted him: in 1860, speaking at the fourth session of the International Statistical Congress, Brougham offended the American minister, Dallas, by ostentatiously pointing out to him the presence of a black person at the congress.

Brougham's later speeches showed his continuing dedication to liberal causes. Criticizing Bentham's view that men made a felicific calculation before deciding to commit crime, he argued that passion, not reason, caused criminality, and that the best antidote to this was education, not imprisonment. Fiercely critical of the married women's property law, which denied married women control of their property, he urged reforms to improve the position of women and to increase their opportunities to work. An admirer of the Rochdale system of co-operatives, Brougham in his eighties was fêted all over the country at mechanics' institutes, which he urged working men to control. At the same time he manifested the limits of his liberalism. Thus, he criticized the American Civil War as showing the evils of unbridled democracy and castigated drink as the source of all evil for the working man.

Retrospect Brougham continued to attend congresses until 1866, but his mental and physical powers began to fade, especially after the death of his great friend Lyndhurst in 1863. He died on 7 May 1868 at Château Eleanor-Louise, Cannes, and was buried on 24 May in the town's cemetery. Tall and thin, with a high forehead, deep-set eyes, and a long, upturned nose, which proved to be the delight of caricaturists, and with a prodigious amount of energy, Brougham was both a congenial and warm-hearted man who could captivate any audience with his wit and learning, and an awkward and abrupt man, who could offend with his eccentric conduct and bore with his vain self-seeking. He aspired to be a polymath who could master science, law, and literature while remaining at the centre of the political stage; but he never stood still long enough to make a permanent impact in any of these fields. As a thinker he cast his net so widely that the vast quantities of print which he produced proved to be of little lasting value. Instead of being a modern Bacon, he gained a more dubious reputation for (in John Morley's phrase) 'encyclopaedic ignorance' (*Studies in Literature*, 1897, 291). As a reformer his successes—in law reform, slavery, and education—came when his restless activity and propagandizing were harnessed to the hard work of more obscure men. As a politician his talent for inspiring distrust ensured that his time in office would be relatively brief. So famous in his day, he was not to be remembered by later generations for any single great achievement: even the Brougham carriage, a small, compact, and manoeuvrable horse carriage to which he gave his name in 1838, was soon superseded, and would not (unlike Wellington's boot) remain in popular culture.

MICHAEL LOBBAN

Sources C. W. New, *The life of Henry Brougham to 1830* (1961) · R. M. Stewart, *Henry Brougham, 1778–1868: his public career* (1986) · A. Aspinall, *Lord Brougham and the whig party* (1927) · R. K. Huch, *Henry, Lord Brougham: the later years, 1830–1868* (1993) · H. P. Brougham, *The life and times of Henry, Lord Brougham*, ed. W. Brougham, 3 vols. (1871) · J. Campbell, *Lives of the lord chancellors*, 8 vols. (1845–69), vol. 8 · M. Lobban, 'Henry Brougham and law reform', *EngHR*, 115 (2000), 1184–215 · R. G. Thorne, 'Brougham, Henry Peter', HoP, *Commons, 1790–1820* · F. Hawes, *Henry Brougham* (1957) · J. B. Atlay, *The Victorian chancellors*, 1 (1906) · UCL, Brougham MSS · BL, Peel MSS · Royal Arch., Melbourne papers · BL, Holland House MSS · BL, Place MSS · *Hansard* · *The Times* · *The Creevey papers*, ed. H. Maxwell, 2 vols.

(1903) · *Brougham and his early friends: letters to James Loch, 1798–1809*, ed. R. H. M. B. Atkinson and G. A. Jackson, 3 vols. (1908) · *The blackmailing of the chancellor: some intimate and hitherto unpublished letters from Harriette Wilson*, ed. K. Bourne (1975) · E. B. Sugden, *Misrepresentations in Campbell's lives of Lyndhurst and Brougham* (1869) · A. Aspinall, *Politics and the press, c.1780–1850* (1949) · [S. Morison and others], *The history of The Times*, 1 (1935) · N. Gash, 'Brougham and the Yorkshire election of 1830', *Pillars of government and other essays on state and society, c.1770 – c.1880* (1986) · J. E. Eardley-Wilmot, *Lord Brougham's acts and bills, from 1811 to the present time* (1857) · V. M. Lester, *Victorian insolvency: bankruptcy, imprisonment for debt and company winding-up in nineteenth-century England* (1995) · J. S. Anderson, *Lawyers and the making of English land law, 1832–1940* (1992) · A. Brundage, *The making of the New Poor Law* (1978) · R. Brent, *Liberal Anglican politics: whiggery, religion, and reform, 1830–1841* (1987) · D. B. Swinfen, 'Henry Brougham and the judicial committee of the privy council', *Law Quarterly Review*, 90 (1974), 396–411 · E. G. Collieu, 'Lord Brougham and the conservatives', *Essays in British history presented to Sir Keith Feiling*, ed. H. R. Trevor-Roper (1964), 195–218 · L. Ritt, 'The Victorian conscience in action: the National Association for the Promotion of Social Science, 1857–1886', PhD diss., Columbia University, 1959 · L. Goldman, *Science, reform, and politics in Victorian Britain: the Social Science Association, 1857–1886* (2002) · W. Bagehot, 'Lord Brougham', in *The collected works of Walter Bagehot*, ed. N. St John-Stevas, 3 (1968), 159–93 · R. Stevens, *Law and politics: the House of Lords as a judicial body, 1800–1976* (1979) · H. Retournay, *Cannes: Lord Henry Brougham et le centenaire* (1879) · 'Select committee ... on the functions of the House of Lords', *Parl. papers* (1856), 8.401, no. 264 [court of appellate jurisdiction] · GEC, *Peerage*, new edn

Archives BL, corresp., Add. MS 59846N · Boston PL, letters and papers · Duke U., Perkins L., papers · DWL, corresp. with Unitarians relating to education bill · Hunt. L., letters · Lincoln's Inn, London, legal papers, judgments · LMA, letters · NL Scot., corresp. and papers · U. Mich., Clements L., corresp. and papers · UCL, corresp. and papers; letters · UCL, letters to Society for the Diffusion of Useful Knowledge | Beds. & Luton ARS, letters to Samuel Whitbread · BL, corresp. with John Allen, Add. MSS 52177–52179 · BL, corresp. with Lord Broughton, Add. MS 47224 · BL, corresp. with W. E. Gladstone, Add. MS 44114 · BL, letters to George Graham, Add. MS 48214 · BL, corresp. with Lord Grenville, Add. MS 58965 · BL, letters to William Hazlitt, Add. MS 38898 · BL, corresp. with Lord Holland and Lady Holland, Add. MSS 51561–51565, 52018–52020, 52125 · BL, letters to Leigh Hunt, Add. MSS 38108–38109 · BL, corresp. with Princess Lieven, Add. MS 47367 · BL, corresp. with Lord Liverpool, Add. MSS 38250–38255, 38369, 38565 · BL, letters to Lord Murray, Add. MS 40687 · BL, letters to Macvey Napier, Add. MSS 35149–35152, 34613–34623, *passim* · BL, corresp. with Sir Robert Peel, Add. MS 40482 · BL, corresp. with Francis Place, Add. MSS 35149–35152, 34613–34623, *passim* · BL, corresp. with Lord Wellesley, Add. MSS 37297–37313, 37416, *passim* · Bodl. Oxf., letters to Sir Francis Burdett · Bodl. Oxf., letters to Lord Clarendon · Bodl. Oxf., letters to Benjamin Disraeli · Bodl. Oxf., letters to S. L. Giffard · Bodl. Oxf., letters to Sir William Napier · Bodl. Oxf., letters to William Somerville · Bodl. Oxf., letters to Samuel Wilberforce · Bodl. Oxf., corresp. with William Wilberforce · Bodl. RH, letters to Zachary Macaulay · Borth. Inst., letters to Sir Charles Wood · Chatsworth House, Derbyshire, letters to duke of Devonshire · CKS, letters to Lord Stanhope · Cumbria AS, Carlisle, corresp. with Sir James Graham · Durham RO, letters to Lord Londonderry · DWL, letters to Henry Crabb Robinson · Exeter Cathedral, letters to Henry Phillpotts · Glamorgan RO, Cardiff, letters to Lord Lyndhurst · Harris Man. Oxf., letters to George Armstrong · Harrowby Manuscript Trust, Sandon Hall, Staffordshire, letters to Lord Harrowby · Herts. ALS, letters to Lord Lytton · HLRO, letters to John Temple Leader · Hunt. L., letters to Zachary Macaulay · Lambton Park, Chester-le-Street, co. Durham, letters to first earl of Durham · Lpool RO, letters to fourteenth earl of Derby · NA Scot., letters to James Loch · NL Scot., letters to J. H. Burton · NL Scot., letters to Edward Ellice · NL Scot., letters to Whitwell Elwin · NL Scot., corresp. with John Lee · NL Scot., corresp. with Lundie family, etc. · NL Scot., corresp. with Robertson-MacDonald family · NL Wales, letters to Sir George Cornewall Lewis · Northumb RO, letters to Thomas Creevey · NRA Scotland, priv. coll., letters to Adam family · NRA Scotland, priv. coll., letters to Lord Moncrieff · Port Eliot, letters to earl of St Germans · priv. coll., letters to Lord Anglesey · priv. coll., letters to Lord Conyngham · PRO, corresp with Lord Ellenborough, PRO 30/12 · PRO, corresp. with Lord John Russell, PRO 30/22 · PRO, letters to Lord Cowley, FO519 · RAS, corresp. with Augustus De Morgan · Royal Arch., Lord Melbourne MSS · Staffs. RO, letters to Lord Hatherton · U. Durham L., corresp. with second Earl Grey · U. Durham L., corresp. with third Earl Grey · U. Durham L., corresp. with Charles Grey · U. Edin. L., letters to John Sainsbury · U. Lpool L., corresp. with John A. Roebuck · U. Mich., Clements L., letters to J. W. Croker · U. Mich., Clements L., letters to Lord Murray · U. Mich., Clements L., letters to Henry Reeve · U. Southampton L., letters to Lord Melbourne · U. Southampton L., corresp. with Lord Palmerston · UCL, corresp. with Sir Edwin Chadwick · UCL, letters to Lord Granton · UCL, letters to Joseph Parkes · UCL, letters to Samuel Rogers · Ushaw College, Durham, corresp. with John Lingard · W. Sussex RO, letters to duke of Richmond · Warks. CRO, letters to Dormer family · Woburn Abbey, Bedfordshire, letters to duke of Bedford

Likenesses S. W. Reynolds, mezzotint, pubd 1820 (after T. Phillips), BM · J. Lonsdale, oils, 1821, NPG; related chalk drawing, NPG · T. Lawrence, oils, 1825, NPG [*see illus.*] · W. Behnes, marble bust, 1830, Lincoln's Inn, London · attrib. J. Francis, circular marble relief, 1831, Yale CBA · bronze bust, 1831, Scot. NPG · J. P. Dantan, caricature, plaster statuette, 1833, Musée Carnavelet, Paris · A. Morton, oils, 1836, Scot. NPG · S. Gambardella, oils, c.1838, Lincoln's Inn, London · S. F. Diez, drawing, 1841, Staatliche Museen zu Berlin · S. Gambardella, oils, c.1845, Wellington Museum, London · D. Macdonald, two sketches, 1847, BM · H. Watkins, albumen print, 1855–9, NPG · C. H. Lear, pen-and-ink drawing, 1857, NPG · D. Macnee, oils, 1863, Parliament House, Edinburgh · J. Mayall, double portrait, oils, c.1864 (with Pierre-Antoine Berryer), Middle Temple, London · M. Noble, marble statue, 1864, Brown's Institute, Liverpool · J. Adams-Acton, marble bust, 1867, NPG; related plaster bust, NPG, Scot. NPG · Cruikshank, caricature, BM · Doyle, caricature, BM · G. Hayter, group portrait, oils (*The trial of Queen Caroline, 1820*), NPG · Heath, caricature, BM · Leech, caricature, BM · D. Maclise, lithograph, BM, NPG; repro. in *Fraser's Magazine* (1831) · J. Stewart, watercolour (after A. Morton), Scot. NPG · medallion (after J. Henning), Scot. NPG · photographs, NPG · wax sculpture, NPG

Wealth at death under £2000: probate, 17 June 1868, *CGPLA Eng. & Wales*

Brougham, John (1810–1880), actor and playwright, was born in Dublin on 9 May 1810. He attended Trinity College, Dublin, and was briefly a student of surgery at the Peter Street Hospital; but an uncle from whom he had expected advancement fell into difficulty, and Brougham, left to his own resources, went to London. A chance encounter with an acquaintance led to his engagement at the Queen's Theatre, Tottenham Court Road (afterwards known as the Prince of Wales's), and there, in July 1830, he made his first appearance on the stage, acting, he claimed, 'some twelve or fourteen parts' in an operatic production of W. T. Moncrieff's *Tom and Jerry*. In 1831 he was a member of the company organized by Madame Vestris for the Olympic Theatre. His first play, a burlesque, was written at this time, for William Evans Burton, who was then acting at the Pavilion Theatre. When Madame Vestris moved from the

John Brougham (1810–1880), by Heath & Beau

Olympic to Covent Garden, Brougham followed her, and there remained as long as she and Charles Mathews were at the head of the theatre.

In 1838 Brougham married the actress Emma Williams, but was separated from her within a few years. On 3 May 1844 he married Annette Hawley, an actress and theatre manager; she died in 1870. In 1840 Brougham became manager of the Lyceum Theatre, which he conducted during summer seasons, and for which he wrote a number of dramatic works. Around this time he collaborated with Dion Boucicault on the comedy *London Assurance*, produced at Covent Garden in March 1841, but in settlement of a dispute with Boucicault he relinquished his share in the authorship, and resigned the part of Dazzle to Mathews.

In 1842 Brougham left England for America, and in October of that year he opened at the Park Theatre, New York, as O'Callaghan in the farce *His Last Legs*. A little later he was employed by W. E. Burton in New York, and wrote for him a number of pieces, including *Bunsby's Wedding* and *The*

Confidence Man. Still later he managed Niblo's Garden, where he produced his fairy tale *Home* and the play *Ambrose Germain*. He opened a new theatre on Broadway, Brougham's Lyceum, in 1850. The Lyceum was at first a success, but the demolition of the building next to it made it appear to be unsafe, and the business declined, leaving him burdened with debts, which, however, he subsequently paid. His next speculation was at the Bowery Theatre, of which he became lessee on 7 July 1856, and where he produced *King John* with superb scenery and a fine company. This was not a commercial success, and Brougham proceeded to write and present a series of sensational dramas, among which were *The Pirates of the Mississippi* and *Tom and Jerry in America*. In September 1860 he returned to London, where he remained for five years, playing at the Lyceum and writing and adapting dramas and opera librettos.

Brougham's reappearance in the USA took place on 10 October 1865 at the Winter Garden Theatre, and he remained thereafter in America. He opened Brougham's Theatre on 25 January 1869, with a comedy by himself called *Better Late than Never*. However, the theatre was soon taken out of his hands by its owner, James Fisk junior, and on 18 May Brougham received a farewell benefit. The attempt to establish Brougham's Theatre was his final effort in management. After that time he was connected with various stock companies, but chiefly with Daly's Theatre and with Wallack's; towards the end of his life he fell into poverty. On 17 January 1878 he received a testimonial benefit at the Academy of Music, at which the sum of $10,278 was received, and this fund, after the payment of incidental expenses, was settled on him in an annuity. His last work was a drama entitled *Home Rule*, and his last appearance on the stage was made as Felix O'Reilly the detective in Boucicault's play *Rescued*, at Booth's Theatre, New York, on 25 October 1879. He died at 60 East Ninth Street, New York, on 7 June 1880, and was buried in Greenwood cemetery on 9 June.

Brougham was the author of more than seventy-five dramatic pieces; most notable were his burlesques, including two on themes of American history, *Columbus* and *Pocahontas*. He published two collections of his miscellaneous writings. As an actor he was remembered for his interpretations of comic Irish characters, among them Sir Lucius O'Trigger in Sheridan's *The Rivals*; he was also famed for his witty curtain speeches. He is said to have been the original of the hero of Charles Lever's novel *The Confessions of Harry Lorrequer* (1903).

G. C. BOASE, rev. JOHN WELLS

Sources W. Winter, ed., *Life, stories and poems of John Brougham* (1881) · C. E. Pascoe, ed., *The dramatic list*, 2nd edn (1880) · Adams, *Drama* · J. N. Ireland, *Records of the New York stage, from 1750 to 1860*, 2 vols. (1866–7) · T. Allston Brown, *A history of the New York stage* (1903) · D. Boucicault, *London assurance*, ed. J. L. Smith (1984) · *Appleton's Annual Cyclopaedia and Register of Important Events*, new ser., 5 (1880), 66 · *DNB*

Likenesses W. Endicott, engraving, Harvard TC · Heath & Beau, photograph, NPG [*see illus.*] · cartes-de-visite, NPG · portrait, repro. in Winter, ed., *Life, stories and poems*

Wealth at death $10,278 raised in a benefit to buy him an annuity a few years before death

Brougham, William, second Baron Brougham and Vaux (1795–1886), law reformer, was born on 26 September 1795 in Edinburgh, the youngest of the five sons of Henry Brougham (1742–1810) and his wife, Eleanor Syme (1750–1839). Henry Peter *Brougham was the eldest of his brothers. He was educated at the high school in Edinburgh and entered Jesus College, Cambridge, in 1813; he graduated BA (senior optime) in 1819 and proceeded MA in 1822. He was called to the bar of Lincoln's Inn in 1823. He remained a fellow of his college from 1821 until his marriage on 12 August 1834 to Emily Frances (d. 1884), daughter of Sir Charles William Taylor MP, first baronet, and his wife, Charlotte.

Brougham was MP in the whig interest for Southwark from 1831 to 1835, when he stood unsuccessfully for Leeds. In the late 1820s and early 1830s he wrote for *The Times*, and acted as a conduit for information between the editor, Thomas Barnes, and Henry Brougham. William remained close to his brother all through his life. Given the age difference and the early death of his daughter, Henry came to regard his brother as almost a son. William was made a master in chancery by his brother in March 1831. The appointment, worth £2500 a year, came in for criticism from the lord chancellor's opponents, but was defended by C. P. Cooper, who noted that William's 'talents and industry had already produced a professional income not very disproportionate to his present salary, and which in a few years it would probably have surpassed' (*A refutation of the calumnies against the Lord Chancellor, contained in the last number of the Quarterly Review in an article upon the pamphlet entitled 'The Reform Ministry and the Reformed Parliament'*, 3rd edn, London, 1833, 95). Like his brother, William was a keen law reformer. As an MP he introduced a bill in May 1833 into the Commons to create a general registry of deeds, having in the previous year chaired a select committee on a similar bill brought by John Campbell. While his initiative failed, he played an important role in the abolition of masters in chancery. In a reply to an enquiry from Lord Langdale in February 1842, Brougham wrote that little could be done to lessen the evils in the offices, which caused much of the delay and expense for litigants in chancery. Instead they should be abolished, and each chancery judge should deal with the whole case before him. However, not expecting much support for this idea, he put forward an alternative notion of giving the masters primary jurisdiction in administrative cases, allowing litigants to bypass the judge. He drew up a bill to this effect which his brother Henry presented in the Lords in 1851. At the same time he published *A letter to Lord Cottenham upon the bill to give primary jurisdiction to the masters in ordinary of the high court of chancery in certain cases* (1850). The subsequent debate over the issue led in 1852 to the abolition of the masters of chancery, which was a crucial step in reforming the court immortalized for its inefficiency in Dickens's *Bleak House*. With the abolition of the office William was granted a pension. In the previous year his brother lobbied hard for William to be appointed to one of the vacant vice-chancellorships. Although Lord Cottenham stated that he had 'always found in him great quickness and a good judicial understanding, and certainly great activity and zeal in the dispatch of business' (University College, London, MS 39788), William was not appointed to the post.

On Henry's death (7 May 1868), some (including Cranworth) felt that William was unsuitable to succeed to a title with a seat in the Lords; but in any event, he played little part in public life, spending most of his time in retirement at Brougham Hall, Westmorland (near Penrith), where he died on 3 January 1886. He was the father of six children. He amassed a considerable fortune, including over 5000 acres of landed property, much of which was acquired through his wife's family.

MICHAEL LOBBAN

Sources GEC, *Peerage* · *The Times* (5 Jan 1886) · C. Carr, 'A Victorian law reformer's correspondence', Selden Society lecture, 1955 · R. K. Huch, *Henry, Lord Brougham: the later years, 1830–1868* (1993) · R. Stewart, *Henry Brougham, 1778–1868: his public career* (1985) · A. Aspinall, *Lord Brougham and the whig party* (1927) · M. Lobban, 'Henry Brougham and law reform', *EngHR*, 115 (2000), 1184–215 · 'Returns showing the date of appointment of each of the present masters in chancery', *Parl. papers* (1847–8), 51.227, no. 132 · Venn, *Alum. Cant.* · W. P. Baildon, ed., *The records of the Honorable Society of Lincoln's Inn: the black books*, 4 (1902) · W. P. Baildon, ed., *The records of the Honorable Society of Lincoln's Inn: admissions*, 2 (1896)
Archives UCL, corresp. | BL, corresp. with W. E. Gladstone, Add. MSS 44403–44488, *passim* · BL, letters to Sir John Archibald Murray, Add. MS 40687 · U. Durham L., letters to Henry George, third Earl Grey · UCL, letters to James Atkinson; letters to James Brougham
Likenesses G. Hayter, group portrait (*The House of Commons, 1833*), NPG
Wealth at death £116,165 11s. 7d.: probate, 15 Feb 1886, CGPLA Eng. & Wales

Brougham and Vaux. For this title name *see* Brougham, Henry Peter, first Baron Brougham and Vaux (1778–1868); Brougham, William, second Baron Brougham and Vaux (1795–1886).

Broughton. For this title name *see* Hobhouse, John Cam, Baron Broughton (1786–1869).

Broughton, Andrew (1602/3–1687), lawyer and politician, was probably the son of Richard Broughton (d. 1635) of Seaton, Rutland, and his wife, whose maiden name was Agard. A younger son, he appears not to have undergone formal education, and his early life remains obscure. He had found his way to Maidstone by 1627, became a freeman in 1630, and obtained election to the common council of the town in 1636. Two years later he served his first term as town chamberlain.

In 1639 Broughton was appointed as clerk of the peace for the county of Kent by the lord chamberlain, Philip Herbert, fourth earl of Pembroke and first earl of Montgomery, lord lieutenant of the county. This appointment came in question in 1642, perhaps owing to the irregularity of his elevation under the auspices of Pembroke's by then defunct lord chamberlaincy, but not impossibly in consequence of Broughton's early entanglement in the partisanship of the Long Parliament. In December 1641 an

Andrew Broughton was involved in some of the controversy surrounding the accusations made by William Chillingworth against the parliamentarian leaders responsible for the impeachment of Strafford and the imprisonment of Geoffrey Palmer for protesting against the grand remonstrance.

Broughton was a member of the Kent county committee from 1643. He acted as attorney on behalf of the corporation of Maidstone during the civil war, and in 1647 he was elected jurat. On 10 January 1649, just two months after his election as mayor of the town, he was chosen to serve as one of two clerks to the high court of justice set up to try Charles I. He was the replacement for one of the trial commissioners' first choices, 'Mr Greaves', probably Richard Greaves, Middlesex clerk of the peace. It was Broughton who read the charge against the king, required of him his plea, and declared the court's sentence of death. Presumably in recognition of his service during the trial, Broughton was appointed clerk of the crown in the upper bench by the Rump Parliament on 1 June 1649. As two of the principal legal officers of the Commonwealth, he and his brother Ambrose, another lawyer, were instructed to assist the attorney-general in the prosecution of radical agitators in September. The following month Andrew was clerk to the court which tried John Lilburne. In 1650 he was called to the bar as an associate of the Inner Temple, where he became an associate to the bench a year later.

Broughton sat in Barebone's Parliament, and has been described by that assembly's historian as an 'ultra-radical'. He was appointed to the council of state on 14 July 1653. In that capacity his responsibilities were numerous, taking in public finance, Irish and Scottish affairs, the administration of the Royal Mint, and a wide range of matters touching on commercial and foreign policy. Despite his very active service he was not reappointed to the council in November 1653. Although he was not one of those nominated to sit in the assembly by the gathered churches of Kent, it was claimed that he was among those religious radicals in the assembly opposed to the formal establishment of a preaching ministry when Cromwell dissolved it. He was elected to Richard Cromwell's parliament, where on one occasion he was vocal in his defence of freedom of conscience, to the point of inflaming some of his less tolerant fellow members, whose indignation he was required to assuage. He was highly critical of 'The humble petition and advice', the other house and the protectoral court. 'Towards Richard himself he was positively insulting' (Woolrych, 222).

Mayor of Maidstone once again in 1659, Broughton fled England the following year. He and his fellow clerk to the high court of justice, John Phelps, came under the terms of the Act of Indemnity and Oblivion, and were marked for punishment falling short of death. Broughton's property in Kent and Rutland was confiscated, including the land he had purchased at the sales of episcopal estate. His house at Maidstone was given to the duke of York, and later conveyed by him to one John Greenhill of New Sarum, Wiltshire, who reconveyed it to Broughton's son,

Andrew Broughton of Seaton in Rutland, whose home was licensed in 1672 for presbyterian worship.

In 1662 Broughton and Phelps were reported to have been at Hamburg. That autumn Broughton joined several regicides at Lausanne in Switzerland, where he and Serjeant Edward Dendy remained when their fellows left for Vevey shortly after. Broughton accompanied Edmund Ludlow and Nicholas Love in their journey to Bern in 1663 to thank the senate of that town for the protection they had been offered during their exile. Broughton died peacefully in 1687, aged eighty-four. His burial on 23 February in the church of St Martin, Vevey, is marked by a memorial inscription.   SEAN KELSEY

Sources G. J. Armytage, ed., *The visitation of the county of Rutland in the year 1618–19*, Harleian Society, 3 (1870), 28–9 • will, PRO, PROB 11/168, fols. 39v–40r [Richard Broughton] • will, PRO, PROB 11/239, fols. 32r–33r [John Broughton] • J. Cave-Browne, ed., *The marriage registers of the parish church of All Saints, Maidstone* (1901), 50 • W. Newton, *The history and antiquities of Maidstone* (1741), 135–6 • J. M. Russell, *The history of Maidstone* (1881), 192–5, 354 • K. S. Martin, ed., *Records of Maidstone* (1926), 98, 102, 113, 116, 119, 120 • E. Stephens, *The clerks of the counties, 1360–1960* (1961), 109 • J. G. Muddiman, *The trial of King Charles the First* (1928) • *CSP dom.*, 1649–50, 315; 1653–4, 45, 47–8, 53, 94, 122, 145, 161, 199, 225; 1672, 78, 199 • *State trials*, 4.1292 • F. A. Inderwick and R. A. Roberts, eds., *A calendar of the Inner Temple records*, 2 (1898), cix, 292, 299, 306 • A. Woolrych, *Commonwealth to protectorate* (1982), 160, 221–3, 412–13 • *Diary of Thomas Burton*, ed. J. T. Rutt, 4 vols. (1828), vol. 4, pp. 144, 292, 325–6, 330 and n. • *The memoirs of Edmund Ludlow*, ed. C. H. Firth, 2 vols. (1894), vol. 1, pp. 214, 215, 218; vol. 2, pp. 276, 343, 344, 347, 357, 513 • J. H. Dixon, 'The regicides', *N&Q*, 5th ser., 6 (1876), 13

Broughton, Arthur (c.1758–1796), physician and botanist, the youngest child of the Revd Thomas *Broughton (1704–1774), vicar of Bedminster, Somerset, and his wife, Anne, daughter of the Revd Thomas Harris, is presumed to have been born in or near Bristol. In 1766 he became a pupil at Bristol Free Grammar School under Charles Lee, recently chosen by the corporation to be its master, and from 1769 to 1776 was apprenticed to William Dyer, apothecary of Bristol. He was noted to have spent all his leisure time on botany. In 1776 he took up medical studies at Edinburgh, graduating MD in 1779 with a thesis 'De vermibus intestinorum' and in 1780 was awarded a prize for an essay 'De sanguinis glutine'. The same year saw him appointed physician at Bristol Infirmary, where he continued his botanical activities, lists of plants prepared by him being included both in Shiercliff's *Bristol and Hotwell Guide* (1789) and in Barrett's *History and Antiquities of the City of Bristol* (1789), while a small flora, *Enchiridion botanicum*, was published in 1782. While at the infirmary, and allegedly as a result of a virulent outbreak of influenza in 1782, Broughton found his health so much impaired that in 1783 he took leave of absence for a recuperative sea voyage, his colleagues covering for him. The change of climate was effective, and he resigned his post to settle in Kingston, Jamaica, where he took on the medical side of a busy and lucrative partnership. Here his botanical work continued, and he produced a *hortus siccus*, 'Herbarium Jamaicense', in 1786 (now in the Bristol Museum), and *Hortus Eastensis, or, A catalogue of exotic plants in the garden of Hinton East Esq in the mountains of Liguanea* (1792), with two later editions.

Broughton died in Kingston, Jamaica, on 29 May 1796. A genus of orchids, *Broughtonia*, was named after him by Robert Brown.   AUDREY LE LIÈVRE

Sources M. D. Crane, 'Arthur Broughton, a late eighteenth century botanist in Bristol and Jamaica', *Archives of Natural History*, 10 (1981–2), 317–30 • A. B. Rendle, 'Three early Jamaican botanists', *Journal of Botany, British and Foreign*, 53 (1915), 104–7

Broughton, Sir (Henry John) Delves, eleventh baronet (1883–1942). *See under* Hay, Josslyn Victor, twenty-second earl of Erroll (1901–1941).

Broughton, Hugh (1549–1612), divine and Hebraist, was born in Oldbury, Shropshire, the son of Robert Broughton of Broughton, Shropshire. He referred to himself as of Welsh descent but nothing more certain is known. He received his early education from Bernard Gilpin, who prepared him for university and sent him to Cambridge, where he found liberal patrons in Henry Hastings, earl of Huntingdon, and Sir Walter Mildmay. He learned Hebrew from Anthony Chevallier, the renowned French Huguenot scholar who was employed by several Cambridge colleges between 1569 and 1572 'to deliver the Hebrew lecture'. After graduating BA from Magdalene College in 1570 Broughton became a fellow of St John's College, but moved to Christ's College in 1572. On his collation as a prebendary of Durham on 13 November 1578 Broughton was obliged to surrender his Cambridge fellowship, and though reinstated in 1581 (having resigned his prebendal stall on 8 November 1580) he did not return to his alma mater. He received the living of Washington, co. Durham, on 6 May 1580 but moved to London in 1583. In exchange for lodgings in the city at the house of his friend William Cotton, a draper, he agreed to act as a private tutor to the family. He distinguished himself through preaching and studied intensely, becoming an outstanding Hebrew scholar.

A disagreement with John Whitgift, archbishop of Canterbury, over the interpretation of scripture, persuaded Broughton to go to Germany in 1589, and apart from brief periodic visits to England he appears to have stayed on the continent until the last year of his life. Early in 1590 he spent some time in Frankfurt, and then in Worms before returning to England for a brief visit in the following year. While Broughton was abroad he engaged in religious discussions with Jews in Hebrew and made the acquaintance of several eminent Christian scholars including Joseph Justus Scaliger. He conducted a debate in the Frankfurt synagogue with a Rabbi Elias. He also records a dispute with Rabbi David Farrar. The close association which he developed with Jews and Christian Hebraists was a significant factor in his linguistic attainments, especially in a grasp of rabbinics unusual for an Elizabethan scholar. During this period he 'took a little soil' (possibly a reference to his wife's property) near Tuam in Ireland, and in a letter to William Cecil, Baron Burghley, lord treasurer, written in London on 16 May 1595, he applied for the bishopric of Tuam. During the 1610s he acted as chaplain to the

Hugh Broughton (1549–1612), by John Payne, 1620

English speaking community in Middelburg in the Netherlands.

Recognition as a scholar It was with his first book, *A Concent of Scripture* (1588), published during the time he spent in London, that Broughton gained recognition as a learned, though controversial, expositor of the Bible. This 'little book of great pains', as he called it (Clarke, 3), is essentially a statement of his belief about the nature of the biblical record. Full of charts and tables, it states dogmatically that holy scripture contains all truth. Since each book agrees with the others on matters of chronology, the whole Bible must be regarded as authoritative. It is far superior to pagan sources, which are to be dismissed whenever they contradict the pure word of God. Its chronology is definitive and should be used to correct the theories of profane writers. Because of the views expressed in it about biblical chronology, the *Concent* was attacked in public lectures by John Rainolds, president of Corpus Christi College, Oxford, and by Edward Lively, regius professor of Hebrew at Cambridge. Broughton defended his standpoint in weekly lectures delivered in St Paul's Cathedral which attracted an audience of up to 100 scholars. Dissatisfied with the way in which his critics were conducting the debate, he wrote to Elizabeth I in 1591, requesting that points of dispute be settled by the ecclesiastical authorities and by the universities. He justified his appeal by claiming that 'while divines jar in their narrations, faith is weakened and all study of scripture; and old, confirmed errors have disgraced all the holy story, that without the enforcement of authority, students will hardly yield to the truth' (*Works*, 1.161). Whitgift and John Aylmer, bishop of London, were chosen as arbitrators and the result went in favour of Broughton. Whitgift changed his opinion of the work and came to accept its conclusions, while Aylmer reiterated his prediction made when the book first appeared 'that one scholar of right judgement would prove all its adversaries foolish' (J. Strype, *Historical Collections of the Life and Acts of … John Aylmer, Bishop of London*, 1701, 249).

Broughton's writings demonstrate that he was an accomplished Hebrew scholar, who may justifiably be regarded as the most proficient English Hebraist of his day. Not only was he able to read the Old Testament in the original, he was familiar at first hand with a wide range of post-biblical Jewish authors. His contribution to Old Testament studies includes a translation of Daniel into English and Latin with explanatory notes and comments (1596), a commentary on Ecclesiastes with an accompanying English translation of the text (1605), an English rendering of Lamentations (1606), and an English version of the book of Job (1610). In what became known as the 'battle of the vowel points' Broughton shared the rabbinic attitude towards the Masoretic vocalization of the Hebrew Bible. He argued against the Catholics that the vowels were a part of the original text, not a late invention of the rabbis and therefore untrustworthy.

In each of these four works the predominating feature was Broughton's extensive use of rabbinic sources. In addition to Targum and Talmud, he insisted that other Jewish writings must be regarded as indispensable to anyone engaged in translating the Bible. In a footnote to his *Treatise of Melchisedek* (1591) he listed no fewer than twenty-two Jewish sources which the serious student of the Hebrew scriptures might consult to his advantage. He referred to David Kimchi as 'the king of grammarians', in *An Epistle to the Learned Nobilitie of England, Touching Translating the Bible* (1597, p. 12). However, he warned that rabbinic writings must not be used indiscriminately. The rabbis were to be quoted only when they supported the Christological interpretation of a given word or phrase: 'when the Jews speak of Christianity then we should cite them, and not cite one's enemies against oneself. There is neither Christianity nor wit in that dealing' (*Works*, 3.558). Isaac Abravanel 'is a rabbi of great pains and wit, but not of grace, and only to be followed when he is on our side' (ibid., 2.215). The use of Jewish sources to confirm Christian truth led him to modify his scholarship to conform to his prejudices.

In addition to rabbinic texts Broughton made frequent recourse to the works of other Christian scholars, and was fulsome in his praise of several prominent intermediaries who helped diffuse Jewish learning among gentiles. The Dominican Sanctes Pagninus's skill in Hebrew 'giveth place to none Italian, former nor later … Montanus, whose like if Spain had bred many, the Pope should have

been closely bitten to the heart'. As for the Latin translation of the Hebrew Bible by Immanuel Tremellius, 'it giveth place to none' (*Works*, 1.257).

A Hebrew translation of the Bible and later works For Broughton, as for many of his protestant contemporaries, fascination with the apocalyptic proved to be a powerful motive for studying Hebrew. In order to unravel the mysteries of the Bible relating to the time of the end, when the last judgment would come, he believed that it was necessary to gain a thorough mastery of Hebrew and take note of traditional Jewish exegesis. His interest in the *Seder 'Olam* (an early medieval Jewish chronology from Creation to the Persian period) is typical of his approach to rabbinic learning in connection with the apocalyptic; he even adopted it as the title of one of his own chronological works. In Christian eschatology the question of the time of the end was closely linked to the hope that the consummation of all things would be preceded by the conversion of the Jews. Broughton not only shared this view, he also took positive steps to effect it. By seeking to provide the Jews with Christian literature in their own language, he hoped to hasten their conversion. He planned to write a treatise in Hebrew proving that Christ fulfilled the Messianic prophecies found in the Old Testament. In 1609 he petitioned James I for a sum of money of between £500 and £1000 per annum to support his projected translation of the New Testament into Hebrew. Two years later he presented the king with another petition, this time seeking authority to expound the book of Revelation in Hebrew and Greek in order to prove to both Jews and gentiles that in it Rome, as empire and church, was damned. Though his schemes never came to fruition, he did try to bring his Hebrew learning to bear on what, for apocalyptists, was an issue of some significance.

Although Broughton had studied Hebrew at Cambridge there is no record that he had taught the language in an official capacity at either of the colleges where he held a fellowship. It was only after his arrival in London in the mid-1580s that his skill as a teacher became apparent. John Lightfoot, who edited his works, described the novel and thorough method Broughton adopted to instruct his pupil Rowland, the son of William Cotton, in biblical languages. Daily Bible readings and conversations in Hebrew were regarded as essential. To facilitate matters the teacher drew up a vocabulary for the young student:

> not in an alphabetical way, as dictionaries and lexicons commonly are. But he first pitched upon a place, or thing more general, and then named all the particulars in it, or belonging to it; as heaven: angels, sun, moon, stars, clouds, etc. So a house: a door, a window, a parlour, a cellar, etc.; a field: grass, a flower, a tree, hedge, furrow, etc. … And to complete all, he had him with him very constantly in his study, where he instilled into him the grammar, and then read to him the Bible. (*Works*, preface, sig. B)

By means of his extensive literary output Broughton communicated his enthusiasm for Hebraica to a far wider audience than a few private tutees. Summing up what he considered to be his contribution to the dissemination of

Hebrew learning, Samuel Clarke claimed that in Broughton's published works:

> the serious and impartial reader will find … a winning and inciting enforcement to the reading of the Scriptures, with a greater seriousness, and more than ordinary searching into them. Among those that have studied his books, many might be named that have grown to be proficients, so far as that they have attained to a most singular, and almost incredible skill … in the understanding of the Bible, though otherwise unlearned men. Yea, some such there were, that being excited and stirred up by his books, applied themselves to the study of the Hebrew tongue and attained to a great measure of skill and knowledge therein. Nay, a woman might be named who did it. (Clarke, 8)

He does not say who 'a woman' was.

For the last twenty years of his life Broughton sought in vain to gain the support of the authorities for a new English translation of the Bible. At the end of the sixteenth century the official version of the scriptures read in churches was the Bishops' Bible of 1568, while the translation used by most people in their homes was the Geneva version of 1560. Because Broughton was unable to find much to commend the Hebrew learning of the translators of the Bishops' Bible, and was so contemptuous of their efforts, he wrote to Burghley in June 1593 requesting financial support for a revised version. He claimed that 'sundry lords, and amongst them some bishops', academics, and others had asked him to undertake a new translation. In response to their request he proposed to invite five other scholars to join him in the enterprise (*DNB*); Burghley refused to approve the venture.

Undaunted Broughton wrote, in Middelburg, *An Epistle to the Learned Nobilitie of England, Touching Translating the Bible* (1597), pressing for a fresh translation. He insisted that the Bishops' Bible be replaced by a superior version, so that the reader would 'in no place be snared by the translator' (facs. edn, 1977, p. 3). He claimed to have the support of Elizabeth:

> They must lay their hande upon their mouth that say the Queene will not have the translation bettered. Her majesties footmen knowe that shee sent an othergates worde to Sir Francis Walsingham even to consider of furthering the matter. And Bishop Elmer [Aylmer] the best Ebrician of all the Bishops, was very earnest with my selfe to take the matter in hande. (ibid., 16)

Once more his plea fell on deaf ears. In a letter to Burghley dated 11 June 1597 he blamed Whitgift for the failure of this second attempt. In 1604 Broughton tried to enlist James's co-operation in the venture by addressing *An Advertisement of Corruption in our Handling of Religion* to a member of the royal court. He warned that 'great and deadlie errors runne current in England as good Divinity. Only his Majestie can and must force the deceavers to confess before all the world how they have been led amisse' (sig. A2). In conclusion he recorded once again his dissatisfaction with the Bishops' Bible and urged the king to instruct those responsible for it to make the necessary emendations.

Although James eventually approved a new translation, he was persuaded to do so not by Broughton but by Broughton's old adversary Rainolds, a leading puritan at

the Hampton Court conference convened in January 1604. By the autumn of that year fifty-four English scholars had been appointed as translators for the new translation, the King James Bible or Authorized Version of 1611. But Broughton, to his chagrin, was not among them. Given the intense disappointment that he felt at being overlooked, it is hardly surprising that he was the first to criticize the new translation. He immediately voiced his disapproval in a short tract, probably written in Middelburg in 1611:

> The late Bible … was sent to me to censure, which bred in me a sadness that will greeve me while I breathe. It is so ill done. Tell his Majestie that I had rather be rent in pieces with wilde horses, then any such translation, by my consent, should bee urged upon poore churches. (H. Broughton, *A Censure of the Late Translation for our Churches*, 1611, no pagination)

He then launched into a vitriolic critique of the new version. Since his learning was beyond question, their refusal to give due recognition to Broughton's merits as a scholar was no credit to the selectors of the Authorized Version. However, it may be justly assumed that he was not invited to co-operate on account of his arrogance and intolerance. Because he was so waspish and cantankerous in controversy, other scholars were unwilling to associate with him. He would have been a troublesome collaborator. Though his criticisms of the Bishops' Bible were largely justified, they were too outspoken for the liking of his contemporaries.

Broughton's personality Examples of Broughton's acerbic temperament abound. In his *Advertisement of Corruption* he engaged in a running battle on matters pertaining to biblical chronology with Lively, regius professor of Hebrew at Cambridge, and one of three individuals appointed by the king to find suitable translators for the new Bible. In his *True Chronologie of the Times of the Persian Monarchy* (1597) Lively rejected Broughton's conclusions about biblical chronology expressed in *A Concent of Scripture*. Criticizing Lively's understanding of the Messianic predictions in Daniel 9: 24–7, Broughton stated that he expected greater learning from a professor of Hebrew of thirty years' standing. In his discussion of the Messiah, 'Mr Liveley sheweth as little learning as ever did any that professed Ebrew, as little Christianity as ever any of faith, and as little modestie as any can shewe' (*An Advertisement of Corruption*, sig. E). He also berated his opponent for slavish adherence to rabbinic exegesis when faced with a difficult passage. The Christian exegete must learn to pick and choose when reading Jewish literature. While the commentaries of Rabbi Ibn Ezra were well worth perusing, Lively 'should have taken all that he speaketh well, and as trueth forced him, and not to follow him where he is most ridiculous' (ibid., sig. F).

In the same tract Broughton castigated Thomas Bilson, bishop of Winchester, for his erroneous interpretation of the clause in the apostles' creed which refers to Jesus's descent into hell. At the end of the sixteenth century the precise destination of Christ after his crucifixion was a topic which engendered lively theological debate. In a pamphlet entitled *A Survey of the Sufferings of Christ for Man's Redemption* Bilson repeated the view, associated with St Augustine of Hippo, that after death Christ descended into hell in order to preach to the souls of the damned, and thereby signal his victory over the powers of evil. Broughton disagreed, insisting that Christ went not to Gehenna (hell) but to Sheol (the unseen world), for the Greek word 'Hades' used in the creed did not signify a place of torment but the abode of the dead. If Bilson would admit that he had misunderstood the original, 'this humilitie would be his high commendation and cut off an infinite company of his errors' (*An Advertisement of Corruption*, sig. A).

Broughton's prospects of preferment must surely have been dashed when he presented *A Petition to the Lords to Examine the Religion and Cariage of Dr Bancroft, Archbishop* in 1608. Richard Bancroft, archbishop of Canterbury, who was initially opposed to the Authorized Version, had carried out the king's wishes and drawn up the instructions for the translators. Broughton castigated him for his support of Lively in the debate on biblical chronology and accused him of being 'an assistant to the unbelieving Jewes'. He was 'a deadly enemy to both testaments, and unallowable in this course to be a teacher or to rule in lerning' (Broughton, *A Petition to the Lords*, 7). In another context Broughton predicted that the archbishop's destination after departing this world would be hell.

Despite his intemperate outbursts, Broughton was a popular teacher beloved of his students. He is said to have been a jovial dinner companion and a loyal friend. He made his final trip to England in November 1611, when he was terminally ill with consumption. He died in London on 4 August 1612 at the house of a draper called Benet in Cheapside. He was buried at St Antholin's Church on the 7th. He was survived by his wife (of whom only her family name, Lingen, is known), a niece of one of his pupils, Alexander Top. On his deathbed Broughton lamented his bad humour and regretted that he was so easily provoked. His reputation endures through the posthumous collecting and reprinting of his works. Most of his published works were collected by Lightfoot in a folio volume and printed in 1662 under the title *The works of the great Albionean divine, renowned in many nations for rare skill in Salems and Athens tongues, and familiar acquaintance with all rabbinical learning, Mr Hugh Broughton*. The collection is prefixed by the editor's 'Life of Broughton'.   G. LLOYD JONES

Sources *The works of the great Albionean divine … Hugh Broughton*, ed. J. Lightfoot (1662) • S. Clark [S. Clarke], *The lives of sundry eminent persons in this later age* (1683) • J. Strype, *Annals of the Reformation and establishment of religion … during Queen Elizabeth's happy reign*, new edn, 1/2 (1824), 612–14 • Venn, *Alum. Cant.*, 1/1.231 • B. Brook, *The lives of the puritans*, 3 vols. (1813) • G. Lloyd Jones, *The discovery of Hebrew in Tudor England* (1983), 164–8, 238–9, 268–70 • A. Kippis and others, eds., *Biographia Britannica, or, The lives of the most eminent persons who have flourished in Great Britain and Ireland*, 2nd edn, 5 vols. (1778–93); repr. (1974)
Archives BL, Sloane MS 3088 • BL, MS Harley 1525 • Bodl. Oxf., corresp.

Likenesses oils, 1588, Christ's College, Cambridge • J. Payne, line engraving, 1620, BM, NPG [*see illus.*]

Broughton, John (*c*.1703–1789), pugilist, was born of unknown parents, probably in London, although claims have been made for Baunton in Gloucestershire. He was apprenticed rather late in life (31 May 1723) to John Martin, a Thames waterman, and assigned the same day to the latter's brother Thomas, a lighterman. On 1 August 1730 he won the annual rowing race held on the River Thames, Doggett's Coat and Badge, against five other watermen who had completed their apprenticeships during the previous twelve months. At the time Broughton was plying his trade at Hungerford Stairs (on the north bank of the Thames where Hungerford Bridge now stands).

Broughton's pugilistic abilities are first reputed to have come to the fore when he comprehensively defeated a waterman following a difference of opinion. By the early 1730s he was contending with some of the country's leading fistic exponents, one of the most skilful of whom was Thomas Allen, a St Giles pipe-maker more usually known as Pipes. In 1730 they engaged in a 55-minute battle, and advertisements in contemporary newspapers show that they were later scheduled to meet again at least three further times. These were at James Stokes's amphitheatre in May 1731 and May 1732, and in November 1734 at Thomas Sibblis's (formerly James Figg's) establishment. Among other pugilists Broughton encountered during that period were the celebrated Westminster cabinet-maker John Gretton (Gretting), a fellow waterman, Thomas Edwards, and Charles Raventon (Reventon), another cabinet-maker. In the second half of the 1730s his most significant contests included those against George Taylor the Barber in May 1737 and a coachman, George Stephenson (Stevenson), in March of the next year. Both matches were for £100 and were attended by a number of persons of distinction. At the latter, which lasted 16½ minutes, a barber was squeezed to death attempting to see the confrontation. During Broughton's career he fought Stephenson on at least two other occasions. Captain John Godfrey, a highly respected contemporary sporting amateur, wrote of witnessing Broughton triumph in a forty-minute battle. Later, in April 1744, Broughton was again victorious in a near nine-minute set-to for a very considerable sum (*Penny London Morning Advertiser*, 23–25 April 1744). One of his bouts against Stephenson was the subject of 'The Gymnasiad, or, Boxing Match: A Very Short, but Very Curious Epic Poem' (1744) by Paul Whitehead, which the satirist dedicated to Broughton.

On 1 January 1743 Broughton set down his proposals for erecting an amphitheatre in London dedicated to boxing and sought contributions towards the cost. He envisaged an establishment where the gentry were not troubled by the populace, and contests were disputed only by those suitably skilled and proven. He suggested that he was the person most qualified to preside over events since he remained undefeated and possessed the physical presence required. On the premises Broughton planned an academy where gentlemen could learn to box with mufflers protecting them from the 'Inconveniency of *black*

John Broughton (*c.*1703–1789), by unknown engraver

Eyes, *broken Jaws*, and *bloody Noses*' (Broughton, 4). The amphitheatre, which he advertised in the press as being in Oxford Road, opened the same year. His regulations for fistic combat there were a significant innovation inasmuch as they constituted the sport's first set of organized rules and remained its guidelines for fair play for almost a century. Besides pugilism, the entertainments at the amphitheatre included occasional contests involving weapons, and even bear-baiting. In 1748 Broughton announced that he had enlarged the amphitheatre's gallery considerably, and proposed opening a boxing academy in the Haymarket (*Daily Advertiser*, 1 Feb 1748).

Broughton's last contest was against John Slack, a butcher who originally hailed from Norfolk. It occurred as a result of an altercation on 8 March 1750 between the two men, and took place at Broughton's amphitheatre on 11 April of that year. An advertisement of two days before the encounter declared that Broughton had enjoyed an 'uninterrupted Course of Victories' for the previous twenty-four years and, having retired, only accepted Slack's challenge because his manhood had been affronted (*Daily Advertiser*, 9 April 1750). For the first two minutes Broughton was the strong favourite, but Slack soon succeeded in temporarily blinding his more seasoned adversary and, after just over fourteen minutes, emerged the unexpected winner. Although it has been suggested that the venue was closed down following Broughton's defeat by Slack, it in fact remained in existence for over three years after the event. During this period the press of the time was largely against the amphitheatre, even going as far as to describe it as a 'Nursery for Tyburn' (*Penny London Post*, 6–8 Feb 1751). However, by

August 1754 the *Gentleman's Magazine* was lamenting the 'cruelty of that law, which has shut up our amphitheatres' and left the fistic 'professors' redundant.

Broughton's height was approximately 5 ft 11 in. and in his prime he was extremely broad-chested and muscular. His development was such that he was one of the models used by the noted sculptor John Michael Rysbrack for his statue of Hercules. Godfrey considered that Broughton owed his position as the premier pugilist of his age to having 'Strength equal to what is human, Skill and Judgement equal to what can be acquired, undebauched Wind, and a bottom Spirit, never to pronounce the word ENOUGH' (Godfrey, 55–6). Broughton himself appeared to have had considerable faith in his own abilities. An anecdote was told of him that when accompanying the duke of Cumberland (with whom he was much in favour at the time) on a military expedition, he was shown a formidable foreign regiment and asserted that he could beat every member of the corps, albeit with a breakfast between each contest.

Broughton was undoubtedly one of the king's bodyguard of the yeomen of the guard and was probably the John Broughton, yeoman (bed) hanger, who accompanied George II to Hanover when the king took command of the army in 1743. Towards the end of 1768 Broughton, described in affidavits published in the *Public Advertiser* (13 December 1768) as 'of Lambeth, in the County of Surry [*sic*], one of his Majesty's Yeomen of the Guards', was actively involved in hiring a gang of ruffians which was sent to Brentford, on behalf of one of the candidates, Sir William Beauchamp Proctor, on the day of the election of a knight of the shire for the county of Middlesex. The purpose of the mob was unclear, being either to preserve order or to impede the election of Proctor's opponent. Following the resulting disturbance on 8 December two men, one of whom was said in court to have been engaged by Broughton, were subsequently found guilty of murder, although later reprieved.

The last remaining exponent of the old school of pugilists, Broughton was still teaching as late as 1787, charging 5*s.* a lesson or 1 guinea if required to stand up to his students. He died on 8 January 1789 at his house at Walcot Place, Kennington Road, Lambeth, where he had kept his coffin in readiness for many years. Although some contemporary journals stated that he was interred in Lambeth church (church of St Mary), it is apparent from the burial records of Westminster Abbey that he was laid to rest there on 21 January. These records confirm that he lies in the west cloister next to his wife, Elizabeth, who passed away, aged fifty-nine, on 7 December 1784 and was buried eleven days later. The fees for Broughton's funeral amounted to £10 4*s.* 3*d.* It appears that the dean at the time objected to the words 'Champion of England' on the gravestone and a gap was left in the inscription. This was not filled until 1988, when in addition to the original proposed wording, 'Prizefighter' was added for clarification. The chief beneficiary of Broughton's estate, which was believed to have been worth upwards of £7000, was his great-niece Catherine Monk, whom he had brought up from infancy and later entrusted with the management of his household. TONY GEE

Sources advertisements, fight previews and reports, *Daily Advertiser* [London]; *Daily Journal* [London]; *Penny London Morning Advertiser*; *Read's Weekly Journal, or, British-Gazetteer*; *London Evening-Post*; *Daily Post* [London] · *London Evening-Post* (1–4 Aug 1730) · *Morning Post, and Daily Advertiser* (9 Jan 1789) · *Scots Magazine*, 51 (1789), 50–51 · J. L. Chester, ed., *The marriage, baptismal, and burial registers of the collegiate church or abbey of St Peter, Westminster*, Harleian Society, 10 (1876), 438, 445–6 [burial] · funeral fee book, 1783–1811, Westminster Abbey Library, 25, 64 · catalogue of gravestones, Westminster Abbey Library · A. P. Stanley, *Historical memorials of Westminster Abbey*, 7th edn (1890), 311 · J. Broughton, *Proposals for erecting an amphitheatre for the manly exercise of boxing* (1743) · apprentice binding register of the Watermen and Lightermen's Company, 1719–25, GL, MS 6289/6 · J. Godfrey, *A treatise upon the useful science of defence* (1747), 55–6, 63–4 · *Whitehall Evening-Post, or, London Intelligencer* (7–10 April 1750) · S. Pegge, *Curialia, or, An historical account of some branches of the royal houshold, &c. &c.*, 3 (1791), 89 · R. Hennell, *The history of the king's body guard of the yeomen of the guard* (1904), 260 · *The World, Fashionable Advertiser* (21 Sept 1787) · *The World, Fashionable Advertiser* (27 Sept 1787) · *The World, Fashionable Advertiser* (29 Oct 1787) · *GM*, 1st ser., 24 (1754) · *Public Advertiser* (13 Dec 1768) · W. Moore, *The infamy of Justice Kelynge, Justice Pell, and John Broughton, bruiser* (1769) · *St James's Chronicle, or, British Evening-Post* (28–31 Jan 1769) · *Daily Advertiser* [London] (1 Feb 1748) · *Penny London Post, or, the Morning Advertiser* (6–8 Feb 1751) · PRO, PROB 18/98 · H. Walpole, *Anecdotes of painting in England: with some account of the principal artists*, ed. R. N. Wornum, new edn, 3 (1849), 756

Likenesses G. Townshend, first marquess Townshend, caricature, pen-and-ink drawing, *c.*1751–1758, NPG · J. Young, mezzotint, 1789 (with George Stevenson; after J. H. Mortimer), BM · R. Cooper, stipple, 1821, BM, Westminster Abbey · F. Ross, lithograph, pubd 1842 (after W. Hogarth), BM, NPG · mezzotint, BM, NPG [*see illus.*]

Wealth at death more than £7000: *London Chronicle* (15–17 Jan 1789); *Scots Magazine* (1 Jan 1789)

Broughton, Rhoda (1840–1920), novelist, was born at Segrwyd Hall, near Denbigh, north Wales, on 29 November 1840, the youngest daughter of the Revd Delves Broughton (*d.* 1863) and Jane, *née* Bennett (*d.* 1860). She had two elder sisters and a younger brother. Broughton's clergyman father was the younger son of an old Staffordshire family, and was given the living of Broughton, in Staffordshire, one of the family seats. She grew up at Broughton Hall, near Eccleshall, an Elizabethan manor house, and was educated by her father, who taught her Latin and Greek and introduced her to Shakespeare. With her literary tastes encouraged by him, she read widely in the good library at the house. Upon the death of her father, she went to live with her sisters in Surbiton, just south of London, until the following year, when one of them, Eleanor, married William Charles Newcombe, of Upper Euarth, Denbighshire; Broughton made her home with them.

Broughton was inspired to write fiction by Anne Thackeray Ritchie's lively novel of girlhood, *The Story of Elizabeth* (1863). She published her first novel, *Not Wisely but too Well* in the *Dublin University Magazine* in 1867, which was edited by the Irish novelist Sheridan Le Fanu, who had married Broughton's maternal aunt, Susanna, in 1843. The same year *Cometh up as a Flower* appeared; it was an immediate best-seller, with its racy story of a young girl who is in love with a handsome, penniless soldier, but who feels obliged to marry a rich but boorish older man in order to support her family after her father's bankruptcy and death. Broughton's fiction is notable for its directness of tone. She often uses a first-person narrator, who addresses the reader with breathless immediacy, combining colloquialisms with a range of literary references, which give an air of cultural respectability to the colloquial intimacy which she seeks to establish. Her heroines are independent-minded, sometimes foolishly over-impetuous, extremely open in voicing their feelings, and deplore all kinds of mid-Victorian stuffiness. Broughton's story-lines and situations were often considered *risqué*. Anthony Trollope, for example, commented that in her 'determination not to be mawkish and missish, she has made her ladies do and say things which ladies would not do and say' (*An Autobiography*, 1883; 1923 edn, 235). Broughton took care, however, that transgression was kept within bounds, and her conclusions are frequently quietly moralistic. But she writes eloquently about the economic pressures upon women, about the ways in which marriage can be a tyranny, and about the often contradictory pulls of love and duty. These issues are reworked in a number of three-volume novels, including *Red as a Rose is She* (1870), *Goodbye, Sweetheart* (1872), *Nancy* (1873), and *Belinda* (1883), all of which she published with the firm of Richard Bentley.

In 1877 Broughton and her sister Eleanor, now widowed, moved to 27 Holywell Street, Oxford, and then, in 1890, to 1 Mansfield Place, Richmond Hill, in Surrey. In *Belinda*, and in *A Widower Indeed* (1891), which she co-authored with Elizabeth Bisland, Broughton expresses some of her exasperation with the close, gossipy world of academic Oxford, where she was ostracized in some circles as a result of her supposedly shocking fiction. *Belinda*'s plot owes something to *Middlemarch*, with its heroine marrying an older scholar—believed, like Casaubon, to have been modelled on Mark Pattison—and finding her emotions and her activities severely restricted. Broughton herself was famous for her conversation, for her tea parties, which amounted to literary salons, and for her entourage of small dogs. Henry James was a good friend; Oscar Wilde, by contrast, allegedly declined to invite her to his parties once her reputation for witty conversation grew. Her depiction of the aesthete Francis Chaloner, in *Second Thoughts* (1880), seems a satiric act of revenge against the young Wilde.

Broughton was a productive novelist, and wrote fast; she could complete a novel in six weeks. After the demise of the three-decker novel in 1894, she took readily to single-volume publication, which suited the punchy and aphoristic qualities of her prose. *A Beginner* (1894) features a young woman who writes a sensation novel, and later fictions contain controversial, less autobiographical elements. *Foes in Law* (1900) ridicules Victorian family life; the heroine of *A Waif's Progress* (1905) flirts throughout with her married guardian; *The Devil and the Deep Sea* (1910) deals with deception, adultery, and embezzlement; and *Between Two Stools* (1910) has a heroine who is tied to a bullying invalid husband while being in love with someone else. Yet Broughton no longer was regarded as particularly controversial, and in some aspects showed herself to be reactionary. *Dear Faustina* (1897), for example, has a heroine ostensibly working for women's causes, but in fact more concerned with self-promotion.

In 1900 Broughton moved back to Oxford to live with a cousin at River View, Headington Hill, but maintained a London flat in Cadogan Gardens, in Kensington, where she spent a period of each year. By the end of her life, she was very infirm, and had been in pain for some years. She died of cancer at her Oxford home on 5 June 1920. Although she had carried on writing until the end of her life, she herself had noted not just her slow decline in popularity, but the shifting judgement on her work. Late in her career, she remarked: 'I began by being the Zola and I have now become the Charlotte Yonge of English fiction' (Earl of Oxford and Asquith, *Memories and Reflections*, vol. 1: 1852–1927, 1928, 217). KATE FLINT

Sources M. Wood, *Rhoda Broughton: profile of a novelist* (1993) · H. C. Black, *Notable women authors of the day* (1893) · 'Miss Rhoda Broughton: a novelist of English character', *The Times* (7 June 1920) · E. Arnold, 'Rhoda Broughton as I knew her', *Fortnightly Review*, 114 (1920), 262–78 · S. M. Ellis, 'Rhoda Broughton', *The Bookman*, 58 (1920), 133–4 · E. L. Linton, 'Miss Broughton's novels', *Temple Bar*, 80 (1887), 196–209 · E. A. Bennett, *Fame and fiction: an enquiry into certain popularities* (1901) · *Diaries and letters of Marie Belloc Lowndes, 1911–1947*, ed. S. Lowndes (1971) · d. cert. · CGPLA Eng. & Wales (1920)
Archives Bodl. Oxf., letters · Ches. & Chester ALSS, corresp. and papers | BL, corresp. with Bentley & Son, publishers, and with Macmillans, Add. MS 54970 · Hove Central Library, Sussex, letters to Viscount Wolseley and Lady Wolseley
Likenesses Barraud, photograph, 1889, NPG; repro. in *Men and Women of the Day*, 2 (1889) · Lord Battersea, photograph, 1890–99, NPG
Wealth at death £6377 9s. 7d.: probate, 11 Aug 1920, CGPLA Eng. & Wales

Broughton [*alias* Rouse], **Richard** (*c*.1561–1635), Roman Catholic priest, was born at Great Stukeley, Huntingdonshire, the son of Edmund and Constantia Broughton, *née* Rouse. His father had been a courtier of Henry VIII's, and he was related to leading Catholic families. He probably matriculated at Pembroke College, Cambridge, in 1577, but took no degree, and next appears as a religious prisoner in the Gatehouse between November 1583 and April 1584. He left England some time later, arriving at Rome on 27 November 1589, under the name Richard Rouse. He began his training as a missionary priest at the English College, Rome, but in 1591 was sent to the seminary at Rheims on account of his health, and was ordained there on 19 December 1592. By November 1593 he was reported to be in England, staying at Thomas Habington's house in Hindlip, Worcestershire. He was a tall man with black hair and a black beard.

Broughton played a prominent role in running the English mission, being appointed an assistant to the archpriest from about July 1613. When the chapter was formed in 1623 he was on it; he was appointed vicar-general in the midlands, and had the title archdeacon of Huntingdon. From at least 1622 he was firmly ensconced in Belvoir Castle as chaplain to the countess of Rutland. When he wished to research his books he went to the Bodleian, registering there in 1626 as a 'minister of God's word',

which suggests a certain panache at a time when it was still a capital offence to be discovered as a Catholic priest.

Broughton was a prolific writer with over twenty titles to his credit. He was an enthusiastic controversialist, always lively and erudite. His favourite controversial device was to use protestant authors against their cause. He attacked the Thirty-Nine Articles, Anglican orders, and the well-worn subject of protestant political loyalty. He did engage in controversy with Catholic authors, in defence of the institution of a Catholic bishop, but he was seldom harsh towards fellow Catholics, and had warm words of praise for both Jesuits and Benedictines, while attempting to correct what he saw as their errors. He also wrote devotional works. His great love was the ancient history of England, where he showed, like many of his contemporaries, more enthusiasm than scepticism. Thus in *The Ecclesiastical History of Great Britain* (1633), perhaps his most ambitious work, he sought to show, among other things, how Christianity had been first planted in this country by a visit from St Peter. In the preface to this work a eulogist describes him as the English Baronius. He died on 18 January 1635 and was buried with his parents in Great Stukeley. PETER HOLMES

Sources G. Anstruther, *The seminary priests*, 4 vols. (1969–77) · *DNB* · R. Webster, 'Richard Broughton', *Downside Review*, 54 (1936), 495–514 · J. Pits, *Relationum historicarum de rebus Anglicis*, ed. [W. Bishop] (Paris, 1619), 815 · R. Broughton, *The ecclesiastical history of Great Britain* (1633), prefaces · Venn, *Alum. Cant.* · Wood, *Ath. Oxon.*: *Fasti* (1815), 428–9 · H. Ellis, ed., *The visitation of the county of Huntingdon … 1613*, CS, 43 (1849) · *The manuscripts of his grace the duke of Rutland*, 4 vols., HMC, 24 (1888–1905), vols. 1, 4 · parish register, Great Stukeley, Cambs. AS [burial] · A. F. Allison and D. M. Rogers, eds., *The contemporary printed literature of the English Counter-Reformation between 1558 and 1640*, 2 vols. (1989–94) · T. H. Clancy, *English Catholic books, 1641–1700: a bibliography* [1974] · Gillow, *Lit. biog. hist.*, vol. 1 · M. Hodgetts, 'Elizabethan priest holes III: East Anglia, Baddesley Clinton, Hindlip', *Recusant History*, 12 (1973–4), 171–97 · A. F. Allison, 'Richard Smith, Richelieu and the French marriage', *Recusant History*, 7 (1963–4), 148–211 · M. C. Questier, *Newsletters from the archpresbyterate of George Birkhead*, CS, 5th ser., 12 (1998)
Archives Archivio Vaticano, Vatican City, Fondo Burghese III, 51c, fol. 137

Broughton, Samuel Daniel (1787–1837), military surgeon, the fourth and youngest son of Thomas Broughton, rector of St Peter's, Bristol, and his wife, Jane, was born in Bristol in July 1787. Thomas Duer *Broughton (1778–1835) was his brother. Samuel was educated at Bristol grammar school under the care of the Revd Samuel Seyer.

After studying at St George's Hospital, London, Broughton became assistant surgeon of the Dorset militia, and in October 1812 he was appointed assistant surgeon of the 2nd Life Guards, of which J. Carrick Moore, elder brother of General Sir John Moore, was then surgeon. Immediately afterwards Broughton was appointed additional surgeon with temporary rank, and placed in medical charge of the service squadrons of the regiment, which was ordered abroad and with which he was present in the Peninsula and south of France until the end of the war. He published his experiences of the fighting from Lisbon to Boulogne in a volume of *Letters from Portugal, Spain, and*

France during the Campaigns of 1812, 1813, and 1814 (1815). He was also with his regiment at the battle of Waterloo.

In July 1821 Broughton succeeded to the surgeoncy of the regiment on the resignation of Moore, who had just been granted a pension of £1000 a year in recognition of the distinguished services of his late brother. Living at Regent's Park barracks, London, with his regiment, Broughton concentrated on his medical and scientific studies and published a number of original papers, chiefly relating to physiological research. Together with a barrister called Mr Wilcox, Broughton delivered some valuable lectures on forensic medicine and toxicology. He was elected a fellow of the Royal Society, in February 1830, and of the Geological Society.

In 1836 Broughton injured his leg in a fall, which resulted in disease of the ankle joint and eventually made amputation necessary. The operation was performed by Robert Liston, but Broughton died at Regent's Park barracks, ten days after the surgery, on 20 August 1837. He was interred in London at Kensal Green cemetery.

H. M. CHICHESTER, rev. PATRICK WALLIS

Sources *GM*, 2nd ser., 8 (1837), 432 · H. J. Rose, *A new general biographical dictionary*, ed. H. J. Rose and T. Wright, 12 vols. (1848), vol. 5, p. 97 · *Catalogue of scientific papers*, Royal Society, 19 vols. (1867–1925)
Archives RS

Broughton, Thomas (1704–1774), Church of England clergyman and author, was born on 5 July 1704 in the parish of St Andrew's, Holborn, London, the elder son and second of six children of the Revd John Broughton DD (*bap.* 1673, *d.* 1720), chaplain to the first duke of Marlborough, lecturer of St Andrew's, Holborn, and vicar of Kingston upon Thames, and his wife, Mary, daughter of Thomas Rutty and his wife, Mary Young. He was educated at St Andrew's School, Holborn (1714–16), Eton College (king's scholar, 1716–20), St Paul's School, London (1720–23), and as a sizar and scholar at Gonville and Caius College, Cambridge (1723–7, MA 1730). His studies at Cambridge were funded by Dr Cave's Charity, administered by the Sons of the Clergy, and he specialized in mathematics and modern languages. Ordained deacon in 1727 and priest in 1728, he was appointed on 24 November 1727 as reader to the Temple Church, in preference to the favoured candidate of the former treasurer of Middle Temple. A few months later (26 February 1728), in a touching letter to Richard Agar, treasurer of Middle Temple, he expressed great concern at having learned that he was displeasing his employers by his apparently negligent reading of prayers and failure to call on the benchers, explaining that he suffered from a speech impediment, which he was aiming to correct with the help of an expensive therapist. Evidently he succeeded, for he remained at the Temple, serving also as rector of Stibbington, Huntingdonshire (1739–44), among other appointments. A staunch upholder of the established church, he published in 1732 *Christianity Distinct from the Religion of Nature*, a three-volume rebuttal of deism, specifically Matthew Tindal's *Christianity as Old as the Creation*; for this the benchers of Inner and Middle

Temples awarded him 20 guineas. On the recommendation of Thomas Sherlock, master of the Temple and bishop of Salisbury, he was appointed on 13 October 1744 to the valuable Salisbury prebendary of the Bristol vicarages of Bedminster, including St Thomas and Abbots Leigh, and St Mary Redcliffe. In 1755 the vestry of St Mary Redcliffe commissioned Hogarth's paintings for the church. By 1750 he had married Anne, daughter of the parish schoolmaster, the Revd Thomas Harris.

A conscientious minister, Broughton was also an industrious and diverse author with a distinct narrative gift. He contributed 120 articles (those signed 'T') to the first three volumes of *Biographia Britannica* (1747–50), mainly on English divines, scholars, and poets, notably Dryden, whose miscellaneous works he edited (*Original Poems and Translations*, 1743). His *Bibliotheca historico-sacra, or, An historical library of the principal matters relating to religion, antient and modern* (1737–9), a two-volume encyclopaedia of world religions in over a thousand pages folio, was reissued in one volume as *An Historical Dictionary of All Religions, from the Creation of the World to this Present Time* in 1742, as *A Dictionary of All Religions* in 1756, and in a Hungarian translation published at Komárom in 1793. His other certain works include further expositions and defences of protestant belief and principles. Kippis lists translations from Greek and Latin and of Bayle and Voltaire and, according to Hawkins, he made the translation of *Don Quixote* attributed to Charles Jervas. According to Kippis his unpublished manuscripts, now lost, included many pieces of verse and two youthful unfinished tragedies, which showed considerable talent. His ready sense of human drama was lastingly realized in his libretto, drawn from Sophocles and Ovid, for 'a work of supreme genius' (Dean, 415), Handel's *Hercules* (1744, first performed King's Theatre, London, 5 January 1745); he had subscribed to Handel's *Atalanta* in 1736. Even in his scholarly works, fielding an impressive quantity and range of references, he is lucid, lively, and modest, and as a minister (notably in *Fifteen Sermons on Select Subjects*, 1778) he promoted Christian virtue at its most generous.

Broughton died in office on 21 December 1774 at Bristol and was buried on 24 December at St Mary Redcliffe. He was survived by his wife and six of their seven children, including Arthur *Broughton, physician and botanist, and in 1811 his widow erected a monument in St Mary Redcliffe to him and some of their children, which, however, was inaccurate as to his early life. 'In private life, he was devoted to the interests and happiness of his family; and was of a mild, cheerful and liberal temper. This disposition, which is not always united with eminent literary abilities, attended him to the grave' (Kippis, 2. x).

RUTH SMITH

Sources J. Venn and others, eds., *Biographical history of Gonville and Caius College*, 2: 1713–1897 (1898), 18 · A. Kippis and others, eds., *Biographia Britannica, or, The lives of the most eminent persons who have flourished in Great Britain and Ireland*, 2nd edn, 2 (1780), ix–x · Honourable Society of Middle Temple, minutes of parliament · Honourable Society of Middle Temple, MT.15/TAM/146 · F. A. Inderwick and R. A. Roberts, eds., *A calendar of the Inner Temple records*, 4 (1933), 185 · St Mary Redcliffe, vestry minutes, Bristol RO · parish register,

St Mary Redcliffe, Bristol RO · J. Foster, 'Index of incumbents since the Reformation', CUL, Add. MSS 6728, 6738 · J. Foster, 'Index to Neve's Fasti', CUL, Add. MS 6746 · G. W. Kendall, 'John Wootton, life and a list of engravings after his pictures', *Walpole Society*, 21 (1932–3), 23–42 · J. Hawkins, *The life of Samuel Johnson, LL.D.* (1787), 216 · E. H. Pearce, *The sons of the clergy*, 2nd edn (1928), 173 · W. Dean, *Handel's dramatic oratorios and masques* (1959), 414–33 · DNB · IGI · 'Bishop Secker's diocese book', ed. E. Ralph, *A Bristol miscellany*, Bristol RS, 37 (1985), 21–69 · R. A. Austen-Leigh, ed., *The Eton College register, 1698–1752* (1927), 46 · M. McDonnell, ed., *The registers of St Paul's School, 1509–1748* (privately printed, London, 1977), 422 · R. Paulson, *Hogarth*, 3 (1993), 202–9 · M. J. H. Liversidge, *William Hogarth's Bristol altar-piece* (1980) · Venn, *Alum. Cant.* · memorial plaque, church of St Mary Redcliffe, Bristol **Archives** Honourable Society of Middle Temple, letter, MT.15/TAM/146 · Honourable Society of Middle Temple, minutes of parliament (MSS), record of appointment

Broughton, Thomas (1712–1777), Church of England clergyman, was born in the parish of St Martin Carfax, Oxford, the son of Thomas Broughton, gentleman, and his wife. He matriculated at University College, Oxford, on 17 December 1731, aged nineteen. In March 1733 he joined a group called 'Methodists' led by John Wesley. He was elected Petreian fellow at Exeter College on 30 June 1733 and full fellow on 14 July 1734. By December 1734 he was increasingly at odds with some of the Methodists, though he remained an ally for some time, even assisting in Wesley's unsuccessful attempt at preferment to the living at Epworth in April 1735.

For a time, beginning in late 1735, Broughton was curate of Cowley, near Uxbridge. In 1736 he became curate at the Tower of London and occasionally rode in the cart with condemned criminals to Tyburn, in the manner depicted by William Hogarth. He took his BA degree on 22 March 1737. A year later he challenged, as too Moravian, Wesley's claims of instantaneous conversion and assurance of faith, and consequently became estranged from the Methodists. Having both obtained and lost a lectureship at St Helen, Bishopsgate, through the influence of George Whitefield, in 1741 he became lecturer of All Hallows, Lombard Street. In July 1741 he resigned his fellowship at Exeter; and in the following year he married a Miss Capel. They had fifteen children; five of them died in infancy.

Broughton was appointed secretary of the Society for Promoting Christian Knowledge on 28 June 1743, a position that occupied him on weekdays for the rest of his life. As the first ordained clergyman to hold the position, he managed the society's publications and assistance to charity schools, missions, and workhouses, but seems to have gained no personal notoriety thereby. A portrait of Broughton by Robert Dunkarton still hangs in the SPCK headquarters. On 7 November 1752 he was installed rector of the church of St John the Evangelist in Wotton, Surrey, a living which also included Oakwood Chapel. Broughton died in London on the morning of St Thomas's day, 21 December 1777, as he was preparing for services; he was found by friends on his knees in clerical attire in the society's house in Hatton Garden. Broughton's published writings include two sermons: *The Christian Soldier, or, The Duties of a Religious Life Recommended to the Army*, preached in

1737 at the Tower, printed in 1738 (12th edn, 1818), and translated into Gaelic (*An saighdear Criosduidh*) in 1797; and *A Serious and Affectionate Warning to Servants* (1746; 9th edn, 1818). RICHARD P. HEITZENRATER

Sources L. Tyerman, *The Oxford Methodists* (1873) · O. Manning and W. Bray, *The history and antiquities of the county of Surrey*, 3 vols. (1804–14) · *The works of John Wesley*, ed. A. C. Outler and others, [26 vols.] (1975–) · Boase, *Mod. Eng. biog.* · Foster, *Alum. Oxon.* · W. K. L. Clarke, *A short history of the SPCK* (1919) · W. O. B. Allen, *Two hundred years: the history of the Society for Promoting Christian Knowledge, 1698–1898* (1898) · VCH Surrey · SPCK early 18th century archives (1976) [microfilm] **Archives** JRL, Methodist Archives and Research Centre, letter to Whitefield **Likenesses** R. Dunkarton, mezzotint (after N. Dance), BM, NPG · R. Dunkarton, oils, Society for Promoting Christian Knowledge, London

Broughton, Thomas Duer (1778–1835), army officer in the East India Company and writer on India, was born in Bristol on 8 March 1778, son of the Revd Thomas Broughton, rector of St Peter's, Bristol, and his wife, Jane; he was great-grandson of the Revd John Broughton, chaplain to the first duke of Marlborough. His younger brother was the military surgeon Samuel Daniel *Broughton. Educated at Eton College (entered 1791, king's scholar 1793), in 1795 he became a cadet on the Bengal establishment. He arrived in India in March 1797. He was actively engaged at the siege of Seringapatam in 1799, and was afterwards appointed commandant of the cadet corps, and in 1802 military resident with the Marathas. For a short time previous to the restoration of Java to the Dutch he held the command of that island. He became a lieutenant on the Madras establishment in October 1797, captain in October 1805, major in March 1816, lieutenant-colonel in June 1822, and colonel in June 1829, after which he returned to England.

Broughton married, in London, on 20 September 1814, Georgiana Sophia, eldest daughter of John Ezechiel Des Champs, afterwards Chamier, of Grosvenor Place, London, member of council at Madras. They had no children. He travelled much in Britain and southern Europe, and was honorary secretary of the Royal Asiatic Society and an active manager of the Mendicity Society and of the Marylebone schools. His publications included *Letters Written in a Mahratta Camp during the Year 1809, Descriptive of … the Mahrattas* (1813) and *Selections from the Popular Poetry of the Hindoos* (1814). Broughton died at his home in Dorset Square, London, on 16 November 1835. THOMPSON COOPER, *rev.* JAMES LUNT

Sources T. D. Broughton, *Letters written in a Mahratta camp* (1813) · GM, 2nd ser., 5 (1836) · *British Museum catalogue of printed books* · W. J. Wilson, ed., *History of the Madras army*, 5 vols. (1882–9) · W. Thorn, *Memoir of the conquest of Java* (1815) · V. C. P. Hodson, *List of officers of the Bengal army, 1758–1834*, 1 (1927) · C. E. Buckland, *Dictionary of Indian biography* (1906) **Archives** U. Southampton L., letters to Arthur Wellesley

Broughton, William Grant (1788–1853), Anglican bishop in Australia, was born at Bridge Street, Westminster, London, on 22 May 1788, the eldest son of Grant Broughton (d.

William Grant Broughton (1788–1853), by William Nicholas, 1843

c.1803) and his wife, Phoebe Ann, daughter of John Rumball of Barnet, Hertfordshire. He attended Barnet grammar school (1794–6) and the King's School, Canterbury (1797–1803). He was to have gone to Pembroke College, Cambridge, but after his father's death financial circumstances prevented this. Through the influence of his paternal uncles and the Cecil family he gained a clerkship in the East India Company treasury department and worked at East India House from 1807 to 1812. A legacy enabled him in 1814 to enter Pembroke College, aged twenty-six. He was sixth wrangler and BA in 1818 (MA, 1823; DD *per saltum*, 1836). From his undergraduate days he was lame and often walked with a stick.

Early career: England, 1818–1829 Broughton was made deacon in 1818 at Salisbury on letters dimissory for the bishop of Winchester, and ordained priest in the same year. He served assistant curacies at Hartley Wespall 1818–27 and Farnham (1827–8). On 13 July 1818 he married Sarah Francis (d. 16 September 1849 in Sydney), eldest daughter of his King's School housemaster, the Revd John Francis, rector of St Mildred's, Canterbury. They had one son, who died in infancy, and two daughters, Sarah and Phoebe. At Hartley Wespall the duchess of Wellington befriended him.

Between 1823 and 1826 Broughton displayed his talent for linguistic textual analysis and published on the Elzevir text of the Greek New Testament and on Bishop Gauden's authorship of the *Eikon basilike*, purportedly Charles I's religious apologia. In both publications he affirmed the canons of tory churchmanship: godly nation, the royal supremacy, and the vocation of empires in the propagation of the Christian gospel. This brought him to the notice of the duke of Wellington who, in 1828, secured

him a chaplaincy to the Tower of London, and, in 1829, the archdeaconry of New South Wales within the diocese of Calcutta. Broughton would have preferred a theological librarianship at the British Museum. Broughton and his family sailed from Sheerness in the convict ship *John*.

Australia: archdeacon, 1829–1834 Everything Broughton believed fitted him for his new post. The archdeaconry had been established in 1825 to secure the Church of England a central place in the new civil order replacing the old convict administration. The archdeacon sat on the executive and legislative councils, and administered a church and schools corporation, to be richly endowed with land, for the expansion of Anglican worship and education. The arrangement was essentially tory, and committed the colonial government to a productive relationship between church and state.

Broughton arrived in Sydney on 13 September 1829, and on 16 September was installed in office at a ceremony in Government House. With his ecclesiastical superior in Calcutta he was *de facto* the autonomous leader of the colonial church within the limits of his priestly orders. He spent his years as archdeacon (1829–36) wrestling with the disparity between the intended influence of his office and the dynamics of colonial change. The projected relationship between church and state did not materialize, and the church and school corporation, which had not been a success, was suspended shortly before Broughton left England, and its charter was revoked in 1833, leaving no funds for churches or schools. These changes stemmed from a local political movement determined to reshape the colony's future civil order in the interests of its settlers, including former convicts, rather than according to the assumptions of the Colonial Office. The colonial-born William Charles Wentworth, a lawyer, publisher, and wealthy pastoralist, towered over local politics at the time of Broughton's arrival. He attacked the office of archdeacon as a novel device for sustaining Colonial Office manipulation of local affairs, and singled out the archdeacon's grand salary and seats on the councils as impositions colonists would remove. Broughton had soon to defend his office and his church against allegations that both were pawns of the Colonial Office, which had nothing to do with religion and everything to do with a political struggle for self-rule.

In 1831 Broughton's position worsened with the arrival of Governor Richard Bourke, an Anglo-Irish whig and liberal Anglican who championed reforms which required a material loss of status for the Church of England in a colony where one quarter of the population was Irish Catholic threatened a repetition of the sectarian discord which cursed Ireland. Broughton was snubbed on the councils, forced to share clerical appointments with Irish Catholics, starved of primary school funds, stripped of his grammar school in Sydney, and denied authority to discipline his clergy without the concurrence of the impossibly distant bishop of Calcutta. He was also maliciously misrepresented to the Colonial Office as a leading exclusive—that is, one of a politically vexatious group of free immigrant settlers who opposed the restoration of full civil rights to former convicts and therefore risked serious social disharmony. Secretly Bourke also angled for his recall to England. By 1833 Broughton considered his role as archdeacon 'very anomalous and personally irksome', and sailed for England in August 1834, having sold his furniture to raise his passage money, and unsure that he would ever return.

Australia again: bishop, 1836–1852 Broughton did return. On 14 February 1836 he was consecrated bishop at Lambeth. The Society for the Propagation of the Gospel (SPG) offered him financial support, and the Colonial Office put his salary on the civil list. He was reappointed to the councils where he could oppose Bourke's religious reforms which were to be settled by a vote of the colonial legislature. While in England he also became acquainted with the Tractarians, whose doctrine of apostolic authority liberated him from thraldom to the royal supremacy. This was the intellectual turning point of his career, and culminated in his later pioneering of the revival of synodical government within the Church of England. He was an older type of high-churchman and—though accused of Puseyite tendencies—never a Tractarian, though he sympathized with them, was a patron of Tractarian clergy, and admired Pusey and Keble. Also in England he met the Revd Edward Coleridge, an Eton housemaster. Coleridge became the bishop's commissary and confidant, and their correspondence is a principal source for the history of the early Australian episcopate.

On 5 June 1836 Broughton was installed as bishop of Australia in St James's Church, Sydney, and immediately confronted Bourke's radical religious and education reforms, although he failed to stop the religious reform embodied in the Church Acts (1836 and 1837), which endorsed a special tie between the civil state and Christianity but allocated religious subsidies to Anglicans, Roman Catholics, Presbyterians, and Wesleyans. Broughton protested, but soon realized his diocese could reap exceptional benefits from the government's offer of a pound-for-pound subsidy. Within a year he had collected £23,000 in cash or pledges, and an alarmed colonial treasury capped religious subsidies at £30,000 annually, two-thirds going to the Church of England. By 1840 parishes had expanded from twelve to thirty-six, and St Andrew's Cathedral was begun. Oxford dons had endowed a diocesan theological library, which was so complete that Origen was said to have been the only patristic text which was not represented. In 1845 he founded St James's Theological College, Sydney, to train local clergy. He had high hopes, but his opponents in the press alleged he was trying to make it a Tractarian stronghold, and it closed in 1849: its failure was a heavy blow to him, and was largely because he failed to gain sufficient support among the laity. He protested against the secular character of the new University of Sydney (1850) and refused a seat on its senate. In 1843 he protested against a Roman Catholic bishop's assumption of the title archbishop of Sydney, and in 1850 against the 'papal aggression' in England.

In 1836 Broughton defeated Bourke's proposal to establish national schools similar to Ireland's. A substitute protestant system might, with support, have been developed, but Broughton insisted upon denominational schools, which Bourke rejected, thus allowing colonial education to remain unfunded for a decade, for which Broughton was unfairly blamed. In 1847 Governor Fitzroy offered to fund national and denominational schools but Broughton mistrusted his resolve and correctly forecast that Fitzroy would leave without providing the money.

After 1837 Broughton's position improved. In December 1837 Bourke left the colony, and the new governor, Sir George Gipps, arrived in February 1838. Gipps, a Canterbury schoolfriend, invited Broughton to draft a free immigration policy to replace the convict labour being withdrawn. Broughton advised giving priority to family immigration to correct the sex imbalance due to many single male convicts. Despite resistance from pastoralists, who favoured the economy of single workers, Gipps adopted Broughton's recommendation. The colony's sex imbalance had almost righted when the 1850s gold rush worsened it again.

Broughton opposed the self-interest of pastoralists on other occasions, largely to prevent the emergence of a super-rich oligarchy of landowners. He championed an artificially high price for crown lands to push settlers onto leases, deeming it important to reserve land to lure future immigrants. He also opposed any resumption of transportation to provide cheap convict labour during a rural depression in the 1840s. Earlier he had defended transportation against its severest critics, Whately in 1833 and Molesworth in 1838, and stressed its record in creating useful colonial citizens. He mixed socially with reformed former convicts, and Moore Theological College was named after a convict benefactor. In 1842 Broughton discredited any revival of transportation as the elevation of money above morals, and turned the issue into a moral crusade.

Broughton did little for the Aborigines, sharing the anthropological assumptions which helped turn the European presence into oppression, but in 1830 he supported Lancelot Threlkeld's translation of the gospels into a tribal dialect, hoping that the Book of Common Prayer would follow. In 1831 he secured approval for a mission at Wellington valley, but the Colonial Office recruited the Church Missionary Society, which undercut his authority. Twice he reported (in 1830 on Van Diemen's Land, in 1838 on New South Wales) to governors on the adverse condition of the Aborigines, and predicted their extinction unless they adopted European habits. In 1850, admitting that his efforts had not borne fruit, he formed the Australian Board of Missions to train Aborigines as evangelists.

Broughton's civil achievements earned him nomination to a personal seat on a reformed legislative council in 1843, but he declined. The *Sydney Morning Herald* hailed this as a selfless gesture to avoid sectarianism, and praised his 'inestimable state papers' on immigration and land as a 'richer collection of facts and a surer guide to accurate conclusions than any other publications that ever came under our notice'. He remained on the executive council until 1847, largely to scrutinize the distribution of religious subsidies.

In 1844 Broughton was notified of the imminent subdivision of his vast diocese of Australia. He surrendered £800 of his salary to quicken results, but it was 1847 before all four posts—Adelaide, Tasmania, Melbourne, and Newcastle—were filled. In 1846 he became bishop of Sydney and metropolitan of Australasia and began to tackle the anomaly of royal supremacy. Neither the British nor the colonial government protected the colonial Church of England, but each wilfully interfered in its affairs. When Broughton proposed appointing an archdeacon the Colonial Office claimed rights of nomination; when he erected a disciplinary court under his letters patent the colonial government refused it recognition, exposing him to civil redress. Robert Lowe (later Lord Sherbrooke), imagining that bishop and clergy had colluded to erect an episcopal monarchism in the diocese, promoted a Church of England Clergyman's Benefice Bill to remove authority over the clergy from the bishop to their congregations. Broughton addressed the legislative council from the bar to defeat the bill. After that he searched for some alternative to the royal supremacy as a foundation to his ecclesiastical authority, and corresponded with W. E. Gladstone and Judge Sir John Coleridge on the issue.

In 1849 Broughton faced personal bankruptcy, being held liable for the debts of the Bank of Australia, of which his diocese was deemed a minor shareholder. He drafted his own defence, which ended the action. In August he fell ill with erysipelas, as did his wife, to whom it proved fatal. Broughton emerged from his anguish with a bolder vision of an autonomous colonial Church of England. He invited the bishops of Australasia to Sydney in 1850 to confer upon uniform solutions to common problems. This meeting made the historic decision to revive synodical government, both diocesan and provincial. He suggested that bishops and clergy constitute a synod to debate doctrine, discipline, and ritual, and for the laity to meet concurrently in a convention to vote only on temporalities or the constitution. No rights were reserved to crown or archbishop, except to acknowledge the traditions of Canterbury.

To remove legal obstacles Gladstone, on Broughton's behalf, approached the British parliament to free colonial dioceses to assemble and by mutual consent draft rules for the internal government of their dioceses, and to prohibit persons who had consented to those rules afterwards appealing against them to English courts. British authorities resisted, fearing a debate might stir demands for genuine convocations in England, but agreed to colonial legislatures taking action. The New South Wales legislature refused, arguing that since the Church Acts the Church of England had no special status requiring extraordinary legislation. Meanwhile Archbishop Sumner signalled Canterbury's opposition to any revival of synods in the Church of England. Broughton wrote immediately to the bishop of Newcastle: 'We must act ourselves.' He circulated for discussion in all parishes a petition requesting the queen to remove all obstacles to clerical synods and

lay conventions as outlined at the bishops' meeting. Then, in April 1852, he summoned the clergy to Sydney: 'Whether I shall call this a Diocesan Synod, I cannot quite determine, but it certainly will be one in effect.' The April meeting disclosed strong clerical support for the American episcopal model, where clergy and laity sat and debated together. Broughton demurred, then compromised. He deplored the concessions other bishops made to greater lay influence. The common model for a colonial synod, as outlined at the bishops' meeting, vanished. Broughton feared this diversity invited rebuff, and removed the debate to London.

Broughton asked the SPG to arrange a meeting with bishops from Canada and South Africa who might join him in drafting a declaration which all colonial churches erecting synods must adopt. He believed that British co-operation would depend on some assurance of uniformity throughout the colonies, and expected such a declaration to transfer appellate jurisdiction from Canterbury to provincial synods.

Last years Broughton sailed for England in August 1852, travelling via South America and arriving, in ill health, in November 1852. The SPG invited Broughton 'as the father of the movement' to preside over a convention of colonial bishops on 25 January 1853, and to draft a document demanding that the colonial churches either be re-established in their individual colonies or be accorded the freedom and independence of other non-established churches. Broughton complied, and the SPG undertook to advertise the document for a month before having the bishops reassemble to formalize their demands, but Broughton was dead before the meeting. He died of bronchitis on 20 February 1853 at the home of Lady Gipps, widow of the former governor, 11 Chester Street, Belgrave Square, London. On 26 February he was buried in the nave of Canterbury Cathedral, the first person so honoured since Cardinal Pole in 1558.

Broughton's burial inside Canterbury Cathedral was an enigma. It acknowledged his heroic struggle to Anglicize the colonial civil order which replaced Australia's convict administration. Contemporary Australian historiography scorns such a goal. Its focus is on 'Australian patriotism', which it portrays as the triumph of Irish settler culture, or sometimes a bush socialism, over the institutions and culture of British imperialism. To dramatize that struggle Broughton has been caricatured to illustrate British arrogance, and thereby marginalized. Broughton will be restored to his rightful place in Australian history when the thoroughly British foundations to Australian civil society are acknowledged as one of the creative dynamics of colonial Australia.

GEORGE P. SHAW

Sources G. P. Shaw, *Patriarch and patriot: William Grant Broughton, colonial statesman and ecclesiastic* (1978) · F. T. Whitington, *William Grant Broughton* (1936) · K. Cable, 'Broughton, William Grant', *AusDB*, 2.196 · Venn, *Alum. Cant.* · Boase, *Mod. Eng. biog.* · *DNB*
Archives Bodl. RH, journals and letters · Mitchell L., NSW, papers · NL Aus., corresp. and papers, Ref. NK 946, 5398, MS 1731 · PRO, series CO. 201, 202, 224, 324, 325 · State Library of New South Wales, Sydney, Dixson Wing, corresp. and papers · U. Birm. L.,

corresp. relating to the New Zealand mission · University of Tasmania, Hobart, corresp. and papers [copies] · London, Australian papers, SPG papers | BL, Gladstone papers · State Archives of New South Wales, Sydney, Colonial Secretary's Office · University of Tasmania, Hobart, Moase collection · Westminster, Overseas Bishopric Fund

Likenesses W. Nicholas, watercolour, 1843, State Library of New South Wales, Sydney, Mitchell and Dixson collections [*see illus.*] · M. Claxton, portrait, 1850?, University of Sydney, St Paul's College · J. Lough, recumbent figure on monument, 1855, Canterbury Cathedral

Broughton, William Robert (1762–1821), naval officer, was a son of Charles Broughton, who died on 27 August 1820, aged eighty-five. After serving as a midshipman on the coast of North America and in the East Indies, and as lieutenant in the *Burford*, in the several engagements between Hughes and Suffren, Broughton was in 1790 appointed to command the brig *Chatham* to accompany Vancouver on his voyage of discovery. He was employed on the survey of the Columbia River and the adjacent coasts. In 1793 he travelled to Vera Cruz, overland from San Blas, on his way to England with dispatches.

On his arrival in England Broughton was made commander, on 3 October 1793, of the *Providence*, a small vessel of 400 tons burden, and was again sent out to the north-west coast of North America. On arriving on the station he found Vancouver gone; and crossing over to the other side, he began, and during the next four years carried out, a survey of the coast of Asia, from lat. 52° N to 35° N, which gained him promotion to post rank on 28 January 1797. On 16 May 1797 the *Providence* struck a coral reef near the coast of Formosa (Taiwan), and was lost. The men, however, were all saved and taken to Macao in the tender, in which Broughton afterwards continued the survey until May 1798, when he was discharged at Trincomalee for a passage to England, where he arrived in the following February. He published the history of this voyage and its geographical results as *Voyage of discovery to the north Pacific ocean … performed in HM sloop Providence and her tender in the years 1795-6-7-8* (1804).

After holding some other commands, Broughton in 1809 commanded the *Illustrious* in the expedition under Lord Gambier against the French Brest fleet in Aix Roads, and at the court martial gave evidence which, so far as it went, implied a general agreement with the charges made by Lord Cochrane. In 1810, still in the *Illustrious*, he went out to the East Indies, and was present at the capture of Mauritius in December. In the following spring he had charge of the expedition against Java, which assembled at Malacca and sailed thence on 11 June 1811. The passage was long, and Broughton, in the opinion of many, was unduly cautious and it was the beginning of August before the troops were landed in the neighbourhood of Batavia. On 9 August 1811 the squadron was joined by Rear-Admiral the Hon. Robert Stopford, who had come to take the command. Broughton was annoyed, and applied for a court martial on the rear-admiral 'for behaving in a cruel, oppressive, and fraudulent manner, unbecoming the character of an officer, in depriving me of the command

of the squadron'. The Admiralty refused Broughton's request, and approved of the course taken by Stopford.

In 1812 Broughton returned to England. He was made a CB at the peace. He had married his cousin Jemima, youngest daughter of the Revd Sir Thomas Delves Broughton, baronet, of Doddington Hall, Cheshire, and they had three daughters and one son, William, afterwards a captain in the navy. During his later years Broughton resided at Florence, where he died suddenly from an attack of angina pectoris on 12 March 1821. He was buried in the English burial-ground at Leghorn. He was survived by his wife. J. K. LAUGHTON, *rev.* ROGER MORRISS

Sources *GM*, 1st ser., 91/1 (1821), 376, 648
Archives British Columbia Archives and Record Service, Victoria, corresp. and logbooks [copies] · NMM, journals | NL Scot., Elliot-Murray-Kynynmound MSS · NL Scot., letters

Broun, John Allan (1817–1879), physicist and meteorologist, was born on 21 September 1817 at Dumfries, where his father kept a school for boys destined for the navy. He entered Edinburgh University in 1837, about the time of his father's death. There his enthusiasm for physical science led to his friendship with Professor J. D. Forbes, who recommended Broun for the post of director of the magnetic observatory newly established by Sir Thomas Brisbane at Makerstoun. After a course of training at Greenwich observatory Broun took up his appointment in April 1842 with a vigour which quickly expanded the role and importance of Makerstoun in the worldwide network of magnetic observatories established in the 1840s. Magnetic and meteorological observations were made hourly (except on Sundays) until 1846, when the term set for concentrated observations expired, after which a limited series continued until 1855. Broun left Makerstoun in 1849 and spent the winter in Edinburgh, assisted by his friend John Welsh, later director of Kew observatory, preparing the results for publication in the *Transactions of the Royal Society of Edinburgh*. In the course of these labours he developed and tested new methods of correcting the values, which were generally adopted elsewhere and brought him some fame as one of the founders of the new observational science of terrestrial magnetism.

In 1850 Broun went to Paris to meet fellow scientists, and while there he met and married Charlotte Marianne Isoline Vallony, daughter of a clergyman of Huguenot extraction from the Swiss canton of Vaud. They had three sons and two daughters. In 1851 he was appointed director of the Trevandrum observatory, founded by the raja of Travancore in 1841, where he arrived in 1852 to oversee both magnetic and meteorological observations. In addition to these duties Broun strove to promote the general welfare of the province. He established a museum, issued an almanac, attempted a reform of weights and measures, and planned and oversaw the construction of public gardens, a road to the mountains, and a sanatorium. The Royal Society elected him FRS in 1853. While he was at Makerstoun Broun had set up a small high-altitude station on the Cheviots to compare magnetic readings at low and high altitude; he now decided to repeat the experiment, choosing to set his station on Agustia Malley, the highest peak of the Travancore Ghats, 6200 feet above sea level. This entailed having to transport huts and apparatus through the forested approaches inhabited by elephants and tigers. During this exercise Broun was afflicted by illness or by altitude and became permanently deaf. In 1860 he went to Europe seeking in vain a cure for his deafness; before returning to Trevandrum, however, he contributed papers on magnetism to the Royal Society of Edinburgh, and for his demonstration that the annual variation of horizontal magnetic force was a global feature he was awarded the society's Keith medal.

In April 1865 Broun left India and with his family lived for some years first at Lausanne, then at Stuttgart, where he was able to indulge his love of music, for he played the violin well and was an admirer of Beethoven. With his own meagre private resources, supplemented by a small pension from the raja of Travancore, he laboured to prepare his voluminous data for publication. In Stuttgart he devised and had made to his design a torsion gravimeter, intended to show the variation with latitude of the earth's gravity field. Broun put it on display at the South Kensington Loan Collection of Scientific Instruments in 1876, but by then it was of small worth because it was recognized that subsurface geology distorted the measured geoid.

In 1873 Broun moved to London, where his first volume of observations made at Trevandrum and Agustia Malley from 1852 to 1869 was published in 1874. It contained upwards of 300,000 corrected values for magnetic declination, with a discussion of the effects of lunar and solar action. This was the only volume to appear, and Broun had the mortification of seeing his thirteen years' work left incomplete. He needed an income, but, as a devoted adherent of the Free Church of Scotland, religious scruples had prevented his taking professional employment in Scotland; now his deafness was an additional handicap. Undaunted, however, and aided by a grant from the Royal Society he undertook to correct the magnetic observations made at the various colonial stations, for which the society awarded him the royal medal in 1878. This was an endless task, and his sense of responsibility added anxiety to Broun's labour. His health began to fail; during a stay in Lynton, Devon, he suffered a nervous attack from which he never fully recovered. A trip to Switzerland helped to rally him, but he died at his London home, 9 Abercorn Place, Maida Vale, on 22 November 1879. He was survived by his wife.

Broun published more than fifty papers, and his work was appreciated at the time, although several of his discoveries were made independently by his contemporaries in other observatories during the intensive global magnetic survey of the 1840s. His careful analyses revealed lunar action on the horizontal magnetic field, as well as the stronger solar diurnal, seasonal, and annual cycles. He was also able to show that large irregular disturbances had their source in the sun, by a means not then understood. An amiable man, endowed with social charm and

integrity, he lacked the self-promotion which might have carried him to a more prominent position in the history of terrestrial magnetism.

A. M. CLERKE, rev. ANITA McCONNELL

Sources B. Stewart, *Nature*, 21 (1879–80), 112–14 · *PRS*, 28 (1878–9), 66 · *PRS*, 30 (1879–80), iii · *The Times* (27 Nov 1879), 6e · *Catalogue of the special loan collection of scientific apparatus at the South Kensington Museum*, 2nd edn (1876), 106–7 · d. cert.
Archives NL Scot., corresp. and papers | CUL, letters to Sir George Stokes · U. St Andr. L., corresp. with James Forbes
Wealth at death under £1500: probate, 13 Feb 1880, *CGPLA Eng. & Wales*

Broun, Sir Richard, eighth baronet (1801–1858), pamphleteer and fraudster, was born at Lochmaben, Dumfriesshire, on 22 April 1801, eldest of the four sons and one daughter of Sir James Broun (1768–1844) of Coalston Park, Lochmaben, and his first wife, Marian, *née* Henderson (d. 1825). The baronetcy of Nova Scotia had been conferred on Sir Richard's ancestor in 1686 and continued until the sixth baronet died without leaving a son, when it passed to a cousin in holy orders who declined to take it up; it was resumed by his eldest son, Sir James, despite doubts being aired about his right to the title. Sir Richard succeeded his father in 1844, and frequently proclaimed himself 'eighth baronet of Scotland and Nova Scotia, feudal baron of Colstoun, Haddingtonshire'.

Nothing is known of Broun's early years. He was in London by 1833, and writing from an address in Wigmore Street in 1839. He soon afterwards moved to Chelsea where he thereafter lived at Sphinx Cottage (later called Sphinx Lodge), in Upper Church Street. One of his earliest schemes was that for a 'line of direct elemental intercourse between Europe and Asia by route of the British North American possessions, and the systematic colonisation of the vacant crown territories over which it will pass' (*DNB*); this was followed by a similar plan for an 'Anglo-Canadian Company, which should outrival in the west the East India Company' (Broun, *British and American Intercourse*). He was on the council of the British–American Association for Emigration and Colonization, an organization set up to pay for emigrants' passages, in 1842, the year it failed. Accusations concerning his role in the matter and others like it, published in *The Globe*, obliged Broun to bring proceedings against its proprietor. At the trial in February 1846 it was said that the newspapermen had failed to locate him at first, but later traced him to a humble lodging in an obscure Brompton street, only to find that he was always 'out'. Broun for his part admitted to not being entitled to call himself 'Sir', and that he had drawn £1000 annually from the British–American Association funds, which themselves had been raised through a loan negotiated by Broun. He was found to be a key instigator of the fraud and the case collapsed.

Broun dabbled in transport and agriculture: in 1834 he was campaigning to nationalize steam-powered road transport for public benefit and government revenue; he was at one time a director of the Paris to Dieppe Railway; and in 1840 he was honorary secretary of the Royal Agricultural Association of England. He was involved with the knights hospitallers of St John of Jerusalem, where he sought to revive the ancient order, and until his death, honorary secretary of the committee of the baronetage for privileges, publishing various pamphlets urging the causes of these two organizations. In one letter he declared himself 'both a consistent Conservative and a consistent protectionist, a stickler for national institutions, whether in Church or State' (Broun, *British and American Intercourse*, 14).

None of these early projects aroused as much public awareness as the proposal by Broun which was first published in 1849 as *The London Necropolis and National Mausoleum*. London's population had increased to the extent that there were some fifty thousand bodies to be disposed of each year, the majority of graveyards were already unhealthily full, and by 1856 the last of the sixty-five city burial-grounds had been closed. Fears of disease were fuelled by the recent cholera outbreaks. There were three possible answers to what was known as 'the dead man's question': additional provision for city burials, favoured by the clergy who were entitled to burial fees; creation of large outer London cemeteries, favoured by the Board of Health; and Sir Richard Broun's vision of 'extramural sepulture' in the shape of a vast new necropolis at Woking, Surrey, served by railway from London, to which bodies could be dispatched in swift and sanitary fashion, avoiding the usual conveyance by hearse through populous streets. A stream of pamphlets and published letters flowed from his pen, some addressed to the hapless earl of Derby and other notables. His vision did come to pass, with the creation of Brookwood cemetery with its train service. Sir Richard died, unmarried and apparently impoverished, at Sphinx Lodge, Upper Church Street, Chelsea, on 10 December 1858. It is not known where he was buried.

ANITA McCONNELL

Sources *British–American Association, and Nova Scotia Baronets: report of the action of damages for alleged libel, Broun (soi-disant) Sir Richard against the "Globe" newspaper*, British–American Association for Emigration and Colonization (1846) • R. Broun, *Appeal to our rulers and ruled, in behalf of a consolidation of the post office, roads, and mechanical conveyance, for the service of the state* (1834) • R. Broun, *British and American intercourse: letter to the Rt Hon. the earl of Derby, on the Imperial Halifax and Quebec railway and Anglo-Asian steam transit project* (1852) • R. Broun, *Extramural interment and the Metropolitan Sanitary Association: letter to the Rt Hon. the earl of Derby and Lord J. Manners, on the dead man's question* (1852) • *The Times* (7 July 1857), 12e • *GM*, 3rd ser., 5 (1858), 216 • *DNB*
Archives Bodl. Oxf., corresp. with Sir Thomas Phillipps
Wealth at death apparently impoverished

Brouncker, Henry, third Viscount Brouncker of Lyons (c.1627–1688). *See under* Brouncker, William, second Viscount Brouncker of Lyons (1620–1684).

Brouncker, William, second Viscount Brouncker of Lyons (1620–1684), mathematician and first president of the Royal Society of London, was born at Castle Lyons, co. Dublin in 1620, probably in April, the eldest son of Sir William Brouncker (1585–1645), gentleman of the privy chamber to Charles I and vice-chamberlain to Charles, prince of Wales, and his wife, Winifred (d. 1649), daughter of Sir William Leigh of Newnham. In 1639 the elder Sir

William Brouncker, second Viscount Brouncker of Lyons (1620–1684), by Sir Peter Lely, c.1674

William had been commissary general of the musters against the Scots; he was made doctor of civil law at Oxford on 1 November 1642. He received a grant of the monastery of Clonnis and was created Baron Brouncker of Newcastle and Viscount Brouncker of Lyons on 12 September 1645. He died in November 1645 at Wadham College, Oxford, and was buried on 20 November in Christ Church Cathedral. His wife died in July 1649 and was buried in London on 10 August 1649. The younger Brouncker succeeded to his father's titles in 1645.

Brouncker was sent to Oxford University at the age of sixteen and graduated MD on 23 February 1647. There is no indication that he practised medicine, but he avoided the turbulent politics of his day by devoting himself to the study of mathematics. In 1653 he published a translation and critique of Descartes's *Musicae compendium* under the pseudonym 'a person of honour', where he proposed to divide the diapason into seventeen equal semitones. In 1657 he started corresponding with fellow mathematician John Wallis, and his discoveries were later published as part of Wallis's work. His most important contribution concerned the quadrature of the circle: Brouncker was the first to express the ratio of the area of a circle to the circumscribed square as an infinite continued fraction. As a mathematician, he enjoyed a good reputation for his abilities—Bishop Burnet, for one, refers to him as a 'profound mathematician' (*Burnet's History*, 1.131). That reputation and his association with Wallis drew Brouncker into the philosophical discussions at Gresham College in the late 1650s, informal gatherings which would eventually grow into the Royal Society of London.

In 1660 Brouncker surfaced as a loyal royalist. In April he signed the 'remarkable declaration' in favour of General Monk and was member of parliament for Westbury, Wiltshire, in the convention parliament of that year. As a reward for his loyalty, on 18 April 1662 Brouncker was appointed chancellor to Queen Catherine and keeper of her great seal. In August 1662 he commissioned and helped design a new yacht for the king. For many years afterwards his relationship with Charles II was cordial, and it was not uncommon for Brouncker to spend time discussing scientific questions with him, often in the company of the diarist John Evelyn or fellow courtier Sir Robert Moray.

The Royal Society of London was incorporated under royal charter, first on 15 July 1662 and again on 15 April 1663. At the time of the second charter Charles II nominated Brouncker as the society's first president, a post he held from 22 April 1663 until 30 November 1677. In that time he continued his interest in mathematics and attempted 'to prove Huygen's assertion of the isochronicity of the cycloidal pendulum' (Whiteside, 157). He also continued his interest in the study of music, and often held musical meetings at his house. In his day he was not known for his experimental research, although he published the results of a series of simple experiments on the recoiling of guns and on the increase in the weight of metals with the application of heat. He was, however, a good administrator: he rarely missed the meetings and regularly paid his dues. Outside the society he was a tireless advocate for the new experimental philosophy. He tried—unsuccessfully—to use his influence at court either to establish a permanent home for the society when it was displaced from Gresham College by the great fire of 1666 or to obtain a grant from the king to cover the society's expenses. As interest in the society waned in the early 1670s many felt that it was time for a change; when it became clear that he would not be re-elected, Brouncker resigned, to be succeeded by Sir Joseph Williamson.

During his presidency Brouncker was also pursuing an active career in the civil service. On 12 November 1664 he was appointed a commissioner of the Admiralty, and it was at this point that he began his long personal and professional relationship with Samuel Pepys. After their first meeting, Pepys described him as a 'modest civil person … wholly ignorant in the business of the Navy as possible, but I hope to make a friend of him, being a worthy man' (Pepys, 5.341). It would seem that Brouncker performed his duties well: from December 1666 to December 1679 he was an assistant comptroller to the treasurer of the Admiralty. After a brief lapse in favour he was reappointed to this post in 1681. He also served as president of Gresham College from 1664 to 1667, and as master of the royal hospital of St Katharine by the Tower from 21 November 1681, after a long battle with judge Sir Robert Atkyns for the post was resolved in court.

Brouncker never married and had no children. He had a number of mistresses, most notably the actress Abigail Williams, his long-time companion. Pepys was not fond of her, but some of his dislike can be attributed to a fire which started in her closet in 1673. The fire spread to some thirty houses, including Pepys's own, and destroyed much of his furniture and works of art. Brouncker died in his house on St James's Street, Westminster, on 5 April 1684 and was buried on 14 April 1684 in the choir of the chapel attached to the hospital of St Katharine.

William Brouncker was succeeded by his brother **Henry Brouncker**, third Viscount Brouncker of Lyons (c.1627–1688), cofferer to Charles II and gentleman of the bedchamber to the duke of York. Henry was created MD on 23 June 1646, took part in the siege of Colchester in 1648, served as the MP for Romney from 1665 to 1668, and was a commissioner of trade and plantation in 1673. According to charges brought against him in the House of Commons in 1668, he ordered the sails of the British fleet to be slackened in the duke of York's name during the battle of Lowestoft in 1664, thereby allowing the Dutch to escape. As a result of the incident he was dismissed from the duke's service and expelled from parliament. He was not well liked, although admired for his skill with chess: Edward, earl of Clarendon, described him as 'a man throughout his whole life notorious for nothing but the highest degree of impudence, stooping to the most infamous offices, and playing chess very well, which preferred him more than the most virtuous qualities could have done' (Clarendon, 2.515). In May 1661 he married Rebecca Rodway, widow of Thomas Jermyn, brother to the earl of St Albans; they had no children, and with his death, on 4 January 1688 at Sheen Abbey, Surrey, the viscountcy and the barony became extinct. He was buried at Richmond, Surrey.

G. S. McINTYRE

Sources J. F. Scott and H. Hartley, 'William, Viscount Brouncker, FRS (1620–1684)', *Notes and Records of the Royal Society*, 15 (1960), 147–56 • Pepys, *Diary* • GEC, *Peerage* • T. Birch, *The history of the Royal Society of London*, 4 vols. (1756–7); repr. with introduction by A. R. Hall (1968), vols. 1–3 • *Bishop Burnet's History of his own time*, new edn (1850) • D. T. Whiteside, 'Brouncker's mathematical papers', *Notes and Records of the Royal Society*, 15 (1960), 157 • T. Sprat, *History of the Royal Society*, ed. J. I. Cope and H. W. Jones (1958) • A. Kippis and others, eds., *Biographia Britannica, or, The lives of the most eminent persons who have flourished in Great Britain and Ireland*, 2nd edn, 2 (1780), 613–14 • Wood, *Ath. Oxon.* • N. Luttrell, *A brief historical relation of state affairs from September 1678 to April 1714*, 1 (1857) • M. Hunter, *The Royal Society and its fellows, 1660–1700: the morphology of an early scientific institution*, 2nd edn (1994) • C. R. Weld, *A history of the Royal Society*, 2 vols. (1848) • *Diary of John Evelyn*, ed. W. Bray, 1–2 (1889) • *The life of Edward, earl of Clarendon … written by himself*, 3 vols. (1759), vol. 2 • J. Dutka, 'Wallis's product, Brouncker's continued fraction, and Leibniz's series', *Archive for History of Exact Sciences*, 26 (1982), 115–26 • C. Jamison, *The history of the Royal Hospital of St Katharine by the Tower of London* (1952) • *The diary of Robert Hooke … 1672–1680*, ed. H. W. Robinson and W. Adams (1935) • *The correspondence of Henry Oldenburg*, ed. and trans. A. R. Hall and M. B. Hall, 13 vols. (1965–86) • 'Brouncker, The Hon. Henry', HoP, *Commons*

Archives Hunt. L., proposal 'on the manning of ships in ordinary' | BL, corresp. with Petty relating to naval matters • RS, letters to Royal Society

Likenesses P. Lely, oils, 1661, RS • P. Lely, oils, c.1674, RS; versions, NPG, Althorp, Northants [*see illus.*] • oils, c.1675 (Henry Brouncker; after P. Lely), NPG • W. Hollar, etching (after J. Evelyn), NPG; repro. in T. Sprat, *History of the Royal Society* (1667)

Brouns [Brown], **Thomas** (d. 1445), bishop of Norwich, was the younger son of William Brouns of Sutton Courtenay and his wife Beatrice. Educated at Oxford, master of arts by 1404, licentiate of laws by 1411, and doctor of both laws by October 1415, he held some lesser benefices while studying, but began his professional career in the chapter of Lincoln as subdean from 1414 to 1419, where he was involved in the notorious lawsuits between the bishop, chapter, and Dean John Macworth, and was regularly a proctor in parliaments for the chapter and diocesan archdeacons, or for the latter alone. He was himself archdeacon of Stow from 1419.

On 9 June 1418 Brouns was appointed to array retinues before Louviers for the king. He was afterwards a councillor in Normandy to Henry V, with a salary of 500 livres tournois and preferment in Rouen Cathedral. Still in France in 1420 he helped to arrange a meeting between Henry V, Charles VI, and the duke of Burgundy in April, and treated with dauphinist envoys about the release of Arthur, duke of Brittany, in July. Between December 1420 and December 1421 he is found arraying various retinues, and was still designated *conseiller du roy* in June 1421.

Then Brouns's career reverted to one in ecclesiastical administration. He was still regarded as an active canon residentiary of Lincoln in 1422 and 1423. He has been said to have begun his services to Archbishop Henry Chichele of Canterbury (d. 1443) in 1419; more certainly he was the archbishop's chancellor by February 1423 (the year he was admitted to the confraternity of Canterbury Cathedral), and thereafter took part in several notable trials of Lollards and worked as auditor of causes. Among other preferments he was archdeacon of Berkshire from June 1427 until his election as dean of Salisbury in July 1431. This latter was compensation because, though in July 1429 Brouns was elected, with royal support, as bishop of Chichester, Pope Martin V, quarrelling with Henry VI's government over other matters, had preferred Simon Sydenham. Characteristically, Brouns seems at this point to have ended his work for Chichele and taken up his duties in Salisbury in person.

However, on 7 January 1433 Brouns left London to attend the Council of Basel as a proctor for both the crown and the province of Canterbury. In September Pope Eugenius IV provided him to succeed Thomas Polton (who had just died at the council) as bishop of Worcester. This time it was the crown that refused him, ostensibly for his disobedience in respect of the statutes against provisors, in reality because the regime, particularly Cardinal Henry Beaufort (d. 1447), was determined to promote the youthful but extremely well-connected Thomas Bourchier (d. 1486). The pope resisted, but gave way in the end; he 'compensated' Brouns, at the government's suggestion and thus saving his own honour, with translation to the much inferior see of Rochester (21 February 1435). Despite such disharmony Brouns had been reappointed to the crown's second delegation to Basel in May 1434, and attended. He withdrew finally with the others in November, and returned home on 12 February 1435. On 19 September 1436 he was translated with unanimous approval to the see of Norwich, superior by far to either Worcester or Rochester.

Until September 1437 Brouns was absent from Norwich, engaged in negotiations with the French. From April to September 1438 he was again in London. On 26 June 1439 he crossed to Calais for peace talks, fell ill, but recovered to continue his work until October. At the same time he was seeking a commercial treaty with Flanders. Otherwise, Brouns was a conscientious resident diocesan, usually based at Hoxne or his palace in Norwich. He compromised a familiar dispute over marks of reverence with the cathedral chapter. The well-known 'Gladman's insurrection' (25 January–4 February 1443) was the violent climax to a long dispute between the cathedral and city of Norwich, in which the laity regarded Brouns as a far from conciliatory face. His register also shows a continued interest in relations between the pope and the Council of Basel.

Brouns's bequests to both Rochester and Norwich cathedrals were gratifyingly handsome to the resident staff, very specific to his own memory, and oblivious or superficial as regards the fabric or function of those places. He devoted more care to endowing a family chantry in Sutton Courtenay. His nephew, Richard Brouns, son of his own elder brother, Richard, was his favourite legatee, and was financed to attend an inn of court for two years. The bishop also remembered young Richard's sister, Alice, and his other nieces, Christina (wife of William Bekyngham, esquire) and Elizabeth (wife of John Cossington, esquire of Kent), as well as two other kinsmen among many servants in his own household, the brothers John and William Herteshorne. The bishop died at Hoxne on 6 December 1445 and requested burial in his designated and designed chantry tomb at the head of Norwich Cathedral nave, near the centre of St William's altar.　　MARGARET HARVEY

Sources Emden, *Oxf.*, 1.281–3 · E. F. Jacob, 'Thomas Brouns, bishop of Norwich, 1436–45', *Essays in British history presented to Sir Keith Feiling*, ed. H. R. Trevor-Roper (1964), 61–83 · E. F. Jacob, 'Two documents relating to Thomas Brouns', *Norfolk Archaeology*, 33 (1962–5), 427–49 · J. Fletcher, *Sutton Courtenay: the history of a Thameside village* (1990) · LPL, register of John Stafford · Norfolk RO, REG/5/10 · D. C. Maddern, *Violence and social order: East Anglia, 1422–42* (1992), 192–204 · HoP, *Commons* · CKS, DRc/R6, fols. 112–19v
Archives CKS, register as bishop of Rochester, DRc/R6 · Norfolk RO, REG/5/10
Wealth at death exact sum unknown: will, Jacob, 'Two documents'

Browell, William (1759–1831), naval officer, son of William Browell, who was a midshipman in the *Centurion* under Commodore Anson, went to sea in 1771 as captain's servant in the sloop *Merlin*; after serving as coxswain, able seaman, midshipman, and master's mate in six other ships, he moved into the *Victory* (100 guns) shortly before the engagement off Ushant.

Browell passed his lieutenant's examination on 5 November 1778, and on 10 November became fourth lieutenant in the *Bienfaisant*; he worked his way up to second lieutenant before joining the *Artois*, on 8 January 1781, in which he was with Captain MacBride at the hard-fought battle of Dogger Bank on 5 August. In 1790 he was for a short time in the *Canada*; when that ship was paid off he was appointed to the *Alcide*, and in early 1793 he moved to the *Leviathan* (74 guns), in which he took part in the British occupation of Toulon under Lord Hood in August–December 1793. On 25 May 1794 he was promoted out of the *Leviathan*; but as she was then at sea he probably remained in her as a volunteer, and was present at the battle of 1 June.

On 29 November Browell received his first command, the yacht *Princess Augusta*, and in June 1795 Lord Hugh Seymour, Browell's captain in the *Leviathan*, now a rear-admiral, hoisted his flag in the *Sans Pareil* (80 guns), and selected Browell as his flag captain. He thus had a distinguished share in the battle off Lorient on 23 June 1795. He remained in the *Sans Pareil* for the next two years, and during this period, on 11 December 1795, at Gosport, he married the daughter of one of his former captains, Admiral Faulknor. She died on 20 September 1809.

In June 1797 the *Sans Pareil* was one of a squadron under Sir Roger Curtis, sent for a few weeks into the North Sea. After its return to Spithead, and while the ship was refitting, Browell, on shore at Gosport, was crushed by a bale of wool falling from a height. The injury to his back was severe and he was never again fit for active service. In 1805 he was appointed one of the captains of Greenwich Hospital, and in 1809 he became lieutenant-governor, a position he held, during a period in which he was also a trustee of the Naval Charitable Society, until his death on 22 July 1831.　　　J. K. Laughton, *rev.* Randolph Cock

Sources commission and warrant books, PRO, ADM 6/21, 22 · lieutenants' passing certificates, PRO, ADM 107/7 fol. 63 · J. Marshall, *Royal naval biography*, 4 vols. (1823–35) [with 4 suppls.] · W. L. Clowes, *The Royal Navy: a history from the earliest times to the present*, 7 vols. (1897–1903) · *Annual Biography and Obituary*, 16 (1832), 106–15 · *GM*, 1st ser., 65 (1795), 1111

Archives PRO, commission and warrant books, ADM 6/21, 22 · PRO, lieutenants' passing certificates, ADM 107/7, fol. 63

PICTURE CREDITS

Briginshaw, Richard William, Baron Briginshaw (1908–1992)—© News International Newspapers Ltd

Brindley, James (1716–1772)—© National Portrait Gallery, London

Brinsmead, John (1814–1908)—© National Portrait Gallery, London

Britannia (*fl.* 1st-21st cent.)—© Copyright The British Museum

Brittain, Vera Mary (1893–1970)—© National Portrait Gallery, London

Britten, (Edward) Benjamin, Baron Britten (1913–1976)—© Cecil Beaton Archive, Sotheby's; collection National Portrait Gallery, London

Britten, James (1846–1924)—by permission of the Linnean Society of London

Britton, John (1771–1857)—© National Portrait Gallery, London

Britton, Thomas (1644–1714)—© National Portrait Gallery, London

Broadbent, Donald Eric (1926–1993)—© Margaret Broadbent

Broadbent, Sir William Henry, first baronet (1835–1907)—© National Portrait Gallery, London

Broadhurst, Sir Edward Tootal, baronet (1858–1922)—The Whitworth Art Gallery, the University of Manchester

Broadhurst, Henry (1840–1911)—© National Portrait Gallery, London

Broadwood, Henry Fowler (1811–1893)—© reserved

Broadwood, John (1732–1812)—© National Portrait Gallery, London

Broadwood, Lucy Etheldred (1858–1929)—© National Portrait Gallery, London

Broccoli, Albert Romolo (1909–1996)—Getty Images - Hulton Archive

Brock, Arthur Clutton- (1868–1924)—by courtesy of the Estate of Sir William

Rothenstein; photograph courtesy of the Tate Gallery, London

Brock, Dame (Madeline) Dorothy (1886–1969)—© National Portrait Gallery, London

Brock, Sir Osmond de Beauvoir (1869–1947)—© National Portrait Gallery, London

Brock, Sir Thomas (1847–1922)—© National Portrait Gallery, London

Brockway, (Archibald) Fenner, Baron Brockway (1888–1988)—© National Portrait Gallery, London

Brodie, Sir Benjamin Collins, first baronet (1783–1862)—© National Portrait Gallery, London

Brodie, Sir Israel (1895–1979)—private collection; photograph National Portrait Gallery, London

Brodum, William (*fl.* 1767–1824)—Wellcome Library, London

Brogan, Sir Denis William (1900–1974)—© National Portrait Gallery, London

Broke, Sir Philip Bowes Vere, first baronet (1776–1841)—© National Portrait Gallery, London

Brome, Alexander (1620–1666)—The Huntington Library, Art Collections and Botanical Gardens, San Marino, CA, USA

Brome, Richard (*c.*1590–1652)—© National Portrait Gallery, London

Bromley, John (1876–1945)—© National Portrait Gallery, London

Bromley, Sir Thomas (*c.*1530–1587)—private collection. Photograph: Photographic Survey, Courtauld Institute of Art, London

Bronescombe, Walter of (*c.*1220–1280)—The Conway Library, Courtauld Institute of Art, London

Bronowski, Jacob (1908–1974)—© National Portrait Gallery, London

Brontë, (Patrick) Branwell (1817–1848)—courtesy of the Brontë Society

Brontë, Charlotte (1816–1855)—© National Portrait Gallery, London

Brontë, Patrick (1777–1861)—reproduced by kind permission of the Dean and Chapter of York

Broodbank, Sir Joseph Guinness (1857–1944)—© National Portrait Gallery, London

Brook, Helen Grace, Lady Brook (1907–1997)—© News International Newspapers Ltd

Brook, Norman Craven, Baron Normanbrook (1902–1967)—© National Portrait Gallery, London

Brooke, Alan Francis, first Viscount Alanbrooke (1883–1963)—© Karsh / Camera Press; collection National Portrait Gallery, London

Brooke, Arthur (1845–1918)—reproduced with kind permission of Unilever Bestfoods from an original in Unilever Corporate Archives

Brooke, Basil Stanlake, first Viscount Brookeborough (1888–1973)—© National Portrait Gallery, London

Brooke, Elizabeth, Lady Brooke (1602?–1683)—© Copyright The British Museum; photograph National Portrait Gallery, London

Brooke, Frances (*bap.* 1724, *d.* 1789)—Read / National Archives of Canada / C-117373

Brooke, George, ninth Baron Cobham (*c.*1497–1558)—The Royal Collection © 2004 HM Queen Elizabeth II

Brooke, Henry (*c.*1703–1783)—by courtesy of the National Gallery of Ireland

Brooke, Sir James (1803–1868)—© National Portrait Gallery, London

Brooke, Rupert Chawner (1887–1915)—© National Portrait Gallery, London

Brooke, Stopford Augustus (1832–1916)—© National Portrait Gallery, London

Brooke, William, tenth Baron Cobham (1527–1597)—reproduced by permission of the Marquess of Bath, Longleat House, Warminster, Wiltshire, Great Britain

Brookes, Joshua (1761–1833)—© National Portrait Gallery, London

Brookes, William Penny (1809–1895)—courtesy of Wenlock Olympian Society

Brooks, (Beatrice) Romaine Mary (1874–1970)—National Museum of American Art, Washington DC / Art Resource, NY

Broome, William (*bap.* 1689, *d.* 1745)—© National Portrait Gallery, London

Brophy, Brigid Antonia (1929–1995)—© Mark Gerson; collection National Portrait Gallery, London

Brothers, Richard (1757–1824)—© National Portrait Gallery, London

Brotherton, Edward Allen, Baron Brotherton (1856–1930)—© National Portrait Gallery, London

Brotherton, Joseph (1783–1857)—© National Portrait Gallery, London

Brougham, Henry Peter, first Baron Brougham and Vaux (1778–1868)—© National Portrait Gallery, London

Brougham, John (1810–1880)—© National Portrait Gallery, London

Broughton, Hugh (1549–1612)—© National Portrait Gallery, London

Broughton, John (*c.*1703–1789)—© National Portrait Gallery, London

Broughton, William Grant (1788–1853)—Dixson Galleries, State Library of New South Wales

Brouncker, William, second Viscount Brouncker of Lyons (1620–1684)—© The Royal Society